MACMILLAN
Collocations
DICTIONARY

MACMILLAN
Collocations
DICTIONARY

Macmillan Education
Between Towns Road, Oxford OX4 3PP
A division of Macmillan Publishers Limited
Companies and representatives throughout the world

ISBN 978 0 230 72403 7

© Macmillan Publishers Limited 2010

First published 2010

Cover design by Liz Faulkner
Typeset by Input Data Services Ltd, Bridgwater, United Kingdom

Printed and bound in Malaysia

10   9   8   7   6   5   4   3
2014   2013   2012

Editor-in-Chief
Michael Rundell

Associate Editor
Gwyneth Fox

EDITORIAL TEAM

Rosalind Combley
Andrew Delahunty
Penny Hands
Lucy Hollingworth
Julie Moore

Elizabeth Potter
Howard Sargeant
Ian Spackman
Jenny Watson
Donald Watt

Laura Wedgeworth

PROJECT TEAM

Publishing Director
Sue Bale

Publisher
Stephen Bullon

Project Manager
Shane Rae

Editor
Sharon Creese

Database management
Edmund Wright

Headword list development
Sarah McKeown

Design
Douglas Williamson
Liz Faulkner

Data input and administration
Beth Penfold
Alona Simister

Sketch Engine corpus software
Lexical Computing Ltd

MACMILLAN DICTIONARY ADVISORY PANEL

INTRODUCTION

MICHAEL RUNDELL

Editor-in-Chief

The *Macmillan Collocations Dictionary* (MCD) provides a complete record of the most typical ways in which common English words combine with one another. These word combinations are known as 'collocations', and this is an important concept for anyone learning, teaching, or using English. According to Professor Michael Hoey, who heads the Macmillan Dictionaries Advisory Panel, collocation is 'the property of language whereby two or more words seem to appear frequently in each other's company'. Long before computer corpora became available, linguists noticed the tendency of some words to 'stick together', in expressions like *conduct a survey, highly effective*, or *rapturous applause*. Nowadays, with a corpus of 1.6 billion words at our disposal, we can reliably identify the most frequent English collocations.

That's the easy part. But lists of collocations on their own are not especially helpful. In order to make this information useful for teachers and students, our team of lexicographers has divided up the various collocations according to the meanings they express. For example, if you are talking about an *argument* (in the sense of 'a set of reasons you use for persuading people'), the corpus provides a long list of words (or 'collocates') which are frequently used with this noun. Our job is to analyse these collocates and sort them into useful sets, such as words meaning 'a strong argument' (*compelling, persuasive, powerful*, and so on), or an argument that is 'sensible and well-argued' (*coherent, rational, well-reasoned* etc) or one that is 'based on incorrect facts' (*spurious, fallacious* etc). For this meaning of *argument*, the MCD provides six sets of adjectives and five sets of verbs, each expressing a different meaning. Every set has its own definition, its own list of collocates, and its own example sentences to show how these combinations work.

Why is collocation so important? Firstly, it is a central feature of language, and – whether you are speaking or writing – it is just as important as grammar. Getting the grammar right is an essential part of producing text which is free of errors. But selecting appropriate collocations is one of the keys to sounding natural and fluent. For this reason, a good collocations dictionary is a valuable resource if you are preparing for IELTS or similar examinations. Secondly, collocation contributes to meaning. Most common words in English have more than one meaning, and we use the surrounding context to indicate (or work out) which meaning is intended. Collocation plays a big part in this process. Consider, for example, the word *goal*, which can mean either something you want to achieve or a point scored in football. When you see *goal* with verbs like *set, achieve,* or *pursue* (or with verbs like *score* or *concede*), you know immediately what is meant, and it is collocation which provides the clue. As the linguist J.R. Firth said, in a famous quotation, 'You shall know a word by the company it keeps'.

Some features of language, such as wordplay, figurative uses, or cultural references, may be seen as 'optional extras' which you can use once you are really fluent. Collocation is not like this. Once you have progressed beyond beginner level, collocation is essential to expressing ideas in the most natural-sounding way. With the *Macmillan Collocations Dictionary*, you have the ideal resource for developing this important skill and using collocation with confidence.

USING THE DICTIONARY IN IELTS

Sam McCarter

ELT Author and Teacher

The *Macmillan Collocations Dictionary* (MCD) is a valuable resource for anyone using English in an academic or professional context. It shows how the most frequent words in English typically combine with each other, and with other words, to form natural-sounding chunks of language – and this is what makes it an especially useful tool for people taking the IELTS exams.

There is an important distinction to be made between IELTS (the International English Language Testing System) and other exams. The purpose of IELTS is not to test students' *knowledge* of the English language, but to assess their *competence* in using it. Students are not awarded a pass or fail, but their scores are reported on a scale ranging from 1 ('Non-User') to 9 ('Expert User').

The word *User* is critical. Rather than testing students' knowledge of grammar or of specific vocabulary items, IELTS evaluates their ability to use the English language in the completion of tasks (within fairly tight time limits) in the four main skills of Listening, Reading, Writing and Speaking. This focus on testing *competence* rather than *knowledge* has implications for students and teachers alike, especially with regard to learning vocabulary.

Let us take, for example, a student who is about to take IELTS, and who has a reasonably large vocabulary of, say, around 7,500 words. A vocabulary of this size is a desirable asset for anyone aiming to achieve a score of 6.5–7 in the academic version of IELTS. But learning words from vocabulary lists is not enough. If our imaginary student has no awareness of how words work naturally together, he/she will be at a disadvantage compared to someone who may have a smaller vocabulary (say 5,000 words), but who is able to use those words effectively by combining them in natural-sounding collocations.

What this illustrates is the importance of learning to use vocabulary, at speed, across tasks within the four main skills. This will improve fluency, clarity of expression, and naturalness – and hence competence in general.

The need for such flexibility in manipulating words to create the kinds of combinations that a fluent speaker would produce naturally is what makes the *Macmillan Collocations Dictionary* an ideal companion for students as they prepare for the IELTS exam.

How producing natural collocations can help IELTS students

There are two aspects of vocabulary that illustrate the relevance of collocation and the value of a dictionary like the MCD:

- the relationship between frequency and 'coverage': research shows that the most common English words make up a high percentage of everything we read or write. The most frequently-used words (the top 2,500) account for almost 80% of all text, while the 7,500 most common words make up over 90%.

- The relationship between frequency and collocation: the more frequent a word is, the more likely it is to enter into 'partnerships' with other words, forming combinations which convey a sense of naturalness and style.

This has implications for *processing information* in the four main skills tested in IELTS.

Processing information: Listening

In the IELTS Listening Module, students

have to be able to process information at natural speed which they hear only once. Grammar and listening skills apart, such processing for students aiming for Score Band 7 requires an ability to identify facts and ideas, to see the relationships between them, and to recognize paraphrases and summaries. From the IELTS student's point of view, the skill of predicting relationships between words in collocations or identifying the paraphrase of one collocation to another at speed is very useful.

At a fairly simple level, this can be illustrated by the alternatives students might have to choose from in a multiple-choice question. As students have to process what they hear while listening, quick understanding of the audio and the questions is essential. Look at the second entry for the word *basic* in MCD:

---

2 of products or services, needed by everyone

● **ADJ+n amenities, essentials, foodstuffs, necessities, needs, sanitation** *Their parents have to work from morning till night to provide the basic necessities.*

A question in the Listening Module might look something like this:
Their parents have to work from morning till night to provide the _____.
  a *basic necessities*
  b *school fees*
  c *expensive clothes*

In the listening module, the speaker might say something like: ... *supply the children with accommodation, food and clothing.* Knowing that the word *basic* is frequently combined with *necessities* to mean things like *accommodation, food and clothing* makes it easier to process information while listening. If students have to think about the meaning of the two words combined, it will slow them down. Furthermore as the vocabulary used in the audio, and in the questions, is likely to be drawn from the most common 2,500 to 7,500 words (either as single items or in combination), then it makes sense to include work on collocation and on possible paraphrases as part of a course.

Processing information: Reading

The reading passages in the academic version of IELTS are long – around 800 words each and up to 2,700 words for the three passages – and students have to answer 40 questions about the passages in one hour. The skills needed for negotiating a text include skimming, scanning, rapid recognition of text type and organization, and the ability to process grammar at speed. But a flexible use of vocabulary can further enhance competence in reading. A good starting point is to acquire a thorough working knowledge of the most frequent English words and – critically – to learn the various ways in which they typically combine to form natural-sounding and predictable collocations.

Reading and processing speeds can surely be enhanced by a detailed understanding of the ways in which words fit together. If we take another entry from the MCD, for the word *significant*, a knowledge of collocation can help students predict as they read. In a text about the important consequences of a policy or decision, for example, the use of the adjective *significant* will 'prime' readers to expect nouns such as *impact* or *effect* to follow:

... *have a significant impact on the economy of the region.*

And collocation manipulation will also help the student to see that the phrase '... *benefit that part of the country considerably*' in a reading passage is being paraphrased by the phrase above in a True/False/Not Given statement or multiple-choice question. As the MCD shows, other words with which *significant* regularly combines, to express the idea of an important result or effect of something, include *implications, consequence, influence,* and *benefit.* These provide yet another rich source of language to manipulate for paraphrasing and summarizing.

The ability to understand and use collocations helps students to increase their speed in processing information as they predict the text that is to cover the blank pages to come.

Building fluency and sounding natural: Writing Task 2

In Task 2 of the academic version of IELTS, students are required to write a minimum of 250 words. A student with a good grasp of collocation has a distinct advantage, as we can see by again looking at the entry for *significant* in the MCD. It shows the nouns and adverbs that most frequently combine with *significant* to express a wide range of ideas. If you want to say something is '*very* significant', there is a choice of typical adverbs. Or again, there are sets of nouns for conveying ideas like 'a significant achievement', 'a significant problem or challenge', or – as discussed already – 'a significant effect or result'. Here we look at the set of nouns frequently used to express the idea of 'a significant event or change':

> • ADJ+n event or change **action, change, decision, development, improvement, initiative, move, trend** *The most significant recent development has been the introduction of an integrated fares and ticketing structure.*

Let's say a student makes a spelling or a grammatical mistake in the sentence (for example, writing *The most significant recent development* or *Most significant recent development*); despite these mistakes, the message is clear. But look at the difference if the student uses words of similar meaning but in unnatural combinations, and writes:

The most key recent act has been the initiative of an integrated fares and ticketing arrangement.

Though the sentence is not 'incorrect', its intended meaning is much less clear, because inappropriate words have been chosen, resulting in untypical collocations. If this is then repeated with the same consistency throughout an essay, with or without grammar or spelling mistakes, it becomes more difficult for the reader (the Examiner), to recover the meaning. Texts like this give the impression the writer lacks fluency and is operating with a limited working vocabulary. Yet, with even quite small changes, the meaning would become more transparent and the text as a whole would feel more natural.

Building fluency and sounding natural: Speaking Parts 2 and 3

The need for fluency becomes even more critical in the Speaking module of IELTS. In Part 2 students are expected to talk about a particular topic: for example, *Describe a recent development in your life that you felt was important.* A good way of demonstrating a wide vocabulary is to employ natural collocations which paraphrase what the Examiner says, rather than just repeating the exact words, for example: *I'm going to talk about a recent change in my life that was very significant.* If students are hesitant as they pick their way through the words that they *know* or simply repeat the words of the Examiner, this will affect their Score Band for vocabulary and fluency. Part 3 covers many abstract topics similar to those covered in Task 2 of the Writing module. Here, students are asked to talk about subjects such as the development of technology and its effects in the workplace or on domestic life. Again, the student who is able, with minimum hesitation, to choose words that fit together to make natural collocations is more likely to achieve a higher Score Band.

The *Macmillan Collocations Dictionary* is a useful companion for anyone working in an academic or professional context or taking exams such as FCE, CAE Proficiency, ILEC and ICFE. For IELTS, it is an especially valuable resource which seems tailor-made to meet the needs of students preparing for this exam.

GUIDE TO THE DICTIONARY

argument N
1 an angry disagreement between people

Headword and word class (N= noun).

2 a set of reasons used for persuading others
- adj+N strong **compelling, convincing, persuasive, powerful, strong, valid** *While it has been claimed that this approach could increase resources for development assistance, there are equally compelling arguments that it may divert scarce aid resources.*
▶ weak **unconvincing, weak** *The proposal is based on an unconvincing argument.*
▶ most important **central, core, main** *Without doubt, the book's central arguments are compelling and backed up with a wealth of evidence.*
▶ sensible or well-argued **cogent, coherent, logical, plausible, rational, reasoned, well-reasoned** *I have seen very cogent arguments for and against the Scottish system of comprehensive education.*
▶ based on incorrect facts or reasoning **fallacious, flawed, spurious** *Sadly, this is a hopelessly flawed argument.*

When a word has more than one meaning, each meaning is shown by a **number**. A **definition** is given for every meaning.

Codes show grammatical relationship between headword and collocates: adj+N means the noun (**N**) **argument** often occurs with the adjectives listed here; v+**N** means the noun is often the object of the verbs listed here.

You can also say that there is **a flaw in** someone's argument: *There are at least two major flaws in your argument.*

▶ about a particular subject **ethical, legal, philosophical, political, theological** *These hypotheses are used as premises in a number of philosophical arguments.*

Note (with grey background): we use these notes when there is a common way of expressing the same idea using a phrase rather than a collocation.

- v+N suggest or use an argument **advance, articulate, deploy, make, outline, present, produce, provide, put forward, supply, use** *There is adequate opportunity to present new arguments and evidence.*
▶ think of or develop an argument **construct, develop, formulate, hone** *I could do with some help formulating my argument.*
▶ not accept an argument **disagree with, dismiss, rebut, refute, reject** *This book rebuts every argument ever offered to 'prove' God's existence.*
▶ make an argument weaker **contradict, counter, demolish, undermine, weaken** *This material goes some way to counter these arguments.*
▶ make an argument stronger **bolster, endorse, lend weight to, reinforce, strengthen, substantiate, support** *It supports our argument that what matters is efficiency, not achieving targets.*

The same **grammatical relation** (like v+**N**) is often used to express different ideas. Each of these sets has a **definition** (like 'think of or develop an argument'), a list of **collocates** (like **construct** or **develop**), and one or more examples.

enhance v
improve something

- adv+V very much **considerably, dramatically, enormously, greatly, immeasurably, significantly, substantially, vastly** *This is an important development which will greatly enhance trade links across Europe.*
- ▶ in a particular way **artificially, chemically, digitally, genetically, nutritionally, surgically** *We have the professional expertise to digitally enhance photos.*

  Usage *Enhance* is often passive in these combinations: *They believe genetically enhanced crops will help poor farmers in developing countries.*

- V+n reputation or appeal **attractiveness, credibility, employability, prospects, reputation** *An award can influence the sales of a book, and enhance the reputation of the author.*

Usage note (with pink background): we use these notes when a collocation needs to be used in a particular way, for example when a verb is often in the passive or a noun usually in the plural.

funding N
money from a government or organization for a particular purpose

- adj+N more **additional, extra, further, increased** *We support increased funding for library services.*
- ▶ enough **adequate, sufficient** *We believe that adequate funding of museums should be continued.*
- ▶ available **available** *Contact your local council for full information on available funding.*
- ▶ types of funding **external, public** *The reality is that without public funding it would be impossible to fully prepare the case for a long trial.*

- n+N from government **government, state** *The charity does not receive any government funding.*
- ▶ source of funding **grant, lottery** *The trust has secured grant funding from the Heritage Lottery Fund and sponsorship for the project.*
- ▶ what funding is used for **project, research** *At the moment we have about £1.2m in research funding.*

- v+N get funding **attract, find, get, obtain, raise, receive, secure, win** *We have already secured funding to help with security and heating.*
- ▶ try to get funding **apply for, bid for, request, seek** *This partnership successfully applied for funding from external sources including the Millennium Commission.*
- ▶ give funding **allocate, approve, award, commit, provide** *The Commission will take the final decision on whether or not to award funding.*
- ▶ increase funding **increase** *They have now increased funding for the immunization programme.*
- ▶ stop or reduce funding **cut, reduce, withdraw, withhold** *The House of Representatives has voted to cut nearly all funding for the program.*
- ▶ decide to use funding for a particular purpose **earmark** *Separate funding has been earmarked for the provision of networked computers.*

When a word is often followed by a particular preposition (such as 'from' or 'for'), we highlight this using bold type in the example.

A a

abandon V
stop doing or planning something or supporting an idea

- adv+V completely **altogether, completely, entirely** *It would not be until the 20th century that science would completely abandon the notion that the universe had always existed.*
- ▶ almost completely **effectively, largely, virtually** *By 1941, the policy of internment had been largely abandoned.*
- ▶ quickly **hastily, quickly** *They quickly abandoned any plans for expanding the business that year.*
- ▶ when something is abandoned **eventually, finally, quickly, soon** *By the 16th century attempts to construct a proper harbour were finally abandoned.*

- V+n **attempt, belief, faith, hope, idea, plan, pretence, principle** *He called on the government to abandon plans to hold a referendum.*

ability N
the power to do something or the skill in doing it

- adj+N very good or impressive **above-average, amazing, exceptional, extraordinary, proven, remarkable, uncanny, unique** *He seems to have an uncanny ability to recognize and develop talented footballers.*
- ▶ natural, rather than learned **innate, instinctive, natural** *George's exceptional natural ability on the piano was soon recognized.*
- ▶ types of ability **academic, cognitive, creative, intellectual, linguistic, mental, musical, organizational, physical, psychic, technical** *Some of these problems arose because a number of the users had limited technical ability.*

- v+N have or show ability **demonstrate, develop, have, possess, prove, show** *The ideal individual will have demonstrated their ability to work independently and as part of a multi-disciplinary group.*
- ▶ not have ability **lack, lose** *We are on the verge of losing our ability to tell one plant or animal from another.*
- ▶ have good or bad effect on ability **affect, enhance, impair, improve, increase, limit, restrict** *How you respond to stress affects your ability to think clearly.*

abnormal ADJ
not usual or typical and possibly harmful

- ADJ+n the way something looks or behaves **behaviour, movement, pattern, reaction, response, result, rhythm** *Many captive elephants appear to display abnormal behaviour.*
- ▶ in medical use, way something develops or occurs in the body **bleeding, cell, discharge, gene, growth, tissue** *Another biopsy revealed more abnormal cells but no cancer.*

abolish V
officially get rid of a law or system

- adv+V **altogether, completely, effectively, finally** *Taxes on savings and dividends will be abolished altogether, except at the higher rate.*

- V+n practice or institution **death penalty, monarchy, poverty, slavery, slave trade** *In 1833 slavery was abolished in all British colonies.*
- ▶ tax or payment **charge, duty, fee, grant, subsidy, tax** *The party has announced its intention to abolish tuition fees if it wins the next election.*
- ▶ rule or law **law, limit, requirement, restriction, rule** *The Bill also abolishes the requirement for private companies to hold an annual general meeting.*

abortion N
an operation that prevents a baby from being born

- adj+N when it is done **early, late, late-term** *She supports a woman's right to decide, but she is not supportive of late-term abortions except in cases where a woman's health is endangered.*
- ▶ types of abortion **backstreet, illegal, legal, medical, unsafe** *The demand for the right to safe and legal abortion was an important issue for the contemporary women's movement.*

- v+N have or perform an abortion **carry out, get, have, perform, seek** *The decision about whether to have an abortion or continue with a pregnancy is not an easy one to make.*
- ▶ allow/not allow legal abortion **allow, ban, legalize, oppose** *Abortion was first legalized in this country forty years ago.*

- N+n relating to the operation **clinic, pill, rate, service** *Legislators have passed a measure which would require abortion clinics to be licensed and regulated by inspectors.*
- ▶ relating to the issue **debate, law, right** *It is well established that women travel abroad to circumvent restrictions in their own national abortion laws.*

absence N
1 not being in usual place

- adj+N length or frequency of absence **frequent, long, long-term, persistent, prolonged, short, short-term, temporary** *Invigilators have been asked to note temporary absences and will record these on script covers when they are collected in.*
- ▶ allowed, or for a good reason **authorized, sickness, unavoidable** *In the case of sickness, or other unavoidable absence, ensure that you obtain a copy of all notes and handouts before the next class.*
- ▶ unreasonable or not allowed **unauthorized, unexplained** *If a student leaves before that date, this may be considered taking unauthorized absence or truancy.*

2 when something does not exist, especially something needed or wanted

- adj+N complete **complete, total** *There is a complete absence of modern teaching aids such as computers.*
- ▶ noticeable or almost complete **apparent, conspicuous, marked, notable, relative, virtual** *This*

author has already noted the conspicuous absence in this report of any consideration of alternative clinical explanations.

- N+of **agreement, data, evidence, explanation, proof, support** *Other scholars would insist that we should follow the biblical text in the absence of contrary evidence.*

absorb V
take in gas, liquid, heat etc

- adv+V **easily, quickly, rapidly, readily, slowly** *Extensive research suggests that a liquid is absorbed far more quickly than tablets or capsules.*

- V+n **carbon, energy, heat, light, liquid, moisture, nutrients, radiation, vitamins, water** *Cotton is a natural fabric which absorbs moisture.*

- V+into **blood, bloodstream, body, cell, skin, tissue** *Alcohol passes through the stomach and small intestine and is absorbed into the bloodstream.*

abstract ADJ
not related to physical objects or real events

- adv+ADJ **fairly, highly, purely, rather** *Each item is liberally illustrated with diagrams making it easier to visualise what is going on in what is often a fairly abstract concept.*

- ADJ+n **argument, concept, idea, notion, principle, reasoning, theory, thinking** *He can express complex abstract ideas in easily comprehensible language.*

abstract N
a summary of a report, speech, or academic paper

- v+N write or send an abstract **provide, send, submit, write** *The deadline for submitting abstracts is February 1st.*
- ▶ examine or accept an abstract **accept, read, referee, review** *All accepted abstracts will be included in the CD-ROM publication of the conference proceedings.*

absurd ADJ
stupid, unreasonable, or silly

- adv+ADJ very or obviously **completely, manifestly, patently, quite, totally, truly, utterly** *To have a city like London with no coherent system of government was manifestly absurd.*
- ▶ rather **faintly, rather, slightly** *His patriotism was so impulsive as to be slightly absurd.*

- ADJ+n **allegation, argument, belief, claim, conclusion, idea, notion, position, situation, suggestion** *We could end up with the absurd situation where government doesn't have anything to do with British business.*

abuse N
1 cruel, violent, or unfair treatment, sometimes involving forced sexual activity

- adj+N **domestic, emotional, physical, psychological, sexual** *Domestic abuse takes many forms, many of them not at all violent in nature.*
- n+N **child, elder, human rights, sex** *Today, we*

would be saying that this is a terrible case of child abuse.

- v+N suffer abuse **endure, experience, suffer** *The British Medical Association estimates that one in four women will suffer physical abuse from a partner during their lives.*
- ▶ commit abuse **commit, perpetrate** *The regime has committed grave human rights abuses.*

- and/or **exploitation, neglect, violence** *Following neglect or abuse, many young people have been in local authority care for a number of years.*

2 the illegal, dishonest, or harmful use of something

- adj+N **appalling, blatant, flagrant, gross, systematic, widespread** *People concerned about ethical issues have formed groups that collectively aim to prevent gross abuses.*

- n+N **alcohol, drug, solvent, substance** *There is an alarming increase in the number of children being treated for alcohol abuse.*

- v+N prevent abuse **combat, curb, prevent, stop, tackle** *Pharmacy bodies have welcomed the Government's recognition of the potential role of pharmacy in tackling drug abuse.*
- ▶ situation in which abuse can happen **be open to** *A system more open to abuse would have been difficult to devise.*

- N+of **authority, position, power, privilege, system, trust** *The UK-wide investigation started earlier this year in the wake of concerns about supermarkets' abuse of power.*

3 angry offensive comments

- adj+N **homophobic, racial, racist, verbal** *Racial abuse was daily directed at residents going about their business.*

- v+N **hurl, scream, shout, subject sb to** *As he left the pitch he hurled some abuse at the referee.* • *Many of these asylum seekers and refugees have been subjected to racial abuse.*

- n+of+N **term** *In Elizabethan England, 'puritan' was a term of abuse.*

abuse V
1 treat someone very badly

- adv+V **emotionally, physically, sexually** *He works particularly with young people who have been sexually abused within their own families.*

2 use something in an illegal, dishonest, or harmful way

- V+n power, position, or system **authority, freedom, position, power, privilege, status, system, trust** *It seems that people in positions of power are, once again, abusing their position.*
- ▶ alcohol or drug **alcohol, drug, substance** *When Hugh left school at 16, he began to abuse alcohol.*

abusive ADJ
1 using offensive or insulting language

- ADJ+n **call, comment, email, language, message** *We will not add comments which use abusive language.*

- and/or **foul, insulting, offensive, threatening, violent** *Any player guilty of using foul and abusive language will be instantly dismissed from the field of play.*

2 involving cruel or violent behaviour

- ADJ+n **behaviour, childhood, conduct, marriage, partner, relationship, situation** *He had a history of violence and of abusive behaviour to women.*
- and/or **controlling, cruel, drunken, neglectful, violent** *She needs help to get away from a violent and abusive relationship.*

academic ADJ
relating to education, especially in colleges and universities

- ADJ+n people **community, department, institution, researcher, staff, tutor** *The college is situated in Bloomsbury, the heart of the academic community in London.*
- ▶ work, achievements, and qualities **achievement, course, discipline, excellence, programme, qualification, research, standards, study, subject, work** *Your CV should clearly set out your skills, experience, academic qualifications and personal details.* ● *Some students do much of their academic work at home using their own computer facilities and so spend less time on campus.*
- ▶ job **career, position, post** *A higher proportion of women hold academic posts at this college than at any other leading U.S. university.*
- ▶ writing **article, journal, paper, publication, writing** *This is a compilation of academic conference papers which explore the relations between critical theory and information technology.*

academic N
teacher at a college or university

- adj+N **distinguished, eminent, leading, prominent, respected, senior, top, world-class** *Astor Visiting Lecturerships provide funding for visits by distinguished academics from the United States for up to one week.*

accelerate V
happen, or make something happen, faster

- adv+V **dramatically, greatly, rapidly, sharply, significantly** *Since Malta's accession to the EU in May 2004, finance sector growth has rapidly accelerated.*
- V+n **decline, development, evolution, expansion, growth, pace, process, progress, rate, trend** *We will use what we have learnt from the inspection process to accelerate the pace of change.*

accent N
pronunciation that shows where someone comes from

- adj+N how strong **broad, heavy, pronounced, slight, strong, thick, unmistakable** *I was served by a woman who spoke English with a very thick accent.*
- ▶ showing where someone is from **foreign, regional, American, English, French etc, northern, southern etc** *Helen calls across to Pat in a broad Scottish*

accent, 'Pat, please turn down the TV'. ● *I dialled the number and a bluff voice with a slight northern accent responded cheerfully.*

- ▶ upper-class **posh** INFORMAL, **upper-class** *With her posh English accent, she isn't quite right in this role.*
- ▶ v+N have or speak with an accent **adopt, do, have, put on, speak in, speak with** *You have a French accent, you cannot deny that.*
- ▶ lose an accent **lose** *His mother hasn't lost her Russian accent.*

accept V
1 take something offered

- adv+V **gladly, graciously, gratefully, reluctantly, willingly** *Contributions will be gratefully accepted.*
- V+n **apology, invitation, offer** *I've accepted her kind offer of hospitality.*

2 agree to or agree with something

- adv+V by all or most people **commonly, generally, universally, widely** *Marketing is a term so widely accepted that we might be tempted to take its meaning for granted.*

Usage **Accept** is almost always passive in these combinations: *It is generally accepted that her work is the most original.*

- ▶ willingly or completely **fully, readily, uncritically** *The City Council readily accepted his objections, and especially when he offered to implement the new design at his own expense.*
- V+n responsibility for something **blame, liability, responsibility** *The trust will not accept responsibility for any loss or damage occurring to vehicles whilst parked on the hospital site.*
- ▶ idea, suggestion, or fact **argument, fact, principle, proposal, recommendation** *The crux of the debate was whether or not to accept the recommendations of the report.*

acceptable ADJ
reasonable or good enough

- adv+ADJ fairly or very **broadly, generally, perfectly, quite** *I believe it's perfectly acceptable to cheat at cooking as long as you don't deceive anyone.*
- ▶ for both people or groups **mutually** *We eventually arrived at a compromise which was mutually acceptable.*
- ▶ from a particular point of view **commercially, culturally, environmentally, ethically, legally, morally, politically, socially** *They want to achieve a change in attitude, so that underage drinking is no longer socially acceptable.*
- v+ADJ **be, become, consider sth, deem sth, find sth, prove, seem** *In the event that a unanimous decision could not be reached, then a majority decision would be considered acceptable.* ● *It remains to be seen if an agreement can be reached that will prove acceptable to both sides.*

acceptance N
1 agreement that something is true or reasonable

- adj+N by many or a growing number of people **broad, general, growing, increasing, public,**

universal, wide, widespread *The technology is now readily available and finding widespread acceptance in the workplace.*
▶ total **unconditional, uncritical, unqualified, unquestioning** *What people often call 'common sense' is the unquestioning acceptance of these notions.*
▶ given unwillingly **grudging, reluctant** *Outright hostility towards the law has been replaced by grudging public acceptance.*
● v+N **achieve, find, gain, win** *None of these proposals has gained acceptance.*

2 agreement to a suggestion or offer
● v+N **confirm, constitute, imply, indicate, show, signify** *Entry into the prize draw implies acceptance of the terms and conditions.*
● N+of **conditions, offer, responsibility, terms** *Contracts should be provided to employees on acceptance of the offer of employment.*

accepted ADJ
which most people consider right or normal
● adv+ADJ **commonly, generally, universally, widely** *The accounting policies contained in the manual follow generally accepted accounting practice for companies.*
● ADJ+n **fact, method, norm, practice, principle, theory, view, wisdom** *It's an accepted fact that memory deteriorates with the passage of time.*

access N
the right or opportunity to have or use something, or the means to go somewhere
● adj+N easily or widely available **direct, easy, free, instant, public, unlimited, unrestricted** *The replaceable screen provides easy access to front panel buttons.*
▶ not allowed **unauthorized** *We protect all customer data against unauthorized access.*
▶ for vehicles or wheelchairs **disabled, vehicular, wheelchair** *The restaurant has full disabled access.*
● v+N have or get access **gain, get, have** *Rabbits must have access to fresh water at all times.*
▶ provide or improve access **afford, allow, enhance, extend, give, grant, improve, provide, widen** *Tenants have an obligation to report repairs and to provide access to allow the work to be carried out.*
▶ prevent or limit access **block, control, deny, limit, prevent, reduce, restrict** *Access is restricted in some parts of the site to registered members only.*

accessible ADJ
1 easy for anyone to obtain and use
● adv+ADJ **freely, publicly, readily, universally, widely** *We aim to make the desired information more readily accessible to the user.*

2 (of a place) easy to find or get to
● adv+ADJ **conveniently, directly, easily, fully, reasonably** *Both airports are conveniently accessible from Miami.* ● *The museum is easily accessible by public transport links or by car.*

accident N
an event or crash that causes damage, injury, or death
● adj+N serious **bad, fatal, horrific, major, nasty, serious, terrible, tragic, unfortunate** *We are working to reduce fatal and serious accidents in Gloucestershire.*
▶ not very serious **minor, non-fatal** *There were scores of minor accidents as vehicles skidded on black ice in the morning rush hour.*
▶ that could be prevented **avoidable, foreseeable, preventable** *Up to a third of all reported medical cases are due to avoidable accidents.*
▶ unusual and unexpected **freak** *He was killed in a freak accident involving a tractor.*
▶ in the home or workplace **domestic, industrial, workplace, work-related** *According to the report, the construction industry suffers from almost 5,000 work-related accidents each year.*
● n+N **automobile, car, cycling, factory, mining, motorcycle, rail, road, road traffic, skiing** *He had a bad car accident a couple of years ago.*
● v+N have an accident **be involved in, have, meet with, suffer, sustain** *Having suffered an unfortunate accident some years ago, Ivan was unable to continue in his career as a chef.*
▶ cause an accident **cause, lead to, result in** *The accident was caused by the driver swerving to avoid a sheep lying dead on the road.*
▶ prevent or try to prevent an accident **avert, avoid, eliminate, minimize, prevent, reduce** *The aim of the plan is to reduce congestion on local roads and minimize accidents.*
● N+v **happen, occur** *More than half of the accidents occur because ladders are not securely placed and fixed.*

accidental ADJ
happening without being planned or intended
● adv+ADJ **almost, completely, entirely, purely** *I can assure you that any omissions are entirely accidental.*
● ADJ+n **breakage, collision, contamination, damage, death, explosion, fire, injury, loss, overdose, spillage** *You are protected against accidental damage, loss or theft for the first 90 days.*

accommodation N
a place where someone stays or lives
● adj+N available for a particular period **emergency, overnight, permanent, temporary** *This is the place to go for further details of the area's visitor attractions and to arrange overnight accommodation.*
▶ types of accommodation **bed-and-breakfast, comfortable, private, rental, rented, residential, self-catering, sheltered, suitable** *The Manor is an ideal place for a conference, offering residential accommodation for up to 60 people.*
▶ cost of accommodation **affordable, budget, cheap, inexpensive, luxurious** *There is a growing need for affordable accommodation in the area.*
● n+N for particlar people **family, graduate, guest, staff, student, tourist, visitor** *The side wing of the*

house offers two separate bedrooms, making it ideal for guest accommodations.

► types of accommodation **bed-and-breakfast, campus, conference, dormitory, holiday, hospital, hotel, office** *Make huge savings on cheap hotel accommodation worldwide.*

● v+N **arrange, book, find, offer, provide, seek** *We offer a range of other services, from finding and booking accommodation to travel insurance and visas.*

accomplish V
succeed in doing something difficult

● adv+V **easily, effectively, quickly, successfully** *There will be more leisure time as more jobs are successfully accomplished by computers.*

● V+n **feat, goal, mission, objective, plan, project, purpose, task** *Each of these tools is used to accomplish a different task.*

accomplished ADJ
very good at doing something

● adv+ADJ **highly, hugely, remarkably, technically, very** *She is a highly accomplished artist.*

● ADJ+n **actor, artist, musician, performer, pianist, player, singer, writer** *Tim is well known locally as an accomplished musician.*

accord N
a formal agreement between countries or groups

● v+N **negotiate, ratify, reach, sign** *As the anniversary passed, 160 states had signed the accord and 63 had ratified it.*

accord V
give someone or something power or respect

● V+n **honour, importance, priority, privilege, protection, recognition, respect, right, status** *He has been accorded near-legendary status in the guitar community.*

account N
1 an arrangement with a bank

● adj+N **checking, current, joint, personal** *Most of our current accounts can be opened online, at a branch or over the phone.*

● n+N **bank, building society, business, credit card, deposit, online, savings** *Check to see if the payment has been deducted from your bank account.*

● v+N **access, close, credit, debit, freeze, manage, open, pay into** *US authorities want to freeze foreign accounts connected with known drug dealers.* ● *We will close the joint account and open an account in the surviving account holder's sole name.*

2 an organization's financial records [always plural]

● adj+N **annual, audited, company** *Your annual accounts have to be filed at Companies House and are available for public inspection.*

● v+N keep or prepare accounts **compile, keep, maintain, prepare** *There is no obligation to prepare*

accounts for the financial period in which a charity ceases to exist.

► make accounts available, publicly or to an official body **file, present, publish, submit** *Under company law, we are obliged to publish our accounts annually.*

► check that accounts are correct **audit, examine, monitor** *We have hired a firm of accountants to audit our accounts and make recommendations for the future.*

3 a report about or description of something

● adj+N **blow-by-blow, brief, detailed, eyewitness, fascinating, first-hand, full** *Sue also offers her first-hand account of what it is like to receive radiotherapy.*

● v+N **give, provide, write** *The possibility of legal proceedings prevented me from providing a detailed account to union officers.*

accountable ADJ
in a position where you must be able to explain your behaviour

● adv+ADJ **democratically, directly, fully, locally, personally, properly, publicly, ultimately** *These reforms would make the criminal justice system directly accountable to the public.*

● v+ADJ **be, become, hold sb, make sb, remain** *Press freedom is a means for holding governments accountable.* ● *However, they remain personally accountable for their decisions.*

● N+for **action, decision, performance** *Now that there is little sense of community for children, they are no longer accountable for their actions.*

● N+to **community, electorate, member, parliament, people, public, shareholder** *In the global economy huge multinationals are only accountable to their shareholders.*

account for PHR VB
be the reason for or explain something

● V+n **change, difference, discrepancy, fact, increase, variation** *Table 4.3 suggests how we might account for seasonal differences in our economic evaluation.*

accumulate V
gradually increase or get more of something

● adv+V **gradually, quickly, rapidly, slowly, steadily** *The fossil remains are believed to have steadily accumulated over thousands of years.*

● V+n money **assets, capital, debt, a fortune, interest, profits, wealth** *The old system of production, based on private property, allowed a minority to accumulate wealth while the majority suffered.*

► knowledge or information **evidence, experience, expertise, knowledge, skill, wisdom** *These reference pages are intended to act as a reference to accumulated wisdom and accepted practice.*

► points **credits, points** *Modules have credit ratings, and students accumulate 120 credits in each year of study.*

● V+over **period, time, years, decades etc** *Your*

greenhouse will probably be full of junk accumulated over recent months.

accuracy N
the quality of being accurate or the ability to be accurate

- adj+N high level of accuracy **absolute, complete, great, high, unerring** It is difficult to quantify the absolute accuracy of the measurements.
- ▶ acceptable or enough **acceptable, reasonable, sufficient** It is difficult to predict with reasonable accuracy which children will develop major problems.
- ▶ types of accuracy **factual, grammatical, historical, scientific, statistical** Every historian worth their salt will tell you that there is no such thing as historical accuracy.
- v+N achieve or improve accuracy **achieve, ensure, guarantee, improve, increase, maintain** Every effort is made to ensure factual accuracy but no responsibility is accepted for the information on these pages.
- ▶ check accuracy **check, confirm, evaluate, measure, monitor, test, verify** He said the BBC had not done enough to check the accuracy of the report before and after it was broadcast.
- ▶ reduce the accuracy of something **compromise, reduce** The management has some concerns with recording information at the end of the shift, which compromises the accuracy of the information being submitted.
- v+with+N **determine, know, measure, predict** I managed to predict with 70% accuracy the winners, just by working out who I felt like supporting.
- n+of+N **degree, level, standard** The age of the universe is a carefully measured number that is now known to a high degree of accuracy.

accurate ADJ
correct or true in every detail

- adv+ADJ very **highly, very** This process offers highly accurate colour reproduction.
- ▶ completely **completely, entirely, perfectly, quite, strictly, totally, wholly** But will the information be entirely accurate?
- ▶ not completely **broadly, fairly, generally, not completely, not entirely, not strictly, not totally, not wholly, pretty** INFORMAL The reports are broadly accurate, though marred by a few errors. ● The picture which Scott painted of Highland life was, however, not entirely accurate.
- ▶ to an acceptable degree **reasonably** He was responsible for providing the first reasonably accurate map of the country.
- ▶ in a particular way **factually, historically, scientifically, technically** This is an enjoyable drama series but it is not historically accurate.
- ▶ in a way that surprises you **amazingly, remarkably, surprisingly, uncannily** His prophecies have turned out to be amazingly accurate.
- ADJ+n information **calculation, data, figure, information, measurement, reading, record** You will have to keep accurate financial records of all transactions.
- ▶ opinion **assessment, diagnosis, estimate, forecast,**

prediction His forecast turned out to be pretty accurate.
- ▶ description **account, depiction, picture, portrayal, reflection, representation** The film, while not the most accurate portrayal of our continent, manages to sum up the general American view of Europe.

accusation N
a claim that someone has done something bad

- adj+N false **baseless, false, groundless, unfounded, unjust, unsubstantiated, untrue** Joan accuses Sonia of making false accusations.
- ▶ serious **serious** That's a very serious accusation you're making.
- ▶ not reasonable **absurd, ludicrous, ridiculous, wild** The desire to find a scapegoat led to wild accusations against foreigners.
- v+N make an accusation **bring, level, make, repeat, throw** Now, who on earth would ever make such an accusation? ● Throwing accusations at each other is not going to help anyone.
- ▶ say an accusation is not true **deny, dismiss, refute, reject** A spokesman for the supermarket denied the accusation of price-fixing that had been levelled at it.
- ▶ take back an accusation **withdraw** She demanded that he withdraw the accusation immediately.
- N+v **fly (around)** The lawsuits and accusations that are flying around are not helping the situation.

accuse V
say that someone has done something wrong

- adv+V wrongly **falsely, unfairly, unjustly, wrongfully, wrongly** Many modern biographies falsely accuse Kipling of racism.
- ▶ in public **openly, publicly** The prime minister publicly accused the organization of inciting unrest.

ache N
a continuous, annoying pain

- adj+N slight **dull, mild, niggling, slight, vague** At first, it was a dull ache, but it gradually worsened and became a sharp pain.
- ▶ continuing for a long time **constant, nagging, persistent** The constant nagging ache made me reach for the painkillers.
- v+N reduce an ache **ease, reduce, relieve, soothe** Massage can help increase circulation and relieve aches.
- ▶ feel an ache **develop, experience, feel, get, have** I have an ache in my shoulder.
- and/or **pains** This website can help with common complaints such as coughs and colds and minor aches and pains.

achieve V
succeed in doing something after trying hard

- adv+V **consistently, easily, fully, successfully** We have now successfully achieved all the targets which we were set at the beginning of the year.
- V+n aim or result **aim, ambition, effect, goal, objective, outcome, result, target** We were more than satisfied that we had achieved our original objectives.

▶ fame **fame, notoriety** *He did not achieve fame until quite late in life.*

▶ success **breakthrough, success, victory** *Customer trust and loyalty are key factors in achieving business success.*

▶ standard **grade, qualifications, standard** *They will be expected to achieve high academic standards as well as developing practical skills.*

▶ position **ranking, status** *Many of these institutions have now achieved university status.*

▶ what is possible **potential** *Our aim is to enable all children to achieve their full potential.*

● V+through **collaboration, co-operation, dialogue, negotiation, participation, partnership** *Wolsey achieved through negotiation what had not been achieved through aggression.*

achievement N

a particular thing that you have achieved; the fact of achieving a particular thing or of being successful in general

● adj+N impressive **amazing, considerable, exceptional, extraordinary, fantastic, great, impressive, major, no mean, notable, outstanding, remarkable, significant, tremendous** *What do you consider are your major achievements?* ● *To do all that before the age of 30 was no mean acheivement.*

▶ most important **crowning, supreme** *This movie is the crowning achievement of the director's career.*

When you are praising something that someone has done successfully, you can use the expression *quite an achievement*: *It's quite an achievement to bring up four children on your own!*

▶ types of achievement **academic, artistic, educational, scholastic, sporting, technical, technological** *His scholastic achievements were not outstanding, although he managed to become sports champion.*

● n+N **business, engineering, research** *Her research achievements were in the field of molecular technology.*

● v+N **acknowledge, celebrate, highlight, honour, mark, recognize, reward** *The International Student Awards are designed to celebrate the achievements of international students studying in the UK.*

acknowledge V

1 accept that something is true or real

● adv+V by many or most people, or in many places **commonly, generally, internationally, universally, widely** *It is widely acknowledged that he is one of the most influential post-war German artists.*

Usage *Acknowledge* is always passive in these combinations.

▶ officially or openly **explicitly, formally, officially, openly, publicly** *They explicitly acknowledged the stress involved in dealing with sick children.*

Usage *Acknowledge* is often passive in these combinations: *It is officially acknowledged as one of the leading research centres in the country.*

▶ without stating it openly **implicitly, tacitly** *The document implicitly acknowledges that no other course of action was possible at the time.*

▶ without hestitation **freely, fully** *She freely acknowledges that much of her success was due to 'being in the right place at the right time'.*

▶ happily **gladly, happily** *He gladly acknowledges his need for help and advice.*

▶ not willingly **grudgingly, reluctantly** *They reluctantly acknowledged that taxes would probably have to rise to pay for the imporvement in services.*

● V+n **difficulty, existence, fact, guilt, importance, influence, mistake, need, responsibility** *I have been assured that the Minister acknowledges the importance of this issue.*

2 tell someone you have received something

● V+n **complaint, letter, receipt** *We hereby acknowledge receipt of your payment.*

3 thank someone for something

● adv+V **gratefully** *We gratefully acknowledge the help of our colleagues in the Computer Science Dept.*

● V+n **achievements, assistance, contribution, generosity, help, support** *The College wishes to acknowledge the generosity of the principal sponsors of the exhibition.*

acquire V

get or develop something

● V+n knowledge or skill **competence, expertise, knowledge, skill, understanding** *Teachers mentioned that such visits enabled them to acquire new skills that they could apply in their classrooms.*

▶ reputation or position **nickname, reputation, status** *Not surprisingly, considering my behaviour, I acquired the nickname 'princess'.*

▶ something that you do or like **habit, taste** *We want people to acquire the habit of using public transport.* ● *He spent some time in Naples, where he acquired a taste for opera.*

You can describe something that you do not like at first, but gradually start to enjoy as an *acquired taste*: *I found the Scottish dish of haggis to be an acquired taste.*

act N

1 a single thing that someone does

● adj+N wrong or illegal **criminal, illegal, immoral, negligent, terrorist, unlawful, wrongful** *She committed a criminal act, but her biggest crime was stupidity.*

▶ very bad **appalling, despicable, heinous, terrible** *Those who carried out these terrible acts were acting as individuals, not on behalf of their country.*

▶ involving force or aggression **barbaric, hostile, violent** *In one hour of television last week over 13 violent acts were shown.*

▶ good **heroic, selfless** *All four soldiers died in selfless acts of sacrifice.*

▶ deliberate **deliberate** *It was not an accident but a deliberate act of violence.*

▶ seeming to have no reason **random, senseless** *The area had suffered random acts of vandalism for a year or more.*

● v+N **carry out, commit, perform, perpetrate** *In*

both those cases, someone else may have committed those acts.

● **N+of** something bad **aggression, cruelty, defiance, disobedience, genocide, revenge, sabotage, terror, terrorism, vandalism, violence** *Furthermore, they carried out acts of terrorism.*
▶ something good **bravery, gallantry, generosity, heroism, kindness** *She is favourably impressed by the act of kindness of a stranger.*

2 a law

● **v+N amend, bring in, contravene, enforce, infringe, introduce, pass, repeal, sign** *Parliament then had to pass an act making it legal to build the railway.*

act V

1 do something for a particular reason; take action

● **adv+V appropriately, decisively, fast, independently, promptly, quickly, swiftly, unilaterally** *We shall review all the evidence and act appropriately in the best interests of all concerned.* • *The Italian authorities had acted quickly once the fraud was discovered.*

● **V+on/upon advice, complaint, evidence, feedback, information, instructions, recommendation, request, suggestion** *Nothing states that Parliament must act upon the recommendations given by the review committee.*

2 behave in a particular way

● **adv+V illegally, impartially, inappropriately, irresponsibly, reasonably, responsibly, strangely, suspiciously, unlawfully, unreasonably** *Police are appealing for any witnesses who may have noticed anyone acting suspiciously in the area on Wednesday 31 May.*

action N

the process of doing something, especially in order to stop a bad situation from developing or continuing

● **adj+N urgent immediate, prompt, swift, urgent** *The EU needs to take urgent action on climate change.*
▶ strong **decisive, effective, positive, strong, tough** *The Council took tough action against people who dumped rubbish.*
▶ involving people working together **concerted** *The report called for concerted action to tackle the problem.*
▶ to prevent or correct something **corrective, preventative, preventive, remedial** *The warning enabled doctors to take preventative action.*
▶ to punish someone **punitive** *The commission has no authority to take punitive action, except for imposing fines.*

● **v+N take action initiate, take, undertake** *The Trust was taking action to prevent racial harassment.*
▶ need or want action **call for, demand, need, require** *More action is needed to tackle the city's housing crisis.*

● **v+into+N** start doing something **come, go, leap,**

spring, swing *The next day the marketing team swung into action.*
▶ make someone do something **force, galvanize, kick, spur** *The government has been forced into action by its defeat in the European Court of Justice.*
▶ make something start being used **put** *These measure were never put into action.*

● **n+of+N course, plan** *Before you decide on a course of action, you need to know the risks involved.*

activity N

1 the fact of people doing something or of something happening

● **adj+N criminal, economic, human, illegal, physical, sexual, terrorist** *Regular physical activity can reduce the risk and severity of conditions such as depression.*

● **v+with+N bustle, buzz** *The main street isn't exactly buzzing with activity these days.*

● **n+of+N burst, flurry, frenzy, level** *Apparently there was a flurry of activity at around five in the morning.* • *Land value changes with time, reflecting the level of general economic activity.*

2 something that you do to achieve an aim, or because it is enjoyable or interesting [usually plural]

● **adj+N** types of activity **creative, criminal, cultural, educational, political, practical, recreational, social, sporting** *Employees should not engage in political activities without express permission from their manager.*
▶ done at a particular time or in a particular place **classroom, day-to-day, everyday, extra-curricular, leisure, outdoor, out-of-school** *The book is full of suggestions for interesting classroom activities.* • *The illness affected her ability to carry out her normal day-to-day activities.* • *The centre offers a wide range of leisure activities.*

● **v+N be involved in, carry out, engage in, indulge in, join in, participate in, undertake** *The types of activities undertaken by mentors and their students have included project work and work shadowing.*

adapt V

1 change your ideas or behaviour in order to deal with a new situation

● **adv+V easily, quickly, readily, successfully, well** *The tigers are adapting well to their new home.*

● **V+to challenge, change, circumstances, climate, conditions, culture, demands, environment, lifestyle, situation, surroundings** *She was not good at adapting to change.*

2 change something in order to make it suitable for a new use of situation.

● **adv+V** easily or successfully **easily, readily, successfully** *The course can be easily adapted to suit levels 3 and 4.*
▶ specially **especially, specially, specifically** *The kitchen and bathroom have been specially adapted for our disabled visitors.*

● V+to **conditions, demands, needs, requirements** *The courses can be adapted to the needs of each individual company.*

adaptable ADJ
able to be used in different situations or for different purposes; able to change your behaviour in order to deal with different situations

● adv+ADJ **easily, extremely, fully, highly, infinitely, readily** *This is a highly adaptable software package that runs independently of the system it monitors.*

● and/or **flexible, resourceful, versatile** *You will need to be flexible and adaptable as things don't always go according to plan.*

● ADJ+to **change, circumstances, needs, range, situation, type, variety** *The system will be flexible and adaptable to the needs of the users.* ● *The building is well planned and adaptable to a wide variety of uses.*

add V
say something more

● adv+V **cryptically, hastily, helpfully, hopefully, ominously, pointedly, quickly, ruefully, thoughtfully, wistfully, wryly** *'Not that I mean he was afraid, of course,' I added hastily.*

added ADJ
present in addition to something else

● ADJ+n good quality or situation **advantage, attraction, benefit, bonus, incentive** *The arrival of the Princess, who spent time talking to the students, was an added bonus and finished off a very exciting day.*
▶ bad quality or situation **burden, complication, disadvantage, poignancy, worry** *After the start of the war they had the added worry of not knowing the fate of the parents they had left behind in their homeland.*

addiction N
a strong need to regularly take a harmful drug or to spend time doing a particular activity

● adj+N **chronic, lifelong, serious** *A lot of people with serious addictions started by taking cannabis.*

● n+N **drug, gambling, nicotine, heroin, alcohol etc** *He spent years struggling with a heroin addiction.*

● v+N cause addiction **cause, lead to** *Gambling can lead to addiction and seriously damage your financial situation.*
▶ fight or deal with addiction **battle, deal with, fight, struggle with** *She is in rehab, battling her addiction to cocaine.*
▶ overcome addiction **beat, break, conquer, cure, kick INFORMAL, overcome** *He has admitted that he needs help in overcoming his addiction.*

addictive ADJ
that you cannot stop doing or taking

● adv+ADJ **completely, dangerously, extremely, highly, horribly, incredibly, powerfully, seriously, strangely, surprisingly, totally INFORMAL, truly** *Nicotine is a highly addictive drug and stopping smoking is not an easy task.* ● *The game is challenging, fun, and strangely addictive.*

addition N
something you add; the act of adding something

● adj+N welcome and useful **excellent, exciting, important, invaluable, significant, useful, valuable, welcome, worthwhile** *The author has produced a valuable addition to the literature in this area.*
▶ made at a particular time **latest, new, recent** *The most recent addition to the building is the installation of air conditioning in all rooms.*
▶ small **minor** *The content of the new article is basically the same as that of the previous one, with a few minor additions.*

● v+N make an addition **make** *No additions can be made to the list once it has been finalized.*
▶ include an addition **include, incorporate, introduce** *Other updates include additions to the website links that are provided.*

address V
try to deal with a problem or question; to discuss something

● adv+V **adequately, directly, effectively, explicitly, fully, satisfactorily, specifically, urgently** *This is an issue we must address urgently.*

● V+n **aspect, challenge, concerns, issue, matter, needs, problem, question, theme, topic** *The paper addresses key aspects of European patent law.* ● *Employers' representatives have made clear their willingness to address concerns raised by the union.*

● v+to-V **aim, fail, seek** *These are some of the questions that this paper seeks to address.*

add to PHR VB
make a feeling, quality, or situation more extreme

● adv+V greatly **considerably, greatly, immeasurably, substantially** *Some of the later modifications to the church add considerably to the building's interest.*
▶ only **merely, only** *Further versions of the document were produced but they merely added to the confusion.*

● V+n positive quality or situation **appeal, attraction, attractiveness, beauty, charm, enjoyment, excitement, fun, pleasure** *A band will be playing throughout the day to add to the fun!*
▶ negative quality or situation **complexity, confusion, problem, woes** *Further storms in the night added to the area's problems.*
▶ atmosphere or feeling **ambience, atmosphere, feel, feeling** *The musical score added to the mysterious feel of the film.*

adequate ADJ
good enough or large enough

● adv+ADJ completely **completely, entirely, fully, perfectly, quite, wholly** *A small suitcase should be perfectly adequate.*

▶ not completely **barely, hardly, not entirely, not wholly** *In many cases, the facilities provided are barely adequate.*

● v+ADJ **be, consider sth, deem sth, prove, seem** *The measures already in place are considered adequate by most experts.* ● *Such a sum should prove adequate for most people's needs.*

● ADJ+for **job, needs, purpose, requirements, task, use** *It is your responsibility to ensure that the insurance cover you purchase is adequate for your particular needs.*

adhere to PHR VB
obey a rule, law or agreement

● adv+V exactly **closely, rigidly, rigorously, scrupulously, strictly, stringently** *Quality standards are set down and strictly adhered to.*
▶ strongly **consistently, faithfully, firmly, religiously, slavishly, steadfastly, strongly** *Maintenance and servicing are also important considerations and should be religiously adhered to.*

● V+n rules or agreements **agreement, guidelines, norms, procedure, protocol, regulations, rules, terms** *Personal supervisors are encouraged to adhere to these guidelines wherever possible.* ● *The unions will ensure that all safety procedures are adhered to and that there will be no risk to the public or employees.*
▶ timetable **deadline, schedule, timescale, timetable** *I should like to stress the importance of adhering to these strict deadlines.*
▶ standard **code, conventions, formula, ideals, principles, standards, tenets** *Rules are best kept to a minimum, but are necessary to ensure we adhere to the highest standards.*

adjourn V
temporarily end something such as a meeting or trial

● V+n **case, debate, hearing, inquest, inquiry, meeting, proceedings, trial** *The trial was adjourned until July 2.*

administer V
1 be responsible for managing the business of an organization, or institution

● V+n **affairs, charity, estate, fund, scheme, trust** *Mr Richards was given responsibility for administering the affairs of the charity.* ● *The council is a registered charity administered by an executive committee.*

2 be responsible for making certain that something is done or provided according to the rules

● V+n **grant, justice, oath, questionnaire, test** *The district council administers house renovation grants.* ● *The courts aim to administer justice as defined by the law.*

3 give someone something

● V+n medicine etc **anaesthetic, antibiotic, dose, drug, first aid, injection, medication, medicine, treatment, vaccine** *Over 100 radiotherapy treatments were administered at the hospital last month.* ● *If the vaccine is administered before infection, it prevents the development of the disease.*

▶ punishment or criticism **beating, caution, punishment, rebuke** *Only the police have the power to administer a caution.*

admirable ADJ
deserving to be admired or respected

● adv+ADJ **particularly, quite, truly, wholly** *The channel's commitment to minority programming is wholly admirable.*

● ADJ+n **aim, attempt, clarity, effort, goal, intention, job, quality, restraint, trait** *He does an admirable job in his first major film role.*

admiration N
a feeling of respect and approval

● adj+N great or very great **boundless, deep, genuine, great, huge, much, profound, tremendous** *She showed a profound admiration for the French education system.*
▶ of many or most people **general, universal** *The new bridge is an object of universal admiration.*
▶ given unwillingly **grudging** *I couldn't help but feel a grudging admiration for what they had achieved.*
▶ of two or more people for each other **mutual** *The two leaders' mutual admiration was evident.*

● v+N have admiration **be filled with, be full of, feel, have** *I was full of admiration for the work the charity did with street children.*
▶ get or deserve someone's admiration **arouse, attract, command, deserve, draw, earn, excite, gain, win** *His ideas and designs drew admiration from all of the experts.*
▶ show admiration **express, show** *In the article he expressed great admiration for the poet's early work.*

● v+in+N **be lost, gasp, gaze, stand, watch** *They gasped in admiration at the view.*

● and/or **affection, awe, envy, gratitude, love, praise, respect, sympathy, thanks, wonder** *She commands the respect and admiration of her fellow council leaders from across Wales.*

admire V
have great respect for someone or something

● adv+V very much **enormously, greatly, hugely, particularly, really** *I have seen and greatly admire the work that the council is doing in this area.*
▶ by all or many people **generally, universally, widely** *As a singer she was universally admired for her highly expressive delivery.*

Usage **Admire** is always passive in these combinations.

admission N
1 permission to join a club or university, or to enter a place

● v+N want or ask for admission **apply for, seek** *To apply for admission to the degree course, you must submit an application form.*
▶ get admission **gain, qualify for** *Season-ticket holders can gain free admission to the game.*
▶ allow admission **grant sb, guarantee (sb)** *Very few asylum seekers are granted admission to the country.*

▶ refuse admission **deny, refuse** *The management reserves the right to refuse admission.*

2 a statement that something is true

● adj+N full and honest **candid, clear, frank, full** *He ended with the candid admission that he did not know what the solution was.*
▶ given unwillingly **grudging** *It was a grudging admission of guilt on the part of the minister.*
▶ not stated directly **implicit, tacit** *The decision is a tacit admission of the failure of the new initiative.*

● v+N **make** *Do not make an admission of guilt before you have contacted a lawyer.*

● N+of **defeat, error, failure, guilt, ignorance, liability, weakness** *This was later interpreted as an admission of guilt.*

admit V

1 agree that something is true or that it exists

● adv+V clearly and willingly **candidly, cheerfully, frankly, freely, happily, openly, readily** *I admitted quite frankly that I did not know much about the case.*
▶ not willingly **grudgingly, reluctantly** *In the end he had to grudgingly admit defeat.*
▶ publicly/not publicly **privately, publicly** *She privately admitted she had been mistaken.*
▶ not directly **tacitly** *The government has tacitly admitted that the official unemployment figures are misleading.*

● V+n **defeat, existence, ignorance, possibility, truth** *He cannot bring himself to admit the truth.*

2 say that you have done something wrong or illegal

● V+n **culpability, error, guilt, liability, manslaughter, mistake, offence** *The teenage killer today admitted manslaughter at a hearing at The Old Bailey.*

adopt V

1 decide to start using an idea, plan, or method

● adv+V by many or most people **generally, universally, widely** *This method has been widely adopted in primary schools.*

Usage **Adopt** is always passive in these combinations.

▶ in a particular area **internationally, nationally** *They proposed that the congestion charge, which had been trialled in London, should be adopted nationally.*

Usage **Adopt** is always passive in these combinations.

▶ with enthusiasm **enthusiastically, with enthusiasm** *Thousands of employees have enthusiastically adopted the new principles.*

● V+n **approach, attitude, measure, method, policy, position, practice, principle, stance, strategy** *It is recommended that a different approach is adopted.*

2 formally accept a proposal, usually by voting

● adv+V **formally, officially, unanimously** *These resolutions were adopted unanimously.*

● V+n **convention, directive, motion, proposal, resolution** *This proposal was adopted by the Commission on 13 June 2000.*

adoption N

1 the process of becoming a child's legal parent

● v+for+N **apply, offer sb, place sb, put sb up** *The new father would then need to apply for adoption and go through the necessary legal steps.* ● *They wanted me to put my baby up for adoption.*

2 the decision to use or accept an idea or method

● adj+N **early, formal, general, rapid, successful, wide, widespread** *We need to assess the impact that widespread adoption of this technology will have on software companies.*

● v+N **consider, encourage, promote, propose, recommend, support** *The study has recommended the adoption of new guidelines.*

advance N

1 progress or an example of progress in science or human knowledge

● adj+N important **considerable, great, huge, important, major, significant, tremendous** *More clinical tests will be necessary before it is clear that the drug represents a major advance.*
▶ types of advance **medical, scientific, technical, technological** *Today we are on the verge of technological advances that will redefine how we wage war.*

● N+in **design, field, genetics, knowledge, medicine, research, science, technique, technology, treatment, understanding** *Advances in medicine mean that the average life expectancy is increasing at a far more rapid rate.*

2 a forward movement towards someone or something

● v+N **block, continue, halt, make, slow, stall, stem, stop** *Reports started to come in that the army had halted its advance.*

3 an attempt to begin a sexual relationship with someone [always plural]

● v+N **make, reject, repel, resist, spurn** *She threatens to report him for making sexual advances to her.*

advance V

1 help something progress and become more developed or successful

● V+n **agenda, career, cause, interest, knowledge, science, understanding** *She was eager to enrol the help of large companies in advancing the environmental agenda.* ● *The Institution plays a major role in advancing public understanding of science.*

2 suggest something for consideration

● V+n **argument, hypothesis, notion, proposition, theory, thesis** *He advanced several theories to account for it.*

advanced ADJ

based on or using the most recent methods or ideas

- adv+ADJ in a particular respect **economically, industrially, politically, scientifically, spiritually, technically, technologically** *The country is usually considered to be less technologically advanced than its neighbours.*
▶ very **extremely, highly** *They have worked closely with the University of Warwick Computer Science Department to develop this new and highly advanced software.*
▶ fairly **fairly, moderately, quite, rather, reasonably, relatively** *Even then they were using some quite advanced technology.*

advantage N
something that makes you more likely to succeed than other people

- adj+N obvious **decisive, definite, distinct, obvious** *The obvious advantage of freeware is that you can try it out as long as you like.*
▶ big **big, considerable, great, huge, major, significant** *One major advantage of digital photography is that the photo can be manipulated readily on the computer.*
▶ extra **added** *You would have the added advantage of meeting people who have some understanding of the subject.*
▶ when you are competing with other people **competitive, tactical** *These new developments are producing opportunities for businesses to gain a competitive advantage.*

- v+N have an advantage **enjoy, have, possess** *The system has some advantages for primary school pupils.*
▶ get an advantage **gain, get, obtain, secure** *Referees must ensure that players do not gain an unfair advantage.*
▶ give an advantage to someone **confer on sb, give sb** *Living in a group confers both advantages and disadvantages.*

If something gives you an advantage, you can also say that it is **to your advantage** to have it or do it

▶ use an advantage **exploit, press home** *We should exploit that advantage before it disappears.*

If you use something because it gives you an advantage, you can also say that you **take advantage of** it

▶ make an advantage less useful **negate, outweigh** *Do the costs involved outweigh the advantages and results?*

- N+over **the competition, competitor, enemy, opponent, rival** *This could give your company a huge advantage over the competition.*

adventure N
an exciting experience

- adj+N amazing **amazing, epic, exciting, great, thrilling, wild** *For me it has been the trip of a lifetime — a truly amazing adventure.*

- v+N tell people about an adventure **chronicle, recount** *A Monkey's Tale recounts the adventures of Kom, a wild monkey living in the jungle.*
▶ begin to have an adventure **begin, embark on, go on, start** *He then embarked on a series of adventures in the remoter areas of Asia.*

▶ want to have adventure **look for, seek** *For those seeking a little more adventure there is canoeing on both these rivers.*

Usage **Adventure** is usually used in the singular and without an article in these combinations: *If you're looking for adventure, you've come to the right place.*

- n+for+N **taste, thirst** *No sailing experience is necessary; all you need is a thirst for adventure and a desire to learn new skills.*

Usage **Adventure** is usually used in the singular and without an article in these combinations: *These holidays will appeal to anyone who has a taste for adventure.*

- n+of+N **sense, spirit** *This is a walk for anyone who is reasonably fit, with a sense of adventure and a love of the English countryside.*

adverse ADJ
negative, unpleasant, or possibly harmful

- ADJ+n effect **consequences, effect, impact, outcome, side-effect** *The replacement of historic features will have an adverse effect on the appearance of the building.*
▶ reaction **reaction** *She had had an adverse reaction to the medication.*
▶ comment **comment, publicity** *This policy has on occasion attracted adverse comments from cinema audiences.*
▶ weather conditions **weather conditions** *Owing to adverse weather conditions, the builders were unable to start work.*

advice N
an opinion about what you should do

- adj+N types of advice **dietary, financial, legal, medical, scientific, technical** *You have the right to ask for medical advice from a doctor at any time.*
▶ fair **impartial, independent, unbiased** *This is a list of organizations that can give you independent advice on your financial affairs.*
▶ from people with special knowledge **expert, professional, specialist** *This is a very complex situation and you need to seek professional advice before making any decision.*
▶ good **good, helpful, invaluable, practical, sound, useful** *Students have access to good information, helpful advice and professional guidance.*

- n+N **business, career, consumer, debt, health, housing, mortgage, safety, tax, travel** *We offer residents basic debt advice.*

- v+N ask for advice **ask for, look for, seek, take** *When should I take professional advice?*
▶ give advice **dispense, give, issue, offer, pass on, provide** *Our consultants offer strategic advice to IT specialists and business managers.*
▶ get advice **get, obtain, receive** *In such cases you should get medical advice.*
▶ accept advice **accept, act on, act upon, follow, heed, listen to, take** *He declined to take their advice, and the situation worsened.*

If you do something because you have accepted someone's advice about it, you can say that you do it **on someone's advice**: *On his advice, she spoke to the manager about it.*

▶ not accept advice **disregard, ignore, reject** *It's my own fault for ignoring your advice.*

If someone tells you not to do something, but you decide not to accept their advice, then you are doing something **against someone's advice**: *You will not be insured if you travel against the advice of your doctor.*

● and/or **assistance, encouragement, guidance, help, information, support** *We will provide confidential encouragement and advice to members.*

adviser N
someone whose job is to give advice

● adj+N giving advice of a particular type **economic, financial, legal, medical, scientific, technical** *As the company's legal adviser, I had all the documents in my care.*
▶ very important **chief, senior, special** *She served for five years as senior adviser to the US chief of staff on health issues.*
● n+N giving advice to the public **business, careers, employment, health, investment, mortgage, safety, tax** *More investment advisers are recommending multi-manager funds to investors.*
▶ giving advice to governments or political organizations **national security, policy** *The comment was made by a senior Green Party policy adviser.*
● v+N **ask, consult, contact, see** *Please contact a qualified financial adviser before making any financial investments.*

advisory ADJ
giving advice

● ADJ+n group **board, body, committee, group, panel, team** *Both parties are guided by relevant advisory committees where necessary.*
▶ job or position **capacity, function, role** *Members of the community were involved in the project in an advisory capacity.*
▶ service **service** *The agency provides partner organisations with advisory services.*

advocate V
support sth publicly

● adv+V **actively, openly, strongly** *We would strongly advocate a review of the proposals.*
● V+n an idea or method **approach, measure, policy, principle, solution, use** *Why do they advocate a policy that is guaranteed to keep the developing world in poverty?*
▶ change **change, reform** *Throughout his political career he has advocated prison reform.*

advocate N
someone giving public support

● adj+N **ardent, enthusiastic, keen, passionate,**

powerful, staunch, strong *He is a passionate advocate for women's sports.*
● N+of **approach, theory, view** *She has always been a strong advocate of the view that smoking should be banned completely.*

affair N
1 events or activities [always plural]

● adj+N relating to politics **current, domestic, foreign, international, national, public, world** *No previous experience of PR is necessary, although an interest in news, current affairs and communications is desirable.*
▶ relating to people or organizations **financial, internal, private** *They should conduct their private affairs so as to minimise the possibility of embarrassment.*
● n+N **business, community, consumer, family, tax** *He is also involved in regional and community affairs.*
● v+N manage affairs **arrange, handle, manage, run** *If your society is a charity, you must help to manage its affairs.*
▶ involve yourself in affairs in an unhelpful way **interfere in, intervene in, meddle in** *America in particular is fond of intervening in the affairs of foreign states.*

2 something that happens in public or political life [usually singular]

● adj+N **family, private** *It was a private affair and I didn't want anybody else to get involved.*
● v+N **deal with, handle, investigate** *I thought he had handled the whole affair extremely well.*

3 a sexual relationship

● adj+N which breaks the trust of your husband or wife **adulterous, extra-marital, passionate, torrid** *He had an extra-marital affair while on holiday in Europe.*
● v+N **begin, have** *The two become intimate and have a passionate affair.*

affect V
change, influence or harm something or someone

● adv+V in a bad way **adversely, badly, deeply, detrimentally, negatively, seriously, severely** *If you felt pain each time you took a step, your quality of life would be severely affected.*
▶ in a major or direct way **directly, greatly, materially, profoundly, significantly** *This national pattern is not significantly affected by local variations.*

affection N
a feeling of liking someone or something

● adj+N **deep, genuine, great, warm** *I remember with great affection the hospitality we received from them.*
● v+N have affection **feel, have** *Toby and Benjamin are opposites and have no affection for each other.*
▶ show affection **demonstrate, display, express, show** *Both men and women show their affection with three kisses on alternate cheeks.*

▸ make other people feel affection towards you **gain, inspire, retain, win** *Professor Blackie soon won the affection of his pupils.*

● N+of **display, expression, mark, outpouring, show, sign** *Parents preferred public displays of affection to be discouraged at school.*

affinity N
a natural feeling of liking and understanding something; a close relationship between two people or things

● adj+N **close, deep, great, natural, particular, special, strong** *Some people say that there is a special affinity between the Welsh and the Irish.*

● v+N have an affinity **feel, have** *The policy also hopes to attract people who have some affinity with the Socialist Party in France.*

▸ show an affinity **demonstrate, display** *Sibelius displayed a strong affinity for music at an early age.*

afternoon N
the time between the middle of the day and the evening

● adj+N described according to the weather conditions **cloudy, hot, rainy, sunny, warm, wet** *The race took place on a hot afternoon in July.*

▸ pleasant **enjoyable, lovely, pleasant, quiet, relaxing** *We enjoyed a relaxing afternoon at one of the many secluded local beaches.*

▸ when you do not do very much **lazy** *She spent a lazy afternoon reading in the garden.*

▸ early/late **early, late, mid** *A series of delays meant that we didn't arrive until late afternoon.*

● N+n sleep **nap, siesta** *We had an afternoon nap in the air-conditioned comfort of our hut.*

▸ food or drink **refreshment, snack, tea** *The Duchess was inviting guests to join her for afternoon tea at 5 o'clock.*

▸ a period of work **briefing, session, workshop** *Afternoon workshops will focus on the difficulties of raising awareness of these problems in schools.*

age N
1 how old someone or something is

● adj+N describing the period of someone's life **advanced, early, middle, old, young** *Her mother had died of a brain tumour at an early age.* ● *The service is aimed at women of middle age and elderly women.*

▸ describing when something is possible or usual **childbearing, marriageable, pensionable, reading, retirement, school-leaving, voting, working** *The offer applies to all men and women of pensionable age.*

● v+N reach an age **approach, attain, get to, live to, reach, survive to** *When the child reached the age of thirteen years, his working life began.*

▸ change the age that someone needs to be **increase, lower, raise** *We hoped that the Government would lower the voting age to 16.*

● and/or **ability, background, ethnicity, gender, nationality, occupation, race, religion, sex, sexuality, sexual orientation** *The course takes into account your child's age and ability.*

2 period of history

● adj+N **bygone, digital, golden, modern** *We're unsure about the long-term future of the music industry in the digital age.*

agenda N
the things that need to be done or thought about

● adj+N relating to a particular area of life **corporate, domestic, political, public, social** *The union is keeping this issue at the top of its political agenda.*

▸ showing particular political opinions **feminist, left-wing, liberal, progressive, right-wing** *The government has various political factions with their own extreme right-wing agendas.*

▸ intended to achieve many things **ambitious, broad, challenging, radical, wide** *The Government has a radical agenda to deliver public services that are not just better than they are now, but truly world-class.*

▸ different **hidden, own** *It is vital that we don't just push our own agenda but actively listen to the needs of those we're seeking to serve.*

● n+N **modernization, policy, reform, research** *These organisations will be key partners in helping to take forward the reform agenda.*

● v+N **advance, deliver, drive, further, have, implement, promote, pursue, push, set** *Parental involvement is an agenda energetically pursued by many schools.*

aggravate V
make something bad become worse

● adv+V **greatly, seriously, severely** *We expect an existing medical condition to be severely aggravated by the physical effects of the work.*

● V+n **condition, injury, pain, problem, situation, symptom** *Changes in temperature may aggravate the symptoms.*

aggression N
1 violent feelings or behaviour

● adj+N using words or actions **physical, verbal** *This is a sign that the customer's verbal aggression is about to become physical.*

▸ expressed strongly **naked** *Here was a moment of sheer, naked aggression.*

● v+N express aggression **display, show** *He suffered hallucinations and displayed aggression as a result of using cocaine.*

▸ not express aggression **control** *He admitted his concern at the player's inability to control his aggression.*

▸ use aggression for another purpose **channel** *Instead of fighting, learn to channel your aggression in a positive way.*

● n+of+N **act** *Acts of aggression against hospital staff are increasingly common.*

● and/or **anger, anxiety, frustration, hostility, violence** *In his therapy sessions James was encouraged to talk about his feelings of aggression and frustration.*

2 the situation when one country attacks another

- adj+N by an army **armed, military** *If a member state is a victim of armed aggression, the other member states can come to its aid.*
▶ started without a reason **unprovoked** *Neutrals saw it as a war of unprovoked aggression.*

- v+N take action against aggression **deter, oppose, resist, stop** *We shall resist all aggression against our territory.*
▶ use aggression **commit, launch** *They have stated that they do not intend to use nuclear weapons to commit aggression.*

- n+of+N **act** *They considered it to be a blatant act of colonialist aggression and occupation.*

agony N
great pain or other unpleasant feelings

- adj+N **absolute, excruciating, great, sheer, terrible** *The pain can vary from mild discomfort to excruciating agony.*

- v+N experience agony **endure, experience, feel, go through, suffer** *For several days she had to go through the agony of not knowing if he was dead or alive.*

> If someone is feeling great pain, you can say that they are *in agony*: This latest injury has left him in agony.

▶ make agony last longer **prolong** *Tell me the worst, why prolong the agony?*

- v+in+N **die, scream, writhe** *Another lad from the ship was screaming in agony because of his terrible burns.*

agree V
1 have the same opinion as someone else

- adv+V completely **absolutely, completely, entirely, quite, totally, wholeheartedly** *I entirely agree with your comments.*
▶ strongly **heartily, strongly** *I described the situation to her and she strongly agreed with our decision.*
▶ to some extent **broadly, largely** *The board largely agreed that changes were inevitable.*
▶ when many people agree **generally, widely** *It is generally agreed that childhood obesity is caused by poor diet.*
▶ when everyone agrees **unanimously** *They unanimously agreed that it had been the right thing to do.*

2 say that you will do what someone suggests or asks

- adv+V when everyone agrees **unanimously** *After a detailed discussion, councillors unanimously agreed to support the proposal.*
▶ without enthusiasm **reluctantly** *The British reluctantly agreed to join in the campaign.*
▶ with enthusiasm **happily, readily** *The company readily agreed to refund the full purchase price.*
▶ kindly **kindly** *Mrs Thomas has kindly agreed to organize next month's meeting.*

3 decide together that something will be done

- V+n plan **arrangement, objective, plan, priority, target** *The new arrangements were agreed at a meeting on 10 November.*

▶ time **date, timescale, timetable** *The work was completed within the timescale that had been agreed.*
▶ conditions **criterion, standard, terms** *It proved very difficult to agree terms for the new project.*
▶ money **budget, fee, price** *They agreed a fee in advance.*
▶ deal **deal** *A deal was agreed soon afterwards.*

agreement N
1 an arrangement about what to do made by two or more people or groups

- adj+N with legal force **binding, contractual, formal, written** *Partner sites will be asked to sign a formal agreement regarding their participation.*
▶ involving or affecting several groups **bilateral, collective, international, multilateral, reciprocal** *In reality, most developing countries have signed up to multilateral environmental agreements.*
▶ made by people before they get married **pre-nuptial** *The increasing incidence of divorce has led to the popularity of pre-nuptial agreements.*
▶ secret **tacit** *There was apparently a tacit agreement to end their opposition to the government's plans.*

- n+N **confidentiality, franchise, licence, licensing, partnership, peace, tenancy, trade** *After intermittent internal fighting a peace agreement was finally signed in 1988.*

- v+N make or arrange an agreement **broker, come to, conclude, enter into, finalize, negotiate, reach, secure** *The failure to come to an agreement was extremely regrettable.*
▶ give an agreement legal force **ratify, sign** *The company has signed an agreement to introduce its technology into Africa and the Caribbean.*
▶ end an agreement **cancel, terminate** *The old rules unfairly prevented the consumer from cancelling the agreement.*
▶ break an agreement **breach, break, go back on, violate** *The troops moved south, breaching the agreement which had been negotiated.*
▶ prepare an agreement in written form **draft** *We give advice on preparing all types of contracts, including drafting informal agreements.*
▶ formally tell people about an agreement **announce** *I'm confident we will soon be in a position to announce an agreement between the club, the landowner and the developer.*
▶ keep to an agreement **abide by, adhere to, comply with, honour, keep to** *We sincerely hope the Government will honour this agreement.*

- N+v begin **come into force** *The agreement will come into force in the next financial year.*
▶ end **expire, terminate** *The present agreement expires in June.*
▶ refer to or include something **concern, cover, relate to, state, stipulate** *Additional agreements covering Canada and Japan are expected to follow.*
▶ make something possible **allow, permit** *The agreement permitted most forms of tobacco advertising except on TV and radio.*

2 a situation when people have same opinion

- adj+N **broad, general, mutual, unanimous** *There appeared to be general agreement on the need for changes to the system.*

If people have the same opinion, you can also say that they are **in agreement**: *All the team is in agreement that the system needs a few alterations.*

aid N

1 money, food etc that is given to help people after a war, flood etc

- adj+N **economic, emergency, foreign, humanitarian, international, medical, overseas** *The number of people seriously affected by the flooding was about two million, around half of whom require emergency food aid.*

- v+N give aid **deliver, give, grant, provide** *The programme was established to provide humanitarian aid to migrants.*
- ▸ increase aid **double, increase** *The EU has also agreed to double its aid to Africa in the next 10 years.*
- ▸ ask for aid **appeal for, apply for, ask for, call for, seek** *They called for humanitarian aid for the earthquake victims.*
- ▸ need aid **depend on, rely on** *The country relies heavily on foreign aid.*

- N+n **agency, budget, convoy, donor, package, worker** *Aid agencies say 6,500 Africans die of preventable diseases daily.*

2 help with doing something

- v+N ask for aid **enlist, seek** *The major method of collection was to enlist the aid of school children.*

If someone gives you help, you can say that they **come to your aid** or **go to your aid** *They have come to the aid of those who needed help.*

3 something that makes it easier to do something

- adj+N **audio-visual, navigational, visual** *It is also a subject that lends itself beautifully to the use of visual aids, including art and videos.*

- n+N **buoyancy, hearing, mobility, navigation, revision, teaching** *Modern navigation aids, particularly radar and the satellite navigator, have diminished the need for the lighthouse.*

AIDS N

a disease that destroys the body's ability to defend itself against infection

- adj+N **full-blown** *Not all those who test positive for HIV go on to develop full-blown AIDS.*

- v+N **be infected with, contract, die of, live with, suffer from** *The hospice cares for children of all ages, all of whom are suffering from AIDS.*

- N+n **awareness, charity, epidemic, orphan, patient** *The singer will donate all future royalties from his singles to AIDS charities.*

- n+against+N **battle, fight** *The UK Government is committed to the fight against AIDS.*

ailment N

an illness, usually not a serious one

- adj+N common **common, everyday** *They have a wide range of products to treat everyday ailments.*
- ▸ serious **chronic, serious** *Elderly drivers often hide*

serious medical ailments in order to retain their driving licences.

- ▸ not serious **minor** *Minor ailments can often be treated without the patient needing to consult a doctor.*

- n+N affecting a particular part of the body **heart, kidney, respiratory, skin, stomach** *They all suffer from respiratory ailments which they blame on air pollution.*

- v+N have an ailment **have, suffer from** *Several of the troops suffered from minor tropical ailments.*
- ▸ make sb have an ailment **cause** *These ailments can be caused by too much sun.*
- ▸ treat an ailment **alleviate, cure, heal, relieve, treat** *The hospital can treat their ailments but not their spiritual needs.*

aim N

the thing that you hope to achieve

- adj+N most important **key, main, overarching, overriding, primary, principal, specific** *The overarching aims of the unit are to reduce crime and the fear of crime in the capital.*
- ▸ first **immediate, initial** *Our immediate aim is to stop the project going ahead.*
- ▸ final **eventual, long-term, ultimate** *The key long-term aim is for the project to be implemented nationally.*
- ▸ stated **avowed, express, stated** *The stated aim of the reforms was to reduce the number of children living in poverty.*
- ▸ good **laudable, legitimate** *I am sure you will agree that this is a very laudable aim: protecting vulnerable people.*
- ▸ general **broad, overall** *He outlined the broad aims of the new procedures.*
- ▸ only **only, sole** *Her sole aim seemed to be to make life difficult for me.*

- v+N achieve an aim **accomplish, achieve, fulfil, meet, realize** *The school has realized its aim of producing students who can make a positive contribution to the community.*
- ▸ help someone achieve an aim **further** *These funds will be used to further the aims of the club.*
- ▸ try to achieve an aim **pursue** *This will assist young people to overcome barriers they face whilst pursuing their personal aims.*
- ▸ describe an aim **clarify, declare, outline, state** *The business plan outlines our strategic aims for the next five years.*

- and/or **ambition, aspiration, goal, objective, outcome, principle, priority, purpose, value** *What are your club's aims and aspirations for the season ahead?*

aim V

intend sth for a particular purpose or group

- adv+V **directly, mainly, particularly, primarily, principally, specifically, squarely** *The course is particularly aimed at those with little coaching experience.*

Usage **Aim** is almost always passive in this meaning: *These conferences are aimed specifically at postgraduate UK researchers.*

air N

1 the mixture of gases that we breathe

- adj+N outside **fresh, open** *It felt good to be out in the open air, enjoying the sunshine.*
- ▶ hot/cold **cold, cool, hot, warm** *They went for a walk in the cool night air.*
- ▶ slightly wet **humid, moist** *As temperatures drop, the moist air condenses into fog.*
- ▶ unpleasant **polluted, stale** *She wanted freedom, an escape from the stale air and the darkness of this room.*
- ▶ pleasant **clean** *After enjoying the clean air of the hills, we crossed the green valley below.*
- ▶ with no wind **still** *The sound of the bird's call travels smoothly in the still air.*
- v+N take air into your body **breathe, inhale, sniff** *I want to see the moon and breathe the evening air.*
- ▶ try and get air **fight for, gasp for** *He was fighting for air as he surfaced out of the water.*
- ▶ move air **blow, expel, pump, suck** *First of all you need to expel all the air from the system.*
- ▶ make air dirty **pollute** *If you're smoking, you're damaging your health and polluting the air.*
- ▶ make air clean **purify** *Some oils actually inhibit airborne bacteria, thus purifying the air in a sickroom.*
- v+in+N **float, fly, hover, stay** *Most of the reports agree that two bright lights appeared close together, hovered in the air for a time, and then rapidly disappeared.*

2 a feeling, atmosphere or attitude

- N+of a strange or unpleasant quality **desperation, menace, unreality** *In this latest novel, there is an air of menace and anxiety from the first page.*
- ▶ an exciting quality **anticipation, excitement, mystery** *It seems there is an air of mystery about the place that attracts them.*
- ▶ an impressive or pleasant quality **calm, confidence, elegance, optimism, respectability, sophistication, superiority** *The town is extremely pleasant and everything has an air of respectable elegance.*

aircraft N

a plane, helicopter etc

- adj+N types of aircraft **cargo, combat, commercial, fighter, jet, military, passenger, transport** *This part of the airport is only used for passenger aircraft.*
- v+N control an aircraft **fly, operate, pilot** *My personal ambition in life is to learn to fly an aircraft.*
- ▶ get onto an aircraft **board** *I finally boarded the aircraft just before midnight and began the long journey home.*
- N+n **engine, factory, hangar, noise** *Hundreds of residents have complained about aircraft noise.*

alarm N

1 fear or worry that something unpleasant or dangerous might happen

- adj+N **undue, unnecessary** *The result, while disappointing, should not be the cause of undue alarm.*

- v+N **cause, express** *Parents obsessed with 'healthy eating' are also causing alarm as their children can grow up feeling guilty about food.*
- n+of+N **cry, feeling, state** *The state of alarm was heightened by every bombing raid.*

2 electrical equipment that makes a sound to warn people

- n+N **attack, burglar, car, emergency, fire, intruder, panic, security, smoke** *The site is fitted with CCTV cameras and intruder alarms.*
- v+N put an alarm in a place **fit, install** *Fit good-quality locks to the windows and doors and install a burglar alarm.*
- ▶ make an alarm ready to work **reset, set** *Don't forget to set the alarm when you leave the house.*
- ▶ cause an alarm to work **activate, trigger** *Steam from irons can trigger your smoke alarm.*
- N+v **go off, ring, sound** *Staff rushed to her room at 9 pm after an alarm had sounded.*

3 warning of danger

- adj+N **false** *The fire service was called to the scene but luckily it was a false alarm.*
- v+N **raise, sound** *A passer-by raised the alarm when he saw smoke coming from the windows of the house.*

alert ADJ

aware of what is happening

- adv+ADJ **constantly, fully, mentally** *All participants must be physically fit and mentally alert.*
- v+ADJ **be, remain, stay** *Officers should remain alert to suspicious objects or individuals within the airport building.*
- ADJ+to **change, danger, fact, needs, possibility, problem, risk, sign** *It is therefore vital that you are alert to such dangers and act accordingly.*

alert N

a warning about something dangerous; a situation when something dangerous could happen

- adj+N **full, high** *After the bomb threats police in the area were put on high alert.*
- n+N **bomb, flood, security, terror, virus** *Several rivers in South Wales were on flood alert.*
- v+N **declare, issue, raise, send, sound** *The alert was declared after amounts of harmful ozone rose almost three times above the highest level considered acceptable by other countries.*
- n+of+N **state** *It had been raining solidly for days and the country was in a state of alert.*

allegation N

statement accusing someone of something bad

- adj+N definitely/possibly not true **baseless, false, unfounded, unproven, unsubstantiated, untrue** *The report contained nothing but unsubstantiated allegations and hearsay.*
- ▶ causing or intending great harm **damaging, defamatory, malicious** *The media should not be*

repeating these highly damaging allegations **about** my client.
▶ serious **serious** *Serious allegations had been made* **against** *medical staff.*

● v+N say or write an allegation **make, repeat** *He made allegations to the police that one of their officers had kicked him.*
▶ say an allegation is not true **contest, deny, dismiss, dispute, rebut, refute, reject** *The Government denies allegations of a secret deal with the industry.*
▶ take back an allegation **retract, withdraw** *Following protests by the workers, the newspaper retracted the allegations.*
▶ check if an allegation is true **investigate** *The police are investigating an allegation of assault on him by a prison officer.*
▶ show or suggest that an allegation is true **prove, substantiate, support** *The company has given the group 14 days to substantiate its allegations.*
▶ have an allegation made against you **face** *The Minister faces allegations that he accepted money in return for his support.*

allege V
claim that something bad has been done

● V+n **abuse, breach, discrimination, fraud, infringement, misconduct, negligence, violation** *The family sued the education authority alleging negligence on the school trip.*

alleged ADJ
claimed but not proved

● ADJ+n something wrong **abuse, assault, breach, conspiracy, crime, fraud, incident, infringement, misconduct, offence, plot, rape, violation** *He is empowered to investigate alleged breaches of the guidelines by the departments listed.*
▶ someone doing something wrong **criminal, harasser, infringer, offender, perpetrator, terrorist** *The alleged offender was not known to the victim.*

alleviate V
make something less painful, severe, or serious

● adv+V **greatly, partially, somewhat** *I have often been able to put my patients at their ease and to dispel or partially alleviate their fears.*
● V+n pain or illness **hunger, pain, suffering, symptoms** *Hot drinks and lots of rest can sometimes alleviate the suffering associated with a cold.*
▶ negative emotion **anxiety, boredom, concern, depression, distress, fear, stress** *A change in routine also alleviates boredom, thereby also reducing psychological fatigue.*
▶ problem or bad situation **burden, congestion, flooding, hardship, plight, poverty, pressure, problem, shortage, unemployment** *This lack of investment in physical activity will do little to alleviate the problems of obesity and poor health.*

alliance N
an arrangement between people, groups, or countries to work together

● adj+N close or successful **close, collaborative, effective, strong, successful** *The government has*

tried to establish a close alliance with different aspects of industry.
▶ weak or not close **broad, loose, uneasy** *They formed an uneasy alliance with other left-wing groups.*
▶ involving unexpected partners **unholy, unlikely** *Opposition to the new law created an unlikely alliance of left-wing activists and Islamic conservatives.*
▶ types of alliance **commercial, defensive, electoral, global, military, political, strategic, tactical** *Security cannot be guaranteed by an increase in arms, nor by military alliances.*

● v+N make an alliance **build, create, enter into, establish, forge, form, make** *Our ability to forge strong alliances gives us a competitive edge.*
▶ make an alliance stronger or bigger **cement, join, strengthen** *These wars helped to strengthen the alliance between the two countries.*

allocate V
officially provide something for a specific purpose

● adv+V **appropriately, fairly, randomly, specifically** *These patients were randomly allocated to one of three groups.*
● V+n money **budget, funding, funds, grant, money, resources, sum** *The Council will allocate an annual budget towards the direct costs of the group's work.*
▶ something of which there is a limited amount **accommodation, land, parking, place, quota, resources, seat, slot, space, ticket, time** *The apartment has single garage plus an allocated parking space.*
▶ person in charge **mentor, supervisor, tutor** *Each student is allocated a personal tutor.*

ally N
a country, organization, or person ready to help you

● adj+N loyal and reliable **close, faithful, firm, loyal, reliable, staunch** *Back in Normandy, Odo became a staunch ally of his nephew, Duke Robert.*
▶ not reliable **unreliable** *They were to prove unreliable allies.*
▶ powerful **key, powerful, strong, valuable** *Our powerful allies are the general public and their growing awareness of the issues.*
▶ previous **erstwhile, former** *The country's attack on its erstwhile allies met with little success.*
▶ how likely **natural, potential, unlikely** *Are there any events or conferences locally where potential allies are likely to be present?*
▶ types of ally **coalition, diplomatic, political, regional, strategic, wartime** *Friendships with the country's diplomatic allies have been consolidated through various official visits.*

● v+N gain an ally **enlist, find, gain, recruit, seek** *The campaign to oppose the airport has gained an unlikely new ally in the form of a former airline boss.*
▶ lose an ally **alienate, betray, lose** *The government says it cannot afford to alienate its most important ally.*
▶ be or become an ally **be, become, prove, remain** *When the two countries were invaded they became allies overnight.*

- N+in **battle, bid, campaign, cause, effort, fight, quest, struggle, war** *They were our key allies in the struggle for better working conditions.*

alter V
make or become different

- adv+V a lot **completely, considerably, dramatically, drastically, extensively, fundamentally, greatly, profoundly, radically, significantly, substantially** *The outside of the church was also radically altered.*
▸ a little **slightly, subtly** *The design was altered slightly from that of the original.*
▸ permanently **forever, irrevocably, permanently** *They arrived just in time to record the landscapes and cultures that would soon be irrevocably altered.*
▸ in a particular way **chemically, genetically, materially, surgically** *You chemically alter the molecules of vegetable oils so that a less viscous product is made: biodiesel.*

alternative N
another possible choice

- adj+N possible **feasible, possible, sustainable, viable, workable** *The method could transform the nuclear energy industry and offer a viable alternative to fossil fuels.*
▸ cheap **cheap, cost-effective, low-cost** *Biking to work is a cheap alternative to going to the gym!*
▸ real **credible, genuine, real, realistic** *So far no credible political alternative to the traditional political parties has emerged.*
▸ good **acceptable, attractive, convenient, effective, healthy, safe, suitable** *This problem has been compounded by the lack of investment in attractive alternatives to car usage.*
▸ extreme **radical** *They have tried to copy the policies of the other two parties rather than offer any radical alternative.*

- v+N provide **offer, present, provide** *The software package offers a viable alternative to competing versions.*
▸ consider **consider, examine, explore, look at, look into** *All manufacturers offer this option, and the majority of customers consider both alternatives.*
▸ look for **develop, find, look for, seek** *This has led scientists to seek less dangerous alternatives.*
▸ suggest **discuss, propose, suggest** *We only offer quality products and will, where possible, suggest suitable alternatives for discontinued components.*

alternative ADJ
1 different but able to be used instead

- ADJ+n method **approach, arrangement, means, method, option, scenario, solution, strategy, suggestion, way** *They will phone you back to discuss what alternative arrangements are available for your own situation.*
▸ way to understand something **explanation, hypothesis, interpretation, view, viewpoint** *He denied that any of these errors had come about deliberately and supplied alternative explanations for them.*

2 different from the conventional type

- ADJ+n **energy, fuel, lifestyle, medicine, remedy, source, therapy, treatment** *We are converting more of the city's fleet to alternative fuels.*

amazing ADJ
very surprising or impressive

- adv+ADJ **absolutely, just, pretty** INFORMAL, **quite, really, simply, so** INFORMAL, **totally** INFORMAL, **truly, utterly** *It's very powerful, very fast and can produce some pretty amazing graphics and sound.* • *Plants are truly amazing and this show explains why.*

ambiguity N
when something has more than one possible meaning

- adj+N basic or essential **deliberate, inherent, systematic** *Some authors indulge in deliberate ambiguity.*
▸ possible **possible, potential** *Any potential ambiguities were resolved with reference to the new guidelines.*
▸ in language **lexical, linguistic, semantic, syntactic** *Another source of syntactic ambiguity is where whole phrases can attach to more than one position in a sentence.*

- v+N cause or increase ambiguity **cause, create, introduce, lead to** *This gives us a more complete document to work with, causing less ambiguity.*
▸ reduce ambiguity **avoid, clarify, eliminate, minimize, reduce, remove, resolve** *Parentheses are used to resolve ambiguities.*
▸ show where ambiguity exists **highlight, identify, reveal** *In some ways the question highlights an inherent ambiguity in his position.*

- n+of+N **amount, degree, element** *The official forecasts of emissions from the transport sector are characterised by a degree of ambiguity and imprecision.*

- and/or **ambivalence, complexity, confusion, contradiction, inconsistency, uncertainty, vagueness** *Avoid ambiguity and confusion in the message you are trying to get over.*

ambiguous ADJ
having more than one possible meaning or difficult to understand

- adv+ADJ rather **potentially, rather, slightly, somewhat** *Ownership of the rights to such material is somewhat ambiguous.*
▸ very **deeply, highly** *Society's attitudes in this regard are highly ambiguous.*
▸ intentionally **deliberately, intentionally** *The word he chooses here is deliberately ambiguous.*
▸ in a particular way **morally, politically, sexually** *His characters are often morally ambiguous.*

- ADJ+n words or language **meaning, phrase, sentence, statement, term, word, wording** *What does its ambiguous wording most probably mean?*
▸ situation **ending, relationship, situation, status** *I'd have preferred a much more ambiguous ending, one in which the future of the world was much more in doubt.*
▸ person or character **character, figure, role** *Padre Pio is an ambiguous figure in the history of the Church.*

▶ information **evidence, findings, results** *The results of the survey were ambiguous, and failed to support our original hypothesis.*

● and/or **complex, confusing, contradictory, obscure, uncertain, unclear, vague** *He feels that many of their requirements were ambiguous and vague.*

ambition N
something that you want to achieve

● adj+N lasting a long time **childhood, lifelong, lifetime, long-held, long-term, ultimate** *His lifelong ambition was to fly a plane.*

▶ quality of ambition **burning, lofty, selfish, unfulfilled** *Perhaps you have unfulfilled ambitions or feel that you are stuck in a rut?*

▶ types of ambition **career, imperial, literary, nuclear, personal, political, territorial** *The course offers a choice of subject pathways to suit a wide range of career ambitions.*

● v+N succeed in an ambition **achieve, fulfil, realize, realize, satisfy** *To realize our ambition, we must develop and sustain a regard for learning at whatever age.*

▶ have an ambition **harbour, have** *Seeing the way the US and Britain attach importance to their nuclear weapons how can we expect other countries not to harbour their own nuclear ambitions?*

▶ block someone's ambition **frustrate, thwart** *It will embolden those who are trying to thwart the ambitions of reformers.*

▶ try to achieve an ambition **further, pursue** *A strong financial position allows us to pursue our ambitions by making the appropriate investments.*

▶ not have any ambition **abandon, lack** *She's young and sophisticated, but thinks her life lacks any real ambition or direction.*

● and/or hopes **aims, aspirations, desires, dreams, goals, hopes** *We believe it is essential to fully understand not only the skills of applicants but also their ambitions and aspirations.*

> Usage ***Ambition*** is usually plural in these combinations.

▶ a positive quality **creativity, determination, drive, enthusiasm, talent, vision** *She loves dealing with people, and has the drive, ambition, and discipline to manage the business and its employees.*

ambitious ADJ
determined to be successful, or needing determination to succeed

● adv+ADJ very **extraordinarily, extremely, highly, hugely, over, overly, too, very, wildly** *The story contained ideas that were once regarded as overly ambitious.*

▶ willing to harm others for your goal **fiercely, ruthlessly** *Underneath his charm and relaxed manner he's ruthlessly ambitious.*

▶ in a particular way **artistically, intellectually, politically, socially** *We are delighted to congratulate this artistically ambitious company on their 21st birthday.*

● ADJ+n project **attempt, initiative, plan, programme, project, proposal, scheme, strategy,**

undertaking, venture *There are ambitious plans to improve facilities at the hospital, some of which are already underway.*

▶ goal **agenda, aim, goal, objective, target, vision** *To achieve an increase in dentist numbers, the Department has set ambitious targets for increasing capacity.*

amend V
make changes to a document or agreement

● V+n **bill, clause, constitution, directive, law, legislation, proposal, regulation, rule** *All motions put forward in the ballot to amend the constitution were carried unanimously.*

amendment N
a change made to a law, agreement, or document

● adj+N major **key, radical, significant, substantial, substantive** *The Energy Bill has completed its committee stage in Congress, with very few substantive amendments.*

▶ minor **minor, slight** *You should therefore be aware that the attached literature may be subject to minor amendments prior to the launch date.*

▶ additional **additional, consequent, further, subsequent** *This decision is made in accordance with the 1997 Education Act and subsequent amendments.*

▶ to the law **constitutional, legislative** *Each constitutional amendment dealt only with specific issues, rather than the Constitution in its totality.*

▶ not final **draft** *The party primarily opposes three aspects of the draft amendment.*

● v+N suggest or support **back, draft, introduce, propose, submit, suggest, support, table** *The bill needs three kinds of safeguard, and I have tabled amendments on three things.*

▶ make **accept, adopt, agree, approve, make, pass** *The Committee examines the bill line by line and can make amendments.*

▶ oppose or stop **defeat, oppose, reject** *For those reasons, I would urge Parliament to reject the amendment.*

▶ need **require** *Early estimates suggest that more than twenty major provisions may require significant amendment.*

● N+to **bill, clause, constitution, directive, draft, law, legislation, motion, regulation, rule** *The bill provides for unknown and unlimited future amendments to the constitution.*

amnesty N
a period in which people who have committed a crime are not punished, or illegal objects can be handed to someone in authority

● adj+N **general, nationwide** *They declared a general amnesty for all political prisoners.*

● n+N **firearms, gun, knife, weapon** *Anyone with an illegal knife or other offensive weapon will be able to hand it in to police without fear of prosecution during a five-week amnesty this summer.*

● v+N **announce, declare, give, grant, offer** *Thus the rebels were able to negotiate good terms and were finally granted an amnesty.*

amount N

a quantity of something, especially money

● adj+N very large **copious, enormous, huge, immense, large, massive, staggering, tremendous, vast** *There was a huge amount of excellent feedback.*
▶ too large **disproportionate, excessive, inordinate, ridiculous** *The job was extremely tedious and took an inordinate amount of time.*
▶ rather large **certain, considerable, fair, significant, substantial** *The task involved a considerable amount of reading, and qualitative analysis.*
▶ small **limited, moderate, reasonable, small, tiny** *The gunman escaped with a small amount of cash.*
▶ equal **equal, equivalent, same** *This album is sure to receive an equal amount of praise.*
▶ at the limit **maximum, minimum** *The large windows ensure that the room receives the maximum amount of light.*
▶ correct **correct, recommended, right, specified** *It is important that children should get the right amount of sleep.*
▶ total **total** *This new facility brings the total amount of storage managed by the company to 150,000 square metres.*

● v+N reduce or limit an amount **decrease, deduct, exceed, fix, limit, minimize, reduce, save** *Medication reduces the amount of work that the heart performs, lowering pressure on the heart and improving pumping ability.*
▶ increase an amount **double, increase** *You need to increase the amount of exercise you take.*
▶ spend or use up an amount **consume, invest, pay, repay, spend** *They wrote telling him that and saying that must pay the amount within seven days.*
▶ borrow an amount **borrow** *If you want to borrow a substantial amount you could consider taking out a cheap personal loan.*
▶ calculate an amount **calculate, determine, estimate, measure** *Using a positive value lets you determine the amount of background light that will always pass through the atmosphere, regardless of its thickness.*

ample ADJ

enough, and often more than you need

● ADJ+n space **accommodation, parking, room, seating, space, storage** *Ample car parking lies within a few steps of the pedestrianised shopping centre.*
▶ opportunity **chance, opportunity, scope** *The sea also provides ample opportunity for the amateur fisherman.*
▶ evidence **evidence, justification, proof, testimony** *There is ample evidence to prove his guilt.*
▶ amount **amount, capacity, quantity, supply** *The area was a major centre for brewing thanks to its ample supplies of good quality water plus the proximity of the large market in London.*

amused ADJ

entertained or interested by something

● adv+ADJ **easily, faintly, highly, mildly, rather** *He sounded faintly amused.*
● ADJ+n expression **expression, eye, glance, look, smile, voice** *He looked up at her again and he found she was regarding him with an amused smile.*

▶ reaction or attitude **condescension, contempt, surprise, tolerance** *I believe the only valid response to behaviour like that is to treat it with amused contempt.*
● v+ADJ **be, keep (sb), look, seem** *We had two teenagers with us to keep amused.* ● *Looking amused, they nodded and went back to their conversation.*

amusing ADJ

funny or entertaining

● adv+ADJ rather **faintly, mildly, moderately, quite, rather, slightly, somewhat, vaguely** *She is given the film's best, though only mildly amusing, joke.*
▶ very **extremely, highly, particularly, very** *There's a highly amusing talk show, where various people talk with members of the public on a range of different topics.*
▶ in a particular way **genuinely, unintentionally, wryly** *The play contained some genuinely amusing dialogue.*
● ADJ+n **anecdote, comment, conversation, incident, scene, story, tale** *If you have any unusual stories or amusing anecdotes, then I want to hear from you urgently.*
● v+ADJ **be, find sb/sth, prove, sound** *I didn't find it very amusing listening to their comments.* ● *It's a story which will no doubt prove amusing to readers of a certain age.*

anaesthetic N

a drug or gas that stops you feeling pain

● adj+N **epidural, general, local, spinal** *The device is implanted under general anaesthetic,*
● v+N give someone an anaesthetic **administer, give, inject, use** *Before treatment, a local anaesthetic is injected into the gum.*
▶ receive an anaesthetic **have, undergo** *When you are undergoing a general anaesthetic your life is in the anaesthetist's hands.*

analogy N

a comparison showing that two things are similar

● adj+N good **appropriate, apt, close, exact, good, helpful, interesting, obvious, perfect, simple, useful** *A more apt analogy would be an aquarium or a zoo: a place for special trips.*
▶ poor **crude, false, imperfect, inappropriate** *The analogy is false, and this misunderstanding can have consequences for the interpretation of the data.*
● v+N make an analogy **draw, employ, make, use** *He drew frequent analogies between Greek literature and modern poetry.*
▶ provide an analogy **propose, provide, suggest** *The name is intended to suggest an analogy with a car engine.*
▶ take an analogy further **continue, extend, press, pursue, stretch** *I won't pursue the analogy but you get the general idea.*

analyse V

study something in order to explain it or find out what it contains

● adv+V carefully **accurately, carefully,**

exhaustively, in depth, in detail, properly, systematically, thoroughly *Contractors should also analyse carefully each of their consultancy contracts.*
▶ in a particular way **chemically, critically, qualitatively, quantitatively, statistically** *It will focus on effective ways of collecting, reviewing and critically analysing the literature relevant to their area of study.*

● V+n information **data, evidence, information, statistics** *The ideal candidate will have sales experience, strong IT skills, the ability to analyse data and excellent administrative skills.*
▶ answers **questionnaire, responses** *You can also try our interactive quiz, which asks you questions, analyses your responses, and gives immediate advice.*
▶ results **findings, results** *Previous studies have analysed results from research over long time spans.*
▶ patterns **patterns, trends** *His job as an industry analyst is to analyse trends in the Telecoms sector.*
▶ effects something has **effects, impact, implications, outcome** *Analysing the outcome of these measures is complex and any conclusion drawn is bound to be highly speculative.*

● and/or find or note **describe, identify, monitor, record, research** *Ensure that all incidents are recorded and analysed.*
▶ collect **collate, collect, gather** *Programmes to detect, collate, analyse and report adverse events must be in place.*
▶ discuss **discuss, evaluate, interpret, report** *The ability to analyse and interpret complex information to a range of audiences is essential.*

analysis N
careful study of something to understand it or learn what it contains

● adj+N careful **careful, detailed, in-depth, rigorous, thorough** *The survey is the first of a quarterly series to provide a detailed, up-to-date analysis of the industry.*
▶ using particular methods **comparative, critical, forensic, functional, numerical, qualitative, quantitative, spatial, statistical, structural, textual, theoretical** *Thirdly, and most important, they did not do a statistical analysis on their data.*
▶ in a particular field **chemical, economic, genetic, linguistic, mathematical, sociological** *The tool is intended for researchers who want to perform a linguistic analysis and store their data in a standard format.*
▶ done at an early stage **initial, preliminary** *Students are taught to make a preliminary analysis of year-end accounts and interpret simple business performance ratios.*
▶ done after the event **retrospective** *Historical information is also an essential component of business planning in general, and especially in retrospective analyses.*

● n+N content, **content, cost-benefit, data, discourse, risk** *Lessons from this study can be applied to further collection of data to improve its quality and to improve methods for data analysis.*

● v+N do an analysis **attempt, carry out, conduct, perform, prepare, undertake** *It is part of their function to undertake risk/benefit analysis of research proposals.*

▶ present an analysis **give, present, provide** *The aim of this paper is to present a short analysis of the change within the power of the state.*

● N+v confirm sth, **confirm sth, demonstrate sth, indicate sth, reveal sth, show sth, suggest sth** *The analysis revealed that 75% of the users were satisfied with the results.*

ancient ADJ
very old, or relating to people who lived very long ago

● adv+ADJ very **extremely, incredibly, particularly, truly, very** *The origins of this myth are extremely ancient.*
▶ rather **pretty** INFORMAL**, quite, rather** *The oil is then sent through a rather ancient pipeline to the refinery, where it is distilled.*

● ADJ+n building, structure, or town **castle, church, city, edifice, monument, ruin, temple, tomb, town** *The ruins of an ancient temple dedicated to Apollo can be found at Didyma.*
▶ belief **custom, legend, myth, mythology, tradition, wisdom** *The ancient Greek myth of the Amazons may have some basis in fact.*
▶ society **civilization, culture, history, kingdom** *Roses were cultivated by the ancient civilizations of China, Asia Minor, Greece and Rome.*
▶ tree or forest **forest, oak, tree, woodland** *Careful landscaping over the past two centuries has ensured that the park is rich in woodland, unspoilt hedgerows and ancient oaks.*
▶ people **Egyptian, Briton etc** *Oak groves were the traditional places of worship for the ancient Celts.*

anecdote N
an interesting or funny story

● adj+N funny **amusing, entertaining, funny, hilarious, humorous, witty** *But by the end, I wanted to hear more than little quips and amusing anecdotes.*
▶ interesting **fascinating, interesting** *The lack of illustrations is relieved by interesting anecdotes and simple diagrams.*
▶ personal **personal** *He kept everyone amused with his store of personal anecdotes.*

● v+N tell an anecdote **recount, relate, tell** *She recounted anecdotes from the time she had spent in Africa.*
▶ tell anecdotes to each other **exchange, share, swap** *We made our way back to the hotel where we spent time in the bar exchanging anecdotes.*

anger N
angry feeling

● adj+N great **deep, fierce, furious, great, intense, seething, violent** *The seething anger is slightly suppressed in this splendid reply.*
▶ for a good reason **justifiable, justified, righteous, understandable** *There is understandable anger at the conditions they are forced to work in.*
▶ among many people **public, widespread** *Widespread anger greeted the news that the factory was set to close.*
▶ strong but under control **controlled, pent-up, repressed, simmering, unexpressed, unresolved**

Is tennis a good way of unleashing all your pent-up anger?

▶ not controlled **unbridled, uncontrollable, uncontrolled** *Uncontrolled anger can lead to arguments and, in the extreme, physical fights.*

▶ real **genuine, real** *His eyes alternated between a normal genial twinkle and flashes of real anger.*

▶ increasing **growing, mounting, rising** *There is growing anger and frustration over housing.*

● v+N express anger **express, show, unleash, vent, voice** *It gave me the chance to find another way of venting my anger.*

▶ cause anger **arouse, cause, fuel, generate, provoke, rouse, spark** *It was unclear precisely what had sparked their anger.*

▶ control or reduce anger **channel, control, defuse, direct, manage, suppress** *We channel our anger into creating positive solutions.*

▶ feel anger **experience, feel** *I felt cheated, more than anything, but never felt anger or any negative emotions.*

● N+v be great or increase **boil (up/over), burn, erupt, explode, grow, mount, rise** *I felt my anger boiling up inside me.*

▶ become less **abate, subside** *In the last two years her confidence has grown and her anger is slowly subsiding.*

● v+with+N have a lot of anger **be filled, be flushed, bristle, burn, explode, seethe, shake** *One person was seething with anger after what he thought was a rip-off.*

▶ show anger **react, respond** *We must not fall into the trap of responding with anger and hate.*

● and/or an angry feeling **aggression, hostility, indignation, irritability, outrage, rage, wrath** *Feelings of irritability or anger are common.*

▶ fear **anxiety, fear** *This is the path to transcending fear and anger.*

▶ hurt **anguish, distress, hurt, pain** *Encourage her to express her hurt and anger.*

▶ a lack of belief **denial, disbelief** *He was staring out of his office window in disbelief and anger.*

▶ confused feeling **confusion, helplessness, shock** *Mutt's feelings of fear, helplessness and anger intensify as his life becomes increasingly restricted by his epilepsy.*

▶ sadness **depression, despair, disappointment, dismay, frustration, grief, sadness, sorrow** *In his letter he expressed his sadness and anger at the fishing methods which cause these dolphin deaths.*

▶ a feeling of strong dislike **bitterness, disgust, hate, hatred, jealousy, resentment** *However, long-term anger and resentment is usually caused by deep insecurity.*

angry ADJ
very annoyed

● adv+ADJ very **bitterly, extremely, furiously, particularly, really, so** INFORMAL, **very** *I was very angry about the decision.*

▶ rather **a little, pretty** INFORMAL, **quite, rather** *He read it out, and at first I was shocked, and then quite angry.*

▶ becoming more angry **increasingly** *The majority of developing countries are increasingly angry that development issues are being sidelined.*

▶ with good reason **justifiably, justly, rightly, understandably** *Members are quite rightly angry about these job cuts and fearful for their future job prospects.*

● ADJ+n group of people **crowd, demonstrators, mob, protesters** *Two soldiers were killed by an angry mob.*

▶ shout **outburst, rant, shout** *Later she was sorry for her angry outburst at her parents.*

▶ protest **demonstration, protest** *There were many angry protests and the dispute reached the national newspapers.*

▶ reaction **feeling, mood, reaction, response** *His appointment as Bishop stirred angry reaction amongst other priests and the laity of the Church.*

▶ sound of your voice **tone, voice** *I was instantly hailed by the chief's deputy, who in an angry voice brought me to a halt.*

● v+ADJ **appear, become, feel, get, grow, look, remain, seem, sound, stay** *His face was bright red and he sounded really angry.*

● and/or rather angry **aggressive, annoyed, irritable** *I have been feeling a bit angry and irritable.*

▶ sad **depressed, sad** *I'm very sad, and angry at those responsible.*

▶ upset **disappointed, distressed, frustrated, upset** *And the Institution at large has felt angry and frustrated by what they saw and heard.*

▶ confused **confused, shocked** *They may feel confused, angry and ashamed.*

▶ afraid **anxious, frightened, scared, worried** *Avoid handling cats that are frightened or angry.*

▶ feeling dislike **bitter, jealous, resentful** *I am so angry and bitter towards him for destroying my life and our marriage.*

anguish N
a feeling of great physical or emotional pain

● adj+N great **deep, extreme, great, terrible** *They spoke with deep anguish about those times.*

▶ personal **personal** *The poem recounts in a minute a spiritual reformation that took days of personal anguish.*

▶ types of anguish **emotional, mental, spiritual** *He suffers much mental anguish during his journey of self-discovery and awareness.*

● v+N feel anguish **endure, experience, feel, suffer** *I looked great physically but mentally I felt anguish and pain.*

▶ cause anguish **cause, fill with** *In addition to the anguish caused by the doctor's mistake, the families were angry at the manner in which the news was broken to them.*

● n+of+N **cry, howl, scream, wail** *He fell to the ground with a howl of anguish, wrongly believing his girlfriend had committed suicide.*

● and/or emotion **anger, despair, fear, frustration, grief, sorrow** *The women's silence represents their view that words can't express the anguish and despair they feel.*

▶ pain or hurt **distress, pain, suffering** *If an event is happening now and manifesting in anguish and pain now, it must be treated now.*

animosity N

a strong feeling of disliking someone or something

- adj+N strong **bitter, deep, great, growing, intense** *At this time there was bitter animosity between the two countries.*
- ▶ started a long time ago **long-standing, old** *The power struggle in the north also could aggravate the long-standing animosity between the two factions.*
- ▶ toward each other **mutual** *Members of different ethnic groups accept each other's individuality with virtually no mutual animosity.*
- ▶ for particular reasons **ethnic, personal, political, racial, religious, sectarian** *These constitutional disagreements were made worse by religious animosities and financial disputes.*
- v+N cause or increase animosity **arouse, cause, create, engender, generate, provoke** *If the employees of the firm are used to receiving 25 days' holiday per year, and you reduce this to 20, you risk creating animosity amongst your workforce.*
- ▶ feel animosity **bear, feel, harbour** *The most amazing thing was that the victim did not harbour any animosity or anger.*

ankle N

the place where the foot joins the leg

- adj+N **bad, damaged, dodgy** INFORMAL**, fractured, injured, sore, sprained, swollen, twisted** *She claimed to have suffered a twisted ankle after she slipped on some stairs at the seafront.*
- v+N **break, damage, dislocate, fracture, hurt, injure, sprain, turn, twist** *His right wrist and ankle were badly sprained and there were contusions to the side of his head.*

anniversary N

date for celebrating when an important event happened

- n+N number of years **centennial, tenth, twenty-fifth etc** *This year also marks another milestone: the thirty-fifth anniversary of the Nuclear Non-Proliferation Treaty.*
- ▶ named major anniversary **diamond, golden, silver** *2006 sees the company celebrate its silver anniversary.*
- ▶ major **landmark, milestone** *If you're booking your honeymoon or landmark anniversary be sure to tell us, as many hotels include extra romantic touches.*
- ▶ wedding **wedding** *Silver is a traditional gift on the 25th wedding anniversary.*
- v+N celebrate an anniversary **celebrate, commemorate, honour, mark** *In 2009 the college celebrated its 100th anniversary.*
- ▶ be about to reach an anniversary **approach** *We are now approaching the tenth anniversary of the founding of the firm.*
- N+n **celebration, edition, event, gift, party, reunion, year** *The Club's 50th anniversary celebrations will take place this June.*

announce V

make a public statement about something

- adv+V officially **formally, officially, publicly** *The news was then officially announced in late January this year.*
- ▶ proudly **proudly, triumphantly** *We can now proudly announce that she will dance a part in The Nutcracker ballet in November.*
- V+n plan **decision, initiative, intention, measures, plan, proposal** *On March 13th the owners announced their intention to close down the whole of their canal.*
- ▶ start of something **availability, creation, formation, launch, publication, release, start** *The Beatrix Potter Society is pleased to announce the launch in April 2005 of an exciting new project.*
- ▶ new person in a job or competition **appointment, candidacy, nomination, signing** *The pharmaceutical resourcing company has announced two further key appointments to its sales recruitment team.*
- ▶ end of a job **closure, departure, redundancy, resignation, retirement** *To the shock of a nation, he announced his retirement from the game at the age of 28.*
- ▶ financial information **cuts, funding, grant, loss, profit** *The finance minister announced spending cuts of almost 20% for the coming year.*

announcement N

a public or official statement providing information

- adj+N type of announcement **formal, government, ministerial, official, public** *No public announcement was made for at least two months.*
- ▶ coming soon **forthcoming, imminent** *There is considerable speculation about the matter but apparently no announcement is imminent.*
- ▶ made early **early, initial, original, preliminary** *The initial announcement of the changes produced so much bad press that they were forced to reconsider the decision.*
- ▶ made recently **latest, recent** *On our website you will find the latest announcement on our activities and campaigns.*
- ▶ additional **further** *A further announcement on the policy change will be made in due course.*
- ▶ important **important, major** *An important announcement regarding the new service will be issued next week.*
- ▶ sudden **dramatic, shock, sudden, surprise, unexpected** *The sudden announcement came as a shock to obervers.*
- v+N make an announcement **issue, make, post** *I hope to be in a position to make an announcement in about two to three months.*
- ▶ receive an announcement **greet, hear, read, receive, welcome** *The announcement was welcomed by environmentalists.*
- ▶ wait for an announcement **await, expect, wait for** *An announcement is expected in the New Year.*
- N+v **come, follow** *The announcement came after much recent speculation that they were to split.*
- ▶ and/or **information, news, notice, update** *See the Work Permits UK website for the latest information and announcements.*

annoyed ADJ

feeling slightly angry or impatient

- adv+ADJ very **extremely, increasingly, really, so**

INFORMAL, **very** *I was becoming increasingly annoyed at the delays.*
▶ rather **a little, mildly, quite, rather, slightly** *I have to tell you that I am rather annoyed with you.*

● v+ADJ **be, become, feel, get, look, seem** *I get very annoyed when websites will not permit you to use the Back button.*

● and/or **angry, frustrated, upset** *When we trip, our heart pounds, and we then feel annoyed or upset.*

annoying ADJ
making you feel slightly angry or impatient

● adv+ADJ **very extremely, incredibly** INFORMAL, **really, so** INFORMAL, **very** *Users will find the pop-up boxes extremely annoying.*
▶ rather **a bit, a little, mildly, quite, rather, slightly, somewhat** *The make-up was a bit annoying because it went into my eyes.*
▶ especially **especially** *This was an especially annoying time to injure myself, just weeks before the big race.*

● v+ADJ **be, become, find sb/sth, get** *This scraping of windscreen wiper against glass became annoying. ● Some people might find the informal style annoying.*

● and/or **distracting, disturbing, frustrating, irritating** *Barking dogs can be disturbing or annoying for neighbours.*

anonymity N
when someone's name is not known or is kept secret

● adj+N complete **complete, strict, total** *Complete anonymity is guaranteed if you want it.*
▶ not complete **relative** *People can be offered relative anonymity by the use of first names only in the telephone conversations.*

● v+N ask for anonymity **insist on, request** *She insisted on anonymity before she would make any statement.*
▶ give or protect anonymity **assure, ensure, give sb, grant (sb), guarantee, maintain, offer (sb), preserve, protect, provide** *I have maintained the anonymity of those who put their complaints to me.*

> When someone agrees to do something only if their name is kept secret, you can say that they do it **on condition of anonymity**: *They agreed to discuss the matter on condition of anonymity.*

▶ remove anonymity **remove, waive** *Removing anonymity from donors may reduce the number of donors willing to come forward.*

anonymous ADJ
without a name being known or mentioned

● adv+ADJ **completely, entirely, totally** *All responses will be completely anonymous.*

● ADJ+n person **author, benefactor, caller, contributor, donor, reviewer, user** *We have received £200 from an anonymous donor.*
▶ communication **complaint, letter, posting, questionnaire, user** *Anonymous postings are not permitted in this forum.*

● v+ADJ **be, keep sth, remain, stay** *The following comments are from a student who prefers to remain anonymous.*

● and/or **confidential, free** *The research is anonymous and confidential.*

answer N
1 a reply to a question

● adj+N short **one-word, quick, short, straightforward, yes/no** *The short answer is "no".*
▶ usual or prepared **pat, stock** *This is obviously the company's stock answer.*
▶ satisfactory **clear, definite, definitive, honest, satisfactory, sensible, straight** *They had not received satisfactory answers.*
▶ not satisfactory **evasive** *They found many of his answers were evasive or ambiguous.*

● v+N give an answer **give, provide, supply** *She never gives a direct answer, even to a direct question.*
▶ receive an answer **find, get, obtain, receive** *When I get an answer from you I will write again.*
▶ want an answer **demand, expect, want** *He demanded a direct answer from him.*

● N+to **inquiry, query, question** *Our online help pages provide answers to your queries quickly and accurately.*

2 a way of dealing with a problem

● adj+N **easy, obvious, simple, straightforward** *Is there a simple answer to this?*

● v+N find an answer **discover, find** *I haven't found any answers yet.*
▶ provide an answer **have, provide, suggest, yield** *A thorough search of our maps did not yield the answer.*
▶ try to find an answer **look for, search for** *I went down to the police station looking for some answers.*

● N+v **depend on, lie in** *The answer lies in feeling confident about yourself.*

● N+to **challenge, conundrum, crisis, dilemma, mystery, problem** *The answer to these problems lies in better fuel efficiency.*

3 a reply to a question in a test

● adj+N correct **correct, right** *Note that there is more than one correct answer.*
▶ incorrect **incorrect, wrong** *Ticks and crosses indicate right or wrong answers.*
▶ types of answer **model, multiple choice, one-word, sample, short** *Here are model answers to the four questions posed.*

● v+N give an answer **give, select, submit, write** *Write your answers on the copy.*

answer V
1 give a reply to a question

● adv+V yes **affirmatively, in the affirmative, positively** *They had answered both requests in the affirmative.*
▶ no **in the negative, negatively** *It would be understandable if you answered in the negative.*
▶ in a satisfactory way **adequately, correctly, definitively, directly, fully, honestly, patiently,**

satisfactorily, truthfully *He asked for his questions to be answered fully.*
▶ in an unsatisfactory way **evasively, incorrectly** *If any questions are answered incorrectly, valuable feedback is provided.*
▶ quickly **immediately, promptly, quickly** *All my queries were answered promptly and efficiently.*

● **V+n** a question **inquiry, query, question, questionnaire, request** *Their national helpline answers employment questions.*
▶ a communication **call, email, phone, telephone** *We normally answer emails within the hour.*

2 explain to someone who has accused you
● **V+n charge, criticism, critics, objection** *How would you answer such criticisms?*

anticipate V
expect or look forward to a future event

● **adv+V** very much or with excitement **eagerly, highly, hotly, hugely, keenly, much** *She has just published her hugely anticipated second novel.*
▶ before, or at the beginning **initially, originally, previously** *So far, more sociologists have volunteered than was originally anticipated.*
▶ by many people **widely** *It is widely anticipated by analysts that house prices will continue to fall.*

Usage Anticipate is almost always passive in all of the adv+V combinations shown above.

● **V+n** possible problem **criticism, delay, difficulty, objection, problem** *Police say they are not anticipating any problems.*
▶ future needs **demands, needs, requirements** *We understand and can anticipate the needs of our clients.*
▶ future event **arrival, change, event, future, growth, increase, outcome, response, trend** *It could help investors anticipate interest-rate changes.*

● and/or **avoid, identify, manage, plan, predict, prepare, prevent, respond to, understand** *Our system anticipates and responds to fluctuating real-time demand on the web.*

anticipation N
excitement about something that is going to happen

● **adj+N** great or increasing **great, growing, high, increasing, mounting, much** *I opened the parcel with great anticipation.*
▶ happy **eager, excited, gleeful, hopeful, joyful, keen, pleasurable** *I wait in eager anticipation!*
▶ nervous **anxious, fearful, nervous** *There's an air of nervous anticipation among the employees.*

● **v+N** increase anticipation **build, heighten, increase** *After a delayed start, the crowd's anticipation was only heightened.*
▶ feel anticipation **feel, sense** *On Thursday night you could sense the anticipation and excitement.*

● **v+with+N await sth, look forward to sth** *They were looking forward to with anticipation to seeing the results of the survey.*

● **n+of+N air, atmosphere, buzz, feeling, sense** *The sense of anticipation in the crowd was almost tangible.*

● and/or happiness **excitement, expectation, hope,** joy *The long drive up Coldwater Canyon was filled with hope and anticipation.*
▶ worry **anxiety, fear, tension, trepidation** *Often emotions can run high in anticipation or fear.*

antipathy N
a strong feeling of dislike

● **adj+N** strong **deep, strong** *Football supporters ofen have a strong antipathy to other teams.*
▶ shared by many people **general, public, widespread** *Plans to open a casino have been abandoned after public antipathy to the scheme.*
▶ between two individuals or groups **mutual, personal** *Theer was a degree of mutual antipathy between the two departments.*

● **v+N** feel antipathy **feel, have, show** *People can feel antipathy towards representatives of authority.*
▶ cause people to feel antipathy **arouse, generate** *It is also the organization which arouses the most antipathy and suspicion.*

anxiety N
a worried feeling that something bad will happen

● **adj+N** strong **acute, considerable, deep, extreme, great, intense, severe** *She complains that she suffered from severe anxiety and depression.*
▶ types of anxiety **parental, public, social** *Parental anxiety and fears concerning surgery are very real.*
▶ that could be avoided **needless, unnecessary** *A few simple precautions can reduce the risk of accidents and prevent unnecessary anxiety.*

● **n+N exam, performance, separation, test** *Many young people suffer from exam anxiety.*
● **v+N** feel anxiety **experience, feel, suffer, suffer from** *It is natural to feel some anxiety when you go into the examination room.*
▶ cause anxiety **arouse, cause, generate, lead to, provoke** *The fear of what might happen sometimes causes anxiety as well.*
▶ increase anxiety **heighten, increase** *Avoid high caffeine and alcohol intake – both can increase anxiety.*
▶ reduce anxiety **allay, alleviate, calm, ease, lessen, minimize, reduce, relieve** *Is there anything that you do that can relieve the anxiety and stress?*
▶ express anxiety **express, voice** *Classroom assistants also expressed anxiety about their job security.*
▶ deal with anxiety **cope with, deal with, dispel, overcome** *He managed to overcome his anxiety over leaving home.*

● **n+of+N cause, degree, feeling, level, sense, source, state, symptom** *Some users report feelings of anxiety and panic.*

anxious ADJ
worried, nervous or impatient about the future

● **adv+ADJ** very **desperately, extremely, particularly, really, so** INFORMAL, **terribly** INFORMAL, **very** *This was important, as everybody was very anxious.*
▶ rather **a little, quite, rather, slightly, somewhat** *I was a little anxious about starting the course.*
▶ as is normal **naturally, understandably** *Patients are understandably anxious to avoid major surgery, if possible.*

- ADJ+n time **moment, time** *There were some anxious moments just before the end of the game.*
▸ person **father, mother, parent, patient, people, relative** *Anxious relatives and friends rushed towards the colliery.*
▸ action **feeling, glance, look, thought** *Anxious glances were exchanged between ministers.*
▸ wait **wait** *There was an anxious wait for the doors to open.*
- v+ADJ be anxious **appear, be, feel, look, remain, seem** *She felt anxious and confused.*
▸ become or make someone anxious **become, get, grow, make sb** *Officers at the top began to get anxious.* • *You may start avoiding the things that make you anxious.*
- and/or **confused, depressed, fearful, nervous, tense, worried** *Many claimants are confused and anxious about the new system.*

apologize V
say sorry for doing something wrong

- adv+V **formally, humbly, in advance, profusely, publicly, sincerely, unreservedly** *I apologize in advance for any omissions.* • *I sincerely apologize to all those who wanted to see us and were unable to do so.*

apology N
a statement saying sorry

- adj+N types of apology **formal, full, official, personal, public, written** *He also won a public apology.*
▸ strongly felt **abject, fulsome, genuine, heartfelt, humble, profound, profuse, sincere, unqualified, unreserved** *If I have missed anybody out, please accept my sincere apologies.*
- v+N want or need an apology **demand, deserve, expect, want** *The prime misister demanded an apology from those who had called him a liar.*
▸ need to make an apology **owe sb** *He felt that they owed him an apology for all the problems he had had with the computer.*
▸ make an apology **issue, make** *The company recently had to make a public apology for inadequate levels of customer support.*
▸ receive or accept an apology **accept, get, receive** *Please accept our apologies for the inconvenience this may cause.*
- n+of+N **letter, word** *I rose and left the table without a word of apology.*

appalling ADJ
very unpleasant and shocking or very disappointing

- adv+ADJ **absolutely, equally, frankly, quite, really, simply, truly, utterly** *I thought the referee was absolutely appalling.*
- ADJ+n event or action **abuse, act, atrocity, catastrophe, crime, cruelty, massacre** *Appalling atrocities were committed by the militia and the armed forces.*
▸ conditions or situation **condition, mess, poverty, situation, state, suffering, tragedy, weather** *The weather was still appalling.*

- v+ADJ **be, find sth, look, sound** *They found their behaviour appalling.* • *His introduction to army life sounds quite appalling.*

apparent ADJ
easy to see or understand, or seeming to exist

- adv+ADJ very **all too, clearly, especially, glaringly, painfully, particularly, quite, readily, so, very** *Their greater acting confidence was readily apparent.*
▸ immediately or soon **immediately, instantly, quickly, soon** *It was immediately apparent that there would be problems with the equipment.*
▸ more and more **increasingly** *It became increasingly apparent that he would have to resign.*
- ADJ+n **anomaly, conflict, contradiction, difference, discrepancy, inconsistency, paradox** *These two facts present an apparent paradox.*
- v+ADJ **be, become, make sth, seem** *The risks are apparent to everyone.* • *She made it very apparent that she did not approve.*

appeal N
1 an urgent request for help, money, information etc

- n+N types of appeal **charity, disaster, earthquake, emergency, fundraising** *We aim to have raised £2000 for our charity appeal.*
▸ style of appeal **direct, emotional, urgent** *Her father made an emotional appeal.*
▸ v+N make an appeal **issue, launch, make, renew** *We've just launched our appeal to raise £12,000 for our charity.*
▸ give to an appeal **contribute to, donate to, give to, respond to, support** *For more details of how to donate to the appeal visit their website.*
- N+v **raise** *Each appeal usually raises around £300.*
- N+for **donations, funds, help, information, support, witnesses** *Again the appeal for funds had a great result.*
- N+to N **contribution, donation, response** *There was a disappointing response to this appeal.*

2 a quality that makes people like or want something

- adj+N types of appeal **aesthetic, emotional, visual** *The wooden floors offer great visual appeal and are also very durable.*
▸ to many people **broad, mass, popular, universal, wide** *This collection of essays is intended to have a wide appeal.*
▸ lasting for a long time **enduring, lasting, timeless** *The design has been created to achieve timeless appeal.*
▸ immediate **immediate, instant** *His delightful drawings had instant appeal.*
- v+N increase appeal **add to, broaden, contribute to, increase, widen** *If they want to attract new members, they will have to widen their appeal.*
▸ lose appeal **lose** *The prospect of two weeks in his company was beginning to lose its appeal.*
▸ have appeal **have, hold** *Following the latest fashions held no appeal for him.*

- N+v **lie in** *Part of his appeal lies in the genuine interest he displays for the subject.*

3 a formal request to change a legal decision

- adj+N **successful/unsuccessful successful, unsuccessful** *If your appeal is successful, you will be entitled to a refund.*
- ▶ sporting appeals **lbw, penalty** *There were penalty appeals at both ends.*

- n+N types of **admission, asylum, employment, enforcement, immigration, penalty, planning** *If my school admission appeal is unsuccessful, can I appeal again?*

- v+N make, or think about making, an appeal **consider, file, lodge, make, submit** *You should lodge your appeal in writing.*
- ▶ deal with an appeal **consider, deal with, decide, determine, hear** *An independent inspector will be appointed to decide the appeal.*
- ▶ allow an appeal **allow, uphold** *The appeal was upheld.*
- ▶ not allow an appeal **dismiss, lose, refuse, reject, withdraw** *The Court of Appeal dismissed an appeal.*

- N+v **fail, succeed** *For all of the reasons given above the appeal succeeds.*

- N+against **conviction, decision, dismissal, notice, order, refusal, ruling, sentence** *They rejected his appeal against his conviction.*

- N+to **adjudicator, commissioner, court, tribunal** *There was no appeal to the federal courts.*

appeal V

1 make an urgent request for help, money, information etc

- adv+V **directly, urgently** *Police are urgently appealing for witnesses.*

- V+for **donation, funds, help, information, money, support, volunteers, witnesses** *We are appealing for more volunteers to come forward.*

2 formally ask a court to change a decision

- adv+V **successfully, unsuccessfully** *She successfully appealed against a jail sentence.*

- V+n **case, conviction, decision, ruling, verdict** *Its manufacturer is to appeal the decision.*

- V+against **conviction, decision, dismissal, notice, order, refusal, ruling, sentence, verdict** *He appealed against his conviction.*

- V+to **adjudicator, commissioner, court, tribunal** *He appealed to a tribunal and lost.*

appealing ADJ

attractive and interesting

- adv+ADJ very **especially, extremely, highly, particularly, so** INFORMAL, **very** *Taking exams is not always very appealing.*
- ▶ rather **quite, rather** *I must admit the idea of three weeks away from the family was rather appealing.*
- ▶ in a particular way **aesthetically, intuitively, strangely, superficially, universally, visually** *a very visually appealing, informative and resourceful website*

- ADJ+n feature **aspect, characteristic, feature** *The recent addition of air conditioning in all bedrooms is an appealing feature.*
- ▶ idea or choice **alternative, idea, option, prospect** *A holiday at home can be an appealing alternative.*

- v+ADJ **be, become, find sth, look, make sth, seem, sound** *Trees and lakes will make your park more appealing to the visitors.*

appearance N

1 the way someone or something looks or seems

- adj+N type of appearance **aesthetic, external, outward, physical, visual** *Her clothes and physical appearance were important to her.*
- ▶ general **overall** *The overall appearance of the site is appealing.*

- v+N have an appearance **assume, give, have, present, take on** *He gave the appearance of being interested in the project.*
- ▶ change the appearance **affect, alter, change, enhance, spoil** *Population growth changed the appearance of the countryside.*
- ▶ keep the appearance **maintain, preserve** *The developers managed to preserve the appearance of the town.*

- N+v **belie, deceive, mislead** *But his appearance belied his words.*

When something is not what it appears to be you can say that **appearances are deceptive**.

2 the time when something starts to exist or when someone appears

- adj+N short **brief, fleeting** *She only had time to make a brief appearance at the party.*
- ▶ unexpected **sudden, surprise, unexpected** *The sudden appearance of a new form of the disease has alarmed scientists.*

- v+N **make, put in** *He finally put in an appearance shortly before lunch.*

appetite N

1 the natural feeling of wanting to eat

- adj+N big **big, enormous, good, healthy, hearty, huge, insatiable, ravenous, voracious** *The fresh air had given us a healthy appetite.*
- ▶ not big **poor** *Weight loss and poor appetite are common as the disease progresses.*

- v+N have or get an appetite **have, work up** *By now you will have worked up an appetite for lunch.*
- ▶ reduce someone's appetite **curb, decrease, reduce, ruin, spoil, suppress** *Eating between meals will spoil your appetite.*
- ▶ lose your appetite **lose** *She had gradually lost her appetite as the depression took hold.*
- ▶ increase someone's appetite **give sb, increase, sharpen, stimulate** *All the training involved gives you an enormous appetite.* • *Sleepiness and increased appetite are common side effects of the drug.*
- ▶ satisfy someone's appetite **sate, satisfy** *Nuts can help to sate the appetite.*

- N+v **grow, increase, return** *Your appetite usually returns as you recover.*

- n+of+N **lack, loss** *Many patients are severely malnourished, owing to loss of appetite.*

2 a feeling of great interest in something

- adj+N big **big, enormous, huge, insatiable, real, voracious** *There seemed to be a real appetite for reform.*
▶ not big **little** *There was little appetite for a strike among the employees.*

- v+N reduce someone's appetite **dull** *Old age had dulled her appetite for change.*
▶ increase someone's appetite **give sb, increase, whet** *Your website gave me a good appetite to discover more of South America.* ● *This fantastic prize has whetted my appetite for more travel.*
▶ lose your appetite **lose** *People have not lost their appetite for libraries.*
▶ satisfy someone's appetite **indulge, sate, satisfy** *Whatever your poetical taste, there is plenty to satisfy your appetite in this volume.*

applaud V

1 show approval by clapping

- adv+V **enthusiastically, generously, heartily, loudly, politely, warmly, wildly** *The audience has risen to its feet, and they are applauding wildly.*

2 praise a decision, action, idea etc

- adv+V **greatly, publicly, roundly, universally, warmly, widely** *This move was widely applauded by experts.*

Usage **Applaud** is usually passive in these combinations.

- V+n **achievement, commitment, decision, efforts, initiative, success, work** *I applaud the efforts you are making to improve performance.*

applause N

the sound of people applauding a performance etc

- adj+N enthusiastic **enthusiastic, generous, great, huge, loud, rapturous, spontaneous, thunderous, tremendous, tumultuous, warm, wild** *Adrian walked onstage, to rapturous applause.*
▶ not enthusiastic **muted, polite** *They left the stage a few songs later to muted applause.*
▶ lasting a long time **prolonged, sustained** *We all erupted into sustained applause.*

- v+N get applause **draw, earn, get, receive, win** *The author received sustained applause.*
▶ deserve applause **deserve, earn** *They were so good to watch and well deserved the applause.*
▶ give applause **break into, burst into, give** *Some songs were given rapturous applause.*
▶ react to applause **accept, acknowledge** *One player hurried off the stage without waiting to acknowledge the applause.*

- N+v start **break out, greet sb/sth** *Their entrance was greeted by polite applause.*
▶ become less **die away, die down, subside** *The crowd's applause died down as the actors took to the stage.*

- n+of+N **burst, ripple, roar, round, storm, thunder** *The drummer got the biggest round of applause.*

applicable ADJ

relevant to a particular situation or group

- adv+ADJ to many situations or groups **broadly, generally, globally, universally, widely** *I think this is useful and widely applicable advice.*
▶ to a particular situation or group **especially, only, particularly** *These methods are only applicable to some chemicals.*
▶ to another situation or group **as, equally** *The book is full of suggestions that are as applicable today as they were in his days.*
▶ at a particular time **currently, immediately, potentially, still** *It aims to provide rapid and immediately applicable results.*
▶ in a particular way **directly, practically, readily** *The project's findings are directly applicable across social work education.*

applicant N

someone applying for a job, loan etc

- adj+N possible **interested, potential, prospective** *Interested applicants can read more details of the programme.*
▶ suitable **eligible, qualified, suitable, well-qualified** *We had a large number of replies from well-qualified applicants.*
▶ successful/unsuccessful **successful, unsuccessful** *Unsuccessful candidates are usually notified within two weeks.*

- n+N **asylum, college, grant, job, licence, loan, university, visa** *There has been a sharp fall in the number of university applicants.*

- v+N asking for applications **invite, look for, welcome** *We welcome applicants from all types of educational background.*
▶ attract applicants **attract** *The campaign hopes to attract 1000 new applicants for social work courses.*
▶ want an applicant to do or be something **expect sb to, require sb to** *Applicants are expected to hold a Master's Degree or equivalent.*
▶ consider an applicant **assess, consider, interview, screen, shortlist, vet** *All suitable applicants are interviewed.*
▶ choose an applicant **accept, choose, select** *Applicants who are selected for the shortlist will be required to sit a short test.*
▶ not choose an applicant **reject** *Unsuccessful applicants are either rejected on the spot or offered a less senior post.*

- N+for **admission, course, employment, job, licence, membership, position, post, registration, vacancy** *Applicants for this course must be 18 or over.*

application N

1 a request for something

- adj+N successful/unsuccessful **successful, unsuccessful** *If your application is unsuccessful, don't be discouraged.*
▶ type of application **formal, online, postal, speculative** *We are always interested in receiving speculative applications.*

- n+N **asylum, funding, grant, job, licence, membership, patent, planning, visa** *Always keep a* *copy of any job application in case you are invited to an interview.*

- v+N make an application **complete, file, fill in, lodge, make, proceed with, put in, send in, submit** *Please contact us to discuss your ideas before making a formal application.*
- ▶ invite or welcome applications **invite, welcome** *The department welcomes applications from mature students.*
- ▶ receive or deal with an application **assess, consider, deal with, process, receive**
- ▶ accept or refuse an application **accept, approve, dismiss, grant, refuse, reject, turn down** *The Court refused her application.*
- N+n **deadline, fee, form, pack, procedure, process** *An application form is available for download.*
- N+for legal processes **adjournment, asylum, bail, injunction, naturalization** *There were no applications for bail.*
- ▶ permission (to do or join something) **admission, approval, authorization, consent, leave, membership, permission, registration** *Applications for membership should be made to the Membership Secretary.*
- ▶ money **funding, grant** *We would encourage more applications for funding for sports.*

2 a particular use something has

- adj+N in particular areas **commercial, industrial, medical, technological** *We expect to develop commercial applications of the technology.*
- ▶ types of application **potential, practical, real-world, specific** *Each chapter highlights practical applications.*
- N+of **concept, knowledge, mathematics, method, methodology, model, principle, rule, science, technique, technology, theory** *There are many potential applications of this methodology.*
- n+of+N **number, range, variety** *These pumps are suitable for a variety of applications.*

3 computer software that does a particular job

- adj+N **desktop, hypermedia, multimedia, software, stand-alone, web, web-based** *Standalone desktop applications are also available.*
- v+N **download, install, launch, run** *I was unable to run the application because there was not enough memory available.*
- N+n **developer, domain, interface, program, programmer, programming, server, software** *It's suitable for anyone who has a basic grasp of web application programming.*

apply V

1 make a request for a job etc

- adv+V **direct, directly, early, online, successfully** *Please apply early to avoid disappointment.*
- V+for a job **job, position, post, vacancy** *The service will allow you to view and apply for current vacancies.*
- ▶ permission to do or have something **bursary, funding, grant, licence, loan, passport, patent, permit, scholarship, visa** *You cannot apply for a passport online.*

- ▶ **accreditation, admission, asylum, exemption, injunction, permission, registration** *students interested in applying for admission to our PhD programme*

2 affect or be relevant to something

- adv+V **equally, irrespective of, only** *This duty applies irrespective of a child's immigration status.*
- n+V a rule **condition, exemption, law, legislation, limit, paragraph, principle, regulation, restriction, rule, section** *Terms and conditions apply.* • *These regulations apply to landlords renting whole properties.*
- ▶ a charge **charge, discount, fee, rate** *Charges apply for this service.*

3 use a method, law, or process

- adv+V **consistently, correctly, inconsistently, rigidly, rigorously, universally** *The system of approvals should be fair, transparent and consistently applied.*
- V+n a rule or idea **criterion, knowledge, principle, rule** *He showed how they had applied design principles.*
- ▶ a method **method, methodology, technique** *You can apply the technique to other services.*

appointment N

1 an arrangement to meet for business or a service

- adj+N made in advance **prior** *We are open most times, but please make a prior appointment.*
- ▶ first/later **first, follow-up, initial** *We shall ask you to attend an initial appointment at which your situation will be assessed.*
- ▶ urgent/not urgent **emergency, routine, urgent** *I told him that I had an urgent business appointment.*
- v+N ask for an appointment **ask for, request** *She requested an appointment with a senior consultant.*
- ▶ make an appointment **arrange, book, confirm, make, schedule** *Telephone reception to make an appointment.*

> You can say that something must be done **by appointment** if you need to make an appointment: *Viewing of the property is by appointment only.*

- ▶ go to an appointment **attend, keep** *I attend regular outpatient appointments.*
- ▶ not go to an appointment **cancel, miss** *They had already cancelled several appointments.*

2 giving someone a job; the job itself

- adj+N in a particular area **academic, judicial, ministerial, political, professional** *He held a number of senior academic appointments.*
- ▶ at a particular level **senior** *Senior appointments are made after a lengthy interview process.*
- ▶ for a particular time **full-time, part-time, permanent, temporary** *This is a temporary appointment for a period of two years.*
- n+N **commission, committee, panel, procedure, process** *A senior Assessor sits on each appointment committee for new academic posts.*
- v+N make an appointment **announce, approve, confirm, make, offer sb** *The committee confirmed his appointment to the post.*

▶ get or have an appointment **hold, obtain, take up** *Her students have obtained appointments in all areas of business.*

▶ end an appointment **terminate** *She was informed that her appointment would be terminated immediately.*

appraisal N
the process of forming an opinion about how effective someone or something is

● adj+N types of appraisal **economic, environmental, financial, technical** *The plan was subject to an environmental appraisal.*

▶ regular **annual, regular** *All doctors will undergo regular appraisal throughout the year.*

▶ full **comprehensive, detailed, full, rigorous, thorough** *This report included a full options appraisal and a full risk assessment.*

▶ honest **honest, independent, objective, realistic** *It was an honest, objective appraisal of the facts.*

● n+N **performance, policy, staff, sustainability**

● v+N **carry out, complete, conduct, make, provide, undertake** *The next stage was to undertake a thorough appraisal of the approach proposed.*

● N+n **criterion, form, interview, meeting, process, report, scheme, system, technique** *Please complete the performance appraisal form.*

appreciate V
1 understand the nature or importance of something

● adv+V well **fully, properly, readily, truly, well** *Being up close to the statues you truly appreciate the scale of work involved.*

▶ by many people **generally, widely** *Its usefulness has not been as widely appreciated as was originally hoped.*

Usage ***Appreciate*** is always used in the passive in these combinations.

▶ enough/not enough **insufficiently, sufficiently** *This is a fact that we did not appreciate sufficiently at the time.*

● V+n **complexity, difference, fact, importance, seriousness, significance, value** *He appreciates the importance of humour in learning.*

● and/or **know, recognize, respect, see, understand** *This considerable convenience for passengers is beginning to be more widely known and appreciated.*

2 recognize the good qualities of someone or something or be grateful for something

● adv+V very much **certainly, deeply, fully, genuinely, greatly, highly, hugely, much, really, truly** *Any contribution that you can make would be hugely appreciated.*

▶ gratefully **gratefully** *Your support would be gratefully appreciated.*

Usage ***Appreciate*** is always used in the passive in this combination.

▶ especially **especially, particularly** *Hikers particularly appreciate the peaceful forests.*

● V+n help **assistance, contribution, effort, help, support** *Your help is greatly appreciated.*

▶ a good quality **beauty, generosity, honesty, kindness, patience** *I very much appreciate your generosity.*

● and/or **acknowledge, admire, enjoy, love, respect, value, welcome** *We welcome and appreciate any new ideas.*

appreciation N
1 a feeling of being grateful

● adj+N **genuine, grateful, sincere, warm** *We record our most sincere appreciation to all those who have made such generous donations.*

● v+N **convey, express, record, show** *Once again I express our appreciation for your support.*

● n+of+N **gesture, token** *Please accept this small gift as a token of our appreciation.*

● and/or **gratitude, love, thanks** *My thanks and appreciation to you for setting up the webpage.*

2 understanding of something and of why it is important

● adj+N good **better, broad, deep, full, genuine, greater, proper, real, thorough, true, wide** *This should give the reader a better appreciation of the geography of the area.*

▶ by many people **public, wide** *We need to promote wider appreciation of the issues involved.*

▶ increasing **growing** *There is growing appreciation of the importance of community.*

● v+N have or get an appreciation **develop, gain, have** *The courses helped me gain an appreciation of management.*

▶ show an appreciation **demonstrate, show** *The article shows a real appreciation of the wider implications of the affair.*

▶ increase someone's appreciation **encourage, enhance, foster, increase, promote** *The project aims to promote an appreciation of the unique local history of this small parish.*

● and/or **awareness, knowledge, recognition, respect, understanding** *A good knowledge and appreciation of current legislation is required.*

apprehension N
a worried feeling that something bad might happen

● adj+N much/not much **considerable, a little, a lot of, serious, slight** *Many of us may have felt in advance a little apprehension.*

▶ at the beginning **initial** *After our initial apprehension we settled in very well.*

● v+N feel apprehension **be filled with, feel** *I waited, filled with apprehension.*

▶ show apprehension **express, show** *Apprehension was expressed by a number of inspectors at the state of the viaduct.*

▶ cause apprehension **cause, increase** *New experiences can cause apprehension.*

▶ feel less apprehension **overcome** *Most people have overcome their initial apprehension about e-learning.*

● n+of+N **degree, feeling, level, sense** *Many students come to the course with some degree of apprehension.*

* and/or **anxiety, doubt, excitement, fear, uncertainty, worry** *There was an air of excitement and apprehension.*

approach N
a way of thinking about or doing something

* adj+N involving different ideas or people **blended, collaborative, coordinated, fresh, holistic, integrated, joined-up, multidisciplinary** *Assessment requires a multidisciplinary approach.*
▶ based on a particular structure or system **analytical, bottom-up, consistent, methodological, strategic, structured, systematic, theoretical, top-down** *It pays to adopt a more systematic approach.*
▶ new or different **alternative, innovative, novel** *This paper presents a novel approach to measuring website performance.*
▶ practical **commonsense, constructive, down-to-earth, flexible, practical, pragmatic, sensible** *It pays to adopt a flexible approach to these matters.*
▶ done in stages **piecemeal** *A piecemeal approach to reform is not acceptable.*

* v+N suggest an approach **outline, propose, suggest** *We therefore suggest an alternative approach.*
▶ use an approach **adopt, employ, follow, pursue, take, use** *Doctors generally take a holistic approach to the condition.*
▶ develop an approach **develop, explore, pioneer** *My company has pioneered this approach for many years.*
▶ like or choose an approach **advocate, agree with, argue for, call for, decide on, endorse, favour, go for, opt for, prefer, recommend** *You can go for a do-it-yourself approach.*
▶ change an approach **change, rethink, revise** *It was time to rethink our approach.*
▶ stop using an approach **abandon** *We eventually had to abandon this approach.*

* n+of+N different types **combination, range, variety** *A diverse range of approaches may be required.*
▶ qualities **advantage, benefit, disadvantage, drawback, effectiveness, feasibility, limitations, validity, weakness** *Advantages and drawbacks of both approaches are discussed.*

* and/or **attitude, method, methodology, principle, strategy, technique, theory** *The course will critically assess and evaluate existing techniques and approaches.*

approach V
1 move closer to someone or something in space or time

* adv+V quickly/slowly **fast, quickly, rapidly, slowly** *The day was fast approaching when the money would run out.*
▶ in a particular way **cautiously, closely, nervously, tentatively** *This bird was giving its warning call so we didn't approach too closely.*

* V+with **caution** *I approached with caution and from a safe distance.*

2 deal with a situation in a particular way

* adv+V **analytically, differently, logically,**

methodically *Dr Fuller emphasises that every site must be approached differently.*

* V+n **issue, problem, question, subject, task, topic** *You can approach the problem two ways.*

* V+with **care, caution** *These questions need to be*

appropriate ADJ
suitable for a particular situation or purpose

* adv+ADJ very **entirely, highly, perfectly, singularly, very, wholly** *It has been a highly appropriate time to undertake this study.*
▶ in a particular way **clinically, contextually, culturally, environmentally, linguistically** *The surgery performed must be clinically appropriate.*

* ADJ+n course of action **action, arrangements, measures, method, precautions, response, safeguards, treatment** *We take appropriate precautions to protect any information you submit using our website.*
▶ things you wear **clothing, dress, footwear**

* v+ADJ **consider sth, deem sth, feel sth, judge sth, regard sth as, think sth** *Please donate any items you deem appropriate.*

* ADJ+for **circumstances, needs, occasion, purpose, setting, situation, task, use** *Not all of the tests mentioned will be appropriate for use with every child.*

* ADJ+to someone's personal situation **ability, age, needs** *Having equipment that is appropriate to the needs of visually impaired pupils is the first step to improved learning.*
▶ general situation **circumstances, conditions, context, location, occasion, purpose, situation, subject, task** *Register is what linguists call a style appropriate to the occasion.*

approval N
1 a positive feeling towards something or someone

* adj+N from people in general **general, unanimous, universal, widespread** *Nuclear power does not enjoy widespread public approval.*
▶ great **hearty, whole-hearted** *He had no doubt but that this would meet with their hearty approval.*

* v+N get someone's approval **earn, gain, get, meet, meet with, win** *If the product does not meet your approval, you can return it for a full refund.*
▶ express approval **express, nod, roar, voice** *The President examined the cartoon, and then nodded his approval.*
▶ want someone's approval **seek, want** *I have never sought approval, I have just done what I've wanted.*

* n+of+N sign of approval **seal, stamp** *Again we get an encore and the song gets the seal of approval.*
▶ actions showing approval **chorus, murmur, nod, roar** *Loud murmurs of approval went up from the audience.*

You can also say that someone does something *in* approval: *He nodded in approval.*

2 official agreement from someone in authority

* adj+N complete **full, official, written** *He led*

Britain into the War of Independence, with the full approval of King George III.

▶ not complete but with conditions **conditional, preliminary, provisional** *The committee agreed to grant the project conditional approval, subject to the provision of additional pre-clinical work.*

▶ formal or official **formal, official, regulatory, statutory** *There are electronic tagging systems available but as yet none of them has official approval.*

▶ given by a particular person or group **committee, congressional, government, ministerial, parental, parliamentary, royal, shareholder** *Parliamentary approval of the regulations is expected shortly.*

▶ given at a particular stage in a process **final, prior, retrospective** *It is his department that has the final approval on the funding for this road.*

● v+N get approval **achieve, gain, get, obtain, receive, secure, win** *The drug AZT gained approval in 1987.*

▶ give approval **confirm, give, grant** *I never gave my approval for these actions.*

▶ try to get approval **apply for, ask for, request, seek** *The club had requested approval to proceed with a revised project.*

You can also say **submit something for approval** or **present something for approval**: *The plans were submitted for approval.*

▶ not give approval **refuse, revoke, suspend, withdraw, withhold** *In one case the centre actually had its approval withdrawn.*

You can also say that something will happen **subject to approval**: *The new course will start in 2011 (subject to approval by the University board).*

approve V

1 have a positive feeling towards someone or something

● adv+V **heartily, thoroughly, wholeheartedly** *Even if I end up disagreeing with the final decisions, I heartily approve of the process.*

2 give official agreement or permission

● adv+V when most people or all people approve **overwhelmingly, unanimously** *The motion was unanimously approved.*

▶ in a particular way **conditionally, formally, officially, personally, provisionally** *You must not start the work before your application for a grant has been officially approved in writing.*

● V+n **amendment, application, appointment, budget, plan, proposal, recommendation, scheme** *The plan was formally approved at the last Budget.*

apt ADJ

suitable

● adv+ADJ **entirely, especially, particularly, peculiarly, perfectly, rather, strangely, very** *This analogy is a particularly apt one.*

● ADJ+n **analogy, comparison, description, metaphor, name, quotation, term, title, word** *Agreeing on an apt title for a new book can be difficult.*

aptitude N

a natural ability to do something well

● adj+N a special aptitude **natural, particular, real, remarkable, special, strong** *She showed a strong aptitude for languages at an early age.*

▶ types of aptitude **academic, intellectual, mathematical, mechanical, musical, technical** *An aural test will show if you have natural musical aptitude.*

● v+N have an aptitude **develop, have, possess** *He discovered he had an aptitude for chemistry.*

You can also talk about people **with an aptitude for** something: *Students with an aptitude for music will enjoy this course.*

▶ show that you have an aptitude **demonstrate, display, show** *Reynolds demonstrated an early aptitude for engineering, and, aged 19, was apprenticed to a well known inventor and mechanical engineer.*

▶ measure someone's aptitude **assess, measure, test** *A written test will be used to assess aptitude for social work.*

arbitrary ADJ

not based on any plan or done for a particular reason

● adv+ADJ rather **fairly, rather, somewhat** *a fairly arbitrary collection of articles*

▶ completely **completely, entirely, purely, quite, totally** *It is a well-argued text which attacks the quite arbitrary division between popular and serious literature.*

▶ seeming arbitrary **apparently, seemingly** *It's a seemingly arbitrary list that has little in the way of logic.*

● ADJ+n **arrest, decision, detention, distinction, execution, limit, number, rule** *Arbitrary arrests and beatings were common.*

archive N

a collection of documents

● adj+N large **comprehensive, extensive, huge, massive, vast** *Each of the towns has an extensive archive and at least one published 'History'.*

▶ stored on computers **digital, electronic, Internet, online, web** *The digital archive has not yet been made accessible to the general public.*

▶ types of archive **archaeological, historical, news, photo, photographic, research, sound, video** *It includes images from the photo archive as well as footage from his other films.*

● v+N look in an archive **access, browse, go to, look at, search, view** *Please feel free to browse our archive of 700 publications.*

▶ create an archive **amass, build, build up, create, generate** *The present owner has amassed a considerable archive relating to the history of his home.*

▶ contain an archive **contain, house** *The Library also houses a separate archive of the University's course materials.*

area N

1 a particular subject or activity

- adj+N difficult **grey, sensitive, specialist, tricky**
INFORMAL *The Green Paper recognises that agriculture remains a sensitive area.*
- ▶ important **core, key, main, priority** *One of the main areas covered is physical activity.*
- N+of type of work or study **expertise, interest, research, responsibility, specialization, work** *His area of specialization was the Victorian period.*
- ▶ something people worry about or disagree about **concern, debate, difficulty, disagreement, uncertainty, weakness** *There are still significant areas of disagreement between us.*

2 part of a city, town, country etc

- adj+N other types of area **built-up, coastal, industrial, inner-city, low-lying, mountainous, populated, remote, residential, rural, upland, urban** *Moor usually occurs in upland areas.*
- ▶ poor **deprived, disadvantaged, slum** *The community was set up specifically to tackle the challenges of deprivation and social exclusion in the most disadvantaged areas.*
- ▶ rich **affluent, upmarket** *They are largely affluent areas and are home to many commuters to London.*

3 space

- adj+N communal, forested, grassy, lawned, paved, shaded, wooded *A door leads outside to a paved area.*
- n+N barbecue, dining, parking, patio, picnic, reception, recreation, seating, sleeping, storage *Within the grounds are numerous nature trails and picnic areas.*

arena N

an area of activity and the people involved in it

- adj+N large **domestic, global, international, world** *The struggle for colonial freedom gathered strength as a powerful independent force in the world arena in this period.*
- ▶ types of arena **business, commercial, competitive, corporate, eduational, financial, policy, political, public, social** *Andy has has worked in the commercial arena for 12 years.*
- v+N become involved in an arena **come into, enter, move into, re-enter, step into** *Judges have to be careful not to step too far into the political arena.*
- ▶ create an arena **create, provide** *It is an opportunity to create an arena in which issues can be discussed.*
- ▶ be involved in an arena **be in, be involved in, compete in, dominate, operate in, work in** *Their objective was to dominate the mobile telecoms arena. • The position would suit someone with previous experience of working in the business arena.*
- N+for **debate, dialogue, discussion** *The classroom provides an arena for direct debate.*

argue V

1 disagree in an angry way

- adv+V loudly or angrily **bitterly, fiercely, furiously, loudly** *Two women began to argue fiercely about who was to blame.*

- ▶ always or frequently **always, constantly, endlessly, frequently** *I'm tired of constantly arguing with my boyfriend.*

2 state a reason or opinion

- adv+V clearly, in a way that persuades people **cogently, coherently, compellingly, convincingly, eloquently, persuasively, plausibly** *There is a full and coherently argued conclusion.*
- ▶ strongly **fiercely, forcefully, passionately, powerfully, strenuously, strongly, vehemently, vigorously** *Two men argued passionately that it would accomplish nothing.*
- ▶ correctly **correctly, reasonably, rightly** *War is a matter of technique, as Trotsky correctly argued.*
- ▶ without changing your opinion **consistently, repeatedly** *The government has consistently argued that everybody who wants to study and who meets the entry level should be able to study, irrespective of his or her financial situation.*
- V+n **case, corner, merit, point, position** *She is feisty and argued her corner eloquently. • I won't be at this rehearsal though, so I won't be forced to argue the merits of my favourite book.*

argument N

1 an angry disagreement between people

- adj+N involving a lot of anger **bitter, fierce, furious, heated, impassioned** *After a heated argument a shot is fired, and one of the professors lies dead!*
- ▶ silly or pointless **petty, pointless, ridiculous, silly** *Please let's not get into a petty argument about American spelling.*
- v+N have an argument **engage in, get into, have** *I overheard all the bridesmaids having a furious argument about who was going to be first to dance with the best man.*
- ▶ become an argument **end in, result in, turn into** *What started out as a minor family difficulty has turned into a bitter argument.*
- ▶ cause an argument or make one worse **be looking for, cause, fuel, provoke** *Eddie's not looking for an argument, but neither is he planning on moving.*
- ▶ involve someone in an argument **draw sb into, embroil sb in, involve sb in** *This could result in you being drawn into arguments.*
- ▶ end an argument **lose, settle, win** *To settle the argument once and for all, what is the song called?*
- ▶ not have an argument **avoid** *Avoid arguments about teenage behaviour.*

2 a set of reasons used for persuading others

- adj+N strong **compelling, convincing, persuasive, powerful, strong, valid** *While it has been claimed that this approach could increase resources for development assistance, there are equally compelling arguments that it may divert scarce aid resources.*
- ▶ weak **unconvincing, weak** *The proposal is based on an unconvincing argument.*
- ▶ most important **central, core, main** *Without doubt, the book's central arguments are compelling and backed up with a wealth of evidence.*
- ▶ sensible or well-argued **cogent, coherent, logical, plausible, rational, reasoned, well-reasoned** *I have seen very cogent arguments for and against the Scottish system of comprehensive education.*

▸ based on incorrect facts or reasoning **fallacious, flawed, spurious** *Sadly, this is a hopelessly flawed argument.*

> You can also say that there is *a flaw in* someone's argument: *There are at least two major flaws in your argument.*

▸ about a particular subject **ethical, legal, philosophical, political, theological** *These hypotheses are used as premises in a number of philosophical arguments.*

● v+N suggest or use an argument **advance, articulate, deploy, make, outline, present, produce, provide, put forward, supply, use** *There is adequate opportunity to present new arguments and evidence.*

▸ think of or develop an argument **construct, develop, formulate, hone** *I could do with some help formulating my argument.*

▸ not accept an argument **disagree with, dismiss, rebut, refute, reject** *This book rebuts every argument ever offered to 'prove' God's existence.*

▸ make an argument weaker **contradict, counter, demolish, undermine, weaken** *This material goes some way to counter these arguments.*

▸ make an argument stronger **bolster, endorse, lend weight to, reinforce, strengthen, substantiate, support** *It supports our argument that what matters is efficiency, not achieving targets.*

arise V
begin to exist or develop

● adv+V **directly, frequently, immediately, independently, inevitably, naturally, spontaneously, unexpectedly** *A mutation of a gene may arise spontaneously in a body cell.*

● n+V something that needs to be discussed **issue, matter, question, situation** *Fox Williams has specialist expertise in advising on legal issues arising from online commerce.*

▸ problems or disagreements **complication, conflict, confusion, controversy, damage, difficulty, dispute, misunderstanding, problem, trouble** *Similar problems arise in some of the other sections.*

▸ opportunity **chance, opportunity, vacancy** *As soon as a suitable vacancy arises, we will let you know.*

▸ something causing worry or uncertainty **concern, doubt, uncertainty** *Doubt has arisen concerning the company's long-term viability.*

arm N
1 body part with your hand at the end

● v+N stretch out your arm **extend, outstretch, straighten, stretch out** *Straighten your arms bringing the bar to waist height.*

▸ move your arms **flail, flap, move, swing, wave** *George jumped up and down waving his arms.*

▸ lift/lower your arms **lift, lower, raise** *I couldn't lift my arms to get dressed.*

▸ cross your arms **cross, fold** *He relapsed into silence, standing with folded arms, staring before him.*

▸ injure your arm **break, fracture, lose, paralyse, sever** *I fell and broke my arm.*

2 part of an organization

● N+of **bank, business, charity, company, government, state** *The president represents the executive arm of government.*

arms N
weapons

● N+n buying/selling of arms **export, industry, procurement, sales, smuggling, trade, trafficking** *In the 19th century Newcastle was an international port and centre of the arms trade.*

▸ people in the arms trade **broker, dealer, exporter, manufacturer, trafficker** *They bought their weaponry from an arms dealer.*

▸ increase in arms **build-up, proliferation, race** *the problem of small arms proliferation*

▸ decrease in arms **limitation, reduction** *Ultimately all countries will have to sign up to an arms reduction protocol.*

▸ ways of reducing arms **control, decommissioning, embargo** *We continue to support international arms control and disarmament initiatives.*

▸ a supply of arms **cache, dump** *A major cave network containing a huge arms cache was discovered.*

army N
1 a large organized group of soldiers trained to fight on land

● adj+N **enemy, guerrilla, rebel, regular, reserve, standing, volunteer** *The enemy army amounted to eight or nine thousand men.*

● v+N join or be in an army **be conscripted into, be drafted into, be recruited into, enlist in, enter, go into, join, serve in** *After graduating he joined the army.*

▸ form or use an army **amass, assemble, deploy, gather, mobilize, muster** *The first battle was with the miners, then the army was deployed against the railworkers.*

▸ leave an army **be discharged from, desert from, leave** *He said he had deserted from the army and wished to surrender himself.*

● N+v when an army attacks **advance, attack (sth), besiege sth, capture sth, invade sth, occupy sth, seize sth, storm sth** *In 1868, the British army invaded Ethiopia.*

▸ when an army stops fighting **flee, retreat, surrender, withdraw** *The French and Spanish were convinced that the Allied army was retreating towards Portugal.*

2 people working or doing sth together

● adj+N **ever-growing, huge, vast, veritable, whole** *Such views are voiced daily by the vast army of EU lobbyists who depend on the EU for their incomes.*

● N+of **bureaucrats, consultants, fans, followers, helpers, lawyers, lobbyists, servants, supporters, volunteers, workers** *Now she is a part of an enthusiastic army of volunteers, each caring for around thirty children.*

arouse V
cause an emotion or attitude

● V+n **admiration, anger, controversy, curiosity, hostility, indignation, interest, jealousy, opposition, resentment, suspicion** *We argued that it was only going to arouse suspicion.*

arrange V

1 make plans for something to happen

- **V+n** appointment, funeral, get-together INFORMAL, interview, meeting, trip, viewing, visit *To arrange a home visit please telephone this number.*
- **V+for** collection, delivery, disposal, inspection, installation, payment, removal, repair, replacement, transfer *The local electricity supplier should arrange for removal of the power supply.*

2 put things in a neat or useful order

- **adv+V** in a particular way beautifully, carefully, cleverly, horizontally, neatly, randomly, symmetrically, tastefully, vertically *Every sort of vegetable was beautifully arranged on a huge plate.*
- ▶ in a particular order alphabetically, chronologically, hierarchically, thematically *They are arranged chronologically and in alphabetical order of the first letter of the surname.*

Usage **Arrange** is often passive in all of the **adv+V** combinations shown above.

3 provide something, by doing what is necessary

- **V+n** accommodation, finance, funding, insurance, loan, mortgage, transport, transportation

arrangement N

a way of organizing things

- **adj+N** alternative, appropriate, existing, financial, flexible, informal, necessary, present, special, temporary *It may be possible to make alternative arrangements.*
- **n+N** catering, childcare, funding, funeral, parking, pension, seating, security, sleeping, travel, working *Please check that the event is happening before making travel arrangements.*

Usage **Arrangement** is always plural in all of the **adj+N** and **n+N** combinations shown above.

- **v+N** make or agree an arrangement agree, come to, confirm, discuss, enter into, finalize, formalize, make, negotiate, put in place *A set of principles was agreed regarding ownership of nuclear weapons, and in 1998 this arrangement was formalized.* • *We will always make an arrangement for someone to call you back if necessary.*
- ▶ change or reconsider an arrangement cancel, change, review, revise, terminate *It is a good idea to review your pension arrangements at least once a year.*

array N

a large group of related people or things

- **adj+N** amazing, bewildering, broad, dazzling, diverse, dizzying, glittering, huge, impressive, vast, wide *A dazzling array of antique pieces can be found in 'The Silver Shop'.*
- **v+N** boast, contain, cover, create, feature, have, offer, present, produce, provide *The city boasts a fantastic array of restaurants in every price range.*

arrest N

an occasion when the police arrest someone

- **adj+N** arbitrary, false, lawful, mass, unlawful, wrongful *Several people complained of arbitrary arrests and shootings.*
- **v+N** arrest someone carry out, effect, make, place sb under, put sb under *More than a hundred arrests were made and hundreds of computers seized.*

When someone has been arrested you can also say that they are **under arrest**.: *You're under arrest.*

- ▶ try to avoid being arrested avoid, escape, evade, resist *At no time did he resist arrest.*
- ▶ be likely to be arrested face, fear, risk *Risking arrest and imprisonment, he smuggles her back to England.*
- **n+of+N** number, series, string, wave *Over the last year there has been a wave of arrests.*

arrival N

when someone or something arrives

- **adj+N** early, eventual, imminent, impending, late, punctual, safe, sudden, timely, unexpected *Mr Arbuthnot apologised profusely for his late arrival.*
- **v+N** wait for the arrival of something anticipate, await, expect *Russ found himself eagerly anticipating her arrival at the studio.*
- ▶ say or show something is arriving announce, herald, mark, signal *A knock on the door heralds the arrival of a magnificent woman in a flowery dress.*
- ▶ be there when something arrives celebrate, greet, welcome, witness *Thirty years ago I witnessed the arrival of the last steam train on this line.*
- ▶ make something's arrival later/earlier delay, hasten *This delayed our arrival at the next lesson.*
- ▶ plan the arrival of something plan, schedule, timetable *Their plane's arrival was scheduled for 12 noon.*

arrive V

reach a place, after being somewhere else

- **adv+V** eventually, finally, promptly, punctually, recently, safely, unexpectedly *Wilson arrived promptly at 4 o'clock.*

arrive at PHR VB

reach a result, decision, or solution

- **V+n** compromise, conclusion, consensus, decision, estimate, interpretation, judgement, solution, truth, understanding, verdict *Paul arrived at his conclusions from reading the committee's report.*

art N

1 painting, drawing, sculpture etc.

- **adj+N** types of art abstract, conceptual, digital, experimental, figurative, fine, folk, graphic, performance, pop, traditional, visual *He studied Fine Art at the Slade School, London.*
- ▶ art of a particular period ancient, classical, contemporary, modern, prehistoric *The Guggenheim Museum is packed with many fine examples of modern art.*
- **v+N** appreciate, commission, create, enjoy,

exhibit, inspire, produce, study, teach *I appreciate art and I want to give other people the opportunity to appreciate it as well.*

2 a special skill, especially one that is useful at work or in business

● **v+N develop, learn, master, perfect, practise** *After 20 years as a union boss, she had perfected the art of compromise.*

● **N+of communication, compromise, conversation, deception, improvisation, leadership, management, negotiation, persuasion** *The workshop was on 'The Art of Persuasion' in business negotiations.*

article N
a piece of writing about a particular subject

● **adj+N good or interesting amusing, excellent, fascinating, informative, insightful, interesting, thoughtful, thought-provoking, well-researched** *The magazine is packed with information and interesting articles on the town.*
▶ **important and influential authoritative, important, influential, major, seminal** *In 1966, Despres, Kindleberger and Salant published a seminal article in The Economist entitled 'The Dollar and World Liquidity—A Minority View'.*
▶ **long or detailed detailed, full-page, in-depth, lengthy, long** *Oppenheimer's article is lengthy, and I cannot begin to summarize it here.*
▶ **short brief, short** *Clearly in a brief article these issues cannot be dealt with.*
▶ **types of article academic, news, online, scholarly, scientific, technical** *These scholarly articles can provide interesting background material for family historians.*

● **n+N encyclopedia, front-page, journal, magazine, newspaper** *Native speakers do read aloud: horoscopes, newspaper articles, poems, etc.*

● **v+N write or publish an article contribute, post, publish, reprint, submit, write** *This article was originally published in 2003 in the Journal of Linguistics*
▶ **discuss or refer to an article cite, discuss, mention, quote (from), refer to, respond to** *In support of her case, Dickson cites two recent articles from The Lancet.*

artist N
a person who makes paintings, sculptures etc

● **adj+N talented accomplished, gifted, outstanding, talented** *The society was established in 1855, to give talented women artists an opportunity to exhibit their work.*
▶ **famous acclaimed, celebrated, famous, influential, popular, renowned, successful, well-known** *It is the first major exhibition in London devoted to this renowned German artist.*
▶ **not yet famous aspiring, budding, unknown, up-and-coming** *It can be hard for an up-and-coming artist to get people to buy his work.*
▶ **working in a particular field or medium ceramic, conceptual, contemporary, graffiti, graphic, performance, pop, tattoo, textile, visual** *The Hayward Gallery's new show draws together work by 50 contemporary artists.*

● **n+N graffiti, installation, landscape, multimedia, portrait, textile, watercolour, wildlife** *She is one of the UK's leading wildlife artists.*

ashamed ADJ
guilty or embarrassed about something

● **adv+ADJ very deeply, really INFORMAL, so, thoroughly, too, utterly, very** *He is deeply ashamed of his actions.*
▶ **slightly or rather almost, a little, quite, rather, slightly, somewhat** *I was a little ashamed of myself for having failed to enjoy his treat sufficiently.*

● **and/or confused, disgusted, embarrassed, frightened, guilty** *A third of people said they would be too ashamed or embarrassed to ask for help.*

ask V
speak or write to get information or make someone give you something

● **adv+V often commonly, constantly, continually, frequently, regularly, repeatedly** *A list of frequently asked questions is given below.*
▶ **in a particular way anxiously, casually, incredulously, innocently, jokingly, kindly, nicely, pointedly, politely, respectfully, rhetorically, sarcastically** *They were asked politely to move their cars.*
▶ **when someone asks a simple question just, merely, simply** *She simply asked whether I would prefer cheque or cash.*

● **V+n advice, blessing, forgiveness, opinion, pardon, permission** *Don't be afraid to ask advice from the people who have already done it.*

ask for PHR VB
● **V+n help or support advice, assistance, forgiveness, guidance, help, permission** *I wrote to the Minister for Culture to point out the anomalies and ask for guidance on how the situation can be resolved.*
▶ **money contribution, deposit, donation, funds, money, refund** *We called them to ask for a contribution towards our travel costs.*
▶ **information or explanation clarification, comment, confirmation, detail, explanation, feedback, information, opinion, proof** *This mailing list will provide a forum where we can share ideas, ask for feedback, and learn from good work going on elsewhere.*

asleep ADJ
not awake

● **adv+ADJ almost, deeply, fast, half, sound** *Opposite me in the armchair, William is fast asleep.*

aspect N
a particular part, feature, or quality of something [usually plural]

● **adj+N many or different different, many, several, various** *The surveys assess various aspects of school quality.*
▶ **important critical, crucial, essential, fundamental, important, key, significant, vital** *Making things by*

hand is still an important aspect of much contemporary craft.

▶ negative or worrying **challenging, controversial, disturbing, negative, problematic, worrying** *The plan has one or two worrying aspects, however.*

▶ positive or interesting **appealing, enjoyable, fascinating, interesting, intriguing, positive, rewarding, striking** *While it has many positive aspects, alternative medicine also contains some very questionable practices.*

▶ types of aspect **commercial, cultural, emotional, environmental, ethical, financial, legal, physical, political, practical, psychological, safety, security, social, spiritual, technical, theoretical** *He has interesting views on the psychological aspects of ill health, and combines physical, mental and spiritual advice in his treatments.* • *Training focuses on technical aspects of plant safety.*

● v+N **address, concentrate on, cover, deal with, discuss, encompass, examine, explore, focus on, highlight, illustrate, investigate, look at, study** *It is important that this aspect is adequately addressed in the case for support of our proposal.* • *This is a two-day short course covering all aspects of product design.*

aspiration N
something you want to achieve [usually plural]

● adj+N in a particular area of life **academic, educational, personal, political, professional, spiritual** *The KLA also developed uncompromising political aspirations.*

▶ for the future **future, longer-term, long-term** *My future aspirations are to exhibit my work here and abroad.*

▶ type of aspiration **democratic, high, legitimate, lofty, low, nationalist, noble, vague** *Shane never really had high aspirations to be famous.*

● v+N satisfy aspirations **achieve, fulfil, match, meet, realize, satisfy** *A third of those interviewed cited a lack of experience as preventing them from achieving their aspirations.*

▶ have or express aspirations **articulate, express, have, reflect, share** *It's a difficult task, and you will benefit tremendously by becoming associated with people who share your aspirations.*

▶ encourage aspirations **encouarge, raise, support** *Becoming involved in their children's development is also beneficial for adults, and can increase confidence and raise aspirations.*

● and/or **achievements, ambitions, attainments, dreams, expectations, hopes, needs** *More than 100 high-quality homes and flats are being built to meet the needs and aspirations of residents.*

assassination N
the murder of someone famous or important

● adj+N **attempted, planned, political, sectarian, targeted** *Most actual or attempted assassinations in history have been the work of crazy fanatics.*

● v+N **attempt, be behind, be involved in, order, plan, plot** *He was accused of plotting the assassination.*

assault N
1 a physical attack on someone

● adj+N **alleged, brutal, criminal, indecent, physical, serious, sexual, unprovoked, vicious, violent** *Police are also investigating another incident of indecent assault on a young girl.*

● v+N **accuse sb of, arrest sb for, charge sb with, commit, convict sb of, experience, investigate, report, suffer, witness** *Drugs are now often being used to commit sexual assault.* • *They were convicted of common assault and gaoled for three months.*

2 a military attack

● adj+N intended to cause a lot of damage **all-out, devastating, direct, fierce, full-scale, massive, relentless** *They launched an all-out assault on the convoy.*

▶ types of assault **air, airborne, amphibious, ground, infantry, military** *This was the largest and most decisive airborne assault of the war.*

● v+N start an assault **launch, lead, mount, plan** *In 1588, a fleet was assembled to mount an assault on France, but, the attempt was thwarted by bad weather.*

▶ not be killed or destroyed in an assault **repel, repulse, resist, survive, withstand** *Senior commanders confirmed Hindenburg's belief that the army would not be able to withstand an Allied assault.*

▶ be attacked **be under, come under** *The border region came under a fierce assault during June, but somehow withstood it.*

3 strong criticism

● adj+N **ferocious, furious, relentless, savage, verbal** *Lenin and his comrades launched a ferocious assault on the economists.*

● v+N **launch, mount, unleash** *Gervais has launched a new assault on the state of British comedy, claiming it doesn't match up to American standards.*

assault V
attack someone violently

● adv+V **brutally, indecently, physically, seriously, sexually, verbally, viciously, violently** *One assistant was physically assaulted.*

assemble V
1 bring people or things together

● adv+V slowly/carefully **carefully, gradually, painstakingly** *He has painstakingly assembled a team of people with great expertise and skills.*

▶ quickly or carelessly **hastily, hurriedly, quickly, rapidly** *They hastily assembled a cast for the new play.*

● V+n a group of people **army, cast, coalition, crew, panel, squad, team** *She has assembled a talented team of dancers, including youngsters from the local area.*

▶ a collection of objects or information **collection, data, evidence, material, package, portfolio, range** *After getting copies of your registered title from the Land Registry, we will assemble a complete package of information and documents to send to your buyer.*

2 come together in a group

- adv+V **hastily, hurriedly, quickly, spontaneously** *The following day, news of his resignation prompted another mass meeting, which assembled spontaneously.*

- n+V **army, congregation, crew, crowd, guests, team, throng** *A large crowd assembled and waited to see if there were any survivors.*

assembly N
a group or meeting of people

- adj+N **consultative, devolved, elected, general, legislative, municipal, national, parliamentary, provincial, regional, unelected** *Yorkshire already had an unelected regional assembly.*

- v+N hold an assembly **call, convene, hold, stage** *The great national assembly was held in August.*

- ▸ elect an assembly **elect, elect sb to** *The assembly was elected in 1992.* • *Only 10 women were elected to the assembly.*

- ▸ end an assembly **abolish, dissolve, suspend** *The Pope was afraid, and in December 1431, he sent a bull to Cardinal Cesarini dissolving the assembly.*

- ▸ speak to an assembly **address, present sth to, report to, speak to** *The Secretary of State accepted an early invitation to address the Assembly.* • *The document presented to the Assembly in mid-December is based on incomplete data.* • *Consider whether any changes are needed and report to the Assembly.*

- N+v **convene, meet, sit** *The Assembly meets today in a state of concern and confusion.*

assert V
1 state firmly that something is true

- adv+V strongly or openly **boldly, confidently, dogmatically, emphatically, firmly, publicly, repeatedly, strongly** *Trade, he has repeatedly asserted, should not be conducted as a form of economic war.*

- ▸ without giving evidence **merely, simply** *The cultural and moral decline of late capitalist civilisation needs to be demonstrated, not merely asserted.*

2 claim a right firmly

- V+n authority **authority, control, dominance, ownership, sovereignty, superiority** *He confided to club management that he found it difficult to assert his authority and control a number of the players.*

- ▸ a right **claim, identity, independence, individuality, right** *You will probably also find that your child uses her new-found vocabulary to assert her independence.*

assertion N
a claim that something is true

- adj+N strongly stated **bald, bold, confident, dogmatic, repeated, sweeping** *This is just one of a number of sweeping assertions with which I do not agree.*

- ▸ untrue or not proved **bare, false, mere, unfounded, unsubstantiated, unsupported** *His attempt to claim that only his own work is correct is something which requires more than mere assertion.*

- ▸ v+N make an assertion **make, repeat** *Before we proceed, we have to make an assertion that affects the forthcoming elaboration.*

- ▸ support or prove an assertion **justify, prove, support** *There is no shortage of statistics to support this assertion.*

- ▸ challenge an assertion or prove it wrong **challenge, contradict, dispute, refute, reject** *'If Shakespeare were alive today, he'd be writing for Hollywood'. Justify or refute this assertion.*

assess V
consider something carefully in order to judge it

- adv+V in a particular way **critically, formally, independently, objectively** *Applications are assessed independently by an international selection panel in consultation with the local organizers of each meeting.*

- ▸ well **accurately, carefully, fully, properly** *The problem needs to be properly assessed.*

- ▸ in education **externally, internally** *One piece of work will be externally assessed.*

- V+n likelihood of success **feasibility, risk, suitability, viability** *The viability of the new system needs to be carefully assessed.*

- ▸ effect **effectiveness, impact, progress** *The effectiveness of the treatment was independently assessed.*

- ▸ needs **needs** *Advice and guidance on how to identify and assess your training needs is available at no cost.*

- ▸ size **extent** *Experts were called in to assess the extent of the damage.*

- ▸ in education **assignment, coursework, essay, module** *We can assess not just students' coursework, but also their role in online discussions.* • *Most University-based modules are assessed on the basis of coursework.*

assessment N
the process of considering something in order to judge it

- adj+N thorough **accurate, comprehensive, detailed, rigorous, thorough** *No detailed assessment of the running costs has yet been made.*

- ▸ done at the beginning **initial, preliminary** *Today I want to give you our preliminary assessment of the measures we need to examine urgently.*

- ▸ in education **continuous, formal, in-course** *Progress on the course is monitored by continuous assessment.*

- n+N **impact, needs, quality, risk, safety** *A needs assessment must be carried out for everyone over the age of 75.*

- v+N **carry out, complete, conduct, make, perform, provide, undertake** *It is recommended that a risk assessment be carried out before embarking on any of these routes.*

- N+of of risk or danger **hazard, risk** *In all cases, an assessment of risks to health must now be undertaken by a competent person.*

- ▸ of performance **effectiveness, performance, progress** *The Government is committed to publishing its own annual assessment of its progress in tackling poverty and social exclusion.*

asset N

1 something that a person or company owns [usually plural]

- adj+N total **total** *Total assets are just over £430 million.*
- ▶ more than you need **surplus** *The company will need to dispose of its surplus assets.*
- ▶ types of asset **business, capital, financial, fixed, intangible, liquid, property, tangible** *Liquid assets at that time were negligible.*
- v+N have or keep assets **hold, manage, own, protect, safeguard** *The Charity's solicitor confirmed that all assets are owned by the Society.*
- ▶ sell or get rid of assets **dispose of, liquidate, realize, sell, transfer** *I wish I had liquidated my assets and gone on one last great journey instead.*
- ▶ take control of assets **freeze, seize** *The police were given new powers to seize criminals' assets in the Proceeds of Crime Act 2002.*
- ▶ buy assets **acquire, purchase** *Gains on assets acquired by taxpayers whilst resident outside the UK will not be included in the new charge.*
- n+of+N **acquisition, confiscation, disposal, ownership, realization, sale, transfer, valuation** *The valuation of assets, both tangible and intangible, is an important element of corporate finance.*

2 a major benefit [usually singular]

- adj+N **great, important, invaluable, priceless, prized, tremendous, valuable** *People are our most valuable asset; they are our biggest investment.*

assignment N

1 work that you do as part of your job

- adj+N **overseas, short-term, temporary, tough** *I wanted to take advantage of being with my husband who is on an overseas assignment.*
- v+N **accept, complete, undertake** *He now works as a freelance independent consultant and has recently completed assignments in the UK, Europe, Asia and Africa.*

2 work that you do as part of your studies

- adj+N **marked, practical, short, tutor-marked, written** *Students are required to submit a written assignment.*
- v+N **assess, complete, do, grade, mark, submit, write** *In order to gain maximum benefit from the distance learning course a planned method of study should be followed with completed assignments being submitted regularly.*

assist V

help someone or something

- adv+V **ably, actively, directly, financially, greatly, materially** *Ably assisted by their friendly staff, they attend to the social needs of their elderly clients.*
- V+in **creation, delivery, development, implementation, management, planning, preparation, production, running** *A group of part-time lecturers assist us in the delivery of the training programme.*
- V+with **development, implementation,**

management, planning, preparation, running *Reporting to the Occupational Health Manager you will assist with the future development of the service.*

assistance N

help that allows someone to do something

- adj+N types of assistance **development, direct, expert, financial, humanitarian, legal, medical, mutual, practical, professional, technical** *There are two ways the College can provide direct financial assistance for students: college loans and college welfare grants.*
- ▶ needed immediately **emergency, immediate, urgent** *Please remember always to dial the Police on 999 if you require urgent assistance.*
- ▶ helpful **generous, invaluable, valuable** *The St John's ambulance service will be on hand in the event of any accidents and we thank them for their invaluable assistance.*
- v+N ask for or need assistance **ask for, need, request, require, seek** *I am also going to seek their assistance with setting up the new system.*
- ▶ get assistance **get, obtain, receive** *There are a series of documents available for external organizations interested in receiving assistance with sports projects.*
- ▶ be grateful for assistance **acknowledge, appreciate, be grateful for** *He will appreciate any assistance with this project.*
- ▶ give assistance **give, offer, provide, render** *Unfortunately, the police seem unable to curb this problem or even offer much assistance.*

assistant N

a person who helps someone in their work

- adj+N types of assistant **administrative, clerical, personal, technical** *In February 1996 I was successful in becoming an administrative assistant in the School.*
- ▶ at a particular level **junior, senior** *I am working as a senior technical assistant in an IT company in Dubai.*
- ▶ working all/part of the time **full-time, part-time** *They recruited a part-time assistant to help on the project.*
- n+N **classroom, laboratory, language, library, research, sales, shop, teaching** *He completed the study while working as a research assistant at the university.*
- v+N **appoint, employ, hire, recruit** *The journal needs to employ an editorial assistant to do this work.*
- N+n **coach, director, editor, manager, professor** *Between 1923–1924 he was the assistant editor of the Transatlantic Review in Paris.*

assortment N

a set of things of various types

- adj+N large **huge, large, rich, vast, wide** *The centre houses a rich assortment of native butterflies, many of which are close to disappearing in the wild.*
- ▶ varied or strange **diverse, eclectic, motley, odd, random, strange, varied** *The square to the west of the building attracts a varied assortment of street performers.*

assume V
1 believe that something is true without proof

- adv+V wrongly **erroneously, incorrectly, mistakenly, wrongly** *Some people miss out on benefits because they wrongly assume they cannot claim anything when they are working.*
- ▶ naturally, without questioning **automatically, implicitly, just, naively, naturally, simply** *We do not automatically assume that all our visitors will come by car.* • *Similarly, individual teachers may teach in ways that reflect their own learning styles and implicitly assume that all their students learn that way.*
- ▶ usually **always, commonly, generally, often, usually, widely** *It is often assumed that air pollution in London is a recent phenomenon.*
- ▶ correctly **correctly, reasonably, safely** *The door beneath, which we may safely assume is original, is probably 12th century.*

Usage In academic writing **assume** is often used in the passive: *It is often incorrectly assumed that ...*

2 start to have control or responsibility

- V+n power or responsibility **command, control, power, responsibility** *In your absence we will assume complete responsibility for your property.*
- ▶ a job or position **chairmanship, leadership, position, presidency, role** *Upon retiring, he embarked upon a couple of coaching stints in Greece before assuming his current position in 2003.*

assumption N
something you consider likely to be true

- adj+N basic **basic, fundamental** *This book challenges basic assumptions about road travel and calls on the government to step in before it is too late.*
- ▶ false **erroneous, false, faulty, incorrect, mistaken, questionable** *Policy has often been based on the false assumption that adults learn foreign languages in the same way that a child learns its native tongue.*
- ▶ reasonable **reasonable** *Is this a reasonable assumption for me to make, do you think?*
- ▶ not examined **implicit, tacit, unexamined, unquestioned, unspoken, unstated** *This presentation challenged many of our often unspoken assumptions regarding the subject.*
- v+N make an assumption **make** *Probably the most important assumptions made in the projections are about future levels of migration.*
- ▶ question an assumption **challenge, examine, question, test** *There is plenty of scope for challenging long-held beliefs and questioning assumptions about the right way to do things.*
- ▶ not accept an assumption **contradict, reject** *Even if we reject this assumption, he is right that there are two clear ways to explain the phenomena.*
- N+v be based on, underlie, underpin *Dave critically evaluated the assumptions underlying this approach.*

You can also say that you do or decide something **on the assumption that**: *We accepted the proposal on the assumption that they would pay the start-up costs.*

assurance N
1 a statement made to remove doubt about something

- adj+N written/spoken **verbal, written** *They have given a written assurance that introducing the new working arrangements will not mean a reduction of staff.*
- ▶ strong **absolute, categorical, repeated, unconditional** *They gave an unconditional assurance that the law would be changed.*
- ▶ not convincing **bland** *Bland assurances that all work is carried out with integrity and objectivity will not suffice.*
- v+N ask for assurance **demand, require, seek, want** *There are around ten countries from whom we are seeking such assurances.*
- ▶ give assurance **give, offer, provide** *The procedures and equipment should be monitored with sufficient frequency to provide assurance that the process is working well.*
- ▶ get assurance **accept, have, obtain, receive, welcome** *We welcome their assurance that the document does not represent University policy.*

2 the fact of being very confident or certain

- adj+N **calm, complete, great, quiet** *To add to an excellent technique, she moves beautifully and dances with charm and calm assurance.*

astonishment N
very great surprise

- adj+N **absolute, complete, great, utmost, utter** *Raymond was staring at us in absolute astonishment.*
- v+N **cause, express** *In legal circles throughout the world, the recognition of the rebel forces caused great astonishment and was condemned.*
- v+in+N **gasp, gaze, stare, watch** *We both stood gazing in astonishment.*
- n+of+N **exclamation, expression, gasp, look** *It was a comment that caused gasps of astonishment around the chamber.*

astute ADJ
good at judging situations and people quickly

- adv+ADJ in a particular way **commercially, financially, politically, psychologically, tactically, technically** *We pride ourselves on being commercially astute, responsive and approachable.*
- ▶ very **exceptionally, particularly, remarkably, very** *He is a very astute player and tactically really aware.*
- ADJ+n person **businessman, businesswoman, investor, observer, politician** *James was an astute businessman who rose to become a leading figure in Darwen at that time.*
- ▶ action **analysis, move, observation** *There are many astute observations about the human condition.*

asylum N
the right to stay somewhere to escape danger

- adj+N **political, temporary** *She claimed political asylum on her arrival in the country.*
- v+N ask for asylum **apply for, claim, request,**

seek *He left a good business behind to seek asylum in England.*
▶ give asylum **give, grant** *We will continue to give asylum to genuine refugees and never play politics with immigration.*
▶ refuse asylum **deny, refuse** *He has been in England for four months and has already been refused asylum and is in the process of appeal.*
● N+n **applicant, application, claim, seeker** *Violet is an asylum seeker who fled her native land after her husband and brother were murdered.*

atmosphere N
the mood that exists in a place

● adj+N friendly **convivial, cosy, friendly, homely, intimate, warm** *A dedicated area especially for children enhances the welcoming and friendly, family atmosphere.*
▶ pleasant; making you feel relaxed **informal, laid-back, peaceful, relaxed, relaxing** *With its laid-back atmosphere and very reasonable prices, Brandnertal ski resort is an ideal family winter destination.*
▶ exciting **electric, lively, vibrant** *Everyone enjoyed the lively atmosphere and good food.*
▶ unpleasant **claustrophobic, tense** *The lush photography and extreme close ups add to the claustrophobic atmosphere.*
● v+N create or add to an atmosphere **add to, capture, contribute to, create, evoke, exude, foster, provide, recreate** *The CD is actually recorded in a studio, but apparently captures the atmosphere of their live performances.*
▶ change an atmosphere **heighten, lighten** *All treatments are carried out in a peaceful environment with calming music to heighten the relaxing atmosphere.*
▶ enjoy or experience an atmosphere **absorb, enjoy, experience, savour** *Ten of us attended and everyone enjoyed the lively atmosphere and good food.*
▶ spoil an atmosphere **spoil** *Although chart music was playing during my lunchtime visit it was very low key and didn't spoil the atmosphere.*
▶ keep an atmosphere **maintain, retain** *The town manages to maintain a village atmosphere and a sense of community.*
● N+of a good atmosphere **calm, peace, tranquillity, trust** *Visitors to the College frequently comment on its atmosphere of calm.*
▶ a bad atmosphere **distrust, fear, hysteria, mistrust, tension** *Not sharing information creates an atmosphere of distrust.*

atrocity N
a cruel and violent act, often in war [usually plural]

● adj+N very bad **appalling, brutal, horrible, horrific, terrible, unspeakable** *Appalling atrocities are caused and driven by the brutality of warfare.*
▶ types of atrocity **terrorist, wartime** *He was found guilty of perpetrating a series of wartime atrocities.*
● v+N **carry out, commit, inflict, perpetrate** *Having committed atrocities, individual soldiers are left with the guilt and the grief to deal with.*

attach V
1 join something to something

● adv+V **firmly, loosely, permanently, securely** *Is the cable securely attached to the appliance?*

2 be connected with something or someone

● n+V **blame, condition, goodwill, liability, stigma** *It may be true that some blame attaches to the management of the place.*

3 to think that something is important

● V+n **importance, significance, value, weight** *We attach particular importance to good diplomatic relations between the two countries.*

attached ADJ
liking someone or something very much, or loving someone

● adv+ADJ **deeply, devotedly, emotionally, sincerely, strongly, too, warmly** *Although their marriage was a political alliance, the pair became deeply attached.*

attack V
1 use violence against someone or something

● adv+V **aggressively, brutally, fiercely, physically, savagely, viciously, violently** *A man was viciously attacked by a gang of youths last night.*

2 criticize someone or something

● adv+V in a particular way **directly, openly, personally, repeatedly, verbally** *In the article he publicly attacked the competence of public sector managers.*
▶ strongly **aggressively, bitterly, fiercely, savagely, strongly, viciously, violently** *I was bitterly attacked and denounced by American radicals of almost every camp.*

attack N
1 a violent attempt to harm someone or something

● adj+N **armed, brutal, frenzied, homophobic, racist, savage, sectarian, unprovoked, vicious, violent** *It was a completely unprovoked attack.*
● n+N **arson, firebomb, revenge** *He was the victim of a firebomb attack on his shop in Whitechapel, London in 1999.*
● v+N **carry out** *It would not be possible for anyone to compose themselves so instantaneously after carrying out such a frenzied attack.*

2 an organized attempt to defeat an enemy

● adj+N **all-out, devastating, pre-emptive, sustained** *A new, radical strategy of pre-emptive attack was outlined to handle terrorists and states who helped them.*

> You can also say that someone or something *is under attack* or that they *come under attack*: *The army headquarters came under sustained attack.*

● n+N using a particular weapon **bomb, gas, grenade, missile, mortar, rocket** *The garrison is on standby but there has not been a rocket attack in weeks.*

▶ using particular people or a particular method
air, guerrilla, infantry, insurgent, suicide, terror, terrorist *It was not a suicide attack, but two car bombs.*

● v+N carry out an attack **carry out, launch, mount, plan** *In retaliation, the army mounted a missile attack on the capital.*

▶ prevent or fight against an attack **counter, deter, repel, repulse, resist, withstand** *The British attack was repulsed but the French made progress in both sectors.*

3 strong criticism

● adj+N **bitter, blistering, concerted, fierce, scathing, stinging, vitriolic** *She launched a scathing attack on the party's campaign tactics.*

● v+N **launch, mount** *Orkney's chief librarian launched an attack on the council after plans for a new Orkney library fell victim to major cutbacks.*

4 the beginning or return of an illness

● n+N **asthma, heart, migraine, panic** *John apparently suffered a major heart attack.*

● v+N **suffer, trigger** *He had suffered a heart attack.*

attain V
succeed in achieving something after much effort; reach something

● V+n state **eminence, enlightenment, maturity, perfection, salvation** *It can be impossible to attain perfection, but with time, effort and the correct approach some progress can be made.*

▶ level or qualification **degree, grade, level, qualification, standard** *Most pupils attain grade A* or A at GCSE.*

attempt N
1 an effort to do something

● adj+N unsuccessful **abortive, botched, bungled, failed, fruitless, futile, misguided, unsuccessful, vain** *He made three unsuccessful attempts to get the right position.*

▶ successful **successful** *The article makes a not entirely successful attempt to explain the new trend.*

▶ determined **brave, concerted, deliberate, desperate, determined, repeated, serious, valiant** *She had made a brave attempt at making herself presentable.*

▶ weak **feeble, half-hearted, pathetic** *She made one final feeble attempt to fight him but her strength had gone.*

● v+N oppose an attempt **block, oppose, reject, resist, undermine** *Most companies are resisting attempts to squeeze cash from them.*

▶ make an attempt **make** *This paper makes an attempt to appraise how successful the new policy has been.*

▶ give up an attempt **abandon** *Unfortunately the Government seems to have abandoned all attempts to limit traffic levels.*

2 an unsuccessful, illegal or wrong act

● n+N **assassination, coup, suicide** *Young people with a past history of suicide attempts are at greater risk of engaging in further suicide attempts.*

▶ v+N **foil, thwart** *Lastly, can I pay tribute to the*

police and security services who have in recent days clearly foiled a serious attempt to commit a terrorist attack in this county.

attempted ADJ
unsuccessful

● ADJ+n **abduction, arson, assassination, break-in, burglary, coup, fraud, murder, rape, robbery, suicide, theft** *A youth was charged with attempted murder for hitting a policeman in South Yorkshire.*

attend V
1 be present at an event or activity

● adv+V **poorly, sparsely, well** *The Christmas party was very well attended.*

> Usage *Attend* is always passive in these combinations.

● V+n meeting **conference, interview, meeting, reunion, session** *Attending networking meetings and 'best practice' seminars is essential.*

▶ event **ceremony, concert, dinner, event, funeral, launch, rally, wedding** *Stunned and shocked, he attended her funeral.*

▶ educational event **lecture, seminar, workshop** *Approximately 4000 children attend orchestra workshops each year.*

2 go regularly to a place

● adv+V **currently, regularly** *Over 1,000 men currently attend our mixed classes every week and enjoy great success.*

● V+n **church, class, clinic, college, course, nursery, school, university** *Several students are now attending the local sixth form college.*

attendance N
the number of people present or the fact of being present

● adj+N good **good, punctual, regular** *Successful completion of the course depends on regular attendance.*

▶ when attendance is necessary **compulsory, full time, mandatory** *School attendance is compulsory between the ages of 5 and 16 years.*

▶ mentioning the number of people attending **average, disappointing, estimated, high, large, record, total** *Average weekly attendance rose by seven per cent during 2002.*

▶ bad **irregular, low, poor, unsatisfactory** *Attendance was unsatisfactory in a quarter of schools.*

● v+N improve attendance **attract, boost, encourage, improve, increase, maximize** *Specialist witness care units in North Wales have improved witness attendance at court by 29%.*

▶ saying attendance is necessary **compel, ensure, require** *Attendance is not required and you may enrol at any time.*

● N+n **figure, rate, record** *Attendance figures at the venue have doubled in the last 4 years.*

● n+in+N **decline, drop, increase** *The public relations exercise paid off and there was a significant increase in attendance figures.*

attention N

1 interest or thought given to something or someone

- adj+N complete **considerable, much, rapt, undivided** *You will have our undivided attention throughout.*
- ▶ little **insufficient, little, scant** *Scant attention was paid to sport.*
- ▶ not wanted **unwanted, unwelcome** *Try not to draw any unwanted attention to yourself.*
- ▶ careful **careful, close, meticulous, particular, special** *We use suppliers who pay careful attention to issues that are important to consumers.*
- v+N get someone's attention **attract, capture, catch, command, draw, grab** INFORMAL, **have, receive** *These are classy boats that will attract attention both when at rest and at speed.*

You can also say that you ***bring something to someone's attention***: *We brought the poor state of the accommodation to their attention.*

- ▶ give attention to **devote, direct, focus, give, pay, turn** *Pay special attention to the kitchen and bathroom.*
- ▶ take attention away from **deflect, distract, divert** *New structures and projects can divert attention away from day-to-day services.*
- ▶ deserve attention **demand, deserve, merit** *One aspect which deserves special attention is media management.*
- N+v when attention changes **focus, move, shift, switch, turn** *Attention now turns to the question of how the plan will be implemented.*
- ▶ when attention goes away **drift, wander** *Turn on the radio and sing to yourself when you find your attention wandering.*
- N+to **aspect, issue, matter, problem** *Thank you most sincerely for your attention to this matter.*
- n+of+N **centre, focus, object** *During the post-war period, the cost of air travel became the focus of attention.*

2 care given to someone or something

- adj+N immediate **immediate, prompt, urgent** *If something requires urgent attention, please contact any member of our Customer Services Team.*
- ▶ medical **medical** *You should be able to get all necessary medical attention if you get into trouble.*
- v+N need attention **demand, need, require** *Dogs are animals that need attention.*
- ▶ give attention **give, lavish** *This is a stunning-looking book that's had a lot of attention lavished on it.*

attitude N

someone's opinions or feelings about something

- adj+N good **can-do** INFORMAL, **caring, enlightened, favourable, liberal, mature, never-say-die** INFORMAL, **positive, right, tolerant** *Pupils showed positive attitudes towards all aspects of their school life.*
- ▶ bad **ambivalent, condescending, contemptuous, defeatist, dismissive, elitist, entrenched, hostile, negative, paternalistic, patronizing, uncaring** *Where the attitudes are negative there are usually*

reasons such as lack of knowledge, over-protection and poverty.

- ▶ relaxed or too relaxed **cavalier, lackadaisical, laid-back, laissez-faire, relaxed** *Stockbridge is a part of the city know for its antique shops and its laid-back attitude.*
- ▶ showing hate or fear **ageist, aggressive, discriminatory, homophobic, hostile, racist, sexist** *It also noted that these discriminatory attitudes go unchallenged.*
- ▶ types of attitude **changing, mental, parental, prevailing, public, societal** *A prevailing attitude of many in our culture is wanting to be clear about everything all of the time.*
- v+N form or change an attitude **challenge, change, develop, influence, shape** *Education is therefore crucial to raising this awareness and changing attitudes and behaviour.*
- ▶ have or show an attitude **adopt, display, express, have, reflect** *I determined that from then on, I should adopt a more positive attitude to life.*
- ▶ examine an attitude **examine, explore** *The module will examine popular attitudes towards post-war social, cultural and political developments.*
- ▶ encourage an attitude **cultivate, encourage, promote**
- N+v **harden, persist, prevail** *This attitude prevailed for a further 40 years.*

attorney N

a lawyer

- adj+N at a particular rank or level **assistant, district, provincial, senior, state** *A lot of assistant state attorneys do their 3-year commitment and then leave.*
- ▶ in a particular area of work **corporate, criminal, defense, divorce, patent, personal, prosecuting** *Prominent criminal attorney Arthur Jamison must plan the perfect murder in this psychological thriller.*
- v+N **appoint, consult, contact, hire, retain** *It is always wise to hire an attorney or broker to look over the final paperwork.*

attract V

make someone want to go somewhere or do something

- V+n people **audience, crowd, delegate, people, recruit, tourist, viewer, visitor** *It is now a Country Park which attracts about 200,000 visitors from the local area.*
- ▶ reaction **attention, criticism, interest, publicity, support** *The idea is already attracting the attention of investors.*
- ▶ business **buyer, clientele, customer, investment, investor, shopper** *I feel that if you get one developer interested in coming to Dover, it will attract other investment.*

attraction N

1 a place or event that is enjoyable to visit

- adj+N how big or important **big, famous, main, major, must-see, popular, premier, star, star, top, world-class** *The main attraction is the string of beaches.*
- ▶ types of attraction **cultural, heritage, historic,**

leisure, local, seaside *Let us discover and support local attractions which may be close to home and yet we have never bothered to visit them.*

- n+N **family, tourist, visitor** *In its day, Belle Vue was one of the premier tourist attractions in the North-West of England.*
- v+N visit or enjoy an attraction **discover, enjoy, experience, explore, visit** *After lunch you will tour Malacca visiting its major attractions.*
- ▸ have an attraction **boast, have, offer** *As well as the animals, the zoo boasted many other attractions.*
- n+of+N **abundance, array, host, multitude, number, variety, wealth** *Warwickshire has a wealth of local attractions to inspire the visitor!*

2 the feeling of liking someone or something

- adj+N **irresistible, mutual, sexual** *Initially, they find that their differences are a source of mutual attraction.*
- v+N **exert, experience, feel, hold** *The mountains exerted their attraction on Brian at an early age.*

attractive ADJ
1 pleasant to look at

- adv+ADJ very **exceptionally, extremely, highly, particularly, strikingly, stunningly, very** *This is a stunningly attractive book.*
- ▸ in a particular way **aesthetically, physically, sexually, visually** *The layout of the garden was aesthetically attractive.*

2 worth having, considering, or doing

- adv+ADJ very **extremely, highly, particularly, very** *The offer of a new car was particularly attractive.*
- ▸ more **increasingly** *Taking the train instead of flying was looking like an increasingly attractive option.*
- ▸ on the surface **superficially** *Although superficially attractive, these arguments pose several problems.*
- ▸ in a particular way **commercially, economically, financially** *It was not a commercially attractive proposition.*
- ADJ+n **alternative, option, proposition, prospect** *The night bus service has also improved hugely, making late nights in town a more attractive proposition*

attribute N
a quality or feature of someone or something

- adj+N good or important **desirable, essential, important, positive, unique** *'People skills' are an essential attribute for a teacher to have.*
- ▸ types of attribute **divine, personal, physical, specific** *What personal attributes make a good dancer?*
- v+N **display, have, possess** *This is an interesting study which has several unique design attributes.*

attribute to PHR VB
believe that something is the result of something else; believe or say that something was written, said, painted etc by someone

- adv+V wrongly **erroneously, falsely, incorrectly,**

mistakenly, wrongly *Her teachers wrongly attributed her learning difficulties to emotional problems.*
- ▸ correctly **correctly, properly** *I had always thought that that particular phrase was properly attributed to Freud.*
- ▸ partly/completely **largely, mainly, partially, partly, wholly** *The differences can be partly attributed to the fact that not all state governments monitor waste disposal closely.*
- ▸ often **commonly, generally, often, usually** *The original concept of satellite television is often attributed to writer Arthur C. Clarke.*
- ▸ by different people **variously** *Vegetation change has been variously attributed to inappropriate grazing and burning regimes, increased atmospheric pollution and climate change.*

Usage **Attribute to** is almost always used in the passive in all of the **adv+V** combinations shown above.

audible ADJ
loud enough to hear

- adv+ADJ difficult to hear **barely, hardly, scarcely** *His voice was barely audible over the drone of the engine.*
- ▸ easy to hear **clearly, distinctly, perfectly** *The music was clearly audible over the noise of the television.*

audience N
1 the people who are present at a concert, play, film etc

- adj+N big **capacity, large, packed** *He received an excellent reception from the capacity audience.*
- ▸ interested **appreciative, enthusiastic, receptive** *The concert took place in front of an enthusiastic audience.*
- v+N entertain an audience **captivate, delight, entertain, enthrall, wow** INFORMAL *Their live sets have wowed audiences all over the country.*
- ▸ make people want to watch, hear etc **attract, pull in** INFORMAL *The show attracted an estimated audience of over 8,000 people.*
- ▸ talk to an audience **address** *Brown addressed an audience of business leaders in Glasgow.*

2 the people who watch, read, or listen to something

- adj+N large or varied **diverse, mass, wide** *The contributions are from American academics but the insights offered are relevant to a much wider audience.*
- ▸ possible audience **intended, potential, target** *The book's intended audience is teenagers.*
- v+N **reach, target** *Joy targets a young adult audience – mostly female in the 25–35 age-range.*

audit N
an official examination of a company's financial records or of the size, number or effectiveness of something

- adj+N done within an organization **internal** *An internal audit found fresh evidence of improper access to confidential computer files.*
- ▸ done by someone outside an organization

external, independent *An independent audit will measure the effectiveness of your company's policies.*

▶ thorough and complete **comprehensive, detailed, full** *A detailed audit of crime was undertaken in the city.*

● v+N **carry out, conduct, do, perform, undertake** *Audits are normally conducted after the end of the financial year in March.*

author N

a person who who writes books, articles etc

● adj+N famous **famous, renowned, well-known** *This is a travel book by one of Germany's best-known authors.*

▶ admired or successful **acclaimed, award-winning, best-selling, popular** *The film is based on a novel by acclaimed Swedish author, Jan Guillou.*

▶ writing many books **prolific** *He was a prolific author, writing many books about the history of Scotland.*

● N+of **abstract, article, bestseller, book, novel, paper, report, study, textbook, work** *Claire is the author of two papers to be presented at the 2010 Digital Humanities Conference in Paris.*

authority N

1 an expert

● adj+N **acknowledged, foremost, leading, respected, ultimate, world** *The author is a leading authority **on** all forms of motorcycle sport.*

2 a public organization with the power to make decisions

● adj+N **local, municipal, public, regional** *Ms Lakeberg worked as a part-time teacher for the regional authority.*

● n+N thing the organization is responsible for **broadcasting, education, funding, health, highways, housing, immigration, planning, police, transport** *The local education authority deals with applications for school places.*

▶ place controlled **airport, city, district, hospital, university** *City authorities across the country are being forced to cut their budgets.*

3 the power and right to do something

● adj+N complete **absolute, complete, supreme** *He said that he was giving Richardson absolute authority in handling the investigation.*

▶ types of authority **judicial, legal, moral** *If another person completes the form on your behalf, they must have the legal authority to do so.*

● v+N give or have authority **delegate, devolve, give, grant, have, hold** *Education policy is an area where authority is devolved to local municipalities.* ● *He did not have the authority to sign the agreement.*

▶ use authority **assert, exercise, exert** *The new Kaiser was determined to assert his authority.*

▶ weaken or question authority **challenge, question, undermine** *Government intervention can undermine the authority of teachers.*

authorization N

official permission to do something

● adj+N **official, prior, proper, written** *Travel or business in the country without prior authorization is banned.*

● v+N get or have authorization **get, have, obtain, receive** *In 1765 the Caribbean islands received authorization for almost unlimited trade with Spanish ports.*

▶ give authorization **give, grant, provide** *Goods should not be returned unless we have given authorization.*

▶ ask for authorization **request, seek** *You need to request authorization to access the files.*

▶ refuse to give authorization **cancel, refuse, revoke, withdraw** *The panel recommended that Mr Donnelly, who previously held this power, should have his authorization withdrawn.*

autonomy N

independence

● adj+N high level of autonomy **complete, considerable, full, greater** *We work closely with other organizations while maintaining complete autonomy.*

▶ types of autonomy **financial, individual, local, national, personal, political, professional, regional** *The guerrillas began fighting for regional autonomy in the north.*

● v+N have or keep autonomy **enjoy, have, maintain, preserve, retain** *She will have greater professional autonomy and be better off financially.*

▶ give or increase autonomy **give, grant, increase, promote** *The school uses IT to promote autonomy in learning.*

▶ limit someone's autonomy **limit, undermine** *Undermining teachers' autonomy forces good teachers to leave the profession.*

autumn N

season between summer and winter

● adj+N late or early **early, late** *The best time to sow your wildflower seeds is in early autumn.*

▶ with a particular type of weather **cool, dry, glorious, mild, sunny, warm, wet** *After a rather dismal summer, we had a glorious autumn.*

● N+n **colour, leaves, months, rain, season, sun, sunshine** *The autumn season generally gives the best mountain views, as the air at this time is crystal clear.*

availability N

how easy it is to get or use something

● adj+N when something is easy to get **easy, general, greater, ready, wide, widespread** *The easy availability of broadband makes working from home a viable option.*

You can also say that something can be bought **subject to availability**: *Tickets may be obtained on the door on the evening of the performance (subject to availability).*

▶ when something is not easy to get **limited, restricted** *Please book early to avoid disappointment as there is limited availability.*

- v+N check or confirm availability **check, confirm, ensure, guarantee** *Please contact your stockist to check the availability of our products before making a special journey.*
- ▶ increase availability **extend, improve, increase** *In order to improve the availability of our service, we offer advice by telephone and email.*
- ▶ reduce availability **limit, reduce, restrict** *Reducing the availability of illegal drugs is a key priority.*

available ADJ
able to be obtained, taken, or used

- adv+ADJ **commercially, commonly, easily, freely, generally, locally, publicly, readily, universally, widely** *Unfortunately, the medicines necessary for treatment aren't readily available in Guatemala.*
- ADJ+for **collection, consultation, download, hire, inspection, purchase, sale, use** *The seminar and lecture facility is available for hire.*

avenue N
1 a wide straight road

- adj+N **broad, leafy, quiet, shady, tree-lined, wide** *The hotel is ideally located on an elegant, tree-lined avenue.*

2 one way of achieving something [usually plural]

- adj+N **alternative, fresh, fruitful, interesting, new, possible, potential, promising** *Explore all possible avenues for a solution before referring any dispute to a higher authority.*

> You can also say that there is an **avenue open to** you: *There are several avenues open to us in this situation.*

- v+N try a way of achieving something **consider, explore, investigate, pursue, try** *The company is exploring avenues to maximize revenue.*
- ▶ provide a way of achieving something **offer, open, provide** *This research opens new avenues that will directly impact patient care.*
- ▶ try every way of achieving something **exhaust** *Prakash has exhausted all legal avenues in the British Courts and is now going to the European Court.*

avert V
prevent something bad from happening

- adv+V **narrowly** *Mercifully, war was narrowly averted.*
- V+n **catastrophe, conflict, crisis, danger, disaster, famine, strike, threat, tragedy, war** *A security guard came outside just as the men were preparing to light the fuse, averting potential disaster.*

avoid V
try to prevent something bad from happening or existing

- adv+V by being careful **carefully, deliberately, scrupulously, studiously** *He studiously avoided all mention of his past or present situation.*
- ▶ only just avoid **narrowly, only just** *The youngster narrowly avoided a collision with a bus coming in the opposite direction.*

- V+n a feeling **disappointment, embarrassment, stress** *Please book in advance to avoid disappointment.*
- ▶ a bad situation **collision, complications, conflict, confrontation, danger, delay, disruption, injury, mistake, pitfall, problem, temptation** *To avoid delays in registration, please complete the application form in full.*
- ▶ confusion **ambiguity, confusion, misunderstanding** *Most of the changes to the text have been made in an attempt to avoid the misunderstandings associated with the use of the first edition.*

await V
1 wait for something

- adv+V **anxiously, eagerly, excitedly, impatiently, keenly, nervously, patiently** *He anxiously awaited more news, fearing he would never see his son again.*

2 when something is going to happen to you

- n+V **adventure, challenge, experience, fate, future, opportunity, shock, surprise, welcome** *After a swift breakfast, they walked back to Lakeside House, where a nasty shock awaited them.* • *A warm and friendly welcome awaits you at all our hotels.*

awake ADJ
not sleeping

- adv+ADJ completely awake **fully, wide** *Now it's 1.17am and I'm wide awake.*
- ▶ only just awake **barely, half** *'Good morning,' said Cole, only half awake himself.*

awaken V
make someone experience a feeling or emotion

- V+n **conscience, curiosity, desire, interest, memory, senses, suspicion, sympathy** *For some people, this anniversary might awaken bad memories.*

award N
1 a prize

- adj+N important and desirable **coveted, major, prestigious, top** *The prestigious award is in recognition of his work in regenerating the town.*
- ▶ when or where the award is given **annual, international, national, regional** *Manufactured in Sweden, these ladders have been the recipient of 10 international awards for innovation.*
- n+N **bravery, design, excellence, gallantry, lifetime achievement** *The ambulance staff who saved a man buried alive have been nominated for a bravery award.*
- v+N win an award **accept, achieve, collect, get, receive, scoop, win** *In its first year of business, the restaurant scooped the silver award in the town's Food and Drink Awards.*
- ▶ give an award **award, give, present** *Recognition of his overall contribution to athletics came when he was awarded the prestigious Olympic Torch award.*
- ▶ be suggested as a possible winner **be nominated**

for, be recommended for, be shortlisted for *The film was nominated for a staggering 125 awards.*

- N+n event when awards are given **ceremony, dinner, evening** *She attended the glittering awards ceremony in London last month.*

Usage **Award** is usually used in the plural in these combinations.

▸ person who wins or may win an award **nominee, recipient, winner** *The award winner is due to be announced on 7 April and the award will be presented in Copenhagen in June.*

2 an amount of money given by a government, organization, or law court

- adj+N **compensatory, discretionary, mandatory** *All awards are discretionary and decisions made by the panel will be final.*

- n+N **compensation, damages, pay** *It is not unusual for the level of fees to exceed the likely compensation award.*

- v+N get an award **get, receive** *An employee will get a special award of two years' salary.*

▸ give an award **grant, make** *Most of the funding bodies have restrictions on granting awards to overseas students.*

aware ADJ
knowing about something

- adv+ADJ knowing a lot **acutely, all too, consciously, fully, increasingly, keenly, painfully, perfectly, well** *We are keenly aware of the challenges that lie ahead for the company.*
▸ knowing a little **dimly, vaguely** *She was vaguely aware of Rena walking around to the bar.*
▸ knowing about a particular subject **commercially, culturally, environmentally, politically, socially** *We want our pupils to develop moral values, and to make them culturally aware.*

- v+ADJ **be, become, grow, make sb, remain, seem** *Consumers are becoming more aware of all the different credit-card offers that are currently available.*

Usage **Make aware** is almost always used in the passive: *Parents and pupils should be made aware of the school's policy on bullying.*

awareness N
knowledge or understanding

- adj+N more awareness **greater, growing, heightened, increased** *There is a need for greater awareness of the disease.*
▸ general awareness **general, public** *Unless public awareness of the importance of preservation is increased, this trend will continue.*
▸ awareness of a particular subject **commercial, cultural, environmental, financial, social, spiritual** *Environmental awareness should have priority in the school curriculum.*

- v+N increase awareness **broaden, build, create, encourage, enhance, foster, generate, heighten, improve, increase, promote, raise, spread** *The charity aims to raise awareness of human rights issues.*
▸ have or show awareness **demonstrate, develop, gain, have, show** *At the end of the course, students should be able to demonstrate an awareness of basic hygiene in food preparation.*

awful ADJ
very bad or unpleasant

- adv+ADJ **absolutely, downright, frankly, pretty** INFORMAL, **really, simply, truly** *The film is truly awful!*

- v+ADJ **look, smell, sound, taste** *I ordered a bottle of dry white wine, which tasted awful.*

awkward ADJ
difficult and embarrassing

- adv+ADJ **a little, particularly, rather, really, slightly, somewhat, very** *It would be a little awkward to admit that their latest technology had fallen into the hands of the enemy.*

- ADJ+n **conversation, moment, pause, position, question, silence, situation** *There was an awkward silence in the room.*

Bb

back V
support someone or something

- adv+V strongly or enthusiastically **enthusiastically, fully, overwhelmingly, strongly, unanimously, wholeheartedly** *He refused to resign and was backed overwhelmingly by the rest of the party.*
- ▶ with money **financially** *The company is financially backing a charity that helps children improve their literacy skills.*
- ▶ very clearly **openly, publicly** *The government needs to publicly back companies that provide clean energy.*

- V+n **bid, call, campaign, claim, decision, effort, initiative, move, plan, project, proposal, scheme** *He is backing a campaign to use low-energy light bulbs to combat carbon emissions.*

backfire V
have the opposite effect to what you wanted

- adv+V **badly, completely, disastrously, horribly, spectacularly** *The Prime Minister's efforts to mend the government's relationship with big business backfired spectacularly.*

- n+V **joke, plan, scheme, strategy, stunt, tactic, trick** *His plan backfired and he was arrested.*

background N
1 the family or social position someone comes from or the education they have had

- adj+N which social class **middle-class, upper-class, working-class** *Students from working-class backgrounds will be most excluded by the new fees.*
- ▶ poor with few opportunities **deprived, disadvantaged, poor** *It is well known that people from disadvantaged backgrounds are less willing to take on debts to go to university.*
- ▶ rich with many opportunities **advantaged, privileged** *He did not come from a privileged background and had to strive hard for what he achieved.*
- ▶ other types of background **academic, cultural, educational, ethnic, professional, religious, social, socio-economic** *We conducted a survey of staff to find out their ethnic background.*

- v+N **be drawn from, come from, have** *Jo comes from a farming background.*

2 information connected with a situation or subject

- adj+N **factual, historical, legal, technical, theoretical** *The chapter provides an interesting account of nineteenth-century biological science, coupled with some historical background.*

- N+n **document, information, knowledge, material, reading, report, research, study** *How much background information is provided for the absolute beginner?*

backing N
support, help, or active approval

- adj+N strong **full, major, overwhelming, powerful, strong, unanimous** *He has the full backing of the US administration.*
- ▶ who is giving backing **government, official, public** *The project has had significant public backing from the outset.*
- ▶ types of backing **commercial, corporate, financial, legal, military, political, scientific** *They enjoyed strong political backing from the ruling party.*

- v+N have backing **enjoy, gain, get, have, receive, secure, win** *The building of the highly controversial tower has won the official backing of the prime minister.*
- ▶ give backing **give, pledge** *The staff were very supportive and gave one hundred percent backing.*
- ▶ obtain or try to obtain backing **get, obtain, secure, seek** *A new sculpture walk is one of the innovative projects to secure financial backing from the North West Tourism Initiative.*

backlash N
a strong negative reaction to something

- adj+N **consumer, political, public, racist, serious, violent** *It is likely that there will be a strong political backlash against this measure.*

- v+N cause a backlash **cause, create, prompt, provoke, spark** *His comments provoked a predictable backlash.*
- ▶ experience a backlash **experience, face** *The government faced a backlash from parents and headteachers.*
- ▶ expect a backlash **anticipate, expect, fear, predict** *Fearing a backlash from customers, the company was forced to apologize.*

backlog N
work that you should already have done, or things that you should have dealt with

- adj+N **considerable, huge, large, massive, significant, substantial** *Past under-investment means there is a massive backlog of repairs.*

- v+N have a backlog **face, have** *I have been ill for three weeks and I have a large backlog of coursework to do.*
- ▶ cause a backlog **cause, create** *The 48-hour stoppage caused a backlog.*
- ▶ deal with a backlog **clear, cope with, deal with, eliminate, reduce, tackle** *I got some stuff done and cleared the mail backlog in the evening but I'm still well behind.*

- N+of **applications, cases, claims, complaints, email, mail, maintenance, paperwork, repairs, work** *At busy periods, a backlog of email developed due to the spam checker taking so long to process messages.*

back up PHR VB
show that an explanation or belief is probably true

- V+n **assertion, claim, findings, view** *These findings are backed up with hard evidence.*

bail N

1 the chance to stay out of prison until a trial

● adj+N **conditional, unconditional** *She was granted unconditional bail and is due to appear at Bristol Crown Court next week.*

● v+N give someone bail **free sb on, give sb, grant sb, release sb on** *Jones pleaded not guilty and was granted bail until January 4.*

▶ refuse someone bail **refuse sb** *Masih has been refused bail since his arrest in April.*

▶ ask to get bail **apply for** *The prisoner applied for bail.*

2 money that is paid to a court so that someone can stay out of prison until their trial

● v+N **pay, post, set** *Bail was set at $1 million for each defendant, police said.*

balance N

a correct relationship between aspects or features

● adj+N good or correct **appropriate, correct, good, healthy, perfect, proper, right** *I wanted to regain a healthy work/life balance.*

▶ needing or created with careful attention **careful, delicate, fine** *Classes involve a careful balance of structured time and free time.*

● v+N reach a balance **achieve, find, strike** *We need to strike a balance between all of these factors.*

▶ change a balance **alter, shift, tilt, tip, upset** *The new Human Rights Act will tip the balance back towards the individual.*

▶ restore a balance **redress, regain, restore** *We need to restore a balance between men's and women's rights.*

● N+v **shift, swing, tilt, tip** *Now the balance has shifted in favour of the Democrats.*

balance V

create a good balance between different things

● V+n balance different needs **demands, desires, needs, rights** *I struggle to balance the demands of my family with my job.* ● *We are trying to balance the needs of the individual against the needs of the population.*

▶ balance money received and money spent **books, budget, checkbook** *Headteachers have been told that they must balance their budgets by next year.*

balanced ADJ

with all aspects existing in fair or correct amounts

● ADJ+n way of looking at things **approach, judgement, perspective, view** *We listen to all opinions and try to reach a balanced judgement.*

▶ reporting **coverage, reporting** *We want fair, balanced coverage in the press.*

▶ diet **diet, meal, nutrition** *A balanced diet is essential for health.*

▶ combination of different types **blend, mix, representation** *The television audience is a well balanced representation of society in general.*

ball N

1 a round object used in games and sports

● v+N strike a ball **head, hit, kick, knock, smash,**
strike, volley *Vickers smashed the ball straight at the goalkeeper.*

▶ throw or catch a ball **bowl, catch, throw** *I always play in goal because I'm good at catching a ball.* ● *The game starts when the teacher throws the ball into the centre of the court.*

▶ hit a ball high or with a sudden movement **chip, clip, flick, lob, loft** *Knox chipped the ball over the back line.*

▶ hit a ball in a skilful way **dribble, pass, play, slip, slot, square** *He dribbled the ball down the pitch.*

▶ fail to hit, catch, or stop a ball **drop, fumble, miss** *The goalkeeper fumbled the ball, and Hamilton scored.*

● N+v **bounce, deflect, hit, rebound, ricochet** *The ball deflected off the goal post.* ● *The ball hit the edge of the goal, then bounced into the net.*

2 any round object or shape

● N+of a substance formed into a round shape **clay, dough, fluff, mud, paper** *Add eggs, and enough water to form a ball of dough.*

▶ thread or wool **string, thread, twine, wool, yarn** *First Knitting Set – complete with knitting needles and six balls of wool.*

balloon N

a coloured bag filled with air

● v+N put air into a balloooon or let air out **blow, deflate, fill, inflate** *We will inflate the balloon of your choice with helium, and decorate it with ribbons.*

▶ send a balloon into the air **fly, launch, release, send** *Thousands of helium-filled balloons were released into the sky.*

▶ burst a balloon **burst, pop** *She burst the balloon with a pin.*

▶ attach a balloon to something **tether, tie** *Each participant ties a balloon around their ankle.*

● N+v when a balloon bursts **burst, pop** *Balloons burst on reaching high levels.*

▶ when a balloon flies in the sky **drift, float, fly, hover, rise, travel** *We looked up and saw a hot air balloon drifting overhead.*

balloon V

suddenly become larger

● n+V **balance, borrowing, debt, deficit, investment** *The company's Chief Executive has just resigned and its financial deficits are ballooning.*

ballot N

the process of voting secretly

● adj+N types of ballot **compulsory, national, postal, presidential, secret** *The whole school takes part in a secret ballot to elect one boy and one girl.*

▶ first, second etc. **final, first, second** *Clarke finishes last, and will not go forward to Thursday's second ballot.*

● v+N organize a ballot **conduct, hold, organize, run** *The union has announced that it will conduct a ballot on strike action.*

▶ demand a ballot **ask for, call for, demand, force** *The union's conference called for a strike ballot on pay.*

● N+for **action, recognition, strike** *Over 20,000*

workers are considering a ballot for industrial action.

● **N+of delegates, employees, members, membership, parents, residents, staff, tenants, union, workers, the workforce** *A ballot of all members will be conducted at the next meeting.*

ban N
an order telling people not to do something

● **adj+N complete absolute, all-out, blanket, complete, outright, total** *A blanket ban on internet use would be out of the question.*
▶ **wide-ranging comprehensive, Europe-wide, global, international, nationwide, world-wide** *The council called for a world-wide ban on biologcal weapons.*
▶ **lasting a particular length of time permanent, temporary, two-year, six-month etc** *He was warned that a second offence could lead to a permanent ban.*

● **v+N introduce a ban implement, impose, introduce** *The government has introduced a ban on the distribution of free disposable bags.*
▶ **support a ban advocate, back, recommend, support, uphold** *Would you advocate a ban on smoking in bars?*
▶ **make sure that a ban continues apply, enforce, maintain** *Water was scarce, and the police used helicopters to enforce a ban on the use of hosepipes.*
▶ **refuse to obey a ban defy, flout, ignore, violate** *Over the last few months, a number of countries have flouted the ban on air travel.*
▶ **end a ban lift, overturn, remove, repeal, rescind** *The judge lifted a press ban on naming the killers.*

● **N+v affect sth, apply to sth, cover sth** *Does the ban on smoking in public places cover private clubs as well?*

bang N
a short, very loud noise

● **adj+N almighty, enormous, huge, loud, massive, mighty, terrific, tremendous** *There was a massive bang and the building shook.*

banish V
try not to be affected by bad thoughts or feelings

● **V+n anxiety, blues, boredom, doubt, fear, feeling, guilt, memory, notion, thought** *His welcoming smile immediately banished my fears.*

bank N
1 a financial institution where people keep their money

● **adj+N types of bank central, clearing, commercial, high-street, investment, merchant, offshore, reserve, savings** *The Bank of England is the central bank of the UK and is not a commercial bank.* ● *Many traditional high-street banks invest in companies that damage the environment.*
▶ **large big, international, large, major, multinational** *By the age of 38, she was already on the board of a multinational investment bank.*

● **N+v charge sth, finance sth, fund sth, issue sth, lend sth, loan sth, offer sth** *The building of the £715m stadium will be financed by a German bank.*

● **N+n account, balance, charge, clerk, loan, statement** *My wages are paid straight into my bank account.*

2 a store of something that can be used when needed

● **n+n blood, data, gene, information, organ, resource, seed, sperm** *The results are collated into a data bank and used to provide national weather forecasts.*

3 a place where things can be recycled

● **n+N bottle, clothing, glass, paper, recycling** *We have a large network of recycling banks throughout the city.*

bankrupt ADJ
1 officially unable to pay money owed

● **adv+ADJ almost, effectively, nearly, officially, practically, technically, virtually** *Within a year the company was technically bankrupt.*

● **ADJ+n person debtor, owner, partner, person** *As a bankrupt person, you may have to sell your home in order to pay your debts.*
▶ **business airline, business, company, firm, industry** *If the company you are dealing with goes bankrupt, you will probably not get your money back.*

● **v+ADJ adjudge sb, be, become, declare sb, go, make sb** *Six hundred firms went bankrupt during this period.*

2 without any good qualities at all

● **adv+ADJ artistically, creatively, culturally, intellectually, morally, politically, spiritually** *The industry has become even more corrupt and morally bankrupt*

bankruptcy N
when a person or organization cannot pay what they owe

● **adj+N about to happen imminent, impending, looming, near, virtual** *In 1977, the whole organization faced imminent bankruptcy.*

When someone is about to become bankrupt, you can also say that they are **on the verge of bankruptcy** or **on the brink of bankruptcy**.

▶ **who is affected corporate, individual, national, personal** *We are currently seeing about 1,500 corporate bankruptcies a month.*

● **v+N be likely or certain to experience bankruptcy face, risk, suffer** *Hundreds of property companies may face bankruptcy this year.*
▶ **officially state your situation declare, disclose, file** *At the age of 19, he became homeless, and was forced to declare bankruptcy.*

banner N
a piece of cloth with a message on

● **adj+N big, giant, huge, large, massive** *The words on the giant banner read 'Fight for your rights'.*

● **v+N carry, hoist, hold, parade, unfurl, wave** *Two students were holding a banner with the words 'Make Poverty History'.*

- **N+v** what is written on a banner **advertise sth, announce sth, bear sth, declare sth, demand sth, depict sth, proclaim sth, read sth, say sth** *Protesters marched into the square, with banners reading 'End state repression' and 'Release political prisoners now'.* • *One banner says 'I'm green and proud of it'.*
- ▶ when a banner is on display **float, flutter, fly, hang** *A banner hung from a bridge saying 'more bike lanes'.*

bare ADJ
basic, with nothing extra

- **ADJ+n** **bones, details, essentials, facts, minimum, necessities, outline, statistics** *Melissa outlined the bare bones of the story.* • *We know only the barest details about his personal life.* • *Only the bare essentials, such as passports and wallets, are permitted.*

bargain N
1 something costing much less than normal

- **adj+N** **absolute, amazing, fantastic, genuine, good, great, real, terrific** *You'll find some amazing bargains here, with up to 50% off some items.*
- **v+N** find or buy a bargain **bag, buy, find, get, grab, pick up, snap up, spot** *Have a look at our sale prices online, and grab a bargain!*
- ▶ like getting bargains **can't resist, like, love** *If you can't resist a bargain, this website is for you.*

  Usage **Bargain** is almost always singular in this use.

- ▶ look for a bargain **hunt for, look for, search for, shop for** *Nearby is the central marketplace, where you can hunt for bargains.*
- **N+n** thing that you buy **accommodation, break, buy, flight, holiday, ticket** *The Travel Shop: get late deals on cheap flights and bargain holidays.*
- ▶ amount that you pay **airfare, deal, fare, price** *We have lots of bargain deals available at the moment: click here for details.*
- ▶ where bargains are displayed **basement, bin, bookshop, bookstore, bucket** *A lot of copies of the book soon ended up in the bargain bins.*

2 an agreement between two people or organizations

- **v+N** **conclude, drive, make, strike** *The union will be driving a hard bargain to ensure that their demands are met.*

  When people strike or drive a *hard* bargain, they argue their case strongly.

baron N
powerful person in a particular type of business

- **n+N** **cocaine, drugs, media, newspaper, oil, press, timber, tobacco** *Recent reports suggest that the drugs barons are gaining power.*

barrage N
criticisms, complaints, or questions directed at someone

- **adj+N** **constant, continuous, endless, non-stop, relentless, steady, sustained** *In the end, the constant*

barrage of negative reporting in the media was bound to affect his popularity.

- **v+N** experience a barrage **face, receive, suffer, survive** *After the show, I received a barrage of letters from American viewers.*
- ▶ direct a barrage at someone **fire off, launch, maintain, unleash** *The association launched a barrage of complaints about illegal file-sharing.*
- **N+of** **abuse, complaints, criticism, emails, insults, mail, propaganda, protests, questions** *She faced a barrage of criticism for her support of the war.*

barrier N
something preventing progress or the achievement of your aims

- **adj+N** difficult or impossible to deal with **formidable, impassable, impenetrable, insurmountable, major, significant** *There are still significant barriers to increased recycling.*
- ▶ types of barrier **attitudinal, cultural, financial, institutional, linguistic, psychological, regulatory, social, technical** *Sawhney's music breaks down cultural barriers, and this has gained him worldwide recognition.*
- **v+N** remove or deal succesfully with a barrier **breach, break down, eliminate, overcome, reduce, remove, smash, surmount, transcend** *As a mature student, it is likely that you have overcome several barriers to achieve your degree.*
- ▶ experience a barrier **encounter, experience, face** *Many young disabled people still face major barriers to achieving their aims.*
- **N+v** **hamper sb, hinder sb, impede sb, inhibit sb, limit sb, prevent sb, restrict sb, stop sb** *The main barrier preventing these children from using the internet is language.*
- **N+to** **development, employment, entry, growth, inclusion, integration, learning, opportunity, participation, progression, success** *For many parents, the cost of childcare is a barrier to employment.*

base on PHR VB
use particular ideas or facts as the basis for a decision, theory etc

- **adv+V** mostly or completely **fundamentally, heavily, largely, mainly, mostly, predominantly, primarily, principally** *The evidence presented in the book seems to be based largely on anecdotes and conversations, rather than on any original research.*
- ▶ using only one set of ideas **entirely, exclusively, purely, solely, wholly** *The inspectors' judgements were based solely on the students' exam results.*
- ▶ partly or to a considerable extent **partially, partly, substantially** *The next chapter provides a summary, based partly on existing published data, of what we know about the organization's aims and leadership.*
- ▶ in a general but not exact way **broadly, loosely** *Her novel is based loosely on a real murder case from the 19th century.*
- **V+on** an idea or belief **assumption, belief, concept, evidence, experience, fact, premise, principle** *Our policy is based on the assumption that the customer is always right.*

▶ a study or analysis **analysis, assessment, interpretation, reading, research, review, study, survey** *Our conclusions are based on a detailed analysis of the carbon content of sediments on the area's shores and beaches.*

▶ information **data, evidence, fact, findings, material, observation, source** *All the information we offer is produced in association with the UK's leading scientific experts, and based on the latest research findings.*

basic ADJ

1 being the most important or necessary part or feature of something

● ADJ+n knowledge or ability **grounding, knowledge, skill, technique, understanding** *The aim of this course is to provide you with a basic knowledge of health and safety in the workplace.*

▶ principle or idea **assumption, belief, concept, criteria, idea, premise, principle, rule, tenet** *His basic premise is that there is one principle cause for all health problems.*

▶ explanation or description **description, explanation, guide, guidelines, introduction, outline, overview** *This excellent book provides a basic overview of microbiology, and gives an up-to-date guide to infections in reproductive medicine.*

▶ part or factor **characteristic, component, element, factor, ingredient, part** *Linguistics has three core areas: sound, grammatical structure, and meaning – the basic ingredients of human language.*

2 of products or services, needed by everyone

● ADJ+n **amenities, essentials, foodstuffs, necessities, needs, sanitation** *Their parents have to work from morning till night to provide the basic necessities.*

basics N

the most important aspects or principles of something

● v+N learn **explore, grasp, know, learn, master, practise, remember, understand** *Just remember the basics of healthy eating: variety and balance are key.*

▶ teach **cover, explain, introduce, outline, present, teach** *This course will introduce the basics of meditation in a simple and practical way.*

● N+of academic or practical subjects **computing, design, grammar, language, law, literacy, management, nutrition, programming, reading, science, theory, writing** *This friendly and practical coursebook offers learners the basics of Russian grammar.*

▶ skills or hobbies **drawing, game, painting, photography, sailing** *You can swim in the sea, learn the basics of sailing, or just relax on the beach.*

basis N

1 a method or system for doing something

● adj+N how often something happens or is done **annual, daily, day-to-day, fortnightly, hourly, month-by-month, monthly, quarterly, regular, weekly, yearly** *Class teachers meet on a weekly basis to plan lessons.*

▶ way of working **freelance, one-to-one, part-time, permanent, pro-rata, temporary, voluntary** *I think*

it's great that there are people who are willing to give us their time on a voluntary basis.

▶ according to individual needs **ad-hoc, as-needed, case-by-case, case-by-case, drop-in, first-come-first-served, individual** *Note that we have limited space and that rooms will be allocated on a first-come-first-served basis.*

● N+of **ability, aptitude, equality, evidence, experience, finding, merit** *Awards are made purely on the basis of academic ability.*

2 ideas or actions from which something develops

● v+N **act as, be, constitute, form, provide, serve as** *A newspaper article can act as a basis for discussion in class.*

● N+for **action, analysis, assessment, calculation, comparison, decision, discussion, negotiation, planning, study** *This course forms an excellent basis for continued study.*

bath N

1 a long container that you wash yourself in

● adj+N **corner, en-suite, freestanding, panelled, roll-top, spa, sunken, tin, walk-in, whirlpool** *Each bathroom contains a shower and a roll-top bath.*

● v+N **clean, empty, fill, run** *How long does it take to fill the bath?*

● and/or **basin, bidet, shower, sink, toilet, washbasin, WC** *The bathroom has a freestanding Victorian bath and WC.*

2 the experience of washing yourself in a bath

● adj+N **cold, hot, nice, relaxing, tepid, warm** *I'm going to have a nice long relaxing bath.*

● v+N have a bath **get into, have, take** *I was looking forward to getting into a hot bath.*

When you are washing yourself in a bath you can also say that you are *in the bath*.

▶ enjoy **enjoy, luxuriate in, relax in, wallow in** *To get a good night's sleep, try luxuriating in a warm bath before you go to bed.*

battery N

an object in a radio, clock etc providing electricity

● adj+N **flat, rechargeable, spare** *Cordless drills run on rechargeable batteries that take 1–3 hours to recharge.*

● v+N add power to a battery **charge, recharge** *The batteries are charged from solar panels on the roof of the boat.*

▶ take power from a battery **discharge, drain** *I have talked for up to 2 hours on the phone, but it does drain the battery.*

▶ take out a battery **change, disconnect, remove, replace** *Is it easy to change the battery without disassembling the unit?*

▶ work using batteries **be powered by, require, run on, use** *The magnifier requires 2 1.5 volt size batteries (not included).*

You can also say that something is *battery powered*.

● N+v **die, fail, run down, run out** *With this wind-up*

torch you don't have to worry about batteries running out in the dark.

- N+n **charger, compartment, life, pack, power** *The notebook weighs 2.1kg and has a battery life of 3.5 hours.*

battle N

1 a fight between armies or people

- adj+N very violent **bloody, ferocious, fierce, hard-fought, pitched** *A pitched battle took place between government troops and rebels.*
- ▶ important **climactic, decisive, famous, final** *On September 3, the final and decisive battle of the Civil War was fought.*
- v+N take part in a battle **fight, join, wage** *The Combined Fleet joined battle with a large Japanese fleet.*
- ▶ win or lose **lose, win** *Charles II lost the Battle of Worcester in 1651.*
- N+v **begin, commence, ensue, rage** *Cars and buildings burned and shops were looted as the battle raged.*

2 a situation in which people try hard to win something or stop something

- adj+N continuing for a long time **long, long-running, ongoing, protracted** *She died on 2 January, after a long battle with cancer.*
- ▶ difficult **bitter, hard-fought, tough, uphill** *The bitter battle between the air industry and environmentalists shows no sign of easing.*

You can also say that someone is *fighting a losing battle*: *We will be fighting a losing battle, in the sense that we will continue to lose habitats and species.*

- ▶ types of battle **boardroom, court, courtroom, legal, relegation, takeover** *The company is now owned by a Spanish-backed consortium after a dramatic takeover battle.*
- v+N **face, fight, lose, wage, win** *Mary won her battle against bureaucracy and red tape.*

battle V

try very hard in a difficult situation

- adv+V **bravely, fiercely, gamely, hard, heroically, valiantly** *But, although they battled gamely, they eventually lost 2–0 to finish as runners up.*
- V+n **addiction, alcoholism, cancer, relegation** *The charity says more needs to be done to help vulnerable people battling drug addictions.*
- V+against **addiction, cancer, disease, illness, injury** *Barry has been battling against cancer for some time.*

bay N

1 an area of the coast where the land curves inwards

- adj+N **beautiful, picturesque, rocky, sandy, secluded, shallow, sheltered, sweeping** *The hotel is set in a secluded bay, fringed with palm trees.*

2 a partly enclosed or marked out area used for a particular purpose

- n+N **bomb, cargo, engine, loading, parking,**

payload *The truck was reversing into a loading bay.*

beach N

an area of sand beside a sea or lake

- adj+N lovely **beautiful, glorious, golden, idyllic, lovely, palm-fringed, stunning, sun-drenched, sun-kissed, superb** *I prefer a holiday somewhere very hot, where I can bask on a sun-drenched beach.*
- ▶ made of a particular material **gravel, pebble/pebbly, sandy, shingle/shingly, stony, white-/black-sand** *We are only a few miles from Brighton with its pebble beaches.*
- ▶ not crowded **deserted, pristine, secluded, uncrowded, unspoilt/unspoiled** *We walked back to the campsite along a deserted beach.*
- ▶ used by a particular group **naturist, nudist, surfing, surf** *If it takes your fancy, then there's even a nudist beach!*

beam N

1 a piece of wood, metal, or concrete that supports a roof

- adj+N as a special feature of a house **exposed, original** *The property has original beams and wooden floors.*
- ▶ made of a material **concrete, oak, steel, wooden** *A 66 foot oak beam supported the ceiling.*

2 a line of light or energy

- n+N **infrared, laser, light, radar, torch** *She transfers these electronic books to students' handheld computers via an infrared beam.*
- N+of **headlights/headlamps, light, sunlight, torch** *Then, in the beam of his torch, he saw a lioness.*

bear V

1 seem to be a particular kind of thing

- V+n similarity **likeness, relation, resemblance, similarity** *The cost of the plane ticket bears no relation to the true environmental cost.*
- ▶ sign **hallmark, mark, scar, sign, stamp, trace** *The book bears some signs of having been written in haste.*

2 take responsibility for something

- V+n **burden, cost, responsibility** *Women have to bear the burden of household work and child-rearing.*

beard N

hair on a man's chin and cheeks

- adj+N styles **bushy, flowing, full, goatee, long, pointed, wispy** *'Ho, ho, ho,' Santa said, smiling behind his big white bushy beard.*
- ▶ colours **black, grey/gray, grizzled, red, white** *He is said to be an old man with a grey beard.*
- v+N have **grow, have, sport, wear** *His hair is long and he wears a beard.*
- ▶ cut **cut, shave (off), trim** *He refuses to shave his beard.*

bearing N

importance to or influence on something

- adj+N **direct, important, indirect, significant** *I am convinced that the numbers in the class have a direct bearing on the achievements of the pupils.*

bear out PHR VB
show that an idea or claim is true

- V+n **claim, conclusion, statement, theory, view** *In the 1980s his theory was borne out by Nobel Prize winning work on fruit flies.*
- n+V **evidence, findings, research, statistics** *A genetic link does seem to be borne out by statistics.*

> Usage *Bear out* is very often used in the passive.

beat V
1 defeat someone or do something better

- adv+V **easily comfortably, comprehensively, convincingly, decisively, easily, hands down, soundly** *Saudi Arabia was comprehensively beaten 4–0 by Ukraine.* • *It beats any standard USB webcam hands down.*

> Usage *Beat* is very often passive in this meaning.

- ▶ by a small margin **just, narrowly** *The total for last year was 195, just beating the previous record of 192.*

2 hit someone or something

- adv+V **badly, brutally, mercilessly, savagely, severely, viciously** *When he tried to run away, he was savagely beaten.*

beating N
the act of hitting someone many times

- adj+N **brutal, savage, severe, terrible, vicious, violent** *Discovery often meant a brutal beating at the hands of the company guards.*
- v+N receive **endure, get, receive, suffer** *Peace activists suffered beatings and arrests.*
- ▶ give **administer, give sb, inflict** *Ravi skipped school regularly, until his father found out and gave him the beating of his life for it!* • *The beatings were inflicted by their husbands.*

beautiful ADJ
extremely attractive or pleasing

- adv+ADJ very **achingly, breathtakingly, exquisitely, hauntingly, outstandingly, ravishingly, spectacularly, staggeringly, strikingly, stunningly** *The island itself was breathtakingly beautiful.*
- ▶ in a particular way **ruggedly, scenically, starkly, strangely** *He produces starkly beautiful monochromatic sculptures.*

beauty N
1 the quality of being beautiful or very pleasing

- adj+N very beautiful **breathtaking, exquisite, great, incredible, outstanding, sheer, stunning, unsurpassed** *Islamic carpets are renowned for their great beauty and technical excellence.*
- ▶ describing the natural world **natural, rugged, scenic, tranquil, unspoiled/unspoilt, wild** *Glasgow acts as the gateway to the scenic beauty of the West Coast.*
- ▶ describing other kinds of beauty **aesthetic, ethereal, feminine, fragile, majestic, serene, stark, timeless** *The image shows the fragile beauty of the young poet's face.*

- v+N enjoy beauty **admire, appreciate, contemplate, enjoy, explore** *Public rights of way allow us to enjoy the beauty and tranquility of our countryside.*
- ▶ help/harm beauty **conserve, enhance, mar, preserve** *The ragged clothes couldn't mar her beauty.*
- ▶ describe or show beauty **capture, celebrate, extol, reveal** *Stunning images reveal the beauty and hidden complexity of dragonflies.*
- ▶ be strongly affected by beauty **be captivated by, be enchanted by, be entranced by, be fascinated by, be mesmerized by, be overwhelmed by, be seduced by, be smitten by, be struck by, be stunned by, be transfixed by** *From the opening bars to the last encore, the audience were captivated by the sheer beauty of her music.*

2 a beautiful woman

- adj+N **great, ravishing, stunning** *At the time of her death in 1929 she was still considered a great beauty.*

beauty ADJ
related to making people look better

- ADJ+n treatment **makeover, product, routine, therapy, tip, treatment** *We are committed to selling truly natural and organic beauty products.*
- ▶ places **parlour/parlor, salon, spa** *Leisure facilities include a gym, a sauna, and a beauty salon.*
- ▶ people **therapist** *During that time, she qualified as a beauty therapist.*

bed N
a piece of furniture for sleeping on

- adj+N types of bed **bunk, divan, double, folding/foldaway/fold-up, four-poster/4-poster, king-size/king-sized, single, sofa, twin** *If you sleep in a double bed up against a wall, ensure you sleep by the wall side.*
- ▶ describing a bed **comfortable, comfy INFORMAL, unmade** *The beds were comfortable and the kitchen had everything we could ever need.*
- v+into+N **climb, collapse, crawl, fall, get, roll, sink, tumble** *We dumped our bags and just crawled into bed.*
- v+to+N **come, crawl, get, go, put sb, retire, send sb** *He was glad to get to bed.* • *Send your child to bed at a regular and reasonable time.*

beg V
ask for something you really want

- adv+V **earnestly, humbly, respectfully** *We earnestly beg you to see that steps are taken to help these families.*
- V+n **favour, forgiveness, mercy, permission, sb's indulgence, sb's pardon** *Years later he returned to his first wife to beg forgiveness.*
- V+for ask someone to do something **attention, forgiveness, help, mercy** *He had sunk to his knees, begging for mercy.*
- ▶ ask for food or money **alms, bread, crumbs, food, money, scraps** *Children were begging for food on the street.*

beginner N
someone starting to learn or do something

- adj+N **absolute, complete, real, relative, total**
*There are ICT programmes for the absolute beginner
or for the more experienced computer user.*

beginning N
1 the first part of something

- v+N **be, herald, indicate, mark, represent, signal,
signify, spell, symbolize** *Easter traditionally marks
the beginning of the holiday season in Cornwall.*

2 the origin or background of a person or thing

- adj+N not very impressive **humble, inauspicious,
lowly, modest, shaky, simple, small, tentative,
unpromising** *He rose from humble beginnings to be
a sought-after club manager.*

Usage **Beginning** is almost always plural in these
combinations.

▶ looking likely to succeed **auspicious, promising**
*Despite this promising beginning, the Blues found
themselves seven points down after ten minutes.*

behave V
do things in a particular way

- adv+V comparing behaviour **differently,
identically, similarly** *Hydrogen and oxygen gases
behave similarly.*
▶ do the right thing **appropriately, ethically,
impeccably, rationally, responsibly, sensibly, well**
*Our view is that the broadcasters behaved
responsibly throughout.*
▶ not do the right thing **aggressively, anti-socially,
badly, improperly, inappropriately, irresponsibly,
unprofessionally, unreasonably** *I just don't want to
be surrounded by other people's children behaving
badly.*
▶ do strange things **erratically, irrationally, oddly,
strangely, unpredictably** *Recently, I have noticed
that my modem has been behaving rather erratically.*

- V+with doing the right thing **decency, decorum,
dignity, integrity, restraint** *You can only have
sensible business arrangements with people who are
trustworthy and behave with integrity.*
▶ showing bravery **bravery, courage, gallantry** *She
behaved with the utmost courage, refusing to
recognise the legitimacy of the court.*
▶ respecting others' feelings **consideration,
courtesy, regard** *We do ask passengers to behave
with consideration for their fellows.*

behaviour N
way someone behaves

- adj+N bad **abusive, aggressive, anti-
social/antisocial, challenging, criminal, deviant,
disorderly, disruptive, inappropriate, loutish,
threatening, unacceptable, unreasonable,
unsporting, violent, yobbish** INFORMAL *Students'
dislike of working in teams could lead to disruptive
behaviour.*
▶ typical way a group behaves **consumer, courtship,
feeding, human, mating, sexual, voting** *Courtship
behaviour in fruit flies has become of particular
interest for neurological researchers.*

- N+n trying to improve behaviour **management,
modification** *We offer workshops on behaviour
management, social skills and confidence building.*
▶ problem **difficulty, disorder, problem** *Sport can be
very important for students with learning difficulties
or behaviour problems.*

belief N
a strong feeling that something is true or good

- adj+N belief in something **Buddhist, Christian,
humanist, Muslim, non-religious, pacifist, pagan,
political, religious, spiritual** *There are a range of
exciting opportunities whatever your age, gender,
race, or religious beliefs.*
▶ strong belief **cherished, deeply-held, firm, long-
held, passionate, strong, strongly-held,
unquestioning, unshakeable** *We share a passionate
belief in the social purposes of adult education.*
▶ wrong belief **erroneous, false, irrational,
misguided, mistaken, superstitious** *Antibiotic
treatment is occasionally given in the mistaken belief
that a sore throat is a bacterial infection.*
▶ held by many people **popular, widely-held,
widespread** *Contrary to popular belief, there is no
real link between Australia and New Zealand.*

- N+in **afterlife, god/God, immortality,
reincarnation, resurrection** *The Egyptians had a
strong belief in the afterlife, which they considered to
be very similar to that of the living.*

believable ADJ

- adv+ADJ very convincing **completely, entirely,
quite, thoroughly, totally, utterly, very, wholly** *The
novel features sympathetic, vividly drawn and wholly
believable characters.*
▶ hard to believe **barely, hardly, scarcely** *It is hardly
believable that he could not support a small family
like his own.*

- ADJ+n **acting, character, characterization,
dialogue, performance, plot, story** *The actors
perform brilliantly and really make the story
believable and life-like.*

believe V
to think that something is true

- adv+V strongly **fervently, firmly, passionately,
strongly, wholeheartedly** *He believes strongly in the
benefits of credit unions to local communities.*
▶ sincerely **genuinely, honestly, sincerely, truly** *I
genuinely believe I am making a difference by being
vegetarian.*
▶ mistakenly **erroneously, mistakenly, wrongly** *He
said teenagers were taking up smoking because they
wrongly believed it would help them lose weight.*
▶ many people believe something **generally, widely**
*It is now widely believed that climate change is
resulting in wetter, colder winters and drier, hotter
summers.*

Usage **Believe** is usually used in the passive
construction 'it is believed that' in these
combinations.

- V+n **hype** INFORMAL, **lie, myth, promise,
propaganda** *23 per cent of children still believe the
old myth that crusts make hair curly.*

- V+in think that something exists **afterlife, fairies, ghosts, god/God, immortality, magic, miracles, reincarnation, resurrection** *In Asian cultures such as China, many people believe in reincarnation.*
▶ think that something is good **democracy, equality, freedom** *I strongly believe in the freedom of the Press, no matter who or what they are.*

believer N
someone who believes in an idea or a religion

- adj+N believing strongly in something **fervent, firm, great, passionate, staunch, strong, true** *Bob is a passionate believer in the importance of early years education.*
▶ religious **Christian, devout, Jewish, Muslim, orthodox** *Natural death is in the patient's best interest and is the most dignified death for a Muslim believer.*

bell N
an object that makes a ringing sound

- n+N **bicycle, church, cow, curfew, door, fire, school, sleigh, wedding** *The front door bell rang and when she answered, there stood a handsome young man.*
- v+N **ring, toll** *The church tolled its bell as a mark of sympathy for farmers yesterday.*
- N+v **chime, clang, jangle, jingle, peal, ring, sound, tinkle, toll** *At nine o'clock the bell rings for morning tea.*

belongings N
the things you own

- adj+N personal **own, personal, worldly** *Nothing compares to the misery of losing all of your worldly belongings in a fire.*
▶ few **few, meagre** *Thousands of people are fleeing the cities with their meagre belongings.*
- v+N get together **collect, gather, pack, pack up, remove, retrieve** *She had less than an hour to gather her belongings before she was bundled onto a plane.*
▶ put somewhere **keep, put, store** *Most hotels have a separate locker room where you can store your belongings.*
▶ protect **cover, insure, protect** *You may find that your household insurance covers your personal belongings while you are on holiday.*
▶ take what belongs to someone **steal, take** *A number of cars were broken into and belongings stolen.*

benchmark N
a standard for judging other things

- adj+N good **agreed, appropriate, clear, good, important, recognized, relevant, useful** *A ratio of one infection control nurse to 250 beds is a good benchmark.*
▶ applying across a particular area **global, industry, international, national** *Energy use is monitored against national benchmarks.*
- v+N set a standard **be, become, create, define, establish, provide, represent, serve as, set** *By carefully setting benchmarks, each agent's performance can be monitored.*

▶ perform in relation to a standard **achieve, exceed, meet, outperform, surpass, underperform** *Organisations who would like to secure approved status would have to meet a fairly high benchmark.*
- N+for **excellence, good/best practice, performance, quality, standards, success** *It will set a benchmark for standards which other manufactures will be measured against.*

bend N
a curve in a road, river etc

- adj+N narrow and dangerous **blind, dangerous, hairpin, sharp, tight** *The vehicle they were passengers in rolled over on a hairpin bend.*
▶ wide **gentle, slight, sweeping** *The roads were great – smooth and dry, with wide, sweeping bends.*
▶ direction **left-hand, right-hand** *Take the track at the sharp right-hand bend in the road.*
- v+N **negotiate, round, take** *Many drivers are taking these bends too fast.*

beneficial ADJ
producing a good effect on someone or something

- adv+ADJ very **enormously, especially, extremely, highly, hugely, immensely, particularly, very** *There was a clear consensus that having a classroom assistant for the first two years of primary school was enormously beneficial.*
▶ from a particular point of view **economically, educationally, environmentally, financially, mutually, socially** *These subsidies should be redirected towards more environmentally beneficial practices.*
- ADJ+n **consequence, effect, impact, outcome, result, side-effect** *Walking not only cuts out pollution, but has the beneficial side-effect of slowing down your lifestyle.*
- v+ADJ **be, prove, seem** *The course will also prove beneficial for experienced managers seeking promotion to more senior positions.*
- and/or **adverse, detrimental, harmful** *Ultraviolet irradiation can be both beneficial and harmful to normal human skin.*

benefit N
1 an advantage or good effect

- adj+N important **enormous, great, lasting, long-term, measurable, obvious, real, significant, substantial, tangible** *These improvements will improve traffic flow and bring real benefits to motorists.*
▶ in addition to something else **added, additional, mutual** *Their local knowledge might well produce useful new leads, with the added benefit that they're on your doorstep.*
▶ of a particular kind **economic, environmental, social, therapeutic** *There is likely to be a significant economic benefit from the development through the creation of jobs.*
- v+N receive **accrue, derive, enjoy, gain, realise, reap** *How they reaped benefits from this approach is explained later.*
▶ provide **bring, confer, deliver, offer, provide, yield**

Charitable status not only confers tax benefits, but also helps encourage individuals to give time or money to causes.

2 government money for people needing financial help

- **n+N** to help with a particular situation **disability, disablement, housing, incapacity, invalidity, retirement, sickness, unemployment** *We aim to reduce by 1 million the number on incapacity benefits.*
- ▶ provided by the state **social security, state, welfare** *Your income, including pensions, annuities and all state benefits, will be taken into consideration.*
- **v+N claim, live on, receive** *Job Centre Plus is a new service for people of working age who are claiming benefits.*

bet N
an agreement in which you risk money on what will happen; the chance of something happening

- **adj+N** safe **best, good, safe, sure** *The Conservatives are looking like a safe bet for the next election.*
- ▶ fairly safe **fair** *It's a fair bet that he's got something to do with this.*
- ▶ not safe **bad, big, outside, risky** *Her run of luck ended just before the biggest bet of all.* • *Gamblers who place even riskier bets should consider seeking help.*
- ▶ type of bet **each-way, spread** *He's a reliable each-way bet.*
- **v+N** make a bet **lay, make, place, put** *The criminals placed bets on the dog fight.*
- ▶ agree to a bet **accept, take** *Bookmakers have stopped taking bets on the race.*
- ▶ reduce the risk of a bet **hedge** *Investors are hedging their bets in the present economic climate.*
- ▶ win/lose a bet **lose, win** *Then he did the round trip in 13 hours, and won the bet.*

betray V
show something, give a sign of something, or make something known

- **V+n** a fault **ignorance, inexperience, lack, misunderstanding, naivety** *Such language is unhelpful and betrays a lack of understanding of the issues involved.*
- ▶ a feeling **emotion, feeling, nervousness** *His hands twitched, betraying the nervousness which didn't show in his voice.*
- ▶ a secret **confidence, secret** *A charge of betraying navy secrets was made against him.*
- **n+V attitude, eye, face, tone, voice** *His beady eyes betrayed no hint of his emotions.*

better ADJ
1 more satisfactory, suitable, pleasant etc.

- **adv+ADJ** a lot **definitely, far, infinitely, much, obviously** *Psychologists tell us active learning is far better than passive learning.*
- ▶ rather **considerably, rather, significantly, somewhat** *The situation in Europe is considerably better than it was two years ago.*
- ▶ slightly **a little, marginally, slightly** *The first half*

was quite bad because it was raining heavily, but the second was marginally better.

- ▶ all the time **consistently** *No one method was consistently better than any other on any test.*

2 healthy again after illness

- **adv+ADJ completely, a little, much** *By mid-March, Mr Pascoe was a little better.*
- **v+ADJ feel, get, look** *If you feel unwell, you take steps to make yourself feel better.*

bewildering ADJ
very large and offering too many choices

- **adv+ADJ** very **completely, utterly** *This is completely bewildering, and I can think of no sane explanation for it.*
- ▶ rather **almost, quite, rather, slightly, sometimes, somewhat** *The interface can be somewhat bewildering to a first-time user.*
- **ADJ+n array, assortment, choice, diversity, mix, range, variety** *Part of the problem is the bewildering array of possibilities on offer.*
- **v+ADJ be, find something, seem** *It was all slightly bewildering.* • *I found the situation completely bewildering.*

bias N
an attitude that makes you treat someone or something in a different or unfair way

- **adj+N** strong **blatant, definite, obvious, overt, strong** *The portals will have a strong bias towards interactive content.*
- ▶ weak **slight** *There is a slight bias against information from local sources.*
- ▶ possible **apparent, possible, potential** *She wanted to avoid accusations of possible bias.*
- ▶ in the system **inbuilt, inherent, institutional, systematic, systemic** *This gives the reader a clue to the bias inherent in the text.*
- ▶ types of bias **age, cultural, gender, ideological, political, racial, sex** *They acknowledged their commitment to eradicate any racial bias.*
- ▶ in politics **left-wing, liberal, right-wing** *At that time, there was a very left-wing bias in TV drama.*
- ▶ not intended **unconscious, unintentional** *Recruiters must take care to monitor a test against unintentional bias.*
- ▶ personal **media, observer, personal** *She did not want personal bias or prejudice to creep into her decision.*
- **v+N** avoid or reduce bias **avoid, correct, counter, eliminate, minimize, overcome, reduce, remove** *The judges are different each year so as to avoid any bias.*
- ▶ cause bias **create, introduce** *Technology is creating a bias towards children of better-off families.*
- ▶ have or show bias **demonstrate, display, exhibit, have, reflect, reveal, show** *It shows an enduring policy bias towards the working class.*
- ▶ notice bias **detect, perceive** *40 per cent of you perceive a gender bias towards men.*
- **N+v** exist or appear **appear, arise, creep in, exist, result from** *This reduces the chances of bias creeping in.*

▶ affect **affect sb/sth, influence sb/sth** *A person's bias influences him to give testimony in his own self-interest.*

● and/or **discrimination, distortion, inaccuracy, prejudice** *All the materials used must be free from bias or prejudice against any particular group.*

biased ADJ
preferring someone or something unfairly

● adv+ADJ very **blatantly, heavily, highly, hopelessly, obviously, severely, strongly, totally** *The whole article was heavily biased in favour of the wife.*

▶ rather **a little, slightly, somewhat** *As you probably realise, I am slightly biased against this view.*

▶ in a particular way **culturally, ideologically, politically, racially** *He has criticised judges for being unrepresentative and politically biased.*

▶ negatively/positively **negatively, positively** *They believe the media are negatively biased in the way they present the events.*

▶ by its nature **inherently** *The present system is seen as inherently biased towards the rich.*

▶ unfairly **unfairly** *As a cyclist, he felt that the law was unfairly biased in favour of the motorist.*

● ADJ+n opinion or report **attitude, coverage, interpretation, opinion, report, reporting, view, viewpoint** *Yes, there has to be regulation to stop biased reporting.*

▶ data **sample, selection** *A biased sample can give a misleading impression of the severity of a problem.*

▶ result **result** *The survey was methodologically flawed, giving biased results.*

▶ person **judge, referee** *They claim that the judge was biased.*

bid V
offer an amount of money for something; offer to do something for an amount of money

● adv+V **competitively, successfully** *She bid successfully for the oak dining table.*

● V+for business or right to do something **business, concession, contract, franchise, licence, project, work** *The companies announced a joint venture to bid for an offshore wind farm project.*

bid N
1 an offer of a particular amount

● adj+N **final, high, initial, low, opening, winning** *If an item doesn't have any initial bids that meet the reserve price, it won't go to auction.*

● v+N make a bid **make, place, prepare, put in, put together, submit, tender** *Four utility companies submitted bids for the business.*

▶ take back a bid **retract, withdraw** *You can retract your bid under certain circumstances.*

▶ agree to a bid **accept** *They have accepted our bid.*

▶ not agree to a bid **reject** *We were severely disappointed that this bid was rejected.*

▶ think about a bid **assess, consider, evaluate** *They had considered bids from companies abroad.*

▶ invite **invite, solicit** *Bids are invited for the assets.*

▶ win **win** *We are serious about winning the bid.*

2 an attempt to do or get something

● adj+N **successful** *Ethical guarantees were built into the successful bid for the games.*

▶ unsuccessful **failed, unsuccessful** *In 1944 there was a failed bid to liberate the city.*

▶ unlikely to succeed **desperate** *In a desperate bid to escape justice, they left behind five wounded officers.*

▶ brave **ambitious, audacious, bold, daring** *The club made an audacious bid for Diego Maradona.*

▶ opposed by the company bid for **hostile** *In June 1995 the company launched a hostile takeover bid.*

▶ types of bid **comeback, election, funding, Olympic, presidential, re-election, takeover** *Radio stations seem to be backing his comeback bid.*

● v+N make a bid **launch, make, mount** *Institutions may consider making a bid for funding.*

▶ win a bid **succeed in, win** *They succeeded in the takeover bid.*

▶ not win a bid **fail in, lose** *He lost his re-election bid for the presidency.*

▶ not accept a bid **reject** *He persuaded the shareholders to reject the bid.*

▶ support a bid **back, support** *Remember to tell others to back their bid.*

● N+v **fail, succeed** *Her bid for recognition finally succeeded.*

● N+for money **funding, funds, grant, money** *Three organisations submitted bids for a grant.*

▶ power **domination, leadership, power, presidency, status, throne** *The event seemed to some like a bid for leadership.*

▶ fame **fame, glory, immortality, recognition, stardom** *The cameras followed the girls as they made their bid for stardom.*

▶ freedom **freedom, independence** *She made a desperate bid for freedom through an open window.*

bill N
1 a statement showing amount of money that you owe

● adj+N occurring regularly **annual, monthly, quarterly, weekly, yearly** *The customer receives a single monthly bill.*

▶ large **hefty, high, huge, large, massive** *He ran up a huge bill which he never paid.*

▶ not paid **outstanding, overdue, unpaid** *He is determined to get payment of outstanding bills from the farmers.*

▶ detailed **itemized** *You will receive a monthly itemised bill showing clearly your usage and charges.*

▶ types of bill **legal, medical** *The insurance will pay all medical bills.*

● n+N **electricity, energy, fuel, gas, heating, household, phone, tax, telephone, utility** *I always make sure we have enough money to pay our mortgage and household bills.*

● v+N pay a bill **foot, pay, pick up, settle, share** *He announced he would be defending himself to save the taxpayer footing his legal aid bill.*

▶ reduce a bill **cut, halve, lower, reduce, slash** INFORMAL *Turning your thermostat down by 1°C can reduce your bill by up to 10 per cent.*

▶ have a bill to pay **face, incur, run up** *We had run up a massive bill for taxis.*

▶ divide a bill **split** *We agreed to split the restaurant bill between the four of us.*

▶ ask or tell somebody to pay a bill **face sb with, hit sb with, land sb with, leave sb with, present, present sb with, saddle sb with** *The real occupant wasn't aware of fraudulent charges until his final bill was presented at checkout.*

▶ be able to pay **afford** *Many in poor areas really cannot afford their energy bills.*

● N+v total **amount to, come to, total** *With a coffee the bill came to £5.00.*

▶ arrive **arrive, come in** *I'll soon run out of money when the bills start coming in.*

2 a written proposal for a new law

● adj+N where bill is debated **congressional, government, parliamentary** *Congressional spending bills will boost funds for some areas of information technology research.*

▶ not final **draft** *The draft bill specifically states that grassland is not to be treated as a crop.*

● v+N suggest a bill **bring, introduce, propose, reintroduce, sponsor** *The government has introduced a mental health bill.*

▶ write a bill **draft** *When we were drafting the Bill we felt that the power should be retained.*

▶ think and talk about a bill **consider, debate** *I do not know why we are even bothering to debate the Bill.*

▶ change a bill **amend, revise** *He said he was considering amending the bill to include the measure.*

▶ support a bill **endorse, support** *For those reasons, we cannot support the bill.*

▶ oppose a bill **oppose** *The new draft mental health Bill was opposed.*

▶ pass a bill **approve, enact, force through, pass, push through, put through, sign** *We are optimistic that another substantial majority will pass the bill.*

▶ not pass a bill **defeat, reject, veto** *The White House has threatened to veto any bill that includes the provision.*

binding ADJ
having to be accepted or obeyed

● ADJ+n promise or agreement **agreement, commitment, contract, document, obligation, promise, treaty, undertaking** *This involves formulating the details to create a binding agreement.*

▶ decision **arbitration, decision, referendum, regulation, ruling** *The courts' rulings are binding and enforceable.*

binge N
an occasion when someone does something, especially drinking, too much

● adj+N on food or drugs **alcohol, alcoholic, drinking, drugs, drunken, eating** *I would wake up with a hangover from hell after a drunken binge.*

▶ spending money **borrowing, shopping, spending** *I was getting desperate for work after a spending binge.*

● N+n person on a binge **drinker, eater** *Binge eaters often eat until they are uncomfortably full.*

▶ types of binge **drinking, eating** *The new law seems to foster the binge drinking culture in this country.*

● v+on+N **be, go** *I once again took to the bottle and went on a binge.*

bird N
an animal with feathers that flies

● N+v fly **circle, flap, flit, flock, flutter, fly, soar, swoop** *Let the birds fly free for long periods every day.*

▶ travel **migrate** *It was the time of year when the birds were migrating to warmer areas.*

▶ make a sound **chirp, sing, tweet, twitter** *At this time of year the birds are singing constantly.*

▶ make a nest **nest** *How do I deal with birds nesting in my roof?*

▶ sleep **roost** *Birds were roosting and feeding on the sandbanks.*

▶ clean itself **preen** *As the bird was preening, we were able to admire the fine plumage.*

▶ lose feathers **moult** *All the birds were moulting and looked in poor condition.*

▶ hit or bite with its beak **peck** *The duck pecked me angrily.*

● n+of+N group **colony, flock** *We saw a flock of about 350 birds just outside the port.*

▶ types of bird **species, variety** *I saw 185 species of bird on this trip.*

birth N
the occasion or process of a baby being born

● adj+N early **premature, preterm** *Premature births are posing a growing burden on families and health services.*

▶ of more than one baby **multiple, twin** *Multiple births are associated with premature and low birth-weight babies.*

▶ when the baby is born alive/dead **live, still** *If the parents are not married to each other the mother can register the still birth on her own.*

▶ planned/not planned **planned, unplanned** *The rate of planned to unplanned out-of-hospital birth is one to one.*

▶ normally impossible **miraculous, virgin** *Old religions have libraries full of parallels to the miraculous birth of Jesus.*

● n+N **home, hospital, water** *After that, the idea of having a home birth began to seem like a real possibility.*

● v+N when a mother has a baby **give** *She gave birth to their first son last year.*

▶ celebrate a birth **celebrate, commemorate, mark** *Naming ceremonies are a lovely way of marking the birth of a baby.*

▶ formally record or announce a birth **announce, register** *She named him Allan and his birth was registered on 14th June.*

▶ help with a birth **attend** *A doctor or midwife attends every birth.*

● N+n at birth **attendant, complication, date, defect, name, weight** *Babies born to poorer families are more likely to be of low birth weight.*

▶ by birth **mother, parent** *I am trying to trace my birth mother.*

▶ of birth **certificate, control, rate** *The registrar will issue a short copy birth certificate.*

▶ caused by birth **injury, trauma** *And many of the*

women with prolonged depression had experienced some birth trauma.

- n+of+N **date, moment, place, time, year** *What is your date of birth?*

bitter ADJ

angry or upset, or involving angry or strong feelings

- adv+ADJ **very extremely, particularly** *There was a particularly bitter dispute over payment for working overtime.*
- ▶ more and more **increasingly** *He became increasingly bitter as the year went on.*
- ▶ rather **a little, rather, slightly, somewhat** *The decision has left her feeling somewhat bitter.*
- ADJ+n disappointment **disappointment** *The trite ending to this film is a bitter disappointment.*
- ▶ conflict **battle, conflict, controversy, dispute, feud, fighting, hatred, quarrel, recriminations, rivalry, row** *The boardroom was the scene of bitter rivalry.*
- ▶ opponent **enemy, rival** *The Bolsheviks were their strongest and bitterest enemies.*
- v+ADJ **become, feel, make sb, remain, seem, sound** *I still feel extremely bitter about the way they had treated me.* ● *That experience has made me very bitter.*
- and/or person **angry, cynical, resentful, sad, twisted** *He became bitter and twisted, unwilling to trust anyone again.*
- ▶ disagreement **acrimonious** *The debate turned bitter and acrimonious at times.*

bitterness N

an angry or upset feeling, especially as a result of disappointment

- adj+N **considerable, great, increasing, intense, little** *An expression of shock and intense bitterness crossed her face.*
- n+of+N hint **feeling, sense, touch, trace** *The events left a sense of bitterness in the community.*
- and/or **anger, hatred, resentment** *This can breed resentment and bitterness at life's unfairness.*

black ADJ

of the darkest colour

- adj+ADJ **glossy, matt** *The cat had glossy black fur*
- adv+ADJ **completely, entirely, solid** *The adult birds are almost completely black.*
- n+ADJ **jet, pitch** *The whole stage was pitch black except for a spotlight in one corner.*

If someone is wearing black clothes, you can say that they are **in black**, **dressed in black**, or **wearing black**: *He asked the name of the woman in black.*

- ADJ+as **coal, ink, night, pitch** *The clouds gathered, black as ink.*

blackmail N

the use of threats to make someone do something

- adj+N **economic, emotional, financial, moral, nuclear** *You use emotional blackmail to manipulate people.*

- v+N use **resort to** *He had achieved what he wanted without resorting to blackmail.*
- N+n **attempt, plot, threat** *She had warned the police about the previous blackmail attempts.*

blame N

responsibility for something bad that has happened

- v+N place the blame **allocate, apportion, assign, attach, lay, pin, place, put** *Don't try and lay the blame on others.*

When you blame someone, you can say that you **lay the blame at someone's door**.

- ▶ get or accept the blame **accept, get, share, shoulder, take** *He denied that he should shoulder any blame for the misery.*
- ▶ move the blame **pass, shift** *This is not trying to shift the blame.*
- ▶ avoid the blame **avoid, deflect, escape** *The senior officers largely escaped blame.*
- ▶ remove the blame **absolve somebody from, absolve somebody of, acquit somebody of, exonerate somebody from, exonerate somebody of** *At the inquest, he was absolved of all blame.*
- N+v **fall on somebody, lie with somebody, rest with somebody** *He said the blame lay with government policies.*
- N+n **culture, game** *There is a blame game about who is most responsible for the dire situation.*
- n+of-N **part, share** *They should take their fair share of the blame.*
- and/or guilty feeling **guilt, responsibility, shame** *This is modern day tragi-comedy about blame, guilt and vengeance.*
- ▶ praise **praise** *Praise or blame would be inappropriate in cases where action is coerced.*

blank ADJ

1 containing no writing, marks, or information

- adv+ADJ **completely, entirely, totally** *You may find that you now have a completely blank screen.*
- ADJ+n surface **card, page, screen, sheet, wall** *At the end of the paper must be added one blank sheet of paper, as a cover.*
- ▶ form or space for information **box, cheque, column, email, field, form, space, template** *You can create your own worksheets, based on the blank templates provided.*
- ▶ object for holding information **cassette, CD, disc, disk, DVD, tape** *Put in a blank CD, plug in a microphone, press record and speak.*
- v+ADJ **be, go, leave something** *Suddenly my mind went blank.* ● *The email subject line was left blank.*

2 showing no emotion or reaction

- adv+ADJ **completely, entirely, totally** *I found it worrying that my memory could be so totally blank.*
- ADJ+n expression **expression, face, look, stare** *We were met with rudeness and blank stares.*
- ▶ feeling or behaviour **amazement, incomprehension, refusal** *He gave her an unaccustomed look of blank incomprehension.*
- v+ADJ **go, look, remain** *My mind went blank.*

blanket N

a thick layer of something; something that makes it difficult to get information or make progress

- N+of something you can see or hear **cloud, fog, mist, smog, snow, sound, star** *We spent the night under a blanket of stars.*
- ▶ darkness or quiet **darkness, silence** *There was a blanket of silence that prevented public discussion of the decisions.*
- ▶ secrets **secrecy, security** *Under a blanket of maximum secrecy, over a million soldiers were gathered.*

blanket ADJ

affecting or aimed at everyone or everything

- ADJ+n when something is not allowed **ban, prohibition, refusal, restriction** *A blanket ban would be impossible to police.*
- ▶ when something is criticized or denied **condemnation, denial** *He issued a blanket denial of all the charges.*
- ▶ protection **amnesty, exclusion, exemption, immunity, protection** *Granting law-enforcement a blanket exemption from charges of terrorism would go too far.*
- ▶ permission **approval, permission** *They benefit from a blanket planning permission granted by government.*
- ▶ plan **approach, policy** *We should not rely on a blanket policy.*
- ▶ information **coverage, statement** *Rare events such as plane crashes or murders receive blanket coverage in the press.*

blast N

1 an explosion

- adj+N cause of blast **atomic, explosive, nuclear** *The effects of a nuclear blast would be lethal for over half the population.*
- ▶ powerful **deadly, huge, powerful** *The group has claimed responsibility for the deadly blast.*
- n+N **bomb, shotgun** *If the man had not ducked, he would have been hit by the shotgun blast.*
- v+N not be destroyed in a blast **survive, withstand** *The walls were designed to withstand bomb blasts.*
- ▶ cause **cause** *It is not known what caused the second blast.*
- N+v **damage sth, destroy sth, hit sth, injure sb, kill sb, occur, rock sth, shake sth, strike sth** *The blasts have reportedly killed at least 25 people.*
- n+of+N **effect, force** *The newsagents' metal shutters blew off with the force of the blast.*

2 a strong current or wave of air, wind, heat etc

- adj+N short **quick, short** *A quick blast with your hair dryer will dry it.*
- ▶ strong **fierce** *The weather lived up to the forecast, with fierce blasts of wind and hard cold rain.*
- ▶ cold **cold, icy** *The wind greeted my arrival on the high ridge with an icy blast.*
- N+of **air, breath, heat, wind, winter** *A few seconds later there was a terrific explosion and a blast of hot air.*

3 a sudden short loud sound

- adj+N short **short** *Three short blasts on the siren signalled danger.*
- ▶ long **long, prolonged** *The signal will be a prolonged blast on the klaxon.*
- ▶ loud **deafening, loud, shrill** *Howard gave three loud blasts on his whistle to let us know he was safe.*
- n+N **horn, trumpet** *Its call resembles a trumpet blast.*
- v+N **blow, deliver, give, sound** *He grabbed the horn and blew a blast.*
- N+on+n **horn, klaxon, siren, trumpet, whistle** *They gave a blast on their horns as they passed.*

blaze N

a large fire

- adj+N **fierce, huge, major, massive, serious** *The cases of vodka helped fuel the massive blaze.*
- v+N start **spark, start a blaze** *An electrical fault started the blaze.*
- ▶ stop a blaze **extinguish, put out** *It took the fire brigade ninety minutes to put the blaze out.*
- ▶ fight a blaze **attend, battle, fight, tackle** *18 firefighters tackled the blaze.*
- ▶ control a blaze **bring under control, contain, get under control** *The blaze was contained before it spread.*
- ▶ escape a blaze **escape, survive** *The family escaped a blaze which ripped the roof off their home.*
- N+v start or grow **break out, spread, start** *A serious blaze broke out on the ship.*

bleak ADJ

seeming cold and unfriendly; unhappy and without hope

- adv+ADJ very **decidedly, extremely, utterly, very** *The outlook for the economy remains decidedly bleak.*
- ▶ rather **fairly, pretty** INFORMAL**, rather** *This all painted a rather bleak picture of the state of higher education.*
- ADJ+n situation **ending, future, outlook, picture, prognosis, prospect, reality, situation** *The outlook was bleak.*
- ▶ place **expanse, hill, hillside, landscape, moor, moorland, mountain, place, spot, surroundings, upland, wasteland** *South of the junction, the road crosses some bleak moorland.*
- v+ADJ **appear, be, look, remain, seem** *The future of the industry remains bleak.*
- and/or lonely **desolate, lonely** *It was a bleak and desolate place, with no signs of human habitation.*
- ▶ cold **cold, exposed, windswept** *The school stands on a very bleak, exposed part of the coastline.*
- ▶ rough **harsh, inhospitable, mountainous, rugged, uninviting, wild** *It is mostly a bleak and mountainous district.*
- ▶ without features **bare, barren, dark, empty, featureless, grey** *The Skeleton Coast seems at first a bleak and featureless region of sand and sea.*
- ▶ without hope **depressing, hopeless** *It is also a rather depressing and bleak look at society.*

bleeding N
process of losing blood from your body

● adj+N in large amounts **excessive, heavy, profuse, severe** *Early symptoms of scurvy include excessive bleeding of the gums.*
▶ inside the body **internal** *The blood vessel ruptured, causing internal bleeding.*
▶ when bleeding does not stop **persistant, prolonged, uncontrollable, uncontrolled** *This condition can lead to heavy, uncontrollable bleeding after surgery.*

● v+N stop or reduce bleeding **control, prevent, reduce, staunch, stem, stop** *He managed to staunch the bleeding.*
▶ cause or increase bleeding **cause, increase** *Sometimes fibroids cause heavy bleeding or pain.*
▶ experience **suffer** *He was suffering internal bleeding from the rupture of a main artery.*

● N+v **continue, persist, stop** *If bleeding persists, a dentist must be contacted.*

blend N
a pleasant combination of different things

● adj+N interesting or unusual **curious, eclectic, exciting, exotic, fascinating, interesting, intriguing, special, unique** *This is a unique blend of country music with a cajun twist.*
▶ good **balanced, delicious, delightful, fine, perfect, rich, right, wonderful** *This film has a balanced blend of comedy and drama.*
▶ delicate, not obvious **harmonious, seamless, subtle** *The style of decoration was a seamless blend of old and new.*
▶ powerful **heady, potent** *He experiences a heady blend of cultures on the island.*

blessing N
1 something good that you feel grateful for

● adj+N both good and bad **mixed** *Knowledge is a mixed blessing.*
▶ great **great, real** *There is no greater blessing than finding what you want to do in life.*

● v+N **count, enjoy** *Keep a positive attitude and count your blessings.*

● N+in **disguise** *The delay could turn out to be a blessing in disguise.*

2 permission or support for something [always singular]

● adj+N **full, official** *The proposal has finally got official blessing.*

● v+N receive blessing **get, obtain, receive** *Three principles received the blessing of the Assembly.*
▶ give blessing **give** *Her mother had given her blessing to the marriage.*

When someone gives or does not give their blessing to something, you can say that it is done **with their blessing** or **without their blessing**: *We sold the house with our parents' blessing.*

▶ not give blessing **withhold** *He was determined to withold his blessing for the proposal.*
▶ have blessing **have** *He has my unqualified blessing.*

blind ADJ
1 unable to see

● adv+ADJ nearly **almost, functionally, nearly, partially, practically, virtually** *My mother is virtually blind now.*
▶ completely **completely, totally** *Our 10-year-old daughter has been totally blind since birth.*
▶ permanently **incurably, permanently** *Our staff can offer incurably blind individuals support.*
▶ not permanently **temporarily** *My mother has gone temporarily blind in one eye.*
▶ since birth **congenitally** *Congenitally blind children have difficulty in making sense of their worlds.*
▶ according to law **legally** *I was registered as legally blind, although I had some peripheral vision in my left eye.*

● v+ADJ **be, be born, go** *She had gone blind in her twenties.*

● and/or **partially sighted, visually impaired** *This highlights the challenges still faced by blind and partially sighted people.*

2 unable to realize, admit, or question the truth about something

● adv+ADJ **morally, spiritually, wilfully** *Only the wilfully blind can claim that this consequence was unforeseen.*

● ADJ+n trust and obedience **acceptance, adherence, faith, obedience, trust** *They demand blind obedience from their members.*
▶ feeling **fury, hatred, love, loyalty, optimism, panic, prejudice, rage** *This setback hadn't sent me into a blind panic.*

● ADJ+to situation **dangers, fact, issue, possibility, problem, reality, truth** *Many people are blind to the fact that they participate in perpetuating racism.*
▶ result **consequences, implications** *They remained blind to the consequences of their actions.*
▶ fault **failings, faults, shortcomings** *While I am not blind to its faults, I still love it.*

● and/or **foolish, ignorant, unquestioning, unreasoning** *The term racism may denote a blind and unreasoning hatred, envy or prejudice.*

blitz N
an organized effort to make sure something becomes publicly known

● n+N **advertising, marketing, media, PR, publicity** *There was no media blitz to accompany the car's launch on the market place.*

● v+N **have, launch, plan** *Sony has launched a TV advertising blitz for its plasma and LCD sets during the Olympics.*

blockade N
an action preventing people or goods moving somewhere

● v+N put a blockade in place **enforce, impose, maintain, tighten** *The British imposed a naval blockade on Italy's coal supplies at the beginning of March 1940.*
▶ end a blockade **end, lift** *The blockade was partially lifted in 1629 when it started to affect Flemish trade.*

▸ get through a blockade **break, break through, run** *That night four ships broke through the blockade of Calvi and landed their cargoes.*

blockage N
something that blocks a tube or pipe

● adj+N **complete, major, partial** *Angina is caused by partial blockage of an artery.*

● v+N cause a blockage **cause, create** *A blood clot can be very serious if it starts to move through your body because it can end up causing a blockage in your heart or lungs.*

▸ remove a blockage **clear, release, remove** *I was kneeling down with one arm in a blocked drain trying to clear the blockage.*

blood N
the red liquid inside your body

● v+N when someone or something makes a person bleed **draw, shed, spill** *The cat scratched me but did not draw blood.* ● *He is a murderer whose main ambition is to shed blood.*

▸ move blood around the body **carry, pump, supply** *The arteries are the tubes that carry blood from the heart to the rest of the body.*

▸ lose blood **lose** *It was a deep wound and she was losing a lot of blood.*

● N+v move around the body **circulate, flow, pump** *Rage flowed through his body faster than the blood pumping through his veins.*

▸ pour quickly from the body **flow, gush, pour, spurt** *A woman was lying in the road with blood pouring from a head wound.*

▸ come out slowly **drip, ooze, seep, trickle** *He was badly injured, and blood was seeping slowly through his shirt.*

● v+in+N **be covered, be drenched, be soaked** *Drenched in blood, the killer ran away across the fields, leaving a trail which police would later follow.*

● n+of+N an amount of blood **drop, pool, trickle** *A few drops of blood are taken from a prick in your finger and dropped into a coloured solution.*

▸ when someone bleeds **loss** *In spite of great loss of blood, he revived.*

blossom V
develop and become more successful

● n+V when a loving relationship develops **friendship, love, relationship, romance** *Before long romance blossomed, and they married the following year.*

▸ when someone's abilities develop **career, talent** *Holbein's talent blossomed as he won commissions to paint the leading figures of the Reformation.*

blow N
1 a hard hit from a weapon or from someone's hand

● adj+N very hard or causing death **fatal, heavy, knock-out, lusty, mighty, mortal, powerful** *A dead dog lay in the gutter, having been struck a fatal blow by a passing car.*

▸ hitting only lightly **glancing** *Thirty seconds later*

Titanic struck the towering iceberg a glancing blow which tore at the ship's hull below the waterline.

● v+N give a blow **deliver, give, land, strike** *He danced around me laughing at my unsuccessful efforts to land a blow.*

You can also say that someone *rains blows (down)* on someone if they hit someone repeatedly: *Police in riot gear rained blows on the unarmed crowd.*

▸ receive a blow **receive, take** *Apparently I received a heavy blow to the head when I hit the road.*

▸ push a blow away **deflect, parry** *Lieutenant Brechar drew his sword just in time to parry a blow.*

▸ when two people hit each other **exchange, trade** *After blows were exchanged in a changing room, both players were fined for alleged misconduct.*

2 something that spoils your chances of success

● adj+N **big, bitter, cruel, crushing, decisive, devastating, fatal, huge, major, massive, serious, severe, shattering, terrible** *The announcement was a devastating blow to the car industry.*

▸ v+N deliver a blow **deal, deliver, inflict** *These crackdowns have dealt a major blow to drug dealers and their networks.*

▸ suffer a blow **suffer, take** *They have suffered a massive blow to their already fragile and emerging economy.*

▸ reduce the effects of a blow **cushion, lessen, soften** *We've been lobbying hard to get some measures in place that would soften the blow for the smallest firms.*

● N+to **confidence, credibility, hopes, morale, prestige, pride** *Failure in these talks would deal a serious blow to hopes of avoiding war.*

blue ADJ
of the same colour as the sky

● adj+ADJ dark **dark, deep, midnight, navy** *The band arrived in a gleaming, midnight blue Rolls-Royce.*

▸ pale **light, pale** *The starling usually lays four to six eggs, which are pale blue.*

▸ bright **bright, brilliant, vivid** *Above, the sky was a clear unbroken vivid blue, the sun almost directly overhead.*

▸ of a particular shade **cobalt, electric, metallic, royal, sapphire, sky, ultramarine** *His eyes were sky blue, and he had flowing hair that reached to his shoulders.*

If someone is wearing blue clothes, you can say that they are *in blue, dressed in blue*, or *wearing blue*: *A tall woman in blue was standing at the back of the room.*

blueprint N
a detailed plan for doing something new

● adj+N **ambitious, clear, detailed, new, original** *No detailed blueprint of how this target could be achieved was ever produced.*

● v+N be a blueprint for something **form, offer, provide, serve as** *This way of working will provide a possible blueprint for other local authorities in how they develop their consultation plans with young people.*

▶ produce a blueprint **create, develop, draw up, launch, produce** *Leaders of the world's richest nations are trying to draw up a blueprint for staving off climate disaster.*

● N+for **action, change, development, future, reform** *A blueprint for the future of Orkney housing was launched at the start of May.*

blunder N
a serious mistake

● adj+N very serious **big, catastrophic, fatal, major, monumental, serious, terrible** *He later claimed it was the biggest blunder of his career.*

▶ in planning **strategic, tactical** *Starting a war at this point would be a serious strategic blunder.*

▶ types of blunder **administrative, cultural, medical, policy** *Hundreds of delegates were denied access to the conference because of massive administrative blunders.*

● v+N **commit, make** *He saw he had made a blunder, so he hastened to explain it away.*

● n+of+N **catalogue, series, string** *A convicted killer walked free from a Scottish court after a series of blunders by security staff.*

blur V
make the difference between things difficult to notice

● V+n **boundary, difference, distinction, divide, line** *The film blurs the boundaries between drama and documentary.*

board N
a senior group with the responsibility to manage something

● adj+N **advisory, editorial, executive, governing, health, supervisory** *He is a member of the editorial board of the British Journalism Review.*

● v+N be or become a member of a board **be appointed to, be elected to, join, serve on, sit on** *He serves on the boards of several companies, as well as working as an independent consultant.*

▶ be in charge of a board **chair** *They are planning to set up a national policing board, to be chaired by a government minister.*

▶ leave a board **resign from, retire from** *She resigned from the board when an agreement couldn't be reached.*

● N+v **convene, meet** *The bank's board convened to discuss ways of handling the crisis.*

● N+n **director, meeting, member, room** *After an 11-hour board meeting, BPI directors voted heavily in favour of the offer.*

> When a matter is dealt with by the board of an organization, you can say it is dealt with *at board level*.

● N+of **directors, examiners, governors, trustees** *The board of directors is responsible for setting the company's strategic aims.*

body N
1 a group of people who work together and have important responsibilities

● adj+N controlling an area of activity **governing, professional, regulatory, ruling, statutory** *The banking crisis results partly from the failure of the relevant regulatory bodies.*

▶ providing money **awarding, funding** *Most of the funding bodies mentioned here have restrictions on granting awards to overseas students.*

▶ providing advice, not taking action **advisory, consultative** *The second chamber should be an advisory body only, with no significant powers.*

▶ acting for a government **government, public** *'Bappenas' is the main government body for economic planning in Indonesia*

▶ types of body **corporate, independent, international, national, voluntary**

● v+N **elect, establish, form, set up** *This has led to more agencies forming regulatory bodies and signing up to their code of practice.*

2 a large amount or collection of knowledge, information, work etc.

● adj+N **considerable, growing, large, substantial, vast** *There is a growing body of evidence demonstrating that, when used well, ICT can raise attainment.*

● N+of **evidence, knowledge, literature, material, opinion, research, work** *The conclusions of this report are drawn from a large body of research from academic institutions all around the world.*

bold ADJ
involving a risk, or not afraid to take a risk

● ADJ+n **action attempt, decision, initiative, move, step** *Capital took the bold move to cut the amount of advertising on the station almost in half.*

▶ statement **assertion, claim, statement** *Smith began with the bold statement 'Scientists are the most important occupational group in the world today'.*

● v+ADJ **become, get, grow** *The sea-raiders were growing bolder in their attacks upon the coast.*

● and/or **ambitious, daring, exciting, imaginative, innovative** *The paper urges the administration to be bold and imaginative in its approach to climate change.*

bomb N
a weapon made to explode

● adj+N types of bomb **atomic, cluster, dirty, high-explosive, hydrogen, incendiary, nuclear, smart** *The Japanese surrendered after America dropped two nuclear bombs on Hiroshima and Nagasaki.*

▶ that has not exploded **unexploded** *The presence of unexploded cluster bombs is a particular hazard for children.*

● v+N put a bomb somewhere **drop, place, plant, throw** *Insurgents planted the bomb on a side road off one of the city's main streets.*

▶ make a bomb explode **detonate, explode, set off** *The U.S. commander on the scene says it is not clear whether it was a suicide bombing or whether the bomb was detonated remotely.*

▸ prevent a bomb from exploding **defuse, disarm** *There is a tenuous plot to do with defusing bombs before they explode.*

● N+v **detonate, explode, go off** *The bed in which he was sleeping was directly over the spot where the bomb went off.*

● N+n explosion or threat **attack, blast, explosion, scare, threat** *In December he survived a bomb blast that destroyed his house.*

▸ damage **crater, damage, site** *The wall near the main entrance shows clear signs of bomb damage.*

bombard V
direct a lot of questions or information at someone
[usually passive]

● adv+V **constantly, continually, daily, relentlessly** *Young women are constantly bombarded with adverts that make them feel inadequate.*

● V+with information **adverts, emails, images, information, messages, propaganda** *Politicians were bombarded with propaganda from the big oil companies.*

▸ questions or requests **calls, questions, requests** *Sorry to hear of your disappointment, but the company is bombarded with requests for work experience.*

bombardment N
an attack on a place with bombs or large guns

● adj+N types of bombardment **aerial, naval** *Under a continuous artillery and aerial bombardment, they have begun to gradually withdraw their forces.*

▸ on a large scale **continuous, heavy, intense, massive, relentless** *Prior to that, the city had been subjected to heavy daily bombardment.*

● v+N begin a bombardment **begin, launch, open** *To pre-empt the attack, the Russians launched a massive artillery bombardment at 02.00 on July 5th.*

▸ suffer bombardment **be subjected to, be under, come under** *As a major port, Liverpool was singled-out for special attention by the Luftwaffe, and it came under heavy bombardment during 1941.*

bombing N
an attack or attacks made using bombs

● adj+N **deadly, heavy, horrific, indiscriminate, intensive** *The government launched a crackdown on militants following three deadly suicide bombings last May.*

● n+N **car, carpet, precision, roadside, saturation, suicide, terrorist** *Fear and anger in London over the suicide bombings is beginning to recede.*

● N+n **attack, campaign, incident, mission, operation, raid, run** *The NATO bombing campaign did cause some damage to the environment.*

bond N
a relationship of love or duty

● adj+N strong **close, strong, unbreakable** *There is a strong bond between him and his classmates.*

▸ types of bond **common, emotional, social, special** *The two families were drawn together by a common bond of affection and sympathy.*

● v+N form a bond **create, develop, establish, forge, form** *Children can form strong bonds with their pets.*

▸ make a bond stronger **cement, strengthen** *Our aim is to strengthen the international bonds of friendship with the working people of all countries.*

▸ break or weaken a bond **break, loosen, weaken** *He also believed that unfaithfulness or intolerable behaviour by either spouse breaks the marriage bond.*

▸ have a bond **be bound by, be linked by, be united by, have, share** *While in India, the Dragoons will be making a special visit to a regiment that they share a special bond with.*

● N+of **affection, friendship, love, trust** *On an individual level extremely strong bonds of friendship are forged, that transcend social barriers.*

bonus N
1 extra money you are paid for your work

● v+N have or get a bonus **earn, get, have, receive** *He will receive the performance-related bonuses in cash.*

▸ give a bonus **award, give, offer, pay** *A Christmas bonus was paid to all employees in the form of a profit-sharing scheme.*

2 an extra, unexpected benefit

● adj+N extra **added, additional, extra, special** *For bird-watchers, these islands provide the added bonus of a selection of species not found anywhere else.*

▸ bringing real benefits **big, definite, great, huge, real** *The car parking facility is a huge bonus when staying in London.*

▸ pleasing to get **nice, unexpected, welcome** *The title story alone is worth the cover price – the high quality of the accompanying tales is merely a welcome bonus.*

booking N
an arrangement made to buy a ticket, stay at a hotel etc

● adj+N made in a particular way **electronic, online, postal, telephone** *There is a €1.50 per ticket fee for online bookings.*

▸ made at a particular time **advance, early, late, prior** *Spaces are very limited and advance booking is essential.*

● n+N **flight, holiday, hotel, room, travel** *I arranged the flights and made my hotel bookings over the internet.*

● v+N make a booking **confirm, make, secure** *All new users must register on the system before they can make a room booking.*

▸ receive a booking **accept, receive, take** *Bookings are only taken for large groups or coach trips.*

▸ cancel a booking **cancel** *To cancel any booking made via the internet, please telephone the centre where the booking was made.*

boom N
a big increase in economic activity

● adj+N lasting a long time **long, prolonged** *The long post-war boom came to an end with the recession of 1974–75.*

▸ on a large scale **big, immense, massive,**

unprecedented *From the year 2000, Ireland enjoyed one of Europe's biggest property booms.*

- n+N **building, construction, consumer, dotcom, export, housing, market, price, property** *The London housing market boom is not only continuing, but is actually getting stronger.*

- v+N experience a boom **enjoy, experience, see, witness** *Germany experienced an economic boom as her economy prospered.* • *The West Coast is witnessing a boom in the development and use of electric vehicles.*

▶ create a boom **create, fuel, lead to, spark, trigger** *These investment analysts are held responsible for fuelling the boom in technology-related stocks.*

- N+in **demand, industry, market, prices, sales, trade, travel** *For those at the bottom of the housing market, a boom in property prices can be a source of particular hardship.*

boom V
experience a period of economic success

- n+V **business, economy, industry, market, sales, trade** *Business has boomed for British design over the past few years.*

boost V
help something to improve or increase

- adv+V **dramatically, greatly, massively, really, significantly, substantially** *These new restaurants will significantly boost the night-time economy of the city centre.*

- V+n positive feelings **confidence, morale, self-confidence, self-esteem** *Even that relatively simple exercise boosted her confidence and morale.*

▶ economic activity and efficiency **competitiveness, economy, efficiency, growth, performance, productivity** *The Commission has awarded €1.6 million to assist farmers in boosting their competitiveness.*

▶ sales and profits **income, profits, revenue, sales** *The price cuts are expected to boost sales this month.*

boost N
something that helps to improve business, confidence etc

- adj+N large **big, great, huge, major, massive, real, significant, tremendous** *Being able to monitor whether a customer is in danger from CO^2 fumes could be a massive boost in the fight to improve safety.*

▶ pleasing **much-needed, timely, welcome** *The chancellor has given charities a welcome boost.*

▶ extra **added, extra, further** *It has given many people the extra boost in confidence they have needed in order to successfully apply for permanent work.*

- n+N **cash, confidence, energy, funding, morale, performance** *Four Sussex-based charities have received a cash boost from the proceeds of the Shoreham Port open day.*

- v+N give a boost **deliver, give, provide** *The scheme has been given another boost by increased government funding.*

▶ get a boost **gain, get, receive** *Labour received a*

boost with a separate poll giving it a ten point lead over the SNP.

bored ADJ
impatient or dissatisfied, because you are not interested in something

- adv+ADJ rather **a bit** INFORMAL, **a little, pretty** INFORMAL, **quite, rather** *The voices are nice, but I got a little bored from the lack of plot.*

▶ very **really, so, thoroughly, very** *I had become so bored with running the same routes on my own that I decided to join a running club.*

> You can also say that you are ***bored stiff, bored to tears, bored to death***, or ***bored out of your mind***.

- v+ADJ **become, feel, get, grow, look** *If a book's too long, I often get bored with it and give up.*

- and/or **depressed, frustrated, lonely, restless, tired** *One can grow bored and frustrated very quickly and lose interest in the entire endeavour.*

boredom N
the feeling of being bored

- adj+N **intense, mind-numbing, sheer, utter** *In many cases, sheer boredom in class causes children to be disruptive.*

- v+N **alleviate, avoid, beat, prevent, relieve** *To relieve the boredom, I counted the cars going in the opposite direction.*

- and/or **anxiety, drudgery, frustration, isolation, loneliness, monotony, stress**

boring ADJ
not at all interesting

- adv+ADJ **very extremely, incredibly, mind-numbingly, plain** INFORMAL, **really** INFORMAL, **so** INFORMAL, **terribly** *His lectures were mind-numbingly boring.*

▶ rather **pretty** INFORMAL, **quite, rather** *It gets quite boring being on your own all the time.*

- ADJ+n **bit, book, job, lesson, life, story, stuff** INFORMAL, **task** *It's a long book, but you can skip the boring bits.*

- and/or **bland, dry, dull, irrelevant, long, old** INFORMAL, **pointless, predictable, repetitive, slow, tedious** *The methods used in teaching English and reading were often dull and boring.* • *Why anyone wants to eat boring old spaghetti bolognese when they could be eating this beats me!*

born ADJ
1 (be born) start to live

- and/or **bred, brought up, educated, raised, reared** *She was born and bred in Oldham, Lancashire.*

- adv+V **early, late, newly, prematurely** *Millions of newly born children every year die from disease, especially in the developing world.*

2 used for emphasizing someone's natural ability to do a particular thing

- ADJ+n **communicator, entertainer, leader, performer, storyteller, winner, worrier** *She's a born* *performer, and went to drama classes from the age of seven.*

3 happening as the result of something

- ADJ+of **desire, desperation, experience, fear, frustration, ignorance, love, necessity** *We need to challenge prejudice, which is so often born of ignorance.*

bother N
trouble or difficulty

- v+N **cause, give sb, go to, have, put sb to, save sb** *To save you the bother of asking, I can now tell you that I have no idea why she would do such a thing.*

- n+of+N **bit** INFORMAL, **lot, spot** INFORMAL *Paul had a bit of bother with his car boot, which wouldn't open.*

bound ADJ
1 having an obligation to do something

- adv+ADJ **by law, contractually, legally, morally** *By using this website you agree to be legally bound by our terms and conditions.*

- ADJ+by **agreement, code, conditions, contract, decision, law, rule, terms** *Solicitors are bound by strict professional rules.*

- ADJ+infinitive **accept, adhere to, comply with, follow, obey, pay, respect** *The Council is not bound to accept the lowest of the bids submitted.*

2 closely connected

- adv+ADJ **indissolubly, inextricably, inseparably** *These two aspects of the problem are inextricably bound up with one another.*

boundary N
1 a line dividing two areas of land

- adj+N types of boundary **administrative, electoral, geographic, geographical, national, territorial** *Communications technology has enabled businesses to operate efficiently across national boundaries.*

- ▶ not natural **artificial** *The boundaries that were drawn between countries by the colonial powers were often artificial.*

- n+N **borough, city, constituency, county, field, parish, ward** *With time, the parish boundaries would change.*

- v+N form or mark a boundary **delineate, draw, establish, form, mark, redraw, set** *The River Lee also marks the traditional boundary between Middlesex and Essex.*

- ▶ go across a boundary **cross, straddle** *The village straddles the boundary between England and Wales.*

- N+n **fence, line, marker, stone, wall** *Ownership of boundary fences may be shown on the deeds of a property.*

2 the limits an of activity or experience [usually plural]

- adj+N **artificial, cultural, departmental, disciplinary, jurisdictional, organizational,**

traditional *The University is supportive of research across disciplinary boundaries.*

- v+N define a boundary **define, establish** *We need to establish the boundaries between the two departments.*

- ▶ push back or go beyond a boundary **cross, cut across, expand, extend, overstep, push, push back, transcend** *The subject cuts across traditional boundaries.*

- ▶ make a boundary less clear **blur** *The work blurs the boundaries between fiction and fact.*

bout N
a short period of illness or sadness

- adj+N serious **bad, long, prolonged, serious, severe** *Throughout his life, Baudelaire suffered from severe bouts of depression.*

- ▶ happening at particular intervals **frequent, occasional, periodic, recurrent, repeated** *Allergic reactions caused recurrent bouts of diarrhoea.*

- v+N **cause, experience, get, have, suffer, suffer from, trigger** *He was not a good sailor and suffered repeated bouts of illness.*

- N+of **depression, diarrhoea, fever, flu, illness, malaria, pneumonia, poisoning, sickness** *It took her a week to get over that last bout of sickness.*

bow to PHR VB
agree to do what someone wants because you are influenced by something

- V+n **authority, demands, experience, knowledge, opinion, pressure, will, wisdom, wishes** *I bowed to her superior knowledge and made changes to the system.*

box N
1 a space on a printed form where you write

- adj+N with nothing inside **blank, empty** *Leave the box blank if you have no additional comments.*

- ▶ relevant **appropriate, relevant** *For more detailed information, tick the relevant box on the form at the end of this booklet.*

- v+N **check, fill in, put sth in, tick, use, write (sth) in** *You must fill in all the boxes on the form.*

2 a space on a computer screen where you read or type something

- adj+N with nothing inside **blank, empty** *Write the expiry date in the blank box.*

- ▶ relevant **appropriate, relevant** *Enter your password in the relevant box, then click OK.*

- n+N **check, dialogue, drop-down, pop-up, search, text, tick** *You'll then see a dialogue box that allows you to select the items you want to view.*

- v+N **check, click, click on, fill in, put sth in, tick, untick, use** *Simply click on the boxes to change your settings.*

boycott N
an act of not buying or using something, as a form of protest

- adj+N in a particular area **global, international,**

national, nationwide, worldwide *A nationwide boycott of the election was called for.*
▸ types of boycott **academic, active, consumer, cultural, economic, mass** *An economic boycott of the Soviet Union would have been pointless.*
● n+N **consumer, store, trade** *The trade boycott was approved by Congress.*
● v+N suggest a boycott **call for, propose, threaten, urge** *Environmental campaigners have urged a boycott of all the company's products.*
▸ organize a boycott **impose, launch, organize** *They organized a successful boycott of a number of the firm's products.*
▸ join a boycott **join, support** *The group actively supported the boycott of the business.*
▸ end a boycott **end, lift** *The boycott was finally lifted in 2007.*
● N+of business **business, company, goods, products, shop, store** *The union proposed a consumer boycott of the shops.*
▸ election **election, referendum** *The party threatened to support a boycott of the referendum.*

boyfriend N
a man or boy in romantic relationship

● adj+N present **current, new** *She brought along her current boyfriend, Jack.*
▸ former **ex-, former, old, then** *Her ex-boyfriend turned up unexpectedly.*
▸ not temporary **long-term, long-time, steady** *None of them has a steady boyfriend.*
▸ acting in a particular way **abusive, jealous** *At that time, she was living with an abusive boyfriend.*

bracket N
1 one of a pair of symbols ( ) [usually plural]

● adj+N **angle, closing, curly, left, opening, right, round, square** *Each answer is followed by the author's initials in square brackets.*
● v+N use brackets **enclose sth in, give sth in, insert, place sth in, put sth in, show sth in, use** *Write the words out in full the first time you use them, and put the abbreviation in brackets.*
▸ open/close brackets **close, open** *Don't forget to close the brackets at the end of your repeat command.*

2 a group you divide people or things into

● adj+N **high, low, middle, top, upper** *This was the movie that placed him in the top bracket of Hollywood stars.*
● n+N **age, income, price, salary, tax** *There are five million people in that age bracket , making it one of the most influential groups in the UK.*

brain N
1 the organ in your head for thinking and feeling

● v+N **activate, affect, damage, injure, stimulate**
● N+n damage or diseases affecting the brain **damage, disorder, haemorrhage, injury, lesion, tumour** *Alexandra's mother died of a brain tumour at the age of 61.*
▸ parts of the brain **cell, stem, tissue** *Alzheimer's disease slowly destroys brain cells.*

▸ medical treatment for the brain **imaging, scan, surgery** *I had to go to hospital for a brain scan.*
▸ activity in the brain **activity, function, waves** *After doing some tests, they found that he had no brain activity.*

2 mental ability or intelligence

● adj+N **quick, sharp** *Her brain was still sharp.*
● v+N **have, pick sb's, rack, take, use** *I racked my brains, trying to think what on earth to do.*

Usage **Brain** is often plural in these combinations.

brake N
1 equipment for slowing down or stopping a vehicle [usually plural]

● adj+N **defective, dodgy** INFORMAL, **faulty** *We see many accidents where the vehicle had faulty brakes.*
● v+N use the brakes **apply, hit, put on, put your foot on, slam on, use** *I slammed on the brakes, stopping just feet from the man.*
▸ stop using the brakes **release, take your foot off** *I released the brakes and put my foot on the accelerator.*
● N+v work/not work correctly **fail, work** *He lost control of the bus after its brakes failed.*
▸ make a noise **screech, squeal** *I heard the brakes squealing, then a loud crash.*

2 something that prevents development or progress

● N+on **development, expansion, growth, progress** *Increased bureaucracy could become a brake on development.*

brake V
stop or slow down a vehicle by using its brakes

● adv+V **early, gently, hard, heavily, late, sharply, suddenly** *I had to brake hard to avoid hitting Luke.*

branch N
1 a part of a tree growing out from its trunk

● adj+N with/without leaves **bare, leafless, leafy** *A bitter wind whistled through the bare branches in the park.*
▸ in a particular position or shape **low, overhanging, spreading, top, topmost**
● v+N **cut, cut back, lop, prune, remove, trim** *They were also asked to cut the branches that were overhanging the main road.*

2 a shop or office representing a large company or organization; the members of an organization

● adj+N **high-street, local, main, nearest** *To find out more, simply book an appointment to speak to an adviser at your local branch.*
● v+N open/close a branch **close, close down, establish, open, open up** *The chain is opening new branches at the rate of one per week.*
▸ visit/contact a branch **contact, visit**
● N+v open/close **close, close down, open, open up** *The local branch closed down last month.*
▸ serve **serve** *It has five branches serving Southampton and the surrounding area.*

- N+n **chairman, committee, manager, meeting, member, office, officer, official, representative, secretary** *They also have a branch office in Nottingham.*

brand N

1 a product with its own name, made by one particular company

- adj+N well-known or popular **established, famous, global, popular, well-known, world-famous** *You will find many famous brands are stocked by the store.*
- ▶ the best quality, or selling most **expensive, leading, luxury, major, premier, premium** *It is Europe's leading brand of gardening equipment and tools.*
- ▶ produced for a particular shop **own** *The supermarket's own-brand products are often considerably cheaper.*
- N+n **awareness, identity, image, leader, loyalty, management, marketing, name, positioning, recognition, value** *Their bread is the brand leader in Lancashire, Yorkshire, and the North East.*

2 a particular type of something

- adj+N **own, particular, peculiar, special, unique** *The band have combined these elements to form their own brand of indie pop.*

brand V

to describe someone or something as a bad person or thing

- V+n **coward, failure, heretic, racist, traitor, troublemaker** *His critical coverage of the conflict infuriated the government, which branded him a traitor.*

brave ADJ

capable of dealing with danger or pain, without being frightened

- adv+ADJ very **exceptionally, extremely, immensely, incredibly, particularly, really, truly** *It was an incredibly brave thing to do.*
- ▶ rather **pretty** INFORMAL, **quite, rather** *It was rather brave of you to ask for a pay rise.*
- ADJ+n people **boy, fellow, fighter, girl, hero, lad, man, serviceman, soldier, warrior** *He was one of the bravest men I had ever met.*
- ▶ actions **attempt, conduct, decision, deed, effort, fight, move, resistance, stand, step** *Several brave attempts were made to save the wounded.* • *The successful entertainment channels will be those taking brave decisions and making fewer compromises.*

bravery N

brave behaviour

- adj+N **conspicuous, exceptional, extraordinary, great, incredible, outstanding, remarkable** *He was also awarded the Victoria Cross for most conspicuous bravery displayed in action.*
- v+N show bravery **demonstrate, display, show** *The British forces have shown great bravery under attack.*

- ▶ require bravery **require, take**
- ▶ recognize or reward someone's bravery **admire, commemorate, honour, praise, recognize, reward**

breach N

1 a failure to follow a law or rule

- adj+N clear or serious **clear, flagrant, grave, serious** *This was a flagrant breach of confidentiality.*
- ▶ possible **alleged, possible, potential, suspected** *The Election Commission should have powers to investigate suspected breaches of electoral law.*
- ▶ not serious **minor** *It was considered to be only a minor breach of regulations.*
- v+N be a breach **constitute** *The disclosure of the information to the public by the university would constitute a breach of confidence.*
- N+of a law or rule **copyright, injunction, law, regulation, reputation, rule, warranty** *He threatened to sue me for breach of copyright.*
- ▶ an agreement or duty **agreement, conditions, confidence, confidentiality, contract, duty, terms, trust, undertaking** *If you don't respond within seven days, you will be in breach of contract.*

2 a serious disagreement

- v+N cause a breach **cause, lead to** *The decision to become an actor caused a breach with his father.*
- ▶ repair a breach **heal, repair** *The situation did little to heal the breach between two opposing sides of his family.*

breach V

break a law, rule, or agreement

- V+n not follow a law or rule **copyright, injunction, law, order, regulation, rule** *It is your responsibility to ensure that you do not breach the rules.*
- ▶ not do what you have promised or agreed to do **agreement, conditions, confidentiality, contract, duty, obligation, terms** *MI6 felt the CIA had breached the secret agreement between the UK and USA.*

bread N

a food made from flour, water, and yeast

- adj+N types of bread **brown, French, granary, home-baked, homemade, naan, organic, pitta, rye, sliced, unleavened, white, wholegrain, wholemeal** *People in poorer households are less likely to eat fresh fruit, wholemeal bread, and other more healthy foods.*
- ▶ fresh **fresh, fresh baked, freshly baked, warm** *There is a delivery of fresh bread to the village every day.*
- ▶ not fresh **mouldy, stale** *This bread is stale already.*
- v+N **bake, butter, cut, eat, make, slice, toast**
- n+of+N **chunk, crust, hunk, loaf, piece, slice** *She had to go out to buy a pint of milk and a small loaf of bread.*

breadth N

a wide range of different things or ideas

- adj+N **considerable, extraordinary, full, great, impressive, sheer, unrivalled, wide** *The university* *has an unrivalled breadth of expertise in the social sciences and humanities.*

● v+N **demonstrate, have, illustrate, increase, offer, provide, reflect, show** *Your essay demonstrates a wide breadth of knowledge.*

● N+of knowledge or experience **experience, expertise, interests, knowledge, skills, understanding, vision** *We value the breadth of experience mature students bring.*

▶ subjects **activities, coverage, subjects, topics** *The strength of the book is the breadth of its coverage.*

breakdown N
a situation in which something fails

● adj+N serious or complete **complete, irretrievable, serious, total** *The turnout in the polls today reflects a serious breakdown in trust between politicians and voters.*

▶ types of breakdown **marital, mental** *Counselling can help in major life events such as marital breakdown.*

● n+N **communication, family, marriage, relationship** *I didn't want the children to suffer in any way because of the breakdown of our marriage.*

● v+N cause a breakdown **cause, lead to** *This decision led to a total breakdown of their relationship.*

▶ prevent a breakdown **avoid, prevent** *The aim is to support you as a family and prevent any family breakdown.*

● N+in **communication, law and order, negotiations, relations, relationship, system, trust** *He denied that there had been a breakdown in communication between himself and his client.*

● N+of relationship **communication, family, marriage, relationship, trust** *Are you struggling with life after relationship breakdown, separation, or divorce?*

▶ discussion **negotiations, talks** *The breakdown of the talks came sooner than had been expected.*

breakfast N
the first meal eaten in the morning

● adj+N including cooked food **cooked, English/Irish/Scottish/Welsh, fried, full, hot, traditional** *Prices from £20 per person/night (includes full breakfast).*

▶ with no cooked food **cold, continental** *A cooked or continental breakfast can be enjoyed in an elegant dining room.*

▶ big **big, hearty, substantial** *They served a hearty breakfast in their sunny dining room.*

▶ small **light, small** *Traditional or lighter breakfasts are available.*

▶ not hurried **leisurely** *We enjoyed a leisurely breakfast on the balcony.*

● v+N eat breakfast **eat, get, have** *Let's get some breakfast before we start.* ● *I had my breakfast before anyone else was up.*

▶ choose not to eat breakfast **miss, skip** *Dwaine quickly put on his school uniform, ran downstairs, skipped breakfast and went off to school.*

▶ cook or serve breakfast **cook, get, make, prepare,**

provide, serve *I had to get my own breakfast that morning.*

break into PHR VB
1 enter a building or vehicle by force, especially in order to steal things

● V+n **apartment, car, flat, home, house, premises, shop, vehicle** *I got back home just in time to catch a burglar trying to break into my house.*

2 start doing something

● V+into **applause, gallop, grin, jog, laughter, run, smile, song, sweat** *We all broke into a sweat as we walked up the steep hill.*

break off PHR VB
1 stop doing something, especially speaking

● V+n **conversation, interview, narrative** *She suddenly broke off the conversation, saying she would have to go.*

2 end a relationship or a discussion

● V+n relationship **connection, contact, engagement, relations, relationship, ties** *'I've broken off my engagement', she said, in a matter-of-fact tone.*

▶ discussion **discussion, negotiations, talks** *The management broke off negotiations when the union refused to compromise.*

break out PHR VB
start

● n+V fighting or violence **fight, fighting, hostilities, rebellion, riot, scuffles, violence, war** *I was eighteen when war broke out.*

▶ a fire **blaze, fire** *The family was asleep upstairs when the fire broke out.*

▶ a disease **cholera, the plague** *Cholera has broken out in the refugee camps.*

breakthrough N
a discovery or achievement that comes after hard work

● adj+N important **big, crucial, great, historic, important, major, real, significant** *This could be the biggest breakthrough in malaria treatment of our generation.*

▶ types of breakthrough **medical, scientific, technical, technological** *Progress toward medical breakthroughs is typically painstaking.*

● n+N **research, technology** *It marks a major technology breakthrough for pupils who are blind or partially sighted.*

● v+N achieve a breakthrough **achieve, make, produce** *Her recent work is making breakthroughs in the investigation of genetic disorders.*

▶ be a breakthrough **be, herald, mark, represent** *The discovery of the first antibiotic marked a breakthrough in modern medicine.*

● N+v **come, happen, occur** *The real breakthrough came when the scientists made a second discovery.*

● N+n for an actor or musician **album, film, hit, performance, role** *In 2002, she starred in her breakthrough film, Blue Crush.*

▸ in science or business **discovery, innovation, product, technology** *This breakthrough innovation allows a car to be driven for 120 miles at 50 mph with a tyre at zero pressure.*

● v+as+N **hail, herald, regard** *These developments are being hailed as major scientific breakthroughs.*

breath N
air going in and out of your body; the act of getting air into your lungs

● adj+N deep or slow **deep, long, slow** *Take another slow breath and release the tension in your body.*

▸ shallow or quick **quick, shallow, sharp** *When people are nervous, they take quick shallow breaths, which makes their voice sound weak.*

▸ having an unpleasant smell **bad, smelly** *She suffered from a digestive disorder that gave her bad breath.*

▸ having a pleasant smell **fresh, sweet** *Good oral hygiene is essential for fresh breath.*

● v+N when you take air into your body **draw, inhale, take** *If you do become anxious, take some deep breaths.*

▸ when you breathe normally again after breathing fast **catch, get back, recover, regain** *I paused to wipe my streaming forehead and recover my breath.*

▸ make breath from your mouth smell pleasant **freshen, sweeten** *Mouthwashes help to control decay and freshen the breath.*

▸ keep breath inside your body **hold** *He could not hold his breath any longer and surfaced for air.*

▸ when you let air out of your body **exhale, let out** *She swallowed hard, and exhaled the breath she'd been holding.*

▸ when you struggle to breathe normally **fight for, gasp for, struggle for** *I was gasping for breath and shaking.*

> If you are struggling to breathe normally, you can say that you are **out of breath** or **short of breath**: *You should walk fast enough to get warm and a little out of breath.*

breathe V
take air into and let it out of your lungs

● adv+V normally **easily, freely, normally, properly** *A decongestant will also help reduce this swelling and help you breathe more easily.*

▸ quietly **quietly, softly** *She sat still, breathing quietly and trying to remain calm.*

▸ taking in a lot of air **deeply, slowly** *I could still breathe deeply without the pain.*

▸ not taking in a lot of air **shallowly** *When you are stressed you tend to breathe shallowly.*

▸ fast **hard, heavily, rapidly** *The other diver was breathing heavily.*

▸ slowly **gently, slowly** *Now, just try to relax and breathe more gently.*

▸ without artificial help **spontaneously** *She began to breathe spontaneously and was taken off the ventilator.*

breathing N
the process of taking air into your body and letting it out again

● adj+N not normal **heavy, irregular, laboured,** **noisy, ragged** *Effects such as nasal bleeding and laboured breathing are all common.*

▸ good or normal **normal, regular** *Listen and make sure the breathing is regular and normal.*

▸ fast/slow **fast, quick, rapid, slow** *Affected animals have a fever, rapid breathing and a nasal discharge.*

▸ taking/not taking a lot of air in **deep, shallow** *Deep breathing calms you and relaxes your body.*

▸ not helped artificially **spontaneous** *Ventilation must be continued until spontaneous breathing is restored.*

● v+N control or improve breathing **assist, control, ease, improve, regulate** *By controlling your breathing, you can influence how relaxed you feel.*

▸ make breathing harder **obstruct, restrict** *Do not put your arm around the patient as this may restrict breathing.*

● N+n **difficulties, exercise, pattern, problems, technique** *When the fumes were released, several people suffered breathing difficulties and eye irritation.* ● *The monitoring device records the patient's breathing pattern.*

● and/or health **circulation, digestion, heartbeat, heart rate, posture, pulse** *His breathing and heartbeat are so slow that they can hardly be detected.*

▸ exercise **exercise, meditation, movement, relaxation** *You will see how breathing, meditation, exercise and sleep can raise mood and energy.*

breathtaking ADJ
1 extremely impressive or beautiful

● adv+ADJ as a sight **scenically, visually** *The informative text is accompanied by visually breathtaking photographs.*

▸ very **absolutely, quite, really, simply, truly** *Some of the landscapes are absolutely breathtaking.*

● ADJ+n **backdrop, beauty, coastline, countryside, display, landscape, panorama, scenery, sight, spectacle, sunset, surroundings, view, vista** *The breathtaking scenery of Scotland presents a fantastic backdrop for a superb range of activities.*

2 extremely bad or shocking

● ADJ+n **arrogance, audacity, cynicism, display, hypocrisy, impertinence** *She accused her opponent of a breathtaking display of arrogance.* ● *This is breathtaking hypocrisy on the part of a government minister.*

breed V
make feelings or situations develop

● V+n negative feelings or situations **anger, complacency, contempt, cynicism, mistrust, resentment, violence** *There is a well-known saying that 'familiarity breeds contempt'.* ● *The study claims that keeping locals apart from the newcomers will only continue to breed resentment.*

▸ positive feelings or situations **independence, success** *Success in one aspect of life can breed success in another.*

breeze N
a light wind

● adj+N slight **gentle, light, slight, soft** *It was still pleasantly warm but with a cooling, gentle breeze.*

▸ powerful **brisk, fresh, stiff, strong** *The course was made more difficult by the stiff breeze.*
▸ pleasant **pleasant** *It was a very warm day, relieved by a pleasant breeze.*
▸ cold **chilly, cold, cool, cooling** *A cool breeze blew in from the moors.* • *The sky is bright blue and a cooling breeze keeps the temperature down.*
▸ warm **balmy, mild, warm** *The wonderful warm weather and balmy sea breezes have given me a real appetite for life.*
▸ from a particular direction **northerly, southerly etc** *A persistent north-westerly breeze continued and gave a fresh feel to the day.*
▸ from/towards the sea **offshore, onshore** *The cliffs provide shelter from the onshore breeze.*

• N+v move **blow, drift, sweep, waft** *A warm sea breeze blew right through the building.*
▸ touch or move something **caress, fan, rustle, stir** *The breeze stirred the trees.*
• v+in+N **blow, dance, flap, flutter, rustle, sway, swing, wave** *The ribbon fluttered and danced in the breeze.*

bribe N
money given to make someone help you by doing something dishonest or illegal

• v+N receive a bribe **accept, receive, take** *She has been charged with taking bribes from a prisoner.*
▸ give someone a bribe **give (sb), offer (sb), pay (sb)** *It is a criminal offence for any person to offer bribes in order to obtain advantage in business.*
▸ ask for a bribe **demand** *The officials demanded a bribe from us before they would let us pass.*

bribery N
the crime of giving someone money for illegal or dishonest help

• v+N **combat, detect, outlaw, resort to, use** *The agency is supporting the government policy of deterring and combating bribery and corruption.* • *In order to do business, they had to resort to bribery and protection deals with local gangsters.*
• N+n **allegation, case, charge, offence, scandal** *The prime minister resigned over a bribery scandal.*
• n+of+N **act, allegation** *The company is facing allegations of bribery in the country's largest smuggling case to date.*
• and/or **coercion, corruption, extortion, fraud, intimidation, theft, threat** *How can the jury be protected from intimidation and bribery?*

bride N
a woman who is getting married

• adj+N pretty **beautiful, blushing, lovely** *Six bridesmaids are attending the blushing bride.*
▸ who will be married to someone in the future **future, intended, prospective** *It is traditional for the man to give his future bride an engagement ring.*
• and/or **bridegroom, groom** *Marriage registers will normally provide the names of the bride and groom, the names of the witnesses, and the name of the officiating priest.*

bridge N
a structure used for crossing a river or road

• v+N cross a bridge **cross (over), go over, pass over** *Cross the suspension bridge and walk back to the city on the other side of the river.*
▸ build a bridge **build, construct, erect** *Years later, a bridge was erected, connecting the park to the town centre.*
• N+v **connect, cross, link, span** *There's a second bridge crossing the river.*

bridge V
make something possible by removing difficulties, disagreements or differences

• adv+V **effectively, successfully** *The centre has successfully bridged the gap between industry and academia.*
• V+n **barrier, chasm, difference, distance, divide, division, gap, gulf** *The project was designed to bridge the language barrier in financial reporting.* • *How far have we succeeded in bridging the gap between prosperous and disadvantaged neighbourhoods?*

brief ADJ
lasting only a short time, or using only a few words

• adv+ADJ when something longer is needed **disappointingly, frustratingly, tantalizingly** *Audiences had a rather frustratingly brief glimpse of him.*
▸ rather **comparatively, fairly, quite, rather, relatively, somewhat** *This number more than quadrupled during a relatively brief period of time.*
▸ very **extremely, very** *This is a very brief summary of the main points of the article.*
▸ which someone is pleased about **mercifully** *The war had been mercifully brief.*
▸ when it is necessary to be brief **necessarily** *A huge range of topics is covered, with the result that each section is necessarily brief and provides only a taster for the reader.*

• ADJ+n period of time **interlude, moment, pause, period, respite, spell, stint** *After a brief stint within the Atomic Energy Commission structure, he moved to the Engineering Research Laboratories.*
▸ use of words **account, biography, description, discussion, explanation, guide, history, introduction, mention, note, outline, overview, résumé, sketch, statement, summary, synopsis** *There is also a brief description of what each newsletter contains next to the link.*

> If you intend to use only a few words to say something, you can say that you will **be brief** or you will **keep this brief**: *I shall be brief as I am aware that we are short of time.* • *I will try to keep this brief, as we all have things to do.*

▸ look **glance, glimpse** *The film gave a brief glimpse into the past glory of the city.*
▸ meeting or visit **encounter, stay, visit** *My life was about to change, starting with a brief encounter in a café in Venice.*

briefing N

a meeting or document to give information or instructions

- adj+N detailed **comprehensive, detailed, full, in-depth, thorough** *Click here for a detailed briefing on the proposed changes.*
- ▶ not detailed or formal **informal, short** *The day started with an informal briefing for journalists from the British ambassador.*
- n+N to journalists **media, news, press** *Initially, media briefings were under the control of the NATO spokesman.*
- ▶ for people taking part in an activity **mission, pre-flight, safety, staff, team** *A full safety briefing is given to passengers.*
- v+N arrange or give a briefing **arrange, conduct, give sb, hold, organize** *They hold briefings for new or inexperienced players.*
- ▶ prepare or publish **issue, prepare, produce, publish** *One of his jobs was to prepare briefings for ministers before they spoke in Parliament.*
- ▶ go to a briefing **attend** *Foreign journalists were allowed to attend the daily briefings on topical issues given by the Prime Minister's official spokesman.*
- N+n meeting **meeting, seminar, session** *Briefing seminars and workshops will be run across the whole country.*
- ▶ document **document, material, note, pack, paper, sheet** *I have read with great interest the background briefing papers provided by the Government.*

bright ADJ

1 shining strongly, or full of strong shining light

- adv+ADJ **blindingly, dazzlingly, exceptionally, extremely, intensely, very** *Even in London, the sun on that summer afternoon was dazzlingly bright.*
- ADJ+n **day, daylight, light, moonlight, morning, sky, star, sun, sunlight, sunshine** *The gardens are bathed in bright Spring sunshine.*
- and/or **airy, cheerful, colourful, crisp, light, spacious, sunny** *There is a large, bright and airy playroom.* • *It was a bright, crisp December morning.*

2 likely to be successful

- adv+ADJ **extremely, very** *The outlook for the industry is very bright.*
- ADJ+n **future, outlook, prospects** *We feel the school has a bright future ahead of it.*

bring V

1 cause a state, situation, or feeling to exist

- V+n something good **benefit, comfort, happiness, hope, joy, peace, pleasure, prosperity, relief, rewards, wealth** *Unfortunately the discussions failed to bring peace between the two factions.*
- ▶ something bad **chaos, misery, shame** *Bad weather brought chaos to the road and rail networks.*

2 start a legal case

- V+n **action, case, charge, claim, proceedings, prosecution** *It is evident that their purpose in bringing this action was to stop production.* • *It is possible to bring legal proceedings against someone who may be misusing the website.*

- V+n+before+n **court, judge, magistrate, tribunal** *Cases can be brought before the tribunal by the tenant.*

bring about PHR VB

make something happen

- V+n situation **situation** *It is human civilization which has brought about the present situation.*
- ▶ change or improvement **change, improvement, regeneration, revival, shift, transformation** *They had helped bring about a shift in the balance of power.*
- ▶ destruction, or loss of power **collapse, destruction, downfall, end, fall, reversal** *The popular uprising had brought about the fall of the government.*
- ▶ peace or agreement **peace, reconciliation** *A national committee was formed to bring about reconciliation and seek solutions to outstanding political problems.*
- ▶ increase/reduction **increase, reduction** *The change brought about a dramatic increase in the population.*

broad ADJ

1 including many different things or people

- adv+ADJ very or sufficiently **exceptionally, impressively, sufficiently, very** *This is an impressively broad collection.*
- ▶ fairly **fairly, pretty** INFORMAL, **quite** *My taste in movies is fairly broad.*
- ADJ+n **appeal, base, category, coalition, consensus, cross-section, range, remit, spectrum, sweep, view** *Oliver advises on a broad spectrum of company law matters.*
- ADJ+in+n **scope** *Some surveys are broader in scope than others.*

2 describing sth in a general way, without many details

- adv+ADJ too **overly, too** *If definitions are too broad they lose their meaning.*
- ▶ rather **pretty** INFORMAL, **rather** *Biotechnology is a rather broad term, and not well defined.*
- ADJ+n **aim, context, definition, generalization, heading, outline, overview, principle, sense, term** *The term 'Decorative Art' is used in its broadest sense.* • *We discussed the issue in very broad terms.*

broadcast N

a programme on radio or television, or seen on the Internet

- adj+N showing events as they happen **live** *It was the first time an opera had been shown in a live broadcast on the Internet.*
- ▶ not made in a studio **outside** *Most of the work is studio-based but it may also include outside broadcasts, depending on the production.*
- ▶ shown on the Internet **online, web** *Our webinars are online broadcasts of seminars covering a wide range of topics.*
- v+N receive a broadcast **hear, receive, see, watch** *One group of strikers was watching a local news broadcast.*
- ▶ make a broadcast **give, make, produce, record** *The group have given regular radio broadcasts.* • *He made several broadcasts for Radio Luxembourg.*

▶ make a broadcast available **beam, show, transmit** *Earlier this year the BBC refused to show the broadcast, which included pictures of the killings.*

broaden V
make something include more things or people

● V+n range **range, reach, remit, scope** *The links page broadens the scope of the site to include other areas that may be of interest.*

▶ knowledge or way of looking at something **awareness, experience, focus, interest, knowledge, mind, outlook, perspective, understanding** *The course has broadened my perspectives on a whole range of issues.*

If you have a lot of new experiences and learn a lot of new things, you can say that you have *broadened your horizons*: *Our organization was established to assist young people in broadening their horizons through cultural exchange programmes.*

▶ when the number of people or things involved is increased **access, appeal, base** *They were determined to broaden access to higher education.* ● *We have entered new markets and broadened our client base.*

▶ definition **definition** *The new act broadened the definition of terrorism to include ordinary political activities, if linked to a banned organization.*

▶ skill **skill** *The course is for fitness instructors who want to broaden their skills to work with children.*

● and/or **deepen, develop, enhance, enrich, expand, extend, improve, increase, strengthen** *This enriches and broadens our students' learning.*

broker V
arrange the details of a deal, plan etc

● V+n **agreement, ceasefire, deal, partnership, peace, relationship, truce** *He brokered a deal on third-world debt relief.* ● *The Scotland Office sees its role partly as brokering relationships between Scottish interests and UK government departments.*

brother N
a boy or man with same parents as you

● adj+N older than you **big, elder, eldest, older** *I live at home with my Mum, Dad and big brother.*

▶ younger than you **baby, kid** INFORMAL, **little, younger** *He was not a gifted player, like his kid brother Bobby.* ● *By this time, my little brother had been born.*

▶ twin **twin** *I had an elder sister and twin brothers who were five years younger than me.*

▶ that you have not seen for a long time **long-lost** *She was finally reunited with her long-lost brother George shortly before she died.*

brow N
1 the line of hair above an eye [usually plural]

● adj+N **arched, arching, bushy, dark, heavy** *She had large, almond-shaped eyes and high arched brows.*

● v+N raise your brows **arch, raise** *'What?' he murmured, arching his brows in surprise.*

▶ move your brows close together **knit** *'I'm not sure,' she answered, knitting her brows.*

2 the part of your face above your eyes

● adj+N hot **fevered, sweaty** *My job was to sit and mop my wife's fevered brow.*

▶ with lines on it **furrowed, wrinkled** *It was a tough question and one that produced a lot of thoughtful faces and furrowed brows.*

● v+N when something gives you a worried or questioning expression **cloud, crease, furrow, wrinkle** *A thought wrinkled his brow.*

▶ wipe your wet brow **mop, wipe** *She used a handkerchief to mop her brow.*

● N+v have a worried or questioning expression **crease, furrow** *People shook their heads and their brows furrowed.*

▶ stop having a worried expression **clear** *Holmes had looked annoyed, but his brow cleared, and he clapped me on the shoulder.*

brown ADJ
having the colour of wood or coffee

● adj+ADJ dark **dark, deep, rich** *Mature birds are dark brown to black.*

▶ pale **light, pale** *A ripe seedpod is pale brown and dry.*

▶ particular shade **chocolate, golden, reddish, yellowish** *Cook until the crust of the pie is golden brown.*

If someone is wearing brown clothes, you can say that they are *in brown*, *dressed in brown*, or *wearing brown*: *She was wearing brown, and it didn't suit her.*

brush aside PHR VB
not accept that something is important or true

● V+n worries or doubts **doubts, worries** *I knew she would just brush aside my worries, as usual.*

▶ criticism or complaint **accusation, complaint, criticism, objection, protest** *The minister brushed aside accusations that he had lied.*

▶ facts, question or suggestion **advice, argument, claim, issue, question, suggestion** *The argument cannot be ignored or simply brushed aside.*

▶ problem **issue, problem** *The problem was largely brushed aside and people's complaints were not taken seriously.*

brutal ADJ
1 extremely violent or cruel

● ADJ+n action or incident **assault, attack, beating, death, killing, massacre, murder, slaying** *In the play she foresees her own brutal death – and that of Agamemnon.* ● *The nation's shock at the brutal murder is now turning to anger.*

▶ system of government **dictatorship, regime** *Under this brutal dictatorship, kidnapping, torture and murder are common.*

▶ quality of something or way of doing something **form, manner, method, nature, way** *There is no more brutal form of warfare than the a siege.* ● *At least 2,000 people were killed in the most brutal way imaginable.*

▶ act or treatment **act, treatment** *Many MPs voiced outrage at the brutal treatment of the students.*

▶ period of cruel treatment **crackdown, occupation, oppression, repression, suppression, war** *For years, nothing was done about the brutal repression in the island.*

▸ person **dictator, killer, murderer, ruler, thug, tyrant** *He is a murderous and brutal dictator who has caused death and destruction to thousands.*

● and/or **barbaric, bloody, corrupt, cruel, harsh, racist, repressive, ruthless, savage, vicious, violent** *They are the victims of a repressive, brutal regime.*

2 so shocking that it seems unkind

● ADJ+n **honesty, reality, reminder, truth** *The article reveals the brutal truth about life in the poorest areas of the country.*

brutality N
extreme and cruel violence

● adj+N very bad **appalling, extreme, sheer, utter** *Discipline is often only held together by extreme brutality.*

▸ done without thinking **casual** *It's a story about the casual brutality to children that often occurs in such places.*

▸ types of brutality **military, physical, police, state** *The Committee have found no evidence of physical brutality.* ● *Its ugly record of police brutality is known in every section of the country.*

● n+of+N **act, allegation, evidence, example, level, victim** *Both units were involved in acts of extreme brutality against civilians.*

● and/or **corruption, cruelty, injustice, oppression, repression, violence** *She was one of more than a million who stood up to defy corruption and brutality.*

bubble N
1 a ball of air or gas

● v+N make bubbles **blow, cause, create, form, produce** *Children love blowing soap bubbles.*

▸ destroy a bubble **burst, pop, prick** *She enjoys bursting the bubbles with her tongue.*

● N+v **burst, float, form, pop, rise** *These bubbles float to the top of the glass and make a froth.*

2 a situation in a particular business when there is a lot of uncertainty

● adj+N **speculative, unsustainable** *A major feature in the last few years was the huge speculative bubble in America in the new technology companies.*

● n+N **dotcom, housing, Internet, property, stock market** *Soaring house prices led to the unsustainable property bubble, which finally burst in 2008.*

● N+v **burst, collapse** *He managed to get his money out before the dotcom bubble burst.*

budget N
the money that a person, organization or government can spend

● adj+N limited **fixed, limited, low, modest, realistic, restricted, shoestring, small, tight, tiny** *Let's discover how to decorate your kitchen on a shoestring budget.* ● *The Production Manager has to work within very tight budgets.*

▸ big **big, huge, large, unlimited** *We don't have an unlimited budget.*

▸ total **overall, total** *The total budget will not exceed £44,000.*

● v+N decide on and manage a budget **agree, allocate, approve, manage, prepare, propose, set** *Just like any other significant purchase, you set a realistic budget.*

▸ manage a budget successfully **balance, control, keep to, keep within, stay within, work within** *Last year we delivered our targets and balanced our budget.* ● *Plan carefully to keep within budgets and deadlines.*

▸ spend a lot of or more than a budget **blow, exceed, go over, overspend, run over, spend, stretch** *It may not be necessary to blow the budget on special equipment.* ● *The production had also gone well over budget.* ● *Having to pay for new flights really stretched our budget.*

▸ change a budget **revise** *We found it necessary to revise the budget halfway through the financial year.*

▸ increase a budget **increase** *The project will fail unless the budget is increased.*

▸ cut a budget **cut, reduce, slash** *Last year we cut the budget by 50%.*

● N+v allows **allow, permit** *If your budget allows, linger here a day or two.*

▸ be used for **go on** *Most of their budget goes on the rent.*

● N+n **cut, deficit, shortfall, surplus** *The Government's annual budget deficit stands at 4 per cent of GDP.*

bug N
1 INFORMAL a minor infectious illness

● adj+N **flu, food poisoning, sickness, stomach, tummy, vomiting** *If you do come down with a food poisoning bug, here's how to spot it.*

● v+N **catch, come down with, get, have, pick up, recover from, suffer from** *Tell her I've got a stomach bug or something.*

2 a minor fault in a computer system or program

● adj+N **known, major, minor, serious** *The user should look for minor bugs in the system.*

● v+N find and tell someone about a bug **discover, encounter, find, report, spot** *How do I report a bug?*

▸ have a bug **contain, have** *If this file contains a bug, you'll have problems.*

▸ fix a bug **correct, eliminate, fix, iron out, remove** *Most programmers I know think it is impossible to totally eliminate bugs.* ● *If the bugs were ironed out, it would be a lot more fun.*

● and/or **error, glitch, problem** *It plays pretty well, with minimal glitches and bugs.*

3 INFORMAL a sudden strong enthusiasm for doing something

● v+N **be bitten by, catch, get** *He grew up without ever catching the video games bug.*

build N
the size and shape of someone's body

● adj+N small or thin **slender, slight, slim, wiry** *She was of very slight build, with delicate features.*

▸ normal **average, medium, normal** *The suspect is described as a man of medium build.*

▸ large or strong **athletic, muscular, powerful, solid,**

stocky, sturdy *He is softly spoken with an athletic build.*

building N
a structure for living or working in

- adj+N old **historic** *There are still a number of historic buildings in the city centre.*
- ▶ how tall **etc, high-rise, low-rise, tall, three-storey, two-storey** *High-rise apartment buildings dominate the landscape.*
- ▶ in bad condition **derelict, dilapidated** *There are a considerable number of derelict buildings in the area.*
- ▶ impressive **grand, handsome, impressive, landmark, magnificent** *The Town Hall is a magnificent building, constructed in Victorian times.*
- ▶ next to another building **adjacent, adjoining** *The fire brigade prevented the fire spreading to adjoining buildings.*
- v+N make a building **build, construct, design, erect** *The building was constructed in the 1990s.*
- ▶ repair or change a building **convert, refurbish, renovate, restore** *Similar buildings are often converted into holiday homes.*
- ▶ destroy a building **demolish, destroy, gut, knock down** *Soon after, the office building was demolished.* • *The 106-year old building was gutted in the blaze.*
- ▶ use a building **occupy** *The school occupies five different buildings.*
- N+v be in a position **occupy, overlook, stand** *The building occupies a prime site in the town centre.*
- ▶ contain **contain, house** *The building houses a number of different businesses.*

build on PHR VB

- V+n success **achievements, progress, reputation, strengths, success** *The club is now hoping to build on the successes of the past, while moving forwards into the future.*
- ▶ knowledge **experience, expertise, knowledge** *Research always builds on previous knowledge.*
- ▶ tradition **foundations, heritage, legacy, tradition** *We have built on our heritage and we're moving forward.*

build-up N
a gradual increase

- adj+N how fast **gradual, rapid, slow, steady** *There was a gradual build-up of tension throughout the movie.*
- ▶ how large **excessive, massive** *Ensure that there is sufficient ventilation to avoid excessive build-up of heat.*
- v+N stop or control build-up **avoid, control, minimize, prevent, reduce, remove** *Chewing gum between meals helps to reduce the build-up of plaque.*
- ▶ cause build-up **allow, cause, lead to** *Criticism can lead to the build-up of hostility.*

bulk N
1 something very large, wide, and solid or the fact of being like this

- adj+N **considerable, enormous, huge, large, massive** *The massive bulk of the mountain loomed above them.*

- v+N add/reduce bulk **add, increase, reduce** *The cover provides protection against scratches and bumps without adding bulk.*
- ▶ move bulk **heave, shift** *The fat man shifted his bulk, moving to the edge of the seat.*
- N+v **dominate, fill, loom** *His large, intimidating bulk filled the doorway.*

2 the largest part of something

- adj+N **great, main, overwhelming, vast** *Some people think of travel as pleasure, but the great bulk of it isn't.*
- v+N **account for, comprise, constitute, form, represent** *In the third part, which represents the bulk of this article, I shall demonstrate the differences between the two systems.*

bullet N
a small piece of metal shot from a gun

- adj+N **fatal, live, speeding, stray** *A stray bullet from a drive-by shooting had hit her in the chest.*
- v+N fire a bullet **aim, fire, put, shoot** *He had put a bullet through his head.*
- ▶ when a bullet hits someone or something **be riddled with, deflect, take** *They had been shot at close range; their bodies were riddled with bullets.* • *By a stroke of good fortune, the bullet was deflected by the camera slung round his neck.* • *The security guard had taken a bullet intended for the president.*
- ▶ get out of the way of a bullet **dodge, duck** *They had to dodge bullets from snipers when they emerged from their homes to get water.*
- N+v move through the air **fly, whistle, whizz** *A bullet whizzed past my head.*
- ▶ hit someone or something **enter, graze, hit, penetrate, pierce, ricochet, shatter, strike, wound** *We could hear the bullets ricocheting off the rocks around us.* • *Her foot was shattered by bullets.*
- ▶ not hit someone or something **miss** *The bullet missed him by an inch or so.*
- n+of+N **hail, stream, volley** *The gang were trapped in a hail of police bullets as they tried to make their escape.*

bulletin N
a short news broadcast, official statement or report giving information

- adj+N how often **daily, hourly, monthly, nightly, quarterly, regular** *View our monthly bulletin online or send for a free printed copy.*
- ▶ how published **electronic, online, printed** *The service includes electronic bulletins delivered to the inboxes of subscribing customers.*
- n+N contents **information, news, security, weather** *The results were broadcast in the evening news bulletin.*
- ▶ method of broadasting or publishing **email, online, radio, television, TV** *Television news bulletins are now available 24 hours a day.*
- v+N send out a bulletin **broadcast, circulate, distribute, issue, post, publish, release** *The unit regularly issues volcano bulletins for monitored active volcanoes.*

▸ read a bulletin **present, read** *She presents weekend news bulletins.*

● N+v **feature, outline, provide, report** *This bulletin provides regular updates on the progress of the project.*

bump up PHR VB INFORMAL
increase something

● adv+V very much **considerably, significantly** *I should be able to bump up the budget considerably.*
▸ not very much **a little, somewhat** *This may bump the numbers up a little.*

● V+n cost **bill, cost, fee, price, rate** *There could be hidden extras that bump up the cost.*
▸ number **amount, count, figures, number, total** *Bumping up the amount of fruit and veg you eat will benefit your health.*

burden N
a serious or difficult responsibility

● adj+N very great **considerable, enormous, heavy, huge, onerous** *These numbers constitute a considerable public health burden.*
▸ too great **crippling, excessive, intolerable, unbearable, unsustainable** *It also places excessive burdens of responsibility on staff.*
▸ unfair **disproportionate, undue, unfair, unnecessary, unreasonable** *Listing them all on the form could be an unreasonable burden.*
▸ extra **added, additional, extra** *He writes of the need to avoid any additional burden on the taxpayer.*

● v+N have a burden **bear, carry, face, shoulder, take on** *Women are still expected to carry the biggest burden in terms of childcare.*

You can also say that someone has a *burden on their shoulders*: *I didn't want to go through life carrying this burden of responsibility on my shoulders.*

▸ put a burden on someone **impose, place, put** *The University acknowledges the financial burden placed upon students.*
▸ make a burden less **ease, lessen, lift, lighten, minimize, reduce, relieve, remove, share** *It is hoped that this report will find ways of easing the burden on poorer families.*
▸ move a burden to someone else **shift** *When someone is struggling, try to shift the burden of responsibility away from them.*
▸ make a burden greater **add to, increase** *This has significantly increased the burden of regulation.*

● N+v **fall on, lie with, rest with** *The financial burden has fallen on a small proportion of the membership.*

bureaucratic ADJ
involving many complicated rules, details, and processes, especially official processes

● adv+ADJ very **extremely, heavily, highly, increasingly, very** *We have highly bureaucratic rules for filling in forms.*
▸ more than necessary **excessively, overly, too, unduly, unnecessarily** *The UN has become excessively bureaucratic and slow.*

● ADJ+n process or system **apparatus, procedure,** **process, structure, system** *Leave all the bureaucratic procedures to our professionals.*
▸ problems or difficulties **bungling, burden, hurdles, inefficiency, inertia, interference, nightmare, obstacles** *We now have a bureaucratic nightmare involving six different departments.*

● v+ADJ **be, become** *In the post-war period, the regime became increasingly bureaucratic.*
● and/or **burdensome, complicated, costly, cumbersome, expensive, slow, unnecessary, wasteful** *The procedure for issuing licences is cumbersome and bureaucratic.*

burglar N
someone who enters a building illegally and steals things

● adj+N possible **potential, suspected, would-be** *It would have been a good opportunity for would-be burglars to get inside.*
▸ who has committed many crimes **professional, prolific, serial** *A prolific burglar was finally arrested, convicted and sent to jail.*
▸ types of burglar **distraction, house, opportunist** *Opportunist burglars are always on the look out for a quick way into your home.*

● v+N prevent burglars **deter, keep sb out, stop** *There are plenty of things you can do to deter a burglar.* ● *Intruder alarms play a significant role in keeping the burglar out.*
▸ meet a burglar stealing something **catch, confront, disturb** *He disturbed a burglar at his home.*

● N+v enter a house **break in/into, enter, get in/into** *Most burglars get in through a back door or window.*
▸ choose who or where to steal from **target** *She has been targeted by burglars in the past.*

burglary N
the crime of entering a building illegally and stealing things

● adj+N happening in a particular place **commercial, domestic, house, household, residential** *This is helping to cut levels of domestic burglary.*
▸ when nothing is stolen **attempted** *There have been two burglaries and one attempted burglary in the area.*

● v+N commit a burglary **carry out, commit** *Most burglaries are carried out by opportunist thieves.*
▸ try to stop burglaries **combat, prevent, reduce, tackle** *Our efforts have paid off in reducing burglary.*
▸ when police deal with a burglary **investigate, record, solve** *Police are also investigating burglaries at two primary schools.*
▸ when someone is stolen from **experience, suffer** *He'd suffered an attempted burglary.*

● N+v **happen, occur, take place** *80 per cent of burglaries occur when the house is empty.* ● *The burglary took place between 5.40am and 5.43am.*

● n+of+N number **number, series, spate** *We have recently had a spate of burglaries.*
▸ victim **victim** *There are simple measures you can take to avoid becoming a victim of burglary.*

burn V
produce heat and light; damage or injure something or someone with fire

- adv+V with a lot of/a little light **brightly, dimly** *The flames burned brightly and steadily.*
- ▸ strongly **fiercely, furiously, intensely, merrily, steadily** *Fires on boats burn fiercely and spread quickly.*
- ▸ in a way that causes serious damage **badly, dreadfully, horribly, severely** *The carpets were badly burned, but no other damage was caused.*
- ▸ so that something is completely destroyed **away, completely, down** *The roof was burned away.* • *Guildford Theatre burnt down in 1963.*

You can also say that a building is ***burned to the ground*** when it is completely destroyed. People who are killed in a fire are ***burned to death***.

burn N
an injury or mark when something burns your skin or a surface

- adj+N from a particular source **chemical, cigarette, electrical, friction, radiation** *Cigarette burns and small rips can also be repaired.*
- ▸ serious **deep, extensive, horrific, nasty, serious, severe, terrible** *She has horrific third-degree burns on her neck, arms, throat and back.*
- ▸ less serious **minor, superficial** *He escaped with superficial burns.*
- ▸ as measured medically **30 per cent, 60 per cent, etc, first-degree, second-degree, etc** *The incident left him with third-degree burns over half his body.* • *He died the following day after suffering 40 per cent burns.*
- v+N cause a burn **cause, inflict, produce** *These chemicals can cause burns to the skin.*
- ▸ have a burn **get, have, receive, suffer, sustain** *William suffered severe burns to his hands.*
- ▸ treat a burn medically **treat** *She underwent a lengthy operation to treat the burns.*
- N+n person **patient, survivor, victim** *the treatment of burns victims*
- ▸ medical treatment **clinic, surgery, treatment, unit** *the burns units of hospitals*

Usage **Burn** is always plural in both of the **N+n** combinations shown above.

burning ADJ
1 felt extremely strongly

- ADJ+n positive feelings **ambition, desire, love, passion** *He was consumed with a burning ambition to become a writer.*
- ▸ negative feelings **anger, hatred, resentment** *I met his eyes with burning hatred .*

2 that people have strong opinions about

- ADJ+n **issue, question** *The burning question is: can the Internet be regulated?*

burst N
a sudden short period of strong emotion, noise or activity

- adj+N short or quick **brief, quick, rapid, short** *The rain started in short bursts that never lasted long.*
- ▸ sudden **spontaneous, sudden** *a sudden burst of music*
- ▸ strong **concentrated, explosive, intense, loud, sharp** *The film contains intense bursts of action followed by long periods where nothing happens.*
- ▸ not happening often or regularly **intermittent, occasional, periodic, sporadic** *There were periodic bursts of popular anger.*
- ▸ first **initial, opening** *Their interest died down soon after the initial burst of enthusiasm.*
- ▸ lasting longer **sustained** *A sustained burst of gunfire wounded four of the youths.*

burst into PHR VB
suddenly start doing something

- adv+V **immediately, promptly, spontaneously, suddenly** *People spontaneously burst into song.*
- V+n a person's action **applause, laughter, song, tears** *She burst into tears.*
- ▸ a plant's growth **bloom, colour, flower, leaf** *Everywhere wildflowers are bursting into bloom.*
- ▸ fire **flames** *Both the car and the motorbike immediately burst into flames.*
- ▸ activity **action, life** *The game was slow to start with but it suddenly burst into life after about 20 minutes.*

bus N
a large road vehicle for passengers

- v+N take a bus **catch, get, go by, go on, ride, take, travel by** *If I go by bus, it takes an hour.* • *The easiest thing would be to go on the bus.*
- ▸ get on a bus **board, climb on/aboard, get on, jump on** *It took several minutes for everyone to board the bus.*
- ▸ wait for a bus **queue for, wait for** *We didn't have to wait long for a bus.*
- ▸ get off a bus **alight from, get off** *It was time to get off the bus.*
- ▸ miss a bus **miss** *Only once did I miss the last bus back to camp.*
- ▸ provide buses **lay on, operate, run** *They even laid on buses to take the children home.* • *We run some 400 buses, mostly on local bus services.*
- N+v travel **go, run, travel** *Buses run every 90 minutes.*
- ▸ go between places **connect, link, operate, serve** *Infrequent buses serve the rural area.*
- ▸ arrive **arrive, pull up, stop** *He ran up to the bus stop just as the bus pulled up.*
- ▸ carry passengers **carry, pick sb up** *At 4 pm the bus picked us up at our hotel.*

business N
1 the work of buying or selling things; how much trade is done

- adj+N when a lot of trade is done **big, brisk, lucrative, profitable** *Language training for business is big business.* • *Business was very brisk all day.*
- ▸ when not much trade is done **slow** *At first business was slow.*
- ▸ main **core** *Your staff are free to concentrate on your core business.*
- v+N do business **carry on, conduct, do, transact**

*I will certainly look forward to doing business **with** you again.* • *More and more business is transacted via the web.*

▸ try to get more business **attract, compete for, tender for** *The choice is growing all the time, with many companies competing for business.*

▸ start business **get into, go into, move into, open for** *He went into business with his cousin.* • *The airport opened for business on 26th October 2007.*

▸ when a business closes **close for, go out of, put sb out of** *The brewery finally closed for business in 1999.* • *Supermarkets finally put him out of business.*

• N+v **boom, flourish, pick up** *Business is slowly picking up.*

• N+n planning **model, objective, opportunity, plan, planning, strategy** *You need to put together a business plan.*

▸ activity **process, venture** *He embarked on his first business venture while still at university.*

▸ ideas **acumen, ethics** *You need to be a fast thinker with good business acumen.*

▸ place **premises** *The tax applies to both residential and business premises.*

• v+in+N be **be, continue, remain, stay** *Farmers and growers are struggling to stay in business.*

▸ succeed **succeed** *There are any number of books available on how to succeed in business.*

2 a commercial organization

• adj+N types of business **family, family-owned, family-run, owner-managed, private, state-owned** *It's a highly successful family-run business producing cheese and yoghurt from local milk.*

▸ doing well or able to do well **flourishing, profitable, successful, thriving, viable** *Before investing you need to convince yourself that the business is viable.*

▸ how big **large, medium-sized, small** *Many small businesses have experienced credit problems recently.*

• v+N start or develop a business **build up, develop, establish, expand, set up** *They had built up the business from a very modest start in rented premises.*

▸ be in charge of a business **manage, operate, run** *She enjoyed running her own business.*

▸ buy/sell a business **buy, sell, take over** *The family business was taken over by an international consortium*

• N+v do well **do well, flourish, prosper, succeed, take off, thrive** *Her business really took off in the second year of trading.*

▸ do badly **collapse, do badly, fail** *The recession has meant that a lot of small businesses have failed.*

businesslike ADJ
dealing with things seriously and effectively

• ADJ+n attitude **approach, attitude, fashion, manner** *A businesslike approach implies sound management principles.*

▸ atmosphere **atmosphere** *The atmosphere is businesslike but very friendly.*

• and/or **brisk, efficient, professional, serious** *The voice on the other end of the line was cool, brisk, businesslike.*

busy ADJ
when there are a lot of things to do

• adv+ADJ very **exceptionally, extremely, frantically, increasingly, incredibly, particularly, really, so, very** *He's an incredibly busy chap.*

▸ rather **fairly, pretty** INFORMAL**, quite, rather** *It has been a fairly busy few months.*

▸ always **always, constantly** *Rick was constantly busy with his recording and acting careers.*

• ADJ+n lifestyle **life, lifestyle, schedule** *These days, most of us have a busy schedule.*

▸ time **day, month, period, time, week, weekend** *As usual I've had a busy weekend.*

• v+ADJ **be, keep, keep sb, look, seem, stay** *You'll feel better if you try and keep busy.* • *The children kept her busy all weekend.*

• and/or negative characteristics **demanding, hectic, stressful, tired** *Things are so busy and hectic here at the moment.*

▸ positive characteristics **active, exciting, productive, varied** *It's important to keep active and busy in retirement.*

buyer N
someone who buys something

• adj+N possible **potential, prospective, would-be** *There has been an increase in the number of would-be buyers registering each month.*

▸ interested in buying **genuine, interested, serious, willing** *More photos are available to serious buyers.*

▸ when someone is buying their first home **first-time** *It is even harder for first-time buyers to enter the property market.*

▸ types of buyer **cash, private, retail, trade** *The writing table was purchased by a private buyer for £1,350.*

• v+N look for or attract buyers **aim at, appeal to, attract, encourage, look for, target** *Make sure your description will attract buyers.* • *We are currently looking for a buyer for the farmhouse.*

▸ find a buyer **find, get** *You have to find buyers for your product.*

▸ discourage buyers **deter, put off** *Buyers were deterred by rising interest rates.*

bypass V
to find a way of not having to pay attention to something

• adv+V **completely, effectively** *The proposal effectively bypassed the statutory planning procedures.*

• V+n **controls, procedures, process, restrictions, security** *They somehow managed to bypass the normal import controls.*

Cc

cab N
a taxi

- v+N stop a cab **flag down, hail, stop** *We hailed a cab in the street outside the hotel.*
- ▶ travel in a cab **catch, get, go by, jump in** INFORMAL, **take** *Have you any objection to taking a cab?*
- ▶ order a cab **book, call, hire, order, phone for** *I'd booked a cab for 4 AM.*
- ▶ share a cab **share** *We decided to share a cab, because her office was on the way.*
- ▶ drive a cab **drive** *He drives a cab by day and works in a hotel by night.*

cabinet N
the senior members of a government

- v+N form or choose a cabinet **appoint, appoint sb to, assemble, choose, elect, form** *The winning party chose its prime minister, who in turn appointed his cabinet.*
- ▶ join or be in a cabinet **enter, join, return to, serve in** *She had served in Bill Clinton's cabinet several years back, and is now back in the administration.*
- ▶ leave a cabinet **leave, quit** INFORMAL, **resign from**
- ▶ change the membership **reshuffle** *He immediately reshuffled his cabinet.*
- N+n members of a cabinet **colleague, committee, member, minister, official, secretary, spokesman** *The initial decision was made by a cabinet committee chaired by the finance minister.* • *Cabinet Members received additional briefings.*
- ▶ a job in a cabinet **position, post, seat** *Why does he feel the need to resign from his cabinet post?*
- ▶ when the members of a cabinet are changed **reshuffle** *In the cabinet reshuffle, home secretary Charles Clarke was replaced by defence secretary John Reid.*

calculate V
1 find out an amount or number by using mathematics

- adv+V accurately **accurately, carefully, correctly, exactly, precisely, with accuracy, with precision** *Is the price to pay calculated correctly?*
- ▶ incorrectly or not exactly **incorrectly, roughly, wrongly** *Housing costs had been incorrectly calculated.*
- ▶ using a particular method **analytically, mathematically, numerically, scientifically, theoretically** *They calculated mathematically the speed of the ball.*

2 make a judgment about what will happen

- adv+V **carefully, coldly, correctly, incorrectly, rightly, shrewdly, wrongly** *He correctly calculated that if they carried on and reached the Pole, they would die of starvation during the return journey.*

calculation N
numbers that you calculate

- adj+N types of calculation **actuarial, arithmetical,** **astronomical, financial, mathematical, numerical, statistical, theoretical** *How could he carry out difficult mathematical calculations without being able to see?*
- ▶ complicated **complex, complicated, detailed** *He is able to do complex calculations in his head.*
- ▶ simple **basic, quick, simple, straightforward** *The problems set will involve simple calculations and logical reasoning.*
- ▶ accurate **accurate, correct, exact, precise** *Animals are weighed to ensure accurate drug dosage calculation.*
- ▶ not exact or not correct **approximate, crude, incorrect, rough** *However, that figure is just a rough calculation.*
- v+N do a calculation **carry out, complete, do, perform, undertake** *He sat performing painstaking calculations by hand.*
- ▶ check a calculation or do it again **check, double-check, redo, revise, verify** *Students are aware of the stategy of checking a calculation, but unwilling to make the effort required.*

call for PHR VB
1 say publicly that something must happen

- V+n end or stop **end, halt, moratorium** *We must unite with others who call for an end to the arms trade.*
- ▶ getting rid of something **abolition, elimination, lifting, removal, repeal, scrapping** *Mr Davis also called for the abolition of tuition fees.*
- ▶ ban or boycott **ban, banning, boycott** *Many people were calling for a ban on smoking in public places.*
- ▶ end to fighting **ceasefire, withdrawal** *The United Nations called for an immediate ceasefire in the Middle East.*
- ▶ investigation or debate **debate, inquiry, investigation** *Christopher's family are calling for a public inquiry into his case.*
- ▶ change **change, overhaul, reform, resignation, rethink, review, shake-up** *The governor of the Fukushima prefecture has called for a review of nuclear energy plans.*
- ▶ vote **referendum, vote** *The opposition have called for a referendum on the issue of the new constitutional treaty.*
- ▶ making something legal **decriminalization, legalisation** *I have not called for the legalisation of drugs.*
- ▶ creation **creation, establishment, setting up** *We have called for the establishment of a Quality Commission to oversee this.* • *Their proposal called for the setting up of an Anglo-Russian trade agreement.*
- ▶ a positive reaction **calm, cooperation, solidarity, unity** *The President called for unity between the Church and State.*

2 require a positive quality

- V+n **ability, imagination, ingenunity, initiative, judgment, knowledge, patience, skill, understanding** *Their continuing life together will* *call for much patience to get over the difficult times.*

call off PHR VB
decide that something will not happen or continue

- V+n event **game, match, meeting, trip, wedding**
  *The pitch was waterlogged and the game had to be
  called off* .
- ▶ military action **attack, campaign** *The French
  mistakenly believed that Prussia had agreed to a
  ceasefire, and called off the attack.*
- ▶ protest **boycott, demonstration, march, protest,
  strike** *It was too late to call off the demonstration,
  which instead turned into a victory celebration.*

calm ADJ
1 not affected by strong emotions

- adv+ADJ very **incredibly, really** INFORMAL, **so, very,
  wonderfully** *She wondered how he could remain so
  calm.*
- ▶ rather **fairly, pretty** INFORMAL, **quite, reasonably,
  relatively** *Pupils learn more effectively in relatively
  calm classrooms.*
- ▶ completely **completely, perfectly, totally** *He was
  perfectly calm, he walked in there without a struggle
  and sat down.*
- ▶ on the outside **outwardly, seemingly** *He remained
  outwardly calm and detached.*
- ▶ surprisingly **remarkably, surprisingly** *The police
  officer said that Mrs Daniels was surprisingly calm
  when he interviewed her.*
- ▶ in a strange way **eerily, strangely, unusually** *I felt
  as if I was caught in a hurricane, and yet I was
  strangely calm.*
- v+ADJ stay calm **keep, remain, stay** *It's important
  to remain calm in situations like this.*
- ▶ feel calm **be, feel** *I feel calmer now that I have
  written all this.*
- ▶ seem calm **appear, look, seem** *The atmosphere in
  the exam room appears calmer.*
- and/or situation or place or atmosphere
  peaceful, quiet, relaxing, tranquil *This is ideal for
  people looking for calm and relaxing holidays in a
  typical French village.*
- ▶ person/animal **confident, contented, cool, gentle,
  measured, rational, serene, unruffled** *The
  elephants are huge animals, but calm and gentle.*

2 with very little wind or movement

- adv+ADJ very **beautifully, really** INFORMAL, **so,
  very, wonderfully** *To my left I saw a golden sunrise
  across the beautifully calm sea.*
- ▶ rather **fairly, pretty** INFORMAL, **quite, reasonably,
  relatively** *Fortunately, the water's pretty calm in
  West India Quay.*
- ▶ completely **completely, dead** INFORMAL, **perfectly,
  totally** *It's perfectly calm, not the slightest breeze.*
- ▶ in a strange way **strangely, unusually** *In the
  morning, as I woke up, the sea was strangely calm.*
- ▶ surprisingly **remarkably** *Enjoy swimming in water
  that is remarkably calm and extremely shallow.*

calm N
a peaceful state or feeling

- adj+N quiet **peaceful, quiet, tranquil** *There is
  lively entertainment during the day and peaceful
  calm at night.*

- ▶ complete or deep **absolute, deep, inner, perfect**
  *Taylor possesses an inner calm, with a cheeky
  confidence which is refreshing.* • *She told me with
  perfect calm that she did not love me any more.*
- ▶ strange **eerie, strange** *An eerie calm descended.*
- ▶ compared to other situations **comparative, relative**
  *Military life has long periods of relative calm
  interspersed with periods of frantic activity.*
- v+N create a calm feeling **bring, create, induce,
  maintain, restore** *Yoga induces calm and relaxation.*
- ▶ spoil a calm feeling **break, disturb, shatter** *A
  massive car bomb shattered the afternoon calm,
  killing at least five people.*
- ▶ enjoy the calm **enjoy** *They enjoy the calm of the
  garden.*
- N+v **descend, pervade sth, prevail, return** *At about
  six in the evening, the streets empty, the beach
  becomes deserted and a calm descends.*

calorie N
a unit for measuring the energy in food, which
affects your weight

- v+N use calories **burn, burn off, expend, use** *Do
  you want to stay fit and healthy, burn calories and
  build muscle?*
- ▶ eat calories **consume, eat, take in** *We put on weight
  when we are eating more calories than our body is
  using.*
- ▶ reduce or try to reduce the calories you eat
  control, count, cut, reduce, restrict, save, watch
  *She's always counting the calories and starting a
  new diet.*
- ▶ provide calories **provide, supply** *A 170g helping of
  boiled potatoes provides about 120 calories.*

camp N
a group of people who share the same beliefs,
political ideas etc

- adj+N **different, opposing, rival** *Here, the
  population is split into three rival camps on the basis
  of religion, and none has an overall majority.*
- v+N **divide into, fall into, form, split into** *With
  regard to the idea of lifelong learning, experts
  broadly fall into two camps.*

campaign N
1 a plan to produce social or political change

- adj+N done with great energy **aggressive,
  concerted, hard-hitting, high-profile, intensive,
  major, mass, massive, relentless, vigorous** *A
  concerted campaign is needed to get rid of negative
  attitudes to mental illness.*
- ▶ successful **effective, successful** *Why was the
  campaign so successful?*
- ▶ long **long-running, ongoing, sustained** *The
  researchers are calling for a sustained public health
  campaign to raise awareness of the link between
  smoking and blindness.*
- ▶ advertising **ad, advertising, marketing, promotion,
  promotional** *The advertisements were released as
  part of the album's promotional campaign.*
- ▶ election **election, electoral, presidential, re-election**
  *Clinton was exhausted in the last days of his
  presidential campaigns.*
- n+N for telling people about sth **awareness,**

awareness-raising, publicity *They want a high profile publicity campaign* **to** *warn of the dangers of driving too fast.*
▶ for giving people false information **disinformation, propaganda, smear, whispering** *In 1917, Grosz joined with John Heartfield in protesting about the German wartime propaganda campaign* **against** *the allies.* • *He says he was the victim of a smear campaign.*
▶ using particular methods **leafleting, letter-writing, media, poster, press** *The newspaper is supporting the hunt for the killer with a poster campaign appealing for witnesses.*
▶ for getting people to work for you **recruitment** *The Department of Health have launched a recruitment campaign to attract people to working in Social Care or Social Work.*
▶ for raising money **fundraising** *Diane and Peter started a fundraising campaign which was widely supported in the town.*
• v+N start a campaign **begin, embark on, implement, initiate, kick-start, launch, mount, start, undertake** *The Department of Health will launch a campaign to encourage people to be tested for hepatitis C infection.*
▶ be involved in a campaign **be involved in, conduct, engage in, fight, help with, join, participate in, take part in, wage** *Students in in Turkey are waging an international campaign for the release of the student leaders.*
▶ lead a campaign **co-ordinate, front, lead, manage, orchestrate, run, spearhead** *She has spearheaded a campaign on food quality and nutritional standards.*
▶ support a campaign **back, endorse, get behind, support** *A leading business pressure group is backing a campaign to safeguard the British honeybee population.*
▶ pay for a campaign **contribute to, finance, fund, pay for** *We rely on the support of people like you to fund our campaign.*
▶ plan a campaign **mastermind, organise, plan** *The campaign was organised by police.*
▶ tell people about a campaign **promote, publicize** *Consider organising public events to publicise your campaign and increase support.*

2 a plan to win a war
• adj+N **aggressive, intensive, major, massive, relentless, sustained** *It is the most sustained bombing campaign since the Second World War.*
• v+N be in involved in a campaign **conduct, continue, engage in, fight, take part in, wage** *U.S. and British forces waged a four-day campaign against Iraq during Operation Desert Fox.*
▶ start a campaign **begin, embark on, launch, mount, start** *Federal forces launched a campaign to re-establish control over the territory.*

campaigner N
someone who tries to produce political or social change
• adj+N experienced **experienced, long-time, seasoned, veteran** *They are seasoned campaigners who spent years documenting and highlighting cases of state abuse.*
▶ hard-working **active, tireless** *Alan was a tireless campaigner for peace.*

▶ for something **animal rights, civil rights, human rights, peace, pro-life, safety** *Despite protests from pro-life campaigners, the legislature voted to allow abortion in a number of cases.*
▶ against something **anti-abortion, anti-fascist, anti-globalization, anti-nuclear, anti-poverty, anti-racist, anti-smoking, anti-war** *Anti-nuclear campaigners are criticising the plan to build more nuclear power plants.*
▶ environmental **environmental, green** *Green campaigners argue the new plane will cause more noise and pollution.*

cancellation N
a decision to stop something that was arranged from taking place
• adj+N late **last-minute, late, sudden** *Even at the busiest of times, there can be last-minute cancellations.*
▶ immediate **immediate** *He requested an immediate cancellation of his membership.*
• v+N make a cancellation **make** *A holiday may be cancelled provided that the cancellation is made in writing.*
▶ cause a cancellation **cause, force, lead to, necessitate, result in** *Snow forced the cancellation of the fun run around Stirling.*
▶ confirm or announce a cancellation **announce, confirm** *Please be sure to confirm a cancellation in writing via email/post.*
▶ request a cancellation **call for, demand, request** *The report calls for full cancellation of Malawi's debt.*

cancer N
a serious illness caused by uncontrolled cell growth
• adj+N not yet serious **early, early-stage, localized, primary** *People with this localized cancer may go on to live normal lives for years.*
▶ able to be treated **curable, operable, treatable** *Bowel cancer is one of the most treatable cancers.*
▶ spreading and dangerous **advanced, aggressive, invasive, secondary** *Invasive breast cancer is cancer that has spread from the breast to the surrounding tissue.*
▶ difficult or impossible to treat **incurable, inoperable, terminal**
• n+N **bowel, breast, cervical, colon, lung, ovarian, prostate, skin, stomach** *She was concerned about her risk of developing ovarian cancer.*
• v+N have cancer **battle, fight, have, suffer, suffer from** *He has cancer and is going to have surgery.*
▶ get cancer **contract, develop, get** *What are my chances of developing cancer?*
▶ cause cancer **cause, induce, lead to, trigger** *These fibres can induce cancer, but it is not known how.*
▶ prevent or help to prevent cancer **combat, prevent, protect against** *There are no magic foods that will prevent cancer.*
▶ find cancer **detect, diagnose, find** *Delay in diagnosing cancer can have serious effects.*
▶ treat or cure cancer **cure, treat** *There have been great improvements in the way cancer is treated.*
▶ recover from cancer **beat** INFORMAL, **overcome, recover from, survive** *She has already beaten cancer once.*

▶ die from cancer **die from, die of, succumb to** *She died from lung cancer 6 months later.*

● N+v appear and develop **arise, develop, grow, occur, spread, strike** *This type of cancer occurs mainly in older people.* ● *The cancer had spread to the surrounding tissues.* ▶ return **come back, recur, return** *His cancer had returned.*

candid ADJ
honest and direct

● adv+ADJ **quite, refreshingly, remarkably, surprisingly, unusually, very** *Harris is refreshingly candid about her feelings toward Hollywood.*

● ADJ+n discussion **conversation, discussion, interview** *In a surprisingly candid interview, she speaks exclusively to Alistair Blake about the pressures of her job.* ▶ admission **admission, confession** *It was a candid admission by the vice-president that the war was out of control.* ▶ account of events **account, autobiography, memoir, reminiscences** *Never before has there been such a fascinating and candid memoir of life behind the diplomatic scenes.*

● and/or **frank, honest, open, revealing** *The need to provide frank and candid advice is important.*

candidate N
a person competing for a job, political position etc

● adj+N successful/unsuccessful **successful, unsuccessful, winning** *The successful candidate will be enthusiastic and work well in a team.* ▶ most likely to be succeed **likely, obvious, preferred, prime** *He is seen as the prime candidate for the position of Chancellor.* ▶ possible **possible, potential, prospective, shortlisted** *We have recently been selecting prospective candidates for the local elections in May.* ▶ good **good, ideal, promising, right, strong, suitable** *I feel that I am an ideal candidate for the job.* ▶ for a particular position **mayoral, parliamentary, presidential, vice-presidential** *Four years later, he became the party's presidential candidate.*

● v+N choose a candidate **choose, elect, select, select sb as, short-list** *Candidates who are short-listed will have to attend an interview.* ▶ offer someone as a candidate **field, stand** *The Green Party is fielding only 114 candidates.* ▶ suggest a candidate **nominate, nominate sb as, recommend, suggest** *We ask you to nominate suitable candidates.* ▶ be a candidate **be, stand as** *He stood as a candidate for the Liberal Party in the last election.*

candle N
a stick of wax burned to give light

● v+N light a candle **light** *Some people like to begin by lighting a candle or saying a prayer.* ▶ put out a candle **blow out, extinguish, put out, snuff out** *We arrived to see her blowing out the candles on her cake.*

● N+v burn **burn, flicker, gutter** *There were candles burning at the front of the church.*

▶ stop burning **burn out, go out** *I carried on reading till the last candle went out.* ▶ light up something **illuminate, light, light up** *The pumpkins are illuminated by candles placed inside.*

cap V
set a limit on an amount

● V+n **charge, cost, fee, liability, price, rate, spending** *Charges are capped at 1.5 per cent.*

capability N
the ability or power to do something, of a person, country, product etc

● adj+N technical **analytical, diagnostic, graphical, multimedia, research, technical, technological** *What are the real technological capabilities of children?* ▶ in the workplace **management, manufacturing, marketing, operational, organizational** *They lack the necessary finance to develop their marketing and management capability to its maximum potential.* ▶ military **combat, defence, deterrent, military, offensive, warfare, warfighting** *We have reduced our deterrent capability to a single nuclear weapons system.* ● *EU governments spend billions of dollars on defense but have very little military capability to show for it.* ▶ advanced **advanced, enhanced, extensive, powerful, superior** *These operating systems offer more advanced capabilities than Windows.3 products.* ● *This requires superior offensive capabilities, including the capacity to project military power rapidly over an extended distance.* ▶ limited **limited** *Pupils with limited academic capability often made very little progress.* ▶ special **unique** *Sophisticated computers and telecommunications have unique capabilities for enhancing learning.*

● v+N have or gain capability **acquire, develop, have, possess** *Singing exercises can help us develop particular vocal capabilities.* ● *Some children do not have the capability to read at a very early age.* ▶ improve capability **boost, build, enhance, expand, extend, improve, increase, stengthen** *Extra funding is necessary to enhance the capability of schools to manage behaviour.* ▶ show that you have capability **demonstrate, prove** *The aim was to demonstrate the capabilities of the digital lecture board to the participants.*

capable ADJ
able to do something

● adv+ADJ very **easily, eminently, extremely, fully, highly, perfectly, quite, very, well** *It is an ambitious programme, but one which we are well capable of achieving.* ▶ rather **reasonably** *If you are reasonably capable at DIY, it undoubtedly costs less to paint a house yourself.* ▶ as capable as someone else **equally** *The two competitors are equally capable of winning.* ▶ in a particular way **academically, intellectually, mentally, physically, technically, technologically** *Many men who are physically capable of fighting are absolutely hopeless at it.*

● and/or **committed, competent, enthusiastic,**

experienced, intelligent, motivated, reliable, willing *There is a shortage of experienced, capable people who have the time to work with volunteers.*

capacity N

the amount something can contain or produce

* adj+N more than is needed **additional, excess, extra, spare** *Some off-street car parks have spare capacity.*
▶ maximum **full, maximum, total** *The maximum seating capacity for the vehicle is eight.*
▶ large **high, large, unlimited** *Their washing machines have a large capacity.*
▶ enough **adequate, sufficient** *The water companies must have sufficient capacity to meet water demand.*

* n+N for containing or carrying something **airport, carrying, holding, load, memory, runway, seating, storage** *Storage capacity must be calculated against the number of animals in the farm.*
▶ for producing something **generating, manufacturing, processing, production, refining** *The government has plans to quadruple its nuclear generating capacity by the year 2020.*

* v+N have capacity **have, possess** *Your hard drive might have a capacity of 10 GB.*
▶ increase capacity **boost, build, develop, double, enhance, expand, improve, increase, strengthen** *They want to extend the length of the pipeline and increase its capacity.*
▶ be larger than available capacity **exceed, outstrip** *The audience greatly exceeded the capacity of the hall.*
▶ reduce capacity **limit, reduce** *As the arteries become diseased, their capacity is reduced.*

capital N

1 money for starting a business or investing

* adj+N for starting a business **initial, seed, start-up, venture** *How do I raise the start-up capital to run a small business?*
▶ for ordinary daily use **working** *More volume can also mean more working capital.*
▶ more than is needed **surplus** *These institutions prefer companies to return surplus capital to shareholders.*

* v+N get capital **accumulate, acquire, borrow, raise** *Both couples sold their homes to raise the capital for the purchase.*
▶ provide or invest capital **allocate, employ, inject, invest, provide** *Will the government refuse to provide the capital for hospital building?*
▶ make capital available **issue, release, unlock** *One of the partners wanted to release her capital from the business.*
▶ make capital unavailable **tie up** *Many retired people have a lot of their capital tied up in property.*
▶ reduce the value of capital **deplete, erode, reduce** *High inflation erodes the capital of financial institutions.*
▶ attract capital **attract** *Russia needed to attract foreign capital to develop its oil and gas industries.*

2 valuable resources apart from money

* adj+N **cultural, human, intellectual, moral, political, social** *This group of interviewees saw*

education in terms of the building of cultural capital.

captivity N

when a person or animal is not free

* v+N be in captivity **be in, endure, live in, remain in** *He was in captivity for 30 years.*
▶ take sb into captivity **bring sb into, carry sb into, take sb into** *Some monkeys are taken into captivity as pets.*
▶ keep sb in captivity **hold sb in, keep sb in** *Polar bears are one of the most unsuitable animals to be kept in captivity.*
▶ escape captivity **escape, escape from** *Being rescued seemed the only way she was going to escape captivity.*
▶ free someone from captivity **free sb from, release sb from, rescue sb from** *The visit is his first to the region since he was released from captivity in Beirut in 1991.*

capture V

clearly express what someone or something is like

* adv+V accurately **accurately, faithfully, precisely** *The Prince and the Pauper is an adventure story that captures amazingly accurately how kids would act if the story actually happened.*
▶ well **neatly, nicely, succinctly, well** *'Parting is such sweet sorrow' neatly captures my feelings on leaving this job.*
▶ very well **beautifully, brilliantly, expertly, perfectly, vividly** *The graphics in 'The Third Age' are very well done and perfectly capture the look and feel of Middle Earth.*
▶ successfully **effectively, really** INFORMAL, **successfully, truly** *See how he successfully captures the mood of the City in one small picture.*

* V+n mood or feeling **atmosphere, essence, feel, feeling, flavour, mood, nuance** *The photographs really captured the mood of the day.*
▶ particular quality **beauty, energy, excitement, magic** *Many great directors have tried to capture the magic of Broadway on a movie screen.*

capture N

1 the act of catching a prisoner

* adj+N at a particular time **eventual, imminent, recent, subsequent** *The DNA evidence led to his eventual capture.*
▶ successful **successful** *The government announced the successful capture of the party's leader.*

* v+N avoid capture **avoid, elude, escape, evade** *Of the seven crew, only two managed to evade capture.*
▶ result in sb's capture **culminate in, lead to, result in** *The operation resulted in the capture of two Israeli soldiers .*

2 the process of recording digital information

* adj+N good or fast **accurate, efficient, rapid, successful** *The accurate capture of customer information is crucial to the success of any organisation.*
▶ electronic **automated, automatic, digital, electronic** *Many companies have moved to electronic capture and processing of paper-based invoices.*

* n+N **audio, data, document, image, video** *Angela is in charge of data capture.*

- v+N **allow, automate, enable, ensure, facilitate, support** *We offer a complete solution for automating the capture and processing of patient data.*

car N
a vehicle for one driver and a few passengers

- v+N drive a car **control, drive, manoeuvre, reverse, steer** *Who was driving the car when the accident happened?*
- ▶ get into/get out of a car **clamber into, climb into, get in, get into, get out of, jump in, jump into, pile into** *A police officer stopped me and asked me to get out of the car.* • *On Sunday evening, we all piled into the car for the journey home to Madrid.*
- ▶ force someone to get into a car **bundle sb into** *We noticed someone being bundled into a police car.*
- ▶ leave a car somewhere **abandon, dump, leave, park** *They park their cars and then walk over the bridge to their offices.*
- ▶ damage or crash a car **bump, crash, damage, dent, overturn, scratch** *I nearly crashed my car this morning.*
- ▶ damage a car so badly that it cannot be fixed **total, wreck, write off** *He and his brother Jake stole and totalled a fancy sports car.*
- ▶ fix a car **fix, mend, repair, tinker with, work on** *I see them tinkering with old cars outside the house.*
- ▶ do something illegal to a car **break into, nick** INFORMAL**, steal, vandalize** *The thief may have lost his hat when breaking into a car.* • *My brothers and sisters were always in trouble – nicking cars, getting into fights, that kind of thing.*
- N+v hit something or someone **collide with, crash into, drive into, go into, hit, reverse into** *We braked suddenly, and the car behind went into the back of us.* • *Mr Evans was crossing the road when he was hit by a car.*
- ▶ go faster **accelerate, speed up** *Suddenly, the car accelerated backwards, straight over the policeman's leg.*
- ▶ go very fast **hurtle, race, speed** *Talbot awakes in the back of a car, hurtling down a deserted road.*
- ▶ move out of control **career, flip over, skid, slide, spin, swerve** *He stepped on the brakes and the car skidded, making a full circle.*
- ▶ go slower or stop **slow down, stop** *She stopped to watch, and saw other cars stop too.*
- ▶ go backwards **back up, reverse** *I was briefly aware of a car reversing out of a driveway.*
- ▶ stop working **break down** *What will we do if the car breaks down?*

carbon N
the gas carbon dioxide, in relation to its effects on the environment

- v+N remove/store carbon **absorb, remove, sequester, store** *Trees remove carbon from the atmosphere.*
- ▶ produce carbon **burn, emit, produce, release** *This car emits more carbon than any other car in the UK.*
- ▶ reduce carbon **cut, reduce, save** *How will reducing their carbon affect the way they use transport?*
- ▶ balance the effect of producing carbon **offset** *If you just have to get away – then there is always the option of offsetting carbon.*
- N+n **capture, credit, economy, emissions,**

footprint, reduction, saving, sink, trading *How can I reduce my carbon footprint?* • *We are producing too much greenhouse gas to be absorbed by plants and other carbon sinks.*

carbon dioxide N
a gas produced by burning fossil fuels, which is damaging to the environment

- v+N take in/remove carbon dioxide **absorb, remove, take in, use** *Forests absorb carbon dioxide and produce oxygen.*
- ▶ produce or form carbon dioxide **emit, form, generate, produce, release** *All fossil fuels produce carbon dioxide and water when they are burned.*
- ▶ reduce carbon dioxide **cut, reduce** *America wishes to move towards the policy of using carbon sinks as a means of reducing carbon dioxide.*
- ▶ balance the effect of producing carbon dioxide **cancel out, offset** *The airport is planting hundreds of trees near to its runway to offset carbon dioxide produced by aircraft.*

care N
1 effort to avoid mistakes or harm

- adj+N great **extra, extreme, great, meticulous, special, the utmost** *These delicate flowers must be treated with the utmost care.*
- ▶ enough **due, proper, reasonable** *Cyclists are required to show due care to pedestrians.* • *Make sure you take proper care of your pet.*
- v+N take care **exercise, take** *Take extra care if anyone in your family is ill.*
- ▶ need care **need, require** *This is an area where extreme care is required.*

2 looking after someone who is sick

- adj+N medical **ante-natal, health, maternity, medical, nursing, post-operative, primary, specialist** *The PCT provides nursing care in patients' homes out of normal working hours.*
- ▶ when someone is dangerously ill **acute, emergency, intensive** *These babies need complex intensive care, specialist equipment and much longer stays in hospital*
- v+N **deliver, offer, provide** *Nurses are accountable to the Chief Nurse, who is responsible for the standards of care delivered to patients.*

care V
to be interested in someone or something

- adv+V very much **deeply, enormously, genuinely, greatly, passionately, really, truly, very much** *I care passionately about this.*
- ▶ almost not **hardly** *At 8.30 a.m. there is another bomb, but people hardly care – they are still paralysed by yesterday's events.*

career N
a job or series of jobs in a profession

- adj+N very successful **brilliant, distinguished, glittering, illustrious, meteoric, remarkable, successful** *He went on to have a distinguished career in politics.*
- ▶ likely to be successful **promising** *He gave up a promising career in football to train as a doctor.*

▶ involving both success and failure **chequered** *Despite a chequered career, he made sure his final performances were his most memorable.*
▶ becoming less successful **flagging** *Damon salvaged his flagging career by starring in the Bourne movies.*
▶ enjoyable or interesting **eventful, fulfilling, rewarding, satisfying, varied** *For anyone who likes the outdoor life farming can offer a rewarding career.*
▶ well-paid **high-flying, lucrative** *She has a brilliant and lucrative career in front of her.*
▶ in a particular profession **acting, broadcasting, footballing, journalistic, managerial, military, musical, nursing, political, recording, singing, teaching** *He worked for a publishing company before embarking on a journalistic career.*

● v+N have a career **follow, have, pursue** *Realising law wasn't for him, he pursued a career in advertising.*
▶ choose or consider a career **choose, consider, contemplate, decide on, plan, think about** *Why did you choose this career?* ● *The careers office offers practical advice for planning your career.*
▶ start a career **begin, commence, embark on, go into, kick-start, launch, start** *He remembers the precise day he began his career in recruitment.*
▶ re-start a career **continue, re-launch, resume, resurrect, revive** *There was no chance of her political career ever being resurrected.*
▶ improve your career **advance, build, develop, enhance, forge, further, progress** *Some people are so desperate to further their careers that they will not criticize their manager.*
▶ end or spoil a career **blight, end, interrupt, ruin** *His footballing career was blighted by injury.*
▶ leave a career **abandon, sacrifice** *She wouldn't sacrifice her acting career to settle down and have a family just yet.*

> When someone leaves a career and starts a new one, you can say that they *change careers*: *People are changing careers several times in their working lifetime instead of sticking rigidly to the same job.*

● N+v **blossom, flourish, progress, take off** *His musical career really blossomed when he was selected as the assistant conductor of the Berlin Philharmonic.*

● N+n advancement **advancement, development, ladder, path, pathway, progression, structure** *What are the prospects for career progression?*
▶ opportunities or goals **ambitions, aspirations, goals, prospects** *Our courses are intended to enhance your career prospects.*
▶ move or change **change, move** *All these career moves have left me in a fairly unique position.*

careful ADJ
taking care to avoid problems or danger

● adv+ADJ very **exceedingly, exceptionally, extra, extremely, really, scrupulously, so** INFORMAL, **very** *I'm a very trustworthy person who is extremely careful with confidential e-mails.* ● *You have to be so careful not to break the fragile parts.*
▶ especially **especially, particularly** *In dry weather please be especially careful about fire.*
▶ rather **fairly, pretty** INFORMAL, **quite, rather, reasonably** *I try to be pretty careful in what I eat.*

● ADJ+n thought or discussion **analysis, assessment, consideration, deliberation, evaluation, thought** *The committee only reached its decision after very careful deliberation.*
▶ study or attention **attention, examination, investigation, monitoring, observation, scrutiny, study, supervision** *Some points made in the document are perfectly acceptable, but others will need careful examination.*
▶ action **handling, management** *This is a sensitive issue which requires very careful handling.*
▶ planning **planning, preparation** *Without careful preparation, there could be major disruption to essential government services.*

● and/or **detailed, diligent, methodical, meticulous, painstaking, systematic, thorough** *The work requires a careful and methodical approach to gathering facts and assessing evidence.*

careless ADJ
not thinking carefully about what you do or say

● adv+ADJ very **downright, so, utterly, very** *I was annoyed with myself for being so careless.*
▶ rather **a little, rather, somewhat** *It seemed a little careless to keep a poisonous liquid within the child's reach.*

● ADJ+n mistake **error, mistake** *At times they played well, but they made too many careless errors.*
▶ something you say **remark, talk, word, wording** *As a politician you have no privacy, and every careless word or rash remark is documented for the world.*
▶ behaviour **attitude, behaviour, manner** *The judge said she had demonstrated a careless attitude to the safety of the children in her care.*

● v+ADJ be or become careless **be, become, get, grow** *Workers were allowed to become careless, for example taking off their headgear in the heat of the day.*
▶ seem careless **look, seem** *He lost his watch, which seemed careless to me.*

● and/or **dangerous, inconsiderate, irresponsible, negligent, reckless, thoughtless** *Rockfalls caused by inconsiderate or careless climbers are unacceptable.*

cargo N
goods sent by ship, plane, train, or truck

● adj+N valuable **precious, valuable** *People cheered as the SS Ohio was towed into harbour with its precious cargo.*
▶ dangerous **dangerous, deadly, hazardous, high-risk** *Ensure the ferry company has been notified of any dangerous substances or hazardous cargoes.*
▶ of people **human** *The slaves were forcibly transported as human cargo across the Atlantic.*
▶ types of cargo **bulk, dry, heavy, liquid** *Approximately 90% of nonbulk, dry and liquid cargo is transported by containers.*

● v+N carry cargo **carry, haul, ship, transport** *The Portuguese and Spanish bosses hired planes to ship their cargoes.*
▶ take cargo off **deliver, discharge, land, offload, unload** *We immediately started unloading cargo once we had tied up.*

▶ put cargo on **load, take on** *The vessel loaded her cargo of corn and proceeded without incident to Russia.*

▶ deal with cargo **handle** *The amount of cargo handled by the airport has doubled to 774 tons.*

● N+n vehicle that carries cargo **aircraft, boat, carrier, liner, plane, ship, truck, vessel** *By the 1860s, cargo ships were being made from iron and powered by steam engines.*

▶ place where cargo is kept **bay, compartment, container, hold** *It was found that water was leaking into the main cargo hold, and from there the disaster developed.*

▶ business of moving cargo **flight, handling, operation, shipment** *More efficient cargo handling meant that costs were reduced and it was safer for both the men and ships.*

carry out PHR VB
do a particular piece of work

● V+n work **work** *They checked that the work had been carried out according to the regulations.*

▶ when you find out about something **experiment, inquiry, opinion poll, poll, research, study, survey, test** *The research carried out here is world-class.*

▶ when you check that something works or is correct **assessment, check, inspection, investigation, review** *Keep a record of all safety checks carried out for at least two years.*

carry through PHR VB
complete something that was planned

● V+n when you bring about change **change, plan, policy, programme, reform, revolution** *Successive governments have lacked the political courage to carry through a necessary reform.*

▶ when you do a piece of work **project, task** *This course is intended to help you as you begin to carry through your project.*

carved ADJ
made by cutting stone or wood

● adv+adj skilfully **beautifully, delicately, elaborately, exquisitely, finely, intricately, ornately, richly** *The exquisitely carved marble temple dates from 1081.*

▶ badly **crudely, roughly** *The figures on the beams of the 15th century roof are crudely carved.*

case N
1 a legal matter for a court to decide

● adj+N types of case **civil, court, criminal, test** *Statements, reports and other documents may eventually be used as evidence in court cases.*

▶ important **high-profile, landmark** *The plaintiff in the landmark case prefers to remain anonymous.*

● n+N **bankruptcy, discrimination, divorce, fraud, libel, murder, negligence** *The trial became one of the most notorious libel cases of the 20th Century.*

● v+N accept a case **handle, take, take on** *If they had known what they were getting into, they would never have taken the case.*

▶ bring a case **bring, investigate, prosecute, pursue**

My job is to investigate and prosecute cases of serious financial and commercial fraud.

▶ try a case in court **consider, hear, try** *If conciliation is not possible, or if it fails, the tribunal will hear the case.*

▶ decide a case **decide, settle** *The case against the newspaper was settled out of court.*

▶ delay or end a case **adjourn, dismiss, drop** *There were no applications for bail and the case was adjourned until May.*

▶ win/lose a case **lose, win** *If you win a case, then you are usually entitled to recover your costs.*

● N+v what a case is about **allege, concern, highlight, involve** *These cases allege that the UK government has breached articles 8, 12 and 14 of the Human Rights code.*

▶ when a case is brought **come before sb, come to court, go to court, go to trial** *When the case came to court, he was acquitted.*

▶ when a case fails **collapse** *I don't think it is right for me to speculate on the reasons why the case collapsed.*

2 the facts and arguments for or against something

● adj+N strong **clear, clear-cut, compelling, convincing, open-and-shut** INFORMAL**, persuasive, powerful, strong, watertight** *Permission will only be granted if a convincing case is made by the student.*

▶ possible **arguable, prima-facie** *There is an arguable case for splitting the walk into two halves.*

▶ weak **weak** *The case against her was weak, to say the least.*

● v+N make a case **argue, make, plead, present, put, state** *I will put the case for a realistic approach to definition and measurement in survey research.*

▶ put a case too strongly **overstate** *Overstating your case is more likely to wreck than to win your argument.*

▶ make a case stronger **bolster, strengthen** *The ruling strengthens the case for equal pension and sickness pay rights for part-timers.*

cash N
1 money in coins or notes

● adj+N **hard, ready, spare** *Shops have always been a target because of the ready cash and shelves of stock.*

● v+N get cash **take out, withdraw** *It is important that people are vigilant when they leave a bank having withdrawn cash.*

▶ pay cash **deposit, pay, pay in** *You can pay us by depositing cash directly to our bank accounts.*

● N+n **deposit, payment, withdrawal** *Of course, a cash deposit is acceptable if booking is made in person.*

2 money in any form, especially money that is available for you to use

● adj+N available **excess, free, hard, spare, surplus** *If you really have debt problems, a budget will show you how much spare cash you have.*

▶ worked for **hard-earned** *In return for parting with their hard-earned cash, investors will expect a stake in the firm.*

▶ needed **much-needed** *Buying locally helps inject much-needed cash back into the rural economy.*

● N+n money used in business **boost, flow, injection** *A cash flow statement is a summary of cash movements for the year.*

▶ money given to someone **advance, donation, payment, windfall** *Four local groups will enjoy a cash windfall thanks to funding from the National Lottery.*

● V+n spend cash **invest, part with** INFORMAL**, spend** *If you won the lottery, what would you spend the cash on?*

▶ earn or save cash **earn, raise, save** *I just want to earn some cash!*

▶ not have enough cash **be short of, be strapped for** INFORMAL *Broadcasters are strapped for cash because of the dramatic fall in their revenues.*

cast N
all the actors in film or play

● adj+N with famous actors **all-star, star-studded, stellar** *Some people have complained that the production does not contain a stellar cast, as promised.*

▶ very good **excellent, impressive, strong, superb, talented, terrific** *The cast are all absolutely terrific, and the script is intelligent and often very funny.*

▶ types of actors **all-female, all-male, ensemble, non-professional, supporting** *The carefully selected supporting cast are also superb.*

● v+N have a cast **boast, feature, have** *Set in Wisconsin in the 1970s, the show boasts a cast of the brightest stars in the business.*

A person in a cast is a *member of the cast*: *Quite a few members of the cast had also starred in the original production.*

▶ lead a cast **head, lead** *The cast is headed by Eva Bartok as Veronique, the mistress of a Balkan king.*

casual ADJ
1 temporary

● ADJ+n worker **labour, labourer, worker** *Other members of his family were also employed from time to time as casual labour.*

▶ work **employment, work** *You can do any temporary or casual employment, and can work with an employer up to a maximum of three months.*

2 relaxed and informal

● ADJ+n clothes **attire, clothes, clothing, dress, wear** *Jeans are standard casual wear.*

▶ feeling **atmosphere** *The atmosphere is very casual – not at all how you'd expect a top restaurant to feel.*

▶ attitude **attitude** *His attitude to his work was criticized as being 'too casual'.*

3 not planned

● ADJ+n **conversation, glance, remark** *It was just a casual throwaway remark.*

4 not regular

● adj+N **gamer, listener, reader, user, viewer, visitor** *The charm and beauty of the old Tudor town are obvious to the casual visitor.*

5 not involved

● ADJ+n **observer, onlooker, passer-by** *Even casual passers-by with no knowledge of the game got swept up in the excitement.*

6 not based on serious feelings

● ADJ+n person **acquaintance** *For several weeks, I stayed with casual acquaintances.*

▶ relationship **encounter, relationship, sex** *A casual encounter might spark a long-term relationship.*

casualty N
1 someone who is injured or killed in an accident or war [usually plural]

● adj+N types of casualty **civilian, military** *Assaults on occupied villages using artillery would inevitably produce civilian casualties.*

▶ many/few **few, heavy, light, many, mass, slight** *The village and the main canal bridge were eventually taken with heavy casualties.*

▶ serious/less serious **fatal, minor, non-fatal, serious** *Since 2000 the number of serious and fatal casualties has halved.*

● n+N types of accident **drink-drive, road, road accident, traffic** *Our society will have to continue to accept a high level of road casualties.*

▶ types of victim **child, cyclist, motorcyclist, pedestrian** *Almost 95% of all older pedestrian casualties are in built-up areas.*

▶ in a war **air-raid, battle, landmine** *Battle casualties amounted to 950 in the final six weeks of the campaign.*

● v+N cause casualties **cause, inflict** *They inflicted heavy casualties on the town before withdrawing to their base in the hills.*

▶ suffer casualties **incur, suffer, sustain** *The division had suffered only light casualties during its time in Normandy.*

▶ reduce casualties **avoid, minimize, reduce** *The coalition claimed to have done its best to minimize civilian casualties.*

▶ remove casualties **airlift, evacuate, recover, rescue** *The casualty was evacuated by stretcher and taken to hospital by road ambulance.*

● N+n **count, figures, rate, toll** *Later reports indicated that the casualty toll might have been much higher*

2 a person or thing that is damaged by something

● adj+N **main, major, notable, significant** *Polar bears are set to become one of the most notable casualties of global warming.*

catastrophe N
an event that causes great damage or sadness

● adj+N serious **appalling, great, major, terrible** *It was a relief to come through without any major catastrophes!*

▶ about to happen **imminent, impending, looming** *Despite predictions of imminent catastrophe, the expected famine failed to materialise.*

You can also say that someone or something is *on the brink of a catastrophe*: *We may well be on the brink of the biggest catastrophe the modern world has ever witnessed.*

▶ types of catastrophe **climatic, ecological, economic, environmental, environmental, global, human, humanitarian, natural, nuclear** *A series of environmental catastrophes has befallen the country.*

● v+N cause a catastrophe **cause, create, provoke, trigger, unleash** *Excesses in the market could trigger a catastrophe at any time.*

▶ avoid a catastrophe **avert, avoid, prevent** *We must take collective action if we are to stand any chance of averting a catastrophe.*

▶ predict a catastrophe **foresee, predict** *Six or eight months ago, many were predicting catastrophe.*

▶ suffer a catastrophe **suffer** *My nation has suffered an appalling catastrophe.*

● N+v when a catastrophe happens **happen, occur, strike, unfold** *On the day of the wedding, several catastrophes struck.*

▶ when a catastrophe affects someone **befall** *Catastrophes have befallen those to whom we had looked most optimistically.*

catastrophic ADJ
causing a lot of damage or suffering; very bad

● adv+ADJ possibly **possibly, potentially** *The earth could warm relatively rapidly, with potentially catastrophic effect.*

▶ very **absolutely, truly, utterly** *The consequences for our way of life – and for the lives of the generations who will follow us – could be truly catastrophic.*

● ADJ+n natural event **earthquake, flood, flooding** *Much of this area was swamped during the catastrophic floods in February 2000.*

▶ failure or damage **collapse, damage, decline, defeat, failure, injury, loss** *House prices will suffer a catastrophic collapse.*

▶ effect **effect** *The low price of coffee had a catastrophic effect on the lives of millions of small farmers.*

▶ event **accident, event, incident** *There is the ever-present danger of a catastrophic accident.*

● v+ADJ be **be, prove** *The decision proved catastrophic.*

cater for PHR VB
provide people with everything they want or need

● adv+V mainly **mainly, mostly, primarily** *The skiing at Bormio is fairly limited, with only 33kms of marked runs catering mainly for beginners and intermediates.*

▶ especially **especially, exclusively, specifically** *A number of specialist hotels around the UK cater specifically for blind and partially sighted people.*

▶ well **adequately, amply, fully, properly, well** *Have the needs of disabled students been adequately catered for?*

● V+n types of people **beginners, children, everyone, groups, parties, pupils, tourists, travellers, visitors** *These trips are of varying standards, but some cater for beginners.*

▶ needs or wants **demand, demands, needs, requirements, tastes** *It is questionable whether the ambulance service will be able to cater for future demand.* ● *The facilities are equipped to cater for the demands of the most discerning tourists.*

▶ different types **level, range, type, variety** *The*

schools have special units which cater for a variety of special educational needs.

cater to PHR VB
provide people with something they want or need

● V+n needs or wants **demands, needs, tastes, whims** *Relax in the bar let the attentive staff cater to your needs.*

▶ types of people **audience, beginners, clientele, crowd, enthusiasts, everyone, the masses, tourists, travellers** *Below are a few ideas to cater to the younger crowd.*

Catholic N
a member of the Roman Catholic Church

● adj+N with a strong belief **devout, good, practising, strict** *As a devout Catholic, she declined to become his mistress.*

▶ former **former, lapsed** *Joseph is a lapsed Catholic.*

● v+N be brought up as, be raised as *I was raised as a Catholic, and once considered becoming a priest.*

cattle N
cows and bulls

● n+N **beef, dairy** *Beef cattle are at greater risk than young dairy cattle.*

● v+N keep cattle **breed, keep, raise, rear** *Townspeople often kept a few cattle on the common land.*

▶ feed cattle **fatten, feed, graze, pasture** *In countries such as Iran, cattle are grazed on fields of wheat in winter.*

▶ move cattle **drive, herd** *He started work at the age of 11 as a farm-worker, herding cattle.*

● n+of+N **head, herd** *They raise 500 head of cattle on their Yorkshire farm.*

cause N
1 a person or thing that makes something happen

● adj+N main or important **common, main, major, number-one** INFORMAL**, primary, prime, principal** *The food we eat has become a major cause of ill health and early death, especially among the poor.*

▶ exact **actual, exact, precise** *The exact cause of the condition is not known.*

▶ basic **fundamental, real, root, underlying** *Until the root cause of the war is correctly identified, the situation remains hopeless.*

▶ possible **likely, possible, probable** *The most likely cause of the accident was engine failure.*

▶ additional **contributory, secondary** *Driver error is found to be a contributory cause in over 90% of accidents.*

▶ single **only, single, sole** *Avoiding milk will only help if milk is the sole cause of the allergy.*

▶ that can be avoided **avoidable, preventable** *Smoking is the single most common preventable cause of premature death and disability.*

▶ known/unknown **known, not known, unknown** *The cause of the fire is not yet known.*

● v+N **ascertain, determine, diagnose, discover, establish, examine, identify, investigate, pinpoint** *A research team has been investigating the causes of large numbers leaving the teaching profession.*

● **N+v** be **lie in** *The root cause of her unhappiness lies in her childhood experiences.*

2 the reason for particular feelings or behaviour

● **adj+N** **good, just, reasonable** *The film has been forgotten for two decades, with good cause.*

You can also say that something happens *not without good cause* to say that it happens for a good reason: *Old Trafford is known to Manchester United supporters as the 'Theatre of Dreams' – and not without good cause.*

● **v+N** **find, give, have** *The most recent developments have given cause for celebration and optimism.*

● **N+for+n** **alarm, anxiety, celebration, complaint, concern, optimism, suspicion** *Lucily it turned out that there was no cause for concern.*

3 an aim or idea that you work for

● **adj+N** **worth supporting charitable, deserving, good, just, noble, worthwhile, worthy** *The annual event helps support many local worthy causes.*

You can also say that something is *all in a good cause* or *all for a good cause*: *So, not only are there celebs, freebies and musical delights, it's also all in a good cause.*

▸ **not worth supporting hopeless, lost** *You can never give up or think of anything as a hopeless cause.*

● **v+N** **advance, champion, espouse, further, promote, support** *We should all be seeking ways to advance the cause of peace.*

cause V
make something happen, usually something bad

● **V+n** physical damage **damage, devastation, harm, problem, trouble** *The damage caused by the earthquake of 1989 is still not restored.*

▸ physical harm to people **discomfort, hardship, injury, pain, suffering** *Any operation is bound to cause some discomfort afterwards.*

▸ confusion or disorder **chaos, confusion, disruption, disturbance, havoc, mayhem, uproar** *A terrific storm blew, causing havoc on land and sea.*

▸ mental harm **alarm, annoyance, concern, consternation, distress, embarassment, nuisance, upset** *Noise nuisance can cause severe distress to people who are subjected to it.*

▸ disagreement **controversy, disagreement** *The president's speech caused controversy among some of his supporters.*

caution N
care that is taken to avoid risks or danger; careful thought before you accept something as being true

● **adj+N** great **considerable, extreme, great, particular, the utmost** *We are once again urging the government to proceed with the utmost caution.*

▸ the correct amount of **appropriate, due, proper, the usual** *You must consider the wider issues associated with what you do and act with due caution.*

● **v+N** advise caution **advise, advocate, counsel, recommend, suggest, urge** *Those who urged caution and asked for more clarity received reprimands.*

▸ use caution **exercise, treat sth with, use** *Parents and guardians should exercise caution when taking under 16s along.* ● *These offers should be treated with caution; most of them are scams.*

▸ need caution **need, require** *Extreme caution is required to get on and off the island even in the best conditions.*

cautious ADJ
careful to avoid problems or danger

● **adv+ADJ** too **excessively, over, overly, too, unduly** *We feel that the Commission may have been overly cautious.*

▸ naturally **naturally, understandably** *Museums are understandably cautious about lending out works.*

▸ very **extremely, very** *Be extremely cautious when stepping on and off trams.*

● **ADJ+n** **approach, assumption, attitude, interpretation, optimism, stance, view, welcome** *Manufacturers expressed cautious optimism for the year ahead.*

● **v+ADJ** **be, become, feel, make sb, remain, seem** *Be cautious about making statements concerning your desire for promotion.* ● *His previous experiences had made him understandably cautious.*

cease V
1 stop happening or continuing

● **adv+V** immediately **forthwith, immediately** *This practice is most undesirable and must cease forthwith.*

▸ suddenly **abruptly, suddenly** *And then the battle ceased as suddenly as it began.*

▸ completely or permanently **altogether, completely, entirely, permanently** *Visibility then became very poor and firing ceased altogether.*

▸ almost **almost, practically, virtually** *Clearance for agriculture has virtually ceased but continues for residential and tourist development.*

▸ in effect **effectively** *With the budget cuts, new building has effectively ceased.*

▸ finally **eventually, finally** *Tin mining only finally ceased at the end of the 20th century.*

▸ for a short time **temporarily** *Weather forecasts temporarily ceased, although storm warnings were continued.*

● **n+V** fighting **bombardment, fighting, firing, gunfire, hostilities, operations** *Once hostilities ceased, we separated and went our own ways.*

▸ activity **activities, activity** *The charity is flourishing, but our fundraising activities never cease.* ● *At the moment of death all brain activity ceases.*

▸ production or trading **operations, production, trading** *Production at the car plant ceased in 2005.*

2 stop doing something

● **V+n** **activity, manufacture, operation, production, trading, work** *The magazine has not ceased production, but has merely been postponed a bit.*

ceasefire N
an agreement to stop fighting temporarily

● **adj+N** **immediate, permanent, temporary, unconditional, unilateral** *The UN General Assembly can demand an immediate unconditional ceasefire.*

- v+N ask for a ceasefire **call for, demand** *In September, the United Nations Security Council demanded an immediate ceasefire.*
- ▶ announce or accept a ceasefire **accept, announce, call, declare, sign** *Two days after my arrival, a ceasefire **between** the warring factions was unexpectedly declared.*
- ▶ get a ceasefire **agree, broker, negotiate, secure** *A ceasefire was agreed following a successful counter-attack.*
- ▶ keep a ceasefire **maintain, observe** *The two groups are currently observing the ceasefire.*
- ▶ end a ceasefire **break, end, violate** *A 1982 ceasefire was broken repeatedly in the years that followed.*
- ▶ see if a ceasefire is being kept **monitor** *2,000 UN troops were now in position to monitor the ceasefire.*
- N+v **break down, come into effect, hold** *She asked what happens if the ceasefires break down.*

ceiling N
an upper limit on a number or amount

- n+N **budget, compensation, loan, price, spending** *Are the spending ceilings likely to be exceeded?*
- v+N **set a ceiling put, set** *Local authorities have put a ceiling on the amount of money per person they are willing to pay.*
- ▶ increase a ceiling **lift, raise** *I invite Ministers to take steps to raise the compensation ceiling in line with inflation.*
- ▶ reduce or get rid of a ceiling **abolish, lower** *We have abolished the ceiling **on** how much money employees can give through the pay packet.*
- N+on amount **amount, number** *In cases of discrimination, there is no ceiling on the amount of compensation payable.*
- ▶ what someone pays **contributions, expenditure, price, spending** *Set a ceiling on the price you are prepared to pay and do not exceed it.*
- ▶ what someone gets **earnings** *The plus side is that the self-employed person has no ceiling on their earnings.*

celebrate V
do something to show that an occasion or event is special

- V+n an important event **anniversary, bicentenary, birth, birthday, coronation, festival, jubilee, occasion, special occasion, wedding** *Why not celebrate your birthday in style with a trip to a top show or concert?*
- ▶ success **achievement, success, victory** *Each school was invited to a special presentation to celebrate their achievement.*

celebrated ADJ
famous and praised by many people

- adv+ADJ rightly **justly, rightly** *He is justly celebrated **as** a comic actor.*
- ▶ by many people **internationally, widely** *In many cases the recipients have been well-known individuals, their achievements already widely celebrated.*
- ADJ+n **actress, architect, artist, author, composer, historian, novelist, painter, photographer, poet,**

writer *The most celebrated modern American poet, is Robert Frost.*

celebrity N
a famous person, especially in entertainment or sport

- adj+N very famous **A-list, famous, high-profile, international, major, top, well-known** *Her glamorous clothes are often worn by A-list celebrities including Kate Winslet and Nicole Kidman.*
- ▶ not very famous **C-list, local, minor** *He went on the road for six months, a minor celebrity touring the country.*
- ▶ suddenly famous **instant, overnight** *Reality TV makes instant celebrities, but their shelf-life is limited.*
- N+n saying what a celebrity does **chef, cook, gardener, hairdresser, presenter, speaker, stylist, supporter** *The original celebrity chef, Mrs Patten has been cooking for nearly 60 years.*
- ▶ involving or done by celebrities **culture, endorsement, guest, interview** *Celebrity endorsements can be two-edged, with the potential to strengthen or weaken political messages.* • *My job is to book the stars and celebrity guests from film, TV, theatre and music.*
- ▶ about celebrities **gossip, magazine** *We have a wide choice of magazines covering topics such as music, current affairs, celebrity gossip, education and employment.*

cell N
the smallest part of a living structure

- adj+N diseased **abnormal, cancer, cancerous, infected, malignant, tumour** *Malignant tumours are made up of cancerous cells.*
- ▶ healthy **healthy, normal** *The aim is to kill the cancer cells without harming the healthy cells.*
- n+N in a particular part of the body **blood, brain, muscle, nerve, skin** *The protein that is produced protects these mature nerve cells from death following an injury.*
- ▶ types of cell **germ, stem** *The male germ cells, called pollen, are produced in a part of the flower called the stamen.*
- v+N damage or destroy cells **attack, damage, destroy, kill** *As well as killing cancer cells, chemotherapy can have other effects.*
- ▶ grow or use cells **culture, harvest, stimulate, transplant** *Stem cell therapies involve more than simply transplanting cells into the body.*
- N+v **die, divide, multiply, proliferate** *The white blood cells divide continuously.*

cement V
make something such as relationship stronger

- V+n a relationship **alliance, bond, friendship, links, partnership, relations, relationship** *Friendships were cemented and energies renewed for the next event to be held in two years time.*
- ▶ someone's position **position, reputation, status** *While the work cemented his reputation for innovation, it didn't really increase his sales.*

censorship N
the process of removing parts of books, films, articles etc that are considered unsuitable

- adj+N severe **heavy, severe, strict** *Strict censorship was used to make sure that opposing views were neither seen nor heard.*
- ▶ types of censorship **government, military, official, political, religious, state** *We should not be surprised at these attempts at political censorship.*
- n+N **film, Internet, press, theatre** *Press censorship was the great issue of the day.*
- v+N use censorship **enforce, impose, introduce** *The government imposed press censorship and suspended many civil liberties.*
- ▶ get rid of censorship **abolish, lift, relax** *After the so-called 'Velvet Revolution' of 1989, censorship was abolished.*

censure N
severe criticism of someone

- adj+N **moral, public, social** *To be an atheist in his time was likely to attract public censure.*
- v+N avoid censure **avoid, escape** *The magazine has escaped censure from the Press Complaints Commission.*
- ▶ deserve or attract censure **attract, deserve, face, incur, risk** *I have no reservations about criticising the police when censure is deserved.*
- n+of+N **motion, vote** *A deliberate breach could result in Council passing a motion of censure.*

census N
the process of officially counting something, especially the number of people in a country

- adj+N types of census **federal, national, official, religious** *The 1901 national census is now available online.*
- n+N **population, traffic, wildlife** *A traffic census was carried out on the roads leading into the city.*
- ▶ periods between censuses **annual, decennial, ten-yearly** *For most people, the ten yearly census is just another form to fill in.*
- v+N **carry out, conduct, hold, take, undertake** *The census is carried out every ten years, but population statistics are required on a more regular basis.*
- N+n person who takes a census **enumerator, taker** *Women census takers first took up posts in 1891.*
- ▶ information from a census **data, figures, records, statistics** *I have used small area census data for 1971 and 1991.*
- ▶ where information is recorded **form, return** *Places of birth are often listed in the census returns.*

central ADJ
1 main or very important

- adv+ADJ **absolutely, increasingly** *As computers become increasingly central to how people work and live, it becomes increasingly essential that they perform as expected.*
- ADJ+n part **aspect, feature, plank, role** *For Luther,*

this teaching had become the central plank of his Christianity.
- ▶ person **character, figure** *There is no central figure in this story, it is divided between several characters.*
- ▶ idea or question **argument, debate, idea, issue, motif, point, question, tenet, theme** *A central theme of our programme is the protection and enhancement of our democracy.*
- ▶ importance **importance** *Listening skills are of central importance to a child's development.*

2 easily reached

- adv+ADJ **conveniently, fairly, pretty** INFORMAL, **quite, reasonably, very** *My accommodation was very central and close to the school.*
- ADJ+n **location** *This central location is easy to travel to, with frequent train services from Edinburgh and Glasgow.*

centralized ADJ
controlled from one place

- adv+ADJ **highly, increasingly, too** *The costs associated with our present highly centralized food system are going to increase.*
- ADJ+n **administration, authority, bureaucracy, control, government, management, organization, planning, system** *The state is a centralized organization of the whole country.*
- and/or **decentralized** *Global control can be either centralized or decentralized.*

centre N
1 the middle part of something

- adj+N exact **dead, exact, very** *Drill a 4mm hole in the exact centre of the circle.*
- n+N **city, town** *The project is looking at the physical regeneration of the two town centres.*

2 an important place for a particular activity

- adj+N types of area **international, local, national, regional, urban** *The incidence of non-employment is higher in urban centres than in rural areas.*
- ▶ types of activity **administrative, commercial, cultural, financial, industrial, tourist** *As a thriving cultural centre, Birmingham has a colourful mixture of entertainment to offer.*
- ▶ important or successful **busy, main, major, thriving, vibrant** *In recent years, the city has undergone an amazing transformation and is now a vibrant cultural centre.*
- N+for+n **commerce, education, industry, manufacture, production, research, shopping, study, teaching, trade** *Narbonne is a busy centre for the wine trade with good shopping.*
- N+of+n **activity, things** *She rented a flat in town to be in the centre of things.*

century N
a period of 100 years

- adj+N which century **19th, 20th, 21st etc, nineteenth, twentieth, twenty-first etc** *The city was first settled by fishermen in the 19th century.*
- ▶ when in the century **early, late, mid-** *The Catholic*

community in Edinburgh began to grow considerably in the mid-19th century.

▶ previous/following **coming, following, last, new, next, previous** *Data suggest that the distribution of wealth has become more equal over the last century.*

▶ coming between **intervening** *The intervening centuries saw the construction of buildings of great importance.*

● v+N **enter, span** *The essays span the late fifteenth century to the middle of the eighteenth century.*

● N+v begin, pass, or end **begin, dawn, draw to a close, elapse, end, pass** *As the twentieth century dawned, the British Empire enjoyed its heyday.*

▶ see **see, witness** *The past century has witnessed tremendous changes in the way we communicate with each other.*

▶ bring **bring** *The 16th and 17th centuries brought a vast increase in trade.*

ceremonial ADJ

done as part of a ceremony, or used in a ceremony

● adv+**ADJ largely, purely** *The role of the mayor is now largely ceremonial.*

● **ADJ**+n events **occasion, parade, procession** *This splendid occasion included ceremonial parades and street performances.*

▶ clothes or objects **dress, robe, sword** *The ceremonial robes are of bright red silk, with the badge on the left breast.*

ceremony N

a formal public event with special traditions

● adj+N big and special **elaborate, glittering, grand, lavish, prestigious, special** *Winners will be announced at a glittering ceremony.*

▶ small or simple **simple** *The couple married last September in a simple ceremony in Cornwall.*

▶ types of ceremony **civil, formal, official, religious, traditional** *Your Aboriginal hosts will welcome you to the region in a traditional ceremony.*

▶ at the beginning/end of an event **closing, opening** *The formal opening ceremony was performed by the Society's president, the Duke of Westminster.*

● n+N **awards, civil partnership, degree, graduation, inauguration, initiation, marriage, naming, prize-giving, unveiling, wedding** *The honorary degrees will be awarded at this year's graduation ceremonies.*

● v+N **attend, conduct, hold, host, perform** *The stadium now has a licence to host civil marriage ceremonies.*

● N+v **celebrate sth, mark sth, take place** *There was a special ceremony to mark the opening of the new department.*

certain ADJ

having no doubts; definitely going to happen

● adv+**ADJ** completely **absolutely, quite** *I'm quite certain that's what she said.*

▶ not completely **fairly, not entirely, pretty** INFORMAL, **reasonably** *By matching this information with our records, we were reasonably certain that Edward was born in 1844.*

▶ almost **almost, virtually** *The process is almost certain to take a couple of years.*

● v+**ADJ appear, be, become, feel, seem** *Scientists became certain that the drug was responsible for these birth defects.*

When you are sure that something is true, you can say that you **know for certain** that it is true.

certainty N

1 a feeling of being certain

● adj+N **absolute, complete, great, reasonable, relative** *What we do know with absolute certainty is that being overweight increases your chances of developing heart disease.*

● v+with+N **know, predict, say, state** *We cannot predict with certainty what will happen now.*

● n+of+N **degree** *Answers cannot be anticipated with any degree of certainty.*

2 something which will definitely happen

● adj+N **absolute, near, only, virtual** *The only certainty in life is death.*

certificate N

an official document stating that facts are true, or that you have a particular qualification or permission for something

● adj+N **medical** *Absences because of illness must be supported by a medical certificate.*

● n+N **birth, death, degree, fire, firearm, first aid, insurance, marriage, safety** *All qualified instructors must be trained and hold a current first aid certificate.*

● v+N have or get a certificate **gain, get, have, hold, obtain, receive** *Students who pass the course obtain a certificate of competency in IT skills.*

▶ give a certificate **award, grant, issue, present** *They were awarded certificates by the exam board for coming in the top five in the country in archaeology.*

chain N

1 a group of businesses belonging to the same company

● adj+N big **big, large, major** *The strategies of the major chains have included intense price competition and loyalty schemes.*

▶ where the chain operates **international, national, nationwide** *So far there are three stores in central London, but the aim is to establish a nationwide chain of 100.*

● n+N **fashion, fast-food, grocery, high-street, hotel, pub, restaurant, retail, supermarket** *Fairtrade fruit is now available in major supermarket chains across the country.*

● N+of+n **hotels, restaurants, shops, stores** *She runs a chain of six hotels in Scotland.*

2 a series of things, people or events

● adj+N long **endless, long, unbroken** *An endless chain of mountains swept towards the horizon.*

▶ of people **human** *We formed a human chain to pass the boxes along out of the way of the fire.*

- v+N **break** *Teachers were trying to break the chain of events that could lead to exam failure.*
- N+of+n things that happen **events** *As an archaeologist, I have come to understand something about the chain of events that have taken us from the Stone Age to the Space Age.*
- ▶ similar objects **beacons, hills, islands, mountains, volcanoes** *Many South American countries are connected by the long chain of mountains known as the Andes Cordillera.*

chair V
be in charge of a meeting or committee

- adv+V **ably, independently, jointly, well** *They agreed that the session should be jointly chaired by a management and a staff representative.*

Usage ***Chair*** is almost always passive in these combinations.

- V+n **board, committee, conference, debate, discussion, event, group, inquiry, meeting, panel, seminar, session** *A question and answer session was chaired by Peter Hughes.*

chairman N
the person in charge of a meeting, committee, or organization

- adj+N types of chairman **deputy, executive, honorary, non-executive, vice** *The chairman and vice-chairman are appointed for a period of three years.*
- ▶ temporary **acting, interim** *He will take over from Paul Smith, who has been acting chairman since June.*
- ▶ leaving **outgoing** *A vote of thanks is due to our outgoing chairman, Stephen Black.*
- n+N **branch, club, committee, company, council, panel, party** *According to the club chairman, the offer made was not enough.*
- v+N choose a chairman **appoint sb (as), elect sb (as)** *He was elected chairman in 1997.*
- ▶ be a chairman **serve as, take over as** *Hunter returned to Chicago and served as chairman of the City Homes Association.*

challenge N
1 something difficult to deal with or achieve

- adj+N big or difficult **big, daunting, difficult, formidable, great, huge, major, real, serious, significant, tough** *This programme helps patients tackle the daunting challenge of giving up smoking.*
- ▶ main or basic **fundamental, key, main** *Securing access to skilled engineering staff is a key challenge.*
- ▶ new **fresh, new** *I am confident that the job will provide me with a fresh challenge.*
- ▶ types of challenge **environmental, intellectual, logistical, physical, technical** *The merger will present some logistical challenges.*
- v+N experience a challenge **face** *New immigrants face cultural challenges.*
- ▶ try to deal with a challenge **address, confront, deal with, embrace, meet, respond to, rise to, tackle**
- ▶ successfully deal with a challenge **overcome, solve**

Only by working together can we overcome the challenges presented by climate change.
- ▶ enjoy a challenge **enjoy, relish** *I would relish the challenge of running a school.*
- ▶ be a challenge **be, create, pose, present** *The disease affects a large number of people and poses a significant challenge to the medical profession.*

2 an action or idea that questions whether something is true or legal; a refusal to accept someone's authority

- adj+N **direct, serious, significant** *The report is a direct challenge to the government's policy.*
- v+N be a challenge **be, constitute, pose, present** *These developing fields of knowledge present a challenge to the old religious patterns of belief.*
- ▶ make a challenge **issue, mount** *Businesses leaders have issued a 10-point challenge to all the main political parties.*
- ▶ accept a challenge **accept, take up** *We must accept the challenge to fundamentally change the way public services are organized.*

challenge V
question whether something is true or legal

- adv+V **directly, effectively, fundamentally, openly, seriously** *Russia has been openly challenging all aspects of the sanctions.*
- V+n **assumption, attitude, belief, claim, decision, idea, notion, perception, preconception, stereotype, thinking, view** *The artist's intention is to challenge perceptions of disability.*

challenging ADJ
difficult, but interesting and enjoyable

- adv+ADJ very **extremely, hugely, really, very** *Treating children with eating disorders can be very challenging.*
- ▶ rather **fairly, quite** *She found the course quite challenging at first.*
- ▶ the way in which something is challenging **intellectually, mentally, physically, technically** *Rescue diving is not only physically demanding but also mentally challenging.*
- ADJ+n **experience, problem, project, question, role, target, task** *Her experience and local knowledge will be invaluable in this challenging role.*
- v+ADJ **be, find sth, make sth, prove** *I found the interview questions very challenging.* • *The task proved to be more challenging than I had expected.*

champion N
the winner of an important competition

- adj+N at present **current, defending, reigning, undefeated** *Their only win was a 2–1 win over reigning champions Chelsea.*
- ▶ in the past **former** *The course was designed by former golf champion, David Jones.*
- ▶ for a particular area or competition **national, Olympic, regional, world, European etc** *Scotland's rowing world champion starts her campaign for Olympic gold tomorrow.*
- ▶ accepted by everyone **undisputed** *Floyd Patterson was the undisputed heavyweight champion of the world.*

- v+N **be, become, be crowned** *The Egyptian youngster swept aside the competition to be crowned champion.*

champion V
publicly support someone or something

- adv+V **actively, consistently, long, successfully** *The Conservative party has long championed the interests of British business.*

- V+n **cause, idea, interests, needs, rights, view** *He has championed animal rights for many years.*

chance N [usually singular]
1 an opportunity to do something

- adj+N good **big, good, great, real** *Don't miss this great chance to buy these popular items at a very special price.*

▸ types of chance **last, only, rare, second** *We both feel privileged to be given a second chance of love.*

- v+N have a chance **get, have** *If you get a chance, read this book. It's great.*

▸ use a chance **grab, jump at, seize, take** *I always wanted to visit Sri Lanka, so when I saw a half price holiday offer, I jumped at the chance.*

▸ waste a chance **blow** INFORMAL**, miss, squander, waste** *Bates blew a great chance to score.*

▸ give someone a chance **give sb, offer (sb)** *The hotel is peaceful and offers a chance to explore the country away from the crowds.*

▸ enjoy the chance **enjoy, relish** *I'm relishing the chance to test myself against some of the best players in the division.*

▸ deserve a chance **deserve** *She deserves a chance to prove that she can do the job.*

2 the possibility something that will happen

- adj+N good **clear-cut, decent, fair, good, great, real, realistic, reasonable, strong** *There was a good chance that the sky would clear later in the day.*

▸ not good **little, outside, remote, slim** *The party never had more than a slim chance of winning.*

▸ how likely a chance is **even, fifty-fifty, 10 per cent, 50 per cent etc, one-in-five, one-in-ten etc** *He had a fifty-fifty chance of survival.*

- v+N have a chance **have** *With sound management, it has every chance of success.*

If you want to talk about the possibility of someone achieving something, you can use the phrases *stand a chance* or *be in with a chance*: *You need to prove that you can sell things, otherwise you don't stand a chance.* • *To be in with a chance of winning, answer these two simple questions.*

▸ increase a chance **improve, increase, maximize** *Research revealed that the drug could increase the chance of developing breast cancer.*

▸ reduce a chance **jeopardize, lessen, minimize, reduce, ruin** *Improving security in your home can help to minimize the chances of a burglary.*

change V
become or make something become different

- adv+V in a big or important way **completely, considerably, dramatically, drastically, fundamentally, radically, significantly,** **substantially** *Conditions in the country have changed radically in the last twenty years.*

▸ slightly **little, slightly, subtly** *Some parts of the film were changed slightly to adapt it for the stage.*

▸ quickly **fast, quickly, rapidly, suddenly** *As is the case with all Mediterranean islands, the weather can change very quickly.*

▸ slowly **gradually, slowly** *Attitudes towards disability are gradually changing.*

▸ all the time **constantly, continually, frequently** *Our landscape is constantly changing and developing.*

▸ forever **forever, irrevocably** *The accident changed her life irrevocably.*

change N
the situation of becoming or being made different

- adj+N big or important **dramatic, drastic, far-reaching, fundamental, lasting, major, profound, radical, significant, substantial, sweeping** *The population problem is going to be difficult to solve, and will involve a major change in social thinking.*

▸ small **minor, slight, small, subtle** *There was a subtle change in the weather.*

▸ fast/slow **gradual, rapid, sudden** *After the war, the shipping industry experienced a rapid change.*

▸ types of change **behavioural, climatic, constitutional, cultural, demographic, environmental, legislative, social, structural, technological** *The behavioural changes that occur in people with Huntington's disease are often very distressing.*

- n+N **career, climate, culture, lifestyle, mood, name, policy, regime, temperature** *Lifestyle changes can help reduce the severity of the illness.*

- v+N suggest a change **propose** *They proposed changes to the school curriculum.*

▸ make a change happen **bring about, cause, effect, implement, initiate, introduce, make** *We've made changes to the way we present information.*

▸ experience a change **experience, undergo** *The website has undergone radical changes in the last year.*

▸ not want a change **resist** *It was inevitable that the policy would be criticized by conservatives within the party who perpetually resist change.*

▸ want a change **embrace, welcome** *The catering staff have embraced the changes.*

▸ be a sign of change **herald** *This new initiative heralds a major change in hospital funding.*

- N+v happen **happen, occur, result from sth, take place** *Major changes resulted from the feedback process.* • *By 1900 many social changes had also taken place.*

▸ have as a result **result in sth** *Recent changes have resulted in a marked increase in production.*

chaos N
a confused situation

- adj+N **absolute, complete, total, utter** *It was complete chaos and there were several scuffles with the riot police.*

- v+N cause chaos **bring, cause, create** *Several centimetres of snow brought chaos to the roads.*

▸ be in chaos **be in, be thrown into, descend into** *The country is in chaos and needs a strong government.*

● *As thousands of women die each year, more and more families are thrown into chaos.*

● N+v **ensue, reign** *Chaos reigned at the airport as fans besieged the singer with requests for her autograph.*

character N

1 the qualities that make up someone's personality

● v+N **reflect, reveal, show** *At the end of the novel her true character is revealed.*

● N+n **defect, flaw, trait** *His kindness was one of his most endearing character traits.*

2 the qualities that make something different

● adj+N **distinct, distinctive, unique** *The city of Rodez boasts a rich and vibrant atmosphere as well as a unique character and charm.*

● v+N keep its character **keep, maintain, preserve, retain** *The picturesque fishing town of Deal has retained its eighteenth century character with quaint alleyways and fisherman's cottages.*

▸ have or give something a character **give sth, have, reflect** *The bars and restaurants give the town a sophisticated character.* ● *All the Cambridge colleges have different characters.*

▸ lose its character **lose** *Are Britain's High Streets losing their character?*

3 someone in a book, film etc

● adj+N main **central, lead, leading, main, principal** *The film's two main characters fall in love.*

▸ less important **minor, supporting** *She played a minor character in the movie.*

▸ types of character **believable, likeable, lovable, sympathetic** *The book is full of totally believable characters.*

● v+N **create, depict, feature, play, portray** *Actors need talent and training that will enable them to portray different characters.*

characteristic N

a typical quality or feature

● adj+N showing that something or someone is different **defining, distinctive, distinguishing, individual, specific, unique** *Distinguishing characteristics of the breed are a flat nose and short ears.*

▸ an important or basic characteristic **basic, essential, fundamental, key, main, salient, typical** *The basic characteristics of the product haven't changed.*

▸ types of characteristic **biological, cultural, general, personal, physical, physiological, racial** *Anyone can achieve success as long as they have the right personal characteristics.*

● v+N **exhibit, have, possess, share** *The two animals have very similar characteristics.*

characteristic ADJ

typical

● adv+ADJ **especially, highly, particularly, quite, so** INFORMAL, **very** *The town is full of the small cottages which are so characteristic of the region.* ● *The scent of the flower is very characteristic – sharp but sweet.*

charge N

1 an amount of money that you have to pay

● adj+N extra **additional, excess, extra** *Rental does not include linen and there is an extra charge for this.*

▸ small **minimum, modest, nominal, small** *Most of our services are provided free or at nominal charge.*

▸ high **extortionate, hefty, high** *The parking charges were extortionate so I wouldn't park there again.*

▸ made how often **annual, daily, monthly, yearly** *There is a daily charge of five pounds for parking.*

▸ fixed or usual **fixed, standard** *There is a fixed service charge of £1,000 a year.*

▸ hidden **hidden** *With car hire there are often hidden charges to look out for.*

● n+N **administration, admission, bank, call, cancellation, delivery, hire, parking, penalty, postage, prescription, service, shipping** *If you cancel your reservation, cancellation charges will be made.*

● v+N involve a charge **incur** *This service incurs a small charge.*

▸ pay a charge **pay** *You will be asked to pay a small charge for the service.*

▸ make a charge **impose, levy, make** *A charge is made to cover the costs of ensuring that the work complies with the regulations.*

▸ start to make a charge **introduce** *Cars have kept off the busiest roads in central London since the charge was introduced in February.*

▸ stop making a charge **abolish** *The government decided to abolish museum charges.*

▸ cancel the usual charge **waive** *The delivery charge is waived on orders over £45.*

> If you want to say there is no charge for something, you can say it is **free of charge**: *You can download the software free of charge.*

2 an official statement accusing someone of crime or of doing something bad [usually plural]

● adj+N **criminal, trumped-up** *He was quite correctly acquitted of the trumped-up charge against him.*

● v+N have a charge made against you **answer, face** *The woman is facing charges of fraud.*

▸ make a charge **bring, press** *He could press charges for assault.*

▸ take back a charge **dismiss, drop, withdraw** *A judge later dismissed the charges because of a lack of evidence.*

▸ deny a charge **deny, reject** *Shah has denied charges of aggravated vehicle taking.*

▸ admit a charge **admit** *The teenager was sentenced last week after admitting 12 charges including theft and robbery.*

▸ be found guilty of a charge **be convicted of** *If convicted of the charges, the actor could face a maximum of seven years in jail.*

▸ be found not guilty of a charge **be acquitted of, be cleared of** *When they went to court, they were cleared of all charges.*

charitable ADJ

intended to help people in need

● ADJ+n organization **body, cause, company,**

foundation, fund, institution, organization, sector, trust *It's a charitable trust dedicated to the long term preservation of Chatsworth House and Park.*
▸ action **activity, donation, gift, giving** *Their holistic care service depends almost entirely on charitable donations and fundraising.*
▸ legal position **status** *It was found that the activities were incompatible with the trust's charitable status.*

charity N
an organization helping people who need money or advice; all these organizations considered as a group

● adj+N **educational, independent, international, local, medical, national, registered** *We are an international charity that aims to improve the detection, care and treatment of heart problems before birth.*

● n+N **animal, cancer, conservation, disability, education, health, homelessness** *He works for a cancer charity that offers information and support to cancer sufferers.*

● v+N start a charity **establish, found, set up** *The charity was set up to help newly arrived asylum seekers and refugees.*

▸ give money to a charity **donate (sth) to, give (sth) to, support** *All profits from the sales of each item will be donated to the charity.*

▸ go to charity **go to** *All the money raised by the event will go to charity.*

▸ run a charity **run** *The charity is run by volunteers who have young children of their own.*

● N+n event or place **appeal, auction, ball, concert, event, fundraiser, shop** *The band performed at a charity concert to raise money for children's charities.*

▸ money **donation** *Centre staff ran a special gift wrapping service in exchange for a charity donation.*

▸ work **work** *Henry was active in charity work for homeless people.*

● v+for+N **raise** *Over £800 was raised for local charities.*

charm N
1 an attractive personal quality that makes people like you

● adj+N **boyish, feminine, great, irresistible, natural, seductive** *He is a slim, cheerful man with a boyish charm.*

● v+N have charm **have, possess** *He has real charm and intelligence.*

▸ have a lot of charm **exude, ooze** *As usual, he oozes charm, and has everyone captivated by his speech.*

▸ resist someone's charm **resist** *How could anyone resist her charm?*

▸ be unable to resist someone's charm **fall for, succumb to** *Despite being portrayed as a hard man, he soon succumbed to Jessica's charms.*

▸ use your charm **turn on** *He can still turn on that special charm whenever he wants.*

● and/or **beauty, elegance, grace, intelligence, personality, warmth, wit** *She had a reputation for her charm, warmth and wit.*

2 a pleasant and attractive quality that something has

● adj+N **old-world, original, rural, rustic, traditional, unique** *This delightful old fishing town still retains much of its original old-world charm.*

● v+N have charm **boast, have, possess** *The property boasts charm and character.*

▸ have a lot of charm **exude, ooze** *The streets of the old port exude a truly Corsican charm.*

▸ lose charm **lose** *These traditional stories have lost none of their charm.*

▸ keep charm **keep, retain** *The village has retained its rural charm despite the onset of tourism.*

● and/or **ambiance, atmosphere, beauty, character, elegance** *It's a 14th century inn of great character and charm.*

chart N
a list, drawing, or graph showing information clearly

● v+N create a chart **compile, create, draw, produce** *The author had compiled charts which compared all the data.*

▸ understand the meaning of a chart **interpret** *The ability to interpret weather charts is a useful skill.*

● N+v **demonstrate, give, illustrate, indicate, reveal, show** *This chart illustrates the relationship between yourself and a common ancestor.*

chart V
record how something develops and changes

● V+n **changes, decline, development, evolution, history, life, progress, rise** *The exhibition charts the history of food and drink from prehistoric times to the modern day.*

charter V
hire a boat, plane, or train

● V+n boat **boat, ship, tanker, vessel, yacht** *You will need to be in a big group; chartering boats is expensive.*

▸ plane or train **aircraft, flight, helicopter, jet, plane, train** *The government chartered the jet because there were no flights to Afghanistan.*

chase N
an attempt to catch someone

● adj+N **dramatic, exciting, frantic, high-speed, mad, spectacular, thrilling** *The movie ends with a dramatic car chase through the streets of Los Angeles.*

● n+N **car, helicopter, motorcycle, police** *The five teenagers were involved in a police chase late on Monday night.*

● v+N take part in a chase **begin, continue, join, start** *He started a high-speed chase across Europe, followed by the police.*

You can also say that someone **gives chase** when they start chasing someone: *Officer Marshall saw the prisoner running away, and he gave chase and secured him.*

▸ not continue with a chase **abandon, give up** *We followed him until night forced us to abandon the chase.*

● N+v **begin, continue, ensue, follow** *The thief tries to escape, and a chase ensues.*

chasm N
a very big difference

● adj+N **gaping, great, growing, huge, unbridgeable, widening, yawning** *Many politicians are not concerned about the gaping chasm between the rich and the poor.*

● N+v **divide, exist, open up, separate** *A communication chasm exists between some teachers and their pupils.*

chat N
1 a friendly conversation

● adj+N informal **cosy, friendly, informal, nice, pleasant** *We were invited in for coffee, and I had a pleasant chat with Madge.*

▸ short **brief, little, quick** *After a quick chat with my parents, I phoned my girlfriend.*

▸ private **confidential, one-to-one, private, quiet** *We can offer you a free confidential chat with one of our experienced advisers.*

2 the exchange of informal written messages using the Internet

● adj+N **instant, live, online, real-time, text-based** *We can provide practical advice by email, instant chat, or telephone.*

● N+n **area, facility, forum, room, session, window** *You can contact the team using the members' online chat facility.*

chatter N
informal talk about things that are not really important

● adj+N **noisy or excited cheerful, excited, noisy** *As the band entered the building, there was a burst of excited chatter.*

> You can also say that a place is *buzzing with chatter* or *filled with chatter*, when a lot of people are talking excitedly.

▸ annoying **constant, endless, incessant** *The children's incessant chatter started to irritate me.*

▸ not interesting or intelligent **empty, inane, mindless** *Elaine's inane chatter drove Kevin mad.*

cheap ADJ
1 not expensive

● adv+ADJ very **amazingly, extremely, fantastically, incredibly, really, ridiculously, unbelievably, very** *By European standards, the cost of medical care here is incredibly cheap.*

▸ rather **fairly, pretty, quite, reasonably** *We stayed at the Hotel Alba, which was clean, friendly, and reasonably cheap.*

▸ in comparisons **considerably, far, a lot, much, relatively, significantly, slightly, substantially** *It's often considerably cheaper to buy online than in the store.*

● and/or in a good way **convenient, easy, efficient, fast, quick, reliable, simple** *The treatment is quick, simple, and cheap.*

▸ of low quality **nasty, shoddy, tacky** *The room was clean, but the furniture looked cheap and tacky.*

2 unfair, unkind, or dishonest

● ADJ+n **jibe, joke, shot, stunt, trick** *I'm not going to listen to him making cheap jibes about my car.*

check V
look at something to make sure that it is right, good, or safe

● adv+V regularly **always, daily, periodically, regularly, routinely** *All the safety equipment is checked daily.*

▸ carefully **carefully, rigorously, thoroughly** *Check the document carefully before signing it.*

▸ before doing anything else **beforehand, first** *If you have any doubts, please check beforehand.*

● V+n **accuracy, authenticity, credentials, eligibility, suitability, validity** *It has not been possible to check the accuracy of this data.*

● V+for being in an acceptable state **accuracy, completeness, compliance, consistency, safety, suitability, validity** *All our employees are checked for their suitability for working with young people.*

▸ problems **abnormalities, contamination, damage, errors, infection, leaks, signs, virus, wear** *The unit should be checked regularly for any signs of damage.*
 ● *The play equipment is checked for wear and damage once a week.*

check N
an examination of someone or something

● adj+N regular **annual, periodic, regular, routine** *We took Jake to the vet for a routine check.*

▸ thorough **rigorous, stringent, thorough** *The safety of your bike is your responsibility, and thorough checks are essential.*

▸ quick **cursory, quick** *Staff should undertake a cursory check of each electrical appliance before use.*

▸ not following a regular pattern **random, spot** *The committee may carry out spot checks to ensure that members are following the rules.*

● n+N **background, credit, health, police, safety, security** *Anyone who works in a school needs a police check.*

● v+N make a check **carry out, complete, conduct, do, make, perform, run, undertake** *You should first run some simple checks to make sure the information is accurate.*

▸ be checked **receive, undergo** *Each member of the team must undergo a medical check.*

● N+v **confirm, indicate, prove, reveal, show** *A quick check confirmed that the battery was dead.*

● N+on **applicant, employee, individual, staff, volunteer** *As an employer, you must carry out checks on all new employees.*

> Usage **Check** is usually plural in these combinations.

check-up N
an examination of a patient by a doctor or a dentist

● adj+N regular **annual, regular, routine, six-monthly, yearly** *It is important to have regular dental check-ups.*

▶ types of check-up **ante-natal, dental, medical, post-natal, veterinary** *When you arrive, you will have a medical check-up.*

● v+N receive a check-up **attend, get, go for, have, receive, undergo** *I went for a check-up at the hospital last week.*

▶ provide a check-up **give, offer, provide** *You will be offered regular check-ups throughout your pregnancy.*

cheek N

1 the soft part of your face below the eyes

● adj+N looking healthy and attractive **chubby, glowing, pink, red, rosy, ruddy** *Ben is 16 months old, with curly brown hair and chubby cheeks.*

▶ looking unhealthy **hollow, pale, pallid, sunken** *He was about 45, with hollow cheeks and pale skin.*

● v+N **brush, caress, kiss, pat, stroke, touch** *Harry bent and kissed her cheek.*

● N+v **burn, flush, glow, redden** *I felt my cheeks redden in shame.*

2 rude and disrespectful behaviour

● adj+N **bare-faced, bloody** INFORMAL, **downright, sheer** *The worst thing of all is the children's sheer cheek.*

cheer V

give a loud shout of approval or happiness

● adv+V **enthusiastically, heartily, loudly, lustily, wildly** *The crowd around me cheered wildly.*

● and/or **chant, clap, shout, wave, whistle, whoop** *People cheered and waved as the Queen's car drove past.*

cheer N

a loud shout of approval or happiness

● adj+N **almighty, big, deafening, huge, loud, massive, rapturous, resounding, rousing, thunderous** *As he stepped onto the stage, there was a massive cheer.*

● v+N give a cheer **give, let out, raise** *The crowd let out an almighty cheer.*

▶ be cheered **be greeted with, elicit, get, receive** *Every speaker was greeted with loud cheers.*

● N+v **break out, erupt, go up, ring out** *A cheer went up when we heard the result.*

● N+from **audience, crowd, fan, public, spectator, supporter** *The band appeared on stage to loud cheers from the audience.*

People say *three cheers for* someone when they want people to cheer three times to show their approval: *Three cheers for the captain and her team!*

cheerful ADJ

happy and friendly

● adv+ADJ always **always, invariably, relentlessly, unfailingly**

▶ very **irrepressibly, remarkably, very, wonderfully** *He was remarkably cheerful, and in excellent health.*

● ADJ+n a way of behaving or feeling **disposition,**

manner, mood, optimism, outlook, personality *Joan has a bright smile and a cheerful outlook.*

▶ the way sb looks or sounds **countenance, face, grin, smile, voice** *He waved good-bye with a cheerful grin.*

● and/or **bright, enthusiastic, friendly, lively, optimistic, outgoing, pleasant** *Applicants will need to be bright and cheerful in their manner.*

chicken N

a bird kept for its eggs and meat

● adj+N reared in a particular way **corn-fed, free-range, organic** *If possible, choose organic eggs that come from free-range chickens.*

▶ cooked in a particular way **barbecued, broiled, chargrilled, fried, grilled, marinated, roast, sweet and sour** *For a healthier meal, try grilled chicken instead of fried chicken.*

● v+N rearing chickens **breed, feed, keep, rear** *For details of how our chickens are reared, click here.*

▶ cooking chicken **barbecue, broil, cook, marinate, roast, stuff** *Marinate the chicken overnight in a mixture of oil, lemon juice and garlic.*

▶ eating chicken **eat** *I prefer to eat chicken or fish when I'm preparing for a race.*

● N+v **cluck, lay, roam, roost, wander** *These chickens lay the most delicious free-range eggs.*

● N+n parts of a chicken for eating **breast, fillet, liver, wings** *Add the chicken breasts and cook gently for 5 minutes.*

▶ pieces of chicken prepared for eating **drumstick, goujons, nuggets** *The dishes appeal to young children – fish fingers, chicken nuggets, sausages.*

▶ dishes containing chicken **broth, korma, salad, sandwich, satay, soup, stock, tikka** *For my main course, I had chicken korma served with rice.*

child N

a person between the age of baby and teenager

● adj+N of a particular age **adolescent, little, newborn, preschool, school-aged, small, teenage, young** *We provide educational services for preschool children.*

▶ with problems **abused, at-risk, disabled, disadvantaged, neglected, special-needs, underprivileged, vulnerable** *We have raised millions of pounds to help disadvantaged children.* ● *The experts say that those who look after pre-school children can take at least two special-needs children in a group of 26 children.*

People also talk about *children with special needs* when referring to children who have physical, emotional, or educational problems, and about *children with learning disabilities* when talking about children whose learning does not progress as fast as that of other children: *Drama can also boost the confidence and communication skills of children with special needs.*

▶ badly behaved **badly behaved, delinquent, difficult, naughty, problem, spoiled** *There are shortages of money, trained staff, and suitable foster carers for difficult children.*

● v+N become the parent of a child **adopt, father,**

give birth to, have *He married twice and fathered nine children.*
▶ be responsible for the care and education of a child **bring up, care for, look after, raise** *The average cost of raising a child has risen to £165,000.*
● N+n relating to the protection of children **care, protection, welfare** *We need a system where child protection comes first.*
▶ relating to social problems some children face **abuse, malnutrition, maltreatment, poverty, trafficking** *Debt is often a major contributing factor to household violence and child abuse.*

childhood N
the time in your life when you are a child

● adj+N happy **carefree, happy, idyllic, privileged** *Scott had an idyllic childhood, growing up on his parents' small farm.*
▶ unhappy **abusive, difficult, lonely, miserable, tough, traumatic, troubled, unhappy** *Peter recalls his miserable childhood in a large, cold, country house.*
● v+N experience your childhood **enjoy, experience, have, spend** *She spent her early childhood in Germany.*
▶ experience your childhood again **recall, recreate, relive, remember, revisit** *Many of us relive our childhood by becoming parents.*
● N+n thoughts and feelings **ambition, dream, innocence, memories** *He may never be able to fulfil his childhood dream of climbing Everest.*
▶ health problems **asthma, blindness, cancer, deafness, disease, epilepsy, illness, leukaemia, obesity** *Childhood obesity is becoming a serious problem in the western world.*
▶ other problems **abuse, depression, trauma** *The report notes an increase in childhood depression, drug abuse, and self-harm.*

choice N
1 the opportunity or right to choose

● adj+N **consumer, parental, patient, personal** *The supermarkets promise us greater consumer choice.*
● v+N have the right to choose **exercise, have** *People can now exercise real choice over where they live.*
▶ give someone a choice **give sb, offer sb, present sb with** *An important principle is to give customers a choice **between** several options.*
▶ give someone more choice **extend, increase, widen** *Some of us disagree with the whole idea of widening consumer choice.*
▶ give someone less choice **constrain, limit, narrow, restrict** *If you have your heart set on staying close to home, this may narrow your choice of university and courses.*

2 a decision to choose someone or something

● adj+N good **excellent, good, ideal, inspired, perfect, right** *Selecting her to lead the team turned out to be an inspired choice.*
▶ based on careful thought **conscious, informed, rational, wise** *They help people to make informed choices regarding healthy eating.*
▶ difficult **difficult, hard, stark, tough** *The church*

gave him a stark choice: stop his political activity or leave.
● v+N make a choice **be faced with, face, make** *Parents face difficult choices when balancing work and family life.*
▶ affect a choice **affect, dictate, guide, influence, inform** *The number of people you invite will dictate your choice of venue.*

3 a range of things for choosing from

● adj+N **good, great, wide** *The old town has a wide choice of shops, bars and restaurants.*
● v+N **have, offer** *The menu offers an impressive choice of dishes for all tastes.*

chore N
a small, ordinary job that you have to do regularly

● adj+N ordinary **daily, day-to-day, everyday, routine** *We recommend some low-cost gadgets which will help you with day-to-day chores.*
▶ unpleasant and boring **menial, mind-numbing, monotonous, mundane, tedious, tiresome** *Revision was a slow and tedious chore, and I never enjoyed it.*
▶ types of chore **administrative, bureaucratic, domestic, household** *Ironing is one of those household chores that most of us hate.*
● v+N **do, perform, undertake** *The domestic servant would perform chores around the house – dusting, cooking and cleaning.*

chorus N
1 part of a song that is repeated several times

● adj+N **catchy, infectious, melodic, memorable, rousing, sing-a-long, strong, upbeat** *The songs on this album all have incredibly infectious choruses.*
● v+N **hum, join in, repeat, sing** *The crowd, with arms waving, joined in the chorus.*

2 a group of people all expressing the same opinion

● adj+N **growing, swelling, vocal** *He has joined the growing chorus of opinion warning against military action.*
● v+N **be greeted by, be met with, lead to, provoke** *The announcement was met with a chorus of disapproval.*
● N+of showing approval **approval, praise** *Hiddink added his voice to the chorus of praise for the fans.*
▶ showing disapproval **complaints, condemnation, criticism, disapproval, jeers, opposition, protest** *Despite the chorus of criticism, the President went ahead with his plan.*

chosen ADJ
when you have decided to have or do something

● ADJ+n subject or area of special interest **area, discipline, field, specialism, speciality, specialty, subject** *The team is made up of professionals who have expertise in their chosen field.* ● *They prepare graduates for a career at the cutting edge of their specialism.*
▶ job **career, profession, vocation** *Will this course help me in my chosen career?*

Christian N

someone whose religion is Christianity

- adj+N active **committed, devout, good, practising** *Ricky's family, who were devout Christians, blamed her when he left the church.*
- ▸ holding very strong beliefs **born-again, evangelical, fundamentalist** *Evangelical Christians believe that sharing their faith is essential.*

chronic ADJ

serious and lasting for a long time

- ADJ+n general illness **complaint, condition, disease, disorder, illness, infection, pain, problem** *The drug is widely used to treat all types of acute and chronic pain.*
- ▸ specific diseases **bronchitis, hepatitis, leukaemia, pancreatitis, sinusitis** *Ferguson died in 1915 from chronic bronchitis.*
- ▸ worry and tiredness **anxiety, depression, fatigue, stress, tiredness** *Low levels of thyroid may result in chronic fatigue, weight gain, or depression.*
- ▸ social or financial problems **lack, problem, shortage, under-funding, under-investment, unemployment** *There is a chronic shortage of doctors and nurses here.*

chronological ADJ

arranged in the order in which events happened

- adv+ADJ **approximately, broadly, largely, roughly, strictly** *The book has a broadly chronological structure.*
- ADJ+n order **arrangement, list, order, sequence, timeline** *Events are listed in chronological order.*
- ▸ description **account, framework, narrative, outline, overview, summary, survey** *Rather than simply provide a chronological survey of musical history, this course will focus on the development of listening skills.*

chunk N

a large piece or amount of something

- adj+N large **big, great, hefty, huge, large, significant, sizeable, substantial**
- ▸ small enough to be dealt with easily **bite-sized, digestible, manageable, small** *The lessons are broken down into bite-size chunks.*
- N+of food **beef, bread, cheese, chicken, cucumber, lamb, meat, pineapple** *Spread the paste thickly onto chunks of fresh crusty bread.*
- ▸ hard, solid substance **concrete, ice, masonry, metal, rock, wood** *Cracks appeared in the walls, and huge chunks of masonry fell to the ground.*
- ▸ time or money **budget, day, money, salary, time** *Driving the kids to school can take a great chunk out of each day – time that not all parents can spare.* • *I have to repay $250 every month, and that's a big chunk of my salary.*

cigarette N

a thin paper tube containing tobacco, for smoking

- v+N light or smoke a cigarette **draw on, light, puff on, smoke** *He sat down in an armchair and lit a cigarette.*
- ▸ finish a cigarette **extinguish, finish, put out, stub**

out *Make sure that cigarettes are firmly stubbed out in ashtrays.*

- N+n what cigarettes produce when smoked **ash, fumes, smoke** *Cigarette smoke contains more than 4,000 different compounds.*
- ▸ part that remains after smoking **butt, end, stub** *Do not throw cigarette stubs or matches on the ground.*
- n+of+N **carton, pack, packet** *She opened her bag and took out a pack of cigarettes.*

circle N

1 a round shape or line

- adj+N **concentric, inner, outer** *The outer circle shows how the appearance of the Moon changes with its position relative to the Earth and the Sun.*
- v+N **create, draw, form** *Press out each piece of dough to form a circle about 6cm in diameter.*

When people form a circle, you can say that they are standing *in a circle*: *The children were standing in a circle, with one of them in the middle.*

2 a group of people

- adj+N large **large, wide** *He will be sorely missed by his large circle of friends.*
- ▸ having influence **inner, policy-making, ruling** *He relied on an inner circle of trusted advisers.*
- ▸ in a particular area of activity **academic, business, financial, literary, political, scientific** *The translation created a stir in Edinburgh's literary circles.*

Usage *Circle* is almost always plural in these combinations.

- ▸ involving someone's personal group **family, social** *A lot of people in my social circle think that I am wasting my time being involved in politics.*
- ▸ close **close, immediate** *No one outside his immediate circle of friends ever really got to know him well.*
- N+of people who know one another **acquaintance, colleague, friend** *For many people, their circle of friends develops in their teenage years and changes little.*
- ▸ supporters **admirer, disciple** *Beethoven very quickly won a large circle of admirers.*
- ▸ artists etc **artist, intellectual** *She was a notable figure in the circle of avant-garde artists in Paris at the turn of the century.*

circuit N

a series of places regularly visited by performers

- adj+N **international, live** *We were lucky enough to see the biggest band on the live circuit.*
- n+N **cabaret, club, comedy, festival, stand-up** *They are five comedians who made a name for themselves on the stand-up circuit.*

circulate V

1 be told or passed to many people

- n+V story **joke, myth, rumour, story** *There is a rumour circulating that the Science Museum might be relocated.*
- ▸ illness **flu, influenza, virus** *Blood tests have confirmed that the virus is circulating in the area.*

2 send a message to all members of group

● adv+V **electronically, internally, widely** *The draft report was circulated widely among local pressure groups.*

● V+n–**copy, document, draft, email, information, leaflet, letter, memo, minutes, newsletter, note, paper, petition, questionnaire, report** *The memo is then circulated to the relevant academic staff.*

circulation N

1 the continuous movement of blood around your body, or of liquid, air etc inside a system

● adj+N **good, poor** *The elderly often suffer from poor circulation.*

● v+N improve circulation **boost, encourage, help, improve, increase, promote, stimulate** *Sauna and steam bathing stimulates blood circulation and relaxes the muscles.*

▶ make circulation worse **impair, impede, restrict** *Make sure none of your clothing is restricting circulation.*

2 the number of newspapers or magazines sold

● adj+N **large, limited, mass, small, wide** *The largest circulations in the UK are of customer magazines, produced by supermarkets.*

● v+N **boost, increase** *The paper needed a publicity coup to boost its circulation.*

● N+v **double, grow, increase, rise** *The Independent's circulation has risen by 11 per cent, faster than that of any other newspaper.*

▶ decrease **drop, fall** *Newspaper circulation has fallen dramatically over the last few years.*

3 the process of passing something from one person to another

● adj+N **general, internal, limited, restricted, wide** *The minister's statement has wide circulation in the media.*

● v+N **come into, put sth into, take sth out of** *Only a few hundred copies of the report were put into circulation.*

circumstance N

a fact or condition that affects something [usually plural]

● adj+N **special, exceptional, extenuating, extreme, mitigating, special, unusual** *The fact that you were using a phone for the purpose of your work whilst driving will not be accepted as mitigating circumstances.*

▶ unexpected **unforeseeable, unforeseen** *Due to unforeseeable circumstances, occasionally your Care Worker may be delayed.*

It is common to talk about circumstances that are **beyond** someone's **control**: *The cancellation of the performance was due to circumstances beyond our control.*

▶ difficult **challenging, difficult, straitened, tragic** *The death of Lorna's father left her family in straitened circumstances.*

▶ particular **certain, individual, particular, personal, specific** *This gives you the flexibility to study at a pace suited to your individual circumstances.*

▶ normal **normal** *Under normal circumstances, this will be credited to your account on the following working day.*

▶ strange **mysterious, suspicious** *When his uncle dies in mysterious circumstances, schoolboy Alex Rider stumbles into a world of mystery and intrigue.*

▶ affecting a particular aspect of life **employment, family, financial, home, household, life, material** *Sometimes a child might come from very difficult home circumstances, and arrive in class in a terrible state.*

▶ very sad **tragic** *The band's lead singer had died under tragic circumstances.*

● N+v cause a particular action **allow sb, compel sb, demand, dictate, force sb, justify, lead to, necessitate, permit sb, prevent sb, require sb, warrant** *If circumstances force you to put off planting them until later, remember to unpack the bulbs as soon as they arrive.* ● *We will seek to implement the change as soon as economic circumstances permit.*

▶ exist **apply, arise, exist, occur, prevail** *The military worth of the target would need to be considered in relation to the circumstances prevailing at the time.*

You can also talk about the circumstances **surrounding** a particular situation: *The inquiry into the circumstances surrouding the death was led by a prominent member of the police force.*

▶ change **alter, change** *His circumstances had changed dramatically in the past year.*

● n+of+N **change, range, set** *The decision will be made according to the set of circumstances in existence at the time.*

cite V

1 mention something or someone

● adv+V **commonly, frequently, oft, often, widely** *Asked why they would like to emigrate, the most oft cited reasons were better quality of life and better weather.*

● V+n **case, evidence, example, instance, precedent, reason, statistics** *More than three quarters of full-time students cited financial reasons as the main obstacle they had to overcome.*

● V+as **cause, evidence, example, factor, influence, justification, precedent, proof, reason, source** *Lack of activity and a sense of belonging are often cited as the root cause of anti-social behaviour.*

Usage **Cite** is very often passive in these combinations.

2 quote from a particular source

● V+n **article, paper, passage, reference, source, study** *Lang cites a German study that found the ingredients in a 50g pot of yoghurt had travelled 1,005 kilometres.*

citizenship N

the legal right to be a citizen of a country

● v+N have citizenship **have, hold** *These children, despite having Irish citizenship, will have to leave the country with their parents.*

▶ gain citizenship **acquire, gain, obtain** *It is now necessary, in order to acquire British citizenship, that people attend a citizenship ceremony.*

▶ grant citizenship **award sb, confer on sb, give sb, grant sb** *They were granted citizenship after ten years' residence in the country.*

▶ refuse citizenship **deny sb, refuse sb, revoke** *Some children born in this country are denied citizenship due to the nationality of their parents.* • *While he was living in Poland, his Canadian citizenship was revoked in 1957.*

▶ give up citizenship **renounce** *Foreigners living in Germany for fifteen years may become German citizens if they have no criminal record and renounce their original citizenship*

civil ADJ
relating to the people in a country

● ADJ+n fighting or disagreement **disobedience, disturbance, strife, unrest** *There were fears that the new law could trigger civil unrest.*

▶ rights **liberties, rights** *If you believe in equal civil rights for all individuals, show your support.*

claim V
state that something is true or that something belongs to you

● adv+V rightly **justifiably, justly, legitimately, rightfully, rightly** *Gaelic can legitimately claim to be Scotland's oldest living language.*

▶ wrongly **falsely, fraudulently, wrongly** *They wrongly claimed that our trade mark infringed their trade mark rights.*

● V+n legal right **allowance, asylum, benefit, compensation, damages, discount, exemption, expenses, rebate, refund, reimbursement, relief** *If someone injures you as a result of deliberate foul play then you will be able to claim compensation for your injuries.*

▶ achievement or praise **credit, victory** *It was not my intention to claim any credit for myself, but for the good work the team has done.*

claim N
a statement that something is true or that you have the right to have something

● adj+N false **absurd, bogus, exaggerated, extravagant, false, fraudulent, outrageous, spurious, unfounded, unsubstantiated** *They defend exploitation by making spurious claims to act in the national interest.*

▶ true **good, legitimate, strong, valid** *These people had a legitimate claim to citizenship.*

● n+N something you want **asylum, compensation, expenses, pay** *She is making a compensation claim for the loss of earnings that her neck injury has caused.*

▶ something that has been done to you **accident, defamation, discrimination, injury, negligence, unfair dismissal** *It can take years for medical negligence claims to reach settlement.*

● v+N make a claim **bring, lodge, make, pursue, stake** *The employees brought a claim of unfair dismissal against the company.*

> You can also say that someone **lays claim to** something: *Milan has long laid claim to the title 'the Italian capital of fashion'.*

▶ support a claim **defend, justify, substantiate, support** *Searches were carried out for evidence to support these claims.*

▶ deny a claim **deny, dismiss, rebut, refute, reject** *The writer's supporters have rejected a claim that she plagiarised a 1916 novel.*

● N+for+n something you want **asylum, benefit, compensation, damages, payment, refund, reimbursement, relief, repayment** *All claims for refunds must be made in writing.*

▶ something that has been done to you **defamation, discrimination, infringement, injury, loss, negligence, non-delivery, unfair dismissal** *The artist had no claim for infringement of copyright.*

clap V
hit your hands together to show you liked or support something

● adv+V with enthusiasm **enthusiastically, loudly, vigorously, wildly** *When I came on stage as the Inspector, they all clapped wildly and roared with laughter.*

▶ without enthusiasm **politely, sarcastically** *Adults sit quietly, though bored, and clap politely at the end.*

● and/or **chant, cheer, dance, laugh, shout, sing, stamp, whistle** *Crowds lined the water's edge, cheering and clapping, shouting words of welcome.*

clarification N
an explanation that makes something clearer

● v+N want clarification **ask for, await, demand, need, request, require, seek, want, welcome** *We would welcome clarification on what should be included in ingredient lists.*

▶ provide clarification **give sb, issue, offer sb, provide sb with** *Perhaps the best course of action would be to issue a clarification of the rules.*

clarify V
explain something more clearly

● adv+V precisely **exactly, precisely** *The government needs to clarify exactly how these agreements will work.*

▶ helpfully **helpfully, usefully** *There are one or two other points that we might usefully clarify.*

▶ enough **adequately, fully, sufficiently** *The definition of what constitutes a 'comprehensive and efficient' service has not been adequately clarified.*

● V+n **ambiguity, confusion, issue, matter, meaning, misconception, misunderstanding, point, position, role, situation** *We would like to clarify our position and are sorry if it was ambiguous before.*

clash N
1 a fight, battle, or angry argument

● adj+N **armed, bloody, fierce, violent** *There were violent clashes between reservists and the riot police.*

● N+v **arise, break out, erupt, occur** *Border clashes still erupt from time to time.*

2 a situation in which things are very different and so cannot exist or work together well

- adj+N **cultural, culture, personality** *Personality clashes can occur between students and teacher.*

- N+of cultures, ideas **civilizations, cultures, ideas, ideologies, interests, opinions** *The author delights in the clash of cultures, stating wryly that England and America have everything in common, except language.*
▸ people **egos, personalities, wills**

class N
1 a social group, based on income, job, education etc

- adj+N poorer **exploited, labouring, lower, oppressed, working** *Health improved for the lower classes, as rationing brought greater equality in food distribution.*
▸ richer or more educated **educated, landowning, leisured, middle, privileged, propertied, ruling, upper, upper-middle** *Historically, women who left home came mainly from the aristocracy and upper-middle class.*
▸ social **social** *Social class influences the educational attainments of pupils.*

- N+n relating to the differences between the classes **conflict, consciousness, differences, divide, struggle** *A class divide soon began to develop between the landed gentry, the factory owners and the workers.*
▸ system **system** *The film is a brilliant satire on the English class system.*

- and/or **age, creed, ethnicity, gender, race, sexuality** *Teachers set high expectations for their pupils, no matter what their class or race.*

2 a group of people learning something together; a lesson or course of lessons

- adj+N types of class **exercise, fitness, keep-fit** *I go to a keep-fit class twice a week.*
▸ level **advanced, beginners, intermediate, introductory, master, mixed-ability** *In a mixed-ability class, high-ability kids can be left to read by themselves, while teachers help the low-ability kids.*
▸ time **evening, weekly, one-hour, two-hour** etc *He is teaching a 10-week course of evening classes, 'Mosaics Made Easy'.*

- v+N give a class **hold, offer, organize, run, teach** *We offer English classes, computer training and careers advice.*
▸ attend a class **attend, do, go to, join, take** *I am taking evening classes in Spanish.*
▸ miss a class **miss, skip** *It won't matter if you miss the occasional class.*

classic ADJ
1 completely typical

- ADJ+n **case, example, symptom** *Aggression is a classic example of anti-social behaviour.*

2 very good and always popular

- ADJ+n film, book, song etc **album, comedy, film, hit, movie, novel, song, tale, text, tune** *The film mixes Jane Austen's classic novel Pride and Prejudice with the glamour and spectacle of Bollywood.*
▸ style **design, elegance, style, styling** *The pots are available in both modern and classic designs.*

classification N
the process of putting things into particular groups

- adj+N **broad, correct, general, standard, systematic** *We compared these society types to a broad classification of language change.*
- v+N suggest or use a classification **adopt, devise, propose, suggest, use** *We propose a classification of these earthquakes on the basis of their waveforms and frequency content.*
▸ be hard to classify **defy** *As a writer, Hare defies easy classification.*
- N+v **be according to, be based on, depend on** *Degree classification is based on performance in the final year.*
- N+n **criteria, method, scheme, system, technique** *This difference is due to the different classification criteria used by the various sources.*

clause N
1 part of a legal document or law

- n+N releasing you from an obligation **escape, exclusion, exemption, get-out, indemnity, opt-out, waiver** *An indemnity clause protects you if you find you've bought a stolen vehicle.*
▸ relating to something **confidentiality, penalty** *There is no penalty clause in the contract for failing to meet the deadline.*
- v+N put a clause in **add, draft, include, insert, introduce** *The union wants to introduce a clause compensating workers for the effects of inflation.*
▸ have a clause within it **contain, include, incorporate** *The contract included clauses that documents must be provided in Welsh.*
▸ change or remove a clause **amend, delete, omit, remove, repeal** *We suggest amending this clause to read 'to encourage compliance' rather than 'to secure compliance'.*
▸ go against a clause **breach, contravene** *The committee ruled that the ad contravened Clause 10 of the Code of Advertising Standards.*
- N+v say something **allow sb, define, permit sb, prohibit, provide that, require sb, specify, state, stipulate** *Most insurance policies include a clause requiring the insured to maintain his vehicle in a safe condition.*
▸ relate to something **apply to, cover, refer to, relate to** *Various clauses cover the respective rights of landlord and tenant.*

2 part of a sentence including a verb and a subject

- adj+N **adverbial, finite, main, non-finite, non-restrictive, relative, restrictive, subordinate** *Relative pronouns introduce relative clauses, and they usually refer back to a noun in the main clause.*

clean ADJ
not dirty

- adv+ADJ very **beautifully, exceptionally, immaculately, impeccably, perfectly, remarkably, scrupulously, sparklingly, spotlessly** *Her home was always spotlessly clean.*
▸ fairly **fairly, reasonably, relatively** *The beach is fairly clean, with a few bits of litter washing ashore.*
- v+ADJ make something clean **rinse, scrape,**

scrub, sweep, wash, wipe *Vinyl floor covering is easy to wipe clean.*

▶ remain or keep something clean **keep sth, stay** *Your cooking area must be kept clean at all times.*

● and/or **bright, dry, fresh, healthy, hygienic, neat, pure, shiny, tidy** *Keep your office clean and tidy.*

clean V
remove the dirt from something

● adv+V thoroughly **carefully, deep, meticulously, professionally, properly, spotlessly, thoroughly** *This facial will deep clean the face.*

> Usage **Clean** is often passive in these combinations: *Her wounds were carefully cleaned and bandages were applied.*

▶ regularly **daily, periodically, regularly, weekly** *The pool is cleaned weekly.*

clear ADJ
obvious and impossible to misunderstand

● adv+ADJ very **absolutely, abundantly, perfectly, very** *A problem that I found totally incomprehensible suddenly became perfectly clear.*

▶ fairly **fairly, pretty INFORMAL, quite, reasonably** *It is pretty clear that there need to be big changes in the way we live.*

▶ in a bad way **painfully** *After Hurricane Katrina, it was painfully clear that the government's emergency response was inadequate.*

▶ not **insufficiently, not, not entirely** *Sales of the product were poor, and the reasons for this are not entirely clear.*

● ADJ+n message **definition, demarcation, distinction, explanation, guidance, guideline, instruction, message, signal, statement** *She doesn't make any clear distinctions between email, the Web, newsgroups – it's all called 'the Net'.* ● *There is a handbook with brief, clear instructions.*

▶ sign of something **evidence, indication, sign** *There is clear evidence that smokefree policies help smokers to quit.*

▶ understanding **idea, picture, understanding, vision** *I meet with the client to get a clear idea of what he or she needs.*

▶ aim **aim, objective** *A team must have clear objectives.*

▶ in competitions etc **mandate, victory, winner** *Neither side had gained a clear victory.*

● v+ADJ **be, become, make sth, seem** *It is clear that bold political leadership will be needed.* ● *The consequences of any actions should be made very clear to the employee.*

● and/or simple **concise, simple, straightforward, succinct, understandable** *In clear and simple language he explains what Reiki is.*

▶ correct **accurate, precise** *The campaign aims to give young people clear and accurate information about drugs.*

▶ logical **coherent, consistent, logical, unambiguous, unequivocal** *Glasgow needs a clear and coherent plan for regeneration.*

clearance N
official permission to do something or go somewhere

● n+N **copyright, customs, entry, security** *Her son's appeal to the Immigration Tribunal was successful, and they were granted entry clearance to the UK.*

● v+N get clearance **be allowed, be given, be granted, gain, get, obtain, receive** *Any aircraft wishing to enter controlled airspace must obtain clearance.*

▶ want or need clearance **await, need, require, seek** *In the early days of the Internet, security clearance was required for access.*

▶ refuse **deny, refuse** *A Customs Officer may refuse clearance of any vessel.*

clear up PHR VB
solve a problem or explain a situation

● V+n confusion **confusion, misconceptions, misunderstanding, mystery** *I would like to take this opportunity to clear up any confusion about the reasons for these changes.*

▶ issue **issue, matter, point, problem, question, situation** *You have raised crucial questions which, if answered, could clear up this matter once and for all.*

clench V
close a part of your body tightly

● adv+V **firmly, tight, tightly** *Michael stood where he was, his fists clenched tight, his breathing quickening.*

● V+n **buttocks, fingers, fist, hand, jaw, muscles, teeth** *Many people clench their jaw when they are concentrating or under stress.*

click V
press a button on a computer mouse

● V+n **arrow, button, checkbox, hyperlink, icon, link, logo, tab** *You can click the icon and hear the mp3 file.*

● V+on+n **arrow, banner, button, hyperlink, icon, image, link, logo, name, picture, symbol, tab, thumbnail, title** *Download the free upgrade by clicking on the link below.*

client N
someone who pays for professional services

● adj+N present or future **existing, new, potential, prospective** *Any time a potential client wants to see your products, simply refer them to your website.*

▶ important **discerning, important, major, prestigious, wealthy** *I was working on a project for a major client.*

▶ an individual or an organization **blue-chip, commercial, corporate, individual, institutional, private** *We advise both those in the voluntary sector and private clients.*

● v+N get clients **take on** *He's got so much work that he can't take on any new clients at present.*

▶ help a client **act for, advise, assist, help, serve, service, support** *The Visa service is able to assist clients with processing British passport applications.*

When somebody is working for a client, you can say that they are working **on behalf of a client**: *We undertake contract research on behalf of Higher Education clients.*

▶ meet with a client **entertain, meet, visit** *We offer an exciting and sophisticated venue for entertaining corporate clients.*

▶ please a client **attract, impress, satisfy** *To impress a potential client, you need both knowledge and experience.*

clientele N
customers of a shop, hotel, restaurant etc

● adj+N loyal **appreciative, devoted, loyal, regular** *The shop has built up a loyal clientele since opening in 2000.*

▶ varied **diverse, mixed, varied, wide** *The restaurant has a mixed clientele of tourists, business people and locals.*

▶ with a lot of money or taste **affluent, discerning, select, sophisticated, trendy, upscale, wealthy, well-heeled** *They supply high quality food products to a discerning clientele.*

▶ from a particular area **international, local, worldwide** *Canada has become a favourite destination for skiers, attracting an international clientele.*

▶ from a particular age group **middle-aged, older, young, youthful** *The marketing was aimed at a new, younger clientele.*

● v+N **attract, cater for, cater to, have, serve** *The bar has live music and attracts an older clientele.*

climate N
1 the weather in a country or region

● adj+N warm/cold **cold, cool, hot, sunny, warm** *This is Scotland, so none of us is used to working in a hot climate.*

▶ wet/dry **arid, dry, humid, wet** *The island's arid climate makes farming difficult.*

▶ moderate/extreme **extreme, harsh, mild, temperate** *New England has a temperate climate with warm sunny summers.*

▶ belonging to a particular type of region **continental, global, maritime, oceanic, sub-tropical, tropical** *Ginger grows in tropical climates.*

● v+N **enjoy, have** *Devon enjoys a mild climate, even during the winter months.*

● N+v **change, cool, shift, vary, warm** *When the climate warms, according to the theory, fresh water from melting Arctic glaciers flows into the North Atlantic*

● N+n **change, model, prediction, scientist, variability** *NASA scientists have discovered new evidence of climate change.*

2 people's attitudes at a particular time

● adj+N in a particular area **business, economic, financial, intellectual, moral, political** *Information is your most valuable asset in today's fast moving business climate.*

▶ current **current, present, prevailing** *The prevailing economic climate presents major challenges for the construction industry.*

▶ helpful **conducive, favourable** *This process establishes a climate conducive to learning.*

● v+N **create, foster** *Instead of setting hospital against hospital, we need to foster a climate of co-operation.*

● N+of+n fear or anger **distrust, fear, hostility, hysteria, insecurity, intolerance, mistrust, paranoia, suspicion, uncertainty** *Terrorism creates a climate of fear.*

▶ trust **openness, tolerance, trust** *The treaty can only work in a climate of openness and mutual trust.*

▶ opinion **opinion** *The climate of public opinion has changed.*

climax N
the most exciting or important moment in something

● adj+N exciting **dramatic, exciting, explosive, gripping, nail-biting, rousing, spectacular, stunning, thrilling** *On stage, there's a subtle tension created that results in a thrilling climax to the show.*

▶ appropriate **fitting** *The fireworks at the end also made for a fitting climax.*

● v+N approach the climax **approach, build to, come to, lead to, near, reach** *She was reaching the climax of her presentation.*

▶ be the climax **be, form, mark, provide, represent** *The World Cup final marked the glorious climax to his dazzling career.*

climb V
1 move up something

● V+n when you use hands and feet **fence, ladder, mountain, peak, rope, stile, tree, wall** *Everest climbers do not climb the mountain for the sake of the view.*

▶ when you walk **hill, slope, stairs, tower** *I climbed the stairs to the third floor.*

● V+over+n **fence, gate, stile, wall** *The boys were caught climbing over a fence into the school grounds.*

2 lead upwards

● V+adv **steeply quickly, rapidly, steeply** *We turned onto a track which climbed steeply upwards.*

▶ gradually **gently, gradually, slowly, steadily** *The road climbs gently for just over a mile.*

▶ up **up, uphill, upwards** *After crossing the stream, the path starts to climb uphill.*

3 become higher in level

● V+adv quickly **quickly, rapidly, sharply, steeply** *World oil prices climbed steeply.*

▶ gradually **gradually, slowly, steadily** *The number of women in the labour market has climbed steadily.*

● n+V **level, price, temperature** *The temperature climbed to around 27°C.*

4 get in or out of something

● V+adv **laboriously, stiffly, wearily** *She yawned as she climbed wearily into bed.*

climb N
an action of moving up, the distance that you have to climb

cling

● adj+N difficult **arduous, awkward, long, steep, stiff, strenuous, tough, vertical** *From here, it is a stiff climb up stairs all the way up to Edinburgh Castle.*

▶ easy **easy, gentle, gradual, short, steady** *The walk starts with a gentle climb to Chapel Farm.*

● v+N try to climb something **attempt, begin, start, tackle** *Do not attempt the climb without a guide.*

▶ succeed in climbing something **complete, make** *Fog prevented us from making the climb to the summit.*

cling V

1 hold onto someone or something tightly

● adv+V when there is a danger of falling **desperately, precariously** *I was clinging desperately to the rockface and trying to make some progress.*

▶ tightly **closely, tightly, together** *Reina clung tightly to her notebook.* ● *There were six people clinging together in the water; three with lifejackets, three without.*

2 try hard to keep something or keep believing something

● adv+V **desperately, doggedly, still, stubbornly, tenaciously** *A large proportion of the people still clung tenaciously to their ancient beliefs.*

Cling on can often be used with the same meaning as *cling*: *She was clinging on desperately to the ledge but she could fall at any second.* ● *For six painful months he managed to cling on to life.*

● V+to an idea or belief **belief, hope, idea, notion** *Martinez is clinging to the hope that he will be fit for the start of the season.*

▶ something you refuse to give up **life, past, power** *His health began to deteriorate, but he clung stubbornly to power.*

clip N

a short part of a film etc

● adj+N **brief, short** *You can view a brief clip of the new video for the single here.*

● n+N **audio, film, movie, mp3, music, news, sound, video** *Photographs and film clips illustrating some of the anecdotes can be found at this address.*

● v+N **download, hear, play, see, show, stream, view, watch** *Visitors to the website will be able to download video clips from the original series.*

clock N

an object that shows the time

● adj+N whether a clock is showing the right time or not **accurate, fast, slow, wrong** *That clock's half an hour fast.*

▶ types of clock **24-hour, atomic, digital, electric, mechanical, quartz** *Each satellite carries an incredibly accurate atomic clock.*

● v+N make a clock ready for use **adjust, reset, set, wind** *I've been gradually setting the alarm clock later and later.*

▶ change the the the time to an earlier or later time **put back, put forward** *Did you remember to put your clocks back?*

▶ make a clock stop working **stop** *He stopped the clock at 4:11:44.*

▶ look at a clock **glance at, keep an eye on, look at, watch** *Have you ever sat by the window in class, idly watching the clock for time to pass?*

● N+v when a clock makes a sound **chime, go off, strike, tick** *The alarm clock went off at seven.* ● *As we crossed the Market Place, the Guildhall clock struck 6 o'clock.*

▶ when everyone changes the time on their clocks **go back, go forward** *Don't forget, tomorrow is the day the clocks go back.*

Clock is always plural in these combinations: *Please note that the clocks go forward this Saturday so it is going to be a very early start.*

▶ when a clock stops working **stop** *The electric clock had stopped at 4.20 p.m.*

▶ show a particular time **say** *The alarm clock said 6.30.*

close ADJ

1 only a short distance away

● adv+ADJ very **really, very** *The office is really close to the airport.*

▶ fairly **fairly, pretty** INFORMAL **, quite, reasonably, relatively** *Salisbury station is quite close to the city centre.*

▶ so close that there is a danger of harm **dangerously, perilously, uncomfortably** *I couldn't get a good view of the waterfall without getting perilously close to the edge.*

▶ in a useful way **conveniently** *The flat is conveniently close to all forms of transport.*

▶ when you are excited about something that you probably cannot get **tantalizingly** *The fish was tantalizingly close but just out of reach.*

● ADJ+n **proximity, quarters, range** *There are two car parks in close proximity to the shopping centre.* ● *This is an opportunity to view wildlife at close quarters.*

● v+ADJ **come, draw, get, move** *Don't get too close to the fire.*

2 careful and involving attention to detail

● ADJ+n look at something **examination, inspection, look, reading, scrutiny** *On closer inspection, the piece of metal proved to be a Roman coin.*

▶ when you watch or pay attention to something **attention, eye, supervision, watch** *From here on we have to keep a close eye on the map and navigate by field boundaries.*

3 similar but not exactly the same

● ADJ+n **approximation, match, parallel, resemblance** *He bore a close facial resemblance to Einstein.*

4 connected by shared interests or feelings

● ADJ+n relationship or working together **association, cooperation, friendship, liaison, link, partnership, relationship** *This has been achieved in close liaison with our colleagues in the marketing department.*

▶ person **associate, friend**

closure N

1 the process of closing a factory, hospital etc permanently; the process of closing a road etc for a time

- adj+N happening soon **imminent** *This is particularly important given the imminent closure of the pit.*
- ▶ happening in the end **eventual** *Business declined, leading to the eventual closure of the factory.*
- ▶ complete/partial **complete, partial, total** *Stockport station re-opened on schedule on 6 September, after complete closure for many weeks for track and signalling work.*
- ▶ for a short time/permanently **emergency, permanent, temporary** *The temporary closure has caused severe disruption for motorists using the busy road.*
- ▶ possible or planned **planned, possible, proposed, threatened** *Renault confirmed its proposed closure of the Vilvorde car plant in Belgium.*
- n+N **branch, factory, hospital, pit, plant, post office, road, school** *Hospital closures have been a massive issue in the region.*
- ▶ v+N be in danger of being closed **be earmarked for, be threatened with, face** *Rural Cornish schools could face closure or amalgamation under plans being drawn up by education bosses.*
- ▶ be responsible for something closing **cause, force** *The snow forced the closure of several roads across Scotland.*
- ▶ say that closure will or should happen **announce, recommend** *The committee recommended the closure of three special schools for the deaf.*
- ▶ stop or try to stop something being closed **oppose, prevent, stop** *Parents from some schools have already organised action groups to oppose closure.*
- N+n **notice, order, plan, programme** *The unions have drawn up an alternative to the management's closure plans.*
- n+of+N **danger, possibility, risk, threat** *Many German departments in the universities are at risk of closure.* ● *Small rural schools are under threat of closure.*

2 the feeling that an unpleasant experience has ended

- v+N **achieve, bring, need, seek** *The discussion even enables Peter to achieve closure on his relationship with Julie.*
- n+of+N **sense** *What's important here is a sense of closure for the families.*

cloud N

1 a mass of water drops in the sky

- adj+N thick or heavy **billowing, heavy, thick** *Websites predicted thick cloud and heavy snow.*
- ▶ colour **black, dark, grey, white** *Low black clouds made photography difficult.*
- ▶ looking as though it will rain soon **ominous, threatening** *Some ominous clouds began to gather over Castle Combe.*
- ▶ high/low **high, low** *The weather was terrible – low cloud and rain, rain, rain.*
- ▶ thin or light **broken, fluffy, light, thin** *It was a day of clear blue sky with a few fluffy clouds overhead.*

- n+N **rain, storm, thunder** *The weather is turning and rain clouds have been passing over us.*
- N+v when clouds form or appear **form, gather, hang, hover, loom, spread, thicken** *Black clouds were gathering over the mountains to the north.*
- ▶ when clouds disappear **clear, disperse, lift, part** *As we started to make our way down into the valley, the clouds parted and there was a brief sunny period.*
- ▶ when clouds move across the sky **drift, float, move, roll, scud** *There was a beautiful crescent moon and clouds scudded dramatically across it.*
- ▶ when clouds hide something **cover, obscure** *The lower hills can provide more attractive walks in poor weather, especially when the higher summits are obscured by clouds.*
- N+n **cover, formation, layer** *The weather was just right for walking, not too hot, with a little cloud cover.*
- n+in+N **break** *Suddenly, there was a break in the clouds and the sun shone.*
- v+in+N **be enveloped in, be shrouded in** *The ridge is often shrouded in thick cloud.*
- n+of+N **band, bank, blanket, layer, mass, patch, veil, wisp** *The bank of clouds which had been steadily rolling in over the last hour arrived, and it started to rain heavily.*

2 a large amount of a substance in the air

- adj+N **dense, great, huge, thick** *A thick cloud of smoke rose over the house.*
- v+N **create, produce** *The impact of the meteorite would create a huge cloud of dust.*
- N+of **ash, dust, gas, smoke, steam, vapour** *The flames spluttered out in clouds of steam.*

club N

an organization for people with a common interest

- adj+N **amateur, exclusive, junior, local, private, social** *She joined the local rowing club.*
- n+N **athletics, fan, health, rowing, sailing, sports, youth, football, golf, etc** *The Students' Union has a large number of social, cultural and sports clubs.*
- v+N start a club **form, start** *We need information on how to start a sports club for the children in the village.*
- ▶ be or become a member of a club **belong to, join** *I decided to join the local youth club.*
- ▶ be responsible for a club **manage, run** *When she was in her 30s, Susan ran clubs for children with learning difficulties.*
- N+v **meet** *Our club meets most Tuesday evenings.*
- N+n **chairman, member, membership, official, secretary** *Club membership has grown over the years.*
- n+of+N **member** *They were all members of the local swimming club.*

clue N

something that helps solve a crime or explain something

- adj+N good or important clue **good, important, useful, valuable, vital** *Any such electrical* abnormalities (which might hold the vital clues to an underlying condition) cannot be detected after death.

▶ clear/not clear **hidden, obvious, subtle** There were obvious clues that something was wrong.

▶ that you can see **visual** A person's expression gives visual clues **about** what they are feeling.

● v+N have or use a clue **follow, have** Following clues obtained from the scene, Italian police have now carried out around 20 searches.

▶ try to find a clue **find, look for, search for** We had to search for clues in an apartment in which a dead body lay.

▶ give a clue **contain, give, hold, leave, offer, provide, yield** The ditch was filled with debris that gave clues to the medieval activities being carried out close by.

● You know the sort of thing, the murderer spiriting himself into thin air leaving no clue **as to** how he committed the crime.

▶ understand clues **decipher, piece together** They had to piece together the clues provided by the objects which had been unearthed at the site.

● n+of+N **number, series, trail** Following a trail of clues which leads from the Deep South to the West Coast, they race against time to find the missing girl.

Usage **Clue** is always plural in these combinations.

coalition N
a temporary union of different political parties or groups

● adj+N involving many parties or groups **broad, global, international** Opposition has come from a broad coalition of humanists, civil libertarians, Conservatives, and even Labour Party rebels.

▶ strong **powerful, strong** A strong coalition of health groups, trade unions, employers and others can help build support for the law.

▶ in control **governing, ruling** The ruling coalition is strongly committed to reform.

▶ not strictly organized **loose** The May Day collective was a loose coalition of left-wing and anarchist protesters.

● n+N **government, opposition** A third candidate of the three-party opposition coalition, the Democratic Union, took less than 100 votes.

● v+N form a coalition **assemble, build, create, forge, form, put together** The goal is to build a coalition of trade union and community groups who will work together to influence government thinking.

▶ join or lead a coalition **join, lead** The general election was narrowly won by the Republican Front, a coalition led by the Socialist Party.

coastline N
the land along a coast

● adj+N impressive or beautiful **beautiful, breathtaking, dramatic, magnificent, spectacular, stunning, unspoiled** The Cinque Terre has a dramatic coastline and is dotted with pretty fishing villages.

▶ not smooth **rocky, rugged** For centuries, Cornwall's rugged coastline was a haven for smugglers.

▶ long **long** The long coastline Turkey has along the

Mediterranean Sea means there is always plenty of fresh sea food on offer.

▶ without buildings on it **undeveloped** Here you can holiday on secluded beaches on a mostly undeveloped coastline.

● v+N move along coastline **follow, hug** If you follow the coastline further south you will reach the historic city of Tarragona. ● The route more or less hugged the coastline until we reached San Francisco.

● N+v **stretch** The coastline stretches for miles with breathtaking views.

● n+of+N **kilometres, length, miles, section, stretch, strip** Our primary function is to conserve this unspoilt stretch of coastline and its communities of plants and animals.

cocktail N
1 a drink made by mixing different drinks together

● adj+N **classic, delicious, exotic, non-alcoholic, pre-dinner** You can lounge in the baking sun while sipping delicious cocktails from their extensive menu.

● v+N make or serve a cocktail **make, mix, serve** The bar staff mixed the most amazing cocktails.

▶ drink a cocktail **drink, have, sip** We drank cocktails by the pool.

● N+n **bar, lounge, party, reception** The hotel also has a restaurant and cocktail lounge.

2 a mixture of different substances, emotions etc, especially a harmful one

● adj+N strong **heady, potent** The music is a potent cocktail of soul and old-fashioned rock.

▶ dangerous **deadly, explosive, lethal** There is a lethal cocktail of gender-based job segregation and sex discrimination in our workplaces.

● N+of **chemicals, drugs, medication, pesticides** Humans and wildlife around the world are exposed to a cocktail of hazardous man-made chemicals.

code N
1 a system for sending secret messages

● adj+N **secret** Daring escapes, secret codes and naval espionage drive a plot that is exciting to the end.

● n+N **Morse** Morse code telegraphy, even in the hands of a very skilled operator, is quite slow.

● v+N learn how to understand a code **break, crack, decipher** Bletchley Park was the largest code-breaking establishment the world had ever seen, where brilliant minds worked to crack German codes.

▶ use a code to write something **write in** It was at Oxford that he started to keep a diary, an old red note book in which he would sometimes write in code.

● N+n **name, word** They would also need to have special code names to protect their identities.

2 a set of rules about how to do something

● adj+N that must be obeyed **strict** Companies follow a strict code of Good Manufacturing Practice.

▶ that people can choose to obey **voluntary** Prior to the passing of the law, tobacco advertising was regulated by a voluntary code of practice agreed between the tobacco industry and the government.

▸ not written down **unwritten** *There is an unwritten code of behaviour at business meetings.*

▸ activity or field in which a code applies **disciplinary, ethical, ministerial, moral, penal, professional** *They have a strict moral code, and will usually try and abide by it.*

● v+N when someone does not obey a code **breach, break, contravene** *Our disciplinary procedures already provide protection for the public against members who breach our strict code of conduct.*

▸ when someone obeys a code **abide by, adhere to, adopt, comply with, follow, keep to** *Schools must comply with a code of practice which says that their admissions process must be clear, fair and impartial.*

▸ when someone makes people obey a code **enforce, introduce** *The restaurant is open to non-residents, but the jacket-and-tie dress code is strictly enforced.*

● N+of **behaviour, conduct, ethics, honour, practice** *Some within the industry are suggesting a voluntary code of conduct.*

coherence N
the fact of fitting or working together in a sensible or pleasing way

● adj+N **intellectual, internal, logical, narrative, structural, textual, thematic** *Units are selected so as to ensure intellectual coherence as well as variety, with a range of cultures and topics covered.*

● v+N give or have coherence **achieve, bring, create, ensure, give, have, maintain, provide** *The discussions were aimed at promoting regional output, and achieving greater coherence in scheduling.*

▸ not have coherence **lack** *Unfortunately, the website design lacks coherence and the information from different museums is structured inconsistently.*

● n+of+N **degree, lack, sense** *A strong sense of coherence within the group is developed on these courses.*

coherent ADJ
reasonable and sensible, with all the different parts fitting together in a sensible way

● adv+ADJ **intellectually, internally, logically, theoretically** *This is a nicely argued, logically coherent article.*

▸ to what degree **entirely, fairly, highly, perfectly, reasonably, remarkably, very** *This has been a difficult chapter to edit into a reasonably coherent form.*

● ADJ+n group of things put together **set, whole** *The result is a work whose strands do not form an entirely coherent whole.*

▸ plan or way of organizing something **approach, framework, plan, policy, programme, strategy, structure, system, vision** *What is needed is a coherent strategy for education outside the classroom that brings together good practice from around the country.*

▸ way **manner, way** *They put forward a plan for operating the railways in a coherent, strategic way.*

▸ argument or description **account, argument, explanation, narrative, picture, theory** *She puts forward coherent arguments and backs them up with evidence.*

▸ piece of writing or speech **sentence** *He is barely capable of forming a coherent sentence.*

● and/or **clear, comprehensive, consistent, effective, logical, systematic** *We need a coherent and comprehensive approach to neighbourhood regeneration.*

coincidence N
a situation where things happen together by chance

● adj+N emphasizing that it is a coincidence **complete, mere, pure, sheer** *It's pure coincidence that I come from the north and the film is set in the north.*

▸ strange or surprising **amazing, bizarre, curious, extraordinary, odd, remarkable, spooky** INFORMAL, **strange, uncanny** *By some strange coincidence, we ended up teaching at the same school.*

▸ when something good or bad happens **fortunate, happy, lucky, unfortunate** *By a happy coincidence (for the broadcasters), the announcement of the election happened during a long newspaper strike.*

● N+v **happen, occur** *Then, in 1850, a very curious coincidence occurred.*

● n+of+N **number, series, string** *The story seems much too far-fetched to ring true, while the plot is driven by a remarkable series of coincidences.*

Usage *Coincidence* is always plural in these combinations.

coincidental ADJ
happening or existing by chance, not planned

● adv+ADJ **entirely, merely, purely** *She claimed that the timing of the visit was purely coincidental.*

● ADJ+n **resemblance, similarity, timing** *McCarthy has never seen any of Graham's work, so the similarities are entirely coincidental.*

cold ADJ
with low or lower than normal temperature

● adv+ADJ very **bitingly, bitterly, extremely, freezing, intensely, really, stone, terribly, very** *It was a bitterly cold afternoon.*

You can also use the expression *cold as ice* to say that something or someone is very cold: *I felt his hands and they were as cold as ice*

▸ rather **a bit** INFORMAL, **a little, pretty** INFORMAL, **quite, rather** *The weather had turned rather cold and windy.*

▸ unusually **exceptionally, unseasonably, unusually** *It was unseasonably cold for the time of year.*

● v+ADJ feel or become cold **become, feel, get, go, grow, turn** *My hands didn't feel cold any more, which was a relief.* ● *The weather was turning colder and animals were starting to hibernate.*

▸ when food is served **eat sth, serve sth** *This dish can also be served cold with salad.*

▸ remain **keep sth, remain, stay** *The boiler came on, but the radiators stayed cold.*

cold N
a minor illness that blocks your nose and may make you cough

collaboration

- adj+N **bad, feverish, heavy, nasty, slight, stinking, streaming** *He had a heavy cold and a bad cough, but he managed to keep working.*
- n+N **head** *I had a streaming head cold.*
- v+N **catch, get, have, suffer from** *She was hardy and never caught a cold, even in the winter.* • *I didn't usually suffer from colds.*

collaboration N
the process of working with someone to produce something

- adj+N close or active **active, close** *Much of the research is carried out in close collaboration with industry.*
- ▶ that has good results **effective, fruitful, productive, successful** *These songs represent another highly successful collaboration for Mancini, this time with lyricist Johnny Mercer.*
- ▶ between countries or academic fields **interdisciplinary, international** *The overall aim of the seminar series is to promote interdisciplinary collaboration.*
- ▶ types of collaboration **artistic, creative, scientific** *Each of these local groups has an issue or theme they want to explore and develop through a creative collaboration with an artist.*
- n+N **inter-institution, research** *Under a research collaboration arrangement, the University and your business jointly carry out the research work.*
- v+N **enable, encourage, facilitate, foster, improve, increase, promote, support** *The festival is a distinctive forum that encourages collaboration among participants and stimulates debate.*
- and/or **communication, cooperation, dialogue, exchange, interaction, networking, partnership, sharing, teamwork** *The purpose of the forum is to encourage collaboration and the exchange of ideas between the two institutions.*

colleague N
someone who works with you

- adj+N when you work closely together **close** *This day will highlight the major contribution made by the late Brian Spencer, with papers from some of his close colleagues.*
- ▶ when you have worked together for a long time **long-time, old** *I would like to thank my mentor and long-time colleague, Professor Brown.*
- ▶ rank, sex, or status of colleague **fellow, female, former, junior, male, senior** *Junior staff work within the department to gain experience from their senior colleagues.*
- ▶ types of colleague **academic, clinical, medical, ministerial, parliamentary, professional** *Librarians should take the role of raising awareness about these issues amongst their academic colleagues.*
- ▶ that you trust or respect **respected, trusted** *There are few more difficult tasks than firing employees, especially those that have been trusted colleagues.*
- ▶ having the same attitudes as you **like-minded** *I discussed the matter with a few like-minded colleagues.*
- n+N **business, work, workplace** *This short story*

regards the aftermath of a violent murder and the shocked reactions of the victim's work colleagues.

collection N
a group of things that someone has gathered together

- adj+N large **extensive, growing, huge, large, small, vast** *The museum's extensive collections of historic photographs are housed here.*
- ▶ of good quality **fascinating, fine, important, impressive, magnificent, outstanding, remarkable, rich, stunning, superb, unique, wonderful** *The house contains one of the finest private art collections in the world.*
- ▶ complete **complete, comprehensive** *Its aim is to collect, preserve and make accessible a comprehensive collection of music from all over the world.*
- ▶ containing different sorts of things **diverse, eclectic, motley, varied** *This is a diverse natural history collection, covering the whole of the animal kingdom.*
- ▶ having a particular status **permanent, private, special** *Many of the loans come from English private collections, which are not open to the public.*
- v+N have a collection **boast, contain, have, hold, house** *Other libraries on campus hold major collections in medical sciences, environmental subjects, law, sciences, and music.*
- ▶ put together a collection **acquire, add to, amass, assemble, build, create, put together** *Over the years, he amassed probably the most important collection of contemporary Austrian art in the country.*
- ▶ make a list of things in the collection **catalogue** *During this time he has catalogued the large collections of the Science Museum in London.*
- ▶ give a collection **bequeath, donate** *When William Cotton died, he bequeathed his collection of paintings by his friend Sir Joshua Reynolds to the museum in Plymouth.*
- ▶ when pieces of writing are published **edit, publish** *She is currently editing a collection of essays.*
- ▶ arrange a collection so people can see it **display, exhibit** *Hallways are perfect for displaying collections of things like maps, framed textiles, plates – anything really!*
- ▶ make a collection complete **complete** *I'm looking for a Tennis programme from the year 1985 to complete my collection.*
- N+v **be made up of, comprise, consist of, contain, cover, include** *The collection also includes work in wood, jewellery, and textiles.*

college N
a place that gives qualifications to students, either below or at degree level

- adj+N **agricultural, local, technical, theological** *Many local amateur radio clubs and societies and technical colleges run courses specifically for the Advanced Radio Communications Examination.*
- n+N **art, community, FE, further education, language, music, sixth-form, sports, teacher-training, technology, university** *Other key partners in this project are the library service and the local FE college.*

- v+N ask to study at a college **apply to** *She applied to the local FE college.*
▶ study at or begin a course at a college **attend, enrol at, enter, go to, start, study at** *More opportunities for school pupils to attend colleges will help increase skill levels in Scotland.*
▶ complete a course at a college **finish, graduate from, leave** *After leaving college, she set up her own studio with the aid of a Crafts Council grant.*
▶ stop going to a college **drop out of** *He dropped out of college in his second year, before he had taken his exams.*

- N+v **offer sth, provide sth, run sth** *The college offers over 400 vocational and educational courses, most leading to a qualification.*

- N+n **campus, course, degree, graduate, leaver, lecturer, library, principal, staff, student, tutor** *This is a buy-and-sell book service for college students.*

collision N

1 an accident involving crashing into something

- adj+N causing death or damage **fatal, serious** *There has been a steady decrease in the number of fatal collisions involving motorcycles over the past three years.*
▶ types of collision **head-on, high-speed, mid-air** *The head-on collision between the two vehicles occurred on the B6052 Chesterfield Road.*
- n+N **road traffic** *At this time of year the number of road traffic collisions on Wiltshire's roads increases.*
- v+N be in a collision **be involved in, have** *He was involved in a collision with a lorry that appeared suddenly in front of him.*
▶ avoid being in a collision **avoid, prevent** *I had to take immediate evasive action to avoid a head-on collision with an oncoming car.*
▶ cause a collision **cause, lead to** *It is not possible to provide exact statistics relating to the number of collisions caused by tired drivers who fall asleep at the wheel.*
- N+v **involve sth, occur** *In 1988 a collision occurred at Clapham involving three trains.*

2 a very serious argument or a great difference between ideas

- adj+N **head-on** *Nor is it right to believe that there has been some seismic shift in union strategy leading to a head-on collision with government.*
- v+N **come into, lead to** *The new Minister is going to come into head-on collision with members of the medical profession.*
- N+n **course** *The unions were set on a collision course with the government.*

colour N

red, blue, green etc

- adj+N bright **bright, brilliant, vibrant, vivid** *The ancient meadows and pastures are at their best in summer, with bright colours, smells and the humming of insects.*
▶ strong **bold, intense, rich, strong** *Cook it over a medium heat, stirring frequently, until it turns a rich golden colour.*

▶ dark **dark, deep** *The meat goes a darker colour very quickly, which customers find unacceptable.*
▶ light **light, muted, pale, pastel, soft** *All the rooms on the ground floor have tiled floors and are painted in white or pastel colours.*
▶ when something is completely in colour **full** *The catalogue features nearly 300 items in full colour, together with a full inventory of the collection.*
▶ types of colour **complementary, matching, natural, neutral, primary, warm** *The costumes of the main characters will be in strong primary colours.*
▶ attractive **beautiful, lovely** *The fish and coral were such beautiful colours.*

- n+N a person's hair, eyes etc **eye, hair, skin** *All over the world people are subjected to cruel treatment because of their race, language, or skin colour.*
▶ set of colours **autumn, rainbow** *Butterflies with rainbow colours wafted on the scented air.*

Usage **Colour** is often plural in these combinations.

- v+N **add, change, match, mix, use** *I love autumn, when the trees start to change colour.*
- N+v **fade, match, range** *He painted in a variety of soft colours ranging from yellows through to greens and browns.*
- N+n **coding, combination, palette, scheme** *The orange-and-red colour scheme is inspired by the decor in my new bedroom, which is lovely and warm and cosy.*
- n+of+N small amount **splash** *They added bulbs in planters for an extra splash of colour.*
▶ many bright colours together **array, blaze, kaleidoscope, riot** *The fruit-and-vegetable markets near the harbour are a riot of colour.*
▶ range **combination, range** *A wide range of colours is available.*
▶ form **shade** *Use several different colours and a variety of shades of those colours.*

colouring N

the colour of someone's hair, skin, and eyes, or of an object, animal, or plant

- adj+N **dark, natural, original, unusual** *Certain shades complement your natural colouring more than others.* ● *The walls of the church still retain their original colouring.*
- v+N **have** *All three brothers had the same colouring and sturdy, muscular build.*

column N

1 a regular article in a newspaper or magazine

- adj+N **editorial, fortnightly, monthly, regular, weekly** *He writes a weekly column for The Independent.*
- n+N **advice, agony, comment, correspondence, gossip, leader, letter, newspaper, opinion** *To get a balanced view of a story, try and read articles and opinion columns from different political perspectives.*
- N+n **inches** *This story amused many and generated lots of column inches.*

2 a long line of people, vehicles, smoke etc

- adj+N **armoured, marching** *We passed marching columns of prisoners-of-war.*

- N+of something rising up **air, smoke, water** *Over to the west, a column of smoke was rising into the air.*
- ▶ people or vehicles **tanks, troops** *First-generation warfare was the era of massed lines and columns of troops.*
- n+of+N **head** *The 4th King's Own regiment was at the head of the column.*

combat V

try to stop something bad from happening or a bad situation becoming worse.

- adv+V **actively, effectively, successfully** *It was a threat that some felt was not being combated effectively.*
- V+n **climate change, crime, discrimination, disease, fraud, global warming, inflation, poverty, problem, racism, terrorism, threat, unemployment, violence** *Schools and colleges have an important role to play in combating everyday racism.*

combination N

something that combines several things

- adj+N best possible **the best, ideal, optimum, perfect, the right, unbeatable, winning** *Human-scale farming and low-impact living are a winning combination.*
- ▶ unusual **rare, strange, unique, unusual** *Carlton Park provides a natural centre for business with its unique combination of an outstanding location, thriving local economy and superb environment.*
- ▶ good or strong **good, interesting, potent, powerful, wonderful** *We have quite a good combination of skills and experience between us.*
- ▶ dangerous **dangerous, deadly, lethal** *As well as being highly-strung with a frightening temper, John was also a heavy drinker – a lethal combination.*
- n+N **colour** *Try out different colour combinations on screen and on paper.*
- v+in+N **be used** *Herbal pills may provide some benefit when used in combination with other techniques.*

comeback N

a period when someone or something becomes successful or popular again

- adj+N great **big, great, impressive, magnificent, spirited, strong, successful, triumphant** *A spirited comeback saw him eventually finish in third place.*
- ▶ surprising **amazing, astonishing, dramatic, remarkable, stunning, surprise, unlikely** *Thirteen points down, the visitors started to mount an unlikely comeback.*
- ▶ late **late, long-awaited** *Although they made a late comeback, there was only ever one side in it,.*
- v+N make a comeback **make, mount, stage** *She made a bid to stage her triumphant screen comeback.*
- ▶ attempt a comeback **attempt, plan** *He attempted a comeback with a little success the following season.*
- N+n musical event or item **album, concert, gig, single, tour** *His much-awaited comeback album only made number 8.*
- ▶ sporting event **game, match, race** *He had been out*

of action with an ankle problem and took a kick on the calf in his comeback match.

come up with PHR VB

think of something such as an idea

- V+n idea or plan **concept, idea, plan, proposal, scheme, strategy, suggestion** *How did you come up with the idea of using a river in this way?*
- ▶ answer **answer, result, solution** *Nobody else has come up with a solution.*
- ▶ explanation **explanation, model, theory** *Astronomers have been attempting to come up with an explanation for this anomaly.*

comfort N

1 a physically relaxed state

- adj+N great **exceptional, great, maximum, optimum, superior, supreme, ultimate, utmost** *Adjust your ironing board to provide maximum comfort for your height.*
- ▶ fair **reasonable, relative** *She will be able to enjoy her retirement in relative comfort.*
- ▶ extra **added, extra** *An adjustable elasticated waistband provides added comfort.*
- v+N provide comfort **guarantee, offer, provide** *It offers superior ride comfort to that of a standard model.*
- ▶ enjoy comfort **enjoy** *They enjoyed the comfort of a stylish Manhattan apartment.*
- ▶ give up comfort **leave, sacrifice** *You can enjoy all this without leaving the comfort of your own home.*
- ▶ increase comfort **enhance, increase** *Many measures are put in place to increase human comfort.*
- N+n **condition, level, temperature, zone** *Fish have an exact comfort zone of temperatures that each species enjoys.*
- v+for+N **build, design, make** *Both houses were designed for comfort.*
- ▶ and/or pleasant feeling **ease, enjoyment, peace, relaxation, warmth** *She cuddled up for comfort and warmth.*
- ▶ safety **safety, security, stability** *We maintain high standards of comfort and safety.*
- ▶ pleasant things **cleanliness, elegance, luxury** *Each room meets the inn's classic style of comfort and luxury.*
- ▶ convenient situation **convenience, practicality** *It had all the comfort and convenience of home.*

2 a feeling of being less sad or worried, or a person or thing that makes you feel that way

- adj+N little **cold, little, scant, small** *It is little comfort that they will see their profits rise marginally.*
- ▶ great **great** *Just reading the reassurances was a great comfort.*
- v+N give comfort **bring, give, offer** *She didn't try to offer any comfort or affection to her father.*
- ▶ take comfort **derive, draw, find, take** *You can take comfort in the knowledge that over 400 families know they will not be affected.*
- ▶ look for comfort **seek** *He does not seek comfort from other female company; he is still in love with his wife.*

- N+n **blanket, eating, food** *As the weather turns colder, soup is a comfort food that is actually good for you.*

- N+in **fact, knowledge, thought** *Some families may find comfort in the fact that something has been learned from the death of their loved one.*

- n+of+N **source** *Knowing his family was safe was a source of comfort to him.*

- and/or **consolation, reassurance, solace** *Without words, comfort and reassurance can be given.*

comic ADJ
funny

- adv+ADJ very **highly, richly, wonderfully** *Tragic facts are fitted around the richly comic character.*
- ▶ rather **rather, slightly** *At times his enthusiasm is slightly comic.*
- ▶ in an unpleasant way **blackly, darkly, grotesquely** *It was billed as a darkly comic thriller.*
- ▶ in a pleasant way **delightfully, gently, lightly** *It is a gently comic take on the human need to reinvent oneself.*
- ▶ accidentally **unintentionally** *The film is unintentionally comic through bad acting and inept direction.*
- ADJ+n **genius, relief, talent, timing, touch** *She has a wonderful sense of comic timing.*

command N
1 an official order

- adj+N whose command **divine, royal** *She believed she was acting on an explicit divine command.*
- ▶ clearly given **explicit, express** *He made it plain he was writing the text at her express command.*
- ▶ in words **verbal** *The dog responds only to verbal commands.*
- v+N give a command **bark, give, issue, shout** *The problem is thinking of morality as a set of commands issued by a deity.*
- ▶ obey a command **carry out, follow, obey** *I obeyed the command and we stopped the engines.*
- ▶ not obey a command **disobey, ignore** *Any baron who disobeyed this royal command would be committing treason.*

2 control of people, especially in the armed forces; control of a situation

- adj+N total **absolute, full, overall, sole, supreme** *Within seconds, I was in full command of the situation.*
- ▶ shared **joint** *They held joint command of the fleet.*
- v+N get or have command **accept, assume, have, hold, resume, take, take over** *He assumed command on the 5th of June.*
- ▶ give up command **relinquish, resign** *That night, the emperor relinquished the supreme command of his army.*
- ▶ give command **give sb** *In 1808 he was given command of the expeditionary forces in Portugal.*
- v+under+N **be, be placed, be put, come** *The Polish Army was evacuated to the Middle East and placed under British command.*

- n+of+N **chain, line** *There must be a single, clearly defined chain of command.*

3 knowledge of something, especially a language

- adj+N **basic, excellent, good, poor** *You will need to demonstrate a basic command of English in order to be accepted for the course.*

- v+N **demonstrate, have, show** *He has a good command of the procedures involved in the selection process.*

> You can also say that someone has a skill **at** their **command**: *She had to use all the tact at her command to persuade them to change their minds.*

commemorate V
show you remember an important person or event by having a special ceremony etc

- V+n a number of years after an event **anniversary, bicentenary, bicentennial, birthday, jubilee** *They were commemorating the 60th anniversary of the ending of the war.*
- ▶ an event **battle, birth, event, founding, occasion, opening, victory, visit** *Many families do this to commemorate a special occasion in their lives.*
- ▶ a death **death, sacrifice** *A coin was struck commemorating the death of the president.*
- ▶ dead person or people **airman, the dead, soldier, victim** *At the centre of the gardens is a plaque commemorating the dead.*
- ▶ what someone has done **achievements, bravery, contribution, life** *Staff were given certificates and vouchers to commemorate their achievements.*

commend V
praise someone or something formally or publicly

- adv+V very much **highly, strongly** *It is an excellent textbook and is to be highly commended.*

> Usage **Commend** is almost always <u>passive</u> in these combinations.

- ▶ in particular **especially, particularly, specially** *The judges particularly commended the participants for the effort they had put in.*
- ▶ with friendly enthusiasm **heartily, warmly, wholeheartedly** *The alterations came in for criticism by some and were warmly commended by others!*

> If something is of little value, you can say that is has **little/nothing to commend it**: *The new system was complex and seemed to have little to commend it.*

commendable ADJ
deserving praise or admiration

- adv+ADJ **highly, particularly, very** *The quality and your attention to detail is highly commendable.*
- ADJ+n performance **attempt, effort, performance** *It ws a commendable effort to stay faithful to the original novel.*
- ▶ quality **clarity, determination, honesty, restraint, speed, spirit** *They led the protest with commendable restraint.*

comment N
a spoken or written remark that gives an opinion

- adj+N useful **constructive, helpful, revealing, useful** *Thanks for your generous and constructive comments.*
- ▶ noticing or understanding well **astute, fair, incisive, informed, insightful, interesting, perceptive, pertinent, thoughtful** *His remarks were accepted as fair comment on the situation.* • *The songs are full of his perceptive comments on society.*
- ▶ not noticing or understanding well **ill-informed, inane, stupid** *Annoyed with inane comments, I posted inane responses myself.*
- ▶ positive **appreciative, favourable, positive** *The monthly policy report continued to receive favourable comment.*
- ▶ negative **adverse, critical, defamatory, derogatory, negative, unfavourable** *No derogatory comments about individuals or groups, please.*
- ▶ offensive **bigoted, libellous, offensive, racist** *Obscenities and offensive comments are banned.*
- ▶ against a group of people **bigoted, racist, sexist** *Rude or racist comments will be erased.*
- ▶ rude **lewd, ribald, rude** *The foul-mouthed audience made lewd comments, trying to provoke me.*
- ▶ unpleasant **caustic, sarcastic, scathing, snide** *She used to make snide comments to our parents if we had misbehaved.*
- ▶ clever or funny **pithy, witty, wry** *Her witty comments and stories were hilarious.*
- ▶ not serious **flippant, throwaway** *A throwaway comment in one film can become central to the next.*
- ▶ careless **offhand, unguarded** *The immediacy of email makes unguarded comments all too easy.*
- ▶ not asked for **unsolicited** *Ten thousand unsolicited comments were received and a content analysis was completed.*
- ▶ at the beginning/end **closing, concluding, final, introductory, opening** *He invited the head of college to make some introductory comments.*
- ▶ more **additional, further** *We may have further comments in the future.*
- ▶ short **brief, quick** *Submit an addition or make a quick comment on this article.*

- v+N make a comment **add, leave, make, offer, post, submit, write** *This is an informal area for visitors to post comments.*

> You can also use the expression **pass comment** meaning to make a comment: *She refused to pass comment on the accusations.*

- ▶ ask for comments **elicit, invite, request, seek, solicit** *We invite comments on the issue of compensation on dismissal.*
- ▶ cause someone to comment **attract, provoke** *I knew my remarks would provoke a comment or two!*
- ▶ welcome **appreciate, value, welcome** *We would sincerely appreciate your comments and feedback.*
- ▶ take back a comment **delete, retract, take back** *The mayor has refused to retract his comment or apologize.*
- ▶ ignore **disregard, ignore** *Ignore any nasty comments.*

- and/or ideas **feedback, ideas, observation, opinions, suggestions, thoughts, views** *Comments and suggestions should be mailed to the following address.*

- ▶ questions **inquiries, queries, questions** *I look forward to any questions or comments you have.*
- ▶ changes **additions, amendments, corrections** *Please contact our website with any comments or corrections.*
- ▶ complaint or criticism **complaint, criticism, objections** *Should you have a comment or complaint to make about a product we provide, then please contact us in writing.*

commentary N
1 a discussion of something

- adj+N short **brief** *She provides a brief commentary on the various chapters in the book.*
- ▶ types of commentary **critical, editorial, political, social, textual** *Write a critical commentary on the following poem.*
- ▶ giving good information **detailed, incisive, informative, insightful** *These volumes contain detailed verse-by-verse commentary.*
- ▶ expert **authoritative, expert** *Expert commentary has ensured the book's leading position.*
- ▶ relevant to the present **topical** *The broadcast provided a topical commentary on America.*

- v+N **give, offer, provide, write** *He has written an expert commentary on the latest economic developments.*

2 a description of an event, for example on radio or television

- adj+N live **live** *I was listening to the live radio commentary on the game.*
- ▶ continuous **running** *The teacher gave a running commentary as he carried out the experiment.*
- ▶ describing how the commentary is provided **audio, live-text, online, radio** *Click here for live-text commentary from the Olympics.*

- v+N **do, give, keep up, provide** *All the news stations provided a commentary on the progress of the talks.*

commerce N
buying and selling goods and services

- adj+N electronic **electronic, online** *We have specialist expertise in legal issues arising from online commerce.*
- ▶ range of commerce **foreign, global, international, local** *They are centres for local commerce.*

- v+N increase commerce **encourage, facilitate, promote, support** *The bridge has connected people and facilitated commerce.*
- ▶ take part in commerce **conduct, engage in** *It considers alternative approaches to taxing commerce conducted electronically.*
- ▶ control commerce **regulate** *He also sought to strengthen and regulate the country's commerce.*
- ▶ affect commerce **affect** *How will the ethnic composition of the area affect local commerce and shopping?*

- and/or **banking, business, finance, industry, trade** *Data mining is a potential source of useful information for industry and commerce.*

commission N

1 an official group that is in charge of something or asked to find out about something

- adj+N types of commission **judicial, parliamentary, presidential, royal, state** *He has been appointed to a parliamentary commission to draw up plans for the reform of the health service.*
- ▶ range of the commission **international, national** *She was released unharmed after members of the international commission intervened.*
- ▶ established by law **statutory** *The new statutory commission will take over this function in May.*
- ▶ giving advice **advisory** *He announced the creation of a presidential advisory commission.*
- ▶ independent **independent** *These functions are carried out by independent electoral commissions.*

- v+N set up a commission **appoint, create, establish, set up** *While in power he created a state road commission.*
- ▶ lead a commission **chair, head** *The judge who chaired the commission warned that the report was an alarm call.*

2 an extra amount of money that you pay for a service or earn when you sell something

- adj+N large **generous, hefty, high, large** *The sellers were mainly interested in collecting hefty commissions.*
- ▶ small **small** *For every item purchased the site receives a small commission of around 5 per cent.*
- ▶ fixed **fixed** *I'd rather the commission were fixed.*

- v+N earn commission **earn, get, receive** *You'll get a small commission on every item you sell.*
- ▶ pay commission **pay** *We pay 20 per cent commission on everything!*
- ▶ charge commission **charge** *You'll get a good exchange rate and we don't charge commission.*
- ▶ take off commission **deduct** *We only received about £100, once the commission had been deducted.*

- N+n rate **percentage, rate** *This leads directly to highly competitive commission rates.*
- ▶ charge **charge, fee, payment** *Commission payments are only one part of the costs of share transactions.*
- ▶ method **basis** *None of our consultants is paid on a commission basis.*

commission V

ask for work to be done or produced for you

- adv+V **especially, specially, specifically** *Almost everything she has written has been specially commissioned.*

> Usage **Commission** is almost always passive in these combinations.

- V+n report **evaluation, paper, poll, project, report, research, review, study, survey** *The agency has commissioned a survey to measure usage.*
- ▶ art **artwork, opera, painting, photograph, piece, play, portrait, sculpture, work** *We are careful when selecting and commissioning artworks for the hospital.*
- ▶ artist **architect, artist, choreographer, composer, designer, sculptor** *He commissioned an artist to prepare designs for his own monument.*

commit V

do something illegal or morally wrong

- V+n when you kill yourself **hara-kiri, suicide** *The situation is complicated when he is arrested and commits suicide in prison.*
- ▶ something against the law **adultery, arson, assault, burglary, crime, felony, fraud, genocide, homicide, murder, offence, perjury, robbery, theft, treason, violence** *If you drive without wearing your lenses or glasses, you are committing an offence.*
- ▶ something wrong **sacrilege, sin** *He begged for forgiveness for the terrible sins he had committed.*
- ▶ an act that is wrong **act, deed** *There were many extremists who were willing to commit acts of violence.*
- ▶ a mistake **blunder, error, mistake** *She committed an error that led to loss of life.*

commitment N

1 a duty, responsibility, or promise

- adj+N earlier **prior** *He had an important prior commitment.*
- ▶ by contract **binding, contractual** *This is manoeuvre to bypass the binding commitments of the treaty.*
- ▶ major **big, considerable, major** *We still have some major commitments to fulfil.*
- ▶ types of commitment **business, family, financial, funding, personal, political, teaching, time, work** *I have family commitments which would make the hours impossible.*

- v+N have or accept a commitment **have, make, take on** *Think carefully before taking on extra financial commitments.*
- ▶ when you do what you have said you will do **deliver on, fulfil, honour, meet** *People know that you fulfil your commitments.*
- ▶ when you do not do what you have said you will do **get out of, renege on, wriggle out of** *I will not renege on that commitment.*

2 enthusiasm, determination, and support for something

- adj+N continuing **continuing, lifelong, long-standing, long-term, ongoing, sustained** *This is part of our ongoing commitment to customer service.*
- ▶ strong **absolute, deep, passionate, real, serious, strong, total, unequivocal, unswerving, wholehearted** *Members' commitment was still strong.*
- ▶ types of commitment **emotional, ideological, moral, political** *The book prickles with fury and political commitment.*

- v+N give your commitment **declare, give, pledge** *All three women pledged their commitment to the party.*
- ▶ repeat your commitment **affirm, confirm, reaffirm, reiterate, restate** *I am happy to reiterate my commitment to a holistic approach.*
- ▶ not have commitment **lack** *You lack commitment to the cause.*
- ▶ show commitment **demonstrate, show, underline** *His work shows his continuing commitment to encouraging new wildlife habitats.*

- n+of+N **degree, lack, level, sense** *Her level of commitment would be difficult to equal.*

committed ADJ
loyal to a belief, organization, or group

- adv+ADJ **absolutely, deeply, fiercely, firmly, fully, highly, strongly, totally, very** *They were both totally committed **to** the aims of the party.*
- ADJ+n **activist, campaigner, enthusiast, fan, follower, supporter** *She is a committed supporter of the disability movement.*

committee N
a group, representing a larger group, which discusses and makes decisions about a particular subject

- adj+N management **executive, management, steering** *An executive committee decides on spending.*
- ▶ advising **advisory, consultative** *Both parties are guided by advisory committees.*
- ▶ of a government **all-party, congressional, cross-party, ministerial, parliamentary, select, senate** *A parliamentary select committee recommended it.*
- ▶ working together **joint** *The two associations set up a joint committee.*
- v+N form a committee **appoint, convene, establish, form, organize, set up** *The two parties agree to form a joint committee.*
- ▶ be in charge of a committee **chair, head** *He chaired the first courses committee.*
- ▶ when a committee's work is stopped **disband** *Its objectives achieved, the committee was disbanded.*
- N+v meet **meet** *These committees meet four times a year.*
- ▶ decide **agree, approve, conclude, decide, determine, recommend** *The committee decided to apply for a loan from the European fund.*
- ▶ discuss **consider, discuss, review** *The executive committee is currently considering options.*
- N+n **chair, chairman, meeting, member** *Each region has its own regional chair and committee members.*
- v+for+N **run, stand** *Members were urged to encourage colleagues to stand for the committee.*
- v+on-N **be, serve, sit, work** *They felt they had been serving on the committee too long.*

commodity N
1 something that can be bought and sold

- adj+N valuable **expensive, valuable** *In the Middle Ages, one valuable commodity was salt.*
- ▶ rare **rare, scarce** *Water is already a scarce commodity worldwide.*
- ▶ important **basic, important, vital** *Basic food commodities include wheat, corn, soybeans, and sugarcane.*
- ▶ in large amounts **bulk, mass-produced** *It is correct that about two thirds of existing rail freight is bulk commodities.*
- ▶ decaying quickly **perishable** *This will maximise the return on a highly perishable commodity.*
- ▶ across the world **global** *Software programming is becoming a global commodity.*
- ▶ able to be sold **marketable, saleable, tradable** *We have to accept that radio is a marketable commodity.*
- v+N trade commodities **buy, new, sell, trade,**

trade in *The main commodities traded were nutmeg and mace.*
- ▶ move between countries **export, import** *The arid climate forced the inhabitants to import most commodities.*
- ▶ produce commodities **produce** *Private funding will be directed toward producing profitable commodities.*
- N+n prices **futures, prices** *The more bullish argue there is scope for rises in commodity prices.*
- ▶ trade **exchange, export, market, trading** *Information on commodity markets is hard to come by.*
- ▶ someone who trades **broker, trader** *He spent several years as a commodity trader.*

2 something that is useful or necessary

- adj+N **precious, rare, scarce, valuable** *With time a very precious commodity, we had to start straight away.*

common ADJ
1 happening frequently or existing in large numbers or amounts

- adv+ADJ very **especially, extremely, particularly, very** *The practice of taking hostages was in former times very common.*
- ▶ rather **fairly, pretty** INFORMAL**, quite, rather, reasonably, relatively** *It's quite common for a child to join a company where a parent works.*
- ▶ unexpectedly **surprisingly** *Accidents in the home are surprisingly common.*
- ▶ becoming more common **increasingly** *Franchising is a business model which is becoming increasingly common.*
- v+ADJ **be, become, prove, remain, seem** *This name remains common in certain areas of the country.*

2 used, done, or shared by a group

- ADJ+n history **ancestor, ancestry, heritage** *All biodiversity is connected through common ancestry of species.*
- ▶ purpose **goal, interest, purpose** *We are all working towards a common goal.*
- ▶ feature **characteristic, feature, theme, thread, trait** *The common theme running through all his work is the anonymity of modern society.*
- ▶ thing that unites **bond** *They recruited troops from localities so that they had a common bond.*

> When two or more people or things share interests or features you can say that they **have something in common**: *We got on very well although we didn't have much in common.* When people agree about something you can say that they are **on**, or **find common ground**: *Audiences enjoy finding common ground with a comedian.*

commonplace ADJ
not unusual

- adv+ADJ very **too, very** *Library web pages are now very commonplace.*
- ▶ rather **fairly, quite, rather, relatively** *It is now quite commonplace for people to work from home.*
- ▶ becoming more commonplace **increasingly** *This*

assumption is now increasingly commonplace in today's commercial arena.

- ADJ+n **assumption, featuer, observation, occurrence, practice** *Such practices were commonplace within the hotel and finance sectors.*

commotion N
noise and confused activity

- adj+N great **considerable, great, huge, much** *He was awakened by the sounds of a great commotion.*
- ▶ minor **minor, slight** *Just then, there arose a slight commotion.*
- ▶ sudden **sudden** *She apologized for the sudden commotion.*

- v+N cause a commotion **cause, create, make** *The announcement of the sentence caused great commotion in court.*

- N+v start **break out, erupt** *A commotion erupted outside the tavern.*
- ▶ stop **die down, subside** *He remained standing until the commotion has subsided.*

communicate V
express thoughts, feelings, or information

- adv+V well **accurately, adequately, appropriately, clearly, effectively, efficiently, meaningfully, powerfully, properly, successfully, well** *Support and advice is available on how to communicate effectively.*
- ▶ ways of communicating **electronically, non-verbally, orally, telepathically, verbally, visually, wirelessly** *We are used to communicating verbally and visually through gestures*
- ▶ directly **directly** *Fans can communicate directly with band members.*
- ▶ easily **confidently, easily, fluently** *They could communicate fluently and effectively with an English speaker.*
- ▶ privately **privately, securely** *This software allows customers to communicate securely with their bank.*
- ▶ quickly **instantaneously, instantly, promptly, quickly** *These notices were communicated almost instantaneously.*

- V+n information or ideas **concept, data, idea, information, knowledge, meaning, message, news, thoughts, truth, understanding, view** *The poet selects language that best communicates his message.*
- ▶ result **decision, findings, outcome, result** *The managers communicated the decision to the staff at a hastily convened meeting.*
- ▶ feeling **emotions, enthusiasm, excitement, feelings, love** *Dogs have a good ability to communicate their feelings and needs.*
- ▶ wishes or plans **intentions, plans, wishes** *He can no longer walk or talk or communicate his wishes to his relations.*

- V+by **email, language, letter, phone, radio, sound, telephone, words** *Only the transport police were able to communicate by radio.*

- V+through **email, Internet, language, medium, music, speech, website, words, writing** *Since the earliest cave dwellers, people have communicated through the medium of art.*

- V+via **email, Internet, mail, telephone, website** *All information about courses and is communicated via email.*

communication N
the expression of thoughts, feelings, or information

- adj+N types of communication **cross-cultural, electronic, intercultural, non-verbal, oral, peer-to-peer, person-to-person, verbal, visual, written** *Such relationships require strategies such the appropriate use of non-verbal communication.*
- ▶ good **effective, excellent, good** *The most important contribution you can make is to ensure good communication.*
- ▶ poor **poor** *IT is plagued by poor communication between engineers and software writers.*
- ▶ quick **instant, instantaneous, real-time** *Miracle mini-gadgets have made instant communication a fact of life.*
- ▶ in two directions **bidirectional, two-way** *Concentrate on ensuring good two-way communication.*
- ▶ safe **secure** *An open channel is unsuitable for secure business communications.*
- ▶ involving many people **mass** *His concern was with mass communication and the cinema was his medium.*

- v+N establish communication **establish, initiate** *Schools should establish clear communication with parents and carers.*
- ▶ improve communication **aid, develop, encourage, enhance, facilitate, foster, improve, promote** *We hope our findings may help to improve communication.*
- ▶ provide communication **ensure, maintain, manage, provide, support** *We pride ourselves on maintaining good communication with our clients.*
- ▶ prevent or interrupt communication **disrupt, hinder, impede, prevent** *Heavy snow disrupted communication with the outside world.*

- N+v **break down, fail** *Communication has failed and the messages that do get through are alarming.*

> You can also talk about a **breakdown in communication**: *They attributed poor staff morale to a breakdown in communication.*

- N+n skill **skill** *It is essential you have excellent written communication skills.*
- ▶ problem **breakdown, difficulties, problems** *Speech therapists can help with communication difficulties.*

- n+of+N **channel, form, line, means, medium, method, mode** *Is a poem the correct means of communication?*

community N
the people who live in a particular area; a group of people who are the same in some way

- adj+N involving a particular area **global, international, local** *The international community was looking at the issue urgently.*
- ▶ whole **entire, whole, wider** *There was also an opportunity to share views with others in the wider community.*
- ▶ work of a community **farming, fishing, mining** *The town was once a farming community.*
- ▶ area of interest **academic, business, healthcare,**

research, scientific *We advise all sectors of the business community involved in construction.*

▶ on the Internet **blogging, Internet, online, user, virtual** *Guidance material will be produced in close collaboration with the user communities.*

▶ of a religion or nationality **ethnic, ethnic minority, faith, indigenous, minority, religious** *The report brings out issues relating to the attitudes of ethnic minority communities.*

▶ from another country **immigrant, migrant, refugee** *Immigrant communities were quickly established in the large industrial cities.*

▶ with a disadvantage **disadvantaged, marginalized** *This paper focuses on disadvantaged ethnic communities.*

▶ successful **sustainable, thriving, vibrant** *This is a thriving community with many village shops.*

▶ closely united **close-knit, cohesive, tight-knit** *You will need the ability to live and work in a small, tight-knit community.*

● v+N help a community **benefit, help, serve, support** *The projects benefits the whole community.*

▶ create a community or make it strong **build, create, empower, revitalize, strengthen, unite, unite** *They work to create communities in which people are proud to live and work.*

▶ involve the community **engage, involve** *We involved the entire community in the decision-making process.*

● N+n activity or feeling **activity, engagement, involvement, participation, spirit** *There should be strong parental and community involvement.*

▶ project **enterprise, initiative, project** *Can a community enterprise be a charity?*

commuter N
someone who travels regularly to and from work

● adj+N **daily, regular** *Regular commuters pay thousands a year just for parking!*

● n+N in a vehicle **bus, car, cycle, rail, train** *For the rail commuter, there is a mainline service taking approximately one hour.*

▶ time of travel **evening, morning, rush-hour** *This is perfect for early-morning commuters.*

● N+n vehicle **bike, bus, car, train** *Three out of twenty commuter trains were cancelled.*

▶ where commuters live **belt, town, village** *They left the commuter belt for a new home close to the coast.*

▶ ways the commuters travel **journey, line, link, railway, route, service, station** *You might find our pubs by a main commuter route.*

▶ for commuters **fare, parking** *These zones seek to control commuter parking.*

company N
1 an organization providing services or making goods

● adj+N large/small **large, major, medium-sized, small** *Large companies and government departments are considering decentralization.*

▶ successful **profitable, successful** *The successful retail company has been trading for over 20 years.*

▶ owned by whom **family-owned, independent, private, publicly owned, state-owned** *He*

highlighted the failed privatization of the state-owned electricity company.

▶ with a good reputation **established, reputable** *This makes it more difficult for new entrants to undercut established companies.*

▶ where a company operates **foreign, global, international, Internet, local, multinational, transnational** *The machine is being bought by a multinational company.*

▶ related to another company **affiliated, holding, parent, sister, subsidiary** *The law does not prevent affiliated companies from sharing customer data with one another.*

▶ for profit **commercial** *The exhibitions present sponsorship opportunities for commercial companies.*

▶ not for profit **not-for-profit** *It is now run as a not-for-profit company.*

▶ doing new things **innovative** *We represent many innovative companies.*

● v+N start a company **establish, form, found, incorporate, launch, register, set up, start, start up** *The company was founded in 1972.*

▶ close a company **dissolve, liquidate, wind up** *When all the assets have been sold, the company is dissolved.*

▶ buy a company **acquire, buy, take over** *It plans to use the money to acquire other companies.*

▶ manage a company **head, manage, run** *He runs his own company, organising events for the IT industry.*

▶ make a company larger **build, expand** *They have plans to expand the company next year.*

▶ work for a company **join, work for** *Finding like-minded designers to join the company was difficult.*

▶ stop working for a company **leave, resign from** *Many of the senior managers were forced to leave the company.*

● N+v make or provide **make, manufacture, produce, provide, sell, specialize in, supply** *The company manufactured motorcycles.*

▶ work **operate** *Today there are still seven companies operating in the zone.*

▶ grow **expand, grow** *The company has expanded both nationally and internationally.*

▶ stop doing business **fail, go bankrupt, go bust** INFORMAL, **go into liquidation, go out of business, go under** *Did the company fail because of the mismanagement by the Directors?*

2 the fact of being with another person or with other people

● adj+N enjoyable **congenial, convivial, good** *This event should appeal to lovers of convivial company and good conversation.*

● v+N enjoy company **enjoy** *She enjoys the company of the other children at playtime.*

▶ look for or need company **need, seek, want** *When you're depressed you need company.* ● *He seeks the company of the older and more sophisticated boys.*

▶ be company for someone **be, keep sb** *Get her a dog. It'll be company for her.* ● *I'll come along to the meeting with you to keep you company.*

3 a group of actors, singers, dancers or soldiers

● adj+N travelling **touring** *The players were drawn from professional touring companies.*

▸ small/large **large, small** *They run one of the most exciting small opera companies in the country.*

● n+N types of company **ballet, dance, repertory, theatre** *The festival will feature 600 theatre companies from all over the world.*

● N+of entertainers **actors, dancers, performers, singers** *A superbly versatile company of eleven actors brought both plays to life.*

▸ soldiers **infantry, soldiers** *A company of infantry was stationed there.*

comparative ADJ

1 judged in comparison to something else

● ADJ+n benefit **advantage** *Factors which produced a comparative advantage in one period can disappear in the next.*

▸ the fact of being easy **ease** *The problem was then solved with comparative ease.*

▸ state of being uncommon or not well known **insignificance, obscurity, rarity** *Today, black and white film is a comparative rarity.*

2 involving the comparison of two or more things

● ADJ+n study **analysis, approach, assessment, evaluation, examination, overview, research, study, survey, test, trial** *The article provides a comparative study of the subject.*

▸ fields of study **anatomy, etc, law, linguistics, philology, politics, religion** *The observation sparked widespread fascination with comparative philology.*

▸ information **information** *The website provides comparative information on a hundred models of car.*

compare V

consider how things or people are similar

● adv+V well **favourably, well** *This compares favourably with the rates in other countries.*

▸ badly **badly, poorly, unfavourably** *Our teaching laboratories compare very unfavourably with those found abroad.*

▸ directly **directly** *Here we directly compare those two possibilities.*

▸ carefully **carefully, systematically** *The data was qualitatively analysed and systematically compared.*

● V+n prices **cost, prices, quotes, rates, savings** *You can't weigh up house values the way you compare petrol prices.*

▸ results **findings, notes, results** *Points are a way of comparing results.*

▸ performance **effectiveness, efficacy, performance** *We want computers to support children's curiosity, not compare their performance.*

▸ data **data, figures** *We will get a clearer picture comparing energy data for June with May.*

● n+V **article, paper, report, study, trial** *The study compares the progress of heart patients undergoing angioplasty.*

● and/or consider differences **contrast** *I tested this hypothesis by comparing and contrasting them with the originals.*

▸ discuss **analyse, assess, describe, discuss, evaluate, examine** *Analyse and compare two print advertisements for similar products.*

comparison N

the process of considering how things or people are similar or different

● adj+N good/bad **favourable, unfavourable, unflattering** *Some of the unfavourable comparisons do not stand up to close examination.*

▸ fair **accurate, apt, fair, meaningful, valid** *We do not believe that this comparison is valid.*

▸ unfair **unfair** *The comparison is unfair: the companies are at different points in their life cycles.*

▸ useful **interesting, useful** *This will provide you with a useful comparison if you decide to employ a builder.*

▸ direct/indirect **direct, indirect, simple** *These are two different platforms, so a direct comparison is difficult.*

▸ detailed **detailed, systematic** *They provide a detailed comparison of the two systems.*

▸ using numbers **quantitative, statistical** *A statistical comparison has been conducted using three years of data.*

▸ based on facts **impartial, objective** *He made objective comparisons of the brightness of stars.*

● v+N make a comparison **do, draw, make, perform, undertake** *The article draws comparisons between this survey and one conducted in 1985.*

▸ allow comparison **allow, enable, facilitate, permit** *It incorporates features allowing comparison of previous versions.*

▸ invite comparison **invite** *The history of those times contains elements that invite comparison with Arthurian romance.*

If something is as good as something else, you can say that it can **bear/stand comparison** with it: *This is a hotel that can bear comparison with the best in the world.* If two things are not similar, you can say that the first **bears no comparison with** the second: *The language of the playground bears no comparison with the language of books.*

▸ provide a comparison **include, involve, provide, show** *Both studies provide a comparison of student performance at a particular moment.*

● v+in+N **fade, pale, suffer** *The first track pales in comparison with the others.*

compassion N

sympathy

● adj+N great **deep, great, immense, profound** *Anger directed toward persons who display great compassion is destructive.*

▸ real **genuine, heartfelt, real, sincere** *Her face seemed full of genuine compassion.*

▸ natural **human, natural** *It is an exquisitely crafted, touching tale of human compassion.*

● v+N show compassion **demonstrate, display, exhibit, express, show** *Does a person need to be religious to show compassion?*

▸ feel compassion **be filled with, feel, have** *You could not help but feel compassion for the victim.*

▸ lack compassion **lack** *No one will ever accuse you of lacking human compassion.*

▸ make someone feel compassion **arouse, excite** *He did not look sufficiently ill to excite our compassion.*

● n+of+N **act, feeling, lack, sense** *She also has a strongly developed sense of compassion for others.*

- and/or kindness **empathy, forgiveness, generosity, kindness, love, mercy, pity, respect** *This requires front-line staff who can demonstrate kindness and compassion.*
- ▶ good judgment **justice, understanding, wisdom** *Wisdom, compassion, and fairness have become the poor relations of electoral expediency.*

compassionate ADJ
feeling sympathy for someone in a bad situation

- adv+ADJ **deeply, profoundly, very, wonderfully** *She seems to have been a wonderfully compassionate woman.*
- ADJ+n reasons **circumstances, grounds, reasons** *We are appealing to him to give her leave to remain here on compassionate grounds.*
- ▶ behaviour or attitude **approach, attitude, manner, response** *Ensure that all persons are dealt with in a caring and compassionate manner.*

- and/or caring **caring, forgiving, generous, gentle, gracious, humane, loving, merciful, sensitive** *He was a brilliant doctor and a caring and compassionate person.*
- ▶ intelligent **considerate, intelligent, just, thoughtful, wise** *You are compassionate and intelligent; you want to do the right thing.*

compelling ADJ
1 very interesting or exciting

- adv+ADJ very **extremely, particularly, so** INFORMAL, **totally, truly, utterly, very** *I found the whole novel utterly compelling.*
- ▶ rather **pretty** INFORMAL, **quite** *That idea of a romantic, glamorous past is quite compelling.*
- ▶ equally **equally** *Her new movie is equally compelling.*
- ▶ in a strange way **oddly, strangely, weirdly** *It's a simple but strangely compelling story about the loss of a parent.*
- ▶ in a particular way **emotionally, intuitively, morally, visually** *Users can explore the museum in a virtual reality that is visually compelling.*

- ADJ+n something written **account, content, narrative, novel, read, reading, story, storyline, tale** *It's a compelling read that you will enjoy from start to finish.*
- ▶ something performed **drama, performance, viewing** *This documentary is compelling viewing.*

2 able to persuade

- adv+ADJ **equally, extremely, logically, particularly, sufficiently** *He produced equally compelling evidence that proved the contrary.*
- ADJ+n **argument, case, evidence, justification, logic, proposition, reason** *There is no compelling reason why this case should go to court.*

- and/or **cogent, coherent, convincing, persuasive** *He presents compelling and convincing evidence that hospitals are failing patients in many respects.*

compensate V
1 change or remove the bad result of something

- adv+V completely **amply, fully** *The weather was awful, but this was more than fully compensated for by the main event.*

- ▶ more than completely **more than** *The tiring day was more than compensated for by the fantastic scenery and sunset.*
- ▶ enough **adequately, effectively, sufficiently** *Sometimes the body cannot compensate adequately.*
- ▶ partly **hardly, partially, partly** *You get a large bedroom, which partly compensates for the lack of storage space.*
- ▶ automatically **automatically** *This system automatically compensates for any change in water pressure.*

- V+for+n low quality or quantity **absence, deficiency, disadvantage, inadequacy, lack, loss, shortcomings, shortfall, weakness** *Quality often compensates for the lack of quantity.*
- ▶ difference **change, difference, distortion, variation** *The machine compensates automatically for the variation in loading position.*
- ▶ fact **fact** *This is to compensate for the fact that there is only one sitting of the examination.*

2 pay someone money for injury or loss

- adv+V completely **fully, in full** *They will fully compensate you if any costs are incurred.*
- ▶ more than the minimum **amply, generously, handsomely** *The class-fee system amply compensated professors with large classes.*
- ▶ enough **adequately, sufficiently** *The agreement ensures that you are adequately compensated for the termination of your employment.*
- ▶ partly **inadequately, partially, partly** *They later partially compensated the complainant for the mistake.*
- ▶ fairly **appropriately, fairly, properly** *You should be compensated fairly for your injuries.*
- ▶ with money **financially** *Senior staff are financially compensated for their lack of job security.*

- V+for+n **damage, injury, loss** *All workers will be compensated for their actual losses.*

compensation N
money that someone receives because something bad has happened to them

- adj+N financial **financial, monetary** *Discrimination is likely to require financial compensation.*
- ▶ that must be paid **due, payable** *Parliament ruled that no compensation was due to investors.*
- ▶ of a large amount **ample, full, maximum, substantial** *The maximum compensation payable is £50.00.*
- ▶ of a reasonable amount **adequate, appropriate, fair, proper, reasonable** *I will continue to fight for full and fair compensation.*

- v+N have the right to compensation **be eligible for, be entitled to, qualify for** *Most of the employees have less than 2 years' service and so are not entitled to compensation.*
- ▶ ask for compensation **apply for, ask for, claim, demand, seek, sue for** *He decided to seek compensation from the holiday company.*

> You say that you are claiming etc a certain amount *in compensation*: *The company demanded $6 million in compensation from the government.*

- ▶ give compensation **agree, award, offer, pay,**

promise, provide *If we cause damage to your vehicle, we will pay reasonable compensation.*

▶ receive compensation **gain, get, obtain, receive, secure, win** *Can I get compensation if I suffer an injury at work?*

● N+n request **claim** *She is making a compensation claim against the company for loss of earnings.*

▶ payment **agreement, award, package, payment, payout, settlement** *The firm has agreed to a compensation package for the victims' families.*

● N+for **accident, damage, discrimination, dismissal, inconvenience, injury, loss, negligence** *Compensation for medical negligence was paid on 1 February last year.*

competence N
the ability to do something well

● adj+N **clinical, communicative, financial, intellectual, linguistic, managerial, organizational, professional, technical** *The team demonstrates a high level of professional competence.*

● v+N develop competence **achieve, acquire, attain, develop, gain, maintain** *The purpose of practice and training is to develop competence.*

▶ show competence **demonstrate, prove, show** *The training programmes allows candidates to demonstrate competence in all areas of ICT skills.*

▶ measure competence **assess, define, evaluate, measure** *There is no magic formula for assessing competence.*

● N+in **area, domain, field, sphere, subject** *Doctors must prove their continuing competence in all clinical areas.*

● and/or **ability, commitment, confidence, experience, expertise, knowledge, skill, understanding** *This course will enable students to develop the knowledge, competence and confidence necessary to perform the tasks effectively.*

competent ADJ
able to do something well

● adv+ADJ very **extremely, fully, highly, thoroughly, very** *Employers want to be sure that their staff are fully competent to deal with their work.*

If you say that someone is *perfectly competent*, you are usually implying that they are good enough but not outstanding: *Every aspect of her work is perfectly competent but that's not necessarily enough.*

▶ fairly **fairly, moderately, reasonably, sufficiently, suitably** *A reasonably competent accountant should easily be able to do this.*

▶ in a specialized way **clinically, culturally, mentally, occupationally, professionally, technically, technologically** *Any technically competent web designer can set this up for you.*

● v+ADJ be **be, become, prove, seem** *Too many drivers on our roads do not seem competent enough.*

▶ judge someone to be **consider sb, deem sb, judge sb** *In order to graduate, students must be deemed competent in a range of areas.*

● ADJ+in **area, discipline, field, matter, role** *It often takes years of hard work to become competent in a particular chosen field.*

competing ADJ
in competition with each other, so that all cannot be true or dealt with in an equal way

● ADJ+n theories **hypotheses, perspectives, theories, views** *In the area of learning styles, many competing theories have been put forward.*

▶ claims **claims, demands, interests, pressures, priorities** *We have to divide our time between the competing demands of work and family.*

competition N
1 when a company or a person is trying to be more successful or better than others

● adj+N strong **cut-throat, fierce, intense, keen, serious, stiff, strong, tough** *The industry faces increasingly tough competition from overseas for the contract.*

▶ fair/unfair **fair, unfair** *We need to encourage fair trade and fair competition between the various suppliers.*

▶ from a particular place **domestic, European, global, international, local** *Taylor fought well against some tough international competition.*

● v+N face competition **be up against, face** *We'll be up against some very tough competition in the finals.*

▶ prevent others from winning **beat off, see off** *The nine-year-old beat off stiff competition from 25 other entrants.*

▶ encourage competition **create, encourage, foster, promote, stimulate** *We're all about promoting serious competition to keep prices low.*

▶ restrict competition **limit, restrict, stifle** *Monopoly is never good because it stifles competition.*

● N+v **heat up, hot up, intensify** *Competition is intensifying as customers demand more online services.*

2 an event when people try to win prizes

● v+N organize a competition **have, hold, organize, run** *A school competition was held to design a poster for the event.*

▶ take part in a competition **be in, compete in, enter, participate in, take part in** *Read the details here and enter the competition today!*

▶ win a competition **win** *The junior boys' teams all won their competitions.*

▶ leave a competition **be banned from, be disqualified from, be eliminated from, retire from, withdraw from** *You will be disqualified from the competition if you break any of these rules.*

▶ judge a competition **judge** *The competition was judged by professional wildlife photographer Michael Leach.*

competitive ADJ
trying to be more successful than others, for example by doing better work or charging lower prices

● adv+ADJ very **exceptionally, extremely, ferociously, fiercely, highly, hugely, incredibly, intensely, so** INFORMAL, **very** *We offer a wide range of services at exceptionally competitive prices.* ● *They are preparing for the intensely competitive university entrance exams.*

▶ in a particular way **commercially, economically**

This service is available at a commercially competitive rate.

▸ in a particular area **globally, internationally** *The Science Faculty undertakes internationally competitive work.*

● ADJ+n advantage **advantage, edge** *These new developments are allowing businesses to gain a competitive advantage.*

▸ price **fee, price, pricing, quote, rate** *The company is known for its quality products and competitive pricing.*

▸ pay **package, rate of pay, salary** *We offer very competitive rates of pay.*

▸ situation or area of work **business, environment, field, industry, marketplace, sector** *The book's aim is to provide information for unsigned bands, helping them get a foot in the door of the highly competitive music industry.*

● v+ADJ **be, become, remain, stay** *These industries must constantly develop new products to stay competitive.*

competitor N

a company that sells the same goods or services as another

● adj+N important **biggest, chief, larger, leading, main, major, serious** *Many of our larger competitors have now gone out of business.*

▸ from another country **foreign, global, international, overseas** *Compare our prices with those of our international competitors!*

▸ very similar **closest, direct, nearest** *The firm is now twice the size of its nearest competitor.*

● v+N be better than a competitor **outperform, outsell, outstrip, overtake, undercut** *We have just succeeded in overtaking our closest competitor.*

▸ start buying from a competitor **switch to** *Poor service is the main reason why customers switch to competitors.*

compile V

make something by bringing together information from different places

● adv+V with care **carefully, lovingly, painstakingly, specially** *This collection of short stories has been specially compiled for young readers.*

▸ without care **hastily** *Their figures were hastily compiled from informal reports.*

> **Usage** *Compile* is usually passive in both of the *adv+V* combinations shown above: *This book of poems is lovingly compiled by teachers and their pupils.*

● V+n list **bibliography, database, index, list, register** *We have compiled a list of useful websites to help you with your studies.*

▸ report **document, dossier, report, statistics** *They are also responsible for compiling management reports.*

▸ published book **anthology, dictionary, publication** *She is currently compiling an anthology of West Indian poetry.*

● V+from several different documents **a number of, a variety of** *The content of the site has been compiled from a variety of sources.*

▸ types of document **documents, records, reports, sources, surveys** *This report has been compiled from various sources.*

> **Usage** *Compile* is usually passive in both of the *V+from* combinations shown above.

complacent ADJ

too confident about how easy something is to deal with

● adv+ADJ very **astonishingly, dangerously, too** *Some candidates are too complacent, and are not doing the necessary preparation.*

▸ rather **a little, rather, somewhat** *I thought his attitude towards the risks of the plan was somewhat complacent.*

● ADJ+n **assumption, attitude, belief** *He said that he was amazed at the complacent attitude to work-place stress in some companies.*

● v+ADJ **appear, become, feel, get, grow, remain, seem** *People are becoming complacent about the potential risks to public health.*

complain V

say you are dissatisfied with something

● adv+V strongly **bitterly, loudly, vociferously** *Customers are complaining vociferously about the quality of the service.*

▸ often **constantly, frequently, often, regularly, repeatedly** *Children frequently complain of boredom on long journeys.*

▸ not often or not much **rarely** *They rarely complained about their heavy workload.*

▸ in a public way **formally, publicly** *The club formally complained to the Football Association.*

> When there is no reason to complain you can say that someone **cannot** or **can hardly complain**: *The solution was my suggestion so I can hardly complain when it didn't work.*

complaint N

1 a statement that you are dissatisfied with something

● adj+N official **formal, official, written** *If the staff are not able to help, the next step is to make a formal complaint.*

▸ based on good reasons **justified, legitimate, well-founded** *The Government did not accept that the complaints from the public were well-founded.*

> If someone has **grounds for complaint** or **cause for complaint**, they have good reasons for complaining.

▸ not very important **minor** *In the case of minor complaints, please speak to a member of staff.*

▸ important **serious** *Any serious complaints should be investigated without delay.*

● v+N make a complaint **file, lodge, make, register, submit, voice** *If you are still not satisfied, you can register an official complaint about the treatment you received.*

▸ deal with a complaint **address, consider, deal with, handle, investigate, log, resolve** *The committee will handle any complaints of discrimination.*

▸ accept that a complaint is reasonable **uphold** *The*

Complaints Committee did not uphold the complaint against the police officer.

▶ refuse to accept a complaint **dismiss, reject** *The reviewer rejected a complaint that the ad was offensive.*

● N+n **mechanism, policy, procedure, process, system** *We have published our complaints procedure on our website.*

> Usage **Complaint** is always plural in these **N+n** combinations: *The council has established a complaints policy. Please click here for further details.*

2 an illness or other medical problem

● adj+N **common, minor** *We can offer advice on common complaints such as coughs and colds.*

● n+N **bowel, chest, heart, kidney, liver, lung, skin, stomach** *She was ill with a stomach complaint.*

● v+N **suffer from** *He's suffering from a chest complaint.*

complete V

1 finish something

● adv+V **on schedule, satisfactorily, successfully** *Postgraduates are students who have successfully completed a first degree.*

● V+n studies **course, degree, diploma, internship, module, PhD, programme, studies, training** *Most students complete the course in one year.*

▶ task **coursework, dissertation, exercise, homework, job, process, project, report, review, study, task, work** *This project was completed early in 2009.*

2 provide the necessary information in an official document

● adv+V **correctly** *We have simplified the form, so it is easier to complete correctly.*

● V+n **application, detail, documentation, form, paperwork, questionnaire, section, survey, worksheet** *Just complete our short online application.*

complete ADJ

1 including everything that is needed, with nothing missing

● ADJ+n **collection, documentation, dsecription, list, package, range, record, sequence, set** *The publication contains a complete record of parliamentary debates in the 18th century.*

● and/or **accurate, authoritative, comprehensive, thorough, up-to-date** *This is a comprehensive and complete on-line cookbook to help prepare any type of meal.*

2 absolute or total – used for emphasis

● ADJ+n something bad or unwanted **collapse, destruction, disaster, disregard, failure, mess, nightmare, nonsense, waste** *No thought had been given to what the aims of the conference were, so it was a complete waste of time and money.*

▶ something positive or good **confidence, freedom, satisfaction, success, support, trust, victory** *Our overall mission is complete customer satisfaction, whatever it takes.*

completion N

the process of finishing an activity or job, or the time when a process is finished

● adj+N **successful satisfactory, successful** *Candidates receive a certificate on satisfactory completion of the course.*

▶ early/late **early, fast, late, timely** *We offer online quotes, fast completion, and competitive rates.*

● v+N plan completion for particular time **expect, plan, schedule** *Construction will start in April with completion scheduled for summer next year.*

▶ when something is expected to be completed **be due for** *The new school buildings are due for completion next year.*

▶ come close to completion **approach, near** *The work is nearing completion.*

▶ achieve completion **achieve, bring sth to, reach** *Of these fifteen projects, eleven will reach completion in March next year*

▶ celebrate completion **celebrate, mark** *We held a party to celebrate completion of the project.*

▶ include completion as a necessary part **include, involve, require** *A PhD requires the completion of an 80,000-word thesis.*

● N+n date **date, day, deadline, time** *The project finished a month ahead of its completion deadline.*

▶ document **certificate, report, statement** *A completion certificate is awarded to all students who attended the course.*

complex ADJ

involving many parts or details and difficult to understand

● adv+ADJ very **extraordinarily, extremely, highly, hugely, immensely, incredibly, particularly, very** *The human brain is an immensely complex organ.*

▶ rather **fairly, quite, rather, relatively, somewhat** *Some methods are fairly complex and others are extremely simple.*

▶ more than necessary **overly, too, unnecessarily** *Some people complained that the process was overly complex.*

● ADJ+n system **arrangement, mechanism, network, process, structure, system** *The climate system is very complex, and understanding it is difficult.*

▶ situation **case, environment, issue, matter, problem, situation** *We can provide advice and guide you through more complex issues.*

▶ task **challenge, operation, project, task** *Most tasks are fairly complex, and they all require a high level of expertise.*

▶ subject **area, phenomenon, subject** *This is a complex area, and we cannot guarantee total accuracy.*

● and/or **challenging, confusing, contradictory, costly, difficult, expensive, subtle, time-consuming, varied** *This project has been a complex and challenging one for the organization.*

complexion N

the appearance of the skin on a person's face

● adj+N light **fair, light, pale, white** *She has a light complexion, brown eyes and long brown wavy hair.*

▸ dark **dark, olive, swarthy** *He was so handsome with his dark hair, dark eyes, and olive complexion.*

▸ red **ruddy** *Bob is heavily built, with a ruddy complexion.*

▸ without marks **clear, flawless, good, perfect, smooth** *The key to a perfect complexion lies in what you eat.*

▸ healthy **fresh, glowing, healthy, radiant** *Each product in the collection is designed to achieve a natural, glowing complexion.*

▸ unhealthy **dull, sallow** *Tiredness, headaches, and a dull complexion are common to sufferers of the condition.*

You can describe someone as being *of* a particular type of *complexion*: *The man was around 45, tall, and of a sallow complexion.*

complexity N
the complicated nature of something

● adj+N great **considerable, enormous, great, high, incredible, real, sheer** *There may be considerable complexity lying behind a seemingly simple statement.*

▸ relating to a particular subject **administrative, computational, legal, logistical, political, psychological, social, structural, technical** *We can give advice in cases involving a high level of legal complexity.*

▸ extra **added, additional, extra, unnecessary** *This method could result in unnecessary administrative complexities.*

▸ becoming greater **growing, increasing** *The report deals with the increasing complexity of crime that the country is facing.*

● v+N understand the complexity of something **appreciate, grasp, recognize, understand** *Most people do not appreciate the complexity of the problem.*

▸ show the complexity of something **demonstrate, explain, highlight, illustrate, reflect, reveal, show** *This chapter highlights the complexity of the process.*

▸ deal with the complexity of something **be faced with, deal with, engage with, grapple with, struggle with** *People do not have the time to engage with the complexity of these issues.*

▸ not understand the complexity of something **underestimate** *Politicians have consistently underestimated the complexity of this issue.*

● N+of situation **case, issue, problem, situation** *Our fees vary according to the length and complexity of the case.*

▸ system **model, operation, process, system** *People often avoid claiming due to the complexity of the process.*

▸ task **procedure, project, task, work** *Because of the size and complexity of the project, we will need to employ extra staff.*

● n+of+N degree, level, measure, scale *Spoken English reaches degrees of complexity that are rarely attained in writing.*

complicated ADJ
difficult to deal with or understand, or consisting of many different parts

● adv+ADJ very **extremely, fiendishly, highly, horrendously, hugely, immensely, incredibly, particularly, really, very** *This immensely complicated process is only partially understood.*

▸ rather **fairly, pretty** INFORMAL**, quite, rather, relatively, somewhat** *The design looks quite complicated, but it's actually very simple.*

▸ too **impossibly, needlessly, overly, too, unnecessarily** *The rules are unnecessarily complicated and difficult to understand.*

● ADJ+n system **procedure, process, rules, system** *He uses simple sketches to explain complicated processes.*

▸ situation **affair, business, case, issue, matter, problem, question, situation, things** *In reality, things are slightly more complicated.*

▸ subject **area, subject** *This is a complicated subject, and it deserves a thorough explanation.*

▸ set of lines, shapes or colours **arrangement, design, pattern** *The model of the ancient city shows complicated arrangements of buildings, trees, and gardens.*

▸ story **plot, story** *This is an excellent but quite complicated story.*

▸ calculation **calculation, equation, formula** *It is very easy to make mistakes if you are working with complicated equations.*

● v+ADJ **appear, be, become, get, grow, look, make sth, prove, seem, sound** *The political situation here will become more complicated.* ● *The process of complaining is made unnecessarily complicated.* ● *This matter is proving more complicated than we expected.*

complication N
1 something making a medical condition worse

● adj+N serious **life-threatening, major, serious, severe, significant** *Severe complications are often restricted to children and the elderly.*

▸ common/rare **common, rare** *Common complications include 'burning' of the skin and nausea.*

▸ possible **possible, potential** *What are the possible complications of surgery?*

▸ relating to a particular medical condition **cardiovascular, diabetic, neurological, obstetric, pulmonary** *Pulmonary complications occur in 50% of cases.*

People often talk about the complications *associated with* or *related to* a particular medical condition.

● v+N experience complications **develop, experience, suffer** *Very few people develop serious complications.*

▸ reduce the chance of having complications **avoid, minimize, prevent, reduce** *Early detection and intervention can minimize complications.*

▸ treat complications **deal with, manage, treat** *Our doctors are fully trained to deal with any complications.*

▸ cause complications **cause, create** *Changes in the heart cause the most serious potential complications.*

▸ die because of complications **die from, die of** *She died of complications *from* a heart complaint.*

● N+v **develop, occur** *See a doctor as soon as possible if you suspect that complications are developing.*

2 something that makes a process or activity more difficult

● adj+N extra **added, additional, further** *There is so much choice of phones, with the added complication of whether to buy one with a a camera or not.*
▶ more than necessary **undue, unnecessary** *Lack of planning can cause unnecessary complications for your loved ones at a difficult time.*
● v+N cause complications **bring, cause, create, involve** *The purpose of this report is to examine areas which caused most complication.*
▶ avoid complications **avoid** *This method avoids complications should the memory card become full.*
● N+v arise, ensue, occur *An ex-girlfriend appears, and predictable complications ensue.*

compliment N
a statement or action that expresses praise of someone

● adj+N making you feel pleased and happy **lovely, nice, wonderful** *We have received wonderful compliments from many people on the performance.*
▶ from someone you have great respect for **big, great, huge, tremendous, ultimate** *The fact that people like our music is the ultimate compliment to the band.*
▶ honest **genuine, sincere** *Only give genuine compliments, and don't overdo it.*
▶ seeming to express admiration, but actually doing the opposite **backhanded** *Saying we'd done better than expected was a bit of a backhanded compliment.*
● v+N make a compliment **give sb, make, pay sb** *Parents who pay compliments to their children will encourage them to behave in the same way.*

> You can say that something was **meant** or *intended as a compliment*: *Don't take it the wrong way. That was meant as a compliment!*

▶ receive a compliment **attract, get, receive** *We are lucky to receive many compliments from customers who have experienced excellent service.*
▶ interpret something as a compliment **take sth as** *I'm not quite sure if you meant it, but I'll take that as a compliment!*
▶ give compliments to each other **exchange** *We exchanged compliments on each other's outfits.*

comply V
obey a rule, law, or request

● adv+V in a willing way **happily, readily, voluntarily, willingly** *Many people resist the commands, whilst others comply willingly.*
▶ not in a willing way **reluctantly** *The owner of the dog reluctantly complied with the court order.*
▶ immediately **immediately, promptly** *If member of staff asks you to be quiet, please comply immediately.*
▶ in a suitable way **adequately, duly, fully, properly, satisfactorily** *We fully comply with all aspects of the Data Protection Act 1998.*
● v+to+V fail, refuse *Your employer has failed to comply with the safety regulations.*
● V+with rules **conditions, guidelines, law,**

legislation, protocol, regulations, rules *Failure to comply with the rules can result in a £5,000 fine.*
▶ something that you have to do **demands, directive, instructions, obligation, order, request, requirement** *Our equipment complies with all safety requirements.*
▶ standard **specifications, standard** *These models do not comply with the revelant safety standard.*
▶ idea or set of plans **policy, principle** *Members are required to comply fully with the club's policy.*

component N
an individual part or feature of something

● adj+N important **core, critical, crucial, essential, fundamental, important, integral, key, main, major, principal, vital** *Pictures are a vital component of a newspaper.*
▶ separate **individual, separate** *Try breaking the problem down into its individual components.*
▶ part of a machine **automotive, electrical, electronic, mechanical, structural** *The development of smaller electronic components is the key to success.*

compose V
write a piece of music or text

● V+n music **melody, music, opera, piece, score, song, soundtrack, symphony, tune, work** *The purpose of this workshop is for students to compose a piece to be performed at the Palace Classics concert.*
   ● *Morricone has composed the scores of more than 500 films and TV series.*
▶ text **letter, message, poem, sentence, text, verse** *Select 'Post' from the web menu to compose the message, then click 'send'.*

composition N
the way that something is formed from separate parts or people

● adj+N including everyone or everything **overall** *The overall composition of the patient's diet is relevant for their health.*
▶ exact **actual, exact, precise** *Manufacturers can control the precise composition of the margarine.*
▶ of a particular type **botanical, chemical, ethnic, mineral, molecular, organic, political** *They studied the chemical composition of stream and soil water in the area.*
● v+N have an effect on the composition of something **affect, alter, change, improve, influence** *Our thoughts and emotions affect the chemical composition in our brain.*
▶ find out the composition of something **determine** *One of the concrete blocks was crushed to determine its exact composition.*
● N+of group of people **audience, community, group, membership, population, team, workforce** *Teachers should think carefully about the size and composition of groups when they are planning their lessons.*
▶ group of people who represent others **board, committee, council, government** *Elections influence the composition of governments at all levels.*
▶ food **diet, food** *The series of lectures covers the chemical composition of foods.*

composure N
the feeling of being calm, confident, and relaxed

- ● adj+N great **admirable, complete, great, perfect, remarkable** *The two women showed remarkable composure in a very frightening situation.*
- ▶ calm **calm, cool, quiet** *With calm composure, he stepped towards the edge of the cliff.*
- ● v+N show composure **demonstrate, display, have, show** *David has great composure, and in a year's time he will be an outstanding footballer.*

> You can also say that someone behaves *with composure*.

- ▶ keep your composure **hold, keep, maintain, retain** *Keep your composure and do not lose your temper.*
- ▶ lose your composure **lose** *'Look, Smith,' he shouted, losing his composure for a moment.*
- ▶ get your composure back **gain, gather, recover, regain, restore** *At first she seemed just a bit nervous, but she quickly gained composure.*

compound N
a chemical substance with two or more elements

- ● adj+N chemical **chemical** *This lesson deals with breaking down a chemical compound using heat.*
- ▶ produced from/not produced from a living thing **inorganic, organic** *The rocks contain organic compounds.*
- ▶ existing naturally/made by people **natural, synthetic** *To increase the range of colours, synthetic compounds are added.*
- ▶ simple/consisting of different parts **complex, simple** *Many simple compounds are liquids or gases at room temperature.*
- ▶ changing or affecting something **active, toxic, volatile** *This is a highly toxic compound that is easily absorbed by the body.*
- ● v+N produce a compound **create, develop, form, make, produce, synthesize** *Compounds are formed when elements join together.*
- ▶ recognize a compound **discover, identify, isolate** *Scientists have isolated active compounds with anti-cancer properties.*
- ▶ contain a compound **be composed of, consist of, contain** *The rocks contain organic compounds.*
- ● N+v start to exist or develop **be derived from, be found, form, occur** *Alum is a compound that occurs naturally in warm, wet climates.*
- ▶ behave **act, behave, interact, react** *The tests show how various compounds behave under different conditions.*
- ▶ contain something **be composed of sth, consist of sth, contain sth** *The simplest aromatic compound contains at least six atoms of carbon.*

compound V
make a problem or difficult situation worse

- ● adv+V just, merely, only, simply *Then people stop exercising, which only compounds the problem.*
- ● V+n problem **difficulty, matter, problem, risk, situation** *The matter is compounded when she discovers that she has failed her exams.*
- ▶ negative feeling **confusion, disappointment, fear, feeling, frustration, misery, uncertainty** *His disappointment was compounded by Kate's refusal to speak to him.*
- ▶ something bad that happens **crisis, disaster, drought, shortage, tragedy** *His tragedy was compounded by the fact that his mother died the following day.*

> Usage **Compound** is usually passive in all of the *V+n* combinations shown above: *The disaster was compounded when Brian was made redundant.* ● *The situation is compounded by the lack of a shared language.*

comprehensive ADJ
including many details or aspects of something

- ● adv+ADJ very **extremely, very** *The index is extremely comprehensive.*
- ▶ completely **fully, thoroughly, totally, truly** *This book is thoroughly comprehensive and a joy to read.*
- ▶ fairly **fairly, pretty** INFORMAL**, quite, reasonably, sufficiently** *Your notes should be accurate, well written and fairly comprehensive.*
- ▶ in a way that surprises and impresses **amazingly, extraordinarily, impressively, incredibly, remarkably** *The range of goods they supply is impressively comprehensive.*
- ● ADJ+n description of the features of something **analysis, assessment, coverage, overview, review, survey** *The course offers extremely comprehensive coverage of the subject matter.*
- ▶ collection of items or services **collection, package, portfolio, range, set** *We offer a comprehensive range of flowering garden bulbs.*
- ▶ list **archive, bibliography, database, directory, glossary, index, list, listing** *Follow this link for a comprehensive listing of all the local activities on offer.*
- ▶ book, document etc telling you about a subject **guide, handbook** *This is a comprehensive guide to soul, funk and hip-hop drumming.*

compromise N
an agreement in which both people or groups give up something

- ● adj+N satisfactory **acceptable, good, reasonable, satisfactory, sensible, workable** *We hope that a satisfactory compromise can be found.*
- ▶ not satisfactory **messy, uneasy, unsatisfactory** *After much discussion, a rather uneasy compromise was reached.*
- ▶ necessary **inevitable, necessary** *This is not an ideal world, and a certain amount of compromise is necessary.*
- ● v+N reach a compromise **accept, achieve, agree, arrive at, find, make, negotiate, reach, strike** *It may be possible to negotiate a compromise with local officials.*
- ▶ suggest a compromise **offer, propose, suggest** *A compromise was suggested: each member would have five minutes to give his or her opinion.*
- ▶ be a compromise **be, represent** *Such an approach represents a compromise.*
- ▶ involve a compromise **entail, involve, require** *The outcome will almost certainly involve compromise **between** the two sides.*

compromise v

1 risk harming or losing something important

- adv+V **deeply, fatally, seriously, severely, significantly** *Standards have been seriously compromised by cuts in funding.*

  Usage ***Compromise*** is usually <u>passive</u> in these combinations.

- V+n safety **safety, security, welfare** *Now delete your password, as it may compromise system security.*
- ▶ quality or effectiveness **effectiveness, performance, quality, standards, validity** *Is it possible to make savings without compromising performance?*
- ▶ independence **independence, neutrality** *No such partnership should be allowed to compromise the independence of the research process.*
- ▶ reputation **reputation** *We will not allow anybody to compromise the excellent reputation of our team's fans.*
- V+on quality **quality, standards** *We will never compromise on quality.*
- ▶ safety **safety** *You can't afford to compromise on safety when children are involved.*

2 act against your beliefs or principles

- adv+V **ethically, morally** *Even the good guys were morally compromised by their own need to survive.*
- V+n beliefs **beliefs, ideals, principles** *Laura realized that she could not compromise her principles.*
- ▶ state of not supporting either side in a disagreement, war etc **impartiality, integrity, objectivity, standards** *To act in any other way would compromise your objectivity.*

compulsion N

a strong feeling that you must do something

- adj+N strong **irresistible, overwhelming, strong** *I felt an overwhelming compulsion to open the envelope.*
- ▶ that you do not understand **strange** *The film is nothing special, but you get a strange compulsion to stay with it to the end.*
- ▶ personal **inner** *I've had an inner compulsion to paint since I was fifteen.*
- v+N feel a compulsion **feel, get, have** *I felt a strong compulsion to laugh.*
- ▶ resist a compulsion **overcome, resist** *Try to resist the compulsion to finish everything on your plate.*
- n+of+N amount **degree, element** *It is important that there is some degree of compulsion on managers to succeed.*
- ▶ feeling **sense** *You may feel a strong sense of compulsion to fall asleep.*

computer N

a machine that stores and processes information in electronic form

- adj+N powerful **fast, powerful** *You need a fast computer to enjoy this game.*
- ▶ connected to the Internet **connected, Internet-connected, Internet-enabled, wireless** *Ensure that Internet-connected computers are equipped with anti-virus software.*
- ▶ designed to be used in the home or office **desktop, home, personal** *Children with access to a home computer do better at school.*
- ▶ with special features **multimedia, touch-screen** *Touch-screen computers enhance the visitor experience.*
- ▶ small and portable **handheld, laptop, netbook, palmtop, portable** *Increasingly, the division between mobile devices and handheld computers is being blurred.*
- v+N start a computer **boot up, log onto, reboot, restart, start up, switch on, switch on** *At the end of the installation you have to restart your computer.*
- ▶ stop using a computer **log off, shut down, switch off** *Always be sure to shut down your computer properly at the end of the day.*
- ▶ use a computer **access, operate, run, use** *Children can touch the screen to operate the computer.*

  When someone is using a computer, you can say that they are doing something ***on a/the computer***: *For most of the lesson the children were working on the computer.*

- ▶ connect computers **connect, link, network** *All students are provided with a networked personal computer.*
- ▶ prepare a computer **configure, program** *We supply, install, and configure computers.*
- ▶ infect/protect a computer **infect, protect** *This virus could infect your computer and cause it to malfunction.*
- ▶ buy a more modern computer **upgrade** *I can't afford to upgrade my computer.*
- N+v work **process, run, work** *I have a new hard drive and my computer is running really well now.*
- ▶ stop working **be down, crash, freeze, go down** *Please could you call back later? All our computers are down.*

conceal v

prevent someone knowing your feelings or information

- adv+V almost not **barely, scarcely** *When she saw Connor, Amy could scarcely conceal her delight.*
- ▶ in a way that works well **effectively, successfully** *How did he manage to conceal his crime so successfully?*
- ▶ in a careful or clever way **carefully, cleverly, deliberately** *This fact was carefully concealed from the public.*
- V+n emotion **contempt, delight, disappointment, emotion, feeling** *'Never mind,' said Anna, concealing her disappointment.*
- ▶ information **evidence, fact, identity, secret, truth** *By shining his torch in their eyes, he was able to conceal his identity.*

concede v

1 admit that something is true

- adv+V willingly **freely, readily, willingly** *He readily concedes that he's not a great singer.*
- ▶ unwillingly **eventually, grudgingly, reluctantly** *They grudgingly conceded that she had not actually broken the law.*

- v+to+V be forced, be reluctant, be unwilling, refuse *He still refuses to concede that what he did was wrong.*

2 stop trying to win something

- adv+V after trying hard to win **eventually, finally, reluctantly** *It was a strong performance, but she eventually had to concede to her rival.*
- ▸ showing good manners **graciously** *He came third, graciously conceding to his fellow team member, Alex.*
- V+n **defeat** *The England team finally had to concede defeat.*
- v+to+V be forced, be reluctant, be unwilling, refuse *Real success never came, and he was forced to concede defeat.*

conceivable ADJ
possible, or possible to imagine

- adv+ADJ almost not **barely, hardly, just, scarcely** *It seems scarcely conceivable that they behaved so badly.*
- ▸ completely **certainly, easily, entirely, perfectly, quite** *It's quite conceivable that a profitable business can be operated successfully by one person.*
- ADJ+n aspect **angle, aspect** *We explore the subject from every conceivable angle.*
- ▸ situation **circumstance, eventuality, occasion, scenario, situation** *Remember: you don't need insurance for every conceivable eventuality.*
- ▸ type **genre, kind, type** *The market is crammed with stalls selling every conceivable type of fish.*
- ▸ subject **subject, topic** *There are blogs covering every conceivable subject, from pets to politics.*

> Usage ***Conceivable*** is almost always preceded by every in all of the ***ADJ+n*** combinations shown above.

conceive V
to imagine or think of something

- adv+V first **first, initially, originally** *The project was originally conceived in 2006.*
- ▸ well **beautifully, brilliantly, carefully, well** *This computer game is well thought out and brilliantly conceived.*
- ▸ not well **poorly** *This film was poorly conceived and poorly directed.*
- V+n idea **concept, idea, notion** *It was in the summer of 2008 that I conceived the idea for this book.*
- ▸ plan **plan, project, scheme** *Their project was conceived as a way to raise money for new equipment.*

concentrate V
1 give all your attention to what you are doing

- adv+V **fully, hard, intensely, intently, properly** *Andrew closed his eyes and concentrated hard.*
- V+on **job, task, work** *I can't really concentrate on my work at present.*

2 give most of your attention to one aim or activity

- adv+V only **entirely, exclusively, only, purely, solely** *In the years that followed, Wegener concentrated solely on his acting career.*

- mainly **largely, mainly, mostly, primarily** *The course concentrates mainly on Britain.*
- V+on activity **activities, business, career, painting, schoolwork, subject, teaching, work, writing** *She gave up teaching in order to concentrate on her writing.*
- ▸ subject **area, issue, matter, subject, theme, topic** *Tthis article will concentrate on an important issue – human rights.*

concentration N
1 giving all your attention to something

- adj+N
- adj+N great **absolute, complete, deep, great, intense, total, utter** *June had a look of deep concentration on her face.*
- ▸ good/bad **good, poor** *One of the most common signs of stress is poor concentration.*
- v+N make concentration better/worse **affect, impair, improve** *A healthy diet can improve concentration.*
- v+N lose concentration **lose** *When carrying passengers, the driver is more likely to be distracted and lose concentration.*
- ▸ need concentration **demand, need, require, take** *It is also a work that demands intense concentration from the audience.*
- ▸ keep concentration **keep, maintain** *It must be very difficult to maintain concentration.*

2 a large number or amount in one area

- adj+N **great, large** *The cliffs are home to some of the greatest concentrations of seabirds in the North Atlantic.*

concept N
an idea of something that exists

- adj+N important **basic, core, fundamental, key** *The book provides students with the basic concepts of economics.*
- ▸ types of concept **abstract, mathematical, philosophical, sociological, theoretical** *As an abstract concept, the notion of time may be difficult for children to grasp.*
- ▸ easy to understand **simple** *Risk Assessment is a simple concept which sounds complicated.*
- ▸ new **innovative, new, original** *I am interested in the ways in which students make sense of new concepts.*
- v+N understand a concept **grasp, understand** *The youngster grasped the concept quickly.*
- ▸ talk or write about a concept **clarify, define, discuss, examine, explain, explore, illustrate, introduce** *Use visual aids and diagrams tol help you to introduce difficult concepts.*

concern N
1 a feeling of worry

- adj+N great **considerable, deep, grave, great, serious** *This is a development that causes grave concern in the Pentagon.*
- ▸ especially great **paramount, particular, special** *However, at the year end there remained two areas of particular concern.*

▸ real **genuine, legitimate, real** *There were grounds for legitimate concern* .

▸ felt by many people **common, general, public, widespread** *There has been widespread concern about the proposals.*

▸ growing, increasing, mounting *However, growing concern focuses on India and China, which currently have 4 million and 1.5 million cases respectively.*

● v+N express concern **articulate, express, voice** *They expressed some concern **about** the rate of progress being made.*

● v+N cause concern **arouse, cause, give rise to, heighten, increase** *Gangs of youths roaming the streets were causing some concern.*

2 something that worries you

● adj+N serious **deep, grave, serious** *We have serious concerns **over** a number of issues.*

▸ main **main, major, overriding, paramount, particular, primary, prime** *The government's main concern is the fact that the current situation is damaging its relations with Spain.*

▸ real **genuine, legitimate, real** *The US government doubtless had genuine concerns **about** weapons of mass destruction.*

▸ needing to be dealt with immediately **immediate, pressing, urgent** *This assumption raises two immediate concerns in my mind, one very obvious the other perhaps not.*

▸ about a particular thing **environmental, ethical, humanitarian** *She believed there were serious environmental concerns.*

● n+N **crime, health, privacy, safety, security** *Spain's oldest nuclear power station was finally closed yesterday following serious safety concerns at the plant.*

● v+N express a concern **air, articulate, echo, express, highlight, outline, raise, reiterate, voice** *The purpose of the meetings is to give local people an opportunity to voice their concerns.*

▸ make a concern seem less serious **allay, alleviate, assuage** *There are social, political and economic issues which need to be addressed to allay concerns **about** inequality.*

3 something you think important

● adj+N **main, major, overriding, paramount, primary, prime** *Remember they are businesses and their main concern is to make money.*

concert N
an event with musical performances for an audience

● adj+N **carol, chamber, chamber music, choral, classical, jazz, orchestral, pop, rock, symphony** *This will be the first rock concert to be held at the new stadium.*

● v+N go to a concert **attend, go to** *I try to attend concerts as often as I can.*

▸ be a performer at a concert **conduct, give, headline, perform, perform at, play, play at** *The choir performs about 13 concerts a year.*

▸ organize a concert **arrange, have, hold, organize, present, promote, put on, sponsor, stage** *The*

concert was staged in a theatre in downtown Los Angeles.

▸ say that a concert will not take place **cancel** *The Rolling Stones were forced to cancel a concert in Spain last night.*

● N+n goer, **hall, performance, platform, programme, promoter, ticket, tour, venue** *He was a frequent concert goer.*

concession N
something given to someone to get an agreement

● adj+N minor **minor, modest, slight, small** *The Committee was not satisfied with those minor concessions.*

▸ major **generous, important, large, major, significant, substantial** *Negotiators feel they have gained major concessions.*

● v+N give someone a concession **allow, extend, give, grant, make, offer** *He is not prepared to make any concessions.*

● v+N get a concession from someone **extract, force, gain, get, negotiate, obtain, receive, secure, win, wrest from sb, wring from sb** *We have been able to win some important concessions through careful negotiations with the government.*

conclude V
1 end

● n+V **article, chapter, paper, report, study** *The report concludes with a discussion of key themes of the analysis.*

● V+with **chapter, discussion, examination, observation, overview, recommendation, reflection, remark, suggestion, summary, words** *The review concluded with recommendations for all levels of government.*

2 end something

● V+n **chapter, discussion, section, speech, talk** *Each chapter is concluded **with** a summary detailing the key points arising from it.*

3 officially make a deal, agreement etc

● V+n **agreement, alliance, armistice, deal, pact, peace, transaction, treaty** *We are delighted to have concluded this important agreement.*

conclusion N
1 something you decide is true

● adj+N correct **correct, logical, obvious, right, valid** *We are delighted that the jury came to the right conclusion.*

▸ incorrect **erroneous, false, hasty, incorrect, wrong** *The report is flawed, its analysis weak, its conclusions wrong.*

If someone reaches the wrong conclusion by not thinking carefully enough, you can say they are ***jumping to conclusions***: *We must be careful not to jump to conclusions.*

▸ definite **clear, definite, firm, inescapable, obvious, robust** *Caution is necessary in drawing definite conclusions from this data.*

▸ not definite **possible, preliminary, provisional,**

tentative *Let us see what provisional conclusions can be drawn at this point in the argument.*

▶ describing your opinion of a conclusion **interesting, significant, startling, surprising, unexpected** *His review of the evidence leads him to quite startling conclusions that will change the character of the current debate.*

● v+N reach a conclusion **arrive at, come to, derive, draw, reach** *In the end, we came to the conclusion that it would be quicker to go by train.* ● *Traditional philosophy derives conclusions about the purpose of life from reflections on the nature of the world.*

> When you are explaining your conclusions, you can also say *in conclusion* or *to conclude*: *To conclude, further work is required if we are to come to a fuller understanding of the importance of this unique site.*

▶ when facts support a conclusion **confirm, justify, lend support to, reinforce, substantiate, support** *This lends support to the conclusions of a recent discussion (White 2006) of the factors contributing to the rise in street crime.*

> You can also say that someone's *conclusion is based on* particular facts: *This conclusion was based on data collected from more than 1,500 monitoring sites around the world.*

2 the ending of something

● adj+N **satisfactory, satisfying, successful** *I regard this as a satisfactory conclusion to the whole investigation.*

● v+N **build to, draw to, near, reach** *The peace negotiations appear to be nearing a conclusion.*

> You can also say that something *leads to* or *results in a conclusion*, or that it *brings* something *to a conclusion*: *He eventually agreed to meet the railway unions, resulting in a successful conclusion to the dispute.* ● *This victory brings to a conclusion a memorable season for the Lions.*

conclusive ADJ
proving something is true

● adv+ADJ rather **fairly, pretty** INFORMAL, **quite** *Hume's argument seems fairly conclusive.*

▶ very **absolutely, completely, entirely, very** *'It's not absolutely conclusive,' says Brown.*

▶ not very **by no means, far from, hardly** *The results are by no means conclusive.*

● ADJ+n **answer, argument, data, evidence, findings, proof, research, result, test** *The findings from these studies do not provide conclusive evidence.*

concur V
agree with someone or something

● adv+V **completely, entirely, fully, heartily, readily, strongly, totally, wholeheartedly** *Councillor McMenamin stated that he concurred wholeheartedly with the views expressed by Councillor Barr.*

● V+with **assessment, comment, conclusion, decision, finding, opinion, recommendation, remark, sentiment, statement, suggestion, view** *The Chairman concurred with these sentiments.*

concussion N
a head injury that makes someone unconscious or confused

● adj+N not serious **mild, minor, slight** *He has missed training this week after being diagnosed with mild concussion by club doctors.*

▶ **bad, serious, severe** *Joe was hospitalized with a severe concussion.*

● v+N **get, have, suffer, suffer from, sustain** *He suffered concussion after his head shattered the windscreen of the car.*

condemn V
criticize someone or something publicly

● adv+V very much **categorically, loudly, outright, roundly, strongly, totally, unequivocally, unreservedly, utterly, vehemently, vigorously, wholeheartedly** *Environmental groups have roundly condemned the scheme.*

▶ by everyone **unanimously, universally** *The 1990 Iraqi invasion of Kuwait was almost universally condemned.*

▶ by many people **widely** *The policy was widely condemned in Britain.*

▶ publicly **openly, publicly** *Neither the Prime Minister nor any politician has publicly condemned the murder.*

▶ for a good reason **justly, rightly** *The proposal was rightly condemned by charities and trade unions.*

● V+n a violent action **act, action, atrocity, attack, bombing, killing, murder, terrorism, violence** *All church leaders have condemned the attacks.*

▶ a bad or wrong action **act, action, move, practice** *The committee also condemned moves to cut the agency's staff by 25%.*

▶ a plan or decision **decision, plan, proposal, scheme** *A senior Labour MP today joined health groups in condemning the Government's decision to delay the Bill to ban tobacco advertising.*

condemnation N
a public statement criticizing someone or something

● adj+N strong **severe, strong** *On September 3, the Russian Foreign Ministry issued its latest strong condemnation of the US and British actions.*

▶ clear or direct **clear, explicit, forthright, outright, unequivocal** *The Cuban Foreign Minister went on to reiterate Cuba's outright condemnation of the terrorist attack.*

▶ by many people in many places **general, international, widespread, worldwide** *There was widespread condemnation yesterday of the brutal treatment of protesters.*

▶ by everyone **unanimous, universal** *The communist state's nuclear test brought universal condemnation from around the globe.*

▶ general **general, sweeping, wholesale** *In his general condemnation of Russian music, he is forced to concede that Glinka has some merit as a composer.*

▶ **absolute, total, utter** *The criticism of American policy stopped short of total condemnation.*

● v+N express condemnation **express, issue, pronounce, reiterate, repeat, voice** *I would like to express my utter condemnation of the attack.*

▶ receive condemnation **attract, bring, draw, provoke, receive** *This shocking comment provoked immediate condemnation across the US.*

condition N

1 the physical state of something

● adj+N bad **appalling, bad, deplorable, poor, terrible, unsafe** *The trucks were in poor condition and prone to breakdown.*

▶ good **excellent, good, immaculate, mint, perfect, pristine, tip-top** INFORMAL *The grounds and building are in immaculate condition.*

2 the physical state of someone

● adj+N serious **critical, serious** *The project is designed to improve the prevention, diagnosis and treatment of cancer, heart disease, diabetes and other serious conditions.*

▶ not changing **stable, unchanged** *The news from the hospital was that her condition was stable.*

▶ physical **physical** *He wanted to get back to scientific work but his physical condition would not allow it.*

▶ medical **medical** *His medical condition was deteriorating.*

● N+v get worse **deteriorate, get worse, worsen** *In the middle of January, Sarah's condition worsened.*

▶ get better **get better, improve** *She visited Albert in hospital and his condition had improved, which made her happy.*

3 the situation or environment in which something happens [always plural]

● adj+N good **excellent, favourable, good, ideal, optimal, optimum, perfect** *He at last found himself working under ideal conditions.*

▶ bad **appalling, atrocious, bad, deplorable, difficult, poor, terrible, unfavourable** *He describes the often appalling conditions on emigrants' ships.*

▶ dirty **insanitary, squalid, unhygienic, unsanitary** *Tens of thousands of people lived there in insanitary conditions.*

● n+N **housing, living, working** *Living conditions were atrocious.*

4 the weather [always plural]

● adj+N good **excellent, favourable, good, ideal** *Generally, conditions were pretty good for the time of year.*

▶ bad **adverse, appalling, atrocious, extreme, harsh, poor, terrible, unfavourable** *I didn't think any boat would have risked coming out to us in such atrocious conditions.*

▶ types of conditions **blustery, damp, dry, freezing, humid, icy, overcast, wet, windy, wintry** *The conditions were quite windy, which made running at an even pace quite difficult.*

▶ relating to the weather **atmospheric, climatic, meteorological, weather** *The weather conditions were terrible.*

5 something needed before another thing can happen

● v+N state that a condition must be accepted **attach, impose, lay down, set, set out, specify** *In granting permission we may impose certain conditions on such things as who does the work and how it is done.*

▶ do what is need by a condition **fulfil, meet, satisfy** *If you satisfy the above conditions, you may be eligible for assistance.*

● and/or **terms** *This should be read in conjunction with our Terms and Conditions.*

6 an illness or health problem that lasts a long time

● adj+N **chronic, debilitating, degenerative, incurable, life-threatening, medical, neurological, pre-existing, rare, serious, treatable** *Always seek the advice of your doctor for any questions you may have regarding a medical condition.*

● n+N **eye, heart, lung, scalp, skin** *He suffered from a heart condition.*

● v+N **be born with, develop, have, inherit, suffer from** *There are probably another million people who have the condition without realising it.*

condolence N

words of sympathy when someone has died [always plural]

● adj+N **deep, heartfelt, personal, profound, sincere** *To her son Patrick and daughter Caroline and family we offer our sincere condolences.*

● v+N gives condolences to sb **add, convey, express, extend, give, offer, pass, pay, send** *We would like to express our condolences to Mr. Robson's family and friends.*

▶ accept condolences from sb **accept** *Please accept my condolences.*

condone V

approve of bad behaviour

● V+n **abuse, act, action, activity, behaviour, killing, murder, practice, terrorism, truancy, use, violence** *I cannot condone those actions, but as a friend I will continue to offer him support on a personal level.*

conducive ADJ

creating a situation that helps something to happen

● adv+ADJ **very, especially, highly, particularly, very** *I've found dog-walking to be especially conducive to creative thinking.*

▶ not very **hardly** *The British climate is hardly conducive to barbecues .*

● ADJ+n **atmosphere, circumstances, climate, conditions, environment, situation, surroundings, weather** *The role of the trainer is to provide an environment conducive to learning.*

● ADJ+to **attainment, development, growth, happiness, health, learning, peace, welfare** *A student's lifestyle is not always conducive to good health.*

conduct V

do something in an organized way

● V+n an activity intended to find out information **experiment, fieldwork, inquiry, interview, investigation, poll, research, review, study, survey, test** *The Council conducted a survey of more than 1,100 businesses as to their future land and building requirements.*

▶ an organized activity **affairs, business, campaign, negotiations, operation** *The attitude to risk of firms within the sector can have a large impact on how its business is conducted.*

conduct N

1 the way someone behaves

● adj+N bad **disgraceful, immoral, improper, unacceptable, unethical, unprofessional, unreasonable, unsporting, unsportsmanlike, violent** *He was sent off later in the match for violent conduct.*

▶ not allowed by the law **criminal, disorderly, negligent, unlawful, wrongful** *The soldiers involved in the incident have not been charged with criminal conduct.*

▶ good **gentlemanly, good, proper** *Offenders may be released early for good conduct.*

▶ types of conduct **ethical, moral, professional** *Members are bound by a strict code of professional conduct.*

2 the way in which a process or activity is managed

● N+of **affairs, business, case, elections, examination, investigation, meeting, operation, proceedings, research, trial, war** *Local residents are entitled to question the council over the conduct of its affairs.*

confer V

give authority, a right, an honour etc to someone

● n+V authority **authority, jurisdiction, legitimacy, power, status** *This bill confers power on Government which no Government ought to have.*

▶ a right **privilege, right** *In the event of death, the Act confers rights of succession to property.*

▶ an honour **award, degree, honour, knighthood** *During the July graduation ceremonies, six honorary degrees were conferred.*

conference N

a meeting to discuss ideas

● adj+N describing how often a conference takes place **annual, biannual, biennial, triennial** *Recent healthcare reforms in England dominated much of the debate at this year's annual conference.*

▶ lasting for a particular time **one-day, three-day, two-day** *The one-day conference attracted nearly forty participants.*

▶ involving people from particular countries or areas **European, international, national, regional** *He has presented papers at international conferences in the United Kingdom, the USA, Australia, and Singapore.*

● n+N **party, peace, sales** *He was a member of the British delegation to the Paris peace conference in 1919.*

● v+N go to a conference **attend, be at, go to** *Teachers from schools across the country attended the two-day residential conference in Cambridge.*

▶ **arrange, call, convene, hold, host, organize, plan, run, schedule, sponsor, stage** *Next year, the EU plans to hold a conference on human rights.*

confess V

1 admit that you have committed a crime

● V+n **crime, guilt, murder** *Half way through the trial, he confessed his guilt to his lawyer.*

● V+to **charge, crime, killing, murder** *Next morning he walks into a Notting Hill police station and confesses to the murder.*

2 admit something bad or embarrassing about yourself

● adv+V **candidly, frankly, freely, honestly, openly, readily** *I freely confess it is quite different from anything I expected to discover.*

● V+n **feeling, ignorance, love, secret** *I have to confess ignorance.*

● V+to **affair, feeling, ignorance** *She also confessed to a feeling of unease about the question of costs.*

confession N

1 a statement in which you admit that you have committed a crime

● adj+N **alleged, false, frank, full, true, written** *After the second murder, a young man was arrested and gave a full confession.*

● v+N say your confession was not true **retract, withdraw** *Downing later tried to retract the confession.*

● v+N make a confession **give, make, write** *He said that the police forced him to make the confession.*

▶ sign a confession **sign** *After 14 hours of continuous interrogation, Brian signed a confession.*

▶ get a confession from sb **elicit, extort, extract, force, get, obtain** *Look, you're not going to get a confession out of me.*

2 a statement in which you admit something bad or embarrassing about yourself

● v+N **make** *I've got a confession to make: I was just trying to impress you.*

confidence N

1 the belief that you can do things well

● adj+N **added, enough, fragile, great, increased, little, new-found, quiet, renewed, sufficient, supreme, unshakeable** *Carol gained greater confidence in her management style and skills.*

● v+N have confidence **be full of, feel, have, possess** *I can drive but don't have a lot of confidence .*

▶ give you more confidence **bolster, boost, build, build up, improve, increase** *An opportunity to perform in this type of environment boosts their confidence.*

▶ start to have confidence **acquire, develop, gain, get** *He may gain confidence as he grows older.*

▶ lack confidence **be lacking in, lack** *I guess I just lacked confidence.*

▶ give you confidence again **give back, rebuild, restore** *The goal may go some way to restoring his confidence.*

▶ give you less confidence **dent, erode, shake, undermine** *He continually seeks to undermine her confidence.*

▶ give you confidence **give, instil** *The experience has*

given me more confidence than I would ever have believed possible.

▶ start to have confidence again **get back, recover, regain** *The course is designed to help them regain confidence and find permanent employment.*

▶ stop having confidence **lose** *Sometimes, after an illness or stay in hospital, older people lose their confidence.*

2 trust in someone or something

● adj+N **absolute, complete, full, great, increased, little, public, renewed, total, utmost** *I have full confidence in my surgeon.*

● v+N have confidence in someone or something **be full of, command, feel, have, possess** *I have complete confidence in my instructor.*

▶ increase confidence in someone or something **bolster, boost, build, build up, improve, increase** *Greater efficiency is necessary for building new confidence in public services.*

▶ lack confidence in someone or something **be lacking in, lack** *Recent elections have shown that Dutch voters lack confidence in their politicians.*

▶ give you confidence in someone or something again **rebuild, restore** *He is widely credited with restoring confidence in the system.*

▶ give you less confidence in someone or something **dent, erode, shake, undermine** *These problems have dented public confidence in the whole NHS.*

▶ give you confidence in someone or something **engender, give, inspire, instil** *A well-designed website instils confidence in your customers.*

▶ stop having confidence in somone or something **lose** *I'll give you one simple reason why people have lost confidence in this government.*

confident ADJ

1 believing in your own abilities and not nervous or frightened

● adv+ADJ fairly **fairly, pretty** INFORMAL**, quite, reasonably** *I'm a fairly confident person but I was nervous before the speeches.*

▶ very **extremely, really, supremely, very** *He looked supremely confident as he strode forward.*

▶ in a way that is not obvious to other people **quietly** *Al is a quietly confident 11-year-old.*

● ADJ+n mood **feeling, mood** *The team will start the season in confident mood on Sunday against Liverpool.*

▶ voice **tone, voice**

▶ behaviour **manner, performance, stride, swagger** *The successful applicant will need to possess a confident telephone manner.*

▶ expression **expression, smile** *She said this with a confident smile.*

▶ statement **assertion, prediction** *All the jury heard was Dr Moore's confident assertion that the forensic evidence virtually proved Andrew guilty.*

▶ person performing a particular activity **communicator, learner, reader, rider, skier, swimmer** *All children taking part must be confident swimmers.*

● v+ADJ **appear, become, feel, get, grow, look, remain, seem, sound** *By 1927 he felt confident enough to expel Trotsky from the Communist Party.*

2 certain that something will happen

● adv+ADJ very **absolutely, completely, entirely, extremely, fully, supremely, totally, very** *But club officials said that they were fully confident that the scheme would go ahead.*

▶ fairly **fairly, pretty** INFORMAL**, quite, reasonably** *I feel reasonably confident that the new building will be ready within the next year.*

▶ in a way that is not obvious to other people **quietly** *I'm quietly confident that things will get better.*

● ADJ+of **future, growth, outcome, progress, prospects, result, success, victory** *Having beaten United already this season, they were confident of victory.*

confidential ADJ

needing to be kept secret

● adv+ADJ **absolutely, completely, entirely, fully, highly, strictly, totally** *All of the information collected on our application form will be kept strictly confidential.*

● ADJ+n **advice, conversation, data, discussion, document, information, report** *The Citizens Advice Bureaux provide free, impartial and confidential advice.*

● v+ADJ **consider sth, keep sth, regard sth as, remain, stay, treat sth as** *All membership details will remain confidential.*

confidentiality N

a situation where something must be kept secret

● adj+N **absolute, complete, full, strict, total, utmost** *Any such information that is received will be handled in strict confidentiality.*

● n+N **client, customer, patient** *Patient confidentiality is respected at all times.*

● v+N no longer protect the confidentiality of sth **breach, break, compromise, undermine, violate** *Occasions may arise where individual advisers feel they need to breach confidentiality.*

▶ protect the confidentiality of sth **assure, ensure, guarantee, maintain, observe, preserve, protect, respect, safeguard** *However, as with all sensitive data there is a need to protect confidentiality.*

confirm V

1 prove that something is true

● V+n **diagnosis, existence, finding, hypothesis, identity, presence, rumour, status, validity** *The latest results confirm this hypothesis.*

2 make you feel sure that an idea or belief is right or true

● V+n **fear, impression, suspicion** *The fact that they knew his name confirmed his worst suspicions.*

● V+in **belief, opinion** *I am confirmed in my opinion that not a moment should be lost in attacking the enemy.*

confirmation N

a statement saying that something is definitely true

● adj+N **formal, further, immediate, independent,**

official *There was no independent confirmation of the incident.*

- v+N get confirmation **get, have, obtain, receive** *So far, the Health Ministry has no confirmation of a radio report of two cholera cases in the northern province of Nampula.*
- ▶ try to get confirmation **request, seek** *I sought confirmation of the precise sequence of events.*
- ▶ wait for confirmation **await, wait for** *I felt confident I had passed the exam, but had to wait for official confirmation.*
- ▶ want confirmation **want** *And if you want confirmation of this, you have only to look at the content of the Bristol report.*
- ▶ give sb confirmation **give, provide** *This correspondence provides confirmation that our high standards are being maintained.*

conflict N

1 angry disagreement between people or groups

- v+N end a conflict **end, resolve, settle, solve** *They provide advice and guidance to help staff work through and solve conflicts.*
- ▶ avoid a conflict **avert, avoid, prevent** *Davies emphasises how to avoid conflict and only deal with it when necessary.*
- ▶ deal with a conflict **deal with, handle, manage** *How good are you at handling conflict?*
- ▶ cause a conflict **cause, create, lead to** *Avoid situations that cause conflict or anger.*

2 fighting between countries or groups

- adj+N **armed, bitter, bloody, ethnic, military, ongoing, sectarian, violent** *There are currently at least 300,000 children under the age of 18 participating in armed conflicts around the world.*
- v+N end a conflict **end, resolve, settle, solve** *Reports the two sides had worked out a deal to end their decades-old conflict were false.*
- ▶ avoid a conflict **avert, avoid, prevent** *The Council of Europe was set up after the Second World War to promote co-operation between European countries and help prevent further conflict.*

3 a situation involving two opposing things

- adj+N **ideological, inherent, internal, irreconcilable** *There was an irreconcilable conflict in the evidence.*

conformity N

behaviour that is similar to the behaviour of everyone else

- v+N **achieve, demand, encourage, enforce, ensure, impose** *Some changes in those arrangements are necessary to ensure their conformity with the new rules of international trade.*
- N+with **contract, law, obligations, policy, principle, provisions, regulations, requirements, rules, standards, will** *Our efforts to fight terrorism will continue to be conducted in conformity with international law.*

confront V

deal with a difficult situation

- V+n **challenge, crisis, demon, difficulty, dilemma,**

fear, issue, past, problem, reality, threat, truth *She was forced to confront her deepest fears.*

confrontation N

a situation in which people are arguing or fighting

- adj+N **armed, bloody, direct, final, inevitable, major, military, nuclear, physical, violent** *She had witnessed the violent confrontations between the rival ethnic and political groups.*
- v+N avoid a confrontation **avert, avoid, prevent** *The police said they wanted to avoid a confrontation.*
- ▶ **cause, force, provoke, spark** *Five hours later, 10 inmates allegedly provoked a confrontation with the prison guards.*

confused ADJ

unable to understand or think clearly; not well organized or explained

- adv+ADJ very **completely, hopelessly, really, thoroughly, totally, utterly, very** *I became totally confused about which way I should go.*
- ▶ rather **a bit INFORMAL, a little, rather, slightly, somewhat** *By now you may be feeling a little confused.*
- v+ADJ **be, become, feel, get, leave sb, look, seem** *I am starting to get very confused about which email address to use. • I was left more confused than ever, trying to work out what I was supposed to do with it.*

confusing ADJ

not easy to understand

- adv+ADJ very **extremely, really, very** *Life can be very confusing sometimes.*
- ▶ rather **a bit INFORMAL, a little, pretty INFORMAL, quite, rather, slightly, somewhat** *The figures are rather confusing and should be treated with some caution.*
- ▶ possibly **potentially** *The combination of drawings and photographs make the pages cluttered and potentially confusing to small children.*
- ADJ+n language **jargon, term, terminology** *A tutor will teach you how to use the internet without confusing jargon or technical details.*
- ▶ situation or issue **issue, matter, message, picture, result, situation, time, world** *Welcome to the confusing world of medicines, where the same basic product is on sale under a variety of different names.*
- v+ADJ **appear, become, find sth, get, seem, sound** *This is a thorough introduction to a subject which many people find confusing. • On first glance, the layout of the chapters seems confusing.*

confusion N

a feeling or state of being confused

- adj+N a lot of confusion **considerable, great, much, total, utter** *There is considerable confusion over what 'enhanced choice' actually means.*
- ▶ involving many people **general, widespread** *The new rules are aimed at ending the widespread confusion over costs.*
- ▶ possible **possible, potential** *He rightly points to the potential confusion of different staff having different pension schemes.*

▶ unnecessary **unnecessary** *To avoid unnecessary confusion the term 'Sub-Committee' is used throughout.*

▶ at the beginning **initial** *After a little initial confusion, a Downing Street spokesman last night confirmed the decision.*

▶ mental **mental** *Even at concentrations as low as 500–1000 parts per million, it can cause headaches, dizziness, and mental confusion.*

● v+N cause confusion **add to, cause, create, lead to, result in, sow, throw sb/sth into** *The wording of the clause has caused some confusion.*

▶ remove confusion **clarify, clear up, eliminate, remove** *It was not until the following day that the confusion was cleared up.*

▶ prevent confusion **avoid, prevent** *To avoid confusion, it should be recognized that there are two products with this name.*

● N+v when confusion exists **arise, reign, surround sth** *Things were somewhat chaotic and confusion reigned for several days.*

● n+of+N **likelihood, risk, source, state** *A further source of confusion is the apparently inconsistent use of symbols.*

congestion N
when people or vehicles block a place

● adj+N bad **bad, heavy, increasing, severe** *Traffic congestion is sometimes heavy on the roads in holiday periods.*

▶ in a city **urban** *Research shows that a national scheme of road pricing could cut urban congestion by half.*

● n+N involving traffic **motorway, road, traffic** *The plans are part of the Council's ongoing efforts to tackle traffic congestion.*

● v+N cause or increase congestion **add to, cause, increase, lead to** *The continued expansion of the market caused severe traffic congestion.*

▶ remove or reduce congestion **alleviate, avoid, cut, ease, minimize, reduce, relieve, tackle** *The new road scheme is a bid to ease congestion and manage traffic incidents.*

congratulations N
an expression of pleasure about someone's success, good luck etc

● adj+N **hearty, sincere, special, warm** *We send our warmest congratulations to them both.*

● v+N give congratulations **extend, offer, send** *I would just like to offer my hearty congratulations to everyone.*

▶ receive congratulations **deserve, receive** *Both teams deserve our warmest congratulations on their achievements.*

● N+v **go to sb** *Our congratulations go to the winning team.*

congress N
a large meeting of members or representatives of a group, especially a political one

● adj+N **annual, international, national, world** *The*

*research was presented **at** the annual congress of the American Epilepsy Society in New Orleans.*

● n+N **party** *At the party congress last December this process continued.*

● v+N organize a congress **convene, hold, organize** *This year's TUC congress was held in Brighton.*

▶ be present at a congress **attend** *Delegates could attend the whole congress or just choose particular morning or afternoon sessions.*

conjecture N
developing a theory or guess without complete information

● adj+N **mere, pure** *This is pure conjecture on my part, as I'm not really qualified to comment.*

● v+N be conjecture **be a matter for, be a matter of, be open to** *The site of the battle is a matter of conjecture.*

▶ show conjecture is right/wrong **confirm, disprove, prove, support** *Unfortunately, no evidence exists to prove the conjecture.*

connection N
1 a relationship between things, events, or people

● adj+N strong or clear **close, deep, direct, intimate, obvious, strong** *The Society has always had a close connection **with** the Library, and the meetings are still held there.*

▶ not strong **tenuous** *There seems to be only a tenuous connection **between** the music used and the influence of the commercial.*

▶ types of connection **causal, emotional, historical, literary, local, logical, personal** *She has a deep emotional connection **with** the land and culture of Spain.*

● v+N have a connection **have, maintain** *We have no connection **with** the hotels and restaurants we review.*

▶ make or recognize a connection **establish, explore, find, forge, make, see** *A real connection was forged **between** the band and its fans.* ● *No one seems to make the connection **between** the two stories.*

▶ no longer have a connection **lose, sever** *Although Mr Gill will be leaving the company, he will not be severing his connections **with** us completely.*

2 people you know who may be useful [usually plural]

● n+N **business, family, personal, political, professional** *He was brought up in the village of Gardenstown, with strong family connections within the fishing industry.*

● v+N **have, use** *She used her connections to help him get a job in the advertising industry.*

connotation N
an additional idea or emotion connected with a word

● adj+N good/bad **negative, positive, unfortunate** *The word 'selection' has unfortunate connotations; 'choice' would be better.*

▶ strong **obvious, strong** *The term has always carried strong connotations of privilege.*

▶ types of connotation **political, religious, sexual** *I*

would blush at the mention of any item that might conceivably have some sexual connotation.

- v+N **acquire, carry, have** It became clear that 'experimental' carried negative connotations.

conscience N
the feeling that tells you whether something you do is right or wrong

- adj+N not feeling guilty **clear, good** Unfortunately, we can make no such claim with a clear conscience.
- ▶ feeling guilty **bad, guilty, troubled** I had a guilty conscience about misleading them.
- ▶ involving one or more people **collective, individual, personal, public** The leadership said this was a matter of individual conscience.
- ▶ types of conscience **moral, political, social** Mo has a social conscience that motivates her to try and make the world a better place.

- v+N have a conscience **have** I have a very clear conscience about doing this.
- ▶ when you feel guilty **awaken, prick, trouble** His conscience was pricked by the sufferings of these starving people.

You can also say that something **is on your conscience**: I don't want another death on my conscience. You can describe feelings of guilt as **pangs of conscience**: A lot of people would have felt real pangs of conscience about what had happened.

- ▶ when you feel less guilty **ease, salve** We may salve our consciences by thinking we give lots of aid to the Third World.
- ▶ when you try to decide what to do **examine, wrestle with** I spent this weekend wrestling with my conscience over the somewhat dubious morality of this situation.
- ▶ do what your conscience tells you **follow** Are there exceptional occasions on which people should follow their consciences, even if it means breaking the law?

- N+v **dictate sth, tell sb to do sth** Our consciences dictate that we must oppose it and that we must attempt to alter it.

conscious ADJ
1 knowing or realizing something

- adv+ADJ **acutely, deeply, extremely, fully, highly, increasingly, painfully, particularly, very** The novel's heroine is acutely conscious of her inferior social status.
- v+ADJ **become, make sb, remain, seem** Everyone should be made conscious of what the issues are. • We remain conscious of the need to avoid undue disruption to passengers.
- ADJ+of+n **danger, fact, importance, issue, need, problem, responsibility** Despite the success of the operation, Wallis remained deeply conscious of the fact that 55 men had died.

2 awake and able to see, hear, and think

- adv+ADJ **barely, fully, still** She was fully conscious the whole time and her condition was not thought to be serious.
- v+ADJ **remain, stay** Nausea came over me and I had to fight hard to stay conscious.

3 done deliberately, knowing what the effect will be

- ADJ+n **act, attempt, choice, decision, effort, intention** I made a conscious effort to make the most of this opportunity.

consciousness N
1 the state of being awake and able to see, hear, and think

- adj+N **full** We're waiting for him to regain full consciousness.
- v+N when someone becomes unconscious **lose** The injured diver collapsed onto the deck and lost consciousness for 10 seconds.
- ▶ when someone becomes conscious again **come to, recover, regain, return to** On regaining consciousness, he was placed in a sitting position.

2 knowledge or understanding of something

- adj+N involving a lot of people **collective, national, popular, public** Her first album dismally failed to register in the public consciousness.
- ▶ increased or growing **growing, heightened, increased, increasing** There is a growing consciousness of the environmental impact of production practices.

- v+N increase consciousness **develop, raise** We must raise consciousness in other countries through Bone Marrow Donors Worldwide.
- ▶ when people start to know about something **enter** But as TV and film gained increasing prominence, new playwrights have struggled to enter our national consciousness.

consensus N
agreement among all the people involved

- adj+N general or strong **broad, clear, common, general, overwhelming, strong, widespread** The general consensus among Egyptologists is that the pyramids were tombs.
- ▶ growing **emerging, growing** Those who deny that climate change is dangerous have chosen to ignore the growing consensus among scientists.
- ▶ among different groups or countries **cross-party, global, international, national** A broad global consensus has emerged that industrial logging of endangered forests is no longer acceptable.
- ▶ types of consensus **political, scholarly, scientific, social** There is a need for as much political consensus as possible on the framework for the pension system.

You can also talk about **a consensus of opinion**: The consensus of opinion was that the idea was viable, provided a suitable site could be found.

- v+N get or develop consensus **achieve, arrive at, build, come to, develop, establish, find, forge, get, reach** Negotiations to finalize the agenda of the summit failed to reach consensus on many major initiatives.
- ▶ try to get consensus **call for, seek** Chancellor Merkel announced that she would seek a broad consensus on how to proceed.
- ▶ show that a consensus exists **reflect** The University's policy on authorship reflects the

consensus on who should be the authors of a paper and what their rights and duties are.

▶ end or damage consensus **break, undermine** They were in danger of breaking the strong political consensus that had been developed over the years.

● N+v **emerge, exist** A growing consensus has emerged regarding the most appropriate forms that ICT education should currently take in early childhood.

● n+of+N **degree, lack** There is diverse opinion and a lack of consensus about how to manage the disease.

consequence N
a result or effect of something [usually plural]

● adj+N bad **adverse, catastrophic, devastating, dire, disastrous, fatal, grave, negative, serious, severe, terrible, tragic, unfortunate** Any miscalculation regarding the dosage could have led to disastrous consequences.

▶ having a large effect over time **far-reaching, important, long-term** 1989 was a momentous year with far-reaching consequences.

▶ happening immediately **direct, immediate** There is little or no quantitative data on how many more students applied as a direct consequence of the advertising campaign.

▶ not intended or expected **unforeseen, unintended** Every war in history has had unintended consequences.

▶ that might happen **possible, potential** Why weren't patients informed of the possible consequences of taking the drug?

▶ expected to happen **inevitable, likely, logical, natural** Breach of confidentiality may well amount to serious professional misconduct, with inevitable disciplinary consequences.

▶ types of consequence **economic, environmental, financial, legal, political, practical, social** My question concerns the economic consequences of implementing these recommendations.

● n+N **health, tax** Even a small amount in the water supply could have had serious health consequences.

● v+N have consequences **have, lead to** Large hydro-electric dams can have serious environmental consequences, such as flooding large areas of land and displacing populations.

▶ experience consequences **accept, deal with, face, reap, suffer, take** The question you must ask is – are you prepared to suffer the consequences of your system failing or malfunctioning?

▶ think or know about consequences **consider, examine, explore, think about, think of, understand** People need to understand the potential consequences of these choices.

▶ say what the consequences might be **foresee, predict, warn of** Is it possible to predict the consequences of transferring a gene from one organism to another?

▶ avoid consequences **avoid, escape** This arrangement enables debtors to reach a compromise with their creditors and avoid the consequences of bankruptcy.

▶ be frightened of consequences **fear** They all feared the consequences of failing to address the problem.

● N+v **arise, follow, result** The company is not liable

for any consequences arising from the use or misuse of the information contained here.

conservation N
1 the careful management of land so that it is not damaged

● adj+N **environmental, marine** She developed her interest in marine conservation at the University of Greenwich.

● n+N **biodiversity, countryside, forest, landscape, nature, rainforest, wetland, wildlife, woodland** These woodlands and green spaces will provide opportunities for recreation, nature conservation, and education.

● N+n area **area** A large part of the centre of Shrewsbury is a conservation area.

▶ action or work **efforts, measures, project, work** Successful seed propagation is part of the conservation work undertaken at Bedgebury.

▶ organization **agency, body, charity, group, organization** Volunteering offers a good way to get a flavour of what working in a wildlife conservation charity is like.

● N+of **biodiversity, environment, habitat, species, wildlife** The prime purpose of our reserves is the conservation of wildlife and habitats.

2 not wasting energy, water etc

● n+N **energy, water** In existing stores, the company is raising employee awareness of energy conservation.

● N+of **energy, fuel, resources** These regulations came into effect earlier in April and are concerned with the conservation of fuel and power.

conservative ADJ
not accepting much change, or traditional in your attitudes

● adv+ADJ very **deeply, extremely, highly, very** Italians are for the most part deeply conservative **in** their approach to bio-ethical issues.

▶ rather **essentially, fairly, quite, rather, relatively** Governments and bureaucracy have a rather conservative attitude towards the role of mass media.

▶ as a basic feature **inherently** These systems are inherently conservative and the pace of change is slow.

▶ in a particular way **politically, socially** She never lost her belief in the staid, socially conservative society of the 1950s, with its traditional family values.

● ADJ+n **approach, attitude, outlook, values, view** Her marriage to a man of conservative views does not seem to have been a happy one.

consider v
think or talk about something carefully, usually before making a decision

● adv+V carefully or thoroughly **carefully, fully, in detail, properly, seriously** Until last week, I would never have given a second thought to the idea, but I am now seriously considering it.

▶ not taking much time **briefly** Let us, then, in conclusion briefly consider the nature of that power.

▶ not all together **individually, separately** Each

application will be considered individually on its merits.

▶ with the aim of making something happen **actively** *They are actively considering a change to the law.*

● V+n question or situation **case, issue, matter, problem, question, situation** *We need to consider the cases in which the usual conditions do not apply.*
 ● *The committee agreed to consider the issues raised in the report.*

▶ facts **evidence, facts** *Let us now consider the evidence that is relevant to our theory.*

▶ request or suggestion **application, proposal, proposition, recommendation, request** *We shall consider your application and respond in seven days.*

▶ effect **effect, impact, implications** *Developers should consider the long-term effects of these proposals before proceeding further.*

▶ choice **alternative, option, possibility** *If you have credit cards with interest rates above 10 per cent, you should consider the possibility of switching the debt to a cheaper loan.*

▶ aspect **aspect, factor** *Consider all these factors carefully, before you come to a decision.*

▶ legal question **case** *The university court meets to consider the cases of students who have appealed against their exam results.*

consideration N
1 careful thought before making a decision

● adj+N careful or thorough **careful, detailed, due, proper, serious** *After careful consideration, we accepted the proposal.*

▶ more **further** *Such appeals are likely to be rejected without further consideration.*

▶ more than usual **special** *We give special consideration to applicants with relevant research experience that may compensate for lack of formal qualifications.*

● v+N give consideration to something **give, take sth into** *The needs and concerns of local residents were taken into consideration.*

When something is being thought about, you can say that it is **under consideration**: *The company wrote to her saying that compensation was still under consideration.*

▶ deserve or need consideration **deserve, merit, need, require, warrant** *Four proposals have been received that merit serious consideration.*

2 something to think about before making a decision

● adj+N important **important, key, main, major, paramount, primary, prime** *For women with dependent children thinking about going out to work, the cost of childcare is a major consideration.*
● types of consideration **economic, environmental, ethical, financial, political, practical, theoretical** *Although emigration did resume in the 1920s, political and economic considerations ensured that it was on a far smaller scale than before.*

Usage **Consideration** is usually plural in these combinations.

● n+N **cost, design, health, safety, security** *Cost considerations are a key issue for most companies.*

Usage **Consideration** is usually plural in these combinations.

● v+N **take into account** *We think the council should take these environmental considerations into account when making a decision on the new road.*

3 thinking about other people's feelings and needs

● v+N behave with consideration **have, show, treat sb with** *Drivers should show consideration for other road users.*

consign to PHR VB
put someone or something somewhere

● V+n **dustbin, dustbin of history, history, history books, oblivion, past, scrap heap** *Such rhetoric seems to be outdated, irrelevant, and destined to be consigned to the dustbin of history.*

consistency N
1 when qualities or behaviour are always the same

● adj+N to a great degree **great, remarkable** *There is a remarkable consistency in the mortality rates for CJD in participating countries.*

▶ considered as a whole **overall** *Remember that overall consistency in your finished work is required.*

▶ relating to how well ideas, arguments, results etc are connected **internal, logical** *You may not agree with him, but there is an internal consistency to his views.*

● v+N when someone makes or keeps something consistent **achieve, ensure, maintain, provide** *Reporting on all departments through the annual report will also ensure consistency in the information provided.*

▶ have consistency **have, show** *In our next twelve games we showed less consistency.*

▶ improve consistency **improve** *Improving consistency in the allocation of costs and expenditure should enable more meaningful financial comparisons to be made.*

● n+of+N how much consistency there is **degree, level** *Try to make sure that there is a degree of consistency between the spelling of hyphenated words.*

▶ no or not enough consistency **lack** *There was a lack of consistency in the tutors' marking of the tests.*

2 how thick or smooth a substance is

● adj+N types of consistency **creamy, smooth, soft, thick, thin** *You may wish to add a little oil or margarine to the mash to give a creamy consistency.*

▶ describing the consistency wanted **the desired, the right** *Add a little water to get the right consistency and cook for two more minutes.*

consistent ADJ
1 not changing in behaviour, attitudes, or qualities

● adv+ADJ very **remarkably, very** *To win 13 out of 16 matches – only losing one – was a remarkably consistent performance throughout the season.*

▶ rather **fairly, quite, reasonably, relatively** *Price rises across the industry were all fairly consistent this year.*

● ADJ+n **approach, level, manner, message,**

performance, policy, quality, standard *A systematic and consistent approach to the issue is important, argue the authors.*

2 containing statements or ideas that are similar

• adv+ADJ completely or mainly **broadly, entirely, fully, perfectly, remarkably, wholly** *These results are entirely consistent with other polling data.*
▸ connected together in a sensible way **internally, logically** *At least the film's plot is internally consistent.*

• ADJ+n **findings, pattern, result** *The authors also compared their results with laboratory studies on how drugs worked and state that their findings are consistent.*

• ADJ+with **aim, data, evidence, findings, hypothesis, objective, policy, principle, requirement, view** *We are concerned that these proposals are not consistent with the stated aim to achieve a clearer focus on regulation.*

consist of PHR VB
be made of particular parts or things

• adv+V mainly **chiefly, essentially, largely, mainly, mostly, predominantly, primarily, principally** *Their natural habitat consists mainly of humid, lowland forests.*
▸ of only one thing **entirely, solely** *His life consists solely of adding numbers at a desk, day in day out, 51 weeks of the year.*
▸ usually **generally, normally, typically, usually** *Withdrawal symptoms usually consist of flu-like symptoms, such as headaches, irritation, depression and anxiety.*

consolidate V
make your power, position, achievements etc stronger or more effective

• V+n power, influence, or position **hold, position, power, reputation** *Labour, on the other hand, will be looking to consolidate its position as the biggest single party.*
▸ what a person learns **knowledge, learning, skills** *My placements have provided the opportunity to consolidate my learning by putting theory into practice.*

conspicuous ADJ
very noticeable or easy to see; very great

• adv+ADJ very **highly, particularly, very** *The flowers are highly conspicuous and are visited by many pollen-collecting bees, flies, and beetles.*
▸ rather **fairly, rather** *I felt rather conspicuous, standing there on my own.*

• ADJ+n feature or example of something **example, feature** *The most conspicuous feature of his paintings is his use of black.*
▸ where something is **place, position** *All players must go out of the room while a thimble or other small object is put in a conspicuous place.*
▸ success/failure **failure, success** *He played for the team for a year, but not with conspicuous success.*

• v+ADJ **become, feel, look** *When I got out of the cab I had to hold my dress together at the back, while trying not to look conspicuous at the same time.*

conspiracy N
a secret plan to do something bad

• adj+N large **grand, great, vast** *They come to believe that there is a vast conspiracy designed to prevent them learning the truth about UFOs.*
▸ involving several countries **global, international** *Davos, high up in the Swiss Alps, is not the centre of a global capitalist conspiracy to divide up the world.*
▸ claimed but not proved **alleged** *The other charges relate to an alleged conspiracy to kill the leader of another church.*
▸ types of conspiracy **criminal, military, political** *Should computer files be private even if they are being used as part of a criminal conspiracy?*

• v+N discover a conspiracy **discover, expose, uncover** *A political journalist uncovers a conspiracy involving the incumbent prime minister.*
▸ be involved in a conspiracy **be involved in, be part of** *There is no way that all these people could be involved in a massive cover-up conspiracy.*
▸ organize a conspiracy **hatch, organize** *Military and political conspiracies were constantly being hatched by the army generals and civilian dissidents.*

constant ADJ
1 continuous or regular over a long period

• adv+ADJ **almost, pretty** INFORMAL, **virtually** *School governance continues to be in a state of almost constant change.*

• ADJ+n something difficult or unpleasant **battle, change, fear, pain, pressure, struggle, threat** *Computer viruses are a constant threat and lead to a lot of wasted time if a virus infects a PC.*
▸ when something reminds you **reminder** *The towering volcano overlooks parts of the island, whilst the vast lava flows are a constant reminder of the destructive power of nature.*
▸ someone or something that is with you **companion, presence** *We lived with death as a constant companion 24 hours a day.* • *He was a constant presence on all the TV chat shows.*
▸ watching or checking **monitoring, supervision, surveillance, vigilance** *The university recognises the need for constant monitoring of its admission policy.*
▸ being present **presence** *The constant presence of a filming team was very disruptive.*
▸ flow or supply of something **demand, flow, source, stream, supply** *Currently, there is a constant stream of information, analysis, and predictions.*

2 continuing at the same rate or level

• adv+ADJ very **remarkably** *The temperature of the body remains remarkably constant.*
▸ completely **absolutely** *Humidity must stay absolutely constant throughout the experiment.*
▸ rather **fairly, pretty** INFORMAL, **relatively** *Manchester's Jewish population has remained fairly constant over recent years.*
▸ not exactly **approximately, broadly, roughly** *Once the sun has set, the temperature drops rapidly and stays roughly constant throughout winter.*

• ADJ+n **pressure, speed, temperature** *Using cruise control on highway trips can help you maintain a constant speed and reduce your fuel consumption.*

- v+**ADJ** remain constant **remain, stay** *The density of newly-built dwellings in England remained fairly constant between 1993 and 2001, at an average of 25 new dwellings per hectare.*
▸ keep something constant **hold, keep** *The glasshouses are fitted with control systems to enable temperatures to be kept constant.*

consternation N
a shocked or worried feeling

- adj+**N** **considerable, general, great, much, widespread** *It was a statement that caused considerable consternation in the press.*
- v+**N** **cause** *The spiralling costs of the new building have caused consternation and anger.*

constitute V
be considered to be something

- V+**n** agreement **acceptance, agreement, contract, endorsement** *Use of the website shall constitute acceptance of these terms and conditions.*
▸ something bad or illegal **breach, discrimination, infringement, nuisance, offence, violation** *Any unauthorized use constitutes an infringement of copyright and may be subject to legal action.*
▸ offer **offer** *Please note that this letter does not constitute an offer of a place on the course.*
▸ danger **danger, hazard, risk, threat** *Racist organisations constitute a threat to the whole community.*

constitution N
1 a set of laws, rules, or principles for a country or organization

- adj+**N** written/unwritten **unwritten, written** *Because Britain has an unwritten constitution, the relationship between central and local government is left to general understandings and customs.*
▸ not in final form **draft, proposed** *The Society's draft constitution also proposed that any person under 30 years should be able to join.*
- v+**N** write or change a constitution **amend, change, draft, draw up, write** *In 1955, Congress amended the constitution to allow his re-election for yet another presidential term.*
▸ have a constitution **have** *Groups must have a constitution, but do not need to be recognized charities.*
▸ formally accept a constitution **adopt, approve, ratify** *A referendum to approve the constitution was held on 15 October 2005 and delivered a majority Yes vote.*
▸ not accept a constitution **reject** *Recent polls suggested that the population would reject the constitution in a referendum.*
▸ be recorded in a constitution **be enshrined in** *The separation of church and state is enshrined in the US constitution.*
- n+to+**N** **amendment, change** *Amendments to the constitution shall be passed by a 60 per cent majority of the votes cast.*

2 your general physical condition, health, and strength

- adj+**N** **delicate, robust, strong, weak** *Those with more delicate constitutions retired to bed.*
- v+**N** be of, have **be of, have** *Fortunately, she was of a stronger constitution than me.*

constraint N
something that limits your freedom

- adj+**N** severe **severe, tight** *The company is working under tight financial constraints.*
▸ major or important **key, main, major, significant** *The main constraint on future tourist development will be a lack of suitable accommodation.*
▸ financial **budgetary, economic, financial** *She explained that the library had to operate within budgetary constraints.*
▸ types of constraint **environmental, legal, operational, physical, practical** *Digital texts are not subject to the physical constraints of printed paper.*
- n+**N** **budget, resource, space, time** *Owing to time constraints, these provisions were not debated during the course of the Bill's passage through the House of Commons.*
- v+**N** put a constraint on someone or something **impose, place, put** *Introducing state funding would impose an even greater constraint on political parties that challenge the prevailing economic order.*
▸ successfully deal with a constraint **overcome, work within** *Scientific research has focused on developing technologies to overcome these constraints in order to improve productivity.*
▸ have a constraint **face** *This is due to the continued budget constraints faced by local authorities.*
▸ remove a constraint **remove** *The aim is to remove the constraints on the growth of the City Centre's key service markets.*

constructive ADJ
intended to be useful or helpful

- adv+**ADJ** **extremely, highly, very** *The planning staff found the meeting very constructive.*
- **ADJ**+n comments **advice, comment, criticism, feedback, suggestion** *Although some comments may be interpreted as somewhat negative, they are meant as constructive criticism.*
▸ discussion **debate, dialogue, discussion** *When tempers have calmed, constructive dialogue might be possible once more.*
▸ behaviour or attitude **approach, contribution, engagement, manner, relationship, response, role, way** *We believe constructive engagement with our customers and shareholders is essential.*
- **ADJ**+in+n **approach, comments, criticism** *The readers were very constructive in their criticism.*
- and/or **helpful, honest, positive, supportive** *The aim is to encourage positive and constructive dialogue between the two groups.*

consult V
1 ask an expert for information or advice

- V+n medical expert **doctor, GP, pharmacist, physician, vet** *If you have problems, consult your doctor.*
▸ legal expert **lawyer, solicitor** *My advice is to consult a solicitor about the matter immediately.*

▶ technical expert **electrician, engineer** *If in doubt, always consult an electrician.*

2 ask people for their opinions

● V+adv **closely, extensively, fully, properly, regularly, widely** *The next step will be to consult as widely as possible on the plans.*

● V+n **colleagues, employees, the public, representatives, residents, staff, stakeholders** *A spokesman said the Council would be consulting local residents about the changes.*

You can also say **consult with** someone: *We shall be consulting with staff to hear their views on the proposed changes.*

3 look at a book or map for information

● V+n **catalogue, dictionary, directory, documentation, map, prospectus, timetable** *At this point, students may consult a dictionary to check spelling or usage.*

consultation N
1 discussions that ask for people's opinions

● adj+N involving many people **extensive, public, wide, wide-ranging, widespread** *There has been extensive consultation with the public on the proposed legislation.*

▶ formal/informal **formal, informal** *An informal consultation started in November 2005 to take forward the second phase of that programme.*

▶ thorough **close, full, in-depth, proper** *Priorities are arrived at after close consultation with business and representative bodies.*

▶ done at the beginning **early, initial, preliminary, prior** *Designs are prepared after initial consultation with residents.*

▶ done later **further, ongoing, regular** *Official policy is decided by the Chairman after a period of ongoing consultation at the annual conference.*

● v+N organize a consultation **begin, carry out, conduct, hold, launch, undertake** *In July 2005, the Assembly Government launched its consultation on the Environment Strategy in Wales.*

● N+n document **document, paper, questionnaire** *We support the ongoing debate on the important issues raised in the consultation paper.*

▶ process or event **event, exercise, meeting, period, phase, procedure, process** *The project has already been through an exhaustive consultation process.*

2 a meeting with someone who gives advice

● adj+N personal or private **face-to-face, one-to-one** *Expert advice is delivered through a series of one-to-one consultations.*

▶ free **free** *For a free consultation and price quote call us on the number below.*

▶ first **initial** *The initial consultation with one of our advisers is free of charge.*

● v+N **arrange, book** *The hospital will then get in touch to arrange a consultation with a relevant specialist if more detailed discussion is needed.*

consumer N
someone who buys goods and services

● adj+N clever **discerning, informed, savvy** INFORMAL *Savvy consumers are always on the lookout for ways to save money.*

▶ rich/poor **affluent, low-income, vulnerable** *The NCC's policy work is focused on the interests of low-income consumers.*

▶ with strong principles **ethical** *Ethical consumers want to have this information.*

● v+N give consumers good information **educate, inform, reassure, warn** *An easily recognisable symbol, it reassures consumers that the food they buy has been produced to exacting standards.*

▶ give consumers bad information **confuse, mislead** *The wording should be altered to avoid confusing consumers.*

▶ help consumers **benefit, empower, help, protect** *What legislation exists to protect consumers?*

▶ sell products to particular consumers **reach, target** *Both companies deny targeting young consumers directly.*

● N+n goods **durables, electronics, goods, products** *Competition will drive down the price of consumer goods.*

▶ actions or attitudes **attitudes, awareness, behaviour, boycott, complaint, confidence, demand, expectations, satisfaction, spending** *Consumer spending increased 5 per cent, the most since 2003.*

▶ something that helps or informs consumers **magazine, protection, watchdog** *The report was produced by the country's consumer watchdog.*

▶ money **credit, debt** *Consumer debt is rising and more people are late paying their bills.*

▶ range of goods and services **choice** *The supermarkets promise us greater consumer choice, but their policies mean that we actually have less choice.*

consumption N
the use of something, or the amount used; the process of eating or drinking something or the amount eaten or drunk

● adj+N too great **excess, excessive, immoderate** *Excessive alcohol consumption is never to be welcomed.*

▶ sensible or controlled **low, moderate, supervised, sustainable** *We need to encourage behaviour that leads to sustainable consumption.*

● n+N energy or fuel **electricity, energy, fuel, oil, oxygen, petrol, power** *The lighter the load, the lower the fuel consumption and emissions.*

▶ food, drink, or tobacco **alcohol, caffeine, cigarette, fish, food, meat, tobacco, vegetable, water** *Some people find it much harder to control their alcohol consumption than others.*

If something is safe to eat or drink, you can say that it is **fit for human consumption**: *Food companies have a legal responsibility to ensure the food they sell is safe and fit for human consumption.* If something is not safe to eat or drink, you can say that it is **unfit for human consumption**.

● v+N reduce consumption **cut, decrease, lower, minimize, reduce** *Water use: how to cut consumption by cutting waste, home gathering and reusing.*

> increase consumption **increase** *For example, driving at higher speeds increases fuel consumption.*

> measure consumption **estimate, measure** *We describe an experiment to measure the consumption of oxygen.*

● N+v increase **grow, increase, rise** *Total energy consumption actually rose with increasing family size.*

> decrease **decline, decrease, drop, fall, reduce** *Consumption fell dramatically and remained low in the depression years.*

● N+n amount or measurement **data, figures, growth, levels, rate** *The books show broad production and consumption data.*

> habits **behaviour, habits, pattern, trends** *On current consumption patterns, this will increase to 48 per cent of the world's projected population by 2025.*

● n+in+N **change, decline, decrease, drop, fall, growth, increase, reduction, rise, trends** *Our target requires a 10 per cent reduction in water consumption.*

● n+of+N **level, pattern, rate** *We aim to record changing patterns of consumption among the ageing population.*

contact N

1 communication between people or groups

● adj+N close **close, direct, face-to-face, intimate, personal** *There is direct and personal contact between the teachers and students.*

> regular **constant, frequent, regular** *He is in regular contact with staff at the Foundation.*

● n+N **email, telephone** *Email contact is also possible.*

● v+N have contact **establish, get in, have, initiate, keep in, maintain, make, re-establish, remain in, renew, resume, stay in** *Large classes means that it is more difficult for the staff to maintain contact with the students.*

The place where someone can make contact, or the person they can contact, can be called the *point of contact*: *The first point of contact for new students should be the international students' centre.*

> not have contact **avoid, lose, sever** *In the intervening years, they lost contact with their former school friends.*

> make someone have contact **bring sb into, put sb in** *I'll put you in contact with a friend of mine.*

● N+n **address, details** *Get in touch with us. Contact details are included below.*

2 the fact that people or things touch

● adj+N **close, intimate, physical, prolonged, sexual** *Diphtheria is also spread by droplet infection through close personal contact.*

If something happens when one thing touches another, you can say that it happens *on contact with* the other: *The cleansing concentrate liquifies on contact with your skin to gently dissolve makeup and dirt.*

● v+N not have contact **avoid, prevent** *Great care*

is required to avoid contact **with** unprotected human skin.

> have contact **come into, make** *Don't allow the two substances to come into contact.*

3 someone you know who may be useful

● v+N **build up, establish, have, make** *The conference has been an invaluable experience and a great chance to see familiar faces and make new contacts.*

● n+of+N **database, list, network** *We can draw on our extensive network of contacts **within** the business community.*

contagious ADJ

1 (used about diseases): spreading through touch or through air

● adv+ADJ very **extremely, highly, very** *Measles is a very highly contagious disease.*

> not very **mildly** *This virus is mildly contagious and can be passed on by direct contact with infected surfaces and towels.*

● ADJ+n **condition, disease, illness, infection, virus** *Contagious diseases such as pneumonia are passed from cage to cage rapidly.*

2 (used about feelings or ideas): spreading quickly among people

● ADJ+n **enthusiasm, laughter, passion** *Even on the phone, his ebullience and enthusiasm were highly contagious.*

contamination N

when something is dirty, polluted or dangerous

● adj+N types of contamination **airborne, bacterial, chemical, faecal, microbiological, radioactive, toxic** *This test gives an indication of the levels of airborne contamination.*

> accidental **accidental, adventitious** *Accidental contamination is becoming very frequent.*

> in many places, in great quantities **excessive, widespread** *The shaft is believed to be responsible for widespread radioactive contamination of the foreshore.*

● v+N stop or reduce contamination **avoid, control, eliminate, limit, minimize, prevent, reduce, remove, stop** *The upper part of the wall must be water-tight to prevent contamination.* ● *Regular training was needed to reduce contamination of organic waste with other waste types.*

> cause contamination **cause, generate, spread** *Pests can also cause physical contamination of foods and should be dealt with immediately.*

> suspect or fear contamination **fear, suspect** *Radioactive contamination is also suspected in some localities.*

contemplate V

to consider something; to consider the possibility of something happening

● adv+V when you are emphasizing something **even** *Have these details clear in your mind before you even contemplate looking at a new property.*

▶ seriously **seriously** *There were times when she seriously contemplated suicide.*

● V+n think about doing something **action, dismissal, divorce, marriage, move, possibility, purchase, retirement, suicide** *A very practical book for people contemplating retirement.*

▶ think about what something is like **beauty, career, fate, future, meaning, prospect** *I devoted only a small amount of time to contemplating my future career.*

● v+to+V **be prepared, refuse** *They refused to contemplate the possibility of defeat.*

If something is so unpleasant that you do not want to think about it, or you do not want to think that it might happen, you can say that it is *too awful to contemplate* or *too horrible to contemplate*: *The impact of another major incident is almost too awful to contemplate.*

contemplation N
the process of thinking about something for long time

● adj+N quiet **deep, peaceful, quiet, silent** *The chapel is available for quiet contemplation during the day.*

▶ types of contemplation **mystical, philosophical, spiritual** *In trying to understand the world around him, the narrator engages in philosophical contemplation.*

● v+N **encourage, invite, provoke** *Challenging artistic material encourages contemplation.*

● adj+in+N **absorbed, lost** *I walked on and on, absorbed in contemplation.*

contempt N
the feeling that someone or something deserves no respect

● adj+N great **absolute, complete, great, profound, total, utter** *She turned to us, a look of utter contempt on her face.*

▶ obvious **flagrant, ill-concealed, undisguised** *What finished his career was his undisguised contempt for the press and his refusal to answer journalists' questions.*

● v+N show or feel contempt **demonstrate, display, express, feel, have, regard sb/sth with, show, view sb/sth with** *Some of these companies have shown only utter contempt for their employees.* ● *She viewed their efforts with contempt.*

▶ feel but not show contempt **conceal, disguise** *He did little to disguise his contempt for his boss.*

▶ treat someone or something with contempt **treat sb/sth with** *Fans are being treated with contempt by the club.*

If someone or something is so bad or unpleasant that they do not deserve any attention, you can say that they are *beneath contempt*.

contender N
someone competing with others for something

● adj+N possible **definite, genuine, likely, major, obvious, possible, real, serious, strong, worthy** *Although a young rider, Jon is a serious contender.*

▶ possibly best **main, prime, top** *The main contenders would appear to be Steve Jones and Dave Wolfin.*

● n+N **championship, leadership, medal, promotion, title** *The Dutchman is always a major championship contender.*

▶ N+for+n **award, championship, crown, honour, job, leadership, position, promotion, throne, title, top spot** *The song will make the top ten, but I can't see it as a likely contender for the top spot.*

content N
the things that a book, programme, or website contains

● adj+N **digital, editorial, factual, graphical, online, textual, video** *To play video content you will need RealPlayer.*

● n+N **curriculum, multimedia, page, syllabus, web** *Multimedia content will be added as authors begin to supply it with their articles.*

● v+N see or read content **access, view** *This allows your readers to view your latest content from the comfort of their desktop.*

▶ create or show content **create, deliver, display** *We use cookies to deliver content that is specific to your interests.*

▶ change content **customize, edit, modify, personalize, tailor, update** *We tailor online content to meet your needs.*

▶ not look at content **skip** *Skip the content and go to the main contact details.*

content ADJ
satisfied with life or with something in particular

● adv+ADJ very **fully, perfectly, quite** *He is now perfectly content in his retired life.*

▶ fairly **broadly, fairly, generally, largely, reasonably** *I'm reasonably content with our day's work.*

● v+ADJ **appear, be, feel, seem** *Sun worshippers on holiday here will be very content.*

contention N
a statement that something is true

● adj+N **basic, central, main, primary** *The article's main contention is that the minister's argument is flawed.*

● v+N disagree with a contention **dispute, reject** *The Panel therefore rejects this contention.*

▶ agree with a contention **accept, uphold** *We cannot accept this contention for two reasons.*

▶ support a contention **support** *This report supports the contention that violence is a usual part of prison life.*

contentious ADJ
causing disagreement between people or groups

● adv+ADJ very **extremely, highly, very** *The proposed merger is likely to become a highly contentious issue.*

▶ in a particular way **politically** *The debate has been academically intense and politically contentious.*

● ADJ+n **area, aspect, debate, decision, issue,**

matter, point, proposal, question, subject, topic *The book bravely tackles some contentious issues.*

- v+ADJ **be, become, prove, remain** *There are growing signs that the issue may prove contentious at October's party conference.*

contest N

a situation or activity in which people compete

- adj+N with no clear leader **close, even, open** *The contest was still wide open.*
- ▶ with one clear leader **one-sided, unequal** *The Bulldogs failed to cope with the speed of the Bears' attack in what turned into a one-sided contest.*
- ▶ types of contest **athletic, electoral, presidential** *The issue of security is likely to play a big role in this year's presidential contest.*
- ▶ exciting **exciting, thrilling** *The game promises to be a thrilling contest between the two league leaders.*

- n+N **beauty, leadership, popularity, sporting, talent** *Good management is not a popularity contest.*

- v+N be involved in a contest **compete in, engage in, enter, participate in, take part in** *I have participated in five contests since I won the parliamentary seat in 1979.*
- ▶ win/lose a contest **lose, win** *She's been winning talent contests since the age of eight.*
- ▶ organize a contest **hold, organize, run** *The problems are the fault of the people who run the contest.*

- N+for+n **control, leadership, place, position, power** *Three years later, however, she was defeated by Alex Salmond in a contest for the leadership of the entire party.*

context N

the general situation that explains why something happens

- adj+N general **broad, general, wider** *Students will have an awareness of how their own work fits into wider musical context of the school and community.*
- ▶ particular **certain, particular, specific** *They examine the specific contexts in which racism emerges in society.*
- ▶ correct **correct, proper** *We ned to study the phenomenon in its proper historical context.*
- ▶ types of context **cultural, educational, global, historical, institutional, organizational, political, social, socio-political** *The article seeks to place the battle in its historical context.*

- v+N create or explain a context **create, define, describe, establish, explain, give, outline, provide, set** *In her introductory chapter, Bush sets the context for the emergence.*
- ▶ think about a context **consider, examine, explore** *Tasks will include looking at details of character and theme, and exploring the contexts in which the play was written.*
- ▶ understand a context **understand** *This ensures the writer is able to understand the context in which their editorial content will be placed.*

- v+in/within+N **consider sth, place sth, see, set sth, understand, view sth** *When viewed in historical context, the event was a minor contamination incident.*

- v+into+N **fit sth, place sth, put sth, set sth** *These research findings should be put into a practical context.*

contract N

a written legal agreement

- adj+N **binding, honorary, lucrative, permanent, short-term, temporary, written** *You are advised to take professional advice before entering into any binding contracts.*

- n+N **construction, employment, maintenance** *Employment contracts, handbooks and policies will need to ensure they reflect changes in the law.*

- v+N try to get a contract **apply for, bid for, compete for, tender for** *We sent these specifications out to firms bidding for the construction contract.*
- ▶ get a contract **secure, win** *The Group has won the contract for a data capture system to support its machines on the London Underground.*
- ▶ discuss or prepare a contract **draft, negotiate, renegotiate** *He even includes guidance on negotiating a contract if you have the good luck to have a proposal accepted.*
- ▶ give someone a contract to do work **award** *They're awarding the construction contract to a French company.*
- ▶ sign a contract **conclude, enter into, sign** *We offer a full service that includes concluding the contract and completing the conveyancing.*

> Before a contract is signed, an agreement is said to be **subject to contract**: *The property is now sold, subject to contract.*

- ▶ break the rules of a contract **breach** *These employees had breached their contract of employment.*
- ▶ keep the rules of a contract **honour** *Failure to honour the contract will result in penalty charges.*
- ▶ end a contract **cancel, rescind, terminate** *The clause allows the employee to terminate the contract with the employer at any time.*

- n+under+N **liability, obligation, responsibility, rights** *A person who is not a party to this agreement has no rights under the contract.*

contradict V

say or show that the opposite of something is true; or that two statements, etc, cannot be true at the same time

- adv+V completely **clearly, completely, directly, flatly, totally** *This flatly contradicted evidence from Government and nuclear industry representatives.*
- ▶ apparently **apparently, seemingly** *The new report apparently contradicts previous assumptions.*

- V+n **assertion, assumption, belief, claim, evidence, findings, notion, opinion, principle, statement, teaching, theory, view** *This apparently contradicted a statement he had previously made to the police.*

- n+V **evidence, facts, findings, results** *These findings contradict current theories on the issue.*

- V+to+v **appear, seem** *This theory appears to be contradicted by the new evidence that has come to light.*

contradiction N

a difference in two or more statements etc that means that both or all of them cannot be true

- adj+N existing within something **inherent, inner, internal** *The research explored the inherent contradictions of the party's policy.*
- ▶ which cannot be dealt with successfully **insoluble, irreconcilable**
- ▶ obvious or major **basic, blatant, complete, direct, fundamental, glaring, obvious, outright** *This was an illustration of the glaring contradiction **between** the needs of the economy and the suffocating grasp of bureaucratic control.*
- ▶ which seems to exist **apparent, seeming** *We need to examine how this apparent contradiction can be resolved.*
- v+N deal successfully with a contradiction **avoid, explain, overcome, a reconcile, resolve, solve** *He explained this apparent contradiction by saying that the situation had now changed.*
- ▶ show that a contradiction exists **expose, highlight, reveal, sharpen** *In the next essay, Dorothy Smith exposes the contradictions **between** the two points of view.*
- N+v **arise, be, exist** *There is a fundamental contradiction in this argument.*
- N+in+n **argument, attitude, evidence, policy, position, statement, system, theory** *There are contradictions in Government policy.*

> If there is a contradiction between things, you can say that one thing is *in contradiction to* another, or *in contradiction with* it: *This response is in blatant contradiction to the statement issued earlier by the exhibition director.*

contradictory ADJ

containing statements or beliefs that cannot all be true; disagreeing with other statements, etc in a way that means that not all of them can be true

- adv+ADJ within itself or between themselves **inherently, internally, mutually** *The two opinions seem mutually contradictory and impossible to reconcile.*
- ▶ very **completely, totally** *The Government's action sends out a completely contradictory message.*
- ▶ apparently **apparently, seemingly** *This apparently contradictory situation can only be understood in the context of the country's recent history.*
- ADJ+n **account, advice, argument, attitude, evidence, feelings, findings, information, message, opinion, position, result, statements, view** *The message they gave was very contradictory and difficult to interpret.* ● *In the face of contradictory statements about the safety of GM foods, the consumer must decide whom to believe.*

contrary ADJ

completely different or opposed to something else

- adv+ADJ **clearly, completely, directly, entirely, quite, totally, wholly** *This is directly contrary **to** government guidance on security.*

- ADJ+n belief or intention **argument, belief, conclusion, opinion, view** *Amid the tidal wave of accolades the film received, there were, of course, contrary opinions.*
- ▶ a fact **evidence, indication**
- ADJ+to+n what people say or think **assertion, assumption, belief, claims, expectations, impression, misconception, myth, opinion, perception, prediction, rumour** *Banks, contrary to popular opinion, do give loans to new businesses.*
- ▶ a rule or agreement **law, principle, spirit** *The effect may well be entirely contrary to the spirit of the treaty.*
- ▶ what people want **intention, interests, wishes** *This was altogether contrary to the wishes of the family.*

contrast N

a great difference, or something very different; a comparison between things

- adj+N great **complete, direct, dramatic, great, marked, sharp, stark, startling, striking, strong, total** *There is certainly a marked contrast **between** the complexity of the website and the simplicity of the newspaper.*
- ▶ pleasant **interesting, pleasing** *The green surroundings of the village form a pleasing contrast to this otherwise bleak, barren district.*

> If two things are very different, you can say that one thing is *in contrast to* the other, or *in contrast with* it: *In contrast to the situation in 1992, we hope that these changes will take place peacefully.* ● *In contrast with the two books discussed earlier, this title is a hugely enjoyable read.* You can also say that one thing *stands in contrast to* another: *These opinions stand in stark contrast to his earlier beliefs.*

- v+N show a contrast **make, offer, present, provide** *The inland towns provide a complete contrast **to** the small coastal villages.*
- ▶ describe a contrast **draw, make** *The writer goes on to draw a contrast **between** the two systems.*

contrast V

be different from something

- adv+V very much **dramatically, greatly, markedly, sharply, starkly, strikingly, strongly, vividly** *The actors' lives contrast starkly **with** their on-screen images.*
- ▶ in a pleasant or interesting way **beautifully, interestingly, nicely, perfectly, wonderfully** *These materials contrast beautifully **with** the grain and colour of the wood.*
- ▶ in a way that is good/bad **favourably, unfavourably** *The situation contrasts very favourably **with** the total lack of initiatives for women and work when the other party was in power.*

contravene V

do something against a rule, law, or agreement

- adv+V **clearly, directly** *The present proposals, if implemented, would directly contravene European Law.*
- V+n **convention, guidelines, law, legislation,**

policy, principle, provision, regulations, requirement, right, rule *This action would contravene the law on discrimination.*

contribute V

1 give money, time etc

● adv+V **equally, financially, generously, substantially**

● V+n **experience, expertise, material, money, resources, suggestions, thoughts, time, views** *We hope that you will be willing to contribute your thoughts and expertise on the subject.*

2 help to achieve something

● adv+V very much **actively, considerably, effectively, enormously, fully, greatly, massively, materially, meaningfully, positively, significantly, substantially** *These strengths contribute significantly to the establishment of an effective climate for learning.*

▶ directly/indirectly **directly, indirectly** *I'd like to thank everybody who has contributed directly or indirectly to the success of this venture.*

▶ equally **equally** *Not everyone contributed equally to the group work sessions.*

contribution N

1 something that helps to achieve something

● adj+N big **big, enormous, great, huge, immense, substantial** *I would like to pay tribute to the enormous contribution that you have made to the success of the department.*

▶ useful and important **important, invaluable, major, meaningful, outstanding, positive, significant, useful, valuable** *The Centre continues to make a very significant contribution to the development of many indigenous Irish companies.*

▶ small **modest, small**

● v+N make a contribution **make** *Such a centre would make a significant contribution to the life of the local community.*

▶ be grateful for a contribution **appreciate, recognize, value** *I don't think the contribution that these young people make is valued nearly highly enough.*

▶ mention a contribution **acknowledge, celebrate, highlight** *They acknowledged the contribution the UK's Guidelines had made to their own recommendations.*

▶ ask people to make a contribution **invite** *The panel has invited contributions from organisations and individuals.*

2 money given to help pay for something

● adj+N **financial, generous, modest, small, substantial** *We would like to thank members for their many generous contributions in the past.*

● v+N make a contribution **make, pay** *The company made a substantial contribution towards funding the Great Exhibition.*

▶ increase a contribution **increase, maximize** *If donors could increase their regular contributions, that would make all the difference.*

▶ ask people to make a contribution **invite, solicit** *To cover the cost of insurance, supervision and training we invite a contribution of £25 to £35 per session.*

contributor N

1 someone who gives money, time, or effort

● adj+N **big, important, key, large, main, major, significant** *Each paper from the main contributors must be 30–40 minutes in length.*

2 someone who writes articles

● adj+N often writing articles **active, frequent, prolific, regular** *She is a regular contributor to Homes and Gardens magazine.*

● N+to+n **book, journal, magazine, newspaper, publication, site, volume, website** *George Orwell was another contributor to the journal.*

contrived ADJ

false or artificial

● adv+ADJ **hopelessly, horribly, obviously, overly, ridiculously** *The cast struggle with the lightweight material, and much of what takes place feels hopelessly contrived.*

● ADJ+n **character, ending, plot, situation, story** *The ending is contrived and unrealistic.*

● v+ADJ **appear, feel, seem, sound** *The writer's style seems rather contrived.*

control N

1 the power to make decisions; power over something

● adj+N complete **absolute, complete, direct, effective, full, overall, total** *The government retains full control of the armed forces.*

▶ types of control **financial, parental, political** *The Finance Service has overall financial control of the Council.*

● v+N have or keep control **assert, have, keep, maintain, retain** *People want to retain control of their own personal data.*

When someone has control of something, you can say that it is **under someone's control**: *The whole organization is now under his control.* You can also say that someone is **in control** or **in control of** a situation etc: *The ruling party was no longer in control of events in the capital.*

▶ get control **assume, gain, seize, take, wrest** *Following Marfleet's death, he assumed control of the business and greatly extended it.*

▶ get control back **reassert, re-establish, regain** *They finally managed to regain control of the islands.*

▶ make control stronger **strengthen, tighten** *They tightened control of labour costs.*

▶ give someone control **give, hand** *He handed control of his affairs to his son.*

▶ use control **exercise, exert** *Their voting rights enabled them to exert control over all aspects of the business.*

▶ lose control **lose, relinquish** *The government was forced to relinquish control over these colonies.*

When someone does not have control of something, you can say that it is **beyond** or **outside someone's control**: *The concert was cancelled for reasons that were beyond our control.* ● *Decisions on financial matters are outside my control.* When people can control a situation you can say that it is **under control**. When they cannot, you can say that it is **out of control**: *Nobody wants to see inflation get out of control.*

2 a law limiting something [usually plural]

● adj+N **strict, stringent, tight** *There are strict controls* **on** *vehicle emissions.*

● n+N **arms, export, gun, immigration** *People are calling for greater gun control.*

● v+N start using controls **enforce, implement, impose, introduce** *The council imposed strict planning controls.*

▶ make controls stricter **strengthen, tighten** *Controls on illegal immigration were strengthened.*

▶ make controls less strict **relax** *The government relented on proposals to relax controls* **over** *advertising.*

▶ remove controls **remove** *Controls on imports were removed.*

control V
keep something at the correct or safe level

● adv+V **adequately, automatically, carefully, strictly, tightly** *Drug dosage is carefully controlled during treatment.*

controversial ADJ
causing disagreement between people

● adv+ADJ very **extremely, highly, hugely, very** *Abortion is a very controversial issue.*

▶ rather **quite, rather, somewhat** *Some quite controversial anti-smoking research has been revealed.*

▶ in a particular way **politically** *Any such tax may be too politically controversial for this government.*

● ADJ+n **decision, issue, plan, proposal, subject, topic** *Controversial plans to convert a derelict church into a nightclub have moved a step closer to completion.*

● v+ADJ **be, become, prove, remain** *The new proposals for tax reform have proved highly controversial.*

controversy N
a disagreement about a public matter which people have strong feelings about

● adj+N much **considerable, great, much** *The drug has been the topic of much controversy in recent times.*

▶ involving strong and angry emotions **bitter, fierce, heated** *There was fierce controversy over the verdict.*

▶ types of controversy **political, religious, scientific** *He was at the centre of a religious controversy which was to prove his eventual downfall.*

● v+N **arouse, attract, cause, court, create,**

generate, provoke, spark *The TV drama courted controversy by featuring underage sex.*

● N+v **arise, continue, rage, surround sth** *No evidence has ever been found and controversy has raged ever since.*

You can talk about the **controversy surrounding** or **concerning** something to say what a controversy is about: *There was great controversy surrounding the introduction of identity cards.*

convention N
1 a way of behaving or doing something that is accepted as normal

● adj+N usual **accepted, standard, traditional, usual** *We follow standard accounting conventions.*

▶ types of convention **artistic, linguistic, literary, social, stylistic, theatrical** *Different types of story have different character, plot and stylistic conventions.*

● v+N follow convention **adhere to, be bound by, conform to, follow** *People are given the freedom to be themselves and to take risks rather than just follow convention.*

▶ not follow convention **defy, flout** *Her work defies all the traditional artistic conventions.*

2 a formal agreement stating how governments should behave

● adj+N **international** *Refugees have a right to petition the government* **under** *international conventions such as the Universal Declaration of Human Rights.*

● v+N make a convention official **adopt, implement, ratify, sign** *North Korea announced it planned to sign several anti-terrorism conventions.*

▶ do something against a convention **breach, contravene, violate** *The recent deportations clearly breach these conventions.*

▶ follow the rules of a convention **accede to, adhere to, be bound by** *The government has agreed to adhere to the convention on chemical weapons.*

● N+v **apply to, define, establish, govern, guarantee, stipulate** *The Dublin convention applies to all EU states.*

It is common to talk about a **convention concerning**, **governing** or **relating to** a particular issue: *They commented on the 1951 convention relating to the status of refugees.*

conventional ADJ
of the usual type

● adv+ADJ very **entirely, highly, utterly, very** *The new sports centre was of an entirely conventional design.*

▶ rather **fairly, pretty** INFORMAL, **quite, rather, relatively** *He adopted a relatively conventional approach to the subject.*

● ADJ+n medicine **medicine, therapy, treatment** *Alternative therapies had helped where conventional medicine had failed.*

▶ ideas or way of doing something **approach, assumption, means, method, morality, notion,** technique, thinking *She had the courage to challenge conventional thinking and strike out on her own.*

When you talk about the **conventional wisdom** on a subject, you mean the beliefs or opinions that most people accept as correct: *The study challenges the conventional wisdom that all exercise is good for you.*

▸ weapons or way of fighting **arms, warfare, weapon** *They differentiated clearly between conventional weapons and nuclear weapons.*

conversation N
(a) private and informal talk between people

● adj+N types of conversation **casual, chance, face-to-face, informal, lively, meaningful, private** *Having a face-to-face conversation is much more personal than a telephone call.*

▸ long/short **brief, long** *Robert and I had a long conversation that day.*

● n+N **email, telephone** *In the course of a telephone conversation he admitted his feelings.*

● v+N have a conversation **be engrossed in, conduct, engage in, have, hold, participate in** *I had an interesting conversation with him about sailing.*

When you talk to someone that you do not know well, in order to be polite you can say that you **make conversation**: *'Nice party, isn't it?' I said, trying to make conversation.* When two people are very involved in a conversation, you can say that they are **deep in conversation**: *I looked across at Mary, who was deep in conversation with her sister.*

▸ start a conversation **enter into, get into, initiate, start, strike up** *We soon got into conversation with our fellow passengers.* ● *Casual jokes helped people to start conversations.*

▸ hear someone else's conversation **overhear** *Our conversation was overheard by fellow travellers.*

▸ try to change the subject of a conversation **steer** *He tried to steer the conversation towards more important matters.*

● N+v **flow, move on (to sth), turn to sth** *Our conversation turned to football.*

● n+of+N subject **subject, topic** *Work seemed to be his only topic of conversation.*

▸ noise **buzz, hum** *The restaurant was filling up and a buzz of conversation filled the air.*

▸ piece **snatches, snippet** *I could hear snatches of conversation through the wall.*

convey V
make ideas, feelings, or information known to someone

● adv+V **accurately, brilliantly, clearly, effectively, explicitly, powerfully, successfully, vividly** *The language used in this poem vividly conveys what it feels like to be dying.*

● V+n **emotion, essence, feeling, idea, impression, information, meaning, message, mood, sense** *Music can convey different moods.*

conviction N
1 a court's decision that someone is guilty

● adj+N criminal **criminal** *Please declare any criminal convictions.*

▸ earlier **previous, prior** *More than one third of women in prison have no previous convictions.*

▸ possibly wrong **unsafe, wrongful** *Amnesty International believes that their trial was unfair and that their convictions are unsafe.*

▸ when the punishment is finished/not finished **spent, unspent** *Information is required about any criminal convictions or cautions, including spent convictions.*

● v+N have a conviction **have** *He had 3 previous convictions for drunk-driving.*

▸ when someone is found guilty **obtain, secure** *The fire investigation team helped find the evidence to secure the conviction of a man for setting fire to his own flat.*

▸ when a court's decision is found to be wrong **overturn, quash** *On appeal, his conviction was quashed by the Court of Appeal.*

▸ when a court's decision is found to be right **uphold** *The Court of Appeal has today upheld the conviction of both men for murder.*

2 a strong belief; the feeling or appearance of being certain about something

● adj+N strong **absolute, deep, firm, profound, strong** *They no longer feel guilt and carry on with absolute conviction that they are right.*

▸ types of conviction **moral, personal, political, religious** *He had strong religious convictions which influenced the way he lived his life.*

● v+N have or express conviction **express, have, hold** *He expressed his conviction that climate change is one of the biggest challenges we face.*

If you say something **with** or **without conviction**, it means that you are confident/not confident about it: *'You may be right,' she said without conviction.*

▸ share conviction **share** *The contributors all share the conviction that the original findings were flawed.*

▸ make conviction stronger **confirm, reinforce, strengthen** *All these points strengthen my conviction that change is inevitable.*

▸ make conviction weaker **shake** *She accepted what they were saying, but it didn't shake her conviction that she was doing the right thing.*

If an argument etc is convincing you can say that it **carries conviction**: *Statements like that would not carry conviction unless they were backed up by evidence.*

convincing ADJ
making you believe something

● adv+ADJ very **completely, entirely, extremely, thoroughly, totally, utterly, very, wholly** *At the trial, the evidence was never wholly convincing.*

▸ rather **pretty** INFORMAL, **quite** *The statistics are pretty convincing.*

▸ not completely **not completely, not entirely** *The plot was full of twists and turns and not entirely convincing.*

● ADJ+n **answer, argument, case, evidence, explanation, proof, reason, story** *The report's authors put together a convincing argument for new legislation.*

● v+ADJ **be, find sth, look, make sth, seam, sound**

You may not find what I have said totally convincing.
● *Her argument didn't sound very convincing to me.*

cool ADJ
1 rather cold, in a pleasant way

● adv+ADJ **pleasantly, refreshingly, relatively** *The temperature was pleasantly cool at night.*

● ADJ+n **air, breeze, climate, conditions, drink, evening, night, place, shade, temperature, water, weather, wind** *Both beaches have bars serving cool drinks.*

● v+ADJ **be, feel, get, keep, keep sth, look, stay** *Keep the food cool until you serve it.* ● *Wear cotton clothes if you want to stay cool.*

● and/or **dark, dry, fresh, nice** *Store in a cool, dry place.* ● *My cats were sleeping somewhere nice and cool.*

2 calm and relaxed

● v+ADJ **keep, stay** *Don't wave your hands about, and stay cool under pressure.*

● and/or **calm** *It is possible to get off a plane looking cool, calm and in control.*

> You can also use the phrase **cool, calm, and collected** to say that someone is calm: *She looked cool, calm, and collected as she responded to their questions.*

cool V
become less strong

● n+V **anger, ardour, enthusiasm, love, passion, temper** *Later, when tempers had cooled, they sat down and talked.*

cooperation N
when people work together to do something

● adj+N complete or active **active, close, effective, full** *Social workers need the full cooperation of family members in order to carry out the assessment.*

▶ types of cooperation **bilateral, cross-border, economic, international, military, multilateral, mutual, nuclear, regional, technical** *The political and military cooperation that had existed prior to the raid now slowly deteriorated.*

● v+N encourage cooperation **encourage, facilitate, foster, promote** *He met with officials to encourage cooperation between American and North Korean organizations.*

▶ increase cooperation **enhance, improve, increase, strengthen** *After a meeting in Washington, the two countries also agreed to improve defence cooperation in the area.*

▶ want cooperation **call for, seek** *In the first project the organization sought cooperation with galleries in and around London.*

▶ need cooperation **need, require** *The operation of such a system requires cooperation between participating sites.*

> You can say that something is done **with/without** someone's **cooperation**: *We would not have achieved such a remarkable result without the cooperation of the public.*

coordinate V
to organize the different parts of a job or plan

● adv+V well **carefully, closely, well** *All elements of the military's fighting capabilities are well coordinated.*

▶ badly **poorly** *International efforts to control drug smuggling were poorly coordinated.*

● V+n **action, activity, attack, campaign, efforts, event, operations, programme, project, research, response, work** *The Education Network coordinates education-related campaigns throughout the university.*

copy N
a document, file etc that is exactly like the original

● adj+N on paper **paper, print, printed** *Printed copies of some parts of the map are on sale.*

▶ electronic **backup, downloadable, electronic** *If you are going to be away from your PC for a long period of time, you can use a file manager program to make a backup copy elsewhere on your memory card.*

▶ exact **exact, identical, perfect** *Make sure that users have an identical copy of the database.*

▶ illegal **counterfeit, illegal, unauthorized, unlicensed** *It is forbidden to make unauthorized copies of software that is stored on the servers.*

● v+N get a copy **download, get, make, print** *He made a copy of the letter and sent it off to his local MP.*

▶ give a copy **attach, distribute, enclose, forward, send** *Attach a copy of the medical certificate to this form.*

▶ keep a copy **keep, save** *Always keep copies of any letters or court forms you send or receive.*

copy V
make a copy of something; do something in the same way as someone else

● adv+V **accurately, blatantly, faithfully, slavishly, verbatim, word for word** *Today, with many bands slavishly copying this style, it has become trite.*

copyright N
the legal right to have control over who uses the work of a writer, artist, musician etc

● v+N have copyright **have, hold, own, retain** *The photographers retain the copyright for all commercial use.*

▶ break copyright rules **breach, infringe, violate** *If you use a sample of someone else's work in your music, you may be infringing their copyright.*

▶ protect copyright **protect** *The publisher was seeking to protect a copyright.*

● N+v **expire, rest with sb** *Copyright expired 70 years after the death of the author.*

● n+of+N **breach, infringement, violation** *Such an action would be regarded as breach of copyright.*

cordial ADJ
friendly

● ADJ+n **atmosphere, invitation, reception, relations, relationship, welcome** *We received a very cordial welcome from the landlord.*

core ADJ
most important, or most basic

- ADJ+n in education **curriculum, module, subject, syllabus, unit** *Music has become part of the core curriculum in the third year.*
- ▶ skill **competence, competency, skill** *The course covers the core competences as specified by the Health and Safety directive.*
- ▶ part **component, element** *The rewards programme is one of the core components of the company's marketing strategy.*
- ▶ activity **activity, business, function** *The organization is being restructured so it can concentrate on its core pharmacy business.*
- ▶ idea **belief, concept, objective, principle, theme, value** *How can we best describe the core values of the civil service?*

corporate ADJ
relating to large companies

- ADJ+n **client, culture, event, finance, hospitality, identity, image, plan, strategy, structure** *Corporate strategy includes a commitment to review customer service standards.*

correct ADJ
right

- adv+ADJ absolutely **absolutely, completely, entirely, perfectly, quite** *I know this statement is difficult to believe, but it is absolutely correct.*
- ▶ not absolutely **basically, broadly, essentially, not strictly, partially** *It is not strictly correct to say that the disease is caused by stress, but stress is an aggravating factor.*
- ▶ in a particular way **factually, grammatically, historically, technically** *All the information is historically correct as far as can be ascertained.*
- v+ADJ **be, be proved, prove** *Is he wrong or will his theories prove correct in time?*
- ADJ+in+n **analysis, assertion, assessment, assumption, belief, view** *The Government is correct in its view that funding must be accompanied by reform.*

correlate V
be connected in a way that is not caused by chance

- adv+V **closely, directly, highly, positively, significantly, strongly, well** *Global warming is undoubtedly caused by some kind of human activity since it correlates strongly with the last century of rapid population and industrial growth.*

correlation N
a connection or relationship not caused by chance

- adj+N strong or important **clear, close, direct, high, significant, strong** *There was a strong correlation between good leadership and successful business outcomes.*
- ▶ positive/negative **negative, positive** *There was a positive correlation between press coverage and sales.*
- ▶ weak **poor, weak** *Only a weak correlation between magnetic fields and cancer incidence was observed.*
- v+N **demonstrate, establish, find, identify,**

observe, show *Doctors found a correlation between blood clot size and the length of time since the last cigarette.*

- N+v **be, exist** *Research shows that a close correlation exists between global GDP growth and carbon emissions.*

correspond V
be the same or similar

- adv+V exactly **directly, exactly, precisely** *The domain name must correspond exactly with the registered name.*
- ▶ approximately **approximately, broadly, closely, roughly** *This ancient kingdom corresponded roughly to the counties of Gloucestershire and Worcestershire.*

correspondence N
1 the process of writing and receiving letters and email; the letters etc that you write and receive

- adj+N personal **confidential, personal, private** *Students may not use the University's address for the purpose of receiving private correspondence.*
- ▶ official **official** *All official correspondence was in Welsh.*
- ▶ lasting a long time **lengthy, protracted, regular** *She kept up a regular correspondence with Brendan for the next few years.*
- v+N send or receive correspondence **address, send** *Please address all correspondence to Head Office.*
- ▶ deal with correspondence **answer, handle** *All correspondence will be answered within 21 days.*
- ▶ have a correspondence with someone **carry on, enter into, keep up** *She refused to enter into any correspondence with the company.*

2 a strong connection between two things

- adj+N **close, direct, exact, one-to-one** *The English alphabet lacks a one-to-one correspondence between sounds and symbols.*

corruption N
dishonest or illegal behaviour by officials

- adj+N when there is a lot of corruption **endemic, rampant, rife, widespread** *Corruption is rife throughout the world.*
- ▶ types of corruption **moral, official, political** *The whole system is open to political corruption.*
- n+N **government, police** *Protesters said they were concerned about widespread government corruption and the lack of jobs.*
- v+N deal with corruption **combat, eliminate, eradicate, fight, prevent, reduce, tackle** *Urgent measures need to be taken to combat corruption.*
- ▶ show corruption **expose** *He exposed the corruption of foreign governments.*
- N+n **allegation, charge, offence, scandal** *Several senior officials were arrested on corruption charges.*

cosmetic ADJ
affecting only the appearance of something

- adv+ADJ **just, largely, merely, only, purely** *These*

were largely cosmetic changes which left the major problems unsolved.

● ADJ+n **change, damage, improvement** *The car suffered only cosmetic damage in the accident.*

cost N

1 the amount of money paid for something

● adj+N total **full, overall, total** *If you are treated privately, you must pay the full cost.*

▶ high **high, huge, prohibitive** *The tennis courts have fallen into disrepair due to the high cost of keeping them maintained.*

▶ becoming higher **escalating, increasing, spiralling** *The escalating cost of gas and electricity is blighting the lives of millions of families.*

▶ low **low, reasonable, small** *There are a range of schemes giving householders an opportunity to improve energy efficiency at a low cost.*

▶ extra **additional, extra** *Other than food, there will be no additional cost.*

▶ average **average** *The average cost of medical care for arthritis was $5,700 per year.*

▶ not obvious **hidden** *But what about some of the hidden costs, such as loss of earnings, travel costs for your family and relatives or extra help around the home?*

● v+N pay the cost **cover, meet, pay** *There was sufficient funds in their budget to cover the cost of any unforeseen repair works.*

▶ have to pay a cost **incur** *Money could be saved by reducing, reusing and recycling waste because that does not incur the cost of landfill tax.*

▶ get back the cost **recoup, recover** *Successful therapists can quickly recoup the cost of their initial training.*

▶ give back the cost **refund, reimburse** *In the event of a return we will refund the total cost of the product.*

▶ reduce the cost **bring down, cut, keep down, lower, reduce** *64 per cent of companies are using e-recruitment in order to cut the cost and time involved in hiring new staff.*

▶ increase the cost **increase, raise** *These additional features will increase the cost.*

▶ pay some of the cost **defray, offset** *The money given to us will help defray the cost of buying new chairs for the centre.*

● N+v become greater **escalate, go up, increase, rise, soar** *The cost of the new system has soared to £2 billion.*

▶ become less **fall, go down** *The cost of food has fallen dramatically in recent months.*

2 damage or loss

● adj+N great **great, heavy, huge, significant, substantial** *They claimed victory, but at great cost because over 1000 soldiers were killed.*

If someone will do something even if it causes damage or loss, you can say that they will do it *at any cost* or *at all costs*: *She was determined to win at all costs.* When there is loss or damage as a result of something, you can say that it has come *at a cost*: *He finished the work but at a cost to his health.*

▶ types of cost **environmental, human, personal,**

social *We cannot underestimate the social cost of mass unemployment.*

● v+N **outweigh** *The economic benefit will far outweigh the human cost of having to relocate staff.*

When someone realizes what has been lost or damaged as a result of something else, you can say that they *count the cost*: *The whole firm is counting the cost of the bombing today.*

3 money spent regularly on electricity, rent etc [always plural]

● adj+N high **high, huge** *This will mean higher energy costs for domestic users.*

▶ becoming higher **escalating, rising, spiralling** *Charities were facing escalating costs due to the introduction of a new tax.*

▶ low **low** *Low costs for software and service operators in India are both an opportunity and a threat to European and US companies.*

▶ types of cost **administrative, fixed, operational, variable** *These charges cover the operational costs of selling and distributing theatre tickets.*

● n+N **administration, childcare, energy, fuel, housing, labour, maintenance, operating, production, running, transport, travel** *Banks want you to access your account online as it costs them less in administration costs.*

● v+N reduce costs **cut, reduce** *As manufacturing industries faced pressure from world competition, they were forced to cut costs on a massive scale.*

▶ make costs as low as possible **keep down, minimize** *Transport costs are minimized by utilising the services of a regular and reliable transport agency.*

● N+v become higher **escalate, go up, increase, rise, soar** *Although visitor numbers only declined slightly, costs escalated, especially for insurance and utilities.*

▶ become lower **fall, go down** *Costs are falling continually.*

▶ be involved **be associated with, be involved in** *There are high costs associated with running this type of business.*

4 money paid for the services of law court [always plural]

● adj+N **legal** *Each party's legal costs will vary depending upon resources used, length of hearing and evidence submitted.*

● v+N **incur, pay** *Failure to do this will result in a summons being issued without further warning, which will incur further costs.*

costly ADJ

costing a lot of money or causing a lot of problems

● ADJ+n **business, delay, error, exercise, mistake, option, process, repair** *Buying your first home can be a costly business.*

● v+ADJ **be, become, prove** *Later changes will prove costly in terms of both time and money.*

● and/or **complex, complicated, damaging, dangerous, difficult, disruptive, lengthy, time-consuming** *The tests are costly and time-consuming to carry out.*

cosy ADJ
warm and comfortable; making you relaxed

- ADJ+n place **accommodation, bar, bed, cottage, lounge, pub, room, surroundings** *Hotel guests can relax in the cosy lounge.*
- ▶ feeling **atmosphere, feel** *The cottage has a very cosy feel.*
- ▶ conversation **chat** *We had a lovely cosy chat over coffee.*
- ▶ fire **fire** *The hotel bar offered a warm welcome and a cosy fire to sit beside.*
- and/or **comfortable, friendly, homely, little, relaxing, romantic, snug, warm** *It was a cosy little bar.* • *I was lying in bed, all warm and cosy.*

cough V
to make a sudden noise by forcing air up through your throat

- adv+V loudly **loudly, violently** *He leaned heavily on his stick, coughing violently.*
- ▶ quietly **discreetly, nervously, politely** *The man paused and coughed nervously before continuing.*
- and/or **choke, sneeze, splutter, wheeze** *I came out of the water coughing and spluttering.*

cough N
the action of coughing or an illness in which you cough

- adj+N types of cough **chesty, dry, hacking, irritating, non-productive, productive, rasping, tickly** *If you have a chesty cough, you will need an 'expectorant' cough medicine.*
- ▶ bad **bad, nasty, severe** *The child was taken to see the doctor with a bad cough.*
- ▶ not very bad **mild, slight** *I am very well, apart from a slight cough.*
- ▶ lasting a long time **chronic, persistent** *He was underweight and suffering from a persistent cough.*
- v+N make a cough better **cure, relieve, soothe, treat** *Drinking lemon juice with honey can relieve your cough.*
- ▶ have a cough **develop, get, have** *Smokers often develop a chronic cough.*
- N+n medicine **linctus, medicine, mixture, remedy, syrup** *The place you buy shampoo and cough syrup is called a pharmacy in America and a chemist in Australia.*
- ▶ sweet **drop, lozenge, sweet** *Try sucking a cough drop.*
- and/or **cold, fever, sneeze** *Like measles, mumps is spread by coughs and sneezes.*

council N
1 elected officials who govern a local area

- adj+N **borough, city, county, district, local, metropolitan, municipal, parish, regional, town** *The houses were built by Surrey county council in the 1920s.*
- v+N **advise, apply to, ask, contact, inform, notify, tell** *People who need to use this service can contact the council using an on-line form.*
- ▶ meet **meet** *The Council meets weekly except during the summer months.*
- ▶ N+v discuss **consider, discuss** *The council is considering applications for grants from local organizations.*
- ▶ agree **adopt sth, agree, approve sth, decide, endorse sth, support sth** *The council agreed to place her in temporary accommodation.*
- ▶ refuse **refuse, reject** *The town council refused his application for planning permission.*
- ▶ pay for **fund, provide** *We are not funded by the council and rely entirely on the services of volunteers.*
- N+n provided by the council **estate, house, housing** *The government has set minimum standards for the condition of council housing.*
- ▶ working for the council **leader, officer, official, spokesman, spokeswoman** *The number of people in Leicester renting allotments has increased, according to a city council spokesman.*
- ▶ paying money to the council **taxpayer, tenant** *As a council tenant, you have the right to have repairs done competently and on time.*
- ▶ tax **tax** *We receive more than half of our funding from central government, the rest coming from council tax.*
- ▶ election **by-election, election** *Public transport is a major issue in the council elections.*

2 a group elected to make decisions

- adj+N ruling **executive, governing, ruling** *The bishop is the president of the governing council of the church.*
- ▶ having a particular role or responsibility **advisory, arts, ecumenical, funding, research, security, skills** *The university attracts sponsorship from research councils, industry, and charities.*
- ▶ for young people **school, student, youth** *Mole Valley Youth Voice is a youth council, consisting of young people between ages 11 and 18*

counsel N
a lawyer representing someone in a court of law

- adj+N defending/prosecuting **defence, defending, prosecuting, prosecution** *An appeal was entered by his defence counsel.*
- ▶ legal **legal, legislative, trial** *He paid a specialist legal counsel to pursue a personal injury claim.*
- ▶ senior/junior **chief, junior, lead, leading, senior** *They paid the fees of the experts, leading counsel and junior counsel.*
- v+N **appoint, instruct** *The costs of instructing counsel and preparing for the hearings will be repaid.*
- N+v represent **act for, advise, appear for, represent** *You have the right to be represented by counsel.*
- ▶ say **argue, conclude, contend, point out, say, submit** *His counsel argued that his case should be considered separately to that of his co-defendant.*
- N+for making an accusation or claim **claimant, plaintiff, prosecution** *Counsel for the prosecution told the court this was a clear case of fraud.*
- ▶ representing the accused **defence, defendant, respondent** *Counsel for the defence asked to see the police officer's notebook.*

counselling N
help with personal problems in the form of talking and listening

- adj+N for emotional problems **bereavement, marriage, relationship, stress, trauma** *After Mum died, I decided to go for bereavement counselling.*
- ▶ for health issues **abortion, genetic, pregnancy** *Women with a family history of haemophilia should be referred for genetic counselling.*
- ▶ for job or money issues **career, debt, workplace** *Debt counselling can help stop you falling further into arrears.*
- ▶ for one person/many people **confidential, face-to-face, group, individual, one-to-one** *The charity offers a telephone helpline, group meetings and one-to-one counselling.*
- ▶ by an expert **professional, specialist** *Specialist counselling and practical advice is available from your local Victim Support scheme.*
- v+N need or get **be referred for, be sent for, go for, have, need, receive, seek** *Eventually, she had to seek professional counselling.*
- ▶ give **give sb, offer (sb), provide, refer sb for** *We offer counselling and support to parents of children with cancer.*
- N+n **service, session** *Contact the student counselling service for advice.*

count N
the process of counting or the amount of something counted

- adj+N low/high **high, low, maximum, peak** *If your blood count is low, you are more vulnerable to infections.*
- ▶ total **final, full, last, total** *Her analysis puts the total death count in the war at 205,000.*
- n+N in the body, in the air etc **blood, cell, platelet, pollen, sperm** *During pregnancy, your blood count may have to be monitored.*
- ▶ number of people **body, head** *While the class read, I did a quiet head count and tick off names.*
- ▶ number of things **calorie, pixel, syllable, vote, word** *Essays should be typed and include a word count.*
- v+N carry out a count **carry out, conduct, do, make** *Wardens on nature reserves conduct regular counts of numbers of seabirds.*
- ▶ reduce the count **lower, reduce** *There is a theory that mobile phones can lower your sperm count.*
- ▶ increase the count **double, increase, raise** *The magazine increased its page count to almost 300 pages.*
- N+v rise **go up, increase, rise** *The unemployment claimant count rose again in November.*
- ▶ fall **decrease, drop, fall, go down** *The average staff count in French companies dropped by 1.8 per cent.*
- ▶ be a particular amount **be at, reach, stand at** *The arrest count stood at 34 last night, most of them drug related.*
- ▶ be more/less than a particular amount **exceed, go above, go below, go over, go under** *I need to adjust my medication if the count goes below 20.*

counter V
to respond to an attack, threat or criticism

- V+n problem **attack, discrimination, extremism, fraud, racism, terrorism, threat** *We must be prepared to counter all possible threats from terrorism.*
- ▶ argument **accusation, argument, claim, criticism, misinformation, objection, propaganda** *The Professor said the study countered the arguments of some educators.*
- ▶ trend **tendency, trend** *More vocational options at school could counter the tendency for young people to drop out at 16 or 17.*
- ▶ effect **effect** *Long, sustained rainfall is needed to counter the effects of the drought.*

counter ADJ
opposite, or with an opposite purpose

- ADJ+n **argument, proposal** *Obviously, there are counter arguments put forward by rural groups.*
- ADJ+to idea or belief **belief, notion, policy, principle, spirit, theory** *This would be counter to the government's policy of involving businesses in these decisions.*
- ▶ aim or advantage **aim, interests, objective** *It would be counter to British interests to destroy that cosy relationship.*

You can also say that something **runs counter** to a belief, principle, etc: *This policy runs counter to the principle of sustainable development.*

counter-attack N
an attack against someone who has just attacked you

- adj+N **aggressive, fierce, immediate, swift** *Their attempt on goal was met with an immediate counter-attack.*
- v+N **conduct, launch, lead, mount** *We should have the legal authority to launch counterattacks against computer hackers.*

country N
1 an area of land with its own government

- adj+N richer/poorer **affluent, high-income, impoverished, low-income, middle-income, poor, prosperous, rich, wealthy** *Rich and middle-income countries are excluded from the agreement.*
- ▶ with/without a lot of industry **advanced, developed, developing, first-world, industrialized, less-developed, third-world, under-developed** *Many developing countries do not have the infrastructure for a successful tourist industry.*

The terms **underdeveloped** and **third-world** are often considered to be offensive. The preferred word is **developing**.

- ▶ where a person comes from **home, mother, native** *Open a UK bank account before you leave your home country.*
- ▶ where a person from another country is living **adopted, host** *You should treat your host country with respect and courtesy.*
- ▶ next to another country **neighbouring** *They are concerned that the dispute could spread to neighbouring countries.*
- ▶ independent **independent, sovereign** *There was a*

policy of non-interference in the affairs of a sovereign country.

▸ not supporting other countries politically **neutral, non-aligned** *The airmen were sent down escape lines to neutral countries like Switzerland.*

2 areas away from cities and towns

● adj+N types of country **hill, hilly, low-lying, mountainous, rugged, wooded** *The road winds through hilly country and crosses several rivers.*

▸ not built on **open, unspoilt** *The country park is a long stretch of open country just a couple of miles from the town centre.*

▸ used for a particular purpose **farming, walking** *This area is mostly farming country.*

countryside N

areas away from cities and towns

● adj+N beautiful **attractive, beautiful, breathtaking, glorious, idyllic, lovely, picturesque, scenic, stunning** *I spent much of my youth wandering in the glorious countryside of the Yorkshire Dales.*

▸ hilly **hilly, mountainous, rolling, rugged, undulating** *The hill offers superb views across the rolling countryside.*

▸ green **lush, verdant, wooded** *The lush countryside produces everything from rice to exotic fruits.*

▸ peaceful **peaceful, tranquil** *Their house was an old mill set in tranquil countryside.*

▸ not built on **open, unspoiled, unspoilt** *Leaving the village, we soon entered open countryside.*

▸ nearby **nearby, surrounding** *They often went for picnics in the surrounding countryside.*

coup N

an occasion when a group takes control suddenly, and usually by force

● adj+N violent **army, bloody, military** *The progressive regime was overthrown by a bloody coup.*

▸ non-violent **bloodless, political** *In 2003 he took power in a bloodless coup.*

▸ unsuccessful **abortive, attempted, failed, unsuccessful** *They were accused of involvement in the abortive coup.*

▸ in a business company **boardroom** *She was sacked last week in a dramatic boardroom coup.*

● v+N plan a coup **attempt, engineer, instigate, launch, lead, mount, orchestrate, organize, plan, plot, stage** *He accused the former president of organising a coup against him.* ● *In 1926, the nationalists staged a coup.*

▸ support a coup **back, support** *They backed the military coup in Chile.*

couple N

two people who are married or in a relationship

● adj+N married/not married **cohabiting, divorced, married, unmarried** *All married couples argue sometimes.*

▸ recently married **bridal, honeymoon, newly married, newly wed**

● of a particular age **elderly, middle-aged, old, retired, young** *In the flat upstairs lived a young couple.*

▸ without children **childless, infertile** *As a baby, he was adopted by a childless couple.*

▸ gay/not gay **gay, heterosexual, homosexual, lesbian, opposite-sex, same-sex** *The number of same-sex couples buying homes together is at an all-time high.*

courage N

the ability to be brave

● adj+N great **considerable, dauntless, enormous, exceptional, extraordinary, great, heroic, immense, indomitable, outstanding, tremendous, undaunted** *Throughout her long illness, she displayed indomitable courage.*

▸ types of courage **moral, personal, physical, political** *It would be an act of political courage to relax retirement laws.*

● v+N show courage **demonstrate, display, have, possess, show** *He showed outstanding courage in coping with his disability.*

▸ manage to find courage **find, gather, muster, pluck up, screw up, summon** *At last I summoned the courage to walk on stage.*

▸ lack courage **lack, lose** *They lack the courage to admit their mistakes.*

▸ praise someone's courage **admire, applaud, celebrate, honour, praise, remember, salute** *He saluted their courage in pursuing a vision that has now become a reality.*

▸ require courage **demand, need, require, take** *Challenging your superiors takes courage.*

● and/or **bravery, determination, dignity, endurance, fortitude, honesty, perseverance, self-sacrifice, strength, tenacity** *He was awarded this medal in recognition of his courage and determination.*

course N

a series of lessons in a subject or skill

● adj+N taking a particular time **full-time, half-day, part-time, short, one-day, two-week, four-year etc** *We were required to attend a one-day management course.*

▸ involving a lot of teaching in a short time **intensive** *This is an intensive course and you should be prepared to work hard.*

▸ at a particular level **degree, diploma, GCSE, honours, MA, postgraduate, pre-sessional, undergraduate** *The university offers graduate and undergraduate courses in a range of disciplines.*

▸ introductory **beginners', foundation, induction, introductory, taster** *We run taster courses for women interested in science and engineering.*

▸ involving training for a job **training, vocational** *To become a healthcare professional, you have to do A levels or take a vocational course.*

▸ improving your knowledge of a subject **refresher** *We recommend that you sign up for a refresher course if you qualified some years ago.*

▸ officially recognized **accredited, certificated** *We have developed an accredited course for library staff.*

▸ taught in a particular way or in a particular place **correspondence, distance-learning, home-study, in-service, modular, residential** *A distance-learning course was introduced, making the qualification available throughout the UK.*

● v+N give a course **deliver, give, offer, run, teach** *I teach courses on archaeology and history.*

▶ attend a course **attend, complete, enrol on, go on, sign up for, take** *Consider going on a computer course at your local college.*

● N+v take place **last, run** *The course runs twice a year, in spring and autumn.*

▶ include or deal with **concentrate on, consist of, cover, examine, explore, focus on, include** *The course examines the role of the state in the postcolonial era.*

● N+v **be aimed at, be designed for, be intended for, be tailored to** *These courses were aimed at adults who want to improve their literacy skills.*

court N
a place where legal trials take place and cases are decided

● v+N attend court **appear in, attend** *Many witnesses are too frightened to attend court.*

▶ be discussed in court **come to, go to** *The case should never have gone to court.*

▶ convince the court **convince, persuade, satisfy** *The newspaper must satisfy the court that there is a public interest in publication of the pictures.*

▶ ask the court for something **ask, petition** *A father petitioned the court for custody of his six-year-old son.*

> You can also say that someone *goes to court* or *takes someone to court* when they ask the court to make someone do or stop doing a particular thing: *A group of parents took a school to court over the teaching of evolutionary theory.*

▶ allow the court to do something **empower, enable, entitle** *The Act empowers the court to seize the assets of someone who has been convicted of a crime.*

● N+v decide or order something **conclude, decide, direct, hold, impose, order, rule** *The court ruled that the inquiry should be in public.*

> When a case is settled before it goes to court, you can say it is *settled out of court*: *Their claim for damages against the travel company was settled out of court.*

▶ disagree with or refuse something **dismiss, overturn, quash, refuse, reject** *A US court rejected his appeal.*

▶ agree with or allow something **accept, award, grant, uphold** *The appeal court upheld a ruling that the company acted unlawfully.*

▶ find someone guilty/not guilty **acquit, clear, convict, sentence** *He was sentenced by a military court to seven years in prison.*

● N+n case **action, battle, case, hearing, proceedings** *The company was threatened with court proceedings if it did not comply.*

▶ decision or order **decision, injunction, judgment, order, ruling, summons** *A federal court ruling held that the police were wrong in arresting him.*

court V
to try to get something, or behave in a way that makes something likely to happen

● adv+V **actively, assiduously, deliberately, openly** *Someone who deliberately courts media attention can hardly complain about being 'hounded'.*

● V+n when you deliberately seek something **attention, controversy, popularity, publicity** *As a critic, he has a reputation for courting controversy.*

▶ when you make something likely **danger, disaster** *To continue to do nothing would be courting disaster.*

courtesy N
polite behaviour that shows respect

● adj+N normal or expected **common, normal, usual** *In Japan, removing your shoes before entering someone's house is common courtesy.*

▶ great **amazing, great, unfailing, utmost** *Every member of the crew treated passengers with the utmost courtesy.*

● and/or **consideration, dignity, friendliness, helpfulness, kindness, politeness, professionalism, respect, tact** *He was an unassuming man, noted for his kindness and courtesy.*

cover V
to include and deal with something

● adv+V **adequately, comprehensively, extensively, fully, in depth, in detail, in full** *This is an excellent book, comprehensively covering a wide range of business topics.*

● V+n subject **aspects, issue, subject, topic** *This section of the book covers the topic of deforestation.*

▶ variety **range, spectrum, variety** *The course covers a range of issues such as population and migration.*

● n+V deal with a subject **book, chapter, course, factsheet, module, section** *The first chapter covers the evolution of the horse.*

▶ apply in a situation **agreement, exemption, guarantee, legislation, licence, regulations, warranty** *The agency has the power to set regulations covering food safety.*

coverage N
attention given to something in the media, or in a book or course of education

● adj+N extensive **blanket, extensive, maximum, saturation, wall-to-wall, widespread** *The trial has been given blanket coverage in the media.*

▶ live **live** *We will bring you live coverage of the final on October 14th.*

▶ detailed **comprehensive, detailed, in-depth** *Clearly students will need more detailed coverage of particular periods, but as a general introduction this book is excellent.*

● n+N types of media **media, news, press, television, TV** *Air disasters receive widespread press coverage.*

● v+N **attract, be given, gain, get, receive** *This year's conference succeeded in attracting far wider media coverage than in the past.*

cover up PHR VB
to hide the truth about something

● V+n truth **evidence, facts, truth** *Ministers and police were involved in plots to cover up the truth and destroy evidence.*

▶ incident **crime, incident, murder** *They decided it would be better to cover up the incident by throwing the body in the sea.*

▸ fault **failure, lack, mistake, problem** *People sometimes try to cover up their own lack of knowledge with confusing terminology.*

cover-up N
an attempt to hide the truth about something bad

- adj+N big **big, elaborate, major, massive** *Campaigners suspect a massive government cover-up.*
- ▸ possible **alleged, attempted** *The government was rocked by claims of an attempted cover-up.*
- ▸ official **government, governmental, high-level, official** *The military denied that there had been any official cover-up of the incident.*

- v+N accuse someone of a cover-up **accuse sb of, allege** *The source telephoned a journalist, alleging a high-level cover-up.*
- ▸ be involved in a cover-up **be engaged in, be involved in** *It was clear that the government had been involved in the cover-up.*
- ▸ reveal a cover-up **expose** *A documentary film-maker tried to expose the cover-up.*
- ▸ organize a cover-up **engineer, orchestrate, organize** *Did the FBI orchestrate a cover-up?*

crack N
a line or opening in a surface

- adj+N thin **faint, fine, hairline, narrow, small, thin, tiny** *An engineer spotted a hairline crack in the fuel tank.*
- ▸ large **deep, large, obvious, wide** *There are obvious cracks in the walls of many houses along this road.*

- N+v **appear, develop, form, open up, run, show** *A crack appeared near the top of the dam.* • *There's a crack running right across the ceiling.*

crackdown N
strong action to stop a particular activity

- adj+N major **major, massive, tough** *This led to a massive crackdown by the authorities, with over 600 people being arrested.*
- ▸ violent **bloody, brutal, military, violent** *What followed was a brutal crackdown on protests by the ruling party.*
- ▸ new or continuing **new, ongoing, recent, renewed** *The alcohol sale restrictions are part of a new crackdown on anti-social behaviour.*

- n+N **government, police** *The police crackdown on vandalism continues.*

- v+N begin a crackdown **announce, begin, launch, order** *Rail bosses this week launched a crackdown on fare dodgers.*
- ▸ continue a crackdown **continue, intensify** *The regime intensified its crackdown on political dissidents.*
- ▸ say you intend a crackdown **pledge, promise, threaten** *Their election manifesto promised a crackdown on companies that pollute the environment.*

- N+on **antisocial behaviour, crime, dissent, drugs, fraud, immigration** *The major cleaned up the city in a major crackdown on crime.*

craft V
to make or produce something skilfully [usually passive]

- adv+V well **beautifully, carefully, cleverly, expertly, exquisitely, finely, lovingly, meticulously, skilfully, superbly, well** *The play features beautifully crafted puppets and live music.*
- ▸ individually **hand, individually, specially** *All our cakes are hand crafted for that special occasion.*

craftsmanship N
the skill of making things using your hands; the quality of work shown in something that has been made by hand

- adj+N **exquisite, fine, intricate, meticulous, outstanding, painstaking, skilled, superb, superior** *The ornamental carvings show superb craftsmanship.*

crash N
1 an accident involving a moving vehicle

- adj+N very bad **horrendous, horrific, serious, terrible, tragic** *He has rebuilt his life since being involved in a horrific motorbike crash.*
- ▸ involving death **fatal** *Investigations are continuing after a fatal crash at a level-crossing near Bath.*
- ▸ involving speed **high-speed, speed-related** *Two cars were involved in a high-speed crash on the motorway.*
- ▸ when the front of one vehicle hits another **head-on** *There was a head-on crash at high speed between the two trains.*

- n+N type of vehicle involved **car, helicopter, motorcycle, plane, train** *Almost 200 people died in the plane crash.*
- ▸ where it happens **air, rail, road** *There will be an inquest into the causes of the rail crash.*

- v+N be involved in a crash **be involved in, have, suffer, survive** *Last year he had a car crash and was seriously injured.*
- ▸ cause a crash **cause** *He was jailed for causing a crash in which two people died.*
- ▸ prevent a crash **avert, avoid, prevent** *She swerved to avoid a crash.*

2 the loud noise of hard things hitting each other

- adj+N **almighty** INFORMAL**, loud, resounding** *The door flew open and hit the wall with an almighty crash.*

- and/or **bang, clang** *We heard a series of bangs and crashes coming from the kitchen.*

craving N
a very strong feeling of wanting something

- adj+N strong **insatiable, intense, strong** *His hunger becomes an insatiable craving: the more he eats, the more he wants.*
- ▸ types of craving **addictive, physical, psychological** *A diet high in fat and sugar may trigger the same addictive cravings as tobacco or drugs.*

- v+N have a craving **experience, feel, get, have** *During the first few weeks of being a non-smoker, you're likely to experience cravings for nicotine at different times of the day.*

▶ control a craving **beat, conquer, control, curb, decrease, eliminate, overcome, reduce, relieve, stop** *You need to learn how to control these cravings with various strategies.*

▶ satisfy a craving **satisfy** *She occasionally has a burger to satisfy her craving for junk food.*

▶ cause a craving **induce, trigger** *Crack appears to induce an intense craving in some users.*

● N+for **alcohol, carbohydrates, chocolate, cigarettes, food, nicotine, sugar, sweets** *Eating fruit can greatly reduce cravings for sugar.*

create V
to make something new or original

● adv+V specially **especially, exclusively, specially, specifically** *Our productions are known for their wonderful visual effects and specially created live music.*

> Usage *Create* is usually passive in these combinations.

▶ newly **newly, recently** *This is a newly created role; your responsibilities will be varied and challenging.*

> Usage *Create* is usually passive in these combinations.

▶ using a particular method **artificially, automatically, digitally, manually** *Virtual reality is the ability to travel into artificially created worlds.*

▶ deliberately/not deliberately **deliberately, inadvertently** *We believe that they have deliberately created an atmosphere of fear in order to intimidate people.*

● V+n feeling **ambience, atmosphere, buzz** INFORMAL**, climate, environment, illusion, impression, mood** *We aim to create an atmosphere where racism is not tolerated.* ● *Leaflets are an excellent way of creating a buzz before the event.*

▶ problem **confusion, havoc, problem, tension** *Winds of more than 70 mph have been creating havoc across the country.*

▶ something positive **chance, incentive, jobs, opportunity, wealth** *I learned some very practical ways to create business opportunities.*

▶ piece of art **artwork, collage, masterpiece, sculpture** *She was commissioned to create artworks for the hospital.*

▶ on a computer **database, directory, file, folder, image, playlist, shortcut, template** *Go to online help to learn how to create a video file.*

creative ADJ
involving imagination and new ideas

● adv+ADJ very **extremely, fantastically, genuinely, highly, incredibly, intensely, really, truly, very, wildly, wonderfully** *Heston is a highly creative and original chef.*

▶ in a particular way **artistically, culturally, musically** *In our opinion, this is the most musically creative and exciting city in the UK today.*

● ADJ+n thinking **idea, solution, thinking** *Our workshops develop creative thinking and research skills.*

▶ talent **flair, potential, talent** *He was a skilled artist, but rarely showed creative flair.*

▶ activity **activity, endeavour** *The regime crushed all attempts at individual freedom and creative endeavour.*

▶ person **genius, thinker** *Nobel was both a creative genuis and an idealist.*

● and/or **dynamic, exciting, expressive, imaginative, innovative, inventive, resourceful, talented** *We are looking for creative and imaginative ways to engage young people.*

creativity N
the ability to create new ideas or things

● adj+N of a person or group **collective, human, individual, personal** *The music we listen to, the books we read, and the computer software we use are all products of human creativity.*

▶ in a particular field **artistic, cultural, literary, musical** *The band demonstrates musical creativity through its freeflowing improvisations.*

● v+N encourage creativity **develop, encourage, enhance, foster, inspire, nurture, promote, spark, stimulate, unleash, unlock** *Drama and role-play can stimulate creativity and enjoyment in learning.*

▶ discourage creativity **inhibit, stifle** *Scientists worry that the emphasis on applied science will stifle creativity.*

▶ direct creativity to a purpose **channel, harness** *Organizations need to develop and harness the creativity of their employees.*

▶ express your creativity **demonstrate, explore, express** *The play centre is a great place for young children to explore their creativity.*

● n+for+N **opportunity, room, scope** *There isn't much scope for creativity in this job.*

● and/or **enthusiasm, flair, imagination, individuality, ingenuity, innovation, inspiration, inventiveness, originality, resourcefulness, spontaneity, talent** *We welcome new ideas, innovation and creativity.*

credentials N
qualities that make someone or something suitable

● adj+N good **excellent, impeccable, impressive, the right, strong** *She has impeccable credentials for the job of heading the US central bank .*

▶ types of credentials **academic, democratic, educational, environmental, ethical, green, liberal, professional, scholarly, scientific** *The car also has impressive green credentials, with very low CO2 emissions.*

● v+N demonstrate your credentials **boost, demonstrate, establish, prove, re-establish, underline** *He had already established his credentials as an economic adviser in the War Cabinet.*

▶ make your credentials stronger **boost, emphasize, improve, reinforce, underline** *The store boosted its ethical credentials by agreeing to sell only ethically sourced products.*

▶ check someone's credentials **check, verify** *Check the company's credentials before you go ahead with building work.*

credibility N
qualities that make people believe someone or something

- adj+N in a particular field **academic, artistic, historical, intellectual, journalistic, political, professional, scientific** *A conference claiming to have some scientific credibility was spoiled by misleading hype.*
- ▶ a lot of **added, enhanced, great, more, much** *A more accurate title would have given this whole article more credibility.*
- ▶ immediate **immediate, instant** *The connection of respected players with the project gave instant credibility with the public.*

- v+N damage credibility **damage, destroy, diminish, question, undermine** *The documents were so obviously false that they totally undermined his credibility as a witness.*
- ▶ improve credibility **add, boost, build, enhance, give, increase, lend, restore** *The clear political independence of the newspaper lends credibility.*
- ▶ have or keep credibility **gain, have, maintain, regain, retain** *Election candidates gain credibility from campaigning on local issues.*
- ▶ lack or lose credibility **lack, lose, strain** *The film is action-packed, but at a certain point it begins to strain credibility.*

- N+n **crisis, gap, issue, problem** *There is a yawning credibility gap between what the Government says in public and its actions.*

credible ADJ
able to be believed or trusted

- adv+ADJ not very **barely, hardly, remotely, scarcely** *Such intolerance is scarcely credible in the 21st century.*
- ▶ very **entirely, extremely, highly, perfectly, quite, totally, utterly, very, wholly** *Evidence for these transactions came from highly credible sources.*
- ▶ in a particular way **academically, politically, scientifically** *A study so narrowly based cannot be scientifically credible.*

- ADJ+n evidence **allegation, evidence, intelligence, source, testimony, witness** *She was not a credible witness.*
- ▶ explanation **argument, explanation, scenario** *No credible explanation is given to support the hype.*
- ▶ another choice **alternative, candidate, opposition** *We need to offer these children credible alternatives to gang membership and violent crime.*
- ▶ threat **deterrence, deterrent, threat** *Airpower has the potential to provide a credible deterrent.*

- v+ADJ **appear, seem, sound** *An author who seems quite credible may be utterly unreliable.*

credit N
1 praise or approval for something you have done

- adj+N great **enormous, full, great, much** *It was a difficult operation, and the whole team deserves enormous credit for its success.*
- ▶ deserved **due, proper** *If you incorporate my maps into other reports, you should give due credit.*

- v+N **claim, deserve, emerge with, get, give, take** *This was a bad-tempered game from which neither side emerged with much credit.* • *He refuses to take credit for much of what he has achieved.*

2 permission to pay for something by borrowing money

- v+N give credit **extend, give sb, offer sb, provide** *The high level of unemployment could make lenders less willing to extend credit.*
- ▶ refuse to give credit **deny sb, refuse sb** *The Enterprise Loan Fund offers loans to small businesses and start-ups which have been refused credit by mainstream lenders.*

- N+n agreement to give credit **agreement, arrangement, facility** *If you do not keep paying the instalments, you will be in breach of the credit agreement.*
- ▶ judgement as to whether someone should be given credit **check, history, rating, record, score** *Generally, a bank will also run an independent credit check before authorizing a loan of this size.*

3 part of an academic course successfully completed

- adj+N **additional, extra, full, partial, transferable** *Stage 2 involves the completion of 120 transferable credits.*

- v+N give credits **award, give, grant** *You have been awarded credit in the module.*
- ▶ earn credits **accrue, accumulate, earn** *You need to accumulate 360 credits to be eligible for an Honours award.*
- ▶ offer credits **carry, offer** *All modules carry 15 credits.*
- ▶ bring credits from somwhere else **transfer** *Students can transfer credit from one institution or programme to another.*

credit card N
a card for buying things and paying later

- v+N pay by credit card **pay by, put sth on, use** *Do I have to pay by credit card?*
- ▶ accept credit cards **accept, take** *Few public phones now accept coins, but many take credit cards.*

- N+n payment **payment, purchase, transaction** *Not all agencies will accept credit card payments.*
- ▶ bill or debt **balance, bill, debt, statement** *I paid this month's credit card bill on Saturday.* • *My credit card debt will be finally paid off in August.*
- ▶ money charged for using a credit card **charges** *Before you travel, it's a good idea to know what your credit card charges are likely to be.*
- ▶ details **details, information, number** *Next you are asked for your credit card details .*
- ▶ company providing credit cards **company, issuer, provider** *Most credit card companies offer you the option of taking out payment protection.*
- ▶ someone who has a credit card **holder, user** *They are planning to reduce the credit limit of many credit card holders.*

credit with PHR VB
say or agree that someone is responsible for an achievement [usually passive]

- adv+V often or by most people **generally, largely, often, sometimes, usually, widely** *She was widely credited with restoring confidence in the banking system.*
- ▶ correctly **correctly, duly, justly, rightly** *He is rightly*

credited with turning the band into global
superstars.
▶ wrongly **incorrectly, mistakenly, wrongly** *Some
critics mistakenly credited her as the narrator.*

creed N
a set of beliefs or principles

● adj+N **official, political, religious** *Amnesty is a
worldwide movement independent of any religious
creed or political ideology.*

● v+N accept a creed **accept, adopt, profess** *His
clerk adopted the same political creed.*

▶ not accept a creed **abandon, reject** *Can these virtues
be found among those who have abandoned the creed
of their fathers?*

● and/or **caste, class, colour, gender, nationality,
race, religion, sex, sexual orientation** *This principle
applies to all members of society, regardless of race,
creed, or gender.*

crime N
an illegal act, or illegal activity in general

● adj+N extremely bad **appalling, atrocious,
despicable, heinous, hideous, horrendous, horrible,
horrific, monstrous, terrible, unspeakable** *We
should do everything possible to protect them against
these heinous crimes.*

▶ impossible to forgive **unforgivable, unpardonable**
His crimes were unforgivable.

▶ minor **low-level, minor, nuisance, petty** *Many
turned to prostitution and petty crime.*

▶ major **grave, major, serious** *Once the only
punishment for major crimes was the death penalty.*

▶ violent/not violent **non-violent, violent** *Viewers
wished to see more sensitivity given to victims of
violent crime.*

▶ involving weapons **armed, gun, gun-related, knife,
knife-related** *Does regulation of firearms affect the
incidence of armed crime?*

▶ involving computers **computer, computer-related,
cyber, high-tech, internet-related** *Computer crime
is a rapidly expanding area.*

▶ relating to vehicles **car, vehicle, vehicle-related**
The number of car crimes solved rose by 60 per cent.

▶ relating to drugs or alcohol **alcohol-fuelled,
alcohol-related, drug, drug-related** *Drug crime is a
cancer in the fabric of our society.*

▶ relating to sex **sex, sexual** *Sex crimes and violence
are on the increase in the area.*

▶ relating to people's race, religion etc **hate,
homophobic, race, racial, racially-motivated, racist,
religious** *We need you to report all incidents of hate
crime.* ● *We have huge under-reporting of racial
crime.*

▶ relating to businesses **business, corporate,
financial, retail, white-collar** *Identity theft is one of
the fastest-growing white-collar crimes.*

▶ committed by well-organized groups **organized**
*Member-states should work together more closely in
the fight organized crime.*

▶ relating to property **acquisitive, property** *Street
level dealing can lead to rises in acquisitive crime,
violence, gun crime, sex markets and begging.*

▶ committed by young people **juvenile, youth** *This
novel has the topical theme of juvenile crime.*

▶ committed in war **war** *Were the shootings a
legitimate reprisal or a war crime?*

▶ in cities **street, urban** *The fear of street crime leaves
people trapped in their homes.*

▶ international **cross-border, international,
transnational** *This requires us to focus on tackling
international crime.*

● v+N commit a crime **be guilty of, carry out,
commit, perpetrate** *We did not commit any crimes.*

▶ try to prevent crime **address, combat, crack down
on, curb, cut, deter, fight, prevent, reduce, tackle**
*Their job involves tackling youth crime and its
consequences.*

▶ solve a crime **detect, investigate, solve** *He helps
the police solve a crime.*

▶ officially accuse someone of a crime **accuse sb of,
prosecute** *Let us co-operate on security and work
together to prosecute terrorist crime.*

▶ officially prove that someone has committed a
crime **convict sb of, find sb guilty of** *The proposal
is to provide anger management courses for people
convicted of crimes against children.*

▶ see or report a crime **report, witness** *A young girl
had witnessed the crime and testified.*

▶ admit a crime **confess, confess to, plead guilty to**
He finally confessed his crime to his family. ● *Some
of the soldiers pleaded guilty to war crimes in return
a reduced jail terms.*

▶ start committing crimes **turn to** *Some have turned
to crime to survive.*

● N+v decrease **decrease, drop, fall** *Overall crime is
falling.*

▶ increase **double, increase, rise, soar** *Street crime
rose in four of the ten areas.*

● N+n dealing with crime **detection, investigation,
prevention, reduction** *We work closely with local
children to teach them about crime prevention and
personal safety.*

▶ people involved in crime **boss, figure, gang, lord,
syndicate** *The drugs trade is hugely profitable for
big crime syndicates.*

▶ where a crime takes place **hotspot, scene** *Officers
use intelligence information to target prolific
offenders and crime hotspots.* ● *This allows digital
reconstructions of crime scenes.*

▶ information about the number of crimes **rate,
statistic, survey, trend** *This report includes a list of
crime statistics.*

▶ a lot of crime happening at one time **spree, wave**
*The presence of one addict can create a
neighbourhood crime spree.*

● n+against+N **battle, fight, war** *The fight against
crime is a moral imperative.*

criminal N
someone who has committed a crime

● adj+N committing minor crimes **common, petty,
small-time, street** *She was a petty criminal who had
no respect for the law.*

▶ dangerous **dangerous, ruthless, serious, violent**
Two-thirds of the convicts were violent criminals.

▶ professional **career, habitual, hardened, persistent,
professional, prolific** *We're dealing with hardened
criminals, not frightened teenagers.*

▶ famous **notorious** *The murdered man turns out to
be a notorious criminal.*

▸ claimed but not proved **alleged, suspected** *The police operation rounded up 617 alleged criminals.*
▸ offically accused **indicted** *Twelve indicted war criminals were sent to The Hague for trial.*
▸ found guilty **convicted** *The convicted criminals could escape the death penalty by volunteering.*

● v+N catch a criminal **apprehend, arrest, catch** *The three criminals were soon apprehended and subsequently convicted of armed robbery.*
▸ try to catch criminals **hunt down, pursue, target** *The investigators specifically target criminals who commit vehicle crime.*
▸ try to prove a criminal is guilty **bring to justice, prosecute** *The government is reformng the laws to bring alleged war criminals to justice.*
▸ make a criminal less likely to commit a crime **deter** *Country people were improving security to deter criminals.*
▸ help a criminal to give up crime **reform, rehabilitate** *Short stays in prison do not rehabilitate criminals.*

crisis N

an urgent, difficult, or dangerous situation

● adj+N major **acute, deep, grave, major, profound, serious, severe** *Meanwhile, the party was going through a deep crisis.*
▸ about to happen **future, impending, looming** *Three million people are at risk from this impending crisis.*
▸ getting worse **deepening, escalating, growing, mounting, worsening** *The debates reflect the deepening crisis in international relations.*
▸ continuing or repeated **ongoing, periodic, perpetual, prolonged, protracted** *We implore them to respond immediately to this ongoing crisis.*
▸ financial **banking, capitalist, currency, debt, economic, financial, fiscal, funding, pension** *The country drifted from one economic crisis to another.*
▸ political **constitutional, political, revolutionary** *This might spark a constitutional crisis.*
▸ related to energy or the environment **ecological, energy, environmental, fuel, oil** *The dominant response to our global ecological crisis is avoiding the issue.* ● *We need other ways to solve the energy crisis.*
▸ personal or emotional **emotional, existential, identity, mid-life, moral, personal, spiritual** *The story is centred on a young woman who's suffering from an identity crisis.*

● v+N experience a crisis **be faced with, experience, face, go through, suffer, undergo** *The university is facing a funding crisis.*
▸ cause a crisis **cause, create, lead to, precipitate, provoke, spark, trigger** *His visit provoked an international crisis.*
▸ make a crisis worse **aggravate, deepen, escalate, exacerbate, intensify, worsen** *It seems irrational that he wants to escalate this crisis.*
▸ handle a crisis **address, alleviate, cope with, deal with, defuse, ease, handle, manage, overcome, resolve, respond to, solve, tackle** *A prisoner exchange is the only way to resolve this crisis.*
▸ avoid a crisis **avert, avoid, prevent** *Appeal funds will also support plans to avert food crises in the future.*
▸ not be badly affected by a crisis **survive, weather** *The company survived the oil crisis.*

▸ N+v happen **arise, erupt, hit, occur, unfold** *Following the elections, a massive political crisis erupted in Florida.*
▸ be about to happen **face sb/sth, loom, threaten (sb/sth)** *As 2005 drew to a close, a major financial crisis loomed.*
▸ have an effect on **affect sb/sth, afflict sb/sth, beset sb/sth, engulf sb/sth, grip sb/sth** *The housing crisis affects us all.* ● *During the 1980s, the country was beset by one economic crisis after another.*
▸ become worse **deepen, escalate, worsen** *The hunt for scapegoats has become widespread as the crisis deepens.*
▸ end **be over, subside** *The immediate crisis was over.*

criterion N

a standard for judging or deciding about something
[usually plural]

● adj+N strict **rigorous, strict, stringent** *We are building a team of first-rate developers and our selection criteria are stringent.*
▸ already decided **predefined, pre-determined, specific, specified** *Performance was scored by predefined criteria.*
▸ only **sole** *The sole criterion for the award of a Scholarship is academic excellence.*
▸ basic **basic, minimum** *Each nominated person has to meet basic selection criteria before they can be considered.*
▸ main **essential, key, main** *Ability to co-operate will be an essential criterion for selection.*
▸ subjective/objective **objective, subjective** *Such criteria are clearly not objective, but require interpretation in context.*

● n+N for being chosen or not chosen **eligibility, exclusion, inclusion, selection** *The national eligibility criteria will be designed to cover all client groups.*
▸ for acceptance **acceptance, admission, entry, membership** *Acceptance criteria for the two-week course are the same as for the six-week course.*
▸ for assessment **assessment, evaluation** *I will discuss the advantages of using assessment criteria, but also the ways in which their use is problematic.*

● v+N satisfy criteria **fit, fulfil, match, meet, satisfy** *Groups must meet specified criteria to successfully apply.*
▸ set criteria **define, establish, lay down, outline, set, specify** *The monies remaining will be distributed in accordance with criteria laid down from time to time.*

critic N

1 someone who states their objection to something they disapprove of [usually plural]

● adj+N major **chief, leading, major, prominent** *He was a prominent critic of the intelligence used before the war.*
▸ expressing severe criticism **bitter, fierce, harsh, hostile, severe, vehement, worst** *She later became a bitter critic of the policy.* ● *Even her harshest critics acknowledge that she has handled the crisis with considerable skill.*

Usage In these combinations the adjective is often in the superlative form: *my most severe critic*

▶ expressing critical opinions directly and clearly **outspoken, strident, trenchant, vocal, vociferous** *He was an outspoken critic of the colonial policies of the period.*
▶ continuing and determined **long-time, persistent, staunch** *He was a persistent critic of conventional thinking.*
● v+N make people less critical, by dealing with their objections **answer, disarm, silence** *The speech is peppered with attempts to answer his critics.* ● *The strength of her track record serves to silence potential critics.*
▶ make critics less unhappy **appease, mollify** *They did nothing to mollify their critics.*
▶ persuade people not to be critical **convince, satisfy** *The company's announcement did not convince some critics.*
▶ prove critics wrong **confound, discredit, prove wrong** *She is delighted with the way they are proving the critics wrong.*

Usage ***Critic*** is usually plural in all of the v+N combinations shown above: *This latest announcement will do little to appease the regime's many critics.*

2 someone whose job is to give opinions about books, films etc

● adj+N respected **distinguished, eminent, influential, perceptive, prominent, renowned, respected** *An eminent art critic described it all as 'putrid filth '.* ● *He may be the most perceptive critic writing about jazz today.*
▶ critic of what **art, cultural, film, literary, music, television, theatre** *He works as a publisher, literary critic, and broadcaster.*
● v+N **divide, impress, satisfy, wow** INFORMAL *It's a novel which has already divided the critics.* ● *Ross Noble has made regular appearances on TV shows and he wowed critics at the Edinburgh Festival.*
● N+v when critics praise something **hail sth, laud sth, praise sth, rave** INFORMAL *The critics hailed her performance as a tour de force.*
▶ when critics say something is bad **deride sth, pan sth** INFORMAL, **savage sth, slate sth** INFORMAL *Critics have panned his latest album.*

critical ADJ

1 stating your objections to something you disapprove of

● adv+ADJ very **deeply, extremely, fiercely, harshly, highly, severely, very** *He continued in the same harshly critical vein.* ● *The article is highly critical of the government's political and economic policies.*
▶ rather **mildly, quite, rather** *They were quite critical, but I think they left with a better understanding of how the business works.*
▶ openly **openly** *The generals were openly critical of government failings.*

2 extremely important, and likely to affect what happens in the future

● adv+ADJ **absolutely, especially, extremely,**

increasingly, particularly, really INFORMAL *Our distant ancestors emerged from the sea, and water is still absolutely critical for our survival.*
● ADJ+n point in time **juncture, moment, point** *The negotiations had been sabotaged at a critical juncture, and war was almost inevitable.*
▶ matter or factor **component, element, factor, issue, role** *We believe that drug testing in the workplace should only be used where safety is a critical issue.* ● *This is not to say that other lines of defense don't have a critical role.*
● v+ADJ **become, prove, remain** *This discovery could prove critical to furthering our understanding of these diseases.*

3 carefully considering and judging something

● ADJ+n ways of thinking **faculties, judgement, reflection, self-reflection, thinking** *The aim of the course is to develop students' critical faculties.*
▶ examination **analysis, appraisal, evaluation, examination, scrutiny** *Professionals should be able to prove that their methods stand up to critical analysis.*
▶ writing or discussion **commentary, debate, discourse, essay, review** *Write a critical commentary on the following poem.* ● *The aim of the seminar is to provide a platform for critical discourse on tourism, politics, democracy, and the resulting web of power relations.*
▶ way of understanding something **appreciation, awareness, understanding** *This course will provide you with a critical understanding of the issues.*
▶ way of thinking about something **approach, perspective, stance, theory** *This scrutiny has produced some very different critical perspectives.*
● and/or **analytical, creative, informed, questioning, reflective, theoretical** *An analytical and critical knowledge of standard grammar is needed.* ● *There are many different ways of stimulating creative, reflective, critical thinking.*

criticism N
bad opinions about something

● adj+N severe **fierce, scathing, serious, severe, stinging, trenchant, vehement** *The police chief faced fierce criticism from civil liberties groups for his handling of the protests.*
▶ negative **adverse, destructive, negative** *The only adverse criticism the film evoked was for its rather sentimental ending.*
▶ positive and helpful **constructive** *Your constructive criticism helps us know when we are not successful.*
▶ fair **justifiable, justified, legitimate, valid** *It is not clear to what extent this criticism is justifiable.*
▶ unfair **unfair, unfounded, unjustified, unwarranted** *I want to go on record as saying that the criticism is totally unjustified.*
▶ public **media, public, widespread** *The reformers point to mounting public criticism.* ● *This has resulted in widespread criticism and heated debate.*
▶ indirect **implicit, implied** *Employees may be reluctant to make suggestions because they fear this may be seen as implied criticism of the management.*
● v+N express criticism **express, make, voice** *Environmental groups have voiced strong criticism of the methods used.*

▶ direct criticism **aim, direct, level, reserve** *You'd have to be very picky to level any criticism at this feature.* • *The strongest criticisms are reserved for regional development agencies.*

▶ attract crtiticsm **arouse, attract, draw, prompt, provoke** *Failure to use funds in accordance with the agreed rules is likely to attract criticism.*

▶ receive criticism **come in for, face, meet with, receive** *The company faced heavy criticism.*

▶ avoid or prevent criticism **avoid, deflect, escape, silence, suppress** *A shameless decision was made to deflect criticism by misleading the public.*

▶ respond effectively to criticism **address, answer, counter, refute, reject, reply to, respond to** *The authors have made an honest attempt to answer the criticisms made of their work.* • *The company rejects this criticism.*

• n+of+N **barrage, chorus, storm, wave** *He faced a barrage of criticism for his support of the war.*

criticize V
say what you think is bad about something

• adv+V severely **bitterly, fiercely, harshly, heavily, roundly, severely, strongly** *Following the release of a Senate report that harshly criticizes US intelligence gathering, lawmakers are shifting their focus.* • *The bank's strategy has been roundly criticized by financial experts.*

▶ fairly **rightly** *The violation of international law was rightly criticized.*

▶ unfairly **unfairly** *If he feels we're being criticized unfairly, he's always ready to respond.*

▶ publicly **openly, publicly** *Anyone who openly criticizes the government faces possible arrest.*

▶ greatly or frequently **constantly, frequently, much, widely** *The cost of parking was widely criticized as extortionate.*

critique N
a careful written examination of subject

• adj+N powerful **damning, devastating, hard-hitting, powerful, scathing, searing, trenchant, withering** *It adds up to a devastating critique of imperialism.*

▶ direct and intelligent **incisive, telling** *He offers an incisive critique of contemporary popular culture.*

▶ detailed **comprehensive, detailed, sustained, systematic, thorough, thoroughgoing** *A detailed critique is available here.*

▶ useful **constructive** *The critique is most constructive and comprehensive.*

▶ types of critique **cultural, feminist, Marxist, political, postmodern, radical, theoretical** *Her book Woman's Evolutio pioneered a feminist critique of the sciences, and is till wide y r *

• v+N **develop, give, ffer, r sen e, publish, write** *Her re erful critique of the youth justice sys*

crop N
a farm plant grown for foou

• adj+N important or main **chief, important, staple, subsistence** *Tax revenues were assessed in quantities of the staple crop, rice.*

▶ large or successful **abundant, bumper, good** *Last year's favourable monsoon resulted in a bumper crop.*

▶ grown for money **cash, commercial, non-food, profitable** *The national economy is mainly dependent on three cash crops, which comprise 95 per cent of their agricultural exports.* • *Reeds, white seed, and oziers were all highly profitable crops.*

▶ grown without chemicals **organic** *At that distance, there is low risk of contamination between GM and organic crops.*

▶ with changed genes **biotech, genetically engineered, genetically modifed, GM, transgenic** *Transgenic crops have been perceived to carry unacceptable risks.*

• v+N plant a crop **plant, sow** *GM crops have been planted at 49 farms.*

▶ grow a crop **cultivate, grow, produce** *Keeping animals requires more land than cultivating crops.*

▶ collect a crop when it has grown **harvest** *The site was excavated directly after the potato crop was harvested.*

▶ destroy a crop **damage, destroy, devastate, ruin** *His family will starve if insects or worms destroy his crops.*

▶ supply water to a crop **irrigate, water** *Farmers use the water from the lake to irrigate their crops.*

• N+v grow successfully **grow, ripen, thrive** *The Joads were lured by the promise of work picking the crops that thrived in the Californian climate.*

▶ fail to grow **fail** *When the potato crop failed, hardship followed.*

• N+n production **cultivation, growth, production, yield** *New agronomic methods will improve crop production.*

▶ failure **damage, failure, loss** *Colder periods have caused crop failures.*

▶ management **husbandry, management, protection, rotation** *Crop management strategies are being developed.* • *Farmers maintain soil fertility by emphasising crop rotation.*

cross-examination N
questions a witness or defendant is asked during a trial

• adj+N **detailed, devastating, hostile, lengthy, pre-trial, rigorous** *His cross-examination was lengthy and extremely detailed.*

• v+N perform a cross-examination **begin, conduct** *The defendant must appoint a legal representative to conduct the cross-examination.*

▶ face cross-examination **be subjected to, face, undergo** *He was ill-prepared to undergo cross-examination.*

▶ not be harmed by cross-examination **stand up to, withstand** *The evidence would not withstand skilful cross-examination.*

• N+of **claimant, complainant, respondent, victim, witness** *There was little cross-examination of these witnesses.*

cross section N
a group containing an example of most types of people or things

• adj+N **broad, good, random, representative,**

typical, wide *There is no suggestion that they are a representative cross section of society.*

- v+N **be drawn from, represent** *Our members are drawn from a broad cross section of society.*
- N+of people in general **community, people, population, public, society** *They represent a wide cross section of society.*
- ▶ particular groups of people **clients, members, residents, staff** *This consultation will include a cross section of residents and staff.*
- ▶ businesses **businesses, companies, industries** *This working party has representatives from a wide cross section of the industry.*
- ▶ organizations **groups, organizations** *She has experience of workshops with a broad cross section of community groups.*

crowd N

1 the audience at a sports game, concert, performance etc

- adj+N large **big, bumper, capacity, good, packed, record, sellout, sold-out** *The Undertones stepped out to a packed, eager crowd ready to be transported back to the 70s.*
- ▶ excited **adoring, eager, ecstatic, excited, expectant, jubilant** *I have rarely seen such a vibrant and ecstatic crowd.* • *He had the expectant crowd hanging onto his every word.*
- ▶ angry **angry, hostile, jeering** *He gets on stage and in front of the hostile crowd completely chokes.*
- ▶ supporting one side in a game **partisan** *They produced some outstanding moments in front of a partisan crowd.*
- v+N entertain a crowd **captivate, dazzle, delight, entertain, enthrall, excite, impress, stun, thrill, wow** *The circus had a huge range of acts to entertain the crowds.*
- ▶ attract a crowd **attract, draw, draw in, pull in** *The shows attract decent-sized crowds.*
- N+n **favourite, noise, pleaser, puller, reaction** *The crowd reaction was extremely positive.*
- n+from+N **applause, cheers, gasps, ovation, reaction, response, roar** *Cheers from the crowd filled her heart with joy.* • *It was a brilliant goal, which drew gasps from he crowd.*

2 a large number of people in one place

- adj+N large **dense, enormous, great, huge, immense, large, sizeable, vast** *There was a large crowd of people near the station.*
- ▶ growing **gathering, growing, swelling** *They kept the attention of the rapidly swelling crowd.*
- ▶ lively and noisy **boisterous, bustling, heaving, jostling, noisy, raucous, rowdy, surging, thronging, vociferous** *Stepping out of the car, I was almost swallowed up in the surging crowd.*
- n+N **evening, holiday, lunchtime, summer, weekend** *There's always a big lunchtime crowd as people escape their offices for an hour or so.*
- v+N **break up, disperse** *The police decided to ride the horses in to disperse this crowd.*
- N+v **assemble, flock, gather, surge, throng** *The glorious weekend weather brought the crowds*

flocking in their thousands to Central Park. • *In the town centre, crowds thronged the streets.*

crucial ADJ

extremely important because of having a major effect

- adv+ADJ very **absolutely, especially, particularly, really, so** INFORMAL, **very** *This is absolutely crucial to the future of the music business.*
- ▶ rather **fairly, pretty, quite, rather** *Knowledge of the operation is fairly crucial in our office.*
- ▶ equally **equally** *Integrated transport systems and good education facilities are equally crucial.*
- ADJ+n aspect or factor **aspect, component, element, factor, ingredient, part, point, role** *The move to digital supply was a crucial factor in enabling better co-operation.*
- ▶ issue **issue, question** *Delegates discussed a number of crucial issues.*
- ▶ decision **decision, vote** *We can help with these crucial decisions.*
- ▶ point in time **juncture, moment, period, phase, stage, timing** *The researcher faces three crucial moments during her work.*
- ▶ importance **importance, significance** *They don't grasp the crucial importance of laws which restrain behaviour.*
- v+ADJ **become, prove, remain** *This may prove crucial in helping to prevent stroke-induced disability.*
- ADJ+to/ADJ+for **development, future, outcome, success, survival, understanding, well-being** *A well-planned implementation is crucial to success.* • *This information is crucial for our understanding of the origin of neutrino masses.*

cruel ADJ

1 getting pleasure from causing physical or emotional pain

- adv+ADJ very **appallingly, downright, extremely, hideously, incredibly, indescribably, particularly, so** INFORMAL, **unbelievably, unspeakably, very** *This type of hunting was banned because it is extremely cruel to the animals.*
- ▶ rather **rather** *I recall a rather cruel comment about her haircut.*
- ▶ deliberately **intentionally** *I am not being intentionally cruel. Just honest.*
- ▶ in an unnecessary way **unnecessarily** *They claim the medical tests are unnecessarily cruel.*
- and/or **barbaric, brutal, degrading, harsh, heartless, inhuman, inhumane, unjust** *Their methods were brutal, cruel, and wholly unacceptable.* • *To starve people deliberately would be cruel and inhumane.*

2 when an event or situation causes great harm, in a way that seems unfair

- adv+ADJ **appallingly, downright, extremely, incredibly, indescribably, particularly, so** INFORMAL, **unbelievably, unspeakably, very** *Death was particularly cruel when it separated the lovers.*
- ADJ+n **blow, fate, irony, twist, twist of fate** *It was a cruel twist of fate that his accomplishment cost him 10 years of imprisonment.*

cruelty N

behaviour that deliberately causes physical or emotional suffering

- adj+N extreme **extreme, unimaginable** *They reserved their most extreme cruelty for their fellow humans.*
- ▶ shocking **appalling, barbaric, barbarous, horrific, terrible, unspeakable** *He was charming most of the time, but with sudden flashes of unspeakable cruelty.*
- ▶ without thought or feeling **bestial, callous, mindless, savage** *She witnessed an act of mindless cruelty.*
- ▶ deliberate **calculated, deliberate, heartless, intentional, ruthless, sadistic** *Most of these injuries are caused not by deliberate cruelty, but by ignorance of modern animal husbandry methods.*
- ▶ unnecessary **gratuitous, needless, unnecessary, wanton** *We hope they will soon be brought to justice for their savage, wanton cruelty.*
- ▶ mental rather than physical **emotional, mental** *The movie deals with mental cruelty and classic love/hate relationships.*

- v+N commit **commit, inflict, perpetrate, practise** *We do not condone cruelty inflicted on any animal.*
- ▶ prevent **end, prevent, stop** *Its mission is to end cruelty to children.*

crusade N

an effort to achieve something morally right

- adj+N personal **lone, lonely, one-man, one-woman, own, personal** *The detective embarks on a one-man crusade to solve the case.*
- ▶ moral or religious **idealistic, moral, religious** *They announced what can only be described as a moral crusade.* • *Many saw the war as a kind of religious crusade against the godless republicans.*

- v+N start a crusade **begin, declare, embark on, initiate, launch, lead, start, undertake** *We have launched an unprecedented crusade to eradicate child poverty.* • *The government must lead a crusade for our environment.*
- ▶ continue a crusade **conduct, continue, fight, pursue, wage** *I've waged a long crusade for rational, scientific thinking.*

crux N

the most important aspect of something

- adj+N **central, main, real, very** *This may be the very crux of our disagreement.*
- v+N **be, form** *These three recommendations form the crux of the report.*
- N+of matter or problem **case, issue, matter, problem, question, story** *The crux of the matter is that few challenges would go to court.*
- ▶ argument or disagreement **argument, debate, disagreement, dispute** *This question – how to reconcile economic development and the reduction of carbon emissions – is at the crux of the debate.*

cry V

have tears coming from your eyes

- adv+V in an uncontrolled way **constantly, excessively, hysterically, incessantly, inconsolably,** **uncontrollably** *I find myself crying uncontrollably, often without reason.*
- ▶ quietly **silently, softly** *David began crying, softly at first and then much louder.*
- ▶ making you feel sympathy **piteously, pitifully** *Some of the men were crying piteously and begging for a drink.*

- V+in **anguish, despair, pain** *People were screaming in pain, relatives crying in anguish.*
- V+with good or happy feelings **happiness, joy, laughter, relief** *The last time I saw him, he actually made me cry with laughter.*
- ▶ painful feelings **frustration, hunger, pain** *There were times when I cried with sheer frustration at the injustice of it all.*

cry N

a loud expression of emotion, pain etc

- adj+N loud **full, great, loud** *I heard a sudden, loud cry of 'BELOW!'*
- ▶ quiet **faint, little, muffled, stifled** *She leaned against a tree with a faint cry of despair.* • *A muffled cry reached me.*
- ▶ high and unpleasant **harsh, high-pitched, piercing, sharp, shrill** *Suddenly a wild, piercing cry sent a feeling of horror through her blood.*
- ▶ sad **agonized, anguished, bitter, desparate, mournful, pitiful, plaintive** *She heard the man's last plaintive cry howling down the wind.*
- ▶ happy **excited, glad, triumphant** *She gave a glad cry of 'Why, it's Father!'*

- v+N give **give, let out, utter** *Maria uttered a small cry of astonishment.*
- ▶ try to stop **muffle, stifle** *He buried his head in his arm, trying to muffle the cry of pain.*
- N+v **echo, go up, ring** *A cry went up that the boat had capsized.*
- N+of pain **agony, pain** *While they were talking, a sudden cry of pain was heard.*
- ▶ emotional pain **anguish, despair, distress, grief, horror, terror** *When Einstein heard the news, he uttered a cry of anguish.*
- ▶ anger **indignation, outrage, protest, rage, vengeance** *He goes down with a cry of rage, fingers reaching towards the shadow.*
- ▶ surprise **alarm, astonishment, surprise** *I gave a cry of surprise.*
- ▶ happiness **delight, joy** *As she opened the door, she let out a cry of joy.*

culmination N

the final result of a process that has continued for a long time

- adj+N **final, fitting, logical, successful, ultimate** *The piece is a fitting culmination of the band's previous work.*
- v+N be the culmination of something **mark, represent** *The development of this service represents the culmination of 36 months of work.*
- ▶ reach a culmination **reach** *They understood how human history would reach its culmination.*
- N+of period of time **decade, lifetime, period, phase, year** *Her suicide was the culmination of thirteen years of mental crises.*

▶ work or effort **campaign, effort, process, project, struggle, work** *The culmination of this process is her precociously mature work.* • *The law represents the culmination of a long struggle for equal rights.*

▶ something you hope for **ambition, dream** *The completion of the new stadium will be the culmination of a dream to bring top-flight football to the city.*

culpable ADJ
responsible for doing something bad or illegal

● adv+ADJ very **especially, highly, particularly** *They are especially culpable since so many of their stores are out of town.*

▶ equally **equally** *The court found each of the defendants equally culpable of the crime.*

▶ in a particular way **criminally, morally** *We consider them to have been morally culpable to some extent.*

● ADJ+n **delay, failure, homicide, ignorance, neglect, negligence** *We found no evidence of deliberate distortion or of culpable negligence.*

culprit N
someone or something that is responsible for something bad or illegal

● adj+N main **biggest, chief, main, major, primary, prime, principal, worst** *As far as superbugs in hospitals are concerned, poor hygiene is the biggest culprit.*

▶ real **real, true** *They then assist Holmes in discovering who the real culprit is.*

▶ likely or suspected **alleged, likely, possible, suspected** *Three persons were identified as the alleged culprits and these were summoned before the Committee.* • *A profile is gradually built up of the likely culprit.*

● v+N catch a culprit **apprehend, arrest, bring to justice, bring to trial, capture, catch, find, trace** *Studying crime reports and identifying patterns helps us catch culprits.*

▶ discover a culprit **discover, identify, name, reveal, uncover, unmask** *By using the latest scientific techniques they are able to identify the culprit.*

cult N
someone or something that is admired in an almost religious way

● N+n story, film, show, or piece of music **classic, comedy, favourite, film, hit, movie, novel, show** *The actress shot to fame in the '80s in a host of future cult classics.* • *To make a cult movie on no money, you need to be a genius.*

▶ person **band, figure, hero, icon, legend** *He was a cult figure of the emerging folk scene.*

▶ status **status** *By this time, the show had been elevated to cult status.*

▶ supporters **following** *The movie inspired a cult following.*

cultivate V
develop an attitude, ability, or relationship

● adv+V carefully **assiduously, carefully, consciously, deliberately, diligently, sedulously** *The image of a decisive and charismatic leader was assiduously cultivated.*

▶ successfully **successfully** *The series successfully cultivated and sustained a viewership of 12 million.*

● V+n relationship **acquaintance, friendship, relationship** *Cultivate friendships with as wide a range of people in the company as possible.*

▶ ability **habit, talent, virtue** *One should cultivate virtues such as honesty, fidelity, and sacrifice.*

▶ attitude **attitude, awareness, taste** *This means cultivating the awareness that human rights are universal.*

▶ image **image** *After several popular albums, she is trying to cultivate a more serious image.*

cultural ADJ
relating to the arts or to a whole culture

● ADJ+n tradition or background **background, heritage, history, identity, tradition** *Our students come from a wide range of educational and cultural backgrounds.*

▶ variety or differences **difference, diversity, pluralism** *Education could be improved if these cultural differences were addressed.* • *The region has some wonderful scenery, and plenty of cultural diversity, too.*

▶ influence or power **hegemony, imperialism, influence** *The human rights movement is sometimes seen as a form of cultural imperialism.*

▶ change **change, renaissance, revolution** *It is a major cultural revolution that will take at minimum 10 to 15 years.*

▶ being sensitive **awareness, sensitivity** *Cultural sensitivity requires a deep intellectual commitment.*

▶ standards **mores, norm** *A neutral dress requirement could run counter to the cultural norms of a particular ethnic group.*

● and/or **artistic, economic, educational, ethnic, historical, intellectual, linguistic, literary, political, religious, social** *His account weaves together intellectual, cultural, and political developments.*

culture N
1 activities involving music, literature, and other arts

● adj+N modern **contemporary, modern, postmodern** *The Mega Mela is a unique festival of traditional and modern Asian culture including fashion shows, music and community events.*

▶ popular **mass, pop INFORMAL, popular** *My interests so far have focused on the links between film, popular culture, and the construction of national and ethnic identity.*

▶ belonging to and typical of a particular place **folk, indigenous, local, native, traditional** *Although a nomadic people, they have managed to hold on to much of their traditional culture despite having settled in towns and villages.*

▶ lively and active **colourful, diverse, rich, vibrant** *The history is told with the music and dance of a rich and vibrant culture.*

▶ types of culture **artistic, literary, musical, visual** *This has led to the focus of Estonians on a literary culture.*

2 the ideas and behaviour of an organization or society

● adj+N main or most common **dominant,**

mainstream, prevailing *Some believe that there was not just one dominant culture in Mexico at this point.*
▶ different **different, diverse** *This question arises wherever people of diverse cultures build new relationships.*
▶ political **political** *A genuinely democratic political culture involves more than simply the periodic casting of votes.*
▶ financial **consumer, enterprise, entrepreneurial, material** *Has the government fostered an entrepreneurial culture in deprived areas?*
▶ in an organization or company **corporate, organizational, workplace** *Are we actively embedding risk management in our organizational culture?*
▶ involving violent, illegal, or anti-social behaviour **binge-drinking, drug, gang, gun, knife, yob** *Alcohol is the mainstay of yob culture, football hooliganism, etc.*
▶ of young people **youth** *Her research analyses the changing attitudes and trends in youth culture.*
▶ in which men have most of the power **male-dominated, patriarchal** *Her story is every woman's search for authenticity in our patriarchal culture.*
▶ emphasizing a particular idea or type of behaviour **blame, celebrity, compensation, dependency, long-hours** *Managers have been responsible for the development of a blame culture: if something goes wrong, it must be someone's fault.*

• v+N create a culture **build, create, develop, engender, establish, foster, promote, strengthen** *We wish to promote a culture of equality throughout the organisation.*
▶ encourage a culture to continue **nurture, perpetuate, preserve, sustain** *Those who call for more stringent controls risk perpetuating a culture of fear and suspicion towards asylum seekers and refugees.*
▶ change a culture **change, influence, shape, transform** *No less important is the task of transforming the culture and standards of education in our major cities.*
▶ accept a new or different culture **absorb, adapt to, adopt, embrace** *The migrants' children tend to embrace the culture and their language skills progress enormously.*

• N+of keeping/not keeping secrets **openness, secrecy** *Laws of this type inevitably lead to a culture of secrecy.*
▶ being/not being held responsible **accountability, impunity** *Only in this way can the culture of impunity be checked.*
▶ negative feelings **blame, cynicism, fear, suspicion** *I'm not interested in continuing this culture of blame.*
▶ taking risks and trying new things **enterprise, entrepreneurship, innovation** *Their aim is to create a culture of entrepreneurship in the university sector.*
▶ improvement **improvement, learning** *Only by building a culture of lifelong learning can this be achieved.*

cunning ADJ
using intelligence to trick or cheat people

• adv+ADJ very **extremely, so, very** *No one realized what he was planning, partly because he was so cunning.*

▶ rather **quite, rather** *They came up with a rather cunning idea to overpower the naive village dwellers.*

• ADJ+n plan **plan, ploy, ruse, scheme, strategy, stunt, tactic, trick** *I've been implementing a cunning plan I had at the beginning of the week.*
▶ disguise **disguise** *They had to adopt cunning disguises so that they could pass into enemy territory unnoticed.*
▶ people **folk, rascal, thief** *Cunning thieves are thought to be using wireless technology to help them find laptops hidden in the boots of cars.*

• and/or **clever, crafty, devilish, devious, ruthless, sly** *If you want to win, you just need to be devious and cunning.*

curb V
control or limit something

• V+n something harmful **abuse, corruption, crime, emissions, global warming, inflation, terrorism** *The president has pushed through legislation to curb corruption.*
▶ rights or power **freedom, power, right** *The union has consistently demanded that legislation be introduced to curb the enormous buying power of the large supermarket chains.*
▶ spread or excess of something **excess, growth, proliferation, rise, spread** *We need to curb the proliferation of small arms and reduce their numbers.*
▶ emotion or physical feeling **appetite, craving, enthusiasm, instinct** *But what can you do to curb those cravings?* • *Consumers seem to have curbed their enthusiasm for shopping.*

curb N
a control that stops or limits something

• adj+N **draconian, strict, tight, tough** *Environmentalists are calling for draconian global curbs on greenhouse gas production.*
• v+N put a curb on something **impose, place, put** *During his chancellorship, he imposed the tightest curbs on public spending since the war.*
▶ lift or ease a curb on something **ease, lift, relax** *They also called for lifting curbs on media.*
▶ call for a curb on something **call for** *Campaigners call for traffic curbs to halt increasing CO2 emissions.*

• N+on **emissions, exports, freedom, immigration, inflation, liberty, spending** *The government's plans to introduce new curbs on civil liberties were condemned.*

cure N
a treatment for a disease or a solution to a problem

• adj+N good **effective, good, great, perfect** *This is the best hangover cure I have ever used!*
▶ magic **magic, magical, marvellous, miracle, miraculous, wonder** *There are no magic or miraculous cures for baldness.*
▶ immediate **instant, overnight, quick** *To make sure none of his affairs become serious, Dr Samir has one instant cure.*
▶ permanent **complete, lasting, permanent** *Unfortunately there is no permanent cure, but it is possible to keep the condition under control.*

▶ eventual or possible **eventual, possible, potential** *We are trying to raise £50,000 for research into the cause and eventual cure of this debilitating illness.*

▶ known **known** *At present, there is no known cure for emphysema.*

● v+N find a cure **discover, find** *It is very important to find a cure for brain tumours.*

▶ promise a cure **guarantee, promise** *The doctor promised a cure for his epilepsy.*

▶ result in a cure **bring about, lead to, result in** *New research may lead to a cure for blindness.*

▶ try to find a cure **look for, research, search for, seek** *The shrine is still used as a place of pilgrimage by those seeking a cure for mental illness.*

▶ develop a cure **develop, devise, invent, produce** *She has developed a cure which has helped herself and other people walk again without pain.*

▶ achieve a cure **achieve, effect, perform** *Achieving a cure takes about six months of daily treatment with antibiotics.*

▶ provide or be a cure **be, offer, provide** *Conventional medicine cannot offer a cure.*

▶ want a cure **hope for, pray for, want** *Over 500 new cases are diagnosed in children in the UK every year and there are many families desperately hoping for a cure.*

cure V
treat an illness or solve a problem

● adv+V magically **magically, miraculously** *Although feng shui can help you in achieving your goals and ambitions, it cannot miraculously cure you of all your problems.*

▶ immediately **instantly, overnight** *The problems in the US will not be cured overnight.*

▶ quickly or easily **easily, fast, quickly** *With modern methods of treatment, ulcers can very often be cured quite quickly.*

▶ permanently or completely **completely, fully, perfectly, permanently** *Most cancers cannot be completely cured once they have spread.*

▶ eventually or possibly **eventually, hopefully, possibly, potentially** *The draught problem was eventually cured by repairing and closing ventilators.*

▶ apparently **apparently, supposedly** *After six treatments of hypnosis she returned home, apparently cured.*

curfew N
a law that prevents people from going outside at night

● adj+N at night **dusk-to-dawn, night, nightly, night-time, overnight** *An overnight curfew was imposed throughout Moscow.*

▶ strict **blanket, strict** *During the day, the offender is free to leave the house, but they are subject to strict overnight curfews.*

● v+N introduce a curfew **declare, impose, introduce, place sth under** *They have imposed a curfew on the 37,000 refugees to be inside their tents by 10pm.*

▶ end a curfew **end, lift** *Officials eventually lifted the curfew in April.*

▶ break a curfew **break, defy, ignore, violate** *Thousands of people defied curfews and took to the streets of the capital.*

▶ enforce a curfew **enforce** *The Army used teargas to enforce the curfew.*

curiosity N
a feeling of wanting to know about something

● adj+N great **boundless, burning, eager, great, inexhaustible, insatiable, intense, real** *They were observing my home, just as I was observing theirs, with that same insatiable curiosity.*

▶ mild **mild** *'What are you doing?' she asked with mild curiosity.*

▶ only **idle, mere, sheer, simple** *They had come first, they said, out of idle curiosity.*

▶ natural **innate, natural** *They have a desire to learn, derived from innate curiosity and a wish for self-development.*

▶ about something unpleasant **morbid** *But you can't help looking back as morbid curiosity makes you wonder if he has died.*

▶ types of curiosity **historical, intellectual, scientific** *An intellectual curiosity and a real desire to learn are important attributes.*

● v+N arouse someone's curiosity **arouse, awaken, excite, fuel, pique, provoke, rouse, spark, stimulate, stir, whet** *When Roland starts sending Cherry coded messages, her curiosity is aroused.*

▶ satisfy someone's curiosity **gratify, satisfy** *To satisfy his own curiosity, Pemberton examines the family's history.*

▶ feel curiosity **be full of, feel** *The emotions I felt when I saw him were surprise and curiosity.*

▶ no longer feel curiosity **deaden, quell, sate, stifle** *In a test-obsessed system, pupils' curiosity is brutally stifled.*

curious ADJ
1 wanting to find out about something

● adv+ADJ very **endlessly, extremely, genuinely, insatiably, intensely, really, terminally, very** *Children are insatiably curious and may well find medicines which are not in a locked cabinet.*

▶ slightly **a little, mildly, slightly** *Clicking this link implies that you are at least mildly curious about me.*

▶ rather **quite, rather, somewhat** *I am somewhat curious as to your reasons for telling people about your diagnosis.*

▶ only **just, merely, plain, simply** *Some requests are from researchers for media programmes and some are from people who are just plain curious.*

▶ naturally **naturally** *I am a naturally curious person.*

▶ about academic work **intellectually** *We are looking for students who are intellectually curious.*

▶ in an unpleasant way **morbidly** *Only the expert, or the morbidly curious, would want to linger in a funeral parlour.*

● v+ADJ be curious **be, feel** *I have always felt curious about other countries.*

▶ become curious **become, get** *He ran off when passers-by became curious.*

● ADJ+infinitive **discover, find, find out, hear, know, learn, note, observe, see** *I'm curious to know why you left the army.*

● and/or **adventurous, enthusiastic, inquisitive, intelligent, interested, open-minded, playful**

Teachers at the High School aim to create inquisitive, curious young people who will always have that desire to find out more.

2 unusual and interesting

- adv+ADJ very **extremely, really** INFORMAL**, very** *He died in very curious circumstances.*
- ▶ rather **quite, rather, somewhat** *It's rather curious, but there isn't any photograph.*
- ▶ slightly **a little, slightly** *It was a slightly curious thing, but on the very first day of the new month the weather settled down and we got a week of hot ish, dry weather.*

- ADJ+n event or situation **case, circumstance, coincidence, incident, phenomenon** *Then again, curious coincidences can just happen.*
- ▶ fact or feature **fact, feature, thing** *But the curious thing I noticed was that about 10 or 15 local lads joined in at the front of the march.*
- ▶ result **effect** *His singing had a curious effect on me.*
- ▶ mixture **blend, combination, mix, mixture** *We'll be following a bridleway through a curious mixture of pasture, woodland and heath.*

- v+ADJ **be, find sth, seem** *Her choice of words seemed curious.*

- and/or **amusing, fascinating, interesting** *It is extremely curious and amusing to listen to the different interpretations or versions of the same thing.*

currency N
the system of money used in a country

- adj+N of a foreign country **foreign** *Purchases and sales of foreign currency were subject to a small tax.*
- ▶ of your own country **domestic, home, local, national** *I had taken a supply of local currency with me as I was not sure how frequent the cashpoints would be.*
- ▶ used all over the world **common, global, international, major** *When going abroad, travellers are advised to take travellers' cheques in a major currency such as Euros, US dollars and Pounds Sterling.*
- ▶ that can be exchanged for other currencies **convertible, hard, reserve** *One of Africa's most unique game parks is being put up for sale to Western buyers in order to raise hard currency.*
- ▶ used by a number of countries **single** *On 1st January 1999, eleven countries joined a European Monetary Union and created a single currency – the Euro.*
- ▶ strong **stable, strong** *The UAE Dirham is a very stable currency.*
- ▶ weak **weak, worthless** *Worthless currency now made food shortages commonplace and severe.*
- ▶ official **official** *The Euro was then the official currency of 12 EU member states (including Finland).*
- ▶ fake **counterfeit, fake** *The change-over will allow people not only to get rid of counterfeit currency, but also to launder cash which has been illegally obtained.*

- v+N exchange a currency **buy, change, convert, exchange, sell** *You should only exchange currency at banks or hotels.*
- ▶ use a currency **adopt, use** *During the 1960s, the*

Irish government decided to adopt a decimal currency like many of its European neighbours.
- ▶ accept a currency **accept** *Unfortunately, we cannot accept any currency other than sterling.*
- ▶ issue a currency **issue** *In most countries it is only the Government, through their central banks, who are permitted to issue currency.*
- ▶ devalue a currency **debase, devalue** *China devalued its currency in 1994.*
- ▶ revalue a currency **revalue** *Will China revalue her currency?*
- ▶ keep one currency the same as another **peg, tie** *Most other East Asian currencies were pegged to the dollar.*

- N+v fall in value **collapse, depreciate, devalue, drop, fall, lose value** *Where a currency depreciates, prices to its farmers and consumers should rise.*
- ▶ rise in value **appreciate, rise** *When the dollar falls, other currencies rise.*
- ▶ change in value **float, fluctuate** *With currencies fluctuating continually, major savings can be made by those that get the financial exchange right.*

current ADJ
happening or existing now

- ADJ+n **arrangement, climate, level, position, practice, rate, situation, state, status, thinking, trend** *If current trends continue, all Americans will be overweight by 2050.*

- and/or future **forthcoming, future, potential, prospective, recent** *Details of current and forthcoming activities are posted on the University website.*
- ▶ past **former, past, previous** *The department has undertaken a review of key previous and current policies in the field of Sustainable Development.*

current N
a strong movement of water in one direction

- adj+N strong or fast **fast, fast-flowing, powerful, strong, swift, swirling, turbulent** *Swim due north for 2–3 minutes if the current isn't strong.*
- ▶ weak **gentle, weak** *These small particles of rock would be easily washed away with even the weakest currents.*
- ▶ in the sea **ocean, oceanic** *Oceanic currents act as a major mechanism for transporting heat.*
- ▶ of the tide **tidal** *A dead body would have turned up by now, due to the tidal currents around the islands.*

- N+v move something **carry sth, pull sth, sweep sth, transport sth** *No place in the world's seas is immune from pollution, as ocean currents transport pollutants to the far corners of the world.*
- ▶ flow **flow** *The current was flowing so fast it was impossible to swim against it.*

curriculum N
the subjects studied by students at a particular school

- adj+N covering many subjects **broad, broad-based, broadly based, varied, wide** *Our broad curriculum covers a wide range of subjects including foreign languages.*
- ▶ with a good mix of subjects **balanced, well-**

balanced *All schools should be funded to allow a broad and balanced curriculum.*
▶ covering a few subjects **narrow** *Teaching and learning should be enjoyable, and not hampered by stress, bureaucracy, and narrow curricula .*
▶ covering too many subjects **crowded** *Teachers may ignore this aspect or find themselves struggling to include it in crowded curricula.*
▶ compulsory **compulsory, prescribed, statutory** *Students follow a compulsory curriculum, which varies according to school type.*
▶ for a whole country **national** *We teach all aspects of the national curriculum and enrich this through such things as visits and special projects.*
▶ basic **basic, core** *Music has become part of the core curriculum.*
▶ fixed **formal, rigid, structured** *The curriculum should not be too rigid.*
▶ not fixed **flexible** *The curriculum is sufficiently flexible to give all pupils the opportunity to excel.*
▶ good **challenging, stimulating** *The school provides a very stimulating curriculum.*
▶ for all kinds of students **inclusive** *All schools are charged with providing an inclusive curriculum which meets the needs of all pupils.*
▶ types of curriculum **academic, vocational** *How can mathematical content be organized in a vocational curriculum?*

● v+N develop a curriculum **create, design, develop, devise** *Our intention is to devise a curriculum that will fit individual children's needs.*
▶ improve a curriculum **enhance, enrich** *This scheme can really enrich your curriculum.*
▶ broaden a curriculum **broaden, supplement** *They want to broaden the post-16 curriculum.*
▶ change a curriculum **adapt, adjust, reform, rethink, revise** *Perhaps we need to rethink our curriculum?*
▶ deliver a curriculum **deliver, teach** *We deliver the curriculum in a variety of teaching and learning styles.*
▶ use a curriculum **access, follow** *Reading skills were identified as crucial to accessing the curriculum.*
▶ exist in a curriculum **permeate, underpin** *The use of ICT permeates the curriculum and is used frequently by staff to engage their pupils.*
▶ personalize a curriculum **personalize, tailor** *We aspire to tailor the curriculum to meet the child's needs.*

cursor N
a small flashing line on a computer screen
● v+N put a cursor somewhere **hold, hover, place, point, position, put** *If you hover your cursor over a match result, an information box will pop up giving details of the match.* ● *Position your cursor over it, and give it a click!*
▶ move a cursor **drag, move, pass** *Hold down the left mouse button and drag the cursor around the image to move.*

curtail V
reduce or limit something, especially something good
● adv+V a lot **considerably, dramatically, drastically, greatly, immediately, seriously,**

severely, sharply, significantly, substantially *The production of harmful materials should be drastically curtailed or stopped.*
▶ slightly **slightly, somewhat** *The bad weather slightly curtailed our climbing activities.*
● V+n particular thing **ability, activity, career, debate, freedom, liberty, power, production, right, use** *Do we really want to give the Government powers that will curtail our freedom in the name of security?*
▶ increase in something **growth, proliferation, spread** *Our planning policies would curtail the spread of out-of-town malls.*

curtain N
cloth hanging from a window to cover it
● adj+N thick **blackout, heavy, plush, thick** *His duties were to inspect houses to see that no chinks of light were showing through the blackout curtains.*
▶ thin **gauzy, sheer** *Sun shone through the white gauzy curtains.*
▶ of a material **cotton, lace, net, silk, velvet** *I decided to put up some net curtains.*
▶ already made **made-to-measure, ready-made** *She creates made-to-measure curtains and Roman blinds in her home workshop.*
▶ patterned **floral, flowery, striped** *She bought a pair of pale blue and gold striped curtains.*
● v+N open the curtains **draw (back), open, pull (back)** *Ask a neighbour to make the house look occupied by closing and drawing the curtains daily.* ● *It is a joy to pull the curtains in the morning!*
▶ close the curtains **close, draw, pull, shut** *He draws the curtains on his bedroom window to block out the view.* ● *Darren threw cushions on the floor and Lisa felt a quick flash of relief that she had pulled the curtains.*
▶ put up curtains **hang, put up** *I lost an earring as I was hanging some new curtains.*

custody N
1 the legal right to look after a child
● adj+N when one person has custody **exclusive, full, sole** *The Superior Court ruled that he deserved sole custody of the couple's two children.*
▶ when two people have custody **joint** *Despite no longer living together, Doug and Alice remain in close contact due to joint custody of their son.*
▶ temporary **interim, temporary** *She has temporary custody of the children until a full divorce hearing is heard.*
● v+N have custody **have** *The judge makes arrangements for one parent to have custody of the child, and the other to have access.*
▶ get custody **gain, get, obtain, win** *The mother got custody of the children.*
▶ give someone custody **award sb, give sb, grant sb** *He is granted temporary custody of her for a further three weeks.*
▶ try to get custody **apply for, ask for, claim, demand, fight for, file for, seek, want** *Within weeks Stephen had decided to seek custody of the children.*
▶ refuse custody **deny, refuse** *The judges decided that adultery was not a reason to deny a woman custody of the children.*
▶ share custody **share** *It was a civilized divorce and they shared custody of their two daughters.*

▶ lose custody **lose** *He feared losing custody of the children.*
▶ keep custody **keep, retain** *They could carry on any legal battle necessary to retain custody of their son.*
▶ transfer custody **transfer** *He wants to transfer custody of his nine-year-old son to his former wife.*

2 when someone is kept in prison until their trial

● adj+N **federal, lawful, legal, military, police, prison, psychiatric** *He escaped from psychiatric custody in 1986 and went into hiding in France.*

● v+N be in custody **be in, remain in, return to** *The suspects remain in custody at a south London police station.*
▶ place someone in custody **commit sb to, place sb in, remand sb in, sentence sb to, take sb into** *She was remanded in custody after being falsely accused of murder.*
▶ keep someone in custody **detain sb in, hold sb in, keep sb in** *If bail is refused, you will be held in custody until your first court appearance.*
▶ leave custody **escape (from), leave** *An investigation has begun after a woman died shortly after leaving police custody.*
▶ release someone from custody **discharge sb from, realease sb from** *The men were released from custody on Thursday morning.*

custom N
a traditional or usual activity

● adj+N old **age-old, ancient, immemorial, old, primitive, time-honoured, traditional** *The ancient customs have been completely abandoned.*
▶ strange or interesting **curious, peculiar, quaint, strange** *These curious old customs still prevail in some parts of western Wales.*
▶ usual or common **common, established, popular, prevailing, usual** *In the early 17th century there was no established custom of using plates, knives and forks as we know them.*
▶ in a particular area **local, native, rustic** *We like staying overnight in village homes, eating local food, and learning the local customs.*
▶ types of custom **burial, marriage, religious, social, tribal** *Social customs differ greatly from one country, region and city to another.*

● v+N follow a custom **adopt, conform to, follow, honour, observe, practise, respect** *While in town it is polite to observe local custom by keeping your knees and shoulders covered.*
▶ revive a custom **revive** *The choir revived the good old custom of going round carol singing.*

customer N
someone who buys goods or services

● adj+N satisfied **delighted, happy, satisfied** *The best form of promotion is recommendation from a satisfied customer.*
▶ not satisfied **angry, awkward, disgruntled, dissatisfied, irate, unhappy** *Only about ten per cent of dissatisfied customers will ever complain to you.*
▶ demanding high quality **demanding, discerning** *We have a wide range of carpet styles to offer the discerning customer.*
▶ loyal **long-standing, long-time, loyal, valued** *When*

we started out in business, we had just a few loyal customers.
▶ regular **regular, repeat** *Many large shopping chains in the UK issue loyalty cards to regular customers.*
▶ possible **potential, prospective, would-be** *This is carried out when we provide potential customers with a quote.*
▶ new/not new **current, existing, new** *This offer is available to new and existing customers.*
▶ important **big, good, important, key, large, major** *The financial sector is a key customer in many developing countries.*
▶ business **business, commercial, corporate, industrial, retail** *Corporate customers' needs are distinct from consumers' needs.*
▶ person **domestic, individual, personal, private, residential** *This service is available to commercial and domestic customers throughout the UK.*

You can also say that a business or service is **customer friendly**: *They aim to provide improved bus services that are both customer friendly and reliable.*

● v+N do something for customers **deal with, give sth, look after, provide, serve, supply, support** *We are committed to providing our customers **with** the highest level of support possible.* ● *We supply customers from all over the world.*
▶ get customers **attract, bring in, draw in, entice, get, result in** *These special offers are intended to attract new customers.*
▶ keep customers **keep, retain** *Whatever your sector, Macromedia Flash helps you attract and retain your customers.*
▶ lose customers **lose** *If your site takes more than a few seconds to load, you're probably going to lose that customer.*
▶ try to get a particular customer **target** *Retailers know how to target their customers and market their products.*

● N+n service **care, service, support** *We pride ourselves on the quality of our customer service.*
▶ satisfaction/dissatisfaction **dissatisfaction, satisfaction** *Each year, we conduct a consumer satisfaction survey.*
▶ needs or wants **demands, expectations, needs, requirements** *Our applications are tailored specifically to customer requirements.*
▶ reactions **comments, complaints, feedback** *Dealing with customer complaints can lead to confrontational situations.*
▶ requests **enquiries, queries, requests** *There used to be a customer service department that dealt with customer enquiries.*
▶ relations **interaction, liaison, relations, relationship** *The company believes in good customer relations.*
▶ choice **choice** *There is relatively little customer choice.*
▶ when customers keep buying from a company **loyalty** *Customer loyalty is the most important factor determining the success or otherwise of a company.*

customs N
the government department that checks goods entering a country

● v+N go through customs **clear, go through, pass through** *When I'd cleared customs, we had another 4 hour car journey.*

▶ notify customs **inform, notify** *As you enter port, fly the yellow quarantine flag and notify Customs of your arrival.*

● N+v **impound sth, seize sth, stop sb** *Customs seize no more than 10 per cent of the total number of cigarettes entering Britain illegally.*

● N+n tax **duty** *Customs duties on telecommunications equipment has been reduced.*

▶ official or organization **agent, authorities, inspector, officer, official** *He was apprehended by customs officers at the airport, in possession of 6,800 ecstasy pills.*

▶ building **control, hall, post** *They were all waiting for us as we came through customs control.*

▶ when something is allowed through customs **clearance** *Delivery will take 2–4 days, customs clearance permitting.*

▶ rules **controls, regulations** *There are no customs controls on wines, spirits and tobacco within the European Union.*

▶ procedures **formalities, procedures** *This leaflet sets out information about customs procedures for the import, export and transit of goods.*

cut N

1 an injury on your skin from something sharp

● adj+N bad **bad, deep, nasty** *He has a very nasty cut on his toe.*

▶ not bad **minor, slight, small, superficial, tiny** *Try to stop the bleeding from a minor cut by pressing it.*

▶ with neat edges **clean** *It was a clean cut, so was bleeding very badly.*

● v+N get a cut **get, suffer, sustain** *The man suffered a cut to his head and was taken to hospital.*

▶ clean a cut **clean, wash** *Cotton wool is good for cleaning cuts and grazes.*

● N+v **bleed, heal** *If a cut bleeds freely, any germs will normally be washed away by the blood.*

● and/or **abrasions, bruises, burns, grazes, scrapes, scratches, sores** *26 people were seriously hurt and the rest suffered minor cuts or bruises only.*

> Usage **Cut** is usually plural in these combinations: *She was covered in cuts and bruises.* ● *The cat ended up with lots of cuts and scrapes.*

2 a reduction in something

● adj+N big **drastic, grave, major, massive, savage, severe, sharp, substantial, sweeping, swingeing** *There have been savage cuts in staff numbers.*

▶ small **small** *There's been a small cut in interest rates.*

● n+N for saying what is cut **budget, funding, job, pay, price, spending, tax, wage** *These kinds of tax cuts do little to stimulate the economy.*

▶ for saying who cuts something **government** *Public services are suffering as a result of government cuts.*

> Usage **Cut** is always plural in this combination: *We can expect more government cuts.*

● v+N **announce, demand, impose, make, oppose, plan, promise, propose, threaten** *A 10 per cent pay cut was imposed on all employees.*

cut V

1 to use a sharp tool to remove part of something

● adv+V in a particular way **carefully, cleanly, diagonally, finely, neatly, thickly** *Carefully cut some wooden kebab skewers down so that they're slightly wider than the shoebox.*

▶ so that something becomes something different **loose, short, straight** *I've decided to have my hair cut short.*

2 to reduce the amount or level of something

● adv+V **dramatically, drastically, radically, severely, subsignificantly, substantially** *Carefully designed traffic calming can dramatically cut road casualties.*

● V+n **budget, bureaucracy, congestion, costs, crime, deficit, emissions, pollution, prices, rate, spending, tax, workforce** *They have set ambitious goals to cut emissions and improve energy efficiency.*

cut back PHR VB

to reduce something

● V+adv slightly **a bit INFORMAL, a little, slightly** *When mum lost her job, we all had to cut back a little.*

▶ a lot **considerably, drastically, a lot, sharply** *Factory workers are now seeing their companies closing or cutting back drastically.*

● V+n **borrowing, budget, emissions, funding, production, spending, workload** *About a third of manufacturers are cutting back production.*

cutback N

a reduction in the amount of money available

● adj+N big **draconian, drastic, huge, major, massive, severe, significant, substantial** *The hospital faces drastic cutbacks or outright closure.*

▶ financial **budget, financial, spending** *The bus service has been withdrawn due to financial cutbacks by the city council.*

● v+N make or tell people about cutbacks **announce, implement, impose, make, propose** *The new government announced a cutback in government expenditure of 200,000 million Pesetas.*

▶ experience cutbacks **be hit by, experience, face, suffer** *The aerospace industry is facing severe cutbacks.*

▶ result in cutbacks **lead to, prompt, result in** *The international debt problem has led to cutbacks in health and education budgets*

cut down PHR VB

to reduce something

● V+adv a lot **considerably, drastically, enormously, a lot, significantly** *This cloth will cut down drastically the amount of cleaning detergents used.*

▶ slightly **a bit INFORMAL, a little, slightly** *Spinning more slowly cuts down energy consumption a little.*

▶ gradually **gradually, slowly** *If you eat too much sugar or salt, cut down gradually.*

● V+n **consumption, drinking, intake, production, smoking, time** *You can customize the large screen to cut down power consumption.*

- V+on+n an activity **drinking, smoking, spending** *Have you ever felt that you should cut down on your drinking?*
- something undesirable **bureaucracy, congestion, costs, waste** *We can all save money by saving energy and cutting down our waste.*
- an amount **amount, degree, number** *My doctor has advised me to cut down on the amount of salt in my diet.*

cut off PHR VB
1 to stop the supply or something, or to stop something working

- V+n money **aid, benefits, financing, funding, subsidies, support, welfare** *Belgium and the Netherlands cut off aid to the Rwandan government.*
- power or water **electricity, gas, power, water** *An electrical storm cut off the mains electricity.*
- in the body **blood, circulation, oxygen** *Ensure that the bandage is not too tight to cut off circulation.*
- supply **flow, supply** *A shortage of freight threatened to cut off supplies of North American maize.*

2 to stop entrance to or communication with a place

- V+n entrance **access, road, route** *She has erected a fence around the land which has cut off access to a historic 16th century tower.*
- communication **communication, contact, negotiations, relations, ties** *Telephone lines snapped, cutting off communication for cities like New York and Philadelphia for weeks.*

cut through PHR VB
to deal quickly and effectively with problems

- V+n **bureaucracy, complexity, confusion, hype, jargon, red tape** *Do you need advice on setting up a business and cutting through the red tape faced by small businesses?*

cutting ADJ
a cutting remark is cruel and intended to upset someone

- adv+ADJ **extremely, particularly, quite, rather, so, very** *Verbally, you can be quite cutting and hurtful.*
- ADJ+n comment **comment, remark, response** *One actress who hadn't done her homework was the object of several cutting remarks from Coward.*
- humour **humour, satire** *Their sketches are a mixture of cutting satire and observational genius.*

cycle N
a repeated series of events

- adj+N continuous or repeated **continual, continuous, endless, never-ending, repeated** *Learning and teaching is a continuous cycle.*
- taking a year, week etc **annual, monthly, seasonal, weekly, yearly** *A yearly cycle is completed between one Christmas and another.*
- normal **natural, normal** *Any scientist will tell you that the weather is just going through a normal cycle.*
- complete **complete, entire, full, whole** *The work will cover the complete software development cycle from user requirements to implementation and testing.*

- where one bad thing leads to another **vicious** *Recent research indicates that contact lens wear and dry eyes can be a vicious cycle.*
- where one good thing leads to another **virtuous** *There is a virtuous cycle of improvement built on high demand.*
- economic **business, economic** *In the previous economic cycle, interest rates remained in double figures for over four years.*
- for creating a baby or living a life **breeding, life, reproductive** *Orang-utans have the slowest reproductive cycle of all the great apes, with an average of eight years between births.*

- v+N complete a cycle **complete, do, follow, go through** *The time it takes a flea to complete this life cycle is extremely variable.*
- repeat or continue a cycle **continue, perpetuate, repeat** *Repeat the cycle as often as you need to.*
- start a cycle **initiate, start** *These recommendations will set the conditions for fast, successful projects and initiate a cycle of ongoing improvement.*
- break a cycle **break, disrupt, end, interrupt, reverse, stop** *We need to break the cycle of poor skills and poverty which many families encounter.*

- N+of bad things **addiction, dependency, deprivation, disadvantage, homelessness, poverty, underachievement, violence** *Together we can break the cycle of deprivation.*
- change **change, development, growth** *Some people felt it was the start of the next big cycle of fashion change.*

cynical ADJ
willing to harm other people to get what you want, or thinking that people are like this

- adv+ADJ very **deeply, extremely, incredibly, so, very** *People in this country are so cynical.*
- rather **fairly, a little, pretty INFORMAL, quite, rather, slightly, somewhat** *It might be rather cynical, but I tend to agree with you on where the funding is going.*
- totally **entirely, totally, utterly** *It was not an entirely cynical decision.*
- too **overly, too, unduly** *One does not have to be unduly cynical to have doubts about the likely success of such a voluntary code of conduct.*

- ADJ+n action or plan **attempt, manoeuvre, move, ploy, tactic** *I was taken in by the cynical marketing ploy of the free CD.*
- behaviour **disbelief, disregard, exploitation, manipulation, opportunism** *His public words were simply a cynical manipulation of the public to promote his reputation.*
- remarks **comment, remark, response** *Try not to make cynical remarks and personal attacks on people's characters.*
- attitude **attitude, view** *The widespread cynical view is that he has simply postponed such increases until after the election.*

- v+ADJ seem cynical **appear, seem, sound** *I don't mean to sound cynical.*
- become cynical **be, become, grow** *Others become cynical because life has worn them down.*
- feel cynical **feel, remain** *Maybe you feel very cynical about this, but wouldn't it be great if it were true?*

- and/or **apathetic, bitter, callous, hypocritical,**

jaded, manipulative, negative, sarcastic, sceptical, world-weary *Those words are clearly the work of a bitter, cynical and extremely unhappy man.*

cynicism N
a belief that people care only about themselves

- adj+N extreme **bitter, considerable, deep, extreme, profound** *Most of us greet new management fads **with** deep cynicism.*
- ▶ pure **pure, sheer, utter** *The sheer cynicism of it amazes me.*
- ▶ increasing **growing, increasing** *My growing cynicism **about** modern music was blown apart by the band's performance.*
- ▶ widespread **general, pervasive, rampant, widespread** *Cynicism was rampant **among** the refugees.*
- ▶ by the public **public** *Today's politicians do not fight against public cynicism, but roll over to accommodate it.*
- ▶ political **political** *Everywhere political cynicism and apathy is growing among the public.*
- ▶ from having a lot of experience **weary, world-**

weary *I prefer her youthful idealism over his world-weary cynicism.*

- ▶ when it is a good thing **healthy** *The Academy will have a healthy cynicism **about** educational jargon and bureaucracy.*
- ▶ when it is a bad thing **corrosive** *Cynicism is corrosive.*
- v+N fight cynicism **combat, counter, fight** *The only way to fight cynicism is to stand up for what we believe in with passion and commitment.*
- ▶ lead to cynicism **breed, feed, generate, lead to** *Such actions merely breed cynicism.*
- ▶ express cynicism **display, express** *Police officers expressed cynicism **about** promotion prospects.*
- ▶ reveal cynicism **expose, reflect, reveal, underline** *Such jokes reflect the cynicism of life in the country at that time.*
- ▶ forgive cynicism **excuse, forgive** *Forgive my cynicism, but if this person exists, where is he now?*
- and/or **apathy, bitterness, despair, disillusionment, distrust, greed, indifference, irony, mistrust, pessimism, scepticism** *Cynicism and apathy **about** politics have increased.*

D d

dam N
a wall built across a river

- adj+N large **giant, huge, large, massive** *The government proposes to build a huge dam on the river.*
- ▶ made of a particular material **concrete, earth, masonry** *The Hoover Dam is the highest concrete dam in the US.*
- ▶ types of dam **hydroelectric, irrigation, mill** *The original lake was flooded by the construction of a hydroelectric dam in 1972.*

- v+N break a dam **breach, break, burst** *A severe storm raised the level of the lake water to the point where it threatened to breach the dam.*
- ▶ build a dam **build, construct, erect** *A model dam was constructed in the fish tank.*

- N+v **break, burst, collapse, flood** *The dam burst and there was mud everywhere.*

damage N
harm

- adj+N a lot **considerable, extensive, great, heavy, much, serious, severe, significant, substantial, untold, widespread** *The allegations caused untold damage to his reputation.*
- ▶ slight **little, minimal, minor, slight** *Minor damage is automatically repaired.*
- ▶ permanent **irreparable, irreversible, lasting, long-term, permanent** *Pollution is causing lasting damage to our environment.*
- ▶ deliberate **criminal, deliberate, malicious, wilful** *Report any incident involving theft, attempted theft or malicious damage to the police.*
- ▶ not deliberate **accidental** *The insurance policy did not cover me for accidental damage to my computer.*
- ▶ to the brain **brain, neurological, psychological** *Exposure to methyl mercury, even in small amounts, can result in devastating neurological damage.*
- ▶ to the environment **ecological, environmental** *Environmental damage is rife as enormous areas of forests are displaced for crops.*
- ▶ types of damage **mechanical, physical, structural** *A sealant does not protect the stone from physical damage.*

- n+N caused by something **bomb, fire, flood, frost, hurricane, smoke, storm** *The wall near the main entrance shows clear signs of bomb damage.*
- ▶ to part of the body **brain, cartilage, kidney, liver, lung, muscle, nerve, skin, tissue** *Tests can establish the presence and severity of the liver damage.*

- v+N cause damage **cause, do, inflict, lead to, result in** *Further damage was caused by a fire which broke out during the repair work.*
- ▶ suffer damage **have, incur, suffer, sustain** *Yvonne sadly suffered brain damage and she subsequently died.*
- ▶ repair or undo damage **repair, reverse, undo** *When you are no longer exposed every day to nicotine, your body begins to repair the damage.*
- ▶ limit damage **limit, minimize, mitigate, reduce** *Treatment must be started early after the initial injury, with the aim of minimizing damage to the spinal cord.*
- ▶ prevent damage **avoid, guard (sth) against, prevent, protect (sth) against, protect (sth) from** *Prevent further damage by making emergency repairs.*
- ▶ look at damage **assess, check sth for, inspect sth for, look at, survey** *A mechanic examined the engine and assessed the damage.*

damage V
to harm something or someone

- adv+V badly **badly, extensively, gravely, heavily, seriously, severely, significantly** *A hurricane in 2002 badly damaged the mangroves and most trees are still dead.*
- ▶ slightly **slightly** *The lifeboat was slightly damaged in a collision with a cruise ship.*
- ▶ permanently **fatally, irreparably, irretrievably, irreversibly, irrevocably, permanently** *Her eyesight was irreparably damaged by this delay in diagnosis.*
- ▶ deliberately **deliberately, intentionally, wilfully** *Anyone who wilfully damages or destroys a tree is guilty of an offence.*
- ▶ not deliberately **accidentally, inadvertently** *If your item is accidentally damaged we'll repair or replace it.*
- ▶ easily **easily** *It is an environment that can easily damage professional confidence.*
- ▶ affecting someone's mind **emotionally, psychologically** *The ordeal has left her psychologically damaged.*
- ▶ affecting an object or someone's body **physically** *It is not possible for a virus to physically damage a computer's processor or hard drive.*

- V+n physically **ecosystem, environment** *They want to live comfortably without damaging the environment of their surroundings.*
- ▶ not physically **business, competitiveness, confidence, credibility, health, image, livelihood, morale, prospects, relationship, reputation** *In the last few weeks a boy wrote to the newspaper saying that unhelpful teachers were damaging his prospects of success in exams.*

damaging ADJ
harmful

- adv+ADJ very **deeply, emotionally, enormously, extremely, hugely, immensely, incredibly, particularly, profoundly, seriously, severely** *Uncertainty would be hugely damaging to economic growth.*
- ▶ possibly **possibly, potentially** *A legal case could attract potentially damaging publicity.*
- ▶ in a particular way **commercially, ecologically, economically, emotionally, environmentally, financially, politically, psychologically, socially** *Less environmentally damaging modes of transport should be promoted.*

- ADJ+n effect **blow, consequences, effect, impact,**

impact, repercussions, result, side-effect *Many drugs that cause damaging side-effects in people have passed animal tests.*

▶ things that are said **allegations, criticism, publicity** *There were damaging allegations made about how he had poisoned his daughter's mind with racism.*

● and/or **dangerous, degrading, disruptive, divisive, hurtful, inappropriate, intrusive, pointless, unnecessary** *Security incidents can be very disruptive and damaging.*

damp ADJ
slightly wet, often in an unpleasant way

● adv+ADJ slightly **a little, slightly** *Wipe any marks or spills with a slightly damp cloth.*

▶ very **extremely, pretty** INFORMAL, **really, very** *It can get pretty damp and windy here.*

▶ rather **fairly, quite, rather, somewhat** *The marquee was a blessing given the rather damp conditions.*

▶ always **constantly, permanently** *Everything is permanently damp with condensation, sweat or saltwater.*

● ADJ+n cloth **cloth, flannel, rag, sponge, tea-towel, towel** *Give it a quick wipe with a damp cloth.*

▶ place inside **cellar, home** *The cellars were sometimes damp and occasionally flooded.*

▶ place outside **grassland, pasture, woodland** *Moss can be found growing in damp or wet places such as beside streams or in damp woodlands.*

▶ ground **grass, ground, sand, soil** *Don't hoe when the soil is damp.*

▶ area **area, patch** *There were damp patches on the walls.*

▶ weather **air, climate, morning, weather** *Damp weather can cause havoc with naturally curly or wavy hair.*

▶ conditions **atmosphere, conditions, environment** *A warm and damp environment accelerates chemical action.*

● and/or of the weather **chilly, cloudy, cold, cool, dismal, dreary, drizzly, dull, foggy, humid, miserable, misty, overcast, wet, windy** *Although the weather was damp and misty, they had a great race.*

▶ of a room or building **cramped, dark, draughty, dusty, musty, smelly** *Too many homes are damp, draughty and hard to heat.*

▶ of an area of ground **boggy, marshy, shaded, shady** *These plants are best suited to damp corners of the garden.*

▶ of a substance **dirty, mouldy, soft** *Store hay carefully to stop it becoming damp and mouldy.*

danger N
a situation with possible harm or damage

● adj+N serious **big, considerable, deadly, extreme, grave, great, mortal, real, serious, terrible** *He realises that he is in grave danger.*

▶ slight **little, slight** *There is relatively little danger from road traffic here.*

▶ always present **constant, ever-present** *The risk of getting bogged down in mud was an ever-present danger.*

▶ possible **possible, potential** *The petrol pumps were banished some years ago because of the potential danger to the public.*

▶ obvious/not obvious **hidden, latent, lurking, obvious, unknown, unseen** *There are obvious dangers if you are a learner or not a strong swimmer – do not get out of your depth.*

▶ now **immediate, present** *I don't think she's in any immediate danger.*

▶ soon **imminent, impending** *She appeared to warn him of impending danger.*

▶ forming part of something **inherent** *I don't need to point out the dangers that are inherent in such a scheme.*

● v+N be a danger **be, constitute, pose, present, represent** *The presence of an asbestos does not in itself constitute any danger.*

▶ be in danger **be exposed to, be in, court, face, flirt with** *Any business that does not protect the security of its data is flirting with danger.*

▶ cause danger **cause, put sb/sth in** *Civilian lives were being put in danger.*

▶ involve danger **be fraught with, involve** *This is a strategy that is fraught with danger.*

▶ avoid danger **avert, avoid, escape (from), prevent** *This leaflet gives advice on spotting the signs of carbon monoxide and avoiding the dangers.*

▶ protect someone or something from danger **guard sb/sth against, protect sb/sth from** *We do not allow smoking on the premises, to protect visitors from the dangers of passive smoking.*

▶ realize or see the danger **appreciate, foresee, perceive, realize, recognize, see, spot, understand** *The boatmen, realising the danger of capsizing, quickly pushed the boat a few feet out from the bank.*

▶ not realize the danger **underestimate** *Don't underestimate the danger of playing with fire.*

▶ reduce or remove danger **eliminate, lessen, minimize, reduce, remove** *Journalists must take hard decisions about the risks they face, although everything is done to minimize the dangers.*

▶ tell someone about danger **alert sb to, highlight, stress, underline, warn sb about, warn sb of** *I'm here to underline those dangers and to help you avoid putting yourself at risk.*

▶ exaggerate a danger **exaggerate** *They tend to exaggerate the dangers in their minds.*

dangerous ADJ
likely to harm someone or cause damage

● adv+ADJ very **downright, exceedingly, exceptionally, exceptionally, extremely, highly, incredibly, positively, pretty** INFORMAL, **profoundly, so, terribly, truly, very** *Nuclear waste is highly dangerous.*

▶ particularly **especially, particularly** *Smoking is especially dangerous if you have a bad cough.*

▶ more and more **increasingly** *The main fear for parents is that their children will be hurt on our increasingly dangerous roads.*

▶ rather **quite, rather** *Surprisingly, many common houseplants are quite dangerous.*

▶ possibly **possibly, potentially** *A pen is a potentially dangerous weapon in the hands of a prisoner.*

▶ as part of its basic nature **inherently, intrinsically** *The Chief Inspector said that this type of driving was inherently dangerous and risked lives.*

▶ when everyone knows something is dangerous **notoriously** *Vinny is making advance preparations* *for crossing a notoriously dangerous part of the ocean.*

▶ in a particular way **physically, politically** *Presumably a study of the evidence would be too politically dangerous.*

● v+ADJ consider something dangerous **consider sth, deem sth, perceive sth as, regard sth as** *Generally biking is considered dangerous on busy or narrow roads.*

▶ be dangerous **be, prove** *Not only was the heating inadequate, but on occasion it proved dangerous.*

▶ seem dangerous **appear, feel, look, seem, sound** *It's difficult to perform a sword fight safely and still make it look dangerous to the audience.*

▶ become dangerous **become, get, grow** *Structures can also become dangerous from lack of maintenance.*

▶ remain dangerous **remain** *Many bombs did not explode, and remain dangerous to this day.*

● and/or **anti-social, damaging, difficult, disruptive, harmful, illegal, irresponsible, unpleasant, violent** *There are children whose disabilities or medical condition leads them to behave in a dangerous or disruptive way.*

darkness N
lack of light

● adj+N total **absolute, complete, impenetrable, pitch, total, utter** *He rubbed his eyes, and soon became aware that he was alone in the church, and in utter darkness.*

▶ almost **near, semi** *The images on this page were taken in near darkness.*

▶ thick **black, deep, dense, inky, thick** *At last the daylight faded and the town was blanketed in inky darkness.*

▶ not clear **murky, smoky** *All the people poured out into the murky darkness of the street.*

▶ increasing **gathering, growing** *Then, in gathering darkness, I drove north.*

● v+N light up darkness **dispel, illuminate, lighten, light up, penetrate, pierce** *The only light that pierces the darkness emits blurrily from the neon sign in the window.*

▶ cause darkness **plunge sth into** *Large parts of the capital were plunged into darkness after the explosion.*

● N+v **approach, close in, descend, engulf sth, envelop sb/sth, fall, shroud sb/sth in, surround sb/sth** *Darkness enveloped him again, but this time there seemed to be lights up ahead.*

dash N
an act of running or hurrying

● adj+N quick and urgent **frantic, mad, quick** *The rain and hail came in again with a vengeance and we were forced to make a mad dash for the cars.*

▶ at a late stage **final, last-minute** *A deputation organized by the Writers' Guild made a last-minute dash to Strasbourg and put the concerns of rights holders directly to MEPs.*

● v+N **make** *The old man made a dash for the door, but was intercepted.*

When you talk about someone hurrying in order to escape from somewhere or reach a place, you can say that they ***make a dash for it***: *He looked at his guards and wondered if he should make a dash for it.*

data N
information used to make calculations or decisions, or used by computers

● adj+N types of data **digital, empirical, experimental, historical, personal, qualitative, quantitative, scientific, statistical** *We do not hold any personal data about customers.*

▶ accurate **accurate, reliable** *Do we have reliable data on the health risks of these chemicals?*

▶ relevant or able to be used **available, relevant** *The council plans to expand the scheme to give doctors' surgeries relevant data about children in care.*

▶ needing to be kept secret **sensitive** *No sensitive data is recorded unless the interviewer has agreed.*

▶ not yet processed **raw** *The raw data needs to be handled and processed before conclusions can be drawn.*

● v+N collect or keep data **capture, collect, contain, gather, hold, obtain, retrieve, store** *Data was collected from the pathology reports of 573 patients.*

▶ deal with or organize data **analyse, extract, handle, interpret, process, protect** *The project will review the relevant literature and gather and analyse the appropriate data.*

▶ look at or use data **access, use** *Only a few people are able to access the client data, for confidentiality reasons.*

▶ move data **download, send, transfer, transmit** *The device enables computers to transmit data across the Internet.*

▶ give or show data **display, generate, present, provide, supply** *The information in this paper was based on raw data supplied to the authors.*

▶ put data in **enter, input, key in, record** *They learnt how to enter data in Excel and how to create a graph from the data.*

▶ be based on data **be based on** *Efforts at comparing UK prices have tended to be based on incomplete data.*

● N+v **indicate, reveal, show, suggest, support** *Our data suggests that our most mature age groups work the highest average number of hours per week.*

● N+n processes or activities **acquisition, analysis, entry, exchange, input, management, processing, protection, storage, structure, transfer** *Data storage gets cheaper every year.*

▶ amount of data **file, set** *Every record in every data file that leaves our processing department gets assigned a sequence number.*

● n+of+N doing something with data **analysis, collection, use** *Systematic collection of clinical data using standardized report forms allows data to be gathered in a uniform way approximately every two years.*

▶ amount of data **amount, collection, piece, set** *You have access to a huge amount of statistical data.*

▶ whether there is data available **lack, source** *It was difficult to explain this result due to a lack of accurate data.*

database N

a large collection of information in a computer

- adj+N type or form of database **central, computerized, electronic, national, online, relational, searchable** *By searching our online vacancy database you will get an idea of the sort of position we can help you with.*
- ▸ size of database **comprehensive, extensive, large** *The Arts Service maintains a comprehensive database of service providers in the arts community.*
- n+N **computer, customer** *It is designed to cover such cases as gaining access to confidential information held on a computer database to use for blackmail.*
- v+N create a database or make changes to it **build, create, develop, maintain, update** *Travel Publishing has created a database of over 5,000 places to visit in the UK.*
- ▸ use a database **access, search, use** *Click on this link to search the database.*
- ▸ put information into a database **add to, enter into, hold in, hold on, store in, store on** *Any personal information that you give, including your email address, is stored in a database for marketing purposes.*
- N+v **contain** *The news database currently only contains items that were added within the past 30 days.*
- N+n **design, entry, management, search, server, system** *It is estimated that the new database system will be complete by the end of September.*

date N

a particular day or year; a particular time when something happens

- adj+N at an earlier or later time **earlier, future, later** *An invoice will be sent to you at a later date.*
- ▸ given exactly or roughly **actual, approximate, exact, precise, provisional, specific, specified** *Please note that the exact date of birth and/or marriage should be provided.*
- ▸ when a baby is due to be born or money is due to be paid **due** *My due date came and I felt fine except for being fed up with everyone asking me if I had had it yet!*
- n+N when something happens **arrival, birth, delivery, departure, launch, publication, release, target** *If you are booking less than 8 weeks before the departure date then we will ask you for payment of the holiday in full.*
- ▸ when something starts or finishes **closing, completion, end, expiry, start** *Applications must arrive before the closing date.*
- v+N when making arrangements **agree, arrange, change, check, choose, confirm, fix, set** *Can we set a date for the next meeting?*
- ▸ when giving a date **announce, give** *She found an inscription giving the precise date for the completion of the mosque.*
- N+of+n **birth, death, meeting, publication** *What is your date of birth?*

dawn N

the beginning of the day, when it begins to get light

- adj+N **bright, early, grey** *At early dawn this morning shots were heard from the direction of the forest.*
- v+N **greet** *We were all up on the observation deck at 6 a.m. to greet the dawn.*
- N+v **break, come** *When dawn broke we had almost emerged from the Nevada desert.*
- N+n **chorus, light, raid** *Why not make the effort to rise early to join us on a guided walk of the bird reserve to listen to the wonderful dawn chorus.*
- N+to+n **dusk** *The estate and grounds are open all year, daily, dawn to dusk.*
- n+of+N **crack** *School trips always start at the crack of dawn, and this one was no exception.*
- and/or **dusk** *The tennis courts are available to the general public between dawn and dusk.*

day N

a period of 24 hours, especially the part when it is light and people are awake

- adj+N next, previous etc **following, next, previous, same** *We were due to leave the following day.*
- ▸ describing the weather **cloudy, cold, fine, glorious, hot, nice, rainy, sunny, warm, wet** *It's the hottest day of the year so far.*
- ▸ enjoyable or important **big, enjoyable, fantastic, fun, good, great, lovely, memorable, perfect, special, wonderful** *I hope you have a really memorable day.*
- ▸ difficult or unpleasant **bad, hard, long** *I think it was one of the worst days of my life.*
- ▸ normal **normal, ordinary, typical** *It is difficult to describe a typical day for me.*
- ▸ busy or not busy **busy, quiet** *We've got a busy day tomorrow.*
- n+N when a particular thing happens **election, feast, opening, polling, school, training, wedding, working** *Payments will be credited to your account the next working day.*
- ▸ seasons **autumn, fall, spring, summer, summer's, winter, winter's** *A glorious summer day helped to make this a very enjoyable occasion for all competitors and spectators.*
- v+N **have, spend, start** *She's spent the last few days in bed, wrapped in her duvet.*
- N+v when a particular day arrives or begins **begin, come, dawn, start** *The day started in a way that no-one wants on their skiing holiday: rain.*
- ▸ happen and come to an end **go, go by, go on, pass, wear on** *The weather improved as the day went on.*
  - *The problem is getting greater as each day passes.*

day-to-day ADJ

happening every day as part of normal life

- ADJ+n work done every day **activities, administration, dealings, management, operation, running, work** *The job of a good manager is not to get too bogged down in the day-to-day running of the firm.*

▸ way things are organized **basis, routine** *You will report to the Research Director on a day-to-day basis.*
▸ responsibility **responsibility** *The job includes taking day-to-day responsibility for student behaviour and welfare.*
▸ life **existence, life** *The programme shows the day-to-day lives of 30 pupils in the London area.*

dead ADJ
no longer alive

● adv+**ADJ** length of time **already, long** *By the time the investigators persuaded the authorities to unload the animals, 40 lambs and 12 sheep were already dead.*
▸ emphasizing that someone is dead **quite** *She entered and saw him lying on his back in a pool of blood, quite dead.*
▸ almost dead **almost, nearly** *There had been a brawl and one man lay almost dead on the street.*

● **ADJ**+n **body** *Police have found a dead body in the house.*
● v+**ADJ** shoot someone **shoot sb** *She was shot dead during an armed raid on her jewellery store.*
▸ when someone is found to be dead **be declared, be found, be pronounced** *She was found dead at her home on Tuesday.*
▸ be dead or die **drop, fall, lie** *A shot rang out and the lion fell dead at their feet.*
▸ pretend to be dead **play** *I was playing dead to avoid getting shot.*

● and/or **alive, injured, live, wounded** *I have a younger brother, but I do not know if he is dead or alive.* ● *The sale of live or dead wild birds is forbidden by law.*

deadline N
the time by which you must do or finish something

● adj+**N** **agreed, final, strict, tight** *I am able to work to tight deadlines and under pressure.*
● v+**N** have a deadline **have, work to** *Whatever you do, have clear deadlines and milestones and stick to them.*
▸ finish something in time **make, meet** *There is still a lot to do to meet the 2011 deadline.*
▸ fail to finish something in time **miss** *It's easy to find that you've missed the deadline for submitting entries.*
▸ tell someone when they must finish something **give, impose, set** *We do not believe that it is sensible for the Government to set an arbitrary deadline for this work.*
▸ make a deadline later **extend** *Luckily my tutor agreed to extend the deadline for handing in the essay.*

● **N**+v when a deadline is getting close **approach, loom** *The application deadline is looming.*
▸ when a deadline has passed **expire, pass** *Once the deadline has passed, you will then have to wait 3–6 months to hear whether your application has been funded.*

deadlock N
a situation in which disagreement cannot be ended

● adj+**N** **current, political** *UN efforts have failed to break the political deadlock between the two camps.*

● v+**N** when a deadlock ends **break** *He described the accord as a landmark document that managed to break the deadlock in global trade talks.*
▸ when a deadlock occurs **end in, reach** *The talks reached deadlock over the question of voting rights for the smaller countries.*

deadly ADJ
able or likely to kill people

● adv+**ADJ** **potentially** *Cheap deals are fuelling the popularity of holidays to countries where this potentially deadly disease is endemic.*
● **ADJ**+n **attack, disease, poison, threat, virus, weapon** *These deadly weapons could end up in the hands of terrorists.*
● v+**ADJ** **be, prove** *The aim is to collect debris and rubbish from the beach that would prove deadly to new-born seal pups and other marine wildlife.*

deaf ADJ
not able to hear anything or hear well

● adv+**ADJ** very or completely deaf **completely, profoundly, severely, totally, very** *He has been profoundly deaf since birth.*
▸ deaf to some extent **partially, slightly** *She is now partially deaf and blind in one eye.*
● v+**ADJ** be or become deaf **be born, become, go** *A child born deaf has immense difficulty in learning speech because the sounds are not there to be heard and repeated.*
▸ make someone deaf **leave sb** *He was very sick when he was two and it left him deaf.*

dealer N
a person who buys and sells something

● adj+**N** with official permission **authorized, franchized, licensed** *Transactions in foreign currency must be through an authorized dealer.*
▸ types of dealer **independent, local, specialist** *Contact your local car dealer for details.*
▸ how honest a dealer is **reputable, unscrupulous** *Are you buying your boat from a reputable dealer?*

● n+**N** **antique, antiques, arms, art, book, car, drug, scrap, used-car** *The campaign aims to increase the number of suspected drug dealers arrested.*

dealing N
1 the business of buying and selling

● n+**N** **drug, property, share** *Regular drug dealing and vandalism added to the city centre's state of decay.*

2 business activities or relationship with someone
[always plural]

● adj+**N** types of dealings **business, commercial, financial** *The Company Accountant controls all the financial dealings of the company.*
▸ nature of dealings **day-to-day, direct, future, personal** *They were able to make themselves understood perfectly efficiently in their day-to-day dealings with one another.*
● v+**N** **have** *The new uniform will be worn by all Air France staff who have direct dealings with customers.*

deal with PHR VB

1 take action relating to something

● adv+V **adequately, appropriately, directly, easily, effectively, efficiently, fairly, promptly, properly, quickly, successfully** *You will need to be able to make quick decisions and deal effectively with unexpected situations.*

● V+n question or comment **complaint, inquiry, issue, query, question** *Our aim is to deal with inquiries, whenever possible, within 24 hours.*

▶ request **application, claim, request** *Your application will be dealt with in 7–10 working days.*

▶ situation **case, consequences, incident, issue, matter, situation** *The unit is equipped with suitable vehicles to deal with major incidents.*

▶ difficulty **challenge, emergency, threat** *She's had a lot of difficulty in her life but she's dealt with all the challenges.*

2 accept and control a difficult emotional situation

● V+n **emotions, grief, stress** *John needs time to deal with his grief in the way that is comfortable for him.*

death N

the state of being dead

● adj+N happening too soon **early, premature, untimely** *Doctors warn him that such a lifestyle will lead to an early death.*

▶ sudden **sudden, unexpected** *He had been called away by the sudden death of his father.*

▶ sad or unpleasant **horrible, painful, sad, tragic** *Her tragic death at such an early age could not have been foreseen.*

▶ describing the cause of death **accidental, mysterious, natural, suspicious, violent** *The jury returned a verdict of accidental death.*

▶ when death seems certain **certain, inevitable** *I knew that staying in this room one second longer would mean certain death.*

▶ about to occur **imminent, impending** *The film forces viewers to confront the possibility of what they would do if faced with their own impending death.*

▶ when someone takes a long time to die **lingering, slow** *Animals caught in snares often suffer a lingering death.*

● v+N cause death **bring, cause, lead to, mean, result in** *Most people felt that a lifelong driving ban was appropriate for motorists who caused death.*

▶ die **die, face, meet, suffer** *He was left, alone, to die a slow death.*

▶ avoid or prevent death **avoid, cheat, escape, prevent** *Four years earlier she had narrowly escaped death when she was involved in a train crash.*

▶ make death come more quickly **hasten** *Was this medical decision either partly or explicitly intended to hasten death?*

▶ feel sad because someone has died **mourn** *Her sudden death is mourned by all who knew her.*

▶ risk death **risk** *The water was so cold that the shipwrecked passengers risked certain death.*

▶ be afraid of death **fear** *I will never again fear death.*

▶ punish someone responsible for a death **avenge** *The widowed Duchess of Gloucester pleads with Gaunt to avenge the death of her husband.*

● N+v occur **come, occur** *Death occurs within minutes unless the normal heart rhythm can be restored.*

▶ be caused by **be due to sth, result from sth** *The body bore no injuries, death having resulted from suffocation.*

● v+to+N how someone dies **bleed, choke, freeze, starve** *The medical staff thought he would probably bleed to death.*

▶ how someone is killed **beat sb, burn sb, crush sb, kick sb, stab sb, stone sb, torture sb** *She was stabbed to death at her home in November 2008.*

▶ punish someone with death **condemn sb, put sb, sentence sb** *The five men were found guilty of high treason and sentenced to death.*

● n+of+N **cause, risk** *In the UK deaths must be registered within five days except where further investigations are needed into the cause of death.*

debate N

a discussion offering different opinions about a subject

● adj+N in which people get angry and excited **fierce, heated, intense, lively, vigorous** *These proposals have been the subject of heated debate over the past few months.*

▶ happening now or over a period of time **contemporary, continuing, current, ongoing** *Despite the ongoing debate surrounding climate change, the UK government is committed to its obligations under the Kyoto Agreement.*

▶ dealing with a variety of subjects **broader, wider, wide-ranging** *We regard the extension of user choice as part of a wider debate about how we can modernize public services.*

▶ involving a lot of people **national, open, public** *What to do next becomes an urgent question of public debate.*

▶ with good arguments **informed, rational, reasoned** *We think it is essential that there is a full and informed debate about these issues in the country before the necessary decision is taken.*

▶ involving a lot of discussion **considerable, endless** *Here we have a truly independent woman film-maker whose films are open to endless debate and interpretation.*

▶ involving a particular way of thinking or subject **academic, critical, intellectual, philosophical, political, scholarly, scientific, theological, theoretical** *There is now considerable political debate within Germany about whether there should be a national minimum wage.*

▶ real or serious **genuine, proper, serious** *The time has come for a proper debate on the issue.*

● v+N start a debate or help it to develop **encourage, fuel, generate, initiate, promote, prompt, provoke, spark, start, stimulate** *The conference aims to stimulate debate about economic regeneration of the region.*

▶ influence a debate **influence, inform, shape** *Scientists have a major role to play in informing the debate on developing and exploiting new technologies.*

▶ take part in a debate **contribute to, engage in, enter, enter into, join, join in** *Do you only engage in debate with those who have the same opinions as you?*

▸ make a debate less limited **widen** *We feel it is important that the energy debate is widened beyond the limited scope of security of supply.*

▸ be pleased that a debate is taking place **welcome** *The debate is greatly welcomed and signals the strength of public concern about this issue.*

▸ stop a debate from developing **stifle** *There is a small band of people who want to stifle informed debate.*

▸ have a debate **have** *He is looking forward to having a wide-ranging debate on the issue.*

● N+v take place or continue **continue, ensue, rage, take place** *Debate has raged on the suitability of this type of news for children ever since.*

▸ be concerned with something **centre around sth, centre on sth, focus on sth** *Debate centred on the potential conflict between the use of the grounds as public spaces and the need for privacy and security.*

● n+of+N **subject** *The connection between his philosophy and his politics has long been a subject of debate among scholars.*

> You can also say that something is *a matter for debate*. If something is not certain because it is possible for people to have different opinions about it, you can say that it is *open to debate*: *Whether or not this is poetry is open to debate.*

debate V
discuss a subject formally before making a decision

● adv+V in an angry or excited way **fiercely, hotly, vigorously** *Ten years later, the issue remains a hotly debated topic.*

▸ with a lot of discussion **at length, endlessly, fully, properly, widely** *Cell phone safety is a topic widely debated around the world.*

▸ publicly **openly, publicly** *The council will not now have the opportunity to force the scheme through without all of the issues being publicly debated.*

● V+n subject or issue **future, issue, matter, merits, question, subject, topic** *We are now in the middle of national men's health week, so there could not be a better time to debate the issue of men and cancer.*

▸ formal proposal that people vote on **amendment, bill, motion** *MPs will get a chance to debate the identity card bill once it has returned to the House of Commons.*

debris N
broken pieces left after something large has been destroyed

● adj+N **falling, flying, loose** *Two of the trapped men were hurt by falling debris.*

● v+N remove debris **clear, clear sth of, remove** *The tunnels were eventually cleared of debris. • It's important that you prepare the soil thoroughly, removing debris and stones.*

▸ cause debris to form **leave, scatter, throw up** *The amount of debris left in the wake of the Great Fire of London must have been great.*

● N+v **block sth, fall, fly** *Bulldozers are working to clear debris blocking roads. • Buildings were blown apart, sending debris flying in all directions.*

● n+of+N **amount, piece, pile** *The wrecked restaurant is still there, as are piles of debris.*

debt N
1 an amount of money owed

● adj+N large debt **crippling, enormous, high, huge, large, massive** *Don't run up a massive debt in the first couple of months.*

> If someone owes a lot of money, you can say that they are *heavily in debt* or *deeply in debt*: *Having lost his job, he was heavily in debt.*

▸ when a debt is getting bigger **mounting** *Mounting debts forced him to sell the estate in 1897.*

▸ not yet paid **outstanding, unpaid** *Your fund could fall short, leaving you with an outstanding debt and no way of paying it off.*

▸ that will never be paid **bad** *The company has experienced a significant rise in bad debts.*

▸ total **total** *She now believes her total debt is £2,000.*

▸ personal **personal** *Nearly three-quarters of the help we give is with welfare benefits and personal debt.*

● n+N types of debt **consumer, credit-card, gambling, household, loan, mortgage, student** *He had gambling debts of over £20,000.*

● v+N have debts **have, incur, run up, take on** *He is fully responsible for any debts incurred while he was a partner.*

▸ pay back debts **clear, pay, pay back, pay off, repay, settle** *The first thing you need to do is to clear your debts.*

▸ make a debt smaller **reduce** *If you've got some extra cash you can make a larger repayment to reduce your debts even quicker.*

▸ say that someone does not have to pay a debt **write off** *They agreed that there would be a part payment of the debts over the specified period, with the remainder of the debts being written off.*

▸ pay interest on a debt **service** *You're spending more on servicing your debts than the thing cost in the first place.*

● n+of+N how much someone owes **amount, burden, level** *We would scrap tuition fees so our young people don't start working life with a huge burden of debt.*

● when money owed is paid back **payment, repayment** *He had borrowed money for it, and he worried on his deathbed over the payment of the debt.*

2 an obligation to be grateful to someone

● adj+N **enormous, great, huge** *We also owe a huge debt to all the local volunteers who helped during the week.*

● v+N have a debt **owe** *I do not think that there has been anyone to whom the Society owes a greater debt of gratitude.*

> You can also say that you are *in someone's debt*: *Vote for me and I'll forever be in your debt.*

▸ say that you have a debt **acknowledge** *Poets as diverse as Auden, Larkin and Walcott have acknowledged their debt to him.*

● N+of+n **gratitude** *My family and I owe a great debt of gratitude to all the hospital staff.*

3 a situation in which you owe money

● v+N **be in, fall into, get into, get out of, go into** *Don't allow your child to get too far into debt.*

> If someone owes a lot of money, you can say that they are **heavily in debt** or **deeply in debt**: *Having lost his job, he was heavily in debt.*

debut N
the first public appearance of a performer or sports player

- adj+N when debut goes well **impressive, promising, successful** *This is a promising debut from McAlevy and I would recommend it to fans of the horror-comedy genre.*
- ▶ types of debut **acting, directorial, international, professional**
- n+N acting and singing **film, screen, singing, solo, stage** *Plummer made her New York stage debut in Artichoke in 1979.*
- ▶ sport **first-team, home, league, Test** *He has yet to make his first-team debut.*
- v+N when someone appears for the first time **make** *He made his debut for Australia in June 2008.*
- ▶ be someone's debut **mark** *The play marks the directorial debut of David Leonard.*

decade N
a period of ten years

- adj+N **coming, following, last, next, past, preceding, previous, recent** *The city's growth in recent decades has been at the expense of the quality of life of most residents.*
- v+N **span, spend** *He is remembered for dozens of stage and screen roles spanning five decades.*
- N+v be the time when something happens **see, witness** *The last decade has seen a massive increase in student numbers.*
- ▶ pass **go by, pass** *A decade has passed since that infamous incident.*

decay N
when something is gradually destroyed by a natural process or gradually gets into a worse state

- adj+N fast/slow **gradual, rapid, slow** *The city's trade and shipping fell into rapid decay.*
- ▶ types of decay **dental, moral, natural, physical, radioactive, social, urban** *Their website features some fascinating images of urban decay.*
- n+N **tooth** *Tooth decay has the highest prevalence of any disease in the world.*
- v+N cause or speed up decay **accelerate, cause** *The micro-organisms which cause decay in organic matter need air to survive.*
- ▶ reach a state of decay **fall into** *The Hall was used as a hospital during the Second World War but has fallen into decay.*
- ▶ prevent or reduce decay **prevent, reduce** *To prevent tooth decay and gum disease it is necessary to have regular dental visits.*
- n+of+N **signs, state** *The timber is showing signs of decay.*

deception N
the act of tricking someone

- adj+N **cruel, deliberate** *She believes this is deliberate deception by the council to conceal the extent of the plans.*
- v+N use deception **obtain sth by, practise, use** *He was convicted of attempting to obtain money by deception.*
- ▶ recognize deception **detect, discover, expose, see through** *Of course it was not long before his deception was discovered.*
- n+of+N **act** *She got the job after a successful act of deception at the interview.*

decide V
1 make a choice about what to do

- adv+V after a long time **eventually, finally, ultimately** *It was finally decided that the Sunderland arts centre was a suitable venue.*
- ▶ how many people decide **unanimously, unilaterally** *The Tribunal unanimously decided to dismiss the appeal.*
- ▶ quickly or suddenly **immediately, quickly, suddenly** *Jim suddenly decided in August 2003 to be a stand-up comedian.*
- ▶ when you do not really want to do something **reluctantly** *They have reluctantly decided to sell the house in order to raise the money to buy a bigger property in Devon.*

2 to affect what will happen, or the result of something

- V+n what will happen **destiny, fate, future, issue, outcome** *Guiding the process does not necessarily mean deciding the outcome.*
- ▶ game **championship, game, match** *A goal in the 90th minute decided the match.*
- ▶ situation or legal case **appeal, case, dispute, question** *An adjudicator was appointed to decide the dispute.*

decision N
a choice made after thinking carefully

- adj+N difficult **difficult, hard, tough** *We have some very tough decisions to make.*
- ▶ good or correct **correct, good, rational, right, sensible, wise** *This was definitely the right decision.*
- ▶ poor or wrong **bad, poor, wrong** *One bad decision was swiftly followed by another.*
- ▶ important **big, important, key, major, momentous** *Within the company there are likely to be several people involved in any key decisions.*
- ▶ based on good information **informed** *University league tables assist students to make informed decisions about where to study.*
- ▶ made quickly **hasty, quick, snap** *Plan ahead and don't make snap decisions.*
- ▶ made by everyone or most people **collective, majority, unanimous** *The jury's decision was unanimous.*
- ▶ done deliberately **conscious** *It was a conscious decision to take control of her life.*
- ▶ that people disagree about **controversial** *This controversial decision led to much protest.*
- n+N **business, investment, management, planning, policy** *Expect to see significant policy decisions in this area.*
- v+N make a decision **arrive at, come to, make,**

reach, take *It didn't take long to make the decision to retreat.*

▸ influence a decision **affect, influence** *When considering a planning application what affects the decision?*

▸ give reasons for a decision **defend, explain, justify** *Whatever method is chosen, the trustees must be able to justify their decision if challenged.*

▸ say or do what you have decided **announce, confirm, implement, issue** *The committee will announce the decision to the parties at the end of the hearing where possible.*

▸ think again about a decision **reconsider, review** *I invite you to reconsider your decision.*

▸ change a decision **overrule, overturn, reverse** *This decision was overturned by the Court of Appeal.*

▸ try to change a decision **appeal against, challenge** *If your application is unsuccessful, you can appeal against the decision.*

▸ when you do not make a decsion until a later time **defer, delay, postpone** *It was agreed to defer a decision on this issue until after Christmas.*

▸ agree with a decision **accept, support, uphold** *Following the result of the ballot, it is clear that the majority do not want to strike, and we accept their decision.*

▸ when you have to make a decision **be faced with, face** *I faced an agonizing decision.*

decisive ADJ
very important for the result of something; making the result of something completely certain

● adv+**ADJ potentially** *Water charge increases are a potentially decisive factor in the business's ability to continue operating.*

● ADJ+n **advantage, battle, factor, goal, influence, moment, role, step** *That was one of the decisive moments of 20th century history, though few realized it at the time.*

● v+**ADJ be, prove** *This added information can prove decisive in the selection process.*

declaration N
an official announcement or important statement

● adj+N **formal, joint, public, solemn** *I am very grateful to the Prime Minister for having agreed to use this occasion to issue a joint declaration.*

● v+N make a declaration **issue, make** *When judges make a formal declaration that a statute is incompatible with the Human Rights Act, this puts considerable pressure on Parliament.*

▸ sign a declaration **sign** *On the eve of the summit, 30 African countries signed a declaration rejecting new powers for the WTO.*

● N+of+n **independence, intent, interest, love, war** *This is tantamount to a declaration of war (at least, a trade war) against its main rivals.*

declare V
announce that something is true or is happening; to state something officially

● V+adj **bankrupt, illegal, invalid, null and void** *He could not see how a marriage of such long standing could be declared invalid.*

● adv+V in public **formally, officially, openly, publicly** *Councillor Denny unveiled the plaque, and officially declared the station open.*

▸ with confidence **boldly, confidently** *She boldly declared that she was quite prepared to take the consequences her actions might have.*

▸ with pride **proudly, triumphantly** *We can now proudly declare that we are officially a good employer!*

● V+n something to other people **intention, interest, love, support** *When she writes him a letter declaring her love for him, she is pointedly rejected.*

▸ winner **winner** *The player with the most points is declared the winner.*

▸ something official **independence, state of emergency, war** *Kazakhstan declared its independence on December 16, 1991.*

decline V
1 become less or worse

● adv+V quickly or to a large extent **considerably, dramatically, drastically, markedly, rapidly, sharply, significantly, steeply, substantially** *In the UK, membership of political parties has declined sharply in recent years.*

▸ gradually or to a slight extent **gradually, slightly, slowly, steadily** *Relative wages for women decline steadily following the birth of a first child.*

● n+V **health, industry, number, population, rate, sales, standards, trade** *Europe's coal and steel industries have declined.*

> Usage *Decline* is often used in the present participle form in these combinations: *Declining birth rates are now common throughout Europe.*

● V+in+n **importance, numbers, popularity** *Why so simple a game without expensive equipment has declined in popularity is puzzling.*

2 say politely that you will not accept something or do something

● adv+V **politely** *My offer to help her was politely declined.*

● V+n **invitation, offer, request** *He declined my invitation to join in the discussion.*

● V+infinitive **answer, comment, say** *Yesterday she declined to comment on the issue.*

decline N
a reduction in amount or quality

● adj+N quick or large decline **dramatic, marked, rapid, serious, severe, sharp, significant, steep** *Recent figures show a steep decline in asylum applications.*

▸ types of decline **economic, industrial, moral** *The town has been in economic decline since the late 1920s.*

▸ when a decline cannot be stopped **inevitable, inexorable, terminal** *The Clyde's salmon fisheries were in terminal decline.*

▸ gradual or slight decline **gradual, slight, slow, steady** *The reality was a steady decline in customer numbers and sales, while costs escalated.*

▸ considered generally or over a long period **general, long-term, overall** *We have seen an overall decline in consumer spending.*

- n+N **population** *A reduced food supply in farmland is insufficient to explain the bird population decline.*
- v+N stop or slow down a decline **arrest, halt, offset, prevent, reverse, slow, stem, stop** *Trade union membership has fallen since the high point of the 1970s and the unions are unable to reverse this decline.*
- ▶ experience a decline **experience, fall into, go into, suffer** *The black rhino population in Africa has suffered a dramatic decline as a result of poaching.*
- ▶ cause a decline **cause, lead to** *The coming of the railways caused a decline in the use of the county's waterways.*
- ▶ speed up a decline **accelerate, hasten** *The episode tarnished Ruskin's reputation, and may have accelerated his mental decline.*
- ▶ be aware of a decline happening **see** *Each time a chain moves in, we see a decline in the volume of coffee sold in independent shops.*

decorate V
make something attractive by putting things on it

- adv+V in an attractive way **attractively, beautifully, nicely** *The church was beautifully decorated with flowers to match the bride's bouquet.*
- ▶ in an expensive way and with many features **elaborately, lavishly, ornately, richly** *Her hat is elaborately decorated with pearls and a star motif.*
- ▶ with bright colours **brightly** *The walls and ceilings were brightly decorated with the children's own work and excellent teaching materials.*

decrease V
become less

- adv+V quickly or to a large extent **considerably, dramatically, greatly, markedly, rapidly, significantly, substantially** *The mortality rates of many cancers have decreased significantly in recent decades.*
- ▶ gradually or to a slight extent **gradually, progressively, slightly, slowly, steadily** *Foreign aid has been steadily decreasing since 1992.*
- V+in+n **number, size, value** *Later that month the pound decreased in value by 20 per cent.*

decrease N
the process of becoming less

- adj+N quick or large decrease **dramatic, great, large, marked, rapid, sharp, significant, substantial** *The results showed a significant decrease in the number of infections in the whole population of children.*
- ▶ gradual or slight decrease **gradual, slight, small, steady** *There has been a steady decrease in the number of fatal collisions involving motorcycles over the past three years.*
- ▶ connected to something else **corresponding** *An increase in expenditure on drugs must be balanced by a corresponding decrease in spending in another area within the NHS cash limit.*
- ▶ considered in general **overall** *This is a decrease of approximately 6.5 per cent, reflecting the overall decrease in energy consumption across the businesses.*
- v+N show that a decrease is happening **indicate, show** *National trends in mortality show a steady*

decrease in death rates from breast cancer in this period.

- ▶ be a decrease **represent** *This represents an overall decrease in purchases of food eaten out.*
- ▶ cause a decrease **cause, lead to, result in** *Intensive agriculture and processing have led to a massive decrease in the nutrient levels in foods.*
- ▶ experience a decrease **experience, have** *Student numbers were similar to last year, when we experienced a significant decrease.*
- ▶ be aware that a decrease is happening **report, see** *I hope that our residents will begin to feel an increased confidence, through seeing real decreases in crime and disorder.*
- N+in+n **level, number, rate, size** *We have not yet*

dedicated ADJ
working very hard on something

- adv+ADJ **extremely, highly, very** *She was a highly dedicated, enthusiastic and popular teacher.*
- and/or **committed, enthusiastic, experienced, hard-working, loyal, professional, skilled, talented** *All food is prepared to the highest standards by our skilled and dedicated staff.*

dedication N
when someone works very hard on something

- adj+N complete **absolute, complete, sheer, total** *His two main strengths are his knowledge and his total dedication.*
- ▶ great **exceptional, extraordinary, great, outstanding** *Chris and Roy have shown great dedication to the Police Force.*
- ▶ continuing unchanged **continued, lifelong, ongoing, tireless, unstinting, unswerving, unwavering** *It's Bob's tireless dedication that keeps this site going.*
- ▶ not selfish **selfless** *The government should recognise the selfless dedication of so many firefighters.*
- v+N show dedication **demonstrate, display, show** *The awards are given to athletes who have shown dedication to their sport.*
- ▶ praise or reward someone's dedication **acknowledge, admire, applaud, appreciate, praise, recognize, reward** *Teachers praised the dedication and hard work of the students who put on the concert.*
- ▶ need dedication **need, require** *These exams are not easy. Hard work and dedication are required.*
- and/or **commitment, courage, determination, enthusiasm, hard work, loyalty, professionalism** *Midwives are well thought of for their professionalism and dedication when working.*

default N
the way something happens unless you choose differently, especially on a computer

- v+N set the default **choose, select, set, specify, supply** *Consider setting the default to double-sided printing.*
- ▶ change the default **alter, change, modify, override, reset** *The program enables you to quickly change the default.*
- ▶ use the default **accept, apply, use** *If you are writing a letter in French, do not use the English defaults.*

- N+n setting **configuration, options, setting, setup** *The default setting in the search box is 'all of the words'.*
- ▶ of text or printing **colour, font, format, size, style** *For me, the default font is a little too small.*
- ▶ computer file **directory, file, location** *Set the default directory as required.*
- ▶ printer **printer** *Click on the OK button to print your document to the default printer.*

defeat N

failure to win or succeed

- adj+N bad **bad, big, heavy, major** *Their heaviest defeat came in 1995 when they lost to Croatia 4–0.*
- ▶ very bad **catastrophic, crushing, devastating, disastrous, dismal, massive** *The British suffered one of their most disastrous defeats of the war.*
- ▶ total or clear **comprehensive, decisive, resounding, total** *A decisive defeat of the enemy was only possible if the Vikings could be brought to battle.*
- ▶ embarrassing or disappointing **disappointing, embarrassing, humiliating, ignominious** *The Social Democrats suffered an ignominious defeat in the regional election.*
- ▶ not bad **narrow** *They were lucky to have escaped with such a narrow defeat.*
- ▶ happening one after the other **consecutive, straight, successive** *The team were desperate to avoid a fourth straight defeat.*
- ▶ unexpected **shock, surprise, unexpected** *They were knocked out of the competition after a shock defeat.*
- v+N suffer a defeat **crash to, face, slip to, slump to, suffer, taste** *The party had suffered four general election defeats.*
- ▶ admit defeat **accept, acknowledge, admit, concede** *He had to admit defeat and accept that he had been wrong.*

Usage **Defeat** is always uncountable in these combinations: *He had to admit defeat. They can choose to concede defeat or fight back.*

- ▶ avoid defeat **avoid** *The first task was to avoid defeat in the opening game.*
- ▶ make someone suffer a defeat **inflict** *They managed to inflict an embarrassing defeat on the Italians.*
- ▶ get revenge for a defeat **avenge** *The world champion avenged her defeat in Melbourne by beating Kitchen 9–6, 4–9, 9–6.*
- ▶ be likely to suffer a defeat **face, stare in the face** *After losing the first two sets, Nadal was staring defeat in the face.*

defeat V

to win against someone or something

- adv+V completely or successfully **completely, comprehensively, decisively, heavily, overwhelmingly, resoundingly, roundly, soundly, successfully** *Wellington decisively defeated Napoleon at the Battle of Waterloo.*
- ▶ easily **comfortably, easily** *The virus is a relentless opponent that will not be easily defeated.*
- ▶ only just **narrowly** *In the election Blaine was narrowly defeated by the Democratic Party candidate.*

Usage **Defeat** is usually passive in this combination: *He was narrowly defeated in the 1995 election.*

- ▶ finally **eventually, finally, ultimately** *In August 1849 Austria had finally defeated Hungary.*

defect N

a fault in a person's body, or in a machine, product etc

- adj+N serious **fundamental, major, serious, severe** *The vehicle has a number of serious defects.*
- ▶ obvious **glaring, obvious** *If there are obvious defects then point them out, as no house is perfect.*
- ▶ not serious **minor, slight, small** *A coat of wax can help conceal minor defects in your paint.*
- ▶ not obvious **hidden, latent, underlying** *They check for latent defects in the construction work.*
- ▶ common **common** *Cleft palate was the most common birth defect.*
- ▶ types of defect **brain, developmental, heart, mechanical, physical, speech, structural, visual** *Depending on the type of visual defect, the child may ignore small toys or always take the brightest ones.*
- ▶ genetic **chromosome, gene, genetic, inherited** *Because it is an inherited defect, affected animals should not be used for breeding.*
- ▶ present from birth **birth, congenital** *Sam was born with a congenital heart defect.*
- v+N have a defect **have, suffer from** *Closer examination revealed both puppies had a serious heart defect.*
- ▶ repair or remove a defect **correct, cure, eliminate, rectify, remedy, remove, repair** *Various surveys were carried out and any defects remedied.*
- ▶ find a defect **detect, discover, find, identify, locate, observe, report** *Researchers cannot yet identify the defect in the gene.*
- ▶ show a defect **indicate, reveal, show** *An inspection revealed 22 major defects, including a faulty emergency door.*
- ▶ discover the cause of a defect **diagnose** *The class will develop your ability to recognize and diagnose common building defects.*
- ▶ cause a defect **cause** *Some insecticides can cause birth defects.*

defective ADJ

not made correctly, or not working correctly

- adv+ADJ very **seriously, severely, very** *Driving with seriously defective eyesight is dangerous as well as illegal.*
- ▶ rather **slightly** *Slightly defective items can be bought at a fraction of the price.*
- ▶ in a particular way **genetically, mentally, morally, physically, structurally** *He was found to be mentally defective.*
- v+ADJ be or become defective **be, become, prove** *The Ctrl key on my keyboard is defective.*
- ▶ consider something defective **consider sth, deem sth, find sth** *No refunds can be given until the goods have been inspected and deemed defective by the manufacturer.*

defence N

1 actions or structures designed to protect someone or something from attack

- adj+N consisting of structures **coast, coastal, flood, makeshift, natural, sea** *We need to improve our flood and coastal defences.*
- ▶ consisting of weapons **air, anti-aircraft, ballistic, missile** *Would the government allow the US to use UK bases for missile defence?*
- ▶ strong **effective, strong** *Our national security depended on effective missile defences.*
- ▶ weak **inadequate, poor, weak** *With poor sea defences, some parts of the region are vulnerable to coastal erosion.*
- ● v+N come to someone's defence **come to, rush to** *The members of NATO committed themselves to come to each other's defence in the event of an attack against any one of them.*
- ▶ be a defence **act as, be, provide** *Fortified walls and watchtowers provide defences against attack.*
- ▶ build a defence **build, construct, erect** *If defences are built in one place, they may increase flood risks elsewhere.* ● *Should the US abandon its plans to build a missile defence?*
- ▶ improve a defence **bolster, improve, reinforce, strengthen** *We propose to strengthen our defences against unfair trade practices.*
- ▶ weaken a defence **weaken** *The Abbey was bombed in 1944, in an effort to weaken the German defences.*
- ▶ break through a defence **breach, break through, penetrate, pierce** *Hackers are managing to breach the defences of large companies' computer systems.*
- ● N+n spending **budget, costs, cuts, expenditure, spending** *Overall, defence spending in the EU is still falling.*
- ▶ policies or plans **pact, policy, programme, scheme, strategy** *Defence policy requires the provision of forces with a high degree of military effectiveness.*
- ▶ abilities **capability** *He believes European nations need to increase their defence capabilities.*
- ▶ companies **company, contractor, industry, sector** *The defence industry is becoming more global.*
- **2** support for a person or idea that is being criticized
- ● adj+N **robust, spirited, staunch, stout, strong, vigorous** *He put up a spirited defence of his views.*

Usage **Defence** is usually singular in these combinations: *The Minister responded with a strong defence of the government's policy.* ● *a vigorous defence of the theory of state capitalism*

- ● v+N **argue in, come to, jump to, leap to, mount, put up, rush to, say sth in, speak in** *The manager leapt to the defence of his players, blaming the defeat on a couple of basic errors.* ● *Despite widespread opposition, he mounted a robust defence of his environmental policies.*

defenceless ADJ
weak and unable to protect yourself

- ● adv+ADJ completely **completely, totally, utterly** *He is curled up asleep, utterly defenceless, utterly trusting.*
- ▶ almost **almost, virtually** *It is wrong to rain rockets and bullets on a virtually defenceless country.*
- ● and/or **helpless, innocent, poor, vulnerable, weak** *This was an unprovoked attack on an innocent and defenceless bystander.*

defend V
1 protect a place or person from attack

- ● adv+V successfully **successfully** *Vauban's lines of fortified towns helped France to successfully defend its northern border.*
- ▶ bravely or well **bravely, fiercely, valiantly, well** *The churchyard was fiercely defended.*
- ▶ with powerful weapons, forces, or structures **heavily, solidly, strongly** *Their mission was to capture the bridge, which was heavily defended.*

2 to support a person or idea that is being criticized

- ● adv+V strongly **fiercely, resolutely, robustly, staunchly, stoutly, strongly, vehemently, vigorously** *This was a man who stoutly defended the policy during the election.*
- ▶ publicly **publicly** *He publicly defended their right to demonstrate.*

defendant N
a person on trial accused of a crime

- ● v+N formally accuse a defendant **accuse, charge, prosecute** *The defendant is charged with theft from a store.*
- ▶ decide a defendant is guilty **convict, fine, sentence** *It is neither moral nor just to convict a defendant on the basis of rumours.*
- ▶ decide a defendant is not guilty **acquit** *Two other defendants were acquitted of terrorism charges.*
- ▶ question a defendant **cross-examine, question** *The prosecution's attorney will have an opportunity to cross-examine the defendant tomorrow.*

defer V
to arrange for something to happen later than planned

- ● adv+V permanently **indefinitely, permanently** *A decision on the new airport has been deferred.*
- ▶ temporarily **temporarily** *If we have to temporarily defer you from giving blood please try and donate again once your deferral period is over.*
- ▶ constantly **constantly, continually, endlessly** *No version of the text is final. Completion may be endlessly deferred.*
- ● V+n decision or action **approval, decision, implementation, matter, payment, sentencing** *It was agreed to defer a decision on this issue until after Christmas.*
- ▶ entry to an institution **admission, application, entry** *Students should inform us at application stage if they are intending to defer entry.*
- ▶ discussion of something **consideration, discussion** *With an election coming soon, it seems prudent to defer consideration of this issue.*

deference N
behaviour that shows respect and willingness to obey

- ● adj+N **due, great, judicial, much, proper, social** *He listened with all due deference.*
- ● v+N **pay, show, treat sb with** *They always treated the priests with great deference.*

defiance N
refusal to obey a person or rule

- adj+N **arrogant, clear, direct, flagrant, heroic, open, outright, wilful** *Such open defiance cannot be tolerated in school.*
- v+N **demonstrate, display, express, show** *The students show their defiance by organizing their own classes outside the college.*
- N+of **authority, law, order, will** *If the tenants remain, in defiance of a court order, the landlord can bring in the police.*
- n+of+N **act, gesture, show, symbol** *In a final act of defiance, the old man refuses to lend them his horse.*

defiant ADJ
refusing to obey a person or rule

- adv+ADJ **almost, grimly, openly, typically** *The tone of this speech is openly defiant.*
- ADJ+n action **act, behaviour, gesture, refusal** *The flag itself has been inverted, a defiant gesture on the part of the artist.*
- ▸ attitude or mood **attitude, mood, spirit, stance, stand** *Wilson maintained a defiant stance, insisting he was determined to move ahead with the office closure.*
- ▸ statement **reply, speech, statement** *In an openly defiant speech, she attacked the military government.*

deficiency N
1 a lack of something the body needs

- adj+N serious **chronic, major, serious, severe, significant** *A severe deficiency of vitamin C will result in a state called scurvy.*
- ▸ not serious **mild, minor** *The white spots on your fingernails are most likely to be caused by a mild zinc deficiency.*
- ▸ common/rare **common, rare** *Vitamin B12 deficiency is relatively common in people aged over 65 years.*
- ▸ relating to food **dietary, nutritional** *Unintended weight loss could signal illness or nutritional deficiency.*
- v+N have a deficiency **have, suffer from** *The doctors thought he had an enzyme deficiency.*
- ▸ correct a deficiency **correct, rectify, remedy** *Hormone Replacement Therapy aims to correct the deficiency of the female hormones that occurs at menopause.*
- ▸ cause a deficiency **cause, induce, lead to, result in** *Incorrect diet causes a deficiency in potassium in the blood.*
- ▸ prevent a deficiency **prevent** *Parrots require highly varied food in order to prevent vitamin deficiencies.*
- ▸ find or show a deficiency **detect, diagnose, show, trace** *It takes two tests to properly diagnose a growth hormone deficiency.*

2 a fault that makes something not good enough

- adj+N serious **major, serious, severe, significant** *Previous research has suffered from two serious deficiencies.*
- ▸ obvious **glaring, obvious** *I was disappointed to note a couple of glaring deficiencies in the book's content.*

- ▸ claimed **alleged** *What do you think about the alleged deficiencies in the medical evidence?*
- ▸ v+N have a deficiency **have** *These boats had many deficiencies, not least their small size.*
- ▸ correct a deficiency **correct, overcome, rectify, redress, remedy** *What action has been taken to remedy the deficiencies we identified?*
- ▸ find or show a deficiency **expose, highlight, identify, indicate, reveal, show** *The appraisal identified serious deficiencies in his work.*
- ▸ deal with a deficiency **address, tackle** *We need to address this deficiency in our knowledge.*

deficient ADJ
lacking the correct amount of something

- adv+ADJ **clearly, genetically, nutritionally, seriously, severely** *People who are severely deficient in vitamin E may suffer degenerative changes in the nervous system.*
- ADJ+in **calcium, iron, minerals, nutrients, protein, vitamins** *Many older people become deficient in vitamin B12.*

deficit N
when a country or business spends more money than it earns or owns

- adj+N large **excessive, huge, large, massive, substantial** *The US has a massive trade deficit.*
- ▸ planned or expected **estimated, forecasted, projected** *The University says its projected deficit has risen this year from £1.5 million to £4.5 million.*
- ▸ increasing over time **ballooning, cumulative, growing, spiralling, widening** *The cumulative deficit continued to grow.*
- ▸ after all amounts have been removed **net, overall** *Our net deficit was £814, but considering we purchased a large amount of equipment during the year, it was a good result.*
- ▸ government **federal, government** *The government deficit is running at 10 per cent of GDP.*
- ▸ types of deficit **balance-of-payments, budget, budgetary, current-account, financial, fiscal, pension, trade** *Fiscal deficits are down and there are much better prospects for growth.*
- v+N have a deficit **be in, face, have, incur, run, show** *Under its constitution California is not allowed to run a deficit.*
- ▸ build up a deficit **accumulate, build up** *The College is believed to have accumulated deficits running into tens of millions of pounds.*
- ▸ cause a deficit **cause, create, lead to, result in** *Expenditure was not monitored, leading to a deficit.*
- ▸ deal with a deficit **address, deal with, tackle** *The company is allowed to continue operating while it addresses its financial deficit.*
- ▸ reduce a deficit **cut, halve, narrow, reduce, trim** *Some schools have already implemented cutbacks to reduce their deficits.*
- ▸ get rid of a deficit **clear, eliminate, get rid of** *The organization has finalised a plan to eliminate its huge pension fund deficit.*
- ▸ correct a deficit **claw back, correct, overcome, plug, remedy, reverse** *The college is struggling to plug an annual deficit of 1.2 million pounds.*
- ▸ pay for a deficit **finance, fund** *To finance its current*

account deficit with the rest of the world, America
has to import $2.6 billion in cash.
▶ say that a deficit is likely **forecast, predict** The
hospital is forecasing a large year-end deficit.

define V
describe clearly and exactly what something is

● adv+V clearly **clearly, explicitly, sharply, well**
Every military operation should have a clearly
defined objective.
▶ exactly **accurately, exactly, precisely** It is not
possible to define precisely what makes up the output
of a plumber.
▶ badly **ill, poorly** Employees should not have ill-
defined, shifting objectives.

Usage **Define** is always passive in these
combinations: The current system is made up of poorly
defined rules. ● ill-defined research methods

▶ strictly **narrowly, rigidly, strictly, tightly** There is a
danger that research may become too narrowly
defined.
▶ not strictly **broadly, loosely, vaguely** Here we will
also broadly define the concept of localization.
● V+n aim **aim, goal, objective** Five key objectives
are defined in their policy statement.
▶ limit **limit, parameters, scope** The constitution
defines the limits of individuals' participation in
political decision-making.
▶ standard that must be achieved **criteria,
requirement, standard** They haven't clearly defined
the criteria by which students are admitted.
▶ purpose **function, role** The charter defines the role
of the mayor and councillors.

definition N
a statement of what a word or expression means

● adj+N clear **clear** Her book provides clear
definitions of the terms used in this field.
▶ general **broad, general, wide**
▶ strict or precise **exact, narrow, precise, rigorous,
strict** The insurance policy refers to 'exceptional
circumstances', but does not give a precise definition.
▶ official or legal **formal, legal, official, statutory**
The new law will propose a statutory definition of
the term 'racial hatred'.
▶ scientific or technical **clinical, mathematical,
scientific, technical** What is the mathematical
definition of 'probability'?
● v+N change a definition **alter, amend, change,
modify, refine, revise, update** The government
changed the definition of joblessness many times in
order to massage the unemployment figures.
▶ make a definition less precise **broaden, expand,
extend, widen** He broadens the definition of
'terrorism' to include any action that has an
'economic impact'.
▶ make a definition more precise **narrow, tighten**
In 2005 we tightened the definition of training to
exclude inductions and workplace briefings.
▶ accept or agree a definition **accept, agree** Would
you accept this definition of poverty?
▶ give a definition **give, offer, propose, provide** My
dictionary gives the definition of 'churlish' as
'boorish or vulgar'.
▶ use a definition **adopt, use** The course adopts a

broad definition of the term 'second language
education'.
▶ produce a definition **establish, formulate, write**
Our definition of an underdeveloped country is based
on the definition formulated by the United Nations.
▶ match or fit a definition **fit, fulfil, satisfy** If a
person satisfies the definition of an employee, he or
she is entitled to certain benefits.

definitive ADJ
final and best

● ADJ+n book or document dealing with facts
**biography, book, collection, document, guide,
history, reference, source, work** This book is the
definitive guide to growing herbs.
▶ version **edition, version** The text was edited as a
definitive version.
▶ answer or conclusion **answer, conclusion,
diagnosis, explanation, interpretation, solution**
I'm not trying to give the definitive answers here.
▶ statement **account, description, statement** Please
treat the specification as a guide rather than a
definitive statement.
▶ proof **evidence, proof** The reference number and
date issued is not definitive proof of exemption.
▶ list **list, record** I would be grateful if you could get
back to me with a simple and definitive list of
requirements.
▶ decision **agreement, ruling** The Court was not
required to make a definitive ruling on this point.

defy V
1 refuse to obey someone or something

● adv+V openly or deliberately **blatantly,
deliberately, openly, publicly** Workers in several
unions openly defied their leaders by taking strike
action.
▶ repeatedly **continually, repeatedly** He argued that
mothers who repeatedly defied court rulings on
access should be jailed.
▶ successfully **successfully** People began to believe
that unjust laws could be successfully defied.

2 be almost impossible to describe, believe, or
understand

● V+n **belief, categorization, classification,
comprehension, definition, description,
expectation, explanation, imagination, logic** Their
claims defy belief.

degrading ADJ
causing you to have less respect for yourself or for
someone else

● ADJ+n **conditions, punishment, treatment** It is
clear that they employed torture, and other forms of
inhuman and degrading punishment.

● and/or **cruel, inhuman, inhumane, offensive** Did
you find the commercial offensive or degrading to
women?

degree N
1 an amount of something

● adj+N large **considerable, great, high, large,
marked, significant, substantial** The leather has to
be measured to a very high degree of accuracy.

▶ extremely or surprisingly large **extraordinary, remarkable, surprising, unprecedented** *There is a remarkable degree of variation in the students' scores.*

▶ fairly large **certain, fair, reasonable** *The emphasis for safe hillwalking is on good navigation and a reasonable degree of fitness.*

▶ slight **lesser, limited, low, moderate, slight** *This method has worked to a limited degree.*

▶ enough **appropriate, requisite, sufficient** *There was no longer a sufficient degree of trust and confidence between them.*

▶ same or similar **equal, same, similar** *Not all students have the same degree of knowledge and skill in using IT.*

▶ different **different, differing, varying** *Ecosystems all over the world have been affected in varying degrees by industrial pollution.*

2 a university course or the qualification it provides

● adj+N at undergraduate level **bachelor's, first, ordinary, undergraduate** *Graduates who have gained first degrees will be presented after those with higher degrees.*

▶ at postgraduate level **doctoral, graduate, higher, master's, postgraduate, research** *Three of my former students are now pursuing doctoral degrees.*

▶ given as a special honour **honorary** *Film-maker Steven Spielberg is to receive an honorary degree at the summer graduate ceremony.*

▶ full-time/part-time **full-time, part-time** *The Department of Management offers two part-time degrees for professionals.*

▶ involving more than one subject **combined, joint** *Combined degrees are designed for students who want the variety of knowledge offered by studying a combination of subjects.*

▶ vocational/non-vocational **non-vocational, vocational** *Some degrees are non-vocational and allow graduate entry to occupations where any degree subject is acceptable.*

▶ with a score **first-class, second-class, third-class** *Applicants must possess a first-class degree in linguistics.*

▶ equivalent **comparable, equivalent** *Ideally, you will have a good media or arts degree or have an equivalent degree in a relevant subject.*

● v+N have a degree **have, hold, possess** *She has a degree in European law.*

▶ do a degree **do, follow, pursue, read for, study for, take** *Are you interested in pursuing a research degree?*

▶ complete a degree **complete, finish** *I completed my degree many years ago.*

▶ give a degree **award sb, confer, give sb, grant sb** *He was recently awarded an honorary degree by the University.*

▶ get a degree **accept, attain, earn, gain, get, graduate with, obtain, receive** *She went on to gain a degree from Cambridge University.*

delay N

when something happens later than expected

● adj+N long **considerable, endless, inordinate, interminable, lengthy, long, serious, significant** *The airport reported lengthy flight delays caused by the snow.*

▶ not necessary or reasonable **avoidable, excessive, inexcusable, unacceptable, undue, unnecessary, unreasonable** *We will carry out the building work without undue delay.*

▶ short **minimal, short, slight** *There may be a slight delay while your details are checked.*

▶ not expected **unexpected, unforeseen** *There are often unforeseen delays and interruptions.*

▶ impossible to avoid **inevitable, unavoidable** *This time limit may only be extended in exceptional cases, where delay is unavoidable due to illness.*

▶ more **further** *Here I am still sitting in the lounge, with further delays caused by an electrical problem on the plane.*

▶ of mail or transport **airport, flight, postal, traffic, train, travel** *She lost two days from her holiday because of flight delays.*

▶ causing loss of money **costly** *Good initial planning will help you avoid costly delays later on.*

● v+N cause a delay **cause, create, introduce, lead to, mean, result in** *Please ask the receptionist to check, even if it means a short delay.*

▶ avoid a delay **avoid, prevent** *To avoid delays in registration please complete the application form in full.*

▶ experience a delay **encounter, experience, face, incur, suffer** *The project has not experienced any major delays.*

▶ reduce delays **eliminate, minimize, reduce** *Waiting lists are kept short in order to minimize delays.*

delay V

to make something happen later than planned or expected

● adv+V a lot **badly, considerably, seriously, severely, significantly, substantially** *The plane we were on was badly delayed by fog.* ● *Significantly delaying the treatment of heat stroke can increase the risk of long-term consequences.*

▶ unnecessarily or unreasonably **unduly, unnecessarily, unreasonably** *Let us know your plans as soon as possible so that work is not unnecessarily delayed.*

▶ slightly **slightly, somewhat** *Nicolette arrived safe and sound, if slightly delayed.*

▶ for ever/not for ever **indefinitely, temporarily** *Plans to install Digital TV in the Grad room have been temporarily delayed.*

▶ when you cannot do anything about it **unavoidably** *If you are unavoidably delayed, please try to contact the school.*

Usage **Delay** is always <u>passive</u> in this combination.

▶ deliberately **deliberately** *They deliberately delayed the conclusion of their work to take into account the findings of a new market research project.*

delegate V

to give part of your work or responsibility to someone else

● V+n power or responsibility **authority, control, decision-making, management, power, responsibility** *The board can delegate powers to make decisions to sub-committees.*

▸ work **duty, job, task, work** *Develop strategies for delegating work within the team.*
▸ role **function, role** *The bishop may delegate his presidential functions to another person.*
▸ decision **decision, matter** *Decisions are not delegated.*

delegation N
a group representing a country or organization

● adj+N important **high-level, high-powered, high-ranking, top-level** *A high-level Russian delegation arrived in Warsaw.*
▸ official **official** *She was part of the official delegation to welcome the returnees.*
▸ government **congressional, government, governmental, parliamentary** *Most major steel producing countries sent industry and government delegations.*
▸ from different political parties **all-party, cross-party** *A cross-party delegation visited Ireland to see how the smokefree law was working there.*

● n+N **business, industry, peace, trade, union** *The Buddhist peace delegation played an important role in settling the conflict.*
● v+N send a delegation **send** *UNISON will send a delegation to this year's Earth Summit.*
▸ lead or organize a delegation **head, lead, organize** *The delegation was led by Barbara Gelb.*
▸ receive or welcome a delegation **host, receive, welcome** *We are hosting a delegation of Chinese business people.*
▸ join or be part of a delegation **be among, be in, join, participate in** *Mr Gerrard was invited to join the delegation by the International Development Minister.*
▸ meet a delegation **meet, meet with** *I met a delegation of children, parents and campaigners to talk about road safety.*

deliberate ADJ
done intentionally, not by accident

● ADJ+n plan or action **act, attempt, effort, ploy, policy, strategy, tactic** *They have made deliberate efforts to improve relations with the United States.*
▸ damage or harm **attack, damage, destruction, harm** *The evidence suggests this was a deliberate attack on one of our ships.*
▸ lying or hiding the truth **concealment, deception, distortion, falsification, lie, manipulation, misrepresentation, omission** *The inquiry revealed that there had been deliberate distortion of intelligence information.*
▸ decision **choice, decision** *In this case, the copyright owner made a deliberate choice to make his books available online.*

deliberation N
long and careful thought or discussions

● adj+N a lot of **considerable, extensive, great, lengthy, long, much** *After much deliberation the winning design was chosen.*
▸ careful or sensible **calm, careful, mature, rational, serious** *Cool and calm deliberation would do them more good than the present infighting.*
▸ enough **due** *After due deliberation, the staff decided*

that the metal should be examined by a qualified laboratory.
▸ more **further** *Further deliberation by the council would be required.*
▸ public/private **internal, public** *The organization's internal deliberations are continuing.*

● v+N start or continue deliberations **begin, continue, resume, start** *Go home and relax and return again tomorrow to resume your deliberations.*
▸ hold deliberations **conduct, hold** *The Committee voted to hold its deliberations in secret.*
▸ complete deliberations **complete, conclude** *The summit conference concluded its deliberations on Wednesday.*

Usage ***Deliberation*** is plural in all of the ***v+N*** combinations shown above: *The legal team have concluded their deliberations.* ● *We will continue our deliberations tomorrow.*

delicate ADJ
1 having small parts or details, and not very strong

● adv+ADJ very **extremely, incredibly, particularly, quite, so** INFORMAL, **very** *Jellyfish are extremely delicate and easily damaged.*
▸ rather **fairly, rather, somewhat** *It is a rather delicate looking butterfly.*
▸ in an attractive way **beautifully, exquisitely, wonderfully** *The veil is made of wonderfully delicate black lace.*
▸ in a surprising way **surprisingly** *He has a surprisingly delicate face, for a man.*

● and/or **beautiful, fragile, intricate, light, pale, soft, subtle, thin** *The fine wire is then shaped into delicate and intricate designs.*

2 needing careful treatment in order avoid problems or embarrassment

● adv+ADJ very **exceptionally, extremely, incredibly, particularly, so, very** *This is a very delicate situation.*
▸ rather **fairly, quite, rather, somewhat** *It is a somewhat delicate matter to refuse a gift.*
▸ politically **politically** *They were discussing the politically delicate question of managing and controlling security.*

● ADJ+n subject that must be discussed or dealt with **issue, matter, question, situation, subject** *We haven't yet discussed the delicate issue of your fee.*
▸ job that must be done **negotiations, operation, process, task** *After delicate negotiations with the government, the project was approved.*

delicious ADJ
with a very pleasant taste or smell

● adv+ADJ **absolutely, mouth-wateringly, particularly, quite, rather, really, simply, truly, utterly** *The restaurant has an extensive menu, and the food was absolutely delicious.*

● v+ADJ **be, look, smell, sound, taste** *The hot chocolate tasted delicious.*

delight N
a feeling of great happiness and pleasure

● adj+N great **absolute, great, intense, pure, sheer,**

utter *The expression on his face was one of sheer delight.*

▶ real **genuine, real, true** *As a nanny, she took a real delight in caring for children.*

▶ obvious **evident, obvious** *His obvious delight was confirmed when he remarked, 'What a splendid show!'*

▶ like a child's **childish, childlike** *Tarantino sets up his cinematic world with an almost childlike delight.*

• v+N experience delight **experience, feel, find, take** *He seemed to take delight in watching me suffer.*

▶ show your delight **convey, express, reveal, show** *They showed their obvious delight throughout the band's set by singing and dancing along with all the songs.*

▶ hide your delight **conceal, contain, hide** *He found it hard to hide his delight.*

▶ share sb's delight **share** *However, Sharon does not share her brother's delight.*

▶ give delight **bring, give** *He liked to dress up as a clown and bring delight to children's faces.*

• v+with+N **beam, laugh, scream, shriek, squeal, whoop** *Why do children laugh and squeal with delight when chased?*

• n+of+N **cheer, cry, scream, shout, shriek, squeal, whoop** *I can hear the shrieks of delight from young children as they unwrap their presents from Santa Claus.*

delighted ADJ
very happy

• adv+ADJ very **absolutely, extremely, highly, really** INFORMAL, **so** INFORMAL, **thoroughly, totally** *I'm absolutely delighted **with** my new earrings.*

▶ particularly **especially, particularly** *That's why we are particularly delighted to be supporting these awards for the second year.*

▶ really **genuinely, truly** *She seemed genuinely delighted by my do-gooding intentions.*

▶ obviously **clearly, obviously** *Peter was his usual modest self but clearly delighted.*

▶ understandably **naturally, understandably** *We are naturally delighted to have won this award.*

delivery N
the process of bringing goods or letters to a place

• adj+N fast **express, fast, prompt, quick, rapid, speedy** *Many thanks for the prompt delivery of our order.*

▶ late **late** *This way we keep the late deliveries to a minimum.*

▶ free **free** *Delivery is free for orders over £50.*

▶ of mail **airmail, mail, parcel, postal** *There is no postal delivery after 13.00 on Saturday.*

▶ next day **next-day, overnight** *If we have the part in stock, it can be sent to you that day for next-day delivery .*

▶ to a particular place **international, local, nationwide, overseas, worldwide** *We can provide both local and worldwide delivery of flowers.*

• v+N accept delivery **accept, receive, take** *We are looking forward to taking delivery of the new machine.*

▶ make sure that delivery happens **ensure,**

guarantee *To ensure rapid delivery we ship the goods by a door-to-door courier service.*

▶ arrange delivery **arrange, arrange for, facilitate, organize, schedule** *Customers are welcome to collect their order or have us arrange delivery.*

▶ refuse delivery **refuse** *If the goods are damaged, we would suggest that you refuse delivery from the courier.*

▶ make or try to make a delivery **attempt, make** *All deliveries are made within 48 hours.*

▶ wait for delivery **await, expect, wait for** *These cars have been purchased and are awaiting delivery.*

▶ delay delivery **delay** *The latest fighting has delayed the delivery of food donations.*

delusion N
1 an idea or belief that is not true

• adj+N affecting many people **collective, mass** *Collective delusion and ignorance often play havoc in society.*

▶ dangerous **dangerous** *The new fatalists believe that we can stop history and that is a dangerous delusion.*

> A person who believes that they are more important than they really are is said to be suffering from *delusions of grandeur*: *He is suffering from delusions of grandeur and an overinflated sense of his own importance.*

• v+N **harbour, have, labour under, suffer (from)** *For years English football had laboured under the delusion that nobody could touch it for class and style.*

2 an idea caused by a mental condition in which you believe things that are not true

• adj+N **paranoid, persecutory** *Elise returns to her childhood home, fleeing from a husband who is suffering from paranoid delusions.*

• v+N **experience, have, suffer (from)** *In some cases of depression people may also experience delusions and hallucinations.*

demand N
1 the amount of a product or service that people want

• adj+N increasing **ever-growing, ever-increasing, growing, increasing, rising, soaring** *Climate change is leading to an increasing demand for water.*

▶ falling **declining, falling** *Falling demand creates tension between firms e.g. during an economic downturn.*

▶ large **great, heavy, high, huge, peak, strong** *Short loan items are in heavy demand and can be booked by other students.*

▶ not satisfied **pent-up, unmet, unsatisfied** *The warmer first half of May allowed pent-up demand for spring/summer ranges to translate into sales.*

▶ large enough **sufficient** *We can lay on extra buses if there is sufficient demand.*

▶ too large **insatiable, overwhelming, unprecedented** *There was an unprecedented demand for tickets for the event.*

▶ types of demand **domestic, global, world** *Output will meet domestic demand, although there may be surplus quantities for export.*

• n+N **client, consumer, customer, passenger** *Fast*

increasing consumer demand is being met with wider availability.

- v+N satisfy demand **accommodate, cope with, fulfil, meet, satisfy** *They always ensured adequate stock was available in their warehouses to satisfy demand.*
- ▶ increase demand **fuel, stimulate** *So what is fuelling this demand for more energy production?*
- ▶ reduce demand **dampen, reduce** *By recovering textiles, merchants are reducing the demand for virgin resources.*
- ▶ predict demand **anticipate, forecast** *Surveys were also used to forecast demand and assist in the development of government policy.*
- ▶ control demand **manage** *We are developing ideas to manage growing demand in the longer term.*
- N+v increase **grow, increase, rise, soar** *We cannot guarantee immediate supply if demand is growing.*
- ▶ be greater than **exceed, outstrip** *Demand far outstrips supply for this product in Europe, Africa and Asia.*
- ▶ fall **fall** *Plantings of red grapes declined in the 1970s as demand fell.*

2 a very firm statement or request that you want something

- adj+N urgent **insistent, urgent** *The dentist was relatively inexperienced and found it difficult to resist Mr M's insistent demand for treatment.*
- ▶ unreasonable **unrealistic, unreasonable** *Special educators are often overworked and face many unrealistic demands.*
- v+N make a demand **make** *The group made a demand for full equality.*
- ▶ satisfy or try to satisfy someone's demands **accede to, accommodate, agree to, comply with, meet, respond to, satisfy** *To meet the demands for improved housing conditions we have developed a new Private Sector Renewal Strategy.*
- ▶ refuse a demand **reject, resist** *Employers resisted the demand for paid educational leave.*

3 the things that need to be done, usually things that are difficult [always plural]

- adj+N great or too great **enormous, excessive, heavy, huge** *In Britain, by comparison with other countries, the teaching demands are excessive.*
- ▶ that cannot all be satisfied **competing, conflicting** *The aim of this service is to assist the athlete to integrate all of the competing demands of their life.*
- ▶ changing or growing **changing, growing, increasing** *Staff are failing to cope with the increasing demands being placed on them.*
- v+N make demands **impose, make, place** *The more complex the score, the greater the demands made on the players.*
- ▶ deal with demands **accommodate, adapt to, balance, cope with, deal with, handle, juggle, meet** *Training days are also kept short to accommodate the demands of childcare.*

demand V

1 say very firmly that you want something; ask a question in a firm or angry way

- adv+V angrily, insistently, loudly, repeatedly,

urgently *The driver angrily demanded the way to Thirsk now that the road was blocked.*

- V+n payment **compensation, money, payment, ransom, refund, repayment** *A large ransom was demanded for his liberty.*
- ▶ words **answer, apology, explanation** *The prime minister demanded an apology from those who had called him a liar.*
- ▶ action **abolition, action, change, inquiry, justice, reform, repeal, resignation, withdrawal** *There was a mass protest demanding his resignation.*

2 say that something is necessary, make something necessary

- V+n **attention, commitment, courage, obedience, respect, sacrifice, skill** *This is a problem which demands urgent attention.*

demanding ADJ
needing much time, ability, and energy

- adv+ADJ very **extremely, highly, particularly, very** *This is a highly demanding position that will require you to meet deadlines.*
- ▶ in a particular way **emotionally, intellectually, mentally, physically, technically** *They performed admirably in a physically demanding competition.*
- ADJ+n job **job, role, task** *Did your boss always give you the most demanding tasks?*
- ▶ situation **conditions, environment, situation** *How do you feel about having to learn something new under such demanding conditions?*
- and/or difficult **complex, difficult, stressful, time-consuming** *Teaching is a demanding, stressful occupation.*
- ▶ interesting or enjoyable **challenging, exciting, interesting, rewarding** *The role can be highly demanding and exciting.*

demise N
the time when something stops existing or someone dies

- adj+N sudden or unexpected **rapid, speedy, sudden, swift** *One of the surprising features of early eighteenth century politics is the sudden demise of the Tory ministry.*
- ▶ happening soon or too soon **early, imminent, impending, premature, untimely** *Predictions of the imminent demise of the party have proven somewhat premature.*
- ▶ sad **sad, tragic, unfortunate** *I bought this car in 2003 following the unfortunate demise of my previous Mini.*
- ▶ final **eventual, final, ultimate** *The oil crisis of the 1970s led to the system's final demise.*
- ▶ unavoidable **inevitable** *Rachel's artwork captures the building's struggle to survive, and its inevitable demise.*
- v+N cause something's demise **bring about, cause, lead to** *The minister's political demise was caused by a letter leaked to the press.*
- ▶ bring forward something's demise **accelerate, hasten** *Ironically, the talks may have hastened the demise of the nationalist party.*
- ▶ predict something's demise **predict** *I've been*

predicting the imminent demise of the company for nearly a decade.

▶ be sad about something's demise **lament, mourn, regret** *I grew up with Thames Television and mourned their demise.*

▶ mark something's demise **herald, mark, signal** *The arrival of the railways in the 1830's heralded the demise of the stagecoach.*

demolish V
prove that something is completely wrong

● adv+V **comprehensively, convincingly, effectively, finally, totally, utterly** *Watson's book effectively demolishes the myth of the impartial scientist.*

● V+n **argument, myth, notion** *The article goes on to analyse and demolish the main economic arguments used in support of the theory.*

demonstrate V
show clearly that something is true or exists

● adv+V in a way that convinces **amply, conclusively, consistently, convincingly, effectively, successfully, unequivocally** *The figures are suggestive, but cannot conclusively demonstrate the reasons for these differences.*

▶ clearly **ably, clearly, dramatically, graphically, vividly** *The authors argue that the failure of this approach has been clearly demonstrated during the last five years.*

▶ in a particular way **empirically, experimentally, practically, scientifically** *The existence of this faculty was first experimentally demonstrated in 1841.*

● V+n usefulness **benefit, effectiveness, efficacy, feasibility, importance, potential, superiority, usefulness, versatility, viability** *The project is to develop a prototype to demonstrate the viability of a European Land Information Service.*

▶ personal quality **ability, aptitude, awareness, commitment, competence, shell, talent, understanding, willingness** *He plans to restore an old pond, demonstrating his continuing commitment to encouraging new wildlife habitats.*

▶ existence **existence, presence** *The blood sample demonstrated the presence of antibodies.*

● n+V article or research **article, book, experiment, paper, project, report, research, study, survey, trial, work** *He said the study demonstrated how incredibly effective cameras are in cutting casualties.*

▶ results **data, findings, results, statistics** *The results demonstrated that the desktop PC is extensively used pre, during and post fieldwork.*

▶ person **author, researcher** *The authors demonstrate the powers of computer simulation when combined with sound scientific theory.*

demonstration N
1 an occasion when a large group of people protests

● adj+N for/against a particular thing **anti-capitalist, anti-globalization, anti-government, anti-war, pro-democracy** *An impressive anti-war demonstration took place in Manchester on Saturday to coincide with International Women's Day.*

▶ peaceful/not peaceful **non-violent, peaceful, violent** *We would never target a group for their peaceful demonstrations.*

▶ large **big, huge, large, mass, massive** *A mass demonstration against the talks attracted over 25,000 trade unionists, workers and residents.*

▶ not planned **spontaneous** *Wide swathes of the population were involved in spontaneous demonstrations and actions.*

● v+N organize a demonstration **call for, hold, organize, plan, stage** *Protesters are planning to stage a demonstration against the new runway.*

▶ go on a demonstration **attend, go on, join, take part in** *The mayor's message is simple and straightforward: do not attend this demonstration.*

▶ refuse permission for a demonstration **ban** *A presidential decree was immediately issued, banning demonstrations until the end of April.*

2 something that proves a fact

● adj+N clear **clear, simple** *Flooding is a clear demonstration of the fact that the climate is changing.*

▶ strong **convincing, graphic, impressive, powerful** *Heal's career was a powerful demonstration of the influential role that a talented and determined shopkeeper can play.*

denial N
a statement that something is not true

● adj+N strong **categorical, emphatic, strenuous, strong, vehement** *The Government has issued a categorical denial of both charges.*

▶ complete **explicit, flat, outright** *The FBI issued a flat denial of the story.*

▶ repeated **repeated** *There is now a well-established pattern of partial disclosures after repeated denials.*

▶ official **government, official** *Both clubs today issued official denials that there has been an approach for the player.*

● v+N **issue, make** *A spokesman issued a vehement denial and said the company was in no way linked to the campaign.*

denounce V
criticize someone or something severely in public

● adv+V strongly **roundly, strongly, vehemently, vigorously** *The book has been roundly denounced by historians as 'a ludicrous and worthless book'.*

▶ publicly **openly, publicly** *Challoner was publicly denounced by Cromwell as a 'drunkard' in 1653.*

▶ angrily **angrily, bitterly** *He bitterly denounced the military leaders who had joined the revolt only to betray it.*

▶ by many people **widely** *The elections were widely denounced as having been marked by intimidation and fraud.*

▶ many times **repeatedly** *Our representatives have repeatedly denounced the kidnapping and killing of civilians.*

dent V
have a bad effect on something

● adv+V badly **badly, seriously, severely** *Turning your new house into a proper home could leave your finances seriously dented.*

▶ a little **slightly** *The recent fiasco has slightly dented their reputation for Teutonic reliability.*

▶ not very much **barely, hardly** *The day's mishaps barely dented the band's morale.*

● V+n feelings **confidence, ego, morale, pride** *Previous employment experiences have dented her confidence.* ● *I came out of it with a few bruises and a dented ego.*

▶ hopes **hopes** *Their hopes were dented when Munster snatched a last minute equaliser to force a 1–1 draw.*

▶ reputation **reputation** *Reports of unreliability severely dented the minister's reputation.*

deny V
say that you did not do something that someone has accused you of; say that something is not true or does not exist

● adv+V strongly **adamantly, emphatically, firmly, stoutly, strenuously, strongly, vehemently, vigorously** *The accusations have reportedly been vehemently denied by officials in Washington.*

▶ at the beginning **initially** *Police initially denied that armed officers had been on the scene.*

▶ angrily **angrily, indignantly** *When Fodor questioned her about it afterwards, she indignantly denied having done such a thing.*

▶ many times **consistently, repeatedly** *Washington has repeatedly denied any intention of an attack.*

▶ completely **categorically, flatly** *He flatly denies that he ever so much as touched any form of illicit narcotic.*

▶ directly/not directly **explicitly, implicitly** *She did not explicitly deny the accusation.*

● V+n accusation **accusation, allegation, charge, claim, rumour** *Elsewhere he has denied allegations that he is a fraud.*

▶ doing something wrong **involvement, wrongdoing** *The school has denied any wrongdoing and is contesting the charge.*

▶ responsibility **liability, responsibility** *As in most medical negligence cases the defendants denied liability.*

▶ the existence or truth of something **existence, fact, possibility, reality, truth, validity** *You cannot discuss the purpose of life with a man who denies the existence of God.*

> You can also say that **there is no denying** something; *There is no denying the fact that she has been a brilliant advocate for her profession.*

departure N
1 an occasion when someone leaves a place

● adj+N sudden or unexpected **abrupt, dramatic, hasty, premature, sudden, surprise, swift** *The sudden departure of their drummer caused the band no end of problems.*

▶ happening soon **imminent, impending** *I just thought I would inform you of my impending departure.*

▶ early/late **early, late** *Guests needing an earlier departure may be catered for by prior arrangement.*

● v+N delay departure **delay, postpone** *She'd heard that I'd had to delay my departure.*

▶ announce departure **announce** *He had already announced his departure earlier this year.*

▶ bring forward departure **hasten** *Her relationships with managers deteriorated, which hastened her departure.*

2 something new or different

● adj+N **dramatic, major, new, radical, significant** *This marks a radical departure from the standard discussion of innovation in health.*

▶ v+N **herald, mark, signal** *Neither case heralds a significant departure from the previous law.*

● N+from **the norm, plan, practice, principle, rule, standards, tradition** *This was a departure from established practice.*

dependable ADJ
able to be relied on

● adv+ADJ very **highly, very** *The recipe database has built up into a highly dependable source of quality dishes.*

▶ always **always, ever** *An ever dependable player, he formed strong partnerships with a number of different players.*

▶ completely **completely, totally, utterly, wholly** *The engine is smooth, powerful and utterly dependable.*

● and/or **reliable, solid, strong, trustworthy** *Wilmer is a solid, dependable actor but he seems out of his depth as the hero.*

dependence N
a situation in which you need someone or something in order to live or succeed

● adj+N complete **absolute, complete, total, utter** *Our total dependence on fossil fuels is like a chemical addiction.*

▶ great **heavy, strong** *With so much of the land unsuitable for crops, there is a particularly heavy dependence on livestock.*

▶ too great **excessive, unhealthy** *Similar problems can be caused by excessive dependence on convenience foods.*

▶ increasing **growing, increasing** *The role of the librarian is changing because of the growing dependence on online resources.*

▶ when two or more people or things are dependent on each other **mutual** *The study stresses the mutual dependence of family members.*

▶ types of dependence **economic, emotional, financial, physical, psychological** *They aimed to reduce local government's financial dependence on central government.*

● n+N on a particular substance or object **car, energy, oil** *Society's ever-increasing car dependence discriminates against those who do not have cars.*

▶ on drugs or a particular drug **alcohol, cocaine, drug, heroin, nicotine, tobacco** *Alcohol dependence leads to potentially fatal physical illness.*

dependent ADJ
needing someone or something to live or succeed

● adv+ADJ completely **completely, directly, entirely, solely, totally, utterly, wholly** *Some 16 million are totally dependent on monthly government-distributed food rations.*

▶ very or mainly **critically, crucially, heavily, highly,**

largely, mainly, primarily, very *I am heavily dependent on lip-reading and cannot do this while taking notes simultaneously.*
▶ in a particular way **economically, emotionally, financially, psychologically** *After exhausting his savings he became financially dependent on his mother.*
▶ partly **partially, partly** *More than two thirds are entirely or partly dependent on benefits.*
▶ when two or more people or things are dependent on each other **mutually** *Industry and academics have become mutually dependent on each other.*

depend on PHR VB
be changed or affected by something

● adv+V very much or mainly **critically, crucially, greatly, largely, mainly, primarily, strongly, very much** *The process will depend crucially on citizen involvement at all levels to make it work.* ● *The position within the class will depend largely on the extent of outside reading.*
▶ partly **in part, partly** *How much we drink depends partly on the genes that we inherit from our parents.*
▶ completely **entirely, solely** *How long it will take you depends entirely on your starting point.*
▶ in the end **ultimately** *Whether a deal can be reached will ultimately depend on what is on offer.*

deploy V
use something

● adv+V in many places **fully, widely, worldwide** *These devices are widely deployed in production networks throughout the world.*
▶ quickly or easily **easily, quickly, rapidly** *New software and updates can therefore be deployed very quickly.*
▶ effectively **effectively, efficiently, successfully** *What renewable energy technologies can be successfully deployed in London?*

● V+n resources or a way of doing something **device, equipment, resources, solutions, strategy, system, tactics, technique** *These pages describe how to deploy data service resources.*
▶ arguments **argument, rhetoric** *He deployed these arguments in his popular writings on the subject.*
▶ soldiers or weapons **missiles, personnel, soldiers, troops, warheads, weapons** *The number of troops they destroyed was at least 40 percent short of the required level.*

depressed ADJ
very unhappy about something that is difficult to change; suffering from depression

● adv+ADJ very **deeply, extremely, severely, very** *He's severely depressed and sleeping about 20 hours a day.*
▶ slightly **mildly, slightly** *She became mildly depressed and miserable.*
▶ with an illness **clinically** *At the extreme end of the spectrum, people can find themselves clinically depressed or even suicidal.*

● v+ADJ **become, feel, get, look, make sb, seem, sound** *When I'm having a bad time or I'm feeling depressed, I let everyone know.* ● *All this talk of recession is enough to make anybody depressed.*

● and/or **angry, anxious, irritable, lethargic, lonely, miserable, sad, suicidal, tired** *For a while she coped, but then she became depressed and anxious.*

depressing ADJ
making you feel very unhappy and disappointed

● adv+ADJ rather **pretty** INFORMAL, **quite, rather, somewhat** *The middle section of the book was rather depressing.*
▶ very **deeply, profoundly, really, thoroughly, very** *Despite lots of fabulous songs, the performances are mostly deeply depressing.*
▶ a little **a little, slightly** *I find it a little depressing that you've lost your objectivity completely.*

● v+ADJ **be, become, find sth, get** *The weather has been pretty depressing since May.* ● *This would have meant doing work that I found totally depressing.*

● and/or dark, dull or sad **bleak, boring, dark, dreary, dull, gloomy, miserable, sad** *Frequently dark and depressing, his stories revolve around tales of honour and betrayal.*
▶ upsetting or annoying **distressing, frustrating, stressful** *Those months in London were a frustrating and depressing time.*

depression N
the feeling or medical condition of being extremely unhappy

● adj+N when depression is an illness **clinical** *The diagnosis of clinical depression is not always straightforward.*
▶ serious/not serious **deep, mild, moderate, severe** *He was diagnosed with severe depression and was off work until July.*
▶ lasting a long time or returning often **chronic** *These feelings of inadequacy can lead to chronic depression.*

● v+N experience depression **develop, experience, fall into, plunge into, sink into, suffer, suffer from** *I feel better than I have felt for years after suffering depression and fatigue.*
▶ cause depression **cause, trigger** *No one is sure how depression is caused.*
▶ treat or cure depression **cure, diagnose, treat** *My depression was not diagnosed until I was 35 and had a breakdown.*
▶ make depression less bad **alleviate, combat, lift, relieve** *If the depression is lifted, the pain often becomes less.*
▶ recover from depression **beat** INFORMAL, **get over** INFORMAL, **overcome, recover from** *The majority of people will overcome their depression completely.*

● n+of+N a time when someone has depression **bout, episode, period** *She's had minor medical problems and one bout of depression.*
▶ when depression starts **onset** *She traced the onset of the depression back to the early deaths of both her parents.*

deprivation N
a situation in which people do not have basic things necessary for a comfortable life

● adj+N severe **acute, extreme, high, relative, severe** *She was working in a school in an area of severe deprivation.*

▶ types of deprivation **economic, multiple, rural, social, socio-economic, urban** *Some areas where there are high levels of social deprivation have relatively few dentists.*

▶ compared with other people's situation **relative** *This is a method of quantifying levels of relative deprivation or affluence in different localities.*

● v+N experience deprivation **experience, face, suffer** *The most severe deprivation is experienced by pensioners living alone who are mainly dependent on state pensions.*

▶ fight deprivation **address, tackle, target** *He gave credit to the government for trying to address deprivation and inequality.*

▶ reduce deprivation **alleviate, overcome, reduce** *The question emerges as to how far the Government can reduce relative deprivation.*

● n+of+N area **area, pocket** *Even idyllic countryside has pockets of deprivation.*

▶ level or measure **extent, index, level, measure** *A number of different measures of deprivation are available.*

▶ series of events **cycle** *Together we can break the cycle of deprivation which at present can persist from cradle to grave.*

● and/or **disadvantage, exclusion, hardship, inequality, isolation, poverty, suffering, unemployment** *Today it is a sprawling estate characterised by acute poverty and deprivation.*

deprived ADJ
lacking the things that are essential for a comfortable life

● adv+**ADJ** in a particular way **culturally, economically, educationally, socially, socio-economically** *The club provides a valuable facility in a socially deprived area of the city.*

▶ very **extremely, severely, very** *Most were living in severely deprived areas where unemployment rates were high.*

▶ compared with others **relatively** *The south coast below the M27 motorway is a relatively deprived area.*

● ADJ+n area **area, district, estate, locality, neighbourhood, region** *Risk factors for involvement in criminality tend to cluster around those who live in the more deprived localities.*

▶ people **children, community, people, population** *Those from deprived communities had the greatest disease burden.*

deputy N
a person who has the second most important job in an organization

● adj+N **authorized, designated** *The Head of Institution or authorized deputy countersigns the form.*

● v+N **appoint (sb as), elect, name, nominate (sb as)** *A District and Divisional Superintendent unable to attend may nominate a deputy.*

● N+n **chairman, chief executive, commander, director, director-general, editor, governor, head, headteacher, leader, mayor, minister** *As has become*

the custom, we were received in Linz Rathaus by the deputy mayor of the town.

derive V
receive or obtain something from something else

● adv+V **chiefly, largely, mainly, mostly, partly, primarily, principally, solely** *These figures are derived mainly from documents found at the house after his death.*

● V+n pleasure or benefit **amusement, benefit, comfort, enjoyment, inspiration, pleasure, satisfaction** *In the past two years of my career I derived very little real satisfaction from my job.*

▶ money **income, profit, revenue** *Some publishers accept advertising and derive revenue from it.*

▶ opinions or facts **conclusion, data, estimate, evidence, facts, figures, knowledge, results** *It is not possible to derive definite conclusions from this data.*

descend into PHR VB
enter a bad state

● adv+V **rapidly** *The situation was rapidly descending into complete chaos.*

● V+n a very bad state **anarchy, chaos, madness, turmoil, violence, war** *They believed that the world was descending into chaos and wickedness.*

▶ a silly state **cliché, farce, parody** *The final part of the story descends into farce and then fantasy.*

description N
a statement about what someone or something is like

● adj+N short **brief, concise, short, succinct** *All you then have to do is enter a brief description of your home.*

▶ long **lengthy, long** *Visitors don't want to read lengthy descriptions.*

▶ detailed **complete, comprehensive, detailed, exhaustive, full, in-depth, thorough** *He showed me the sale catalogue with its detailed descriptions of all the farms.*

▶ not detailed **general, vague** *She could only provide them with a vague description of her attacker.*

▶ with unpleasant details **graphic** *His novels contain graphic descriptions of sexual violence.*

▶ exact or clear **accurate, apt, clear, good, precise** *Full and accurate descriptions of courses must be provided.*

▶ powerful **powerful, vivid** *The description is so vivid, it makes you want to head for the island immediately.*

▶ spoken/written **verbal, written** *A written role description can be given to the volunteer when they start volunteering.*

● v+N give a description **give, issue, provide** *The police have issued a description of the men they want to interview.*

▶ match a description **fit, match** *If you provide details of an image you are searching for, we will endeavour to match your description.*

▶ be impossible to describe **beggar, defy** *The sensation I felt at that moment defies description.*

● N+v **apply to, correspond to, fit, match** *If any of these descriptions apply to you then we can help.*

deserve V

if you deserve something, it is right that you get it

- adv+V very much **fully, justly, richly, rightfully, rightly, thoroughly, truly, well** *Sarah gets the full marks and recognition she so richly deserves.*
- ▶ definitely **certainly, definitely, really, undoubtedly** *He certainly deserved this reward.*
- ▶ not at all **hardly, scarcely** *The present castle scarcely deserves the name.*

- V+n praise or thanks **acclaim, accolade, award, congratulations, credit, honour, mention, a pat on the back** INFORMAL, **plaudits, praise, recognition, thanks** *The developers deserve a pat on the back.*

> You can say that someone **deserves better** if you feel that they have not been treated fairly: *Lone fathers and their children deserve better.*

- ▶ applause **applause, ovation** *All those involved deserve tremendous applause.*
- ▶ victory **victory, win** *Leeds thoroughly deserved their victory against a hard-working Liverpool side.*
- ▶ support **support** *Our children's work belongs to the whole congregation and so deserves its support.*
- ▶ attention **attention** *Right then, onto a topic that really deserves your attention.*
- ▶ respect **consideration, respect** *Animals should be regarded as sensitive living beings who deserve respect and consideration.*
- ▶ punishment **punishment** *In either case a grave crime has been committed which deserves a grave punishment.*

design N

the way something is made and how it looks and works; the process of deciding how something will be made

- adj+N types of design **architectural, computer-aided, graphic, interior, urban** *Rob returned to academic studies, gaining honours in graphic design and illustration.*
- ▶ elegant **elegant, sleek, stylish** *Our sleek design neatly conceals a critical network of wires and connectors.*
- ▶ original or modern **contemporary, innovative, original** *It's an original Danish design in cherry wood, from the 1970s.*
- ▶ simple and always fashionable **classic** *They insist on good classic design and excellent materials.*
- ▶ easy to use **ergonomic** *The innovative ergonomic design of the handle ensures the cup is easy to hold.*

- N+n **concept, element, fault, feature, flaw, process** *The new road layout incorporates design features to assist cyclists and pedestrians.*

desirable ADJ

something that is desirable has qualities that make you want it

- adv+ADJ very **eminently, extremely, highly, very** *For the urban poor, anything that lowers the price of basic foods is highly desirable.*
- ▶ clearly **clearly, obviously** *Mobility of researchers and students is clearly desirable.*
- ▶ in a particular way **educationally, environmentally, morally, socially** *Although travelling by bus, cycle or foot is environmentally desirable, many people must use a car.*

- ADJ+n characteristic **attribute, characteristic, feature, quality, trait** *When wireless networks started out, high security was a long way down the list of desirable attributes.*
- ▶ result **outcome, result** *These kinds of learning are desirable outcomes of any educational process.*
- ▶ ability **ability, skill** *Project management skills are hugely desirable for managers at all levels of an organization.*

- v+ADJ **be, become, consider sth, deem sth, seem, think sth** *For some people the virtual world becomes more desirable than the real world.* • *It was not considered desirable to inform the public at this stage.*

desire N

a strong feeling of wanting something

- adj+N strong **ardent, burning, deep, fervent, insatiable, intense, overwhelming, passionate, strong** *There is a very strong desire among many of the younger people to speak their native tongue.*
- ▶ sincere **earnest, genuine, sincere** *The leadership has responded with a genuine desire to work together for the good of the country.*
- ▶ not satisfied **unfulfilled, unsatisfied** *Try and free yourself from unfulfilled desire for what you can't afford.*
- ▶ not expressed **hidden, secret** *In this article Warner examines the secret desires behind such fears.*

- v+N express a desire **express, indicate, show** *A lot of people also express a desire to start a new career.*
- ▶ satisfy a desire **fulfil, gratify, indulge, satisfy** *Maybe nothing will satisfy my desire for the perfect magazine.*
- ▶ have a desire **feel, have** *I have little desire to pay into a fund that won't be there when I retire.*
- ▶ stop yourself feeling a desire **curb, repress, suppress** *It was a critical moment, but I managed to suppress any desire to leave.*
- ▶ make a desire stronger **arouse, fuel, stimulate** *She grew up in South Africa, which fueled a desire to write about the injustices there.*

- v+from+N **arise, come, derive, spring, stem** *This practice stemmed from a desire to give a sense of order to the world.*

desolate ADJ

empty, without people or pleasant features

- adv+ADJ **rather, utterly, very** *Bus stations can be rather desolate places, and indeed there was no nearby cafe that was open.*

- ADJ+n land **land, landscape, region, waste, wasteland, wilderness** *For hundreds of miles to the south there was nothing but desolate wasteland.*
- ▶ types of area **moor, moorland, plain, valley** *The scenery is varied, taking in picturesque harbours, ruined castles and desolate moorland.*
- ▶ place **place, spot** *When you think of a wilderness, more than likely the image of some desolate place comes to mind.*

- and/or **barren, bleak, dark, empty, lonely, remote, wild** *To the west is some of the most desolate and lonely coastline in the world.*

despair N

the loss of hope in a very bad situation

- adj+N **absolute, black, complete, dark, deep, total, utter** *The letters kept Marina's mother from utter despair.*
- v+N **be driven to, be plunged into, fall into, sink into** *She was driven to despair by the circumstances in which she found herself.*
- and/or sad feelings **anguish, despondency, distress, fear, grief, hopelessness, loneliness, misery, sadness** *It was a desolate-looking place, a fitting refuge for despair and misery.*
- ▶ angry feelings **anger, frustration, rage** *About a third of the visitors came over to share their rage and despair.*
- ▶ happy feelings **elation, hope** *In the end the enduring message of the Bishop's lecture was one of hope, not despair.*

desperate ADJ

1 extremely worried or extremely serious

- adv+ADJ **absolutely, increasingly, pretty** INFORMAL, **quite, rather, really** *I think the situation's pretty desperate – time's running out for those trapped people fast.*
- ADJ+n **circumstances, desire, need, plight, poverty, shortage, situation, struggle** *There is a desperate need for more science teachers.* • *We need to highlight the continuing, desperate plight of the refugees.*

> You can also say that someone or something is *in desperate need of* something: *The whole area is in desperate need of regeneration.*

- v+ADJ **be, get, grow, look, sound** *By this time the girl's family was starting to get desperate.*

2 having little hope of success; done because no other way is possible

- adv+ADJ **absolutely, increasingly, pretty** INFORMAL, **quite, rather, really** *This represents a rather desperate attempt to gain more popularity.*
- ADJ+n **attempt, bid, effort, measures, plea, search, struggle** *Millions fled their homes in a desperate search for food.*

despicable ADJ

extremely unpleasant

- adv+ADJ **absolutely, totally, utterly** *His comments are absolutely despicable.*
- ADJ+n **act, attack, behaviour, character, crime** *The Council of Europe called the racist attack a despicable act.*
- and/or **cowardly, vile** *This was a cowardly and despicable crime.*

destination N

the place where someone or something is going

- adj+N popular **major, popular, premier, top** *In summer, Switzerland is a popular destination for hikers.*
- ▶ far away **exotic, far-flung, long-haul** *Florida is the UK's favourite long-haul destination.*
- ▶ perfect **ideal, perfect** *Scotland is an ideal destination for a break of any length.*
- ▶ final **final, intended, ultimate** *We reached our final destination in the evening.*
- n+N **holiday, honeymoon, leisure, shopping, short break, ski, tour, tourism, tourist, travel, vacation, visitor** *Devon is one of Europe's most popular holiday destinations and enjoys a mild climate even during the winter months.*
- v+N travel to a destination **travel to** *Children travelling to an international destination are required to travel with necessary documents.*
- ▶ arrive at a destination **arrive at, reach** *Packages can take between 1 and 5 days to reach their destination from leaving our premises.*

destiny N

the things that you will do, or the things that will happen in the future

- adj+N whose destiny **human, individual, personal, your own** *I felt I was not in control of my own destiny.*
- ▶ in the future **final, future, ultimate** *Who knows what will be the ultimate destiny of the Internet?*
- ▶ types of destiny **economic, historical, political** *They felt they had little control over the economic destiny that had been decided for them.*
- v+N **change, control, decide, determine, fulfil, influence, shape** *We have been given the freedom to shape our own destiny.*
- N+v **await sb, depend on sth, lie** *Does the same destiny await you?* • *After a year or so working as much as I could, I decided that my destiny lay in travelling.*

destroy V

cause damage so severe that something stops existing

- adv+V completely **completely, totally, utterly** *A member of staff was wounded in the blast, which totally destroyed the vehicle.*
- ▶ partly **partially, partly** *In 1760 the Abbey was partially destroyed by a hurricane, leaving the ruin that we see today.*
- ▶ almost **almost, effectively, nearly, virtually** *The affair nearly destroyed my marriage.*
- ▶ carefully and thoroughly **systematically** *Far from saving the club, they have systematically destroyed it.*
- ▶ deliberately **deliberately** *Some of the records had been deliberately destroyed to prevent people's identities becoming known.*
- ▶ for no good reason **wantonly** *They wantonly destroyed cities like Rotterdam for no military purpose.*
- ▶ in the end **ultimately** *Constant criticism ultimately destroys any confidence or optimism that you may have.*

destruction N

damage that is so severe that something no longer exists

- adj+N complete **complete, total, wholesale** *The ensuing explosion resulted in the complete destruction of a patrol vehicle.*

▶ great **massive, widespread** *Typhoons can cause massive destruction, flooding and landslides.*

▶ unnecessary **wanton** *Over the last 30 years we have seen the wanton destruction of forests.*

▶ deliberate **deliberate, systematic, wilful** *The worst act of vandalism was the deliberate destruction of the Library in Alexandra.*

▶ types of destruction **ecological, environmental, physical** *Human action causes ecological destruction.*

● v+N cause destruction **cause, wreak** *The terrorist attacks were calculated to wreak terrible destruction.*

▶ stop destruction **prevent, stop** *The land was purchased by Nottinghamshire County Council to prevent further destruction to the house and parkland.*

detail N

1 a small fact or piece of information

● adj+N small or not important **minor, small, tiny** *It's just a tiny detail, but we want to get it right.*

● v+N **discuss, finalize, work out, worry about** *The committee met to finalize the details of the arrangements for the summer party.*

Usage **Detail** is almost always plural in these combinations: *Don't worry about the details; we can sort them out later.*

2 information [always plural]

● adj+N more **further, more** *For further details please contact Diane Montgomery on extension 920.*

▶ complete **full** *You can find out full details of all the courses by clicking one of the links above.*

▶ unpleasant **gory, graphic, sordid** *The journal gives gory details of frostbite damage.*

▶ exact **exact, precise, up-to-date** *You get precise details when you enrol.*

▶ basic and short **basic, brief, sketchy** *Brief details are given below.*

▶ types of detail **biographical, personal, technical** *Your personal details held on our database will be destroyed after 21 days.*

● v+N give details **announce, disclose, divulge, enter, give, pass on, provide, publish, reveal, send, submit, supply** *Enter your address details and e-mail address.* ● *I have a couple of gig venues in mind, I'll pass the details on to Stewart.*

▶ get details **get, obtain, receive** *You can obtain details of the courses on our website.*

▶ change details **amend, update** *To add or remove yourself from the list, or amend your details, please email us.*

▶ make sure details are correct **confirm** *A security check will be made to confirm your details.*

▶ have details **contain** *The booklet contains details of charities which may be able to help.*

3 all the small aspects or features that something has, considered all together [always singular]

● adj+N exact or careful **considerable, great, meticulous, minute** *They went into the arrangements for the day in minute detail.*

You can say that someone who is careful about every detail has **attention to detail**: *His essays are good but he lacks attention to detail.*

● v+in+N **analyse, comment, cover, describe, discuss, examine, explain, report, review, study, talk** *We'll need to discuss the matter in detail later.*

● v+into+N **go** *I felt the lecturer hadn't gone into enough detail.*

detailed ADJ

including many small facts

● adv+ADJ very **extremely, highly, incredibly, very** *The analysis was extremely detailed and informative.*

▶ rather **fairly, quite** *This page is fairly detailed, giving the reader a clear idea of the topics covered.*

▶ enough **sufficiently** *Are the instructions sufficiently detailed to allow students to complete the work?*

● ADJ+n **account, analysis, assessment, description, discussion, examination, explanation, information, instructions, investigation, knowledge, plan, proposal, report, study** *Police have issued a detailed description of the suspect.*

● and/or **accurate, analytical, clear, comprehensive, full, informative, lengthy, thorough** *Chapter 2 provides a clear and detailed overview of the structure of the industry.*

detection N

the process of proving that something is present or of finding out about someone or something

● adj+N early **early** *The cervical smear test has been a great help in the early detection of cervical cancer.*

▶ quick **rapid** *The company is developing a device for rapid detection of viruses.*

▶ correct **accurate, reliable** *This filter provides more accurate detection of spam emails.*

● v+N avoid detection **avoid, escape, evade** *In order to avoid detection, all work had to be carried out at night.*

▶ allow detection **allow, enable, permit** *This method allows early detection of infected animals and therefore early treatment.*

▶ improve detection **improve** *We are an international charity that aims to improve the detection, care and treatment of heart problems.*

detention N

being held by the police or in prison

● adj+N **arbitrary, continued, illegal, indefinite, preventive, unlawful** *People's mental health will be badly affected by continued detention.*

● v+N **be in, hold sb in, remain in** *At least 1,000 people are held in detention without trial.* ● *Fewer than 20 prisoners remain in detention at the camp.*

● N+n **camp, centre, facility** *He was being held prisoner at a detention facility.*

● and/or **arrest, deportation, imprisonment** *The arrest and detention of many of these men was arbitrary and unjustifiable.*

deter V

make someone decide not to do something

- adv+V **effectively** *People who have no real aptitude for the work will then be effectively deterred from entering the profession.*

- V+n criminal **burglar, criminal, intruder, offender, thief, vandal** *Well-lit areas deter car thieves.*

▶ crime **attack, crime, fraud, theft** *Many people argue that tougher punishments deter crime.*

deteriorate V

become worse

- adv+V quickly **fast, quickly, rapidly** *By this time the weather was deteriorating rapidly and a storm was rolling up the valley.*

▶ slowly **gradually, slowly, steadily** *His condition gradually deteriorated and he sadly died on 26 January 1998.*

▶ noticeably **dramatically, markedly, noticeably, sharply, significantly, visibly** *The military situation has deteriorated sharply over the past year.*

▶ badly **badly, seriously, severely** *Many of the drawings were on paper which was now deteriorating badly.*

- n+V **condition, eyesight, health, hearing, performance, quality, relationship, sight, situation, weather** *Eyesight and hearing deteriorate with age.*

deterioration N

the fact of becoming worse

- adj+N gradual **gradual, progressive, steady** *There has been a steady deterioration in relations between the two countries.*

▶ quick **rapid, sudden** *Any sudden deterioration in vision should be taken seriously.*

▶ serious or noticeable **marked, noticeable, serious, severe, significant** *Doctors were concerned by the significant deterioration in her condition.*

▶ not serious **slight** *There is the possibility of a slight deterioration in the weather over the next few days.*

▶ types of deterioration **general, mental, physical** *Auguste had died after several years of progressive mental deterioration.*

- v+N **accelerate, cause, prevent** *As water on the fruit accelerates deterioration, do not wash it until you are ready to use it.*

determination N

the refusal to be prevented from doing something

- adj+N **absolute, dogged, fierce, great, grim, gritty, ruthless, sheer, single-minded, steely** *Without his steely determination and charismatic leadership, the organization would never have existed.*

- v+N show determination **demonstrate, show** *The team began to show more determination and this was rewarded with a goal.*

▶ express determination **express, reflect, signal, underline** *The prime minister signalled his determination to move the process forward.*

▶ need determination **require** *There are still some technical difficulties ahead that will require determination to overcome.*

- and/or **commitment, courage, dedication, drive, enthusiasm, grit, perseverance, persistence, resolve, tenacity** *This gave them the courage and determination to tackle the problems that beset them.*

determined ADJ

letting nothing prevent you from doing what you want to do

- adv+ADJ **absolutely, grimly, quite** *She was absolutely determined that she would get her own way.*

- ADJ+n **attack, attempt, campaign, effort, opposition, resistance** *But despite her determined efforts, Rita never again matched her original achievement.*

deterrent N

something that makes someone less likely to do something bad

- adj+N **effective, good, major, powerful, strong, visible** *Mechanical immobilisers act as a visible deterrent to the opportunist car thief and most fit across the steering wheel.*

- v+N **act as, provide, serve as** *Security marking your property acts as a deterrent against theft.*

- N+n **effect** *The presence of CCTV can have a strong deterrent effect on a wide range of offences.*

detour N

a longer or unusual way to go somewhere

- adj+N short **brief, quick, short, slight, small** *On the way a short detour can be made to visit the impressive monastery at St Florian.*

▶ long **lengthy, long** *I made detours, sometimes quite long detours, to avoid the ice.*

▶ not planned **unplanned, unscheduled** *We made an unscheduled detour into Ghent, to have a look at the new museum.*

- v+N **make, take** *I brought Anni home, taking a detour to stop at the office and collect some things.*

detrimental ADJ

harmful or damaging

- adv+ADJ **extremely, highly, seriously, very** *Smoking is seriously detrimental to health.*

- ADJ+n **consequences, effect, impact** *The proposed bypass would have a large and detrimental impact on an unspoiled area of forest.*

- v+ADJ **be, consider sth, prove** *They identified a specific problem that is proving detrimental to their core business.*

devastating ADJ

causing a lot of harm or damage

- adv+ADJ **absolutely, potentially, quite** *The company sought to implement IT systems that would be immune to the potentially devastating consequences of hardware failure.*

- ADJ+n result **blow, consequences, effect, impact** *The floods had a devastating impact on crops and food production.*

▸ event **attack, disease, earthquake, fire, flood, war** *A devastating earthquake in the state of Gujarat killed more than 20,000 people.*

devastation N
damage affecting a large area or many people

● adj+N great **great, total, utter, widespread** *The tsunami has caused widespread devastation impacting many countries.*

▸ types of devastation **ecological, economic, environmental, social** *Many African countries may lose one fifth of their population within a decade, causing economic and social devastation.*

● v+N **cause, wreak** *Storms and gales wreaked devastation in Latin America and Europe at the end of 1999.*

● n+of+N place **scene** *What greeted me was a scene of utter devastation.*

▸ amount **trail** *A hurricane hit Northern England leaving a trail of devastation in its wake.*

▸ extent **extent, scale** *She spoke about the scale of the devastation she had encountered in the worst-hit areas.*

develop V
1 become bigger or more successful

● adv+V quickly **quickly, rapidly** *The school developed rapidly through private donations.*

▸ slowly **gradually, slowly** *There is currently a niche market which is gradually developing.*

2 get or improve abilities, skills, or knowledge

● V+n **ability, awareness, capability, expertise, knowledge, skills, understanding** *On both of these courses you will develop your understanding of how schools operate.*

development N
change, growth, or improvement over time; the creation of something

● adj+N continuing **continued, continuing, continuous, ongoing** *We are committed to the continued professional development of all our employees.*

▸ quick **rapid** *The organization has recently gone through a period of change and rapid development.*

▸ able to continue **sustainable** *Mainstream industry needs to be convinced of the need for sustainable development and the benefits of cleaner production and pollution control.*

▸ types of development **economic, industrial, personal, professional** *Japan began its industrial development after the Meiji restoration in 1868.*

● n+N **business, career, community, skills, staff, workforce** *The scheme aims to facilitate the study of courses which aid career development.*

● v+N help development **aid, encourage, facilitate, foster, promote, stimulate, support, undergo** *The organization aims to promote the development of a multicultural inclusive society through sport and art.*

▸ make development less quick **hinder, impede, inhibit** *Poor diet inhibits the development of healthy muscles and bones.*

▸ make development quicker **accelerate** *The book gives you ways in which to accelerate the development of your business.*

▸ prevent development **prevent** *Extreme jealousy can prevent the development of healthy relationships.*

▸ watch and check development **monitor, oversee** *A committee has been appointed to oversee the future service development.*

▸ see and describe development **trace** *From these texts, it is possible to trace the development of the Hebrew language.*

▸ influence development **influence** *Our role is to influence the development and implementation of European policy.*

▸ form the basis for development **underpin** *The region's universities and land-based colleges will be essential to underpin skills development.*

▸ when development happens **undergo** *The country is undergoing rapid development at the present time.*

● N+n **aid, opportunity, plan, process, programme** *Since 1985, the country has benefited from over 335 million euros of development aid.*

devise V
invent a method of doing something

● adv+V specially **specially, specifically** *The office layouts have been specifically devised to facilitate communication.*

▸ cleverly **carefully, cleverly, ingeniously** *The system was cleverly devised to appeal to participants of widely varying abilities.*

Usage ***Devise*** is usually passive in the ***adv+V*** combinations shown above.

● V+n **means, mechanism, method, plan, plan, policy, programme, scheme, solution, strategy, system, technique, way** *Scientists hope to devise better methods for predicting potential outbreaks of disease.*

● and/or **deliver, develop, implement** *We help clients devise and implement appropriate strategies to enter and develop new markets.*

devoid ADJ
lacking something, especially a good quality

● adv+ADJ completely **completely, entirely, totally, utterly** *I believe that people who are entirely devoid of imagination never can be really good gardeners.*

▸ almost **almost, largely, practically, virtually** *The first half of the game was largely devoid of excitement.*

● ADJ+of meaning or importance **content, meaning, merit, sense, significance, substance** *He talked in clichés, devoid of any real content.*

▸ quality or emotion **character, emotion, excitement, humour, ideas, imagination, personality** *The new housing development is devoid of any distinctive character.*

▸ life **life** *The North Sea may become a desert, totally devoid of any life.*

devoted ADJ
liking or loving someone or something very much

● adv+ADJ completely, totally *Although his life was focused on his work, he was completely devoted to his family.*

- ADJ+n **couple, fan, follower, following, servant, supporter, wife, son etc** *The singer has a devoted following among folk fans in the US.* • *Ted will be greatly missed by his devoted wife of 57 years.*

- and/or **faithful, loving, loyal** *David was a devoted and loyal son.*

devote to PHR VB
spend time or effort doing something

- V+n **attention, effort, efforts, energy, life, resources, time** *He has devoted much energy to supporting his chosen charitable causes.*

devotion N
great love, admiration, or loyalty; spending a lot of time or energy on an activity

- adj+N not thinking of yourself **selfless, unswerving** *He showed selfless devotion to his sick wife.*
- ▶ strong or too strong **deep, fanatical, great, passionate, single-minded, slavish, total, unswerving** *Both players showed unfailing loyalty and a total devotion to the team.*
- v+N **show** *Special thanks to Newark Hospice, especially the care workers who showed great devotion and care.*

diagnosis N
a statement about what disease someone has

- adj+N definite **definite, definitive, positive** *Even when there is no definite diagnosis, information could be given, including some idea of the nature of the illness.*
- ▶ not definite **provisional, tentative** *A doctor called back, made a provisional diagnosis of pneumonia and arranged a home visit.*
- ▶ early **early, prompt, rapid** *Many sufferers fail to get an early diagnosis from their doctors, and this can result in a worsening of symptoms.*
- v+N make a diagnosis **establish, make, reach** *In order to make a diagnosis, the doctor relies on what you say.*
- ▶ help to make a diagnosis **aid, facilitate** *Chest X-rays are sometimes used to aid the initial diagnosis.*
- ▶ support a diagnosis **confirm, support** *An ultrasound may confirm the diagnosis.*
- ▶ prove that a diagnosis is wrong **exclude** *Most tests are not 100 per cent specific and therefore a negative result does not exclude the diagnosis.*

dialogue N
a process of discussion in order to solve problems

- adj+N useful **constructive, effective, fruitful, informed, meaningful** *The organization aims to promote meaningful dialogue between different regions and communities.*
- ▶ continuing **constant, continuing, ongoing** *Our aim is to bring this ongoing dialogue to the attention of our participating educational communities.*
- ▶ open or direct **open** *This is achieved through open dialogue with our local research ethics committee.*
- ▶ with both groups talking and listening **interactive, two-way** *Peace will only be possible if both sides are prepared to enter into a genuine two-way dialogue.*

- ▶ types of dialogue **intercultural, interfaith, political** *In addition to political dialogue between Brussels and national capitals, the EU must foster people-to-people contact.*
- v+N start a dialogue **begin, create, develop, enter into, establish, initiate, open, start** *Librarians need to establish a dialogue with academics to address these issues.*
- ▶ have a dialogue **engage in, have, participate in** *The Islamic Society wishes to spread the truth about Islam and does this by engaging in dialogue with Muslims and non-Muslims alike.*
- ▶ encourage a dialogue **encourage, facilitate, promote, stimulate** *We provide an advocacy service which aims to encourage and facilitate dialogue between parents and teachers.*
- ▶ continue a dialogue **maintain** *Media relations officers maintain a regular dialogue with journalists.*

diary N
a book etc, for recording what has happened to you each day

- adj+N daily/weekly **daily, weekly** *Keep a daily diary of how you feel, including every ache and pain.*
- ▶ private **personal, private, secret** *Jennie kept private diaries and Mitchell was also allowed to read these.*
- ▶ using a particular medium **online, video** *Create a free online travel diary to record all your experiences.*
- v+N write a diary **complete, keep, write** *Each member of the family is asked to complete a diary about their eating habits.* • *She kept a diary of her visit.*
- ▶ write something in a diary **note sth in, record sth in, write sth in** *Each patient noted the severity of the pain in a diary.*
- N+n **entry, extract** *I read some of my diary entries from when I was younger.*

dictate V
influence or control how something is done

- adv+V **largely, otherwise, partly** *Wedding style will be largely dictated by your personality.* • *This is the preferred method, unless local circumstances dictate otherwise.*

> **Usage** *Dictate* is usually passive in the last two *adv+V* combinations shown above: *The approach taken will be partly dictated by student preference.*

- n+V **circumstances, common sense, conditions, custom, fashion, logic, the market, reason, tradition** *Tradition dictates that the bridegroom's speech is kind and polite about the bride.*

diet N
1 the type of food someone eats

- adj+N healthy **balanced, healthy, nutritious, varied, well-balanced** *A balanced diet is essential for health.*
- ▶ unhealthy **poor, unhealthy** *Unhealthy diets, which tend to include too much sugar, salt and fatty foods, are linked to cancer and heart disease.*
- ▶ types of diet **gluten-free, high-fat, high-fibre, high-protein, low-calorie, low-fat, macrobiotic, vegan,**

vegetarian *Eat a sensible low-fat diet so the liver doesn't have to process lots of fat.*

▸ usual **staple** *Today rice is the staple diet of over 1.5 million people.*

▸ not eating some things **restricted, special, strict** *Special diets such as kosher, halal, and vegan can be catered for on request.* • *She ate a strict vegetarian diet.*

● n+N **fad** *The fad diets can often exclude entire food groups, such as wheat or dairy products.*

● v+N **eat a diet be on, eat, follow, have** *Try to eat a balanced diet.*

▸ improve a diet **improve** *The doctor told me I need to improve my diet.*

▸ change a diet **change** *I gave up all sweet things and changed my diet.*

▸ keep to a diet **keep to, stick to** *Coeliac disease is a very serious disease, so you must stick strictly to a gluten-free diet in order to feel better.*

2 when someone is trying to lose weight

● adj+N **strict** *He went on a strict diet of 1200 calories a day to try and lose some weight.*

● v+N **be on, go on, keep to, stick to** *I'm won't have any more, thank you. I'm on a diet.*

differ v
be different from something else

● adv+V very much **considerably, dramatically, enormously, greatly, markedly, radically, sharply, significantly, substantially, vastly, widely, wildly** *The two cultures differ markedly in relation to men's role.*

▸ not very much **little, slightly, somewhat** *Modern man (homo sapiens) emerged between 30,000 and 40,000 years ago, differing little in intellectual capacity and physique from today.*

▸ in a basic way **fundamentally, materially** *This war differed fundamentally from any previous conflict.*

difference N

1 something that makes one person or thing different from another; the amount by which something is different from something else

● adj+N big **big, considerable, enormous, huge, major, marked, massive, substantial, vast** *There is a huge difference between the abilities of a six-month-old baby and a two-year-old child.*

▸ small **little, minor, slight, subtle** *The two models are basically the same machine, but there are some slight differences.*

▸ clear and easy to see **appreciable, distinct, notable, noticeable, obvious, striking** *It was interesting to see the obvious differences between the east and west sides of the country.*

▸ basic **essential, fundamental** *Invited to compare the two, most people soon spot the essential difference.*

▸ important **crucial, important, significant** *There are two important differences between buy-to-let mortgages and standard mortgages.*

▸ main **key, main** *Read this paper to understand the key differences between spyware and viruses.*

▸ types of difference **cultural, genetic, individual, racial, regional** *Another area of misunderstanding is cultural differences in lifestyle.*

● n+N **age, class, gender, price, sex, temperature, time** *We need to address gender differences in attainment at school.* • *There's a three-hour time difference between London and Moscow.*

● v+N recognize that there is a difference **detect, identify, know, notice, see, spot, tell** *I don't see a big difference between this act and a knife-throwing act.* • *It's hard to tell the difference between the low-fat and high-fat versions.*

> When something has a big effect, you can say that it **makes a difference**: *Having two assistants instead of one will make a big difference.*

▸ emphasize a difference **emphasize, highlight, stress** *The novel highlights the differences between romance and courtship today and how it was in the past.*

▸ discuss a difference **examine, explore, look at** *This study aims to explore the differences in achievement between the two groups of students.*

▸ explain a difference **account for, explain** *It is difficult to know how to account for the differences shown in the statistics.*

● N+v **arise from, emerge, lie in** *The main difference lies in the type of merchandise sold.*

● and/or **similarity** *The article talks about the differences and similarities between life in Britain and life in the US.*

> Usage **Difference** is always plural when used with **similiarities**: *The children were asked to identify the differences and similarities between the two pictures.*

2 disagreements about something [always plural]

● adj+N **irreconcilable** *Gilbertson resigned due to irreconcilable differences with the committee.*

● v+N have differences **have your** *I know Coxsone and I had our differences, but I'm sad to see him go.*

> When people disagree you can also say that they have **a difference of opinion**: *We had a difference of opinion about the best way to proceed.*

▸ end differences **overcome, reconcile, resolve, settle, transcend** *Both countries need to start discussions and resolve their differences.*

● N+v **arise, emerge, persist, remain** *We have resolved most issues, but some outstanding differences remain.*

different ADJ
not the same as someone or something

● adv+ADJ very **altogether, completely, entirely, quite, radically, totally, vastly, very, wholly, wildly** *The University is completely different from how I imagined.* • *The new chairman has a radically different approach to his predecessors.*

▸ noticeably **distinctly, markedly, strikingly** *The three songs are all markedly different in character.*

▸ in important ways **fundamentally, qualitatively, significantly, substantially** *Human language is qualitatively different from animal communication.*

▸ in a good way **refreshingly** *The story is familiar, but the author's style is refreshingly different.*

● ADJ+n method **approach, method, strategy** *The*

study showed how different approaches to achieving equal opportunities can be equally successful.

▶ way of thinking **angle, interpretation, perspective, position, slant, standpoint, viewpoint** *In the story,Tyler is a charismatic salesman who has a whole different slant on life, which captivates Jack.*

● v+ADJ **appear, be, feel, look, seem, smell, sound, taste** *Colours look different against different backgrounds.*

difficult ADJ
not easy to do or understand

● adv+ADJ very **especially, extraordinarily, extremely, incredibly, particularly, so, surprisingly, terribly, too, very** *Things can be extremely difficult when family members have to be separated.*

▶ rather **a little, quite, rather** *The office is rather difficult to reach by car, so we recommend the bus.*

▶ in a way that makes you annoyed or impatient **fiendishly, frustratingly, impossibly, unreasonably** *The book includes some fiendishly difficult puzzles.*

▶ more than before **doubly, increasingly** *The team's task became doubly difficult when they had a player sent off after 25 minutes.*

▶ in a way that is well known **notoriously** *It is notoriously difficult to get healthcare messages across to men.*

▶ in a particular way **logistically, technically** *The music is not technically difficult, but still satisfying to play.*

● v+ADJ be or become difficult **be, become, get, prove, remain** *Persuading these people to leave is proving difficult.*

▶ seem difficult **appear, seem, sound** *For some children learning to swim seems much more difficult than for others.*

▶ make something difficult **make sth, render sth** *Rescue operations were rendered difficult by the enemy shelling the area.*

▶ think something is difficult **consider sth, find sth** *It's one of those books which you'll find difficult to put down.*

difficulty N
a problem or the fact of finding something difficult

● adj+N serious **considerable, enormous, extreme, great, major, serious, severe** *I had great difficulty in persuading him I was telling the truth.*

▶ impossible to overcome **insuperable, insurmountable** *The difficulties with enforcing this law are major, but certainly not insuperable.*

▶ in a particular area **behavioural, emotional, financial, logistical, mental, practical, technical** *The company was in financial difficulty and there wasn't enough money to cover the wages.*

▶ particular to someone or something **inherent, particular, specific** *There are inherent difficulties in trying to manage such a large volume of data.*

● v+N have difficulties **encounter, experience, face, have, run into** *We offer psychological help for young people experiencing difficulties in their personal lives.*

▶ overcome difficulties **avoid, overcome, resolve, surmount** *We had to overcome a few technical difficulties at the beginning.*

▶ cause difficulties **cause, create, pose, present** *The*

*new development could cause difficulties **with** parking.*

▶ make difficulties worse **compound, exacerbate** *Disabled people's difficulties are compounded by a lack of understanding of their needs.*

▶ predict or fail to predict difficulties **acknowledge, anticipate, foresee, recognize, underestimate** *I do not foresee any difficulty **in** completing the work on time.*

● N+v face someone **beset sb/sth, confront sb/sth, face sb/sth, surround sb/sth** *There are many difficulties besetting the Northern Ireland administration.*

▶ relate to something **arise, lie in, lie with** *The difficulty lies in fixing the budget.*

dignity N
respect from others or respect for yourself

● adj+N as part of a person's character **essential, human, inherent, innate, personal** *We want a society in which the inherent dignity and worth of every individual is respected.*

▶ quiet **calm, quiet** *She replied **with** quiet dignity.*

▶ great **great, immense, such** *He worked through difficult circumstances **with** great dignity and humanity.*

● v+N show or keep your dignity **affirm, maintain, regain, retain, show** *Throughout his captivity he maintained his dignity as a human being and soldier.*

▶ defend someone's dignity **defend, preserve, promote, protect, respect, restore, uphold** *Hospital staff will make every effort to respect your dignity and privacy.*

▶ destroy someone's dignity **compromise, offend, strip sb of, undermine, violate** *In their opinion, the poster violated the dignity of women.*

● and/or **courage, honour, independence, privacy, respect, self-respect, worth** *She faced her death with astonishing courage and dignity.*

dilemma N
a situation when you must make a difficult decision

● adj+N serious **acute, difficult, painful, real, terrible** *The spread of armed conflict presents us with a real dilemma.*

▶ basic **age-old, classic, fundamental** *It's the age-old dilemma: how to find a holiday that all the family will enjoy?*

▶ types of dilemma **ethical, legal, moral, philosophical, social** *He discusses philosophical dilemmas such as whether assassination can ever be morally right.*

● v+N face a dilemma **confront, deal with, face, find yourself in, grapple with, have, wrestle with** *All religions face the dilemma of balancing individual salvation and social engagement.*

▶ create a dilemma **create, pose, present** *The humanitarian situation in the country poses a moral dilemma for the United Nations.*

▶ resolve a dilemma **address, overcome, resolve, solve, tackle** *He finally resolved the dilemma by deciding to accept both invitations.*

● N+v **arise, confront sb, face sb** *Many ethical dilemmas confront documentary film makers.*

dimension N
an aspect of a situation

- adj+N new or different **added, additional, different, extra, further, new** *Recordings can give your learning of French an extra dimension.*
- ▶ types of dimension **cultural, ethical, historical, moral, political, psychological, religious, social, spiritual** *Religious or not, many of us feel that our lives have a spiritual dimension.*
- ▶ affecting a particular area **European, global, international, regional** *Through contacts abroad our work has developed an international dimension.*
- v+N give something a dimension **add, bring, give (sth), introduce, provide** *Her involvement will add a valuable new dimension to the project.*
- ▶ have or develop a dimension **acquire, assume, develop, have, take on** *The present-day carnival has assumed a modern dimension.*

diminish V
become less, or to make something become or seem less

- adv+V very much **considerably, dramatically, drastically, greatly, markedly, much, seriously, severely, significantly, substantially, vastly** *The value of his assets has greatly diminished.* • *Ministers worry that their power will be much diminished.*
- ▶ not very much **slightly, somewhat** *My enthusiasm has been somewhat diminished lately.*
- ▶ quickly **fast, rapidly, sharply** *The number of large employers is rapidly diminishing.*
- ▶ gradually **gradually, progressively, slowly, steadily** *They tried to cling on to their gradually diminishing empire.*
- V+n importance or power **importance, power, role, significance, value** *Most of these observations are simple common sense, which does not diminish their significance.*
- ▶ effects **effect, impact, influence** *The company will take all practical steps to prevent or diminish harmful impacts on the environment.*
- ▶ usefulness **ability, credibility, effectiveness, usefulness** *There is evidence that smoking diminishes the effectiveness of this form of therapy.*
- ▶ enthusiasm **appetite, enjoyment, enthusiasm** *The bad weather in no way diminished our enjoyment of the festival.*
- ▶ popularity **credibility, popularity** *The stories about the affair did nothing to diminish his popularity.*
- ▶ likelihood **chances, likelihood, risk** *Choosing the wrong agent greatly diminishes your chances of getting a good deal on your house.*
- n+V power **effect, importance, influence, power, threat** *While their influence has much diminished since 1997, it remains substantial.*
- ▶ amount **capacity, number, resource, supply** *His oxygen supply was diminishing fast.*

> Usage In the **n+V** combinations shown above, **diminish** is often used as a present participle adjective: *His book recognises the diminishing power of religion.* • *We can all help preserve the world's rapidly diminishing resources.*

- V+in **importance, number, size, stature, value**

Traditional metal industries have diminished in importance.

diploma N
a course of study at a college or university

- adj+N at a particular level **advanced, foundation, graduate, postgraduate** *She graduated with first-class honours and is currently studying for a graduate diploma in law.*
- ▶ taking a particular time **full-time, one-year, part-time, two-year** *The course is aimed at students who have completed a two-year diploma.*
- ▶ preparing for a job **professional, vocational** *The government plans to introduce new vocational diplomas aimed at 16–18 year olds.*
- v+N study for a diploma **do, study for** *I decided to do a postgraduate diploma in journalism.*
- ▶ get a diploma **attain, be awarded, complete, earn, gain, obtain, receive** *He was awarded his teaching diploma in 2005.*
- ▶ have a diploma **have, hold** *He holds a diploma in management studies.*

diplomatic ADJ
relating to the profession of diplomacy

- ADJ+n efforts or activities **channels, efforts, initiative, manoeuvrings, means, mission, negotiation, niceties, offensive, pressure, solution, wrangling** *We seek to resolve disputes through political, economic and diplomatic means.*
- ▶ relating to diplomacy **ally, incident, isolation, recognition, relations, representation** *In 1924 Britain reopened diplomatic relations with the Soviet Union.*
- ▶ relating to diplomats **corps, immunity, post, source** *Some diplomats have used their diplomatic immunity to avoid paying fines.*

direct ADJ
involving only the things or people mentioned and nothing in between

- ADJ+n contact **access, communication, contact, intervention** *Infection is through direct contact with contaminated blood.*
- ▶ result **consequence, outcome, result** *These additional sales occurred as a direct result of our efforts.*
- ▶ influence **bearing, control, impact, influence** *The decisions of politicians have a direct bearing on people's lives.*
- ▶ relationship **comparison, connection, correlation, involvement, link, relevance** *The course was interesting, but it had no direct relevance to the work that we do.*
- ▶ something opposite or completely different **contradiction, contrast, contravention, opposite** *This would seem to be a direct contradiction of Freud's view that dreams are there to preserve sleep.*

direct V
aim something [usually passive]

- adv+V mainly **largely, mainly, primarily, principally** *The marketing of crafts is primarily directed at tourists.*
- ▶ specifically **exclusively, particularly, solely,**

specifically *The last section is directed specifically at parents of children with eating disorders.*

● **V+n** efforts **activities, attention, efforts, energy, focus, resources** *We should be directing our efforts towards the preservation of the environment.* ● *We need to ensure that resources are directed to improving educational standards in the school.*

▶ anger **anger, attack, criticism** *His anger was directed at his own players rather than the opposition.*

direction N

1 the path someone or someone moves along

● adj+N right/wrong **right, wrong** *I'm looking for the bathroom. Can you tell me if I'm going in the right direction?*

▶ same/different **different, opposite, reverse, same** *The route is slightly easier in the reverse direction.*

▶ general **general, overall** *Keep walking in the general direction of the line of trees.*

▶ particular directions **anitclockwise, clockwise, downward, easterly, forward, northerly, perpendicular, southerly, upward, vertical, westerly** *Turn the dial in a clockwise direction.*

● v+N move or be in a direction **face, go in, move (sth) in, point (sth/sb) in, take** *Turn 180° to face the opposite direction.*

▶ change direction **change, reverse, switch** *The wind was constantly changing direction.*

2 instructions for doing something or getting somewhere [always plural]

● adj+N **clear, detailed, step-by-step** *Ensure that candidates are provided with clear directions to the venue for the interview.*

● v+N **follow, obey, do what directions say** *You can find the site by following the directions above.*

▶ give, issue, provide, give directions *Take the medication according to the directions given on the box.*

3 the general development or progress of someone or something

● adj+N good or right **positive, promising, right** *You have taken a big step in the right direction by coming to us for help.*

▶ same/different **different, new, opposite, reverse, same** *While charitable donations increased in the US, the trend in the UK went in the opposite direction.*

▶ future **future, strategic** *His role is to shape the strategic direction of the company.*

▶ general **general, overall** *The document outlines our priorities and general direction.*

▶ unexpected **unexpected** *At this point, her career took a new and totally unexpected direction.*

● n+N **career, policy, research** *The government has presented a new policy direction on transport.*

● v+N move in a direction **go in, move in, take** *One day she meets a young man and her life takes a new direction.*

▶ control something's direction **control, determine, dictate, influence, set, shape, steer** *Citizens can help shape the future direction of their society through political debate.*

▶ show something's direction **indicate, predict,**

suggest *Our aim was to indicate possible directions for future research.*

▶ change something's direction **alter, change** *You may decide to change your career direction.*

disability N

a condition that affects the body or brain

● adj+N affecting part of your body **hearing, mobility, neurological, physical, sensory, visual** *The school has been adapted for children with physical disabilities.*

▶ affecting your mental abilities **cognitive, communication, developmental, intellectual, language, learning, mental, reading** *Donna has a mild learning disability.*

▶ severe **complex, lifelong, long-term, multiple, permanent, profound, serious, severe** *These children have a range of special needs, and in some cases profound disabilities.*

▶ mild **mild, moderate, temporary** *Even students with moderate intellectual disabilities succeeded under the program.*

● v+N have a disability **experience, have, suffer from** *The treatment can reduce long-term disability experienced by patients with arthritis.*

▶ overcome a disability **overcome** *Her fight to overcome her disabilities made her an inspiration for millions of blind people.*

▶ cause disability **cause, lead to, result in** *A ruptured tendon can occasionally cause permanent disability.*

● N+n for supporting people with disabilities **awareness, campaigner, charity, movement, organization, rights** *We try to educate the public in disability awareness.*

▶ discrimination **discrimination** *I have personal experience of disability discrimination.*

▶ payments **allowance, benefit, premium** *The service is free to anyone receiving any form of disability allowance.*

disabled ADJ

having a mental or physical disability

● adv+ADJ in a particular way **developmentally, intellectually, mentally, physically, visually** *A new unit has been built at the school so that physically disabled pupils can take full advantage of mainstream secondary education.*

▶ seriously **badly, chronically, permanently, profoundly, seriously, severely, significantly** *There are several thousand servicemen who are severely disabled.*

▶ not very seriously **partially, temporarily** *He was injured in a car accident, leaving him partially disabled.*

● v+ADJ **be, be born, become, be left** *The woman was left disabled after an alleged medical mistake.*

disadvantage N

something that makes someone or something less effective, successful, or attractive

● adj+N big or important **big, considerable, distinct, great, huge, major, obvious, particular, serious, severe, significant, substantial** *One of the major disadvantages of this treatment is it can lead* to kidney infection. • *The lack of river crossings put East London **at** a substantial disadvantage.*

▶ main **main, primary, principal** *The primary disadvantage of these tests is the time it takes to develop questions which really probe the student's learning.*

▶ not big **slight** *Although there is a slight cost disadvantage, the installation is quicker and easier.*

▶ types of disadvantage **competitive, economic, educational, employment, market, racial, social, socio-economic, tax** *Socio-economic disadvantages such as poverty have an impact on learning.*

▶ possible **possible, potential** *We discuss some of the potential disadvantages **for** employees of flexible working hours.*

▶ impossible to avoid **inherent** *Convertibles have some inherent disadvantages, such as noise and vulnerability to theft.*

• v+N have a disadvantage **experience, face, have, suffer** *Despite its beauty and charm, the village does face some disadvantages from its proximity to a major city.*

▶ deal with a disadvantage **address, alleviate, avoid, combat, counter, eliminate, minimise, overcome, reduce, tackle** *There have to be further opportunities for people to overcome economic disadvantage.*

▶ outweigh a disadvantage **counteract, counterbalance, offset, outweigh, redress** *In a life-threatening situation, the advantages of a blood transfusion outweigh the disadvantages.*

• v+at+N put someone or something **leave sb/sth, place sb/sth, put sb/sth** *Traditional working patterns place women at a particular disadvantage.*

▶ be **be, feel, remain, start** *Small independent shops often feel at a disadvantage.*

• and/or **advantage, benefit, merit** *There are advantages and disadvantages **to** working from home.*

disadvantaged ADJ
lacking the advantages that other people have

• adv+ADJ from a particular point of view **economically, educationally, financially, socially, socio-economically** *There is a higher incidence of behavioural problems in children from economically disadvantaged populations.*

▶ seriously **doubly, especially, particularly, seriously, severely, significantly, substantially** *Some minority groups have prospered in Britain, but others remain severely disadvantaged.*

▶ unfairly **disproportionately, relatively, unfairly** *Ensure that the disabled student is not unfairly disadvantaged by selection procedures.*

• ADJ+n a person or group or the situation they live in **background, child, circumstances, community, group, household, individual, minority, youth** *As the city's wealth and reputation has grown, so has the gap between its prosperous and disadvantaged communities.*

▶ place or area **area, neighbourhood, region** *The Groundwork team has a long-term commitment to supporting people in disadvantaged neighbourhoods.*

disagree V
have a different opinion from someone else's

• adv+V completely **completely, entirely, fundamentally, profoundly, totally, wholeheartedly** *People on the same side of the debate may still disagree quite fundamentally **on** the best tactics to adopt.*

▶ strongly **passionately, strongly, vehemently, violently** *I strongly disagree **with** animal experimentation of any kind.*

▶ politely **politely, respectfully** *His attorney said, 'We respectfully disagree **with** the judge's decision'.*

▶ openly **openly, publicly** *To disagree publicly with his father was a declaration of rebellion.*

• V+about **cause, meaning, nature** *If scholars disagree about the very nature of their subject, they cannot claim that the subject is a science.*

• V+on **detail, issue, matter, point, question, thing** *Although my colleague and I disagree on certain details, our attitudes are very similar.*

• V+with statement **assertion, comment, conclusion, contention, decision, finding, policy, premise, proposal, proposition, recommendation, statement, suggestion** *He believed these people were real scientists, however much he disagreed with their conclusions.*

▶ idea **idea, interpretation, notion, opinion, sentiment, stance, view, viewpoint** *We disagree with the view that it is schools' sole responsibility to educate children, not parents'.*

disagreement N
a situation in which people disagree

• adj+N serious **considerable, deep, major, serious, significant, strong, substantial, widespread** *These proposals are likely to cause significant disagreement among party members.*

▶ too basic to be resolved **fundamental, irreconcilable, irresolvable, profound, unresolved** *When faced with a fundamental disagreement **between** two scientists, what are we to conclude?*

▶ not very serious **minor, slight** *Disputes with neighbours can range from minor disagreements to serious harassment.*

▶ angry **bitter, sharp, violent** *He had a sharp disagreement **with** John Wesley **over** doctrinal matters.*

▶ about particular subjects or issues **doctrinal, moral, political, theological** *Even within major faiths there are moral disagreements.*

• v+N have a disagreement **be in, have** *Of course we have disagreements from time to time.*

▶ resolve or avoid disagreement **avoid, handle, resolve, settle, solve** *It is important to resolve any disagreements through discussion.*

▶ cause disagreement **cause, provoke** *The question of whether Britain could join the European single currency is causing disagreement again.*

▶ express disagreement **air, express, voice** *Some colleagues have expressed disagreement **with** this view.*

• N+v happen **arise, emerge, erupt, exist, occur** *Both parties agree that it is in their interest to deal speedily with any disagreement that arises.*

▶ continue or get worse **escalate, persist, remain** *Deep disagreements remain **over** any future UN role in Iraq.*

- and/or argument **argument, conflict, confusion, controversy, criticism, difference, dispute, dissent, division, misunderstanding, tension, uncertainty** *We have to identify areas of conflict and disagreement and find a way to resolution.*
- ▶ agreement **agreement** *Your agreement or disagreement with that statement will partly depend on your general prejudices.*

disappearance N

when someone or something disappears

- adj+N mysterious **inexplicable, mysterious, strange, unexplained, unsolved** *According to local folklore, there have been several mysterious disappearances in the wood.*
- ▶ sudden **abrupt, rapid, sudden, swift** *There will be a dramatic temperature rise accompanied by the rapid disappearance of snow.*
- ▶ gradual **eventual, gradual** *We have seen the gradual disappearance of the gramophone record.*
- ▶ complete **complete, total** *Nine out of ten patients reported a complete disappearance of the symptoms.*
- ▶ almost complete **near, virtual** *The near disappearance of shipbuilding attests to the decline of British manufacturing industry.*
- v+N cause a disappearance **cause, lead to, mean** *Will this mean the disappearance of products people value?*
- ▶ regret a disappearance **lament, mourn, regret** *Many inhabitants mourn the disappearance of small family-run shops from the town.*
- ▶ explain a disappearance **explain, investigate, solve** *The boys wondered how to explain the car's disappearance to their parents.*

disappointed ADJ

dissatisfied with someone or something

- adv+ADJ very **bitterly, deeply, desperately, extremely, hugely, really, sadly, so, sorely, very** *I am bitterly disappointed, because I felt the deal was very close*
- ▶ rather **a little, pretty** INFORMAL**, quite, rather, slightly, somewhat** *I'm a little disappointed at how few cinemas are showing the film.*
- ▶ v+ADJ be or seem disappointed **be, become, feel, get, look, remain, seem, sound** *I felt disappointed that no one seemed to offer any hypothesis on why this was happening.*
- ▶ be made disappointed **be left, come away, end up, go away** *It was the first time I'd ever been to a concert and come away disappointed.*
- and/or **angry, bitter, confused, distressed, embarrassed, frustrated, sad, sorry, upset** *Her family were extremely angry and disappointed with her.*

disappointing ADJ

not as good as wanted or expected

- adv+ADJ very **bitterly, crushingly, deeply, desperately, doubly, especially, extremely, hugely, massively, particularly, profoundly, really, terribly, very** *We came away with a bitterly disappointing 0–0 draw. • It was very disappointing to see an increase in offences last year.*
- ▶ rather **a bit, a little, mildly,** INFORMAL**, quite,**

- rather, slightly, somewhat, a tad INFORMAL *We had a nice drive there and back, but the show itself was a little disappointing.*
- ADJ+n result **defeat, end, ending, finish, news, outcome, result** *I took lots of photographs but the results were disappointing.*
- ▶ performance **display, performance, season, showing, start** *They discussed the party's disappointing showing in the local elections.*
- ▶ amount or number **attendance, figure, response, sales, turnout** *The album's disappointing sales led to many rumours concerning the future of the group.*
- v+ADJ **be, prove, remain, seem, sound** *In the end, the much-anticipated conference proved disappointing.*

disappointment N

1 a disappointed feeling

- adj+N **bitter, considerable, crushing, deep, extreme, grave, great, immense, intense, massive, profound, severe, utter** *He expressed extreme disappointment in the company's performance. • I found to my great disappointment that the book was out of print.*
- v+N feel disappointment **experience, feel, share, suffer** *I share your disappointment that more girls are not choosing careers in science.*
- ▶ hide your disappointment **conceal, hide** *'It wasn't too bad,' said Rory, trying to conceal his disappointment at not being closer.*
- ▶ show your disappointment **express, voice** *Davies was quick to voice his disappointment with the referee.*
- ▶ cause disappointment **cause, compound** *Sorry for any disappointment caused to regular visitors.*
- ▶ reduce or deal with disappointment **avoid, offset, overcome, temper** *You have to be able to overcome minor disappointments.*
- N+v **arise, await sb, follow** *Disappointment awaits the overconfident!*
- and/or **anger, discouragement, disillusion, disillusionment, dismay, frustration, grief, hurt, regret, sadness, sorrow, surprise, vexation** *Frustration and disappointment with the service could lead customers to go elsewhere.*

2 someone or something disappointing

- adj+N big **big, bitter, considerable, crushing, great, huge, major, massive, profound, severe, terrible** *This came as a bitter disappointment to all involved. • It is a great disappointment that Government has refused to act.*
- ▶ small **slight** *The one slight disappointment was the lack of original material.*
- v+N **be, come as, prove** *He rehearsed very hard for the concert, which unfortunately proved a great disappointment.*

disapproval N

a feeling of not approving of someone or something

- adj+N strong/not strong **deep, mild, severe, stern, strong** *The United States has expressed its strong disapproval at these moves.*
- ▶ clearly expressed/not clearly expressed **implicit,**

obvious *She set out to overcome his obvious disapproval of her.*

▶ among a lot of people **general, public, universal, widespread** *Despite overwhelming public disapproval, some cosmetic companies continue to test their products on animals.*

You can also say that there is *a chorus of disapproval* when a lot of people express disapproval of something: *When it was reported that the government was considering such a change, there was a chorus of disapproval.*

▶ from a particular source **official, parental, social** *The best deterrents to youth crime are detection and parental disapproval.*

▶ for moral or religious reasons **moral, religious** *More couples now cohabit, free of the social and religious disapproval of past generations.*

● v+N show disapproval **evince, express, indicate, mark, register, show, vent, voice** *She immediately voiced her disapproval of what I was wearing.*

▶ be the object of disapproval **arouse, earn, face, incur, provoke, risk** *New or higher taxes always incur the disapproval of the people.*

disapproving ADJ
showing someone does not approve of something

● adv+ADJ very **very** *They were giving me very disapproving looks.*

▶ not very **faintly, rather, vaguely** *Her tone when she spoke to me was vaguely disapproving.*

● ADJ+n expression **face, frown, gaze, glance, look, stare** *I didn't get any disapproving stares, just sympathetic smiles.*

▶ remark **comment, noises, tone, voice** *Everyone stood around making disapproving noises but nobody actually complained.*

disaster N
1 something causing great damage or killing many people

● adj+N very bad **catastrophic, major, terrible, worst** *A relatively small incident was turned into a major disaster when the mine manager insisted on sending men back into the mine.*

▶ likely to happen **imminent, impending, looming, potential** *Humanitarian agencies are warning of an impending disaster in the city.*

▶ caused by weather and other natural events **earthquake, flood, humanitarian, hurricane, natural, quake, tsunami** *The devastation caused by this terrible natural disaster is becoming apparent.*

▶ affecting the environment **climate-related, ecological, environmental** *There is no doubt that the our over-dependence on oil led to this ecological disaster.*

▶ causing great human suffering **humanitarian** *Following the war and the famine, the country was on the brink of a humanitarian disaster.*

▶ involving transport **air, ferry, maritime, rail, shipping, tanker, train** *This was the worst rail disaster in Ireland's history.*

▶ at a mine **colliery, mining, pit** *82 people were killed in a mining disaster.*

● v+N suffer a disaster **be affected by, be**

devastated by, be hit by, experience, face, suffer *There was a massive effort to help the millions of people affected by the disaster.*

▶ cause or be a disaster **be, bring, cause, mean, spell** *This monopoly spells disaster for the ill and the poor in developing nations.*

▶ avoid disaster **avert, avoid, prevent** *A guard prevented the men from lighting the fuse, averting potential disaster.*

▶ predict disaster **foresee, foretell, portend, predict** *Scientists predict environmental disaster if we do not act now.*

▶ do something that makes disaster likely **court, invite, risk** *By ignoring his generals' warnings, Napoleon was simply courting disaster.*

● N+v happen **befall sb/sth, engulf sb/sth, happen, occur, overtake sb/sth, overwhelm sb/sth, strike, unfold** *Then, the day before the ceremony, disaster struck.*

▶ threaten to happen **await sb/sth, loom, threaten sb/sth** *There were concerns that another humanitarian disaster was looming.*

You can also say that something is *a disaster waiting to happen*: *According to the report, stored nuclear waste is a disaster waiting to happen.*

● N+n to combat disaster **appeal, fund, management, mitigation, plan, planning, preparedness, prevention, recovery, reduction, relief, response** *The Red Cross is working with the Government to develop disaster preparedness plans.*

▶ affected by disaster **area, victim, zone** *There have been outbreaks of cholera in the disaster zone.*

2 something completely unsuccessful

● adj+N complete **absolute, complete, total, unmitigated, utter** *Their previous league game had been an unmitigated disaster.*

▶ types of disaster **box-office, electoral, fashion, financial, public relations** *Buying a property to let can be a good investment, or it can be a financial disaster.*

disastrous ADJ
causing a lot of damage or harm

● adv+ADJ very **absolutely, particularly, so, totally, truly, utterly** *This was absolutely disastrous for businesses and homeowners.*

▶ rather **fairly, pretty INFORMAL, quite, rather** *To be 4 points down compared with the last poll is pretty disastrous.*

▶ possibly **possibly, potentially, ultimately** *The new rules will have potentially disastrous implications for poor countries.*

▶ in a particular way **ecologically, economically, environmentally, financially, politically, socially** *Building the new road would be not only prohibitively expensive, but environmentally disastrous.*

● ADJ+n consequence **consequence, effect, impact, result** *He pressed the button again, this time with disastrous results.*

▶ decision or action **attempt, campaign, decision, failure, miscalculation, mistake, policy** *We must not repeat the disastrous mistakes of the 1930s.*

▶ event **battle, defeat, earthquake, fire, flood,**

marriage, start, war *About 100 years ago, a disastrous fire swept through the building.* • *Their voyage got off to a disastrous start.*

- v+ADJ **be, prove** *The campaign against the Russians in the early months of 1915 proved disastrous.*

disbelief N
the feeling of not believing someone or something

- adj+N complete **absolute, complete, sheer, total, utter** *We looked on in utter disbelief.*
- ▶ shocked **horrified, open-mouthed, shocked, stunned** *She listened with stunned disbelief as he explained that the crash had not been an accident.*
- ▶ among many people **general, widespread** *There was widespread disbelief that ordinary people like us could make any difference.*
- v+N express disbelief **declare, express, voice** *Some people express disbelief at their diagnosis.*
- ▶ put aside disbelief **suspend** *This is extremely unlikely, but let us suspend our disbelief and ask what impact it might have.*
- v+in+N **gasp, groan, listen, look, stare, watch** *This recording had me gasping in disbelief, and then laughing out loud at the sheer audacity of it all.*
- and/or **amazement, anger, denial, despair, disgust, dismay, horror, numbness, shock** *No words can convey the shock, horror and disbelief at what has taken place.*

discernible ADJ
able to be seen, noticed, or understood

- adv+ADJ almost not **barely, faintly, hardly, just, scarcely** *The sign has a turquoise stripe with a barely discernible logo in the corner.*
- ▶ very **clearly, easily, immediately, plainly, readily** *His influence on the policy is clearly discernible.*
- ADJ+n change or difference **change, difference, improvement, shift** *You could run your car on the oil with no discernible difference in its performance.*
- ▶ effect **benefit, effect, impact, influence** *The US government has been waging a high profile war on opium production, but with no discernible impact.*
- ▶ pattern **connection, logic, pattern, relationship, tendency, theme, trend** *There is a discernible pattern linking inequality with environmental damage.*

Usage **Discernible** is very often used in negative constructions in all of the **ADJ+n** patterns shown above: *There has been no discernible adverse effect on employment.* • *We saw no discernible trend in the mortality rate.*

discharge V
to perform a duty

- adv+V **effectively, efficiently, faithfully, properly, satisfactorily** *Probation officers say they lack the resources to be able to properly discharge their duties.*
- V+n **duty, function, obligation, responsibility** *Members of staff must discharge their responsibilities in accordance with the law.*

discipline N
control over people's behaviour by making them obey rules

- adj+N strict **rigid, strict** *They were offered shelter and food, but under a regime of strict discipline.*
- ▶ in a particular place **classroom, prison, school** *The teacher must be able to maintain classroom discipline.*
- ▶ not strict **lax** *The report criticizes the management for 'lax discipline' in the use of explosives in the mine.*
- v+N impose discipline **enforce, exercise, impose, instil, maintain, practise, restore** *The expedition was run in military style, with discipline imposed from the top.*
- ▶ require discipline **involve, require, take** *Putting these principles into practice takes discipline.*
- ▶ lack discipline **lack** *Although he had the skill to achieve great things, he admits that he lacked the discipline.*
- and/or **dedication, patience, restraint, rigour, self-control** *We can help to instil the dedication and discipline the children need in order to achieve their goals.*

disclose V
to give information to people

- adv+V to everyone **clearly, fully, openly, publicly** *The judge stunned Africa when he publicly disclosed that he was living with Aids.*
- ▶ deliberately **knowingly, voluntarily, wilfully** *Information we hold about you will not be voluntarily disclosed to any third party.*
- ▶ carelessly **inadvertently, recklessly** *If you inadvertently disclose your password to anyone, you should change it immediately.*
- ▶ according or not according to law **improperly, lawfully, properly, unlawfully** *This is yet more evidence that was not properly disclosed.*
- V+n facts **address, content, data, detail, existence, fact, information, transaction, whereabouts** *There are situations in which a teacher may have to disclose information told to them in confidence.*
- ▶ something that has been secret **identity, name, password, secret** *He reportedly disclosed secrets of his country's military capability.*
- ▶ information about yourself or your past **conviction, disability, misconduct, sexuality, status, wrongdoing** *There is no obligation to disclose your marital status.*
- ▶ document **documents, papers** *In litigation, parties must disclose all documents that are relevant to the issues.*

disclosure N
the process of giving information to people

- adj+N open and honest **frank, full, public** *There should be full public disclosure of the resulting report.*
- ▶ not allowed or not right **improper, inappropriate, unauthorized, unlawful, unwarranted** *Encryption on data files does help against the threat of unauthorized information disclosure.*

▶ not deliberate **accidental, inadvertent** *Accidental disclosure of personal information is not uncommon.*

▶ made willingly **discretionary, voluntary** *Officials needed guidance when deciding whether or not to make a discretionary disclosure of secret government information.*

▶ made because a law or rule forces you **mandatory** *We want the government to make environmental disclosure mandatory for British companies.*

● v+N make a disclosure **make** *Laws exist to protect employees who make a disclosure of wrongdoing to their employer.*

▶ allow or order disclosure **authorize, compel, force, order, permit, require** *This rule requires the disclosure of all relevant personal, financial or other business interests.*

▶ ask for disclosure **demand, request, seek** *They sued the bank and sought disclosure of numerous documents.*

▶ prevent disclosure **avoid, prevent, prohibit, refuse** *They were accused of deliberately destroying records to prevent their disclosure.*

● N+of of information **data, evidence, facts, identity, information** *There will be no disclosure of the identity of the donor.*

▶ of financial information **asset, interest, ownership, transaction** *Divorce procedure requires both parties to make full disclosure of their financial assets.*

▶ of something about yourself **conviction, disability** *One of the main reasons for non disclosure of a disability is fear of discrimination.*

▶ of a document **document, documentation, material, records, report** *The judge may order disclosure of material which the prosecution is not willing to disclose.*

discomfort N
a feeling of slight pain or unhappiness

● adj+N severe **acute, considerable, extreme, much, obvious, severe** *The accident left him unable to walk without severe discomfort.*

▶ slight **a little, little, mild, minimal, minor, moderate, momentary, slight, temporary** *You may feel a little discomfort in the arm at first.*

▶ in a body part **abdominal, breast, chest, pelvic, physical, stomach, visual** *He was suffering from abdominal discomfort and weight loss.*

● v+N cause discomfort **cause (sb)** *His old injury still causes him some discomfort.*

▶ feel discomfort **experience, feel, suffer, tolerate** *If you feel any discomfort or pain when you exercise, do not continue.*

▶ reduce or prevent discomfort **alleviate, avoid, ease, minimize, prevent, reduce, relieve, spare sb** *She was given a pain killer to relieve any discomfort from her swollen eye.* ● *If he had pleaded guilty to start with, it would have spared the jury the discomfort of sitting through hours of testimony.*

● N+v **accompany sth, arise from sth, be associated with sth, follow sth, result from sth** *Little or no discomfort is associated with this form of the disease.*

discontent N
the feeling of not being satisfied with something

● adj+N widespread **general, mass, popular, public, universal, widespread** *This widespread discontent came to a head with a two month long strike in 1812.*

▶ strong **bitter, considerable, deep, great, profound, seething** *Corruption creates profound discontent among citizens.*

▶ increasing **growing, increasing, rising, simmering** *There is increasing discontent among Internet users with Web advertising.*

▶ types of discontent **economic, political, social** *Religious and ethnic strife has continued, fuelled by economic discontent.*

● v+N express discontent **express, register, voice** *Voters may come to the polls with the sole intent of registering their discontent with the administration.*

● cause discontent **arouse, breed, cause, engender, foment, fuel, provoke** *Economic stagnation has fuelled popular discontent.*

● N+v **arise, grow, rise, spread** *Discontent steadily grew among the people.*

discount N
a reduction in the price of something

● adj+N large **big, generous, hefty, huge, massive, significant, substantial** *Large retailers can use their buying power to obtain substantial discounts.*

▶ special **exclusive, introductory, online, preferential, special** *Sign up to our newsletter to receive exclusive discounts on hundreds of gardening products.*

● v+N offer a discount **allow, give sb, grant sb, offer** *We are often able to offer further discounts to our web customers.*

▶ get a discount **attract, be entitled to, claim, earn, enjoy, get, obtain, qualify for, receive** *Members receive a 10 % discount off ticket prices.*

▶ agree a discount **arrange, negotiate, secure** *The college has arranged a discount for its students at a local fitness centre.*

discourse N
language or discussion of a particular type

● adj+N written/spoken **spoken, written** *We studied the frequency of occurrence of certain words in spoken discourse.*

▶ in a particular field **academic, critical, cultural, feminist, ideological, literary, mathematical, moral, philosophical, political, religious, scholarly, scientific, theological, theoretical** *She argues that women have been excluded from academic discourse.*

▶ generally used **contemporary, dominant, mainstream, public** *Although highly mathematical, these concepts have entered public discourse.*

● v+N analyse discourse **analyze, examine, explore** *Researchers analyzed the discourse of the interviewers and the participants.*

▶ influence discourse **construct, dominate, enter, frame, permeate, shape** *Political discourse is now dominated by moralizing.*

discovery N
the process of learning something new or finding something hidden or lost

● adj+N new **latest, new, recent** *Another recent discovery, made just a few days ago, is that there is a tree growing out of the stonework.*

▶ surprising or interesting **amazing, exciting, interesting, remarkable, shocking, startling, surprising, unexpected** *But workers have encountered a number of problems, including the unexpected discovery of electricity cables.*

▶ important **great, groundbreaking, important, major, significant** *Cinchona, or 'Quinine Bark' is one of the rainforest's most famous plants and most important discoveries.*

▶ types of discovery **academic, archaeological, mathematical, scientific** *Founded in 1920, Swansea is a vibrant, research-led university at the forefront of academic and scientific discovery.*

▶ v+N make a discovery **make** *Scholars have dreamt of making such discoveries for centuries.*

▶ cause a discovery to take place **lead to** *A search of the surrounding area led to the discovery of a possible crime scene.*

▶ after making a discovery **follow** *The police have now called off the search following the discovery of a body.*

▶ tell people about a discovery **announce, describe, report** *Archaeologists have announced the discovery of one of the largest prehistoric hill forts in Britain.*

▶ wait for a discovery to take place **await** *Of the 1.5 million species of animal that have been described, 1 million are insects (and there are many more that await discovery and naming).*

discredit V
make people stop respecting someone or trusting something [usually passive]

● adv+V **completely, increasingly, largely, thoroughly, totally, utterly, widely** *The current drug testing regime is thoroughly discredited.*

● V+n **argument, evidence, idea, theory** *Modern science has discredited theories of biological racial superiority.*

discrepancy N
a difference between things that should be the same

● adj+N when a discrepancy seems to exist **apparent, unexplained** *How do you explain the apparent discrepancy between the two sets of figures?*

▶ large or important **big, great, huge, large, major, marked, obvious, serious, significant, wide** *There was a significant discrepancy between the two figures.*

▶ small or not important **minor, slight, small** *There are some minor discrepancies in the ages of the dead according to different sources.*

● v+N explain a discrepancy **account for, explain** *Can you explain the discrepancy between the experimental and the theoretical value?*

▶ notice a discrepancy **detect, discover, find, find, identify, note, notice** *If you notice any discrepancies in any of the data, please inform us so that we can amend our records.*

▶ show a discrepancy **highlight, point out, reveal, show** *The paper highlights the discrepancy between the share of the vote for the main parties and their representation in the House of Commons.*

▶ deal with a discrepancy **correct, resolve** *The best way of resolving any discrepancy between my memory and the official records would have been to show me the latter.*

● N+v **arise, exist, occur** *Should errors or discrepancies arise, there should be agreed processes which deal with claims or complaints.*

discretion N
1 the right or ability to make a decision

● adj+N when one person or group has complete discretion **absolute, complete, entire, sole, unfettered** *The implementation of controls is at the absolute discretion of Immigration Officers.*

▶ over a range of areas **broad, wide** *The court retains a wide discretion when it comes to deciding who should get what.*

▶ types of discretion **judicial, local** *This is ultimately a matter for local discretion.*

● v+N use discretion **exercise, use** *In all other respects he was allowed to exercise his discretion as he saw fit.*

▶ have discretion **have** *Officers have the discretion to decide what is reasonable in the circumstances.*

▶ give someone discretion or let them use it **give sb, leave sth to** *The government has proposed to give local authorities discretion to negotiate these contracts.* ● *Payment terms shall be left to the discretion of the Board.*

● and/or **confidentiality, flexibility, judgment** *The government wants to give greater discretion and flexibility to the regions.*

2 careful and sensitive behaviour

● adj+N **great, utmost** *Your personal information will be treated with the utmost discretion.*

● v+N **call for, need, require** *These are important occasions that require discretion and privacy.*

discriminate V
treat someone unfairly because of their race, religion etc

● adv+V not in a direct way **indirectly** *She claimed that she had been indirectly discriminated against by being required to work full-time.*

▶ in a direct way **actively, directly** *Scotland is now actively discriminating against students from the rest of the UK.*

▶ happening frequently **systematically** *Some governments use the law to establish authoritarian states which systematically discriminate against minority groups.*

▶ in an unfair or illegal way **unfairly, unlawfully** *He felt that he had been unfairly discriminated against because of his disability.*

▶ because of someone's race **racially** *He claimed that he had been racially discriminated against between July 1999 and September 2002.*

▶ in a way that gives special benefits to someone **positively** *More and more investors and customers are positively discriminating in favour of green companies or organizations.*

discrimination N
unfair treatment because of religion, race etc

● adj+N types of discrimination **ethnic, racial, religious, sexual** *The Commission for Racial Equality exists to tackle racial discrimination and promote racial equality.*

▶ obvious or direct **blatant, direct, overt** *Direct discrimination occurs when a person is treated less favourably than others on grounds of sex or on racial grounds.*

▶ not direct **indirect** *Companies may be guilty of indirect discrimination without knowing it.*

▶ unfair or illegal **unfair, unjustifiable, unjustified, unlawful** *All advertisements must be free from any unlawful discrimination.*

▶ giving special benefits to someone **positive** *It is possible to offer more favourable treatment to disabled people and students as long as this does not take the form of positive discrimination.*

▶ claimed but not proved **alleged** *You must make your complaint no later than three months after the date of the alleged discrimination.*

▶ happening frequently **systematic** *Women are everywhere victims of systematic discrimination, oppression and sexual abuse.*

▶ in a particular company or profession **institutional** *The Disability Discrimination Act calls for the public sector to root out institutional discrimination and create positive attitudes towards disabled people.*

● n+N **age, disability, employment, gender, race, sex, sexual-orientation** *He has recently appeared in cases of sex discrimination, disability discrimination and whistle-blowing.*

● v+N experience discrimination **experience, face, suffer** *One mother thought she faced discrimination because she was too old, and one because she was too young.*

▶ end or prevent discrimination **avoid, challenge, combat, eliminate, end, fight, outlaw, prevent, prohibit, tackle** *Two weeks ago the government announced draft legislation to outlaw age discrimination in the workplace.*

▶ allow discrimination to continue **institutionalize, justify, perpetuate, tolerate** *The bill actually perpetuates existing discrimination by religious organizations.*

▶ be considered discrimination **amount to, constitute** *Where an employer refuses a request for part-time working, a refusal may amount to indirect sex discrimination.*

● n+of+N **form** *Sussex Police prides itself on being an equal opportunity employer, encouraging diversity and working hard to stamp out any form of discrimination.*

● and/or **abuse, bias, harassment, intolerance, oppression, persecution, prejudice, racism, stigma** *He collected evidence of numerous incidents of persecution and discrimination against Christians.*

discuss V
talk or write about something

● adv+V thoroughly or in detail **at length, endlessly, extensively, fully, in detail, thoroughly, widely** *These considerations are discussed in more detail below.*

▶ for a short time **briefly** *We did briefly discuss the question of costs.*

▶ not hiding anything, or in public **freely, openly, publicly** *The school should discuss openly and honestly any bullying or other problems with parents of the pupils involved.*

▶ in a way that is relaxed and not official **informally** *Applicants wishing to informally discuss the post prior to application may ring Clive Hutton on the number below.*

▶ in an official way **formally** *Each topic is methodically and formally discussed and recommendations are made.*

▶ in a careful and considered way **explicitly, rationally, seriously, specifically** *Can globalization be discussed rationally without bringing politics into it?*

● V+n **idea, issue, matter, plan, possibility, problem, proposal, question, situation, subject, topic** *Many of these issues are discussed in the next chapter.*

discussion N
a conversation about something, usually something important

● adj+N long or detailed **detailed, extensive, full, in-depth, lengthy, long, ongoing** *We can put you in touch with relevant tutors for more detailed discussion of available courses.*

▶ short **brief** *The Committee then held a brief discussion about the content of an application under Article 14.*

▶ general **general** *He tried to draw everyone into a general discussion.*

▶ informal **informal** *I have had informal discussions with the project manager and she is optimistic that they will complete the project by September.*

▶ describing the character of the discussion **constructive, frank, heated, interesting, lively, open, serious** *The two talks were followed by very lively discussion in the seminar room.*

▶ taking place on the Internet **online** *It is recommended that you have regular access to a computer so that you can get involved in online discussions.*

● n+N **class, group, panel, round-table** *Students will be expected to take part in class discussions.*

● v+N have a discussion **have, hold** *We are currently having discussions about what exactly we will put on the site.*

▶ take part in a discussion **be involved in, engage in, enter into, join in, participate in, take part in** *He was pleasant and entered into the discussions along with everyone else.*

▶ encourage a discussion to take place **encourage, facilitate, initiate, promote, prompt, provoke, stimulate** *Humour is used to stimulate discussions and writing.*

▶ start or continue a discussion **begin, continue, open, start** *We have started discussions with the council about the future of the racecourse, but we are at the very early stages of consultation.*

● N+v when a discussion takes place or continues **continue, ensue, take place** *Detailed discussions have taken place with the Department of Health at the highest level.*

▶ when a discussion ends or after something happens **conclude, follow, summarize** *The working group has been set up to conclude discussions by next June.*

▶ be the main person in a discussion **dominate, guide, lead** *There was a general discussion led by*

Professor Ward in relation to the library development.

▶ what a discussion is about **centre on sth, focus on sth** *The fact that the discussion centred largely on drug abuse is a reflection of the level of public concern on the issue.*

disdain N

the feeling that someone or something does not deserve respect

● adj+N **great, lofty, utter** *His utter disdain for economists and economics is well known.*

● v+N show disdain **display, express, show** *He attempts to show his disdain for social conventions by adopting a bizarre mode of dress.*

▶ have disdain **have, treat sb/sth with** *Her remarks were treated by the press with complete disdain.*

● n+of+N **look** *The cat paused and gave me a look of monumental disdain.*

● and/or **arrogance, contempt, scorn**

disease N

an illness affecting people or animals

● adj+N describing how a person or animal gets a disease **contagious, genetic, infectious** *Ornithosis is an infectious disease that affects many bird species worldwide.*

▶ serious **chronic, fatal, incurable, serious, severe** *Malaria is a serious and sometimes fatal disease transmitted by mosquitoes.*

▶ where the disease comes from **airborne, food-borne, fungal, seed-borne, soil-borne, waterborne** *Good practices will help reduce infant and child mortality by eradicating waterborne diseases that flourish in unsanitary conditions.*

● v+N get a disease **acquire, catch, contract, develop, get** *It is believed the man, who has not been named, caught the disease while on holiday.*

▶ have a disease **harbour, have, suffer from** *She suffers from chronic respiratory disease.*

▶ die from a disease **die from, die of** *His father died of heart disease at the age of 56.*

▶ cause or spread a disease **carry, cause, spread, transmit** *The disease is caused by a deficiency of vitamin B in the diet.*

▶ find out what disease someone has **detect, diagnose** *The prognosis is good if the disease is diagnosed and treated early*

▶ cure or treat a disease **cure, treat** *The improved survival rates are a result of the advances that have been made in successfully treating this disease.*

▶ work to get rid of a disease **combat, conquer, control, eradicate, fight, prevent** *Thanks to modern science, we have conquered the smallpox disease and it no longer occurs naturally.*

● N+v **affect sb, spread** *Other statistical techniques can use patient data to understand how a disease spreads, without testing it on animals.*

▶ n+of+N **outbreak, risk, spread, treatment** *The government is taking positive steps to prevent the spread of the disease and fight its effects.*

disgrace N

1 the loss of other people's respect

● v+N bring disgrace **bring** *She'd brought disgrace on her family, shame, indeed, on the whole village.*

▶ be in disgrace **be in, fall into** *I was in disgrace at the time, because I had set the dormitory on fire the night before.*

2 someone or something very bad

● adj+N complete **absolute, complete, total, utter** *It is an absolute disgrace that she didn't win.*

▶ involving people in general **national, public** *The performance of our privatized railways is, by common consent, a national disgrace.*

● N+to **country, family, humanity, name, profession** *In my opinion he is a disgrace to the legal profession.*

disgraceful ADJ

extremely bad or shocking

● adv+ADJ **absolutely, quite, utterly** *It's absolutely disgraceful the way Michael has been treated.*

● ADJ+n how someone behaves **behaviour, conduct, manner, treatment** *This was quite disgraceful behaviour, especially as it involved people in the emergency services.*

▶ result of someone's actions **incident, scene, state** *She complains very bitterly in her diary of the disgraceful state of the roads.*

disguise V

hide your feelings, intentions etc

● adv+V **barely, thinly** *'Look,' he said, with barely disguised exasperation.*

● V+n what is true or real **fact, reality, truth** *I tried to sound casual to disguise the fact that I was having a ridiculously wonderful time.*

▶ what you intend to do **intentions** *Both parties endeavoured to disguise their real intentions.*

▶ why you do something **motive** *He accused board members of disguising their real motives for introducing the policy.*

> Usage **Motive** is almost always plural in this combination.

▶ lack of respect **contempt** *Hunter replied with barely disguised contempt.*

disgust N

a strong feeling of not liking something or being angry about something

● adj+N complete **absolute, much, outright, total, utter** *She looked at him in utter disgust.*

▶ great **deep, great** *He insisted on smoking throughout the journey, to the great disgust of his fellow passengers.*

● v+N express disgust **express, register, show, voice** *The reason that I am contacting you is to express my utter disgust at your current advertising campaign.*

▶ feel disgust **demonstrate, feel** *Like everyone else who witnessed these scenes, I felt total disgust.*

▶ not show disgust **conceal, hide** *Erasmus did not conceal his disgust at being excommunicated.*

● n+of+N **expression, feeling, look, sense** *She put*

the glass to her lips, but, having tasted the liquor, she returned it with a look of disgust.

dishonest ADJ
willing to do things that are not honest

- adv+ADJ completely **downright, thoroughly, utterly** *Any introduction agency that claims that they will definitely find your perfect partner is being unrealistic or downright dishonest!*
- ▶ in a basic way **fundamentally** *There is the perception that the government is fundamentally dishonest and politicians are not to be trusted.*
- ▶ when discussing ideas **intellectually** *His blind assertion that 'prison works' appears as empirically untrue as it was always intellectually dishonest.*

- ADJ+n behaviour **behaviour, claim, conduct, practice** *Such cynical and essentially dishonest behaviour brings shame on the whole profession.*
- ▶ people **dealer, employee, trader** *Legislators can play an important part in protecting the public from dishonest traders.*

disillusioned ADJ
disappointed by someone or something

- adv+ADJ very **completely, deeply, totally, very** *Pollsters report that the public is totally disillusioned **with** politics and political campaigns.*
- ▶ more and more **increasingly** *With people becoming increasingly disillusioned **with** supermarkets, traditional markets could be poised for a revival.*

- v+ADJ become **become, get, grow** *As a result of a number of serious work-based assaults she grew disillusioned **with** her chosen vocation.*
- ▶ feel **feel** *If people feel disillusioned **about** politics, they are less likely to go out and vote.*

- and/or **bored, disappointed, frustrated** *She became increasingly disillusioned and frustrated **with** her role as a teacher.*

dislike V
not like someone or something

- adv+V strongly **actively, greatly, intensely, particularly, really, strongly** *His middle name was Arthur, which he disliked intensely.*
- ▶ by many people **generally, universally, widely** *The new shopping centre is almost universally disliked.*

- and/or **like** *Tell us what you like and dislike **about** our new website.*

dislike N
a feeling of not liking someone or something

- adj+N strong **deep, great, intense, strong** *She had an intense dislike of cats.*
- ▶ immediate **instant** *The two take an instant dislike to one another, but have to find ways to coexist.*
- ▶ between two people **mutual, personal** *These allegations could have been motivated or exaggerated by personal dislike.*

- v+N feel dislike **have, share, take** *It seems that my new boss has taken a dislike to me.*
- ▶ show dislike **express, show** *Some boys actually expressed a strong dislike of reading.*

- and/or **likes** *She went out of her way to find out his likes and dislikes.*

> Usage ***Dislike*** is always plural in this combination.

dismay N
a worried, disappointed, or sad feeling about something

- adj+N great **deep, great, much, utter** *To my great dismay, this useful service is no longer available.*
- ▶ felt by many people **widespread** *This decision was met with widespread dismay.*

- v+N express dismay **express, voice** *I would wish to express my dismay **at** the editor's decision to allow publication of this letter.*
- ▶ react with dismay **greet sth with, react with** *The news was greeted with dismay by wildlife campaigners.*
- ▶ cause dismay **cause** *The court's decision will cause dismay among broadcasters.*
- ▶ feel dismay **feel** *I felt their dismay as they travelled home having lost 2–0.*

- and/or **anger, concern, disbelief, horror, shock, surprise** *Human rights groups have reacted with anger and dismay at the decision to build the new oil pipeline.*

dismiss V
refuse to accept that something might be true or important

- adv+V quickly or immediately **immediately, quickly, summarily** *Beth quickly dismissed the notion **as** absurd.*
- ▶ completely **out of hand** *This suggestion was dismissed out of hand.*
- ▶ without difficulty or careful thought **casually, easily, lightly, simply** *These fears should not be dismissed so lightly.*
- ▶ in a way that shows lack of respect **arrogantly, contemptuously** *They contemptuously dismissed warnings about spiralling costs.*

- V+n what is being said or written **accusation, allegation, claim, complaint, concern, criticism, report, rumour, speculation, suggestion** *A spokeswoman dismissed the claim that the show was in bad taste.*
- ▶ an idea or argument **argument, evidence, idea, notion, possibility, theory** *He dismissed the idea that a change in the leadership would be desirable or even possible.*
- ▶ what people worry about **concern, fear, worry** *Scientists have dismissed fears of a 'Brave New World' of cloned superhumans.*

dismissal N
an act of making someone leave their job

- adj+N unfair or illegal **constructive, unfair, unlawful, wrongful** *She claimed that the company's conduct amounted to unfair dismissal.*
- ▶ happening immediately **automatic, immediate, instant, summary** *Failure to comply with these regulations will result in instant dismissal.*
- ▶ fair or legal **disciplinary, fair, statutory** *The arbitrator will come to a decision as to whether the dismissal was fair.*

● v+N claim dismissal of a particular type **claim** *You are entitled to claim unfair dismissal if your employer sacks you without a good reason.*
▶ experience dismissal **be threatened with, face** *The five members of staff involved were disciplined and could have faced dismissal.*
▶ cause a person's dismissal **lead to, result in** *Accepting a job offer having lied on your application form can lead to dismissal.*
● n+for+N **reason** *You are entitled to written reasons for dismissal from your employer.*

> Usage You can also talk about **the grounds for someone's dismissal**: *He claimed unfair dismissal on the grounds of age.* • *Supplying false information could be grounds for dismissal.*

dismissive ADJ
refusing to consider something as important

● adv+ADJ rather **quite, rather, somewhat** *Geser is rather dismissive of museums' attempts to foster e-learning.*
▶ very **so, very** *There was no mention of his colleagues except in very dismissive terms.*
▶ to the same degree **equally** *She is equally dismissive of modern ballet.*
● ADJ+n what someone says or feels **attitude, comment, remark, response** *I have been pretty disgusted at the dismissive attitude of most of the doctors I have encountered.*
▶ hand movement **gesture, wave** *He did not look up from his papers but made a dismissive gesture with his hand.*

disperse V
1 when a crowd separates and people go in different directions

● adv+V **gradually, quickly, quietly, rapidly, soon** *The soldiers succeeded in capturing 11 of the ringleaders and the rest quickly dispersed.*
● V+n **crowd, demonstrators, group, rioters, settlement** *The police attempted to disperse the crowd.*
● n+V **army, crowd, mob** *The small crowd dispersed, looking worried.*

2 spread, or make things spread, over an area

● adv+V **evenly, geographically, globally, widely** *In comparison with all ethnic groups, the Chinese community is diverse and widely dispersed across Britain.*
● V+n **population, seeds, smoke, spore** *Fruit bats once lived on the island, dispersing seeds and pollinating the island's forests.*
● n+V **cloud, mist** *By evening most of the cloud had dispersed but it was still very hazy.*

display V
show a feeling, quality, or attitude by the way you behave

● adv+V **openly, publicly** *Kerry openly displayed a dislike of Dean on a personal level.*
● V+n **attitude, behaviour, characteristic, courage,** **ignorance, sign, symptom, talent** *The role allowed her to display her considerable comic talents.*

display N
1 an arrangement or performance for people to see

● adj+N very good or impressive **amazing, brilliant, colourful, dazzling, eye-catching, fantastic, fascinating, fine, impressive, magnificent, spectacular, stunning, superb, wonderful** *The concert was finished off with a spectacular firework display.*
▶ for the public to see **permanent, public, static, temporary** *The gallery has a new permanent display of local artists' work.*
▶ forms of display **3D, audio-visual, computer-generated, digital, electronic, graphical, interactive, LED, photographic, video, visual** *The museum's interactive displays allow you to learn about the intricacies of bank note design and production.*
▶ types of display **aerial, floral** *Stafford is famous for its award-winning floral displays.*
● n+N types of display **air, falconry, firework, flower, flying, parachute** *Attractions include a flying display by vintage aircraft.*
▶ where a display can be seen **exhibition, museum, window** *Come and see our window display of craftwork and jewellery.*
● v+N create a display **arrange, create, make, mount, organize, produce** *When creating and mounting displays, use the expertise of support staff..*
▶ produce a display for people to see **give, perform, produce, put on, treat sb to** *The girls emerged victorious, having put on an exemplary display of attacking play.* • *We were treated to a display of traditional Polish folk dancing.*
▶ be able to be seen in a display **be on, be put on, go on** *The new collection will be put on display in the gallery next month.*
▶ have a display **exhibit, feature, feature, have, host** *The gallery has the largest display of contemporary craft work in the country.*
▶ see a display **see, view, watch** *Huge crowds gathered to watch the excellent air display.*

2 when someone shows a particular feeling, quality etc

● adj+N that people can see **open, public** *His public display of gratitude will be seen as a significant political gesture.*
▶ intended to impress people **impressive, ostentatious** *Avoid ostentatious displays of wealth and keep expensive jewellery, watches and cameras out of sight.*
● N+of **affection, anger, courage, emotion, grief, power, wealth** *Several parents said they would prefer public displays of affection to be discouraged at school.*
● V+n **witness** *This was the only time he had witnessed a display of such anger.*

displeasure N
the feeling of being annoyed or unhappy

● adj+N great **considerable, evident, extreme, great**

*The government has done nothing to conceal its great displeasure **with** these developments.*

▶ of God **divine** *Floods are less likely to be associated with divine displeasure than with greedy property developers building on flood plains.*

● v+N experience someone's displeasure **incur** *He incurred the displeasure of his family when he gave up a business career and took up boxing.*

▶ express one's displeasure **express, register, show, signal, vent, voice** *The medical profession has expressed its displeasure **at** its exclusion from these discussions.*

disposition N
how someone normally thinks and behaves

● adj+N nervous **nervous** *It's gruesome and very graphic, so don't buy this DVD if you are of a nervous disposition!*

▶ happy or friendly **affectionate, amiable, cheerful, cheery, friendly, sunny** *Don was always of a cheerful disposition, and he will be missed.*

▶ quiet or gentle **calm, gentle** *He had a kindly and gentle disposition.*

▶ willing to give time, money etc **benevolent, generous** *He was a man of generous disposition and highly respected.*

● v+N have a particular disposition **have, show** *She has a sunny disposition and a lot of patience.*

dispute N
a serious disagreement

● adj+N with angry feelings **acrimonious, bitter, heated** *This was one of the longest running and most bitter industrial disputes in the history of labour relations.*

▶ serious **fierce, major, serious** *WTO rules have led to a major dispute **between** the EU and the United States over banana imports.*

▶ over a long period **lengthy, long-running, long-standing, ongoing, prolonged, protracted** *Bus drivers are holding a ninth strike in a long-running dispute **over** pay.*

▶ within a group **domestic, internal** *The government is now riven by internal disputes.*

▶ between countries **international** *Countries should try to resolve international disputes through peaceful dialogue and negotiation.*

▶ unimportant dispute **minor, petty** *He bought the land and almost immediately encountered a petty dispute over boundaries.*

▶ types of dispute **civil, commercial, contractual, industrial, legal, matrimonial, political, territorial, theological** *Territorial disputes led to a costly war in which thousands were killed.*

● n+N involving an area of land **border, boundary, land** *I have a boundary dispute **with** a neighbour and need to know the exact area of land that my property occupies.*

▶ types of dispute **contract, employment, family, labour, pay, property, trade** *University lecturers have finally settled their pay dispute.*

● v+N end a dispute **end, resolve, settle, solve** *The vast majority of these disputes are resolved within months.*

▶ have a dispute with someone **be involved in, have**

*For the last two years the company has been involved in a legal dispute **with** a coffee store chain over the use of its logo.*

▶ cause a dispute **cause, lead to** *Parking is an issue that has led to unpleasant neighbourhood disputes.*

▶ deal with a dispute **deal with, handle** *Her caseload includes dealing with commercial disputes.*

▶ try to solve a dispute **adjudicate, arbitrate, decide, determine, mediate** *For over ten years she has mediated disputes involving parties at all educational levels for the Los Angeles courts.*

▶ avoid a dispute **avoid, prevent** *The maintenance of proper records will avoid any dispute as to the amount to be charged.*

● N+v when a dispute happens **arise, erupt, occur** *Any dispute arising from the use of this website shall be governed by the laws of Scotland.*

▶ what a dispute is about **concern sth, involve sb/sth, relate to sth** *The current dispute concerns actors' employment status.*

disregard N
a lack of respect for something

● adj+N complete **absolute, complete, total, utter, wholesale** *She had a total disregard **for** the welfare of the animals in her care.*

▶ not caring or thinking about the effects **arrogant, blatant, callous, cynical, flagrant, reckless, wanton** *The organizers showed a blatant disregard **for** everyone's safety.*

▶ seeming to show disregard **apparent** *We noted the sheer volume of traffic and the apparent disregard **for** the road space of other drivers.*

● v+N show a disregard for something **demonstrate, display, show** *Not only does their behaviour show a disregard **for** the law and other people's property, but also for their own personal safety.*

▶ have a disregard for something **have** *He had a disregard of petty administrative rules.*

● N+of **danger, duty, law, rules** *His conduct throughout showed great courage and absolute disregard of danger.*

disregard V
not consider something important

● adv+V completely **completely, entirely, totally, utterly** *The company seems to have completely disregarded the industry code of practice with regard to health and safety.*

▶ in an obvious way **blatantly, deilberately, flagrantly** *Very few of us drive with the intention of blatantly disregarding speed limits.*

● V+n **advice, evidence, fact, law, right, rule, warning** *Even if we dislike their message, we cannot disregard the fact that millions of people feel strongly enough about it to take to the streets.*

disrespect N
lack of respect for someone or something

● adj+N complete **complete, total, utter** *His act demonstrates a total disrespect **for** women.*

▶ good and sensible **healthy** *She clearly has a healthy disrespect **for** authority.*

- v+N show disrespect **show, treat sb/sth with** *How dare he show such disrespect to his audience.*
- ▶ intend disrespect **intend, mean** *I don't mean any disrespect to the author, but I cannot agree with these comments.*

disruption N
when a problem stops something continuing

- adj+N great or serious **considerable, major, serious, severe, significant, widespread** *The temporary closure has caused severe disruption to motorists using the busy road.*
- ▶ as small as possible **minimal, minimum** *Surveys of the clinics are being carried out to decide how these moves should be managed in order to create minimum disruption.*
- ▶ that cannot be avoided **inevitable, unavoidable** *Some disruption is inevitable with a project of this nature.*
- ▶ not lasting long **short-term, temporary** *We are doing everything we can to minimise any short-term disruption and impact on the environment.*
- ▶ not expected or necessary **unexpected, unnecessary, unplanned** *Employees have the right to take unpaid time off to deal with family emergencies such as illness or the unexpected disruption of childcare arrangements.*
- ▶ types of disruption **economic, social** *The instability of energy supplies may cause serious social disruption.*
- n+N **business, family, network, service, supply, traffic, transport** *A full closure of the central bridge was considered, but severe traffic disruption would have resulted.*
- v+N cause disruption **cause, ensure, lead to** *Further strike action was expected to cause severe disruption during the busy summer months.*
- ▶ experience disruption **experience, face, suffer** *Thousands of bus passengers face disruption if a threatened strike by drivers goes ahead.*
- ▶ avoid disruption **avoid, prevent** *If the work goes ahead as planned, this will prevent major disruption at the beginning of the new term.*
- ▶ reduce disruption **lessen, limit, minimize, reduce** *The work has been scheduled to take place during quiet periods, in order to minimize disruption for road users.*

disruptive ADJ
causing difficulties that prevent something continuing properly

- adv+ADJ very **extremely, highly, seriously, very** *These long working hours can be very disruptive to your home life.*
- ▶ possibly **potentially** *We set out to produce a secure system that alerts airlines to potentially disruptive passengers.*
- ADJ+n behaviour or effect **behaviour, effect, influence** *Support staff will need training in dealing with disruptive behaviour in schools.*
- ▶ people **child, passenger, prisoner, pupil** *Disruptive children in classes damage the education of others.*
- and/or expensive **costly, expensive** *If disputes arise, they can be disruptive and expensive to deal with.*
- ▶ violent or unfriendly **abusive, aggressive, anti-social, destructive, violent** *He was extremely aggressive and disruptive in class.*

dissatisfaction N
a feeling of not being satisfied with something

- adj+N involving many people **general, public, widespread** *There was widespread dissatisfaction with the outcome of these negotiations.*
- ▶ great **considerable, deep, great, much, profound** *The May elections underlined deep dissatisfaction with Labour.*
- ▶ growing **growing, increasing** *There is a growing public dissatisfaction with politicians and politics.*
- n+N **consumer, customer, job** *Working with IT support staff to eliminate problems that cause customer dissatisfaction is a top priority of the Helpdesk.*
- v+N express dissatisfaction **express, voice** *He wrote to the chief executive to express his dissatisfaction with the way the complaint had been handled.*
- ▶ cause dissatisfaction **cause, lead to** *Low morale and increased pressure on remaining staff can cause further dissatisfaction among the work force.*
- ▶ show dissatisfaction **indicate, reflect, reveal** *A recent study revealed widespread dissatisfaction with news coverage.*
- n+of+N cause of dissatisfaction **cause, source** *If your job is a source of dissatisfaction, the signs are probably clear.*
- ▶ expressing or feeling dissatisfaction **expression, feeling, mood, sense** *Their experience has left them feeling a profound sense of dissatisfaction with themselves.*
- ▶ amount of dissatisfaction **degree, level** *The level of student dissatisfaction with library facilities is high.*

dissatisfied ADJ
not satisfied with something

- adv+ADJ very **deeply, increasingly, thoroughly, very** *She had become increasingly dissatisfied with the limited range of roles available to women.*
- ▶ still **still** *If you are still dissatisfied, you can make a formal complaint.*
- ADJ+n **complainant, customer** *Dissatisfied customers who have to wait a long time on jammed phone lines might take their business elsewhere.*
- v+ADJ **become, feel, remain** *If you have already complained to the relevant mobile operator and remain dissatisfied with their response, you can complain to us.*

dissent N
disagreement with the ideas of people in authority

- adj+N types of dissent **political, religious** *The extension of security policies in many countries has been used to suppress political dissent.*
- ▶ within an organization **internal** *Some of the main political parties have been affected by internal dissent.*
- ▶ legal or sensible **legitimate, rational** *The definition of terrorism in the Act is so wide as to endanger legitimate dissent.*

- **v+N** stop dissent **crush, quell, repress, silence, stifle, suppress** *This ban was an attempt to silence all dissent within the party.*
- ▶ allow dissent **tolerate** *It is an ideology that tolerates no dissent.*
- ▶ express dissent **express, show** *Literature is an important way of expressing dissent or criticism.*
- **n+of+N** **expression, suppression, voice** *All the while he has kept his colleagues in their places, stifling any voices of dissent.*

dissertation N
a long piece of writing for a university degree

- **adj+N** as a stage in a person's studies **doctoral, final, final-year, undergraduate** *David is completing a doctoral dissertation on the eighteenth-century British novel.*
- ▶ of a particular length **15,000-, 20,000-word etc** *In the summer term, each student prepares a 10,000-word dissertation.*
- ▶ not published **unpublished** *This account is based on Gorton's unpublished doctoral dissertation at Columbia University.*
- ▶ based on research **research-based** *Part-time students must submit a research-based dissertation of not more than 15,000 words.*
- ▶ that you have to/do not have to do **compulsory, optional** *Assessment includes a compulsory 10,000-word dissertation.*
- **v+N** do a dissertation **do, prepare, produce, undertake, work on, write** *All students undertake a compulsory dissertation on a topic related to their programme of study.*
- ▶ do research for a dissertation **plan, research** *Jessie spent one month researching her dissertation in Japan.*
- ▶ present a dissertation **defend, present, submit** *Candidates are required to submit a dissertation on a subject of their choice.*
- ▶ complete a dissertation **complete, finish** *She has recently completed her PhD dissertation.*
- ▶ be the teacher in charge of a student's dissertation **supervise** *I have supervised MA dissertations on a number of topics, including testing and error analysis.*
- **N+v** **describe sth, examine sth, explore sth, investigate sth** *This dissertation examines the cultural impact of postwar immigration in Great Britain.*
- **N+n** **outline, project, proposal, subject, topic** *Click here to see some of the dissertation topics that students have completed in the last few years.*
- **N+on** **aspect, subject, theme, topic** *The MA also requires a dissertation on a topic of the student's choice.*

distance N
the space between two people, things, or places

- **adj+N** long **considerable, a fair, a good, great, long, vast** *We can provide transport for patients who live a long distance from the hospital.*

When something is a long way from you it is ***in the distance***: *The peaks of the Pyrenees would be seen in the far distance.* If you are a long way from something or someone you may see them ***at/from a distance***: *I've only ever seen him from a distance, never close up.*

- ▶ not very long **reasonable, short, small** *As it was a warm night, they walked the short distance home.*

If you say that a place is ***within walking/driving/cycling distance***, you mean that it is easy to reach by walking, driving, or cycling.

- ▶ not too close **comfortable, discreet, respectful, safe** *Photographs were taken at a respectful distance.*
- **v+N** travel a distance **cover, travel** *We had to travel the whole distance on foot.*
- ▶ travel a distance in a particular way **cycle, drive, swim, walk** *You should be able to swim a distance of 400m with ease.*
- ▶ keep a certain amount of distance between two things **keep, maintain** *Try to maintain a safe distance between your car and the vehicle in front of you.*

distaste N
a feeling of not liking someone or something

- **adj+N** strong **considerable, deep, great, profound, strong** *She was very clear about her profound distaste for politics.*
- ▶ obvious **apparent, clear, evident, obvious** *He looked at the painting with obvious distaste.*
- ▶ felt by a large number of people **general, popular, public, universal, widespread** *The case has highlighted a growing public distaste for performing animals.*
- **v+N** feel distaste **develop, feel, have** *I've always had a deep distaste for the hierarchical structure of most companies.*
- ▶ show distaste **demonstrate, express, show** *The public has shown consistent distaste for factory farming.*
- ▶ hide distaste **conceal, hide** *She made no effort to conceal her distaste for him.*

distinction N
1 a difference between two things

- **adj+N** clear **clear, clear-cut, marked, sharp** *It is important to make a clear distinction between fact and fiction.*
- ▶ important **crucial, fundamental, important** *Robson notes the crucial distinction between political activity and organized violence.*
- ▶ not obvious **fine, subtle** *It's a subtle distinction, but it's a very important one.*
- ▶ false **artificial, false** *Williams makes an artificial distinction between grammar and usage.*
- **v+N** recognize or state a distinction **clarify, draw, make, recognize** *Employers must recognize the distinction between academic success and practical experience.*
- ▶ make sure a distinction remains **keep, maintain, preserve, retain** *To maintain the distinction between judicial and political decisions, the Founding Fathers insisted that the judiciary should be free of political interference.*
- ▶ cause a distinction to become less clear **blur,**

confuse, erode *As a result of the information revolution, the old distinctions **between** different types of media are increasingly being blurred.*
▶ remove a distinction **abolish, challenge, erase, remove** *We want to erase the distinctions **between** learning at school or home.*

2 excellent qualities, skills, or features [always singular]

● adj+N great **considerable, great, high, particular, some** *He's also an academic, and a professor of great distinction.*
▶ not great **dubious** *There were distinguished guests, and there were guests of dubious distinction.*
● N+in **field, sphere, subject, literature, science, engineering etc** *We have two research scholars of the highest distinction in their respective fields.*

distinctive ADJ
easy to recognize because of being different

● adv+ADJ very **extremely, highly, particularly, quite, truly, utterly, very** *Each character in the book is unique and highly distinctive.*
▶ in a particular way **architecturally, culturally, visually** *Our websites are visually distinctive, and our prices are the cheapest you'll ever see.*
● ADJ+n flavour **flavour, taste** *Each dish has its own distinctive flavour and aroma.*
▶ smell **aroma, smell** *The flowers come in a range of colours, and have a very distinctive smell.*
▶ appearance **appearance, lines, look, shape** *One of our strengths is our product's distinctive look.*
▶ pattern or design **livery, mark, marking, pattern, styling** *The airline has its own distinctive green and white livery.*
▶ sound **sound, vocals, voice** *The unique combination gives the band its own distinctive sound.*
▶ characteristic **characteristic, feature, quality, trait** *One of the most distinctive characteristics of the book is the attention to detail.*
▶ character **character, feel, identity, personality, style** *The distinctive character of this place and its people is under threat.*

distinguished ADJ
successful and respected by many people

● adv+ADJ very **eminently, exceptionally, highly** *The book is written by a team of highly distinguished academics.*
▶ known by people around the world **internationally** *The project is led by two internationally distinguished historians.*
● ADJ+n academic **academic, professor, scholar, teacher, economist, historian, scientist etc** *Professor Scruton is a distinguished academic, author, and composer.*
▶ expert **actor, architect, artist, conductor, expert, lawyer, musician, painter, philospher, statesman, writer** *Temirkanov is one of the world's most distinguished conductors and musicians.*
▶ person who attends an event **guest, speaker, visitor** *They invited a wide variety of distinguished speakers to the conference.*
▶ life or work **career, history, past, record** *She went on to have a long and distinguished career in politics.*

▶ opinion that people have **reputation** *Professor Davis enjoys a very distinguished reputation as a historian of religion.*

distort V
make something no longer true or accurate

● adv+V to a great extent **grossly, seriously, severely, significantly** *An error in punctuation can significantly distort the meaning of a sentence.*
▶ completely **completely, totally** *Their remarks appeared in the newspapers in a totally distorted form.*
▶ intentionally **deliberately, systematically, wilfully** *The term 'bias' refers to anything that systematically distorts the results of a research study.*
▶ not very much **slightly** *The programme slightly distorted the evidence in the interests of entertainment.*
● V+n truth or facts **evidence, facts, findings, reality, results, truth** *They have a reputation for lying and distorting the facts.*
▶ how people understand something **meaning, perception, understanding, view** *Translation involves transferring a message into another language without distorting the meaning.*

distortion N
a change making something no longer true

● adj+N extreme **gross, grotesque, serious, severe, significant** *These figures are a gross distortion.*
▶ intentional **deliberate, systematic** *He insisted that there had been no deliberate distortion of the truth.*
● N+of **facts, figures, history, reality, truth** *Many of these media reports are grotesque distortions of reality.*
● and/or **exaggeration, half-truths, inaccuracies, lies, misrepresentation, omissions** *The site contained a number of factual inaccuracies and distortions.*

distraction N
something preventing you concentrating on something else

● adj+N not wanted or needed **annoying, irritating, unhelpful, unnecessary, unwanted, unwelcome** *Many teachers see mobile phones as an unwelcome distraction.*
▶ pleasant **pleasant, welcome** *Rob's arrival came as a welcome distraction from studying.*
▶ not important or lasting only a short time **minor, momentary** *Apart from these minor distractions, my impressions of the book are positive.*
▶ happening often or all the time **constant** *The noise of traffic is a constant distraction.*
● v+N get rid of distractions **avoid, eliminate, minimize, reduce, remove** *As far as possible, try to minimize distractions while you work.*
▶ ignore distractions **ignore, resist** *Successful distance learners can resist constant distractions.*
● N+from activity **activity, business, job, task, work** *They argue that local projects are a distraction from more important tasks.*
▶ aim **focus, goal, objective, purpose** *All this*

paperwork is a distraction from the main purpose of schools: teaching children.

distress N
an unhappy, worried, or upset feeling

- adj+N severe **acute, considerable, deep, extreme, great, severe, significant, substantial** *Noise from neighbours can cause severe distress to people who have to listen to it.*
- ▶ unnecessary **undue, unnecessary** *I would like to offer my sincere apologies for causing you any undue distress.*
- ▶ emotional **emotional, mental, psychological** *We can help you to cope with any emotional distress that may arise during treatment.*
- v+N cause distress **cause (sb), inflict, occasion** *The distress occasioned by his situation could make him very ill.*
- ▶ experience distress **endure, experience, feel, suffer** *I very much regret the distress suffered by Mrs Atkinson, and the sadness caused to her family.*

If you are **in distress**, you are feeling very unhappy, worried, or upset: *When she arrived, she was in obvious distress.*

- ▶ reduce distress **alleviate, ease, minimize, reduce, relieve** *The aim is not to cure the patient, but to alleviate distress and pain.*
- ▶ increase distress **aggravate, exacerbate, increase** *This change has greatly increased the distress caused to victims.*
- n+of+N **cry, expression, feeling, sign, signal, symptom** *The child showed no signs of distress when her mother left.*

distressing ADJ
making you very unhappy, worried, or upset

- adv+ADJ very **deeply, extremely, particularly, profoundly, very** *The death of a close relative can be a deeply distressing time.*
- ▶ rather **quite, rather** *The whole incident has been quite distressing for me.*
- ADJ+n experience **circumstances, event, experience, incident, ordeal, situation, time** *Jenny found the whole experience extremely distressing.*
- ▶ illness **condition, disorder, illness, problem, symptom** *New medicines may relieve the symptoms of this distressing condition.*
- ▶ something that you see **scene, sight** *We were met with the distressing sight of people sleeping on the streets.*
- ▶ news **news** *In episode 2, Rick and Debbie receive distressing news from London.*
- v+ADJ **be, become, find sth** *These symptoms are very distressing to the patient.* • *This report contains photographs which some people may find distressing.*
- and/or **difficult, frightening, painful, stressful, traumatic, unpleasant** *The drug's side effects can be unpleasant and distressing.*

distribution N
1 the process of supplying goods or essential items from a central place to many places or people

- adj+N without limits **free, general** *Ensure that*

your CV is appropriate for general distribution and is not too job-specific.

- ▶ without cost **free** *The leaflet is available for free distribution to schools and colleges.*
- ▶ over a particular area **global, international, local, national, regional, worldwide** *The movie is now enjoying international distribution.*
- v+N **control, ensure, facilitate, handle, manage, organize, oversee** *Our principal task is to handle the distribution of food aid in the affected regions.*
- N+n place or method **centre, chain, channel, depot, network, system** *The efficient management of distribution chains will provide rapid delivery of growth.*
- ▶ agreement **agreement, arrangement, deal, rights** *This move will have no impact on our existing UK distribution agreements.*

2 the way that something is present or available in different amounts over an area

- adj+N equal or fair **equal, equitable, even, fair** *How can we ensure an equitable distribution of the earth's resources?*
- ▶ not equal or not fair **patchy, skewed, unequal, uneven, unfair** *The unequal distribution of wealth excludes millions of people from the globalized world.*
- ▶ over an area **geographic, geographical, global, local, regional, worldwide** *The study aims to establish the geographical distribution of the insect in the British Isles.*
- ▶ in many places **broad, wide, widespread** *In Egypt the plant seems to have had a wider distribution.*
- ▶ in few places **restricted** *The other two species had a much more restricted distribution.*

distrust N
a feeling of not trusting someone or something

- adj+N strong **deep, extreme, great, intense, profound** *He had a deep distrust of wealth and power.*
- ▶ becoming stronger **deepening, growing, increasing** *There is an increasing distrust of public institutions.*
- ▶ felt by many people **general, public, widespread** *There was a general distrust of all strangers.*
- ▶ felt in the same way by each of two or more groups or people **mutual** *These differences of opinion led to mutual distrust between the two nations.*
- ▶ sensible and based on good reasons **healthy** *I had always had a healthy distrust of anyone trying to sell me something.*
- v+N cause distrust **arouse, cause, create, engender, foster, inspire, provoke, sow** *This report has provoked a distrust of doctors by some patients.*
- ▶ feel distrust **have** *My parents had a deep distrust of all things foreign.*
- ▶ show distrust **display, express, reveal, show** *They expressed their extreme distrust of politicians.*
- ▶ stop feeling distrust **overcome** *The course aims to help beginners overcome their distrust of computers.*
- n+of+N **atmosphere, climate, feeling** *Their refusal to share information created an atmosphere of distrust.*

disturb V
stop a situation being pleasant or peaceful

- V+n peace **calm, peace, silence, tranquillity** *There is no traffic to disturb your peace.*
- ▸ sleep **repose, sleep, slumber** *Pain is something that often disturbs sleep.*
- ▸ balance **balance, equilibrium, harmony** *Bringing up old memories of the past could disturb your equilibrium.*
- ▸ thoughts **concentration, reverie** *Joshua's reverie was disturbed by a knock at the door.*

disturbance N
when people are noisy or violent

- adj+N important or serious **major, significant, violent, widespread** *Introduction of the new law resulted in major civil disturbances.*
- ▸ not serious **minor** *There were a number of minor disturbances in the area.*
- ▸ involving the public **civil, public** *They may be called to assist with road accidents or public disturbances.*
- v+N cause a disturbance **cause, create, give rise to, trigger** *At 2pm he saw the defendant creating a disturbance in the street.*
- ▸ stop a disturbance **deal with, put down, quell, suppress** *Police officers from six counties were brought in to quell the disturbances.*
- ▸ take part in a disturbance **be involved in, participate in, take part in** *He spent 60 days in jail for taking part in the disturbances.*
- N+v happen **begin, happen, occur, take place** *The disturbances occurred both before and after the match.*
- ▸ happen as a result of something **arise from sth, follow sth, result from sth** *Civil disturbance followed, and several protestors were arrested.*

disturbed ADJ
affected by mental or emotional problems

- adv+ADJ very **acutely, deeply, highly, profoundly, seriously, severely, very** *Some of the patients are acutely disturbed and unable to communicate.*
- ▸ relating to illness of the mind **behaviourally, emotionally, mentally, psychologically** *The woman, who is mentally disturbed, was taken to a secure hospital for treatment.*
- ADJ+n **adolescent, child, individual, patient, teenager** *After university, I worked as a psychiatric nurse with disturbed adolescents.*

disturbing ADJ
making you feel shocked, worried, or upset

- adv+ADJ very **deeply, extremely, genuinely, highly, particularly, profoundly, very** *Many people find this a profoundly disturbing book.*
- ▸ rather **a little, quite, rather, slightly, somewhat** *These very short dream-like stories are a little disturbing.*
- ▸ in a way that is difficult to define **strangely, vaguely** *I found the exhibition astonishing and fascinating, and strangely disturbing.*
- ADJ+n tendency **tendency, trend** *Over the last few years a rather disturbing trend has emerged.*

- ▸ news **footage, news, report** *In episode 4, Stephen gets some disturbing news.*
- ▸ feature **aspect, feature, quality** *The inexperience of the care staff was a particularly disturbing feature of the evidence.*
- ▸ fact **evidence, fact, findings, statistic, thing, truth** *It's a disturbing fact that the UK is top of the list for cocaine use.*
- ▸ picture **image, picture** *The economic forecasts for this year paint an even more disturbing picture.*
- ▸ experience or situation **event, experience, incident, situation** *All in all it was a slightly disturbing experience.*

diverge V
be different or become different

- adv+V to a great extent **considerably, markedly, radically, sharply, significantly, substantially, widely** *Since 2006, prices of the two products have diverged sharply.* • *You will not be permitted to diverge significantly **from** these guidelines.*
- ▸ slightly **slightly, somewhat, to some extent** *These views diverge somewhat **from** those expressed in earlier articles.*
- n+V **claims, opinions, viewpoints, views** *Views diverge widely **on** whether children should be permitted to attend.*

diverse ADJ
including people or things that are different from each other or of different kinds

- adv+ADJ very **amazingly, enormously, extraordinarily, extremely, highly, incredibly, remarkably, richly, very, wonderfully** *East London is one of the most richly diverse parts of the capital.*
- ▸ in a way that relates to race **ethnically, racially** *The school serves an ethnically diverse community.*
- ▸ in a way that relates to human behaviour **culturally, linguistically, socially** *Working in such a linguistically diverse nation is a challenge.*
- ▸ in a way that relates to the physical features of an area **geographically** *Each island has an individual identity and they are very geographically diverse.*
- ADJ+n group of people **audience, community, group, population, society, workforce** *Many employers understand the benefits of having a diverse workforce.*
- ▸ range or selection **array, collection, mix, portfolio, range, selection** *The programme covers a diverse range of topics.*
- ▸ types of culture **backgrounds, cultures** *We encourage people of diverse backgrounds to apply.*
- and/or **colourful, complex, cosmopolitan, exciting, rich, varied, vibrant** *New York is one of the most vibrant and diverse cities in the world.*

diversity N
the existence of different people, things, or features within a group

- adj+N great **amazing, considerable, enormous, great, huge, immense, incredible, infinite, rich, sheer, wide** *This scheme offers young people a fantastic opportunity to experience the rich diversity of American culture.*

▸ relating to race **ethnic, racial** *We must ensure that the workforce reflects the ethnic diversity of the local community.*
▸ relating to human behaviour **cultural, linguistic, religious** *We celebrate Scotland's linguistic diversity.*
▸ relating to biology **biological, botanical, ecological, genetic** *Mountains are an important source of biological diversity.*

● v+N show respect for diversity **appreciate, celebrate, embrace, respect, value, welcome** *Our organization celebrates the diversity of cultures within today's society.*
▸ encourage or support diversity **encourage, promote, recognize, support** *Our aim is to promote cultural diversity.*
▸ keep diversity from being lost **conserve, maintain, preserve, protect** *Be environmentally responsible – preserve diversity and reduce climate change.*
▸ show that diversity exists **demonstrate, highlight, illustrate, reflect, represent, show** *The educational environment reflects the diversity of society.*

divert V

use something for a different purpose, or take attention away from something

● V+n money **cash, funding, funds, investment, money, resources, revenue, wealth** *Why are they planning to divert resources away from schools and hospitals?*
▸ effort **effort, energy** *These targets could divert effort from solving immediate problems.*
▸ thoughts or attention **attention, focus, mind, thoughts** *The phone rang, diverting my thoughts from the essay I was writing.*

● V+n+from **duty, mission, purpose, task** *There is a significant cost to the health service as nurses are diverted from other tasks.*

divided ADJ

affected by major disagreements between people

● adv+ADJ deeply **bitterly, deeply, hopelessly, sharply** *The Republican Party was deeply divided on the matter.*
▸ within itself **internally** *The Empire ws internally divided, with extremes of wealth and poverty.*
▸ in a particular way **ethnically, politically, racially, socially** *This illustrates the difficulty of working in a politically divided society.*

● ADJ+n **city, community, country, nation, party, society, state** *Divided communities have united in working together to slow down climate change.*

● ADJ+on **issue, matter, point, question, subject** *Opinions are sharply divided on this issue.*

● and/or **confused, fragmented, weak** *This is a weak and divided government whose future is uncertain.*

division N

1 separating people, things, or ideas into smaller groups or parts

● adj+N equal **equal, fair** *Anne insisted on an equal division of the money.*
▸ unequal **unequal, unfair** *Her study examines the consequences for women's health of the unequal division of household labour.*

▸ basic or clear **basic, clear, clear-cut, fundamental, natural, obvious, simple, strict** *There is no simple division into academic and non-academic subjects.*
▸ not detailed **broad** *In literature the broadest division is between poetry, prose and drama.*
▸ not taking facts into account **arbitrary, artificial** *Often a quite arbitrary division is made between popular and serious interests.*

2 a disagreement between people, especially within a group [usually plural]

● adj+N very serious **bitter, deep, huge, sharp** *The conference revealed deep divisions within the Democratic Party.*
▸ within a group **communal, domestic, internal** *The government's internal divisions have weakened it considerably.*
▸ relating to race **ethnic, racial** *These ethnic divisions between the groups led to years of civil war.*
▸ relating to society or politics **cultural, political, social** *What are the main causes of social division and violence in this country?*

● v+N cause divisions **cause, create, produce, promote** *We were saddened to see the divisions caused by religious belief.*
▸ make divisions worse **deepen, exacerbate, perpetuate, reinforce** *The possibility of links with the Greens have deepened divisions within the party.*
▸ overcome divisions **heal, overcome, transcend** *We will do our best to overcome the religious divisions that threaten our peace.*

divisive ADJ

likely to cause arguments or differences between people

● adv+ADJ very **bitterly, deeply, extremely, highly, very** *Immigration on this scale is highly divisive.*
▸ possibly **potentially** *Teachers complain that the scheme is potentially divisive.*
▸ relating to social class **socially** *Schools are more socially divisive than ever.*
▸ relating to politics **politically** *Any kind of politically divisive discussion was forbidden.*

● ADJ+n subject for discussion **argument, debate, issue** *Even on this extremely divisive issue, we respect each other's views.*
▸ political action or system **campaign, measure, policy, politics, system, tactics** *Their divisive policies are destroying communities.*
▸ effect **effect, influence** *Their actions are likely to have a deeply divisive effect.*
▸ quality **nature** *They commented on the divisive nature of the country's education system.*

divorce N

a legal way of ending a marriage

● adj+N difficult or unpleasant **acrimonious, bitter, difficult, messy, nasty, painful** *Their first marriage ended in acrimonious divorce.*
▸ easy or not unpleasant **amicable, easy, quick** *We have been married for one year, and we both want an amicable divorce.*
▸ not opposed by one of the partners **uncontested** *This procedure speeded up uncontested divorces.*

● v+N officially ask a court for a divorce **apply**

for, ask for, file for, initiate, petition for, seek, sue for *I will be seeking a divorce on the grounds of unreasonable behaviour.*

> The word **grounds** is used when talking about the reasons for a divorce: *She felt that his behaviour gave her grounds for divorce.* • *He sought a divorce on the grounds of incompatability.*

▸ agree to a divorce **agree to, consent to** *Your husband or wife must consent to the divorce in writing.*
▸ allow a divorce **grant** *The court granting the divorce may also deal with the future of any children.*
▸ experience a divorce **experience, go through** *Support is available for children who are experiencing parental divorce.* • *I am going through a divorce right now.*
▸ complete the divorce process **finalize, get, obtain** *My parents got a divorce, and since then I've been really unhappy.*
▸ have divorce as the final result **end in, result in** *Increasing numbers of marriages are ending in divorce.*

● N+n **decree, law, lawyer, petition, proceedings, process, settlement** *Can I start divorce proceedings without my husband's consent?*

doctorate N
the highest qualification given by a university

● v+N do a doctorate **do, study for, undertake, work on, write** *I did my doctorate on 20th-century American literature.*
▸ finish a doctorate **complete, finish** *I successfully completed my doctorate in the summer of 2005.*
▸ gain a doctorate **achieve, attain, earn, gain, obtain, receive** *Peter obtained his doctorate from Oxford in 1992.*
▸ officially give a doctorate **award, confer, grant** *Rebecca was awarded a doctorate from the University of Michigan for her research.*
▸ have a doctorate **have, hold, possess** *He holds a doctorate from the London School of Economics.*

doctrine N
a set of principles or beliefs

● adj+N basic **basic, central, essential, fundamental** *Reincarnation is one of the central doctrines of Buddhism.*
▸ the most important at the moment **current, prevailing** *We believe that the current doctrine serves to preserve the peace.*
▸ generally accepted **accepted, classical, established, orthodox, traditional** *We disagree with the traditional doctrine that nothing can ever justify dying.*
▸ relating to a particular subject **economic, legal, military, philosophical, political, religious, theological** *In this course, little time is spent on developing an understanding of legal doctrine.*

● v+N tell other people about a doctrine **expound, preach, proclaim, propound, teach** *They preached the doctrine of peace and stability.*
▸ support or believe in a doctrine **adhere to, affirm, believe, believe in, defend, espouse, subscribe to, uphold** *The present government claims to espouse*

the doctrine of 'zero-tolerance' towards any form of corruption.
▸ say that a doctrine is not true **deny, refute, reject, undermine** *Berkeley rejected Locke's doctrine of abstract ideas.*

document N
1 a piece of paper or set of papers containing official information

● adj+N official **administrative, formal, legal, official, statutory** *I use my full name when I'm signing official documents.*
▸ relating to a particular subject **related, relevant, supporting** *Please bring any relevant documents with you to your first appointment.*
▸ not copied **original** *Please do not send original documents.*
▸ secret **confidential, secret** *We have obtained a confidential document revealing plans to sell off the company.*
▸ very important **core, crucial, definitive, important, key, major** *Our department is responsible for preparing key planning documents.*
▸ connected with the past **ancient, archival, early, historical** *The book is illustrated with an interesting selection of historical documents.*
▸ finished **complete, final, revised** *I'll send you a copy of the final document.*
▸ not finished, and for discussion **consultative, draft, initial** *This draft document has been prepared as a first stage in the production of the city's five-year development plan.*

● n+N **background, briefing, consultation, discussion, planning, policy, research, strategy** *A strategy document concerning the new initiatives is available to schools upon request.*

● v+N prepare a document **compile, draft, draw up, prepare, produce, work on** *They drew up a document containing a list of points for discussion*
▸ sign a document **sign** *Once you have signed the document, please send it to us at the following address.*
▸ publish a document **circulate, distribute, issue, publish, release** *We plan to publish a more detailed document later this year.*
▸ make a secret document public **disclose, leak** *Do you know who leaked this document?*

● N+v describe or explain **describe sth, detail sth, explain sth, outline sth, reveal sth, set out sth, state sth, summarize sth** *We are circulating a document outlining the new procedure.*
▸ be about a subject **concern sth, contain sth, pertain to sth, relate to sth** *The collection includes documents relating to history and film.*

2 a computer file you can write in

● v+N work on a document **format, modify, print, print out, save, scroll through** *For safety, we suggest that you save the document to your hard disk.*
▸ get a document from a computer **access, download, retrieve, view** *Click here to download the document.*
▸ send a document with an email **attach** *Don't forget to attach the document.*

● N+n **collection, exchange, format, management,**

processing, retrieval, storage *Add value to your business with an efficient document management system.*

document V
record something in writing or on film

- adv+V well **carefully, comprehensively, exhaustively, extensively, fully, meticulously, thoroughly, well, widely** *The impact of the project has been extensively documented.*
- ▶ badly **inadequately, poorly** *The development of the language in the Middle Ages has been poorly documented.*

> Usage **Document** is usually passive in all of the **adv+V** combinations shown above.

- V+n facts **case, evidence, fact, findings, information** *Students must carry out a survey and document their findings.*
- ▶ experiences or actions **activities, details, event, experience, history, incident, life** *They have documented their everyday lives with families and friends.*
- ▶ process **procedure, process** *We plan to document this procedure more fully in the near future.*

documentation N
official written material

- adj+N connected with what is being discussed **appropriate, associated, related, relevant** *You will be required to produce relevant documentation confirming that you are the legal owner of the vehicle.*
- ▶ provided with something else **accompanying, supporting** *You should read the accompanying documentation before you install the software.*
- ▶ giving a lot of information **complete, comprehensive, detailed, extensive** *In our detailed documentation, we include full directions to each hotel.*
- ▶ available on the Internet **online** *Where is the latest online documentation?*

- v+N produce documentation **compile, create, draft, prepare, produce** *We can help you to produce useful and complete documentation for your product.*
- ▶ provide documentation **provide, submit, supply** *Please ensure that a copy of the correct documentation is supplied.*
- ▶ look at or check documentation **check, consult, refer to, review** *Please refer to the accompanying documentation for more details.*
- ▶ change or improve documentation **improve, revise, update** *The job includes creating and revising documentation such as staff handbooks.*

dominance N
influence or power over others

- adj+N very strong or powerful **overwhelming, total, unchallenged, unquestioned** *How do you explain their overwhelming dominance in basketball?*
- ▶ affecting the whole world **global, world** *The book examines the history behind the country's global political dominance.*
- ▶ relating to politics and society **cultural, economic,** **market, military, political, territorial** *The ruling classes maintained economic dominance and power.*
- ▶ by men **male** *This type of behaviour is aimed at maintaining male dominance over women.*
- ▶ becoming stronger or more powerful **growing, increasing** *The increasing dominance of the supermarkets is affecting small retailers everywhere.*

- v+N achieve dominance **achieve, assert, assume, attain, establish, gain, have** *Britain established dominance over the globe during the 19th century.*
- ▶ cause dominance to continue **confirm, continue, ensure, maintain, reinforce, retain** *The government's policy is to ensure that military dominance is maintained.*
- ▶ cause dominance to end or become weaker **challenge, counter, end, erode, reduce** *The aim was to reduce the dominance of cars over pedestrian traffic.*
- ▶ achieve dominance again **reassert, re-establish** *In the final race, the top three teams reasserted their dominance.*

dominant ADJ
more important, powerful, or successful than others

- adv+ADJ very or completely **completely, overwhelmingly, particularly, totally, utterly, very** *Women were always overwhelmingly dominant in our family.*
- ▶ more and more **increasingly** *The supermarkets have become increasingly dominant in recent years.*
- ▶ in a particular way **culturally, economically, militarily, politically, socially** *Under such a system, the middle class is economically dominant.*

- ADJ+n set of ideas **approach, discourse, idea, ideology, paradigm, theory** *The dominant ideology in the US and Europe is capitalism.*
- ▶ part or aspect **element, factor, feature, theme** *The weather has been the dominant feature in the media for the last two weeks.*
- ▶ position **position, role** *How have Germany, Japan and the US developed such dominant positions?*
- ▶ person, group, or country **class, figure, force, group, nation, party, player, power** *She became one of the dominant figures on the London art scene.*

dominate V
be more important, powerful, or successful than other people or things

- adv+V very much **completely, heavily, largely, overwhelmingly, totally** *The menu here is heavily dominated by pizza.*

> Usage **Dominate** is usually passive in these combinations: *The world of comedy is almost completely dominated by men.*

- ▶ more and more **increasingly** *Peace and security increasingly dominate the political agenda.*
- ▶ at the present **currently, presently** *China currently dominates world badminton and table tennis.*

domination N
power over other people or things

- adj+N complete **complete, total** *We had total domination in the first half of the game.*

▸ over the whole world **global, world** *The story follows their progress from the early days through to global domination.*

▸ by one country over another **colonial, foreign, imperial, imperialist, territorial** *The current situation is one of lack of security and foreign domination.*

▸ relating to politics and society **cultural, ideological, military, political** *This chapter explores the correspondence between globalization and American cultural domination.*

▸ in economic terms **capitalist, corporate, economic** *This form of economic domination by a few rich nations is no longer acceptable.*

▸ by men and boys **male** *The report calls for an end to male domination in the ICT classroom.*

● v+N achieve domination **achieve, establish, impose, secure** *In order to achieve their domination, the invaders destroyed the local religion.*

▸ be under someone's domination **be under, come under** *The surrounding kingdoms had come under the domination of Rome.*

▸ cause domination to continue **continue, extend, increase, maintain, perpetuate** *The women's team continued their domination of college hockey with three wins last week.*

▸ oppose domination **avoid, oppose, prevent, resist** *There are many voices opposing supermarket domination.*

▸ cause domination to end **break, end** *Goldman was on the U.S. team that ended Italian domination of the game.*

donation N
1 money or goods given in order to help people

● adj+N large **generous, handsome, large, sizeable, substantial** *Thank you for your very generous donation to the charity.*

▸ small **modest, small** *You may use the library in return for a small donation to the Society.*

▸ consisting of money **financial, monetary** *You can now make financial donations towards the cost of research through our website.*

▸ made once or regularly **annual, monthly, one-off, regular** *Members support us by means of a one-off donation, or by setting up a monthly payment.*

▸ intended to help people or an organization **charitable** *These charitable donations keep the universities going.*

▸ given by someone whose name is not known **anonymous** *We asked people to give an anonymous donation in a sealed envelope.*

● v+N ask for a donation **appeal for, apply for, ask for, call for, look for** *We are asking for donations to help us reach our £90,000 target.*

▸ give a donation **give, make** *There will be an opportunity to make a donation to the church.*

▸ receive a donation **accept, collect, get, receive** *Amnesty International does not accept donations from governments.*

▸ be happy to receive a donation **appreciate, welcome** *Admission is free, although donations are appreciated.*

▸ need donations in order to survive **depend on, rely on, run on, survive on** *The shop relies on donations, so please donate any items that you can spare.*

2 blood, body parts etc given by one person to help someone who needs them

● n+N **blood, bone marrow, egg, organ, sperm, tissue** *Much of modern medicine is only made possible because of blood donation.*

donor N
1 someone who gives blood etc for medical use

● n+N **blood, bone marrow, egg, kidney, organ, sperm, tissue** *The scheme aims to increase the number of kidney donors available.*

▸ v+N try to get donors **appeal for, attract, call for, look for, recruit, search for** *We are always looking for egg donors.*

▸ test donors to check for illness **screen, test** *All donors are screened before giving blood.*

2 someone who gives money or goods to help a charity, political party etc

● adj+N giving large amounts of money **big, generous, international, major, wealthy** *He was, and remains, a generous donor to the Labour Party.*

▸ not giving their name **anonymous, unknown** *We have received £200 from an anonymous donor.*

▸ relating to large organizations **corporate, institutional** *One-third of the Party's funds now comes from corporate donors.*

▸ relating to individual people **individual, private** *We have received generous support from several private donors.*

● N+v promise to give money or goods **commit sth, pledge sth, promise sth** *In all, donors pledged $452.9 million.*

▸ give money or goods **contribute sth, donate sth, give sth** *An anonymous donor has contributed £1000 to the appeal.*

▸ pay for something **fund sth** *The yearly award is funded by generous institutional donors, including one of our largest insurance companies.*

doom N
destruction, death, or complete failure that cannot be avoided

● adj+N going to happen soon **imminent, impending** *I also share her sense of impending doom.*

▸ certain to happen **certain, inevitable** *I was sure that any minute I would fall to certain doom.*

● v+N **meet, predict, prophesy, seal, spell, threaten** *Scarce rain spelled doom for villages reliant on producing crops.*

● n+of+N a feeling of doom **feeling, sense** *Their sense of doom is understandable.*

▸ something or someone that is a sign of doom **harbinger, portent, sign** *The raven was seen as a harbinger of doom.*

▸ a prediction of doom **prediction, prophecy** *Despite his sister Cassandra's prophecies of doom, Hector goes into battle and is treacherously murdered by Achilles.*

▸ someone who says that something bad will happen **prophet, voice** *I don't want to be a prophet of doom, but the forecast says it will rain all weekend.*

door N
an object that you open to enter place

- v+N open a door **fling open, open, pull open, push open** *My father enters the room, pushing the door open with his back.*
- ▸ close a door **close, pull to, push to, shut** *Before I had time to protest, he pulled the door to, and I heard him lock me in from the outside.*
- ▸ close a door with a loud noise **bang, slam** *I ran to my room and slammed the door.*
- ▸ lock a door **bar, bolt, lock, secure** *Always secure outside doors, even when you're in.*
- ▸ use a key to open a door **unlock** *She took a key and unlocked the door that led into the garden.*
- ▸ use force to open a door **break down, force, kick down, smash down** *Police broke the door down and found her lying on the floor.*
- ▸ try a door to see if you can open it **try** *I went and tried the door, but of course it was locked.*
- ▸ open a door to see who is knocking on it **answer, get** *Ben and I answered the door and let her in.*
- ▸ go through the space when a door is open **enter, go through, step through, walk through** *On entering the main door, there are two round blue glass windows, one on either side.*
- ▸ knock on a door so people know you are there **bang on, hammer on, knock at, knock on** *There's someone knocking at the door.*
- ▸ use an object to keep a door open **prop open, wedge open** *Never wedge fire doors open.*

dose N
an amount of medicine ready to take

- adj+N large **big, heavy, high, large, massive** *They put me on a very high dose of medication, which almost killed me.*
- ▸ small **low, small** *It is advisable to start with a low dose.*
- ▸ enough to kill you **fatal, lethal** *The day after her funeral, he took a fatal dose of sleeping tablets.*
- ▸ correct **correct, optimal, optimum, recommended** *It is important not to exceed the correct dose.*
- ▸ the most/the least **maximum, minimum** *She was taking the maximum daily dose of ibuprofen.*
- ▸ taken at specific times **daily, weekly** *You can take a daily dose of thyroxine tablets to keep your blood level of thyroxine normal.*
- ▸ one or two **double, single** *The drug is given as a single dose.*
- v+N give someone a dose **administer, deliver, give sb** *Children are given two doses of vaccine about four weeks apart.*
- ▸ take a dose **receive, take** *Children should take the maximum recommended dose of paracetamol for their age group.*
- ▸ take a dose regularly **be on** *He is on a low dose of anti-depressants.*
- ▸ increase a dose **increase** *Your doctor will gradually increase your dose, until the ideal dose is established.*
- ▸ reduce a dose **decrease, reduce** *If you are feeling better, your doctor will tell you how to reduce the dose gradually.*
- ▸ change a dose **adjust, alter, change** *The dose is adjusted to suit individual patient requirements.*
- ▸ tell someone what dose he or she needs **prescribe** *75mg is the average dose prescribed.*
- ▸ forget to take a dose **miss** *If you miss a dose, take the dose as soon as you remember.*
- ▸ take a bigger dose than you should **exceed** *Don't exceed the doses recommended on the packet.*

doubt N
a feeling of not being certain about something

- adj+N serious **considerable, genuine, grave, great, major, much, real, serious, severe, significant, strong** *There are grave doubts about whether the schemes would do much to address climate change.*
- ▸ slight **slight, small** *There is a slight doubt about whether he will be fit enough for Saturday's game.*
- ▸ new **fresh, new** *This evidence raises fresh doubts about cloning animals for use in human transplants.*
- ▸ slight but you think about it a lot **lingering, nagging, niggling** *I thought our relationship was good, but there was a niggling doubt in my mind.*
- ▸ becoming stronger **growing, increasing** *There are growing doubts about Brown's suitability for the job.*
- v+N have doubt **entertain, feel, harbour, have** *I felt considerable doubt as to whether a simple rule could be formulated.* • *She harboured very considerable doubts about the validity of the advice she had received.*
- ▸ cause doubt **cause, create, raise, sow, throw** *The jailing of a corrupt detective has raised doubts about 22 other cases.*

> You can say that someone or something **casts doubt on** something when that thing is made less certain, less good, or less real: *Police are investigating cases of postal vote fraud that could cast doubt on today's elections.*

- ▸ get rid of doubt **avoid, dispel, eliminate, overcome, remove, resolve** *Writing a will removes any doubt as to what your intentions are.*
- ▸ say what your doubts are **express, raise, voice** *Representatives of Iraq's ethnic Turk and Christian minorities all voiced doubt about the U.S. plans.*
- and/or **anxiety, concern, confusion, difficulty, fear, question, suspicion, uncertainty, worry** *If you have any doubts or worries, feel free to discuss these with your instructor.*

doubt V
think that something is unlikely

- adv+V **highly, rather, seriously, sincerely, strongly, very much** *We seriously doubt whether that date is achievable.*
- V+n truth **accuracy, authenticity, claim, sincerity, truth, validity, veracity, word** *Personally, I doubt the truth of this story.*
- ▸ that someone or something exists **existence** *He doubted the existence of God, and could argue his case.*
- ▸ an ability **ability, power** *I started to doubt my abilities as a teacher.*
- ▸ a quality **commitment, honesty, integrity, sanity, value, wisdom** *I do not doubt their commitment, however, nor the strength of their relationship.*

downfall N

a sudden loss of power, status, or success

- adj+N **eventual, final, ultimate** *Napoleon's ultimate downfall was due to the forces that the Revolution had unleashed and Napoleon accelerated.*
- v+N cause someone or something's downfall **bring about, cause, hasten, lead to, prove** *He was at the centre of a religious controversy which was to prove his eventual downfall.*
- ▶ plan secretly to cause someone or something's downfall **engineer, plot** *Many of the group's members had been actively plotting his downfall.*

downpour N

a large amount of rain that falls quickly

- adj+N **heavy, steady, sudden, torrential, tropical** *Low cloud and torrential downpours meant that views over Loch Lomond were limited.*

downturn N

a reduction in economic or business activity

- adj+N serious **major, serious, severe, sharp, significant** *Sweden has recently suffered its most severe economic downturn since the 1930s.*
- ▶ economic **economic** *The club had been hit very hard by the country's economic downturn.*
- ▶ happening around the world **global, worldwide** *In the event of a global downturn, the country's economy is more exposed and more vulnerable than most.*
- ▶ long **prolonged, sustained** *Japan's hotel industry is a victim of the prolonged economic downturn.*
- v+N experience a downturn **experience, face, see, suffer** *Like the economy, the property market saw a downturn in 2001 and 2002.*
- ▶ cause a downturn **cause, precipitate** *Stock investors may sell off their holdings, causing a downturn in the stock market and the national economy.*
- ▶ be successful in spite of a downturn **survive, weather** *We have probably weathered the downturn better than other countries.*
- N+in **business, demand, the economy, industry, market, sales, trade** *The Governor of the Bank of England warned of a possible downturn in the housing market.* • *Because we'd kept our costs down, we survived the downturn in sales.*

draft N

a preliminary version of a plan or letter

- adj+N first or early **early, first, initial, original, preliminary** *This is an early draft of the work, complete with the author's corrections, additions and deletions.*
- ▶ final **final, last** *Draft documents have been circulated for discussion pending a final draft.*
- ▶ likely to be changed **rough, working** *Before filling out the application form, it is a good idea to write a rough draft first.*
- ▶ having been changed **amended, revised** *You can then submit an amended draft.*
- v+N write a draft **create, prepare, produce, write** *When you have an idea of what you want to say, write a rough draft.*

- ▶ read a draft **proofread, read** *The editor suggested some changes when he read my draft.*
- ▶ finish a draft **complete, finalise, finish** *Once the first draft is completed, set it aside for the few days so that you can return to it with a fresh eye.* • *I was just finishing the final draft of a very complicated book.*
- ▶ let other people see a draft **circulate, issue, present, publish, submit** *We were able to submit the most recent draft to Sport England for comment.*
- ▶ agree to a draft **agree, approve** *In 2008, the committee approved the final draft.*
- ▶ make changes to a draft **amend, revise** *After lengthy discussions, the draft was revised.*
- ▶ look at a draft in order to see if it needs to be changed **consider, review** *The current drafts were reviewed at the Ottawa project meeting.*
- N+n law or rule **bill, clause, constitution, directive, guidance, guidelines, law, legislation, order, regulation, rule** *Draft legislation is expected, and must be implemented by 2015.*
- ▶ agreement **agreement, contract, treaty** *Advice and a draft childminding contract are available from the Scottish Childminding Association.*
- ▶ plan **plan, policy, proposal, resolution, strategy** *Draft management plans have been completed for Mungo National Park.*
- ▶ document **copy, document, letter, manifesto, paper, report, statement, version** *The draft document is now ready for circulation among the wider membership.*

draft V

write a preliminary version of a plan or letter

- adv+V well **carefully, properly, well** *Such a clause would have to be carefully drafted.*
- ▶ badly **badly, poorly** *Solicitors make a lot of money sorting out poorly drafted home-made wills.*
- ▶ first **initially, originally** *This legislation was originally drafted in 1946.*
- V+n a law or rule **amendment, bill, clause, constitution, guidance, guidelines, law, legislation, regulation, rule** *We have drafted two bills that are currently undergoing authorisation by the Parliament.*
- ▶ a document or piece of writing **article, document, documentation, letter, memo, note, paper, report, statement, will** *The working group was drafting a report that would be circulated for comment within the next two months.*
- ▶ a plan **plan, policy, proposal, resolution, strategy** *The next step would be to draft a management strategy.*
- ▶ a reply **reply, response, treaty** *Mr Vaz was not involved in drafting the reply to this letter, but he had seen a copy of it.*
- ▶ draft an agreement **agreement, contract** *You need to ensure that your employees have signed properly drafted contracts of employment.*

drain V

use too much money, resources etc

- V+n **funds, money, reserves, resources** *A flu epidemic would drain the country's scarce resources.*

drain N

something that uses too much money, resources etc

- adj+N big **big, heavy, huge, major, massive, serious, significant** *If your pet becomes ill unexpectedly, treatment can a be a big drain on your savings.*
- ▶ always happening **constant, continual, steady** *Increasing imports of continental goods meant there was a steady drain of cash out of Scotland.*
- ▶ of money **economic, financial** *We're bracing ourselves for the financial drain which seems inevitable.*
- ▶ of energy or power **battery, energy, power** *For night time use there is a lamp with a timeout of about 6 seconds to prevent undue battery drain.*

> If a lot of skilled people leave one place to go and work in another, it is referred to as a **brain drain**: *Local business owners are concerned about the brain drain.*

- v+N be or become a drain **become, prove, represent** *Persistent performance issues can become a serious drain on business resources.*
- ▶ cause a drain **cause** *Deliberate countryside fires cause a drain on the resources of the Fire and Rescue Service.*
- ▶ reduce or stop a drain **prevent, reduce, stop** *Because this oil is vegetable based, it reduces the drain on our valuable fossil fuel resources.*
- N+on on wealth or income **budget, the coffers, the economy, the exchequer, funds, income, profit, reserves, sb's finances, sb's pocket, taxpayers** *Education is an investment, not a drain on the economy.*
- ▶ on energy or resources **energy, resources** *An unhealthy spine can be a drain on your energy and vitality.*

drama N

a play for theatre, television, or radio

- adj+N modern **contemporary, modern** *Wooldridge was also very keen on contemporary American drama, particularly plays by Tennessee Williams.*
- ▶ set in the past **costume, epic, historical, period** *The BBC has always done good period dramas.*
- ▶ exciting and keeping your attention **compelling, engaging, gripping, riveting** *Lawn Dogs is a well written, subtle yet compelling drama.*
- ▶ showing life as it really is **gritty, real-life** *Six Bend Trap is a gritty northern drama, set in a world of greyhound racing.*
- ▶ having a strong effect **hard-hitting, intense, poignant, powerful** *The plot to this powerful drama revolves around a car accident that brings the three characters together.*
- ▶ types of drama **classic, classical, medical, musical, political, popular, psychological, romantic, serious, tragic** *Shakespeare's tragic drama of the 'star-crossed' young lovers is seen to be an extraordinary work.*
- n+N on television or radio **radio, television, TV** *Watch out for this brand new TV drama.*
- ▶ the people who the drama is intended for **adult, family, teen** *Laura Wade's beautifully poised family drama was first performed at Soho Theatre, London, in 2005.*
- ▶ the subject or type of drama **comedy, courtroom, crime, hospital, police** *This comedy drama is refreshingly honest without being dark, witty without being silly, and most of all compulsive.*
- v+N be a performer in a drama **appear in, be in, perform, star in** *Tim Holt stars in this classic drama.*
- ▶ write a drama **devise, write** *Forster had written a drama set in the English Civil War.*
- ▶ make a drama ready for television or stage **direct, produce** *She has directed television drama and award-winning short films.*
- ▶ watch a drama **watch** *He likes watching Shakespearean drama.*
- ▶ put on a drama **broadcast, put on, stage** *The Pavilion Theatre staged some great dramas.*
- and/or **art, comedy, dance, documentary, literature, music, poetry, singing** *I've always loved dance, drama, music and literature.*

dramatic ADJ

1 sudden and easy to notice

- adv+ADJ very **really, truly, very** *The council's proposals to step up recycling during the next twelve months could bring about a very dramatic increase to 45 % or more.*
- ▶ rather **fairly, pretty** INFORMAL**, quite, rather** *The population of the world has shown a fairly dramatic increase in recent times.*
- ADJ+n change **change, development, difference, shift, transformation, turnaround** *The past five years have seen a dramatic change in the ethos and mission of Australian universities.*
- ▶ increase or improvement **advance, expansion, growth, improvement, increase, rise** *With dramatic increases in energy, fuel and raw material prices, additional pressures are being placed on businesses.*
- ▶ decrease **cut, decline, decrease, drop, fall, loss, reduction** *As a result of people giving up smoking, there has been a dramatic reduction in deaths in many countries.*
- ▶ effect **consequence, effect, impact, result** *A new programme for tackling crime was introduced, with dramatic results.*

2 exciting and impressive

- adv+ADJ very **intensely, powerfully, really, truly, very** *The building will be a very dramatic addition to the London skyline.*
- ▶ rather **fairly, pretty** INFORMAL**, quite, rather** *He escaped in a quite dramatic fashion.*
- ADJ+n event or situation **action, display, event, experience, incident, moment, situation, victory** *It was another dramatic victory for the team.*
- ▶ natural feature **cliff, coastline, landscape, mountain, scenery, setting** *For dramatic scenery, tranquil lakes and great walks you can't beat the Lake District.*
- ▶ something you look at **image, picture, scene, view** *The book is packed with dramatic images. • It's a private hotel with dramatic views over the bay and harbour.*
- ▶ story **account, monologue, narrative, story** *State-of-the-art displays in the new visitor building tell the dramatic story of the Battle of Hastings.*

▶ end **climax, finale** *The game was a dramatic finale to a championship that had plenty of thrills and some excellent football.*
▶ way **fashion** *He was leading the race until he flew over the handlebars of his bicycle in dramatic fashion.*

draw V
consider the ways in which things are different or similar

● V+n compare and show similarities **analogy, comparison, connection, parallel** *The article draws comparisons between the results of this survey and one conducted in 1985.*
▶ compare and show differences **boundary, contrast, distinction, line** *He draws a contrast between the situation then and the situation now.*

drawback N
a feature that makes something less useful

● adj+N only or main **main, only** *The only drawback is that it shuts at 10pm.*
▶ serious **big, great, major, real, serious, significant** *One of the major drawbacks of this movie is the number of characters the viewer is expected to keep track of.*
▶ not very serious **minor, slight** *A slight drawback for UK readers is the fact that the author says things which do not quite work for the UK.*
▶ possible **possible, potential** *Sarah also mentions some of the potential drawbacks to the programme.*
▶ easy to notice **obvious** *This book's obvious drawbacks are its size and cost.*

● and/or **advantages, benefits, difficulties, limitations, merits** *There are benefits and drawbacks to leasing.*

draw on PHR VB
use something gained or saved

● V+n information or ideas **advice, approach, data, evidence, example, information, insight, material, method, principle, resources, support, theory** *The panel will draw on advice from subject experts as necessary.* ● *The authors draw on evidence from an international survey of the largest 200 airlines.*
▶ knowledge, experience, or skills **experience, expertise, knowledge, memory, skill, strengths, understanding, wisdom** *The programme will draw on the strengths of staff within The School of Healthcare to provide relevant teaching.*
▶ tradition **heritage, history, tradition** *His figurative art drew on Spanish tradition, but was informed by an understanding of modernist practice.*
▶ work or research that has been done **findings, research, study, survey, work** *Each workshop is led by an experienced facilitator, drawing on their own research and consultancy.*

draw up PHR VB
prepare and write something

● V+n a plan or list **agenda, framework, list, plan, policy, programme, proposal, schedule, scheme, shortlist, strategy, timetable** *The company is drawing up detailed proposals for upgrading the sewer networks.*

▶ rules, laws etc **code, constitution, guidance, guidelines, legislation, recommendations, regulations, rules, specifications, standards** *We recommend that the Department of Health draws up guidelines for the management of obese patients.*
▶ an agreement **agreement, contract** *Once the proposal is agreed we will draw up a contract which will indicate the specific terms and agreements.*
▶ a document **budget, charter, document, draft, report, response, statement, will** *The committee drew up a report and submitted its findings to the club committee.*

dream N
1 something experienced in your mind during sleep

● adj+N strange **bizarre, strange, weird** *When I do get to sleep I have a strange dream involving chasing people down fire escapes.*
▶ bad **bad, disturbing, horrible** *I keep having bad dreams in which I am falling from a cliff.*
▶ nice **nice, pleasant** *I awoke from a pleasant dream.*
▶ in which you see what is going to happen in the future **prophetic** *He had had a spookily prophetic dream about death.*
▶ involving sexual thoughts **erotic** *She had been having erotic dreams about a stranger she had met only a few days ago.*
▶ very clear **lucid, vivid** *18.3 per cent of patients who took the drug reported having had vivid dreams.*
▶ happening many times **recurrent, recurring** *Jane and I have both had strange, recurring dreams about death.*

● v+N have a dream **dream, have** *People often dream vivid recurrent dreams of events in the past.* ● *I had a bad dream last night.*
▶ wake from a dream **awake from, wake from** *He looked slightly disorientated, as if he had just woken from a dream.*

2 something good that you hope to achieve

● adj+N not likely to be achieved **crazy, distant, elusive, impossible, romantic, unattainable, utopian** *In our culture we are continually tempted to pay money for an elusive dream of satisfaction.*
▶ that you have had for a very long time **lifelong, long-held** *She was an ambitious mother, whose lifelong dream was for all four daughters to become accomplished musicians.*
▶ big and ambitious **big, great** *Kapoor was a small time filmmaker with big dreams.*
▶ not achieved **broken, shattered, unfulfilled** *He was left with nothing but his memories and shattered dreams.*
▶ happening at the end of a process **ultimate** *My ultimate dream is to have a farm of my own.*

> If something is *beyond your wildest dreams*, it is much better than you imagined: *In a few years he will be rich beyond even his wildest dreams.*

● n+N **boyhood, childhood** *Smithy said 'It was my childhood dream come true to fly this iconic British fighter'.*
● v+N have a dream **have** *Quite a few people have a dream of running a hotel, but then find they hate the lifestyle having taken the plunge.*
▶ try to achieve your dream **chase, follow, pursue** *A*

therapist convinced Cate to pursue her dream of becoming a singer.

▶ achieve your dream **achieve, fulfil, live, realize** He's living his dreams.

> You can also say that someone's **dream turns to reality** or someone's **dream comes true**: His Olympic dream turned to reality when he won a gold medal in Beijing.

▶ end someone's dream **destroy, end, shatter** Aidan badly injured his knee, which effectively ended his dreams of football stardom.

● and/or **ambitions, aspirations, desires, goals, hopes, visions** You may also like to mention your hopes and dreams for the future.

dress V
wear clothes

● adv+V in clothes that are tidy and smart **beautifully, elegantly, immaculately, impeccably, neatly, nicely, smartly, well** Where no uniform is provided, you should dress smartly.

▶ in clothes that look untidy **badly, shabbily** There were lots of shabbily dressed women and girls, and seemingly hordes of young children around.

▶ in clothes that are suitable **accordingly, appropriately, properly, suitably** If you dress appropriately, you'll feel more comfortable.

▶ in clothes that are not suitable **inappropriately, provocatively** Students who are inappropriately dressed may be withdrawn from lessons until the situation is remedied.

▶ in clothes that are formal or informal **casually, formally** This is the place to dine if you don't want to dress formally.

▶ in clothes that are traditional and not offensive **conservatively, decently, modestly, respectably** She dresses very conservatively and always keeps her head covered.

▶ in clothes that do not have a lot of decoration **plainly, soberly** Danni is more soberly dressed in a grey and black ensemble.

▶ in clothes that are fashionable **fashionably** She began to dress more fashionably.

drink V
drink alcohol

● adv+V a lot or too much **excessively, freely, heavily, regularly** If you drink heavily and smoke, your chances of developing oral cancer are 15 times higher.

▶ in a sensible way **healthily, moderately, responsibly, safely, sensibly** The campaign aims to encourage people to drink sensibly over Christmas and New Year.

● and/or **chat, drive, eat, smoke** If you hold a driving licence, do not drink and drive.

drinker N
someone who often drinks alcohol

● adj+N drinking a lot of alcohol **big, frequent, hard, hardened, heavy, regular** Heavy drinkers often develop fatty change in the liver.

▶ drinking too much alcohol **binge, dependent, excessive, problem** Official statistics show that

women are becoming problem drinkers more quickly than men.

▶ drinking a little alcohol **light, moderate, occasional** Moderate drinkers – people who have an alcoholic drink or two a day – are 54 per cent less likely than non-drinkers to be obese.

▶ drinking alcohol only at social occasions **social** He was a non-smoker and a social drinker.

▶ too young to drink alcohol legally **underage** Underage drinkers and those who serve them will face fines.

drinking N
the activity of drinking alcohol

● adj+N a lot **hard, heavy, regular** He died from liver disease which could have been caused by regular heavy drinking.

▶ too much **binge, excessive, harmful, hazardous, irresponsible, problem** An advertisement campaign to show people the dangers of binge drinking was also launched.

▶ not too much **moderate, responsible, safe, sensible** The importance of sensible drinking cannot be over-estimated.

▶ causing problems for other people **anti-social** There is a problem of anti-social drinking on the streets of the town.

▶ when you are legally too young **underage** Vandalism, graffiti, underage drinking, drug misuse and threatening behaviour are all serious problems.

● v+N stop drinking **quit, stop** Even in advanced liver disease, it is still beneficial to stop drinking.

▶ reduce drinking **control, curb, reduce** Many people reduce their drinking as they get older for a variety of health reasons.

▶ deal with drinking **combat, tackle** This is an innovative scheme to tackle street drinking.

▶ start drinking **start** Middle-class women who are becoming socially successful have started drinking.

▶ go somewhere for drinking **go, go out** The most popular place to go drinking in Bristol is Clifton Village.

● N+n habit or problem **habit, problem** She has sought treatment for her drinking problem.

▶ someone you often drink with **buddy, companion, partner** He came home drunk tonight, and he brought a couple of his drinking buddies with him.

▶ time when you drink **binge, bout, session** Remember you might be over the limit for driving the next morning after a heavy drinking session.

▶ the belief that drinking is important and part of society **culture** We don't think that the drinking culture which is causing health problems in the UK can be turned around overnight.

drive V
control a vehicle so that it moves somewhere

● adv+V quickly **fast, quickly** You should never think it is safe to drive fast on rural roads just because there is less traffic.

▶ slowly **slowly** She had to drive slowly through the steep cobbled streets of the town.

▶ carefully **carefully, safely** Please drive carefully along this road as it is used by children, pedestrians and horses.

▶ dangerously **dangerously, recklessly** Police chased

the vehicle which was being driven recklessly through the streets of South London.

● and/or **drink** *Don't guess at the safe alcohol level, leave the car at home and don't drink and drive.*

drive N
determination

● v+N **have, possess** *If you have the drive, ambition and determination to succeed in the hectic world of modelling then contact us now.*

● and/or **ability, ambition, commitment, determination, energy, enthusiasm, initiative, motivation, passion, skill, vision** *Without Gerry's drive and enthusiasm, the organization would probably never have been formed.*

driving N
the activity of controlling a vehicle so that it moves somewhere

● adj+N bad **aggressive, bad, careless, dangerous, erratic, inconsiderate, irresponsible, negligent, poor, reckless** *Bad driving and excess speed were the cause of 95 per cent of these collisions.*

▸ good **careful, good, safe, skilful** *The training focuses on safe driving.*

▸ involving a driver who has drunk alcohol or taken illegal drugs **drink, drug, drunk** *Most of us are well aware of the problems of drink driving, but little is said about the perils of drunk pedestrians.*

● v+N **do** *Jane did the driving because I was tired.*

● N+n **ban, conditions, experience, instructor, lesson, licence, offence, test** *Most people feel that a lifelong driving ban is appropriate for motorists who cause death.* ● *Freezing fog caused some nasty driving conditions.*

drop N
a fall in amount or value

● adj+N large **big, considerable, dramatic, great, huge, large, marked, massive, sharp, significant, steep, substantial** *There has been a sharp drop in imports.*

▸ small **slight, small** *The number of motorists arrested saw a slight drop, with 28 this month compared to 32 last month.*

▸ sudden **sudden** *If there is a sudden drop in pressure, the motor can stall.*

● v+N **cause, experience, suffer** *The company had suffered an 11.2 per cent drop in sales.*

● N+in an amount of money **income, price, profit, revenue, salary, value** *The drop in oil prices hasn't led to a reduction in the price of petrol.*

▸ temperature or pressure **pressure, temperature** *Hypothermia is a potentially serious condition caused by a drop in body temperature.*

▸ the number of people who want or use something **consumption, demand, sales, trade** *The figures show a further drop in sales.*

▸ quality or standards **quality, standards** *He believed there had been a drop in standards in our schools.*

▸ the amount produced **output, performance, production** *This policy triggered a sharp drop in production of agricultural goods.*

▸ a number of people or things **crime, level, number, rate** *Police have reported a massive drop in the number of drink related incidents this year.*

drought N
a long period without rain, causing great harm

● adj+N severe **bad, devastating, extreme, major, serious, severe** *After a summer of severe drought and hardship for coffee farmers in Honduras, the autumn rains have begun.*

▸ continuing for a long time **extended, long, prolonged** *Long droughts also affect crops and water supplies.*

▸ happening often **frequent, periodic, recurrent** *Mauritania is a country that suffers from recurrent drought.*

● v+N have a drought **experience, face, have, suffer** *Africa will suffer both more frequent droughts and more serious floods.*

▸ cause a drought **cause** *Climate change in Australia is predicted to cause worse droughts and bushfires.*

▸ survive a drought **survive, withstand** *The plants are adapted to survive frequent droughts and survive in poor-quality soil.*

● N+v **affect sth, hit sth** *The drought has hit much of Northeast Asia, including northern China and Mongolia.*

drug N
an illegal substance that changes the body and mind [usually plural]

● adj+N illegal **illegal, illicit** *The possession of illicit drugs in some countries carries very severe penalties.*

▸ types of drug **hard, recreational, soft** *As with alcohol abuse, recreational drugs are thought to have a damaging effect on the nervous system.*

● v+N take drugs **abuse, be involved in, do** INFORMAL, **experiment with, inject, take, use** *There is often total disbelief when parents are told that their son or daughter is involved in drugs.* ● *Up to half of young people may have experimented with illegal drugs or solvents by the time they are 16.*

> If someone takes drugs regularly, you can also use the phrase **be on drugs**: *He was on drugs, and stole to feed his habit.*

▸ sell drugs **deal, deal in, peddle, push, sell, supply** *He has admitted dealing drugs to pay for prostitutes.*

▸ be unable to stop using a drug **be addicted to, be dependent on, be hooked on** INFORMAL *Having spent most of his adult life addicted to drugs, Barber didn't know how to function without them.*

▸ make a drug which was illegal become legal **legalize** *Cannabis use has rocketed since the drug was legalized in the Netherlands.*

▸ take drugs away using official power **seize** *Officers raided the flat to seize illegal drugs.*

▸ bring drugs into a country illegally **smuggle** *He had smuggled drugs between Mexico and the US.*

● N+n someone who takes drugs **abuser, addict, misuser, user** *Drug addicts will steal from friends and family to buy drugs.*

▸ the use of drugs **abuse, misuse, taking, use** *Health professionals can help to identify problem alcohol and drug use as early as possible.*

▸ someone who sells drugs **baron, dealer, lord, smuggler, trafficker** *Police are targeting drug dealers.*

▸ the act of selling drugs **deal, dealing, smuggling, trade, trafficking** *At the hearing, they will be able to apply to seize money they believe to have been earned from drug deals.*

▸ the problem of being unable to stop taking drugs **addiction, dependence, dependency, habit, problem** *Many prisoners have a drink or drug addiction.*

▸ crime related to drugs **charge, crime, driving, offence** *Two men have been arrested on suspicion of drug offences.*

▸ an official attempt to take drugs away **bust** INFORMAL, **raid** *Police seized heroin and cocaine in a drugs bust.*

▸ an occasion when someone takes too much of a drug **overdose** *Reeves died of a drug overdose.*

drunk ADJ
uncontrolled because of drinking too much alcohol

● adv+ADJ very **completely, extremely, really, very** *All the men kept buying Dan beer and he was very drunk!*

▸ rather **pretty** INFORMAL, **quite, rather, slightly** *We were in a bar in Glasgow after a gig, and we got pretty drunk.*

● v+ADJ **be, become, feel, get** *On their first date Alan got so drunk that he couldn't remember the way home.*

● and/or **disorderly, incapable, rowdy, sober** *Geoffrey was in custody charged with being drunk and disorderly the previous night.* ● *I never could tell if she was drunk or sober.*

dry ADJ
when there is no rain

● adv+ADJ rather **fairly, reasonably, relatively, somewhat** *It was fortunate that the weather remained relatively dry during the winter.*

▸ in most places or at most times **generally, mainly, mostly** *The weather was mostly dry except for a heavy downpour during the latter part of the visit.*

▸ in a way that is different from usual **exceptionally, surprisingly, unusually** *The exceptionally dry weather is responsible for the dry riverbed.*

● v+ADJ **be, become, keep, remain, stay, turn** *I hope it stays dry for another week.*

● and/or **cloudy, cold, cool, crisp, hot, mild, sunny, warm, wet, windy** *In May the weather is mild and generally dry, making the walking conditions good.*

due ADJ
according to the usual standards or rules

● ADJ+n **acknowledgment, allowance, attention, care, consideration, diligence, notice, process, regard, respect** *Due consideration will be given to needs in relation to culture, race, religion and disability.*

dull ADJ
boring

● adv+ADJ very **extremely, incredibly, mind-numbingly** INFORMAL, **plain, really, terminally, terribly, very** *He was good at chemistry but found it mind-numbingly dull.*

▸ rather **fairly, a little, pretty** INFORMAL, **quite, rather, slightly, somewhat** *I thought the ending was very predictable and the storyline was a little dull.*

● v+ADJ **be, become, get, look, seem, sound** *The film sounds very dull.*

● and/or **boring, dreary, lifeless, monotonous, predictable, repetitive, tedious** *I find their songs dull and repetitive.*

duty N
a moral or legal obligation

● adj+N by a law or rule **fiduciary, legal, statutory** *There is a statutory duty to replace the trees which are removed or destroyed to build something.*

▸ by moral or religious beliefs **Christian, ethical, moral, religious, religious, spiritual** *I felt that I had a very strong moral duty to stand up and say: 'This is wrong'.*

▸ by the rules of your job **administrative, contractual, professional** *All counsellors have a professional duty to arrange external supervision.*

▸ that helps society **civic, public** *She felt that it was her civic duty to vote.*

● v+N have a duty **have, owe** *We have a legal duty to provide you with advice and assistance.* ● *Councils owe a duty to their tax payers to recover unpaid rents.*

> You can also say that someone is ***under a duty***: *Tour operators are under a duty to ensure that accommodation is safe and hygienic.*

▸ do a duty **carry out, discharge, do, exercise, fulfil, meet, perform, undertake** *He called for a report into the way the company was performing its duty, not just to shareholders, but to workers and consumers too.*

▸ not do a duty **avoid, breach, evade, neglect** *The council had neglected its duty to keep the drains clear, thus causing the water build up.*

▸ make someone have a duty **impose, place, put** *The law imposes a duty on employers to ensure the health and safety of all employees.*

▸ start to have a duty **assume, take on** *He temporarily assumed the duty of chairman.*

● N+of **care, confidence, confidentiality, faith** *The Government has placed an increased duty of care on employers for staff health problems.*

● n+of+N the act of not doing a duty **breach, dereliction, neglect** *The employers were not in breach of duty by exposing him to brick dust.*

▸ a feeling of duty **sense** *He was a committed Christian with a strong sense of public duty.*

● and/or **obligation, power, privilege, responsibility, right** *All citizens, wherever they are located, have certain responsibilities and duties.*

Ee

earn V
get something from your own efforts or behaviour

- V+n a name **name, nickname, title** *The bird is most vocal at dawn and dusk which has earned it the nickname 'six o'clock bird'.*
- ▶ praise, respect, etc **acclaim, accolade, admiration, applause, gratitude, plaudits, praise, recognition, reputation, respect, trust** *She has earned an international reputation for her achievements in opera.* ● *She has a lot of authority and has earned much respect from her employees.*
- ▶ a degree, award etc **award, degree, distinction, doctorate, medal** *She earned a degree from Bristol University.*
- ▶ a right **right** *Cafe Maitreya has definitely earned the right to call itself the best vegetarian restaurant.*
- ▶ a victory **victory, win** *They earned the victory, but Scotland made them work for 80 minutes.*
- ▶ a position **place, position, status** *The score was enough to earn them a place in the finals.*

earthquake N
a sudden shaking movement of the ground

- adj+N big **big, great, huge, large, major, massive, powerful, severe, strong, violent** *A massive earthquake registering 9.0 on the Richter scale struck off the west coast of Indonesia.*
- ▶ causing a lot of damage **bad, catastrophic, destructive, devastating, disastrous, terrible** *A devastating earthquake in the state of Gujarat killed more than 20,000 people.*
- ▶ small **minor, small** *Minor earthquakes rumble beneath Britain every day, although we seldom feel a thing.*

easy ADJ
not difficult, or not needing much work

- adv+ADJ very **dead** INFORMAL, **exceptionally, extremely, incredibly, particularly, really, remarkably, ridiculously, very, wonderfully** *The website was really easy to use and I quickly found what I wanted.*
- ▶ rather **comparatively, fairly, pretty** INFORMAL, **quite, reasonably, relatively, slightly** *Once I made the commitment to losing weight, it was relatively easy.*
- ▶ in a way that surprises you **amazingly, surprisingly** *The cake was surprisingly easy to make.*
- ▶ but not as easy as it first seems **deceptively** *The book is a deceptively easy read, and repays more careful attention than the style would suggest.*
- v+ADJ **be, become, feel, find sth, look, make sth, seem, sound** *Planning of the project was made easier through regular communication between the people involved.*

eater N
someone who eats in a particular way

- adj+N only eating a few foods and refusing to try others **faddy, finicky, fussy, picky** *Many young children are picky eaters.*
- ▶ eating a lot of food **big, good, hearty, heavy, voracious** *He used to be a very good eater, but around four months ago he started to go off his food.*
- ▶ unable to stop eating **compulsive** *Compulsive eaters try diet after diet in an attempt to lose weight.*
- ▶ eating healthy food **healthy** *I'm a very healthy eater and do plenty of exercise.*
- ▶ making a mess when you eat **messy** *My little boy is such a messy eater and gets his food everywhere.*

eat into PHR VB
use more time or money than intended

- V+n **budget, income, profit, resources, savings, time** *Many professional musicians make up their incomes through teaching, which inevitably eats into their own practice time.*

eat up PHR VB
use large amounts of time, money, or other resources

- V+n **bandwidth, capital, cash, funds, memory, money, profits, resources, space, time** *The program will eat up valuable space on your hard drive.*

echo N
a repeated noise caused by sound hitting a surface

- adj+N clear **booming, clear, distinct, strong** *A booming echo answered each bang and filled the cave with sound.*
- ▶ not clear **distant, faint, hollow** *I heard four planks fall down with a hollow echo.*
- ▶ strange **curious, eerie, ghostly, strange** *Her voice cast strange echoes in the empty room.*

ecological ADJ
relating to the environment

- ADJ+n effect **consequences, effect, footprint, impact, implications** *One way to find out how green you are is to see what kind of ecological footprint you are creating.*
- ▶ damage **collapse, damage, degradation, destruction, devastation** *Global warming threatens catastrophic climate change and ecological damage.*
- ▶ disaster **catastrophe, crisis, disaster** *Chernobyl and Bhopal are just two of the ecological disasters of recent decades.*
- ▶ importance **importance, significance, status, value** *We are interested in the ecological status of rivers, that is, what plant, fish and other life can be supported.*
- ▶ balance **balance, integrity, stability** *The inappropriate usage of mountain areas is causing the ecological balance in these areas to collapse.*
- ▶ differences **diversity, variation** *We want to preserve ecological diversity.*
- ▶ area **corridor, niche, zone** *This is the core of a large project to establish ecological corridors in the Brazilian rainforests.*
- ▶ study **study, survey** *Ecological surveys are conducted to ensure that the impact of the scheme is minimised.*

▶ ability to continue **sustainability** *The Green Party is committed to ecological sustainability.*

economic ADJ
relating to a country's or region's economy

- adv+ADJ **essentially, primarily, purely, solely, strictly** *In this article he shifts the definition of growth from a purely economic standpoint to one based on welfare, health etc.*
- ADJ+n improvement **boom, growth, recovery, revival, upturn** *China's economic boom transformed Shanghai into a twenty-first century global city.*
▶ good situation **prosperity, stability, viability, vitality** *Public transport plays an important part in the economic prosperity of the area.*
▶ worsening **collapse, crisis, decline, downturn, slowdown, slump** *Falling attendances at industrial trade shows are partly as a result of the economic downturn.*
▶ bad situation **crisis, depression, inactivity, recession, stagnation** *In the mid-1980s, Europe was gripped by economic stagnation.*
▶ difficulty **backwardness, deprivation, hardship** *Many people are leaving their communities, only to face economic hardship in the cities.*
▶ activity or development **activity, development, regeneration** *The government is committed to the economic regeneration of its market towns.*
▶ protest actions **blockade, embargo, sanction** *Many children died as a result of the economic sanctions imposed on the region.*
▶ change **reform** *The Egyptian economy has been undergoing economic reforms.*
▶ regular changes **cycle** *We aim to reduce the unemployment rate over the economic cycle.*
▶ situation **climate, situation** *The economic climate in the Netherlands is hard right now.*
▶ future **outlook, prospects** *What are your thoughts about the economic outlook?*
▶ sign **indicator** *Economic indicators include household income and business performance.*
▶ policy or theory **policy, theory** *Our economic policy is based on getting the best out of all our people and all their potential.*

economical ADJ
not costing or spending much money

- adv+ADJ very **exceptionally, extremely, highly, so** INFORMAL, **very** *As well as being highly economical, natural gas is less harmful to the environment than petrol and diesel.*
▶ rather **fairly, quite, reasonably, relatively** *Hiring a car is a convenient and fairly economical way of getting around.*
- ADJ+n way or method **manner, means, method, way** *Previously developed built-up areas must be developed in an economical way.*
▶ solution or idea **proposition, solution** *We are committed to supplying the most economical solutions to our customer's power problems.*
▶ choice **alternative, choice, option** *Charter airlines offer an economical alternative to scheduled airlines.*
▶ action **operation, production, use** *Learning from notes can be an economical use of time.*
- and/or **convenient, easy, effective, efficient,**

practical, reliable *The fragrance lingers much longer in the air and it is therefore much more effective and economical than normal air fresheners.*

economy N
a country's system of organizing trade, industry, and money

- adj+N strong **booming, buoyant, dynamic, healthy, robust, stable, strong, thriving, vibrant** *It is one of the most dynamic economies in the region.*
▶ weak **ailing, faltering, fragile, sagging, sluggish, stagnant, vulnerable, weak** *They are attempting to rebuild the country's fragile economy.*
▶ types of economy **advanced, capitalist, global, hi-tech, industrial, knowledge-based, low-carbon, market, mixed, planned, post-industrial, rural** *They aim to develop a world-class knowledge-based economy by supporting hi-tech innovative companies.*
- v+N make an economy stronger **boost, develop, kick-start, regenerate, revitalize, revive, stimulate, strengthen, transform** *The export of grain and coal helped to kick-start Russia's economy after the war.*
▶ make an economy worse **cripple, damage, devastate, harm, undermine** *Any extra regulation could further damage an already weak economy.*
- N+v when an economy improves **boom, expand, grow, pick up, rebound, recover** *During the early 1920s the Italian economy expanded dramatically.*

To describe an economy which is improving, you can also talk about *an upturn in an economy* or *an economic upturn*: *Experts are optimistic about an early upturn in the world economy.*

▶ when an economy gets worse **collapse, contract, decline, falter, shrink, slow (down), stagnate** *Without access to its key markets, the economy would rapidly collapse.*

To describe an economy which is getting worse, you can also talk about *a downturn* or *slowdown in an economy* or *an economic downturn/slowdown*: *The recession has tested the ability of management to cope with a period of economic downturn.*

education N
the activity of educating people

- adj+N good **decent, good, high-quality, proper** *We all have views on what constitutes a good education.*
▶ general or basic **all-round, basic, broad, general** *The course provides a broad education for those who take up other occupations.*
▶ for young children **early-years, elementary, nursery, primary** *The game is aimed at pupils who are leaving primary education and are about to start at secondary school.*
▶ for older children **post-primary, secondary** *Within secondary education, all pupils up to 16 years of age study English, maths, and science.*
▶ for adults **adult, continuing** *Many local centres offer continuing education programmes for adults.*
▶ at college or university **college, further, higher, tertiary, university** *Most of those who leave university do not return to higher education after a year.*
▶ for children with/without special needs **mainstream, special** *Such pupils often have needs that are ignored in mainstream education.*

▶ where different groups learn together **comprehensive, inclusive, integrated** *State comprehensive education was introduced in Britain in the 1960s, enabling children with different levels of ability to be taught together.* • *The move towards inclusive education has begun.*

▶ in private schools **independent, private, public-school** *There has been a move by more affluent people towards private education.*

▶ in government schools **public, public-school, state** *Good state education and clean hospitals are very important to people.*

In the UK a **public-school education** refers to education in one of the country's leading private schools for children between the ages of 13 and 18 (known as 'public schools'). In the US, **public** or **public-school education** is provided in schools that are paid for from taxes and free for children to attend. This is called **state education** in the UK.

▶ types of education **classical, liberal, traditional** *The school has always believed in the value of a broad liberal education.*

▶ for everyone **universal** *Literacy and universal education is being promoted worldwide.*

▶ in preparation for a particular job **vocational** *Vocational education covers subjects such as maths, technology and information technology.*

▶ in a particular subject **legal, medical, religious, sex** *Happily in this country we have an excellent tradition of religious education in schools.*

▶ full-time/part-time **full-time, part-time** *Most children's full-time education is confined to less than nine years.*

▶ in schools/not in schools **formal, informal, non-formal** *They received no formal education.*

● v+N give an education **deliver, give sb, offer sb, provide** *The play group provides pre-school education to under fives.*

▶ get an education **access, benefit from, get, receive** *The goal of so many students is to get an education so that they can get a real job and make some real money.*

▶ be in education **be in, continue in, remain in, stay in** *All her children are still in full-time education.*

▶ enter education **come into, enter, go into, pursue, re-enter, return to, undertake** *Each year applications are received from students entering further education and needing extra help with computers, wheelchairs or other equipment.*

▶ continue or complete your education **complete, continue, finish** *People who have just started work after completing their education are particularly vulnerable.*

▶ leave education **leave** *Fewer Scottish teenagers leave education at 16, and many more go on to university than in England.*

▶ deny someone an education **deny sb, deprive sb of, exclude sb from** *Many children are denied education because they cannot afford the uniform.*

eerie ADJ
strange and mysterious, and sometimes frightening

● ADJ+n sound **echo, silence, sound** *The others disappeared, leaving an eerie silence in the yard.*

▶ light **glow, light** *A full moon bathed everything in a strange, eerie glow.*

▶ atmosphere **atmosphere, calm, feeling** *People say they find the atmosphere very eerie late at night and have to get off the hill.*

▶ similarity **resemblance, similarity** *He was fascinated by her eerie resemblance to a character in his latest novel.*

● and/or **atmospheric, dark, strange, unsettling** *A strange and eerie calm settled over the park.*

effect N
a change produced in one person or thing by another

● adj+N bad **adverse, damaging, deleterious, detrimental, devastating, harmful, ill, negative, undesirable** *Changes were about to occur that would have adverse effects on his career.*

▶ good **beneficial, positive** *Evidence can be seen of the beneficial effects of a cut in the drink-drive limit.*

▶ wanted **desired** *The video had the desired effect. It made the audience think about the consequences of bad behaviour.*

▶ big **dramatic, far-reaching, major, profound, serious, significant, substantial** *Motorcycles and scooters can have a dramatic effect on reducing congestion.*

▶ small **little** *He prescribed medication to lower my blood pressure, but this had little effect.*

▶ unintended **unintended** *The reform of any law may have unintended effects.*

An additional effect that is not intended and that could be unpleasant is a **side effect**: *The treatment has no significant side effects.*

▶ indirect **indirect, knock-on** *When you run a small business everything that happens in your private life has knock-on effects on your business.*

▶ gradually increasing **cumulative, snowball** *Laser treatments have cumulative effects, which means that the dose from one treatment lasts for some time and what remains will be added to the dose delivered in the next treatment.*

▶ causing a series of events **domino, ripple** *Some diplomats pointed to the domino effect non-US participation might create: without the United States, China and Russia and others would be unlikely to join.*

▶ future **long-term** *The study was to investigate the long-term effects on monkeys when they were separated from their mothers when only six months old.*

▶ types of effect **calming, depressant, sedative, stimulant, warming** *This kind of chanting has a deeply calming effect on mind and body.*

● v+N have an effect **cause, exert, have, produce, result in** *Nutrition has a major effect on the body.*

▶ experience an effect **cope with, deal with, experience, reel from, suffer, suffer from** *The country was still reeling from the effects of war.*

▶ increase an effect **enhance, increase, magnify**

▶ reduce an effect **lessen, minimize, reduce** *How can we minimize the effects of stress?*

▶ reduce an effect by doing something with an opposite effect **compensate for, counter, counteract, mitigate, offset** *You will be taught about the effects of diving on your body and how to mitigate these effects.*

▶ study an effect **assess, consider, evaluate, examine, investigate, look at, observe, quantify, study** *The aim was to investigate the effects of tourism in the Mediterranean.*

● N+v happen **arise from, last, occur, result from** *The survey focuses on air-quality effects which arise from the increase in road traffic.*

▶ become less strong **disappear, wear off** *The effects of the drug usually wear off after a few hours.*

effective ADJ
working well and producing the intended result

● adv+ADJ very **devastatingly, extremely, fully, highly, hugely, pretty** INFORMAL**, really** INFORMAL**, truly, very** *David has a highly effective way of engaging the listener.*

▶ rather **moderately, partially, quite, reasonably** *The previous treatment has been ineffective or only partially effective.*

▶ more and more **increasingly, more and more** *As you become increasingly effective in your role you will become more valued as an employee.*

▶ in a surprising way **amazingly, extraordinarily, incredibly, remarkably, surprisingly** *I have now developed a beautifully simple but amazingly effective strategy.*

▶ equally **equally** *Both forms of treatment have proved equally effective.*

▶ in a particular way **clinically, economically, educationally, operationally, pedagogically** *Is multimedia educationally effective?*

● ADJ+n way or method **alternative, manner, means, mechanism, method, solution, strategy, tool, way** *Combining diet with exercise is a far more effective means of losing weight.*

▶ actions or activities **communication, control, intervention, leadership, learning, management, teaching, teamwork, use** *We need to ensure the most effective use of buildings.*

▶ treatment **remedy, treatment, vaccine** *No effective malaria vaccine has yet been developed.*

▶ weapon, or something that stops someone doing something **deterrent** *Highly visible locks have proved very effective deterrents in blocks of garages.*

effectiveness N
the quality of being effective

● v+N examine effectiveness **analyse, assess, compare, determine, evaluate, examine, gauge, investigate, judge, look at, measure, monitor, test** *It is important to keep evaluating the effectiveness of educational methods.*

▶ improve effectiveness **enhance, improve, increase, maximize, optimize, strengthen** *This policy improves the effectiveness of ads.*

▶ reduce effectiveness **compromise, decrease, diminish, limit, lose, reduce, undermine** *The recent threat to email from computer viruses has seriously reduced its effectiveness.*

▶ show effectiveness **confirm, demonstrate, prove, show, verify** *New drugs need to undergo rigorous trials to prove their effectiveness and safety.*

▶ ensure effectiveness **ensure** *The Bank of England's main job is to ensure the effectiveness of the UK financial system.*

▶ doubt effectiveness **doubt, question** *This study was*

not undertaken to question the effectiveness of trades unions.

efficiency N
the ability to work well and produce good results

● adj+N types of efficiency **administrative, economic, mechanical, operational, organizational, technical** *A major advantage of upgrading our system is improved operational efficiency.*

▶ greatest **maximum, optimal, optimum, utmost** *All wording in any advertising campaign is carefully calculated for maximum efficiency.*

▶ great **great, high** *Greater efficiency means reduced costs.*

▶ at a low level **low** *British housing has low thermal efficiency, and thus offers poorer protection against cold.*

▶ of a person **calm, ruthless** *He set about regaining his throne with ruthless efficiency.*

● v+N improve efficiency **boost, encourage, enhance, improve, increase, maximize, optimize, promote** *In the last Parliament we focused on ways to improve the efficiency of Government.*

▶ reduce efficiency **affect, compromise, decrease, impair, reduce** *Dirt reduces lighting efficiency, encouraging people to turn more lights on.*

▶ achieve efficiency **achieve, attain, ensure, maintain** *You need to clean the filters regularly to ensure total efficiency.*

▶ measure or test efficiency **assess, evaluate, measure, test** *For secondary, university and technical education, efficiency is measured by the number of graduates who find jobs.*

efficient ADJ
working well and producing good results

● adv+ADJ very **extraordinarily, extremely, highly, incredibly, remarkably, ruthlessly, very** *It is an extremely efficient and well-run organisation.*

▶ rather **fairly, reasonably, relatively** *Halogen dynamos are reasonably efficient and cheap to run.*

▶ in a particular way **computationally, economically, environmentally, operationally, technically, thermally** *We should encourage people to use the most environmentally efficient way to travel.*

● ADJ+n way or method **manner, means, method, process, system, way** *We aim to deal with any complaints in a professional and efficient manner.*

▶ action or activity **delivery, handling, management, running, service, use** *Hydroponics makes very efficient use of resources.*

▶ working **functioning, operation** *It is important for the efficient operation of any pharmacy business for the head office to be able to communicate with the branches.*

effort N
an attempt to do something

● adj+N big **all-out, big, concentrated, concerted, considerable, determined, great, massive, strenuous** *A concerted effort has been made to clean up the area.*

To say that someone makes a big effort to do something, you can say they *spared no effort* in doing it: *No effort was spared in maintaining clean attractive stations.*

▶ very good **brave, heroic, sterling, valiant** *The Net was a valiant effort by the BBC to put together a programme about the Internet.*

▶ continuing **sustained, tireless, unstinting, untiring** *I would like to thank thank the organizers for their tireless efforts to ensure the smooth running of the conference.*

▶ enough **all reasonable, every** *All reasonable efforts have been made to contact the current copyright holder.*

▶ small **feeble, little** *He made a feeble effort to move, staggered, then fell to the ground.*

▶ conscious **conscious** *Make a conscious effort to slow down your breathing.*

▶ desperate **desperate, frantic** *They were making frantic efforts to save the injured passengers.*

▶ unsuccessful **futile, vain, wasted** *I wrote down my thoughts in a vain effort to get rid of them by sharing them with the world.*

▶ worthwhile **worthwhile** *I felt as though all my efforts had been worthwhile.*

▶ at the end **final, last, last-ditch** *The UN is trying to secure talks between the two sides in a last-ditch effort to avoid war.*

▶ by a group **collaborative, combined, cooperative, joint, team** *This book is a collaborative effort involving several researchers.*

▶ by one person **individual, solo** *We must all make our individual effort to care for our world and encourage others to do the same.*

● v+N make an effort **make** *The employee should make all reasonable efforts to attend the interview.*

▶ make a bigger effort **intensify, redouble, renew** *We redoubled our efforts, and were soon rewarded.*

▶ continue making an effort **continue** *Around 30 firefighters are continuing their efforts to put out the fire.*

▶ stop making an effort **abandon** *We will never abandon our efforts for the elimination of nuclear weapons.*

▶ focus your effort **concentrate, direct, focus, target** *We must concentrate our efforts on the big issues that cause real harm.*

▶ make someone's efforts less successful **block, frustrate, hamper, hinder, impede, sabotage, thwart, undermine** *Other colleagues may be trying to undermine your efforts.*

▶ reward or support someone's efforts **reward, support** *Their efforts were rewarded when their striker scored.*

● N+v fail **come to nothing, fail, prove unsuccessful** *All their efforts had failed and they felt there was little more that they could do.*

▶ succeed **pay off, prove successful, succeed** *My efforts finally paid off and I got the job I wanted.*

effortless ADJ
done well or successfully and without effort

● adv+ADJ completely **absolutely, completely** *The movements appeared very relaxed and completely effortless.*

▶ almost **almost, virtually** *A totally professional bar manager makes quality service look almost effortless.*

▶ in a way that seems effortless **apparently, seemingly** *Rachel is now singing with seemingly effortless skill.*

● ADJ+n **charm, control, cool, ease, elegance, grace, power, style, superiority** *Hilary has made the transformation from TV star to recording artist with effortless ease.*

● and/or **easy, natural, quick, smooth** *The style of playing is smooth and effortless.*

ego N
the opinion that you have of yourself and your own importance

● adj+N when you think you are very good **big, enormous, huge, inflated, massive, over-inflated** *The band have some of the biggest egos in rock music.*

▶ when you need people to say you are good **fragile** *Fragile egos don't respond too well to criticism.*

● v+N when you make someone feel more important **bolster, boost, feed, inflate, massage, pander to** *They only invite to meetings the people who make them feel comfortable and massage their egos.*

▶ when you make someone feel less important **bruise, deflate, dent** *I wanted to punish someone who had bruised my ego.*

elaborate ADJ
very detailed and complicated

● adv+ADJ very **extremely, highly, very** *Its language is highly elaborate, full of puns and other wordplay.*

▶ rather **fairly, quite, rather, somewhat** *It seems a rather elaborate way of saying something that is basically very simple.*

▶ too **over, too** *The presentation is elegant rather than over elaborate.*

● ADJ+n trick **charade, hoax, joke, plot, scam, scheme** *At first I thought that it was an elaborate hoax.*

▶ ritual **ceremony, ritual** *The male fruit fly has an elaborate courtship ritual.*

▶ decoration **decoration, design, ornamentation, pattern** *All the carvings were two dimensional designs with little elaborate decoration.*

elation N
a feeling of great happiness and excitement

● adj+N **great, pure, sheer** *When I finished the marathon I felt a combination of exhaustion and pure elation.*

● n+of+N **feeling, moment, mood, sense, state, wave** *There's a shared sense of elation that the theatre is now open.*

elect V
choose someone by voting

● adv+V in fair elections **constitutionally, democratically, freely, legitimately** *The next step in the process is to democratically elect a Regional Council to oversee and run the region.*

▶ when everyone votes for someone **unanimously**

The board unanimously elected its chief executive to succeed Mr Weill as chairman.

▶ by the people in a particular area **locally, nationally, regionally** *They were locally elected officials who listened to the people and gave them what they wanted.*

▶ at the correct time or according to the correct procedure **duly, formally** *Councillor Bresland was duly elected and took up the position as Chairman.*

▶ when most people vote for someone **by a landslide, overwhelmingly** *He was overwhelmingly elected president of the new republic.*

▶ directly/indirectly **directly, indirectly** *The parliament represents the EU's citizens and is directly elected by them.*

election N
an occasion when people vote

● adj+N fair **democratic, fair, free** *The Prime Minister was appointed after a democratic election.*

▶ sudden **snap** *The government is keen to call a snap election because there are a whole number of financial scandals which might implicate ministers next year.*

▶ types of election **congressional, council, general, leadership, local, mayoral, municipal, national, parliamentary, presidential, state** *People tend to vote differently in general and local elections.*

▶ part way through a government's time in power **midterm** *The Democrats made major gains in the 1930 midterm elections.*

● v+N hold an election **conduct, have, hold** *The Committee resigned and elections were held for the Committee positions.*

▶ win an election **be elected in, defeat sb in, win** *Labour won the election with the votes of 22 percent of the electorate.*

▶ lose an election **lose** *Mr. Gore lost the 2000 election.*

▶ fight an election **contest, fight, participate in, stand in** *He stood in the election as an independent candidate.*

▶ vote in an election **cast a vote in, vote in** *Fewer than half of the electroate voted in yesterday's local elections.*

▶ call an election **call** *He resigned as Prime Minister in December and called an immediate election.*

▶ try to influence the result of an election **interfere in, rig** *For over 20 years he has maintained control by rigging elections.*

▶ not take part in an election **boycott** *They urged Nicaraguans to boycott the election.*

▶ see whether an election is fair **monitor** *The Electoral Commission is an independent body set up by Parliament to monitor elections.*

electricity N
energy that produces light, heat, and power

● v+N produce electricity **convert sth into, create, generate, make, produce** *Electricity was generated by turning the handle of the machine.*

▶ use electricity **consume, run on, use** *Diesel cars can be converted to run on electricity.*

▶ provide electricity **distribute, provide (sb with), supply (sb with)** *The wind turbine will supply enough electricity for over 2,200 homes.*

▶ stop providing electricity **cut (off), disconnect**

Their electricity was cut off because they didn't pay their bills.

▶ waste/not waste electricity **conserve, save, waste** *To save electricity use low energy light bulbs.*

▶ let electricity pass through **conduct** *Plastic doesn't conduct electricity.*

● N+from+n **coal, fossil fuels, gas, renewables, solar power, sunlight, waste, wind** *The government wanted to get 10 percent of electricity from renewables by 2010.*

elegance
the quality of being beautiful in a graceful or simple way

● adj+N simple **cool, natural, quiet, restrained, simple** *Our designs feature clean lines and a simple elegance.*

▶ great **great, sheer, supreme** *The whole of the rooms were re-papered, and were furnished with great elegance.*

▶ old/new **classic, classical, contemporary, modern, timeless, traditional** *Their timeless elegance and unrivalled culinary performance have made them a legend.*

▶ types of elegance **architectural, sartorial** *Having taken his sister's advice, Danny was a figure of sartorial elegance.*

● and/or beauty **beauty, charm, glamour, grace, style** *Enjoy our stylish setting, and surround yourself in elegance and style.*

▶ comfort **comfort, luxury** *Natural colours create a cosy ambience, reflecting luxury and elegance.*

▶ simplicity **clarity, lightness, purity, simplicity** *The ultimate goal should always be speed, simplicity and elegance.*

▶ refinement **finesse, poise, precision, refinement, sophistication, taste, wit** *Deborah Bull danced with elegance and precision.*

elegant ADJ
1 beautiful in a graceful or simple way

● adv+ADJ very **beautifully, extremely, incredibly, rather, remarkably, so** INFORMAL**, strikingly, supremely, truly, very, wonderfully** *It is a wonderfully elegant building.*

▶ in a particular way **casually, classically, coolly** *The room is decorated in classically elegant rich burgundy colours.*

▶ in someone's style of clothes **sartorially** *Bugs Bunny is a sartorially elegant but rather naughty cartoon rabbit.*

● and/or **beautiful, graceful, refined, sophisticated, stylish** *The hotel has all the ingredients for an elegant and stylish wedding.*

2 impressive because of being simple and effective

● adv+ADJ very **extremely, incredibly, particularly, rather, supremely, very, wonderfully** *The result is a wonderfully elegant and rigorous system.*

▶ in a particular way **mathematically, technically, theoretically** *Scientists have have to devise solutions that are not only technically elegant but also cost effective.*

● ADJ+n **prose, solution** *The article is written in clear, readable, and elegant prose.*

element N

an important basic part of something complicated

- adj+N important **critical, crucial, essential, important, integral, key, major, significant, vital** *Parents' involvement is a key element in the success of their children's learning at school.*
- most important **central, core, main** *The student should be able to identify the main elements of climate.*
- basic **basic, fundamental** *There are four basic elements of a story – a beginning, a middle and an end, together with some sort of credible plot.*
- individual **constituent, discrete, individual** *Think of it as a coherent system, not a series of individual elements.*
- different **different, disparate** *All of those seemingly disparate elements are blended into one coherent whole.*
- types of element **decorative, graphic, graphical, structural, visual** *The main structural elements of the house simply rest on the concrete blocks.*

eligible ADJ

allowed to do or receive something

- ADJ+for consideration for a job or position **consideration, election, nomination, re-appointment, re-election** *Any ex-members of the committee shall be eligible for re-election.*
- membership or inclusion **admission, entry, inclusion, membership** *Only persons aged 16 years or over shall be eligible for membership of any lottery.*
- money **aid, assistance, benefit, funding, help, loan, support** *If you are eligible for help towards the cost of school uniform, we will send you a voucher.*
- money for education **bursary, grant, scholarship** *Students from the poorest backgrounds are eligible for a bursary.*
- money off something **concession, discount, relief** *If your vehicle is 1200cc or less, you may be eligible for the discount.*
- money you get back **compensation, rebate, refund** *Soiled goods will not be eligible for refund or exchange.*
- permission to leave prison early **parole** *UK prisoners are eligible for parole after they have served half their sentence.*
- ADJ+infinitive **apply, claim, compete, enter, join, participate, play, receive sth, register, serve, stand, vote, work** *Who is eligible to apply for the course?*

eliminate V

get rid of something

- adv+V completely **altogether, completely, entirely, totally** *I didn't totally eliminate all the wheat from my diet, but cut way back.*
- almost completely **almost, effectively, essentially, largely, practically, virtually** *The measures have virtually eliminated illegal parking in the area.*
- gradually **gradually, progressively** *Many people believed that nuclear weapons were being gradually eliminated.*
- permanently **for ever, permanently** *He will announce a plan to permanently eliminate the threat of terrorism.*
- according to a careful plan **systematically** *These practices systematically eliminate biodiversity from farmland.*

- V+n problems **ambiguity, confusion, duplication, error, hassle, problem, waste** *We should work together to eliminate the duplication of effort.*
- unfairness or suffering **discrimination, hunger, illiteracy, inequality, poverty, racism** *New legislation is aimed at eliminating sex discrimination.*
- risk **possibility, risk** *The box helps you keep your cupboards tidy and eliminates the possibility of bottles being knocked over*

elite N

a small group of people with a lot of advantages

- adj+N with a high social position **aristocratic, educated, landed, privileged, wealthy** *Power and wealth is in the hands of the privileged elite.*
- powerful **powerful** *Disputes about national economic policy arose between these powerful elites.*
- small **small** *Art is not just for a small wealthy elite.*
- in charge of an area or country **governing, ruling** *A small number of families traditionally formed the core of the country's ruling elite.*
- in a particular area **local, urban** *Piped water supply in most poor countries is only available to a small urban elite constituting a tiny proportion of the population.*
- types of elite **bureaucratic, business, capitalist, cultural, economic, intellectual, liberal, military, political, social** *This plan has been made by political elites against the interests of the common people.*

eloquent ADJ

expressing what you mean clearly and effectively

- ADJ+n what someone says **defence, plea, sermon, speech, statement, testimony, tribute** *The conclusion of this paper is an eloquent testimony to the value sometimes added by rigorous economic theory.*
- person **advocate, critic, preacher, speaker, witness** *He was respected as an eloquent local preacher.*
- and/or **entertaining, erudite, passionate, persuasive, witty** *Hansen is a very erudite and eloquent speaker who doesn't fumble or hesitate.*

embargo N

a government order preventing trade with another country

- adj+N total **absolute, complete, total** *He supported a total embargo on trade.*
- strict **comprehensive, crippling, strict, tight** *The army is roughly half the size it was during the recent war and remains under a tight arms embargo.*
- not total **partial** *President Eisenhower responded by declaring a partial embargo on trade with Cuba.*
- types of embargo **arms, economic, export, international, military, oil, trade** *Gasoline prices fell lower than they had been at any time since the oil embargo of 1973.*
- v+N put an embargo on something **declare, impose, lay, place, put** *The government had placed an embargo on the export of raw nuts because it could not believe the low prices that the exporters were quoting.*
- make sure that an embargo is obeyed **enforce** *They were not able to guarantee that the embargo would be strictly enforced.*

▶ be affected by an embargo **be affected by, be under** *At that time both countries were under US trade embargos.*

▶ end an embargo **end, lift, remove** *They decided to lift the arms embargo **on** the region.*

▶ not end an embargo **maintain, prolong** *France's decision to maintain the embargo caused a trade row.*

▶ make an embargo more/less strict **ease, tighten** *It also tightened the weapons embargo and cracked down hard on the oil-smuggling trade.*

▶ break an embargo **be in breach of, breach, break, bypass, circumvent, violate** *International arms embargoes are systematically violated.*

▶ not break an embargo **respect** *They declared in July that they would no longer respect the trade embargo.*

embark on PHR VB
start major new project or activity

● V+n **campaign, career, course, degree, initiative, mission, policy, process, programme, project, series, study, venture** *He decided to go to university and embark on a career in law.* ● *This year, we embarked on a series of roadshows to teach children about healthy eating.*

embarrassed ADJ
ashamed and worried what people will think

● adv+ADJ **very acutely, almost, deeply, extremely, really INFORMAL, so INFORMAL, terribly, thoroughly, too, utterly, very** *As a teenager, I was acutely embarrassed **by** my parents.* ● *People are also often too embarrassed to talk to their doctor about these symptoms.*

▶ rather **faintly, a little, mildly, quite, rather, slightly, somewhat** *Although I felt a little embarrassed **about** all the compliments, I was beginning to enjoy it.*

● v+ADJ **appear, be, become, feel, get, look, seem, sound** *If students feel embarrassed, ask them to write questions on pieces of paper and hand them in anonymously.* ● *When she laughs at my spelling mistakes I get very embarrassed **about** it.*

● and/or **afraid, angry, ashamed, awkward, nervous, shy, uncomfortable** *Most people feel awkward and embarrassed sitting in front of a camera.*

embarrassing ADJ
making you feel nervous, ashamed, or stupid

● adv+ADJ **very acutely, deeply, downright, excruciatingly, extremely, highly, hugely, intensely, painfully, really INFORMAL, terribly, toe-curlingly, too, very** *It must have been excruciatingly embarrassing for you to have had to go through this.*

▶ rather **faintly, a little, quite, rather, slightly, somewhat** *The crowd seemed to love it, but looking back it's rather embarrassing.*

▶ when something could be embarrassing **potentially** *Reporters were not permitted to ask potentially embarrassing questions.*

▶ politically **politically** *Refusal to disclose the figures could be politically embarrassing.*

● and/or **awkward, difficult, inconvenient, painful,**

shameful, uncomfortable *The situation was awkward and even embarrassing.*

embarrassment N
a feeling of being nervous or ashamed; something that makes you embarrassed

● adj+N **serious acute, considerable, extreme, great, huge, major, much, serious, severe** *The defeat is a major embarrassment for the administration.* ● *His stammer was a source of much embarrassment.*

▶ possible **possible, potential** *If you are inexperienced in business, overcome potential embarrassment and ask for help.*

▶ slight **mild, slight** *His head lowered through slight embarrassment, he admitted to having piano lessons for two years but failing to achieve grade 1!*

▶ total **complete, sheer, utter** *The reaction of the players seemed to range from dismay to sheer embarrassment.*

▶ types of embarrassment **financial, personal, political, professional, social** *His visit is causing political embarrassment in Italy.*

● v+N **experience embarrassment cringe with, die of, experience, feel, squirm with, suffer** *Cringing with embarrassment, he got up to sing a song.*

▶ cause embarrassment **cause (sb), lead to, result in** *The news has caused serious embarrassment for the Prime Minister.*

▶ not cause embarrassment **avoid, minimize, prevent, save (sb), spare (sb)** *To spare the embarrassment of those who do not know the answer, the child is allowed to nominate another to answer the question instead.*

▶ stop experiencing embarrassment **get over, overcome** *Now I have got over the embarrassment of telling people what my problem is.*

▶ hide your embarrassment **cover, hide** *He stood up quickly, trying to hide his embarrassment.*

embody V
be an excellent example of a principle or quality

● V+n **idea or principle concept, ethos, idea, ideal, notion, principle, truth, value** *Where the challenge is greatest, reform must be boldest – and academies embody that principle.*

▶ quality **essence, spirit** *He manages to embody the spirit of a man on the verge of a great change with ease.*

embrace V
welcome and completely accept a belief, method etc

● adv+V **fully or enthusiastically actively, eagerly, enthusiastically, fully, heartily, readily, uncritically, wholeheartedly, willingly** *He enthusiastically embraced new technology, and in particular the Internet.*

▶ publicly **openly, publicly** *Hollywood is still reluctant to publicly embrace homosexuality.*

● V+n **challenge, change, concept, diversity, ethos, idea, innovation, notion, opportunity, principle, technology** *She embraces diversity, and believes that all students should have an opportunity to contribute to music lessons.*

emerge V
become known

- adv+V slowly **gradually, slowly** *Startling findings are gradually emerging from the archives.*
- quickly or suddenly **quickly, rapidly, suddenly** *We are well equipped to deal with these rapidly emerging issues.*
- clearly **clearly, strongly** *What had happened clearly emerges from a document that was published later.*
- naturally **naturally, spontaneously** *A number of issues emerged spontaneously at this conference.*
- later **later, subsequently** *It subsequently emerged that they had been in possession of the facts all along.*
- in the end **eventually, ultimately** *Like it or not, the truth will eventually emerge.*
- n+V **conclusion, consensus, details, evidence, fact, findings, idea, issue, pattern, picture, story, theme, theory, trend, truth** *In recent years, a consensus has emerged about the Government's current approach.*

emergence N
the process of appearing or becoming recognized

- adj+N **eventual, gradual, possible, rapid, recent, slow, subsequent, sudden** *Look at the public and political stresses caused by the sudden emergence of genetic engineering into unprepared societies.*
- v+N see the emergence of something **see, witness** *The last decades of the previous century witnessed the emergence of several new diseases.*
- signal the emergence of something **herald, mark, signal** *Wind energy could herald the emergence of Britain as a leading player in the green industrial revolution.*
- study the emergence of something **examine, explore, investigate, look at, study** *This article examines the emergence of a pro-strike press.*
- follow the emergence of something **chart, follow, trace, track** *In Control and Freedom, Chun traces the emergence of the Internet as a mass medium.*
- cause the emergence of something **bring about, contribute to, culminate in, lead to, result in** *This has led to the emergence of organised criminals who made fortunes supplying illegal alcohol.*
- prevent or delay the emergence of something **block, delay, inhibit, prevent** *Preventing the emergence of a 'digital divide' between business in different parts of the country must be a top policy priority.*
- encourage the emergence of something **encourage, facilitate, foster, promote, stimulate, support** *The availability of funds encouraged the emergence of new initiatives and new organisations.*
- be before the emergence of something **precede, predate** *The interest in consumer health information predates the emergence of the Internet.*
- be at the same time as the emergence of something **coincide with** *His appointment coincided with the emergence of soul as the preferred dance music of black teenagers.*

emergency N
an unexpected dangerous situation requiring immediate action

- adj+N very serious **dire, extreme, life-threatening, major** *Only use this number in cases of extreme emergency.*
- real **genuine, real** *Call 999 if you have a genuine emergency requiring the attendance of the emergency services.*
- types of emergency **dental, domestic, family, health, medical, surgical** *Only call your doctor at the weekend in a genuine medical emergency.*
- v+N be an emergency **be, constitute** *This situation could hardly be said to constitute an emergency.*
- deal with an emergency **cope with, deal with, handle, manage, respond to** *We are set up to handle emergencies quickly and efficiently.*

emergency ADJ
involving or used in an emergency

- ADJ+n situation **situation** *The appointed person will have the skills necessary to give first aid in an emergency situation.*
- action **measure, plan, procedures, response** *The International Energy Agency outlined emergency measures that could be implemented if oil supplies fell by 1–2 million barrels a day.*
- help **aid, assistance** *We are providing emergency assistance to many affected communities.*
- medical treatment **operation, surgery, treatment** *He had to undergo an emergency operation on his leg.*
- services **services** *All the emergency services were present at the scene.*

emission N
a substance that goes into the air [usually plural]

- adj+N **harmful, noxious, toxic** *We aim to implement a 45 per cent reduction in harmful emissions by 2020.*
- n+N consisting of a particular substance **carbon, carbon dioxide, CO2, greenhouse gas, methane, particulate, pollutant, sulphur** *The UK's Environment Minister said yesterday that cutting carbon emissions should become the European Union's primary purpose.*
- from a particular source **aviation, exhaust, tailpipe, vehicle** *In fact, some of these products cause substantial increases in exhaust emissions.*
- v+N reduce emissions **control, curb, cut, halve, limit, lower, minimize, reduce, regulate, restrict, slash** *The Kyoto Protocol set targets for reducing emissions by 2008–2012.*
- measure the amount of emissions **calculate, estimate, measure, monitor** *As a company we will record and monitor our carbon emissions on an annual basis.*
- N+n reduction and control of emissions **control, limits, reduction, regulations, standards, targets** *What is needed is a longer-term plan for emission reductions.*
- amount of emissions **levels, rates** *Like many other companies, it was looking for ways to increase production while keeping emission levels to a minimum.*

emotion N
a feeling such as love or fear

- adj+N strong **deep, extreme, heightened, intense, overwhelming, powerful, strong** *These are issues which arouse strong emotions.*
- ▶ harmful **destructive, negative** *Laughter provides a harmless outlet for these negative emotions.*
- ▶ various **conflicting, contradictory, mixed** *She admitted to having mixed emotions about the situation.*
- ▶ not allowed to be expressed **pent-up, repressed, unexpressed** *Like crying, laughter allows the release of pent-up emotions.*
- ▶ real **genuine, heartfelt, real** *I thought I caught a hint of genuine emotion in his voice.*
- v+N feel an emotion **experience, feel** *I felt every emotion imaginable, from guilt to stupidity and fear.*
- ▶ feel a lot of emotion **be choked with, be filled with, be overcome with, be overwhelmed with** *He was completely overcome with emotion.*
- ▶ show emotion **betray, communicate, convey, display, express, portray, show** *The prisoner showed no emotion as he was led away.*
- ▶ cause emotion to be felt **arouse, elicit, evoke, provoke, stir, trigger** *Music has a particularly important role in evoking emotion in film viewers.*
- ▶ control your emotions **control, hide, repress, suppress** *She would be unable to control her emotions in an encounter with him.*
- n+of+N mixture **gamut, mixture, roller coaster, spectrum** *The whole two days were a roller coaster of emotions which ranged from sadness to elation.*
- ▶ expression **display, expression, outpouring** *Art is the expression of emotion in a controlled form.*

emotional ADJ
1 relating to emotions and their effect on your life

- ADJ+n **abuse, attachment, distress, state, stress, support, trauma, turmoil, upset, well-being** *Our emotional well-being isn't something that any of us should take for granted.*
- and/or **behavioural, cognitive, intellectual, mental, physical, practical, psychological, sexual, social, spiritual** *Many pupils have severe emotional and behavioural difficulties.*

2 affected by and expressing strong emotion

- adv+ADJ very **deeply, extremely, highly, intensely, quite, really, so** INFORMAL, **very** *Joey is in a highly emotional state.*
- ▶ rather **a little, rather, somewhat** *He looked a little emotional at the end.*
- ADJ+n **appeal, experience, farewell, journey, moment, outburst, reunion, roller coaster, scene, state** *When you have your first child it's an emotional roller coaster of an experience.*
- and/or **expressive, heartfelt, powerful** *This is a powerful emotional book which will involve readers immediately.*

emotive ADJ
causing strong feelings

- adv+ADJ **deeply, extremely, highly, particularly,**

powerfully, very *Both writers and actors have handled the highly emotive subject with sensitivity.*
- ADJ+n subject **issue, subject, topic** *The use of animals in medical research is an emotive issue.*
- ▶ word or words **argument, expression, language, phrase, rhetoric, term, word** *The debate will certainly not be advanced by the use of emotive language.*

empathy N
the ability to understand how someone feels

- adj+N great **deep, great, much, strong, total** *I have great empathy **with** the person who wrote it.*
- ▶ real **genuine, natural, real, true** *Really understanding someone else's needs requires genuine empathy and respect.*
- v+N have empathy **feel, have** *I always felt a certain empathy **with** him as our personal circumstances were similar.*
- ▶ show empathy **demonstrate, display, express, show** *Good leaders can be tough and take decisions as well as showing empathy and humility.*
- ▶ cause empathy **build, create, encourage, establish, evoke** *Each of the characters evoked our empathy in different ways.*

emphasis N
special attention given to one thing

- adj+N **considerable, great, heavy, the main, much, particular, special, strong** *The first chapter explores information systems, with particular emphasis **on** hospital information systems.*
- v+N give emphasis to something **give, lay, place, put** *Special emphasis is placed **on** the core subjects of English, Mathematics and Science.*
- ▶ change the emphasis to something else **change, shift, switch** *The Government has been switching the emphasis from the state to the individual to provide for retirement.*

emphasize V
give particular importance or attention to something

- adv+V **consistently, constantly, continually, particularly, repeatedly, rightly, strongly** *This is something we can't emphasize too strongly.*
- V+n importance **importance, significance, uniqueness, value** *I can't emphasize the importance of this enough.*
- ▶ need **necessity, need** *She emphasized the need to protect the country's infant democracy.*
- ▶ fact **aspect, fact, point** *He emphasized the fact that the objective of the sanctions was not to hurt ordinary people.*
- ▶ difference/similarity **difference, distinction, similarity** *The results emphasize the differences between the two approaches.*

emphatic ADJ
with a very clear result

- ADJ+n **defeat, success, victory, win** *Manchester maintained last week's form with an emphatic victory over Chelsea.*

empire N

1 a number of countries ruled by one government

● adj+N **far-flung, huge, large, mighty, sprawling, vast** *Under Charles V, Austria was part of a vast empire.*

● v+N increase the size of an empire **expand, extend** *At that time European powers fought brutal battles throughout Africa to expand their empires.*

▶ establish an empire **build, create, establish, forge, found** *Ur-Nammu founded the empire, which stretched into Iran.*

▶ rule an empire **control, govern, rule** *We are going to examine how Britain, a small country, came to rule a huge empire.*

▶ destroy an empire **destroy, dismantle, overthrow** *In the year 1532, the Inca empire was destroyed by the Spaniards.*

● N+v be destroyed **collapse, come to an end, crumble, decline, disintegrate, fall, fall apart** *The Western empire finally crumbled in the fifth century AD.*

▶ increase in size **expand, grew, spread** *The Russian empire expanded gradually.*

▶ continue for a particular distance **extend, reach, stretch** *They became intent on creating a new empire stretching from the Caucasus all the way to central Asia.*

● n+of+N **break-up, collapse, downfall, fall** *The gradual and messy collapse of the Empire is a complex story.*

2 a group of companies controlled by one company

● adj+N large **huge, large, vast** *Having built up a vast empire, he disposed of it to the US Steel Corporation in 1901.*

▶ types of empire **business, commercial, fashion, financial, industrial, media, newspaper, property, publishing, trading** *He then moved to the Bahamas, from where he controls his business empire.*

● v+N create an empire **build, build up, create, found** *I admire the way he has built his enormous media empire.*

▶ increase the size of an empire **expand, extend** *This profit will obviously increase their bank balance and enable them to progressively expand their empire.*

▶ control and organize an empire **control, rule, run** *She continues to run her empire from a home office.*

empirical ADJ

based on real experience or scientific experiments

▶ ADJ+n facts **data, evidence, findings** *I am struck by how little empirical evidence supports their claims.*

▶ study **analysis, investigation, observation, research, study** *These assertions have not been backed up by any large-scale empirical studies.*

▶ method **approach, method** *He contributed much to the development of empirical methods in the social sciences.*

employ V

use something for a particular purpose

▶ V+n **means, method, methodology, strategy, tactics, technique** *Different schools will employ different means to achieve the same result.*

employee N

someone who is paid regularly to work

● adj+N working for a particular time **full-time, part-time, permanent, temporary** *They now have 14 full-time employees.*

▶ in the past/present/future **existing, former, potential, prospective** *At present employees and prospective employees have protection against discrimination.*

● N+n **benefits, contributions, involvement, morale, productivity, relations, representative, satisfaction** *Are your pension costs affecting your ability to offer other employee benefits?*

employer N

a person or company that employs workers

● adj+N possibly going to employ someone **potential, prospective** *Your main aim is to convince a prospective employer that you have the skills, experience and enthusiasm to do the job.*

▶ past/present/future **current, former, future, previous** *He said that despite his sacking he had no hard feelings towards his former employers.*

▶ employing a particular number of people **large, major, small** *We are the third largest employer in the county.*

employment N

work that you are paid regularly for; a situation when a person or people have paid work

● adj+N for a particular time **casual, continuous, full-time, part-time, permanent, regular, secure, temporary** *The programme also provides the opportunity to study part time while in full-time employment.*

▶ past/present/future **current, future, previous** *Please give a description of your previous or current employment.*

▶ paid, or paid badly/well **gainful, low-paid, paid, salaried, well-paid** *We need to give young people opportunities to secure gainful employment.*

● v+N try to get employment **look for, seek** *How many recent graduates will decide to seek employment elsewhere?*

▶ get employment **find, gain, get, obtain, secure** *Other employees are being helped by various agencies to find alternative employment.*

▶ end someone's employment **terminate** *You will also be given a notice in writing terminating your employment.*

▶ leave employment **give up, leave** *She received a letter from his employer saying that he had left their employment on 16 August.*

▶ provide or increase employment **create, generate, guarantee, increase, promote, provide** *This new initiative will create employment in a very depressed area.*

● N+n legal matters **contract, law, legislation, rights, status, tribunal** *Employment legislation is extremely complicated.*

▶ opportunities **opportunities, options, possibilities, prospects** *We aim to ensure that local people benefit from the employment opportunities generated by construction work in the borough.*

empty ADJ

containing nothing

- adv+ADJ half **half** *Some reservoirs across Britain are half empty after the driest August and September since records began.*
- ▶ almost **almost, nearly, practically, virtually** *The pub was almost empty.*
- ▶ to a large degree **largely, mostly** *The harbour is tiny and is now mostly empty.*
- ▶ completely **completely, quite, totally** *Most of the buildings appeared completely empty.*
- ▶ rather **fairly, pretty** INFORMAL, **rather, relatively** *Much to my surprise, the departure lounge is relatively empty.*
- adv+ADJ **eerily, strangely** *The streets were strangely empty of traffic.*
- v+ADJ **leave sth, lie, remain, sit, stand, stay** *After the war, the Hall stood empty for almost twenty years.*

encounter N

a meeting, especially one that was not planned

- adj+N close **close, face-to-face, intimate** *He survived a close encounter with a polar bear when on an Arctic expedition.*
- ▶ unexpected **casual, chance, random, unexpected** *A chance encounter with a girl on the bus changed the course of his life.*
- ▶ short **brief** *The memories of our brief encounter were beginning to fade.*
- v+N **experience, have, survive** *During our drive through the country we had several encounters with the police.*

encounter V

experience a problem

- V+n **challenge, difficulty, hostility, obstacle, obstruction, opposition, prejudice, problem, resistance, situation** *We have tested this system but if you encounter any problems please email us.*

encourage V

suggest that someone does something that you believe would be good; provide conditions that help something to happen

- adv+V **actively, especially, particularly, positively, strongly** *She has responsibility for actively encouraging the involvement of minorities in the programme.*
- V+n use or activity **adoption, development, growth, involvement, participation, take-up, uptake, use** *We are developing initiatives in this field as a means of encouraging greater participation by young people.*
- ▶ working together **collaboration, cooperation, dialogue, sharing** *Anything that encourages dialogue between parents and the school has to be good.*
- ▶ new ideas **creativity, innovation** *The aim of the proposal is to encourage creativity and problem-solving skills.*
- ▶ spending **investment, spending** *The town is a good example of how planning can encourage long-term investment in the infrastructure.*

encouragement N

words or actions that give someone confidence or hope, or that help something to happen

- adj+N great **active, considerable, constant, great, much, strong, tremendous** *The School offers great encouragement for boys to develop an interest in the arts.*
- ▶ a little **gentle, a little** *With a little encouragement, she could achieve much better grades.*
- ▶ shared with other people **mutual** *In situations like this you can provide mutual encouragement to each other.*
- v+N give someone encouragement **give, lend, offer (sb), provide (sb with)** *I have not been given any encouragement whatsoever.*
- ▶ shout encouragement **scream, shout, yell** *Crowds lined the bank and shouted encouragement.*
- ▶ need encouragement **need, require** *Whether we write or draw, sing or dance, we all need encouragement.*
- ▶ get encouragement **draw, gain, get, receive, take** *He received very little encouragement from his parents, even though he was obviously a natural performer.*
- and/or **advice, assistance, guidance, help, hope, inspiration, praise, reassurance, support** *I would never be where I am today without your support and encouragement.*

end N

the final part of a period of time, situation, or event

- adj+N sudden, or happening too soon or in a bad way **abrupt, premature, sudden, tragic, untimely** *The band's playing days came to an untimely end in 1997.*
- ▶ absolute **very** *I left the most important points to the very end of my speech.*
- ▶ suitable **fitting** *It was a fitting end to the career of a great champion.*

> When you continue until the end, even if the situation is difficult or unpleasant, you can do something **to** or **until the bitter end**: *She remained loyal to her husband until the bitter end.*

- v+N reach an end **approach, come to, draw to, get to, near, reach** *Now the war is coming to an end.*

> You can also say that something is **at an end**: *Finally the cold weather was at an end.*

- ▶ show that the end has been reached **mark, mean, signal, signify, spell** *The festival marks the end of the fast of Ramadan.*

> You can say that something **brings a situation to an end**: *The court case brought his career to an end.*

end V

reach a final point

- adv+V suddenly **abruptly, immediately, quickly, suddenly** *Her career ended very abruptly after ten years following a knee injury.*
- ▶ finally **at last, eventually, finally** *The wars with France had finally ended, and hundreds of thousands of soldiers and sailors had returned to the home country.*

▸ early or too early **early, prematurely** *Unfortunately, the press conference was forced to end prematurely.*
▸ well **happily, peacefully, well** *The plot has twists and turns but, of course, ends happily.*
▸ badly **badly, disastrously, tragically, unhappily** *It'll all end badly.*

endanger V
put someone or something into a dangerous situation

● V+n **existence, future, health, liberty, life, peace, safety, security, stability, survival** *It can never be acceptable to resort to violence that endangers innocent lives.*

A type of animal or plant that may become extinct (that is, it may disappear from the world) is known as an ***endangered species***: *The Scops owl is now a seriously endangered species.*

endeavour N
an effort to do something new or difficult

● adj+N involving a particular subject or activity **academic, artistic, athletic, creative, intellectual, journalistic, scholarly, scientific** *Their organisation exists to promote artistic endeavour, to relieve poverty, and to promote youth education.*
▸ involving people working together **collaborative, collective, joint** *The programme represents a collective endeavour to eradicate childhood disease.*
▸ deserving praise **heroic, worthwhile** *All these initiatives are worthwhile endeavours.*
▸ unsuccessful **fruitless, vain** *You can try keeping the garden weed-free, but this is likely to be a fruitless endeavour.*

end in PHR VB
have something as a final result

● V+n a bad situation **death, disappointment, disaster, divorce, failure, tragedy** *The rescue attempt ended in disaster.*
▸ a particular result in a competition **defeat, draw, victory** *Cambridge retained the title in a thrilling match that ended in a draw.*

ending N
the way in which something ends

● adj+N happy **fairy-tale, happy, perfect, satisfying, upbeat** *Luckily there is a happy ending to this story.*
▸ sad **downbeat, sad, tragic, unhappy** *Like almost all of Conrad's work it has a tragic ending.*
▸ different **alternate, alternative** *Apparently the director had planned two alternate endings to the movie.*

endless ADJ
seeming to have no end or limit

● adv+ADJ **almost, apparently, potentially, practically, seemingly, virtually** *If you're looking for accommodation, you will be bombarded with a seemingly endless list of choices.*
● ADJ+n possibilities **choice, opportunities, permutations, possibilities, variations** *You can learn a new hobby, acquire new skills to further your*

career or begin to plan a new career altogether – the possibilities are endless.
▸ number or supply **array, list, series, supply, variety** *There are a wide variety of jobs within the food industry, from suppliers to retailers as well as magazines, research organisations etc. – the list is endless.*
▸ something that keeps coming or happening **procession, repetition, stream, succession** *The shop is busy all day with an endless stream of visitors.*
▸ time **hours** *All these artists have provided endless hours of listening pleasure.*

endorse V
publicly express support for someone or something

● adv+V strongly **enthusiastically, heartily, strongly, warmly, wholeheartedly** *The Borough Council strongly endorses this policy.*
▸ completely **entirely, fully, thoroughly** *The National Union of Students fully endorsed this recommendation.*
▸ officially **formally, officially** *G8 leaders are expected to officially endorse the plan.*
▸ with everyone agreeing **unanimously** *The agreement was then unanimously endorsed by last year's party conference.*
▸ publicly **openly, publicly** *She publicly endorsed an online campaign to back local farmers.*

● V+n **action, approach, decision, idea, plan, policy, principle, proposal, recommendation, statement, view** *A meeting on May 19 enthusiastically endorsed the proposal.*

endorsement N
an occasion when someone gives public support to someone or something

● adj+N strong **clear, enthusiastic, full, glowing, overwhelming, positive, resounding, ringing, strong, wholehearted** *It cannot be said to be a ringing endorsement of the party's policies.*
▸ official **formal, official** *It was an initial step in the process of gaining official endorsement for reform.*

● v+N mean that an endorsement exists **constitute, imply, indicate, represent** *A link from this website to another does not imply an endorsement of that site or its contents.*
▸ get an endorsement **gain, get, obtain, receive, secure, win** *Our courses have received endorsements from many professional bodies.*
▸ give an endorsement **dispense, give, provide** *The Chancellor gave his wholehearted endorsement to the project.*
▸ have an endorsement **enjoy, have** *The pipeline didn't have official US endorsement.*

endurance N
the ability to continue doing something difficult, especially something physical

● adj+N types of endurance **human, mental, physical** *He is keen to improve his physical endurance in preparation for this year's British Championships.*
▸ great **great, heroic** *We read of feats of great endurance, daring and bravery.*

endure

- v+N improve endurance **build, build up, develop, enhance, improve, increase** *To increase endurance, eat more sweet, juicy fruits, and more protein.*
▶ find out how good someone's endurance is **test** *The course was far too short to test the endurance of the competitors.*
▶ have endurance **have, possess** *He had the endurance but lacked the speed needed for cross-country.*

- N+n person **athlete, cyclist, racer, rider, runner** *Is there any real benefit to be gained from weight training if you are an endurance athlete?*
▶ activity **activity, event, exercise, race, racing, ride, riding, running, sport, training, workout** *Both groups also continued with their normal endurance training.*
▶ test **test** *This really became something of an endurance test because the thing went on for so long.*

- and/or **courage, fitness, patience, perseverance, power, speed, stamina, strength** *These exercises aim to increase muscular strength and endurance.*

endure V
suffer something unpleasant over a long period

- adv+V **bravely, patiently, stoically** *He always looked on the bright side and stoically endured the appalling conditions.*

- V+n **agony, conditions, hardship, horror, humiliation, misery, pain, persecution, privations, suffering, trials** *The early settlers endured untold hardships during their first year here.*

enemy N
1 someone who is opposed to someone else and who tries to harm them

- adj+N very determined **bitter, deadly, great, implacable, mortal, sworn** *Emily and Ralph are bitter enemies.*
▶ dangerous **dangerous, formidable, powerful** *He has made powerful enemies.*

- v+N **have, make** *Mr. Wilson did not have an enemy in the world.*

2 a country that is fighting another country in a war

- v+N attack an enemy **attack, confront, encounter, engage, face, fight, fight against** *They advanced boldly to attack the enemy.*
▶ defeat an enemy **annihilate, conquer, crush, defeat, destroy, kill, rout, slay, subdue, vanquish** *They succeeded in completely defeating the enemy.*

- N+n armed forces **aircraft, combatants, forces, troops** *The division's first encounter with enemy forces was on 14 June.*
▶ attack **action, attack, bombing, fire, raid** *We ran up the slope in the face of heavy enemy fire.*

energy N
1 the supply of physical power or enthusiasm that you have

- adj+N very great or intense **boundless, inexhaustible, pure, raw, sheer, tremendous** *Gerry's enthusiasm and boundless energy will be missed by everyone at the school.*
▶ too much **excess, surplus** *Let the kids work off their excess energy with a few races.*
▶ emotional **emotional, manic, nervous** *I expended a lot of nervous energy on the day of the wedding.*
▶ not expressed **pent-up** *Now was the time to release all that pent-up energy.*
▶ types of energy **creative, youthful** *Their youthful energy was just what the project needed.*

- v+N put energy into something **channel, concentrate, devote, direct, focus, put, throw, turn** *His conducting is always fun to watch because he puts so much energy into it.*
▶ use energy **expend, invest, use** *So Guido has decided that he'd rather people expended their energy on something a little more productive.*
▶ have a lot of energy **be brimming with, be bursting with, be buzzing with, be filled with, be fizzing with, be full of, be overflowing with** *She seemed to be bursting with energy throughout the show.*
▶ have energy **have, possess** *I still feel I have the energy and enthusiasm I always had.*
▶ get energy **summon, summon up** *They couldn't summon up the energy for a game of football.*
▶ save energy **conserve, save** *Should they run more slowly to conserve energy?*
▶ not have energy **be drained of, lack** *I gain weight extremely easily and lack energy.*
▶ waste energy **waste** *I'm sure I made those complaints last time, so I won't waste energy repeating them.*
▶ get rid of energy **release, work off** *I need to work off all this surplus energy I've got.*

- and/or **commitment, enthusiasm, excitement, imagination, passion, talent, time, vitality** *It all takes time and energy.*

2 a form of power such as electricity

- adj+N provided by a particular form of power **atomic, geothermal, nuclear, solar, thermal, tidal, wave, wind** *By 2075, the uranium used for nuclear energy will be running out.*
▶ less harmful to environment **alternative, clean, green, renewable, sustainable** *Many countries are turning to renewable energy to supplement traditional power generation.*

- v+N save energy **conserve, save** *In addition, the technology uses cold water, which also saves energy.*
▶ produce energy **generate, produce** *Several thousand wind turbines would be needed to produce the same energy as a conventional power station.*
▶ waste energy **waste** *We need to educate our children to understand the importance of not wasting energy.*
▶ use energy **consume, use** *In a typical city, 47 per cent of all energy is consumed by buildings.*

- N+n use **consumption, usage, use** *The threat of global warming means we should be decreasing our energy use, not increasing it.*
▶ careful use **conservation, saving** *Energy saving is often the easiest way to cut carbon emissions.*
▶ cost **bill, costs, expenditure, prices** *Initial estimates suggest that they could reduce energy costs by 30–50 per cent.*

▶ production **generation, production** *We must explore ways of developing renewable forms of energy production.*

enforce V
make sure that a law or rule is obeyed, or that something happens

● adv+V strictly **aggressively, fully, rigidly, rigorously, strictly, stringently, strongly, vigorously** *A recent survey found almost two-thirds of Edinburgh residents think parking restrictions should be strictly enforced.*

● correctly **adequately, correctly, effectively, properly** *He stated that, in many developing countries, environmental protection legislation is not properly enforced.*

▶ V+n a law or rule **law, legislation, order, regulations, rule, standards** *At present it is very difficult to enforce the law in such cases.*

▶ an order to stop doing something **ban, blockade, curfew, embargo, prohibition, restriction, sanctions** *There are fears that little is being done to enforce the ban.*

▶ agreement **agreement** *You need to ensure that the tenancy agreement is enforced.*

▶ something that is wanted **conformity, discipline, obedience, uniformity, will** *In the past, corporal punishment was used to enforce discipline.* ● *They were prepared to use military force to enforce their will.*

engage in PHR VB
take part in a particular activity

▶ V+n a discussion **conversation, debate, dialogue, discussion, negotiations** *We are keen to engage in a genuine debate on the issue.*

▶ a particular activity **activity, agriculture, exercise, manufacture, pursuit, research, trade, work** *After breakfast, patients engage in a range of activities from 9.30am to midday.*

▶ fighting **battle, combat, conflict, fighting, struggle, war, warfare** *The Scottish warriors were about to engage in battle with a Northumbrian force.*

▶ a type of behaviour or an action **act, behaviour, conduct** *Many of the children are engaged in anti-social behaviour.*

engagement N
a formal agreement to get married

▶ v+N announce an engagement **announce** *About a month later they announced their engagement.*

▶ celebrate an engagement **celebrate** *Most couples celebrate their engagement with some form of party for family and friends.*

▶ end an engagement **break, break off, cancel, end, terminate** *Gwyneth broke off her engagement to the actor in 1997.*

engage with PHR VB
try to understand and deal with something

▶ V+n **agenda, argument, concept, debate, idea, issue, problem, process** *It goes on to suggest how the voluntary sector might engage with the issue.*

You can say that someone **engages in** conversation, dialogue, research, combat, conduct etc, or that they **are engaged**: *You are encouraged to engage in a dialogue with your manager.* ● *We are also actively engaged in dialogues with academics and educationalists.* You can also say **engage someone in** (a) conversation, a debate, a discussion etc: *I suspect that she doesn't want me to engage her in conversation about her children's problems at school.*

engrossed ADJ
completely involved or very interested in something

● ADJ+v completely **completely, entirely, fully, totally, utterly, wholly** *His grandfather was totally engrossed in his work.*

▶ very **deeply, quite, thoroughly** *She was apparently deeply engrossed in a newspaper.*

enhance V
improve something

● adv+V very much **considerably, dramatically, enormously, greatly, immeasurably, significantly, substantially, vastly** *This is an important development which will greatly enhance trade links across Europe.*

▶ in a particular way **artificially, chemically, digitally, genetically, nutritionally, surgically** *We have the professional expertise to digitally enhance photos.*

Usage **Enhance** is often passive in these combinations: *They believe genetically enhanced crops will help poor farmers in developing countries.*

● V+n reputation or appeal **attractiveness, credibility, employability, prospects, reputation** *An award can influence the sales of a book, and enhance the reputation of the author.*

▶ effectiveness **competitiveness, effectiveness, efficiency, performance, productivity, quality** *There are ways to boost the speed of your PC and enhance its performance.*

▶ how safe something is **security** *We've compiled a list of tips on how you can enhance your security when using the Internet.*

▶ ability or knowledge **ability, capability, capacity, learning, skill, understanding** *A diverse workforce enhances the ability of a business to innovate.*

▶ enjoyment **enjoyment, experience** *Knowing your guests are entertained can only enhance your enjoyment of your wedding day.*

▶ personal qualities **beauty, self-esteem, vitality** *Involving pupils in decision-making enhances their self-esteem.*

enjoy V
1 to get pleasure from something

● adv+V very much **enormously, greatly, hugely, immensely, really, thoroughly, tremendously, truly** *I thoroughly enjoyed the performance and thought all the cast were excellent.*

▶ rather **quite, rather** *We were very busy that day and, to my surprise, I rather enjoyed it.*

▶ particularly **especially, particularly** *The girls seemed to particularly enjoy the trip.*

▶ obviously **clearly, obviously** *The author obviously enjoys surprising the reader.*

2 to have something as a benefit or advantage

● V+n **advantage, benefit, popularity, prestige, privilege, reputation, status, support** *The university enjoys an international reputation for excellence in social sciences and humanities.*

enjoyable ADJ
something that is enjoyable gives you pleasure

● adv+ADJ very **enormously, extremely, fantastically, highly, hugely, immensely, incredibly, really, so, supremely, terrifically, thoroughly, tremendously, truly, very, wonderfully** *The visit of the exchange students has been hugely enjoyable for all those involved.*

▶ rather **fairly, quite** *Building the walls was quite enjoyable work.*

▶ particularly **especially, particularly** *Today's meeting was particularly enjoyable.*

● v+ADJ **be, become, find sth, prove** *What is it about reading that you find so enjoyable? ● As ever the trip proved very enjoyable for everybody concerned.*

enjoyment N
pleasure that you get from something

● adj+N great **great, maximum, much** *I remember all those superb athletes who have given me such great enjoyment through the years.*

▶ pure **pure, sheer** *Whether you read for self-improvement or just for sheer enjoyment, this book is for you.*

▶ of a particular kind **aesthetic, sensual** *Artists have a sensual enjoyment of colour and texture.*

▶ obvious **evident, obvious** *The musicians' obvious enjoyment produces a fantastic stage show.*

▶ of one or more people **mutual, personal, public, shared, sb's own** *What brought them together was almost certainly their mutual enjoyment of music. ● Cycle at your own pace, for your own enjoyment.*

● v+N get enjoyment **derive, gain, get** *Members of the choir derive great enjoyment from their informal rehearsals.*

▶ give enjoyment **bring (sb), give (sb)** *This delightful production will bring enjoyment to children of all ages.*

▶ increase enjoyment **enhance, ensure, heighten, increase, maximize, multiply** *This beautifully illustrated book will enhance readers' enjoyment of wild flowers.*

▶ lessen enjoyment **affect, diminish, disrupt, hamper, impair, impede, lessen, mar, ruin, spoil** *It was fairly busy, but that didn't spoil our enjoyment of this lovely spot.*

▶ encourage enjoyment of something **encourage, promote** *We aim to promote the enjoyment and understanding of cinema throughout the UK.*

enormity N
the extremely large, bad, or serious nature of something

● adj+N **full, sheer** *The police are challenged by the sheer enormity of the crime wave.*

● v+N understand the enormity of something **appreciate, comprehend, grasp, realize, recognize, understand** *I now realize the enormity of the problems they are facing in developing countries.*

▶ describe the enormity of something **bring home, capture, convey, express, illustrate** *How can you convey the enormity of what happened during World War II?*

▶ think about the enormity of something **consider, contemplate** *The future may seem overwhelming when we contemplate the enormity of the task before us.*

● N+of a bad situation **calamity, catastrophe, crisis, disaster, horror, loss, problem, suffering, threat, tragedy** *By then the enormity of the tragedy was beginning to become clear from news reports.*

▶ a bad deed **crime, offence, sin** *No one can fail to be shocked by the enormity of his crimes.*

▶ a task **challenge, project, task, undertaking** *Recent events have only highlighted the enormity of the challenges we face in tackling global warming.*

enormous ADJ
very large in size or quantity

● adv+ADJ very **absolutely, simply, so, truly** *The amount of money they can make is absolutely enormous.*

▶ possibly **potentially** *When the oil slick reaches the coast it will inflict potentially enormous damage.*

● ADJ+n quantity **amount, number, quantity, sum, volume** *The work required an enormous amount of time and energy.*

▶ good quality **advantage, fun, pleasure, potential, wealth** *The country has enormous potential for eco-tourism.*

▶ importance **importance, significance** *The year 1994 was one of enormous significance for Northern Ireland.*

▶ effect on something **benefit, boost, contribution, damage, impact, implications, influence, power** *Weather has enormous influences on society.*

▶ pressure **burden, pressure, strain** *Even under the most enormous pressure, they remained calm and controlled.*

▶ difference **difference, gulf** *It seems that no one has taken into account the enormous difference in body weight between a human and a mouse.*

▶ task **challenge, effort, task, undertaking** *Widespread deprivation still imposes enormous challenges.*

▶ success or improvement **popularity, progress, strides, success** *Medical science has made enormous strides in tackling the disease.*

▶ variety **diversity, range, scope, variety** *They sell an enormous variety of crafts, jewellery and other accessories.*

entail V
involve having or doing a particular thing

● adv+V always or naturally **always, automatically, inevitably, invariably, logically, naturally, necessarily, obviously** *His job necessarily entails him visiting some remote places.*

▶ usually **generally, normally, often, probably, typically, usually** *Participation in the seminars usually entails some preparatory work.*

enter into PHR VB

1 start to take part in an official discussion or other formal activity

▸ V+n **conversation, correspondence, debate, dialogue, discussion, negotiations, relationship, talks** *Our office will not normally be able to enter into any correspondence about tax matters.*

2 sign an official agreement

▸ V+n **agreement, alliance, arrangement, contract, partnership, transaction, treaty** *Some people try to plan for the risk of divorce by entering into pre-nuptial agreements.*

entertain V

1 provide an enjoyable experience for someone

▸ adv+V generously **handsomely, hospitably, lavishly, royally, splendidly, sumptuously** *We were royally entertained by our hosts who had laid on a splendid buffet supper.*

▸ very much **certainly, highly, hugely, thoroughly, well** *I didn't know what to expect from the show but was thoroughly entertained all the way though.*

Usage ***Entertain*** is usually passive in all the ***adv+V*** combinations shown above.

▸ and/or be informative **challenge, edify, educate, enlighten, inform, inspire, instruct, motivate, stimulate** *The magazine's remit is to entertain and educate.*

▸ be fun or surprising **amaze, amuse, captivate, delight, engage, engross, enthral, excite, fascinate, surprise, thrill** *Town centre shoppers will be entertained and amused by street performers.*

2 consider an idea or feeling

▸ V+n **doubt, hope, idea, illusion, notion, possibility, suspicion, thought** *Even at 30, I still entertain notions of playing for Scotland at football.*

entertaining ADJ

enjoyable or fun to do

▸ adv+ADJ very **brilliantly, delightfully, extremely, fabulously, highly, hugely, immensely, marvellously, richly, terrifically, thoroughly, vastly, very, wildly, wonderfully** *It's easy to read and hugely entertaining.*

▸ rather **mildly, moderately, quite, reasonably** *The film is hardly a masterpiece, but it's mildly entertaining.*

▸ v+ADJ **be, find sth, prove** *I found the film much more entertaining than the book.* • *The multiplayer game proved very entertaining.*

▸ and/or educational **educational, enlightening, informative, instructive, thought-provoking** *It is your job to present facts in an entertaining and informative way.*

▸ interesting **challenging, engaging, exciting, fascinating, inspiring, interesting, intriguing, lively, provocative, stimulating** *His style is a lively and entertaining mixture of poetry, music and comedy.*

▸ amusing **amusing, enjoyable, funny, witty** *She stars in a fast-paced, entertaining and witty drama.*

▸ easy to understand **accessible, readable, watchable**

This is a highly entertaining and readable book about a complex subject.

enthusiasm N

the feeling of being very interested in something or excited by it

● adj+N great **boundless, considerable, enormous, genuine, great, much, real, sheer, such, tremendous, unbounded, unbridled** *Their common bond is their boundless enthusiasm for film.* • *People set to work with such enthusiasm that the job was completed on time.*

▸ not great **little** *The students showed little enthusiasm for the subject.*

▸ affecting others **contagious, infectious** *All the instructors really enjoy their work, and their enthusiasm is infectious.*

▸ obvious **evident, obvious, palpable** *With obvious enthusiasm, she talked about her career so far.*

▸ typical of young people **boyish, childlike, youthful** *Those who have met him comment on his engaging warmth and youthful enthusiasm.*

▸ lasting a long time, or coming back **continued, new-found, renewed, tireless, undiminished, undimmed, unflagging** *The dawn brought with it a renewed enthusiasm and we started to climb again.*

▸ not lasting **initial** *My initial enthusiasm was tempered when I realized the game was going to take place 500 miles away.*

● v+N show enthusiasm **communicate, convey, demonstrate, display, express, exude, show** *Both schools expressed great enthusiasm for putting on a shared drama production.*

▸ feel enthusiasm **be full of, experience, feel, have, share** *It is lovely to get amongst the children and share their enthusiasm about books.*

▸ create enthusiasm **arouse, engender, fire, foster, generate, kindle, rekindle, renew, spark** *The whole experience rekindled my enthusiasm for music in a major way.*

▸ lessen someone's enthusiasm **curb, dampen, temper** *The rain poured down but could do nothing to dampen our enthusiasm.*

▸ direct enthusiasm to a purpose **capture, channel, harness** *If you could harness this enthusiasm, what changes could be brought about!*

▸ try to feel enthusiasm **muster, summon** *I'm afraid I could muster very little enthusiasm for the play.*

▸ lose/not lose your enthusiasm **lose, maintain, retain** *We came home from holiday early, having lost all enthusiasm.*

▸ be affected by someone's enthusiasm **be delighted by, be encouraged by, be impressed by, be infected by, be overwhelmed by** *We are constantly encouraged by the enthusiasm of young people for our project.*

● N+v become less **dwindle, wane** *I have done this job for seven years and my enthusiasm is waning.*

▸ affect others **inspire, rub off on** *Harry is such a positive character that his enthusiasm rubs off on everyone.*

● and/or determination or energy **commitment, confidence, dedication, determination, drive, energy, excitement, motivation, optimism, passion, verve, vigour, warmth, willingness** *We look for candidates with enthusiasm and commitment.*

▶ skill, knowledge or ability **creativity, expertise, flair, knowledge, professionalism, skill, talent** *He praised the professionalism and enthusiasm of his team.*

▶ interest or enjoyment **enjoyment, interest** *The enthusiasm and enjoyment shown by all the youngsters on the course was inspiring.*

enthusiastic ADJ
very interested in or excited by something

● adv+ADJ very **extremely, genuinely, highly, hugely, incredibly, really, so, tremendously, very, wildly** *I am very enthusiastic about science and I would encourage everybody to study it.*

▶ not very **not over, not overly, not too** *To be frank I wasn't over enthusiastic about the idea at first.*

▶ particularly **particularly** *The children were particularly enthusiastic about using the computer.*

▶ in a way that affects others **infectiously** *The lecturer is infectiously enthusiastic.*

▶ too **over-, overly, too** *I must confess that I'm not over-enthusiastic about washing the car.* ● *My sometimes overly enthusiastic approach to life annoys some people.*

● v+ADJ **be, become, feel, get, remain, seem, sound** *We try to encourage young people to engage with books and become enthusiastic about reading.*

entrepreneur N
someone who starts new businesses

● adj+N hoping to be successful **aspiring, budding, nascent, potential, wannabe** INFORMAL, **would-be** *Are you a budding entrepreneur with an idea that you believe can make you millions?*

▶ successful **millionaire, multimillionaire, successful, wealthy** *Like many successful entrepreneurs, she comes from a tough working-class background.*

entry N
1 the act of going into a place; the right to enter a place

● adj+N free **free** *The London Pass gives you free entry to over 60 favourite attractions.*

▶ without permission **forced, forcible, illegal, unauthorized** *The entrance should normally be kept locked to prevent unauthorized entry.*

● v+N manage to enter **force, gain** *If we cannot establish your whereabouts, we will contact the Police who will force entry into your home.* ● *Refugees have made perilous trips to gain entry to the United Kingdom.*

▶ refuse to allow someone to enter **deny sb, refuse sb, restrict** *Anyone found to be under the minimum age will be refused entry.*

▶ allow someone to enter **allow, facilitate, permit** *The joint ticket allows entry to both museums for a full year.*

2 the process of becoming involved in or part of something

● v+N try to enter **apply for, seek** *He has some advice for those seeking entry into the acting profession.*

▶ delay entering **defer, delay** *We welcome applications from students who wish to defer entry to their chosen course for one year.*

● N+n qualifications **criteria, qualifications, requirements** *We can tell you more about the content of courses and the entry requirements.*

▶ form **form** *If you would like to take part then please complete and return the entry form below.*

▶ method **point, route** *The project aims to provide an entry route to undergraduate study for students with non-standard qualifications.*

● N+into work or area of work **employment, field, industry, politics, profession, service, world** *There are no standard qualifications that guarantee entry into the media industry.* ● *This was the work that marked her entry into the literary world.*

▶ education **higher education, school, university** *The number of applicants for entry into higher education rose.*

▶ market **market, marketplace** *Following our entry into this market in January, we now serve 890,000 retail energy customers.*

▶ war **war** *The USA's entry into the war signalled the arrival on the world stage of a new great power.*

environment N
1 the place and conditions in which people live and work, or things exist

● adj+N in which a particular activity takes place **business, learning, living, manufacturing, trading, work, working** *Every organisation must undertake an assessment of fire risks in order to maintain a safe working environment.*

▶ natural **natural** *This will give you the opportunity to see animals in their natural environment.*

▶ in a particular place **classroom, office, workplace** *Children have many important learning experiences outside a classroom environment.*

▶ across the whole world **global** *These changes will affect the global business environment.*

▶ in a town/the country **rural, urban** *Most new houses will be built in what is essentially a rural environment.*

▶ safe or stable **controlled, safe, secure, smoke-free, stable** *It is essential that an adopted child be placed in a secure environment.*

▶ friendly or pleasant **caring, conducive, friendly, non-threatening, nurturing, pleasant, relaxed, supportive** *Trainees will work in a supportive environment that encourages open-mindedness and co-operation.*

▶ not easy to live in **harsh, hostile, inhospitable** *They are researching the creation of GM crops that can withstand harsh environments.*

▶ suitable for **conducive to** *Generally our aim is to provide a learning enviroment that is conducive to discovery and discussion.*

▶ exciting or stressful **challenging, changing, competitive, dynamic, fast-paced, pressurized, stimulating** *In an increasingly competitive business environment, companies want fast results.*

▶ physical **external, physical** *The child's circumstances will be assessed, including the physical environment in which they are being brought up.*

● v+N create an environment **build, create, provide** *We have used technology to create a unique learning environment.*

▶ improve an environment **enhance, improve** *Our*

responsibility is to maintain and improve the environment in which members of the university study, work and live.

2 the natural world

- adj+N natural **global, natural, physical** *It's madness that the destruction of the natural environment continues unhindered.*
- ▶ types of environment **aquatic, coastal, desert, marine, rainforest** *Every country has an interest in the sustainable management of the marine environment.*
- v+N protect the environment **conserve, preserve, protect, safeguard** *We need to develop the land in a responsible way which protects the environment.*
- ▶ harm the environment **affect, damage, degrade, destroy, harm, pollute** *In most cases waste products are burned, polluting the environment.*

environmental ADJ

relating to humans' effect on the natural world; intended to protect the environment

- ADJ+n damage **catastrophe, damage, degradation, hazard, impact, pollution** *She takes a strong interest in the environmental impact of aviation.*
- ▶ protection **benefits, improvements, protection, stewardship** *We all recognise the need for environmental protection and the desirability of preserving wildlife habitat.*
- ▶ issues **concerns, considerations, factors, issues** *Chloroflurocarbons (CFCs) are being phased out due to environmental concerns.*
- ▶ awareness **assessment, awareness, credentials, sustainability** *Environmental assessment should be integrated into health service planning, for example when constructing new hospitals.*
- ▶ policy **legislation, policy** *Environmental legislation places strict controls on emissions from industry.*
- ▶ campaigner **campaigner, protester** *Plans to build a new airport have been slammed by environmental campaigners.*

envisage V

to have something as a plan or intention

- adv+V at or from the beginning **always, first, hitherto, initially, originally, previously** *The development took a little longer than originally envisaged.*
- ▶ now **currently, now, presently** *We currently envisage that this will be complete two years after the start of the contract.*

> Usage **Envisage** is often passive in all the **adv+V** combinations shown above.

- ▶ clearly **clearly, explicitly** *The legislation clearly envisages that there will be some cases that do not qualify.*

envy N

an unhappy feeling of wanting what someone else has

- v+N cause envy **arouse, attract, cause, draw, excite, inspire, provoke** *Beauty was one of the few powers that women possessed and, naturally, power always arouses envy.*

- ▶ feel envy **be consumed by, be filled with, be green with, feel** *Watching them, Nicky was consumed by envy.*
- ▶ express envy **express, show** *Several people expressed considerable envy of her not having to go to school.*
- ▶ overcome your envy **overcome, swallow** *I tried to swallow my envy and feel happy for him.*
- v+with+N **look, watch** *Those on the lowest incomes look with envy at this sort of salary.*

epidemic N

a situation in which a disease quickly infects many people

- adj+N across a large area **global, widespread, worldwide** *We are concerned with raising awareness of the global HIV/AIDS epidemic.*
- ▶ serious **deadly, devastating, disastrous, major, serious, severe** *At that time, plague and other devastating epidemics were a constant threat.*
- ▶ not talked about **hidden, silent** *Hepatitis C has been called the silent epidemic because people are not aware of the problem.*
- n+N of a particular disease **cholera, flu, smallpox etc** *He died in the typhus epidemic that was raging at the time.*
- ▶ of other harmful things **crime, drug, obesity, smoking, tobacco** *America and Europe face an obesity epidemic which will shorten the lives of today's children.*
- v+N fight an epidemic **address, combat, control, cope with, curb, deal with, eradicate, fight, halt, prevent, stop, tackle** *We need a sustained programme to try to combat the epidemic of binge drinking.*
- ▶ cause an epidemic **cause, drive, fuel, prolong** *Poverty and poor living conditions are fuelling the epidemic.*
- ▶ experience an epidemic **be affected by, be hit by, be in the grip of, experience, face, have, suffer** *The area is suffering a measles epidemic.*
- N+v start **begin, break out, occur** *The disease is very widespread in South East Asia, with epidemics breaking out every few years.*
- ▶ continue **continue, rage, spread, worsen** *At this time a smallpox epidemic was raging in the town.*
- ▶ affect a place **affect sth, devastate sth, hit (sth), ravage sth, strike (sth), sweep (through) sth** *Influenza epidemics sweep the world every year, killing the very young and the very old.*
- N+of disease **disease, cholera, flu, smallpox etc** *Vaccines prevent epidemics of diseases such as measles and smallpox.*
- ▶ other harmful things **obesity, suicide** *The World Health Organisation identified the epidemic of obesity as one of the world's most serious health problems.*
- n+of+N start **beginning, onset, outbreak, start** *The onset of cholera epidemics after 1831 added another killer disease to the world.*
- ▶ spread **extent, impact, spread** *These measures were effective in stopping the spread of the epidemic.*
- ▶ highest point **peak** *Even at the peak of the epidemic, influenza accounted for only four per cent of all deaths.*

equal ADJ

1 the same in value, amount, or size

- adv+**ADJ** approximately **about, almost, approximately, broadly, fairly, nearly, relatively, roughly, virtually** *We take approximately 170 students, with roughly equal numbers of boys and girls.*
- ► exactly **exactly** *The two gardens are exactly equal in size.*
- **ADJ**+n size or amount **amount, size** *The land is broken down into 3 areas of roughly equal size.*
- ► quality or value **quality, value** *The Medicines Controls Agency ensures that generic medicines are of equal quality.*
- ► importance **importance, prominence, weighting** *The four elements of assessment receive equal weighting, 25 per cent each.*

When you say that two things have an equal effect or importance, you can use the phrase *in equal measure*: *The puzzles are frustrating and rewarding in equal measure.*

- ► part or share **instalment, proportion, share** *Students can pay in full at the start of the academic year, or in two equal instalments.*
- ► probability **chance, probability** *There is an equal chance of either of these events happening.*
- v+**ADJ** **be ranked, finish, rank** *The two teams finished equal on points.*

2 having or deserving the same as others; giving people the same rights or opportunities

- adv+**ADJ** **absolutely, genuinely, truly** *Here women and men are truly equal.*
- **ADJ**+n opportunities or treatment **access, chances, opportunities, pay, rights, treatment** *The University is committed to equal opportunities.*
- ► status **footing, status** *This attitude puts doctors on an equal footing with their patients.* • *Women should have equal status as citizens to men.*
- ► person **partner** *Children should be treated as equal partners in their education.*
- v+**ADJ** **be born, become, be considered, be created** *My mother was born and raised in East Germany where, for all its faults, women were considered equal with men.*

equality N

the state of being equal

- adj+**N** in a particular area **economic, legal, political, racial, religious, sexual, social** *Recent research has shown that there is a real lack of social equality in rural communities.*
- ► complete **absolute, complete, full, genuine, perfect, real, true** *Measures are proposed to create genuine equality of educational opportunity for all children.*
- n+**N** for a particular group **disability, gay, gender, race, sex** *This important document sets out our commitment to race equality.*
- ► in employment **employment, pay, workplace** *Disability campaign groups are clamouring for legislation to enforce workplace equality.*
- v+**N** support equality **advance, advocate, affirm, champion, deliver, embrace, ensure, guarantee,**

improve, promote, provide, support *As an organisation we promote equality.*
- ► achieve equality **achieve, secure** *She is committed to achieving full equality for Irish Travellers.*
- ► demand equality **assert, demand** *People have come together to demand equality and freedom for all.*
- **N**+of **access, opportunity, rights, status, treatment** *Our policy for the development of the arts is based on equality of access and celebration of diversity.*

equilibrium N

a state of balance or calm

- v+**N** achieve equilibrium **achieve, attain, establish, find, reach** *We need to achieve a new equilibrium between our species and the rest of the planet.*
- ► keep or regain equilibrium **maintain, recover, re-establish, regain, restore** *The global climate restores the equilibrium by either heating up or cooling down.*
- ► disturb equilibrium **disrupt, disturb, upset** *An injury upset his equilibrium, and he finished seventh.*

equip V

provide a person or place with things they need

- adv+**V** well **adequately, beautifully, comfortably, comprehensively, excellently, extensively, fully, generously, lavishly, luxuriously, properly, superbly, thoroughly, well** *The kitchen is fully equipped with cooker, fridge, microwave, etc.*
- ► badly **badly, ill, poorly** *Their fire crews were unskilled, untrained and badly equipped.* • *We were ill-equipped to deal with the challenges that lay ahead.*
- ► for a particular purpose **appropriately, specially, suitably, uniquely** *The instrument is uniquely equipped to pick up heart, lung and other body sounds.*

Usage *Equip* is usually passive in all of the *adv+V* combinations shown above: *The fitness centre is superbly equipped.* • *They can capture video evidence in specially equipped vans.*

era N

a period of time with a particular quality or character

- adj+**N** new or present **current, modern, new, present** *In this modern era of electronic publishing, the printed book is still as popular as ever.*
- ► old **bygone, long-gone, past** *The Victorian dolls' house is a wonderful record of a bygone era.*
- ► great or greatest **golden, great** *The Electric Picture Palace is a re-creation of the golden era of cinema.*
- ► exciting **exciting** *We're looking forward to an exciting new era in translation technology.*
- v+**N** be the start of an era **begin, herald, inaugurate, mark, open, signal, usher in** *Completion of the human genome sequence heralded a new era in medicine.*
- ► enter an era **enter, move into** *We're moving into an era of renewable energy.*
- ► be typical of an era **characterize, define, epitomize, reflect** *These classic songs define a golden era in pop music history.*

▸ remember an era **evoke, recall, recapture, recreate, relive** *The house has been decorated in a style that recalls the graceful Edwardian era.*

● N+v begin **arrive, begin, come, commence, dawn, emerge, open, start** *A new era dawned with the accession of Queen Victoria in 1838.*

▸ end **end, pass** *The Puritan era had passed and religious fervour died down.*

▸ n+of+N beginning **beginning, dawn, start** *With the dawn of the new era of technology, anything seems to be possible.*

▸ end **end, passing** *We wanted to do a big charity gig to mark the end of an era for the band.*

eradicate V
get rid of something bad completely

● adv+V completely **completely, effectively, entirely, finally, fully, permanently, successfully, systematically, totally** *It is almost impossible to totally eradicate smuggling.*

▸ almost **almost, largely, virtually** *He claims that long-term youth unemployment has been virtually eradicated.*

● V+n problem **discrimination, hunger, illiteracy, poverty, prejudice, problem, racism, terrorism** *Too much human ingenuity is channelled into developing new weapons, and not enough into eradicating poverty.*

▸ disease **disease, polio, smallpox, virus** *Smallpox was completely eradicated from the natural environment by 1980.*

▸ living creature **infestation, pest, weeds** *Armstrong was a keen gardener, and was obsessed with eradicating garden weeds.*

error N
a mistake in a calculation or decision

● adj+N serious **fatal, glaring, grave, gross, obvious, serious** *Such a glaring error in style and grammar can cause a reader to switch off instantly.*

▸ not serious **minor, slight** *I only spotted one or two minor errors in the whole essay.*

▸ basic or common **common, fundamental, schoolboy** *Another common holiday error is overlooking the car.*

▸ types of error **clerical, factual, grammatical, printing, spelling, tactical, typographical** *As an editor, you are responsible for eliminating typographical errors.*

▸ by a person **driver, human, pilot** *It was human error, due to the stress he was under.*

▸ unintentional **accidental, inadvertent, unintentional** *The author apologizes for any inadvertent errors or omissions in the acknowledgements.*

● v+N make or cause an error **cause, commit, generate, introduce, make** *She realised she had made a grave error.*

▸ contain an error **contain** *The text contained grammatical errors.*

▸ notice an error **detect, discover, encounter, identify, notice, realize, spot** *This pilot fortunately realized his error.*

▸ correct an error **correct, rectify, remedy** *Individuals are permitted to know what personal information is held about them and to correct any errors.*

▸ avoid errors **avoid, eliminate, minimize, prevent, reduce** *This saves having to re-type everything and eliminates errors.*

▸ make an error worse **compound, repeat** *They then compounded the error by telling customers that they were mistaken.*

● N+v **appear, arise, creep in, happen, occur, result** *In spite of the extreme care taken in copying the manuscripts, minor errors inevitably creep in.*

erupt V
start suddenly, with a lot of violence or noise

● adv+V suddenly **spontaneously, suddenly** *Applause suddenly erupted from one side of the auditorium.*

▸ violently **violently** *A few months ago the problem erupted violently.*

▸ from time to time **occasionally, periodically, sometimes** *Epidemics of the plague erupted periodically throughout the late Middle Ages.*

● n+V violence or conflict **chaos, conflict, crisis, dispute, fighting, fury, pandemonium, protests, rioting, riots, row, tension, trouble, violence, war** *Violence has erupted again in the region and there are fears of civil war.*

▸ scandal **controversy, furore, scandal** *He was set to become prime minister when a bribery scandal erupted.*

● V+into violence or anger **chaos, frenzy, fury, pandemonium, rage, riots, violence, war** *The simmering frustration erupted into riots.*

▸ cheers or laughter **applause, laughter** *The crowd erupted into applause.*

escalate V
increase or become worse

● adv+V quickly or very much **dramatically, hugely, massively, quickly, rapidly, sharply, significantly** *The level of traffic could escalate very rapidly.*

▸ gradually **gradually, slowly, steadily** *For many people, occasional drug use will gradually escalate into addiction.*

▸ in a worrying way **alarmingly, dangerously** *If such problems are not considered, costs can escalate alarmingly.*

● n+V violence or conflict **conflict, confrontation, dispute, fighting, protests, row, tension, trouble, unrest, violence, war** *The violence escalated rapidly as police began firing tear gas and charging the march.*

▸ problem **crisis, incident, problem, situation** *Early recognition and intervention will help to prevent problems escalating.*

▸ amount of money **cost, debt, price** *With fuel prices escalating, transport represents a substantial cost.*

> **Usage** *Escalate* is very often used as a present participle adjective in all of the *n+V* combinations shown above: *Many people have been displaced as a result of the escalating conflict.* ● *There is concern about escalating oil prices.*

escalation
a sudden increase in something bad

- adj+N large **dramatic, further, major, massive, serious, significant** *I doubt there will be any significant escalation in our local crime-rate.*
- ▶ sudden or quick **rapid, sharp, sudden** *There was a sudden escalation in police activity with the arrival of four extra police vans.*
- ▶ military **military, nuclear** *We fear a military escalation of the conflict.*
- N+of of violence **aggression, attack, conflict, hostilities, violence, war** *The escalation of violence in recent months poses an increased threat to UK troops.*
- ▶ of a problem **crisis, dispute, hostility, tension** *A convincing argument backed by a previously stated policy may limit escalation of a crisis.*
- v+N prevent or stop escalation **avoid, halt, limit, prevent, stop** *Our first task is obviously to stop the escalation of violence.*
- ▶ indicate escalation **mark, represent** *This represents an escalation of outside intervention, with all the problems that entails.*
- ▶ cause escalation **cause, lead to** *The Government's tobacco tax policy is causing a huge escalation in smuggling.*

escape V
avoid death, injury, damage, or something unpleasant

- V+adj **alive, unharmed, unhurt, uninjured, unpunished, unscathed** *The bed was blown to bits, but he escaped unhurt.*
- adv+V only just **barely, just, narrowly** *She narrowly escaped being thrown into jail.*
- ▶ luckily **fortunately, luckily, miraculously** *The Croatian coastline has miraculously escaped the overdevelopment of some Mediterranean holiday destinations.*
- V+n punishment **censure, detection, justice, liability, prosecution, punishment** *The speeding driver escaped prosecution because it was too late to send him a ticket.*
- ▶ death, injury or damage **death, destruction, fate, injury, ravages** *The island has escaped the ravages of modern tourism.*

escape N
the act of avoiding or getting away from someone or something unpleasant

- adj+N lucky **amazing, fortunate, lucky, miraculous, narrow, remarkable** *Looks like we had a lucky escape from nearly buying that heap of junk.*
- ▶ exciting **daring, dramatic** *The ship made a daring escape under cover of darkness.*
- ▶ quick **hasty, hurried, quick** *You may need your back door keys to make a hasty escape in case of a fire.*
- ▶ eventual **eventual, ultimate** *The second half of the film concerns itself with his flight for survival and eventual escape to Mexico.*
- ▶ attempted **attempted** *He was shot during an attempted escape to Spain.*
- v+N make an escape **effect, make, make good** *They effected their escape by sea.* ● *He made good his escape when he was left unattended by the guards.*
- ▶ try to escape **attempt, plan, plot, seek** *If any prisoner was thought likely to attempt an escape, he was set to work in chains.*
- ▶ help someone escape **aid, arrange, assist, engineer, facilitate, provide** *He aided their escape from the firing squad.*
- ▶ prevent an escape **block, impede, prevent** *When I tried to leave, the staff surrounded me to prevent my escape.*
- N+n way to escape **route** *People should be aware of the location of fire alarms, extinguishers and escape routes.*
- ▶ attempt **attempt, bid, plan** *He made two escape attempts from Prisoner Of War Camp.*
- n+of+N **chance, hope, means** *Do not use the lift as a means of escape during a fire.*

essay N
a short piece of writing on a particular subject

- v+N produce an essay **contribute, prepare, publish, submit, write** *I have written an essay on the history of science.*
- ▶ read an essay **assess, mark, read** *This workshop will help students understand what tutors are looking for when they are assessing essays.*
- N+v be about something **address, be about, concern, deal with, discuss, examine, explain, explore, focus on** *This collection of essays examines the identity of science fiction cinema.*
- ▶ say something **argue, conclude, demonstrate** *The essay argues that our obsession with convenience damages the environment.*
- ▶ have a particular title **be called, be entitled, be titled** *George Orwell wrote an essay entitled The Art of Donald McGill.*

essence N
the most important part or aspect of something

- v+N be the essence of something **be, constitute, contain, define, embody, epitomize, represent** *This brutality is entirely against the moral values constituting the essence of the religion.*
- ▶ capture or convey the essence **capture, communicate, convey, distil, encapsulate, evoke, express, reflect, reveal** *His ability to capture the essence of the animals he draws sets him apart.*
- ▶ not lose the essence **preserve, recapture, retain** *The old town has somehow preserved its essence and charm and is worth visiting.*
- ▶ understand the essence **grasp, understand** *Grasping the essence of the document is not an easy task.*

essential ADJ
necessary and basic

- adv+ADJ absolutely **absolutely, really, so, truly, utterly** *The computer is absolutely essential to our mode of working.*
- ▶ almost **almost, pretty** INFORMAL**, usually, virtually** *A car is almost essential for getting around the island.*
- ▶ obviously **clearly, obviously** *It is obviously essential that you include an email address.*
- ADJ+n part or aspect **aspect, attribute,**

characteristic, component, element, feature, ingredient, part, role *We asked him to identify the essential components of a great online business.*

▶ skill **skill** *The course is for students who need to develop essential skills before moving on to the next level.*

▶ tool **companion, equipment, guide, information, tool** *It is the one reference tool that is essential for everyone in the writing industry.*

▶ something you must read, see, buy etc **item, listening, purchase, reading, viewing** *Needless to say this book should be considered essential reading.*

▶ condition **criterion, precondition, prerequisite, requirement** *Good literacy and numeracy skills are an essential requirement.*

▶ nutrients **fats, mineral, nutrient, vitamin** *These foods fill children up, but do not provide the essential nutrients they need for healthy development.*

● v+ADJ **be, become, consider sth, deem sth, prove, regard sth as, remain, seem** *Charging for road use will become essential as the number of vehicles on the roads grows.* ● *In this profession it is deemed essential to work very long hours if you want to be successful.*

establish v
create something, or make it known or accepted

● adv+V **well definitively, firmly, fully, long, successfully, well** *The project successfully established certain principles.*

▶ recently **newly, recently** *We have recently established a bursary scheme for students from low-income families.*

> Usage **Establish** is often passive in these combinations: *The scheme offers business advice to newly established firms.*

▶ quickly **quickly, rapidly** *You must be able to quickly establish good working relationships with a diverse range of people.*

● V+n reputation **authority, credentials, credibility, legitimacy, reputation** *We have established a reputation for truly outstanding professional results.*

▶ relationship **connection, link, partnership, rapport, relationship** *This is the artist's attempt to establish a rapport with the viewer.*

▶ presence **bridgehead, foothold, presence** *They can use technology to create new markets or establish a foothold in existing markets.*

▶ basis or principle **base, baseline, benchmark, criterion, foundation, framework, precedent, principle, procedure** *The aim was to establish benchmarks for water consumption in different types of buildings.*

▶ identity **identity** *This card is widely used as a way of establishing identity.*

estimate N
an amount that you guess using the available information

● adj+N approximate **approximate, crude, rough** *They will produce a rough estimate of what they think the work will cost.*

▶ accurate or reasonable **accurate, realistic, reasonable, reliable, unbiased** *Exit polls have*

traditionally been the most accurate estimate of voters' intentions.

▶ cautious **cautious, conservative** *At a conservative estimate, around 100,000 have been killed in the war so far.*

▶ made at the beginning **initial, original, preliminary, previous, provisional** *Initial estimates suggest that they could reduce energy costs by 30–50 per cent.*

▶ made recently **current, latest, recent, revised, updated** *Current estimates show that just 5 per cent of people over 65 live in sheltered housing.*

▶ official **official** *Official estimates of the national population have been significantly revised since the Census.*

● v+N make an estimate **arrive at, give (sb), make, prepare, present, produce, provide, publish, submit** *It is not difficult to arrive at a rough estimate of the cost.* ● *All departments were asked to provide provisional estimates for the cost of replacing equipment.*

▶ get an estimate **get, obtain** *More data is needed to get reliable estimates.*

▶ change an estimate **refine, revise, update** *The International Monetary Fund revised its estimate for annual growth.*

● N+v show **indicate, place sth at, predict, put sth at, show, suggest** *Estimates indicate that the average household size in England is 2.37 people.* ● *Estimates put the figure at closer to £1 million.*

▶ vary **differ, range, vary** *Estimates vary, but usually range from 3–8 per cent of the male population.*

ethical ADJ
involving the principles of right and wrong

● ADJ+n issue or aspect **aspects, concerns, considerations, dilemma, dimension, implications, issue, questions** *The ethical implications of making this information available need to be considered.*

▶ principles **code, framework, guidelines, imperatives, norms, policy, principles, standards, theory** *The business is run according to clear ethical principles.*

▶ behaviour **behaviour, conduct, practice, stance** *Professionals must maintain a high standard of ethical conduct.*

ethnic ADJ
relating to groups who have the same culture

● ADJ+n group **community, group, grouping, minority, population** *There was no evidence of inequality relating to social class, educational attainment, income or ethnic group.*

▶ when different groups exist **composition, diversity, make-up** *Efforts should be made to ensure that the composition of the workforce reflects the ethnic diversity of the local community.* ● *London is proud of the extraordinary complexity of its cultural and ethnic make-up.*

▶ origin **background, identity, origin** *Of the 18 new appointments made during 2003/4, 16 were white, one was Asian and one was of another ethnic origin.*

▶ disagreement or fighting **conflict, hatred, strife, tension** *They were active in several projects which aimed to defuse the ethnic tension in the area.*

etiquette N

a set of rules for correct social behaviour

- adj+N good **correct, good, proper** *Whatever amount you give as a tip, the proper etiquette is to do it subtly.*
- ▶ bad **bad, poor** *Shouting unnecessarily is considered bad etiquette and may spoil other golfers' concentration and enjoyment.*
- ▶ types of situation **professional, social** *Professional etiquette dictates that these teachers remain anonymous.*
- n+N **business, court, email, forum, golf, wedding** *If you want to post a message, please observe the forum etiquette.* ● *We can also advise on all aspects of wedding etiquette and traditions.*
- v+N **follow, observe** *We kindly ask all our participants to follow our on-site etiquette to ensure a smooth-flowing and pleasant event.*
- N+v **demand, dictate, require** *At dance events like this, etiquette dictates that a lady will never decline an invitation to dance.*
- n+of+N **point, rule** *There are a few points of etiquette associated with this game.*

> If someone breaks a rule about correct behaviour, you can call their bad behaviour a ***breach of etiquette***: *It was considered a breach of etiquette for players at the lower end of the social order to win the game.*

evade V

1 avoid doing something, paying something or dealing with something

- V+n something that you ought to do **duty, obligation, responsibility** *The county council is evading its legal duty to reopen the route.*
- ▶ something that you must pay **duty, tax** *Attempts to evade excise duty and VAT are taken very seriously.*
- ▶ question or problem **issue, question** *He managed to evade the question about how much the new scheme would cost.*

2 avoid being caught or punished

- adv+V **just, narrowly, successfully** *The winger hit a low ball across goal that just evaded his onrushing teammates.*
- V+n when you have done something wrong **arrest, the authorities, justice, law, prosecution** *We want to stop these offending employers from evading justice.*
- ▶ when someone is trying to catch someone or something **capture, detection, predator, pursuer, sb's clutches** *I broke my arm jumping off a shed in an attempt to evade my pursuer.* ● *The servants tried to catch it, but the mysterious creature skilfully evaded their clutches.*

evaluate V

think carefully about something in order to make a judgment or decision about it

- adv+V in a careful, organized, or scientific way **carefully, critically, empirically, formally, fully, properly, rigorously, scientifically, systematically,** **thoroughly** *Students need to reflect on and critically evaluate their own work.*
- ▶ in a fair or independent way **independently, objectively** *The trial is now being evaluated independently by the Institute of Human Ageing at Liverpool University.*
- ▶ in relation to numbers or amounts **numerically, quantitatively** *These schemes will be quantitatively evaluated regarding, for example, effect, costs, maintenance, and visual impact.*
- ▶ all the time **constantly, continually, regularly** *We are constantly evaluating and updating our IT training courses and would like to hear from you.*
- V+n how good, useful or successful something is **adequacy, appropriateness, effectiveness, efficacy, performance, progress, quality, success, suitability, use, usefulness** *Experienced mentors evaluate the teaching performance of trainees.*
- ▶ the effect or importance of something **effect, impact, significance** *You must evaluate the impact of these resources on student learning.*
- ▶ the result of something **outcome, result** *The agent evaluates the likely outcome of pursuing each possible course of action.*
- ▶ whether something can be done or used **feasibility** *An experimental study is planned to evaluate the feasibility of these techniques.*
- ▶ what has been written, said, or done **argument, evidence, information, research, work** *The task is to analyse and evaluate the evidence, and then draw and justify conclusions.*
- ▶ suggestion for doing something, or way of doing something **approach, method, option, policy, proposal** *We need to understand and critically evaluate the data-analysis methods that are proposed.*
- ▶ risk **risk** *These are quick and cost-effective procedures for evaluating the risks and costs involved in implementing new systems.*
- n+V project or document **paper, project, report, study, trial** *The report evaluates the key broadcasting technology developments that are taking place.*
- ▶ person or group **expert, panel, participant, researcher, student, teacher, team** *The proposals were evaluated by an independent panel.*

evaluation N

the process of making a judgment or decision about something

- adj+N **careful, critical, detailed, formal, rigorous, systematic, thorough** *All pesticides are subject to rigorous scientific evaluation before approval for use is given.*
- ▶ fair or independent **external, independent, objective** *There was no formal, objective evaluation of the assignments.*
- ▶ comparing things **comparative** *The institute also carries out comparative product evaluations that facilitate selection of the best products.*
- ▶ looking at cost **economic** *We are undertaking technical and economic evaluations of a number of novel technologies.*
- ▶ early **initial, preliminary** *The initial evaluation revealed the potential usefulness of this technique.*
- n+N something that is being judged **job,**

performance *Employees' salary was linked to the results of job evaluation.*

▶ someone who is judging people or things **peer** *Workers don't talk talk to each other, and there is little quality control through peer evaluation.*

● v+N make an evaluation **carry out, complete, conduct, perform, provide, undertake** *The college will conduct a long-term evaluation of how students have developed their careers.*

If something is being considered and judged, you can say that it is *under evaluation*: *The project under evaluation aims to study ways of making contact more accessible for these groups.*

▶ be the subject of an evaluation **undergo** *The service has undergone a three-month evaluation.*

● N+v **conclude, confirm, demonstrate, find, highlight, indicate, reveal, show, suggest** *Evaluation has shown positive outcomes for the children.*

● N+n process **exercise, procedure, process, study** *Developing a rigorous evaluation process was not an easy task.*

▶ method **method, methodology, strategy, technique, tool** *Explain your evaluation methodology, and explain how the necessary data was collected.*

▶ document **form, questionnaire, report, sheet, summary** *We would be grateful if you could complete this evaluation form to help us in planning future events.*

▶ points to consider **criteria** *Examples of additional evaluation criteria can be found below.*

evening N
the period between afternoon and night

● adj+N described according to the weather **balmy, chilly, cold, sunny, warm** *They had a picnic in the park on one of the few balmy evenings of that summer.*

▶ pleasant **convivial, enjoyable, entertaining, lovely, magical, pleasant, relaxing, romantic, wonderful** *It was such an enjoyable evening, an experience never to be forgotten.*

▶ early/late **early, late** *We expect to arrive in the early evening.*

▶ that you remember **memorable** *This was a truly memorable evening for all concerned.*

● v+N **enjoy, spend** *We spent the evening in a strange little pub near Guildford.*

● N+v **come, draw on, wear on** *I got more and more tired as the evening wore on.*

When you talk about an evening ending, you can use the expression *draw to a close*: *As the evening drew to a close, the crowd started heading for the exits.* When you are talking about the evenings becoming shorter in the autumn, you can use the expression *draw in*: *I can't go out running for so long after work now that the evenings are drawing in.*

● N+n event **buffet, class, concert, entertainment, meal, meeting, reception, session** *Breakfast and evening meals are included in the cost.*

▶ weather **sky, sun, sunshine** *There followed a photo call in the glorious evening sunshine.*

▶ clothes **dress, gown, wear** *It was a very fancy occasion with everyone in their best evening wear.*

event N
1 something that happens

● adj+N bad **adverse, cataclysmic, catastrophic, tragic, traumatic** *The patient should avoid situations that remind him of the traumatic event.*

▶ important **great, historic, important, major, momentous, significant** *This is the first trial on a charge of genocide in history, which is a momentous event in international law.*

▶ happening now/recently/in the past/in the future **current, future, historical, past, recent** *Most historical events fade from memory with the passage of time.*

▶ happening afterwards **subsequent** *They changed their mind about the policy in the light of subsequent events.*

● v+N see an event **witness** *The world of sport witnessed many important events this year.*

▶ record or describe an event **depict, describe, record, recount** *This ancient document does not record events chronologically.*

▶ remember or celebrate an event **celebrate, commemorate, mark, recall, remember** *The festival commemorated significant events in the history of the town.*

● N+v happen **happen, occur, take place, transpire, unfold** *It may be that a particular event occurred that damaged profits for that year.*

▶ cause something **lead to, lead up to, trigger** *The article examines all the events leading up to the outbreak of war.*

When you are talking about events connected with something, you can use *surrounding*: *Police questioned witnesses about the events surrounding his death.*

● n+of+N **chain, course, sequence, series** *He felt that he himself had set in motion the chain of events that killed her* ● *She was one of those people who, in the normal course of events, look to other people to make decisions.*

2 an organized occasion such as a party or sports competition

● v+N **arrange, attend, host, organize, plan, promote, publicize, run, sponsor, stage** *The museum will continue to host many special events throughout the year.*

● N+v **take place** *The hour-long event takes place at the Town Hall on 23 March.*

● n+of+N **programme, range, series, variety** *There will be a programme of events, such as workshops, masterclasses and seminars*

evidence N
facts or physical signs that help to prove something

● adj+N giving clear proof **ample, clear, compelling, conclusive, convincing, credible, hard, incontrovertible, irrefutable, overwhelming, strong** *There is overwhelming evidence of the benefits that Intelligent Buildings can deliver.*

▶ giving only limited proof **anecdotal, circumstantial** *These stories provide only circumstantial evidence and need to be backed up with documentary proof.*

▶ agreeing/disagreeing **conflicting, contradictory, corroborative, supporting** *There is conflicting evidence on the effectiveness of this therapy.*

▶ in the form of documents **documentary, written** *The Institute will examine documentary evidence acquired throughout this period.*

▶ of a scientific type **empirical, forensic, scientific** *There is support for the theory, but there is also empirical evidence against it.*

▶ proving that someone committed a crime **incriminating** *According to these sources, the president knew of the existence of this document and the incriminating evidence it contained.*

• v+N look for or get evidence **collect, find, gather, look for, marshal, obtain, uncover** *It is important to obtain this evidence as soon after the accident as possible.*

• show evidence **give, present, produce, provide, submit** *You will need to produce evidence of income and submit this with the application form.*

▶ look at evidence **consider, evaluate, examine, review** *Examine the evidence and decide for yourself.*

▶ find meaning of evidence **interpret** *Candidates should be able to interpret evidence from historical documents.*

▶ get rid of evidence **destroy** *The vehicle had been left burnt out in a fire aimed deliberately at destroying any scientific evidence of the crime.*

• N+v show something **confirm, demonstrate, indicate, point to, prove, show, suggest, support** *Evidence shows that millions of jobs have been created in telecommunications.*

▶ exist **exist** *If no evidence exists then the lack of evidence itself might be included as a weakness.*

▶ become known **come to light, emerge** *Evidence has also emerged that farmers continued to use the deadly substance for a further 10 years.*

▶ increase **accumulate, mount** *Objective evidence has steadily accumulated to confirm this hypothesis.*

• N+for **assertion, claim, effectiveness, efficacy, existence, hypothesis, presence** *There is some evidence for the existence of such an organisation in Scotland in the fourteenth century.*

If something exists, or if people can see it, you can say that it is *in evidence*: *The day I met the writer V. S. Naipaul his books were everywhere in evidence.*

• n+of+N **piece, shred** *The police investigation was proceeding without a shred of evidence.*

If people say or think something because of evidence, you can use the phrase *in the light of the evidence*: *This conclusion was reasonable in light of the medical evidence available.*

evident ADJ
easy to see, notice, or understand

• adv+ADJ very **clearly, immediately, plainly, quite, very** *This trend is clearly evident not only in Britain but in many other EU countries.*

▶ particularly **especially, particularly** *Racism is a serious problem in the area and is particularly evident in the larger towns.*

▶ more **increasingly** *It has become increasingly evident from their actions that the councils and their officials have scant regard for local people's welfare.*

▶ in an obvious and unpleasant way **painfully** *By 1979, the need for drastic measures had become painfully evident to all concerned.*

• v+ADJ **be, become, make sth, seem** *This fact was made evident in all our communications on the subject.*

evil ADJ
doing bad or cruel things; deliberately causing great harm

• adv+ADJ very or completely **thoroughly, truly, utterly, wholly** *His opinion was that all nuclear weapons are utterly evil.*

▶ because of what it is **inherently, intrinsically** *Racism is intrinsically evil and destructive.*

evoke V
bring an emotion, idea, or memory into your mind

• adv+V **beautifully, brilliantly, immediately, perfectly, powerfully, strongly, vividly** *Vividly evoking landscapes, people and his daily life, the letters offer revealing glimpses into Chekhov's preoccupations.*

• V+n **atmosphere, emotion, feeling, image, memory, mood, reaction, response, sense, spirit, sympathy** *It is a familiar song that evokes memories of times past in the audience.*

exaggerate V
describe something in a way that makes it seem better, worse, more important etc than it really is

• adv+V very much **greatly, grossly, hugely, vastly, wildly** *Fears about the safety of the beef were grossly exaggerated.*

▶ a little **slightly, somewhat** *This may sound somewhat exaggerated but it reflects the true situation.*

Usage *Exaggerate* is usually <u>passive</u> in all of the *adv+V* combinations shown above.

• V+n importance, size, or seriousness **extent, importance, scale, seriousness, significance** *I do not want to exaggerate the scale of the problem.*

▶ problem or danger **danger, problem, risk, threat** *We don't believe that we have exaggerated the threat that is posed to our national security.*

▶ effect **effect, impact** *These studies tend to exaggerate the effects of diet on health.*

▶ difference **difference** *She might have exaggerated differences, forgetting the considerable similarities.*

exaggeration N
a description that makes something seem better, worse, more important etc than it really is

• adj+N great **great, gross, wild** *That last comment was a gross exaggeration.*

▶ not great **a bit of an INFORMAL, slight** *Well, maybe 'terrible' is a bit of an exaggeration, but that's how it felt at the time.*

If you want to emphasize that something extreme is true, you can use the expression **I can say without exaggeration that...**: *I can honestly say without exaggeration that this is the worst club I have ever been to.*

- N+of **facts, risk, threat, truth** *We are concerned about these stories which seem to be a gross exaggeration of the facts.*

exam N
an important test of a student's knowledge

- adj+N happening at a particular stage **end-of-semester, end-of-term, end-of-year, final, first-year, second-year etc** *She passed all her first-year exams.*
- ▶ types of exam **external, internal, mock, multiple-choice, oral, practical, professional, written** *Please note that a mock exam will be held in the spring term to prepare you for the real thing in the summer.*
- ▶ lasting a particular time **one-hour, two-hour etc** *The final test will be a three-hour written examination.*

- v+N put someone's name on a list for an exam **enter (sb), register (sb)** *All of the classes were entered for the Spanish GCSE exam.* • *You will be given guidance on what to do and how to enter for the exam.*
- ▶ prepare an exam for students **set** *Who sets the exams? Is there an external exam board?*
- ▶ do an exam **do, sit, take** *This is the career he will pursue after he sits his exams and leaves school.*
- ▶ do an exam again after failing **resit, retake** *Students that missed passing by a few marks will be given the opportunity to resit exams.*
- ▶ prepare for an exam **cram for, prepare for, revise for, study for** *There are times when I don't want to cook, like when I'm cramming for exams.*
- ▶ be successful in an exam **do well in, pass** *She did well in her French exam.* • *If I pass these exams I can follow my ambition to become a doctor.*
- ▶ be unsuccessful in an exam **do badly in, fail, flunk** INFORMAL *If they fail their final exams, their prospective careers as lawyers will be over.*

- N+n question or set of questions **paper, question** *It is now possible to access exam papers and electronic course material articles from the college website.*
- ▶ student's set of written answers **script** *Your completed exam script should be submitted to the School Office by 16.00 on the same day.*
- ▶ preparation for an exam **preparation, revision** *Tutors offer study skills advice, particularly concerning exam revision.*
- ▶ student's score in an exam **grade, mark, results** *Students were being admitted to these colleges despite having achieved lower exam grades.*

examination N
1 an important test of a student's knowledge

- adj+N happening at a particular stage **final, preliminary** *The students all scored high marks in their final examinations.*
- ▶ types of examination **external, formal, mock, multiple-choice, oral, practical, professional,**

public, written *At the school, success in public examinations is considered essential.*
- ▶ lasting a particular time **one-hour, two-hour etc** *You will be assessed by a three-hour written examination.*

- v+N prepare an examination for students **hold** *Most of the university examinations are held in May.*
- ▶ do an examination **sit, take** *The students normally sit the final examination at the age of 17 or 18.*
- ▶ do an examination again after failing **resit** *In this case, you are likely to have to resit the examination or complete another assignment.*
- ▶ be successful in an examination **pass** *You may be required to pass an examination.*
- ▶ be unsuccessful in an examination **fail** *If you fail an examination or coursework, you are required to take a resit in that subject at the next available session.*
- ▶ prepare for an examination **prepare for, revise for, study for** *Good short-term memory is useful for students when studying for examinations.*

- N+n set of questions **paper, question** *The assessment consists of an examination paper covering all three units of the course.*
- ▶ student's set of written answers **script** *It is University policy not to return examination scripts to students.*
- ▶ preparation for an examination **preparation** *Do you need help with your examination preparation?*
- ▶ student's score in an examination **grade, mark, results** *The prize is awarded for the highest examination mark in History.*

2 a careful look at something to find out about it

- adj+N done carefully and completely **careful, close, critical, detailed, full, in-depth, rigorous, systematic, thorough** *Mr Robertson had made a thorough examination of the deceased woman's home shortly after her death.*
- ▶ done quickly **brief, cursory, superficial** *A cursory examination of related works may clarify this point.*
- ▶ done early/later **further, initial, preliminary, subsequent** *Initial examination of the pottery suggested an Iron Age date.*
- ▶ done in a particular way **clinical, forensic, medical, microscopic, physical** *The next day the car was taken to a police garage and a full forensic examination was done.*

If something is being considered or checked carefully, you can say that it is **under examination**: *Many of the articles focus on the specific issues under examination.*

- v+N do an examination **carry out, conduct, do, make, perform, undertake** *Ideally, a cardiologist should perform the examination to increase the chances of detection.*
- ▶ have an examination **undergo** *All candidates will be required to undergo a medical examination.*
- ▶ need or deserve examination **deserve, merit, need** *All these points need close examination.*

- N+v **confirm, indicate, reveal, show, suggest** *Superficial examination showed obvious similarities between the suspect's handwriting and that in the letter.*

examine V
look at something carefully to find out about it or check it

- adv+V carefully or in great detail **carefully, closely, critically, fully, in depth, in detail, minutely, properly, rigorously, systematically, thoroughly** *Let us continue then by carefully examining Lenin's writings on peaceful revolution.*
- ▶ not great detail **briefly** *The appeals process will be briefly examined.*
- ▶ separately **individually, separately** *Each case will be examined individually and its merits assessed.*

- n+V **article, author, chapter, expert, module, paper, project, report, research, researcher, study, thesis** *This paper examines the literature on the ethics of marketing.*

- V+for **evidence, presence, signs** *The tissue obtained can then be examined for evidence of genetic or metabolic disorders.*

You can also **examine whether** something is the case: *This article examines whether developments in genetic technology result in changes in public expectations and fears.*

example N
1 something that you mention to help explain what you are talking about

- adj+N very good or clear **classic, clear, excellent, fine, good, obvious, perfect, prime, typical** *Peru provides a prime example of how hurricane forecasts can be valuable.*
- ▶ unusual or interesting **notable, outstanding, striking** *The free exchange of data is an outstanding example of international cooperation.*
- ▶ not good **bad, glaring** *This is another glaring example of the company's inefficiency.*
- ▶ common/rare **common, rare** *Common examples are fear of snakes, birds, or insects.*

- v+N **cite, give, highlight, provide, quote** *To cite a popular example, Europe has 73 air-traffic control centres, whereas the USA has only 20 to manage twice as many flights.*

- N+v **assume, demonstrate, illustrate, indicate, point to, refer to, show, suggest** *The above example assumes that each task will be done by a separate person.* ● *Here is an example showing the sequence of things to be done.*

2 a person or way of behaving that is considered as a model that other people should copy [always singular]

- adj+N good **excellent, fine, good, shining** *John is a shining example of how to take control of one's own career.*
- ▶ bad **bad, poor** *They accused her of setting a bad example to the rest of the staff.*

If you think someone's good behaviour deserves to be copied, you can say that it is *an example to* someone: *Turkey is a shining example to the world of the virtues of cultural diversity.*

- v+N give or be an example for others to copy **be, set** *She has a very good subject knowledge and sets an excellent example in her own teaching.*

- ▶ follow someone's good example **follow, imitate** *The Welsh body is encouraging more environmental organisations to follow its example.*

If people show others how to behave by behaving well themselves, you can say that they lead *by example*, or that others learn *by example*: *The captain has led the team by example and is definitely the player to watch for next season.*

exasperation N
an annoyed feeling you have because something is not right

- adj+N **sheer, total** *I am writing this letter to express my total exasperation* **with** *your venue.*

- v+N **express** *The Secretary of State expressed exasperation* **at** *the Minister's remarks.*

- v+in+N **ask, exclaim, say** *She exclaimed in exasperation that their presence was more of a hindrance than a help.*

- and/or **anger, frustration** *He couldn't hide his frustration and exasperation when he finally got through to the Customer Services Department.*

exceed V
be greater than a number or amount; go above an official limit

- adv+V by a large amount **comfortably, considerably, far, greatly, significantly, substantially, vastly** *There have been very significant increases over the last few years, far exceeding national averages.*
- ▶ by a small amount **slightly** *As a result, expenditure may slightly exceed income, but not by a significant amount.*

- V+n **amount, average, budget, capacity, demand, limit, quota, speed limit, supply, target, threshold** *You will be required to develop business to exceed sales targets whilst providing a high level of customer service.*

If something is much better or much more than you expected, you can say that *it exceeds your expectations*: *The attendance figure of more than 12,000 exceeded all our expectations.*

excellent ADJ
extremely good

- adv+ADJ very **absolutely** INFORMAL, **quite, really, simply, truly** *Not everything was good, but much of the work was truly excellent.*
- ▶ rather **rather** *This new album, far from being a disappointment, is really rather excellent.*
- ▶ mostly or usually **generally, mostly, usually** *The quality of the food is generally excellent, and beats comparison with that in more expensive restaurants.*
- ▶ when everything or everyone is excellent **uniformly** *The performances of the cast are uniformly excellent.*
- ▶ all the time **consistently** *This is one of the most consistently excellent small hotels in Scotland.*
- ▶ in a particular way **academically, musically, technically** *This was technically excellent playing of a beautiful piece of music.*

- v+ADJ **be, judge sb/sth, look, prove, sound** *Much of the teaching was judged excellent by the school inspectors.* • *The new system has proved excellent at solving many of our problems.*

exception N
something that is not included in a general statement

- adj+N single **only, sole** *I also understand that, with the sole exception of training days, my work will be done in this office.*
- ▸ obvious **clear, conspicuous, glaring, notable, obvious** *With a few notable exceptions, historians know very little about the festivals in this period.*
- ▸ existing in a few cases **few, occasional, odd, rare** *At the start of every day – with the odd exception, because of my travelling – I read a few pages of the Bible.*
- ▸ important **important, major** *This is an important exception to the general rule.*
- ▸ not important or bad **minor** *One pleasant surprise was that biting insects were virtually absent throughout our stay (with one or two minor exceptions).*
- ▸ possible **possible** *House prices have fallen in every region, with the possible exception of London.*
- ▸ limited to one case **specific** *There are specific exceptions to these conditions for those people working with children.*
- ▸ much better than all others **honourable** *The performances were, with a few honourable exceptions, rather dull.*

If you allow something for a particular person, for a special reason, you can say that you are **making an exception for** them: *The committee cannot make an exception in Lara's case, just because he is famous.* If you want to emphasize that there are no exceptions to a statement, you can use the phrase **without exception**: *Over the years our students, without exception, have really enjoyed the experience.*

exceptional ADJ
1 extremely good or impressive; much more or greater than usual

- adv+ADJ **highly, quite, truly** *We provide a truly exceptional service and are proud of our customer loyalty.*
- ADJ+n good quality or achievement **ability, achievement, clarity, contribution, performance, quality, service, skills, standard, talent, value** *The judges were greatly impressed by the exceptional talent of the winner.*
- ▸ difficult situation **hardship** *Help is available if you are suffering exceptional hardship.*

2 very unusual

- adv+ADJ **highly, wholly** *These items may be permitted in highly exceptional cases.*
- ADJ+n **case, circumstances, reason, situation** *Such grants will only be awarded in exceptional circumstances.*

exchange N
1 a situation in which one person gives another person something and receives something similar in return

- adj+N between two groups **mutual, reciprocal, two-way** *This programme is set up to facilitate a two-way exchange of information between the departments.*
- ▸ honest or bringing good results **frank, fruitful** *Many thanks to all participants in what was a very fruitful exchange of ideas.*
- v+N **encourage, facilitate, foster, promote, stimulate** *The aim of the meeting is to promote the exchange of ideas between teachers at the various colleges.*
- N+of ideas or information **ideas, information, knowledge, views** *Ample opportunity will be provided for the exchange of ideas and discussion of the issues involved.*
- ▸ letters, emails or words **correspondence, emails, letters, messages, words** *Keep a note of all exchanges of correspondence between you and the company.*
- ▸ shooting **fire, gunfire, shots** *The United Nations troops resisted and an exchange of fire ensued.*

2 an angry conversation or argument

- adj+N **acrimonious, angry, brief, frank, heated, verbal** *The two became involved in a heated exchange and it seemed as though a fight might break out.*

excite V
make someone have a particular feeling or reaction

- V+n feeling **admiration, astonishment, curiosity, imagination, interest, suspicion, sympathy** *My letter had clearly excited his curiosity.*
- ▸ reaction **comment, speculation** *Like every new initiative, it will excite the usual comments from the usual suspects.*

excitement N
the feeling of being excited

- adj+N **breathless, considerable, feverish, genuine, great, intense, much, palpable, real, sheer, tremendous** *Then she smiled, and he felt his heart give a bound of feverish excitement.*
- v+N create excitement **bring, cause, create, generate** *A group's lead singer must generate excitement on stage.*
- ▸ feel excitement **enjoy, experience, feel, share** *The group is experiencing the excitement of crossing international cultural barriers.*
- N+v become greater **build, grow, mount, rise** *Excitement mounts as the great white limousine glides into view – and stops just in front of you!*
- ▸ stop **die down, subside, wear off** *Once the excitement of the victory has subsided, we will carefully analyse the team's performance.*

You can also feel excitement **at** something: *The whole island is buzzing with excitement at the prospect of having the world's finest players on its doorstep.*

- v+with+N **be bursting with, be filled with, buzz, tremble** *His was a life that was filled with excitement, opportunity and wonder.*

- n+of+N **buzz, feeling, flurry, frenzy, frisson, ripple, rush, tingle** *You could feel the buzz of excitement from the young people as they climbed aboard the coaches.*

- and/or **adventure, anticipation, enthusiasm, fear, fun, glamour, joy, suspense, thrill** *So it was with mixed feelings of anticipation, excitement and fear that I set off.*

exciting ADJ
making you feel excited

- adv+ADJ very **extremely, fantastically, genuinely, hugely, incredibly, particularly, really, terribly, tremendously, truly, very** *We have a tremendously exciting programme of change over the next few years as we redevelop the museum.*
- ▶ rather **pretty** INFORMAL, **quite, rather** *I found the prospect of moving house rather exciting.*
- ▶ in a particular way **intellectually, visually** *Newcastle is one of the most visually exciting of all the great industrial cities of the north.*

- v+ADJ **be, become, feel, find sth, get, look, make sth, prove, seem, sound** *The things you find most exciting are those that are unexpected.* • *The next few weeks are sure to prove very exciting for the club.*

- and/or **challenging, diverse, dynamic, fresh, innovative, interesting, new, rewarding, stimulating, varied, vibrant** *He has taken up his job as head of an exciting new business project.*

exclusion N
a situation in which someone is deliberately prevented from having something, being involved in something

- adj+N **economic, financial, social** *We welcome the government's agenda for tackling social exclusion and increasing employment opportunities.*

- N+from **education, membership, participation, school, society** *These children face exclusion from society, health, education and employment, and their needs should be addressed.*

- v+N deal with exclusion **address, combat, reduce, tackle** *Local facilities, such as public libraries, play a key role in tackling exclusion in modern societies.*
- ▶ experience exclusion **experience, face, suffer** *They criticized the serious level of unfair treatment and exclusion experienced by disabled people.*

excuse N
an explanation for your failure or mistake; a reason for something

- adj+N good **acceptable, good, great, reasonable** *Birthdays are always a great excuse for a party!* • *Those people who fail to attend without giving a reasonable excuse may have their benefit cut.*
- ▶ that suits you **convenient** *The government is using the recession as a convenient excuse for cutting aid budgets.*
- ▶ bad **feeble, flimsy, lame, pathetic, poor, weak** *He made some lame excuse about why he couldn't do the work in time.*

- v+N **find, give, have, invent, make, offer, provide,**

use *Do your customers avoid your calls or give excuses when you chase them for payment?*

execute V
do or perform something

- V+adv well **beautifully, brilliantly, efficiently, expertly, professionally, skilfully, successfully** *The graphics, the buttons, and the general design are all professionally executed.*
- ▶ badly **badly, poorly** *She writes lines that actors couldn't possibly deliver without them sounding badly written and poorly executed.*

> Usage **Execute** is often passive in these combinations.

- V+n movement **manoeuvre** *The aircraft executed a daring rolling manoeuvre.*
- ▶ task **mission, operation, plan, task, work** *The young lady who had executed the work told me that it had been a painstaking process.*

exemplify V
be a typical example of something; show something using an example

- adv+V **clearly, perfectly, strikingly, well** *The story of Manchester United perfectly exemplifies the appeal of competitive sport.*

- V+n **approach, attitude, point, practice, principle, spirit, tradition, trend** *We can exemplify this point by the use of case-study evidence.* • *He exemplifies the singer-songwriter tradition at its best.*

exemption N
permission to ignore a rule, obligation, or payment

- v+N give someone an exemption **allow, give (sb), grant (sb), permit, provide** *Washington finally granted a special exemption on exports to Britain.*
- ▶ have the right to an exemption **be eligible for, be entitled to, qualify for** *Families with young children qualify for an exemption from the tax.*
- ▶ get an exemption **gain, obtain** *Note: if you already have a degree in a suitable subject, you may gain exemption from one or more years of study based on your previous qualifications.*
- ▶ try to get an exemption **apply for, claim, seek** *We are horrified that the churches are seeking exemptions from European law.*
- ▶ complete **absolute, full, unconditional** *The degree provides full exemption from the professional examinations of the Law Society.*
- ▶ not complete **conditional, limited, partial** *Certain people will be eligible for full or partial exemption from the tax.*

exercise N
physical activity

- adj+N physically difficult **intense, strenuous, vigorous** *It is essential to drink plenty of fluids during periods of strenuous exercise.*
- ▶ physically easy **gentle, light, moderate** *Gentle exercise in water is relaxing at any time.*
- ▶ done regularly or for a long time **daily, prolonged, regular** *Regular aerobic exercise encourages a better night's sleep and is very good for your general health and well-being.*

▸ types of exercise **aerobic, cardiovascular** *An effective and practical all-over body workout, featuring aerobic exercise and muscle toning.*

● v+N **do, get, take** *Alan also used to be very active, but as he got older he did less exercise.*

● N+n **class, programme, regime, regimen, routine, session** *If you suffer from a medical condition, you should consult your doctor before starting a new exercise regime.*

exercise V

1 use your power or rights

● adv+V **freely, fully, lawfully, properly** *In the present climate, the public cannot lawfully exercise those rights.*

● V+n **authority, choice, control, influence, jurisdiction, power, prerogative, right, sovereignty, veto** *She told her granddaughter at an early age that she must exercise her right to vote.*

2 use a skill or quality to avoid problems

● V+n **care, caution, control, discretion, judgment, responsibility, restraint, self-restraint, skill, vigilance** *Parents should exercise caution when taking under 16s into this area.*

exert V

use your influence or authority to achieve or affect something

● V+n **control or influence authority, control, dominance, influence, power, pressure** *The social and cultural demands of childhood were shown to be exerting very heavy pressures on children.*

▸ attraction **attraction, fascination, pull** *The 'American Dream' continues to exert a powerful pull on many people outside America.*

exhaust V

use all that you have of something

● adv+V almost **almost, nearly, practically** *By then my patience was nearly exhausted.*

▸ quickly **quickly, rapidly** *Stocks of the antiviral drug were quickly exhausted.*

Usage **Exhaust** is usually passive in all the *adv+V* combinations shown above.

● V+n supply of something **ammunition, fuel, reserves, resources, stock, supply** *The allied forces soon exhausted their supplies.*

▸ personal quality **patience, strength** *She had soon exhausted the patience of her new boss, and was sacked.*

▸ possible methods or solutions **avenue, possibilities** *We must be prepared to exhaust all avenues to achieve that.*

exhausted ADJ

extremely tired and without any energy

● ADV+adj very **absolutely, completely, thoroughly, totally, utterly** *I woke up later than intended, due to being absolutely exhausted from lack of sleep. • These young pilots might return from their flights completely exhausted after a difficult and dangerous time.*

▸ in a particular way **emotionally, mentally, physically** *By the end of the day I was mentally exhausted, trying to arrive at the best solution for the clients' problems.*

exhausting ADJ

making you feel extremely tired

● adv+ADJ very **absolutely, completely, totally, utterly** *Though it wasn't a demanding class, I found it utterly exhausting.*

▸ rather **pretty, quite, rather, somewhat** *Life is now utterly different and pretty exhausting.*

▸ in a particular way **emotionally, mentally, physically** *Simultaneous interpretation is a very stressful and mentally exhausting activity that requires a high level of concentration.*

● and/or bad in another way **dangerous, difficult, frustrating, long, painful, stressful** *I'd had an exhausting and stressful day at work.*

▸ good in another way **exciting, inspiring, rewarding** *The experience of collaborating with so many individuals on a project was both inspiring and exhausting.*

exhaustion N

the feeling of being extremely tired

● adj+N extreme **complete, extreme, severe, sheer, total, utter** *The dance went on until the dancers dropped out from sheer exhaustion.*

▸ types of exhaustion **emotional, mental, nervous, physical** *His wife was suffering from nervous exhaustion brought on by poverty.*

● v+from+N **collapse, die, drop, suffer** *Several refugees collapsed from exhaustion at the border crossing.*

● n+of+N **brink, a feeling, point, state** *He entered the room in a state of apparent exhaustion. • We are willing to work hard, to the point of exhaustion if need be.*

exhaustive ADJ

thorough or complete

● adv+ADJ **by no means, hardly, neither** *This book is by no means exhaustive, but it provides a very informative overview of the Russian Revolution. • The coverage is neither exhaustive nor uniform; there is a bias towards the history of statistics.*

● ADJ+n document **bibliography, catalogue, checklist, documentation, guide, list, listing** *This is not intended to be an exhaustive list.*

▸ actions or words **account, analysis, description, examination, inquiry, investigation, notes, research, review, search, study, survey, testing** *This information was gained after an exhaustive inquiry by the Dutch government. • Dr O'Brien made an exhaustive study of the topic for his new book.*

● and/or **complete, comprehensive, definitive, detailed, exclusive, long, thorough** *This document outlines the duties required of the post holder, but is not a comprehensive or exhaustive list. • This isn't intended to be an exhaustive or definitive guide; if in doubt, consult a specialist.*

exhibit   266

exhibit V
show a particular feeling, quality, or ability

- ● V+n **behaviour, characteristic, sign, symptom, tendency, trait** *Some patients begin exhibiting violent tendencies.*

exhibition N
a public event where interesting things are shown

- ● v+N organize an exhibition **arrange, curate, hold, host, mount, organize, stage** *The school will mount two exhibitions of pupils' work.*
- ▶ make an exhibition start to be available to people **inaugurate, launch, open, present** *The group launched their first exhibition at Centrespace Gallery in Bristol.*
- ▶ go to an exhibition **attend, view, visit** *Delegates were able to visit the exhibition and pop into the sessions that were of interest to them.*
- ▶ contain an exhibition **house** *We stop off at the memorial to Che Guevara in Santa Clara, which houses a fascinating exhibition of his life.*

exorbitant ADJ
much more than is reasonable

- ● ADJ+n an amount of money that someone charges or pays **bill, charge, cost, fare, fee, price, rent** *Passengers are simply fed up with paying exorbitant rail fares.*
- ▶ an amount of money in general **amount, increase, rate, sum** *They were able to sell the building for an exorbitant sum.*
- ▶ an amount of money that someone earns **salary** *No footballer is worth the exorbitant salary they are paid.*
- ▶ something that someone asks for **demand** *The project suffered as a result of exorbitant demands made by local landowners.*

expand V
become a bigger business or organization

- ● adv+V **considerably, constantly, continuously, dramatically, exponentially, gradually, greatly, massively, quickly, rapidly, significantly, slowly, steadily, substantially** *The global market for these products has expanded exponentially.*
- ● n+V **business, company, economy, empire, firm, market** *US software and IT firms are expanding into Europe.*

expanse N
a large area of land, water, or sky

- ● adj+N very large **boundless, broad, endless, huge, infinite, large, vast, wide** *There they gazed upon a vast expanse of dusty land.*
- ▶ empty **barren, bleak, desolate, featureless, treeless** *The road crosses the bleak expanse of Rannoch Moor.*

expansion N
the process of making a business or activity grow

- ● adj+N large **considerable, dramatic, huge, limitless, major, massive, significant, substantial, vast** *There has been a massive expansion of air services over recent decades.* ● *The company is currently undergoing a vast expansion in its agricultural activities.*
- ▶ continuing **continual, continued, continuing, further, ongoing, relentless, steady, sustained** *The relentless expansion in worldwide demand for energy has had huge consequences on the regional economy.* ● *The UK economy has experienced the longest sustained expansion since quarterly records began in 1955.*
- ▶ happening quickly or slowly **gradual, rapid, sudden** *Rapid expansion has seen the chain increase from 860 to nearly 1400 shops over the last three years.*
- ▶ happening in the future **future, planned** *The planned expansion will see over 100 new offices opening in the next 10 years.*
- ● v+N make an expansion happen **accelerate, accommodate, aid, facilitate, favour, fuel, undergo** *The investment expansion was fuelled by expanding credit and a strong stock market.*
- ▶ prevent an expansion **halt, hinder** *The ring road currently acts as a 'concrete collar', hindering the expansion of local markets.*
- ● N+into **market, sector** *Since then, the company has achieved rapid expansion into all sectors of the fashion and retail industries.*
- ● N+of **agriculture, airport, capacity, commerce, economy, education, empire, industry, network, production, sector, trade** *The long-term prospects for the expansion of British agriculture have never been better.* ● *The expansion of the Chinese economy has enabled many students from China to seek higher education in other countries.*
- ● and/or **consolidation, continuation, diversification, growth** *The post-war period saw an expansion and diversification of courses.*

expectation N
a belief that something should happen, or will happen, in a particular way

- ● adj+N not reasonable **exaggerated, false, unreal, unrealistic, unreasonable** *We want the company to provide the service we are paying for; this is not an unreasonable expectation.*
- ▶ reasonable **legitimate, rational, realistic, reasonable** *Were customers' expectations realistic in relation to quality and value for money?*
- ▶ expecting things to be good **high, optimistic, sanguine** *Today's young Scots have high expectations of college courses.*

> Usage In most combinations, *expectation* is plural: *When customers have too many expectations, they are inevitably disappointed.*

- ▶ expecting things to be bad **low** *Only people with low expectations will find this show entertaining.*

> If you are talking about things that people do because they expect something else to happen, you can use the phrases *in the expectation of* and *in the expectation that*: *We pay a higher price in the expectation of better service.*

- ● v+N be better than people expected **exceed, outperform, outstrip, surpass** *The public's response to the music outstripped the band's initial expectations.*

▶ be worse than people expected **dampen, dash, disappoint, fall below, fall short of** *Their supporters' high expectations were dashed.*

▶ be different to what people expected **confound, contradict, defy, shatter, subvert** *Short films work best when they subvert audience expectations.*

▶ be the way people expected it to be **come up to, fulfil, live up to, match, meet, satisfy** *The Council strives to meet the expectations and aspirations of the community in delivering top-quality services.*

> If something happens the way you expect it to, you can say that it is *in line with expectations*: *It was the right decision and was wholly in line with people's expectations.*

▶ have expectations **have, hold** *The two groups have completely different expectations.* • *Now teachers have the expectation that girls will achieve higher examination grades.*

expedition N

a journey, especially a long journey that has been carefully planned

● adj+N for a particular purpose **archaeological, exploratory, marine, military, naval, scientific** *The fjord was unexplored until the Spanish led a scientific expedition there in 1793.*

▶ exciting or dangerous **adventurous, daring, gruelling** *He planned the diets for gruelling expeditions to the North Pole and Everest.*

▶ unsuccessful **doomed, ill-fated** *He was a member of Ernest Shackleton's ill-fated expedition to cross the Antarctic.*

▶ to a particular or distant place **overland, overseas, polar** *By the age of 24, he had been on four long overseas expeditions.*

● n+N **backpacking, camping, caving, diving, fishing, hunting, kayaking, mountaineering, shopping, whaling** *The Cuillin Ridge is definitely the finest mountaineering expedition in Britain.*

● v+N make an expedition **embark on, go on, make, participate in, undertake** *In the early 1900s, a small group of British explorers made several expeditions to the polar regions of the Arctic and the Antarctic.*

> If someone is making an expedition, you can say that they are *on an expedition*: *I was 2,000 miles away on an expedition of my own.*

▶ organize or lead an expedition **command, conduct, lead, mount, organize, plan** *When in Norway, he heard the Germans were to mount an expedition to the Antarctic.*

expenditure N

money that is spent

● adj+N expected **anticipated, estimated, planned, projected** *Projected expenditure for 2004/05 was £3.821m, well within the target figure.*

▶ total **actual, annual, gross, total** *Gross expenditure on the NHS increased by 8 per cent in the last financial year.*

● n+N by a particular group **consumer, government, household** *Reductions in tax often lead to increases in household expenditure.*

▶ on a particular thing **advertising, defence, energy, healthcare, NHS** *We share Labour's desire to limit defence expenditure.*

▶ money spent to earn more money **capital** *Capital expenditure is required for initial equipment and land.*

● v+N control or reduce expenditure **control, curb, curtail, cut, monitor, reduce** *The new regulations are designed to curb public expenditure, not to increase it.*

▶ allow expenditure **approve, authorize** *The committee approved the expenditure of £20,000 for a new computer-based system.*

▶ have to spend money **incur** *Generally, it is better to incur expenditure just before the end of your accounting year.*

▶ pay money back **defray, offset, reimburse** *These savings will successfully offset any significant additional expenditure.*

● N+v be more than before **go up, increase, rise** *Total expenditure increased by 23 per cent.*

▶ be less than before **decline, decrease, fall, go down** *One item on which expenditure has declined very strikingly has been insurance.*

expense N

1 money that you spend when you buy something

● adj+N additional and minor **added, additional, extra, incidental, miscellaneous** *This sum is intended to cover the cost of evening meals, drinks and snacks, and other incidental expenses.*

▶ major **considerable, enormous** *The car had been restored at enormous expense by the former owner.*

▶ types of expense **administrative, legal, medical, operational** *Clients will not be liable for any legal expenses.*

● v+N spend money **incur** *Students also incur expenses for the following: photocopying, stationery, and printing.*

> If you cause someone to spend money, you can say that you *put them to expense*: *We didn't want to put you to any extra expense.* If someone spends money on themselves or on your behalf, you can say that they *go to some expense* or *they go to the expense of* doing something: *If your computer is still working, why go to the expense of buying a new version?*

▶ have or give money to pay for something **afford, cover, meet** *The council has granted £1,600 to meet these expenses.*

▶ avoid spending money **avoid, save, spare** *The original idea was to put our catalogue on the Web and save some printing expense.*

> If people have spent a lot of money on providing or organizing something, you can say that *no expense was spared*: *No expense was spared when it came to choosing the correct mix of software applications.*

2 money that you spend when you do your job

● v+N pay money back **pay, pay back, refund, reimburse** *The company will refund reasonable travel expenses.*

▶ ask someone to pay money back **claim, reclaim** *If you are on a low income, you may be entitled to reclaim your travel expenses.*

Usage In most combinations, **expense** is used in the plural: *The money goes towards rent and other living expenses.*

expensive ADJ
costing a lot of money

- adv+ADJ too **overly, prohibitively, too** *Other types of CD printers can be prohibitively expensive.*
- ▶ very **enormously, extremely, hideously, horrendously, hugely, ludicrously, massively, outrageously, ruinously, very** *The hotel restaurant was outrageously expensive.*
- v+ADJ **appear, be, become, look, prove, remain, seem, sound** *This system can prove very expensive.*

experience N
1 knowledge and skill that you gain while you do something

- adj+N much **considerable, extensive, vast** *We have vast experience in handling contracts for both employers and employees.*
- ▶ direct **direct, first-hand, hands-on, practical** *Apprenticeships are a great way to go straight into the workplace and get real hands-on experience.*
- ▶ not much **limited** *The majority of the actors had very limited experience.*
- ▶ useful or appropriate **educational, professional, relevant, valuable** *The post requires at least 3 years' relevant experience.*
- v+N have or provide experience **bring, have, offer, provide** *She has considerable experience in managing organisational cultural change.*
- ▶ get experience **acquire, broaden, gain, get** *The post-holder will be expected to undertake research in company law and to gain some experience of teaching for the Law Faculty.*

2 knowledge that you gain from life

- N+v **confirm, illustrate, indicate, prove, show, suggest, teach, tell sb** *Our experience indicates that professionals working in the criminal justice system find part-time study particularly attractive.*
- v+from+N **come, derive, draw, gain, know, learn** *We all make mistakes and and we can all learn from experience.*
- v+on+N **depend, draw, rely** *It is also important for the UK to draw on the experience of other countries.*

3 something that happens to you

- adj+N pleasant **enjoyable, memorable, positive, rewarding, wonderful** *It has been an interesting and rewarding experience.*
- ▶ unpleasant **bad, frightening, harrowing, painful, strange, traumatic, unpleasant** *Finding out that your child has a disability is a very painful and traumatic experience for most parents.*
- v+N talk about an experience **discuss, explore, recount, share** *She recounts her experiences and the different methods employed compared with those in Britain.*
- ▶ have an experience **have** *It seems that many children had the same experience.*

experience V
if you experience something, it happens to you

- adv+V **actually, directly, first hand, personally** *Members of the group had experienced first hand the effects of living with people with mental health problems.*
- V+n something unpleasant **abuse, decline, delay, deprivation, difficulty, disadvantage, discomfort, discrimination, distress, frustration, harassment, hardship, pain, problem, stress, symptom, trauma, violence** *You should always consult your doctor if you experience any discomfort.*
- ▶ something pleasant **joy, thrill** *Experience the joy and wonder of seeing the world from the treetops.*

experiment N
a scientific test done to find out something

- adj+N **behavioural, computational, genetic, numerical, psychological, scientific** *Psychological experiments can produce theories of human nature that do not coincide with the actual experience of any subject.*
- v+N do an experiment **carry out, conduct, do, perform, run, undertake** *The experiment was carried out on white rats.*
- ▶ design an experiment **design, devise, plan** *The NASA research group is devising experiments for the International Space Station.*
- N+v **confirm, demonstrate, illustrate, indicate, prove, reveal, show, suggest, verify** *Experiments have demonstrated eating such contaminated fish may increase the risk of developing cancer.*

experimental ADJ
used in or obtained from scientific experiments

- ADJ+n information **data, evidence, observations, results** *To date, experimental observations have been limited due to the severe weather conditions.*
- ▶ tools or methods **apparatus, measurement, technique** *We established a new experimental technique, whereby cancer cells were distributed in thin collagen gel.*

expert N
someone with great knowledge or skill

- adj+N **acknowledged, distinguished, eminent, foremost, renowned, respected** *Nick is one of Madagascar's foremost wildlife experts.*
- N+v **advise, agree, argue, believe, claim, conclude, disagree, predict, reckon, say, suggest, tell, urge, warn** *Global warming is weakening more forests through disease and drought, experts warn.*
- and/or **beginner, enthusiast, non-expert, novice, specialist** *The success will depend upon the quality and effort put in by enthusiasts and experts in the marine world.*

expertise N
skill or knowledge obtained from long experience

- adj+N great **considerable, extensive, in-depth, unparalleled, unrivalled, wide-ranging** *Our unparalleled expertise in competitive energy markets* *gives us an outstanding foundation for expansion overseas.*

▶ types of expertise **clinical, culinary, professional, scientific, technical, technological** *Our 'in-house' engineering services teams include engineers who have a wide range of experience and technical expertise.*

● v+N use expertise **access, bring to bear, call on, contribute, draw on, lend, offer, pool, provide, share, utilize** *We were very lucky to have someone of his calibre who was able and willing to lend his expertise.*

▶ have expertise **demonstrate, possess** *Overall, the team possesses expertise in several key fields.*

▶ get expertise **accumulate, acquire, develop, gain** *You will then be given the chance to develop expertise and knowledge through on-the-job training.*

▶ not have expertise **lack** *Companies often lack the expertise to create a really successful website.*

● and/or other forms of ability **advice, experience, know-how, knowledge, professionalism, talent** *There is no greater concentration of talent, expertise and resources in the field of Scottish studies anywhere in the world.*

▶ other things needed **equipment, resources, technology** *Tests that require special equipment and expertise may be done in a different laboratory.*

expire V

1 if an official document expires, it can no longer be used

● n+V **certificate, contract, copyright, lease, licence, passport, patent, permit, visa, warranty** *People whose passports had expired were not allowed to cast their vote.*

2 if a point in time expires, it passes and some action must be taken

● n+V **deadline, period** *Plans are being prepared for strike action before the legal deadline expires.*

explain V

give someone a reason or make someone understand something

● adv+V **well adequately, fully, in detail, properly, satisfactorily, thoroughly** *What has not been satisfactorily explained is why this situation was allowed to exist for so long.*

▶ clearly **carefully, clearly, exactly, precisely, simply, succinctly** *Each recipe is pictured and succinctly explained.*

▶ not completely **partially, partly** *His damaged reputation could partially explain his long years in opposition.*

▶ in a calm way **calmly, patiently, politely, rationally** *I reply by politely explaining their error and asking them to remove me from their database.*

▶ V+n **idea, meaning, motivation, nature, principle, process, purpose, rationale, reason, reasoning, significance, thinking** *She explained the rationale behind the precautions that are recommended.*

explanation N

a reason you give for something

▶ adj+N likely to be true **adequate, convincing,**

convincing, likely, logical, obvious, plausible, probable, rational, reasonable, satisfactory *I can give no rational explanation for why these boats were so fast.*

▶ giving many details **detailed, full, thorough** *A full explanation for both of these tests will be given before the procedure commences.*

▶ giving few details **brief, concise** *We include a brief explanation of how to obtain information from the selected links.*

● v+N give an explanation **furnish, give, offer, propose, provide** *Is it impossible to furnish an explanation which would cover both of these facts?*

▶ ask for an explanation **demand, need, request, require, seek, want** *We have written to the Council seeking an explanation for the cuts.*

If it seems impossible to explain why or how something happened, you can say that it **defies explanation**: *Just because an event seems to defy explanation, there is no reason to class it as a miracle.*

explode V

burst with great force

● n+V **bomb, device, grenade, mine, missile, rocket, shell** *Shells were exploding around and behind the gunners.*

exploit V

1 treat someone unfairly to get benefits for yourself

● adv+V **cruelly, cynically, mercilessly, ruthlessly, sexually, shamelessly, unfairly** *Many countries have cynically exploited migrants.* ● *Innocent children are groomed for prostitution and sexually exploited by adults.*

● V+n **labour, masses, worker, workforce** *Big business is profiting from exploiting cheap labour in the region.*

2 use a situation to get benefits yourself

● adv+V in a particular way **commercially, economically, financially, industrially, industrially, profitably** *The programme was globally exported but never commercially exploited.*

▶ well **brilliantly, cleverly, effectively, fully, profitably, skilfully, successfully, usefully** *We want companies to fully exploit the advantages that information systems can offer.*

● V+n **advantage, fear, flaw, gap, loophole, opportunity, possibility, weakness** *Insurance salesmen are exploiting fears of job losses to dump unsuitable policies on unwary customers.*

exploitation N

unfair treatment of people or resources

● adj+N cruel **brutal, cynical, ruthless** *There still exists brutal exploitation by a class which constantly squeezes workers.*

▶ types of exploitation **capitalist, colonial, economic, imperialist, sexual** *The struggle against the imperialist exploitation of the big global corporations will continue.*

● v+N stop exploitation **abolish, avoid, combat, eliminate, end, fight, prevent, prohibit, stop** *It is*

our aim to end the exploitation and alienation of young people.
▶ say that exploitation is wrong **condemn, denounce, expose** We condemn the exploitation of the young and weak.
▶ continue exploitation **encourage, facilitate, intensify, permit, perpetuate** The trade in ivory is encouraging illegal exploitation of vulnerable populations in parts of Africa.

exploration N
a thorough examination or discussion of something

● adj+N thorough **deep, detailed, in-depth, systematic, thorough** Follow these hyperlinks for a thorough exploration of the subject.
▶ interesting **fascinating, imaginative, stimulating** The resulting book is a fascinating exploration of the nature of creativity.
● v+N be worth exploring **deserve, merit, warrant** He notes some other areas which merit further exploration.
▶ give useful results **repay, reward** This is a fascinating area of study that repays exploration.
▶ start, continue, and end **begin, commence, conclude, conduct, continue, initiate** On this course you will conduct in-depth explorations of the language of particular authors.
● N+v **discover, encourage, highlight, reveal** Our exploration highlights the possibility that some systems might be capable of predicting individual health problems.

explore V
examine or discuss something thoroughly

● adv+V thoroughly **comprehensively, extensively, fully, systematically, thoroughly** This book systematically explores all the key areas and issues involved.
▶ in a particular way **creatively, critically, independently** This is something that might be explored creatively in the context of this present discussion.
● V+n possibility or choice **avenue, feasibility, opportunity, option, possibility, potential** The committee is exploring the feasibility of providing services for other ethnic minority communities.
▶ subject **aspect, concept, idea, issue, nature, notion, relationship, theme, topic** This term the history workshop will be exploring the theme of gender and labour.

explosion N
energy released by a bomb or something similar

● adj+N **loud, massive, terrific, tremendous, violent** He was wakened by a terrific explosion and found himself on the floor.
● v+N **cause, detonate, lead to, result in, set off, trigger** A cigarette lighter may have triggered a fatal explosion in Dunkirk, Indiana.
● N+v **destroy, occur, rip through, rock, shake, shatter, tear through** A huge explosion shook the ship.

exponent N
someone who is good at doing something

● adj+N **best-known, chief, distinguished, finest, foremost, notable, prime, principal, prominent, supreme** They are among the foremost exponents of contemporary folk music in Britain today.

express V
tell someone about your feelings by speaking or writing

● adv+V clearly **clearly, eloquently, explicitly, forcefully, freely, openly, publicly, strongly** The law established a new framework for people to freely express their political opinions.
▶ using few words **precisely, simply, succinctly** It is not likely that the question will be simply expressed.

express ADJ
very clear

● ADJ+n permission **agreement, authorisation, consent, permission** We will not use your contact details for any other purpose without your express permission.
▶ wish or request **aim, intention, order, provision, purpose, wish** The society was formed with the express aim of encouraging the writing of poetry.

expressive ADJ
clearly showing your thoughts or feelings

● adv+ADJ very **deeply, extremely, highly, intensely, powerfully, richly, very** The pieces are written in a richly expressive style.

If something expresses a feeling or quality, you can say that it is **expressive of** that feeling or quality: Duncan's dancing was characterized by free, flowing movements expressive of inner emotion.

▶ in an impressive way **beautifully, wonderfully** This sensitive, beautifully expressive film is a most affecting experience.

extension N
extra time given to someone to allow them to finish something

● v+N ask for an extension **apply for, ask for, call for, request, seek** Austria is seeking an extension of the September deadline from the United States.
▶ give someone an extension **grant, offer, permit** Nick Barmby looks set to be offered a one-year extension to his contract.
▶ get an extension **get, negotiate, receive** Hand your work in on time, or negotiate extensions with your tutor.

extensive ADJ
including or affecting a lot of things

● ADJ+n a set or number of things **archive, array, collection, coverage, database, library, list, menu, network, portfolio, range, repertoire, selection** Our website is intended as an overview of our extensive product range.
▶ involving a lot of thinking, writing, or talking **consultation, discussion, documentation, investigation, research, review, survey** Almost all medications go through many years of extensive

research before they are considered safe and effective.
► personal qualities **experience, knowledge** *We have gained extensive knowledge of the stairlift market.*
► bad effect **damage, flooding** *The fire had caused extensive damage in the past.*
► use **use** *We also make extensive use of email.*
► changes or improvements **alteration, refurbishment, renovation** *The centre has recently undergone extensive refurbishment and offers quality training and conference facilities.*

● and/or **costly, detailed, thorough, up-to-date, varied, wide-ranging** *The menu was surprisingly varied and extensive.*

extent N
the size and importance of a problem or situation

● adj+N **actual, exact, full, precise, true** *The true extent of the computer virus threat is unknown because most infections are not reported to some central body.*

> You can use the phrase **to a ... extent** to indicate how true a particular statement is: *The complaints were to a large extent valid.* | ● *To a certain extent I was relieved.*

● v+N measure extent **ascertain, assess, determine, establish, estimate, examine, explore, gauge, investigate, measure** *The research aimed to assess the extent of atmospheric damage by aircraft.*
► show extent **demonstrate, indicate, reveal, show** *A hospital examination revealed the extent of the problem and an emergency operation was scheduled.*
► limit extent **limit** *The overriding aim, then, was to limit the extent of any war.*
► think extent is less than it really is **underestimate** *These figures underestimated the true extent of mental illness amongst young people in prison.*
► think extent is greater than it really is **overestimate, overstate** *It is impossible to overestimate the extent to which language difficulties can influence learning outcomes.*

exterior N
the way that someone appears and behaves

● adj+N **tough gruff, rough, tough** *He is a very nice person beneath the gruff exterior.*
● **calm, cool** *Maintaining a calm exterior in that situation was a very hard thing to do.*

● N+v **belie, conceal** *The house's quaint chocolate-box exterior belies its cool contempoary interior design.* ● *This light-hearted exterior conceals an inner determination to succeed.*

extinction N
the situation of no longer existing

● adj+N **total complete, mass, total** *The loyalists who remain are dwindling in number and face total extinction.*
► **near near** *Unsustainable harvesting practices resulted in near extinction of the species by the mid-20th century.*

● v+N be close to possible extinction **be threatened with, face** *Many world languages face extinction.*

> If something may soon become extinct, you can use the phrases **be in danger of** or **be on the brink/verge of extinction**: *Some species are in danger of extinction.* | ● *Financial problems mean the club is now on the brink of extinction.*

► cause extinction **cause** *Human predation caused the extinction of the great auk.*
► prevent extinction **prevent** *If we are to save the future of our planet and prevent the extinction of the human race, all nations must work together.*

extradition N
the process of sending an accused person back to the country where a crime was committed so they can be tried

● v+N ask for someone's extradition **demand, request, seek** *By this time the true extent of his war crimes was well known, and he was arrested after Germany requested his extradition.*
► try to stop extradition **fight** *The man accused of the bombing is fighting extradition to Britain.*
► be facing extradition **await, face** *She is currently awaiting extradition to Thailand on fraud charges.*

● N+n agreement **agreement, arrangement, treaty** *The country has no extradition treaty with the United States.*
► order or request **order, request, warrant** *He was arrested in Kensington under an extradition warrant issued by Bow Street magistrates court.*
► process **procedure, process** *Lawyers say the extradition process can take many months.*
► legal case **case, hearing, proceedings** *Extradition proceedings are due to start in late September.*
► law **law** *We will bring forward a bill to modernise our extradition law.*

extraordinary ADJ
very unusual and surprising

● adv+ADJ **absolutely, pretty INFORMAL, quite, rather, really, truly, very** *The BBC's political editor described Sir Richard's remarks as 'quite extraordinary'.*

● v+ADJ **consider sth, find sth, seem, sound** *What I do find extraordinary is that they provide no email contact details either on their website or their stationery.* ● *It seems extraordinary that the emphasis on finance and quality is not matched by similar attention to the allocation of workloads to staff.*

extreme ADJ
very unusual

● adv+ADJ **very particularly, very** *Surgery is only used in very extreme cases, when all ordinary courses of treatment have failed.*
► **rather quite, rather, relatively** *These events are relatively extreme, and very rare in Britain.*

● ADJ+n **case, circumstances, conditions, event, example, form, measure, version** *Except in extreme circumstances, penalties when incurred are not waived.*

eye N

the part of the body in your face that you use for seeing with

- adj+N colours of eyes **blue, brown, dark, green, grey, hazel** *He had brown eyes and brown hair.*
- ▶ red where it should be white **bloodshot, red** *The infection causes bloodshot eyes with a sticky discharge.*
- ▶ the way your eyes look and your expression **beady, piercing, sparkling, staring** *The dog then turned its beady black eyes to me.*
- ▶ looking tired **bleary, sleepy, tired** *I stumbled off the plane, with crumpled clothes and bleary eyes.*
- ▶ close together, far apart or deep in your face **close-set, deep-set, sunken, wide-set** *He had a thin nose and close-set eyes.*
- ▶ sticking out **bulging, protruding** *This breed of dog has noticeably protruding eyes.*

> You can use the expression **the naked eye** to refer to seeing things without the help of a microscope etc: *The eggs are so small that they cannot be seen with the naked eye.*

- v+N close your eyes **close, shut** *Lucy closed her eyes again and tried to sleep.*
- ▶ open your eyes **open** *Christie opened her eyes but she remained silent.*
- ▶ protect your eyes from light **shade, shield** *Meg was shading her eyes against the morning sun.*
- ▶ make your eyes move upwards **roll** *He sighed and rolled his eyes at the question.*
- ▶ rub your eyes **rub** *The boy was sleepy and rubbing his eyes.*

- ▶ turn your eyes away **avert** *I averted my eyes as he was getting dressed.*
- ▶ open and shut your eyes quickly **blink** *He blinked his eyes again, forcing them to focus.*
- N+v look at something **catch sth, fall on sth, gaze, look at, scan sth, stare** *My eyes were staring into the gloom.*
- ▶ look shiny **flash, gleam, glow, light up, shine, twinkle** *Her eyes twinkled with pleasure.*
- ▶ become more open/less open **narrow, widen** *Frank's eyes narrowed as he tried to work out the difference in the man's appearance.*
- ▶ when you look in different directions quickly **dart** *My eyes quickly darted around the room to see if Jane was there.*
- ▶ when your eyes show that you are bored or tired **glaze, glaze over** *When people started talking about house prices, her eyes glazed over.*
- ▶ when your eyes open and shut quickly **blink** *She looked up at him, her eyes blinking rapidly.*

eyesight N

the ability to see

- adj+N bad **bad, failing, poor** *Many people with poor eyesight will be able to read large print.*
- ▶ good **excellent, good** *To drive a car, you must have good eyesight.*
- ▶ perfect **perfect** *My eyesight is perfect.*
- v+N **damage, improve, lose** *Staring directly at the sun can permanently damage eyesight.*
- N+v **deteriorate, fail** *Our eyesight deteriorates as we get older.*

Ff

face N

1 the front part of the head; the expression on someone's face

- adj+N looking pale **ashen, pale, pallid, sallow, white** *She looked anything but healthy with her pale face and deep-set eyes.*
- describing the shape of a face **chubby, heart-shaped, oval, round, thin** *He had a thin face and hollow cheeks.*
- describing the expression on a face **beaming, blank, contorted, expressionless, expressive, impassive, smiling** *Her face was contorted with anger.* • *He raised his head to see more, and saw the smiling face of Tom.*
- with lines **lined, wrinkled** *This woman is evidently old, which can be read from her hunched posture and wrinkled face.*
- attractive **handsome, pretty** *She was a small girl with wiry black hair and a pretty face.*
- looking tired or ill **haggard, pinched** *A pale and haggard face looked back at me.*
- with freckles **freckled** *Amy had a sweet freckled face and looked too young to be consumed by such grief.*
- with a beard **bearded** *I can picture his bearded face from the newspaper.*
- red **flushed, red** *Her face was red and blotchy with tears.*

> When you want to emphasize the fact that someone looks young and healthy, you can use the expression **fresh-faced**: *This is a photo of me when I was a fresh-faced boy.*

- N+v become red **flush, redden** *Her face flushed at the slight awkwardness of the meeting.*
- look more cheerful **brighten, light up** *I put the rod in his hand and when he caught a fish his face lit up.*
- look serious **darken** *He looked down at the body and his face darkened.*

2 the way something looks or appears

- adj+N **changing, public** *The film examined the changing face of Britain's towns and cities over the past fifty years.* • *The article discusses both the public face and the behind-the-scenes activities of the company.*
- v+N **change** *In the 1950s there was one musician who helped change the face of the British music.*

face V

have to deal with a problem that is likely to happen

- V+n problem or difficult situation **challenge, competition, consequences, crisis, difficulty, dilemma, discrimination, eviction, hardship, issue, problem, shortage** *Schools are left to face the dire consequences of this policy.* • *The article discusses the problems faced by disabled people.*
- punishment **charges, fine, penalty, prosecution** *Those caught fishing illegally face tough penalties.*
- something bad that may happen **prospect, threat** *The country is facing the prospect of a severe drought.*
- losing your job **redundancy** *More than a thousand workers at the factory are facing redundancy as the crisis talks with management continue.*
- something that prevents you from doing what you want **barriers, obstacle, opposition** *Women tended to face greater barriers in the workplace.*
- something difficult **challenge, difficulty, dilemma, issue, problem, threat** *The question of waste management is perhaps the greatest challenge facing local government today.*

2 accept that a bad situation exists

- V+n **fact, reality, truth** *As Christians, we have to face the reality that many people are cynical about the church.*

> Usage In this meaning, you can use **face up to** in the same way as **face**: *She had to face up to the fact that she still missed him.*

facilitate V

make it easier for something to happen

- adv+V **actively, directly, greatly** *The research programme is greatly facilitated by strong collaboration with over 60 countries around the world.*
- V+n **access, collaboration, communication, development, dialogue, discussion, exchange, learning, process, understanding** *It was designed as a web-based news server to facilitate communication within the company.*
- and/or **encourage, promote, stimulate, support** *We aim to encourage and facilitate constructive and positive dialogue between the various faith groups.*

facility N [usually plural]

a room, equipment etc provided for people to use

- adj+N good **excellent, good, superb, world-class** *The call centre has excellent facilities such as free parking and staff canteen.*
- modern **modern, state-of-the-art** *The school has state-of-the-art sports facilities.*
- built for a particular purpose **purpose-built** *The modern purpose-built facility offers a range of storage solutions.*
- shared with other people **communal, shared** *Other communal facilities include indoor and outdoor swimming pools and green areas.*
- for disabled people **disabled** *What disabled facilities are there?*
- inside/outside **indoor, outdoor** *Hotel guests can take advantage of our excellent indoor leisure facilities.*
- types of facility **medical, recreational** *Are there medical facilities on campus?*
- many **extensive** *There are extensive facilities already available in the main building.*
- n+N for sport and leisure **leisure, recreation, sporting** *The Moorland Hotel has an excellent choice*

of leisure facilities, including an all-weather tennis court and golf course.
▸ for cooking or providing food **catering, cooking, kitchen** Full catering facilities are available for lunch and general refreshments.
▸ other types of facility **baby-changing, childcare, conference, parking, recycling, shopping, toilet** A national park substation and toilet facilities are provided at the mountain summit.
● v+N have facilities **boast, have, offer, provide** The city boasts many excellent facilities for sport. ● The factory has excellent facilities.
▸ use facilities **make use of, use** Students are free to use any of the facilities on campus.
▸ improve facilities **improve, refurbish, upgrade** We have an ongoing programme to upgrade our facilities.
● N+v **be on offer, cater for, include, offer, provide** Our conference facilities cater for up to 40 delegates.

fact N
a piece of true information
● adj+N impossible to argue with **hard, incontrovertible, indisputable, inescapable, irrefutable, proven, relevant, true, undeniable, undisputed** This sound investment is backed up by hard facts. ● This is an undeniable fact which no-one is disputing.
▸ basic **bare, basic** These are the bare facts of the case in question, and further details will be found in the evidence.
▸ that people may not like **plain, simple** It is a plain fact that ageing increases the likelihood of developing cancer.
▸ describing how well-known a fact is **known, little-known, well-known** It is a little-known fact that he was a successful footballer in his youth.
▸ important **important, key** The key facts of the case are as follows.
▸ interesting or surprising **amazing, astonishing, fascinating, interesting, remarkable, shocking, startling, striking, surprising** The book contains some fascinating facts. ● The article reveals some startling facts about the history of theme parks.
▸ worrying **alarming, disturbing, worrying** It is a disturbing fact that the UK is top of the list for asthma sufferers.
▸ types of fact **empirical, historical, scientific** A closer study of historical facts shows that this accusation is ill-founded.
● v+N ignore a fact **ignore, overlook** It is quite unrealistic now to ignore these facts.
▸ hide a fact **conceal, hide, obscure** In the House of Lords, one of the older peers was asleep, with no attempt to hide this fact.
▸ say that a fact is not true **deny, dispute** It would be hard to dispute the fact that we live in an increasingly stressful world.
▸ state a fact **state** I'm simply stating the facts.
▸ tell someone a fact that was not known before **disclose, reveal** The origin of a street name often reveals unsuspected facts about the history of the area.
▸ find out a fact **discover, establish, uncover** We need to establish the facts behind the killings.

▸ know a fact **know** A number of facts are known with certainty.
▸ accept a fact **accept, acknowledge, recognize** We need to acknowledge the fact that this plan would involve extra costs.
▸ think about facts **consider** You need to consider the facts before making a decision.
● and/or **fiction, figures** It was a documentary-style programme that mixed fact and fiction. ● All the facts and figures are then compiled into reports.

factor N
something that influences an event
● adj+N causing or helping to cause something **causal, contributing, contributory, motivating** Debt is often a contributing factor in household violence and child abuse.
▸ important **critical, crucial, important, key, major, significant** 88 per cent of students say price is the most important factor in their lunch-buying decisions.
▸ deciding something **deciding, decisive, determining** Your academic qualification, while important, may not be the deciding factor.
▸ making something seem worse **aggravating** His total lack of remorse is an aggravating factor in this case.
▸ making something seem less bad **mitigating** The court accepted Tan's medical condition as a mitigating factor.
▸ making something more complicated **complicating** The dispute could be a complicating factor for the US.
▸ basic but not obvious **underlying** The simulator has been designed to inform understanding of the underlying factors affecting risk from flooding.
▸ coming from outside **external** External factors, such as the weather, can also affect the volume of sales.
▸ types of factor **demographic, economic, environmental, genetic, psychological, social, socio-economic** Genetic factors do not cause drug dependence, but they increase the risks for some individuals.
● n+N **lifestyle, risk** Lifestyle factors such as poor diet and lack of exercise predispose to osteoporosis. ● Untreated high blood pressure has been identified as a risk factor for strokes.
● v+N consider factors **consider, examine, investigate, take into account** A large number of factors are considered during the site selection process.
▸ identify factors **identify** The study will also identify the psychological factors which may influence how dentists work.
● N+v **affect, cause, contribute to, control, determine, drive, govern, influence, shape** The research shows that early childhood factors strongly influence mental health throughout life.

When you are talking about factors over which you have no influence, you can say that the factors are **beyond** someone's **control**: Pupil absence is linked to factors beyond the control of individual schools.

● n+of+N **combination, number, range, variety** This

situation is due to a number of factors, the most important of which is a lack of funds.

factual ADJ
based on facts or containing only facts

- adv+ADJ completely **entirely, purely, strictly** *Ensure that reports are purely factual.*
- ▶ mostly **essentially, largely** *Science subjects are essentially factual even though those facts are initially dependent on an accumulation of evidence.*
- ADJ+n information **account, content, description, evidence, information, knowledge, programme, report, statement** *Factual knowledge is still essential to most kinds of thinking, and lies at the core of history.*
- ▶ mistake **error, inaccuracy, mistake** *The report contained a number of factual inaccuracies.*
- ▶ correctness **accuracy** *Every effort is made to ensure factual accuracy, but no responsibility is accepted for this information.*

fade V
become less and disappear

- n+V **colour, dream, hope, image, light, memory, music, smile, voice** *Just as hope was fading, the boy was found alive and well.* • *The light was fading, and we had no time to explore the trackside forest.*
- V+into **insignificance, oblivion, obscurity** *Most of the contestants in such talent shows quickly fade into obscurity.*

fail V
1 be unsuccessful

- adv+V very badly **abysmally, completely, conspicuously, dismally, miserably, singularly, spectacularly, totally, utterly** *We set ourselves some defensive targets and we failed miserably.*
- ▶ only just fail **narrowly** *He narrowly failed to qualify for the Olympics.*
- ▶ fail after a period of time **ultimately** *However, like so many other well-intentioned approaches in this area, it ultimately failed.*
- n+V **appeal, application, attempt, negotiations, plan, scheme, venture** *There was no way of clearing the site and all attempts failed.*
- V+in **attempt, bid, efforts, mission, objective, quest, task** *He dived into the water but failed in his attempt to save the boy.*

2 not do something expected

- adv+V in a noticeable way **signally, singularly** *A senior officer signally failed to assess the situation properly.*
- ▶ many times **consistently, persistently, repeatedly** *Banks are consistently failing to inform disabled customers that they can choose to continue using signatures rather than chip and pin.*
- V+in **duty, obligation, responsibility** *The national broadcaster had failed in its duty to cover this major international event.*

failing N
a fault or a weak point

- adj+N serious **major, serious, significant** *The report highlights serious failings in the system.*
- ▶ of a person or people **human, moral, personal** *They are human beings and they have human failings and prejudices.*
- ▶ of a system **administrative, procedural, systemic** *She identified administrative failings on the part of the company.*
- v+N have a failing **have** *If the movie has any failings, it's that the plot may be a bit confusing for children.*
- ▶ show a failing **expose, highlight, identify** *The girl's murder exposed serious failings by the Child Protection Services.*
- and/or **fault, shortcomings, weakness** *They will be responsible for tackling failings and shortcomings in their services.*

failure N
1 lack of success; someone or something that is not successful

- adj+N complete or very bad **catastrophic, complete, dismal, miserable, total, utter** *The policy has been a dismal failure.* • *Yet another blow to the movement came from the utter failure of mass migration in the year 1920.*
- ▶ over a period of time **persistent, repeated** *Regrettably, under the current Government it has all too often been a story of repeated failure.*
- v+N result in failure **end in, result in** *20 out of 36 missions to Mars have ended in failure.*
- ▶ admit failure **admit** *In trying to find something about the production to criticise, I have to admit failure.*
- ▶ be or call someone or something a failure **be, deem sb/sth, prove** *Society has deemed these children failures, before they even leave school.* • *The appeal for volunteers to help with the work proved a failure.*
- ▶ seem certain to result in failure **be doomed to** *The health service is doomed to failure without radical changes in funding and approach.*
- N+n **rate** *Efficacy was high, with a failure rate of only 0.7 per cent.*

2 when someone does not do something that they are expected to do

- adj+N **persistent, repeated, systematic** *The report was highly critical of the repeated failure of the police to ensure continuity in local policing.*
- n+N **government, management** *Legal action may be successful if it can be shown that management failures were a cause of the death concerned.*
- v+N admit failure **acknowledge, admit** *The Home Office has admitted a failure to protect him whilst he worked at the prison.*
- ▶ give good reasons for failure **excuse, explain, justify** *This does not excuse the failure to adopt adequate strategies for the care of these patients.*

3 a situation where something stops working correctly

- adj+N relating to a body part **cardiac, renal, respiratory** *Patients with suspected renal failure are referred for renal investigation.*

▶ relating to a machine **mechanical, structural** *This is a much better design as it is less prone to mechanical failure.*

▶ having a very bad result **catastrophic** *The engines suffered catastrophic failures.*

● n+N body part **heart, kidney, liver, organ** *Kidney failure, if it occurs, leads to an almost 100 per cent mortality rate.*

▶ equipment or system **brake, engine, equipment, hardware, software, system** *One would think the only reason an airplane could crash was engine failure.*

▶ power **power** *The power failure was blamed on a fault between the railway lines and the national grid.*

● v+N **experience, suffer** *Rubens suffered an engine failure just 18 laps into the race.*

● N+v **occur** *Subsequent examination indicated that mechanical failure had occurred.*

faint ADJ
slight and not strong or clear

● ADJ+n smell **smell, whiff** *I noticed a faint smell of smoke.*

▶ light **glimmer, glow, light** *Alder could just make out a faint glow, which he hoped was lamplight.*

▶ sound **cry, echo, hum, sound, voice, whisper** *A faint sound reached my ears from the veranda outside.*

▶ expression **smile** *She looked at me with suspicion; then a faint smile crossed her face.*

▶ hope **hope** *He entered the competition in the faint hope of winning.*

▶ amount **hint, trace** *"You look lovely," he said with a faint hint of sarcasm.*

● v+ADJ **become, grow** *I heard the sound of footsteps grow faint in the distance and die away.*

fair ADJ
treating people equally; reasonable and morally right

● adv+ADJ very **absolutely, completely, entirely, perfectly, quite, scrupulously, very** *This is a scrupulously fair and well-reasoned account.* ● *The teacher was strict but very fair.*

▶ not **hardly, not really** *It is hardly fair to keep it a secret from him.*

▶ quite **pretty** INFORMAL, **reasonably** *The report contained a reasonably fair and balanced description of the case.*

● v+ADJ **consider sth, seem, sound** *This system is usually considered fairer to both management and employees.*

> When you are saying that something is reasonable and likely to be true, you can use the expression *it's fair to say/assume/conclude that*: I think it's fair to say that people are not happy about the tax rise.

● and/or **balanced, equal, equitable, free, honest, open, reasonable, transparent, true** *Managers should make sure companies have fair and transparent recruitment procedures.*

faith N
strong belief or trust in someone or something

● adj+N strong **great, implicit, strong, unshakeable** *We have great faith in the players that are at the club at the moment.*

▶ not questioned **blind** *He had blind faith in the homeopath who had eliminated his eczema.*

▶ real **genuine, real** *I was amazed – here was a woman who I didn't know showing genuine faith in me.*

● v+N have faith **have, place, put** *I have a lot of faith in him and know he won't let me down.* ● *People put their faith in the wonder-drugs such as penicillin and cortisone.*

▶ weaken faith **destroy, shake, undermine** *Poor care, even for short periods, can seriously undermine faith in community services.*

▶ lose faith **lose** *How am I going to get out of this situation without them losing faith in me?*

▶ make faith strong again **restore** *The person who returned my stolen purse has restored my faith in human nature.*

fall V
1 become lower in amount, level, or value

● adv+V by a large amount **dramatically, drastically, sharply, significantly, steeply** *In early October the dollar fell sharply against the yen.*

▶ quickly **quickly, rapidly, suddenly** *Temperatures fell rapidly overnight.*

▶ slowly **gradually, steadily** *Student numbers are falling steadily.*

▶ by a small amount **slightly** *Figures show that crime fell very slightly between 2001–02 and 2002–03.*

● n+V **crime, income, level, population, price, profit, rate, sales, temperature, unemployment** *Unemployment fell from about 3 million in 1993 to under 2 million in 1999.*

2 belong to particular group or activity

● V+into **category** *Those who do not fall into this category tend to make a slow and limited recovery.*

● V+outside **criterion, definition, range, remit, scope, terms** *They added that military action would fall outside the criteria for a "just war".*

● V+within **ambit, area, category, criterion, definition, jurisdiction, paragraph, range, remit, scope, terms** *It is generally recognised that all of these activities fall within the remit of child protection.*

3 change into another (negative) state

● V+into **abeyance, decay, disfavour, disrepair, disrepute, disuse, neglect, oblivion** *The building fell into disuse and was eventually pulled down in 2001.*

fall N
1 when someone or something falls to the ground

● adj+N **bad, heavy, nasty** *Charles had strained his back in a heavy fall and couldn't help with the lifting.*

● v+N **have, suffer, take** *If he has a fall when he's on his own he finds it hard to get back up.*

▶ make a fall less bad **break, cushion** *The majority*

of falls also result in wrist pain as we naturally outstretch our hands to cushion our fall.

2 when an amount, level, or value falls

- adj+N large **big, dramatic, large, marked, sharp, significant, steep, substantial** *The sharp fall in the world market price of cotton in recent years has hit peasant incomes.*
- ▶ small **slight, small** *There was a slight fall in output during the early years of the First World War.*
- ▶ quick or sudden **rapid, sudden, unexpected** *There was a sudden fall in pressure and temperature.*
- v+N experience a fall **experience, see, suffer** *Executive directors saw falls in their overall remuneration packages last year.*
- ▶ cause a fall **cause, lead to** *The difficulty with this strategy is that it would probably cause a further fall in the yen.*
- ▶ be a fall **represent** *This represents a 50 per cent fall in the death rate since the new medication was introduced.*

fall down PHR VB
fail because of weak points

- ▶ n+V argument or ideas **analogy, argument, comparison, report, theory** *But the debtor analogy falls down because it assumes the debtors acknowledge the debt, which they don't.*
- ▶ system **scheme, system** *Where the system fell down is in the response to these plans.*

fall through PHR VB
fail to happen

- ▶ n+V **deal, plan, project, sale** *The plans fell through, so we were left with some free time.*

false ADJ
not true, or based on wrong information

- ▶ adv+ADJ completely **absolutely, completely, entirely, totally, utterly** *It is unbelievable that anyone could make this utterly false allegation.*
- ▶ obviously **blatantly, manifestly, obviously, patently** *Needless to say, both are denying all allegations, describing them as 'patently false'.*
- ▶ in a way that you can prove **demonstrably** *The key claims that they made were demonstrably false.*
- ▶ ADJ+n **accusation, allegation, assumption, belief, claim, description, impression, statement** *The campaign seeks to highlight the damage that false accusations can do to teachers' careers.* • *These methods are used in the false belief that children will benefit from them.*
- ▶ and/or **true** *Read the sentences and decide if they are true or false.*

fame N
the state of being famous

- ▶ adj+N where someone is famous **international, national, worldwide** *Knock is only a small town, but it gained international fame when an apparition of the Virgin Mary turned it into a place of pilgrimage.*
- ▶ a lot of fame **considerable, great** *This performance earned him great fame.*

- ▶ coming immediately **instant** *This is the age of reality TV when kids want instant fame.*
- ▶ coming recently **new-found** *Her new-found fame was difficult to deal with at first.*
- ▶ continuing for a long time **enduring, lasting** *Owen achieved lasting fame with his war poetry.*
- v+N achieve fame **achieve, earn, enjoy, find, gain, win** *Some people will do anything to achieve fame and celebrity.*

> If you want to talk about the reason why someone has achieved fame, you can use the phrase *claim to fame*: *Perhaps his best claim to fame was as the writer of the soul classic 'Go Now' in 1964.*

- ▶ achieve fame quickly **rise to, shoot to** *The actress shot to fame after appearing in several cult classics.*
- ▶ try to be famous **seek** *He was just sixteen when he travelled to London to seek fame as an actor.*
- ▶ bring someone fame **bring sb** *Her Oscar-winning performance in the film 'A Love Story' brought her international fame.*
- N+v **grow, rest on, spread** *His fame rests on his reputation as a poet and landscape gardener.*
- and/or **celebrity, fortune, money, notoriety, wealth** *He dreams that his proposed children's book will bring him fame and fortune.*

familiar ADJ
known to you, or recognized by you; common or happening often

- adv+ADJ very **extremely, very** *She mentioned names which were all very familiar to me.*
- ▶ a little **fairly, pretty** INFORMAL**, quite, reasonably, vaguely** *Some of the stories will be vaguely familiar to you, and some may seem slightly strange.*
- ▶ in a strange way **eerily, oddly, strangely** *The voice was squeaky and oddly familiar.*
- ▶ in a pleasant way **reassuringly** *It looks subtly different yet reassuringly familiar.*
- ▶ immediately **immediately, instantly** *Emmental, with its huge marble-sized holes, is now an instantly familiar cheese around the world.*
- ▶ in a bad way **all too, depressingly, horribly** *We have the all too familiar situation where the evidence is made to fit the theory rather than the other way around.* • *We were greeted with the depressingly familiar sight of no coffee and no food.*
- ADJ+n person **face, figure** *Looking around the room and seeing so many familiar faces I felt suddenly at home.*
- ▶ place **environment, landmark, surroundings, territory** *Your recovery will be faster in familiar surroundings with the support of your family and friends.*
- ▶ sound **song, sound, tune, voice** *I listen to these old, familiar songs and find myself floating back in time to my youth.*
- ▶ something you see **scene, sight** *The distinctive yellow and black signs for special events remain a familiar sight at the roadside.*

family N
a group of people who are related to each other

- adj+N poor **disadvantaged, low-income, needy,**

poor *The grant is awarded to students from low-income families.*

▶ rich **rich, wealthy, well-off, well-to-do** *He came from a wealthy family.*

▶ having two parents living together **two-parent** *Unfortunately, the report concludes that many fathers in two-parent families have low involvement with their children's education.*

▶ where one parent is responsible for the family **lone-parent, one-parent, single-parent** *One-parent families still have the greatest risk of poverty of any family type.*

▶ loving and caring **close-knit, loving** *We are a very close-knit family and spend a lot of time together.*

▶ having problems **dysfunctional** *I was a lonely young man from a dysfunctional family.*

▶ including aunts, uncles, cousins etc **extended** *Balinese communities function more like large, extended families than the disconnected societies of the West.*

▶ including just parents and children **immediate, nuclear** *This is a free confidential telephone help line, which is available to all staff and their immediate family.* • *There is a decline in the number of traditional nuclear families.*

▶ big **big, large** *Ann then married Thomas Kennedy and had a large family.*

▶ when a child has been adopted or is being cared for by a family that is not its own **adoptive, foster** *We are always looking for adoptive families for children aged between four and nine.* • *She lived with various foster families in the 1980s.*

• v+N feed, clothe, educate etc children **bring up, feed, raise, support** *Most of the group were widows, many struggling to support large families.*

▶ have children **start** *In the past, women gave up their jobs when they started a family.*

famine N

lack of food causing many people to be ill or die

• adj+N **devastating, great, severe, terrible** *Twenty years ago much of the country was gripped by a terrible famine.*

• v+N suffer a famine **face, suffer** *It is estimated that nearly 13 million people in the region will face famine in the coming months.*

▶ lessen the effect of a famine **relieve** *Millions of pounds were raised to help relieve famine worldwide.*

• N+v **hit, occur, strike, threaten** *The pandemic will amplify the impact of the famine which is threatening the southern areas of the country.*

• N+n **relief, victim** *Generous Americans give over one million items of unwanted clothing to the famine relief effort.*

• and/or **disease, drought, war** *As drought and famine continue to plague the country, the average life expectancy has dropped to 46 years.*

fan N

someone who likes a sport, famous person etc very much

• adj+N **adoring, ardent, avid, big, devoted, diehard, hardcore, huge, loyal** *He is an avid fan of musicals and often employs musical numbers in his work.*

• v+N please fans **delight, thrill, wow** *Kylie Minogue wowed fans last night with a sensational performance.*

▶ disappoint fans **alienate, disappoint** *The absence of any interviews with the cast will disappoint fans of the movie.*

• N+n website or place for fans to meet **club, forum, site** *This is an independent fan site dedicated to Arsenal FC.*

▶ letters from fans **mail** *She was able to boast more fan mail than any other female stage star.*

▶ all fans **base** *By promoting gigs and being close to their fan base, the band has ensured they never experience the disappointment of playing to an empty venue.*

fantasy N

an experience that you imagine happening to you; a state or situation that is not real

• adj+N sexual or romantic **erotic, romantic, sexual** *She contrasts the woman's romantic fantasies with the reality of motherhood.*

▶ strange **wild** *You couldn't imagine such a thing even in your wildest fantasies.*

▶ complete **complete, pure, sheer** *This story is pure fantasy. There's no truth in it at all.*

• n+N **childhood** *I guess that childhood fantasies stay pretty strong.*

• v+N have a fantasy **have** *I have a fantasy I might have held down a sensible job and been very rich.*

▶ make a fantasy happen **fulfil, indulge, live** *You may even fancy fulfilling your childhood fantasy of being a Princess for the day.* • *In this movie three young girls get to live their fantasies.*

fare N

money paid for a journey

• adj+N cheap **cheap, low** *The website finds you the cheapest fares on all airlines.*

▶ expensive **expensive, high** *This country has some of the most expensive train fares in Europe.*

▶ cheaper than usual **concessionary, discount, discounted** *Concessionary fares are available for students and people over 65.*

▶ for travel to a place but not back again **one-way, single** *The one-way fare is £5.50.*

▶ for travel to and back from a place **return, round-trip** *Return fares start from £149.*

▶ usual **full, standard** *The Bahncard is aimed at the frequent rail traveller, offering a 50 per cent discount on the standard fare.*

▶ a fare that is the same for everyone **flat** *You will be charged a flat fare of 50p per single journey.*

• v+N pay a fare **pay** *Passengers must pay the correct fare or leave the vehicle.*

▶ charge a fare **charge** *The city's transport system is a service, and the fares charged are lower than that required to pay for the system.*

• N+n someone who tries to avoid paying a fare **dodger** *There are regular blitzes on the underground to catch the fare dodgers.*

▶ the crime of not paying a fare **evasion** *Many instances of fare evasion or travelling on invalid tickets were also detected.*

fascination N

the power to interest or attract people very strongly; the state of being interested in or attracted by something

- adj+N lasting for a long time **abiding, constant, continued, continuing, enduring, eternal, lasting, lifelong, ongoing, perennial** *This experience may help to explain his lifelong fascination with the sea.*
- strange **peculiar, strange** *Why do men have that strange fascination with model railways?*
- connected with unpleasant things **morbid, unhealthy** *Some of the exhibits (internal organs in a jar etc) proved to have a morbid fascination for our students.*

- v+N have a fascination **exercise, exert, have, hold, retain** *The plays of Samuel Beckett hold a strange fascination for modern theatre audiences.*
- feel or show a fascination **feel, have, show** *Americans have a fascination with automobiles and guns.*
- share a fascination **share** *Most people don't share my fascination with insects.*

- N+v **lie in** *Much of the novel's fascination lies in observing how the characters react differently to events.*

- v+in+N **stare, watch** *As a child, he used to watch in fascination as his father carved wood into figures.*

- v+with+N watch
- listen **I listened with fascination to the account of his early life in Russia.**

fashion N

a style of dress or an activity that is popular at a particular time; the fact of something being popular

- adj+N popular now **contemporary, current, the latest, modern** *She was always dressed in the latest fashions from Paris and Milan.*
- changing **changing** *He outlined the changing fashions in economic policy over the past decade.*

- v+N when something is or becomes fashionable **be (back) in, become, come (back) into** *Short skirts are back in fashion.* • *At that time it became the fashion for city-dwellers to go to the seaside.*
- when something is not or stops being fashionable **be out of, fall out of, go out of** *Jeans never go out of fashion.*
- start a fashion **set, start** *The first Queen Elizabeth started a fashion for pale skin.*
- follow a fashion **follow, keep up with** *I can't keep up with all the latest fashions.*

- N+v **change, come and go** *Fashions change regularly.*

fat ADJ

having too much flesh on your body

- adv+ADJ very **enormously, extremely, hugely, immensely, incredibly, really, very** *They watched the procession, which included the enormously fat Queen of Tonga.*
- rather **pretty** INFORMAL**, quite, rather** *He had a rather fat red face.*
- too **grossly, too** *Don't let your dog get too fat.*

- v+ADJ **become, get, grow, make sb** *British children are getting fatter according to a study published in the British Medical Journal.* • *Too many sweets will make you fat!*

fatal ADJ

1 causing someone to die

- ADJ+n event **accident, collision, crash, fall** *He met with a fatal accident at the colliery yesterday.*
- when someone is ill **cancer, complications, disease, haemorrhage, heart attack, illness, infection, stroke** *This is a rare but often fatal disease.*
- when someone is hurt **attack, blow, injury, shooting, shot, wound** *There was never any evidence to suggest that he had actually fired the fatal shot.*

- v+ADJ **be, prove** *The snake's bite rarely proves fatal to humans.*

2 with very serious negative effects

- ADJ+n event **blow** *They received a fatal blow with the loss of their top scorer after eight minutes.*
- fault **flaw, weakness** *Unfortunately, there is a fatal flaw in the argument.*
- mistake **blunder, error, mistake** *Never underestimate me, because you will be making a fatal error.*

- v+ADJ **be, prove** *Such errors of judgment could prove fatal in the current economic climate.*

fate N

1 the things that happen to someone

- adj+N unpleasant **awful, cruel, dreadful, grisly, horrible, ignominious, miserable, terrible, unhappy** *Huge shipments of food aid were needed to save the population from a terrible fate.*
- sad **sad, tragic** *The young soldier suffers a tragic fate in horrifying circumstances.*
- final **eventual, final, ultimate** *Mystery surrounds the ultimate fate of William Lees.*

- v+N control what someone's fate will be **decide, determine, dictate, seal** *A major defeat in Normandy sealed King John's fate.*
- experience a fate **experience, have, meet, suffer, undergo** *Other species of seabirds on the island suffered a similar fate.*
- avoid a fate **avoid, be spared, escape** *Born in Berlin, he died on the Spanish border while trying to escape the fate that awaited most of his fellow Central European Jews.*
- share a fate **share** *Many others deserted, fearing that they would share the fate of their comrades.*
- have to deal with a fate **face** *Most are either killed or face an even worse fate.*
- accept a fate **accept, resign yourself to** *To her credit she accepted her fate with great humour.*

- N+v happen to or be waiting for someone or something **await, befall, lie in store for** *The same fate befell most of the competitors.*
- not be decided **be uncertain, hang in the balance** *Despite intense negotiations, the company's fate is still hanging in the balance.*
- depend on someone or something **be in the hands of, depend on** *The fate of the area's wildlife depends on the town planners.*

2 the power that some people believe controls everything that happens

- adj+N **cruel, kind** *Fate was kind to me that day.*
- v+N **believe in, tempt** *It would be tempting fate to say that I've got a good chance of getting promoted.*
- N+v **conspire against, decide, decree, intervene** *They must have felt that fate was conspiring against them.*
- n+of+N **quirk, turn, twist** *By a cruel twist of fate, he ended up as Anne's stepson.*

fatigue N
a feeling of being extremely tired

- adj+N lasting for a long time **chronic, constant, persistent, prolonged** *One of my symptoms is chronic fatigue.*
- ▶ severe **extreme, great, overwhelming, profound, severe** *Extreme fatigue can sometimes be a symptom of anaemia.*
- ▶ types of fatigue **general, mental, muscle, muscular, physical** *I was also feeling just a bit of muscular fatigue.*
- v+N experience fatigue **experience, feel, suffer, suffer from** *It is extremely important to visit a doctor if you experience fatigue that seems to have no specific cause.*
- ▶ cause fatigue **cause, induce, produce** *Diabetes is another illness that can cause fatigue.*
- ▶ reduce fatigue **alleviate, decrease, minimise, reduce, relieve** *In China, the root is often used to reduce fatigue and boost energy levels.*
- ▶ try hard to prevent fatigue **combat, fight, fight off, resist** *These stimulants act on the nervous system and help combat fatigue.*
- ▶ prevent fatigue **avoid, prevent** *The good news is that there are steps you can take to help prevent fatigue.*

fault N
1 the fact of being responsible for something bad

- adj+N **sb's own, stupid** *I am sorry for them, but it's all their own fault; why didn't they take more care?*

> If someone is reponsible for a bad or unpleasant situation, you can say that they are **at fault**: *When a marriage breaks up it is very hard to say who is at fault.*

- N+v **lie with** *It may be that, in some cases, the fault lies with individual schools.*

2 a feature or problem that makes something less good or effective

- adj+N minor **minor, slight** *These are minor faults considering this is the company's first online game.*
- ▶ serious **dangerous, glaring, major, serious** *The enquiry found that there was a serious fault in one of the engines.*
- ▶ most serious **main** *The main fault with your essay is that it is too short.*
- ▶ types of fault **design, electrical, hardware, manufacturing, mechanical, software, structural, technical** *The fire was caused by an electrical fault.*
- v+N have or start to have a fault **develop, have** *The current system has faults.*

- ▶ deal effectively with a fault **correct, cure, fix, rectify, remedy, repair, resolve** *He spent over an hour attempting to fix the fault.*
- ▶ find or tell someone about a fault **detect, diagnose, discover, find, identify, report, spot, trace** *It was found that 67 per cent of garages failed to spot common faults.*

> When you criticise someone for the mistakes they have made, you **find fault** with them or with something they have done: *My manager was always finding fault with my work.*

- N+v **arise, lie in, occur** *They discovered that the fault lay in a blocked air vent.*

favour N
1 something done in order to help someone

- adj+N big **big, great, huge, massive** *The waitress seemed to think she was doing us a big favour taking our order.*
- ▶ small **little, slight, small** *I have a little favour to ask.*
- ▶ special **special** *As a special favour the children were allowed to stay for free.*
- ▶ for a particular person **personal** *He took on the case as a personal favour to her family.*
- v+N do a favour **do (sb)** *I thought I was doing him a favour, letting him live here.*
- ▶ do a favour for someone who has done one for you **reciprocate, repay, return** *I'm sure you'll return the favour one day.*
- ▶ ask someone to do a favour **ask (sb), beg, request, seek** *I would like to ask a favour.*
- ▶ think someone should do a favour for you **expect, look for** *I have already told them not to expect any favours.*
- ▶ have an obligation to do a favour **owe** *She then reminds Terry that he owes her a favour.*

> You can say that someone does something **as a favour**: *I'm only going as a favour to my parents.* | • *He didn't want any payment; he said he'd done it as a favour.*

2 support or admiration from people

- adj+N great **considerable, great, high, much, particular, special** *The concept has gained considerable favour in recent years.*
- ▶ types of favour **divine, political, popular, public, royal** *In 1485, he returned to royal favour.*
- v+N try to gain favour **court, curry, seek** *She accused the Prime Minister of trying to curry favour with the US administration.*
- ▶ gain favour **earn, find, gain, obtain, receive, secure, win** *Such an approach has found favour among some in the UK.*
- ▶ lose favour **be out of, fall from, fall out of, lose** *The two companies have lately lost favour with investors.*
- ▶ have someone's favour **be in, enjoy, have** *The right to hold a market was a privilege granted by the monarch to nobles who enjoyed his favour.*

favourable ADJ
1 showing approval of someone or something

- adv+ADJ very **exceptionally, extremely, highly, overwhelmingly, particularly, very** *Comments from my own patients have been highly favourable.*

▶ mainly **broadly, generally, largely, mainly, mostly** *However, the reception was generally favourable.*

▶ rather **quite, rather, reasonably, relatively** *Feedback has been quite favourable.*

● ADJ+n statement **comment, coverage, publicity, report, review** *The series gained favourable reviews from the very first episode.*

▶ reaction **reaction, reception, response** *It has already received a favourable response from critics.*

▶ opinion **attitude, opinion** *She formed a very favourable opinion of the area, which she spent a week exploring.*

2 giving someone or something an advantage or a benefit

● adv+ADJ very **exceptionally, extremely, highly, particularly, very** *This environment was exceptionally favourable to the development of revolutionary scientific ideas.*

▶ rather **quite, rather, reasonably, relatively** *Spain wants to maintain the relatively favourable position it was granted by the treaty.*

● ADJ+n situation **circumstances, conditions, environment, position, situation** *The plan aims to create favourable conditions for a strong, varied, and sustainable economy*

▶ treatment **terms, treatment** *There are also companies in the list who appear to have received favourable treatment.*

▶ result **outcome, result** *None of these actions guarantees a favourable outcome.*

● v+ADJ **appear, be, become, look, prove, remain, seem** *The area proved highly favourable for agriculture.* ◗

favourite N

1 the person or thing you like the best

● adj+N great **absolute, all-time, big, definite, firm, great, particular, real, special** *The main character has the potential to become a firm favourite with young readers.*

▶ for a long time **established, long-standing, long-time, old, perennial, traditional** *They played all their old favourites and the crowd loved them.*

▶ of particular person or group **audience, crowd, family, fan, personal, popular** *Scott enjoyed writing 'The Antiquary' more than its predecessors, and it remained his personal favourite among his novels.*

2 the person or animal that is expected to win a race or competition

● adj+N clear **clear, hot, odds-on, overwhelming** *They went into the World Cup as clear favourites for the title.*

▶ with another person or animal **joint** *The two bands are the joint favourites to win the coveted music award next month.*

● N+v **be tipped as, emerge as, start as** *The film is tipped as a favourite to do well at this year's Oscars.*

fear N

1 the feeling of being frightened

● adj+N real **genuine, real** *I lived in real fear of that teacher until I left that school.*

▶ always present **constant, nagging** *Whilst Anne was*

in hiding she kept a diary describing the isolation that they felt and their constant fear of discovery.

▶ great **deep, great, intense, mortal, terrible** *There is great fear in the community about the level of burglaries, attacks on the elderly, and anti-social behaviour.*

● v+N feel fear **experience, feel, have** *Strange as it all was, I felt no fear.*

▶ control fear **conquer, overcome** *I decided I had to overcome my fear and learn to swim.*

▶ cause fear **arouse, cause, create, engender, evoke, generate, incite, induce, inspire, instil, provoke, strike** *The outbreak of the French Revolution struck fear into the heart of every ruler in Europe.*

● v+with+N shake with fear **quake, quiver, shake, shiver, tremble** *She was so nervous that she was shaking with fear.*

▶ be unable to move because of fear **be frozen with, be paralysed by/with** *About halfway down the cliff he became paralysed with fear.*

▶ feel a lot of fear **be filled with, be gripped by/with, be overcome by, be seized with** *The city was gripped by fear and most of the inhabitants had left.*

2 something bad you are afraid might happen [usually plural]

● adj+N unreasonable **groundless, irrational, paranoid, unfounded, unjustified** *Of course, all my fears were unfounded.*

▶ reasonable **justified, legitimate, understandable, well-founded** *These fears are understandable but in many instances misguided.*

▶ real **genuine, real** *There are genuine fears that GM crop production might have an adverse effect on our wildlife.*

▶ greatest **biggest, deepest, greatest, worst** *X-rays this morning confirmed our worst fears.*

● v+N make fears go away or become less strong **allay, alleviate, assuage, banish, calm, dispel, ease, overcome, quell, reduce, soothe** *I shall be happy to give him a copy of the report, which will doubtless allay those fears.*

▶ express fears **express, voice** *Local residents expressed fears that the scheme would devalue local properties.*

▶ cause fears **arouse, cause, prompt, provoke, raise, spark** *A powerful earthquake struck near the Indonesian island of Sumatra yesterday, sparking fears of another tsunami.*

▶ increase fears **heighten, increase, stoke** *Continued economic uncertainty continues to stoke fears of redundancy amongst UK employees.*

feasibility N

the chance that something has of happening or being successful

● v+N examine feasibility **ascertain, assess, consider, determine, discuss, establish, evaluate, examine, explore, investigate, study, test** *The study investigating the feasibility of providing major new cultural facilities in Leeds has now been completed.*

▶ prove feasibility **confirm, demonstrate, prove, show** *The objective of the project is to demonstrate the feasibility of such a system.*

▶ doubt feasibility **doubt, question** *The review body*

questioned the feasibility of keeping all three colleges open.

- N+n **assessment, report, study** *The first stage, a feasibility study, started in October 2009.*

- N+of **approach, concept, idea, measure, option, project, proposal, scheme, system** *You will need to provide technical evidence supporting the feasibility of the project.*

feasible ADJ
possible or likely to succeed

- adv+**ADJ** in a particular way **commercially, computationally, economically, financially, operationally, politically, practically, technically, technologically, theoretically** *I have no reason to doubt the author's statement that the scheme is technically feasible.*
- ▶ completely **eminently, entirely, perfectly, quite** *Most people nowadays have access to a computer, but it is perfectly feasible to do the course without one.*

- **ADJ**+n **alternative, approach, idea, method, option, plan, project, proposal, proposition, solution, system, way** *With the limited resources available, this is not a feasible option.*

- and/or **affordable, appropriate, desirable, possible, practicable, practical, realistic, viable** *We estimate that it is desirable and feasible to have a 30 per cent reduction in carbon dioxide emissions by this date.*

feat N
an impressive and difficult act

- adj+**N** difficult or impossible **difficult, impossible, no easy, no mean, no small, tricky** *To truly excel, companies need to perform strongly across a range of areas – no mean feat in today's tough business climate.*
- ▶ impressive **amazing, astonishing, extraordinary, great, heroic, impressive, incredible, miraculous, outstanding, prodigious, remarkable, spectacular** *Brunel's bridge is still one of the most remarkable feats of engineering in the British Isles.*
- ▶ types of feat **acrobatic, architectural, engineering, gymnastic, intellectual, logistical, organizational, physical, technical, technological** *The dancers will amaze you with their acrobatic feats.*

- v+**N** perform a feat **accomplish, achieve, complete, do, manage, perform** *After performing many feats of courage, he was killed by Achilles.*
- ▶ copy a feat someone else has performed **emulate, match** *He was hoping to emulate the feat of his hero and win three successive titles.*

feature N
1 an important part or aspect of something

- adj+**N** special **defining, distinctive, distinguishing, identifying, interesting, notable, special, striking, unique, unusual** *A distinctive feature of the building is its unusual green roof.*
- ▶ important **central, dominant, important, key, main, major, prominent, salient** *A key feature of such initiatives is the focus on previously neglected groups such as women.*

- ▶ usual or essential **basic, crucial, essential, standard** *Air conditioning is a standard feature across our cars.*
- ▶ useful **handy, nifty** INFORMAL, **useful** *This is a very useful feature, which allows you unlimited email access.*
- ▶ that stops something from being completely bad **redeeming** *She considered him to be a horrible man, with few, if any, redeeming features.*
- ▶ types of feature **archaeological, architectural, geological, physical, structural, topographical** *These are the only architectural features to survive the restoration.*

- n+**N** **design, multimedia, navigation, safety, search, security** *It boasts a range of safety features to ensure maximum protection for driver and passengers.*

- v+**N** **boast, contain, have, include, incorporate, offer, possess** *It incorporates several new features specifically designed for the American market.*

- **N**+v **characterize, distinguish** *To summarize, the following features charaterize information retrieval systems.*

2 a part of your face such as your eyes or mouth [usually plural]

- adj+**N** **attractive, chiselled, distinctive, nice, prominent, regular, striking, strong** *He is a young man of medium height, with regular features, blond hair, and blue eyes.*

feature V
be a part of something

- adv+**V** **extensively, heavily, highly, largely, prominently, strongly** *The legendary actor featured prominently in the final Star Wars movie.*

fee N
money paid for professional services; money paid to do or join something [usually plural]

- adj+**N** low **low, modest, nominal, reasonable, small** *For a small fee you can upgrade your room.*
- ▶ high **exorbitant, extortionate, fat** INFORMAL, **hefty, high, huge, large, substantial** *Specialists are able to demand high fees for their expertise.*
- ▶ additional **additional, extra, top-up** *Students marched in protest against top-up fees.*
- ▶ charged for particular services **legal, medical, professional, veterinary** *I can't afford the legal fees.*
- ▶ fixed **fixed, flat, set** *Tax advisers will charge per hour or a pre-arranged flat fee.*
- ▶ charged for a particular time **annual, daily, hourly, monthly, yearly** *Our annual fee for gym membership is very reasonable.*
- ▶ charged only once **one-off** *For a one-off fee of £200 you can enjoy the benefits of membership for two years.*

- n+**N** **administration, admission, affiliation, booking, cancellation, course, entrance, entry, membership, registration, renewal, subscription, transfer, tuition** *The government is likely to raise the current level of tuition fees.*

- v+**N** charge a fee **charge, impose, levy** *The amount is roughly similar to the fees charged by many independent schools.*

▶ when a fee has to be paid **attract, incur** *Any change to the reservation will incur a fee.*

▶ earn a fee **command, earn, receive** *Bands like that can command huge fees.*

▶ agree on a fee **negotiate, set** *We are prepared to negotiate a reasonable fee for the right candidate.*

▶ pay a fee **pay** *This agreement means you only pay your solicitor's fees if they are successful in obtaining compensation for you.*

▶ give back the money paid as a fee **refund, reimburse** *We will refund any course fees paid.*

▶ not charge a fee **waive** *During the month of May hundreds of solicitors will waive their usual fees for drawing up a will.*

▶ reduce a fee **lower, reduce** *Not surprisingly, the client asked us to reduce our fees.*

▶ increase a fee **increase, put up, raise** *How long can the profession continue to increase its fees significantly ahead of inflation?*

● **N+v be due, be payable** *Tuition fees are due at the start of the academic year.*

feedback N

comments on how good something was, or how well or badly someone is doing something

● adj+N useful **constructive, effective, invaluable, useful, valuable** *We are grateful for the constructive feedback we received during the year.*

▶ praising someone or something **encouraging, favourable, positive** *So far there has been very positive feedback from the public.*

▶ criticizing someone or something **negative** *Never give negative feedback, even if students haven't done so well.*

▶ immediate **immediate, instant** *You will be given instant feedback on your answers.*

▶ given early on **initial** *Initial feedback from conference delegates on the sessions has been excellent.*

● v+N give feedback **give (sb), offer, provide, send (sb), submit** *They recognized the benefits of providing feedback to students on their performance in these tests.*

▶ get feedback **gain, get, have, obtain, receive** *We are really keen to get feedback on how useful you find the toolkit.*

▶ like feedback **appreciate, like, value, welcome** *We welcome feedback from people making use of these features.*

▶ ask for feedback **ask for, encourage, invite, request, seek, solicit** *The questionnaire is a familiar method of seeking feedback from students.*

▶ gather feedback **collect, gather** *Detailed feedback is gathered from both candidate and client after an interview.*

● N+v **confirm, highlight, indicate, show, suggest** *She reported that initial feedback suggested that the residents were pleased with the new facilities.*

feeling N

1 something that you feel

● adj+N strong **deep, intense, strong** *The feeling of loneliness was incredibly intense.*

▶ bad **bad, horrible, uncomfortable, uneasy, unpleasant** *It is the worst feeling I've ever experienced.*

▶ strange **eerie, strange** *She still had that strange feeling about the man.*

● v+N **experience, get, have** *They may also experience feelings of guilt or anger.*

2 emotions or opinions [always plural]

● adj+N of different types **ambivalent, mixed** *I viewed the changes that were coming with mixed feelings.*

● v+N have feelings **harbour, have** *Remember that I have feelings too.*

▶ express feelings **express, give vent to, share, vent, voice** *Psychotherapy provides a client with the opportunity to express their feelings.*

▶ stop yourself having feelings **repress, suppress** *There are others who tell no one, suppressing their real feelings.*

▶ hide your feelings **hide** *Boys are supposed to hide their feelings more than girls.*

▶ hurt someone's feelings **hurt** *You really hurt my feelings.*

▶ have the same feelings as someone else **reciprocate, return, share** *She also fancies Danny but her feelings are not reciprocated.*

● N+v **change, run high** *Feelings on the issue are running high in the town.*

3 an opinion based on general thoughts rather than definite reasons

● adj+N definite **definite, distinct, overwhelming, strong** *I have this strong feeling that I have met them before.*

▶ felt very strongly, in a way that you cannot explain **gut** *My gut feeling is that we shouldn't agree to do it.*

▶ not fully formed **nagging, sneaking, sneaky, vague** *I have this nagging feeling that there's something I've forgotten.*

▶ shared by many people **general, widespread** *There is a widespread feeling that the banks have become too powerful.*

● v+N **get, have** *Anna got the feeling that he was rather cross.*

fend off PHR VB

defend yourself against an attack or criticism

● V+n an attack **attack, blow, challenge, tackle** *The British had just managed to fend off the attack.*

▶ someone who attacks you **attacker, boarder, intruder, mugger, pursuer** *She tried to fend off the attacker with kicks.*

▶ criticism **accusation, attack, challenge, claim, criticism, objection** *US officials tried to fend off growing criticism for the latest security lapse.*

▶ question **query, question** *He now had to fend off questions about whether he'd resign over the matter.*

ferry N

a boat that makes short regular journeys

● v+N travel on a ferry **catch, get, go by, take, use** *There's time for a swim before we catch the ferry to Athens.*

▶ get onto a ferry **board, get on, get onto** *At Rosslare we board the ferry back to Wales.*

- N+v leave **depart, go, leave, sail** *Ferries depart every half an hour to Capri.*
- ▶ exist and be available **operate, run** *Ferries run daily to the neighbouring island of Kalymnos from the small harbour.*
- ▶ go across an area of water **cross** *Twenty ferries cross each day from Larne and Belfast to Stranraer.*
- ▶ arrive **arrive, berth, come in, dock** *The ferry arrives in France at 12.30pm.*

fertility N

the ability of the soil to produce crops or of people or animals to produce babies

- ● v+N reduce fertility **decrease, lower, reduce** *You can reduce fertility by stripping off the top 5–10cm or so of topsoil.*
- ▶ increase fertility **aid, boost, build, enhance, improve, increase, restore** *Organic farmers use crop rotations to improve the fertility of their soil.*
- ▶ prevent fertility from being destroyed **maintain, preserve** *Compost is applied to our fields to maintain fertility.*
- ● N+v **decline, fall** *These figures include older women whose fertility is declining.*

fervour N

very strong feeling or enthusiasm

- ● adj+N great **great, intense** *It was a time of intense nationalist fervour.*
- ▶ types of fervour **evangelical, moral, national, nationalist, nationalistic, patriotic, political, religious, revolutionary, spiritual** *In the year 1557 religious fervour gripped England.*
- ● v+N **arouse, increase, stoke up** *The song aroused great patriotic fervour among the spectators.*

festival N

1 a series of performances or events held somewhere each year

- ● adj+N happening at particular intervals **annual, biennial** *In July, hordes of rock fans arrive for the town's famous annual festival.*
- ▶ lasting a particular time **month-long, week-long, one-day, three-day etc, one-week, three-week etc** *The summer highlight, however, is the three-day festival starting on August 2nd.*
- ▶ types of festival **cultural, literary** *He has given poetry readings at literary festivals.*
- ● n+N **arts, comedy, dance, drama, film, folk, jazz, music, pop, rock** *It has been shown at various international film festivals, winning an award in Chicago.*
- ● v+N organize a festival **have, hold, host, organize, run, stage** *A huge medieval festival is held here every August.*
- ▶ help pay for a festival **sponsor** *The university is involved in sponsoring local arts festivals.*
- ▶ go to a festival **attend, go to, visit** *People come from all over Europe just to attend the festival.*
- ● N+v **run, take place** *This year's festival runs from 22 September to 22 October.*
- ● N+n **audience, director, -goer, organizer** *The band drove the crowd wild and got festival goers to their feet dancing.*

2 a religious celebration or public holiday

- ● v+N **celebrate, observe** *Hindus celebrate a spring festival called Holi at this time.*
- ● N+v **celebrate, commemorate, mark** *Some religious festivals mark the sowing, rather than the harvesting, of crops.*

feud N

an angry disagreement that lasts a long time

- ● adj+N having continued for a long time **long, long-running, long-standing, old** *The incident was part of a long-running feud.*
- ▶ still happening **continuing, ongoing, running** *The ongoing feud between the board of directors and the local businessman became public again last week.*
- ● v+N end a feud **end, settle** *The Prince of Verona commands the families to end their feud.*

fever N

1 a medical condition in which the temperature of your body is very high

- ● adj+N severe **acute, high, raging, severe** *Billy ran a high fever for days.*
- ▶ not severe **mild, slight** *Other symptoms may include mild fever, tiredness and headache.*
- ● v+N have a fever **have, run, suffer from** *Tell your doctor immediately if you have a fever or other signs of infection.*
- ▶ get a fever **develop, get** *Unfortunately I developed a fever that night.*
- ▶ cause a fever **cause, induce, produce** *It causes fever, shaking, and headaches.*
- ▶ reduce a fever **bring, down, ease, reduce, relieve** *Paracetamol is used to treat headaches or to reduce fever.*

2 strong excitement and enthusiasm affecting many people

- ● n+N **election, football, war, wedding** *Election fever began to sweep the country.*
- ● v+N **be gripped by** *At the time, the country was gripped by election fever.*
- ● N+v **grip, hit, sweep** *Football fever once again gripped the nation, with a World Cup on the horizon.*

fictitious ADJ

not real or true; invented for a book, play, or film

- ● adv+ADJ completely **completely, entirely, purely, totally, wholly** *I am not suggesting that this eminent historian published an account that was entirely fictitious.*
- ▶ mainly **largely** *The profits it had declared were largely fictitious.*
- ● ADJ+n **account, character, claim, company, example, identity, name, scenario, story** *He is accused of making 145 false tax returns using fictitious names and Social Security numbers.*

field N

1 a subject that you study or a type of work that you do

- ● adj+N **chosen, particular, related, respective,**

specialist, specialized *You will have the chance to work closely with leading specialists in your chosen field.* • *They were both experts in their own respective fields.*

● v+N deal with a field **cover, survey** *In this course we shall survey the entire field of political economy.*

▶ make a field smaller **narrow** *Graduates are encouraged to narrow their field of interest and concentrate on two main topics.*

● n+in+N **expert, innovator, leader, pioneer, practitioner, professional, researcher, scholar, specialist** *Occasional seminars and workshops with experts in various fields were also organised.*

● N+of **endeavour, expertise, inquiry, research, study** *This is an active and exciting field of study.*

2 the people or organizations taking part in a competition or business [always singular]

● v+N lead the field **dominate, head, lead** *We lead the field in our chosen markets.*

▶ make the field smaller **narrow** *His resignation narrowed the field of candidates down to five.*

fieldwork N

work involving studying something in its environment

● adj+N **anthropological, archaeological, ethnographic, geographical, geological** *She still does archaeological fieldwork in the area.*

● v+N **carry out, conduct, do, engage in, participate in, take part in, undertake** *Students are required to undertake fieldwork.*

fierce ADJ

1 involving very strong feelings; very angry or ready to attack

● ADJ+n argument **argument, battle, controversy, debate, disagreement, fight** *The film became the centre of a fierce debate about censorship.*

▶ fighting **attack, battle, fight, fighting, resistance, struggle** *Warsaw was the scene of fierce fighting between occupying German forces and the Polish resistance.*

▶ criticism **attack, criticism, denunciation** *The company has come under fierce criticism in recent weeks over its policy to axe services to rural areas.*

▶ person **defender, enemy, fighter, opponent, warrior** *These fierce Germanic warriors had hunted wild boar with nothing but spears.*

▶ feeling **determination, loyalty, pride** *The poulation had shown a fierce determination to resist the invaders.*

2 involving a lot of force or energy

● ADJ+n competition **competition, rivalry** *British companies are facing fierce overseas competition.*

▶ opposition **fight, opposition, resistance, struggle** *Plans to build a new American-style restaurant in the area have met with fierce opposition.*

fight V

1 use a weapon against someone; hit, kick, or bite other people or animals

● adv+V in a brave way **bravely, courageously,**

gallantly, heroically, resolutely, valiantly *The soldiers, though outnumbered, fought bravely and finally defeated their attacks.*

▶ with great effort **bitterly, desperately, ferociously, fiercely, hard, tenaciously, vigorously** *He had fought hard in the battle.*

● V+n **battle, skirmish, war** *In 1868, the British army invaded Ethiopia and fought a battle at the town of Maqdala.*

2 try hard to prevent something from happening or getting worse

● V+n(+against) **corruption, crime, discrimination, fascism, injustice, oppression, poverty, racism, terror, terrorism** *No one questions the determination of the White House to fight terrorism.*

3 try hard to achieve something

● adv+V **constantly, desperately, doggedly, effectively, energetically, hard, strenuously, stubbornly, successfully, tenaciously, tirelessly, vigorously** *She fought tirelessly for decent pay and conditions for women.*

● V+for **compensation, equality, justice, recognition, reform, rights** *She will do a fine job fighting for the rights of disabled people.*

4 try not to show or do something

● V+n **desire, emotion, feeling, impulse, urge** *There were moments where I had to fight the urge to give in.*

5 compete to win or get something

● adv+V **bitterly, closely, hard, keenly, tightly** *The first two games were closely fought.*

● V+n **contest, election, game, match** *He says Labour needs more funding to fight the next election.*

● V+for **place, position** *There were quite a few people fighting for a place on the course.*

fight N

1 a situation in which people hit each other

● adj+N **big, bloody, brutal, drunken, fair, real, vicious** *A real fight is nothing like a kung-fu movie!*

● v+N start a fight **pick, provoke, start** *He tried to pick a fight with me for no reason.*

▶ have a fight **be in, have** *Police were called following reports of two men having a fight.*

▶ become involved in a fight **engage in, get in, get into, get involved in** *He was constantly getting into fights in his youth.*

▶ want a fight **be looking for, be spoiling for, want** *I could tell from his tone of voice that he was spoiling for a fight.*

▶ stop a fight **break up, stop** *She tried to stop the fight between the two men.*

2 an attempt to win something that others want

● adj+N **brave, courageous, desperate, gallant, good, spirited, valiant** *When Alger served for the match it looked like Johnson's brave fight was over.*

● v+N **face, have, lose, put up, win** *They had lost in the final, despite putting up a tremendous fight.*

● N+for **championship, control, dominance, place,**

supremacy, victory, votes *The fight for control of Russia's second biggest oil company is far from over.*

3 a determined attempt to prevent something bad happening or getting worse; a determined attempt to achieve something

- adj+N **brave, courageous, desperate, hard, long, valiant** *She passed away on 4th September after a brave fight against cancer.*

- v+N **back, continue, join, lead, lose, put up, spearhead, support, win** *There are many protest groups that are willing to put up a strong fight against any expansion of the country's airports.*

- N+against **cancer, crime, discrimination, disease, drugs, fascism, fraud, poverty, racism, terror, terrorism** *We consider the fight against terrorism to be our absolute priority.*

- N+for **democracy, equality, justice, life, rights, socialism, survival** *The fight for equality still has some way to go.*

fight back PHR VB

try hard not to show a feeling

- V+n **anger, impulse, pain, panic, rage, sleepiness, tears, urge, yawn** *It was very emotional and I had to fight back the tears.*

fighting N

a situation in which soldiers or armies use weapons against each other, or people hit, kick, or bite each other

- adj+N fierce **bitter, desperate, fierce, hard, heavy, intense, serious, severe** *Heavy fighting is continuing in the town.*

- ▶ happening occasionally or in some places **intermittent, sporadic** *They wrecked the concert hall and sporadic fighting then broke out around the village.*

- ▶ between individual soldiers etc **hand-to-hand** *Hand-to-hand fighting went on in every street.*

- ▶ starting again **renewed** *Renewed fighting broke out at the very moment when peace seemed to be in sight.*

- v+N stop fighting **end, halt, stop** *The Treaty of Amiens (1802–03) temporarily ended the fighting between England and France.*

- ▶ avoid fighting **avoid, escape, flee** *There are now 200,000 refugees who have fled the fighting and are without food, water or shelter.*

- N+v start **begin, break out, commence, erupt, start** *Fighting broke out throughout the country.*

- ▶ take place **occur, take place** *Most of the fighting took place on the Western Front.*

- ▶ continue **continue, go on** *The fighting continued into the late afternoon.*

- ▶ happen after something **ensue, follow** *Some desperate hand-to-hand fighting ensued before the city was captured.*

- ▶ continue with a lot of force and violence **rage** *Reports said intense fighting is raging along the border.*

- ▶ become worse **escalate, intensify** *During March fighting escalated again when the army launched another offensive against the rebels.*

- ▶ stop **cease, end, stop** *On November the 11th 1918, at 11am, all fighting ceased on the Western Front.*

fight off PHR VB

1 stop someone who is trying to attack you

- V+n **army, assailant, attacker, enemy, gang, invaders, mugger, rapist** *They were ambushed, but managed to fight off their attackers.*

2 prevent an illness from affecting you

- V+n **bacteria, cold, depression, disease, flu, germs, illness, infection, virus** *Even when symptoms do occur, the body can often fight off the infection.*

figure N

1 an official number that has been counted or calculated

- adj+N official **official** *Official figures have not yet been released.*

- ▶ final/not final **final, provisional** *The final figure will probably be closer to one million dollars.*

- ▶ exact **accurate, actual, exact, precise, reliable** *The actual figures involved are likely to be substantially higher.*

- ▶ not exact **approximate, ballpark, rough** *We're only able to give you a ballpark figure at this stage.*

- ▶ high/low **high, low** *As expected, the figures are higher for women.*

- ▶ average **average** *The analysis tool compiles an average figure for each of the six management standards.*

- ▶ including everything **total** *The total figure owed to the company exceeded 10 million dollars.*

- n+N **attendance, audience, casualty, census, circulation, crime, inflation, performance, population, sales, unemployment, viewing** *Sales figures were down again.*

- v+N **calculate, compare, compile, estimate, give, obtain, produce, publish, record, release, report, revise** *Table 3 gives figures for each local authority.*

- and/or **facts** *This site contains facts and figures about tourism in Britain.*

2 someone who is important in some way

- adj+N important **central, eminent, important, influential, key, leading, major, pivotal, prominent, seminal, senior, towering** *She was a prominent figure in the local community.*

- ▶ respected **respected** *She was one of the most respected figures in British architecture.*

- ▶ that people disagree about **controversial** *He has always been a controversial figure in rock-climbing circles.*

- ▶ that people know well **familiar, legendary, well-known** *The website lists some legendary figures associated with the area.*

- ▶ in a particular area of activity **historical, literary, political, religious** *She was a wife, mother, and social commentator as well as a leading literary figure.*

figure V

be an important part of something

- adv+V very much **heavily, highly, largely, prominently, significantly, strongly** *The UK has a long history of sports, having figured prominently in their world-wide development.*

▸ not very much **barely, hardly** *Climate change has barely figured in the election campaign.*

file N

1 a set of information on a computer

● adj+N types of file **backup, data, digital, downloadable, executable, program, read-me, self-extracting, temporary** *You are recommended to save your references periodically by creating a backup file.*

▸ containing particular kinds of data **audio, graphic, image, MP3, sound, text, video** *The first thing is to decide what type of sound file you want to create.*

● v+N open/close a file **close, open** *You need a special piece of software to open this file.*

▸ get a file so that you can open it **access, download, locate, retrieve** *You will need a password to download these files.*

▸ look at a file **view** *To view a PDF file, locate the file on your computer, and double click it.*

▸ make or copy a file **copy, create, generate** *The user should create a new file with the same name as the existing file.*

▸ change a file **convert, edit, modify, overwrite, rename, update** *Any attempt to overwrite the file will result in an error message.*

▸ keep a file **hold, keep, save** *Sometimes you will want to let the user save a file to disk.*

▸ get rid of a file **delete** *You may think that emptying the Recycle Bin will finally delete the files but it doesn't.*

▸ make a file secret **encrypt** *Data in these files is encrypted, securing your information against unsanctioned users.*

▸ return a file to the place where it belongs **upload** *To upload your files to the website, you can use an FTP program.*

● and/or **directory, folder, subdirectory** *Add a comment to each file, folder and disk.*

2 a set of papers, documents, or records

● v+N have/keep a file **hold, keep** *Personal data in files held by such organisations must be accurate, up to date and accessible.*

▸ keep information in a file **keep sth on file, record sth on file, retain sth on file, sth remains on file, store sth on file** *The photograph will be kept on file and you will be offered a copy as a souvenir.* ● *We shall contact you after a year to ask if you would like your details to remain on file.*

▸ start/complete a file **close, open** *The responsible officer will open a file on the complaint.*

fill V

1 when a sound, smell etc is very noticeable

● n+V smells **aroma, fragrance, scent, smell** *The smell of fresh flowers filled the air.*

▸ sounds **birdsong, cries, laughter, sound, whispers** *Roaring laughter filled the stuffy conference room.*

▸ light **glow, light, sunlight** *An extraordinary blaze of coloured light fills the view.*

▸ smoke **smoke** *Pearl sat up in bed and realised that smoke was filling her room–the house was on fire.*

2 make you feel an emotion strongly

● V+n+with happiness or positive feelings

admiration, awe, excitement, hope, joy, laughter, wonder *Our hearts were filled with admiration for our dear friend.*

▸ sad feelings **longing, remorse, sadness** *Mary couldn't wait to get away, yet now as she recalled the day when she left her home, she was filled with remorse.*

▸ angry feelings **anger, hate, rage** *The play explores the motives of men so filled with rage that they turn their weapons against their own families.*

▸ fear **dread, fear** *That scenario leaves me filled with dread.*

> Usage **Fill** is usually passive in all of the **V+n+with** combinations shown above: *I was filled with more hope and optimism than I had felt for a very long time.*

3 give someone a job or position

● V+n **position, post, vacancy** *There was not much unemployment and it was hard to fill vacancies.*

film N

a series of moving pictures with sound

● n+N types of film **animated, avant-garde, classic, documentary, feature, feature-length, full-length, live-action, low-budget, silent** *Are you not tempted to make a live-action film with real actors?*

▸ genres of film **arthouse, blockbuster, gangster, horror, porn, science-fiction, sci-fi, slasher, vampire, zombie** *Scorsese has shown that he is capable of so much more than the gangster films that have made his name.*

● v+N make a film **make, remake, shoot** *It is always hard when you try to remake a classic film, and this was no exception.*

▸ take part in the making of a film **direct, edit, produce** *The film is directed by Mike Nichols, one of whose first films was The Graduate starring Dustin Hoffman.*

▸ make a film available for the public to see **distribute, release, screen, show** *Redbus Film Distribution will release the film in the United Kingdom.* ● *From time to time we will screen films more informally in the cafe.*

▸ watch a film **see, view, watch** *I don't watch films much.*

▸ be an actor in a film **appear in, be in, co-star in, star in** *She started as a child actor, and has been in dozens of films.*

● N+n people who work in the film industry **crew, director, maker, producer, star** *This festival showcases the work of Turkey's leading film makers.*

▸ the business of making films **industry, production, studio** *Customers include sports teams, theatrical companies, film studios and conference organisers.*

▸ an occasion when a film is shown **premiere, screening, showing** *We will now be negotiating with the new owners to ensure that film screenings remain available at the venue.*

▸ people who are very interested in films **buff, fan** *He is a huge film buff with a collection of over 3,000 videos and DVDs.*

▸ pieces of film **clip, footage** *Not only does the show feature a great live band but lots of film footage as well.*

final ADJ

1 at the end of a series of things

- ADJ+n in a book or document **chapter, paragraph, section** *The final chapter contains more detailed background information for the teacher.*
- ▶ in a play or film **episode, instalment, scene** *There's a very creepy, very spine-tingling sequence at the end of this final episode.*
- ▶ in a competition **game, match, play-off, round, set** *This sets both teams up nicely to face each other in the final play-offs.*

2 at the end of a process or event

- ADJ+n last event or product **draft, exam, report, version** *Projects typically end with a reflective final report.*
- ▶ last part or stage **part, phase, stage** *You should be reaching the final stages of planning.*
- ▶ result **mark, outcome, placings, reckoning, result, score, tally, verdict** *As a group you should always be optimistic about the final outcome.*
- ▶ in a war, argument etc **battle, confrontation, showdown**

3 when a decision, offer etc cannot be changed

- ADJ+n **answer, decision, offer, say, settlement** *You'll have 30 seconds to select your responses and to confirm that it's your final answer.* • *The referee's decision is final.*

finale N

the last in a series of events

- adj+N exciting **dramatic, exciting, exhilarating, explosive, rousing, thrilling** *How could this fantastic band say goodbye after such a rousing finale?*
- ▶ impressive **fantastic, glorious, grand, spectacular, stunning** *The scene was now set for a fantastic finale to an already exciting evening.*
- ▶ tense **gripping, tense** *The production concentrates on building up the atmosphere to a gripping finale.*
- N+to to a period **day, evening, season, week, year** *Winning the bronze was an exciting finale to a superb season.*
- ▶ to an event **festival, meal, programme, show, trip** *This dramatic area should make a grand finale to our trip.*

finance N

1 decisions on how money is spent or invested

- adj+N **consumer, corporate, government, international, local government, personal** *He has written several books on trade policy and international finance.*
- N+n person in charge of finance **chief, director, manager, minister, officer** *Peter was appointed finance director of the trust in November 2002.*
- ▶ group in charge of finance **committee, department, ministry, team** *The finance department are now holding weekly meetings.*

2 money used to pay for major projects, investments etc

- adj+N types of finance **bank, capital, commercial, external, private, private sector, public, public sector, start-up, structured** *The sum is expected to raise a further £46 million of private sector finance.*
- ▶ extra **additional, extra** *Of course, additional finance is being put into tourism at the moment.*
- n+N for a particular purpose **car, housing, mortgage, motor, project** *They are a company that provides car finance for most people, regardless of their credit history.*
- ▶ for a particular type of borrower **business, consumer, family, household, student** *In response to increasing demand, we are able to offer funding through a leading provider of consumer finance.*
- v+N arrange, attract, obtain, raise, secure, seek, sort out *Producers have failed to raise the finance for the movie.*
- N+for **business, development, enterprise, expansion, project, purchase, start-up** *Finance for the purchase was provided by a leading merchant bank.*

finance V

provide money for something such as a large project

- adv+V in what way **independently, jointly, locally, privately, publicly, solely** *Some of the costs of research and development are publicly financed.*
- ▶ to what degree **entirely, fully, largely, mainly, partially, partly, wholly** *Amnesty International is financed largely by subscriptions and donations from its worldwide membership.*
- ▶ properly **adequately, properly, well** *We must ensure that our athletes are properly financed to achieve medal success.*

> Usage **Finance** is usually passive in all the **adv+V** combinations shown above.

financial ADJ

involving money

- ADJ+n help or support **advice, aid, assistance, backing, support** *There are two ways the College can provide direct financial assistance for students.*
- ▶ encouragement/rewards **incentives, rewards** *People will always respond to financial incentives.*
- ▶ likelihood of continued success **stability, sustainability, viability** *The safety of the banking system is fundamental to long-term financial stability.*
- ▶ people or organizations involved in finance **adviser, advisor, analyst, backer, institution, services** *If you are still unsure, please contact your financial adviser.*
- ▶ management **management, planning, projection** *The plan outlines our strategic direction and provides financial projections for the next five years.*
- ▶ bad or dishonest management **irregularities, mismanagement, scandal** *He was eventually expelled from the board amid allegations of financial irregularities.*
- ▶ problems **burden, difficulties, hardship, straits, stringency** *Is there anything I can do to safeguard against this type of financial hardship?*
- ▶ crisis **crisis, meltdown** *By this time, the US car industry was facing financial meltdown.*

find V

1 discover a solution or way of doing something

- V+n **alternative, answer, compromise, method, solution, way** *The challenge now is to find lasting solutions to the problem of climate change.*

2 achieve a state of happiness/satisfaction

- V+n **comfort, fulfilment, happiness, inspiration, peace, pleasure, relief, satisfaction** *Instead of pursuing material goals, they found fulfilment in spending more time with their friends and families.*

find N

something interesting or valuable, especially something from the past

- adj+N interesting or exciting **exciting, important, interesting, rare, significant, spectacular** *It's too early yet to report any interesting finds.*
- ▶ of a particular type or period **archaeological, medieval, prehistoric** *There had been recent archaeological finds in and around the car park.*
- v+N make a find **detect, discover, excavate, make, recover, uncover, unearth** *No archaeological deposits or finds were recovered.*
- ▶ record a find **identify, record, report** *It is quite clear that many finds are not recorded at present.*

findings N

information that you discover after doing research

- adj+N main **key, main, principal** *The event featured key findings from research carried out by the project.*
- ▶ important **important, significant** *Keep people informed of any significant findings in your assessment.*
- ▶ interesting or surprising **interesting, startling, striking, surprising, unexpected** *To many students, this exercise brings about unexpected findings and surprises.*
- ▶ shocking or worrying **alarming, disturbing, shocking, worrying** *Scientists describe the findings as both surprising and alarming, because they suggest global warming could be accelerating.*
- ▶ not final **initial, interim, preliminary, provisional** *This paper reports on the initial findings of the evaluation team.*
- n+N **audit, poll, project, report, research, study, survey** *Thousands of professional journals spread new research findings worldwide.*
- v+N record findings **describe, outline, record, report, summarize** *A newsletter summarising the key findings is available.*
- ▶ make findings public **communicate, disseminate, present, publicize, publish, share** *This talk presented the findings of a national survey into the final year at medical school.*
- ▶ examine findings **analyse, compare, discuss, interpret, review** *They will then be inputting their data into a computer before interpreting their findings.*
- ▶ confirm or repeat someone else's findings **confirm, corroborate, replicate, substantiate, validate** *In 2009, a new study confirmed earlier findings on leukaemia in the region.*

- N+v show **demonstrate, highlight, imply, indicate, reveal, show, suggest, underline** *The findings suggest that people are generally honest about money matters.*
- ▶ support other findings **confirm, reinforce, support, underscore** *The findings confirm predictions of the Big Bang theory.*
- ▶ contradict other findings **challenge, contradict** *The researchers say that their findings contradict the idea that drinking too much beer makes people obese.*
- N+from **consultation, experiment, investigation, project, questionnaire, report, research, review, study, survey** *The book concludes with a summary of the main findings from this research.*
- N+of **audit, consultation, inquiry, inspection, investigation, poll, project, questionnaire, report, research, review, study, survey** *The findings of the survey are described on page 4.*

fine N

money you must pay for breaking the law

- adj+N immediate **automatic, instant, on-the-spot** *Individuals who defy the legislation face on-the-spot fines of £50.*
- ▶ large **crippling, enormous, heavy, hefty, large, massive, stiff, substantial, swingeing, unlimited** *Hefty fines will be levied against anyone breaching the restrictions.*
- ▶ not yet paid **outstanding, unpaid** *Many people are in prison because of unpaid fines.*
- v+N get a fine **face, get, incur, receive, risk** *They will face unlimited fines and possible imprisonment.*
- ▶ make someone pay a fine **give sb, impose, issue, levy** *There were concerns about the low level of fines imposed by magistrates' courts.*
- ▶ pay a fine **pay** *He said he would go to court rather than pay the fine.*

finger N

one of the long thin parts on your hands

- adj+N fat **chubby, fat, podgy, stubby** *A child with short stubby fingers will struggle to play the double bass but may find a brass instrument presents no problems.*
- ▶ not straight or healthy **arthritic, bent, crooked, gnarled, swollen** *My fingers are really swollen.*
- ▶ thin **bony, delicate, slender, thin** *Her slender fingers were never without a cigarette.*
- v+N point a finger **jab, point, poke** *He jabs a finger at a paragraph in one of his books.*
- ▶ move your fingers **flex, wag, waggle, wiggle** *'This is your fault, young lady,' he said, wagging a finger in Michelle's face.*
- ▶ make a noise with your fingers **click, snap** *'Don't click your fingers at me, I'm not a dog,' Hannah continued.*

finish N

1 the end of a race, game etc

- adj+N exciting **dramatic, exciting, nail-biting, tense, thrilling** *The game built to a thrilling finish.*
- ▶ close **close, tight** *Sandown is the racecourse which is the most likely to end in a tight finish.*

2 the appearance of a surface

- adj+N smooth or shiny **glossy, metallic, polished, satin, shiny, smooth** *Then rub clean vigorously for shiny finish.*
▶ not smooth or shiny **matt, textured** *The matt black finish means that finger prints are no longer an issue, the cover refusing to retain greasy finger marks for more than a few seconds.*
▶ attractive **attractive, decorative, superb** *The process, which provided an attractive finish was known as japanning.*
▶ long-lasting **durable, tough** *The top and bottom plates were given a more durable finish.*

fire N

1 flames and heat from something that is burning

- adj+N causing a lot of damage **catastrophic, destructive, devastating, disastrous, major, serious** *A disastrous fire swept through the monastery, necessitating considerable reconstruction.*
▶ not accidental **deliberate, malicious, suspicious** *The attack, on Saturday, was the second deliberate fire at the building.*
▶ burning strongly **fierce, intense** *We also visited the crash site, still very hot from the intense fire.*
- n+N **bush, chimney, domestic, forest, house, warehouse** *The walker is reminded of the need to take special care to prevent the outbreak of forest fires.*
- v+N put out a fire **douse, extinguish, put out, quench** *The fire was extinguished with a fire extinguisher from one of the other boats.*
▶ try to put out a fire **fight, tackle** *Before the arrival of the brigade there had been no attempt to fight the fire.*
▶ start a fire **start** *The fire was started after a side window was smashed at around 2 a.m.*

> You say that someone **sets fire to** something when they deliberately make something burn. You say that something **catches fire** when it starts to burn.

- N+v start **break out, burn, erupt, start** *Fire broke out and escaping gas soon ignited the wreckage.*
▶ burn strongly **blaze, crackle, rage** *An intense fire was raging by the time the firemen arrived on the scene.*
▶ move quickly **engulf sth, spread, sweep through sth** *The fire spread rapidly to an adjacent building.*
▶ cause great damage **consume sth, damage sth, destroy sth, devastate sth, gut sth** INFORMAL, **ravage sth** *The fire gutted the interior of the building.*
- N+n **detection, hazard, precautions, prevention, protection, safety, suppression** *Are wooden beams in our chimney a fire hazard?*

2 a pile of burning wood etc for producing heat

- adj+N types of fire **coal, electric, gas, log, open, peat, wood** *There is another open fire in the dining/living space.*
▶ giving warmth **blazing, cosy, crackling, glowing, roaring, warm** *I'm glad too that you've got a cosy fire to warm yourself.*
- v+N **build, lay, light, make, stoke** *The fire was lit and the smell of wood smoke pervaded the room.*

firm N

a business or company

- adj+N with a good reputation **established, leading, prestigious, reputable, respected** *By using the Internet I made a list of the reputable firms.*
▶ how large a firm is **international, large, medium-sized, multinational, small** *Smaller firms are often well behind the market leaders.*
- n+N involved in finance **accountancy, accounting, brokerage, consulting, equity, insurance, investment, manufacturing** *Though only 37, she is already a partner in a local accountancy firm, heading a team that advises medical practitioners.*
▶ involved in the law **law** *The men are represented by the head of the human rights department at a leading London law firm.*
▶ involved in building, manufacturing etc **construction, engineering, haulage, manufacturing** *On leaving school he joined an electrical engineering firm at Rugby.*
- v+N create a firm **establish, found, set up, start** *He founded a building firm in 1860 and was later joined by a partner named Wilcock.*
▶ run a firm **manage, run** *I plan to run my own engineering firm when I graduate next May.*
- N+v when a firm employs someone **employ, hire, recruit** *These firms employ graduates from any degree discipline.*
▶ what firms do **act for, manufacture, operate, specialize in, supply** *Our 217 member firms operate on more than 500 sites and employ 21,000 staff.*
▶ when a firm fails **close down, fail, go bust** INFORMAL, **go under** INFORMAL, **shut down** *After a few months the firm failed and the family again experienced great hardship.*

firm ADJ

definite, and unlikely to change

- ADJ+n basis **base, basis, footing, foundation** *The time has come to put consumer representation onto a firmer footing.*
▶ person who believes in something **advocate, believer, supporter** *We're firm believers in the concept that business travel can be a pleasure.*
▶ feeling or belief **belief, commitment, conviction, resolve, stance** *The party likes to portray him as a man of firm moral convictions who is, above all, trustworthy .*
▶ evidence **evidence** *There was no firm evidence to prove that the request received proper consideration.*
▶ understanding **grasp, grounding** *To do the job well, you need a firm grasp of how international banking works.*

firm up PHR VB

make something more definite

- V+n plans **arrangements, booking, date, details, plans, programme, schedule, timetable** *We have not firmed up a date yet, but are looking at end of April.*
▶ ideas **ideas, proposals, suggestions, views** *These workshops will be really useful in terms of helping you firm up ideas for your final project.*

fist N
your hand when your fingers are closed tightly

- adj+N **clenched, closed, tight** *Clench your hands into tight fists.*
- v+N form a fist **clench, make** *Her nerves were numb and she could barely make fists.*
- ▶ move your fist in a threatening way **raise, shake, wave** *They shook their fists, shouted obscenities, and threatened to kill her.*
- ▶ hit something with your fist **bang, beat, slam, smash** *I want to scream and beat my fists against the wall.*

fit V
be the right size or shape

- adv+V tightly **neatly, securely, snugly, tightly** *The unit is powered by 2 AA batteries which fit snugly into the top.*
- ▶ exactly or correctly **exactly, like a glove, perfectly, properly** *Jerry tried on the suit, and it fitted like a glove.* • *If you do wear a helmet, make sure it fits properly.*
- ▶ comfortably **comfortably, nicely, well** *Necklaces need to be the right length in order to fit comfortably.*

fit ADJ
1 healthy, strong, and regularly taking exercise

- adv+ADJ very **extremely, incredibly, really, remarkably, supremely, very** *Above all else we were supremely fit.*
- ▶ rather **averagely, fairly, moderately, pretty** INFORMAL**, quite, reasonably, relatively** *In order to become a diver, you need to be reasonably fit and healthy.*
- ▶ physically **physically** *Applicants must aged 20–65 and be physically fit.*
- ▶ completely **fully, perfectly** *Both of them are fully fit and will line up in the Wolves side tonight.*
- v+ADJ appear fit **feel, look** *The weight started coming off and I was feeling much fitter.*
- ▶ get fit **become, get** *As you get fitter, you'll gain muscle mass, which is more dense than fat.*
- ▶ stay fit **keep, stay** *To keep fit, Shelley takes part in several half marathons each year.*
- and/or **active, athletic, healthy, lean, strong** *I look fit and healthy now, but four years ago everything was different.*

2 of a good enough standard for a purpose or use

- ADJ+n **condition, state** *They examined the mine to determine whether it was in a fit state to be entered with safety or not.*
- ADJ+for **consumption, habitation, purpose, use** *The house has been extensively refurbished to ensure that it is fit for purpose.*

fit N
1 a strong sudden reaction that you cannot control

- adj+N **coughing, giggling, screaming, sneezing** *What causes sneezing fits?*
- v+N **have, throw** *The Secretary General would throw a fit if he said yes.*
- N+of laughter **giggles, hysterics, laughter** *It's*

both inventive and very funny – the audience were in fits of giggles.

- ▶ angry feelings **anger, jealousy, passion, petulance, pique, rage, temper** *A spare racket is a good idea if you are prone to fits of on-court pique.*
- ▶ sad or hopeless feelings **depression, despair, desperation, remorse** *He shot himself in a fit of depression.*

2 whether something is the right size and shape

- adj+N tight **close, snug, tight** *These items have been designed to be a tight fit.*
- ▶ loose or comfortable **comfortable, loose** *A slightly looser fit looks good on everybody.*
- ▶ exact **exact, excellent, good, perfect** *Finally, everything is assembled to ensure a perfect fit prior to despatch.*

fitness N
1 the state of being physically healthy and strong

- adj+N types of fitness **aerobic, cardiorespiratory, cardiovascular, physical** *Whether you want to lose weight or improve your cardiovascular fitness, we have a selection of classes suited to you.*
- ▶ levels of fitness **average, full, peak, reasonable, superior** *She eats a mere 2,000 calories a day when she is at peak fitness.*
- ▶ general **all-round, general, overall** *Doing aerobic exercise can improve your overall fitness.*
- v+N achieve or keep fitness **achieve, gain, maintain** *Circuit training is one of the best ways to achieve all-round fitness.*
- ▶ improve your fitness **boost, enhance, improve, increase** *I am a committed and determined personal trainer, dedicated to improving your fitness.*
- ▶ get your fitness back **get back to, regain, return to** *He was looking at the possibility of a special practice session to continue regaining full fitness.*
- ▶ test someone's fitness **assess, measure, monitor, test** *We would welcome any journalist to come along and test their fitness in the gym challenge.*
- N+n places for improving your fitness **centre, club, facilities, room, studio, suite** *A fitness suite with separate changing facilities will also be introduced.*
- ▶ people who teach fitness **coach, instructor, professional, trainer** *Two qualified fitness instructors manage the gymnasium.*
- ▶ people who are interested in fitness **enthusiast, fanatic** *The needs of sports and fitness enthusiasts are met by the Abbey Fit Centre.*
- ▶ activities for improving fitness **class, programme, regime, training** *We would advise that you always consult your GP before embarking on any fitness regime.*

2 whether someone or something is suitable or of a good enough standard

- v+N **assess, demonstrate, determine, evaluate** *In the UK, the General Medical Council requires that doctors demonstrate their continued fitness to practise by the process of revalidation.*
- N+for **consumption, habitation, purpose, use** *We can give no guarantees as to the fitness for purpose of the information or advice we give.*

fix V

1 make a firm decision about a price or amount, and not allow it to change

- V+n **amount, fee, limit, price, quota, rate, remuneration, rent** *The head of department has discretion to fix the fees charged for work on private contracts.*

2 arrange for something to happen at a particular time or place

- V+n **appointment, date, meeting, time, venue** *If you are happy, we agree a contract with you, and fix some dates.*

> In this meaning, you can use *fix up* in the same way as *fix*: *I'll try and fix up a meeting with the principal.*

fix N

a solution to a problem

- adj+N quick **immediate, instant, quick** *There is no quick fix for the problems facing the car industry.*
- ▶ easy **easy, simple** *The problem is certainly solvable, although not with any simple technological fix.*
- ▶ temporary **short-term, temporary** *The budget was a short-term fix, designed to get the party through the next election.*
- ▶ permanent **permanent** *The repairs are really just an interim measure, pending a more permanent fix.*

fixed ADJ

agreed in advance, and not changing

- ADJ+n price or charge **charge, cost, fee, price, rate, repayment** *At government-run handicraft stores, the prices are fixed.*
- ▶ amount **amount, percentage, quota, sum** *The annual increase in benefits is normally based on a fixed percentage, or on the retail price index (RPI).*
- ▶ income **income, salary** *As I am self-employed, I don't have a fixed salary, and my earnings tend to vary.*
- ▶ period **period, term** *This arrangement allows the banks access to money market rates for a fixed term at a fixed interest rate.*
- ▶ punishment **fine, penalty** *Failure to submit the form will incur an automatic fixed penalty.*

fizzle out PHR VB INFORMAL

gradually fail, become less enthusiastic, or disappear

- n+V events or activities **attack, campaign, career, game, match, season** *While his singing career was fizzling out, his writing career was just beginning.*
- ▶ feelings or relationships **excitement, passion, relationship, romance** *After that relationship fizzled out she took up various office jobs.*
- ▶ protests **fight, protest, revolution, strike** *At last year's conference, small-scale protests fizzled out.*

flag N

a piece of cloth representing a country or organization

- v+N raise a flag **hoist, raise** *Many peals were rung throughout the day and flags were hoisted on all the church towers.*
- ▶ take down a flag **lower** *The U.S. flag over the White*

House along with flags elsewhere was lowered to half-staff.

- ▶ show a flag **display, fly, hang out, unfurl, wave** *We formed in full procession and unfurled our flags once more.*
- N+v **flap, flutter, fly, hang, wave** *At the South Pole, a tent was left behind, with the Norwegian flag flying from a four-metre pole.*
- v+with+N **adorn, bedeck, deck, decorate, drape, festoon** *The train was gaily decorated with flags.*

flag up PHR VB

mention something in order to draw attention to it

- V+n **area of concern, concern, importance, issue, need, problem** *The specific issues flagged up in the meeting included the need for more staff.*

flair N

a way of doing something that shows confidence, skill, and imagination

- adj+N great **great, natural, real, tremendous** *You must possess a natural flair for the subtlety of colour.*
- ▶ in a particular subject or activity **artistic, cinematic, creative, design, entrepreneurial, imaginative, individual, journalistic, theatrical, visual** *They bring a mix of specialist skills and entrepreneurial flair to the project.*
- v+N have or show flair **demonstrate, display, have, possess, show** *You must be able to demonstrate genuine flair and enthusiasm for working within retail.*
- ▶ lack flair **lack** *Jack was well-organized, but he lacked business flair.*
- and/or **creativity, enthusiasm, expertise, imagination, originality, panache, passion, skill, style, talent** *The brief allowed students to show imagination and flair in their work.*

flame N

the brightly burning gas that comes from a fire

- adj+N not covered **naked** *Never eat, smoke or use naked flames when carrying out procedures involving these kits.*
- ▶ strong or bright **bright, fierce, roaring** *Five fire crews battled fierce flames for almost an hour.*
- v+N light a flame **ignite, light** *I was there in Atlanta when he lit the Olympic flame.*
- ▶ put out a flame **douse, extinguish, quench, smother** *We had quite a hectic time extinguishing the flames.*
- ▶ make flames burn more strongly **feed, fuel** *He fed the young flame with wisps of dry grass and with the tiniest dry twigs.*
- ▶ when flames start burning strongly **burst into, erupt in, go up in** *The wooden stairs of the house had burst into flame.*
- N+v burn **burn, consume sth, crackle, flicker, leap, lick sth, rise, roar, shoot** *A policeman had seen flames leaping through the roof, and raised the alarm.* • *We saw flames shooting out of the back of the plane.*

Usage Except when talking about a single flame (for example, the flame of a candle), **flame** is usually used in the plural.

▸ spread **engulf sth, spread** *A family was forced to flee when flames engulfed the historic pub where they lived.*

▸ die down or go out **die, die down, go out, subside** *The flames subsided, and smoke billowed from the smouldering brands.*

flare V

when fighting, disagreements etc get worse or more violent

● n+V trouble or fighting **conflict, tension, trouble, violence** *Five years later he was forced to flee the country on horseback when trouble flared between the rebels and the government.*

▸ disagreements **dispute, row** *Fresh rows flared up in the countdown to the talks.*

▸ anger **anger, temper** *John felt his temper flare once again.*

In all these meanings, you can use **flare up** in the same way as **flare**: *Since the end of the war, tensions have flared up periodically.*

flash N

1 a bright light that appears for short time

● adj+N **blinding, brief, bright, brilliant, intense, momentary, quick, sudden, vivid** *A vivid orange flash, followed immediately by another, appeared over the park.*

● N+of **fire, flame, light, lightning, sunlight** *There was a flash of bright light and thunder rumbled in the distance.*

2 a sudden understanding, idea, or emotion

● adj+N **brief, momentary, occasional, odd, quick, sudden** *The writing shows occasional flashes of his trademark ironic humor.*

● N+of of understanding **insight, intuition, recognition** *By some flash of intuition, I knew what he intended.*

▸ of anger **anger, temper** *For a moment his face showed a flash of anger, but this soon melted away into a broad smile.*

▸ of cleverness **brilliance, genius, humour, inspiration, wit** *Previous albums have all shown flashes of brilliance but have been uneven.* ● *There were flashes of humour and outbursts of anger.*

flavour N

1 the particular taste that food or drink has

● adj+N mild **delicate, mellow, mild, subtle** *Compared to other beans, Arabica gives a more delicate flavour.*

▸ strong **intense, pungent, rich, strong, tangy** *Bay leaves can be used whole, cut up or ground to give a strong and pungent flavour.*

▸ good **delicious, fine, good** *The flesh is said to be very sweet, with a delicious flavour.*

▸ spicy **aromatic, peppery, spicy** *Since there is a lot of water, put in lots of herbs, for that aromatic flavour.*

▸ unusual **distinctive, exotic, unique** *Make sure the fruit is really ripe to get the benefit of the wonderful exotic flavours.*

▸ tasting of a particular thing **creamy, earthy, fruity, gamey, nutty, smoky** *Spelt is an ancient variety of wheat with a delicious, nutty flavour.*

● v+N have a particular flavour **have** *The fruit has a good flavour and has a slightly orange-yellow smooth skin.*

▸ give flavour to something **add, bring out, give, impart** *Add extra flavour to potato salad and rice dishes with crushed fennel seeds.*

▸ keep flavour **preserve, retain** *When lightly steamed, the leaves retain their flavour and texture well.*

▸ improve flavour **complement, enhance, improve, intensify** *Look for good-quality flour, as this will improve the flavour of the rolls*

▸ mix flavours **blend, combine, mix** *Cook over low heat for 2 to 3 minutes to blend the flavours.*

2 a particular quality that is typical of something

● adj+N **authentic, exotic, international, strong, unique** *The lively street market has a strong continental flavour.*

● v+N **add, capture, convey, have, retain** *The track and pit area were carefully restored for the film, to capture the original flavour of motor racing in the 1930s.* ● *The titles given to these myths convey the general flavour.*

flaw N

a mistake or fault in something

● adj+N serious **basic, big, critical, fatal, fundamental, inherent, major, serious, significant** *Uncertainty of outcome is often a fatal flaw in a research proposal.*

▸ small **minor, slight** *There are still some minor flaws but overall this is a great picture.*

▸ types of flaw **logical, methodological, structural, technical** *Most of the existing trials have serious methodological flaws.*

▸ obvious **glaring, obvious** *Are there glaring architectural flaws that I've just missed?*

▸ that destroys someone **tragic** *He is a great man brought down by a tragic flaw.*

● n+N in a system **design, security, software** *Unfortunately, this study had serious design flaws.*

▸ in a person's character **character, personality** *Traits that some might call personality flaws can also be seen as a source of strength.*

● v+N find a flaw **discover, find, identify, spot** INFORMAL, **uncover** *Always quick to spot any flaws or problems, he is equally ready to provide solutions.*

▸ reveal a flaw **demonstrate, expose, highlight, point out, point to, reveal** *Critics have pointed to flaws in the technology used in the cards.*

▸ fix a flaw **address, correct, fix** INFORMAL *Why can't programmers just fix the flaws these viruses exploit?*

● N+in idea or argument **argument, logic, reasoning, theory** *There are a number of flaws in your argument that are based on this same misconception.*

▸ method or system **approach, design, methodology, plan, process, system** *Their review has identified serious flaws in the methodology of the animal tests.*

flawed ADJ

1 not satisfactory or successful, because of something wrong or something missing

- adv+ADJ very **badly, deeply, fatally, fundamentally, hopelessly, inherently, seriously** *The US government also condemned the elections as 'fundamentally flawed'.*
- ▶ in a particular way **conceptually, methodologically, scientifically** *Scientifically flawed research is immoral, and could in no way be considered legal.*
- ADJ+n thinking **argument, assumption, concept, logic, premise, reasoning, thinking** *He has little mercy on flawed arguments, wherever they originate.*
- ▶ process or system **analysis, methodology, model, process, system** *The reviews sometimes reveal poor quality of analysis, or flawed methodology.*
- ▶ suggestion **policy, proposal** *I urge government to reassess these flawed proposals before it is too late.*

2 a flawed person has serious faults in their character

- ADJ+n **character, genius, hero** *He may have been a flawed genius – but a genius nonetheless.*

flexibility N

the ability to make changes or deal with a changing situation

- adj+N great **considerable, great, tremendous** *Although this organization structure provides you with great flexibility, it is quite complex.*
- ▶ more **added, additional, greater, increased, more** *A bespoke itinerary very often costs no more than an escorted group tour, and will offer more flexibility.*
- ▶ total **complete, maximum, total, ultimate** *I am self-employed, which gives me maximum flexibility in organising my schedule around my other interests.*
- ▶ the best **unparalleled, unrivalled** *Internet shopping gives you the unrivalled flexibility and speed that is sometimes required when making a purchase.*
- ▶ enough or necessary **enough, necessary, sufficient** *Employees should be allowed sufficient flexibility to organise their own work.*
- ▶ built-in **built-in, inbuilt, inherent** *Modern aircraft have an inherent flexibility that allows them to be used in different roles.*
- v+N have or show flexibility **be characterized by, demonstrate, have** *It is an approach to learning that is characterised by flexibility, in the sense that it can be implemented in a variety of ways.*
- ▶ not have flexibility **lack** *An electronic system would lack the flexibility to deal with errors in a human organization.*
- ▶ give flexibility **afford (sb/sth), allow (for), ensure, give (sb/sth), introduce, offer (sb/sth), provide (sb/sth with)** *Our members should be afforded some flexibility within the proposed schemes.*
- ▶ increase flexibility **add, add to, enhance, improve, increase, maximize** *We want to increase the flexibility of work and loosen the traditional ties between work and location.*
- ▶ need or want flexibility **need, require, want** *You need a clear plan, but you also need flexibility.*

flexible ADJ

able to make or deal with changes

- adv+ADJ very **extremely, highly, incredibly, infinitely, remarkably, very** *Workers support each other in highly flexible teams.*
- ▶ completely **completely, entirely, fully, totally** *This is a totally flexible training programme that our homeworkers can fit in around their existing commitments.*
- ▶ rather **fairly, pretty** INFORMAL, **reasonably** *As I am self-employed, I can be flexible about the hours I work.*
- ▶ enough/not enough **insufficiently, sufficiently** *The LLM programme is sufficiently flexible to make it appropriate for many different career paths.*
- ▶ in a way that nothing else is **uniquely** *Our employees are offered a uniquely flexible working environment, with home working positively encouraged.*
- ▶ as part of something's basic nature **inherently** *Timetables are largely irrelevant in the more informal and inherently flexible home education setting.*
- ADJ+n activity **learning, working** *Flexible working may be essential for employees who have a disabled child.*
- ▶ system or attitude **approach, arrangement, attitude, programme, solution, system** *He has a positive flexible approach to his work and is committed and hardworking.*
- ▶ people working **workforce** *Business looks to create a more skilled and flexible workforce.*
- ▶ and/or **adaptable, cost-effective, efficient, innovative, responsive, versatile** *This service is adaptable and flexible to meet the needs of very diverse individuals.*

flight N

a journey on a plane

- adj+N long-distance **long-distance, long-haul** *Hub airports are mainly used by travellers making long-haul flights in large aircraft.*
- ▶ short-distance **short-haul** *High-speed rail could be used as an alternative to short-haul flights.*
- ▶ within a country **domestic, internal** *There are numerous internal flights within Croatia.*
- ▶ between countries **intercontinental, international, transatlantic, transcontinental** *There have been a series of cancellations of international flights bound for the United States.*
- ▶ direct **direct, non-stop** *Icelandair operates non-stop flights to Reykjavik.*
- ▶ to a place and back **return, round-trip** *Expect to pay around £390 for a return flight in February.*
- ▶ going to/returning from a place **homeward, inbound, incoming, outbound, return** *We depart from Santander Airport for our return flight to London.*
- ▶ after another flight **connecting, onward** *After lunch, transfer to the airport for your onward flight.*
- ▶ cheap **bargain, cheap, low-cost, no-frills** *Low-cost flights have led to heavy air traffic increases.*
- ▶ regular **regular, scheduled** *A number of new scheduled flights have also started this summer.*
- ▶ provided by a holiday company **charter** *Thomas Cook Airlines operate charter flights to Florida.*

▸ lasting a particular time **one-hour, four-hour, etc**
*She had just stepped off a ten-hour flight from Los
Angeles.*

● v+N book a flight **arrange, be booked on, book
(on), get** *Please book a flight with an arrival time
of between 8.30 – 9.30am.*

▸ catch a flight **catch, get, take, travel on** *We caught
an early morning flight back to London.*

▸ not catch a flight **miss** *He was almost certainly
going to miss his flight.*

▸ get on a flight **board, get on** *He can't convince her
to stay, and she boards the flight.*

▸ book too many people onto a flight **overbook** *Our
flight was overbooked, so we volunteered to go on
the next one.*

▸ tell an airline you will definitely be travelling on
a flight **reconfirm** *Do I need to reconfirm each flight
shown on my itinerary before departure?*

● N+v **arrive, be bound for, depart, land, operate**
*Charter flights operate from some UK airports to
both Girona and Barcelona.*

flood v

1 to cover something with water

● adv+V partly **partially, partly** *A heavy shower
partially flooded the road leading to the Post Office.*

▸ badly or completely **badly, completely, severely**
*The footpath in Wellworth Park has been badly
flooded in recent weeks.*

▸ often **frequently, often, regularly** *Many villages were
regularly flooded in winter.*

▸ sometimes **occasionally, periodically** *This part of
the moors was periodically flooded by sea tides up
to 400 years ago.*

▸ always **permanently** *The Barrage will permanently
flood the estuary, in order to hide unsightly mudflats
and create a lake.*

▸ at particular times of the year **seasonally** *There
are plans for houses designed to float on seasonally
flooded areas.*

2 to fill a place with a bright light

● n+V **light, moonlight, sunlight** *There is plenty of
natural light flooding the apartments.*

● V+with **daylight, light, moonlight, sunlight,
sunshine** *The market square, flooded with sunshine
and framed by clear blue skies, looked beautiful.*

Usage ***Flood*** is usually <u>passive</u> in these
combinations.

3 to arrive in large numbers

● n+V people **immigrants, refugees, tourists**
Refugees were flooding over the border.

▸ things **donations, emails, imports, memories,
messages, money, tributes** *Memories flooded back
of that time in London in 1988.*

● V+with **calls, complaints, messages, requests** *After
the programme, the organization was flooded with
calls from people wanting to help.*

Usage ***Flood*** is usually <u>passive</u> in these
combinations.

flood N

1 a lot of water covering a previously dry area

● adj+N bad **bad, great, heavy, huge, major, serious,
severe** *In 1882 the flood was especially severe and
one man drowned.*

▸ very bad **catastrophic, devastating, disastrous,
massive, terrible** *Devastating floods in the rainy
season washed away most of the year's rice harvest.*

▸ sudden **flash, sudden** *Be wary of flash floods in
mountain ranges where streams can suddenly turn
into 5m of water with almost no warning.*

● v+N cause a flood **bring, cause, lead to, result in,
trigger, unleash** *Floods triggered by torrential rain
have killed at least 24 people.*

▸ survive a flood **survive, withstand** *The bridge has
stubbornly survived floods which have demolished
other structures.*

▸ experience a flood **be devastated by, be hit by, be
ravaged by, experience, suffer** *Parts of the Czech
Republic have been devastated by floods.*

● N+v get less **recede, subside** *When the flood
subsides, the Nile Valley is thoroughly fertilised and
crops may be grown there.*

▸ happen **come, rise** *Floods were rising in the
Dortmund area.*

When a river has a lot more water than usual in it,
you can say it is ***in flood***: *The river was in flood and
things were starting to look dangerous.*

▸ take someone or something away **sweep sb/sth
away, wash sb/sth away** *Smallwood Bridge was
swept away by a flood.*

2 a large number of people or things that arrive at
the same time

● adj+N **great, unprecedented, veritable** *Over the
last twenty years a veritable flood of reports on racism
against black and ethnic staff has been published.*

● v+N cause a flood of things or people **bring,
cause, prompt, provoke, trigger, unleash** *Scenes of
sex and violence prompted a flood of complaints to
the BBC.*

▸ stop a flood of people or things **prevent, stem,
stop** *Law enforcement agencies are struggling to
stem the flood of illegal narcotics coming into the
United States.*

● N+of people **immigrants, migrants, refugees,
tourists** *The country was unable to cope with the
flood of refugees.*

▸ letters or messages **applications, calls, claims,
complaints, emails, letters, requests, spam** *His
article provoked a flood of emails.*

▸ products **imports** *Indian coffee prices have collapsed
under pressure from a flood of cheap imports.*

▸ memories **memories** *Your message brought back a
flood of memories which I thought were long
suppressed!*

flout v

to deliberately refuse to obey a rule or custom

● adv+V openly or deliberately **blatantly, clearly,
deliberately, flagrantly, openly** *Many overseas
companies are openly flouting the law and attempting
to fix the prices at which their products are sold in
Britain.*

▶continually or regularly **consistently, constantly, continually, frequently, persistently, regularly, repeatedly, routinely, systematically** *Laws on the size of fish catches are routinely flouted.*

▶by many people **widely** *Speed limits are widely flouted by drivers.*

● V+n law or rule **ban, guidelines, law, principle, regulations, rule** *We intend to clamp down on those who flout the law.*

▶normal behaviour **convention, expectations, norms, stereotype** *Mary is a girl in a man's sport, flouting convention to achieve her ambitions.*

▶authority **authority** *They can imprison anyone who flouts their authority.*

flow N

a continuous movement of liquid, traffic, or people; a supply of something that continues without stopping

● adj+N constant **constant, continuous, steady, uninterrupted** *The brain is dependent on a continuous flow of blood.*

▶in one/both directions **one-way, two-way** *We need a two-way flow of information and ideas.*

▶not blocked **free, smooth** *The air cleaner ensures a smooth flow of air in the carburettors.*

● n+N of a substance or object **aid, air, blood, cash, energy, gas, heat, lava, river, traffic, water** *Blood flow to the finger is faster than it is to other areas of the body.*

▶of ideas or an activity **data, information, work** *Using the most appropriate work flow processes and communication technology will speed up the project.*

● v+N stop, reduce, or block the flow **block, disrupt, impede, interrupt, obstruct, reduce, restrict, staunch, stem, stop** *A dam is built across a river to restrict the flow of water.*

▶keep, improve, or increase the flow **ease, facilitate, improve, increase, maintain, stimulate** *The arrangement will facilitate a free flow of information to all parties.*

▶control the flow **control, manage, regulate** *Chakras regulate the flow of energy around our energy system.*

flow V

1 to move somewhere smoothly and continuously; to continue being supplied without stopping

● adv+V **directly, easily, fast, freely, gently, nicely, smoothly, steadily** *There was no congestion and the traffic always flowed freely.*

2 to follow in an easy natural way

● adv+V **easily, effortlessly, freely, logically, naturally, nicely, seamlessly, smoothly** *Your conclusion must flow naturally from the arguments in your essay.*

flower N

the attractive coloured part of a plant, or a plant that has these

● adj+N wild/not wild **garden, wild** *The park is full of wild flowers, and home to over 60 species of birds.*

▶with a beautiful appearance or smell **beautiful, bright, colourful, delicate, fragrant, lovely** *It*

flowers over a long period from late summer into autumn, and its flowers are fragrant.

▶used for decoration **cut, fresh** *Log fires burn throughout the winter and fresh flowers add colour and warmth.*

● v+N produce flowers **bear, carry, have, produce** *In summer the plant has small white flowers that are followed by bright red berries.*

▶grow flowers **cultivate, grow, plant** *We endeavour to grow flowers that attract butterflies.*

▶make flowers fertile **pollinate** *Hummingbirds have an important role in pollinating flowers.*

● N+v **appear, bloom, come, fade, grow, open** *Under his skilled care, vegetables thrived and flowers grew in profusion.*

flu N

a common infectious disease causing a fever and weakness

● adj+N **avian, bird, pandemic, seasonal, swine** *Tests showed that 500 people had been infected with swine flu.*

● v+N get flu **catch, contract, develop, get** *If you do catch flu, stay home.*

▶have flu **be in bed with, be infected with, fight, have, suffer from** *At first I thought I had the flu.*

▶spread or cause flu **cause, spread** *Flu is spread by coughs and sneezes from people who are already infected with the virus.*

▶prevent flu **immunize sb against, prevent, protect sb against, vaccinate sb against** *Will you get your kids vaccinated against the flu?*

● N+n injection or medicine **immunization, injection, jab, shot, vaccination, vaccine** *Does the flu vaccine work?*

▶when a lot of people have flu **epidemic, outbreak, pandemic** *We cannot prevent a flu pandemic, but we can reduce its impact.*

▶virus **bug, virus** *How are bird flu viruses different from human flu viruses?*

▶symptoms **symptoms** *I had flu symptoms and was feeling a bit down.*

To describe symptoms that are typical of flu you can also talk about **flu-like symptoms**: *Not having the drug often makes the user feel ill with flu-like symptoms.*

● n+of+N type **form, strain, type** *Outbreaks of various strains of bird flu are regularly detected around the world.*

▶case **bout, case, dose, touch** *After a bout of flu, you can feel tired for a couple of weeks.*

▶when flu affects many people **outbreak, spread** *The government has made plans for dealing with the outbreak of flu in the UK.*

fluctuate V

to change frequently

● adv+V very much **considerably, dramatically, enormously, greatly, markedly, rapidly, significantly, widely, wildly** *The weather that day fluctuated wildly between extremes.*

▶slightly **slightly, somewhat** *The numbers, whilst fluctuating slightly from year to year, show no sign of decline.*

▶ in an irregular way **erratically, randomly, unpredictably** *Numbers of applicants fluctuate unpredictably from one year to another.*
▶ always **constantly, continually** *The price of oil on world markets fluctuates constantly.*
▶ according to the time of year **seasonally** *Groundwater levels fluctuate seasonally in response to changes in rainfall.*

● n+V **currency, income, inflation, level, market, membership, number, population, price, rate, temperature, unemployment, value, weight** *Customers should be aware that the exchange rate fluctuates daily.*

fluctuation N
frequent changes in amount, value, or level

● adj+N large or rapid **considerable, dramatic, extreme, large, marked, rapid, wide, wild** *Fairly extreme temperature fluctuations can occur in a conservatory.*
▶ small **minor, small, tiny** *The share value has risen promisingly with some minor fluctuation.*
▶ sudden or irregular **random, sudden** *I was warned that sudden fluctuations in alcohol consumption could be fatal.*
▶ constant or repeated **constant, cyclical, periodic** *Sound is a periodic fluctuation of air pressure.*
▶ according to the time of year **seasonal** *Growth in this sector has not been continuous, even when seasonal fluctuations are taken into account.*
▶ natural **natural** *The current warming of our planet has exceeded the natural fluctuations.*
▶ types of fluctuation **climatic, economic, hormonal, statistical, thermal** *Hormonal fluctuations may cause headache or migraine.*

● n+N **climate, currency, exchange rate, price, temperature** *The price is subject to currency fluctuations.*

● N+in level or number **level, number, rate, value** *What might be behind these large fluctuations in crime levels?*
● climate or weather **climate, humidity, rainfall, temperature** *Dramatic fluctuations in climates around the world have led to increased disruption in weather patterns.*
▶ economic factors **demand, income, market, output, price, supply** *The country's economy is vulnerable to fluctuations in the price of oil.*

flurry N
1 a short period of activity or emotion

● adj+N **brief, initial, minor, occasional, small, sudden** *There may be an initial flurry of interest in your property when it first goes on the market for sale.*
● v+N **bring, cause, create, produce, prompt, provoke, spark, trigger, unleash** *This hostage crisis sparked a flurry of activity amongst politicians and peace campaigners.*
● N+of activity **action, activity** *Watching the flurry of activity at our bird table every morning is a charming way to begin the day.*
▶ excitement or interest **excitement, interest, publicity, speculation** *There was a brief flurry of excitement when the gifts were first discovered.*

▶ events **announcements, attacks, lawsuits** *Landmines and a flurry of attacks killed 12 soldiers last week.*
▶ communications **announcements, calls, correspondence, emails, letters** *I sent a frantic flurry of emails.*

2 a small amount of something blown around

● adj+N **brief, light, occasional, small, sudden** *You can see the frost and a light flurry of snow in one or two of the photos.*
● N+of **feathers, rain, sleet, snow, snowflakes** *It was a cold January day, with flurries of snow in the air.*

flush V
if someone flushes, their face becomes red

● V+adj **crimson, pink, red** *Signs of overheating are: ears flushing red and rapid shallow breathing.*
● adv+V **angrily, deeply, guiltily, a little, slightly** *'I'll be glad to be of service, sir,' he said, flushing slightly.*
● V+with **anger, embarrassment, enthusiasm, excitement, joy, pleasure, pride** *I felt my face flushing with anger as I was forced to listen to his comments.*

> You can also say that someone or something **is flushed** with anger, excitement etc: *She was flushed with pride as she went up to receive her prize.*

focus V
to give attention, effort etc to a particular subject

● adv+V mainly **especially, largely, mainly, mostly, particularly, predominantly, primarily, principally** *This project will focus primarily on scientific and technical data.*
▶ a lot **firmly, heavily, strongly** *Most dance instructors focus heavily on the teaching of moves.*
▶ only **entirely, exclusively, purely, solely, specifically, totally** *It is not enough to focus solely on performance – price is also important.*
▶ on one or a few things **clearly, closely, narrowly, sharply, tightly** *Many researchers are dissatisfied with narrowly-focussed research.*
▶ more and more **increasingly** *Cultural activity in the 21st century is increasingly focussing on commerce.*
▶ in a particular way **clinically, commercially, vocationally** *This is a commercially-focussed company, but it's not just about making money.*

> Usage **Focus** is always passive in these combinations: *The courses for nurses are clinically-focussed.* ● *a commercially-focussed business*

● V+n **attention, efforts, mind, thoughts** *It is important that we focus our efforts on change-management issues.*
● n+V **article, book, conference, debate, module, paper, project, research, seminar, session, study, work** *The conference focusses on public-sector reform in the UK.*

focus N
special attention or concentration on something, or the thing being concentrated on

● adj+N main **central, core, key, main, major,**

primary, prime, principal *The main focus of the visit was for the team to learn the techniques of caving and mountaineering.* ● *The role of women in the workplace was a primary focus for our discussions.*

▶ only **exclusive, sole** *Give your child some 'quality time' when he is the sole focus of your attention.*

▶ strong or clear **clear, intense, sharp, strong** *In her book, the issue of food safety is given a sharp focus.*

▶ special or important **important, particular, real, special, specific** *This year's film festival has a special focus on the Nigerian film industry.*

▶ more **greater, increased, more, renewed** *There should be a greater focus placed during teacher training courses on identifying children with learning difficulties.*

▶ on a small number of things **narrow, tight** *There has been a very narrow focus to the research, concentrating mainly upon the health needs of a small group of people.*

▶ on a large number of things **broad** *The report has too broad a focus to deal with all our questions.*

▶ types of focus **geographical, international, regional, strategic, vocational** *Many of our courses have a vocational focus.*

● v+N move the focus **change, move, redirect, shift, switch** *People should shift their focus away from material possessions to personal fulfilment.*

▶ keep the focus **maintain** *Maintaining our focus on value is crucial to the success of the company.*

▶ put the focus on something **bring sth into, place, put, throw sth into** *The case brings into focus the importance of patients being able to make fully informed decisions about their care and treatment.*

▶ come into focus **come into** *Various areas of disagreement have come into focus.*

▶ give something a clearer focus **sharpen** *We are revising and sharpening the focus of our business plan.*

▶ broaden the focus **broaden, widen** *I chose to broaden the focus of my research to make it more applicable to a wider audience.*

▶ narrow the focus **narrow** *According to one theory, a nation should narrow its focus of activity, abandoning certain industries while developing those in which it has the greatest comparative advantage.*

● N+v **be on, change, remain on, shift, turn to** *In the third year of the course the focus shifts to contemporary literature.*

● N+of attention or interest **attention, concern, interest** *During the post-war period, the cost of air travel became the focus of attention and prices fell.*

▶ activity **activity** *This area was a focus of activity in the Bronze Age.*

▶ discussion **debate, discussion** *Where these homeless people are to be housed will be the focus of debate in the coming months.*

▶ investigation or study **article, inquiry, investigation, paper, project, research, study, work** *A prime focus of genetic research is on crops intended for animals.*

fog N

thick cloud close to the ground

● adj+N thick **dense, heavy, impenetrable, thick** *The fog was so thick you couldn't see anything.*

▶ moving around **swirling** *The mist around the town*

had thickened into a dense swirling fog that drifted across the surrounding countryside.

▶ cold **cold, freezing** *The airport was closed because of freezing fog.*

▶ in some places but not others **patchy** *It will be a bright day with plenty of sunshine for most places and some patchy fog.*

▶ near the coast **coastal, sea** *The top of the cliffs is shrouded in coastal fog.*

▶ continuing **persistent** *Persistent fog can be a maritime hazard from May to September.*

● N+v appear **close in, come in, descend, roll in** *A thick fog descended.*

▶ disappear **clear, lift** *By now most of the fog had lifted and the sun was getting a bit warmer.*

▶ cover something **cloak, cover, envelop, shroud, surround** *A thick white fog cloaks the rooftops.*

▶ get thicker/less thick **thicken, thin** *The fog thickened and visibility was reduced to fifty metres or so.*

▶ be present **hang, linger** *The fog hung in the air like cotton wool.*

● n+of+N **bank, blanket, layer, patch, veil** *The rain has stopped and a thick blanket of fog has settled over the river.*

foil v

to prevent someone from doing something they are trying to do

● V+n **attack, attempt, plan, plot, robbery** *The security services have foiled a serious attempt to commit a terrorist attack in this county.*

folk N INFORMAL

people in general

● adj+N ordinary **common, everyday, ordinary** *Roseanne proved that ordinary folks could create extraordinary comedy.*

▶ old/young **elderly, old, young** *Most of the old folk stayed indoors in bad weather.*

▶ good or friendly **decent, fine, friendly, good, honest, kind, nice** *Most of the people in the neighbourhood are decent folk.*

▶ from the country/city **city, country, farming, rural** *Country folk were encouraged to come to the city.*

follow v

1 to walk, drive etc behind someone

● adv+V closely **closely** *A neighbour saw him dashing into the Smiths' house, followed closely by Emily.*

▶ quickly **quickly, speedily, swiftly** *The betrayed husband swiftly followed the couple and found them in a hotel.*

▶ obediently **dutifully, meekly, obediently** *Some dogs obediently follow their owners.*

2 to happen or come after something else

● adv+V soon or immediately **closely, directly, immediately, quickly, shortly, soon, swiftly** *There was a small explosion, followed immediately by a larger one.*

▶ naturally or logically **inevitably, logically, naturally** *Each section follows logically from the previous one, telling a story, rather than being a collections of facts.*

▶ if needed or wanted **optionally** *The final school qualification is split into two parts, AS followed optionally by A2* .

3 be true as a result of something else

● adv+V **automatically, logically, necessarily** *It doesn't necessarily follow that clever parents have clever children.*

4 to obey an order or take someone's advice

● adv+V closely **carefully, closely, exactly, faithfully, rigidly, rigorously, strictly** *If you faithfully follow the procedures in this article there is almost nothing that can go wrong.*

To say that someone follows something closely, you can also say that they follow it *to the letter*: *I followed the recipe to the letter, but still my cake sank in the middle.*

▶ not closely **broadly, roughly** *The policy set out below broadly follows their recommendations.*

▶ without thinking **blindly, slavishly, without question** *Their experience is recorded, not to be followed blindly, but in the hope that it may help someone else as they think through the issues.*

▶ obediently **dutifully, meekly, obediently** *Field marshals dutifully followed his orders on when and where armies should move.*

● V+n rules or orders **command, orders, rules** *Many people do not follow basic hygiene rules.*

▶ advice **advice, guidelines, recommendation, suggestion** *By following these five simple guidelines you could help reduce climate change.*

▶ instructions **directions, instructions, recipe** *Open the application and follow the on-screen instructions.*

▶ correct way of doing something **procedure** *If you have sent us a complaint we will follow our complaints procedure.*

5 to do the same as someone else

● V+n follow someone's example **example, lead** *Those who possess nuclear weapons can no longer condemn other countries for following their example and developing their own.*

You can also say that someone *follows suit*: *They began to offer takeaway food, and other restaurants followed suit.*

▶ follow usual behaviour **convention, fashion, precedent, tradition** *People are given the freedom to take risks and not just follow convention.*

follower N

someone who believes what a system of ideas teaches

● adj+N faithful **close, dedicated, devoted, devout, faithful, loyal, true** *At the funeral he preached to an audience of devoted followers.*

▶ enthusiastic **ardent, avid, enthusiastic, fanatical, keen** *Tom Cruise is an avid follower of Scientology.*

following N

people who support or admire a person or organization

● adj+N large **big, considerable, large, sizeable, strong, substantial** *The band soon had a strong following of loyal fans wherever they went.*

▶ very large **enormous, huge, massive, tremendous** *Manchester United is a big club with a huge following.*

▶ loyal **dedicated, devoted, faithful, loyal** *The market was established in the 1930s and still attracts a loyal following of shoppers.*

▶ enthusiastic **enthusiastic, fanatical** *There are examples where a TV series or a film has created its own fanatical following.*

▶ in many countries **international, worldwide** *The magazine has a worldwide following and is well respected in and outside the art world.*

▶ within a small group of people **cult** *Reviled by critics, Highlander inspired a cult following.*

● v+N have a following **command, have** *He commanded a huge following both in his own lifetime and down to the present day.*

▶ get a following **achieve, acquire, amass, attract, build up, find, gain, get, inspire** *The system has achieved a worldwide following through reputation, excellence of product and amazing results.*

fond ADJ

1 happy or loving

● ADJ+n memory **memory, recollections, remembrance, reminiscence** *I have many fond memories of my time at university.*

▶ goodbye **farewell** *It was time to say a fond farewell to the Japanese students.*

▶ love **affection, love** *They still talk about the festival with fond affection.*

▶ action or expression **embrace, smile** *'I think you've been dreaming, Daniel,' Janet said with a fond smile.*

2 that you want very much to happen

● ADJ+n **dream, hope, wish** *It is my fond hope that he will grow up to be a healthy young man.*

fool N

someone who does not behave sensibly

● adj+N when criticizing someone in a gentle way **old, poor** *Oh, don't listen to that old fool.*

▶ believing something that is not true **deluded, gullible, misguided, naive** *He says that people who think fishing is cruel are misguided fools.*

▶ stupid or crazy **crazy, mad, silly, stupid** *What crazy fool would bring a van onto the beach?*

▶ complete **complete, utter** *John reacted in a way that made him seem a complete fool.*

▶ sentimental **sentimental** *Being a sentimental old fool, I cried all the way through the film.*

▶ not good at something **bumbling, incompetent** *How could such a bumbling fool get to this position?*

● v+N behave like a fool **act (like), behave like, grin like, play, talk like** *He was always playing the fool.*

▶ seem like a fool **feel (like), look (like), sound like** *I would have looked a fool if I'd been wrong.*

▶ say or think that someone is a fool **call sb, take sb for** *I get the horrible feeling I'm being taken for a fool.*

foot 300

When you **make a fool out of someone**, you deliberately make them seem stupid: *I felt that they had made a fool out of me at the interview.* When you **make a fool of yourself**, you make yourself seem stupid by behaving in a silly or embarassing way: *He made a fool of himself by turning up drunk to a TV chat show.*

foot N
the part of your body at the end of your leg

- adj+N uncomfortable or injured **aching, blistered, numb, sore, swollen, tired, weary** *My feet were sore from walking so far.*
▸ sweating or smelling **smelly, sweaty** *People who go barefoot most of the time don't suffer from smelly feet.*
▸ without shoes or socks on **bare** *I sat at the water's edge just letting the sea flow over my bare feet.*
▸ at the back/front of an animal **back, fore, front, hind** *The dog was standing up on its hind feet.*
▸ of a particular shape or appearance **big, broad, dainty, little, narrow, small, tiny, wide** *The children's feet were very broad and it was difficult finding shoes to fit them.*

- v+N make a noise with your foot or feet **stamp, stomp, tap** *Elizabeth pouted and argued and stamped her feet.*
▸ move your foot or feet **dangle, flex, kick, shuffle, stick out** *They shuffled their feet slowly in time to the music.*

- N+v **ache, hurt, swell** *I took my shoes off because my feet were aching.*

When people's feet are hurting, they often use the informal expression: **My feet are killing me**: *I'll have to sit down. My feet are killing me.*

foothold N
a position from which you can become more successful [always singular]

- adj+N strong **good, secure, significant, solid, stable, strong** *Britain wanted to establish a strong foothold in the Eastern Mediterranean.*

- v+N have a foothold **have** *Britain no longer has a strong foothold in the region.*
▸ gain or keep a foothold **establish, find, gain, get, maintain, obtain, secure, take** *When anger and fear have gained a foothold, they can stay quietly in the background for a long time.*
▸ give someone or something a foothold **give sb/sth, provide (sb/sth with)** *Try not to give the opposing team a foothold in the game.*
▸ lose a foothold **lose** *The company's results show it is losing its foothold on the domestic market.*

footing N
1 a firm position for your feet on a surface [always singular]

- adj+N **firm, secure, solid, sound, stable** *The surface is a combination of sand and plastic granules, to provide both a soft landing and a secure footing for the horses.*

- v+N lose your footing **lose, miss** *She lost her footing and fell, injuring her arm.*

▸ get or keep your footing **find, get, keep, regain** *It snowed until just before the race and the athletes were unable to keep their footing even when wearing spikes.*

2 the basic conditions in which something operates; the position of one person or group in relation to another [always singular]

- adj+N strong **firm, secure, solid, sound, stable, strong, sure** *He intends to set the nation's economy on a firmer footing.*
▸ equal **equal, even, level, same** *All staff should be treated on an equal footing for health and safety.*
▸ formal or correct **formal, proper** *Ollie reasoned that this was just the time to put their relationship on a proper footing.*
▸ permanent or continuing **permanent, sustainable** *Community banking is helping local traders to organise their finances and put their lives on a more sustainable footing.*
▸ types of footing **commercial, financial, legal, scientific, statutory, war** *Ministers were reluctant to put the army on a war footing.*

- v+N have a footing **be on, compete on, have, stand on** *I would be interested to know if it is illogical research or if it has a solid footing.*

Compete on is always used with one of the adjectives **equal, same, even**, or **level**: *Women are encouraged to achieve and compete on an equal footing with men.* ● *Companies can't afford to compete on a level footing.*

▸ get or keep a footing **establish, find, gain, get, get back on, keep, obtain, regain** *The tour enabled him to pay off his debts and regain his financial footing.*
▸ give someone or something a footing **get sth back on, give sb/sth, place sb/sth on, provide (sb/sth with), put sb/sth on** *He believes that the sanctions against drugs in sport should be put on a legal footing.*

footstep N
the sound your feet make when you walk [usually plural]

- adj+N loud **heavy, loud** *I could hear heavy footsteps coming up the stairs.*
▸ quiet **light, quiet, soft** *What attracted her attention was hearing soft footsteps going up the stairs.*
▸ quick **hasty, hurried** *They had only gone a few metres when there was a sound of hurried footsteps behind them.*

- N+v make a noise **crunch, echo, ring, sound** *She could hear her footsteps ringing on the cobbles and the pounding of her breath.*
▸ approach **approach, come** *As they talked, they heard footsteps approaching.*
▸ move further away **die away, fade away, recede, retreat** *Then I heard him walk away, his footsteps receding.*

footwork N
1 the way you move your feet in dancing or sport

- adj+N complicated **complicated, fancy, intricate** *Each player in control of the ball does some fancy footwork before passing it on to another.*
▸ quick or skilful **dazzling, deft, excellent, fast, neat,**

niftyINFORMAL **, nimble, perfect, precise, quick** *With their great vocals and nifty footwork, the band had the crowd standing with their first number.*

2 quick clever actions to deal with a problem

● adj+N **clever, deft, fancy, nifty, nimble** *The disciplinary panel was confused by some fancy legal footwork.*

forbid V
to state that something is not allowed

● adv+V definitely **explicitly, expressly, positively, specifically, strictly** *Reproduction of any part of the website without permission is strictly forbidden.*

▶ completely **absolutely, altogether, completely, totally** *Climbing on the ship's rails was absolutely forbidden.*

▶ legally or officially **by law, legally, officially** *In Spain, it is forbidden by law not to attend school if you are under 16.*

> Usage **Forbid** is usually passive in all of the *adv+V* combinations shown above: *In some places, beach vendors are forbidden by law.* ● *It is expressly forbidden to use petty cash to pay for entertainment expenses.*

force N
1 physical strength or violence

● adj+N great **brute, full, great, overwhelming, sheer** *Any challenge to the leader is crushed with brute force.* ● *They tried to lower the sails before the full force of the wind hit them.*

▶ too great **excessive** *The police were accused of using excessive force to disperse the demonstrators,*

▶ reasonable **reasonable** *Reasonable force can be used to make an arrest.*

● v+N **employ, resort to, use** *We will not use force or resort to aggression in order to achieve our objectives.*

> If you want to say that someone uses force to do something, you can also say that they do it *by force*: *The elected government was removed by force in 1962.* ● *Many Africans were brought to Britain by force in the 17th and 18th centuries.*

2 someone or something that has a big influence

● adj+N strong **formidable, irresistible, powerful, strong, unstoppable** *Fear is the most powerful force in the universe.*

▶ important **dominant, major** *America is the dominant force in the process of globalisation.*

▶ that makes something happen **driving, motivating** *UNICEF is a driving force for people throughout the world working to ensure a better future for children.*

▶ bad **dark, demonic, destructive, evil, hostile, lethal, malevolent** *For some people, food can become a destructive force that can completely dominate their thoughts, feelings and actions.*

▶ having a good effect **guiding, liberating, unifying** *Should television act as a unifying force for the country, bringing us all together in a great community of viewers sharing a common experience?*

▶ invisible **invisible, mysterious, unseen** *Bells would ring, doors open of their own accord and bedclothes would be moved by an unseen force.*

▶ from outside **external** *Financial success is not based not upon external forces, but on your own abilities to keep what you have in your wallet, and not in someone else's.*

▶ opposite **opposing** *The Chinese believe that two opposing forces exist in every living thing.*

▶ types of force **creative, political** *He was the creative force behind many Broadway shows.*

3 a group of people doing military or police work

● v+N create a force **assemble, create, mobilize** *They had orders to assemble a rescue force immediately.*

▶ use a force **deploy** *We are always prepared to deploy British forces to evacuate UK nationals in an emergency.*

▶ put a force in a place **station** *US forces were stationed in Britain during and after the war.*

▶ take a force out of a place **withdraw** *Both countries have now withdrawn their forces from the area.*

forecast N
a statement about what is likely to happen

● adj+N correct or realistic **accurate, correct, exact, realistic, reliable** *Whether or not it is an accurate forecast of future scenarios is yet to be seen.*

▶ that something good will happen **good, optimistic** *In 2000 violence erupted again, despite optimistic forecasts of peace by the president.*

▶ that something bad will happen **dire, gloomy, grim, pessimistic, poor** *Many newspaper headlines concentrated on the gloomy economic forecasts.*

▶ incorrect **inaccurate, wrong** *Most forecasts turn out to be inaccurate.*

▶ long-term/short-term **long-range, long-term, short-range, short-term** *The rain is starting now, but long-range forecasts predict more sunshine in the second half of August.*

▶ types of forecast **economic, financial, meteorological** *It is important to note the reasons why economic forecasts are so inaccurate.*

● n+N **cash-flow, inflation, profit, sales, traffic, weather** *Your sales forecasts should be as realistic as possible.*

● v+N make a forecast **give, issue, make, prepare, present, produce, provide** *It is not possible at the moment to make an exact forecast.*

▶ change a forecast **adjust, revise, update** *The International Monetary Fund has revised downwards its growth forecast for the area.*

▶ raise a forecast **improve, raise** *The company raised its forecast for operating profits this year.*

▶ reduce a forecast **downgrade, lower, reduce** *We are concerned that a low return could reduce savings forecasts.*

▶ be the same as/more than a forecast **be in line with, exceed, meet** *These traffic figures are in line with the forecasts in our master plan.* ● *Sales so far have exceeded initial forecasts.*

● N+v **assume, indicate, predict, say, show, suggest** *The Bank's forecast suggests that inflation may rise above ten per cent.*

forefront N
a leading or important position [always singular]

● v+N be at the forefront **be at, be in, be positioned**

at, operate at, stand at, stand in, work at *Our research interests are positioned at the forefront of academic debate.*

▶put or keep someone or something at the forefront **bring sb/sth to, keep sb/sth at, keep sb/sth in, place sb/sth at, place sb/sth in, push sb/sth to** *It is the students' strengths that are brought to the forefront and developed.*

▶stay at the forefront **remain at, remain in, stay at, stay in** *We remain at the forefront of chemical research.*

▶start to be at the forefront **come to, move to** *The relationship between Holmes and Mary Russell comes to the forefront, but in a romantic way.*

● N+of something that is happening **campaign, change, debate, development, efforts, fight, innovation, research, revolution, struggle, technology** *The German economy remains at the forefront of innovation.*

Usage *Forefront* is always preceded by *the*. *The forefront* is usually preceded by *at* or sometimes *in*: *We are at the forefront of AIDS research.* ● *Asian Cinema has been in the forefront of all that's new and dynamic in world cinema.*

▶someone's thinking **consciousness, mind, thinking** *These are questions that are at the forefront of most people's minds.*

foresight N
the good judgment to plan before an event

● adj+N great, and deserving praise **admirable, commendable, great, remarkable** *The local council, showing remarkable foresight, took steps to acquire land for use as public open space.*

▶little **little** *It was a ruling made with little foresight.*

● v+N have/not have foresight **have, lack** *Parliament does not always have the foresight to limit risk in advance.*

▶show foresight **demonstrate, display, show** *They showed great foresight in investing in emerging technologies.*

▶require foresight **require, take** *For a computer network to give the best results, a lot of detailed planning and foresight is required before installation.*

● and/or **courage, imagination, inspiration, intelligence, planning, vision, wisdom** *He's had the courage and foresight to plan further ahead than many politicians usually do.*

forge v
to successfully create something

● V+n relationship **alliance, bond, coalition, connection, consensus, contact, friendship, links, partnership, relationship, ties** *The school is forging links with universities in Russia, Canada, India and China.*

▶reputation **reputation** *She has forged a reputation as a highly-regarded coach.*

▶career **career** *He now hopes to forge a career in the digital media industry.*

forget v
to not remember a fact or not remember to do something

● adv+V completely **completely, entirely, totally** *I've completely forgotten what we were talking about.*

▶for a short time **momentarily, temporarily** *He relaxed for a second and momentarily forgot about the problem.*

▶in a way that gives you an advantage **conveniently** *She conveniently forgets to mention that it was her who caused the problem in the first place.*

▶almost **almost, nearly** *I almost forgot to mention the most important point!*

▶by most people **all but, largely** *The details of the incident are now largely forgotten.*

Usage *Forget* is usually passive in these combinations.

▶soon **easily, promptly, quickly, soon** *This is a rewarding experience that you won't soon forget.*

You can also say that something is *easy to forget*: *It's easy to forget the dangers of too much sun.*

● v+V often forget **seem to, tend to** *Users tend to forget passwords they don't routinely use.*

▶want to forget **try to, want to** *It happened soon after, when people were trying to forget the war.*

forgiveness N
the action or feeling of forgiving someone

● adj+N complete **complete, genuine, total, true, unconditional** *Can there be true forgiveness without true repentance?*

▶from God **divine** *They repent their misdeeds before the Almighty, and beg divine forgiveness.*

● v+N ask for forgiveness **ask (for), beg (for), implore, pray for, seek** *I was not willing to ask for forgiveness.* ● *He begged her forgiveness for the betrayal.*

▶give someone forgiveness **grant sb, offer (sb)** *She was mugged and badly injured, but she wrote to her attacker offering forgiveness.*

form N
1 a particular type of something, or a particular way something appears

● adj+N common **common, popular** *The most common form of heart disease is coronary heart disease.*

▶uncommon **rare, unusual** *Chronic myeloid leukaemia (CML) is a rare form of cancer.*

▶basic **basic, canonical, simple, standard** *In its most basic form, the dance is done with a simple wooden pole with ribbons attached.*

▶different **alternative, different, modified, variant, various** *Various forms of surgical treatment have been tried.*

▶not serious **mild** *She suffered from a mild form of anaemia.*

▶severe **extreme, severe** *The regime permitted physical abuse, detention, and other extreme forms of punishment.*

▶old **original, traditional** *Traditional forms of worship are failing to meet the needs of our generation.*

▶new **new, present** *New forms of competition are likely to result from technological change.*

● v+N assume, have, take *Domestic abuse takes many forms.*

2 an official document with spaces for information

- adj+N for a particular purpose **application, booking, claim, consent, enquiry, enrolment, entry, evaluation, feedback, membership, nomination, order, registration, request** *Enclosed is a booking form which should be returned by 31 August.*
▸ electronic or paper **downloadable, electronic, online, printable, printed** *Simply fill in the online registration form.*
▸ completed **completed** *Completed response forms should be sent to the project administrator.*

- v+N complete a form **complete, fill in, fill out, sign** *If you would like one of our team to contact you, please complete the enquiry form.*
▸ enclose a form **attach, enclose** *An entry form for the competition is enclosed with this Newsletter.*
▸ send back a form **return, send, submit** *You can register your interest by completing and returning the form.*

3 how well someone is performing

- adj+N good **fine, good, great, rare, top, winning** *She has been in fine form this season.* • *Bill Murray is on top form throughout the film and extremely funny.*
▸ bad **bad, poor** *United's poor form continued as they were beaten 1–0 by Arsenal.*

- v+N stay in good form **find, maintain, regain, return to** *The Tigers struggled to maintain their form, and they finished 14th in the Second Division.*

> You can also say that someone has *a return to form*: *The movie represents a welcome return to form for George Lucas.*

▸ not stay in good form **lose** *Leeds, who have not won in five games, appear to have lost form.*

> You can also say that someone has *a loss of form*: *His loss of form this season is very worrying.*

formal ADJ

1 official

- ADJ+n procedure or action **agreement, approval, assessment, caution, complaint, consultation, investigation, method, notice, notification, procedure, recognition, specification** *If you wish to make a formal complaint, please put your concerns in writing to the Admissions Tutor.*
▸ in education **education, examinations, qualifications, schooling, training** *We will consider applicants without formal qualifications who can show they have ability and commitment.*

2 traditional or conservative in style

- adv+ADJ very **highly, very** *Although the garden was nice, it was a bit sparse and very formal.*
▸ rather **fairly, a little, quite, rather, relatively, somewhat** *Pleated wool skirts can look rather formal.*
▸ too **overly, too** *Meetings between parents and teaching staff should not be overly formal.*

- ADJ+n dress **attire, dress, wear** *Staff sometimes dress in more formal business attire as appropriate.*
▸ occasion **dinner, occasion** *You can choose between a cafeteria meal and a more formal dinner by candlelight.*

▸ arrangement of something **arrangement, garden, layout** *In the traditional, formal arrangement there is a top table where the bride and groom sit.*

formidable ADJ

very impressive or difficult to deal with

- adv+ADJ very **so, truly, very** *They have built up a truly formidable reputation as the hottest live band in Britain.*
▸ rather **fairly, pretty** INFORMAL**, quite, rather** *The foothills of the Italian Alps form a pretty formidable barrier.*

- ADJ+n opponent **adversary, competitor, enemy, foe, opponent, opposition, rival** *He is a formidable opponent for anyone daring to break the law.*
▸ obstacle **barrier, obstacle** *There are formidable obstacles to such claims ever succeeding in court.*
▸ task **challenge, task** *Caring for a seriously injured casualty in a remote area is a formidable challenge.*
▸ quality **intellect, presence, reputation, talent** *Their set featured Bob singing solo, showcasing his formidable singing talent.*
▸ group **array, line-up** *There will be a formidable array of top speakers at the conference.*
▸ power or powerful person or group **force, power** *Carthage had become the most formidable force in the Western Mediterranean.* • *The article demonstrates the formidable force of modern multinational corporations.*

formula N

a plan or method for dealing with something

- adj+N successful **proven, successful, tried-and-tested, winning** *There is no proven formula for motivating staff, but there are a number of methods which you might consider.* • *We can help you come up with a winning business formula.*
▸ usual or basic **basic, standard** *There is no standard formula for designing such layouts.*
▸ easy/not easy **complex, complicated, simple** *The market potential of an area is determined according to a simple formula.*
▸ mysterious **magic, magical, secret** *There are no magic formulas that will solve all our financial troubles.*

- v+N find a formula **come up with, create, develop, devise, discover, find, hit on, perfect** *They soon realized that they had hit on the perfect formula for ski holidays.*
▸ use a formula **adopt, apply, follow, stick to, use** *The speeches after dinner followed the usual conventional formula.*

formulate V

to carefully develop or express a plan, idea, or statement

- adv+V carefully **carefully, clearly, correctly, precisely, properly** *They will have to carefully formulate their strategy to ensure that their constituents' needs are addressed.*
▸ recently/at first **initially, newly, originally** *The idea was originally formulated by mathematician A.W.Tucker.*

● V+n plan **plan, policy, proposal, recommendation, strategy** *The government will need to formulate a plan to deal with this extra waste.*

▶ theory or idea **argument, concept, doctrine, hypothesis, opinion, problem, proposition, theory** *Care and thought must be exercised in formulating the problem.* ● *Isaac Newton formulated the theory of universal gravitation.*

▶ question or statement **idea, query, question, reply, response, statement** *It will help you formulate questions you want the lecturer to answer.*

▶ rule or guidelines **criteria, guidelines, law, model, principle, rule** *One doesn't make wars less likely to happen by formulating rules of warfare.*

forthright ADJ
speaking directly and honestly

● adv+**ADJ** typically **characteristically, typically** *Fred was typically forthright **about** the problems he encountered during filming.*

▶ especially or unusually **particularly, unusually** *Some members were particularly forthright **in** their criticism.*

▶ in a good way **refreshingly, wonderfully** *What some regard as refreshingly forthright, others will regard as opinionated ranting.*

● ADJ+n manner **approach, manner, style, tone** *Most students discuss their strengths and weaknesses in a very open and forthright manner.*

▶ criticism or statement **condemnation, criticism, declaration, statement** *Farmers applauded his forthright condemnation of the action.*

▶ view **opinion, view** *She is known for her forthright views and her sense of humour.*

● and/or **blunt, courageous, frank, honest, no-nonsense, open, opinionated, outspoken** *Mr. Willis was frank and forthright **in** his answers to the questions raised.* ● *She has a forthright no-nonsense approach to business.*

fortune N
1 a very large amount of money [usually singular]

● adj+N large **absolute** INFORMAL**, considerable, enormous, great, huge, immense, large, vast** *It must have cost an absolute fortune – but then, they can afford it.* ● *He had inherited a considerable fortune from his aunt.* ● *Vast fortunes have been made from the trade of cotton, tobacco and sugar.*

The expression **a small fortune** means 'a lot of money': *We paid a small fortune for this holiday.*

▶ small **small** *It cost me a small fortune to get all the photos developed.*

▶ belonging to the person **personal** *She has a personal fortune of over a million dollars.*

● v+N get or save a fortune **accumulate, acquire, amass, earn, inherit, make, save** *By living economically they amassed a considerable fortune.* ● *Save a fortune by not driving.*

▶ spend or lose a fortune **lose, pay, put at stake, spend, squander** *The company has spent a fortune researching and developing new treatments.*

▶ cost a fortune **cost** *This is a practical car that doesn't cost a fortune to run.*

2 the good and bad things that happen to someone [always plural]

● adj+N changing **changing, fluctuating, mixed** *The theatre opened in 1815 and continued with fluctuating fortunes until 1908.*

▶ getting worse **ailing, declining, flagging** *He aims to revive the party's flagging fortunes.*

▶ different to others **contrasting** *It is interesting to consider the contrasting fortunes of the two clubs.*

▶ in a particular area **economic, electoral, political** *A downturn in your economic fortunes can offer a valuable opportunity to rethink your priorities.*

● v+N change fortunes **change, restore, reverse, revive, transform** *It is part of an attempt to revive the fortunes of central Birmingham.*

▶ follow fortunes **follow** *The play follows the fortunes of two young women, Fatima and Laura.*

● N+v decline **decline, dwindle, ebb, wane** *The town's fortunes declined from the start of the 17th century.*

▶ improve **improve, revive** *With the publication of his novel his fortunes improved.*

▶ change **change, fluctuate, swing, turn** *Since the newspaper began measuring the popularity of politicians, his fortunes have fluctuated.*

● n+in+N **change, decline, downturn, improvement, resurgence, turnaround, upturn** *The opening of the new arts centre signalled an upturn in the fortunes of the town.*

▶ n+of+N **reversal** *The economy had suffered a dramatic reversal of fortunes.*

3 luck, especially good luck

● adj+N good **good** *I had the very good fortune to have a job that was both challenging and fun.*

▶ bad **bad, ill** *Some people think this award brings bad fortune.*

● v+N bring (sb), give (sb) *The spirit of the well is supposed to give good fortune to those who throw in coins.*

● N+v favour sb, smile on sb *For years, fortune favoured him, and everything he touched succeeded.*

▶ n+of+N occasion when something good happens **piece, stroke** *We did have one piece of good fortune when someone offered us a flat to rent at a reasonable price.*

Usage **Fortune** is almost always preceded by **good** in these combinations: *By a stroke of good fortune I was in the right place at the right time.*

▶ change **change, reversal** *They were still hoping for a change of fortune in the business.*

forum N
an event, website, newspaper etc where people have the opportunity to discuss something

● adj+N electronic **electronic, interactive, online, web-based** *We have set up an online forum where children from participating schools can share their ideas.*

▶ open to everyone **open, public** *This public forum*

is designed to provide a platform for you to ask questions.

▶ appropriate for something **appropriate, ideal** *This hearing is not an appropriate forum for the discussion of detailed technical issues.*

▶ involving a particular geographical area **international, local, national, regional** *We propose to create a new international forum addressing Internet governance issues.*

▶ with a particular purpose **consultative, debating, discussion** *New consultative forums will be established so we can find out what staff think of changes.*

▶ v+N provide a forum **create, establish, launch, organize, provide** *We hope to provide a forum for discussions of methods and approaches.*

▶ be in charge of a forum **chair, host, moderate** *After the keynote speech, there will be an open forum chaired by the Vice Chancellor.*

▶ take part in a forum **access, attend, browse, join, visit** *You will have to register to join the forum.*

▶ N+for **communication, consultation, debate, dialogue, discussion, dissemination, exchange, sharing** *This is a forum for the exchange of news and views about Medieval and Baroque music.*

foster V
o encourage something to develop

▶ adv+V deliberately **actively, carefully, deliberately** *Community organisations can actively foster good neighbourly behaviour.*

▶ successfully **effectively, successfully** *We believe that many essential life skills are effectively fostered through sport.*

▶ V+n relationship or links **collaboration, cooperation, dialogue, friendship, interaction, links, partnership, relations, relationship** *The new programme will foster collaboration between researchers.*

▶ attitude or atmosphere **atmosphere, attitude, culture, environment, ethos, spirit** *We have a reputation for fostering a culture of diversity.*

▶ awareness **appreciation, awareness, sense, understanding** *Our volunteers fostered a sense of community among the participants.* • *The aim of the tutorial is to foster an understanding of online publication.*

▶ growth **development, growth** *We must foster the growth of a new generation of architects.*

▶ particular positive qualities **creativity, entrepreneurship, excellence, innovation, talent, teamwork** *We aim to foster creativity and self-expression in young people.*

▶ learning **learning** *This is a highly structured programme designed to foster independent learning.*

▶ illusion **illusion** *These are stories that foster our illusions of immortality.*

oundation N
he most basic part of something, from which it evelops

▶ adj+N strong **deep, excellent, firm, secure, solid, sound, stable, strong** *The programme provides a solid foundation for the development of business skills.*

▶ weak **shaky, shallow, weak** *His claims seem to be built on shaky foundations.*

▶ based on a type of thinking **biblical, conceptual, empirical, logical, mathematical, philosophical, religious, theological, theoretical** *There is no biblical foundation for this view.* • *We are interested in practical applications rather than the theoretical foundations of the topic.*

• v+N be or provide a foundation **build, constitute, create, establish, form, lay, provide, set** *We hope to lay the foundations of a low-carbon economy.*

▶ weaken the foundations **destroy, rock, shake, threaten, undermine, weaken** *The disease has shaken the foundations of rural communities.*

▶ strengthen the foundations **reinforce, strengthen, underpin** *These developments will strengthen the foundations for building world peace.*

▶ lack foundation **lack** *The proposals lack a foundation of public trust and confidence.*

• N+for **development, the future, growth, improvement, learning, research, study, success, understanding, work** *The course provides a foundation for further study at a higher level.* • *This is a mainly theoretical module which builds the foundation for future work in several disciplines.*

fragile ADJ
easy to break or damage; not strong or healthy

• adv+ADJ very **extremely, incredibly, so, too, very** *The bacteria is extremely fragile and does not live outside the body.*

▶ rather **a little, quite, rather, relatively, somewhat** *I didn't get much sleep last night and I feel a little fragile.* • *The magazine was printed on rather fragile paper.*

▶ from a particular point of view **ecologically, economically, emotionally, environmentally** *The islands are ecologically fragile and vulnerable to environmental degradation.*

• ADJ+n environment **ecology, ecosystem, environment, habitat** *Deforestation and heavy farming seriously damage fragile mountain ecosystems.*

▶ peace **ceasefire, peace, truce** *The ceasefire restored a fragile peace in the area.*

▶ situation of a country etc **democracy, economy** *The income generated by tourism is essential in the fragile rural economies.*

▶ relationship **relationship** *The play deals with the fragile relationship between a father and his step-daughter.*

▶ confidence **confidence, ego, psyche** *A person with low self-esteem and a fragile ego has an overwhelming need to be the centre of attention.*

▶ state or condition **balance, condition, nature, state** *They did not want to destroy the fragile ecological balance that had developed over the years.* • *When artefacts are discovered, they are often in a very fragile state.*

framework N
ideas used for forming decisions and judgments

• adj+N general or shared **broad, common, comprehensive, general, overall, overarching, unified, unifying** *Within the broad framework of* *'inclusive education', there are some clear underlying principles.*

▶ clear **clear, coherent, logical, robust, structured** *A clear and coherent policy framework is required.*

▶ types of framework **analytical, conceptual, constitutional, contractual, ethical, fiscal, institutional, legal, legislative, methodological, national, regulatory, statutory, strategic, theoretical** *The legislation was aimed at harmonising the regulatory framework within which firms operate.*

● v+N develop or provide a framework **agree, build, come up with, construct, create, define, describe, design, develop, devise, establish, formulate, introduce, outline, present, propose, provide** *This constitution provided the first framework for democratic governance in the modern world.*

▶ use a framework **adopt, implement, use** *The paper attempts to implement a logical framework for the resolution of ethical issues.*

▶ be a framework **constitute, form, offer** *The charter contains six statements which form the framework of an overall policy.* ● *The 5–14 curriculum offers a framework within which such skills can be developed.*

franchise N
an agreement for someone to sell a company's products or run a business in a particular place

● v+N have or get a franchise **acquire, be awarded, be granted, buy, operate, own, purchase, run, win** *In 1955 Independent Television was awarded a franchise for broadcasting to the nation.*

▶ sell a franchise **award, grant, sell** *They have opened 350 stores and sold franchises to create another 1,000.*

▶ renew a franchise **extend, renegotiate, renew** *The company can refuse to renew the franchise of any contracting company.*

▶ lose a franchise **lose** *The train company could lose its franchise if targets are not met.*

● N+n agreement or deal **agreement, arrangement, bid, contract, deal, fee, package** *The fashion retailer is to open stores in the Middle East under a franchise agreement .* ● *What do I receive for the franchise fee?*

▶ holder **holder, operator, owner, partner** *The soft drink is sold though a local franchise holder in Burma.*

▶ business **business, network, operation, opportunity, store** *Central to the success of any franchise operation is the support of the franchisor.*

frank ADJ
honest and clear

● adv+ADJ very **absolutely, brutally, perfectly, quite, very** *To be brutally frank about it, the negatives far outweigh the positives.* ● *I'm going to be quite frank with you.*

▶ surprisingly **astonishingly, remarkably, startlingly, surprisingly, unusually** *In a remarkably frank interview he reveals why he left his wife.*

▶ in a good way **admirably, disarmingly, refreshingly** *Her disarmingly frank account of her illness is both harrowing and brave.*

● ADJ+n discussion **conversation, debate,**

discussion, exchange (of views), interview *There must be a free and frank discussion of the issue.*

▶ admission or statement **acknowledgement, admission, avowal, confession, disclosure, statement** *He made some astonishingly frank admissions to the budget committee.*

▶ description **account, depiction** *The book's frank description of drugs and sexuality is startling, considering it was written in the 1950s.*

▶ opinion **assessment, opinion** *The chairman asked for individuals to give their frank opinions on what needs to be done.*

▶ manner **manner** *The Minister finally talked directly about the issues in a frank manner.*

● and/or **candid, fearless, forthright, free, full, honest, open, outspoken, revealing, sincere** *We had a full and frank discussion of the problems involved.* ● *You will probably have many questions for your doctor that require frank and honest answers.*

frantic ADJ
done in a very urgent way or full of activity; very worried

● adv+ADJ very **absolutely** INFORMAL, **very** *It was past midnight and her parents were feeling absolutely frantic.*

▶ rather **almost, pretty** INFORMAL, **quite, rather, slightly** *He was almost frantic in his efforts to persuade me to go.*

▶ increasingly **increasingly** *He made a series of increasingly frantic telephone calls.*

● ADJ+n effort **attempt, effort** *His frantic efforts to avoid blame indicate a man under great stress.*

▶ rush **dash, rush, scramble** *The expedition ended with a frantic dash to reach their pick-up point in time.*

▶ phone call **(phone) call** *Her frantic phone call to the emergency services had been recorded and was played at the inquest.*

▶ activity **activity** *Last week was relatively quiet, after all the frantic activity at the beginning of the month*

▶ search **search** *When she discovers that her daughter is missing, she embarks on a frantic search for answers.*

▶ speed **pace** *The game started off at a frantic pace.*

fraud N
the crime of obtaining something by tricking someone or producing false information

● adj+N possible **alleged, attempted, potential, suspected** *The Benefits Agency were investigating a suspected fraud.*

▶ large or serious **complex, large-scale, massive, serious, widespread** *The company recently collapsed after an alleged massive fraud.*

▶ deliberate **deliberate, outright** *He has clearly been guilty of mismanagement, if not outright fraud.*

● v+N fight or stop fraud **combat, counter, deter, eliminate, fight, prevent, reduce, stamp out, stop, tackle** *We believe ID cards will not help to combat identity fraud.*

▶ discover fraud **detect, discover, expose, investigate, uncover** *Internal auditors detected a possible fraud.*

▶ commit fraud **commit, perpetrate** *For those*

committing benefit fraud, the penalties can include imprisonment.

▶ think or say there is fraud **allege, report, suspect** *There may be some institutions who would rather not report fraud, in case it reflects badly on them.*

● N+n **detection, investigation, prevention, protection** *These measures are intended to assist fraud prevention.*

● n+for+N **opportunity, potential, scope** *With more people buying goods online, the opportunities for Internet fraud are increasing.*

freak ADJ
extremely unusual and unexpected

● ADJ+n weather conditions **conditions, gust, rainstorm, snowstorm, storm, thunderstorm, tornado, wave, weather, wind** *The town was hit by a freak storm of heavy snows and sub-zero cold.*

▶ accident **accident, injury** *A freak accident left him paralysed.*

▶ event **event, incident, occurrence, result** *Apparently it was likely that this was a freak occurrence and would never happen again.*

free ADJ
1 not costing anything

● adv+ADJ completely **absolutely, completely, entirely, totally** *We know just how important this service is to keep your PC secure – that is why we provide it completely free.*

▶ almost **almost, generally, mostly, practically, usually, virtually** *There is lots of software you can download for free or almost free.* ● *In Germany, higher education is virtually free.*

2 not in prison, or not held or trapped somewhere

▶ v+ADJ move around **be, roam** *Fights often take place when dogs are allowed to roam free.*

▶ get free **break, wriggle** *I wriggled free of the heavy backpack and stretched myself.*

▶ be set free **be set, go, walk** *She had already served her sentence, so she walked free from the court.*

▶ allow someone to be free **set sb** *He was questioned by an officer who then set him free.*

3 not limited or restricted by something

▶ adv+ADJ completely **entirely, genuinely, perfectly, totally, truly, wholly** *The Audit Office is totally free to decide upon the schedule.*

▶ mostly **almost, comparatively, essentially, fairly, generally, largely, mostly, relatively, virtually** *The USA needs to be more vigilant to remain a relatively free society.*

▶ in a good way **blessedly, mercifully, refreshingly, remarkably** *The language is mercifully free from unnecessary jargon.*

● ADJ+n activity **access, elections, speech, trade** *Visitors are not allowed free access to the building outside normal working hours.* ● *They challenged a law restricting free speech on the Internet.*

▶ choice **choice, will** *He argues that humanity has free will in choosing good or evil.*

▶ place **country, society** *The idea is disgusting, and in a free society it is our right to say so.*

> You can use the expression **feel free** when you are encouraging someone to do something: *Please feel free to leave a comment in the visitors' book.*

● ADJ+from interference from outside **constraint, distraction, encumbrance, harassment, interference, intimidation, obstruction** *We argue for an independent service, free from political interference.*

▶ negative feelings **fear, guilt, worry** *People have the right to live their lives free from fear.*

▶ discrimination **bias, discrimination, prejudice** *A pay system should be based on objective criteria and free from gender bias.*

free V
to make someone or something available for use

● V+n resources **resources** *The Police hope this will free their resources to deal with more serious crimes.*

▶ space **memory, space, storage** *Try freeing some space or using another disk.*

> **Free up** has the same meaning and can be used in the same combinations: *The system would ease the burden on the health service and free up more resources.* ● *We moved the journals into an archive, freeing up shelf space.*

freedom N
1 the right or ability to do what you want or go where you want

● adj+N in a particular area of activity **academic, artistic, creative, democratic, economic, editorial, financial, intellectual, media, political, press, religious, sexual, spiritual** *Britain is a multi-faith society in which everyone has the right to religious freedom.*

▶ complete or great **absolute, complete, considerable, genuine, great, maximum, total, true, unlimited** *We offer complete freedom from party dogma.*

▶ fairly great **relative** *Their sacrifices enabled future generations to live a life of relative freedom.*

▶ basic **basic, fundamental, human** *He argues that basic human freedoms entail knowledge and education.*

▶ individual **individual, personal** *The courses allow students individual freedom to devise and follow their own study patterns.*

▶ new **new-found, unprecedented** *She relishes her new-found freedom from family obligations.*

● v+N have freedom **enjoy, exercise, have** *It is important to protect the freedoms enjoyed by the people of the UK.*

▶ get freedom **gain, regain, secure** *We campaign to help those convicted unjustly to regain their freedom.*

▶ give someone freedom **allow sb, give sb, grant sb** *Signatories to the arrangement were granted complete freedom of religion.*

▶ restrict freedom **curb, curtail, deny sb, infringe, limit, restrict, suppress, threaten, undermine** *The legislation restricts the freedom of choice of employees.*

▶ value freedom **cherish, love, relish, respect, value, want** *Ours is an individualistic culture, that values freedom and creativity.*

▸ protect freedom **defend, enshrine, guarantee, preserve, protect, safeguard, uphold** *We must vigorously defend press freedom.*

▸ give up freedom **give up, sacrifice** *Government policies must protect us, without sacrificing too much freedom.*

● N+of to say what you want **expression, speech** *Under a totalitarian regime there is no freedom of speech.*

▸ to have information **information, the press** *We need to balance protecting privacy against the freedom of information.*

▸ to believe what you want **belief, conscience, religion, thought, worship** *The Toleration Act of 1690 allowed freedom of worship.*

▸ to go where you want or meet who you want **assembly, association, movement** *Freedom of movement inside the EU means that you have the same rights as a national of the State in which you work.*

▸ to do what you want **action, choice, will** *The hunting debate is a matter of freedom of choice.*

2 a situation in which you are not affected by something unpleasant

● N+from **discrimination, disease, fear, hunger, interference, oppression, pain, poverty, tyranny, want** *The charter demands freedom of speech, freedom of belief, freedom from want and freedom from fear.*

freeze N
an official decision preventing an increase in something

● n+N **pay, price, recruitment, spending, wage** *The Chancellor of the Exchequer has called for a three-year public sector pay freeze.*

● v+N impose a freeze **announce, implement, impose, introduce, put on** *The postal services regulator imposed a two-year price freeze on stamps.*

▸ ask for a freeze **call for, demand, propose** *They are demanding a freeze on any increase in boat traffic.*

▸ end a freeze **end, lift** *We urge the Agency to lift its freeze on grants for maintenance work.*

frenzy N
great or uncontrolled activity or emotion

● adj+N types of frenzy **bidding, buying, football, patriotic, religious, sexual, shopping, speculative** *The system encourages speculative frenzies and market bubbles rather than investment in real assets.*

▸ in the media **media, press, tabloid** *There is a tabloid frenzy surrounding the actor and his pregnant wife.*

▸ mad **ecstatic, insane, mad, wild** *In a mad frenzy, we dashed around the room, drunkenly thanking everyone for coming, and kissing all our guests.*

● v+N **cause, create, drive sb into, fuel, generate, prompt, send sb into, spark, throw sb into, trigger, unleash, whip sb into** *His arrest sparked a worldwide media frenzy.*

● N+of **activity, excitement** *Last year, in a frenzy of activity, I visited most of the capital cities of Europe.*

fresh ADJ
new and different

● adv+ADJ very **completely, entirely, genuinely, really, totally** *The project will take a completely fresh approach to the provision of local travel facilities.*

▸ rather **fairly, pretty INFORMAL, quite, reasonably, relatively** *I feel I have created something relatively fresh and vibrant and exciting.*

▸ in a good way **delightfully, fantastically, wonderfully** *I was inspired by his wonderfully fresh angle on these traditional stories.*

▸ in a surprising way **amazingly, remarkably, startlingly, surprisingly** *Her insights and imagery are startlingly fresh.*

● ADJ+n **approach, impetus, insight, look, perspective, start, thinking** *Why not visit the areas featured on this site and take a fresh look at London today?*

friction N
disagreement

● adj+N great **constant, much** *There was a constant friction within their partnership.*

▸ unnecessary **unnecessary** *If we talked things over, we could avoid all this unnecessary friction.*

▸ within a group **family, internal** *Poor communication within a company could result in internal friction.*

● v+N cause friction **cause, create, generate, lead to, result in** *Money problems can cause friction in a relationship.*

▸ make friction worse **exacerbate, increase** *Such a move could exacerbate frictions **between** the two groups.*

● n+of+N **cause, source** *This uncertainty is a source of friction and bitterness.*

friend N
someone you know well and like

● adj+N close **beloved, best, bosom, close, dear, good, great, intimate, trusted** *He was a close friend of Dr Barry.*

▸ closest **best, closest** *She's been my best friend since I was a girl.*

▸ from long ago **boyhood, childhood, college, girlhood, lifelong, long-lost, long-time, old, school** *James and Ed were old friends, and for a time had lived in the same Cambridge street.*

▸ loyal **faithful, loyal, true** *He was a loyal friend and colleague who was much loved through the world of theatre.*

▸ new **new, new-found** *By the end of the night, Holly had made a lot of new friends.*

▸ that two or more people share **mutual** *I met him through a mutual friend.*

▸ referring to pets **canine, feline, four-legged, furry** *You are advised to check that your lease allows pets before becoming attached to a furry friend.*

● v+N make friends **find, make, win** *He had no difficulty in making friends **with** other young people.*

▸ be or become friends **be, become** *In 1622 he met Vandyck and the two became intimate friends.*

▸ have a friend **have** *I like to have male friends.*

▸ lose a friend **lose** *I'd lose too many friends if I started criticizing their work.*

▸ remain friends **remain, stay** *I hope the friends I have made at Cambridge will remain friends long after I leave.*

● n+of+N **bunch, circle, group, network** *She had a very wide circle of friends, from all stages in her life.*

friendly ADJ
pleasant and helpful

● adv+ADJ very **exceptionally, extremely, genuinely, incredibly, particularly, really, very** *Everyone was very friendly and helpful.*

▸ rather **pretty** INFORMAL **quite** *They shook hands and became quite friendly.*

▸ in a good way **delightfully, fantastically, wonderfully** *The people are so wonderfully friendly and that is the most important thing.*

▸ always **always, unfailingly** *It's a beautiful city and the locals are unfailingly friendly.*

▸ too **overly, too** *Parents warn their children about overly friendly strangers in the street.*

● ADJ+n atmosphere or manner **atmosphere, environment, manner, personality** *We offer training and careers advice in an informal and friendly atmosphere.*

▸ person or people **bunch, locals, staff** *My colleagues are a friendly bunch, always ready to help.*

▸ behaviour **banter, chat, face, greeting, service, smile, welcome** *It was good to see a friendly face when I finally arrived at my destination.* ● *A friendly welcome awaits you at our Bed and Breakfast.*

▸ competition **rivalry** *There is much friendly rivalry between the two bands.*

● v+ADJ **appear, be, become, feel, look, seem, sound** *I don't think he was feeling very friendly towards me!*

● and/or welcoming **approachable, hospitable, informal** *The Texan people were very friendly and hospitable.*

▸ lively **chatty, cheerful, enthusiastic, lively, outgoing, sociable** *So if you have an outgoing and friendly personality, apply now!*

▸ polite **courteous, pleasant, polite** *You will be impressed by our polite friendly customer service.*

▸ caring **attentive, caring, helpful, supportive, warm** *We have tried to create a warm and friendly environment in which you can relax.*

▸ professional **efficient, experienced, informative, knowledgeable, professional, reliable** *Ordering was easy, and the service was efficient and friendly.*

friendship N
the relationship between people or groups who are friends

● adj+N close, strong **close, deep, firm, intense, intimate, passionate, strong, warm** *At this time many adolescents form close friendships.*

▸ lasting a long time **childhood, enduring, lasting, lifelong, long, long-lasting, long-standing, old, undying** *It aims to foster lasting friendships between scouts of all races, religions and cultures.*

▸ sincere **genuine, real, sincere, true** *Genuine friendship is easy to find among these hospitable people.*

▸ new or developing **blossoming, growing, new** *This*

gives people the opportunity to develop new friendships within their own community.

▸ surprising **unlikely** *In many ways ours is an unlikely friendship.*

▸ non-sexual **platonic** *There was one aspect of our relationship which I found unsettling – his platonic friendships with his ex-girlfriends.*

▸ personal **personal** *He has put a personal friendship at risk for political reasons.*

● v+N form a friendship **begin, build, establish, forge, form, make, strike up** *The two men forged a friendship during the World Cup.* ● *Team sport is a healthy way to have fun and make lifelong friendships.*

▸ look for friendship **seek** *The club is for singles seeking friendship, love or just a fling.*

▸ encourage friendship **cultivate, encourage, foster, nurture, promote** *We are dedicated to promoting friendship and cooperation between China and the UK.*

▸ strengthen a friendship **cement, deepen, strengthen** *Voluntary work can help you make new friends or cement existing friendships.*

▸ renew a friendship **reaffirm, rekindle, renew** *Their friendship was renewed after the break-up of her marriage.*

▸ weaken or damage a friendship **betray, ruin, test** *We hope that 10 days in each other's company doesn't test our friendship too much!*

▸ keep a friendship going **maintain, sustain** *It is important to be able to build and sustain friendships **with** other people.*

● N+v begin **begin, start** *An unusual friendship began **between** these two very different people.*

▸ develop or become stronger **blossom, deepen, develop, flourish, grow** *I'm sure many friendships have blossomed from the experience.*

▸ last **last, survive** *Their friendship lasted until Crisp's death.*

frightening ADJ
making you feel afraid

● adv+ADJ very **deeply, extremely, particularly, really, so, terribly, too, very** *Panic attacks are extremely frightening, but remember: no-one has ever died from one.*

▸ genuinely **downright, genuinely, positively, truly** *Hallowe'en has become a genuinely frightening time for some.*

▸ rather **almost, a little, pretty** INFORMAL **quite, rather, slightly, somewhat** *For a moment it was quite frightening as they stood above us shouting something that we couldn't understand.*

● v+ADJ **be, find sth, look, seem, sound** *She needs a lot of support to do things that she finds frightening.* ● *While this might sound frightening, it can actually be helpful.*

fringe N
1 the outer edge of something

● adj+N outer **extreme, outer** *The outer fringes of the planet's atmosphere reach almost 600 kilometres into space.*

Usage *Fringe* is usually plural in these combinations.

▸ of a particular type **coastal, rural, suburban, upland, urban** *Erosion threatens the coastal fringe of the park.*

2 the more strange or extreme parts of a group, organization or subject

● adj+N extreme, **loony** INFORMAL, **lunatic, outer, radical, wilder** *There is a lunatic fringe in any statistically large group of people.* ● *They were discussing subjects* **on** *the wilder fringes of their discipline.*

● N+n group **element, group, party** *They are a fringe group that has no mainstream role in Swedish politics.*

▸ event or activity **event, meeting, theatre** *He attended a Campaign for Electoral Reform fringe meeting at the Labour Party conference.*

front N
an attempt to give a particular impression, that may not be sincere

● adj+N united **unified, united** *We need to present a unified front in response to these attacks.*

▸ brave **bold, brave** *I saw through the brave front to the scared child beneath.*

● v+N present, **put on, put up, show** *People think I'm so confident, but I'm just putting on a front.*

frontier N
the most advanced or recent ideas about something [usually plural]

● adj+N last **final, furthest, last** *Oceans are one of the last great frontiers for environmental science.*

▸ new **new, next** *He described their research into the next frontiers of printing and imaging.*

● v+N when new discoveries are made **advance, expand, extend, push back, push forward, roll back** *Exploration pushed back the frontiers of science.*

▸ explore the frontiers **explore** *Our organization is dedicated to exploring new frontiers of mind, body, and health.*

● N+of knowledge **knowledge, research, science, technology** *Every day we expand the frontiers of medical research.*

▸ a subject **discipline, subject** *Our academic staff are working at the frontiers of their subjects.*

frost N
a thin white layer of ice; a period of cold weather when frost forms

● adj+N severe **bitter, hard, heavy, prolonged, severe, sharp, thick, widespread** *On Christmas morning there was a hard frost.*

▸ mild **light, moderate, slight** *There was a thin sheet of ice on the windscreen, so there must have been a slight frost in the night.*

▸ on the ground/in the air **air, ground** *The following morning there was brilliant blue sunshine and a ground frost.*

▸ at a particular time of day **morning, night, overnight** *Even in April we still have the occasional night frost.*

▸ at a particular time of year **autumn, early, first, late, spring, winter** *Cold springs with late frosts in May and early June cause problems.*

● v+N survive, **tolerate, withstand** *The plant is hardy and withstands frost.*

● N+n damage, **protection** *The farmers have insurance against storm and frost damage.*

frosty ADJ
1 cold enough to produce frost

● ADJ+n time of day **day, morning, night** *It was a clear, frosty night.*

▸ weather **air, conditions, weather** *The ground can be very hard in frosty weather.*

● and/or **bright, clear, cold** *We set off on a cold and frosty morning.*

2 unfriendly and showing lack of approval

● ADJ+n **atmosphere, reception, response** *She thinks they are likely to get a frosty reception.*

frown V
move your eyebrows down and closer together, because you are annoyed or worried or are thinking hard

● adv+V not very much **slightly** *She frowned slightly at the memory.*

▸ very much **deeply, heavily** *He read the letter again, frowning heavily.*

▸ when you are thinking seriously about something **thoughtfully** *Blake frowned thoughtfully as he put the phone down.*

fruitful ADJ
producing good results

● adv+ADJ very **extremely, particularly, very** *It is a strategy that has proved to be very fruitful.*

▸ possibly **potentially** *Potentially fruitful avenues of inquiry were being neglected.*

● ADJ+n relationship **collaboration, partnership, relationship** *A year ago the two musicians began a very fruitful collaboration.*

▸ when people discuss ideas **dialogue, discussion, exchange** *The visit was a great success and fruitful discussions took place with respect to future projects.*

▸ way of doing something or finding something out **approach, area, avenue, source, way** *This promises to be a fruitful area of future research.*

● v+ADJ **be, prove** *This research proved particularly fruitful.*

● and/or **enjoyable, happy, interesting, long, new, productive** *That was the beginning of a long and fruitful relationship.*

fruitless ADJ
producing no good results

● adv+ADJ apparently **apparently, seemingly** *It took many months of seemingly fruitless experiments before a breakthrough was finally made.*

▸ to a great extent **largely** *After a largely fruitless morning, we retreated back to the hotel.*

▸ in the end **ultimately** *We spent another hot, sticky, and ultimately fruitless day looking at houses.*

- ADJ+n **attempt, effort, exercise, journey, search, task, trip** *There is nothing more annoying at the start of a day than the fruitless search for a parking space.*
- v+ADJ **be, prove** *Several hours of waiting proved fruitless, so I headed back home.*

frustrate v
prevent someone or something from succeeding

- V+n attempt to do something **attempt, efforts** *He single-handedly frustrated all my attempts to bring this company's IT infrastructure up to date.*
- ▶ intention to do something **ambitions, intentions, plan, purpose** *Bad weather frustrated their plans to finish the work on time.*

frustrated ADJ
annoyed because of not achieving something

- adv+ADJ very **extremely, really, very** *He became very frustrated at the lack of response he was getting.*
- ▶ more and more **increasingly** *I became increasingly frustrated by my lack of progress.*
- ▶ slightly **a bit** INFORMAL, **a little, quite** *I was now getting a little frustrated with the delay.*
- ▶ clearly **clearly** *He left soon afterwards, clearly frustrated and upset with the decision.*
- ▶ sexually **sexually** *Audra Lindley played his sexually frustrated wife Helen.*

- v+ADJ **be, become, get, grow, leave sb** *It's easy to get frustrated if you are stuck at traffic lights. • The large crowd was left frustrated when the singer did not put in an appearance.*
- ▶ **feel** *I came away from the meeting feeling somewhat frustrated.*

- and/or **angry** *I have had so many calls from people who are frustrated and angry because software has not been installed properly.*

frustrating ADJ
annoying you by preventing you achieving something

- adv+ADJ very **deeply, extremely, immensely, incredibly, particularly, really, very** *Buying presents should be fun, but it can be incredibly frustrating.*
- ▶ rather **a bit** INFORMAL, **a little, quite, rather, somewhat** *It is quite frustrating to spend all afternoon stuck in traffic.*
- ▶ in the end **ultimately** *They had found the whole process interesting but ultimately frustrating.*

- ADJ+n **aspect, day, experience, task, thing, time** *Attempting to lose weight can be a frustrating experience.*
- v+ADJ **be, become, find sth, get, prove** *I couldn't even get an interview, which I found very frustrating. • The software may prove frustrating for the average computer user.*

frustration N
an annoyed feeling you get when you cannot achieve your aim

- adj+N complete **sheer, utter** *Any moment now, I'm going to thump the monitor out of sheer frustration.*
- ▶ great **big, considerable, deep, great, much** *It is a source of great frustration to see all this funding go to ineffective programmes.*
- ▶ increasing **growing, increasing, mounting** *There is a growing frustration with the slow progress of the trial.*
- ▶ not expressed and difficult to control **pent-up** *She needed an outlet for the pent-up frustrations that had developed over time.*
- ▶ sexual **sexual** *It is a song about lust and sexual frustration.*

- v+N express frustration **express, show, take out, vent** *He is making daily calls to express his frustration at the lack of progress. • Many seemed keen to take their frustration out on the police.*
- ▶ feel frustration **experience, feel** *We have all experienced the frustrations of having new equipment arrive faulty.*
- ▶ cause frustration **cause, lead to, result in** *Expectations that are unfulfilled can too easily lead to frustration.*
- ▶ understand someone else's frustration **share, understand** *I understand frustrations about the slow progress in dealing with this issue.*

- N+v start being felt **creep in** *At times, frustration crept in and we wondered if we had done the right thing.*
- ▶ become stronger **boil over, mount** *His frustration mounted as he struggled to teach himself to walk again.*

- n+of+N when someone feels frustration **feeling, sense** *By now, about an hour had gone by and the sense of frustration was beginning to grow.*
- ▶ where frustration comes from **source** *It has become a source of frustration that there is no basic standard for transcribing data of this kind.*

- and/or **anger, anxiety, boredom, confusion, disappointment, fear** *Many residents feel frustration and anger about not being able to find a parking space near their home.*

fuel v
make something increase or become worse

- V+n ideas or discussion about something **debate, rumours, speculation** *Todd was appointed as manager within days, fuelling speculation that a deal had been done before Quinn's departure.*
- ▶ bad feelings or bad situation **conflict, controversy, criticism, fears, hatred, resentment, suspicion, tension** *The population has been forced to drink untreated water, which has fuelled fears of an outbreak of cholera.*
- ▶ economic increase **boom, demand, growth** *Additional growth in wireless communication will fuel a strong demand for encryption hardware and software.*
- ▶ what someone expects or wants **desire, expectations** *We must also guard against fuelling unrealistic expectations.*

fulfil v
carry out or achieve a particular task, wish or standard

- adv+V **adequately, admirably, effectively, properly, successfully** *They must have proper* training if they are to fulfil their role as advisers effectively.

- V+n purpose or job **function, purpose, role** As an introduction to health care economics, this book fulfils a useful function.
- ▶ what people need **need** Such buildings fail to fulfil the real needs of the people who live and work in them.
- ▶ what someone wishes to achieve **ambition, aspirations, desire, dream, expectations, hope, wish** Another reason for going was to fulfil a lifelong ambition and see wild animals on the plains of Africa.
- ▶ aim **aim, mission, objective, task** The book admirably fulfils its main objective, which is to provide an informative guide for the linguistics undergraduate.
- ▶ what someone is capable of achieving **potential** Aren't we supposed to be trying to get all children to fulfil their potential?
- ▶ duty or obligation **commitment, duty, obligation, responsibility** We have to consider whether we have a legal duty towards you, and, if so, how we will fulfil that duty.
- ▶ something you have said you will do **pledge, promise** The government will be forced to rely on administrative savings to fulfil their election promises.
- ▶ particular standard **conditions, criteria, requirements** The centre provides educational material to schools to help them fulfil the requirements of the national curriculum.

fulfilment N

1 happiness and satisfaction obtained from doing something

- adj+N personal **individual, personal** We hope children will discover the joys of reading and the personal fulfilment that that can bring.
- ▶ great or complete **complete, great, true** We all wish Adam and Barbara great fulfilment in this next exciting phase of their careers.
- ▶ types of fulfilment **emotional, human, sexual, spiritual** Down through the ages, Man has trodden many pathways to spiritual fulfilment and still not found the answer to the eternal questions.
- v+N **achieve, bring, ensure, experience, find, seek** Without a proper relationship to our environment, we cannot find any true fulfilment.
- n+of+N **feeling, sense** We encouraged people to question whether shopping gave them any great sense of fulfilment.
- and/or **happiness, satisfaction, success** Finding inner peace is a key to happiness and fulfilment.

2 doing or achieving something promised or expected

- adj+N **partial** This thesis is submitted in partial fulfilment of the requirements for the degree of Master of Philosophy.
- N+of what needs to be or must be done **condition, objective, purpose, requirement** The research was undertaken in partial fulfilment of the requirements for an MSc in painting conservation at the Courtauld Institute of Art.

- ▶ obligation or promise **duty, obligation, promise** She wrote to explain the delay in the fulfilment of her tax obligation.
- ▶ what someone wishes to achieve **aim, ambition, desire, dream, vision** Working here is the fulfilment of a lifelong dream.
- ▶ what someone is able to achieve **potential** Our aim is ensure equality of opportunity and the fulfilment of individual potential.

full ADJ

1 containing the largest amount that will fit somewhere, or a lot of something

- adv+ADJ almost **almost, nearly, virtually** Wait until the bath is almost full before adding 5–10 drops of your chosen oil.
- ▶ not nearly **nowhere near** The cinema was nowhere near full and we got a good seat near the back.
- ▶ partly **half, two-thirds etc** Never fill a pan more than one-third full of fat or oil.
- ▶ completely **completely** The car park was completely full.

> You can also say that a container is **full to the brim** or that a room or other place is **full to capacity**: The hall is full to capacity. A container, room, or piece of writing can be **packed full** or **crammed full** of something: The book is packed full of useful information on the area.

- ▶ very **very** There is a very full bibliography, which is invaluable for the researcher working on Russian history.
- ▶ rather **fairly, pretty** INFORMAL, **quite** The restaurant can get quite full at the weekend, so be sure to book a table in advance.
- v+ADJ **be, become, get, look, seem** It doesn't take long for these disks to get full.

2 complete

- ADJ+n something good gained or received **advantage, potential, recovery, refund** If this is not satisfactory to you, you will be given a full refund.
- ▶ something written or said **description, details, name, report, story, text, version** Full details of terms and conditions are available on request.
- ▶ range or set of things **extent, list, range, set** The arts centre offers a full range of classes for children and teenagers.

3 as loud, powerful, fast etc as possible

- ADJ+n **speed, strength, volume** They drove away at full speed.

fumes N

smoke or gas with an unpleasant smell

- adj+N **dangerous, harmful, hazardous, noxious, poisonous, toxic** Toxic fumes pose a health and safety danger to people, equipment and the environment.
- n+N **car, diesel, exhaust, petrol, traffic** Children being driven to school may be exposed to higher levels of traffic fumes than those children walking or cycling to school.
- v+N breathe in fumes **breathe, breathe in, inhale** When birds sit on top of chimneys for warmth, they can inhale toxic fumes.

▶ produce fumes **emit, give off, produce, release** *Do not burn waste which gives off fumes and gases.*

▶ be affected by fumes **be overcome by** *The children were overcome by fumes from the fire and died in their bedrooms.*

fun N

enjoyment; an enjoyable activity; a person whose company is enjoyable

● adj+N great **enormous, fantastic, good, great, tremendous** *Why don't you invite Alison? She's good fun.* ● *It's hard work, but great fun.*

▶ complete **pure, sheer** *We want children to experience the sheer fun of learning.*

▶ harmless **clean, harmless** *The programme is good, harmless fun for children of all ages.*

● v+N have fun **have** *I was having so much fun.*

▶ be, or seem to be, fun **be, look (like), sound (like)** *She says she's joined a band, which sounds fun.*

If something is not enjoyable, you can say that it is **no fun**: *It's no fun living on your own.*

▶ provide fun **bring, offer, provide** *This challenging activity will provide fun and exhilaration for active minds and bodies.*

▶ join in fun **enjoy, join in** *Come along and join in the fun.*

▶ spoil fun **ruin, spoil** *It may not be great weather but don't let that spoil your fun!*

▶ n+of+N how much **a bit, a lot, lots, plenty** *We've had mist and rain, we've had hot sun, but most of all we've had lots of fun!*

▶ ability to have fun **sense** *Marianne has a great sense of fun.*

function N

1 the job or responsibility that something or someone has

● adj+N main or essential **basic, essential, key, main, primary, vital** *The main functions of this council are to set national security policies and assist in planning security strategies.*

▶ important **important, useful** *One of the liver's most important functions is to break down food and convert it into energy when needed.*

▶ specific **specific** *The projects have served three specific functions within the formal research process.*

▶ to do with the body **bodily** *He suffered some loss of control over bodily functions.*

● n+N **brain, liver etc** *Dialysis may be necessary until kidney function has returned.*

▶ v+N have or perform a particular function **carry out, discharge, exercise, fulfil, have, perform, serve, undertake** *Some of these functions are carried out by members of the department.* ● *Flood plains perform the essential function of storing water during flood events.*

2 a social event, especially one for a large number of people

● adj+N **official, social** *Her company specialized in organizing charity events and large social functions.*

▶ v+N **attend, go to, hold** *He had attended any number of official functions over the years.*

function V

work or operate correctly or in a particular way

● adv+V correctly **correctly, normally, properly** *This test will give an indication of whether the liver is functioning properly.*

▶ well **effectively, efficiently, perfectly, satisfactorily, smoothly, well** *The Commission is losing staff and its ability to function effectively is seriously in question.*

▶ not well **poorly** *She was constantly ill because of her poorly functioning immune system.*

▶ with all aspects working as they should **fully** *The product acts as a fully functioning multimedia website on a DVD-ROM.*

▶ in a way that is not dependent on someone or something else **autonomously, independently** *Local government cannot function independently of central government.*

● v+to-V **be able to, be unable to, cease to, continue to** *The club cannot continue to function in its current form.*

functional ADJ

doing something well or operating in the correct way

● adv+ADJ doing all it should **fully** *They have managed to build a fully functional system in only three months.*

▶ doing several things well **highly, very** *We have over ten years' experience in designing quick-to-load, easy-to-navigate, highly functional websites.*

▶ only functional, nothing else **merely, purely, strictly** *The stadium is purely functional and of no architectural merit.*

fund N

1 an amount of money collected, saved, or invested

● adj+N **central, charitable, general, special** *We operate a charitable fund that donates approximately £85,000 a year to support charitable causes.*

● n+N **contingency, hardship, investment, pension, prize, relief, trust** *All deposits are kept in a trust fund and will be returned to you if the product you booked cannot be provided.*

● v+N start a fund **create, establish, launch, set up** *A public fund has been set up to raise money for victims of the earthquake.*

▶ manage a fund **administer, manage** *The Council was administering the fund on behalf of the victims.*

2 a large supply of something

● adj+N **great, huge, rich, vast** *We have accumulated a vast fund of knowledge on the subject.*

● N+of knowledge **experience, information, knowledge** *His friend had a fund of obscure knowledge about space travel.*

▶ stories **anecdotes, stories** *She has a rich fund of funny stories.*

3 money available to spend [always plural]

● adj+N enough **sufficient** *Get a design agency to design your newsletter if you have sufficient funds.*

▶ not enough **insufficient** *There are insufficient funds in the estate to repay the debt.*

You can also say that someone is **short of funds** or **low on funds** or has **run out of funds** or that there is **a lack of funds**: *The school is desperately short of funds.*

▶ a lot **substantial** *Substantial funds have been invested in upgrading facilities at the sports centre.*

▶ not a lot **limited** *Enrolled graduate students are eligible for limited funds to support travel to conferences.*

▶ available **available** *We can only continue to help her if the funds are available to pay for the bills.*

▶ necessary **much-needed, vital** *We rely on the generosity and enthusiasm of the public to raise the vital funds needed to continue our important work.*

▶ extra **additional, extra** *Residents on all the estates helped to raise additional funds.*

▶ public or private **private, public** *The City of Hamburg supported the restoration with public funds, because the hotel is defined as a historical landmark.*

● n+N **government, lottery** *Around £1.6 million of government funds are provided each year for UK Sport to run the testing programme.*

● v+N get or collect funds **raise, receive** *He is planning to walk across the islands to raise funds for the Multiple Sclerosis Trust.*

▶ have funds **have** *The health service is constantly complaining that it doesn't have enough funds.*

▶ give someone funds **allocate, distribute, provide** *Some funds are provided for scientific travel and other support costs.*

▶ use funds **spend, use** *We have a responsibility to ensure that funds are used effectively in the provision of public transport.*

▶ take funds **withdraw** *You cannot normally begin to withdraw funds until age 50 at the earliest.*

fund V
provide money for something expensive

● adv+V how something is funded **centrally, commercially, directly, externally, federally, jointly, privately, publicly** *This is a publicly-funded service costing £200 million.*

▶ partly/completely **entirely, fully, partially, partly** *The development of this website has been partly funded with a grant from Arts Council England.*

▶ with enough/not enough money **adequately, generously, inadequately, poorly, properly** *The new department was poorly organized and inadequately funded.*

Usage **Fund** is usually passive in all the **adv+V** combinations shown above: *A commercially funded initiative.* ● *The organization is entirely funded by voluntary donations.*

● V+n **programme, project, research, scheme, service, study, work** *The project is funded by the Economic and Social Research Council.*

fundamental ADJ
relating to the basic nature or character of something; essential to the existence or success of something

● adv+ADJ very or completely **absolutely, quite, very** *The second point is absolutely fundamental.*

▶ rather **fairly, pretty** INFORMAL, **rather** *The company was forced to undergo fairly fundamental changes.*

● ADJ+n idea or issue **issue, principle, question** *The political will to use nuclear weapons against another nuclear-armed state raises many of the fundamental questions of nuclear deterrence.*

▶ right **right** *This new legislation removes fundamental rights, such as the right to protest.*

▶ change or difference **change, difference** *Over the last 30 years, Manchester has experienced a fundamental change in the structure of its economy.*

▶ fault or problem **flaw, problem, weakness** *It appears that there is a fundamental flaw in the current proposal.*

● v+ADJ **be, become, consider sth, regard sth as, remain** *Other industries which have long been regarded as fundamental to the town's success fared no better.* ● *These questions remain fundamental to political, and indeed everyday, life.*

● ADJ+to **development, life, process, success, understanding, work** *Their broad-based capability and expertise is fundamental to their success.*

fundamentals N
the most basic and important aspects of something

● adj+N basic **basic, underlying** *The author takes a complex science and explains the underlying fundamentals in a way that anyone can understand.*

▶ reliable **good, sound, strong** *Sound fundamentals mean the economy is well placed to respond positively when the world economic recovery gathers pace.*

● v+N learn the fundamentals **grasp, learn, understand** *Once you have learned the fundamentals of programming, this is a good book to have.*

▶ teach or discuss the fundamentals **address, cover, examine, explore, teach** *The aim of the course is to teach the fundamentals of occupational hygiene to those considering a career in this discipline.*

● n+in+N **grounding** *This course provides a thorough grounding in the fundamentals of chemical engineering.*

● n+of+N **appreciation, grasp, knowledge, understanding** *This seminar is designed to provide participants with an understanding of the fundamentals of e-learning.*

funding N
money from a government or organization for a particular purpose

● adj+N more **additional, extra, further, increased** *We support increased funding for library services.*

▶ enough **adequate, sufficient** *We believe that adequate funding of museums should be continued.*

▶ available **available** *Contact your local council for full information on available funding.*

▶ types of funding **external, public** *The reality is that without public funding it would be impossible to fully prepare the case for a long trial.*

● n+N from government **government, state** *The charity does not receive any government funding.*

▶ source of funding **grant, lottery** *The trust has secured grant funding from the Heritage Lottery Fund and sponsorship for the project.*

▶ what funding is used for **project, research** *At the moment we have about £1.2m in research funding.*

● v+N get funding **attract, find, get, obtain, raise, receive, secure, win** *We have already secured funding to help with security and heating.*

▶ try to get funding **apply for, bid for, request, seek** *This partnership successfully applied for funding from external sources including the Millennium Commission.*

▶ give funding **allocate, approve, award, commit, provide** *The Commission will take the final decision on whether or not to award funding.*

▶ increase funding **increase** *They have now increased funding for the immunization programme.*

▶ stop or reduce funding **cut, reduce, withdraw, withhold** *The House of Representatives has voted to cut nearly all funding for the program.*

▶ decide to use funding for a particular purpose **earmark** *Separate funding has been earmarked for the provision of networked computers.*

▶ N+n organization that gives funding **agency, body** *Where a group was affiliated to a particular organization such as a church, funding bodies were hesitant in providing financial support.*

▶ source or flow of funding **source, stream** *Academics are increasingly keen to access new funding streams.*

▶ request for funding **application, bid** *Funding applications are currently being prepared to finance future phases of work.*

● n+in+N **change, cut, increase, reduction, shortfall** *There will be a massive shortfall in funding for schools in the next few years.*

● n+of+N **application, bid, request** *Their application for funding from the Research Council was turned down.*

● n+of+N **lack, level, source** *Possible sources of funding will also need to be identified and applied to.*

funeral N
a ceremony after someone dies

● adj+N **elaborate, private, public, simple** *A private funeral will be held on 19 September, followed by a memorial service at Wakefield Cathedral on 24 October.*

● n+N **family, state** *He received a state funeral and was buried at Westminster Abbey.*

● v+N go to a funeral **attend, go to** *She had to attend the funeral of a close relative.*

▶ arrange or carry out a funeral **arrange, conduct** *The funeral was arranged for the following Wednesday.*

▶ have a funeral **have** *He will have a private family funeral in accordance with his wishes.*

● N+v take place **be held, take place** *His funeral was held at St Paul's Church, Heaton Mersey.*

● N+n **ceremony, procession, service** *Several days later, a simple funeral service was held.*

funny ADJ
1 that makes you laugh

● adv+ADJ very **brilliantly, extremely, genuinely, hilariously, hysterically, incredibly, really,**

riotously, uproariously, very, wickedly *As a live performer he manages to be incredibly surreal and hysterically funny at the same time.*

▶ rather **pretty** INFORMAL**, quite, rather** *My son thought the film was pretty funny.*

▶ not intentionally **unintentionally** *The play is so melodramatic that it is unintentionally funny.*

● ADJ+n joke or story **anecdote, joke, story** *A joke isn't funny if you have to explain it.*

▶ something performed or written **book, comedy, film, movie, play, show** *It's the funniest film of the year.*

▶ part or aspect of something **bit, moment, scene, side, stuff** *The movie has some very funny moments in it.*

● v+ADJ **be, find sb/sth, look, seem, sound** *Everyone seemed to find my singing extremely funny. ● It was pretty terrifying at the time, although it seems pretty funny now.*

● and/or **clever, entertaining, moving, poignant, sad, scary, touching, witty** *The film is, for the most part, a funny and touching story.*

2 strange, or unusual

● ADJ+n **feeling, look, noise, thing, way** *The funny thing is that nobody said anything about what happened in the bar.*

● v+ADJ **be, feel, look, seem, smell, sound, taste** *This tea tastes funny.*

● ADJ+infinitive **hear, see, think** *I used the first edition of the dictionary as an undergraduate student, and it's funny to think that I am now one of its authors.*

furious ADJ
extremely angry

● adv+ADJ very **absolutely** *The damage to the cars was quite minor, but I feel absolutely furious about it.*

▶ still **still** *Kathy is still furious with Sid.*

▶ in a way that you can understand **understandably** *They were understandably furious at the comments and asked for them to be withdrawn.*

● ADJ+n **argument, attack, debate, reaction, response, row** *The bombing has already provoked a furious reaction.*

furnished ADJ
with furniture in it

● adv+ADJ completely **fully** *All these flats are fully furnished.*

▶ in an attractive or pleasant way **attractively, beautifully, comfortably, elegantly, tastefully, well** *All our rooms are comfortably furnished, with central heating and colour TV.*

▶ in a simple way **simply** *The servants' hall was a large but simply-furnished room, near to the main kitchen.*

● ADJ+n **accommodation, apartment, bedroom, house, property, room** *The apartment is fully furnished and central heating is installed.*

● and/or **unfurnished** *Should I let my property furnished or unfurnished?*

furore N

great anger, excitement, or activity

- adj+N happening now or a short time ago **current, recent** *The recent furore over party funding has obscured other issues.*
- ▶ political or public **political, public** *These indiscretions caused a minor political furore.*
- ▶ big/not big **considerable, great, huge, minor** *She has spoken out today amid the great furore about MP's expenses.*
- n+N **media** *The media furore around this case prompted the police to issue a statement on Wednesday.*

> You can use **surrounding** to say what a furore is about: *He left the government in the furore surrounding his million-pound loan to another government minister.*

- v+N **cause, create, provoke, spark** *A few months later his donation became public knowledge, and the revelation caused a furore in Parliament.*

fury N

very strong anger

- adj+N **blind, cold, full, great, intense** *She turned on him in a blind fury.* • *The minister will face the full fury of the teachers' representatives at their conference tomorrow.*
- v+N express your fury **express, react with, unleash, vent** *Tenants have expressed fury at sudden sharp rises in leases.*
- ▶ cause someone's fury **cause, provoke, spark** *The Court of Appeal decision sparked fury from the relatives of the four people who died in the tragedy.*
- N+v **boil over, erupt, subside** *Fury erupted in the court after the judge passed sentence.*
- v+with+N **react, repond** *The students reacted with fury at the decision.*

fuss N

much unnecessary worry or excitement about something

- adj+N a lot **big, great, huge, a lot of, much** *He always kicks up a huge fuss about what he wears.*
- ▶ not much **little, minimal, minimum** *A good company should pay a genuine claim promptly and with minimum fuss.*

> When something happens **without (a) fuss**, there is no unnecessary worry or excitement: *The children went off to bed without a fuss.* When you are commenting on unnnecessary fuss, you can use the expression **a fuss about nothing**: *If you ask me, the whole thing is a fuss about nothing.*

- v+N **cause, create, kick up** INFORMAL, **make** *Stop making a fuss about it; it really isn't a problem.*
- n+of+N **minimum** *We'll identify your needs and meet them with the minimum of fuss.*

futile ADJ

unsuccessful, or useless

- adv+ADJ in the end **ultimately** *People ran in a desperate and ultimately futile attempt to escape the fire.*
- ▶ completely **completely, quite, utterly** *Boycotting the company's products was seen as an utterly futile gesture.*
- ▶ to some or a great extent **largely, rather, somewhat** *Attempts to change the situation proved largely futile.*
- ADJ+n **attempt, debate, discussion, effort, exercise, gesture, search, struggle** *Many feel that voting changes nothing and is a futile exercise.*
- v+ADJ **be, prove, seem** *The police did their best to maintain control, but their attempts proved futile.*

future N

the time following the present time; what will happen to someone or something at a later time

- adj+N coming soon **foreseeable, immediate, near, not-too-distant** *Mortgage rates are more likely to go down rather than up in the foreseeable future.*
- ▶ far off in time or over a long time **distant, long-term** *The film is set in the distant future.*
- ▶ when good things happen **better, bright, exciting, promising, prosperous, successful** *Our team of specialists are working together to build a brighter future for the town.*
- ▶ when you are not sure what will happen **uncertain, unknown** *The immediate future is uncertain.*
- ▶ when bad things happen **bleak, grim** *This play is set in a bleak urban future where packs of young men hunt beggars in the streets.*
- v+N say what will happen in the future **foretell, look into, predict, see, see into** *You cannot afford to look too far into the future.*
- ▶ plan what to do in the future **face, look to, plan for** *Let us face the future with optimism.* • *We are focussed on helping our members to save, to get the protection they need, and to plan for the future.*
- ▶ have a particular kind of future **face, have** *The company faces an uncertain future.* • *He has a bright future ahead of him.*
- ▶ influence the future or someone's future **decide, determine, shape** *Tourism is playing an increasing role in shaping the economic future of the area.*
- ▶ protect the future **ensure, safeguard, secure** *Nobody has done more to secure the future of the charity in recent years.*
- ▶ be a danger to something's future **threaten** *Peat extraction threatens the future of these habitats.*
- ▶ work to make something good happen **build, create** *Our communities need to move forward to build a more secure future.*
- ▶ talk or think about the future **consider, discuss, think about** *This was an opportunity to discuss the future of regional broadcasting.*
- N+v **await sb, bring, hold** *These are brilliant results and a bright future awaits the students of 2009!* • *Does anyone really know what the future holds?*
- n+for+N **aspirations, hope, plan, prospect, vision** *What are your plans for the future?*
- v+for+N **augur well, bode well, plan, prepare** *The performances of the players bode well for the future of the sport in this country.*

Gg

gadget N
a useful small tool or piece of equipment

- adj+N electronic **electronic, high-tech** *There's pressure on young people to have the latest designer clothes and electronic gadgets.*
- ▶ new **latest, new** *He has all the latest gadgets and home entertainment.*
- ▶ clever and useful **clever, cool** INFORMAL, **handy, must-have** INFORMAL, **nifty** INFORMAL *This handy gadget allows you to record a voice message of up to 70 seconds long.*
- ▶ small **little** *It is a useful little gadget and would make a great gift.*
- n+N **household, kitchen** *There is a wonderful selection of interesting kitchen gadgets on display.*
- v+N **have, use** *Matt used a gadget that involves a laser projecting the image of a keyboard onto a flat surface.*

gain V
get or achieve something; get a benefit or advantage

- adv+V **fast, quickly, rapidly** *The Maudsley Hospital rapidly gained an international reputation for psychiatric teaching and research.*
- ▶ gradually **gradually, slowly, steadily** *Aromatherapy has been steadily gaining credibility among the general public.*
- ▶ successfully **successfully** *At the age of 15, he successfully gained a scholarship to the local art college.*
- ▶ very much **considerably, enormously** *Britain has gained enormously from the skills and dedication of its immigrant workers.*
- V+n when you know or learn something **experience, idea, information, insight, knowledge, qualification, understanding** *Join us for a week to gain an idea of what it is like to work in a big office.* • *Students will be given the chance to gain an insight into business and entrepreneurship.*
- ▶ recognition **acceptance, credibility, popularity, recognition, reputation** *This is a technique that is gaining popularity in this country.*
- ▶ confidence **confidence** *I have gained more confidence since acting on stage.*
- ▶ right to go somewhere **access, entry** *Hackers can gain access to data on files and read or tamper with confidential data.*
- ▶ speed, progress or development **momentum, speed** *The conspiracy soon gained momentum.*
- ▶ weight or strength **strength, weight** *He still needs to gain more weight and build up his muscles.*
- ▶ advantage **advantage** *The seminar will focus on how innovation in design can help your business gain a competitive advantage over your competitors.*
- V+in+n **confidence, importance, popularity, strength** *This event is gaining in popularity every year.*

gain N
1 an improvement, increase, or advantage

- adj+N large **big, great, huge, large, real, significant, substantial** *Significant performance gains have been recorded at all five UK sites.*
- ▶ small **modest, small** *Both newspapers have made modest gains in circulation recently.*
- ▶ total **net, overall, total** *In that period, there had been a net gain of 27,000 nurses and midwives.*
- ▶ in the future **long-term, potential, short-term** *However, it's important to remember that short-term pain could lead to very important long-term gains.*
- n+N **efficiency, health, heat, performance, productivity, weight** *There is the prospect of some efficiency gains, but the benefits are unlikely to be passed on to consumers.*
- v+N make a gain **achieve, make** *Students participating in paired bilingual programs made the most dramatic gains in reading performance.*
- ▶ bring a gain **bring, deliver, produce** *The revolution of 'scientific' farming has undoubtedly brought huge gains in productivity.*
- ▶ make a gain larger **increase, maximize** *Online brokers can provide strategies to limit your losses and maximize your gains.*
- ▶ make a gain smaller **reduce** *This tinted glass reduces solar heat gain.*
- ▶ make sure you keep gains you already have **consolidate** *He provides detailed guidance on collecting and using data, piloting your ideas, and consolidating the gains you make.*
- ▶ show there is a gain **show** *The share price showed a modest gain yesterday.*

2 money or other benefits from something

- adj+N financial **commercial, economic, financial, material, monetary** *Use of the archive must be for the purpose of study and under no circumstances for any commercial gain.*
- ▶ for your own benefit **personal, private** *She accused him of abusing his position for personal gain.*

gait N
the way someone walks, especially when it is unusual

- adj+N **awkward, mincing, rolling, shambling, shuffling, staggering, unsteady** *He was a stout man, with a rolling gait.*

gale N
a very strong wind

- adj+N strong **fierce, furious, heavy, howling, severe, strong, terrible, terrific, violent** *Through the night we had severe gales that rocked the ship.*
- ▶ from a particular direction **northerly, south-easterly, etc** *The ships sheltered in the bay from the howling westerly gales.*
- N+v when a gale blows **blow, rage, sweep across sth** *There was an easterly gale blowing.*

You can also say that *it is blowing a gale* when there is a very strong wind: *It was blowing a gale and impossible to stand upright.*

▸ hit sth **batter sth, buffet sth, lash sth** *Gales frequently lash the western coast.*
▸ become weaker **abate** *The next day, when the gale had abated, we were able to cross the bay.*

gamble N
an action involving risks but possible benefits

● adj+N big **big, enormous, huge, major, massive** *I quit my job and took a massive gamble.*
▸ very risky **dangerous, reckless, risky** *The government embarked on a reckless gamble.*
▸ when you have almost no hope left **desperate** *Our only hope lies in one last, desperate gamble.*
▸ when you consider the risks **calculated** *It was a calculated gamble designed to restart negotiations.*

● v+N take a risk **take** *They took a huge financial gamble by publishing the book themselves.*

● N+v be successful **pay off** *The gamble paid off and the company sold thousands of these products.*
▸ be unsuccessful **fail** *He left the band to become a solo performer, but the gamble failed.*

gambler N
someone who regularly risks money on the result of a game or competition

● adj+N gambling frequently or in large amounts **hardened, heavy, inveterate, notorious** *He was known to be a heavy gambler, and was declared bankrupt when he failed to meet a tax demand.*
▸ as a job **professional** *Black made a good living as a professional gambler, backing horses or playing poker.*
▸ using a computer **online** *Statistics suggested that online gamblers were predominantly women.*
▸ unable to stop **compulsive, pathological, problem** *Nine out of ten problem gamblers are men.*
▸ someone who has given up gambling **recovering, reformed** *As a recovering gambler, I can tell you that once this illness gets hold of you, you lose all thought for anyone else.*

gambling N
an activity in which people risk money on the result of a game or competition

● adj+N uncontrolled **compulsive, excessive, heavy, pathological** *He has a weakness for excessive gambling.*
▸ using a computer **online, remote** *The Gambling Commission will also regulate remote gambling.*
▸ illegal **illegal, underage** *Are there adequate safeguards to prevent underage gambling on the Internet?*

● n+N using a computer **cyber, Internet, mobile** *She spent vast amounts on cyber gambling.*
▸ when gambling is a problem **problem** *They fund research into problem gambling.*

● v+N control **regulate** *The Government expressed its intention to regulate online gambling.*
▸ allow **legalise, permit** *The state of Nevada legalised gambling in 1931.*
▸ not allow **ban, forbid, prohibit** *Gambling is prohibited in the University buildings and grounds.*
▸ someone stops **quit, stop** *I have tried various methods of quitting gambling.*

● N+n a place for illegal gambling **den** *Police raided a gambling den in London.*
▸ using a computer **site, website** *This is an online gambling site.*
▸ when gambling is a problem for someone **addiction, debt, habit, problem** *He steals to feed his gambling habit.*
▸ someone who cannot stop **addict** *Gambling addicts could be barred from casinos.*

● and/or alcohol or drugs **alcohol, drink, drinking, drugs, drunkenness, smoking** *Alcohol and gambling are prohibited.*
▸ illegal or immoral activities **pornography, prostitution, racketeering** *Some people feel very strongly about gambling and pornography.* ● *He subsequently accused of racketeering and gambling.*

gang N
a group of criminals or people who cause trouble

● adj+N violent **armed, ruthless, vicious, violent** *Armed gangs shot at military helicopters.*
▸ young **teen, teenage** *Violent teenage gangs wander the streets looking for trouble.*
▸ well-known **notorious** *He was part of a notorious gang of thieves.*
▸ fighting against each other **rival, warring** *The fight was a clash between two rival gangs.*

> Usage *Rival* and *warring* always come before *gang*.

● n+N **crime, drugs, kidnap, murder, terror, trafficking** *The police never charged the vicious kidnap gang.*
● N+n someone who is in a gang **member** *He is a former gang member.*
▸ the leader of a gang **boss, leader, lord** *In the story, the gang leader takes revenge on someone who informed on him.*
▸ beliefs of gang members **culture, mentality** *More and more young people are involved in gang culture.*
▸ fighting between gangs **fight, rivalry, violence, war, warfare** *His friend became part of the cycle of crime, violence and gang warfare.*

● N+of thieves **bandits, burglars, looters, murderers, pickpockets, pirates, poachers, shoplifters, thieves** *Oliver gets involved with a gang of pickpockets.*
▸ violent people **assassins, hooligans, ruffians, skinheads, terrorists, thugs, toughs, yobs** *He was the victim of a vicious assault by a gang of drunken yobs.*
▸ criminals **criminals, crooks, outlaws, smugglers** *Gangs of criminals target bank customers when they are making cash withdrawals.*
▸ young people **boys, kids, teenagers, youths** *As they were leaving, they saw a gang of youths attacking another lad.*

● n+of+N someone who is in a gang **member, part** *He was part of a gang raiding identities throughout Britain.*

> You can also say that someone *is in a gang*, or *belongs to a gang*.

gap N
1 a space or opening between things

● adj+N small **little, narrow, small, tiny** *He has a little gap between his front teeth.* ● *These creatures can squeeze through tiny gaps.*

▶ large **big, enormous, large, massive, wide** *There are wide gaps between the floorboards.*

● v+N **fill in, leave, seal** *Leave a gap of 2 inches.*

2 something missing that prevents something from being complete

● adj+N **big, considerable, enormous, large, massive, serious, significant, substantial** *These new discoveries fill a significant gap in the historical record.*

● n+N **financing, funding, knowledge, skills** *Establishing specialist schools would help to plug the skills gap.*

● v+N see or show what is missing **highlight, identify, recognise, reveal, spot** *Identify gaps in your skills base.*

▶ provide what is missing **address, eliminate, fill, overcome, plug, tackle** *Nurses are being used to fill the gaps left by the shortage of doctors.*

▶ cause something to be missing **create, leave** *His sudden death leaves an enormous gap.*

● N+in in information **coverage, evidence, knowledge, literature, records, research, understanding** *There is a gap in knowledge here which can never be filled.*

▶ in providing a service **provision, service** *We are trying to identify gaps in the provision of healthcare services.*

▶ in a market for goods or services **market** *They had identified a gap in the market for fairly-priced organic food.*

> A **gap in** something is nearly always bad. However, a **gap in the market** is usually good, because it provides an opportunity for someone to **fill the gap**.

● and/or **deficiencies, inconsistencies, omissions, shortfalls, weaknesses** *There are gaps and deficiencies at the moment and these need addressing.*

> Usage **Gap** is usually plural in these **and/or** combinations.

3 a large difference between things or groups

● adj+N large **enormous, ever-widening, gaping, glaring, huge, large, massive, unbridgeable, wide, yawning** *There is a yawning gap between the rhetoric and the reality.*

▶ based on people's ages **generational** *The explanation is more complex than a generational gap.*

● n+N a difference between situations **affordability, attainment, income, pay, productivity, research-practice, theory-practice, wage** *The wider the income gap, the greater the unhappiness at seeing ourselves being poorly rewarded.*

▶ a difference between people **age, gender, generation** *There was a massive age gap between them and he'd been married before.*

● v+N reduce the difference **bridge, close, halve, narrow, redress, reduce** *These changes will narrow*

the gap **between** the best and the worst local councils.

▶ increase the difference **increase, widen** *These factors were widening the gap between rich and poor.*

● N+v when a difference appears or exists **appear, exist, open up, persist** *A significant gap persists between those with the best and worst dental health.*

▶ when a difference increases **grow, widen** *The gap grows as the child grows older.*

▶ when a difference is reduced **close, narrow** *These gender pay gaps have narrowed in recent years.*

● N+in **attainment, life expectancy, performance** *This gap in attainment widens with age.*

4 a period when something does not happen

● adj+N **huge, long, unexplained** *There was a long gap between lunch and dinner.* ● *Your CV should show no unexplained gaps.*

● v+N **leave** *Leave a suitable gap (normally a week) before administering a second dose of the medicine.*

● N+of **one week, three days etc** *There will be a gap of several months before the building can be completed.*

gas N
a non-solid, non-liquid substance like air

● v+N produce gas **emit, exhale, form, give off, produce, release** *The waste emits gases like ammonia and methane.*

▶ take in gas **absorb, adsorb, breathe in, inhale** *Each time you smoke a cigarette you breathe in a gas called carbon monoxide.*

▶ burn gas **burn, ignite** *There is the danger of a spark igniting flammable gas.*

▶ supply gas **pipe, pump, supply** *Gas is piped to the terminal.*

▶ become aware of gas **detect, smell** *If you smell gas, turn off all gas supplies immediately.*

● N+v **escape, leak, seep** *The gas seeps through cracks in the rocks and soil.*

● N in containing or delivering gas **canister, cylinder, pipe, pipeline, piping, tanker** *Empty gas cylinders should be returned.*

▶ production or supply **production, reserves, supply** *Algeria has vast oil and gas reserves.*

▶ when gas comes out by accident **emissions, leak** *The explosion may have been caused by a gas leak.*

● n+of+N **accumulation, bubble, build-up, cloud, concentration, presence, release, smell** *Gas detection equipment is installed to help warn of accumulations of gas.*

gasp V
breathe in suddenly, expressing surprise, shock, fear etc

● adv+V **audibly, incredulously, loudly, suddenly** *I heard audience members audibly gasping at the film's visuals.*

● V+in **admiration, amazement, astonishment, awe, disbelief, horror, pain, shock, surprise, wonder** *When she saw who it was, she gasped in shock.*

● V+with **admiration, amazement, delight, shock**

She literally gasped with delight when she saw the view.

- and/or **choke, cough, groan, laugh, moan, pant, splutter, wheeze** *I was coughing, choking and gasping for air.*

gasp N
a sudden noisy breath, expressing surprise, shock, fear etc

- adj+N from a group of people **collective** *A collective gasp rose from the onlookers.*
- ▶ loud **audible, loud** *As he demonstrated the trick, there were audible gasps from the audience.*
- ▶ quiet **faint, little, muffled** *She gave a little gasp when she saw his injuries.*
- ▶ showing surprise or shock **horrified, shocked, startled** *The baby reacted with a startled gasp.*

- v+N **be greeted with, bring, draw, elicit** *The photographs drew gasps of amazement from admiring audiences.*

- N+v **go up, rise** *A gasp went up from the audience.*

You can also say that *there are gasps*: *There were gasps of horror from everyone in the room.*

- N+of **admiration, amazement, astonishment, awe, delight, disbelief, horror, incredulity, surprise, wonder** *The film drew gasps of admiration when it was screened at the festival.*

gather V
1 collect information

- adv+V secretly **covertly** *Spyware can covertly gather data.*
- ▶ carefully **carefully, painstakingly, systematically** *They had spent a year painstakingly gathering information on the case.*
- V+n **data, evidence, feedback, information, intelligence, material, statistics** *Data was gathered through a structured questionnaire.* ● *The information gathered from this survey will be used to inform the other studies.*

2 increase force, speed, strength etc

- adv+V **gradually, quickly, rapidly, slowly** *Parental criticisms rapidly gathered momentum.*
- V+n **force, momentum, pace, speed, steam, strength** *Economic growth is likely to continue as globalization gathers pace.*

gathering N
1 a group of people meeting together

- adj+N of important people **distinguished, important, prestigious** *Dr Davies has been invited to speak at a number of prestigious gatherings.*
- ▶ of different types of people **international, local, national, public** *Trafalgar Square is used for many public gatherings.*
- ▶ large **big, huge, large, largest-ever, mass** *At mass gatherings, such as musical or sporting events, provision of medical services is essential.*
- ▶ small **intimate, select, small** *This room is also suitable for more intimate gatherings.*
- ▶ happening for a particular reason **celebratory,**

farewell, political, religious, social *A farewell gathering was held in the hall.*
- ▶ informal and enjoyable **convivial, festive, impromptu, informal** *It's a very informal gathering over a sandwich lunch.*
- ▶ happening at regular times **regular, annual, weekly, etc** *We also organise monthly social gatherings.*
- N+N church, clan, community, family, youth *They weren't invited to family gatherings.*
- v+N organize a gathering **arrange, convene, hold, host, organize** *Two or three social gatherings are arranged each year.*
- ▶ be present at a gathering **attend, be at, be invited to, come to, go to, participate in** *50,000 persons attended the various gatherings.*
- ▶ give a speech at a gathering **address, speak at, speak to, tell (that)** *He told the gathering that everyone must play a part.*
- N+of **believers, clan(s), experts, friends, leaders, musicians, people, scholars** *I am delighted to address such a distinguished gathering of people.*

2 the process or activity of collecting information

- n+N **data, evidence, information, intelligence, news, opinion** *The BBC has a reputation for reliable news gathering.*
- N+of **data, evidence, information, intelligence** *The process will include wide consultation and the gathering of evidence.*
- and/or **analysis, collation, dissemination, evaluation, interpretation, processing, sharing** *This module concerns the gathering, collation and evaluation of information.*

gathering ADJ
gradually increasing

- ADJ+n **darkness, dusk, gloom, storm, twilight** *We spotted two elephants in the gathering dusk.*

Usage *Gathering* is used <u>before</u> the noun in all these combinations.

gauge V
make a judgment about something using available information

- adv+V **accurately, correctly, exactly, precisely, quickly** *This helps you and your students to quickly gauge their understanding.*
- V+n people's opinions **attitudes, feeling, interest, mood, opinion, reaction, response** *We surveyed the membership by email to gauge interest.*
- ▶ success **effectiveness, impact, progress, success** *These quizzes will help you gauge your progress.*
- ▶ level or amount **degree, demand, extent, level, strength** *A referendum or postal vote has proved a good way of gauging the strength of local opinions.*

You can also say that you *gauge whether* something happens: *The results can be tracked over time to gauge whether changes have occurred.*

gaze V
look for a long time

- adv+V looking in a particular direction **around, back, down, downward(s), out, skyward(s), upward(s)** *The fishermen gazed upwards.*
- ▶ while thinking **abstractedly, dreamily, thoughtfully** *Jeff gazed thoughtfully at Caroline.*
- ▶ not thinking **blankly, vacantly** *He sat gazing vacantly at the floor.*
- ▶ feeling sad **enviously, forlornly, mournfully, sadly, wistfully** *He gazed forlornly across the bay for several seconds.*
- ▶ with love **adoringly, fondly, longingly, lovingly, tenderly** *The two lead characters gaze lovingly into one another's eyes.*
- ▶ with admiration **admiringly, wonderingly** *You can gaze admiringly at the luxury yachts.*
- ▶ with interest **curiously, eagerly** *The children stopped their game to gaze curiously at us.*
- ▶ without stopping **earnestly, fixedly, intently, long, steadfastly, steadily** *He gazed steadily into her soft brown eyes.*
- ▶ without talking **silently** *They gazed silently at the desert.*
- V+in in admiration **admiration, awe, rapture, wonder, wonderment** *I gazed in rapture at this beautiful scene.*
- ▶ feeling surprised **amazement, astonishment, surprise** *It was the first time the children had seen the sea, and they gazed in amazement.*
- ▶ feeling shocked **disbelief, horror** *The two lads could only gaze in disbelief.*

gaze N
a way of looking at someone or something

- adj+N not moving away **penetrating, piercing, steady, steely, unflinching, unswerving, watchful** *She fixes them with her steely gaze.*
- ▶ showing your feelings **critical, disapproving, wistful** *They enjoy themselves, free from the disapproving gaze of others.*
- v+N move your gaze towards someone or something **cast, direct, fix, turn** *Julian sat silently waiting, his gaze fixed on the door.*
- ▶ move your gaze away from someone or something **avert, draw, lower, shift, tear** *We sat in horror, unable to tear our gaze away from his gun.*
- ▶ look/do not look at someone who is looking at you **avoid, hold, meet, return** *Even then, the boy wouldn't meet his gaze.*
- N+v **drift, fall on sb/sth, sweep sth, wander** *His gaze drifted back to the game.*

gem N
something very special

- adj+N not well-known **forgotten, hidden, lesser-known, little-known, lost, obscure, overlooked, underrated, undiscovered, unexpected, unreleased** *This island is the last undiscovered gem of the Caribbean.* • *We still find old master tapes with the occasional unreleased gem buried in them.*
- ▶ types of gem **architectural, cultural, historical, musical, scenic** *Each original song is a musical gem.*
- ▶ emphasizing that something is a gem **absolute, glittering, little, priceless, rare, real, sparkling, true** *With its white beaches and crystal-clear waters, Sardinia is a rare gem.*

Usage *Gem* is used after the adjective in all of the **adj+N** combinations shown above.

- n+N **comedy, horror, indie, pop, punk, soul** *There are plenty of great lost punk gems out there.*
- v+N find a gem **come across, discover, find, stumble across, stumble upon, uncover, unearth** *This disc of their early recordings unearths some absolute gems.*
- ▶ contain gems **be filled with, be littered with, be packed with, contain, feature, include** *The album is packed with gems.* • *Tours of the castle are fascinating, and feature many hidden gems.*
- N+of **information, wisdom** *It's packed with little gems of wisdom.*

gender N
the fact of being either male or female

- adj+N male/female **female, feminine, indeterminate, male, masculine** *While there are midwives of both genders, the female gender has been used throughout.*
- ▶ same/different **different, mixed, opposite, same** *You may have an advisor of the same gender if you request this.*
- N+n gender issues **issues, politics, relations, studies** *Looking at the way in which different societies approached gender issues could be very important.*
- ▶ considering men and women in a particular way **identity, stereotype, stereotyping** *Do you agree that society imposes gender stereotypes?*
- ▶ treating men and women differently **bias, differences, discrimination, disparity, divide, divisions, gap, imbalance, inequality, inequity, split** *She faces many challenges, including the fight against gender discrimination.*
- ▶ treating men and women fairly **balance, equality, equity, parity** *Further action needed to be taken to address the gender balance.*
- n+of+N how gender is considered **issue, notion, question** *How is the issue of gender handled in the film?*
- ▶ how gender is shown **portrayal, representation** *This film is such an ambiguous portrayal of gender.*
- ▶ because of gender **in terms, on the basis, on the grounds** *No one is treated less favourably on the grounds of gender.*
- and/or family background or personal characteristics **age, background, caste, class, culture, marital status, occupation, status** *Mental health problems can affect anyone, regardless of age, race, gender or social background.*
- ▶ race **colour, ethnicity, ethnic origin, nationality, race** *There are perceived differences in socio-economic status, ethnicity and gender.*
- ▶ beliefs **beliefs, creed, political affiliation, politics, religion, religious affiliation** *We have a commitment to all people, regardless of race, religion, creed, gender or culture.*
- ▶ sex **masculinity, sex, sexuality, sexual orientation** *Certain individuals are discriminated against on factors such as gender, sexual orientation, religious affiliation and age.*

▶ disability **disability** *We deal with people who have been discriminated against on various grounds, including gender and disability.*

general ADJ

1 not specific, exact, or detailed

● ADJ+n advice **advice, guidance** *This article offers general guidance and is not intended to be a substitute for professional advice.*

▶ description **account, description, introduction, overview** *For a general overview of this semester's programme, see our website.*

▶ idea or principle **idea, principle, rule** *The document outlines some general principles for dealing with toxic waste.*

2 true for most people, things or situations

● ADJ+n belief or feeling **assumption, concern, feeling, opinion, presumption** *The general feeling in the industry is that these tax rises will discourage investment.*

▶ agreement **agreement, consensus** *There was a general consensus that the crisis had been caused by irresponsible speculation in the financial markets.*

▶ way things are developing **direction, pattern, trend** *This policy is unlikely to reverse the general trend towards higher unemployment.*

generalization N

a statement that is true in most situations

● adj+N too general, and not considering specific cases **broad, dangerous, gross, misleading, sweeping, vague** *Their report is badly-researched and full of broad generalizations.*

▶ useful and appropriate to most situations **abstract, appropriate, empirical, inductive** *How robust is this as an empirical generalisation?*

● v+N make a generalization **draw, make** *On the basis of this survey, the authors draw some interesting generalizations about the link between poverty and ill-health.*

▶ avoid making generalizations **avoid** *Avoid sweeping generalisations and dogmatic statements.*

generate V

1 to produce feelings, opinions, or information

● V+n **controversy, debate, discussion, enthusiasm, excitement, ideas, interest, publicity, support** *His music was generating greater interest than his paintings.*

2 to create money, jobs, or business

● V+n money, income etc **cash, income, output, profit, revenue, surplus, wealth** *Last year, its 70,000 employees helped generate pre-tax profits of $350m.*

▶ business activity **business, employment, jobs, sales, traffic** *Specialists in search engines can help you generate traffic to your website.*

generation N

the members of a family, society, or other group who are of a similar age

● adj+N older or earlier **older, past, preceding, previous** *The older generation loves those songs.* ●

People are spending a smaller proportion of their lives in work than previous generations did.

▶ younger or present **current, new, present, young, younger**

▶ next or future **coming, emerging, future, later, new, next, rising, subsequent, succeeding** *Inspiring and helping to shape the coming generation is a noble task.* ● *Some art should be protected for future generations.*

▶ existing at a particular time **baby-boom, post-war** *This reaction is typical of this post-war generation.*

▶ all of a generation **entire, whole** *An entire generation is growing up without parents.*

● v+N influence a generation **educate, influence, inspire, introduce to sth, nurture, shape, train** *He influenced a whole generation of younger pianists.* ● *This is the music that shaped a generation.*

▶ create a generation **breed, produce, spawn** *If we breed a future generation of academics, who will be the plumbers, carpenters, road sweepers etc?*

▶ involve more than one generation **be passed (down) from... to..., be passed (on) through, skip, span** *The condition can be passed from one generation to the next.* ● *These recessive diseases often skip generations.*

● n+between+N **bridge, conflict, gap, relations, relationship, understanding** *The purpose is to bring youngsters and older people together by building bridges between the generations.*

generic ADJ

suitable for a range of similar things

● ADJ+n word **description, name, term, title, word** *This is a generic term that is used to refer to both groups.*

▶ skill **competency, skill** *Many generic skills can be developed through working in the leisure industry.*

▶ method **approach, method, principle, solution** *We are developing a generic approach to data-transfer between the different government departments.*

▶ product **drug, medicine, model, package, software, version** *Generic software is available which can run on a variety of computers.*

generosity N

kindness, especially in giving things to people

● adj+N **amazing, continued, enormous, extraordinary, incredible, kind, overwhelming, selfless, unbounded** *What touched me most was the overwhelming generosity of the people.*

● v+N feel grateful for someone's generosity **appreciate, be overwhelmed by, be touched by** *I have been deeply touched by the generosity of many people.*

▶ depend on someone's generosity **be dependent on, benefit from, depend on, rely on** *The charity receives no government funding, so is dependent on the generosity of its supporters.*

● N+of **benefactors, donors, individuals, members, the public, sponsors, supporters** *As a charity, we are entirely dependent on the generosity of our supporters.*

● and/or **goodwill, hospitality, kindness, selflessness, support, warmth** *We'll remember you always for your warmth and generosity.*

generous ADJ
giving a lot of time or money

- adv+ADJ very **amazingly, exceedingly, exceptionally, extraordinarily, extremely, hugely, incredibly, very**
- ▶ more than is needed **excessively, overly, too** *Their pay policy tends to be overly generous towards senior management.*
- ADJ+n person **benefactor, donor, sponsor, supporter** *We would like to thank the many generous sponsors who supported the team.*
- ▶ amount of money **allowance, bequest, donation, endowment, entitlement, gift, grant, salary, sponsorship** *Your generous donation is very much appreciated.*
- ▶ kindness **gesture, hospitality, offer** *Few will forget his generous hospitality.*
- ▶ help **assistance, help, support** *The new library could not have been built without the generous support of former students.*
- and/or **compassionate, hospitable, kind, loving, thoughtful, warm, warm-hearted** *People were unfailingly kind and generous to us.*
- N+with **help, money, time** *He was generous with his time and money towards those needing help.*

genetic ADJ
relating to genes or the study of genes

- ADJ+n change **alteration, engineering, manipulation, modification, mutation** *The book covers the ethics of genetic engineering.*
- ▶ variety **diversity, variability, variation** *The aim is to safeguard the genetic diversity of crops.*
- ▶ problem or illness **abnormality, condition, defect, disease, disorder** *He suffers from a rare genetic disorder which affects his eyes.*
- ▶ characteristics **inheritance, make-up, marker, predisposition, susceptibility** *It could be due to a genetic susceptibility.*
- ▶ test **diagnosis, screening, test, testing** *In the future, genetic tests might be a valuable technique.*

genius N
a very high level of skill or ability, or a person who has this

- adj+N having a particular skill or ability **artistic, cinematic, comedic, comic, creative, inventive, literary, lyrical, mathematical, musical, poetic, scientific** *Oscar Wilde was a literary genius.* • *The way Darwin developed his idea showed real scientific genius.*
- ▶ very great **absolute, inspired, pure, real, sheer, true** *It's a work of sheer genius.*
- ▶ also having bad qualities **eccentric, evil, flawed, mad, maverick, tortured** *He may have been a flawed genius – but a genius nonetheless.*
- n+N **chess, comedy, computer, engineering, footballing, guitar, marketing, mathematics, maths, pop, songwriting** *The plot is pure comedy genius.*
- v+N show great ability **demonstrate, display, reveal, show** *In the final, Federer once more displayed his tactical genius.*
- ▶ be recognized for one's ability **be hailed as, be**

recognised as, be regarded as *He was hailed as a genius throughout Europe.*
- n+of+N a sign or example of genius **flash, mark, sign, spark, stroke, touch** *The real stroke of genius is his pricing strategy.*
- ▶ a piece of work that shows genius **feat, piece, work** *She deserves a lot of credit for this piece of cinematic genius.*

genocide N
the murder of large numbers of people from a particular race

- adj+N **mass, systematic** *He has been taken to the international war crimes court, and faces a charge of mass genocide.*
- v+N be responsible for **commit, perpetrate** *She claimed to have known nothing about the genocide perpetrated by the Hutus.*
- n+of+N **act, crime, perpetrator, survivor, victim** *A tribunal was created to deal with the perpetrators of the genocide.*

genre N
a style in cinema, writing, or art

- adj+N well-known **classic, established, traditional** *She brings new ideas to the traditional genre of landscape painting.*
- ▶ popular **favourite, popular** *These books about people's awful childhoods became a popular genre in the 1990s.*
- ▶ types of genre **cinematic, comic, documentary, dramatic, literary, musical** *The show is a blend of musical genres.*
- n+N **action-adventure, detective, fantasy, film noir, gangster, horror, indie, non-fiction, sci-fi, spy, superhero, thriller, vampire, zombie**
- v+N create a genre **develop, establish, invent, spawn** *Tolkien's world of Middle-Earth spawned an entire genre of fantasy writing.*
- ▶ change or improve a genre **redefine, reinvent** *'Reservoir Dogs' is a classic which redefines a genre.*
- ▶ involve more than one genre **combine, cross, mix, span, transcend** *Her vocals transcend musical genres.*

germ N
a form of bacteria that spreads disease [usually plural]

- adj+N **dangerous, deadly, drug-resistant, harmful, infectious, nasty** *Infection occurs when harmful germs present on the hands are accidentally swallowed.*
- v+N contain germs **carry, contain, harbour** *Toys can harbour germs if they are not regularly cleaned.*
- ▶ destroy germs **destroy, eliminate, fight, kill, remove** *Simple hand washing removes most germs effectively.*
- ▶ spread germs **spread, transmit** *Wear a facemask to avoid transmitting airborne germs.*
- N+v **attack sth, cause sth, enter sth, multiply, spread** *Germs multiply rapidly in warm milk.*
- n+of+N **presence, spread, transmission** *Take these steps to limit the spread of germs.*

• and/or **bacteria, dirt, disease, infection, virus** *The plaster lets in air, but keeps dirt and germs out.*

gesture N
1 a movement communicating feeling or instruction

• adj+N unpleasant **angry, obscene, offensive, rude, threatening** *The driver and her passenger made offensive gestures and shouted obscenities.*

▶ done in an extreme way, using your face, hands, and arms **exaggerated, expansive, expressive, extravagant, sweeping, theatrical** *He waved his arm in an expansive gesture.*

2 something that you do which shows what you think or intend

• adj+N not effective **empty, futile, pointless, symbolic, token** *In every sense it was a futile gesture against the government.*

▶ generous **extravagant, generous, grand, magnanimous, thoughtful** *He can repay your generous gesture next time you're dining out.*

▶ showing feelings **conciliatory, defiant, kind, romantic** *Bill thanked the Mayor for his kind gesture.*

• N+of positive feelings **appreciation, friendship, goodwill, gratitude, respect, solidarity, support** *He has been refusing food and drink as a gesture of solidarity.*

▶ negative feelings **contempt, defiance, despair, protest** *Crowds came out on the streets in a gesture of protest over the election results.*

get across PHR VB
make people understand something

• V+across **facts, feelings, ideas, meaning, message, point, point of view** *It was difficult to get new ideas across to senior staff.* • *He tried to get across his point.*

get over PHR VB
recover from a bad situation, or find a way to deal with it

• V+over feeling **disappointment, excitement, feeling, shock, surprise** *Once you've got over the initial shock, consider your plan of action.*

▶ illness **cold, illness, injury, jet lag** *First, he's got to get over the injury.*

▶ fear **fear, phobia** *I really want to get over my phobia of snakes.*

▶ difficulty **barrier, difficulty, hump, hurdle, problem** *We know we will get over these hurdles.*

▶ unpleasant event **break-up, crisis, death, loss, trauma** *It takes a long time to get over a marriage break-up.*

ghost N
the spirit of a dead person that someone sees

• adj+N **ancestral, evil, friendly, headless, mischievous, resident, shadowy, vengeful** *The house had a friendly ghost which used to switch on the lights.*

• v+N make a ghost disappear **banish, exorcise, lay, summon** *The clergy were called in to exorcise the ghost.*

▶ make a ghost appear **conjure, invoke, summon** *The trees are believed to conjure female ghosts.*

▶ see a ghost **encounter, meet, see, witness** *She claims that she saw the ghost of a young airman in uniform.*

• N+v **appear, haunt sth, roam, vanish, wander** *They say her ghost haunts the room!*

giant N
a very large organization, or a very successful, influential person

• adj+N organization **corporate, industrial, international, multinational, pharmaceutical, retail** *The new mall has attracted a number of well-known retail giants.*

▶ person **intellectual, literary, musical, political** *The course begins with a lecture on Aristotle, Plato, and other intellectual giants from Classical Greece.*

• n+N **banking, computer, construction, electronics, insurance, oil, software, supermarket, technology, telecoms** *We're getting news of job losses at Japanese telecoms giant NTT.*

gift N
1 something that you give as a present

• adj+N completely right for someone **ideal, perfect** *This software is the perfect gift for anyone interested in mixing and editing original tracks.*

▶ better or more expensive than usual **generous, lavish, luxury, special** *Thank you for sharing our day and for your generous gifts.*

▶ not costing a lot **small** *If you're invited to someone's home for a meal, you could take a small gift.*

▶ valued highly **precious** *Friendship is a very precious gift.*

▶ given free by a company **free** *You will receive a free gift when you renew your subscription.*

▶ unusual **unique, unusual** *This colourful apron makes an unusual gift for anyone who cooks.*

• n+N **anniversary, birthday, farewell, retirement, wedding** *Why don't you ask them what they would like as a wedding gift?*

• v+N give someone a gift **bring, buy, give, make, send** *It's hard to buy gifts for someone with no specific hobbies.* • *If you would like to make a gift to the charity, please fill in a donation form.*

▶ be suitable as a gift **make** *Concert tickets make a great surprise gift.*

▶ receive a gift **accept, get, receive** *Please accept this small gift as a token of our appreciation.*

▶ put paper round a gift/take paper off a gift **unwrap, wrap** *We will wrap your gift in an attractive package at no extra charge.*

▶ when people give each other gifts **exchange** *At this time gifts are exchanged and festive meals prepared.*

• v+as+N **give sth** *The vouchers can be given as gifts or used to discount the weekly classes that we run.*

2 a natural ability to do something well

• adj+N extremely good or unusual **extraordinary, great, rare, special, wonderful** *Rogers was a man of extraordinary gifts in many fields, and everything he did, he did well.*

▶ natural **god-given, natural** *Oakes displays a natural gift for suspense.*

- v+N **have, possess** *She has the rare gift of presenting difficult concepts in everyday terms.*

gifted ADJ
with an impressive natural ability

- adv+ADJ very **exceptionally, extremely, highly, naturally, supremely, truly, very** *He is exceptionally gifted in mathematics.*
- ▶ in a particular subject or activity **academically, intellectually, mathematically, musically, technically** *Will was also musically gifted, developing a fine tenor voice.*
- ADJ+n young person **child, pupil, student** *How does the school support gifted children?*
- ▶ artist, writer, performer etc **actor, actress, artist, athlete, musician, performer, player, teacher, writer** *She is the most naturally gifted player I have ever seen.*

giggle V
laugh in a nervous, excited, or silly way

- adv+V **helplessly, hysterically, nervously, uncontrollably** *Within seconds, my husband and I were giggling uncontrollably.*
- V+with **delight, glee** *The children were giggling with delight at the clown's antics.*

giggle N
a high and nervous or silly laugh [usually plural]

- adj+N **girlish, little, nervous** *There were lots of nervous giggles.*
- v+N be unable to stop giggling **get, have** *We got the giggles on stage and started poking each other.*
- ▶ try to stop giggles **stifle, suppress** *'Hi, Mum,' I said, trying to stifle giggles.*
- make someone giggle **give sb** *Something has given her the giggles.*
- v+into+N **collapse** *We had to sit at the back because we kept collapsing into giggles.*
- n+of+N **fit** *John and James were having a fit of the giggles.*

girlfriend N
a woman or girl in a romantic relationship

- adj+N present **current, new** *He turned up with Anna, his current girlfriend.*
- ▶ former **ex-, former, old, then** *His ex-girlfriend appeared at the wedding too.* • *My then girlfriend came from Ireland.*
- ▶ not temporary **long-term, long-time, steady** *None of them have steady girlfriends.*
- ▶ beautiful **beautiful, gorgeous, lovely, pretty** *I met up later with my gorgeous girlfriend.*
- v+N have or get a girlfriend **find, get, have** *I haven't had a girlfriend for several years.*
- ▶ finish relationship with a girlfriend **dump** INFORMAL *He is said to have dumped his pregnant girlfriend via a text message.*

the gist N
the main idea or most important point

- adj+N **general** *I'm simplifying a lot, naturally, but that's the general gist.*

- v+N understand the gist **catch, get, understand** *It was a bit of a convoluted explanation, but I hope that you got the gist of it.*
- ▶ give someone the gist **convey, give (sb)** *I took no notes and therefore I can give only the gist of what she said.*
- N+of **argument, article, conversation, matter, reply, story, text** *If the gist of the argument can be described in a couple of pages, then why bother with the remainder?*

glad ADJ
happy and pleased about something

- adv+ADJ very **extremely, only too, really, so, very** *If you have any further queries, we are only too glad to help.* • *I am so glad you were able to come.*
- ▶ rather **quite, rather** *Children's parties like this make you quite glad birthdays come round only once a year.*
- ▶ simply **just** *I'm just glad we got here in time.*
- ▶ always **always** *I'm always glad to see you.*
- v+ADJ **be, feel, make sb, seem** *There's nothing like hill-walking to make you feel glad to be alive.* • *It's sites like this that make you glad that the web exists.*
- ADJ+infinitive **announce, be, have, hear, know, learn, report, say, see** *I'm glad to hear you're feeling better.*

glamour N
a quality of being exciting, attractive, and fashionable

- v+N have glamour **have** *Australia's second city does not have the glamour of Sydney.*
- ▶ not have glamour **lack** *Although buses may lack the glamour of rail transport, they do matter.*
- ▶ add glamour **add, bring** *A classy hat can add glamour.*
- n+of+N **bit, touch** *A cocktail bar can add a touch of glamour to the evening.*
- and/or **elegance, excitement, glitz, luxury, romance, sophistication, style, style** *We hope the glitz and glamour of the opening night will bring with it much-needed funds for the good work of this great charity.*

glance V
look somewhere quickly and then look away

- adv+V showing someone's feelings or manner **anxiously, casually, fearfully, furtively, nervously, sharply** *From time to time he glanced furtively over his shoulder at the door.*
- ▶ quickly **briefly, quickly, swiftly** *She glanced briefly at our passports.*
- ▶ almost did not **barely** *He barely glanced at her and sat down.*
- ▶ in a particular direction **around, back, down, up** *Glancing back, they saw a huge cloud of dust.*

glance N
a quick look at someone or something

- adj+N lasting only a short time **brief, casual, cursory, fleeting, passing, quick** *He gave her no more than a cursory glance.*

You can use the expression *at a glance* when you mean that you can see something very easily: *I could see at a glance that it wasn't his own work.*

▶ to the side or behind **backward(s), sidelong, sideways** *'He's gorgeous,' she thought, as she cast a sidelong glance his way.*

▶ showing someone's feelings or manner **admiring, amused, curious, disapproving, nervous, sharp, worried** *She wore a low-cut black dress, and drew many admiring glances.*

▶ trying not to be noticed **furtive** *The boy began to steal furtive glances at the girl.*

▶ showing you know about something **knowing, meaningful** *They tried hard not to exchange knowing glances.*

▶ trying to express a warning **warning** *She shot him a warning glance and hissed 'Don't say anything'*

• v+N give someone or something a glance **cast (sb), give (sb), have, shoot (sb), steal, take, throw (sb)** *I cast a quick glance back, expecting to see the dog following us.* • *She shot me a surprised glance.*

▶ give someone or something a glance without others seeing **sneak** *His eyes were glazing over and he kept sneaking glances at the clock.*

▶ when people look at each other **exchange** *Nervous glances were exchanged as everyone wondered who was going to be next.*

▶ see someone's glance **catch** *Martin caught several glances being thrown his way, few of them friendly.*

glare V
look at someone or something very angrily

• adv+V glare in return **back** *Orlando glared at the cat, the cat glared back at him.*

▶ glare and nothing else **just** *I said hello but she just glared at me.*

▶ in an angry way **accusingly, angrily, fiercely, furiously** *He clenched his fists and glared fiercely.*

glare N
1 an angry look

• adj+N angry or threatening **angry, baleful, fierce** *He bared his yellow crooked teeth at me, as I cowered underneath his baleful glare.*

▶ hard and unfriendly **steely** *This remark was met with a steely glare.*

• v+N **fix sb with, give sb** *He fixed her with a steely glare.*

2 unpleasant bright light

• adj+N **bright, dazzling, fierce, full, harsh, intense** *Some walkers were out early, avoiding the full glare of the afternoon sun.*

• v+N reduce or get rid of glare **avoid, eliminate, reduce** *Some modern cars have a metallic windscreen coating to reduce glare.*

▶ cause glare **cause** *Lower the window blinds if sunlight is causing glare.*

▶ reflect glare **reflect** *The monitor should be tilted towards the pupil and should not reflect glare.*

• N+of **headlights, light, sun, sunlight** *A red deer, transfixed with fear in the glare of the headlights, stood quivering.*

gleam V
shine brightly

• V+adj **white** *We could see the church gleaming white on the hill.*

• adv+V **brightly, palely, softly** *The boats gleamed brightly in the sun.*

• n+V **eyes, light, sun, teeth** *Her teeth gleamed and her eyes shone.*

• V+in **light, sun, sunlight, sunshine** *Ely Cathedral was clearly visible on the skyline, gleaming in the sunlight.*

gleam N
1 a light

• adj+N **bright, faint, pale** *A faint gleam of moonlight pierced the blinds and curtains.*

• v+N see a gleam **catch, see** *I saw the gleam of the gun barrel.*

• N+of **light, sunshine** *A gleam of sunshine fell between two immense pinnacles of rock.*

2 a look of excitement or another emotion in someone's eyes

• adj+N **evil, manic, wicked** *He was smiling again, with just a hint of the old wicked gleam in his eyes.*

• v+N **have** *Kevin and Ian had a dangerous gleam in their eyes as they came in.*

glide V
move smoothly and easily with no noise

• adv+V smoothly **easily, effortlessly, gracefully, smoothly** *The man doesn't merely walk – he effortlessly glides across the floor.*

▶ quietly or slowly **gently, noiselessly, silently, slowly** *Birds and other wildlife are undisturbed by the silent canoes gliding gently by.*

▶ in an impressive way **majestically** *The sleek white ship glided majestically through the water.*

glimmer N
1 a soft weak light that is not steady

• adj+N very weak **faint, feeble, tiny** *I saw a faint glimmer of light piercing through the darkness.*

▶ first **first** *The boats were ready to launch at the first glimmer of daylight.*

• N+of **dawn, light** *I saw a glimmer of light, and headed towards it.*

2 a small amount or small sign of something

• adj+N **faint, slight, small, tiny** *There wasn't the slightest glimmer of interest in his reply.*

• N+of **excitement, hope, interest, recognition, understanding** *There's a glimmer of hope that the project might go ahead after all.*

glimpse N
an occasion when you see something for a moment; an experience that gives you an impression of something

• adj+N for only a short time **brief, fleeting, quick**

The crowd parted and I caught a fleeting glimpse of the dancers.
▸ happening sometimes but not frequently **occasional, rare** *The air became brown with dust, allowing only occasional glimpses of the blue sky above.* • *When Joe talks you get a rare glimpse into a world when horses still worked on farms.*
▸ when you see something you cannot get **tantalizing** *It is a city of high walls and tantalizing glimpses through doorways.*
▸ interesting or exciting **exciting, fascinating, interesting, intriguing** *The site offers a fascinating glimpse into the daily lives of ordinary Egyptians.*
▸ first **first** *We reached the Causeway Coast at last and got our first glimpse of the Atlantic Ocean.*

• v+N get a glimpse **catch, get, have, see** *If you're lucky, you might catch a glimpse of an otter.*
▸ provide a glimpse **afford (sb), allow (sb), give (sb), offer (sb)** *Back on the North Col, we were afforded a brief glimpse of Everest before the snow set in once again.* • *The book gives a wonderful glimpse into life in a remote Greek village at that time.*

glint N
1 a quick flash of light

• v+N **catch, see** *He caught a glint of silver as they passed.*

• N+of shiny metal **gold, metal, silver** *A glint of metal caught his eye, and he turned his head to look.*
▸ light **light, sunlight** *Glints of light from his sword danced across his face and reflected in his eyes.*

2 a sudden quick appearance of an emotion expressed in someone's eyes

• adj+N **evil, mischievous, steely, wicked** *He quietly mentioned this, with a slightly evil glint in his eye.*
• v+N **have** *She had a mischievous glint in her eyes.*
• N+in **eye** *He laughed, but there was a glint in his eye that showed he was serious.*

glitter V
shine with a lot of small quick flashes of light

• adv+V **brightly** *The tall spires of the royal palace glittered brightly against the blue sky.*
• n+V **stars** *Half an hour later, the fog had lifted, and the stars were glittering in the September sky.*
• V+in **light, sun, sunlight, sunshine** *There were acres of parked cars glittering in the sunshine.*

global ADJ
including or affecting the whole world

• adv+ADJ **increasingly, truly** *Markets are becoming increasingly global, or at least multinational.*
• ADJ+n community **community, society**
▸ economic or business situation **capitalism, economy, market, marketplace, trade** *Once the global economy begins to show signs of recovery, we can seize upon that opportunity.*
▸ group, organization or system **conglomerate, corporation, network** *The agency works through a global network of not-for-profit organizations.*
▸ problem **catastrophe, disaster** *The book predicts*

that there will be a global catastrophe if these warnings are not heeded.
▸ when the economy has problems **downturn, recession, slowdown** *The global economic slowdown has affected every part of their lives.*
▸ poverty **poverty** *In a fairer world, can tourism help global poverty?*
▸ disease **epidemic, pandemic** *AIDs is a global pandemic that is having devastating consequences.*
▸ size or extent **reach, scale** *We are concerned about the global scale of the epidemic.*
▸ way of thinking about a situation **context, dimension, perspective** *This is an article for teachers who want to bring a global dimension to their teaching.* • *The report looks at road accidents from a global perspective.*
▸ climate **climate, climate change, environment, temperature** *The gradual rise in global temperature has been attributed to the release of greenhouse gases into the atmosphere.*
▸ successful company **leader** *The company is a global leader in consumer and digital electronics.*
▸ brand **brand** *Amazon's headquarters are in the USA, but it is a global brand.*

• v+ADJ **be, become, go** *The festival will go global, with digital live events to be streamed over the web.*

global warming N
the increase in the Earth's temperature, caused by humans

• v+N cause global warming or make it worse **accelerate, cause, contribute to** *Burning fossil fuels contributes to global warming.*
▸ stop or try to stop global warming **combat, halt, tackle** *Radical cuts in UK carbon emissions are required to combat global warming.*
▸ reduce global warming **reduce, slow** *By reducing global warming you are helping biodiversity because climate change can adversely affect habitats and species.*

• n+of+N **cause, challenge, consequences, effect, impact, problem, rate, result, threat** *The effects of global warming, have become more and more apparent.*

• and/or **climate change, pollution** *There is still much scepticism over the extent of global warming and climate change.*

globe N
the world [always singular]

• adj+N **entire, whole** *Our map collection consists of more that 15,000 maps from the 16th to the 18th century, covering the entire globe.*

• v+N spread across the globe **span, spread across** *London was once the centre of a trading Empire that spanned the entire globe.*
▸ travel around the globe **circle, circumnavigate, travel** *Just think, you could travel the globe and never stop partying.*

• n+across+N **country, people** *We currently have staff and students from over 100 different countries across the globe.*
• n+around+N **country, people** *The efforts of talented*

and skilled people around the globe have made our success possible.

- n+of+N **corner, part, side** *Students have come from all corners of the globe, including Africa, Asia, the Indian subcontinent and other parts of Europe.* ● *This enables you to work efficiently with people on the other side of the globe.*

gloom N

1 a feeling of having little hope

- adj+N strong or getting stronger **deep, deepening** *By Saturday, Kate was plunged into a deep gloom.*
- ▶ general **general** *Given the general gloom, it's worth pointing out a bit of good news.*
- ▶ economic **economic** *Companies have cut back on staff in response to the growing economic gloom.*
- v+N cause gloom **cast** *The tragedy has cast a gloom over the whole village.*
- ▶ make gloom worse **add to** *A diagnosis of ME added to the gloom for Lisette and her family.*
- ▶ get rid of gloom **dispel, lift** *A victory in the cup match lifted the gloom at the pub.*
- N+v **deepen, descend, lift** *Gloom descended on to the entire doomed production.*
- and/or **despondency, doom** *However, it is not all doom and gloom.*

2 darkness that makes seeing difficult

- adj+N getting darker **deepening, gathering** *We finally arrived at our destination in the gathering gloom of an autumn evening.*
- ▶ very dark **deep** *The hills and lakes were shrouded in a deep gloom.*
- v+N try to see or be able to see **adjust to, peer into, pierce** *It took a while for my eyes to adjust to the gloom of the cave.* ● *We made our way to the entrance and peered into the gloom.*
- ▶ appear **emerge from** *We emerged from the gloom of the church into bright sunlight.*

gloomy ADJ

1 showing that things are not going well

- adv+ADJ **decidedly, pretty** INFORMAL**, rather, very** *The outlook for the firm was decidedly gloomy.*
- ADJ+n statement about what is likely to happen **forecast, prediction, prognosis** *Despite the gloomy forecast, there are reasons to be hopeful.*
- ▶ what a situation is like or what might happen **outlook, picture, prospect** *The report painted a gloomy financial picture.*
- v+ADJ **look** *The future is looking even gloomier for their children.*

2 dark in a sad or depressing way

- adv+ADJ **pretty** INFORMAL**, rather, very** *The wood is lovely on a sunny day, though in dull weather it tends to be a rather gloomy place.*
- ADJ+n **day, interior, sky, weather** *It was a bleak, gloomy day in January.*
- and/or **cold, dark, depressing, dull, wet** *The kitchen and hallway were dark and gloomy.*

glorious ADJ

1 extremely successful and likely to be remembered

- ADJ+n **future, moment, past, victory** *The country was still clinging to the memories of its glorious imperial past.*

2 very beautiful or (of the weather) sunny and warm

- adv+ADJ **absolutely, simply, truly** *It was an absolutely glorious day.*
- ADJ+n weather **day, summer, sunshine, weather** *Not that we can really complain, with the glorious weather we've had for the last two days.*
- ▶ natural things **beach, coastline, countryside, garden, scenery, sunset, view** *The Isle of Wight has some glorious countryside with spectacular views.*
- ▶ colour **colour** *Their leaves display glorious autumn colours.*

glory N

1 admiration and praise from other people

- adj+N because of someone else's success **reflected** *She was still basking in the reflected glory of her husband's success.*
- ▶ personal **personal** *They are both very involved in my success but neither of them is trying to get any personal glory out of it.*
- v+N bring glory **bring** *I recall being amazed at the hardships the climbers endured to bring glory to France.*
- ▶ get glory **cover yourself in/with, get, take** *He has hardly covered himself in glory during his few matches this season.* ● *Someone else may get all the glory, but you'll learn an invaluable lesson.*
- ▶ enjoy glory **bask in, revel in** *The town was basking in the glory of winning the 'best-kept town or village' competition.*
- n+of+N **blaze** *She decided to go out in a blaze of glory.*
- n+of+N **moment** *He was enjoying his moment of glory.*

2 great beauty

- adj+N as it was in the past **former** *The garden has been restored to its former glory.*
- ▶ full **full** *The pictures above show the full glory of the new staircase.*

> You can also talk about something *in all its glory*: *We could now see the mountains in all their glory.*

- ▶ most impressive **crowning** *Monument Valley is the area's crowning glory.*
- v+N **restore sth to** *We would all love to see the Roman Baths restored to their former glory.*

glossy ADJ

1 shiny in an attractive way

- ADJ+n **finish, foliage, hair, leaves, paper, surface** *The glossy dark-green leaves are sharp and prickly.*
- and/or **black, green, shiny, smooth, thick** *Her daughter was tall and slender, with a cascade of glossy black hair tumbling over her shoulders.*

2 printed on shiny paper

- ADJ+n **brochure, cover, leaflet, magazine, publication** *His photographs regularly appear in leading glossy magazines throughout the world.*

glow V

1 shine with a soft or steady light

- V+adj **blue, golden, green, orange, red** *As darkness fell, the sky glowed red from the fires which were still raging.*
- adv+V **brightly** *The logs were glowing brightly on the hearth.*
- ▸ not brightly **dimly, faintly, softly** *The lamp glows dimly when the system is off.*
- n+V **fire, lamp, light, sky, sun** *She had childhood memories of the red safety light glowing in the attic darkroom at home.*
- V+in **dark** *I've got a pen that glows in the dark.*

2 show strong and happy emotion, especially in your face

- adv+V **positively** *When he speaks about his daughter, he positively glows with pride.*
- n+V **eyes, face** *Her face glowed with happiness.*

3 look pink or red

- n+V **cheeks, face, skin** *Regular exercise is an absolute must if you really want to ensure your skin is glowing.*
- V+with **health** *She was glowing with health.*

glow N

1 a soft or steady light

- adj+N **warm** *Inside, the warm glow of the log fire provides an inviting welcome.*
- ▸ not bright **dim, dull, faint, gentle, pale, soft** *He could just make out a faint glow, which he hoped was lamplight.*
- ▸ bright **bright** *A bright, greenish glow is emitted for up to 15 minutes.*
- ▸ colour of glow **blue, golden, green, orange, red** *In the distance, she could see the field covered with a golden glow.*
- ▸ strange **eerie** *A full moon bathed everything in a kind of eerie glow.*
- v+N make a glow appear on something **cast, give (sth)** *Madge lit the candles and their light reflected in the silver and glass, casting a soft glow over the table.*
- ▸ produce or send out a glow **create, emit, make, produce** *The buttons on the front panel emit a sharp glow when active.*
- ▸ be filled with a glow **be bathed in** *By this time, it was light and the view of the world below was opening up, bathed in the orange morning glow.*
- N+v **emanate, light sth, surround sth** *That night, an eerie glow lit the sky across the world.*

2 a healthy or embarrassed pink skin colour

- adj+N **healthy, rosy, warm** *Her face had a rosy glow and her eyes sparkled.*
- v+N have a glow **have** *She still has a healthy glow.*
- ▸ bring a glow **bring, give (sb/sth)** *On most nights there's a roaring log fire to bring a glow to your cheeks!*

3 a strong pleasant feeling

- adj+N **rosy, warm** *I emerged from the theatre with a warm glow of delight and satisfaction.*
- v+N feel a glow **bask in, feel, have** *They are still basking in the glow of their remarkable election success.* ● *I began to feel a glow of pride.*

go about PHR VB

do something that you normally do, in your usual way

- V+n **activities, business, duties, job, life, routine, task, work** *Try to stay relaxed as you go about your daily activities.* ● *I sat on the bench watching people going about their business.*

go against PHR VB

oppose someone or something

- V+n **advice, nature, opinion, principles, recommendation, spirit, teaching, trend, view, wishes** *He claimed that their actions, while not illegal, went against the spirit of the original guidelines.* ● *Decisions that go against the wishes of local communities can have very damaging effects.*

goal N

1 something that you hope to achieve

- adj+N over a long period **long-term, ultimate** *Winning is always the ultimate goal, but I did not expect it to happen.*
- ▸ over a short period **short-term** *Set yourself realistic short-term goals that will help you regain your confidence.*
- ▸ most important **main, primary** *Our primary goal is to maximize our returns to shareholders.*
- ▸ clearly stated **clear, specific, stated** *This operation had the stated goal of reducing crime in the city centre.*
- ▸ that can be achieved **achievable, attainable, realistic** *Set yourself small, achievable goals with specific timescales, rather than trying to take on everything at once.*
- ▸ difficult or impossible to achieve **ambitious, unattainable, unrealistic** *Cataloguing each of our estimated 100,000 genes is the ambitious goal of the Human Genome Project.*
- ▸ shared **common, shared** *We will work actively to promote collaboration between all parties in the healthcare system in order to achieve our common goals.*
- ▸ your own **personal** *We do everything in our power to help you achieve your personal goals.*
- ▸ carefully planned **strategic** *These intensive courses help individuals to develop professional skills, and businesses to achieve their strategic goals.*
- n+N **business, career** *If you know what your career goals are, it makes it so much easier to make the right choices along the way.*
- v+N achieve a goal **accomplish, achieve, attain, meet, reach** *How does the company intend to achieve this goal?*
- ▸ try to achieve a goal **pursue, work towards** *We are all working towards the same goal.*

▸ have or decide on a goal **establish, have** *A good first step is to establish realizable goals.* • *You might have long-term goals which can take a year or more to complete – for example, a change in career or location.*

▸ give someone a goal **set (sb)** *Managers can set new performance goals and give agents incentives to meet them.*

2 when the ball is put into the net in games such as football

• adj+N that wins a match **decisive, winning** *Kluivert scored the winning goal in the 1995 European Cup final when he was only 18.*

▸ that makes the score level **equalizing** *Another defensive error led to the equalizing goal.*

▸ showing skill **well-taken** *Danny Crow scored with a well-taken goal.*

▸ scored because of careless play **sloppy** *We gave away two sloppy goals.*

▸ accidentally scored against your own team **own** *Wolves got back into the match via an own goal.*

▸ late/early in a match **early, late, opening** *Auxerre nearly snatched a late goal but the match ended 1–1.*

• v+N score a goal **get, score** *He scored two fantastic goals.*

▸ have a goal scored against you **concede, give away, let in** *We might concede a few goals, but we are likely to score a few too.*

▸ score a goal when you are losing **pull back** *Montrose pulled a goal back early in the second half.*

▸ not allow a goal **disallow** *A perfectly good goal was disallowed because the ref didn't see the ball had crossed the line.*

goods N
objects produced for sale

• adj+N electrical **electrical, electronic** *Many people replace even expensive electrical goods rather than having them repaired.*

▸ made in a factory **manufactured** *A majority of our food, manufactured goods and raw materials are imported.*

▸ staying in good condition for a short/long time **durable, perishable** *You will be refunded the full amount minus the cost of any perishable goods which cannot be resold.*

▸ not working properly **damaged, defective, faulty** *If your goods are faulty you may request a refund.*

▸ involving crime **counterfeit, stolen** *Several men were arrested in connection with allegations of handling stolen goods.*

▸ not expensive **cheap** *This is a great place to get cheap goods.*

• n+N **consumer, household, luxury** *Measures include the discouraging of excessive packing of consumer goods.*

• v+N sell goods **sell, supply** *Selling goods in global markets is complicated.*

▸ buy goods **buy, order, purchase** *Try to buy goods with less packaging.*

▸ make goods **make, manufacture, produce** *All goods manufactured by us are guaranteed.*

▸ sell goods to/buy goods from another country **export, import** *Wool and woollen goods were exported all over Europe.*

▸ send goods **deliver, return, ship, transport** *If goods are not delivered, it is essential that you contact us within 30 days of the dispatch of your order.*

• and/or **services** *Some taxes, like VAT, are added to the price you pay for the goods or services.*

gorgeous ADJ
very beautiful or pleasant

• adv+ADJ **absolutely, drop-dead** INFORMAL, **really, simply, utterly** *The boys are all young and drop-dead gorgeous.*

• ADJ+n person **boy, girl, girlfriend, guy, woman** *Fashion photographers are always on the lookout for gorgeous young girls to shoot.*

▸ weather or surroundings **beach, coastline, countryside, garden, scenery, sunshine, surroundings, weather** *We keep going back to Scotland for our holidays because of the gorgeous scenery.*

• v+ADJ **be, look, smell, sound** *She was looking as gorgeous as ever.*

gossip N
conversation about people's private lives

• adj+N interesting **hot, interesting, juicy, salacious** *Do you want to hear some juicy gossip?*

▸ unkind **malicious, vicious** *It turned out to be nothing but malicious gossip.*

▸ most recent **latest** *He always has all the latest gossip.*

▸ lacking any purpose or reason **idle** *I'm not usually one for idle gossip.*

▸ local **local** *Malkerns is a small town whose heart is based around the local pub, where you can get a good meal or catch up with the local gossip.*

▸ relating to a particular area of activity **cultural, literary, political** *If you like political gossip, you might be amused by this blog.*

• n+N about famous people **celeb, celebrity, showbiz, soap** *The government's latest tax plans just aren't as interesting to most people as the latest celebrity gossip.*

▸ about people in a particular place **office, town, village** *He never listens to office gossip.*

• v+N exchange gossip **exchange, listen to, swap** *We exchange gossip and enjoy a coffee in the sun.*

▸ tell gossip to someone else **pass on, share, spread** *Ben accuses Ron of spreading malicious gossip.*

▸ hear gossip **hear, listen to** *She's surprised that Caroline hasn't heard the latest gossip.*

• n+of+N **bit, item, piece, snippet** *She can't resist passing on this juicy piece of gossip to her cousin.*

government N
1 a group running a country, region, or town

• adj+N **central, city, federal, local, national, provincial, regional, state** *We receive more than half of our funding from central government.*

• n+N **caretaker, coalition, minority, national unity, power-sharing, puppet, unity** *The new coalition government lasted only two weeks.*

• v+N elect a government **elect** *Voters were ready for a change and eager to elect a new government.*

▶ form a government **form** *When Balfour resigned in 1905, Edward VII invited Henry Campbell-Bannerman to form a government.*

▶ force a government from power **bring down, oust, overthrow, topple** *He called for an armed uprising to overthrow the government.*

▶ criticize a government **accuse, blame, condemn, criticize, denounce, slam** *The newspaper blames the Government for the current crisis.*

▶ try to influence a government **lobby, press, pressure, pressurize** *We must lobby the government for urgent legislation to end this discrimination.*

▶ ask a government to do something **petition** *The Council began to petition Government for additional finance to progress its regeneration plans.*

● N+v start work as a government **come into office, come into power, come to office, come to power, take power** *The Labour government came to power in 1997.*

● be forced from a position of power **collapse, fall** *The government could fall as soon as Friday.*

● N+n a part of a government **agency, body, department, ministry, quango** *The committee includes members from all government departments with an interest in science, engineering, and technology.*

▶ someone working for a government **adviser, appointee, employee, minister, official, representative, spokesperson, statistician** *Doctors' leaders are holding emergency meetings with government officials this week to try to resolve the problem.*

▶ a plan by a government **initiative, legislation, measure, plan, policy, programme, proposal, reform** *It is government policy that has led to the present situation.*

▶ money spent by a government **expenditure, spending** *A substantial increase in government spending is planned over the next three years.*

▶ money from a government **funding, grant, subsidy** *The Charity does not receive any government funding.*

▶ support by a government **approval, backing, support** *We were delighted that our plans won government backing.*

2 the process, method, or effects of governing

● adj+N types of government **authoritarian, democratic, representative, totalitarian** *The country has experienced both military dictatorship and democratic government.*

● with all the parts working well together **joined-up** *There is also a need for joined-up government.*

● strong **firm, strong** *It is the best voting method available and one which guarantees strong government.*

● good **effective, good** *Both parties claimed to be the champions of liberty and good government.*

● weak **weak** *Proportional representation could lead to weak government, with many small parties having to form a coalition.*

● having too much control over people's lives **big** *In one respect, this is the usual Republican message about getting rid of big government.*

● avoiding having too much control over people's lives **small** *Americans have seen where small government leads.*

grab V

1 take hold of something quickly or roughly

● V+n a part of someone's body **ankle, arm, hand, shoulder, wrist** *I managed to grab her arm, but then she fell onto the rocks below.*

▶ a bag **bag, handbag, rucksack** *If someone attempts to grab your bag, it may be best to let them take it rather than risk confrontation or injury.*

▶ a piece of clothing **coat, jacket** *He grabbed his coat and ran out of the house to his car.*

▶ a piece of equipment **binoculars, camera, microphone, mike**

▶ a weapon **gun, knife**

2 succeed in getting something, especially by acting quickly

● V+n a goal **equalizer, goal, hat-trick, try, winner** *Jones grabbed his second goal in the 59th minute.*

▶ someone's attention **attention, imagination** *Time and effort needs to be spent on producing a CV which will grab the interviewer's attention.*

▶ something costing less than usual **bargain** *Save yourself $20 and grab a bargain with our low price of $9.99.*

▶ an opportunity **chance, opportunity** *We wanted to go, so we grabbed the chance.*

▶ a seat **seat** *Jack pushed in front of Elizabeth and Callum and grabbed the last seat.*

▶ a victory in sports **victory, win** *They grabbed their first win of the season with a 3–1 triumph yesterday.*

▶ a share of something **share** *The company is making a bold attempt to grab a share of the UK market.*

graceful ADJ

attractive in shape, appearance, or movement

● ADJ+n shape **figure, form, lines, shape** *The car's graceful lines, high speed, reliability and performance have made her a legend in her own lifetime.*

▶ object **arch, architecture, bridge, neck, tree** *The famous, graceful arch of St. Louis rises high above the Mississippi.*

▶ movement **arc, bow, curve, dance, motion, movement** *Her eyes were bright and expressive, her movements graceful.*

▶ person, animal, or bird **bird, creature, dancer, swan** *He has developed into a very refined and graceful dancer.*

● and/or **beautiful, charming, delicate, effortless, elegant** *Graceful and elegant, Stockholm is built on fourteen islands.*

grade N

a letter or number showing the quality of a student's work

● adj+N good **excellent, good, high, top** *I left school with good grades.*

▶ bad **bad, low, poor** *Despite her high intelligence, she received poor grades.*

▶ average **average** *Traditionally, girls achieve higher average grades than their male counterparts.*

▶ final **final, overall** *There are three coursework assignments which count for 50 per cent of the final grade.*

● v+N get a grade **achieve, attain, earn, gain, get,**

have, obtain, receive, score, secure *I had to work hard to ensure I got the grades required for Medicine.*
▶ give someone a grade **award, give** *Grades for practice essays are given so that you can assess your own progress.*
▶ improve a grade **boost, improve, raise** *You can resit any module to improve your grade.*

gradual ADJ

1 happen slowly and by small amounts

● ADJ+n change **change, evolution, shift, transformation, transition** *The sex hormones are chemicals which bring about gradual changes in the body.*
▶ improvement **improvement, progress** *There was a gradual improvement in his work.*
▶ change to a worse state **decay, decline, deterioration** *There has been a gradual decline in the patient's health.*
▶ increase **accumulation, build-up, increase, rise** *We have seen a gradual increase in the price of oil.*
▶ reduction **decrease, diminution, erosion, loss, reduction** *The Bank of England must consider a gradual reduction in interest rates.*
▶ process **process** *The company recognises that changing the workplace culture is a gradual process.*

2 not steep

● ADJ+n **ascent, climb, descent, slope** *The hotel is 200 metres from the beach, up a gradual slope.*

graduate N

someone with a degree from a university

● adj+N **new, recent** *The post might suit a recent graduate.*
● n+N in a particular subject **science, history, economics etc** *The demand for chemical engineering graduates remains high.*
▶ with a particular level of degree **honours** *She is an honours graduate of the University of Western Australia and the Open University, co-author and photographer of Great Irish Houses and Castles and Dublin, a Grand Tour, and photographer of Ancient Ireland.*
▶ from a particular type of institution **art school, business school, college, law school, medical school, university** *The objective is to double the number of university graduates in the information technology sector as quickly as possible.*
● N+n study **course, programme, school, studentship, study** *The two-year graduate programme leads to an MA in Environmental Studies.*
▶ training **apprenticeship, placement, training** *The company has a prestigious graduate training scheme.*
▶ jobs or employment **career, employment, job, recruitment, vacancy** *Around 50 per cent of graduate vacancies do not require a specific subject or discipline.*
▶ workers **entrant, recruit, trainee** *We provide comprehensive training for all new graduate entrants.*

grand ADJ

very impressive

● adv+ADJ **awfully, rather, really, terribly, very** *They*

live in a rather grand house with its own tennis court.
● ADJ+n occasion or event **affair, banquet, finale, opening, procession** *Dinner was a very grand affair.*
▶ plan **design, plan, scheme, vision** *This event put an end to Bonaparte's grand plan to invade Great Britain.*
▶ place **ballroom, house, mansion, palace** *Until 1938, a grand mansion stood on this site.*
▶ size **scale** *The Colosseum was built on a grand scale.*
▶ style **style** *The choir celebrated its thirtieth anniversary in grand style by making its first foreign concert tour.*
▶ action **gesture** *The chance has been missed to make a grand gesture that would show the fundamental difference between the two parties.*

grandeur N

the impressive quality of a place, object, or occasion

● adj+N describing beautiful or wild areas of land **natural, rugged, scenic, wild** *You will stand in awe of the natural grandeur of Niagara Falls.* ● *The resort provides an ideal base from which to explore the rugged grandeur of this part of Wales.*
▶ past **ancient, faded, fading, former, original, past** *The ruins of the ancient castle give an idea of its former grandeur.*
▶ impressive **awe-inspiring, majestic** *The Grampians in the distance tower above them in majestic grandeur.*
● very great **sheer** *The landscapes of mainland Norway are breathtaking in their sheer grandeur.*
● N+of of an area **landscape, mountains, scenery, surroundings** *I love walking in the Alps, because of the grandeur of the scenery.*
▶ of a building **architecture, building, palace** *The museum would be worth visiting just for the grandeur of the building itself.*

grant V

let someone have or do something

● V+n permission **access, approval, authorization, concession, consent, leave, permission** *In 1994, permission was granted for a large housing development on the land.*
▶ a document giving someone permission to do something **charter, lease, licence, patent, permit, visa, warrant** *The register should contain particulars of the premises for which the licences were granted.*
▶ what someone wants or has asked for **application, petition, request, wish** *If you were granted one wish, what would it be?*
▶ freedom from something **amnesty, bail, dispensation, exemption, immunity, pardon, reprieve** *It makes much more economic sense to grant an amnesty to illegal immigrants than to try to deport them.*
▶ right **asylum, privilege, right** *The user is granted the right to use the software within the terms of the licence agreement.*

graph N

a picture using lines to show the relationship between numbers

- v+N **construct, create, draw, plot, produce** *Draw a graph of the results.*

- N+v **demonstrate, depict, display, illustrate, indicate, represent, show** *The graph below shows the amount of waste produced in Grampian each year since 2000.*

graphic ADJ

1 described in great detail, often unpleasant detail

- ADJ+n detail **detail** *Terry goes into graphic detail about his addiction.*
- ▶ description in words or pictures **account, depiction, description, image, portrayal, scene** *It provides graphic accounts of the crimes, including murder, carried out by these gangs.*
- ▶ example **example, illustration** *Almost half of all children are born to unmarried parents, a graphic illustration of rapidly-changing social attitudes.*
- ▶ action **sex, violence** *Sweden banned the film because of its graphic violence.*

2 relating to drawing

- ADJ+n drawing **illustration, image, imagery, representation** *The book contains graphic illustrations of the technical process.*
- ▶ novel **novel** *Graphic novels, magazines and comics are available at some libraries.*
- ▶ artist **artist, designer** *Our team of graphic designers can prepare electronic media, exhibition materials or questionnaires for you.*
- ▶ art **art, arts, design** *She studied graphic arts and photography.*

> Usage ***Graphic*** always comes before the noun in all of the ***ADJ+n*** combinations shown above: *Icons on a screen are graphic representations of files or programs.*

graphics N

pictures produced by computers

- adj+N impressive **amazing, excellent, high-end, high-quality, stunning, superb** *It is a very impressive game and the graphics are stunning.*
- ▶ impressive but without real value **fancy, flashy, slick** *They don't waste time with flashy graphics.*
- v+N produce graphics **create, design, generate, produce** *We use the best technology available to create our graphics specifically for our clients.*
- ▶ have or use graphics **contain, feature, include, use** *Consider highlighting key points of your lecture using graphics and animations.*
- ▶ show graphics **display** *Not all browsers display graphics or run scripts.*
- N+n **card, editor, package, program, software** *If you look in any computer magazine, you will see long lists of graphics packages in the advertisements.*

grasp V

1 take and hold someone or something tightly

- adv+V **firmly, tightly** *She sat on her horse, grasping the reins tightly in her hands.*
- V+n a part of someone's body **arm, elbow, hand, shoulder, wrist** *Catherine got up, but Fiona grasped her hand.*

- ▶ a weapon **knife, stick, sword** *He grasped his sword in order to slay him.*
- V+by **arm, hand, shoulders, wrist** *A tall, fierce-looking woman came up to her and grasped her by the wrist.*
- V+in **arms, claws, hand, paws** *I grasped the stick firmly in my right hand.*

2 understand something

- adv+V completely **fully** *Heisenberg soon showed that he fully grasped the implications of the new ideas.*
- ▶ quickly **immediately, instantly, quickly** *The chapter summaries allow the main points to be grasped quickly.*
- ▶ easily **easily, readily** *It's an idea that makes sense and is easily grasped.*
- ▶ without thinking about it **instinctively, intuitively** *Most early societies intuitively grasped the idea that the sun was the source of all life.*
- V+n an idea **concept, idea, point, principle** *The youngster quickly grasped the concept.*
- ▶ the meaning of something **essence, implication, meaning, nature, significance** *He immediately grasped the meaning of his companion's troubled look.*
- ▶ the basic aspects of something **basics, essentials, fundamentals, rudiments** *Once you have grasped the basics you are ready to go.*
- ▶ the importance of something **importance, seriousness** *Historians were quick to grasp the importance of the Kennedy assassination.*
- ▶ a fact **fact, reality, truth** *I still can't grasp the fact that he's never coming back, that I'll never hear his voice again.*

3 take advantage of an opportunity

- adv+V **eagerly, enthusiastically** *I eagerly grasped this opportunity of earning my living.*
- V+n **chance, opportunity** *She grasped the chance to train as a professional photographer.*

grasp N

1 the ability to understand something

- adj+N good **clear, comprehensive, excellent, firm, good, impressive, profound, real, remarkable, solid, sound, strong, sure, thorough** *It sounds like she has a good grasp of the basics.*
- ▶ not good enough **inadequate, limited, poor, shaky, tenuous, weak** *Children sometimes have a tenuous grasp of where food comes from.*
- ▶ basic **basic, rudimentary** *She had only a rudimentary grasp of English.*
- ▶ fairly good **decent, fair, reasonable** *As a biologist, I've got a reasonable grasp of how the human body works.*
- ▶ achieved because of a natural ability **instinctive, intuitive** *Matthew clearly has an intuitive grasp of film making.*
- v+N get a grasp of something **acquire, develop, gain, get** *It is important to get a grasp of some of the economic concepts that affect the markets.*
- ▶ have a grasp of something **have, possess** *As long as you have a basic grasp of arithmetic and a bit of common sense, you can get by in most workplaces.*

▶ show a grasp of something **display, reveal, show**
*The film shows a remarkable grasp of the reality of
life in Nazi Austria.*
▶ need a grasp of something **need, require** *You will
need a solid grasp of the techniques for creating
stories, poems, and scripts.*
▶ give someone a grasp of something **give (sb)** *The
accompanying CD gives the student a thorough
grasp of the spoken language.*

2 a very tight hold of someone or something

● adj+N **firm, tight** *The infant's grasp is firm.*

● v+N **elude, escape, evade, slip from, slip out of**
*The girl escaped his grasp and ran down the
alleyway.*

grass N
a common plant with thin leaves that covers the
ground

● adj+N long **long, tall** *The children played around
a bit in the long grass.*
▶ short **short** *Simon knelt on the short grass.*
▶ wet **damp, dewy, sodden, wet** *She slipped on the
wet grass and broke her ankle.*
▶ dry **dry, parched** *Someone had carelessly thrown
away a lit cigarette end, setting the dry grass alight.*
▶ thick or growing well **dense, lush, thick** *The grass
was lush after the recent rain.*
▶ thin or not growing well **patchy, sparse**

● v+N cut grass **clip, cut, mow, trim** *He was
employed to cut the grass at the golf course.*
▶ eat grass **chew, eat, graze, munch, nibble** *Asian
elephants eat grass, roots, leaves, twigs, bark, and
fruit.*
▶ grow grass **grow, plant, sow** *We want to persuade
landowners and cattle ranchers not to chop down
trees to grow grass.*

● N+n covered with or consisting of grass **bank,
court, path, pitch, track, verge** *We parked on the
grass verge by the church.*
▶ consisting of cut grass **clippings, cuttings,
mowings** *The council will only collect grass cuttings
if they are placed in green plastic bags provided by
them.*

● n+of+N a single piece of grass **bit, blade, piece,
stalk** *The horse was nibbling at some long blades of
grass.*
▶ a group of pieces of grass growing close together
clump, tuft, tussock *A few clumps of grass cling to
its steep sides.*
▶ an area covered with grass **area, bit, expanse,
patch, piece, stretch, strip** *My garden is nothing
more than a patch of grass.*

grate V
rub food against a grater to cut it into small pieces

● adv+V recently **freshly** *Add a little freshly grated
nutmeg to the onion mixture.*
▶ into very small pieces **finely** *Finely grate the
potatoes and place in a bowl of water for 10 minutes.*
▶ into large pieces **coarsely, roughly** *Coarsely grate
the zest from the lemon and squeeze the juice.*

● V+n cheese **cheese** *Sprinkle the top with grated
cheese.*

▶ a vegetable **carrot, courgette, cucumber, onion**
Next, wash and grate the carrots.
▶ a fruit **apple, coconut** *Serve topped with grated
apple.*
▶ a substance from a plant added to provide a
particular flavour **ginger, horseradish, nutmeg**
*You can also grate some ginger over the top of the
dish.*
▶ chocolate **chocolate** *Decorate with grated chocolate
and chill before serving.*
▶ the outer skin of a fruit **peel, rind, zest** *Mix this
with two teaspoons of chopped parsely and the grated
rind of half a lemon.*

grateful ADJ
feeling that you want to thank someone

● adv+ADJ very **deeply, enormously, especially,
extremely, immensely, most, particularly,
profoundly, really, so** INFORMAL, **very** *We are
extremely grateful for their support.*
▶ for a very long time **always, eternally, forever** *I
will be eternally grateful to him for that.*
▶ in a sincere way **genuinely, truly** *We are truly
grateful for this wonderful gift.*

● ADJ+for help **assistance, contribution, help,
support, work** *I would be very grateful for any help.*
▶ money **contribution, donation, generosity** *The
school is enormously grateful for the donation.*
▶ opportunity **chance, opportunity** *I am really
grateful for the opportunity to visit India, not just
for my research.*
▶ advice **advice, comments, suggestion** *I'd be grateful
for any advice you could give me.*
▶ information **information** *We were so grateful for the
information she gave us about our mother.*

gratitude N
a feeling of being grateful

● adj+N sincere **heartfelt, sincere** *The family would
like to express their sincere gratitude to all relatives,
friends, and neighbours for the many messages of
sympathy received at this sad time.*
▶ great **deep, enormous, immense, profound** *He
leaves with our profound gratitude for all that he
has done.*
▶ continuing for a very long time **eternal,
everlasting, undying** *These men deserve the nation's
undying gratitude.*

● v+N express gratitude **convey, express, extend,
offer, record** *I don't know how to express my
immense gratitude.*
▶ show gratitude **show** *They naturally wished to show
their gratitude.*
▶ feel gratitude **feel** *She felt no gratitude to him.*
▶ receive someone's gratitude **earn, receive, win** *He
quickly earned the gratitude of his team-mates.*
▶ deserve gratitude **deserve** *For that, they deserve
our gratitude.*

If you think that someone deserves your gratitude,
you can say that you *owe them a debt of gratitude*:
*We owe a debt of gratitude to the college for the use
of its facilities during filming.*

● N+for help **assistance, contribution, help, support**
*They would like to record their gratitude for the help
they've received.*

▶ kind behaviour **kindness** *I often think of him with gratitude for his kindness to me.*

▶ work **efforts, service, work** *They deserve our respect and gratitude for the work they do.*

● n+of+N a way of showing gratitude **expression, tears, words** *He put the money in his pocket, without any expression of gratitude.*

▶ a feeling of gratitude **feeling, sense** *I was filled with a deep sense of gratitude.*

greatness N
a position of power, success, or respect

● adj+N real **real, true** *This is a band destined for true greatness.*

▶ future **future, potential** *She dreams of future greatness.*

▶ past **former, past** *No traces of the city's former greatness remain.*

▶ in a particular area of activity **artistic, literary, musical** *He realized his pursuit of literary greatness was incompatible with the obligations of marriage.*

● v+N **achieve, aspire to, be destined for** *He believed everyone was capable of achieving greatness.*

greed N
a wish for more money or possessions than you need

● adj+N emphasizes the degree of greed **naked, pure, sheer, simple, unadulterated** *This is just another example of pure greed by the banks.*

▶ by companies **capitalist, commercial, corporate** *There is too much corporate greed in the world.*

▶ uncontrolled **insatiable, rampant, unbridled** *These people were largely motivated by insatiable greed.*

▶ by people in general **human** *The planet is suffering from the disastrous effects of human greed.*

▶ by an individual person **individual, personal, private** *Most people are driven by personal greed.*

● v+N **feed, satisfy** *They seek to satisfy their own greed and their own ambitions.*

● v+by+N **be driven, be fuelled, be motivated** *They deny the possibility of any alternative to a society fuelled by greed.*

green ADJ
like grass in colour

● adj+ADJ dark **dark, deep, rich** *A small bird, it has a mixture of light brown and deep green feathers.*

▶ pale **light, pale** *Each window contains sections of pale green glass resembling jade.*

▶ bright **bright, glossy, vibrant, vivid** *The region has beautiful scenery, with vivid green valleys dotted with small villages.*

▶ particular shade **bluish, greyish, leafy, lime, metallic, olive** *He was dressed immaculately in his smart olive green uniform.*

If someone is wearing green clothes, you can say that they are *in green*, *dressed in green*, or *wearing green*: *Smart crew members dressed in green guided us up to our seats.*

greet V
be polite or friendly when meeting someone

● adv+V in a friendly way **cordially, enthusiastically, warmly** *We were greeted warmly by my father-in-law.*

▶ not by a representative **personally** *You will be personally greeted on arrival.*

● V+with **hug, kiss, smile** *Mrs Bowler was greeted with a hug by her daughter.*

2 react to something in particular way

● adv+V **enthusiastically, positively, rapturously** *The suggestion was greeted enthusiastically.*

● V+n statement **announcement, suggestion** *The announcement was greeted coolly by business leaders.*

▶ news **news** *Aid agencies greeted the news of a possible peace deal with caution.*

● n+V **applause, cheer, chorus, laughter, roar, silence** *Thunderous applause greeted the winners.*

● V+with positive reactions **delight, enthusiasm, excitement, joy** *The news was greeted with delight by his followers.*

▶ negative reactions **anger, derision, dismay, hostility** *The president's decision was greeted with dismay by many Democrats and even some Republicans.*

▶ silence **silence** *The offer was greeted with silence.*

▶ shouting **chorus, cry, howl, roar** *This was greeted with cries of outrage from delegates.*

▶ refusal to believe something **disbelief, incredulity, scepticism** *The claims were greeted with scepticism.*

▶ shock **horror, shock** *His execution was greeted with horror by his family.*

greeting N
1 polite or friendly words or actions when meeting someone

● adj+N friendly **affectionate, cheery, cordial, friendly, hearty, warm** *Whenever I met him, he always offered a cheery greeting.*

▶ formal **formal, polite** *'It is a pleasure to meet you,' he said, extending a hand in polite greeting.*

▶ usual **standard, usual** *I walked into the class and gave my usual greeting.*

▶ traditional **traditional** *She smiled widely and clasped her hands in the traditional greeting.*

● v+N **exchange, give (sb), offer (sb), return, shout** *Recognising each other from university, we exchanged greetings.*

2 a friendly message sent to someone for their birthday, Christmas etc [usually plural]

● adj+N friendly **cordial, warm** *I would like to extend my warmest greetings to everyone, with best wishes for 2010.*

▶ connected with Christmas and the New Year **festive, holiday, New Year, seasonal, season's** *Cards bearing messages of love and festive greetings have been sent since Roman Times.*

▶ connected with someone's birthday **birthday** *Birthday greetings to a very special dad, father-in-law and grandad.*

● v+N **bring, convey, extend, send (sb)** *We send seasonal greetings to all, and our best wishes for health and happiness in the New Year.*

grey ADJ

1 black mixed with white

- adj+ADJ dark **dark** *The sky was dark grey, and it was starting to rain.*
- ▶ pale **light, pale, soft** *Their website has a soft grey background, with very readable black text.*
- ▶ in a particular shade **ashen, bluish, brownish, metallic, pinkish, silvery, steely** *Her large, steely grey eyes stared at him calmly.*

If someone is wearing grey clothes, you can say that they are *in grey*, *dressed in grey*, or *wearing grey*: *The castle is supposedly haunted by a Victorian lady in grey.*

2 having hair that is becoming whiter

- adv+ADJ fairly **quite, slightly** *Captain Bedford was a tall, slightly grey man of fifty.*
- ▶ earlier than usual **prematurely** *I was putting on weight, and beginning to go prematurely grey.*
- ▶ completely **completely** *By that time, you'll probably be completely grey.*
- v+ADJ **be, go, turn** *I seem to be going grey very quickly.*

grief N

a strong feeling of sadness

- adj+N great **bitter, deep, great, intense, overwhelming, profound, untold** *We all feel deep grief when those who are dear to us die.*
- ▶ real **genuine, real** *Catherine's grief at the loss of this husband who had never loved her was genuine.*
- ▶ private **personal, private** *Everyone has to learn how to ease their own private grief.*
- ▶ public **collective, public** *Intense public grief had attended the death of President Nasser in 1970.*
- v+N show or express grief **display, express, show** *They need to know that it is all right to be upset and express their grief.*
- ▶ experience grief **experience, feel, share, suffer** *All of America must feel enormous grief at that appalling event.*
- ▶ succeed in dealing with grief **heal, overcome** *I cannot seem to overcome the grief.*
- ▶ understand someone's grief **understand** *All volunteers undertake a training course on understanding grief and loss.*
- ▶ accept grief **bear** *They bore their grief with immense dignity.*
- n+of+N an act of expressing grief **display, expression, outpouring** *Verdi's death in January 1901 resulted in a national outpouring of grief.*
- ▶ a feeling of grief **feeling, sense** *In that situation, a feeling of grief often begins long before the actual death.*

grievance N

feeling that you have been treated unfairly or a complaint about this

- adj+N real **genuine, just, legitimate, real, valid** *Despite their legitimate grievances, these movements are no longer portrayed as resistance movements.*
- ▶ having existed for a long time **long-standing, old** *This will tackle a long-standing grievance of many pensioners.*

- ▶ reasonable **reasonable** *We will endeavour to resolve any reasonable grievance as soon as possible.*
- ▶ types of grievance **economic, political** *The agitation seems to have been concerned solely with the redress of economic grievances.*
- ▶ relating to a single person **individual, personal** *The document also proposes removing the right to take individual grievances to external arbitrators.*
- v+N state a grievance **air, articulate, express, raise, state, voice** *You need to create a secure environment where colleagues feel able to air their grievances and discuss problems.*
- ▶ find a solution to a grievance **address, redress, resolve, settle** *Grievances are usually best resolved through direct dialogue between the employee and the relevant manager.*
- ▶ officially present a grievance **bring, file, lodge, present, pursue, submit** *There is a minimum 28-day period after lodging the grievance before an employee can make his claim to an employment tribunal.*
- ▶ listen to a grievance **hear, listen to** *The manager hearing the grievance may decide to see individuals separately.*
- ▶ feel a grievance **feel, harbour, nurse** *Even in families, grievances are nursed, sometimes for years.*
- n+of+N cause, matter, **sense, source** *The Treaty of Versailles left Germany with a sense of grievance.*

grim ADJ

1 unpleasant, without hope, and causing worry

- adv+ADJ rather **fairly, pretty** INFORMAL, **quite, rather, somewhat** *This all sounds pretty grim and hopeless but it is really not.*
- ▶ very **particularly, really, truly, very** *Life is really grim around here.*
- ADJ+n situation **conditions, scenario, situation** *They both agreed that the situation is grim.*
- ▶ future **future, outlook, prospect** *Whoever wins the election, the outlook is grim.*
- ▶ statement about the future **forecast, prognosis, warning** *Even with antibiotics, the prognosis is fairly grim.*
- ▶ account **news, reading, story, tale** *The list made grim reading.*
- ▶ fact **fact, reality, statistic, truth** *In the 1930s, Americans longed to escape the grim realities of the Depression.*
- ▶ work **job, task, work** *The grim task of removing bodies from the scenes of London's bomb blasts has been completed.*
- ▶ something reminding you of a past event **reminder** *We were taken to the cemetery at Thiepval, a grim reminder of the horrors of war.*
- v+ADJ **look, seem, sound** *Things are looking grim for the music industry as a whole.*

2 describing ugly and unpleasant places

- adv+ADJ rather **fairly, pretty** INFORMAL, **quite, rather, somewhat** *This is a rather grim building inside.*
- ▶ very **particularly, really, truly, very** *The surroundings were very grim.*
- ADJ+n **block, building, estate, fortress, surroundings** *She grew up on a grim housing estate in Wembley.*

grin V

smile showing your teeth

- adv+V with a big smile **broadly, widely** *Mike opened the door, grinning broadly.*
- in a silly way **inanely, madly, maniacally, wildly** *Des, Mick and Wayne just grinned inanely.*
- in an embarrassed way **sheepishly** *He grinned sheepishly at the polite applause.*
- in a satisfied way **smugly** *The boy grinned smugly at him and strolled nonchalantly to the door.*
- with a lack of respect **cheekily, impishly, mischievously, wickedly** *Two of the students were grinning mischievously across their desks.*
- in a nervous way **nervously** *Andy caught my eye and grinned nervously.*

grin N

a big smile that shows your teeth

- adj+N big **beaming, big, broad, huge, wide** *I saw him coming back with a big grin on his face.*
- showing a lot of teeth **toothy** *He favoured them with a toothy grin.*
- satisfied **satisfied, smug** *'I'm afraid so, Jack,' Daniel replied with a slightly smug grin.*
- showing a lack of respect **cheeky, devilish, impish, mischievous, sly, wicked** *He'd always have a twinkle in his eye and a cheeky grin.*
- silly **cheesy** INFORMAL**, goofy** INFORMAL**, inane, manic, silly, stupid** *He had an inane grin on his face.*
- showing sadness or disappointment **rueful, wry** *She remembered the experience with a rueful grin.*
- embarrassed **embarrassed, sheepish** *Quickly hiding my embarrassment with a sheepish grin I dashed back up the stairs.*
- happy **cheery** *John will always greet you with a cheery grin.*
- evil **evil** *There was an evil grin on her face when she looked over at us.*
- permanent **fixed, permanent** *Most of us at the party were walking around with permanent grins on our faces because we were having such a good time.*
- v+N **flash, give (sb), grin, have, smile, sport, wear** *Miss Gold suddenly flashed a broad, cheerful grin at the audience.*

grip N

a firm, strong hold

- adj+N strong **firm, good, powerful, secure, strong, tight, vice-like** *He has a vice-like grip on her arm.*
- weak **loose, weak** *As well as having a weak grip, I cannot move my fingers properly in that hand.*
- v+N make a grip stronger **strengthen, tighten** *He tightened his grip on the kid's arm.*
- make a grip weaker **loose, loosen, relax, release** *He pulled at her fingers, trying to loosen her grip.*
- have or keep a grip **have, keep, maintain** *Ensure you have a secure grip on the device when using it.*
  - *Keep a firm grip on handbags and shoulder bags in crowded places.*
- lose a grip **lose** *He was losing his grip on the boxes under his arm.*
- get a grip **get, take** *I grabbed him by the hair, got a grip on his shirt with my other hand, and pulled him out of the water.*

2 power and control over someone or something

- adj+N strong **firm, iron, powerful, strong, tight, vice-like** *Despite calls for him to relinquish some control over institutions, he has maintained his tight grip.*
- weak **loose, tenuous, weak** *The church has a much looser grip here than in Poland.*
- v+N have a grip **have, hold** *By November the government believed that it now had a grip on the situation.*
- get a grip **get, take** *You really ought to get a grip on your own finances.*
- make a grip stronger **strengthen, tighten** *The King has sought to tighten his grip on the country by increasing the presence of police on the streets.*
- make a grip weaker **loosen, relax, release, relinquish** *France and Spain have relaxed their grip on public sector pay rises.*
- keep a grip **exert, keep, maintain, retain** *Montrose kept a firm grip on the match.*
- lose a grip **lose** *The nobility began to lose their grip on power.*

grip V

1 hold something tightly

- adv+V **firmly, hard, tightly** *The baby gripped my finger tightly.*
- V+n part of the body **arm, finger, hand, shoulder, throat, wrist** *Louise suddenly gripped my arm and stared at me with wild eyes.*
- object **bar, handrail, rail, seat, sword, wheel** *I was gripping the steering wheel very hard.*

2 have a strong effect on someone

- V+n **city, country, nation, region, world** *Some 80 years ago, the Great Depression gripped the country.*
- n+V strong emotion **excitement, fear, fever, panic** *Football fever is gripping the nation.*
- situation **crisis** *A crisis is gripping the education system.*

groan N

a long low sound of pain, sadness, or disappointment

- adj+N loud **loud** *He gave a loud groan.*
- deep **deep, low** *She was interrupted by a deep groan from her husband.*
- able to be heard **audible** *She let out an audible groan.*
- by everyone **collective** *There was a collective groan from the crowd.*
- v+N produce a groan **emit, give, let out, utter** *She shuddered and uttered a little groan.*
- stop yourself producing a groan **suppress** *I suppressed a groan, blinked and yawned widely.*

gross ADJ

extremely bad and deserving disapproval

- ADJ+n illegal or unacceptable behaviour **abuse, indecency, injustice, misconduct, mismanagement, violation** *Following an investigation, the agency has dismissed 14 members of staff for gross misconduct.*
- lack of skill or good judgement **incompetence, inefficiency, mismanagement, negligence** *Three top*

*managers have been charged with gross
mismanagement of public funds.*

▸ statement or claim **distortion, exaggeration,
oversimplification** *I think your argument is a gross
oversimplification of the case against capital
punishment.*

ground N

1 a reason for saying or doing something [usually
plural]

● adj+N good **good, reasonable, strong, sufficient,
valid** *There were reasonable grounds to believe that
he was involved with the deception.*

> You can use the phrases *on grounds of* and *on the
> grounds that* to talk about the reason for
> something: *The company will approve a request for
> early retirement on grounds of ill-health.*

▸ types of grounds **compassionate, economic,
financial, legal, medical, moral, political** *She was
released early on medical grounds.*

● v+N **be, give sb, have, provide** *They know that
they do not have any valid grounds for complaint.*

2 a subject or idea being talked about [always
singular]

● adj+N **familiar, new, old, safe, the same** *No useful
purpose would be served by going over old ground.*
● *The new article covered pretty much the same
ground as the old one.*

> You can say that something *breaks new/fresh
> ground* when it is completely different from what
> has gone before: *This book breaks new ground in the
> scientific study of phobias.*

● v+N **cover, go over, tread** *But these new
regulations cover the same ground.*

ground V

base an idea or decision on something [usually
passive]

● adv+V well **firmly, solidly, thoroughly** *The policy
is solidly grounded in economic theory.*
▸ in a particular respect **empirically, historically,
scientifically, theoretically** *Financial economists
will at last be able to offer relevant and scientifically
grounded investment advice.*

grounding N

a basic knowledge of a subject

● adj+N good **excellent, firm, good, solid, sound,
strong, thorough** *Although GCSE music provides a
solid grounding for study of the subject at a higher
level, it is also a stimulating course in its own right.*
▸ basic **basic** *We are looking for people who have at
least a basic grounding in the sciences.*
● v+N get a grounding **acquire, gain, get** *Students
get a thorough grounding in software development.*
▸ give someone a grounding **ensure, give (sb), offer
(sb), provide (sb with)** *The course offers an intensive
grounding in one of the major non-European
civilizations of the world.*
▸ have a grounding **have** *These courses are for
learners who have a basic grounding in English
and want to improve their communication skills.*

groundless ADJ

not based on evidence or good reasons

● adv+ADJ **entirely, totally, utterly** *Such claims are
utterly groundless, as anyone who attended our
previous meetings can testify.*
● ADJ+n **accusation, allegation, claims, doubts,
fears, rumour, suspicions** *I hope I'm exaggerating
and my fears prove groundless.*
● v+ADJ **be, prove** *Luckily, the rumour proved
groundless and things continued as normal.*

groundwork N

work done in order to prepare for something

● adj+N necessary **essential, necessary** *This two-
stage approach looks shrewd, with the working
paper laying the essential groundwork.*
▸ basic **basic, fundamental, initial** *Advice was
provided by the National Gallery, where much
fundamental groundwork was accomplished.*
● good **excellent, solid, valuable** *The trip was a
consolidation exercise which will provide valuable
groundwork for future years.*
▸ types of groundwork **diplomatic, intellectual,
theoretical** *The first two chapters lay the theoretical
groundwork for the rest of the book.*
● v+N **do, form, lay, prepare, provide** *The review
was intended to lay the groundwork for progress.* ●
*The chapter provides very valuable groundwork for
the rest of his discussion.*

group N

a set of people or things

● adj+N types of group **demographic, ethnic, racial,
religious, social, socio-economic** *The legislation
promotes equality of opportunity between people in
different racial groups.*
▸ in a particular area **local, national, regional** *The
Victorian Society is a nationwide organization with
a London headquarters and eight regional groups.*
▸ of a particular size **big, finite, large, select, small**
*The student will be a member of a large group of
graduates involved in biochemical analyses of lake
sediments.* ● *Only a select group of artists will be
asked to participate.*
▸ with members who are similar to/different from
each other **disparate, diverse, heterogeneous,
homogeneous, mixed** *This year a mixed group of
pupils and teachers undertook an exchange with a
Chinese school.*
▸ consisting of people with problems
disadvantaged, marginalized, vulnerable *The
scheme should be extended to other vulnerable
groups, particularly to those households who
currently receive Income Support payments.*
● n+N consisting of a particular type of person
client, consumer, terrorist, user, youth *As a
Government, we always work in partnership with
consumer groups.*
▸ defined with regard to a particular feature **age,
faith** *The Forum has membership from the following
faith groups: Christian, Buddhist, Hindu, Islamic,
Jewish and Sikh.*
▸ concerned with a particular activity **discussion,
lobby, pressure, research, self-help, support** *There*

are also support groups that offer advice and counselling to bereaved people.

● v+N organize a group **chair, establish, head, lead, organize, run, set up** *The counsellors who lead the groups are experienced in setting up a safe and trusting atmosphere.*

▶ form a group; be or become a member of a group **form, join** *I'd really like to form a group with others, so we can work together.* ● *These languages form a group with many features in common.* ● *If you are interested in joining the group, email us at the address below.*

● v+into+N divide things or people into groups **categorize, classify, divide, organize, put, sort, split, subdivide** *These substances can be classified into three groups, depending on their solubility in water.* ● *The students were split into two groups of six.*

▶ when people or things form a group or groups **break, fall, form** *After the introduction, we broke into groups to discuss the issues among ourselves.* ● *The replies to the questionnaire fell into three distinct groups.*

group V
out people or things into groups [usually passive]

▶ adv+V broadly **broadly, loosely, roughly** *The company offers a wide range of services, which can be broadly grouped into four categories: web development, creative services, recruitment and hosting.*

▶ when things are similar, or close together **closely, tightly** *In an alphabetical scheme, closely grouped items may have nothing in common, beyond the fact that their names begin with the same letter.*

▶ according to a particular feature **alphabetically, thematically** *Words and pictures are grouped thematically and feature favourite topics such as toys, animals and parts of the body.*

▶ in a sensible or convenient way **conveniently, logically, sensibly** *Our site allows you to look at products that are grouped together logically.*

▶ V+by+n **ability, category, region, subject, theme, topic, type** *To assist with searching, the information is grouped by theme and date of release.*

▶ V+into+n **areas, categories, classes, clusters, regions, sections, sets, themes, types, units** *These issues can be grouped into three main sections.*

▶ V+under+n **categories, headings, themes** *Soils are grouped under three headings: Sand, Loam and Clay.*

grouping N
set of people or things considered as group

▶ adj+N types of grouping **ethnic, political, professional, regional, religious, social, socio-economic, tribal** *The sample covered people in all socio-economic groupings and included unmarried women who had opted to remain childless.*

▶ clearly/not clearly defined **broad, distinct, informal, loose** *Thinking of a spectrum, rather than distinct groupings, may be more useful.* ● *The organization is an informal grouping of UK companies, launched in 2008.*

▶ v+N make a grouping **create, establish, organize**

She creates small groupings within mixed-ability classes, with each working at their own pace.

▶ be a grouping **form, represent** *The Department of Neuroscience (DNS) represents the other significant grouping of neuroscientists.*

▶ identify or suggest a grouping **describe, identify, propose, recognize, suggest** *Aristotle identifies three main groupings in Attica, and two are set around important aristocratic clans.*

grow V
increase or become stronger

● adv+V fast or by a large amount **apace, considerably, dramatically, enormously, exponentially, rapidly, significantly, strongly, substantially** *The Catholic community in Edinburgh began to grow considerably in the mid-19th century.*

▶ in a steady way **constantly, continually, gradually, slowly, steadily** *The numbers of people taking the course have grown steadily over the past few years.*

● V+in **confidence, importance, maturity, popularity, size, stature, strength** *I hope this tournament will be run again next year, as I can only see it growing in stature.*

growing ADJ
becoming bigger, more frequent, or more serious

● adv+ADJ **fast, rapidly** *Newcastle University offers a rapidly growing and vibrant Business School, located in the centre of one of the UK's friendliest cities.*

● ADJ+n number or amount **number, percentage, proportion** *Growing numbers of older people are likely to place intolerable strain on our health and social care services.*

▶ business, economy or place **brand, city, company, economy, sector** *At that time, Republic of Ireland was one of the world's fastest growing economies.*

Usage ***Growing*** is very often preceded by ***fastest*** in these combinations: *It is now the UK's fastest growing confectionery brand.*

▶ feelings **awareness, concern, discontent, interest, popularity, realization, recognition, trend, unrest** *I began to have growing concerns over the non-development of her verbal communication.*

▶ importance **importance** *It is a seaside town of rapidly growing importance.*

▶ when someone wants something **demand** *There is a growing demand for this type of product.*

growth N
an increase in the importance, success, or size of something; an increase in the size or development of a living thing

● adj+N fast or great **explosive, exponential, fast, massive, rapid, significant, strong, substantial, unprecedented** *The latter half of the twentieth century saw exponential growth in air travel.*

▶ steady **continued, steady, sustained** *Our purpose is to secure the long-term success of the club by sustained growth in membership numbers and subscription income.*

▶ slow **slow, sluggish** *For example, countries such as Japan and Switzerland are low-spending nations but* have had slow growth **in** GDP per head in recent years.

▶ normal or healthy **healthy, normal** The range of cereals offers a complete balanced diet for healthy growth.

▶ types of growth **economic, industrial** Britain's rate of expansion and industrial growth had continued to fall behind that of other countries.

● v+N cause growth **accelerate, boost, contribute to, drive, encourage, facilitate, foster, lead to, promote, stimulate** You will walk away with useful ideas to accelerate the growth of your business.

▶ stop growth or make it slow **inhibit, prevent, restrict, slow, stunt, suppress** The government has tried for some years to inhibit traffic growth. ● The children's mental and physical growth was stunted by malnutrition.

▶ see or show growth **see, show, witness** The UK has witnessed dramatic growth **in** income inequality over the past 20 years.

● N+v **accelerate, fall, occur, outstrip, slow** Bone growth occurs most quickly during foetal life, infancy and puberty. ● Consumption growth has far outstripped population growth.

● N+n **potential, prospect, rate, spurt, strategy** Larger companies increasingly recognise the growth potential of environmental markets. ● Growth spurts could cause certain teenage cancers.

● n+in+N **decline, increase, slowdown** The current slowdown in economic growth has had a significant impact on business confidence.

grudge N
an angry feeling because of something wrong or unfair

● adj+N **long-held, long-standing, old, personal** He had complex, long-standing grudges **against** nearly every tenant.

● v+N **bear, carry, harbour, hold** Bobby has reasons of his own for harbouring a grudge **against** Glen.

guarantee V
1 make certain that something will happen or exist

● adv+V almost **almost, practically, virtually** If you make the booking yourself, you almost guarantee that you'll not pay the high prices routinely charged to tourists.

▶ completely **absolutely, fully** No checking system can fully guarantee that a newly-downloaded file is fully safe.

▶ in effect **effectively** His presence effectively guarantees an entertaining broadcast.

▶ automatically **automatically** Join our loyalty scheme, which automatically guarantees you a 30 per cent saving on all purchases.

● V+n **accuracy, freedom, independence, safety, security, stability, success, survival** These services guarantee the security of your transactions over the Internet.

2 to promise that something will happen, or that someone will get something

● adv+V **absolutely, personally, unconditionally**

The trustees will personally guarantee any loans required for the purchase of the site.

● V+n **confidentiality, delivery, privacy, safety, satisfaction** We guarantee your complete satisfaction.

guarantee N
1 an agreement protecting someone buying goods

● adj+N **cast-iron, insurance-backed, lifetime, money-back, no-quibble, 30-day, one-year etc** These genuine parts come with a two-year guarantee **against** defects.

● v+N have **carry, come with, have** All sales and repairs carry a three-year guarantee.

● N+v protect **apply to, cover, protect** All subscribers are protected by this guarantee.

▶ be no longer valid **expire, run out** Technology has made it possible to design things to last just long enough until the guarantee expires.

● N+of **authenticity, quality, reliability** A guarantee of authenticity will accompany each item.

2 a promise that something will happen

● adj+N **absolute, cast-iron, unconditional** I realise no professional footballer can be given a cast-iron guarantee of first-team football.

● v+N give a guarantee **give (sb), offer (sb), provide (sb with)** We had to give a guarantee that we could pay that amount.

▶ ask for a guarantee **ask for, seek** The country is seeking a guarantee that it will have a say in how the oil revenue is spent.

▶ make a guarantee no longer valid **invalidate** If you modify the equipment in any way, you may invalidate the guarantee.

● N+of+n **anonymity, confidentiality, privacy, satisfaction, success** Each respondent was given guarantees of anonymity and confidentiality.

guard V
1 protect a place or thing [usually passive]

● adv+V **carefully, closely, heavily, tightly** We were sitting in a building more heavily guarded than any other in the UK.

2 try hard to keep something, or keep something secret [usually passive]

● adv+V **carefully, closely, fiercely, jealously, strictly, tightly** It was a jealously guarded secret.

guard against PHR VB
try to prevent something from happening

● V+n **abuse, attack, complacency, danger, error, fraud, possibility, risk, temptation, threat** There is still a need to guard against complacency, and more must be done to reverse the rising trend in reported crimes. ● We had to guard against the possibility that future trustees might decide to sell the collection.

guess N
an opinion about what could be true

● adj+N made without careful calculation

random, rough, wild *At a rough guess, the value could not be much under £5,000.*

▶ based on intelligent thought **best, educated, informed, intelligent** *He made a best guess based on his observations at the time.* • *I don't know for certain, but I can make an educated guess.*

▶ probably fairly accurate **fair, good, reasonable** *It's a fair guess that most new immigrants already have friends or family here.*

▶ correct/not correct **correct, incorrect** *One point is awarded for each correct guess.*

▶ correct, in a lucky way **inspired, lucky** *'How did you know?' 'I didn't. It was a lucky guess.'*

> If you want to emphasize how uncertain you are about something, you can use the phrase **anybody's guess**: *What the future holds for the family is anybody's guess.*

▶ v+N **have, hazard, make, take** *I imagine – but I'm only hazarding a guess – that more than 50 per cent of the people that come here actually come for the good weather.*

guesswork N
attempts to find an answer by guessing

▶ adj+N complete **pure** *Everything I've written so far is pure guesswork.*

▶ based on intelligent thought **educated, informed, intelligent** *A little educated guesswork had led me to this conclusion.*

▶ v+N use guesswork **base sth on, rely on, resort to** *I'm not going to make promises based on guesswork.*

▶ get rid of guesswork **eliminate, remove, take out** *LoanPayment is an easy-to-use tool that takes the guesswork out of calculating loan repayments.*

guest N
someone invited to your home, or to a party, meeting or other event

▶ adj+N that you have invited/not invited **invited, unexpected, uninvited, unwanted, unwelcome, welcome** *The spectacle was witnessed by 2000 invited guests.* • *He managed to evict the unwanted guest.* • *The sign was intended to deter unwelcome guests.*

staying the night **overnight** *There is a spare bedroom for overnight guests.*

famous or special **celebrity, distinguished, famous, important, special** *The audience included many distinguished guests from business and academia.*

▶ v+N invite a guest **invite** *They were not sure how many guests they should invite to their wedding.*

welcome a guest **greet, receive, welcome** *On arrival, guests are welcomed in the main reception area.*

entertain a guest **amuse, delight, entertain** *The guests were entertained by amusing speeches and a band.*

be able to hold a particular number of guests **accommodate, hold, seat** *The restaurant comfortably seats 100 guests.*

▶ v+with+N **chat, interact, mingle, mix, socialize** *We then got the chance to mingle with the celebrity guests.*

guidance N
advice about what to do

● adj+N good **authoritative, clear, detailed, expert, full, practical, useful** *He is the person to whom members turn for authoritative guidance on a wide range of initiatives.*

▶ types of guidance **academic, educational, official, parental, professional, spiritual, statutory, technical, vocational** *We advise you to seek professional guidance on matters such as these.*

● v+N give guidance **deliver, give (sb), issue, offer (sb), provide (sb with)** *The association offers financial guidance on benefit issues.*

▶ publish guidance **develop, draft, issue, prepare, produce, publish** *There are also numerous examples of departments producing their own guidance on environmental issues.*

▶ change guidance **amend, review, revise, update** *The Local Authority also said it would amend its guidance to referees, in order to encourage a more open approach in the future.*

▶ need or ask for guidance **ask for, look for, need, require, seek, want** *It is no surprise that children need guidance to deal with these issues.*

▶ get or receive guidance **get, obtain, take** *New members should take guidance from experienced members as to whether conditions are suitable for skiing.*

▶ wait for guidance **await, wait for** *We are waiting for government guidance to see what the effects of the new law will be.*

▶ follow guidance **follow** *When choosing your courses, you should follow the guidance contained in this guide.*

● v+under+N **act, operate, train, work** *Junior hospital doctors work under the guidance of the consultants.*

guide N
1 a book etc that gives information about something

● adj+N good or useful **essential, good, handy, helpful, indispensable, practical, reliable, useful** *This useful guide to events in the area can be downloaded as a pdf file.*

▶ short or simple **basic, brief, quick, short, simple** *The following is a brief guide to English pronunciation:*

▶ detailed or complete **comprehensive, detailed, in-depth** *Their website is a comprehensive guide to various environmental issues.*

▶ easy to follow **step-by-step** *Here is our step-by-step guide to completing the form.*

▶ better than all the others **definitive** *Her new book is the definitive guide to careers in the music industry.*

▶ in a particular form **audio, downloadable, hands-on, interactive, online, photographic, printed** *Their website includes a handy interactive guide to removing stains.*

2 something that helps you to make a judgment

● adj+N good **good, helpful, reliable, useful** *Academic achievement is not a wholly reliable guide as to who will succeed.*

▶ approximate **approximate, general, rough** *As a*

rough guide, you'll probably take about two hours to complete each batch.

- v+N **give (sb), intend sth as, provide (sb with), use sth as** *This picture can be used a good guide to the structure and layout of the old Globe Theatre.*

guide v
teach someone or help someone make decisions

- adv+V **ably, expertly, gently, personally** *She ably guided us through a series of examples to demonstrate her points.*

- V+through **procedure, process, series, stage** *The user is guided through the process step by step.*

guidelines N
official instructions or advice about something
[always plural]

- adj+N types of guidelines **clinical, dietary, ethical, nutritional, official, professional, regulatory, technical** *Some credit card companies have ethical guidelines about the companies and industries they support.*

- ▶ clear or strict **clear, detailed, prescriptive, strict, stringent** *Some organisations may have quite stringent guidelines on who can volunteer with them.*

- v+N make or give people guidelines **develop, draw up, establish, give sb, issue, lay down, lay out, produce, propose, publish, set out** *The organization should issue more definite guidelines on what owners' responsibilities are.*

- ▶ do what guidelines say **abide by, adhere to, adopt, apply, comply with, conform to, enforce, follow, implement, meet, operate within, stay within, stick to, work to, work within** *How do we ensure that members follow the guidelines?*

- ▶ not do what guidelines say **breach, break, flout, go against, ignore** *The FSA can heavily fine firms breaching its guidelines.*

- N+v **advise, apply, indicate, recommend, require, say, set out, state, stipulate, suggest** *The following guidelines on homework apply to secondary school pupils. • The guidelines stipulate that a student nurse must work at least 50 % of their placement hours with their mentor.*

- n+of+N **list, series, set** *UNESCO is developing a set of guidelines for planners in the Ministry of Education.*

guilt N
1 the ashamed, unhappy feeling you get after doing something bad

- adj+N **overwhelming, terrible** *She was unable to cope with the overwhelming guilt she felt.*

- v+N feel guilt **be consumed by, be racked by, be tormented with, experience, feel, suffer from** *Parents may feel guilt about what genes they have transmitted.*

- ▶ get rid of guilt **assuage, ease, relieve** *People often try to assuage the guilt of wrongdoing by doing right.*

- n+of+N **burden, feeling, pang, sense, twinge** *I feel a burden of guilt that I'm alive and he's dead. • I couldn't help but feel a twinge of guilt.*

2 the fact that someone has committed a crime or done something wrong

- v+N admit guilt **acknowledge, admit, confess** *The defendants all confessed their guilt in the opening days of the trial.*

- ▶ deny guilt **deny** *Five of those charged have denied their guilt.*

- ▶ show that someone is guilty **establish, prove** *Helen suspects him all along and eventually proves his guilt.*

- ▶ have guilt **bear** *The judge felt that Jones bore little guilt in the collapse of his firm.*

- N+v **lie** *There was no doubt where the main guilt lay.*

- n+of+N **admission, burden, confession** *His apology was tantamount to an admission of guilt. • She must bear the burden of guilt for her brother's death in the crash.*

guilty ADJ
1 ashamed and sorry for doing something wrong; making you feel like this

- adv+ADJ very **deeply, extremely, so, terribly** INFORMAL, **very** *I felt terribly guilty that I had let her down.*

- ▶ rather **a little, rather, slightly, somewhat** *Most of us left the room feeling silghtly guilty and determined to do better next time.*

- ADJ+n **conscience, feeling, pleasure, secret, silence** *New Year offers from gyms make the most of our guilty consciences from eating all that Christmas food. • I indulged in a few guilty pleasures, like watching trashy films on the TV.*

- v+ADJ **feel, look** *The redundancies left remaining workers feeling guilty about keeping their jobs.*

2 having committed a crime or done something wrong

- adv+ADJ **clearly, equally, obviously** *If two people take part in a murder, then both of them are equally guilty, no matter who actually did the killing.*

- ADJ+n person **defendant, party, person, prisoner, suspect** *The guilty party turned out to be a 13-year-old child.*

- ▶ decision **verdict** *Emily remained calm as the foreman of the jury gave the guilty verdict.*

- ▶ statement **plea** *He formally entered a guilty plea on Friday.*

- v+n+ADJ **be, consider sb, declare sb, deem sb, find sb, hold sb, judge sb, plead, presume sb, pronounce sb, prove sb** *Anyone driving above those limits is deemed guilty of 'excessive speed'. • He pleaded guilty to driving without due care and attention.*

gulf N
a great difference between people or groups

- adj+N big **deep, enormous, great, huge, impassable, unbridgeable, vast, wide, yawning** *There was an unbridgeable gulf between the world of the miners and that of the educated gentlemen.*

- ▶ becoming bigger **growing, widening** *It was clear that the growing gulf between the US and Europe on this subject is becoming an increasing problem.*

▸ types of gulf **cultural, ideological, philosophical, psychological** *Between the two parties there was a fundamental philosophical gulf.*

● v+N close a gulf **bridge, close, cross, fix** *In fact, the gap between politics and people is getting wider and the big question is how to bridge that gulf.*

▸ make a gulf bigger/smaller **narrow, widen** *Climate change will widen the gulf between rich and poor.*

● N+v exist or appear **exist, open (up)** *A huge gulf has opened up between the lives of politicians and those of ordinary people.*

▸ separate people **divide, separate** *A deep gulf separates primitive from modern democracy.*

gun N
a weapon that shoots bullets

● v+N shoot a gun **discharge, fire, shoot** *New recruits are taught how to drive a tank, fire a gun and march in step.*

▸ have a gun with you **carry** *He feels safest when he's carrying a gun.*

▸ hold a gun and be ready to use it **aim, brandish, cock, draw, hold, level, point, pull out, train, wave, wield** *One lad brandished an imitation plastic gun and waved it in a threatening manner.*

▸ put bullets etc in a gun **load** *The men who load the guns cannot see the ships they are firing at.*

● N+v **blast, blaze, fire, go off, open fire, open up, sound** *In the altercation, the gun went off and the driver was killed.*

● N+n **battle, control, crime, culture, law, lobby, ownership, violence** *I wholly support the Home Secretary's commitment to tackling gun crime.* ● *The drug culture spawns the gun culture, and both help create the culture of violence.*

gunfire N
shots from guns

● adj+N **distant, heavy, sporadic** *Apart from sporadic gunfire, the day was pretty quiet.*

● v+N when someone or something is hit by gunfire **be damaged by, be destroyed by, be hit by, be killed by, be wounded by** *An American child is killed by gunfire every 2 hours and 40 minutes.*

▸ when two groups shoot at each other **exchange** *The people had taken to the streets and they exchanged gunfire with the police units who had been drafted in.*

● N+v **erupt, ring out, sound** *Automatic gunfire rings out at night throughout town.*

● n+of+N **barrage, burst, exchange, hail, sound, volley** *Then a hail of gunfire splattered the wall behind him.*

Hh

habit N
something you do often or regularly; a physical need to do something regularly

- adj+N unpleasant **annoying, bad, dirty, disgusting, filthy, irritating, nasty, unfortunate, unhealthy** *Auden's slovenliness and disgusting habits somehow emerge as charming eccentricities.*
- ▶ strange **curious, peculiar, strange** *The creatures have the peculiar habit of making sudden long leaps as they trot along.*
- n+N **drinking, driving, eating, feeding, reading, shopping, sleeping, spending, surfing** *Some Internet users may have unwittingly downloaded spyware which reports on their surfing habits.*
- v+N have a habit **have** *The chimpanzees have a nasty habit of throwing things at you.*

> If you do something regularly, you can say that you are **in the habit** of doing it or that you **make a habit** of doing it: *I'm not in the habit of gossiping about my friends.* If you have been doing something regularly for a long time, you can say that you do it **out of habit** or do it **from habit**: *Heading back to the park gates, we made an obligatory stop at the drinking fountain, out of habit rather than necessity.*

- ▶ start having a habit **acquire, adopt, cultivate, develop, fall into, get into** *As you discipline your life and begin to cultivate good habits, you get your life under control.* • *Get into the habit of using the stairs rather than the lift.*
- ▶ stop having a habit **break, kick, overcome, quit** *Drug abusers are being helped to overcome the habit rather than being jailed.*
- ▶ change your habits **alter, change** *To lose weight, you must aim to change your eating habits.*

habitat N
the usual home of an animal or plant

- adj+N in danger **fragile, rare, threatened** *Lowland heath is a rare and threatened habitat.*
- ▶ natural or suitable **ideal, native, natural, preferred, suitable** *The best information comes from the people who saw the bird in its native habitat.*
- v+N cause harm to a habitat **damage, degrade, destroy, disturb, threaten** *The roadbuilding programme threatens wildlife habitats in the whole East Thames Corridor.*
- ▶ keep a habitat safe or make it better **conserve, enhance, preserve, protect, restore, safeguard** *The Trust aims to safeguard this fragile habitat and its indigenous wildlife through a number of conservation measures.*
- ▶ create or provide a habitat **create, provide** *These forests provide a habitat utilized by many species.*
- ▶ be found in a habitat **live in, occur in, thrive in** *More than half of British butterfly species occur in this habitat.*
- N+v grow smaller **decline, disappear, shrink** *Numbers of cheetahs are dwindling because their natural habitat is shrinking.*

- ▶ contain animals or plants **attract, include, support** *Each habitat usually supports a fairly diverse group of organisms.*
- N+n creation or improvement **conservation, creation, enhancement, improvement, management, restoration** *They have encouraged wildlife through habitat creation and conservation.*
- ▶ destruction **degradation, destruction, disturbance, fragmentation, loss** *Historical declines of many species can be attributed in part to habitat loss.*
- ▶ type or range of types **diversity, type** *Habitat diversity is important since the number of habitat types has been shown to be a good represenation of species diversity.* • *Savannah is the primary habitat type in two large national parks in South Africa.*
- n+on+N **effect, impact, pressure** *These pollutants have a direct impact on habitats and species.*
- n+to+N **damage, disturbance, threat** *Key threats to grassland habitats include fertiliser application and overgrazing.*

hail V
say publicly that someone or something is good

- adv+V **immediately, often, recently, rightly, universally, widely** *The movie is rightly hailed as a classic of the genre.*

> Usage **Hail** is usually passive in these combinations: *Automatic Speech Recognition is often hailed as the most natural interface between humans and machines.*

- V+as **breakthrough, classic, genius, hero, masterpiece, saviour, success, triumph, victory** *When the book was first published, it was hailed as a masterpiece of comic satire.*

hair N
the mass of fibres that grows on your head

- adj+N of a particular colour or shade **auburn, black, blonde, brown, dark, fair, ginger, golden, grey, light, red, white**
- ▶ straight/not straight **curly, frizzy, straight, wavy** *Her soft wavy hair was grey and she wore elegant pearl earrings.*
- ▶ long/short **cropped, flowing, long, short, shoulder-length** *Not everyone with cropped hair is a hooligan.*
- ▶ thin/thick **fine, thick, thin** *My hair is really fine and difficult to style.*
- ▶ shiny or soft **glossy, shiny, silky, sleek, soft** *She looked stunning with her mane of glossy black hair.*
- ▶ looking untidy **messy, shaggy, straggly, tangled, tousled, unkempt, untidy, windswept** *He was about 20, with unkempt hair and a beard.*
- ▶ looking unpleasant **greasy, lank, matted** *The old woman's hair was lank and unwashed and her skin was pallid.*
- v+N have your hair in a particular style **grow, have, plait, tie back, wear** *I'm growing my hair long again.* • *He had his hair in a ponytail.* • *She wore her hair in long curls at the sides.*

▶ cut hair **crop, cut, shave (off), trim** *Where do you have your hair cut?*

▶ arrange your hair **brush, comb, do** *She wanted to buy some new clothes and get her hair done.* • *I must do my hair before I go out.*

▶ change the colour of your hair **bleach, colour, dye** *His hair was still so dark; we wondered if he dyed it.*

● N+v be very long **cascade, fall, hang, tumble** *As she leant back in the chair her long dark hair cascaded over her shoulders.*

▶ become less thick **thin** *I was putting on weight and my hair was thinning.*

halt N
a temporary or permanent stop in a process or movement

● adj+N **abrupt, complete, grinding, premature, screeching, sudden, temporary** *The house-building boom came to an abrupt halt at the start of the recession.*

● v+N ask for a halt **call for, demand, order** *They called for an immediate halt to the deportation of asylum seekers.*

▶ when somebody or something makes something stop **bring, call, force, put** *Lack of funds brought a halt to a number of initiatives.* • *The campaign put a halt to further expansion of the town.*

▶ v+to+N when somebody or something makes something stop **bring** *Work was brought to a halt by the appalling weather.*

▶ come to a halt **come, draw** *Last year, my career came to an abrupt halt, as a result of a serious back injury.*

▶ come to a halt in a particular way **grind, screech, shudder, skid** *The talks went on for several weeks and then finally ground to a halt.* • *The car screeched to a halt, narrowly avoiding a wall.*

hamper V
prevent something from happening or progressing normally

● adv+V **badly, greatly, seriously, severely, significantly** *Research has been severely hampered by the costs of obtaining data.*

Usage **Hamper** is usually passive in these combinations.

▶ V+n **ability, attempt, development, effectiveness, effort, growth, investigation, operation, progress, recovery** *But the popularity of four-wheel drive 'sports utility vehicles' is hampering efforts to cut air pollution on Britain's roads.*

hand N
the part of your body at the end of your arm

● v+N when you greet someone **shake, wave** *I had to shake hands with everyone in the room.* • *She shook my hand and welcomed me warmly.*

▶ move your hand out or up **extend, hold out, outstretch, raise** *As a man approached, she extended her hand for the ticket.*

▶ have someone's hand in yours **clasp, hold, squeeze, take** *The child held his mother's hand tightly and wouldn't let go.* • *It's unusual to see an elderly couple holding hands.*

You can also say that two people who are holding each other's hand are **hand in hand**: *They walked off down the street, hand in hand.*

▶ rub or twist your hands together **rub, wring** *I rubbed my hands together to try and keep warm.* • *He was wringing his hands nervously as the interviewer's questions became more aggressive.*

▶ close your hand **clench, squeeze** *Clench your hands into tight fists, hold for a few seconds, then slowly spread your fingers.*

● N+v hold something or someone **clasp, close around, clutch, grasp, grip, hold** *Suddenly, a strong hand clasped his arm and drew him into the darkness.*

▶ shake **shake, tremble** *My hands were trembling so much that they were impossible to control.*

▶ close **clench, close around sth, close over sth** *Peter tensed, his hands clenching tight.* • *The man's hands closed around her throat.*

handicap N
a disadvantage preventing you from doing something well

● adj+N serious **grave, permanent, profound, serious, severe, terrible** *The time and effort involved in individual evaluation can present a severe handicap.*

▶ additional **added, additional** *Sykes had the added handicap of being dismissed by his teacher as 'not likely to get much further'.*

● v+N be a handicap **be, become, constitute, present, prove** *Lack of communication proved a major handicap to the commanders on the ground.*

▶ have a handicap **face, have, suffer** *Agriculture in these mountainous areas suffers a permanent natural handicap.*

▶ overcome a handicap **overcome** *The young Charles was determined to overcome these childhood handicaps.*

handle V
1 deal with or be responsible for something

● adv+V well **competently, deftly, easily, efficiently, expertly, professionally, skilfully, superbly, well** *Using this system, frequently changing data can be handled efficiently.* • *I'm certain that the changes will be well handled by the teaching staff.*

▶ correctly **appropriately, correctly, properly** *Allegations must be taken seriously and handled properly.*

▶ carefully **carefully, securely, sensitively** *These are very delicate problems and must be handled sensitively by parents or carers.*

▶ not well **badly, poorly** *Complaints about abuse are often handled badly.*

▶ in a different way **differently, separately** *We accept in hindsight that it might have all been handled differently.* • *Energy use is handled separately on this site.*

Usage **Handle** is usually passive in all of the **adv+V** combinations shown above.

● V+n situation **affair, dispute, incident, matter, situation** *It was obvious the attendant was distraught and unable to handle the situation on her own.*
▶ task or case **case, caseload, claim, task** *Currently, they are looking for a solicitor to handle a mixed caseload.*
▶ complaint or request **call, complaint, enquiry, query, request** *Some traditional brokers can only handle phone enquiries.*
▶ data **data, traffic, transaction** *They have the ability to handle transactions in many different currencies.*
▶ stress **stress** *Read our handy hints on revision, handling stress and coping with exams.*
▶ feature **aspect** *Trained electricians will handle all aspects of the electrical installation of the appliances.*

● V+with skill **aplomb, confidence, ease, efficiency, professionalism** *It is a crucial role which he handled with aplomb.*
▶ care **care, caution, delicacy, discretion, respect, sensitivity** *There is one subject we wish to touch on, though it needs to be handled with delicacy.*
▶ humour **humour** *The bleak subject matter is handled with wonderful humour.*

Usage **Handle** is usually passive in all of the **V+with** combinations shown above.

2 touch or hold someone or something

● adv+V correctly **correctly, properly, safely** *If discs are not handled correctly, air and moisture can penetrate.*
▶ carefully **carefully, with care** *If using pesticides at home, handle with care.*
▶ not carefully **roughly** *These are stressful places, with animals often being handled roughly.*
▶ by hand **manually** *The system allows panels to be moved directly into position without having to be handled manually.*

Usage **Handle** is usually passive in all of the **adv+V** combinations shown above.

handsome ADJ
with a very attractive face

● adv+ADJ very **devastatingly, exceedingly, exceptionally, extremely, impossibly, incredibly, remarkably, singularly, unbelievably, unusually, very** *Although married, she falls in love with the devastatingly handsome Count Vronsky.*
▶ fairly **fairly, quite, rather** *She met a rather handsome Irish gentleman, and hoped to see him again.*
▶ in a very noticeable way **strikingly, stunningly** *His charisma and strikingly handsome features held television audiences spellbound.*
▶ looking slightly rough or badly behaved **darkly, dashingly, devilishly, ruggedly** *He was a tall man with ruggedly handsome good looks.*
▶ looking young **boyishly** *He is boyishly handsome in a way that guarantees him slots on TV.*
▶ in a traditional way **classically** *Not classically handsome, he is thin and wears glasses.*

● and/or tall or strong **athletic, tall** *There in the doorway stood a tall handsome young man.*
▶ charming **agreeable, charismatic, charming, debonair, gentlemanly** *Handsome and debonair, he sweeps Cornelia off her feet.*
▶ intelligent **intelligent, witty** *He is a gifted scholar, a first-rate sportsman, and handsome and witty too.*
▶ brave **brave, dashing** *The hero is usually a brave, handsome young man.*
▶ well-dressed **well-dressed** *A handsome, well-dressed gentleman asked what was troubling her.*
▶ young **young** *She fell in love with a handsome young man.*
▶ with particular colour hair **blond, dark** *George Clooney is tall, dark, handsome – and like a wine, he seems to be getting better with age.*

handwriting N
how someone writes using a pen or pencil

● adj+N not clear **appalling, atrocious, awful, cramped, illegible, messy, poor, shaky, spidery, terrible, unclear, untidy** *The completed forms contained spelling mistakes and illegible handwriting.* ● *There was a note from her in very shaky handwriting.*
▶ clear **legible, neat, tidy** *Please ensure that the handwriting is legible, by using block capitals.*
▶ flowing **fluent, joined-up** *Children need to be taught that legible, fluent handwriting serves their own interests.*
▶ in a particular style **cursive, italic, old-fashioned** *They are taught cursive handwriting around the age of 8.*
▶ belonging to someone **own** *The collection contains Forster's own copy, annotated in his own handwriting.*

● v+N understand someone's handwriting **decipher, interpret, read, recognize** *By peering very hard, I could decipher her handwriting.*
▶ not understand someone's handwriting **misread** *The use of Mobile Data Terminals would avoid errors caused by typists misreading handwriting.*
▶ practise your handwriting **improve, practise** *I really must get her to practise her handwriting, as that's what is holding her back.*
▶ study someone's handwriting **analyse, compare** *If you send a hand-written application, beware – they may analyse your handwriting.*
▶ make your handwriting look different **disguise, forge** *Nick received a card from his mum, who'd disguised her handwriting.*

handy ADJ
useful

● ADJ+n advice **hint, tip** *There are plenty of handy hints to help improve your skills.*
▶ tool **checklist, gadget, guide, tool** *This is a handy gadget which fits into the palm of your hand.*

● v+ADJ **be, come in, prove** *The log splitter will prove extremely handy for anyone who has open fire in their home.*

hang V
remain in the air

● n+V **cloud, mist, smoke** *The weather is wretched, dark clouds hanging ominously over the city.*

haphazard ADJ

not planned or organized

- adv+ADJ rather **fairly, largely, a little, often, pretty** INFORMAL**, quite, rather, relatively, slightly, sometimes, somewhat** *Do they follow a structured approach to their work or do things appear somewhat haphazard?*
- ▶ very **completely, extremely, totally** *The organisation in the park was totally haphazard, with a queue of cars blocking the way of the coaches.*
- ▶ apparently **apparently, seemingly** *To fully understand the characters' seemingly haphazard behaviour, you have to be familiar with the book.*
- ADJ+n way of doing something **approach, fashion, manner, nature, way** *Our booking policy has operated in a slightly haphazard fashion in the past.*
- combination **arrangement, jumble, mixture, pile** *He pulled a few books from the shelves and placed them in a haphazard pile.*
- and/or **casual, chaotic, confusing, idiosyncratic, inconsistent, ineffective, random, uncontrolled, uncoordinated, unpredictable, unsatisfactory, unstructured** *A common complaint has been the apparently haphazard and uncoordinated way that employment legislation has been brought in.*

happen V

take place, usually without being planned

- adv+V really **actually, really** *I can see no evidence of this actually happening.*
- quickly **overnight, quickly, suddenly** *Organisational and cultural change never happens overnight.*
- often or usually **always, everywhere, frequently, normally, usually** *Women are designed to have babies one at a time, and with natural conception, this is what usually happens.*
- rarely or occasionally **occasionally, rarely, sometimes** *Some film critics say great cinema happens only rarely.*
- by itself **automatically, naturally** *Data backups on laptops do not happen automatically.*
- again **again** *What can be done to ensure that disasters like this don't happen again?*
- n+V accident or bad event **accident, attack, catastrophe, collision, crash, disaster, earthquake, event, explosion, incident, mistake, seizure, tragedy** *Did you know that most children's accidents happen at home?*
- magical event **magic, miracle** *I do believe that miracles happen.*
- change **change, evolution, revolution** *It is only through the efforts of everyone that changes happen.*
- something or nothing **anything, everything, nothing, something** *Any proposals have got to get the consent of all the parties, otherwise nothing happens.*

happiness N

the feeling of being happy

- adj+N complete **perfect, pure, sheer, supreme, true, unalloyed** *For the two sisters, the years of unalloyed happiness and contentment were gone.*

- ▶ not real **illusory** *We spend our time rushing around, chasing after illusory happiness.*
- ▶ long-lasting **eternal, everlasting, lasting** *With all your heart, you wish them sincere and lasting happiness.*
- ▶ brief **fleeting, fragile, short-lived** *Drugs are an expensive way to buy a little fleeting happiness.*
- ▶ at home **domestic, marital** *His infatuation destroyed his domestic happiness and tarnished his name.*
- ▶ on earth **earthly, worldly** *He loses his fiancée and the chance of earthly happiness.*
- ▶ new or future **future, new-found** *Should they tell her, and risk ruining her new-found happiness?*
- v+N seek happiness **desire, pursue, seek** *They sought happiness through their community, friends and family, rather than through material possessions.*
- ▶ find happiness **achieve, attain, experience, find** *She has been driven to despair by her inability to find happiness with her husband.*
- ▶ increase happiness **maximize, promote, spread** *He argues that a good action is one that promotes happiness.*
- ▶ bring someone happiness **bestow, bring (sb), guarantee** *The sad fact is that money does not bring happiness at all.*
- ▶ spoil or destroy happiness **destroy, disturb, mar, ruin, shatter** *His happiness is shattered when he discovers that she is already married.*
- ▶ show signs of happiness **exude, radiate** *Adam was still laughing, his face radiating happiness.*
- ▶ deserve happiness **deserve** *You fully deserve the happiness that has come your way.*
- ▶ sacrifice happiness **sacrifice** *He sacrifices his happiness to make sure I am happy.*
- N+v **come from, consist in, depend on, lie in** *Your happiness lies in using your creativity to communicate something meaningful.*
- and/or **contentment, fulfilment, joy, love, peace, prosperity, sadness, sorrow, unhappiness, wealth, well-being** *May the holiday season bring only happiness and joy to you and your family.*

happy ADJ

1 feeling pleased and not sad

- adv+ADJ very **blissfully, completely, deliriously, extremely, perfectly, very** *For the first year after their marriage the two of them were blissfully happy.* • *These were very happy days and I made some great friends.*
- ▶ truly **genuinely, really, truly** *He was really surprised, but really happy, about the job.*
- ▶ fairly **fairly, generally, pretty** INFORMAL**, reasonably** *This will help you become generally happier and more effective in all that you do.*
- v+ADJ be happy **be, feel** *We all know that if we feel happier, our families feel happier.*
- ▶ appear happy **appear, look, seem, sound** *What's the matter? You don't sound very happy.*
- ▶ remain happy **remain, stay** *I just need to stay happy and in a positive frame of mind.*

2 satisfied that something is good or right

- adv+ADJ very **extremely, perfectly, quite, very** *A large crowd were quite happy to stay outside and try* and see the act free of charge. • I'm very happy **with** what I've seen of the preparations.

▸ not very **not completely, not entirely, not particularly, not too, not totally** They were not too happy **about** newcomers trying to occupy their territory.

▸ fairly **fairly, generally, pretty** INFORMAL, **reasonably** Most people are reasonably happy **with** the result.

● v+ADJ be happy **be, feel** Once everyone is happy **with** the choice, the booking is made.

▸ seem happy **appear, look, seem, sound** They didn't look too happy **about** having their business displayed everywhere.

▸ keep someone happy **keep sb** Different sizes, different tastes, how can you keep everyone happy?

harass V
keep annoying or upsetting someone

● adv+V repeatedly **constantly, continually, continuously, often, persistently, repeatedly, routinely, systematically** You can obtain a legal injunction against the perpetrators if they are persistently harassing you.

▸ deliberately **deliberately** The charity believes the authorities are deliberately harassing Dr Mudawi.

▸ in a particular way **physically, verbally** A group of drunk men were verbally harassing every woman who walked past them.

▸ because of a particular characteristic **racially, sexually** Soon after the takeaway opened, local youth began to racially harass Mr Zhang.

● and/or threaten **bully, humiliate, intimidate, threaten** He condemned militant anti-vivisectionists who harass and intimidate researchers.

▸ follow or annoy **annoy, pester, stalk, torment** He approached her with the intention of harassing and pestering her.

▸ attack **assault, attack, molest** 40 per cent of nurses reported that they have been harassed or assaulted by patients or their relatives.

▸ insult **abuse, defame, insult** Under no circumstances should you abuse or harass other players online.

▸ treat unfairly **discriminate against, oppress, victimize** If you feel you are being harassed or discriminated against in any way, please let us know.

▸ pursue or arrest **arrest, detain, hound, imprison, persecute** His security forces have harassed, imprisoned and tortured with impunity.

harassment N
regular annoying or unpleasant behaviour towards someone

● adj+N repeated **constant, continual, continued, ongoing, persistent, sustained, systematic** He was evicted following persistent harassment of his neighbour.

▸ types of harassment **homophobic, racial, racist, sectarian, sexual, verbal** A member of staff left her post amid claims of racial harassment.

● v+N experience harassment **be subjected to, endure, experience, face, suffer** We will provide help for members if they are experiencing harassment or discrimination at work.

▸ allege harassment **allege** I recently acted on behalf of a female employee alleging sexual harassment.

▸ try to stop harassment **combat, eliminate, prevent, stop, tackle** New guidance on tackling the harassment of staff was announced last week.

harbour V
keep a thought or feeling in your mind

● adv+V **knowingly, long, secretly** Turkey has long harboured an aspiration to join the European Union.

● V+n anger or dislike **animosity, bitterness, dislike, distaste, grudge, hatred, resentment** People tend to harbour grudges over the most trivial of things.

▸ suspicion or doubt **doubt, misgivings, suspicion** Many continued to harbour suspicions as to his true whereabouts.

▸ ambition or hope **ambition, hope** They harbour totalitarian ambitions while pretending to be democrats.

▸ illusion **delusion, illusion** None of us harbour any illusions about doing this as a career.

▸ desire **crush, desire** He secretly harbours a crush on the receptionist at the clinic next door.

▸ secret **secret** His eldest son harbours a guilty secret.

hard ADJ
difficult

● adv+ADJ very **awfully, desperately, exceedingly, extremely, really, so, terribly, tremendously, very** Mining for tin was a very hard and dangerous occupation.

▸ rather **fairly, a little, moderately, pretty** INFORMAL, **quite, rather, reasonably, relatively, slightly, somewhat** This is a claim that is pretty hard to justify.

▸ sometimes **often, sometimes** It was sometimes hard to know whether she was suffering or not.

▸ more than usually **doubly, especially, exceptionally, extraordinarily, particularly** Meeting all my deadlines has been particularly hard this month.

▸ surprisingly **incredibly, surprisingly, unbelievably** The band handled this incredibly hard piece with ease. • These birds can be surprisingly hard to see amongst the treetops.

▸ according to what is always said **notoriously, traditionally** The target group for the project is men under 45, who are notoriously hard to reach.

▸ in a particular way **physically** Although the work is physically hard, he enjoys it.

● ADJ+infinitive understand **comprehend, fathom, figure out, grasp, read, see, understand** This play, though hard to understand at times, is probably one of Shakespeare's best.

▸ believe **accept, believe, swallow** It is hard to believe that this peak was first climbed only a hundred years ago!

▸ say exactly what, who, how many etc **define, describe, gauge, guess, judge, know, pin down, pinpoint, predict, quantify, say, tell** It is hard to predict what might happen in the future. • It's hard to tell if this is due to the translation or the original Japanese text.

▸ think or imagine **imagine, think** It's hard to imagine a low-calorie fat.

▸ deny or avoid **avoid, deny, escape, ignore, miss, resist** It's hard to avoid comparing the new version

with the old. ● *You are starving hungry and the lure of fast food is just too hard to resist.*
▶ argue **argue (with), convince sb, disagree** *At the time it was hard to argue with Burns' decision to let him go.*
▶ find or spot **detect, discern, distinguish, find, spot** *Many of the woodland species are hard to find.*
▶ reach or achieve **achieve, reach** *We secured a 'Very Good' award, which is extremely hard to achieve.*
▶ cope **cope (with)** *She finds the divorce very hard to cope with.*
▶ explain **explain, justify, reconcile** *Some experiences are so powerful, they are hard to explain.*
▶ choose **choose, pick** *It's hard to pick highlights from such a collection of success.*
▶ remember **remember** *This may seem complicated and hard to remember, but it isn't.*

hardship N
suffering or difficulties, especially because of lack of money

● adj+N very bad **acute, appalling, considerable, enduring, exceptional, extreme, grave, immense, incredible, severe, terrible, unbearable, unimaginable, untold, widespread** *Some of the people who reach the UK have suffered unimaginable hardship in their country of origin.*
▶ real **genuine, real** *Financial support is available for those able to demonstrate genuine financial hardship.*
▶ unreasonable **undue, unjustifiable, unnecessary** *It is necessary to plan for change in the best way for the community as a whole, without causing undue hardship.*
▶ unexpected **unexpected, unforeseen** *Bursaries may be awarded in cases of unforeseen hardship or temporary difficulty.*
▶ types of hardship **economic, financial** *Many students face financial hardship.*

● v+N experience hardship **encounter, endure, experience, face, suffer, undergo** *They were the faithful followers who endured hardship and privation with the king.*
▶ cause hardship **bring, cause, impose on sb, inflict on sb, perpetuate** *Many people thought sanctions merely inflicted hardships on ordinary people.*
▶ reduce hardship **alleviate, ease, minimize, relieve** *We are able in some instances to make additional payments to alleviate hardship.*
▶ avoid or overcome hardship **avoid, overcome, withstand** *They have shown such determination to overcome the hardships they faced on their journey.*

harm N
injury, damage, or problems you cause

● adj+N serious **grave, immense, serious, significant, substantial** *The directive could do serious harm to the development of electronic commerce in the European Union.*
▶ not very serious **minimal** *Some of these techniques have positive effects, or at least do minimal harm.*
▶ permanent or lasting **irreparable, irreversible, irrevocable, lasting, long-term** *If adopted, the policy could cause irreparable harm to the national security of the United States.*
▶ unnecessary or unacceptable **disproportionate,**

unacceptable, undue, unnecessary *Any further delay means more unnecessary harm to your health.*
▶ impossible to calculate **incalculable, untold** *The policy has visited untold harm on the poor in tropical climates.*
▶ possible to predict **avoidable, foreseeable, potential** *We hope that doctors can all prevent avoidable harm to patients.*
▶ possible to prove **demonstrable** *There was no demonstrable harm from folic acid supplementation.*
▶ deliberate **deliberate, intentional** *There are a number of public services designed to protect children from deliberate harm.*
▶ types of harm **bodily, emotional, environmental, pecuniary, physical, psychiatric, psychological** *A bad experience with drugs can lead to psychological harm.*

● v+N cause harm **cause, do (sb), inflict (on sb), occasion** *Trials of the treatment look promising, and it certainly seems to do no harm.* ● *These weapons inflict significant harm on civilians.*
▶ intend harm **intend (sb), mean (sb), wish (sb)** *While these people may have meant no harm, their actions threaten the community.*
▶ suffer harm **suffer** *If a child appears at risk of suffering significant harm, he/she may be removed from the parents.*
▶ risk harm **risk** *Academics who disagree risk harm to their careers.*
▶ avoid harm **avert, avoid, escape, prevent** *Rapid treatment for depressed mothers can prevent harm to children.*
▶ reduce harm **alleviate, minimize, mitigate, reduce** *We can study how other countries minimize the harm of drugs.*
▶ repair harm **redress, repair, undo** *No amount of supplements can undo the harm done by an unhealthy diet!*
▶ balance harm **balance, outweigh** *In these cases, benefits of surgery probably outweigh harm.*

harm V
injure, damage, or hurt someone or something

● adv+V seriously **gravely, seriously, severely** *This could seriously harm our ability to attract foreign capital.*
▶ in an important way **materially, significantly, substantially** *We will act if we consider that an organization is significantly harming the interests of a consumer.*
▶ deliberately **deliberately, intentionally, knowingly** *Although the dog would never intentionally harm them, she is best kept away from small children.*
▶ not deliberately **accidentally, indirectly, unintentionally** *Families can unintentionally harm their community's prosperity by having more children.*
▶ permanently or for a long time **irreparably, permanently** *This development would irreparably harm the natural environment of the region.*
▶ in an unnecessary or unacceptable way **unacceptably, unduly, unnecessarily** *We need to be sure that participants are not unduly harmed as a result of the research.*
▶ possibly **potentially, ultimately** *These areas should be protected from practices which could potentially harm the environment.*

▶ in a particular way **emotionally, physically, psychologically, sexually** *If the client was physically harmed, a physiotherapist may be needed.*

harmful ADJ
causing harm

● adv+ADJ seriously **deeply, extremely, seriously, significantly** *Modest alcohol intake may be beneficial, although excess is extremely harmful.*
▶ definitely **actively, definitely, downright, genuinely, overtly, positively** *Much of the material on the Internet is misleading or positively harmful.*
▶ particularly **especially, particularly** *This can be especially harmful because increased fat around the waist is linked to heart disease.*
▶ always, by its nature **inherently, intrinsically, necessarily** *We think of bacteria as intrinsically harmful.*
▶ possibly **possibly, potentially** *Organic food is free of potentially harmful pesticide residues.*
▶ in a particular way **environmentally, physically, psychologically, sexually, socially** *The waste emits gases like ammonia and methane that can be environmentally harmful.*
● v+ADJ be or become harmful **be, become, prove** *Taken in excess, salt can prove harmful.*
▶ consider harmful **consider, deem, regard** *Many chemicals have potential health threats and are considered harmful to the environment.*

harmless ADJ
not likely to cause harm or problems

● adv+ADJ completely **completely, entirely, perfectly, quite, totally, utterly** *The spots are perfectly harmless and I would advise no treatment for them.*
▶ fairly **comparatively, fairly, pretty** INFORMAL, **reasonably, relatively** *Most ocean waves are relatively harmless because their energy spreads rapidly.*
▶ mostly or basically **basically, essentially, mostly, ultimately, virtually** *He was well known as an often drunk but essentially harmless young idiot.*
▶ usually **normally, usually** *An allergy occurs when the body's immune system over-reacts to normally harmless substances.*
▶ apparently **apparently, ostensibly, seemingly** *Seemingly harmless alterations may have undesired effects.*
▶ from a particular point of view **biologically, environmentally, politically** *It generates electric power by combining hydrogen and cheap, environmentally harmless methanol.*
● v+ADJ be or become harmless **be, be rendered, prove** *The weapons should be removed and rendered harmless.* ● *The bacteria proved harmless to humans.*
▶ seem harmless **appear, look, seem, sound** *In its early stages, diabetes is often not diagnosed because its symptoms seem harmless.*

harmony N
when people live and work well together

● adj+N perfect **perfect, universal** *They long to live in the wild, in perfect harmony with nature.*

▶ happy **blissful** *I hope you spend the rest of your lives together in blissful harmony.*
▶ relative **relative** *A feeling of ease and relative harmony gradually replaces the arguments.*
▶ types of harmony **communal, inter-ethnic, marital, racial** *There must be more action at national and local level to promote racial harmony.*
● v+N create harmony **achieve, attain, create, cultivate, foster, promote** *We strive to create harmony by forgiveness, not by seeking retribution.*
▶ bring back harmony **re-establish, restore** *We must do all that we can to restore harmony in the community.*
▶ disturb harmony **disrupt, disturb** *No arguments ever disturbed the harmony of their household.*

harness V
control something so that you can use it

● adv+V **effectively, efficiently, fully, properly, successfully, truly** *The new site allowed the organization to effectively harness the potential of the web.*
● V+n power **energy, potential, power, strength** *We haven't yet harnessed the full power of science in our quest to crack crime.*
▶ knowledge or skill **capability, expertise, resources, skill, talent, technology** *Businesses need to harness the latest technology to enhance their potential.*
▶ personal quality or emotion **anger, creativity, diversity, enthusiasm, goodwill, imagination, intelligence, passion** *We help organisations to develop and harness the creativity of their employees.*

harsh ADJ
1 conditions or places: unpleasant to be in

● adv+ADJ very **notoriously, unbelievably** *They were fighting over unbelievably harsh terrain in foul weather and at night.*
▶ more than usual **exceptionally, particularly, unusually** *An unusually harsh winter led to a famine in which 30,000 people died.*
● ADJ+n environment **desert, environment, terrain** *They will have to trek across the harsh Namibian desert.*
▶ conditions **conditions** *People questioned the contrast between the vast wealth of the ruling class and the harsh conditions of the working class.*
▶ weather **climate, weather, winter** *In the mountainous interior, the climate is harsher and the soil poorer.*
▶ light **glare, lighting, spotlight, sunlight** *He preferred candles to the harsh glare of electric lighting.*
● and/or **arid, barren, bleak, inhospitable** *The landscape we pass through is harsh, barren and empty.*

2 very strict and unkind

● adv+ADJ excessively or unreasonably **exceptionally, excessively, extremely, overly, particularly, too, unacceptably, unbelievably, unduly, unnecessarily, unreasonably, unusually** *Sending a player off for celebrating a goal seems unbelievably harsh.* ● *His comments can seem scathing and unduly harsh.*
▶ rather **a little, pretty** INFORMAL, **quite, rather,**

slightly, sometimes, somewhat, a tad INFORMAL
Perhaps I'm being a tad harsh.

● ADJ+n punishment or discipline **critique,
discipline, penalty, punishment, regime, reprisal,
retribution, sanction, sentence, sentencing, verdict**
*The students were subjected to harsh military
punishment.* ● *She was locked in a hospital with a
harsh prison regime.*

▶ criticism **criticism, judgement** *The manager came
in for some harsh criticism after the game.*

▶ treatment **repression, treatment** *There were many
rumours regarding her harsh treatment of her
daughter-in-law.*

▶ comment **tone, words** *Katie had some harsh words
for Debbie.*

▶ person **critic** *In many cases, the artist is his own
harshest critic.*

● and/or unsympathetic **judgmental, punitive,
uncompromising, unsympathetic, unyielding** *He
depicts the priests as harsh and unyielding.*

▶ cruel **brutal, cruel, inhumane, oppressive,
repressive** *Prison conditions were undeniably brutal
and harsh.*

▶ unfair **unfair, unjust** *The proposed ban is harsh and
unjust.*

3 not sounding pleasant or gentle

● and/or **abrasive, discordant, dissonant, grating,
guttural, hoarse, loud, metallic, shrill, strident**
Then I heard a harsh, grating voice.

4 facts: unpleasant but true

● ADJ+n fact **fact, reality, truth** *The harsh financial
reality is that we have to cut our expenditure on
services.*

▶ lesson **lesson, reminder** *The harsh lesson of his
theory was that we are just like the rest of the animal
kingdom.*

▶ realism **realism** *Harsh realism forces us to
contemplate an alliance.*

harvest N
a crop that is collected

● adj+N good or large **abundant, bountiful,
bumper, plenteous, plentiful, record, rich** *Dettor
irrigation and high-yielding varieties led to
increasingly bountiful rice harvests.*

▶ bad or small **bad, disastrous, failed, meagre, poor**
*More than 10 million people are in urgent need of
food because of meagre harvests.*

● v+N collect the harvest **bring in, garner, gather,
gather in, get in, pick, reap** *Peru's coffee farmers
should be smiling, having reaped record harvests
last year.*

▶ produce a harvest **produce, yield** *An increasing
proportion of the UK's vegetable harvest is produced
using irrigation.*

▶ destroy the harvest **decimate, destroy, devastate,
ruin** *There is a locust swarm threatening to devastate
harvests across West Africa.*

▶ expect a harvest **anticipate, expect, forecast,
predict** *The Ivory Coast is forecasting a bumper
cocoa harvest.*

hassle N INFORMAL
a situation that causes problems or annoys you

● adj+N big **enormous, major, real** *The installation
is not quite straightforward, but it's not a major
hassle.*

▶ small **less, little, minimal, minimum, minor, slight**
*You want to sell your home quickly, with minimal
hassle.*

> You can also say that something is *hassle free* or
> *free from hassle*: *Choosing and buying insurance
> should be as hassle free as possible.* ● *The club brings
> together people who want to enjoy an evening free
> from hassle.*

▶ regular or usual **daily, everyday, usual** *You can
avoid many of the everyday hassles faced by workers
in large organisations, such as sitting in endless
meetings.*

▶ happening all the time **constant, endless** *The
country was beautiful despite the endless hassle and
the heat..*

▶ additional or unnecessary **added, extra,
unnecessary** *If the bus service is reduced then it will
mean added hassle.*

▶ types of hassle **administrative, bureaucratic** *I gave
up the idea of flying around the world because of the
bureaucratic hassles involved.*

● v+N **avoid, eliminate, escape, lessen, minimise,
reduce, remove, save** *You will avoid the hassle of
securing your wheels every time you lock your bike.*

> You can also say that something *takes the hassle
> out of* doing something: *This takes the hassle out of
> selling things online.*

haste N
great speed in doing something

● adj+N not appropriate **indecent, undignified,
undue, unseemly** *There has been criticism following
the unseemly haste with which his successor was
appointed.*

▶ great **breathless, desperate, feverish, great** *The
rescuers worked with feverish haste in trying to
reach the other men.*

● v+N make haste **make** *It was difficult to make
much haste in the soft sand.*

hate V
dislike someone or something very much

● adv+V very much **absolutely, bitterly, cordially,
heartily, intensely, mortally, passionately, utterly**
The cat absolutely hates being picked up. ● *Speed
bumps tend to be cordially hated by cyclists.*

▶ really **positively, really** *If there is one thing I
positively hate, it's pointless arguing.*

▶ secretly **secretly** *They secretly hate you and want
your job.*

▶ openly **openly** *And he openly hates children.*

▶ personally **personally** *I personally hate filling in
forms.*

▶ universally **universally** *The military was
universally hated, but also feared.*

● and/or **despise, detest, dread, envy, fear, loathe,
scorn** *A tax collector was the most hated and despised
human being in society at that time.*

hate N

the feeling of hating someone or something

- v+N **feel, peddle, preach, spread** *The mayor accused the National Party of peddling hate.*
- N+n expressing or trying to spread hate **campaign, mail, mob, propaganda, speech** *He has been subject to a barrage of hate mail about the show.*
- ▶ caused by hate **crime, incident** *We collect information about religiously motivated hate crime.*
- ▶ the object of hate **figure** *The player has become a hate figure to Liverpool fans.*
- and/or **anger, bigotry, bitterness, disgust, enmity, envy, fear, intolerance, jealousy, prejudice, racism, violence** *These people have absolutely nothing to offer Northern Ireland except hate and bigotry.*

hatred N

the feeling of hating someone or something

- adj+N very strong **bitter, burning, ferocious, fierce, implacable, intense, inveterate, mortal, seething, venomous, virulent** *This fact helps explain the bitter hatred and rivalry that developed between the brothers.*
- ▶ unreasonable **blind, fanatical, indiscriminate, irrational, obsessive, pathological, unreasoning** *After a day at work, I am now developing an irrational hatred of the telephone.*
- ▶ lasting for ever or for a long time **abiding, undying** *The men are filled with undying hatred for the officers and the war.*
- ▶ deep or instinctive **deep-rooted, deep-seated, ingrained, instinctive, visceral** *A lifetime of abuse has created a deep-seated hatred of men.*
- ▶ violent **deadly, genocidal, murderous** *He spoke of the murderous hatred dividing people of different religions.*
- ▶ not hidden **naked, outright, sheer, utter** *We have faced suspicion and at times outright hatred.*
- ▶ mutual **mutual** *Though these groups profess deep mutual hatred, they actually have a lot in common.*
- ▶ types of hatred **anti-gay, class, ethnic, homophobic, race, racial, racist, religious, sectarian, tribal** *Black and Asian people have been driven from their homes after vicious campaigns of racial hatred.*
- v+N cause or encourage hatred **arouse, breed, engender, foment, foster, fuel, incite, inflame, intensify, peddle, preach, provoke, spread, stir up, whip up** *Extremists should not be allowed to use this as an excuse to foment hatred.*
- ▶ feel hatred **feel, harbour** *I still harbour hatred for the sports teacher who forced us to have cold showers.*
- ▶ express hatred **vent** *The Internet is a perfect place to anonymously vent hatred.*
- ▶ overcome hatred **combat, overcome** *It is our responsibility to combat hatred, intolerance and prejudice.*
- and/or anger **anger, bitterness, fury, rage, resentment, venom** *Her deception blew her family apart in hatred and bitterness.*
- ▶ dislike **animosity, dislike, enmity, hostility, ill-will, loathing, malice** *These reactions should never be allowed to turn into blind hatred and enmity.*
- ▶ violence or cruelty **bloodshed, brutality, cruelty, persecution, violence** *People must not be able to whip up hatred and violence by playing on people's religious beliefs.*
- ▶ prejudice **anti-Semitism, bigotry, intolerance, prejudice, racism, xenophobia** *They are supporting policies that can only increase the hatred and prejudice suffered by asylum seekers.*
- ▶ jealousy or rivalry **envy, greed, jealousy, rivalry** *Their success in business has attracted hatred and jealousy.*
- ▶ ridicule or disgust **contempt, disgust, revulsion, ridicule, scorn** *He stood up for his beliefs despite the hatred and ridicule poured upon him.*
- ▶ fear or suspicion **distrust, fear, mistrust, suspicion** *All his policy was dictated by his fear and hatred of the French Revolution.*
- ▶ revenge **revenge, vengeance, vindictiveness** *There was a vile campaign of vindictiveness and hatred focused on us.*
- ▶ ignorance **ignorance, misunderstanding** *His piece is designed to stir up misunderstanding and hatred.*
- ▶ extremism **extremism, fanaticism** *We need to stop them from teaching extremism and hatred.*

haunt V

continue to cause problems or make someone feel worried or upset for a long time

- adv+V **continually, eternally, forever, perpetually, persistently, still** *I am eternally haunted by the thought that I could have saved her.*
- n+V vision or possibility **apparition, demon, nightmare, spectre, vision** *A growing population of old people has become the spectre haunting global capitalism.*
- ▶ memory or past **ghost, memory, past** *His past constantly haunts him.*
- ▶ emotion **fear, guilt** *She has been haunted by guilt ever since Vic died.*
- ▶ event **disappearance, tragedy** *She is still haunted by the disappearance of her twin sister.*

haunt N

a place that someone likes and visits often

- adj+N regular **accustomed, favourite, regular, usual** *Everyone expects to see him regularly at his usual haunt in the College bar.*
- ▶ former **boyhood, childhood, former, old** *It will be interesting to visit old haunts and discover what has changed.*
- v+N go to **frequent, visit** *The rockers frequented haunts such as the Ace Cafe in north London.*
- ▶ go back to **go back to, rediscover, return to, revisit** *We've had a great time revisiting old haunts, and exploring new places.*

haven N

a place where people or animals are safe and happy

- adj+N peaceful **idyllic, peaceful, quiet, relaxing, restful, secluded, serene, sheltered, tranquil, unspoilt** *Step into the tranquil haven provided by the Royal Highland Hotel.*
- ▶ safe **safe** *Canada acted as a safe haven for loyalists fleeing from the rest of the Americas.*
- ▶ true **perfect, veritable** *Their garden is a veritable haven for birds.*
- n+N for tourists **backpacker, holiday, tourist** *The*

islands' reputation as a tourist haven was established in the 1960s.

▶ for lovers of food **foodie, gourmet** *The town is fast gaining a reputation as a bit of a foodie haven.*

▶ for rich people **tax** *The business is based in the British offshore tax haven of Jersey.*

▶ for animals **wildlife** *Esteros do Ibera in Argentina is a wildlife haven of marshes, forests and savanna.*

havoc N

a situation where things are damaged, destroyed, or very badly organized

● adj+N terrible **dreadful, fearful, sad, terrible, untold** *We need to understand the decisions and actions that wrought such terrible havoc in Europe between 1939 and 1945.*

▶ much **absolute, much, such, widespread** *Rabbits can cause absolute havoc in just a couple of days in a garden.*

● v+N bring, **cause, create, inflict, play, spread, unleash, wreak** *The sun can play havoc with your skin.* ● *A serious outbreak of the disease wreaked havoc amongst the poultry industry.*

hazard N

something that could be dangerous

● adj+N serious **lethal, major, particular, serious, significant, specific** *When used in schools solvent-based paints are a particular hazard to children.* ● *Car fires do not present an especially serious hazard to those tackling the fire.*

▶ possible **possible, potential** *No warning is given by manufacturers of this potential hazard.*

▶ immediate **immediate, imminent** *If a food ingredient poses an imminent hazard to public health, it must be withdrawn.*

▶ expected **associated, foreseeable, inherent, obvious** *The production of hydrocarbons carries inherent hazards.*

▶ not expected **hidden, unexpected, unforeseen** *There are unforeseen hazards, such as blind bends or animals in the road, that could lead to crashes.*

▶ happening in nature **natural** *Some areas are particularly vulnerable to erosion, floods, landslides and other natural hazards.*

▶ types of hazard **biological, chemical, climatic, electrical, environmental, geological, moral, navigational, occupational, radioactive** *Workplace asthma is the fastest growing occupational hazard in the UK.*

▶ n+N risk of a particular event **accident, avalanche, choking, contamination, drowing, earthquake, explosion, fire, flood, landslide, radiation, tripping, tsunami** *They refused to install sound-proofing material, as they considered it to be a potential fire hazard.*

▶ threat to something **health, safety, traffic** *Bird strike represents one of the major safety hazards to aircraft at take-off and landing.*

▶ risk in a particular place **workplace** *Classify your work activities in order to identify workplace hazards.*

● v+N be or create a hazard **be, cause, constitute, create, pose, present, represent** *Small quantities of the substance shouldn't pose a safety hazard if handled carefully.*

▶ face a hazard **encounter, face** *Along the way, they will encounter hazards like wild animals and robbers!*

▶ be aware of a hazard **anticipate, assess, identify, perceive, recognize, spot** *A childminder's job includes identifying these hazards and removing them.*

▶ get rid of hazards **eliminate, remedy, remove** *Apart from eliminating the radiation hazard, an MRI scan offers other advantages over X-rays.*

▶ reduce hazards **control, minimize, mitigate, reduce** *Science education should include learning how to minimize hazards when carrying out experiments.*

▶ avoid hazards **avoid, dodge, negotiate** *Suddenly having to swerve to avoid a hazard can result in a fatal crash.*

▶ reveal a hazard **highlight, reveal** *Any incidents that reveal a potential hazard should be reported.*

hazardous ADJ

dangerous, especially to people's health or safety

● adv+ADJ possibly **possibly, potentially** *Radar could alert you to a potentially hazardous situation.*

▶ very **extremely, highly** *The rescue services had to work in extremely hazardous conditions.*

▶ too **too, unacceptably** *Trees may be removed if they are felt to be unacceptably hazardous to property.*

▶ especially **especially, particularly, unusually** *The broken pavements around St Pauls Square are particularly hazardous.*

▶ rather **moderately, somewhat** *Liquid crystals are considered moderately hazardous and should be handled with care.*

▶ by its nature **inherently** *Genetic engineering biotechnology is inherently hazardous.*

▶ in a particular way **biologically, environmentally** *We aim to avoid batteries containing environmentally hazardous materials.*

● v+ADJ be hazardous **be, prove** *These missions prove hazardous, owing to difficult terrain and bad weather.*

▶ be considered hazardous **be classed as, be classified (as), be considered, be deemed** *The conditions were deemed too hazardous to use the helicopter.*

haze N

an unclear atmosphere because of smoke or mist in the air

● adj+N thick **thick** *Visibility was poor in the thick haze of smoke.*

▶ of smoke **smoky** *He suddenly spoke up from across the table through the blue smoky haze.*

▶ in particular weather **foggy, misty, moonlit** *On the horizon, a mountain emerges above the moonlit haze.*

▶ unpleasant or poisonous **acrid, noxious** *The fire created a cloud of noxious yellow haze.*

● N+v cover something **envelop sth, hide sth, obscure sth, shroud sth, surround sth** *The pollution haze usually obscures the mountains.*

▶ be present **float over sth, hang over sth** *A grey haze hangs over the factories.*

▶ come down **descend** *A haze descends upon the valley.*

▶ disappear **clear, lift** *The early morning haze cleared to reveal beautiful snow slopes.*

hazy ADJ

1 not clear because of smoke, mist etc

- ● ADJ+n light **glow, moonlight, sun, sunlight, sunshine** *The sky is pale blue, with hazy sunshine.*
- ▶ cloud or mist **cloud, fog, mist** *The scene was veiled in a hazy fog.*
- ▶ sight **glimpse, outline, visibility** *We caught a hazy glimpse of the Pennines in the distance.*
- ▶ sky or air **atmosphere, horizon, sky** *The weather was fine, but the atmosphere remarkably hazy.*
- ▶ time of day **afternoon, morning** *I first met him on a hazy autumn afternoon.*

2 not very clear in your memory or mind

- ● adv+ADJ rather **a little, rather, slightly, somewhat** *He was somewhat hazy on the subject of whether they had met before.*
- ▶ very **distinctly, very** *The details of what happened are distinctly hazy.*
- ▶ in a way that is understandable **understandably** *After all this time, their memories are understandably hazy.*
- ● ADJ+n **flash-back, memory, recollection** *Alan had only hazy recollections of their meeting.*

head N

1 the top part of your body, containing your brain

- ● adj+N with little or no hair **bald, balding, shaven** *He had a large, bald head and pale, protruding eyes.*
- ▶ injured or in pain **sore, swollen** *I have a bit of a sore head because we drank too much last night.*
- ▶ with no hat or scarf **bare** *When she drives off, her head is still bare, but seen from behind in the next shot, the hat is back.*
- ▶ not attached to a body **decapitated, disembodied, severed** *I looked up to see a giant disembodied moose's head above the fireplace.*
- ● v+N move your head **bob, jerk, nod, shake, toss (back), turn** *They nodded their heads and said they agreed with the proposal.* ● *I asked her if she could help but she shook her head and said 'No'.* ● *Bob just stood there, shaking his head in disbelief.*
- ▶ lower your head **bend, bow, droop, duck, hang, lower** *Let us bow our heads and pray.*
- ▶ raise your head or move it to one side **cock, incline, lift, raise, tilt** *He cocked his head on one side and looked at me with some curiosity.*
- ▶ hold your head up **hold up** *He was so weak that he had a difficult time holding his head up.*
- ▶ move your head so that you can look somewhere **poke, pop** INFORMAL**, put, stick** INFORMAL *He called out to her and poked his head around the bathroom door.*
- ▶ injure your head **bang, bash, bump, hit, knock, smash** *Had she fallen down the cellar steps and banged her head or something?*
- ▶ scratch your head **scratch** *She scratched her head and looked puzzled.*
- ● N+v hurt **ache, explode, hurt, pound, throb** *My head still ached and bled from the blow.*
- ▶ hang down **droop, fall, hang, loll** *A drunk, with his head lolling, approached us.*
- ● n+of+N **nod, scratch, shake, toss** *The suggestion was greeted by tuts, raised eyebrows and shakes of the head.*

2 your mind and thoughts

- ● adj+N **clear, cool, level** *She always kept a cool head in a crisis.*
- ▶ v+N be in someone's head **be in, be inside** *It is not all in your head – the pain you feel is real.*
- ▶ get into someone's head **come into, enter, get inside, get into** *A strange thought had just come into my head.* ● *Historians need to get into the heads of the people they are writing about.*
- ▶ put something into someone's head **drum sth into, put sth into** *Who put that idea into your head?*
- ▶ get something out of someone's head **get sth out of** *I still can't get that image out of my head.*
- ● N+v **buzz, reel, spin, swim** *My head is still reeling from the shock of finding out the truth about my mother.*

head V

to be in control of a group

- ● V+n **commission, committee, consortium, delegation, department, division, group, inquiry, team** *The University of Leicester heads the project consortium.*

> In this meaning, you can use **head up** in the same way as **head**: *They appointed Paul Richards to head up the new department.*

headache N

1 a pain in your head

- ● adj+N bad **bad, blinding, chronic, pounding, severe, splitting, terrible, throbbing, thumping** *I've got a splitting headache – I'm going upstairs for a nap.*
- ▶ not bad **mild, slight** *After taking the medication, some people feel sick or have a mild headache.*
- ▶ regular, repeated, or lasting a long time **constant, episodic, frequent, persistent, recurrent, recurring** *Depression can cause frequent headaches.*

> Usage **Headache** is usually plural in these combinations: *He suffers from persistent headaches.* ● *Doctors are trying to find the cause of her recurrent headaches.*

- ● n+N **migraine, tension** *About 7 years ago, my sister started getting migraine headaches.*
- ● v+N cause a headache **bring on, cause, give sb, induce, lead to, trigger** *Cheap sunglasses will strain the eyes and eventually cause a headache.*
- ▶ relieve or prevent a headache **alleviate, cure, ease, prevent, relieve, soothe, treat** *Meadowsweet tea can help relieve headaches.*
- ▶ have or get a headache **complain of, develop, experience, get, have, suffer (from)** *I felt tired and shaky and I had a headache.*

2 INFORMAL something that causes you lots of problems

- ● adj+N **big, constant, logistical, major, real** *Why is watering the plants such a major headache?*
- ● v+N be or become a headache **be, become, cause, create, pose, prove** *Assessment always proves our biggest headache.*
- ▶ experience a headache **experience, face, have,**

suffer *You can enjoy the entire day in one place without having the headache of driving from place to place.*
▶ reduce or remove a headache **alleviate, avoid, reduce, remove, solve** *To alleviate cash-flow headaches, investors can opt for an interest-only loan.*

heading N
a title or general description

● adj+N general **broad, general, generic, main** *Websites are indexed under broad category headings.*
▶ specific **specific** *The report is written in chapters with specific headings.*
▶ clear or useful **appropriate, clear, relevant** *Use clear headings, sub-headings and cross-references so people can find their way round the document.*
▶ types of heading **descriptive, thematic** *The module will explore specific problems in the context of four thematic headings.*

● n+N **category, chapter, column, menu, page, paragraph, section, subject, table, topic** *Click on the column heading to sort the list by that column.*

● v+under+N group something under a heading **arrange, categorize, classify, group, list, organize, present, summarize** *Soils are grouped under three headings: Sand, Loam, and Clay.*
▶ be under a heading **appear, come, fall** *The recommendations fall under four broad headings.*

headline N
1 the title of a newspaper story in large letters

● adj+N dramatic **dramatic, lurid, sensational, sensationalist, shock** *The next morning, newspaper headlines were even more sensational.*
▶ short and clever **catchy, snappy** *Think of a snappy headline for your article.*
▶ easily noticed **attention-grabbing, eye-catching** *His reports usually start with a brief attention-grabbing headline.*
▶ causing strong emotion **alarmist, emotive, hysterical** *There was another rash of hysterical headlines when the police found a girl wandering the streets in the middle of the night.*
▶ main **banner, main** *The main headline on the front of the paper is what mostly attracts the consumer.*
▶ misleading **misleading** *Despite the misleading headline 'acupuncture can ease the pain of childbirth', the newspaper article then goes on to report the research accurately.*

● n+N **front-page, media, newspaper, tabloid** *The newspaper ran a huge front-page headline: 'Millions will die'.*

● v+N have a headline **carry, have, run** *All of the late papers in the U.S. carried headlines similar to those in the Louisville Courier.*
▶ look at headlines **scan, see** *Flip the pages, scan the headlines and highlight the articles you want to read in greater depth.*

● N+v **announce, claim, declare, proclaim, read, refer to, say, scream, suggest** *Only a month or so ago, the headlines screamed 'Swine Flu!'*

2 the most important stories in the news [always plural]

● n+N **news** *Here are the news headlines.*
● v+N be in the headlines **attract, be in, capture, catch, get, grab, hit, make** *Footballers are always hitting the headlines for fighting on the pitch.*
▶ dominate the headlines **dominate, hog, steal** *The subject currently dominating headlines around the world is terrorism.*

head off PHR VB
to prevent something from happening or someone from doing something

● V+n difficult situation **clash, crisis, problems, revolt, war** *Greater use could be made of mediation to head off potential court clashes.*
▶ comment **accusations, criticism** *The company is trying to head off accusations that its efforts to comply with the terms of the settlement are inadequate.*
▶ possibility **possibility, threat** *We must extend our use of renewable sources of energy if we are to head off the threat of devastating climate change.*
▶ when someone wants something **demands** *The government tried to head off demands for more general access to confidential information.*

headquarters N
the place where an organization has its main offices

● adj+N of part of an organization **branch, divisional** *She was offered a job at divisional headquarters.*
▶ of a business **company, corporate** *London is home to many UK corporate headquarters.*
▶ for managing something **administrative, operational** *At the administrative headquarters of the President, there are two guards inside and two outside.*
▶ military or police **army, military, police** *The police headquarters are in the centre of the city.*
▶ main **central, main** *The company's main headquarters are located in Mannheim, Germany.*
▶ for a particular area **district, global, international, national, regional** *More than 275 global corporations have already chosen Sydney as their regional headquarters.*
▶ permanent/temporary **permanent, temporary** *The Group has no permanent headquarters and the staff is purely voluntary.*

● v+N be or become a headquarters **act as, be, become, house, serve as** *This Spanish castle now serves as the prime minister's headquarters.*
▶ establish a headquarters **build, establish, locate, use sth as** *Multinational companies tend to establish their headquarters in major European cities.* ● *Over 150 major companies chose to locate their headquarters in the area last year.*
▶ move a headquarters **move, relocate** *Hubbard moved his headquarters from Pheonix to Washington DC.*

● N+v be somewhere **be based, be located, be situated** *Their headquarters are located in tiny offices in London.*

heal V
1 if an injury or emotional problem heals, it gets better; to make an injury or emotional problem, or a person, better

- adv+V completely **completely, fully, properly, totally, truly** *The ulcers on my legs have now healed completely.*
- ▶ well **nicely, normally, properly, well** *The bruises should heal nicely in a few days.*
- ▶ quickly/slowly **fast, quickly, rapidly, slowly** *To his surprise, the burns healed quickly, with very little scarring.*
- ▶ without treatment **naturally, spontaneously, without treatment** *Most spinal fractures will heal spontaneously after traction and a suitable period of bed-rest.*
- ▶ physically **physically** *Two years may be roughly the length of time necessary for brain tissue to heal physically.*
- ▶ emotionally **emotionally, spiritually** *When I came back from the pilgrimage I felt emotionally healed.*
- ▶ in a surprising way **magically, miraculously** *After bathing it in the water of the well, his wound was miraculously healed within a few days.*
- V+n injury **burn, fracture, injury, scar, sore, ulcer, wound** *A drug is being pioneered that heals wounds without leaving a scar.*
- ▶ emotional problem **heartache, hurt, pain** *Time will heal our hurt.*
- ▶ disease or pain **ailment, disease, illness, pain, sickness** *Mint is said to be able to heal the pain of a bee sting.*
- ▶ sick person **the sick** *Hospitals are not businesses in the commercial sense – they are there to heal the sick.*
- n+V injury or emotional problem **blister, bruise, cut, fracture, injury, lesion, scar, sore, ulcer, wound** *The emotional scars have never healed.* • *Why do stomach ulcers not heal very well?*
- ▶ bodily substance **bone, skin, tissue** *He will need to be immobilised using a cast while the important bones heal.*

2 to make people stop fighting and improve their relationship

- V+n **breach, divide, division, rift, schism, split** *These approaches can heal rifts and lead to reconciliation.*

health N
the physical and mental condition of someone's body; the fact of being strong and well; the job of providing medical care

- adj+N bad **bad, ill, poor** *He was forced to retire because of ill health.*
- ▶ good **excellent, full, good, optimum, perfect, robust, rude** *You appear this evening to be in rude health!*
- ▶ general **general, overall** *Walking is a great form of exercise if you want to improve your general health.*
- ▶ mental **emotional, mental, psychological, spiritual** *Mental health is about how we think, feel and behave.*
- ▶ physical **physical** *It is stupid not to take medical advice when it will lead to physical health.*
- ▶ sexual **reproductive, sexual** *Her research interests are in the areas of sexually-transmitted infections and reproductive health.*
- ▶ of teeth or mouth **dental, oral** *Recent scientific research has shown a link between poor oral health and other conditions such as heart and lung disease.*

- of people in general **community, public** *The agency's primary objective is to protect public health.*
- ▶ of a particular group **animal, child, employee, human, men's, women's** *The levels of contamination are too low to pose a danger to human health.*
- ▶ long-term **long-term** *It is important to safeguard the long-term health of your eyes.*
- v+N improve your health **benefit, boost, enhance, improve** *Giving up smoking is probably the greatest single step you can take to improve your health.*
- ▶ damage your health **damage, harm, ruin** *Occasional intense exercise when you're unfit can damage your health further.*
- ▶ risk your health **compromise, endanger, jeopardize, risk, threaten** *She recklessly and foolishly endangered her health by deliberately starving herself.*
- ▶ protect your health **look after, maintain, protect, safeguard** *No charge will be made for items necessary to safeguard your health or safety.*
- ▶ affect your health **affect, influence** *The way we live can affect our health*
- ▶ recover your health **recover, regain, restore** *He has recovered his health after having a heart attack last year.*
- N+v get worse **decline, deteriorate, fail, worsen** *His health deteriorated rapidly during the final six months of his life.*
- ▶ get better **improve** *I hope your health improves.*
- N+n connected with medical care **care, check, professional, service, worker** *The country offers its residents free health care.*
- ▶ problem or danger **hazard, problem, scare, warning** *The service is aimed at vulnerable people with mental or physical health problems.*
- n+to+N **damage, danger, harm, hazard, risk, threat** *Air pollution causes damage to health.*
- v+to+N **nurse sb (back), restore sb, return sb** *Some cats are injured or ill and are nursed back to health before being homed.*
- and/or **fitness, happiness, hygiene, safety, vitality, well-being** *Each level of management is responsible for the health and safety of staff under their command.*

healthy ADJ
strong and not sick or weak

- adv+ADJ very **extremely, perfectly, positively, remarkably, very** *When the baby was born he was perfectly healthy.*
- ▶ fairly **fairly, generally, pretty** INFORMAL, **reasonably, relatively** *I've always been fairly healthy.*
- ▶ apparently **apparently, seemingly** *Apparently healthy pigs may be incubating disease.*
- ▶ mentally **emotionally, mentally, psychologically, spiritually** *One of the key aims of Mental Health Week is to raise awareness about staying mentally healthy.*
- ▶ physically **physically** *Keeping physically healthy helps protect against many conditions.*
- ▶ financially **financially** *The company must be able to show that it is financially healthy.*
- v+ADJ **appear, be, become, feel, get, keep, look,**

remain, seem, sound, stay *We have to do more to help young people get healthy.* ● *There are hints on how to keep healthy, through diet, exercise and relaxation.* ● *How can a heart be kept healthy?*

● and/or of a person **active, fit, happy, normal, safe, strong** *I look fit and healthy now, but four years ago everything was different.*
▶ of an economy, business etc **productive, prosperous, vibrant, vigorous** *We need a healthy and vibrant farming sector.*

heap V
to give something to someone

● V+n bad things **abuse, blame, criticism, pressure, ridicule, scorn** *During her speech, she heaped particular scorn on the former Prime Minister.*
▶ good things **accolades, adulation, praise** *He would always heap generous praise on his wife.*

heart N
1 the organ that makes blood flow round your body

● adj+N **diseased, enlarged, healthy, weak** *X-rays will often show that the heart is enlarged.*
● N+v beat **beat, flutter, hammer, pound, pump, race, thump** *My heart began to beat faster.*
▶ not beat **fail, miss a beat, skip a beat, stop** *If the patient's heart has stopped, then cardiac massage may help.*
● N+n disease or problem **abnormality, condition, defect, disease, murmur, trouble** *Some babies are born with heart defects.*
▶ when the heart stops working properly **attack, failure** *Every 2 minutes in the UK, someone has a heart attack.*
▶ operation **bypass, operation, surgery, transplant, transplantation** *He had a successful heart transplant in 2001.*
▶ beating **beat, palpitations, rate** *Several drugs can be used to slow the heart rate down.*

2 your feelings

● adj+N good **big, brave, generous, good, kind, loving, pure, sincere, tender, warm** *Giving up your own time to help someone like this shows dedication and a big heart.*
▶ bad **deceitful, evil** *You're a bad man with an evil heart.*
▶ sad, lonely, or sorry **contrite, heavy, lonely, sad, troubled** *So with slightly heavy hearts we started trying to make compromises.*
▶ happy or thankful **glad, joyful, merry, thankful** *Help them to look back at Stuart's life with a smile and a thankful heart.*
▶ unfeeling **cold, stony** *The movie has some tender moments that will bring a tear to all but the coldest heart.*
● v+N when you make someone happy **gladden, lift, warm** *The very sight of you gladdens my heart.*
▶ when you make someone sad **break, grieve, tear out, trouble** *Katie had her heart broken once, and she's not going to let it happen again.*
▶ when you make someone feel something **melt, soften, stir, touch** *If you recite your sermon in a monotone and have no passion, it will rarely touch peoples hearts.*

▶ when you make someone love you **capture, win (over)** *The first part of the romance deals with Guy's attempts to win the heart of Roband's daughter.*
▶ open your heart **open, pour out** *I wanted to open my heart to him and tell him all that I was feeling.*
▶ have a particular kind of heart **have** *He had a big heart as well as delightful manners.*
▶ follow your heart **follow** *Follow your heart and do what you feel is right.*

> When you want something very much, you can say that you **have your heart set on it**: *He's got his heart set on spending a year or so in France.*

● N+v when you are happy **leap, overflow, rejoice, sing, soar, swell** *Her heart leapt with joy.*
▶ when you are sad **ache, bleed, break, sink** *His heart sank. He knew it was going to be a long night.*
▶ when you want someone or something **yearn** *My heart yearns to see him again.*
▶ when you like or pity someone **melt** *My heart just melts when I see these angelic and innocent faces.*
● v+from+N come **come, flow, spring** *His generosity comes from the heart, and is never a token gesture.*
▶ do something **sing, speak, write** *Speak from the heart about what makes you angry or sad.*

> You can use the expression **from the bottom of my heart** to emphasize that you are sincere about something: *I'm sorry, and I mean that from the bottom of my heart.*

3 the central or most important part of something

● adj+N **very** *The hotel is located in the very heart of the city centre.*
● v+at+N **be, be located, be placed, be positioned, be situated, lie, lie, remain, sit, stand** *It was confusion over standards that lay at the heart of this summer's problems.*
▶ strike **strike** *A spate of brutal murders starts to unfold, striking at the heart of village life and casting suspicion on everyone.*
● v+in+N **be based, be located, be set, be situated, be tucked, lie, lurk, nestle** *This tiny village nestles in the heart of the hills.*
● v+into+N **delve, descend, enter, go, penetrate, plunge, reach** *The river plunged straight into the heart of the forest.*
● v+through+N **flow, go, pass, run** *The famous National Road ran through the heart of that region.*
● v+to+N **come, cut, get, go, penetrate** *We want you to get right to the heart of the matter.*

heat N
1 the quality of being hot

● adj+N extreme **burning, extreme, fierce, intense, searing, white** *A blast of searing heat came to meet him as the furnace door was opened.*
▶ of weather **baking, blistering, oppressive, scorching, stifling, sweltering, unbearable** *He had both windows open because of the sweltering heat.*
▶ from the sun **solar** *Materials with high mass are particularly good at absorbing the solar heat entering a building.*
▶ dry **dry** *Excessive dry heat can build up if too many machines are placed in a small area.*

▶ too much **excess, excessive, surplus** *Sunstroke is caused by excessive body heat and dehydration.*

● v+N produce heat **generate, produce** *Wood burns readily and produces heat.*

▶ give out heat **conduct, emit, give out, radiate, reflect, release, transfer** *The floor becomes warm and in turn radiates heat.*

▶ take or keep in heat **absorb, conserve, keep in, retain, store, trap** *When a lizard is feeling cold they will find a safe place to rest in the sun and absorb its heat.* ● *Better insulation helps a home to retain heat and use less fuel.*

▶ lose heat **dissipate, lose** *A large amount of heat was lost up the chimney.*

▶ withstand heat **tolerate, withstand** *These tiles are engineered to withstand heat.*

● N+v come from something **escape from, evaporate from, radiate from** *I could feel the heat radiating from his body as I did my best to cool him down.*

▶ damage something **damage, destroy, melt, scorch** *The heat scorched her face even from 10 feet away.*

▶ heat someone or something **warm** *They used their body heat to warm each other.*

▶ increase **build up, intensify, rise** *Very soon the heat builds up again.*

▶ decrease **abate, dissipate, subside** *Within seconds of our leaving the coast, the heat abates.*

2 warmth produced by an oven or heating system

● v+N reduce the heat **lower, reduce, turn down** *Mix well, reduce the heat and simmer for 10 minutes.*

▶ increase the heat **increase, turn up** *Turn the heat up to the highest setting.*

▶ turn on the heat **put on, switch on, turn on** *The device turns on the heat if it is too cold.*

▶ turn off the heat **switch off, turn off** *Switch off the heat to rooms you are not using.*

heated ADJ
angry and excited

● adv+ADJ very **very** *This contribution prompted a very heated discussion.*

▶ rather **quite, rather** *What followed was a rather heated exchange between the two heads of department.*

▶ slightly **a little, slightly** *Our conversation got slightly heated at one point.*

▶ increasingly **increasingly, more and more** *The debate over drug laws is becoming increasingly heated.*

● ADJ+n **argument, controversy, debate, discussion, exchange** *Heated arguments broke out as the locals tried to stop the relief trucks from leaving.*

● v+ADJ **be, become, get, grow** *The debate about what to do lasted weeks and got quite heated.*

heavy ADJ
used to say that there is a lot of something or that something is severe

● adv+ADJ very **especially, exceptionally, excessively, extremely, particularly, really, unusually, very** *Traffic was unusually heavy all day and evening.*

▶ rather **fairly, moderately, pretty** INFORMAL**, quite, rather, relatively** *The workload is fairly heavy – with not only lectures but also practicals.*

● ADJ+n rain or snow **downpour, rain, rainstorm, showers, snow, thunderstorm** *The water level rises up during heavy downpours.*

▶ traffic **traffic** *Heavy traffic and frequent stoplights slowed progress to a crawl.*

▶ work **workload** *Many students found it difficult to cope with the heavy workload.*

▶ when something is used very much **emphasis, reliance** *Singapore is a very open economy (meaning a heavy reliance on international trade).*

▶ defeat or loss **casualties, defeat, losses** *The enemy inflicted heavy casualties on the Allied troops.* ● *Their heaviest defeat came in 1995 when they lost to Croatia 4–0.*

> You can say that something **takes a heavy toll** on something when it affects a situation very badly: *The recession has taken a heavy toll on many of our high-street stores.*

▶ responsibility **burden, load, responsibility** *Many staff complained about the heavy administrative burden of keeping records that to them had no obvious purpose.*

▶ medical problem **bleeding, cold** *Sometimes fibroids cause heavy bleeding or pain.*

▶ activity **drinking, fighting, smoking** *From the 17th to the 19th heavy fighting took place in the city.*

height N
1 how high or tall something is; the distance above the ground etc

● adj+N maximum **full, maximum** *He drew himself up to his full height and cleared his throat.*

▶ average **average** *She was twelve years old and of less than average height.*

▶ great **considerable, great, towering** *He was looking down at it from a very great height.*

▶ correct or enough **correct, right** *The seat is at the right height for elderly patients.*

● n+N body parts **chest, head, knee, shoulder, waist** *To arrive at this position, the athlete must first deadlift the bar to waist height.*

▶ building parts **ceiling, roof** *The tower is low, standing at just above roof height.*

● v+N be at a height **be at, be positioned at** *Make sure that the saddle of your bicycle is at the correct height.*

▶ reach a height **attain, climb to, reach, rise to** *Why do snails climbing a wall only ever reach a certain height, about 8 feet, from the ground?*

▶ change the height of something **adjust, alter, change, vary** *The canal bridges all had their height altered to accommodate steam trains.*

▶ measure or guess a height **calculate, determine, estimate, measure** *A mathematician, a physicist and an engineer are each given 50 pounds to measure the height of a building.*

▶ increase the height of something **increase, raise** *They are increasing the height of the existing building by one storey.*

▶ reduce the height of something **lower, reduce** *Reducing the vehicle's chassis height achieves a low centre of gravity, which improves road holding.*

▶ gain height **gain, regain** *The path gains height pretty quickly.*
▶ lose height **lose** *The aircraft started to lose height as it approached Heathrow.*

2 the time or level when something is at its greatest [always singular]

● N+of success **fame, glory, popularity, power, prosperity** *When Elvis was at the height of his fame, he enjoyed a high-rolling lifestyle.*
▶ situation **boom, career, crisis** *The magazine hit the news stands at the height of the dotcom boom.*
▶ bad quality **folly, hypocrisy, irresponsibility** *It will be the height of irresponsibility for the Government to permit airport expansion.*
▶ good quality **fashion, luxury, sophistication** *Their Italianate-style bathroom is the height of luxury.*

3 a high level of success or activity [usually plural]

● adj+N great **commanding, dizzy, dizzying, giddy, great, heady, lofty** *The next ten years saw the group release a number of albums, all of which failed to reach the dizzy heights of their earlier successes.*
▶ new **new** *Innovation and drive are critical to take any business to new heights.*

● v+N **achieve, ascend to, attain, climb to, reach, rise to, scale, soar to, take sth to** *Princess Anne reached the heights of sportsmanship by representing Britain in the Olympics.*

heighten V
to make a feeling or emotion stronger

● adv+V **considerably, dramatically, greatly, really, significantly** *The number of fatalities greatly heightened public concern about food safety.*
▶ V+n awareness **awareness** *Coming away to college can often heighten your awareness about how you look.*
▶ worry or fear **anxiety, concern, fear, tension** *The attacks were designed to heighten tensions between the two communities.*
▶ feeling or emotion **atmosphere, emotion, feeling, sense** *All treatments are carried out with calming music to heighten the relaxing atmosphere.*
▶ enjoyment **enjoyment, pleasure** *Try to heighten children's enjoyment of stories.*
▶ interest **interest, speculation** *Warnings about the dangers of drugs can heighten interest and use.*
▶ anticipation or suspicion **anticipation, expectation, suspense, suspicion** *Anticipation was heightened by the fact Janet Jackson was on the bill.*
▶ effect **effect, impact** *Excellent performances from the cast heighten the effect of the excellent script.*

heir N
someone who will receive money, property or a title when another person dies; someone who will have a particular job next

● adj+N legally accepted **lawful, legitimate, rightful, true** *The book details Frederick's struggle to be recognized as the rightful heir to the Bohemian crown.*
▶ only **last, sole** *He died leaving an infant son, Thomas, as his sole heir.*
▶ remaining **surviving** *Queen Anne had no surviving heirs.*

● v+N produce an heir **bear, produce** *She does her duty and produces an heir.*
▶ make someone an heir **appoint (as), declare (as), designate (as), name (as), nominate (as)** *He was named as a possible heir to the post of Governor General.*
▶ have an heir **have, leave** *When he died in 1957 he left no heirs.*
● N+v survive someone **succeed, survive** *Their eldest son had no male heirs who survived him.*
▶ inherit something **inherit** *Property could only be inherited by male heirs.*

help V
to make a situation better or make it easier to achieve something

● adv+V very much **considerably, enormously, greatly, immensely, a lot, really** INFORMAL, **significantly, tremendously** *Learning how to relax your muscles and get the tension out of your body can help enormously with pain.*
▶ not very much **hardly, not at all** *It hardly helped matters when he revealed that he hadn't done what he had promised to do.*
▶ a little **a bit** INFORMAL, **a little** *It helped a bit just knowing she was there.*
▶ definitely **certainly, definitely, undoubtedly** *Enjoyment certainly helps to pass the time.*

help N
the process of helping someone, a person or thing that helps

● adj+N great **a big** INFORMAL, **considerable, enormous, great, immense, invaluable, real, tremendous** *The computer has been a great help to do my homework on.*
▶ a little **a bit of** INFORMAL, **a little, some** *The children were able to communicate with a little help from translators.*
▶ given generously **unstinting** *I couldn't have managed it all without Lucy's unstinting help.*
▶ extra **additional, extra, further, more** *The library offers extra help if you are a distance learner.*
▶ urgent **emergency, immediate, urgent** *The woman clearly needed urgent medical help.*
▶ from a qualified person **expert, outside, professional, specialist, specialized** *You may decide it is wise to use professional help with your accounts.*
▶ types of help **financial, medical, practical, psychiatric, secretarial, technical** *Our team provides practical help to young, physically disabled people.*

● v+N get help **enlist, find, get, obtain, receive** *Juliet enlists the help of her nurse to find Romeo.*
▶ try to get help **appeal for, ask for, beg for, plead for, request, seek, solicit** *It is advisable to seek professional help.*
▶ call for help **call for, cry for, scream for, shout for** *There have been reports that the man was crying for help throughout the night.*
▶ need or want help **need, require, want, would like** *We need your help to spot problems as they happen.*
▶ appreciate someone's help **acknowledge, appreciate, value** *She really appreciates your help.*
▶ give help **give, offer, provide** *If you could offer some help, it would be most appreciated!*

▶ refuse help **refuse** *Susan convinces Dr Weissman she's rational, and refuses psychiatric help.*

▶ accept help **accept, welcome** *Her own experience of cancer teaches her to accept the help offered by family and friends.*

● n+for+N call **call, cry, shout** *Their shouts for help were heard by people outside a nearby pub.*

▶ request **appeal, plea, request** *The organization has made many appeals for financial help.*

● and/or **advice, assistance, cooperation, encouragement, guidance, kindness, patience, reassurance, support** *Get help and advice from sensible people.*

helpful ADJ
providing help

● adv+ADJ very **enormously, extremely, immensely, incredibly, really, so** INFORMAL, **terribly** INFORMAL, **tremendously, very** *Most of the time he was extremely helpful, haggling over prices and finding out information.*

▶ particularly **especially, particularly** *Illustrations of pupils' work and commentary on their work is particularly helpful to teachers.*

▶ always **always, unfailingly** *She was unfailingly helpful in giving advice.*

● v+ADJ **be, consider sth, find sb/sth, prove, seem** *Thanks for lending me the book. I found it very helpful.* ● *I hope these comments will prove useful to the committee when they're making their decision.*

● and/or **approachable, cheerful, considerate, constructive, courteous, efficient, friendly, kind, knowledgeable, pleasant, polite, supportive** *All the staff are friendly and helpful.*

helpless ADJ
1 not able to do anything without help

● adv+ADJ completely **absolutely, completely, quite, so** INFORMAL, **totally, utterly** *I felt utterly helpless in the face of such tragedy and started to cry.*

▶ almost **almost, nearly, practically, virtually** *In the last decade of her life, almost helpless, Rita was cared for by her daughter.*

● v+ADJ **be, feel, leave sb, lie, look, render sb, seem, sit, stand** *They were responsible for thousands of job losses and then did nothing to help those who had been left helpless.* ● *He lay helpless on the ground from a shot in the knee.*

● and/or **hopeless, innocent, poor, powerless, vulnerable, weak** *Getting into credit card debt can leave you feeling helpless and hopeless.*

2 impossible to control

● ADJ+n laughter **giggles, laughter, mirth** *His stories reduce children to helpless laughter.*

▶ sadness **grief, misery** *The repeated lines in the first stanza reveal her helpless misery and her sense of life as repetitive and meaningless.*

▶ anger **rage** *Filled with helpless rage after the denial of the permit, Nina began to cry.*

heritage N
the art, buildings, traditions, and beliefs that a society considers important to its history and culture

● adj+N varied **diverse, multicultural, rich, varied** *The district has a very rich heritage of landscapes, buildings, museums, villages and towns.*

▶ shared **common, shared** *This event encourages cross-border links and brings together our communities in a shared heritage.*

▶ of a country **national, the nation's** *Exmoor is one of our finest landscapes and an important part of our national heritage.*

▶ good or special **precious, priceless, proud, strong, unique** *London has a unique heritage of traditions that stretches back over a thousand years.*

▶ types of heritage **archaeological, architectural, artistic, cultural, geological, industrial, literary, maritime, mining, musical, natural, sporting** *It's a city with a great cultural heritage.*

● v+N have a heritage **be steeped in, enjoy, have** *The goal was to take a brand steeped in heritage and make it relevant to youth today.*

▶ protect a heritage **conserve, defend, maintain, preserve, protect, restore, safeguard** *Perpignan has managed to preserve its Spanish heritage.*

▶ explore or discover a heritage **discover, explore** *'Flavours of Chile' is a series which explores the heritage and cuisine of one of the world's most inaccessible countries*

▶ appreciate a heritage **appreciate, celebrate, respect, value** *We need young people to appreciate more fully the rich heritage that we have in Northern Ireland.*

hero N
1 a brave person or someone that you admire

● adj+N popular or famous **famous, popular** *He is one of our most popular sporting heroes.*

▶ real **great, real, true** *Real heroes are often ordinary people you would never expect to have extraordinary qualities.*

▶ forgotten or not known about **forgotten, unsung** *Community leaders are the unsung heroes in youth groups that inspire young people to believe in themselves.*

▶ unexpected **unlikely** *In some ways, he seems an unlikely hero.*

▶ not willing **reluctant** *Ned is the kind of bewildered, reluctant hero who'd rather be sitting at home with a book.*

▶ in a country or area **local, national** *Now a national hero, Horatio was showered with honours.*

▶ dead **fallen** *Cenotaphs to fallen heroes sprang up in every town square and village green.*

▶ brave **brave, intrepid** *We took photos of our intrepid heroes before they set off on the climb.*

▶ winning **conquering** *He entered the town like a conquering hero.*

● n+N in a particular activity **football, footballing, guitar, sporting, war** *Muhammed Ali is my favourite sporting hero.*

▶ from childhood **boyhood, childhood, schoolboy** *I finally got the chance to meet my boyhood hero.*

● v+N consider or treat someone a hero **hail sb**

(as), regard sb as, see sb as, treat sb as *The victorious Alexander is hailed a hero on his return.*
▸ become a hero **become, turn into** *Donovan soon became a hero of the hippy generation*
▸ copy a hero **emulate** *The world turned its back on them when they tried to emulate their heroes.*
▸ honour a hero **celebrate, commemorate, honour** *The awards are to honour these unsung heroes.*

2 the main male character of a book etc
● adj+N **comic, dashing, eponymous, fictional, flawed, legendary, mythical, romantic, tragic** *Robinson Crusoe is the eponymous hero of the book.*

heroic ADJ
very brave or determined

● adv+ADJ very **genuinely, positively, truly** *Smugglers are often erroneously depicted as positively heroic and even admirable.*
▸ rather **pretty** INFORMAL, **quite** *It was a pretty heroic effort, considering that one set of instruments didn't work.*
● ADJ+n action **achievement, act, action, deed, endeavour, exploit, feat** *He was awarded the Victoria Cross for his heroic deeds.*
▸ effort or attempt **attempt, effort, struggle** *I'd like to thank my legal team for their heroic efforts in court.*
▸ personal quality **courage, virtue** *Your heroic courage will never be forgotten.*
▸ resistance **defiance, resistance** *For years they maintained a heroic resistance against tyranny.*
▸ failure **failure** *The book tells the tale behind one of the UK's most heroic failures.*
● and/or **brave, courageous, daring, noble, selfless** *The emergency services performed countless selfless and heroic acts.*

heroine N
1 the main female character of a book etc
● adj+N **beautiful, eponymous, feisty, fictional, literary, romantic, spirited, tragic, young** *Shirley was a masculine name until Charlotte Brontë used it for the eponymous heroine of her novel 'Shirley'.*

2 a brave woman or a woman that you admire
● adj+N forgotten or not known about **forgotten, unnamed, unsung** *Hannah is one of Scotland's unsung heroines of climbing.*
▸ in an area **national** *Florence Nightingale returned to England as a national heroine.*

heroism N
impressive actions that prove someone is brave

● adj+N **extraordinary, genuine, great, individual, outstanding, selfless, true** *He saved the lives of his comrades with selfless heroism.*
● v+N show heroism **demonstrate, display, exhibit, show** *The full scale of the heroism shown by the emergency services has finally emerged.*
▸ recognize someone's heroism **acknowledge, applaud, celebrate, praise, recognize** *We applaud their heroism, their bravery, and their commitment to democracy.*
● n+of+N act **act, deed, example, feat** *Morgan's act*

of heroism put him in newspapers all over the country.
▸ story **story, tale** *Graphic battle scenes and tales of heroism will appeal to military historians and readers of adventure stories alike.*
● and/or **bravery, courage, determination, devotion, sacrifice, self-sacrifice** *Saving Private Ryan is a story of heroism and sacrifice.*

hesitation N
a pause before doing something or a feeling that you should not do something

● adj+N slight or occasional **brief, little, momentary, occasional, slight** *Without the slightest hesitation and with scant regard for his own safety Des entered the bloodied scene.*

> You can use the expression **have no hesitation in doing something** when you mean that you would be willing to do it: *I would have no hesitation in recommending him for the job.*

▸ a lot **considerable, great, long, a lot of, much** *After much hesitation, it was decided to use Josef as a double agent.*
▸ more **further, more** *More hesitation about the scheme would send out the wrong message.*
▸ at the beginning **initial** *After initial hesitation, she allowed the stitches to be removed.*
▸ with bad results **fatal** *They must act now, hesitation could be fatal.*
● v+without+N **accept sb/sth, answer, do sth, recommend sb/sth, reply, say sth** *I am saying without hesitation that that will not happen.*
● n+of+N **moment, period, second** *He stopped, and that moment of hesitation saved his life.*

hidden ADJ
not easy to find, see, or know about

● adv+ADJ until now **hitherto, previously** *The council agreed to make public previously hidden details.*
▸ mainly or completely **completely, deeply, largely, well** *The views and experiences of those who choose not to have children have remained largely hidden.*
▸ partly **partially** *Drivers are distracted by partially-hidden cameras.*
▸ cleverly or carefully **cunningly** *The plug sockets are cunningly-hidden beneath hatches on the floor.*
● ADJ+n something valuable or good **gem, talent, treasure** *There are many hidden treasures just waiting to be discovered.*
▸ costs **charges, costs, extras** *There are no hidden extras payable on arrival.*
▸ reason **agenda, motive** *The government has denied there is any hidden agenda behind the plan.*
▸ secret or information **secret, truth** *She has a lot of dark, hidden secrets in her young life.*
▸ meaning or message **meaning, message** *There are quite a few possible hidden meanings to this film.*
▸ danger or problem **danger, flaw, menace** *Mother was always warning us about the hidden dangers of being out late at night.*
● v+ADJ **be, keep, keep sb/sth, lie, remain, stay** *And then a secret that he has kept hidden all his life is revealed.* ● *Stella remained hidden in the bushes.*

- ADJ+from **sight, view** *The path to full integration is no longer hidden from public view.*

hide V
to not allow someone to know the truth or what you are feeling

- adv+V well **deliberately, effectively, well** *She hides her problems very well.*
- ▶ not easily **barely** *He could barely hide his disappointment at the news.*
- V+n secret **fact, secret, truth** *He's hiding a terrible secret – one that's been tearing him apart for years.*
- ▶ feeling **delight, disappointment, embarrassment, emotions, feelings, sadness, shame** *He stood up quickly, trying to hide his embarrassment.*
- ▶ action or expression **blushes, smile, tears** *I'm sure I saw her put her hand over her mouth to hide a smile.*
- ▶ something about yourself **identity, sexuality, talent** *Spammers can use various methods to hide their identities.*

hide behind PHR VB
to use something to hide the truth

- V+behind **cloak, excuse, facade, mask, smokescreen, veil, wall** *He preferred to hide behind the cloak of anonymity.*

hierarchical ADJ
considering differences in status very important

- adv+ADJ **extremely, highly, rigidly, strictly, strongly, very** *The ruling party was remade by Stalin into a rigidly hierarchical structure similar to a military institution.*
- ADJ+n **arrangement, classification, level, model, order, organization, relationship, society, structure, system** *The hierarchical structure of medieval society is well documented.*
- and/or **authoritarian, bureaucratic, rigid, traditional** *Their views represented a rejection of the top-down, hierarchical and authoritarian models of political organization.*

hierarchy N
a system of organization involving different levels

- adj+N strict or clear **clear, rigid, strict** *Wolves work in a strict hierarchy of power.*
- ▶ complex **complex** *The major religions all have complex hierarchies.*
- ▶ traditional **established, traditional** *In urban areas, the traditional caste hierarchy is not as clear.*
- ▶ types of hierarchy **bureaucratic, caste, church, class, management, military, organizational, racial, religious, social** *Social class matters, because your position within the social hierarchy strongly influences the kind of life you can lead.*
- ▶ for classifying things **classification, taxonomic** *The names of 4,629 species of mammals are given in a taxonomic hierarchy that includes Order, Family, Subfamily, and Genus.*
- v+N **arrange sth in, construct, create, develop, establish, form, impose** *The files are arranged in a hierarchy of files and folders.*

high ADJ
great in amount, standard, or importance

- adv+ADJ very **exceptionally, extraordinarily, extremely, incredibly, particularly, ridiculously, significantly, very** *Their products are of exceptionally high quality.*
- ▶ fairly **fairly, moderately, quite, relatively, slightly** *Many of our students come from less well-paid families and have relatively high levels of deprivation.*
- ▶ unusually **anomalously, surprisingly, unexpectedly, unusually** *Temperatures have been unusually high this summer.*
- ▶ too **abnormally, dangerously, excessively, prohibitively, too, unacceptably, unnecessarily, unrealistically, unreasonably** *Some drugs can cause your blood pressure to go dangerously high.*
- ▶ worryingly **alarmingly, worryingly** *Deforestation continues at an alarmingly high rate.*
- ▶ compared to other things **comparatively, disproportionately, proportionately** *Young people are at a disproportionately higher risk of being victims of crime.*
- ADJ+n level or amount **concentration, degree, dose, level, number, percentage, proportion, rate, volume** *The University takes in a high proportion of students from disadvantaged backgrounds.*
- ▶ how often something occurs **incidence, prevalence** *The incidence was particularly high between 1985 and 1991, when there were 99 cases.*
- ▶ money **costs, prices, taxes, wages** *Why put up with high prices when you don't have to?*
- ▶ physical quality **density, frequency, humidity, pressure, temperature** *The strengths of both steel and concrete are considerably reduced at high temperatures.*
- ▶ medical condition **blood pressure, cholesterol** *What causes high blood pressure?*
- ▶ unemployment **unemployment** *It is very difficult to get a job in these times of high unemployment.*
- ▶ risk **risk** *Temporary workers face a higher risk of accidents than those on a permanent contract.*
- ▶ standard or quality **calibre, quality, standard** *We strive to maintain the highest standards of service.*
- ▶ expectations **expectations, hopes** *We have high hopes of winning this game.*
- ▶ opinion **esteem, opinion, regard** *He was held in high esteem as an energetic, friendly, unassuming and entertaining companion.*
- ▶ position **position, rank, status** *Such clothes were expensive to produce at the time and a symbol of high status.*
- ▶ importance **importance, priority** *Appearance is not a high priority for some people.*

highlight V
to describe something in a way that makes people notice it

- adv+V well **clearly, dramatically, effectively, explicitly, helpfully, interestingly, perfectly, starkly** *Our results clearly highlight the need for phonics instruction for children in their first two years at school.*
- ▶ repeatedly **consistently, continually, repeatedly** *A shortage of medical consultant staff was highlighted repeatedly.*

▸ particularly **particularly, specifically** *The effect of poverty on their social involvement was an area particularly highlighted by children.*

● V+n importance or need **importance, need** *He highlighted the importance of sharing our research findings with others.*

▸ fact or problem **area, aspect, danger, difficulty, fact, issue, pitfall, plight, problem** *I think you've highlighted a critical issue.* ● *We have been working with many other European zoos to highlight the plight of these beautiful animals.*

▸ difference **difference** *This highlights an interesting cultural difference between the US and the UK.*

▸ bad qualities **deficiencies, failings, flaws, inadequacies, inconsistencies, lack, shortcomings, weaknesses** *Don't highlight your inadequacies.* ● *The report highlighted the lack of progress that had been made in most areas.*

▸ good qualities **achievements, benefits** *Highlight the health benefits of living in a home which is not too hot and not too cold.*

hill N
an area of high land smaller than mountain

● adj+N steep/not steep **gentle, steep** *You go up a very steep hill to a set of lights.*

▸ high/low **big, high, low, small** *Harrow is a little town set on a very high hill.*

▸ going up and down gently **rolling, undulating** *There are picturesque villages nestling amongst rolling hills.*

> Usage **Hill** is always plural in these combinations: *It is a magical land of mountains, gently undulating hills, open plains and lush valleys.*

covered in grass or trees **forested, grassy, green, lush, verdant, wooded** *Backed by fields and wooded hills, it is a very attractive property.*

▸ rocky or with few plants **barren, rocky, rugged** *Mountain rescue teams searched the rugged hills, but found no one.*

▸ where there is a lot of wind **windswept** *We parked at the top of a windswept hill, with a spectacular 360 degree view.*

▸ v+N go up a hill **ascend, climb (up), go up, walk up** *We climbed the hill back up to the church.*

go down a hill **descend, go down, walk down** *Descending the hill, we enter a dense mass of forest.*

go over the top of a hill **come over, crest, walk over** *As you crest the hill, take the left hand filter lane.*

be amongst hills **be set amongst, be surrounded by, nestle amongst, nestle between, nestle in** *Many towns and villages nestle amongst the Tuscan hills and valleys.*

be on the top of a hill **be perched on, crown, stand on** *Close to the border, wooded valleys give way to green rolling hills crowned by medieval towns.*

n+of+N top **brow, crest, summit, top** *Over the crest of a distant hill they saw a procession moving toward them.*

bottom **base, bottom, foot** *Small villages with churches cluster around the foot of the hill.*

hillside N
the land on a hill below the top

● adj+N covered in trees or grass **forested, grassy, green, lush, verdant, wooded** *The valley winds its way between wooded hillsides and spectacular cliffs.*

▸ steep/not steep **rolling, sloping, steep** *Set on a gently sloping hillside with the impressive Mount Ponoig as its backdrop, the village is an impressive development.* ● *The track descends a steep hillside in a series of hairpin bends.*

▸ rocky or with few plants **barren, craggy, rocky, stony** *Its preferred habitat is thick woodland or rocky hillsides.*

▸ with few plants **bare, barren, scrubby** *A side-track leads across the scrubby hillsides overlooking the town.*

▸ where there is a lot of wind **windswept** *They searched the barren windswept hillsides for the body, but found nothing.*

● v+N cover the hillside **cover, dot** *As darkness fell, a few isolated lights dotted the opposite hillside.*

▸ be in the hillside **be built into, be carved into, be cut into** *White horses carved into hillsides can be found in several places in the West of England.*

▸ be on the hillside **be perched on, be set on, perch on, sit on, stand on** *Their tiny cottage sits on the hillside, with uninterrupted views.*

hinder V
stop someone or something from making progress

● adv+V very much **greatly, seriously, severely, significantly** *Men established rules and customs that severely hindered women from inheriting, owning or earning wealth.*

▸ not very much **slightly, somewhat** *His research efforts are somewhat hindered by living in Leeds.*

● V+n progress **development, growth, progress, recovery** *Further progress was hindered by severe financial problems.*

▸ attempts **attempts, efforts** *I hope my constant interruptions did not hinder their efforts too much.*

▸ act or process **ability, investigation, operation, performance, process** *What helps and what hinders the change process?*

▸ movement **access, movement** *His movement was hindered by the splint strapped to his leg.*

▸ communication **communication, understanding** *Poor spelling and an inability to write clearly hinders communication.*

● and/or help **aid, facilitate, help** *Software can help or hinder your aim.*

▸ harm **delay, obstruct, prevent** *He conceals his own failure by hindering and obstructing the creative work of others.*

hint N
1 an indirect comment

● adj+N direct **broad, heavy, strong** *Meg sends for some brochures about retirement villages as a strong hint to Ettie.*

▸ indirect **gentle, little, slight, subtle, tantalizing, vague, veiled** *She spends the week dropping subtle hints, which I totally fail to notice.*

● v+N give a hint **drop, give, offer** *Let us drop the hint to let someone know what you desire!*

▸ understand a hint **get, take** *Is it not about time she took the hint, and realised what harm she is doing?*

▶ include a hint **contain, provide** *The article contains no hint that such questions are being asked.*

2 a useful suggestion or piece of advice

● adj+N **handy, helpful, practical, useful, valuable** *I would be grateful for any kind of helpful hints and tips.*

● v+N **give hints contain, give, include, offer, provide** *The booklet provides hints for parents and teachers.*

▶ find hints **find** *Here you will find many useful hints to help answer your questions.*

● and/or **advice, clues, suggestions, tips, tricks** *For more hints and tips about filling in the form, visit our website.*

3 a small amount of something

● adj+N **faint, gentle, little, mere, the merest, slight, the slightest, subtle, vague** *We were the only customers there, and there was not even the slightest hint of music.*

● v+N **notice a hint of something detect** *Do I detect a hint of sarcasm?*

▶ show a hint of something **betray, reveal, show** *David shows a hint of sympathy, but no more.*

▶ contain a hint of something **contain, offer, provide** *The booklet contains hints on how to avoid catching flu.*

▶ add a hint of something **add** *The trumpet solo added a hint of sadness to the music.*

● N+of of a feeling **bitterness, desperation, irony, menace, nostalgia, sadness, sarcasm** *'I make soul music,' he says without even a hint of irony.*

▶ of a flavour **bitterness, smokiness, spice, sweetness** *The food is French, with a subtle hint of north African spice.*

▶ of an expression **a smile** *The hint of a smile came across the old man's lips and he nodded.*

▶ of a colour **colour** *The flowers are closed, just showing a hint of colour.*

historic ADJ

1 important because of being old and interesting

● adv+ADJ **richly, truly, very** *Enjoy a visit to the richly historic and exciting capital city of Madrid.*

● ADJ+n building **building, castle, house, inn, landmark, monument, site** *Find out about the historic landmarks in your area.*

▶ place **capital, city, port, street, town, village** *Annecy is an historic town of cobbled streets, tiled roofs and beautiful canals.*

▶ area **district, environment, landscape, quarter** *The area also benefits from various historic landscapes which the Council is keen to safeguard.*

2 that will be recorded in history

● adv+ADJ **richly, truly, very** *This is a truly historic moment for the UK.*

● ADJ+n importance **importance, significance** *This is a year of historic significance for the school.*

▶ event **achievement, agreement, battle, decision, meeting, moment, occasion, victory** *Entry is free to all supporters wishing to attend the historic occasion.*

historical ADJ

1 connected with history or with the past

● ADJ+n relating to historical study **background, basis, context, debate, dimension, interpretation, investigation, perspective, precedent, research** *All art is best understood in terms of the historical context that produced it.*

▶ evidence **document, evidence, fact, material, record** *Preservation of historical records is the duty of a museum.*

▶ person **figure, personage** *If you were able to spend an hour with one dead, historical figure, who would it be and what would you ask them?*

▶ truth **accuracy, truth** *Every historian worth their salt will tell you that there is no such thing as historical accuracy.*

▶ importance **importance, significance** *Included in this volume are 72 papers, selected for their historical importance and continuing significance.*

▶ description **account, introduction, narrative, overview, survey** *The book gives a historical survey of five major topics, with an overview of the relevant research.*

● and/or **archaeological, architectural, biographical, contemporary, cultural, geographical, literary, philosophical, political, social, sociological** *The building is of outstanding historical and architectural significance.*

2 based on people or events in the past

● ADJ+n **epic, fiction, novel, romance** *Not many people read Sir Walter Scott's historical novels these days.*

history N

the past, or the study of it

● adj+N types of history **ancient, contemporary, human, local, medieval, modern, oral, recent, recorded** *Capturing oral history is a vital part of research.*

▶ about particular countries **British, Irish, American etc** *Both local and Scottish history really only began to flourish from the 1960s.*

▶ about particular subjects **architectural, cultural, ecclesiastical, maritime, military, naval, social** *Cultural history and social history are particular areas of staff interest.*

● n+N **art, aviation, church, cinema, family, mining, railway, world** *Other options include art history classes and wine tasting.*

● v+N discover history **chart, explore, reconstruct, teach, trace** *This book traces the history of the guilds and liveries.*

▶ write history **chronicle, document, record, recount, rewrite, write** *The book chronicles the history of the Association from its origins to the modern day.*

▶ study history **learn, read, study** *Two-thirds of the students who come to us have not studied art history before.*

● N+v **demonstrate sth, prove sth, reveal sth, show sth, suggest sth, teach sb, tell sb** *History has shown that creativity and imagination can lead to incredible success.*

● N+n involved with history **department, faculty,**

society *Before joining the History Faculty of the University of Cambridge, he taught at Stanford University.*

▶ what is taught **curriculum, syllabus** *Learning how to be a historian is one of the main features of the History syllabus.*

▶ about history **book, lesson, textbook** *If I want know what happened in the past, I read a history book.*

▶ people **buff** INFORMAL, **lecturer, professor, student, teacher** *History buffs will enjoy the 14th century church with its famous sundial.*

● N+of **art, Christianity, cinema, mathematics, medicine, philosophy, photography, science, thought, warfare** *He chose to embark on a history of science by beginning with a history of electricity.*

hit N
a song, film, play, or show that is very successful

● adj+N big **big, blockbuster, great, greatest, huge, massive, runaway, smash, sure-fire, top-ten, worldwide** *Subtitled Why Try Harder, this features all his biggest hits and a couple of sublime remixes.*

▶ types of hit **box-office, chart, comedy, crossover, dance, disco, indie, pop** *This thriller became one of France's biggest box-office hits of last year.*

▶ immediate **immediate, instant** *Tim Burton's much-loved film became an instant hit in 1990.*

● N+n song **album, record, single, song** *A succession of hit singles and albums followed.*

▶ show **comedy, film, movie, musical, series, show, sitcom** *I have lost track of just how many seasons of this hit show have been shown on TV.*

hitch N
a problem that is not very serious

● adj+N small **little, minor, slight, small** *After this minor hitch, the remainder of the journey went smoothly.*

If there are no problems at all, you can say that something happens **without a single hitch**: *The whole night went off without one single hitch.*

▶ big **major** *This year's Festival went off **without** any major hitches.*

▶ types of hitch **last-minute, technical** *There were a couple of technical hitches during the first half.*

▶ v+without+N **go, pass, proceed, run** *My postgraduate year at Jordanstown went without a hitch.*

HIV N
a virus that can cause aids

▶ v+N test for HIV **be screened for, be tested for** *We know that being tested for HIV and hepatitis is stressful.*

▶ catch HIV **acquire, be infected, catch, contract, get** INFORMAL *I got HIV from my first boyfriend.*

▶ have HIV **have, live with, suffer from** *Many people living with HIV have never taken an HIV test.*

People can be **HIV positive** or **HIV negative**: *Within Europe there are no restrictions on travel if you are HIV positive.*

▶ n+of+N spread **spread, transmission** *There is no law in this country against transmission of HIV.*

▶ frequency **incidence, prevalence** *In the meantime, incidence of HIV amongst young gay men in the UK is not falling.*

hoax N
a dishonest trick

● adj+N **big, cruel, elaborate, gigantic, great** *One wonders whether the pair were the victims of an elaborate hoax.*

● v+N carry out a hoax **perpetrate** *The letter turned out to have been a hoax perpetrated by pupils at the school.*

▶ reveal a hoax **expose, reveal** *He once exposed a spectacular hoax solely through phone interviews.*

● N+n act **bomb, call, email, message, virus, warning** *How can I spot a hoax email or fake offer?*

▶ person **caller** *Hoax callers are also prosecuted.*

hobby N
something you enjoy doing when you are not working

● adj+N interesting **absorbing, fascinating, interesting** *Here you will find everything you need for the fascinating hobby of quilting.*

▶ enjoyable **enjoyable, favourite, fun, great, rewarding** *Candlemaking is an easy and rewarding hobby.*

▶ unusual **peculiar, strange, unusual** *John had quite unusual hobbies as a child.*

▶ expensive **expensive** *Dirt biking is a relatively expensive hobby.*

● v+N do a hobby **enjoy, have, indulge, pursue** *Housesitting has provided them with the time to pursue hobbies and special interests.*

▶ start a hobby **start, take up** *Start a new hobby, volunteer, or take a class yourself.*

hold V
1 organize an event

● V+n for discussion **conference, meeting, seminar, session, symposium, talks, workshop** *The association holds seminars and conferences, and compiles statistics.*

▶ ceremony or celebration **ceremony, dinner, event, funeral, reception, wedding** *An awards ceremony was held and the winning team left in a limousine.*

▶ election **election, referendum** *Any resident can stand as a director and elections are held every two years.*

▶ competition **audition, championship, competition, raffle** *We will be holding auditions in early July.*

▶ inquiry **hearing, inquest, inquiry** *Public inquiries were held in 1992 and 1995.*

▶ protest **demonstration, protest, rally, vigil** *A dozen peace activists held a vigil before the Fort for over one month.*

2 have a particular quality

● V+n interest **appeal, fascination, interest** *The plays of Samuel Beckett hold a strange fascination for modern theatre audiences.*

▶ hope **hope, promise** *The scheme is very successful and holds great hope for future development.*

hold N

1 the fact of holding someone or something

- adj+N tight or strong **close, firm, secure, strong, tenacious, tight** *This time the bird seemed to have a firmer hold on its prey.*
- ▸ weak or loose **loose, precarious** *The buddy follows, keeping a loose hold on the line.*
- v+N take hold **catch, gain, get, grab, seize, take** *I shoved my torch in my pocket, grabbed hold of the rope and stepped out into the dark.*
- ▸ keep hold **keep, maintain, retain** *Keeping hold of the strap, support the baby with that hand.*
- ▸ tighten/loosen a hold **loosen, tighten** *Rose tightened her hold on Eve's hand.*
- ▸ release or lose a hold **lose, release, relinquish** *He somehow lost his hold and fell off the waggon.*

2 power or control over a situation, area or person

- adj+N strong **firm, good, powerful, secure, strong, tenacious, tight** *The rich countries kept a pretty tight hold on their wealth.*
- ▸ weak **fragile, loose, precarious, slender, tenuous** *Democracy has only had a tenuous hold in the South.*
- v+N take control **catch, gain, get, grab, seize, take** *In a very short time the fire took hold and the mill became a raging inferno.*
- ▸ keep control **consolidate, keep, maintain, retain** *Liverpool maintained their slender hold on second position in the Group with a 3–2 win.*
- ▸ tighten/loosen control **loosen, tighten** *Positive feedback reinforces particular ideas; negative feedback loosens their hold.*
- ▸ lose or give up control **lose, release, relinquish** *The state is relinquishing its hold on the bank.*

hole N

a space in the surface of something

- adj+N big **big, deep, gaping, huge, large, massive** *A huge hole suddenly appeared about thirty feet below the dam's parapet.*
- ▸ small **small, tiny** *The edges of each tiny hole are slightly frayed.*
- ▸ of a particular shape **circular, rectangular, round, square** *The top of the cage has two circular holes in it.*
- n+N made by a particular thing **bullet, drill, screw** *Every morning they wake up to fresh bullet holes along the street.*
- ▸ for a particular purpose **drain, drainage, nest, ventilation** *Unless you are creating a bog garden, the container must have drainage holes.*
- ▸ where an animal lives **mouse, rabbit** *He would promptly explore anything resembling a rabbit hole.*
- v+N make a hole **bore, burn, cut, drill, make** *Drill a hole in the side of the drum at the bottom.*

> If something has a lot of holes in it, you can say it is **riddled with holes**: *Why are our streets riddled with holes?*

- ▸ make a hole using force **blast, blow, poke, punch** *Press the button again and it will blow a hole in the wall.*
- ▸ fill a hole **fill, fill in, plug** *Clean off the surfaces and plug the holes with a water-proof plug.*
- ▸ dig a hole **dig, excavate** *Jim, Alison and her daughters dug holes for the trees to go in.*

home N

the place where you live

- adj+N with particular characteristics **affordable, comfortable, decent, luxurious, permanent** *The number of new, affordable homes being built is not keeping up with demand.*
- ▸ types of home **detached, semi-detached, single-family, starter, three-bedroom, four-bedroom etc** *I well remember with what pride I carried our baby daughter into our starter home.*
- ▸ safe or happy **caring, happy, loving, safe** *A loving, caring home is one of the most important influences in the life of a child.*
- ▸ for holidays **holiday, second, vacation** *The deposit for holiday home bookings is £50.00 per week.*
- ▸ who lives there **family, marital, matrimonial** *They're looking for the perfect family home.*
- v+N go home **come, go, head, return** *Mr Smith is in the Navy and only comes home once a year.*
- ▸ leave your parent's home **leave** *Her elder sisters have left home.*
- ▸ buy/rent a home **buy, rent** *John Morgan, who has bought a new home in the Cleveland Park development, added: 'I want to stay in the neighbourhood, close to my friends and relatives, but I need a modern property that's safe, warm and comfortable'.*
- ▸ leave your home **get away, go away, leave** *She couldn't get away from home and go off to University.*
- ▸ be forced to leave your home **abandon, flee** *Up to 1,000 were killed, with many more forced to flee their homes.*
- ▸ arrive home **arrive, get** *I got home at about 6.*

homeless ADJ

without a place to live

- adv+ADJ deliberately/not deliberately **intentionally, unintentionally** *What if you decide I am intentionally homeless?*
- ▸ officially **legally, officially, statutorily** *The Council has accepted you as statutorily homeless.*
- ▸ for a short time **temporarily** *6,000 residents were made temporarily homeless.*
- v+ADJ **become, be left, be made, be rendered, end up** *The young people have become homeless for a variety of reasons.*

homework N

work students must do at home

- v+N do homework **complete, do, finish** *Doing homework is important: it makes a difference to learning.*
- ▸ set homework **assign, give, set** *There is no legal requirement for a school to set homework.*
- ▸ mark homework **grade, mark** *Homework is marked according to the general school marking policy.*
- ▸ give homework in **give in, hand in, submit** *How often do I have to submit homework?*
- ▸ be given homework **get, have** *Some days you don't get much homework.*
- N+n task **activity, assignment, exercise, task** *This written work was set as a homework task.*

▶ for organizing homework **diary, timetable** *Make sure the pupil has a copy of the homework timetable.*

honest ADJ
not lying or cheating, and obeying the law

● adv+ADJ completely **absolutely, completely, entirely, perfectly, scrupulously, totally** *To be perfectly honest, I think she may be asked to leave her position.*

▶ in a way that pleases you **disarmingly, refreshingly** *He was refreshingly honest about his disappointment.*

▶ in a way that may upset people **brutally, painfully, ruthlessly, searingly, unflinchingly** *His words were painfully honest; his performance was open and brave.*

▶ in a particular way **emotionally, intellectually** *They are intellectually honest without being condescending.*

● ADJ+n opinion **advice, answer, appraisal, assessment, feedback, opinion** *Please leave your honest opinion of the service received.*

▶ discussion **communication, debate, dialogue, discussion** *The unity of the Socialist Alliance can only be strengthened through honest debate.*

▶ mistake **mistake** *It was an honest mistake, honestly made and included in good faith.*

● and/or **decent, fair, frank, open, reliable, sincere, trustworthy, truthful** *He is a decent, honest and trustworthy individual.*

honesty N
an honest way of behaving, speaking, or thinking

● adj+N complete **absolute, complete, scrupulous, total** *I want to face the feelings inside of me with complete honesty.*

▶ that pleases people **admirable, commendable, disarming, refreshing** *The book is written with a refreshing honesty that makes it easily readable.*

▶ that may upset people **brutal, stark, uncompromising, unflinching** *He acted with uncompromising, even brutal honesty.*

▶ types of honesty **emotional, intellectual** *Courage and intellectual honesty are essential qualities in politics.*

● v+N appreciate **admire, appreciate, respect, value** *I appreciate the honesty and openness shown during the interviews.*

▶ expect or need **demand, encourage, expect, require, want** *Science is a profession that demands honesty.*

▶ doubt **doubt, impugn, question** *I have no reason to doubt your honesty.*

▶ have **have** *Teachers must have the personal honesty to acknowledge their limitations.*

● and/or **courage, decency, fairness, frankness, humility, integrity, openness, probity, reliability, sincerity, trust, trustworthiness, truth, truthfulness** *I believe in honesty and integrity in all things.*

honour N
1 something that makes you proud

● adj+N great **great, huge, major, rare, tremendous** *It's usually seen as a great honour to be chosen as a baby's godparent.*

▶ not an honour **dubious** *Some states can claim the dubious honour of having failed to ratify either convention.*

● v+N **be given, do sb, have** *Sadly I never met him, although I do have the honour of knowing Annette.*

2 a prize for achievement

● adj+N important **coveted, prestigious** *The most coveted honour for soldier or sailor is the Victoria Cross.*

▶ high **high, major, top** *Top honours were shared between the east-west rivals.*

● v+N give an honour **award, bestow, confer, grant** *Susan is extremely delighted by the honour bestowed on her.*

▶ receive an honour **accept, be given, gain, receive, scoop** INFORMAL**, share, take, win** *Wigner received many honours for his outstanding work.*

▶ deserve an honour **achieve, deserve, earn** *We offer our congratulations on this well-deserved honour.*

honour V
do what you promised to do

● V+n promise **commitment, guarantee, obligation, pledge, responsibility, undertaking** *We hope that the Government will decide to honour its pledge to hold a full review.*

▶ agreement **agreement, contract, deal** *This union has a proud record of honouring agreements.*

▶ request **request, wish** *In retrospect, I should never have honoured your request.*

hope V
want and expect something to happen

● adv+V very much **dearly, desperately, earnestly, fervently, really, sincerely, very much** *I sincerely hope you begin to feel better soon.*

▶ definitely **certainly, truly** *This is the first time I have exhibited my work in a gallery, but I certainly hope it won't be the last.*

▶ secretly **secretly** *I had been secretly hoping that some kind of a compromise might be found.*

● and/or wish **pray, wish** *We sincerely hope and pray common sense and justice will prevail.*

▶ think **believe, think** *I hope, and think, that we all enjoyed the trip.*

▶ expect **anticipate, expect, intend, trust** *We hope and trust that our prayers will be answered.*

hope N
1 the feeling or belief that something you want will happen

● adj+N weak **faint, false, forlorn, little, pious, slim, vague, vain** *I hope he's right – although it's a forlorn hope, I admit.*

▶ sincere **earnest, fervent, fond, sincere** *My sincere hope is that this petition will help secure a future for the children of this area.*

▶ great **best, great, real** *There are great hopes for a revolution in cancer treatment in the next few years.*

▶ last **last** *I choked back a cry, my last hope gone.*

● v+N damage or destroy hope **dash, dent, destroy, end, extinguish, shatter** *Hopes were dashed when plans for a stadium were refused.*

▶ create hope **bring, give, offer, raise** *Civil resistance offers the one slim hope of avoiding all-out civil war.*

▶ have hope **cherish, entertain, harbour, have** *The young are supposed to cherish vain hopes and go to the barricades for foolish causes.*

▶ lose hope **abandon, give up, lose** *At last, he lost heart, and abandoned all hope of escape.*

● n+of+N small amount **flicker, gleam, glimmer, ray, spark** *When I phoned her, I felt as if there was a tiny glimmer of hope.*

▶ someone or something that gives hope **beacon, flame, sign, symbol** *She had been a symbol of hope for the world.*

2 something that you wish for [usually plural]

● adj+N disappointed **desperate, disappointed, futile, unfulfilled, unrealistic** *Do you have any unfulfilled hopes and ambitions?*

▶ ambitious **high** *We have high hopes that the competition will become a flagship event.*

▶ optimistic **optimistic, sanguine** *Its success ought to exceed even the sanguine hopes of the promoters.*

horizon N

1 a line in the distance where the sky meets the earth

● adj+N distant/close **distant, far, near** *It is the land of far horizons.*

▶ wide **broad, endless, infinite, limitless** *The rolling hills in the distance make the view appear like a seascape with an infinite horizon.*

▶ in a particular direction **eastern, western etc** *The man's eyes were fixed upon the northern horizon.*

● v+N **dominate, scan, sweep, watch** *As you look westward from the city, Mount Fuji dominates the horizon.* ● *Look out of the corner of the eyes when scanning the horizon.*

2 the limits of your experience [usually plural]

● adj+N wide **broad, endless, infinite, limitless, wide** *One would hope scholars might have wider horizons.*

▶ narrow **limited, narrow, restricted** *Horizons were narrow and opportunities limited.*

▶ new **new** *One trip led to another, with breaks in between that opened up new horizons.*

▶ types of horizons **artistic, cultural, educational, historical, intellectual, musical, social** *Seeking to broaden his musical horizons, he took an interest in early music.*

● v+N widen someone's horizons **broaden, enlarge, expand, extend, open, open up, widen** *My year in Salzburg really broadened my horizons.*

▶ limit someone's horizons **limit, narrow** *Their horizons are limited by terms of office that last five years at most.*

● N+v **expand, extend, open up, widen** *Times move on, however, and horizons expand.*

horrific ADJ

shocking and upsetting

● adv+ADJ **absolutely, particularly, pretty INFORMAL, quite, truly** *Her experience was truly horrific.*

● ADJ+n crime **abuse, act, attack, crime, murder**

This horrific murder has shattered pupils at the school that the boys attended.

▶ accident or harm **accident, crash, death, injury, tragedy** *The Spaniard was lucky to escape from an horrific crash.*

▶ incident **event, experience, incident, ordeal** *Their work helped expose the truth about this horrific event.*

horror N

a strong feeling of shock or fear

● adj+N **abject, absolute, indescribable, sheer, unimaginable, unspeakable, utter** *His images present figures caught in a landscape of unspeakable horror.*

● v+in+N **gasp, recoil, stare, watch** *Some of you may recoil in horror at this idea.*

● v+with+N **be filled, react** *British consumers will react with horror.*

● and/or **despair, disbelief, disgust, fear, shock, terror** *The papers all spoke of the shock and horror on the faces of the bystanders.*

hospital N

the place where ill or injured people are treated

● v+N leave hospital **be discharged, come out of, leave** *She left hospital on January 3 and continued her drugs at home.*

▶ go to a hospital **attend, go into, visit** *I have been attending hospital for tests on my heart.*

● N+n **admission, discharge, stay** *In general, women were satisfied with the length of their hospital stay.*

● v+to+N **be admitted, be airlifted, be readmitted, be rushed, be taken, be transferred, go** *20,000 children are admitted to hospital in Britain each year with a head injury.*

hospitality N

1 generous behaviour towards visitors and guests

● adj+N generous **generous, lavish** *Everywhere, we received generous hospitality.*

▶ kind **friendly, genuine, gracious, warm** *This family-run restaurant offers award-winning cuisine, combined with friendly hospitality.*

▶ very good **excellent, great, superb, wonderful** *Once again, we enjoyed some wonderful hospitality.*

▶ traditional or famous **legendary, traditional** *Indian hospitality is legendary and gracious.*

▶ in a particular place **Scottish, Irish, Welsh etc** *Try a taste of Southern hospitality in Savannah, New Orleans or Nashville.*

● v+N receive hospitality **accept, appreciate, enjoy, experience, receive** *You will experience traditional Siberian hospitality in the last week of the tour.*

▶ give hospitality **extend, give, offer, provide, show** *We look forward to extending this hospitality to you.*

▶ return someone's hospitality **repay, return** *Henry repaid their hospitality by inviting them to his house in France.*

● and/or **comfort, friendliness, friendship, generosity, kindness, warmth, welcome** *For his* kindness and hospitality we owe him our sincerest thanks.

2 entertainment of customers by a company

- adj+N **corporate, matchday, pre-match** Why not treat your family or friends to a great day's entertainment with our matchday hospitality packages?

- N+n business **business, industry, sector, trade** The hospitality business is all about dealing with people.

▶ location **area, facility, marquee, suite, tent, venue** The show was very well attended and our hospitality suite was very busy throughout the three days.

▶ event **event** The Theatre is pleased to present our Hospitality Events and can be booked for most shows.

- and/or **catering, entertainment, leisure, retail, tourism** The College is focussed on the hospitality, tourism, leisure and services to people sectors.

host N
a person, place or organization that entertains people

- adj+N **friendly, generous, genial, gracious, hospitable** Bill was a most gracious host and very personable.

- v+N **act as, play** Dartford is to play host to its first farmers market on Friday 11 November.

- N+n **city, country, family, institution, nation, organization** We must point out that not all of our host families are qualified teachers.

hostage N
a prisoner kept by someone who wants something

- v+N take or hold a hostage **hold sb, keep sb, take sb** The U.S. did not publish the fact that an American citizen had been taken hostage.

▶ release or rescue a hostage **free, release, rescue** After 9 months, the hostage was released.

▶ kill a hostage **execute, kill, shoot** If the demands are not met, the hostages are usually executed.

▶ N+n person **negotiator, -taker** One further crew member remains in the hands of the hostage takers.

▶ act or situation **crisis, drama, negotiation, rescue, situation, taking** As in any hostage situation, you have to be careful not to encourage hostage taking

hostile ADJ
1 difficult or dangerous

- adv+ADJ **extremely, very** The soldiers were ordered to operate a fuel supply convoy through 200 miles of extremely hostile terrain.

- ADJ+n **climate, environment, terrain, territory, world** The Defence Secretary did not pretend that our forces were going into particularly hostile territory.

2 unfriendly, critical, or threatening

- adv+ADJ very **actively, bitterly, deeply, downright, extremely, implacably, increasingly, very** Most Scottish newspapers were downright hostile to independence.

- openly **openly, overtly** Some people are supportive and understanding, others are openly hostile.

- ADJ+n in business **bid, takeover** Last year, they launched a hostile takeover bid for another software company.

▶ action or attitude **act, attack, attitude, intent, reaction, reception, response, threat** He is being watched, but not with hostile intent.

▶ situation **atmosphere, circumstances, climate, situation** The atmosphere was decidedly hostile and unfriendly.

▶ person or group **army, audience, critic, crowd, faction, forces, regime** The soldiers came under attack from a hostile crowd throwing petrol bombs and other missiles.

▶ comment or criticism **comment, criticism, propaganda, question** Ignoring a great deal of hostile criticism, Bennett went ahead with his plan.

- v+ADJ **be, become, feel, remain, seem, turn** It is quite clear I am hostile to your theory and practice.

hostility N
1 fighting between enemies in a war [always plural]

- v+N end hostilities **cease, end, suspend** The hostilities were ended by a truce on 3 January 1992.

> To say that hostilities start, you can talk about the **outbreak of hostilities** or the **commencement of hostilities**. To say that hostilities end, you can talk about the **cessation of hostilities** or the **end of hostilities**.

- N+v hostilities start **begin, break out, commence, erupt, start** In May 1803 hostilities broke out again.

▶ hostilities stop **cease, end** Once hostilities ceased, we separated and went our own ways.

▶ hostilities continue or start again **continue, renew, resume** If open hostilities resume, it will hurt everyone, especially the poorest.

2 opposition or unfriendly behaviour

- adj+N open **active, open, outright, overt** The other ministers varied in attitude from outright hostility to neutrality.

▶ strong **bitter, deep, downright, extreme, implacable, intense, unremitting** She noted the extreme hostility between the mother and the father.

▶ shared **mutual** Rivalry or even mutual hostility is not uncommon.

▶ general **considerable, public, widespread** When the Act was first introduced there was widespread public hostility to it.

- v+N cause hostility **arouse, attract, generate, incur, provoke** His enquiries did nothing but arouse hostility among the English residents.

▶ face hostility **encounter, face** We encountered considerable hostility, but it was an important learning experience.

▶ express hostility **demonstrate, express, show** In these pamphlets, Ward expressed his hostility towards other religious sects.

▶ overcome or end hostility **end, overcome, suspend** The challenge has been to overcome the hostility to trade unions in general.

hot ADJ
very high in temperature

- adv+ADJ very **baking, blazing, blisteringly,**

boiling, burning, extremely, incredibly, really, scorching, scorchingly, searingly, swelteringly, very** *On a blisteringly hot day in July, the air con packed in.*
- ▶ too **excessively, oppressively, stiflingly, too, unbearably, uncomfortably** *I woke up gasping for breath in a stiflingly hot tent.*
- ▶ rather **moderately, pretty INFORMAL, quite, rather** *Bake in a moderately hot oven for 30 mins.*
- ▶ used about food and liquids **piping, scalding, smoking, steaming** *Sprinkle with toasted flaked almonds and serve piping hot.*

hour N
the time when you do a particular thing [always plural]

- ● adj+N when someone works **flexible, long, unsociable, unsocial** *Unsocial hours, evening and weekend work is a regular part of a stage actor's life.*
- ▶ when a place is open **extended, licensing, normal, office, opening, operating, trading** *Opening hours are 9am to 5pm Monday to Friday.*
- ▶ when someone is awake **waking** *Children spend 85 per cent of their waking hours outside of school.*
- ● v+N **keep, work** *British men work the longest hours in Europe – and professional women are catching up.*

housing N
buildings for people to live in

- ● adj+N cheap/expensive **affordable, cheap, low-cost, unaffordable** *A quarter of the homes will be affordable housing.*
- ▶ good/bad quality **adequate, decent, inadequate, overcrowded, poor, slum, substandard, suitable** *People who came in those days faced social problems – there was no decent housing.*
- ▶ types of housing **private, public, sheltered, social** *Many local councils provide sheltered housing for the elderly, with a warden on site for emergencies.* ● *Low pay, job insecurity, lack of decent social housing and poor community facilities affect working-class young people.*
- ▶ where housing is **rural, suburban, urban** *Bay windows were a common feature of UK suburban housing until the late 1930s.*
- ● v+N build housing **build, provide** *It's costing more and more to build housing – and particularly social housing.*
- ▶ improve housing **improve, rebuild, refurbish** *Care and Repair is a charity set up to improve the housing of older and disabled people.*
- ● N+n **boom, crisis, market, provision, shortage** *The housing crisis affects us all.*

hug N
the action of putting your arms round someone

- ● adj+N big **big, huge, massive** *Because I am injured, he gives me a big hug.*
- ▶ quick **quick** *She gave me a quick hug and went slowly and sadly down the stairs.*
- ▶ friendly or loving **affectionate, friendly, loving, warm** *My dad gave me a warm hug and said goodbye.*
- ▶ giving sympathy **comforting, reassuring,**

sympathetic *After such a hard day, it was nice to get a sympathetic hug.*
- ● v+N **get, give sb, have, need** *We had a hug and he kissed me on both cheeks.*

huge ADJ
extremely large in amount or degree

- ● adv+ADJ very **absolutely, really, so, unimaginably** *The store has an absolutely huge range of kitchenware.*
- ▶ rather **pretty INFORMAL** *The cost of this whole process can be pretty huge.*
- ▶ possibly in the future **potentially** *If they get the contract there are potentially huge financial rewards.*
- ● ADJ+n amount **amount, chunk, number, pile, profit, quantity, sum** *A huge chunk of the money they needed was provided by a single wealthy investor.*
- ▶ effect **boost, difference, impact** *Interactive whiteboards have had a huge impact on teaching across all areas of the curriculum.*
- ▶ increase/improvement **increase, leap, strides, surge, upsurge** *The company has made huge strides in terms of its environmental impact.*
- ▶ success **acclaim, hit, popularity, success** *Her latest book has earned her huge critical acclaim, including a Booker Prize nomination.*
- ▶ task **challenge, task, undertaking** *The census is a huge undertaking, involving every house in the country.*
- ▶ variety **range, variety** *The Diploma has helped me acheive my goals by opening up a huge range of opportunities.*
- ▶ something disappointing **blow, disappointment, setback** *His recent injury has come as a huge blow to the whole team.*

humanitarian ADJ
involving people affected by war, flood etc

- ● ADJ+n bad situation **catastrophe, crisis, disaster, emergency, situation, tragedy** *This silent humanitarian crisis is killing 6000 children daily.*
- ▶ food, supplies etc **aid, assistance, relief, supplies** *She reports here from Fallujah, where she is helping to deliver humanitarian aid.*
- ▶ attempt to give help **effort, intervention, mission, operation, programme** *It was officially described as a humanitarian mission, carrying medicine and other aid to Iraq.*
- ▶ organization or person providing help **agency, organization, worker** *It is a social justice and humanitarian organization that has helped thousands of people in war-torn countries.*

humiliate V
make someone feel embarrassed and ashamed [usually passive]

- ● adv+V in front of other people **publicly** *Even the distinguished general was publicly humiliated.*
- ▶ very much **completely, deeply, totally, utterly** *Matilda is deeply humiliated, as Cassie ushers her out the door.*
- ● and/or **belittle, embarrass, hurt, insult, patronize**

Patients are often humiliated and embarrassed by incontinence.

humiliating ADJ
making you feel embarrassed and ashamed

- ● adv+ADJ **completely, deeply, totally, utterly, very** *Being in debt can be very humiliating and embarrassing, and can lead to stress and other health problems.*
- ● ADJ+n experience **experience, treatment** *For a woman in her position, being made redundant was a humiliating experience.*
- ▶ defeat **defeat, retreat, surrender** *It was a humiliating defeat for the once-great champion.*
- ▶ change of mind or policy **climbdown, U-turn** *Bank bosses have been forced to make a humiliating U-turn.*

humiliation N
an ashamed and embarrassed feeling

- ● adj+N complete **abject, complete, deep, total, utter** *I thought your weight would be publicly announced, which would be total humiliation!*
- ▶ more **further, repeated** *The scandal heaped further humiliation on the government.*
- ▶ worse than anything before **final, ultimate** *The final humiliation came after his death, when it was revealed that, despite his claims, he had never won any bravery medals.*
- ▶ public **public** *Winning the boat race is ecstasy, losing is public humiliation.*
- ▶ v+N suffer humiliation **endure, face, suffer, undergo** *In 1908 they faced the humiliation of a 9–1 defeat.*
- ▶ avoid humiliation **avoid** *We avoided total humiliation, but we did not make the hoped-for breakthrough.*
- ▶ make someone suffer humiliation **heap on, inflict on** *After dropping out of college, he was arrested for a drug offence, heaping further humiliation on his parents.*

humorous ADJ
funny

- ▶ adv+ADJ very **delightfully, very, wickedly, wonderfully** *Both are wickedly humorous yet disturbing tales in which laughter seems to well up and then freeze in one's throat.*
- ▶ rather **gently, mildly, quite, rather, slightly** *The book features Cartwright's gently humorous illustrations.*
- ▶ in a rather frightening way **blackly, darkly, grimly** *This darkly humorous novel involves plenty of blood and gore.*
- ● ADJ+n story or poem **anecdote, poem, story, tale, verse** *Miles captivated his audience with humorous tales of his experiences while climbing the Himalayas.*
- ▶ event **incident, interlude, moment** *It's a rather grim drama, but there are a few humorous moments.*
- ▶ manner **style, tone, touch** *He gave his lectures with a light, humorous touch.*
- ▶ comment **aside, quip, remark** *Serious political commentary is interspersed with humorous asides.*
- ● and/or **engaging, irreverent, light-hearted, lively,**

playful, quirky, satirical *It's a show that takes a light-hearted and humorous look at the week's news.*

humour N
a funny quality that makes people laugh

- ● adj+N slightly frightening **black, dark, gallows, grim, macabre, morbid** *There's actually a certain amount of black humour in this film.*
- ▶ unusual and slightly crazy **off-the-wall, quirky, surreal, wacky, zany** *Monty Python films offered a similar style of surreal humour.*
- ▶ about sex or body functions **bawdy, smutty, toilet** *The foundation of British comedy is toilet humour.*
- ▶ not obvious or direct **gentle, subtle, tongue-in-cheek** *He also showed that he hadn't lost his knack for gentle humour.*
- ▶ expressed without laughing or smiling **deadpan, dry, wry** *I have long been a fan of his deadpan humour.*
- ▶ showing a lack of respect **ironic, irreverent, sarcastic, sardonic** *This was done with his usual dose of irreverent humour, never considering whether it would get back to his parents.*
- ▶ making jokes about yourself **self-deprecating** *Her ability to see her own imperfections, coupled with her self-deprecating humour, make her all the more likable.*
- ▶ based on physical actions such as falling over **slapstick** *The dame is crucial to pantomime's slapstick humour.*
- ● n+of+N **brand** *His special brand of humour has made his show essential viewing.*

> If you want to talk about someone's ability to find situations funny and make other people laugh, you can use the phrase *sense of humour*: *She has a great sense of humour and always makes me laugh.*

hunger N
1 a lack of food that can cause illness or death

- ▶ v+N try to prevent or deal with hunger **alleviate, combat, fight, reduce, relieve** *The aim is to alleviate world hunger and enhance food security in developing countries.*
- ▶ end hunger **eliminate, end, eradicate** *The first goal of eradicating hunger depends on sustainable and productive agriculture.*
- ▶ die because of hunger **die of** *Global capitalism means that a large part of the population are dying of hunger, while a few have all the wealth.*
- ● and/or **destitution, disease, homelessness, misery, poverty** *This simple strategy could help eradicate hunger and poverty.*

2 the feeling that you need food

- ● v+N **alleviate, assuage, satisfy** *The fruit satisfied her hunger.*
- ● n+of+N **feeling, pangs** *I ate some bread to stave off the pangs of hunger.*
- ● and/or **exhaustion, fatigue, thirst, tiredness** *The tablets can cause mood swings and feelings of hunger and thirst.*

3 a feeling of wanting something very much

- ● adj+N **great, insatiable, sheer, unsatisfied** *News*

channels have an insatiable hunger *for dramatic images and sound bites.*

● v+N **appease, satisfy** *To satisfy our hunger for details about the tragedy, news reports were fleshed out with details about the girls' lives.*

● N+for **justice, knowledge, power, revenge, success, truth** *We need somebody with initiative and a real hunger for success.*

hungry ADJ
1 feeling that you want food

● adv+ADJ **constantly, desperately, ravenously, really, so, very** *It was two o'clock when I awoke ravenously hungry.*

● v+ADJ **be, feel, get, go** *Shockingly, there are still places in Britain today where mothers go hungry so they can feed their families.*

● and/or **cold, desperate, homeless, poor, sick, thirsty, tired, weary** *By teatime I was tired and hungry.*

2 wanting something very much

● ADJ+for success **success, victory, a win** *Dixon, competing in her fourth Olympic Games, is hungry for success.*

▶ information **information, knowledge, news** *I'm hungry for knowledge and eager to learn more.*

▶ power **power** *Wimund sought greater acclaim and was hungry for even more power.*

hunt N
a search for someone

● n+N **murder, police** *The murder hunt is being led by Detective Superintendent Steve Bolam.*

● v+N start a hunt **begin, launch** *Police have launched a hunt for the missing chef.*

▶ join others in the hunt **join** *Several villagers joined the hunt for the girls.*

▶ organize a hunt **conduct, lead, organize** *The detective leading the hunt said the man who attacked Nadia would have been heavily bloodstained.*

● N+for **culprit, killer, murderer, perpetrator, rapist, terrorist** *This has become Scotland's largest-ever hunt for a serial rapist.*

hurdle N
one of several problems to solve

● adj+N big **big, formidable, major, significant** *Despite major legal hurdles which still need to be overcome, the company is confident that the project will be a success.*

▶ first **first, initial** *It is at this first hurdle that most would-be decision-makers fall.*

▶ last **final, last** *Most applicants for the fire service fail before reaching the last hurdle.*

▶ impossible to deal with **insurmountable** *With correct planning and supervision, these hurdles are not insurmountable.*

▶ types of hurdle **administrative, bureaucratic, financial, legal, planning, regulatory, technical** *Even after solving the technical challenges, there are also legal hurdles.*

● v+N experience a hurdle **encounter, face** *Immigrants faced huge hurdles in the job market.*

▶ successfully deal with a hurdle **clear, get over, jump, negotiate, overcome, surmount** *He has overcome the first hurdle, which is to be selected for interview.*

▶ fail because of being unable to deal with a hurdle **fall at** *Unfortunately, the scheme fell at the first hurdle through lack of finance, and was temporarily abandoned*

hurt V
1 feel pain

● adv+V very much **badly, like hell** INFORMAL, **really, terribly** *My leg really hurts.*

▶ a little **slightly** *By the end of the film, my head hurt slightly.*

2 cause physical pain

● adv+V very much **badly, seriously** *She hurt herself quite badly on some broken glass.*

▶ a little **slightly** *He fell and slightly hurt his hip.*

3 cause someone emotional pain

● adv+V **badly, deeply, emotionally, really** *The remarks about her weight deeply hurt her.*

hurt ADJ
1 injured or feeling physical pain

● adv+ADJ badly **badly, seriously, severely** *I wasn't badly hurt and I saw the driver of the other car and she looked okay.*

▶ slightly **slightly** *I was slightly hurt by flying glass.*

▶ v+ADJ **get** *He fell off the bike and was lucky he didn't get hurt.*

2 upset

● adv+ADJ very **deeply, really, terribly, very** *He was deeply hurt by her comments.*

▶ rather **quite, slightly** *I was slightly hurt that she didn't invite me to her wedding.*

● v+ADJ **feel, get, look, sound** *I didn't want another relationship because I didn't want to get hurt again.*

● and/or **angry, disappointed, embarrassed, upset** *Misunderstandings like this can leave people feeling hurt and angry.*

hush N
a sudden silence

● adj+N **breathless, deathly, eerie, expectant, reverential** *There was a deathly hush and a little voice said 'Are you alright John?'*

● N+v **descend, fall** *A hush descended over the hall as the moment arrived for the painting to be revealed*

hygiene N
the practice of keeping things clean

● adj+N good **good, meticulous, proper, scrupulous, strict** *Advice about the importance of good hygiene should be given.*

▶ bad **inadequate, poor** *The link between poor hygiene and disease transmission is well known.*

▶ basic **basic** *Washing hands after using the toilet is a matter of basic hygiene.*

▶ types of hygiene **dental, oral, personal** *Personal hygiene is important to stop the spread of disease.*

▪ n+N in a place **dairy, hospital, kitchen, washroom** *Hospital hygiene has been a matter for concern recently.*

▶ with your hands **hand** *Hand hygiene is a key priority in fighting infection.*

▪ when dealing with food **food** *Staff are first given basic training in food hygiene.*

▪ v+N **improve, maintain, observe, practise, promote** *What other measures should we consider to improve hygiene in our hospitals?*

▪ N+n **legislation, measures, precautions, procedures, regulations, standards** *Restaurants which fail to meet statutory hygiene standards will be closed down.*

hype N INFORMAL
clever use of advertising and the media to create interest

▪ n+N using the media **advertising, Internet, marketing, media, press** *Do not believe all the marketing hype on the covers.*

▶ before an important event **pre-launch, pre-match, pre-release, pre-season** *The movie never really lived up to the pre-launch hype.*

▶ v+N believe hype **believe, swallow** *People just seemed to swallow all the hype and hand over their money.*

not believe or be influenced by hype **cut through, forget, ignore** *This book is intended to cut through the hype and answer the questions which really matter.* • *Forget the media hype – it's just a mediocre record that's been very well promoted.*

be as good as hype claims **justify, live up to, match** *There are a couple of good tracks, but really not enough to justify all the hype.*

N+v **surround** *The amount of hype surrounding the release of a new Harry Potter book seems to grow with each release.*

hypothesis N
an idea being used to explain something

adj+N reasonable **plausible, reasonable, valid** *It is unjustified to reject this quite plausible hypothesis on the basis that some inconclusive evidence implies that all evidence is spurious.*

not proved, but being tested **speculative, tentative, unproven, untested, working** *This is, of course, only a tentative hypothesis, but there is a fair bit of supporting evidence.*

capable of being tested **falsifiable, testable** *He provides no testable hypotheses, only a lot of vague, unscientific speculation.*

v+N form a hypothesis **advance, develop, form, formulate, propose, suggest** *You might like to formulate a hypothesis to investigate this.*

▶ test a hypothesis to see if it is correct **consider, evaluate, examine, explore, investigate, test** *This is a practical demonstration of how corpora can be used to investigate a particular linguistic hypothesis.*

▶ prove a hypothesis is not correct **contradict, disprove, explode** *Scholars doubt and disprove hypotheses until they are upheld by the evidence.*

▶ prove a hypothesis is correct **confirm, prove, support, verify** *Their results partly supported these hypotheses.*

▶ say you think a hypothesis is probably not correct **refute, reject** *When religious hypotheses are refuted by scientists, the theists will go on believing anyway.*

▶ say you think a hypothesis is probably correct **accept** *Now, for the sake of argument we will accept the hypothesis that he is right.*

• N+v **concern sth, explain sth, predict sth, suggest sth** *The data will be used to test further hypotheses concerning how household division of labour reproduces gender inequities.* • *Finally, the hypothesis explains some curious features of early Christianity.*

hypothetical ADJ
possible, but not actual

• adv+ADJ **entirely, largely, merely, purely** *Of course, such assertions are purely hypothetical.*

• ADJ+n **case, example, question, scenario, situation** *He said that he was not going to get into answering hypothetical questions about when an election might or might not be called.*

hysteria N
uncontrolled excitement or extreme fear

• adj+N **collective, mass, public** *Objectivity should be sought and public hysteria should not determine news coverage.*

• n+N **media, press, tabloid** *Given all the press hysteria, it is surprising that there are only 50 asylum seekers in the whole town.*

• v+N **cause, create, fuel, generate, incite, whip up** *There is no need for the hysteria being whipped up about health workers who have HIV.*

• n+of+N **atmosphere, climate, outbreak, wave** *In the 16th century, a wave of hysteria about witchcraft swept Europe.*

hysterical ADJ
behaving in an uncontrolled way and very emotional

• adv+ADJ **absolutely, almost, downright, increasingly, slightly** *An increasingly hysterical Mrs Pemberton begged the man for help.*

• v+ADJ **be, become, get, sound** *At this, his wife became almost hysterical, waving her hands in the air and yelling loudly.*

Ii

icon N

famous person who is regarded as representing an area of life or culture

- n+N **cultural, fashion, feminist, gay, pop, rock, sporting, style** *This biography casts new light on Frida Kahlo, who is widely celebrated as a feminist icon.* • *This is the largest under-cover arena in Europe, and has hosted shows by some of the world's biggest pop and rock icons.*

idea N

1 a plan, purpose, or suggestion

- adj+N good or clever **brilliant, clever, excellent, fantastic INFORMAL, good, great** *The teachers are full of enthusiasm and good ideas to make learning fun for children.*
- ▷ showing imagination and original thinking **creative, imaginative, ingenious, original** *It was an ingenious idea which eventually saved the company a great deal of money.*
- ▷ new **fresh, new, novel** *We're always keen to try new ideas.*
- ▷ new and involving major changes **innovative, radical, revolutionary** *At this time, people were discovering Freud's revolutionary ideas about the unconscious.*
- ▷ bad or stupid **bad, half-baked, impractical, silly, stupid** *They came up with a half-baked idea for expanding the business.*
- ▷ crazy and completely impractical **crazy, fanciful, hare-brained, ludicrous, outlandish, preposterous, ridiculous, utopian, wacky** *Their solution is to build more airports – the whole idea is ludicrous.*
- ▷ types of idea **creative, practical** *It's ideal for serious writers who want to get the most from their creative ideas.*
- n+N **business, design, fundraising, gift, recipe** *This magazine will help anyone looking for gift ideas.*
- v+N have an idea **come up with, conceive, have, hit on** *He hit upon the wonderful idea of publishing old maps.*

If someone has a lot of ideas, you can say they are **full of ideas**: *Ben was full of ideas about how to make money.*

- ▷ develop an idea **develop, formulate** *His subsequent book, Cities for a Small Planet, developed these ideas in greater depth.*
- ▷ encourage new ideas to develop **generate, spark, stimulate** *The purpose of the worksheet is to generate new ideas about alternative energy.*
- ▷ talk about ideas with other people **bounce around, bounce off sb, discuss, exchange, share, swap** *This is an ideal opportunity to try out new technologies and bounce ideas off other practitioners.*
- ▷ try to find an idea **look for** *I am looking for ideas on how to run the workshop in an interesting way.*
- ▷ consider an idea as possible **consider, entertain, experiment with, explore, play with, toy with** *Initially, I toyed with the idea of doing it myself.*

If someone is willing to consider any ideas, you can say they are **open to ideas**: *We are open to ideas and willing to discuss any suggestions.*

- ▷ try to get people to accept your idea **promote** *We'll need to be bolder in promoting our ideas.*
- ▷ tell people what your ideas are **articulate, communicate, convey, expound, express** *They looked for for simple and effective ways to communicate environmental ideas with a mass market appeal.*
- ▷ suggest an idea for people to consider **contribute, float, introduce, meet, pitch, present, suggest** *We meet monthly to discuss important issues and to float new ideas.*
- ▷ like an idea **embrace, like, welcome** *We welcome new ideas, innovation and creativity.*
- ▷ decide an idea is not practical **abandon, dismiss, reject** *I temporarily abandoned the idea of going to college.*
- N+v when someone suddenly has an idea **hit sb, occur to sb** *Suddenly, an idea hit him and he rushed over to Krodders excitedly.*
- ▷ when an idea comes from something **come from sth, originate, stem from sth** *The idea stemmed from a conversation I had with Jane.*
- ▷ when an idea starts to develop **arise, develop, emerge, evolve** *Some excellent ideas have emerged from our questionnaires.*
- and/or **concept, experience, information, opinion, suggestion, thought** *New ideas and suggestions are welcomed.*

2 information or thoughts you have about something

- adj+N not clear **basic, faint, rough, vague** *They had only a vague idea of its location.*
- ▷ clear **clear, definite** *Start with a clear idea of your needs.*
- ▷ formed before you have enough information or experience **pre-conceived** *People came with pre-conceived ideas about what children with Down's Syndrome were like.*
- ▷ impossible to change **fixed** *He has very fixed ideas about the role of women.*
- v+N have an idea **have** *I had no idea who had attacked John.*
- ▷ get an idea **get** *Anyone got any idea what's the cause of this?*
- ▷ give an idea **give** *To try to give some idea of the height.*

ideal N

an idea about what is good and right

- adj+N based on high moral standards **high, lofty, noble** *The Mother's Union has high ideals, supporting family life and those who are married.*
- ▷ based on a perfect situation that does not really exist **romantic, unrealistic, utopian** *Why is an educated adult still holding on to a romantic ideal that only exists in fiction?*

▶ impossible **unattainable** *This progressive aim proved for the most part an unattainable ideal.*

▶ moral or religious **ethical, humanistic, moral, religious, spiritual** *She wouldn't do anything that conflicted with her moral ideas.*

● political **democratic, egalitarian, liberal, political, republican, socialist** *The society promotes democratic ideas of tolerance and equality.*

● v+N believe in an ideal **embrace, espouse, uphold** *He espoused the ideals of peace and tolerance.*

▶ achieve an ideal **achieve, attain, realize** *Of course, we do not live in an ideal world and it may never be possible to fully achieve these ideals.*

▶ represent an ideal **conform to, embody, represent** *Individual soldiers, most notably Henry Havelock, came to embody the evangelical ideal of a Christian soldier.*

▶ try to make people accept an ideal **disseminate, promote** *The temperance movement promoted anti-alcohol ideals.*

▶ stop believing in an ideal **abandon, betray, compromise, sacrifice** *By this time, the party had abandoned its egalitarian ideals.*

identical ADJ
exactly the same

● adv+ADJ almost **almost, largely, nearly, practically, virtually** *Venus has a dense atmosphere and is almost identical in size to the Earth.*

▶ in the most basic ways **basically, essentially** *These fish are essentially identical in terms of upkeep.*

▶ in every way **absolutely, exactly** *These cakes are handmade and no two cakes will be absolutely identical.*

▶ in a genetic, chemical etc way **chemically, genetically, physically, structurally** *Cloning creates a genetically identical copy of an animal or plant.*

● v+ADJ **appear, be, look, seem, sound** *His symptoms sounded identical to mine.*

▶ ADJ+in **appearance, design, shape, size, structure** *The crystals produced are identical in appearance.*

identification N
an official document that proves who you are

▶ adj+N personal **personal** *In order to claim the dog, the owner must provide a description together with personal identification.*

▶ types of identification **biometric, electronic, photographic** *Photographic identification will be required to gain entry.*

▶ correct or acceptable **proper, valid** *To enter the building, you need to provide valid identification.*

● v+N carry identification with you **carry** *Legitimate callers should carry identification.*

▶ show identification **provide, show** *You will need to provide identification such as a student card or credit card.*

▶ check someone's identification **check, verify** *Whenever anyone calls to your home to carry out work, always check their identification carefully.*

● N+n **badge, card, code, document, number, tag, wristband** *Every volunteer is required to have a police check and wear an identification badge.*

● n+of+N **form, means, proof** *You need to show two forms of identification.*

2 the action of recognizing someone or something

● adj+N correct **accurate, correct, precise, proper** *Remember, the more detailed the description, the greater the chance of an accurate identification.*

▶ quick **instant, quick, rapid** *Fast tracking of forensic samples will aid the rapid identification and arrest of offenders.*

▶ definite **conclusive, positive, unambiguous** *The bird's plumage and song were sufficiently distinctive to allow a positive identification.*

▶ early **early** *Screening is used for early identification of metabolic diseases.*

▶ formal or official **formal, official** *The body of Sergeant Williams was recovered, and after formal identification was buried at sea.*

▶ easy **easy** *Ensure all stewards are wearing the correct clothing for easy identification.*

● v+N allow identification **allow, enable, permit** *Patients can be screened at home, which allows the rapid identification of serious sleep disorders.*

▶ help identification **aid, assist, facilitate** *The surnames have been put in capitals to aid identification.*

▶ make an identification **make** *Always use a good field guide to make your identification.*

▶ prove an identification is correct **confirm, support** *The book does not have a botanical key to support identification of more unusual specimens.*

identify V
1 recognize someone or something and know who or what they are

● adv+V correctly **accurately, correctly, properly, reliably, rightly, successfully** *It is vital to accurately identify the copyright owner of each item.*

▶ not correctly **falsely, incorrectly, mistakenly, wrongly** *The man on the supermarket checkout incorrectly identified a piece of broccoli as cabbage.*

▶ easily **easily, readily** *Each child has a dedicated, numbered seat so the supervisor can easily identify any absentees.*

▶ quickly **quickly, rapidly** *Our consultants are able to quickly identify the key issues.*

▶ definitely **clearly, positively, precisely, specifically, unambiguously** *The Local Authority is expected to clearly identify where changes and amendments have been made.*

▶ not definitely **tentatively** *The animal was tentatively identified as a brown rat on the basis of size, but it could have been a different type of rat.*

▶ formally or officially **formally** *The body has been formally identified as that of James Smith.*

2 to recognize something that needs dealing with

● V+n problem or fault **deficiencies, failings, problem, shortcomings, shortfall, weakness** *Both studies have identified the same weakness with the method of measuring pollution.*

▶ danger **danger, hazard, risk** *The report identifies the business risks and shows how they can be minimised.*

▶ cause **cause, factor, source** *This chapter explains how to identify factors that may interfere with normal wound healing.*

▶ something that needs to be done **needs, priorities,**

requirement *There are a number of areas where the company has identified the need for further improvements.*

- and/or **address, assess, evaluate** *Its recommendations had strongly urged farmers to identify and address hazards on their farms.*

identity N

1 who someone is, their name, address etc

- adj+N incorrect **mistaken** *Police believe the shooting was a case of mistaken identity.*
- ▶ true **true** *Though he is pressed to reveal his true identity, he tells only the king.*
- ▶ not true **assumed, false, stolen** *He had registered under an assumed identity.*
- v+N prove your identity **authenticate, confirm, prove, verify** *He was released, after the police verified his identity.*
- ▶ check that someone is who they say they are **check** *You should always check the identity of any caller.*
- ▶ show your identity **disclose, divulge, reveal** *The graffiti artist 'Banksy' has been pressed to reveal his identity.*
- ▶ take someone else's identity for criminal purposes **assume, steal** *Any personal documents you throw away can be used to steal your identity.*
- ▶ discover someone's identity **ascertain, discover** *Police are trying to discover the identity of a woman whose body was found in woodland last night.*
- N+n something that proves your identity **badge, card, document, tag** *If a caller asks to come in, request to see their identity card.*
- ▶ crimes related to identity **fraud, scam, theft** *I am moving house and I am worried about the next occupants using my mail for identity theft.*
- ▶ check **check** *We carry out identity checks on all new staff.*

2 the qualities that make someone what they are and make them different from others

- adj+N of a nation, place, or people **cultural, ethnic, national, racial, regional, tribal** *The community is well-integrated but has also retained its distinctive cultural identity within Birmingham.*
- ▶ of an organization **corporate** *In today's business world it is important to develop an effective corporate identity.*
- ▶ shared by a large group **collective, common, communal, shared** *The women had forged a collective identity as young feminists.*
- ▶ personal **individual, own, personal** *He had a strong sense of personal identity.*
- ▶ clearly different from others **distinct, distinctive, separate, strong, unique** *Scotland has a distinct identity.*
- v+N create or develop an identity **construct, create, define, develop, establish, forge, shape** *The company has firmly established its identity on the British high street.*
- ▶ keep your identity and not change it **maintain, preserve, retain** *Many people moving to Britain feel it is important to retain their own cultural identity.*
- ▶ lose your identity **lose** *She felt she had lost some of her identity since getting married.*

▶ make your identity clear to other people **affirm, assert** *They have tried to assert their own regional identity.*

ideology N

a system of ideas and principles

- adj+N current and main **dominant, hegemonic, prevailing, ruling** *The dominant ideology in the US and Europe is capitalism.*
- ▶ with extreme or unacceptable ideas **extremist, fascist, fundamentalist, perverted, racist, totalitarian** *This is a far right white supremacist party with a fascist ideology.*
- ▶ relating to business or economics **capitalist, consumerist, free-market, market, neo-liberal** *The recent economic downturn has weakened the dominance of neo-liberal economic ideologies.*
- ▶ religious/not religious **religious, secular** *The predominantly secular ideology of western Europe is being challenged.*
- ▶ political **bourgeois, communist, conservative, liberal, Marxist, socialist** *What is the place of the individual in conservative ideology?*
- v+N have an ideology **adopt, embrace, espouse, share** *How can the state be racist and espouse an ideology of multiculturalism?*
- ▶ disagree with an ideology **challenge, oppose, reject** *Marxism and feminism both challenge this ideology.*
- ▶ try to make more people agree with an ideology **peddle, promote, propagate, spread** *You're promoting an egalitarian ideology and you have to convince people.*

idle ADJ

1 not being used

- v+ADJ **be left, lie, remain, sit, stand** *There's even a built-in screensaver if the screen sits idle for too long.*

2 without real purpose or effect

- ADJ+n talk **banter, chatter, chit-chat, gossip, talk** *There was no time for idle chatter.*
- ▶ wondering if something is true **curiosity, speculation** *They had come to look out of idle curiosity.*
- ▶ statement **boast, threat** *She talked about taking legal action, and this was no idle threat.*

ignite V

to cause conflict, strong feelings etc

- V+n debate or criticism **controversy, debate, outrage, protest** *The announcement has ignited an intense public debate.*
- ▶ war **revolution, war** *He blamed foreign terrorists for trying to ignite civil war.*
- ▶ thoughts and feelings **enthusiasm, imagination, passion, spark** *This trip ignited in me a passion for travel.* • *It was my English teacher who first ignited a spark of interest in languages.*

ignorance N

a lack of knowledge or information

- adj+N great or complete **complete, profound,**

sheer, total, utter *Inaccurate information is more dangerous than total ignorance.*

▸ shocking **abysmal, astonishing, gross, inexcusable, lamentable, staggering, woeful** *The author displays a staggering ignorance of the subject.*

▸ deliberate **wilful** *These people refuse, through wilful ignorance, to take the trouble to understand science.*

▸ on the part of many people **general, widespread** *There is widespread ignorance about the causes of the disease.*

Blissful ignorance is a state in which you do not know about something unpleasant, so it does not make you unhappy: *It is better to know the unpleasant truth than to live in blissful ignorance.*

▸ v+N show ignorance **betray, demonstrate, display, reveal, show** *Their attitudes reveal a profound ignorance of the countryside and agriculture.*

▸ claim or admit ignorance **admit, claim, confess, plead, profess** *Don't be afraid to admit your ignorance by asking questions.*

You say **Excuse my ignorance** or **Forgive my ignorance** when you are asking a question that someone might expect you to know the answer to: *Excuse my ignorance, but what does 'PCD' stand for?*

▸ when someone pretends not to know something **affect, feign, pretend** *He feigned ignorance when she asked him about the letter.*

▸ try to stop ignorance **combat, eradicate, fight, overcome** *They understand the importance of education in combating ignorance.*

▸ be caused by ignorance **be based on** *Negative stereotypes are most often based on ignorance.*

▸ N+of fact or existence **existence, fact, reality, truth** *For six months, we remained in complete ignorance of the fact.*

▸ subject **affair, issue, matter, subject** *He freely admits his ignorance of such subjects as the arts.*

▸ law or rules **law, procedure, regulation, rules** *Ignorance of the law is no excuse.*

▸ v+in+N **act, be kept, leave sb, live, remain** *The country has been kept in ignorance for too long.* ● *I allowed her to remain in ignorance of his intentions.*

▸ n+of+N **admission, amount, degree, display, level, sign** *The statement shows a profound level of ignorance about the role of the Welsh language in our society.*

gnorant ADJ

ot knowing something you should know, or not nowing the right way to behave

▸ adv+ADJ very or completely **entirely, profoundly, totally, utterly, wholly** *So many people are totally ignorant of the real situation.*

▸ in a way that shocks **abysmally, appallingly, deplorably, grossly, woefully** *Most of these politicians are woefully ignorant of the countryside and its wild animals and birds.*

▸ deliberately **wilfully** *Many are wilfully ignorant; others know the truth and do not care.*

▸ to a great extent **largely** *The public is still largely ignorant of this controversy.*

If you say that someone is **blissfully ignorant**, you mean that they do not know an unpleasant fact, and so they do not worry: *Juliet's father was blissfully ignorant of his daughter's condition.*

● ADJ+n ordinary people **masses, people, public** *The ignorant masses blame the scientists for inventing these weapons.*

▸ stupid person **fool, idiot** *We country people are not all ignorant fools, you know.*

● v+ADJ **appear, be, be kept, feel, remain, seem** *Why are ordinary people kept ignorant of what is happening in the world?* ● *The general public remains largely ignorant about environmental awareness.*

ignore V

not consider or pay attention to someone or something

● adv+V completely **altogether, completely, entirely, totally** *Parents' views were completely ignored.*

▸ almost **almost, virtually** *The press virtually ignored the story as not being newsworthy.*

▸ deliberately or in a way that shows you do not care **blatantly, blithely, deliberately, flagrantly, pointedly, studiously, wilfully** *The facts have been blithely ignored by politicians and the media.*

▸ just **just, simply** *They ask a lot of questions, and then simply ignore the answers.*

▸ by most people or in most cases **generally, largely, mostly, universally, widely** *Notices about not leaving litter are largely ignored.*

▸ often, and in a systematic way **persistently, systematically** *The research literature has systematically ignored these findings.*

▸ in a way that suits someone well **conveniently, quietly** *His article conveniently ignores the fact that many of those interviewed expressed no preference.*

● V+n fact or existence **evidence, existence, fact, possibility, reality** *It is quite unwise to ignore these facts*

▸ advice **advice, warning** *It is clear that many people ignored the safety warnings.*

▸ request, order, or rule **demand, instruction, order, plea, question, regulation, request** *My father was obviously in distress, but his pleas were ignored.*

▸ remark **comment, insult, remark** *Ignoring these remarks, I got into the car and drove away.*

▸ protest **protest** *'Be quiet,' he said, ignoring her protests.*

▸ threat **threat** *Just ignore any threats and don't respond to emails from strangers.*

▸ problem or danger **danger, issue, problem, risk** *Their transport policies blithely ignore the risk of environmental disaster.*

ill ADJ

not healthy; having a medical condition

● adv+ADJ very **critically, dangerously, desperately, extremely, gravely, really, seriously, severely, very** *He phoned, saying that his wife had been taken seriously ill.*

▸ rather **pretty** INFORMAL**, quite, rather** *By that stage I was feeling quite ill.*

▶ in a way that cannot be cured **fatally, incurably, mortally, terminally** *The centre offers care for terminally ill children.*

▶ in the mind **mentally** *Many mentally ill patients are cared for in the community.*

▶ when someone becomes ill very quickly and seriously **acutely** *Elderly people were blocking beds that were needed for acutely ill patients.*

▶ when someone is ill for a long time **chronically** *The work involved in caring for a chronically ill relative may lead to family conflicts.*

● v+ADJ **become, be taken, fall, feel, get, make sb** *My father fell seriously ill last month.* ● *All the stress at work had made her ill.*

illegal ADJ

not allowed by the law

● adv+ADJ completely **completely, highly, totally** *In the United Kingdom, all handguns are completely illegal.*

▶ according to a strict understanding of the rules **strictly, technically** *The sale of this type of meat is technically illegal.*

▶ in an obvious way **blatantly, clearly, patently** *We need to fight this type of blatantly illegal behaviour.*

▶ possibly **possibly, potentially, probably** *These activities are potentially illegal – and certainly dangerous.*

● v+ADJ **be, become, consider sth, declare sth, deem sth, make sth, remain, rule sth** *In 2002, it became illegal for schools to discriminate against students with disabilities in any way.* ● *The demonstrations were declared illegal on election day.*

illicit ADJ

not approved of, or not allowed by the law or rules

● ADJ+n activity or use **activity, use** *The organization's funds come from illicit activity.*

▶ particular activity **copying, distillation, import, manufacture, trade, traffic, trafficking** *The music industry is experiencing serious harm from illicit copying of online music.*

▶ item **arms, drug, heroin, imports, substance, weapons, whisky** *He moved to Scotland, where he began to produce illicit whisky.*

▶ relationship **affair, liaison, sex** *He had allegedly conducted an illicit affair with a married woman.*

illiteracy N

inability to read or write

● v+N **combat, eliminate, eradicate, reduce, tackle** *In 2008 the charity received a UNESCO award for its work in combatting illiteracy across the world.*

● and/or **disease, ignorance, poverty, unemployment** *They launched a huge education program to tackle widespread illiteracy and ignorance.*

illness N

the state of being ill or a period of being ill

● adj+N serious **critical, debilitating, life-threatening, serious, severe** *Have you had a serious illness in the past six months?*

▶ not serious **mild, minor** *Many minor illnesses, such as colds and flu, are caused by a virus.*

▶ becoming serious very quickly **acute** *There was a special area where accidents and cases of acute illness could be treated.*

▶ lasting a long time **chronic, lingering, long, long-standing, long-term** *Nocturnal enuresis (bed-wetting) is the most common chronic childhood illness.*

▶ that cannot be cured **fatal, life-limiting, terminal** *Hospices are institutions that care for people with terminal illnesses.*

▶ getting worse over time **degenerative, progressive** *Alcoholism is a progressive illness, which only gets worse.*

▶ affecting your mind **depressive, mental, psychiatric, psychotic, stress-related** *Most people are likely to suffer mental illness at some point in their lives.*

▶ affecting children **childhood** *The leaflet gives information on how to deal with minor childhood illnesses.*

● v+N have an illness **experience, have, suffer, suffer from** *Over half a million people in the UK suffer from stress-related illness.*

▶ start to have an illness **catch, contract, develop, get** *He died shortly after the war from an illness he had contracted in the prisoner-of-war camp.*

▶ bear an illness **bear, endure** *She died after a long illness which she bore with great patience and dignity*

▶ recognize and treat an illness **cure, diagnose, manage, treat** *Managing chronic illness in elderly patients is one of the main tasks of the general practitioner.* ● *The pharmacist can give you advice on treating minor illnesses.*

▶ fight or recover from an illness **cope with, deal with, fight, get over, overcome, recover from** *I am taking vitamin and zinc tablets to get over this illness.*

▶ pretend to have an illness **fake, feign** *She took time off work, feigning illness and not answering the phone.*

▶ die as a result of an illness **die from** *Pearson died from a long-term illness in 1998.*

● N+v happen **arise, occur, strike** *Accidents and illnesses often occur when people are stressed.*

▶ affect someone **affect sb, afflict sb** *Asthma is the most common chronic illness affecting children worldwide.*

▶ cause someone to be unable to live normally **handicap sb, incapacitate sb, weaken sb** *How will you manage financially if you are incapacitated by illness?*

▶ have a particular effect **cause sth, mean sth, result in sth** *Serious mental illness often results in social isolation.*

▶ happen as a result of something **be caused by sth, result from sth** *He died after a short illness resulting from an accident.*

▶ become worse **progress, worsen** *The pain usually gets worse as the illness progresses.*

▶ cause a lot of problems for someone **beset sb, blight sth, plague sb** *Since March last year, he has been plagued by two serious illnesses.*

● n+of+N **bout, case, episode, onset, outbreak, period, recurrence** *He has suffered from several* *episodes of mental illness over the past two years.* • *Children will be infectious for quite some time after the onset of the illness.*

illusion N
a false belief or idea, or an effect that is different from what is real

● adj+N relating to the senses **auditory, optical, perceptual, sensory, visual** *You will be amazed by optical illusions such as the 'floating finger' and the impossible triangle.*
▶ presented to an audience **magical, spectacular, theatrical** *Messel was a master of theatrical illusion.*
▶ when something is only an illusion **mere, pure, simple** *Is the concept of choice a mere illusion?*
▶ false **false** *Don't be under any false illusions. This is going to be hard work!*
▶ relating to a belief that things are better than they really are **comforting, grand, romantic, vain** *Fortunately, when they chose life on the farm, they had no romantic illusions.*

● v+N create an illusion **create, give** *'Perspective' is the way that artists create an illusion of a three dimensional image on a two-dimensional surface.*
▶ have an illusion **be under, cherish, entertain, foster, harbour, have, labour under** *I harbour no illusions about the time and effort needed to solve this problem.* • *Please don't labour under the illusion that you can always join the union 'when something goes wrong'.*
▶ destroy an illusion **destroy, dispel, shatter, spoil** *The attack destroyed any illusion that we are safe in the world.*
▶ make sure that people continue to have an illusion **maintain, perpetuate, preserve, reinforce, sustain** *They want to sustain the illusion that they are in control.*

illustrate V
show what something is like or that something is true

● adv+V **above, amply, below, clearly, dramatically, effectively, neatly, nicely, perfectly, starkly, vividly, well** *The information is illustrated in the table below.* • *This novel illustrates perfectly how money does not create happiness.* • *The study starkly illustrates the problems facing younger workers today.*
▶ V+n idea, fact, or opinion **argument, aspect, concept, fact, point, principle** *Two examples from my own experience will illustrate my point.*
▶ how important something is **importance** *These results illustrate the importance of the Web in Higher Education.*
▶ how difficult something is **complexity, difficulty** *I mention this fact only to illustrate the complexity of the situation.*
▶ problem **danger, dilemma, problem** *The results of the study illustrate the dilemmas faced by primary school teachers.*
▶ way of doing something **approach, method** *In each section, the author has given practical examples to illustrate the methods he describes.*
▶ v+to+V **attempt, seek, serve, try** *The following images attempt to illustrate this point.* • *An example*

will serve to illustrate how this process can be of help.

2 provide the pictures for a book

● adv+V in an attractive way **attractively, beautifully, colourfully, sumptuously, superbly** *She edited a series of books on ceramics, all superbly illustrated.*
▶ with a large number of illustrations **copiously, fully, generously, lavishly, liberally, profusely, richly** *The volume is lavishly illustrated with 175 photos, most in colour.*

Usage ***Illustrate*** is almost always passive in the ***adv+V*** combinations shown above.

illustration N
an example that shows that something is true or that makes something easier to understand

● adj+N **clear, excellent, good, graphic, perfect, practical, striking, useful, vivid** *The huge interest in the creature was a vivid illustration of the British love of animals.*

● v+N give an illustration **give, offer, present, provide** *The author gives us helpful illustrations of the problems involved and ways to solve them.* • *The project provides a good illustration of how people can learn to work together effectively.*
▶ use something as an illustration **give sth as, offer sth as, take sth as, use sth as** *I will take a recent incident as an illustration of my point.*
▶ be an illustration **be, serve as** *This is not an exhaustive list but it can serve as an illustration of the way in which sport can promote community spirit.*

image N
1 other people's opinion of something, or the opinion that you try to create in other people's minds

● adj+N good **positive, the right** *We produce books which give positive images of disabled people.*
▶ bad **negative, poor, tarnished, the wrong** *All these news stories have given the industry a tarnished image.*
▶ relating to work or a company **brand, corporate, professional** *Your website should closely reflect your corporate image.*

● v+N present an image **convey, have, maintain, present, project** *It is important that we project the right image.*
▶ encourage an image **promote** *The aim of the club is to promote a positive image of motorcycling.*
▶ get rid of an image **rid yourself of, shake, shed** *Cornell is trying to shed his rock star image.*

● N+n **problem** *The nuclear industry has always had an image problem.*

2 a picture or idea in your mind [usually singular]

● adj+N in your mind **mental** *Having learnt the word 'dog', we now have a mental image of a dog every time we hear the word.*
▶ clear **powerful, vivid** *I still have a vivid image of my grandfather reading me a story.*
▶ lasting for a long time **enduring, indelible** *One of the most enduring images of London is of a city wrapped in a blanket of fog.*

▶ held by many people **popular, stereotypical** *For many people, the word 'granny' brings to mind the sterotypical image of an old lady who stays at home baking cookies and knitting.*

▶ making you remember something **evocative** *The book is packed with evocative images of the past.*

▶ ideal **ideal** *Every culture has a different ideal image of beauty.*

● v+N have an image in your mind **have** *I still have the image of her sweet little face in my mind.*

▶ make an image appear in your mind **bring to mind, call to mind, conjure, conjure up, evoke, summon up** *The guitar music conjures up images of a warm summer night in Spain.*

3 a picture

● adj+N impressive **dramatic, enduring, evocative, iconic, memorable, powerful, striking, stunning, vivid** *The judges are looking for striking images: pictures that tell a story.*

▶ disturbing or unpleasant **disturbing, shocking, violent** *Parents will want to discuss any disturbing images on the news with their children.*

imagery N
pictures, objects or the use of words that represent an idea

● adj+N strong **evocative, powerful, startling, striking, stunning, vivid** *We're using striking imagery to create maximum impact.*

▶ religious **biblical, religious** *Some of the larger paintings use religious imagery as a source.*

▶ relating to how people see things in their minds **mental, symbolic, visual** *The process of translating words on a screen into mental imagery has the same effect as the magic that happens in a theatre.*

▶ expressing ideas with imagination **lyrical, poetic** *He doesn't use poetic imagery and metaphor for its own sake – only when it enhances the narrative.*

▶ produced using electronic equipment **computer-generated, digital, photographic, satellite, video** *High-quality photographic imagery will be used in the hunt for weapons.*

● v+N use imagery **draw on, employ, use, utilize** *Old family photographs and more recent imagery are utilized as source material.*

● N+v **conjure up, evoke** *The stunning visual imagery evokes visions that can be interpreted by the spectator.*

imagination N
the ability to think of clever and original ideas, or form pictures in your mind

● adj+N strong **active, creative, fertile, lively, rich, vivid** *Children have vivid imaginations.*

▶ too strong **fevered, overactive, wild** *They are the product of overactive imaginations.*

▶ relating to poetry and art **artistic, poetic, romantic** *The workshops focus on creative linguistic play and poetic imagination.*

▶ relating to what you see in your mind **visual** *Closing your eyes for this exercise will help the visual imagination.*

▶ relating to people in general **collective, human, popular, public** *Star Wars continues to capture our*

collective imagination. ● *What she had witnessed was a hell beyond human imagination.*

● v+N have/not have a good imagination **have, lack** *Good science fiction writers often have rich and active imaginations.* ● *Her work is pedestrian and lacks imagination.*

▶ use your imagination **use** *The classes encourage pupils to use their imagination to develop characters and stories.*

▶ cause someone to use their imagination more **exercise, stretch** *I soon learnt how to tell stories in a way that stretched people's imagination.*

▶ encourage people's imagination to work **engage, excite, fire, fuel, ignite, inspire, spark, stimulate, stir, trigger, unlock** *Drawing is a great way to fire your imagination.*

▶ when people become interested in something **captivate, capture, catch, grab, grip** *This is a fantastic product that has caught consumers' imagination.*

▶ when something goes beyond what people can imagine **defy** *It was a decidedly hair-raising story that defied the imagination.*

▶ N+v bring images into your mind **conjure up sth** *My imagination conjured up a thousand images to torment me.*

▶ get out of control **play tricks on you, run away with you, run riot, run wild** *The fancy-dress party is an opportunity to let your imagination run wild!*

▶ n+of+N **lack** *There is a curious lack of imagination in this novel.*

When someone says that something is *all in your imagination* or is *a figment of your imagination*, they mean that you have imagined it, and therefore it does not really exist: *Bobby doesn't really exist; he's just a figment of Poppy's imagination.* If something is not the case *by any stretch of the imagination*, it is not the case at all: *This was not acceptable behaviour by any stretch of the imagination.*

imaginative ADJ
involving new, different, or exciting ideas

● adv+ADJ **brilliantly, extraordinarily, extremely, highly, hugely, particularly, really, richly, truly, very, wildly, wonderfully** *Visually, the play is stunning, and extraordinarily imaginative.*

● ADJ+n way of thinking about or doing something **approach, idea, method, proposal, response, solution, thinking, way** *Pupils gain from imaginative teaching approaches.* ● *Several imaginative solutions to these problems have been suggested.*

▶ literature **fiction, literature, storytelling, writing** *I get much of my reading enjoyment from imaginative fiction.*

● and/or **bold, creative, exciting, innovative, inventive, stimulating** *Television is filled with creative, imaginative people.*

imbalance N
a situation in which the balance between two things is not equal or fair

● adj+N serious **chronic, gross, growing, massive,**

serious, significant *There is a serious regional imbalance **in** education for the disabled.*

▸ not serious **slight** *There was a slight imbalance bewteen the soloist and the orchestra.*

▸ economic **demographic, economic, financial, fiscal** *The Regional Development Agency aims to address social and economic imbalances.*

▸ relating to chemicals in the body **chemical, hormonal, metabolic** *His depression was caused by a chemical imbalance **in** the brain.*

▸ relating to substances in food **dietary, nutritional** *If children are allowed to only eat their favourite foods, nutritional imbalances may occur.*

▸ between different places **global, regional** *This course will address the question of global imbalance of power.*

● v+N cause an imbalance **cause, create, lead to** *If we eat a lot of fatty foods while doing little activity outdoors, we create an imbalance.*

▸ try to deal with an imbalance **address, tackle** *We need leaders who can address the imbalances that cause poverty.*

▸ correct an imbalance **correct, eliminate, offset, overcome, rectify, redress, reduce, remedy, resolve** *A vitamin and mineral supplement would correct any dietary imbalance.*

▸ cause an imbalance to continue or get worse **aggravate, grow, perpetuate, worsen** *The excess fat tissue aggravates the hormonal imbalance.* ● *The current situation has worsened the imbalance **between** supply and demand.*

▸ notice that an imbalance exists **detect** *A regular check-up with a qualified practitioner can help you detect imbalances.*

imitation N

1 an act of copying someone's behaviour

● adj+N good or quite good **close, fair, good, great, passable, perfect** *'One has to live and learn,' she remarked, with a passable imitation of her father's manner.*

▸ bad **bad, feeble, poor** *All they could manage was a poor imitation of the Rolling Stones.*

▸ v+N **do, give, perform** *Jacob can do a great imitation of Jim Carrey.*

2 a copy of something that is usually not as good as the original

● adj+N good or quite good **close, exact, good, passable** *I think that it is a very good imitation of my handwriting.*

▸ bad **cheap, inferior, mere, pale, poor, second-class** *Their advice is: 'beware of cheap imitations'.*

▸ v+N produce an imitation **create, make, produce** *You can produce a fairly good imitation of a restaurant pizza in a domestic oven.*

▸ cause many imitations to be made **spawn** *It is a novel that has spawned numerous imitations.*

▸ avoid buying imitations **avoid, beware of** *Cheap imitations are best avoided.*

▸ N+n weapon **firearm, gun, handgun, weapon** *Carrying an imitation firearm in a public place is an offence.*

▸ jewellery **diamond, gold, jewellery** *In the jeweller's, I bought a necklace and earrings in imitation diamonds.*

▸ leather **leather** *You can get an imitation leather jacket if you do not like the idea of real leather.*

immediate ADJ

1 happening or done now, without any delay

● ADJ+n action **action, measures, reaction, response, steps** *My immediate reaction was to say 'No'.* ● *People with genuine emergencies expect an immediate response.*

▸ danger or worry **concern, danger, threat** *The committee will first of all examine the areas of immediate concern.* ● *Doctors told him that his life was in no immediate danger.*

▸ need **need, requirement** *First there will be an informal chat to assess the immediate needs of the family and the child.*

▸ aim **aim, concern, objective, priority** *Our immediate concern now is to get the website up and running.*

▸ result of something **aftermath, consequence, effect, impact** *In the immediate aftermath of a disaster, we provide medical care, water, food, and shelter.*

▸ end to fighting or holding of prisoners **ceasefire, release** *An immediate ceasefire is necessary to stop the needless loss of lives.*

▸ stopping something or taking something back **ban, halt, withdrawal** *There must be an immediate halt to all military aid to the region.*

▸ future **future** *This situation is unlikely to change in the immediate future.*

2 close in distance or relationship

● ADJ+n people **family, neighbours** *Only immediate family attended the funeral.*

▸ place **environment, environs, locality, neighbourhood, surroundings, vicinity** *There are a number of car parks in the immediate vicinity.*

immense ADJ

extremely large

● adv+ADJ **absolutely, potentially, simply, truly** *The scale of the project is truly immense.*

● ADJ+n amount **amount, number, quantity, range** *He did an immense amount of research before writing the book.*

▸ importance **importance, power, significance, value** *National Parks are of immense importance to our country*

▸ effect or influence **benefit, impact, implications, influence** *Sociological analyses acknowledge that new technology has an immense impact on the way we live our lives.*

▸ pleasure **fun, pleasure, satisfaction** *His painting has given immense pleasure to people across the world.*

▸ pressure or suffering **difficulty, pressure, sadness, suffering** *This attitude to work causes immense pressure on family life.*

▸ positive quality **charm, courage, popularity, potential, talent** *Showing immense courage, the girl ran to call the police.*

▸ wealth **wealth** *Both Edinburgh and Glasgow were cities of immense wealth.*

immigrant N

someone from another country who comes to live in a country

- adj+N legal/illegal **illegal, legal, undocumented** *All illegal immigrants can claim asylum.*
▶ recent **new, newly arrived, recent** *Like many recent immigrants to the country, he is driving a taxi for a living.*
- v+N encourage or allow immigrants into a country **attract, integrate, welcome** *During the nineteenth century, Argentina was eager to attract immigrants from Europe.*
▶ stop immigrants from entering a country **arrest, detain, exclude, restrict** *Authorities may detain immigrants for a 'reasonable' period of time.*
▶ send immmigrants away **deport, expel, repatriate** *The new policy seeks to deport immigrants without trial.*
▶ employ immigrants **employ, hire** *What is the penalty for an employer who hires illegal immigrants?*
▶ treat immigrants unfairly **exploit** *Abbott wrote an article about the way immigrants were exploited.*
- n+of+N **flood, influx, wave** *The influx of immigrants has had a great impact on schools.*

immigration N
the process of coming into a country to live there permanently

- adj+N legal/illegal **clandestine, illegal, legal** *The government plans to introduce tougher measures on illegal immigration.*
▶ involving large numbers **large-scale, mass, massive** *The 1950s saw the start of large-scale immigration from the Caribbean.*
▶ not controlled **uncontrolled, unlimited, unrestricted** *Uncontrolled immigration is putting a strain on our public services.*
- v+N control immigration **control, curb, limit, reduce, restrict, tackle, tighten** *The arguments for curbing immigration are well known.*
▶ try to stop immigration **combat, oppose** *Those who oppose large-scale immigration want to establish 'Fortress Britain'.*
▶ stop immigration **halt, stop** *They are the only party proposing to stop unlimited immigration to this country.*
▶ encourage immigration **encourage, facilitate, increase** *The aim of the programme is to facilitate the immigration of experienced business people.*
- N+n rules or control **control, law, legislation, policy, restrictions, rules** *Under U.S. immigration law, immigrants may obtain a green card by marrying a U.S. citizen.*
▶ person in authority **adjudicator, authority, minister, officer, official** *When he arrived in Britain, he was given a certificate stamped by an immigration officer.*
- n+on+N **controls, crackdown, limit, restriction** *There will be a crackdown on immigration in the run-up to the election.*
- n+of+N **influx, tide, wave** *The third great wave of immigration into the United States occurred in 1884.*

immoral ADJ
morally wrong

- adv+ADJ extremely **deeply, grossly, highly,**

profoundly, totally *A lifestyle that does not consider future generations is profoundly immoral.*
▶ basically **fundamentally, inherently, intrinsically** *The waste of life in war is inherently immoral.*
- ADJ+n **act, action, activity, behaviour, conduct, lifestyle, practice** *Recent business scandals involved a large measure of immoral conduct.*
- v+ADJ **be, consider sth, seem** *This modern form of slavery is simply immoral.* • *Until the 1950s it was considered immoral to use the corneas of dead people for transplant.*

immune ADJ
not influenced or affected by something

- adv+ADJ almost **almost, largely, practically, relatively, virtually** *Our teak outdoor furniture is virtually immune to the stresses of the British climate.*
▶ completely **completely, entirely, totally** *The south of France isn't entirely immune to the effects of winter.*
▶ based on how something appears **apparently, seemingly** *Waugh was apparently immune to fear.*
- v+ADJ **be, become, prove, remain, seem** *The company claimed that their I.T. systems were immune to hardware failure.*
- ADJ+from **law, liability, prosecution** *No person should be immune from prosecution for war crimes.*
- ADJ+to **attack, criticism, effects, influence, interference, pressure, stress, temptation** *The higher education sector can hardly be immune to the effects of a 10% cut in funding.*

immunity N
1 a special right not to be affected by a law

- adj+N **diplomatic, parliamentary, presidential** *Some diplomats have used their diplomatic immunity to avoid paying parking fines.*
- v+N have immunity **benefit from, enjoy** *Embassy staff will enjoy diplomatic immunity so long as they are in this country.*
▶ claim immunity **claim** *She claimed parliamentary immunity and refused to stand trial.*
▶ give immunity **grant (sb), guarantee (sb), promise (sb)** *Together with their families, they have been granted diplomatic immunity.*
▶ remove immunity **lift, waive** *His parliamentary immunity was lifted and he was sentenced to 16 years in prison.*
- N+from **action, jurisdiction, liability, proceedings, prosecution** *Prosecutors will now be able to offer immunity from prosecution.*

2 the body's protection against disease or a particular disease

- adj+N weak **compromised, decreased, depressed, impaired, lowered, suppressed** *You should avoid people with a lowered immunity if you have shingles.*
▶ lasting a long time **lifelong, long-lasting** *One infection is thought to confer lifelong immunity.*
▶ present at birth **maternal, newborn** *The puppy has received adequate maternal immunity to enable it to resist disease for some weeks.*
- v+N give immunity **confer, induce** *The new*

vaccine can confer immunity following just one dose.
▶ get immunity **acquire** *Those who work with the varnish seem to acquire immunity to its actions.*
▶ make immunity stronger **boost, stimulate** *The high vitamin and mineral content helps to boost immunity and energy levels.*
● N+against/to **disease, infection, virus** *In childhood, the adenoids are probably useful in developing immunity against infections.* ● *Do adults acquire immunity to the virus?*

impact N
1 an effect or influence [usually singular]

● adj+N strong **dramatic, enormous, huge, major, maximum, powerful, profound, significant** *The machine includes prominent branding for maximum impact at the point of sale.* ● *This important musician had such a profound impact on my life.*
▶ not strong **limited, marginal, minimal, negligible** *The factory is designed to operate with minimal impact on the environment.*
▶ positive **beneficial, positive** *It is not clear whether these activities have a positive impact on children's reading skills.*
▶ negative **adverse, damaging, detrimental, devastating, disastrous, negative, serious, severe** *For the local community, the environmental impact of these new mines will be devastating.*
▶ direct **direct, immediate** *The results will have an immediate impact on the care that patients receive.*
▶ lasting a long time **lasting, long-lasting, long-term** *If we act now, we could make a lasting impact on poverty.*
▶ affecting your mind or emotions **emotional, psychological** *The psychological impact of living with HIV is an issue that affects both long-term survivors and the newly-diagnosed.*
▶ relating to money and business **commercial, economic, financial** *The study assesses the commercial impact of new information systems and the Internet.*
▶ relating to a particular subject **cultural, ecological, environmental, political, social, socioeconomic** *This process will inevitably have some ecological impact.*
● v+N have an impact **create, have, make** *The funding is vital for the us to be able to make a real impact on the community.*
▶ reduce impact **absorb, cushion, lessen, limit, minimize, mitigate, reduce, soften** *Use your spending power to reduce your impact on the environment.*
▶ examine impact **analyse, consider, examine, explore, investigate, understand** *This paper examines the impact of new teaching methods that were introduced a year ago.*
▶ measure impact **assess, calculate, estimate, evaluate, measure, quantify** *In the next chapter, we assess the impact of the minimum wage on individuals and firms.*
2 an occasion when one object hits another [usually singular]

● v+N receive an impact **take** *The ball of the foot should take the initial impact.*
▶ make an impact less strong **absorb, cushion,**

lessen, soften *Inflatable balloons cushion the impact of the controlled crash landing.*
▶ survive an impact **survive, withstand** *Cycle helmets are designed to withstand impact at speeds of around 13mph*
● v+on+N explode **detonate, explode** *The bombs are intended to detonate on impact.*
▶ break **break, shatter** *Casey's neck broke on impact.*

impair V
make something less good or effective

● adv+V greatly, markedly, profoundly, seriously, **severely, significantly, substantially** *His disability severely impairs his ability to walk.*
● V+n ability, concentration, effectiveness, **function, judgement, memory, mobility, performance** *The drug impairs mental functions such as attention and memory.*

impaired ADJ
prevented from using a particular ability fully

● adv+ADJ relating to the brain **cognitively, intellectually, mentally, neurologically** *The majority of children here are severely mentally impaired.*
▶ relating to sight **visually** *Reading web content can be especially problematic for visually-impaired users.*
▶ relating to hearing **aurally** *The system is designed to help aurally-impaired people*

You can also use the expressions *hearing-impaired* and *sight-impaired*: *Signing will be provided at the meeting for the hearing-impaired.*

▶ seriously **profoundly, seriously, severely, substantially** *We work with the most profoundly impaired children.*
▶ for ever **permanently** *Now her memory is permanently impaired.*
▶ not seriously **mildly, slightly** *I am fine, apart from a slightly impaired memory function.*
● ADJ+n ability to see **eyesight, sight, vision** *If your vision is impaired and you'd appreciate a large print version, please phone our Customer Services Department.*
▶ ability to hear **hearing** *Any child who has impaired hearing can join this group.*
▶ ability to walk **mobility** *This equipment helps us deal with patients whose mobility is impaired.*

impartial ADJ
not connected to or influenced by a particular person or group

● adv+ADJ completely **absolutely, completely, entirely, strictly, totally** *Our aim is to provide completely impartial advice.*
▶ really **genuinely, truly** *We offer genuinely impartial advice.*
▶ in a way that relates to politics **politically** *A politically impartial civil service is a great national asset.*
▶ as some people believe **so-called, supposedly** *I cannot fully share his admiration for the supposedly impartial civil service.*
● ADJ+n person or group that judges **adjudicator,**

assessor, judge, panel *Entries will be judged by a panel of impartial adjudicators.*

▶ person or group that settles disagreements **arbitrator, mediator, tribunal** *The mediator is impartial: he or she does not take sides.*

▶ person who makes sure people obey rules in sports **referee, umpire** *The lack of impartial referees allowed players to break the rules.*

▶ advice **advice, guidance** *The service offers impartial advice to new businesses.*

▶ journalism **journalism, reporting** *We are committed to honest and impartial reporting of the news.*

● and/or **balanced, fair, objective, unbiased** *Members of the panel must be impartial and unbiased.*

impatience N
the annoyed feeling you have when something does not happen as quickly as you would like

● adj+N **growing, mounting** *His growing impatience with Robert began to show.*

● v+N show impatience **display, express, reveal, show** *Maintain normal eye contact and do not show impatience.*

▶ control impatience **conceal, control, curb, restrain** *I could no longer control my impatience at the delay; I climbed the stairs and opened the door.*

● n+of+N **feeling, gesture, sign** *I detect a feeling of growing public impatience.*

impede V
make it more difficult for something to happen or be done

● adv+V seriously **greatly, seriously, severely, significantly** *This situation could seriously impede economic growth.*

▶ in a way that is not necessary or reasonable **unduly, unfairly, unnecessarily, unreasonably** *We provide security without unnecessarily impeding users' ability to perform their job.*

● V+n movement **circulation, flow, mobility, movement, passage, progress** *No sofas, chairs, or other furniture impeded the free circulation of the guests.*

▶ ability **ability** *All of these factors impede the ability of the blood to absorb oxygen.*

▶ action or progress **action, development, effectiveness, efforts, implementation, innovation, performance, progress** *Progress was impeded by problems of planning permission.*

▶ economic performance **growth, recovery, trade** *At first, worries about the safety of online transactions impeded the growth of e-commerce.*

impetus N
a force that makes something happen or develop
[always singular]

● adj+N strong **considerable, dramatic, enormous, great, powerful, strong, tremendous** *The railway gave a powerful impetus to the prosperity of the town.*

▶ most important **main, major** *The main impetus behind the rise in inflation comes from the impact of higher food prices.*

▶ new and different **fresh, new, renewed** *This news lends fresh impetus to the union's campaign.*

▶ given at the beginning **initial, original** *The initial impetus for a literacy project came from a local literacy training day.*

▶ extra **added, additional, extra, further** *Recent legislation has brought further impetus to this project.*

● v+N be an impetus **act as, serve as** *The building project served as an impetus for regeneration.*

▶ give impetus **bring, give, inject, lend, provide** *Economic factors are providing the impetus for more automated solutions.*

▶ create impetus **create, generate** *The interest shown in our town has served to create a renewed impetus in the project.*

▶ gain impetus **acquire, derive, gain, receive** *This strategy is gaining impetus globally.*

▶ lose impetus **lose** *The songs cause the film to lose impetus.*

implement V
make an idea, plan, system or law start to work

● adv+V successfully **correctly, effectively, efficiently, properly, rigorously, successfully** *We successfully implemented the scheme on 17 February 2009.*

▶ completely **fully** *The planned changes have not yet been fully implemented.*

▶ immediately **immediately, quickly, swiftly, with immediate effect, without delay** *The adjudicator's decision is final and must be implemented immediately.*

▶ over a particular area **locally, nationally, widely** *National contracts will be locally implemented.*

▶ badly **badly, poorly** *Legislation which is poorly implemented is not acceptable.*

Usage *Implement* is usually passive in all of the *adv+V* combinations shown above: *Their advertising campaign was badly implemented.* ● *We are now working to ensure that the recommendations are effectively implemented.*

● V+n something that tells people how to deal with a problem **guidelines, recommendations** *The government now aims to implement the recommendations of the safety review.*

▶ way of dealing with a problem **measures, policy, solution, strategy** *One purpose of implementing these measures is to control the flow of traffic.*

▶ law or rule **directive, law, legislation, provisions, regulations, ruling** *The legislation was fully implemented in July 2005, when international tobacco advertising was banned.*

▶ plan **plan, programme, proposal, scheme, system** *The committee agreed to implement the plan as soon as possible.*

▶ official agreement **accord, agreement, resolution** *He visited the US and Europe, promising to implement the peace accord.*

▶ change **change, improvements, reform** *There has been steady progress in implementing reforms in the police force.*

● v+to-V agree to implement something **agree, promise** *The management apologized and agreed to implement the recommendations.*

▶ try to implement something **attempt, try** *Many school teachers are attempting to implement the reform proposals.*

▶ have to implement something **be forced, be obliged, have** *You may be forced to implement change by internal factors.*

▶ fail or refuse to implement something **fail, refuse** *The council has refused to implement the ruling, due to budget cuts.*

implementation N
the process of implementing something

● adj+N successful or complete **effective, efficient, full, proper, smooth, successful** *We will consult widely to ensure smooth implementation of the legislation.*

▶ quick **immediate, rapid, speedy, timely** *Establish a timetable for the speedy implementation of recommendations.*

▶ covering a wide area **full-scale, large-scale, widespread** *The widespread implementation of the new methods is encouraging.*

▶ actual **actual, concrete, practical** *The actual implementation of a new policy can be challenging.*

▶ in stages **phased, step-by-step** *The phased implementation will be carried out in seven police forces.*

● v+N achieve implementation **achieve, ensure** *Regular meetings are held to ensure the smooth implementation of policy.*

▶ manage implementation **coordinate, manage, monitor, oversee, supervise** *The Department has a responsibility for overseeing implementation of EU directives.*

▶ help implementation **accelerate, aid, assist in, contribute to, facilitate, simplify, support** *This company was chosen to facilitate the implementation of the project.*

▶ delay implementation **defer, postpone** *Permission was granted to postpone implementation.*

● N+n **date, phase, plan, process, schedule, stage, strategy, timetable** *The implementation process required close collaboration between the various departments.*

● n+to+N **barrier, delay, obstacle** *The group will research the barriers to implementation of change in the industry.*

implication N
1 a possible effect or result [usually plural]

● adj+N important **considerable, enormous, important, profound, significant** *These differences have significant implications for growth and development.*

▶ negative **devastating, negative, serious** *This ruling could have devastating implications for thousands of people.*

▶ possible **possible, potential** *The potential legal implications of this approach are enormous.*

▶ affecting a large number of people or things **broad, far-reaching, wide, wide-ranging** *The legislation has far-reaching implications for property owners in the UK.*

▶ over a long period of time **long-term** *We need to carefully consider the long-term implications of development.*

▶ relating to a real situation **practical** *This report has practical implications for our work in the classroom.*

▶ relating to money **budgetary, economic, financial** *You should consider carefully the financial implications of studying for a higher degree.*

▶ relating to a theory or method **methodological, theoretical** *In this chapter, we discuss the methodological implications of two theoretical frameworks.*

▶ relating to a particular subject **environmental, ethical, legal, moral, pedagogical, philosophical, political** *Many decisions doctors take have ethical implications.*

● n+N **cost, health, policy, resource, safety, security, tax, welfare** *They also identify the cost implications of achieving improved energy ratings.*

● v+N have implications **carry, have** *Some of these changes carry more wide-ranging implications.*

▶ consider implications **consider, discuss, examine, explore, investigate, ponder, reflect upon, think about** *The paper discusses the implications of our findings in relation to students' learning.*

▶ make a judgment about implications **assess, evaluate** *Most users do not consciously assess the privacy implications of every online situation they encounter.*

▶ understand implications **appreciate, grasp, realize, understand** *We have failed to realize the wider implications of these events.*

2 something that you suggest is true [usually singular]

● adj+N **clear, obvious, underlying, unspoken** *The obvious implication was that Simon was lying.*

● v+N **deny, reject, resent** *She resented his implication that she was a cheat.*

implicit ADJ
not stated directly

● ADJ+n something that people understand and accept or agree to **acknowledgement, agreement, assumption, recognition, understanding** *There is an implicit assumption among the community that these issues will be resolved.*

▶ criticism **condemnation, criticism, critique, rebuke** *Throughout the report there was implicit criticism of the council's actions.*

▶ threat **challenge, threat** *We had to accept peace on their terms, or the implicit threat of renewed violence.*

imply V
suggest that something exists or is true, without saying so directly

● adv+V clearly **clearly, plainly, strongly** *The report clearly implied a growing need for new tests.*

▶ wrongly **falsely, incorrectly, misleadingly, wrongly** *The broadcast falsely implies that cycling is an unusually dangerous activity.*

▶ as a logical result **automatically, inevitably, logically, necessarily** *If we teach writing more effectively, does that logically imply that our students will becoming better writers?*

▶ not necessarily or not at all **in no way, not necessarily** *Autonomy does not necessarily imply unlimited freedom.*

● V+n the fact that you approve of something **acceptance, approval, consent, endorsement** *A link* to another website does not imply endorsement of the material on that site.

▶ the fact that you do not approve of something **contradiction, criticism, rejection** *Inclusion on the Register does not imply criticism of the person in question.*

▶ the fact that something exists **existence** *A positive result does not necessarily imply the existence of the disease.*

• **n+V** information that you discover **data, evidence, findings, study** *Our findings imply the presence of liquid water on Mars.*

▶ something that is said or written **comment, definition, language, narrative, phrase, statement, wording** *This statement implies that we might as well just accept things as they are.*

▶ theory **hypothesis, theorem** *This hypothesis implies that when something occurs, it has more chance of happening again.*

importance N

the fact of being important

• adj+N great **considerable, enormous, extreme, great, huge, immense, key, major, much, profound, tremendous** *These findings are interesting but they are not of much importance at this stage.*

▶ essential **critical, crucial, decisive, fundamental, key, vital** *People must understand the vital importance of these resources for future generations.*

▶ more than anything else **cardinal, especial, first, highest, overriding, overwhelming, paramount, particular, primary, prime, special, supreme, utmost** *I believe motivating students to learn is of paramount importance.*

▶ little **little, minor** *Compared to health, education, and taxes the issue is of minor importance.*

▶ relative to something else **equal, less, lesser, relative, secondary** *We assessed the relative importance of different factors in predicting whether young people would use drugs.* • *Winning is of secondary importance, although it is very nice.*

▶ becoming more/less **declining, diminishing, growing, increased, increasing** *His growing importance in shaping policy became clear during the strike.*

▶ types of importance **archaeological, architectural, ecological, economic, historic, historical, strategic, symbolic** *The river port gave the city a special strategic importance.*

▶ in a particular geographical area **international, national** *This is a list of sites considered to be of national importance for nature conservation.*

• v+N be or become important **assume, have, take on** *Air power has assumed a greater military importance in recent times.*

▶ give something importance **accord sth, ascribe, attach, attribute, give sth, place** *Do not attach too much importance to the differences in admissions procedures between the Colleges.* • *Their business strategy places great importance on IT.*

▶ understand something's importance **acknowledge, appreciate, be convinced of, grasp, note, perceive, realize, recognize, understand** *We understand the importance of keeping you informed of progress.*

▶ emphasize something's importance **affirm, assert,**

emphasize, highlight, reaffirm, reassert, reinforce, reiterate, stress, underline, underscore *Dr Connolly stresses the importance of being open and honest with children.*

▶ exaggerate something's importance **exaggerate, overemphasize, overestimate, overstate** *We cannot overstate the importance of this point.*

▶ deny or forget something's importance **deny, downplay, ignore, overlook, underestimate, underplay, understate, undervalue** *The Minister seemed to be downplaying the importance of the inquiry.*

▶ show something's importance **confirm, demonstrate, explain, illustrate, indicate, point to, reflect, reveal, show** *The report points to the importance of patients being able to access the service quickly.*

▶ discuss how important something is **assess, discuss, evaluate, examine** *This lecture will discuss the importance of patents to the pharmaceutical industry.*

• **N+v** **be in, lie in** *The unit's importance lies in the pioneering work it is doing with children who have been excluded from mainstream schools.*

• **v+in+N** **decline, gain, grow, increase** *The town grew in importance in the late 18th century.*

important ADJ

having a major effect on someone or something

• adv+ADJ very **critically, crucially, enormously, extremely, fundamentally, highly, hugely, immensely, incredibly, massively, profoundly, really, so, terribly, very, vitally** *During their captivity, that friendship was vitally important to them.*

▶ especially **especially, particularly, supremely** *This advice is especially important for younger women.*

▶ rather **pretty** INFORMAL, **quite** *Listen carefully. This is quite important.*

▶ possibly **potentially** *Anxiety was recognized as a potentially important factor.*

▶ relative to something else **doubly, equally, increasingly, most, too** *It is equally important for Government Offices to monitor and review progress.* • *Our friendship is too important to risk over something so silly.*

▶ clearly **clearly, obviously** *It is obviously important to liaise with the owner of the land.*

The expression *the single most important* is very common: *This was probably the single most important factor in the decision.*

▶ in a particular way **architecturally, biologically, clinically, commercially, economically, historically, industrially, medically, strategically** *All the churches on the list are architecturally or historically important.* • *This report highlights the decline in strategically important areas of industry.*

▶ across a particular geographical area **globally, internationally, locally, nationally, regionally** *The island is home to internationally important seabird populations.*

• ADJ+n factor or aspect **aspect, component, consideration, element, facet, factor, feature, thing** *Socioeconomic deprivation is an important risk factor for heart disease.* • *Music is the most important thing in the world to me.*

▶ role **contribution, part, role** *Carbohydrates play an important role in maintaining health.*

▶ point or issue **issue, point, question** *The website explains why climate change is such an important issue and what you can do to help.*

▶ difference **difference, distinction** *There is an important distinction to be made between cosmetic surgery and reconstructive surgery.*

▶ decision or action **decision, milestone, step** *Volunteers from across the country gathered to mark this important milestone for the organization.*

▶ something you learn **discovery, lesson** *What is the most important lesson you've learned in your professional life?*

● v+ADJ **be, become, consider sth, deem sth, feel, prove, remain, seem** *Knowledge of foreign languages is becoming increasingly important to businesses.* ● *It is considered important that feedback is given immediately after the session.*

impose V
to force people to accept something

● adv+V from outside **centrally, externally** *They have to make difficult choices within externally imposed budget constraints.*

Usage ***Impose*** is usually passive in these combinations: *Don't insult their professional judgement with a lot of centrally imposed regulations.*

▶ in an unreasonable way **arbitrarily, artificially, heavy-handedly, rigidly, simply, unilaterally** *No one was consulted in any way about the scheme, it was simply imposed.* ● *Agreement means consent from both parties, not one side unilaterally imposing its view.*

▶ using force **aggressively, forcefully, forcibly, physically** *In seeking to forcibly impose a belief system on everyone else, they display cultural intolerance.*

● V+n punishment **fine, penalty, punishment, sanctions, sentence** *The judge said she had no option but to impose a custodial sentence.*

▶ restriction or limit **condition, constraints, curfew, deadline, limit, limitation, moratorium, quota, requirement, restraints, restriction** *Section 23 imposes various restrictions on the Parliament's powers.*

▶ tax or charge **charge, levy, surcharge, tariff, tax** *Some Scandinavian countries impose much higher taxes on car ownership than does the UK.*

▶ ban **ban, blockade, embargo, prohibition** *They imposed an embargo on all exports to the area.*

▶ rule **regulation, rule** *The landlord is entitled to impose parking regulations on his tenants.*

▶ duty **duty, liability, obligation** *The Directive imposes obligations on public bodies with regard to how they use personal information.*

▶ burden **burden, strain** *The emissions from aircraft impose a great burden on the world's climate.*

▶ will **will** *It is wrong to impose the will of a small elite on the majority.*

impossible ADJ
unable to be done or to happen

● adv+ADJ completely **absolutely, completely, downright, quite, simply, totally, utterly** *I realized that it was absolutely impossible to get a job without a proper work permit.*

▶ almost **all but, almost, nearly, practically, virtually, well-nigh** *It's all but impossible to have a rational discussion about the issue.* ● *The prison cells were so overcrowded that it was almost impossible for prisoners to sit down.*

▶ obviously **clearly, manifestly, obviously** *Bringing a life-sized tree onto the stage was obviously impossible.*

▶ apparently **apparently, probably, seemingly** *We should be grateful for his tireless efforts against seemingly impossible odds.*

▶ in a particular way **humanly, logically, logistically, mathematically, morally, physically, politically, technically** *It would have been physically impossible to read them all, even if you did nothing else for a week.*

● v+ADJ **appear, be, become, be rendered, look, prove, seem, sound** *The game was rendered impossible by the wintry conditions.* ● *It proved impossible to reach an agreement.* ● *Telling your life story in 20 seconds sounds impossible.*

impractical ADJ
not sensible, or not likely to be effective or successful

● adv+ADJ very **highly, hopelessly, quite, ridiculously, simply, totally, utterly, wholly, wildly** *Without technology, these activities would be totally impractical.*

▶ rather **probably, rather, somewhat** *These cars are regarded as somewhat impractical, with little carrying capacity and poor fuel consumption.*

▶ obviously **clearly** *Building such a large single telescope is clearly impractical.*

● v+ADJ **be, become, be considered, be rendered, prove, seem** *Exchanging large files was rendered impractical by the low speed of the modem.* ● *It may prove impractical to move large quantities of fresh water.*

impression N
an opinion or feeling about something or someone

● adj+N good **favourable, good, positive, the right** *The food and service all made favourable impressions.*

▶ bad **bad, negative, poor, unfavourable** *It is regrettable that a negative impression has been created.*

▶ incorrect **erroneous, false, incorrect, mistaken, wrong** *Whoever is paying you is doing so under the mistaken impression that you're actually doing some work!*

▶ that deceives someone **deceptive, misleading** *A biased sample can give a misleading impression of the severity of the problem.*

▶ accurate **accurate, the right** *Your CV should convey an accurate impression of what you have achieved.*

▶ general **general, overall, overriding** *The picture gives an overall impression of peace and serenity.*

▶ strong **big, clear, deep, distinct, overwhelming, powerful, profound, striking, strong, vivid** *The visit made a deep impression on me.* ● *I got the distinct impression they were tired of being there.*

▶ lasting a long time **abiding, indelible, lasting** *No*

matter how old you are, this film will leave a lasting impression.

▶ vague or brief **fleeting, vague** *Many people have no idea what we do, beyond a vague impression that it is 'good work'.*

▶ immediate **first, immediate, initial, instant** *His first impression of the party was not a very positive one.*

● v+N create an impression **convey, create, give, leave, make, produce** *His account is incomplete and gives the wrong impression.*

▶ get or have an impression **form, gain, get, have** *I had the impression of a settled and happy community.*

▶ correct an impression **correct, counter, dispel** *I would like to correct the impression you may have got that I can't play.*

▶ confirm an impression **confirm, reinforce** *Evidence confirms our earlier impression that the effect is small.*

impressive ADJ
very good, large etc in a way that you admire

● adv+ADJ very **deeply, enormously, especially, extremely, genuinely, highly, hugely, immensely, incredibly, massively, mightily, mighty** INFORMAL, **particularly, really, so, truly, very** *As a committed supporter of the disability movement, she is a mightily impressive individual.*

▶ rather **fairly, pretty** INFORMAL**, quite, rather** *It must have once been a rather impressive town house.*

▶ certainly **admittedly, certainly, undeniably** *Their live performances are said to be exhilarating, and this debut album is certainly impressive.*

▶ compared with something else **doubly, equally, similarly** *To achieve such subtlety with such a young cast is doubly impressive.*

▶ in a particular way **architecturally, technically, visually** *Even after all these years, the film is still visually impressive.*

● v+ADJ **be, become, look, prove, remain, sound** *The results so far have proved impressive.*

imprisonment N
the punishment of being put in prison

● adj+N illegal **arbitrary, false, illegal, unjust, unlawful, wrongful** *He would like to thank everyone who has supported him over his 8 long years of wrongful imprisonment.*

▶ long **continued, indefinite, long, long-term** *Those who went against the authorities could find themselves facing execution or indefinite imprisonment.*

▶ for a particular length of time **life, 12 months', 5 years' etc** *The prisoner was fined and sentenced to 28 days' imprisonment for possession of drugs.*

● v+N when someone is imprisoned **receive, serve, suffer, undergo** *He was told he had to serve eight months' imprisonment.*

▶ avoid imprisonment **avoid, escape** *Although she was heavily fined, she managed to escape imprisonment.*

▶ risk imprisonment **face, risk** *Some risked imprisonment and even death to take part in the protest.*

▶ impose imprisonment **impose, sentence sb to** *A*

sentence of imprisonment was imposed by the magistrate.

improve V
to make something better or to become better

● adv+V a lot **considerably, dramatically, drastically, enormously, greatly, hugely, immeasurably, immensely, massively, radically, remarkably, tremendously, vastly** *In the second half of the game, his concentration seemed to improve greatly.*

> If something has improved a lot, you can say that it is ***much improved***: *The bus services in this area are now much improved.*

▶ a little **marginally, slightly, somewhat** *Road conditions improved slightly today.*

▶ noticeably **demonstrably, markedly, materially, measurably, notably, noticeably, significantly, substantially, tangibly, visibly** *These developments will significantly improve healthcare facilities in the area.*

▶ certainly **certainly, definitely, undoubtedly** *The use of the program definitely improved the general understanding of the class.*

▶ all the time **consistently, constantly, continually, continuously** *He continually improves his performance by setting more and more challenging goals.*

▶ slowly or gradually **gradually, progressively, slowly, steadily** *Employment rates for older people have steadily improved.*

▶ quickly **fast, quickly, rapidly** *Current computing technology is rapidly improving.*

▶ generally **generally, overall** *Results have generally improved this year.*

▶ in this way **consequently, hence, thereby, therefore, thus** *More and more trees are being planted to provide green areas, thereby improving air quality.*

● V+with **age, experience, practice, time, use** *It is a complex skill and, like all skills, it improves with practice.*

improvement N
the process of becoming better or making something better

● adj+N great **big, considerable, dramatic, drastic, great, huge, major, massive, radical, remarkable, substantial, tremendous, vast** *England's 10-year-olds have shown a dramatic improvement in maths tests over the past decade.*

▶ small **marginal, minor, modest, slight** *I had an X-ray and the doctor said there was a slight improvement already.*

▶ noticeable **appreciable, definite, demonstrable, distinct, genuine, marked, measurable, notable, noticeable, real, significant, tangible** *These proposals will make a significant improvement to the current position.*

▶ continuing **constant, continual, continued, continuous, lasting, long-term, ongoing, sustainable, sustained, year-on-year** *It is clear that results have risen again this year, demonstrating the continued improvements in education.*

▶ slow or gradual **gradual, incremental, progressive,**

steady *Then there was a gradual improvement in his work, particularly in science.*
▸ rapid **immediate, rapid** *After a few sessions of therapy there was a rapid improvement in his condition.*
▸ general **general, overall** *The inspectors noted an overall improvement on the previous year.*
▸ necessary **much-needed, necessary, needed, welcome** *The revenue raised would go into much-needed improvements in public transport.*
▸ recent **recent** *Recent technical improvements mean that a better solution is available.*
▸ possible or planned **further, future, planned, possible, potential, suggested** *Other suggested improvements included a greater police presence and better street lighting.*
▸ types of improvement **agricultural, cosmetic, environmental, genetic, operational, technical, technological** *Recycling has the potential to create jobs and achieve environmental improvement.*
● v+N make an improvement **achieve, effect, implement, introduce, make, secure** *Her mission is to achieve a lasting improvement in her quality of life.*
▸ cause an improvement **bring, bring about, deliver, enable, produce, yield** *None of these variations of the basic design yielded any great improvements.*
▸ notice an improvement **identify, measure, note, notice, report, see** *The doctor said that if I didn't notice an improvement we would try a different drug.*
▸ show an improvement **demonstrate, show** *The overall pass rates showed a marginal improvement.*
▸ be an improvement **represent** *This represented a 13 per cent improvement in profitability.*
▸ experience an improvement **experience, undergo** *The area around the harbour is currently undergoing improvement.*
▸ want or need improvement **demand, expect, need, require, seek** *The actual wording of the report needs improvement.*
▸ suggest an improvement **plan, propose, recommend, suggest** *If you would like to suggest improvements to our website, we would be happy to hear from you.*
▸ encourage improvement **encourage, ensure, facilitate, promote, support** *Feedback should promote learning and facilitate improvement.*
▸ promise an improvement **promise** *I can report today that the promised improvements in the system are being delivered.*
● n+for+N **need, opportunity, room, scope** *The present service is good, but there is always room for improvement.*

impulse N
a sudden strong feeling that you must do something
● adj+N sudden **sudden** *On a sudden impulse, I rode after him.*
▸ first **first, initial** *My first impulse was to go out and buy a whole new set of clothes.*
▸ strong **irresistible, powerful, strong** *There came to him an irresistible impulse to pray.*
▸ natural **natural, primitive, spontaneous** *Our natural impulses can be altruistic and cooperative as well as selfish.*
▸ violent, destructive **aggressive, anarchic,**

destructive, murderous, sadistic, self-destructive, suicidal, violent *His life is a constant struggle to control his destructive impulses.*
▸ generous **charitable, generous** *On a generous impulse, he gave the man his coat.*
▸ creative **artistic, creative** *The exhibition is a celebration of the creative impulse, which we all possess but which is so often stifled.*
▸ not rational **contradictory, irrational** *She will always be a woman of contradictory impulses.*
▸ not expressed **repressed** *Hidden motives, repressed impulses, and secret passions are revealed in the course of the play.*
● v+N have an impulse **feel, have** *He felt an impulse to assist her.*
▸ fight an impulse **control, fight, repress, resist, restrain** *She resisted the impulse to give him a hug.*
▸ obey an impulse **follow, obey** *What I really want to do is just obey my own impulses.*

inability N
the fact that you cannot do something
● adj+N complete **complete, sheer, total, utter** *What this indicates is their utter inability to deal with any policy issue.*
▸ apparent **apparent, seeming** *He deplores humanity's seeming inability to love selflessly.*
▸ very bad or unfortunate **chronic, pathological, woeful** *There is a woeful inability to learn from past experience.*
● v+N show inability **demonstrate, highlight, prove, reflect, reveal, show** *This simply demonstrates an inability to work together effectively.*
▸ overcome inability **overcome** *Helen Keller was a deaf and blind girl who overcame her inability to communicate.*

inaccurate ADJ
not accurate or correct
● adv+ADJ very **completely, grossly, highly, hopelessly, totally, very, wholly, wildly** *Many of the forecasts made about life in the future were wildly inaccurate.*
▸ rather **quite, rather, slightly, somewhat** *This is a slightly inaccurate quotation from Rudyard Kipling's poem If.*
▸ in a bad way **unacceptably, woefully** *The economic predictions made by those computer models were unacceptably inaccurate.*
▸ in a particular way **factually, historically, scientifically, technically** *His writing was criticized as being unoriginal and factually inaccurate.*
● ADJ+n information **data, information, record** *If our invoice has been based on inaccurate information, we shall submit a revised invoice.*
▸ description **description, portrayal, report, reporting, representation** *An observer condemned the international media for its inaccurate reporting of events.*
▸ when someone says what will happen **estimate, forecast, prediction** *We understand that some of the estimates are grossly inaccurate.*
▸ when someone believes something **assumption, interpretation, perception** *We often make inaccurate assumptions about people if we are unaware they have a hearing problem.*

▶ statement **claim, statement** *If concerns are raised that our claims are inaccurate or unfounded, we will investigate.*

▶ result **result** *Review of medical papers must be meticulous to prevent false or inaccurate results being published.*

● and/or unfair **distorted, unbalanced, unfair, unfounded** *To equate this great religion with backwardness is totally unfair and inaccurate.*

● incorrect **exaggerated, false, imprecise, incorrect, unreliable, untrue** *The claims made in the book are untrue and inaccurate.*

▶ incomplete **inadequate, incomplete** *You should be aware that at times the information may be incomplete, inaccurate or may have become out of date.*

▶ outdated **outdated, out-of-date** *If anything in the data is inaccurate or out-of-date, let us know and we will amend our records.*

▶ confusing **confusing, contradictory, inconsistent** *We believe that the use of the word 'racial' is in itself inaccurate and confusing, because we all belong to one human race.*

▶ unhelpful **irrelevant, unhelpful** *We cannot be held responsible if any advice you are given proves to be inaccurate or unhelpful.*

inadequacy N

a failure or fault that makes something or someone not good enough

● adj+N serious **serious, total, utter, woeful** *Why do we accept the woeful inadequacy of our public transport system?*

▶ not proved **alleged, apparent** *The claim was based on the alleged inadequacy of the repairs.*

▶ personal **own, personal** *He at least recognizes his own inadequacy, and has a sense of responsibility.*

▶ types of inadequacy **conceptual, emotional, methodological, nutritional, sexual, structural, technical** *We should take into account the methodological inadequacies of the studies reporting the results.*

● v+N reveal inadequacy **demonstrate, expose, highlight, illustrate, prove, reveal, show** *The dispute has exposed serious inadequacies in UK employment law.*

▶ admit inadequacy **acknowledge, admit, confess, realize, recognize** *Reading my own paper again, I realize its many inadequacies.*

▶ do something about inadequacy **address, overcome** *Senior officers must address these staffing inadequacies.*

▶ hide inadequacy **hide** *We hide our own inadequacies by blaming others.*

inadequate ADJ

not good enough

● adv+ADJ very **completely, entirely, profoundly, quite, seriously, so, thoroughly, totally, utterly, very, wholly** *Their current email system is wholly inadequate for their requirements.*

▶ in a very bad way **desperately, grossly, hopelessly, miserably, pathetically, pitifully, ridiculously, woefully** *The guidance on this topic is still woefully inadequate.*

▶ rather **rather, somewhat** *We had to work with our somewhat inadequate resources.*

▶ obviously **clearly, demonstrably, manifestly, obviously, plainly** *However, this expenditure was clearly inadequate.*

▶ generally **altogether, generally** *Parents felt that complaints procedures were generally inadequate.*

▶ in a particular way **nutritionally, socially** *High-fat, low-carbohydrate diets are nutritionally inadequate.*

● v+ADJ appear, be, **become, be considered, be deemed, feel, prove, seem** *The funds for this work are deemed inadequate.* ● *The operation of the market has proved inadequate as a means of assuring quality.*

inappropriate ADJ

not suitable in a particular situation

● adv+ADJ very **completely, entirely, grossly, highly, particularly, quite, singularly, totally, utterly, wholly, wildly** *Motor traffic is wholly inappropriate in parks.*

▶ rather **rather, somewhat** *The scientific name is somewhat inappropriate, as the beetle is all one colour.*

▶ obviously **clearly, obviously** *The current system is clearly inappropriate for the future.*

▶ in some way **otherwise, somehow** *Staff must not send email messages which are in any way defamatory, obscene or otherwise inappropriate.*

▶ generally **generally** *It is generally inappropriate to bring disciplinary proceedings against workers because they took part in industrial action.*

▶ in a particular way **aesthetically, clinically, culturally, developmentally, morally, sexually, socially** *Children should not be given activities that are developmentally inappropriate to them.*

● v+ADJ appear, be, **consider sth, deem sth, prove, seem** *We can help Internet users avoid content that they deem inappropriate for their children.* ● *Guidelines appropriate to industrialised countries may prove inappropriate in poorer countries.*

incentive N

something that encourages people to do something or to work harder

● adj+N strong, great **attractive, big, generous, great, powerful, strong** *The aim of this system is to give suppliers a strong incentive to reduce costs.*

▶ not great **less, little** *For too many people, there is little incentive to stay in the area of their birth.*

> When you say that there is little or no incentive, you can use the expression *a lack of incentive*: There will be a lack of incentive for consumers to switch to the new technology if it is not made cheaper.

▶ additional **added, additional, extra, further** *He has an added incentive to ensure the works are finished on time.*

▶ enough/not enough **adequate, insufficient, sufficient** *We know that it is possible for people to change, given sufficient incentive to do so.*

▶ genuine **clear, positive, real, tangible** *As money follows the patient, hospitals will have real incentives to improve.*

▶ types of incentive **cash, commercial, economic, financial, monetary, tax** *We are introducing tax* incentives **for** companies to install energy conservation measures.

- v+N have an incentive **have** *The supplier has an incentive to overestimate costs in order to set a higher price.*
- ▸ provide an incentive **act as, be, create, give sb, introduce, offer, provide** *The vouchers provide an excellent incentive for children to visit their local library.*
- ▸ reduce an incentive **reduce, remove, undermine** *This can reduce the incentive to give up smoking.*
- ▸ increase an incentive **improve, increase** *The exam performance of schools outside the city continues to improve, further increasing the incentive for families to move out.*
- ▸ need an incentive **need** *We need greater incentives for households to invest in renewable energy.*
- N+n system **framework, mechanism, plan, programme, scheme, structure** *We are putting in place a new management incentive scheme.*
- ▸ payment **bonus, package, payment** *Small employers will receive incentive payments if they file their tax returns electronically.*

incidence N

the number of cases of an illness or condition; the number of times something happens

- adj+N high or higher **elevated, greater, high, higher, increased** *The study showed elevated tumour incidence in the groups exposed to high radiation.*
- ▸ low or lower **low, lower, reduced** *Studies have demonstrated that there is a lower incidence of the disease in older horses.*
- ▸ general **average, cumulative, overall** *The cumulative incidence of gout in a population of caucasian US men was 8.6 per cent over a 29-year period.*
- ▸ annual **annual, yearly** *Primary brain tumours are relatively rare, with the annual global incidence ranging from six to 12 per 100,000 population.*
- ▸ reported **recorded, reported** *This was the first reported incidence of skin tumours believed to be caused by Papova Virus.*
- ▸ estimated **estimated** *Williams syndrome is a rare condition with an estimated incidence of 1 in 35,000.*
- ▸ actual **actual, true** *Fear of crime exceeds the actual incidence.*
- v+N have a particular incidence **have, show** *People with autism have a higher incidence of epilepsy.*
- ▸ reduce the incidence **decrease, lower, minimize, reduce** *The trial will determine whether antibiotics reduce the incidence of miscarriage.*
- ▸ study the incidence **compare, examine, investigate, monitor** *Several studies have examined the incidence of malnutrition in the UK.*
- ▸ find out the incidence **calculate, determine** *The study set out to determine the incidence of depression among the patients of a particular medical practice.*
- ▸ estimate the incidence **estimate, underestimate** *The study estimated the overall incidence to be one suicide per 1200 patients.*
- N+v rise **increase, rise** *The incidence of stroke rises with increasing age.*
- ▸ fall **decrease, fall** *The global incidence of leprosy is decreasing rapidly.*

- ▸ vary **vary** *This is one of the most common cancers in the world, but its incidence varies widely.*
- n+in+N **change, decline, decrease, difference, increase, reduction, rise, variation** *There was a significant increase in the incidence of football hooliganism during that period.*

incident N

something that happens, especially something violent or dangerous

- adj+N serious **adverse, catastrophic, critical, fatal, horrific, major, serious, traumatic, violent** *The directive is aimed at serious incidents of environmental damage.*
- ▸ minor **minor, trivial** *Even relatively minor incidents can damage business performance.*
- ▸ related/not related **isolated, one-off, related, separate, similar, unrelated** *A peaceful and festive protest, it was marred by a few isolated incidents.* • *Troops have shot dead four armed men in two separate incidents overnight.*
- ▸ strange or amusing **amusing, bizarre, curious, embarrassing** *One amusing incident I remember involved a package which had to be delivered to Liverpool.*
- ▸ that you regret **regrettable, tragic, unfortunate, unpleasant, unsavoury, untoward** *This was a tragic incident in which a child has needlessly lost his life.*
- ▸ reported **recorded, reported** *The most serious types of incidents accounted for the smallest percentage of reported incidents.*
- ▸ possible **alleged, suspicious** *When and where did the alleged incident occur?*
- ▸ involving an attack on a group **antisemitic, homophobic, racial, racist** *It is our duty to encourage the reporting of racist incidents.*
- n+N **bullying, contamination, domestic violence, firearm, flooding, poisoning, pollution, security, stabbing, terrorist, traffic** *Victims should keep a diary of all bullying incidents.*

> When an event takes place without anything bad happening, you can say that it ***passes without incident***: *The anniversary of the massacre passed without incident.*

- v+N officially report or record an incident **document, log, record, report** *The victim's parents have reported the incident to police.*
- ▸ describe an incident **describe, discuss, mention, recount, relate** *She described the incident in her journal.*
- ▸ see an incident **witness** *We would like to hear from anyone who was travelling on that bus and witnessed the incident.*
- ▸ deal with an incident **attend, handle, investigate, manage, resolve, tackle** *Officers from the Crash Investigation Unit will attend such incidents to examine the scene.* • *We aim to prevent crime through effectively resolving minor incidents.*
- ▸ prevent incidents **prevent, reduce** *The Food Hygiene Campaign aims to reduce incidents of food poisoning by 20 per cent.*
- ▸ cause an incident **cause** *A single insecure computer can cause a major security incident.*
- N+v happen **arise, happen, occur, take place** *I'd*

like to remind the public to lock car doors when possible, to stop such incidents occurring.
► cause something **cause, prompt, result in, spark, trigger** *This incident sparked concerns about security at the airport.*
► involve someone or something **involve** *Terry was arrested after an incident involving his former partner.*
► get worse **escalate** *The incident escalated to the extent that the police were called.*

incite V
to make people do violent or criminal things

● adv+V deliberately **actively, deliberately, openly** *These marches are staged to antagonize people and deliberately incite trouble.*
► indirectly **indirectly** *It will also be illegal to publish material that indirectly incites terrorist acts.*

● V+n incite violence or hatred **hatred, murder, mutiny, racism, rebellion, riot, terrorism, unrest, violence** *Those that try to incite hatred or engage in violence have no place here.*
► incite people **crowd, mob** *In 1559, a sermon preached by John Knox incited a mob to ransack Scone Abbey.*

inclination N
a feeling that you want to do something; a tendency to do something

● adj+N personal **natural, personal, sb's own** *There's obviously a natural inclination to be a teacher in me.* ● *My own inclination is to ignore the matter completely.*
► strong **strong** *Most of us have strong inclinations to preserve our lives.*
► not strong **the slightest** *It is disappointing that they show not the slightest inclination to compromise.*
► types of inclination **amorous, artistic, musical, religious, sexual** *His early musical inclinations were encouraged by his father.*

● v+N have an inclination **feel, have, show** *You can learn a lot, if you have the inclination to do so.*
► follow your inclinations **follow** *I firmly believe in allowing the learner to follow his/her own inclinations as far as is possible.*
► resist your inclinations **curb, resist** *We must resist the inclination to romanticize the past.*

inclusion N
the action of including someone or something

● adj+N possible **eventual, possible** *Send us your articles for possible inclusion in our newsletter.*

● v+N deserve inclusion **deserve, justify, merit, warrant** *In truth, every one of his poems merits inclusion in this anthology.*
► make inclusion certain **ensure, guarantee** *Acceptance does not automatically guarantee inclusion in the final publication.*
► allow inclusion **allow, permit** *Modifications have been made to the study to allow the inclusion of patients over 65 years old.*
► prevent inclusion **preclude, prevent** *We regret that lack of space has precluded the inclusion of some photographs.*

● n+for+N **criteria** *They had a set of criteria for the inclusion or not of items in the database.*

● v+for+N **consider sb/sth, qualify, select sb/sth** *If you'd like to be considered for inclusion in the next show, please send us your details.* ● *Most of the articles did not qualify for inclusion in the journal.*

income N
money obtained from working or from investments

● adj+N high **high, substantial** *Around half of those with the highest incomes say they want to reduce their working hours.*
► low or moderate **insufficient, limited, low, meagre, middle, moderate, modest** *Families on very low incomes will receive extra money as well.*
► additional **additional, extra** *We have been able to afford a new car because of the extra income.*
► regular **guaranteed, regular, secure, stable, steady** *It provides the charity with regular income, enabling us to plan long-term.*
► estimated or future **anticipated, estimated, expected, future, notional, projected** *A major development scheme will go ahead on the basis of projected income.*
► average **average, median, per-capita** *Average incomes grew by 36 per cent during this period.*
► increasing **rising** *It was a time of low inflation and rising incomes.*
► total **combined, family, household, joint, national, total** *Work out your total income for a week or a month, then take away the expenditure.*
► remaining or available **disposable, excess, residual, surplus** *Women now have far greater disposable incomes than in the past.*
► taxed/untaxed **gross, post-tax, pre-tax, taxable, taxed, tax-free, undeclared, untaxed** *The amount you get depends on the gross income for your household.*
► basic **basic, minimum** *People want to know that they have a decent minimum income in retirement.*
► lost **lost** *The TV company collapsed, costing the football club around £4 million in lost income.*
► during a particular period **annual, monthly, weekly, yearly** *Any young person who lives in a household with an annual income of £30k or less should apply for an allowance.*
► not earned **unearned** *Unearned income from savings should also be declared.*

● v+N earn an income **derive, earn, have, receive** *Neither of his sons earned an income from the farm.*
► increase your income **augment, boost, increase, maximize, raise, supplement** *To supplement his meagre income in the shipyards, Charlie worked as a waiter.*
► reduce your income **lose, reduce** *The rise in interest rates reduces the available income that people have to buy things.*
► produce an income **generate, guarantee, pay, provide, yield** *Increased visitors will generate income to support the rural economy and help to sustain jobs.*
► declare an income **declare** *It is your responsibility to keep records of your financial affairs and to declare your income.*

● N+v increase **grow, increase, rise** *Profits increased by 32 per cent and total income rose by 28 per cent.*
► decrease **decline, drop, fall, plummet** *As people come off benefits and go into work, they can actually find their incomes fall.*

▶ change **fluctuate** *It can be difficult for customers to budget when their income fluctuates in such an unpredictable manner.*

▶ be more than **exceed, outstrip** *If your trading income exceeds £58,000 you should register for VAT.*

● n+in+N **change, decline, drop, fall, growth, increase, reduction, rise** *After her illness and a drop in income, she fell into debt.*

● n+of+N **source** *We can only ensure the service is maintained if there is a regular source of income.*

● and/or **expenditure, expenses, outgoings** *You must keep a record of income and expenditure.*

incompatible ADJ
unable to work or exist with something

● adv+ADJ completely **absolutely, completely, entirely, quite, simply, totally, utterly, wholly** *His claims were completely incompatible with the facts I observed.*

▶ not **not, not necessarily** *The two systems have quite different, but not necessarily incompatible, agendas.*

▶ basically **fundamentally, inherently, intrinsically** *The assumption was that belief in God and belief in science are fundamentally incompatible.*

▶ clearly **clearly, manifestly** *These ideas are clearly incompatible with Buddhist teaching.*

▶ at times **largely, often, potentially** *The two theories seem largely incompatible.*

▶ apparently **apparently, seemingly** *These seemingly incompatible elements are woven together deftly in the book.*

▶ disagreeing with something else **mutually** *A range of sometimes mutually incompatible viewpoints coexist.*

● v+ADJ **appear, be, become, be considered, be declared, be deemed, prove, seem** *This description appears incompatible with what we know of human development.* ● *At that time, homosexuality was considered incompatible with service in the Armed Forces.*

incompetence N
lack of skill or ability to do something well

● adj+N very bad **bungling, crass, gross, sheer, shocking, staggering, total, utter** *Through its sheer incompetence, the Government could be endangering people's lives.*

● types of incompetence **administrative, bureaucratic, managerial, military, ministerial, official, professional** *These were 'friendly-fire' casualties, victims of military incompetence.*

● v+N show incompetence **demonstrate, display, prove, reveal, show** *He said the case revealed gross incompetence by Ministers.*

▶ accuse someone of incompetence **accuse sb of, allege** *They sued the company, alleging incompetence on the part of the managers.*

▶ hide incompetence **hide** *The company is using the Data Protection Act to hide its own incompetence.*

inconclusive ADJ
not producing a definite result or complete proof

● adv+ADJ rather **fairly, pretty INFORMAL, rather,**

somewhat *The results of the test were interesting, but somewhat inconclusive.*

▶ mostly **generally, largely, often** *The debate so far has been largely inconclusive.*

● v+ADJ **be, prove, remain** *Further investigations were made, but they proved inconclusive.*

● and/or **ambiguous, conflicting, confusing, contradictory, uncertain, unclear, unresolved** *The evidence on complementary therapies remains inconclusive or contradictory.*

inconsistency N
something that does not match something else; the fact of not matching something or of not always being the same

● adj+N apparent or possible **alleged, apparent, perceived, possible, potential, seeming** *Can you clarify the apparent inconsistencies between these assessments of the number of civilian deaths?*

▶ obvious **blatant, glaring, obvious** *In spite of obvious inconsistencies in his story, the police did not consider it necessary to detain him.*

▶ serious **considerable, gross, major, serious, significant** *How, without gross inconsistency, can you allow one and not the other?*

▶ slight **minor, occasional, slight** *There is a slight inconsistency in the difficulty of the exercises.*

▶ basic **inherent, internal, logical** *The logical inconsistency between these objectives is clear.*

● v+N show inconsistency **demonstrate, expose, highlight, identify, illustrate, reveal, show, uncover** *This report highlighted major inconsistencies in the way job roles are classified.*

▶ notice inconsistency **detect, find, note, notice, perceive, spot** *Some people perceive inconsistencies in the approach taken towards different countries.*

▶ deal with inconsistency **address, avoid, correct, eliminate, overcome, reconcile, remove, resolve** *The two benchmarks would need to be agreed together to avoid inconsistency between them.* ● *The principles set out in this document will help to remove the inconsistencies that arise from the absence of a defined standard.*

▶ contain inconsistency **contain** *She referred to the inconsistencies contained in the medical report.*

▶ explain inconsistency **explain** *The police should be asked to explain any inconsistencies in the statements.*

● N+v **arise, exist, occur** *Inconsistencies exist in the definitions of 'a career'.*

inconsistent ADJ
not matching, not always behaving in the same way or producing the same results

● adv+ADJ completely **completely, entirely, totally, utterly, wholly** *In Britain, we claim to be compassionate to animals, and this practice is wholly inconsistent with that claim.*

▶ very **hopelessly, so, very, wildly** *The accessibility of information on the web can be very inconsistent.*

▶ rather **a little, quite, rather, somewhat** *Some of his current policies are somewhat inconsistent with those principles.*

▶ obviously **clearly, plainly** *We believe such a treaty*

is plainly inconsistent **with** our fundamental obligations.
- ▶ in a way that annoys or surprises you **frustratingly, strangely** *Despite some frustratingly inconsistent performances, he still produces moments of magic.*
- ▶ disagreeing with itself or something else **internally, mutually** *They offered varied and mutually inconsistent interpretations of the data.*
- ● and/or confusing **ambiguous, conflicting, confused, confusing, contradictory, illogical, incoherent, unclear** *Current legislation was said to be confusing and inconsistent.*
- ▶ unfair **arbitrary, unfair, unjust** *The current system is inconsistent and unfair.*
- ▶ not reliable **erratic, unpredictable, unreliable** *The children were often exposed to erratic and inconsistent adult behaviour.*
- ▶ not correct **inaccurate, incorrect** *Duplication of documents can lead to inconsistent and inaccurate records.*
- ▶ not complete **inadequate, incomplete, patchy** *The medical evidence presented to the Inquiry is incomplete, inconsistent, and inadequate.*

inconvenience N
an annoying problem or situation

- ● adj+N great **considerable, great, gross, major, serious, significant** *Staff are expected to use public transport, unless its use results in considerable inconvenience.*
- ▶ minor **mere, minor, slight, temporary, trifling** *Changing the clocks twice a year is little more than a minor inconvenience.*
- ▶ too much **too much, undue, unnecessary** *It is possible for us all to reduce our carbon footprint without undue inconvenience.*
- ▶ minimum **the least, minimal, minimum** *We will carry out the work in a way which causes you the least possible inconvenience.*
- ● v+N regret inconvenience **apologize for, regret** *We regret the inconvenience and assure our customers that normal service will be resumed as soon as possible.*
- ▶ cause inconvenience **cause (sb), occasion, put sb to** *We realise that these arrangements may cause some inconvenience and thank you for your co-operation. ● The guests should not be disappointed or put to any inconvenience.*
- ▶ experience inconvenience **experience, suffer** *They may make compensation payments to those who have suffered severe inconvenience.*
- ▶ prevent or reduce inconvenience **avoid, eliminate, minimize, obviate, prevent, reduce, save (sb), spare sb** *Care must be taken to avoid inconvenience or disturbance to neighbours.*
- ▶ compensate for inconvenience **compensate (sb) for, outweigh, remedy** *The factory's cheap fuel supply outweighed the inconvenience of its location.*

incorrect ADJ
wrong, or not accurate or true

- ● adv+ADJ completely **completely, entirely, fundamentally, quite, simply, totally, wholly** *Many of the policies that have been proposed are based on totally incorrect assumptions.*

- ▶ obviously **blatantly, clearly, demonstrably, manifestly, obviously** *The claim that 'quantum theory needs no interpretation' seems to me to be obviously incorrect.*
- ▶ partly **partly, slightly** *The information I was given was slightly incorrect.*
- ▶ in a particular way **chronologically, factually, grammatically, historically, legally, mathematically, scientifically, syntactically, technically** *His statement is factually incorrect and logically absurd.*

The expression **politically incorrect** refers to language or behaviour that may be offensive to people who have been affected by discrimination, for example women or ethnic minorities: *She's intelligent and – forgive me for being politically incorrect – she doesn't look too bad either!*

- ● v+ADJ **be, consider sth, deem sth, prove** *They were working with figures which are now considered incorrect. ● Their early forecasts proved incorrect.*

increase V
to become larger or make something larger in amount or number

- ● adv+V very much **considerably, enormously, greatly, hugely, immeasurably, massively, significantly, substantially, tremendously, vastly** *The number of children who are overweight has increased significantly in the past decade.*
- ▶ a little **marginally, moderately, modestly, slightly, temporarily** *Viewing figures were low, although they did increase slightly as the season progressed.*
- ▶ noticeably **appreciably, markedly, noticeably** *The programme has noticeably increased students' final grades.*
- ▶ suddenly or quickly **dramatically, drastically, rapidly, sharply, steeply** *The number of vehicles having to be removed and disposed of has increased dramatically.*
- ▶ steadily or gradually **gradually, slowly, steadily** *Gradually increase your level of activity and you will enjoy the health benefits.*
- ▶ by a particular factor **exponentially, incrementally, progressively, twofold, threefold etc** *Complaints about male stereotypes in ad campaigns have increased tenfold since 1995.*
- ▶ all the time **constantly, continually, continuously** *The demand for these services is constantly increasing.*
- ▶ because of something else **accordingly, consequently, correspondingly, inevitably, therefore** *If the post is full-time then the budget will be correspondingly increased.*
- ● V+by **average, factor, rate, five, ten per cent etc** *The risk was increased by a factor of ten for adults in the older age range.*

increase N
a rise in number, amount, or degree

- ● adj+N big **big, considerable, enormous, huge, large, massive, significant, substantial, vast, whopping (great)** INFORMAL *The long-term data suggest a decline, although we have seen a significant increase in recent years.*
- ▶ small **marginal, modest, slight, small** *In 2008 the*

company recorded just 29 complaints, a slight increase **on** the 16 recorded the previous year.

▶ noticeable **marked, noticeable** We have noticed a marked increase **in** the numbers of birds in our garden.

▶ sudden or quick **dramatic, rapid, sharp, steep, sudden** The rapid increase **in** the local population put a strain on our services.

▶ steady or gradual **gradual, progressive, steady, year-on-year** After decades of steady increases, the number of bicycles on China's streets has begun to fall.

▶ continuing **continual, continued, sustained** An online ticketing system has enabled us to handle a continued increase **in** ticket sales.

▶ predicted or suggested **anticipated, planned, projected, proposed** We believe that the network has sufficient capacity to handle the anticipated increases **in** email volumes.

▶ apparent/actual **actual, apparent, observed, real** Naturally, we are disturbed by any suggestion of an apparent increase **in** crime.

▶ connected with something else **consequent, corresponding, proportional, resultant** This could result in a dollar sell-off and a corresponding increase **in** oil and gold prices.

▶ surprising or worrying **alarming, unprecedented, worrying** There has been an alarming increase **in** injuries and deaths among young drivers in the region.

▶ average **average, overall** This equates to an average increase **in** tax of 4.1 per cent.

▶ by a particular factor or amount **double-digit, exponential, five, ten etc per cent, incremental, twofold, threefold etc** During that period there was a fivefold increase **in** the number of patients presenting with asthma.

● v+N show an increase **demonstrate, experience, indicate, reveal, show** Turnover is expected to show an increase of over 45 per cent this year.

▶ be an increase **represent** This represents an increase in real terms.

You can also say that something is **on the increase**: Crime in the area is on the increase again.

▶ cause an increase **achieve, bring about, cause, lead to, produce, result in** Darkness causes an increase **in** the release of the body's sleep hormone.

▶ involve an increase **be accompanied by, involve, mean** The shortage of teachers was accompanied by an increase in class sizes.

▶ notice an increase **note, notice, see, witness** You have probably seen an increase **in** the amount of 'junk mail' showing up in your email box.

▶ report an increase **announce, record, report** They have reported an increase of 208 per cent **in** people visiting their website.

▶ predict an increase **anticipate, envisage, expect, forecast, predict** The US Energy Information Administration predicts a 43 per cent increase **in** carbon emissions by 2030.

▶ ask for an increase **call for, demand, recommend, suggest** The report recommended an increase **in** the state pension.

▶ deal with an increase **absorb, accommodate** The new road will accommodate the increase **in** vehicular traffic.

● N+v **come, occur** Much of the increase comes from burning fossil fuels. ● Almost all of the increase occurred between the late 1970s and mid 1990s.

increased ADJ
greater in size, amount, or degree

● ADJ+n amount that is produced or ability to work well **efficiency, productivity** Employers will achieve increased productivity by allowing employees to focus on their work rather than family concerns.

▶ spending **expenditure, funding, investment** She called for increased investment by the council in roads and schools.

▶ possibility of something happening **frequency, incidence, risk** Women who carry this gene are living with an increased risk of breast cancer.

▶ level or rate **level, rate** Increased traffic levels will be detrimental to both pedestrians and cyclists.

▶ being aware of something **awareness, understanding** Increased awareness of new technologies in retailing is essential.

▶ amount that is wanted **demand** As the population grows there will be an increased demand for food.

▶ good quality in a person **concentration, confidence, flexibility, motivation, satisfaction, self-esteem** The course will give you increased confidence and skills in using information technology.

incur V
1 to have to pay something [usually passive]

● V+n expense **costs, expenditure, expenses** You will be reimbursed for any reasonable expenses incurred in attending the hearing.

▶ charge or penalty **charge, debt, fee, fine, penalty, punishment, surcharge, tax, VAT** Please note credit cards incur a 3 per cent surcharge.

▶ financial loss **deficit, loss** The insurance policy covers losses incurred as a result of forced entry.

2 experience something unpleasant as a result of your actions

● V+n someone's anger **disapproval, displeasure, enmity, hostility, wrath** The company might be trying to stall its creditors as long as possible without incurring their wrath.

▶ damage **casualties, damage, injury** The doctor said I must have incurred a head injury.

▶ delay **delay** Samples which are incorrectly labelled will incur needless delays.

▶ risk **risk** To stray from these pathways incurred a serious risk of drowning in mud and water.

independence N
freedom from the control of another country, organization, or person

● adj+N complete **absolute, complete, full, genuine, outright, total, true** The nationalist movement demanded complete independence.

▶ not complete **conditional, nominal, relative** The two states had British Governors while retaining their nominal independence.

▶ more **greater, more** At thirteen years plus, the child moves towards greater independence.

▶ new or recent **new-found** Leaving family behind can be exciting but also quite stressful as you learn to cope with your new-found independence.

▶ that you have to fight for **hard-won** *She was unwilling to give up her hard-won independence.*
▶ determined **fierce, sturdy** *The stories reflect the unique character of the Yorkshire Dales, and the fierce independence of their inhabitants.*
▶ types of independence **economic, editorial, financial, intellectual, journalistic, judicial, legislative, national, operational, personal, political** *The company claims to follow a policy of editorial independence for all its newspapers.*

● v+N declare independence **assert, declare, proclaim** *On November 3, 1903, Panama declared its independence from Colombia.*
▶ achieve or have independence **achieve, attain, gain, regain, secure, win** *When I gave up my job to become a mum, I didn't know how I could regain my financial independence.*
▶ give independence **give sb, grant sb, recognize, restore** *In 1960, Belgium decided to grant its colony independence.*
▶ encourage independence **advocate, develop, encourage, foster, increase, maximize, promote, respect, strengthen, support** *We work to promote independence and equal opportunities for deaf people.*
▶ protect independence **defend, ensure, guarantee, protect, safeguard, uphold** *The unions must at all times defend their complete independence from the employers.*
▶ reduce independence **compromise, undermine** *It would gravely compromise the independence of the organization if its director were appointed by Ministers.*
▶ want and try and get independence **call for, demand, fight for, seek, struggle for, want** *The main reason she left home was that she was seeking her independence.*
▶ value independence **cherish, enjoy, value** *Teenagers really value their independence.*
▶ keep independence **maintain, preserve, retain** *The tenants live in a secure setting, while maintaining their independence in their own apartments.*
▶ lose or lack independence **give up, lack, lose, sacrifice** *Older people are often fearful of losing their independence.*

● n+for+N **battle, call, campaign, demand, desire, fight, struggle** *The book examines Gandhi's role in the struggle for Indian independence.*

● n+of+N **degree, feeling, lack, loss, measure, sense** *The living arrangements enabled the elderly people to retain a degree of independence.*

independent ADJ
1 ruled by its own government

● adv+ADJ **fully, genuinely, newly** *Survival was no easy task for the newly independent state.*

● ADJ+n **country, nation, republic, state** *Croatia received international recognition as an independent republic.*

● v+ADJ **be, become, feel, make sb, remain, stay** *Losing her mother so early had made her very independent.* ● *Many people manage to stay independent until well into their eighties.*

● v+ADJ **be, become, declare sth, make sth, remain, stay** *India became independent from Britain in 1947.* ● *South Arabia was declared independent in 1967.*

2 fair because not influenced by anyone else

● adv+ADJ completely **completely, entirely, fully, genuinely, totally, truly, wholly** *Governments are sometimes hesitant about setting up truly independent bodies, in case their recommendations conflict with government policy.*
▶ to some extent **fairly, relatively** *The legal system of the country remained relatively independent.*
▶ in a particular area of activity **editorially, legally, politically** *The TV channel is funded by government money, but is editorially independent.*

● ADJ+n expert **adviser, assessor, auditor, consultant, expert, observer** *Their independent financial advisers look at your current financial situation and then suggest which products you should consider.*
▶ examination of a situation **inquiry, review, verification** *The government initially refused to hold an independent inquiry into the circumstances that led to the war.*
▶ organization **body, charity, judiciary, organization, panel, regulator, thinktank, tribunal, watchdog** *The Electoral Commission, an independent body set up by Parliament to monitor elections, confirmed that it was investigating irregularities.*
▶ help **advice, arbitration** *The Citizens Advice Bureau service offers free, confidential, impartial and independent advice.*

3 not depending on other people for help or money

● adv+ADJ in a determined way **fiercely, proudly** *He is a fiercely independent 88-year-old, still living in his own home.*
▶ very or completely **completely, quite, very** *Cats are very independent animals.*
▶ rather **fairly, quite, relatively** *In Africa, women traditionally led relatively independent lives.*
▶ concerning money **economically, financially** *They appreciated the opportunity to become financially independent of their parents.*

index N
1 an alphabetical list at the back of a book

● adj+N alphabetical **alphabetical** *Almost all non-fiction books provide an alphabetical index.*
▶ complete **complete, comprehensive, detailed, extensive, full** *It also includes a comprehensive index.*
▶ types of index **author, online, searchable, subject, thematic** *The subject index will make the use of the book easier.*

● v+N create an index **compile, construct, create, generate, produce** *She is compiling an index to the correspondence of Sir Walter Scott.*
▶ use an index **check, look in, search, use** *Use the index to look up key words.*
▶ include something in an index **include sth in, list sth in, mention sth in** *This topic is not mentioned frequently enough to be included in the index.*
▶ look for something in an index **look sth up in** *When you look up a subject in the index, you will find the page numbers where that subject is mentioned in the body of the book.*

- N+v **contain, cover, give, have, include, list, provide** *This index gives the first line of each hymn.*

2 a number showing a value compared with something else

- n+N **consumer-price, cost-of-living, inflation, market-share, price, retail-price, stock, stock-market** *The current rate of increase in the retail price index is around 1.9 per cent.*
- N+v become higher **climb, rise** *The index rose 0.2 per cent last month after a 1.2 per cent decline in June.*
- ▶ become lower **drop, fall, slip** *From March 2000 to March 2001 the index fell from 4500 to 1750.*
- ▶ have a particular value at the end of a day **close** *The Nikkei index closed on Monday at a five-year high.*
- ▶ have a particular value at the beginning of a day **open** *The index opened down 60, but recovered slightly to be only lower by 40 points mid-morning.*

indicate V

1 express something

- V+n willingness to do or accept something **acceptance, agreement, assent, readiness, willingness** *He has indicated his willingness to negotiate treaty changes with Russia.*
- ▶ unwillingness **reluctance, unwillingness** *She indicated her reluctance to take on the assignment.*
- ▶ wish **desire, wish** *He has already indicated his desire to leave the club.*
- ▶ preference **preference** *Please indicate your preference for a particular type of accommodation.*
- ▶ intention **intention** *She has indicated her intention to retire from the Board in September.*

2 show that something exists or will happen

- adv+V clearly **clearly, explicitly, plainly, strongly** *This study clearly indicated that the scheme would save lives.*
- ▶ not always **not necessarily** *We must remember that lowest price does not necessarily indicate best value.*
- V+n existence **existence, presence** *Preliminary field tests indicated the possible presence of a biological toxin.*
- ▶ degree **degree, extent, level** *The study aims to indicate the extent to which religious discrimination overlaps with racial discrimination.*
- ▶ importance **importance, status** *This indicates the importance of looking at population mobility in a wider context.*
- ▶ need **need** *Changing circumstances indicate a need for more flexible approaches.*
- ▶ possibility **likelihood, possibility, potential** *Recent work indicates the possibility of a link between long-term exposure and a range of chronic illnesses.*

indication N

a sign or statement that something exists, happens, or is true

- adj+N clear **clear, definite, obvious** *There are clear indications that some equipment manufacturers are aware of the need for change in design.*
- ▶ happening at the beginning of a process **early, initial, preliminary** *Early indications are promising.*
- ▶ strong **firm, good, positive, strong** *Often, the initial response of a cancer to radiotherapy is a good indication of how successful the treatment will be.*
- ▶ first **first** *The first indication of the apparent success of this strategy came in October 1982.*
- ▶ accurate **accurate, precise, reliable** *It is recognised that few students regard their exam performance as an accurate indication of their ability.*
- ▶ not exact **approximate, broad, general, rough, vague** *Cast and crew were legally obliged to keep plot details absolutely confidential except for the vaguest indications about how the story would evolve.*
- ▶ quite good **fair** *The pictures were taken a short while ago and are a fair indication of the overall condition of the car.*
- ▶ slight **slight** *Today, the building gives not the slightest indication of its former history.*
- ▶ using only a few words **brief** *Only a brief indication of the progress of the patient will be given.*
- ▶ useful **useful** *The results of the survey provided a useful indication as to which methods of recycling are used most by householders.*
- ▶ not much **little** *There is little indication at the moment that market conditions will change.*
- ▶ some **some** *The fact that this CD is the third to be released in the series is some indication of how successful the concept has been.*
- v+N give someone an indication **give (sb), offer (sb), provide** *He gave no indication that he shares this view.*
- ▶ get an indication **get, obtain, receive** *It is helpful for us to get an indication of what people feel about this situation.*
- ▶ have an indication **have** *It would be a good idea to have some indication of how long it lasts.*
- ▶ understand something as an indication **interpret sth as, regard sth as, see sth as, take sth as** *These figures should be taken as an indication of how much the project might cost overall.*
- N+v **be, point to sth, show sth, suggest sth** *All the indications are that is will be another successful year.* • *The initial indications point to a victory for the ruling party.*

Usage *Indication* is almost always plural in these combinations.

indictment N

something that shows how bad or wrong something is

- adj+N expressing strong criticism **damning, devastating, powerful, savage, scathing, searing** *This new book is a damning indictment of the economic policies of the government over the past 20 years.*
- ▶ making you feel upset **sad, shocking, terrible** *The editorial says this is 'a sad indictment of our education system'.*

indifference N

lack of interest or sympathy

- adj+N complete **absolute, complete, supreme, total, utter** *It is a matter of complete indifference to me.*
- ▶ not sympathetic **callous, cold** *She shows a callous indifference to the suffering of others.*

▶ felt by most people **general, public** *Efforts to start a boycott are handicapped by public indifference.*

▶ seeming to exist **apparent, seeming** *Some of us were not a little wounded by the apparent indifference of the public.*

▶ deliberate **studied** *I adopted a pose of studied indifference.*

● v+N show indifference **demonstrate, display, express, show** *Her tone expressed her entire indifference.*

▶ feel indifference **feel** *He seemed to be a man who felt total indifference to everything going on around him.*

▶ pretend to feel indifference **feign** *Of course, I feigned complete indifference.*

▶ treat something with indifference **treat sb/sth with** *They were accused of treating the wefare of the elderly with indifference.*

▶ experience indifference **be met with** *The suggestion met with indifference on the part of most members of the team.*

indispensable ADJ

that you need in order to exist, or to be able to do something

● adv+ADJ **absolutely, completely, quite, truly, utterly** *This dictionary is absolutely indispensable for any serious student of the language.*

● ADJ+n source of information **aid, book, companion, guide, reference, resource, source** *The book is an indispensable guide to understanding the relationship between law and politics in Northern Ireland.*

▶ item or piece of equipment **aid, resource, tool** *Millions of people around the world now view their mobile phone as an indispensable tool when travelling abroad.*

▶ part **addition, component, element, feature, part, role** *Postgraduate students are now an indispensable part of the teaching force at almost all universities.*

individual N

a person, considered separately from their society or community

● adj+N emphasizing that an individual is not part of a group **private, single** *Grants are made to corporations as well as to private individuals.*

▶ thinking in the same way as other people **like-minded** *People tend to seek advice from like-minded individuals.*

▶ particular **certain, particular, specific** *The services will work best if they target specific individuals in a specific way.*

● v+as+N treat someone as an individual **respect, treat, value** *It felt good to be treated as an individual at last.*

▶ become more of an individual **develop, grow** *The time away from family helped her develop as an individual.*

individuality N

the things that make someone or something different from all others

● v+N show individuality **assert, express, reflect, show** *Some, however, did take the opportunity to express their individuality from time to time.*

▶ have or develop individuality **develop, have** *The architects intend each school to be unique and have its own individuality.*

▶ give individuality to someone or something **add, bring, give** *Pictures are a wonderful way to give your home individuality.*

▶ help individuality to develop **encourage, promote** *Our aims are to respect the individual and encourage individuality.*

▶ keep individuality **maintain, preserve, retain** *The villages have practically merged into one urban area, although each retains its own individuality .*

▶ lose individuality **give up, lose, sacrifice** *Members of a crowd lose their individuality.*

▶ show that you understand the importance of individuality **celebrate, recognize, respect, value** *Managers are working to develop a culture where diversity and individuality are valued.*

● n+of+N **expression, loss, sense** *She felt that how she dressed should be an expression of her individuality.*

indulge V

allow yourself to have or do something enjoyable

● V+n **appetite, curiosity, desire, fancy, fantasy, interest, love, obsession, passion, taste, whim** *His father decided to allow him to indulge his new-found passion for acting.*

● V+in something that you like doing **activity, hobby, pastime, pleasures** *Retirement gave him the opportunity to indulge in his favourite leisure activities.*

▶ something you feel **fantasy, nostalgia, passion** *She indulged in elaborate fantasies of success and achievement.*

▶ luxury **luxury** *He privately indulged in every luxury that he forbade to others.*

▶ thinking **speculation, thinking** *I don't mind indulging in a little speculation.*

industry N

the production of goods, especially in factories; the people and organizations involved in making products or providing a service

● adj+N producing large/small goods **heavy, light** *A variety of new light industries have been attracted to the area.*

▶ successful **booming, expanding, flourishing, growing, profitable, thriving** *Mumbai is the home of India's thriving film industry.*

▶ not successful **ailing, declining, loss-making** *The measures were designed to boost Britain's ailing manufacturing industry.*

▶ owned/not owned by the state **nationalized, private, privatized, state-owned** *The general strike paralysed both private industry and government departments for ten days.*

▶ types of industry **high-tech, knowledge-based, manufacturing, science, traditional** *The firm provides advice to high-tech industries such as those producing computer software and semiconductors.*

● v+N encourage and support industry **benefit, help, promote, protect, subsidize, support** *Currently* *the government supports the rail industry to the extent of four billion pounds.*

▸ damage industry **cripple, damage, destroy** *The threat of disease has certainly damaged the tourist industry in the area.*

▸ make industry obey rules **regulate** *They accused the government of failing to regulate the banking industry adequately.*

▸ take away rules relating to industry **deregulate** *Recently, Japan has been deregulating its industries and privatizing state-owned businesses.*

▸ organize industry in a different way **restructure** *They put forward proposals for restructuring the road-haulage industry.*

▸ when governments/private people take control of industry **denationalize, nationalize, privatize** *After the war, many key industries were nationalized.*

● N+v be successful **expand, flourish, grow, thrive** *As the coal industry expanded, the problems of flooding increased.*

● not be successful **collapse, decline, struggle** *Currently, as fewer people move house, the home-improvement industry is struggling.*

▸ face something **experience, face, suffer** *The tourist industry has suffered a steady decline in recent years.*

inefficient ADJ
not working in the best possible way

● adv+ADJ very **extremely, grossly, highly, hopelessly, hugely, incredibly, very** *Our huge power stations are grossly inefficient: they waste two thirds of the energy that they produce.*

● in comparison with someone or something similar **comparatively, relatively** *In fact these methods are relatively inefficient.*

▸ rather **fairly, quite, rather** *While this system is certainly an improvement, it is still quite inefficient.*

● ADJ+n way of doing something **method, practice, procedure, process, system, technique** *We are cutting costs by getting rid of inefficient practices.*

● use **They** *are planning campaigns to educate the public on the consequences of inefficient energy use.*

● management **management** *In the private sector, when companies are in financial difficulty it is often as a result of inefficient management.*

● v+ADJ **be, become, prove, seem** *Their method of calculating the average price of corn proved inefficient.*

● and/or not effective **ineffective** *Our system may be complex, but it is neither ineffective nor inefficient.*

● costing too much **costly, expensive, wasteful** *Court procedures are inefficient and costly.*

● old **old, outdated** *They continue to use outdated and inefficient techniques.*

● slow **slow** *A new search engine will replace this slow and inefficient one.*

inequality N
a situation in which people are not equal

● adj+N types of inequality **economic, educational, environmental, ethnic, geographical, racial, sexual, social, socioeconomic, structural** *The region has the highest rates of social inequality in the world.*

▸ great **extreme, glaring, great, gross, huge, massive, stark** *We believe that the gross inequalities in UK*

society damage not only the poorest in society, but everyone.

▸ relating to a particular area **global, regional** *Children in the countries we work in are severely at risk as a direct consequence of poverty; poverty that is the consequence of global inequalities which need to be addressed at the highest levels.*

▸ continuing to exist **entrenched, persistent** *Health Action Zones will be concentrated in areas of pronounced deprivation and poor health, reflecting the Government's commitment to tackle entrenched inequalities.*

▸ existing now **current, existing** *And since the worse off tend to be disadvantaged in this area – in terms of motivation and information, as well as resources – it is likely to exacerbate existing inequality.*

▸ becoming greater **growing, increasing, rising, widening, worsening** *The growing inequality in our society has been highlighted over the past year.*

● n+N relating to money **earnings, income, pay, wage, wealth** *Income inequality was greater in the mid-1990s than at any time since the late 1940s.*

▸ relating to health **health** *Further progress in the elimination of health inequalities is crucial.*

▸ relating to social class **class** *This book focuses on the ways in which class inequalities manifest themselves in Britain today.*

▸ relating to race **race** *More work is needed to overcome race inequality in public services.*

▸ relating to the fact of being male or female **gender** *During this time she was actively campaigning on the issue of gender inequality.*

● v+N try to deal with inequality **address, challenge, combat, confront, redress, tackle, target** *The project offers a range of services designed to tackle inequality and disadvantage in the labour market.*

▸ reduce inequality **lessen, reduce** *Is the government really serious about reducing inequalities within our society?*

▸ increase inequality **exacerbate, increase, reinforce, widen** *They concede that globalisation has increased inequality between rich and poor.*

▸ get rid of inequality **eliminate, end, overcome, remove** *The Council is committed to eliminating inequality and discrimination wherever it can.*

▸ experience inequality **experience, face** *There is no evidence that the general improvement in living standards has lessened the inequality experienced by the majority of African Americans.*

▸ cause inequality **cause, create, lead to** *The goverment is working to tackle the social, educational and economic barriers that create inequality and poverty.*

▸ allow inequality to continue to exist **maintain, perpetuate** *The current system only perpetuates inequality.*

● N+v continue to exist **continue, persist, remain** *Huge inequalities persist.*

▸ exist **exist** *We must recognize that inequalities exist and take steps to address them.*

▸ become greater **grow, increase, rise, widen** *Existing regional inequalities are widening.*

inevitable ADJ
impossible to avoid or prevent

- adv+ADJ almost **almost, virtually** *A strike is now almost inevitable.*
- ▶ perhaps **perhaps** *His parents were farmers, so it was perhaps inevitable that he would spend most of his working life connected with the land.*
- ▶ probably **probably** *The eventual outcome was probably inevitable.*
- ▶ according to what seems to be true **apparently, seemingly** *The new training programme aims to break this seemingly inevitable decline.*
- ▶ rather **fairly, pretty** INFORMAL, **somehow** *Living so close to the sea, I guess it was fairly inevitable that I'd develop an interest in sailing.*
- ▶ completely **absolutely** *It's absolutely inevitable that it's going to happen at some point.*
- ▶ in a way that you think is bad or wrong **sadly** *The result was sadly inevitable.*

- ADJ+n result **consequence, corollary, outcome, result** *She said this criticism and interference was the inevitable consequence of giving more power to judges.*
- ▶ decision **conclusion** *This line of argument leads to the inevitable conclusion that military force is the only solution to this conflict.*
- ▶ fighting **clash, conflict, confrontation, war** *It now seems certain that war is inevitable.*
- ▶ problem **delay, disruption** *Whilst some disruption is inevitable with a project of this nature, we will endeavour to keep inconvenience to a minimum.*
- ▶ bad situation **collapse, death, decline, defeat, demise, fate** *As a society, we must innovate or face inevitable economic decline.*
- ▶ change **change** *Change is inevitable and the school must embrace that process and see it as an opportunity.*
- ▶ mistake **mistake** *Mistakes are inevitable in an operation on this scale.*
- ▶ disappointment **disappointment** *Such disappointments are inevitable in any market economy.*
- ▶ loss **loss** *The airlines are streamlining their businesses, and job losses are inevitable.*

- v+ADJ **appear, become, look, make sth, seem, see sth as** *When the talks collapsed, the closure of the firm became inevitable.* • *A general lowering of standards seems inevitable.* • *Some unhappiness can be seen as natural and inevitable.*

- and/or **desirable, natural, necessary, unavoidable** *Change, in one form or another, is both inevitable and desirable.*

inexhaustible ADJ
never completely used up, and always available

- adv+ADJ almost **almost, virtually** *She has an almost inexhaustible passion for her work.*
- ▶ according to what seems to be true **apparently, seemingly** *A man of seemingly inexhaustible vitality, Prior made an excellent teacher.*

- ADJ+n supply **fund, quantity, reserve, resource, source, store, supply** *He's also got an inexhaustible supply of similar stories.*
- ▶ quality **energy, enthusiasm, patience** *He possessed the organising ability and inexhaustible energy to carry on the good work of his predecessor.*

infection N
the process of becoming infected with a disease

- v+N prevent or try to prevent infection **avoid, guard against, prevent, protect against, stop** *To avoid infection, try to follow these simple rules.*
- ▶ cause infection **cause** *The cracks in the skin may allow bacteria to enter and cause infection.*
- ▶ attempt to get rid of infection **combat, control, fight, resist, treat** *Positive thinking has been found to boost the body's immune system so we can better fight infection.*
- ▶ get rid of infection **eliminate, eradicate** *There is no intention to continue vaccination beyond what is necessary to contain the epidemic and eliminate infection.*
- ▶ reduce infection **reduce** *The first national campaign to encourage hand cleaning by hospital staff in order to reduce infection has been announced.*
- ▶ spread infection **spread** *Good hygiene can cut down the risk of spreading infection.*
- ▶ prove that infection is present **detect** *By doing both tests simultaneously, it should be possible to detect infection in these animals.*

- N+v **arise, cause sth, clear up, occur, persist, spread** *Acute infections cause a very high body temperature.* • *Most skin infections clear up with no permanent adverse effects.*

- n+against+N **defence, fight, immunity, protection** *With this condition, the body's defence against infection is severely impaired.*

inference N
an opinion you form about something based on information you already have

- adj+N reasonable **logical, reasonable, valid** *He presents a set of statistics from which valid inferences can be drawn.*
- ▶ clear **clear, obvious** *The clear inference is that they were the first people to realize the mistake.*
- ▶ wrong **false, incorrect, mistaken** *The statement is wrong and would always lead to false inferences.*

- v+N make an inference **draw, make** *Critical reading has been defined as learning to evaluate, draw inferences and arrive at conclusions based on the evidence.*
- ▶ make an inference possible or acceptable **allow, justify, permit, support** *This action by itself is not sufficient to justify an inference of racial bias.*

inferior ADJ
not as good or of such a high a status, as someone or something else

- adv+ADJ very **decidedly, far, greatly, markedly, much, noticeably, significantly, vastly, very, very much** *Their weaponry is vastly inferior to ours.*
- ▶ rather **rather, slightly, somewhat** *Their second half performance was slightly inferior to their first half efforts.*
- ▶ in a particular way **genetically, intellectually, morally, numerically, racially, socially, technically, technologically** *He confesses that he still feels a bit socially inferior to his wife.*

- ADJ+n status **grade, position, rank, status** *Every day they are reminded of their inferior status.*

▶ quality **performance, quality** *Forgeries are often of inferior quality.*

▶ product **product** *I can't really see the point in paying the same sort of money for an inferior product.*

▶ copy **copy, imitation, sequel, version** *Inferior copies of our products have been flooding onto the European market from the Far East.*

▶ person **being** *Isabella grew up in a period when society regarded women as inferior beings.*

▶ group **race** *Racism is the belief that there are superior and inferior races.*

▶ v+ADJ **be, consider sb/sth, deem sb/sth, feel, regard sb/sth** *Garnett's translation is generally considered inferior to Magarshack's.* ● *He couldn't help feeling inferior to most of his colleagues.*

inflated ADJ
higher than it should be; made to seem more important than it really is

■ adv+ADJ **greatly, grossly, hugely, vastly** *There is no way he can justify such a vastly inflated fee.*

Over-inflated can be used in the same way as *inflated*: *Investors should be wary of over-inflated property prices in some parts of London.*

■ ADJ+n price, number, or pay **cost, fee, figure, price, rate, salary, wages** *Liquor was only available on the black market, and at hugely inflated prices.*

▶ opinion of yourself **ego, opinion, sense** *Footballers have an inflated sense of their own importance.*

▶ claim or expectations **claim, expectations** *The danger of such inflated expectations is that they can lead to disappointment.*

inflation N
an economic process in which prices increase so money loses value

■ adj+N low **low, moderate** *Although inflation is low, you will still feel your spending power reduce year after year.*

▪ high **double-digit, high, massive** *High inflation eroded the value of savings.*

▪ becoming higher **accelerating, galloping, increasing, rampant, rising, runaway, soaring, spiralling** *Rampant inflation and high unemployment might result.*

▪ calculated for a particular period **annual, quarterly** *The rate of annual inflation reached 14 per cent in March 2006.*

▪ happening quickly **rapid** *With rapid inflation, cash values of assets increase rapidly.*

■ v+N cause inflation **cause** *Their spending plans are likely to cause runaway inflation.*

▪ control inflation **bring under control, combat, control, curb, fight, keep down, keep in check, keep under control** *We are doing everything in our power to curb inflation.*

▪ increase more quickly than inflation **outpace, outstrip** *Average house prices are still outpacing inflation.*

▪ increase inflation **fuel, increase, push up** *They argue that high consumer spending is in danger of fuelling inflation.*

▪ be equal to inflation **keep pace with, keep up with, match** *The average wage increase matched annual inflation at around 1.8 per cent.*

▶ reduce inflation **bring down, get down, reduce** *The government's main aim is to keep down public expenditure so as to reduce inflation.*

● N+v become higher **accelerate, increase, rise, soar, spiral** *Inflation has now risen to 8 per cent.*

▶ become lower **drop, fall** *Inflation has fallen sharply in India.*

▶ reduce something **erode, reduce** *Inflation has eroded workers' salaries to a degree not seen since the 1980s.*

▶ slow down **ease, slow, slow down** *Inflation slowed to 0.1 per cent, from 1.1 per cent in March.*

▶ be higher than something **exceed** *The Bank of England will take whatever action it thinks necessary to stop inflation exceeding its target.*

▶ be at something **average, reach, remain at, run at, stand at, stay at** *Inflation reached a new record level in June.*

● N+n **figures, forecast, outlook, rate, report, target** *For the first time in three decades the inflation rate is in single digits.*

● n+against+N **battle, fight, protection** *Tax policy also plays a role in the fight against inflation.*

● v+against+N **protect sth** *All the benefits are protected against inflation.*

● n+of+N **level, measure, rate** *There are a number of measures of inflation in use today.*

inflict V
cause something unpleasant to happen

● V+n damage **damage, destruction, devastation** *The damage inflicted on London had been enormous.*

▶ harm **atrocities, cruelty, death, harm, horrors, injury, pain, suffering, torture, trauma, violence, wound** *Reprisals are an extreme measure because in most cases they inflict suffering on innocent persons.*

▶ defeat **defeat** *They succeeded in inflicting a 1–0 defeat on Woking.*

▶ punishment **penalty, punishment** *The government had stated that it would inflict penalties on any company that allowed a pay rise above 5 per cent.*

▶ problems **hardship, misery** *Of course, there are unfortunate occasions when we have to inflict hardship on innocent people to achieve something vital.*

▶ deaths of people **casualties, losses** *With the aid of accurate artillery fire, they managed to inflict heavy casualties on the Americans.*

influence N
the effect that a person or thing has on someone or something; a person or thing that has an effect on someone or something

● adj+N great **big, considerable, decisive, enormous, great, important, major, profound, significant** *He wrote a great deal and had an enormous influence on a number of very important people.*

▶ strong **powerful, strong** *The media has a powerful influence on public opinion.*

▶ good **good, positive** *Sally was a good influence on her friend Harry.* ● *We work closely with young people in the area and try to have a positive influence on them.*

▶ bad **bad, evil, negative, pernicious** *That group of boys were a bad influence* **on** *my son.* ● *They argue that film and television can exert a negative influence* **on** *our children.*

▶ affecting a particular area of activity **cultural, political** *Russian cultural influence has been relatively small.*

▶ by people who do not belong to a particular group **external, outside** *They must exercise independent judgement, and must not be subject to any outside influence.*

▶ unreasonable **undue** *The Government stands accused of trying to exert an undue influence* **over** *the judicial process.*

▶ continuing for a long time **lasting** *Debussy's methods were to have a lasting influence* **on** *the direction of 20th Century music.*

▶ direct **direct** *She argues that the Vatican had little direct influence* **on** *the course of events in the years that followed the Second World War.*

▶ making people feel calmer **calming, steadying** *He had a steadying influence* **on** *his younger, less experienced, colleagues.*

▶ making someone's character develop **formative** *He has been a formative influence* **on** *a generation of German artists.*

● v+N have or use influence **exercise, exert, have, use, wield** *His writing was to exert great influence on Gandhi.*

▶ increase influence **extend, increase, spread, strengthen** *Both countries were attempting to extend their influence* **in** *the area.*

▶ reduce influence **diminish, reduce, undermine, weaken** *Constitutional changes were designed to weaken Russian influence in the country.*

▶ examine the influence of someone or something **examine, explore, investigate, trace** *This course will examine the main influences* **on** *Puccini's musical style.*

▶ gain influence **gain** *Operating in this way, large firms are able to gain still greater influence* **in** *related markets.*

▶ oppose the influence of someone or something **counter, counteract, resist** *One way to counter the influence of unhealthy food advertising would be to use the same techniques to promote healthier options.*

▶ show the influence of someone or something **reflect, show** *His work reflected the influence of Soviet filmmakers, particularly Eisenstein.*

▶ admit that the influence of someone or something exists **acknowledge** *Whistler and Monet both initially acknowledged the profound influence of Turner.*

● N+v grow **continue, extend, grow, remain** *Those were the years when British influence around the world was growing steadily.*

▶ become less **decline, diminish, wane** *After several hundred years, Rome's influence waned.*

● v+under+N start being influenced by someone or something **come, fall** *At university he came under the influence of various radical political thinkers.*

▶ drive or act **act, drive** *She was charged with driving under the influence of alcohol.*

influence V

affect a situation or someone's behaviour

● adv+V very much **deeply, greatly, heavily, hugely, powerfully, profoundly, significantly, strongly, substantially** *Blackmore claims to be heavily influenced by Bach.*

▶ in a good way **positively** *New research claims that interaction with pets can positively influence children's physical and emotional development*

▶ in a bad way **adversely, negatively** *You must avoid those things which negatively influence your thinking.*

▶ clearly **clearly, obviously, undoubtedly** *The idea has clearly influenced the current government agenda.*

▶ mainly **largely, mainly** *Venezuela's culture is largely influenced by its North American neighbour.*

▶ directly **directly** *By working closely with the artist, the children will be able to contribute ideas and opinions which will directly influence the development of the work.*

▶ indirectly **indirectly** *Many of these ideas indirectly influenced thinkers like Nietzsche and Heidegger.*

▶ in an unreasonable way **unduly** *There is a risk of the private sector unduly influencing the drafting of the new legislation.*

● V+n decision **choice, decision, decision-making** *There will be numerous factors which will influence your choice of car*

▶ behaviour **behaviour** *An important part of this study is the extent to which the media influences our behaviour.*

▶ opinion **attitude, opinion, perception, thinking** *He is willing to use his vast wealth to try and influence public opinion.*

▶ result **outcome** *It was, however, too late to influence the outcome of the election.*

▶ process **change, development, direction, process** *These are the priorities which are likely to influence the direction of government policy.*

▶ work **work, writing** *These authors were to influence her own writing later on.*

▶ the future **future** *By participating and making your views known, you can influence the future.*

▶ design **design, shape** *The trip made pupils more aware of how the local environment influences the design of buildings.*

▶ plan **agenda, plan, policy** *The organization also aims to influence government policy in this area.*

▶ debate **debate** *This is your chance to influence the debate.*

influential ADJ

able to influence the way people think and behave

● adv+ADJ **deeply, enormously, especially, extremely, highly, hugely, immensely, incredibly, massively, particularly, profoundly, very** *Like his friend and contemporary, Andy Warhol, he was hugely influential both during his life and after his death.*

● ADJ+n person with a particular skill **artist, commentator, critic, designer, journalist, leader, musician, philosopher, player, politician, thinker, writer** *He was hailed as 'one of the most influential thinkers of the 20th century'.*

▶ person **figure, voice** *His writings attracted the*

attention of influential figures in the Church of England.

▶ published piece of writing **book, newspaper** *The Washington Post is a highly influential newspaper.*

▶ group **band, group** *The Government's approach has come in for strong criticism from an influential group of MPs.*

▶ organization **body, organization** *This body was very influential in shaping the direction of full-time professional education for librarians.*

▶ part **factor, role** *The successful candidate will have an influential role in shaping the company's long-term strategy.*

▶ job **position** *Last week I was talking to someone who now has a very influential position.*

▶ v+ADJ **be, become, prove, remain** *She remains enormously influential, even ten years after her death.*

influx N

a large number of people or things coming into a place

▶ adj+N large **big, enormous, great, huge, large, major, massive, significant, vast** *The club has had a huge influx of new members.*

▶ recent **fresh, new, recent** *China's booming economy has also contributed strongly to the recent influx of Chinese students pursuing academic qualifications in the UK.*

▶ sudden **sudden** *A sudden influx of migrant workers has led to a revival of extreme right-wing nationalism.*

▶ quick **rapid** *There is huge population growth in this area through the rapid influx of families from rural areas.*

▶ continuous **constant, regular, steady** *We need a constant influx of immigrants to do the jobs we don't want to, and to make up for the fall in population.*

▶ v+N get an influx **experience, receive, see** *The firm has just received an influx of investment from its parent company.*

▶ deal with an influx **cope with, deal with, handle** *The universities struggled to cope with the influx of new students.*

N+of people **foreigners, immigrants, members, migrants, players, refugees, settlers, students, tourists, visitors, workers** *The influx of refugees would probably be more than Mali could cope with.*

money **capital, cash, investment** *The economy is stable and benefiting from an influx of foreign investment.*

informal ADJ

relaxed and friendly; not official

▶ adv+ADJ very or completely **completely, extremely, quite, totally, very** *This gives us the opportunity to discuss the topic in a very informal way.*

rather **fairly, pretty INFORMAL, quite, rather, relatively** *Many research collaborations are fairly informal and simply involve two or more members exchanging information occasionally.*

ADJ+n mood in a place **atmosphere** *Dining is available in the informal atmosphere of our excellent restaurant.*

▶ place **setting** *It is always useful to meet potential employees in an informal setting, before the actual interview.*

▶ conversation **conversation, interview** *It was a friendly and fairly informal interview.*

▶ social occasion **gathering, get-together** *The magnificent state dining room can be used for special dinners or the family dining room for more informal gatherings.*

▶ way **manner, style, way** *Class sizes are small, with teaching taking place in an informal style.*

▶ arrangement **arrangement** *There are currently some informal arrangements for sharing equipment among participants.*

▶ talks **chat, consultation, discussions, talks** *Informal talks between union bosses and Tube management, aimed at averting a strike, broke down.*

▶ meeting **meeting, session** *The delegation will hold other informal meetings outside of the official agenda.*

▶ meal **dinner, lunch** *Prior to the meeting, members and guests attended an informal dinner held in honour of the speaker.*

▶ question **inquiries** *Informal inquiries and requests for further details are encouraged.*

information N

knowledge or facts about someone or something

● adj+N more **additional, further, more, new, supplementary** *I can give you more information if you need.*

▶ correct **accurate, correct, precise, reliable** *The author has consulted original documentary evidence to ensure that the information is accurate.*

▶ incorrect **erroneous, false, inaccurate, incorrect, misleading** *You mustn't deliberately mislead the police, give them false information, waste their time or obstruct them.*

▶ recent/not recent **new, out-of-date, up-to-date, up-to-the-minute** *The writing style is clear throughout and the information is up-to-date.*

▶ about what has happened in the past **background** *Let me give you some background information on the case.*

▶ useful **pertinent, relevant, useful, valuable** *You will also find details of bus routes to schools and colleges in the area, and other useful information.*

▶ basic **basic** *The publication provides basic information for carers about services that exist in the local area.*

▶ secret **classified, confidential, inside, sensitive** *They believe they have acted in the public interest by disclosing confidential information.*

▶ available **available** *No information regarding troop losses is currently available.*

▶ containing only facts **factual** *Read this book for its factual information, not its analysis.*

▶ detailed **detailed, in-depth** *More detailed information can be found on the universities' websites.*

▶ complete or enough/not complete or enough **complete, comprehensive, full, incomplete, insufficient, sufficient** *We do not have sufficient information to make a decision at the present time.*

When something provides a lot of information, you can say that it is **packed with information**: *The guide is packed with information about what to do in the area.*

▶ types of information **bibliographic, biographical, economic, genetic, geographic, historical, practical, statistical** *It also contains much new biographical information **about** the artist.*

• v+N have information **have, possess** *Police are appealing for any witnesses, or anyone who may have any information in connection with this crime.*

▶ need information **need, require** *Should you require any further information **about** this event, please do not hesitate to contact us.*

▶ provide information **communicate, convey, disclose, divulge, give (sb), provide, supply, transmit** *In order to provide information more relevant to you, we need to learn more about you.*

▶ tell private or secret information **leak** *It may well have been Downing Street itself that leaked the information to the newspaper.*

▶ get information **access, acquire, elicit, extract, find, get, glean, obtain, receive, retrieve** *You can obtain further information from your Local Authority.*

▶ ask for information **appeal for, ask for, request** *Click here to request information **on** any of the courses listed above.*

▶ look for information **gather, look for, search for, seek** *The Colonel moved from group to group, seeking information **about** the unknown lady.*

▶ contain information **contain** *The following links are to pages that contain information **on** this subject.*

▶ make information contain the most recent facts **update** *Members and customers who have registered online with us may update their account information at any time.*

▶ deal with information **process** *Here the computers process all the information coming in by satellite from all over the world.*

▶ interpret information **analyze, interpret** *Our role is to collect and analyze information, which will be used to help make decisions.*

▶ keep information **keep, store** *Make sure you store private information in a directory that isn't accessible to others.*

▶ exchange or share information **exchange, share** *They agreed to exchange information **on** this matter.*

▶ deliberately not provide information **withhold** *Do you believe that the company is withholding information **about** its assets?*

▶ collect information **collect, gather** *Companies want to collect information **about** their customers for various reasons.*

• n+of+N piece **piece, snippet** *This was an important piece of information, as it confirmed our original suspicions. • The little snippets of information about his personal life made the interview more interesting.*

▶ large amount **wealth** *This is a beautifully illustrated book, giving a wealth of information **on** the flowers of the area.*

▶ source **source** *The Internet is likely to be the most useful source of information for the project.*

informative ADJ
giving a lot of helpful information

• adv+ADJ **extremely, highly, particularly, really, so** INFORMAL, **very, wonderfully** *The lectures were highly informative and interesting.*

• ADJ+n piece of writing **article, book, booklet, guide, introduction, leaflet, magazine, newsletter, text** *She has written many amusing and informative articles for various national newspapers and magazines.*

▶ talk **commentary, lecture, presentation, talk** *The new footage is nice, as is the interesting and informative commentary.*

▶ event **seminar, session, workshop** *The sessions were very informative and efficiently run.*

▶ website **site, website** *I found the website informative and easy to use.*

• v+ADJ **be, find sth, prove** *The answers to the questionnaire proved very informative. • This is a new course which we found very informative, especially for new recruits.*

• and/or **enjoyable, entertaining, helpful, interesting, stimulating, useful** *Journalists aim to provide articles that are both entertaining and informative.*

informed ADJ
based on good knowledge of something; having a good knowledge about something

• ADJ+n decision **choice, decision** *The area of study must be clearly defined so that students can make an informed choice at the outset.*

▶ opinion **assessment, judgment, opinion, view** *It is the job of a columnist to have an informed opinion.*

▶ agreement **consent** *The practice of obtaining informed consent is often left to the most junior and least experienced member of staff.*

▶ knowledge **understanding** *The government needs a more informed understanding of childhood poverty, or policies designed to improve the lives of poor children run the risk of failing.*

▶ advice **advice** *Our experience of the food industry enables us to provide objective and informed advice based on up-to-date knowledge.*

▶ guess **guess** *You have to make an informed guess.*

▶ comment **comment** *You will acquire knowledge an understanding of a wide range of issues and gain the ability to express your opinions and give informe comments.*

▶ person or people **citizen, consumer, observer, public, reader** *As science advances, the necessity for a more informed public becomes increasingly urgen • This book is designed for the informed reader.*

ingenious ADJ
based on new and clever ideas

• adv+ADJ very **highly, truly, very** *He used a very ingenious method to photograph snow crystals.*

▶ rather **quite, rather** *Her theory was quite ingenious but she was unable to back it up with evidence.*

• ADJ+n machine **contrivance, device, gadget, invention, machine** *More and more ingenious wireless devices are being introduced all the time.*

▶ plan or method **method, plan, ploy, solution, system, way** *They have come up with a very ingenious solution.*

▶ idea **idea** *This ingenious idea saved a massive amount of labour.*

▶ use **use** *This new production of the play makes ingenious use of simple resources.*

▶ design **design** *The frame is strong and light, thanks to its ingenious design.*

▶ argument **argument** *The defence countered with an ingenious argument.*

ingenuity N
the ability to solve problems in new and clever ways

● adj+N great **considerable, great, much** *Much ingenuity went into improvising the necessary components.*

▶ not much **a little** *Billions can be made with a little ingenuity and clever marketing.*

▶ human **human** *Human ingenuity will always find a way around the law.*

▶ types of ingenuity **creative, mechanical, technical, technological** *The technical ingenuity and combination of materials are typical of much of the furniture shown in the Exhibition.*

● v+N need ingenuity **need, require, take** *Cooking fish and meat using a minimal amount of fat, yet getting the maximum flavour, takes ingenuity.*

▶ show ingenuity **demonstrate, display, show** *Considerable ingenuity was shown in the design of these early systems.*

▶ use ingenuity **use** *He was forced to use his ingenuity to survive.*

▶ have ingenuity **have** *We also have the ingenuity to make them much more energy-efficient.*

● and/or **creativity, determination, energy, imagination, inventiveness, skill** *Artistic people are characterized by creativity, ingenuity and inspiration.*

ingrained ADJ
having existed for a long time and difficult to change

▶ adv+**ADJ** **deeply** *Their television viewing habits are deeply ingrained.*

▶ **ADJ**+n behaviour **behaviour, culture, habit, pattern** *Dishonesty is now an ingrained habit with this government.*

▶ opinion **attitude, belief, prejudice, sense** *We all have ingrained prejudices that we find it hard to overcome.* ● *He needed to overcome an ingrained sense of failure before he could feel content.*

ingredient N
something that gives something else its character or that makes it effective

▶ adj+N important or essential **crucial, essential, important, key, necessary, vital** *Don't forget the other vital ingredient in a successful relationship – fun.*

▶ main **main, principal** *The two main ingredients are time and advertising.*

▶ special **magic, secret, special** *They possessed that secret ingredient that only a handful of bands are capable of producing.*

▶ basic **basic, staple** *The basic ingredients of a good life are very similar in all cultures.*

inhabitant N
a person or animal that lives somewhere

● adj+N original or early **aboriginal, ancient, early, first, indigenous, native, original** *The indigenous inhabitants of Latin America exerted a great influence on the Spanish language.*

▶ present **current, present** *The present inhabitants are of Scandinavian stock.*

▶ local **local** *This phenomenon is well known to most of the local inhabitants.*

▶ previous **former, previous** *The new settlers made use of the places of worship which the former inhabitants had erected.*

inhabited ADJ
lived in by people

● adv+ADJ by few people **sparsely, thinly** *Tilos is a large but sparsely inhabited island.*

▶ by many people **densely** *The large oil and gas fields are close to densely inhabited areas.*

▶ continuously **continuously** *Damascus claims to be the oldest continuously inhabited city in the world.*

▶ permanently **permanently** *It is officially one of the hottest permanently inhabited places on the planet.*

▶ in the beginning **originally** *Haiti was originally inhabited by the Arawak, an Amerindian race.*

▶ mainly **chiefly, mainly, mostly** *The village was chiefly inhabited by workers employed in the weaving trade.*

inherent ADJ
basic or essential, giving something its character

● ADJ+n fault **ambiguity, bias, complexity, contradiction, defect, flaw, limitation, tension, weakness** *She pointed to the contradictions inherent in Government policy.*

▶ danger **danger, risk** *Keep in mind that there are inherent dangers in consuming excessively high amounts of protein.*

▶ problem **difficulty, problem** *However, there are inherent difficulties in providing the services they recommend.*

▶ quality **characteristic, quality** *It is also an inherent characteristic of the subject that an individual student's performance might vary greatly over different modules.*

▶ tendency **tendency** *The general tendencies inherent in capitalism are brilliantly analysed by Marx and Engels.*

▶ ability **ability, strength** *One of the inherent strengths of the Internet is the access it affords to up-to-date information.*

▶ quality of not being certain **uncertainty** *A major area of his research is to understand how the brain deals with the uncertainty inherent in the world.*

inheritance N
property or money you receive from someone when they die

● adj+N **large, small** *He used a small inheritance to help finance his studies.*

● v+N leave an inheritance **leave (sb)** *People hoping to leave a sizeable inheritance could see a large chunk of it disappear in tax.*

▶ claim or receive an inheritance **claim, receive** *She*

was due to receive a large inheritance in the next ten years.

▶ waste an inheritance **squander** *If there are concerns that a child may squander the inheritance, the money can be put into a trust fund.*

● N+n **laws, tax** *Politicians did not want to abolish inheritance tax.*

initial ADJ
happening at the beginning of a process

● ADJ+n time **period, phase, stage** *There were delays during the initial stages of the case.*

▶ idea **advice, aim, analysis, concept, estimate, idea, proposal, thoughts** *The document sets out some initial thoughts for consideration.*

▶ feeling **enthusiasm, reluctance, scepticism, shock** *After the initial shock, I'm now really looking forward to it.*

▶ reaction **assessment, diagnosis, evaluation, feedback, impression, reaction, response, review** *The initial impression is of a very well-made item.*

▶ result **findings, indications, results, success** *The initial results of this work will be presented.*

▶ way of getting information **discussion, inquiry, investigation, survey** *Initial inquiries about research degrees should be addressed to the departmental office.*

▶ meeting **consultation, contact, interview, meeting** *An initial meeting was held in the autumn of 2009.*

▶ payment **cost, deposit, fee, investment, outlay** *An initial deposit will be required.*

initiative N
1 an important action intended to solve a problem

● adj+N important **ambitious, bold, exciting, high-profile, key, major, successful** *We are delighted to announce another major initiative to enhance access to the Library's archives.*

▶ new **groundbreaking, innovative, new, pioneering** *This is an exciting new initiative from the Government.*

▶ happening in a particular area **global, international, local, national, nationwide, regional, community-based, school-based, UK-based, etc, UK-wide, city-wide, industry-wide, etc** *It has grown from a regional initiative to a national project.*

▶ happening with support from others **collaborative, joint** *The new service is a joint initiative by the health service and local councils.*

▶ paid for by a particular organization **government-funded, EU-funded, council-funded, etc** *The council-funded initiative will help pay for athletes' training.*

▶ to raise money **fundraising** *The match is a fundraising initiative to raise money for disaster victims.*

● n+N **community, government** *This is a community initiative to tackle the problem of litter in the town.*

● v+N start an initiative **announce, introduce, launch** *We are about to launch a major initiative to find out your views.*

▶ support an initiative **back, encourage, fund, promote, sponsor, support, welcome** *We are delighted to back the initiative.*

▶ make an initiative happen **coordinate, develop, drive, implement, lead, spearhead, undertake** *He*

has worked in both sectors and is coordinating the initiative.

▶ take part in an initiative **be involved in, contribute to, participate in, take part in** *Fifty three establishments are now involved in the initiative.*

● N+v **aim, focus on, include, involve, seek, target** *This national initiative aims to reduce the occurrence of motorcycle crashes on Scotland's roads.* ● *The initiative focuses on raising aspirations among young people.*

● n+of+N **number, raft, range, series** *This is one element in a whole raft of initiatives designed to improve the overall quality of education.*

2 the ability to decide independently what to do [always singular]

● adj+N **his own, her own, etc** *We are looking for someone who can work on their own initiative.*

● v+N use initiative **demonstrate, show, use** *Candidates should demonstrate initiative and flexibility.* ● *They will need to use their initiative.*

▶ encourage initiative **encourage** *The staff plan encourages initiative and the taking of responsibility.*

● and/or **courage, creativity, drive, enthusiasm, flexibility, resourcefulness, responsibility** *Experience is not essential if the candidate can show initiative and drive.*

3 the opportunity to take action before others do

● v+N **have, lose, regain, seize, take** *He didn't sit around waiting for someone else to take the initiative.*

> Usage ***Initiative*** is always used with the in these combinations: *The party seized the initiative on key election issues such as tax and immigration.*

injunction N
a court order that stops someone from doing something

● v+N ask for or get an injunction against someone **apply for, bring, obtain, seek, take out, win** *The university applied for an injunction against the protesters.* ● *They won an injunction to prevent the government from terminating the contract.*

▶ give an injunction **grant (sb), issue** *The court refused to grant the injunction, citing a lack of evidence.*

▶ not pay attention to an injunction **be in breach of, breach** *Those who breach the injunction could face arrest.*

▶ stop an injunction **lift** *The judge ordered that the injunction be lifted.*

● N+v **ban, order, prevent, prohibit, require, restrain** *He issued an injunction restraining the BBC from publishing of the names of the two social workers.*

injure V
cause damage to someone's body

● adv+V **seriously badly, critically, fatally, gravely, permanently, seriously, severely** *They are not believed to have been seriously injured in the crash.*

slightly **slightly** *41 passengers were slightly injured or suffered from shock.*

> Usage *Injure* is usually passive in all the *adv+V* combinations shown above.

V+n person who is not directly involved in a situation **bystander, civilian, member of the public** *Six civilians were injured in the attack.*

person involved in a traffic accident **cyclist, driver, motorcyclist, passenger, pedestrian** *Most cyclists who are injured or killed are hit by motor vehicles.*

body part **ankle, knee, wrist, shoulder, etc** *He fell at work and injured his back.*

and/or **kill, maim** *This is a home for children who have been injured and maimed by landmines.*

njury N

physical damage done to a person

adj+N affecting a body part **facial, physical, spinal** *He miraculously escaped serious physical injury.*

to several parts of the body **multiple** *He was struck by a passing car, sustaining multiple injuries, from which he later died.*

serious **fatal, horrific, life-threatening, major, nasty, painful, serious, severe, terrible** *She suffered a serious injury to her head.*

not serious **minor, niggling, slight** *Two people were treated in hospital for minor injuries.*

caused by work **industrial, occupational, work-related** *Manual handling is a cause of many work-related injuries.*

caused accidentally/not accidentally **accidental, non-accidental** *Falls are the main cause of accidental injury to children.* • *It is quite likely that the injuries were non-accidental, and that the child was, in fact, assaulted.*

n+N affecting a body part **ankle, knee, head etc** *He has sustained a brain injury.*

caused by a particular action or activity **repetitive strain, sports, whiplash** *Whiplash injury is a very common consequence of car accidents.*

v+N receive an injury **acquire, incur, pick up, receive, suffer, sustain** *He had picked up a back injury during training.* • *No other injuries were sustained.*

have an injury **be hampered by, be nursing, be plagued by, have** *Dave was nursing a hand injury.* • *She was plagued by injury all season.*

pretend to have an injury **feign** *He feigned injury to get a medical certificate.*

cause an injury **cause, inflict** *Fireworks can inflict terrible injuries.*

deal with an injury **overcome, treat** *He may play this weekend after overcoming an ankle injury.*

make an injury worse **aggravate, exacerbate** *Do not attempt to move them: this could exacerbate the injuries.*

avoid or reduce injury **avoid, escape, prevent, reduce** *Several men escaped injury in the explosion.* • *Cycle helmets may reduce head injury by up to 80 per cent.*

N+v happen **happen, occur** *Don't continue to exercise if an injury occurs.*

be a result of **arise from, result from** *We will not pay compensation for any injury, unless it results from our negligence.*

> get better **heal** *Although her physical injuries have healed, the trauma of that day will remain with her for a long time.*

and/or **damage, death, disability, ill-health, illness, loss** *The club shall not be liable for loss, injury or damage resulting from the use of this information.*

injustice N

failure to treat someone fairly; an unfair action or event

adj+N very bad **appalling, blatant, cruel, glaring, grave, gross, monstrous, outrageous, terrible** *This would be a grave injustice.*

> types of injustice **racial, social** *We will continue our fight against all forms of social injustice.*

v+N commit an injustice **commit, inflict, mete out, perpetrate, perpetuate** *Even in modern times, terrible injustices have been perpetrated.*

> work against or correct injustice **challenge, combat, correct, expose, fight, rectify, redress, remedy, right, tackle** *He became well known for exposing injustice and fearlessly criticizing the government.*

> suffer injustice **be a victim of, suffer** *I felt angry that I had been the victim of an injustice.*

innocence N

1 the state of not being guilty of a crime or of doing something wrong

v+N claim someone's innocence **assert, claim, declare, maintain, plead, proclaim, profess, protest** *Although he protests his innocence, he remains a discredited figure.*

> when someone pretends to be innocent **feign** *It is unacceptable for these people to feign innocence and try and shift the blame onto others.*

> prove or decide on someone's innocence **decide on, prove** *He had a good case to prove his innocence.*

and/or **guilt** *It is the job of the court to decide on guilt or innocence.*

2 the state of being like a child, having little experience of the world and trusting other people

adj+N **childish, childlike, naive, playful, sweet, touching, wide-eyed, youthful** *The movie combines childlike innocence with the darker emotions of adulthood.*

N+of **childhood, youth** *His work portrays the innocence of childhood.*

n+of+N state or appearance **air, look, state** *There has always been an air of innocence about the girl – that's her charm.*

> loss **loss** *The theme of the book is treachery and the loss of innocence.*

> If you do something *in all innocence*, you do it without intending to upset or harm someone: *I asked him about his wife in all innocence.*

innocent ADJ

1 not guilty of a crime, or of doing something wrong

- adv+**ADJ completely, entirely, totally, wholly** *He was completely innocent of the charge.*
- **ADJ**+n person harmed **bystander, citizen, civilian, passer-by, victim** *They were the innocent victims of terrorist separatists.*
- ▶ animal **animal, creature** *The production of fur coats is not a reason to kill an innocent creature.*
- v+**ADJ be, be declared, be found, be presumed, be proven/proved** *He was declared innocent of any crimes by the court.* • *The defendant is presumed innocent until proven guilty.*

2 not intended to harm or upset anyone

- adv+**ADJ** seeming **apparently, ostensibly, seemingly** *It was a seemingly innocent question.*
- ▶ completely **completely, entirely, perfectly, quite, totally** *They were probably quite innocent stories.*

innovation N

1 a new idea, method, machine etc

- adj+**N** new or different **cutting-edge, exciting, groundbreaking, the latest, radical, recent** *Once in a lifetime we see groundbreaking innovations such as these.*
- ▶ important **exciting, major, outstanding** *Find out about a range of exciting innovations.*
- ▶ in a particular area **artistic, educational, methodological, scientific, technical** *They earned £300,000 through a company that made money out of scientific innovations from the university.*
- v+**N introduce, showcase** *The company will be showcasing the latest innovations during the event.*

2 the invention or use of new ideas, methods, equipment etc

- adj+**N** types of innovation **artistic, educational, industrial, methodological, organizational, scientific, technical, technological** *These organisations foster technological innovation in healthcare.*
- ▶ happening quickly or without stopping **constant, continual, continued, continuous, rapid** *The 19th century was a time of rapid innovation and change in Britain.*
- v+**N** encourage innovation **be committed to, drive, embrace, encourage, facilitate, foster, invest in, nurture, promote, reward, spur, stimulate, support** *The funding has driven innovation.*
- ▶ stop innovation **discourage, inhibit, stifle** *Our aim is not to stifle innovation.*
- and/or **creativity, efficiency, enterprise, entrepreneurship, excellence, flexibility, imagination, improvement, invention, research** *Creativity and innovation are at the heart of a successful business.*

innovative ADJ

new, original, and advanced

- adv+**ADJ** in a particular way **technically, technologically** *We pride ourselves on providing technically innovative engineering solutions.*
- ▶ very **extremely, genuinely, highly, strikingly, truly, wonderfully** *This is truly innovative music.*
- **ADJ**+n method or use **approach, method, methodology, practice, technique, technology, use, way** *His innovative techniques made him a leader in his field.* • *They won an award for the innovative use of IT in schools.*
- ▶ project or course **campaign, course, initiative, programme, project, research, scheme, strategy, work** *You will be working on innovative projects, breaking new ground and sharing your learning with others.*
- ▶ idea or solution **concept, design, idea, solution, strategy, thinking** *We deliver cost-effective, innovative solutions founded on technical competency.*
- ▶ product or tool **device, product, tool** *The company has quickly developed a reputation for its innovative products.*
- ▶ feature **aspect, feature** *The new software has many useful and innovative features.*
- ▶ person **designer, thinker, writer** *The country's most innovative young designers will show off their creations.*
- and/or **bold, creative, exciting, fresh, groundbreaking, imaginative, new, progressive** *Dubai has developed a reputation for its bold and innovative approach in creating architectural wonders.*

input N

help consisting of ideas, advice, or information

- adj+**N** important **invaluable, significant, valuable** *Additional thanks to Peter and Stephen for their invaluable input to the workshop.*
- ▶ a lot **considerable, significant, substantial** *Responses require a considerable input of time.*
- ▶ not much **minimal** *The students worked on their own and required minimal input from staff.*
- ▶ more or extra **additional** *The report was prepared by the City Council, with additional input from environmental organizations.*
- ▶ types of input **artistic, constructive, creative, parental, technical** *The sessions will encourage creative input from participants.*
- v+**N** ask for or want input **appreciate, need, require, seek, welcome** *We value your feedback and welcome your input into the process.*
- ▶ think input is important **value** *We are committed to continuous improvement of our services and we value your input and contributions.*
- ▶ give input **provide** *Visiting professionals provide specialist input throughout the course.*
- ▶ get input **get, receive** *The Education department is keen to receive input from local businesses.*

inquest N

an official attempt by a court to find the cause of someone's death

- v+**N adjourn, conduct, hold, open** *An inquest into the death was opened and adjourned.*
- **N**+v receive information **be told (that), hear (that)** *The inquest heard that large quantities of alcohol were found in his blood.*
- ▶ decide **conclude (that), record a verdict, return a**

verdict, rule (that) *The inquest recorded an open verdict.*

▶ start **open** *An inquest will open this week.*

inquiry N

1 an official examination of a crime, accident etc

● adj+N **full, independent, internal, judicial, parliamentary, public** *She has been suspended by her employers pending an internal inquiry.* ● *The paper is calling for an independent public inquiry.*

● n+N **government, murder, police** *The organisation has demanded a government inquiry into the matter.*

● v+N ask for an inquiry **ask for, call for, demand** *The parents are right to demand a full inquiry into the death of their son while he was in custody.*

▶ say that an inquiry will take place **announce** *The minister will announce an inquiry into the effect of the ban.*

▶ hold an inquiry **conduct, hold, launch, undertake** *Police have launched a murder inquiry.*

2 a question intended to get information

● adj+N done first or later **further, initial, preliminary, subsequent, urgent** *He is now on police bail pending further inquiries.* ● *Preliminary inquiries into their finances have begun.*

Usage **Inquiry** is often plural in these combinations

▶ general/specific **general, routine, specific** *Please do not address routine inquiries to the Emergency Service.* ● *If you have a specific inquiry, please complete this online form.*

▶ urgent **urgent** *If your inquiry is urgent, you may prefer to phone the helpline.*

▶ asking carefully **confidential, discreet, tentative** *I started making a few tentative inquiries.*

▶ using a particular form of communication **house-to-house, postal, written** *Police carried out house-to-house inquiries.*

● n+N **email, media, press, telephone** *We were instructed not to respond to media inquiries.*

▶ v+N make inquiries **carry out, make** *To make inquiries about meetings, please contact the Administrator.*

▶ send an inquiry to someone **address to, direct to, email, send, submit** *Any inquiries relating to this should be addressed to Computing Services.*

▶ welcome an inquiry **welcome** *The library welcomes inquiries by phone, email or letter.*

▶ receive an inquiry **get** INFORMAL, **receive** *We received a huge number of inquiries.*

▶ have a lot of inquiries **be inundated with** *After the programme the BBC was inundated with inquiries about the case.*

▶ deal with an inquiry **answer, deal with, field, handle, reply to, respond to** *The Council has not responded to our inquiry concerning planning permission.*

insane ADJ

very stupid or crazy; suffering from severe mental illness

● adv+ADJ completely **absolutely, completely, quite, totally, utterly** *Are they totally insane?* ● *The whole idea is utterly insane.*

▶ rather **rather, slightly, somewhat** *It all sounded slightly insane.*

▶ in a particular way **clinically, criminally** *He was in a prison for the criminally insane.*

● v+ADJ **be, be certified, become, be declared, be driven, go, seem, sound** *She knew she must get help or she would go insane.* ● *This probably sounds insane from a common-sense point of view.*

inscription N

writing that is cut into or written on a surface, or a special message written on a page

● v+N have an inscription **bear, carry** *The book bears the inscription 'Printed in Newark in 1778'.*

▶ when an inscription is cut into a surface **be carved, be cut, be engraved, be etched** *There are two inscriptions carved on the plinth.*

▶ read an inscription **decipher, read** *The inscription was deciphered; the stone was a Roman milestone.*

● N+v **commemorate, date from, read, record, refer to, say** *The Greek inscription reads 'The best things are laid up for us in heaven.'*

insecure ADJ

not confident, strong or safe

● adv+ADJ in a particular way **economically, emotionally, financially, socially** *In the current situation, millions of people feel financially insecure.*

▶ very **deeply, desperately, extremely, very** *Mike has become very insecure about his relationship with his wife.*

▶ rather **a little, rather, slightly, somewhat** *It feels a little insecure giving our credit card details electronically.*

● ADJ+n **employment, job, network, status** *This is a tool for secure remote login over insecure networks.*

● v+ADJ **be, become, feel, remain** *Householders feel increasingly insecure, and vulnerable.* ● *Their financial situation remained insecure for many years.*

insecurity N

the feeling of not being confident or safe

● adj+N types of insecurity **economic, emotional, financial, global, national, personal, political, social** *Do you face financial insecurity?*

▶ deep **deep, deep seated, fundamental, inherent** *This desire to project one's own values onto other people masks a deep-seated insecurity.*

▶ great **acute, extreme, great, huge** *There was a feeling of great insecurity among tenants, given their few legal rights.*

▶ felt by a lot of people or all the time **chronic, constant, endemic, general, pervasive, widespread** *The violence and rape continues, and there is widespread insecurity.*

● n+of+N feeling **feeling, sense, sign** *Graffiti, litter and criminal damage heighten communities' feelings of insecurity and fear of crime.*

▶ state **climate, state** *The end result is a society threatened in its core values, a state of social insecurity.*

▶ cause **cause, source** *The causes of insecurity must be tackled rather than simply responding after a problem has arisen.*

▸ sign **sign, symptom** *Mr Hastings said that displaying the flag was a sign of insecurity.*

insight N

the opportunity or ability to notice and understand things; something that you notice or understand

- adj+N interesting **fascinating, interesting, intriguing** *He presents fascinating insights into historical figures.*
▸ different or unusual **fresh, further, new, rare, unique** *This will be a rare insight into a very interesting part of the world.*
▸ showing or allowing great understanding **clear, considerable, deep, detailed, great, penetrating, perceptive, profound, real, remarkable, revealing** *Her article contains some profound insights.*
▸ useful **important, invaluable, powerful, useful, valuable** *The powerful insights gained from this process enable you to make positive changes.*
- v+N get an insight **acquire, gain, get, obtain** *Work experience is an opportunity for young people to gain an insight into the world of work.*
▸ give an insight **afford (sb), give (sb), offer (sb), present, provide, reveal, share, yield** *This survey will provide fresh insights into public attitudes.*
▸ show insight **display, show** *She displays considerable insight.*

insist V

say very firmly that something is true or must happen

- adv+V often or continuously **always, often, repeatedly, resolutely, still** *Officials have repeatedly insisted that such an incident was impossible.* ● *But he still insists it is a bargain.*
▸ in a determined way **adamantly, doggedly, strongly, stubbornly, vehemently** *My mother stubbornly insisted on trying to do everything herself.*
▸ completely **absolutely** *They absolutely insist on it; they won't take no for an answer.*

> People often start a statement with *I must insist...* instead of *I insist...: I must insist that you respect the terms of our arrangement.*

▸ correctly **rightly, wisely** *My teacher rightly insisted I do it.*

inspection N

the process of checking something; an occasion when something is checked officially

- adj+N unexpected **random, unannounced** *There were further unannounced inspections in September.*
▸ happening often or at set times **annual, frequent, periodic, programmed, regular, routine, yearly** *The Commission carries out an annual inspection to monitor standards and premises.*
▸ happening at the beginning/happening later **further, initial, preliminary** *Further inspection revealed that the work had not been carried out to the requested standard.*
▸ done by a particular group **external, independent, joint, public** *The shop must pass a rigorous independent inspection to ensure it meets the high standard of service laid down in the code of practice.*
▸ careful/not careful **careful, close, cursory, detailed, full, quick, rigorous, thorough, visual** *On closer inspection, the damage was not as bad as I had thought.*
▸ when an organization passes an inspection **positive, satisfactory, successful** *Accreditation normally follows two satisfactory site inspections.*
- v+N do an inspection **carry out, conduct, do, make, perform, undertake** *Regular inspections were carried out.* ● *When work is complete, a detailed inspection of the premises will be made.*
▸ have an inspection **undergo** *The vehicle has undergone an inspection.*
▸ pass/fail an inspection **fail, pass** *There was an increase in the number of schools that failed inspections.*
- N+v happen **take place** *He assured her that inspections had taken place and the equipment was safe.*
▸ involve **cover, involve** *The inspection covers hygiene, safety, quality and service.*
▸ show **confirm, highlight, identify, indicate, reveal, show** *The inspection identifies strengths and areas for improvement.* ● *Close inspection revealed fingerprints.*

inspiration N

a sudden feeling of enthusiasm, or a new idea; someone or something that gives you new ideas

- adj+N types of inspiration **artistic, culinary, divine, musical, poetic** *All these features make London a source of artistic inspiration.*
▸ new or original **fresh, original** *We're always open to fresh inspiration.*
▸ great **great, real, true** *He was a real inspiration.* ● *His life-saving actions are a true inspiration to others.*
- v+N get inspiration **derive, draw, find, gain, get, take** *He drew inspiration from classical tales.* ● *She finds inspiration in the shapes and colours of these beautiful objects.*
▸ need or look for inspiration **lack, look for, need, seek, wait for** *I needed some inspiration.*
▸ provide inspiration **act as, provide, serve as** *These experiences provide inspiration for his poetry.*
- N+v **come, strike** *Most of my inspiration comes from traditional stories.* ● *But then inspiration struck!*
- n+of+N **burst, flash, moment, source, spark, vein** *The answer came to me in a flash of inspiration.* ● *There were three main sources of inspiration for her art: the sea, the landscape, and wild flowers.*

inspire V

give people a particular feeling

- V+n **affection, awe, confidence, devotion, envy, loyalty, passion, respect, terror** *It's not hard to see why the band inspires such passion in their fans.*

instance N

an example of something happening

- adj+N many **innumerable, many, multiple, numerous, several** *There have been many instances of Members using Scots words in their debates.*
▸ few **few, rare** *Please note, there are a few instances of strong language.*

▶ first, second etc **first, second** *The second instance is of a more tragic, as well as of a more striking, nature.*

▶ remarkable **remarkable, striking** *We have heard of two rather remarkable instances of this lately.*

▶ particular **particular, specific** *Could the term have another connotation in this particular instance?*

▶ only **only, single, solitary** *We shall confine ourselves to a single instance.*

● v+N be an instance **be, represent** *To be fair, there are instances where the melodies do not vary much from track to track.*

▶ find or record an instance **find, identify, record** *I found several instances of the phrase being quoted on CNN.*

▶ mention an instance **cite, give, mention, provide, report** *I give one instance, typical although extreme.*

● N+of **abuse, brutality, cruelty, fraud, harassment, malpractice, misconduct, misuse, non-compliance, plagiarism, theft, vandalism** *We know that there were instances of fraud under the previous system.* ● *It is necessary to give this warning because instances of plagiarism have been detected in the past.*

instant ADJ
immediate

● adv+ADJ **almost, virtually** *The impact was almost instant.*

● ADJ+n feeling **dislike, gratification, liking, rapport, reaction** *They took an instant dislike to one another.* ● *Most people have been trained to expect instant gratification these days.*

▶ success **bestseller, classic, fame, hit, success** *His novel became an instant success.*

▶ communication **answer, communication, confirmation, feedback, information, message, notification, response** *This program gives you instant feedback.* ● *If you receive emails or instant messages that upset you, just try to ignore them.*

▶ access **access** *The service is designed to provide instant access to colleagues who have similar problems.*

▶ result or solution **answer, result, solution** *There are not always instant solutions to life's problems.*

instinct N
a natural tendency to act in a particular way; a natural ability to know what to do in a particular situation

▶ adj+N basic **base, basic, primal, primeval, primitive** *The primal instinct of self-preservation takes over.*

▶ natural **human, innate, natural** *It's human instinct to be suspicious.*

▶ for protecting or fighting **aggressive, predatory, protective** *He's going to have to curb his aggressive instincts.*

▶ like a mother or father **maternal, motherly, paternal** *She has strong maternal instincts.*

▶ n+N types of instinct **herd, homing, hunting, killer, survival** *This dog still has a very strong hunting instinct.*

▶ basic **animal, gut** *Follow your gut instincts.*

● v+N follow instincts **follow, obey, trust** *You've always told me to trust my instincts.*

▶ not follow instincts **curb, fight, ignore, overcome, suppress** *We should make the effort to overcome our basic animal instincts.*

▶ produce or develop an instinct **arouse, develop, hone** *Her motherly instincts were instantly aroused.* ● *I had already developed a finely-honed instinct for survival.*

● N+v cause someone to do something **drive, guide, lead, prompt, say, tell, warn** *We are all animals, driven by instincts little changed by civilisation.* ● *Let your instincts guide you.* ● *Some instinct warns her not to reveal her feelings.*

▶ start working **kick in, take over** *A survival instinct kicks in.*

instinctive ADJ
done naturally and without thinking

● adv+ADJ **almost, completely, largely, purely** *It was a purely instinctive thing that made me love him.*

● ADJ+n feeling or understanding **dislike, fear, feel, feeling, grasp, hatred, sense, sympathy, understanding** *He had an instinctive feel for what was important and what was not.*

▶ behaviour **ability, behaviour, reaction, response, tendency** *The instinctive response to such a dilemma is to try and find a course of action that doesn't make it worse.*

institution N
a large organization such as a bank, university, or hospital

● adj+N types of institution **academic, charitable, educational, financial, political, private, professional, public, tertiary** *The hospital was founded in 1771 as a charitable institution.*

▶ existing in a particular area **global, local, regional, international, European, British etc** *The University would be the only Scottish institution taking part in the pilot.*

▶ well-known or prestigious **established, important, leading, major, prestigious, well-known** *He received honorary degrees from many prestigious institutions, including Cambridge University.*

● n+N money **banking, finance, lending** *Banks and other lending institutions offer funding solutions.*

▶ education **further education, higher education, research, teaching, university** *This is principally a teaching institution.*

▶ working with others **host, partner** *Scholarships are made on the basis of the host institution providing matching funds.*

▶ government **government, public-sector** *Public-sector institutions are better equipped to absorb the costs.*

● n+with+N **collaboration, connection, cooperation, link, partnership, relationship** *The university maintains research links with similar institutions worldwide.*

instruction N
1 a statement about something that must be done [usually plural]

- adj+N clear **clear, explicit, precise, specific**
Councils were given clear instructions on how to put the proposals into practice.
▶ detailed **comprehensive, detailed, full** *He gave me detailed instructions on what to do in his absence.*
▶ firm **firm, strict** *He is under strict instructions to say nothing.*
▶ given in a particular way **verbal, written** *Keep any verbal instructions short and simple.*
- v+N give instructions **give, issue, leave, send** *He sent instructions to his son to buy the land.*
▶ wait for instructions **await** *I await your instructions.*
▶ receive instructions **get, receive** *Students will receive detailed instructions on how to present their work.*
▶ follow/not follow instructions **act on, comply with, disobey, disregard, follow, obey** *Why didn't you follow my instructions?*

2 information explaining how to do or use something [always plural]

- adj+N clear or easy **clear, easy-to-follow, simple, step-by-step** *Our step-by-step instructions will help you install the software successfully.*
▶ detailed **detailed, full** *Each unit comes with detailed instructions on assembly.*
- v+N give instructions **give, provide** *We provide instructions for use with all our equipment.*
▶ read and follow instructions **follow, read** *Click on the link and then follow the instructions.* • *Always read the instructions before lighting fireworks.*

You can also say that you do something *according to the instructions* or *in accordance with the instructions*: *I assembled the furniture according to the instructions supplied by the manufacturer.*

instrument N
something that is used in order to make something happen

- adj+N financial **economic, financial** *There will be more use of economic instruments such as pricing and taxation.*
▶ legal **legal, legally binding, statutory** *The Treaty is a legally binding instrument.*
▶ effective/not effective **blunt, effective, powerful** *Using criminal law to control human behaviour is using a blunt instrument against a sophisticated problem.* • *Education is probably the most powerful instrument of change that we have.*
- v+as+N **act, be used, function, serve** *In order to serve as an instrument of communication, language must be bound by rules.*

insufficient ADJ
not enough

- adv+ADJ **clearly, grossly, quite, wholly** *He said their plans were 'grossly insufficient'.*
- ADJ+n information **data, evidence** *There is insufficient evidence to draw clear conclusions.*
▶ care **attention, emphasis** *Insufficient attention is paid to what is going on outside this academic discipline.*

▶ space **space** *If there is insufficient space, please continue on a separate sheet.*
▶ computer memory **memory, RAM** *Applications work slowly or keep saying 'insufficient memory'. What's wrong?*
▶ resources **funding, funds, resources, supply** *Insufficient resources were made available to facilitate this process.*
- v+ADJ **be, become, be considered, be deemed, prove, remain** *The firm's assets proved insufficient to meet his costs and remuneration.*

insult N
an offensive remark; something that shows a lack of respect

- adj+N **deliberate, the final, gratuitous, grave, gross, personal, racial, racist, the ultimate** *The final insult is that now we, the taxpayers, have to rescue the banks that caused the problem.* • *This is a grave insult to all decent people.*

To add insult to injury is used to talk about an additional problem: *They are treated badly and, to add insult to injury, receive appallingly low wages.*

- v+N shout insults **hurl, shout, throw** *They hurled insults at me.*
▶ when two people or groups insult each other **exchange, trade** *The two politicians used the broadcast to exchange insults.*

Usage *Insult* is usually plural in these combinations.

insulting ADJ
offensive

- adv+ADJ very **deeply, downright, extremely, highly** *They found her behaviour deeply insulting.*
▶ rather **mildly, pretty** INFORMAL**, rather, slightly, vaguely** *Praising a book as a 'quick read' seems to me to be mildly insulting.*
- ADJ+n **behaviour, comments, language, remarks, words** *He admitted abusive and insulting behaviour towards staff.*
- and/or **abusive, aggressive, offensive, rude, threatening** *Material which contains abusive or insulting language will be banned.*

insurance N
an arrangement with a company in which you give them money regularly, and receive money from them if something bad happens

- n+N vehicle **auto, automobile, car** *It is an offence to drive without car insurance.*
▶ travel **holiday, travel** *It is strongly recommended that you take out holiday insurance.*
▶ personal **health, home, household, life** *We could save you up to 25 per cent on your home insurance.*
- v+N have or get insurance **be covered by, buy, get, have, obtain, take out** *The cost of treatment will be covered by your insurance.* • *It is sensible to take out insurance against cancellation.*
▶ make insurance not valid **invalidate** *Failure to disclose a pre-existing medical condition may invalidate your insurance.*
▶ when someone makes a claim **claim on** *When the*

kitchen was flooded, we claimed for the damage on our insurance.

● N+v **cover sb/sth, pay out** *Check if your insurance covers you for legal costs.* ● *Make sure the insurance covers dentist's costs too.* ● *General insurance only pays out when the insured event occurs.*

● N+n arrangement **cover, plan, policy** *You are required to take out insurance cover.*

▶ money **costs, premium, quote** *Insurance premiums have risen by ten per cent this year.*

▶ person or organization **broker, company** *He worked as an insurance broker.*

▶ claim **claim** *Use this form if you need to make an insurance claim.*

insurmountable ADJ
impossible to deal with successfully

● adv+ADJ **almost, apparently, seemingly** *It is a seemingly insurmountable problem.*

● ADJ+n problem **barrier, challenge, difficulty, hurdle, obstacle, problem, task** *This may seem like an insurmountable task to other people.*

● chance of something happening **odds** *He overcame seemingly insurmountable odds to achieve his dream.*

● v+ADJ **appear, be, prove, seem** *You must be prepared to be flexible if the problems prove insurmountable.*

intact ADJ
not harmed, damaged, or lacking any parts

● adv+ADJ to a particular extent **almost, largely, reasonably, relatively, substantially, virtually** *The bridge is still largely intact.*

▶ completely **completely, fully, perfectly** *We are now able to move large trees with the root system almost completely intact.*

▶ still **still** *The buildings had survived, with many of the original walls still intact.*

● v+ADJ **arrive, be, keep sth, leave sth, preserve sth, remain, survive** *The Welsh have preserved intact their language and music.* ● *This unique little church survived intact until 1757.*

intake N
1 the amount of something you eat or drink

● adj+N high or too high **excess, excessive, high** *A high intake of green vegetables is associated with a reduced risk for bowel cancer.*

▶ moderate or adequate **adequate, average, moderate** *Choose a balanced diet and focus on moderate fat intake.*

▶ low or inadequate **inadequate, insufficient, low** *People in poorer households have lower nutritional intakes than people in richer households.*

▶ happening regularly **daily, regular** *A diet that includes regular intake of spices can help maintain resistance to infection.*

▶ types of intake **caloric, calorific, dietary, nutritional** *Which food provides 15 per cent of our daily dietary calcium intake?*

● v+N reduce intake **cut, decrease, limit, lower, moderate, reduce, restrict** *Reducing calorie intake during pregnancy is generally not recommended.*

▶ increase intake **boost** INFORMAL, **double, increase, up** INFORMAL *I've upped my daily fruit intake considerably.*

▶ control or check intake **control, monitor, regulate** *I am taking steps to control my alcohol intake, but I find the thought of not drinking pretty tough.*

▶ exceed intake **exceed** *It is inadvisable to exceed the recommended daily intake.*

2 the number of people accepted by an institution

● adj+N **annual, current, estimated, new** *The MBA International has an annual intake of 75 students.*

● v+N increase intake **boost** INFORMAL, **double, increase** *The Committee advised the Government to increase student intake nationally by 1000 per year.*

▶ reduce intake **cut, reduce** *Both schools were considering reducing their intake for future years.*

integration N
the process of combining things; or of becoming, or allowing someone to become, a full member of society

● adj+N effective or complete **close, complete, effective, seamless, successful** *The judges were particularly impressed by their seamless integration of live and recorded music.*

▶ types of integration **economic, global, political, racial, regional, social**

● v+N encourage or increase integration **accelerate, encourage, enhance, facilitate, foster, improve, increase, promote, support** *This policy encourages integration of research and collaboration across traditional boundaries.*

▶ achieve integration **achieve, allow, bring about, enable, ensure** *This plan should achieve successful integration **between** the two departments.*

▶ prevent integration **hinder, impede** *Central government should ensure that integration is not impeded by factors that lie within its control.*

● N+into **community, economy, society, system** *Membership of the World Trade Organization is a linchpin of our integration into the world economy.*

● n+towards+N **move, progress, step** *They resisted all moves towards further European integration.*

integrity N
1 the quality of always following your moral principles

● adj+N great or complete **absolute, great, high, unimpeachable, unquestionable, the utmost** *Stan is well known to be a person of unimpeachable integrity.*

▶ types of integrity **academic, artistic, editorial, journalistic, moral, personal, professional, scientific** *Courtesy, tolerance and personal integrity are esteemed qualities.*

● v+N have or keep your integrity **have, maintain, retain** *Can he maintain his integrity and still remain silent when this is going on?*

▶ damage someone's integrity **compromise, undermine** *For years, I have argued that this state of affairs compromises our intellectual integrity.*

▶ not have integrity **lack** *Their leaders were all felt to lack integrity.*

▶ respect someone's integrity **respect** *Even those who disagree will respect her integrity.*

▶ question someone's integrity **doubt, question** *I'm not asking you to support me, but I don't think that anyone can question my integrity.*

● and/or **competence, courage, dignity, fairness, honesty, impartiality, openness, probity, professionalism, selflessness, sincerity, uprightness** *Honesty, integrity and professionalism underpin everything that we do.*

2 the quality of being complete or whole

● adj+N **physical, structural, territorial** *The item must also be inspected to ensure its structural integrity.*

● n+N **data, database, document, system** *Pages can be checked on-screen for data integrity and colour matching.*

● v+N keep integrity **ensure, guarantee, maintain, preserve, protect, retain, safeguard** *They took careful steps with the evidence to preserve its integrity.*

▶ damage or threaten integrity **compromise, jeopardize, threaten, undermine, violate** *The defect did not threaten the integrity of the building.*

▶ check integrity **check, verify** *Use this report to verify the integrity of your external links.*

● and/or **accuracy, authenticity, confidentiality, consistency, reliability, security, sovereignty** *This was considered a threat to the country's sovereignty and territorial integrity.*

intellectual ADJ
relating to the ability to think intelligently

● adv+ADJ very or too **highly, overly, too, very** *Seigl, highly intellectual and wealthy, is struggling to come to terms with his background.*

▶ only **merely, purely** *His earlier work tended towards purely intellectual puzzle pictures.*

● ADJ+n good qualities **challenge, curiosity, honesty, integrity** *What do I enjoy most about my job? The intellectual challenge.* ● *An intellectual curiosity and a real desire to learn are also important attributes.*

▶ bad qualities **dishonesty, laziness, snobbery, superiority** *You might accuse me of intellectual snobbery.*

▶ ability **ability, capacity** *The primary purpose is to develop your intellectual capacity.*

▶ something that people do **achievement, pursuit** *He participated in a number of cultural and intellectual pursuits.*

▶ tradition or general situation **climate, life, tradition** *The subject known as 'Cultural Studies' draws on the Marxist intellectual tradition.*

● and/or **aesthetic, artistic, creative, cultural, emotional, moral, physical, political, practical, sensory, social, spiritual** *The social, intellectual, spiritual and emotional needs of the pupils drive our educational agenda.*

intelligence N
1 the ability to understand and think about things

● adj+N low/average/high **above-average,**

average, high, low, superior *Most children with epilepsy are of average intelligence.*

▶ great **considerable, great** *She's a writer of great intelligence and vitality.*

▶ types of intelligence **emotional, human, innate, interpersonal, intrapersonal** *What, if anything, is meant by 'emotional intelligence'?*

● v+N have or show intelligence **possess, show** *Why do human beings possess intelligence so superior to that of our nearest relatives?*

▶ use your intelligence **apply, use** *Try and teach children to use their intelligence.*

▶ insult someone's intelligence **insult, underestimate** *This report insults the intelligence of the public.*

▶ measure someone's intelligence **measure** *IQ or Intelligence Quotient is an attempt to measure intelligence.*

▶ lack intelligence **lack** *He much resembled his father, but lacked his sharp intelligence.*

2 information about secret activity

● v+N get intelligence **collect, gain, gather, obtain, receive** *They had received little intelligence that such an attack would take place.*

▶ provide or share intelligence **disseminate, provide, share** *Russia can give the US a great deal of help by sharing intelligence on terrorist groups.*

● N+n person **agent, analyst, chief, officer, official, operative, source** *The brothers were debriefed by Western intelligence officials.*

▶ organization **agency, community, service** *The intelligence agency says it will pay for information that is valuable to the U.S. government.*

▶ activity **gathering, operations, sharing** *They are providing a valuable source of intelligence gathering.*

intelligent ADJ
good at thinking clearly and quickly

● adv+ADJ very **exceptionally, extremely, fiercely, highly, incredibly, very** *Thinking up something highly intelligent, witty and relevant is a difficult thing to do.*

▶ fairly **fairly, moderately, quite, reasonably** *Some of the people who contact us seem reasonably intelligent and articulate.*

▶ with regard to feelings **emotionally** *Happiness requires emotionally intelligent attitudes and behaviour.*

● ADJ+n living being **animal, being, creature, layman, man, person, woman** *Nicely written for the intelligent layman, this is a good all-round introduction to what stone circles are all about.*

▶ machine **device, machine, robot, system** *When intelligent robots are sent into hazardous situations, fewer human lives are put at risk.*

● and/or **bright, creative, funny, informed, perceptive, sensitive, thoughtful, witty** *He struck me as an intelligent and thoughtful person.*

intelligible ADJ
clear or simple enough to understand

● adv+ADJ completely **fully, perfectly** *Her speech is not perfect, but she is perfectly intelligible.*

▶ hardly **barely, scarcely** *The Latin text is scarcely intelligible.*
▶ easily **easily, readily** *The discussion will be readily intelligible to a broad readership.*
▶ when two people or groups can understand each other **mutually** *Swedish is closely related to, and often mutually intelligible with, Danish and Norwegian.*

● ADJ+n **account, explanation, language, sentence, speech, word** *The language is intelligible even to a child.*

● v+ADJ **be, become, make sth, render sth** *His statement only becomes intelligible when we acknowledge that he is using irony.* ● *The EU can be made to work, and its workings can be made intelligible.*

intense ADJ
very great or extreme; done with a lot of effort or attention

● adv+ADJ **very extraordinarily, extremely, incredibly, really, so, too, very** *Extraordinarily intense flavours are found in every dish.*
▶ rather **fairly, pretty INFORMAL, quite, rather** *The sun can be quite intense and you should take care to drink plenty of fluids.*
● especially **particularly** *The main focus of the meeting was on the drug industry, which is under particularly intense scrutiny at the moment.*

● ADJ+n physical sensation **aroma, cold, flavour, heat, pain** *We have cooler springs and less intense heat during the summer.*
▶ feelings **desire, dislike, emotion, excitement, feeling, longing** *Don't feel embarrassed about crying, as it helps when you release these intense emotions.*
▶ when something is considered or discussed **debate, scrutiny, speculation** *The bank was subject of intense speculation yesterday, with analysts suggesting it would be nationalized.*
▶ when someone is thinking hard **concentration** *This work demands intense concentration and it is very tiring.*
▶ pressure **pressure** *Ministries will now come under intense pressure to change the law.*
▶ fighting **bombardment, fighting** *The Allies attacked under cover of an intense bombardment.*
▶ competition **competition, rivalry** *Intense competition ensures that only a few actors reach star billing.*

● v+ADJ **be, become, get, grow, remain** *The pressure got more intense in the second year of the course.*

intensify V
become or make something greater, stronger, or more extreme

● adv+V **dramatically, greatly, sharply** *First of all, exploitation of the colonies will become greatly intensified.*
▶ V+n activity **activity, campaign, competition, cooperation, effort, pressure** *We agreed to increase and intensify our efforts in the security area.*
▶ conflict **battle, conflict, crackdown, offensive, struggle, violence** *He announced his intention to intensify the conflict.*

● n+V activity **competition, fighting, pressure** *From 1985 to 1987, fighting intensified, with heavy casualties.*
▶ physical sensation **heat, pain** *As the heat intensified, the trucks became like ovens.*

intensive ADJ
1 involving a lot of effort, energy, or attention

● adv+ADJ **very extremely, highly, particularly, really, very** *Listening to a foreign language is a very intensive and demanding activity.*
▶ rather **fairly, pretty INFORMAL, quite, rather** *I presented my Interim Report this morning and we had a fairly intensive discussion.*
● ADJ+n study or training **course, programme, study, training, tuition** *Many postgraduate courses are very intensive and can be extremely hard work.*
▶ treatment or care **care, chemotherapy, intervention, physiotherapy, support, therapy, treatment** *Having undergone months of intensive chemotherapy, Mollie felt weak and depressed.*
▶ attempt **effort** *The press generally praised the intensive efforts on the part of the government to secure the hostages' freedom.*
▶ use **use** *There is still little experience of the intensive use of Information Technology in the ordinary classroom.*

2 producing as much food as possible

● ADJ+n **agriculture, cultivation, farming, grazing, methods, production, rearing** *The book is about social injustice as well as intensive farming.* ● *Many health scares have been linked to intensive farming methods.*

intention N
a plan in your mind to do something

● adj+N good **the best of, good, honourable, noble, peaceful** *I know you had the best of intentions, but you should have consulted me first.* ● *She said that everything she had done had been done with good intentions.*
▶ bad **bad, evil, murderous** *Euthanasia of any form would inevitably be corrupted by those with evil intentions.*

> **Usage** *Intention* is usually plural in the *adj+N* combinations shown above: *You can only talk of sin when a person's intentions are bad.*

▶ stated or clear **avowed, clear, conscious, deliberate, express, stated** *The stated intention of the changes is to deliver improved services for patients.*

> If someone does not intend to do something, you can say that they *do not have the slightest intention of* doing it: *He was an armchair rebel and had not the slightest intention of going to jail.*

▶ real **real, true** *By the time Rick realised Tony's real intentions it was too late.*
▶ first **original** *The original intention had been to climb Helvellyn as well, but I decided to cut the route short.*
▶ only **sole** *This was done with the sole intention of causing controversy.*

● v+N have an intention **have** *In the future I have every intention of aiming higher.*

You can say that you **have no intention of doing** something to emphasize that you do not intend to do it: *We have no intention whatsoever of placing restrictions on the sports of angling and shooting.*

▶ state an intention **announce, communicate, declare, express, indicate, signal, state** *She has indicated her intention to retire from the Board.*

▶ confirm an intention **confirm, reaffirm, reiterate** *He confirmed his intention to come to Moscow for the event.*

interest N

1 a feeling of wanting to know about something

● adj+N strong **active, avid, considerable, deep, great, keen, passionate, special** *He has a keen interest in sailing and also enjoys fishing.*

▶ lasting a long time **abiding, lifelong, long-standing** *This early introduction to languages laid the foundations of his abiding interest in all languages.*

▶ real **genuine, real** *My real interest in railways dates from a visit to the Bluebell Railway in 1974.*

● v+N have or show interest **express, feel, have, show, take** *Peter was soon making contact with medical men who had an interest in hypnosis.*

▶ create interest **arouse, attract, generate, rekindle, spark, stimulate** *The demonstrations were very well supported and much interest was generated.* ● *Others who had already used the technology said the seminar had rekindled their interest.*

▶ keep interest **keep, maintain, sustain** *It's absolutely essential to maintain the audience's interest throughout your speech.*

▶ lose interest **lose** *I lost interest in music generally for many years.*

● N+v **grow, wane** *His interest in music has waned since he left university.*

● n+of+N **lack, level** *The students' lack of interest made teaching them hard work.*

2 a quality that makes you notice something

● adj+N great **considerable, especial, great, particular, special** *Of great interest to coin collectors is the reign of James II.*

▶ little **little** *Generally, this type of research is of little interest to the average reader.*

▶ when something is interesting in itself **intrinsic** *Students found that the intrinsic interest of the material justifies the work involved in studying it.*

▶ types of interest **archaeological, architectural, historic, historical, local, scientific** *The building is considered of significant historical interest.*

● v+N **be of, have, hold no, lack** *This specific issue will continue to be of interest in Scotland and throughout the UK.* ● *The topic held no interest for me.*

3 something you enjoy doing or learning about

● adj+N main **main, principal** *Ian's main interests are in cultural theory and gender studies.*

▶ wide **broad, wide, wide-ranging** *His scholarship and interests were wide-ranging.*

▶ of a person **personal, sb's own** *Construct an entirely customised itinerary, to suit your own interests and idiosyncrasies.*

▶ in a particular area **leisure, outside, sporting** *It is important to have outside interests apart from your work.*

▶ academic **academic, research, scholarly, specialist, teaching** *The group comprises researchers and scholars with a range of specialist interests.*

4 money charged or paid for lending money

● v+N charge interest **charge** *You will continue to be charged interest during any period of deferment.*

▶ pay interest **pay** *Mostly, the interest is paid without tax being deducted.*

▶ earn interest **earn** *If you save money on deposit with a bank or building society, you will earn interest.*

● N+v **accrue** *Interest accrues on a daily basis from the date of your purchase.*

● N+n **charge, payment, rate, repayment** *The interest payments are exempt from income tax.*

● n+of+N **rate** *What rate of interest will be charged?*

5 an advantage or benefit to someone or something

● adj+N now, or in the future **long-term, short-term** *We have to look after the long-term interests of the college.*

▶ personal **personal, private, selfish, sb's own** *He put his private interests above those of the residents.*

▶ types of interest **commercial, economic, financial, national, political, public** *We reserve the right to publish your views if there is an overriding public interest.*

If something is **in someone's best interests**, it brings an advantage to them: *It's in your best interests to resign now.* If someone has **somebody's (best) interests at heart**, they want to help them: *He claims he has only my best interests at heart.*

● v+N represent or help someone's interests **act in, further, look after, promote, represent, serve** *She claimed to be acting in the interest of the company.* ● *Pressure groups seek to represent the interests of a particular section of society.*

▶ defend someone's interests **defend, protect, safeguard** *They were searching for the best way to defend the interests of the nation.*

interested ADJ

wanting to know about or do something

● adv+ADJ very **deeply, especially, extremely, greatly, intensely, keenly, particularly, passionately, really, very** *I was particularly interested in what she had to say about diabetes and insulin.*

▶ slightly **fairly, mildly, not terribly, vaguely** *I was vaguely interested in what he had to say.*

▶ only **only, simply** *He was only interested in how many of them I could sell for him.*

▶ not at all **not at all, not in the least, not remotely, not the least bit** INFORMAL *The public is not remotely interested in media ethics.*

▶ mainly **chiefly, mainly, primarily, principally** *The services are primarily interested in expanding in ways which fit with their existing business.*

▶ truly **genuinely, seriously, truly** *Please only reply if you are genuinely interested – thanks.*

● v+ADJ **appear, be, become, feel, get, get sb,**

remain, seem, sound *If you are interested in sport, Birmingham has plenty of facilities.* • *We need to get more people interested in taking part.*

interesting ADJ
making you want to know about it

- adv+ADJ very **especially, extremely, genuinely, intensely, particularly, really, terribly** INFORMAL, **very** *Combined degrees can be particularly interesting and challenging for students.*
- ▶ not at all **not remotely, not terribly** INFORMAL, **not very** *There's nothing remotely interesting or original going on in this storyline.*
- ▶ rather or not very **fairly, mildly, moderately, pretty** INFORMAL, **quite, rather, vaguely** *This is his own account of those years, an account I found quite interesting.*
- ▶ because of what it is **intrinsically** *You'll find the novel intrinsically interesting and also important for the light it sheds on the period.*
- ▶ in a particular way **architecturally, historically, philosophically, scientifically, theoretically, visually** *There were lots of large, modern office blocks and they really were very architecturally interesting.*
- v+ADJ **be, become, find sb/sth, look, make sth, prove, seem, sound** *You don't want to spend a year on something that you don't find at all interesting.* • *The answers to the questionnaire proved very interesting.*
- and/or useful **enlightening, informative, instructive, relevant, useful, worthwhile** *We hope that you will visit the site and find the project interesting and informative.*
- enjoyable **amusing, engaging, enjoyable, entertaining, rewarding** *It was interesting and amusing to hear his experiences.*
- ▶ exciting **challenging, exciting, lively, stimulating, thought-provoking** *I'd describe the working environment here as continually interesting and challenging.*

interminable ADJ
continuing for a long time in a boring way

- adv+ADJ **seemingly** *Their war service was a seemingly interminable succession of physically and mentally punishing patrols.*
- ADJ+n wait **delay, wait** *After an interminable wait instructions were given to board a train which had just steamed alongside our ship.*
- discussion **argument, debate, discussion** *I never wanted to get involved in interminable arguments.*
- meeting **meeting** *I wasn't sorry not to have to attend any more of those interminable meetings when I retired.*
- v+ADJ **be, seem** *The journey through the night seemed interminable.*

the Internet N
the computer system that allows people across the world to exchange information

- adj+N **broadband, high-speed, mobile, wireless** *All students must have access to a computer which has broadband Internet.*
- v+N have or use the Internet **access, be**

connected to, be linked to, connect to, go on, link to, use *There is no question that consumers want to access the Internet at high speeds.*
- ▶ search the Internet **explore, scour, search, surf, trawl** *I surf the Internet and do most of my work online.*
- ▶ regulate the Internet **censor, police, regulate** *The government uses filtering systems to police and censor the Internet.*
- v+on+N **advertise, buy, find, look, post, publish, search, sell, shop** *The results will be published on the Internet.* • *I enjoy shopping on the Internet.*
- v+via/over+N **access, broadcast, communicate, deliver, order, purchase, sell, send** *The course is delivered via the Internet, using a Virtual Learning Environment.* • *Most of our products are sold over the Internet.*

interpret V
understand or explain something

- adv+V correctly/wrongly **accurately, correctly, incorrectly, mistakenly, properly, rightly, wrongly** *They had not interpreted the evidence correctly.*
- ▶ broadly/narrowly **broadly, flexibly, liberally, literally, loosely, narrowly, restrictively, strictly, widely** *The term 'language' is interpreted broadly to include all human communication.*
- ▶ cautiously **carefully, cautiously, tentatively** *The results of this analysis should be cautiously interpreted.*
- ▶ by a lot of people **widely** *This decision was widely interpreted as an admission of failure on the government's part.*
- ▶ in different ways **variously** *The name of the village has been variously interpreted.*

> Usage ***Interpret*** is usually passive in all of the ***adv+V*** combinations shown above: *The results need to be carefully interpreted.* With ***widely*** and ***various***, interpret is always passive.

- V+n information **data, evidence, findings, information, results** *There is concern that current requirements lead to a rather artificial approach to analysing and interpreting data.*
- ▶ writing **brief, passage, scripture, text** *Only the Pope or the top hierarchy could interpret the holy scriptures.*
- ▶ symbols or dreams **dream, parable, prophecy, symbol** *For many years, scholars interpreted these symbols as letters in Phoenician script.*
- ▶ law **law, legislation** *It is for the courts to interpret law, not the regulator.*
- ▶ visual information **chart, diagram, graph** *An added bonus is that pupils develop their ability to interpret graphs in a meaningful context.*

interpretation N
an explanation of the meaning of something

- adj+N wide/narrow **broad, liberal, literal, narrow, selective, strict** *Some religious groups argue for a literal interpretation of the Bible.*
- ▶ correct/wrong **accurate, authoritative, correct, false, incorrect, valid, wrong** *Will you confirm whether my interpretation is more correct than the one that you offered?*

▶ possible **plausible, possible** *We put forward possible interpretations of these results.*
▶ personal **sb's own, subjective** *His reading is based on a highly subjective interpretation.*
▶ different **alternative, conflicting, contradictory, different, differing, divergent** *The tradition of law is an ongoing process of conflicting interpretations.*

If something is *open to interpretation*, its intended meaning is not clear and people may have different opinions about it: *Beckett's play is open to various interpretations.*

● v+N give an interpretation **give, offer, present, propose, provide, suggest** *The advice and interpretation given is useful, wise and appropriate.*
▶ accept an interpretation **accept** *Sometimes their new interpretations were readily accepted by their peers.*
▶ reject an interpretation **challenge, dispute, reject** *The doctors are challenging the strict interpretations of the guidelines.*
▶ support an interpretation **confirm, favour, support** *The underlying Greek text does not support this interpretation.*
▶ need interpretation **need, require** *Data requires interpretation before it becomes 'information'.*
▶ when something is difficult to interpret **defy, resist** *There are some place names which defy interpretation.*
▶ make an interpretation possible **allow** *Satellite images allow the interpretation of habitats, population and industry.*

● n+of+N **matter, method, problem, process, question, range, variety** *The meaning of race is a matter of social interpretation, not a fact of biology or genetics.* ● *These facts are open to a variety of interpretations.*

interrupt V
stop someone speaking or make something stop for a time

● adv+V often/not often **constantly, continually, frequently, occasionally, periodically, repeatedly** *According to one observer, he was unable to answer without being constantly interrupted.*
▶ for a short time **briefly, temporarily** *A mini stroke occurs when the blood supply is briefly interrupted.*
▶ suddenly or violently **abruptly, rudely, suddenly** *When I was 11, our quiet lives were rudely interrupted by World War II.*

● V+n **career, conversation, flow, proceedings, sleep, speech, studies, supply, thoughts** *All this running around interrupts the flow of the game.*

interruption N
something that stops someone speaking or something happening for a time

● adj+N frequent/not frequent **constant, frequent, occasional** *They had difficulty working in that office because of frequent interruptions.*
▶ short or unimportant **brief, minimal, minor, short, slight, temporary** *62 Roper Road was to be my home, with a few short interruptions, for nine years.*
▶ planned/not planned **planned, unplanned, unscheduled** *IT services are subject to unplanned interruption from time to time.*

▶ sudden or rude **rude, sudden, unexpected** *There is a sudden rude interruption as the narrator dashes on stage and yells to the speaker.*

● v+N cause interruption **cause** *There is considerable engineering work that may cause interruption in your area.*
▶ avoid or reduce interruptions **avoid, minimize, prevent, reduce** *Steps should be taken to avoid unnecessary interruptions to consultations.*
▶ experience interruption **experience, suffer, tolerate** *Users will not experience any interruption in service.*
▶ ignore interruptions **ignore** *Ignoring the interruption, he continued.*

intervene V
become involved in a situation, in order to change it

● adv+V directly **actively, directly, personally, positively** *Will the Prime Minister personally intervene to defend our grammar schools?*
▶ quickly **early, immediately, promptly, quickly** *It is important to intervene early before problems become serious.*
▶ effectively **decisively, effectively, successfully** *We will intervene decisively and effectively where councils are failing local people.*
▶ in a particular way **militarily, physically** *There is already a general reluctance amongst states to intervene militarily.*

● V+in a process **affairs, case, debate, matter, proceedings, process, situation** *US administrations keep finding new excuses for intervening in Latin American affairs.*
▶ a fight **conflict, dispute, fight, row, struggle, war** *He intervened in a dispute which took place in a local shop.*

intervention N
when someone becomes involved in something

● adj+N early **early, timely** *With early intervention, disabled children's lives can be transformed.*
▶ not much **minimal** *The children work on their own or in groups, with minimal intervention from teachers.*
▶ effective **effective, targeted** *To be effective, interventions need to be customer-oriented.*
▶ medical **medical, pharmacological, surgical, therapeutic** *When other treatments have failed, surgical intervention is possible.*
▶ by an army or government **armed, government, humanitarian, military, state** *Government intervention in the media varies across countries.*
▶ human/not human **divine, human, manual** *Service has been patchy where the failure of IT has meant reliance on human intervention.* ● *Mostly, this process will happen automatically, but sometimes manual intervention is required.*

● v+N need or ask for intervention **call for, necessitate, need, require** *Within a couple of years she felt that further surgical intervention was required.*
▶ justify intervention **justify, warrant** *The problem is not serious enough to warrant intervention.*

interview N
a formal meeting in which someone asks another person questions

- adj+N for research **face-to-face, follow-up, in-depth, one-on-one, one-to-one, qualitative, semi-structured, structured, unstructured** *Data was collected using semi-structured interviews and questionnaires.*
- ▶ for the public **candid, celebrity, exclusive, live, revealing** *In an exclusive interview **with** our paper, Daniel admitted that he had taken drugs.*
- ▶ for a job **job** *Hopefully, your job interviews will all go well.*
- ▶ using a particular medium **broadcast, newspaper, phone, radio, telephone, television, TV** *After you have submitted the application form there will be a telephone interview.*
- ▶ formal/informal **formal, informal** *Entry to this course is through an informal interview **with** the course manager.*
- ▶ with the police **police** *Police interviews **with** detainees should not be interrupted to facilitate visits.*

- v+N conduct an interview **carry out, conduct, do, hold** *In the majority of cases the interviews were conducted in the respondent's home.*
- ask for or arrange an interview **arrange, request** *The newspaper requested an interview **with** the minister.*
- give an interview **do, give, grant** *Bonney loves giving interviews and is exuberant and bubbly.*
- get or attend a job interview **attend, be called for, be invited for, be selected for, be shortlisted for, come for, go for, have** *Interested applicants are asked to attend an interview.*

- N+n material **data, transcript** *Actual quotations from interview transcripts are given in italics.*
- process **preparation, process, question, skills, techniques, tips** *What is the application and interview process?*
- recording of interview **clips, footage, snippets** *The clips were punctuated by interview footage of those who had been affected by the disaster.*

- n+from+N **excerpt, extract** *This is an excerpt from a 2008 interview **with** the party leader.*

intimidating ADJ
making you feel nervous or frightened

- adv+ADJ rather **a little, pretty INFORMAL, quite, rather, slightly, somewhat** *The sound of splintering glass was quite intimidating.*
- very **extremely, very** *Large fairs can be very intimidating.*

- ADJ+n place or situation **atmosphere, environment, experience, place, process, prospect, situation** *Being interviewed by a panel of five people was an intimidating prospect.*
- a person's behaviour **behaviour, manner, presence** *Even as a 16-year-old he had an intimidating physical presence.*

- and/or **abusive, aggressive, frightening, hostile, malicious, offensive, threatening, violent** *Intimidating or abusive behaviour just won't be tolerated.*

intolerable ADJ
impossible to bear or deal with

- adv+ADJ completely **absolutely, completely, quite, simply** *I found this situation quite intolerable.*
- ▶ almost **almost, increasingly** *I meet people daily who find facets of their lives almost intolerable.*

- ADJ+n situation **burden, conditions, pressure, strain, stress** *Both the Prison and Probation Services are under near intolerable pressure.*
- ▶ behaviour **behaviour, interference, nuisance** *This sort of behaviour is intolerable.*
- ▶ suffering **pain, suffering** *His face expressed intolerable suffering.*
- ▶ level **level** *Local campaigners claim the new road will create intolerable noise levels.*

- v+ADJ **be, become, find sth, make sth, prove, seem** *The situation is becoming intolerable for the residents.* • *Thousands of young women face challenges every day that most of us would find intolerable.*

intolerance N
the refusal to accept behaviour or beliefs that are different from your own

- adj+N types of intolerance **racial, religious** *Modern audiences may find the issues of religious intolerance and xenophobia rather close to home.*
- ▶ increasing **growing, increasing** *These developments are taking place in the context of growing intolerance and racism in Europe.*

- v+N cause intolerance **breed, cause** *These fears breed intolerance, discrimination and racism.*
- ▶ show intolerance **display, show** *He despaired that such a traditionally liberal country would show such intolerance of different points of view.*

- and/or feelings **bigotry, fanaticism, hatred, ignorance, prejudice, racism, xenophobia** *That kind of bigotry and intolerance **towards** minorities ought to be unacceptable.*
- ▶ acts **discrimination, persecution, violence** *Early modern Europe was noted for its religious intolerance, persecution and division.*

intricate ADJ
very detailed in design or structure; very complicated

- adv+ADJ very **amazingly, beautifully, extremely, highly, incredibly, very** *China's craftsmen create incredibly intricate ornaments and jewellery from jade.*
- ▶ rather **fairly, quite, rather** *The walls are covered with designs and patterns, many quite intricate.*

- ADJ+n object **carving, embroidery, tapestry** *The variety of materials and themes for these intricate carvings is astonishing.*
- ▶ pattern **decoration, design, detail, mosaic, pattern, shape** *You do not have the skill to paint the intricate designs.*
- ▶ structure **maze, network, web** *Once the heart of the old fishing town, Brighton's historic quarter is an intricate maze of twisting alleyways.*
- ▶ in music **harmony, melody, rhythm** *The intricate melodies and interwoven harmonies will repay careful and repeated attention.*

▶ plot **plot** *This is high-quality writing: the plot is intricate but coherent, and the characterization is excellent.*

intriguing ADJ
very interesting, and often strange or mysterious

● adv+ADJ very **endlessly, especially, highly, particularly, very, wonderfully** *Afghanistan is an amazing and endlessly intriguing place.*
▶ rather **quite, rather** *On paper, the character twists that emerge sound quite intriguing.*
▶ truly **certainly, genuinely, truly** *For adventurous diners, it offers some genuinely intriguing dishes.*
▶ equally **equally** *Act II of Richard and Anne's story is as intriguing and heartbreaking as the first.*

● ADJ+n mixture **blend, combination, mix, mixture** *Hobart itself is an intriguing blend of heritage and lifestyle, scenery and culture.*
▶ idea or possibility **concept, idea, possibility, premise, prospect** *This apparently simple provision raises a number of intriguing possibilities.*
▶ story **character, plot, story, tale, title** *The characters are developed and engaging, the plot is intriguing.*
▶ look at something **glimpse, insight** *The biography offers an intriguing insight into his early life.*
▶ mystery **mystery, puzzle, question** *The identity of the young woman remains an intriguing mystery.*

● v+ADJ be, **become, find sth, look, remain, seem, sound** *What aspects of Japanese culture do you find most intriguing?* ● *That sounds intriguing. Tell me more!*

introduce V
bring something into existence or start to use something

● adv+V first **first, initially, originally** *When civil partnerships were first introduced, many people tended to regard them as just a formality.*
▶ slowly **gradually, progressively** *Once we have discovered if the child can see at all, we can gradually introduce different stimuli.*
▶ successfully **successfully** *The right of access was successfully introduced two months ahead of target.*
▶ accidentally/not accidentally **accidentally, deliberately, inadvertently** *The water hyacinth was accidentally introduced to Lake Victoria in 1988.*

● V+n law or rule **bill, legislation, measure, reform, regulation** *There was a firm belief that the new Government would introduce legislation against age discrimination.*
▶ idea or subject **concept, idea, notion, topic** *Ideas and concepts introduced to you in your first year will be developed later in the course.*
▶ system or policy **change, initiative, method, policy, procedure, scheme, system** *We introduced the mentoring system into the college last year.*

introduction N
1 the process of bringing something into existence or use for the first time

● adj+N gradual **gradual, phased** *He is reassured by the idea of a gradual introduction.*
▶ recent **recent** *Its recent introduction has raised questions about whether the drug is effective and cost-effective.*

▶ in many places **widespread** *Pilot schemes are essential before widespread introduction.*

● v+N bring about the introduction of something **announce, facilitate, oversee, pioneer, propose** *The university has pioneered the introduction of the four-day timetable.*
▶ delay or advance the introduction of something **accelerate, bring forward, delay, postpone** *The government decided to postpone the introduction of the system.*
▶ oppose or support the introduction of something **oppose, prevent, support, welcome, would like to see** *I oppose the introduction of the euro on principle.*
▶ when something is introduced **herald, see** *That year saw the introduction of free bus passes for pensioners.*

2 a first opportunity to learn or experience something

● adj+N short or simple **accessible, basic, brief, concise, general, gentle, practical, quick** *The Ibsen workshop was a brief introduction to his work.*
▶ good **excellent, good, ideal, informative, perfect, readable, sound, useful** *This is an easy route, and an excellent introduction to the area.*
▶ complete **comprehensive, thorough** *The Handbook is a comprehensive introduction to health and safety.*
▶ expressing opinions **critical** *The book is called The New Media: a critical introduction.*

● v+N **give, include, offer, provide** *This book provides a sound introduction to economics, organization and management.*

intruder N
someone who should not be in a place

● adj+N unwanted **uninvited, unwanted, unwelcome** *The spiny branches are a useful deterrent against unwanted intruders.*
▶ possible **possible, potential, would-be** *The tannoy system has been effectively employed to scare off would-be intruders.*
▶ with particular characteristics **armed, malicious, masked** *Along the frontier, soldiers killed 34 armed intruders.*

● v+N keep intruders away **deter, keep out, repel, scare off, stop** *The presence of effective security measures strongly deters intruders.*
▶ find or catch intruders **catch, confront, detect, discover, disturb, identify, tackle** *They believe that the dog's barking disturbed the intruders.*

intrusion N
someone or something that interrupts; the act of becoming involved in something in a way that is not wanted

● adj+N not wanted or not reasonable **unacceptable, unauthorized, unnecessary, unwanted, unwarranted, unwelcome** *This is a piec of unnecessary intrusion into our national life.*
▶ sudden or violent **sudden, violent** *These films are based upon the sudden intrusion of modern life into a small rural Scottish community.*
▶ types of intrusion **government, media, press** *He says that media intrusion has played a big part in the collapse of the marriage.*

- v+N reduce or avoid intrusion **avoid, minimize, prevent, reduce** *The design places great emphasis on minimizing intrusion **on** the landscape.*
▶ dislike intrusion **resent** *He seemed to resent the intrusion of a human being in such an unfrequented spot.*
▶ notice intrusion **detect** *I have a CCTV system with movement detection to transmit video when an intrusion is detected.*

intuition N
the ability to know or understand things through your feelings

- adj+N **female, feminine, human, sb's own** *Here are some examples to check against your own intuitions.*
- v+N use or develop intuition **develop, follow, rely on, trust, use** *I'm sure it will work out – trust your intuition.*
▶ confirm someone's intuition **confirm** *The results of the survey confirmed our intuitions.*
- N+v **guide, suggest, tell sb** *What is your intuition telling you about this relationship?*
- n+of+N **flash, power** *By some flash of intuition, I knew what it was that he intended.* • *We believe in the power of intuition and common sense.*

intuitive ADJ
based on feelings rather than on facts

- adv+ADJ very **deeply, highly, very** *She was observant, very intuitive and creative.*
▶ completely **completely, entirely, totally** *We can learn about beauty, but the concept itself is entirely intuitive.*
- ADJ+n understanding **ability, feel, grasp, insight, perception, sense, understanding, wisdom** *Most people have an intuitive grasp of the social meaning of genetics.*
▶ approach **approach, way** *What unites many of these bands is an organic, intuitive approach to music making.*

invalid ADJ
not true or legally effective

- adv+ADJ in a particular way **legally, scientifically, statistically, technically** *The marriage was ruled to be legally invalid.*
▶ completely **completely, totally** *If the earthing is faulty, this test should not be performed as the results would be totally invalid.*
- ADJ+n in an election **ballot, vote** *Any system should have live checking for invalid ballots.*
▶ idea **argument, assumption, conclusion** *The premise is true and no doubt comforting; but the conclusion is invalid.*
▶ document **permit** *Inaccurate details may render a permit invalid.*
- v+ADJ **be, become, be considered, be declared, be deemed, be held, be rendered, be ruled** *The vouchers they sent me are invalid!* • *Consequently, the cheque was returned and the 79 votes declared invalid.*

invaluable ADJ
extremely useful

- adv+ADJ very **absolutely, particularly, quite, totally, truly** *British History Online is an absolutely invaluable source of British historic information.*
▶ possibly **often, potentially** *The service is potentially invaluable **to** companies who want to target a particular market.*
- ADJ+n tool **aid, asset, resource, source, tool** *The archive is an invaluable resource for educators.*
▶ help or contribution **addition, advice, assistance, contribution, feedback, guidance, help, input, service, support, tip** *Thank you once again for the invaluable contribution you are making.*
▶ knowledge or understanding **experience, expertise, information, insight, knowledge, skill** *I got an invaluable insight into the workings of an international current affairs magazine.*
▶ opportunity **opportunity** *The Congress offers invaluable networking opportunities.*
▶ document **book, companion, guide, reference, sourcebook** *This book is an invaluable guide to the Stanislavski system.*
- v+ADJ **be, become, find sth, prove** *Here are three books you'll find invaluable.* • *Luckily, I had an old portable microscope, which proved invaluable.*

inventory N
a list giving details of everything in a place

- adj+N full or complete **accurate, complete, comprehensive, detailed, exhaustive, extensive, full, thorough** *Once the leases are signed, a detailed inventory is agreed between the landlord and tenants.*
▶ up-to-date **current, up-to-date** *My job is to keep an up-to-date inventory of all the school's Digital Media equipment.*
- v+N make an inventory **compile, complete, conduct, create, make, prepare, produce, take, undertake** *The executors had to compile an inventory of all of the deceased's possessions.*
▶ keep an inventory **keep, maintain, update** *You need to maintain an inventory of equipment, furniture etc.*

invest V
spend money on something with the aim of making a profit; to use something for a particular purpose

- adv+V a lot **aggressively, heavily, massively, significantly, substantially** *We invest heavily **in** training and talent development.*
▶ carefully **ethically, prudently, strategically, wisely** *Our research demonstrates how crucial it is that these resources are used to invest wisely **for** the future.*
▶ outside your own country **abroad, internationally, offshore, overseas** *More and more Taiwanese businesspeople are investing overseas.*
▶ directly/indirectly **directly, indirectly** *We do not have money to invest directly **in** these ventures, but we can offer support and training.*
▶ using your own money **personally** *All three managers have invested personally **in** the business.*
- V+n money **amount, assets, billions, capital, cash,**

money, **savings, sum** *People are investing huge sums of money* **in** *property.*
▶ time or effort **effort, energy, time** *We have invested considerable energy* **in** *developing good relations with the local community.*

investigate V
try to learn the true facts about something

● adv+V fully or thoroughly **actively, adequately, carefully, extensively, fully, in depth, in detail, properly, rigorously, seriously, systematically, thoroughly, vigorously** *Any suspected case of bacterial contamination must be thoroughly investigated.*
▶ in a fair way **appropriately, formally, impartially, independently** *The External Auditor also has powers to independently investigate fraud and corruption.*
▶ using a particular method **archaeologically, critically, empirically, experimentally, numerically, scientifically** *This study investigated experimentally* **whether** *stress alters food choice during a meal.*
▶ immediately **immediately, promptly, urgently** *Complaints from students should be investigated promptly.*
▶ personally **personally** *He has many years' experience as a detective and has personally investigated over 100 murders.*

● V+n incident or crime **accident, case, crime, death, disappearance, fraud, homicide, incident, matter, miscarriage of justice, murder, robbery** *Kitson says he is willing to cooperate with authorities investigating the incident.*
▶ theory or claim **allegation, claim, complaint, hypothesis** *We investigate complaints about food premises within the Surrey Heath area.*
▶ issue **aspect, issue, phenomenon, problem** *The Government is investigating the issue of deteriorating health amongst older drivers.*
▶ cause **cause** *The body investigates the causes of all serious air accidents.*
▶ possibility **feasibility, possibility, potential** *We are investigating the feasibility of a new network for measuring air pollution.*
▶ effect **effect, impact** *The study investigated the effect of taking aspirin alone or in combination with ibuprofen.*
▶ effectiveness **applicability, effectiveness, efficacy, use** *A randomised controlled trial investigated the effectiveness of the drug in preventing cardiovascular disease.*

investigation N
the process of trying to find out about something

● adj+N full or careful **detailed, full, in-depth, lengthy, painstaking, proper, rigorous, systematic, thorough** *There must be a thorough investigation* **into** *any case where a child is harmed by a parent.*
▶ fair **impartial, independent** *Forensic scientists carry out impartial investigations on behalf of the prosecution or defence.*
▶ official **formal, official** *He wrote to the police requesting that they begin a formal investigation* **into** *the affair.*
▶ internal **internal** *The college launched an internal investigation* **into** *her complaint last year.*

▶ happening now **ongoing, underway** *Police said that the operation was part of an ongoing investigation* **into** *serious and organised crime.* ● *An investigation is underway after an outbreak of botulism which killed 40 cows.*
▶ early **initial, preliminary** *Preliminary investigations indicate that this looks promising.*
▶ later **further, subsequent** *If the doctor feels that your dizziness requires further investigation, she will refer you to the Audiology department.*
▶ types of investigation **archaeological, criminal, empirical, epidemiological, experimental, forensic, laboratory, philosophical, police, radiological, scientific, undercover** *This first phase of the work will include archaeological investigations.*

● n+N **accident, crime, fraud, murder** *The murder investigation must be reopened immediately with a new police team.*

● v+N carry out an investigation **carry out, conduct, continue, pursue, undertake** *The tramway has been closed while the Health and Safety Executive conducts an investigation.*
▶ need or deserve investigation **deserve, merit, need, require, warrant** *This area warrants some serious scientific investigation.*
▶ begin an investigation **begin, commence, initiate, instigate, launch, reopen** *Startling new information on her family's past spurs Anya to launch her own personal investigation.*
▶ finish an investigation **complete, conclude, discontinue** *The advertisement must be withdrawn until an investigation is completed.*
▶ ask for an investigation **call for, commission, demand, order** *The Community Fund ordered an investigation* **into** *the organization's political activities.*
▶ cause an investigation to be started **prompt, trigger** *This information prompted an investigation* **into** *the child's home circumstances.*
▶ be in charge of an investigation **lead, supervise** *Detective Sergeant Steve Parker has been leading the investigation.*
▶ get in the way of an investigation **hamper, prejudice** *I am not at liberty to disclose my reasons because it could prejudice the investigation.*
▶ be the subject of an investigation **be under, undergo** *They were aware of the seriousness of the matter that was under investigation.* ● *All water-pipes, flues, cisterns, and sewers underwent an investigation.*

● N+v show something **conclude, confirm, demonstrate, disclose, discover, establish, find, identify, indicate, prove, reveal, show, suggest, uncover, unearth** *Its investigation had revealed that the fake drug had come from outside the European Union.*
▶ take place **be carried out, continue, proceed, progress, take place** *It would be inappropriate to go into further detail whilst the criminal investigation is continuing.*
▶ begin **begin, commence** *Investigations have begun* **into** *the cause of the fire.*
▶ involve someone or something **concern, focus on, include, involve** *The investigation included detailed inspections inside the tunnel.*

investment N

money spent on something with the aim of making a profit; the process of spending money; something that will give you benefits in the future

- adj+N large **considerable, enormous, heavy, huge, large, large-scale, major, massive, significant, substantial** *They know their company makes a substantial investment in the community.*
- ▶ not very large **minimal, minimum, modest** *The album sold well and soon recovered its modest investment.*
- ▶ risky **risky, speculative** *Fraudsters had promised them lucrative returns on risky investments.*
- ▶ sensible or good **good, productive, profitable, responsible, shrewd, sound, wise, worthwhile** *With a recommended retail price of £180 they are a very worthwhile investment.*
- ▶ public/private **private, private-sector, public** *The government is keen to encourage private investment in the renewal of disadvantaged neighbourhoods.*
- ▶ additional **additional, extra, further, future** *We are putting substantial extra investment into schools.*
- ▶ over a long period **continued, long-term, ongoing, sustained** *The compensation award is needed to fund the basics of life, leaving nothing available for long-term investment.*
- ▶ initial **initial, up-front** *Investors get their initial investment back plus 75 per cent of profits.*
- ▶ types of investment **capital, equity, ethical, financial, housing, infrastructure, property, stockmarket, transport** *Ethical property investment offers the investor a financial, social and environmental return.*

- v+N make an investment **make, put into** *It is better to be aware of possible failure than to make a rash investment.*
- encourage or get investment **attract, boost, encourage, facilitate, promote, secure, stimulate** *China attracts more foreign investment than any country except the United States.* • *It can be difficult for small business to secure investment.*
- discourage investment **deter, discourage** *He says entering the single currency would discourage investment.*
- increase an investment **double, increase** *There was a call for rich countries to double their investments in poor nations.*
- get or pay back what you invested **recoup, recover, repay** *They are convinced that the band has a following and that they stand a good chance of recouping their investment.*
- make the most of an investment **maximize, optimize** *After investing millions in new technology, businesses are looking to maximise their investment.*
- pay for an investment **finance, fund** *There was a discussion on how to appropriately finance property investments.*
- protect an investment **manage, protect, safeguard** *Regular servicing will help maintain your vehicle's value and protect your investment.*
- need or ask for investment **need, require, seek** *The harbour area desperately requires investment.*

invitation N

a request to someone to do something or spend time with you

- adj+N friendly or kind **cordial, gracious, kind, polite, warm** *The letter contained a cordial invitation to stay with his uncle for as long as he wished.*
- ▶ formal **formal, official** *Formal invitations had been sent out to the various ministries and embassies.*
- ▶ open to everyone **general, open** *The BBC placed an open invitation for tenders in the Official Journal of the European Communities.*
- ▶ personal to someone **exclusive, personal, special** *You can only get in by personal invitation.*
- ▶ with no fixed date **long-standing, open, standing** *Will he remind them of our long-standing invitation to the Prime Minister's wife to visit Fairfield hospital?*

- v+N receive an invitation **get, receive** *I received an invitation to the 10th Anniversary Meeting of the Society.*
- ▶ send an invitation **extend, issue, send, send out** *The advertisement extended an invitation to other businesses to join the ever-growing club.*
- ▶ accept an invitation **accept** *Leading figures in the industry have accepted an invitation to address the conference.*
- ▶ refuse an invitation **decline, refuse, reject** *He declined my invitation to join in the discussion.*
- ▶ take back an invitation **cancel, withdraw** *If you cannot attend within this time, we may have to withdraw your invitation.*
- ▶ want an invitation **request, welcome** *We welcome the invitation from the Commission on Environmental Pollution to respond.*

invite V

1 ask someone to do something or spend time with you

- adv+V kindly **cordially, generously, graciously, kindly, respectfully, warmly** *You are cordially invited to attend the 4th International Conference on Advanced Engineering Design.*
- ▶ formally **formally, officially** *Applicants selected will be formally invited to attend an interview.*
- ▶ specially **especially, expressly, particularly, personally, specially, specifically** *We were delighted to welcome the Mayor and his wife along with other specially invited guests.*
- ▶ regularly **annually, frequently, occasionally, often, regularly** *She is regularly invited to contribute to scientific journals.*
- ▶ openly **explicitly, openly** *We openly invite anyone seeking help to contact us.*

2 say that you would like to receive something from someone

- V+n opinions or comments **comments, contributions, feedback, responses, views** *Contributions to the debate are invited from both architects and historians.*
- ▶ suggestions **offers, proposals, suggestions** *Offers over £2000 are invited.*
- ▶ applications **applications** *We invite applications from all members of staff, regardless of where they are based.*
- ▶ academic article or talk **paper** *For the seminar, papers are invited on the following topics:*

involved ADJ

1 affected by, included in, or taking part in something

- adv+ADJ **actively, closely, deeply, directly, fully, heavily, intimately, personally** *Our feedback indicates that the project works best where students are actively involved (ie not just listening).* • *Inaccurate reporting affects not just those directly involved, but also those who read what is written.*

- v+ADJ **be, become, feel, get, remain** *I wish I had got more involved in sport at college.*

2 complicated and difficult to understand

- and/or complicated **complex, complicated, detailed, difficult, intricate** *Management of an event can be a complex and involved task.*

- ▶ long **lengthy, long** *He was in the middle of a long, involved story.*

involvement N

the act of taking part in something; the interest that you feel for something

- adj+N direct **active, close, day-to-day, direct, hands-on, personal** *In psychiatry, getting better involves the patient's active involvement.*

- ▶ when someone's feelings are involved **emotional** *She learned to avoid emotional involvement with the children who passed through her care.*

- ▶ continuing for some time **continued, continuing, long-standing, ongoing, sustained** *The company's reputation was being damaged by his continued involvement.*

- ▶ real or effective **effective, meaningful, significant** *There should be meaningful involvement by all those with an interest in the future development of the area.*

- ▶ great or increased **extensive, full, greater, increased, increasing** *My increased involvement in the running of the club took up all my spare time.*

- ▶ little **minimal** *The Government takes a laissez-faire approach to offshore business, and its involvement is minimal.*

- ▶ not proved **alleged** *The charges relate to his alleged involvement in an illegal sports betting enterprise.*

- v+N encourage involvement **encourage, ensure, facilitate, foster, maximize, promote, secure, seek, stimulate, strengthen, support, value, welcome** *The Regeneration Team encourages community involvement in its projects.*

- ▶ increase involvement **deepen, enhance, extend, improve, increase, widen** *The University plans to deepen its involvement in the life of the city.*

- ▶ reduce or stop involvement **avoid, cease, limit, preclude** *Certain definitions of God and religion may preclude the involvement of those of a different faith.*

- ▶ continue involvement **continue, maintain** *He expects to continue his involvement with the work of the Crisis Centre in Bristol.*

- ▶ admit involvement **admit, confirm** *A 34-year-old man has admitted his involvement in a worldwide software counterfeiting scam.*

- ▶ deny involvement **deny** *When later questioned by police, he denied any involvement in the accident.*

irony N

a funny situation in which something is the opposite of what is intended or expected; a form of humour in which words are used to express the opposite of what they really mean

- adj+N sad **bitter, cruel, grim, poignant, sad, savage, terrible, tragic** *It is a bitter irony that James was able to leave the country unhindered by the secret police – only to be shot and killed weeks later.*

- ▶ pleasing or amusing **bittersweet, comic, delicious, delightful, nice, wry** *By a delicious irony, it was his own comments that were used to condemn him.*

- ▶ great or greatest **deep, final, great, profound, supreme, ultimate** *It is a great irony that he himself is the commissioner responsible for rooting out corruption.*

- ▶ slight **certain, gentle, subtle** *There is a certain irony to a web-based project promoting an Internet-free day.*

- ▶ expressed strongly **heavy** *'You'll no doubt want to congratulate me,' she said with heavy irony.*

- ▶ strange **curious, strange** *One of the strange ironies of life is that while you need determination to succeed, too much determination leads to failure.*

- ▶ not deliberate **unintended, unintentional** *The film's unintentional irony is that we have to believe that a 40-year-old and a 29-year-old are the same age.*

- ▶ part of something **inescapable, inherent** *The inescapable irony is that the US desperately needs to revitalize the democratic process at home.*

- n+of+N **hint, touch, trace** *'Perfect technique,' he commented, without a hint of irony.*

irrational ADJ

done or happening without sensible reasons

- adv+ADJ apparently **apparently, seemingly** *Fear attaches itself to new technology for seemingly irrational reasons.*

- ▶ completely or very **completely, deeply, entirely, highly, quite, totally, utterly, wholly** *Joining the Euro now would be completely irrational.*

- ▶ basically **essentially, fundamentally** *Most hatred is essentially irrational and based on ignorance.*

- and/or not reasonable or logical **absurd, illogical, perverse, stupid, superstitious, unreasonable, unscientific** *To apply the same rules to all countries, however different, is illogical and irrational.*

- ▶ not fair **arbitrary, unfair, unjust** *Penalising them in this way is irrational and unjust.*

- ▶ bad, cruel, or violent **destructive, immoral, vindictive, violent** *The government took us into a war that was illegal, immoral and irrational.*

- ▶ not controlled **chaotic, emotional, uncontrollable, wild** *Advertising tries to exploit the emotional and irrational drives of young children.*

- ▶ hard to explain or predict **inexplicable, unpredictable** *He was prone to irrational and unpredictable behaviour.*

irreconcilable ADJ

so opposed that agreement is impossible

- adv+ADJ apparently **apparently, seemingly** *The problem is that they must now do two apparently irreconcilable things at once.*

- ▶ totally **totally, utterly** *Those tests were totally*

*irreconcilable **with** their claims to be committed to nuclear disarmament.*

- ADJ+n **conflict, contradiction, differences, disagreement** *She felt that there were irreconcilable differences between her public and her private life.*

irrelevant ADJ
not important or not relevant

- adv+ADJ completely **absolutely, completely, entirely, quite, simply, totally, utterly, wholly** *It's true, but completely irrelevant **to** the discussion.*
- ▶ mostly or almost **almost, increasingly, largely, mostly, often, practically, virtually** *The output of academic research is considered as mostly irrelevant to the real world of marketing.*
- ▶ rather **fairly, pretty** INFORMAL**, rather, somewhat** *We now read this letter as an interesting but somewhat irrelevant piece of history.*
- ▶ basically **basically, essentially, ultimately** *In science the individual scientist is basically irrelevant.*
- ▶ apparently **apparently, seemingly** *People were put off by the number of seemingly irrelevant questions you had to answer.*

- v+ADJ **appear, be, become, consider sth, deem sth, prove, regard sth as, seem** *In the age of the Internet, distance is becoming irrelevant. • The actual text of an advertisement is often considered irrelevant.*
- and/or not interesting **boring, dull, uninteresting** *Is the Bible boring and irrelevant **to** children today?*
- wrong or false **erroneous, false, inaccurate, unsubstantiated, untrue** *You need to be wary of false or irrelevant information on the Internet.*
- old-fashioned **dated, obsolete, outdated, out-dated, outmoded, out-of-date** *Has public ownership become outdated and irrelevant?*
- not helpful or useful **meaningless, redundant, superfluous, unhelpful, unnecessary, useless** *He took out his phone and made a series of totally irrelevant and unnecessary calls.*
- not important **immaterial, inconsequential, superficial, trivial, unimportant** *The students are warned not to ask trivial or irrelevant questions.*

irreversible ADJ
impossible to change or bring back

- adv+ADJ possibly or probably **possibly, potentially, probably, seemingly** *Nutritional deficiencies in a baby's diet have potentially irreversible consequences.*
- effectively **effectively, essentially** *The decisions made on the basis of this report will be effectively irreversible.*
- ADJ+n change or effect **change, consequences, effect, process, shift** *Mankind has always made irreversible changes to his habitat.*
- damage or destruction **damage, destruction, harm, loss** *Degenerative brain diseases are marked by progressive, irreversible damage to cells of the central nervous system.*
- process of getting worse **decline, degradation, deterioration** *By 1998 it was clear that their market share was in irreversible decline.*

irritating ADJ
making you feel annoyed or impatient

- adv+ADJ very **deeply, downright, extremely, highly, hugely, immensely, incredibly, intensely, particularly, really, so, very** *I found her comment intensely irritating at the time.*
- ▶ rather **a bit** INFORMAL**, faintly, a little, mildly, moderately, quite, rather, slightly, somewhat** *The only mildly irritating aspect of the evening was the fact that people were allowed to smoke indoors.*
- ▶ more and more **increasingly** *David found the noise increasingly irritating as the night progressed.*

- v+ADJ **be, become, find sth, get** *The hard drive makes a rattling noise which becomes very irritating. • Some people like his writing style, but I find it highly irritating.*

isolated ADJ
1 alone, or a long way from other places or people

- adv+ADJ very **completely, extremely** *She was among people, but she felt completely isolated.*
- ▶ rather **quite, relatively** *The university campus can seem relatively isolated and insular.*
- ▶ more and more **increasingly** *His behaviour, which was at times bizarre, left him increasingly isolated.*
- ▶ in a particular way **geographically, politically, socially** *They organize activities for socially isolated and lonely older people.*

- v+ADJ **be, become, feel, leave sb, remain** *Participating in a group or workshop helps students to feel less isolated. • Many older people are left isolated when they finish working.*

2 happening only once

- ADJ+n **case, incident, instance, occurrence, outbreak, phenomenon** *The committee hope this was an isolated incident but will continue monitoring the situation.*

isolation N
the state of feeling alone or being separated from other people

- adj+N complete or great **complete, extreme, total** *The scribes worked day and night in complete isolation.*
- ▶ relative **comparative, relative** *For over sixty years she has lived and written in relative isolation.*
- ▶ chosen/not chosen **enforced, self-imposed** *Japan opened up to the outside world in 1854 after more than 200 years of self-imposed isolation.*
- ▶ types of isolation **cultural, emotional, geographical, intellectual, professional, social** *Their physical and social isolation makes it difficult for disabled women to break out of their situation.*

- v+N prevent or stop isolation **avoid, break, end, overcome, prevent** *Talking to others is the best way to prevent isolation and maintain perspective.*
- ▶ reduce or combat isolation **alleviate, combat, counter, lessen, reduce, relieve, tackle** *For deaf people, learning to lipread reduces isolation.*
- ▶ increase isolation **increase, intensify** *Such behaviour can increase the isolation and sense of despair felt by an individual.*
- ▶ experience isolation **experience, face, feel** *With the loss of a loved one, we experience pain and isolation.*

issue N

a subject that people discuss or argue about; a problem

- adj+N important **big, central, critical, crucial, fundamental, important, key, main, major, pressing, real, serious, special, substantive** *The key issue is that it all depends on the quality of the data.*
- ▸ that people feel strongly about **burning, contentious, controversial, divisive, emotive, sensitive, thorny, vexed** *Darwin's theory of evolution seems to be a much more contentious issue in the USA than in Europe.*
- ▸ complicated **complex, complicated, difficult, problematic** *Tax is a complex issue.*
- ▸ current **contemporary, current, topical** *In our regular newsletter we draw attention to topical issues.*
- ▸ related **pertinent, related, relevant** *We provide information and advice on disability and related issues.*
- ▸ not yet settled **outstanding, unresolved** *Underlying the violence is the continuing, unresolved issue of the country's political future.*
- ▸ general/specific **broader, general, particular, specific, wider** *If there are specific issues that you want to cover, then let me know.*
- ▸ affecting a particular area **global, local** *Climate change is a global issue.*

- v+N deal with an issue **address, approach, confront, deal with, face, grapple with, handle, pursue, tackle, wrestle with** *The curriculum should address the real issues affecting young people's lives.*
- ▸ settle an issue **decide, overcome, resolve, settle, solve** *If customers complain, we will seek to resolve the issue as quickly as possible.*
- ▸ discuss or investigate an issue **analyse, consider, cover, debate, discuss, examine, explore, investigate, look at, outline, research** *The goal of this workshop was to discuss the issue of bilingual development.*
- ▸ look at an issue again **readdress, review, revisit** *It will be interesting to revisit this issue at the end of the year.*
- ▸ mention or point out an issue **bring up, broach, highlight, identify, mention, raise** *The Board discussed some of the issues regarding copyright that were raised at the Media Forum Seminar.*
- ▸ explain an issue **clarify, explain, summarize** *The book does a good job of clarifying the fundamental issues.*
- ▸ avoid an issue **avoid, dodge, duck, evade, ignore,**

sidestep *Political parties cannot afford to duck this issue; they must face it head on.*
- ▸ make an issue less clear **cloud, complicate, confuse, fudge** *The press has clouded the issue by stirring up emotions.*
- ▸ understand an issue **grasp, understand** *We can help you understand the complex legal issues involved in exporting overseas.*

- N+v have to do with something or someone **be associated with, be involved in, be related to, concern, involve, relate to, revolve around, surround** *The clinic offers advice on obesity, alcohol and other issues surrounding men's health.*
- ▸ affect someone or something **affect, confront, face, impact on** *This article looks at some of the issues facing Scottish artists.*
- ▸ occur **arise, emerge** *The editors intended to include the feature until a copyright issue arose.*

- n+of+N **number, range, variety** *The public willl be consulted on a range of issues affecting the local community.*

issue V

to officially give something or make something available

- V+n a statement or announcement **alert, apology, declaration, notice, reminder, statement, ultimatum, warning** *The Environment Agency issued a flood warning for the area.*
- ▸ a document giving information **bulletin, circular, communiqué, document, guidance, guidelines, invoice, leaflet, letter, manifesto, pamphlet, press release, prospectus, questionnaire** *When we despatch the item, we issue a final invoice which must be paid within 30 days.*
- ▸ a document giving permission or proof **badge, card, certificate, invitation, licence, passport, permit, prescription, receipt, ticket, visa** *They issue parking permits for access to University areas.*
- ▸ an order **command, decree, edict, fatwa, injunction, instructions, order, proclamation, ruling** *In 1290, King Edward I issued an edict ordering Jews to leave Britain.*
- ▸ legal document **subpoena, summons, warrant, writ** *If the individual fails to appear in court on the appointed day, a warrant is issued for their arrest.*
- ▸ money or something worth money **banknote, bond, cheque, coin, refund, shares, stamp, token, voucher** *If, for any reason, you are not happy with the goods you have purchased, we will issue a full refund.*

Jj

jail N
a place where people have to stay as punishment for a crime

- adj+N very secure **maximum-security, top-security** *Elite units guard the top security jail.*
- ▶ with bad conditions **notorious, overcrowded** *These executions took place in the dictator's most notorious jail.*
- ▶ outside the normal system **military, secret** *There are reports of the CIA operating secret jails for terrorism suspects.*
- v+N go to or be in jail **be in, be put in, be sent to, be thrown in, go to, languish in** *He committed a burglary, for which he went to jail for six months.* • *Thousands of political prisoners are still languishing in jail.*
- ▶ risk going to jail **face, risk** *Two drivers involved in a high-speed car race have been warned they may face jail.*
- ▶ avoid going to jail **avoid, be spared, escape** *Her family spoke out yesterday after hearing her attacker was spared jail.*
- ▶ leave jail **be freed from, be released from, get out of, leave** *Kate is grateful to her mother, who helped her once she left jail.*
- N+n **sentence, term** *Those found guilty of harassment now face a five-year jail sentence.*

jargon N
words that are used only by people doing particular work

- adj+N complicated or hard to understand **arcane, complex, complicated, confusing, impenetrable, incomprehensible, meaningless, obscure** *A tutor will teach you how to use the Internet without confusing jargon.*
- ▶ new **current, fashionable, modern** *Green is used unless there is some reason to change. It's the default colour, to use modern jargon.*
- ▶ types of jargon **academic, bureaucratic, financial, legal, marketing, medical, military, scientific, technical** *We will simplify the legal jargon by clearly explaining any obligations or restrictions that may be relevant to you.*
- v+N use jargon **contain, spout** INFORMAL**, talk, use** *This is not a book where the authors simply spout theoretical jargon.*
- ▶ avoid jargon **avoid, banish, eliminate, remove** *Avoid jargon and abbreviations – they send out the message that your site is for an exclusive group of users.*
- ▶ understand jargon **know, understand** *Many people cannot understand the jargon and technical terms used by computer manufacturers.*
- ▶ explain jargon **decipher, demystify, explain, translate** *The author has a unique talent for demystifying medical jargon.*

jaw N
the part of the face that includes the chin and bottom teeth

- adj+N **chiselled, jutting, protruding, square, strong** *Daniel is a hunky actor with designer stubble on his chiselled jaw.*
- v+N **clamp shut, clench, lock, snap** *He clamped his jaw shut as he felt the point of the knife.*
- N+v **drop** *When I heard the song for the first time, my jaw dropped in amazement.*

2 [always plural] the mouth

- adj+N dangerous **powerful, slavering, snapping** *She was saved from the slavering jaws of a guard dog.*
- ▶ open **gaping, open** *The picture showed a savage wolf with gaping jaws.*
- v+N **prise open** *The jaws of the shark were prised open.*
- N+v **clamp, lock, snap** *A crocodile came onto the shore, jaws snapping.*

jealous ADJ
unhappy because someone has something you want, or because someone you love seems attracted to another person

- adv+ADJ very **bitterly, dead** INFORMAL**, deeply, extremely, fiercely, incredibly, intensely, really, so, terribly, very** *Seeing her husband kissing other women in film roles makes her extremely jealous.*
- ▶ unreasonably **absurdly, exceedingly, insanely, pathologically** *She became insanely jealous when he socialized with other people.*
- ▶ rather **a little, quite, rather, slightly, somewhat, a tad** INFORMAL *I imagine his brothers were a little jealous of his good fortune.*
- ▶ more and more **increasingly** *I am increasingly jealous about my partner's ex-wife.*
- v+ADJ **be, become, feel, get, make sb** *They may feel jealous of the attention the other child is getting.* • *I always looked so happy, it made him jealous.*

jealousy N
an unhappy feeling because someone has something you want, or because someone you love seems attracted to another person

- adj+N strong **bitter, extreme, fierce, sheer** *It's the story of Salieri and his bitter jealousy of Wolfgang Amadeus Mozart.*
- ▶ unreasonable or silly **insane, irrational, obsessive, petty, unhealthy** *They find the academic world to be riddled with petty jealousies.*
- ▶ of a particular type **professional, sexual** *Infidelity and sexual jealousy seem to be universal elements of human sexual behaviour.*
- v+N cause jealousy **arouse, awaken, cause, engender, excite, incur, inflame, inspire, provoke, spark** *The king's generosity towards him had aroused the jealousy of some courtiers.*
- ▶ feel jealousy **be consumed with, experience, feel** *He says he never felt any jealousy of other players.*
- n+of+N **feeling, fit, pang, tinge, twinge** *He*

experienced pangs of jealousy when he discovered
she had asked Ned to go with her instead.

jeopardize V
risk damaging or destroying something important

- adv+V seriously **gravely, seriously, severely** The
students' safety is being seriously jeopardized by
heavy traffic through the car park.
▶ possibly **possibly, potentially** New laws could
potentially jeopardize jobs.
- V+n safety or health **health, safety, security,
welfare, well-being** Her friends are worried her
severe exercise regime is jeopardizing her health.
▶ opportunity or future success **chances, future,
prospects, success, survival, viability** Don't
jeopardize your chances at interviews by being
unprepared.
▶ relationship **friendship, relationship** Germany did
not want to jeopardize its relationship with Russia.
▶ job **job, livelihood** Illegal copying jeopardizes the
livelihoods of artists and song writers.

jerk V
move very suddenly, or make something move
suddenly

- adv+V suddenly **abruptly, suddenly** A whiplash
injury occurs when the neck is jerked suddenly and
the muscles are strained.
▶ violently **uncontrollably, violently** As soon as it took
off, the aircraft started to jerk violently, which caused
a panic.
▶ in a particular direction **upright, forward,
backwards etc** I pulled the ripcord and was jerked
back by the parachute as it opened.
▶ awake **awake** I jerked awake in the chair, startled.

job N
1 work that you do to earn money

- adj+N interesting or well-paid **better-paid,
decent, good, high-powered, plum, rewarding,
top, well-paid** Jennifer gave up her well-paid job to
start a magazine.
▶ not interesting or well-paid **boring, dead-end, low-
paid, menial, tedious, unskilled** His prospects were
limited to a low-paid job in the civil service or the
military.
▶ working particular hours **full-time, nine-to-five,
part-time** I'd had part-time jobs in bars and cafés
when I was a student.
▶ perfect **dream, ideal, perfect** Think about the future:
what's your ideal job?
▶ difficult or skilled **demanding, difficult, skilled,
stressful** Stressful jobs can increase the risk of heart
disease.
▶ easy **cushy** INFORMAL, **easy** I have a cushy office job
and feel I can continue to work past 65.
▶ new/old **current, first, new, old, previous** I have a
lot of responsibility in my current job.
▶ permanent or secure **permanent, proper, secure,
steady** At the end of the maternity cover assignment
she was offered a permanent job.
▶ temporary **holiday, summer, temping, temporary,
vacation** More people are likely to take temporary
jobs over the festive period.
▶ types of job **blue-collar, cleaning, desk, graduate,
office, secretarial, teaching, white-collar** She is

moving to London, where she will begin a teaching
job in September.

- v+N have or start a job **have, start, take, take on,
take up** She now has a job with the council.
▶ get a job **be offered, find, get, land** After a few
months he was offered a job as a legal assistant. •
After graduating I was really confident that I could
get a good job.
▶ do a job **carry out, do, perform, work** You have
shown that you can do the job well.
▶ keep a job **hold down, keep** She's very unstable and
has never been able to hold down a job.
▶ lose or leave a job **change, leave, lose, quit, resign
from** If things at work don't improve soon, I'm going
to have to change jobs. • Thousands of car workers
are set to lose their jobs.
▶ make someone leave their job **dismiss from, fire
from, sack from** Last week he was fired from a job
he'd held for nearly three years.
▶ get rid of jobs **axe, cut, shed, slash** The ferry
company says it wants to axe 1,200 jobs.
▶ when jobs are in danger of being lost **jeopardize,
threaten** Cutbacks in funding will threaten jobs at
the local council offices.
▶ create or protect jobs **create, defend, generate,
protect, safeguard, save** Every year, around 600,000
jobs are created in the IT sector worldwide.

- N+v **entail, pay** What exactly does the job entail? •
Unfortunately my new job doesn't pay very well.

- N+n availability **creation, market, offer, vacancy**
Get details of job vacancies by email or text.
▶ opportunities **opportunities, prospects** They live in
squalor, with little education or health care, and few
job prospects.
▶ person who has or wants a job **applicant, holder,
hunter, seeker, sharer** The program includes
vocational training for job seekers.
▶ search **hunting, search** Job websites can assist you
in your job search.
▶ happiness or security in your job **insecurity,
satisfaction, security** Small rises in job satisfaction
give us as much happiness as a big rise in salary.
▶ loss of jobs **cuts, losses** Organizational change has
led to job losses.
▶ description or features of a job **description,
profile, role, spec** INFORMAL, **specification, title** The
job description included database design.

2 a task or piece of work

- adj+N done well **amazing** INFORMAL, **brilliant,
excellent, fantastic, fine, good, great, magnificent,
marvellous, splendid, sterling, superb, terrific,
tremendous, wonderful** May I say what a fantastic
job you have done with your website.
▶ not done well **bad, bodged** INFORMAL, **botched** Afte.
completing a botched job, the builders demanded
four thousand pounds from the elderly couple.
▶ difficult **difficult, hard, not easy, thankless, tough,
unenviable** They have the unenviable job of trying
to motivate a team with no money available.
▶ big/small **big, little, long, small** It's a big job and
it'll take a long time.
▶ of various kinds **odd** Volunteers are needed for
helping with publicity, making coffee and doing
other odd jobs.

7

9 **joke**

Usage **Job** is always plural in this combination.

- v+N accept or do a job **carry out, do, get on with, take on** *There are several freeware applications which will do the job just as well.*
- finish a job **complete, finish** *The job was completed in one and a half days to the satisfaction of the customer.*
- get a job **be given, get** *I was given the job of holding the ladder.*
- give someone a job **allocate (sb), give sb** *He spends a lot of his time allocating jobs to members of his team.*

jog N
a run at a slow, steady speed

- adj+N slow **easy, gentle, light, slow, steady** *Keep going at a gentle jog for 5–10 minutes.*
- quick **brisk, quick** *There's nothing like a quick jog around the field to make you feel awake.*
- regular **daily, morning** *I saw him out on his morning jog.*
- v+N **break into, go for** *At the top of the hill I broke into a jog.* • *Every day I exercise, swim or go for a jog.*

join V
become a member of an organization or club

- adv+V at a particular time **eventually, immediately, recently, subsequently** *This page is to welcome the new members who have recently joined us.*
- at first **initially, originally** *Jarrod initially joined the bank in a technology role.*
- officially **formally, officially** *In May 1997, China sent observers to attend a meeting, and formally joined the committee later that year.*
- because you want to **voluntarily** *We believe that children benefit from out-of-school clubs that they join voluntarily.*
- V+n group or club **band, choir, club, forum, group, gym, party, team, union** *Anyone who might be interested in joining a school tennis team should sign up here.*
- company **company, firm** *He joined the firm in 1998 and became a Partner in 2003.*
- armed forces **army, battalion, navy, RAF, regiment** *He joined the army and served in Northern Ireland, Kosovo and Iraq.*
- queue or list **list, queue** *Click here to join our mailing list.*

join in PHR VB
start an activity with others who are already doing it

- V+adv **eagerly, enthusiastically, happily, heartily** *Someone started to applaud, and I enthusiastically joined in.*
- V+n fun or celebration **activities, celebrations, festivities, fun, game** *Local pubs joined in the fun with a beer festival, music and a barbecue.*
- discussion, argument, or fight **banter, conversation, debate, discussion, fight, fray** *Choose a book from the list below, read it and join in the discussion.*

- dancing, singing, laughing etc **applause, chorus, dance, dancing, laughter, singing** *The teacher starts the song and asks the children to all join in the chorus.*
- procession or protest **condemnation, procession, protest** *People joined in the procession as it wound through the town.*
- search **hunt, search** *The public were invited to join in the hunt for mediaeval treasure.*

joint ADJ
involving two or more people or groups

- ADJ+n effort or work **action, bid, effort, endeavour, initiative, operation, project, venture, working** *Members of the Rugby Club visited the school and donated rugby kit in a new joint venture.*
- ownership or responsibility **authorship, custody, ownership, responsibility, tenancy** *Doug and Alice remain in close contact, as they have joint custody of their nine-year-old son Joe.*
- owner or controller **editor, owner, tenant** *She is joint editor of the journal, Eurasian Studies.*
- statement or agreement **agreement, communiqué, declaration, statement** *After the meeting, the leaders issued a joint communiqué.*
- meeting or group **committee, conference, meeting** *This weekend, two media studies associations held a joint conference.*
- winner or possible winner **favourite, winner** *The two teams were declared joint winners.*

joke N
something that is funny or intended to make people laugh

- adj+N good or funny **funny, good, hilarious** *A joke isn't funny if you have to explain it.*
- bad or not funny **awful, bad, feeble, lame, silly, stupid, terrible, unfunny** *Dad used to embarrass me with his lame jokes.*
- well-known **corny, favourite, old** *There is plenty of audience participation, along with the usual corny jokes and slapstick.*
- offensive **crass, cruel, off-colour, offensive, racist, sexist, sick, tasteless** *Is this some kind of sick joke?*
- about sex **bawdy, crude, dirty, filthy, risqué, rude, smutty** *Most of the birthday cards contain smutty jokes.*
- complicated **elaborate** *There is a myth that contemporary artists are somehow indulging in an elaborate joke at the expense of the public.*
- types of joke **inside, visual** *This book is like an inside joke for anyone who loves Japan.* • *The film is full of marvellous visual jokes.*

A **practical joke** is a trick that is intended to surprise someone or make them look silly: *April Fools' Day is the classic occasion for playing practical jokes on your family and colleagues.*

- v+N when someone says or does something to make other people laugh **crack, have, make, play, repeat, share, swap, tell** *Most of the officers were well liked by the men, and they even cracked jokes with us.* • *He played a practical joke on Mervin by putting salt in the sugar bowl.*
- enjoy jokes **appreciate, enjoy, like** *I am very friendly and enjoy a good joke and a good laugh.*

▶ understand a joke **get, understand** *Philip got the joke and laughed heartily.*

▶ know a joke **hear, know, remember** *Remember the old joke about paying people to dig holes and then getting others to fill them?*

● N+v be told to many people **circulate, go around** *Jokes circulated widely about how there were 50 million suspects for the crime.*

● go wrong **backfire, fall flat** *The joke backfired badly on the girls when someone told the teacher what they had done.*

jolt N
a sudden violent movement, shock, or feeling

● adj+N sudden **sharp, sudden** *They were blown backward by a sudden jolt of energy.*

▶ violent **almighty, massive, severe, violent** *This came as a severe jolt to my pride.*

▶ unpleasant **nasty, sickening** *Suddenly there was a sickening jolt as the ship ran into the submerged rock.*

▶ slight **little, slight** *The cars stopped with a slight jolt.*

● v+N experience a jolt **feel, get, receive, suffer** *I felt a jolt of recognition when I first read his poetry.*
● *Edward's confidence received a jolt.*

▶ give a jolt **give (sth/sb)** *The bus gave a jolt and stopped.*

journal N
a magazine relating to a particular subject or profession

● adj+N academic **academic, learned, peer-reviewed, scholarly** *Papers presented at the seminar have since been published in peer-reviewed journals.*

▶ respected **august, esteemed, leading, prestigious, reputable, respected** *The New England Journal of Medicine is arguably one of the most prestigious medical journals.*

▶ not well-known **obscure** *His work was largely unpublished or published in some obscure journals that nobody read.*

▶ specialized **specialist, specialized** *Matthew writes regular articles for specialized journals and the general press.*

▶ for members of a particular company or profession **in-house, official, professional, trade** *This is the official journal of the American College of Sports Medicine.*

▶ published in a particular form **electronic, online, printed** *The library makes a wide range of electronic journals available to readers.*

▶ published at particular times **bimonthly, monthly, quarterly, twice-yearly, weekly** *The Cheshire Genealogist is the quarterly journal of the South Cheshire History Society.*

▶ relating to particular subjects **literary, medical, scientific** *Homeopathic remedies are no more beneficial than placebos, a leading medical journal has said.*

● v+N produce a journal **edit, found, produce, publish** *He is the only scientist ever to edit the literary journal Granta.*

▶ buy or read a journal **browse, read, subscribe to** *The tool allows you to explore research topics and browse scientific journals.*

▶ write for a journal **contribute to, submit sth to** *She has contributed to professional journals and published articles on teaching and learning.*

▶ be published in a journal **appear in, be cited in, be published in, be reported in, feature in** *His essays have appeared in many leading international journals.*

● N+v be about **be devoted to, cover, focus on** *We have an extensive database of journals devoted to the study of history.*

▶ contain **contain, feature, include, publish** *This journal includes articles on applied physiology.*

● n+of+N **copy, issue, volume** *The article appears in the current issue of the journal.*

journalism N
the activity of reporting the news for newspapers, radio, or television

● adj+N of a good quality **good, incisive, responsible, serious** *The best journalism has always come from dissidents.*

▶ trying to change bad things **campaigning, crusading, hard-hitting** *Her articles about the health service were crusading journalism at its best.*

▶ trying to find out facts **investigative** *Clever investigative journalism and many leaked stories led to a call for something to be done.*

▶ popular or not serious **gutter, mainstream, muckraking, popular, sensational, sensationalist, tabloid** *Maybe this is just another case of sensationalist, tabloid journalism.*

▶ when people are paid money for information to be used in newspaper stories **chequebook** *Paying the rapist for his story was an outrageous case of chequebook journalism.*

▶ not good or accurate **irresponsible, lazy, shoddy, sloppy, unethical** *News releases are helpful, but it's lazy journalism just to print everything they say.*

▶ fair or objective **independent, objective** *In the interests of objective journalism, a balanced article should have been printed.*

▶ modern **contemporary, modern** *These pamphlets represented the forerunners of modern British journalism.*

▶ of a particular type **literary, political, sports** *Generally, I think the standard of political journalism is poor in this country.*

▶ in a particular form **broadcast, magazine, online, photographic, radio, television** *There are obvious signs that the style of newspapers is being influenced by online journalism.*

journalist N
a person whose job is to report the news for a newspaper, radio, or television

● adj+N admired by many people **distinguished, respected** *Penny is a respected journalist with her own column in design magazine Intra.*

▶ well-known **prominent, well-known** *He is a well-known journalist specializing in archaeological news.*

▶ given an important prize **award-winning, prize-winning** *Roger Hutchinson is an award-winning journalist and author.*

▶ reporting on a particular area of activity **environmental, financial, political** *There are now*

nearly 300 political journalists based at Westminster.
▶ travelling with an army and reporting on what it does **embedded** *What embedded journalists write is controlled by the military, who thus feed their own version of the facts to the world.*
▶ experienced **experienced, veteran** *The veteran journalist was killed in the Gambia last week.*
▶ not permanently employed by a particular company **freelance, independent** *She has also had work published as a freelance journalist.*
▶ trying to find out the facts about something **investigative** *Gareth Jones was one of Wales' finest investigative journalists.*
▶ trying to achieve political or social change **campaigning, crusading** *In his work as a campaigning journalist, he exposed the use of torture in the country's police cells.*

● n+N using a particular means of communicating information **broadcast, magazine, newspaper, print, radio, tabloid, television, TV** *She cut her teeth as a newspaper journalist in her home town of Weston-super-Mare, in South West England, after training in Wales.*
▶ reporting on a particular area of activity **fashion, football, music, news, science, sports, travel** *Like many music journalists, I was really just a frustrated musician.*
▶ when a private person reports on an event **citizen** *In the age of blogs and digital photos, the phenomenon of the citizen journalist has become a force to be reckoned with.*

● N+v write, or report on something **cover, describe, report (on), specialize in, write (on)** *West is a journalist writing on health issues.*
▶ ask someone questions **interview** *Peters is a journalist who has interviewed many of the country's top football stars.*
▶ make something publicly known **expose, uncover** *Journalists who expose corrupt practices often find their lives under threat.*
▶ try to find out about something **investigate** *Lawyers have acquired notes made by two journalists who investigated the killings in 1972.*

ourney N

an occasion when you travel from one place to another

▶ adj+N in a particular direction **homeward, onward, outward, return** *We had to go through the same ordeal on our homeward journey.*
▶ when you go and return **return, round-trip** *In the terrible conditions, it took them eight hours to make a four-mile round-trip journey.*
▶ long **epic, lengthy, long, long-distance** *It was a long journey of about 6 hours.*
▶ short **short** *After lunch, we got back on the coach for the short journey to Dartington.*
▶ difficult or tiring **arduous, difficult, exhausting, gruelling, hard, harrowing, nightmare, tiring** *In 1132, the monks embarked on the arduous journey to Yorkshire.*
▶ pleasant **enjoyable, pleasant** *They wished us a pleasant journey.*
▶ interesting **adventurous, eventful, exciting, fascinating, incredible, unforgettable** *Travelling by rail, you will have an unforgettable journey through the French countryside.*

▶ without anything unusual or exciting happening **tedious, uneventful** *We had a fairly uneventful journey.*
▶ dangerous **dangerous, hazardous, perilous** *She wrote a letter to her father telling him why she was undertaking this perilous journey.*
▶ safe **safe** *They said goodbye and wished us a safe journey home.*
▶ lasting for a particular time **five-minute, twenty-minute etc, two-hour, five-hour etc** *London Waterloo to Portsmouth Harbour Station is only a ninety-minute journey.* • *Going to the nearest big town meant a four-hour journey by road and ferry.*
▶ being a particular distance **three-mile, ten-mile etc** *After their seventy-mile journey, Custer's men were too tired to fight effectively.*
▶ going across land **overland** *This is a classic overland journey to the roof of the world.*

● n+N **boat, bus, car, coach, ferry, plane, rail, railway, sea, taxi, train** *Barrow is located an hour's train journey from here.*
● v+N make a journey **go on, make, take, undertake** *He made the journey every day.* • *We took a thrilling snowmobile journey across one of Europe's biggest glaciers.*
▶ start a journey **begin, commence, embark on, set off on, set out on, start** *Litvinov then sets out on his journey back to Russia.*
▶ start a journey again **continue, resume** *Their injuries were not serious and they were able to continue their journey to Newark.*
▶ finish a journey **complete, end, finish** *The representatives later transferred to a jet to complete their journey to Bonn.*
▶ stay alive despite a journey **survive** *He knew they wouldn't survive the 40-mile journey back to their ship.*
▶ stop a journey for a short time **break** *We broke our journey at Pittlochrie for breakfast around ten.*

● N+v **begin, continue, end, go, last, start, take, take sb** *They say that the longest journey begins with one small step.* • *The whole journey took about four hours.* • *Our journey took us through some spectacular scenery.*

joy N

a feeling of great happiness; something that makes you feel very happy

● adj+N great **deep, great, immense, intense, much, overwhelming** *In a very short time she learned to walk, to the great joy of her mother.*
▶ impossible to describe **indescribable, inexpressible, unspeakable** *We went through an experience that ranged from pure terror to indescribable joy.*
▶ lasting for a long time **eternal, everlasting, lasting, unending** *The believer will know eternal joy in heaven.*
▶ without a limit **boundless, unbounded, unbridled** *Nothing else brings such unbridled joy to so many people.*
▶ complete **pure, real, sheer, true, unadulterated, unalloyed, utter** *The band get together for the sheer joy of making live jazz happen.*
▶ lasting for a short time **short-lived** *But the joy was*

short-lived as the home side drew level six minutes later.

- v+N feel joy **experience, feel, get, know, take** *We experienced both joy and sadness as we listened.* • *She took joy in everything she did in her life.*
▶ cause joy **bring (sb), give** *It is clear that he brought joy to many.*
▶ discover joy **discover, find** *It was a great thrill to watch so many children discover the joy of performing.*
▶ discover joy again **rediscover, relive** *I've rediscovered the joy of doing nothing.*
▶ express joy **convey, express** *The music expresses joy, love, and life.*
▶ remember joy **recall, remember** *I remember the joy that reading gave me.*
▶ cause many people to feel joy **spread** *They find a pleasure in spreading joy around them.*
▶ share joy **share** *Her neighbours and friends share her joy.*
▶ imagine someone's joy **imagine** *Imagine my joy when I heard the news.*
▶ show joy **radiate** *She radiates joy and vivacity as well as a profound sense of innocence.*

judge N
1 someone who makes decisions in a court of law

- adj+N important **distinguished, eminent** *Britain's most eminent judges have warned politicians that they will fight for their independence.*
▶ experienced **experienced** *He is one of the most experienced judges dealing with criminal cases in England and Wales.*
▶ senior **senior** *A senior judge has described the treatment of the prisoners as 'monstrous'.*
▶ highest in authority **chief** *He is a former chief judge of the U.S. Court of Appeals for the Seventh Circuit.*
▶ not elected **unelected** *Law in Britain is not just made by Parliament; it is also made by unelected judges.*
▶ in charge of a trial **presiding, trial** *He refused to answer questions put to him by the presiding judge.*

- N+v make a decision about something **conclude, decide, find, hold, rule** *The judges ruled that Mr Khan had not been given an adequate opportunity to respond to the allegations against him.*
▶ be in charge **hear, preside (over), sit** *Mr Justice Johnson, the judge who is presiding over the appeal, has asked for further medical opinion.* • *She told reporters that she believed the judge who was sitting in the case had ignored important defence evidence.*
▶ not agree to something **refuse, reject** *The judge had refused her application to have her case dealt with by arbitration.*
▶ accept something **accept, admit, agree, allow** *The judge accepted that the firm took its tax obligations seriously.*
▶ allow something to be done **grant** *On 11 August 1997 a judge granted the extradition of all three men.*
▶ state officially that something is wrong **dismiss, overrule, overturn, quash** *A judge later dismissed the charges for lack of evidence.*
▶ order someone to do something **direct, order** *The trial judge directed the jury that they should acquit the defendant.*
▶ officially state what someone's punishment will

be **sentence** *The Virginia circuit judge has sentenced him to nine years in jail.*
▶ give a summary of the evidence in a case **sum up** *After the prosecution and defence had been completed, the judge summed up the case for the jury.*
▶ state officially that something is right **uphold** *The judges upheld the verdict of the original jury.*
▶ officially decide to give someone something **award** *The judge awarded £200,000 to each claimant.*
▶ consider something **consider** *The judge considered the submissions that had been made to him.*

- v+before+N **appear, come, go** *The boys appeared before the judge after spending a night in jail.*

2 someone who decides who the winner of a competition will be

- v+N **dazzle, impress, wow** INFORMAL *A number of aspects of the project particularly impressed the judges.*

- N+v choose someone or something as the winner **choose, decide, decide on, pick, vote for** *After hours of deliberation, the judges decided on the winner.*
▶ praise someone or something **commend, praise** *The judges praised the 'consistently high standard of gardening' achieved by each of the finalists.*
▶ give something **award** *Judges awarded the 'Free Newspaper of the Year' title to the Milton Keynes Citizen.*

- n+of+N **group, panel, team** *The panel of judges were unanimous in deciding who should win this highly coveted prize.*

judge V
form an opinion about something after considering the facts

- V+n success **effectiveness, success** *Visitors' figures alone are not sufficient to judge the success of an exhibition.*
▶ the degree to which something is suitable **acceptability, appropriateness, suitability** *It provides the employer with an opportunity to judge your suitability for the job.*
▶ the degree to which something is correct **accuracy, correctness** *I am unable to judge the accuracy of this claim.*
▶ the degree to which something is good enough **adequacy, validity** *Not having read Browne's book, I am in no position to judge the validity of his arguments.*
▶ quality **merit, quality** *No attempt is made here to judge the quality of that work.*

judgment N
1 an opinion formed after thinking carefully about something

- adj+N final **definitive, final** *We have not yet reached a final judgment.*
▶ based on someone's own feelings and opinions **personal, subjective** *This is an entirely subjective judgment, I realize.*
▶ not based on someone's own feelings and opinions **impartial, independent, objective** *You must make an objective judgment of the evidence.*
▶ based on good knowledge or careful thought

about something **balanced, considered, informed, reasoned** *It is too early to make an informed judgment about the impact on the UK economy.*
▶ made too quickly **hasty, snap** *Avoid making snap judgments about people.*
▶ unfair **harsh** *He is inclined to harsh judgments about his former colleagues.*

● v+N make a judgment **come to, form, make, reach** *I can make no judgment on that issue.*
▶ base a judgment on something **base on** *These are the criteria on which we base our judgments of students' performance.*
▶ express a judgment **deliver, give, pass, pronounce, render** *You are always so quick to pass judgment.*
▶ not make a judgment **reserve, suspend, withhold** *I am reserving judgment for the time being.*

● N+v **be based on** *Their judgment was based on a broad range of evidence.*

2 your ability to understand a situation well and make good decisions

● adj+N types of judgment **aesthetic, clinical, critical, editorial, ethical, moral, political, professional** *Some put it down to a lapse of editorial judgment.*
▶ good **fine, good, shrewd, sound** *She succeeded, more by luck than good judgment.*
▶ bad **bad, poor** *Perhaps this is a case of bad judgment on her part.*
▶ not influenced by someone else **impartial, independent** *He works with minimal supervision and exercises independent judgment.*

● v+N use judgment **exercise, use** *If only the government would trust him and leave him to exercise his own judgment.*
▶ affect judgment **affect, colour, influence** *You are allowing personal opinions to influence your judgment.*
▶ affect judgment in a bad way **cloud, distort, impair** *I suspect that prejudice sometimes clouds their judgment.*
▶ trust someone's judgment **respect, trust** *She found herself afraid to trust her own judgment.*
▶ feel doubt about someone's judgment **doubt, question** *Accidents occurred because more junior staff did not want to question the judgment of their superiors.*
▶ show judgment **display, show** *Her conduct showed bad judgment on her part.*

● n+of+N **error, lapse** *She made a further error of judgment by appointing him as a minister in her cabinet.*

ump at PHR VB
ake an opportunity in a very enthusiastic way

● V+n opportunity **chance, opportunity** *We jumped at the chance of a trip to Sri Lanka.*
▶ offer **offer** *Although he was just a few months short of retirement, Rogers jumped at the offer.*
▶ idea **idea** *Harry asked me if I could supply the music for his films and I jumped at the idea.*

unior ADJ
without a lot of responsibility or power

● ADJ+n worker or workers **clerk, colleague,**

doctor, member of staff, minister, officer, partner, reporter, staff *The British Medical Association reports that there are 21,000 junior doctors competing for 9,500 jobs.* ● *This scheme is about the observation of junior staff by their seniors.*
▶ job **job, position, post, rank** *Grace worked in the same department as Ann, but in a junior post.*

2 intended for or involving young people

● ADJ+n person taking part in a sport **athlete, champion, player** *They have produced some outstanding junior athletes in the past.* ● *He was British junior champion in 1998.*
▶ team **squad, team** *Luke was captain of the junior squad that travelled to Germany.*
▶ group of teams **league** *There are many international soccer players who made it to the professional game through the junior leagues.*
▶ club **club** *The Trust's junior club has over 1500 members.*
▶ member of a club **member** *Clubs may, if they so desire, accept junior members.*
▶ competition **championship, tournament** *Adam came second in the junior championship.*
▶ part of a club **section** *The Club does not have a junior section.*

junk N
old, broken, or useless things

● adj+N **assorted, old, unwanted, useless** *Use this as an excuse to get rid of any old junk.*

● v+N **accumulate, collect** *Your attic will probably be full of junk that you have accumulated over the years.*

● n+of+N pile **heap, pile** *On the right of the bed is a pile of junk.*
▶ amount **amount, load** *Judging by the amount of junk in our house, I don't think we throw anything away.*
▶ piece **bit, piece** *Skilled craftsmen take pieces of junk and transform them into useful items.*

jurisdiction N
the right or power to make legal decisions

● v+N have jurisdiction **have, possess, retain** *An award can be attacked on the grounds that the adjudicator had no jurisdiction to make it.*
▶ use jurisdiction **exercise** *He sought to defend the right of the civil power to exercise jurisdiction in ecclesiastical matters.*
▶ give jurisdiction **confer, give, grant, transfer** *The Act of 1932 transferred jurisdiction to county courts.*
▶ lack jurisdiction **lack** *Judge Sirica ruled that the Federal District Court lacked jurisdiction to comply with the Senate Committee's request for the tapes.*
▶ claim jurisdiction **assert, claim** *African bishops have claimed jurisdiction over the three parishes.*
▶ refuse to accept the jurisdiction of someone or something **challenge, contest, dispute** *I intend to contest the jurisdiction.*
▶ accept the jurisdiction of someone or something **accept** *The parties shall accept the exclusive jurisdiction of the English Courts.*
▶ limit the jurisdiction of someone or something **limit** *The Presidential Decree limits the jurisdiction*

of the court to those cases that took place after 30 August 1999.

▶ increase jurisdiction **extend** *The Ombudsman's jurisdiction was extended to include complaints about the care and treatment of patients.*

▶ go beyond jurisdiction **exceed** *The adjudicator has exceeded his jurisdiction.*

▶ have to accept the jurisdiction of someone or something **be subject to, come under** *She argues that a wide range of current domestic policies will gradually come under the jurisdiction of the European Commission.*

jury N

a group of members of the public who decide in a court of law whether someone has committed a crime

● v+N speak to a jury **address** *The prosecutor addressed the jury of six men and six women.*

▶ order a jury to do something **direct, instruct** *She directed the jury to return a not guilty verdict.*

▶ persuade a jury **convince, impress, persuade, satisfy, sway** *Forensic evidence convinced the jury that he had murdered the three women.*

▶ make a jury give a formal promise **swear in** *The jury was sworn in today and the prosecution started to present its case.*

▶ be part of a jury **serve on, sit on** *Anyone aged 18–70 can be summoned to serve on a jury.*

▶ officially allow a jury to leave **discharge, dismiss** *The jury was discharged after failing to reach a verdict.*

▶ choose a jury **select** *Reporting restrictions were lifted and a jury was selected.*

▶ warn a jury **warn** *It may be appropriate for the judge to warn the jury to exercise caution before acting upon the unsupported evidence of a witness.*

▶ remind a jury **remind** *The judge normally reminds the jury of their oath.*

● N+v make a decision about whether someone has committed a crime **deliver a verdict, give a verdict, reach a verdict, return a verdict** *The jury returned a verdict of accidental death.*

▶ officially decide that someone has not committed a crime **acquit, clear, find sb not guilty** *He was acquitted unanimously by a jury of nine women and three men.*

▶ officially decide that someone has committed a crime **convict, find sb guilty** *The jury swiftly convicted her of murder.*

▶ decide something **decide, find** *The jury has decided that there was insufficient evidence to persuade them of the defendant's guilt.*

▶ officially decide to give someone something **award** *The next day, the jury awarded her record damages of £600,000.*

▶ officially discuss whether someone has committed a crime **be out, consider its verdict, deliberate** *The jury had deliberated for six hours before finding Elmore guilty.*

▶ consider something **consider** *The jury considered the evidence and returned the verdict that she had accidentally drowned.*

▶ go to a private room to decide whether someone has committed a crime **retire** *The jury retired to consider their verdict.*

justice N

1 fair and moral treatment of people

● adj+N **divine, economic, environmental, natural, racial, social** *The Report recommended that arrangements for handling complaints should reflect the principles of natural justice.*

▶ v+N want or try to get justice **ask for, demand, pursue, seek, want** *They carried posters demanding justice for pensioners.*

▶ get justice **achieve, get, obtain, secure** *She believed in the power of politics to achieve social justice.*

▶ support justice **promote, serve, uphold** *We are responsible in government for upholding justice, civil rights, and democracy.*

▶ stop someone getting justice **deny sb** *Miners with these terrible illnesses were denied justice for years.*

▶ make certain that someone gets justice **ensure** *This is the best prospect of ensuring justice for those who died.*

● n+for+N **call, campaign, demand, desire, fight, quest, search, struggle** *He launched a campaign for justice for all Britain's 300,000 Travellers.*

2 the legal process of judging and punishing people

● adj+N **civil, criminal, juvenile, restorative, retributive** *The book is an ideal text for students taking courses in criminal justice.*

▶ v+N provide justice **administer, deliver, dispense, mete out** *Our object has been to establish an independent judiciary capable of dispensing justice effectively and efficiently.*

> When justice has been provided, you can say that *justice has been done*: *The family was delighted that she had been convicted and that justice had thus been done.*

▶ avoid justice **avoid, escape, evade** *The real killer escaped justice, while two innocent men had their lives destroyed.*

▶ try to prevent justice being provided **obstruct** *They have been found guilty by a US court of obstructing justice.*

▶ have to experience justice **face** *He will never face justice in his home country.*

▶ cause someone to have to experience justice **bring sb to** *We will find these people and we will bring them to justice.*

justifiable ADJ

that has a good reason for being done

● adv+ADJ in a particular way **commercially, economically, ethically, legally, morally, objectively, rationally** *She argues that the war is morally justifiable.*

▶ completely **entirely, fully, perfectly, quite, wholly** *If it has happened to you, don't be upset by the strength of your reactions, for they are perfectly justifiable.*

● ADJ+n feeling **anger, pride** *All those who took part can feel justifiable pride in what was achieved.*

▶ action **act, action, measure** *You will admit that the action was morally justifiable, if technically criminal.*

▶ reason **argument, case, cause, grounds, reason**

They may have valid and justifiable reasons for wanting to remain anonymous.

▶ criticism **complaint, criticism** *There is justifiable criticism of the police for their failure to act quickly.*

▶ worry or fear **concern, fear** *There are, of course, many justifiable concerns about the proposals.*

▶ claim **claim** *Both could make a justifiable claim to being France's most picturesque village.*

▶ decision **decision** *We decided that it was a justifiable decision on the evidence available.*

▶ use **use** *I don't think it's a justifiable use of taxpayers' money.*

● v+ADJ **be, consider sth, seem** *In some circumstances it was considered justifiable not to pursue the complaints.* ● *For these reasons, it seems justifiable to argue that the facility should continue to exist.*

justification N
a reason why something is right

● adj+N types of justification **economic, ethical, ideological, intellectual, legal, moral, philosophical, rational, scientific, theological, theoretical** *The core of Dostoevsky's novel is Raskolnikov's attempt to find a moral justification for his crime.*

▶ some or enough **adequate, ample, proper, sufficient** *They argue that the United States would seem to have ample justification for an attack under international law.* ● *Some people argued, with some justification, that we did not get it right yesterday.*

▶ not enough **insufficient, little** *There seems little justification for such a policy.*

▶ only **only, sole** *The only justification for breaching a young person's confidentiality is if they are at serious risk of immediate harm.*

▶ strong **clear, compelling, convincing, strong** *Nowhere does he give a convincing justification for his decision.*

▶ reasonable **reasonable, valid** *Many had been arrested and detained without reasonable justification.*

▶ not based on personal feelings **objective** *That is not an objective justification, because it is itself rooted in discrimination.*

v+N provide a justification **give (sb), offer (sb), provide (sb with)** *While various justifications are offered for this, they are all irrelevant.*

need a justification **need, require** *He evidently felt that fighting the evil of Nazism required no justification beyond the fact that it was the right thing to do.*

find a justification **find** *It is hard to find a justification for his actions.*

understand a justification **see** *I can see no justification for this at all.*

▶ have a justification **have** *The practice has no scientific justification.*

justified ADJ
doing something for good reasons, or done for good reasons

● adv+ADJ completely **completely, entirely, fully, perfectly, quite, totally, wholly** *I feel fully justified in expressing a personal opinion about the matter.*

▶ in a particular way **economically, legally, morally, scientifically** *Do you think you are morally justified in downloading music illegally?*

▶ partly **partially, partly** *We can feel partially justified at least.*

▶ very **well** *Howie felt well justified in having invested $2m to treble capacity at his processing plant last year.*

▶ in a way that is not based on personal feelings **objectively** *The new law will prevent discrimination on the basis of age, unless that can be objectively justified.*

● v+ADJ **appear, be, feel, prove, seem** *The fears she had expressed were to prove justified.*

justify V
show that there is a good reason for something

● V+n action **act, action, intervention** *The evidence justifying intervention is simply not provided.*

▶ decision **choice, conclusion, decision** *Can you justify your choice?*

▶ belief **belief, faith** *They do not believe they need to justify their beliefs.*

▶ money spent on something **cost, expenditure, expense, investment, outlay, spending** *The rail company was unable to justify the expenditure on a line which carried so few people.*

▶ existence **existence** *In order to justify their existence, all branches of government have to be seen to be doing things.*

▶ claim **assertion, assumption, claim** *The research carried out on behalf of the advertisers was not rigorous enough to justify the claims made in their ads.*

▶ refusal **refusal** *It will be harder for an employer to justify a refusal of flexible working if the worker has suggested practical solutions to the employer's concerns.*

● v+to-V be used to **serve** *The figures served to justify planned cutbacks in state pensions.*

▶ seem to **appear, seem** *Some of his statements seem to justify such criticism.*

▶ try to **attempt, seek, struggle, try** *I tried to justify my actions to myself.*

▶ need to **have, need** *Don't feel you have to justify your decision to anyone.*

K k

keen ADJ

1 wanting to do something

- adv+ADJ very **desperately, especially, extremely, particularly, really, so** INFORMAL**, terribly, very** We are particularly keen to encourage more girls and young women to consider a career in construction.
- ▶ not very **not at all, not exactly, not overly, not that** INFORMAL**, not too** I'm not too keen **on** the idea.
- ▶ rather **pretty** INFORMAL**, quite** I'm quite keen on learning more about photography.
- ▶ in a way that is easy to understand **naturally, understandably** The Prime Minister was understandably keen to stress the improvements in the economy since they gained power.

- v+ADJ **appear, be, feel, look, remain, seem, sound** She seemed keen to join the club.

2 very strong or very effective

- ADJ+n interest or awareness **anticipation, appreciation, awareness, interest, sense** Although Pepys had no scientific training, he took a keen interest in science and joined the Royal Society in 1665. • She was a woman with a keen sense of public duty.
- ▶ physical ability **eye, eyesight, hearing, sense of hearing, sense of smell** You need keen eyesight to spot it.
- ▶ mental ability **brain, insight, intellect, mind, wit** She is a woman of keen intellect.

keep V

1 store information by writing it or putting it into a computer

- V+n **accounts, archive, blog, diary, file, journal, log, note, record, register** During that time she kept a diary which I am now preparing for publication.

2 make something stay within a limit

- V+within **boundaries, bounds, budget, confines, limits, parameters, range** We need to ensure expenditure is kept within budget.

keep to PHR VB

1 prevent an amount or number from passing a limit

- V+n **level, limit, maximum, minimum** The number attending will be kept to a maximum of 40.

2 follow an agreement or rule

- V+n plan **deadline, plan, schedule, timetable** The contractor will be required to keep to this schedule.
- ▶ agreement **agreement, promise, terms** If he failed to keep to the agreement, they would take immediate action through the courts.
- ▶ rule **guidelines, rule** Make sure the child is rewarded for keeping to the rules.
- ▶ amount **budget** This arrangement is perfect if you want to keep to a strict budget.
- ▶ limited amount of food **diet** I've been keeping strictly to my new diet.

keep up PHR VB

continue to do something

- V+n work **good work** You're doing great! Keep up the good work!
- ▶ rate **momentum, pace** He can't keep that pace up forever.
- ▶ payment **payment, repayment** She had been unable to keep up payments on the new loan.
- ▶ communication **commentary, conversation, correspondence** We met in 1997 and since then we've kept up a correspondence.
- ▶ effort **effort, fight** The longer-term answer must be to keep up the fight to repeal all the anti-union laws.
- ▶ opposition **opposition** She called on them to keep up their opposition to the war.
- ▶ pressure **pressure, tension** Unfortunately, Wales could not keep up the pressure in the second half.

key N

1 a metal object for locking a door or container or operating a vehicle's engine

- adj+N spare **duplicate, spare** Who has a spare key to the flat?
- ▶ that fits many locks **master, skeleton** He let them in **with** a master key.
- v+N use a key **turn, use** She jumped into her car, turned the keys in the ignition, and set off for work.
- ▶ put a key into a lock **insert, put in** You may start to find it difficult to hold a cup or insert a key into a lock.
- ▶ take a key out of a lock **remove, take out** Check that you have locked the back door and removed the key.
- ▶ cause keys to make a noise **jangle, jingle** We heard keys being jangled and a heavy door being opened.

> When you have a key made, you **get a key cut**: When we rented out our flat, we needed to get some duplicate keys cut.

- N+v open something **open, unlock** Neil found that one of the keys opened the hut where the equipment was kept.
- ▶ lock something **lock** The biggest key locks the side door.
- ▶ be operated **turn** She heard the key turn in the lock.
- ▶ make a noise **jangle, jingle** His keys jingled in his pocket.
- n+of+N **bunch, set** He reached in his pocket and took out a bunch of keys.

2 the main thing helping you to achieve somethin [usually singular]

- v+N **have, hold** Wireless technology holds the key to further developments in the industry.
- ▶ N+to success **prosperity, success, victory** The executive producer of the show says audience participation is the key to its success.
- ▶ state of continuing to exist **survival** Care for the natural environment is the key to the survival of lif on earth.

▶ development **development, growth, improvement** *The key to small business growth is specialisation.*
▶ future **future** *So we have to make it a priority as a nation to invest in what is the key to our whole economic future.*
▶ happiness **happiness** *Big houses and fast cars are not the key to happiness.*
▶ knowledge **understanding** *It is the key to an understanding of this great world religion.*

3 a part of a keyboard pressed to produce a letter, number etc
● v+N press a key **depress, hit, hold down, press, tap, use** *Initially, the children's fingers struggled to hit the correct keys.*
▶ stop pressing a key **release** *As soon as you release the key, the image stops scrolling.*

key ADJ
very important

● adv+ADJ **absolutely, clearly, obviously, potentially** *Training is clearly key to success in this project.*
● ADJ+n part of something **aspect, component, element, factor, feature, ingredient, part** *One of the key elements of highly effective teams is clearly defined roles and responsibilities.*
▶ person **figure, player** *Paul was a key player in the development of the training scheme.*
▶ idea **concept, idea, point, principle** *Use coloured pens to highlight key points.*
▶ role **part, role** *Both played key roles in Queensland's victory over Victoria yesterday.*
▶ issue **area, issue, theme** *This paper outlines the Association's views on key issues relating to English teaching.*
▶ aim **aim, goal, objective, priority** *The strategy sets out four key objectives which need to be met.*
▶ information **findings, information** *Below is a summary of some of the key findings.*
▶ skill **skill** *There are five specific key skills which were identified during the consultation process.*
● v+ADJ **be, consider sb/sth, prove, remain, seem** *Sea grass is considered key to the health of coral reef habitats.* ● *January's election may prove key to the future direction of the country.*

kick V
it someone or something with your foot

V+adj **closed, open, shut** *The door was kicked open, and Phil rushed in.*
adv+V violently **brutally, hard, viciously, violently** *He also viciously kicked a boy of just seventeen.*
accidentally/deliberately **accidentally, deliberately** *She was accidentally kicked on the back of the head by her opponent.*
many times **repeatedly** *He was repeatedly kicked and stamped on.*
and/or **beat, bite, hit, punch, stamp** *They kicked and punched him, demanding his wallet, which he handed over.*

kick N

1 a hit with your foot
● adj+N **hard, hefty, powerful, sharp, swift, vicious** *A vicious kick in the stomach left him desperately gasping for breath.*
● v+N get a kick **get, receive** *He had to be carried off in the 20th minute after getting a kick on the shin.*
▶ give someone or something a kick **deliver, give (sb/sth), land, plant** *I had an overwhelming urge to give my motorcycle a hefty kick.*
▶ aim a kick **aim, take** *I took a kick at the front door of the flat.*

2 INFORMAL a feeling of excitement or pleasure
● adj+N **big, great, huge, real** *In 1999 I broke the college record, and that gave me a real kick.*
● v+N **get, give sb** *She seemed to get a big kick out of it.*

kid N INFORMAL
a child

● adj+N **big, cool, little, local, poor, rich, young** *Whether you're young or just a big kid at heart, there's plenty for you to do in the area.* ● *He spots this young kid walking up the road with something under his arm.*
● n+N **city, neighbourhood, school, street** *The aim is to encourage school kids to take up the sport.*
● v+like+N **act, behave, feel, look** *I'm really excited. I feel like a kid again.*
● n+of+N **bunch, crowd, gang, group, load** *They clearly thought we were just a bunch of kids on a school excursion.* ● *There were a load of kids there, out in canoes from the Activity Centre.*

kill V
make a person or other living thing die

● adv+V in a way that causes as little pain as possible **humanely, painlessly** *Any animals showing symptoms will be humanely killed without delay.*
▶ very quickly **instantaneously, instantly, outright** *Six of the drivers were killed outright.*
▶ nearly **almost, nearly** *Leslie was returning home late at night when he was almost killed in a car crash.*
▶ finally **eventually, finally** *Harold was mortally wounded by an arrow which struck him in the eye and eventually killed him.*
▶ slowly **slowly** *The disease is slowly killing her.*
▶ deliberately **deliberately, intentionally** *They are claiming allied forces deliberately killed innocent people.*
▶ accidentally **accidentally, inadvertently** *He had forgiven the man who accidentally killed his eldest son.*
▶ illegally **illegally, unlawfully** *An inquest jury ruled that he had been unlawfully killed by officers from the Metropolitan Police.*
▶ in a cruel way **brutally** *This is what the journalist was investigating when he was kidnapped and brutally killed.*
▶ without caring who dies **indiscriminately** *The*

rebels were killing men, women, and children indiscriminately.
▶ in a way that causes great sadness **tragically** *Stephen was tragically killed in a road accident in 1989.*
▶ in a way that is not necessary **needlessly** *Far too many people are needlessly killed or injured in crashes on our roads.*

killer N
someone who kills another person

● adj+N mentally ill **crazed, deranged, mad, psychopathic, psychotic** *A psychopathic killer viciously attacked a woman journalist returning home from a TV broadcast.*
▶ killing several people one after another **serial** *At the same time, another serial killer also began killing women in the Yorkshire area.*
▶ cruel **brutal, sadistic, vicious** *He's then sent to track down the sadistic killer.*
▶ real **real** *Is the real killer still out there?*
▶ lacking sympathy **cold-blooded, cold-hearted, merciless, ruthless** *Ripley is an unscrupulous art dealer and also a cold-blooded killer.*
▶ famous **infamous, notorious** *Is it possible that the infamous killer, never captured by the London police, has made his way to the streets of New York City?*
▶ claimed to be a killer **accused, alleged, suspected** *The alleged killers, three policemen, are in jail.*
▶ paid to be a killer **contract, hired, professional** *The suspect is known to have approached a contract killer a month before her murder.*

● v+N catch a killer **apprehend, arrest, catch, find, stop** *The parents of the schoolboy say they will not rest until their son's killers are caught.*
▶ try to catch a killer **hunt, trace, track, track down** *Murder squad police are still hunting the killer of the two young men.*
▶ find out who the killer is **identify** *After three months, however, police have not identified his killer.*
▶ make a killer have a trial **bring sb to justice** *So began a long investigation to bring her killer to justice.*

● N+v kill someone **kill, murder, strike** *When he finds his parents have been murdered by vicious killers, he sets out to track them down.* ● *The killer had struck again, this time murdering a woman who was out walking a dog.*
▶ move around in a place **roam, stalk** *Will they find the identity of the killer stalking the streets, before any more young women are slaughtered?*
▶ try to find someone in order to kill them **hunt, stalk** *Meanwhile, he's being stalked by a killer.*
▶ try to kill someone **attack, target** *When Paige discovers that the killer is targeting children, she knows that she cannot just stand and watch as more die.*

killing N
an act of deliberately killing someone

● adj+N illegal **extrajudicial, illegal, unlawful** *The inquest jury recorded a unanimous verdict of unlawful killing.*
▶ deliberate **deliberate, intentional, systematic, targeted, wilful** *The targeting and deliberate killing of civilians is unacceptable.*

▶ accidental **accidental** *Military officials are investigating the accidental killing of nine children during an air attack on an alleged terrorist hideout.*
▶ cruel **brutal** *The government is committed to a thorough investigation of the events behind the brutal killing.*
▶ showing a lack of sympathy **cold-blooded** *An ex-soldier has been arrested for the cold-blooded killings of four members of his family.*
▶ causing many people to die **mass** *Government soldiers have also been responsible for mass killings.*
▶ done because of religious differences **sectarian** *The bombing sparked a wave of sectarian killings.*
▶ done without caring who dies **indiscriminate** *The international community cannot permit the indiscriminate killing of civilians.*
▶ done for no reason **needless, random, senseless, wanton** *He was brutally murdered in a senseless killing.*
▶ very unpleasant **gruesome** *It turns out to be the first of a series of gruesome killings.*
▶ causing as little pain as possible **humane** *Inspectors have the power to require the humane killing of any protected animal they consider to be suffering excessively or unnecessarily.*
▶ involving a series of people **serial** *This is a well performed, thought-provoking film about the investigation into Korea's first serial killings.*

● n+N **contract, gangland, honour, mercy, revenge** *From physical abuse to forced marriages and honour killings, domestic violence continues to be frighteningly common in many communities.*

● v+N stop a killing **end, halt, prevent, stop** *The UN forces were unable to stop the brutal killings.*
▶ say that a killing is wrong **condemn** *No one has yet condemned the killing of an innocent man.*
▶ order a killing **order** *The three men were convicted in January of ordering the killing.*
▶ say that a killing is not allowed **forbid, prohibit** *The 1928 law forbade the killing of bulls in bullfights.*
▶ approve of a killing **condone** *I, of course, don't condone the killing of innocent people.*
▶ commit a killing **be reponsible for, carry out, commit** *Such killings are carried out by the security services.*
▶ try to find out about a killing **investigate** *A special commission was announced to investigate the killings.*
▶ see a killing **witness** *He had witnessed the killing of a detainee by a guard.*
▶ say that there is a good reason for a killing **justify** *They will probably try to justify the killing by saying that he was resisting arrest.*

kind N
a type of person or thing

● adj+N different **different** *This site has good guides to grammar and different kinds of writing.*
▶ particular **certain, distinct, particular, special, specific** *It is an advanced vocational course designed to prepare you for a particular kind of work.*
▶ various **several, various** *There are cages with monkeys and apes of various kinds in them.*
▶ strange **funny, odd, peculiar, strange, weird** *The man was playing a strange kind of instrument.*

▸ same **same, similar** *The British army conducted similar kinds of operations there in the 1950s.*
▸ usual **common, normal, typical, usual** *Amy is definitely not your usual kind of heroine.*
▸ right/wrong **right, wrong** *Our guide will help you choose the right kind of drill for the job.*
▸ best/worst **best, worst** *Swimming is probably the best kind of exercise you can take during pregnancy.*
 ● *These people are racists of the worst kind.*

kind ADJ
behaving in a way that shows you care about other people

● adv+ADJ **extremely, incredibly, really, so, too, very** *He was always extremely kind to her.*
▸ and/or **caring, considerate, friendly, generous, gentle, good, helpful, loving, nice, thoughtful** *'He was probably the kindest, gentlest soul you'd ever want to meet,' she said.*

kindness N
kind behaviour, or kind feelings

▸ adj+N **extraordinary, great, human, loving, real, unfailing, utmost** *He spoke rather quietly, and was a man of great kindness.*
v+N show kindness to someone **show (sb), treat sb with** *I would like to thank all my friends and neighbours, who showed me such kindness in my sad loss.*
reward someone for their kindness **repay, return** *How can she truly repay his kindness?*
receive kindness **meet with, receive** *Her mother had received so much kindness from the Deanes.*
remember someone's kindness **never forget, remember** *I shall never forget your kindness.*
be grateful for someone's kindness **appreciate** *Their kindness is very much appreciated.*

N+v **overwhelm, touch** *I was overwhelmed by their kindness and thoughtfulness.*

and/or **compassion, friendship, generosity, goodness, patience, sympathy, thoughtfulness, warmth** *We continue to rely on the kindness and generosity of our sponsors in order to keep the centre open.*

king N
the senior male member of a royal family

v+N make someone king **anoint, appoint, crown, proclaim** *He was crowned king in 1306.*
force a king from his position of power **depose, overthrow** *Shakespeare's Richard II was considered a highly political play, since it shows a king being deposed.*
become king **become** *Edward III had become king in 1326 at the age of 14.*
perform duties for a king **serve** *He thought of becoming a monk there when he could no longer serve the king.*

N+v rule **command, reign, rule** *From the mid 6th century BC, Persian kings ruled over peoples and territory stretching from Northern Libya to Central Asia.*
officially give up power **abdicate** *The king abdicated and was imprisoned in Pontefract Castle.*

kiss V
touch someone with your lips because of love or sexual feelings, or when you say hello or goodbye

● adv+V with strong sexual feelings **passionately** *A surge of desire swept through me as we kissed passionately.*
▸ gently **gently, lightly, softly, tenderly** *He smoothed her hair from her forehead and kissed her very tenderly on the lips.*

● and/or **caress, cuddle, embrace, hug** *Then we all hugged and kissed and said goodbye.*

kiss N
an act of kissing someone

● adj+N involving strong sexual feelings **passionate** *She surprised Ian by giving him a passionate kiss.*
▸ first **first** *Holly visits him in the hospital, and they share their first kiss.*
▸ last **final, last** *I just want him back, to give him one last kiss.*
▸ big **big** *He pulled her towards him and gave her a big kiss.*
▸ little **little** *I just gave her a little kiss on the forehead.*
▸ showing that you like or care about someone **affectionate, loving, tender, warm**
▸ gentle **gentle, soft** *I planted a gentle kiss on Daniel's head and pulled him even closer.*
▸ quick **quick** *She greeted me with a quick kiss on the cheek.*
▸ wet **sloppy** INFORMAL, **wet** *I miss the way you'd wake me in the morning with a sloppy kiss.*
▸ lasting a long time **lingering, long** *But this time we shared a tight hug and a long kiss.*
▸ without any sexual feeling **chaste, innocent** *He merely planted a chaste kiss on her forehead, instead of her lips as she'd expected.*

● n+N **farewell, goodbye, goodnight** *Natalie was hoping for a goodnight kiss.*
● v+N place a kiss **drop, place, plant** *She leaned forward and planted a kiss on his cheek.*
▸ give someone a kiss **give** *She gave me a kiss and touched my cheek with her hand.*
▸ give someone a kiss unexpectedly **snatch, steal** *He grabbed her from behind and stole a kiss.*
▸ get a kiss **get, receive** *He was hoping to get a kiss from her.*
▸ give someone and be given a kiss **exchange, share** *They exchanged a quick kiss.*
▸ kiss your hand and pretend to blow the kiss to someone **blow (sb)** *He blew her a kiss as he left.*

● and/or **cuddle, hug** *The couple finally paused in the deserted bus shelter, for a kiss and a cuddle.*

knack N
a skill or ability

● adj+N **amazing, extraordinary, great, happy, incredible, real, special, uncanny, unerring, wonderful** *He has the uncanny knack of noticing when someone is upset, or in need of support, or simply just wants to talk.*
● v+N have a knack **have** *She seemed to have a knack for being in the right place at the right time.*

▸ get a knack **acquire, develop, get, learn** *It is relatively easy, once you have got the knack.*
▸ lose a knack **lose** *It seems that I've not lost the knack completely.*
▸ show a knack **demonstrate, display, show** *James shows a real knack for composing simple yet fantastic melodies.*

knead V
prepare dough or clay by pressing it

● adv+V gently **gently, lightly** *Knead the mixture lightly until it forms a smooth dough.*
▸ thoroughly **thoroughly, well** *Place the dough on a floured surface and knead it well until it feels elastic.*
▸ for a short time **briefly** *Briefly knead the dough to release some of the air.*

● V+n **bread, clay, dough, mixture, pastry** *On a board sprinkled with flour, knead the dough for 10–15 minutes.*

knife N
1 an object with sharp blade for cutting food

● adj+N sharp/not sharp **blunt, sharp** *Using a sharp knife, slice the aubergines lengthwise.*
▸ with a row of points along the edge **serrated** *With a serrated knife cut off the top and bottom of the orange.*

● n+N for cutting a particular food **bread, butter, steak, vegetable** *She threatened to stab him with the bread knife.*
▸ used in a kitchen **kitchen** *We have a wide range of kitchen knives available.*
▸ made of steel **stainless steel, steel** *He bought a set of twelve stainless steel knives.*
▸ for cutting meat **carving** *Why do we need an electric carving knife?*

● v+N **sharpen** *A flat stone was used for sharpening knives or tools.*

● n+of+N **blade, handle, set** *Keep the blade of your knife sharp at all times.* ● *I had bought myself a set of chef's knives.*

2 an object with a sharp blade used as a weapon

● v+N carry a knife **be armed with, carry** *Most of the young men were carrying knives.*
▸ take out a knife **produce, pull, pull out, take out** *She pulled a knife on me!*
▸ point or wave a knife **brandish, point, wave, wield** *They were robbed by two men brandishing knives.*
▸ threaten or attack someone with a knife **attack sb with, stab sb with, threaten sb with** *She had been repeatedly stabbed with a knife.*
▸ put a knife in someone **plunge, stick INFORMAL, thrust** *He grabbed him by the hair and plunged a knife into his back.*

● N+n **attack, crime, cut, fight, wound** *The reported levels of knife crime in the area are low.*

knot N
a point where something is tied

● adj+N **loose, tight** *Be careful to check that the knots are tight and the tension is correct.*

● v+N tie a knot **make, tie** *He tied a knot in his silk scarf.*

▸ untie a knot **undo, untie** *Stan was fumbling to undo the knot around the sack.*
▸ make a knot tighter/looser **loosen, tighten** *Now pull the ends of the yarn to tighten the knot.*

knowledge N
what someone knows about a particular subject, or what is known generally about different things or about life

● adj+N when someone knows a lot **detailed, encyclopaedic, extensive, good, in-depth, intimate, sound, thorough, unrivalled, vast** *The exhibition was greatly facilitated by Rosenthal's encyclopaedic knowledge of current British art.*
▸ basic **basic, limited, superficial** *He had a basic knowledge of French.*
▸ knowing the most recent facts **up-to-date** *They need to be good communicators and have up-to-date knowledge of the legal requirements.*
▸ gained through doing or hearing something yourself **direct, first-hand** *The students on work experience will gain first-hand knowledge about the police.*
▸ given by someone who knows a lot **expert, inside, specialist** *Health and safety advisers offer expert knowledge and skills in order to generate and promote a positive health and safety culture.*
▸ types of knowledge **factual, local, mathematical, medical, practical, professional, scientific, technical, theoretical** *We live on site and can help with any enquiries and share our local knowledge with you.* ● *I didn't have enough medical knowledge to know what was wrong with him.*

● n+N what has happened in the past **background** *The studies can be challenging and can require more background knowledge about the subject.*

● v+N have knowledge **have, possess** *All our drivers are familiar with the handling and control of the vehicles and possess a good knowledge of mechanics should this be needed.*
▸ not have knowledge **lack** *Some of the staff lacked appropriate knowledge of the patients' specific care needs.*
▸ get knowledge **accumulate, acquire, gain, glean** *You will gain practical knowledge of all aspects of the job as well as recognised qualifications.*
▸ improve knowledge **advance, broaden, build on, deepen, develop, enhance, expand, extend, further, improve, increase, widen** *I hope to further my knowledge of languages by studying Spanish at university.*
▸ use knowledge **apply, draw on, use** *We apply our practical knowledge of what actually works in this field, to make your adverts stand out from the crowd.*
▸ share knowledge **disseminate, impart, pass on, share** *Workers in both organizations had established practices for sharing knowledge which were informal and unstructured.*
▸ test knowledge **test** *Children can take part in a quiz that will test their wildlife knowledge.*
▸ show knowledge **demonstrate, show** *All applicants will be required to demonstrate knowledge of legal requirements.*

● and/or **ability, confidence, experience, expertise, insight, skills, understanding** *The social work*

*department provides ongoing support and training
to help carers develop their knowledge and skills.*

knowledgeable ADJ
knowing a lot

- adv+ADJ very **extremely, highly, very** *The staff
seemed very knowledgeable and up to date with the
technology.*
▸ enough **sufficiently** *There will always be someone
on the staff who is sufficiently knowledgeable **about**
every individual student to provide a worthwhile
reference.*

- ADJ+n person **audience, expert, guide, person,
professional, speaker, staff, team** *A knowledgeable
guide accompanies all our cruises.*
▸ advice **advice** *Thank you for your prompt service
and knowledgeable advice.*

- v+ADJ **appear, be, become, seem, sound** *Patients
are bcoming more knowledgeable **about** the range
of treatment that is open to them.*

   and/or **enthusiastic, experienced, friendly,
   helpful, professional, skilled** *Our helpful and
   knowledgeable staff are ready and waiting for your
   call or email.*

known ADJ
that people know about

- adv+ADJ known about by many people
commonly, generally, well, widely *The author does
little more than take widely-known ideas and
regurgitate them under new headings.*
▸ known about by few people **little** *He played for a
little-known band called 'Plastic Dog'.*

- ADJ+n **cause, cure, example, fact, problem, risk
factor** *At present, there is no known cure for
emphysema, which causes advanced damage to the
lungs and can eventually kill sufferers.*

kudos N
praise and respect because of an achievement

- adj+N much **great** *His is a name that adds great
kudos to any racing championship.*
▸ extra **added, extra** *A teaching assistant gains extra
kudos and respect for being in charge of doling out
the sweets!*

- v+N have kudos **have** *He also has the added kudos
of having been part of the triumphant English team.*
▸ get kudos **earn, gain, get** *She earned further kudos
by being the only girl in the class who could speak
Spanish.*

Ll

labour N

1 workers considered as group

- ● adj+N relating to the amount of skill that workers have **semi-skilled, skilled, unskilled** *The emphasis was on skills, as the need for skilled labour was clearly there.*
- ▶ relating to the amount of money that workers earn **cheap, unpaid** *They were criticized for using unpaid labour.*
- ▶ relating to whether the workers are temporary or not **casual, organized** *The mechanisation of farming began to reduce the need for casual labour.*
- ● n+N **child, immigrant, migrant, slave, sweatshop, volunteer** *We all want to see an end to child labour and to secure adherence to core labour standards across the world.*
- ● v+N employ labour **employ, hire, use** *David employs local labour to repair an outhouse at the farm.*
- ▶ treat labour badly **exploit** *Big businesses are profiting from exploiting cheap labour.*
- ● N+n group of workers **force, market, supply** *The UK has a highly skilled and flexible labour force.*
- ▶ when workers are unhappy **dispute, unrest** *The arbitration scheme deals with labour disputes.*
- ▶ movement of workers **flexibility, migration, mobility** *This rise in the standard of living is both a main cause and a main effect of labour migration.*
- ▶ when there are not enough workers **shortage** *The labour shortages in the booming economy of south-east England have attracted many workers from abroad.*
- ▶ cost **costs** *Redundancies are one way of reducing labour costs.*
- ▶ law **law** *Under UK labour laws, industrial action must commence within four weeks of a ballot closing.*
- ▶ organizations **movement, union** *The labour movement tries to protect workers' rights.*

2 work, especially hard physical work

- ● adj+N **back-breaking, forced, hard, manual, physical** *The Geneva convention bans the use of forced labour for prisoners of war.*
- ● v+N **withdraw** *The cleaners threatened to withdraw their labour after the informal talks with management broke down.*

labour under PHR VB

- ● V+n **delusion, illusion, impression, misapprehension, misconception** *For a long time, Garth had laboured under the misapprehension that the two men were related.*

lack N

a situation when there is not enough of something

- ● adj+N complete **complete, sheer, total, utter** *There appears to be a complete lack of interest in athletics.*
- ▶ very serious **chronic, profound, serious, severe,**

woeful *She suffers from a chronic lack of self-confidence.*
- ▶ easy to see **conspicuous, distinct, marked, notable, noticeable, obvious, singular** *There's a distinct lack of modestly priced housing in the area.*
- ▶ making you feel worried, angry or surprised **alarming, appalling, remarkable, shocking, surprising, worrying** *There was a surprising lack of people in the 25 – 34 age range.* ● *The food hygiene survey uncovered a worrying lack of knowledge of basic hygiene which is putting people at risk.*
- ▶ relative **comparative, relative** *Despite his relative lack of formal education, he was very successful.*
- ▶ apparent **apparent, seeming** *In reality, it was the tedium of his life that had resulted in his apparent lack of memory.*
- ▶ general **general, overall** *There were complaints about the general lack of cleanliness.*

lack V

not have any or enough of something

- ● adv+V **clearly, completely, entirely, totally** *Her new book completely lacks the originality of her first novel.*
- ● V+n ability or knowledge or experience **ability, capacity, experience, knowledge, skill** *He lacked the experience necessary to do the job.*
- ▶ a special quality **finesse, originality, pace, punch, sophistication, spark, sparkle** *The film lacks the punch of films such as Memento and Jacob's Ladder.*
- ▶ power or strength **power, resources, strength** *This song could find itself inside the top three, but might just lack the strength to make it to number one.*
- ▶ personal quality **ambition, charisma, confidence, courage, imagination, motivation, sense, wisdom** *He confessed freely that he lacked the courage to speak out.*
- ▶ quality that makes something believable **conviction, credibility** *We were creating chances, but too many of our shots lacked any conviction.*
- ▶ clear quality **clarity, coherence** *The argument presented lacked any coherence.*
- ▶ thorough and careful quality **depth, rigour** *The work was generally good throughout, although it lacked rigour at times.*

lacking ADJ

that does not exist or is not available

- ● adv+ADJ in a way that is serious or sad **sadly, seriously, severely** *The film is quite exciting, but surprisingly lacking in plot.*
- ▶ clearly **clearly, conspicuously, distinctly, noticeably, obviously, singularly** *These 'life skills' were distinctly lacking in disadvantaged groups.*
- ▶ completely **completely, entirely, totally, wholly** *H is almost entirely lacking in emotion.*
- ▶ rather **rather, somehow** *This is an attitude which has been rather lacking in recent years.*

land N

an area of ground, especially one used for a particular purpose

- adj+N used for farming **agricultural, arable** *84 per cent of agricultural land in the country is polluted by acid rain.*
- used for businesses or factories **industrial** *Details of council-owned industrial land available for sale can be found on the website.*
- not used **bare, derelict, disused, uncultivated, unused, vacant, waste** *Parks were built on derelict land, canals cleaned up and car-free days implemented.*
- that has never had buildings on it **greenbelt, greenfield, undeveloped** *And even if there is a need, such homes can be built elsewhere without spoiling greenfield land.*
- that has had buildings on it before **brownfield, previously developed** *The development is being built on a 70-hectare site, which is primarily brownfield land.*
- good for growing crops **fertile, rich** *Some Egyptians grew wheat and barley on the fertile land of the Nile valley.*
- not good for growing crops **barren, infertile** *Several years of drought have made the land even more barren.*
- dirty or polluted **contaminated, polluted** *He's heading a project to clean up contaminated land.*
- owned by a particular person or company **private** *The path is on private land and so is not accessible to the public.*
- types of land **arid, flat, hilly, low-lying, marshy** *It's a winding road that cuts across the flat land of the estuary.*
- n+N **farm, farming, grazing, pasture** *This is grazing land where livestock can wander freely.*
- N+n **management, reclamation** *He has been involved in brownfield land reclamation and redevelopment on sites formerly occupied by collieries and gas works.*
- n+of+N **area, expanse, parcel, patch, piece, plot, portion, stretch, strip, tract** *He bought a plot of land to build the house on.*

landing N
the process of moving a plane etc down onto the ground

- adj+N smooth **perfect, smooth** *The pilot managed to make a very smooth landing.*
- not smooth **bumpy, rough** *We were rather shaken up after a bumpy landing on a small grass airstrip.*
- safe **safe, successful** *The plane made a safe landing after a problem with one of its engines.*
- because of a problem **emergency, forced** *A charter jet carrying 237 passengers has made an emergency landing after it appeared to suffer engine trouble.*
- n+N **crash** *Two men were injured when their helicopter made a crash landing following technical difficulties.*
- v+N **attempt, make** *American Airlines and British Airways make routine landings there.*

landmark N
an easily noticed famous building or object

- adj+N famous **familiar, famous, iconic, recognizable, well-known** *The Eiffel Tower is arguably the most famous landmark in Paris.*
- easy to see **distinctive, notable, prominent** *The spire, standing 56 metres high, is still the most prominent landmark in Bishop's Stortford, and can be seen from virtually every part of the town.*
- old **historic, historical** *Clifton is famous for its plethora of shops and its historical landmarks, such as Brunel's famous Clifton Suspension Bridge.*
- in the place that you are **local** *Kendal Castle is an important local landmark and historical building.*
- N+n **building** *There are many landmark buildings, including the Stadium of Light – the home of Sunderland Football Club.*

2 a major event or achievement in a process

- adj+N **great, important, major, significant** *The adoption of the National Policy on Education by the Parliament in 1986 is a major landmark in the history of education in independent India.*
- v+N **celebrate, pass, reach** *The company celebrated a landmark in 1979 when over one million passengers were carried for the first time in a single year.*
- N+n **achievement, case, decision, event, judgment, ruling, study** *The court overturned the decision, making this a landmark ruling which will have a far-reaching effect for insurers.*
- N+in **development, history** *The event was a landmark in the history of the women's movement.*

landscape N
a beautiful area of land or one that has a particular type of feature

- adj+N beautiful **beautiful, breathtaking, dramatic, idyllic, picturesque, scenic, spectacular, stunning** *The Costa Calida's beautiful landscapes provide opportunities for a range of outdoor activities.*
- not developed **unspoilt** *This peaceful, unspoilt landscape supports a wealth of birdlife.*
- empty **barren, bleak, desolate, harsh, stark, wild** *The road changes character here, and the landscape is quite bleak.*
- with mountains or hills **hilly, mountainous** *The holiday villas are in an ideal location amongst the breathtaking, mountainous landscapes of Andalucia.*
- without hills **flat** *The city of Ely rises above the flat landscape of the East Anglian fens.*
- with a lot of gentle slopes **rolling, undulating** *Our route to Coniston took us through an undulating landscape.*
- with rocks **rocky, rugged** *People come to Cheddar Gorge because of its extraordinary rocky landscape.*
- with a lot of trees **wooded** *Wooded landscapes help to release rainwater more slowly, and this in turn means fewer floods.*
- city/country **rural, urban** *The UK has a rich variety of rural landscapes, from sweeping moorland to pretty hamlets.*
- very green **green, lush** *This is one of the Caribbean's most popular islands, with lush landscapes and stunning beaches.*
- with different types of features **diverse, varied** *New Zealand is a large country with a varied landscape.*
- n+N **desert, moorland, mountain** *It is a region of*

rocky plains and desert landscape broken by the fertile wine-growing areas.

● v+N be the main feature in a landscape **dominate** *On the road to the village, a striking nineteenth-century church dominates the landscape.*

▶ be present in a landscape **dot, litter** *Enormous craters dot the landscape in many areas.*

▶ form a landscape **create, form, shape** *Farming plays a crucial role in shaping the landscape.*

▶ change a landscape **alter, change, transform** *The removal of hedges changed the landscape of the area completely.*

▶ spoil a landscape **blight, scar** *Rubbish clogs the waterways and blights the landscape.*

▶ protect or improve a landscape **conserve, enhance, protect** *Their aim was to enhance and conserve typical English landscapes.*

language N

1 human communication using spoken or written words; the style or type of words used by a person or group

● adj+N rude **abusive, bad, foul, obscene, offensive, strong** *Thomas was sent off for using foul and abusive language towards the referee.*

▶ ordinary **everyday, ordinary, plain, simple** *Use plain language and avoid jargon and technical terms.*

▶ suitable **appropriate, suitable** *Always use language that is appropriate for the situation.*

▶ describing the level of formality **colloquial, formal, informal**

▶ types of language **descriptive, figurative, literary, non-technical, poetic, racist, sexist, spoken, technical, written** *Poetic language is often figurative, with ideas condensed for maximum impact.*

● v+N use language **adopt, use** *Try not to adopt the language of the tabloid press.* ● *He then began to use some very bad language.*

▶ get language **acquire** *This module examines how children acquire language and learn to communicate.*

▶ be careful with the language you use **mind, watch** *You are a role model for the children and we ask you to mind your language at all times of day.*

● N+n **acquisition, development, learning, proficiency, skills** *Nursery rhymes encourage language development, imagination and a sense of rhythm.*

2 the particular form of words and speech that is used by the people of a country or area

● adj+N first **first, native** *If your native language is not English, you may be required to do a short test of proficiency in English.*

▶ second **foreign, second** *The ability to speak at least one foreign language is essential.*

▶ used in official contexts **official** *The material is available in both French and English, which are both official languages in Canada.*

▶ still spoken/no longer spoken **dead, modern** *Dead languages such as Latin are still taught in many schools.*

▶ originally used in a place **indigenous** *Welsh, the indigenous Celtic language of Wales, is the linchpin of national identity.*

▶ only spoken by a minority of people **minority** *Minority languages, such as Gaelic and Scots in Scotland, have received more attention in recent years.*

▶ spoken by two or more people or groups **common, shared** *The Old Slavs shared a common language, known as Old Slavonic.*

● v+N speak a language **speak** *He speaks four languages fluently.*

▶ learn/teach a language **learn, study, teach** *It's not easy to learn a new language as an adult.*

▶ when someone learns a language without being taught **acquire** *Children acquire the language of the community they are in.*

▶ know a language well **master** *It took me several years to master the language when we moved to Spain.*

lapse N

a period of not doing something in the right way

● adj+N lasting for a short time **momentary, temporary** *He had a momentary lapse of concentration and ran into the back of the car in front.*

▶ happening occasionally **occasional, odd** *Despite the odd lapse in concentration, her playing was pretty good on the whole.*

▶ serious **serious** *It was a serious lapse of judgement that would later almost destroy his career.*

▶ not serious **minor, slight** *I would hope that this is a minor lapse and does not indicate a lack of new ideas.*

● n+N **memory, security** *There have been security lapses at the prison in which prisoners have been able to escape.*

● N+in **concentration** *A lapse in concentration allowed Stevenage to score.*

● N+of **concentration, memory** *We all have lapses of memory occasionally, and this book will help improve your memory.*

large ADJ

bigger than usual in size or amount

● adv+ADJ very **exceptionally, extremely, impossibly, very** *There is a smaller bedroom which has an exceptionally large and comfy double bed.*

▶ rather **fairly, pretty** INFORMAL**, quite, rather, reasonably** *Sound files can be quite large and will therefore take longer to download.*

▶ unusually **abnormally, disproportionately, unusually** *The group included an unusually large quotient of female composers.*

▶ large when compared to others **comparatively, relatively** *Owners do not often look in their pets' mouths, so many mouth tumours are comparatively large when first seen.*

▶ large enough **sufficiently** *The print is sufficiently large so they won't need their reading glasses on.*

▶ in a way that surprises you **surprisingly, unexpectedly** *A surprisingly large crowd made it out of bed in time for the start.*

● v+ADJ **appear, be, become, figure, get, grow, look, loom, seem** *Mirrors make a room appear larger than it really is.* ● *Several issues have loomed larged in their discussions.*

laugh V

make a noise when you find something funny

- adv+V loudly, or so that people can hear **aloud, loudly, out loud, uproariously** *I laughed aloud when I saw what he was wearing.*
- quietly **quietly, softly** *'He is really rather naughty sometimes,' said Mary, laughing softly.*
- when someone laughs a lot in a way that they cannot control **hard, helplessly, hysterically, uncontrollably** *I was laughing so hard at the joke that my face was hurting.*

> When someone suddenly starts to laugh, you can say they **burst out laughing**: *We looked at each other and burst out laughing.*

- in a happy, enthusiastic way **gleefully, heartily, merrily** *Philip gets the joke and laughs heartily.*
- in a nervous way **nervously** *Professor Baldwin laughed nervously and glanced at the stage area.*
- showing regret **ruefully** *'I shouldn't have gone,' she said, and laughed ruefully.*

laugh N

the sound you make when you laugh

- adj+N loud **big, hearty, huge, loud** *Hudson greeted the question with a huge laugh.*
- making other people laugh too **infectious** *John's infectious laugh made everyone feel that he was nothing more than a mate playing a few tunes for you.*
- showing someone's feelings or attitude **embarassed, jolly, merrily, nervous, scornful** *He gave a nervous laugh and looked down at the floor.*
- sounding sad, not happy **hollow** *When you tell teachers that standards are rising, the most usual reaction is a hollow laugh.*
- v+N when people laugh **get, raise** *His speech got a few laughs.*

> You can also use the expression **make someone laugh**: *The story was a familiar one but it made the audience laugh.*

- make the sound of a laugh **give** *Debbie gave a reluctant laugh and shook her head.*
- stop a laugh from being heard **stifle, suppress** *She had to stifle a laugh by hiding her face in Bob's coat.*

laugh off PHR VB

joke to show something is not important

- V+n **criticism, reports, rumours, suggestions** *He laughed off suggestions that he had become a sex symbol.*

laughter N

the sound of someone laughing

- adj+N loud **hearty, loud, raucous** *The whole class erupted in loud laughter.*
- quiet or not expressed **gentle, muffled, polite, silent** *She was shaking with silent laughter.*
- impossible to control **helpless, hysterical, maniacal, uncontrollable, wild** *The characters would burst out into maniacal laughter for no reason.*
- nervous **nervous** *There was nervous laughter as we donned our safety helmets.*

- showing that you think someone or something is stupid **derisive, scornful** *Facing the ordeal, he arrived at the door only to be met by the derisive laughter of two of his so-called friends.*
- making other people laugh too **infectious** *He was an affable listener and greeted other people's jokes with hearty and infectious laughter.*
- v+N cause laughter **bring, cause, prompt, provoke** *The remark provoked laughter in the courtroom.*
- stop laughter **stifle, suppress** *He put his hand over his mouth to stifle his laughter.*
- N+v fill a place **fill sth, ring out** *Their happy laughter rang out around the house.*
- become quieter **die down** *When the laughter died down, he resumed his speech.*
- v+into+N **break (out), burst** *He suddenly burst into hysterical laughter for no apparent reason.*
- v+with+N **cry, howl, roar, scream, shake** *The audience thought it was part of the act and roared with laughter.*
- n+of+N sudden attack **fit** *This last remark sent Alice into a fit of laughter.*
- when laughter is loud **gale, hoot, howl, peal, roar, shriek** *The question was met with a gale of laughter.*
- when laughter spreads around a group of people **ripple** *There was a faint ripple of laughter from the audience.*

launch V

start a major activity or start selling a product

- adv+V officially **formally, officially** *The health minister officially launched the campaign.*
- recently **newly, recently** *The University of St Andrews is one of four Scottish universities, which recently launched an innovative partnership with Edinburgh Zoo.*

> Usage **Launch** is always passive when used with **newly**: *The club's newly launched website is packed with useful information.*

- successfully **successfully** *The product has already been successfully launched in the US.*
- V+n business, product, or service **book, brand, business, magazine, newspaper, paper, product, service, website** *Low-cost airline bmibaby has launched services from Cardiff International Airport.*
- attack **assault, attack, invasion, offensive** *A head teacher has launched a stinging attack on the Government's policy of sending special needs pupils to mainstream schools.* • *It was the year that King Harald of Norway launched his invasion of England.*
- attempt to achieve something **appeal, bid, campaign, initiative, petition, programme, project, scheme** *The Department of Health has announced that it will launch a campaign to encourage people to be tested for hepatitis C infection.*
- investigation **inquiry, investigation, study, survey** *Detectives in Armagh have launched a murder inquiry after a man died having sustained a number of gunshot wounds.*
- career **career** *We'll give you as much support as we can in launching your catering career.*

▶ competition **competition** *A competition was launched to name the staff magazine.*

launch into PHR VB
start something with a lot of enthusiasm

● V+n angry speech **attack, diatribe, monologue, rant, tirade** *He launched into a serious diatribe about how important it was for me to keep accurate records.*

▶ song **rendition, song** *He launched into a jaunty rendition of 'When The Saints Go Marching In'.*

lavish V
give someone a lot of something

● V+n **attention, care, love, money, praise** *Children do not need lots of money lavished on them – what they want is lots of your time and attention.*

lavish ADJ
in large amounts, or costing a lot of money

● ADJ+n event or entertainment **celebration, ceremony, entertainment, party, production, reception, wedding** *They wed at a lavish ceremony in Malibu.*

▶ meal **banquet, dinner, lunch, meal** *Our flexible facilities can accommodate a variety of requirements, from small intimate dinners to large lavish banquets.*

▶ decoration **decoration** *The manuscript is of great significance, owing to its lavish decoration and the fact that it is the only preserved illustrated chronicle of the Byzantine era.*

▶ way of living **lifestyle** *He has been living a lavish lifestyle, with fast cars and magnificent homes.*

▶ gift **gift** *He spent thousands on lavish gifts for his girlfriends.*

▶ surroundings **surroundings** *The premises provide excellent facilities in lavish modern surroundings.*

▶ praise **praise** *The school has received lavish praise from the inspectors.*

law N
an official rule or system of rules that people must obey

● adj+N strict **draconian, restrictive, strict, stringent, tough** *Due to strict libel laws in the UK, the scientist identified will not be named in this article.*

▶ wrong or unfair **discriminatory, oppressive, repressive, unjust** *The white regime had no intention of changing the unjust laws of apartheid.*

▶ relating to a country, state etc **federal, international, national, state** *Anyone possessing marijuana for medicinal purposes would be breaking federal law.*

▶ types of law **civil, commercial, constitutional, criminal, electoral, environmental, humanitarian, matrimonial** *There are a number of criminal and civil laws to protect ownership.* ● *The team deals with all aspects of matrimonial law, with particular expertise in domestic violence.*

● v+N obey a law **obey, observe, respect, uphold** *When Crandall refused to obey the law she was arrested and imprisoned.*

You can describe someone who obeys the law as *law-abiding*: *The vast majority of our law-abiding customers appreciate our tough action against fare cheats.*

▶ not obey a law **breach, break, contravene, disobey, flout, infringe, transgress, violate** *Breaching copyright law is an offence.*

▶ make something become a law **adopt, enact, implement, impose, introduce, pass** *The government wants to introduce tougher laws on crime.*

▶ change a law **alter, amend, change, reform, review, revise** *The Scottish Executive is committed to reforming the law as soon as reasonably practicable*

▶ make sure that people obey a law **administer, apply, enforce** *These laws are rarely enforced for SUVs, however, since these vehicles are seen as passenger vehicles instead of commercial trucks.*

▶ become a law **become** *When the Sunday Trading Act became law in 1994, there was protection for those who didn't want to work on Sundays.*

▶ get rid of a law **abolish, overturn, repeal** *The league was disbanded in 1846 when the laws were repealed.*

▶ make a law stricter **strengthen, tighten** *The government plans to tighten the law in order to protect the public from sex offenders.*

▶ make a law less strict **liberalize, relax** *Britain's licensing laws have been relaxed.*

▶ make a law clearer **clarify, interpret** *Where there is no clear statute law, the courts have to interpret and clarify the law.*

▶ make a law deal with more things **extend** *There are plans to extend laws against inciting racial hatred to include religious hatred.*

▶ publicly disagree with a law and ask for it to be tested in a court **challenge** *The two men successfully challenged laws which prevented workers over 65 claiming full employment rights.*

▶ decide what a law will be **formulate, make** *The law was formulated before the advent of the Internet*

● N+v control something **control, govern, regulate** *The laws governing adoption in Wales are very similar to the laws in England.*

▶ allow something **allow, authorize, permit** *Charity law currently allows charities to undertake some trading activity.*

▶ not allow something **ban, forbid, prevent, prohibit, regulate** *Spain's government introduced a law banning mistreatment of pets.*

▶ say you must do something **dictate, force, oblige sb, prescribe, require (sb)** *All UK employers are required by law to register with a health and safety enforcing agency.*

▶ say something **say, state, stipulate** *The law states that the education and support of children and young people is primarily the responsibility of parents.*

▶ limit something **limit, restrict** *The law limits the number of pupils in an infant class with one qualified teacher to a maximum of 30.*

▶ affect someone or something **affect, apply to, cover** *The law applies to charities.*

▶ accept something **recognize** *The law already recognizes that this sort of evidence can be relevant*

▶ change **change** *The law changed a few years ago and now part-time workers enjoy exactly the same rights.*

- N+n **enforcement, enforcer, reform** *Police and other law enforcers are under pressure to counter rising levels of violent gun crime.*

lawsuit N

a legal case involving disagreement between two people

- v+N start a lawsuit **bring, file, issue, launch** *The Hollywood movie studios have filed a lawsuit **against** 22 websites which they claim encourage and facilitate movie piracy.*
- ▶ be going to have a lawsuit **face** *The charity is facing three lawsuits from volunteers claiming unfair dismissal.*
- ▶ end a lawsuit by reaching a decision **settle** *Bates has settled his lawsuit **with** Chelsea following his acrimonious departure from the club.*
- ▶ win/lose a lawsuit **lose, win** *Eight families who have won lawsuits will receive more than $213 million.*
- ▶ decide not to go ahead with a lawsuit **drop** *They have dropped the multi-million dollar lawsuit **over** the title of the movie.*
- ▶ say a lawsuit cannot continue **dismiss** *A federal judge dismissed the copyright infringement lawsuit because there was not enough evidence to prove any melody had in fact been stolen.*
- N+v **accuse sb of sth, allege, claim, say** *21 people have filed a lawsuit accusing the government of negligence.* • *The lawsuit alleges that the company failed to disclose vital information about the drug.*

lay down PHR VB

state officially what someone must do

- V+n **conditions, criteria, guidelines, legislation, principles, procedures, regulations, requirements, rules, standards** *The directive lays down rules governing the collection, processing, and transfer of personal data for marketing purposes.*

layer N

an amount or sheet of a substance that covers a surface or that lies between two things or substances

- adj+N thick **deep, dense, thick** *The glass may be wrapped in a towel or thick layers of paper tissue.*
- ▶ thin **fine, thin** *There was a thin layer of dust on the shelf.*
- ▶ not allowing a substance to pass through **impermeable, protective, waterproof** *When hiking, it's always advisable to wear a waterproof top layer or anorak.*
- ▶ single/double **double, single** *The first thing to do is to insulate the greenhouse with a double layer of polythene.*
- ▶ extra **additional, extra, second** *We recommend an extra layer of lacquer in kitchens and halls, where there is a greater risk of water spillage.*
- ▶ on the outside **outer, outermost** *Cork is the spongy outer layer of the bark.*
- ▶ on the top **top, topmost, upper** *Even a few weeks of very hot, dry weather can dry out the upper layers of the soil.*
- ▶ in the middle **inner, middle** *Halfway through the process, the cheese usually has three bands, the two outer layers where the cheese has ripened and a middle layer where the cheese is still white.*
- ▶ on the bottom **bottom, lower** *It is important that the pond has a good bottom layer of mud and other sediment.*

- v+N form a layer **form** *Esters are virtually insoluble in water and tend to form a thin layer on the surface.*
- ▶ add a layer **add, apply, place, put** *She applied a thin layer of cream all over her face and neck.*
- ▶ remove a layer **remove** *The outer plaster layer was completely removed.*

lead N

first position in a race or competition; the distance etc by which someone is winning

- adj+N big **clear, comfortable, commanding, decisive, healthy, strong, substantial, unassailable** *New Zealand now had a commanding 26-point lead.*
- ▶ small **narrow, slender, slim** *Bristol took a slender lead at 21–19 but were unable to close out the game.*
- ▶ how big **5-point, 10-point etc, one-goal, two-goal etc** *A 69th minute header from Foley gave Ireland a three-goal lead.*
- ▶ early in the game etc **early** *After taking an early lead, Roma were beaten 3–1.*
- ▶ v+N have the lead **have** *Liverpool had the lead at the end of the first half.*

> If someone has the lead, you can also say they are **in the lead**: *Ryder was in the lead at the end of the first week of the competition.*

- ▶ take the lead from someone else **gain, grab, seize, snatch, steal, take** *Livi almost snatched the lead when Alan Main made an error.*
- ▶ take the lead again after not having it for a time **regain, retake** *Tattenhall, however, continued to win more of the midfield battle and regained the lead just before half time.*
- ▶ make the lead greater **consolidate, double, extend, increase, open up, stretch** *In the second quarter, the team extended their lead to seven points.*
- ▶ not have the lead anymore **lose, squander, surrender** *Southall's problems continued when they surrendered a three-goal lead to eventually lose 5–4.*
- ▶ keep the lead **defend, hold, maintain, retain** *Fergus retained his one-game lead to take the cup.*
- ▶ take the lead gradually **edge into, establish, go into, move into** *They edged into the lead in the tenth minute and never looked back.*
- ▶ take the lead very quickly in a game or race **race into, storm into, surge into, sweep into** *Felce stormed into the lead and set a blistering pace.*

leader N

1 a person who is responsible for or in control of a group, country etc

- adj+N types of leader **civic, military, political, rebel, religious, spiritual, tribal** *Religious leaders are urging Western nations and bankers to cancel the debt owed by the world's poorest nations.*
- ▶ good, or inspiring others **charismatic, great, inspirational, visionary** *He has proved himself an inspirational leader.*
- ▶ having a lot of power **influential, prominent, senior**

The course will provide training opportunities for senior leaders and governing bodies.

▶ natural **born, natural** *Some people are natural leaders, but leadership skills can also be learnt.*

▶ in the past or future **former, future** *Neil Kinnock is a former leader of the Labour party.*

● v+N choose a leader **appoint sb (as), choose sb (as), elect sb (as), recruit** *The party has changed its rules on electing leaders.*

▶ become a leader **become** *William Hague became party leader at the age of 36.*

▶ get rid of a leader **depose, topple** *They are prepared to go to war, if necessary, to topple the country's leader.*

2 a person, company or product that is more successful than others

● adj+N certain **acknowledged, undisputed** *With headquarters in London, we are the UK's undisputed market leader in executive recruitment and coaching.*

▶ in the whole world **global, worldwide** *With over thirty years' experience, REL are considered the global leaders in working capital consultancy.*

● n+N **brand, industry, market, world** *Mackie's ice cream is now well established as brand leader in Scotland.*

● N+in in an area of industry **area, field, industry, market, sector** *We're a powerful player in the publishing industry and a leader in our field.*

▶ in a particular process **design, development, education, manufacture, provision, research, technology** *We're leaders in the manufacture and supply of mattresses.*

leadership N

the position of being leader of something; the qualities of a good leader

● adj+N good or that inspires others **charismatic, clear, courageous, decisive, effective, excellent, firm, good, inspirational, inspiring, strong, visionary** *I want to see strong leadership with the mandate to make tough decisions.*

▶ bad **poor, weak** *Improvements had been hampered in a few schools because of weak leadership.*

▶ types of leadership **academic, civic, managerial, military, moral, political, spiritual, strategic** *The rebels lacked unity and political leadership, and after eighteen months the mutiny was crushed.*

● n+N **business, church, community, government, party, project, research, school, team, union, world** *The course considers the key requirements of team leadership.*

● v+N get the leadership **assume, gain, win** *Following Milner's death in 1925, he assumed the leadership of the group.*

▶ give up the leadership **relinquish, resign** *He resigned the party leadership after the electoral defeat of 1987.*

▶ show leadership **demonstrate, exercise, provide, show** *As a company, we demonstrate leadership from the top and we expect our managers to manage.*

▶ need leadership **need, require** *We have our goals, but setting them requires strong leadership.*

▶ not have leadership **lack** *They had the experience but they lacked leadership and courage.*

● N+n someone who wants to have the leadership **candidate, contender** *The three leadership contenders will be appearing on a discussion programme.*

▶ competition to decide who will have the leadership **battle, contest, election** *He is the favourite to win the forthcoming Conservative Party leadership contest.*

▶ attempt to persuade people to give you the leadership **bid, campaign, challenge** *She launched her leadership campaign today.*

▶ job **position, post, role** *He took on a leadership role in the church.*

▶ the way someone leads **style** *The course enabled him to assess his leadership style and develop strategies to manage his workload more effectively.*

▶ the ability to lead well **ability, capability, qualities, skills** *The development of leadership skills across the whole staff is seen as a priority.*

lead to PHR VB

begin the process that causes something to happen

● adv+V afterwards or in the end **eventually, finally, subsequently, ultimately** *The condition damages blood vessels and organs, and can ultimately lead to diabetes.*

▶ possibly **possibly, potentially** *The policy could potentially lead to divisions between students and lecturers.*

▶ directly/not directly **directly, indirectly** *This meeting led directly to my being offered a job.*

▶ in a way that is certain and cannot be prevented **automatically, inevitably, inexorably, invariably, necessarily** *Rampant consumerism has led inexorably to gross inequalities in our society.*

▶ not always **not necessarily** *A university degree does not necessarily lead to higher earnings, though this is usually the case.*

▶ easily or quickly **easily, quickly** *Fatigue can so easily lead to unsafe driving.*

▶ naturally **naturally** *This topic naturally leads to discussion of assessment procedures.*

● V+n something positive **creation, discovery, dismissal, emergence, formation, founding, improvement** *It was the study of human white blood cells that eventually led to discoveries of current treatments in fighting AIDS.*

▶ something negative **arrest, closure, collapse, confusion, death, decline, delay, demise, destruction, deterioration, downfall, failure, loss, misunderstanding** *It was greed which led to his downfall.*

▶ increase or growth **growth, increase** *Research showed that a drop in oxygen levels in the blood can lead to an increase in blood clotting.*

▶ decrease **decrease, reduction** *These measures led to a 60 per cent reduction in overall accident frequency.*

leap N

a sudden increase, improvement, or change

● adj+N big or important **big, dramatic, enormous, giant, great, huge, major, massive, quantum, significant, tremendous** *With a willingness to change, we could still make the quantum leap to eliminate poverty.*

▶ small **small** *My reason for doing this course was to make a small leap forward in my professional life.*

▶ in your mind and thoughts **conceptual, imaginative, intuitive, mental** *Lewis-Williams suggests it is a conceptual leap to make 2D drawings from 3D life.*

▶ types of leap **evolutionary, qualitative, technological** *There have been giant technological leaps in the computer industry.*

● v+N make a leap **make, take** *The team has taken a major leap forward today, with the appointment of a new manager.*

▶ be a leap **be, represent** *This development represents a massive leap in the use of web-based technology.*

▶ need a leap **require** *It requires a leap of imagination to fully understand what she was going through at that time.*

leave N

1 a period of time away from your job

● adj+N **annual, extended, paid, parental, unpaid** *A pilot is entitled to 20 days' annual leave.* ● *Employees can have unpaid leave of up to 12 months.*

● n+N leave because you have a new child **adoption, maternity, paternity** *It was David's first day back from paternity leave and he brought photos of his new baby.*

▶ leave because you want to study **sabbatical, study** *The current director is taking six months sabbatical leave from the organization.*

▶ leave because you are ill **sick, sickness** *She's on sick leave due to stress.*

▶ leave because someone in your family is ill or has died **bereavement, compassionate** *Her mother died and she took five days' bereavement leave.*

● v+N have or take leave **go on, have, take, use** *He's already taken all his leave.*

▶ give someone leave **give sb, grant (sb)** *Departments may grant additional leave, which will normally be unpaid or taken as annual leave.*

▶ increase leave over a period of time **accrue** *An employee continues to accrue annual leave while on paternity leave.*

● N+n **allowance, entitlement, period** *If the employee wants to take her full leave entitlement, she does not need to give you notice.*

2 permission

● v+N give leave **give sb, grant (sb)** *They will only be granted leave to enter in very limited circumstances.*

▶ refuse leave **refuse (sb)** *Mr and Mrs Reeman were refused leave to appeal to the House of Lords.*

▶ get leave **obtain** *The creditor must obtain the leave of the court to present a winding-up petition.*

▶ try to get leave **apply for, seek** *He was seeking leave to enter the United Kingdom.*

lecture N

1 talk to a group about a particular subject

● adj+N introducing a subject or series of lectures **inaugural, introductory, keynote** *The day started with a lively keynote lecture by Professor John Gaffney.*

▶ for everyone **plenary** *Lynn Abrams has been invited to give the plenary lecture at the Scottish History conference at the University of Guelph, Canada.*

▶ given each week or year **annual, weekly** *Since 1968, when Professor Bernal retired from Birkbeck, the College has sponsored an annual lecture in his memory.*

▶ traditional or formal/informal in style **formal, informal, traditional** *The teaching methods will consist of formal lectures, case study analysis, practical workshops and discussion groups.*

▶ public **public** *This is a public lecture, open to all, and will be held at 7.00 p.m. in the main lecture theatre.*

▶ with pictures **illustrated** *Antonia Swinson is planning an illustrated lecture on her findings.*

▶ to honour someone who has died **memorial** *I am extremely honoured to have been invited to give this year's James Smart memorial lecture.*

▶ interesting **fascinating, informative, interesting, thought-provoking** *Mr Sampson gave an interesting lecture on 'How to Choose a Picture'.*

● n+N **guest** *In December, students attended a guest lecture given by Jean Bennett.*

● v+N give a lecture **deliver, give, present** *He has recently given a lecture to the Royal Society entitled 'Why We Co-operate'.*

▶ go to a lecture **attend, go to, listen to** *I went to a lecture about the history of British landscape painting.*

▶ not go to a lecture **miss** *Are lecture notes available if I've missed a lecture?*

▶ have a lecture to go to **have** *I only have one lecture today.*

▶ organize a lecture **hold** *Lectures are held on Thursday evenings and Friday mornings.*

● N+v **be entitled sth** *Dr Helen Mason will give a lecture entitled 'Our Dynamic Sun' at 9.15 a.m. on Saturday 23rd September.*

● N+n where a lecture takes place **hall, room, theatre** *The lecture theatre is on the ground floor of the Harris Building.*

▶ written information **handout, material, notes** *Printed lecture notes are made available and given out in class.*

▶ series of lectures **course, programme, series** *All lecture courses have weekly tutorials.*

> You can also talk about *a series/course/programme of lectures*: *The course will be taught through a series of lectures and tutorials.*

▶ travelling around giving lectures **tour** *He has recently been on lecture tours in the USA, Canada, and throughout the UK.*

● n+of+N **outline, recording, summary, text, transcript** *These are explanatory notes, not a transcript of the lecture.*

leg N

a part of the body

● adj+N **left/right** **left, right** *Straighten the right leg and swing the left foot forward.*

▶ front/back **back, front, hind, rear** *Unlike most other dinosaurs, it had front legs longer than the hind ones.*

▶ long/short **long, short** *He is a tall, thin man with long legs.*

▸ fat/thin **fat, slender, spindly** *She says he has little spindly legs and a huge belly.*

▸ that hurt **painful, sore** *We hurried down the mountain as quickly as our sore legs would carry us.*

▸ with hair on them **hairy** *Shorts aren't a good look if you have hairy legs.*

▸ not straight **bandy** *She had bandy legs from doing so much horse riding.*

> You can also say that someone is **bandy-legged** or **bow-legged**: *I watched the slight, bandy-legged figure move towards me.*

▸ not covered **bare** *Her bare legs were tan.*

▸ strong/weak **muscular, strong, sturdy, weak, wobbly** *These birds have thick strong legs and powerful feet.*

▸ part of leg **lower, upper** *She had a fracture to her lower leg.*

● v+N stretch or bend your leg **bend, straighten, stretch** *He stretched out his legs under his desk.*

> You can also say that someone's legs are **straight**: *For these exercises, lie on your back with your legs straight.*

▸ move your leg **lift, raise, swing** *I swung my legs out of bed and went to the kitchen to make breakfast.*

▸ sit with one leg over the other **cross** *Jan crossed his legs and leaned back in the chair.*

▸ kick your legs **kick** *That's it son, kick your legs – well done!*

▸ break your leg **break, fracture** *I broke my leg playing football.*

● N+v hurt **ache, hurt** *My legs were aching after I had been standing up all day.*

▸ bend or shake **bend, buckle, give way, shake** *He got out of the wheelchair and tried to stand up, but his legs gave way under him.*

▸ hang down **dangle, hang** *I sat at the front of the boat with my legs dangling over the side.*

legacy N
something that exists because of a past event or what someone achieved

● adj+N lasting a long time **enduring, lasting** *Sam Cooke is one of those artists who died young but left a lasting legacy.*

▸ that is impressive **great, rich** *Cambridge is an ideal place in which to study History of Art, since it has a rich legacy of architectural masterpieces.*

▸ connected with culture or the past **cultural, historical** *The island's turbulent history and rich cultural legacy are seen in the many archaeological remains.*

● v+N leave or create a legacy **create, leave behind, leave (sb)** *His playing left a large legacy with fellow musicians, not only in terms of his choice of format, but in terms of style.*

▸ receive a legacy from someone **have, inherit** *We inherited a legacy of high crime and underinvestment.*

● N+v **live on, remain** *Elvis Presley died in 1977, but his legacy lives on.*

legal ADJ
1 relating to the law or lawyers

● ADJ+n advice **advice** *He said the council had taken legal advice on the matter.*

▸ lawyers or the legal system **framework, profession, system** *She is researching students' attitudes to the law and the legal system.*

▸ when a case is brought to court **action, challenge, proceedings** *Such action is essential if providers are to avoid facing possible legal action.*

▸ costs **costs, fees** *If you do not win your case, the court may ask you to contribute to the other side's legal costs.*

2 allowed by the law or according to the law

● adv+ADJ **completely, entirely, perfectly, strictly, totally** *It is perfectly legal to form a new company from the remnants of a failed company.*

● ADJ+n limit **limit, minimum** *Check that you are driving within the legal speed limit.*

▸ right **right** *Under employment legislation, there is a legal right not to be unfairly dismissed.*

▸ what you must do **duty, obligation, requirement, responsibility** *There is a legal obligation for an appropriate adult to be present to look after the welfare of the young person.*

● v+ADJ **be, become, make sth, remain** *Some people feel that cannabis should be made legal.* ● *Slavery remained legal in British colonies until 1833.*

legality N
the fact that something is legal

● adj+N **doubtful, dubious, questionable** *This was an act of dubious legality.*

● v+N **challenge, contest, determine, dispute, question, uphold** *Union members are questioning the legality of the University's actions.*

legislation N
a law, or a set of laws

● adj+N current **current, existing** *Under current legislation, they have limited powers to act.*

▸ new **new, recent** *Apparently, the new legislation on this issue will not be retrospective.*

▸ suggested **draft, proposed** *The Times says that the proposed legislation will be good for rural drivers.*

▸ strict **draconian, repressive, strict, stringent, tough** *A further raft of draconian anti-terror legislation was announced by a Home Office minister.*

▸ that people argue about **controversial** *This controversial new legislation would decriminalize the possession of small guns.*

▸ valid for what has happened in the past **retrospective** *This legislation is not retrospective and applies only to cases that occurred after 1 December 2008.*

● v+N make legislation official **adopt, approve, enact, introduce, pass, push through** *Legislation was introduced that gave tenants the right to purchase their home at a discounted price.* ● *They pushed through legislation to allow the police more powers.*

▸ suggest or plan legislation **announce, bring forward, call for, plan, propose, put forward** *Each*

member-state can both propose legislation and veto anything.
▶ prepare and write legislation **draft, draw up** The proposed assembly would not have the ability to draft legislation.
▶ change legislation **amend, change, reform, revise, strengthen, tighten** There have been recent discussions about amending this legislation.
▶ obey legislation **abide by, comply with** Your supplier should be able to demonstrate that they comply with the legislation.
▶ not obey legislation **breach, contravene** The restaurant pleaded guilty to breaching food safety legislation.
▶ make sure that legislation is obeyed **enforce, implement** The RSPCA has considerable experience of enforcing animal welfare legislation.
▶ need legislation **need, require** Out of the 61 recommendations, the Strategy Unit envisaged that 35 of them would require legislation.
● n+of+N **piece, raft** Some pieces of legislation are easier to draft than others. ● MPs are debating another raft of legislation relating to dangerous dogs.

legislative ADJ
relating to laws or the process of making new laws
● ADJ+n process of making laws **change, framework, power, process, programme, proposal, requirement** These documents must be reviewed regularly and revised in the light of legislative changes.
▶ people who make laws **assembly, authority, body** The legislative assembly has 50 members elected to serve a five-year term.

legitimate ADJ
fair and reasonable
● adv+ADJ **absolutely, entirely, perfectly, quite, totally** His reasons for refusing to take part were perfectly legitimate.
● ADJ+n **aim, claim, concern, expectation, interest, purpose, reason, right, target** Society has a legitimate interest in procedures that may ultimately influence the genetics of the human race.
● v+ADJ **appear, be, consider sth, deem sth, seem** The trial could not be considered legitimate in the these circumstances. ● In brief, it seems legitimate to group the results as follows:

leisure N
activities you do to relax or enjoy yourself
● N+n business of providing such activities **centre, complex, facilities, industry, opportunities, services** The Moorland Links Hotel has an excellent choice of leisure facilities.
▶ taking part in such activities **activity, pursuit, time** Most of the major retailers are striving to promote shopping as an enjoyable leisure activity.

lend V
give something a particular quality
● V+n making an idea seem more correct **credence, credibility, plausibility, support, weight** These latest findings lend credence to his theory.

▶ feeling given by a place or situation **air of sth, charm, dignity, sense of sth** The crisp black-and-white cinematography helps lend an air of classic style to the whole affair.

lengthy ADJ
long, often longer than you want
● adv+ADJ very **extremely, very** Here are a few examples from the extremely lengthy list:
▶ rather **fairly, quite, rather, somewhat** It turned out that applying for a visa was a fairly lengthy process.
● ADJ+n way of doing something **procedure, process** These regulations are the product of a detailed and lengthy consultative process.
▶ when someone is away **absence** She finally returned to work after a lengthy absence.
▶ wait **wait** We then had a lengthy wait at the doctor's surgery.
▶ period of time **delay, pause, period, spell** There will be lengthy delays while the road remains closed.
▶ time spent talking **debate, discussion, interview, negotiations** After lengthy negotiations with the government, an agreement was reached.
▶ something written **article, document, list, report** At over 500 pages long, the report is a lengthy document.
● and/or expensive **costly, expensive** Our advice is not to get involved in lengthy and costly litigation.
▶ complicated or taking a long time **complex, complicated, detailed, difficult, laborious, time-consuming** Where our advice is complicated or lengthy, it will be provided in writing.

lenient ADJ
punishing someone less severely than expected
● adv+ADJ **too, unduly** In the past three years, 339 cases have had their sentences referred to the court of appeal for being unduly lenient.
● ADJ+n punishment **penalty, punishment, sentence, sentencing** He received a lenient sentence because of his disability.
▶ opinion of something or way of dealing with someone **approach, attitude, treatment, view** The magistrates took a lenient view of the case.

lessen V
become smaller or make something smaller
● adv+V very much **considerably, greatly, significantly** Support for continuing the war now lessened considerably.
▶ gradually **gradually** Social tensions have gradually lessened in the region.
▶ a little **slightly, somewhat** The impact of this announcement was lessened somewhat by the events which were to follow.
● V+n effect of something **burden, effect, impact** This dramatically reduces transport costs, lessens the impact on the environment and diverts waste away from landfill sites.
▶ chance of something happening **chance, likelihood, risk** By incorporating a day of rest into your training, you lessen your chance of injury.
▶ unpleasant situation or feeling **disruption, pain, stress, suffering, tension**

lesson N
something you learn from life or experience

- adj+N important **important, salutary, useful, valuable, vital** *I lost the bet, but learned a valuable lesson.*
- ▶ unpleasant or difficult **bitter, hard, harsh, painful** *The whole experience was a hard lesson in humility.*
- ▶ moral **moral** *A parable is a story whose purpose is to teach a moral lesson.*

- v+N be a lesson **be, serve as** *It's a sad story and should serve as a lesson to the young people of today.*
- ▶ learn a lesson **draw, learn** *We will listen and learn, and draw lessons from other people's experiences.* • *I learnt this lesson very early in my career.*
- ▶ teach a lesson **give sb, teach (sb)** *Their loss taught me an important lesson about making the most of time that we have with people.*
- ▶ use a lesson **apply** *He shows how we can apply the lessons learned on the rugby pitch to a business environment to achieve better performance.*
- ▶ identify a lesson **identify** *The review has identified five important lessons for improving our service to customers.*

- N+from **experience, history, past** *We have to learn the lessons from the past.*

- N+of **history, past** *Those who ignore the lessons of history are doomed to repeat them.*

lethal ADJ
very dangerous and able to kill you

- adv+ADJ possibly **possibly, potentially** *Fireworks are potentially lethal, and experience tells us that young people especially are at risk.*
- ▶ very **extremely, highly** *Pancreatic cancer is a highly lethal disease.*

- ADJ+n something that affects or harms the body **disease, dose, force, injection, weapon** *He was exposed to a lethal dose of radiation.*
- ▶ combination **cocktail, combination** *She was found dead in her kitchen, having taken a lethal cocktail of alcohol and weedkiller.* • *As well as being highly-strung with a frightening temper, John was also a heavy drinker – a lethal combination.*
- ▶ effect **effect** *The lethal effects of the gas are well known.*

- v+ADJ **be, prove** *This strain of bird flu has proven especially lethal to humans, with a mortality rate approaching 70 per cent.*

let out PHR VB
make a noise

- V+n loud noise **cry, howl, roar, scream, shriek, whoop, yell** *She let out a piercing scream.*
- ▶ quieter noise **gasp, sigh** *He let out a huge sigh of relief.*

letter N
a written message that is sent to someone

- adj+N published, so everyone can read it **open** *In an open letter, the Foreign Secretary said the visit would have many benefits for the UK.*
- ▶ sent to a lot of people **circular** *A circular letter*

about *the merger was sent to shareholders on 27 May.*
- ▶ written as a reply to many people **standard** *I had a feeling that this was just a standard letter.*
- ▶ formal **formal** *Present employer reference and final security checks will be completed before a formal letter of appointment is sent to you.*
- ▶ personal **personal** *We received a personal letter of congratulation from the mayor.*
- ▶ sent with something else **accompanying, cover** AME, **covering** *To apply, please forward a full CV and covering letter to this address.*
- ▶ not in its final form **draft** *The Council agreed the contents of a draft letter.*
- ▶ not signed **anonymous** *Then an anonymous letter arrived, telling him he had a grown-up son who was looking for him.*

- n+N **acceptance, acknowledgement, confirmation, follow-up, reminder, resignation, thank-you, warning** *A second, follow-up letter was sent to all those who had failed to respond to the first one.*

- v+N write a letter **compose, dictate, draft, type, write** *Local people were urged to write a letter each to the company.*

> You can use the expression *by letter* to say that someone communicates using a letter: *All bookings must be confirmed by letter or email.*

- ▶ send or deliver a letter **circulate, deliver, forward, post, send, submit** *A letter on the subject was circulated to all head teachers.* • *She sent a letter of apology to Mr Payne.* • *Please submit a letter of application to our Human Resources department.*
- ▶ receive a letter **get, receive** *Did you receive my letter?*
- ▶ read a letter **read** *Thank you for letting me read these letters.*
- ▶ reply to a letter **answer, reply to, respond to** *We aim to answer letters within 20 working days of receiving them.*
- ▶ say you have received a letter **acknowledge** *They acknowledged his letter of 6 April, but said that they were unable to help any further.*
- ▶ sign a letter **sign** *A total of 23 Senators have signed a letter supporting the proposal.*
- ▶ write someone's name and address on a letter **address** *The letter is addressed to 'The Occupier'.*
- ▶ send a letter with something else **attach, enclose** *Our reasons for not attending are given in the enclosed letter.*

- N+v have a date on it **be dated** *I provided this information in my letter dated 15 March 2009.*
- ▶ say **advise, confirm, explain, indicate, inform sb, outline, state** *The letter stated that no further money was available for the project.*
- ▶ end **conclude (with), end (with)** *The letter concluded with the following sentence:*

- N+of **acceptance, apology, application, appointment, complaint, condolence, congratulation, invitation, objection, recommendation, resignation, support, sympathy, thanks** *The neighbours sent formal letters of complaint to the local council.*

level N

1 the amount of something that can be measured

- adj+N high/low **high, low** *High levels of poverty in this community lead to many young people dropping out of school.*
- ▶ increasing **increasing, rising** *People have experienced rising levels of stress since last month's terrorist attacks.*
- ▶ highest/lowest **maximum, minimum, record** *Introducing minimum pay levels for apprenticeships would encourage participation in the scheme.*
- ▶ average or normal **average, normal** *He argues that rising affluence in the developed world has not increased average levels of happiness.*
- ▶ suitable or acceptable **acceptable, appropriate, the right** *Stocks have now fallen to below the acceptable level.*
- ▶ current **current, present** *I believe that a decline in prices from their current levels is necessary.*
- ▶ general **general, overall** *These statistics show what has happened to the general level of unemployment over the past year.*

- n+N **blood-sugar, cholesterol, energy, fitness, noise, staffing, stress, traffic** *Traffic levels will inevitably continue to increase, and road capacity must meet the demand.*
- ▶ v+N reach a level **achieve, reach** *The tension again grew, reaching its highest level of the afternoon.*
- ▶ increase a level **improve, increase, raise** *Saturated fats raise your cholesterol level.*
- ▶ reduce a level **lower, reduce** *These properties have been double-glazed to reduce noise levels.*
- ▶ stay at a particular level **remain at** *House prices remain at the level they were at in 2008.*
- ▶ make a level stay the same **maintain** *To maintain the current levels of service, council tax is expected to rise by 2.5 per cent.*
- ▶ measure or check a level **assess, determine, measure, monitor** *How are we to determine the appropriate level of compensation for these kinds of personal disadvantage?*
- ▶ decide on a level **set** *Their report set minimum levels for the nutritional content of school meals.*
- ▶ be more than a level **exceed** *Exhaust emissions must not exceed prescribed levels.*

- N+v become higher **go up, rise, soar** *Over recent years, business investment levels have risen significantly.*
- ▶ become lower **drop, fall, go down, plummet** *Burglary levels have fallen steadily.*
- ▶ change **fluctuate, vary** *Employment levels varied significantly within the UK.*

2 the standard of someone's ability or their position in an organization

- adj+N relating to a particular area **global, international, local, national, regional** *The results will inform management decisions made at local, regional, and national levels.*
- ▶ high or advanced **advanced, high, senior, top, upper** *You should have experience of dealing with clients at a senior level.*
- ▶ below advanced **intermediate** *Classes are for beginner to intermediate level.*
- ▶ low or basic **basic, elementary, entry, low** *In the*

first chapter, the concept of scale is introduced at a basic level.

- n+N **degree, postgraduate, undergraduate, university** *This book will be of interest to all students of literature at undergraduate level and above.*
- ▶ v+N **achieve, attain, reach** *I have attained the entry level required for the part-time Masters Degree course in Business Information Technology.*

leverage N

the power to make someone do what you want

- adj+N great **considerable, great, maximum** *Wallace is now a deputy First Minister with much greater political leverage than before.*
- ▶ types of leverage **diplomatic, economic, financial, political** *The EU should not hesitate to use this economic leverage for political purposes.*

- v+N have leverage **have** *Small retailers will see a much higher rise in cost because they don't have the leverage to negotiate.*
- ▶ get leverage **gain, get** *She used this incident to gain political leverage.*
- ▶ give leverage **give sb, provide** *Their position as junior partner in the Scottish Government coalition has given them the leverage to push the legislation through.*
- ▶ use leverage **exert, use** *If we fail to use our leverage in a positive way to bring about peace, the conflict will widen.*

liability N

legal responsibility for causing damage, or for paying for something

- adj+N full/not full **full, limited, strict** *This directive imposes strict liability on the producer of a defective product for damage caused by it.*
- ▶ types of liability **criminal, legal, personal** *The criminal liability of individual directors is usually limited.*

- v+N accept liability **accept, admit, assume** *We do not accept any liability for the content of external websites.*
- ▶ have liability **have** *We have no liability to pay you back any money by way of compensation or refund.*
- ▶ not accept liability **deny, disclaim** *Court proceedings would need to be issued if the other party denied liability for the accident.*
- ▶ reduce level of liability **limit** *Clauses have been included in most policies to limit insurance liability to a single policy year.*
- ▶ avoid liability **avoid** *Such a contract may be regarded as an attempt by the employer to avoid liability for death or personal injury.*

- N+for damage or injury **accident, damage, death, injury, loss** *We will not accept liability for any loss or damage incurred due to the details produced on this site.*
- ▶ mistakes **error, negligence** *The author cannot accept liability for errors or omissions.*
- ▶ cost of something **cost** *The task of the court is to decide the parties' liability for costs.*
- ▶ content **content** *The Trust accepts no liability for the content of the website.*
- ▶ result **consequences** *Neither we, nor any*

contributor, can accept any liability for the future consequences of your actions.

liable ADJ
legally responsible for causing damage or injury; responsible for paying or doing something

- adv+**ADJ** in a particular way **criminally, financially, legally** *The Appeal Court hearing ruled that the company was not legally liable for her death.*
- ▶ with/without someone else **individually, jointly, personally, solely** *You are solely liable for all your activities while using our equipment.*
- ▶ completely **fully, strictly** *Each individual is fully liable for any debt that is incurred.*
- **ADJ**+for damage or loss **damage, injury, loss** *Students will be liable for any damage done by them to University property.*
- ▶ money **cost, debt** *I understand that I will be liable for any such costs caused by my negligence.*
- **ADJ**+to **fine, imprisonment, penalty, prosecution, punishment, tax** *Any landlord who flouts these regulations will be liable to a fine up to a maximum of £1000.*

liaison N
the exchange of information between people or organizations

- adj+**N** **close, effective, good, ongoing, regular** *We are working in close liaison with the police in an attempt to improve the working environment for our staff.* • *As part of its ongoing liaison with the local community, the centre offers a regular drop-in session open to all.*
- **n+N** **client, community, customer, family, police, school** *You will be responsible for customer liaison for commercial customers.*
- v+**N** **encourage, ensure, establish, facilitate, improve, maintain, promote, provide** *We will also maintain effective liaison with our colleagues in the Housing Advice Team.*
- **N+n** person **officer** *She regularly works with police liaison officers.*
- ▶ group or organization **committee, group, meeting, service, team** *Every academic department has a staff-student liaison committee.*

liar N
someone who tells lies

- adj+**N** describing someone who cannot stop telling lies **compulsive, habitual, pathological** *Jenkins was described in court as a compulsive liar.*
- ▶ emphasizing that someone is a liar **big** *Don't believe him – he's the biggest liar in the school.*
- ▶ good/bad at telling lies **bad, good** *Poor Milly is not a very good liar.*
- v+**N** **be, call sb** *Are you calling me a liar?*
- and/or **cheat, fool, hypocrite, thief** *The play portrays all politicans as cheats and liars.*

liberty N
the freedom to behave how you want

- adj+**N** of all citizens **civil** *He believes this is an attack on civil liberties.*

- ▶ individual **individual, personal** *A recent poll shows that the majority of voters believe that the Government is introducing too much legislation which infringes personal liberty.*
- ▶ religious or political **political, religious** *Since 1945 the country has enjoyed political liberty and a democratic constitution.*
- ▶ human **human** *The human liberties which we all hold dear need to be defended against flagrant abuse by any dictatorship.*
- ▶ basic **basic** *The most basic liberty of all is the right of the ordinary citizen to go about their business free from fear or terror.*
- v+**N** protect liberty **defend, guarantee, preserve, protect, safeguard** *He has led the campaign to protect religious liberty in the wake of a series of parliamentary and legal threats.*
- ▶ limit or reduce liberty **curtail, destroy, erode, infringe, restrict, undermine** *A growing climate of mistrust and fear in the country is damaging national unity and eroding civil liberties.*
- ▶ threaten liberty **endanger, threaten** *The new anti-terrorism laws threaten liberties that people take for granted.*
- ▶ give someone liberty **allow sb, give sb** *Students are given considerable liberty to manage their own time.*
- ▶ have liberty **enjoy, have** *As a writer, I have the artistic liberty to use the material as I see fit.*
- ▶ lose liberty **lose** *We are at risk of losing not just our civil liberties but our very lives through the actions of terrorists.*
- **n+on+N** **attack** *Detention is now regarded by some as an attack on the civil liberties of pupils!*
- **n+to+N** **right, threat** *Everyone has the right to liberty and security.* • *She believes that ID cards are a threat to civil liberties.*
- **n+of+N** **infringement** *The author argues that the new Act constitutes a gross infringement of civil liberties.*

licence N
a document giving you permission to do something

- adj+**N** types of licence **full, provisional, special** *You must be aged 21 or over and have had a full driving licence for at least three years.*
- ▶ officially accepted **valid** *It is illegal to drive on the highways without a valid licence.*
- **n+N** **driving, entertainment, export, import, liquor, operating, software, TV, user** *We will need some ID, e.g. driving licence or council tax letter.*
- v+**N** give someone a licence **award (sb), grant (sb), issue** *The Coal Authority grants licences for coal exploration and extraction.*

> If a product is made or sold **under licence**, it is made or sold with the permission of the company that usually makes it: *The majority of aircraft were manufactured under licence in the United States.*

- ▶ get a licence **buy, get, obtain, purchase, receive** *If you want to do street collections, you are required to obtain a licence from the local authority.*
- ▶ ask for a licence **apply for** *If you are applying for a provisional licence, you should indicate this on the application form.*

▶ have a licence **have, hold** *If you hold a licence for the most recent version of the software, you can purchase a licence upgrade.*

▶ officially say a licence is no longer legal **revoke, take away** *The channel was told it would have its broadcasting licence revoked unless drastic measures were taken.*

▶ lose a licence **lose** *Drivers whose breath tests are positive face losing their licence for 12 months.*

▶ ask for a licence to continue longer **renew** *The hotel's application to renew its entertainment licence is due to be heard on December 14.*

▶ need a licence **need, require** *If you have a mains-operated television in your home, you need a licence for it.*

● N+v allow **allow (sb), authorize (sb), enable (sb), permit (sb)** *This licence allows you to make a specified number of digital copies of the document.*

▶ apply to **apply to, cover** *The licence also applies to titles published in the last five years.*

▶ be officially acceptable **be valid** *The licence will be valid for 12 months from the date of issue.*

▶ be no longer officially accepted **expire** *The current licence expires in January 2011.*

lie V
exist or consist of something

● n+V answer **answer, solution** *The answer lies in the fact that the diet prohibits nearly all carbohydrates.*

▶ problem **difficulty, problem** *In part, the problem lies in the fragmentary nature of the subject matter.*

▶ responsibility for something **blame, fault, responsibility** *The fault lies with society in general.*

▶ quality **difference, interest, power, strength** *The department's key strength lies in having a substantial and experienced team.*

▶ future **future** *Where do you think your future lies?*

lie N
a deliberately untrue statement

● adj+N complete or obvious **barefaced, blatant, complete, downright, outright** *This is a blatant lie and you know it.*

▶ serious **big** *They have been caught out in a big lie.*

▶ told to avoid upsetting someone **white** *It might be better to tell a little white lie.*

▶ deliberate **deliberate** *I do not believe that the Prime Minister stands up there and tells us deliberate lies.*

● v+N tell a lie **spread, tell** *She accused Susan of spreading vicious lies about her.*

▶ believe a lie **believe** *Perhaps he started to believe his own lies.*

▶ make a lie known **expose** *We have had to fight a battle to expose the lies of our leaders.*

● n+of+N **pack** INFORMAL**, tissue, web** *This unfortunately turned out to be a pack of lies. • The case against him was based on a tissue of lies.*

life N
1 the time from someone's birth to their death

● adj+N entire **entire, whole** *I have lived in this region my entire life.*

▶ long/short **long, short** *Throughout his long life, he used literature as a means of escape.*

▶ later part of life **later** *This may cause mental problems in later life.*

> You can also say *late in life*: *He married late in life.*

▶ earlier part of life **early** *In early life he was a keen chemist, but soon devoted himself to the teaching of surgery.*

● n+N **adult** *I had been in retail for most of my adult life.*

● v+N live your life **go through, live, spend** *She spent her whole life fighting for racial equality.*

▶ spend a lot of your life doing something **dedicate, devote, give** *He was able to devote his life to intellectual pursuits.*

▶ make your life last longer **prolong** *Public health is concerned with preventing disease, prolonging life and promoting health.*

▶ make your life shorter **shorten** *The dosage of painkillers necessary to control a patient's pain may have the side effect of shortening his life.*

▶ come to the end of your life **end** *She ended her life a contented woman.*

2 a particular way of living and the experiences you have [usually singular]

● adj+N common or normal **daily, day-to-day, everyday, normal, ordinary** *The decisions made by our elected representatives affect everybody's daily lives.*

▶ real **real** *I'm much less witty in real life than I am on my blog.*

▶ personal **personal, private** *He believes people have a right to a private life as long as it does not affect their public duties.*

▶ relating to work **professional, working** *Ken has been a journalist for most of his working life.*

▶ relating to particular activities or situations **cultural, political, public, religious, social** *In those days, women were effectively excluded from political life.*

▶ new **new** *Many people move to the city to start a new life.*

▶ modern **modern** *Few aspects of modern life remain unaffected by the use of email and the Internet.*

▶ when you are married **married** *They settled down to married life in Inverness.*

▶ easy/not easy **difficult, easy, hard** *Life wasn't easy at school for him.*

▶ busy **active, busy** *What a busy life we lead!*

▶ healthy **healthy** *We try to help people to live a healthier, less stressful life.*

▶ happy **happy** *Why does the education system so often fail to equip children to lead happy lives?*

▶ in the town/countryside **rural, urban** *It's not a realistic depiction of rural life in Denmark.*

● n+N **city, community, family, home, school, student, university, village** *Academics are being lured away from university life into research, development, and consultancy.*

● v+N lead a particular life **enjoy, have, lead, live** *I lead a very busy life.*

▶ change or affect your life **affect, change, improve, rebuild, transform** *That song changed my life forever.*

3 the state of being alive

- v+N lose your life **lose** *More than 300 people lost their lives in the disaster.*
- ▶ save someone's life **save** *The drink-driving campaign has undoubtedly saved lives.*
- ▶ put someone's life in danger **endanger, put at risk, risk, threaten** *These men and women risk their lives to save others at sea.*
- ▶ take someone's life **claim, end, take** *The disaster claimed 85 lives.*
- ▶ when someone chooses to die **give** *She gave her life to save her son.*

lifeline N
a person or thing that you depend on very much

- adj+N important **important, real, vital** *Village shops provide an important lifeline to rural communities.*
- ▶ financial **economic, financial** *Many small businesses provide a vital economic lifeline to local neighbourhoods.*
- v+N give a lifeline **give (sb), hand (sb), offer (sb), provide, throw (sb)** *The company would have collapsed, but was thrown a financial lifeline by a consortium of investors.*
- ▶ be a lifeline **act as, be, become, prove, serve as** *The Internet is becoming a lifeline for me because I work from home.*
- ▶ have a lifeline **have** *United had a lifeline and they looked like grabbing it with such intent that a shock victory was on the cards.*

lifespan N
the length of time that a person or animal lives or something continues to exist

- adj+N normal or average **average, expected, natural, normal** *One estimate of the average lifespan of the Snowy Owl is five years.*
- ▶ of a particular length **10-year, 20-year etc** *During its five-year lifespan, the centre has developed its own unique character.*
- ▶ short/long **limited, long, short** *Recent research has shown that their long lifespan is, at least in part, as a result of good diet.*
- ▶ human **human** *Resources that accumulated over eons of geological time are being consumed in a single human lifespan.*
- v+N have a lifespan **have** *These penguins have a lifespan of 15–20 years.*
- ▶ increase a lifespan **extend, increase, lengthen, prolong** *Some packaging is necessary to protect products and prolong their lifespan.*
- ▶ reduce a lifespan **reduce, shorten** *Some researchers warn, however, that taking the drug in high doses may actually reduce lifespan.*

lifestyle N
the type of life you have

- adj+N healthy/not healthy **healthy, unhealthy** *Fruit and vegetables are key to a healthier lifestyle.*
- ▶ active/not active **active, inactive, sedentary** *Back pain is often brought on by a sedentary lifestyle and an inability to relax.*
- ▶ spending a lot of time outside **outdoor** *If you enjoy the outdoor lifestyle, Swaziland is a great place to be.*
- ▶ busy **busy, hectic** *A new online language tuition service has been launched to assist people wanting to fit in language lessons around a busy lifestyle.*
- ▶ traditional/not traditional **alternative, modern, traditional** *The Bedouin who live here are no longer able to follow their traditional nomadic lifestyle.*
- ▶ able to pay for nice and expensive things **comfortable, extravagant, lavish, luxurious, luxury** *She struggles to maintain the family's lavish lifestyle on their income.*
- ▶ moving from place to place **nomadic** *Mongolia is a country where approximately half of the population still leads a nomadic lifestyle.*
- v+N have a particular lifestyle **enjoy, have, lead, live** *He continued to enjoy a lifestyle of luxury yachts and holiday homes in Monaco.*
- ▶ start having a particular lifestyle **adopt, choose** *We have helped over 600 children lose weight, increase fitness levels, and adopt a healthy lifestyle.*
- ▶ continue having a particular lifestyle **maintain** *This is on the assumption that his pension will not be sufficient for him to be able to maintain his current lifestyle.*
- ▶ change or improve your lifestyle **change, improve** *I was told to change my lifestyle or I would very soon be dead.*
- ▶ encourage people to have a particular lifestyle **encourage, promote** *The Government has launched new guidelines aimed at promoting healthier lifestyles for children.*
- ▶ be suitable for your lifestyle **suit** *Learn at home at your own pace to suit your lifestyle.*
- N+n **advice, change, choice, magazine, modification** *Research suggests a person's quality of life directly reflects health-related lifestyle choices as opposed to genetic factors.*
- n+in+N **change** *This huge expansion in the market reflects the change in consumer lifestyles and shopping patterns.*

lifetime N
the period of time when someone is alive or the length of time that something exists

- adj+N whole **entire, whole** *It would probably take a whole lifetime to get to know Cairo.*
- ▶ short/long **long, short** *She has already achieved a lot in her short lifetime.*
- v+N **have, last, seem like, spend, take** *These artificial joints have a lifetime of about twenty years.*
  - ● *He has spent a lifetime in the food business.*
- N+of something that is planned or exists **building, contract, parliament, plan, product, project** *Frequent update meetings will be held during the lifetime of the project to ensure communication channels are kept open.*
- ▶ experience **experience** *The conductor of the choir has a lifetime of experience in teaching music.*

> You can also say *a lifetime's experience*: *She has a lifetime's experience of working with animals.*

- n+of+N **adventure, chance, experience, holiday, opportunity, trip** *Win an all-expenses-paid trip of a lifetime to the rainforests of Brazil!*

lift V

1 officially end a rule or law stopping something

- adv+V **completely, partially, temporarily** *Recent moves to partially lift the ban on ivory trade are eroding its effectiveness.*
- V+n **ban, blockade, curfew, embargo, restriction, sanction** *Several governments are now urging the UN to lift the sanctions.*

2 when someone starts to feel happier or the weather improves

- V+n way someone is feeling **heart, mood, spirit** *It's amazing how a bit of sunshine can lift the spirits, isn't it?*
- ▶ something that causes trouble or difficulty **burden, weight** *We will lift the suffocating burden of regulation and allow business to breathe again.*
- n+V weather **cloud, fog, mist** *By now, most of the fog had lifted and the sun was getting warmer.*
- ▶ way someone is feeling **spirits** *When I saw the children so happy, my spirits lifted for a while.*

light N

1 brightness from the sun, a fire, a piece of equipment etc

- adj+N bright **bright, brilliant, good, intense, shimmering, strong** *The light became brighter and I could distinctly see three shapes.*
- ▶ not bright **bad, dim, fading, faint, poor, weak** *I couldn't really see his expression in the dim light.*
- ▶ natural **natural** *The dining room has no natural light.*
- ▶ artificial **artificial, electric** *In 1895, Chester's streets were lit for the first time with electric light.*
- ▶ having a particular colour **golden, white, yellow** *The stage was flooded with bright white light.*
- v+N provide light **cast, emit, give, give out, provide** *An intensely white light was emitted by the object.*
- ▶ reflect light **reflect** *The two sides are white, to reflect the light.*
- N+v be produced **gleam, glow, shine** *On my way upstairs, I saw light shining through a chink in the door of a room which I knew to be unoccupied.*
- ▶ make something bright **illuminate** *The scene was illuminated by the midday light.*
- ▶ become less bright **fade, fail, go** *By the time I'd got there, the light was already fading fast.*
- ▶ shine from or in a particular direction **come from, emanate from, fall, stream** *There's also a lot of light coming from above.*
- ▶ fill a place **fill, flood** *The door suddenly opened and light flooded the scene.*
- ▶ make someone temporarily blind **blind, dazzle** *She was blinded by the light.*
- n+of+N line of light **beam, ray, shaft, streak** *Rays of light broke through chinks in the clouds and lit up the hills and lakes.*
- ▶ amount of light that appears **blaze, burst, chink, flash, gleam, glimmer, patch, pool, pulse** *There was a flash of bright light, and thunder rumbled in the distance.*
- ▶ quality **brightness, glare, glow, intensity** *The warm glow of the lights made the room homely and inviting.*

- and/or **dark, darkness, heat, shade, shadow, warmth** *The canopy of trees gives patches of light and shade in the forest.*

2 a piece of electrical equipment producing brightness

- adj+N bright **bright** *Local fishermen shine bright lights on the waters to attract squid.*
- ▶ flashing **blinking, flashing, flickering, pulsing, twinkling** *The flashing lights of the disco were a little overwhelming at first.*
- ▶ making someone temporarily blind **blinding, dazzling** *Suddenly, a blinding light flashed and a thunderous blast was heard.*
- v+N switch on a light **flick on, flip on, put on, switch on, turn on** *He came straight upstairs into the bedroom and put the light on.*
- ▶ switch off a light **extinguish, flick off, flip off, put off, put out, shut off, switch off, turn off, turn out** *Will the last one out please switch the lights off?*
- ▶ use a light **have on** *He was scared of the dark and always had a light on when he slept.*
- ▶ continue to use a light **keep on, leave on** *When you go out at night, close all the curtains and leave the lights on.*
- ▶ make a light brighter **turn up** *There can be a really long wait at the bar and they turn the lights up at the stroke of 11pm.*
- ▶ make a light less bright **dim, turn down** *Try turning down the lights and playing some atmospheric music.*
- ▶ direct a light somewhere **flash, shine** *Jim shone his light in Ron's face and then mine.*
- N+v flash **blink, flash, flicker, twinkle** *Two police cars sped by with their blue lights flashing.*
- ▶ become less bright **dim, go down** *The lights dimmed and the orchestra began to play.*
- ▶ shine **glow, shine** *He led them quietly towards the house where a few lights shone from windows.*
- ▶ make something bright **illuminate** *Suddenly, the road ahead was illuminated by lights bearing down on them.*
- ▶ make someone temporarily blind **blind, dazzle** *I was blinded by the strong theatre lights and I could not see the audience.*
- ▶ be shining **be on** *I went along Ingram Street, where few lights were on.*
- ▶ not be shining **be off, be out** *All the lights were off and the place was silent.*
- ▶ start to shine **come on, go on** *Get some timer switches so that lights come on automatically in the evening.*
- ▶ stop shining **go off, go out** *Half way through the gig, all the lights went out.*

light ADJ

bright because of light from the sun

- adv+ADJ very **extremely, very** *It was an extremely light and spacious fourth-floor flat.*
- ▶ fairly **fairly, quite** *The room was painted in a fairly light colour.*
- v+ADJ **be, become, get, grow, remain, stay** *It was just getting light outside when we set off.*
- and/or **airy, bright, spacious** *The rooms are light and airy.*

light V
make a place brighter by giving it light [usually passive]

- adv+V with not much light **dimly** *She led me through the dimly lit corridors.*
- ▶ well **properly, well** *Always park somewhere that is well lit and preferably somewhere with CCTV.*
- ▶ badly **badly, poorly** *The way to the station is so badly lit, it is unsafe at night.*
- ▶ brightly **brightly, brilliantly** *We all received a very warm welcome as we entered the brightly lit hall.*

lighting N
light of a particular type or quality

- adj+N artificial **artificial, electric, fluorescent** *The salon is illuminated by fluorescent lighting.*
- ▶ creating a particular mood or feeling **atmospheric, moody** *The atmospheric lighting gave a spooky feel to the whole play.*
- ▶ natural **natural** *Unfortunately, the lack of budget means natural lighting only, so the indoor scenes are very dark.*
- ▶ outdoor **exterior, external, outdoor** *There is ample parking and also exterior lighting.*
- ▶ indoor **indoor, interior** *The remote control will switch on all of the car's lights, as well as the interior lighting.*
- ▶ bright **bright** *The building has been modernised, with spacious entrances, bright lighting, and underfloor heating among the improvements.*
- ▶ not too bright **low, soft, subdued, subtle** *Watch the DVD in a room with subdued lighting.*
- ▶ not bright enough **bad, dim, poor** *The lighting is so dim in Act 2 that it is difficult to see all the figures on stage.*
- ▶ enough **adequate, good, proper** *There should be adequate lighting in all urban streets and parks.*
- ▶ on ceiling **overhead** *You can use desk lamps in place of overhead lighting.*

lightning N
flashes of light in the sky during a storm

- N+v hit someone or something **hit, strike** *The house was seriously damaged after being struck by lightning.*
- ▶ flash **flash** *The lightning flashed for a third time.*
- ▶ make something brighter **illuminate, light, light up** *A spectacular thunderstorm built up, with lightning lighting up the sky.*
- N+n **bolt, flash, strike** *Many fires are due to natural events such as lightning strikes.*
- n+of+N **bolt, flash, steak** *Then came a flash of lightning followed by a loud peal of thunder.*

likelihood N
the chance that something might happen

- adj+N less or smaller **decreased, less, lower, reduced** *In small villages, there is less likelihood of properties becoming available to let.* • *Girls in the group that did regular exercise had a lower likelihood of becoming obese.*
- ▶ more or greater **greater, increased, more** *Unfortunately, people with diabetes have a greater likelihood of increased blood pressure.*

- ▶ not much **little, not much, remote** *The population of the world shows little likelihood of decreasing.*
- ▶ strong **every, high, real, significant, strong, substantial** *There is every likelihood that we will be successful.* • *This is a high risk strategy with a strong likelihood of failure.*
- ▶ some **reasonable** *Nowadays, most forms of cancer can be treated with a reasonable likelihood of a satisfactory outcome.*

- v+N increase the likelihood of something **enhance, improve, increase, maximize** *The incident had increased the likelihood of military action against the regime.*
- ▶ reduce the likelihood of something **decrease, diminish, lessen, minimize, reduce** *Wearing a cycle helmet reduces the likelihood of serious head injury.*
- ▶ affect the likelihood of something **affect, influence** *A pregnant mother's diet can affect the likelihood of health problems in her babies.*
- ▶ make a judgment about the likelihood of something **assess, calculate, consider, determine, estimate, evaluate, predict** *We will be able to better predict the likelihood of an individual responding to a particular course of drug treatment.*

likely ADJ
probably going to happen, or probably true

- adv+ADJ very **all too, entirely, especially, extremely, highly, more than, overwhelmingly, particularly, very** *It is highly likely that the treaty will be endorsed by an overwhelming majority of member countries.*
- ▶ rather **fairly, pretty** INFORMAL**, quite, reasonably** *This is a fairly likely scenario given that they have lost their last 10 matches.*
- ▶ almost not at all **hardly, remotely, scarcely** *If he was supposedly illiterate in his own language, Arabic, it is hardly likely that he would have been able to read Hebrew.* • *We never looked remotely likely to score even one point.*
- ▶ more or less than is right **disproportionately** *This group is also disproportionately likely to have a low income.*
- ▶ more and more **increasingly** *Millwall now look increasingly likely to be relegated.*
- ▶ equally **equally** *Men and women are equally likely to be in work prior to having children, but this changes after childbirth.*
- ▶ when you are asking whether something is likely **at all** *Is it at all likely that he would have left without saying goodbye?*
- ▶ not **not at all** *She's not at all likely to take over the leadership if the present leader resigns.*

- ADJ+n result **consequence, outcome, possibility, result, scenario** *What would be the likely outcome of this situation?*
- ▶ effect **effect, impact** *Students will be expected to be able to analyse the likely impact of these trends on the performance of the business.*
- ▶ person or thing that will probably achieve something **candidate, contender, winner** *He now looks like the most likely winner of the championship.*
- ▶ explanation **explanation, reason** *The most likely explanation for this is an increase in population.*
- ▶ cause **cause** *Most learner drivers are within the age limits when the most likely cause of accidental death is in a road traffic accident.*

▶ reaction **reaction, response** *Particular attention should be paid to the likely reaction of customers to any changes in services.*

▶ origin **origin, source** *The most likely source is thought to be Asia.*

▶ cost **cost** *It is important you have a clear idea of the likely overall cost of studying in the UK.*

● v+ADJ **appear, consider sb/sth, look, make sth, regard sb/sth as, seem, sound, think sb/sth** *The artist signs himself 'W. de Brailes' and it seems very likely that he was the William de Brailes who lived in Catte Street in Oxford around 1230–1260.* ● *They thought it likely that he was involved in planning the robbery.*

likeness N

the quality of being similar to someone or something

● adj+N **exact, excellent, good, incredible, perfect, remarkable, striking, strong, true, uncanny** *They felt that the portrait was a good likeness of their daughter.* ● *You must admit the likeness is uncanny.*

● v+N **have a likeness bear, have** *He bears a remarkable likeness to Freddie.*

▶ show a likeness **capture, catch, show** *The painting is perfect, and you have captured his likeness so well.*

▶ see a likeness **see** *She saw no likeness between the friend of her youth and the prince who stood before her.*

liking N

a feeling of enjoying or liking something

● adj+N **strong great, particular, real, special, strong** *She admits to having a great liking for the music of Shostakovich.*

▶ immediate **immediate, instant** *We first met her at Jonathan's graduation, and took an instant liking to her.*

▶ sincere **genuine** *He acted out of a genuine liking for the man.*

● v+N **have a liking for someone or something have** *I have a liking for old films, preferably in black and white.*

> You can also say that something is **to someone's liking**: *I'm afraid that the music they played wasn't really to my liking.*

▶ start to have a liking for someone or something **develop, take** *For some unknown reason, she took an immediate liking to the old man.*

▶ express a liking for someone or something **express** *He expressed his liking for New Zealand and its mountains.*

▶ show a liking for someone or something **show** *German audiences showed no liking for it.*

▶ share a liking for someone or something **share** *We both share a liking for the good things in life.*

the limelight N

attention from newspapers, television etc

● adj+N **international, media, political, public** *The former council leader was propelled back into the political limelight last night.*

● v+N **try to have all the limelight grab, hog**

INFORMAL, **steal** *Jim Carrey has a tendency to steal the limelight, which we can see on the DVD extras.*

▶ like the limelight **bask in, enjoy, love** *She is someone who enjoys the limelight.*

▶ want or try to have the limelight **seek, want** *A woman of humility and modesty, Paula never sought the limelight.*

▶ avoid the limelight **avoid, shun** *Leroy Burgess is an unusual artist, in as much as he shuns the limelight.*

▶ share the limelight **share** *For once, however, he will have to share the limelight.*

▶ have the limelight **be in** *Apparently, she wanted to be in the limelight for once in her life.*

▶ not have the limelight **be out of** *From then on, Byron was never out of the limelight.*

▶ start to have the limelight **come into, step into** *A new generation of young Arab women writers are stepping into the limelight.*

▶ be forced to have the limelight **be propelled into, be thrown into, be thrust into** *It has also been a time when Africa has been thrust into the limelight.*

limit V

prevent a number, amount, or effect from increasing past a particular point; reduce someone's ability to be effective

● adv+V **drastically, seriously, severely** *The wartime measures severely limited the opening hours of pubs.*

● V+n amount **amount, capacity, intake** *Limit the amount you take to what you actually need.*

▶ number **capacity, intake, number** *We need to limit the number of new countries developing nuclear weapons.*

▶ size **extent, magnitude, scope, size** *These birds have relatively small feet, which limits the size of prey that they can catch.*

▶ growth **growth, spread** *These plans will aim to limit the spread of disease.*

▶ damage **damage** *The Italian government is said to be anxious to act quickly to limit the damage caused by such a revelation.*

▶ power **power** *He attempted to limit the power of the Supreme Court.*

▶ effect, impact **effect, impact** *There is surely enough popular support behind measures to limit the impact of climate change.*

▶ usefulness **effectiveness, usefulness** *These are all factors which can limit the usefulness of this approach.*

▶ someone's freedom to do something or go somewhere **ability, access, freedom** *The law severely limited the freedom of the press.*

▶ possibility or choice **choice, opportunity, options, possibility** *Think carefully before you decide which subjects to take. Don't limit your options.*

limit N

the largest or smallest amount of something that is allowed

● adj+N upper **maximum, upper** *There is a fixed upper limit to the amount of interest charged on your home loan.*

▶ lower **lower, minimum** *Most buyers have a minimum limit on the number of bedrooms they need and want the maximum space they can afford.*

▶ strict **severe, strict, stringent, tight** *For this reason, strict limits are set on the levels of lead in drinking water.*

▶ safe **safe** *There is no known safe limit to exposure to asbestos.*

▶ not based on any particular facts **arbitrary** *Arbitrary limits on immigration would damage our economy and push up taxes.*

▶ legal **legal, statutory** *You may still be affected by alcohol the next day and could lose your licence if you drive and are still over the legal limit.*

▶ fixed or agreed **agreed, established, prescribed, recommended, set, specified** *The recommended daily limit for a woman is 70g of fat.*

▶ acceptable **acceptable** *What are the acceptable limits of individual freedom in a civilized country?*

▶ normal **normal** *His hearing is within normal limits so he does not need a hearing aid.*

● n+N relating to money **borrowing, cash, credit, earning, expenditure, overdraft, spending** *Don't go over your agreed overdraft limit.*

▶ relating to speed, time, size, age, weight **age, size, speed, time, weight** *A speed limit of 10 miles per hour must be observed in the University grounds.*

▶ relating to alcohol **alcohol** *The report has called for an alcohol limit to be applied to boat users along the lines currently applied to drivers.*

● v+N not obey a limit **breach, break, exceed, go over** *It is likely that the total level of salt in the water could exceed this limit.*

▶ obey a limit **obey, observe** *Simply obey the limit and you are doing all that is necessary for road safety.*

▶ establish a limit **agree, define, determine, fix, impose, introduce, place, prescribe, propose, put, set, specify** *There are now no limits imposed on importing tobacco and alcohol products from one EU country to another.*

▶ increase a limit **extend, increase, raise** *Ask your credit card provider to temporarily increase your limit.*

▶ reduce a limit **lower, reduce** *The government has resisted calls to reduce the limit.*

▶ make sure that a limit is obeyed **enforce** *The program will automatically enforce this limit for you.*

limitation N

1 a rule or situation that puts a limit on something

● adj+N strict **serious, severe, strict** *In addition, there was a strict limitation on the number of foreign players who could play for a club.*

▶ major **important, major, significant** *There would, therefore, be significant limitations on any fiscal expansion.*

▶ current **current** *Current limitations on funding for small voluntary organisations are unfair.*

▶ financial **budgetary, financial** *We tailor our service to the budgetary limitations of our clients.*

● n+N **budget, resource, size, space, time** *Because of space limitations we may be unable to print every letter we receive.*

● v+N put a limitation on something **impose, place, put** *They may also impose a limitation on the types of investment you are allowed to make.*

▶ get rid of a limitation **remove** *The Act removed the limitation on the use of Welsh in the courts.*

2 a disadvantage or weak point [usually plural]

● adj+N types of limitations **functional, methodological, physical, practical, technical, technological** *We ensure there is no discrimination toward applicants, based on age, sex, religion, marital status, sexual preference or physical limitations.*

▶ existing as a permanent feature of something **inherent, intrinsic** *The methodology has inherent limitations.*

▶ serious **serious, severe** *The existing machines are over 40 years old and have been demonstrated to have serious limitations.*

▶ major **important, major, significant** *Although the model has been used successfully to provide initial estimates, it has important limitations.*

▶ current **current** *The authors discuss some current limitations of the system.*

▶ basic **basic, fundamental** *These are engineering issues, not fundamental limitations, and have been dealt with in a recently published design for a new system.*

▶ obvious **obvious** *However, this approach has obvious limitations.*

● v+N understand or accept limitations **accept, acknowledge, appreciate, know, note, realize, recognize, understand** *It is difficult for some older people to acknowledge their limitations.*

▶ try to deal with limitations **address** *In this paper, we discuss three experiments that address the limitations of our previous studies.*

▶ succeed in dealing with limitations **circumvent, overcome, transcend** *The Museum welcomes disabled visitors and tries to overcome the limitations of a historic building that does not provide easy access for people with disabilities.*

▶ have limitations **have** *We recognise that our current method does have limitations.*

▶ show limitations **expose, highlight, identify, reveal** *The report highlights the limitations of this approach.*

▶ consider limitations **consider, discuss** *We should be considering the limitations of polls like these.*

limited ADJ

not allowed to go above a particular level; not very good, or great in amount

● adv+ADJ very **extremely, seriously, severely, strictly, very** *Staff time is extremely limited, so we ask you to phone only at certain set hours.*

▶ rather **fairly, quite, rather, relatively, somewhat** *The rail network in Scotland is relatively limited in extent.*

● ADJ+n amount **amount, budget, capacity, quantity, resources, supply** *Unfortunately, I only have a limited amount of time to spend answering these questions.*

▶ number **number, range** *Please book early, as there is only a limited number of places available.*

▶ time **duration, period, time** *This offer is for a limited time period only.*

▶ space **space** *Some airlines have decided on slightly smaller bag sizes because of the limited space in the aircraft.*

▸ size **extent, scope, size** *At the same time, the limited size of groups allows each individual to contribute fully to discussions.*

● v+ADJ **appear, be, become, remain, seem** *The commercial applications of the product remain limited.*

line N

an imaginary limit or border between two situations or conditions

● adj+N **fine, thin** *So remember that there is a fine line **between** helping the bride make her choice and imposing your choice upon her.*

● v+N **blur, cross, draw, straddle, tread** *I cannot help feeling that, with this legislation, our society has crossed a line.* ● *It's hard to draw a line **between** sadness and depression.*

linger V

last or continue for a long time

● n+V doubt **doubt, question, suspicion** *But a doubt lingers in my mind.*

> Usage **Linger** is usually used as a present participle adjective in these combinations: *A clear answer would help to dispel any lingering suspicions as to his honesty.*

▸ memory **memory** *Memories of the attack still linger for most New Yorkers.*
▸ taste **flavour, taste** *Let the flavours linger on your tongue.*
▸ smell **aroma, odour, perfume, scent, smell** *That wonderful smell still lingers.*
▸ tradition **tradition** *Indeed, in all the Celtic parts of Britain, living traditions still linger.*
▸ feeling **pain, pain** *This was several years ago, but the pain still lingers!*

> In this meaning, you can use **linger on** in the same way as **linger**: *Ten years later, the memory still lingers on.*

link V

people, things, or events: be related [usually passive]

● adv i V so as to be impossible to separate **indissolubly, inextricably, inseparably, intrinsically** *Although these aspects are all inextricably linked, it can be useful to consider them separately.*
▸ strongly **firmly, strongly** *Social group and housing type are strongly linked in Britain.*
▸ directly **directly, explicitly** *Death from malaria in Africa is thus directly linked **to** poverty.*
▸ closely **closely, intimately** *These two factors are, of course, closely linked.*
▸ clearly **clearly, obviously** *Tourism and holiday trends are clearly linked to consumer confidence and the economy.*

link N

1 a connection between people, things, or events

● adj+N clear **clear, definite, explicit, obvious** *Were we missing some obvious link?*
▸ direct **direct** *Quite clearly, there is a direct link **between** population growth and energy demand.*
▸ weak **tenuous, weak** *It feels like a tenuous link **between** two unrelated subjects.*

▸ showing that one thing causes another **causal** *There was very little evidence of a causal link.*
▸ strong or close **close, strong** *There is often a strong link **between** depression and problems at work.*
▸ important or very important **important, key, vital** *The Liaison Officer provides a vital link **between** the community and the site team.*

● v+N **establish, find, prove, see** *It is the job of the forensic scientist to establish a link **between** the perpetrator and the crime on the basis of scientific evidence.*

2 a relationship between people, organizations, or countries [usually plural]

● adj+N **close, strong** *We have close links **with** the parish of St Joseph's.*
● n+N **business, sporting, trade, trading** *The Australian economy is flourishing, not least because of trading links **with** its Asian neighbours.*
● v+N create links **build, create, develop, establish, forge, foster** *Over the years, we have forged close links **with** business and the professions.*
▸ end links **break, cut, sever** *Activists warned the company to sever links **with** a firm which carries out medical experiments on animals.*
▸ continue links **maintain** *The Association maintains links **with** related professional organizations.*
▸ have links **have** *He pointed out that he was the first Asian member of the Government and obviously had links **with** the Asian community.*
▸ make links stronger **strengthen** *I am looking forward to helping the college strengthen its links **with** employers.*

3 (in computing) a connection between one file or section and another

● n+N **download, email, hypertext, Internet, navigation, text, Web, website** *Listed here are a number of useful contact addresses and Web links.*
● v+N use a link **click, click on, follow, see, use** *Follow the link **to** the online form and send us your details.*
▸ have a link **contain, have, include** *Each job title has a link **to** the advertisement for that vacancy and further information if available.*
▸ create a link **add, build, create, post** *I have taken the liberty of building a link **to** your site from my own.*
▸ provide a link **provide** *Links are provided at the right hand side of this page.*
▸ add the most recent information to a link **update** *Now all you have to do is to update the link **to** your blog archives.*
▸ check a link **check** *This article was added to our website on 25/01/09, at which time all links were checked.*
▸ send someone a link **send** *To send a link for the car you are viewing to a friend, simply click 'Send to a friend'.*

lip N

the top or bottom edge of your mouth

● v+N press your lips together **compress, press together, purse** *She pursed her lips and frowned like a doctor considering a case.*

▶ bite your lips **bite, chew** *Her father bit his lip and gazed at the floor.*
▶ open your lips **open, part** *I opened my lips to speak.*
▶ close your lips **close** *She closed her lips and folded her hands before her.*
▶ make your lips wet **lick, moisten, wet** *He moistened his lips with the tip of his tongue.*
▶ push your lips together and forwards **pout, pucker** *She tossed her head and pouted her lips.*
▶ make a noise with your lips **smack** *Then the stranger tasted a spoonful of the soup and smacked his lips and said, 'Ah, delicious!'*
▶ pull your top lip upwards at one side **curl** *They curled their lips in contempt and turned away.*

● N+v open/close **close, open, part** *His lips opened, and he whispered, 'Kiss me.'*
▶ shake **quiver, tremble** *Her lips quiver as she searches for the right words to say.*
▶ move **move** *I was so overcome with emotion and feeling that, although my lips moved, no sound escaped my throat.*
▶ be pressed together **purse, tighten** *His lips tightened, and he frowned with solemn resolution.*
▶ be pulled upwards at one side **curl** *Her lips curled with scorn.*

liquid N
a substance that flows

● adj+N burning easily **flammable, inflammable** *Never use petrol or other flammable liquids to light fires.*
▶ thick **thick, viscous** *Each bottle contained a viscous liquid.*
▶ thin **thin** *Add more cold water a little at a time until it forms a thin liquid with the consistency of milk.*
▶ resembling oil **oily** *Vegetable fats tend to be oily liquids.*
▶ having no colour **colourless** *Formaldehyde is a colourless liquid used to preserve dead bodies.*
▶ transparent **clear** *Shake until the liquid is completely clear.*

● v+N pour a liquid **pour** *Next, he poured the liquid into the bowl and added the herbs.*
▶ accidentally pour a liquid out of its container **spill** *Take care not to spill the liquid.*
▶ let a liquid flow away from something **decant, drain, drain off, strain, strain off** *First, you need to begin draining the liquid in the tank.*
▶ heat a liquid **boil, bring to the boil, heat** *Heat the liquid to just below boiling point.*
▶ when a dry substance takes in liquid **absorb, soak up** *Simmer for 10 more minutes until the rice is tender and all the liquid is absorbed.*

● N+v move somewhere **drip, flow, pour, seep, spurt, trickle** *Thicker liquids, like syrup, flow more slowly.*
▶ become thicker **reduce** *Boil vigorously until the liquid has reduced to a thick sauce.*

liquidation N
a situation in which a business closes and sells everything

● adj+N **compulsory, voluntary** *They have a duty to investigate the affairs of companies in compulsory liquidation.*

▶ v+N experience liquidation **be forced into, be placed in, be put into, enter, enter into, go into** *Work halted on the project a month ago, after the firm went into liquidation.*
▶ avoid liquidation **avoid** *The directors ought to have known that the company could not realistically avoid liquidation.*
▶ be likely to experience liquidation **face** *Unless a buyer is found, the football club faces liquidation.*

list N
a set of names, numbers etc one below another

● adj+N complete **complete, comprehensive, exhaustive, full** *The above list is not exhaustive.*
▶ not complete **incomplete, non-exhaustive, partial** *This is a non-exhaustive list of topics that may be covered.*
▶ long **extensive, huge, long** *I could probably come up with a long list of possible reasons.*
▶ short **brief, short** *The list is short, because these sites themselves provide links to many others.*
▶ detailed **detailed** *It is now possible to publish a detailed list of the coins in the Museum Collection.*
▶ ordered in a particular way **alphabetical, chronological** *Below is an alphabetical list of the bills which the Committee has considered so far this session.*
▶ seeming to have no end **endless** *We have members from all communities: Sikh, Hindu, Muslim, Afghan, Iranian, Kurdish... the list is endless.*
▶ impressive **impressive** *There was an impressive list of backers for the project.*
▶ certain, and not likely to change **definitive** *Consult the handbook for the definitive list of current course requirements.*

● v+N make a list **compile, create, make, prepare, produce** *Make a list of all the reasons why you want to stop smoking.*
▶ publish a list **publish** *The Tribunal will then publish a list of the names of the witnesses that it proposes should be called to give evidence.*
▶ provide a list **provide** *The search engine will provide a list of documents where your keyword occurs.*
▶ add the most recent information to a list **update** *I hope to update the list at fairly regular intervals.*

listen V
pay attention to or try to hear a sound

● adv+V carefully **actively, attentively, carefully, closely, hard, intently, properly, with care** *Obviously, we listened very carefully to what he had to say.*
▶ in a patient way **patiently** *Peter listened very patiently until Jake was finished.*
▶ politely **politely, respectfully, with respect** *They listened very politely to our explanation.*
▶ in a sympathetic way **sympathetically, with understanding** *I moaned about it to her for a while, and she listened sympathetically.*
▶ in a keen or interested way **avidly, eagerly, with attention, with interest** *All of them listened eagerly to him.*
▶ quietly **in silence, quietly, silently** *The whole audience listened quietly to her speech.*

listener N
someone who listens to a person speaking

- adj+N good **good, great, sensitive** *Are you a good listener and sympathetic to others?*
- ▸ careful **attentive** *He found in Mrs Phillips a very attentive listener.*
- ▸ sympathetic **sympathetic** *A sympathetic listener is always there if you need someone to talk to.*
- ▸ patient **patient** *Both he and his wife were wonderfully patient listeners.*

literacy N
the ability to read and write; the ability to understand a particular area of knowledge

- adj+N in a particular area **cultural, digital, emotional, financial, functional, mathematical, musical, political, scientific, visual** *Emotional literacy includes the ability to understand, express and manage our own emotions and respond to the emotions of others.* ● *He reported on the work that is currently taking place to upgrade standards of financial literacy in the UK.*
- basic **basic, general** *Seven million adults have their opportunities for learning and employment reduced because they lack basic literacy.*
- relating to everyone **mass, national, universal** *Before universal literacy came in the years after 1870, spelling tended to follow local pronunciations.*
- low in quality **poor** *This new booklet is designed for practitioners who work with parents with poor literacy.*
- n+N in a particular area **computer, information, media** *Computer literacy and good administration skills are essential.*
- relating to a particular group **adult, female, male** *The borough has one of the lowest levels of adult literacy in the country.*
- v+N improve literacy **boost, develop, encourage, enhance, foster, improve, increase, promote** *It encourages all schools to focus on these approaches to improving literacy.*
- teach literacy **teach** *She is conducting research into improving methods of teaching literacy to boys.*
- achieve literacy **achieve, acquire, learn** *These people are not achieving literacy at a level adequate for functioning in today's society.*
- N+n skills **skills** *The school has seen improvements in these children's literacy skills.*
- education **education, instruction, teaching, training** *A small number of carefully picked pupils will have extra literacy teaching.*
- development **development** *The courses help parents to support their children's reading and literacy development.*
- level **level, rate, standard** *The country has a literacy rate of around 79 per cent.*
- project **initiative, programme, project, strategy** *The money will be spent on running women's literacy programmes.*
- n+of+N level, standard *A good standard of literacy and numeracy, supported by a good general education, is essential.*
- and/or **numeracy** *Approximately 20 per cent of adults report difficulties with literacy and numeracy.*

literary ADJ
involving the activity of writing or reading books

- ADJ+n expert **critic, scholar** *He is literary critic of the New York Times.*
- ▸ study **criticism, study, theory** *Her academic interests include literary theory and women's literature.*
- ▸ work of literature **classic, masterpiece, text, work** *He is best known for his television dramatizations of English literary classics.*
- ▸ magazine **journal, magazine** *I also edited the school's literary magazine that year.*
- ▸ tradition **heritage, history, tradition** *Dublin is home to a great literary tradition.*
- ▸ writer **figure, giant** *Forster was also an influential critic who helped to establish younger literary figures, such as the poet Robert Browning.*
- ▸ festival **festival** *Just a short drive away is Hay-on-Wye, famous for its annual literary festival.*
- ▸ type of literature **genre** *This course gives students the opportunity to study a wide range of texts from different literary genres and periods of time.*
- ▸ style **style** *His literary style is remarkably fine.*
- ▸ stories about imaginary events and people **fiction** *We have the widest range of titles of any UK publisher, from children's books to literary fiction.*

literate ADJ
having a good understanding of a particular subject

- adv+ADJ **digitally, economically, emotionally, financially, mathematically, musically, scientifically, technically, technologically, visually** *The growing importance of scientific issues in our daily lives demands that everyone is scientifically literate.*

literature N
1 stories, poems, and plays

- adj+N relating to a particular language or country **English, American, Latin etc** *She's also started an Open University degree in Spanish literature.*
- ▸ relating to a particular period **classical, contemporary, medieval, modern, Victorian** *She has edited an anthology of contemporary literature in translation.*
- ▸ relating to a particular century **eighteenth-century, nineteenth-century etc** *I teach Victorian and twentieth-century literature, at both undergraduate and postgraduate levels.*
- ▸ very good, and having been popular for a long time **classic** *She directed a series of movies based on classic literature.*
- v+N **publish, read, study, teach, write** *He was educated at the Tokyo Imperial University, where he studied English literature.*
- n+of+N **piece, work** *Pushkin's Eugene Onegin is the first great work of Russian literature.*

2 all the books, papers etc, about a particular academic subject

- adj+N types of literature **academic, medical, peer-reviewed, scholarly, scientific** *The book's weak point is that it ignores so much of the most important scientific literature.*
- ▸ current **current, existing, recent** *This book fills a gap in the existing literature.*

▶ available **available** *We will review all the available relevant literature.*

▶ large in amount **extensive, vast** *It includes discussion of the extensive literature which has been published recently on film and religion.*

● v+N **analyse, appraise, evaluate, examine, read, review, study, summarize, survey** *The report surveys the literature on the effects of EU regulation on economic activity.*

● N+n **review, survey** *Students will be assessed on the basis of a 5000-word literature review.*

● n+in+N **confusion, debate, gap, omission** *There is debate in the literature about what constitutes a valid task.* ● *There would appear to be a gap in the literature here, and a need for further research.*

● n+of+N when someone studies the literature **appraisal, overview, review, survey** *Her dissertation included a review of the literature and current research on the subject.*

▶ amount **body, wealth** *There is a vast body of literature on this topic.*

litigation N
the use of the legal system to settle a disagreement

● adj+N types of litigation **civil, commercial, criminal** *Increasing efforts are being made to streamline civil litigation.*

▶ expensive **costly, expensive** *What can managers and employers do to protect themselves from costly litigation?*

▶ possible **possible, potential** *The field of medicine is a growing source of potential litigation as patients become more aware of their rights.*

▶ complicated **complex** *With extensive experience of all areas of complex litigation, we have particular expertise in cross-border claims.*

▶ continuing for a long time **endless, lengthy, protracted** *Most claims get caught up in protracted litigation.*

▶ current **current, ongoing** *The mayor's spokesperson said she was unable to comment on ongoing litigation.*

▶ unnecessary **unnecessary** *The great difficulty in introducing such a scheme was perceived to be the danger of encouraging unnecessary litigation.*

▶ successful **successful** *She has been interviewed and filmed for broadcasts in relation to successful litigation she has handled.*

● v+N take part in litigation **be engaged in, be involved in, bring, conduct, pursue, undertake** *We conduct litigation in all areas of law, particularly banking and insurance disputes.*

▶ avoid litigation **avoid, prevent** *We are conscious that our clients frequently prefer to avoid litigation.*

▶ start litigation **commence, initiate, launch, start** *What advice should a solicitor give to a client commencing litigation?*

▶ encourage litigation **encourage** *Some witnesses argued that this encouraged litigation in Scotland.*

▶ try to prevent litigation **discourage** *Our aim is to resolve disputes early on and to discourage litigation.*

▶ consider starting litigation **consider, contemplate** *The company is contemplating further litigation.*

▶ threaten to start litigation **threaten** *The slightest derogatory statement was enough to provoke a letter*

from his lawyers threatening litigation and demanding an apology.

▶ pay for litigation **finance, fund** *He had provided money to fund the litigation.*

▶ settle litigation **end, settle** *We do not know the precise terms on which that litigation was settled.*

▶ have to become involved in litigation **face** *If we are not to face litigation in the future, we must implement what the law requires from us in this area.*

▶ deal with litigation **handle, manage** *We also have an extensive track record of successfully handling litigation in a number of foreign jurisdictions.*

litter N
rubbish on the ground

● v+N drop litter **drop, dump, throw** *There is no excuse for dropping litter.*

> You can also talk about litter being **strewn**: *When I walk around the town, I see litter strewn around everywhere.* ● *I was disgusted by the litter-strewn streets of the capital.*

▶ leave litter **leave, leave behind** *Don't leave litter – use the bins provided.*

▶ pick up litter **clean up, clear up, collect, pick up, remove** *They will also be able to fine shops selling take-away food if they refuse to clear up litter outside their premises.*

▶ reduce litter **reduce** *Everyone needs to do their bit to reduce litter.*

live V
have a particular kind of life

● adv+V in a peaceful way **harmoniously, in peace, peaceably, peacefully** *Its inhabitants live harmoniously in a peaceful and unique multicultural society.*

▶ without help from other people **independently** *Social Services can help you to continue to live independently in your home.*

▶ happily **happily** *Everyone has a right to live happily and free from discrimination.*

▶ well **comfortably, well** *These people lived quite comfortably, pursued professional careers, and in some cases were quite wealthy.*

▶ in a healthy way **healthily** *The majority of older people have too small an income to live healthily.*

▶ without spending much money **frugally** *In this cold and inhospitable house, the sisters lived frugally.*

▶ without enough money **below the poverty line, in poverty** *His book was dedicated to the 'wretched of the earth', who were condemned to live in poverty.*

livelihood N
something that provides the money you need to live

● adj+N good and secure **decent, secure, sustainable, viable** *They highlighted the plight of the poor, who were denied sustainable livelihoods by unfair trade.*

▶ not good or secure **meagre, precarious** *The communities earned a precarious livelihood from the few tourists to the area.*

● v+N earn a livelihood **achieve, derive, earn, gain,**

make, secure *The two girls had no immediate means of earning a livelihood.*

▸ be likely to harm a livelihood **jeopardize, threaten** *The policy threatens the livelihoods of thousands of fishermen.*

▸ harm a livelihood **affect, damage, destroy, ruin, undermine** *It is hoped that the big multi-national businesses can be pressurised into changing practices that seriously affect the livelihoods of the world's most vulnerable communities.* ● *By doubling its cotton exports, the USA will destroy the livelihoods of 250 million African cotton farmers.*

▸ protect a livelihood **defend, maintain, protect, safeguard, support** *This is a beautifully written and well-acted play about two families struggling to maintain their livelihoods.*

▸ make sure a livelihood is possible **assure, ensure, guarantee** *In such a society, everyone is guaranteed a livelihood.*

▸ lose a livelihood **lose** *Several projects were set up to help the many people who had lost their livelihoods during the disaster.*

▸ try to find a livelihood **seek** *These women were, in consequence, obliged to seek a livelihood elsewhere.*

▸ provide a livelihood **provide** *Today, agriculture provides a livelihood for about 60 per cent of Madagascar's population of 12 million.*

▸ improve a livelihood **improve** *Public funding of their work is a good way to improve the livelihoods of the poor in low-income countries.*

N+v depend on *The farmers' livelihoods depended on being able to harvest their crops in time.*

ively ADJ
involving many people giving their opinions

adv+ADJ very **extremely, very** *Their differing viewpoints led to some extremely lively debates.*
rather **fairly, pretty INFORMAL, rather** *The session turned out to be rather lively, with many conflicting opinions being expressed.*

ADJ+n **controversy, conversation, correspondence, debate, discussion, exchange, forum, messageboard, session** *Mr. McGlinn's paper generated a lively discussion.*

and/or **informative, stimulating, thought-provoking** *There then followed a lively and stimulating question-and-answer session.*

ve through PHR VB
till be alive after experiencing a dangerous or unpleasant situation

V+n event **revolution, war** *My grandfather lived through two world wars, and served in the first.*
experience **change, experience, horror** *People in the nineteenth century lived through tremendous changes.*
period **age, century, decade, era, period, time, year** *He lived through that period as a young man.*

ving N
money that you earn to live on

adj+N good **comfortable, decent, good** *It's still possible to earn a decent living as a contractor.*
likely to change without warning **precarious** *He lived for a year in the United States, where he earned*

a precarious living as a journalist and short story writer.

▸ not good enough **meagre** *Many village residents eke out a meagre living by raising chicken and sheep.*

● v+N earn a living **earn, make** *A year after his release from prison, Lane was making a good living through a range of business ventures.*

▸ have difficulty in earning a living **eke out, scrape, scratch** *Aldington managed to scrape a living as a freelance writer and translator.*

▸ provide a living **provide** *He'd worked so hard to provide a living for his family.*

▸ do something as a job in order to earn a living **do sth for** *What do you do for a living?*

load N
an amount of work to be done; a problem or responsibility that you have to deal with

● adj+N large **full, heavy** *She could cope with a heavy load of work without any apparent falling off in quality.*

▸ types of load **administrative, legislative** *The increasing administrative load of the committee had led the Chairman to propose that the number of members should be raised to eight.*

▸ small **light** *Those research students who have taken fewer courses will normally be expected to add an additional 4,000 words to their dissertation to make up for the lighter load.*

▸ extra **additional, extra** *Staff members may require help to deal with the additional load.*

● n+N **course, teaching, work** *His teaching load was extremely heavy.*

● v+N reduce a load **ease, lessen, lighten, reduce** *It will help lighten the load on our systems at this peak time.*

▸ share a load **share** *We can always use more volunteers to share the load.*

▸ divide and share a load **spread** *This proposal would spread the load much more widely.*

▸ increase a load **increase** *This will inevitably increase the load on Directors.*

loan N
an amount of money that is borrowed

● v+N get a loan **arrange, get, obtain, raise, receive, take out** *I need to get a loan to pay for my holiday.*

▸ give someone a loan **arrange, extend, give sb, grant (sb), make (sb), offer, provide** *They also offer loans, and they have a low rate of interest.*

▸ pay back a loan **pay back, pay off, repay** *You only start repaying this loan once you have finished studying and are earning more than £15,000 a year.*

▸ agree to give someone a loan **approve, sanction** *The bank will not approve the loan.*

▸ refuse to give someone a loan **refuse** *If a loan is refused, a clear reason will be given to the customer.*

▸ make sure that a loan will be paid **back, guarantee, secure, underwrite** *The loan is secured against your property.*

▸ ask for a loan **apply for, ask for, negotiate, request** *The first stop was Washington, to negotiate a loan to prop up the ailing economy.*

lobby N

a group which is trying to influence politicians about a particular issue; a protest by a lobby

- adj+N **powerful, strong, vociferous** *The whisky distillers have a very powerful lobby for their product, and urge every government to keep down the tax on whisky.* • *The agricultural lobby is vociferous, in the face of declining incomes on family farms.*

- v+N **form, join, lead, organize** *Four MPs joined the lobby **against** the ban, forcing the government to review the case in the High Court.*

- N+n **group, organization** *A smokers' lobby group sent messages to politicians urging them not to support a total ban on smoking in public places.*

lobby V

try to influence powerful people about a particular issue

- adv+V using a lot of effort **actively, hard, heavily, strongly, vigorously** *We have lobbied hard to have this ban overturned.*
- ▶ successfully **effectively, successfully** *The group successfully lobbied for the introduction of women-only wards in hospitals.*

- V+n **authority, company, council, councillor, government, minister, MP, parliament, politicians** *The group is calling for people to lobby the government for urgent legislation to end this discrimination.*

- V+for **amendment, change, funding, improvement, introduction of sth, legislation, right, support** *We have actively lobbied for a change in the law.*

location N

the place or position of someone or something

- adj+N perfect **ideal, perfect, prime** *The area's outstanding natural beauty makes it an ideal location for a well-earned break.*
- ▶ good or suitable **accessible, appropriate, convenient, excellent, good, great, suitable, superb** *The company is based at a convenient location just off the motorway.*
- ▶ beautiful **attractive, beautiful, idyllic, picturesque, scenic, spectacular, stunning** *The houses are in a beautiful location on the banks of the Conwy river.*
- ▶ quiet **peaceful, quiet, tranquil** *The hotel stands in its own garden in a wonderfully quiet location.*
- ▶ exact **exact, precise, specific** *The tracking device gives information on the car's exact location.*
- ▶ secret **secret, undisclosed** *He is being held by U.S. intelligence agents at an undisclosed location.*
- ▶ in relation to other places **geographic, geographical, physical** *Haddington's early prosperity was almost entirely due to its geographic location.*
- ▶ far from other places **isolated, remote, secluded** *His ashes were scattered at a remote location on Dartmoor.*
- ▶ unusual and interesting **exotic** *I'm envious because he's always jetting off to exotic locations!*
- ▶ popular **popular** *Cardiff is a popular location for call centres, with a number of large organizations having offices within the city.*

- n+N **beachfront, beachside, city-centre, countryside, downtown, hillside, riverside, roadside, seafront, seaside, waterfront, waterside** *The town is famous for its lovely riverside location and annual arts festival.*

- v+N **confirm, determine, discover, establish, find, identify, indicate, mark, pinpoint, show, specify** *GPS uses satellites to pinpoint your location anywhere on the planet to within a few feet.*

lodge V

formally make a complaint, claim etc

- V+n **amendment, appeal, application, case, claim, complaint, grievance, motion, objection, petition, protest, request** *Neighbours have lodged objections to the plans to erect five CCTV cameras around the grounds of her house.*

logic N

the way someone connects ideas when they are explaining something; the fact of being a reasonable explanation

- adj+N basic **basic, cold, inherent, pure, simple** *Simple logic says that making fuels from crops can reduce lethal greenhouse gas emissions.*
- ▶ incorrect **faulty, flawed, perverse, twisted, warped** *A little close scrutiny soon reveals the twisted logic of racism.*

- v+N use logic **apply, be based on, employ, use** *I used the same rather obvious logic in selecting Frankie as you did with David .*
- ▶ understand or accept someone's logic **accept, appreciate, follow, see, understand** *I appreciate the logic **behind** this line of thought.* • *I am trying to follow the logic of why the health service should be run like a supermarket.*
- ▶ have doubts about someone's logic **question** *He questioned the logic of pushing through changes in time for a general election.*
- ▶ be the opposite of what logic makes you think **defy** *It defies logic to say that the beliefs of a theist and an atheist are equally valid.*
- ▶ explain logic **explain** *Let me try to explain the logic underlying the decision-making process.*

- N+v say **dictate, say, suggest** *There is a mismatch between what logic dictates is good for our health, and what we actually do.*
- ▶ be relevant **apply** *The same logic applies in the case of smaller organizations.*

logical ADJ

connecting ideas in sensible way

- adv+ADJ very or completely **completely, entirely, only, perfectly, purely, quite, strictly, very** *It seemed only logical that we investigate all the options open to us.* • *They can't see themselves, and their behaviour seems to them perfectly logical.*
- ▶ rather **fairly, pretty** INFORMAL *The book is arranged in a fairly logical sequence.*

- ADJ+n decision or result **conclusion, consequence, outcome** *The logical conclusion of this research is to bring back the grammar school, so that all really smart kids can profit from this experience.*

▶ stage or development **development, extension, progression** *Smith said that genetic modification was a logical extension of natural plant breeding.*

▶ order **order, sequence, structure** *The chapters follow a logical sequence.*

▶ thoughts or arguments **analysis, argument, deduction, reasoning, thinking, thought** *I thought she presented a sound and logical argument.* ● *Being capable of logical thinking does not exclude appreciation of poetry, art, or music.*

▶ method or action **approach, process, step, way** *This is a natural and logical step for the society to take.* ● *Telephone groups are a logical way to build on the success of Parentline Plus.*

▶ reason **explanation, reason** *This must have a logical explanation, which at the moment eludes me.*

▶ choice **choice** *With all his experience, Ben was the logical choice for the job.*

● ADJ+infinitive **assume, conclude, expect, say, suggest, suppose, think** *It is logical to assume that the general results would not necessarily be different for larger populations.*

● and/or **coherent, methodical, rational, sensible** *Aim to communicate information in a logical and coherent fashion.*

long ADJ
asting a large amount of time

▶ adv+ADJ very **awfully, extremely, incredibly, really, very** *I think we are in for a very long wait.*

▶ rather **comparatively, fairly, pretty** INFORMAL, **reasonably, relatively** *It was a pretty long match, at nearly three hours.*

▶ too **excessively, overly, unacceptably, unnecessarily, unreasonably** *Under this system, approval takes an unacceptably long time.*

▶ long enough **sufficiently** *Performance should be assessed over a sufficiently long period.*

▶ longer than usual **exceptionally, surprisingly, unusually** *We've had an unusually long spell of dry weather.*

▶ so long that it seems almost silly **impossibly, inordinately, ridiculously** *The drive to Prague was easy, even including a ridiculously long stop in Dresden.*

longing N
strong feeling of wanting someone or something

adj+N great **deep, great, intense, passionate, profound** *I came back here, feeling an intense longing to see the place again.*

secret **secret** *Even the most relaxed parents have secret longings for their children to do well.*

for the past **nostalgic** *Overall, there is a nostalgic longing to regain lost innocence.*

v+N have a longing **be filled with, feel, have** *We all have longings for joy and satisfaction.*

satisfy a longing **satisfy** *The trip had satisfied her longing for adventure.*

and/or **desire, loneliness, nostalgia, regret, yearning** *We tend to look back on our lives with regret, or longing for the old days to come back.*

long-standing ADJ
having existed for a long time

● ADJ+n relationship or connection **association, collaboration, connection, friendship, link, partnership, relationship** *The university has long-standing links with Turin university.*

▶ problem or illness **illness, injury, issue, problem** *Midfielder Damian Lacey is another definite absentee after his long-standing foot problem flared up again.*

▶ person **client, customer, friend, member, partner, supporter** *He is an active and long-standing member of the golf club.*

▶ interest or involvement **commitment, concern, interest, involvement** *We have a long-standing commitment to education.*

▶ way of doing something **policy, practice, tradition** *The long-standing tradition of giving sweets to celebrate special occasions such as weddings was started centuries ago in Italy.*

▶ an opinion, based on what you have done **history, record, reputation** *This hotel has a long-standing reputation for good food and wine.*

▶ disagreement/agreement **agreement, debate, dispute** *The invasion was the result of a long-standing territorial dispute.*

▶ experience or knowledge **experience, expertise** *She has long-standing experience of project development.*

long-term ADJ
1 continuing to exist or be relevant for a long time in the future

● ADJ+n result or effect **consequences, effect, impact, outcome** *She is conducting research into the long-term effects of antenatal stress.*

▶ plan **plan, planning, policy, solution, strategy** *We're involved in the development of a long-term marketing strategy.*

▶ aim **aim, goal, objective, vision** *We need to ensure that the UK's long-term goal of reducing carbon emissions is met.*

▶ success, health etc **benefit, development, growth, health, preservation, stability, success, survival, sustainability, viability** *Addressing these challenges is crucial for long-term commercial success.*

▶ damage, problems etc **complications, damage, problem, risk** *Excessive exposure to the sun can cause long-term skin damage.*

▶ future **future, prospects** *The long-term future of the club remains uncertain.*

▶ relationship **relationship** *We aim to establish long-term relationships with all our clients.*

2 having existed for a long time

● ADJ+n **illness, relationship, unemployment** *Both our children are in long-term relationships but show no sign of getting married.* ● *The government has introduced new training schemes in a bid to tackle long-term unemployment.*

look V
1 move your eyes to see someone or something

● adv+V directly **directly, straight** *Looking directly at the sun can cause serious damage to your eyes.*

▶ carefully **carefully, closely, hard, intently, properly** *If you look carefully, you should be able to find evidence of foxes in the area.*

▸ quickly **briefly, quickly** *She looked quickly toward the other person.*
▸ with a particular feeling **anxiously, eagerly, earnestly, enviously, fondly, longingly, nervously, suspiciously, wistfully** *He looked anxiously over his shoulder as he spoke.*

2 be planning to do something

● V+infinitive employ someone **appoint, employ, hire, recruit, take on** *Our client is looking to recruit an experienced training manager to work as part of the training team.*
▸ start something **create, establish, start** *He was looking to start a new career.*
▸ improve or increase something **add sth, build up sth, develop sth, enhance sth, expand (sth), extend sth, improve (sth), increase sth, strengthen sth** *The company is looking to expand its overseas operations.* ● *We shall be looking to expand in the new financial year.*
▸ buy/sell something **acquire, buy, get, invest, purchase, sell** *I'm looking to buy a digital camera for my travels.*
▸ move to a different place **move** *They are looking to move to the South West for a change of lifestyle.*

Usage Look is used in the form **be looking to** in this meaning.

look N

1 an act of looking at someone or something

● adj+N careful **careful, close, good, proper, thorough** *This bird was too shy for me to get a proper look.*
▸ quick **brief, cursory, quick** *He turned, gave me a quick look and asked 'Which way did you come?'*
▸ long **lingering, long** *I took one last lingering look at the house, then turned and left.*
▸ pretending that you are not interested **casual** *I took a casual look inside, and saw that Caroline was already there.*

● v+N have a look **get, have, take** *He moved forward to get a closer look.*
▸ have a quick look **cast, shoot** *Jack shot a quick look at Daniel, whose expression was unfathomable.*
▸ have a look secretly **sneak** *I remember as a child, I used to sneak a look at their letters which my mother had kept.*

2 an expression on your face or in your eyes

● adj+N strange **funny, odd, strange** *He had a funny look on his face – I just knew he was in on the plot.*
▸ showing that you want more information **questioning, quizzical, searching** *Curtis glanced at it and gave him a quizzical look.*
▸ showing that you are thinking carefully **thoughtful** *The question provoked many thoughtful looks among the audience.*
▸ showing that you do not approve **angry, dark, dirty, withering** *Ann gave me a dirty look and left the room.*
▸ showing that you do not understand something **blank, puzzled** *There was a puzzled look in her eyes.*
▸ showing that you know about something **knowing** *'Anything to do with the smugglers?' inquired the boy, with a knowing look.*

▸ showing worry **anxious, serious, worried** *She noticed the worried look on his face as his wife was put into the ambulance.*

● v+N **cast sb, give sb, shoot sb** *She gave me an anxious look.*
● N+of surprise or shock **amazement, astonishment, disbelief, shock, surprise** *There were looks of surprise when the winner was announced.*
▸ confusion **bewilderment, confusion, glazed** *There was a look of confusion on her face when I announced who I was.*
▸ negative feelings **despair, disappointment, disgust, fear, horror, panic, terror** *I will never forget the look of sheer terror on the face of that animal as it was being tortured.*
▸ positive feelings **concern, love, relief, triumph** *There she stood, with a look of triumph on her face.*

3 an act of thinking carefully about something

● adj+N involving a lot of facts and details **careful, comprehensive, detailed, in-depth, informative, thorough** *The talk provided an informative look into the world of caravanning.*
▸ involving a few facts and details **brief, cursory, quick** *Here we take a brief look at a couple of alternatives, and how one family is tackling the problem head on.*
▸ considering something as it really is, even if unpleasant **critical, hard, honest, realistic, serious** *The first step is to take an honest look at your financial situation.*
▸ new **fresh, new** *We need to take a fresh look at the situation.*
▸ interesting or unusual **fascinating, interesting, offbeat, refreshing, unique** *This site also includes an interesting look into the history that dictates which side of the road different countries drive on.*
▸ involving humour **entertaining, humorous, irreverent, light-hearted, satirical, wry** *The magazine offers a humorous look at women's lives.*
▸ considering facts that only people involved will know **behind-the-scenes, inside** *This is a behind-the-scenes look at the restaurant industry.*
▸ making you remember happy times in the past **nostalgic** *The film is a nostalgic look at Britain's steam trains.*

● v+N have a look **have, take** *We need to have a look at the way we deal with customer complaints.*
▸ provide a look **offer, provide** *Her book offers a fascinating look at life in the 19th century.*

look into PHR VB

try to discover the facts about something

● V+n a situation or problem **case, issue, matter, problem, situation, subject** *There is real anger among the public, and the minister must look into the issue immediately.*
▸ a part of a situation **aspect, cause, circumstances detail** *The Hutton inquiry was set up to look into the circumstances surrounding the death.*
▸ a complaint **allegation, claim, complaint** *Greater Manchester police were looking into allegations of malpractice.*
▸ a possibility **feasibility, idea, option, possibility, question** *We are looking into the possibility of maintaining a local archive.*

▶ an effect **effect, implications** *A Parliamentary committee has been appointed to look into the effects of changing the law.*

loophole N
a way of avoiding obeying a law etc

● adj+N legal **legal** *Too often, we hear of employers who use legal loopholes to abuse the rights of workers.*

▶ serious **glaring, major, serious** *The organization has campaigned for the registration of nannies, to close a major loophole in the regulatory system.*

▶ possible **possible, potential** *The new amendment clsoed a potential loophole in the legislation.*

● n+N **security, tax** *We need to close the tax loopholes that allow the rich to avoid paying tax altogether.*

● v+N use a loophole **exploit, take advantage of, use** *Some drivers have exploited the legal loophole by 'transferring' penalty points on their licences to relatives or friends.*

▶ create a loophole **create, leave** *Critics argue that introducing this type of ID card would create loopholes which terrorists can exploit.*

▶ get rid of a loophole **block, close, plug** *The shake-up will close the loopholes which allowed the killer to get a job as a school caretaker.*

▶ find a loophole **discover, find, identify** *The company found a planning loophole that has allowed it to double the size of its existing stores by building a mezzanine level within the store.*

● N+in **law, legislation, regulations, system** *There are loopholes in the current law that still leave people vulnerable.*

ose V
top having a positive feeling, quality, or attitude

▶ V+n **confidence, faith, hope, interest, patience, respect, trust** *People were beginning to lose hope of finding him alive.*

oss N
money that is lost in business

adj+N large **big, considerable, enormous, heavy, huge, large, massive, severe, significant, substantial** *A hostile takeover would be likely if they suffered huge losses and their share price collapsed.*
small **small** *The business is scheduled to make a small loss in its first year.*
financial **economic, financial** *Financial loss forced the corporation to reorganize its business.*
total **overall, total** *Overall losses are reckoned at more than $2 billion.*
before paying tax **pre-tax** *The takeover announcement came as the company announced a pre-tax loss of £1.4 million.*
in a year **annual** *They posted the largest annual loss in US corporate history.*

v+N suffer a loss **incur, make, suffer, sustain** *The company made a loss before tax of £0.4 million.*
reduce a loss **minimize, reduce** *An effective disaster recovery plan can reduce losses by 90 per cent.*
announce a loss **announce, post, record, report** *The property company has reported a loss of GBP21.4m for the year to the end of June.*

▶ get back a loss **recoup, recover** *We're hoping to re-open in August, but we'll never recoup our losses.*

▶ balance out the effect of a loss **cover, offset** *These payments will help offset the loss of earnings.*

2 the death of someone

● adj+N **devastating, sad, terrible, tragic** *The family wish to thank all who have given help and support following the sad loss of Jo.*

● v+N feel sad because of a loss **grieve, mourn** *We mourn the loss not only of a good soldier, but of a good comrade as well.*

▶ experience the loss of someone **experience, suffer** *She suffered the loss of her grandmother in 2004.*

loud ADJ
used to describe a sound that is strong and easy to hear

● adv+ADJ very **deafeningly, extremely, incredibly, really, very** *There was a very loud explosion.*

▶ rather **fairly, pretty** INFORMAL, **quite, rather** *At this speed, the fan was rather loud.*

▶ too **excessively, overly, too, uncomfortably** *Damage to hearing caused by excessively loud music adds up over the years.*

love V
be very strongly attracted to someone; to care very much about someone

● adv+V deeply **dearly, deeply, greatly, passionately, really, truly, unconditionally** *He loves his family deeply.*

▶ in a way that is easy to see **clearly, obviously** *She clearly loved Sidney as more than a conventional friend.*

▶ secretly **secretly** *Mary secretly loves Edward, but he thinks of her as a friend.*

▶ in a way that is sincere **genuinely** *Jim does genuinely love Karen, there's no doubt about it.*

> When someone loves another person, you can say that they are **in love** (with them): *I was in love with my best friend's brother.* ● *We were young and we were in love.* When someone starts to love with another person, you can say that they **fall in love** (with them): *She had fallen in love with James the first time she met him.*

love N
a strong emotional and sexual feeling for someone; the feeling of liking or caring for someone or something very much

● adj+N lasting forever or for a long time **abiding, enduring, everlasting, steadfast, undying, unfailing** *They had declared their undying love for each other.*

▶ strong **boundless, deep, intense, passionate, profound, strong** *He has a deep love for the English countryside.*

▶ sincere **genuine, real, sheer, true** *But true love is strong and speaks the truth.*

▶ when you are young **first, young** *Young love can be intensely passionate.*

▶ without demanding anything from the other person **selfless, unconditional** *My parents have given me unconditional love and support.*

▶ not felt by the other person **unrequited** *This is a*

touching story of unrequited love developing into friendship.
▶ too strong and involving jealous feelings **jealous, obsessive** *This is a tale of a man's obsessive love for a woman who has no love for him.*

> You can talk about someone being ***deeply/madly/head over heels in love*** with someone: *After ten years of marriage they were still madly in love.* If someone loves someone else from the first time they see them, you can talk about ***love at first sight***: *It was love at first sight when I met Alan.*

● v+N feel love **be in, experience, feel, have** *I didn't feel any instant love for Flynn.*
▶ start to feel love **fall in** *She had fallen in love with one of her teachers.*
▶ show love **demonstrate, express, show** *Words couldn't ever express my love for you.*
▶ tell someone you love him or her **confess, declare, proclaim, profess** *In a moving scene, Brad declares his love for Lucy.*
▶ look for someone who will give you love **look for, pursue, seek** *Many people join dating agencies looking for love.*
▶ find someone who will give you love **discover, find** *Both women found love on their travels.*
▶ tell someone that you do not want their love **reject** *He was downcast because she had rejected his love.*

● N+v **blossom, grow** *They kept in touch after their first meeting in Berlin, their love grew and they married.*

● and/or **affection, attention, care, compassion, devotion, faith, friendship, happiness, joy, respect, sex, support, understanding** *Thank you to Paul for his love and support.*

low ADJ
small in amount or level

● adv+ADJ very **exceptionally, extremely, incredibly, remarkably** *Medical supplies are already extremely low.*
▶ rather **fairly, pretty** INFORMAL, **quite, slightly** *Her blood pressure was quite low.*
▶ when compared to other similar things **comparatively, relatively** *This is a good product at a relatively low price.*
▶ in a way that is dangerous **dangerously, perilously** *The oxygen level in the pond could drop to dangerously low levels.*
▶ in a way that is different from usual **abnormally, artificially, unusually** *She maintained an abnormally low weight for her height.*
▶ in a way that seems surprising or silly **ridiculously, surprisingly** *He was driving at a ridiculously low speed.* ● *Off season, the weekly rates are surprisingly low.*
▶ in a way that is not as good as it should be or not as good as you want **disappointingly, unacceptably** *The level of response was disappointingly low.*

● v+ADJ **be, become, get, keep sth, remain, run, stay** *The college has kept course fees as low as possible.* ● *We need more blood donors as stocks are running dangerously low.*

loyal ADJ
always willing to support someone, even in difficult times

● adv+ADJ **absolutely, extremely, fiercely, intensely, totally, very** *I am fiercely loyal to my friends, and would do almost anything for them.*
● ADJ+n person or animal **ally, citizen, client, companion, customer, dog, employee, fan, follower, friend, member, reader, servant, soldier, subject, supporter** *He has been a loyal friend.*
▶ group **audience, clientele, fan base, following, staff, workforce** *Not surprisingly, the restaurant has acquired a loyal following over the years.*
▶ service or support **service, support** *Whoever is the new leader, they can count on my loyal support.*

loyalty N
support for someone or something

● adj+N strong **absolute, fierce, great, strong, total, undying, unswerving** *The girls have a fierce loyalty to their mother.*
▶ not thinking about whether someone or something deserves loyalty **blind, unquestioning** *This is not blind loyalty to the Party, but a recognition that we are a collective movement.*
▶ giving loyalty to someone or something that does not deserve it **misplaced** *Reluctance to give information to the police may be out of a misplaced loyalty.*
▶ types of loyalty **personal, political, tribal** *The sense of ethnic identity and tribal loyalty of many remains strong.*
▶ real and sincere **true** *You showed me what true loyalty meant.*

● v+N show loyalty **demonstrate, display, prove, show** *Fortunately for Mary, Joseph would later demonstrate his loyalty to her.*
▶ increase loyalty **build, create, encourage, increase, strengthen** *By giving employees some responsibility for the organization's direction, you are encouraging loyalty at a grass-roots level.*
▶ make someone feel loyalty **command, engender, foster, gain, generate, inspire, secure, win** *Motivated people inspire loyalty and that leads to excellence in what we do.*
▶ feel loyalty **develop, feel, have** *Some breeds of dog develop a strong loyalty to members of the family and are rather wary of strangers.*
▶ keep someone's or your loyalty **retain** *We must demonstrate our commitment to retaining the loyalt of our customer base.* ● *Few, if any, of the original members retained their loyalty to the party.*
▶ give someone something in return for their loyalty **repay, reward** *She rewarded his loyalty by making him a Privy Councillor.*
▶ make a statement expressing loyalty **declare, express, pledge, swear** *The book tells the tale of th great warriors Kuan Gung and Chang Fei, who pledged their loyalty to Liu Pei.*
▶ want loyalty from someone **demand, expect** *The leadership is very quick to demand loyalty from party members.*
▶ test someone's loyalty **test** *This is a strategy that is certain to test the loyalty and commitment of staf*

● N+v **lie** *I feel completely confident in him and I feel my loyalty lies with him.*

● n+of+N **declaration, expression, feeling, sense** *She refused to betray him out of some misguided sense of loyalty.*

uck N

n influence that seems to make things happen, specially good things; success that you have by hance

adj+N complete and pure **blind, plain, pure, sheer** *By sheer luck he survived the war unharmed.*
good **good, great** *They wished us good luck for the future.*
bad **bad, cruel, ill, rotten, terrible** *Marco's run of rotten luck continues.*

v+N get or have luck **get, have** *It's about time we got some good luck.*
bring luck for someone **bring** *The four-leaved clover is supposed to bring luck and love.*
need luck **need, require** *All singers need a degree of luck in order to succeed.*
deserve luck **deserve** *I'm so pleased for you, you really deserve some good luck!*
wish someone else luck **wish sb** *We wish her luck in her new job.*
feel annoyed because you have had bad luck **curse** *Sarah stopped at the red light, cursing her bad luck.*

N+v change **change, turn** *His luck changed when he landed a job with Hippo books.*
end **run out** *On 39 minutes, our luck eventually ran out and their other team scored.*
continue **continue, hold** *Luck held for Hawkins and Drake, as they were able to escape.*

n+of+N a time when several lucky things happen **run** *He is like a gambler whose run of luck ends just before the biggest bet of all.*
a degree of luck **amount, degree, element** *In many cases, however, there will be an element of luck as to the results that are obtained.*
a time when a lucky thing happens **bit, piece, slice, stroke** *It was a deserved piece of luck for Bell and the whole team.*
a situation in which luck rather than skill controls what happens **matter** *Winning the lottery is simply a matter of luck.*

cky ADJ

you are lucky, something good happens to you a result of luck

adv+ADJ very **exceptionally, extraordinarily, extremely, incredibly, really, very** *Under the circumstances, I was very lucky to survive.*
rather **fairly, pretty** INFORMAL, **quite** *We were fairly lucky with the weather, so it all went well.*
v+ADJ **be, consider yourself, count yourself, feel, get, strike** *I consider myself really lucky to be in such a beautiful place, working with a brilliant bunch of people.* ● *I waited less than a minute for both transfers, so I guess I got lucky.* ● *We struck lucky with the hotel we had chosen – it was excellent.*

crative ADJ

nging a lot of money

adv+ADJ very **extremely, highly, very** *This led to*

a desperate scramble for highly lucrative oil contracts.
▶ possibly in the future **potentially** *They are promoting Scotch Whisky as a worthwhile and potentially lucrative investment for individuals.*
● ADJ+n job or opportunity **career, employment, job, opportunity, position, post, work** *The film opened the gateway to a lucrative career in TV.*
▶ business **business, industry, market, trade, venture** *Gaming is becoming a more lucrative business every day.*
▶ deal **bid, contract, deal, investment, offer** *Both groups are likely to get lucrative record deals.*

luggage N

bags and suitcases for a journey

● adj+N heavy or large in size **bulky, heavy, oversize** *If you have heavy luggage, it is best to take a taxi.*
▶ carried on to a plane with you **carry-on, hand** *Carry important medications in your hand luggage.*
▶ put in the hold of an aircraft **checked-in** *The airline will start charging for each piece of checked-in luggage.*
● v+N carry luggage **carry, transport** *Porters are hard to find, so you will be the one responsible for carrying your luggage.*
▶ give luggage to someone at an airport so it can be put on the plane **check (in)** *You can check your luggage in at the airline counter.*
▶ load/unload luggage **load, stow, unload** *Unload your luggage, and an official will safely park your car for you.*
▶ get your luggage back **collect, reclaim, retrieve** *I had to dash back to the station, retrieve my luggage and then hurry to the airport.*
● n+of+N **item, piece** *Please make sure all items of luggage are securely stowed in the overhead lockers.*

lukewarm ADJ

not very enthusiastic or interested

● adv+ADJ **decidedly, distinctly** *The movie may get better reviews here than in America, where it attracted a decidedly lukewarm response.*
● ADJ+n **reaction, reception, response, review, support** *Her last film got a lukewarm reception.*

lull N

a quiet period during an active or violent situation

● adj+N **brief, momentary, short, slight, temporary** *In the spring of 1942, there was a brief lull in fighting.*
● N+in **action, activity, conversation, fighting, proceedings, storm, violence** *During a lull in the conversation, I asked Irving about a comment he'd made earlier.*

lunch N

a meal in the middle of the day

● adj+N good **delicious, excellent, good, great, lovely, nice, superb, tasty, wonderful** *After an excellent lunch, some of us went to look round the museum.*

▶ lasting a long time **lazy, leisurely, long, relaxed** *The hotel terrace is ideal for long, lazy lunches.*
▶ lasting only a short time **quick** *We'll have a quick lunch then get back to work.*
▶ eaten early/late **early, late** *We then headed back down the valley for a late lunch.*
▶ hot/cold **cold, hot** *We serve a variety of hot and cold lunches.*
▶ involving only a little food **light** *The Verandah serves light lunches around the pool.*
▶ involving good food or a lot of food **full, gourmet, hearty, lavish, sumptuous** *We stopped at a pub and enjoyed a hearty lunch.*
▶ in order to celebrate something **celebration, celebratory, special** *She joined the rest of the family for a celebratory lunch.*
▶ formal/informal **formal, informal** *The meeting finished with an informal lunch.*
▶ consisting of sandwiches that you take with you and eat somewhere **box, pack, packed, picnic** *Packed lunches are available on request.*
▶ consisting of a lot of alcohol **boozy** INFORMAL, **liquid** *My boss always went out to lunch, and on his return it was obvious they were very liquid lunches!*

● n+N the place where you have lunch **bar, pub, school** *We stopped for an excellent pub lunch at the Malt Shovel.*
▶ the type of food you eat for lunch **buffet, sandwich, snack** *The launch will be followed by a buffet lunch.*
▶ the number of parts that a lunch has **three-course, two-course** *The price includes two-course lunch and coffee.*
▶ that you combine with business **business, networking, working** *There will be a networking lunch before the seminar.*

● v+N have lunch **eat, get, grab** INFORMAL, **have** *Chris and I headed off to Interlaken to get some lunch.*
▶ make lunch **cook, fix, make, prepare** *I then went to the kitchen to prepare the lunch.*
▶ not have lunch **miss, skip** *We'd skipped lunch to go to a show.*
▶ meet someone and have lunch with them **do** INFORMAL, **go for, meet for** *Tell him to call me – we'll do lunch.*
▶ provide lunch **provide, serve** *Lunch is served between 12.00pm and 3.00pm.*

● N+n the period when you stop work and eat lunch **break, hour, period** *I went for a walk during my lunch break.*
▶ the act of stopping doing something in order to eat lunch **halt, stop** *A lunch stop is often made at a public house, although not always.*
▶ an event that involves eating lunch **date, meeting, party** *They agree on a lunch date, but Martha fails to show.*
▶ a list of food that is available for lunch in a restaurant **menu** *The lunch menu is based around baguettes, salads, and burgers.*
▶ a place where you can eat lunch **spot, venue** *Just to the south is Port au Moulin, another great lunch spot.*

● n+of+N **bite** INFORMAL, **spot** INFORMAL *We ran for an hour, then returned home for a spot of lunch.*

lure N
something that attracts someone [usually singular]

● adj+N **irresistible, tempting** *The stunning coastline is an irresistable lure for yachtsmen.*
● v+N **be attracted by, be seduced by, be tempted by, resist, succumb to** *Customers can't resist the lure of a free gift.*
● N+of **fame, gold, money, profit, the sea, the stage, wealth** *For ordinary people, the lure of fame can be all too tantalising.*

lush ADJ
lush plants and places look very green and health

● ADJ+n **countryside, field, foliage, forest, garden, grass, greenery, hill, hillside, island, jungle, landscape, meadow, mountain, pasture, rainforest scenery, valley, vegetation** *We stayed in a hotel set amongst lush tropical gardens.*
● and/or **beautiful, fertile, green, tropical, verdant** *We explored the lush green landscape and picturesque sandy beaches.*

lust N
1 a strong feeling of wanting to have sex

● adj+N **carnal, insatiable, sexual, unbridled** *Sexual lust will never banish our yearning for love.*
● v+N **be driven by, indulge, satisfy** *He acted with no regard other than to satisfy his own sexual lust.*

2 great enthusiasm for something

● adj+N **insatiable** *He was obsessed by an insatiabl lust for power and money.*
● n+N **blood** *They would start beating him up and would not stop until they had satisfied their blood lust.*
● v+N **be driven by, have, indulge, satisfy** *Throughout the play, he is shown as being driven by his lust for revenge.*
● N+for **adventure, blood, fame, gold, life, money, power, profit, revenge, violence, wealth** *What I love about Charlotte is her lust for life. ● I have se what the lust for money brings out in people and i is not nice.*

luxury N
1 something that is expensive or enjoyable but unnecessary; something that you would like to do or have but that is not necessary

● adj+N expensive or impossible to afford **expensive, unaffordable** *Oysters have become scarce, and thus an expensive luxury.*
▶ not too expensive **affordable** *Handbags count as one of those affordable luxuries that will make or break an outfit.*
▶ little **little, small** *Other little luxuries such as refrigerators, irons, hairdryers or Internet access c available on request.*
▶ unnecessary **unnecessary** *Advertising constantly tries to convince us that we really need one unnecessary luxury after another.*
▶ rare **rare** *Permanent chauffeurs are a rare luxury these days.*

▸ real **real, true** *There is electricity and running water which, to Mike, is a real luxury.*

▸ extra **added** *The chalet also boasts the added luxury of a sauna.*

▸ v+N **afford, enjoy** *Employees can no longer afford the luxury of feeling loyal to their employers.* ● *If you enjoy the luxuries in life, why not upgrade to one of our executive rooms.*

▪ a very comfortable situation surrounded by the best and most expensive things

▹ adj+N great **five-star, great, real, true** *Their Christmas hampers are a taste of real luxury at very reasonable prices.*

complete **absolute, complete, pure, sheer, total, ultimate** *He lives in absolute luxury.* ● *For ultimate luxury, the hotel offers a spa.*

when compared to other things **comparative, relative** *I checked into the relative luxury of a Super 8 Motel.*

that you can/cannot afford **affordable, unaffordable** *Our boutique shops offer affordable luxury.*

▸ attractive and not trying to impress **discreet, refined, understated** *Eight bedrooms provide classic understated luxury with private balconies overlooking the lush gardens.*

▸ trying to impress **extravagant, ostentatious, unashamed** *A third of the population lived at subsistence level, while the court lived in ostentatious luxury.*

● v+N offer luxury **offer, provide** *This is a stunning, romantic hotel offering sophisticated luxury, surrounded by glorious natural beauty.*

▸ enjoy or experience luxury **enjoy, experience, indulge in, live in** *If you enjoy discreet luxury, look no further than this resort.* ● *We invite you to experience the luxury of being treated like royalty.*

● n+of+N **bit, lap, life, touch** *He was a rich, spoiled brat who had been brought up in the lap of luxury.* ● *Tom works long hours as an aeroplane repairman so Leeza can live the life of luxury at home.* ● *Our bedrooms are tastefully decorated to add a touch of luxury to your stay.*

M m

mad ADJ
1 very silly or stupid; mentally ill

- adv+**ADJ** completely **absolutely, barking**
INFORMAL, **completely, quite, raving** INFORMAL, **really,
totally** *Everyone thought I was barking mad to leave
my job.*
▶ rather **pretty** INFORMAL, **slightly** *The organization
also attracted some slightly mad people.*
- v+**ADJ be, drive sb, go, seem** *The constant ringing
of her phone was driving her mad.* • *I'd go mad if I
had to stay in bed for a week.*

2 done quickly and without thinking or organizing

- **ADJ**+n **dash, panic, rush, scramble** *At the end of
the film, there was a mad rush for the doors.*

madness N
actions showing a lack of careful thought

- adj+**N absolute, complete, pure, sheer, total, utter**
All this seems to me sheer madness.
- v+**N be madness be, seem (like)** *It's a big river
and it would be madness to try and cross it in the
dark.*
▶ stop madness **end, stop** *We will end the madness of
police officers having to fill in forms every time they
stop someone.*
- n+of+**N act, bout, fit, minute, moment, touch**
*Robert, in a moment of madness, tried to climb a
ladder that wasn't leaning on anything.*

magnet N
something that attracts people very strongly

- v+**N act as, act like, become, behave like, be (like),
prove, remain** *For much of the 20th century, the
USA acted like a magnet for people facing oppression
in their own homelands.*
- **N**+for people **artists, climbers, enthusiasts,
migrants, tourists, visitors, walkers** *The beaches
and waters adjacent to the coast act as a magnet for
tourists.*
▶ activity **crime, investment, talent, tourism** *Many of
the high-rise developments became magnets for
crime.*

magnify V
to make something bigger, worse, more severe etc

- adv+**V** a lot **considerably, enormously, greatly,
massively, significantly, tenfold** *Small differences
that appear insignificant against an average player
are magnified tenfold when you play against the best
players in the world.*
▶ just **just, only, simply** *Avoiding relationship
breakdown problems will not make them go away,
but only magnify them.*
- **V**+n **difference, difficulty, effect, importance,
power, problem, scale** *In large groups these
problems are magnified.*

magnitude N
the great size, importance, or effect of something

- adj+**N** great **considerable, great, high, large,
sheer, unimaginable, unparalleled** *You cannot visit
the Eden Project without being amazed at the sheer
magnitude of it all.*
▶ small **low, small** *Similar effects, although of a
smaller magnitude, were observed for a second defec
in the gene.*
- v+**N** reduce the magnitude of something **limit,
reduce** *The size of the pins limits the magnitude of
the load that can be carried.*
▶ become greater in magnitude **grow in, increase in**
*The automobile engine produces heat, increasing in
magnitude with increasing speed and load.*
▶ differ in magnitude **differ, vary** *This effect varies
in magnitude for different reasons.*
▶ guess or calculate the magnitude of something
**assess, calculate, determine, estimate, measure,
predict, quantify** *Population pressure needs to be
taken into account in predicting the magnitude of
the expected migration.*
▶ realize the magnitude of something **appreciate,
grasp, realize, understand** *He gradually comes to
realise the magnitude of what he is being asked and
goes to the police.*
▶ not realize the magnitude of something
underestimate *I think that we underestimate the
magnitude of what we are attempting.*
- **N**+of **achievement, change, difference, disaster,
effect, error, problem, response, risk, task, threat**
*When it comes to lung cancer, the magnitude of the
effect of cigarette smoking far outweighs all other
factors.*

mailing list N
a list of people who receive letters or emails from
a company

- v+**N** create a mailing list **build up, create,
generate, set up** *How do I set up a mailing list?*
▶ put someone on a mailing list **add sb to, put sb
on** *Email or phone with your postal address and w
will add you to the mailing list.*
▶ be on a mailing list **be included on, be on** *Unless
you are on the mailing list, it's easy to find that
you've missed the deadline for submitting entries.*
▶ join a mailing list **go on(to), join, register with,
sign up to, sign up to, subscribe to** *Hundreds of
people have signed up to the mailing list.*
▶ take someone off a mailing list **remove sb from,
take sb off** *To be removed from the mailing list,
reply to this message.*
▶ take yourself off a mailing list **unsubscribe from
withdraw from** *You can unsubscribe from our
mailing list at any time.*

main ADJ
most important, largest, or most frequently used

- **ADJ**+n point or theme **concern, point, theme,
thrust** *The main thrust of their work has been on
geography.*

▸ aim **aim, focus, objective, priority, purpose** *The main objectives are to develop new research collaborations with Japanese companies.*

▸ reason or cause **cause, culprit, factor, reason, source** *The main reason behind their decision to move abroad is that they have had enough of life in the UK.*

▸ feature **attraction, feature** *The main attraction of Skiathos is the abundance of excellent beaches along the island's coastline.*

▸ problem **disadvantage, drawback, obstacle, problem** *The main drawback of bitumen is that it turns to a dull greyish colour over a period of time.*

▸ finding **conclusion, finding** *This article covers the main findings of our research.*

▸ difference **difference** *There isn't much that can be achieved in one platform that can't be on the other one. The main difference is how the end is achieved.*

mainstream ADJ

considered ordinary or normal by most people

adv+ADJ fairly **fairly, quite, relatively** *Guitar bands are back in vogue and rock is fairly mainstream again.*

very **completely, truly, very** *His films were popular but too cutting and socially conscious to be truly mainstream.*

increasingly **increasingly** *The generation of energy from solar panels is becoming increasingly mainstream.*

v+ADJ **be, become** *This idea met with staunch criticism when it was introduced because it was not mainstream.*

maintain V

to keep something the same

adv+V **constantly, continuously, indefinitely, steadfastly, successfully** *We ensure that safety and hygiene standards are continuously maintained.*

V+n standard or level **level, performance, quality, standard** *The University aims to maintain a high standard of academic scholarship and research.*

situation **balance, consistency, continuity, control, momentum, stability, status quo** *If environmentalists are to maintain their current momentum, they will need to switch from defensive to offensive strategies.*

secrecy **confidentiality, secrecy** *Secrecy is often maintained by the use of threats.*

personal qualities **composure, dignity, integrity** *Try to maintain your composure during the interview.*

qualities of an organization **competitiveness, independence, reputation** *Only by bringing together science and business more effectively will we maintain our competitiveness.*

communication or relationship **contact, dialogue, links, network, relations, relationship** *All phone and Internet lines used by the troops to maintain contact with relatives have been shut down.*

level of interest or enthusiasm **commitment, interest, morale** *He played a major role in maintaining the army's morale during a difficult period.*

control **control, vigilance** *It's important to maintain*

constant vigilance, in order to ensure that the final product is as good as it can be.*

2 to keep a building, road etc in good condition

● adv+V well **beautifully, immaculately, successfully, superbly, well** *The house has been very well maintained.*

▸ badly **badly, inadequately, poorly** *Scooters and motorcycles are frequently unstable on poorly maintained roads.*

▸ carefully **carefully, lovingly, meticulously** *Smartly furnished and meticulously maintained, Adelphi House has ten comfortable guest bedrooms.*

▸ properly or well enough **adequately, correctly, fully, properly** *A full service history shows a car has been properly maintained.*

▸ regularly **regularly** *Automatic equipment must be regularly maintained and an alarm fitted to alert staff in the event of breakdown.*

Usage **Maintain** is usually passive in all of the **adv+V** combinations shown above.

maintenance N

work done in order to keep a building, machine etc in good condition

● adj+N regular or planned **annual, periodic, planned, regular, routine, scheduled** *A conventional power station is often shut down for routine maintenance.*

▸ not planned **unplanned, unscheduled** *The only unscheduled mechanical maintenance required was the replacement of an erratic oil pressure unit.*

▸ done to prevent problems **preventative, preventive** *Preventative maintenance is always better than cure.*

▸ continuing **constant, day-to-day, ongoing** *The Council runs a programme of ongoing maintenance which specifically deals with improving homes over a longer period of time.*

▸ little **little, low, minimal** *The benefit of kiosks is that they are smaller, cheaper, need little staff intervention and minimal maintenance.*

▸ good/bad **poor, proper** *Proper maintenance is important to ensure reliability of the apparatus when running unattended.*

▸ general **basic, general** *Most of the work we did was centred around general maintenance of the station.*

▸ necessary **essential, necessary** *The railway is currently closed for essential maintenance.*

● v+N need maintenance **need, require** *The instrument is easy to operate and requires no maintenance.*

▸ do maintenance **assist with, carry out, do, help with, perform, provide, undertake** *We need to clear overhanging branches in the car park and do some maintenance in the playground.*

▸ not do maintenance **neglect** *Maintenance of the road network was neglected during the war.*

▸ ensure maintenance is done correctly **ensure, oversee, supervise** *When in port, the mate will supervise deck maintenance, cargo operations, and general ship's business.*

▸ receive maintenance **receive, undergo** *We try to minimise the number of aircraft undergoing maintenance at any one time.*

▸ improve maintenance **facilitate, improve, simplify** *This additional revenue will be used to improve maintenance of existing sites.*

▶ pay for maintenance **contribute towards, cover, finance, fund, pay for** *There is a subscription to cover maintenance and upgrade.*

● and/or **cleaning, construction, improvement, installation, operation, renovation, repair, restoration, servicing, upgrade, upkeep** *Structures can become dangerous from lack of maintenance and repair.*

major ADJ
important, serious, or large

● adv+ADJ fairly **fairly, pretty** INFORMAL**, quite, rather** *Publishing a book is a fairly major undertaking.*

▶ very **particularly, really** INFORMAL**, very** *You could go through a very major operation, only to find that the cancer started to grow somewhere else.*

▶ potentially **potentially** *They were trying to prevent the spread of a potentially major problem.*

● ADJ+n problem **challenge, concern, drawback, flaw, hurdle, obstacle, problem, setback** *The negative attitude of the students proved to be a major obstacle to success.*

▶ process of change **change, overhaul, redevelopment, refit, refurbishment, shake-up, upgrade** *The graphics have had quite a major overhaul.*

▶ cause or effect **cause, factor, impact, influence, source** *Few would disagree that money is a major cause of stress in today's family.*

▶ role or part **component, contribution, part, role** *The papers published here together form a major contribution to the study of Burma.* ● *Market research plays a major part in understanding customers' needs.*

▶ event **development, incident** *The Government is investing a huge amount of money in the emergency services to enable them to better respond to major incidents.*

▶ medical operation **operation, surgery** *I had to have major surgery to both eyes.*

▶ important point or stage in something **breakthrough, milestone** *The opening of the Research Institute represents a major milestone in the history of scientific and medical research.*

▶ project or course of action **programme, project, scheme, undertaking** *During the 1990s, the area underwent a major programme of redevelopment.*

majority N
1 most of the people or things in a group [always singular]

● adj+N large **great, large, overwhelming, significant, substantial, vast** *The vast majority of women in prison are serving sentences for non-violent offences.*

▶ not expressing their views **silent** *A well-organized minority can often get more attention than the silent majority.*

▶ clear, and impossible to doubt **clear** *We believe these values are shared by a clear majority of the public.*

● v+N form the majority **be in, comprise, constitute, form, make up, represent** *In this part of the workforce, women are in the majority.*

▶ suit or satisfy the majority **benefit, satisfy, suit** *Moderate the pace to suit the majority of the group.*

● N+n opinion or decision **approval, decision, judgment, opinion, view** *They promised the plan would not go ahead if it was against the majority opinion.*

▶ ownership **holding, ownership, share, shareholding, stake** *The British Airports Authority agreed a deal for a majority stake in Budapest airport.*

▶ owner **shareholder, stockholder** *He is executive chairman and majority shareholder of Lunar Energy.*

2 the number of votes by which a person or party wins

● adj+N large **clear, huge, landslide, large, massive, substantial** *Any Government with a large majority can force things through the House.*

▶ when one person or group gets more votes than all the others **absolute, outright, overall** *The process continues until one candidate has an absolute majority.*

▶ small **narrow, slim, small** *In the national congress, the right still enjoys a slim majority in the upper house.*

▶ of a particular size **64/10/144 etc seat, 73/54/60 etc per cent, one/600/13,000 etc vote, two-thirds/three-quarters etc** *We voted by an 85 per cent majority to adopt the resolution.* ● *Amendments to the Constitution shall only be made by a two-thirds majority of members present at the Annual General Meeting.*

▶ not large, but large enough **comfortable, solid** *S. held on to her seat in Congress with a comfortable majority.*

● v+N have a majority **command, have** *In order to be Prime Minister, you have to be able to command a majority in Parliament.*

▶ win a majority **attain, gain, obtain, secure, win** *T. film opens in 1920, two years after Sinn Fein had won a huge majority in the new Irish parliament.*

▶ keep a majority **retain** *ZANU-PF therefore still retains a majority of the seats in the 150-seat parliament.*

▶ increase a majority **increase** *As a consequence of this hard work, he has substantially increased his majority at each election.*

▶ reduce a majority **overturn, reduce, slash** *At the last election, his majority was slashed from appro. 20,000 to a couple of hundred votes.*

▶ lose a majority **lose** *The Liberals also lost their majority in the national assembly.*

● v+by+N decide or agree to something **approve sb/sth, carry sth, decide sth, elect sb, endorse sb/sth, pass sth, ratify sth, vote sth** *This motion must be passed by a 75 per cent majority of the committee present at two consecutive meetings.*

▶ not agree to something **reject sb/sth** *The committee report was rejected by a majority of conference.*

▶ defeat someone or something **defeat sb/sth** *The motion was defeated by a large majority.*

make-up N
1 substances for adding colour to someone's face

● adj+N very neat **flawless, immaculate** *Her hair and make-up were always immaculate.*

▸ a lot **heavy, loads of** INFORMAL *Students are not allowed to wear jewellery or heavy make-up.*

● v+N wear make-up **wear** *Not all women wear make-up.*

▸ put on make-up **apply, do, put on** *I was driven up the road to the beauticians to have my make-up done.*

▸ take off make-up **remove, take off, wipe off** *It may be helpful to remove any make-up, so that your doctor can see your skin properly.*

the people or things that form a single group or whole

adj+N of a group of people **cultural, demographic, ethnic, racial, religious, social, socio-economic** *What is the ethnic make-up of the school?*

of a person **genetic, physiological, psychological** *Every human being's genetic make-up has a similar structure.*

of a substance **chemical, geological** *Soil chemistry is about the chemical make-up of soils and sediments.*

with many different types of people **cosmopolitan, diverse, multi-cultural** *The vibrant cosmopolitan make-up of London means we have over 12,000 restaurants selling produce from over 60 different cuisines.*

N+of **audience, committee, community, council, household, population, society, squad, team, workforce** *Changes in the make-up of the workforce reflect an increase in women workers.*

malice N

strong feeling of wanting to be unkind

adj+N **deliberate, pure, sheer** *There really is such a thing as sheer motiveless malice.*

v+N **bear (sb), be motivated by, do sth out of, intend (sb)** *He was a man who bore no malice.*

and/or **cruelty, envy, greed, hatred, jealousy, revenge, spite** *It was an ufairly critical review full of spite and malice.*

malicious ADJ

owing deliberate cruelty

adv+ADJ **deliberately, intentionally, particularly, truly** *The judge described it as an unpleasant and particularly malicious attack on an innocent person.*

ADJ+n remarks or criticism **accusation, allegation, attack, claim, criticism, falsehood, gossip, rumour** *Huw dismissed these comments as malicious gossip.*

intention **intent, purpose** *Children usually play with fire out of curiosity rather than malicious intent.*

and/or **defamatory, deliberate, false, insulting, intimidating, spiteful, threatening, unfounded** *Every criticism was malicious and unfounded.*

malnutrition N

ness caused by lack of food

adj+N severe **acute, chronic, serious, severe** *The ack of variation in people's diets has led to chronic malnutrition.*

▸ in children or unborn babies **foetal, infant** *The identification of babies who suffered from foetal malnutrition is not easy.*

▸ widespread **common, rampant, rife, widespread** *Malnutrition was rife, causing many children to have rickets.*

> Usage The adjectives in these combinations come after the noun: *Malnutrition was rampant.* | ● *In some parts of India, malnutrition is extremely common.*

● v+N have malnutrition **face, have, suffer (from)** *One in five children suffers malnutrition on a daily basis.*

▸ prevent or reduce malnutrition **alleviate, combat, correct, prevent, reduce, tackle, treat** *Current advances in rice technology may be able to alleviate the severe malnutrition currently experienced.*

▸ cause malnutrition **cause, contribute to, lead to** *Mothers often give babies solid food too early, causing malnutrition.*

● and/or physical or medical problems **dehydration, disease, hunger, ill-health, malaria, starvation** *Most importantly, we want to end starvation and malnutrition, which affects billions of people.*

▸ social problems **illiteracy, insecurity, poverty** *The prosperous countries need to help the developing countries to overcome poverty, illiteracy and malnutrition.*

management N

1 control and operation of a business or organization

● adj+N good **effective, efficient, good, proper, sound, successful, sympathetic** *Integral to effective management is developing appropriate forms of evaluation.*

▸ bad **bad, poor** *Poor management will always impact a service regardless of size.*

▸ general **general, overall** *Many managers have moved on from accounting roles to general management .*

▸ everyday **day-to-day** *The board will endorse long-term direction rather than provide day-to-day management.*

▸ business **business, corporate** *Ann has over 26 years experience in corporate management.*

▸ dealing with a particular area of work **economic, environmental, financial, operational, strategic** *She is responsible for the company's strategic management and future planning.*

● N+n system or method **plan, practice, solution, strategy, system, technique, tool** *As with any management plan, actual performance should be regularly measured and monitored.*

▸ structure **framework, structure** *A new management structure was designed to speed up decisions.*

▸ job **function, position, role** *I went from supervisor to a management role.*

▸ skills or experience **experience, expertise, skills** *He is ex-Navy and brings with him all the management skills you'd expect from his background.*

▸ style **style** *People either like my management style or they don't.*

▸ responsibility or decision **decision, issue, policy, responsibility** *Management responsibilities increase with seniority.*

▶ training **training** *His original management training was gained from Manchester Business School.*

▶ company or person **company, consultancy, consultant** *In 1987, he left the Ministry of Defence to start his own management consultancy.*

2 the people who manage a business or organization

● adj+N at a particular level **middle, senior, top** *11 per cent of senior management are women.*

▶ new **new** *The company opened under new management and is going strong to this day.*

● N+n group of people **board, committee, team** *The test results were welcomed by the management team.*

3 the process of controlling or dealing with something

● n+N personal problems or injuries **anger, pain, stress, weight, wound** *He had been on several anger management courses.*

▶ public problems **disease, flood, pest, traffic, waste** *Congestion has been reduced in urban areas through traffic management.*

▶ project **project** *Discover how you can really put your project management skills to work.*

▶ money **asset, debt, fund, investment, money** *Scottish Widows is one of Britain's largest asset management groups.*

▶ difficult or risky situations **crisis, disaster, risk** *It might be helpful to view Monday's events as a test in crisis management.*

▶ resources **energy, housing, resource, water** *Our advice on energy management can help you prepare for a low-carbon future.*

manager N
someone whose organizes and controls part or all of an organization

● adj+N of a particular level **assistant, deputy, junior, middle, senior, top** *Responsibilities would include keeping board members and senior managers up to date with government policies.*

▶ immediately above you in an organization **line** *If you need time off work, please ask your line manager.*

▶ experienced **experienced** *We are currently looking for an experienced manager for our Canterbury store.*

▶ good **effective, good, successful** *To be an effective manager, you must have a degree of freedom in how you use your time.*

▶ of a whole business **general** *The company has recently recruited Ian Welsh to be general manager of the motors business.*

▶ of part of a business **departmental, divisional, local, regional** *Ross Twyford is the Regional Manager of Interfleet's New Zealand office.*

▶ temporary **interim, temporary** *Our clients require talented interim managers for a wide variety of situations.*

▶ of a particular area of work **catering, commercial, financial, marketing, production, project, retail, sales, strategic, technical** *Please contact our Commercial Manager for a tailored quotation based on your specific needs.*

● n+N **bank, farm, hospital, shop, store, theatre** *Patients can also apply to the hospital managers to review their case.*

managerial ADJ
relating to the job of manager

● adv+ADJ **predominantly, purely** *Initially, her role was that of a tax specialist, but in recent years she has moved into a predominantly managerial role.*

● ADJ+n job **career, job, occupation, position, post, role** *He has a managerial position within the security profession.*

▶ responsibilities or qualities **accountability, discretion, responsibilities, responsiveness, skills, style** *My day is split between my clinical work and my managerial responsibilities.*

▶ bad qualities **incompetence** *There are few automatic checks to managerial incompetence.*

● and/or **administrative, clinical, financial, operational, organizational, professional, supervisory, technical** *Many managerial and supervisory jobs are suitable for job sharing.*

mandate N
the authority of an elected government to do thing

● adj+N given in an election **constitutional, democratic, election, electoral, popular** *With less than 30 per cent of the vote, they can hardly claim a popular mandate.*

▶ clear **clear, convincing, decisive, overwhelming, strong, sweeping** *The people have given us a clear mandate to be a voice on their behalf.*

▶ new **fresh, new, renewed** *The next election is abou winning a renewed mandate to shape a future in which opportunities are available to everyone.*

● v+N fulfil a mandate **complete, discharge, exercise, fulfil** *We have no budgets of our own to fulfil the mandates we were elected on.*

▶ extend a mandate **extend** *The UN Security Counc passed a resolution extending his mandate for 12 months.*

● N+v **end, expire** *He will not stand in next year's elections, and will retire when his mandate expires*

● N+for **action, change, reform** *The new president took office in January, with a clear mandate for change.*

manifest ADJ
obvious and easy to notice or understand

● adv+ADJ **clearly, fully, increasingly, patently** *Their influence is clearly manifest in our religious literature.*

● ADJ+n **absurdity, contempt, disregard, injustice, nonsense, unfairness** *The present system is a manifest absurdity, which discredits Europe and i institutions.*

manifesto N
a formal statement expressing the plans or aims an organization, especially a political party

● v+N prepare a manifesto **draft, draw up, prepar produce** *We drafted a manifesto and got it accepte by the Party.*

▶ publish a manifesto **issue, launch, present, publi unveil** *Their election manifesto was launched on 1. April.*

▶ do what your manifesto says you will do **carry out, carry through, implement** *We are determined to carry through the manifesto we were elected on.*

● N+v **call for sth, commit sb to do sth, outline sth, pledge sth, promise sth, say sth, set out sth, state sth** *The BNP's election manifesto pledged to 'encourage' immigrants to return to their country of origin.*

● N+n **commitment, pledge, promise** *The government failed to meet its manifesto commitments on public service reform.*

manner N

1 the way in which something is done

● adj+N efficient or effective **constructive, cost-effective, effective, efficient** *The main use of the plough is to clean snow from roads in an efficient manner.*

▶ similar **analogous, like, same, similar** *Each policy area is treated in a like manner.*

▶ good enough **acceptable, satisfactory** *We have not yet had our questions answered in a satisfactory manner.*

▶ usual **normal, traditional, usual** *Run the presentation in the usual manner, using the screen icon at the bottom left of the window.*

▶ orderly **controlled, orderly, structured, systematic** *Cars must be parked in an orderly manner.*

▶ unplanned **ad hoc** *Too often, testing is done in an ad hoc manner and too late in the development cycle.*

▶ sensible **appropriate, rational, responsible, safe, sensible** *The garbage collected was disposed of in a responsible manner.*

▶ kind or fair **equitable, humane, impartial, sensitive, sympathetic** *The policy is to deal with all calls in an understanding sympathetic manner, whilst offering the best possible advice.*

▶ correct **correct, proper** *You must use things like equipment in the proper manner.*

▶ clear or simple **accessible, concise, easy-to-read, easy-to-understand, logical, step-by-step, straightforward** *Colours, shapes, and graphics can be used to express ideas in a concise manner.*

▶ at the right time **timely** *In most cases, forces cannot be deployed abroad in a timely manner.*

someone's way of behaving or speaking

adj+N polite **courteous, polite, respectful**

professional **business-like, professional** *The ideal person will be of smart appearance with an outgoing but professional manner.*

bad **anti-social, disorderly** *Teenagers were hanging around street corners, behaving in an anti-social manner.*

confident **confident, outgoing** *She has a confident manner and loads of personality.*

calm **calm, dignified, gentle** *Underneath this calm manner, there was a very strong sense of loyalty to those with him.*

bad **aggressive, disparaging, patronising** *They try to intimidate you with an aggressive manner.*

friendly **engaging, friendly, pleasant** *His friendly manner helped put me at ease.*

n+N **bedside, telephone** *Any good doctor knows that his or her bedside manner is as important as any medicine.*

3 accepted forms of polite behaviour [always plural]

● adj+N good **excellent, exquisite, good, impeccable, perfect** *He seems a charming, gentlemanly sort with impeccable manners.*

▶ bad **bad, poor** *In certain countries, it is considered bad manners to make eye contact with a woman.*

manoeuvre N

an action or movement that needs skill

● adj+N done in order to avoid something **defensive, evasive** *Someone had put a line across the canal to snag our propeller, but we saw it in time and made an evasive manoeuvre.*

▶ difficult or dangerous **awkward, complex, complicated, difficult, risky, tricky** *He was excellent, taking us safely in to locks and doing all of the tricky manoeuvres.*

▶ brave **brave, daring** *Eventually, he took the lead with a brave manoeuvre at Paddock Hill Bend.*

▶ types of manoeuvre **bureaucratic, diplomatic, legal, political** *There have been desperate bureaucratic manoeuvres to try and deal with the crisis.*

▶ done in order to get advantage for yourself **clever, cynical** *The opposition saw the president's pledges as a cynical manoeuvre to allow him to retain his grip on power.*

▶ of an aircraft **acrobatic, aerial, aerobatic** *Once at a safe height, your instructor will demonstrate some basic aerobatic manoeuvres.*

▶ of a vehicle **braking, overtaking, reversing** *The crash was the result of an overtaking manoeuvre that went wrong.*

● v+N **carry out, complete, execute, perform** *Road safety campaigns need to focus on how to negotiate bends and junctions, and how to carry out overtaking manoeuvres.*

manpower N

all the people who work in a particular place

● adj+N trained or skilled **experienced, qualified, skilled, trained** *Our greatest problem was a lack of trained manpower.*

▶ a lot **abundant, ample, considerable, unlimited** *We have abundant manpower due to massive unemployment.*

▶ available for work **available** *By 1917, the army was using all of the available manpower.*

▶ enough **enough, necessary, sufficient** *Here, anyone who has the necessary manpower can plough land freely.*

▶ not enough **insufficient, limited, scarce** *After consideration, the YMCA decided that they had insufficient manpower to run the scheme.*

▶ extra **additional, extra, surplus** *Extra manpower from neighbouring fire stations was drafted in.*

▶ types of manpower **clerical, medical, military, police, technical, veterinary** *National Service provides military manpower relatively cheaply.*

● v+N use manpower **allocate, deploy, employ** *More than a quarter of their IT manpower is permanently deployed in non-productive 'fix and maintain' roles.*

▶ reduce manpower **budget, halve, reduce** *He promptly cut the army and navy and reduced manpower in both services.*

▶ supply or recruit manpower **provide, recruit, supply** *Imigration has supplied the manpower necessary for economic growth.*

▶ need manpower **need, require** *Enforcing department policy is an extensive task, which requires additional manpower.*

▶ lack manpower **lack** *They'd been told repeatedly the police lacked the manpower to pursue particular lines of inquiry.*

● N+n shortage **crisis, deficiency, shortage** *The manpower shortage caused by increased military drafts could no longer be filled.*

▶ how manpower is used **deployment, planning** *The key to proper manpower planning is to give staff enough incentive to work unsocial hours.*

▶ needs **requirements** *Many European countries still have military structures geared to territorial defence, with massive manpower requirements.*

▶ supply **reserves, resources** *Russia's manpower reserves were virtually limitless.*

▶ costs **costs** *One of the first things to break down in society was the criminal justice system, because of the manpower costs.*

● n+of+N supply **pool, reserve, reservoir, supply** *The dominions were important to Britain as they could provide a valuable reservoir of manpower.*

▶ shortage **lack, shortage** *There was a desperate shortage of medical manpower.*

march N
a walk by a group of people protesting

● n+N **anti-war, gay pride, hunger, peace, protest** *Campaigners fighting to save a North Wales hospital staged a protest march through a seaside resort.*

● v+N go on a march **attend, go on, join (in), participate in, take part in** *Along with more than a million others, I went on the peace march in London.*

▶ lead a march **lead** *John Burns, carrying a red flag, led a march through the capital.*

▶ organize or hold a march **hold, organize, plan, stage** *We have organised marches with thousands of people demanding that these multinationals are not given access to our lands.*

▶ stop a march **abandon, cancel, end, halt, stop** *The march was halted en route by the police.*

▶ ban a march **ban** *The Commissioner of the Metropolitan Police banned the march as politically motivated.*

margin N
1 the amount a competition or election is won by

● adj+N small **narrow, slender, slim, small, tight** *He was elected by only a narrow margin.*

▶ large **ample, comfortable, considerable, convincing, generous, huge, substantial, wide** *Estonia's 2001 win was by a very wide margin.*

▶ winning **winning** *Lindley scored a fine victory, extending his winning margin to almost seven seconds.*

2 the difference between what a business pays for something and what they sell it for

● adj+N before tax **gross, pre-tax** *Increasing gross margin entails increasing sales revenue or reducing the cost of the merchandise.*

▶ after tax and other expenses **net, operating** *The duty will wipe out any net margin made on shoe sales.*

▶ small **low, slim, small, tight** *The margins are low for tour operators.*

▶ large **fat** INFORMAL**, good, healthy, high, large** *These markets allow small producers to sell directly to consumers, giving them better margins.*

▶ fairly large **reasonable** *These prices should provide a reasonable profit margin for farms.*

● v+N reduce a margin **decrease, depress, diminish, erode, narrow, shrink, squeeze** *Rising rents squeezed margins for Dorfman's stores.*

▶ increase a margin **boost, improve, increase, maximise** *These notebooks are important for PC companies looking to boost their margins.*

▶ maintain a margin **maintain** *Maintaining an average gross margin of 25 per cent is very realistic.*

▶ achieve a margin **achieve, make** *By the third year, they were achieving a healthy margin of 30 per cent.*

mark N
1 a small dirty, damaged, or coloured area

● adj+N difficult or impossible to remove **permanent, stubborn** *On really stubborn marks, use a little neat ammonia on a damp cloth.*

▶ dirty or unpleasant **dirty, greasy, oily, unsightly** *There were greasy marks all over the windows.*

▶ distinctive **characteristic, distinctive** *The Jackdaw had a distinctive white mark on its neck.*

▶ faint or small **faint, slight, tiny** *The only visible remains were some very slight marks where the droplets had been.*

▶ large or obvious **big, dark, visible** *I have a big black mark from his tyre on my leathers.*

● n+N types of mark **bite, scorch, scratch, scuff, skid** *There were no skid marks or other signs on the roadway to indicate what had happened.*

● made by a particular thing **brush, bullet, claw, finger, grease, nail, paint, paw, teeth, tyre** *To remove grease marks from paper, sprinkle talcum powder over the grease mark and leave overnight.*

● v+N make a mark **leave, make** *You can chop vegetables or put a hot saucepan on it without leaving a mark.*

▶ carry **bear, carry, have** *All the fragments bear the unmistakable marks of machine saw cutting along their edges.*

2 a particular level, stage, total etc that is reached [usually singular]

● v+N reach a mark **hit, reach** *Troop levels at one stage had reached the 30,000 mark.*

▶ pass a mark **exceed, pass, surpass, top** *What's more interesting is that the figure nationally has passed the 50 per cent mark, at 61 per cent.*

▶ be close to reaching a mark **approach, near** *His CD and video sales are fast approaching the five million mark.*

3 something showing a particular quality

● N+of high quality or achievement **achievement, distinction, excellence, greatness** *This award is widely recognized as a mark of excellence.*

▶ thanks **appreciation, gratitude** *As a mark of*

gratitude for his service to the Club, the Directors awarded him a lifetime membership.

▶ positive feelings **affection, approbation, esteem, honour, respect, trust** Both teams will wear black armbands as a mark of respect.

▶ negative feelings **contempt, displeasure, disrespect** Prolonged eye contact when greeting the Chinese for the first time may be seen as a mark of disrespect.

marked ADJ

clear and noticeable

● ADJ+n difference **contrast, difference, discrepancy, disparity, variation** This pattern stands in marked contrast to the national trend.

▶ similarity **resemblance, similarity** They found a 'marked similarity' in the responses of those who chose to continue on into higher education and those who did not.

▶ decrease or worsening **decline, decrease, deterioration, drop, reduction, slowdown** This year, the entries fell from 400 to 130, a marked decrease.

▶ increase or improvement **improvement, increase, rise, upturn** The additional measures put in place in December had resulted in a marked improvement in the company's performance.

▶ tendency to do/not do something **preference, reluctance, tendency, trend** In the Cambrian pronunciation, there is a marked tendency to contract, or shorten the words.

● effect **effect, impact, influence** His plays had a marked influence on the development of French drama.

market N

1 trade in goods of a particular kind

● adj+N with a lot of competition **competitive, crowded, tough** In a highly competitive market, pharmaceutical companies are under intense pressure to increase efficiency.

● successful **booming, buoyant, healthy, profitable, thriving** People are rebuilding MGs again and the spares market is booming.

● not successful **depressed, sluggish, weak** When the market is in a depressed state, properties can be difficult to sell.

● changing often **volatile** The market was initially extremely volatile, with sales swinging wildly from year to year.

● with no restrictions **free, open** There is no way of controlling a free market.

● illegal **black, illegal** There is a growing trade in illegally obtained fish, and some large specimens may fetch as much as £1000 each on the black market.

● worldwide **global, worldwide** The pace of change in global financial markets is accelerating.

● overseas **foreign, international, overseas** If you want to service overseas markets, you'll have to think about using foreign language pages on your website.

● in your own country or area **domestic, home, internal, local** We are a small family business which specialises in better quality carpets for the domestic market.

● types of market **commercial, export, financial, rental, retail** Why have the various sections of the retail market retained 'old-style' pricing strategies?

● n+N **advertising, car, energy, housing, insurance,**

labour, livestock, mortgage, oil, property, software The Internet advertising market is growing rapidly.

● v+N enter a market **break into, enter, get into, move into, penetrate, re-enter** Digisoft announced plans to enter the computer games market.

▶ be the most powerful company in a market **capture, corner, dominate, lead, monopolize** As an after-work drinking spot, Occo is pretty much cornering the local market.

▶ put a product on the market **bring sth to, put sth on** Just over one in ten properties are put on the market by corporate landlords.

▶ take a product off the market **take sth off, withdraw sth from** The drug has now been withdrawn from the market for safety reasons.

▶ become available on the market **appear on, come on, come onto, hit, reach** You might have heard of a few great offers coming on the broadband market recently.

▶ come onto a market in large quantities **flood, saturate** We need to stop goods which are inefficient in energy flooding our markets.

▶ supply a market **serve, service, supply** Birds like these have a high commercial value and are often taken to supply the falconry market.

▶ make rules that control a market **regulate** It is essential that this market is regulated efficiently and effectively.

▶ remove rules that control a market **deregulate, liberalize** The Government's action plan takes on board the OFT's recommendations for liberalising this important market.

▶ find out about a market **analyse, look at, research, test** Take the time to research the car insurance market for the best deals.

▶ make a market operate in a wrong or harmful way **disrupt, distort** It's not the market itself which is the problem, but the market distorted by banks and monopolies.

▶ make good use of a market **capitalize on, exploit, tap into** The company needs to be applauded for exploiting a new market.

▶ make a market more stable **stabilise** The objective behind capping the rent is to stabilise the market.

● N+v get bigger **expand, grow, open up** The market in postal services opened up to competition.

▶ improve **pick up, recover, rise, stabilise** What happens next will depend very much on whether the market picks up in August.

▶ get smaller **be down, shrink** Both domestic and foreign markets shrank because of a lack of money.

▶ get worse **be down, decline, fall, slow** The traditional soft drinks market is down 8 per cent.

▶ fail **collapse, crash, fail** The company was initially very successful, but the motorcycle market collapsed after the first world war.

Another way of saying that a market fails is to say that *the bottom drops out of the market* or *the bottom falls out of the market*: The bottom fell out of the market due to changes in leisure interests.

▶ change **evolve, mature** The market is continuously evolving to ensure magazines carry on appealing to their target audience.

▶ make sth happen **demand sth, dictate sth, force sth** You have to go with what the market dictates.

● N+n share **penetration, position, share** A supplier

that charges significantly more than its rivals is likely to lose market share.

▶ leader **leader** *We are the market leaders in the sale and acquisition of leisure businesses.*

▶ economy or economics **economics, economy** *The market economy is able to respond more easily to the wishes of the consumers than the large official health care systems.*

▶ value or price **price, value** *The property was offered under market value for a quick let.*

▶ research or information **analysis, data, intelligence, knowledge, research, testing** *Your market research should contain details of many target companies.*

▶ conditions or demand **conditions, demand, failure, forces, trends** *Farmers were guaranteed a price for their crops regardless of market forces.*

▶ part or area **area, sector, segment** *The downturn has affected almost every market segment.*

2 all the people who buy a product

● adj+N new **emerging, new, potential** *With over 40 million people worldwide with Scottish roots, there is a sizeable potential market.*

▶ growing **burgeoning, expanding, growing** *Computer companies are beginning to realize that the elderly population is a growing market.*

▶ large **big, huge, large, mass, sizeable** *China has the potential to become a huge market for the company.*

▶ specialized **niche** *Their organic products supply a fast-growing niche market.*

● v+N try to sell things to a particular market **aim at, cater for, target** *The company has been targeting the Chinese market.*

▶ create or expand a market **build, develop, expand, grow, open, open up** *Jeremy spends much of his time overseas, developing new markets.* ● *They believe they can grow the market by 80 per cent in two years.*

market V
to use advertising and other methods to sell something

● adv+V a lot **actively, aggressively, heavily** *A low quality product aggressively marketed will often outsell a high quality product with passive marketing.*

▶ well or successfully **cleverly, effectively, properly, successfully** *The end result has been successfully marketed and sold into many high street retail chains.*

▶ in many countries **globally, internationally, worldwide** *The software will be marketed worldwide.*

▶ commercially **commercially** *Senior politicians and business figures are joining forces to devise and commercially market environmental initiatives.*

marketable ADJ
a marketable product or person is one that people want to buy or have

● adv+ADJ **easily, extremely, highly, hugely, readily** *Graduates from these courses are highly marketable.*

● ADJ+n product **asset, commodity, product** *Radio is a marketable commodity and programme controllers are fighting for listeners.*

▶ skill or qualification **qualification, skill** *As an LLB graduate, you will be in possession of a very marketable qualification.*

marketing N
a company's ways of encouraging people to buy its products or services

● adj+N good **clever, creative, innovative, shrewd, slick, sophisticated** *Is this really going to benefit the learner, or is it just more clever marketing?*

▶ successful **effective, successful** *Successful marketing relies on effective targeting.*

▶ using all possible methods **aggressive, vigorous** *There must be aggressive marketing to ensure that drivers are made aware that the train offers a viable alternative.*

▶ carefully planned **strategic, targeted** *We specialize in strategic marketing and corporate communications.*

▶ aimed at many people **mass** *The use of the mobile phone as a mass marketing tool has not gone unnoticed over the years.*

▶ not asked for **unsolicited** *Your email address will not be circulated and we will not use it for unsolicited marketing.*

▶ types of marketing **direct, in-store, interactive, internet, mobile, on-line, viral** *Online marketing begins with the initial concept and design of your website.*

● N+n plan **campaign, effort, initiative, plan, programme, strategy** *A high-profile marketing campaign appears to be showing early signs of success.*

▶ method or idea **concept, gimmick, ploy, tactic, technique, tool** *Too many companies offer 'green' electricity tariffs that are little more than marketing gimmicks.*

▶ people **assistant, consultant, department, director, guru, manager, professional, specialist, team** *For years now, marketing gurus have been trying to improve on the world's best-seller, the Bible.*

● company **agency, company, consultancy, firm** *In 1996, he co-founded a marketing consultancy in Sydney.*

▶ written material **brochure, literature, material** *We do not send out unsolicited marketing material to anyone.*

▶ excitement and interest **hype** *Do not believe all the marketing hype on the covers.*

marketplace N
an area of business activity

● adj+N with many companies competing **competitive, crowded, huge, overcrowded, saturated** *How do you distinguish yourself in a crowded marketplace?*

▶ international **global, globalized, international** *The legislation would be a further blow to European business in a demanding global marketplace.*

▶ changing a lot **changing, ever-changing, evolving, volatile** *The International Cocoa Organisation was set up to encourage price stability in a historically volatile marketplace.*

marriage N
the relationship between people who are married to each other

- adj+N unhappy **disastrous, loveless, stormy, tempestuous, troubled, unhappy** *She is tired of being in a loveless marriage.*
▶ violent **abusive, violent** *With more financial independence, women would not have to be trapped in a violent and abusive marriage.*
▶ ending in divorce **failed** *Apart from his failed marriage, Maurice was relatively successful with women.*
▶ not producing children **childless** *She was brought up by Tom and his second wife Laura, whose marriage was childless.*
▶ not real **sham** *A woman who had set up sham marriages to help Indian men skip immigration procedures was sentenced to 10 years' imprisonment.*
▶ happy **happy, perfect, stable, strong** *We wish them well for the future and hope they enjoy a long and happy marriage.*
▶ between people of different faiths or races **interfaith, interracial, mixed, mixed-faith, mixed-race** *Judaism did not permit mixed marriages.*
▶ between gay people **gay, same-sex** *In October 2004, the Spanish government approved a draft law to legalise same-sex marriage.*
▶ arranged by parents **arranged** *She married for love at a time when arranged marriages were the norm.*
▶ when one partner does not want to be married **forced** *A marriage which takes place without the permission of the two people involved is defined as a forced marriage.*

- v+N end a marriage **annul, dissolve, end, terminate** *She appealed to the Pope to annul her marriage.*
▶ destroy a marriage **destroy, doom, ruin, wreck** *His obsessive behaviour was wrecking his marriage.*
▶ save a marriage **save** *In a last ditch attempt to save their marriage, they went to counselling.*
▶ consider marriage **contemplate, intend, talk about, think about** *In the summer of 1928, Jim was contemplating marriage to a local girl.*
▶ propose marriage **propose** *She has many admirers, including the wealthy Lord Augustus who proposes marriage to her.*
▶ make a marriage legal or official **consummate, legalize, solemnize** *The marriage was consummated and on 7 January 1796 a daughter, Charlotte, was born to the couple.*
▶ ban a type of marriage **ban, forbid, prohibit** *In 1950, Mao introduced the Marriage Reform Law which banned forced marriages.*
▶ recognize a type of marriage **recognize** *He also criticised the government's refusal to recognise same-sex marriages.*

- N+v fail **break down, break up, collapse, crumble, disintegrate, end, fail, founder** *When Billy was three, his parents' marriage broke down and his father left.*
▶ survive or last **last, survive** *My father had many affairs, but somehow his marriage survived.*

- N+n **breakdown, break-up, ceremony, certificate, contract, guidance, license, proposal, vows** *The stress stemming from job insecurity was found to be a major factor in marriage breakdown.*

married ADJ
having a husband or wife

- adv+ADJ happily/unhappily **happily, unhappily** *I am a happily married man with three children.*
▶ recently **newly, recently** *Everyone present at the wedding ceremony walks up to the front to congratulate the newly married couple.*
▶ legally **lawfully, legally** *This pension will only be paid to legally married partners.*

marshal V
gather and organize people or things effectively

- adv+V ably, expertly, superbly, well *Tate's return was a welcome one, and he dominated a well-marshalled defence.*

- V+n facts or thoughts **arguments, evidence, facts, thoughts** *He has collected and marshalled his evidence well and presents it in a persuasive manner.*
▶ resources **resources** *We are by the side of Britain in marshalling all resources to fight the menace of terrorism, no matter where it is.*
▶ people for defending **defence** *He captained the side and marshalled the defence superbly.*
▶ people for fighting **army, forces, troops** *The 33rd Division was marshalling its troops along the western bank of the river.*

marvel V
show or feel surprise or admiration

- V+at sight **architecture, scenery, sight, spectacle, vista** *We were able to marvel at this sight for several minutes before the group of lions moved off.*
▶ positive quality **beauty, brilliance, grandeur, magnificence, wonders** *I never fail to marvel at the wonders of technology!*
▶ skill **ability, ingenuity, skill** *Museums display early motor engines and people can marvel at their ingenuity.*

- v+V **can only, continue to, have to** *You could only marvel at the organisation and planning involved.*

mass N
1 a large number or amount of people or things; an amount of a substance without a clear shape

- adj+N when many people are close together and moving about **heaving, seething, teeming** *The crowd was now a sweating, seething mass of bodies pressing up against the stage.*
▶ when people or things are very similar **broad, undifferentiated** *This idea would be rejected by the broad mass of people.* • *It is important not to treat the sales force as an undifferentiated mass.*
▶ confused or vague **amorphous, confused, shapeless, swirling, tangled** *Polymers consist of a tangled mass of very long molecules in which the atoms are joined by strong covalent bonds.*
▶ stretching over a wide area **sprawling** *They looked down at the sprawling mass of the city below them.*
▶ solid **dense, solid** *A blood clot is a solid mass of blood.*
▶ very large **great, huge, large, vast** *Though the greatest mass of nerve cells is collected in the brain, the nervous system links all parts of the body.*

- N+of of people in general **humanity, mankind, people, the population** *I could see no individuals, just a mass of humanity following orders.*
▶ of particular classes **the peasantry, the peasants,**

the proletariat, the workers *The success of the revolution depended on the working class being able to win the mass of the peasantry.*

▶ of information **evidence, information, material** *The mass of material to be considered is overwhelming.*

2 ordinary people who are not rich or famous [always plural]

● adj+N **downtrodden, exploited, huddled, oppressed, proletarian, toiling, uneducated, unwashed** *The oppressed masses rose up in a bid to secure justice for themselves.*

● v+N **entertain, rally, reach, rouse** *The leaders began rallying the masses in their cause.*

mass ADJ
affecting a large number of people

● ADJ+n movement of people **emigration, exodus, immigration, migration, mobilization, movement** *There was much suffering and loss of life and a mass exodus.*

▶ killing or death **destruction, execution, extermination, extinction, killing, murder, slaughter, suicide** *Mass murder by the state is not rare.*

▶ grave **grave** *90 or more soldiers were buried in a mass grave in a field at St Venant.*

▶ protest or fighting **demonstration, movement, protest, struggle** *The regime organised mass demonstrations.* ● *They called for the formation of a new party based on the mass anti-war movement.*

▶ feeling **hysteria** *In some areas there were deep social crises and a few outbreaks of mass hysteria.*

▶ unemployment **unemployment** *He was brought up in a community in which there was mass unemployment.*

▶ tourism **tourism** *It was a wonderful area, largely unspoilt by mass tourism.*

▶ audience **audience** *His plays failed to reach a mass audience as he had hoped they might.*

massive ADJ
very large or great; very severe

● adv+ADJ very **absolutely, quite, really, so, truly** *The BBC Internet infrastructure is absolutely massive – it's actually a network unto itself.*

▶ fairly **fairly, pretty** INFORMAL *Their product range is pretty massive, and they sell just about everything.*

▶ possibly **potentially** *The workload is potentially massive, but all workloads are.*

● ADJ+n amount **amount, quantity** *The program can deal with massive amounts of data.*

▶ increase or decrease **boost, expansion, growth, hike** INFORMAL**, increase, influx, rise** *There have been massive increases in the prices of many journals.*

▶ task **effort, task, undertaking** *The compilation of such a comprehensive guide is a massive undertaking.*

▶ effect **effect, impact** *Her resignation had a massive impact on the organisation.*

▶ amount of money **cuts, debt, investment, saving, subsidy** *Don't run up a massive debt in the first couple of months.*

▶ success **hit, success** *The event was a massive success.*

▶ event that causes problems or sadness **blow**

Losing a second match would be a massive blow to his world title hopes.

▶ attack or explosion **bombardment, earthquake, explosion, retaliation** *Suddenly, there was a massive explosion.*

▶ medical event **bleeding, haemorrhage, heart attack** *In the early hours of the morning, she had a massive brain haemorrhage.*

master V
learn something or control something

● adv+V quickly or easily **easily, quickly** *He exhibited widely and quickly mastered new technical advances.*

▶ completely **completely, fully, properly, really, successfully, thoroughly, truly** *I never fully mastered the technique, but the theory was fine.*

▶ in the end **eventually, finally** *I had done it! I had finally mastered the art of making bread.*

● V+n the basics **basics, essentials, fundamentals** *Having mastered the basics of guitar playing, you quickly realise what a versatile instrument the guitar is.*

▶ a skill **art, craft, knack, skill, trick** *I just can't master the art of multi-tasking!*

▶ task **challenge, task** *Our course will help you identify your strengths and master the challenges of your new job.*

▶ idea or subject **concept, material, subject** *Maths tutorials are designed to help you master the material in the introductory coursebook.*

▶ language **grammar, language, vocabulary** *For someone who learnt slowly, she did well to master one language and have an understanding of a second.*

▶ something complicated **complexities, intricacies** *Sailors master the complexities of navigating their ships through various weather and sea conditions.*

masterpiece N
an excellent painting, book, piece of music etc

● adj+N types of masterpiece **architectural, artistic, choral, cinematic, comic, culinary, literary, musical, operatic** *Cambridge has a rich legacy of architectural masterpieces.*

▶ recognized/not recognized **acknowledged, forgotten, lost, neglected, undisputed** *Titus Andronicus is Shakespeare's neglected masterpiece.*

▶ lasting **enduring, timeless** *Few now challenge the fact that he wrote some of the enduring masterpieces of the late 19th and early 20th centuries.*

▶ small or minor **mini, miniature, minor** *'My Dark Life' and 'The Bridge I Burned' are both miniature pop masterpieces.*

▶ complete **absolute, great, true** *This film is an absolute masterpiece.*

● v+N create a masterpiece **compose, create, paint, produce, write** *Now you can create your own culinary masterpiece.*

▶ be recognized as a masterpiece **be considered, be hailed as, be recognized as, be regarded as** *I kept asking myself why this book is considered a masterpiece.*

● N+of **architecture, art, cinema, comedy, craftsmanship, design, engineering, fiction, literature, painting, writing** *The Palace is a masterpiece of English baroque architecture.*

mastery N
great knowledge or skill

- adj+N complete or great **absolute, consummate, great, perfect, supreme, total** *It is not his style that is so amazing, but his absolute mastery of it.*
- ▶ showing no effort **effortless** *Soderbergh's seemingly effortless mastery of his medium goes from strength to strength.*
- ▶ types of mastery **intellectual, musical, technical, technological** *Her technical mastery is unquestionable.*
- v+N get or have mastery **achieve, acquire, attain, develop, gain, have, obtain** *Information and skills will be repeated until mastery is achieved.*
- ▶ show mastery **demonstrate, display, show** *The topic must allow you to make a contribution to existing knowledge and demonstrate your mastery of the subject.*

match N
1 a game in which players or teams compete

- adj+N types of match **away, first-class, friendly, home, live, one-day, testimonial** *In a mark of gratitude for his service to the Club, the Directors awarded him a testimonial match.*
- ▶ in a competition **final, qualifying, quarter-final, semi-final, first-round, second-round** etc *She won her third-round match against Davis.*
- ▶ close **close, competitive, hard-fought, tense, tight, tough** *Our last game, a friendly against a Scottish team, was an extremely close match.*
- ▶ very important because it decides something **crucial** *This will be a crucial match that we must win!*
- ▶ enjoyable **entertaining, exciting, good, thrilling** *A draw was a fair result in an entertaining enough match given the soft ground.*
- v+N win, lose or draw a match **concede, draw, level, lose, win** *The first team to capture the flag will win the match.*
- ▶ decide how a match ends **clinch** INFORMAL, **decide** *That was the point that finally clinched the match.*
- ▶ play a match **play** *We have played some friendly matches at the new Sports Centre this term.*
- ▶ be in charge of a match **referee, umpire** *You are refereeing a first-round match.*

2 a thing that combines with or looks the same as something else

- adj+N **approximate, close, exact, good, ideal, perfect, suitable** *Exact colour match cannot be guaranteed.*
- v+N **find** *If you are looking for something in particular, just give us a ring and we will try to find your ideal match.*

match V
1 be the same as something; to combine well with something else

- adv+V closely or exactly **closely, equally, evenly, exactly, perfectly, precisely** *Even though the music was improvised, it perfectly matched the action on the screen.*
- ▶ approximately **broadly, roughly** *Professor Reynolds said: 'Our findings broadly match those from other countries'.*
- V+n **criteria, demand, description, expectations, needs, profile, requirements, specification** *You can set up a free Email Alert to tell you when a job matching your criteria is advertised.*

2 achieve the same amount or level as something; to provide something that is equal in amount or level to something else

- V+n money **donation, funding, funds** *Certain companies are prepared to match donations to a charity by their employees.*
- ▶ growth or speed **growth, increase, pace, rise** *Our office failed to match the growth of the rest of the company.* • *The pace of reform has to match the pace of change.*

material N
1 a substance

- adj+N in a natural state **raw** *As industry gathered pace, good sources of raw materials and power could turn a small town into a city.*

  Usage *Material* is usually plural in this combination.

- ▶ waste **waste** *The amount of recycling of waste material has increased hugely.*

  Usage *Material* is usually plural in this combination.

- ▶ dangerous or radioactive **hazardous, radioactive, toxic** *Radioactive materials are used extensively in medicine, agriculture, research, and manufacturing.*
- ▶ recycled or recyclable **recyclable, recycled** *Wherever possible, recycled materials were used.*
- ▶ likely to catch fire **combustible, flammable, inflammable** *Building sites contain a lot of highly flammable material.*
- ▶ living or from something that was alive **genetic, natural, organic** *Within each organism lies a unique set of genetic material that encodes the characteristics of that organism.*
- ▶ artificial **artificial, man-made, synthetic** *The cover is made of synthetic material.*
- n+N **building, construction, insulation, packaging, roofing, writing** *Alternative roofing materials were sought and the demand for slate never again recovered its former level.*
- v+N **dispose of, reclaim, recycle, reprocess, reuse, use** *There's still some debate as to how best you dispose of biodegradable materials.*

2 information, ideas or documents

- adj+N in a particular form **audio-visual, electronic, interactive, online, photographic, printed, unpublished, video, web-based** *Students are expected to work through the various online material that is provided.*
- ▶ of a particular type or for a particular purpose **educational, historical, illustrative, pornographic, promotional** *The promotional material from the company implied that the product was available now.*
- ▶ secret or private **confidential, sensitive** *Do not send sensitive material in email.*
- ▶ not suitable **inappropriate, indecent, unsuitable** *He was sacked for downloading inappropriate material from the Internet.*

▶ real or original **authentic, original** *The Internet is an excellent source of authentic language material for teaching purposes.*

● n+N for business **marketing, publicity** *Ideas for new publicity materials are welcome.*

▶ for education or research **background, course, reading, reference, self-study, source, teaching, training** *The walls and ceilings were brightly decorated with the children's own work and excellent teaching materials.*

▶ types of material **archive, copyright** *The precious collections of books and archive material published during the bombardment.*

material ADJ
relating to money and possessions, not emotions

● ADJ+n **gain, goods, possessions, prosperity, resources, rewards, wealth** *We have the human and material resources available to achieve sustainable development.*

matter N
1 something being discussed, considered, or dealt with

● adj+N serious or urgent/not serious or urgent **important, minor, pressing, routine, serious, trivial, urgent** *Obviously, if the matter is urgent, it will be attended to as soon as possible.*

> You can say that something is **no laughing matter** to emphasize that it is serious: *Whilst the image conjured up may be amusing, on reflection it's hardly a laughing matter.*

▶ easy/difficult **complex, complicated, contentious, easy, no easy, no simple, simple, straightforward** *How best to tackle this is no simple matter.*

● v+N raise a matter **bring before sb, bring to sb's attention, bring up, raise, refer to sb, report** *Is there anyone else I can refer the matter to?*

▶ discuss or consider a matter **consider, consult (sb) on, debate, discuss, talk about, think about** *The Committee discussed this matter at its meeting on 14 February.*

▶ deal with a matter **address, deal with, handle, intervene in, investigate, look into** *He/she will listen to your concerns, investigate the matter, and then report back to you.*

▶ decide a matter **clarify, decide, resolve, settle** *This resolves a matter which has been of concern for a number of years.*

▶ involve a matter **relate to** *This question will not be discussed at the meeting as it relates to a matter that is outside the department's concern.*

> You can use **concerning** and **regarding** to mean 'about a matter': *For further details regarding this matter, please contact our Head Office.*

▶ take a matter further **pursue, take further** *We might have to pursue the matter through the courts.*

> You can use the expression **let the matter drop** when someone is not taking a matter further: *We decided to let the matter drop and said no more about it.*

● N+v **affect, appertain to, concern, pertain to, relate to** *It is important to understand that matters*

which relate to children can be brought before a court at any time.

2 a particular type of substance

● adj+N physical **dry, inorganic, organic, solid, vegetable** *All soils contain some percentage of nitrogen, which is obtained from the organic matter.*

▶ for reading **printed, reading** *A number of countries require imported printed matter to be marked with the country of origin.*

mature ADJ
grown to adult size or behaving in a sensible way, like an adult

● adv+ADJ in a particular way **emotionally, physically, sexually, spiritually** *I was of the opinion that he was an emotionally mature, intelligent man of the world.*

▶ very or surprisingly **astonishingly, incredibly, particularly, remarkably, surprisingly, truly, very** *If you ask what they like, you get a range of surprisingly mature responses.*

▶ completely **fully** *Most of the trees are now fully mature.*

▶ fairly **fairly, quite, reasonably, relatively** *You need to be a fairly mature reader to cope with the ideas discussed.*

mature V
1 become adult or start behaving like an adult

● adv+V quickly/slowly/early/late **early, fast, late, quickly, rapidly, slowly** *Children who mature late, comparatively speaking, are generally smaller than their peers.*

▶ in a particular way **emotionally, intellectually, physically, psychologically, sexually, spiritually** *As she continued to mature spiritually, the poems continued to flow.*

2 to develop a pleasant strong flavour

● adv+V quickly/slowly **fast, quickly, slowly** *The wine is left to mature slowly in the cellars.*

▶ naturally or well **beautifully, naturally, nicely, traditionally** *Cheese requires time to mature naturally.*

● n+V **cheese, whisky, wine** *Wines mature in either stainless steel tanks or large oak vats.*

maturity N
1 the qualities and behaviour of a sensible adult

● adj+N types of maturity **emotional, intellectual, moral, psychological, spiritual** *Spiritual maturity isn't like chronological age.*

▶ great **astonishing, remarkable** *Children understand the message with astonishing maturity.*

● v+N get or have maturity **achieve, attain, gain, possess, reach** *He possesses a maturity well beyond his years.*

▶ lack maturity **lack** *If we lack the maturity and wisdom to act wisely, then we ask for help.*

▶ show maturity **demonstrate, display, show** *Sixth-form students demonstrate considerable maturity.*

2 full growth or completed development

● adj+N **full, physiological, reproductive, sexual,**

skeletal *Males reach sexual maturity at 5–6 years old, females at 3–5 years.*

- v+N reach maturity **achieve, attain, gain, reach** *It takes 3 to 4 years for the spider to reach maturity.*
- ▶ approach maturity **approach, near** *A tree such as this, nearing maturity, would not be growing as rapidly as a younger specimen.*

maximize V
make something as large as possible

- V+n money or value **gains, profitability, profits, return, revenue, value, yield** *The methods used are designed to maximize profits, always at the expense of the animals.*
- ▶ chances **chances, likelihood** *To truly maximize your chances of getting interviews, the time to act is now.*
- ▶ how well something works **effectiveness, efficiency, performance, potential, productivity, throughput** *Colleges have been driven by new public management practice in an attempt to maximize efficiency.*
- ▶ extent to which people take part in something **attendance, participation** *We hope to maximize employee participation by giving them direct access to information about the scheme.*
- ▶ sales **sales** *Using the Internet as a marketing tool will help your company maximize sales.*

maximum ADJ
the largest possible in amount, size, or number

- ADJ+n measurements **depth, height, length, speed, temperature, weight, width** *Remember that the maximum length of any consultation should be no more than 20 minutes.*
- ▶ punishment **fine, penalty, sentence** *The maximum penalty is an unlimited fine.*
- ▶ amount or number **amount, capacity, dose, limit, number, score, size, value** *The maximum score that could be achieved was 35.*
- ▶ abstract qualities **advantage, benefit, comfort, efficiency, enjoyment, flexibility** *The vouchers come in £5, £10 & £25 denominations for maximum flexibility.*
- and/or **allowable, permissible, possible, recommended** *Note that the upper voltage line of each pair shows the maximum allowable current under ideal conditions.*

maximum N
the largest possible number, amount, or degree

- adj+N recommended or allowed **allowable, legal, permitted, recommended, statutory** *All offenders will be prosecuted to the maximum allowable under current copyright laws.*
- ▶ fixed **absolute, specified, stated** *Rent is paid according to the number of moorings within the specified maximum.*
- v+N reach or exceed a maximum **attain, exceed, reach** *Average sales volumes are 1.6 tonnes per year and reach a maximum of three tonnes per year.*
- ▶ set a maximum **allow, permit** *A maximum of 2 hours is permitted for each customer.*

meal N
an occasion when you eat, such as breakfast, lunch, or dinner

- adj+N good **decent, delicious, excellent, gourmet, lovely, sumptuous, tasty** *After our delicious meal, we prepared for the afternoon excursion.*
- ▶ small/large **big, hearty, heavy, light, slap-up** INFORMAL, **snack, square** *The Green Lounge Cafe is the ideal place for a hearty meal, cup of tea or a quick snack.* • *School dinner is often the only square meal they get in the day.*
- ▶ biggest meal in the day **main** *We have our main meal in the evening.*
- ▶ healthy **balanced, healthy, nourishing, nutritious** *A consistent effort to eat healthy meals is the key to losing weight.*
- ▶ how many courses **two-course, 3-course etc** *The price for the four-course meal (excluding wine) has been set at £35.*
- ▶ fresh/not fresh **frozen, home-cooked/prepared, ready-cooked, ready-made** *The company is also looking into the provision of ready-cooked frozen meals.*
- ▶ cooked and served hot **hot** *We will ensure that a hot meal is delivered to every old person every day.*
- ▶ where people serve themselves from a table **buffet** *A buffet meal will be served in the course of the evening.*
- ▶ served on a plane **in-flight** *Huge savings can be made by not serving in-flight meals.*

- v+N cook a meal **cook, prepare** *Everyone takes a turn in helping to cook one evening meal.*
- ▶ eat a meal **digest, eat, have, snatch** *Be regular in your meal times and eat your main meal in the middle of the day.* • *I usually snatched my meals in the canteen, when time allowed.*
- ▶ order a meal **order** *I can read a newspaper in French and order a meal in a French restaurant.*
- ▶ miss a meal **miss, skip** *Eat regularly and do not skip meals.*
- ▶ provide a meal **provide, serve** *A total of some 400 meals are served each working day.*

meaning N
the thing, action, feeling, or idea that a word or words represent

- adj+N basic **basic, literal, ordinary, original, plain** *The words have a literal meaning that we can easily understand.*
- ▶ hidden or deep **deep, hidden, inner, metaphorical** *There are quite a few possible hidden meanings to this film.*
- ▶ when words are not used in their normal meaning **figurative, metaphorical, symbolic** *Some words have both literal and metaphorical meanings, for example 'to hammer'.*
- ▶ more than one **double, multiple** *The project aims to cast new light on the multiple meanings of democracy.*
- ▶ clear **clear** *He didn't express himself too well, but the meaning was clear: he did not want to come with us.*
- ▶ exact **exact, precise** *You must give the precise meaning of what you are being asked.*
- ▶ true **actual, intended, real, true** *The real meaning of Christmas is so much more evident in a smaller community.*

▶ same or different **different, same** *Sometimes different words will carry the same meaning.*

● v+N give meaning **ascribe, assign, attach, give** *There may be more than one symbolic meaning attached to the lighthouse in the novel.*

▶ have or get meaning **acquire, get, have, take on** *Viewed from this perspective, the issues take on a whole new meaning.*

▶ find meaning **discover, find** *Help your children to find the meanings of words by showing them how to use a dictionary efficiently.*

▶ understand meaning **catch, decipher, determine, get, grasp, guess, infer, understand** *The dog must be able to understand the meaning of the word 'no'.*

▶ explain meaning **clarify, define, explain, interpret** *The draft policy guidance is also welcome in that it helps to clarify the meaning of social inclusion.*

▶ communicate meaning **communicate, convey, express** *In art, images need to be read and understood if they are to communicate their meaning.*

meaningful ADJ
serious, useful or important; having a meaning

● adv+ADJ in a particular way or area **biologically, clinically, personally, physically, semantically, socially, statistically** *Only three trials were of sufficient power to detect a clinically meaningful difference.*

▶ very **deeply, highly, profoundly, really, truly, very** *Listening to music is profoundly meaningful.*

● ADJ+n discussion **consultation, conversation, dialogue, discussion** *You may find yourself having deep and meaningful conversations with total strangers.*

▶ relationship **interaction, relationship** *Some people felt that their disability prevented them from having meaningful social relationships with their peers.*

▶ activity **contribution, engagement, involvement, occupation, participation** *Below are 3 examples of projects which have used meaningful occupation to help change peoples lives.*

▶ conclusion or comparison **comparison, conclusion** *The response was large enough to draw meaningful conclusions about local views.*

▶ result **result** *We shall not get any meaningful results form this flawed piece of research.*

▶ way **manner, way** *Finally, the seventh phase is to synthesise the data in a meaningful manner.*

▶ when a meaning is expressed without words **gesture, glance, look** *He gave me a meaningful glance, as if to say 'That's enough'.*

● v+ADJ **be, become, consider sth, prove, seem** *Her life only became meaningful when she was able to make decisions for herself.* ● *This data was ignored for the purposes of the analysis as it was considered less meaningful.*

means N
a method for doing or achieving something

● adj+N effective **cost-effective, effective, efficient, excellent, powerful, reliable** *Massage is itself a powerful means of relaxation.*

▶ main **chief, dominant, primary, prime** *Councils still rely on landfill as the primary means of waste disposal.*

▶ only **only, sole** *CVs will not be accepted as a sole means of application.*

▶ useful or essential **convenient, essential, invaluable, key, useful, valuable, vital** *Taxis are an invaluable means of door-to-door transport for many people.* ● *'Park and Ride' is used a key means of reducing congestion on the roads.*

▶ reasonable or legal **acceptable, legal, legitimate, proportionate, viable** *Due to economic and environmental reasons, the canal is no longer a viable means of transporting goods.*

▶ preferred **preferred** *When travelling further afield train travel is the preferred means of transport.*

▶ not using force **non-violent, peaceful** *They hoped to achieve their objectives by peaceful means.*

▶ different **alternative, different, other** *I had no other means of repaying them for the help they had given me.*

● v+N find or look for a means **devise, discover, find, seek** *In 1819, Sir John Herschel discovered a means by which photographs could be fixed and therefore stored.*

▶ provide a means **afford, establish, offer, provide** *College grades afford a means of recording intellectual efficiency.*

▶ be or become a means **be, become, constitute** *Previously a community relations site, it became an invaluable means of communicating with interested clients.*

> If something is done purely in order to achieve an aim, you can refer to it as *a means to an end*: *We monitor the projects that deal with standards, either as a means to an end, or an end in itself.*

▶ have/not have a means **lack, possess** *Even had they possessed the means to help, they lacked the will.*

measure N
1 an action to achieve or deal with something [usually plural]

● adj+N that prevent or protect something **precautionary, preventative, preventive, protective** *The company is withdrawing the drug as a precautionary measure.*

▶ severe **draconian, drastic, harsh, punitive, severe, stringent, strong, tough** *Drastic measures must be taken to reduce the overall use of toxic substances.*

▶ temporary **interim, short-term, temporary** *It was decided to freeze the Charity's bank accounts as a precautionary, interim measure.*

▶ necessary, suitable or effective **appropriate, effective, necessary** *Modern pest control measures are effective, but cannot be relied upon entirely.*

▶ special or extra **additional, special** *The programme will involve special measures to challenge the gifted and talented students.*

▶ to correct something **corrective, remedial** *If you take corrective measures, you can bounce back from exhaustion in a week or two.*

▶ to save money, energy or water **cost-cutting, cost-saving, energy-saving, water-saving** *In view of the budget deficit, a wide range of cost-cutting measures was introduced.*

● n+N **austerity, conservation, efficiency, emergency, safety, security** *The additional security measures, imposed last year, remain in place.*

- v+N introduce or suggest measures **announce, identify, introduce, outline, recommend** *The Chancellor announced measures to boost funds for health research.*
▶ use measures **adopt, implement, take, undertake** *Drastic measures were taken to improve the situation.*
▶ make someone use measures **enforce, impose** *We will continue to take, and enforce, national measures to conserve stocks.*
▶ oppose measures **oppose** *We oppose any measures which will further erode the traditionally superb standards of animal and plant health.*
▶ include measures **incorporate** *Developers will be encouraged to incorporate measures to enhance biodiversity.*

2 an amount that is neither large nor small

- adj+N large or quite large **considerable, large, reasonable, significant, substantial** *Caution and common sense can provide a large measure of protection for sensitive documents.*
▶ small **limited, small** *Such a limited measure of reform is a mere farce.*

- N+of **autonomy, certainty, independence, protection, self-government, success** *The National Assembly provides a limited measure of autonomy for Wales.*

medal N

an object that you are given for winning a competition or being brave

- adj+N important or that people want very much **coveted, prestigious** *The garden was judged to be one of the best in the show, and was just points away from a coveted gold medal.*
▶ for a person or team **individual, team** *If he runs to form, he has an outside chance of an individual medal.*
▶ deserved **well-deserved** *All of the competitors went home with a well-deserved medal.*
▶ marking an event **commemorative, souvenir** *Players receive a commemorative medal.*

- v+N win a medal **claim, clinch** INFORMAL, **earn, gain, scoop** INFORMAL, **secure, snatch** INFORMAL, **win** *Several women have won the class medal in recent years.*
▶ be given a medal **be awarded, be given, be presented with, collect, get** INFORMAL, **receive** *Frank was awarded the military medal in 1918.*
▶ give a medal **award (sb), present (sb with)** *The chairman at the sponsoring company presented the medals.*
▶ deserve a medal **deserve** *The mastermind who invented low-fat chocolate mousse deserves a medal.*

- N+n possible winner **contender, hope, hopeful, prospect** *The aim of the programme is to identify and develop medal hopefuls aged between 13–16 years.*
▶ winner **winner** *It was the end of an era for the five times Olympic Gold Medal winner when she retired from the sport last week.*
▶ number of medals won **haul, tally** *The final medal haul for the team was 3 gold, 2 silver and 5 bronze.*

the media N

radio, television, newspapers, the Internet, and magazines

- adj+N types of media **corporate, mainstream, mass, news, tabloid, traditional** *One fairly obvious constraint of the mass media is that most of us don't have access to them.*
▶ in a particular area **foreign, local, national** *Most of them, of course, were Londoners – where the national media is based.*
▶ methods of delivery **broadcast, digital, electronic, interactive, online, print, printed** *All electronic media is afforded the same copyright restrictions as a literary or artistic work.*

- v+N control the media **control, dominate, manipulate** *They think they can control the Internet the way they try to control the print media, but they will fail.*
▶ use the media **exploit, handle, use** *Handled well, the media is a useful vehicle for getting your message across.*
▶ blame the media **accuse, blame** *He accused the media of creating a 'frenzy' during the A-level scandal this summer.*

- N+v **focus on, pick up on, portray, report** *Thankfully, the media didn't pick up on the story until much later.* • *The media reports that house prices are rising again now.*

- N+n people who own the media **baron, mogul, tycoon** *I am not sure whether it is better to be called a 'media mogul' or a 'paper tiger'.*
▶ people who work in the media **commentator, correspondent, pundit, regulator** *Now a respected media pundit, he writes an exclusive column for Liverpoolfc.tv each week.*
▶ media company or companies **conglomerate, empire, giant, industry**
▶ excitement **circus, frenzy, hype, hysteria** *We do not know what caused this minor media frenzy, but we tried our hardest to take advantage of it.*
▶ what the media does or says **campaign, coverage, enquiry, speculation** *There will be a media campaign from both the police and the local council.*
▶ attention **attention, exposure, spotlight** *Although the service has developed rapidly, its development has not been in the media spotlight.*
▶ when the media is not allowed to comment **blackout** *She is responsible for the media blackout on reports about her brother.*

medical ADJ

relating to medicine and the treatment of conditions

- ADJ+n person or job **adviser, doctor, expert, officer, personnel, practitioner, profession, professional, researcher, staff, student** *Please consult your own medical practitioner for advice specific to yourself.*
▶ condition or problem **condition, emergency, problem** *If you are on medication or suffer from a medical condition, it is best to discuss your plans with your doctor.*
▶ treatment **attention, care, intervention, procedure, supervision, therapy, treatment** *In 1948, the National Health Service was formed and for the first*

time everyone was entitled to free medical treatment.

▶ examination **check-up, consultation, examination** *You must also pass a medical examination.*

▶ advice **advice** *If you experience any of these symptoms you should seek medical advice within 24 hours.*

▶ progress **advance, breakthrough** *The paper gives an overview of recent medical advances that benefited from research on animals.*

medication N
a drug you take to treat an illness

● adj+N **non-prescription, oral, over-the-counter, prescribed, prescription, preventive** *Many people take prescribed medication on either a short-term or long-term basis.*

● v+N take medication **receive, take** *Some simply forget to take their medication unless reminded.*

You can say that someone is **on medication** when they are regularly taking medication: *Please take care when driving if you are on medication, as it can have side-effects.*

▶ give medication **administer, dispense, prescribe** *A doctor can prescribe medication to prevent or reduce the frequency of headaches.*

▶ need medication **require** *Do any of the pupils require medication for asthma?*

▶ change medication **adjust, change, review** *It is useful to review all medication regularly.*

▶ stop or refuse medication **discontinue, refuse, stop, withdraw** *You should not discontinue this medication without first consulting your doctor.*

medicine N
the treatment and prevention of illnesses and injuries

● adj+N traditional **conventional, orthodox, traditional** *Aromatherapy should be regarded as complementary to conventional medicine.*

▶ alternative **alternative, complementary, homeopathic, unconventional** *Most people using complementary medicine do so in conjunction with conventional medicine.*

▶ from a particular area **Western, Oriental etc** *Acupuncture is an alternative therapy based on the principles of traditional Chinese medicine.*

● v+N **graduate in, practise, qualify in, study, train in, work in** *He is currently studying medicine at Birmingham University.*

● n+of+N **aspect, branch, field** *They specialize in developing technologies in the fields of medicine and healthcare.*

meet V
do what is necessary in order to deal with a situation or to do what you planned

● adv+V **adequately, consistently, effectively, successfully** *The corresponding demand in England was adequately met.*

● V+n what is needed or asked for **demands, need, needs, requirements** *The council proposes to meet this need by building two new sports facilities.* ● *We have tailored the course to meet the needs of our students.*

▶ amount that is wanted **demand** *It will not be possible to meet the demand for new houses in the next few years.*

▶ a standard **condition, criterion, expectation, specification, standard** *Any who did not meet the set criteria were set to work on farms or left to fend for themselves.*

▶ an aim **aim, challenge, commitment, deadline, goal, objective, target** *They only care about meeting their own deadlines and scoring the best marks.*

● and/or **exceed, surpass** *This target was met and subsequently exceeded.*

meeting N
an occasion when people gather to discuss things

● adj+N previous, next etc **first, forthcoming, last, next, previous, recent, upcoming** *They asked for improved attendance at the next meeting.*

▶ how frequent **annual, monthly, quarterly, regular, weekly** *We shall discuss these issues in our annual meeting.*

▶ formal/informal **formal, informal** *The matter will be discussed first at an informal meeting.*

▶ public/private **confidential, open, private, public, secret** *This is an open meeting, which anyone is welcome to attend.*

▶ first or early **first, founding, inaugural, initial, preliminary, preparatory** *The inaugural meeting of the new association will be held on 20 January.*

▶ talking directly to a person or people **face-to-face, one-to-one** *Face-to-face meetings remain the most effective method of communicating.*

▶ where something is achieved **constructive, positive, productive, successful** *Thank you all for a very productive meeting.*

▶ types of meeting **consultation, consultative, emergency, extraordinary, planning, special** *The next monthly planning meeting will be on Thursday 5th.*

● v+N ask for a meeting **ask for, call for, demand** *The unions have called for a meeting with the Minister.*

▶ hold a meeting **arrange, call, convene, hold, organize, plan, request, schedule** *The formal meetings with the staff are held every six months at set times of the year.*

▶ run a meeting **chair, conduct, host, preside at, preside over** *The British Film Commission hosts regular meetings of the UK Film Commission Network.*

▶ delay or cancel a meeting **call off, cancel, defer, postpone** *In the event, the meeting was postponed pending clarification of the Council's budget cuts.*

▶ start or end a meeting **adjourn, bring to a close, close, draw to a close, end, open** *She thanked the speakers and brought the meeting to a close at 10pm.* ● *The Chairman opened the meeting and made a short statement about the Club Knock-Out Competition.*

▶ speak at a meeting **address, inform, remind, report to, speak at, tell** *Each meeting is usually addressed by an invited speaker.*

▶ go to or take part in a meeting **attend, go to, participate in, take part in** *Delegates from all the major national and regional bodies are attending the meetings.*

- N+v start or end **begin, break up, close, commence, conclude, end, finish, open** *The meeting officially broke up at around ten o'clock.*
- discuss or decide **approve, decide, discuss, ensorse** *The application was approved by the planning meeting.*

meet with PHR VB
get a particular result or reaction

- V+n approval or success **acclaim, applause, approbation, approval, enthusiasm, success** *Both of these superb albums met with high acclaim and commercial success.*
- opposition or criticism **criticism, derision, disapproval, hostility, opposition, protest, resistance, scepticism** *The proposals for the multiplex development have met with widespread opposition.*
- response **response** *If you can say a few words in Arabic, you will usually meet with an enthusiastic response.*
- when someone does not believe you **disbelief, incredulity** *This theory initially met with disbelief on the part of most researchers.*
- little or no reaction **indifference, silence** *Our proposition continues to meet with a resounding silence.*

Meet is used with the same meaning: *He met resistance from the local Police force, who didn't like him poking his nose around the place.*

mellow ADJ
relaxed, soft, or smooth

- ADJ+n sound or music **jazz, sound, tone, tune, vocal** *Bassoons have a rich and mellow sound.*
- mood **mood** *Luckily, I'd caught him in a mellow mood.*
- flavour **flavour** *Heating tends to reduce the acidity, so if a more mellow flavour is required, cook it.*
- and/or **rich, smooth, soft, sweet, warm** *They manufactured a very popular, sweet, mellow cider.*

melody N
a tune or song

- adj+N beautiful **beautiful, enchanting, gorgeous, soft, sweet** *Here the album reaches its peak and the band create some gorgeous melodies and heartfelt lyrics.*
- making you feel emotional **haunting, lyrical, soaring, soulful, sublime, sweeping, uplifting** *This is a thoughtful song with a haunting melody that I can listen to over and over again.*
- easy to sing or remember **catchy, hummable, infectious, memorable** *Jam-packed with intensely catchy melodies, their guitar-driven rock is guaranteed to get you on your feet.*
- with a rising and falling sound **lilting** *The gently plucked guitars and lilting vocal melodies conjured up the atmosphere of the Islands.*
- v+N perform a melody **hum, play, sing, whistle** *I used to hum melodies from Louis Armstrong.*
- write a melody **compose** *The haunting melodies were especially composed for the production by Martin Phipps.*

member N
someone who belongs to a club, organisation, or group

- adj+N original **founder, founding, original** *She was a founder member of the local Bridge club.*
- new/present/former **current, former, new, past, present** *A list of past and present members of the Board can be accessed online.*
- senior/junior **junior, rank-and-file, senior** *Rank-and-file members of the party felt they were being ignored by government ministers.*
- with a particular status **affiliate, associate, ex-officio, full, honorary, ordinary, voting** *Only full members will be entitled to vote on the issue.*
- important **important, key, leading, prominent** *Mark has been a key member of a story management team.*
- n+N **audience, band, board, cabinet, cast, church, club, committee, council, crew, faculty, family, gang, group, party, squad, staff, team, trade union, union** *I am looking forward very much to meeting the staff, tenants and board members when I take up my new post in January.* • *Most weavers are taught to weave at an early age by a family member.*
- v+N make someone a member **appoint, elect, nominate** *Committee members are appointed for two years as a general rule.*
- get a new member or members **recruit** *This is our main chance to recruit new members for the year.*
- be or become a member **be, become** *How did you become a member?*
- N+v **attend, join, participate (in), serve, vote** *The session was attended by all the members of the team.* • *Members who join during the year will receive all the publications published that year.*

membership N
the fact of belonging to an organization or group

- adj+N types of membership **affiliate, associate, corporate, full, honorary, individual, joint, ordinary** *Honorary membership will only be awarded to members who have made a considerable contribution to the advancement of the Association*
- length of membership **annual, temporary** *A 9-hole golf course is ¼ mile away, where temporary membership is readily available.*
- being very involved in the organization you have membership of **active** *Requests for cruiser moorings are not normally considered from members who have not had five years active membership of the Club.*
- n+N that will continue for all of your life **life, lifetime** *If you are a member of a club, consider taking out lifetime membership.*
- for a short period to see if you like it **trial** *For all these pilots, learning to glide started with a trial membership.*
- v+N when someone becomes or asks to become a member **apply for, register for, seek, take out** *If you wish to apply for membership, you should fill in this form.*
- have membership **have, hold** *He also holds membership of the Royal Society of Chemistry.*
- end your or someone's membership **cancel, resign,**

suspend, terminate, withdraw *You have the right to cancel your membership at any time.*
▶ arrange for membership to continue **renew** *If you renew your membership before the end of the month, you will be entitled to a 10 per cent discount.*
▶ say someone cannot have membership **deny sb, refuse sb** *The Committee may refuse membership to any person without being required to provide a reason.*
▶ allow someone membership **approve, award, grant (sb), offer** *For applicants under 16, we require that a parent or guardian sign a permission form before we grant membership.*
▶ fulfil the conditions for membership **qualify for** *11–16 year olds qualify for junior membership, and this costs just £26 per year.*
▶ get membership **gain, obtain** *In April 2005, RSIN successfully gained full membership of the Telephone Helpline Association*
▶ keep membership **retain** *Other party members have retained their membership, but are sorely disappointed in their party.*

● N+n money you pay for membership **dues, fee, subscription** *The annual individual membership fee is £10 for adults and £5 for juniors.*
▶ things given to you when you get membership **card, number, pack** *All you need to do to benefit from member prices is show us your membership card.*
▶ person who deals with membership issues **secretary** *For full details, contact the membership secretary.*

memo N
a short note you send to a colleague

● adj+N secret **confidential, secret** *A confidential memo of a conversation between the US president and the British Prime Minister was leaked to the press.*
▶ within an organization **internal** *An internal police memo said that the suspects were professional and respectable.*
▶ given to journalists or the public even though it should be secret **leaked** *Details of the schemes emerged in a leaked memo last night, causing anger among MPs .*

● v+N write or send a memo **circulate, draft, issue, send, write** *The Head of Security issued a memo advising that the old security passes will expire at the end of the month.*
▶ make a memo public even though it is secret **leak** *Shortly after the memo was leaked to the press, the chief executive of the bank resigned.*

memorable ADJ
worth remembering or easy to remember

● adv+ADJ very **extremely, highly, really, truly, very** *Walking trips with your family make truly memorable holidays.*
▶ particularly **especially, particularly** *The bar is particularly memorable for its warm friendly atmosphere.*
▶ immediately **instantly** *The chorus is instantly memorable, creating the feeling that the song is familiar to the listener in a very short time.*

● ADJ+n event **encounter, event, experience,**

holiday, journey, occasion, performance, stay, trip, victory, visit, win *Whether you are touring Cornwall or visiting for business, we promise you a happy, relaxed and memorable stay.*
▶ time **day, evening, moment, night, weekend** *My sincere thanks go to them both for a memorable evening.*
▶ music **chorus, melody, song, tune** *Mendelssohn's Violin Concerto is packed full of memorable tunes.*
▶ words **line, phrase, quote, words** *Tony Blair's most memorable phrase from the 1997 election was 'Education, Education, Education'.*
▶ something you see **image, scene** *The magazine has undoubtedly produced some iconic and memorable images.*

● v+ADJ **be, make sth, prove, remain** *The hotel aims to make your stay truly memorable.* ● *The match proved memorable, but for all the wrong reasons.*

memorandum N
a short written statement containing information about an official issue

● adj+N containing information that should not be made public **confidential, secret** *This plan was first presented in a confidential memorandum sent to the Cabinet secretary.*
▶ made public even though it should be kept secret **leaked** *We know from a leaked memorandum that the army had been planning the raid for some time.*
▶ within an organization **internal** *The staff are kept informed by internal memorandums and briefing meetings.*
▶ prepared by two or more groups or organizations **joint** *A joint memorandum was then signed by the two ministers.*

● v+N write a memorandum **draft, prepare, write** *Fleming wrote a lengthy memorandum describing the structure and functions of the organization.*
▶ send a memorandum **issue, send, submit** *The management company issued a memorandum to each of its vessels highlighting the lessons to be learned from the accident.*
▶ sign or put the date on a memorandum **date, sign** *A number of academic economists signed a memorandum calling on the British government to abandon the theories of hardline monetarism.*

● N+v **outline, set out, state** *This memorandum sets out the terms and conditions of the agreement.*

memorial N
a structure built to remind people of a famous person or event

● adj+N permanent **everlasting, lasting, permanent** *Dartmouth Hospital was opened in 1877 as a permanent memorial to Queen Victoria's Jubilee.*
▶ suitable **fitting, suitable** *The grave was cleaned and restored in 1993 and is a fitting memorial to the founder of the church.*
▶ making you feel sad **poignant** *The windows are a poignant memorial to the thousands of Allied servicemen who lost their lives in the Battle of Normandy.*

● v+N build a memorial **build, create, erect, put up** *The memorial was erected here following the South African War (1899–1902).*

▶ show a memorial for the first time at a special ceremony **unveil** *The Prince of Wales unveiled a British memorial near Ground Zero.*

▶ say officially that a memorial is for someone **dedicate** *The memorial was dedicated at a moving ceremony last week.*

● N+v **be dedicated to, commemorate, mark, record** *The memorial commemorates those who lost their lives in the last war.*

● N+to **casualties, the dead, soldiers, sb's memory, victims** *After the disaster, the people of Coventry paid for a playground to be built as a lasting memorial to the dead.*

memory N

1 something you remember

● adj+N good **fantastic, favourite, fond, good, happy, lovely, sweet, wonderful** *He still has very fond memories of his days here.*

▶ bad **bad, bitter, haunting, painful, traumatic, unhappy, unpleasant** *Training may bring back unpleasant memories for some members of staff.*

▶ clear **clear, strong, vivid** *Ali said he still had vivid memories of the night when his parents were killed.*

▶ not clear **dim, distant, fading, faint, hazy, vague** *I have vague memories of my childhood.*

▶ special to you **cherished, precious, special, treasured** *Auntie Catherine died too young but left us precious memories.*

▶ lasting for a long time **abiding, enduring, lasting, unforgettable** *My abiding memory will be of a sunny Sunday morning by the Seine.*

▶ that stays with you for a long time in an unpleasant way **haunting** *She was still tortured by haunting memories of life in the death camps.*

▶ that you try to forget **repressed** *I hoped that the therapy would unlock repressed childhood memories of the time when my sister disappeared.*

▶ first **earliest, first** *My earliest memory was having to shelter under the table at the age of three during the blitz of 1940.*

● n+N **childhood, family, holiday, wartime** *It's strange how vivid some childhood memories are.*

● v+N have or provide a memory **have, hold** *She has many happy memories of her time in Seattle* ● *Leeds holds many good memories for me and it will be nice to return.*

▶ make a memory come into your mind **awaken, bring back, conjure up, evoke, invoke, prompt, rekindle, revive, spark, stir (up), trigger** *Our sense of smell has the ability to evoke memories – both visual and emotional.*

▶ get rid of a memory **block out, bury, erase, repress, suppress** *She decided to move house to erase her painful memories of him.*

▶ make a memory continue **keep alive, perpetuate, preserve** *Writing a diary is a wonderful way to preserve your cherished memories.*

▶ talk or write about a memory **recall, recount, share** *He recounts his memories of Nazi persecution with extraordinary courage and compassion.*

▶ remember a memory with affection **cherish, treasure** *We will cherish the memories from our first visit to Scotland and hope to come back soon.*

▶ do something which makes a memory come back

relive *They decided to relive the memories of their special wedding by returning to the Cayman Islands.*

▶ do something which will make a memory **create** *School trips can create lasting memories of school life.*

● N+v stay in your mind **linger (on), live on, remain, stay** *The memory of that night lingered in my mind.*

▶ disappear from your mind **fade** *Most memories fade with time.*

▶ give you unpleasant feelings for a long time **haunt** *Years later, Laura is still haunted by memories of her childhood.*

▶ suddenly come into your mind **flood back** *Memories flooded back of his years at Oxford and his girlfriend there.*

2 ability to remember things

● adj+N bad **bad, impaired, poor, short, terrible** *I have a terrible memory for books I've read.*

▶ good **good, long** *People with long memories will remember that before 1971 a pound was divided into twenty shillings.*

▶ for things that happened a long/short time ago **long-term, short-term** *Symptoms of dementia can be loss of short-term memory, confusion and disjointed conversations.*

▶ remembering only some things and not others **selective** *Humans have a selective memory which is susceptible to distortion.*

● v+N improve your memory in general **enhance, improve, strengthen** *In some patients, these drugs help to improve memory and concentration.*

▶ improve your memory about a particular thing **jog, refresh** *This photo may help refresh your memory.*

▶ make your memory worse **impair** *Different types of encephalitis can impair memory and understanding of words, amongst other things.*

▶ lose your memory **lose** *Ali was knocked unconscious in an accident and lost his memory.*

▶ stay in someone's memory **be etched in, haunt, linger in, live (on) in, remain in, stay in** *His tremendous skill is still etched in my memory.* ● *Her mother's beautiful face still haunted her memory for years afterwards.*

▶ not stay in people's memory **fade from** *After that, Mary Seacole faded from memory.*

> If you cannot remember a particular fact, you can use the phrase *escape your memory*: *He was a tall man, but his name escapes my memory.*

● N+v **fail (you), go** *My memory fails me on certain things.* ● *My balance, perception and memory have gone and I have a weakness on my left side.*

> If you do not remember things correctly, you can also say that your *memory plays tricks*: *Maybe my memory's playing tricks, but I'm sure we went there once before.* When you are saying that you think that you have remembered something correctly, you can use the expression *if my memory serves me well/right/correctly*: *They won the title in 1997, if my memory serves me correctly.*

menace N

1 someone or something that is dangerous or annoying

- adj+N great **great, real, serious** *The noise and mess seagulls produce is a real menace.*
- ▶ becoming greater **growing** *Vandalism is a growing menace, which the legal establishment does not seem to take very seriously.*
- ▶ existing all the time **constant** *Electricity pylons are a constant menace to paraglider pilots and have been responsible for a number of deaths.*
- v+N be or become a menace **become, constitute, prove** *Drugs are becoming a menace in parts of Wales.*
- ▶ deal with a menace **combat, fight, tackle** *All eight Scottish police forces will be tackling the menace of drink drivers.*

2 a threatening quality or feeling

- adj+N **brooding, hidden** *There was an atmosphere of brooding menace.*
- n+of+N **air, atmosphere, hint, sense** *When I went on, the footsteps started again and with them a sense of menace I cannot describe.*

menacing ADJ

intended to threaten or frighten someone

- adv+ADJ very **deeply, extremely, genuinely** *This was a genuinely menacing thriller, with a good sense of place.*
- ▶ rather **rather, slightly, somewhat, vaguely** *One of the cats sat facing me, giving me a slightly menacing look.*
- ADJ+n **atmosphere, character, look, presence, threat, tone** *He gives the film a truly menacing tone as the creepy host of the party.*

mental ADJ

relating to the mind

- ADJ+n illness or problem **breakdown, condition, difficulty, disability, disorder, handicap, illness, impairment, instability, problem, retardation** *He was suffering from mental illness.*
- ▶ health **health, state, wellbeing** *Positive and negative forces at home impact on a child's mental wellbeing.*
- ▶ ability/inability to do things **ability, agility, capacity, faculties, function, functioning, incapacity** *It quickly became clear that he lacked the mental capacity to do the job.*
- ▶ activities done or happening in your mind **activity, arithmetic, attitude, awareness, calculation, challenge, effort, image, note, picture, process** *There is also a need for more work focused on mental arithmetic.* • *I enjoy challenges, and climbing has proved a new physical and mental challenge.* • *Those three words will evoke a string of mental images.* • *They studied the activity of the brain as humans engaged in various mental processes.*
- ▶ bad feelings **anguish, confusion, distress, stress, suffering** *Children who were being bullied showed high levels of mental distress.*
- ▶ positive qualities **alertness, energy, stimulation, strength, toughness** *Children are calmer if given enough exercise and mental stimulation.*

- and/or **bodily, emotional, physical, psychological, spiritual** *If you are taking care of another person, you need a break occasionally, for the sake of your physical and mental wellbeing.*

mention N

the act of referring to someone or something

- adj+N quick **brief, cursory, passing, quick** *The exhibition receives only cursory mention in the last chapter.*
- ▶ special or praising someone **favourable, honourable, special** *I would like to make special mention of the unsung heroes who support the playing side of the club.*
- ▶ particular **explicit, particular, specific** *There is no specific mention of legal action in the report.*
- ▶ not much **little, scant** *In the past, hypnotism as a form of medical treatment fell out of favour and received scant mention in the medical journals.*
- ▶ used for emphasizing the big effect that mentioning something has **the mere, the very** *If the very mention of the gym makes you reach for the chocolate biscuits, try to find a sport or fitness class that you enjoy.*

- v+N give a mention **give, make** *I must give a special mention to the title track because it's a great song.* • *Mention was made of all his exploits.*
- ▶ get a mention **earn, get, receive** *His most recent film doesn't even get a mention in the article.* • *The clinic's treatment and research work received a special mention in the report.*
- ▶ deserve a mention **deserve, merit, rate, warrant** *The final two songs here deserve an extra-special mention.*

> When you are praising or thanking someone, you can say *special mention goes to*: *A special mention goes to Hannah Brown, who completed the course in very difficult circumstances.*

- ▶ make no mention **avoid, omit** *His autobiography omitted any mention of his career in the IRA.*

> You can also say *there is no mention of*: *There is no mention of any such costs in the contract.*

- ▶ read or hear a mention **find, hear** *I could find no mention of them in the guide.*

menu N

1 a list of food available in restaurant etc

- adj+N with many choices **extensive, full, varied** *There is a varied menu, including a variety of fish or cheeses and continental cold meats.*

> You can say that something is *on the menu* when it is available: *We've got fresh lobster on the menu tonight.*

- ▶ with food that sounds good **excellent, exciting, imaginative, impressive, mouth-watering, superb, tasty, tempting** *There is a tempting menu to suit all palates.*
- ▶ types of menu **à la carte, fixed, fixed-price, seasonal, set, table d'hôte, traditional, vegetarian, three-course etc** *There is a choice of four dishes per course and a separate vegetarian menu is available.* • *The two-couse menu is only £15 at lunchtimes.*

- v+N look at a menu **look at, peruse, read, study**

We managed to find a table outside and settled down to peruse the menu.

▶ create a menu **create, devise, plan, prepare** *He regularly devised new menus, and trained chefs.*

▶ change a menu **change, vary** *We vary our menus frequently to keep our regular customers inspired and to make the most of seasonally available produce.*

▶ choose what you want from a menu **choose from, order from, select from** *Children under 12 can select from the children's menu.*

● N+v **boast, feature, offer** *The hotel's menu boasts a selection of delicious dishes.*

2 a list of choices on a computer screen

● adj+N **drop-down, interactive, main, navigation, on-screen, pop-up, pull-down** *The text is small, but a navigation menu remains present at the top of the page.*

● v+N show or use a menu **access, activate, browse, display, navigate, view** *Hold the right mouse button down to activate the pop-up menu.*

▶ choose from a menu **access sth from, choose (sth) from, select (sth) from** *Select from the menu on the left to learn more about the various courses on offer.*

mercy N

an act of forgiving or not punishing someone

● adj+N **divine, great, infinite** *The letters bear witness to God's infinite mercy.*

● v+N **ask for, beg for, cry for, plead for, pray for, seek** *He had sunk to his knees, begging for mercy.*

● show mercy **grant (sb), show (sb)** *They showed little mercy to their prisoners.*

> You can also use the expression *have mercy on someone*: *They prayed that God would have mercy on them all.* When something or someone shows no mercy, you can say that they act *without mercy*: *The original inhabitants of the islands were hunted down and shot without mercy.*

● receive mercy **obtain, receive** *He had received mercy and grace from God for his sins.*

● and/or **compassion, forgiveness, goodness, grace, justice, love** *Quite often these solutions are based on threat and force, rather than considerations of mercy and compassion.*

merger N

the process of combining two companies or organizations

● adj+N possible or planned **planned, possible, potential, proposed** *The proposed merger between Volvo and Saab-Scania was the most discussed business deal of the year.*

● complete **complete, full** *The sheer size of these firms would make a full merger difficult.*

● between big companies **big, major** *The deal between the two British providers is the fourth major merger this year for the European hosting market.*

● v+N be in charge of a merger **oversee** *Having successfully overseen the merger of Coca-Cola UK and Schweppes, she was appointed Commercial Director.*

▶ announce a merger **announce** *Hewlett-Packard (HP) and Compaq announced a merger to form a new company.*

▶ say that a merger can happen **agree, approve** *The Secretary of State has been asked to approve the merger.*

▶ say that a merger cannot happen **block, prohibit** *The Competition Commission has only ever blocked 18 mergers outright.*

▶ complete a merger **complete** *The Incentive Travel and Meetings Association has finally completed its merger with the Corporate Events Association to form an organization named Eventia.*

● N+n discussions about a merger **discussions, negotiations, talks** *Merger talks between the two companies continued, but they too failed eventually.*

▶ plan for a merger **plan, proposal** *The civil aviation ministry is planning to seek the views of various ministries on the merger proposal.*

▶ agreement on a merger **agreement, deal** *Under the terms of the merger agreement, shareholders will receive $12.50 per share in cash.*

merit N

an advantage or good quality; the fact of having good qualities

● adj+N great **considerable, exceptional, great, outstanding** *We conclude that there is considerable merit in implementing such a proposal.*

▶ not certain **dubious, questionable** *He was droning on about the dubious merits of bathing in olive oil.*

▶ when compared with others **comparative, relative** *There was much discussion of the relative merits of the two schemes.*

▶ relating to one person or thing **individual, personal** *The qualifications and individual merits of each candidate will also be taken into account.*

▶ essential and part of someone or something **intrinsic** *Tourists use the town as a base from which to explore the south of the island rather than for any intrinsic merit.*

▶ types of merit **academic, aesthetic, architectural, artistic, literary, scientific, technical** *I think the novel is entertaining, but has no literary merit whatsoever.*

● v+N discuss merits **argue, debate, discuss** *Today colleges debate the relative merits of the humanities and the sciences.*

▶ judge merits **assess, compare, consider, determine, evaluate, examine, investigate, judge, weigh (up)** *The proposals are collected together below so that you can assess their merits.*

▶ have merits **have, possess** *Each of these strategies possesses respective merits.*

▶ see that someone or something has merits **acknowledge, appreciate, recognize, see** *He suddenly saw the merits of Cabinet decision-making.*

▶ tell other people enthusiastically about merits **extol** *She was reading the travel section of the newspaper which was extolling the merits of the latest fashionable ski resort.*

▶ express doubts about merit **question** *The ombudsman is not able to question the merits of any decision by the local council, but can investigate the way in which the decision has been taken.*

merit V

deserve or be worth something

- adv+V a lot **fully, well** *The orchestra well merited the encore it received for the three dances.*
- ▶ not much **hardly** *If the mountains had been just below 3,000ft rather than just above, they would hardly merit a mention.*

- V+n being looked at, discussed or mentioned **attention, consideration, discussion, examination, exploration, inclusion, investigation, a mention, study** *Four proposals have been received that merit serious consideration.*
- ▶ treatment or action **action, treatment** *He said that criminals fully merited the harsh treatment they received.*
- ▶ protection **protection** *Who is to decide which species of animal merit protection?*
- ▶ recognition or praise **award, name, place, praise, recognition, title** *She was a key figure, who merited a place in any list of major photographers.*

mess N

a dirty or untidy place or person; a difficult situation caused by people making mistakes

- adj+N very bad or unpleasant **appalling, awful, big, dreadful, horrible, huge, sorry, terrible, unholy** *Despite all that happened, some good has come out of the whole sorry mess.* ● *How can you find anything in this unholy mess?*

  People often use the expression *a fine mess* to describe a difficult situation: *What a fine mess the Borough Council has got itself into again!*

- ▶ complete **absolute, complete, real, right** INFORMAL, **total, utter** *I'd just got up and I looked a right mess.* ● *20 years of underfunding has left the system a total mess.*
- ▶ types of mess **gooey, soggy, sticky, tangled** *Kate's hair was a tangled mess.*

- v+N cause a mess **cause, create, leave, make** *It is the government that has created this whole mess.* ● *He was very tidy and made sure he left no mess at all.*

  You can also say leave something *in a mess*: *Try not to leave your room in such a mess.* ● *When he retired, we found that he had left the accounts in a mess.*

- ▶ deal with a mess **clean up, clear up, sort out** *Mum ordered them to clean up the mess.* ● *If the government doesn't sort out this mess, the electorate will turn to extreme parties.*
- ▶ be in or get into a mess **be in, get into** *They had been eating chocolate and were in a terrible mess.* ● *How did the department get into this mess?*
- ▶ look a mess **look** *I tried to tidy the kitchen, but it still looked a mess when they arrived.*

message N

1 a piece of information you send to someone when you cannot speak to them directly

- adj+N **brief, cryptic, important, secret, urgent** *There was a cryptic message left at the scene of the crime, which the police were unable to decipher.*
- n+N **answerphone, email, mail, phone, radio, SMS, telephone, text, voice, voicemail** *I had a voicemail message from my mother saying that she was arriving that evening.*

- v+N send a message **leave (sb), post, record, send (sb)** *He had left me a message on my voicemail asking me to call him immediately.* ● *You can send messages to his family and friends through his tribute website.*
- ▶ get a message **get, receive** *Callers phoning out of hours will receive a message asking them to phone back within normal working hours.*
- ▶ write a message **compose, write** *He wrote a wonderful little message for the children on the back of the postcard.*
- ▶ read or listen to a message **listen to, open, read, retrieve** *Simply open your message and you will notice two options side by side towards the bottom.* ● *To retrieve your voicemail messages, dial 2580.*
- ▶ pass a message to someone else **forward, give sb, pass on, relay, take** *I'm afraid John's not here. Can I give him a message?* ● *She's out of the office. Can I take a message?*
- ▶ see if anyone has left a message for you **check** *He had been too busy check the messages on his phone.*
- ▶ take a message from one place to another **carry, convey, transmit** *His job was to carry messages from the general to the troops.*

- N+v say something **ask (sb), confirm, contain, indicate, say, state, tell sb** *If you have no items in your basket, you will see a message stating the basket is empty.*
- ▶ arrive **arrive, come, pop up** *The messages pop up automatically when a user is logged in, making them harder to ignore.*
- ▶ get to someone **reach** *Unfortunately, the message didn't reach me in time.*

- N+of **condolence, congratulation, support, sympathy, thanks** *Thank you to everyone who sent messages of condolence and sympathy, which were gratefully received and appreciated.*

2 the main idea that you want people to remember

- adj+N strong **powerful, strong** *The demonstration sent a powerful message to the government that war is not wanted.*
- ▶ clear **clear, consistent, simple, stark, unambiguous** *The government wants to send out a clear message on the importance of school attendance.*
- ▶ not clear **conflicting, confusing, contradictory, mixed** *We are constantly bombarded with conflicting messages regarding image and diet.*
- ▶ main **basic, core, key, main** *The handbook draws together the key messages in the new legislation.*
- ▶ important **important, serious** *The presentation had a number of important messages.*
- ▶ hidden **hidden, subliminal** *There is a hidden message that lots of young people commit antisocial behaviour, when in fact it is only a tiny minority.*
- ▶ negative/positive/the wrong/the right **negative, positive, the right, the wrong** *A poor display gives potential customers negative messages about product quality and is worse than no display at all.* ● *We help you communicate the right message about job cuts, both inside and outside your organization.*

- v+N communicate a message **carry, communicate, convey, get across, give, present, put across, send (out)** *The story carries a message*

about the power of friendship and community. •
*They may be small-scale studies, but they convey a
clear message.*

▶ emphasize a message **bring home, highlight,
promote, ram home, reinforce** *The campaign aims
to reinforce the message that drinking and driving
is dangerous.*

▶ spread a message to a lot of people **disseminate,
preach, proclaim, spread** *We firmly believe that the
most effective way to spread the message about
animal cruelty is through the work of local activists.*

messy ADJ
complicated, difficult, and unpleasant to deal with

▶ ADJ+n **affair, business, compromise, divorce,
process, reality, situation** *A messy divorce had left
him with a rather low opinion of marriage.* • *This
novel is about the painful, messy reality of family
life.*

metaphor N
a way of referring to one thing as another, in order
to show how they are similar

▶ adj+N suitable **appropriate, apt** *The 'urban
jungle' is an apt metaphor for modern city
environments.*
· having a strong effect **potent, powerful** *The great
statues were toppled over and mutilated, providing
a powerful metaphor for the end of a 'golden age '.*
· types of metaphor **extended, mixed, poetic, visual**
*Extended metaphors are particularly useful. These
are metaphors developed through more than one
point of comparison.* • *What McKenna doesn't do is
explain that he's got an uphill struggle on his hands
(excuse the mixed metaphor).*
main **central** *The central metaphor of the book is
indebtedness.*
complicated **elaborate** *The author introduces
repetitive strain injury as an elaborate metaphor
for her character's sense of frustration.*

▶ v+N **create, develop, employ, provide, use** *His
extraordinary ability to use metaphors really
brought the subject alive for people.*

▶ N+v **describe, imply, represent, suggest** *The coin
metaphor suggests that both sides are necessary at
some level.*

method N
a way of doing something

▶ adj+N traditional or normal **common,
conventional, normal, standard, traditional, usual**
*Traditional methods of repair have to be used in
order to preserve the character of a building.*
new **innovative, new, novel** *At The Prince's Trust,
we are using innovative methods to reach and
support the hardest to help young people.*
good **acceptable, accurate, convenient, effective,
efficient, good, practical, proven, reliable, tried-
and-tested, useful** *Trailers are a proven method of
advertising a film's genre, stars and storyline to an
audience.*
main or favourite **preferred, principal** *Everyone
has his or her preferred method of making tea.*
different **alternative, different** *E-learning provides
an alternative method of learning.*

▶ easy **easy, simple** *The Internet offers a simple method
for the exchange of information during the lengthy
process of public consultation.*

▶ using the most modern ideas and equipment
advanced, modern, sophisticated *Very
sophisticated screening methods are used to
determine the size of the tumour.*

• n+N **collection, communication, construction,
cooking, farming, learning, manufacturing,
payment, production, research, selection, teaching,
training, treatment, working** *Use low fat cooking
methods such as grilling, barbequing, stir-frying, dry
roasting or poaching.* • *This page confirms your
address and asks you to choose your preferred
payment method.*

▶ v+N use a method **apply, employ, use, utilize** *They
use methods of assessing vision that are most
suitable for young children.*

▶ start to use a method for the first time **adopt,
choose, implement, introduce, pioneer** *Tens of
thousands of farmers have adopted the method in the
years since researchers introduced it to Cambodia in
2001.*

▶ discover a method **develop, devise, discover,
establish, find, identify, invent** *Scientists and
engineers have devised several methods to clean up
oil spills.*

▶ change a method **change, improve, revise** *Lessons
from this study can be applied to improve methods
for data analysis.*

meticulous ADJ
thorough and paying attention to detail

• ADJ+n **analysis, approach, attention, attention to
detail, care, detail, examination, planning,
preparation, record, research, study, work** *The book
examines all aspects of English grammar in
meticulous detail.* • *All school trips and visits require
meticulous planning and organization.*

• and/or **careful, detailed, methodical, painstaking,
thorough** *Only by meticulous, painstaking research
can we hope to establish the truth.*

migrant N
someone travelling to another place to work

• adj+N **economic, illegal, rural, skilled,
undocumented** *He believes that identity cards would
not deter terrorists, criminals, or illegal migrants.*

• N+n a group of migrants **community, population**
*The organization supports refugee and migrant
communities in the UK.*

▶ working **labour, labourer, worker** *Migrant labour
provides an important part of the village income.* •
*A sudden influx of migrant workers led to a revival
of extreme right-wing nationalism.*

mild ADJ
not serious or not severe

• adv+ADJ very **very** *Typically, the illness is very
mild and most patients do not need to consult their
doctor.*

▶ rather **fairly, quite, rather** *I'm lucky, my asthma is
quite mild.*

▶ usually **generally, usually** *Psoriasis is a long-term
condition, but in most people it is usually mild.*

▶ when compared to others **comparatively, relatively** *The seizures are brief, and the epilepsy is relatively mild.*

● ADJ+n illness or disability **attack, condition, disability, disease, illness, impairment, infection, injury, problem, virus** *Flu can vary from a very mild illness to a very severe one.* ● *Cognitive behavioural therapy can be useful in treating mild to moderate mental health problems.*

▶ particular illness or condition **asthma, depression, discomfort, fever, headache, pain, rash, stroke** *Paracetamol should be their first choice of drug for mild pain.*

▶ a form or case of an illness **case, dose, form, strain, version** *She suffered from a mild form of anemia characterized by a folic acid deficiency.*

▶ effects of an illness **effects, reaction, symptoms** *Most people in the UK who have dysentery only have mild symptoms.*

▶ feeling **annoyance, interest, irritation, panic, shock, surprise, upset** *There was mild panic when I couldn't find the passports.*

▶ punishment or criticism **criticism, punishment, rebuke** *Remember that even the mildest criticism can be very hurtful.*

milestone N

an event or achievement that marks a stage in a process

● adj+N important **big, critical, crucial, great, historic, huge, important, key, major, real, significant** *The next key milestone comes tomorrow, with completion of the eagerly waited Southwater Community Centre.*

▶ types of milestone **developmental, personal** *From ages four to five, parallel play and learning to share with others are developmental milestones.*

● v+N reach a milestone **achieve, hit, meet, pass, reach** *Fifty years old this year, the organization has reached a major milestone.*

▶ celebrate a milestone **celebrate, mark** *To mark the milestone in her career, colleagues presented her with a beautiful bouquet of flowers.*

▶ be a milestone **be, represent** *This award represents a milestone in the development of the division.*

● N+in **career, development, history, life, process** *Delmedigo's book can be regarded as a milestone in the history of Jewish thought.*

military ADJ

relating to armies or armed forces

● ADJ+n activity **action, activity, attack, campaign, conflict, coup, effort, exercise, intervention, invasion, mission, operation, presence, response, strike** *He took part in military campaigns against France and its allies in Hanover (1805–6).*

▶ group **force, organization, unit** *In 1747, he was commander in chief of all military forces in India and the Far East.*

▶ people **authorities, commander, leader, officer, official, personnel** *At the time, there were 22,000 U.S. military personnel in Afghanistan.*

▶ place where a military organization is based **base, installation, site** *He had taken photographs of Soviet military installations and airfields.*

▶ equipment and facilities **aircraft, cemetery, equipment, facility, hospital, training, uniform, vehicle** *About a quarter of the world's jet fuel is used by military aircraft.*

▶ power **capability, might, power, strength** *No nation has ever had as much military power as the United States.*

▶ service **service** *As soon as he was released from military service, he left England aboard a ship bound for Spain.*

▶ when a military force controls a place **government, occupation, regime, rule** *East Timor won its independence in 2002 after a long struggle against military occupation*

▶ a place that a military organization is trying to attack **target** *The insurgents have recently increased attacks on police and military targets in the area.*

mimic V

copy someone or work in the same way as something else

● adv+V **accurately, closely, effectively, exactly, perfectly** *This immune system is too complex to be accurately mimicked either in the laboratory or by computer simulation programmes.*

● V+n **action, behaviour, condition, effect, movement, process, sound, structure, style** *The drug appears to mimic the action of human oestrogen hormones.*

mind N

the part of you that thinks, knows etc; your intelligence and ability to understand things

● adj+N mind **human** *Both the human body and the human mind are constructed to need daily rest.*

▶ with a lot of ideas **active, creative, fertile** *The Mini was created by the fertile mind of Alec Issigonis.*

▶ clever **bright, brilliant, intelligent, keen, lively, quick, sharp** *Mr Howard's sharp, lawyerly mind would have been perfectly suited to these disputes.*

▶ wanting to know things **enquiring, inquisitive** *To be a good journalist, you need an enquiring mind.*

▶ full of thoughts **crowded, full** *His mind was full of schemes for keeping us out of mischief.*

▶ thinking in a logical way **analytical, logical, rational** *She had a cool, logical mind, and a quick, ready wit.*

▶ having bad or unpleasant thoughts **dirty, sick, troubled, twisted** *It becomes clear that his ingratiating good manners hid a deeply troubled mind.*

▶ not willing to accept new ideas **closed** *As a journalist, I learned early on that it was unwise to have a closed mind.*

▶ willing to accept new ideas **open** *You will enjoy the stay if you go with an open mind and not with any preconceived notions.*

▶ suspicious **suspicious** *She had a suspicious mind and was inclined not to believe him.*

▶ the part of the mind that you are aware of **conscious** *There is always dynamic interaction between the conscious mind and the subconscious mind.*

▶ the part of your mind that you are not aware of **subconscious, unconscious** *A dream is your unconscious mind processing your hopes and fears.*

- v+N come into your mind **come into, come to, cross, enter, go through** *A sudden thought crossed my mind.*
▶ fill your mind **fill, occupy** *Floods of painful memories filled my mind.*
▶ develop and improve your mind **broaden, challenge, develop, exercise, improve, stimulate, stretch, train** *Travel helps to improve your confidence and broaden your mind.*
▶ make your mind think about one thing **concentrate, direct, fix, focus** *Awareness of breathing is central to all forms of yoga and promotes calmness, helping to focus the mind and relieve stress and mental fatigue.*

> You can also use the expression **keep your mind on**: *It was difficult to keep my mind on my work with all that was going on around me.*

▶ stop your mind from having particular thoughts **clear, empty, free** *I know it sounds stupid but when I'm running it clears my mind.*
▶ make your mind feel more relaxed **calm, relax** *Meditation is a way to calm the mind.*
▶ use your mind **engage, use** *Using the subconscious mind is the fastest way to create calm.*
▶ confuse or surprise your mind **boggle** *How that will happen boggles my mind.*
▶ know what someone else has in their mind **read** *He had a seemingly uncanny ability to read minds.*
▶ lose **lose** *Often we are reluctant to talk about such fantasies, fearing that we are losing our mind.*

- N+v work **work** *These notes offer an unrivalled glimpse into how his mind worked.*
- start **turn to sth** *With that immediate matter resolved, Julian's mind turned again to escape.*
- start to think about other things that are not relevant **drift, wander** *Her mind wandered too, back to happier times.*
- have a lot of thoughts **buzz, race** *My mind raced for a few moments, trying to rationalise the situation.*
- feel confused or surprised **boggle, reel, spin** *My mind boggled at the implications of what he was saying. ● Her mind was reeling with the effort of keeping up with everything that had happened to her in the last fortnight.*

> You can also use the expression **mind-boggling** to say that something is hard to imagine; *Footballers now earn a mind-boggling amount of money.*

minefield N
situation with many possible problems or dangers

- adj+N possible **potential** *Customers face a potential minefield when trying to select a reputable supplier.*
- real **veritable** *The Internet is a veritable minefield of things that can invade your computer and affect your data.*
- in a particular area **ethical, legal, moral, political** *The speaker painted a picture of the legal minefields associated with GM crops.*

- v+N **avoid, enter, face, navigate, negotiate, prove** *Practical advice can be provided for negotiating the minefield of employment regulations. ● The practice of medicine on cruise ships can prove a legal*

minefield, with doctors being sued in countries that they never visited.

minimal ADJ
extremely small, or as small as possible

- ADJ+n amount or cost **amount, cost, level, number, use** *We can easily provide this service for you at minimal cost. ● We aim for minimal use of chemicals.*
▶ bad effect **damage, delay, disruption, disturbance, loss, risk** *The ship had been hit but had suffered minimal damage.*
▶ effect **change, effect, impact** *The design of the building will have a minimal impact on the environment.*
▶ work or effort **effort, input, intervention, involvement, maintenance, supervision, support, training, work** *Researchers are able to access information with minimal effort.*

minimize V
reduce something to the smallest amount or degree

- V+n amount or cost **amount, cost, need, number, time** *Businesses aim to maximize profits and minimize costs.*
▶ something bad **burden, damage, danger, delay, disruption, errors, harm, loss, noise, problem, stress, waste** *The works have been scheduled to take place during quiet periods, in order to minimize disruption for road users.*
▶ the possibility of something bad happening **chance, possibility, risk, threat** *Good personal hygiene minimizes the chances of spreading the disease.*
▶ effect **effect, impact** *Making payments over a longer period of time can minimize the effect on your budget.*

minimum ADJ
as small as necessary or possible

- ADJ+n amount **age, amount, level, number, period, time** *The minimum age for Junior Diving membership has been set at 14 years of age.*
▶ amount of money **charge, cost, payment, price, rate, value** *We apply a minimum charge of £150, however short the let.*
▶ measurement of something **distance, height, length, score, size, speed, temperature, weight, width** *Hutches should be a minimum size of 4 feet x 2 feet x 2 feet, with larger ones for bigger breeds.*
▶ something bad or unwanted **delay, disruption, disturbance, effort, fuss, loss, risk** *A good company should pay a genuine claim promptly and with minimum fuss.*
▶ standard **criteria, requirement, standard** *The minimum requirements are a year's experience within a legal environment and a sound administrational background.*

minimum N
the smallest amount or degree necessary or possible

- adj+N absolute **absolute, bare, basic, very** *The bare minimum needed is the computer itself, a monitor, and a keyboard.*
▶ legal **legal, statutory** *Our training is very rigorous*

and far exceeds the legal minimums adopted by many airlines.

▶ definite **guaranteed** *The size of the jackpot is determined by the number of people who participate in each draw but there is a guaranteed minimum of 1.27 million euros.*

▶ advised **recommended** *There is a recommended minimum of one toilet, one hot shower and one washbasin for every twelve persons catered for.*

● v+N **keep sth to, reduce sth to** *Costs are kept to a minimum.*

● N+of **delay, disruption, disturbance, fuss, hassle** INFORMAL, **inconvenience, interference** *The new system allows appointments to be changed with the minimum of fuss.*

minister N
an official in charge of a government department

● adj+N **chief, junior, senior** *The junior minister for Italy's civil protection has attacked the UN and other countries for failing to keep their promises.*

● n+N **cabinet, government** *The news sparked a national row and government ministers promised to examine the case.*

● v+N give someone the job of minister **appoint sb (as), elect sb (as)** *Hilbrand Nawijn was appointed minister for asylum and immigration.*

▶ get rid of a minister **dismiss (sb) as, sack** *He appointed and dismissed his ministers at his own will.*

▶ try to influence a minister **lobby, urge** *Campaigners are lobbying ministers to upgrade the road.*

minor ADJ
not very important in comparison with others

● adv+ADJ very **extremely, very** *All of the above are very minor problems, and solutions have already been found for most of them.*

▶ rather or compared with something else **comparatively, fairly, rather, relatively** *A large proportion of women in jail are there for comparatively minor offences.*

▶ apparently **apparently, seemingly** *A seemingly minor glitch can cause a computer to crash.*

● ADJ+n change **adjustment, alteration, amendment, change, correction, modification, repair, revision, tweak, variation** *They made only minor amendments to the text.*

▶ problem or fault **blip** INFORMAL, **bug, defect, drawback, error, fault, flaw, inconvenience, mistake, problem, setback** *For most of us, changing the clocks twice a year is little more than a minor inconvenience.*

▶ illness or injury, or when somebody is operated on **ailment, illness, injury, operation, surgery** *Pharmacists are a good source of advice about minor ailments.*

▶ complaint or criticism **complaint, gripe, irritation, quibble** *Still, these are minor quibbles with what is otherwise a very enjoyable film.*

▶ illegal activity **breach, crime, offence** *She said that most women were in prison for minor offences and should instead be rehabilitated within the community.*

▶ something that happens **accident, incident** *They managed to prevent a minor incident turning into a major blaze.*

▶ road **road** *The map is very detailed, with all paths, minor roads, campsites etc shown.*

▶ difference **difference, discrepancy** *Although there are some minor differences in the system, the principles are the same.*

minority N
a smaller, different group within a larger group

● adj+N large **significant, sizeable, substantial** *A sizeable minority of respondents, about 20 per cent, felt that people from other religions were treated better.*

▶ small **insignificant, small, tiny** *The party represents the interests of a tiny minority of the electorate.*

▶ badly or unfairly treated **disadvantaged, oppressed, persecuted, under-represented** *Diabetes is a particular threat to disadvantaged minorities in industrialized nations.*

▶ with advantages **elite, over-represented, privileged, wealthy** *This rotten system only benefits a privileged minority.*

▶ aggressive or complaining a lot **militant, vocal, vociferous** *The campaign appears to be led by a vociferous minority.*

▶ types of minority **ethnic, linguistic, racial, religious, sexual** *The University will especially welcome applications from women and ethnic minorities.*

● v+N be a minority **be, constitute, represent** *The problem of students with such problems varies from institution to institution. But even where they constitute a small minority, it is important that their needs are met.*

▶ treat a minority badly or unfairly **discriminate against, exclude, persecute**

● N+n group **background, community, culture, faction, group, nationality, party, population, sect** *Police met with representatives from the many minority groups that make up the community.*

▶ believed or held by a minority **faith, opinion, religion, viewpoint** *We want to overcome our differences without silencing minority viewpoints.*

▶ done, used etc by a minority **interest, language, sport** *Minority languages used within the EU include Croatian, Romani, Slovak, Romanian, Serbian and Slovene.*

▶ owning a minority of something **holding, shareholding, stake** *He will keep a minority stake in the company.*

minute N
a period of 60 seconds; a short period of time

● adj+N a few **a few, several** *Download the pack by clicking on the icon below – this may take a few minutes.*

▶ first or early **early, first, opening** *The first goal came in the opening minute of the match.*

▶ last **closing, dying, final, last** *The closing minutes of the game were unbearably tense.* ● *They came away with a disappointing 2–2 draw after missing penalty in the last minute.*

▶ spare **spare** *Have a look at our website when you've got a few spare minutes.*

You can also say *a few, etc minutes spare*: *Have you got a few minutes spare to hear about the new system?*

‣ v+N take a minute **last, take** *This test takes 15–20 minutes.* • *Could I have a word with you? It'll only take a minute.*

‣ spend a minute **spend, wait, waste** *We had to wait 30 minutes for the car to come and pick us up.*

‣ allow a minute **allow, spare** *Please allow a minute or so for this page to load.*

‣ N+v pass **elapse, fly by, pass, tick by** *Perhaps five minutes had elapsed before the man turned around.*

‣ remain **be left, remain** *The match was abandoned with 18 minutes remaining.*

minute ADJ
very small

‣ ADJ+n object or piece **droplet, particle, speck, trace** *Many marine species are now affected by minute toxic particles from plastic bags.*

‣ quantity **fraction, quantity** *This only represents a minute fraction of total education spending.*

‣ detail **detail** *He wanted to know about everything in minute detail.*

miracle N
an extraordinary or impossible event, especially one considered an act of God

‣ adj+N great **amazing, astonishing, mighty, stupendous, wondrous** *It was an astonishing miracle – I have never seen anything like it.*
small **minor, small** *In the last two years a minor miracle has taken place.*
performed by God **divine** *Some believe this to be a divine miracle.*
types of miracle **economic, medical** *The growth of China in recent years has been described as an economic miracle.*

‣ v+N perform a miracle **accomplish, perform, work** *The teachers were being asked to perform miracles with limited resources.*

Usage **Miracle** is usually plural in these combinations: *Successive governments have worked miracles in creating a modern, vibrant and successful economy.*

see or experience a miracle **witness** *Many people claim that they have witnessed a miracle either in their own life or another person's.*
want or expect a miracle **expect, hope for, pray for** *You can't expect miracles overnight.*
promise a miracle **promise** *We are not promising miracles; but there is a great deal that can be done.*

‣ N+v happen **happen, occur** *I do believe that miracles happen, but in this case I would ask people to use their common sense.*
be called **be hailed as** *The 'weeping' statue is being hailed as a miracle by some.*

‣ N+n solution **cure, diet, drug** *There is no magic pill or miracle diet for losing weight.*
person who can do miracles **worker** *He was not a miracle worker, but he was a great teacher.*

miraculous ADJ
extremely lucky and unexpected

‣ adv+ADJ apparently **allegedly, apparently, seemingly, supposedly** *Her family and friends rejoiced at this seemingly miraculous recovery.*

‣ truly **truly** *The survival of the gardens over so many centuries is truly miraculous.*

‣ almost **almost** *It will be a tremendous and almost miraculous achievement if they succeed.*

‣ ADJ+n escape or recovery **escape, recovery** *Villagers had a miraculous escape when a fighter jet crashed into the village just yards away from a loaded petrol tanker.*

‣ cure **cure, healing** *There are no miraculous cures for baldness.* • *Many people, from different Christian traditions, believe that miraculous healing continues to take place.*

‣ action or event **deed, feat, occurrence, transformation** *How did he accomplish this miraculous feat?*

miscalculation N
when a mistake is made

‣ adj+N big **disastrous, grave, gross, serious, tragic** *They made a grave miscalculation.*

‣ small **slight** *Even a slight miscalculation at this sensitive juncture could cause discord.*

‣ v+N make **make** *The alternative explanation is that someone made a simple miscalculation.*

miscarriage N
the process of giving birth to a baby before it has developed enough to live

‣ adj+N repeated **frequent, recurrent, repeated** *Twenty women with a history of recurrent miscarriage took part in the study.*

‣ with an unknown or accidental cause **spontaneous, unexplained** *Many spontaneous miscarriages are connected to potential birth defects.*

‣ early in pregnancy **early** *Mrs Peters has had two early miscarriages.*

‣ possible **threatened** *Herbs were used to treat specific conditions such as threatened miscarriage.*

‣ v+N have a miscarriage **experience, have, suffer** *She revealed that she had suffered five miscarriages.*

‣ cause a miscarriage **cause, induce** *These chromosomal abnormalities may be severe enough to cause a miscarriage.*

‣ prevent or avoid a miscarriage **avoid, prevent** *More frequent scanning is not going to prevent a miscarriage.*

‣ n+of+N **cause, history, likelihood, risk** *Women who smoke face an increased risk of miscarriage or stillbirth.*

misconception N
a wrong belief caused by not understanding something

‣ adj+N common **common, popular, prevalent, widespread** *It is a common misconception that an unsecured loan is less risky than a secured loan.*

‣ bad or unfortunate **damaging, gross, serious, unfortunate, worrying** *Many in the West harbour gross misconceptions regarding Islam.*

▶ basic **basic, fundamental** *There is a fundamental misconception about the art of Tracey Emin, Rachel Whiteread and their generation.*

● v+N have a misconception **harbour, have, hold, labour under** *There are many misconceptions held by teachers and parents about careers in the arts.* ● *Some boys labour under the misconception that carrying a knife will make them seem 'cool'.*

▶ correct or get rid of a misconception **allay, clarify, correct, dispel, overcome, redress, refute** *We are holding a series of meetings to dispel misconceptions surrounding our intentions.*

▶ take action against a misconception **address, challenge, combat, confront, counter, tackle** *The paper is focused on addressing public misconceptions about mental illness.*

▶ cause a misconception **give rise to, lead to, perpetuate, reinforce** *The lack of archaeological data has perpetuated misconceptions about this period.*

▶ be based on a misconception **be based on** *This theory is based on several misconceptions about the nature of modern society.*

● N+v **abound, arise, persist** *The misconception arose chiefly because they had been supplied with incomplete information.*

> You can use *surrounding*, *regarding* or *concerning* to say what a misconception is about: *The fears and misconceptions surrounding the disease mean that those with early symptoms are reluctant to come forward.*

misconduct N
bad or dishonest behaviour, especially in your job

● adj+N serious **criminal, grave, gross, serious** *Accusations of gross misconduct were levelled against the Finance Officer.*

▶ deliberate **deliberate, flagrant, wilful** *Security was so lax that it amounted to wilful misconduct.*

▶ types of misconduct **academic, professional, scientific, sexual** *University staff should see plagiarism as a significant form of academic misconduct.*

▶ suspected **alleged, suspected** *A confidential report about the minister's alleged sexual misconduct was leaked to the press.*

● v+N say that there is misconduct **accuse sb of, admit, allege, report, suspect** *Where there are grounds to suspect serious misconduct, the University reserves the right to record telephone calls.*

▶ commit misconduct **be guilty of, commit** *A lawyer could be accused of stealing client funds or otherwise committing professional misconduct.*

▶ deny misconduct **deny** *The Doctor, an official government adviser, denies professional misconduct.*

▶ investigate or prove misconduct **investigate, prove** *The Commissioners investigate misconduct and abuse.*

▶ when someone loses their job **dismiss sb for, sack sb for** *It is not appropriate for employers to dismiss an employee for alleged gross misconduct without a hearing taking place.*

miserable ADJ
extremely unhappy or uncomfortable

● adv+ADJ very **absolutely, downright, so, thoroughly, truly, utterly** *One quarter of the population believe life is unfair, and one in three feel downright miserable.*

▶ rather **fairly, pretty** INFORMAL, **rather** *It is always pretty miserable driving alone through the outskirts of London.*

● ADJ+n life or experience **childhood, existence, experience, fate, life, plight** *Peter, now a very old man, recalls his miserable childhood in Ireland.*

▶ conditions **conditions** *Animals suffer miserable conditions on factory farms.*

▶ state **condition, state** *When I left him he was in a miserable state.*

▶ person **creature, wretch** *We were all arrested, including those miserable wretches who had just been freed from decades of incarceration.*

▶ place **hovel, hut, slum** *Millions flee the poverty of rural life to the equally miserable city slums.*

▶ weather **afternoon, drizzle, weather** *It is an attractive place, even on a miserable afternoon.*

● v+ADJ **be, feel, look, seem, sound** *Nearly a million young people have felt so miserable that they have considered suicide.*

misery N
the state of being extremely unhappy or uncomfortable

● adj+N very great **abject, appalling, indescribable, squalid, unspeakable, untold, utter** *Taking this lifeline away from people with Alzheimer's will cause untold misery to patients and their families.*

▶ absolute **absolute, sheer** *Bullying can make life at work sheer misery.*

▶ hopeless **helpless, hopeless** *Men stood on the deck of the sinking ship in helpless misery.*

▶ of people **human** *The government promised a crackdown on traffickers who profit from human misery.*

● v+N cause misery **bring, cause, herald, inflict (on sb), spell** *These are the prolific offenders who inflict misery on the law-abiding majority.* ● *High fuel bills spell misery for the poor.*

▶ make misery worse **aggravate, compound, deepen, heap on sb, perpetuate, pile on sb, spread** *The Chancellor was accused of piling misery on bereaved families by increasing inheritance tax.*

▶ stop or reduce misery **alleviate, ease, end, relieve** *He had a desperate need to earn money to alleviate his family's economic misery.*

▶ suffer misery **endure, suffer** *Commuters will continue to suffer the misery of long traffic queues.*

misfortune N
bad luck, or something unpleasant that happens

● adj+N very bad **cruel, dire, dreadful, grave, great, terrible** *What dreadful misfortune had befallen him?*

▶ personal **personal** *We tend to assume that all personal misfortune must be someone's fault.*

● v+N suffer misfortune **endure, experience, have, suffer** *He suffered the misfortune of being declared bankrupt and losing his business.*

▶ bring misfortune **bring** *In some parts of the country, people with red hair were thought to bring misfortune.*

suffer a lot of misfortune **be dogged by, be plagued by** *The ship finally docked after a voyage that had been dogged by misfortune.*

N+v **befall sb/sth, happen, occur, overtake sb/sth, strike** *Misfortune struck, and the building was destroyed by fire.*

n+of+N **catalogue, run, series** *It seemed that there had been a run of misfortune in the village and a number of children had died.*

misgivings N
doubts about something

adj+N serious **considerable, deep, grave, profound, serious, severe, strong** *I have grave misgivings about the practical implications of these arguments.*

slight **slight** *I must admit to slight misgivings when I bought my ticket.*

at first **early, initial** *Despite initial misgivings, I have come to like the book a lot.*

about what is right or wrong **ethical** *Many researchers have ethical misgivings about doing applied research.*

v+N have misgivings **entertain, feel, harbour, have** *I have some misgivings about the plan to knock down the main building.*

> You can use **concerning** or **regarding** to say what misgivings are about: *There are many groups which have serious misgivings concerning commercial genetic testing.*

express misgivings **express, voice** *The Irish Farmers Association has voiced misgivings.*

overcome misgivings **allay, overcome** *If you overcome your misgivings and visit an auction, you will find yourself hooked.*

cause misgivings **arouse** *This new form of surveillance aroused misgivings in the public.*

misguided ADJ
based on wrong judgments or opinions

adv+ADJ in a very bad or unfortunate way **dangerously, sadly, terribly, tragically, woefully** *The idea that it is in their interest to continue fighting is woefully misguided.*

completely **completely, deeply, fundamentally, profoundly, totally, utterly** *It is a well-meaning thought, but utterly misguided.*

rather **a little, rather, somewhat** *There is a somewhat misguided obsession with celebrity in the art world.*

ADJ+n attempt **attempt** *Their misguided attempts to tell everyone how to live their lives have the opposite effect.*

belief **assumption, belief, idealism, notion** *He had the misguided belief that the band could not continue without him.*

impression **impression, perception** *There is a misguided perception among young people that cannabis is harmless.*

emotion **hope, loyalty** *People sometimes protect an incompetent colleague out of misguided loyalty.*

and/or **dangerous, ignorant, naive, wrong** *To suggest that all video games are 'evil' is ignorant and misguided.*

mishap N
a minor mistake or accident

adj+N small **minor, slight** *You need to cope with minor mishaps such as losing your mobile phone.*

> serious **major, serious, unfortunate** *One major mishap occurred when a videotape was accidentally wiped.*

> funny or embarrassing **amusing, comic, embarrassing, hilarious** *All this leads to an extremely entertaining comedy with hilarious mishaps and witty dialogue.*

> occasional **occasional** *Even the most experienced translator has an occasional mishap.*

> types of mishap **mechanical, medical, technical** *The charity offers help to the victims of medical mishaps.*

v+N prevent or avoid a mishap **avoid, prevent** *The article was entitled 'How to avoid holiday mishaps'.*

> have a mishap **have, suffer** *If a child does suffer a mishap during lessons or at playtime, prompt treatment is essential.*

N+v **befall sb, occur** *An unfortunate mishap befell one of the cast members.*

n+of+N **catalogue, series** *The first in a series of mishaps occurred when a train hit the buffers at Lime Street station.*

misinformation N
false or incorrect information

adj+N **deliberate, intentional** *The media had been fed deliberate misinformation.*

v+N spread misinformation **circulate, disseminate, feed sb, peddle, propagate, spread** *Having lost the arguments, our opponents are now reduced to peddling misinformation.*

> correct misinformation **correct, counter, counteract, dispel** *When invited to correct this misinformation at interview, he simply confirmed it.*

n+of+N **amount, piece** *The book manages to correct some pieces of misinformation concerning the history of the school.*

misinterpret V
understand or explain something wrongly

adv+V deliberately **deliberately, wilfully** *They have ignored or wilfully misinterpreted the evidence we have provided.*

> badly **completely, grossly, wildly** *The remarks I made on News 24 about this were grossly misinterpreted.*

> always or often **consistently, frequently, often** *Do you feel that you are consistently misinterpreted or misrepresented by journalists?*

> by many people **commonly, widely** *This was widely misinterpreted as forcing employees to work until their 70th birthday.*

> Usage **Misinterpret** is usually passive in these combinations.

> easily **easily** *Many of the instructions are misleading or easily misinterpreted.*

Usage **Misinterpret** is usually passive in these combinations.

- V+n word or statement **comment, instructions, meaning, message, phrase, remark, words** *He accused the foreign press of misinterpreting his remarks.*
▸ intentions **intentions, motives** *I could tell her everything without fear that she would misinterpret my motives.*
▸ signal **sign, signal** *I thought he wanted to kiss me, but I could have misinterpreted the signs.*
▸ facts **evidence, facts, statistics** *Anybody who thinks I have misinterpreted the facts can check them out.*

misjudge V
make a wrong judgment about a person or situation; make an incorrect calculation

- adv+V **badly, completely, fatally, grossly, horribly, seriously, sorely, totally, woefully** *The new minister appeared with his beautifully crafted speech, but fatally misjudged the mood of Parliament.*
- V+n speed or movement of something **bounce, distance, speed, timing** *The goalkeeper misjudged the bounce and the ball went over his head.*
▸ mood or situation **mood, situation** *He took too much notice of the press and completely misjudged the situation.*

misleading ADJ
intended or likely to make someone believe something incorrect or false

- adv+ADJ seriously or completely **completely, dangerously, downright, grossly, highly, profoundly, seriously, totally, wholly, wildly** *This statement is either grossly misleading or completely false.*
▸ deliberately **deliberately, intentionally, knowingly, wilfully** *The way in which he had filled out his form was deliberately misleading.*
▸ not deliberately **inadvertently, unintentionally** *Computer-generated displays can be unintentionally misleading.*
▸ clearly **blatantly, frankly, positively** *To publish the research in this form would be positively misleading.*
▸ rather **a little, rather, slightly, somewhat** *The title may be slightly misleading.*
▸ possibly **possibly, potentially** *He commented on the potentially misleading nature of the scores.*
- ADJ+n advertisement **advert, advertisement, advertising, propaganda** *The document lays down rules concerning misleading advertisements.*
▸ title **headline, title** *Despite the misleading headline, the article did go on to represent the research accurately.*
▸ statement or claim **assertion, claim, statement, wording** *Many of the studies are full of misleading statements unsupported by data.*
▸ impression **impression** *A biased sample can give a misleading impression of the scale of a problem.*

mismanagement N
the process of managing something badly

- adj+N very bad **appalling, disastrous, gross,** **serious** *Every shareholder lost money thanks to the gross mismanagement of the company.*
▸ possible **alleged** *Detectives are investigating the alleged mismanagement of a lottery competition at the club.*
▸ types of mismanagement **bureaucratic, economic, financial, governmental, ministerial** *This town has suffered over the years from bureaucratic mismanagement.*
- and/or **corruption, fraud, incompetence, inefficiency, misconduct, neglect, waste** *The Commission is satisfied that there has been no misconduct or mismanagement in the administration of the charity.*

miss V
1 not notice or understand something

- adv+V completely **completely, entirely, totally** *The article completely misses the fact that fresh research has been done since that time.*
▸ somehow **somehow** *All these years I've somehow missed what a fantastic drummer he is.*
▸ easily **easily** *These are details that are easily missed.*
- V+n **clue, joke, point** *I think you've missed my point.*

2 fail to take advantage of something; fail to do something in time

- adv+V not often **never, rarely** *The government never miss an opportunity to make political capital out of the company's problems.*
▸ unfortunately **unfortunately** *I unfortunately missed the closing date for entries.*
▸ not deliberately **accidentally, inadvertently** *What happens if you inadvertently miss a dose of your medication?*
- V+n miss an opportunity **chance, opportunity** *Your numbers are automatically entered every single week, so you never miss a chance to win.*
▸ when you do not do something that you have arranged **appointment, deadline** *It has a handy alarm that means I don't miss my deadlines!*

3 feel sad because someone is not with you

- adv+V **badly, dearly, deeply, desperately, greatly, really, sadly, sorely** *We will sorely miss him, as will his thousands of devoted fans around the world.*

mission N
1 an important piece of work for a government or large organization, or a military operation

- adj+N secret **covert, secret, top-secret, undercover** *Special Forces operatives risk their lives on undercover missions around the world.*
▸ difficult **dangerous, daring, perilous** *Kerensky had set out on a dangerous mission to bring loyal troops from outside the city.*
▸ types of mission **diplomatic, humanitarian, military, tactical** *He described the trip as a humanitarian mission aimed at setting up a blood bank in Baghdad.*
▸ with a particular purpose **bombing, fact-finding, outreach, peace-keeping, reconnaissance, rescue, spying, trade** *The Mayor is flying to the earthquake zone on a fact-finding mission.*

‣ v+N carry out a mission **conduct, execute, further, participate in, perform, pursue, undertake** *We will fund other costs where it helps us to further our charitable mission.*

‣ complete a mission **accomplish, achieve, complete, fulfil** *They rely on local people for the information they need to accomplish the mission.*

‣ stop a mission **abort** *A severe storm blew up and the mission was aborted.*

‣ be given a mission **be assigned, be charged with, be entrusted with, be given, be sent on** *Each field artillery unit is assigned a tactical mission.*

‣ go on a mission **begin, embark on, go on** *Together they embarked on a daring mission to save her.*

an important goal for a person or organization

‣ adj+N most important **core, main, primary** *The targets that we have set all aim towards our core mission: to build a safe, just and tolerant society.*
general **overall** *The overall mission of the Library Service is to bring knowledge and enjoyment to as many people as possible.*
publicly stated **stated** *Its stated mission is to promote and support science in Scotland.*

v+N achieve your mission **achieve, fulfil** *We will endeavour to fulfil our mission by inviting and welcoming artists into membership.*
have a mission **have** *IT Services have a mission to provide ICT solutions which enable and support the University's learning community.*
carry out your mission **pursue** *In pursuing this mission, we must work in close partnership with local healthcare teams.*

N+n **statement** *Our mission statement is 'to produce outstanding products that genuinely make a difference'.*

ıist N

mass of small drops of water in the air close to the ground

adj+N thick **dense, impenetrable, thick** *We set off for the moor, driving straight into dense mist.*
thin **hazy, thin, wispy** *We walked in bright sunshine, with a few strands of wispy mist.*
soft **gentle, soft** *The sun shone through the soft silvery mist that hung in patches over the sea.*
making things look mysterious **atmospheric, eerie, ghostly** *You can see for miles and eerie mists around Glastonbury Tor offer an atmospheric walk to the top.*
of a particular colour **grey, silvery, white** *The track is swathed in a grey mist.*
low **low-lying** *There is background of high hills, their peaks rising clear above low-lying mist.*
moving **rolling, swirling** *Troops landed on the beach in the swirling mist of a grey dawn.*
only present in some places **patchy** *The night will be cold and clear but patchy mist may develop by morning.*
seen at a particular time **autumn, autumnal, dawn, early, evening, morning, winter** *Once the early autumn mist had cleared, it was a beautiful late September day.*
in or from a particular place **moorland, mountain, sea** *A dense moorland mist had settled, reducing visibility to a few feet.*

‣ N+v surround or cover something **cling to, envelop, hang over, obscure, shroud, veil** *The day turned out dull and cold, with a mist shrouding the bare limestone edge.*

You can also say that something is ***shrouded in mist***: *Behind us rose the bulk of Elephant Island, shrouded in mist.*

‣ move **drift, rise, roll, swirl** *We stood on the cliffs and watched as the mist rolled in from the sea.*

‣ disappear **clear, disperse, lift** *By the time I got there, blue patches of sky were appearing and the mist had cleared.*

‣ come down **come down, descend, settle** *A thick mist soon descended, so we had to turn back.*

‣ be over somewhere **hang, lie** *The day dawned sunny, with a light mist hanging over the valleys.*

● v+into+N **disappear, vanish** *I tried to keep him in sight, but then he disappeared into the mist and I was alone.*

● n+of+N **bank, blanket, cloud, patch, veil** *We ran into a bank of sea mist that reduced the visibility to fifty metres.*

mistake N

1 something you do, say, write, or think that is not correct

● adj+N silly **careless, embarrassing, foolish, silly, sloppy, stupid** *The misnaming of the defendant in the claim form was a silly mistake by the claimant's solicitors.*

‣ serious **bad, serious** *There are often bad mistakes in job descriptions.*

‣ not serious **minor, slight** *There are one or two minor mistakes and misspellings in the subtitles, but nothing serious.*

‣ happening occasionally **occasional, odd** *He makes the odd mistake simply because he's so keen, but overall he's coming on great.*

‣ common or basic **classic, common, elementary** *So many people make one or more of these common mistakes on their CV.*

‣ not deliberate **genuine, honest, innocent, unintentional** *Many discounts are issued incorrectly because of genuine mistakes made by claimants.*

‣ deliberate **deliberate** *This reminds me of adverts for proofreaders that are filled with deliberate mistakes.*

‣ obvious **glaring** *I have seen glaring mistakes in expensive magazine ads.*

‣ types of mistake **copying, factual, grammar, grammatical, printing, punctuation, spelling, translation** *I apologise for any factual or grammatical mistakes.*

● v+N make a mistake **make** *They made a mistake in the original certificate of registration.*

‣ notice a mistake **discover, find, notice, realize, spot** *If you spot a mistake, please send us the details and we will pass it on to the people responsible for maintaining the data.*

‣ correct or get rid of mistakes **correct, eliminate, fix, rectify, remedy, undo** *The present edition improves on its predecessors by correcting a few minor mistakes.* ● *Before submitting your work, use the checklist to eliminate common mistakes.*

‣ contain a mistake **contain** *The list clearly still contains mistakes.*

▶ admit or apologize for a mistake **acknowledge, admit** *As regular readers will know, I do like to admit my mistakes and rectify them before they do too much damage.*

▶ forgive a mistake **excuse, forgive** *Please forgive any mistakes, broken links, and the like.*

● N+v **arise, creep in, happen, occur** *The mistake crept in because the Korean numbering system is different to the European one.*

2 something you wish you had not done, because it causes a lot of problems

● adj+N serious **awful, bad, big, disastrous, dreadful, fatal, ghastly, grave, grievous, horrible, huge, serious, terrible, tragic** *The opinion became firmly established that the last war was a grave mistake.*

▶ costing a lot of money **costly, expensive** *Get advice from the professionals and avoid costly mistakes.*

▶ types of mistake **defensive, fashion, tactical** *It was, as many US officials now concede, a tactical mistake.*

● v+N make a mistake **commit, make** *They made the mistake of assuming that all users will have a broadband Internet connection.*

▶ avoid mistakes **avoid, prevent** *In order to prevent any future mistakes, we need to have a clear agreement.*

▶ make the same mistake again **repeat** *They risk repeating the mistakes of the past by building large housing estates.*

▶ realize or regret a mistake **acknowledge, admit, regret** *As I look back on my life, I realize that I don't regret a single life-changing mistake.*

▶ forgive a mistake **excuse, forgive** *As he was very young at the time, perhaps he can be excused this mistake.*

mistaken ADJ
wrong, not correct

● adv+ADJ **fundamentally, gravely, grossly, much, profoundly, sadly, seriously, very much** *They would be profoundly mistaken if they thought so.* ● *Unless I'm very much mistaken, this will prove to be a bestseller.*

● ADJ+n belief **assumption, belief, conclusion, explanation, idea, impression, interpretation, notion, perception, view** *Normandy villages were destroyed in the mistaken belief that they housed the German army.*

▶ identity **identification, identity** *He felt that it was a case of mistaken identity, but could not find the real culprit.*

● v+ADJ **be, prove** *This idea later proved seriously mistaken.*

misunderstanding N
a failure to understand someone or something correctly; a small argument

● adj+N serious **complete, fundamental, gross, profound, serious, terrible** *A critic claimed the poet's popularity was based on a complete misunderstanding of what his poems are about.* ● *The reason is the persistent and gross misunderstanding of Darwinian evolution.*

▶ not very serious **slight** *There had been a slight misunderstanding with Smith over funding arrangements.*

● common **common, widespread** *There continues to be a widespread misunderstanding that the term 'common law wife/husband' has legal significance.*

▶ unfortunate **tragic, unfortunate** *Say it now. That may save a tragic misunderstanding later on.*

▶ unnecessary or silly **ridiculous, unnecessary** *Hasty messages sent without due consideration can cause unnecessary misunderstandings.*

▶ amusing **comic, comical, hilarious** *That small lie turns into a bigger one, and soon Paul's life is a series of comical misunderstandings.*

▶ deliberate **intentional, wilful** *This is a wilful misunderstanding of gambling as a harmless hobby rather than an addiction.*

▶ genuine **genuine** *Often the issue at the heart of the argument turns out to be a genuine misunderstanding.*

▶ on both sides **mutual** *I write about the Irish/British relationship and all its mutual attractions and mutual misunderstandings.*

▶ between different cultures **cross-cultural, cultural, inter-cultural** *Cultural misunderstandings can lead to the loss of business deals.*

● v+N be based on a misunderstanding **arise from, be based on, result from, stem from** *In my view, the concerns are based on a misunderstanding about the nature of our proposal.*

▶ resolve or correct a misunderstanding **clarify, clear up, correct, dispel, eliminate, overcome, resolve** *The report dispels the common misunderstanding that chronic diseases mainly affect people in wealthy countries.*

▶ avoid a misunderstanding **avoid, minimize, prevent** *In future, we are asking people to confirm in writing, to avoid any misunderstandings.*

▶ cause misunderstandings **cause, lead to** *Cultural differences in behaviour can cause misunderstandings.*

▶ reveal a misunderstanding **betray** *The language used betrays a misunderstanding of geology and geological processes.*

● N+v **arise, lead to sth, occur** *Sometimes difficulties and misunderstandings arise between parents or guardians and teachers.* ● *A misunderstanding has led to a misinterpretation of the facts.*

mix V

1 combine activities, ideas, styles etc

● adv+V cleverly **cleverly, deftly, effortlessly, expertly, skilfully** *The film deftly mixes fact and fiction.*

▶ without showing that things are mixed **seamlessly** *DJs like to mix one track into another seamlessly.*

▶ randomly **randomly** *His surrealist poetry creates poems by randomly mixing together newsfeeds from online news sources.*

▶ freely **freely, liberally** *Media coverage of popular science is often liberally mixed with myth.*

2 meet people socially and talk to them

● adv+V socially **informally, socially** *Their visit also gave them an important opportunity to mix informally with their fellow candidates.*

▶ freely **freely** *The College is one of Cambridge's*

friendliest, with undergraduates, graduates and Fellows mixing freely.

mix N

a particular combination of objects, qualities, substances, or a combination of different types of people

● adj+N right or well balanced **appropriate, balanced, even, good, healthy, the optimum, perfect, the right** *The school has a balanced socio-economic mix.* ● *He plays the role with just the right mix of charm and malice.*
▸ exciting **exciting, exhilarating, heady, intoxicating, lively, potent, stimulating, vibrant** *The coast of Tanzania offers a heady mix of east African and Arabian cultures.*
▸ dangerous **explosive, volatile** *The website contains a volatile mix of apocalyptic religious and conspiracy theories.*
▸ varied **broad, cosmopolitan, diverse, eclectic, rich, varied** *Universities offer a wider range of courses than ever before, suiting a much broader mix of abilities.* ● *Daniel has done well to assemble such an eclectic mix of works by local artists.*
▸ unusual or interesting **bewildering, bizarre, complex, curious, fascinating, interesting, intriguing, odd, strange, unique, unusual, weird** *The magazine is a unique mix of news and gossip.*
▸ usual **usual** *Before that there is the usual mix of bureaucracy and builders to deal with.*
▸ pleasing **clever, delicious, delightful, nice, pleasing, refreshing, wonderful** *His new book is a clever mix of reporting and theory.*
▸ types of mix **cultural, ethnic, racial** *The ethnic mix within the Company is extremely diverse.*

● v+N contain or consist of a mix **boast, combine, comprise, consist of, contain, feature, incorporate, offer, provide** *The event was a great success, combining the right mix of new and existing customers.* ● *This day workshop will comprise a mix of presentations and case studies.*
▸ create a mix **bring together, create** *Employ people of all ages to create a mix of skills and experience that benefit your business.*
▸ attract a mix **attract** *We hope to attract a good mix of creative people and technologists.*
▸ show that there is a mix **reflect** *Guatemala's culture reflects the fascinating mix of influences on the country's turbulent history.*

mixed ADJ

partly good and partly bad

● adv+ADJ very **decidedly, distinctly, very** *The album was greeted with decidedly mixed reviews upon its original release.*
▸ rather **fairly, pretty** INFORMAL**, rather, somewhat** *The figures suggest that the economic forecast is somewhat mixed.*
▸ strangely **curiously, strangely** *It describes the strangely mixed emotions of so many middle-aged parents whose children are leaving home.*
▸ not surprisingly **predictably** *On the topic of the Millennium Centre, opinions are predictably mixed.*

● ADJ+n something that is present or happens **blessing** *Knowledge can be a mixed blessing – sometimes it's better not to know.*
▸ success **fortunes** *The year has been one of mixed fortunes for the netball team.*
▸ emotions **emotions, feelings** *It was with mixed feelings that I learned I was to meet him again.*
▸ reaction **reaction, reception** *The proposal met with a mixed reception from residents.*

mixture N

a combination of different things, people, qualities etc

● adj+N varied **complex, eclectic, rich** *The architecture of the centre is an eclectic mixture of contemporary and traditional styles.*
▸ good or balanced **balanced, delightful, judicious** *The album is a perfectly balanced mixture of slow, tender songs, and upbeat rock songs.*
▸ strange **bizarre, curious, odd, strange, uneasy** *His work is a curious mixture of the old and new methods of inquiry.*
▸ interesting **fascinating, intriguing** *The book is an intriguing mixture of theory, practice, and case history.*
▸ powerful **heady, potent** *The show contains a potent mixture of dreams and sacrifices, family rebellion and romance.*
▸ dangerous **combustible, explosive, incendiary, volatile** *They had chosen the most combustible mixture of personalities they could possibly find.*

● v+N **be, comprise, consist of, contain, include, provide** *The newsletter provides a mixture of local news plus guides to entertainment and shopping in the area.*

mob N

a crowd that is dangerous or difficult to control

● adj+N angry or excited **angry, enraged, excited, frenzied, furious, hostile, infuriated** *The building was torn down by an angry mob.*
▸ violent **armed, bloodthirsty, violent** *Dickens wrote A Tale of Two Cities from the point of view of the aristocrat as victim of the bloodthirsty mob.*
▸ badly behaved **drunken, rioting, riotous, rowdy, unruly** *The military were called in to help clear the neighbourhood of the unruly mob.*
▸ making a noise **baying, braying, howling, jeering, noisy** *She was almost dragged out of her car by the baying mob.*
▸ hungry **hungry** *With bread prices at record levels, hungry mobs attacked the gates of Paris.*
▸ stupid **ignorant** *An ignorant mob slaughtered most of a family because they were 'witches'.*

● n+N wanting to kill or punish someone **lynch, vigilante** *Feelings were running high and she feared her son might become the victim of a lynch mob.*

● v+N encourage or excite a mob **incite, rouse** *He accused the newspaper of trying to incite vigilante mobs with sensationalist stories.*
▸ calm or break up a mob **calm, disperse, quell** *Troops were called in to quell a mob attacking a meeting at the Courthouse.*

● N+v attack someone or something **assail, assault, attack, besiege, chase, storm** *The police station was besieged by a mob and its windows smashed.*
▸ kill someone **lynch, murder** *In 1736 an Edinburgh*

mob lynched Captain Porteous, the commander of the Town Guard.

▶ damage or steal property **loot, plunder, ransack, smash** A mob had ransacked the Colonial Building.

▶ throw things **pelt, stone** A 50-strong mob pelted police with bottles and broken glass.

▶ come together **gather** A mob gathered outside the prison.

▶ break up or go away **disperse** He was asked to remain behind for his own safety, until the mob dispersed.

● N+n **justice, mentality, rule, violence** Only hate-filled racists want to see mob rule, lynchings and persecutions.

mobility N

1 the ability to move your body or to travel from one place to another

● adj+N restricted **decreased, impaired, limited, restricted** The whole of the Conference Centre is easily accessible for people with impaired mobility.

▶ getting worse **declining, decreasing, deteriorating** Advancing years and declining mobility obliged him to sell the boat.

▶ improved **increased** The benefits of massage include increased mobility in the neck and shoulders.

● v+N reduce mobility **affect, compromise, constrain, hinder, impede, inhibit, limit, reduce, restrict** She has leg and hip problems that have affected her mobility. ● Corded phones restrict your mobility while you talk.

▶ increase mobility **aid, enhance, facilitate, improve, increase** This session comprises 30 minutes of gentle exercises to increase mobility in muscles and joints.

▶ get back, give back, or keep mobility **maintain, regain, restore** Despite moments of great pain and despair, he worked hard to regain full mobility.

2 a tendency to move between places, jobs, social groups etc

● adj+N to a higher or lower social class **downward, upward** The number of state-educated entrants to our top universities has risen, a potent symbol of upward mobility.

▶ types of mobility **geographic, geographical, occupational, social** Traditionally, western Europe has had a very low rate of geographic mobility.

● n+N **job, labour, population, staff, student** The 'Erasmus' scheme encourages greater student mobility between participating universities.

● v+N increase or encourage mobility **aid, ease, encourage, facilitate, promote** The scheme also aids staff mobility because employees can move to other participating employers and stay in the same pension scheme.

▶ limit or discourage mobility **impede, limit, restrict** The housing market is making inequality wider and further impeding social mobility.

mobilize V

to bring together something such as a large group of people or money and support, in order to achieve something

● adv+V quickly **immediately, quickly, rapidly** He

quickly mobilized the public to collect money and materials.

▶ successfully **effectively, successfully** The union has successfully mobilized **against** the government.

● V+n people to fight **army, forces, masses, troops** Germany invaded the Soviet Union on the very same day, mobilizing the largest army (3,500,000 men) ever known.

▶ supporters **allies, electorate, voters** He used the Internet to mobilize voters.

▶ support or resources **public opinion, resources, votes** This can be used to predict high-risk years for malaria with sufficient time to mobilize resources to reduce the impact of epidemics.

▶ opposition **opposition, protest** The focus of the campaign is to mobilize local opposition to the development.

mock V

laugh at someone or something and make them look stupid

● adv+V in an unkind way **cruelly, mercilessly** Everybody else in the house mercilessly mocked me.

▶ in a kind way **affectionately, gently, lightly** They gently mock people for being too young, too posh, or too Australian.

▶ openly **openly** People openly mocked the singer's voice as shrill, piercing and annoying.

● and/or **belittle, deride, despise, insult, jeer, persecute, ridicule, scorn, sneer at, tease** Are you being mocked or ridiculed at school?

mode N

a particular way of doing something or of operating something

● adj+N usual **dominant, main, normal, standard, traditional, usual** Verbal speech remains our usual mode of communication.

▶ only **only, sole** The car does not need to be your sole mode of transport.

▶ best **best, preferred** Our preferred mode of communication is email.

▶ different **alternative, different, new, other, various** You will experience different modes of behaviour when you travel abroad.

● v+N use a particular mode **activate, choose, operate in, run in, select, switch to, unlock** The device can operate in several different modes. ● Next, select an appropriate screen mode for your program.

▶ use one mode and then another **switch between, toggle between** You can toggle between modes with the control lever.

● N+of transport **transport, transportation, travel** Cycling is a sustainable mode of transport and an effective means of exercise.

▶ communication **communication, expression, interaction** Images, rather than words, have become the dominant mode of communication.

model N

a way of behaving or doing something, especially one which other people copy

● adj+N simple or usual **basic, common, conventional, dominant, simple, standard,**

traditional *We follow the traditional comprehensive model of secondary schooling.*

▸ good **excellent, good, positive, successful** *It is particularly important that the staff work well as a team and provide a good model.*

▸ different **alternative, different, innovative, new** *In this section we consider an alternative trading model.*

▸ relating to society, business, or the economy **business, economic, financial, management, social** *The European economic model itself is now under criticism.*

▸ v+N create a model **build, create, design, develop, introduce, produce, provide** *The company provides a positive model for businesses in the region.*

▸ use a model **adopt, apply, follow, use** *The model that we are currently using is not suited to children with special needs.*

▸ fit a model **conform to, fit** *In your research, do not force language data to fit your model.*

▸ N+of **behaviour, best practice, excellence, good practice** *The organization is a model of best practice.*

moderate ADJ
not very great or very small; not extreme

▸ adv+ADJ when compared with others **comparatively, relatively** *Reactions to the announcement were relatively moderate.*

▸ very **very** *She congratulated him on his very moderate speech.*

▸ relating to politics **politically** *I would vote for any politically moderate party at the moment.*

▸ rather **fairly, quite** *The path can be muddy, even after quite moderate amounts of rainfall.*

▸ surprisingly **surprisingly** *Toronto has a surprisingly moderate climate.*

▸ ADJ+n number, degree, or size **amount, degree, level, number, size** *Eat only moderate amounts of dairy products.*

▸ speed **pace, speed** *The tour pace is moderate with generally easy walking.*

▸ increase or growth **growth, increase** *In horses, a moderate increase in body temperature is not a disadvantage.*

▸ money paid, earned, or charged **charge, cost, fee, income, price, rent, tax** *They have a good selection of wines at moderate prices.*

▸ eating food or drinking alcohol **consumption, drinking, intake** *Most people suffer no ill effects from the moderate consumption of alcohol.*

▸ weather **breeze, climate, rain, rainfall, temperature, visibility** *Areas of yellow on the map indicate moderate rainfall.*

▸ exercise **activity, exercise** *Adults should take half an hour of moderate exercise five times a week.*

modest ADJ
fairly small, unimportant, or inexpensive

▸ adv+ADJ when compared with others **comparatively, relatively** *Many of our managers earn a relatively modest salary.*

▸ very **extremely, remarkably, very** *The director's office is remarkably modest.*

▸ rather **fairly, pretty INFORMAL, quite, rather** *From pretty modest beginnings, he's gone on to work with some of the most respected names in the business.*

▸ in a way that you do not expect **surprisingly** *These wines are available for surprisingly modest prices.*

● ADJ+n money to pay **amount, charge, cost, fee, outlay, premium, price, sum** *There is a modest entrance fee to the centre.*

▸ amount of money someone has or earns **budget, grant, income, means, profit, salary, savings** *They had a very modest budget for the film.*

▸ amount **amount, number** *Only a modest amount of coal is still produced.*

▸ increase or improvement **gain, growth, improvement, increase, rise** *There has been a modest increase in revenue from membership fees.*

▸ size or rate of something **scale, size** *Expansion of the factory took place on a modest scale.*

▸ success **success** *The new service met with modest success.*

▸ change **change** *Even this modest change in the law has had some unexpected consequences.*

▸ effect **benefit, effect, impact** *Some people take Vitamin E, which may have a modest effect on the progression of the illness.*

2 not liking to talk about your achievements

● adv+ADJ typically **characteristically, typically** *She was characteristically modest about her achievements.*

▸ too **overly, too, unduly** *Don't be unduly assertive, but don't be unduly modest, either.*

● and/or **humble, self-effacing, shy, unassuming** *Modest unassuming folk rarely get the success they deserve.*

modesty N
a tendency not to talk about your achievements

● adj+N greater than is necessary **excessive, extreme, undue** *Excessive modesty has no place in a job interview.*

▸ false **false, mock** *This is no time for false modesty: you need to be honest about what you can do.*

▸ typical of someone's character **characteristic, innate, natural, typical** *With characteristic modesty, Brian did not mention the award at all.*

modification N
a change to something

● adj+N great **drastic, extensive, major, radical, significant, substantial** *The building must undergo extensive modification before it can be used.*

▸ small **minimal, minor, simple, slight, small** *Minor modifications can be made to accommodate changes in temperature.*

▸ necessary or important **important, necessary** *Any necessary modifications to play equipment must be carried out before the park opens.*

▸ more **further, subsequent** *The building was erected in the 13th Century, with subsequent modifications in the 15th Century.*

▸ to the genes of something **gene, genetic** *Genetic modification of plants allows much greater control over the features of any crop.*

● v+N make modification **carry out, implement, make, perform, undertake** *Some further bodywork modifications were carried out in the workshop.*

▸ need modification **entail, involve, need, require**

The advantage of this kind of building was that it did not require major modification.
▶ receive modification **receive, undergo** *The ship is currently undergoing modifications in Poland.*
▶ include modification **include, incorporate, introduce** *The second edition includes several minor modifications.*

modify V
change something

● adv+V to a great extent **considerably, drastically, extensively, greatly, heavily, profoundly, radically, substantially** *The church was extensively modified between 1300 and 1310.*
▶ to a small extent **slightly, somewhat, subtly** *The pictures above have been slightly modified for demonstration purposes.*
▶ according to particular needs **accordingly, appropriately, specially, suitably** *The software has been suitably modified for use in a classroom context.*
▶ in a scientific way **chemically, genetically** *About one third of all the corn has been genetically modified.*

> **Usage** *Modify* is usually passive in all of the *adv+V* combinations shown above: *If your car has been heavily modified, you should seek a specialist.* ● *It is important to keep up with changes in the law, so that plans can be modified accordingly.*

module N
a unit of a course of study

● adj+N that you must study **compulsory, core, mandatory, obligatory, required** *In your first year, you follow compulsory modules in your specialist language.*
▶ that you can choose to study **elective, optional** *Many of these optional modules will be available by distance learning.*
▶ taken during a particular period **introductory, first-year, second-year etc** *I failed one of my final-year modules.*
▶ gaining a particular number of points or credit **double, single, 10-credit, 20-credit etc** *Students taking our MA courses must complete four double modules over two years.* ● *Each 15-credit core module is taught over a period of five weeks in twenty hours of lectures.*
▶ taken after/before completing a degree **postgraduate, undergraduate** *I teach three undergraduate modules at the University of Cardiff.*
▶ separate **individual, self-contained, separate, single, stand-alone** *To attend an individual module, the student must be registered for it.* ● *It is possible to apply for single modules.*
▶ available on the Internet **online** *Online learning modules are free to anyone visiting the site.*
▶ involving more than one subject **interdisciplinary** *The module is interdisciplinary, taught by faculty members from the schools of English and History.*

● v+N teach a module **deliver, offer, teach** *The module is delivered through lectures, seminars and presentations.*
▶ study a module **complete, do, study, undertake, work through** *Computing and business awareness modules are studied in the first year.*

▶ choose a module **choose, opt for, select, take** *Students can choose a module on French cinema.*
▶ decide whether someone has passed a module **assess** *The module is assessed through a coursework essay and an examination.*
▶ pass/fail a module **fail, pass** *What happens if I fail one module?*

● N+v **be composed of sth, be divided into sth, be split into sth, comprise sth, consist of sth** *The programme consists of four modules and five compulsory weekend sessions.*

moisture N
a small amount of water or other liquid in or on something

● adj+N too much **excess, excessive** *Dehumidifiers work by removing excess moisture from the air.*
▶ that remains somewhere **residual, trapped** *Trapped moisture on the floor covering is a breeding ground for micro-organisms.*
▶ in the air **ambient, atmospheric** *Many of these plants have aerial roots to absorb atmospheric moisture.*

● v+N take moisture out of something **absorb, draw, extract, pull, remove, suck** *A sheet of kitchen paper will help to absorb any moisture.*
▶ hold moisture **conserve, lock in, retain, seal in, trap** *Trees are important as they conserve moisture and protect the landscape.*
▶ stop moisture entering something **displace, repel, resist** *The material repels moisture, maintaining its effectiveness in outdoor conditions.*

● N+v turn into steam **evaporate** *Continue to fry the mushrooms until all the moisture has evaporated.*
▶ turn back into water **condense** *The air cools, and the moisture condenses.*

● N+n amount of moisture in something **content** *The increased moisture content leaves the skin soft and supple.*
▶ small drops **droplets, vapour** *The wool fibres pull the moisture vapour away from the skin.*

moment N
a point in time or a short or important period of time

● adj+N important **critical, crucial, decisive, defining, important, key, pivotal** *The computer crashed at a critical moment.*
▶ very good or enjoyable **glorious, great, magic, magical, memorable, special, wonderful** *Describe special moment in your life.*
▶ giving you a particular feeling **embarrassing, funny, poignant, proud** *What was the most embarrassing moment in your career?*
▶ when you are not doing anything else **odd, spare** *She wrote the story at odd moments when the children were out of the house.* ● *I worked on it every spare moment.*
▶ suitable **good, opportune, perfect, right** *The offer came at an opportune moment in my career.*
▶ exact **exact, particular, precise, very** *They are playing live in Glasgow at this very moment.*
▶ lasting a short time or not happening frequently **brief, fleeting, odd** *For a fleeting moment, he*

believed her. • *There was the odd moment of brilliance in what was otherwise quite a dull movie.*

• v+N enjoy a moment **cherish, enjoy, revel in, savour** *'Aah,' sighed Sarah, savouring the moment.*

▸ act quickly to take advantage of a moment **capture, seize** *A good photographer can capture these magical moments of nature.*

▸ remember a moment **recall, reflect on, relive, remember, return to** *Do you recall any moments of rebellion in your youth?*

▸ wait for a moment **hang on (for), hesitate (for), hold on (for), pause (for), wait (for)** *Ellie cleared her throat and paused a moment.*

▸ choose a moment to do something **choose, pick** *My mother always picks the worst moments to call me.*

▸ wait for a moment with fear **dread** *I dreaded the moment when she would find out what had been going on.*

▸ N+v happen **arrive, come, occur** *Finally, the moment came and we were off.*

▸ stop happening **pass** *Fortunately, those difficult moments soon pass.*

▸ N+of happiness **glory, joy, magic, triumph** *I was in the changing room, enjoying a brief moment of triumph.*

▸ great skill or intelligence **brilliance, genius** *The performance showed several real moments of brilliance.*

▸ silence **calm, silence, stillness** *After a moment of silence, she shyly spoke.*

▸ when you are not thinking clearly **madness, panic** *In a moment of madness, I agreed to go with her on the trip.*

▸ when you find out the truth **clarity, revelation, truth** *The moment of truth has arrived.*

> If you do something *on the spur of the moment*, you do it suddenly, without taking the time to plan it: *I decided on the spur of the moment to invite him.* If you do something *in the heat of the moment*, you do it at a time when you are too excited or angry to think carefully: *I said things I didn't mean in the heat of the moment.*

momentary ADJ
lasting for a very short time

▸ ADJ+n period when nothing happens **hesitation, hush, lull, pause, respite** *There were several gunshots, with a momentary pause between each.*

▸ when you fail to do something correctly **aberration, lapse** *The driver of the car had a momentary lapse of concentration and ran into the back of the bike.*

▸ excited or nervous state **flicker, flutter, frisson, pang, panic, shudder, thrill** *Not even a momentary flutter of interest stirred her face.*

▸ when you see something for a very short time **glimpse** *I only managed to get a momentary glimpse of the photo before she snatched it away from me.*

momentum N
progress or development that is becoming faster or stronger [always singular]

• adj+N strong **considerable, great, high, real, strong** *We enter the new year with considerable momentum and exciting new products.*

▸ becoming stronger **gathering, growing, increasing** *These profits reflected growing momentum in business markets.*

▸ that cannot be stopped **inexorable, irresistible, irreversible, unstoppable** *Over the past few years, this concept has developed an irresistible momentum.*

▸ happening again with more energy **fresh, new** *A new momentum has been established in our business.*

• v+N create momentum **build (up), create, generate** *We need to build some momentum before the semi-final.* • *The fear is that the momentum which we have built up over the past three years will be lost.*

▸ gain momentum **acquire, develop, gain, gather** *In 1997, the first wave of Internet fever was starting to gather momentum.*

▸ keep momentum at the same level **conserve, keep going, keep up, maintain, sustain** *He could not keep the momentum going, and eventually finished third.*

▸ use momentum **build on, capitalize on** *Hopes that manufacturing companies could build on the momentum established at the turn of the year have been dashed.*

▸ lose momentum **lose** *The Government cannot afford to lose momentum at this stage.*

• N+v **build (up), continue, gather, grow** *Then, just as momentum was gathering, the group split.*

• N+for **action, change, improvement, reform** *I am confident that the momentum for change can be maintained.*

monarchy N
a form of government in which a king or queen rules the country; the royal family of a country

• adj+N **absolute, constitutional, hereditary, parliamentary** *Absolute monarchy in France was established during the 17th century.* • *Today, Thailand is a constitutional monarchy comprising 76 provinces.*

• v+N force a monarchy out of power **abolish, depose, destroy, end, overthrow, reject, remove, topple** *The monarchy was abolished in 1889, and a republic was established.*

▸ bring back a monarchy **re-establish, restore** *In 1660, the monarchy was restored in a period of history known as the Restoration.*

▸ establish a monarchy **establish, found, set up** *A constitutional monarchy was established in 1993.*

• n+of+N **abolition, collapse, downfall, fall, overthrow** *Conrad accepted the collapse of the monarchy without particular emotion.*

monetary ADJ
relating to money and financial systems

• ADJ+n set of plans or actions agreed by government **economics, mechanism, policy, reform, regime, rules, target** *Responsibility for monetary policy was transferred to the Bank of England in 1997.*

▸ when money is earned or paid **compensation, discipline, donation, gain, incentive, recompense,**

reward *An online business can earn you big monetary rewards.*

▶ how much money something is worth **valuation, value** *Art finds its true monetary value from what the experts say.*

▶ situation in which there are no sudden changes **stability** *Long-term monetary stability is essential for economic success.*

money N

what you earn and buy things with

● adj+N enough **enough, sufficient** *I haven't got enough money to go out tonight.*

▶ extra **additional, extra, more** *Families on very low incomes will receive extra money as well.*

▶ available to be spent **spare, unspent** *Have you got any spare money?*

▶ in a large amount **big, serious** *Magazine work: this is where the really big money is.*

When someone has or gets a large amount of money, you can say that they are *in the money*: *He doesn't want to know me any more now he's in the money.*

● v+N spend or invest money **invest, pay, pay out, spend** *Don't spend too much money!*

▶ waste or lose money **fritter away, lose, squander, throw away** INFORMAL, **waste** *If you buy this phone, you'll be wasting your money.*

▶ earn or receive money **borrow, bring in, collect, earn, get, make, raise, receive** *I want to earn money and travel abroad.*

▶ give or lend money **donate, give, lend, loan** *They donated part of the money to a charity.*

▶ use money for a particular purpose **allocate, earmark** *Money is allocated to schools according to how many pupils they have.*

▶ cost money **cost, set sb back** *Do your piano lessons cost much money? ● The holiday set us back a lot of money.*

▶ owe money **owe** *I had to work in the evenings because I owed money.*

▶ put money away to spend later **save** *We're trying to save our money so we can have a holiday.*

▶ steal money **embezzle, extort, siphon off, steal** *The money was stolen from a car in Millgate last night.*

▶ take money out of a bank account **access, draw out, take out, withdraw** *You can withdraw money using a cash-machine.*

● N+v be spent on or given to **go on sth, go to sth** *The money went to the French government.*

▶ have as a source **come from sth** *Most of our money comes from charitable donations.*

▶ be earned or received in large amounts **come in, flow in, pour in, roll in** INFORMAL *Business improved, and money started pouring in.*

● N+n problems **problems, worries** *Money worries cause more stress than anything else in our daily lives.*

▶ hiding origins of money **launderer, laundering** *The two men were arrested for money laundering.*

monitor V

regularly check something or watch someone

● adv+V in a thorough way **accurately, carefully, closely, properly, rigorously, strictly** *The new*

system creates opportunities for managers to closely monitor work.

▶ regularly **annually, constantly, continually, continuously, daily, monthly, periodically, regularly, routinely, systematically** *Experts continually monitor the volcano for signs of activity.*

● V+n how something changes **change, progress, progression, trend** *Monitor your progress in order to keep yourself motivated.*

▶ how good something is or how well it is done **delivery, effectiveness, implementation, performance, quality, standard** *The law requires public authorities to monitor delivery of their services, and respond to findings. ● The Quality Assurance Team monitors the quality of the service.*

▶ what is happening **activity, behaviour, movement, situation** *We will continue to monitor the situation.*

▶ how much is being spent or used **expenditure, usage** *The school governors are responsible for setting the school budget each year and monitoring expenditure.*

▶ effect or result **effect, impact, outcome, success** *The committee was asked to monitor the effects of these changes.*

monologue N

a long speech by one person

● adj+N funny **amusing, comic, hilarious, humorous** *She had a gift for comic monologues.*

▶ dramatic **dramatic** *His verse ranges widely, from dramatic monologues to love lyrics and poems about public events.*

▶ expressing what a person is thinking **inner, interior, internal** *The film was one of the first to use a voice-over to denote an internal monologue.*

▶ lasting a particular amount of time **hour-long, ten-minute, two-hour, etc** *He launched into an hour-long monologue about the company's past achievements. ● The discussion ended with a five-minute monologue from the chairman.*

▶ long **extended, lengthy, rambling** *The essays take the form of an extended monologue.*

● v+N perform a monologue **deliver, perform, recite, speak** *By the age of eight, Paul was writing poetry and reciting monologues.*

▶ start a monologue **launch into, open** *She launched into a dramatic monologue about how beautiful life is.*

monopolize V

control something and not let others be involved in it

● adv+V almost, nearly, practically, virtually *The fishing industry here is nearly monopolized by one company.*

● V+n trade **market, marketplace, trade** *A small number of supermarkets monopolize the retail trade.*

▶ conversation **conversation** *Don't monopolize the conversation; you will learn more by letting others talk.*

▶ attention **attention** *Newborn babies tend to monopolize their parents' attention, leading to jealousy on the part of older siblings.*

monopoly N
the only company providing a product or service, or the control that one company has

- adj+N owned by the government **public, state, state-owned, state-run** *The school is a state-owned monopoly, and it once controlled all ski instruction in France.*
- private **capitalist, commercial, corporate, private** *Commercial monopolies are not generally good for consumers.*
- large **big, giant, global, powerful** *At that time, he was head of Russia's giant gas monopoly.*
- almost total **effective, near, virtual** *In 1840, the company had a virtual monopoly of all the waterways in the area.*

- v+N create a monopoly **create, establish, secure, set up** *A merger between the two companies would create a monopoly in this sector.*
- have a monopoly **enjoy, exercise, have, hold, possess** *One local paper enjoys a near monopoly on the publication of local news.*
- continue to have a monopoly **keep, maintain, preserve, retain** *It is not sensible to retain a state monopoly in telecommunications.*
- get rid of a monopoly **abolish, break, challenge, end** *The party is committed to ending the monopoly of the postal service.*

monotonous ADJ
boring and unpleasant because not changing

- adv+ADJ **fairly, rather, somewhat** *This piece of music starts off with a somewhat monotonous drum beat.*
- ADJ+n voice **drawl, tone, voice** *I could hear Ray's monotonous tones in the next room.*
- sound **drone, hum, sound** *The engine resembles the monotonous drone of a tractor.*
- when something is repeated many times **regularity, repetition, routine, uniformity** *We can go back twenty years and find that the same issues are raised with monotonous regularity.* • *Many people are happy to accept the idea of living the same monotonous daily routine.*
- work **chore, drudgery, task** *Boring or monotonous tasks may increase fatigue.*
- landscape **landscape, scenery** *The highway runs dead straight for mile after mile, through one of the most monotonous landscapes on Earth.*
- and/or **boring, dull, repetitive, tedious** *For some people, endless hours in a gym become monotonous and boring.*

monumental ADJ
used for emphasizing how big, bad, or important something is

- adv+ADJ **absolutely, truly** *We have been given the opportunity to create a truly monumental work.*
- ADJ+n mistake or failure **blunder, error, failure, folly** *On some occasions he showed great skill, but on others he committed monumental blunders.*
- task or achievement **achievement, challenge, effort, feat, task, work** *The event was a monumental feat of organization.*

> You can also say that something happens **on a monumental scale**, or talk about a mistake or achievement **of monumental proportions** to emphasize how big or important something is: *The movie is about men in power committing fraud on a monumental scale.* • *This was a disaster of monumental proportions.*

- change **change** *The Inuit way of life faces monumental changes in the next decade or so.*

mood N
the way a person or group of people feels

- adj+N good **buoyant, good, jovial, playful, upbeat** *The country was in a positive, upbeat mood.*
- very good **ecstatic, euphoric, jubilant** *The team flew home yesterday in euphoric mood.*
- bad **bad, depressed, foul, melancholic, sombre** *The Queen's death cast a sombre mood over the nation.*
- when someone is thinking deeply **contemplative, pensive, reflective** *In reflective mood, she thought back over her achievements of the past year.*
- having good feelings about the future **bullish, confident, optimistic** *We're all in confident mood after some good results.*
- relaxed **mellow, relaxed** *I'm in a mellow mood and I've been playing some great songs on the guitar.*
- of people in general **general, national, popular, prevailing, public** *The popular mood is to resist government policy and to force change.*
- celebrating an event **celebratory, festive** *The news put us in celebratory mood.*

> Usage **Mood** is often used without an article in these **adj+N** combinations: *A successful deal had been done, and they left the meeting in buoyant mood.*

- v+N experience a particular mood **be in, feel in** *Despite the weather, I still feel in the mood for an adventure.*
- improve someone's mood **brighten, elevate, heighten, lift, lighten** *Sport can lift your mood and make you sleep like a baby.*
- spoil someone's good mood **dampen, kill, spoil** *Don't let a bit of rain dampen your mood.*
- make people think of or experience a particular mood **capture, cast, catch, convey, encapsulate, evoke** *Music can convey different moods.*
- create a mood **create, establish, set** *The decor sets the mood for serene and lazy days.*
- go well with a mood **go with, match, reflect, suit** *Choose the colour that best suits your mood.*

- N+v improve **brighten, lighten** *He grinned, and Elizabeth's mood lightened.*
- become worse **darken, deepen, descend, worsen** *In the later years of the century the public mood darkened.*
- change **alter, change, shift, swing, turn, vary** *Our mood naturally varies from day to day.*

- N+of bad feeling **anger, cynicism, depression, despair, despondency, disappointment, pessimism** *There is a general mood of pessimism about the future.*
- good feeling **anticipation, optimism** *There is a real mood of optimism amongst our members.*

moon N

the object that goes around the Earth and that can be seen shining at night

- • adj+N of a particular shape **crescent, full, half** *A full moon was rising over the town.*
- ▶ of a particular colour and brightness **bright, glowing, luminous, pale, silvery** *A pale yellow moon hung above a vast empty land.*
- • v+N hide the moon **cover, eclipse, hide, obscure** *At the time of his birth, the moon was eclipsed.*
- ▶ look at the moon **observe, see, view, watch** *We can easily observe the moon and its phases.*
- • N+v be in the sky **appear, come up, hang, rise** *This evening, the moon appeared above the horizon at 9 pm.* • *A slender crescent moon hung low in the sky.*
- ▶ produce light **cast sth, glow, illuminate sth, light sth, light sth up, shine** *The full moon cast a silvery light over the beach.*
- ▶ get bigger/smaller **wane, wax** *Most herbs are more powerful when the moon is waxing or full.*

moral ADJ

relating to right and wrong

- • adv+ADJ **deeply, highly, intrinsically, profoundly, purely, strictly, truly** *Her autobiography has a profoundly moral message.*
- • ADJ+n right or duty **duty, imperative, obligation, responsibility, right** *We have a moral duty to help those who are poorer than we are.*
- ▶ difficult decision **choice, dilemma** *Many countries are posed with a moral dilemma when asylum seekers arrive on their shores.*
- ▶ good qualities **courage, superiority, virtue** *Is moral virtue the principal goal of Buddhism?*
- ▶ judgment **judgment** *A doctor should work to cure someone without forming a moral judgment about their activities.*
- ▶ rules or principles **beliefs, code, norms, precept, principle, standards, values** *They have a strict personal moral code, and they try to abide by it.*
- ▶ criticism **indignation, outrage** *They were quick to express their moral outrage at the government's policies on refugees.*

morals N

generally accepted principles of right and wrong [always plural]

- • adj+N good or strict **good, high, pure, religious, strict, traditional** *He was a man of integrity and high morals.*
- ▶ not strict **dubious, lax, loose, questionable** *Our lives are too often influenced by the lax morals of our society.*
- ▶ personal/public **personal, public** *They accused him of attempting to corrupt public morals.*
- ▶ relating to sex **sexual** *Drugs, alcohol, and the decline in sexual morals are all worries faced by parents.*
- • v+N have/lack morals **have, lack** *Joe lacks morals, and doesn't care about betraying those who trust him.*
- ▶ teach morals **teach (sb)** *Children should be taught morals and ethics from the start.*
- ▶ cause morals to be lost or risk being lost

compromise, corrupt, endanger, undermine *Bad language corrupts the morals of our children.*

morale N

the amount of enthusiasm that is felt in a group at a particular time

- • adj+N good **enhanced, excellent, good, high, improved** *Morale is generally better when you have a casual dress code.*
- ▶ bad **damaged, low, poor** *The report noted poor performance and low morale in most departments.*
- ▶ becoming worse **flagging, plummeting, sagging** *The win boosted the team's sagging morale.*
- ▶ felt by the people of a country **civilian, domestic, internal, national, public** *The government quickly realized the importance of good public morale.*
- • n+N **crew, employee, staff, troop, workplace** *Staff morale has been really high this month.*
- • v+N affect morale **affect** *These cuts have affected morale in the public sector.*
- ▶ improve morale **bolster, boost, improve, raise, restore, revive** *A win against Barcelona will boost morale in the UK.*
- ▶ make morale weak **damage, dent, erode, lower, sap, undermine, weaken** *Repeated attacks on the city had sapped morale.*
- ▶ destroy morale **destroy** *Members of the team who aren't pulling their weight can destroy the morale of the rest of the team.*
- ▶ not lose morale **foster, maintain, sustain** *Keeping your goal in mind will help you to maintain your morale when times are hard.*
- • N+v get worse **collapse, drop, fall, plummet, sink, slump, worsen** *Production dropped, morale plummeted and many people left the company.*
- ▶ get better **improve, rise** *Morale has improved and attendance is up.*

> You can also talk about something being **morale boosting**: *They realized the importance of providing the troops with morale-boosting music.*

moratorium N

an official agreement to stop an activity temporarily

- • adj+N lasting for a particular period **90-day, 6-month, 5-year, etc** *The country has declared a two-year moratorium on some of its foreign debt repayments.*
- ▶ covering a particular area **EU-wide, global, international, worldwide** *In 1986, the worldwide moratorium on commercial whaling came into force.*
- ▶ declared by one country or group **unilateral** *They have announced a unilateral moratorium on further testing.*
- ▶ starting immediately **immediate** *There should be an immediate moratorium on the trade of any object appearing on this list.*
- ▶ done by choice **self-imposed, voluntary** *Their voluntary moratorium on nuclear testing was universally welcomed.*
- ▶ lasting for a limited period **temporary** *The City Council has placed a temporary moratorium on all planning applications.*
- • v+N want or ask for a moratorium **argue for,**

ask for, call for, demand, vote for *Switzerland voted for a five-year moratorium* **on** *the planting of GM crops.*

▶ introduce a moratorium **announce, declare, impose, institute, introduce** *The EU introduced a moratorium* **on** *the drug until 2015.*

▶ increase the period of a moratorium **extend** *The moratorium was extended for two additional years in 2007.*

▶ end a moratorium **end, lift, overturn** *The moratorium was lifted in May this year.*

morning N
the period from midnight, or from when the sun rises, until midday

● adj+N at the beginning, middle, or end of the morning **early, late, mid** *I usually have a small glass of fruit juice with breakfast, and an apple mid morning.*

If you do something ***first thing in the morning***, you do it at the very beginning of the day: *Drink the juice of fresh lemon in a glass of warm water first thing in the morning*

▶ with good weather **beautiful, bright, glorious, lovely, sunny, warm** *On Saturday we awoke to a lovely sunny morning.*

▶ with wet weather **damp, foggy, misty, rainy, wet** *The morning was wet and foggy, but we decided to go ahead with the trip anyway.*

▶ with cold weather **chilly, cold, crisp, frosty** *It was a fine crisp early morning just before Christmas when we first noticed the change.*

▶ without sun **cloudy, dreary, dull, grey, overcast** *The morning was overcast with a little rain from time to time.*

▶ relaxed **lazy, leisurely** *We spent a leisurely morning looking around the old town.*

● N+v begin **arrive, begin, break, dawn, start** *Saturday morning dawned clear and bright.*

▶ continue **pass, progress, wear on** *As the morning progressed, the crowd grew.*

mortality N
the fact of dying, or number of deaths within an area, group etc

● adj+N high/low **great, high, low, significant** *Mortality* **among** *transplant patients is high.*

▶ of babies **infantile, neonatal, perinatal, premature** *These children are at increased risk of neonatal mortality.*

● v+N reduce mortality **cut, decrease, improve, lower, reduce** *We aim to reduce mortality from cancer by three-quarters.*

▶ experience mortality **experience, suffer** *This species suffers heavy mortality when winters are severe.*

▶ study mortality **analyse, assess, examine, explain, monitor, observe, record** *The aim of the study was to assess mortality* **among** *single mothers.*

● N+v become less **decline, decrease, drop, fall** *Infant mortality has fallen, and average height has increased.*

▶ increase **increase, rise** *This area is the only part of the world where child mortality is rising.*

● N+n rate **pattern, rate, ratio, risk, trend** *The maternal mortality rate is high.*

▶ information **data, figures, statistics** *The mortality figures are available sorted by age, sex, cause, and area.*

mortgage N
a legal agreement to borrow money to buy a house

● v+N arrange to have a mortgage **apply for, arrange** *How do I go about arranging a mortgage?*

▶ get a mortgage **get, obtain, secure, take out** *Taking out a mortgage is a big decision.*

▶ have a mortgage **have** *Do you have a mortgage* **on** *your home?*

▶ pay back money borrowed on a mortgage **clear, pay, pay off, redeem, repay** *There are various ways to repay your mortgage.*

▶ change to a different mortgage **change, switch** *Many people regularly switch their mortgage to take advantage of better deals.*

● N+n person or organization that gives or arranges mortgages **adviser, broker, intermediary, lender** *I would advise you to go through an independent mortgage broker.*

▶ amount of money paid back **payment, repayment** *Londoners spend an average of 22.8 per cent of their salaries on mortgage repayments.*

▶ money that a person has failed to pay back **arrears** *Mark describes how the loss of his job led to mortgage arrears.*

▶ cost of mortgage **rate** *We can find you the best mortgage rates in the UK.*

motion N
1 a formal proposal to discuss and vote on

● v+N suggest a motion **file, introduce, lodge, move, propose, put, put forward, submit, table** *Councillor Goodman put forward a motion stating that cyclists should not be permitted use of pedestrian areas.*

▶ discuss a motion **consider, debate, discuss** *The committee agreed to consider any motion submitted by any member.*

▶ support a motion **argue for, back, be in favour of, second, sign, speak for, speak in favour/support of, support, vote for** *The motion was seconded by Nick Jones and unanimously approved by the committee.*

▶ oppose a motion **argue against, be against, oppose, speak against, vote against** *I strongly oppose this motion.*

▶ vote on a motion **vote on** *The council then voted on the motion, which was approved by a majority vote.*

▶ vote for and accept a motion **accept, adopt, approve, carry, pass** *There were no speeches against, so the motion was passed.*

▶ vote against and not accept a motion **defeat, reject** *The motion was overwhelmingly defeated by doctors attending the conference.*

2 the process or action of moving [usually singular]

● adj+N well controlled **controlled, fluid, gliding, smooth, steady** *Follow the swing through with your arms and shoulders, all in one smooth motion.*

▶ not smooth **bouncing, jerky, wobbling** *Trevor shrieked with horror, swiping at the creature with a jerky motion.*

▸ quick **quick, rapid, swift** *She took hold of his hand gently in one swift motion.*

▸ circular **anticlockwise, circular, clockwise, rotary, rotational, spinning, swirling, twisting** *Apply the cream using a circular motion on the forehead and neck.*

▸ from one side to another **rocking, rolling, swaying, swinging** *My baby loved the music and the rocking motion.*

▸ in a particular direction **backwards, downward, forward, horizontal, sideways, upward, vertical** *The viewer has a sense of continuing forward motion.*

▸ continuing all the time **constant, continuous, perpetual** *Liquids consist of particles that are in constant motion.*

● v+N perform a motion **make, perform** *He began to perform a circular motion with his right hand.*

▸ copy motion **mimic, simulate** *The children moved backwards and forwards to mimic the motion of the waves.*

▸ feel motion **detect, feel** *When motion is detected, the alarm will sound.*

motivate V
make someone feel determined or enthusiastic

● V+n people at work **colleagues, employees, staff, team, workforce** *Flexible working conditions and training can help to motivate your workforce.*

▸ learners **learners, pupils, students** *This series of lessons will interest and motivate pupils.*

▸ people in general **individuals, others, participants, youngsters** *Lisa is a capable leader with the ability to motivate others.*

● and/or **empower, encourage, energize, engage, enthuse, excite, inspire, stimulate** *This fascinating CD will inspire and motivate all pupils of mathematics.*

motivated ADJ
1 enthusiastic and determined to succeed

● ADJ+n person or people at work **employee, professional, staff, team, workforce** *Your organization will benefit from a more motivated workforce.*

▸ learner **graduate, learner, pupil, student** *Individuals in the 12–15 age group are well motivated, enthusiastic learners.*

▸ person **individual, person** *Are you a dynamic and motivated individual?*

● v+ADJ **be, become, get (sb), keep (sb), stay** *Keep your staff motivated by giving regular feedback.* ● *Staying motivated can often be a real challenge.*

● and/or **ambitious, committed, dynamic, energetic, enthusiastic, skilled, talented** *Our staff are motivated, enthusiastic and committed to delivering high quality care.*

● adv+V very **highly, strongly, well** *This approach to learning encourages students to be highly motivated.*

▸ not very **poorly** *He described the army as 'poorly equipped, poorly trained, and poorly motivated'.*

2 caused, or made to act, by a particular belief or emotion

● adv+V only or mainly **primarily, purely, solely** *We are motivated solely by our desire to help.*

▸ relating to race **ethnically, racially** *Two hundred racially motivated attacks were reported between January and September.*

▸ relating to politics **ideologically, politically** *We believe that the accusations against all these men were politically motivated.*

▸ relating to religion and morals **ethically, religiously, theologically** *The police want to improve their service for people who are victims of religiously motivated crime.*

▸ relating to money **commercially, financially** *Company goals are normally financially motivated.*

motivation N
enthusiasm and determination to do something

● adj+N strong **great, high, strong** *Motivation among the staff is high.*

▸ low **low, poor** *Poor motivation can lead to poor attendance at classes.*

▸ extra **extra** *The sessions should give you extra motivation when you see how far you have come since the beginning.*

▸ personal **personal** *Much depends on each boy's personal motivation: if he wants to work, he will make progress.*

● v+N have motivation **find, have** *Without her, I could never have found the motivation to carry on.* ● *Teachers need to find out why these students have poor motivation.*

▸ not have motivation **lack, lose** *Often, young athletes will lose motivation or drop out of a sport when they suffer their first injury.*

▸ give someone motivation **generate, provide** *For others, the office environment can provide the motivation and interaction that people need to work effectively.*

▸ keep and increase motivation **boost, build, encourage, enhance, improve, increase, keep, maintain, raise, sustain** *Students said that they learnt a huge amount on placement and it increased their motivation for the final year.* ● *Praise is important to keep motivation high.*

▸ make someone's motivation less strong **reduce** *When asked to name factors whcih reduced motivation, 56 per cent mentioned 'workload'.*

● n+of+N **lack, level, source** *Often pupils do not see the purpose of what they are being taught and so display an apparent lack of motivation.*

● and/or **ability, attitude, commitment, confidence, enthusiasm, interest, morale, skill** *We aim to improve the motivation and skills of our workforce.*

motive N
the reason you do something

● adj+N not obvious **hidden, underlying** *Greed and revenge are her underlying motives.*

▸ thinking about other people/about yourself **altruistic, pure, selfish** *Apart from the altruistic motive of sharing your knowledge and ideas with others, there is much to be gained from publishing.*

▸ giving an advantage **ulterior** *It soon emerges that he has an ulterior motive.*

▸ bad/good **bad, good, right, sinister, wrong** *I know*

it was done for the best of motives. ▪ *It now seems evident that there was some much more sinister motive behind the timing of this announcement.*

▶ main **main, primary, prime** *Persistent questioning led to a confession that the primary motive for the move was economic.*

▶ real **real, true** *The police doubt whether car theft was the real motive for the murder.*

▶ types of motive **economic, political, religious** *The campaign was inspired by purely political motives.*

● n+N **profit** *It appears that the profit motive was put before miners' lives.*

● v+N have a motive **have** *It transpires that Mary had her own motives for bringing Jane along to the meeting.*

▶ look at or have doubts about someone's motive **consider, doubt, examine, question, suspect** *I question the motives of those who wish to restrict particular areas of work to particular groups.*

▶ find out someone's motive **establish, find, find out** *No motive for the crime was clearly established.*

▶ understand or explain someone's motive **explain, understand** *Although the audience cannot condone what he has done, they must understand his motives.*

▶ say that someone has a motive **attribute** *You must stop attributing sinister motives to those around you.*

motley ADJ
consisting of many different types

● ADJ+n group of people **band, bunch, crew, crowd** *Gathered together in the hall, we looked a motley crew.*

▶ group of things **assortment, collection** *They travelled about the country in a motley collection of old vans, lorries and buses.*

mount V
1 when a feeling gets stronger over time

● V+adv **rapidly, steadily** *The mystery is entertaining and the suspense rapidly mounts into a terrific climax.*

● n+V **concern, excitement, fears, pressure, speculation, suspense, tension** *Tension had been mounting in the town for most of the day.*

2 prepare for and begin an activity or event

● V+n **assault, attack, campaign, challenge, defence, exhibition, investigation, operation, opposition, protest, resistance, response** *It is essential that we mount a vigorous campaign to remove the restrictions.*

mountain N
a very high hill

▶ adj+N high **high, huge, lofty, tall, towering** *They climbed the three highest mountains in Scotland, England and Wales in 25 hours 45 minutes.*

▶ steep **steep** *The steep mountains and treacherous ravines render much of the Islands inaccessible.*

▶ impressive and beautiful **beautiful, dramatic, magnificent, majestic, spectacular** *The road gives the visitor a high-level view of the majestic mountains to the west.*

▶ with rough rocks **craggy, rocky, rugged** *He set out*

from his family's home in the rugged Basque mountains of northern Spain.

▶ with snow on top **snow-capped, snow-covered, snowy** *She could see the towering snow-capped mountains in the distance.*

▶ covered in mist **misty** *The view was spectacular, with the misty mountains in the background.*

▶ with forests on it **forested** *The two birds of prey were seen flying high above the forested mountains.*

▶ near/far **distant, nearby, remote** *Looking south, you see the snowy peaks of a distant mountain.*

▶ surrounding **surrounding** *On a clear day, the views of Mont Blanc and the surrounding mountains are simply awe-inspiring.*

● v+N go up a mountain **ascend, climb, go up, scale, walk up** *His hobbies include collecting Japanese pottery and climbing mountains.*

▶ come down a mountain **come down, go down** *Watch the film carefully, and you may see us coming down the mountain.*

▶ cross mountains **cross** *Today we cross the mountains into Italy.*

● N+v be tall and easy to see **rise** *Sheer cliffs and steep rugged mountains rise on either side of the turbulent river.*

▶ surround a place **surround** *It is a colourful town surrounded by beautiful mountains.*

● N+n group **chain, range** *Karakoram in Pakistan is one of the highest mountain ranges of Central Asia.*

▶ area or view **landscape, region, scenery, terrain, view** *Take a mountain bike to the top of the cable car and enjoy the exhilarating descent through spectacular mountain scenery.*

▶ top **peak, summit, top** *Eagles soar over the mountain peaks.*

▶ part **crag, ridge, slope, valley** *The wall here follows a narrow mountain ridge that gives spectacular views over the surrounding area.*

▶ town or valley **resort** *Our school in the mountain resort of Zell am see offers German-language courses for beginners.*

mounting ADJ
increasing

● ADJ+n money to pay **costs, debts** *With mounting debts, the business is heading for trouble.*

▶ something bad **anger, anxiety, concern, crime, criticism, frustration, pressure, problems, tension** *The UK government will face mounting pressure this week to review the laws on cannabis.*

▶ excitement **excitement** *We waited in the Arrivals Lounge with mounting excitement.*

▶ evidence **evidence** *There is mounting evidence that fatigue is associated with poor immune function.*

mount up PHR VB
increase or get larger

● n+V evidence **evidence** *Evidence is mounting up that the situation is rapidly getting worse.*

▶ problems **problems** *Looking after your house regularly will make sure that problems do not mount up.*

▶ money to pay **bills, costs, debts** *Small debts can easily mount up.*

mouth N

the part of the face that is used for eating and speaking

- ● **adj+N** open/closed **closed, gaping, open, wide-open** *This announcement was met with gaping mouths and amused glances.*
- ▶ big **big, large, wide** *High cheekbones and a wide mouth give her a permanent air of faint amusement.*
- ▶ small or thin **small, thin** *These fish have quite small mouths.*
- ▶ dry **dry** *Her mouth was too dry for her to spit.*
- ▶ sore **sore** *Some chemotherapy drugs can make your mouth sore and cause small ulcers.*
- ▶ full **full** *Don't talk with your mouth full.*
- ● **v+N** open your mouth, especially to speak **open** *She is not very interesting to talk to since she rarely opens her mouth.*
- ▶ close your mouth and not speak **close, keep closed, keep shut, shut** *Keep your mouth shut, do not volunteer any information.*
- ▶ cover your mouth **cover** *It is sometimes necessary to cover your mouth with your hand to avoid inhaling the insects that hover beneath the trees.*
- ● **N+v** open or be open **drop open, fall open, hang open, open** *I stepped into the room and my mouth fell open.*
- ▶ close **close** *The woman's eyes began to flutter and her mouth closed.*
- ▶ when water forms in your mouth **water** *I passed a house where they were cooking curry, and by the time I got to the end of the street my mouth was watering.*
- ▶ have little water in it **go dry** *He swallowed and his mouth instantly went dry as he panicked at the thought of leaving the ground.*
- ▶ move, and show a particular expression **curl, tighten, turn up/down, twitch** *Her mouth turned down in a look of disgust.*
- ● **n+of+N** **back, corner, roof, side** *A half- smoked cigar hung from the corner of his mouth.*

move N

something done to achieve something; or a change in something

- ● **adj+N** good or clever **clever, good, positive, right, sensible, shrewd, smart, welcome, wise** *It is a wise move to make sure your anti-virus program is bang up-to-date.*

> You can also talk about *a move in the right direction*: *These proposals represent a move in the right direction.*

- ▶ brave **bold, brave** *This is a bold move, and one that should be supported.*
- ▶ bad or wrong **bad, wrong** *Reducing staffing levels at train stations is a bad move.*
- ▶ important **big, significant** *Although the overall system remains segregated, there have been significant moves towards a more inclusive approach.*
- ▶ when it happens **first, latest, next, recent** *Union leaders will meet on Friday to discuss their next move.*
- ▶ unusual **unprecedented, unusual** *In an unprecedented move, the police issued the images of 31 protesters they wanted to interview.*

- ▶ planned **planned, proposed** *In a carefully planned move, the union decided that they would ask their members to strike for a period of four hours.*
- ▶ carefully planned to achieve an aim **strategic, tactical** *This merger represents the best strategic move for both companies.*
- ● **n+N** **career** *You will receive expert advice on your next career move from our recruitment consultant.*
- ● **v+N** make a move **make** *At the moment they daren't make a move against their enemies.*
- ▶ plan or consider a move **announce, consider, contemplate, plan** *Focus on what you want to achieve and plan each move carefully.*
- ▶ support a move **back, support, welcome** *We welcome any moves to encourage industry to support postgraduate students.*
- ▶ oppose a move **be opposed to, block, condemn, oppose, reject, resist** *I pointed out that the University opposed any move to take selection away from College tutors.*
- ▶ lead to a move **prompt** *These problems prompted moves to reform the entire system.*
- ▶ be a move **be, be seen as, represent** *The reclassification of the drug in no way represents a move towards decriminalization or legalization.*
- ● **N+v** **come, follow, involve, mark, mean, prove, reflect** *The move follows mounting criticism of the level of ministers' pay.*

movement N

1 a group of people with the same aim

- ● **adj+N** involving many people **global, international, mass, national, popular** *Change has come from mass social movements exerting pressure on the ruling class.*
- ▶ involving ordinary people **grass-roots** *'Stop the War' began as a grass-roots movement and its strength has remained at its roots.*
- ▶ growing **emerging, growing** *There is a growing movement against corporate globalization.*
- ▶ types of movement **anti-capitalist, anti-war, environmental, nationalist, political, religious, revolutionary, social, socialist** *She soon became a leading figure in the socialist movement.*
- ● **n+N** **animal rights, civil rights, independence, labour, peace, resistance, trade union** *Many of the most enthusiastic supporters of the proposals come from the senior ranks of the trade union movement.*
- ● **v+N** start or organize a movement **build, create, found, launch, organize, start** *The modern Olympic movement was founded by Baron Pierre de Coubertin.*
- ▶ support or be part of a movement **be engaged in, be involved in, be part of, join, support** *He became increasingly involved in the civil rights movement.*
- ▶ lead a movement **lead** *She led the movement for independence.*
- ▶ make a movement stronger **encourage, strengthen** *We need to strengthen the fair trade movement in this country.*
- ▶ oppose or destroy a movement **crush, oppose, suppress** *They did everything they could to crush the rebel movement by repression.*
- ● **N+v** begin **arise, begin, emerge, start** *Why did the*

women's movement emerge from the middle of the 19th century in so many countries?
▶ grow **grow, spread** The international anti-war movement grew on an unprecedented scale.

> You can also say that a movement **gains momentum**, **ground**, or **strength**, or that it **gathers momentum** or **strength**: The environmental movement is gaining strength at an increasing rate.

▶ be against/for something **oppose, support** The disability rights movement strongly opposed this approach.

2 a change in the position of your body; an act of moving

● adj+N in a particular direction **backward, downward, forward, lateral, upward** Remove the mascara **in** an upward movement of the lashes to avoid irritating the eye.
▶ slight **slight** The outside light reacts to the slightest movement.
▶ quick **quick, rapid, sudden** Neck strain can be caused by a sudden movement of the head, backward, forward or sideways.
▶ smooth **fluid, smooth** Simply press the key and the front can be opened **in** a smooth movement.
▶ not smooth or controlled **involuntary, jerky** There may be twitching or jerking of the arms or legs, or involuntary eye movements.
▶ of your body **bodily, physical** Playing a stringed instrument involves physical movement.

● n+N **arm, body, eye, hand, head, limb, muscle** After each set of eye movements, the therapist will ask the client what they noticed.

● v+N make a movement **make, perform** Do not make any sudden movements.
▶ limit a movement **limit, restrict** My hip is painful and restricts my movement.
▶ control a movement **control, direct** A motor nerve is one that runs down to a muscle and controls its movement.
▶ notice a movement **detect, feel, notice, sense** Sensors can detect the slightest movement.

movie N
a film shown in a cinema or on television

● adj+N coming soon **forthcoming, upcoming** He also talked about his upcoming movie and the launch of his autobiography.
▶ costing/not costing a lot of money **high-budget, low-budget** There has been a boom in low-budget horror movies for home rental.
▶ making you feel frightened **horror, scary** Are you terrified of scary movies? Do you hide behind the sofa?
▶ making you feel happy **feel-good** This is not a feel-good movie; it is a deeply sobering wake-up call.
▶ with a lasting value **classic** She loved classic movies such as The Maltese Falcon and Casablanca.
▶ very successful **blockbuster** He was known mainly for blockbuster movies like Alien or True Lies.

● v+N watch a movie **go to, see, watch** I first saw this movie when I was twelve.
▶ make a movie **create, direct, film, make, produce, shoot** You can make the scariest movie without a single drop of blood.

▶ make a movie available **release** I am looking forward to the movie being released in the UK.
▶ show a movie **show** Built in 1913, The Empire Picture Playhouse was used for showing silent movies.
▶ show a movie on a DVD player or computer **play** Click on the image to play the movie.
▶ appear in a movie **act in, appear in, co-star, feature in, star in** Since then she has starred in several successful movies.

● N+v have in it **co-star, feature, star** Michael Mann's spectacular 1992 movie starred Daniel Day-Lewis.
▶ take place **be set in** Dog Soldiers is a horror movie set in Scotland but filmed in Luxembourg.

moving ADJ
making you feel emotional

● adv+ADJ **deeply, incredibly, intensely, profoundly, quite, very** It was a poignant and deeply moving end to the day.

● ADJ+n **account, experience, moment, speech, story, tribute** This is a very moving story of a woman who struggles to come to terms with her father's death.

● v+ADJ **be, find sth** I found the whole experience deeply moving.

● and/or **funny, inspiring, poignant, powerful** Over the past 30 years, he has created some of the most moving and powerful music ever written.

muddled ADJ
not clear or effective

● adv+ADJ very **hopelessly, very** This hopelessly muddled thinking was typical of the department at that time.
▶ rather **a little, rather, slightly, somewhat** The arguments they presented were somewhat muddled.

● ADJ+n **thinking, thought** We take the view that this proposal is the product of muddled thinking and must be revisited.

muffled ADJ
not easy to hear because the sound is blocked by something

● ADJ+n **cry, footsteps, laughter, noise, roar, sob, sound, thud, voice** There was a muffled cry and the sound of a body hitting the floor.

multilateral ADJ
involving three or more groups

● ADJ+n agreement **agreement, treaty** Most developing countries have signed up to multilateral environmental agreements.
▶ discussion **diplomacy, negotiations, talks** The deal had been the result of more than six years of multilateral negotiations.
▶ organization **agency, institution, organization** It also works with multilateral institutions, including the World Bank, United Nations agencies, and the European Commission.
▶ way of doing something **approach, disarmament, system** They demanded that the government should

support the multilateral approach to international
policy-making.
▸ getting rid of weapons **disarmament** *There had
been limited success in multilateral disarmament
and arms control.*

● and/or **bilateral, unilateral** *Governments in the
region are increasingly forming bilateral and
multilateral alliances to combat terrorist activity.*

multinational ADJ
having offices, shops, factories etc in several
countries

● ADJ+n **company, conglomerate, corporation,
enterprise, firm, giant, group, manufacturer,
organization** *As with all major high-technology
industries, it is now dominated by large
multinational companies.*

multiply V
increase in number or by a large amount

● adv+V quickly **quickly, rapidly, uncontrollably**
*Because orders were multiplying rapidly, they
decided to build a new plant on the site of the existing
works.*
▸ by a large amount **exponentially, greatly** *The
number of complaints during this year has
multiplied greatly.*
▸ to a particular degree **fivefold, tenfold etc** *They
estimated that the number of operations carried out
had multiplied fourfold.*

● n+V **bacteria, cell, germs, parasites, virus** *Storage
temperature affects the speed with which harmful
bacteria multiply.*

mumble V
speak in quiet way that is not clear

● adv+V **incoherently, quietly, softly** *Groups of
adolescents can often be seen loitering around
shopping arcades, mumbling incoherently to each
other.*

● V+n **apology, excuse, nonsense, something,
words** *Rob arrived, mumbling something about the
alarm not working.*

mundane ADJ
ordinary and not interesting or exciting

● adv+ADJ rather **fairly, pretty INFORMAL, quite,
rather, relatively, somewhat** *This is, of course, a
fairly mundane use of the new technology.*
▸ very **extremely, incredibly, positively, utterly, very**
*Unfortunately, some photos of such ghostly mists
have very mundane explanations.*
▸ appearing to be mundane, but perhaps not
apparently, seemingly *Rubber is a seemingly
mundane substance that comes to life through its
social history.*

● ADJ+n what someone does or how they live
**activity, chore, existence, job, life, reality, task,
world** *For Miles, the trip represents an opportunity
to get away from his mundane existence.*
▸ fact or aspect of a situation **detail, explanation,
level, matter, thing** *More mundane matters also
occupied the committee – on 6th May the librarian
was authorized to obtain a new doormat!*

▸ something that happens **event** *Good writing
enables the most mundane event to be transformed
into something significant, exciting even.*
▸ object **item, object** *The camera avoids their faces,
focusing on mundane objects such as a bowl of cereal,
an alarm clock, a fish tank.*

● and/or **boring, dull, everyday, ordinary, routine,
trivial** *His paintings are rooted in the everyday,
mundane aspects of life.*

murder N
the crime of killing someone deliberately

● adj+N extremely violent and unpleasant **bloody,
brutal, gruesome, horrific** *She was the victim of a
brutal murder.*
▸ when two or more people are killed **double, mass**
*Nelson was sentenced to 35 years in prison for the
double murder.*
▸ deliberately planned or showing no emotion **cold-
blooded, premeditated, wilful** *This was no
accident – it was cold-blooded murder.*
▸ when someone tries to murder someone but does
not succeed **attempted** *She faced charges of
attempted murder and abduction.*
▸ when the person responsible has not been found
unsolved *In various newspapers he was linked to
other unsolved murders.*
▸ because of someone's race **racist** *Police believe this
was a racist murder.*

● v+N commit a murder **carry out, commit** *It's
about a group of teens who conspire to commit
murder.*
▸ see someone commit a murder **witness** *The child
had witnessed the brutal murder of two gang
members.*
▸ find out who committed a murder **investigate,
solve** *Police investigating the murder of the 13-year-
old girl have spoken to thousands of people in the
area.*
▸ be involved in a murder **be implicated in, be
involved in** *They were suspected of being involved
in the murder of the leader of the opposition.*
▸ when someone says that they have committed a
murder **confess to** *She confessed to the murder of
her husband under extreme provocation.*
▸ say that someone has committed a murder **accuse
sb of, arrest sb for, charge sb with, convict sb of** *So
far, nobody has been arrested for this murder.*

● N+v **occur, take place** *This was the same weekend
that the murders took place.*

● N+n relating to the police and courts of law
case, charge, conviction, inquiry, investigation, trial
*The cause of death was violent and we are treating
the investigation as a murder inquiry.*
▸ person **suspect, victim** *A body found in a peat bog
in northern Germany was first thought to be a
murder victim.*
▸ weapon or scene **scene, weapon** *The murder
weapon has never been recovered.*
▸ story about a murder **mystery** *His latest film is a
psychological murder mystery set in Victorian
London.*

● n+in+N **complicity, involvement, part** *He is also
charged with complicity in mass murder.*

- n+to+N **conspiracy, incitement** *He pleaded guilty to five charges of conspiracy to murder.*

- n+of+N **allegation, charge, series, spate, suspicion, verdict** *This was the latest in a spate of murders involving supervised offenders.* • *She was arrested on suspicion of murder.*

murder V
commit the crime of killing someone deliberately

- adv+V in a cruel way **brutally, cruelly, gruesomely, in cold blood, savagely, viciously** *Her brother was murdered in cold blood.*

  Usage *Murder* is usually passive in these combinations.

- in a planned or organized way **deliberately, systematically** *The brutal regime systematically murdered thousands of its citizens.*

murderer N
someone who commits murder

- adj+N killing several or many people **mass, serial** *He was indeed a mass murderer and a tyrant, but he was not alone.*
- thought to be guilty **alleged, suspected** *The young woman, an alleged child murderer, was treated brutally by the other inmates.*
- proved to be guilty **convicted** *The agreement resulted in the release of many terrorists, including convicted murderers.*
- showing no emotion **cold-blooded, ruthless** *Why are you mounting a campaign in support of cold-blooded murderers?*
- very cruel **brutal, sadistic** *He had brought to justice some of America's most brutal murderers.*
- well known **infamous, notorious** *Crippen is one of the most notorious murderers in the history of Scotland Yard.*

- v+N **arrest, bring to justice, catch, convict, find** *The murderer was never caught.*

murmur V
say something in a very quiet voice

- adv+V **apologetically, appreciatively, quietly, softly** *'Wake up, please,' I murmured softly.*

- V+n **greeting, prayer, reply, something, thanks, words** *She murmured some words of sympathy.*

murmur N
something said in a quiet voice; a quiet expression of a feeling, or a low sound

- adj+N quiet **faint, gentle, indistinct, low, slight** *She spoke in a low murmur.*
- with many people speaking **general** *There was a general murmur of approval from those present.*
- loud or that you can hear **audible, loud** *There was an audible murmur of discontent when the news was announced.*
- N+of showing people's feelings **agreement, approval, disapproval, discontent** *This speech was met with murmurs of agreement from around the room.*
- sound of voices **conversation, voices** *A murmur of voices came from behind that door.*

muscle N
a piece of flesh that connects one bone to another, used for moving a part of your body

- adj+N stretched tight **tense, tight** *Some of my muscles were very tense and others were weak.*
- when a muscle hurts or is damaged **aching, damaged, pulled, sore, stiff, strained, tired, torn, weak** *Warming up is important, especially in cold weather, to avoid strains and pulled muscles.*
- strong and healthy **lean, strong** *Strong muscles are less prone to sprains.*
- sticking out **bulging** *He is in perfect health, with huge bulging muscles.*

- v+N make a muscle tight or less tight **contract, flex, relax, stretch, tense, tighten** *Stretch the cramped muscle by pulling or pushing your toes towards your shin.*
- damage a muscle **damage, pull, strain, tear** *He pulled a muscle in his back and had to leave the field.*
- make your muscles stronger **build, strengthen, tone** *You can use weights to strengthen your arm muscles.*
- exercise your muscles **exercise** *Walking around and stretching exercises muscles and increases blood circulation.*

- N+v become tight/less tight **contract, cramp, flex, relax, tense, tighten** *The dog's eyes gleamed and its leg muscles tensed, ready to spring.*
- hurt or become weak or damaged **ache, waste (away), weaken** *My chest is becoming congested and my muscles are wasting away.*
- move or stick out **bulge, ripple, twitch** *Have you watched weightlifters and seen how their muscles bulge and eyes pop?*

music N
a pleasant arrangement of sounds made by voices and instruments

- v+N play music **make, perform, play** *They mainly played music from the 70s and 80s.*
- write music **compose, create, write** *The theme music was composed by John Williams.*
- listen to music **hear, listen to** *Take your child to hear live music being played.* • *My only form of entertainment is to listen to music and go on the Internet.*
- be filled with music **be filled with** *It was an evening that was filled with the most delightful music.*
- record music **record** *Most of this music was recorded between 1997 and 2003.*
- write music to go with something **set sth to** *There will be a fantastic firework display set to music with Preston docks as a backdrop.*
- understand the symbols of written music **read** *I learned to play the piano and read music early in life.*

- N+v be heard **blare (out), blast (out), come, flow, play** *Music was playing quietly in the background.*
- sound **sound** *The title music sounds menacing and mysterious.*
- float through the air **drift, waft** *Music drifted up from the village in the evenings.*
- be heard with something **accompany** *The film is accompanied by the music of Bach.*

▶ stop or start **begin, fade (away), start, stop** *The Cuban people are incredibly welcoming, so don't expect to stay seated when the music starts!*

● n+of+N piece of music **piece** *What is your favourite piece of music?*

▶ type of music **kind, style, type** *He is extremely experienced in all styles of music, ranging from Classical to Pop.*

musician N
a person performing or writing music

● adj+N very good **accomplished, brilliant, excellent, fine, gifted, outstanding, talented, virtuoso** *The orchestra features some of London's most talented young musicians.*

▶ professional/not professional **amateur, professional** *We perform at least four concerts each year, regularly engaging professional musicians and soloists.*

▶ famous and respected **acclaimed, distinguished, eminent, famous, influential, leading, legendary, renowned, respected, top** *The ensemble brings together internationally renowned musicians from the UK and South Africa.*

▶ having experience **experienced, trained** *Only 13 per cent of trained musicians enter 'performance related' employment.*

▶ having a range of different skills **multi-talented, versatile** *He is a versatile musician, having learnt to play piano, flute and saxophone at an early age.*

▶ hoping to be successful **aspiring, budding** *We have many budding musicians and singers at our school.*

muster V
try to produce enthusiasm or determination

● V+n **courage, energy, enthusiasm, strength, support, will** *She finally mustered the courage to speak up.*

muted ADJ
not as strong or extreme as usual

● adv+ADJ **curiously, rather, slightly, somewhat, strangely, very** *A significant factor has been the rather muted response of the moderates in the party.*

● ADJ+n reaction **applause, criticism, reaction, response** *There has been a surprisingly muted response to the proposed changes in the law.*

▶ colours **colour, palette, shade, tone, grey, green etc** *The rooms are decorated in muted shades.*

▶ sound **sound** *We stood outside the church, listening to the muted sound of hymn-singing from inside.*

● v+ADJ **be, become, remain, seem** *The response to the new arrangement remained muted, to say the least.*

mutter V
talk quietly, especially when annoyed or embarrassed

● adv+V in an angry or threatening way **angrily, darkly** *'I won't be responsible for what I do to that cat if he comes back,' she muttered darkly.*

▶ quietly **quietly, under your breath** *A visitor was heard to mutter under his breath that he did not believe a word of it.*

● V+n apology, **curse, expletive, oath, prayer, remark, something, threat, word** *He was last seen wandering towards the exit, muttering something about trying to hire a car.*

mutual ADJ
done in the same way by each person, or belonging to each person

● ADJ+n feeling **admiration, appreciation, attraction, distrust, love, recognition, respect, suspicion, tolerance, trust, understanding** *A way to stop all these conflicts is to start developing a level of mutual respect for each other.*

You can say **the feeling is mutual** to say that one person dislikes someone as much as that person dislikes them: *I didn't like her much when I first met her, and I am sure the feeling was mutual.*

▶ agreement **agreement, consent** *The parties have agreed by mutual consent to conclude the contract between them.*

▶ help or advantage **advantage, assistance, benefit, cooperation, interest, support** *The committee provides a forum where issues of mutual interest can be explored.*

▶ dependence **dependence, dependency, interdependence** *It was a close community, supported by mutual dependence.*

▶ feeling of worry **concern** *The two organizations met to discuss issues of mutual concern.*

▶ friend **friend** *They first met through a mutual friend.*

mystery N
something you cannot explain or understand

● adj+N not yet explained or not able to be explained **enduring, insoluble, unexplained, unfathomable, unsolved** *The issue of consciousness is considered by many to be the most important unsolved mystery of modern science.*

▶ great **big, deep, great, profound** *They all shared a consuming desire to understand the deepest mysteries of life.*

▶ complete **complete, total** INFORMAL *The cause of this is still a complete mystery to me.* ● *What really happened remains a total mystery.*

▶ little **little** *It was obviously another of life's little mysteries, that we would never explain.*

▶ interesting **intriguing** *Inspector Wallander has yet another intriguing mystery to solve in this new novel by Mankell.*

● v+N explain a mystery **explain, reveal, solve, uncover, unlock, unravel** *The novel is about the attempts of a young journalist to unravel the mystery of a young girl's murder 25 years previously.*

▶ try to understand a mystery **explore, ponder, understand** *Now science has given us the tools to understand the mystery of healing foods and nutrients.*

▶ be or remain a mystery **be shrouded in, remain** *His early life is shrouded in mystery.*

● N+v **deepen, remain, surround sth, unfold, unravel** *The mystery deepens when another intelligence officer is murdered in the same way.* ● *Mystery still surrounds the causes of this disease.*

You can use **surrounding** or **regarding** to say what a mystery is about: *Police are no closer to solving the mystery surrounding the young man's death.*

- n+of+N quality or feeling **air, aura, sense** *It seems there is an air of mystery about the place that attracts them.*
▶ to some extent **a bit, something** *Just how advertising works continues to be something of a mystery.*

myth N
something wrongly believed to be true

- adj+N that many people believe **common, popular, urban, widespread** *Contrary to popular myth, not everyone wants to go to university.*
▶ modern/old **modern, old** *This raises another old myth about rail freight: that freight trains are slow and that road freight transportation is faster than rail.*
▶ lasting for a long time **enduring, persistent** *One of the most enduring myths about Manchester is that is always rains there.*
▶ dangerous **dangerous** *The idea that nuclear power is the solution to climate change is a dangerous myth.*

- v+N prove or show a myth is not true **counter, debunk, demolish, destroy, dispel, disprove, explode, expose, scotch, shatter** *'Real Nappy Week' is all about dispelling the myths about modern re-usable nappies.*
▶ create or spread a myth **create, peddle, perpetuate, propagate** *Women's magazines perpetuate the myth that thin is beautiful.*
▶ believe a myth **believe, buy into** *Far too many people believe the myth that modern languages are superfluous because 'the whole world speaks English'.*
▶ question whether a myth is true **challenge** *The report challenges myths about food and poverty.*
▶ be based on a myth **be based on** *The belief that all political careers end in failure is based on the myth that all MPs hope to become Prime Minister.*

- N+v **abound, grow up, persist, remain** *A myth has grown up over the last two years that this is a unilateralist administration.*

You can use **surrounding** or **regarding** to say what a myth is about: *This article aims to dispel the myths surrounding refugees and migrant workers.*

Nn

naive ADJ
lacking experience of life and believing things too easily

- adv+ADJ very **extremely, hopelessly, incredibly** INFORMAL, **so, very** *I can't believe I was so naive.*
- ▶ rather **a bit, a little, quite, rather, somewhat** *I was under the rather naive impression that people would gladly pay for you to help them out in this way, but I was wrong.*
- ▶ in politics **politically** *I may be accused of being politically naive, but I always mistrust suggestions that one votes according to the way one thinks the vote will be received.*

- ADJ+n idea or method **approach, assumption, belief, notion, question, theory, view** *We tend to adopt a naive view, assuming that pictures in books and magazines tell a simple truth.*
- ▶ feeling that things will go well **optimism** *Young people tend to display a naive optimism about human nature and human society.*

- and/or **foolish, gullible, idealistic, innocent, simplistic, young** *He was a competent teacher, but very young and naive.*

naked ADJ
1 not wearing any clothes

- adv+ADJ completely **completely, entirely, quite, stark, totally** *The door closed behind me and I was now standing stark naked in the corridor.*
- ▶ almost **almost, half, nearly, practically, virtually** *The miners worked, almost naked, for up to twelve hours a day in filthy conditions. • She's always wandering around half naked.*

- ADJ+n person **boy, child, figure, girl, lady, man, model, woman** *I stopped beside a sculpture of a naked woman.*
- ▶ part of the body **breast, foot, shoulder, torso** *The hot sand burned his naked feet.*
- ▶ skin **flesh, skin** *The softness of the fabric felt nice against her naked flesh.*
- ▶ body **body, form** *Her naked body was found by her cleaner in the bathroom.*

- v+ADJ **be, pose, strip (sb), run, swim, walk** *They were made to strip naked and their heads were shaved.*

2 not covered

- ADJ+n **bulb, flame, light, sword** *Close all doors and windows, extinguish all naked flames and switch off the gas supply.*

3 very strong, not controlled or limited

- ADJ+n **aggression, ambition, greed, hatred, self-interest** *While he was in office, his unscrupulousness and naked ambition brought about his downfall.*

name N
a word or set of words by which a person or thing is usually known

- adj+N that is given to you **Christian, first, given** *We called each other by our first names.*
- ▶ of your family **family, last, second** *The practice of using a surname or family name is relatively recent.*
- ▶ middle **middle, second** *'Have you got a middle name?' 'Yes, it's Elizabeth – Mary Elizabeth Jones.'*
- ▶ that a woman uses before/after she gets married **maiden, married** *What was your mother's maiden name?*
- ▶ that someone uses instead of their own name **assumed, false, pen** *He signed the letter using an assumed name. • She wrote the book under the pen name George Eliot.*

- v+N change your name **change** *She didn't change her name when she got married.*
- ▶ take and use a name **adopt, assume, take** *The school adopted its current name in 1954.*
- ▶ have the name **be known by, go by, have** *I know there was a family going by the name of Griffin in the area at the time.*

narrative N
a story or account of something

- adj+N that holds your attention **compelling, engaging, gripping, vivid** *Her latest novel is a complex and compelling narrative that weaves together many strands of plot.*
- ▶ complicated/not complicated **complex, conventional, detailed, multi-layered, simple, straightforward** *In the documentary there is no conventional narrative, just a collection of filmed scenes.*
- ▶ in which the parts fit together well **coherent** *He looks at a number of different cases and they are tied into a coherent narrative.*
- ▶ told in a particular order **chronological, linear, non-linear** *The film is a chronological narrative of her life, from a traumatic birth to a contented old age.*
- ▶ told from a particular point of view **first-person, third-person** *I chose a first-person narrative, because that made it sound like something you might be hearing spoken aloud.*
- ▶ types of narrative **autobiographical, biblical, biographical, fictional, historical, personal, poetic, traditional** *She mixes passages of autobiographical narrative with polemical discussion.*

- v+N create a narrative **construct, create, develop, produce, shape, weave, write** *Archaeologists can learn from historians that we should use our findings to create good narratives and engaging stories about the past and its people.*
- ▶ offer a narrative **give, offer, present, provide** *He has skilfully mastered the evidence to provide a coherent narrative.*

- N+v **emerge, flow, progress, unfold** *As the narrative gradually unfolds, the nature of the relationship between mother and daughter becomes clearer.*

- N+n **account, film, form, history, poem, strand,**

structure, style, thread, voice *The book has a complex narrative structure, flowing backwards and forwards in time.*

narrow ADJ

1 limited in range or variety

● ADJ+n range or situation **confines, focus, range, scope** *On the courses, teachers get to know their pupils as people, beyond the narrow confines of the classroom.* ● *The report suggested that small schools limited pupils to a narrow range of opportunities.*

▶ view **definition, interpretation, perspective, sense, view** *One would have to have a very narrow view of the world to not see the value of this.*

2 achieved with difficulty

● ADJ+n **defeat, escape, majority, margin, victory** *He knew what a narrow escape he had had.* ● *They won the semi-final by a very narrow margin.*

nasty ADJ

unpleasant to experience; unkind or offensive

● adv+ADJ very **downright** INFORMAL**, especially, extremely, particularly, plain** INFORMAL**, really, truly, very** *The boys were being cheeky, rather than downright nasty.* ● *I cannot help feeling that this must have been a particularly nasty way to die.*

▶ rather **fairly, pretty** INFORMAL**, quite, rather** *It left a rather nasty brown stain.*

● ADJ+n surprise **shock, surprise** *Some of them are likely to be in for a nasty surprise.*

▶ situation **business, situation** *It was a nasty business, from any point of view.*

▶ period **moment** *He still winces as he recalls that nasty moment.*

▶ smell **smell** *There was a nasty smell in the building which no one had ever been able to identify.*

▶ taste **taste** *My daughter now takes half a tablet instead and prefers this as there is no nasty taste.*

▶ experience **experience** *She'd had a nasty experience the day before.*

▶ noise **noise** *A nasty noise started coming from the gearbox.*

▶ statement **attack, comment, letter, message, stuff, thing** *She made a really nasty comment about his wife.*

▶ person **character, man, person, piece of work** INFORMAL *John shouts after Ken, 'You're a nasty little man!'* ● *She is a throughly nasty piece of work.*

▶ action **trick** *She decided it was time to play a nasty trick on him after what he did last week.*

▶ part of someone's personality **side** *There is a nasty, vicious side to him.*

▶ injury **bite, cut, gash, injury, wound** *He suffered a nasty injury to his leg.*

▶ illness **bug, cold, cough, disease, infection, virus** *It's a very nasty disease you don't want to get.*

▶ accident **accident, fall** *Toby has a nasty accident in the kitchen.*

▶ effect **effect** *We are constantly bombarded with information about the nasty effects of climate change.*

▶ problem **problem** *It caused a very nasty problem for the government.*

▶ case **case** *She thought she had a nasty case of flu.*

v+ADJ **be, get, look, smell, sound, taste, turn** *I*

had an experience which, in retrospect, could have turned very nasty indeed.

nation N

a country that has its own land and government; the people of a particular country

● adj+N poor **developing, impoverished, poor** *The G8 Summit meets this week to decide the fate of the world's poorest nations.*

▶ rich **affluent, prosperous, rich, wealthy** *The rich nations are still negotiating primarily in the interests of their major multinationals.*

▶ strong **great, leading, major, powerful, strong** *They argued that these were the qualities that had made their nation great.*

▶ suffering unfair treatment **oppressed** *The nationalism of oppressed nations is an inevitable reaction to colonialism.*

▶ industrial **industrial, industrialized** *The rapid rate of growth in all the major industrial nations has led to a considerable shortage of IT specialists.*

▶ advanced **advanced, developed** *There is global trend towards an ageing population in developed nations.*

▶ independent **free, independent, sovereign** *The period ended with Mexico becoming an independent nation.*

▶ democratic **democratic** *In democratic nations, national laws are also driven to a large extent by public opinion.*

▶ new **emerging, new, young** *The capital of the new nation was named Washington in his honour.*

▶ behaving in a dangerous way **rogue** *There is a growing threat of missile attacks from rogue nations.*

▶ whole **entire, whole** *He apologized in the name of the whole nation.*

▶ with people sharing the same aims or beliefs **united** *We are no longer a united nation.*

▶ with people disagreeing about aims and beliefs **divided** *The Britain of 1974 was a much more divided nation than a decade earlier.*

● v+N govern a nation **govern, lead** *He has shown he is no longer fit to lead our nation.*

▶ defend a nation **defend, protect, save** *The whole concept of dying to defend a nation is almost alien to modern minds.*

▶ create a nation **build, create** *The UN has had the momentous task of trying to build a nation from scratch.*

▶ destroy a nation **destroy** *They are determined to fight the evil that threatens to destroy their nation.*

▶ affect a nation **shock, sweep** *Her horrific murder shocked the nation.* ● *World Cup fever was sweeping the nation at the time.*

▶ cause a nation to disagree about aims and beliefs **divide** *Many issues divided the nation.*

▶ unite a nation **unite** *Royalists say that this week has shown the royal family can still unite the nation like nothing else.*

▶ speak to a nation **address, tell** *Addressing the nation, the Prime Minister called the attack mass murder.*

▶ represent a nation **represent** *The Queen represents the nation at times of great celebration or sorrow.*

▶ serve a nation **serve** *When War was declared in August 1914, many British women demanded the right to serve the nation.*

nationalist N

someone who believes that their nation should be independent, or that their nation's interests are more important than those of other nations.

- adj+N considered reasonable **moderate** *There was now a belief that moderate nationalists and unionists could now work constructively together.*
- ▶ considered unreasonable **extreme** *The extreme nationalists of the Scottish Republican Socialist Movement are also unrepresented.*
- ▶ with very strong beliefs **ardent, fervent, radical** *He was a fervent nationalist and a supporter of the Welsh deciding their own destiny.*

nationalist ADJ

trying to achieve political independence for a particular nation; believing that your nation's interests are more important than those of other nations

- ADJ+n set of things that need to be done or that you want to achieve **agenda, aspirations** *He dealt with nationalist aspirations by creating a federation of six republics.*
- ▶ aim or fight **cause, opposition, struggle** *He took up the nationalist cause, becoming the champion of the poor tenant farmers against their absentee English landlords.* • *The traditional nationalist opposition to British rule is thus seen by unionists as incompatible with the survival of their own sense of identity.*
- ▶ tradition **tradition** *Both books sought to deny the importance of the nationalist tradition in Irish history.*
- ▶ opinion **feeling, sentiment** *The war was preceded by a rise in nationalist feeling.*
- ▶ system of ideas **ideology, policy** *The movement was a reaction against attempts to poison the minds of young workers with bourgeois nationalist ideology.*
- ▶ style of speaking or writing **rhetoric** *The EU disapproved of his authoritarian politics and nationalist rhetoric.*

nationalistic ADJ

extremely proud of your own nation and believing that it is better than other nations

- adv+ADJ **aggressively, fervently, fiercely, highly, intensely, strongly** *Chopin's music with its strongly nationalistic character was bound to fall under suspicion in certain quarters.*
- ADJ+n **attitude, feelings, fervour, pride, sentiment** *The atmosphere of nationalistic fervour which they encouraged may well have hastened the conflict.*
- and/or **chauvinistic, militaristic, patriotic, xenophobic** *The idea that the English national identity has to be nationalistic, xenophobic and racist has completely gone now.*

nationality N

the legal status of being a citizen of a particular country

- adj+N relating to a particular country **British, French etc** *Under Irish law, any person born on the island of Ireland may obtain Irish nationality.*
- ▶ relating to two countries **dual** *Dual nationality can only be acquired in accordance with the laws of both Finland and the other state in question.*
- ▶ mixed **mixed** *Groups are of mixed nationality but the main language spoken is English.*
- ▶ foreign **foreign** *With regard to the amount of tax, persons of foreign nationality are required to pay the same as citizens of the country.*
- v+N get a particular nationality **acquire, adopt, assume, obtain, take** *Rupert Murdoch was born in Australia, but took US nationality.*
- ▶ give someone a particular nationality **grant sb** *He took up residence in Britain but was not granted British nationality.*
- ▶ have a particular nationality **have, hold, possess** *Generally, an English person is someone who lives in England and holds British nationality, regardless of their racial origin.*
- ▶ change nationality **change** *I arrived in 1960, and I changed my nationality in 1963 from Pakistani to British.*
- ▶ lose a particular nationality **lose** *So, if you get another nationality, you will not lose your British nationality.*
- ▶ keep a particular nationality **keep, retain** *Charlie Chaplin retained his British nationality throughout his life.*
- ▶ claim a particular nationality **claim** *Claiming French nationality, he was transferred to a camp near Marienburg for French prisoners of war.*

natural ADJ

1 existing in nature and not produced or caused by people

- adv+ADJ **completely, totally** *It is made from completely natural ingredients.*
- ADJ+n substance **ingredients, material, product, resources, substance** *They stressed the need for using natural resources in a sustainable way.*
- ▶ surroundings **ecosystem, environment, habitat, landscape, setting, surroundings, world** *Article 55 states: Care shall be taken in warfare to protect the natural environment against widespread, long-term and severe damage.*
- ▶ beauty **beauty** *Everyone was amazed by the island's natural beauty.*
- ▶ process **process** *Germination is a natural process that depends on the right supply of moisture, light, and air.*
- ▶ state **state** *Large areas of the park have been left in their natural state.*
- ▶ event **phenomenon** *It is generally agreed that the vast majority of UFO reports can be explained as misidentifications of aircraft or natural phenomena.*
- ▶ causes **causes** *He died of natural causes, and there are no suspicious circumstances.*
- ▶ feature **feature** *We will work with the local community to safeguard coastal wildlife and the coastline's unique natural features.*
- ▶ choice **alternative, choice** *Herbal medicines offer a natural alternative to conventional medicines.*

2 reasonable or expected in particular situation

- adv+ADJ completely **completely, entirely, perfectly, quite, totally** *It was perfectly natural always to have your gas mask with you when you went to school.*

▶ very **very** *In these circumstances, it is very natural to feel fear, anxiety, and despair.*

▶ only **only** *When we see our friends in trouble, it's only natural to want to help.*

● ADJ+n reaction or result **consequence, reaction, response** *I fully agree with Elaine; it is a natural reaction to retaliate when hit.*

▶ thing **thing** *To want a quiet life is the most natural thing in the world.*

▶ choice **choice** *He was the natural choice for the part of Johnny.*

3 existing in someone from early age

● ADJ+n ability **ability, talent** *He has a tremendous amount of natural ability.*

▶ tendency **inclination, instinct, tendency** *All this goes against the natural instincts of the Chancellor.*

nature N
a basic quality or feature of something

● adj+N real **real, true** *His expression immediately indicated the true nature of his feelings.*

▶ exact **exact, precise** *There is a debate amongst historians as to the precise nature of Charles II's intentions at this time.*

▶ same **same, similar** *There are no other commercial sites of a similar nature in the West Midlands.*

▶ different **different** *Colin, however, had problems of a different nature.*

▶ basic **basic, essential, fundamental** *We must first be clear about the essential nature of democracy.*

You can use the expression *by its (very) nature* to describe a quality that something has because of what it is: *Medical records, by their very nature, contain sensitive information.*

▶ general **general** *This booklet contains information of a general nature about the school.*

▶ complicated **complex, complicated** *The involvement of the African Union in the mediation effort is especially important because of the complicated nature of the crisis.*

▶ technical **technical** *Some of the information is of a highly technical nature.*

▶ serious **serious** *The serious nature of some offences may mean that they cannot be dealt with in this court.*

▶ private or needing to be dealt with carefully **confidential, personal, private, sensitive** *Page 1 of the letter was of a personal nature, so it has been omitted.*

▶ very special **unique** *The unique nature of the university has attracted a diverse range of students.*

▶ containing different elements **diverse** *The diverse nature of the party's electoral support needs to be underlined.*

▶ v+N know the nature of something **know, recognize, understand** *Perhaps the best way to try to understand the nature of this problem is to take a familiar modern analogy – that of doctor and patient.*

▶ examine the nature of something **analyse, consider, discuss, examine, explore, investigate** *The book seeks to explore the nature of religious belief and practice in fourteenth-century England.*

▶ establish the nature of something **assess, define,**

determine, establish** *We will work with your business to establish the exact nature of your finance requirements.*

▶ change the nature of something **alter, change, transform** *The Act will fundamentally change the nature of higher education.*

▶ keep the nature of something **keep, preserve** *We wanted to preserve the informal nature of our meetings.*

▶ show the nature of something **emphasize, reflect, reveal, show** *We wanted to create a website that reflected the nature of the business in a clear and uncomplicated manner.*

▶ explain the nature of something **explain** *Physics endeavours to explain the nature of the physical world from sub-atomic particles to the whole universe.*

▶ describe the nature of something **describe** *In his introduction to the book, John describes the complex nature of his relationship with his mum.*

nausea N
the feeling that you are going to vomit

● adj+N severe **acute, severe, violent** *Chemotherapy can have serious side effects such as hair loss and severe nausea.*

▶ not severe **mild, slight** *Twelve of the nineteen participants reported feelings of mild nausea at some time during the trial.*

▶ lasting for a long time **chronic, persistent** *Chronic nausea can significantly impair a patient's quality of life.*

● v+N cause nausea **bring on, cause, induce, produce** *High doses of iron can cause nausea.*

▶ experience nausea **experience, feel, have, suffer (from)** *As many as 90 per cent of pregnant women will experience some nausea and vomiting.*

▶ prevent nausea **combat, control, prevent** *There are now new drugs to control nausea which can be very effective, so do ask your doctor or nurse.*

▶ reduce nausea **alleviate, ease, reduce, relieve** *Ginger tea or ginger tablets can help reduce nausea.*

▶ cure nausea **treat** *The drug has been used in the UK for over 30 years to treat nausea in cancer patients.*

● n+of+N **bout, feeling, onset, sensation, wave** *I felt weak and had to fight off occasional waves of nausea.*

navigate V
choose a path for a ship, plane, or car to go along, find a path through a difficult place or a way of dealing with a difficult situation

● adv+V successfully **effectively, efficiently, smoothly, successfully** *Ten days later, he successfully navigated the lifeboat on the epic sixteen-day journey from Elephant Island to South Georgia.* ● *He helped his clients successfully navigate UK immigration laws.*

▶ in a safe way **safely** *These notes will help you navigate your way safely through the complex decisions that you will have to take.*

▶ easily **easily** *There is a site map to help you navigate easily around the website.*

▶ accurately **accurately** *You need to be able to navigate accurately in fine weather and foul.*

▶ confidently **confidently** *By the end of the workshop,*

*you will be able to navigate confidently **around** the Internet.*

▸ skilfully **skilfully** *Anyway, he safely got us airborne and skilfully navigated **across** the featureless wastes below.*

navy N
the part of a country's armed forces that fights at sea

● adj+N **large, modern, strong** *In 1629, Richelieu decided that France needed a proper and modern navy.*

● v+N join/leave the navy **enter, join, leave** *He joined the navy at the age of twelve, and was a captain at 26.*

▸ create a navy **build, create** *The United States used its economic supremacy to build a strong navy.*

▸ defeat a navy **defeat** *Their aim now was to defeat the Egyptian navy.*

▸ have a navy **have** *Switzerland doesn't have a navy.*

▸ increase the size of a navy **expand** *From Britain's point of view, Germany's desire to expand her navy was unacceptable.*

▸ continue to have a navy **maintain** *Even weaker countries tried to maintain a navy.*

▸ serve in the navy **be in, serve in** *He served in the French navy for a time.*

necessary ADJ
essential or needed for something

● adv+ADJ very or exactly **absolutely, entirely, really, strictly, very, vitally** *A qualification in this area will be helpful although it's not strictly necessary.*

▸ scarcely **hardly, scarcely** *It's hardly necessary to stress that these facts should not be disclosed to the public.*

▸ more and more **increasingly** *It has become increasingly necessary for the industry to establish standards of practice.*

▸ clearly **clearly** *It is clearly necessary to involve parents at the planning stage.*

▸ equally **equally** *Resources are essential, but equally necessary is the will to succeed.*

▸ in a particular way **clinically, legally, logically, medically, politically** *The surgery must be medically necessary; cosmetic surgery does not qualify.*

● v+ADJ consider something **believe sth, consider, deem, feel sth, find sth, judge sth, regard sth as, see sth as, think sth** *The Inspector was given powers to do anything he considered necessary.*

▸ be or become **be, become, remain** *Occasionally, surgery may become necessary.*

▸ seem **appear, seem** *The measures that he recommended do not seem necessary at this stage.*

▸ make something **make sth, render sth** *The act makes it necessary for employers to ensure that employees have a safe environment in which to work.*

▸ be shown to be **prove** *Ambulances have been put on standby in preparation for a full-scale evacuation, should it prove necessary.*

necessity N
1 the fact of a process, thing, or action being needed in a situation

● adj+N types of necessity **commercial, economic,**

financial, historical, legal, logical, medical, military, operational, political, social *Throughout her life, she would insist that she became an artist **through** economic necessity.*

▸ urgent **dire, immediate, urgent** *Do not use this technique except in cases of dire necessity. ● We should draw attention to the urgent necessity to change what is happening in that country, for the benefit of its own citizens.*

▸ great **absolute, great, sheer, vital** *Local residents use the road for vehicles only in cases of absolute necessity. ● I had to go out to work **from** sheer necessity.*

▸ practical **practical** *As a matter of practical necessity, non-EU parts of Western Europe comply with many EU regulations.*

● v+N avoid or get rid of necessity **avoid, eliminate, obviate, remove** *The new line into London obviated the necessity to run trains over the North Kent line.*

▸ stress necessity **assert, emphasize, highlight, stress, underline** *They stressed the necessity **for** groups to keep their records up to date.*

▸ realize or accept necessity **accept, acknowledge, perceive, realize, recognize, understand** *We recognize the necessity of reaching young people through other young people.*

▸ question or deny necessity **deny, question** *She questioned the necessity of so many advisers being present.*

2 something that you must have in order to live, work, or do something

● adj+N basic **bare, basic** *Their parents have to work from dawn to dusk to provide the basic necessities.*

▸ great **absolute, vital** *Things that are luxuries are often presented to the consumer as absolute necessities.*

▸ needed every day **daily** *He's talking here about food, clothing, daily necessities.*

● v+N **have, lack** *We lived in poverty and lacked even the basic necessities.*

neck N
the part of the body that joins the head to the body

● adj+N painful or injured **bad, broken, fractured, painful, sore, stiff** *I've had a bad neck for years.*

▸ short/long **long, short** *He was small and stocky, with a short neck.*

▸ thick **fat, thick** *He craned his thick neck to glance back over his shoulder.*

▸ thin **scraggy INFORMAL, scrawny, slender, slim, thin** *She was a tall girl with a slender neck.*

▸ not covered **bare** *He could feel the draught on his bare neck.*

● v+N stretch your neck **bend, crane, extend, strain, stretch** *She craned her neck to see what was going on.*

▸ break your or someone's neck **break, snap** *In a freak accident in February 1940, Leonard broke his neck.*

▸ injure your neck **crick, hurt, injure, strain, twist** *In the warm-up, Ferdinand cricked his neck, so couldn' play.*

▸ twist an animal's neck **twist, wring** *They killed the chickens by wringing their necks.*

need V

when it is necessary to have or do something

- adv+V very much **badly, desperately, really, sorely, urgently** *In order to achieve this, we desperately need your help.*
- not always or not in every situation **not necessarily** *You don't necessarily need to be present in person.*
- in fact **actually, really** *For such short trips, do you really need to take the car?*
- only **just, only, simply** *I only need glasses for reading.*
- clearly **clearly, obviously** *The woman clearly needed urgent medical help.*
- certainly **certainly, definitely** *This old hotel certainly needs a facelift.*
- usually **generally, normally, usually** *A schoolchild usually needs to sleep about 10 hours every night.*
- almost not **hardly** *These fears, I need hardly say, are completely unjustified.*

need N

1 a situation in which it is necessary for something to be done

- adj+N great or urgent **desperate, dire, great, immediate, pressing, urgent** *The school was in desperate need of refurbishment.* • *There was a pressing need for such a facility in the area.*
- increasing or continuing **constant, continuing, growing, increasing** *We have been unable to meet the increasing need for training.*
- clear **clear, obvious** *The project identified a clear need for flexible training opportunities.*

- v+N show or emphasize the need for something **emphasize, highlight, show, stress, underline, underscore** *These figures highlight the urgent need for tougher action on climate change.*

> You can use the expression *in need of* to say that something is necessary: *The system was in need of updating.* The phrase *there is no need* means that something is not necessary: *There was no need for the computers to be replaced.*

feel the need of something **feel, have** *I felt the need to speak out.*
get rid of the need for something **avoid, eliminate, obviate, remove** *We do not claim that GM crops will eliminate the need for economic, political or social change, or that they will feed the world.*
see or accept the need for something **accept, acknowledge, perceive, recognize, see, understand** *We all recognize the need for greater environmental protection.*
satisfy the need for something **address, fulfil, meet, satisfy** *This chapter addresses the need for alternative research strategies.*
reduce the need for something **reduce** *Better treatment techniques may further reduce the need for surgery for patients with these cancers.*
increase the need for something **increase** *Slow economic growth has increased the need for public expenditure.*
show the need for something **demonstrate, reflect, show** *The international conflicts of recent years have clearly demonstrated the need for better understanding between different cultures.*
create the need for something **create** *This

expansion has created the need for larger office facilities.

2 something that someone requires [usually plural]

- adj+N basic **basic, essential, fundamental** *We are not meeting the basic needs of some of the most disadvantaged groups in society.*
- great or urgent **immediate, pressing** *50,000 tonnes of grain would be enough to satisfy the immediate needs of the population.*
- special or particular **individual, particular, special, specific** *We realize that you have very specific needs, so we will tailor the course to you.*
- not satisfied **unmet** *There is now a range of innovative therapies to satisfy unmet needs in cancer patients.*
- different **conflicting, different, diverse** *It is often difficult to cater for the conflicting needs of diverse groups.*
- types of need **dietary, economic, educational, financial, health, human, medical, nutritional, physical, psychological, social, spiritual** *Different criteria apply for children with special educational needs.*

- v+N identify or consider need **assess, consider, identify** *Training needs will be identified at each stage.*
- satisfy or try to satisfy need **accommodate, address, cater for/to, focus on, fulfil, meet, provide for, respond to, satisfy, suit, support** *We will use our resources to respond effectively to the diverse needs of the pupils in our care.* • *We offer three packages to suit your particular needs.*
- when needs decide something **be determined by, be dictated by, be driven by, be geared to/towards, be tailored to** *We are driven by the needs of our customers in every situation.* • *This service is tailored to the needs of individual small companies.*
- balance needs **balance** *Each headteacher must balance the needs of the troublesome pupil along with the needs of the rest of the children in the school.*

negative ADJ

1 expressing disagreement, criticism, or opposition; giving more attention to bad possibilities than to good ones

- adv+ADJ very **extremely, highly, overwhelmingly, strongly, very** *Several patients expressed strongly negative reactions.*
- rather **quite, rather, somewhat** *Sometimes the remarks of our closest friends and family can at first be quite negative.*
- completely **completely, entirely, purely, totally, wholly** *Stevenson's message was not totally negative.*
- mainly **generally, largely, mostly, predominantly** *I'm amazed at how the reviews on this page seem to be largely negative.*

- ADJ+n reaction **reaction, response** *The paper was prepared and submitted, but the group received a negative response.*
- statement **comment, feedback, remark** *I was shocked at some of the negative comments.*
- emotion **emotion, feeling** *One of the best ways to avoid succumbing to negative emotions is to be focused on the task.*
- thought **thought** *Do you suffer from negative thoughts about your body and health?*

▶ view **attitude, perception, stereotype, view** *Youngsters from poorer backgrounds can develop negative attitudes to learning early on.*
▶ image or description **image, portrayal** *Do social workers really deserve the negative image the media give them?*
▶ attention in magazines or newspapers, or on television or radio **coverage, publicity** *The Conference aimed to counteract much of the negative publicity surrounding migrant workers.*
▶ idea **association, connotation** *The term 'asylum seeker' carries many negative connotations.*

2 harmful or bad

● adv+ADJ very **extremely, highly, overwhelmingly, profoundly, strongly, very** *Such a proposal could have extremely negative implications for the BBC.*
▶ rather **quite, rather, somewhat** *In fact, she got over this rather negative feeling very quickly*
▶ completely **completely, entirely, purely, totally, wholly** *A ban would also have an entirely negative effect.*
▶ mainly **generally, largely, mostly** *World War I had a generally negative impact on Honduras.*
▶ possibly **potentially** *The report focuses on the potentially negative results for future welfare services .*

● ADJ+n effect **effect, impact** *The survey found that 60 per cent of respondents thought the current tax system was having a negative impact on their international competitiveness.*
▶ result **consequences, implications, repercussions, result** *Significant numbers still choose not to disclose this information because they fear negative consequences.*
▶ aspect **aspect, side** *Modern historians have been quick to emphasize the negative aspects of the period.*
▶ experience **experience** *For most people, serving on a jury is a negative experience.*

neglect V
1 fail to do something you should do

● V+n duty **duty, responsibility** *He had been neglecting his duties as a director.*
▶ work **schoolwork, task, work** *So concentrate on your football, but don't neglect your schoolwork.*
▶ education **education** *He has neglected the education of his children and spoiled them by indulging all their wishes.*
▶ health **health** *She neglected her health and became seriously ill.*

● V+infinitive say **explain, inform, mention, point out, report, tell** *He neglected to mention that he was already married.*
▶ pay **pay** *The record company had neglected to pay the studio and the tapes were confiscated until payment was received.*
▶ ask **ask** *I spoke to a young woman who I think was Mr Woolley's daughter, though I neglected to ask.*
▶ bring **bring** *Then darkness descended, and we realized that we had neglected to bring a torch to look at our map.*
▶ consider **consider** *Of course, he neglects to consider the actual consequences of his action.*

2 fail to pay attention to something

● adv+V often or to a great extent **largely, often** *She looks at poetry that has been largely neglected by scholars.*
▶ to some extent **relatively, somewhat** *This aspect of local studies has been somewhat neglected.*
▶ unfairly or sadly **sadly, unfairly, unjustly** *This is an unjustly neglected masterpiece of 18th century prose.*

> **Neglect** is usuallly plural in all of the **adv+V** combinations shown above.

● V+n subject **field, issue, subject, topic** *Literary scholars have rather neglected the whole issue.*
▶ importance **importance, role** *Sometimes, in our preoccupation with government and politics, we neglect the importance of civil institutions.*
▶ piece of work **work** *Professor Friedman completely neglects the work of Herman Daly, Robert Costanza and other ecological economists.*
▶ aspect **aspect** *But she neglects the darker aspects of the drama.*
▶ fact **fact** *The book neglects the fact that the operation of markets and of government are entirely interdependent.*

neglect N
the failure to give someone or something the care or attention they need

● adj+N deliberate **deliberate, wilful** *Parents can be prosecuted for wilful neglect if they leave a child unsupervised in a manner likely to cause unnecessary suffering or injury to health.*
▶ serious **gross, serious, severe** *The case revealed gross neglect within the CIA.*
▶ types of neglect **emotional, physical** *What they experienced was clearly emotional neglect and physical abuse.*
▶ by parents **parental** *Parental neglect can cause lasting damage.*
▶ complete **complete, total** *Since his death, he has suffered almost total neglect as a composer.*
▶ kind and not intended to be harmful **benign** *The administration is now following a policy of benign neglect, allowing market forces to push down the dollar's value internationally.*
▶ relative **comparative, relative** *This is reflected in the relative neglect of the study of legislation.*
▶ general **general** *These days, the buildings suffer from general neglect.*
▶ seeming to exist **apparent** *It's quite true that she was deeply wounded by the king's apparent neglect.*
▶ criminal **criminal** *Whether this constitutes criminal neglect is not for me to judge.*

● v+N experience neglect **experience, suffer, suffer from** *The city suffers from comparative neglect.*
▶ deal with neglect **address, tackle** *The local authority has a moral and legal responsibility to address the neglect of our local heritage and environment.*
▶ make people notice neglect **highlight** *The report highlights the shameful neglect of this vulnerable and often isolated group of people.*

neglected ADJ
1 not given attention

● ADJ+n **area, aspect, classic, dimension, element,**

field, masterpiece, subject, topic *The article concludes by suggesting that it would be fruitful for more research to be done in this largely neglected area.*

2 not cared for

● ADJ+n person **child, wife** *The King spent very little time with his neglected wife.*
▶ place **building, garden** *All this is a far cry from the dark and somewhat neglected garden that Michael and Caryl took over in 1983.*

negligence N

failure to give necessary care or attention

● adj+N serious **gross, serious** *The Government also proposes three new offences designed to make individuals in an organization accountable for serious acts of gross negligence which result in death.*
▶ deliberate **deliberate, wilful** *Welsby thinks that I may have a case if I were to sue for wilful negligence.*
▶ involving guilt or a crime **criminal, culpable** *He said even if Dr Norris made an error of judgement it did not amount to criminal negligence.*
▶ personal **personal** *Members will be charged for loss or damage resulting from personal negligence.*
▶ for which you are partly responsible **contributory** *A finding of contributory negligence is highly likely.*
▶ types of negligence **clinical, corporate, medical, professional** *He has written on issues related to clinical negligence and personal injury.*

● v+N **accuse sb of, admit, allege, arise from, claim, establish, involve, prove, result from** *A private prosecution brought by the father alleged negligence on the part of the travel company.* ● *They claimed for injury resulting from the firm's negligence.*

negligent ADJ

failing to give necessary care or attention

adv+ADJ **allegedly, criminally, grossly, potentially, professionally** *The Security Council was grossly negligent in not monitoring the effects of sanctions.*

v+ADJ **be, consider sb, deem sb, find sb, prove sb** *The court found that he had been criminally negligent.* ● *You could be convicted if you are proved negligent in a court of law.*

negligible ADJ

very unimportant or small

adv+ADJ almost **almost, virtually** *The cost of such items is almost negligible.*
fairly **fairly, pretty** INFORMAL *While the books get an undeniable boost in sales from the films, it's usually fairly negligible compared to the overall sales.*

ADJ+n amount **amount, content, level, proportion, quantity** *Pesticide levels are reduced during washing, cooking, or processing fruits and vegetables, with negligible amounts remaining in the final product.*
effect **effect, impact, influence** *Present policies seem to be having a negligible effect on getting more people to cycle.*
cost **cost, overheads** *The overheads are negligible and the benefits considerable, even when it appears*

that a machine has vast resources; rarely are you the only user!

▶ risk **chance, risk** *Very low doses of radiation are used, which pose a negligible risk to health.*
▶ importance **importance** *In virtually all cases, these differences are of negligible importance.*
▶ increase **increase, rise** *There has been a negligible increase in public investment in these sectors since 2005.*
▶ difference **difference** *The price difference was negligible, so we went ahead and bought it.*
▶ loss or damage **damage, loss** *A negligible loss to a large company, for example, could be catastrophic for a private individual or small business.*
▶ help or benefit **benefit, contribution** *Pacific Island countries make a small or negligible contribution to greenhouse gas emissions.*
▶ rate **rate** *The drop-out rate is negligible for these courses.*

● v+ADJ **be, become, consider sth, seem** *Their contribution to the event was negligible.* ● *In this case, the risk is considered negligible.*

negotiate V

1 try to reach agreement by discussing something in a formal way

● adv+V successfully **effectively, successfully** *Trade unions still successfully negotiate wage settlements for whole sectors of industry.*
▶ separately **individually, separately** *Directors' contracts must be negotiated individually.*
▶ directly **directly** *In the summer of 1647, Cromwell and his senior army colleagues decided to negotiate directly with the King.*
▶ for a particular area **locally, nationally** *The report also called for women to be able to negotiate locally for more flexible working practices.*

● V+n agreement **agreement, arrangement, ceasefire, contract, deal, package, peace, purchase, sale, settlement, terms, treaty, truce** *A union often negotiates agreements with employers on pay and conditions.*
▶ price **discount, fee, price, rate, salary** *Taxis fares are fixed, but it is a good idea to negotiate a price before getting in.*
▶ solution or change **change, solution** *Either negotiate changes with your lender or refuse the loan.*
▶ right **right** *The company negotiated exclusive rights to import and distribute his products within the UK.*

2 successfully travel along a path or road; get past something that is in your way or stopping you doing something

● adv+V **carefully, safely, skilfully, successfully** *After safely negotiating the road, we then had to cross a railway line.*

● V+n route **path, road, route, way** *We all have to negotiate our way through public spaces in our everyday lives.*
▶ obstacle or danger **bend, hazard, maze, minefield, obstacle, roundabout, stairs** *We successfully negotiated the minefield of regulations relating to the employment of young people.* ● *You will need to help elderly residents to negotiate the stairs on their way to the meeting.*

negotiation N

formal discussions in which people or groups try to reach an agreement [usually plural]

- adj+N relating to a particular area **international, local, national** *The EU has played a significant role in international negotiations on climate change.*
- ▶ types of negotiation **contractual, diplomatic, political** *There have been incidents where political negotiations have floundered because of careless reporting.*
- ▶ involving a particular number of groups or countries **all-party, bilateral, multilateral, multi-party** *We have made clear our readiness to engage in multilateral negotiations.*
- ▶ involving people at a high level **high-level** *In this job you will be involved in high-level negotiations with leading retailers.*
- ▶ lasting for a long time **lengthy, prolonged, protracted** *A deal was signed yesterday after weeks of protracted negotiations.*
- ▶ current/future **current, forthcoming, future, ongoing** *They are worried about the possible failure of the current negotiations.* • *She had been involved in ongoing negotiations since the middle of December.*
- ▶ complex or difficult **complex, detailed, difficult, intense, intensive, tough** *Detailed negotiations with Swansea Council are underway to finalize the arrangements.*
- ▶ formal/informal **formal, informal** *Formal negotiations are scheduled to start next week.*
- ▶ direct **direct, face-to-face** *There is no reason not to explore the alternative option of direct negotiation with the employer.*
- n+N **climate (change), contract, disarmament, pay, peace, trade** *Trade ministers will discuss launching a new round of trade negotiations.*
- v+N start negotiations **begin, commence, enter, enter into, initiate, open, start** *The Government said it would enter into negotiations with the unions on their plans.*
- ▶ continue negotiations **continue** *The EU urges the parties to continue negotiations in order to arrive at a peaceful settlement.*
- ▶ organize negotiations **conduct, hold, pursue, undertake** *We have conducted negotiations with the manufacturers on behalf of the client.*
- ▶ deal with negotiations **handle** *Devon County Council will be handling the negotiations with landowners along the route of the line.*
- ▶ be in charge of negotiations **lead, oversee** *The union's deputy general secretary will lead the negotiations.*
- ▶ finish negotiations **complete, conclude** *China remains optimistic about concluding the negotiations before the deadline.*
- ▶ stop negotiations **break off, suspend, terminate** *Then the three senior executives got up and strode angrily out of the room, breaking off negotiations.*
- ▶ start negotiations again **reopen, restart, resume, revive** *He expressed deep concern over the violence and urged both sides to resume negotiations.*
- N+v start **begin, commence, start** *Negotiations began with a financial institution last December, but an agreement over the price hasn't been reached.*

If something is **open to negotiation**, it is able to be changed after discussion: *The union said that everything is open to negotiation.* When something is **subject to negotiation**, it may be changed after discussion: *We've reached a broad agreement but the details are subject to negotiation.*

- ▶ continue **continue, go on, proceed** *Although the pay dispute has not been settled, nurses are continuing to work while the negotiations continue.*
- ▶ take place **take place** *The committee chairman said negotiations were still taking place over the purchase.*
- ▶ fail **break down, collapse, fail, stall** *At the end of June, negotiations broke down.*

neighbourhood N

a particular area of a city or town

- adj+N local **immediate, local, surrounding** *Improve your local neighbourhood by renovating disused premises so that they can be used as a base for community activities.*
- ▶ good **good, nice** *Every one wants and is entitled to live in a good neighbourhood.*
- ▶ bad **bad, dangerous, rough, tough** *As a child I grew up in a very bad neighbourhood.*
- ▶ rich **affluent, wealthy** *Children in England's poorest areas are three times as likely to be hit by a car as those in more affluent neighbourhoods.*
- ▶ poor **deprived, disadvantaged, low-income, poor, run-down** *We all know the problems of our poorest neighbourhoods – decaying housing, unemployment, street crime, and drugs.*
- ▶ quiet **quiet** *This quiet neighbourhood is just 5 minutes' walk from the town centre.*
- ▶ safe **safe** *He argues that local communities want CCTV because they believe it will reduce crime, and make their neighbourhood safer.*
- ▶ in a particular area **city, inner-city, suburban, urban** *The report recommended solutions to bring people back into urban neighbourhoods.*
- ▶ containing a particular social class **middle-class, working-class** *They own a large comfortable house in a middle-class neighbourhood.*
- ▶ containing a mixture of different types of people or buildings **mixed** *We lived in a mixed neighbourhood – black, white and Mexican – and many of the houses were rundown.*
- ▶ consisting mainly of houses **residential** *The streets in the residential neighbourhood are eerily empty.*
- v+N make a neighbourhood **create, establish** *One of our aims is to create safer neighbourhoods and healthier workplaces.*
- ▶ improve a neighbourhood **improve, regenerate, renew, revitalize, transform** *We are working to regenerate some of the most disadvantaged neighbourhoods of the city.*

neighbouring ADJ

near each other

- ADJ+n area **area, borough, county, district, parish, region** *The benefits of using the same system in neighbouring areas are clear.*
- ▶ country **country, state** *The majority of refugees go to neighbouring countries.*
- ▶ town or village **city, community, resort, town,**

village *The situation in the neighbouring villages is no better.*

▶ organization **authority, council, local authority** *A neighbouring authority, Lambeth Council, demanded an environmental assessment.*

▶ piece of land **farm, farmland, field, land, property** *The house and grounds were scoured but there was no sign of the lad and so the neighbouring fields were searched.*

▶ building or street **building, house, property, school, street** *The fire in the shop caused damage to a neighbouring property.*

▶ island **island** *There is a plan to build Britain's biggest wind farm on the neighbouring island of Lewis.*

▶ person or people **farmer, land owner, resident, tribe** *The land around the canal was sold off to a variety of neighbouring landowners following closure.*

nerve N

1 a worried feeling that you will fail [always plural]

▶ v+N have nerves **get, have, suffer from** *Afterwards, she reportedly admitted that she had suffered from nerves.*

▶ calm nerves **calm, ease, settle, soothe, steady** *He gave Atherton some pills to calm his nerves.*

▶ control nerves **control, deal with, overcome, steady** *Trying hard to overcome her nerves, she strode into the main building.*

2 the ability to control your fear and remain determined in a difficult or dangerous situation

▶ v+N have nerve **have** *I'm glad I had the nerve to talk to you that day.*

▶ keep your nerve **hold, keep** *England can win if they hold their nerve.*

▶ lose your nerve **lose** *I lost my nerve when I realised how high up I was.*

▶ need nerve **need, require, take** *It takes a lot of nerve to make the jump.*

▶ lack nerve **lack** *This government lacks the nerve to make tough decisions.*

▶ show nerve **show** *He showed the nerve and composure that fans have become accustomed to.*

▶ find your nerve **find** *I'm still not sure where I found the nerve to do it.*

▶ find out how good someone's nerve is **test** *Abseiling will really test your nerve.*

nervous ADJ

feeling excited and worried, or slightly afraid

▶ adv+ADJ very **extremely, highly, incredibly, particularly, really, so** INFORMAL, **very** *On the first day of filming I was really nervous.*

▶ slightly **a little, slightly** *I was a little nervous to start with, but now I'm fine.*

▶ rather **pretty** INFORMAL, **quite, rather, somewhat** *She had been quite nervous about performing in front of more than 100 people.*

▶ clearly **clearly, obviously, visibly** *Mrs. Gough was obviously nervous and very shy.*

▶ more and more **increasingly** *Demand will often drop significantly during downturns as buyers become increasingly nervous.*

▶ in a way that is normal and reasonable

understandably *Staff are understandably nervous about the future.*

● v+ADJ **appear, become, feel, get, grow, look, make sb, remain, seem, sound** *I was starting to feel very nervous about the exams.* ● *Sit down: you're making me nervous walking up and down like that.*

● and/or **anxious, apprehensive, edgy, excited, frightened, jumpy, scared, shy, tense, worried** *I didn't sleep well and woke up at five with a nervous excited feeling in my stomach.*

nervousness

being nervous

● adj+N slight **certain, slight** *There was a slight nervousness about our play last weekend.*

▶ natural **natural, understandable** *I detect an understandable nervousness on your part.*

▶ early or apparent **apparent, initial** *Despite her apparent nervousness, she had a deep assurance about her.*

● and/or **anxiety, excitement, irritability, restlessness, tension** *The most common side effects are restlessness, nervousness, and headaches.*

● n+of+N **degree, feeling, sign, trace** *In most cases, outward signs of nervousness evaporate within two or three minutes of starting the interview.*

● v+N hide or overcome nervousness **hide, overcome** *In the end, I overcame my initial nervousness.*

▶ show nervousness **betray** *Sue was quiet, and when she did speak her voice betrayed a slight nervousness.*

▶ cause nervousness **cause** *Caffeine can elevate blood pressure, and cause nervousness or irritability.*

network N

1 a system of connected roads, wires etc

● adj+N relating to a particular area **global, international, local, national, nationwide, regional, worldwide** *Each of these airports will be linked to its region by regional high-speed train networks.*

▶ large **extensive, large, wide** *An extensive network of canals waters the fertile fields.*

● n+N for transport **bus, motorway, rail, railway, road, train, transport** *The EU will be providing structural funds for improving our transport network.*

▶ for communication **broadband, mobile phone, mobile telephone, phone, telecommunications, telephone** *Your computer is connected to the telephone network to access remote computers and online services.*

● v+N create a network **build, construct, create, develop, establish** *Over the next three years, the project aims to develop a network of paths and cycleways through these woodland areas.*

▶ operate a network **manage, operate, run** *Until then, the coach network was managed by the National Bus Company, a state-owned business.*

▶ form a network **form** *These fallen trees formed a network of bridges that we regularly crossed on our adventures.*

▶ keep a network operating **maintain** *They maintain a network of footpaths, providing access to the gorge.*

► make a network increase in size **expand** *The £33.5bn is part of a ten-year transport plan, which the committee believes is not enough to expand the network.*

2 a group of people, organizations, or places that are connected or that work together

● adj+N relating to a particular area **global, international, local, national, nationwide, regional, worldwide** *It sells a wide range of financial products direct to the public through its national network of branches.*

► large **extensive, large, wide** *They are the country's largest network of independent estate agents.*

► complex **complex** *There is a complex network of subsidies and quotas, which supposedly protects farmers by guaranteeing prices.*

► social **social** *Contact with children from different cultural and socio-economic backgrounds enhances children's capacity for developing wider social networks.*

► informal **informal** *This is an informal network which meets in order to share ideas about the important issues of the day.*

► support **support** *We have set up a learning and support network that is open to all students.*

● v+N create a network **build, construct, create, develop, establish, set up** *We have also established a network of distributors in over 20 countries, where customers can purchase our materials in local currency.*

► operate a network **manage, operate, run** *The Forestry Bureau operates a network of hostels in forest areas that are more than a day's journey from any city.*

► form a network **form** *Officials of the ancient Egyptian bureaucracy were highly trained individuals who ran all the major state institutions and formed a network of highly motivated and powerful people.*

► join a network **join** *You will be joining a network of like-minded individuals, all of whom are passionately committed to providing pre-school children with a positive introduction to sport.*

► use a network **use** *Always keep your CV up to date and use your existing network of contacts, as well as developing new ones, to create opportunities for career development.*

► keep a network operating **maintain** *The organization maintains a network of regional offices across the UK.*

► have a network **have** *We have a network of experienced professionals who will guide you in choosing the right solution for you.*

► provide a network **provide** *The agreements we have with universities in over 20 countries provide a network of educational opportunities to satisfy the most ambitious student.*

► support a network **support** *An international fund was set up to support a global network of public research institutions.*

► make a network increase in size **expand** *The Alumni Association is continuously expanding its network of contacts all over the world.*

neutral ADJ
not supporting a particular side in an argument or disagreement

● adv+ADJ **ethically, ideologically, politically, religiously** *The monarch is supposed to be politically neutral and represent the whole nation.*

● ADJ+n opinion or attitude **approach, attitude, evaluation, point of view, position, stance, view, viewpoint** *If you feel unable to support us openly, then you must take a neutral position.*

► person **arbiter, mediator, observer, party, person, third party, umpire** *As a neutral observer, I recently attended the Public Inquiry on the proposed bus route.*

● v+ADJ **appear, be, remain, stay** *Sweden's comments reflect its attempts to appear neutral in international affairs.*

neutrality N
the state of not supporting either side in a war, disagreement etc

● v+N continue your neutrality **maintain, observe, preserve, retain, uphold** *Hitler believed that neither Belgium nor Holland would long maintain their neutrality.*

► make sure neutrality continues **ensure, guarantee** *Mr. Chen has also ensured the neutrality of the civil service.*

► announce your neutrality **declare, proclaim** *On the outbreak of World War I, Norway declared its neutrality.*

► give up your neutrality **abandon** *The West might succeed in forcing them into abandoning their neutrality.*

► not accept someone's neutrality **violate** *Which of the belligerent nations had been first to violate the neutrality of Europe's non-combatant states?*

► damage your neutrality **compromise** *They run the risk of compromising their neutrality and thus jeopardizing their traditional humanitarian role.*

new ADJ
1 recently made

● adv+ADJ very **brand, spanking** INFORMAL**, very** *The company offers a comprehensive service whether you are looking for a brand new car or a used vehicle.*

► fairly **comparatively, fairly, quite, relatively** *They were living in a relatively new house.*

2 replacing something

● adv+ADJ **completely, entirely, genuinely, quite, radically, totally, wholly** *The development of quantum mechanics led to some radically new ideas about the behaviour of matter.*

news N
1 information about something that has happened recently

● adj+N good **excellent, fantastic, good, great, positive, welcome, wonderful** *Joe has good news for Pauline – his daughter Megan can attend the wedding.*

► bad **awful, bad, disturbing, shocking, terrible** *So you're suggesting that next year we say to them: 'We have some bad news for you.'*

► exciting **exciting, interesting** *You might think that this is not very exciting news.*

► sad **devastating, sad, tragic** *He received letters next* *day from his wife and sister, conveying the same sad news.*

▸ v+N get news **get, have, hear, receive** *I was so very sorry to hear the news of Carl's death yesterday.*

▸ give someone news **announce, break, bring, deliver, give sb, tell sb** *We were worried about breaking the news to our friends and families.*

▸ share news **share, spread** *Sheila hurried back to the room to share her news.*

▸ be pleased to get news **welcome** *We welcome the news that the project has received funding from the Home Office.*

▸ wait for news **await, respect, wait for** *The family anxiously awaits news of their son James, who is away at war.*

▸ N+v arrive **arrive, come, reach** *But during the day worrying news arrived that the Duke of Cumberland's army was already at Lichfield.*

▸ become known by more people **spread** *The news spread quickly.*

▸ n+of+N **bit, piece, snippet** *As Elinor and Marianne were walking together the next morning, the latter communicated a piece of news to her sister.*

information about recent events reported in newspapers, television, radio, the Internet etc

▸ adj+N recent **breaking, hot** INFORMAL**, latest, recent, up-to-the-minute** *Here is a round-up of the latest news.*

relating to a particular area **domestic, foreign, global, international, local, national, regional** *We will also keep you updated on local news and events.*

relating to a particular subject **corporate, economic, financial, political** *Bloomberg is a large-scale provider of financial news and information.*

important **front-page, headline, important, major** *When this story gets out, it will be headline news in the financial press.*

▸ n+N relating to a particular subject **business, celebrity, company, entertainment, football, health, industry, market, music, science, sports, technology, travel** *Aside from specialized content, such as crosswords, or business news on the Financial Times's FT.com, newspapers offer their content free.*

relating to a particular area **home, world** *In November, one story will dominate world news more than any other: the American Presidential Election.*

▸ v+N announce news **announce, break, broadcast, post, print, publish, report** *The Washington Post was first to break the news of Saylor's plans.*

contain news **carry, contain, cover, feature, include** *The news was covered in the Saturday edition of the paper.*

become news **become** *Two years ago she became front-page news when her boyfriend was sentenced to two years in jail after a horribly bizarre series of events.*

provide news **deliver, provide** *Many organisations now provide news in this format.*

pay attention to the development of news **follow** *I followed the news on Reuters and the Internet.*

▸ N+v **break, come in, emerge** *The news broke in Thursday's local evening press.*

▸ N+n piece of news **flash, item, release, story** *You

can view older news items by using the links at the bottom of the page.*

▸ broadcast that gives news **briefing, bulletin, programme, report** *The site offers subscribers a discussion forum, and a daily news briefing on developments in the stock market.*

▸ n+of+N **item, snippet** *It seems every week now there's some item of news about how we need to reduce our dependence on cars.*

newspaper N

a set of large printed sheets of folded paper containing news

▸ adj+N relating to a particular area **foreign, international, local, national, provincial, regional** *She decided to put an advert in the local newspaper.*

▸ published at a particular time **daily, evening, morning, Sunday, weekly** *Berlin's largest daily newspaper publicised the event.*

▸ published in a particular size **broadsheet, tabloid** *Four things sell tabloid newspapers on a Sunday in South Africa – sex, drugs, music, and soccer.*

▸ dealing with serious/entertaining news **popular, serious** *Why did he make this important announcement, not in Congress, but in a popular newspaper?*

▸ n+N **business, community, company, sports, student, university** *She got a taste of journalism while working on the university newspaper.*

nice ADJ

1 attractive, enjoyable, or pleasant

▸ adv+ADJ very **awfully, especially, extremely, particularly, perfectly, really, so** INFORMAL**, very** *I just relaxed, got a video, and had a really nice meal.*

▸ rather **fairly, pretty** INFORMAL**, quite, rather** *Where we live is quite nice.*

▸ v+ADJ **feel, look, seem, smell, sound, taste** *You look so nice in that dress.*

2 friendly, kind, and pleasant

▸ adv+ADJ very **awfully, especially, extremely, incredibly, particularly, perfectly, really, so** INFORMAL**, thoroughly, very** *When I got back, he was particularly nice to me.*

▸ rather **pretty** INFORMAL**, quite** *The teachers are all quite nice*

▸ in a sincere way **genuinely, truly** *You get the impression he is a genuinely nice guy.*

▸ v+ADJ **seem** *They were really reserved and quiet but seemed very nice.*

niche N

1 a job or activity that you are good at and that is very suitable for you

▸ v+N carve, carve out, find *Rich could never find the niche where he felt he belonged.*

2 a market for a specific product or service that no one else is providing

▸ v+N find a niche **discover, find, identify, recognise, spot** *Their rapid expansion is proof that they have identified a niche in the market.*

▸ establish a niche **carve, carve out, create, develop,**

establish *It has carved a niche for itself servicing firms with between 50 and 500 employees, who tend to spend £1,000 to £10,000 a month.*

▶ have a niche **fill, occupy** *Firms may respond to this pressure by specialising and deliberately occupying different niches.*

▶ use a niche in order to get an advantage **exploit** *The company has excelled at exploiting niches in the past.*

▶ provide what a niche needs **fit, serve** *It was keen to develop more products to serve this lucrative niche.*

▶ try to sell to a niche **target** *He hopes not to target just one specific niche but an entire cross-section of markets.*

● N+n market **area, industry, market, sector** *The private sector has also developed niche markets, such as cosmetic surgery, which are either limited or unavailable on the NHS.*

▶ company **business, channel, company, consultancy, firm, operator, player, practice** *She unveiled the company's plans to concentrate on building niche businesses around its existing specialities.*

▶ product **brand, magazine, model, product, publication, title** *Companies include major international players and small organisations manufacturing niche products.*

▶ use of advertising to sell products **marketing** *Specialist sites could be used to support niche marketing.*

▶ people watching or listening to something on television or radio **audience** *I think this is going to appeal to a very small niche audience.*

night N
the part of a day when it is dark

● adj+N dark **black, dark** *It is said that on dark nights, when the wind blows gently through the ruins, the hideous shrieks of the monk can be heard.*

▶ cold **chilly, cold, cool, frosty** *The nights are still cool, even when the days are scorching.*

▶ warm **hot, mild, warm** *It was another warm night in southern California.*

▶ with a lot of wind **stormy, wild, windy** *On a stormy night, she and Clifford escaped from the castle on horseback.*

▶ with a lot of clouds **cloudy** *After a mainly cloudy night, the sky will clear around dawn.*

▶ with light from the moon **bright, moonlit** *It was a moonlit night, so he decided to take his wife on a romantic boat ride on the lake.*

▶ with no light from the moon **moonless** *He kept his eyes fixed on the dark road, his mood as black as the moonless night.*

▶ with no clouds or rain **clear, dry, fine** *On a clear night, sit on the veranda and be amazed by the brightness of the twinkling stars.* ● *To the north it will be a dry night with clear skies and some patchy, shallow, ground fog will develop in the valleys.*

▶ wet **damp, rainy, wet** *We woke after a very wet night to a slight drizzle.*

▶ beautiful **beautiful** *It had been a gorgeous spring day and as the sun sank slowly, there was the promise of a beautiful night too.*

▶ with a lot of stars **starlit, starry** *I confess to being spellbound when I stand outside on a starry night and simply gaze upwards.*

nightmare N
an extremely difficult or frightening situation

● adj+N complete **absolute, complete, real, total** *My search for a nanny for my two girls is proving to be an absolute nightmare.*

▶ worst **biggest, ultimate, worst** *It turned out to be their worst nightmare.*

▶ types of nightmare **administrative, bureaucratic, environmental, financial, legal, logistical** *Planning a wedding can be a logistical nightmare.*

● v+N **endure, experience, face, live, suffer** *With a shortage of radiotherapists, thousands of patients are living a nightmare, waiting for their treatment to begin.*

● N+n **journey, scenario, season, situation, start, vision, world** *That is the nightmare scenario research scientists warned of this week.*

nod V
move your head downwards and then upwards, to show you agree or understand

● adv+V slowly **slowly** *He nodded slowly, starting to understand.*

▶ quickly **quickly** *The woman nods quickly, and point to the building opposite.*

▶ in a way that shows you are worried **gravely, grimly, seriously, solemnly, thoughtfully** *He nodded gravely at intervals as they told their story.* ● *He nods thoughtfully while considering the question.*

▶ in a way that shows you are wise **sagely, wisely** *Another general sat nodding sagely at every remark that Hitler made.*

▶ in a way that shows you understand **knowingly, sympathetically, understandingly** *I explained the situation to a receptionist, who nodded knowingly.*

▶ in a way that shows you agree **approvingly, enthusiastically** *Campbell and Milburn, who were listening attentively, nodded approvingly.*

▶ in a way that shows you are sad **sadly** *When he asked if he knows what happened to her, Willard nods sadly.*

▶ slightly **gently, imperceptibly, slightly, weakly** *He nodded slightly at his superior, but said nothing.*

▶ politely **politely, respectfully** *The councillors I was addressing nodded politely and pretended to have understood what I was saying.*

▶ without saying anything **quietly, silently** *He pointed this out to Thomas, who nodded silently.*

▶ with a strong movement **emphatically, furiously, vigorously** *I could not help nodding vigorously in agreement.*

noise N
a loud or unpleasant sound

● adj+N loud **deafening, loud** *Persistent exposure to loud noise can result in deafness.*

▶ too much **excessive, too much** *Excessive noise is also a significant hazard for site workers.*

▶ unpleasant **horrible, terrible** *Inside the capsule the noise is terrible, but the rocket is still held on the launch pad.*

▶ present around you **ambient, background, extraneous, general** *I found the background noise unbearable.*

▶ continuous **constant, incessant** *The constant noise of machinery was deafening.*

▶ not wanted **unwanted** *Our system is designed to eliminate unwanted noise.*

▶ types of noise **banging, buzzing, clicking, hissing, humming, rattling, rumbling** *The transformer makes a slight humming noise.*

▶ v+N make noise **cause, create, generate, make, produce** *We were careful not to make too much noise.*

▶ make less noise **control, keep down, keep to a minimum, reduce** *Oi, you lot, keep the noise down!*

▶ reduce the effect of noise **deaden, drown out, minimize, reduce**

▶ get rid of noise **eliminate, stop** *This has the advantage of eliminating any noise coming from the main house.*

▶ increase noise **increase** *Bringing traffic into a place where no traffic exists will greatly increase noise.*

▶ N+n amount of noise **level** *Campaigners said the new road would create intolerable noise levels.*

▶ controlling the amount of noise **abatement, control, management, reduction, suppression** *Electric vehicles have environmental benefits, but will also bring about noise reduction.*

▶ bad effects of noise **impact, nuisance, pollution, problem** *Cycling can help reduce traffic congestion and noise pollution.*

noisy ADJ
making a lot of noise

adv+ADJ very **extremely, incredibly, particularly, really, so** INFORMAL, **terribly, very** *If your neighbour is particularly noisy, it may be worth having a word with them anyway .*

rather **fairly, a little, pretty** INFORMAL, **quite, rather, slightly, somewhat** *They can be quite noisy for such tiny birds.*

full of noise

adv+ADJ very **extremely, incredibly, particularly, really, so** INFORMAL, **terribly, very** *The interior of the aircraft was extremely noisy.*

rather **fairly, a little, pretty** INFORMAL, **quite, rather, slightly, somewhat** *Rooms overlooking Green Street can be a little noisy.*

and/or full of people or activity **boisterous, busy, chaotic, crowded, lively** *The place was very busy and noisy.*

large **big, large** *I left the large noisy nightclub with a couple of friends, having danced a bit.*

small **cramped, little, small** *Forty minutes sitting alone with a drink in a small, noisy café is not much fun.*

dirty **dirty, dusty, polluted** *The city itself is noisy and dirty.*

having an unpleasant smell **smelly** *The laundry is noisy and smelly, and not unlike a factory.*

hot **hot** *New York is noisy and hot and I lie awake for much of the night.*

nominal ADJ
very small and much less than something is really worth

ADJ+n **amount, charge, cost, fee, price, rate, rent, sum, value** *Copies can be obtained from the address below for a nominal fee of £10.*

nomination N
an official suggestion that someone should get a job or a prize

● adj+N **Democratic, presidential, Republican** *She has already established herself as the early frontrunner for the Democratic nomination.*

● n+N **Academy Award, Emmy, Grammy, Oscar, party** *Both the director and the film itself are definitely in line for Oscar nominations.*

● v+N get a nomination **earn, gain, get, receive, secure, win** *He tried to win the Republican nomination for the presidency of the United States, but failed.*

▶ make a nomination **make, put forward, send, submit** *Members are invited to make nominations for this year's awards, which will be presented at a special event on 22nd March.*

▶ ask for nominations **ask for, encourage, invite, request, solicit, welcome** *Nominations are invited for the following posts: President, Vice-President, Secretary, and Treasurer.*

▶ say that you no longer want a nomination **withdraw** *The election was postponed and James was persuaded to withdraw his nomination.*

▶ try to get a nomination **seek, stand for** *It is important that all members should feel free to seek nomination or to nominate others.*

▶ accept a nomination **accept** *Miss Pamela Henry accepted the nomination for President and was duly elected.*

▶ announce a nomination **announce** *Bardem could well be in the running again for an Oscar when the nominations are announced on January 25th.*

▶ consider a nomination **assess, consider, review** *The Committee considered 37 nominations for honorary degrees.*

▶ support a nomination **endorse, support** *He joined the Republican Party and in 1860 supported the nomination of Abraham Lincoln.*

▶ give official agreement to a nomination **approve** *The Board shall approve the nomination to the Chairmanship.*

● N+n documents relating to nomination **document, form, letter, papers** *The committee now has 60 days to check the nomination papers for any irregularities.*

▶ process **arrangements, criteria, procedure, process** *The nomination procedure has been kept as simple as possible to encourage participation.*

nonchalance
being relaxed and not worried

● adj+N **airy, apparent, carefree, deceptive, seeming, studied** *The air of nonchalance is very deceptive, however, since the strength and skill needed are enormous.*

● v+N **fake, feign** *His opponent was leaning against the wall, unsuccessfully feigning nonchalance.*

nonsense N
ideas, behaviour, or statements that are not true or sensible

● adj+N complete **absolute, arrant, complete, plain, pure, sheer, total, utter** *The police said that the claims were 'utter nonsense'.*

▶ such **such** *I've never heard such nonsense in all my life.*

● v+N talk or write nonsense **peddle, speak, spout** INFORMAL**, talk, write** *You're talking complete nonsense.*

▶ believe nonsense **believe, be taken in by** *You don't want to believe that nonsense.*

norm N

1 something that is usual or expected

● adj+N **accepted, established, existing, expected, prevailing** *The nuclear family has been the firmly established norm for the past fifty years or so.*

● n+N **industry, market, sector** *The results obtained were consistent with industry norms.*

● v+N establish a norm **create, establish, set** *All the law can do is set a norm and enforce it equally.*

▶ become a norm **become** *These things have become the norm in academic life today.*

▶ obey a norm **accept, conform to, follow, observe** *I'm afraid I have always been a bit of a rebel and don't like to conform to the norm.*

▶ refuse to obey a norm **break from, challenge** *It is important to continually challenge the norm.*

▶ be different from a norm **depart from, deviate from, differ from, diverge from, vary from, violate** *He has composed a unique score which dares to deviate from the accepted Hollywood norm.*

▶ continue to be a norm **remain** *Once established, this type of architecture remained the norm for over a millennium.*

▶ think that something is the norm **consider sth** *For most positions, one month's notice is considered the norm.*

2 standards of behaviour accepted in a particular society [always plural]

● adj+N social **cultural, social, societal** *Throughout our life, we belong to a number of social groups with differing social norms.*

▶ moral or religious **ethical, moral, religious** *Moral norms are taken to be universal and to exercise some constraint on conduct.*

▶ traditional **traditional** *Two hundred and sixteen children described living with parents who insisted on traditional norms.*

● n+N **community, gender, group** *Such a person will by and large not have his/her attitudes determined mainly by group norms.*

normal ADJ

not unusual or surprising in any way

● adv+ADJ completely **absolutely, completely, entirely, perfectly, quite, totally** *To the people living 50 years ago this would have seemed perfectly normal.*

▶ rather **fairly, pretty** INFORMAL**, relatively** *They appeared to lead fairly normal lives.*

● ADJ+n method **manner, method, mode, practice, procedure, process, routine, system, way** *If you want to do a PhD, you need to go through the normal application process.*

▶ situation **circumstances, conditions, course of events, development, situation, state** *In normal circumstances, this is a very safe and routine operation.*

▶ amount or measurement **amount, cost, fee, level, pressure, price, range, rate, size, speed, temperature, value, weight** *The background radiation level remained more or less normal.*

● v+ADJ seem normal **appear, look, seem** *The guard checks the monitor, but everything looks normal.*

▶ consider something normal **accept sth as, call sth, consider sth, regard sth as, view sth as** *It is considered normal to gain 10 to 12kg during pregnancy.*

normality N

a situation in which everything is normal

● adj+N relative **comparative, relative** *The new King and Queen and the Princesses had only two years of comparative normality before the outbreak of World War II.*

▶ seeming to exist **apparent, seeming** *His music establishes the film's tone, which discourages us from trusting the apparent normality and tranquillity of this small town.*

● v+N go back to normality **regain, resume, return to** *With the removal of Milosevic from his presidency the Balkans were slowly returning to normality.*

▶ make normality exist again **re-establish, restore** *Today, the city is trying to restore some normality after the attack.*

▶ seem like normality **approach, resemble** *I just want to get my life back to something approaching normality.*

● n+of+N a kind of normality **degree, kind, semblance, sort** *Finally, the markets seem to have returned to some semblance of normality.*

▶ a feeling of normality **feeling, sense** *This is an important way of helping restore a sense of normality to the community.*

nose N

the part of your face above your mouth that you use for smelling and breathing

● adj+N large and noticeable **big, large, long, prominent** *Jon has the biggest nose I've ever seen.*

▶ small **button, little, short, small** *It would be nice to have a smaller nose, but I don't think I'd seriously consider cosmetic surgery.*

▶ pointed **pointed, pointy** INFORMAL**, sharp** *She wasn't exactly pretty: her nose was too sharp for that.*

▶ flat **flat, pug, snub** *He was a handsome, blond man with deep-set eyes, a snub nose, and a small moustache.*

▶ straight **straight** *His nose was straight with rather flared nostrils.*

▶ curved downwards **aquiline, hook, hooked** *His hair was grey, his forehead high, and his nose aquiline.*

▶ curved upwards **turned-up, upturned** *Her sister had a dear little upturned nose.*

▶ preventing you from breathing well **stuffy** *Take hot showers to clear a stuffy nose.*

▶ with liquid coming from it **runny, snotty** INFORMAL *It's that time of year when every child seems to constantly have a runny nose.*

▶ covered in blood **bleeding, bloodied, bloody** *The young man appeared to sustain a bloody nose during the attack.*

nostalgia N

thoughts about happy times in your past

- adj+N complete **pure, sheer, unashamed** *The reunion in May assembled nearly 40 old members for an evening of pure nostalgia.*
- when you remember something as being better than it really was **misty-eyed, romantic, rose-tinted, sentimental** *The number of truly dire 'vintage' shows is too easily forgotten by those who cling to their rose-tinted nostalgia for yesteryear.*
- slightly sad **wistful** *The music for this beautiful film is filled with a wistful nostalgia.*
- for a particular period **50s, 60s, 70s etc** *He is clearly not returning to the music scene to cash in on 80s nostalgia.*

- v+N produce a feeling of nostalgia **bring, bring back, evoke** *Such footage is included to add historical authenticity to the piece, but often evokes the most nostalgia in the viewer.*
- feel nostalgia **feel** *This little restaurant is definitely worth a visit, especially if you have visited Spain recently and are feeling nostalgia for the food or culture.*
- enjoy nostalgia **enjoy, indulge in, wallow in** *They seem to do nothing but wallow in nostalgia for the good old days.*

- N+for **age, childhood, days, era, past** *If you fancy an unusual day out, or have the faintest bit of nostalgia for a more civilized age of travel, then this is definitely worth trying.*

- n+of+N a feeling of nostalgia **feeling, mood, pang, sense, wave** *For you, those three words will evoke a string of mental images, but more importantly a sense of nostalgia, and also, a sense of outrage.*
- a little nostalgia **bit, hint, touch** *There is nothing wrong with a bit of nostalgia.*
- a period of nostalgia **bout, evening, moment, night** *For classic rock fans, this was going to be a night of nostalgia.*
- an example of nostalgia **dose, piece, slice** INFORMAL *It was a classic piece of nostalgia from when the show was arguably at the height of its powers.*

notable ADJ

unusual or interesting enough to be mentioned or noticed

- ADJ+n achievement **accomplishment, achievement, feat, success, victory, win** *There have been a number of notable successes recently.*
- action that helps to achieve something **contribution** *This is an excellent resource and a notable contribution to Puerto Rican studies.*
- someone or something that is different from the rest **exception** *East Asian economies (with the notable exception of Indonesia) have been slowly recovering.*
- example **case, example, exponent, instance** *The Town Bridge is a notable example of a fine medieval bridge.*
- feature **feature** *The two most notable features of the July weather were the extreme heat over most of the month, and then the severe thunderstorm on 26th.*
- person **figure, personality** *He was a notable figure in the history of nineteenth-century Africa.*
- building **building** *Other notable buildings include the church of St Peter and St Paul, one of the most beautiful in the county.*
- piece of work **work** *Some of his most notable works include the themes to Star Wars, Superman, Jaws, and E.T.*
- difference **difference** *The most notable difference between the two coinages was the twenty pence coin, the Irish coin being circular as opposed to the seven-sided British version.*
- change **change, departure, improvement** *This announcement represents a notable departure from earlier policy statements.*
- something that is expected, but missing **absence, omission** *There were some notable omissions in the paper's list of 'the 100 best novels'.*

note N

1 short pieces of information that you write in order to remember something, especially when studying [usually plural]

- adj+N in detail **comprehensive, copious, detailed, extensive, extensive** *I made copious notes in the reference library.*
- short and without much detail **brief, rough** *Just have a quick look through your brief notes, diagrams or lists, test yourself on a couple of topics, then relax.*

- n+N **course, discussion, field, lab** INFORMAL, **laboratory, lecture, research, revision** *There is more to revision for an examination than memorising your lecture notes.*
- v+N write notes **make, scribble, take, write, write down, write up** *I sit in the lecture theatre for an hour taking notes and copying down diagrams from the overhead projector.*
- read notes **go through, look through, read, read through** *The waiting area is comfortable and quiet enough if you want to read through notes before the exam.*

2 a particular mood or style

- adj+N positive **brighter, happier, hopeful, lighter, optimistic, positive** *On a positive note, customer reaction has been good.*
- serious **serious, sombre** *Unusually, this comedy ends on a serious note.*
- sad **sad** *However, I have to finish on a very sad note.*

Usage In all of the **adj+N** combinations shown above, **note** usually appears in the pattern **on a ... note**.

note V

notice or realize something

- V+n **change, difference, importance, lack, need, problem, progress, use** *Please note the changes of venue for these meetings.*

noted ADJ

well known for a particular quality or ability

- ADJ+n **architect, artist, author, authority, composer, critic, expert, historian, scholar, writer** *The book was selected by noted historian Paul Johnson as one of his three favourite books of the year.*

noteworthy ADJ
worth giving special attention or praise to

- adv+ADJ **especially, particularly** *In terms of the town's history, however, 1848 was particularly noteworthy.*
- ADJ+n aspect of something **aspect, example, fact, feature, item** *A noteworthy feature of the Department is the relative youth of its members.*
- ▶ event **event, incident** *The most noteworthy event of the winter of 1915/16 was a successful British raid on the trenches at Gommecourt.*
- ▶ achievement **accomplishment, achievement, contribution, performance, success** *Through her various books and papers, she has made a noteworthy contribution to contemporary philosophy.*

notice V
become conscious of someone or something by seeing, hearing, or feeling

- adv+V almost not **barely, hardly, not really, scarcely** *It's very light and you will hardly notice you are wearing it.*
- ▶ not even **not even** *Three of us had our bags stolen without even noticing that anything had happened.*
- ▶ immediately **at once, immediately, instantly** *I entered my room and immediately noticed my laptop was gone.*
- ▶ quickly **quickly** *By doing these exercises on a regular basis you will soon notice a difference.*
- ▶ just **just, only just** *I've just noticed that on every page on the site I spelled 'World' as 'Wold'.*
- ▶ only **only** *His absence was only noticed at eleven pm.*
- ▶ suddenly **suddenly** *He was preparing lunch when he suddenly noticed a strange figure standing behind some bushes in the garden.*
- ▶ first **first** *I first noticed that I was losing my hair at the age of 18.*
- ▶ never **never** *I must have driven past it so many times, but I had never noticed it before.*

notice N
information or a warning about something that is going to happen

- adj+N given previously **advance, previous, prior** *All prices are subject to change without prior notice.*
- ▶ written **written** *The student concerned shall be given written notice of the complaint.*
- ▶ enough **adequate, reasonable, sufficient** *With sufficient notice, we can prepare menus for those with special diets.*
- ▶ according to the usual rules **due** *Organizers had to provide local magistrates with due notice of the time and place of the meeting.*
- ▶ a particular amount of time before something happens **a week's, 21 days', three months' etc** *Staff were given only one month's notice of the decision to close the factory.*
- N+v have notice **get, have, receive** *You'll want everyone to have notice of the event well in advance.*
- ▶ give notice **give, send** *Each party must be given notice of the hearing date.*
- ▶ need notice **need, require** *We require notice of cancellation before 2pm on the day prior to delivery.*
- N+of a plan or planned event **date, decision,**

event, intention, meeting *You must give your employer 4 weeks' notice of the date you intend to leave.*
- ▶ a change in something planned **cancellation, change, termination, withdrawal** *A full refund will be given, provided we receive notice of cancellation seven days before the event.*

noticeable ADJ
easy to see, hear, or feel

- adv+ADJ very **especially, particularly, quite, really, so, very** *In Britain, increased alcohol consumption is particularly noticeable in young women.*
- ▶ almost not **barely, hardly, scarcely** *The engine noise is barely noticeable.*
- ▶ clearly **clearly, easily, readily** *The swelling on my face was easily noticeable.*
- ▶ immediately **immediately, instantly** *What was immediately noticeable was the far lower police presence than usual.*
- ADJ+n difference **difference** *You will soon see a noticeable difference in your dog's behaviour.*
- ▶ effect **effect, impact, result** *Higher prices have had a noticeable effect on demand.*
- ▶ change **change, shift, variation** *This change is noticeable in all major towns and cities.*
- ▶ improvement **improvement** *However, a few areas had not shown a noticeable improvement from the previous survey in 2001.*
- ▶ increase **increase, rise** *There has been of late a very noticeable increase in the number of accidents on this stretch of road.*
- ▶ reduction **decline, drop, reduction** *The police report a noticeable reduction in the amount of graffiti.*
- ▶ tendency **tendency, trend** *By 2010, one of the most noticeable trends will be an ageing population.*
- ▶ lack **absence, lack** *There is still a noticeable lack of black and minority ethnic people in NHS leadership and management positions.*
- ▶ feature **aspect, feature** *Perhaps the most noticeable feature of the church is the elaborately carved gilt altar.*

notification N
an official announcement that something has happened or will happen

- adj+N previous **advance, early, previous, prior** *The University reserves the right to withdraw or amend a scholarship without prior notification.*
- ▶ immediate **immediate, instant, prompt** *Once I had placed my order I got an immediate notification.*
- ▶ in a particular form **electronic, email, written** *You have the right to cancel your order, without giving a reason, providing that we receive written notification of cancellation within 7 days of the receipt of your order.*
- ▶ official **formal, official, statutory** *Formal notification will be sent to members nearer the time.*
- ▶ automatic **automatic** *You can ask for automatic notification by email.*
- v+N get a notification **get, have, receive** *You can register on our website to receive notification of all our new publications.*
- ▶ give someone a notification **give, issue, provide,**

send, submit *Councillor Bresland had not been given notification of the meeting.*

▶ need or ask for a notification **request, require** *Many mortgage lenders require notification that commercial activities are being undertaken at the property.*

● N+of something that has happened or will happen **appointment, decision, event, meeting, outcome, result** *We are awaiting notification of the results of a recent school inspection.*

▶ a change **cancellation, change** *You must give the Benefits Agency notification of any changes in your circumstances.*

notify V

inform someone officially about something [usually passive]

● adv+V immediately **forthwith, immediately, instantly, promptly** *Ensure all customers are immediately notified of any new properties that may be suitable.*

▶ officially **formally, officially** *You will be formally notified of the result of your examination by the Examinations Office.*

▶ automatically **automatically** *Please complete your details here to be automatically notified when new items are added to the website.*

▶ before sth happens **beforehand, in advance** *Anyone wishing to attend on the night needs to notify us in advance.*

▶ directly **directly** *Winners will be notified directly and details of all winners will appear on our website.*

▶ according to agreed rules **accordingly, duly, properly** *We are investigating this problem, and customers will be notified accordingly.*

● V+by **email, letter, mail, phone, post, telephone** *You will be notified by email when this has been done.*

● V+of change **amendment, change, update** *I have tried to ensure that all details are updated as soon as I'm notified of any changes.*

decision or result **decision, outcome, result** *A senior officer will consider your application and you will be notified of the outcome in writing.*

date **date** *They were then notified of the date of the hearing before the judge.*

event **event, incident** *If you register your email address with us, you will be notified of all future events.*

meeting **meeting** *He complained that he had not been notified of the meeting.*

request **application** *Neighbours will be notified of your application and asked for objections.*

notion N

an idea, opinion, or belief

adj+N silly **absurd, crazy, foolish, ridiculous, romantic, silly, strange** *That's a ridiculous notion.*

traditional **accepted, conventional, prevalent, traditional** *As a result, traditional notions of the classroom have begun to undergo a radical change.*

not clear **vague** *Some of us have known from a very early age what career we want to pursue; others have only a vague notion.*

clear **clear** *Alice had no very clear notion of how long ago it had happened.*

▶ incorrect **false, misguided, mistaken** *Is it a misguided notion to believe in the goodness of humanity?*

▶ basic **basic, fundamental** *She seems to be questioning the basic notion that political legitimacy comes from democratic elections.*

▶ important **central, important, key** *This is a central notion in Wittgenstein's later thinking.*

▶ general **broad, general** *The introduction to the report will give you a general notion of some of the many problems we faced.*

▶ modern **contemporary, current, modern** *But from the 1870s onwards, the modern notion of addiction began to take shape.*

▶ simple or too simple **simple, simplistic** *Their approach is based on the simple notion that it is more cost-effective to get it right first time than correct mistakes later.*

▶ old **old, old-fashioned, outdated, primitive** *We should move away from the outdated notion that education is only for the young.*

▶ particular **particular** *But it was more than twenty years earlier that he had come to accept this particular notion of perfection.*

▶ common **common, popular, widespread** *This is very different from the common notion of God.*

▶ whole **entire, whole** *The whole notion of celebrity has changed.*

▶ existing as a thought in the mind **abstract, theoretical** *The acceptance of the abstract notion of an 'afterlife' is still a very powerful impulse in directing individual action.*

▶ slightest **faintest, foggiest, slightest** *I didn't have the faintest notion of who she was!*

▶ strange **bizarre, fanciful, odd, strange** *There was no medical evidence to support such a fanciful notion.*

▶ difficult to understand or deal with **complex, problematic** *Governments favour the idea of 'sustainability', but it is a complex notion.*

● v+N have a notion **have** *At the time I had no notion of where this would lead.*

▶ support a notion **reinforce, support** *Other studies support the notion that exercised muscles need protein very rapidly.*

▶ express doubts about a notion **challenge, question** *Some scholars have rightly questioned this notion.*

▶ accept a notion **accept, embrace, entertain** *We cannot accept the notion of time-travelling.*

▶ refuse to accept a notion **abandon, dismiss, dispel, reject** *Beth quickly dismisses the notion as absurd.*

▶ discuss a notion **consider, discuss, examine, explore** *This paper will discuss these two notions from a theoretical and historical point of view.*

▶ offer a notion so that it can be considered **introduce, put forward** *The final story introduces the notion of immortality.*

▶ add details to a notion **develop** *He does not develop further his notion of how full European integration might be achieved.*

▶ explain the meaning of a notion **define** *We must first define the notion of public interest.*

notoriety N

the state of being famous for doing something bad or shocking

● adj+N some **a certain, some** *He has a certain notoriety in his home town.*

▸ a lot of **considerable, great, much, widespread** *He wrote several works on social issues which attained considerable notoriety.*
▸ in a particular place **international, national, worldwide** *In real life, Coach Carter achieved national notoriety when he made the controversial decision to bench the whole of his team.*
▸ immediate **instant, sudden** *The book gained instant notoriety because of its assertion that Hitler knew nothing of the Holocaust.*
▸ lasting for a long time **lasting** *The name Fletcher Christian has obtained a lasting notoriety through its connection with the Mutiny on the Bounty.*
▸ public **public** *Stevenson would have revelled in such public notoriety.*

• v+N achieve notoriety **achieve, acquire, attain, earn, gain, win** *Jenny and her gang rapidly achieved notoriety.* • *In the 1930s, it gained notoriety as one of the few churches in London where divorced people could get married.*
▸ have notoriety **enjoy, have** *Perhaps one of the most famous prisoners held in the Tower of London, Walter Raleigh enjoyed notoriety throughout his life.*
▸ cause notoriety **bring** *The murder brought notoriety to the small village.*

notorious ADJ
famous for something bad

• ADJ+n person who commits a crime **bandit, criminal, gangster, highwayman, killer, murderer, pirate, robber, smuggler, terrorist, thief, villain** *Here is where the most notorious criminal of all, Jack the Ripper, carried out his crimes.*
▸ person **character, figure** *That night he went to visit a couple of notorious characters who would do literally anything for money.*
▸ crime **crime, murder** *A man jailed almost 50 years ago for one of the province's most notorious murders has had his name cleared.*
▸ event or action **case, episode, example, incident, scandal** *In a notorious incident in 1860, British and French soldiers ransacked the imperial summer palace outside Beijing.*
▸ place **blackspot, camp, district, estate, jail, prison, road, slum, spot** *Conditions in the notorious camp were becoming increasingly appalling.*
▸ reputation **reputation** *The Glasgow audience had a notorious reputation for being the most difficult in the country.*
▸ group **band, gang** *Cruz was a former member of one of New York's most notorious gangs.*
▸ film **film** *The scene has clearly been included purely to generate some publicity for the film – a ploy which has worked for some of the most notorious films in history.*
▸ court case **case, trial** *Many significant legal reforms were influenced by notorious cases.*

nourishment N
1 food or the substances in food that are necessary for life, growth, and health

• adj+N not much **insufficient, little** *These high-calorie foods provide very little nourishment for you and your baby.*
▸ enough **adequate, enough, proper, sufficient** *Pandas need to eat up to 18kg of food a day to get enough nourishment.* • *Cancer patients must be diligent about getting the proper nourishment.*
▸ extra **extra** *Cakes, biscuits, chocolate, puddings and crisps are an easy way of getting extra nourishment.*
▸ essential **essential, vital** *It provides the nourishment essential to a baby's healthy and sustained growth.*

• v+N provide nourishment **provide, supply** *It has food value and is intended to provide nourishment.*
▸ get nourishment **derive, gain, obtain, receive** *During his last few weeks, he could only receive nourishment through a tube.*
▸ need nourishment **need** *Food supplements can be helpful if you need extra nourishment.*
▸ try to get nourishment **seek** *These monks, observing their order's rule against meat, sought nourishment in milk, butter, and cheese.*
▸ take nourishment **draw, take** *The root is the only place through which the whole tree can draw nourishment.*

2 something that encourages the development of ideas, feelings, abilities etc

• adj+N **emotional, intellectual, spiritual** *These volumes provide plenty of intellectual nourishment.*
• v+N provide nourishment **provide, supply** *He claims that the normality and remoteness of Minneapolis provided just the artistic nourishment he needed.*
▸ get nourishment **derive, draw, gain, obtain, receive, take** *Goodall enjoys listening to pop and classical, but as a composer he derives more nourishment from the latter.*
▸ need nourishment **need** *We need spiritual nourishment if we are to live as God's people in this world.*
▸ try to get nourishment **seek** *In some cultures, they seek nourishment in some form of New Age spirituality.*

novel N
a long written story about imaginary characters and events

• adj+N types of novel **classic, comic, contemporary, epic, Gothic, graphic, historical, romantic, satirical, Victorian** *Not many people read Sir Walter Scott's historical novels these days.*
▸ popular **best-selling, blockbuster, popular, successful** *He has produced a string of best-selling novels.*
▸ regarded as very good **acclaimed, award-winning important** *The movie is an adaptation of her award winning novel.*
▸ exciting **compelling, exciting, gripping, unputdownable** *Full of drama, passion and mystery, her novel is completely unputdownable.*
• n+N **adventure, crime, detective, fantasy, horror, mystery, science fiction, sci-fi, spy** *Linda is an avid reader of crime novels.*

novel ADJ
new or unusual

• adv+ADJ very **completely, entirely, genuinely, truly** *The book introduces an entirely novel concept in linguistics.*
▸ fairly **fairly, quite, rather, relatively** *They came up with a rather novel approach to the problem.*

- ADJ+n way **approach, form, method, model, process, solution, strategy, technique, way** *We have devised a unique Student Learning Programme, which offers students a completely novel approach to study.*
- ▸ system **system** *The transfer involved the creation in Hong Kong of a novel system of government.*
- ▸ idea **concept, idea** *Here's a novel idea to help keep the kids amused during those long summer holidays.*
- ▸ technology **technology** *Collaboration with pharmaceutical companies will be necessary to enable this novel technology to be rigorously tested on a wide range of animals and humans.*

nuance N
a slight difference that is fairly important

- adj+N slight **delicate, fine, slight, subtle** *Young children do not understand the subtle nuances of more sophisticated stories.*
- ▸ of language **linguistic, semantic, verbal** *Remember, these guys are lawyers, attuned to every verbal nuance.*
- ▸ of music **musical, rhythmic, tonal, vocal** *The subtle vocal nuances of the singer are less noticeable on the DVD.*
- ▸ types of nuance **contextual, cultural, emotional, stylistic** *In order for a PR campaign to be successful abroad, an appreciation of the target language and its cultural nuances is necessary.*
- v+N capture a nuance **capture, convey, master, reflect, reveal** *Rosemary Edmonds's classic translation fully captures the subtle nuances of Tolstoy's writing.*
- ▸ understand or notice a nuance **appreciate, detect, grasp, hear, understand** *He liked to scoff at Danny for his failure to grasp the nuances of thuggish etiquette.*
- ▸ not capture a nuance **lack (in), lose, miss** *Pitt gives this performance his all, not missing a nuance of Bishop's layered personality.*
- ▸ add nuance **add** *His book adds nuance to a debate that is often depicted in stark or simplistic terms.*
- and/or **ambiguity, complexity, subtlety** *Good interpreters are alert to nuances and subtleties of meaning in both languages.*

numb ADJ
having no feeling, or unable to react because of shock

- adv+ADJ completely **completely, pretty** INFORMAL, **totally** *My limbs were completely numb.*
- slightly **a little, quite, rather, slightly** *I walked down the stairs, feeling slightly numb, and then I saw a familiar face outside the hotel.*
- emotionally **emotionally** *Feeling emotionally numb is often the first reaction to the death of a loved one.*
- ADJ+with cold **cold** *It is hard to work when your hands and feet are numb with cold.*
- emotion **fear, grief, shock** *Sitting in Europe and hearing about the earthquake in my home town left me feeling powerless and numb with shock.*

number N
quantity of people or things

- adj+N large **considerable, great, high, large,** **sheer, significant, substantial** *In 2005, there were 128 women elected to the UK Parliament, the highest number ever.*
- ▸ very large **enormous, huge, infinite, massive** INFORMAL, **overwhelming, record, unlimited, vast** *BMX is a sport enjoyed by a huge number of young people.*
- ▸ surprising or unexpected **surprising, unprecedented** *Due to the unprecedented number of applications received, we will not be able to reply to unsuccessful applicants.*
- ▸ fairly large **fair** INFORMAL, **good** INFORMAL, **reasonable** *About 60 people attended in the end which was a fair number.*
- ▸ small **limited, low, small, tiny** *Please note there are only a limited number of seats available.*
- ▸ same or similar **equal, same, similar** *The condition affects approximately 2 per cent of the population, and men and women are affected in equal numbers.*
- ▸ enough **adequate, sufficient** *The creche is offered subject to there being sufficient numbers of children.*
- ▸ too big **disproportionate, excessive** *A disproportionate number of accidents involve child cyclists.*
- ▸ total **final, overall, total** *The home page indicates the total number of visitors to the site.*
- ▸ real or exact **actual, exact, real** *The actual number of women who have experienced domestic violence is far more than that.*
- ▸ correct or exact **correct, right** *Although their current residence had the right number of rooms, the bathrooms were too small.*
- ▸ not exact **approximate, estimated** *These figures have been used to calculate approximate population numbers.*
- v+N increase the number of something **double, increase, raise** *The airline wants to increase the number of flights to Maputo to three or four a week.*
- ▸ reduce the number of something **cut, limit, reduce** *Our aim is to reduce the number of cars on the road.*
- ▸ give the number of something **give, indicate, list, specify** *The figure in brackets gives the number of students in the class.*
- ▸ count or guess the number of something **count, determine, estimate, identify, record** *A wildlife survey of 1979 estimated the number of elephants in Mozambique at over 54,000.*
- ▸ be more than the number of something **exceed** *The Romans lost about four hundred men, and the wounded did not exceed that number.*
- N+v increase **double, grow, increase, rise, soar, swell** *Student numbers have grown rapidly in recent years.*
- ▸ decrease **decline, decrease, drop, dwindle, fall, plummet** *Although the class was well attended at first, numbers soon dwindled and the class had to close.*
- ▸ change or be different **change, differ, fluctuate, vary** *Rabbits can quickly disappear during a hard winter, with the result that numbers fluctuate widely over time.*
- ▸ used for saying what a number is **approach sth, exceed sth, reach sth** *Airport passenger numbers exceeded 1 million for the first time.*

numerous ADJ
existing in large numbers

- adv+ADJ very **exceedingly, extremely, pretty**
  INFORMAL, **very** *These soft-bodied beetles may be very numerous on flower heads in summer.*
- ▶ fairly **fairly, quite, rather, relatively** *The benefits of keeping the hospital open were fairly numerous.*
- ▶ more and more **increasingly** *He was returned to office at the election, despite increasingly numerous allegations of corruption.*
- ▶ enough **sufficiently** *The communities are never sufficiently numerous to constitute a village.*
- ▶ especially **especially, particularly** *They were all over North America, but were particularly numerous in the Rocky Mountains.*

nursing N
the job, skills, or training of nurses

- adj+N **community, district, intensive care, medical, mental health, orthopaedic, paediatric, psychiatric, veterinary** *I deeply admire his commitment to psychiatric nursing.*
- v+N do nursing **do, practise, specialize in** *She is registered to practise nursing in the UK.*
- ▶ study nursing **learn, study, train in** *The best decision I ever made was to study nursing.*
- ▶ decide to do nursing as a career **choose, enter, pursue** *We are delighted to be awarding prizes to young people who wish to pursue nursing as a career.*

nutrition N
food, or the science of food

- adj+N good **adequate, balanced, correct, good, healthy, proper** *Adequate nutrition is essential if a child is to enjoy a healthy childhood.*
- ▶ bad **inadequate, poor** *Poverty means not only low incomes but also lack of education and poor nutrition and health.*
- v+N improve nutrition **boost, enhance, improve** *It is important that nutrition is improved in hospitals and in care homes.*
- ▶ provide nutrition **deliver, ensure, provide** *The emphasis is on providing basic affordable nutrition for less well-off people.*
- ▶ receive nutrition **receive** *To progress and succeed in your training, your body must receive the proper nutrition and rest it requires to recover.*

nutritious ADJ
providing the substances needed for good health

- adv+ADJ **extremely, highly, incredibly, particularly, very** *Bread is highly nutritious and provides a good source of vitamins and minerals.*
- ADJ+n **breakfast, diet, food, lunch, meal, recipe, snack** *Don't forget to include some nutritious snacks, such as dried fruit, cereal bars or oatcakes.*
- and/or **appetising, balanced, delicious, healthy, palatable, satisfying, tasty, well-balanced, wholesome** *It is important that the foods eaten should be wholesome and nutritious.*

Oo

oath N
a formal promise

- adj+N **binding, holy, judicial, sacred, solemn, sworn** *The speech should probably end with Hal on his knees, making a solemn oath before the king.*
- v+N make an oath **sign, swear, take** *People holding public office were required to swear an oath of loyalty to the Crown.*
- ▶ break an oath **break, refuse, renounce, violate** *I hope you are not asking me to break my oath.*
- ▶ not break an oath **fulfil** *The President has promised to fulfill his oath to protect this and future generations of Americans.*
- ▶ make someone make an oath **administer** *The Clerk administers the oath to the Jury.*
- N+of **allegiance, loyalty, obedience, office, secrecy** *Many people who live in Britain would not want to take the proposed oath of allegiance.*

obedience N
doing what someone tells you to do

- adj+N without thinking **blind, implicit, passive, slavish, unquestioning** *Robin, accustomed to unquestioning obedience, turned and went immediately up the stairs.*
- ▶ total **absolute, perfect, strict, unconditional** *The government of North Korea is based on an ideology of absolute obedience to the supreme leader Kim Jung Il.*
- ▶ showing a good quality **dutiful, faithful, humble, loving, sincere** *He sat down with humble obedience.*
- v+N demand or expect obedience **command, compel, demand, expect** *There was something in his stern face and resolute action which compelled obedience.*
- ▶ promise or show obedience **owe, promise, swear, vow, yield** *The friars who have already vowed obedience wear a particular type of tunic.*
- ▶ enforce or reward obedience **enforce, reward** *The magistrate who would reward obedience must punish rebellion.*
- ▶ refuse obedience **refuse** *If people refuse that obedience, then they cut themselves off from the Church.*

obey V
to do what a law or person says you must do

- adv+V without thinking **blindly, implicitly, slavishly, unquestioningly, without question** *The father who is blindly obeyed is obeyed from sheer weakness.*
- ▶ in a willing way **cheerfully, gladly, willingly** *The children willingly obeyed their elders, and toddlers played peacefully together without arguing.*
- ▶ in a loyal way **dutifully, faithfully, loyally** *Under hypnosis, Bill dutifully obeyed.*
- ▶ in a reluctant way **reluctantly** *I reluctantly obeyed, because he threatened me with dire consequences if I didn't.*
- ▶ quickly **immediately, instantly, promptly, without**

hesitation *He gave the order for his men to run into the castle, which they instantly obeyed.*

- V+n **command, instruction, law, order, rule, summons** *If the patient is awake enough to obey commands ask them to lift their head off the pillow for 5 seconds.*

object N
the person or thing that people have a particular feeling about

- N+of love or admiration **admiration, adoration, affection, desire, reverence, veneration, worship** *The object of his affections was a girl whom he had met at a school dance.*
- ▶ dislike or pity **derision, hatred, pity, ridicule, scorn** *It treats the rich and powerful as objects of ridicule rather than objects of reverence.*
- ▶ interest **curiosity** *We had become objects of curiosity to the people on the quay.*

object V
to be opposed to something, or to express opposition to something

- adv+V a lot **bitterly, fundamentally, greatly, strenuously, strongly, vehemently, vigorously, violently** *When he realized what the medical data was being used for, he objected strenuously.*
- ▶ in a particular way **formally, legally, publicly** *All the affected local authorities formally objected to the proposals.*
- ▶ consistently **consistently** *In these discussions, he consistently objected to any directives that were clearly in contravention of existing international law.*
- ▶ loudly **loudly, vociferously** *The defence lawyers objected vociferously to the display of the money, saying that the prosecution had not proved its origin.*
- ▶ at first **initially** *Even the men who initially objected to doing manual work eventually helped out.*
- ▶ when you think someone is right **conscientiously, rightly** *Feminists rightly object to such demeaning portrayals of their sex.*

objection N
a reason for disagreeing with a plan, or a statement expressing your disagreement

- adj+N main **chief, main, primary, principal** *My main objection to hunting is that it is cruel.*
- ▶ strong **fundamental, serious, strenuous, strong** *There are fundamental objections to human reproductive cloning.*
- ▶ reasonable or valid **principled, valid** *She doesn't think there are any valid objections he can raise.*
- ▶ not reasonable **frivolous, spurious** *This sort of spurious objection is being allowed to obscure a very serious issue.*
- ▶ formal **formal, written** *You will be given 6 weeks from the date of publication to make formal objections on the finalised plan.*
- ▶ not dealt with or impossible to deal with **insuperable, unresolved** *Any unresolved objections will be considered at a public inquiry.*

▶ types of objection **ethical, ideological, moral, philosophical, religious, theological** *Some people have an ethical objection to birth control.*

● v+N have an objection **have** *They can then write to the planning committee if they have any objections.*

▶ make an objection **express, make, outline, raise, state, voice** *No one present voiced any objections.*

▶ make a formal objection **lodge, register, submit** *Once an application has been received you have 28 days in which to lodge an objection.*

▶ withdraw an objection **drop, withdraw** *For these reasons, the committee has decided to withdraw its objections.*

▶ answer an objection **answer, counter, deal with, meet, reply to, respond to** *It is often better to answer an objection before a customer even thinks of it.*

▶ not accept or ignore an objection **dismiss, ignore, refute, reject** *He dismisses objections that Web-based systems are not fast or secure enough for automation applications.*

objective N
something you plan to achieve

● adj+N main **core, first, key, main, major, overall, overarching, overriding, primary, prime, principal** *The overriding objective is getting it right first time.*

▶ clear **clear, explicit, stated** *Teachers plan carefully, and lessons have clear objectives.*

▶ not specific **broad** *Their broad objective is to enrich the education of the student in the widest cultural sense.*

▶ for the future **long-term, ultimate** *The union of the Arab world is the ultimate objective.*

▶ for now **immediate, short-term** *Our immediate objective is to reduce the rate of growth of smuggling.*

▶ shared **common, shared** *The club has grown to approximately 40 members with one common objective, to have fun running.*

▶ different **conflicting** *In radiotherapy two conflicting objectives must be reconciled for each patient.*

▶ only **sole** *Over time his sole objective became extending his own life.*

▶ able to be measured **measurable** *The success of training should be assessed against measurable objectives.*

▶ able to be achieved **achievable, realistic, sustainable** *I believe our objectives are realistic and achievable.*

▶ difficult to achieve **ambitious** *The government has set itself the ambitious objective of making the UK the world's most favourable environment for e-commerce.*

▶ types of objective **business, corporate, educational, environmental, learning, military, organisational, policy, strategic** *Here is a list of your learning objectives for this term.*

● v+N achieve an objective **accomplish, achieve, attain, fulfil, meet, reach, realize, satisfy, secure, succeed in** *Reason and science cannot always tell us the best course of action to achieve our objectives.*

▶ try to achieve an objective **further, pursue** *Are other organisations working in your field or pursuing similar objectives?*

▶ set or state an objective **agree, clarify, define, identify, outline, set, state** *Allow a coach to help you set objectives to achieve the best impact on your performance.*

objective ADJ
based only on facts

● adv+ADJ completely **absolutely, completely, entirely, purely, totally, truly, wholly** *The assessment of a candidate's suitability is rarely wholly objective.*

▶ fairly or partly **essentially, fairly, partly, reasonably, relatively** *Select information in order to give a comprehensible and reasonably objective account.*

▶ when something may not be objective **apparently, ostensibly, seemingly, supposedly** *The supposedly objective assessment of the outcomes of medical interventions is increasingly popular in the Health Service.*

● ADJ+n assessment **account, analysis, appraisal, assessment, evaluation, judgement, measurement, reasoning, study, testing** *The independent expert's report is intended to be an objective assessment of the scheme.*

▶ journalism **journalism, reporting** *The newspaper gives fairly balanced objective reporting of the news.*

▶ viewpoint **stance, standpoint, view, viewpoint** *From an objective standpoint, there is nothing unusual about the present case.*

obligation N
something you must do

● adj+N legal or contractual **constitutional, contractual, legal, legislative, regulatory, statutory** *Where a tour operator has failed to honour its contractual obligations to a customer, it may be liable to pay compensation.*

▶ moral **ethical, moral** *With ownership comes the moral obligation to share it.*

▶ strict **absolute, onerous, solemn, strict** *These companies are under a strict obligation to protect your data.*

▶ most important **overriding, primary** *The Court has an overriding obligation to be fair.*

▶ that must be fulfilled **binding, enforceable, mandatory** *At this stage, there is no binding obligation on you or us.*

▶ that two people have to each other **mutual, reciprocal** *The agreement we sign with partners reflects our mutual obligations.*

▶ that cannot both be fulfilled **conflicting** *The different aims of medical practice and scientific research generate potentially conflicting obligations for physicians who engage in clinical research.*

▶ to other countries **international** *Failure to implement the treaty would result in the United Kingdom being in breach of its international obligations.*

▶ types of obligation **disarmament, financial, lease, pension, planning, religious** *If you own your house, then obviously your biggest financial obligation is your mortgage.*

● v+N have an obligation **be under, feel under, have, owe** *We all owe obligations to each other.*

▶ give someone an obligation **impose, place, place sb under** *Obligations are placed on broadcasters to deliver services in the public interest.*

▶ accept or understand an obligation **accept, acknowledge, recognise, respect, understand** *It is* *difficult to imagine them accepting an obligation to take out further insurance.*

▸ fulfil an obligation **comply with, discharge, fulfil, honour, meet, observe, perform, satisfy, undertake** *Society must fulfil its obligations to those unable to help themselves.*

▸ not fulfil an obligation **avoid, be in breach of, breach, disregard, evade, flout, ignore, violate** *The authorities had breached their obligations under international law by banning the march.*

▸ make someone fulfil an obligation **enforce** *There are no legal grounds to enforce this obligation.*

▸ define an obligation **define, outline** *There is a growing battery of legislation that defines your obligations to your workforce.*

▸ behave as though you have an obligation **assume** *The press assumes a curious obligation to inform us about matters relating to firearms.*

▸ be more important than an obligation **override** *The obligation to help my child overrides my obligation to meet you for lunch.*

obliterate V
to get rid of something completely

● adv+V completely **completely, entirely, totally** *The runway has completely obliterated the next section of the old A9 road.*

▸ almost **almost, largely, nearly, virtually** *Then they spent a week demolishing the wall stone by stone and virtually obliterating any sign of its existence.*

▸ partly **partially, partly** *A steep pathway, now worn with age and partially obliterated, remains.*

oblivion N
the state of having no memory or consciousness or of being totally forgotten

● adj+N total **complete, total, utter** *Then the visions disappeared and left me in utter oblivion.*

▸ almost **near** *The Liberal Party rose to supremacy in the mid eighteen-hundreds, only to disappear into near oblivion by the 1960s.*

▸ when this is a good thing **comfortable, merciful, sweet** *The unaesthetic finally brought merciful oblivion.*

▸ caused by alcohol **alcoholic, drunken** *Everyone was obviously well on their way to alcoholic oblivion.*

● v into+N **disappear, fade, fall, pass, sink, slip** *It is unbelievable that an artist of such talent and ability should slip into almost total oblivion.*

oblivious ADJ
not noticing or knowing about something

● adv+ADJ totally **absolutely, completely, entirely, totally, utterly** *He wanders through life totally oblivious to the problems he causes for everyone.*

▸ fairly or mainly **fairly, largely, quite, somewhat** *A few groups of younger people were chatting at a large table, fairly oblivious to how obnoxious they sounded.*

▸ almost **almost** *Many of these fascinating creatures seem almost oblivious to our presence.*

▸ happily **blissfully, happily** *The crowd had surrendered to the passion and joy of the day and seemed blissfully oblivious of the cameramen.*

▸ seemingly **apparently, seemingly** *This man has no principles and is seemingly oblivious to shame.*

obscene ADJ
offensive in a sexual or moral way

● adv+ADJ very or completely **absolutely, downright, particularly, truly** *A name may translate into something funny or downright obscene in another language.* ● *To welcome the use of this technology for beer and drugs, while denying it to those in need of food, seems to me to be truly obscene.*

▸ fairly or almost **almost, quite, rather, vaguely** *Viz's writers would latch onto any vaguely obscene street slang and print it.*

● ADJ+n sexually obscene **abuse, call, gesture, graffiti, joke, language** *He made an obscene gesture to Radebe's back as he walked away.*

▸ morally obscene **amount, inequality, profit, wealth** *A small minority at the top enjoy obscene wealth while a massive majority exists in abject poverty and misery.*

● and/or **abusive, defamatory, indecent, lewd, libellous, offensive, pornographic, profane, racist, threatening, vulgar** *The contents of the message were described by the judge as 'obscene and defamatory'.*

obscenities N
sexually offensive words or actions

● v+N **mouth, mutter, scream, shout, yell** *They shook their fists, shouted obscenities, and threatened to kill her.*

obscurity N
when someone or something is not known or remembered

● adj+N almost **comparative, relative, virtual** *Animation attracts people who are happy to work away in relative obscurity.*

▸ total **complete, sheer, total** *From total obscurity they made a great leap to national fame and superstardom.*

● v+from+N bring someone out of obscurity **pluck sb, rescue sb** *Rakhmonov was plucked from relative political obscurity to become Chairman of the Supreme Soviet.*

▸ come out of obscurity **emerge, rise** *Tanzania has emerged from comparative obscurity to stand as one of Africa's most popular travel destinations.*

● v+in+N **be lost, die, languish, live, remain** *An influx of well-paid U.N. employees and foreign diplomats has revived the careers of some painters who had been languishing in obscurity.*

● v+into+N **disappear, drift, fade, fall, sink, slip, vanish** *Many of his films have faded into obscurity.*

observant ADJ
noticing everything that happens

● adv+ADJ **acutely, extremely, keenly, sharply, shrewdly, very** *He was keenly observant, and he noticed the changes in the creek.*

observation N
1 the process of watching

● adj+N careful or continuous **accurate, acute, careful, close, continuous, detailed, precise,**

systematic *Careful observation over a period of time will show the effects quite clearly.*

▶ not careful **casual** *Let me give a couple of examples, drawn from casual observation.*

▶ done yourself **direct, first-hand, personal** *First-hand observation gives an account a certain authenticity.*

▶ types of observation **behavioural, classroom, clinical, ethnographic, experimental, scientific, visual** *Meteorology is based on the scientific observation of the Earth's atmosphere.*

● v+from+N know something from observation **deduce sth, draw sth, infer sth, know sth, learn sth, obtain sth** *Some observers assume they know from observation alone what is happening, and why.*

▶ come from observation **arise, come, derive, result, stem** *All the sound medical knowledge of today stems from observations carried out on human beings.*

● v+under+N **keep, place** *Children must be kept under close observation at all times.*

2 a written or spoken comment

● adj+N clever or interesting **accurate, astute, insightful, interesting, perceptive, pertinent, sharp, shrewd** *He makes some startlingly astute observations during the discussion.*

▶ funny **humorous, witty, wry** *Waugh's rich language and witty observations make Brideshead Revisited an essential part of any book lover's collection.*

▶ general **general** *There are a couple of general observations that are worth making.*

● v+N **make, offer** *If you would permit me, I'd like to make an observation.*

observe V

1 to accept and obey a rule, agreement, custom etc

● adv+V **correctly, duly, faithfully, impeccably, keenly, scrupulously, strictly** *When you are driving, always wear a safety belt and strictly observe speed limits.*

● V+n rule or precaution **limit, ordinance, precaution, restriction, rule** *Failure to observe parking restrictions could result in the clamping of unauthorised vehicles.*

▶ custom **convention, custom, ritual** *Even secular Jews still observe many customs that are of a religious origin.*

▶ something that has been agreed **ceasefire, confidentiality, silence** *Before kick-off a minute's silence was observed in memory of a former member of the club who had recently died.*

2 to make a comment

● adv+V in a clever or funny way **astutely, drily, perceptively, shrewdly, wryly** *As Mortlock wryly observes, the subject was the cause of some agitation at the time.*

▶ in a casual way **casually** *At the awards ceremony, one of the judges casually observed that, as a bass, I had 20 years to wait before reaching vocal maturity.*

▶ when someone is right **correctly, justly, rightly** *Jo rightly observed that it was "a lovely drying day".*

▶ when someone's comments are famous **famously** *Alfred Hitchcock famously observed that movies should be more than just picture postcards of people talking.*

observer N

someone who watches or sees something, but does not take part

● adj+N with no special interest or involvement **casual, passive** *But the Empress was more than just a passive observer.*

▶ impartial **disinterested, dispassionate, external, impartial, independent, neutral, objective, outside, unbiased** *What seems criminality on a grand scale to the impartial observer was to the British simply a matter of getting on with the job.*

▶ clever **acute, astute, intelligent, keen, perceptive, shrewd** *Astute observers have commented on the strangely close relationship between corporate culture and counterculture.*

▶ with a particular attitude **cynical, sympathetic** *Other more cynical observers have accused Bush of trying to buy votes in the UN to gain more support for the war against Iraq.*

▶ experienced or trained **experienced, expert, informed, seasoned, trained** *He is a seasoned observer of the international scene who has worked in 59 countries.*

▶ not experienced or trained **inexperienced, novice, untrained** *When an experienced surgeon operates he or she is using many small 'tricks', which may not be obvious to the inexperienced observer.*

▶ types of observer **climatological, election, industry, meteorological, military** *Germany also provides military observers for UN peacekeeping missions.*

obsession N

too much thought about someone or something

● adj+N not good **unhealthy, worrying** *I think you may be developing an unhealthy obsession with shopping.*

▶ strange **bizarre, morbid, unnatural, weird** *We're no: alone in our unnatural obsession with food and weight.*

▶ not sensible **excessive, irrational, neurotic** *People with OCD are aware that their compulsions and obsessions are irrational or excessive.*

▶ extreme **compulsive, fanatical, single-minded** *Because they're not allowed to travel into the West it becomes an almost fanatical obsession to do it.*

▶ about sex **erotic, sexual** *Asylum is a dark psychological thriller of sexual obsession set in the 1950s.*

▶ continuing for a long time **lifelong, longstanding** *His lifelong obsession was the idea that there could be life on other worlds in our solar system.*

▶ increasing **growing** *We live in a materialistic age where there seems to be a growing obsession with money.*

● v+N have an obsession **have, suffer from** *A local 16-year-old known as the Insect Boy has an obsessio: with bugs.*

▶ have the same obsession **share** *I'm very lucky to have a partner who shares the obsession of my life!*

▶ be an obsession **amount to, be** *His love for the har, amounted to an obsession.*

▶ almost be an obsession **border on** *She has a likin, for cream cakes that borders on obsession.*

▶ become an obsession **become, develop, turn into** *Coffee has become an obsession for Kiwis in recent years, in particular the search for the perfect 'flat white'.*

▸ satisfy an obsession **feed, indulge, satisfy** *The library gives me access to all the books necessary to indulge my obsession **with** the Great War.*

▸ overcome an obsession **overcome** *We need to overcome our obsession **with** material things.*

▸ show an obsession **reflect, reveal** *Jenni Sinclair's art reflects her obsession **with** people and the nature of humans.*

obsolete ADJ
replaced by something newer and better

● adv+ADJ almost **almost, effectively, essentially, largely, nearly, practically, virtually** *Paper communication between staff is virtually obsolete, with email the preferred medium of internal communication.*

▸ completely **completely, entirely, thoroughly, totally, wholly** *Manpower will not become totally obsolete, but its use will be substantially reduced.*

▸ partly **partially** *We will see mobile learning applications make the classroom partially obsolete.*

▸ more and more **increasingly** *The rise of solar and other renewable industries worldwide could make oil an increasingly obsolete fuel.*

● v+ADJ be or become obsolete **be, become, seem** *15 per cent of what you buy can suddenly become obsolete.*

▸ make something obsolete **make sth, render sth** *Many road maps have been rendered obsolete by changes in the road network.*

▸ say that something is obsolete **declare sth** *This weapon was declared obsolete in 1947, having been in service since 1915.*

▸ consider something obsolete **consider sth, deem sth** *His tier of management has apparently been deemed obsolete.*

obstacle N
a difficulty or problem that prevents you from achieving something

▸ adj+N large **big, daunting, enormous, formidable, major, serious, significant** *Despite the formidable obstacles in her path, she allowed nothing to deter her from meeting the needs of sailors and their families.*

▸ impossible to overcome **immovable, impassable, insuperable, insurmountable** *The mental health practitioner is faced with seemingly insurmountable obstacles, especially the stigma associated with mental health problems.*

▸ main **chief, greatest, main, principal** *The chief obstacle, of course, was money.*

▸ types of obstacle **bureaucratic, legal, logistical, procedural** *Many farmers find that they face many costly and bureaucratic obstacles. ● Removal of legal obstacles leads to easier divorce.*

▸ v+N overcome an obstacle **overcome, surmount** *Young people from impoverished areas often have to surmount additional obstacles to gain a better education.*

▸ encounter an obstacle **be confronted by, be confronted with, come across, encounter, face, run into** *Your parents knew they were going to encounter obstacles from both cultures when they decided to marry.*

▸ remove an obstacle **clear, eliminate, remove** *We*

need to be providing real opportunities for women in this field, offering more training and removing the obstacles to their success.

▸ be an obstacle **act as, be, constitute, pose, present, prove** *The lack of effective judicial procedures poses a further obstacle to securing remedies for unacceptable conduct.*

▸ avoid or deal with an obstacle **avoid, deal with, negotiate, tackle** *The mentoring process helps teachers to tackle obstacles they face.*

● N+v **block, hamper, hinder, impede, prevent** *What do prisoners get out of learning and what obstacles hinder their progress?*

> You can also say that ***an obstacle stands in someone's way*** or ***an obstacle stands in the way of something***: *These people didn't let any obstacles stand in their way. ● A number of obstacles stand in the way of our country's advancing to the next stage in terms of human rights.*

obstruct V
to take action to prevent something from happening

● adv+V deliberately **deliberately, intentionally, wilfully** *They were not intentionally obstructing lawful work.*

▸ often **constantly, frequently, repeatedly** *The Baghdad regime repeatedly obstructed efforts to resume monitoring of its program to produce weapons of mass destruction.*

● and/or **delay, disrupt, hinder, impede, interfere with, prevent** *It is an offence to obstruct or impede firefighters or ambulance workers.*

obstruction N
something blocking a path, passage, door etc, or the act of blocking it

● v+N cause an obstruction **cause, create, lead to, result in** *Many of the bins stay out all day, causing an obstruction.*

▸ encounter an obstruction **encounter, hit** *He only changed direction when he encountered an obstruction.*

▸ remove an obstruction **clear, relieve, remove** *Nasal decongestants such as ephedrine can help relieve nasal obstruction.*

▸ avoid an obstruction **avoid, bypass** *I follow the path and am careful to avoid obstructions.*

▸ prevent or minimize an obstruction **minimize, prevent** *Parking is no longer permitted on the north side of Bradford Street to prevent obstruction to through traffic.*

▸ be an obstruction **amount to, constitute** *Any protrusion was so minimal that it could not be said to amount to a physical obstruction of the highway.*

obtain V
to get something you want or need

● adv+V illegally or dishonestly **dishonestly, falsely, fraudulently, illegally, improperly, unfairly, unlawfully** *He had obtained the cash by fraudulently obtaining a number of bank loans.*

▸ legally or honestly **fairly, lawfully, legally** *Personal data should be fairly and lawfully obtained.*

▸ easily or quickly **easily, quickly, readily** *All of the new forms can be easily obtained from the website.*

▸ for little or no money **cheaply, free (of charge)** *Tickets to the village swimming pool can be obtained free of charge from the hotel reception.*

▸ separately **independently, separately** *The two samples were obtained independently.*

▸ directly **directly** *A solicitor must take all reasonable steps to obtain directly from a witness the potential evidence in a case.*

▸ from somewhere **abroad, locally** *More and more HIV positive people are appreciating the help that can be obtained locally, including in their own homes.*

▸ in a particular way **commercially, electronically, experimentally** *It was possible to plot a graph in a few minutes using a computer that would have required days to obtain experimentally.*

● V+n permission **approval, authorisation, clearance, confirmation, consent, permission** *The wedding couple had obtained special permission from the Bishop to use the church.*

▸ information **advice, estimate, evidence, feedback, information, quotation, quote, result** *Where can I obtain further advice?*

▸ money **compensation, credit, funding, loan, mortgage, relief** *Participants will learn how schools obtain funding and prepare their budgets.*

▸ official document **degree, grant, injunction, license, permit, qualification, warrant** *Would you like to obtain a qualification for the work that you do?*

▸ for work to be done **estimate, quotation, quote** *You will need to obtain an estimate from two or three different builders before you decide to do the work.*

obvious ADJ
clear to almost anyone

● adv+ADJ very **abundantly, blatantly, blindingly, glaringly, immediately, intuitively, painfully, patently, perfectly, plainly, pretty INFORMAL, so INFORMAL, very** *You may have missed something blindingly obvious.*

▸ fairly **fairly, quite, rather** *The turn is right, not left, off the main road (as there is no left turn this will be fairly obvious!)*

▸ more and more **increasingly** *Towards the end of the 18th Century, it became increasingly obvious that nobody had any idea about the number of people living in the British Isles.*

● ADJ+n reason or result **answer, explanation, implication, reason** *The majority of companies have restrictive contracts for obvious reasons.*

▸ difference/similarity **difference, exception, parallel, similarity** *There are the obvious parallels with what happened in America during the fifties*

▸ good thing **advantage, attraction, benefit** *The most obvious advantage of a caravanning holiday is financial.*

▸ bad thing **danger, disadvantage, flaw, limitation, mistake** *The obvious flaw in this film is the lack of Kevin Bacon.*

▸ choice **choice** *I was interested in finance and banking was the obvious choice after university.*

● v+ADJ seem obvious **appear, look, seem, sound** *It would seem obvious that resources should be weighted to the areas where there is greatest need.*

▸ be or become obvious **be, become** *By the 1830's it had become obvious that Queen Adelaide was not going to produce a living child.*

▸ make something obvious **make sth** *They made it obvious they didn't like me.*

occasion N
1 a time at which something happens

● adj+N few **a few, the odd, rare** *Even if you do not wish your child to have a meal at school every day there is always the odd occasion when you do.* ● *It was one of those rare occasions when we all disagreed with him.*

▸ different **different, other, separate** *Harold considered the harassment so serious that he reported it to the police on three separate occasions.*

▸ previous **earlier, previous** *Pupils from our school have visited the home on three previous occasions.*

▸ subsequent or future **future, subsequent** *He again on a subsequent occasion showed supreme courage in tending wounded soldiers under heavy shell fire.*

▸ one **the only, particular** *This was the only occasion on which Johnson was ever moved to reply to an attacker.*

▸ many **countless, frequent, many, numerous** *She is a skilled healer and has helped me on numerous occasions.*

▸ several **several, various** *That they are spending such a large amount of money has been confirmed to me on several occasions.*

▸ one after the other **consecutive, successive** *Roosevelt was elected on four successive occasions as US President.*

> Usage Occasion is always <u>plural</u> in the last three ***adj+N*** combinations shown above: *Liverpool won the League Cup on four consecutive occasions.* ● *There will be countless occasions when things go wrong.*

● V+N recall, recount, **remember, remind sb of, talk about, think of** *I was reminded of a previous occasion when we had a chapel outing there years ago.*

2 a special or important time or event

● adj+N special **auspicious, big, glittering, historic, landmark, memorable, special, unique** *Messages for special occasions can be read out over the tannoy system during the half-time interval.*

▸ formal **ceremonial, civic, formal, official, royal, state** *For ceremonial occasions, the regiment dresses in absolutely authentic uniforms.*

▸ happy **enjoyable, happy, joyful, joyous** *They provided champagne and the lunch was a joyous occasion.*

▸ sad **sad, solemn** *Warn children that the funeral will be a sad occasion.*

▸ for celebrating or socializing **festive, social** *Meals are also social occasions.*

● n+N **family, sporting** *Weddings are family occasions.*

● v+N mark or celebrate an occasion **celebrate, commemorate, honour, mark, record** *A plaque marking the occasion will be erected at a later date.*

▶ spoil an occasion **mar, ruin, spoil** *Special occasions were usually ruined by his drinking.*
▶ suit an occasion **befit, fit, suit** *We have menus to suit every occasion.*
▶ attend an occasion **attend, grace, participate in, witness** *Many illustrious nobles and generals of the Empire graced the occasion with their presence.*

occupant N
someone who uses a place or has a particular job for a period of time

● adj+N original or previous **former, last, original, previous** *Nigel was the previous occupant of the office that I now use.*
▶ current **current, present** *A quick way to judge the suitability of a property is to talk to the current occupants and neighbours.*
▶ future **future, next** *Properties should be left as found, ready for next occupant.*
▶ only one **only, sole** *Are you the sole occupant of the flat, or do you have tenants?*

● N+of **apartment, building, car, chair, flat, house, post, premises, property, room, vehicle** *The occupants of the house were not injured in the explosion.* ● *She will be the first female occupant of this important government post.*

occupation N
1 a job

● adj+N types of occupation **clerical, industrial, managerial, manual, non-manual, professional, skilled, technical, unskilled** *The last decade has witnessed a huge increase in the number of people employed in managerial and professional occupations.*
▶ done for the whole week etc **full-time** *She combines coaching gymnastics with her full-time occupation as a teacher.*
● v+N have a particular occupation **follow, pursue** *Many of the unemployed had no hope of following their normal occupation in mining or shipbuilding.*
▶ start a particular occupation **enter** *Research showed that the majority of students entered professional occupations.*
▶ write down what your or someone's occupation is **give, list** *In the 1041 census, Edward's occupation was given as a clerk.*

2 going into a place and taking control away from the people or government there

● adj+N types of occupation **brutal, colonial, foreign, illegal, imperialist, military** *The country finally won its independence after a long struggle against military occupation.*
▶ continuing to exist **continued, continuing** *They protested at the continuing occupation of their country by foreign powers.*
● v+N oppose an occupation **fight, oppose, resist** *We support the right of the people to resist occupation but oppose methods of individual terror.*
▶ end an occupation **end** *The campaign to end the occupation will continue in this country and abroad.*
▶ N+v **begin, end, last** *As soon as the occupation began, it was clear that the occupiers had given no thought to civil society.*

occur V
happen or exist

● adv+V often **commonly, frequently, regularly, repeatedly** *Droughts are likely to occur more frequently in the south east of the country.*
▶ mainly **generally, largely, mainly, mostly, normally, predominantly, primarily, typically, usually** *Abuse is known to occur primarily within families.*
▶ rarely **infrequently, rarely** *Osteoarthritis rarely occurs before the age of 40.*
▶ sometimes, but not in a predictable way **by chance, occasionally, sporadically** *The probability of such improvements occurring by chance was found to be less than one in a thousand.* ● *This error may first occur only sporadically.*
▶ suddenly or quickly **immediately, quickly, rapidly, suddenly, without warning** *Such a condition can occur suddenly, as a result of an accident, or can develop more slowly.*
▶ naturally **naturally, spontaneously** *These flu viruses occur naturally among birds.*
▶ at the same time as something else **simultaneously, together** *These processes occur simultaneously.*

● n+V problem or mistake **difficulty, error, failure, fault, mistake, problem** *Problems normally occur when helicopters stray from designated routes or fly too low in the sky.*
▶ damage or loss **damage, loss** *We do not accept responsibility for any damage which occurs to vehicles in this car park.*
▶ delay **delay** *Considerable delays usually occur before the application is finally processed.*
▶ event or situation **activity, event, incident, opportunity, phenomenon, situation** *In the middle of winter, an exciting event occurred.*
▶ change **change, development, growth, transformation** *Huge changes have occurred.*
▶ accident or disaster **accident, collision, crash, crisis, disaster, emergency, explosion, fire, tragedy** *More than half of all fatal crashes occur on rural roads.*
▶ crime **attack, crime, murder, offence, theft** *Many of the offences occurred overnight when the homeowner was asleep.*
▶ something bad affecting your body **complications, condition, death, disease, illness, injury, pain, symptom** *Death usually occurs within two years of the symptoms appearing.*

occurrence N
something that happens

● adj+N happening often **common, daily, everyday, frequent, regular, widespread** *This problem is a frequent occurrence in those who are just taking up diving.*
▶ rare **freak, infrequent, isolated, rare, uncommon, unique, unusual** *In the past few years, weather events which would once have been written off as freak occurrences have become more and more frequent.* ● *Whilst drain failure is a very rare occurrence, it can cause major disruption to production.*
▶ strange **odd, strange, unexpected** *Strange occurrences begin happening.*
▶ natural **natural, normal** *Blackheads are unpleasant, but they are a natural occurrence.*

odd ADJ
unusual or unexpected

- adv+ADJ very **extremely, really, very** *Harriet's behaviour was extremely odd.*
- ▶ rather **a bit, a little, pretty** INFORMAL**, quite, rather, slightly, somewhat** *The structure of the book is a bit odd and did not encourage me to read further.*
- ▶ definitely and simply **decidedly, distinctly, downright, plain** *If you do come across anything broken or just plain odd, please let me know.*

- v+ADJ **appear, be, feel, find sth/sb, look, seem, sound** *Their methods may seem odd, but we are assured that they are extremely effective.*

> If you think something is odd, you can also say that it **strikes you as odd**: *It struck me as odd that he didn't even reply to the letter.*

- ADJ+infinitive **hear, say, see, suggest, think** *It's odd to think that the events that happened a week ago could alter our lives forever.*

odds N
1 the chances of something happening

- adj+N when it is likely something will happen **good, great, high, short** *The game offers players 27 times better odds of winning a jackpot than the National Lottery does.* • *They laid short odds on another attack taking place very soon.*
- ▶ when it is not likely something will happen **long, low** *Only Portugal at 200 to 1 have lower odds.*

> If there is not much chance of something happening, you can also say **the odds are stacked against someone/something**: *Some smokers do live long lives, but the odds are still heavily stacked against it.*

- v+N when you make something more likely **improve, increase, shorten** *The article tells you how to increase your odds of getting a loan.*
- ▶ when you make something less likely **reduce** *By controlling your blood pressure, you are reducing your odds for having a stroke.*
- ▶ go against the odds **beat, defy, overcome** *Several small companies have beaten the odds and stayed in business.*
- ▶ say what the odds are **give, lay, offer, set** *The bookmaker, however, has offered odds of 2 to 1.*

2 difficulties or conditions that make success unlikely

- adj+N **impossible, insurmountable, overwhelming, tremendous** *He has shown great courage in the face of overwhelming odds.* • *They managed to cling to life against tremendous odds.*

odour N
a smell

- adj+N unpleasant **bad, foul, musty, offensive, stale, unpleasant** *Soiled garments and perspiration caused bad odours.*
- ▶ strong **pungent, strong** *Fats should be stored in a cool place and away from strong odours.*
- ▶ not strong **faint, slight** *It was a pale yellow liquid with a faint odour of fruit.*
- ▶ staying in a place for a long time **lingering** *Try and eliminate any lingering odours from the dustbins.*

- ▶ easy to recognize **characteristic, distinctive** *Allicin is one of the compounds that gives garlic its characteristic odour.*

- v+N produce an odour **emit, give off, produce** *This species of plant emits a strong odour.*
- ▶ cause an odour **cause, create** *Street urination causes an unpleasant odour and health risks.*
- ▶ reduce or get rid of an odour **control, eliminate, neutralize, reduce, remove** *It is gently scented and eliminates odours very effectively.*
- ▶ notice an odour **detect, smell** *Approximately 53 minutes into the flight, the flight crew smelled a strong odour of burning in the cockpit.*

offence N
1 a crime or illegal activity for which there is a punishment

- adj+N serious **grave, major, serious** *Throwing or letting off fireworks in a public place is a serious offence, which can result in a fine of up to £5,000.*
- ▶ not serious **minor, petty, trivial** *Every year the police record a whole range of minor and petty offences.*
- ▶ types of offence **drug-related, non-violent, sexual, terrorist, violent** *Most women in prison are there for non-violent offences, most commonly shoplifting.*
- ▶ describing what the result or punishment could be **arrestable, bookable, disciplinary, imprisonable, indictable, punishable, sackable** *Possession of the drug is no longer an arrestable offence.* • *He was sent off for a second bookable offence.*
- ▶ said to have happened but not yet tried in a court **alleged** *If you wish to contest the alleged offence, you may request a court hearing.*
- ▶ according to the law **statutory** *It is a statutory offence to drive a vehicle along a bridleway in the absence of a private right to do so.*
- ▶ according to a criminal/civil law **civil, criminal** *In the UK, infringement of copyright is a civil offence and the remedy has to be found in the civil courts.*

- n+N **driving, drug, firearms, motoring, parking, public order, sex, traffic** *Community officers have powers to deal with some traffic offences such as illegal parking.*

- v+N **accuse sb of, admit, be convicted of, commit, constitute, investigate** *The company admitted 20 offences of illegally employing children aged 13.* • *He was convicted of a drink-driving offence and lost his licence.* • *The consequences for staff who commit an offence are potentially very serious.* • *Failure to register contitutes a criminal offence.*

2 the feeling of being angry, upset, or insulted

- adj+N **great, widespread** *They concluded that the poster was distressing and likely to cause widespread offence.*

- v+N cause offence **cause, give** *The TV station apologized for causing offence with its report on the dead singer.*
- ▶ feel offence **take** *Mr Gabb took offence at the accusation.*
- ▶ intend offence **intend, mean** *I'm sorry, I didn't intend any offence.*

offend V
make someone angry or upset

- adv+V very much **deeply, greatly, seriously** *I've only been here a day and he's already deeply offended me.*
- ▶ easily **easily** *If you're easily offended, then you probably shouldn't watch this programme.*
- and/or **hurt, insult, shock, upset** *Movies have a great power to shock and offend as well as entertain and inspire.*

offender N
someone who has committed a crime

- adj+N having committed more than one crime **persistent, prolific, repeat, serial** *Custodial sentences should be imposed for serious, persistent offenders.*
- ▶ having committed a crime for the first time **first, first-time** *First-time offenders can be sentenced to up to three years in prison.*
- ▶ young **juvenile, young** *This project aims to help young offenders or those at risk of offending.*
- ▶ having committed a serious crime **dangerous, serious** *The police force has a good record of catching serious offenders, including those involved in burglary and drug crime.*
- ▶ having committed a crime that is not serious **minor, petty** *He believed that prison for minor offenders was a waste of money.*
- ▶ having committed a particular type of crime **sexual, violent** *It's the government's job to protect the public from violent offenders.*
- ▶ believed to have committed a crime **alleged, suspected** *The alleged offender is known to the victim.*
- ▶ having been found guilty in a court of law **convicted** *If convicted offenders feel they didn't receive a fair trial, they are entitled to appeal.*
- n+N **drink-drive, drug, sex** *Convicted drug offenders are referred for treatment.*
- v+N catch an offender **apprehend, arrest, catch, detain** *Police are appealing for help in catching the offenders responsible for breaking into the home of an elderly lady.*
- punish an offender **imprison, prosecute, punish, sentence** *The police try to prosecute offenders wherever possible.*

offensive ADJ
unpleasant or insulting

- adv+ADJ very **deeply, downright, extremely, grossly, highly, very** *That suggestion was not only deeply offensive, but also wrong.*
- in a way that seems unnecessary **gratuitously** *He condemned the gratuitously offensive and indeed racist remarks.*
- in a particular way **morally, racially** *I find your views morally offensive and totally reprehensible.*
- likely to be offensive **potentially** *Filtering can also protect you from potentially offensive material which may be contained within spam emails.*
- ADJ+n writing or remarks **comment, content,** graffiti, joke, language, material, message, **remark, word** *Employees who use company email to share offensive jokes or obscene images with friends will be dealt with severely.*
- ▶ behaviour **behaviour, gesture, manner** *Avoid insulting or offensive behaviour – this includes swearing and insulting others.*
- v+ADJ **be, be deemed, consider sth, find sth, seem** *Many of the pictures could be deemed offensive.*
  - *It is his hypocrisy which I find offensive.*
- and/or **abusive, defamatory, illegal, inappropriate, indecent, insulting, obscene, pornographic, threatening** *Please don't make offensive or defamatory posts on our forum.*

offer V
to give someone something or let them know that you will do something

- adv+V kindly **generously, kindly** *Stuart kindly offered to swap seats with me so I could sit next to my wife.*
- ▶ willingly **freely, willingly** *He willingly offered his time and money to help the charity.*
- v+to-V seem to offer something **appear, seem** *Bespoke software, written for your organization, may appear to offer advantages.*
- ▶ not offer something **fail** *He criticized the main parties for failing to offer voters a genuine choice on tax and spend.*
- ▶ to have to offer something **be compelled, be forced, be obliged** *All schools will be obliged to offer part-time school attendance.*

offer N
a statement in which you offer someone something

- adj+N kind **generous, kind** *This generous offer was immediately accepted.*
- ▶ good **attractive, exciting, fantastic, good, tempting** *It was a tempting offer which I just couldn't refuse.*
- ▶ formal or official **formal, written** *Two references will be taken up prior to all successful candidates prior to a formal offer of employment.*
- ▶ with/without conditions **conditional, unconditional** *She had been given an unconditional offer of a place at the college.*
- v+N make an offer **make (sb), put in** *When you place an order you are making an offer to buy the goods, which the company can refuse to accept.* • *Seven bidders are thought to have put in offers for the UK grocery business.*
- ▶ get an offer **get, have, receive** *I received an offer to buy out my business.*
- ▶ refuse an offer **decline, refuse, reject, turn down** *He asked her to go to Hong Kong with him, but she rejected his offer.*
- ▶ accept an offer **accept, take, take up** *The minister accepted an offer to visit Sheffield.*
- ▶ think about an offer **consider** *We will consider offers to tour to any location in the UK or abroad.*
- ▶ say an offer is no longer available **withdraw** *We will withdraw the offer of a place if we find that you have given fraudulent or misleading information.*

offset V

balance effects so that there is no advantage or disadvantage

- adv+V to a certain extent **partially, partly, slightly, somewhat** *Increases in the retail sector were partially offset by a fall in the motor trades.*
- ▶ completely **completely, fully** *The reduced turnover costs would not be sufficient to offset completely the higher wage bill.*
- ▶ very much **largely** *Cost saving initiatives and selling price increases has largely offset cost inflation.*
- V+n cost or amount **cost, expenditure, expense, fee, payment, price, savings** *To offset these costs, many small recycling businesses pool resources with other companies.*
- ▶ increase **gain, growth, increase, rise** *However, increased utility costs and business rates are likely to more than offset these gains.*
- ▶ loss or decrease **decline, deficit, fall, loss, reduction, shortfall** *Any development will need to contribute significant economic and environmental benefits to offset the loss of greenfield land.*
- ▶ effect **benefit, effect, impact** *Sports drinks have been designed to offset the impact of dehydration by replacing both the fluids and body salts that are lost during exercise.*
- ▶ risk **risk** *Cycling has health benefits which can offset the risks attached to it.*
- V+against **cost, income, profit, tax** *The group's losses can be offset against future taxable profits.*

omission N

someone or something not included

- adj+N obvious **glaring, notable, obvious, striking** *There are some glaring omissions, and some odd inclusions.*
- ▶ important **important, major, serious, significant** *I believe that there is an important omission from the current proposals, something that I consider to be an essential point.*
- ▶ not important **minor** *This has nothing to do with the main story, so it is a very minor omission.*
- ▶ strange and unexpected **curious, strange, surprising** *There is no diesel model, which is a surprising omission in a car of this class.*
- ▶ deliberate/not deliberate **deliberate, inadvertent, intentional** *I understand that any false information or deliberate omissions will disqualify me from employment.*
- ▶ that you regret **regrettable, unfortunate** *Readers must be aware of some unfortunate omissions in the article.*
- v+N notice an omission **identify, note, notice, spot** *If you spot any omissions that you think should be included, please let us know.*
- ▶ correct an omission **correct, rectify, remedy** *To correct that omission we provide the details here – see below.*

omit V

fail to include someone or something

- adv+V deliberately **deliberately, intentionally, purposely** *These letters were deliberately omitted from the autobiography in order not to cause offence.*
- ▶ not deliberately **accidentally, inadvertently** *These figures were accidentally omitted from the calculations.*
- ▶ in a way that is to someone's advantage **carefully, conveniently** *Mr. Arnold conveniently omitted his political title when replying to a letter in the newspaper.*
- ▶ completely **altogether, completely, entirely, totally** *Several passages were altered and some were omitted altogether.* • *Increase water intake and totally omit starches, sugars, processed foods from your diet.*
- V+n information **details, fact, information, mention, name, reference** *She had omitted a few minor details about her husband.* • *The statement omitted any mention of responsibility for the war.*
- ▶ part of some writing **letter, line, paragraph, passage, section, verse, word** *In reading, young children may sometimes omit words.*
- V+infinitive **add, ask, mention, say, state, tell** *My only slight criticism is that the reviewer omitted to mention the excellent cinematography.*

one-sided ADJ

in which one person, opinion etc has more influence

- adv+ADJ very or completely **completely, totally, very** *The review was very one-sided and failed to do justice to the novel.*
- ▶ rather **pretty** INFORMAL, **rather, somewhat** *In the second half, two further goals ended a rather one-sided match.*
- ▶ in a bad way **embarrassingly, grossly, hopelessly, horribly** *The report is selective and grossly one-sided.*
- ADJ+n **affair, approach, argument, contest, conversation, game, match, relationship, view** *The negotiations should not be a one-sided affair.*

onset N

the beginning of something, especially something bad [always singular]

- adj+N sudden or quick **abrupt, rapid, sudden** *People who have a stroke experience a sudden onset of disability.*
- ▶ slow **gradual, insidious, slow** *Symptoms begin with a gradual onset of breathlessness.*
- ▶ early/late **delayed, early, late** *Building was delayed by the early onset of winter.*
- v+N cause the onset **cause, trigger** *This hormone is important in triggering the onset of labour.*
- ▶ delay or prevent the onset **delay, postpone, prevent, slow** *There are treatments that can control HIV and delay the onset of AIDS.*
- ▶ mark the onset **herald, mark, signal** *Primroses, daffodils, bluebells and wild orchids herald the onset of the main holiday season.*
- N+of illness **condition, disease, illness, pain, symptoms, dementia, diabetes etc** *The onset of a mental illness is often heralded by being unable to fulfil roles that had previously been carried out successfully.* • *For some, the onset of schizophrenia will be rapid, with family members noticing psychotic symptoms.*
- ▶ process in the body **labour, menstruation, puberty** *Teenagers with the disease frequently experience a delay in the onset of puberty.*

▶ problem or event **crisis, problem, war** *Both Tamara and Isaac had fled Poland with the onset of war, and had met as exiles in London.*

▶ weather or season **rain, season, weather, winter** *Try and arrive before the onset of the hurricane season.* • *The containers should be well watered before the onset of bad weather.* • *Food shortages will become more acute with the onset of winter.*

onslaught N
large numbers of people or things coming at the same time; an attack

• adj+N **constant, relentless** *As the blog grows, under the relentless onslaught of my posts and project updates, the good stuff tends to get buried.*

• v+N **start or continue an onslaught continue, launch, mount, unleash** *Domestically, he launched an onslaught on civil liberties.*

▶ have to deal with an onslaught **face** *People in Britain are facing an onslaught of cuts in local council services.*

• deal with an onslaught successfully **resist, survive, withstand** *Email servers should be secure enough to withstand the onslaught of email-borne threats like viruses and spam.*

ooze V
show a particular quality in an obvious way

• adv+V **just, positively, simply** *The cottages are in a charming rural location that simply oozes character and atmosphere.*

• V+n **atmosphere, character, charisma, charm, class, confidence, quality, sex appeal, style** *It's a classy bar and restaurant that oozes style.*

open ADJ
1 honest and not keeping things secret

• adv+ADJ very or completely **completely, entirely, genuinely, quite, totally, truly** *They were quite open about it.*

• to some extent **fairly, relatively** *The management had been fairly open about its intentions.*

• and/or **fair, frank, friendly, honest, transparent** *Couples must be open and frank with each other.*

2 willing to consider different things

• adv+ADJ **genuinely, refreshingly, surprisingly** *They have a refreshingly open approach to solving the company's problems.*

• ADJ+to **ideas, offers, possibilities, suggestions** *Munro is a man who is open to all possibilities.*

3 when it is possible or reasonable to do something

• ADJ+to **abuse, argument, attack, criticism, debate, discussion, exploitation, interpretation, negotiation, question** *The system is poorly designed and open to abuse.*

open V
begin a discussion, trial etc

• V+n **campaign, debate, discussion, inquiry, investigation, meeting, negotiations, proceedings, session, talks** *Prosecutors have opened a criminal investigation over the jailbreak.*

opening N
1 an occasion when a new place is open to the public for the first time

• adj+N **formal, grand, official, public** *The venue's official opening will take place on Saturday 17 June.*

• v+N celebrate an opening **celebrate, commemorate, mark** *The prince unveiled a plaque to mark the opening of the garden centre.*

▶ go to an opening **attend** *More than 250 guests attended the official opening of the hospice.*

• N+n **ceremony** *The opening ceremony was a fantastic extravaganza with balloons, singing and dancing.*

2 an opportunity to do something

• adj+N **new, possible** *We need to examine not just the problems encountered with the current state of affairs, but also possible new openings.*

• v+N **create, give sb, provide** *The changes have created welcome openings for foreign companies.*

openness N
honesty, when you do not try to hide information; willingness to accept new ideas

• adj+N more **greater, increasing, more** *Although the responses show increasing openness, a culture of secrecy still prevails in some institutions.*

▶ new **new** *The underlying reason for this new openness, which grew through the 1980s, was the change of generations.*

▶ complete **absolute, complete, total** *My policy has always been one of complete openness with the staff.*

▶ types of openness **emotional, intellectual, political** *Intellectual openness is the prerequisite for all scientific work.*

• v+N show openness **demonstrate, show** *He also showed an openness with his party.*

▶ encourage openness **encourage, promote** *The Act aims to promote greater openness between employers and staff*

• and/or **accountability, fairness, flexibility, honesty, integrity, respect, transparency, trust** *I also appreciate the honesty and openness shown during the interviews.*

operate V
if an organization operates, it does its work; to run an organization

• adv+V **well effectively, efficiently, satisfactorily, smoothly, successfully** *Good PAs are an invaluable asset, and few companies can operate efficiently or effectively without them.*

▶ in a particular area **globally, internationally, locally, nationally, nationwide, overseas, worldwide** *Established in 1992, the company now operates internationally.*

▶ in a way that makes a profit **commercially, profitably** *The theatre operated quite profitably for many years.*

▶ independently **autonomously, independently** *The two organizations operate independently, within the National Health Service.*

operation N

1 a set of actions to achieve something; the fact of something functioning

- adj+N large **big, large, large-scale, major, massive** *A British soldier was killed and another was injured yesterday during a major operation.*
- ▶ secret **clandestine, covert, secret, undercover** *Hundreds of senior officers had been involved in this covert operation.*
- ▶ difficult or dangerous **complex, dangerous, hazardous** *It was a complex operation involving more than 400 staff from over 20 prisons.*
- ▶ done with someone else **joint** *The area was cleaned up through a joint operation between the police and the Environment Agency.*

- n+N to find or get back someone or something **recovery, rescue, salvage, search** *We returned to duty to continue the recovery operation at the aircraft crash scene.*
- ▶ to increase security **intelligence, security, surveillance** *He was involved in planning the security operation for the Olympc Games.*
- ▶ to stop fighting **peace, peacekeeping** *United Nations peacekeeping operations began in 1948.*
- ▶ to make a place clean again **clean-up** *This clean-up operation is very necessary to tackle Balsall Heath's rat problem.*
- ▶ to help people in need **relief** *We have launched relief operations in the east of the island district, where the majority of houses have been completely destroyed.*

- v+N start an operation **launch, mount** *Villagers launched a clean-up operation after homes and gardens were left covered in straw.*
- ▶ carry out an operation **carry out, conduct, perform, run, undertake** *There are publications about how to properly conduct covert operations.*
- ▶ lead an operation **direct, lead** *Mr Jack Clark was also on the scene directing operations.*
- ▶ check an operation is being done correctly **monitor, oversee, supervise** *Someone in authority must supervise any digging-out operation.*
- ▶ organize an operation **coordinate, organize** *Superintendent Bartlett is coordinating the police operation.*
- ▶ stop or interrupt an operation **cease, disrupt, suspend** *The company suspended drilling operations because of the extreme cold.*
- ▶ start an operation again **resume** *They resumed the search operation at first light.*

2 the medical process of cutting into a person's body

- adj+N big **major, serious** *My father has been in hospital for the last five weeks recovering from a major stomach operation.*
- ▶ small **minor, routine, small** *Unless your operation is very minor, you will undergo some routine tests.*
- ▶ done to find out what is causing a problem **exploratory** *The surgeon may suggest an exploratory operation **on** your ankle to check on the state of the joint.*
- ▶ that saves someone's life **emergency, life-saving** *James needed a life-saving operation when one of his lungs collapsed.*

- v+N have an operation **have, undergo** *He was taken to hospital where he underwent an operation under full anaesthetic.*
- ▶ do an operation **carry out, do, perform** *The surgeon who did my operation did a wonderful job and saved my life.*
- ▶ need an operation **need, require** *Unfortunately, at the end of September, Diana fell in the street and broke her hip and required an operation.*
- ▶ get better after an operation **recover from** *Jones is at home recovering from an operation.*

3 a company or part of a large company

- adj+N operating in a particular place **global, international, multinational, national, offshore, overseas, regional, worldwide** *They began extensive reviews of the company's global operations.*
- ▶ large **big, large** *It is the largest automotive transport operation of its type, and has 37 locations around Europe.*
- ▶ small **small** *The range of goods was impressive for such a small operation.*
- ▶ types of operation **commercial, retail** *In 1966, HMV began expanding its retail operations in London.*

- v+N start an operation **establish, set up, start** *After the massive stampede to set up offshore operations, things have stabilised.*
- ▶ manage an operation **manage, run** *This course focuses on the logistical skills necessary to run a watersports operation.*
- ▶ make an operation bigger **expand** *The company has announced new initiatives to expand its operations in the UK and the USA.*

operational ADJ

working

- adv+ADJ **currently, fully** *Lerwick's new international ferry terminal became fully operational in October 2002.*
- ADJ+n ability or level of success **activity, capability, effectiveness, efficiency, level, performance** *These tools will help businesses make further improvements to their operational efficiency.*
- ▶ costs **costs** *The provision of high levels of quality will have a significant impact on operational costs.*
- ▶ needs **needs, requirements** *Any arrangement that you choose must be agreed with your Head of Department so that it fits into the operational requirements of the department.*
- ▶ method **practice, procedure, process** *Operational procedures typically need to be tailored to fit the needs of the particular environment.*
- ▶ problem **difficulty, issue, problem** *These incidents must be resolved promptly as security incidents can cause operational problems, damage reputations or even have legal implications.*

- v+ADJ **be, become, declare sth, keep sth, remain** *The system was declared operational after extensive testing.* • *The station had to remain operational at all times during the contract.*

opinion N

the attitude that you or a group of people have towards something

- adj+N good **favourable, good, high, positive** *He always had a high opinion of Rhodri's talents.*

▸ bad **low, negative, poor** *I'm afraid I have a low opinion of taxi drivers whether I'm driving or cycling.*

▸ strong **strong** *Some strong opinions have been voiced about the issue.*

▸ honest **honest** *If you can, speak to the existing tenants and get their honest opinion of the house.*

▸ different **conflicting, different, mixed** *There were decidedly mixed opinions on this wine.*

When people disagree, they have a *difference of opinion*: *Despite our many differences of opinion, we remained good friends.*

▸ based on good knowledge **expert, informed, professional, specialist** *This was the expert opinion of an eminent neuro-surgeon who gave evidence at the trial.*

▸ of one person **personal, sb's own, subjective** *We are all entitled to our own opinions!*

▸ of most people **general, popular, public** *The Prime Minister would be foolish to ignore public opinion.*

▸ types of opinion **legal, medical, political, religious, scientific** *If someone posts a political opinion that you disagree with, please feel free to comment.*

▸ from someone else **second** *When you're dealing with doctors, it's sometimes better to get a second opinion on your diagnosis.*

● v+N have an opinion **have, hold** *Email me if you have any opinions on the design.*

You can also use the expressions *in someone's opinion* and *be of the opinion that*: *People don't take enough exercise, in my opinion.* ● *The board was of the opinion that further cuts would need to be made.*

▸ begin to have an opinion **develop, form, formulate** *The tribunal formed the opinion that there was a serious risk to the well-being of the residents in Hillside Manor.*

▸ say what your opinion is **air, express, give, offer, provide, state, venture, voice** *Herbert thought about the situation for a while before venturing an opinion.*

▸ ask for people's opinions **ask (for) sb's, canvass, seek, solicit** *The review team sought opinions from a wide range of those who were affected by the decision.*

▸ get someone's opinion **get sb's, obtain sb's** *It is useful to get someone else's opinion.*

▸ change your opinion **alter, change, revise** *I've revised my opinion of Jacques.*

▸ have the same opinion as someone else **share** *The police didn't seem to share that opinion.*

▸ respect other people's opinions **respect, value** *We really value your opinion and want to hear it.*

▸ influence people's opinion about something **influence, shape, sway** *The war had shaped voters' opinions.*

▸ show that someone's opinion is correct **confirm, support** *Is there any information that would confirm this opinion?*

● N+v exist **prevail** *On this point, three different opinions prevail.*

▸ differ **differ, diverge, vary** *Opinions on the procedure differ widely among doctors.*

▸ change **change, shift** *As I get older, I find my opinions are changing.* ● *US public opinion on the war has shifted in the past year.*

You can use *regarding* or *concerning* to say what an opinion is about: *I strongly disagreed with the writer's opinion concerning the underlying cause of the catastrophe.*

opponent N

someone who competes or argues against you; someone who disagrees with something

● adj+N difficult to beat **dangerous, formidable, powerful, strong, tough** *We will come up against stronger opponents, but Ealing never field a bad side.*

▸ not difficult to beat **weak** *Our opponents were surprisingly weak by their usual high standards, and we enjoyed a runaway victory.*

▸ main **chief, leading, main, prominent** *She was one of the main opponents of the war.*

▸ political **political** *The government acted in a repressive manner towards its political opponents and critics.*

▸ having qualities that make you respect them **worthy** *I think Gosport will prove to be worthy opponents.*

▸ expressing an opinion often and strongly **bitter, fierce, outspoken, staunch, vocal** *They have both been vocal opponents of government plans for privatization.*

● v+N face an opponent **face** *But in all these areas Britain faces tough opponents.*

▸ defeat an opponent **beat, crush** INFORMAL**, defeat, overcome** *As long as you stay within the rules, there are loads of ways in which you can try to defeat your opponent.*

▸ be cleverer than your opponent **outwit** *In race after race he outwits opponents by overtaking them when they are stationary in the pits.*

opportunity N

a chance to do something

● adj+N good **amazing, excellent, exciting, fantastic, golden, good, great, huge, invaluable, major, superb, tremendous, valuable, wonderful** *This is a very exciting opportunity to be part of the leadership team.* ● *This presents a great opportunity for us to show what we can do.*

▸ special or unusual **exceptional, historic, once-in-a-lifetime, outstanding, rare, unique, unparalleled, unrivalled** *A hot air balloon ride provides you with a unique opportunity to see tourist attractions from thousands of feet up in the air!*

▸ perfect **heaven-sent, ideal, perfect** *This meeting will be the perfect opportunity for them to find out more.*

▸ genuine **real, significant** *These agreements offer a real opportunity to improve the relationship between central and local government.*

▸ new **new, unprecedented** *There are new opportunities for collaboration between biologists, programmers and engineers.*

▸ first **earliest, first** *You should discuss this with your tutor at the earliest opportunity.*

▸ many **ample, endless, many, numerous** *As well as the organised events, there is ample opportunity to just chat.*

▸ available **available, every** *Check out the newspapers to see what opportunities are currently available in your local area.*

▶ more **additional, further, more** *Field trips provide further opportunities to develop specialist skills and knowledge.*

▶ possible **future, possible, potential** *The management were unwilling to give any guarantees about future employment opportunities.*

▶ missed **lost, missed, wasted** *Your days at school may be remembered as a time of prejudice, frustration and lost opportunities.*

▶ equal **equal** *Employers should ensure they are offering equal opportunities for any job.*

▶ types of opportunity **business, career, commercial, creative, economic, educational, employment, funding, investment, job, learning, networking, professional, promotional, recreational, scoring, training** *Free travel to the Museum would improve educational opportunities for a significant number of children.* • *This property presents a terrific investment opportunity.*

● v+N have an opportunity **get, have** *You will have the opportunity to try different styles of writing including novels, plays, poems, and magazine articles.*

▶ provide an opportunity **afford (sb), allow sb, bring (sb), create, give sb, offer (sb), present (sb with), provide (sb with), represent** *Members will be given the opportunity to ask questions at the end.*

▶ take an opportunity **embrace, exploit, grasp, seize, take** *People would seize any opportunity to ease their miserable lives.*

▶ fail to take an opportunity **lose, miss, pass up, squander, waste** *Don't miss this rare opportunity to see and hear the best of world music all on one stage.*

▶ appreciate an opportunity **appreciate, embrace, enjoy, relish, welcome** *We would welcome an opportunity for further discussion.*

▶ offer more opportunity **develop, enhance, expand, extend, improve, increase, maximize, promote** *Our economic policy is based on maximising economic opportunity for all.*

▶ not allow someone an opportunity **deny sb, limit, reduce** *At that time, Chinese people were denied the opportunity to buy homes outside the Chinatown ghetto.*

▶ notice or point out an opportunity **find, highlight, identify, see, spot** *We can identify job opportunities and match them with the right people.*

▶ look for an opportunity **pursue, seek** *We are actively seeking opportunities to extend our market reach.*

oppose V
not approve of a plan or policy

● adv+V strongly **actively, adamantly, bitterly, fiercely, firmly, strenuously, strongly, vehemently, vigorously, violently** *I strongly oppose these proposals and I have made my views known to the Commission.*

▶ completely **absolutely, totally, utterly** *A resolution totally opposing war was overwhelmingly passed.*

▶ by a large majority **overwhelmingly** *The American Black community overwhelmingly opposed Bush.*

▶ openly **openly, publicly** *Church leaders were faced with the decision of whether to openly oppose the totalitarian regime.*

▶ at first **initially** *Residents of the village came to value the building which they had initially opposed.*

▶ without ever changing **consistently, resolutely, steadfastly** *The Tories have resolutely opposed proposals of this kind in government and in opposition.*

opposed ADJ
not wanting something to happen

● adv+ADJ strongly **bitterly, fiercely, strongly, vehemently, violently** *He was vehemently opposed to factory reforms.*

▶ completely **fundamentally, totally, utterly** *These people are fundamentally opposed to the use of animals in research.*

▶ in a determined way **adamantly, firmly, implacably, resolutely** *The Church was implacably opposed to such marriages.*

▶ by a large majority **overwhelmingly** *There is no doubt that the Turkish people are overwhelmingly opposed to war.*

▶ in a particular way **ideologically** *There must be thousands of people who resort to private medicine despite being ideologically opposed to it.*

opposite ADJ
completely different

● adv+ADJ completely **completely, diametrically, directly, entirely** *They feel they are being asked to do two diametrically opposite things at the same time.*

▶ exactly **exactly, precisely** *His views on society were exactly opposite to those expressed by Julius Caesar.*

▶ apparently **apparently, seemingly** *This was a wonderful mix of music and science, two seemingly opposite disciplines.*

● ADJ+n position or direction **corner, direction, end, extreme, polarity, pole, side** *While donations have risen sharply in America, the trend in Britain has gone in the opposite direction.* • *Each new theory was a reaction against the one before, and would go to the opposite extreme.*

▶ effect **effect, reaction** *Some people have the opposite reaction: 'Yes, this is the job for me!'*

▶ conclusion **conclusion** *On similar facts the Court of Appeal came to the opposite conclusion.*

opposition N
strong disagreement with a plan or policy

● adj+N strong **bitter, considerable, fierce, formidable, implacable, intense, stiff, strong, tough, vehement, vigorous, vocal, vociferous** *The bill is still not signed and still faces stiff opposition.* • *Local parents are united in their vehement opposition to the plan.*

▶ by many people **concerted, mass, massive, overwhelming, united, widespread** *The Minister decided to push ahead with the code despite widespread opposition.*

▶ growing **growing, increasing, mounting** *He faced increasing opposition even within his own party.*

▶ open **open, outright** *Respondents expressed views ranging from concern to outright opposition.*

▶ political **democratic, parliamentary, political** *Denmark had to scale back its military deployment because of parliamentary opposition.*

▶ based on principles **ideological, principled** *He was known for his principled opposition to corruption.*

▶ violent **armed, violent** *A campaign of violent opposition by the nationalists led to the suspension of the constitution.*

● v+N express opposition **declare, express, state, voice** *They appeared on national TV to voice their opposition to the legislation.*

▶ repeat your opposition **reaffirm, reiterate, restate** *He reiterated his opposition to any expansion of Birmingham Airport.*

▶ experience opposition **encounter, face, meet, meet with** *The government is proposing new anti-terrorist laws, but they are already encountering fierce opposition.*

▶ create opposition **arouse, draw, provoke** *The coming of the motor car aroused opposition from pedestrians and cyclists alike.*

▶ organize opposition **galvanize, mobilize, organize, rally** *Loyalist groups attempted to mobilize opposition to the peace process.*

▶ stop opposition **crush, overcome, repress, silence, stifle, suppress** *He has used death squads to crush opposition.*

> You can also say that someone **brooks no opposition**: *He has demonstrated time and time again that he will brook no opposition to his vision.*

▶ give up opposition **drop, withdraw** *They urged him to drop his opposition to reform.*

▶ control opposition **counter, overcome** *Medicine was her choice from an early age and she had to overcome family opposition in order to achieve her goal.*

oppression N
unfair and cruel treatment by a powerful person or government

● adj+N cruel **brutal, cruel, grievous, ruthless, tyrannical** *The play is a celebration of individual virtue in the face of tyrannical oppression.*

▶ never stopping **continued, relentless, systematic** *Martin Luther King preached against the systematic oppression of African Americans.*

▶ types of oppression **colonial, feudal, imperialist, patriarchal, racial, racist** *Imperialist oppression and exploitation created the conditions for terrorism.*

● v+N experience oppression **endure, experience, face, suffer** *Lesbians and gay men had suffered oppression before the change in the law.*

▶ fight oppression **challenge, combat, end, fight, fight against, overcome, overthrow, resist, struggle against** *Islam, Christianity and Judaism all call on their followers to resist oppression.*

▶ escape from oppression **escape (from), flee** *People wrongly believe most of them are not fleeing political oppression but are economic migrants.*

▶ defend oppression **justify** *Physical and cultural differences are used to justify oppression.*

● and/or **brutality, cruelty, discrimination, domination, exploitation, humiliation, injustice, persecution, poverty, racism, slavery, subjugation, tyranny** *The constitution should offer safeguards against tyranny and oppression.*

optimism N
a tendency to expect good things to happen

● adj+N cautious **cautious, guarded, reserved** *Fears of a drought gave way to cautious optimism.*

▶ great **boundless, eternal, heady, irrepressible, unbridled, unfailing, unqualified** *My father's boundless optimism was strong enough to give me and my sister a better life.* ● *The book reflects the heady optimism of the early 1960s.*

▶ not reasonable **blind, excessive, facile, misplaced, naive, undue, unfounded, unrealistic, unwarranted** *They tend to display a naive optimism about human nature and human history.*

▶ cheerful **buoyant, cheerful, cheery, infectious** *A spirit of cheery optimism and confidence animates all his letters.*

▶ typical of the young **bright-eyed, youthful** *He plays the role of a politician whose youthful optimism has long since died.*

▶ new **renewed** *The second half of the year has started well, with renewed optimism about the state of the global economy.*

● v+N express optimism **express, exude, radiate** *He believed it was the duty of a leader to always exude optimism.*

▶ cause optimism **engender, instil** *His appointment engendered optimism that more enlightened policies could emerge.*

▶ reduce or destroy optimism **dampen, shatter, temper** *Increasing unemployment across the UK has failed to dampen the optimism of recruitment firms.*

● N+v disappear **evaporate, wane** *But Robert's initial optimism has already waned.*

▶ be common **abound, prevail** *I feel a sense of optimism is prevailing in Japan.*

▶ be justified **be justified, be rewarded** *We started the season with high hopes, and this optimism was soon rewarded.*

optimistic ADJ
hopeful and confident about the future

● adv+ADJ excessively **absurdly, excessively, falsely, hopelessly, hugely, naively, over, overly, ridiculously, a tad** INFORMAL, **too, unduly, unrealistically, wildly** *Budget estimates were overly optimistic.* ● *Perhaps I was a tad optimistic to hope for 300 competitors to turn up.*

▶ carefully **cautiously, guardedly, moderately, quietly** *Of course he could still withdraw, but I feel cautiously optimistic that he will buy the flat.*

▶ always **determinedly, eternally, relentlessly** *The Bank of England remains determinedly optimistic about growth prospects.*

▶ strangely or surprisingly **extraordinarily, remarkably, strangely** *This is a strangely optimistic book, set in very grim times yet leaving you with a sense of dignity and hope.*

▶ by a large majority **overwhelmingly** *Respondents to the survey were overwhelmingly optimistic about the future of the sector.*

▶ calmly **moderately, quietly** *As a politician who*

remained committed to peaceful change, he was
quietly optimistic of the future.

- ADJ+n attitude **attitude, outlook, view** *The
entrepreneur has an optimistic outlook on life.*
▸ prediction or estimate **assumption, estimate,
expectation, forecast, prediction, projection,
scenario, vision** *This growth rate is above even the
most optimistic forecasts for developing countries.*
▸ conclusion **conclusion, prognosis** *There is another
way of assessing the work that leads to a less
optimistic conclusion.*
▸ hope **hope** *I have finished my novel and have
optimistic hopes of getting it published.*
▸ mood or tone **mood, note, tone** *There is a slightly
more optimistic mood in the music industry.*

- v+ADJ be or feel optimistic **be, become, feel** *Now
I feel more optimistic about my future.*
▸ remain optimistic **remain, stay** *Despite falling
listeners and fewer ads, the station remains
optimistic.*
▸ seem optimistic **appear, look, seem, sound** *I do not
wish to sound too optimistic, but everything is falling
into place.*
▸ prove too optimistic **prove** *Even that lower figure
may prove optimistic.*

option N
something you can choose in a particular situation

- adj+N good or attractive **attractive, easy, good,
preferred, safe** *After School Clubs are usually the
easiest option for school-age children.* • *Please let us
know your preferred option.*
▸ practical or sensible **realistic, sensible, viable** *Solar
energy could become a viable option for energy
production.*
▸ cheap/expensive **cheap, expensive** *For a cheaper
option, buy a model with rechargeable batteries.*
▸ available **available, open, possible** *You need to
accurately compare the costs of all the available
options.* • *This should be considered as a last resort
if no other treatment options are open.*
▸ various **additional, alternative, different,
following, other, several, various** *In Appendix 1, a
number of alternative options are detailed for
comparison.*
▸ only **only** *For many, low skilled, low paid jobs are
their only option.*

- n+N **accommodation, career, childcare, dining,
housing, payment, transport, travel, treatment** *It's
never too late to start thinking about your career
options.* • *We've been tackling congestion by giving
people better information about their travel options.*

- v+N have an option **have** *Little more than five
years ago, web developers had just one option when
creating online shopping sites.*
▸ choose an option **choose, exercise, favour, pursue,
select, specify** *Those who wish to exercise this option
should contact their personal tutor.*
▸ discuss or consider options **assess, consider,
discuss, evaluate, examine, explore, investigate,
review** *Currently, the Council is considering two
options.*
▸ give someone an option **give sb, grant sb, offer
(sb)** *We offer the option of receiving all the news as
a single daily digest.*

▸ describe options **identify, list, outline** *The paper
outlined three possible options.*
▸ reduce options **limit** *I realise that working from
home limits my options somewhat.*
▸ in computing **set** *The Job Wizard allows you to set
many options and is very easy to use.*

optional ADJ
available or possible if wanted

- adv+ADJ **completely, entirely, purely, strictly** *The
project is entirely optional and students may form
any group of people to undertake the research.*

- ADJ+n additional feature **accessory, add-on,
extra** *You can also purchase optional accessories
including a travel charger and a wireless keyboard.*
▸ part of course of study **dissertation, module,
subject, unit** *Optional modules include: advanced
research methods; medical law and ethics; Freud and
Psychoanalysis.*
▸ trip **excursion, tour** *We can organise your choice of
accommodation, optional tours and transfers.*

ordeal N
a very unpleasant experience

- adj+N terrible **appalling, awful, distressing,
dreadful, excruciating, frightening, grim,
gruelling, harrowing, hideous, horrendous,
horrible, horrific, painful, terrible, terrifying,
traumatic** *She managed to escape after her horrific
ordeal and called the police.*
▸ long **entire, lengthy, prolonged, whole** *Passengers
and crew suffered a prolonged ordeal while they
waited to be rescued.*

- v+N suffer an ordeal **endure, experience, face,
suffer, undergo** *Then he had to endure the terrifying
ordeal of a press conference with a barrage of hostile
questions.*
▸ survive an ordeal **survive** *Many animals are dead,
and those that have survived the ordeal are in a
terrible condition.*
▸ avoid an ordeal **be spared, escape** *She was spared
the ordeal of having to identify the bodies.*
▸ describe an ordeal **describe, recount, relive** *The
director persuaded the two men to relive their ordeal
for the camera.*

order N
1 the way things are arranged or done

- adj+N sensible or correct **correct, logical, natural,
right** *Then draw up an agenda by putting everything
into a logical order.*
▸ from highest/lowest or first/last **ascending,
descending, reverse** *Hotels are listed in descending
order of price per room.* • *Let me take things in
reverse order and deal with the last point first.*
▸ not in order **random** *The shuffle function plays all
the songs from that year in a random order.*

> You can also say that something is **in no particular
> order**: *The artists featured are listed in no particular
> order.*

▸ types of order **alphabetical, chronological,
numerical, rank, sequential** *The bibliography is
arranged in alphabetical order according to author
surnames.* • *The criteria to be applied are listed in
rank order.*

v+N put things in an order **arrange sth in, list sth in, put sth in** *Can you put them in the order in which they occurred?*

▸ change an order **change, reverse** *If you change the order of words in a sentence, you change the meaning.*

▸ **N+of** **importance, precedence, preference, priority, seniority** *There are three possible solutions, listed here in* no specific *order of preference.*

2 a request for a product

▸ **adj+N** large **bulk, large, major** *We offer discounts on bulk orders, so it makes sense to stock up.*

▸ new **new** *Do you have the resources to cope with new orders and enquiries that come in?*

▸ special **special** *They had received a special order for a different version of the design.*

▸ placed in a particular way **mail, online, telephone** *When you place an online order, we will send a confirming email message.*

▸ **v+N** make an order **make, place, put in, submit** *The matching headcover is included free when you place your order through the website.*

▸ get or accept an order **accept, confirm, get, receive, secure, take** *We accept orders only with a UK-based billing address.* • *The waiter asked, 'Can I take your order?'*

▸ deal with an order **complete, fulfil, process** *We aim to process your order by the end of the next working day.*

▸ send what has been ordered **deliver, dispatch, send, ship** *International orders are sent by Air Mail.*

▸ change or cancel an order **amend, cancel, change** *You may cancel or amend your order prior to checkout.*

an instruction from someone in authority

adj+N strict **strict** *Agamemnon had given him strict orders to guard his wife when he left for Troy.*

temporary **interim, temporary** *The tribunal will make an interim order that he remains employed until the full hearing.*

types of order **court, military** *The device was used to encode military orders during World War II.*

for a particular thing to be done **adoption, banning, closure, confiscation, disqualification, preservation, purchase, restraining, winding-up** *Compulsory liquidation is where a person, usually a creditor, petitions the court to make a winding-up order.*

v+N give an order **give (sb), grant (sb), issue, send, sign** *A possession order was granted by the Court.* • *Robert issued orders for pits to be dug beside the road.*

obey an order **carry out, execute, follow, obey** *The soldiers had no choice but to obey orders.*

disobey an order **breach, disobey, refuse** *He said Mr Field had breached the court order by returning to the flat.* • *They were prosecuted for inciting soldiers to disobey orders.*

be given an order **get, have, receive** *The troops received orders to march immediately on the town.*

obtain an order **obtain, secure** *Residents secured a closure order last month forcing the tenants out of the area.*

change an order **change, revoke** *The judge may at*

any time revoke an order committing a person to prison.

▸ ask for an order **ask for, seek** *The lender can seek a court order to recover the debt.*

● **N+v** state or specify something **prescribe sth, require sth, specify sth, state sth** *An enforcement order specifies the steps the company has to take to comply.* • *The orders stated the attack would take place the following day.*

▸ forbid something **ban sth, forbid sth, prohibit sth** *These orders ban certain football supporters from attending matches.*

▸ allow something **authorize sb/sth** *The Minister gave an order authorizing the carrying out of the works.*

4 a situation in which people obey laws and rules

● **adj+N** public **civil, public** *Sensationalist news coverage can itself be a threat to public order.*

● **v+N** create or bring back order **impose, restore** *He was tasked with restoring order at the end of the civil war.*

▸ keep order **keep, maintain** *I had to maintain order, so after two warnings I sent her out of the classroom.*

order V
tell someone they must do something

● **adv+V** immediately **immediately, promptly** *The French court immediately ordered her release.*

▸ specifically **expressly, specifically** *Some Generals specifically ordered bombings of civilian villages.*

▸ according to reports **allegedly, reportedly** *He allegedly ordered that payments be misrecorded in the company books.*

orderly ADJ
well organized, or well-behaved

● **ADJ+n** manner **fashion, manner** *Luggage should be collected in an orderly fashion.*

▸ working **conduct, functioning** *The government has a duty to ensure the orderly functioning of the economy.*

▸ change **handover, succession, transition** *The retiring chairman will remain at the company until the AGM in order to assist in an orderly transition.*

▸ queue **procession, queue** *People are blocking entrances to the loos by not forming an orderly queue.*

▸ leaving somewhere **evacuation, retreat, withdrawal** *Fire Stewards will ensure the orderly evacuation of the building.*

▸ sensible order **progression, sequence** *Teaching skills in an orderly sequence usually has the best results.*

organ N
a body part that does a specific job

● **adj+N** of the body **bodily, internal** *A mouse has a similar set of bodily organs and muscles to a human.*

▸ needed for life **major, vital** *The body's vital organs cannot function without water.*

▸ with a particular function **digestive, reproductive, sense, sensory, sex, sexual** *In fact, the reproductive organs do not start to function until puberty.*

▸ in a particular place **abdominal, genital, pelvic** *Sometimes, other pelvic organs such as the bladder and bowel are injured during a hysterectomy.*

▶ diseased **diseased** *Stem cell treatments have the potential to regenerate damaged and diseased organs.*

▶ transplanted **transplanted** *The drug helped to overcome the problem of the patient's body rejecting the transplanted organ.*

● v+N damage **affect, damage** *This bacteria can also cause septicemia and damage the internal organs.*

▶ remove **remove, transplant** *The main problem in transplanting organs is rejection.*

▶ donate **donate** *Discuss your wishes with your relatives if you wish to donate your organs.*

● N+n transplant **donation, transplant, transplantation** *Our teaching hospitals provide advanced care, such as organ transplants, cancer and cardiac care.*

▶ problem **damage, failure, rejection** *He died of multiple organ failure.*

▶ donor **donor** *Not everyone is a suitable organ donor.*

organize V
prepare or arrange an activity or event

● V+n conference or meeting **conference, meeting, seminar, symposium, workshop** *The Art History Department is organizing a conference on conservation.*

▶ protest **boycott, demonstration, march, protest, rally** *The Black community was outraged, and quickly organized a boycott of the buses in protest.*

▶ trip **expedition, tour, trip** *The Artsline Youth Project organizes trips to cinemas, theatres, and gigs.*

▶ event or show **competition, contest, event, exhibition, tournament** *Barbara organizes our annual poetry contest.*

▶ something written **petition, referendum, rota** *Liberal Democrats are organizing a nationwide petition to scrap council tax.*

organized ADJ
showing careful planning

● adv+ADJ well **brilliantly, efficiently, highly, well** *This is a highly organized and well-run department.*

▶ not very well **loosely, poorly** *It seems to be a loosely organized group with no single identifiable leader.*

origin N
the place, time, situation etc where something or someone comes from or begins to exist [usually plural]

● adj+N not known or understood **dubious, mysterious, obscure, uncertain, unknown** *The origins of the word are unknown.*

▶ types of origin **biological, ethnic, genetic, geographical, national, racial** *A government survey has found that ethnic origin plays a big part in the sort of ill health someone will suffer.*

▶ from a particular time **ancient, medieval** *Longton is another village of ancient origin.*

▶ not rich **humble** *He was a wonderful man, full of humanity, who never forgot his humble origins.*

▶ not from this world **divine, extraterrestrial, mythical, supernatural** *His right to rule was believed to be of divine origin.*

● v+N have a particular origin **have, owe, trace** *It is said these Games owe their origins to tests of*

strength and skill set by Highland chiefs. ● *The Liberal Party traces its origins to the 18th century.*

▶ discover someone's or something's origins **ascertain, determine, discover, pinpoint, uncover, unravel** *When a pain is felt internally, it can be difficult to pinpoint its origin.*

▶ investigate someone's or something's origins **examine, explore, investigate** *The course explored the origin and development of Darwin's evolutionary theory.*

▶ reveal someone's or something's origins **betray, indicate, reveal, suggest** *This is the family name and indicates the Persian origin of the family.*

▶ hide someone's or something's origins **belie, conceal, disguise, obscure** *His tanned skin and dark, curly hair belie his German origins.* ● *The money is passed through a series of transactions to obscure its origin.*

▶ explain someone's or something's origins **explain, understand** *The goal of the research was to seek to understand the origin of life.*

● N+of **civilization, consciousness, cosmos, galaxy, species, universe** *Professor Stephen Hawking is a theoretical physicist noted for his research into the origin of the universe.*

original ADJ
new, interesting, and different from anything else

● adv+ADJ very or completely **completely, entirely, genuinely, highly, hugely, totally, truly, utterly, wholly, wildly** *Steve has developed a highly original songwriting style.*

▶ in a surprising or exciting way **amazingly, breathtakingly, powerfully, remarkably, startlingly, strikingly, stunningly, thrillingly** *It is a work of great poetic beauty, written in a startlingly original voice.*

▶ in a good way **brilliantly, fantastically, refreshingly, wonderfully** *This is the most refreshingly original book about British politics that I have read for som time.*

▶ not very **hardly, not terribly** *While the plot isn't terribly original, the central characters are interesting.*

originality N
the quality of being new and interesting, or the ability to think of new and interesting ideas

● adj+N great **genuine, great, much, outstanding, real, sheer, utmost** *There was always much originality and ingenuity in what he did.* ● *The shee originality of this comedian will ensure that you wi see no other performer like him.*

▶ surprising or exciting **astonishing, compelling, daring, remarkable, startling, striking** *This is an unclassifiable work of startling originality.*

▶ types of originality **artistic, creative** *The judges will be particularly looking for artistic originality and innovation.*

● v+N show originality **demonstrate, display, exhibit, exude, possess, show** *Our musical style is eclectic, experimental at times, and exudes originality.*

▶ lack originality **lack, lose** *He was a learned man, but he lacked originality.*

▶ keep originality **maintain, retain** *His poems still*

*retain their originality, freshness, and often
humorous content.*

ornate ADJ
decorated with complicated patterns or shapes

- adv+ADJ very **extremely, highly, incredibly,
  lavishly, richly, very** *The concert hall is renowned
  for its lavishly ornate interior.*
▶ in a good way **beautifully, fantastically,
  wonderfully** *Within the gardens are many
  wonderfully ornate fountains and ponds.*
▶ excessively **excessively, over, overly, rather** *The
  clothing was of good quality, but overly ornate and
  overpriced.*

- ADJ+n object **balcony, balustrade, buckle,
  canopy, ceiling, chandelier, cornice, facade,
  fireplace, fountain, frieze, lamppost, pulpit, railing,
  reredos, urn, valance** *The lavishly decorated
  banquet hall is complete with ornate chandeliers and
  panelled walls.*
▶ work **carving, decor, ironwork, plasterwork,
  stonework** *The building has soaring ceilings with
  ornate plasterwork.*

orthodox ADJ
generally accepted as correct, usual, or traditional

▶ adv+ADJ strictly **rigidly, strictly** *He was as rigidly
  orthodox as Mark Twain was revolutionary.*
▶ in a particular way **doctrinally, theologically** *Like
  Newton, most scientists at this time were
  theologically orthodox.*

- ADJ+n religious belief system **creed, doctrine,
  dogma, theology, Judaism, Christianity etc**
  *Orthodox Protestant theology counts among its
  central doctrines the primacy of the individual
  conscience.*
  believer **believer, rabbi, theologian, Jew, Muslim
  etc** *Both parties were orthodox Jews and were
  required, under Jewish law, to refer their disputes to
  a Beth Din.*
  political or scientific system **medicine, Marxism,
  Darwinism etc** *There are already more alternative
  'healers' in Britain than practitioners of orthodox
  medicine.*

orthodoxy N
an idea, practice, or set of beliefs that is traditional,
usual, or generally considered correct

  adj+N current or accepted **accepted, established,
  fashionable, prevailing, reigning, ruling** *This was
  the accepted academic orthodoxy until the 1930s.*
  strict **dogmatic, rigid** *There were times, however,
  when his seriousness degenerated into dogmatic
  orthodoxy.*
  religious **doctrinal, religious, theological, Catholic,
  Protestant etc** *Franciscans believe in simplicity,
  obedience and doctrinal orthodoxy.*
  political, economic etc **feminist, ideological,
  liberal, modernist, Keynesian, Marxist etc** *France
  in the 1990s saw a tremendous backlash against the
  liberal economic orthodoxy of the 1980s.*

  v+N **accept, challenge, defy, question, reject,
  subvert** *We need MPs like him who remain willing
  to challenge current orthodoxy.*

outbreak N
the sudden start of war, disease etc

- adj+N very bad **devastating, severe, virulent**
  *There was devastating outbreak of cholera which
  killed many in the 1830s.*
▶ happening occasionally or again **periodic,
  renewed, sporadic** *The East End has seen sporadic
  outbreaks of mob violence.*
▶ possible/definite **confirmed, suspected** *Three
  toddlers have been taken to hospital after a suspected
  outbreak of the E coli virus.*
▶ sudden **sudden** *There was a sudden outbreak of
  theft, and Roddy was suspected.*
▶ of a particular disease **cholera, flu, foot-and-
  mouth, influenza, measles, salmonella, smallpox,
  typhoid** *England is experiencing its biggest measles
  outbreak in 20 years.*
▶ worldwide **pandemic** *There is currently a significant
  risk of a worldwide pandemic influenza outbreak.*
▶ infectious **communicable, infectious** *Nationally and
  internationally infectious disease outbreaks in farm
  animals can have devastating results.*
▶ how caused **foodborne, waterborne** *Gastroenteritis,
  the illness most often cause by waterborne outbreaks,
  is not uncommon and has many causes.*

- v+N cause an outbreak **cause, precede,
  precipitate, trigger** *Many believe that it was military
  and strategic factors that precipitated the outbreak
  of war in 1914.*
▶ deal with or stop an outbreak **combat, control,
  eradicate, halt, investigate, prevent, tackle** *There
  is a detailed contingency plan to eradicate any
  outbreak of avian flu in poultry.*
▶ say there is or will be an outbreak **detect, fear,
  predict, report** *Police feared outbreaks of violence
  between the contending factions.*

- N+of disease **cholera, diarrhoea, disease, fever,
  flu, foot-and-mouth, influenza, measles,
  meningitis, mumps, plague, poisoning, rabies,
  scabies, smallpox, typhus** *In the 13th Century, a
  terrible outbreak of the plague, known as the Black
  Death, hit London.*
▶ violence **hostilities, violence, war** *He was in Paris
  just before the outbreak of hostilities in 1939.*

outburst N
a sudden spoken expression of strong feeling

- adj+N aggressive or violent **abusive, aggressive,
  angry, drunken, intemperate, petulant, violent** *He
  had a tendency toward violent outbursts and an
  admitted drink problem.*
▶ very emotional **emotional, hysterical, impassioned,
  indignant, irrational, uncontrollable** *A letter of
  complaint would surely have been more effective than
  this hysterical outburst.*
▶ occasional/frequent **frequent, occasional, sporadic**
  *Despite recent elections, there are still sporadic
  outbursts of conflict.*
▶ sudden or surprising **explosive, spontaneous,
  sudden, uncharacteristic, unexpected** *He has a
  hair-trigger temper which often leads to sudden
  outbursts of violence.*

- v+N **cause, prompt, provoke, trigger** *The
  television drama provoked an outburst from the
  Unionist leader.*

- N+of anger or emotion **anger, emotion, grief, indignation, rage, temper, violence, wrath** *My family suffered through my drinking and outbursts of temper.*
▶ laughter or applause **applause, laughter** *There were occasional outbursts of laughter from the audience.*

outcome N
the final result of something

- adj+N good **beneficial, favourable, optimal, positive, satisfactory, successful** *This practical step-by-step guide will help you to achieve a successful outcome.*
▶ bad **adverse, disappointing, fatal, negative, poor, tragic, unsatisfactory** *The review calls for more clinical trials on the adverse outcomes of treatment.*
▶ after some time **eventual, final, longer-term, long-term, overall, ultimate** *There is acute uncertainty about the eventual outcome of global financial instability.* • *The earlier treatment begins, the better the long-term outcome.*
▶ immediate or not likely to last **short-term** *The short-term military outcome may not be in doubt, but questions remain regarding broader political outcomes.*
▶ known/not known **anticipated, expected, inevitable, logical, predictable, uncertain, unexpected** *From that point on, the outcome was inevitable.*
▶ wanted/not wanted **agreed, desirable, desired, intended, undesirable, unintended** *It was vital to be clear from the start about intended outcomes.*
▶ possible or likely **likely, possible, potential, probably** *As has been said very often, life is a terminal illness with only one possible outcome.*
▶ that can be clearly seen **actual, measurable, tangible** *Most charity trustees want to see immediate and tangible outcomes of the funding they provide.*
▶ most important **key, main, primary** *A key outcome of the study was the recognition that more investment was needed.*
▶ of a particular type of process **birth, clinical, educational, health, learning, pregnancy, surgical, treatment** *Access to computers can enhance educational outcomes for socially disadvantaged learners.*

- v+N produce an outcome **achieve, deliver, ensure, guarantee, know, optimise, produce, secure, yield** *Prospects for diplomacy to deliver a satisfactory outcome were undermined.*
▶ decide the outcome **decide, determine, predetermine** *This debate will be crucial in determining the outcome of the election.*
▶ affect the outcome **affect, alter, improve, influence, shape** *Teachers are being asked to improve academic outcomes for all their students.* • *Local people felt they were not given any chance to influence the outcome of the process.*
▶ analyse the outcome **analyse, assess, compare, discuss, evaluate, examine, measure, monitor, review** *He evaluates the likely outcome of pursuing each possible course of action.*
▶ predict or expect an outcome **anticipate, envisage, expect, predict** *The results will improve our ability to predict the outcome of a stroke.*
▶ describe an outcome **define, detail, identify, record, report, specify, summarise** *This section summarises the main outcomes of the discussions which took place.*
▶ make assumptions about an outcome **pre-empt, prejudge** *The investigation is at an early stage and it would be wrong to prejudge the outcome.*
▶ wait for the outcome **await** *The agency houses asylum seekers while they await the outcome of their residency applications.*

- N+of **consultation, discussion, experiment, investigation, negotiation, process, project** *The town council was delighted with the outcome of the negotiations and readily agreed to them.*

outcry N
an angry reaction by many people

- adj+N public **open, popular, public** *If a school had such unstable, inconsistent leadership there would be a public outcry.*
▶ large **great, huge, massive, much** *There would be a massive outcry if such a scheme were proposed now.*
▶ in a particular area **international, national** *The community are convinced that an international outcry will stop this tourist development.*
▶ angry **furious** *Plans for a mobile phone mast have sparked a furious outcry from people in the area.*
▶ immediate **immediate** *There was an immediate outcry which led to the building plans being scrapped.*

- v+N cause an outcry **cause, prompt, provoke, spark, trigger** *When the government announced a slight rise in social security payments, it provoked an outcry.*
▶ make an outcry **raise** *Everyone remembers the furious outcry raised by the press.*

outlay N
money needed for a new business or project

- adj+N small **little, minimal, minimum, modest, small** *For a minimal outlay, your site content remains fresh and relevant to your customers.*
▶ large **considerable, hefty, huge, large, significant, substantial** *Shareholders are unlikely to sanction a further hefty outlay on new players this summer.*
▶ at the beginning **initial** *The initial outlay is so small it is only a matter of weeks before you are in profit.*
▶ total **total** *Our total outlay on paper, printing and other expenses was £429.*
▶ financial **capital, cash, financial** *For charities, it's an opportunity to have a piece of work done with no financial outlay.*

- v+N get back an outlay **recoup, recover, repay** *At $99, you'll easily recoup the outlay in your increased productivity.*
▶ be able to afford an outlay **afford, justify** *Many supporters cannot afford the outlay for a season ticket.*
▶ require an outlay **incur, involve, require** *You may be looking at ways to expand your business whilst incurring little capital outlay.*
▶ reduce an outlay **minimize, reduce** *Users can adopt a pay-as-you-use approach to minimise their outlay.*

outlet N
a way of expressing feelings not normally expressed

● v+N find an outlet **find** *His anger and hatred had been brewing for twenty-five years and now it had found an outlet.*

▸ want an outlet **need, seek** *These young men seek an outlet for their aggression.*

▸ be an outlet **act as, be, provide (sb with)** *Music provides an invaluable outlet for safe expression of feelings and emotions.*

● N+for anger **aggression, anger, frustration** *Most games simply act as an outlet for our frustrations.*

▸ creativity **creativity, self-expression, talent** *Rapping can be an excellent outlet for self-expression.*

▸ energy or enthusiasm **energy, passion** *Young people need an organisation that provides adequate outlets for their energies.*

▸ feelings **emotion, feelings, instinct** *Laughter provides a harmless outlet for these negative emotions.*

outline V

ive the main ideas without giving all the details

adv+V briefly **briefly, succinctly** *This book starts by outlining briefly the type of world in which Margaret lived.*

clearly **clearly, eloquently** *A booklet supplied with the video case clearly outlines the key messages.*

generally **broadly** *The new structure of the school is broadly outlined below.*

V+n plan **framework, measures, plan, proposal, vision** *I have asked the architects to outline their proposals for environmental sustainability in the design of the new building.*

principles or rules **basics, criteria, principles, requirements** *The paper outlines the principles which lie behind Labour's new policy making processes.*

method **approach, methodology, procedure, steps, strategy** *Employees should use the procedure outlined in their contract to pursue grievances.*

aim **aim, objectives, priorities** *This report will outline our objectives for the coming year.*

results or findings **findings, progress, recommendations** *This document outlines the main findings from the research.*

reasons **background, rationale, reasons** *The union outlined its initial reasons for opposing the sell-off.*

outline N

explanation including general points but not tails

adj+N brief **brief, succinct** *Applicants are initially invited to provide a brief outline of their idea.*

vague **bare, sketchy, vague** *The town has an interesting history, of which I know only a sketchy outline.*

general **broad, rough** *This article gives a rough outline of what you need to get yourself online.*

basic **bare, basic** *Let me give you a basic outline of the project.*

detailed **detailed** *For a more detailed outline of this course, go to our Courses page.*

not yet definite **provisional, tentative** *A provisional outline of the programme follows – please note that this is subject to revisions.*

v+N prepare an outline **draft, prepare, sketch** *I*

have sketched the outline of my argument in favour of a written constitution.

▸ provide someone with an outline **give (sb), present (sb with), provide (sb with), submit** *Authors wishing to contribute are encouraged to submit an outline of a prospective paper.*

▸ change an outline **revise** *You will probably need to revise your outline as you plan your essay.*

outlook N

an idea about what something will be like, or a general attitude to things

● adj+N positive or optimistic **bright, cheerful, optimistic, positive, rosy, sunny** *Political stability has given Cambodia a more optimistic outlook.*

▸ negative or pessimistic **bleak, gloomy, grim, pessimistic** *Many of the students believe they have failed and that their outlook is bleak.*

▸ uncertain **uncertain** *Despite an uncertain outlook at the beginning of last year, we managed to turn a small operating profit.*

▸ reflecting someone's age **mature, youthful** *I enjoyed reading this collection of poems, particularly for its refreshing, youthful outlook.*

▸ over a particular time period **long-term, medium-term, short-term** *Sources are optimistic about the medium-term outlook for growth.*

▸ types of outlook **conservative, economic, humanistic, liberal, materialistic, philosophical, reactionary, religious, secular, theological** *This change was a shift in his basic philosophical outlook.*

● v+N change **alter, change, shape, transform** *She accepts that prices will fall, but that does not change her positive outlook.*

▸ make better/worse **improve, worsen** *These cuts have further worsened the economic outlook.*

▸ make broader **broaden, widen** *We must broaden our outlook by listening to other cultures as well.*

▸ share **share** *They shared a radical outlook and became conscientious objectors during the war.*

▸ reflect **reflect** *His policy of hiring people who were bilingual was because he felt bilingualism reflected a broader outlook on life.*

output N

the amount produced by a person, organization etc

● adj+N large **large, massive, prodigious, prolific** *The stories he wrote for use in the classroom were the beginning of a prolific output of children's writing.*

▸ total **combined, entire, gross, total** *The share of total economic output accounted for by industry has declined in recent decades.*

▸ maximum **maximum, peak** *This system has a maximum output of 500 kW.*

▸ that can be measured **measurable, tangible** *One of the major difficulties is in defining the measurable outputs of the organisation.*

▸ types of output **agricultural, creative, electrical, industrial, literary, musical** *Why did agricultural output in Africa decrease between 1980 and 2001?*

● v+N give a particular output **achieve, deliver, generate, produce** *He admitted they had absorbed a lot of money and as yet produced little valuable output.*

▸ increase output **boost, double, increase, maximize,**

optimize *We provide all the necessary information on how to maximise output and contain costs.*
▶ decrease output **decrease, reduce** *This can reduce the output of blood from the heart.*
▶ control or measure output **control, measure, monitor, restrict** *First, we have to do more to control our own output of greenhouse gases.*

outrage N

1 a strong feeling of anger and shock

● adj+N moral **moral, righteous** *His innocent suffering excites the audience's pity and moral outrage.*
▶ easy to understand **justifiable, justified, understandable** *Whatever the motivation behind his comment, it caused understandable outrage in Northern Ireland.*
▶ easy to notice **palpable** *The anger and outrage were palpable, but there seemed to be nothing anyone could do.*
▶ from many people **public, widespread** *There has been widespread outrage at his remarks.*
▶ pretended **mock** *'Put that down,' he orders in mock outrage.*

● v+N cause outrage **arouse, cause, ignite, prompt, provoke, spark, trigger** *His comments on race relations in Britain have frequently sparked outrage.*
▶ feel outrage **feel, share** *If you share our outrage at this barbaric practice, please help us with a donation.*
▶ express your outrage **express, voice** *The UN High Commissioner on Human Rights has also expressed outrage at the attacks.*
▶ pretend to feel outrage **feign** *They feign outrage over the slightest perceived insult.*

● and/or **anger, condemnation, derision, disgust, dismay, horror, incomprehension, incredulity, indignation, shock** *Revelations about how the children were treated have provoked outrage and disgust.*

2 an event causing strong anger and shock

● adj+N violent **brutal, murderous** *He must do everything in his power to stop these murderous outrages.*
▶ extremely bad **appalling, unspeakable** *Perpetrators of unspeakable outrages are being allowed to go free.*
▶ real **absolute, utter** *This is an absolute outrage and completely unacceptable.*
▶ by terrorists **terrorist** *London is on alert for a possible terrorist outrage.*

● v+N commit an outrage **commit, perpetrate** *Atrocities and outrages were perpetrated by both sides during the civil war.*
▶ condemn an outrage **condemn** *The Prime Minister was quick to condemn the outrage.*

outrageous ADJ

very shocking or unreasonable

● adv+ADJ completely **absolutely, completely, quite, so, totally, truly, utterly** *The prices were completely outrageous, and I couldn't understand how a normal family could afford them.*
▶ rather **pretty** INFORMAL *He's pretty outrageous at times.*

▶ in a particular way **morally** *One might well argue that such treatment of him would be morally outrageous.*

● ADJ+n behaviour **antics, behaviour, stunt** *Certain stunts are so outrageous or strange that they deserve celebrating in their own right.*
▶ clothes **clothes, costume, outfit** *We are still planning to have some fun on Christmas Eve as we do our pub run in some outrageous outfits.*
▶ entertainment **comedy** *Her breakout role came as the choirgirl in the outrageous teen comedy hit 'American Pie'.*
▶ lie or accusation **accusation, claim, lie, slur, story** *That's an outrageous slur!*

outset N

the start of something

● v+at+N say **declare, emphasize, mention, say, specify, state, stress** *As stated at the outset, there is a vast array of advantages to building sustainable, low emissions buildings.*
▶ decide **decide, determine, establish** *The precise curriculum will be determined at the outset by detailed discussion between the tutor and the student concerned.*
▶ agree **acknowledge, agree, recognize** *We recognise at the outset that this was a very small sample and there were good reasons for this.*
▶ make clear **clarify** *The costing of projects must be clarified at the outset.*

● v+from+N be damaged or likely to fail **be doomed, be flawed** *She now claims that the scheme was doomed from the outset.*
▶ say **acknowledge, state, stress** *You must state from the outset what you are including with the house.*
▶ think about **consider** *All design details should be considered from the outset, and not as an afterthought.*

outspoken ADJ

stating your opinion honestly

● ADJ+n critic **critic, opponent** *She is well known as an outspoken critic of bureaucracy.*
▶ supporter **advocate, defender, proponent, supporter** *He is an outspoken advocate for public education.*
▶ criticism **attack, criticism, opposition** *He used a radio interview to launch an outspoken attack on the government.*

● and/or **controversial, forthright, frank, independent, opinionated** *He was opinionated and outspoken, but he was honest and truthful.*

outstanding ADJ

extremely good or impressive

● adv+ADJ very **absolutely, particularly, quite, really, simply, truly** *These cottages offer truly outstanding accommodation and are within an easy drive to places of historical interest.*
▶ in a particular way **academically, internationally, technically** *Academically outstanding students can realize their full academic potential through the Honors Program.*
▶ over a period of time **consistently, still** *Staff are encouraged to submit a nomination for an award*

for any employee who offers consistently outstanding service.

- ADJ+n achievement **achievement, contribution, merit, performance, record, reputation, result, success** *We are ready to use many of the outstanding achievements of European social democracy as our model.*
▶ ability **ability, talent** *At the Jesuit College, Torricelli showed that he had outstanding talents.*
▶ feature or quality **beauty, feature, quality, scenery** *The scenery is outstanding, and has given the name 'Little Switzerland' to this part of Hampshire.*
▶ example **example** *The Pompidou Centre in Paris is an outstanding example of the effect of urban regeneration.*

outweigh V
be more important, useful, or valuable than something

▶ adv+V very greatly **decisively, far, greatly, heavily, hugely, massively, vastly** *The benefits far outweigh these obstacles, he says, adding that the main challenge is training.*
▶ considerably **considerably, significantly, substantially** *The cost of filming in Scotland considerably outweighed the cost of filming in New Zealand.*
▶ certainly or probably **certainly, clearly, definitely, easily, probably, surely** *The benefits can certainly outweigh the difficulties.*

V+n advantages **advantage, benefit, gains, pluses, positives, pros INFORMAL, rewards** *To be brutally frank, however, the negatives far outweigh the positives.*
disadvantages **cons INFORMAL, disadvantages, drawbacks, harm, negatives** *If the gains clearly outweigh the drawbacks, carry on with this process.*

ovation N
act of clapping to express approval or enjoyment

adj+N enthusiastic **enthusiastic, huge, loud, rapturous, rousing, spontaneous, thunderous, tremendous, tumultuous, warm** *Eminently moving in places, the film 'Tarnation' received a rapturous ovation, and with good reason.*

A **standing ovation** is an occasion when an audience stands and applauds at the same time: *At the end there was a standing ovation for him and the whole cast.*

long **long, prolonged, five minute, ten-minute etc** *Clinton's appearance on stage brought the crowd to its feet for a prolonged ovation.*
deserved **deserved, well-deserved** *The lads got a terrific and well-deserved ovation.*

v+N **be given, earn, get, receive, win** *We received a standing ovation and a personal letter of congratulation on behalf of the King.*

overall ADJ
considering or including everything

adv+ADJ **2nd, 3rd, 4th etc** *I limped to the finish line 10 seconds behind Joe, happy with a placing of 5th overall.*

ADJ+n aim **aim, objective, strategy** *Our overall*
aim is to provide teaching of excellence, to students of high calibre from a wide range of backgrounds.
▶ result **mark, rate, rating, score** *Each assignment is equivalent to 1000 words and counts for 5 per cent of the overall marks.*
▶ outcome **conclusion, effectiveness, performance, satisfaction** *Our overall conclusion is that this is a competitive market.*
▶ effect **effect, impression** *The overall impression is of a warm and light-filled openness.*
▶ cost **budget, cost** *Use of lower cost services did not necessarily reduce overall costs.*
▶ responsibility **responsibility** *The Board has overall responsibility for the Group's system of internal control.*
▶ winner **winner** *Choosing the overall winner was a difficult task for the judging panel.*
▶ feeling **feel, picture** *The course aims to give an overall picture of the framework of the law relating to charities.*

overcome V
1 succeed in dealing with a problem

- adv+V partly/completely **completely, largely, partially, partly** *Some of these difficulties can be partially overcome by using calculators.*
▶ finally **eventually, finally, ultimately** *The boy eventually overcame the mental block and told me about it.*
▶ quickly/slowly **gradually, quickly, soon** *The aim of the treatment is to help the person to gradually overcome their addiction.*
▶ successfully **successfully** *No other paper has reported this approach to successfully overcome this problem.*

- V+n a problem **adversity, barrier, challenge, constraint, difficulty, hurdle, obstacle, prejudice, problem** *Can you identify ways to try to overcome those barriers?*
▶ a lack or weakness **disadvantages, fear, inertia, limitations, reluctance, shortcomings, weakness** *I am using excitement to overcome my fear.*
▶ opposition **objection, opposition, resistance** *High-density housing must overcome cultural resistance and a negative historical legacy.*

2 make someone very emotional, weak, or ill [usually passive]

- n+V emotion **anger, curiosity, emotion, excitement, fear, greed, grief, guilt** *I am overcome by my curiosity about one point.*
▶ smoke or gas **fumes, gas, smoke** *The men in question were overcome by the fumes.*
▶ sleep **sleep** *Sleep overcame a few of the party on the return to London that evening.*

overdose N
too much of a drug taken at once

- adj+N fatal/not fatal **fatal, lethal, non-fatal** *Fatal overdose of stimulant drugs is usually linked with cardiac depression and arrest.*
▶ accidental/deliberate **accidental, deliberate, intentional** *Deliberate or accidental overdoses were not included; nor were patients who were not admitted overnight to hospital.*
▶ very large **massive** *I took a massive overdose and was devastated when I woke up 4 days later.*

▶ suspected **suspected** *Any patient with a suspected paracetemol overdose should be taken to hospital immediately.*

● v+N **die from, die of, take** *On the day they were to leave for Ibiza, she took an overdose of pills and died.*

overdraft N

an agreement with a bank allowing you to spend money from an empty account

● adj+N not charged for **fee-free, interest-free** *Most banks now offer interest-free overdrafts of up to a few hundred pounds to all students.*

▶ allowed/not allowed **agreed, authorized, unauthorized** *Take care not to run up an unauthorised overdraft.*

▶ big **big, hefty, huge** *I've lots of plans for the summer, mainly paying off my huge overdraft.*

● v+N arrange or have an overdraft **arrange** *How quickly can an overdraft be arranged?*

▶ allow an overdraft **agree, authorize, offer** *The basic bank account does not offer an overdraft, a cheque book or a debit card.*

▶ pay back an overdraft **clear, pay off, reduce, repay** *He suggested that we should be trying to repay the overdraft, not increase it.*

▶ increase an overdraft **extend, increase** *Extending your overdraft may be an option, but your bank may not agree to this.*

overestimate V

consider something to be better or bigger than it is

● adv+V greatly **greatly, grossly, seriously, significantly, substantially, vastly** *Such writers tend to vastly overestimate the uniqueness of their ideas.*

▶ to some degree **slightly, somewhat** *The title 'New Media' slightly overestimates the scope of the book.*

● V+n importance **extent, importance, significance** *It would be as well not to overestimate the significance of the discontent.*

> You can say that it is **impossible, hard** or **difficult to overestimate** something when you want to stress its extent or significance: *It is impossible to overestimate the importance of the contribution made by Britain's iron-masters.*

▶ influence **impact, influence** *Many persons are inclined to overestimate the influence of inheritance in determining success in business.*

▶ risk **risk** *People tend to overestimate risks that have received a lot of media attention.*

▶ ability **ability** *In general, they overestimate the abilities of children at any given age.*

overhaul V

completely change a system to make it work better

● adv+V **completely, extensively, fully, radically, substantially, thoroughly, totally** *Over the course of the year, we had to radically overhaul our systems of accounting.*

● V+n **law, legislation, procedures, regulations, structure, system** *The proposals will completely*

overhaul chemicals safety legislation. ● *The postal service plans to overhaul its pricing structure as it faces increased competition.*

overhaul N

thorough changes to a system

● adj+N changing many things **drastic, fundamental, radical, thorough** *The EU budget needs a thorough overhaul, the report says.*

▶ large in scale **comprehensive, extensive, major, massive, total** *The Ford Motor Company is planning a major overhaul of its largest plant, which will revolutionize the way it makes cars.*

● v+N need an overhaul **need, require** *The current rules now need an overhaul.*

▶ carry out an overhaul **carry out, undertake** *As Home Secretary, he undertook an overhaul of the prisons.*

▶ have an overhaul **undergo** *Norwich International Airport is set to undergo a major overhaul.*

overheads N

the regular costs of a business or organization

● adj+N low **low, minimal, negligible** *The administration is run on a voluntary basis, so overheads are minimal.*

▶ high **costly, excessive, expensive, high, huge, significant** *The problem is that a business like this requires large, central locations with massive overheads.*

▶ extra **additional, extra, increased** *You incur no additional overheads other than to meet your advertising costs.*

▶ unnecessary **unnecessary** *The coalition also tries to avoid incurring unnecessary overheads.*

▶ types of overheads **administrative, bureaucratic, computational, institutional, organizational** *This is part of an effort to spend as little as possible on bureaucratic overheads.*

● v+N reduce overheads **eliminate, minimize, reduce** *Your sales strategy should be based on minimizing overheads.*

▶ have to pay overheads **incur** *Projects such as the Wellcome Trust Building and the Cancer Centre incur significant overheads.*

overlook V

fail to do something or ignore something

● adv+V often or sometimes **frequently, often, sometimes** *The needs of disabled people from black and ethnic minority groups were often overlooked.*

▶ mainly or completely **completely, entirely, largely** *It is unsurprising that the findings of the Report were largely overlooked.*

▶ deliberately/accidentally **conveniently, inadvertently** *This is a scientific fact conveniently overlooked and denied by many male scientists.*

▶ easily **easily** *If you don't get it right, you'll be easily overlooked.*

● V+n **distinction, fact, importance, possibility, shortcomings, significance** *These arguments overlook a fact which we neglect at our peril.*

overriding ADJ
more important than anything else

- ADJ+n aim **aim, goal, objective** *The overriding objective should be to provide high quality public services.*
- factor or idea **factor, principle, theme** *The overriding factor is the rise in uncertainty in life.*
- concern **concern, consideration, preoccupation, priority** *The overriding consideration should be to keep the size and complexity of plans manageable.*
- impression **impression** *The overriding impression she gained from this was that she and the child were safe.*
- duty **duty, obligation** *Expert witnesses owe their overriding duty to the court, not the client.*
- importance **importance** *The course emphasises the overriding importance of initiative and creativity.*
- longing **ambition, desire, passion** *His overriding desire was to have a brief period alone.*

oversee V
watch something to check it happens correctly

- V+n creation or development **construction, creation, development, expansion, preparation, production, progress, transformation, transition** *Sir David oversaw a tremendous expansion of the institute's research activities.*
  operation **administration, conduct, operation, running** *I am responsible for overseeing the running and management of the building itself.*
  delivery **delivery, implementation** *The group will set up an action plan and oversee its delivery.*
  feature **aspect** *We can save you time and money by overseeing each aspect of running an event.*
  project **project** *The librarian will continue to oversee the project and maintain the website.*
- and/or manage **coordinate, direct, manage, monitor, regulate, supervise** *The success of the website illustrates my ability to coordinate and oversee this kind of project.*
  enforce **enforce, implement** *The Information Commissioner's Office is the Government department that oversees and enforces freedom of information.*

oversight N
the job of checking that something works well

- adj+N types of oversight **democratic, editorial, judicial, pastoral, regulatory, strategic** *There is no provision for judicial oversight.*
  by a particular body or group **civilian, congressional, episcopal, parliamentary** *These efforts will merit close congressional oversight as they are implemented.*
  effective **independent, rigorous** *Birkbeck College maintains its own internal rigorous oversight of standards.*
- v+N have oversight **exercise, have, include, provide** *We also have oversight from an equipment technician and educational audiologist.*
  keep or improve oversight **ensure, improve, maintain, retain, strengthen** *A Finance Committee has been established to improve financial oversight.*
  give oversight to someone **delegate, give** *The Governing Body has delegated the oversight of this policy to its Curriculum Committee.*

- need oversight **require** *He has suggested that independent oversight is now required.*
- N+of **activity, arrangements, implementation, matters, operation, programme, regulation** *The Audit Committee provides independent oversight of audit activities.*

2 something you do not notice that causes problems later

- adj+N **administrative, glaring, slight, unfortunate** *Please let me know if there are any glaring oversights or errors in this.*
- v+N **correct, rectify, remedy** *A three-year research project aims to remedy this oversight.*

overthrow V
force a leader or government from power

- adv+V **completely, eventually, finally** *The regime was finally overthrown by its regional opponents in 1991.*
- V+n a leader **dictator, king, leader, president, ruler, tsar, tyrant** *If it is possible, should a tyrant be overthrown?*
- a government or political system **capitalism, democracy, dictatorship, dynasty, government, imperialism, monarchy, regime, tyranny** *At meetings, Edwards constantly called for an armed uprising to overthrow the government.*

overtones
noticeable but not obvious qualities

- adj+N types of overtones **emotional, moral, political, racial, racist, religious, romantic, sexual, supernatural** *Her music is laden with heavy emotional overtones.* • *This is a rip-roaring adventure story with political overtones.*
- strong or clear **clear, heavy, obvious, strong** *The idea of spreading the word carries obvious religious overtones.*
- slight **slight, subtle** *In addition to its avowed purpose, marriage has acquired subtle overtones as a sign of maturity.*
- negative or frightening **dark, negative, pejorative, sinister** *It's a pity that the word mythology has the negative overtones that it has.*
- v+N **carry, have** *Like many Arabic words, 'Illya' carries multiple overtones, making it difficult to translate.*

overturn V
officially change a decision or law [usually passive]

- adv+V later **subsequently** *Only one case was subsequently overturned.*
- completely or successfully **completely, successfully** *The Review Commission has seen 50 per cent of the convictions it has referred being successfully overturned on Appeal.*
- V+n legal decision **acquittal, conviction, decision, injunction, judgement, ruling, sentence, verdict** *His conviction was overturned in 1995.*
- law **ban, law** *No EU law has ever been successfully overturned by Parliament.*

overview N

a description or knowledge of the main features of something

- adj+N short **brief, concise, introductory, quick, succinct** *This Handbook provides an introductory overview to the subject.*
- ▸ long or detailed **comprehensive, thorough** *Chapter two gives a particularly thorough, comprehensive overview of assessment procedures.*
- ▸ good **excellent, useful** *This revised paperback version provides an excellent overview of the fundamentals of exercise physiology.*
- ▸ general **broad, general** *The aim is to give you a broad overview of the types of content available.*
- ▸ types of overview **detailed, historical, impartial, strategic** *The University has produced a strategic overview of learning.*
- v+N give an overview **give, include, offer, present, provide** *A brief overview is provided in Appendix One.*
- ▸ get an overview **gain, get, obtain** *Students will gain an overview of one of the central branches of Western philosophy.*
- ▸ include an overview **feature, include** *This is a research guide featuring concise overviews of historical periods and chronologies.*
- N+of **concepts, issues, subject, theories, topic** *Read these pages for an overview of each topic.*

overweight ADJ

heavier than you should be

- adv+ADJ very **dangerously, excessively, extremely, grossly, seriously, severely, significantly, very** *Figures show that one in five adults is dangerously overweight.*
- ▸ slightly or moderately **slightly, somewhat** *He was a classic candidate for a heart attack, somewhat overweight, a smoker and a drinker.*
- and/or **inactive, obese, underweight, unfit** *Today's youth are getting rapidly overweight and seriously unfit.*

overwhelm V

affect someone's emotions in a very powerful way

- adv+V completely **absolutely, completely, quite, simply, totally, utterly** *Such incidents and feelings have the effect of completely overwhelming our coping resources.*
- ▸ almost **almost** *I looked in the window and nausea almost overwhelmed me.*
- n+V something someone does **enthusiasm, generosity, kindness, response** *We have been overwhelmed by your enthusiasm for Fairtrade.* • *I have been overwhelmed by the generosity and support of so many people.*
- ▸ feelings or a feeling **emotion, feeling, grief, sadness** *Unexpectedly, I had been overwhelmed by emotion on seeing Applecross again.*
- ▸ a quality **beauty** *He was so overwhelmed by her beauty that he asked Griselidis to marry him.*

> Usage ***Overwhelm*** is usually passive in all of the ***n+V*** combinations shown above: *Tina has lost her son Sam, and is overwhelmed by grief.*

- V+with **emotion, feeling, gratitude, grief, joy, sadness, sorrow** *I was overwhelmed with gratitude at such concern.*

overwhelming ADJ

1 much larger, stronger etc than anything else

- adv+ADJ completely or very **absolutely, completely, quite, so** *In the case of the firefighters, opposition to the government was absolutely overwhelming.*
- ▸ apparently **seemingly** *A brilliant strategist, he won many battles, often against seemingly overwhelming odds.*
- ▸ rather **pretty INFORMAL** *He said: 'I expected to win because the evidence was pretty overwhelming'.*
- ADJ+n numbers or strength **firepower, majority, odds, preponderance, superiority, vote** *The overwhelming majority of the jobs created were in the private sector.*
- ▸ acceptance/rejection **consensus, endorsement, opposition, rejection** *These results reveal an overwhelming consumer endorsement for face-to-face service.*
- ▸ success **popularity, success, victory** *The campaign was an overwhelming success.*
- ▸ evidence **evidence, impression** *There is no overwhelming evidence to support this and information has been anecdotal and subjective.*
- ▸ response **response** *We had an overwhelming response to the survey and would like to thank all who took part.*
- v+ADJ **appear, be, become, prove, seem** *Here he argues that the statistics demonstrating the futility of wind power are now overwhelming.*

2 an overwhelming emotion is very strong

- adv+ADJ completely or very **completely, quite, so, too, totally, truly, utterly** *To hear how loyal the fans are, it's truly overwhelming.*
- ▸ almost **almost, nearly** *Number 4 is a work of enormous strength and passion almost overwhelming in its intensity.*
- ▸ rather **pretty INFORMAL, rather, somewhat** *The whole experience can be somewhat overwhelming.*
- ▸ slightly **a little, slightly** *Initially, the number of characters we are introduced to can seem a little overwhelming.*
- ▸ in a particular way **emotionally** *Heartbreak Productions bring their unique style of storytelling to a new production of this emotionally overwhelming play.*
- ADJ+n feelings **desire, emotion, feeling, urge** *My overwhelming feeling is sadness.*
- ▸ a particular feeling **grief, guilt, joy, sadness** *For some considerable time, you may have moments of overwhelming sadness.*

owner N

someone who owns something

- adj+N present, previous or future **current, former, new, original, present, previous, prospective, would-be** *Holland House is named after a former owner in Sir Henry, Earl of Holland.*
- ▸ only or joint **joint, principal, sole** *The joint owner of the newspaper decided to close it down.*

▶ legal **legal, rightful** *All materials and images on this site are considered to be copyrighted to its rightful owner.*

▶ proud **proud** *It seems that the hard work has been worth it and Collingwood will be the proud owner of a brand new gym.*

ownership N
legal possession of something

● adj+N legal or complete **freehold, legal, outright, rightful** *During the building contract period, legal ownership of the building site transfers to our Contractor.*

▶ public/private **private, public** *It was proposed that the company should be converted to public ownership.*

▶ only or shared **joint, shared, sole** *Click here for more information on shared ownership.*

▶ belonging to everyone **collective, common, communal** *Work, production and ownership were all communal.*

● v+N claim ownership **assert, claim** *The law should prevent squatters from claiming ownership of your farmland.*

▶ prove ownership **confirm, establish, prove, verify**

To obtain the permit, you must prove ownership of the vehicle.

▶ take or keep ownership **acquire, assume, establish, retain, take** *There are areas in which foreign citizens may not acquire ownership of real property.*

▶ give up ownership **relinquish, transfer** *I relinquish all ownership!*

▶ dispute ownership **dispute** *Where ownership is disputed, ask for written evidence to prove ownership.*

ozone N
oxygen existing high in the Earth's atmosphere

● adj+N **atmospheric, ground-level, stratospheric** *An accurate way of measuring atmospheric ozone is by using an Ozone Monitor.*

● v+N create ozone **create, form, generate, produce** *Ozone is formed in the stratosphere by free radical reactions.*

▶ destroy ozone **deplete, destroy** *What is the evidence that stratospheric ozone is destroyed by chlorine and bromine?*

● N+n **depletion, hole, layer** *Global warming could increase ozone depletion.*

Pp

pace N
the speed at which something happens

- adj+N slow **gentle, leisurely, sedate, slow, unhurried** *Trade unions will still be disappointed at the slow pace of change.*
- ▶ moderate **even, moderate, relaxed, steady** *It is a village that is growing at a steady pace.*
- ▶ fast **brisk, fast, quick, rapid** *Refugee returns continued at a brisk pace last year.*
- ▶ very fast **blistering, breakneck, cracking, electrifying, ferocious, frantic, frenetic, furious, hectic, relentless, tremendous** *The second half began at the same frantic pace.*

- v+N make the pace faster **accelerate, force, quicken** *The book is written in short, sometimes very short, chapters that serve to quicken the pace.*
- ▶ make the pace slower **slacken, slow** *The conflict almost certainly would slow the pace of the global economic recovery.*
- ▶ keep the pace the same **keep, maintain, match, sustain** *During the past 40 years, food production has kept pace with global population growth. • We are willing to put forth our most concerted effort, in order to maintain a steady pace of reform.*
- ▶ set the pace **set** *Our laser technology continues to set the pace for other companies to meet.*
- ▶ have no or little pace **lack** *The film feels slow and lacks the pace needed to keep your interest.*

> You can also say that something **gathers pace** when it happens more quickly: *Once agreement has been reached, the financial and legal procedures will gather pace.*

- N+v increase **accelerate, hot up** INFORMAL, **increase, pick up** INFORMAL, **quicken** *Gradually the pace quickens and the activity increases.*
- ▶ decrease **slacken, slow** *Although the pace slackens somewhat in the second half, this is a pleasing, cosmopolitan film.*

- N+of of change **change, development, globalisation, growth, innovation, progress** *There is every reason to believe that the pace of change will remain intense.*
- ▶ of life **life** *The pace of life here is very slow.*

pact N
an agreement between people or groups to do something

- adj+N **electoral, military, nuclear** *In entering into this agreement, we are clear that this is not an electoral pact.*
- n+N **cooperation, defence, growth, non-aggression, security, stability, trade** *We have always declared our readiness to conclude a non-aggression pact with any state.*
- v+N make a pact **agree, conclude, enter, make, sign** *As for anyone who reads this – let's make a pact that we'll never forget him.*
- ▶ break a pact **break, violate** *I thought the band was over as we'd broken the pact we formed when we started.*

pain N
a feeling that you have in your body when you are hurt or ill

- adj+N in a particular part of the body **abdominal, back, chest, joint, muscular, neck, stomach** *There is a lot you can do to prevent back pain in your workplace.*

> You can refer to pain that has no single location as **aches and pains**: *I had aches and pains that continued into the next day.*

- ▶ lasting for a long/short time **acute, chronic, constant, persistent** *It is sometimes possible to treat the cause of chronic pain.*
- ▶ very bad **agonizing, excruciating, extreme, much, severe, terrible, unbearable** *The pain was excruciating.*
- ▶ not bad **mild, moderate, slight** *Paracetemol should be the first choice for mild pain.*
- ▶ intense **burning, intense, searing, sharp, stabbing** *I feel a sharp pain in the side of my arm.*

- v+N reduce pain **alleviate, control, decrease, dull, ease, lessen, reduce, relieve, soothe, treat** *Soon after injury, an ice bag may be applied to relieve pain and swelling.*
- ▶ cause pain **cause, inflict** *Possibly nothing inflicts more intense pain than fire.*
- ▶ feel pain **endure, experience, feel, suffer** *He suddenly felt a terrific pain in his head as though a nail had been driven into it.*
- ▶ help to prevent pain **eliminate, minimize** *Hypnosis can be used to minimize the pain of dental surgery.*

- N+n control of pain **control, management, relief** *Advice may need to be sought from the pain management team.*
- ▶ tolerance of pain **threshold, tolerance** *There is considerable variation in individual pain thresholds.*
- ▶ medicine for pain **medication, meds** INFORMAL *Over the-counter pain medications are recommended to relieve minor pain from tension headache.*

- and/or **aches, discomfort, distress, suffering** *People with epilepsy say that they do not experience pain or distress before or when they have seizures.*

painful ADJ
1 making you feel upset, ashamed, or unhappy

- adv+ADJ very **acutely, agonizingly, exceedingly, excruciatingly, extremely, incredibly, intensely, terribly, too, unbearably, very** *Parents have recognised that embarrassment is excruciatingly painful for adolescents.*
- ▶ rather **quite, rather** *That was the best team I have ever swum with and it was rather painful to lose.*
- ▶ in a particular way **emotionally** *While paranoia can be treated by analysis, it is a difficult and emotionally painful process.*

- ADJ+n event, experience, or situation **choice,**

circumstances, decision, dilemma, episode, experience, ordeal, scene, shock, situation *Nobody wants to prolong the painful ordeal of a divorce.*

▸ memory **memory, recollection, reminder** *Some painful recollection had stolen across his mind, and driven him into silence.*

▸ feeling **emotion, feeling** *He learned to welcome his painful feelings during meditation.*

● v+ADJ **be, prove, seem** *Perhaps things that once brought her pleasure now seem painful.*

2 feeling pain

● adv+ADJ very **acutely, agonizingly, exceedingly, excruciatingly, extremely, incredibly, intensely, terribly, too, unbearably, very** *Death from cholera is quick and agonizingly painful.*

▸ rather **quite, rather** *For a few years, several of these joints were quite painful and often red and tender.*

● ADJ+n **condition, contraction, cramp, sensation, spasm** *This can make normal mobility impossible and can also cause painful muscular spasms.*

● v+ADJ **be, become, feel, look, sound** *As time went by, the knee became quite painful on exercise.*

painless ADJ
1 not causing any physical pain

● adv+ADJ almost **almost, virtually** *Many people are worried about this, but acupuncture is usually almost painless.*

▸ rather **fairly, pretty** INFORMAL, **relatively** *As this form of glaucoma is relatively painless, a person can lose up to 60 per cent of vision and not know.*

● completely **completely, entirely, quite, totally** *The whole process takes around 20 minutes and is completely painless.*

● ADJ+n **operation, procedure, process, treatment** *Radiotherapy is a painless procedure but can have uncomfortable side effects.*

● and/or quick **fast, quick, rapid, swift** *He was reassured that his friend would have experienced a swift and painless death.*

● easy **simple, smooth, straightforward** *The measurement of blood pressure is a painless and simple process.*

▸ safe **safe** *The flu vaccine is safe, painless and effective.*

less difficult or unpleasant than you expect

adv+ADJ almost **almost, relatively, virtually** *Even changing money at the bank was an almost painless experience.*

rather **fairly, pretty** INFORMAL *The Bank believes that such an adjustment should be fairly painless.*

completely **completely, entirely, quite, totally** *Economic experts did not expect this process to be entirely painless.*

ADJ+n **operation, procedure, process, transition** *If you are buying a direct flight, then booking online is a painless process.*

and/or quick **fast, quick, rapid, swift** *As noted before, plugging everything together was fairly quick and painless.*

easy **simple, smooth, straightforward** *The relatively painless and smooth transition was in no small part due to Janice's hard work.*

palate N
the ability to taste and judge flavours

● adj+N refined **discerning, discriminating, refined, sophisticated** *Our menus are designed to delight the most discerning palate.*

▸ tired **jaded** *With over 500 restaurants, Birmingham is certain to be able to satisfy even the most jaded palate.*

● v+N tempt someone's palate **tempt, tickle** *Pasta is a versatile food and can make hearty suppers or light dishes to tempt the palate.*

▸ satisfy someone's palate **delight, refresh, satisfy** *A little green salad on the side is quite nice as it helps to refresh the palate.*

▸ take away tastes **cleanse** *After testing wine, drink some water to cleanse the palate.*

pale ADJ
having lighter than usual skin

● adv+ADJ very **extremely, very** *Lucy turned very pale and slumped motionless over a table.*

▸ rather **fairly, a little, quite, rather, slightly, somewhat** *Apart from looking slightly pale, he seemed his usual self.*

▸ unusually **abnormally, unusually** *Tell your doctor if the child looks unusually pale or bruises more easily than usual.*

● v+ADJ **be, become, go, grow, look, seem, turn** *'You look pale, my child,' said her father.* ● *His face turned pale and he was struggling for air.*

● ADJ+as **death, ghost, sheet** *Then, looking pale as a ghost, Amelia crept warily into the kitchen.*

● and/or **gaunt, haggard, sickly, thin, wan** *Day by day, his face was growing pale and wan.*

panel N
a group of people who make decisions or discuss things

● adj+N of experts **distinguished, expert** *Abstracts will be reviewed by an expert panel.*

▸ independent **independent** *In July each year, an independent panel of judges shortlist 12 albums which they believe to be the 'Albums of the Year'.*

▸ types of panel **advisory, disciplinary, editorial, interviewing, judging** *A course may be substituted by a programme of directed reading if the advisory panel considers this more appropriate.*

● n+N **adjudication, adoption, appeals, arbitration, interview, review, selection** *If you are unhappy with the school allocated to your child, you can appeal to an independent appeals panel.*

● v+N be on a panel **be on, be represented on, serve on, sit on** *Members are invited to consider who should sit on the panel.*

▸ be in charge of a panel **chair** *Damien Hirst chaired the panel of judges.*

▸ establish a panel **appoint, assemble, convene, establish** *An independent panel convened by the American Council on Science and Health reviewed the health risks of DINP, the plasticiser used most frequently in toys.*

● N+of **academics, adjudicators, advisers, assessors, examiners, experts, interviewers, judges, speakers**

The winner and runners up will be selected by a panel of judges.

- v+to+N **appeal, present sth, put sth, refer sth, submit sth** *Each entry was photographed and submitted to a panel of judges who will select seventeen national winners.*

- n+of+N **chair, chairman, member** *I am sure that other members of the panel will agree.*

pang N

a sudden strong and unpleasant pain or emotion

- adj+N brief or slight **little, momentary, slight** *A slight pang of jealousy overcame Leah.*
- ▶ strong or sudden **bitter, sharp, sudden** *I felt a blow and then a sharp pang, and there I was pinned by the shoulder to the mast.*

- v+N feel a pang **experience, feel, suffer** *Later, I suffered pangs of guilt for what I had done.*
- ▶ make a pang less strong **allay, relieve** *The berries relieved their pangs of hunger for a time.*

- N+of emotion **conscience, disappointment, guilt, jealousy, loneliness, nostalgia, regret, remorse, sympathy** *Her tears and sorrow looked so realistic that I almost felt a pang of remorse.*
- ▶ physical feeling **hunger, pain, thirst** *But suddenly he felt a pang of hunger, got the box out of his satchel and opened it up.*

panic N

a sudden very strong feeling of fear or worry [always singular]

- adj+N brief or slight **mild, momentary** *'Nothing,' Rhanda said, feeling foolish for her momentary panic.*
- ▶ extreme **blind, full-blown, mad, sheer, utter** *I was pleased that this little setback hadn't sent me into a blind panic.* • *He had a moment of sheer panic at what he had done.*
- ▶ by a lot of people **mass, widespread** *When the disease broke out in the Far East last year, there was widespread panic.*
- ▶ sudden or just before something **last-minute, sudden** *I decided that pre-booking a place would avoid any last-minute panic.*
- ▶ unnecessary **unnecessary** *This has helped to quash silly rumours and quell unnecessary panic among divers.*
- ▶ moral **moral** *Is the current moral panic over young offenders misplaced?*

- v+N cause or spread panic **cause, create, induce, lead to, provoke, spark, spread, throw sb into, trigger** *The engine failed, sparking panic in the cockpit.*
- ▶ calm panic **calm, quell** *I tried to focus on my breathing, trying to slow it down and calm the panic that was beginning to take hold.*
- ▶ prevent panic **avoid, prevent** *He explains that he wants to keep the incident a secret to avoid panic.*
- ▶ feel panic **experience, feel, fly into, get in, get into** *At some time or other, most people experience panic, and when this happens we notice changes in our body.*

- N+v happen or spread **break out, ensue, grip sb, rise, seize sb, set in, spread, strike (sb), sweep**

through sb/sth *Suddenly faced with reality, panic set in.*
- ▶ become less **subside** *After the panic had subsided, she managed to get herself free.*

- n+of+N **air, atmosphere, feeling, fit, look, moment, sense, state, surge, wave** *He felt a huge wave of panic ripple up through his whole body.*

paper N

an academic piece of writing or a talk on an official or academic subject

- adj+N types of paper **academic, consultative, official, research, scholarly, scientific, technical** *A standard scientific paper in most journals will contain around 6 figures or tables.*
- ▶ important **seminal** *The article has become a seminal paper for researchers in the field.*
- ▶ written with someone else **joint** *They published a joint paper on this subject in 2008.*
- ▶ when someone who is an expert comments on a paper **peer-reviewed** *He has actually never published a peer-reviewed paper on climate change.*

- n+N for an occasion or publication **conference, journal, keynote, seminar** *A list of publications, abstracts and published conference papers are given below.*
- ▶ for discussion **consultation, discussion, working** *This prompted us to examine the issue and offer our explorations as a discussion paper.*
- ▶ not final **draft** *She asked me to read her draft paper before she submitted it to a journal.*

- v+N write a paper **draft, prepare, produce, write** *This paper was originally drafted in 2000.*
- ▶ write a paper with someone else **co-author, contribute to** *This work is introduced in a paper co authored with Ian Stark.*
- ▶ present a paper **deliver, give, present** *I travelled to San Francisco to present my paper at the 5th International Conference of Sports Engineering.*
- ▶ publish a paper **issue, print, publish** *She has published papers on a wide range of topics.*
- ▶ submit a paper **submit** *Students can submit papers only with the approval of their supervisors.*
- ▶ mention a paper **cite, quote** *If no one has cited a paper within two or three years of publication, the work it contains is very likely to be lost.*
- ▶ write about a paper **comment on, respond to, review, summarize** *We aim to secure the participation of a set of world-class experts to comment on the papers presented.*

- N+v present or describe something **address, consider, describe, discuss, examine, explore, focus on, outline, present** *He was the author of another influential paper describing computer security issues.*
- ▶ state or suggest something **argue, propose, state, suggest** *This paper argues that the trend of a shorter average length of hospital stay is likely to continue.*

paperwork N

the part of a job that involves producing reports, records, and letters

- adj+N necessary **necessary, relevant, required** *You will be responsible for ensuring that all required paperwork is completed to deadline.*

▶ excessive **endless, excessive, unnecessary** *We want to cut down on unnecessary paperwork for police officers.*

● v+N complete paperwork **complete, finalize** *Individual staff should complete their paperwork in advance of the review meeting.*

▶ involve paperwork **involve, require** *In some situations registering a death may involve more paperwork, so it will take a bit longer.*

▶ deal with paperwork **check, deal with, handle, organize, process, sort out** *The paperwork was sorted out quickly and efficiently and the customer service was excellent.*

▶ reduce or get rid of paperwork **cut, cut down on, eliminate, reduce** *Our aim is to reduce paperwork and bureaucracy to the absolute minimum.*

● n+of+N **backlog, mass, mountain, pile, reams** *Each meeting involves a mountain of paperwork.*

paradox N

a situation with features that do not normally exist together

● adj+N apparent **apparent, seeming** *They have achieved the seeming paradox of combining exciting modern design at low cost.*

▶ strange or interesting **curious, interesting, strange** *It is a curious paradox of our age that, at a time when we are confronted with global issues, we tend to attach great importance to small matters.*

● v+N present a paradox **pose, present** *These two facts present an apparent paradox.*

▶ solve a paradox **explain, resolve, solve** *How does she resolve the paradox that she makes use of the very technologies that she is criticizing?*

parallel N

a similarity, or something or someone that is similar; a comparison

● adj+N obvious **obvious, striking** *This model offers a striking parallel to the situation in the Shetland Islands today.*

▶ close or exact **close, exact** *The word 'Weltanschauung' has no exact parallel in English.*

● v+N **draw, find, note, reveal, see, suggest** *Dufton draws interesting parallels between the treatment and education of the deaf in Paris, Dresden and Prague.* ● *The film, though set in the past, reveals obvious parallels with our own times.*

paralysis N

the loss of the ability to move your body

● adj+N partial/total **partial, total** *A brain tumour has left her with partial paralysis and loss of vision.*
temporary/permanent **permanent, temporary** *During this phase of sleep, our closed eyes dart rapidly about and our muscles suffer temporary paralysis.*

● v+N cause paralysis **cause, lead to, result in** *Paralysis is caused by something being wrong with the nerves that activate muscles.*
suffer paralysis **be affected by, suffer (from)** *Not all the victims of polio suffered paralysis.*

parameter N

a limit affecting how something can be done [usually plural]

● adj+N particular **certain, specific, specified** *The partnerships will operate within specified parameters.*

▶ broad/strict **broad, strict** *The broad parameters of the inquiry will be set by academic staff.*

▶ important **basic, critical, important, key, relevant** *Uncertainty has been identified as one of the key parameters limiting the development of brownfield sites.*

● v+N set parameters **define, determine, establish, set, specify** *By setting the parameters for discussion in this way, the debate has been skewed.*

▶ change or vary parameters **adjust, alter, change, modify, vary** *We are already changing the parameters by which we judge legitimate interpretations.*

▶ choose or use parameters **choose, use** *These parameters are used to classify stars into different types.*

● v+within+N **fall, operate, work** *The changes fall within the parameters of the original plans.*

paranoia N

the feeling that people do not like you and are trying to harm you, although there is no proof for this

● adj+N extreme **acute, deep, extreme, intense, rampant, severe** *The film accurately portrays Hitler's acute paranoia and his sense of being betrayed by a number of his generals.*

▶ slight **mild, slight** *I suffered a lot of nervous tension, with slight paranoia.*

▶ increasing **creeping, escalating, growing, increasing, mounting** *Soon he starts to wonder about his own growing paranoia – who can he trust?*

▶ not based on fact **unfounded** *It turned out that Ian's paranoia was not unfounded, when a soldier broke into their hotel room.*

▶ of a lot of people **collective, mass, widespread** *Why was there a widespread paranoia about Catholicism in late seventeenth century England?*

▶ caused by drugs **drug-fuelled, drug-induced** *After two decades of drug-fuelled paranoia and erratic behaviour, the singer was back on track.*

● v+N suffer from paranoia **experience, suffer (from)** *Vince is experiencing intense paranoia at work, petrified that Rosalie has revealed his secret.*

▶ cause paranoia **fuel, generate, induce** *Cocaine damages the heart, can lead to strokes, and can induce paranoia.*

● n+of+N **atmosphere, climate, feeling, mood, sense, state** *In a complete state of paranoia, the police quickly cordoned off the area outside the gates.*

pardon N

a decision to forgive someone for a crime

● adj+N with no conditions **free, full, general, unconditional** *In prisoner amnesties, convicted criminals are granted full pardons.*

▶ with conditions **conditional** *He was given a conditional pardon that meant he could leave Tasmania but could never return to England.*

▶ given to someone who has died **posthumous** *Was Hanratty the victim of a miscarriage of justice and should he receive a posthumous pardon?*

● v+N give a pardon **give sb, grant (sb), issue** *The Secretary of State is now re-considering whether to grant a pardon.*

▶ receive **get, obtain, receive, secure** *Fifteen officers sentenced to death received a royal pardon.*

parental ADJ
involving or provided by parents

● ADJ+n permission **consent, permission** *Our group leaders provide extra activities for students who do not have parental consent to go off campus.*

▶ responsibility or rights **duties, responsibility, rights** *Desperate for money and unable to face his parental responsibilities, Bruno gives his son away.*

▶ choice **choice, preference** *Parental preference cannot always be met.*

▶ involvement **involvement, participation** *We want to encourage greater parental involvement in school matters.*

▶ help **guidance, support** *A key factor for success at school is parental support.*

▶ feelings **affection, anxiety, approval, disapproval, expectations, wishes** *Parental anxiety about daughters studying abroad was identified as an influence in dissuading some girls from the study of modern European languages.*

parliament N
an elected group of people who make the laws of a country

● adj+N **devolved, hung** *This would have produced a hung parliament, with Labour as the largest party.*

● v+N enter parliament **enter, go into** *Mussolini entered parliament in 1921.*

▶ try to be elected to a parliament **run for, stand for** *What made you decide to stand for parliament?*

▶ elect someone to parliament **elect sb to** *She later went to prison, but was ultimately elected to the Indian parliament.*

▶ elect a parliament **elect** *Voters went to the polls in September 2005 to elect a new parliament.*

▶ present something to parliament **lay sth before, present sth to, put sth before** *The legislation was finally laid before parliament in 2002.*

▶ ask parliament for something **lobby, petition** *Their MP was with them when they came to London to petition parliament.*

▶ formally end parliament **dissolve, suspend** *A general election is called when the queen dissolves parliament on the advice of the Prime Minister.*

● v+through+N go through parliament **go, pass, progress** *A new broadcasting Bill is currently going through parliament.*

▶ make something go through parliament **force, push, rush** *The bill was rushed through parliament with very little debate.*

parody N
1 a humorous copy of a literary or musical work

● adj+N funny **amusing, comic, funny, hilarious, witty** *His tale takes the form of an amusing parody.*

▶ affectionate **affectionate, gentle** *The two comedians*

play a host of characters from gangland bosses to useless detectives in an affectionate parody of the gangster movie.

● v+into+N **descend, slip** *He gives a terrific performance as a complex and untrustworthy politician, without descending into parody.*

2 something done so badly that it seems like a parody

● adj+N unpleasant **cruel, grim, grotesque** *He described the book as 'a grotesque parody of scientific inquiry devoid of intellectual credibility or literary merit'.*

▶ only **mere** *In his mind, this act created a mere parody of freedom.*

parole N
permission to leave prison before the official time

● v+N get parole **get** *How are these prisoners expected to get parole when they are required to acknowledge an offence that they have in fact not committed?*

▶ try to get parole **apply for** *Brady accepted his fate and has never applied for parole.*

▶ grant someone parole **grant sb, release sb on** *The century's most notorious child killer has been granted parole after twenty-five years.*

▶ think about granting someone parole **consider sb for** *The offender will qualify to be considered for parole at the half-way point of the sentence.*

▶ refuse someone parole **deny, refuse** *The vast majority of offenders had been refused parole.*

▶ break your parole **breach, break, violate** *Later released, she was re-arrested for violating parole.*

part N
1 an individual piece, section, or aspect of something

● adj+N important **core, crucial, essential, important, integral, key, main, major, vital** *A web operation should always be an integral part of any business.*

▶ large **big, great, large, significant, substantial** *A large part of my thesis concerns Shakespeare's tragedies.*

▶ small **minor, small, tiny** *Only a small part of the old city still stands.*

▶ late or last **final, latter, second** *The latter part of the 19th century was one of relative economic decline.*

▶ early or first **early, first** *The parish register begins in 1570, but the early part is very imperfect.*

▶ difficult **difficult, hard, tricky** *Not being able to see what they were doing was the hardest part.*

▶ separate **different, distinct, individual, separate** *The module is split into two distinct parts.*

▶ making a whole **component, constituent** *The whole team is greater than its constituent parts.*

● v+N be a part of something **be, become, constitute, form, remain, represent** *Motor racing will remain a big part of his life.*

▶ have a number of parts **be composed of, be comprised of, be made of, consist of, fall into, have** *The study falls into two principal parts.*

● v+into+N **break, divide, separate, split, subdivide** *The paper is divided into four parts.*

2 the way in which someone or something is involved in an activity or event [always singular]

- adj+N important or most important **big, important, large, leading, major, significant** *He took a leading part in the campaign for greater staff involvement.* • *Counselling can play a significant part in helping families face loss.*
- ▶ small **minor, small** *We can play a small part in helping the charity raise the money it needs.*
- ▶ active **active** *Members are encouraged to take an active part in the running of the club.*
- v+N have, play, take *All the staff had an important part in the achievement of our target.*

participant N
someone who takes part in something

- adj+N enthusiastic or willing **active, eager, enthusiastic, keen, willing** *Church leaders were not merely pawns in a political game; they were active participants.*
- ▶ unwilling **reluctant, unwilling** *A small team of committed staff would be preferable to a larger team, some of whom are reluctant participants.*
- ▶ potential **potential, prospective, would-be** *It is important that prospective participants provide us with the relevant information.*
- ▶ taking part at the same time **fellow** *I found that most of my fellow participants were about 20 years older than me.*
- v+N get participants **attract, recruit, select** *Test participants were recruited at random.*
- ▶ motivate participants **encourage, engage, motivate** *By breaking down inhibitions and focusing energy, Anjali inspires and motivates workshop participants.*
- ▶ ask participants to do something **ask, invite** *The participants were invited to suggest topics for discussion.*
- ▶ allow participants to do something **allow, empower, enable, equip, help** *The scheme enables participants to spend a day a week at college.*

participate V
to take part in something

- adv+V enthusiastically or fully **actively, enthusiastically, freely, fully** *Our aim has been to encourage every member to participate actively in our community.*
- ▶ willingly **voluntarily, willingly** *They participated willingly in the class discussions.*
- ▶ in a useful way **constructively, meaningfully** *Occupational therapy helps patients participate meaningfully in activities of daily life.*
- ▶ successfully **effectively, successfully** *Our organization works to promote equality of opportunity for women and enable them to participate effectively at all levels.*
- ▶ directly **directly** *She assisted with the preparation of the report but did not participate directly in the writing of it.*

participation N
the process of taking part in something

- adj+N enthusiastic **active, enthusiastic** *Active participation in political life is the mark of a good citizen.*
- ▶ useful or effective **effective, meaningful** *How do we ensure full and meaningful participation in education?*
- ▶ voluntary **voluntary** *Will you tell participants that their participation is voluntary?*
- ▶ by a lot of people **full, mass, maximum, wide** *Mass participation in the Internet in this country has become a reality.*
- ▶ more **increased, more, widening** *Increased participation in decision making is a desirable goal.*
- ▶ by a particular group **audience, employee, parental, public, pupil, youth** *The first set is traditional Bavarian music, with a lot of audience participation.*
- v+N encourage participation **encourage, facilitate, foster, promote** *Were there attempts to encourage participation from those parents who would most benefit?*
- ▶ increase participation **boost, broaden, enhance, increase, maximize, stimulate, strengthen, widen** *How do we maximize participation in recycling schemes?*
- ▶ discourage participation **discourage, inhibit** *Peer attitudes towards students from marginalised groups can be critical in either encouraging or inhibiting active participation.*
- ▶ enable participation **enable, ensure, secure** *We hope to secure the participation of a set of world-class experts to comment on the papers presented.*

particular ADJ
especially great

- ADJ+n attention **attention, emphasis, focus, reference** *Chris will be teaching a karate course, with a particular focus on realistic fighting methods.* • *She gave a paper on trends in agriculture, with particular reference to sustainable production methods.*
- ▶ interest or importance **concern, importance, interest, relevance, significance** *The talk on newspaper design was of particular interest.*

parting ADJ
done or said when someone is leaving

- ADJ+n **comment, gesture, gift, message, shot, thought, words** *As a parting shot, the secretary hoped that more of the committee would attend the next meeting.*

partnership N
a relationship between people in business or in another activity, or an organization formed through this relationship

- adj+N successful or useful **beneficial, effective, fruitful, productive, successful** *The company has a long and fruitful partnership with a leading German security software firm.*
- ▶ close or real **close, genuine, solid, strong, true** *Our approach to research is based upon a spirit of close partnership with our clients.*
- ▶ long or long-lasting **lasting, long, long-standing, long-term, sustainable** *From Shanghai, the airline offers convenient connections to several cities within*

China through its long-standing partnership **with**
China Eastern Airlines.
▶ equal **equal, joint** *We should be working together* **in**
an equal partnership, not pushing apart.
▶ in business **business, commercial, corporate,**
professional *They formed a corporate partnership*
with *the company several years ago.*
▶ for working together **collaborative, working** *She*
believed that a collaborative partnership would
benefit both institutions.
▶ for doing something creative **creative** *Braque is*
the only artist ever to sustain a creative partnership
with *Picasso.*

● v+N form a partnership **build, cement, create,**
develop, embark on, establish, forge, form, launch
This new type of school will run on independent lines,
but forging strong partnerships throughout its
community.
▶ break up a partnership **break up, dissolve,**
withdraw from *One partner can rescind the contract,*
effectively dissolving the partnership.
▶ encourage a partnership **encourage, facilitate,**
foster, promote *The scheme is designed to foster*
partnerships **between** *university academics and*
industry.

● v+in+N **act, deliver sth, develop sth, operate,**
organize sth, run sth, work *The programme is run*
in partnership **with** *a neighbouring college.* ● *We*
work in partnership **with** *a wide range of*
organizations across the country.

● v+into+N **enter, go** *William went into partnership*
with his father at the age of 22.

party N
1 a social event at which people celebrate
something or have fun

● v+N hold a party **arrange, give, have, hold, host,**
organize, organize, stage, throw *It will be the*
biggest party ever thrown.
▶ invite someone to a party **invite sb to** *I've been*
invited to John's retirement party.
▶ go to a party **attend, come to, go to** *Nearly a*
thousand guests attended house parties there.
▶ go to a party uninvited **crash** INFORMAL, **gatecrash**
The uninvited guests jump over a wall to gatecrash
the party.

● N+n **atmosphere, mood** *The music gives the place*
a real party atmosphere.

2 a political group that people can vote for in
elections

● adj+N political **political** *They did not organise as*
a political party until 1885.
▶ main **main, mainstream, major** *All the major*
political parties support a cut in climate-change gases.

● n+N in government **governing, ruling** *This was a*
way of keeping the peasants dependent on the state
and harvesting their votes for the ruling party.
▶ in opposition **opposition** *The Government and*
opposition parties say they are serious about
addressing the health threat posed by obesity in
young people.
▶ with few or fewer votes **minority** *The Liberal Party*
has been a minority party for most of this century.

● v+N **divide, elect, expel sb from, form, join, lead,**

leave, represent, resign from, unite, vote for *You*
can further help our campaign by making a donation
or joining the party.

● N+n politics **politics** *What we really need is an end*
to party politics.
▶ people **activist, chairman, faithful, leader,**
leadership, member, membership, official *His*
comments angered the party faithful.
▶ support **affiliation, loyalty** *What were her political*
party affiliations?

pass V
1 to be successful in a test or examination

● adv+V successfully or easily **easily, successfully,**
with ease *All children who successfully passed the*
test received a certificate.

> If someone passes a test very easily, you can say that
> they *pass with flying colours*: *We all passed the*
> *assessment with flying colours.*

▶ in the end **eventually, finally** *She took her driving*
test three times before eventually passing.

● V+N **assessment, audition, exam, examination,**
inspection, test *Before a shop is accepted into the*
scheme, it must pass a rigorous independent
inspection.

● V+with+n **distinction, merit** *In total, 8 students*
passed with distinction.

2 to make a law, proposal etc official

● adv+V **overwhelmingly, unanimously** *A resolution*
totally opposing war was overwhelmingly passed.

● V+n **act, amendment, bill, law, legislation,**
motion, ordinance, resolution *There were no*
speeches against, so the motion was passed.

passion N
1 a powerful emotion

● adj+N real **genuine, heartfelt, true** *He plays and*
sings the blues **with** *genuine passion.*
▶ great **deep, fierce, great, intense, raw, strong,**
unbridled, violent *Fierce passions were aroused by*
the debate.
▶ negative or violent **destructive, violent** *She believes*
that humans are driven by self-interest, greed and
other destructive passions.

● v+N cause passion **arouse, excite, fuel, ignite,**
inflame, rouse, stir *The presence of foreign troops*
arouses strong passions in the region.
▶ show someone's passion **convey** *She does a*
wonderful job of conveying the passion and
dedication of these volunteers.

2 a strong enthusiasm or interest, or something
that produces this interest

● adj+N strong **all-consuming, burning, consuming,**
real, ruling *Photography gradually developed for*
him from a casual interest to a consuming passion.
▶ lasting a long time **abiding, enduring, lifelong** *His*
thesis was on American cars, one of his lifelong
passions.

● v+N **develop, discover, harbour, have, indulge,**
pursue, share *Andrea is based in San Jose and*

*indulges her passion **for** the outdoors by regular treks in the mountains.*

passionate ADJ
showing or expressing strong beliefs, interest or emotions

- adv+ADJ very **absolutely, deeply, extremely, incredibly, intensely, really** INFORMAL, **very** *He gave an intensely passionate vocal performance.*
- ▶ genuinely **genuinely, truly** *The staff were very helpful, the chef genuinely passionate **about** the food.*
- ADJ+n people **advocate, believer, campaigner, fan, supporter** *The Chief Constable is a passionate advocate of speed cameras.*
- ▶ feeling or belief **belief, commitment, desire, devotion, interest, longing, love, opposition, support** *I have been inspired by your passionate devotion to your children.*
- and/or **committed, dedicated, energetic, enthusiastic, knowledgeable, motivated** *I know how committed and passionate our nursing team is.*

passport N
an official document used when travelling to foreign countries

- adj+N full or valid **full, valid** *A full passport is required for entry, but there is no need for a visa.* • *You cannot travel abroad without a valid passport.*
- ▶ not valid **expired, invalid** *How do I renew an expired passport?*
- ▶ false **counterfeit, fake, false, forged** *He was arrested trying to leave Heathrow airport **on** a fake passport.*
- ▶ replacing another passport **replacement** *Any replacement passport that is issued will have the same expiry date as your existing passport.*
- ▶ types of passport **biometric, machine-readable** *For entry to the US, you must have a machine-readable passport.*
- ▶ v+N have a passport **be in possession of, carry, have, hold, travel on** *They were accepted into the country reluctantly, even though they carried British passports.* • *She generally travels on her Irish passport rather than her British one.*
- ▶ get a passport **apply for, get, renew** *You will need to obtain a renewal form in order to renew your passport.*
- ▶ give someone a passport **issue (sb with)** *Please state the place where your passport was issued.*
- ▶ check or mark a passport **check, endorse, stamp** *Bring your offer of employment, plus a suitably endorsed passport.*
- ▶ take someone's passport away **confiscate** *Their passports were confiscated and they were unable to leave the airport.*
- ▶ give up your passport **surrender** *Some fans have been ordered to surrender their passports in a bid to stop hooligan problems at the World Cup.*
- ▶ N+v be valid, expire **expire** *As a rule, passports expire after ten years.*

  N+n **applicant, application, check, fraud, holder, renewal, stamp** *US passport holders currently require a Tourist Visa.*

password N
the series of numbers or letters that you need in order to get into a computer system

- adj+N incorrect/correct **correct, incorrect, invalid, valid** *Each incorrect password entered is logged, showing the time, and the password supplied.*
- ▶ secure/not secure **secure, strong, weak** *These passwords are usually very secure, but can be very hard to remember.*
- ▶ secret **confidential, secret** *You must keep these passwords secret as if anyone else knows them they will be able to rewrite your page.*
- ▶ temporary **temporary** *You must change your temporary password when logging in for the first time.*
- v+N enter a password **enter, re-enter, type** *If the correct password is typed, then the screen is unlocked.*
- ▶ change a password **change, reset** *How do I reset my password?*
- ▶ protect a password **encrypt, protect** *eBay's security policy states that they always encrypt your password.*
- ▶ tell someone a password **disclose, divulge, reveal** *We never ask you to divulge your password via email.*
- ▶ confirm a password **confirm, verify** *The next window asks you to verify your password.*
- ▶ give a password **allocate, assign, generate, issue, set, specify, supply** *A secure password is automatically generated for you.*
- ▶ get a password **recover, retrieve** *To retrieve your password, follow the steps outlined here.*
- ▶ find out someone's password **crack** *They were able to crack user passwords and access personal accounts.*

past N
the things someone has done or that a place has experienced

- adj+N with problems **tragic, traumatic, troubled, turbulent, violent** *She had a troubled past; her father had left the family home when Sarah was only ten.*
- ▶ when bad things happened **dark, murky, shady, sordid** *They immediately fall in love and Alma confesses her slightly murky past to him.*
- ▶ when good or interesting things happened **colourful, fascinating, glorious, illustrious, rich** *To stay at the Savoy Hotel is to experience London's illustrious past.*
- ▶ when both good and bad things happened **chequered** *The island has had a chequered past, as have many regions in this part of the world.*
- ▶ with a particular government or economy **colonial, imperial, industrial, maritime** *There are still signs of Hong Kong's colonial past.*

pastime N
something you do regularly for fun

- adj+N enjoyable **enjoyable, pleasant, pleasurable, popular, relaxing, rewarding** *Seen as a pleasurable pastime, gardening can be fraught with danger.*
- ▶ harmless **harmless, innocent** *Gambling can be a harmless pastime for the majority but a terrible addiction for a few.*

▸ done in your spare time **leisure, recreational** *A huge selection of recreational pastimes are offered in and around the resort.*

● v+N **engage in, enjoy, indulge in, pursue** *Most people indulged in that favourite holiday pastime – lying on a sunbed basking in the Mediterranean sun.*

patch N
an area different from what surrounds it

● adj+N wet/dry **damp, dry, icy, wet** *Building surveyors will be able to tell you whether the damp patch is due to a roof leak.*

▸ hair **bald, bare** *He took the hat off that was covering his bald patch.*

▸ colours **pale, white, brown etc** *It is a common condition that causes pale, white patches to develop on the skin.*

● N+of **colour, ice, mud, rust, skin, sky, snow** *By the time I got there, blue patches of sky were appearing and the mist cleared.*

patch up PHR VB
become friends again after a disagreement

● V+n **differences, relations, relationship, things** *It's time the leaders got together in an attempt to patch up their differences.* ● *He needs to patch things up with his father.*

> Usage When used with *things*, the word *things* always comes between *patch* and *up*: *He realises he may have left it too late to patch things up with his father.*

patchy ADJ
1 happening or existing only in some places

● adv+ADJ rather **rather, somewhat** *Below this lodge, the forest becomes somewhat patchy, punctuated by areas of secondary growth and clearings.*

▸ very **extremely, very** *Last year the rains in Ghana were very late, and extremely patchy when they did arrive.*

● ADJ+n weather **cloud, drizzle, fog, mist, rain, snow** *The weather was bright and sunny with some patchy clouds.*

▸ way something is shared or spread around **coverage, distribution, provision** *These birds live all around Britain, but their distribution is patchy.*

2 not complete, or only good in parts

● adv+ADJ rather **a bit, rather, somewhat** *The information in this section is somewhat patchy: we have tried to make sure that it is accurate but we may have made mistakes.*

▸ very **decidedly, extremely, very** *Her education has been extremely patchy and consists mainly of fluency in foreign languages.*

● ADJ+n **affair, album, evidence, performance, picture, quality, record, results** *The production was a patchy affair, reliant on the comic talents of a few individual actors.*

path N
a way for walking from one place to another

● adj+N ways of describing a path **long, long-distance, narrow, short, steep, well-trodden, well-worn, winding** *At the gate, we turned right along a narrow path.*

▸ main **main** *Retrace your steps to the main ridge path and head southeast.*

▸ surface **grassy, muddy, paved, rocky, rough, stony** *The only way up to it is by a steep and muddy path.*

▸ beside the sea **coastal** *The Pembrokeshire coastal path runs right past the house.*

● n+N surface **concrete, grass, gravel, tarmac** *The lake is available for fishing and is bordered by a tarmac path for easy access.*

▸ where the path is **cliff, coast, forest, mountain, riverside, woodland** *The route follows a series of cliff paths linking coastal towns and villages.*

● N+v **climb, continue, descend, follow sth, fork, go, lead to sth, leave sth, pass, run, turn, wind** *The path follows the contours of the field edge going around a house and garden.* ● *The path runs due northeast for another kilometer or so.*

patience N
doing something or waiting for a long time without losing interest or becoming angry

● adj+N seeming to have no limit **endless, inexhaustible, infinite, limitless, unfailing, unlimited** *He was a fantastic teacher with infinite patience.*

▸ a lot/not much **considerable, great, little, much, not much** *You showed great patience when we were being particularly slow on the uptake.*

● v+N have or show patience **display, have, show** *United showed patience in waiting for their chance.*

▸ lose patience **lose, run out of** *Web users are often impatient and, if a page takes a long time to appear, they will lose patience and look elsewhere.*

▸ make someone lose or nearly lose patience **exhaust, test** *He had been more than usually annoying and my patience was exhausted.*

> You can say that someone *tries your patience* when they are very annoying and you are beginning to get angry with them.

▸ need patience **need, require, take** *This trick might require some patience, but is well worth it.*

▸ reward patience **reward** *It is a game that rewards patience and thought, rather than speed and reflexes.*

▸ be patient **be, exercise, practise** *Learning to drive can be frustrating and requires you to exercise considerable patience.*

● N+v **run out, wear out** *Our patience is running out and we need you to make a decision.*

> You can say that someone's patience *is wearing thin* when they are no longer willing to do or accept something: *My wife has been hugely patient, but her patience is wearing thin.*

patriotic ADJ
feeling love and duty towards your country

● adv+ADJ **fiercely, very** *The Irish, Scots and Welsh can also be fiercely patriotic.*

● ADJ+n feelings **feeling, fervour, pride,**

sentiments, spirit, zeal *People took to the streets in an outpouring of patriotic fervour.*
▶ duty **duty** *He believes it is a citizen's patriotic duty to question the government.*

pattern N
a series of actions showing how things normally happen

● adj+N same/different **different, same, similar** *A similar pattern of violence was seen in other parts of the region.*
▶ usual or fixed **basic, common, familiar, habitual, normal, predictable, set, traditional, typical, usual** *There is no set pattern for feeding a normal healthy baby in the first 24 hours.*
▶ regular **consistent, regular** *The results did not seem to settle down into any regular pattern.*
▶ that changes **changing, flexible, shifting** *These figures show changing patterns in drink consumption and production throughout the world.*
▶ general **general, overall** *While some indicators are clearly getting better, there is no general pattern of improvement.*
▶ clear **clear** *There was no clear pattern as to which characteristics were likely to be associated with problems.*
▶ of behaviour **behavioural** *The study will specifically examine the behavioural patterns of scent communication in foxes.*

● n+N **behaviour, consumption, shift, sleep, travel, usage, weather, working** *Appetite and sleep patterns may be disrupted.*

● v+N follow or agree with a pattern **conform to, fall into, fit, fit into, follow, repeat** *This collection of stories follows the pattern of his best work: believable story lines with low-key descriptions.*
▶ establish a pattern **establish, set** *Momentum is key to establishing the pattern of the campaign in its early stages.*
▶ show a pattern **exhibit, reveal, show** *These results show a similar pattern to those given in table 3.*
▶ recognize a pattern **find, identify, recognize, see** *Studying crime reports and identifying patterns helps us catch culprits.*
▶ change a pattern **alter, change, disrupt, shift** *One of the consequences of climate change may be to alter the pattern of migration for birds and fish.*

● N+v **change, emerge** *Over and over again, the same pattern emerges.*

● N+of **behaviour, consumption, employment, growth, interaction, usage, use** *By monitoring monthly usage, a pattern of consumption can be identified.*

pause N
when someone stops doing something before starting again

adj+N for a short time **brief, momentary, short, slight** *There was a brief pause while he did some mental arithmetic.*
for a long time **lengthy, long, prolonged** *After a long pause, Michael said 'Yes, I'll come.'*
having a particular effect or meaning **awkward, dramatic, pregnant, uncomfortable** *'I need to*

straighten some things out,' she said, after an awkward pause.
▶ how often **frequent, occasional** *Keep sentences short, with frequent pauses.*

pay N
money you receive for doing your job

● adj+N amount you receive **average, gross, net, take-home, total** *Sales commissions still account for a significant proportion of take-home pay.*
▶ full/half **full, half** *In times of ill-health, a teacher can receive full pay for six months.*
▶ without any extra payments **basic** *We have been able to secure a 2.2 per cent increase in basic pay.*
▶ high/low **good, high, low, poor** *Although the job security was good, the pay was poor.*
▶ equal **equal** *You have the right to equal pay with members of the opposite sex doing the same or a comparable job to you.*
▶ controlled by law **contractual, statutory** *During pregnancy you are eligible for statutory maternity pay.*

> **Sick pay** is money you are entitled to when you are ill and off work: *A company refused to pay a worker sick pay because they thought he was not genuinely ill.*

● n+N **holiday, maternity, paternity, redundancy** *Since 1993, all temporary workers are entitled to holiday pay.*
● v+N receive pay **earn, get, receive** *If you are an extra in a student movie, don't expect to get any pay.*
▶ give sb pay **give sb, pay (sb)** *Redundancy pay is paid gross without deduction of tax and national insurance.*
▶ reduce pay **cut, reduce** *Margaret's pay was cut and holidays reduced when a new company took over the running of the business.*
▶ increase pay **improve, increase** *Academics from two unions have voted to strike unless their pay is increased.*

payment N
money that you pay or receive, or the process of paying money

● adj+N at regular times **annual, monthly, quarterly, regular, weekly, yearly** *Her monthly mortgage payment is £700.*
▶ single **lump-sum, one-off, single** *This is a one-off payment only and not an annual requirement.*
▶ needing to be paid now **due** *Full payment is due prior to delivery of the goods.*
▶ paying on time or late **immediate, late, overdue, prompt** *There are fines for late payment.*
▶ paying the full amount or part of it **full, part, partial** *For bookings cancelled with less than 48 hours' notice, full payment will be required.*
▶ by electronic means **electronic, online** *We accept online payment in a secure environment by debit and credit card.*

● n+N **compensations, debt, dividend, mortgage, redundancy, royalty** *The International Monetary Fund urged Aregntina to set aside more cash for debt payments.*
● v+N make a payment **make, send** *If you experience*

a problem making your online payment, you can email or telephone us for advice.

▶ continue to make regular payments **keep up, meet** *Use our budget calculator to work out whether you'll have enough to meet your monthly payments.*

▶ fail to make a regular payment **miss** *Any missed payments are chased on the lender's behalf by a debt collections agency.*

▶ accept or receive a payment **accept, receive, take** *We accept payment using the following credit cards.*

▶ say a payment can be made **approve, authorize** *When the budget holder is satisfied with the invoice, they should authorize payment and pass it to finance for processing.*

▶ stop a payment being made **cancel, defer, delay, stop, withhold** *The insurance company withheld payment.*

▶ deal with a payment **process** *Payments are usually processed within two working days.*

▶ ask for a payment **demand, request** *He has received four letters demanding payment.*

pay off PHR VB
pay money that was borrowed to buy something

● V+n **amount, balance, credit card, debt, loan, money, mortgage** *There are no charges if you want to pay the loan off early.*

peace N
a situation in which there is no war

● adj+N that lasts **durable, enduring, lasting, permanent, perpetual** *After centuries of conflict and war, lasting peace can now finally be achieved.*

▶ that might not last long **fragile, uneasy** *The agreement brought a fragile peace to the region.*

▶ relative **relative** *With relative peace in Scotland during the 18th century, the population of the town doubled.*

▶ world **global, international, world** *Children are our best hope for world peace.*

● v+N bring peace **bring, build, make, secure** *The international community has played a major role in bringing peace and stability back to the countries of the region.*

▶ keep peace **keep, maintain, preserve, safeguard** *These operations support diplomatic efforts to maintain peace in an area of potential conflict.*

▶ make peace exist again **re-establish, restore** *In the meantime the revolt collapsed, thus briefly restoring peace to the country.*

▶ achieve peace **achieve** *Negotiation can achieve peace on honourable terms.*

▶ encourage peace **negotiate, promote** *The agreement would serve the interests of both sides and promote regional peace and security.*

▶ harm the chances of peace **endanger, threaten** *Terrorism gravely threatens international peace.*

● N+n agreement **accord, agreement, deal, settlement, treaty** *Wars go on and on beyond the signing of international agreements and peace treaties.*

▶ discussions **negotiations, process, talks** *The peace talks have stalled again.*

peaceful ADJ
1 not involving war or violence

● adv+ADJ completely **entirely, exclusively** *We are committed to exclusively peaceful means of resolving political issues.*

▶ mainly **largely, relatively** *Despite growing unrest, the presidential elections were relatively peaceful and fair.*

● ADJ+n **coexistence, demonstration, means, protest, resolution, settlement, solution** *We will support and defend the right to peaceful protest.*

2 calm and quiet

● adv+ADJ **delightfully, quite, so, truly, very, wonderfully** *It is completely surrounded by trees, and is a wonderfully peaceful place.*

● ADJ+n **atmosphere, location, place, setting, spot, surroundings** *Although within easy reach of major routes, the farm is in a delightfully peaceful spot, overlooking rolling countryside.*

● and/or **beautiful, calm, idyllic, picturesque, quiet, relaxing, secluded, tranquil, unspoilt** *Throughout my visit a peaceful and relaxing atmosphere prevailed.*

peak ADJ
highest, or involving the largest number of people

● ADJ+n time **hours, months, period, season, time** *There will be a shortage of parking spaces at peak periods.*

▶ amount wanted or done **demand, output, performance** *Last year the company recorded its highest ever peak demand for water.*

▶ level **level, rate** *No need to compromise web browsing speed – we deliver quick responses even at peak traffic levels.*

peer V
look carefully at something that is difficult to see

● adv+V closely or with interest **closely, curiously, intently** *He sat down opposite me, peering intently into my eyes.*

▶ in a worried or careful way **anxiously, cautiously, nervously** *I waited for him at a coffee shop, nervously peering up over the top of my book.*

▶ direction **about, ahead, back, down, inside, out, up** *He opened the box slightly and peered inside before shutting it quietly.*

penalty N
a punishment for breaking a rule or law

● adj+N severe **draconian, harsh, heavy, hefty, severe, stiff, tough** *There are severe penalties for making a false declaration.*

▶ most severe possible **maximum** *The maximum penalty is up to two years' imprisonment.*

▶ fixed **fixed** *Failure to submit the form will incur an automatic fixed penalty.*

▶ legal **civil, criminal** *The company or its directors may face criminal penalties.*

▶ financial **financial** *In one country, energy regulators have imposed financial penalties when investment commitments were not fulfilled.*

● n+N **cost, tax, time** *Courts have the power to impose*

cost penalties on parties who unreasonably refuse to
mediate.

- v+N give someone a penalty **exact, give, impose,
  introduce** If the tax office finds that there are errors
  in your tax return, they are likely to impose penalties.
- ▶ receive a penalty **face, incur, receive, suffer** If you
  fail to comply with these responsibilities, you are
  likely to incur financial penalties.
- ▶ lead to a penalty **carry, prescribe** Non-compliance
  with the safety regulations is a criminal offence and
  carries monetary penalties or imprisonment.
- ▶ avoid a penalty **avoid** Filing online could help you
  to avoid late-payment penalties.
- ▶ make someone pay money **charge, levy** Any student
  who registers late will be charged a late registration
  penalty.
- ▶ make a penalty more severe **increase** Despite moves
  to increase penalties for gun crime, the illegal
  possession of firearms is becoming a significant
  threat.

pension N
money received regularly after you stop working

- adj+N types of pension **basic, occupational,
  personal, private** Many higher-paid workers can
  afford to retire earlier **on** private pensions.
- ▶ paying well **decent, generous** The money is
  available to ensure that all people receive a decent
  pension when they come to retire.
- ▶ whole amount **full** She has recommended increasing
  the age at which retired people become entitled to a
  full state pension up from 65 to 67.
- ▶ each year **annual, yearly** Retirement benefits consist
  of an annual pension paid for life and a tax-free lump
  sum.
- n+N **company, retirement, state** He received a state
  retirement pension from October 1996 onwards.
- v+N receive a pension **collect, draw, get, receive**
  He may be able to start drawing his pension early.
- ▶ have the right to receive a pension **be entitled to,
  qualify for** I do not qualify for a state pension.
- ▶ officially ask for a pension **claim** Ministers have
  been told that one in five men will not live long
  enough to claim a state pension if the retirement age
  is raised to 70.
- ▶ no longer receive a pension **lose** We need to find a
  just solution for those who have lost their pensions,
  many of whom are suffering real hardship.
- ▶ pay a pension **grant, pay** Any pensions paid to
  partners or dependants will be subject to income tax
  in the normal way.
- ▶ increase a pension **increase, raise** The government
  has committed to raise pensions in line with prices,
  not earnings.
- ▶ make payments to pay for your pension
  contribute to, fund A member of an occupational
  pension scheme cannot contribute to a personal
  pension.
- N+n **age, arrangement, benefit, contribution,
  fund, plan, provision, scheme** The income generated
  within a pension scheme is tax-free.

perceive V
understand something in a particular way

- adv+V in general **commonly, generally, widely**

The main political parties are widely perceived to be
too similar.

> Usage **Perceive** is usually in the passive in these
> combinations.

- ▶ clearly **clearly** He received what he clearly perceived
  to be threatening phone calls.
- ▶ only slightly **dimly** The extent to which their own
  economy is propped up by public money is only dimly
  perceived, if at all.
- ▶ in different ways **differently** The circumstances
  surrounding the breakdown may be perceived
  differently by the patient and the doctor.
- V+as **problem, threat** Parking is generally not
  perceived as a problem in the town.

perceived
thought to be real

- V+n problem or danger **bias, danger, failure,
  inadequacy, injustice, lack, risk, shortcomings,
  threat, unfairness, weakness** There are constant
  complaints about a perceived lack of proper medical
  care. ● He argues that the perceived threat of
  communism created a new interest in human rights
  in Western democracies.
- ▶ need **necessity, need** There was also a perceived
  need for Norfolk to be more aggressive in promoting
  its attractions.
- ▶ benefit **benefit, usefulness** This chapter involves a
  detailed analysis of the perceived benefits of using
  computer-generated displays in the courtroom.
- ▶ wisdom **wisdom** For too long the perceived wisdom
  has been that UK farmers must compete at world
  prices.

percentage N
part of a total divided by 100

- adj+N high **great, high, large, significant,
  sizeable** Young people make up a large percentage
  of new drivers.
- ▶ low **low, small, tiny** Our income from circulation is
  just a small percentage of the newspaper's income.
- ▶ total **overall** The report reveals that the overall
  percentage of female engineers has actually declined.
- ▶ average **average** The average percentage of pupils
  having to share books is just over 44 per cent.
- v+N calculate a percentage **calculate** Now
  calculate the percentage of time spent on each subject.
- ▶ put an amount in the form of a percentage
  calculate sth as, express sth as Marks are expressed
  as a percentage.
- ▶ be a particular percentage **represent** The products
  available on-line represent only a small percentage
  of those in our shop.
- ▶ increase/reduce a percentage **increase, reduce** A
  bus interchange is being built at the airport in order
  to increase the percentage of passengers using public
  transport.

perceptible ADJ
able to be noticed

- adv+ADJ almost not **barely, hardly, scarcely** For
  a time progress was slow, in fact barely perceptible.
- ▶ clearly **clearly** This research suggests that technology
  needs to have a clearly perceptible benefit before it
  will be adopted.

- ADJ+n **change, difference, effect** *Even a fairly big jump in disk performance might not make a perceptible difference to the overall speed of your system.*

perception N
a way of understanding or thinking about something

- adj+N shared by many people **common, general, popular, public, widespread** *There continues to be a widespread perception that large-scale international fraud is victimless.*
- ▶ negative/positive **negative, positive** *The new campaign launched today aims to reverse negative perceptions of the region.*
- ▶ not true **distorted, false, misguided, mistaken** *Such stories tend to instil a false perception that offending by young people is rising.*
- v+N change or influence a perception **affect, alter, change, influence, shape** *I think becoming parents has also changed our perception of TV.*
- ▶ change a perception so that it is not true **colour, distort** *Companies who are unresponsive or take too long distort customer perceptions in a way which impacts on the whole profession.*
- ▶ create a perception **create** *Attacks of this sort create a perception of vulnerability and loss of control.*
- ▶ make a perception stronger **heighten, reinforce** *Some of the proposals may simply reinforce negative perceptions of young people.*
- ▶ improve a perception **enhance, improve** *If we work together to drive up performance across the sector, we can improve public perception of our service.*
- ▶ question or examine a perception **challenge, counter, examine, explore, investigate** *The film challenges perceptions of disability.*
- N+of **beauty, reality, risk, safety, self** *The exhibition examines perceptions of beauty in the built environment.*

perceptive ADJ
noticing or understanding things quickly

- adv+ADJ **extremely, highly, unusually, very** *Her act is filled with intelligent and highly perceptive observations.*
- ADJ+n something said or written **analysis, article, comment, insight, observation** *This essay shows good organization, and offers perceptive comments on the text.*
- ▶ person **critic, reader** *He may be the most perceptive critic writing about jazz today.*

perfect ADJ
completely good, correct, or accurate

- adv+ADJ completely **absolutely, just, quite, simply, utterly** *The weather was absolutely perfect, without a cloud in sight.*
- ▶ almost **almost, near, nearly, practically, virtually, well-nigh** *Three swans came around the point, their wings beating in almost perfect unison.*
- ▶ appearing to be perfect **seemingly** *It is a seemingly perfect society, but just crack the surface and you find chaos and corruption lying underneath.*
- ▶ apart from that **otherwise** *It is the only flaw in an otherwise perfect tale.*

- ▶ in a particular respect **aesthetically, morally, technically, theoretically** *The singing is without doubt technically perfect.*
- v+ADJ **be, become, look, make (sth), seem, sound** *The proposition looks perfect on paper.*

perfect V
make something completely free from faults

- V+n **art, method, skill, technique** *Having undertaken no formal musical training, he spent the next few years practising and perfecting his technique.*

perfection N
a state of being perfect

- adj+N complete **absolute, sheer** *Her standard of absolute perfection never changes.*
- ▶ almost complete **near** *His last album was a work of near perfection.*

> You can also say that a person or thing is *close to perfection*: *They came as close to perfection as any team had ever done.*

- ▶ types of perfection **moral, physical, spiritual, technical** *She became addicted to a quest for physical perfection in place of her self-esteem.*
- v+N achieve perfection **achieve, attain, reach** *It's unrealistic to expect that we will ever achieve perfection.*
- ▶ want or try to achieve perfection **demand, expect, seek, strive for** *Having grown up as an internationally competitive gymnast, Allie strives for perfection in all that she does.*

perform V
1 complete a complicated action or activity

- V+n something you have to do **duty, obligation, service, task** *Employees may be required to perform tasks beyond their strict job description.*
- ▶ job a person or thing has **function, role** *The second chamber needs the legitimacy to perform its functions – revision, scrutiny, and constitutional oversight – effectively.*
- ▶ operation or activity **action, activity, exercise, manoeuvre, operation, procedure, surgery** *Sometimes surgeons find cancer when they are performing a routine gall bladder operation.*
- ▶ experiment or test **check, experiment, test** *The rovers will land at separate sites and perform detailed geological experiments on the surface of Mars.*
- ▶ ceremony **ceremony, ritual** *Councillor Denny performed the opening ceremony by unveiling a suitably inscribed plaque.*
- ▶ calculation or examination **analysis, calculation, examination, measurement, search** *Perform a post-code search to find your nearest branch.*

2 do something with a particular amount of success

- adv+V **well admirably, brilliantly, effectively, efficiently, excellently, flawlessly, strongly, superbly, well** *The software is reliable and always performs well.*
- ▶ well enough **adequately, consistently, satisfactorily** *Our other regional offices continue to perform satisfactorily.*

▸ not well **badly, poorly** *My digital camera performs badly in very bright sunshine, rendering shadows pitch black.*

performance N

1 performing a play, dance, or other entertainment

● adj+N given before an audience **live, public** *She began recording some of her live performances.*

▸ performing alone **solo** *In this solo performance, Faith Brook takes on the most challenging role of her career.*

▸ very good **brilliant, excellent, fine, good, great, impressive, memorable, outstanding, stunning** *Ian McKellan's performance is outstanding and fully deserved the standing ovation at the end.*

▸ types of performance **musical, theatrical, vocal** *Emma Williams delivers a dazzling vocal performance.*

● n+N time of the day **evening, matinee** *Prices are often reduced for matinee performances.*

▸ types of performance **concert, dance, music, stage, theatre** *The hall is used for theatre performances and musical productions.*

● v+N give a performance **deliver, give** *Tom Hanks gives the funniest performance of his career.*

▸ organize a performance **produce, put on, stage** *The theatre regularly puts on performances of Shakespeare and well known musicals.*

▸ watch a performance **attend, go to, see, watch** *Later she took ballet classes, although she had never seen a live performance.*

▸ be part of a performance **feature** *The show will feature a performance from the winner of the 2009 competition.*

2 how well or effectively someone or something does something

● adj+N very good **excellent, fine, good, great, impressive, outstanding, strong, superb** *Both sides produced excellent team performances in a match that was 'an advert for football'.*

▸ very fast or powerful **high** *This chip has been proved through testing to achieve high performance and stability.*

▸ not good **bad, disappointing, poor** *How would you account for the party's poor performance in the election?*

▸ as a whole **overall** *Progress to the MSc depends on overall performance in assignments and examinations.*

▸ types of performance **academic, economic, environmental, financial** *These measures are intended to improve the economic performance of the region.*

● n+N **business, sales, school** *Our sales teams receive quarterly bonuses based on sales performance.*

● v+N improve performance **boost, enhance, improve, increase** *Sports science support can help to improve athletic performance.*

▸ affect performance **affect** *Too much stress can affect your performance at work.*

▸ make performance as good as possible **maximize, optimize** *We provide expert support to extend the life of your systems and optimize their performance.*

▸ measure or check performance **assess, evaluate,**

measure, monitor *We monitor our performance frequently to ensure the continuous improvement of our services.*

▸ produce a performance **achieve, deliver, give, produce, put in** *Supermarkets delivered a strong trading performance during the first half of the year.*

perfume N

the pleasant smell of something

● adj+N **delicate, exotic, heady, rich, sweet** *There was the heady perfume of honeysuckle in the air.*

peril N

danger

● adj+N great **deadly, dire, extreme, grave, great, mortal, serious** *Your father is in great peril.*

▸ happening soon **imminent** *Rescue parties worked in imminent peril from a dangerous roof to recover the bodies from the debris.*

▸ your own **own** *Anyone who ignores these warnings does so at their own peril.*

● v+N **be in, encounter, face** *The penguins face many perils as they seek their traditional breeding grounds.*

permission N

the right to do something given by someone

● adj+N stated clearly **explicit, express, specific** *We will not approach a current employer for a reference without the express permission of the candidate.*

▸ written or formal **formal, official, written** *It is illegal to copy any of the content on this site without written permission from the editor.*

▸ already obtained **prior** *Any motor vehicle left on a University car park overnight without the prior permission of the Security Officer will be removed.*

▸ special **special** *Former students have special permission to use a number of the University's facilities.*

▸ complete **full** *We will only reveal personal information to anyone else with your full permission.*

▸ necessary **appropriate, necessary, relevant** *Unfortunately, we do not have the necessary permission to publish the presentation.*

▸ from a child's parents **parental** *If you're under 16, you may need parental permission, so go with one of your parents.*

▸ for building or changing a building **planning** *Some types of development do not need planning permission.*

● v+N have permission **have** *Do you have permission to take photographs?*

▸ get permission **gain, get, obtain, receive** *You must obtain permission for the use of these photographs.*

▸ give permission **give (sb), grant (sb)** *Unless you give your explicit permission, we will not print your address.*

▸ refuse permission **deny (sb), refuse (sb)** *Maria was refused permission to change her course.*

▸ ask for permission **apply for, ask, ask for, request, seek** *I contacted the owners and asked for permission to use their pictures.*

▸ need permission **need, require** *You may need permission to build an extension to your home.*

permit N

an official document giving permission to do something

- adj+N **necessary, special, temporary, valid** *Visitors should report to reception on arrival for a temporary parking permit.*
- n+N **fishing, parking, residence, work** *Overseas graduates must be in possession of a valid work permit.*
- v+N let someone have a permit **authorize, grant, issue** *The River Kelvin Angling Association (RKAA) issues season permits, which cost £15 for a year.*
- ▶ get a permit **apply for, buy, get, obtain, renew** *How do I obtain a resident's parking permit?*
- ▶ have a permit **have, hold** *University personnel not holding a permit may use the parking facilities on a day-to-day basis.*
- ▶ need a permit **need, require** *Do you have a car park and do I need a permit?*
- ▶ show a permit **display** *Make sure your permit is clearly displayed in the nearside of the vehicle's windscreen.*

perpetuate V

make a bad situation or process continue

- adv+V **merely, only, simply, unwittingly** *Retribution and vengeance simply perpetuates the cycle of violence.*
- V+n idea or belief **idea, lie, myth, stereotype** *Television perpetuates the myth that science is all-knowing.*
- ▶ bad or unfair situation **cycle, division, inequality, injustice, poverty, violence** *Does the largely segregated education system in the country perpetuate community divisions?*

persecution N

extremely bad treatment of someone

- adj+N severe **brutal, cruel, fierce, intense, ruthless, severe, terrible** *In the meantime, my proposal should be accepted and the cruel, wasteful persecution and jailing of of seriously ill people should end.*
- ▶ done in a thorough and continuous way **relentless, renewed, repeated, systematic** *He has overseen systematic persecution of the Basques since he came to office.*
- ▶ types of persecution **political, racial, religious** *Many of these people have left their country because they were direct targets of political, religious or racial persecution.*
- v+N suffer persecution **be subjected to, endure, experience, face, suffer, undergo** *All of the early converts faced persecution, and some were put to death.*
- ▶ escape from persecution **avoid, escape, flee** *Britain should be a safe refuge for those genuinely fleeing persecution.*
- ▶ be frightened that you might suffer persecution **fear** *People can seek asylum in the UK if they fear persecution in their own country.*
- and/or **death, discrimination, imprisonment, intolerance, oppression, poverty, prejudice, repression, suffering, violence, war** *No decent country wishes to send genuine asylum seekers back to persecution or death.*

perseverance N

determination to continue doing something difficult

- adj+N **dogged, indomitable, patient, sheer, steady** *They fought for freedom with a dogged perseverance and indomitable endurance that can only be termed heroic.*
- v+N **demand, demonstrate, need, require** *You need perseverance to push through those moments of frustration.*
- N+v **be rewarded, pay off** *Eventually, his perseverance paid off and he found a job.*
- and/or **commitment, courage, dedication, determination, effort, energy, hard work, patience, skill** *Hard work and perseverance will pay off.*

persist V

continue to exist

- adv+V **indefinitely, still** *This belief still persists to this day.*
- n+V problem or illness **condition, difficulty, pain, problem, symptom** *If your symptoms persist, please contact your doctor.*
- ▶ feeling **doubt, fear, feeling** *Where doubts persist, it is very important for tutors not to brush these aside as something everyone experiences.*
- ▶ situation **difference, effect, inequality, situation, trend** *Income inequalities persist and grow.*
- ▶ belief **attitude, myth, rumour** *Rumours persist that she's expecting her first baby, but she's not confirming or denying anything.*

persistent ADJ

1 continuing

- ADJ+n illness **cough, diarrhoea, headache, infection, inflammation, injury, pain, symptom, vomiting, weakness** *Smoking can cause a persistent cough.*
- ▶ problem **breach, difficulty, failure, harassment, problem** *Where there are persistent problems, the council could take over management of the property.*
- ▶ bad weather **drizzle, fog, rain** *Persistent rain throughout the morning resulted in this match being abandoned.*
- ▶ belief **belief, myth, reports, rumour** *There are persistent rumours that within the grounds of two country parks in Scotland are mass-graves.*

2 continuing to do something in a determined way

- ADJ+n behaviour or actions **attack, attempt, call, demand, effort, refusal** *The BBC's persistent refusal to cover absolutely anything to do with the Election campaign raised much criticism in 1955.*
- ▶ criminal or person doing something bad **criminal, offender, shoplifter, troublemaker, truant** *Custodial sentences should be imposed for serious, persistent offenders.*

personality N

someone's character

- adj+N good **good, great, pleasant** *I meet a guy,*

he's lovely, attractive, great personality, open, intelligent, amazing.

▶ strong **big, dominant, forceful, larger-than-life, powerful, strong** *He was a man with a happy disposition and a big personality.*

▶ lively **charismatic, colourful, dynamic, flamboyant, lively, vibrant** *Jose's lively personality and sense of humour got us all through many a challenging day!*

▶ not easy to understand **complex** *She has a complex personality and is so sensitive, she gets hurt very easily.*

▶ friendly and liking to be with other people **bubbly, friendly, outgoing, warm** *I have a bubbly personality and like good conversation and a laugh or two.*

▶ interesting and attractive **charming, engaging, likeable, magnetic** *We found him a man of charming personality, and an excellent speaker.*

▶ your own **individual, unique** *Tony has been at the group for 9 years and his unique personality and charm will be very much missed.*

▶ addictive **addictive** *I have an addictive personality and intend to steer clear of drugs.*

● v+N show what someone's personality is like **express, reflect, reveal, show** *The interior decor of your home should reflect your personality.*

▶ not have much of a personality **lack** *Vanna and Nella share their mother's beauty, but lack her strong personality.*

● N+n personality type **type** *People of different personality types are better at different tasks.*

▶ part of someone's personality **characteristic, quirk, trait** *Personality traits such as determination, motivation, and curiosity all contribute to the success of students.*

▶ personality problem **defect, disorder, problem** *Stone's case was complex because of a personality disorder combined with drug and alcohol abuse.*

▶ a test to discover what someone's personality is like **profile, questionnaire, test** *Online personality tests aren't really the best judges of character.*

▶ the situation when two people argue because they have very different personalities **clash, conflict, difference** *Due to the nature of the business, personality clashes can occur between students and teacher.*

personnel N
people in a company, organization, or military force

● adj+N having a lot of experience or training **competent, experienced, qualified, skilled, trained** *The application of herbicide should be carried out only by trained personnel.*

▶ most important **key, senior** *It is essential that key personnel are on site to assist before the incident escalates.*

▶ types of personnel **administrative, armed, civilian, medical, military, naval, operational, professional, supervisory, technical** *2,800 medical personnel were mobilised at short notice to support 467,000 British troops.*

perspective N
way of thinking about something

● adj+N new **fresh, new** *The challenges gave me a new perspective on my own role.*

▶ different **alternative, contrasting, different, differing** *The film is made up of stories told by people with differing perspectives.*

▶ in terms of a particular place **global, international, local, national, regional** *The report provides a genuinely international perspective, showing how people all over the world were affected by the war.*

▶ involving many ideas **broad, wide** *Staff will also have to consider their own personal development and skills, and have a broad perspective of the council's business.*

▶ reasonable and considering all possibilities **balanced, holistic, proper** *If you feel it is appropriate, try talking to other people to help you get a balanced perspective on which are the most likely explanations.*

▶ your own perspective **personal, sb's own** *From a personal perspective, doing this work has given me a renewed confidence in my abilities.*

▶ not the same as anyone else's **unique** *Their unique perspectives and input created an exhibition that was exciting and educational.*

▶ types of perspective **critical, cultural, economic, financial, historical, human, philosophical, political, practical, psychological, public, religious, social, sociological, theoretical** *We examine how the problem can be dealt with from a practical perspective.*

● v+N have a perspective **embrace, have** *These are just my thoughts and I'm sure some people will have a different perspective.*

▶ offer a perspective **bring, give, offer, present, provide** *Tillerson provided an industry perspective on the impact of shifts in the global energy sector.*

▶ discuss or analyse a perspective **consider, discuss, examine, explore** *This module explores two complementary perspectives.*

▶ get a perspective **develop, gain, get** *Try and get a genuine perspective of what the job is like from people who work in the industry.*

▶ use a particular perspective in a piece of writing **adopt, take** *Her recent work on conflict and development takes a cross-sectoral perspective to explore agency responses to war and violent conflict.*

▶ change a perspective **change, shift** *Also, this changed my perspective on what I want to do in the future.*

▶ have the same perspective as someone else **share** *There are allies who share our perspective and will work with us to secure common objectives.*

▶ make your perspective include more ideas **broaden, widen** *The course should help broaden your perspectives on different areas of plant biology.*

▶ include a perspective **incorporate** *The course is an ideal opportunity for EU studies to incorporate perspectives from many disciplines.*

persuasive ADJ
good at making people do or believe what you want

● adv+ADJ **gently, highly, very** *The case for the Lord Chancellor to set a figure below 3 per cent is highly persuasive.*

● ADJ+n writing, speech, argument **account, argument, case, communication, evidence,** language, message, monologue, presentation, rationale, reason, reasoning, speech, writing *This programme offers the most persuasive evidence of success in reducing recidivism.*

▸ power or skill **force, power, skills** *The persuasive powers of these individuals are incredible.*

● v+ADJ **be, prove, seem, sound** *There is one piece of evidence that at first glance seems persuasive.*

pertinent ADJ
relevant to something

● adv+ADJ **especially, extremely, highly, particularly, very** *This issue is particularly pertinent to North East London, which has some of the most deprived boroughs in the country.*

● ADJ+n **comment, data, detail, example, fact, factor, information, issue, observation, point, question, topic** *This book contains a wealth of helpful material, with pertinent observations and practical suggestions.* ● *Hopefully, patients will be better informed and able to ask pertinent questions at their consultation.*

● v+ADJ **be, become, consider, remain, seem** *The company will have to take the decisions it considers pertinent.*

pervasive ADJ
spreading through the whole of something

● adv+ADJ **all, increasingly** *Visiting some Asian cities, one becomes aware of the all pervasive influence of American globalization.*

● ADJ+n **effect, influence, nature, presence, problem, sense, smell, theme, use** *We need to deal with the pervasive influence of drugs and crime.* ● *With the all pervasive nature and rapid development of the Internet, educational products will also begin to trade as global commodities.*

pessimism N
the belief that the worst will always happen

● adj+N **deep, deep-seated, extreme, growing, profound** *She carried into adulthood a profound pessimism about human relationships.*

● v+N **express, reflect** *The article expresses a deep-seated pessimism about the potential of art to effect radical change.*

● and/or **cynicism, despair, fear, optimism** *He was obviously trying to be funny, but his statement reflects the despair and pessimism of our times.*

pessimistic ADJ
thinking that the worst will always happen

● adv+ADJ very **deeply, extremely, profoundly, very** *He's extremely pessimistic about what will happen in the world generally.*

▸ rather **rather, somewhat** *I was somewhat pessimistic about getting a draw let alone a win!*

▸ too **overly, too, unduly** *But perhaps I'm being overly pessimistic here.*

● ADJ+n attitude or belief **assessment, assumption, attitude, conclusion, outlook, view** *There is a*

pessimistic view that the group can never develop into a mass organisation.

▸ forecast **estimate, forecast, prediction** *The crisis is even more severe than the most pessimistic forecasts from a year ago.*

▸ situation **scenario** *The scientists are emphasizing the most pessimistic scenario in order to attract public attention.*

pest N
an insect or animal that damages plants or food

● v+N get rid of a pest **combat, control, destroy, eradicate, kill, suppress** *A biopesticide will control only the pest for which it has been developed.*

▸ attract a pest **attract** *Shrinkage in timber which has not properly been dried will open gaps that can attract pests.*

▸ not attract a pest **deter, prevent, resist** *Crops that are genetically modified to resist a pest do not need to be sprayed with pesticides to control that pest.*

● N+n things done to deal with pests **control, management, resistance** *Biological control is an increasingly important area of modern pest management.*

▸ a time when pests attack something **attack, infestation, problem** *Considerable financial loss is incurred by pest infestations in food and packaging materials.*

petition N
a document signed by many people who want something

● n+N **email, Internet, online** *Over 900 people have signed the online petition at the campaign's website.*

● v+N sign a petition **sign** *When people saw this, they signed a petition objecting to planning permission.*

▸ give a petition to someone in authority **deliver, hand in, lodge, present, send, submit, table** *We demonstrated in Leicester Square and then we presented a petition to the Prime Minister.*

▸ start and organize a petition **circulate, launch, organize, raise, start** *Scotland's churches have launched a joint petition urging the UK Government not to replace the Trident nuclear weapons system.*

▸ write a petition **draft, word** *The Clerk is available to give advice to Members drafting petitions.*

▸ reject a petition **dismiss, reject** *Parliament rejected a massive petition calling for the adoption of the Charter.*

● N+v a petition asks for something **ask for sth, call for sth, demand sth, request sth, urge sth** *Campaigners collected 8,500 signatures on a petition calling for a referendum.*

▸ a petition supports something **support sth** *Thousands of locals have signed petitions supporting the development.*

▸ a petition opposes something **oppose sth, protest against sth** *Over 40,000 people signed a petition opposing the scheme.*

petty ADJ
about things that are not important

● ADJ+n argument **argument, bickering, dispute,**

squabble *Please let's not get into petty arguments about spelling.*

▶ rule **regulation, restriction, rule** *Mack hates the children's home that he lives in, with its petty rules.*

▶ feeling **concerns, jealousy, rivalry** *He wanted to demonstrate his distance from petty concerns.* ● *The academic world was riddled with petty jealousies, rumours of love affairs and swindled funds.*

phase N

a period during the development of something

● adj+N coming at or near the beginning **developmental, early, first, initial, preliminary, preparatory, primary, second, start-up** *Work started on the first phase of the rail link in October 1998.*

▶ coming at or near the end **final, last, later, subsequent, successive** *The final phase of development at Meridian is nearing completion.*

▶ important **critical, crucial, important, key, major** *The project is now entering a critical phase before full launch later this year.*

▶ when activity takes place **operational** *The operational phase continued for approximately 21 weeks during which 41,232 cubic metres of water was treated.*

▶ different **different, distinct** *The process of digestion can be thought to have three distinct phases: ingestion, digestion and egestion.*

▶ lasting only for a short time **passing, transient** *In the early days, some thought his obsession with computer games was just a passing phase.*

▶ moving from one phase to another **transitional** *The Egyptians also believed that the precision of the equinoxes triggered the various transitional phases in both civilization and the natural world.*

● v+N enter a phase **begin, enter, start** *After a rolling programme of art fairs in London since March, we now enter a quieter phase over the summer.*

▶ make a phase start to happen **initiate, launch** *The company has launched the next phase of demolition at Longbridge.*

▶ go through a phase **go through** *Many children go through phases of refusing to eat certain foods.*

▶ end a phase **complete** *We completed the research phase of the project on time.*

mark a phase **mark** *This marks an exciting phase in the development of one of the UK's most strategically important waterfront sites.*

phenomenal ADJ

extremely impressive or surprising

adv+ADJ **absolutely, quite, simply, truly** *The campaign attracted a truly phenomenal level of support.*

ADJ+n increase **growth, increase, rise** *In the 1980s and 1990s, the Southeast Asian countries saw phenomenal economic growth.*

ability **ability, memory, power, talent** *I have never ceased to be amazed by Cardinal Martin's phenomenal memory.*

achievement **achievement, performance, result, success** *The phenomenal success of online auctions is unprecedented.*

speed at which something happens **pace, rate,**

speed *The club grew at a phenomenal pace through the late 1990's.*

amount of something **amount, demand, response** *We have had a phenomenal response and there are only a limited number of places still available.*

phenomenon N

something that happens or exists

● adj+N rare **isolated, rare, unique** *It is a unique phenomenon – no other theatre in Britain attempts this extraordinary turnover of plays.*

▶ common or known about **common, familiar, well-known** *The teachers found specific learning disability a less familiar phenomenon than intellectual disability.*

▶ becoming more common **growing** *Home education of children is a growing phenomenon in the UK.*

▶ strange **bizarre, curious, extraordinary, mysterious, peculiar, strange, unexplained, unusual** *The strange phenomenon was discovered in the corner of a field.*

▶ interesting **fascinating, interesting, remarkable** *An interesting phenomenon which happens at sea is that time can simultaneously progress incredibly quickly and tortuously slowly.*

▶ relating to things that do not seem to have a scientific or natural explanation **paranormal, psychic, supernatural** *Do you believe in psychic phenomena, and have you had any personal experience of ghosts?*

▶ natural **natural** *He believed that climate change was a natural phenomenon, and not caused by the way we live.*

▶ able to be seen **observable, observed** *The theory of evolution is an attempt to explain observed natural phenomena.*

▶ happening everywhere **global, international, universal, widespread, worldwide** *Terrorism is an international phenomenon and requires an international response.*

▶ new or recent **emergent, modern, new, recent** *Racial hatred resulting in abuse and vicious murderous attacks is not a new phenomenon.*

▶ types of phenomena **astronomical, biological, celestial, cultural, economic, historical, linguistic, mental, physical, political, psychological, religious, scientific, social** *Globalisation is not merely an economic phenomenon, and that is why our response cannot simply be an economic one.*

● v+N understand a phenomenon **explain, understand** *To understand this phenomenon, one must first grasp the inextricable connection that exists between magnetism and electricity.*

▶ study a phenomenon **analyse, examine, explore, investigate, research, study** *There are groups which investigate the phenomenon of UFOs.*

▶ discover a phenomenon **discover** *These ideas have helped scientists to formulate specific questions and discover new phenomena.*

● n+of+N **explanation, interpretation, investigation, nature, observation, understanding** *You will never be able to ensure that your interpretation of the phenomenon is the right one.*

phobia N

a very strong fear of something

● adj+N **dental, social, specific** *People with a social*

phobia have a fear of embarrassing themselves or of being humiliated in public.

- v+N have a phobia **experience, have, suffer from** *I have had a phobia of spiders since childhood.*
- ▶ start to have a phobia **develop** *I started to develop phobias about walking up and down stairs.*
- ▶ deal successfully with a phobia **overcome** *She's also overcome her phobia of water and enjoys swimming now.*
- ▶ give medical help to someone with a phobia **cure, treat** *Hypnotherapy can be an effective way of treating phobias.*
- and/or **anxiety, depression, disorder, fear** *Hypnosis can very effectively help with fears and phobias.*

phone N
a telephone

- v+N use a phone **get on** INFORMAL**, use** *What are you waiting for? Get on the phone and book your flights!*
- ▶ pick up a phone when it rings **answer, get** INFORMAL**, pick up** *Ellie rushed to answer the phone.*
- ▶ talk to someone using a phone **be on, chat on, speak on, talk on** *A couple of nights ago I was talking on the phone to my father.*
- N+v **go, ring** *A minute later the phone rang again.*

physique N
the shape of someone's body, especially a man's

- adj+N **athletic, balanced, fine, great, lean, magnificent, muscular, powerful, strong** *In both of these films, Pitt's muscular physique was on display.*

picture N
a description or idea of what someone or something is like

- adj+N clear **clear, coherent, vivid** *We can provide a clear picture of your financial performance.*
- ▶ general **general, overall** *The overall picture is therefore rather bleak for the American armed forces.*
- ▶ including many details **balanced, broad, comprehensive, detailed, rounded** *The film presents a comprehensive picture of life in China.*
- ▶ including all details **big, complete, full, whole** *Be careful when comparing the performance of individual schools based only on these results – they don't give you the full picture.*
- ▶ not correct **distorted, false, misleading** *Official figures can sometimes give a distorted picture.*
- ▶ correct **accurate, real, realistic, true** *If you want an accurate picture of just how evil and deceived he was, read this book.*
- ▶ showing that a situation is not good **bleak, depressing, disturbing, gloomy, grim** *The report paints a gloomy picture of the organization's current position.*
- ▶ showing that a situation is good **positive, rosy** *It was an upbeat presentation which painted a positive picture for the future.*
- ▶ in your own mind **mental** *Mental pictures rarely match the reality.*
- v+N give a picture **create, give, offer, paint,**

portray, present, provide *History, however, paints a different picture of the reasons behind the wall's existence.* ● *The book presents an accurate picture of rural life.*
- ▶ get a picture **build, form, gain** *If they come and speak to me, it will help me to build a wider picture of what is happening.*
- ▶ make a picture complete **complete** *The property is newly furnished, and the log fire completes the picture of a tranquil and picturesque holiday home.*
- N+v **emerge** *A clearer picture is also emerging of Chester's place in the hierarchy of Roman Britain.*

piece N
a piece of writing, art, or music

- v+N write a piece of music or writing **compose, produce, write** *I would like to write a bass trombone piece with orchestra.*
- ▶ play a piece of music **perform, play** *We are quite happy to play any piece of music which is not already in our repertoire, given sufficient notice.*
- ▶ make a piece of art **craft, create, make, produce** *This piece is crafted in sterling silver.*
- ▶ record a piece of music **record** *We recorded the last piece of music for the last scene of the film.*
- ▶ publish a piece of writing **publish** *This is an edited version of a piece originally published in the British Medical Journal.*

pinnacle N
the most successful part of something

- adj+N **absolute, very** *Barenboim was at the very pinnacle of his profession.*
- v+N **achieve, mark, reach, represent, rise to** *This song doesn't quite reach the same pinnacle of excellence as the title track.* ● *The Olympic Games represent the pinnacle of sporting achievement.*
- N+of job **career, profession** *Footballers at the pinnacle of their careers earn huge amounts of money.*
- ▶ achievement or success **achievement, excellence, fame, power, success** *Frankie Howerd rose to the very pinnacle of comedic success.*

pinpoint V
discover or explain exactly what something is

- adv+V **accurately, exactly, precisely** *Technicians need to accurately pinpoint the location of the leak before repairs can begin.*
- V+n a place **area, location, position, spot** *GPS uses satellites to pinpoint your location to within a few feet.*
- ▶ a time **date, moment** *Many people can pinpoint the precise moment when their interest in mathematics was awakened.*
- ▶ a cause or reason **cause, factor, reason, source** *Many people are simply not able to pinpoint the source of their stress.*
- ▶ a problem **problem, weakness** *Detailed records about each piece of equipment help our engineers to pinpoint any possible problems.*

pint N INFORMAL
a pint of beer

- **v+N** drink a pint **consume, down, drink, have, knock back, sink, sip, sup** *The toilets were out of order, which made things very uncomfortable for those of us who had downed a pint or two.*
▶ buy a pint **buy, get, grab, order** *Grab a pint and join us for the Oktoberfest celebration.*
▶ serve a pint **pour, pull, serve** *As a child she lived in a pub, and she still remembers how to pull a pint.*
▶ like a pint **enjoy, like** *He still enjoys a pint in the area's excellent pubs.*

pioneering ADJ
done for first time using new methods

- **ADJ+n** work **course, development, effort, experiment, initiative, programme, project, research, scheme, service, study, system, work** *A pioneering programme to help stop young people falling into a life of crime is proving a success.* • *Enzo Tiezzi has carried out pioneering work on sustainable development and ecological problems.*
▶ method or idea **approach, design, idea, method, solution, technique, technology, way** *Leeds Metropolitan University has developed a pioneering approach to tackling obesity in young people.*
▶ medical treatment **surgery, treatment** *Patients will benefit from pioneering treatments in world-class facilities.*

pipe N
a tube that carries liquid or gas

- **adj+N** broken **broken, burst, cracked, fractured, leaking, leaky, perforated** *A large amount of water is lost through leaking pipes.*
▶ what pipe is made of **clay, concrete, copper, earthenware, iron, lead, plastic** *The water is transported by plastic pipes from the filter tank to the village.*
▶ **v+N** put a pipe somewhere **connect, fit, install, lay, run** *In 1919, a pipe was laid to supply water to the new houses.*
▶ mend damage to a pipe **fix, repair** *He was on the road outside the house fixing the burst water pipe.*
▶ stop a pipe being connected **disconnect** *The worst part of the job is the moment when you disconnect the fuel pipe.*
▶ put material around a pipe to prevent heat loss **insulate, lag** *The fuel pipes have been insulated.*
▶ prevent liquid or gas running freely through a pipe **block** *We had to remove a tree root which was blocking the drainage pipe.*
▶ **N+v** a pipe goes somewhere **go, lead to sth, run** *The pipes run under the floor.*
▶ a pipe bursts or leaks **burst, fracture, leak** *If your pipes burst, then your priority will be to minimize any damage from escaping water.*
▶ a pipe has a particular liquid flowing through it **carry sth** *Several of the original pipes still carry water.*

pitch N
flat area for playing particular sports on

- **n+N** sport played on a pitch **baseball, cricket, football, hockey, rugby, soccer, sports, training** *The school has excellent sports facilities with two football pitches and a gym.*
▶ made from grass **grass, turf** *The stadium has a retractable roof, and a grass pitch.*
▶ made from an artificial material **all-weather, artificial, astro, astroturf, synthetic** *Through the winter, good use has been made of the new all weather pitch at the leisure centre.*

pitfall N
a problem that is likely to happen

- **adj+N** possible **possible, potential** *Despite all these potential pitfalls, most whirlpools are successfully installed.*
▶ most likely to happen **common, main, major** *Here are some common pitfalls to avoid when using the Internet, and suggestions for how to cope with them.*
▶ obvious **obvious** *Another obvious pitfall at a job interview is forgetting what you wrote on your application form.*

- **v+N** have a pitfall **have** *As laudable as the clinical programme is, it has some pitfalls.*
▶ have a lot of pitfalls **be fraught with, be full of** *It is a difficult process which is fraught with pitfalls.*
▶ avoid a pitfall **avoid, overcome** *Try to avoid the pitfalls that so many people fall into when writing their CV.*
▶ not avoid a pitfall **fall into** *I believe that the Prime Minister is in danger of falling into the very pitfalls highlighted in this book.*
▶ know about a pitfall **know, understand** *Get advice from someone who has already bought a house and knows the pitfalls.*
▶ find a pitfall **identify, recognise** *The project began with research to identify any potential pitfalls.*

pity N
a feeling of sympathy for someone

- **adj+N** deep, genuine, great, much, real** *He feels great pity for animals that are mistreated.*
▶ **v+N** have pity **be filled with, be full of, feel, have** *He was quite unmoved; he had no pity for me.*
▶ show pity **show** *There were some nice moments of O'Sullivan showing pity for his victims.*
▶ deserve pity **deserve** *The weak deserve our pity; the wicked our contempt.*
▶ arouse pity **arouse, evoke, excite** *What we fear for ouselves excites our pity when it happens to others.*

- **and/or** anger, compassion, horror, mercy, sympathy** *She became aware, for the first time, of the sympathy and pity that disabled people have to face every day.*

place N
an opportunity to be a member of a sports team, organization, college etc

- **v+N** get a place **clinch, earn, gain, get, obtain, secure, win** *His form suggests that he will be one of the favourites to win a place in the Great Britain team.*
▶ give someone a place **award sb, give sb, offer sb** *National Scholarships will be provided to all those who are offered a place at a Higher Education institute.*
▶ say someone cannot have a place **deny sb, refuse sb** *He was refused a place at his first choice of university because his grades were too low.*

▸ accept a place **accept, take up** *The number of people taking up places on HND courses rose by 2.5 per cent.*

place V

1 put something somewhere

● adv+V **carefully, firmly, gently, neatly, randomly** *I carefully placed my poppy wreath at the foot of the column and left the cemetery.* ● *Take the needle out of its wrapping and place it firmly onto the tip of the syringe.* ● *Twenty-four colourful carpet tiles have been placed randomly on the floor.*

2 to have a particular attitude to someone or something

● V+n importance **emphasis, importance, value** *The dental practice places a special emphasis on preventive care.*

▸ hope or trust **confidence, faith, hope, reliance, trust** *Going through the process several times is necessary before we can place any confidence in our methodology.*

▸ blame **blame** *She placed the blame squarely on her brother.*

plan N

actions that help you achieve something

● adj+N future **future, long-term, overall** *Future plans at the Eden Project include a hotel and an Education Centre.*

▸ with many details **comprehensive, detailed** *Clearly you cannot make any detailed plans now, as the project will need to be discussed in depth with your supervisor.*

▸ big and possibly difficult to achieve **ambitious, big, grand, grandiose, great, major, radical** *The school had ambitious plans to develop the site.*

▸ likely to succeed **coherent, definite, realistic, sound, viable** *Sound plans are in place to sustain the steady growth achieved over more than 85 years.*

▸ clever **brilliant, clever, cunning, elaborate** *Will their cunning plan succeed?*

▸ involving disagreement between people **controversial** *Controversial plans to convert a derelict chapel into a nightclub have moved a step closer to completion.*

▸ clear **clear** *The report includes clear plans for retaining and developing teachers.*

▸ involving strategy **strategic** *The strategic plans of the University of Glasgow place great importance on collaboration.*

● v+N make a plan **construct, create, develop, devise, draw up, figure out, form, formulate, hatch, make, prepare, produce, put together, work out** *The industry will develop a plan for in-house supplementary training.*

▸ have a plan **have** *Do you have a contingency plan for just such an emergency?*

▸ tell people what the plan is **announce, launch, outline, present, publish, reveal, set out, unveil** *Ministers have already announced plans to recruit 20,000 teaching assistants.*

▸ implement a plan **adopt, carry out, execute, implement, introduce, pursue** *The local history society adopted his plan to hold a 65km race in traditional wooden boats.*

▸ decide not to continue with a plan **abandon, cancel, drop, reject, scrap, shelve** *The television company abandoned plans to broadcast the show.*

▸ support a plan **support, welcome** *We welcome the plans to build a new community hospital.*

▸ approve a plan **agree (to), approve** *Father Tunstall approved the plans for the church but had retired before the official opening.*

▸ oppose a plan **fight, oppose** *Campaigners are fighting plans to turn Elvaston Castle into a luxury hotel.*

▸ think about a plan **consider, discuss** *The company is considering plans to launch a franchise operation to sell its drinks in the US.*

▸ change a plan **alter, amend, change, modify, review, revise** *The council hastily changed the plans after protests from the public.*

▸ decide the final details of a plan **finalize** *They needed longer to finalize their plans.*

▸ stop a plan from being successful **derail, foil, scupper** INFORMAL, **thwart** *These plans were thwarted by much opposition.*

● N+for **development, expansion, future, growth, improvement, redevelopment, reform** *There are now detailed plans for the redevelopment of children's services in the borough.*

plan V

think carefully about actions you will take

● adv+V for the future **ahead, in advance** *Planning ahead is essential for your organization's success.*

▸ carefully **carefully, meticulously, thoroughly** *I had been carefully planning this trip for so long.*

▸ badly **badly, poorly** *The war was never necessary and was turning out to be badly planned.*

▸ well **effectively, properly, successfully, well** *To plan effectively, we need to know where the gaps in provision lie.*

● V+n travel **expedition, holiday, journey, route, tour, trip, visit, walk** *Always use an Ordnance Survey map to help you plan your route.*

▸ event **conference, event, party, wedding** *We look forward to helping you plan the wedding of your dreams.*

▸ what you will do during a particular time **day, itinerary, schedule, week, weekend, your time** *He had a breakfast of bread and fruit, eaten while mentally planning his day.* ● *You are free to plan your own itinerary.*

▸ activity **activity, campaign, lesson, operation, programme, project** *There is a separate teachers' section to help you plan your lessons.* ● *Police officers used video footage from the game and local intelligence to plan the operation.*

▸ career or life **career, life** *The centre offers information and practical advice for planning your career.*

plane N

an aircraft with wings

● v+N travel somewhere on a plane **catch, get on, jump on** INFORMAL, **take** *Jon immediately caught a plane to Pennsylvania when he heard his mother was sick.*

▸ get on a plane **board, get on** *He forgot his passport and wasn't allowed to board the plane.*

▸ get off a plane **get off, leave, step off** *The heat hit me as I stepped off the plane at Delhi.*
▸ arrive too late to get a plane **miss** *We almost missed the plane because the car broke down on the way to the airport.*
▸ fly a plane **fly, pilot** *The pilot was drunk and shouldn't have been flying the plane.*
▸ make a plane come down to the ground **land** *She managed to land the plane safely.*
▸ take control of a plane illegally while it is flying **hijack** *On September 11, 2001, four planes were hijacked over American skies.*

● N+v a plane comes down to the ground **arrive, land, touch down** *I was asleep and didn't feel the slight bump as the plane touched down.*
▸ a plane leaves the ground and moves up into the sky **take off** *At 12:25 our plane took off for Stavanger.*
▸ a plane has people or things in it **carry sb/sth** *A UN plane carrying one U.S. citizen and two Philippine nationals crashed in a field earlier today.*
▸ a plane moves through the sky **fly, travel** *The plane flew over the city.*
▸ a plane hits something by accident **crash** *The plane crashed in Wales, killing all on board.*

● N+n trip **flight, journey, ride, trip** *We took a forty-minute plane ride over the Canyon.*
▹ ticket **ticket** *You can save money by buying plane tickets online.*
▹ accident **crash** *He was killed in a plane crash.*

planning N
the process of deciding how to do something or how something should be

● adj+N careful or good **careful, detailed, effective, efficient, meticulous, proper, thorough** *All school trips require meticulous planning and organization.*
▹ poor **inadequate, poor** *Traffic chaos results from poor town planning.*
▹ future **forward, future, long-term, strategic** *The following quotes show the value of forward planning and organisation.*
▹ types of planning **environmental, financial, regional, urban** *A fundamental requirement of sound financial planning is having an up-to-date will.*

● N+N **business, career, contingency, emergency, family, inheritance, land, retirement, tax, transport, wedding** *The report has brought the crucial topic of retirement planning into the public spotlight.*
▹ N+n request/permission **application, approval, consent, decision, permission** *The Secretary of State has formally refused planning permission for the 5,000 dwelling scheme.*
▹ process **framework, guidance, policy, process, stage, system** *We are arguing for the right of third parties to have an enhanced role within the planning process.*
▹ authority **authority, committee, department** *Your local authority's planning department will be able to provide you with the forms you need.*
▹ rules or laws **enforcement, guidelines, law, legislation, regulations** *Property owners should always check that planning regulations do not apply to changes they want to make.*

plant N
a factory that produces or processes things

● adj+N for making things **assembly, chemical, industrial, manufacturing** *Honda were losing over 1,000 workers from their manufacturing plant in Yokohama.*
▸ for producing power **coal-fired, generating, nuclear, power** *The nuclear plant has not been generating power since early 2002.*
▸ for processing things **desalination, incineration, processing, recycling, refrigeration, sewage** *Arguments for higher landfill taxes often come from those who run incineration plants.*

● v+N open or shut a plant **close, close down, open, shut, shut down** *When a plant is shut down, all the steam condenses in the pipework.*
▸ run a plant **operate, run** *There comes a time when it is no longer economic to operate the plant.*

platform N
a chance to express something or for something to happen

● adj+N strong **profitable, robust, solid, stable** *He said that now we had a stable platform, we could address our priorities for the future.*
▸ very good **ideal, perfect** *Major sporting events provide a perfect platform for creative media ideas.*

● v+N **build, create, provide** *The main target is to provide a platform where French researchers and foreign guests will learn to work together.*

● N+for for discussion **debate, dialogue, discussion, exchange, networking** *The success of this year's event has established Orkney as a major international platform for scientific debate. ● The purpose of the forum is to provide a platform for the exchange of ideas.*
▸ for growth or change **delivery, expansion, the future, growth, innovation, integration** *She would be concentrating on keeping costs to a minimum and building a platform for growth.*
▸ for cooperation **collaboration, cooperation, sharing** *I want this to be a platform for collaboration.*
▸ for types of people **artist, designer, musician, talent** *Scotland has a thriving art scene and Glasgow is a great platform for new artists.*

plausible ADJ
likely to be true or effective

● adv+ADJ very/not very **entirely, not remotely, perfectly, remotely, superficially, utterly** *I presented him with this perfectly plausible theory and he threw it back in my face.*
▸ rather **quite, reasonably** *Although I am unable to verify this story, I find it quite plausible.*
▸ in a particular way **biologically, intuitively, physically, psychologically, scientifically** *There is enough evidence for evolution to make it scientifically plausible.*

● ADJ+n suggestion **argument, assumption, hypothesis, scenario, suggestion, theory** *The most plausible scenario was thought to be connected with the volcanically active moon Io.*
▸ explanation **explanation, interpretation, mechanism** *They argued that they could find no*

plausible mechanism which would be responsible for the effect.

- v+ADJ **appear, be, look, remain, seem, sound** *The significance of these observations is unclear, and it remains plausible that this is simply an effect of differences in the sleep/wake cycle.*

play N
a piece of writing that is intended to be performed

- adj+N types of play **classic, comic, morality, musical, mystery, one-man, one-woman** *This is an action-packed historical mystery play, with Elizabethan writer and poet Sir Francis Bacon as its central character.*
- ▶ for a particular medium **radio, stage, television, TV** *Do you think we'll see a new stage play from you at some point?*
- ▶ of a particular length **full-length, one-act, short** *By the end of the semester, students will have a developed idea for their full-length play.*
- ▶ good or successful **acclaimed, award-winning, brilliant** *Throughout his career he has directed numerous critically acclaimed plays and musicals.*
- v+N prepare a play **direct, produce, rehearse** *On weekdays, you will often find a theatre group rehearsing an upcoming play in the church hall.*
- ▶ perform a play **broadcast, perform, present, put on, stage** *The total number of plays performed is vast, and many lack real merit.*
- ▶ create a play **adapt, commission, devise, write** *Stuck at home full-time with kids, she wrote her first play, Mummy Make it Better, in 2003.*
- ▶ watch a play **see, watch** *We might go to a theatre to watch a play.*

plea N
1 an urgent or emotional request for something

- adj+N strong **earnest, eloquent, emotional, heartfelt, impassioned, passionate, plaintive** *He was an extraordinary figure whose passionate plea for liberty has relevance for every generation.*
- ▶ urgent **anguished, desperate, urgent** *Even the title of the new album seems an almost desperate plea for a new beginning.*
- ▶ repeated **constant, repeated** *Despite repeated verbal pleas from the police to put the weapon down, the man refused.*
- ▶ made at a particular time **final, last-minute, timely** *Just one final plea, don't forget to tell us if you change your address!*
- v+N make a plea **issue, make** *This gives me the opportunity to make a plea to parents to stand as school governors.*
- ▶ repeat a plea **repeat** *He repeated his plea for the decriminalisation of cannabis.*
- ▶ accept a plea **answer, hear, heed** *The majority heeded our plea following last year's event to clean up after your dogs.*
- ▶ reject or ignore a plea **dismiss, ignore, reject, resist** *The King ignored her pleas; he was blind to the passion of her feelings.*
- N+for **clemency, forgiveness, leniency, mercy** *He has a sense of fair play and justice, but he's not easily swayed by pleas for mercy.*

2 when someone says if they are guilty or not

- adj+N **guilty, not-guilty** *The acquittal rate for not-guilty pleas was around 40 %.*
- v+N **change, dismiss, enter, offer, submit, tender** *He has vowed not to enter a plea in protest at a law he describes as 'corrupt'.*
- N+of **ignorance, innocence, insanity** *The Bench accepted his plea of ignorance and dismissed the case.*

plead V
1 ask for something in an urgent or emotional way

- adv+V **desperately, earnestly, eloquently** *Alexander pleads eloquently for an education in both the sciences and the humanities.*
- V+for mercy **forgiveness, mercy, pardon, sb's life** *The farmer's face turned as white as milk, and he began to plead for pardon.*
- ▶ help **assistance, help** *The regional authorities in the Azores are pleading for help.*

2 say in court if you are guilty or not

- V+adj **guilty, not guilty** *The prisoner pleaded guilty.*
- V+n **ignorance, innocence, insanity** *He pleaded insanity at the trial, but it was rejected and he was sentenced to death.*

pleasure N
a feeling of happiness, enjoyment, or satisfaction

- adj+N strong **absolute, enormous, great, immense, intense** *His painting has given immense pleasure to people across the world.*
- ▶ physical or not spiritual **carnal, earthly, hedonistic, sensual, sensuous, sexual, worldly** *The advocate generosity to the poor, and they rebuke all worldly pleasures.*
- ▶ not normal or healthy **dubious, guilty, perverse, sadistic, vicarious** *It's a dreadful movie, but there's a certain perverse pleasure to be taken in its sheer awfulness.*
- ▶ simple **genuine, innocent, pure, sheer, simple** *I think there is a case for doing subjects that simply stretch the mind, for the sheer pleasure of learning.*
- ▶ types of pleasure **aesthetic, aural, dining, driving, listening, reading, shopping, viewing** *Lucio selects the best new music for your aural pleasure.*
- v+N give pleasure **afford, bring, give** *It gives me great personal satisfaction to create jewellery which then brings pleasure to other people.*
- ▶ get pleasure **derive, discover, experience, feel, find, have, take, taste** *We take particular pleasure in sharing your visit and helping you make the mo. of it.*
- ▶ show that you feel pleasure **communicate, expres show** *The Director expressed her pleasure at being asked to take over the project.*
- ▶ increase pleasure **enhance, heighten, maximize** *The pleasure is heightened by the fact that it is the middle of a British winter.*
- and/or **comfort, delight, enjoyment, excitement, happiness, joy, pride, satisfaction** *Ducks and geese are delightful birds and can give their owners muc pleasure and enjoyment.*

pledge N

a serious and public promise to do something

- adj+N serious or important **firm, historic, personal, solemn** *The first priority is the fulfilment of our solemn pledge to rid the world of nuclear weapons.*
- ▶ in politics **campaign, election, manifesto, pre-election** *Their manifesto pledges are like a litany of broken promises.*
- v+N make a pledge **affirm, make** *Last week, the party made a firm pledge that they would cancel the incinerator.*
- ▶ keep a pledge **fulfil, honour, meet, redeem** *We want the Government to honour its pre-election pledge and set a target for reducing packaging.*
- ▶ break a pledge **abandon, break, drop, violate** *The General Council promptly broke its pledge, to the delight of the mineowners.*
- ▶ repeat a pledge **reiterate, repeat** *I reiterate our pledge to reduce our own nuclear arsenal.*
- N+of **allegiance, love, loyalty, support** *We received strong pledges of support for our campaign.*

plight N

a sad, serious, or difficult situation

- adj+N very bad **desperate, dire, perilous, pitiful, sad, sorry, terrible** *Meanwhile, the B team knew nothing of the desperate plight of the main expedition.*
- ▶ current **current, present** *Like many Leeds fans, I would gladly trade those dark days for the reality of our current plight.*
- ▶ types of plight **economic, financial** *News of the club's financial plight was broken to the players on Wednesday.*
- v+N improve someone's plight **address, aid, alleviate, ease** *It requires a common will to alleviate the plight of the people.*
- explain someone's plight **explain, expose, highlight, illustrate, publicize** *The film highlights the plight of high school students in the Richmond area.*
- ignore or make worse someone's plight **ignore, neglect, worsen** *Does development improve or worsen the plight of third-world peoples?*
- N+of **asylum seekers, the homeless, orphans, pensioners, the poor, refugees** *This year, we run a day focussing on the plight of the homeless.*

plot N

a secret plan to do something bad

- adj+N evil **dastardly, devious, fiendish, sinister** *Their dastardly plot was ready for execution.*
- complicated **complex, elaborate** *The police concoct an elaborate plot to reveal the killer.*
- n+N **assassination, bomb, murder, revenge, terror, terrorist** *Air travellers face further delays after this morning's foiled bomb plot.*
- v+N create a plot **concoct, hatch** *A plot is hatched to restore Richard to the throne.*
- ▶ discover a plot **uncover, unravel** *In 1861, Pinkerton uncovered a plot to assassinate Abraham Lincoln.*
- make a plot fail **foil, thwart** *Haven't we foiled countless terrorist plots since 9–11?*

2 the main story of a book, film etc

- adj+N complicated **complicated, convoluted, intricate, labyrinthine** *The traditional convoluted plot has been replaced by a more simple storyline.*
- ▶ appealing **clever, gripping, intriguing** *Great stories, gripping plots and characters you really care about make these books ideal for the older child.*
- ▶ boring **predictable** *The early shows reflected the lack of cash, with predictable plots and relatively low production values.*
- N+v be about something **concern sth, hinge on sth, involve sth, revolve around sth** *The opera's plot hinges on the feigned death of one of the characters.*
  - *I have to stress that the plot revolves around a historical murder mystery, but religion and politics certainly play an important role in the unfolding of the story.*
- ▶ get more complicated **thicken, twist, twist and turn** *When the ex-wife of the doctor, Sarah, turns up, the plot thickens.*
- ▶ progress **move along, move forward, move towards, progress, unfold, unravel** *The problem lies in the film's inability to establish the main characters before the plot progresses.*

ploy N

a way of tricking or confusing someone

- adj+N clever or cunning **clever, cunning, cynical, deliberate** *I don't believe there is any attempt to mislead here, nor is the title a cynical marketing ploy.*
- ▶ obvious or usual **cheap, common, obvious, usual** *He expects his readers to have forgotten, or not noticed, his cheap ploy.*
- ▶ types of ploy **advertising, marketing, propaganda, psychological, tactical** *Is this just another marketing ploy, or is customised skincare really the future?*

plunge V

1 fall quickly from a high position

- adv+V down **down, downwards, headfirst, headlong** *The front of the boat plunged downwards and disappeared.*

2 if an amount or level plunges it suddenly becomes much lower

- n+V **price, profits, shares, temperature** *In winter, temperatures plunge to minus 36 degrees Celsius.*

3 suddenly go into a bad situation

- V+into **chaos, conflict, crisis, debt, depression, despair, poverty, recession, turmoil** *The thirties saw the world plunged into an economic depression.*

poem N

a piece of writing arranged in fixed lines

- adj+N types of poem **dialect, epic, lyric, lyrical, narrative, nonsense, satirical** *Why do we associate the epic poem with Homer?*
- ▶ short/long **long, short** *The interview will include discussion of a short poem which they will be given one hour beforehand.*
- ▶ funny/sad **funny, humorous, poignant, sad, touching** *One of the saddest poems was that on the cruel murder of his son.*

▶ about love **erotic, love, romantic** *Burns was writing his romantic poems all **about** shepherdesses and the grandeur of nature.*

▶ well-known/not well-known **famous, unpublished, well-known** *His most famous poem, A Drunk Man looks at a Thistle (1926), examined the spiritual nature of his home country.*

▶ favourite **favourite** *It would be hard to select a favourite poem from such an altogether pleasing book.*

● v+N write a poem **compose, craft, pen, write** *Paradise Lost may be one of the greatest poems ever written.*

▶ publish a poem **print, publish, reprint** *A book of his poems was published in 1919.*

▶ say a poem **read, recite** *Read your poems to the class or display the poems in a class book.*

▶ refer to a poem **quote** *Click here for references to the poems quoted in this article.*

▶ dedicate a poem **dedicate** *Even after their final separation in 1926, he was to continue to dedicate his poems to Gabrielle.*

poignant ADJ
giving you feelings of sadness

● adv+ADJ very **deeply, especially, extremely, particularly, unbearably, very, wonderfully** *There is something particularly poignant about Christmas time for the bereaved.*

▶ rather **quite, rather** *I also found Mahmut's relationship with his ex-wife to be quite poignant.*

● ADJ+n work of art **ballad, drama, lyric, memoir, poem, tale, tragedy** *The title piece is a poignant memoir of his family and of growing up in Leeds.*

▶ reminder **memorial, reminder, tribute** *It was a poignant reminder of how life could be nasty, brutish and short.*

▶ moment **moment** *Certain moments are nicely poignant, others are wonderfully funny.*

▶ ending **ending, farewell** *There's some delightful writing in this piece, with something of a poignant ending.*

▶ portrait **portrait, portrayal** *It's a poignant portrait of the innocence of a child caught in an tragedy created by adults.*

point N
1 an idea or opinion

● adj+N main **central, crucial, essential, important, key, main, major, salient, vital** *The key point is that your body views any change as stressful.*

A **moot point** is one that is open to discussion and cannot easily be decided: *How any undergraduate could possibly be expected to be 'original' in any meaningful sense is surely a moot point.* A **talking point** is one that people are eager to discuss: *The factory workforce all turned out to witness the move of the aircraft that had been the talking point of everyone since its inception back in 1944.*

▶ good **excellent, good, interesting, valid, valuable** *Mr Carr put forward some very interesting points in response to correspondence received.*

▶ first/last **final, first, last** *That brings me to my final point, which is how do we help give the Climate Group the focus that it needs?*

▶ not important **minor, trivial** *However, there are some minor points to be made.*

● v+N make a point **make, put forward, raise** *He raises some very good points, which I've seen before elsewhere.*

▶ explain a point **clarify, get across, illustrate, summarize** *You are very welcome to ask me to clarify any points or questions when you next see me.*

▶ discuss or prove a point **address, argue, discuss, prove** *The content analysis undertaken here cannot solidly prove this point one way or the other.*

▶ understand/not understand a point **get, miss, see, understand** *I thought maybe it was me who was missing the point.*

▶ emphasize a point **drive home, emphasize, hammer home** INFORMAL**, highlight, labour, reinforce, reiterate** *Good PowerPoint slides emphasise the points that you are making.*

2 an aspect or feature

● adj+N good **good, high, strong** *The section on interpersonal skills is obviously not the author's strong point.*

The **finer points** of something are the most important or interesting aspects of it: *Post match, there will be a bar and light refreshments for those who want to discuss the finer points of the game.*

▶ bad **low, weak** *It will probably become necessary to work on your weak points.*

pointless ADJ
lacking any purpose or use

● adv+ADJ completely **absolutely, completely, entirely, totally, utterly** *The film starts off with a completely pointless opening sequence aboard a boat.*

▶ rather **almost, fairly, largely, pretty** INFORMAL**, rather** *Such speculation is pretty pointless.*

▶ slightly **a little, slightly, somewhat** *Now that I think about it, that does seem a little pointless.*

▶ apparently **apparently, seemingly** *Despite the seemingly pointless situation of the entire protest, the day must be considered a success.*

● ADJ+n action or activity **activity, exercise, experiment, gesture, pursuit, task, waste** *This may all seem like a pointless exercise.*

▶ discussion or comment **argument, comment, debate, discussion, question, review** *The committee got bogged down in a pointless debate about why each drug is in a particular class.*

● v+ADJ be or become **be, become, be rendered, prove** *If no one buys the new products, then the recycling process becomes pointless.*

▶ seem **feel, seem** *In fact, it seems pretty pointless to try and duplicate his advice here.*

point of view N
a way of judging a situation

● adj+N a particular point of view **aesthetic, business, commercial, economic, environmental, historical, legal, military, moral, philosophical, political, practical, scientific, technical, theoretical** *When evaluating a project, organisations often want to establish whether it is worthwhile from an economic point of view.* ● *I think they are getting better advice, certainly from a moral point of view.*

▶ personal **personal, subjective** *This website is written from a personal point of view and not a medical one.*

● v+N have a point of view **adopt, have, take** *A journalist is, after all, entitled to have a point of view.*

▶ understand a point of view **see, understand** *We expect you to try to understand other people's point of view.*

▶ express a point of view **express, present, put across, put forward** *Show respect and sympathy to the customer by listening patiently, and then put forward your point of view.*

point to PHR VB
show the truth or importance of something

▶ V+n fact or possibility **existence, fact, possibility, reality** *All the evidence pointed to the fact that Danielle was the only one who could have done this dreadful act.*

▶ problem **danger, flaw, lack, shortcoming, weakness** *Scholars have rightfully pointed to flaws in survey research into attitudes of EU citizens.*

▶ difference/similarity **contradiction, discrepancy, inconsistency, similarity** *Sceptics take great delight in pointing to the obvious contradiction.*

▶ need **necessity, need** *Above all, they point to the need for regular oversight of these centres.*

▶ conclusion **conclusion** *I think the work of several of our leading developmental psychologists points to this conclusion.*

poised ADJ
about to do or achieve something

ADJ+for breakthrough, comeback, expansion, growth, success, victory *The business is – or should be – poised for explosive growth.*

ADJ+on the brink of, the edge of, the threshold of *In short, the climate system as we know it is poised on the edge of a profound transition.*

ADJ+infinitive attack attack, invade, strike *Rommel had driven the British out of Libya and stood poised to invade Egypt.*

poison N
substance that can harm or kill people

adj+N dangerous **dangerous, deadly, fatal, lethal, potent, powerful, toxic** *Almost all cyanide compounds are extremely deadly poisons.*
slow **slow** *Slow poison was so much more subtle: by the time it could be detected it was too late.*

v+N take poison **drink, eat, ingest, swallow** *The symptoms usually begin half an hour to an hour after ingesting the poison.*
give poison **administer, give sb, inject** *She made an impassioned speech for her own defence, in which she totally denied administering poison.*
put down poison **lay, spread** *Instructions for laying the poison are clearly printed on each packet and should be followed carefully.*

police N
people who try to catch criminals

n+N with a particular job **border, riot, security,** **traffic** *They blocked the roads around the plant and fought a long battle with the riot police.*

▶ in uniform/not in uniform **plain-clothes, uniformed** *Plain-clothes police officers targeted traders selling pornography.*

▶ types of police **armed, civilian, military, neighbourhood, paramilitary, secret, undercover** *The gunman was killed by armed police the next day.*

● v+N contact the police **alert, contact, inform, notify, summon, tell** *I would stress she does not have to contact the police if she does not wish to do so.*

▶ phone the police **call, phone, ring, telephone** *Over thirty people witnessed the attack on her, but not one of them came to her aid or even phoned the police.*

▶ help the police **assist, help** *When members of the public wish to assist the police, they can do so by contacting their local police station.*

▶ blame or not help the police **accuse, blame, criticise, obstruct, sue** *The doctors protested their innocence and accused the police of using torture.*

● N+n action or activity **bail, check, custody, investigation, raid** *We are protesting because we believe police raids could happen to anyone.*

▶ person **escort, patrol, spokesman** *A police spokesman said the farmers were not part of the protest.*

▶ vehicle **car, helicopter, van** *I was thrown against the police van while they frisked me.*

police V
use police officers to control something

● adv+V effectively **effectively, properly, well** *Only by effectively engaging with our diverse communities will we be able to police effectively.*

▶ severely **heavily, rigorously, strictly** *They strictly policed the demonstration, removing placards that were deemed inappropriate.*

● V+n event **parade, protest** *A huge security presence is required to police the parade through the town.*

▶ area **district, neighbourhood** *Find out more about those policing your neighbourhoods.*

policy N
plans agreed by a government, party, or business

● adj+N areas of policy **agricultural, economic, educational, employment, energy, environmental, fiscal, foreign, monetary, planning, public, security, social, transport** *It's hard enough for a British government to frame an economic policy for all of Britain.*

▶ national or local **domestic, local, national, regional** *The consultation claims that the government's regional policies are delivering results.*

▶ current or future **current, future** *It helps if you are aware of current policies affecting your area.*

▶ official **federal, government, official, state** *Her responsibilities include keeping senior managers up to date with government policies in the area of green technology.*

▶ clear or effective policy **clear, coherent, deliberate, effective** *The total lack of any coherent policy has been apparent to all.*

● v+N create policy **design, develop, devise, draft,**

formulate, make, plan *We have ensured that the medium of Welsh is considered when formulating new policies.*

▶ introduce or follow a policy **adopt, apply, follow, implement, impose, introduce, propose, pursue** *It would probably benefit all concerned to adopt a policy of cooperation.*

▶ decide policy **decide, determine, set** *All of these aspects need to be considered in detail before deciding future policy.*

▶ change policy **amend, change, reverse, review, revise, update** *It is your responsibility to review this policy from time to time.*

▶ influence policy **affect, influence, inform, shape** *The discussion forum enables us to influence policy both locally and nationally.*

● N+n making policy **decision, initiative, making, recommendation** *Expect to see significant policy decisions in this area.* ● *The European Women's Lobby Aims to increase women's impact on European policy making.*

▶ people who make policy **advisor, analyst, maker** *One aspect of this work has led to an IT based checklist for policy makers.*

▶ statement of policy **document, formulation, framework, paper, statement** *You can read our views on natural resources in our policy statements.*

▶ policy aims **goals, objectives** *Taken together, these two responses will help Ministers set policy objectives for the industry.*

▶ policy change **changes, reform, review** *The Party will lobby for a balanced package of policy reforms.*

polite ADJ
behaving towards other people in a pleasant way

● adv+ADJ very **extremely, incredibly, scrupulously, so, terribly, very** *The service was swift and the staff incredibly polite and efficient.*

▶ always **unfailingly** *Whatever you want, he is unfailingly polite.*

▶ rather **generally, perfectly, quite, rather** *I was only asking you in a perfectly polite way a simple rational question.*

▶ too **too** *She is not impressed by my materialism, but is far too polite to comment.*

● ADJ+n behaviour **gesture, manner, smile** *Polite manners are essential in company.*

▶ writing **letter, reminder, reply, request** *A polite letter to them to ask them if they would be willing to give a talk to your Group will do wonders.* ● *I have to take the time to write a polite reply that I can't do it.*

● and/or pleasant **charming, considerate, courteous, friendly, pleasant, respectful, well-mannered** *Our pupils are well behaved, polite and courteous.*

▶ helpful or efficient **attentive, competent, efficient, helpful** *Ensure your waiting staff are polite and attentive, yet not overbearing.*

political ADJ
relating to politics, or involved in politics

● adv+ADJ openly/not openly **blatantly, explicitly, inherently, intrinsically, openly, overtly** *The group said that their new album would see a return to their overtly political songs.*

▶ partly or mainly **essentially, fundamentally, mainly, partly, primarily** *Their main functions are religious and military, not primarily political.*

▶ very or completely **deeply, highly, intensely, profoundly, purely** *This seemingly trivial issue has become profoundly political.*

● ADJ+n thought or discussion **culture, debate, discourse, ideology, opinion, philosophy, power, theory, thought** *We will engage in and encourage the process of political debate.*

▶ people **activist, elite, leader, leadership, opponent** *There was a top-down democracy run by and for the political elites.*

▶ situation **climate, context, landscape, situation** *Has the political climate made us forget humanity?*

▶ conflict **instability, struggle** *France seems to be undergoing a period of intense political instability.*

▶ organization **institution, party** *The experience of urban parish councils is that political parties often control them.*

politics N
ideas and activities for getting political power

● adj+N for a particular cause **democratic, left-wing, nationalist, progressive, radical, revolutionary, right-wing, socialist** *He became involved in progressive politics.*

▶ relating to gender **feminist, gender, sexual** *To conclude, I reflect briefly on the implications of her work for feminist identity politics.*

▶ in a particular area **domestic, global, internal, international, local, national** *The whole book is a valuable source on the current activities and concern of NGOs in global politics.*

▶ types of politics **electoral, mainstream, parliamentary, partisan, sectarian** *He came to parliamentary politics relatively late.*

● v+N to into politics **enter, go into, practise** *In entering politics he was following in the footsteps of his father.*

▶ leave politics **denounce, quit, reject, shun** *Mowlan who quit politics in the last election, said the Prime Minister had become more presidential than she liked.*

▶ talk about politics **debate, discuss, talk (about)** *Robinson's main hobby was talking politics.*

▶ change politics **influence, shape, transform** *It is common to observe that British politics was enduringly transformed by the reign of Queen Victoria.*

poll N
an occasion when many people are asked their opinions

● adj+N recent **the latest, recent** *According to the latest polls, the percentage of Christian marriages ending in divorce is around 50 %.*

A *poll* is often called an opinion poll: *A recent opinion poll revealed that more than 80 per cent of people in Catalonia agree that bullfights are cruel.*

▶ types of poll **national, nationwide, public, reader, viewer** *A nationwide poll suggests most people would like the government to take more action to improve public health.*

- how the questions are asked **online, phone, telephone** *Have your say in this week's online poll.*
- informal **informal, quick, straw** *Feelings are mixed, as a pavement straw poll outside the office revealed.*
- how often **monthly, weekly** *You can have your say in our weekly poll.*
- v+N carry out a poll **carry out, conduct, do, hold, organise, run, take, undertake** *A poll was conducted during the program in which more than 8,000 people took part.*
- publish a poll **post, publish, release** *The National Institute for Mental Health has posted a poll on the members' discussion zone inviting your views.* ● *The five main UK polls published on the morning of the general election predicted a Labour lead of 0.8%.*
- pay for a poll **commission** *The BBC commissioned a telephone poll of viewers to find the greatest Briton of all time.*

pollution N

the process of damaging the environment, or the substances that do this

- adj+N affecting something **atmospheric, environmental, groundwater, marine, water** *Atmospheric pollution is global, and affects all soils, as does climate change.*
- caused by something **agricultural, airborne, carbon, carbon dioxide, chemical, industrial, light, noise, pesticide, radioactive, sewage, smoke, traffic** *To minimise light pollution, careful consideration has been given to the external lighting.*
- v+N cause or increase pollution **cause, emit, generate, increase** *The pollution is caused mainly by traffic emissions.*
- reduce or prevent pollution **avoid, control, curb, cut, eliminate, minimize, prevent, reduce, tackle** *Isn't the aim to reduce pollution?*
- check pollution **measure, monitor** *Many local councils monitor urban pollution to determine, for example, the effects of local traffic congestion.*
- N+n **abatement, control, emission, level, monitoring, prevention, reduction** *Substantial financial savings can be made from pollution prevention measures.*

ponder V

think carefully about something before reaching a decision

- adv+V with time expressions **again, awhile, ever, long, often, still** *My friends and I often pondered on the possibility of marriage and a family.*
- deeply **deeply, seriously** *He pondered deeply on all matters of seafaring.*
- V+n a mystery **conundrum, enigma, mystery** *I got on my bike, still pondering the mystery of the missing tombstone.*
- the meaning of something **implications, meaning, significance** *We should all ponder the implications of this.*
- a question or problem **fact, matter, possibility, problem, question** *Philosophers and scientists have been pondering this question for centuries.*
- the future **fate, sb's future, sb's next move** *Michelle is pondering her future in education.*

popular ADJ

1 liked by many people

- adv+ADJ very **enormously, exceedingly, exceptionally, extremely, highly, hugely, immensely, incredibly, massively, particularly, so, tremendously, universally, very, wildly** *Sandra has run hugely popular Dance and Yoga Holidays for the past five years.* ● *Colin was charming, universally popular with colleagues and adored by his patients.*
- increasingly **increasingly** *Nowadays, it is increasingly popular to ask candidates to fill in on-line application forms.*
- fairly **fairly, pretty** INFORMAL, **quite, relatively** *Ethical investments are now a relatively popular way of making money.*
- ADJ+n place **attraction, destination, location, resort, spot, venue** *Germany is becoming an increasingly popular holiday destination.*
- activity **game, pastime, sport** *Denmark has a long history of sea faring, and sailing is a popular pastime.*
- choice **choice, option** *Renting a holiday cottage is a popular choice for many people during the Summer.*
- culture **culture, entertainment, fiction, genre, magazine, music, series, show, song** *A writer in a popular magazine once described what she thought a perfect world would be like.*
- v+ADJ be or stay popular **be, prove, remain, stay** *Tuesday coached sessions are proving popular with members.*
- become popular **become, be made, get, grow** *High diving became popular amongst a small circle of enthusiasts.*
- seem popular **appear, seem** *So far, these sessions appear popular, with good attendances.*

2 held by many people

- ADJ+n **belief, misconception, myth, opinion, perception** *You seem to subscribe to the popular misconception that science is arbitrary.*

The expression ***contrary to popular belief/opinion etc*** is used to say that what many people believe is not actually true: *Contrary to popular opinion, a wedding isn't the end of anything but a new start.*

popularity N

the situation of being popular with many people

- adj+N great **enormous, huge, immense, incredible, overwhelming, renewed, tremendous** *We have a perpetual backlog of submissions due to the enormous popularity of the site.*
- growing **burgeoning, ever-growing, ever-increasing, increasing, rising, soaring** *Because of the ever-increasing popularity of aromatherapy, the demand for practitioners has never been greater.*
- recent **new-found, sudden** *Verdi's new-found popularity sprang not least from his own identification with the nationalist movement.*
- longlasting **continued, continuing, enduring, lasting** *No wonder this show has enjoyed such enduring popularity.*
- in many places **widespread, worldwide** *Salsa has origins in Cuban music but credit for its worldwide popularity belongs to the Puerto Ricans of New York.*
- decreasing **declining, waning** *The declining*

popularity of school meals is placing a strain on local authorities

- v+N gain, keep, or increase popularity **attain, boost, gain, increase, regain, retain** *Laser hair removal is gaining popularity as a method of permanent hair removal.*
- ▶ lose or reduce popularity **diminish, lose** *He began to lose popularity among his people.*
- N+v increase **grow, increase, rise, soar, spread** *Her album Fever sent the Melbourne-born singer's popularity soaring around the world.*
- ▶ decrease **decline, plummet, wane** *With a career spanning some 30 years, Paul's popularity has never waned.*
- and/or **fame, importance, influence, reputation, success** *Hunt was invited to give the sermon because of his current popularity and fame.*

populated ADJ
a populated area has people living there

- adv+ADJ heavily **densely, heavily, highly** *We live on a heavily populated island, and create a lot of waste.*
- ▶ lightly **sparsely, thinly** *This is considered a good little school in a very thinly populated district.*
- ADJ+n **area, city, country, island, region** *Toronto is Canada's largest and most populated city.*

population N
the people who live in a particular area

- adj+N types of population **civilian, ethnic, general, human, indigenous, native, resident** *Pro-government militias then launched reprisals against the civilian populations.*
- ▶ in a particular area **local, rural, urban** *The Town Council recognises that rural populations have special transport needs.*
- ▶ whole **entire, total, whole** *The municipality has a total population of around 25,000 inhabitants.*
- N+v increase **double, expand, explode, grow, increase, rise** *The background is that the population is rising by over 3 per cent per year.*
- ▶ decrease **decline, decrease, fall, shrink** *The population declined markedly from 1,460 in 1861 to 919 in 1961.*
- N+n increase or decrease **decline, explosion, growth, increase** *There are environmental arguments for population stability, but we do not need population decline.*
- ▶ figures **census, estimates, projections, statistics, trends** *The Home Office noted the need for population estimates by ethnic group and religion.*
- ▶ size **density, size** *The list does not take into account the population sizes of the areas.*

portfolio N
the set of investments or other things belonging to a person or company

- adj+N varied **balanced, broad, comprehensive, diverse, diversified, varied, wide, wide-ranging** *The UK needs a balanced portfolio of energy generating capacity from numerous sources.*
- ▶ large **enviable, extensive, impressive, large** *They*

recently announced a new addition to their already extensive product portfolio.

- n+N **asset, bond, client, equity, investment, loan, patent, product, property, share** *The company has a $400 million investment portfolio.*
- v+N expand a portfolio **broaden, develop, diversify, expand, grow, strengthen** *A good independent financial adviser will show you how you can diversify your portfolio.*
- ▶ put together a portfolio **assemble, build, construct** *We have assembled an exciting portfolio of investments.*
- ▶ manage a portfolio **manage** *As property managers we manage a portfolio of properties.*
- N+v a portfolio includes **consist of, contain, include** *The portfolio consists of more than 100 hospital sites across England and Wales.*

portrait N
1 a picture of someone, especially their face

- adj+N using a particular medium **engraved, pastel, photographic** *There is a black and white photographic portrait of him in 1937.*
- ▶ large/small **full-length, life-size, miniature** *Whistler alternated between small painting and full-length portraits.*
- ▶ making someone look more/less attractive **flattering, idealized, unflattering** *His more recent paintings include a rather unflattering portrait of the Queen.*
- ▶ looking real **lifelike** *A lifelike portrait by Hans Holbein hangs in the city museum.*
- v+N create a portrait **create, draw, paint, sketch** *Peter has painted iconic portraits of rock stars.*
- ▶ have a portrait done **commission** *Her husband commissioned the portrait to celebrate her 70th birthday.*

2 a description of someone or something

- adj+N showing affection **affectionate, sympathetic** *The book provides an affectionate portrait of this underrated artist.*
- ▶ including many personal details **candid, intimate, revealing** *This film is an intimate portrait of three generations of one family.*
- ▶ with strong details **vivid** *His report presents a vivid portrait of a political system under pressure.*
- ▶ making someone seem more/less attractive **flattering, idealized, unflattering** *His reminiscences also include unflattering portraits of his political colleagues.*
- ▶ sad **haunting, poignant** *It's a poignant portrait of the innocence of a child caught in a tragedy he cannot comprehend.*
- ▶ critical **satirical** *This novel includes a satirical portrait of Stalin.*
- v+N **craft, create, draw** *The director crafts a beautiful portrait of Cuban culture.*

portray V
show or describe someone or something in a particular way

- adv+V very clearly **graphically, powerfully, starkly, vividly** *The writer vividly portrays the dangers of the harsh Arctic environment.*

▸ very well **brilliantly, eloquently, excellently, magnificently, memorably, skilfully, superbly** *He lost several stone in weight to brilliantly portray a factory worker with insomnia.*

▸ in a way that seems real **convincingly, realistically, subtly** *He is a director with a talent for convincingly portraying human emotion.*

▸ showing sympathy for the subject **sensitively, sympathetically** *The film sympathetically portrays a lesbian relationship.*

▸ in a way that touches the emotions **movingly, touchingly** *The plight of young homeless people is movingly portrayed.*

> **Portray** is usually passive in these combinations: *Their marriage is touchingly portrayed.*

▸ accurately **accurately, faithfully** *We have taken great trouble to ensure that this Parents' Guide accurately portrays the school.*

▸ not accurately **falsely, misleadingly** *The advert falsely portrayed Roberts as a supporter of violent acts.*

▸ not in a positive way **negatively, stereotypically** *Many faith groups feel that religion is portrayed negatively in the media.*

n+V media **media** *The media habitually portrays young people in a negative light.*

actor **actor, actress** *How many actors have portrayed the Doctor in the series?*

artist **artist, author, cartoonist, painter** *He had been upset by the way he was portrayed by political cartoonists.*

work **advert, advertisement, cartoon, film, movie, novel, painting, photograph, poster** *Advertisements portraying an environmentally-friendly image are part of their strategy.*

ortrayal N

e way that something or someone is portrayed

adj+N honest, even about bad things **frank, gritty, truthful, uncompromising, unflinching** *'Mean Streets' is Scorsese's brutal, unflinching portrayal of violence.*

seeming real **convincing, realistic, vivid** *Wright's vivid portrayal of growing up makes compelling reading.*

accurate/not accurate **accurate, inaccurate** *It's a more accurate portrayal of the legal system than most thrillers.*

negative or unfair **negative, stereotyped, stereotypical** *The stereotypical portrayal of a drink-driver is as a man in middle age.*

showing affection or understanding **affectionate, sympathetic** *As a director, he is known for his sympathetic portrayal of women.*

skilful or subtle **masterful, masterly, nuanced** *Newman earned an Oscar nomination for his nuanced portrayal of the former sports hero.*

revealing many personal details **intimate** *The 90-minute film is an intimate portrayal of the Cuban leader.*

sad **moving, poignant, touching** *I found the novel a poignant portrayal of the effects of war.*

shocking or frightening **chilling, harrowing, haunting, searing** *This is a witty but chilling portrayal of the last decadent days of the French aristocracy.*

▸ in a particular form **cinematic, fictional, film, media, on-screen, screen, television** *The movie is a fictional portrayal of a modern-day Robin Hood.*

pose V

create or present something difficult that someone has to deal with

• V+n threat or danger **danger, harm, hazard, menace, risk, threat** *Members of the public may very occasionally pose a threat to staff.*

▸ obstacle or difficulty **barrier, challenge, constraint, difficulty, obstacle, problem** *Antarctica poses logistical challenges for researchers.*

▸ question **query, question** *Dennis then posed the question of what the next step should be.*

▸ difficult question **conundrum, dilemma, headache, paradox, puzzle, riddle** *This particle poses a serious puzzle in astrophysics.*

▸ something worrying **concern** *The effects of cyanides on human health pose concerns.*

position N

1 the way someone or something is placed, or the place where they are

• adj+N good or important **central, prime, prominent** *A placard hangs in a prominent position on the wall of the dressing room.*

▸ correct **correct, right** *The aircraft was now several miles off from its correct position.*

▸ exact **exact, precise** *They were able to locate their precise position using GPS.*

▸ horizontal, vertical etc **horizontal, upright, vertical** *He leaned to the left before returning to an upright position.*

▸ not moving **fixed, permanent** *Weights can be used to hold the patient's spine in a fixed position.*

▸ before being moved **neutral, original, starting** *Hitting this icon will restore the window to its original position and size.*

▸ same **same, similar** *He takes a photograph every morning from exactly the same position.*

▸ comfortable **comfortable** *Sit quietly, in a comfortable position with a straight back.*

▸ high **commanding, elevated, high** *The cottage is situated in a wonderful elevated position.*

▸ performing a particular action **driving, lying, lying-down, riding, sitting, standing** *You may feel dizzy when you get up quickly from a lying or sitting position.*

▸ in the world, in a country etc **geographical** *Apart from its strategic geographical position, Bulgaria is also famous for its exceptional natural landscape.*

▸ in sport **defensive, offside, pole** *He got caught in an offside position.*

▸ in war **commanding, defensive, offensive, strategic** *The ridge provided a natural defensive position and the Germans decided to dig in.*

• v+N get into a position **adopt, assume, get into, take, take up** *The seat allows the rider to adopt a natural, upright sitting position.*

▸ be in a position **occupy** *The group of islands occupies a very central position in the Indian Ocean.*

▸ change a position **adjust, alter, change, shift** *The referee will need to adjust his position throughout the game.*

▸ show or find a position **determine, indicate, mark** *These mark the positions of the roof timbers.*

2 the situation that someone or something is in

- adj+N strong or good **dominant, good, important, prominent, strong** *As market leader, we will strive to remain in this prominent position.*
- ▶ very special **enviable, ideal, privileged, unique** *You are in a unique position to help us.*
- ▶ not strong **weak** *Farmers are in an extremely weak bargaining position.*
- ▶ difficult or dangerous **awkward, compromising, dangerous, difficult, precarious** *If you are a teacher, you must tread very carefully so as not to put yourself in a difficult position.*
- ▶ current **current, present** *The documents relate to the current financial position of Thames Trusts.*
- ▶ same **same, similar** *Unfortunately, Northern Ireland did not make it to the World Cup, and Scotland and Wales were in the same position.*
- ▶ types of position **bargaining, competitive, financial, legal, market, negotiating, strategic, tax** *A solicitor can advise you about your legal position.*

- v+N be in a position **be in, hold, occupy** *Military factors still occupy an important position in state security.*
- ▶ reach a position **attain, establish, gain, reach, regain** *We are not yet at crisis point, but much work needs to be done to stop us reaching that position.*
- ▶ keep or strengthen your position **cement, confirm, consolidate, defend, improve, maintain, reinforce, retain, secure, strengthen** *Sales are up 9 per cent, confirming our position as the country's leading brand.* • *The supermarket continued to match competitor prices order to maintain its competitive position.*
- ▶ weaken a position **undermine** *Britain's global position was fatally undermined by the incident.*
- ▶ explain the position **explain, outline, state** *He outlined the position and told them what he intended to do.*
- ▶ change or consider changing your position **change, consider, review** *We met to review the position and to consider what lessons could be learnt.*

3 someone's opinion about an important issue

- adj+N official **official** *These comments do not reflect the official position of the U.S. Government.*
- ▶ common **common** *We are collaborating with other professional bodies to establish a common position on copyright law.*
- ▶ clear **clear** *The international community has a very clear position on the nature of his regime.*
- ▶ neutral **neutral** *'We have a neutral position,' said a spokeswoman.*
- ▶ types of position **ideological, philosophical, political, theoretical** *This work contains the fullest statement of his political position.*

- v+N take a position **adopt, assume, reach, take** *Mr Michel has tried in vain to push the EU into adopting a common position over Iraq.* • *We take the position that so-called 'crimes of honour' should be treated like any other acts of violence.*
- ▶ change your position **alter, change, reconsider, shift** *Jeffreys appears to have changed his position on the study.*
- ▶ explain your position **clarify, defend, explain, reverse, state, summarize** *In an interview shown on News at Ten, he explained his position.*

positive ADJ

1 expecting or indicating something good, or believing that something is good

- adv+ADJ very **enormously, exceptionally, extremely, highly, hugely, incredibly, really, strongly, tremendously, very** *We have had extremely positive talks with the city council.*
- ▶ rather **fairly, mildly, pretty** INFORMAL, **quite** *With the possibility of a record deal in the future, things are looking fairly positive.*
- ▶ mostly **broadly, generally, largely, mainly, mostly, overwhelmingly, predominantly** *The impact of the scheme on the local economy has been generally positive.*
- ▶ completely **completely, consistently, entirely, unambiguously, unanimously, unequivocally, uniformly, universally, wholly** *83 people attended, and feedback was almost universally positive.*
- ▶ compared with something else **equally, similarly** *Emiliana's endearing personality has evoked an equally positive response from the media.*
- ▶ in a way that is surprising **amazingly, refreshingly, remarkably, surprisingly, wonderfully** *The scheme has had a remarkably positive impact on young people.*

- ADJ+n attitude or mood **attitude, emotion, ethos, feeling, note, outlook, thinking** *In this session, we have aimed at fostering positive attitudes to learning* • *On a positive note, the treatment did not make an patients worse, although it does not seem to have worked for them.*
- ▶ reaction **comment, feedback, reaction, response** *The initial response from employees was overwhelmingly positive.*
- ▶ effect or influence **effect, impact, influence** *The positive effects of eating fresh fruit and vegetables as part of a healthy diet are well proven.*
- ▶ result **outcome, result, sign** *The team's first tournament of the season ended with a positive resul when they came second.*
- ▶ way of doing something **approach, manner, way** *We are looking for someone who thrives on change, with a flexible, positive approach.*
- ▶ contribution **benefit, contribution** *They have proved that they can make a positive contribution t the community.*
- ▶ action **action, move, step** *There are several positi steps you can take to improve the situation.*
- ▶ change **change, difference, trend** *Some companies reported positive changes, for example increased productivity.*
- ▶ aspect **aspect, attribute** *One of the positive aspects of the Scottish education system is that there is less social segregation than in England and Wales.*
- ▶ experience **experience, relationship** *The staff wor at developing a positive relationship with their customers.*
- ▶ encouragement **affirmation, encouragement, reinforcement** *Positive encouragement from you w contribute to the children's enjoyment and self-estee.*
- ▶ impression **image, impression** *The media should encouraged to portray positive images of disabled people.*
- ▶ message **message, publicity, spin** *The film puts across a positive message about tolerance.*

- v+ADJ feel **be, feel, think** INFORMAL *I began to feel*

very positive – convinced I had made the right decision. ● *I don't often despair about anything – think positive!*

▸ seem **appear, look, seem, sound** *The vast majority of those I have talked to seem very positive about the future.*

▸ remain **keep, remain, stay** *As professionals, we stay positive and we get on with the job of teaching.*

▸ be **be, prove** *Hopefully this change will prove positive, although it's too early to tell.*

2 completely sure

▸ adv+ADJ completely **absolutely, quite** *Are you absolutely positive about that?*

▸ not completely **almost, fairly** *I'm almost positive that it shouldn't cost £15 to travel from Euston to Soho.*

possess V

⊃ own or have an object, quality or ability

V+n characteristic **attribute, characteristic, personality, quality, trait** *If you believe that you possess the necessary attributes for this role, apply now.*

ability **ability, capability, capacity, faculty, power, skill, talent** *He possessed the ability to immediately grasp complex situations.*

knowledge **expertise, knowledge** *They possess an in-depth knowledge of client affairs, often gained over many years.*

good quality **charm, courage, merit, virtue** *Despite its many problems, the city possesses a natural charm.*

educational qualification **degree, qualification** *You must possess a relevant technical qualification.*

personal property **property, wealth** *Those who possess wealth possess political influence.*

something that may be illegal **arsenal, cannabis, firearm, weapon, WMD** *The police may revoke a certificate if they believe the holder no longer has good reason to possess a firearm.*

possession N

⊃ something you own

adj+N very valuable to someone **cherished, precious, prized, treasured, valuable, valued** *The painting of his son soon became his most prized possession.*

material **earthly, material, worldly** *We were marching with all our worldly possessions on our backs.*

personal **personal, private** *There was no storage space for his personal possessions.*

possibility N

⊃ the chance that something might happen or be true

adj+N strong or definite **definite, distinct, real, realistic, strong** *There is a distinct possibility that the virus may change into a very virulent form.*

obvious **obvious** *Cardboard coffins are an obvious possibility for people selecting woodland burials.*

great or many **endless, immense, infinite, limitless, tremendous, unlimited** *Combining and manipulating these images on my computer, I find the possibilities are endless.*

Usage *Possibility* is usually plural in these combinations: *As an artist, he explores the infinite possibilities of a world without boundaries.*

▸ slight **remote, slight, slim** *The clear benefits of breast-feeding should be weighed against the remote possibility of adverse effects.*

▸ exciting or interesting **exciting, interesting, intriguing** *This approach has exciting possibilities for researchers.*

Usage *Possibility* is usually plural in these combinations: *The idea raises interesting possibilities in terms of product placement.*

▸ existing in theory **future, logical, mere, theoretical** *The mere possibility of prosecution was likely to lead to more self-censorship.*

▸ different **alternative, different** *An alternative possibility is a commentary guiding the student through the text on an audio-cassette.*

▸ types of possibility **creative, practical, technological** *I find the creative possibilities the game offers utterly wonderful.*

● v+N discuss or examine a possibility **discuss, examine, explore, investigate** *The Board has explored the possibility of the sale of the company.*

▸ consider or admit a possibility **admit, concede, consider, contemplate, entertain** *He began to contemplate the possibility of meeting her by chance.*

▸ rule out a possibility **eliminate, exclude, exhaust, preclude, rule out** *The system eliminates the possibilities of cross contamination between patients.* ● *We should not blame a staff member before exhausting every technical possibility.*

▸ refuse to admit a possibility **deny, dismiss, ignore** *We cannot ignore the possibility that migratory birds played a part in transmitting the virus.*

▸ avoid a possibility **avoid, minimize, reduce** *This will minimize the possibility of anything going wrong with our service.*

▸ offer a possibility **allow (sb), offer (sb), open, raise** *This raises the possibility of future drugs being able to provide a cure.*

▸ mention a possibility **mention, suggest** *He didn't mention the possibility of deliberate abuse of the system.*

▸ face a possibility **face** *Many regions face the possibility of droughts.*

▸ take advantage of a possibility **exploit** *Military forces understandably seek to exploit the possibilities of cutting-edge technology.*

possible ADJ

⊃ something that is possible can be done

● adv+ADJ perfectly **certainly, entirely, perfectly, quite** *He accepts it is perfectly possible that evolutionary change moved faster at some times than others.*

▸ logically **logically, theoretically** *Isn't it logically possible that the universe should have contained nothing but two exactly similar spheres?*

▸ according to what is reasonable **humanly, reasonably** *The band like to play as many gigs as humanly possible.*

▸ equally **equally** *Although it is likely that many will prove to be correct, it is equally possible that some will be proved wrong.*

▶ from a particular point of view **physically, practically, technically** *It was technically possible to take the information from the database.*

▶ not likely or not often **rarely, remotely, scarcely** *Contrary to popular myth, it is rarely possible to state an exact time of death.*

> *Remotely* is often used with a negative word such as *never* or *not*: *It never seemed remotely possible that I would go to university.*

▶ only just **hardly** *I had such severe knee and joint pain that it was hardly possible to do my job.*

● ADJ+n explanation **cause, explanation, reason, source** *There are only two possible explanations to this case.*

▶ solution **answer, solution** *The concepts shown are amongst a number of possible solutions for the business.*

▶ result **consequence, outcome** *The table summarises what actions need to be taken and indicates possible outcomes.*

▶ effect **effect, impact, implication** *The report into possible effects on children living near the site has yet to be completed.*

▶ situation **combination, scenario** *The first task is to list all the possible combinations of 0s and 1s.*

▶ alternative **alternative, option** *There is time for you to get more information about possible alternatives.*

▶ way **means, route, way** *Our goal will be to support them in every way possible.*

▶ exception **exception** *He is the best tennis player I have ever seen, with the possible exception of Federer.*

● v+ADJ be or become possible **be, become, be made, be rendered, prove, remain** *Using genetic techniques, it has proved possible to pinpoint the genetic abnormality responsible for causing a rare disease.*

▶ seem possible **appear, look, seem** *It seems possible that he was in the Navy.*

▶ believe something is possible **believe sth, consider sth, deem sth, dream sth, imagine sth, think sth** *I soon found myself working harder than I'd ever done in my life, but also having more fun than I'd thought possible!*

> **Usage** In these combinations, *possible* usually directly follows the verb, referring back to the object which is a construction with a comparative, 'ever' or 'never': *Conditions got worse faster than I could ever believe possible.* ● *You will be challenged in ways you never imagined possible.*

post N
a job

● adj+N available **vacant** *The post of director of finance is vacant currently.*

▶ senior/not senior **junior, senior** *We plan to create two new senior teacher posts.*

▶ permanent/not permanent **fixed-term, locum, permanent, temporary** *Temping for a charity can open doors into permanent posts.*

▶ full-/part-time **full-time, part-time** *There are 21 full-time posts within the Fire Control Department.*

▶ types of post **academic, administrative, diplomatic, lecturing, managerial, ministerial, teaching** *An increasing proportion of women now occupy academic posts.*

● v+N have a post **hold, occupy** *He has held a postgraduate training post at The Royal London Hospital.*

▶ get a post **accept, secure, take, take up** *If the successful candidate accepts the post, she will not be able to start work until December.*

▶ leave a post **quit, relinquish, resign** *Curry unfortunately had to resign his post as Station Manager.*

▶ find someone for a post **advertise, appoint sb to, fill** *If a Nurse left the Trust, it would take a minimum of 12 weeks to fill the post.*

▶ pay for a post **fund** *Only one local school for children with learning disabilities currently funds a music therapy post.*

postpone V
decide something will be done later

● adv+V for a long time or permanently **forever, indefinitely** *She was under suspicion of murder, and her release was postponed indefinitely.*

▶ temporarily **provisionally, temporarily** *The planned surgery has been provisionally postponed.*

▶ more than once **again, repeatedly, twice** *The completion of the work has been repeatedly postponed.*

● V+n life event **honeymoon, parenthood, retirement, wedding** *People now need to work longer and postpone retirement.*

▶ election or competition **election, fixture, match, referendum** *We have decided to postpone the election until the Autumn.*

▶ start or departure **commencement, departure, launch** *The launch was postponed on 13 July after a problem with a hydrogen tank sensor.*

▶ decision or judgement **decision, hearing** *The hearing is now postponed to September 25.*

▶ meeting **AGM, meeting** *The board were forced to postpone the AGM.*

● and/or **abandon, adjourn, cancel, defer, delay, rearrange, reschedule** *The organisers reserve the right to postpone, cancel, or abandon the race in bad weather or bad light.*

posture N
1 the position of someone's body when sitting, standing, or walking

● adj+N upright **alert, erect, upright** *She should sit in an upright posture, with the chair supporting her lower back.*

▶ standing or sitting **seated, sitting, standing** *I slowly raised myself into a sitting posture.*

▶ lying down **reclining, recumbent** *In the painting the Bishop is represented in a recumbent posture, dressed in his robes.*

▶ good or comfortable **correct, good, neutral, relaxed, resting** *You need to pay attention to correct posture.* ● *The comfortable, arched shape holds your hand in a natural resting posture.*

▶ not good or comfortable **abnormal, awkward, contorted, poor, unnatural** *There were ceramic figurines of ballet dancers in various contorted postures.* ● *Poor posture and unsuitable seating often result in back, neck or shoulder pain.*

▶ bent **hunched, stooped** *The woman's great age co*

be guessed from her hunched posture and wrinkled
face.

▶ not moving **static** The photograph, judging by the
static postures of the figures, is a reconstruction after
the event.

▶ typical **characteristic** Weight gain at the front of the
body encourages the characteristic posture adopted
by most pregnant women.

▶ of the body **bodily** Humans have certain bodily
postures that we associate with aggression.

▶ v+N take up a posture **adopt, assume, take, take
up** Your physiotherapist will help you to adopt good
posture.

▶ change your posture **adjust, improve** Before you
step out, adjust your posture – knees bent, body
straight.

▶ keep or return to the same posture **maintain,
resume** The guard waved them through and
resumed his posture of vigilance.

● attitude or behaviour towards other people

▶ adj+N aggressive **aggressive, threatening**
Governments, through adopting threatening
postures, endanger the whole world.

▶ not aggressive **defensive, neutral, submissive** We
strive for a neutral posture and have appointed an
American-Palestinian as our Director.

potential ADJ
possible or likely in the future

ADJ+n danger or harm **damage, danger, harm,
hazard, liability, loss, risk, threat** Building sites are
full of potential hazards that can present a real
threat to personal safety.
problem **barrier, conflict, difficulty, pitfall,
problem** The joy of coming parenthood is often
coupled with fear about potential problems.
benefit **advantage, benefit, gain, saving, solution**
People need to understand the potential economic
benefits that can result from environmental
protection.
effect **consequence, effect, impact, implication** The
police were concerned at the potential impact of a
march on good community relations.
provider of something **bidder, buyer, client,
customer, donor, employer, funder, investor,
partner, purchaser, source, sponsor, supplier, user**
She was showing a potential buyer around the house.
receiver of something **applicant, audience,
beneficiary, candidate, employee, recruit, target**
We are responsible for selecting new students from
potential applicants.

potential N
the future possibility to develop or achieve
something

adj+N great **considerable, enormous, great, huge,
immense, incredible, massive, tremendous, vast**
There is enormous potential for the waterways to
play a vital role in the regeneration of the city.
maximum **full, maximum** We aim to encourage every
pupil to develop his or her full potential.
unlimited **infinite, limitless, unlimited** Every
human life represents almost unlimited potential.
real **real, significant, true, undoubted** If they are
not fit, they cannot play to their true potential.

▶ future **future, long-term** Increasing participation in
the labour market will help to raise the economy's
long-term growth potential.

▶ unused **unfulfilled, untapped** We should be more
innovative with our marketing, as there is great
untapped potential.

▶ of people **human** The fulfilment of human potential
is what all great schools should be aiming for.

▶ types of potential **academic, archaeological, comic,
commercial, creative, destructive, economic,
educational, expressive, productive, therapeutic**
There is a need for workspaces that make the most
of people's creative potential.

● n+N to earn or make money **earning, export,
investment, money-making, profit, revenue, yield**
The right qualifications can make a big difference to
your earning potential.

▶ to grow **expansion, growth** We see our biggest
growth potential in eastern Europe.

▶ personal qualities **leadership, sporting** Candidates
will have the chance to display their leadership
potential.

● v+N have or show potential **demonstrate, have,
offer, show** This is their chance to demonstrate
academic potential. ● I believe that I have the
potential to make it big within the film industry.

▶ use one's potential **achieve, fulfil, reach, realize**
Our aim is to ensure that every student realizes his
or her full potential.

▶ make the most of potential **develop, enhance,
exploit, harness, increase, maximize, optimize, tap
into, unleash, unlock, utilize** The task of harnessing
the potential of all staff in the creative process is
particularly difficult. ● The strategy aims to
maximise the development potential of areas of East
London.

▶ study potential **assess, consider, evaluate,
examine, explore, investigate** We are exploring the
potential of hand held devices with wireless internet
facilities for staff and students.

▶ recognize potential **appreciate, highlight, identify,
identify, recognize, see, spot, understand** He
recognized the potential for disaster was enormous.

● N+for growth **expansion, growth** There is still
great potential for growth in the market.

▶ improvement or advantage **collaboration,
improvement, savings** The report identified the
potential for further savings.

▶ problem **conflict, contamination, damage, disaster,
disruption, duplication, harm** Many substances have
the potential for harm if not used appropriately.

▶ use or abuse **abuse, exploitation, fraud, misuse**
These are interesting and unusual properties with
potential for commercial exploitation.

▶ confusion or error **confusion, error,
misunderstanding** Electors casting votes in order of
preference removes the potential for confusion.

poverty N
the situation of not having enough money

● adj+N very bad **abject, appalling, crippling,
crushing, desperate, dire, extreme, grinding,
severe, terrible** These are countries rich in resources,
but their people are suffering abject poverty.

▶ affecting very many people **endemic, mass, rife,
widespread** Unemployment is high and poverty is

---

rife. • *There is widespread poverty among mountain inhabitants.*

▶ hard to get rid of **chronic, entrenched, persistent** *The charity was established in response to the chronic poverty and environmental crisis in Africa.*

▶ in a particular area **global, rural, urban** *The idea is a series of concerts to highlight global poverty.*

▶ compared to others **absolute, relative** *In Nigeria, 75 million people live in absolute poverty.*

● v+N fight poverty **address, combat, fight, overcome, tackle** *We are asking candidates what they and their party would do to tackle poverty.*

▶ reduce poverty **alleviate, halve, reduce, relieve** *Increasing home ownership won't alleviate poverty, he says.*

▶ get rid of poverty **abolish, eliminate, end, eradicate** *Our goal is eradicating child poverty.*

▶ increase poverty **deepen, exacerbate, perpetuate, worsen** *Water related diseases exacerbate poverty and threaten lives.*

▶ experience poverty **experience, live in, suffer** *Lone parents and their children are more likely to experience poverty and ill health.*

▶ escape from poverty **escape, flee** *Emma dreams of escaping the poverty of the East End.*

● and/or additional problems **famine, homelessness, hunger, illiteracy, starvation, underdevelopment, unemployment** *World leaders committed to halving extreme poverty and hunger by 2015.*

▶ inequality or unfairness **exclusion, inequality, injustice, oppression** *The new president expressed his intention to deal with poverty and inequality in Brazil.*

▶ suffering or bad conditions **degradation, deprivation, destitution, hardship, misery, squalor** *He was horrified at the poverty and misery of these women.*

power N
the ability to influence or control others

● adj+N great **absolute, awesome, great, immense, mighty, sheer, supreme** *The UN has immense power; they can send troops anywhere in the world.*

▶ supernatural or magic **divine, magical, miraculous, psychic, superhuman, supernatural** *Prospero's magical powers allow him to take control of the island.*

▶ types of power **executive, expressive, judicial, legal, legislative, military, political** *This is an abuse of political power.*

▶ to do a particular thing **bargaining, decision-making, healing, law-making, purchasing, sentencing, spending, veto** *The system is less democratic because decision-making powers are held by one person.*

● v+N have power **have, hold, possess** *A mother has power over her child.*

▶ use power **abuse, exercise, exert, harness, use, wield** *In a democracy, judges must be able to exercise their judical powers independently.*

▶ give power **confer (on sb), give (sb), grant (sb), hand** *The Act conferred power on the authorities to prohibit public gatherings.*

▶ get power **acquire, gain, get, seize, take, usurp** *He seized power in a bloody coup.*

▶ lose or lack power **lack, lose** *Those who lack power are often silenced.*

▶ share or give away power **cede, decentralize, delegate, devolve** *Central government refuses to devolve power to local government because it thinks it is inefficient.*

▶ increase power **centralize, consolidate, increase, leverage** *Our aim is to increase people's power over their own lives.*

▶ reduce power **curb, reduce** *He failed in his attempt to curb the power of the Church.*

powerful ADJ
able to influence or control people

● adv+ADJ very **amazingly, awesomely, enormously, extremely, hugely, immensely, incredibly, massively, pretty INFORMAL, tremendously, very** *He sees global culture as driven by a few immensely powerful corporate interests.*

▶ unusually or particularly **especially, exceptionally, extraordinarily, particularly** *Television is an exceptionally powerful medium.*

▶ in a particular way **economically, emotionally, politically** *The number of women in politically powerful positions has not increased significantly.*

▶ really **really, truly** *Harper Lee's 'To Kill a Mockingbird' is a truly powerful and important masterpiece.*

practicable ADJ
able to be done or used successfully

● ADJ+n action **measure, precaution, step** *The company must take all reasonably practicable steps to ensure the health and safety of employees.*

▶ solution **remedy, solution** *Putting up a wall seems like the only practicable solution to the problem.*

▶ choice **alternative, option, proposition** *A bonfire may be the best practicable option for disposing of garden waste.*

▶ way **means, method, way** *Use all practicable mean to reduce risks.*

practical ADJ
involving or relating to real situations

● adv+ADJ very **eminently, extremely, highly, immensely, incredibly, intensely, perfectly, supremely, thoroughly, totally, uniquely, very** *The material is not merely very readable but eminently practical.*

▶ fairly or mostly **essentially, mostly, predominantly, reasonably** *The course is essentially practical, and skills will be acquired by doing rather than by listening.*

▶ in a good or surprising way **refreshingly, superbly, surprisingly, wonderfully** *Her approach is refreshingly practical.*

▶ strictly or completely **entirely, purely, severely, strictly, utterly** *When they planned the garden, the impetus behind it was purely practical.*

▶ really **really, truly** *Focus recently has been upon creating a truly practical signing system for babies*

● ADJ+n help or advice **advice, assistance, guidance, guide, help, suggestion, support, tip** *offer practical advice on issues such as careers, housing, and health.*

▶ knowledge or experience **experience, knowledge**

skill *Our advice comes from people with practical experience as volunteers.*

▶ solution or action **approach, solution, step, way** *The journal focuses on practical solutions rather than theory.*

▶ use or effect **application, implementation, implication, importance, purpose, signficance, use** *Are these notions just academic waffle, or do they have some practical implications?*

▶ aspect **aspect, consideration, reason** *The module concentrates on the practical aspects of solar astronomy.*

▶ problem **difficulty, issue, problem** *There may be practical difficulties in getting to the clinic.*

▶ example **example** *The delegates were shown practical examples of how enzymes are being used.*

▶ class or exercise **activity, class, demonstration, exercise, session, training, workshop** *The workshop will use a mix of presentations, practical exercises, and group discussion.*

● and/or not practical **academic, conceptual, creative, emotional, ethical, intellectual, moral, spiritual, theoretical** *Success is demonstrated through the practical and intellectual capability to both design and make quality products.*

▶ realistic **down-to-earth, everyday, hands-on, manual, proven, realistic, sensible, simple** *The Food Doctor for Babies and Children provides sensible, practical aid to ensure that your child has a balanced diet.*

practice N

1 way of doing something

● adj+N good **best, effective, good, recommended, safe, sound** *There are many excellent teachers and many examples of good practice.*

▶ usual **common, established, everyday, normal, routine, standard, traditional, usual** *It is standard practice to ensure candidates agree each application.*

▶ current **actual, current, existing, modern** *We feel some of the initiatives are no improvement on our current practice.*

▶ bad **bad, poor** *The majority of car accidents are caused by poor driving practices.*

▶ unfair **discriminatory, unfair** *The agency will consider whether unfair business practices have been used.*

▶ types of practice **agricultural, artistic, clinical, commercial, cultural, educational, environmental, legal, medical, religious** *The Government uses this judgement as the basis for accepted medical practice.*

▶ doing a particular thing **accounting, driving, employment, farming, management, nursing, teaching, working** *The Association offers advice on safe working practices.*

● v+N use a practice **adopt, continue, demonstrate, employ, follow, implement, introduce** *If more people adopted this practice, we would have fewer security problems.*

▶ share or encourage a practice **disseminate, encourage, promote, share, spread** *We will encourage sustainable land management practices.* ● *Members work together as a team to share best practices.*

▶ examine practice **evaluate, examine, review** *I would encourage all departments to review their practices and procedures regularly.*

▶ influence practice **influence, inform, underpin** *Further research is required to inform nursing practice.*

▶ improve practice **change, develop, enhance, improve** *This is a very useful document and I'm sure it will improve environmental practice at airports.*

▶ identify practice **highlight, identify** *We will produce a Household Waste Disposal guide highlighting best practice.*

▶ say what practice must be **ensure, prescribe** *Our staff comprises experienced therapists whose work is supervised to ensure good practice.*

● and/or **idea, policy, principle, research, theory** *The course is a stimulating blend of theory and practice designed to create graduates with the necessary skills to manage a business.*

practise V

1 repeat an activity regularly so you get better

● adv+V carefully **assiduously, diligently, hard** *On most days he practised assiduously, preparing for his violin lessons.*

▶ regularly **daily, regularly** *These exercises are easily taught by a physiotherapist and should be practised daily at home.*

2 work in a particular profession

● V+as legal jobs **advocate, attorney, barrister, lawyer, mediator, notary, solicitor** *Cole became the first Black African to practise as a barrister in the English Courts.*

▶ medical jobs **counsellor, doctor, GP, midwife, nurse, physician, psychotherapist, surgeon, therapist** *Val has been practising as a midwife for the last 13 years.*

▶ other professions **accountant, architect** *She originally trained and practised as an architect.*

pragmatic ADJ

emphasizing practical results or reasons

● adv+ADJ very **eminently, extremely, highly, very** *The book is highly pragmatic in its approach.*

▶ entirely or only **entirely, merely, purely, wholly** *The choice of what type of building to live in is not merely pragmatic.* ● *Humane treatment of political prisoners is preferable, even for purely pragmatic reasons.*

▶ mostly or rather **essentially, fairly, largely, pretty** INFORMAL, **rather** *The arguments in favour of the change are largely pragmatic.*

▶ in a way that is typical **typically** *Roger is typically pragmatic about the problem.*

● ADJ+n approach or attitude **approach, attitude, perspective, stance, view** *A pragmatic stance, rather than a humanitarian one, seems to have dominated their response to the deportations.*

▶ solution **compromise, response, solution** *We believe in pragmatic compromises rather than dogmatic ideology.*

▶ reason **argument, consideration, reason** *Our agreement should be based on pragmatic considerations of mutual benefit and not on a political agenda.*

● and/or **flexible, practical, realistic, sensible** *With their pragmatic and flexible approach, British troops demonstrated admirable peacekeeping skills.*

praise v
express strong approval or admiration

- adv+V enthusiastically **enthusiastically, extravagantly, highly, lavishly, roundly, warmly** *He had had two novels published, both of which had been lavishly praised by critics.*
- ▶ by everyone or many people **consistently, unanimously, universally, widely** *The symphony was almost universally praised.*
- ▶ by critics **critically** *He is the author of critically praised books about Fidel Castro and Pope John Paul II.*

> Usage *Praise* is usually passive in the three *adv+V* combinations shown above: *It was the most highly praised biography of the year.* • *The company was widely praised for its response to the crisis.*

- ▶ in a way that is deserved **justly, rightly** *She rightly praises the efforts of local people.*
- ▶ in public **openly, publicly** *Since taking office, he has publicly praised the insurgency.*

praise N
an expression of strong approval or admiration

- adj+N great **effusive, exaggerated, extravagant, fulsome, glowing, gushing, hearty, high, lavish, sincere, unqualified** *Since opening in 2003, the hotel has garnered lavish praise from travel magazines.*
- ▶ not great **faint** *They issued a statement that damns the new alliance with faint praise.*
- ▶ by everyone or many people **unanimous, universal, widespread** *The book has deservedly received almost unanimous praise.*
- ▶ deserved/not deserved **deserving, undeserved, well-deserved** *The composer joined those on stage to receive well-deserved praise.*
- ▶ types of praise **critical, verbal** *He won critical praise for his smaller independent films.*
- v+N give praise **bestow on sb/sth, heap on sb/sth, lavish on sb/sth, shower on sb/sth** *The manager heaped praise on his side after they came from behind to win the game.*

> You can also say that someone *sings the praises of* someone or something: *I have been singing your praises to all my friends and they want to meet you.*

- ▶ receive praise **attract, earn, garner, receive, win** *Despite these problems, the conference earned praise for its organisation.*
- ▶ deserve praise **deserve, merit** *The medical profession deserves the highest praise for this astonishing achievement.*

pray v
very strongly wish or hope for something, or ask God for something

- adv+V sincerely **earnestly, honestly, humbly, sincerely** *Peter was kept in jail, but the church prayed earnestly to God for him.*
- ▶ enthusiastically **devoutly, fervently, heartily** *He most devoutly prayed that his government might be prosperous.*
- ▶ quietly/loudly **aloud, loudly, privately, quietly, silently** *She raced down the stairs, silently praying that her feeling of foreboding might be unfounded.*
- ▶ all the time **constantly, incessantly, unceasingly**

She would pray incessantly that the real murderer might give himself up.

prayer N
words spoken to God

- adj+N **contemplative, earnest, fervent, silent** *Cromwell regarded the manoeuvre as the answer to his fervent prayers.*
- ▶ v+N say a prayer **offer, read, say, utter** *The whole school had an assembly and said some prayers.*
- ▶ repeat a prayer **chant, intone, recite, repeat** *They are told to recite Christian prayers six times a day.*
- ▶ say a prayer quietly **mumble, murmur, mutter, whisper** *I closed my eyes and whispered a prayer for a successful outcome to my journey.*
- ▶ answer someone's prayer **answer, hear** *Her prayers are answered and her son is safely returned.*

precaution N
something that is done to protect against possible harm

- adj+N sensible **common-sense, prudent, sensible, wise** *This may be a wise precaution under certain conditions.*
- ▶ good enough **adequate, appropriate, necessary, proper, reasonable, suitable** *The judge found that the company failed to take reasonable precautions against the risk of accident.*
- ▶ usual or basic **basic, elementary, simple, usual** *Too many people do not follow simple precautions to protect their property.*
- ▶ strict **elaborate, strict, stringent** *Elaborate precautions are taken to ensure that there is no fraud of any kind.*
- ▶ additional **added, additional, extra, special** *Police are urging residents to take extra security precautions following a spate of burglaries.*
- ▶ types of precaution **fire, hygiene, safety, sanitary, security** *Legislation requires that adequate fire precautions are in place.*
- v+N take precautions **adopt, exercise, follow, observe, take** *The best way to keep yourself safe when you're out is to take sensible precautions.*
- ▶ put precautions in place **implement, institute, put in place** *He instituted air-raid precautions including a black-out of London.*
- ▶ describe precautions **detail, outline** *This Code outlines sensible precautions for those visiting the countryside.*
- ▶ require precaution **need, require** *This task may require additional precautions, such as the wearing of gloves.*
- ▶ advise precaution **advise, recommend** *The guidelines recommend precautions for avoiding static electricity problems.*
- ▶ ignore precautions **neglect** *Target-obsessed executives have neglected elementary precautions in order to maximise output.*

precedent N
a past action as an example or reason for doing something

- adj+N bad **bad, dangerous, disastrous, disturbing, ominous, unacceptable, undesirable, unfortunate, unwelcome, worrying** *These sackings represent a very worrying precedent.*

▶ good **encouraging, useful** *His success in securing permission to write his finals in Scots is an encouraging precedent.*

▶ plenty **ample** *There is ample precedent for producing films for children with well-written dialogue and convincing characters.*

▶ types of precedent **artistic, biblical, classical, historic, historical, judicial, legal, scriptural** *His speech invoked historical precedents for the union of kingdoms.*

● v+N create a precedent **create, establish, set** *He warned that using force to impose democracy sets a dangerous precedent.*

▶ be a precedent **act as, become, constitute, provide, serve as** *This could serve as a precedent for other cases where 'crimes of opinion' are punished.*

▶ follow a precedent **follow** *Following a precedent set by the US, the EU announced a ban on 23 organizations.*

▶ refer to a precedent **cite, invoke** *He could cite various Biblical precedents for the use of song in the service of God.*

precise ADJ
exact and accurate

● adv+ADJ very **absolutely, exceptionally, exquisitely, extremely, highly, infinitely, perfectly, quite, surgically, very, wonderfully** *He was engaged in an exquisitely precise examination of the details of linguistic usage.* ● *What she means by this is something quite precise.*

▶ surprisingly **amazingly, incredibly, remarkably, surprisingly** *She spent, apparently, an incredibly precise 43 per cent of her time with her father.*

▶ rather **fairly, rather, reasonably, relatively** *Some students already have a fairly precise idea of the research topic which they intend to pursue.*

▶ enough/not enough **insufficiently, sufficiently** *The use of the words 'seven days' is insufficiently precise, and it would be preferable to stipulate 'seven working days'.*

in a particular way **historically, mathematically, scientifically, technically** *We take the photographs in a consistent and scientifically precise way.*

ADJ+n description or words used **description, detail, formulation, specification, wording** *We spent days haggling over the precise wording of our declaration.*

meaning **definition, meaning, semantics** *Uncertainty over the precise meaning of 'serious misconduct' is an area of concern.*

instructions **instruction** *It is difficult to give precise instructions covering all situations, so we have provided some general guidelines.*

estimate or calculation **calculation, estimate, figure, measurement, prediction** *These are difficult tasks requiring precise measurements.*

time or position **date, extent, location, moment, timetable, timing** *For urgent deliveries where precise timing is required, we can use an express courier service.*

movement or change **adjustment, alignment, positioning** *The cooker includes child safety knobs that allow precise adjustment.*

nature of something **mechanism, nature** *There are many diseases where the precise mechanism is not understood but the cause is established.*

▶ opposite **opposite** *Replacing human contact with computerised phone lines is the precise opposite of personalising public services.*

▶ cause or reason **cause, circumstance, diagnosis** *As for the precise cause of the accident, that is something that the coroner will decide.*

preconception N
an opinion formed without much information or experience

● adj+N false or negative **erroneous, false, negative, stereotypical** *The racial politics that inform his outlook are based on stereotypical preconceptions.*

▶ deep in a person or culture **cultural, ingrained** *Our preconceptions about groups of people are deeply ingrained.*

● v+N question or overcome preconceptions **abandon, challenge, confound, defy, discard, dispel, overcome, puncture, question, rethink, shatter, subvert** *The module aims to challenge preconceptions of what music is.*

▶ have preconceptions **have** *I'm sorry to say I had a very false preconception of how Africa and African people would be.*

▶ fit preconceptions **fit, match, suit** *It was obvious that he rejected the information because it did not fit his preconceptions.*

predicament N
an unpleasant situation that is not easy to escape

● adj+N very bad **appalling, desperate, dire, dreadful, perilous, precarious, terrible** *We can feed the vulnerable children, but food alone will not solve their dire predicament.*

▶ difficult or embarrassing **awkward, embarrassing, unfortunate, unpleasant** *He has put himself in a very awkward predicament.*

▶ current **current, present** *Indeed, she is partly responsible for the country's present predicament.*

● v+N be in a predicament **be caught in, be in, be stuck in, face** *Midwives face an appalling predicament when women refuse a caesarean in the late stages of labour.*

▶ understand a predicament **appreciate, realize, understand** *We then realized our unfortunate predicament: there was no way we could get back in time.*

▶ describe a predicament **describe, explain** *I called the breakdown service and explained my predicament.*

▶ solve a predicament **escape, overcome, solve** *She offered him an opportunity to escape his predicament.*

▶ make a predicament worse **worsen** *The company's predicament was worsened by delivery problems.*

predict V
say what you think will happen

● adv+V correctly **accurately, correctly, realistically, reliably, rightly, successfully** *He has made a name for himself by accurately predicting election results.*

▶ precisely **exactly, precisely** *You won't be able to predict exactly what will appear on your exam paper.*

▶ wrongly **incorrectly, wrongly** *Currently, around 50 per cent of students have their A level grades incorrectly predicted.*

▶ with confidence **boldly, confidently, safely** *The coach boldly predicted that his side would win the World Cup.* • *These are the people who we can safely predict will turn out to vote.*

▶ by many people **consistently, widely** *This did not constitute the severe earthquake which had been widely predicted.*

Usage **Predict** is usually passive in these combinations.

▶ using a particular method **mathematically, theoretically** *This effect was predicted theoretically using basic cell biology.*

● V+n result **consequence, effect, outcome, prognosis** *Cost analysis can help to predict the outcome of different policies.*

▶ fall/rise **fall, growth, increase, rise, shortfall, trend** *The British Airports Authority has predicted a rise in the number of passengers over the next ten years.*

▶ how likely something is **likelihood, occurrence, probability** *It's hard to predict the likelihood of your pet becoming ill or being injured.*

▶ how bad something is **collapse, severity** *Researchers are hoping to develop simple blood tests which could predict the severity of osteoarthritis.*

▶ future **future** *He said that the best way to predict the future is to create it.*

▶ behaviour **behaviour, performance** *If a child has a good understanding of emotions, then they are more likely to be able to predict the behaviour of others and respond appropriately.*

predictable ADJ
happening in the way you would expect

● adv+ADJ very **completely, eminently, entirely, highly, totally, utterly, wholly** *There were two overwhelming and entirely predictable responses.*

▶ in a bad way **boringly, depressingly, disappointingly, horribly, painfully, sadly, tediously** *It is depressingly predictable that there should be resistance to this proposal.*

▶ rather **fairly, largely, a little, pretty** INFORMAL, **rather, reasonably, relatively, slightly, somewhat** *Most of his stories were fairly predictable, with clear-cut heroes and villains.*

● ADJ+n result **consequence, outcome, result** *These were the predictable consequences of their policies, which were actually fuelling crime.*

▶ way of doing something **manner, pattern, routine** *Customers don't behave in a predictable manner.*

▶ reaction **reaction, response** *This was another predictable reaction from resentful locals.*

▶ story **ending, plot, storyline** *The ending is somewhat predictable, but the high quality acting compensates for this.*

prediction N
a statement about what will happen in the future

● adj+N accurate **accurate, correct, good, precise, reliable** *Her astonishingly accurate predictions are an invaluable asset to the American business world.*

▶ incorrect **false, inaccurate, incorrect, wrong** *All the experts' predictions were wrong.*

▶ specific **specific** *Specific predictions of tsunamis are not going to be possible in the foreseeable future.*

▶ about natural events **climate, tidal, weather** *Although they are made by the same sort of mathematical model, weather forecasts and climate predictions are really quite different.*

▶ involving amounts **mathematical, numerical, quantitative, statistical** *We have reached the very interesting point where we can compare the numerical predictions with the experimental observations.*

▶ saying that something very bad will happen **dire, gloomy, grim, pessimistic** *Despite dire predictions of a devastating wave of human disease, very few humans have contracted the infection.*

● v+N make a prediction **give, make, offer, provide** *In that article, I made a prediction which turned out to be drastically incorrect.*

▶ show that a prediction is correct **confirm, fulfil, support, validate, verify** *These computations have so far confirmed the predictions of her hypothesis.*

▶ produce a prediction **generate, model, produce** *Different numerical techniques now produce the same predictions.*

▶ make a prediction possible **allow, enable** *Newton's laws of motion generally do not allow precise predictions except in the simplest cases.*

▶ obtain a prediction **get, obtain** *The program offers users the ability to obtain tidal predictions for over 6,000 ports worldwide.*

▶ match a prediction **match** *As the images above show, the actual eclipse matched the predictions very closely.*

▶ improve a prediction **improve, refine, revise** *An understanding of how the infection is transmitted will improve predictions of how the epidemic will develop.*

preferable ADJ
more suitable or useful than something else

● adv+ADJ to a large degree **far, greatly, highly, infinitely, much, vastly** *Having 70 people moving smoothly and quickly on a bus is far preferable to having 70 single-occupant cars blocking the whole road.*

▶ clearly **clearly, obviously** *Wilhelm Stekel's method of psychoanalysis is, in my experience, often clearly preferable to Freud's or Adler's.*

▶ in a particular way **environmentally, morally** *The aim is to identify environmentally preferable products that meet basic quality specifications.*

▶ usually **generally, normally, often, usually** *Paracetamol is usually preferable, as it is less likely to have unwanted side effects, and costs less.*

▶ definitely **certainly, definitely, surely** *But if we allow ourselves to be influenced by the convenience argument, some methods are certainly preferable to others.*

preference N
a feeling of liking or wanting someone or something more than someone or something else

● adj+N personal **individual, personal** *In the end it all comes down to personal preference.*

▶ definite **clear, marked, particular, strong** *There was no single view but a strong preference for (b).*

▸ relating to a particular subject or activity **constitutional, cultural, ideological, political, racial, sexual** *In December 2003, the government introduced legislation making discrimination in the workplace over sexual preference illegal.*

▸ showing position in a series **first, second etc** *The voter may express a third preference, so that if the Liberal Democrat candidate is eliminated, then the voter can still influence whether a Labour or a Conservative candidate is elected.*

▸ general **general** *There was a general preference for the small group sessions rather than the set-piece lectures.*

▸ shown by a particular group **parental, patient, public** *It is unrealistic – and unfair to parents – to give the impression that parental preference can always be met.*

▸ different **different** *At the end of the day, different people have different preferences.*

● v+N have a preference **have** *If you have a preference, please let me know which day you prefer.*

▸ show a preference **exhibit, indicate, reflect, reveal, show** *In the first six weeks, babies show no preference for a particular person.*

▸ state a preference **declare, express, specify, state** *This section of the form allows you to express a preference for the school you want your child to go to.*

▸ give preference to someone or something **give** *The College gives preference to applicants with Mathematics at A level.*

▸ suit someone's preference **match, meet, suit** *There is a range of lodging in the village to suit all preferences and budgets.*

▸ know someone's preference **know** *Please let us know your preference when making your reservation.*

▸ on a computer **change, configure, reset, set** *Under the Options menu you can set various preferences for display.*

▸ choose **choose, select** *The restaurant can send a menu so we can choose our preferences beforehand.*

pregnancy N

the condition of being pregnant, or the period when a woman is pregnant

▸ adj+N affecting girls who are teenagers **teen, teenage, underage** *The UK has the highest rate of teen pregnancies in western Europe.*

▸ not wanted **unintended, unplanned, unwanted** *Contraception is really important as it can prevent unplanned pregnancy.*

▸ early **early** *Women need to take folic acid supplements during early pregnancy to help give their babies the best start in life.*

▸ late **late** *Researchers warned that scans in late pregnancy were now routine in many countries.*

▸ involving more than one baby **multiple, twin** *The first edition of this book was a landmark publication in establishing the study of multiple pregnancy.*

▸ involving a baby growing outside the organ in which babies grow **ectopic** *Tests over several days may be requested to rule out an ectopic pregnancy.*

▸ normal **healthy, normal, uncomplicated, uneventful** *Providing your pregnancy is normal,*

you can continue to exercise throughout the nine months.

▸ successful **successful** *From what you say, there seems every chance of a successful pregnancy.*

● v+N have a pregnancy **experience, have** *She had had a trouble-free pregnancy.*

▸ end a pregnancy **abort, end, terminate** *Women now have the well-established right to terminate an unwanted pregnancy.*

▸ prevent a pregnancy **avoid, prevent** *The following figures will give you some idea of which methods are best at preventing pregnancy.*

▸ plan a pregnancy **plan** *Most of them had not planned their pregnancies.*

▸ prove that a pregnancy exists **confirm** *The doctor called to confirm her pregnancy .*

▸ reduce the number of pregnancies **reduce** *For those interested in reducing teenage pregnancy the message is bleak.*

● N+n **advice, care, kit, problem, rate, symptom, test, testing** *I decided to do a pregnancy test as I felt that I was pregnant.*

pregnant ADJ

having a baby developing inside the body

● adv+ADJ very **heavily, hugely, very** *He travelled to Washington with his heavily pregnant wife and their two small children.*

▸ clearly **visibly** *It had only been 7 months since her last pregnancy and she was already visibly pregnant.*

▸ recently **newly, recently** *Benjamin drops out of high school to set up home with his newly pregnant girlfriend.*

▸ unexpectedly **unexpectedly** *When Eileen finds herself unexpectedly pregnant, her husband is determined the family should move to more spacious accommodation.*

▸ for a particular period of time **eight weeks, five months etc** *Lisa is four months pregnant and is said by friends to be 'thrilled'.*

● v+ADJ become pregnant **become, fall, get** *Joanne got pregnant at 17 while still at school.*

▸ look pregnant **look** *Does Melissa look pregnant to you in that picture?*

▸ make someone pregnant **get sb, make sb** *When Briony started being sick, he thought he'd got her pregnant.*

prejudice N

an unreasonable opinion or feeling, especially the feeling of not liking a particular group of people

● adj+N types of prejudice **cultural, national, political, racial, racist, religious, social** *In far too many firms, technicians and technologists, designers and production engineers are held back by the social prejudices and anti-scientific bias of the 'old boy' network.*

▸ personal **individual, personal** *What people say is rarely objectively factual, because the person's background, knowledge and individual prejudices and preoccupations usually determine it.*

▸ strong **deep, deep-rooted, deep-seated, ingrained, strong** *There was a strong prejudice against Government aid.*

▶ common **common, popular, widespread** *As well as coping with popular prejudice and frequent racism, asylum seekers arriving in Scotland face a real risk of falling into poverty.*

▶ unreasonable **blind, extreme, ignorant, irrational, unfair** *It should be a civilized and grown-up debate based on facts rather than blind prejudice.*

▶ not deliberate **unconscious, unwitting** *Steps will be taken to eradicate all forms of unwitting prejudice.*

▶ obvious **blatant** *When faced with blatant prejudice, don't be afraid to challenge it.*

● v+N have a prejudice **have, hold** *Do you think employers have a prejudice **against** young people who live on inner-city housing estates?*

▶ succeed in dealing with prejudice **counter, eliminate, overcome, remove** *We need to work hard to overcome the prejudice faced daily by people living with HIV.*

▶ experience prejudice **encounter, experience, face, suffer** *They remain a minority that has suffered racial prejudice for over 400 years.*

▶ fight prejudice **challenge, combat, confront, fight, reduce, tackle** *The association also aims to challenge prejudice within society against people with mental health issues.*

▶ make a prejudice stronger **confirm, reinforce** *It is important to understand that there are some widely used words and actions that are offensive because they reinforce prejudice and negative stereotypes.*

▶ show prejudice **reflect, show** *These views may be based on out-of-date knowledge or on rumour, or may reflect personal prejudices.*

● and/or **bias, bigotry, discrimination, fear, hatred, ignorance, racism** *If you have evidence of bias or prejudice, you should present this to your head of department.*

prejudice V
make someone form an opinion about someone or something before they have enough information

● adv+V unfairly **unduly, unfairly, unreasonably** *It could well be that the two women's costumes unfairly prejudiced us against them from the outset, but their performance left us rather cold.*

▶ seriously **seriously, substantially** *The trial was dramatically halted after the Sunday Mirror published an article which, the judge said, risked 'seriously prejudicing' the jury.*

● V+n **employer, jurors, jury** *Everybody would agree that disability should not prejudice an employer against recruiting or retaining someone.*

preliminary ADJ
coming before the most important part of something

● ADJ+n results **conclusions, findings, observations, results** *The preliminary results obtained show the effectiveness of our approach.*

▶ study **analysis, assessment, examination, investigation, research, study, survey, test, trial** *Hitler commissioned a preliminary study of the problems the military would experience in an attack on Norway.*

▶ data **data, evidence** *Preliminary data on the reliability and validity of the procedure are reported,*

and its potential applications in the care of the long-term mentally ill are discussed.*

▶ stage **round, stage** *The original fourteen teams had competed in two preliminary rounds earlier in the term.*

▶ design **design** *This is a very preliminary design, and the size and shape have yet to be finalized.*

▶ report **report** *The committee made no significant changes to the proposals outlined in its preliminary report issued last August.*

▶ meeting **discussions, hearing, talks** *An LG spokesman told Mobile: 'We have no comment on the reported interest in acquiring Siemens' handset unit.' However, LG is understood to have entered into preliminary discussions with Siemens.* ● *The new rules apply to any criminal proceedings such as a preliminary hearing, trial or sentencing.*

▶ act of reading **reading** *Ideally, they should come to the lecture having done some preliminary reading.*

▶ in a court of law **injunction, ruling** *The case was referred to the European Court for a preliminary ruling as to whether it was contrary to the Equal Treatment Directive.*

preoccupation N
1 a state in which you think about something so much that you do not think about other things

● adj+N current **contemporary, current, modern, ongoing, present** *The current preoccupation with terrorism risks overshadowing the need to eradicate poverty.*

▶ continuing for a long time **constant, lifelong** *His lifelong preoccupation with death became acutely personal in the 1980s when he became seriously ill.*

▶ much more than is reasonable **excessive, obsessive** *He has shown excessive preoccupation with the purely administrative side of the work.*

2 something that you think about and want to do because it is important

● adj+N main **central, chief, main, major, overriding, primary** *To provide for defence in a way that is not seen by neighbours as aggressive has been a major preoccupation of arms control over the last fifteen years.*

▶ current **contemporary, current, modern, ongoing, present** *Canadian music is one of my current preoccupations.*

▶ continuing for a long time **constant, lifelong** *In the camps, keeping up the spirits of the sick was a constant preoccupation.*

▶ common **common, usual** *A common preoccupation of much contemporary writing about world politics concerns the relationship between continuity and change.*

▶ only **sole** *Cuts in public expenditure seem to be almost the sole preoccupation of both national and local government.*

▶ relating to a particular subject **cultural, political, thematic** *These products embody many of our deepest cultural preoccupations.*

preparation N
1 the process of making someone or something ready for something

● adj+N good **effective, excellent, good, ideal, proper** *Good preparation helps you manage your* nerves and shows the employer that you really want the job.

▶ enough **adequate** The key here is adequate preparation and ensuring everyone knows what they need to do.

▶ not enough **inadequate, poor** Some barristers were criticized for last-minute or poor preparation of cases.

▶ careful **careful, thorough** He has already put months of careful preparation into this project.

▶ types of preparation **mental, physical** My role here will be to co-ordinate the physical preparation of the players.

▶ necessary **essential, necessary** Morton argues that four months is not enough time for the necessary preparation.

▶ much **a lot of, much** Much preparation has already been done for the audit, which will take place in the week commencing 26 April.

▶ not much **little, not much** In all too many cases, they have had little preparation for the task.

● v+N do preparation **do, undertake** Did you do any preparation for the role?

▶ need preparation **need, require** Good meetings don't just happen – they require a lot of preparation and planning.

▶ be in charge of preparation **coordinate, facilitate, oversee, supervise** She is responsible for overseeing the preparation of the advertising campaign.

▶ provide preparation **give, offer, provide** The course provides a valuable preparation for a wide variety of careers.

● and/or **cooking, implementation, planning, presentation, research, storage, training** Some time spent in preparation and planning is vital – but not to the extent that no real work gets done.

2 things that you do so that you are ready for something [always plural]

● adj+N final **final, last-minute** Final preparations are getting under way in London today for a spectacular £1 million firework display to mark the New Year.

▶ necessary **essential, necessary** The Board instructed him to make whatever preparations were necessary.

▶ special **special** Do I need to make any special preparations for your visit?

▶ military **military** The military preparations of the United States were in the initial stages.

▶ detailed **detailed, elaborate, extensive** Extensive preparations have been made to minimize any disruption to the public.

▶ v+N make preparations **make** Anna was making her preparations for going to Southend as had been arranged.

▶ start preparations **begin, commence, start** In June the 4th Army, under General Sir Henry Rawlinson, began preparations for an Allied counter-offensive on the Somme.

▶ complete preparations **complete, finalize, finish** The team are completing their preparations in Ulster this week.

▶ continue preparations **continue** Meanwhile, Bulgaria was continuing its preparations for accession to the EU.

▶ be in charge of preparations **coordinate, oversee**

The music was conducted in turn by three senior boys who had overseen the final preparations in the absence of the musical director, injured in a car accident.

prerequisite N

something that must exist before something else is possible

● adj+N essential **absolute, crucial, essential, indispensable, necessary, vital** Good comprehensive insurance cover is an essential prerequisite of any winter holiday.

▶ important **important, key, main** The ability to relate to customers from a diverse range of cultures is a key prerequisite for this position.

▶ basic **basic, fundamental** A basic prerequisite for doing business in any country is that you agree to abide by that country's laws.

● N+for development **development, growth, progress** Promote modernization of India's infrastructure as a prerequisite for the continued growth of the Indian economy.

▶ course of study **course, module** Many second-year courses are prerequisites for later modules.

▶ permission to take a course of study **admission, entry** Formal qualifications in mathematics are not a prerequisite for entry to the course.

▶ employment **employment** Knowledge of both Italian and German is a prerequisite for all employment in state administration and public corporations in South Tyrol.

▶ success **achievement, success** Investment in a well-educated workforce is now accepted as a prerequisite for economic success.

▶ process of taking part in something **membership, participation** Membership of the United Nations, furthermore, is not a prerequisite for membership of the WHO.

▶ peace **peace** The independence and territorial sovereignty of all nations is a prerequisite for peace in the world.

▶ democracy **democracy** A fundamental prerequisite for democracy is the principle of freedom of expression.

presence N

1 the existence of someone or something in a particular place

● v+N show the presence of someone or something **betray, demonstrate, indicate, reveal, show, signal, suggest** Finds of pottery, flint and stone axes indicate the presence of Neolithic communities in the 5th and 4th millennia BC.

▶ ask for the presence of someone or something **request, require** She was not continuously seen in the series but was only brought in when a particular storyline required her presence.

▶ feel the presence of someone or something **feel, sense** I could feel her presence.

▶ discover the presence of someone or something **detect, determine, establish, identify** When tests have established the presence of a kidney stone, the next step is to determine treatment.

▶ prove the presence of someone or something **confirm** The study confirmed the presence of two populations of wild boar living in Britain.

► explain the presence of someone or something **explain** *How else can we explain the presence of plant species found nowhere else in the world?*

► notice the presence of someone or something **note, notice** *Vigilance should be exercised in noting the presence of strangers or of unusual parcels or packages in the building.*

► show someone that you have noticed their presence **acknowledge** *The man acknowledges their presence but doesn't look directly at them.*

2 a group of people who are in a place for a particular purpose

● v+N establish a presence **create, establish** *Attacking Afghanistan would also help to establish an American presence in Central Asia (with its vast oil reserves).*

► increase a presence **build, develop, expand, increase, strengthen** *The King has sought to tighten his grip on the country by introducing daily curfews and increasing the presence of police on the streets.*

► continue a presence **continue, maintain** *We will maintain an appropriate military presence for as long as is necessary.*

► have a presence **have** *What other European countries does your company have a presence in?*

present ADJ
existing or happening now

● adv+ADJ **naturally, physically, regularly** *History staff regularly present research papers at leading national and international conferences around the world.*

● ADJ+n time **day, moment, time** *The museum tells the story of flight up to the present day.*

► situation **arrangements, circumstances, conditions, position, situation** *He went to see Mr Osman and told him what the present situation was.*

► person or group **government, member, occupant, owner** *The kitchen is in a single-storey extension added by the present owners.*

► system **arrangement, system** *We are working hard to make the present system more efficient.*

► level **level** *I would be extremely concerned if there were a reduction in the present level of service.*

► state **condition, form, state, structure** *He described the Church at the time as small, but very light, airy and neat, which is a fair description of its present state.*

● v+ADJ be present **be, become, remain** *Witnesses are not allowed to remain present in the proceedings after they have given evidence.*

present V
cause something such as a problem, threat, or opportunity

● V+n problem **challenge, difficulty, problem** *International operations, on any scale, can also present problems.*

► danger **danger, hazard, risk, threat** *The research concluded that, for adults, the normal use of mobile phones does not present a measurable risk to the health of the individual.*

► opportunity **chance, opportunity** *The scheme presents a significant opportunity to contribute to the long term regeneration of the town.*

presentation N
a formal talk in which you describe or explain something to a group

● v+N make a presentation **deliver, do, give, make** *She gave a brief presentation on a proposed scheme for developing the area.*

► be at a presentation **attend, hear, see, view** *In the afternoon, the meeting heard short presentations from four invited speakers.*

► prepare a presentation **prepare** *A colleague and I prepared a presentation about our project.*

preserve V
1 take care of a place or building in order to prevent it from being harmed or destroyed [usually passive]

● adv+V well **beautifully, excellently, perfectly, superbly, well, wonderfully** *Skara Brae is a well preserved village dating from 2500BC.*

► carefully **carefully, faithfully, lovingly** *The city possesses a wealth of superb architecture that has been carefully preserved.*

► badly **badly, poorly** *The wood contains evidence of shell holes and trenches, though these are poorly preserved.*

2 keep something from changing or being lost

● V+n **character, freedom, heritage, history, identity, integrity, life, memory, peace, right, tradition** *Perpignan, once the capital of the kingdom of Majorca, has managed to preserve its Spanish heritage.*

press N
newspapers and news magazines

● adj+N for a particular area **foreign, international, local, national, provincial, regional** *We will be inviting the local press along to report on the day.*

► relating to a particular subject **financial, music, trade** *She also writes about pensions for the financial press.*

► having a particular quality **gutter, left-wing, mainstream, popular, quality, right-wing, tabloid** *This appalling racism is encouraged by right-wing politicians and sections of the popular press.*

► not controlled by government **democratic, free, independent, liberal** *They have rule of law, and protection of minorities, a free press, and a viable political opposition.*

► published every day **daily, monthly, weekly** *A lot of nonsense has appeared in some of the British daily press recently.*

● N+n **briefing, campaign, clipping, coverage, enquiry, freedom, report, statement** *Air disasters receive widespread press coverage, which often causes people to cancel flights.*

press for PHR VB
try in a determined way to achieve something

● V+for **action, ban, change, improvements, legislation, measures, meeting, reduction, reform, solution** *A group called the Chartists, which developed in the late 1830s, pressed for sweeping changes to the political system.*

pressure N

1 attempts to persuade, threaten, or force someone to do something

- adj+N great **considerable, enormous, great, intense, maximum, strong** *His father was himself an outstanding musician and exerted great pressure on the young Wolfgang to develop his musical abilities.*
- ▶ too much **excessive, extreme, heavy, undue** *Radio and television stations should be free to report news, comments and opinions without undue pressure from any quarter.*
- ▶ types of pressure **commercial, economic, financial, political, social** *We want to put political pressure on the government to end the deportations.*
- ▶ continuous **constant, continued** *Continued popular pressure led to the eventual suspension of the project.*
- ▶ increasing **growing, increasing, mounting** *Mounting international pressure soon forced an early end to the the fighting.*
- ▶ public **popular, public** *Don't underestimate the power of public pressure.*
- ▶ international **diplomatic, international** *International pressure will be essential to ensuring that this happens.*
- ▶ from outside a place or organization **external** *We also face external pressures to compromise.*
- v+N put pressure on someone **apply, bring to bear, exert, place, put** *Did they mean that the US was not putting enough pressure on the Israeli prime minister to make concessions for peace?*
- ▶ increase pressure on someone **add to, heighten, increase, intensify** *Consumer groups are also increasing the pressure on mobile phone companies to take action.*
- ▶ reduce pressure on someone **alleviate, ease, lessen, reduce** *School uniforms can be helpful in reducing the pressure on parents to buy expensive designer clothes for their children.*
- ▶ continue pressure on someone **keep, maintain, sustain** *We must ensure that the EU maintains pressure on the Peruvian government and offers support when appropriate.*
- ▶ resist pressure **resist, stand up to, withstand** *President Kennedy resisted pressure to intervene in Laos in 1961–62.*
- ▶ experience pressure **be under, come under, experience, face** *The Home Secretary faces irresistible pressure to comply with today's Supreme Court ruling.*
- ▶ fail or be unable to resist pressure **bow to, buckle under, give in to** *This is a fantastic band who do not bow to the commercial pressures of the music industry.*

2 a worried feeling that you get when dealing with a difficult or complicated situation

- adj+N great **considerable, enormous, extreme, great, heavy, immense, intense, severe** *It was apparent that she was under considerable pressure.*
- continuous **constant** *People feel overworked, under constant pressure, and inadequately rewarded for their increased efforts.*
- v+N experience pressure **be under, come under, experience, feel** *He was feeling the pressure in his new post.*

- ▶ understand pressure **understand** *They understand the pressures and pace of such organizations.*
- ▶ cause pressure **cause, create** *Working part time can create added pressure for international students, as studying in a different language and in a different academic tradition can be more time-consuming than for a UK student.*
- ▶ deal with pressure **cope with, deal with, handle, stand, take** *He simply could not handle the pressures of being a head coach at this level.*

prestige N

a good reputation caused by impressive achievements

- adj+N great **considerable, enormous, great, high, immense** *Men have much greater prestige and authority in the village.*
- ▶ low **low** *The artillery had the lowest prestige of all branches of the armed forces.*
- ▶ types of prestige **academic, cultural, moral, political, social** *A state grant allows her to study at university and thereafter to acquire social prestige as a secondary-school teacher.*
- ▶ in a particular place **international, national** *At that time, the U.S. feared that it was falling behind the U.S.S.R. both in technological advances and international prestige.*
- ▶ personal **personal** *Nevertheless, his office does not automatically confer influence or personal prestige.*
- v+N have prestige **enjoy, have** *For two thousand years, Egypt had enjoyed a prestige throughout the known world second to none.*
- ▶ increase prestige **boost, enhance, increase, raise** *It was not an essential building and it is thought that it was constructed in order to enhance the prestige of the abbey.*
- ▶ give prestige **add, attach, bestow, bring, carry, confer, lend** *The Festival's standing as a major UK arts event brings enormous prestige to our City.*
- ▶ get prestige **acquire, gain, get, win** *People in this category often join gangs to gain prestige in their peer group.*
- ▶ keep prestige **maintain** *Throughout the later centuries the village has always maintained a certain prestige, owing to its past history.*
- ▶ get or give prestige again **recover, regain, restore** *The ports of the East of Scotland never recovered the prestige they had in the Middle Ages.*
- ▶ want prestige **seek, want** *He had always wanted prestige and power and now his dreams were going to come true.*

prestigious ADJ

admired and respected by people

- adv+ADJ very **extremely, highly, hugely, particularly, truly, very** *Her performance earned her a highly prestigious Tony Award.*
- ▶ rather **fairly, quite, rather** *I was Captain of the Wales Youth side, which is quite prestigious.*
- ▶ in a particular way **internationally, socially** *They were mentioned in a recent edition of The Mathematical Gazette, the internationally prestigious publication of the Mathematical Association.*
- ADJ+n event **ceremony, competition, conference, contest, event, festival, tournament** *This*

prestigious event takes place at the National Exhibition Centre in Birmingham.

▸ prize **accolade, award, medal, prize, title, trophy** *The RIBA Stirling Prize is the UK's most prestigious architectural prize.*

▸ institution **institution, school, university** *It is one of the oldest and most prestigious universities in Greece.*

▸ publication **journal, publication** *The results of the research have been published in the most prestigious journal in the field.*

▸ organization **brand, client, company, organization** *Ballet Nacional de Cuba is one of the world's most prestigious dance companies.*

▸ place **location, venue** *Claire has played at various prestigious venues in and around London.*

▸ project **contract, development, project** *We are delighted to be working with the British Olympic Association on such a prestigious project.*

pretence N
behaviour that does not honestly express your real feelings, thoughts, or intentions

● adj+N **elaborate, fair, mere, plausible, specious, vain** *Union leaders accepted defeat in advance, with a mere pretence of consulting the rank and file.*

● v+N make a pretence **make** *She made no pretence of despair at the loss of his affection.*

▸ end a pretence **abandon, destroy, drop, end, give up, stop** *It's time to drop the pretence.*

▸ continue a pretence **keep up, maintain, sustain** *He kept up the pretence for the rest of his life.*

● N+of **democracy, impartiality, justice, neutrality, objectivity, piety** *The US failed to maintain any pretence of neutrality.*

pretext N
a reason you pretend to have in order to hide your real reason

● adj+N false **false, spurious** *New legislation is needed to protect consumers from individuals and companies who attempt to obtain personal or financial information under false pretexts.*

▸ slight or difficult to believe **flimsy, slight, thin** *The police constantly harass them and demand their identity papers on the slightest pretext.*

▸ providing an advantage **convenient** *He was executed using some convenient pretext.*

▸ difficult to believe **flimsy** *His view is that Britain and America invaded Iraq on the flimsiest pretext.*

▸ when emphasizing that something is just a pretext **mere** *The claim that nuclear deterrence is needed to avoid biological and chemical attacks is understood by many as a mere pretext to retain nuclear weapons forever.*

▸ likely to be true **plausible** *I managed to find a plausible pretext to see him.*

● v+N provide a pretext **afford, furnish, provide** *A 4-0 home defeat by Manchester United provided the pretext for sacking him.*

▸ find a pretext **discover, find** *He would usually find some pretext to go upstairs when I was around.*

▸ look for a pretext **seek** *Are the U.S. and Britain seeking a pretext for intervention in order to take advantage of Sudan's oil?*

▸ create a pretext **create, fabricate, invent** *They must not appear to be deliberately creating a pretext for war.*

prevailing ADJ
1 existing at a particular time or place

● ADJ+n situation **circumstances, climate, conditions, environment, situation** *So it was a question of making the best of the prevailing conditions.*

▸ rate **price, rate, value** *All our prices are subject to VAT at the prevailing rate.*

2 most common, or having most influence

● ADJ+n opinion **assumption, attitude, ideology, mood, opinion, orthodoxy, trend, view, wisdom** *The prevailing mood is summed up by a headline in the Baghdad edition of the London-based daily.*

▸ culture **culture** *We must recognize the prevailing secular culture of our society.*

▸ style **style** *About a century afterwards, the house underwent alterations, in conformity with the prevailing style of architecture.*

▸ practice **custom, practice** *He called upon the bishops of the province of Asia to abandon their custom and to accept the prevailing practice of always celebrating Easter on Sunday.*

prevent V
stop something from happening or someone from doing something

● adv+V **completely, easily, effectively, hopefully, necessarily, permanently** *The emergency measures put in place by the government effectively prevented this, however.*

● and/or **control, cure, delay, detect, manage, minimise, reduce, treat** *They recommend the use of the drug as a means of preventing and treating obesity.*

preventable ADJ
capable of being prevented

● adv+ADJ completely **completely, entirely, totally, wholly** *Most health conditions being treated by medicine today are entirely preventable.*

▸ easily **easily** *The message is that most fires in the home are easily preventable.*

▸ mostly **largely, mostly** *Problems with the teeth and gums in cats are largely preventable if you feed the correct diet from a young age.*

▸ possibly **potentially** *Even more tragically, 90 per cent of these cancers are potentially preventable.*

● ADJ+n disease **blindness, cancer, condition, disease, illness, infection, problem** *Aid agencies say 6,500 Africans die of preventable diseases daily.*

▸ accident or injury **accident, disaster, fire, incident, injury** *Every year, thousands of children are injured in preventable accidents involving toys.*

▸ death **death, mortality** *Obesity is the second biggest cause of preventable death in the United States.*

▸ mistake **error** *We have seen an increasing number of preventable errors within the NHS this year.*

▸ cause **cause, factor** *Most newborn deaths are the result of preventable causes such as infections, complications at birth and low birth weight.*

- and/or **avoidable, curable, predictable, treatable** *Millions of people in remote rural populations die every year from preventable or treatable diseases.*

price N
the amount of money that something costs to buy

- adj+N good **affordable, competitive, fair, good, great, reasonable** *Book in advance to get the best price.*
- ▶ low **cheap, low, minimum** *Online stores can sell these products at much lower prices and still make a profit.*
- ▶ high **high, inflated** *So don't put up with second-rate service and high prices when you don't have to.*
- ▶ special **special, unbeatable** *These posters are now available to our supporters at a special price of £1 each.*
- ▶ complete **full** *All tickets bought on the day will be at the full price.*
- ▶ usual **normal, usual** *Subscribe to the magazine today and save 28 per cent off the normal price.*
- ▶ including all costs **inclusive** *The Hotel is offering a special 3-course lunch served between 12 noon-2pm for an inclusive price of £16.95 every day of the Festival.*
- ▶ reduced **discounted, reduced** *I got another 20 per cent off the discounted price.*
- ▶ total **total** *When we accept your order we will confirm the total price that you will be asked to pay.*
- ▶ for goods sold in large quantities to shops **wholesale** *Power companies will, of course, seek to justify the increases by pointing to the steep rise in wholesale prices.*
- ▶ for goods sold directly to the public **retail** *Royalties usually pay around 2 per cent to 5 per cent of the retail price.*
- ▶ average **average** *In the district, the average price of a house has risen by around 40 per cent since 2001.*
- ▶ right or true **actual, correct, realistic, right** *We provide our clients with common-sense marketing advice and guidance to help them sell their property promptly and at the right price.*
- ▶ n+N **admission, bargain, commodity, house, market, property, purchase, share, ticket** *Average house prices increased by around 25 per cent between 2001 and 2005.*

> **Usage** *Price* is usually plural when used with *house* and *property*.

- ▶ v+N increase a price **double, increase, put up, raise** *The UK government recently increased the price of student visas.*
- ▶ reduce a price **bring down, cut, drop, keep down, lower, reduce, slash** *Just last week, we saw several leading supermarkets reduce the price of bananas by 21 pence per kilo.*
- ▶ pay a price **pay** *Their customers are used to paying really low prices.*
- ▶ agree a price **agree, agree on, guarantee, negotiate** *The difference with us compared with most other firms is that we will always agree the price in advance with you.*
- ▶ charge a price **charge, fix, set** *Rich countries set low prices for the goods that poor countries produce.*
- ▶ compare prices **check, compare** *Read product reviews and compare prices on over a million products.*

- ▶ offer a price **give, offer, quote** *We can offer very competitive prices.*
- ▶ be sold for a price **achieve, command, fetch, get, go for, obtain** *Rare and collectable toys have been going for record prices over the last decade or so.*
- ▶ want to sell for a price **ask, ask for** *We could ask a considerably higher price.*
- n+in+N **drop, fall, fluctuation, increase, reduction, rise** *Inflation is expected to decline because of a slower econnomy and a drop in fuel prices.*

pride N
a feeling of pleasure and satisfaction that you get when you, or someone connected with you, have achieved something special

- adj+N much **considerable, enormous, great, immense, much, particular** *You ought to take great pride in what you have achieved here tonight.*
- ▶ real **real** *There is a firm but exceedingly friendly relationship between teachers and pupils, and there is a real pride in the school.*
- ▶ strong **fierce** *The village has a strong sense of community spirit and a fierce pride in its history.*
- ▶ some **a certain, little, some** *German President Horst Koehler said: 'That a fellow countryman has become Pope fills us with a special joy in Germany – and also a little pride.'*
- ▶ reasonable **justifiable** *Mr Lambert told me with justifiable pride that this wine had recently won several awards.*
- ▶ easy to see **obvious** *The students' obvious pride in their achievement spoke volumes.*
- v+N have pride **feel, have, take** *You should have pride in what you do.*
- ▶ express pride **express** *Coach Craig Dowd expressed his pride in such a courageous performance by his young team.*
- ▶ share pride **share** *We do hope you will consider coming to Edinburgh, and share our pride in our city and our college.*
- ▶ give pride back **regain, restore** *By driving crime out we will be encouraging more people to shop locally, helping to restore pride and prosperity in our communities.*
- ▶ make someone feel pride **engender, foster, instil** *Her aim is to look after the area and to foster community pride.*
- ▶ damage someone's pride **bruise, dent, humble, hurt, wound** *The sinking of the Titanic humbled the pride of the British people.*
- ▶ not be too proud to change your mind **swallow** *The Government should swallow its pride and scrap their road-building scheme.*
- N+in achievement **achievement, performance, quality, success** *The UK fire service can take pride in its many successes.*
- ▶ appearance **appearance** *All staff take a pride in their appearance and ensure that they are well groomed when they arrive for work.*
- ▶ place **area, city, community, country, environment, neghbourhood, school, surroundings, town** *Only together can we crack this type of crime and restore genuine pride in our communities.*
- ▶ history **culture, heritage, history, tradition** *This is*

an opportunity to regain our pride in our heritage and our powerful links with the past.
▶ ability **ability** *We are constantly updating the product range and take pride in our ability to meet clients' ever-changing needs.*
▶ work **job, work** *There certainly was pride in a job well done.*

primary ADJ
most important

● ADJ+n aim **aim, goal, objective, purpose** *The primary aim of the report was to contribute information on the research findings from various mental health programmes.*
▶ cause or reason **cause, motivation, reason** *Councillor Ingram cited the war as his primary reason for leaving Labour and joining the Greens.*
▶ thing you are most interested in or concerned about **concern, consideration, focus, interest** *Here Kant shows awareness of the range of the world's religions, but his primary focus continues to be upon Christianity.* ● *Her primary research interests are Caribbean, African, South Asian and Black-British writers.*
▶ duty **duty, responsibility** *The fundamental principle of our approach to postgraduate training is that the student has the primary responsibility for her/his own learning.*
▶ job **function, role** *The primary role of the review has been to look at how effective the Council's legal services are.*
▶ method **means** *Ten years ago, the company moved to email as a primary means of communication.*
▶ where something comes from **source** *Plants are not only the primary source of food on earth, but they also supply oxygen to the air we breathe.*

prime ADJ
1 most important

● ADJ+n aim **aim, goal, objective, purpose** *Reduced energy consumption was one of the prime objectives of the project.*
▶ cause or reason **cause, driver, factor, motivation, motive, reason** *Human activities are the prime reason the world's oceans have slowly warmed over the past 40 years.*
▶ thing considered important **concern, consideration** *Animal welfare and the enrichment of their lives will always be our organization's prime concern.*
▶ thing concentrated on **focus** *These courses cover a wide range of language skills for non-native speakers, with the prime focus being on oral and writing skills.*
▶ thing providing information **source** *They should therefore be considered prime sources for the military historian and author.*
▶ job or duty **duty, function, responsibility, task** *The Air Force had the prime responsibility for UFO investigation.*
▶ importance **importance** *It is their editorial skills which are of prime importance when it comes to giving authors really practical help.*
▶ influence **influence, mover** *He was the planner and prime mover in the military and diplomatic preparation for war.*

▶ job **function, role** *The Wolves front line failed in its prime function of scoring goals.*

2 of the highest quality

● ADJ+n place **area, land, location, position, site, spot** *The main campus is an ideal venue, taking full advantage of the University's prime location in Cardiff's civic centre.*
▶ example **example** *Academies are a prime example of the innovation we seek.*

principle N
1 a basic belief, theory, or rule that influences how something is done

● adj+N basic **basic, elementary, first, fundamental, underlying** *The need for a thorough grounding in the basic principles of mathematics and statistics has never been more important.*
▶ important **core, guiding, important, key, overarching, overriding, underlying** *The University's animal research work is governed by four key principles.*
▶ general **broad, general** *The general principle in employment tribunal cases is that each party has to pay their own costs whether they win or lose.*
▶ main **essential, main** *One of the Government's main principles for addressing family issues has been that paid work is the route out of poverty for families.*
▶ from the beginning **founding** *One of the founding principles of the National Health Service was that health care should be provided free at the point of use.*
▶ types of principle **democratic, legal, scientific** *There is considerable discussion at the moment in the UK about the wisdom of adopting some legal principles developed in the United States.*

● v+N establish a principle **develop, establish, identify** *This report established some important principles.*
▶ explain a principle **cover, explain, illustrate, outline, set out** *The following example illustrates some of the principles set out in this article.*
▶ use a principle **apply, follow, use** *The problems of applying such principles in practice are therefore familiar.*
▶ support a principle **support, uphold** *The Council supports the principle of meeting a proportion of energy needs from renewable sources.*
▶ accept a principle **accept, adopt** *The government had finally accepted the principle that 'society should include in its economic structure some form of direct financial provision for the maintenance of children'.*
▶ make a principle less important **abandon, compromise, undermine** *Bukharin blamed Lenin for undermining the principles of the revolution.*

2 a basic moral rule or belief that influences your behaviour [usually plural]

● adj+N moral **ethical, moral** *In planning the study, ethical principles and cultural norms were carefully specified.*
▶ very good **high** *He was a man of high principles.*
▶ for everyone **universal** *Responsibility for one's own actions is a universal principle that we should not change.*

● v+N have principles **have** *He has been accused of*

having no principles because he changed his mind over three important issues.
▶ give up principles **abandon, betray, compromise** They seemed to have totally abandoned their principles in order to hang on to power.
▶ continue to have principles **adhere to, stand by, stick to** You have to admire them for sticking to their principles.

prior ADJ
happening, existing, or done before a particular time

● ADJ+n knowledge **experience, knowledge** Even those without any prior knowledge should pick up the basic skills in just one day.
▶ arrangement **agreement, arrangement, booking** Orders may be collected from our premises by prior arrangement.
▶ permission **agreement, approval, authorization, consent, permission** Your details will not be passed onto any third parties without your prior consent.
▶ warning **notice, notification, warning** Timings may alter without prior notice.
▶ meeting or arrangement **appointment, commitment, engagement** He had an important prior commitment, of course.
▶ discussion **consultation** Banks and credit card companies change conditions without prior consultation.
▶ achievement **attainment, qualification** Teaching should address the preferred learning styles of pupils as well as their prior attainment.

priority N
1 something important that must be done first

● adj+N important **absolute, clear, first, great, high, important, key, main, major, top** Burglaries are not always treated as a high priority.
▶ urgent **immediate, urgent** Our immediate priority at the moment must be to boost student numbers both at undergraduate and postgraduate level.
▶ not important **low** Many people in the local community viewed those issues as a low priority.
▶ relating to a particular area **local, national, regional** We believe that local people are best placed to decide local priorities.
▶ types of priority **corporate, political, strategic** Tackling child poverty is one of our top political priorities.
▶ relating to a particular time **current, future** This policy document seeks to identify future priorities.
▶ v+N establish priorities **define, establish, set** This approach sets out a clear framework for making choices and setting priorities.
▶ recognize priorities **decide, determine, identify** At the conference a number of priorities were identified.
▶ make someone or something a priority **consider sb/sth, make sb/sth** We need to make tackling corruption a priority.
▶ be a priority **be, become, remain** The need for speedy communications became a priority in Elizabeth I's reign.
▶ show priorities **highlight, reflect** The NHS of the future must reflect those priorities.
▶ agree priorities **agree** Bear this in mind when discussing treatment options and agreeing priorities and goals with the patient.

▶ deal with priorities **address, deliver** The aim is to give hospitals more freedom to address local priorities.

2 the importance that you give to something that must be done

● adj+N important **absolute, great, high, top** The government attaches a high priority to effective public involvement in local transport policies.
▶ urgent **urgent** It seems highly unlikely that the EU itself will take appropriate action, unless a conscious decision is made to give this matter the urgent priority it deserves.
▶ not important **low** As a result, projects given lower priority by the committee did not receive immediate funding.
● v+N have priority **have** People with disabilities can join the programme immediately and have priority for suitable training places.
▶ get priority **get, receive, take** In times of water shortage, newly planted trees and shrubs should take priority over established plants.
▶ give priority to someone or something **assign, give, place, put** The Council tries to help as many people as possible, but has to give priority to those in the greatest need.

prison N
an institution where people are kept as punishment for committing a crime

● v+N leave prison **be discharged from, be let out of, be released from, come out of, get out of, leave** Our aim must be wherever possible that those leaving prison have a job on release.
▶ avoid prison **avoid, escape** Some footballers have escaped prison simply because they were high-profile professional sportsmen.
▶ go to prison **enter, go to** Key recommendations include early interventions to prevent young people with a mental illness entering prison.
▶ send someone to prison **put sb in, send sb to, throw sb in, throw sb into** More women are sent to prison for shoplifting than anything else.
▶ escape from prison **break out of, escape from** Marsh's wife helps the criminal duo to escape from prison.
● N+n official **authorities, governor, guard, officer, official, staff, warden, warder** Rioting left ten prison officers and three inmates injured.
▶ period of punishment **sentence, term** A Spanish court has condemned an employer to a three-year prison sentence following a fatal accident for which he was held responsible.
▶ person being punished **inmate, population** The total prison population of this country is about 75,000.
▶ room **cell** The prison cells smelt of damp.
▶ conditions **conditions, life** Prison conditions are growing progressively worse as the government fails to tackle overcrowding.

privacy N
the freedom to do things without other people watching you or knowing what you are doing

● adj+N complete **absolute, complete, maximum,**

strict, total *The Mountain View Suite is for those looking for complete privacy.*
▶ personal **individual, personal** *Britain's first law protecting personal privacy on a more general basis was included in Queen's Speech in May 1997.*
▶ more **added, extra, greater, more** *They aim to ensure better facilities for patients with a comfortable environment and more privacy.*
▶ not much **little, not much** *There's little privacy and, at busy times, it can be difficult for people to concentrate.*

● v+N protect privacy **ensure, guarantee, maintain, preserve, protect, respect, safeguard** *Those people who wish to protect their privacy may use a Box Number for their correspondence.*
▶ spoil someone's privacy **breach, compromise, disturb, infringe, intrude on, invade, violate** *It is not our intention to invade your privacy in carrying out such checks.*
▶ provide privacy **afford, allow, give, offer, provide** *Screens were used from early on in China as decorative items and to provide privacy within a living area.*
▶ consider privacy important **value** *Keane rarely courted publicity and was famed for valuing his privacy.*

privilege N
a special benefit or right available only to some people

● adj+N great **absolute, enormous, extraordinary, great, huge, immense, real, tremendous** *It is an immense privilege to accept this award.*
▶ not as good as it seems **doubtful, dubious** *Alan has the dubious privilege of being the person I'm going to work with.*
▶ for only one person or group **exclusive, monopoly, peculiar, unique** *Certain English kings granted exclusive trading privileges to favoured merchants.*
▶ rare **rare** *It is a rare privilege to have an audience with a king.*
▶ special **special** *We want civil and religious liberty for all and special privileges for none.*

● v+N have a privilege **benefit from, enjoy, have, possess** *The wealthy and powerful enjoy many privileges.*
▶ be given a privilege **be entitled to, gain, get, receive** *Older students receive many privileges.*
▶ use a privilege **claim, exercise** *Previously, free postage had been available to Members of Parliament, who could exercise their privilege for official purposes.*
▶ give someone a privilege **afford sb, assign (sb), confer, give (sb), grant sb** *Membership of the club confers enormous privileges.*
▶ not give or take away a privilege **deny sb, revoke, withdraw** *This child is being denied the privilege of seeing his father .*
▶ abuse a privilege **abuse** *Everyone has my number in case they need to contact me in between visits, but they hardly ever abuse the privilege.*

privileged ADJ
having special advantages and opportunities

● adv+ADJ very **enormously, extremely, highly,**
immensely, incredibly, really INFORMAL, **very** *I feel immensely privileged and honoured to be invited.*
▶ rather **quite, relatively** *In the UK, we enjoy a relatively privileged position in the world.*
▶ having a privilege that no one else has **uniquely** *You could say that the 'modern' period begins in 1969, when a uniquely privileged man put his lonely footprint on the moon.*

● ADJ+n group **caste, class, elite, minority** *All such information should be made available to everyone, and not just to a privileged elite.*
▶ childhood or family **background, childhood, upbringing** *He was born into an aristocratic family and had a highly privileged upbringing.*
▶ position **position, status** *We're in the privileged position of being able to pay the loan back early.*

prize N
a reward for success in a sport or competition

● adj+N important or special **amazing, big, coveted, fabulous, fantastic, generous, glittering, major, prestigious, special, ultimate** *We are delighted that the Museum has been shortlisted for this prestigious prize.*
▶ first **first, jackpot, top** *The regional winners will go through to the next round, and have the chance to win the top prize of £25,000.*
▶ second **runner-up, second** *Winner and runner-up prizes will be awarded in each of the two age categories 7–10 and 11–14.*
▶ for coming last **booby, consolation** *Dusty Bin was the booby prize on which TV gameshow?*
▶ in the form of money **cash, monetary** *A competition with cash prizes for the highest scores adds a little zest to the proceedings.*

● v+N win a prize **claim, clinch, collect, land, receive, scoop, win** *The competition is open to everybody, and there is the opportunity of winning some amazing prizes.*
▶ give a prize **award, give, offer, present** *Prizes were awarded for the best poster.*
▶ deserve a prize **deserve** *I think everyone that stops smoking deserves a prize.*

● v+for+N **compete, consider, nominate, qualify, shortlist** *She was shortlisted for the Turner prize in 1987.*

probability N
a measure of how likely something is

● adj+N high **great, high, real, reasonable, significant, strong** *There is a high probability that any soya-bean meal imported into the EU will be from GM sources.*
▶ low **low, small** *There was a low probability of the information being true.*
▶ equal **equal** *All anwers have an equal probability o, being correct.*
▶ based on scientific methods **mathematical, statistical** *The hospital uses a program that calculates the patient's statistical probablity of dying*

● v+N calculate or guess the probabilty of something **assess, calculate, determine, establish, estimate, evaluate, find, predict, quantify** *He was one of the first to calculate the probability of* *collisions between the asteroids and the major planets.*

▶ increase the probability of something **enhance, improve, increase, maximize, raise** *The key question is how to increase the probability of success in this competitive environment.*

▶ reduce the probability of something **decrease, lessen, lower, minimize, reduce** *Race alone does not directly increase or decrease the probability that a child will be poor.*

▶ affect the probability of something **influence** *Similar factors are found to influence the probability of both boys and girls attending and completing school.*

▶ show the probability of something **indicate** *The volcano's condition indicates a high probability for an eruption to occur in the immediate future.*

probable ADJ
likely to happen or be true

● adv+ADJ **entirely, equally, extremely, highly, increasingly, quite, reasonably, statistically, very** *At some point in your family's past, it is highly probable that a direct ancestor arrived from overseas.*

● ADJ+n result or effect **consequence, effect, impact, outcome, result, scenario** *It is too early to forecast the probable outcome of their efforts.*

● cause or reason **cause, diagnosis, explanation, reason** *That doesn't seem to me a very probable explanation.*

● origin **origin, source** *Central Africa was the most probable source of the infection.*

● number or amount **cost, date, loss, value** *The company faces collapse, with the probable loss of 10,000 jobs.*

problem N
something that causes trouble or difficulty

● adj+N serious **acute, big, fundamental, huge, major, real, serious, severe, significant, urgent** *The risk of flooding is a major problem in this area.*

● main **central, key, main** *I think the main problem is that we have too many overpaid players.*

● not serious **little** INFORMAL**, minor, slight, small** *He had slight problems with some of the hard to pronounce names.*

● difficult **complex, difficult, intractable** *In practice, most problems are too complex for this approach.*

● common **common, global, widespread** *Shrinkage and cracking in concrete flooring is a common problem facing the builder.*

● possible **possible, potential** *A fire-detection system will identify and deal with potential problems at a very early stage.*

● not obvious **hidden, underlying** *There may be an underlying problem that is causing your illness or making it worse.*

● types of problem **behavioural, debt, economic, emotional, environmental, financial, health, logistical, mechanical, medical, practical, psychological, social, technical, traffic** *Any technical problems associated with installing the system should be referred to the technical support unit.*

● continuing for a long time **chronic, long-term, ongoing** *She was suffering from chronic health problems.*

▶ happening at the beginning of something **initial, teething** *Despite a number of teething problems, the project was a great success.*

● v+N cause a problem **cause, create, lead to, result in** *Water shortages could lead to environmental problems.*

▶ solve a problem **combat, correct, cure, fix, get around, get over, overcome, rectify, remedy, resolve, solve, sort out** *Violence should never be an accepted way to solve problems.*

▶ deal with a problem **address, approach, confront, deal with, handle, respond to, tackle, treat** *Over the past few years there have been several attempts to tackle these problems.*

▶ try to solve a very difficult problem **grapple with, struggle with, wrestle with** *Researchers have been grappling with the problems associated with the collection of accurate data.*

▶ make a problem worse **add to, compound, contribute to, exacerbate, increase** *Flood alleviation works need to be planned carefully to ensure that they do not exacerbate problems elsewhere.*

▶ make a problem less serious **alleviate, ease, help with, minimise, reduce** *This lack of investment in physical activity will do little to alleviate the problems of obesity and poor health.*

▶ experience a problem **develop, encounter, experience, face, have, run into, suffer (with)** *If you encounter problems while trying to view the full size images, please read the help page.*

▶ experience a lot of problems **be beset by, be beset with, be blighted by, be dogged by, be dogged with, be hampered by, be plagued by, be plagued with** *The service has been beset by problems and delays.*

> Usage In these combinations, **problem** is always plural: *The estate was badly designed and dogged by problems from the beginning.* ● *The whole production has been beset with problems.*

▶ be a problem **be, become, pose, present, remain** *International operations, on any scale, can present problems.*

▶ avoid or prevent a problem **avoid, eliminate, guard sb/sth against, prevent, protect sb/sth against** *The advantage of headsets over conventional speakers is that they eliminate any problem of feedback.*

▶ find out about a problem **come across, detect, diagnose, discover, identify, spot** *Any problems were quickly identified.*

▶ investigate a problem **investigate, look at, look into** *Call our helpline and we will look into the problem for you.*

▶ show that a problem exists **alert sb to, highlight, indicate, point to** *This disorder doesn't generally point to psychological problems.*

● N+v happen **arise, emerge, occur, start** *The problem arises when plants and animals are introduced to garden ponds that are from a different area.*

▶ exist or be caused by something **exist, lie, stem from** *The problem lies not with the public but with governments.*

▶ remain **persist, remain** *If the problem persists, then please contact us.*

● n+to+N **answer, approach, reaction, remedy,**

resolution, response, solution *Many ideas have to be considered before a good solution to any problem can be found.*

- v+as+N **identify sth, perceive sth, regard sth, see sth, treat sth, view sth** *An ageing population should be regarded not as a problem but as an asset.*

procedure N

a way of doing something, especially the correct or usual way

- adj+N normal or usual **established, normal, routine, standard, usual** *Standard procedures were used to withdraw people from the situation.*
- ▶ correct **appropriate, correct, formal, proper** *Problems can occur if you do not follow the correct procedures.*
- ▶ required by law **legal, statutory** *If formal permission is required, there is a statutory procedure for applying to undertake the work.*
- ▶ strict **rigorous, robust, strict** *Due to rigorous checking procedures, errors in the data are extremely rare.*
- ▶ complicated or long **complex, complicated, detailed, lengthy** *The analysis of the results is a complicated procedure.*
- ▶ simple **simple, step-by-step, straightforward** *If all this sounds a bit technical, it isn't, it's a really simple procedure.*
- ▶ types of procedure **administrative, bureaucratic, disciplinary, legislative, parliamentary** *Employers must inform staff about disciplinary procedures.*

- n+N for making a complaint **complaints, grievance** *The independent review is the final stage of the complaints procedure.*
- ▶ for ensuring safety **evacuation, safety, security** *All the staff and students need to know about safety procedures.*
- ▶ for deciding who to choose **admissions, recruitment, selection** *The admissions procedures for children with special educational needs are different from those for other children.*
- ▶ for checking or testing something **assessment, checking, evaluation, monitoring, testing** *The professional institutions will have to make sure that they have proper assessment procedures in place.*
- ▶ for applying for something **application** *We've covered how to find a course and the application procedure.*

- v+N follow a procedure **adhere to, comply with, follow, go through, use** *If you follow the safety procedures when you dive, you are unlikely to suffer a serious accident.*
- ▶ start to use a procedure **adopt, implement, introduce** *We have introduced a new simple procedure for student assessment.*
- ▶ make a procedure better **simplify, standardise, streamline** *We need to simplify the procedures for testing new students.*
- ▶ describe a procedure **define, describe, detail, explain, outline, set out** *This book of guidance sets out the Department's procedures for dealing with poor performance.*
- ▶ develop a procedure **develop, establish, set up** *To address these issues, we have developed a screening procedure.*
- ▶ change a procedure **change, revise** *The department recommends that child protection procedures should be revised.*

proceedings N

actions taken to settle a legal matter

- adj+N **civil, court, criminal, disciplinary, judicial, legal** *Legal proceedings may be the only method of resolving some disputes.*
- ▶ n+N **adoption, arbitration, bankruptcy, defamation, disqualification, divorce, extradition, impeachment, infringement, insolvency, libel** *Can I commence divorce proceedings straight away?*
- ▶ v+N start proceedings **bring, commence, initiate, instigate, institute, issue, start** *The Attorney-General instituted proceedings against the Editor of that newspaper.*
- ▶ stop or delay proceedings **adjourn, delay, discontinue, disrupt, halt, interrupt, terminate** *The proceedings were formally discontinued at Camberwell Youth Court on 29 July 1993.*

process N

a series of actions or events that are designed to have a particular result

- adj+N slow or long **drawn-out, gradual, lengthy, long, slow** *It can be a very long, slow process to develop a relationship of trust.*
- ▶ difficult or complicated **complex, complicated, difficult** *The complex process of testing the new drug had begun.*
- ▶ simple **simple, straightforward** *Life coaching is a fairly simple process.*
- ▶ continuing or continuous **continuous, ongoing** *We would like feedback to be an ongoing process, and we welcome all your comments – positive or negative.*
- ▶ done with great care **rigorous** *All applicants have to undergo a rigorous interview process.*
- ▶ types of process **biological, creative, democratic, evolutionary, industrial, legal, natural, physical, physiological, political** *Fumes and odour are produced in many industrial processes.*

- n+N for choosing someone **admissions, appointment, interview, recruitment, selection** *Personal qualities and experience are taken into account in the selection process.*
- ▶ for achieving peace **peace** *If it really wants to relaunch the peace process, it must stop acts of terror.*
- ▶ for finding out if something is good **appraisal, assessment, evaluation** *The person is at the centre of the whole assessment process and their 'needs' are its focus.*
- ▶ for making something **design, manufacturing, production** *The entire manufacturing process is carefully controlled and monitored.*
- ▶ for deciding or planning something **consultation, decision-making, planning** *We want staff to be more involved in decision-making processes.*
- ▶ for looking at past decisions **appeals, review** *The review process had revealed the need to revisit and clarify some of the earlier provisions.*
- ▶ for applying for something **application, registration** *Is the application process the same for mature applicants?*
- ▶ in the body **aging, healing** *Wrinkles are a normal part of the aging process.*

● v+N be involved in a process **be involved in, go
through, participate in, undergo** *Belfast is going
through a process of continuous regeneration and
development.*

▸ speed up a process **accelerate, drive, speed up** *The
process is accelerated by heat, light, and the presence
of water.*

▸ slow down a process **delay, slow (down)** *One thing
that slows the process down is having to go through
so many checks.*

▸ improve a process **enhance, improve, simplify,
streamline** *There has been a lot of discussion about
streamlining the processes of the EU so that the
system can work properly.*

▸ help a process to be successful **aid, assist, ease,
facilitate, help** *It works with nature's ability to heal
the body and aids this healing process.*

▸ interfere with a process **complicate, disrupt,
interfere with, undermine** *A number of substances
interfere with physiological processes in the body.*

▸ start a process **begin, embark on, initiate, start**
*They took the top floor of the buildings over and
began the slow process of turning it into a home.*

▸ continue or complete a process **complete, continue**
Step 6 completes the online payment process.

▸ repeat a process **repeat** *Repeat this process until
the cabbage is all used up.*

▸ check on a process **monitor, oversee, review** *A
second office in Hong Kong oversees the production
process.*

process V
ɔ deal officially with a document, request etc

adv+V well **correctly, efficiently, properly,
securely, successfully** *This will ensure that your
delivered manuscript can be efficiently processed.*
quickly **immediately, promptly, quickly** *The order
was processed very quickly and you kept me informed
of its progress.*
by hand/computer **automatically, digitally,
electronically, manually** *It was recognised that
manually processing cheques was simply not an
efficient use of time.*
separately **individually, separately** *All applications
will then be processed separately from all general
enquiries.*

V+n **application, booking, cheque, claim, enquiry,
invoice, order, payment, refund, request** *Rachel
Todd is in charge of processing grant applications.*

roclaim V
▸ announce something publicly

adv+V **boldly, confidently, loudly, openly,
proudly, publicly, repeatedly** *The department loudly
proclaimed its latest successes in seizing smuggled
drugs.*

V+n information **fact, message, news** *Many zoos
proclaim a 'conservation' message, but does their
performance reflect this?*
a fact about yourself **allegiance, commitment,
innocence, intention** *He continues to proclaim his
innocence after 20 years in jail.*

▸ a feeling or belief **belief, faith, love** *In his speech,
de Gaulle proclaimed his faith that France would
eventually be liberated.*

▸ a successful result **independence, liberty, peace,
victory** *In 1813, Colombia proclaimed its
independence from Spain.*

proclamation N
an official announcement about something
important

● adj+N **formal, official, presidential, public, royal,
verbal** *The original flag was set out by royal
proclamation on 12 April 1606.*

● v+N **issue, make, publish, sign** *Important public
proclamations were made here.*

produce V
to make or grow something

● adv+V in a particular way **automatically,
cheaply, commercially, easily, naturally,
organically, professionally, quickly, sustainably**
*Today, coal and textiles can be produced more
cheaply in other countries.*

▸ in a particular place **domestically, locally** *Support
local business by purchasing locally produced goods.*

produce N
fruit, vegetables and other things that farmers
produce

● adj+N types of produce **agricultural, dairy, farm,
fresh, garden, horticultural, organic, seasonal**
Consumers are buying more organic produce.

▸ produced nearby **local, locally-grown** *There are
weekly markets selling local produce.*

▸ of good quality **fine, quality** *Growers are
recognising there is a market for quality produce.*

● v+N sell or supply **export, market, promote, sell,
stock** *The National Milk Bar idea was developed by
a Welsh dairy farmer as a way to market his produce.*

▸ buy or produce **buy, grow, import, purchase, source**
*The problem is that most of their produce is imported
from all over the world.*

product N
1 something made, grown, or obtained for sale

● adj+N new or special **exciting, innovative, new,
unique** *Organisations have been reluctant to devote
precious resources to developing innovative new
products.*

▸ not new **existing, traditional** *Which of the company's
existing products are really working for them?*

▸ recycled or organic **natural, organic, recycled,
sustainable** *Here are some samples of our recycled
products.*

▸ not working properly **defective** *One customer
claims the company makes defective products and
values profits over safety.*

▸ specialist **niche, specialist** *We sell organic wine and
other niche products.*

▸ types of product **agricultural, beauty, cleaning,
commercial, cosmetic, dairy, digital, electrical,
electronic, food, industrial, medicinal,
pharmaceutical** *Avoid consumption of alcohol and
medicinal products containing alcohol.*

▶ finished **end, final, finished** *I have seen a review copy of the book but not the final product.*

> Usage **Product** is usually <u>singular</u> in these combinations: *Were you happy with the finished product?* ● *The final product looks very much like a dustbin lid.*

● v+N design a product **design, develop** *These products are designed for a variety of customers.*

▶ produce a product **create, make, manufacture, produce, supply** *All our products are individually manufactured from high quality timber.*

▶ advertise a product **advertise, endorse, market, promote** *Focus on the price of the product and not all the fancy advertising promoting the product .*

▶ sell a product **distribute, sell, stock** *These products are sold in Spain and in the Canary Islands, mainly to tourists.*

▶ start to sell a product **launch, release** *We will be launching some exciting new underfloor heating products in the near future.*

▶ buy a product **buy, order, purchase** *To order these products, please contact your local HP sales representative.*

▶ import/export a product **export, import** *We have now started to export our products to the Far East.*

● n+of+N **choice, line, number, range, selection, variety** *We offer a full line of affordable products to decorate your home.*

2 the result of something

● N+of thoughts **fantasy, imagination, mind, thinking** *Supernatural creatures are products of the imagination.*

▶ natural process **evolution, nature** *We are products of nature, but we also create ourselves through our own activity in shaping the world.*

▶ political process **capitalism, globalization** *He was a strong opponent of Marxist theories that war was the product of capitalism.*

▶ relationship **collaboration, fusion, interaction, interplay, partnership** *Knowledge is the product of the interaction of a person's skills and experience with information.*

▶ culture **civilization, culture, tradition** *She argued that 'femininity' may be more a product of culture than of biology.*

▶ upbringing **background, upbringing** *My first marriage was to Matsui-san, who was the product of a middle class upbringing in Japan.*

▶ time **decade, era, period** *The tradition is the product of a bygone era.*

▶ hard work **effort, labour, research, work** *This stunning piece of software is the product of a major collaborative effort.*

production N

the process of making things in large quantities

● adj+N in factories **commercial, factory, industrial** *The product goes into commercial production later this year.*

▶ on farms **agricultural, farm** *The challenges to increasing agricultural production are too great for most farmers.*

▶ in one country/the world **domestic, global, international, national, regional** *For global oil production, the peak is predicted to come sometime between 2007 and 2020.*

▶ in large quantities **bulk, intensive, large-scale, mass** *Mass production and increasing competition is all good news for you, the consumer, as you get improved products at a cheaper price.*

▶ in small quantities **limited, low, small-scale** *Some climates can support only low production of crops.*

▶ too much **excess, surplus** *Waste is defined as any activity that adds cost but not value to the end product such as excess production, stock, and idle work in progress.*

▶ efficient **efficient, lean, successful** *Lean production is a philosophy and a way of working involving eliminating all forms of waste.*

▶ producing little pollution **clean, renewable, sustainable** *Industry needs to be convinced of the benefits of cleaner production and pollution control.*

▶ without using chemicals **organic** *During the two years of conversion to organic production, the farm hosted more than 400 visitors.*

● v+N stop production **cease, discontinue, end, halt, stop** *Production was halted and advertising of the drug was withdrawn.*

▶ start production **begin, commence, go into, put sth into, start** *Their latest model is due to go into production in December.*

▶ restart production **restart, resume** *There are no plans to restart production.*

▶ cause problems for production **affect, delay, disrupt, interfere with** *The occupations are disrupting the production of tobacco and other agricultural crops.*

▶ increase production **boost, double, expand, improve, increase, maximise, stimulate** *New technologies can help rice farmers boost production.*

▶ reduce production **cut, decrease, limit, reduce, restrict** *10 OPEC countries reduced oil production by 640,000 barrels a day.*

▶ move production to another place **move, shift, switch, transfer** *Capitalists threaten to shift production abroad if workers do not agree to everything they demand.*

▶ make production more automatic **automate, mechanize** *We are now in a position to automate the production of our magazine.*

productive ADJ

producing a lot of something or achieving good results

● adv+ADJ very **enormously, extremely, highly, incredibly, remarkably, very** *Bees are highly productive workers.*

▶ rather **fairly, quite, reasonably** *I then went to work and had a reasonably productive day.*

▶ to both people **mutually** *The university has a mutually productive relationship with local industries.*

▶ in a particular way **agriculturally, biologically, economically, scientifically** *Kelp forests are among the most biologically productive habitats in the marine environment.*

● ADJ+n people **employee, force, labour, worker, workforce** *Excessive hours working is no recipe for a healthy, productive workforce.*

▶ relationship **collaboration, interaction, links,**

partnership, relationship *I am very pleased to be working with them and look forward to a very productive relationship.*

▸ discussion **dialogue, discussion** *We had a useful and productive discussion on that subject.*

▸ something you own **asset, capital, resource** *For many people, good health is probably also the only productive asset they have.*

▸ for saying how productive something is **capacity, efficiency, potential, power** *A business can improve productive efficiency by producing output at the lowest cost possible.*

▸ v+ADJ **be, become, prove, remain, stay** *The mines in this area were re-opened, and proved remarkably productive.*

productivity N
the rate at which goods are produced

▸ adj+N high **excellent, high, maximum, optimum** *You should ensure that your business maintains maximum productivity at all times.*

▸ low **low, poor** *It is a myth that low productivity is caused by excessive regulation of the labour market.*

▸ total **net, overall, total** *The project will help to achieve the Government's target of improving the overall productivity of small firms.*

▸ types of productivity **agricultural, economic, industrial** *The contribution this department makes to the country's economic productivity and prosperity is ever more important.*

▸ lost **lost** *Polio places a burden on populations in terms of suffering, lost productivity and increased need for medical resources.*

v+N increase productivity **boost, drive, enhance, improve, increase, raise** *We recognise that enhancing productivity is a continuing challenge to firms.*

increase productivity to the maximum level **maximize, optimize** *Maximize your productivity with a fast, reliable internet connection.*

reduce productivity **compromise, decrease, diminish, hamper, hinder, reduce** *We have always said that long hours working can hinder productivity.*

affect productivity **affect, impact (on), influence** *Phishing attacks can seriously impact business productivity.*

N+v increase **double, grow, improve, increase, rise** *Today's figures show that productivity has risen by nearly a fifth.*

decrease **decline, fall** *In some areas, productivity is declining as soil degrades or erodes.*

be less than someone or something **lag behind sb** *Overall our productivity lags behind our main competitors.*

n+in+N increase **gain, growth, improvement, increase, rise** *Wage increases can only be justified by improvements in productivity.*

decrease **decline, decrease, drop, fall, reduction** *How can this decline in productivity be turned around?*

profession N
job that needs special skills and qualifications

adj+N respectable **honourable, noble,**

respectable, respected *Journalism is often seen as an honourable profession, with a mission to keep the public informed.*

▸ well-paid **financially rewarding, lucrative, well-paid** *Music is a lifetime of hard study, and it can be one of the least financially rewarding professions there is.*

▸ with mainly men **male-dominated** *Although photography is still quite a male-dominated profession, Liz hasn't really had any problems.*

▸ types of professions **accountancy, acting, architectural, dental, financial, journalistic, legal, medical, teaching** *I look upon the general practitioner as the most important man in the medical profession*

Usage In these combinations, **profession** is singular: *She works in the legal profession.* ● *I have been in the teaching profession for 20 years.* However, when you are talking about professions such as nursing and social work, you can refer to these as a group as **the caring professions**: *Many people in the caring professions put other people's needs above their own.*

● v+N enter a profession **choose, enter (into), go into, join** *To enter certain professions, it is necessary to take a course of study.*

▸ leave a profession **abandon, leave, quit** INFORMAL, **retire from** *A worrying number of student teachers are quitting the profession shortly after qualifying.*

▸ work in a profession **belong to, engage in, exercise, follow, practise (in), pursue, work in** *Librarians belong to a profession that values and insists on systematic skills updating.*

▸ control a profession with rules **govern, regulate** *Lawyers are currently awaiting publication of draft legislation governing the way the legal profession is regulated.*

professional ADJ
1 showing a high level of skill or commitment

● adv+ADJ **extremely, highly, incredibly, really** INFORMAL, **thoroughly, totally, truly, utterly, very** *I have always found them to be highly professional individuals, offering their clients an excellent service.*

● ADJ+n **approach, attitude, behaviour, conduct, manner** *Players are expected to compete in a professional manner.*

2 involving work needing special skills and qualifications

● ADJ+n help **advice, assistance, guidance, help** *Every business needs professional help.*

▸ skill or knowledge **competence, experience, expertise, knowledge, skill** *We have used our professional expertise to help many organizations with specific projects.*

▸ opinion **judgement, opinion** *In my professional opinion, you do not need an antibiotic.*

3 relating to the rules, standards, and arrangements or a profession

● ADJ+n qualification or training **accreditation, degree, development, qualification, training** *If you want to improve your business skills, you can choose a professional qualification in a management or marketing area.*

▸ organization **association, body, institute, organization, society** *The Association of Lighting Designers is the professional body representing lighting designers.*

▸ standards **code, ethics, integrity, standards** *He believed that many problems were due to a lack of professional ethics among civil servants.*

▸ responsiblities **duties, obligations, responsibilities** *Staff must be adequately trained to carry out their professional duties.*

▸ bad behaviour **misconduct, negligence** *She was dismissed because of serious professional misconduct.*

proficiency N

a high degree of ability or skill

● adj+N reasonable **adequate, intermediate, reasonable, sufficient** *All students must demonstrate adequate proficiency in the English language.*

▸ good **advanced, considerable, great, high** *At nine years of age, he attained a great proficiency in the Greek language.*

▸ not good **basic, limited** *Most people can quickly gain basic proficiency with the software without doing a course.*

▸ types of proficiency **academic, linguistic, mathematical, musical, technical** *There is great skill and technical proficiency in Croft's poetry.*

● v+N achieve proficiency **achieve, acquire, attain, develop, gain** *He had already attained the highest proficiency in kung fu techniques.*

▸ improve proficiency **enhance, improve, increase** *The best way to improve your proficiency in English is to read as much as you possibly can.*

▸ maintain proficiency **maintain** *Like any newly learnt skill, to maintain proficiency, one must practise.*

▸ show proficiency **demonstrate, prove, show** *You will need certificates demonstrating proficiency in fire-fighting, survival and first aid.*

● n+of+N **degree, level, standard** *Achieving high levels of proficiency in any type of task requires an effective training strategy.*

proficient ADJ

very skilful at something you have learned

● adv+ADJ very **extremely, fully, highly, very** *Diane is a highly proficient software developer.*

▸ rather **fairly, quite, reasonably, sufficiently** *I was becoming reasonably proficient at recognizing different species of trees.*

▸ technically **technically** *He was interested in photography from an early age and was very technically proficient.*

● and/or **confident, experienced, knowledgeable, professional, skilled** *We support a number of training courses to help our members become more knowledgeable and proficient.*

profile N

1 the public image of a person or organization

● adj+N getting a lot of/little attention **high, low, strong** *The company's owner has always tried to keep a low profile.*

▸ good **excellent, favourable, good, positive** *David Beckham is clearly craving a more favourable media profile.*

▸ public **media, public** *He spends as much time working on his public profile as he does on his business interests.*

▸ of a person **own, personal** *We can provide you with an opportunity to raise your personal profile.*

▸ of an organization **company, corporate** *Expect to dramatically boost your company's corporate profile with our professional sign solutions.*

▸ in a particular area of life or business **academic, economic, online, political, social** *His political profile has fallen recently.*

▸ in a particular place **international, local, national** *Previous hosts of the conference have found that it can be an opportunity to raise the international profile of their own institution.*

● v+N improve your profile **boost, elevate, enhance, heighten, improve, increase, raise** *The main aim of the project is to raise the profile of beaches along this stretch of coastline.*

▸ keep your profile **keep, maintain** *Ruth has been keeping her profile high with appearances on TV.*

▸ change your profile **alter, change** *By the early 19th century, the town's status had deteriorated badly, and its profile subsequently was altered out of all recognition by new building.*

▸ establish a profile **build, develop, establish, gain** *It is difficult for organizations such as Greenpeace to establish a high profile in some countries.*

2 a description of a person, group, or organization

● adj+N detailed or complete **complete, comprehensive, detailed, full, in-depth** *I researched and prepared detailed profiles of people the Prime Minister was to meet.*

▸ not detailed **brief, short** *Please email a brief profile of yourself to me.*

▸ accurate **accurate** *A business starts with an accurate profile of each and every customer.*

▸ of one person **individual, personal** *You can update your personal profile at any time.*

▸ of someone's mind or character **personality, psychological** *I read a newspaper article outlining psychological profile of the serial killer.*

▸ of someone's genes **DNA, gene, genetic** *We compared the genetic profiles of Polynesians with people from mainland China.*

▸ of the people in an area **demographic, population** *The demographic profile of the area shows an ageing population.*

▸ of someone's work or achievements **academic, career, professional** *Parents are kept infomed or the child's progress through academic profiles.*

▸ of someone's social position **social, socio-econom** *The groups in the three areas exhibited different socio-economic profiles.*

▸ of a company **company, corporate** *Click here to view the company profile.*

● v+N create a profile **build (up), compile, construct, create, generate, produce, write** *We are hoping to build profiles of listeners to our radio station.*

▸ change a profile **alter, change, edit, modify, upda** *Most of the people have only updated their profile every few years or so.*

▶ match a profile **fit, match** *You tell us the type of events you're interested in and you'll receive a regular email detailing those which match your profile.*

profit N

extra money earned after costs are paid

● adj+N large **big, considerable, decent** INFORMAL, **fat** INFORMAL, **good, handsome, healthy, hefty** INFORMAL, **high, substantial, tidy** INFORMAL *It was said that he made quite a tidy profit with the tales of his story.*

▶ very large **enormous, huge, massive, record, vast** *Huge profits were reaped by the pharmaceutical companies which sold these drugs.*

If you disapprove of the fact that a company makes very large profits, you can say that they make **obscene profits**: *While many local sports clubs are barely surviving, big multi-national companies are making obscene profits.*

▶ more than is reasonable **excess, excessive** *If anything, the scope for making excess profit has narrowed.*

▶ small **low, meagre, modest, reasonable, small** *We still intend to make a profit; albeit a relatively modest one.*

▶ before tax **gross, pre-tax, taxable** *During 2008/9, the company reported pre-tax profits of $1.8 million.*

▶ after tax **after tax, clear, net, overall, post tax** *Net profit is the balance of the gross profit once operating expenses are deducted.*

▶ possible in the future **future, potential** *The costs of building a global brand would far outweigh the potential profits.*

▶ expected **expected, forecast** *Shares have been falling, along with forecast profits.*

▶ lost **lost, unrealized** *The lender will at least recoup some of their lost profits through the exit fee.*

▶ from normal business **operating** *Operating profit was up by 11 per cent.*

▶ v+N make profit **bring (in), deliver, derive, earn, extract, generate, make, realize, reap, return, take, turn, yield** *Building companies are there to make a profit.*

▶ increase profit **boost, double, increase, maximize** *To boost profits, many supermarkets have taken on additional roles as pharmacies, clothes stores and petrol retailers.*

▶ announce or show a profit **announce, post, report, show** *We are delighted to announce pre-tax profits of $116.8 million for the six months ended October 31st.*

▶ share profit **share, split** *We set up a joint venture where we would split the profits.*

▶ N+v rise **climb, double, go up, grow, increase, jump, leap, rise, soar, surge** *While supermakets' profits soar, farmers and growers are struggling to stay in business.*

▶ fall **come down, decline, drop, fall, plummet, plunge, slump** *The electronics group's profits slumped from $21.6m to $2.4m last year.*

▶ equal an amount **amount to, equal, total** *Pretax profit amounted to 90.72 billion yen.*

profitability N

the degree to which something is profitable

● v+N increase profitability **boost, enhance, improve, increase, maximize, raise** *Her replacement will be charged with improving profitability.*

▶ reduce profitability **reduce** *Imposing a tax would push up our costs and reduce our profitability.*

▶ maintain profitability **maintain, sustain** *Profitability must be maintained whatever the circumstances.*

▶ achieve profitability **achieve, ensure, reach** *You will never achieve profitability that way.*

▶ affect profitability **affect, compromise, impact (on), influence** *Profitability was impacted by the increase in energy costs.*

▶ bring back profitability **restore** *They have taken vigorous steps to restore profitability.*

profitable ADJ

making a profit

● adv+ADJ very **enormously, extremely, highly, hugely, immensely, very** *Mumbai is the home of India's hugely profitable movie-making industry.*

▶ rather **fairly, quite** *Now it is quite profitable to collect personal data.*

▶ slightly **barely, marginally** *Marginally profitable mines became unprofitable and ceased production.*

▶ potentially **potentially** *You will have drawn up a 'business plan' which shows that your business idea is potentially profitable.*

▶ financially **commercially, economically, financially** *It is important that the service is carefully monitored to ensure it remains commercially profitable.*

● ADJ+n **business, company, enterprise, industry, investment, market, operation, venture** *David built Impressions into a very successful and profitable enterprise.*

profound ADJ

very great

● ADJ+n effect **consequence, effect, impact, implications, impression, influence, ramifications, repercussions** *The battle would have a profound effect on the rest of the war.*

▶ feeling **contempt, disagreement, disappointment, feeling, gratitude, grief, ignorance, impression, regret, sadness, sense, shock, sorrow, sympathy** *Once he'd gone, I felt a profound sense of failure.*

▶ disability **deafness, disability, impairment** *She had problems at school due to her profound deafness.*

▶ change or difference **change, difference, shift, transformation** *This era witnessed profound transformations in the American industrial labour market.*

▶ problem **crisis, difficulty, problem** *The government was unable to cushion them from the profound economic crisis.*

▶ quiet or stillness **silence, stillness** *A profound silence reigned throughout the assembly.*

▶ knowledge **awareness, grasp, knowledge, understanding** *She was a distinguished academic, with a profound grasp of the economic issues.*

program N

instructions making a computer work or perform an action

- v+N start or operate a program **execute, initiate, invoke, launch, open, restart, run, start** *Make sure you run your anti-virus program every time you switch on the computer.*
- ▶ write a program **compile, create, design, develop, write** *It is worth your while trying to write the program yourself.*
- ▶ load a program **download, install, load** *Then run the file to install the program and to add an entry to your Start Programs menu.*
- ▶ edit a program **configure, edit, modify** *It is not possible to edit the program.*
- ▶ end a program **close, exit** *You'll have to exit the whole program and start again.*

programme N
a plan of activities for achieving something

- adj+N full or varied **complete, comprehensive, extensive, full, intensive, varied, wide** *We are planning a comprehensive programme of presentations and publicity.*
- ▶ well-organized **structured** *Our structured training programme is unique to us.*
- ▶ flexible **flexible** *The college's flexible programmes allow you to tailor your studies to your individual interests.*
- ▶ new **innovative, new** *The ski school has an innovative learn-to-ski programme.*
- ▶ important or special **ambitious, exciting, major, special** *In 1998, there was a major programme to refurbish and enlarge the building.*
- ▶ continuous or long-term **long-term, ongoing, rolling** *After a rolling programme of art fairs since March, we now enter a quieter phase over the summer.*
- ▶ with someone else **collaborative, integrated, joint** *This is a joint programme between Edinburgh and Cambridge Universities.*
- ▶ educational **academic, college, degree, education, educational, graduate, research, school, training, undergraduate** *An educational programme for dancers, ballet teachers and choreographers needs to be established to decrease the incidence of ballet injuries.*
- ▶ in a particular place **international, local, national, regional** *There is no national screening programme.*

- n+N training or education **degree, education, graduate, induction, leadership, literacy, mentoring, postgraduate, skills, study, teaching** *For more information on our graduate programmes, see the online prospectus.*
- ▶ medical or health-related **drug, health, immunization, recovery, rehabilitation, screening, treatment, vaccination** *Cancer rates have fallen thanks to the new screening programme.*
- ▶ for improving something or somewhere **modernization, reform, refurbishment, regeneration** *The area remains problematic, despite a multi-million pound regeneration programme.*
- ▶ exercise or sport **coaching, exercise, fitness, sports** *Money has been made available to fund a sports programme for the under-12s.*

- v+N design a programme **design, develop, devise, draw up, establish, plan, set up** *This part-time programme is designed for students already working in health care.*

- ▶ run or manage a programme **conduct, co-ordinate, deliver, implement, manage, offer, organize, oversee, run, undertake** *Five institutions are already delivering professional development programmes to staff.*
- ▶ take part in a programme **attend, complete, follow, join, pursue, undergo** *You may be completing a training programme or starting your first job.*
- ▶ start a programme **begin, initiate, introduce, launch, start** *The programme was launched in 1998 by the United Nations.*

- N+of study or training **education, lectures, research, study, teaching, training, work** *The undergraduate degree is a three-year programme of study.*
- ▶ change or improvement **change, development, expansion, improvement, maintenance, modernization, reform, refurbishment, regeneration, rehabilitation, renewal, renovation, restoration** *The government began an ambitious programme of land reform.*
- ▶ action or activities **action, activities, measures** *You need to draw up a programme of action to tackle the issues you have identified.*
- ▶ providing money **investment, support** *Our ongoing programme of investment across our business ensures we can deliver the right solutions to our clients.*

progress N
the process of developing or improving something

- adj+N gradual **gradual, incremental, smooth, steady** *The team made steady progress to the semi-finals.*
- ▶ fast **fast, rapid, speedy, swift** *This enables our teachers to develop each student's abilities so that they make rapid progress.*
- ▶ slow **slow** *Dissatisfied with the slow progress being made, Alan resigned.*
- ▶ a lot **considerable, dramatic, encouraging, enormous, excellent, genuine, good, great, impressive, real, remarkable, significant, substantial, tremendous** *Significant progress has been made over the past three years.*
- ▶ a little **limited, little** *There is little progress on environmental reforms.*
- ▶ satisfactory **adequate, satisfactory, solid, sufficient** *The trainee must maintain satisfactory progress at all times.*
- ▶ not satisfactory **insufficient, unsatisfactory** *Departments prepare reports on the progress of all students whose progress is unsatisfactory.*
- ▶ continuing **continued, further, future, sustained** *The latest sales figures demonstrate the continued progress of the business.*
- ▶ types of progress **academic, economic, educational, industrial, medical, scientific, social, technical, technological** *We live in a world of unprecedented wealth and technological progress.*

- v+N make progress **achieve, make** *We continue to make good progress across all of our planned development areas.*
- ▶ follow something's progress **chart, follow, monitor, oversee, trace, track, watch** *They will use the new camera it to chart the progress of building works currently being carried out at the school.*

▶ slow down something's progress **delay, hamper, hinder, hold back, impede, inhibit, slow (down), undermine** *Progress was impeded by problems of access and planning permission.*

▶ speed up something's progress **accelerate, facilitate** *The company said it was examining all options to accelerate its progress.*

▶ measure or check something's progress **assess, check (on), evaluate, gauge, measure, review** *This survey will provide hard facts for us to measure our progress.*

▶ stop something's progress **arrest, block, halt, stop** *There are treatments to stop the progress of the condition and help relieve symptoms.*

▶ show something's progress **demonstrate, mark, show** *The photos show the progress of the restoration.*

▶ continue something's progress **continue, maintain** *Scholarships can be held for up to three years, subject to satisfactory progress being maintained.*

progress V
to continue to develop or move forward

▶ adv+V well **favourably, nicely, satisfactorily, smoothly, successfully, well** *She goes to school, where she is progressing nicely.*

▶ quickly **apace, fast, quickly, rapidly, swiftly** *Fundraising is progressing apace.*

▶ slowly or gradually **gradually, slowly, steadily** *Paralysis associated with the disease progresses steadily, though the rate differs between individuals.*

▶ a lot **considerably, enormously, significantly** *Since then, the band has progressed significantly and has recently performed at various venues around the region.*

progression N
gradual change or development

adj+N natural **automatic, inevitable, logical, natural** *So when the job came up, it seemed the natural progression and I jumped at the opportunity.*

fast **quick, rapid** *Hudson attributes her rapid progression through the sport to the goals she set herself from the beginning.*

slow or gradual **gradual, slow, steady** *Critics see in his work a steady progression from lighter, frivolous work to darker, more serious plays.*

smooth and without breaks **seamless, smooth** *To enable the smooth progression of research grant applications, the following procedures have been established.*

more **further, future, incremental** *Even if you do develop eye disease, it can be managed and treated to prevent any further progression.*

satisfactory **positive, satisfactory, successful** *The curriculum is designed to ensure satisfactory progression to college education.*

v+N slow down a progression **delay, hinder, inhibit, retard, slow (down)** *There are drugs that slow the progression of heart disease.*

speed up a progression **accelerate, aid, encourage, enhance, facilitate, promote, support** *These reports, together with your record of achievement and development, facilitate your progression as a teacher.*

stop or prevent a progression **block, halt, prevent, reverse, stop** *The chairman's ego refused to give in*

and foolish pride has halted the progression of the football club.

▶ affect a progression **affect, determine, influence** *Education is important because it influences career progression and earnings once in work.*

▶ monitor a progression **chart, follow, monitor, track** *The book charts the progression of this republican movement from the 1920s to today.*

▶ ensure a progression **allow, enable, ensure, guarantee** *Successful completion of the course guarantees progression to the first year of a degree course.*

▶ show a progression **demonstrate, show** *The old boatyard now houses an array of boats, showing the progression to modern day vessels.*

▶ make a progression **make** *Steve made the natural progression from modeling to television by becoming the presenter of 'The Popfactory'.*

prohibit V
to officially stop something from being done [usually passive]

● adv+V **absolutely, completely, effectively, explicitly, expressly, generally, legally, specifically, strictly, totally** *Cheating is strictly prohibited.*

prohibition N
a law or rule that prevents something

● adj+N complete **absolute, blanket, complete, outright, total** *In some workplaces, there may be an absolute prohibition on possession of alcohol.*

▶ extremely clear **explicit, express** *There is an express prohibition on discrimination on the ground of pregnancy.*

▶ general **comprehensive, general** *The Bill created a general prohibition of smoking at work.*

▶ supported by laws **legal, legislative, statutory** *National parliaments should examine whether they have adequate legal prohibitions against using statistical information to bring harm on individuals.*

● v+N introduce a prohibition **impose, issue** *The final section of the Act gives the police power to impose parking prohibitions and restrictions.*

▶ make sure a prohibition is obeyed **enforce** *The Tobacco Control Agency enforces prohibitions on the advertising of tobacco products in Ireland.*

▶ remove a prohibition **end, lift, relax, remove, repeal** *This provision would lift the current prohibition on imported meat.*

▶ not obey a prohibition **breach, contravene, infringe, violate** *In 1987, US courts ruled that the Office of Public Diplomacy had violated a prohibition against using federal funds for domestic propaganda.*

prohibitive ADJ
too expensive to buy or use

● ADJ+n **cost, expense, fee, premium, price, tariff** *The prohibitive cost of childcare will make it uneconomical for these women to continue working for the company.*

project N
a planned piece of organized work

- adj+N large or important **ambitious, big, important, large, large-scale, major** *Some schools have undertaken very ambitious projects, such as building their own wind turbines.*
  - ▶ small **short, small** *There is a growing interest in smaller community-based projects.*
  - ▶ involving groups working together **collaborative, joint** *The study is an outcome of a collaborative research project between the Universities of Berlin and Oxford.*
  - ▶ involving new and exciting ideas **creative, exciting, innovative, pioneering** *You will be working on innovative projects and sharing your learning with others.*
  - ▶ successful **successful** *Overall, the project was very successful in meeting the objectives originally set.*
  - ▶ continuing **ongoing** *Police say the operation is part of an ongoing project to crack down on drug use in schools.*
  - ▶ involving research **research** *At the end of this period, students are expected to complete a short research project.*
  - ▶ done for a short time as a test **pilot** *The initial results from this pilot project were presented by the design team.*
- v+N be responsible for a project and do it **carry out, conduct, embark on, undertake** *Many projects are undertaken each year where students work with commerce and industry.*
  - ▶ be in charge of a project **lead, manage, organize, oversee, run, supervise** *This project is run to provide gardening maintenance and care for the elderly and disabled of Newstead Estate.*
  - ▶ start a project **implement, initiate, launch, set up, start** *The project was set up to record the memories and experiences of the Vietnamese living in the UK.*
  - ▶ complete a project **complete, deliver** *The team was able to complete both projects to time and on budget.*
  - ▶ plan a project **design, develop, plan** *It took a year to plan the project and find the money to make it happen.*
  - ▶ provide the money for a project **finance, fund, support** *These projects are funded by a range of sources, including the EU, industry, and UK and overseas governments.*
  - ▶ judge the quality of a project **assess, evaluate, monitor, review** *The project was extensively evaluated by researchers from the Department of Public Health.*

projection N
a calculation about how something will develop

- adj+N in the future **forward, future, long-term** *The falling birth rate is also reflected in the future projection of the number of children under 16.*
  - ▶ based on good evidence **accurate, detailed, realistic** *The Chairman insisted on the importance of making realistic cost projections.*
  - ▶ too confident **optimistic** *Growth rates have exceeded our most optimistic projections.*
  - ▶ types of projection **demographic, economic, financial, fiscal** *It may prove impossible to meet the financial projections.*
- n+N **cash flow, growth, income, population, revenue, spending** *She prepared a business plan, including cash flow projections for a full year.*

- v+N make a projection **make, outline, prepare, produce** *Starting with population data from 1650 to the present day, projections are made for the future.*
  - ▶ base a projection on something **base on sth** *All projections are based on a set of assumptions.*
  - ▶ make changes to a projection **revise, update** *The company has revised downwards its market growth projection.*
  - ▶ be greater than a projection **exceed** *The report states that last year market growth exceeded all projections.*
- N+v when a projection shows something **indicate sth, predict sth, show sth, suggest sth** *All our projections indicate that the demand for university education will continue to grow.*
  - ▶ when a projection depends on something else **assume sth, depend on sth** *Current population projections assume that immigration will continue at the same level.*

prolific ADJ
producing many books, works of art etc

- adv+ADJ **extremely, highly, hugely, incredibly, quite, very** *Haydn was an extremely prolific composer.*
- ADJ+n writer, musician, or artist **artist, author, composer, journalist, novelist, painter, poet, songwriter, writer** *Adrian is the prolific author of poetry, novels, and plays.*
  - ▶ football player **goalscorer, scorer, striker** *Van Basten proved to be a prolific goalscorer.*
  - ▶ criminal **burglar, offender, thief** *Burglary levels have fallen steadily as the police target prolific offenders.*
  - ▶ what someone produces **output** *For almost 20 year his orchestral output was prolific.*
  - ▶ time when someone is prolific **career, life, period** *His most prolific period as a painter came after the end of World War One.*

prolong V
make something last longer

- V+n life **life, life expectancy, lifespan, survival** *According to the experts, a diet that is high in nutrition and low in fat can actually help prolong your life.*
  - ▶ time spent in a place **stay** *I was keen to prolong m stay in the city.*
  - ▶ pain or suffering **agony, suffering** *In some cases, restarting the patient's heart leaves them with a severe disability, and only prolongs their suffering.*
  - ▶ war or serious disagreement **conflict, dispute, wa** *The UN accused the warring parties of deliberately prolonging the war as they looted gold, diamonds, and other goods.*

prominence N
the state of being important or well known

- adj+N more **greater, increased, increasing** *Women characters have taken on increasing prominence in his work.*
  - ▶ equal **equal, same** *Signs must be fully bilingual, giving equal prominence to both English and Wels*
  - ▶ appropriate or deserved **appropriate, deserved, due** *In our view, significant risk factors were not given due prominence.*

▸ not deserved or necessary **undue** *Our view is that these statistics are unreliable, and have been given undue prominence by the news media.*

▸ involving a lot of people **global, international, national, public** *Rob admitted that the speed of his rise to national prominence has stunned him.*

▸ v+N give prominence **accord, give sb/sth** *We were of the view that this story was given too much prominence in the news bulletin.*

▸ have or achieve prominence **achieve, acquire, assume, come into, come to, enjoy, gain, rise to** *The young forward rose to prominence in the 1982/3 season.*

▸ n+to+N **rise** *The city's rise to prominence began in the 12th century with the founding of the Cathedral.*

prominent ADJ
important and well known

adv+ADJ **especially, increasingly, particularly, very** *This school of thought is becoming increasingly prominent in the USA.*

ADJ+n influence in a situation **part, role** *The Welsh language plays a prominent part in the teaching and in the everyday life of the school.*
feature **feature** *One of the most prominent features of the blogging phenomenon is that anyone can do it.*
person **artist, businessman, campaigner, figure, lawyer, leader, member, name, politician, scholar, scientist** *She is one of the broadcasting industry's most prominent figures.*
issue **factor, issue, theme** *A prominent theme in Shakespeare's plays is the unjust accusation of infidelity.*

ADJ+in+n **campaign, circles, field, movement** *She comes from a family that is prominent in local business circles.*

promise V
tell someone you will definitely do something

adv+V strongly **faithfully, repeatedly, solemnly** *Unwilling to let him go, his wife consents on condition he promises faithfully to return to her.*
at first **first, initially, originally** *Only 5,000 tickets were available for fans – far fewer than the number that was initially promised.*

promise N
a statement that you will definitely do something

adj+N not sincere **empty, false, hollow** *Without change, these targets are little more than empty promises.*
that is not kept **broken, unfulfilled** *People are sick and tired of the government's broken promises.*
that you must keep **binding** *A binding promise does not have to be made in writing on headed notepaper.*
not clearly explained **vague** *Such vague promises were unlikely to satisfy the workforce.*
serious **solemn** *Solemn promises were made to increase aid and support development in Africa.*

v+N make a promise **give, make** *Leaders around the world have made endless promises to end poverty.*
keep a promise **deliver, deliver on, fulfil, honour,**

implement, keep, meet *I'm sorry, I couldn't keep my promise.*

▸ break a promise **break, go back on** *Cecil promised the conspirators they would be allowed to escape or pardoned, and then broke his promise.*

▸ make someone keep a promise **hold sb to** *We are determined to hold the new BBC leadership to that promise.*

▸ receive a promise **be given, receive** *They had received vague promises of support from the Secretary of State.*

▸ persuade someone to give you a promise **extract, obtain, secure** *According to legend, the dying queen extracted a promise from Shah Jahan that he would build a magnificent mausoleum.*

2 signs that someone or something will be successful

● adj+N great **considerable, enormous, exceptional, great, much, real** *She was immediately recognized as a writer of great promise.*

> You can also say that something is ***full of promise***: *The day started full of promise.*

▸ early **early, initial** *The heyday of steam ploughing came at the beginning of the 20th century, but it never quite fulfilled its early promise.*

▸ not achieved **unfulfilled** *I do have a sense of unfulfilled promise when reading this book.*

● v+N show promise **hold, show** *I look forward to seeing more mature work from him, as his prose shows great promise.*

▸ be as good as expected **confirm, fulfil, live up to, realize** *The second half didn't quite live up to the promise of the early chapters.*

promising ADJ
likely to be successful

● adv+ADJ very **exceptionally, extremely, highly, really, very** *Kempson's performance against Northampton was highly promising.*

▸ fairly **fairly, quite, rather** *At first sight, the new software looked rather promising, but we soon began to see its weaknesses.*

● ADJ+n beginning **beginning, debut, start** *The home team got off to a promising start with a goal in the first five minutes.*

▸ chance of future success **career, future, prospects** *Why would a man give up a promising literary career to become a sportswriter?*

▸ person **candidate, newcomer, player, prospect, talent, youngster** *Eventually, the choice was whittled down to a small number of promising candidates.*

▸ way of doing something **approach, avenue, direction, line, method, route, strategy, technique, way** *Genetically engineering rice is seen as a promising approach to tackling food shortages.* ● *Darwin's research suggested several promising lines of investigation.*

▸ evidence of success **results, sign** *The drug has shown promising results in mice with Type 2 diabetes.*

● v+ADJ **appear, be, look, seem, sound** *The day was already looking very promising.*

● and/or **bright, exciting, new, young** *She is one of European cinema's most promising new talents.*

promote V
support or encourage something

● adv+V strongly **aggressively, heavily, strongly, vigorously** *We believe that micro-enterprises deserve to be strongly promoted in the UK.*

▶ in an active way **actively, positively** *Schools which have actively promoted cycling have been successful in increasing the numbers of children who cycle to school.*

▶ effectively **effectively, successfully** *Solutions do exist and, if promoted effectively, can go a long way to solving management problems.*

▶ in a lot of places **widely** *The philosophy of inclusive education has been widely promoted in Canadian schools.*

● V+n knowledge or understanding **awareness, education, interest, learning, study, understanding** *The aim of the project was to promote awareness of energy conservation in the home and school.*

▶ development or increase **development, growth** *The Chancellor announced today a series of measures to promote productivity growth.*

▶ equal rights and treatment **access, diversity, equality, opportunity, rights** *The programme is designed to promote equal access to education and employment for all.* ● *The government claims it is committed to promoting the rights of people with disabilities.*

▶ involvement by many people **collaboration, co-operation, integration, involvement, participation, partnership** *We want to promote greater participation by local people in the planning process.*

▶ discussion **debate, dialogue, discussion** *The aim of the conference is to promote dialogue between scientists and religious leaders.*

promotion N
1 a move to a higher level in an organization, group of sports teams etc

● v+N get promotion **achieve, clinch, earn, gain, get, receive, secure, win** *The club's main focus this season is on winning promotion.*

▶ try to get promotion **seek** *The qualifications gained will assist you when you seek promotion.*

● n+of+N **chance, hope, possibility, prospect** *If we win this game, then we have a very good chance of promotion.*

2 activity to help sell products, increase business etc

● n+N **business, export, product, sales, trade** *The company has experienced teams dedicated to sales promotion.*

● v+N **do, launch, organize, run** *We are currently running a consumer promotion offering a free trial to new customers.*

prompt V
cause something to happen or be done

● V+n ideas or discussion about something **call, debate, discussion, investigation, question, speculation** *The company prompted speculation*

about its future by suspending its shares on Tuesday.

▶ worry **concern, fears** *The discovery of a flock of dead swans prompted fears that the virus was spreading.*

▶ change **change, development, review** *Eventually, pressure from the public prompted a change in government policy.*

▶ reaction **reaction, response** *The employees have refused to raise their offer, prompting an angry reaction from the teaching union.*

▶ action **action, move** *What prompted the move into theatre?*

prompt ADJ
immediate or quick

● ADJ+n **action, attention, delivery, diagnosis, payment, reply, response, service, treatment** *Thank you very much for your prompt reply.*

● and/or **accurate, courteous, effective, efficient, friendly, helpful, professional, reliable** *Feedback on the assessment was prompt and helpful.*

prone ADJ
likely to do or experience something

● adv+ADJ **especially, extremely, increasingly, notoriously, particularly, very** *Small businesses and sole traders are particularly prone to stress.*

● n+ADJ **accident, crisis, disease, error, injury** *We are introducing a computerized system that will automate many tasks that were previously tedious and error prone.*

● v+ADJ **be, become, remain, seem** *Despite all these improvements, the area remains prone to drought and famine.*

● ADJ+to natural disasters **drought, earthquake, famine, flooding** *The area is still prone to flooding.*

▶ physical or mental illness **allergy, anxiety, cancer, depression, disease, disorders, illness, infection** *People who are overweight are more prone to sleep disorders.*

▶ problems or lack of proper functioning **breakdown, damage, error, problems** *Most of the trucks were in poor condition and prone to breakdown.*

proof N
information showing that something is definitely true

● adj+N that cannot be doubted **absolute, conclusive, definitive, final, incontrovertible, irrefutable** *There is speculation as to how old the carvings are and who carved them, but there is no conclusive proof.*

▶ likely to persuade people **clear, convincing, positive** *He claims these images are the most convincing proof yet of UFOs.*

▶ based on facts **concrete, real, solid, tangible** *She suspects that her husband had a hand in her son's death, but there is no tangible proof.*

▶ enough **ample, sufficient** *Their financial success is ample proof that they are offering a service that people enjoy.*

▶ more **additional, further** *It is further proof, if needed, that keeping an open mind is essential when listening to music.*

▸ types of proof **documentary, experimental, formal, mathematical, scientific** *Is there any scientific proof of the effectiveness of aromatherapy?*

▸ v+N give someone proof **furnish, give sb, offer (sb), present, produce, provide (sb with), show (sb), submit, supply** *To be eligible, you will need to provide proof of residency.*

▸ have proof **have** *The bar staff have the right to refuse to serve you if you have no proof that you are over 18.*

▸ need or ask for proof **ask for, demand, need, request, require, seek, want** *Orders made from countries outside the UK may require further proof of identity to support the card transaction.*

▸ be proof **be, constitute** *Anecdotal evidence does not constitute scientific proof.*

▸ get proof **find, get, obtain, see** *How do I obtain proof of my student status?*

propaganda N

information spread by a government or organization to influence people

adj+N deliberately dishonest **blatant, false, misleading, pure** *There would be an outcry if such blatant political propaganda was introduced into schools.*

types of propaganda **extremist, political, racist, religious, right-wing, socialist, sorporate** *Her article set out to attack corporate propaganda that climate change was not a serious issue.*

n+N **enemy, government, state, war, wartime** *Despite government propaganda, news of the hellish reality of the war was well known in Britain due to returned wounded servicemen.*

v+N spread propaganda **broadcast, disseminate, distribute, issue, peddle, publish, spread** *The movement spreads its propaganda mainly via radio and TV.*

reply to propaganda **counter, counteract** *Be prepared to counter any anti-union propaganda that the management may distribute.*

believe propaganda **accept, believe, swallow** *There is every sign that he came to believe his own propaganda.*

N+n system or process for spreading propaganda **campaign, effort, exercise, war** *The union does seem to be winning the propaganda war*

people responsible **department, machine, machinery, ministry** *In 1929, he had been given overall charge of the party's propaganda machine.*

purposes **purposes** *The media was used during the conflict for propaganda purposes.*

methods or materials used **broadcast, film, leaflet, material, messages, poster** *He also appeared as the devil, complete with horns and tail, in a number of short propaganda films.*

n+of+N **barrage, form, means, piece** *The pamphlet is nothing but a nasty piece of propaganda.*

proper ADJ

right, correct, or morally good

adv+ADJ completely or very **entirely, perfectly, quite, very, wholly** *He argues that in many cases it 's perfectly proper to withhold or withdraw life-preserving treatment.*

▸ no more than what is right **only** *I am usually quick to complain if I receive poor service, so I feel it only proper to compliment good service.*

● and/or **effective, fair, reasonable, right** *Many hours had been spent discussing the issue, as was entirely right and proper.*

proportion N

a quantity forming part or share of whole

● adj+N large **considerable, great, high, huge, large, significant, sizeable, substantial** *A high proportion of the town's residents work in the capital.*

▸ larger or increasing **greater, higher, increasing** *Populations in the West are shifting towards a greater proportion of older people.*

▸ small **low, small, tiny** *Only a tiny proportion of party members ever got involved in the policy-making process.*

▸ fairly large **fair, good, reasonable** *A fair proportion of the revenue raised from the scheme is to be spent on making the streets more accessible.*

▸ equal **equal** *Where these repairs are undertaken, the costs are divided amongst all properties on the estate in equal proportions.*

▸ same **same, similar** *Only 12 per cent consumed the recommended amount of five a day or more, while the same proportion consumed none at all.*

▸ certain **certain, specified** *He would like all electrical generation to have a certain proportion from wind farms.*

proposal N

a plan or suggestion to be considered

● adj+N detailed **detailed, full** *I will consult all interested parties before we bring forward detailed proposals for this new body.*

▸ not detailed or in its final form **draft, outline** *The architect had submitted draft proposals by fax for security fencing at the front of the building.*

▸ previous or current **current, initial, latest, new, original, recent, revised** *The Government's initial proposals for reform were published in October 2002.*

▸ practical or specific **concrete, specific** *The report is rather vague when it comes to making concrete proposals.*

▸ causing disagreement **controversial** *The Association of British Insurers plans to reveal these controversial proposals at a conference later this month.*

▸ involving major changes **ambitious, exciting, innovative, radical** *Some of the transport proposals are radical and will require a separate public consultation.*

▸ formal **formal, written** *A formal proposal will now be presented to English Nature, and a public consultation exercise will take place.*

▸ relating to a law **legislative** *We look forward to working closely with the Government on legislative proposals to implement this Directive.*

▸ important **important, major, significant** *The talks eventually led to some significant new proposals.*

● v+N make a proposal **bring forward, make, present, put forward, submit** *Short-listed applicants will be invited to submit full proposals by the end of March.*

▸ develop a proposal **develop, draft, formulate,**

prepare *The next stage will be to develop some specific proposals **for** improvements to the park.*

▶ give the main ideas of a proposal **outline** *The parking proposals are outlined in section 4G.*

▶ support a proposal **endorse, support, welcome** *I am sure that good businesses are going to welcome the proposals to strengthen industry codes of practice.*

▶ accept a proposal **accept, adopt, approve** *If your proposal is approved, you will be notified by e-mail.*

▶ not accept or support a proposal **oppose, reject** *The Labour Government will continue to oppose any proposals to increase the permitted maximum weight limit for heavy lorries.*

▶ discuss or consider a proposal **assess, consider, discuss, evaluate, review** *I have been travelling the country to discuss the proposals with students.*

propose v
suggest a plan, idea, or actions

● V+n plan or action **approach, measure, mechanism, plan, programme, scheme, solution, strategy** *We propose a number of measures to create jobs and clean up the environment.*

▶ change **amendment, change, reform** *The Government has proposed widespread changes to the taxation of trusts.*

▶ law or rule **directive, law, legislation, regulation, standards** *The law proposes tough new standards for nutrition in school meals.*

proposition N
1 an offer or suggestion

● adj+N interesting or worth doing **attractive, compelling, exciting, tempting** *We have given much thought to Mr Engelman's submission, but have to say that we do not find it an attractive proposition.*

▶ likely to be successful **feasible, practical, realistic, viable** *Loans can be provided to help applicants who have a viable business proposition.*

▶ in business **business, commercial** *Had the channel been considered as a commercial proposition, it would never have been launched.*

● v+N make a proposition **make, put to sb** *He then made a startling proposition: that they start a new life in Africa.* ● *Before I put this proposition to you, I must ask for your solemn promise to be discreet.*

▶ accept/not accept a proposition **accept, reject** *Where referenda have been held on the creation of directly elected mayors, voters have often rejected the proposition.*

2 someone or something that must be dealt with

● adj+N difficult or causing problems **difficult, expensive, risky, serious, tough, tricky** *Taking on a whole new workforce of 20,000 people from scratch would be a tough proposition.*

▶ attractive **attractive, exciting, interesting** *The night bus service has also improved hugely, making late nights in town a more attractive proposition.*

▶ different **different** *We easily beat them last season, but they are likely to be an entirely different proposition this time around.*

prose N
written language that is not poetry

● adj+N clear **clear, lucid, readable** *The book is thoroughly researched and written in the lucid prose we expect from the author.*

▶ well written **beautiful, elegant, poetic** *Written with all his characteristically elegant prose, this short biography is still perhaps the best introduction to Newton and his work.*

Purple prose is written in a very emotional or complicated style: *How do you convey the essential nature of music without resorting to highly technical jargon or purple prose?*

▶ describing something or telling a story **descriptive, narrative** *To support the descriptive prose there are numerous excellent photographs.*

prosecution N
the process of formally accusing someone of a crime

● v+N be likely to suffer prosecution **be liable to, face, risk** *You could face prosecution if smoke from your bonfire causes a nuisance.*

▶ avoid prosecution **avoid, escape** *A number of police officers were caught speeding but escaped prosecution*

▶ cause a prosecution to happen **bring, initiate, mount, pursue** *The Inspectorate will bring prosecutions if it believes that it has evidence that water unfit for human consumption was supplied.*

▶ result in a prosecution **lead to, result in** *Failure to comply with the above terms may result in prosecution **for** unauthorized use of copyrighted material.*

● N+n people **advocate, counsel, lawyer, team, witness** *They argued they did not receive a fair trial and claimed prosecution witnesses had been coached*

▶ facts or claims **case, claim, evidence** *Police Officer Hadley rejected prosecution claims that he had destroyed vital evidence.*

prospect N
the possibility that something will happen, or the thought of it happening

● adj+N likely to happen or succeed **excellent, good, realistic, reasonable** *There is no longer a realistic prospect of conviction.*

▶ immediate **immediate** *We regret to report that there is no immediate prospect of her return to work.*

▶ not much **little** *Students are leaving school with little prospect of getting a job because they lack basic literacy skills.*

▶ worrying or frightening **alarming, bleak, daunting, frightening, grim, terrifying** *It was a daunting prospect and I did have to think about it, but it was a once in a lifetime opportunity.*

▶ interesting or exciting **attractive, exciting, interesting, tantalizing, tempting** *I will be travelling to China for the first time, an exciting prospect.*

● v+N provide the prospect of something **offer, provide, raise** *The elections do not offer any prospect of change.*

▶ have to deal with a prospect **be faced with, face** *Many of our young people face the prospect of years of unemployment.*

▶ be happy about a prospect **be excited about, be excited at, relish, welcome** *She did not relish the* *prospect of all the administrative work she would have to do.*

▸ make a prospect more likely **boost, enhance, improve** *A period of voluntary work could boost your long-term career prospects.*

prosperity N
the situation of being successful and rich

● adj+N economic **commercial, economic, financial, material** *It was a time of relative economic prosperity.*

▸ continuing in the future **continued, future, lasting, long-term** *These new conference and exhibition facilities are essential to the city's future prosperity.*

▸ increasing **growing, increased, increasing, rising** *There is more work to do to ensure everyone can share in the growing prosperity of the country.*

▸ great **great, unparalleled** *I predict a year of great prosperity and success.*

▸ relative **relative** *Aberdeen has enjoyed three decades of relative prosperity and low unemployment.*

▸ experienced by most people **general, national, shared** *Enterprise is the key to our national prosperity.*

● v+N bring prosperity **bring, build, create, deliver, ensure, promote, spread** *Shipbuilding, manufacturing and trading brought prosperity to Inverclyde in the 19th and 20th centuries.*

▸ experience or achieve prosperity **achieve, enjoy** *Britons today enjoy prosperity far greater than that of previous generations.*

▸ increase the level of prosperity **boost, enhance, increase** *It is hoped that investment in green technologies will enhance the prosperity of the region.*

protect V
keep someone or something safe from harm [usually passive]

● adv+V completely **completely, fully** *We can assist you in making sure your rights are fully protected.*

▸ well **adequately, effectively, properly, well** *Despite high levels of anxiety over online security, many computers aren't adequately protected against infection.*

▸ not well enough **inadequately, poorly** *Experts who examined the site concluded that the uranium was inadequately protected.*

▸ by laws or rules **constitutionally, legally, specially, statutorily** *Confidentiality of medical information is legally protected.*

protection N
the process of keeping someone or something safe

● adj+N good enough **adequate, effective, proper, sufficient** *Every business should have adequate protection against viruses and data loss.*

▸ better **better, greater, improved** *The junction needs to be redesigned to provide better protection for cyclists and pedestrians.*

▸ additional **added, additional, enhanced, extra, further** *The shelter is erected on a solid surface, and then covered in sandbags to provide added protection.*

▸ complete **complete, comprehensive, full, maximum** *He should be kept away from other cats for 10 days after the second injection to ensure maximum protection.*

▸ special **special** *Children and young people have a right to special protection.*

▸ legal **legal, statutory** *We believe that children have a right to the same legal protection from violence as adults.*

▸ environmental **environmental** *Environmental protection cannot be successfully achieved without tackling the accompanying social issues.*

● n+N data and computers **anti-virus, copyright, data, firewall, password** *They are a major London law firm advising clients in all aspects of data protection.*

▸ people **child, consumer** *We provide training in topics such as child protection and food hygiene.*

▸ money or property **income, mortgage, payment, property** *The mortgage includes an income protection plan, in case you lose your job.*

● v+N give protection **afford (sb), give (sb), offer (sb), provide (sb with)** *A large golf umbrella certainly affords greater protection from the rain.*

▸ make sure someone or something has protection **ensure (sb), guarantee (sb)** *The vaccination is usually effective, but it does not guarantee protection.*

▸ need or try to get protection **need, require, seek** *Hanging baskets will need protection over the winter.*

▸ have or receive protection **enjoy, have, receive** *Because of its vulnerable status the dormouse receives legal protection under the Wildlife and Countryside Act.*

● n+of+N **degree, level, standard** *The anti-virus software provides a high level of protection.*

protective ADJ
wanting to protect someone from harm

● adv+ADJ very **extremely, fiercely, very** *She is fiercely protective of her step-daughter.*

▸ more than is reasonable **over, overly, too** *Parents who drive their children to school are sometimes seen as over-protective.*

● v+ADJ **be, become, feel** *She's so vulnerable and trusting that you're immediately drawn into her character and feel hugely protective towards her.*

protest N
1 a strong complaint or disagreement

● adj+N angry or strong **angry, loud, strong** *My argument was greeted by a storm of angry protest.*

▸ formal **formal, official** *I am writing to register a formal protest regarding the treatment that I received recently at your store.*

● v+N make a protest **lodge, make, register, voice** *After the race, the Spanish team lodged an official protest.*

▸ make a protest happen **prompt, provoke, spark** *The referee awarded the goal, sparking vociferous protests from United.*

▸ ignore a protest **ignore** *Ignoring the drunken protests of the girls, she heaved herself to her feet.*

● n+of+N **howl, storm** *Any calls to reduce the danger posed by motor vehicles, such as actually enforcing legal speed limits, lead to howls of protest from drivers.*

2 public actions designed to show strong disagreement

- adj+N peaceful/violent **non-violent, peaceful, violent** *The invasion triggered violent protests across the world.*
▸ involving many people **global, international, mass, massive, popular, public, widespread** *There had been an outbreak of popular protest **against** the tax.*
▸ political **political** *The regime attempted to pass a bill banning all political protest.*
- v+N organize a protest **hold, launch, organize, stage** *Supporters staged a brief sit-down protest before the game.*
▸ make a protest happen **lead to, spark** *Allegations of vote-rigging sparked massive protests.*
▸ support or take part in a protest **join, lead, support** *Over 100 people joined a protest last Saturday **against** the government's harsh treatment of asylum seekers.*
▸ try to stop people protesting **ban, prevent, stifle, suppress** *The law gives police the power to impose no-go zones and to ban peaceful protest.*
- N+n **demonstration, group, march, meeting, movement, rally** *Sunday's protest march drew thousands of people into the capital.*
- n+of+N **act, campaign, storm, wave** *A wave of protests erupted across France.*

protest v
express strong disagreement with something, especially as a group and in public

- adv+V loudly or strongly **loudly, strongly, vehemently, vigorously** *Why didn't people protest more vigorously **against** such treatment?*
▸ in a peaceful way **peacefully** *We are determined to continue peacefully protesting outside parliament.*

protester N
someone who publicly shows opposition to something

- N+v come together **demonstrate, gather, march, occupy sth** *Hundreds of protesters had gathered to prevent work starting on the controversial rail tunnel.*
▸ make demands **call for sth, chant sth, demand sth, shout sth** *Outside the court, protesters chanted anti-war slogans.*

proud ADJ
happy about your achievements, possessions, family etc

- adv+ADJ very **enormously, especially, extremely, fiercely, immensely, incredibly, particularly, really, so** INFORMAL, **truly, very** *We are immensely proud of Paula and all she has achieved.*
▸ with a good reason for being proud **justifiably, justly, rightfully, rightly** *They ought to feel justifiably proud of their efforts.*
▸ rather **quite, rather** *I'm feeling quite proud of myself as I never used to run more than 2 miles when I was at school.*
- v+ADJ **be, feel, look, seem, sound** *We all felt incredibly proud that the students had achieved such excellent results.*

prove v
1 provide evidence which shows that something is true

- adv+V so that there is no longer any doubt **beyond a doubt, beyond the shadow of a doubt, categorically, conclusively, definitively, without a doubt, without the shadow of a doubt** *Genetic testing can prove conclusively whether someone has the disease or not.*
▸ in a scientific way **clinically, mathematically, scientifically, statistically** *It was a long time before the benefits of tea to health would be scientifically proven.*
▸ only **just, merely, only** *This decision only proves tha[t] the World Trade Organization is unqualified to dea[l] with complex scientific and environmental issues.*
- V+n a claim **allegation, case, claim, point** *'That, Peter,' I replied, 'proves my point.'*
▸ fact of being guilty/not guilty **guilt, innocence** *They destroyed any piece of evidence that might prove his innocence.*
▸ fact of who you are **identity** *You will need to provid[e] original documents proving your identity.*
▸ value **value, worth** *He has to be given a chance to prove his worth.*
▸ existence **existence** *Modern science has not yet proved existence of intelligent life on other planets.*
▸ ability **ability, capability, competence, fitness, skil[l]** *He is an actor who has proved his ability in a number of important films.*
▸ a theory **hypothesis, theory** *The class introduces students to the scientific method, helping them creat[e] tests to prove their hypotheses.*

2 be shown to have a particular quality

- V+adj useful **advantageous, beneficial, fruitful, helpful, invaluable, useful, valuable** *This file contains tips and suggestions that might prove useful.*
▸ popular **popular** *The conference has proved very popular, and we regret to inform you that all available spaces have now been taken.*
▸ difficult **challenging, difficult, problematic, tough, tricky, troublesome** *Documentary evidence has proved difficult to find.*
▸ easy **easy** *Finding suitable accommodation in the area proved easy.*
▸ interesting **interesting** *I thought it might prove interesting to compare their different approaches to the problem.*
▸ expensive **costly, expensive** *Any later changes to the design will prove costly in both time and money[.]*
▸ successful **effective, successful** *The plan was well thought out and immediately proved successful.*
▸ unsuccessful **disastrous, inadequate, ineffective, unsuccessful, unworkable** *His efforts proved unsuccessful.*
▸ causing someone to die **fatal** *In the UK there are 65,000 cases of skin cancer each year, with 2,000 proving fatal.*
▸ necessary **necessary** *The Government intends to u[se] its powers to cap local authority budgets, should that prove necessary.*
▸ impossible **impossible** *Getting a visa proved near[ly] impossible.*
▸ possible **possible** *The intention had been to intervi[ew]*

three separate groups of parents at each school but this proved possible in one school only.

▶ true or correct **accurate, correct, true** *If these rumours prove true, she will be forced to resign.*

▶ untrue or incorrect **false, incorrect, unfounded, wrong** *What protection does the buyer have if the seller's information proves incorrect?*

proven ADJ
shown to be true, real, or effective

● ADJ+n method **approach, method, methodology, procedure, solution, strategy, system, technique, way** *Proven, old-fashioned methods are the most successful.*

▶ ability **ability, capability, competence, expertise, skills, talent** *Our reputation for integrity and our proven ability to deliver high quality work to a very high standard were also key factors in winning this contract.*

▶ experience **background, experience** *Ideally, you will have at least five to eight years proven experience of communicating ideas and information in a highly competitive commercial environment.*

▶ benefit **advantage, benefit** *There are definite and proven health benefits from simply drinking more water.*

▶ record of achievements **pedigree, record, reputation, track record** *Course tutors have a proven track record in teaching science to non-specialist adults.*

▶ connection **connection, link** *However, there is as yet no proven link between the use of mobile phones and brain cancer.*

▶ results **results** *These methods are simple and give proven results.*

▶ fact **fact** *All I'm saying is, I don't think it's a good idea to say something is a proven fact when it is not.*

▶ technology **technology** *The lower the amount of proven technology involved in the project, the greater the difficulty in raising finance.*

▶ product **design, product, tool** *The system has been developed using widely available and proven software tools.*

▶ success **success** *These unique study guides are a proven success in helping students achieve their maximum potential.*

▶ quality of being reliable **reliability** *Because of its small size, ease of use, and proven reliability, the stove has been the choice of campers and hikers worldwide for many years.*

provide V
give someone something that they want or need

● V+n information **analysis, background, data, details, evidence, explanation, information, summary** *The site provides information on its three major research programmes.*

▶ help **aid, assistance, care, help, support** *The government is providing further support for those parents with particular needs.*

▶ advice **advice, feedback, guidance** *Once you've made your choice, we can provide advice on how best to set up your system.*

▶ education **education, teaching, training** *Our aim is to provide practical training which gives students the skills they need.*

▶ protection **protection** *The system is designed to provide protection from terrorist attacks.*

▶ service **service** *We also provide a service specifically for South Asian women.*

▶ place to live or work **accommodation, environment, facility, space** *The library is housed in a chapel that has been refurbished to provide modern facilities in beautiful surroundings.*

▶ range **range** *The Institute provides a range of undergraduate and graduate programmes.*

2 cause something to exist or be available

● V+n opportunity **opportunity** *The work provided the opportunity for students to enjoy being physically active out in the fresh air.*

▶ way of understanding something **insight, overview** *This Report provides a very useful insight into the range of activities undertaken by the Fund.*

▶ answer **answer, solution** *The same approach also provides the practical answer to forging a new relationship between scientists and the public.*

▶ way of doing something **basis, framework, mechanism, system** *Each chapter would provide the basis for a term's work.*

▶ way of using something **access** *Our reference libraries provide access to a wide range of information.*

▶ opportunity for discussion **forum, platform** *The website provides a forum for you to exchange ideas with other researchers.*

provider N
an organization that provides a service to the public

● n+N Internet **broadband, Internet, Internet service, network, service** *We are currently acting for a number of well established IT businesses, including Internet service providers and software companies.*

▶ information **content, data, information** *Information providers are responsible for the content they publish.*

▶ technology **applications, software, technology** *Check with your software provider for these updates regularly.*

▶ care **care, childcare, healthcare, treatment** *The purpose of the Act is to improve the regulation of healthcare providers.*

▶ education **course, education, training** *We work in partnership with the voluntary sector, education providers, and employers.*

▶ financial service **credit card, finance, insurance, loan, mortgage, pension** *In most instances, we can get a better rate than your existing pension provider.*

▶ place to live **accommodation, housing** *The website is a useful resource, and we urge housing providers, tenants, and community groups to use it.*

▶ service **service, support** *The Disability Discrimination Act makes it unlawful for a service provider to discriminate against a disabled person.*

▶ transport **transport** *Our aim is to work in partnership with transport providers to achieve an efficient and affordable transport system.*

▶ solution **solution** *They have already established themselves as an innovative solutions provider.*

provision N

1 the act of providing something that someone needs

- adj+N relating to time **current, existing, future** *Respondents were also invited to provide comments on the current provision of the service.*
- ▶ relating to education **educational** *The overall quality of educational provision is improving.*
- ▶ public **public** *In housing, the role of public provision, and even public finance, may diminish.*
- ▶ private **private** *With the move to increased private provision of previously public tasks, the non-profit sector has grown steadily.*
- ▶ local **local** *Local provision of suitable facilities is also very patchy.*
- ▶ required by the law **legal, statutory** *What are the rules governing the statutory provision of childcare facilities?*

- v+N improve provision **enhance, improve** *This report makes recommendations on how to improve the provision of care.*
- ▶ make certain that there is provision **ensure** *To ensure the provision of up-to-date information, the details on this site are maintained by the retailers themselves.*
- ▶ increase provision **develop, expand, extend, increase** *The Association was formed in 1967 to increase the provision of low-cost affordable housing in the district.*
- ▶ say that provision is necessary **require** *The Broadcasting Act requires the provision of high-quality national and international news during peak time.*
- ▶ consider provision **consider, review** *The school should consider the provision of better, more secure facilities for bicycle storage.*
- ▶ encourage provision **encourage, support** *The Green Party supports the provision of good-quality subsidized public transport for all students who do not live within a short distance of their school.*

2 plans or preparations for future needs

- adj+N special **special, specific** *Despite representations from various bodies, the Government has, at least so far, declined to make special provision for such insurance.*
- ▶ additional **additional, further** *This issue obviously arose years before we came into office, but we have made additional provision for research.*
- ▶ good or enough **adequate, effective, good** *We hope that adequate provision will be made in the spending review now being conducted by the Government.*
- ▶ not good enough **inadequate, poor** *Their forecasts made inadequate provision for the effects of inflation.*
- ▶ suitable **appropriate, proper** *Appropriate provision must be made for research.*

- v+N make **All airlines make provisions for travellers with diabetes if you inform them at the time of booking.*
- N+for **access, development, education, needs, parking, payment, protection, retirement, service, use** *They can then assess the individual early in the process and begin to make provision for their needs at an early stage.*

provisional ADJ

intended to be temporary, and not yet finally agreed or settled

- adv+ADJ **merely, only, still** *Please note that this timetable is only provisional, and subject to change.*
- ADJ+n information **data, figures** *Provisional figures showed that the number of nurses and midwives had increased by over 10,000 in the last year alone.*
- ▶ decision **conclusion, decision** *The ombudsman made provisional decisions on both cases in July and received a significant number of comments in response.*
- ▶ results **findings, results** *The main trends were published as provisional results in December 2008, but the latest bulletin includes final figures.*
- ▶ suggestion **recommendation** *Of all the Commission's provisional recommendations, this one has perhaps been the most controversial.*
- ▶ plan or system **arrangement, measure, plan, programme, timetable** *However, provisional arrangements are already being made for next year's conference.* • *Please be aware that these plans are provisional and may change.*
- ▶ statement **diagnosis, estimate, report, statement** *A provisional diagnosis of inflammatory bowel disease was made.*
- ▶ title **title** *The provisional title for this publication is 'Lessons from the South'.*
- ▶ list **list** *A provisional list of topics for discussion is given below.*
- ▶ agreement or approval **agreement, approval** *Ankara and Damascus signed a provisional agreement in 1987.*
- ▶ arrangement to buy something **booking, reservation** *We can hold a provisional booking for two weeks.*
- ▶ date **date** *A provisional date of 12 March has been set for the partners' meeting.*
- ▶ offer **offer** *She had received a provisional offer of employment.*
- ▶ request for permission **application** *It is appreciated that many students will not have finalized plans by that date, but a provisional application should be submitted.*

provocation N

something that causes you to react in an angry or violent way

- adj+N very little **least, slight** *She loses her temper at the slightest provocation.*
- ▶ extreme **extreme** *Our police officers have behaved in a measured and professional way despite extreme provocation.*
- ▶ clear and intentional **blatant, deliberate, direct** *This resolution is a direct provocation to the government of Iraq.*
- ▶ serious **serious, severe** *North Korea's nuclear test was a 'serious provocation', the US Secretary of State said at a press conference.*

- v+N **avoid, condemn, constitute, react to, respond to** *The way in which some officers responded to provocation was clearly an important issue.*

provocative ADJ

intended to annoy or upset people or to cause discussion or disagreement

● adv+ADJ very **extremely, highly, particularly, very** *The Committee considered that her comments had been highly provocative and very inappropriate.*
▶ deliberately **deliberately, intentionally** *Some of the articles are deliberately provocative.*
▶ rather **rather, somewhat** *The anti-American sentiment completely undermines the film's rather provocative message.*
▶ slightly **slightly** *Some of his remarks could have been misinterpreted as being slightly provocative.*

● ADJ+n piece of writing **article, book, essay, piece, read, title** *It is certainly an original and provocative book, though at times extraordinarily difficult.*
▶ statement or speech **claim, comment, remark, speech, statement** *You made a very provocative statement in your New York Times interview.*
▶ question **question** *But the passage raises some provocative questions which are as relevant for us today as they were then.*
▶ language **language** *Prior to the England v. Germany game, some newspapers used provocative language in their headlines.*
▶ action **act, action, visit** *We are working with the international community for a decisive response to this provocative act.*
▶ behaviour **attitude, behaviour, manner** *The police behaved in a highly professional way in the face of extremely provocative behaviour.*
▶ idea **idea** *This is a rich book, full of provocative ideas, which should appeal to any reader concerned about the future of human rights law and practice.*
▶ film or other artistic production **film, image, play** *Now five of his most provocative, thought-provoking films are available in one collection.*
▶ argument **argument** *Philosophy abounds with provocative arguments in which apparently simple assumptions lead to unexpected and often baffling conclusions.*
▶ and/or **challenging, controversial, entertaining, funny, informative, interesting, original, powerful, stimulating, thoughtful** *This is a challenging and provocative work, and recommended to anyone interested in the subject.*

provoke V

cause a reaction, especially an angry one

● adv+V deliberately **deliberately** *They claim that the police deliberately provoked disorder to discredit the protestors and their cause.*
▶ easily **easily** *Such rumours could easily provoke financial chaos in the markets.*
▶ finally **eventually, finally** *History says that the murder of Calvo-Sotelo, a right-wing leader, was what finally provoked the conflict.*
▶ immediately **immediately** *The announcement immediately provoked an angry response from some of the leading names in French film-making.*
▶ in a way that is impossible to avoid **inevitably** *Hume's omission from the team inevitably provoked debate among supporters.*

▶ V+n reaction **reaction, response, retaliation** *The subject is complex and provokes strong reactions.*

▶ anger **anger, fury, outrage, resentment, wrath** *The news has provoked outrage amongst the thousands of travellers who rely on this service.*
▶ discussion **debate, discussion** *His talk should be very entertaining and provoke much discussion.*
▶ violent action **attack, conflict, confrontation, rebellion, resistance, riot, violence, war** *The government's decision to suspend elections will provoke violence from militants.*
▶ opposition **attack, backlash, criticism, opposition, outcry, protest, resistance** *Naturally, this provoked widespread opposition from other Bishops and Archbishops.*
▶ feeling **emotion, feeling** *The case has provoked strong feelings all round.*
▶ thought **reflection, thought** *It is an engaging drama, and one that provokes much thought.*
▶ question **question** *Our short courses are designed to stimulate thinking, provoke questions, and provide opportunities for our students to explore ideas.*
▶ disagreement **controversy, disagreement, dispute** *Proposals to redevelop this site have provoked considerable local controversy.*
▶ worried feeling **anxiety** *Final-year examinations in particular tend to provoke great anxiety amongst students.*
▶ difficult situation **crisis** *The news that Chen had gone over to the opposition provoked a crisis in the party.*
▶ comment **comment, remark** *I knew my remarks would provoke a comment or two from you.*
▶ interest **interest** *These projects have provoked much public interest.*

prowess N

great skill or ability

● adj+N physical **physical** *Gifted with a laser-sharp mind and extraordinary physical prowess, she rose quickly through the ranks.*
▶ at thinking or studying **academic, intellectual, mental** *Why does the school give so much priority to sporting activities and not enough to academic prowess?*
▶ at sport **athletic, batting, footballing, goal-scoring, sporting** *Liddell is best known for his athletic prowess immortalized in the film 'Chariots of Fire'.*
▶ sexual **sexual** *Rumours were already spreading of Finch's sexual prowess.*
▶ at fighting **martial, military** *There was never any doubt about the military prowess of the soldiers of both countries.*
▶ at music **instrumental, lyrical, musical, vocal** *We were impressed by their professionalism and musical prowess.*
▶ at art or literature **artistic, creative, literary** *At that moment I wished for some artistic prowess, so that I could have painted the image.*
▶ at cooking food **culinary** *Use these recipes to impress dinner guests with your culinary prowess.*
▶ technical **technical, technological** *What they lack in technical prowess, they certainly make up for in enthusiasm.*

● v+N show prowess **demonstrate, display, show** *Britain's young riders showed their prowess in the finals, as they took home the team gold medal.*
▶ test someone's prowess **test** *The aim of the*

competition is to test the prowess and agility of the dogs.

▶ prove your prowess **prove** *Nikola proved his prowess in mathematics at school, and entered the Technical University at Graz in order to study electrical engineering.*

prudent ADJ
careful and using good judgment

● adv+ADJ very **extremely, very** *We have approved what we believe to be a very prudent budget that will enable us to maintain an effective service.*

▶ fairly **reasonably** *The return to the idea of a transfer of emphasis from nuclear to conventional forces appears reasonably prudent.*

▶ in a particular way **commercially, economically, financially, fiscally, politically** *You have a duty to ensure that the club's business is operated in a financially prudent way.*

● ADJ+n course of action **course, course of action, measure, move, step** *Mr Soames agreed that this was a prudent course of action to take.*

▶ plan **policy, provision, strategy** *The International Red Cross maintained a prudent policy of discreet diplomacy and aid.*

▶ decision **assumption, decision** *It's often a prudent decision to invest no more than 25 per cent of your portfolio in the riskiest assets.*

▶ management **management** *Through the prudent management of its finances in recent years, the College has been steadily improving its financial position.*

▶ financial behaviour **borrowing, budgeting, investment, spending** *Prudent investment, notably in British and American railways, greatly increased his fortune.*

▶ method **approach** *And, in the light of recent experience, we have adopted a more prudent approach to forecasting income tax revenues.*

▶ planning **planning** *Time will tell what the results of this prudent planning will achieve.*

▶ use **use** *There is now a conscious regard for protecting the environment through prudent use of energy.*

▶ advice **advice** *When out Christmas shopping, the most prudent advice is to park in a well-lit, security-patrolled area.*

▶ level **level** *The Minimum Wage was set at a cautious and prudent level so as not to undermine competitiveness.*

● v+ADJ be or seem prudent **appear, be, seem** *It would seem prudent to spend money on technologies that have less harmful side effects.*

▶ think something prudent **consider sth, deem sth, think sth** *It is considered prudent to control the kinds of development permitted in the vicinity of these installations.*

▶ be shown to be prudent **prove** *It may prove financially prudent to review your investments at this time.*

psychological ADJ
involving or affecting your mind

● ADJ+n problem **condition, disorder, issue, problem** *There are some claims that cannabis use*

can lead to psychological problems like schizophrenia.

▶ aspect **aspect, factor** *He argues that it is psychological factors which influence adults' willingness and ability to learn.*

▶ health **health, well-being** *Social isolation can have a detrimental effect on psychological well-being.*

▶ harmful effects **damage, distress, harm, stress, trauma** *It is far too early to say what psychological damage has been done in the long run.*

▶ need **need** *Such commitment between two people meets a deep-rooted psychological need.*

▶ condition **condition, state** *Alex is asked to evaluate her psychological state.*

▶ help **help, support, therapy, treatment** *Priority should be given to providing psychological support to children and their families.*

▶ effects **consequences, effects, impact** *The research deals with refugees and the psychological effects of the traumas they had been through.*

puberty N
the period when a child changes physically into an adult

● v+N start puberty **attain, enter, hit** INFORMAL, **reach** *The girls are married off when they reach puberty, often at the age of 12.*

▶ be about to start puberty soon **approach** *I was now in the period when I was fast approaching puberty.*

▶ experience puberty **go through, undergo** *Many young people go through puberty and adolescence with few problems; for others it is a time of uncertainty and anxiety.*

▶ delay puberty **delay** *Excessive exercise tends to delay puberty by about five months for every year of training.*

● n+of+N **age, onset, sign** *This disease mainly affects women, usually just after the onset of puberty.*

public N
people in general

● v+N involve the public **engage, involve** *Part of the Planning department's role is to involve the public and enable them to have a say in what is being planned.*

▶ tell the public **inform, tell, warn** *The police defended their decision not to inform the public of his escape.*

▶ ask the public for its opinion **ask, consult** *The government actively seeks to consult the public on certain pieces of legislation.*

▶ protect the public **protect** *What changes do you think should be made to the criminal justice system to protect the public better?*

▶ educate the public **educate** *The campaign will be aimed at educating the public and informing MPs and other decision-makers.*

▶ work for the public **serve** *Members of Congress would do well to remember that they are there to serve the public, not to dictate to us.*

▶ persuade the public **convince, persuade, urge** *The nuclear industry has some serious work to do to convince the public that it can be trusted.*

▶ make the public feel less worried **assure, reassure** *I'd like to reassure the public that they have nothing to fear.*

▶ give the public false information **deceive, misinform, mislead** *The government has misled the public on this highly controversial issue.*

publication N

1 producing a book, magazine, report etc and making it available to the public

● v+N start/stop publication **begin, cease** *The magazine ceased publication in December 2006.*
▶ prevent or delay publication **delay, prevent, prohibit** *The Inquiry's report is complete, but it is feared that the government will delay publication.*
▶ be the time when publication happens **mark, see** *1859 saw the publication of Darwin's famous book.*
▶ welcome the publication of something **welcome** *Friends of the Earth have welcomed the publication of a report on the power of supermarkets.*
▶ wait for publication **await, wait for** *Children were eagerly awaiting the publication of the next Harry Potter book.*
▶ announce publication **announce** *We are very pleased to announce the publication of our new series of business books.*

● v+for+N accept something for publication **accept, approve, select** *Over 120 papers from 10 countries were accepted for publication.*
▶ offer something for publication **submit** *This article was submitted for publication earlier this year.*
▶ prepare something for publication **edit, prepare** *During that time, she kept a diary which I am now preparing for publication.*
▶ consider something for publication **consider** *All submissions will be considered for publication.*
▶ intend something for publication **intend, plan, schedule** *Raphael's notebooks were never intended for publication.* ● *His latest thriller is scheduled for publication soon.*
▶ make arrangements for the publication of something **arrange** *In 1786, he arrived in Edinburgh to arrange for the publication of his poetry.*

2 a book, magazine, article etc

● adj+N new **forthcoming, new, recent** *For details of forthcoming publications, see our website.*
▶ important **important, key, major** *Her new book is a key publication which sums up recent work in the field.*
▶ useful **relevant, useful** *Your course leader will circulate a list of relevant publications.*

publicity N

attention in magazines, newspapers, or television

● adj+N positive **excellent, favourable, good, great, positive** *Think of the good publicity that will bring the school.*
▶ negative **adverse, bad, damaging, negative, unfavourable** *He proves that there is no such thing as bad publicity.*
▶ a lot **considerable, great, massive, much** *The Awards have had considerable publicity on both sides of the Atlantic.*
▶ in a particular area **international, local, national** *This year's event attracted less national publicity than usual.*
▶ everywhere **extensive, wide, widespread** *Recent*

reports of accelerating rates of ice melting across the Arctic have received widespread publicity.
▶ free **free** *The media give terrorists free publicity for which commercial advertisers would pay literally millions of pounds.*
▶ as much as possible **maximum** *The Board emphasised that maximum publicity should be given to the new arrangements.*
▶ recent **recent** *Given the recent publicity around identity theft, it would be wise to prevent your information falling into the wrong hands.*

● v+N get publicity **gain, garner, get, receive** *The band is getting much more publicity now.*
▶ give someone or something publicity **give, provide** *The story was given wide publicity in the press.*
▶ create publicity **attract, bring, create, generate** *The tour generated plenty of positive publicity.*
▶ avoid publicity **avoid, shun** *He always tried to avoid any publicity.*
▶ try to get publicity **seek, want** *The lottery winners wanted no publicity and I promised them that they would get none.*
▶ need publicity **need** *I don't need the publicity.*
▶ like publicity **enjoy, revel in, welcome** *She seemed to revel in all the publicity she received during the court case.*

publish V

1 produce many copies of a book, magazine, or newspaper

● V+n book **book, edition, journal, magazine, newspaper, paper, work** *This journal is published twice a year by the Faculty of Economics in Ljubljana, Slovenia.*

2 make information available to the public, in a report, newspaper, website etc

● V+n piece of writing **article, document, guidance, paper, report, study** *The study was published last year by the German Institute for Economic Research.*
▶ information **data, details, figures, findings, information, list, material, research, results** *New figures published by the industry regulator confirm the company has met its target for the year.* ● *Her recent research was published in the Journal of Comparative Psychology.*

pull in PHR VB

attract a large number of people

● V+n audience **audience, crowd, listeners, punters, tourists, viewers, visitors** *They are hoping the town's new literary festival will help to pull in the tourists.* ● *His talk show regularly pulled in 3.5 million viewers on Friday nights.*

pulse N

the regular movement of blood pumped round the body

● adj+N fast **fast, racing, rapid** *He found Martin in bed, with a severe fever and a very rapid pulse.*
▶ slow **slow** *The first signs are low blood pressure and a slow pulse.*
▶ strong **strong** *His pulse is still strong.*
▶ weak **faint, weak** *She had a suspected fracture of the skull and her pulse was weak.*

▶ regular **regular, steady** *His blood pressure is 180/90mmHg and he has a regular pulse with a rate of 55 bpm.*

▶ not regular **irregular** *I seem to have an irregular pulse.*

● v+N check a pulse **check, take** *To see if she really had malaria, I took her pulse.*

▶ feel a pulse **feel** *She could feel no pulse and thought that the man must have died.*

▶ find a pulse **find** *Workers rushed to his aid, but he was unconscious and they could not find a pulse.*

▶ have a pulse **have** *Mouth-to-mouth is simple and works really well for people who still have a pulse but aren't breathing well or easily.*

▶ make a pulse become faster **quicken** *Studies have shown that the colour red can quicken the pulse and breathing rate, as well as increase appetite.*

▶ check whether someone has a pulse **check for, feel for** *When checking for a pulse, use the carotid artery in the neck.*

● N+v make strong regular movements **beat, pound, throb** *I felt my flesh tingle with excitement, and my pulse beat rapidly.*

▶ become faster **quicken** *I felt my pulse quicken as I scanned the pages.*

▶ be very fast **race** *Her pulse raced as her instinct told her that something was not right.*

▶ slow down **slow, slow down** *His pulse slowed and his blood pressure showed a reduction.*

punch N
when you hit someone or something with your closed hand

● adj+N strong **big, hard, heavy, mighty, powerful, solid, strong** *Then half way through the third round, I caught him with three hard punches in succession.*

▶ first **first** *The old man had always said, 'Son, always get the first punch in'.*

▶ making someone fall and be unable to get up **killer, knockout** *Barnes landed a knockout punch in the first round.*

▶ weak **weak** *He was totally off balance and only able to throw weak punches.*

▶ single **single** *He was laid out with a single punch.*

● v+N aim a punch **aim, swing, throw** *He clearly threw the first punch.*

▶ hit someone or something with a punch **deliver, give sb, land** *He grabbed Harry's shirt and landed a punch in his face.*

▶ hit each other with punches **exchange, trade** *Williams was sent off after exchanging punches with one of the other players.*

▶ prevent a punch from hitting you **block, dodge** *Alan swung at Steve, who blocked the punch and connected with a blow of his own to Alan's face.*

▶ have a strong punch **pack** *Tyson packed a powerful punch.*

punish V
make someone suffer for doing something wrong or illegal

● adv+V severely **harshly, heavily, severely** *He was caught trying to break out of prison and he was severely punished.*

▶ in a cruel way **brutally, cruelly, ruthlessly** *Some of the workers went on strike, and were brutally punished for it.*

▶ properly **accordingly, duly, properly** *We will ensure that those who are dealing drugs are properly punished.*

▶ fairly **fairly, justly** *Justice means ensuring people who break the law are punished fairly and rehabilitated if possible.*

▶ unfairly **unfairly, unjustly** *Who doesn't remember being unfairly punished by their teachers?*

▶ physically **physically** *The study found that children who were smacked were more likely to display aggression than those who were never physically punished.*

● V+n person **criminal, culprit, murderer, offender, perpetrator, wrongdoer** *The key question to ask is whether punishing offenders actually reduces crime.*

▶ bad or illegal act **behaviour, crime, infringement, offence, transgression** *The role of the criminal justice system is, of course, to detect and punish crimes.*

▶ act that is against religious laws **evil, sin** *God's justice demands that sin be punished.*

▶ failure **failure** *Their position is that we should reward success and punish failure.*

● V+for illegal act **contempt, crime, offence** *It is vitally important that, as well as being punished for their crimes, fraudsters are deprived of their criminal gains.*

▶ bad act **act, action, behaviour** *Several of the villagers were punished for their actions in the Civil War.*

▶ act that is against religious laws **sin** *The Bible says that each person will be punished for their own sin.*

▶ mistake **mistake** *Should I be punished for a mistake which was clearly not my fault?*

punishment N
the action of punishing someone or of being punished

● adj+N severe **draconian, harsh, heavy, serious, severe** *Punishments were very severe for protesters.*

▶ suitable **appropriate, due, fitting, suitable** *There needs to be appropriate punishment for such a terrible crime.*

▶ fair **just** *She asked that she should be sent to prison as a just punishment for her wickedness.*

▶ continuing for ever **eternal, everlasting** *He thinks she deserves eternal punishment for what she did.*

▶ worst **worst** *The worst punishment we can give someone in this country is to sentence them to life imprisonment.*

● v+N give someone punishment **administer, give sb, impose, inflict, mete out** *The judge imposed the maximum punishment of three months' imprisonment.*

▶ accept punishment **accept, bear, take** *He should just shut up and take his punishment like a man.*

▶ receive punishment **face, receive, suffer** *Youngsters will still need to face punishment whether it is a fine, caution, or work in the community.*

▶ avoid punishment **avoid, escape** *Members of privileged groups often escape punishment.*

▶ deserve punishment **deserve** *She knows she deserved punishment, but argues that the sentence was too hard.*

▶ state what punishment should be given **prescribe**
*The law prescribes harsh punishments for those
convicted of such activities.*

pure ADJ

1 not mixed with anything that might spoil the
quality or effect

● adv+ADJ very **extremely, remarkably, very**
*Diamonds are made of carbon, and are extremely
pure.*

▶ completely **absolutely, perfectly** *The magnesium in
the samples analysed was absolutely pure.*

▶ fairly **quite, relatively** *Many of their components
have now been isolated in a relatively pure form.*

▶ almost **almost, nearly, virtually** *Previously, gold
coins were made from almost pure gold.*

2 used for emphasizing the amount or degree of
something

● ADJ+n enjoyment or pleasure **bliss, delight,
enjoyment, entertainment, fun, happiness, joy,
magic, pleasure** *Driving the car is just pure joy.*

▶ luck **chance, coincidence, luck** *It was pure chance
that we eventually found the car again.*

▶ statements about a possible situation **conjecture,
speculation** *Bear in mind, though, that this is pure
speculation.*

▶ statements that are not true **fantasy, fiction,
invention** *The prosecution showed that several of
these claims were pure fantasy.*

▶ evil **evil** *Hitler still, more than anyone else, embodies
pure evil.*

▶ love **love** *It's the nearest thing to pure love I've ever
experienced.*

▶ very high level of skill or ability **genius** *All six
episodes from this series are pure genius.*

purpose N

the aim someone wants to achieve

▶ adj+N main **chief, main, primary, prime, principal**
*The primary purpose of chemical weapons is to deter
their use by others.*

▶ useful **practical, useful** *This is a fun project with a
practical purpose.*

▶ specific **particular, special, specific** *Charles said
that some of these funds were given for specific
purposes.*

▶ common **common, shared** *A confederation is a group
of states united for a common purpose.*

▶ general **general** *For many years it has been part of
Crystal Palace Park and is used by local people for
general recreational purposes.*

▶ original **original** *It is the only medieval monastery
in Britain still being used for its original purpose.*

▶ only **only, sole** *This we are told is the sole purpose
of existence.*

▶ types of purpose **administrative, charitable,
commercial, educational, military, political** *Any use
of this material for commercial purposes of any kind
is strictly forbidden.*

▶ real or intended **intended, real, true** *Of course, the
real purpose of the race was to raise money for
charity.*

▶ n+N **business, information, insurance, marketing,
reference, research, security, tax, teaching, training**
*All businesses, including sole traders, need to register
for tax purposes.*

Usage ***Purpose*** is usually plural in all of the ***n+N***
combinations shown above: *A lot of businesses now
use Twitter for marketing purposes.*

● v+N achieve a purpose **accomplish, achieve,
fulfil** *A great deal of aid has been sent to the region,
but without really achieving its purpose.*

▶ make it possible to achieve a purpose **answer,
meet, serve** *This meeting has served no useful
purpose.*

▶ prevent a purpose from being achieved **defeat**
*This, of course, defeats the entire purpose of the
exercise.*

▶ suit someone's purpose **suit** *The US sold weapons
to Iraq when it suited their purpose.*

▶ explain a purpose **explain, outline** *The
questionnaires clearly explained the purpose and
nature of the research.*

▶ have a purpose **have, share** *The Bill has three main
purposes.*

pursue V

follow a course of activity

● adv+V actively **actively, energetically,
enthusiastically, vigorously** *For several years, they
vigorously pursued the objective of eliminating
poverty.*

▶ with great determination **doggedly, relentlessly,
systematically** *They are still doggedly pursuing
policies which will cause huge environmental
damage.*

● V+n course of action **course, course of action, line**
*Only one bank seems seriously interested in pursuing
this course of action.*

▶ policy or plan **approach, initiative, path, policy,
programme, strategy** *There is no justification for
changing a policy pursued by successive Governments
for nearly fifty years.*

▶ career **career** *I was already sure that I wanted to
pursue a career in law.*

▶ study **course, course of study, research, study**
*Postgraduates often work directly with companies
whilst pursuing their research.*

▶ activity **activity, interest, opportunity, project** *He
announced he would be leaving the company to
pursue other projects.*

▶ legal case **action, case, claim** *She is pursuing an
action for damages in the courts.*

▶ aim or ambition **aim, ambition, dream, goal,
objective** *They fear that those who have used
violence to pursue political objectives in the past will
do so again in the future.*

pursuit N

1 the process of trying to achieve something

● N+of aim **aim, ambition, dream, goal, objective,
purpose, vision** *He was to devote the next ten years
of his life to the pursuit of this goal.*

▶ happiness **happiness, pleasure** *Life, liberty, and the
pursuit of happiness are at the top of America's list
of rights.*

▶ money **money, profit, wealth** *With any large
corporation, pursuit of profit is the prime motivation.*

▶ knowledge or truth **knowledge, truth,
understanding** *All members of the university, both*

academic staff and students, share a common aim: the pursuit of knowledge.
▸ peace **peace** *The UN Secretary-General said that 'there are times when the use of force may be legitimate in the pursuit of peace'.*
▸ justice or fairness **equality, justice, rights** *He is a detective who is dogged in his pursuit of justice.*
▸ quality **excellence, quality** *As an artist, she is more interested in the pursuit of excellence than in financial reward.*
▸ power or success **power, success** *She is driven by the pursuit of power for its own sake.*

2 an activity you enjoy [usually plural]

● adj+N types of pursuit **academic, artistic, creative, cultural, intellectual, literary, scientific** *Born into a wealthy family, he was able to devote his life to intellectual pursuits.*
▸ outdoor **country, outdoor** *Inverclyde is a centre for numerous outdoor pursuits and activities.*
▸ popular **favourite, popular** *Diving is a particularly popular pursuit on the Cayman Islands.*
▸ active **active, energetic, sporting** *Cycling is one of the few active pursuits that you can all do as a family and all enjoy.*
▸ traditional **traditional** *On Exmoor, hunting, shooting, and fishing are traditional pursuits enjoyed by a large number of local people.*
▸ done for enjoyment **leisure, recreational** *Walking and swimming are his main recreational pursuits.*

● v+N like particular pursuits **enjoy, love, prefer** *Never a star pupil in academic subjects, he preferred pursuits such as photography and carpentry.*
▸ take part in particular pursuits **be engaged in, be involved in, engage in, follow, indulge in, participate in, take part in** *You will be able to take part in a variety of creative pursuits.*
▸ provide particular pursuits **offer** *Glengarry is the ideal base for a Highland holiday, offering many leisure pursuits.*

push for PHR VB
try hard to get or achieve something

● V+n change **action, change, improvement, reform** *We are organizing demonstrations to push for change.*
▸ position **place** *He is pushing hard for a place on the team.*
▸ law **amendment, law, legislation** *Senators are pushing for speedy legislation to protect endangered animals in the area.*
▸ increase **increase** *At the same time, the Civil Service is pushing for an even bigger increase in pay.*
▸ agreement **agreement** *The charity is pushing for trade agreements to benefit poor people.*
▸ official statement that something must not be

done **ban** *Campaigners are urging the President to push for a complete ban on chemical weapons.*
▸ war **war** *The prime minister pushed for a war which three-quarters of the UK population opposed.*
▸ official decision or action **adoption, implementation, introduction** *Most of the poorer countries were pushing for a rapid implementation of low-carbon policies.*

put aside PHR VB
stop being affected by a problem, argument etc so that you can achieve something more important

● V+n **concerns, differences, prejudices, rivalries, thoughts** *We now feel that we can put aside these rivalries and work together to rebuild the party.*

put forward PHR VB
offer an idea, opinion, reason etc

● V+n proposal **plan, proposal, proposition, recommendation, suggestion** *At the UN General Assembly in 1996, China put forward a five-point proposal on nuclear disarmament.*
▸ opinion **opinion, point of view, view** *The conference is also an opportunity for members of the public to put forward their opinions about the way forward for the city.*
▸ idea **argument, hypothesis, idea, theory** *Tutorials give students a chance to put forward ideas that are sometimes new to the tutor.*
▸ reason **reason** *At a Congressional Inquiry, the Association put forward seven reasons why the proposals should be scrapped.*

put in PHR VB
make an official request, claim, offer etc

● V+n offer **bid, offer** *Manchester United had put in a bid of more than £7.5 million.*
▸ request **application, request** *It is worth putting in an application as you can always withdraw it later if you really have to.*
▸ claim **claim** *We decided to demand compensation from the holiday company, and put in a claim.*

puzzle N
someone or something you cannot understand

● adj+N **challenging, complex, complicated, difficult, hard, tough** *The disease presents a complex biochemical puzzle.*

● v+N solve a puzzle **crack, piece together, solve, unravel** *They have been trying to solve the puzzle of where the 20,000–30,000 laborers who built the pyramids lived.*
▸ be or continue to be a puzzle **pose, present, remain** *His complex theories as well as his enigmatic personality also pose a puzzle.* ● *The source of the problem remains a puzzle, airline officials say.*

Qq

qualification N
something you obtain after successfully finishing an educational course

- adj+N educational **academic, educational, postgraduate** *He felt that in the UK education system there was too much focus on academic qualifications.*
- professional **financial, professional, technical, vocational, work-related** *The truth is that 33 per cent of asylum seekers have degrees or professional qualifications.*
- suitable for a purpose **appropriate, relevant, suitable** *An appropriate qualification in the subject to be taught is a prequisite.*
- basic **basic** *Some offenders gained basic qualifications while in prison.*
- additional **additional, further** *Further qualifications can enhance careers, or open up whole new ones.*
- officially recognized **accredited, formal, recognized** *Formal qualifications are preferable but not vital.*
- special **special, specialist, specific** *While no specific qualifications are needed, many companies like a graduate or someone with A levels.*
- necessary in order to do a job **essential, mandatory, minimum, necessary** *Only half the staff have the necessary qualifications.*
- with the same value **equivalent** *You should have GCSEs or equivalent qualifications in English Language and Mathematics.*

- n+N for teaching a subject **coaching, teaching, training** *Some roles will also require a recognized teaching qualification.*
- for a particular job **accountancy, business, childcare, engineering, IT, management, marketing, nursing, social work** *Steve currently holds three management qualifications including an MA in management studies.*
- allowing you to take a course **entrance, entry** *The University claims it is attracting more students with better entry qualifications.*
- in a language **English language, language** *Employers appreciate a language qualification, even when the jobs they seek to fill require no special language ability.*

- v+N have a qualification **have, hold, possess** *Almost three-quarters of staff in care homes have no qualifications.*
- get a qualification **achieve, acquire, gain, get, obtain, secure, take** *I hope to gain further qualifications and eventually become a teacher.*
- offer a qualification **offer, provide** *The college offers vocational qualifications in subjects such as travel and tourism, computing and business.*
- complete a qualification **complete** *The programme is organized so that participants can complete the qualification in approximately three months .*
- give a qualification **award** *You must pass all the internal assessments in order to pass the course and be awarded the appropriate qualification.*
- accept that a qualification is valid **recognize** *In France, they tend not to recognise non-French qualifications.*

- need a qualification **need, require** *You don't need any special qualifications, just an ability to listen and a desire to help.*
- study for a qualification **pursue, study for, train for, undertake** *You will enhance your career prospects if you pursue a professional qualfication.*
- and/or **degree, education, experience, expertise, knowledge, skill, training** *A lack of appropriate qualifications and experience is, in practice, an obstacle to employment.*

qualified ADJ
thoroughly trained for a particular job

- adv+ADJ properly **fully, properly** *In this course, you will be trained by a fully qualified instructor.*
- well **highly, well** *Students work with highly qualified staff, most of whom have worked in industry.*
- recently **newly, recently** *Organizations recruiting newly qualified graduates are often looking for very specific skills.*
- to a suitable standard **appropriately, suitably** *We will normally interview all suitably qualified applicants.*
- to a professional standard **professionally** *The Centre's Director and counsellors are all professionally qualified.*
- in a particular area of activity **clinically, legally, medically, technically** *Each tribunal is headed by a legally qualified chairperson who sits with two independent members.*
- well enough **adequately, sufficiently** *It is becoming increasingly hard to recruit sufficiently qualified engineers.*
- not well enough **insufficiently, poorly** *There remains the significant problem of poorly qualified school leavers.*
- with formal educational qualifications **academically** *The admissions process is fair and open, with all academically qualified candidates receiving equal consideration.*

qualify V
1 become a member of a particular profession after a period of training or study

- V+as **accountant, architect, barrister, dentist, doctor, engineer, instructor, lawyer, midwife, nurse, physiotherapist, pilot, solicitor, surveyor, teacher, therapist** *Simon qualified as a solicitor in 1994.*
- V+in **dentistry, law, medicine, nursing, psychology, science** *She qualified in medicine at the University of London.*
- V+infinitive **act, practise, teach, undertake, work** *The programme allows graduates to qualify to teach while doing 'on the job' training.*

2 have the right qualities to be allowed to do something or have something

- V+for financial help **aid, allowance, assistance, award, benefit, funding, grant, help, loan,**

payment, pension, support *Carers on low incomes may qualify for benefits such as Income Support.*
▶ reduction in charge **discount, reduction, relief** *Investors in venture capital trusts will qualify for income tax relief of 30 per cent.*
▶ permission not to pay something **exemption** *Which items qualify for exemption from VAT?*
▶ special price **rate** *You need to be a student over 50 per cent of the time in order to qualify for a student rate.*
▶ right to do something or join something **admission, entry, membership** *Completed forms must be returned before 31st March to qualify for entry into the draw.*
▶ programme **programme, scheme** *You will also need proof that you qualify for the scheme.*
▶ entry to a competition **championship, competition, event, race, tournament** *She had qualified for the event by setting a time of 12.3 seconds in the trials.*

quality N

● adj+N good **excellent, exceptional, fine, good, great, high, outstanding, superb, superior, top** *Australian wheat is of higher quality than ours.*
▶ bad **inferior, low, poor** *The result is usually a product of poor quality that weighs more than most adult bikes.*
▶ general **general, overall** *The potential impact of a weak teacher on the overall quality of a school can be considerable.*
▶ fantastic INFORMAL
▶ good enough **adequate, reasonable, satisfactory, sufficient** *Their range of computers provides reasonable quality at an affordable price.*

● v+N improve quality **develop, enhance, improve, increase, promote, raise** *The aim is to improve the quality of decision-making throughout the company.*
▶ reduce quality **degrade, reduce** *A supplier may seek to reduce quality of service in order to increase profits.*
▶ check quality **assess, check, evaluate, monitor** *The panel is supposed to assess the quality of the content of each journal article submitted for publication.*
▶ affect quality in a negative way **affect, compromise, sacrifice** *Budget cuts are affecting the quality of education students are receiving.*
▶ achieve quality **achieve, deliver** *Our aim is to achieve the highest possible quality in research at the international level.*
▶ make sure that quality stays the same **assure, ensure, maintain, preserve, protect** *In order to increase volume, while maintaining quality, we began forging links with other organic farms in the area.*

● N+n **assessment, assurance, control, management, monitoring, standards** *The research has been conducted by a senior manager with responsibility for quality assurance.*

quality ADJ
of a high standard

● ADJ+n product **craft, food, furniture, goods, produce, product, software, toy, wine** *Established in 1985, the company has grown to become a leading manufacturer of quality electrical products.*
▶ service **advice, care, service, solutions, support** *Rushforth said the continued growth of the company*

was down to 'providing a very professional, quality service'.*
▶ company supplying a product **supplier** *We always try to buy from quality local suppliers.*
▶ material **material** *Manufactured from quality raw materials, it is built for strength and durability.*
▶ places to live or work **accommodation, houses, housing, offices** *The Council recognises it has a duty to provide safe, quality housing where residents can feel secure.*
▶ education or training **education, research, teaching, training** *We have a proven track record of delivering quality training in management.*

quantity N
the amount of something

● adj+N large **copious, enormous, generous, great, high, huge, immense, large, massive, substantial, unlimited, vast** *Deciduous trees can drop vast quantities of leaves in autumn.*
▶ quite large **considerable, moderate, reasonable, significant** *An abundance of corn grows in this area, and a considerable quantity of it is exported.*
▶ too large **excessive** *Eating excessive quantities of food leads to obesity and health problems.*
▶ small **limited, low, minute, small, tiny** *A post-mortem revealed tiny quantities of arsenic in his body.*
▶ enough **adequate, sufficient** *Many people in the world do not have access to sufficient quantities of food.*
▶ the least possible **minimum** *The minimum quantity you can order by post is 200g.*
▶ the most possible **maximum** *This is the maximum quantity of information that the device is capable of storing.*

quarrel N
an argument

● adj+N serious and angry **bitter, deadly, fierce, serious** *It was during this period that Scott had a bitter quarrel with his mother.*
▶ about something unimportant **petty, silly, unseemly** *She got involved in a petty quarrel with one of her housemates.*
▶ between members of a family or other group **domestic, internal, personal, private** *I was dragged into a domestic quarrel between Jane and her mother.*

● v+N have a quarrel **become involved in, be involved in, get involved in, have** *He got involved in a quarrel with his cousin, who was staying at the same hotel.*
▶ try to start a quarrel **pick, provoke** *He had a tendency to take offence and to pick quarrels with people.*
▶ end a quarrel **end, patch up, resolve, settle** *They tried to let the children settle their own quarrels without taking sides.*

● N+v **arise, break out, erupt** *A quarrel broke out between Olga and her sister.*

quarrel V
have an argument

● adv+V **bitterly, constantly, frequently, violently** *He was always in trouble at school, constantly* *quarrelling and getting into fights with other children.*

quash V

officially say a court's decision was wrong

- V+n **acquittal, conviction, decision, indictment, order, sentence, verdict** *He was found guilty but, on appeal, his conviction was quashed by the Court of Appeal.*

query N

a request for information or an explanation

- adj+N easy to deal with **minor, quick, small** *I have sent Mr Blake a few small queries, which I am sure he will be able to deal with.*
- ▶ more **additional, further, more, other** *For any further queries, please email the conference organizer.*
- ▶ about one particular thing **specific** *I was researching a holiday and had a specific query about flight times.*
- ▶ general **general** *If you have a general query, and are unsure who to contact, the administrator will be able to help.*
- ▶ not yet dealt with **outstanding** *The insurance company still had to resolve a number of outstanding queries before they could issue a policy.*
- v+N have a query **have** *If you have any further queries, please do not hesitate to contact us.*
- ▶ tell someone what your query is **pose, raise, submit** *Check the details, and raise any queries immediately.*
- ▶ deal with a query **deal with, handle, process** *Please e-mail us and we will respond to your query as soon as we can.*
- ▶ give information in response to a query **answer, resolve, solve** *We aim to answer your email queries within 2 working days.*
- ▶ get a query from someone **get, receive** *We have received many queries about the date of the next concert.*

quest N

a long difficult search

- adj+N continuing for a long time **constant, endless, eternal, long, never-ending, relentless, unending** *She is engaged in a constant quest to find clothes that fit.*
- ▶ happening now and continuing **continuing, ongoing** *The ongoing quest for safer food has meant that increasing numbers of consumers view supermarkets with suspicion.*
- ▶ unlikely to be successful **fruitless, futile, hopeless, impossible** *The novel centres on her futile quest to find a job she enjoyed.*
- ▶ types of quest **intellectual, personal, religious, scientific, spiritual** *What had begun as a personal quest had grown into a very promising research project.*
- v+N start a quest **begin, embark on, start** *A third coalition was necessary because Napoleon began a quest for military empire in Europe.*
- ▶ be involved in a quest **be engaged in, continue, go on, pursue, undertake** *The book is about one man pursuing his quest for what he believes to be right.*

- ▶ end a quest successfully **achieve, complete, end** *After two months, I had completed my quest of visiting every single church in Suffolk.*
- ▶ end a quest before you have completed it **abandon** *At the age of forty six, and in failing health, he had to abandon his quest for power.*
- N+for for information **answer, enlightenment, knowledge, meaning, solution, truth, understanding** *The quest for answers goes on.*
- ▶ for a particular state **freedom, justice, love, peace, perfection, revenge** *If your quest for love has so far proved fruitless – how about spending a night speed dating?*
- ▶ for success or power **domination, excellence, glory, power, success** *He has agreed to help the club in its quest for success.*

question N

1 a request for information

- adj+N good and worth asking **fair, good, interesting, intriguing, pertinent, reasonable, relevant, valid** *That's a good question and I'm not sure what the answer is.*
- ▶ silly **silly, stupid** *He's always pestering me with stupid questions.*
- ▶ difficult to answer **awkward, challenging, difficult, hard, tough, tricky** *This is a really hard question to answer.*
- ▶ easy to answer **basic, easy, quick, simple** *Answer a simple question for your chance to win a fantastic family holiday at Center Parcs.*
- ▶ not yet answered **outstanding, unanswered** *If you still have any unanswered questions, please contact us and we'll do our best to help.*
- ▶ asking for an opinion and not an answer of 'yes' or 'no' **open, open-ended** *Ensure there is no presumption of guilt and ask open questions.*
- ▶ designed to discover the truth **probing, searching** *Howard asked me a lot of probing questions about our chances of success.*
- ▶ direct because you want to get information **direct, pointed** *The Minister was ruffled by some very pointed questions.*
- ▶ designed to make someone give a particular answer **leading, loaded, trick** *Advocates should not be permitted to ask their witnesses leading questions.*
- ▶ about your private life **personal** *She didn't want to answer personal questions about her family life.*
- v+N have a question **have** *If you have any questions about the services we offer or would like to place an order then please contact us.*
- ▶ ask a question **ask (sb), pose, put** *Young children ask a lot of questions.*
- ▶ officially ask someone to answer a question **submit, table** *He has tabled questions to the defence secretary asking what plans were drawn up to evacuate British nationals.*
- ▶ answer a question **answer, reply to, respond to** *The teacher was on hand to answer questions.*
- ▶ try to avoid someone's question **avoid, dodge, evade, ignore, sidestep** *Politicians are often accused of trying to avoid questions.*
- ▶ express a question in a particular way **formulate, frame, phrase** *In an investigation of this type, you need to take great care in the way you frame your questions.*

▶ express a question in a different way **rephrase** *If your students do not understand what you are talking about, then you should try to rephrase the question.*

▶ have to deal with questions **face, field** *After the break, Robinson fielded questions on his career.*

2 an issue needing to be discussed and solved

● adj+N important **basic, big, burning, central, critical, crucial, fundamental, important, key, main, major, serious, vital** *The critical question is whether they will be able to cope.*

▶ difficult **challenging, complex, controversial, difficult, thorny, tough, tricky, vexed** *Whether Mr Brooks should or should not have been prosecuted is a vexed question.*

▶ that has not been dealt with **unanswered, unresolved** *His presidency was very controversial, and there are still many unresolved questions.*

▶ types of question **constitutional, environmental, historical, moral, philosophical, political, scientific, social, theological** *The role of the church in politics raises important constitutional questions.*

● v+N make people start to think about a question **bring up, highlight, pose, prompt, raise** *This raises the question of how representative the data is.*

▶ think about or discuss a question **consider, debate, discuss, examine, explore, investigate, ponder** *These questions are considered in the next two essays of the collection.*

▶ deal with a question **address, confront, deal with, handle, tackle** *Some hospitals have not addressed the question of the management of emergency admissions.*

▶ solve a question **answer, resolve, settle, solve** *DNA research has finally resolved the question of the dodo's ancestry.*

▶ avoid a question **avoid, ignore** *In an age of many beliefs and none, the church cannot avoid the great theological questions.*

question V
have or express doubts about something

● adv+V strongly **seriously, strongly** *I seriously question the legality of this move.*

▶ often **constantly, continually, increasingly** *The effectiveness of this approach is, however, increasingly questioned.*

▶ not often **rarely** *The need for a professional police force is rarely questioned.*

▶ correctly **rightly** *Some scholars have rightly questioned this notion.*

▶ in a public way **openly, publicly** *They will openly question the referee's decisions.*

● V+n an idea or belief **assumption, attitude, belief, claim, existence, faith, idea, notion, view** *As I grew older, I began to question the existence of God.* ● *I've always questioned the idea of music as 'entertainment' but it's really difficult to define it as anything else.*

▶ whether it is good, right, or legal to do something **accuracy, effectiveness, legality, legitimacy, merit, validity, value, wisdom** *Senior politicians were privately questioning the wisdom of appointing him to such a role.*

▶ an aspect of someone's character **ability,** **commitment, integrity, sanity, sexuality** *I feel unsure of myself; I constantly question my own ability, and my self-confidence is rock-bottom.*

▶ a way of doing something **approach, decision, policy, practice, technique, use, way** *All organizations need to question the way they do business.*

▶ the reason why someone does something **aim, motivation, motives, purpose** *She has questioned their motives for this decision.*

▶ whether something is needed **need** *Local residents question the need for yet another runway.*

▶ someone's right or power **authority, right** *During the Reformation, people questioned the authority of the Pope.*

▶ what someone or something does **role** *The community has begun to question the role of the security forces.*

questionable ADJ
possibly not good, right, or true

● adv+ADJ very **extremely, highly, very** *The country has developed a highly questionable asylum policy, built on shaky evidence.*

▶ rather **rather, somewhat** *His management of the team was somewhat questionable.*

▶ in a particular way **ethically, legally, morally** *Some genetic research is ethically questionable.*

● ADJ+n usefulness or relevance **benefit, relevance, utility, value** *Their advice on agricultural methods is of questionable value for subsistence farmers in developing companies.*

▶ action or decision **action, activity, decision, method, practice, procedure** *The discussion ended with a highly questionable decision regarding the funding of basic research.*

▶ belief or claim **argument, assertion, assumption, claim** *Her theory is based on several rather questionable assumptions.*

▶ correctness **legitimacy, validity** *Opponents of these plans produced some statistics of questionable validity.*

● v+ADJ **appear, be, become, remain, seem** *It remains questionable whether these measures will bring a return to economic stability.*

questioning N
a situation in which someone is asked questions

● adj+N **aggressive, close, further, tough** *The parents are being held for further questioning.*

● v+N **be brought in for, be detained for, be held for, be wanted for, face, undergo** *The two men are wanted for questioning in connection with a burglary at a superstore.*

questioning ADJ
showing that you want more information or that you have doubts

● ADJ+n **approach, attitude, glance, look, mind** *Students are adopting a more questioning approach in lectures.*

queue N
a line of people waiting for something

- adj+N long **big, endless, enormous, huge, large, lengthy, long, massive** *At weekends there are often huge queues at the checkouts.*
▶ short **short, small** *Maurice joined a short queue of people at the reception desk.*
▶ well-behaved and well-controlled **orderly** *He made them all stand in an orderly queue, and anyone who pushed was sent to the back.*
- v+N be in a queue **be in, stand in, wait in** *We got fed up with waiting in the queue so we just went home.*
▶ join a queue **join** *You can buy tickets at the venue. However, be prepared to join the queue.*
▶ form a queue **form** *People are blocking entrances by not forming an orderly queue.*
▶ reduce the length of a queue **cut, reduce** *Self check-in was designed to cut queues at the airport.*
▶ move in front of people who have been waiting longer than you **jump** *Jumping the queue is considered extremely impolite in Britain.*
- N+v when a queue forms **build up, form** *Outside the theatre a large queue had formed.*
▶ when people in a queue move forward **move** *Queuing didn't take too long as the queue moved quite quickly.*
▶ when a queue is very long **snake, stretch** *Queues snaked around the building.*

quick ADJ
fast

- adv+ADJ very **exceptionally, extremely, incredibly, really, very** *Cataract surgery is an extremely quick and effective operation which can be performed on almost every patient.*
▶ rather **fairly, pretty** INFORMAL, **quite, reasonably, relatively** *When he lost the first set 15/4, I thought the match was going to be pretty quick.*
▶ in a way that is surprising **amazingly, remarkably, surprisingly** *A surprisingly quick train journey got me to Cardiff for mid-morning.*
- ADJ+infinitive **acknowledge sth, condemn sb/sth, criticize sb/sth, defend sb/sth, dismiss sh/sth, judge (sb), point out sth, praise sb/sth, react, realize sth, recognize sth, respond, spot sth** *As US officials were quick to point out, details of the offer were extremely sketchy.*
- and/or and easy **convenient, easy, painless, simple, straightforward** *The recipes are all quick and easy to cook.*
▶ and good **accurate, effective, efficient, good, reliable, safe** *We are a small company, dedicated to providing a quick and efficient service.*
▶ and cheap or free **cheap, cost-effective, free, inexpensive** *Try our quick and free assessment to see if the programme could help you.*

quiet ADJ
1 making little or no noise

- adv+ADJ very **exceptionally, extremely, perfectly, really, very** *The engine is smooth and very quiet.*
▶ rather **fairly, a little, pretty** INFORMAL, **quite, rather, reasonably, relatively, somewhat** *Despite being fairly quiet while walking, the girls soon bounced back to their happy noisy selves shortly after reaching the hut.*

▶ in a way that is unusual or surprising **remarkably, strangely, surprisingly, unusually** *Prescott was strangely quiet that day.*
- v+ADJ stay quiet **keep, remain, stay** *Keeping quiet for a minute or two is easy.*
▶ become quiet **become, fall, go, grow** *The room fell quiet as we waited for the big announcement.* • *He grew quiet when he joined them in the kitchen.*
▶ seem quiet **appear, seem** *The other cat seemed pretty quiet in comparison.*

2 with little activity

- adv+ADJ very **dead** INFORMAL, **exceptionally, extremely, perfectly, really, very** *The Canaletto Hotel is an elegant, family run hotel situated in a very quiet residential area.*
▶ rather **fairly, a little, pretty** INFORMAL, **quite, reasonably, relatively, somewhat** *In the neighbourhood where we live, life is relatively quiet.*
▶ in a way that is unusual or surprising **remarkably, strangely, surprisingly, unusually** *The windows are open to the evening, the street below us strangely quiet.*
▶ in a way that is slightly frightening **deathly, eerily, suspiciously, uncannily** *The streets were eerily quiet after the explosions.*
- ADJ+n place **area, backwater, location, neighbourhood, place, resort, road, room, setting, spot, street, suburb, surroundings, town, village** *The cottage is located in a quiet road in this charming village.*
▶ time **day, evening, moment, month, night, period, time, week, weekend** *We were tired so decided to have a quiet day.*
▶ occasion or event **affair, drink, game, holiday, life, meal** *This unique atmosphere makes it a perfect setting for a quiet drink after work.*
- and/or **calm, clean, comfortable, lovely, nice, peaceful, relaxing, rural, secluded, tranquil, unspoiled** *The hotel was nice and quiet.* • *The quiet, peaceful life in the warm climate of Guernsey suited her.*

quirk N
a strange or annoying habit or feature

- adj+N strange or unusual **bizarre, funny, interesting, odd, strange** *Apart from a few odd quirks, I haven't found any significant problems with the new software.*
▶ annoying **annoying, unfortunate** *The CD also has some annoying quirks; one song sounded as if it has been recorded in a shower room.*
▶ little **little, minor** *Children can develop all sorts of little quirks, most of which are perfectly normal parts of growing up.*
▶ of one person or thing **individual, personal** *Much like people, aircraft also have their own individual quirks.*
- and/or **foible, oddity** *For all of his foibles and quirks, Partridge can be quite a funny and interesting personality.*

quit V
leave a job, school etc permanently

- adv+V **finally, immediately, recently, suddenly** *By*

the time I finally quit five years ago, the decision came naturally, and I had the strength to do it.

- V+n **band, business, club, game, job, post, profession, role, school, show, sport, work** *I hated working with him so much that I quit my job.*

quota N
an officially allowed amount of something

- adj+N full **full, maximum** *The full quota of ten teams participated.*
- ▶ not changing **fixed, strict** *With the exception of a quota of seven in Medicine imposed by the University, we have no fixed quotas in any subject.*
- ▶ relating to a particular time period **annual, daily, monthly, weekly** *There is an annual quota of 9,000 New Zealand working holiday visas for British passport holders.*
- ▶ large **high, large** *It may be difficult to achieve high quotas of affordable housing.*

- v+N decide what a quota should be **allocate, establish, impose, introduce, set** *Universities set quotas for the number of undergraduates they accept.*
- ▶ increase a quota **double, increase, raise** *Canada has gradually increased the quota on harp seal hunts, allowing up to 350,000 a year to be killed.*
- ▶ reduce a quota **cut, reduce** *The EU decided today to cut fish quotas by up to 55 per cent.*
- ▶ reach a quota **achieve, fulfil, meet, reach** *In order to meet the production quotas, employees will have to work harder.*
- ▶ have or do more than a quota allows **exceed** *If you exceed your email quota you will be unable to receive any new messages.*

quotation N
1 words taken from book, play, film etc

- adj+N using exactly the same words **direct, exact, verbatim** *Verbatim quotations should be in inverted commas, and directly acknowledged.*
- ▶ short **brief, short** *Short quotations should, as far as possible, be included in the text and enclosed in single quotation marks.*
- ▶ long **lengthy, long** *There were too many lengthy quotations.*
- ▶ well-known **famous, well-known** *The French satirist Voltaire's famous quotation – 'Work banishes those three great evils: boredom, vice and poverty' – was widely propagated.*

- v+N give a quotation **cite, include, use** *In his book on Russia, he cites a quotation from The Revolution Betrayed.*
- ▶ get a quotation from somewhere **take** *The following quotation is taken from the 1995 report.*
- ▶ say who first said something **attribute** *Make sure you attribute quotations, ideas and theories to the people who came up with them.*

- N+v a quotation comes from something **come from sth** *The quotation comes from Shakespeare's Macbeth.*
- ▶ a quotation shows or suggests something **illustrate sth, indicate sth, show sth, suggest sth** *As this quotation suggests, the UK tends to do relatively well in international comparisons of student retention.*

- N+from **article, book, interview, letter, paper,**

play, poem, source, speech, text *Your dissertation should be in English, but quotations from primary sources must be in the language of the original.*

2 the price someone offers to do some work for someone

- adj+N **competitive, detailed, free, full, no-obligation, online, personal, written** *Written quotations are available on request.*

- v+N give someone a quotation **give (sb), issue, offer (sb), provide (sb with), supply** *Quotations are provided on request.*
- ▶ get a quotation **get, obtain** *Do get an accurate written quotation for all work required.*
- ▶ ask for a quotation **request, seek** *The secretary was asked to seek quotations for carpeting the office.*
- ▶ agree to the price in a quotation **accept** *If you accept our quotation, we will then inform you of when work is likely to proceed.*

quote V
1 say or write someone else's words

- adv+V often or in many places **commonly, extensively, freely, frequently, publicly, widely** *He is a regular guest on business television and he is frequently quoted in newspapers and periodicals.*
- ▶ using the exact words that were said **accurately, correctly, directly, verbatim** *Readers' comments are quoted verbatim from a recent readership survey.*
- ▶ using only some words or ideas **selectively** *Naturally, I have selectively quoted the statistics that promote this school's academic strengths.*
- ▶ in a way that shows you like what someone said **approvingly** *When the leader of a party of 'the left' approvingly quotes Republicans, something very odd is going on.*

- V+n **author, message, paragraph, passage, phrase, remark, sentence, text, verse, word** *It is not necessary to quote a passage in full.*
- V+from **article, book, document, letter, material, paper, poem, publication, report, review, source, speech, text** *She quotes from a well-known paper about how children acquire language.*

2 give something as an example to support a statement

- adv+V **commonly, extensively, frequently, often, widely** *Another frequently quoted investment is your own home, but the prime reason for owning your home should be the convenience and pleasure you get from living in it.*
- V+n **case, evidence, example, figure, number, research, statistic, study, work** *Figures were quoted which showed the extent of the decline.*

quote N
1 a quotation from a book, play, speech etc

- adj+N using exactly the same words **direct, exact** *I'm struggling to remember the exact quote.*
- ▶ well-known **classic, famous, memorable, quotable, well-known** *There are famous quotes from all of the popular Shakespeare plays.*
- ▶ long/short **brief, long, short** *Only short quotes are included.*
- ▶ good or interesting **good, great, inspirational,**

interesting, wonderful *Inspirational quotes provide comfort in difficult times.*

● v+N **attribute, take, use** *Ceefax reported the result with a quote attributed to Tony Blair.* ● *The quotes below are taken from the research survey in response to a question about community living.*

● N+v a quote comes from somewhere **come from sth** *The quotes come from a wide variety of sources and backgrounds.*

▶ a quote shows or suggests something **illustrate sth, indicate sth, show sth, suggest sth** *The following quotes show the value of forward planning and organization.*

2 the price someone offers to do some work for someone

● adj+N offering a low price **affordable, cheap, competitive, low, reasonable** *Motorists should not only search for a competitive quote, but also for the best insurance cover.*

▶ with full details **detailed, full** *Please contact us for a full quote.*

▶ not costing anything **free** *We'll offer you a free website design quote, including your requirements and budgets.*

▶ given online or in writing **online, written** *Visit several garages and get them to provide you with a written quote.*

▶ given very quickly **instant, quick** *You can get an instant online quote.*

▶ done especially for you **individual, personal** *We are happy to send you a personal quote to suit your requirements.*

● v+N get a quote **get, obtain** *Before you get started, obtain several quotes and compare terms.*

▶ give someone a quote **give (sb), offer (sb), provide (sb with)** *We will provide a free quote, with a breakdown of all costs.*

▶ ask for a quote **request, seek** *The Clerk has been asked to seek quotes for this.*

▶ agree to the price in a quote **accept** *Don't accept the first quote you get.*

▶ compare different quotes **compare** *Compare these quotes with your current home insurance policy to see if you are over-paying.*

Rr

race N
a competition, especially in sports or politics

- v+N take part in a race **be in, compete in, contest, enter, join, participate in, run in, take part in** *Four riders contest a race, usually in pairs from opposing clubs.*
- ▶ win/lose a race **lose, win** *He felt cruelly disappointed to lose the race when victory had been in sight.*
- ▶ decide to stop taking part in a race **drop out of, pull out of, retire from, withdraw from** *He considered withdrawing from the leadership race.*
- ▶ do things so you are ready for a race **prepare for, train for** *We are preparing for the opening race of the season.*
- ▶ organize a race **have, hold, organize, stage** *This year they will be staging an extra race for runners in the under-15 category.*
- ▶ complete a race **complete, finish** *She entered and completed the race in 3 hrs 23 mins.*
- ▶ be winning a race **dominate, lead** *Corser led the first race from start to finish.*

racial ADJ
happening between people of different races

- ADJ+n good or fair treatment and relationships **equality, harmony, justice, tolerance** *He spent his whole life fighting for racial equality.* • *These values of racial tolerance are very much part of Muslim teaching.*
- ▶ unfair treatment **bias, discrimination, inequality, prejudice** *There is no doubt that racial discrimination exists and that current legislation is insufficient to tackle it.*
- ▶ violent or threatening behaviour **abuse, attack, crime, harassment, hatred, incident, slur, violence** *Most of the residents reported experiencing racial abuse.*
- ▶ social divisions and lack of trust **conflict, division, intolerance, tension** *In many cities, explosive urban riots sparked by racial tensions have shattered community relations.*

racism N
failure to respect people of other races

- adj+N very obvious **blatant, overt** *Today, overt racism is rare in schooling.*
- ▶ in every part of an organization, society, etc **endemic, ingrained, inherent, institutional, institutionalized** *Institutionalized racism and social exclusion are facts of life in modern Britain.*
- ▶ existing, but not intentional or openly expressed **covert, subtle, unconscious, unwitting** *In some cases, covert racism is expressed through criticism of religious practices.*
- ▶ of the most extreme kind **extreme, vicious, violent, virulent** *The party's virulent racism has been linked to a rise in attacks on ethnic minorities.*
- v+N suffer racism **encounter, experience, face, suffer** *Of 85 people interviewed, 43 experienced racism on a regular basis.*
- ▶ deal with the problem of racism **address,**
challenge, combat, confront, deal with, fight, tackle *The union is committed to tackling racism, fascism and other forms of bigotry in the workplace.*
- ▶ get rid of racism **counter, eliminate, end, eradicate, stamp out** *The police are working hard to eradicate racism – and to control crime.*
- ▶ encourage racism **encourage, fuel, promote** *This wave of hysteria about asylum seekers has fuelled racism in every corner of society.*

radiation N
energy produced during nuclear reaction or sent out by the sun

- adj+N high/low in amount **high-level, intense, low-level** *While the dangers of high-level radiation have been more obvious, the hazards of low-level radiation are increasingly coming to light.*
- ▶ dangerous **dangerous, deadly, harmful** *In the worst-case scenario, this could lead to a nuclear explosion, unleashing deadly radiation.*
- v+N produce or give off radiation **emit, generate, produce, release, transmit** *There's little danger to human health from the relatively weak radiation generated by mobile phones.*
- ▶ take in radiation **absorb** *Triple-glazed windows are coated to absorb infrared radiation in the winter and reflect it in the summer.*
- ▶ measure radiation **detect, measure** *When measuring the radiation, meters measure the electric or the magnetic field, and then it is converted into the power density.*

radical ADJ
new and very different from usual

- ADJ+n change **change, departure, improvement, overhaul, reform, restructuring, rethink, review, revision, shake-up, shift, transformation** *The Government must work for a radical reform of the world's financial system.*
- ▶ idea or plan **agenda, alternative, approach, idea, programme, proposal, solution** *The political class proved too weak to adopt radical solutions to the threat of climate change.*

raft N
a very large number of people or things

- adj+N huge, new, whole **huge, new, whole** *To start with, there's a whole raft of programmes that have had to be approved.*
- N+of **benefits, changes, features, improvements, initiatives, issues, laws, legislation, measures, policies, proposals, regulations** *There is a raft of new policies and initiatives designed to tackle the problems of disadvantaged areas, schools and pupils*

rage N
a very strong feeling of anger

- adj+N very great **blind, boiling, furious, great, jealous, murderous, uncontrollable, violent** *Thomas cut her throat in a jealous rage.*

▸ but unable to do anything **frustrated, impotent** *I am one of those listeners who frequently find themselves shouting at their radios in impotent rage.*

▸ when drunk **drunken** *His father tried to shoot him while in a drunken rage.*

● v+N feel rage **be consumed with, be filled with, feel, seethe with** *In the story, he is consumed with rage and sets out to kill his sister's murderer.*

▸ control rage **channel, control, suppress** *I could no longer suppress the rage that burned within me.*

▸ express or show rage **explode with, express, unleash, vent** *They vented their rage by breaking the windows and shutters of the house.*

▸ cause rage **cause, provoke** *This decision will provoke rage from smokers.*

▸ make rage worse **fuel** *These revelations fuelled the rage of an already angry electorate.*

● and/or **anger, despair, fear, frustration, fury, grief, hatred, jealousy, pain, violence** *Rage and jealousy overwhelm him, and trouble ensues.*

rage V

continue with force, violence, or angry arguments

● adv+V **fiercely, furiously** *The storm raged furiously.*

● n+V argument **argument, battle, conflict, controversy, debate** *Debates are raging about the best way to tackle global warming.*

▸ war or fighting **battle, fighting, struggle, war** *There were unwinnable wars raging on two continents.*

▸ natural event **epidemic, fire, gale, storm, tempest** *An intense fire was raging by the time firefighters arrived on the scene.*

raid N

a sudden short military attack

● adj+N big **big, heavy, large, major, massive** *There was a heavy raid on Coventry, with over 400 bombers destroying a large part of the city centre.*

▸ brave **daring** *Ireton led a daring raid on the Royalists' quarters and took a number of prisoners.*

▸ causing a lot of damage **devastating** *Roxanne worked in Liverpool during the devastating air raids.*

▸ done without warning, to surprise your enemy **lightning, surprise** *Huge damage was done by their lightning raids on our shipping.*

▸ n+N types of raid **air, bomber, bombing, commando, enemy** *The bridge was destroyed by the RAF during a bombing raid.*

▸ time when a raid happens **dawn, daylight, morning, night, night-time, pre-dawn** *Daylight attacks gradually gave way to night raids.*

▸ v+N make a raid **carry out, conduct, execute, launch, make, mount, stage** *The US airforce launched bombing raids on Basra, destroying a radar system.*

▸ be in charge of a raid **lead** *He was killed in action while leading a raid on enemy trenches at Loos, in October 1916.*

▸ experience a raid **experience, suffer** *On September 1, 1939, as the war broke out, Warsaw suffered the first air raids on a major city.*

rain N

water falling in drops from the sky

● adj+N heavy **drenching, driving, hard, heavy, horizontal, pouring, torrential** *The lifeboat battled in strong winds, driving rain and poor visibility to bring the man to safety.*

▸ light **drizzling, drizzly, fine, gentle, light, slight, soft** *Northern Scotland had a mostly mild night with some light rain.*

▸ continuing for a long time **constant, continual, continuous, endless, incessant, persistent, prolonged, relentless, steady** *Building work was halted in December after weeks of incessant rain.*

▸ happening for short periods **intermittent, occasional, showery** *It was a dull and damp morning with intermittent light rain and poor visibility.*

▸ happening in some places **patchy** *A large area of patchy rain was over Northern France.*

● N+v rain falls **beat down, come down, descend, fall, lash down, pelt down, pour down** *The traffic was awful and the rain was lashing down.*

▸ rain stops **cease, clear, stop** *The rain quickly cleared and the garden produced a myriad of birds.*

▸ rain becomes less **ease (off), let up** *Once the rain had eased, we returned to the field.*

▸ rain starts **arrive, begin, come, start** *The heavy rain arrived a little sooner than predicted.*

▸ rain seems likely to start **threaten** *The nature trail is also a good option if rain is threatening, since it is easy to get back to the hotel.*

▸ rain seems likely but does not happen **hold off** *The rain held off too – most of the time.*

▸ rain makes someone or something very wet **drench sb/sth, flood sth, soak sb/sth** *The rain drenched not only my clothes, but also my spirits.*

▸ rain hits a place **hit sth, sweep sth** *Glasgow was hit by heavy rain, leaving the organisers no alternative but to call off proceedings.*

rain V

when water falls in drops from clouds

● adv+V a lot **hard, heavily, torrentially** *It rained hard all night.*

▸ a little **lightly** *It was only raining lightly so we set off for our walk.*

▸ all the time **constantly, continuously, incessantly, non-stop, solidly, steadily** *It rained continuously for three days.*

rainfall N

amount of rain during particular time

● adj+N high **above average, excessive, extreme, heavy, high, intense, prolonged, significant, substantial, torrential** *The period since 30th October has seen significant rainfall across northern China, with scores of rivers having burst their banks.*

▸ low **below average, light, little, low** *The region enjoys a relatively mild climate and low rainfall.*

▸ not high and not low **moderate** *In the east of the country, there is moderate rainfall throughout the year.*

▸ average **average, mean, normal** *Between 18th and 23rd June we had 1½ times the normal rainfall for the whole of June.*

▸ typical of a particular season **autumn, seasonal,**

spring, summer, winter *Seasonal rainfall over the highlands of Ethiopia controls the flow of the Blue Nile.*
► enough for a country's needs **abundant, plentiful** *In good years, abundant rainfall guarantees a good rice crop.*
► not enough **inadequate, limited, poor** *In recent years, poor rainfall and persistent drought have caused widespread misery.*
► each year, month etc **annual, daily, monthly** *Annual rainfall is high (1700mm), but there is a dry season from May to September.*
● v+N have rainfall **experience, have, receive** *The east-coast city of Edinburgh receives much less rainfall than the west of Scotland.*
► measure or record rainfall **measure, record** *12.7mm of rainfall was recorded over 7.5 hours at Pitsford Hall.*

rainforest N
a forest in hot countries where it rains a lot

● adj+N **ancient, dense, lowland, lush, pristine, temperate, tropical, virgin** *Green iguanas live in tropical rainforests.*
● v+N protect a rainforest **protect, save** *The website provides details of their work to protect the rainforests, marine ecosystems and wildlife.*
► destroy or be likely to destroy a rainforest **destroy, threaten** *Today agriculture and logging are not destroying the rainforest at the same rate as 40 years ago.*
● N+n **canopy, conservation, destruction, ecosystem, environment, habitat, species** *White-faced monkeys live in small family groups in the rainforest canopy.*
● n+of+N **area, patch, swathes, tract** *Demand for soya crops led to the destruction of vast swathes of rainforest.*

raise V
cause a particular feeling or reaction

● V+n **alarm, awareness, concerns, consciousness, doubts, fears, hopes, interest, suspicion, tensions** *Thousands of events have been organised to raise awareness of the disease.* ● *This decision will raise fears that some patients will not be given the best treatment.*

rally N
a public meeting showing support, or as a protest

● adj+N large **major, mass** *The general strike ended with a mass rally in the capital city.*
► not violent **peaceful** *Anti-war groups are calling for a peaceful rally and a march on parliament.*
► with a particular purpose **anti-war, election, peace, pre-election, protest** *She was speaking at a Conservative Party pre-election rally last night.*
● v+N organize a rally **hold, organize, stage** *It was here that the suffragettes staged their rallies in support of votes for women.*
► take part in a rally **attend, join, take part in** *He attended an anti-vivisection rally in Trafalgar Square.*
► speak at a rally **address, speak at** *Union leaders*

*will address a rally **against** the proposed new legislation.*

random ADJ
chosen or happening without any particular method or pattern

● adv+ADJ completely **completely, entirely, genuinely, purely, totally, truly, utterly** *Perhaps the selection of the dates is purely random.*
► apparently **apparently, seemingly** *There were row upon row of books in seemingly random order.*
► almost or rather **almost, essentially, fairly, pretty** INFORMAL, **quite, rather, slightly, somewhat** *These devices create passwords that are essentially random but easy for you to remember.* ● *They gave me a lot of slightly random questions which I had to answer.*
● ADJ+n sample or choice **choice, sample, sampling, selection** *This is a random selection some of my favourite photos.*
► check or test **check, test, testing** *Since random testing has been introduced into the sport there has been a reduction in the number of positive samples.*
► order **order** *The device plays the 100 songs you listen to most in a random order.*
● v+ADJ **appear, be, look, seem** *The whole process seems completely random.*

range N
a number of different things, numbers, measurements etc included within a category or limit

● adj+N large **broad, comprehensive, enormous, extensive, huge, large, massive, vast, wide** *We provide a wide range of training opportunities to meet the needs of teachers and classroom assistants.*
► varied **diverse, varied** *He has had an impressive film career, portraying a diverse range of characters.*
► full **complete, entire, full, whole** *Throughout this website, the term 'deaf' is used to cover the whole range of hearing loss.*
► impressive or good **excellent, exciting, fantastic, good, great, impressive, superb** *They make an impressive range of furniture from a variety of woods.*
► small **limited, narrow** *We have wetsuits for hire, but in a limited range of sizes.*
► normal **normal** *All these children are within the normal range of intelligence.*
● v+N have a range **boast, demonstrate, display, have, show** *Our menu boasts a range of expertly prepared dishes.*
► produce or create a range **develop, introduce, manufacture, produce** *The archive produces a range of audio and print publications related to its collections.*
► include a range **contain, cover, embrace, encompass, feature, include, incorporate, reflect, represent, span** *The course has covered a good range of topics.*
► offer or provide a range **bring, deliver, launch, offer, provide, sell, supply** *We can help you launch a new product range.* ● *The school offers a full range of options for postgraduate study.*
► examine a range **address, consider, discuss, examine, explore, study, view** *You will explore a range of computing platforms and electronic media.*

▶ use a range **access, choose from, enjoy, experience, select from, use** *Guests can enjoy a wide range of leisure activities.*

▶ increase a range **broaden, expand, extend, increase, widen** *The course is ideal for managers seeking to extend their range of skills.*

rapid ADJ
happening, moving, or acting quickly

● adv+ADJ very **exceedingly, excessively, extremely, spectacularly, very** *His recovery was extremely rapid.*

▶ surprisingly **amazingly, astonishingly, remarkably, surprisingly, unexpectedly** *There have been astonishingly rapid technological developments in broadcasting.*

▶ unusually **abnormally, exceptionally, extraordinarily, unusually** *This followed a long period of unusually rapid economic growth.*

▶ rather **comparatively, fairly, quite, reasonably, relatively** *At first, they made fairly rapid progress.*

● ADJ+n growth or increase **expansion, growth, increase, rise, spread** *During the nineteenth century there was a rapid expansion of large-scale industry.*

▶ start **onset** *'Acute' describes a disease of rapid onset, severe symptoms and brief duration.*

▶ improvement or progress **advance, progress, progression, recovery** *This enables our teachers to develop each student's abilities so that they make rapid progress.*

▶ getting less or worse **decline, deterioration** *There was a rapid decline in the fortunes of the British film industry.*

▶ change **change, evolution, turnaround, turnover** *We are living in a time of incredibly rapid change.*

▶ speed **acceleration, pace** *Our Internet service is growing at a rapid pace.*

▶ sequence of events **succession** *The family moved several times in very rapid succession.*

rapidity N
speed

adj+N great **extraordinary, extreme, great** *Several new settlements sprang up with great rapidity.*

> Usage These *adj+N* combinations are usually in the form *with+adj+rapidity*: *His moods would change with great rapidity.* ● *The men work with astonishing rapidity.*

surprising **amazing, astonishing, startling, surprising** *The flames spread with amazing rapidity.*

frightening **alarming, disturbing, frightening** *Such an infection can develop with alarming rapidity.*

rapport N
relationship in which people like and understand each other

adj+N natural or immediate **easy, genuine, immediate, instant, instinctive, intuitive, natural** *There was an instinctive rapport between the two musicians that comes across in every note.*

close **close, friendly, intimate, warm** *Her reserve and caution make it difficult for her to build a close rapport with others.*

good **excellent, extraordinary, fantastic, good,** **positive, remarkable, strong, superb, terrific, tremendous, wonderful** *The two actors have a terrific rapport, coming to life in their scenes together.*

● v+N have a rapport **enjoy, have** *He enjoyed a good rapport with the rest of the team.*

▶ develop a rapport **achieve, build, create, develop, establish, strike up** *She always established a wonderful rapport with her pupils.*

▶ maintain a rapport **maintain** *They maintained a strong rapport with the audience throughout the set.*

● N+with audience **audience, crowd, fans, viewers** *The success of the gig was due to their rapport with the crowd.*

▶ customer etc **clients, customers, patients, pupils** *We are looking for someone with good interpersonal skills, who is able to build rapport with customers.*

▶ people at work **colleagues, staff** *His rapport with his colleagues makes him an excellent role model.*

rare ADJ
not happening, seen, or found very often

● adv+ADJ very **exceedingly, exceptionally, extremely, impossibly, rather, vanishingly, very** *It is an area of outstanding beauty and home to extremely rare wildlife.*

▶ rather **comparatively, fairly, pretty INFORMAL, quite, relatively, somewhat** *Childhood leukaemia is a comparatively rare disorder.*

▶ fortunately **fortunately, mercifully, thankfully** *Child abduction makes the headlines but is fortunately rare.*

▶ surprisingly **extraordinarily, incredibly, surprisingly** *Cases of aggression after playing violent games are surprisingly rare.*

▶ more and more **increasingly** *Vinyl records are increasingly rare in homes.*

● ADJ+n case or event **event, example, exception, instance, occasion, occurrence** *With a few rare exceptions, these researchers work in university laboratories.* ● *On the rare occasions that they had people for dinner my mother might cook 'Boeuf Bourgignon'.*

▶ opportunity **chance, opportunity** *This is a rare chance to see these world-renowned performers in the UK.*

▶ sight **appearance, sight** *These fish are now a fairly rare sight in our waters.*

▶ look **glimpse** *In the film we get a rare glimpse into a world that remains intensely private.*

▶ thing **commodity** *We pride ourselves on our personal service – a rare commodity nowadays.*

▶ medical condition **complication, condition, disease, disorder** *Another rare complication is that surgery can cause damage to the spinal cord.*

▶ animal, plant etc **bird, breed, butterfly, plant, species** *The park is a haven for the rarest species of Scottish wildlife.*

rash ADJ
acting or done too quickly

● adv+ADJ **rather, somewhat, too** *It would be somewhat rash to assert that the recession is now behind us.*

● ADJ+n **assumption, conjecture, decision,**

prediction, presumption, promise *He made the brave, if maybe rash, decision to appear on BBC News.*

● ADJ+infinitive **argue, assert, assume, attempt, attribute, deny, dismiss, predict, presume** *It would be rash to assume that the trial judge will agree.*

rate N
the number of times something happens, or the speed at which it happens, during a particular period

● adj+N high or fast **alarming, fast, high, rapid** *They claim that the Earth is heating up at an alarming rate.* ● *In addition, occupying troops suffer very high injury rates.*

▶ low or slow **low, slow** *Prosperous countries tend to have lower birth rates.*

▶ maximum/minimum **maximum, minimum** *You should exercise at 50–60 per cent of your maximum heart rate.*

▶ average **average, overall** *Average vacancy rates dropped to 13.89 per cent.*

● n+N **birth, crime, death, detection, growth, mortality, pass, response, success, survival, unemployment** *10-year survival rates with this form of cancer are as low as 10 per cent.*

● N+v rise **double, increase, rise, soar** *The death rate has risen even more in recent months.*

▶ fall **decline, decrease, drop, fall, plummet, slow** *The inflation rate has fallen dramatically over the past 5 years.*

▶ change or vary **fluctuate, vary** *Questionnaires are commonly used, but response rates vary greatly.*

▶ be average, be, remain **be, remain** *Over the years, our repayment rate has averaged 98 per cent.*

▶ be more than **exceed** *In maths the pass rate exceeds 88 per cent.*

rating N
a measurement of how good or popular something is

● adj+N high **high, maximum, top** *Twenty-four of the college's 37 subject areas have been awarded the highest rating.*

▶ low **low** *The government has slipped to its lowest poll rating since 2005.*

▶ average **average, overall** *The album has an average rating of 8 out of 10 based on 8 reviews.*

● n+N approval **approval, popularity, satisfaction** *Our aim is to achieve at least an 80 per cent satisfaction rating from our clients.*

▶ by particular people **customer, user** *You can check user ratings for all these products online.*

● v+N get or have a rating **achieve, earn, gain, get, have, obtain, receive** *We have achieved a top research rating, one of only three departments in the country to do so.*

▶ give someone or something a rating **assign, award (sb/sth), give (sb/sth)** *Participants were asked to assign a rating of 1–7 to each of the photos.*

● N+v rise **go up, rise, soar** *His performances sent the show's audience ratings soaring.*

▶ fall **decline, drop, fall, go down, plummet, slip,**

slump, tumble *Her approval ratings have plummeted in recent months.*

▶ vary **depend on, range from** *The ratings range from Very Useful to Useless.*

▶ show or mean something **demonstrate, indicate, mean, reflect** *What do the star ratings mean?* ● *His rating reflects the huge improvement in performance this year.*

ratio N
a relationship between numbers or amounts

● adj+N high **high** *These plants maintain a high ratio of carbon dioxide to oxygen within photosynthetic cells.*

▶ low **low** *For this group the success ratio was even lower.*

▶ good **favourable, optimum** *Small groups enable us to provide a favourable pupil:teacher ratio.*

● n+N of staff to customers etc **staffing, staff-patient, staff-student, student:staff** *Day nurseries have more intensive staffing ratios depending on the ages of children being cared for.*

▶ of males to females **male:female, sex** *The department has a male:female ratio of 65:35.*

▶ of deaths **mortality, survival** *We measured five-year survival rates and relative survival ratios.*

▶ in economics **benefit/cost, cost-benefit, price/earnings** *The benefit/cost ratio is predicted to be 1.3 to 1.*

> The noun modifiers in this group can be written with a slash, a hyphen, a colon, or separated by the word 'to': *staff/student ratio,* ● *price-earnings ratio,* ● *cost:benefit ratio,* ● *male to female ratio.*

● N+v go up **increase, rise** *Within 10 years the firm's debt-equity ratio had risen to 570 per cent.*

▶ go down **decline, decrease, drop, fall, halve** *The se ratio declined further to 719 girls to every 1,000 boys*

▶ get better/worse **improve, worsen** *Staff/student ratios have worsened.*

▶ vary **differ, range from sth** *Mortality ratios range from approximately 0.5 to 0.8.*

▶ be more than something **exceed sth** *This shows that the patient:staff ratio exceeds that recommende in 2005.*

▶ indicate something **indicate, mean** *A low ratio indicates that the dividend is at an unsustainable level.*

rational ADJ
based on sensible practical reasons

● adv+ADJ very **eminently, perfectly** *This is a perfectly rational response to the situation.*

▶ entirely **entirely, purely, rigorously, strictly, wholl** *An attacked nation is unlikely to act in a purely rational way.*

▶ mostly **essentially** *We have an image of the self as an essentially rational being.*

▶ apparently **apparently, seemingly, supposedly** *It for this reason that theories of aliens continue to gain support among seemingly rational people.*

▶ from a particular point of view **economically, scientifically** *You could argue that young people wh are choosing to go to university are being economically rational.*

● ADJ+n ability to think **faculty, thinking, though**

Our rational faculties also allow us to think abstractly. • *He seemed to have lost the power of rational thought.*

▸ argument or analysis **analysis, argument, debate, discourse, discussion** *Inspectors' decisions must be backed up by rational argument.*

▸ way of doing something **approach** *Research showed that donors adopt a rational approach to their giving, tending to donate to charities where they can see how their money is used.*

response **response** *This technology is the only rational response to abrupt climate change.*

explanation or reason **basis, explanation, justification** *The majority of alternative medicines have no rational scientific basis.* • *I can give no rational explanation for why these boats were so quick.*

choice or conclusion **calculation, choice, decision** *This assumes that people make a rational financial calculation about whether to take a job or remain on benefit.*

view or theory **assessment, hypothesis, theory, view** *I like the eminently rational view that Peterson takes.*

person **being, creature, thinker** *His theory assumes that people are rational creatures who plan long-term goals.*

each V

achieve something after discussion or thought

V+n agreement **agreement, compromise, consensus, settlement** *Trained mediators help those involved to reach an agreement which everyone can live with.*

decision **conclusion, decision, verdict** *Reviews over the past 25 years have reached different conclusions.*

react V

behave in a particular way when something happens

adv+V positively **enthusiastically, favourably, positively** *This workshop will look at how managers can help their staff to react positively to change.*

negatively **adversely, badly, defensively, negatively, unfavourably** *It seems inconceivable that anyone could react negatively to this decision.*

angrily or violently **aggressively, angrily, furiously, sharply, violently** *Parents of children at the school have reacted angrily to the proposals.*

quickly **immediately, instantaneously, instantly, promptly, quickly, rapidly, swiftly** *We will be able to react more quickly to customers' needs.*

calmly or carefully **calmly, cautiously** *Although clearly upset, she reacted calmly and without fuss.*

emotionally **emotionally, instinctively, spontaneously** *You should avoid reacting emotionally to anything that is said in the interview.*

strongly **strongly, vigorously** *A normal adult reacts strongly to any suggestion of violence being directed at a baby.*

appropriately **accordingly, appropriately** *The character is placed in extraordinary circumstances and he reacts accordingly.*

differently **differently** *Would the referee react differently if this incident happened in the last minute of the game?*

● V+in **fashion, manner, way** *Different people react in different ways to a sudden shock.*

● V+with anger or shock **anger, disdain, dismay, fury, horror, hostility, indignation, outrage, scorn** *Conservationists reacted with fury after the land was sold for development.*

▸ surprise or disbelief **amazement, astonishment, disbelief, incredulity, scepticism** *Officials have reacted with incredulity to the latest claims.*

▸ pleasure **glee** *Academics reacted with unconcealed glee to the news of his resignation.*

reaction N

1 the way you react to something

● adj+N positive **favourable, positive** *We have never had such a positive reaction to a guest speaker before.*

▸ negative **negative** *We all have a fear of failure or of a negative reaction.*

▸ mixed **mixed** *Published in 1972, the book drew a very mixed reaction.*

▸ angry or violent **angry, defensive, hostile, violent** *The slow progress of reform led to a violent reaction from the nationalists.*

▸ strong **extreme, hysterical, strong** *It is a film that tends to prompt extreme reactions.*

▸ emotional **emotional** *If you receive a threatening phone call, don't say anything – the caller wants to get an emotional reaction.*

▸ immediate or first **immediate, initial, instant** *He said that his inital reaction was shock.*

▸ done quickly without thinking **gut, instinctive, knee-jerk, spontaneous** *The chairman insisted this was not a knee-jerk reaction and took into account the views of the fans.*

▸ normal **natural, normal, understandable** *Worry is an understandable reaction to change.*

● v+N cause a reaction **cause, draw, elicit, evoke, lead to, produce, prompt, provoke, result in, spark, trigger** *The subject is complex and provokes strong reactions.*

▸ get a reaction **get, receive** *She did not receive quite the reaction that she had expected.*

▸ observe or measure a reaction **gauge, observe** *Extensive market research was carried out to gauge the reactions of consumers.*

▸ expect a reaction **anticipate, expect** *They anticipate very cautious reactions to their suggestions.*

2 a bad effect on the body caused by something

● adj+N negative **adverse** *Adverse reactions to the drug include headaches and gastro-intestinal disturbances.*

▸ very bad **acute, fatal, life-threatening, serious, severe** *Several reports have been published of severe reactions in people with no previous psychiatric symptoms.*

▸ possible **suspected** *Suspected adverse reactions in children should always be reported.*

▸ not immediate **delayed** *Travel should be avoided within 14 days of the treatment in case a delayed reaction occurs.*

▸ types of reaction **allergic, anaphylactic, immune, inflammatory, systemic, toxic** *This provokes an immune reaction that includes chronic inflammation.*

● v+N have a reaction **experience, show, suffer**

(from), undergo *A clear procedure must be followed when a patient undergoes a serious reaction.*
▸ cause a reaction **cause, induce, lead to, produce, provoke, result in, stimulate, trigger** *Researchers have identified a type of protein that triggers allergic reactions.*
▸ report or notice a reaction **observe, report** *Several city residents reported allergic reactions after recent crop dusting on nearby farms.*

read N
something that you read; an act of reading something

● adj+N good **cracking** INFORMAL, **good, recommended, terrific** *This is a terrific read for those interested in the real Venice.*
▸ holding your attention **compelling, compulsive, engrossing, enthralling, fascinating, gripping, riveting, thrilling** *I found the book to be an extremely gripping read, as well as being very informative.*
▸ interesting or informative **informative, interesting, stimulating, thought-provoking** *His blog is a very interesting read.*
▸ amusing or enjoyable **amusing, engaging, enjoyable, entertaining, rollicking** INFORMAL *Sharp, witty and fast-paced, this is an undemanding but thoroughly enjoyable read.*
▸ worth reading **rewarding, satisfying, worthwhile** *It is a worthwhile read for pharmacists and for those interested in herbal remedies.*
▸ easy **easy, quick** *This is a small volume, with large type and a lot of white space that make it a quick read.*

reader N
someone who reads

● adj+N keen **avid, interested, voracious** *Although I was an avid reader, I never thought of myself as a writer.* ● *Interested readers may contact me for a copy of the list.*
▸ regular **faithful, loyal, regular** *As a regular reader of Gardening Review, I will miss her column.*
▸ ordinary **casual, general, ordinary** *To a casual reader, these are just numbers.*
▸ clever or careful **alert, astute, critical, discerning, observant** *Astute readers will have spotted the deliberate mistake by now.*
▸ good or confident **competent, confident, experienced, fluent** *Using this system, the children have become more fluent and confident readers.*
▸ not keen or confident **reluctant** *They have published a new range of short, fast-paced books aimed at adult reluctant readers.*

readiness N
the state of being ready, or willing to deal with something

● v+N express readiness **announce, declare, express, imply, signal, stress** *Several candidates have signalled their readiness to stand.*
▸ confirm readiness **confirm, reaffirm** *The EU reaffirmed its readiness to contribute to a multilateral diplomatic solution.*
▸ show readiness **demonstrate, indicate, show** *Candidates enrolling on the programme must demonstrate readiness to undertake doctoral-level work.*

▸ make sure of someone's readiness **assure, ensure, maintain** *Pre-season exercises will help ensure your readiness for the season itself.*
▸ assess someone's readiness **assess, determine** *Monitor your progress and assess your own readiness to sit the exam.*
▸ increase readiness **enhance, increase** *They have the overall goal of increasing the school readiness of young children.*

reading N
something that you read; the act of reading something

● adj+N compulsory **compulsory, essential, required** *It will be essential reading for everyone involved in teaching or learning economic theory.*
▸ recommended **recommended, suggested** *A list of recommended reading accompanies your module material.*
▸ additional **additional, further, supplementary** *This site also provides links to further reading.*
▸ to prepare for something **background, introductory, preliminary, preparatory** *Doing preparatory reading will make it easier for you to follow the lecture.*
▸ interesting **compelling, compulsive, fascinating, interesting** *They make interesting reading as they tell us so much about the daily life of our ancestors.*
▸ worrying or shocking **depressing, grim, uncomfortable** *The report will make uncomfortable reading for the Government.*
▸ careful **careful, close, critical** *I should like to thank Professor Jones for his careful reading of the first draft of this paper.*

real ADJ
having the true qualities of particular type of thing

● ADJ+n problem or difficulty **challenge, concern, difficulty, issue, need, problem** *We know that anti-social behaviour causes real problems.*
▸ danger **danger, risk, threat** *Climate change is a real threat to the future of humanity.*
▸ change or effect **change, difference, impact** *You could make a real difference to the lives of people touched by cancer.*
▸ benefit or improvement **advantage, benefit, improvement, progress, value** *These grants have brought real benefit to local communities.*
▸ chance **chance, opportunity, possibility, prospect** *There is also the very real possibility of injury.*
▸ choice **alternative, choice** *She opposed their policies without proposing any real alternative.*
▸ pleasure **pleasure, treat** *It was a real treat to be able to sit in the sunshine.*
▸ something unfortunate **pity, shame** *It's a real shame for students who are really quite gifted not to have this opportunity.*
▸ feeling **feeling, sense** *Recycling gives us a real sense that we are doing something for the environment.*

realism N
the ability to accept or see situations as they really are

● adj+N gritty **gritty, stark, unflinching** *In its depiction of the urban working classes, the film lacked the gritty social realism that was later pioneered by directors such as Loach.*

- v+N add realism **add, bring, increase, inject, introduce, lend** *The Institute has made efforts to inject some realism and clarity into the debate.*
- show realism **achieve** *The actors commented that it had been hard to achieve realism in the fight scenes.*
- reject realism **abandon, reject** *Atkinson abandons realism in favour of demonstrating the possibility of achieving happiness after loss.*
- lack realism **lack** *Capable of great inspiration and idealism, they are often accused of lacking realism.*
- n+of+N feeling **sense** *Attention to historical detail added a sense of realism to the display.*
- amount **air, degree, dose, element, level, touch** *Optimism, tempered by an element of realism, will help you ensure that your dream becomes a reality.*
- *These new simulations achieve an unprecedented level of realism.*

realistic ADJ
based on facts and situations as they really are

- ADJ+n chance or hope **chance, expectation, hope, possibility, proposition, prospect** *There is no realistic prospect of any action.*
- alternative or solution **alternative, option, solution** *Public transport is not a realistic alternative for many of these journeys.*
- goal or plan **aim, goal, plan, target** *It is most important to set realistic goals in relation to children's weight.*
- time or money allowed **budget, timeframe, timescale, timetable** *The problem was the absence of a sensible and realistic timescale for implementation.*
- assessment of something **appraisal, assessment, assumption, estimate** *Figures must be based on realistic estimates.*
- attitude **attitude, view** *This attitude is simply not realistic.*
- and/or **accurate, achievable, attainable, believable, credible, deliverable, honest, manageable, meaningful, measurable, practical, pragmatic, sensible, workable** *Are the aims of the project realistic and achievable within the proposed timeframe?*

seeming very like real life

- adv+ADJ very **amazingly, completely, incredibly, intensely, remarkably, strikingly, stunningly, vividly** *A strikingly realistic wax mask of King George will be on display.*
- in a frightening or shocking way **brutally, chillingly, disturbingly, frighteningly, grimly, grittily, horribly, scarily** *Her emotionally disturbed cellmate is played in a frighteningly realistic portrayal by Gillian Wright.*
- in a good way **brilliantly, impressively, wonderfully** *With brilliantly realistic models, the animated dinosaurs really bring this story to life.*

- ADJ+n picture **depiction, picture, portrayal** *Viewers were invited to witness a realistic portrayal of the often unglamorous daily lives of police detectives.*
- animation **animation, simulation** *Motion capture allows for realistic animations of human movement.*
- situation **scenario, situation** *Trainees are tested in realistic scenarios by the Ambulance Service.*

- effect **effect** *The sound effects were amazingly realistic.*

reality N
the real character of things, not what is imagined or possible; a fact, event etc as it really exists

- adj+N sad or difficult **brutal, grim, gritty, harsh, sad, stark** *The harsh financial reality is that we have to reduce our spending on services.*
- of every day; ordinary **day-to-day, everyday, mundane** *The exhibition explores everyday realities of life in a war zone.*
- actual **physical, practical** *Imagination is a link between the outer world of physical reality and our inner world.*
- objective/not objective **objective, subjective** *This all comes down to belief, not objective reality.*
- types of reality **commercial, economic, historical, political, practical** *The courts must understand commercial realities and not impose excessive regulation.*

- v+N accept or deal with reality **accept, acknowledge, confront, experience, face, recognize** *I seek to understand why events occurred, even if this means confronting unpleasant realities.*
- understand reality **grasp, understand** *He seemed to have an inability to grasp reality.*
- reflect or show reality **depict, mirror, portray, reflect** *The programme-makers would argue that they were merely trying to portray reality.*
- deny or ignore reality **deny, doubt, escape, ignore** *We cannot deny the reality that, in our modern world, the principle of a job for life is dead.*
- try to hide reality **disguise, distort, obscure** *The ad distorts reality by using stereotypes and simplifications.*
- become reality **become** *If we work together, we can ensure that this dream becomes a reality.*

realization N
the process or moment of understanding something

- adj+N coming gradually **dawning, gradual, growing** *There has been a gradual realization that people within very different communities nevertheless want very similar things.*
- sudden **sudden** *The sudden realization of my own ignorance came home to me.*
- frightening or worrying **awful, chilling, sobering, stark** *Our satisfaction with these achievements is matched by the sobering realization that much remains to be done.*
- v+N arrive at, **come to** *We all need to come to the realization of what trouble we're in.*
- N+v **come, dawn (on sb), hit sb, spread** *The realization dawns that there is money left and a short time to spend it.*

realize V
1 know and understand something

- adv+V quickly or at once **immediately, instantly, quickly, soon** *But I soon realized that this wasn't the case.*
- suddenly **suddenly** *I suddenly realized that I had been talking out loud to myself.*

▶ first **first** *When did you first realise you wanted to write fiction?*

▶ slowly or later **afterwards, belatedly, eventually, finally, gradually, slowly** *You eventually realize that they are not just giving you knowledge, but teaching you how to think.*

▶ completely **fully** *I wonder if these sportsmen fully realize the enormous responsibility they have to young players.*

● V+n importance **importance, significance** *It is possible that journalists don't themselves realize the importance of this fact.*

▶ seriousness **enormity, extent, seriousness** *I now realize the enormity of the problems they are facing in developing countries.*

▶ mistake **error, folly, mistake** *They missed the turning and didn't realise their mistake till they were nearly back in Toddington!*

▶ problem **danger, futility, limitations** *She stopped, realizing the futility of the question.*

▶ truth **truth** *It seems incredible that those close to her did not realize the truth.*

2 achieve something planned or hoped for

● V+n hope or dream **ambition, aspiration, dream, ideal, vision** *At long last he was able to realize his ambition to become a painter.*

▶ goal **goal, objective** *The group met to decide the best way of realizing their objectives.*

▶ possibility **potential** *She is a very capable woman who is gradually realizing her full potential.*

▶ money **gain, profit, saving** *Car manufacturers could realize savings of $2,700 per vehicle produced.*

reappraisal N

an occasion when you consider an attitude or situation again

● adj+N complete **complete, fundamental, radical, thorough, total** *The decline in funds will require a radical reappraisal of the way in which teaching and research are conducted.*

▶ urgent **urgent** *There needs to be an urgent reappraisal of bed numbers in all new hospitals.*

▶ occasional **periodic** *The conditions of the code of professional conduct are subject to periodic reappraisal.*

▶ critical **critical** *It's time for a critical reappraisal of new age music.*

● v+N **demand, force, invite, lead to, necessitate, prompt, require, trigger** *Increasing membership necessitated reappraisal of the services offered.*

reason N

a fact or situation that explains why something happened or is true; a cause for doing or thinking something

● adj+N good **compelling, good, legitimate, logical, right, sound, sufficient, valid** *There could be compelling social reasons for a person to live in a particular area.*

▶ not good **wrong** *Young people are always making the headlines – often for the wrong reasons.*

▶ main **fundamental, key, main, major, primary, prime, principal** *Survey results show farmers choose to grow biotech crops for two main reasons.*

▶ only **only, sole** *We believe that the only reason the*

system has not collapsed completely is the diligence of staff.

▶ obvious **obvious** *The majority of companies have restrictive contracts, for obvious reasons.*

▶ common **common** *The most common reasons for needing to work away from the office were business trips and meetings.*

▶ real **genuine, real, underlying** *Citizens were probably unaware of the real reasons why the government decided to go to war.*

▶ simple **simple** *There are very simple reasons for this.* ● *We don't provide accommodation for the simple reason that most people prefer to find their own.*

▶ various **different, many, several, various** *For various reasons, sales of DAB digital radios have been poor.*

▶ same **same, similar, very** *Avoiding clutter is the very reason why many people buy a laptop in the first place.*

▶ possible **possible** *The sample should be examined to identify a possible reason for these low moisture levels.*

▶ unknown **strange, unknown** *For some unknown reason she took an immediate liking to him.*

You can also say that something is done **for no apparent reason, for no particular reason,** or **for reasons unknown:** *The bass player wandered off stage for no particular reason.*

▶ types of reason **commercial, economic, financial, historical, legal, medical, operational, personal, political, practical, technical** *The results may be unavailable for some technical reason.*

● n+N **business, confidentiality, conservation, copyright, family, health, hygiene, privacy, safety, security, tax, timetabling** *This cannot be dealt with over the phone for obvious security reasons.*

Usage In all of these combinations, **reason** is usually plural and preceded by **for:** *The owner was wealthy enough to live abroad for tax reasons.*

● v+N have a reason **have** *Our cleaning staff have every reason to be proud of the role they perform.*

▶ give a reason **cite, give (sb), indicate, list, mention, offer, provide, reveal, specify, state, suggest** *If the form has been rejected, you will be given the reason why.* ● *Can you suggest any reasons for these differences?*

▶ explain or describe the reason **articulate, describe, detail, explain, highlight, outline, set out** *It might help allay your concerns if I explain the reasons why the regulations were published.* ● *The adverts are aimed at highlighting the reasons for speed limits.*

▶ examine the reasons **address, analyse, consider, discuss, examine, explore, investigate** *This new research explores the reasons why children run away from home.*

▶ discover the reason **ascertain, discover, find, identify, pinpoint, uncover** *Discovering the reason for certain behaviour can improve your relationship.*

▶ know or understand the reason **guess, know, see, understand** *At least I now know the real reason.* ● *I apologise about this in advance and I hope you understand my reasons.*

▶ not accept a reason **question** *More and more people questioned his reasons for becoming involved.*

If you do not think that there is any reason for something, you can say that you **see no reason** for it: *I see no reason to change the rules at this time.*

▶ be the reason **be, constitute, seem to be** *She seems to think her desire to hurt his reputation constitutes a genuine reason for doing so.*

▶ think something is the reason **believe, suppose, suspect** *I suspect his real reason for going on the show was to find fame.*

▶ v+as+N **cite, give, quote, regard, see, suggest, use** *Lack of motivation is usually cited as the reason for students failing to complete the course.*

reasonable ADJ
sensible and fair

▶ adv+ADJ very or completely **eminently, entirely, extremely, perfectly, very** *There is no simple answer to your perfectly reasonable question.*

▶ rather **fairly, pretty** INFORMAL, **quite** *I have tried to present my arguments in a fairly reasonable and open style.*

ADJ+n explanation **excuse, explanation** *Illness will only be considered a reasonable excuse if the person can produce a doctor's note.*
expectation **assumption, expectation, request** *We are committed to providing our customers with the standard of service that meets their reasonable expectations.*
agreement **compromise** *The deal seemed a reasonable compromise in the circumstances.*
cause **cause, grounds** *There are reasonable grounds for suspecting that there is a risk to public safety.*
chance **chance, prospect** *He ruled that the appeal had no reasonable prospects of success.*
action or effort **attempt, care, effort, precaution, step** *We have taken every reasonable precaution to ensure the accuracy of information on this website.*
guess **estimate, guess** *This method gives a reasonable estimate of the body size.*
belief **belief, doubt, suspicion** *It is for the prosecution to prove beyond a reasonable doubt that the defendant committed the crime.*
time period **notice, period, timescale** *Alternative vegetarian menus are available, given reasonable notice.*

v+ADJ **be, consider sth, deem sth, look, regard sth as, seem, sound, think sth** *This level of expenditure was considered reasonable.* • *It seems reasonable to conclude that most people are in favour of the changes.*

ADJ+infinitive **argue, assume, believe, conclude, deduce, expect, hypothesize, infer, presume, speculate, suggest, suppose, suspect** *It is reasonable to assume that cats may have acquired some resistance to common diseases of rats and mice.*

reasoning N
the process of thinking in an intelligent sensible way

adj+N types of reasoning **causal, deductive, inductive, logical, mathematical, non-verbal, verbal** *Business relies heavily on inductive reasoning, which assumes that the future will resemble the past.*
good **clear, correct, sound** *There was sound*

reasoning behind the choice of a woman as a candidate for the post.*

▶ bad **circular, false, faulty** *Her argument was based on faulty reasoning.*

● v+N explain the reasoning **explain, justify, outline** *Lesley explained the reasoning behind her choices.*

▶ question the reasoning **query, question** *Mr Thomas questions the reasoning behind such a conclusion.*

▶ understand the reasoning **understand** *The main aim is to learn what people have to say about a topic and understand their reasoning.*

▶ use reasoning **apply, employ** *You can apply the same reasoning to other cases.*

● N+behind **choice, decision, move, recommendation** *In the event that institutions choose to differ from this guidance, the reasoning behind the decision should be stated.*

reassurance N
the act of making someone feel less worried; an explanation that helps someone to feel less worried

● adj+N not worth very much **bland, false** *I expressed my concerns, only to be met with bland reassurances that, to me, were unconvincing.*

▶ constant **constant, repeated** *I felt the need for constant reassurance that I was doing the right thing.*

▶ additional **added, additional, extra** *Participants have the added reassurance that a 300-person trial showed the vaccines were safe.*

▶ public **public, visible** *There is a need to communicate successes and to provide public reassurance.*

▶ spoken **verbal** *This time the government will not settle for verbal reassurances but will have to see concrete action.*

● v+N need or want reassurance **need, require, seek, want** *We therefore seek reassurances that the company's commitment to regional planning will be maintained.*

▶ give reassurance **give (sb), offer (sb), provide (sb with)** *Additional scrutiny provides reassurance that marking has been carried out appropriately.*

▶ receive reassurance **receive** *Until we receive reassurances that this has been done, we will remain concerned.*

rebate N
money that is officially given back to someone

● v+N have the right to a rebate **be eligible for, be entitled to, be owed, be promised, qualify for** *She was promised a 10 per cent rebate if she changed suppliers.*

▶ ask for a rebate **claim** *This enables us to claim a tax rebate of 28 pence for every pound you donate.*

▶ get a rebate **get, negotiate, receive, secure** *A full time student will receive a 25 per cent rebate.*

▶ give someone a rebate **grant (sb), offer (sb), pay (sb)** *The government pays a rebate of National Insurance contributions to your pension provider.*

rebellion N
an occasion when people refuse to obey, or attempt to remove, their government or leaders

- v+N stop a rebellion **crush, defeat, quash, quell, repress, subdue, suppress** *The government sent in troops to quell the rebellion.*
- ▶ encourage rebellion **foment, incite, instigate** *He was court-martialled and executed on charges of fomenting rebellion.*
- ▶ organize and take part in a rebellion **join, launch, lead, participate in, stage** *Employees staged a successful rebellion* **against** *the appointment of a new Chief Executive.*
- ▶ cause a rebellion **precipitate, provoke, spark, trigger** *This action sparked an anti-government rebellion.*

rebuild v

make a situation as good as it was previously

- V+n confidence **confidence, self-confidence, self-esteem, trust** *To counter negative media coverage, the agency was commissioned to rebuild consumer confidence.*
- ▶ life or means of living **life, livelihood** *Small producers organised themselves into co-operatives in order to begin the process of rebuilding their livelihoods.*
- ▶ economy **economy** *After the war, the first priority was to rebuild the shattered economies of Europe.*

rebuke N

an occasion when someone is told they have behaved badly

- adj+N strong **furious, indignant, scathing, severe, sharp, stern, stinging, strong** *The head of the UN delivered a stern rebuke to both states over the breaking of international law.*
- ▶ weak **gentle, mild** *There was not even a mild rebuke for the huge losses that had been sustained.*
- v+N give a rebuke **administer, deliver, issue** *The European Parliament issued a stinging rebuke to the British government for its handling of the crisis.*
- ▶ earn or receive a rebuke **draw, earn, provoke** *That provoked a sharp rebuke from the US Secretary of State.*

recall v

remember something

- adv+V very well **accurately, clearly, distinctly, precisely, vividly** *I can still vividly recall the smell of damp plaster which seemed to pervade the building.*
- ▶ not very well **barely, dimly, not exactly, vaguely** *I vaguely recall a comment from one of his novels.*
- ▶ with affection **fondly, lovingly, with affection, with fondness** *She fondly recalls her students' enthusiasm for the subject.*
- ▶ with regret **bitterly, ruefully, sadly** *He still ruefully recalls the opportunities that he failed to take advantage of.*

recede v

to move back from a high point, or become less strong

- adv+V quickly **dramatically, fast, quickly, rapidly** *Young people are seeing the prospects of home ownership receding fast.*
- ▶ slowly **gradually, slowly** *The pain in his tooth gradually receded over the course of the day.*

- n+V water **flood, flood water, sea, tide, water, wave** *When the water finally receded, we were left with the job of cleaning up the house.*
- ▶ something bad **danger, fear, menace, pain, threat** *The threat of an imminent attack seems to have receded, but we must all remain vigilant.*

recent ADJ

happening or starting a short time ago

- adv+ADJ rather **comparatively, fairly, pretty** INFORMAL, **quite, rather, reasonably, relatively** *Diving as we know it today is of comparatively recent origin.*
- ▶ very **especially, so, too, very** *All presentations were based on research that was either very recent or still under development.*
- ▶ in a particular way **geologically, historically** *Most of the geologically recent eruptions are due to the nitrogen and methane on Triton.*
- ADJ+n study **article, paper, poll, publication, report, research, review, study, survey** *A recent survey showed that 60 per cent of churchgoers in this country never read their Bibles outside church.*
- ▶ change **advance, change, development, trend** *We're hoping to increase understanding of recent changes in demography and family structure.*
- ▶ event **announcement, conference, discovery, event, meeting, trip, visit** *Our only regret is that we didn't stay longer as part of our most recent visit.*
- ▶ period **decade, history, month, past, week, year** *There have been many cutbacks over recent years in every unit, not just ours.*
- ▶ decision **decision, judgment** *There have been many articles about the recent court decision that email is not private.*
- ▶ discovery **discovery, findings** *In this workshop, I will summarize some of the recent findings from neuroscience that I think are useful.*

reception N

the way someone or something is received

- adj+N very good **cordial, ecstatic, enthusiastic, favourable, rapturous, rousing, tumultuous, warm** *Tonight, I think we got it right; the song received a rapturous reception.*
- ▶ very bad **frosty, hostile** *They were going home very likely to a hostile reception.*
- ▶ neither very good nor very bad **cool, lukewarm, mixed** *Her last film got a lukewarm reception.*
- v+N be given, get, meet with, receive *The former Burnley captain led Luton out and received the most incredible reception.*

recession N

a period of economic problems and high unemployment

- adj+N bad or longlasting **bad, deep, full-blown, prolonged, severe, sustained** *We had just come through a full-blown official recession.*
- ▶ happening everywhere **global, international, world, worldwide** *These factors increase the risks another worldwide recession.*
- ▶ economic **economic** *Few people could have imagined that an international economic recession was just around the corner.*

▶ about to happen **impending** *If I believe in a property market crash then I must believe in an impending recession.*

▶ getting worse **deepening** *Last year was also marked by a deepening global recession.*

■ v+N face or experience a recession **be hit by** INFORMAL, **enter, experience, face, move into, suffer** *I agree that we are now entering a recession.*

▶ cause a recession **cause, precipitate, trigger** *Worsening problems for the world's largest economy could trigger a worldwide recession.*

▶ avoid or survive a recession **avoid, prevent, survive, weather** *Linda started her business in 1990 and immediately had to weather the recession of the early 90s.*

▶ predict a recession **predict** *Some observers predict a recession of 1930s proportions, but lasting much longer.*

■ N+v be about to start **loom** *I could see a recession looming and I'd been offered a teaching post at Princeton.*

▶ start **begin, hit** INFORMAL *When recession hit just a few months later in 1989, they went under.*

▶ get worse **bite, deepen** *Brazil's recession deepened, and eventually it too faced a currency crisis.*

ecipe N
instructions for preparing a particular dish

■ adj+N delicious **delicious, fabulous, flavourful, mouth-watering, tasty, yummy** INFORMAL *The first is a tasty recipe for almond macaroons.*

types of recipe **authentic, favourite, savoury, seasonal, secret, traditional, vegetarian** *For more traditional Spanish recipes see our recipe for Spanish paella.*

healthy **healthy, nutritious** *I have come up with many delicious, nutritious recipes any school age child can follow and enjoy.*

■ v+N create a recipe **concoct, devise, invent, perfect** *We had great fun concocting different recipes and eating them.*

change a recipe **adapt, recreate** *They started work on trying to recreate the recipe from memory.*

follow a recipe **cook, follow, test, try** *Why not try this classic recipe?*

something that makes it very likely that another thing will happen

■ N+for bad things **anarchy, confusion, disaster, paralysis, stagnation** *Consuming non-renewable fossil fuels is generally accepted as a recipe for global disaster.*

good things **fairness, happiness, success** *Like many other recipes for instant success, this new world order proved to be built on sand.*

cognition N
aise, respect, or admiration

■ adj+N official or formal **explicit, formal, institutional, legal, official, statutory** *A number of individuals have been identified as deserving formal recognition.*

among particular people or in certain places **international, national, professional, public, social, wide, worldwide** *When she met him, Robert Graves had achieved international recognition.*

▶ deserved **growing, overdue, proper, well-deserved** *Many congratulations to Philip on this well-deserved recognition.*

● v+N get recognition **achieve, attain, earn, enjoy, gain, get, obtain, receive, secure, win** *By the mid sixties he was gaining recognition as a virtuoso folk guitarist.*

▶ deserve recognition **deserve, merit** *Thank you, keep up the excellent work, you deserve recognition for such a contribution.*

▶ want recognition **seek** *Agnes was a modest woman who never sought recognition or reward.*

▶ give recognition **confer, give sb** *We have an honours system designed precisely to confer public recognition on acts of personal good.*

● N+for **achievement, commitment, contribution, effort, excellence, success, work** *He received little recognition for his achievements during his lifetime.*

recognizable ADJ
able to be recognized

● adv+ADJ immediately **immediately, instantly** *Sheltered beneath the familiar shape of Table Mountain, this historic city is instantly recognizable.*

▶ easily **clearly, easily, readily** *They are generally evergreen and have easily recognizable needle-like leaves.*

▶ with difficulty **barely, hardly, scarcely** *The city is hardly recognizable since I last visited it in 1986.*

recognize V
accept that someone or something is true, important or good

● adv+V among particular people **generally, officially, publicly, universally, widely** *The need for an up-to-date study of the place names of the area is widely recognized.*

▶ in particular places **globally, internationally, nationally, worldwide** *The University of Alabama at Birmingham is nationally recognized.*

▶ directly/indirectly **explicitly, implicitly** *The Conventions explicitly recognize that drugs should be available for medical purposes.*

▶ clearly **clearly, fully, readily** *It is readily recognized by almost all biblical students that the Gospel of John was the last of the Gospels written.*

Usage **Recognize** is usually passive in all of the **adv+V** combinations shown above.

● V+n importance or excellence **achievement, excellence, greatness, importance, significance** *As time goes on, major companies are beginning to recognize the true importance of podcasting.*

▶ need **necessity, need** *Christians generally recognize the necessity for the believer to live a holy life.*

▶ problems **dangers, limitations, problems, risks** *If you recognize your limitations and ask for assistance, you will do much better than even you anticipated.*

▶ truth **legitimacy, truth, validity** *Indonesia accepts and recognizes the universal validity of basic human rights and fundamental freedoms.*

recoil V
be upset by something frightening or unpleasant

- V+in horror **disgust, horror** *Even as I recoiled in horror, the courtyard became flooded with intense light.*
▶ shock **shock, surprise** *He awoke with a start and recoiled slightly in surprise.*
▶ fear **fear, terror** *They had glimpsed the terrible prospect of civil war and recoiled in terror.*

recollection N
a memory of something that has happened

- adj+N clear **clear, distinct, vivid** *Eliza West was my grandmother and I still have a very vivid recollection of her in her eighties.*

> You can use the expression **to the best of my recollection** to say that you think you remember something but are not entirely sure: *To the best of my recollection, the officer's name was Jackson.*

▶ vague **dim, faint, hazy, imperfect, vague** *I have a vague recollection of a cloakroom in a house.*
▶ pleasant/unpleasant **distressing, fond, painful, pleasant** *Painful recollections will intrude which cannot be repelled.*
▶ personal **autobiographical, personal** *A whole generation has now reached adulthood without any personal recollection of either World War.*
▶ from a long time ago **childhood, distant, early** *His earliest recollections as a child are of singing simple pop songs around the house.*

- v+N have/not have a recollection **have, have no** *I have a pleasant recollection of an incident so many years ago.*
▶ share a recollection **share** *We would like to thank everyone who has shared their recollections.*
▶ keep a recollection **cherish, preserve, record** *To the last, he cherished fond recollections of his student days in Glasgow.*

- N+of **childhood, event, incident, life, past** *The most chilling section of the book contains his recollections of his childhood with his father and brother.*

recommend V
1 advise someone to do something

- adv+V strongly **highly, strongly, unanimously** *We strongly recommend that you only run software with a good security track record.*
▶ certainly **certainly, definitely** *I would definitely recommend giving her a call.*
▶ especially **especially, particularly, specifically** *Helmets and gloves are particularly recommended for off-road riding.*
▶ usually or always **always, normally, often, usually** *We normally recommend a taxi, of which there is a never-ending supply at the front of the station.*

2 say someone or something is good

- adv+V strongly **heartily, highly, thoroughly, unreservedly, warmly, wholeheartedly** *'The Fall of Paris' is an excellent book which I can thoroughly recommend.*
▶ definitely **certainly, definitely, particularly** *The lodge was great and I will certainly recommend it to anybody who is looking to stay there.*
▶ willingly **happily, unreservedly** *I would happily recommend you to anyone needing your services.*

▶ personally **personally** *I can personally recommend Southampton as a great place to study Geology.*

recommendation N
a suggestion about how to deal with something

- adj+N final/not final **final, interim, preliminary, provisional** *The recommendations are provisional and may change after consultation.*
▶ main **key, main, principal** *A key recommendation was made that disabled people be involved throughou the development of the website.*
▶ definite **concrete, definite, detailed, formal, specific** *These are still immature technologies and few definite recommendations can be made.*

- v+N produce a recommendation **come up with** INFORMAL, **formulate, produce, put forward** *The paper has drawn out the factors that influence successful partnership working and has produced recommendations.*
▶ make a recommendation **issue, make, outline, present, propose, submit** *This wide ranging review made two key recommendations on regional data.*
▶ discuss a recommendation **consider** *The group will consider recommendations from the committee.*
▶ accept or adopt a recommendation **accept, adopt agree, approve, endorse, follow, implement, ratify welcome** *If you follow our recommendations, you can minimise the risks of security problems occurring.*
▶ reject a recommendation **ignore, overturn, reject** *The government rejects this recommendation but accepts that the Code of Practice needs amendment.*

recompense N
payment for injury or loss caused

- adj+N fair **adequate, fair, just, proper, reasonable** *It is an offence for an officer to receive anything beyond the proper recompense for doing his or her job.*
▶ financial **financial, monetary** *If you have been in a car accident that was not your fault, we can help you to get financial recompense.*
▶ generous **ample** *The hill-lover will discover ample recompense for the time spent in an exploration of these hills and dales.*

- v+N ask for recompense **claim, demand, seek** *There was one occasion when someone did try to seek recompense for advice.*
▶ be given recompense **be given, get, receive** *In return, authors and publishers will receive fair recompense for this secondary use of their materia.*

reconciliation N
a new friendly relationship after arguing or fighting

- adj+N final **complete, eventual, final, ultimate** *Her vision is one of ultimate reconciliation betwee Ulster's two peoples.*
▶ true **genuine, true** *He stressed the need for toleran and for genuine national reconciliation.*
▶ national **national** *These recommendations were meant to promote national reconciliation.*

- v+N try to get reconciliation **attempt, seek** *We should seek reconciliation and a good-neighbor policy.*

▶ achieve reconciliation **achieve, bring about, effect** *Nothing more can be done to effect the reconciliation.*
▶ encourage reconciliation **encourage, facilitate, foster, promote** *Is it possible for outsiders to foster reconciliation and peacebuilding?*
▪ and/or peace or forgiveness **forgiveness, healing, mediation, peace, redemption, repentance** *In his life he worked for peace and reconciliation and unity.*
▶ cooperation or justice **cooperation, justice, reconstruction, unity** *We are committed to a non-violent struggle for peace, justice and reconciliation.*

reconstruct V
build something again

▪ adv+V carefully **carefully, meticulously, painstakingly** *Over the next two years, the building was painstakingly reconstructed.*
▪ exactly **accurately, exactly, faithfully** *In 1965 the Suspension Bridge was faithfully reconstructed by Buckinghamshire County Council.*
▪ partly **partially, partly, substantially** *It was possible to partially reconstruct the sequence of events.*
  completely **completely, entirely** *Her knee has had to be completely reconstructed.*
  mentally **imaginatively, mentally** *The pictures are inspired by fragments that are imaginatively reconstructed.*

reconstruction N
the process of building something again

  adj+N physical **3D, full-scale, full-size, life-size, three-dimensional** *The 3D reconstruction includes the Loyn Bridge which is also an ancient monument.*
  mental **hypothetical, imaginative** *There are many different ways of using language: for example, description, analysis, storytelling and imaginative reconstruction.*
  after a disaster **post-conflict, post-flood, post-war** *A donor conference on post-flood reconstruction should be held in Maputo later in May.*
  accurate **accurate, faithful, meticulous** *The uncompressed images are a faithful reconstruction of the originals.*
  types of reconstruction **climatic, dramatic, forensic, historical, virtual** *The jury, wearing special goggles, were able to watch a virtual reconstruction of the operating theatre.*
  v+N attempt or suggest reconstruction **attempt, propose** *Some scholars have attempted a reconstruction of what the document might have contained.*
  allow reconstruction **allow, enable, facilitate, permit** *This data can enable a fairly accurate historical reconstruction of this formative time period.*
  carry out reconstruction **perform, undertake** *Work began in the C11th, additions and reconstructions being undertaken in subsequent centuries.*

record N
information kept about something that has happened

  adj+N types of record **academic, accounting, administrative, archaeological, bibliographic, criminal, historical, medical, official, patient** *The*

role of plant foods in prehistoric diets is seriously under-represented owing to its scarcity in the archaeological record. ● *Patients can apply for access to their medical records.*
▶ in a particular form **electronic, manual, photographic, written** *A written record of the bullying makes it easier to prove what has been going on.*
▶ true or accurate **accurate, correct, true** *The minutes were then agreed as a true and accurate record.*
▶ complete or detailed **complete, comprehensive, detailed, extensive, full** *Please see Charles and Susan's website for a much more detailed record of progress.*
▶ permanent **permanent** *A permanent record of this spectacular exhibition will appear as the next issue.*
▶ secret **confidential, secret** *When the judge asked him how he had gained access to confidential phone records, he refused to reply.*

● v+N keep a record **hold, keep, maintain, preserve, retain, store** *Keep an accurate record of past exam results.*
▶ look at a record **access, check, consult, examine, inspect, retrieve, review, search, view** *We will then contact you to make arrangements to access the records.*
▶ make a record **compile, create, place sth on, put sth on** *Before it is too late, I shall endeavour to place on permanent record all such notices of our town music.*

> You can say that someone ***goes on record*** when they say something that will be officially recorded: *The library committee went on record more than once to express their satisfaction with his services.*

▶ publish a record **publish, release** *Thanks to the Freedom of Information Act, the security forces were forced to release secret records which revealed the use of torture.*
▶ change a record **amend, update** *These credit records are updated monthly to show whether you keep payments up to date.*
▶ destroy a record **delete, destroy** *The decision to reverse the policy and reinstate deleted records came in June.*

2 the best achievement in an activity, especially sport

● adj+N at a particular level **British, club, county, national, Olympic, world** *She improved the junior women's club record by 4 seconds.*
▶ not beaten **unbeaten** *That result was good news for Helen, who maintained her unbeaten record.*
● v+N set a record **establish, set** *His determination to set the record shines through.*
▶ hold or keep a record **hold, maintain, retain** *The family now holds world records in both Hardball and Softball.*
▶ beat a record **beat, break, smash** INFORMAL *We later found out he smashed his own record by 0.6 of a second.*

3 the things someone has done, giving an idea of what they are like

● adj+N good **enviable, excellent, good, impressive, outstanding, proven, strong** *Our graduates have an impressive record of obtaining work with a wide range of employers.*

> A record in this sense is often referred to as a **track record**: *The ideal candidate has a proven track record in business-to-business sales.*

▶ bad **appalling, bad, poor** *The two candidates of the left have poor records of supporting industrial action.*

• n+N **accident, attendance, employment, human rights, safety, voting** *Although Britain has one of the best road safety records in the world, ten people die on the roads every day.*

record V
make a record of something that has happened

• adv+V accurately **accurately, carefully, correctly, properly** *Parents were unable to record accurately the quantities of food consumed by their children.*
▶ regularly **annually, daily, faithfully, regularly, routinely** *A lot of athletes keep a training diary, faithfully recording everything they do.*
▶ in a particular form **digitally, electronically, manually** *We visit your home and digitally record your possessions.*
▶ in a particular way **automatically, formally, officially, systematically** *Over the last four years, there have only been around 200 to 250 officially recorded strikes each year.*

recount V
say what happened

• adv+V with a particular feeling **gleefully, happily, proudly** *He gleefully recounts every personal detail.*
▶ causing a particular reaction **movingly, vividly** *Local characters and customs are vividly recounted.*
▶ briefly **briefly** *Let me briefly recount Cartwright's view as I see it.*
• V+n story **anecdote, legend, saga, story, tale** *A story-teller will recount traditional Indian tales, and there will be Indian music.*
▶ event **deed, encounter, episode, incident** *Later in the same letter, his friend recounted an episode of almost suicidal courage.*
▶ adventure **adventures, exploits** *In the classical texts, her mythological exploits are recounted.*
▶ experience **conversation, dream, experience, memory** *The Vice Chairman recounted this conversation to the Chief Executive of the Trust.*

recover V
become healthy and strong again after illness or problems

• adv+V quickly **quickly, rapidly, speedily** *He recovered rapidly, and Edith decided to train as a nurse.*
▶ slowly **gradually, slowly** *He was slowly recovering from his wounds.*
▶ completely **completely, fully, properly, successfully** *All will change when I fully recover from my surgery.* • *Despite initial problems in the banking sector, the economy recovered successfully from one of the worst recessions in the last 100 years.*
▶ after a certain period **eventually, never, soon** *It is important to note that most people eventually recover from the illness.*

▶ partly **enough, partially, sufficiently** *Four months after my stroke, I was recovered enough to take on voluntary work.*
• V+from from illness, injury, or medical treatment **anaesthetic, illness, infection, injury, operation, stroke, surgery, trauma, wounds** *People recover from most minor illnesses by themselves and don't need to be seen by a doctor.*
▶ from a difficult or bad experience **crash, crisis, disaster, ordeal, recession, setback, shock, war** *Manufacturing industry has never fully recovered from the setbacks of recent years.*

recovery N
the process of getting back to normal after illness or problems

• adj+N quick **fast, quick, rapid, speedy, swift** *We send all our best wishes for a speedy recovery.*
▶ slow **gradual, slow** *Emma's recovery was quite slow with intensive physiotherapy while still in hospital.*
▶ in the economy **economic, gradual, modest, partial, seasonal, slow, sustained** *Scotland's traditional textiles industry is making a remarkable and sustained recovery.*
▶ unexplained **miraculous, remarkable, spontaneous** *Maybe you have had a miraculous recovery, I don't know.*
▶ complete **complete, full** *When identified and treated early, more than half of the cases made a full recovery.*
• v+N help recovery **aid, assist, drive, encourage, ensure, facilitate, promote, revive** *You can play your part in reducing the stress for the patient and aiding their recovery.* • *It will be a tough challenge to revive economic activity and promote the recovery of agricultural production.*
▶ make a recovery **make** *He was expected to make a full recovery.*
▶ make recovery quicker **accelerate, hasten, speed** *What can be done to hasten recovery?*
▶ prevent recovery or make it happen more slowly **delay, hinder, limit, prevent** *The dry soils could delay the seasonal recovery in eastern England.*
▶ make recovery as large as possible **maximize** *Targeted measures could improve the situation and help maximize economic recovery.*
• N+from from illness, injury, or medical treatment **addiction, anaesthesia, depression, illness, infection, injury, operation, stroke, surgery, wounds** *It is never too late to begin recovery from alcohol addiction.*
▶ from a difficult or bad experience **crisis, damage, failure, recession** *The ERM collapse saw a reduction in interest rates and the beginnings of a recovery from deep recession.*

recruitment N
the process of finding people to join an organization

• adj+N temporary/permanent **permanent, temporary** *For specific examples of how we deliver temporary recruitment give us a call.*
▶ fair or careful **fair, rigorous, selective** *Lewisham puts great importance on ensuring that every stage in our recruitment process is fair.*
▶ international **international, overseas** *Since 1997, Britain has relied heavily on overseas recruitment.*

▸ large-scale **large-scale, mass** *Mass recruitment by the IRA began only after Bloody Sunday.*

● n+N **donor, graduate, postgraduate, staff, teacher, trainee, trustee, volunteer** *This month is volunteer recruitment month*

● v+N increase recruitment **aid, boost, encourage, improve, increase, stimulate** *The on-site gym is likely to boost recruitment at the hospital.*

▸ manage recruitment **co-ordinate, facilitate, oversee** *The Human Resources Department co-ordinates all recruitment.*

▸ check recruitment **monitor** *The University will continue to monitor its recruitment of students from ethnic minorities.*

N+n company **agency, consultancy, firm** *Speak to recruitment consultancies to get their view on what the organisation is like.*

process **procedure, process, strategy** *What is the recruitment process for a graduate applying for work with your organisation?*

problems **crisis, difficulties** *First of all there is the recruitment crisis confronting the service at large.*

campaign **campaign, drive** *We will shortly be launching a recruitment drive for more members.*

recur V
happen again

adv+V often **commonly, frequently, often, regularly** *The unfortunate result is that the back-ache regularly recurs.*

all the time **constantly, continually** *Modest is the word that constantly recurs in tributes.*

n+V **disease, pain, problem, symptom** *If symptoms recur within 2 months, consult a medical practitioner.*

recurring ADJ
happening again, especially several times

ADJ+n pattern **motif, pattern, phrase, refrain, theme** *The need for cooperation between specialists was a recurring theme.*

dream **dream, nightmare** *The book begins with Nick's attempts at communicating the horrors of his recurring nightmare to his closest friend.*

problem or illness **headache, illness, infection, problem** *Doctors advise regular examinations for patients with a history of recurring ear infections.*

recycle V
change waste materials so that they can be used again

adv+V safely or carefully **economically, efficiently, responsibly, safely** *Make sure you recycle responsibly.*

many times **continuously, endlessly, infinitely, repeatedly** *Aluminium cans can be recycled infinitely.*

and/or use again **reclaim, recover, refurbish, repair, reprocess, reuse** *Much of the waste that we produce can be reused or recycled.*

get rid of **discard, dispose of** *You can use our household waste and recycling sites to recycle and dispose of household rubbish.*

recycling N
the process of changing waste materials to use again

● n+N from a place **doorstep, household, kerbside** *In 2002 just over half of households had a doorstep recycling service.*

▸ of a product or material **aluminium, cardboard, cartridge, glass, plastic, rainwater, waste** *A cardboard recycling scheme is being considered for the future.*

● v+N increase recycling **boost, expand, improve, increase, maximize** *Ultimately, the goal is to reduce waste production and to maximize recycling and reuse.*

▸ encourage recycling **encourage, facilitate, promote** *We are delighted to help the Council to promote its recycling, reuse and composting initiatives.*

▸ introduce recycling **introduce** *Paper was being recycled as early as 1690, while New York introduced metal recycling in 1776.*

red ADJ
of the same colour as blood

● adj+ADJ bright **bright, brilliant, fiery, vibrant, vivid** *Your minimum requirements should be a front light with distinct beam and a bright red rear light.*

▸ light **light, pale** *The prevalent colouring of the decorations was grey blue, lemon yellow and pale red.*

▸ dark **dark, deep, dull, dusky, rich** *She wore a tiara and veil in her hair and carried a bouquet of deep red roses.*

▸ types of red **carmine, cherry, crimson, pinkish, poppy, purplish, ruby, rust, scarlet** *As castings are removed from the moulds, they are often still glowing cherry red with heat.*

● v+ADJ become red **become, flush, glow, turn** *As darkness fell, the sky glowed red from the fires which were still raging.*

▸ make something red **colour sth, dye sth, paint sth, stain sth** *The approximate extent of the estate is coloured red on the map below.*

reduce V
make something less in size, amount etc

● adv+V greatly **considerably, greatly, markedly, much, seriously, significantly, substantially** *With so many parents both working, time with their children has been greatly reduced.*

▸ very greatly **dramatically, drastically, massively, radically, severely, sharply, vastly** *On Sundays and public holidays, schedules are drastically reduced.*

▸ gradually **gradually, progressively, steadily** *In Britain the monarch's absolute power has been gradually reduced over time.*

▸ slightly **slightly** *A Zip file of the document has been created to slightly reduce the file size for downloading.*

reduction N
the process or result of making something smaller

● adj+N large **considerable, marked, significant, substantial** *The very significant reduction in grants was not thought through.*

▶ very large **dramatic, drastic, huge, massive, sharp** *We should like to see drastic reduction in rates of perinatal and infant death.*

▶ small **modest, slight** *The agreement also provides for a very slight reduction in annual hours.*

▶ gradual **gradual, progressive, steady, sustained** *We must therefore plan today for a gradual reduction of our bases in the Far East.*

▶ quick **rapid** *A rapid reduction can lead to a physical withdrawal syndrome in up to 40 per cent of cases.*

▶ overall **overall** *The overall reduction in car mileage travelled was 17 per cent.*

● n+N of a social problem **crime, debt, poverty, traffic** *This section provides residents with a wealth of information about community safety and crime reduction.*

▶ of a problem people have **harm, risk, stress** *Others had worked specifically testing the impact of the arts on stress reduction.*

▶ of a substance **carbon, emission, greenhouse gas, pollution, waste** *Rewarding carbon reduction is vital to enable the sensible investment and policy decisions we need.*

● v+N suggest or announce a reduction **announce, negotiate, propose, recommend** *The European Commission's reaction was to propose the most drastic reductions we have yet seen.*

▶ cause or make a reduction **achieve, bring about, cause, deliver, effect, make, secure** *How has this reduction been achieved?*

▶ experience a reduction **experience, face** *The Group experienced a significant reduction in output without a comparable reduction in energy use.*

▶ show a reduction **demonstrate, show** *They were able to demonstrate an 84 per cent reduction in hospital admissions from those who attended the Project.*

● N+in rate or severity **frequency, incidence, number, prevalence, rate, severity, size** *The new directives will see a reduction in the number of different polymers used.*

▶ money paid or received **cost, duty, expenditure, fee, funding, income, price, spending, tax** *The company has been able to maximize the efficiency of its workforce and make significant reductions in expenditure.*

▶ death **casualty, fatality, mortality** *The largest reduction in mortality was seen in patients with progressive heart failure.*

redundancy N

a situation where a worker is no longer needed

● adj+N compulsory/voluntary **compulsory, enforced, planned, voluntary** *Managers are under instructions to avoid compulsory redundancies wherever possible.*

▶ large-scale **collective, large-scale, mass, massive, widespread** *Large-scale redundancies and industrial action affected many workers.*

▶ coming soon **imminent, impending, inevitable** *The effect of an impending redundancy on an individual may be significant.*

▶ possible **potential, threatened** *The employees sought advice about their potential redundancy.*

▶ unfair **unfair** *Grievances dealt with include unfair*

dismissal, unfair redundancy, harassment and discrimination.

● v+N plan or suggest redundancies **plan, propose, threaten** *Representatives said they were horrified by the level of redundancies proposed.*

▶ expect redundancy **be faced with, be threatened by, be threatened with, expect, face** *Are you facing redundancy, early retirement, or just looking for a change?*

▶ accept redundancy **accept** *They want the dockers to accept compulsory redundancies.*

redundant ADJ

no longer needed

● adv+ADJ mainly or partly **largely, partially, pretty INFORMAL, somewhat, virtually** *Child fares ar largely redundant now but are available for those children who don't have a Photocard.*

▶ completely **completely, effectively, entirely, totally, utterly** *Is the notion of style as a sign of personal expression completely redundant?*

▶ increasingly **increasingly** *The traditional model is becoming increasingly redundant.*

● v+ADJ make something redundant **declare sth, render sth** *The church was declared redundant in the early 1970s, and has been closed ever since.*

▶ be or seem redundant **be, become, seem** *Reviewir the film itself seems pretty redundant.*

reference N

1 a mention of someone or something

● adj+N clear **direct, explicit, particular, specific** *Research the course thoroughly so you can make specific reference to areas which interest you.*

▶ not clear **oblique, obscure, vague, veiled** *They laugh at the jokes and they pick up on obscure references too.*

▶ detailed or numerous **constant, detailed, frequer numerous, repeated** *There were of course numero references to Nottingham in the text.*

▶ short or infrequent **brief, occasional, passing** *Br references are made to medication review.*

▶ types of reference **biblical, cultural, historical, literary, visual** *I think there are a lot of cultural references here which don't translate well.*

● v+N contain a reference **contain, include** *Paragraphs 8.3 and 8.13 contain additional references to the company.*

▶ make a reference **make** *The Government's latest evidence made no explicit reference to procuremen costs.*

2 a statement giving information about you, use when you are applying for a job

● adj+N good **excellent, glowing, good, satisfactor** *All appointments are subject to the receipt of satisfactory references.*

▶ types of reference **academic, character** *You need include two academic references and copies of you qualifying certificates.*

● v+N ask for a reference **request, require** *The H. Department will normally request references prior to interview.*

▶ provide a reference **provide, supply** *Can you provide references?*

give someone a reference **give sb, write** *The Personal Supervisor would normally be expected to write a reference for a student if requested to do so.*

check a reference **check, follow up, obtain, take up** *All our staff are checked through the Criminal Record Bureau and all references are followed up.*

3 a mention in writing of a writer or piece of work

adj+N **bibliographic, bibliographical, selected, useful** *From the beginning you should ensure you record complete bibliographical references.*

v+N give references **cite, give, include, list, quote, supply** *Where multiple references are cited, they should be in numerical order irrespective of chronology.*

contain references **contain** *Each section is illustrated by examples and contains references for further information.*

eferendum N

n opportunity for people to vote on one subject

adj+N types of referendum **binding, constitutional, consultative, national, nationwide, presidential** *The result of the referendum is not legally binding.*

coming soon **forthcoming, upcoming** *The money will support the forthcoming constitutional referendum.*

v+N have a referendum **call, conduct, have, hold, organize** *At least nine countries are committed to holding a referendum on the new treaty.*

want a referendum **call for, demand, propose, want** *We demand a referendum on this fundamental shift in the way we are governed.*

win/lose a referendum **lose, win** *There is little likelihood that he can win a referendum on giving up the pound.*

efer to PHR VB

nd someone or something to another person or ace

V+n a question **enquiry, query** *Please do not refer routine enquiries or non-urgent items to the Emergency Service.*

a problem or case **case, complaint, dispute, matter, merger** *Subsequently, Britain referred the dispute to the League of Nations.*

a person **caller, client, enquirer, journalist, offender, patient, reader** *The callers are referred to the appropriate organisation for support.*

fine V

prove something by making small changes

adv+V all the time **constantly, continually, continuously** *This technology was developed in-house and is continuously refined.*

gradually **gradually, progressively** *These first establish broad outlines of the embryo body plan, which are progressively refined as the embryo develops.*

v+n method **methodology, technique** *One enters into research not only to gain credentials but to refine methodology and present findings.*

theory **concept, criteria, definition, estimate, hypothesis, model, parameters, specification** *As*

the web technology spread, his initial specifications were refined.

skill **skills, understanding** *She chose to refine her translation skills by taking a post-graduate diploma in Technical and Specialised Translation.*

reflect V

show the existence or nature of something

adv+V correctly **accurately, correctly, exactly, faithfully, properly, truly** *I did not think the newspaper article accurately reflected my views.*

completely **certainly, fully, obviously, perfectly** *Improvements in the quality of teaching are fully reflected in pupils' performance.*

more or less **adequately, broadly, largely, partially, partly, probably** *These three projects broadly reflect the areas of research central to the company.*

necessarily **necessarily** *The article does not necessarily reflect the views of the government.*

V+n **change, commitment, concern, difference, diversity, fact, importance, interest, need, opinion, priority, reality, trend, view** *The very low figure reflects the fact that people are spending less on eating out.*

reflection N

1 careful thought about something

adj+N calm **mature, quiet, sober, sombre, thoughtful** *On sober reflection, it would appear that this element of the design was a mistake.*

types of reflection **critical, personal, philosophical, prayerful, theological** *The candidate needs to be able to demonstrate a high level of critical reflection.*

v+N cause reflection **encourage, prompt, provoke, stimulate** *Each section is followed by questions to prompt reflection and suggestions for further reading.*

help reflection **aid, facilitate** *Some questions are designed to aid reflection on past experiences.*

N+v **reveal, show, suggest** *Yet a moment's reflection reveals that this too is unlikely.*

2 something that clearly shows something

adj+N accurate **accurate, clear, fair, true** *The eventual 6–2 scoreline provides a fair reflection of the balance of play.*

causing regret **poor, sad** *This is a sad reflection on our legal system.*

not accurate **distorted** *The political instability at the top is a distorted reflection of the general instability in society.*

reform N

a change that is intended to improve a system or correct faults

adj+N making major changes **far-reaching, fundamental, radical, sweeping, wide-ranging** *The system dated back to the Second World War and needed radical reform.*

types of reform **agricultural, constitutional, democratic, economic, educational, electoral, institutional, judicial, legislative, liturgical, monetary, parliamentary, penal, regulatory, social** *The conquest of inflation is the most visible sign of economic reform.*

- n+N **curriculum, immigration, justice, law, NHS, pension, police, prison, tax, voting, welfare** *The Democratic National Platform in 2000 criticised the Republicans' proposed tax reform.*

- v+N support reform **advocate, back, embrace, favour, propose** *Our parliamentary party will back reforms that help people find work.*

▶ make reform happen **announce, bring about, carry out, carry through, drive through, effect, enact, implement, initiate, introduce, push through, undertake** *We have recently introduced the largest reforms of NHS dentistry in over 50 years.*

- N+n **act, agenda, bill, effort, initiative, legislation, measure, movement, package, process, programme, proposal** *Under the reform package, our farmers will be required to compete globally with foreign farmers.*

reform V
improve a situation by correcting bad things

- adv+V **completely, drastically, fundamentally, radically, totally** *The Government had promised to radically reform public services.*

refreshing ADJ
welcome because of being different or exciting

- adv+ADJ **delightfully, surprisingly, thoroughly, truly, wonderfully** *It was wonderfully refreshing to walk in the sand and to feel the cool sea washing over our feet.*

- ADJ+n **alternative, antidote, candour, change, honesty, simplicity, take** *His inventive humour provides a refreshing take on the insanity of modern life.*

refuge N
protection from dangerous or unpleasant things

- v+N give someone refuge **afford, give, grant, offer, provide** *The room gave refuge from the pressures of school life.*

▶ get refuge **find, take** *More than 33,000 people took refuge in storm shelters across the state.*

▶ try to find refuge **seek** *He agrees to shelter his wife's cousins who are seeking refuge in New York as illegal immigrants.*

- and/or **asylum, safety, sanctuary, shelter** *The government aims to recognise the rights of those seeking asylum, refuge and a better life.*

refugee N
a person who leaves their country because of danger

- v+N send refugees away **deport, disperse, evacuate, expel, force out, relocate, repatriate, return** *It is the policy of the government to repatriate the refugees in a gradual manner.*

▶ give refugees a place to live **house, resettle, shelter** *Authorities have begun resettling refugees in cities across the country.*

▶ put refugees in prison **detain** *The refugees were detained at the police station because their documents were not in order.*

- N+v come to a place **arrive in, enter, flood into, flow into, pour into, settle in, stream into** *More than 3,000 Kosovo refugees streamed into Albania.*

▶ leave a place **depart, escape, flee** *More than 100,000 refugees have fled to Thailand.*

- N+n place or group **camp, community, convoy, hostel, population** *Kenya also has a refugee population of 180,000, mainly from the Sudan and Somalia.*

▶ organization helping refugees **agency, organization** *He found out through the UN refugee agency that resettlement to Chile was an option.*

▶ movement of refugess **exodus, influx** *It was the scene of a massive refugee exodus following an uprising that was crushed in 1991.*

▶ legal position **status** *The US soldier attempted to claim refugee status in Canada.*

▶ problem **crisis** *The EU donated US$633,500 in emergency aid to help deal with the Kosovo refugee crisis in Albania.*

refund N
money you paid that you get back

- adj+N **complete, due, full, immediate, partial** *If a refund is due, we will credit your credit card within twenty four hours.* • *If this is not satisfactory to you you will be given a full refund.*

- v+N ask for a refund **apply for, ask for, claim, demand, request** *You may be able to claim a refun for travel costs to the hospital.*

▶ get a refund **get, obtain, receive** *How can I obtain a refund for faulty goods bought from a market trader?*

▶ give sb a refund **arrange, give, grant, issue, offer, process** *We will issue a full refund of the price you paid for the item, and the return postage.*

refusal N
the act of refusing to do something

- adj+N firm **adamant, outright, point-blank, resolute, steadfast** *Their stance is characterised by an almost point-blank refusal to consider other points of view.*

▶ repeated **continued, persistent, repeated** *Shell's repeated refusal to deal with these issues shows the need for Government intervention.*

▶ unfair **obstinate, stubborn, unreasonable, wilful** *The only obstacle to a totally harmonious society is the stubborn refusal of its inhabitants to embrace the virtues of the market.*

- v+N get a refusal **meet with** *So far our requests have met with a refusal.*

▶ try to change a refusal **appeal, appeal against, challenge** *If an applicant wishes to challenge a refusal, he or she should in the first instance apply to the department concerned.*

▶ change a refusal **override, overturn, quash** *Recently, another inspector overturned a refusal of planning permission for a car showroom.*

refuse V
say you will not give, accept or do something

- adv+V firmly **absolutely, adamantly, bluntly, categorically, flatly, outright, point-blank, resolutely, simply, steadfastly** *They flatly refused increase their pay offer any further.*

▶ unfairly **obstinately, stubbornly, unfairly, unreasonably, wilfully, wrongfully, wrongly** *The organization wilfully refused to believe what was clearly true.*

▶ several times **consistently, continually, persistently, repeatedly** *They have consistently refused to listen to students' concerns over the library closure plans.*

● V+n permission in general **consent, leave, permission** *They were refused leave to appeal to the House of Lords.*

▶ permission to enter a place **admission, admittance, entry** *He has received an apology from the US government after he was refused entry to the country.*

▶ something that someone asks for **application, bail, licence, parole, registration, request, visa** *More than 500 drivers were refused licences last year.*

▶ something that someone offers **invitation, mediation, offer, treatment** *Joyce refuses his invitation to dinner.*

regain V
get something again that you lost

▶ adv+V completely **completely, fully** *It may be some time before he fully regains the strength he has lost.*

▶ quickly **immediately, quickly, rapidly** *John rapidly regained his mental faculties and his physical health improved dramatically.*

▶ slowly **eventually, finally, gradually, slowly** *Liberating forces are gradually regaining control of parts of the occupied territory.*

V+n behaviour or mental state **composure, confidence, consciousness, credibility, dignity, fitness, popularity, sanity, self-confidence, self-respect, strength** *This setback rocked the home side and they struggled to regain their composure for at least twenty minutes.*

possession **control, crown, independence, lead, possession, sovereignty, throne** *Portugal had regained its independence from Spain the previous year.*

regard V
consider someone or something in a particular way

adv+V with a good opinion **favourably, highly, well** *Lee, a highly regarded stand-up comedian, speaks with measured, deadpan precision.*

by most or all people **commonly, generally, normally, universally, usually, widely** *Stars from the earliest days of British rock 'n' roll gathered at the spot widely regarded as its birthplace.*

which is fair or correct **justly, rightly** *The clinic is quite rightly regarded throughout Europe as the most progressive of its kind.*

for a long time **long, traditionally** *Mickelson was long regarded as the best modern-day player not to win a major tournament.*

V+with **affection, awe, caution, contempt, disdain, favour, horror, hostility, indifference, respect, scepticism, suspicion** *This adversarial style of debate is regarded with disdain by New Labour women.*

regard N
attention or care given to something or someone

adj+N not enough **insufficient, little, scant, slight**

It has become increasingly evident that the councils and their officials have scant regard for local people's welfare.

▶ which the situation deserves **due, positive, proper, sufficient** *Due regard must be paid to such policies, and authorities must not appoint unqualified staff.*

▶ special **particular, special** *Landscape policies for the coast also need to pay particular regard to how development is viewed from the sea and along the coastline.*

● v+N **demonstrate, give, have, pay, show** *Hospitals need an approach that pays regard to patients' wishes.*

2 respect and admiration for someone or something

● adj+N high, mutual, utmost *It was characteristic of Carr that this did not alter his high regard for Orwell.*

● v+N **demonstrate, have, hold sb/sth in, show** *Today, many years after the end of the Second World War, Winston Churchill is still held in high regard.*

regime N
1 a government, especially a strict or unfair one

● adj+N **authoritarian, brutal, corrupt, dictatorial, fascist, oppressive, repressive, strict, totalitarian, tyrannical** *These companies also sell arms to repressive regimes.*

● v+N get rid of a regime **change, depose, destabilize, oust, overthrow, topple** *The US determined to topple the Iraqi regime.*

▶ make a regime stronger **bolster, strengthen** *Oil companies were accused of bolstering a repressive military regime.*

▶ make a regime less strict **liberalize, modernize, reform** *He needed to clear the baggage of Stalin as a way of modernising the regime.*

▶ establish a regime **establish, set up** *When the communist regime was established in 1940, art became subordinate to politics.*

▶ criticize a regime **challenge, criticize, discredit, oppose** *The delegates did not fear to criticize the Bolshevik regime and present the demands of the workers.*

● N+v stop existing **collapse, crumble, fail, fall** *The Shah of Iran's westernised regime had collapsed and given way to a theocratic Islamic state.*

▶ treat people badly **oppress, persecute** *The majority of Iraq's population are Shi'ite Muslims, but the Sunni Muslim regime has brutally oppressed them.*

● N+n **change, shift** *The film documents the way in which female citizens of Afghanistan were positively affected by the regime change.*

2 a system of rules controlling something

● adj+N **fiscal, regulatory** *We need a regulatory regime which takes a direct interest in public services.*

● n+N **enforcement, inspection, licensing, tax, testing, verification** *In the 1970s, the burden of UK taxation drove her to Ireland which had a more favourable tax regime.*

● v+N make a regime exist **establish, implement, impose, institute, introduce** *We are now over a year* *into the new family-friendly regime introduced by the Government.*

▶ make a regime simpler **simplify** *We should be simplifying the tax regime and providing incentives for people to save.*

region N

a large area with particular politics, geography, or culture

● adj+N **arid, coastal, mountainous, polar, remote, temperate, tropical** *The coastal regions of east Malaysia have some of the best diving sites in the world.*

● n+N **border, desert, frontier, highland, mountain** *Huge amounts of solar energy fall on desert regions.*

register V

1 show your feelings about something

● V+n **disgust, interest** *Her eyes registered a sudden interest in this unusual visitor.*

2 make your opinion known publicly or officially

● adv+V **formally, officially** *There will be a period when members of the public get the chance to formally register their objections to the proposed rail link.*

● V+n **complaint, intention, objection, opposition, protest, vote** *A boycott of imported products is an effective way of registering a protest about the policies of the government concerned.*

register N

an official list or record of something

● adj+N types of register **baptismal, burial, electoral, episcopal, parochial, statutory** *We need to ensure that everyone who has the right to vote is on the electoral register.*

▶ applying to a whole country or organization **central, national** *The government plans to introduce a new national register of competent contractors.*

● v+N have a register **compile, hold, keep, maintain** *The University is required to maintain a register of equipment assets.*

▶ set up a register **create, establish** *The Agency has established a register of how many of its staff speak Welsh.*

▶ look at a register **access, check, consult, inspect, search, view** *I took a trip to Northampton Record Office to consult the original parish registers.*

▶ change a register **amend, edit, update** *He instructed the elections department to update its register of eligible voters.*

● v+from+N take someone or something off a register **delete, erase, remove, strike** *He was guilty of breaching the rules and was erased from the medical register.*

● v+in+N **enter, hold, include, keep, list, mention, note, place, record** *When he was christened at twelve days old, he was mistakenly entered in the register as a girl.*

● v+on+N be on a register **appear, go, remain, stay** *'Member' means any person whose name appears on the register.*

▶ put someone or something on a register **enter, hold, include, list, place, put, record** *Their names are placed on the Church register.*

registration N

the process of recording information on an official list

● v+N end the registration of someone or something **block, cancel, invalidate, suspend, terminate, withdraw** *There was no appearance from the couple and in their absence a decision was made to cancel the registration.*

▶ register someone or something **complete, confirm, effect, grant, process, renew** *Follow the on-screen instructions to complete your registration.*

● N+n document **card, certificate, document, form** *Simply click on the 'Sign In' button and complete the registration form.*

▶ process **procedure, process, scheme** *The details will not be passed to any party not involved in the registration procedure.*

▶ number, symbol, or other detail **code, detail, mark, number, status** *How do I enter my registration code?*

regret V

feel sorry or sad that something has happened

● adv+V **bitterly, deeply, greatly, much, profoundly, seriously, sincerely, truly** *We deeply regret any inconvenience that this possible compromise may cause you.*

● V+infinitive **announce, inform, report, say** *The conference has proved very popular, and we regret to inform you that all available spaces have now been taken.*

regret N

sadness about something that has happened

● adj+N **considerable, deep, great, much, profound, sincere** *All casualties suffered by the UK Armed Forces are a source of profound regret.*

● v+N show regret **express, show, voice** *Israel's leaders had voiced their deep regret for the civilian deaths and injuries.*

▶ feel regret **feel, harbour, have** *Reflecting on his previous career, it is clear that he harbours regrets.*

● n+of+N small amount of regret **hint, pang, sense, tinge, twinge** *I felt a slight pang of regret that I wouldn't be visting them this summer.*

▶ feeling or expression of regret **expression, feeling, sense** *Expressions of regret started to pour in after his death.*

▶ matter of regret **matter** *It is a matter of regret that the Government refuses to do the right thing.*

▶ cause of regret **cause, source** *She said it was a source of great regret that nine firefighters had lost their lives as a result of the explosion.*

● and/or **apology, bitterness, disappointment, grief, guilt, longing, remorse, resentment, sadness, shame, sorrow, sympathy** *Holding onto regrets and bitterness will only keep your life from moving forward.*

regrettable ADJ
making you feel sad or sorry

- adv+ADJ **deeply, extremely, highly, particularly, profoundly, very** The Minister said any job losses would be 'deeply regrettable'.
- ADJ+n **accident, consequence, decision, delay, fact, incident, mistake, omission, situation** The bombing of the Chinese Embassy was a deeply regrettable mistake.

regulate V
control an activity, process, or industry

- adv+V very well **carefully, closely, heavily, highly, strictly, tightly** These 'adult' channels are much more tightly regulated here than in other parts of Europe.
- not very well **minimally, poorly, weakly** Meals in many schools are poorly regulated and of low nutritional value.

regulation N
official rules controlling how things are done

- adj+N strict **strict, stringent, tight, tough** These properties have to comply with stringent legal regulations **regarding** fire safety and facilities supplied.
- too strict **burdensome, excessive, restrictive, unnecessary** They promised not to impose burdensome regulations on business.
- types of regulation **economic, environmental, federal, financial, legal, statutory** Air France has been gradually phasing out its Boeing 747-200Fs to comply with environmental regulations.
- that must be obeyed **binding, disciplinary, prescriptive** The UK government is pushing for voluntary controls rather than binding regulations on business.
- v+N make regulations exist **adopt, enact, introduce, issue, lay down** Members must accept the will of the majority where specific regulations are not laid down.
- fail to obey regulations **breach, contravene, flout, infringe, violate** The employee has a right of appeal if the employer has breached the regulations.
- make people obey regulations **enforce, implement, impose** These officers are fully trained to deal with public order situations and enforce traffic regulations.
- change regulations in some way **amend, harmonize, revise, simplify, tighten** A revised proposal from the Netherlands did little to tighten regulations.
- obey regulations **adhere to, comply with, conform to, satisfy** The prospective employer must make a formal application, which must satisfy the appropriate regulations.

N+v state something **define, mean, prescribe, state, stipulate** EU regulations state that researchers must assess the pain that an animal may feel during an experiment.
not allow something **outlaw, prohibit, restrict** The regulations outlaw discrimination on grounds of (among other things) a philosophical belief.
allow something or make something necessary

allow, impose, permit, require Mexican regulations permit the owner of an automobile to import it into Mexico for a period of six months.
- refer to something or control something **affect, apply, concern, cover, govern, pertain, regard, relate** This review will look at the regulations governing those activities.

reign N
the period when a king or queen rules

- adj+N bringing wars or problems **bloody, disastrous, inglorious, troubled, turbulent** It was a very troubled reign, and insurrections took place in this country against Roman rule.
- bringing peace or comfort **glorious, illustrious, peaceful, prosperous** Louis Philippe's reign was prosperous but uneventful, as his ministers pursued cautious policies.

reinforce V
make an idea, belief, or feeling stronger

- adv+V very much **powerfully, strongly** This image was powerfully reinforced by the popular television series entitled Roots by Alex Hailey.
- often **constantly, continually, continuously** The habit of making firm decisions continuously reinforces the sense of personal growth.

- V+n idea or belief **belief, commitment, notion, prejudice, stereotype, tendency, view** Your answer should avoid stereotyping or reinforcing prejudices.
- feeling **feeling, impression, message, perception, suspicion** Lambert's illustrations reinforce the impression of a lazy afternoon in summer.

reject V
not accept something

- adv+V firmly **categorically, comprehensively, decisively, emphatically, explicitly, firmly, flatly, outright, overwhelmingly, roundly, summarily, totally, unanimously, unequivocally, utterly, vehemently** In many cases the deportees' claims have been rejected outright as 'manifestly unfounded'.
- angrily **angrily, contemptuously, indignantly, scornfully** The King contemptuously rejects the Parliamentary proposals.

- V+n statement or opinion **accusation, allegation, argument, assertion, belief, claim, contention, hypothesis, idea, notion, proposition, suggestion** We also reject the shallow notion that those who carry out terrorist attacks are motivated by evil.
- suggestion **bid, invitation, offer, proposal, proposition, suggestion** He was the only man able to persuade shareholders to reject the bid from Mr Green.
- attempt **attempt** The UK must reject any attempt to undermine environmental legislation.
- request **application, call, demand, plea, request** Nato rejects call to cut nuclear arms.

rejection N
a refusal to accept something or someone

- adj+N **decisive, explicit, outright, overwhelming, utter, wholesale** Representatives voted for outright rejection of the management's proposals.

- **v+N** advise people to reject something
recommend, urge *Many in the Church are urging the rejection of the arguments of the extremists.*
▶ when rejection is possible **fear, risk** *Patients with this condition commonly fear social rejection.*
▶ experience rejection **cope with, deal with, endure, experience, suffer** *Inevitably, your paper may be rejected – many are, and all academics have suffered rejection at some time.*

relapse N
a return to illness or another bad state

- **v+N** cause a relapse **cause, precipitate, trigger** *Even moving house can precipitate a relapse in some people.*
▶ experience a relapse **experience, suffer** *Two patients experienced a relapse.*
▶ prevent a relapse **avoid, prevent** *Longer-term preventive therapy aims to prevent relapses.*

relate V
be about something, or be connected to something

- **adv+V** only or mainly **especially, exclusively, mainly, mostly, particularly, primarily, principally, solely, specifically** *This section relates solely to unincorporated charities.*
▶ closely **clearly, closely, directly, strongly** *Scientists are interested in the viscoelasticity of cells, since it directly relates to their biological functioning.*
▶ not closely **loosely** *I suspected that the first and second halves might only loosely relate to each other.*

- **n+V** subject **discipline, issue, issue, matter, theme, topic** *This web page will include features and articles on a wide range of topics relating to Latin and Roman culture.*
▶ question or action **complaint, enquiry, query, question** *There were complaints relating to defective goods and faulty installation.*
▶ law or rule **enactment, law, legislation, provision, regulation, rule** *This legislation relates to offshore and non-resident business.*
▶ document **article, correspondence, data, document, documentation, material, paper, record, statistic** *The police can require a mobile-phone operator to provide traffic data relating to a suspect's use of a mobile phone.*
▶ argument **dispute** *Our lawyers are able to advise on disputes relating to website and partnering agreements.*
▶ crime **offence** *The ambulance driver was subsequently convicted for a driving offence relating to the accident.*

related ADJ
1 connected

- **adv+ADJ** closely, directly *The two matters are not directly related.*

- **ADJ+n** subject **discipline, issue, item, matter, subject, topic** *We deal only with divorce and related issues.*
▶ document **article, document, documentation, link, material, site, websites** *The last part of each page consists of a number of related links to other information held on the web site, or links to external resources.*

2 belonging to the same family

- **adv+ADJ** closely, distantly *Members within each superfamily are distantly related to each other.*

relation N
1 the relationship between countries, people, or organizations [always plural]

- **adj+N** types of relations **diplomatic, industrial** *Blair had transformed Labour's approach to industrial relations.*
▶ international **bilateral, foreign, international, transatlantic** *Bilateral relations between Saudi Arabia and Iran deteriorated to the point of confrontation.*
▶ friendly **friendly, harmonious** *The new approach of the Natural Law Party simultaneously strengthens sovereignty while promoting constructive and harmonious relations with all European nations.*
▶ getting worse **deteriorating, worsening** *The expulsion of two diplomats added to the worsening relations between the two countries.*

- **v+N** improve relations **cement, improve, promote, strengthen** *This event aims to cement relations between Scotland and Catalunya.*
▶ create relations **establish, forge, foster** *They were attempting to forge better relations between the trade unions and employers.*
▶ make relations worse **damage, sour, strain, worsen** *But his rhetoric also soured traditional relations with the United States.*
▶ end relations **sever** *Iraq was likely to sever all relations with Australia.*
▶ make relations good again **normalize, re-establish, restore, resume** *We are exploring ways to normalize relations with China.*
▶ change relations **alter, transform** *Some sociologists believe that the purpose of learning is to transform social relations.*

2 a connection between people or things

- **adj+N** types of relation **causal, logical, semantic, spatial** *Our theoretical framework describes how visual and textual information combine in terms of semantic relations between images and texts.*
▶ close **close** *The close relation of urology and transplant surgery means that some of the staff work in both departments.*

relationship N
1 the way in which things are connected

- **adj+N** causal, close, complex, direct, strong, symbiotic *There is often a symbiotic relationship between the data and the hardware/software system that provides access to it.*

- **v+N** consider a relationship **examine, explore, investigate** *He was keen to explore the relationship between literature and theology.*
▶ describe a relationship **clarify, define, describe, understand** *This formal document clarifies the relationship between the Council and community and voluntary sectors.*

2 people's behaviour towards each other

- **adj+N** close, intimate, lasting, long-standing, loving, personal, sexual, stable *We're beginning a* process of continuous involvement in projects to build long-lasting relationships **between** European and Brazilian partners.

- v+N create a relationship **build, develop, establish, forge, form, foster** *By forging strong relationships **with** private landowners and environmental organisations, the company has a unique take on the island.*
- ▶ make a relationship better **cement, deepen, improve, repair, strengthen** *Music is very important to most E4 viewers and we hope this new programming will help strengthen our relationship **with** our existing audience as well as attract a new one.*
- ▶ make a relationship worse **damage, ruin, strain, undermine** *An atmosphere of suspicion can ruin relationships and undermine confidence.*

relative ADJ
having a particular quality when compared with something

- ADJ+n positive aspect **abundance, calm, importance, merit, stability, strength** *There was a discussion on the relative merits of different logos.*
- ▶ negative aspect **decline, deprivation, isolation, lack, obscurity, paucity, poverty, risk** *The Council's grants programme is now more targeted at socially excluded groups and areas of relative deprivation.*

relative N
a member of your family

- adj+N **close, dead, deceased, dependent, distant, elderly, living, long-lost, near** *The wedding party was made up of distant relatives and slight acquaintances.*
- and/or **friend, neighbour** *Also thank you to the many friends and relatives who attended her funeral.*

relax V
1 rest and allow yourself to become calm

- adv+V just **just, simply** *You can sit outside to eat or just relax and admire the spectacular view.*
- ▶ completely **completely, totally** *She finds it difficult to 'switch off' and completely relax.*
- ▶ slightly **a bit, a little, slightly** *Once we knew we weren't going to be late, we relaxed a bit.*
- ▶ in a way that can be seen **visibly** *With each puff on her cigarette she visibly relaxed.*
- ▶ v+to+V **begin to, help sb (to), learn to, make sb, need to, start to, try to** *Playing quiet, calming music can prove soothing and help you to relax.* ● *The audience are already on your side so try to relax.*
- and/or **chat, enjoy sth, rest, sit, unwind, watch sth** *This is the ideal place to relax and unwind after a busy day.*

2 make less strict

- V+n law or rule **constraint, control, law, regulation, requirement, restriction, rule** *We have now relaxed our restrictions on imports from Europe.*
- ▶ way of thinking about something **approach, attitude, policy, stance** *For a time the government relaxed its stance on the use of soft drugs.*

relaxed ADJ
calm, informal, and comfortable

- adv+ADJ very or completely **completely, totally, very, wonderfully** *The day's travelling was very relaxed, and the scenery was absolutely spectacular throughout.*
- ▶ rather **fairly, pretty** INFORMAL**, quite, relatively** *There is a fairly relaxed but disciplined attitude towards training which makes it very enjoyable to learn.*
- ▶ in a pleasant way **pleasantly** *Most patients feel pleasantly relaxed after treatment and there are no side-effects.*
- ADJ+n mood or feeling in person or a place **ambience, atmosphere, environment, feel, feeling, mood, setting, surroundings** *The Guildford campus offers a friendly and relaxed atmosphere.*
- ▶ way of doing or thinking about something **approach, attitude, manner, style** *The residential nature of the school allows a chance to discuss the issues raised in a relaxed manner.*
- v+ADJ **appear, be, feel, keep sb, look, seem** *She appeared completely relaxed and seemed to be enjoying herself.* ● *It's important to keep everybody relaxed and happy.*

relay V
communicate information to someone; receive and send a broadcast signal

- V+n **footage, image, information, instructions, mail, message, news, signal, story** *There were several large screens relaying images of the festivities from around the world.* ● *The results are confidential and no information is relayed to third parties.*

release V
make information or documents, or a film, CD, software etc, available

- adv+V recently **newly, recently** *That's the conclusion to be drawn from recently released statistics.*
- ▶ officially or publicly **officially, publicly** *Details of the proposed changes have yet to be officially released.*
- ▶ in the past **originally, previously** *This remastered version was originally released in 1982.*
- V+n information **details, document, figures, information, report, statement, statistics** *Applications are up by nearly 5.8 per cent on last year, according to new figures released today.*
- ▶ film, CD, software etc **album, CD, DVD, edition, film, movie, recording, single, software, song, track, update, version** *The young band is about to release its debut album.* ● *New software updates for the phone will be released soon.*

release N
1 the act of letting someone leave

- adj+N **early, immediate, imminent** *The US President demanded the immediate release of the 39 sailors.*
- v+N **demand, negotiate, secure** *The government of France has sent diplomatic envoys to try to secure the release of the two men.*

2 the act of making information or documents, or a film, CD, software etc, available

- adj+N **forthcoming, future, latest, original, previous, upcoming** *Fans are looking forward eagerly to the forthcoming release of the band's new album.*

- n+N **news, press** *Click here to link to the full press release.*

- v+N **anticipate, authorize, await, delay, postpone, prevent** *There are safeguards to prevent the unauthorized release of personal information.*

relevance N
the quality of being directly connected with and important to something else

- adj+N specific **particular, special, specific** *I now turn to a subject which is of particular relevance to Northern Ireland, namely veterinary education.*
- ▶ direct **direct, immediate** *Much of the report will be of direct relevance to parents.*
- ▶ relating to real or modern situations **contemporary, practical** *We should not think that his work is of no contemporary relevance just because he got his predictions wrong.*
- ▶ great or greater **considerable, great, obvious, wider** *The researchers conclude that the findings of this work have wider relevance.*
- ▶ limited **limited, little** *Much of the course was of limited relevance to some of the participants.*
- ▶ continuing **continued, continuing** *Reading these poems demonstrates the continued relevance of Classics in the modern world.*
- ▶ possible **possible, potential** *Other general topics of potential relevance to prospective travellers are covered very briefly here.*
- ▶ when something is probably not relevant **dubious, marginal, questionable** *Much of the material on such websites may be of questionable relevance.*

- v+N have relevance **be of, have, retain** *Chapters 1 and 11 are of particular relevance to this case.*
- ▶ not have relevance **lack, lose** *Things that once seemed so important to me have begun to lose their relevance.*
- ▶ show relevance **demonstrate, emphasize, show, underline, underscore** *Competitions like this deserve to be well supported, to demonstrate the relevance of chemistry to the wider community.*
- ▶ make certain of relevance **ensure** *All the modules have been developed in co-operation with leading industrialists, to ensure relevance and currency.*
- ▶ consider relevance **assess, consider, determine, evaluate, explore, gauge, judge** *Look at the references to assess the relevance of the results of each search.*
- ▶ have doubts about relevance **question** *They questioned the relevance of listing outdated achievements.*
- ▶ understand relevance **see, understand** *It is often difficult for students to see the relevance of statistics to their degree subject.*
- ▶ increase relevance **increase** *The UK pages option increases the relevance of returned pages for the UK searcher.*

relevant ADJ
directly connected with something being discussed

- adv+ADJ very **clearly, entirely, especially, extremely, highly, particularly, very** *This is an interesting question and highly relevant to the discussion.*
- ▶ more and more **increasingly** *These skills are highly valued and increasingly relevant to today's society.*
- ▶ not, or not very **not entirely, not necessarily, not strictly** *The data that is not strictly relevant to the research project is not discussed here.*
- ▶ directly **directly, immediately** *Applicants ideally should have some directly relevant conservation experience.*
- ▶ still/no longer **no longer, still** *Although the opera was written in the mid-19th century, its themes are still relevant today.*
- ▶ in a particular way **clinically, commercially, culturally, locally, morally, personally, professionally, socially** *Is there a morally relevant distinction between the two cases?*

- v+ADJ **be, become, consider sth, deem sth, regard sth as, remain, seem, see sth as** *Give details of anything not included elsewhere in this form which you consider relevant to your application* • *Today the novel seems more relevant than ever.*

- N+to **circumstances, debate, discussion, investigation, issue, job, needs, situation, study, subject, theme, topic** *Please keep the message relevant to the subject of the article.*

reliability N
the quality of being reliable

- adj+N high **high** *We can arrange delivery of your purchases worldwide, with reasonably low prices and high reliability.*
- ▶ more **greater, improved, increased** *The new computer system offers improved performance, as well as increased reliability.*
- ▶ low **poor** *Passengers continue to complain of high prices, poor reliability, and dirty, old trains.*
- ▶ shown to be the case **proven** *Our equipment is now used worldwide and has a proven reliability.*

- v+N improve reliability **enhance, improve, increase** *We aim to reduce operating costs and improve reliability.*
- ▶ judge reliability **assess** *It is impossible to objectively assess the reliability and validity of the research.*
- ▶ make certain of reliability **ensure** *Proper maintenance is important to ensure reliability of the apparatus when running unattended.*
- ▶ express doubts about reliability **question** *The report questions the reliability of the tests' results.*

- N+of information **data, evidence, information, results** *There have also been concerns about the reliability of the data.*
- ▶ how something works or is done **service, supply, system** *While overall reliability of service has improved, punctuality is still disappointing.*

reliable ADJ
that can be trusted to be accurate

- adv+ADJ very **extremely, highly, very** *The tests were considered to be extremely reliable indicators of fitness.*

▶ completely **completely, totally, utterly** *I suggest they are the very best of witnesses and that their testimony is utterly reliable.*
▶ rather **fairly, pretty** INFORMAL**, reasonably** *The number of unique visitors provides a reasonably reliable measure of a web page's popularity.*
▶ in a particular respect **historically, statistically** *A statistically reliable test must await a larger sample size made up of more valid data.*
● ADJ+n information **data, estimate, evidence, figures, indicator, information, measure, measurement, result, statistics, test** *There is a shortage of reliable information on the issue.*
▶ source of information **guide, source, witness** *But don't forget that the Internet is not always a reliable source.*

reliance N
the state of depending on a person or thing

● adj+N great **great, heavy** *Singapore has a heavy reliance on international trade.*
▶ increasing **growing, increased, increasing** *Growing numbers of people in their 20s and 30s are suffering from severe memory loss because of increasing reliance on computer technology.*
▶ too much **excessive, too much, undue** *Much confusion can be created by undue reliance on anecdotal evidence.*
▶ total **exclusive, sole, total** *Recent events make it evident that an exclusive reliance on military force will not bring about a fundamental solution.*
▶ continuing **continued, continuing** *Continued reliance on these fossil fuels could delay the development of renewable technologies.*
● v+N place reliance on something **place** *The tribunal was unable to place much reliance on what he said.*
▶ increase/reduce reliance **increase, reduce** *These crops really help us to reduce our reliance on imports.*

reliant ADJ
depending on someone or something

▶ adv+ADJ to a great degree **heavily, increasingly** *Those without access to a car were heavily reliant on costly and inadequate public transport.*
▶ completely **completely, entirely, totally, wholly** *When you are totally reliant on your pension, you are less likely to take risks with your pension fund.*

relief N
the happy feeling that something bad has not happened, or the reduction of pain

▶ adj+N great **enormous, great, huge, immense** *I've been told there's nothing to worry about, which is a huge relief.*
▶ just what you need **blessed, much-needed, welcome** *It is a welcome relief that this potential loophole has been so firmly closed.*
▶ for a short time **short-term, temporary** *Applying local heat to a painful joint often gives short-term relief.*
▶ immediate **immediate, instant** *These tablets produce immediate pain relief.*
▶ effective **effective** *The drug can give effective relief for a range of conditions with minimal side effects.*

● n+N **pain, stress** *She is refusing any form of pain relief.*
● v+N give relief **bring (sb), give (sb), offer (sb), provide (sb with)** *Seasonal rains brought relief to some areas during April and May.*
▶ be a relief **come as** *The news came as a huge relief.*
▶ look for or get relief **find, get, seek** *Many people find crying an outlet for grief, whilst others find relief for their sadness in other ways.*
▶ express or feel relief **express, feel** *At first I was nervous, but walking in I felt sheer relief.*
● n+of+N **feeling, sense, sigh** *Jeff breathed a sigh of relief.*

2 help given to people in a bad situation

● adj+N **humanitarian** *The emphasis has shifted from simple humanitarian relief to broader economic assistance and the rebuilding of infrastructure.*
● n+N **disaster, emergency, famine, flood, tsunami** *We raised £1.4 million for the appeal, which was spent entirely on emergency relief.*
● v+N provide relief **give sb, provide (sb with)** *The charity provides relief to victims of natural disasters and violent conflicts.*
▶ receive relief **receive** *One year after the disaster, tens of thousands of people have received emergency relief.*
● N+n work done **effort, operation, programme, work** *Volunteers are helping with the relief efforts by distributing food and medicines.*
▶ people **agency, fund, organization, worker** *The mountainous nature of the land made the aid effort very difficult for emergency relief agencies.*
▶ help given **aid, supplies** *The city's traumatized survivors are living in roadside tents and relying on relief supplies.*

relieve V
make pain, a problem, or a bad situation less unpleasant or serious

● V+n pain **discomfort, pain, symptoms** *Nitrous oxide is now widely used to relieve pain, during childbirth in particular.*
▶ something bad **anxiety, boredom, burden, congestion, poverty, pressure, stress, suffering, tension** *Laughter is great for bonding and relieving stress.*

relieved ADJ
happy because something bad has not happened

● adv+ADJ very **greatly, mightily, very** *We were mightily relieved to hear the half-time whistle.*
▶ rather **quite, somewhat** *She was somewhat relieved when she finally learnt that he had merely broken his arm.*
● ADJ+infinitive **discover, find, hear, know, learn, see** *We are all relieved to see that Janice has made a full recovery.*

religion N
the belief in the existence of a god or gods

● v+N belong to or believe in a religion **belong to, embrace, practise, profess** *Do any family members practise a religion?*

▸ not agree with a religion **reject** *It hurt his parents to see him openly rejecting their religion.*

▸ change your religion **change** *He had persuaded her to change her religion and marry him.*

▸ start a religion **found** *Jainism is a religion founded in India in the 6th century BC.*

▸ teach or study a religion **study, teach** *The course will introduce different ways of studying religion and theology.*

religious ADJ

1 relating to religion or a particular religion

● adv+**ADJ** expressed in an open way **explicitly, overtly** *Few of the quotations were overtly religious.*

▸ only or exactly **purely, specifically, strictly** *This is a political rather than a purely religious issue.*

▸ mostly **essentially** *Whilst some war memorials were essentially religious in character, others were primarily secular.*

● **ADJ**+n belief **affiliation, belief, conviction, faith, tradition** *I can understand the strength of feeling with which many people hold religious beliefs.*

▸ group of people **community, denomination, group, institution, minority, movement, sect** *The Christian Union is the largest religious group on the campus.*

▸ activities and duties **ceremony, festival, observance, practice, ritual, worship** *Sharia is the sacred law of Islam, and applies to all aspects of life, not just religious practices.*

▸ bad feelings or treatment **discrimination, hatred, intolerance, persecution** *Legislation has been introduced to tackle religious discrimination in employment.*

▸ right to have beliefs **freedom, liberty, tolerance** *This law is meant to promote religious freedom.*

▸ teaching **education, instruction** *The government has scrapped a proposal to drop religious education from the school curriculum.*

▸ leader **leader** *The country's efforts to ensure inter-religious harmony have been fully approved by international religious leaders.*

2 believing strongly in your religion

● adv+**ADJ** very **deeply, devoutly, intensely, profoundly, very** *She was a deeply religious woman.*

relinquish V

give up power, position, or an advantage

● V+n **control, position, post, power, responsibility, right, role** *It soon became clear that the ruling class did not want to relinquish control.*

● v+to-V **be forced to, be reluctant to, refuse to** *He was ultimately forced to relinquish power.*

relish V

get great pleasure or satisfaction from something

● V+n **challenge, chance, idea, opportunity, prospect, role, thought** *The girls relished the opportunity to practise their language skills and enjoy the culture of these cities.*

reluctance N

being unwilling to do something

● adj+N great **considerable, extreme, great, marked** *She accepted his resignation with great reluctance.*

▸ that can be understood **natural, understandable** *There is an understandable reluctance of people, particularly older workers, to move long distances to take up work.*

▸ seeming to exist **apparent** *The reason for her apparent reluctance to co-operate has not been explained.*

▸ at first **initial** *In spite of their initial reluctance, they had worked very hard.*

▸ shared by many people **general** *This is the result of men's general reluctance to undergo regular health checks.*

● v+N show reluctance **express, show** *Some of these dogs take easily to water but others show a reluctance to get more than their feet wet.*

▸ deal with your reluctance **overcome** *The Harry Potter books have persuaded huge numbers of children to overcome their reluctance to reading.*

▸ understand someone's reluctance **understand** *We are sure the Court will understand our reluctance to incur further legal costs at this stage.*

reluctant ADJ

unwilling to do something

● adv+**ADJ** very or rather **extremely, increasingly, somewhat, very** *The police were extremely reluctant to take action.*

▸ at first **initially** *Although we were initially reluctant to go to the street party, it turned out to be great fun.*

▸ when it is not surprising **understandably** *Prison medical staff are understandably reluctant to prescribe these kinds of drugs too freely.*

▸ when it is surprising **strangely** *Dr Fleming seemed strangely reluctant to discuss his research.*

rely on PHR VB

trust someone or something to do something for you, or need someone or something

● adv+**V** very much **heavily** *In the past, Kent's economy has relied heavily on the growing of hops for the production of beer.*

▸ completely **completely, entirely, exclusively, solely, totally** *We receive no government or charitable funding, and rely solely on donations.*

▸ mainly **largely, mainly, primarily** *The Panamanian economy relies primarily on the service sector, which accounts for 75 per cent of national income.*

▸ more and more **increasingly** *As a nation we are increasingly relying on credit to finance our lifestyles.*

▸ only **simply** *Do not simply rely on your memory to store all the strands of information you come across.*

● V+n help or money **donations, generosity, goodwill, support, volunteers** *The museum is short of funds, relying on private donations and voluntary unpaid trustees and guides.*

▸ your opinion, memory, or ability **ability, assumption, expertise, judgement, memory** *I was always prepared to go into hospital if the doctors said so – I relied on their judgement.*

▸ information **evidence, fact, source** *Historians do not rely on single sources.*

▸ other people **others** *While I was ill, I had to rely on others to do the simplest of tasks.*

remain V

continue to be in a situation or condition

- V+adj **anonymous, constant, high, intact, low, open, silent, stable, strong, true, unchanged, unclear, unknown** *Her weight has remained relatively constant for the past five years.* • *It remains unclear to me what the benefits are.*

remark N

something that someone says

- adj+N coming at the beginning/end **closing, concluding, introductory, opening, preliminary** *If your project is focussed on one particular industry or technology, you might include introductory remarks about this here.*
- ▶ without thinking about it first **casual, chance, off-the-cuff, throwaway** *I'm surprised this generated so much correspondence, as it was just a throwaway remark.*
- ▶ brief **brief, passing** *Let me conclude with some brief remarks about the country's defence industry.*
- ▶ unpleasant or insulting **cutting, defamatory, derogatory, disparaging, insulting, offensive, rude, sarcastic, snide** *She did make a few derogatory remarks about economists.*
- ▶ insulting someone's race or sex **racist, sexist** *Ferdinand has called for tough penalties for players who make racist remarks during matches.*
- ▶ kind **complimentary, kind** *I want to thank Professor Briggs for the complimentary remarks he makes about my book in his review.*
- ▶ not serious enough **flippant** *That was a very flippant remark to make if you don't mind me saying so.*
- ▶ clever and funny **witty** *Sophie made some witty remark on the subject.*
- v+N make a remark **make** *People on the team were making uncomplimentary remarks about each other.*
- ▶ hear a remark **hear** *He felt irritated when he heard such glib remarks.*
- ▶ begin/end remarks **conclude, preface** *She prefaced her remarks with greetings from the King.*
- ▶ repeat a remark **quote** *The remarks were widely quoted in newspapers and on the broadcast media.*

remark V

say a few words about something

- adv+V **casually, drily, famously, jokingly, pointedly, wryly** *Ruth casually remarked that she thought her arm was broken.*

remarkable ADJ

unusual in a surprising or impressive way

- adv+ADJ very **absolutely, quite, truly, very** *The results were truly remarkable.*
- ▶ rather **pretty** INFORMAL, **rather, somewhat** *I think it's a pretty remarkable book.*
- ▶ equally **equally** *His second novel, following shortly after his first, was equally remarkable.*
- ▶ especially **especially, particularly** *There was nothing particularly remarkable about her two-bedroom bungalow.*
- ADJ+n something done or achieved

achievement, career, feat, progress, recovery, success *We raised the money in six months, a remarkable achievement.*

- ▶ event, account, or fact **coincidence, discovery, fact, feature, phenomenon, story** *Bede's World tells the remarkable story of the life and times of the Venerable Bede, one of the greatest scholars of the Early Middle Ages.*
- ▶ being similar **resemblance, similarity** *The room bears a remarkable resemblance to the one in the painting.*
- ▶ ability **ability, talent** *She is largely self-taught and has a remarkable ability for learning music by heart.*
- ▶ person or people **man, people, woman** *He was, indeed, one of the most remarkable men of his generation.*
- ▶ example **example, instance** *Kew gardens are also home to two remarkable examples of Victorian glass technology.*

remedy N

a solution to a particular problem

- adj+N good or effective **effective, perfect** *The most effective remedy to ITV's audience decline will be increased investment in original programming.*
- ▶ legal **judicial, legal** *We always prefer to enter into agreements rather than being forced to resort to legal remedies.*
- ▶ suitable **adequate, appropriate** *The court ruled that judicial review was not the appropriate remedy, as other means of redress had not been tried.*
- ▶ possible **available, possible** *A landowner faced with squatters has a number of remedies available to him.*
- ▶ simple **simple** *If suppliers don't like the prices they are paid by supermarkets, the remedy is simple: don't deal with them.*
- v+N provide or suggest a remedy **offer, propose, provide, suggest** *How well does the Code provide remedies for borrowers' legitimate grievances?*
- ▶ find a remedy **find, pursue, seek** *I could claim damages and seek a legal remedy.*
- ▶ use all remedies **exhaust** *It is important to exhaust all local remedies to the situation before taking serious international action.*
- ▶ have a remedy **have** *Do you have any remedy for loss of business or inconvenience suffered while you wait for these repairs?*

remember V

have an image in your mind of something in the past

- adv+V clearly **clearly, distinctly, vividly, well** *She vividly remembered the day the news of his death arrived.*
- ▶ not clearly **barely, dimly, hardly, vaguely** *It made no impression on me and I can barely remember what happened.* • *I vaguely remember realizing that something wasn't right.*
- ▶ correctly **correctly, rightly** *It was Saturday morning, at about 11.30, if I remember correctly.*
- ▶ exactly **exactly** *It's hard to remember exactly, but I think there were around a dozen or 15 people there.*
- ▶ with positive feelings **affectionately, fondly, lovingly** *I have always fondly remembered those days in Manchester.*

▶ always or still **always, forever, still** *I still remember how excited I was when I first heard that record.*

● V+with **affection, fondness, gratitude, love, pleasure, pride, sadness** *She will be remembered with affection by many past students.*

reminder N
something that reminds you of something in the past or of something you need to do

● adj+N existing for a long time or happening often **constant, daily, frequent, lasting, permanent** *The vast lava flows are a constant reminder of the destructive power of nature.*

▶ coming at a very suitable time **timely** *This incident served as a timely reminder that mishaps can occur, regardless of the experience of the diver.*

▶ felt strongly and clearly **powerful, sharp, stark, vivid** *The deaths in West Virginia have been a stark reminder of how dangerous an operation coal mining can be.*

▶ that you can see **visible** *Today there are few visible reminders of what the town was like in medieval times.*

▶ giving you sad or unpleasant feelings **chilling, grim, painful, poignant, salutary, sobering, unwelcome** *The cemetery and museum remain as a poignant reminder of these events.*

▶ done gently or quickly **brief, gentle, little, quick, subtle** *This is a gentle reminder to all those who've yet to book that the deadline is 30 June.*

▶ useful **useful** *The checklists are designed to be useful tick-box reminders to help you put good practice into action.*

● v+N be a reminder **act as, be, provide, serve as** *Christopher's death and today's convictions serve as a reminder of the potential consequences of carrying knives.*

▶ give a reminder **give (sb), issue, send (sb)** *Halfway through the year, now is probably the time to give a brief reminder of forthcoming events on the calendar.*

▶ receive a reminder **get, receive** *Every summer, I get a fortnight-long reminder of what city life is like.*

▶ need a reminder **need** *Sometimes I need a little reminder of the good things in life.*

reminiscent ADJ
reminding you of something

● adv+ADJ very **strongly, very** *The guitar work is well executed and strongly reminiscent of the classic Rainbow sound.*

▶ rather **faintly, rather, slightly, somewhat, vaguely** *Many of the young trees have a conical shape, vaguely reminiscent of conifers.*

▶ in a strange way **curiously, eerily, oddly, strangely** *The route features scenery eerily reminiscent of that at Land's End over a thousand miles behind you.*

remorse N
a strong guilty feeling about something that you have done

● adj+N **deep, genuine** *Wallis, on the other hand, had shown signs of genuine remorse.*

● v+N show remorse **express, show** *The defendants have shown no remorse for their conduct.*

▶ feel remorse **be filled with, be full of, feel** *Mary couldn't wait to get away, yet now as she recalled the day when she left her home, she was filled with remorse.*

● n+of+N feeling **feeling, pang** *Polly felt a sudden pang of remorse.*

▶ lack **lack** *Parole was refused because of his lack of remorse.*

remove V
take someone or something out or away or get rid of it

● adv+V completely **altogether, completely, entirely, totally** *This paragraph should be removed altogether.*

▶ without difficulty **easily** *You can easily remove sticky fingerprints in traditional varnish using white spirit.*

▶ carefully or gently **carefully, gently** *Carefully remove the tree from its pot, protecting the roots while doing so.*

▶ using force **forcibly, physically** *He was forcibly removed for attacking the security guard.*

▶ using your hands; not automatically **manually, physically** *You can set dates for content expiry so that members of staff don't need to manually remove details of an out-of-date event, etc.*

▶ automatically **automatically** *Normally tax is removed automatically before you receive the interest.*

▶ safely **safely** *The data storage device can now be safely removed from the system.*

▶ quickly **immediately, quickly** *It is the job of the Environment Agency to make sure such obstructions are removed quickly to keep the river flowing.*

▶ for a short time for ever **permanently, temporarily** *Click on the delete button to permanently remove information you no longer want on the website.*

▶ by a medical operation **surgically** *Currently, the only way to prevent the disease spreading is by surgically removing the colon.*

● V+n difficulty or problem **barrier, obstacle, restriction** *As a means of removing barriers to learning, ICT has a great deal to offer.*

▶ something that blocks something else **obstruction** *Gently tilt the person's head back and remove the obstruction in their throat.*

▶ need **need** *The Council will ensure that all reasonable steps will be taken to remove the need for court action to recover possession of a property.*

▶ mark or what is left **debris, dirt, stain, trace** *What is the best method to remove tea stains from a carpet?*

▶ something said or written **material, reference** *Steps will be taken where possible to remove any inappropriate material posted on the message board.*

renaissance N
new interest that makes something popular again

● adj+N **cultural, economic, urban** *The station's redevelopment will also aid the urban and economic renaissance of that area of the city.*

> You can say that a place or thing is experiencing **something of a renaissance**: *Patchwork is enjoying something of a renaissance, increasingly seen as an exciting contemporary art form.*

● v+N experience a renaissance **enjoy, experience,**

see, undergo *In Argentina, documentary film-making is enjoying a veritable renaissance.*
▶ cause a renaissance **achieve, create, initiate, spark, stimulate** *He was part of the group that sparked a renaissance in traditional cuban music.*

render V
cause to be something

● V+adj not useful **ineffective, obsolete, redundant, unusable, useless** *Electronic resources can be rendered obsolete by rapidly changing hardware and software.*
▶ without meaning or value **invalid, irrelevant, meaningless, worthless** *If you do this, your will may be rendered invalid in the eyes of the law.* ● *Copyright protection will be rendered meaningless if it is not backed up by legal enforcement.*
▶ difficult or not possible **difficult, impossible** *Further attempts were rendered impossible because of the lack of money available.*
▶ not able to speak **speechless** *I am rendered speechless by the insensitivity of such remarks.*

renew V
do or have something again after a pause

● V+n relationship **acquaintance, friendship** *I am looking forward to meeting new friends and renewing old acquaintances at the conference.*
▶ interest **enthusiasm, interest** *The course will offer teachers an opportunity to refresh their skills and renew their enthusiasm for their subject.*
▶ attack **attack** *The media renewed their attack on the prime minister in the papers today.*
▶ when someone asks for something **appeal, call** *The Conservative party renewed its call for a public inquiry into the affair.*
▶ when someone does something **effort** *We shall have to renew our efforts in an attempt to fill the vacancy.*
▶ when someone promises something **commitment, promise** *The company has renewed its commitment to education by doubling the number of scholarships it is offering.*

renovate V
repair and improve a building [usually passive]

▶ adv+V recently **newly, recently** *We stopped off at the newly renovated Olympic stadium.*
▶ completely or to a large degree **completely, extensively, fully, totally** *The property was completely renovated in 2007.*
▶ in a way that is attractive or shows good judgement **beautifully, carefully, sympathetically, tastefully, thoughtfully** *The house has been sympathetically renovated in keeping with the original style.*

renovation N
the repairing and improving of a building

▶ adj+N large in degree **extensive, major** *The building underwent extensive renovation in 2009.*
▶ complete **complete, total** *The farmhouse is in need of complete renovation.*
▶ recent **recent** *The Park Plaza Hotel has undergone a very recent renovation.*

● v+N experience renovation **undergo** *The facility has recently undergone a major renovation.*
▶ need renovation **need, require** *The ground floor is completely unfinished and needs total renovation.*
▶ do renovation **carry out, complete, undertake** *In 2004 a complete renovation of the hotel was carried out.*
▶ be closed while renovation is done **be closed for** *The theatre is currently closed for major renovations.*

● N+n **programme, project, scheme, work** *They are looking to buy a house as a renovation project.*

● and/or **construction, conversion, extension, maintenance, refurbishment, repair, restoration** *The property could benefit from some renovation and refurbishment.*

rent N
money paid regularly for using a building

● adj+N how often rent is to be paid **annual, monthly, weekly, yearly** *Her monthly rent is £525.*
▶ low/high **affordable, high, low** *Dundee has a wide choice of properties available at affordable rents.*
▶ very small **nominal, peppercorn** *The Council leased the land to the community group for 21 years at a peppercorn rent.*
▶ fair or usual **fair, market** *Each tenant pays a fair rent, which is used to cover maintenance costs and to repay the mortgage.* ● *The flats will be let out at the market rent.*
▶ due to be paid **due, payable** *All rents are due on the 1st of each month.*
▶ not yet paid **unpaid** *The deposit may also be retained to cover unpaid rent or bills.*

● v+N pay rent **pay** *Students will be more inclined pay higher rents for warm, well-maintained accommodation.*
▶ charge rent **charge** *The monks became greedy and charged excessive rents, and the townspeople protested.*
▶ receive or get rent **collect, receive** *When the first houses were built on the estate, he was put in charge of collecting rents and electricity payments from residents.*
▶ have or be enough money to pay the rent **afford, cover** *For people on low incomes, housing benefit continues to cover the rent.*
▶ owe rent **owe** *The tenant still owes two months' rent.*
▶ say what the rent is **fix, set** *The tenancy of a unit is renewable every three years and the rent is fixed for that period.*
▶ increase/ reduce the rent **increase, raise, reduce** *Is the landlord able to increase my rent?*

reorganization N
the process of organizing something in a different way

● adj+N bringing major changes **complete, comprehensive, major, massive, radical, significant, wholesale** *A major reorganization of hospital services has occurred.*
▶ types of reorganization **corporate, departmental, internal, structural** *Performance slipped last year due to internal reorganization following a reduction in staff numbers.*

● v+N experience reorganization **undergo** *During*

2009, the faculty and departmental structure of the University underwent major reorganization.
- ▶ carry out reorganization **carry out, implement, undertake** As profits plunged, the company's board undertook a radical reorganization.
- ▶ plan or announce reorganization **announce, discuss, plan, propose** The Administration is proposing a major reorganization of its secret services.

repair N
work done to fix something damaged

- ● adj+N big **extensive, major, significant, substantial** Over £2 million will be spent on major repairs and improvements over the next six years.
- ▶ small **minor, small** The ground floor remained almost the same for the next 500 years, although there were minor repairs and alterations.
- ▶ needing to be done immediately **emergency, immediate, urgent** Urgent repairs had to be carried out on the ceiling, which had become dangerous.
- ▶ necessary **essential, necessary** We will carry out any necessary repairs within 24 hours if it is an emergency.
- ▶ temporary **running, temporary** They made temporary repairs to the roof in appalling conditions.
- ▶ permanent **permanent** A temporary repair can be effected until a permanent repair is possible.
- ▶ usual and not done for a specific reason **general, routine** The county council spends around £15 million a year on routine housing repairs.
- ▶ types of repair **electrical, mechanical, structural, surgical** Structural repairs to 500 sewers started in April 2005.
- ● v+N do a repair **carry out, do, effect, make, perform, undertake** Repairs were carried out on the clock in 1998.
- ▶ have a repair done **undergo** The building is currently undergoing extensive external repair.
- ▶ need repair **be in need of, need, require** Don't be fooled by doorsellers calling and suggesting your property needs urgent repairs.
- ▶ organize or give permission for repairs **arrange, authorize, manage, organize** We're waiting for our insurance company to authorize the repairs.

Usage **Repair** is usually plural in all of the **v+N** combinations shown above.

- ● N+n work **job, work** This is a list of the repair work needed to bring your property up to a reasonable standard.
- ▶ cost **bill, costs** The total repair bill will run into many millions of pounds.
- ▶ place where repairs are done **centre, facility, shop, workshop** He also started the first motorcycle repair shop in Wolverhampton.
- ▶ company that does repairs **business, company** She runs a shoe repair business.
- ▶ person who does repairs **man** The washing machine repair man is coming to the house.
- ▶ service **service** Your warranty says the company will provide an on-site repair service within 24 hrs of calling.
- ▶ a set of tools to make small repairs **kit** An emergency repair kit is included.

- ● and/or **alteration, construction, improvement, maintenance, modification, refurbishment, renovation, replacement, restoration** Structures can also become dangerous from lack of maintenance and repair.

repay V
1 give someone money you borrowed from them

- ● adv+V **fully, immediately, promptly** The loan must be fully repaid within a year.
- ● V+n **amount, balance, capital, cost, debt, fee, grant, interest, investment, loan, money, mortgage, overpayment, sum** You only start repaying this loan once you have finished studying and are earning a salary.

2 reward someone who has helped you

- ● adv+V **amply** I had shown her some acts of kindness, for which she amply repaid me.
- ● V+n **compliment, faith, favour, hospitality, kindness, loyalty** Now I want to repay the club's faith in me by scoring goals.

repayment N
an amount of money you pay a person or bank after you have borrowed from them

- ● adj+N how often the payment is made **annual, monthly, weekly** In the early years, the monthly repayment consists almost entirely of interest.
- ▶ complete **full, total** You can insist on full repayment.
- ▶ paid before you need to **early** Your existing loans may have penalties for early repayment.
- ▶ the least amount that is possible **minimum** A borrower making the minimum repayments each month will take 32 years to repay the average credit card debt.
- ▶ low enough to be easy to make **affordable, easy, low, manageable** Our Homeowner loan plans could help make your monthly repayments more affordable.
- ● v+N make a repayment **make, pay** If you've got some extra cash, you can make a larger repayment to reduce your debts more quickly.
- ▶ make all the repayments needed **keep up, meet** If a lender is to finance your business, they must be sure that you can meet the repayments.
- ▶ arrange for repayments to be made later **defer** Repayments are often deferred until your first job commences.
- ▶ make repayments over a particular period **spread** You have the flexibility to spread your repayments over one to ten years.
- ▶ have enough money to make repayments **afford** Be sure you can afford the repayments before entering into any credit agreement.
- ▶ ask for repayment **claim, demand, seek** The lender is not obliged to renew your loan, and may demand repayment at the end of the original period.
- ▶ increase/reduce a repayment **increase, reduce** You don't have to remortgage to reduce your repayments.
- ▶ calculate a repayment **calculate** Use this Mortgage Calculator to calculate approximate mortgage repayments.
- ▶ fail to make a repayment at the agreed time **miss** If you miss a repayment, the bank will make every effort to assist you.

repeat V

1 say or write something again

- adv+V using exactly the same words **exactly, faithfully, verbatim** *I won't repeat verbatim what has been said elsewhere.*
- ▶ many times and in a way that continues for too long **ad nauseam, constantly, continually, continuously, endlessly, over and over (again)** *With Inspector Charlton continually repeating her threats, I reluctantly signed the form.*
- ▶ often **frequently, often** *My own name I heard frequently repeated, with, 'Bring him out, bring him out!'*
- ▶ just **merely, simply** *This involves much more than simply repeating words.*
- ▶ one more time **again, once more** *'Can I talk to the police officer?' the boy repeated again in a low whisper.*

2 do something again

- adv+V often **frequently, often, regularly** *When the same muscular action is frequently repeated, injuries sometimes follow.*
- ▶ just **merely, simply** *To invite more people, simply repeat the above process as many times as you like.*
- ▶ many times, and in a way that continues for too long **constantly, continually, continuously, endlessly, indefinitely** *If an employee continually repeats an offence then it is a case of gross misconduct.*
- ▶ how often someone repeats something **annually, daily, periodically** *It is hoped that this event will be repeated annually.* • *The review will be repeated periodically.*
- ▶ one more time **again** *He was concerned to see the same approach being repeated again.*
- ▶ in exactly the same way **exactly** *Every detail of the experiment has to be given, so that somebody else can repeat exactly what was done.*

repeated ADJ

done many times

- ▶ ADJ+n something you say or write **assertion, assurance, call for sth, claim, complaint, question, reference, request, statement, warning** *I have not received a copy, either, even after repeated requests.*
- ▶ attempt to do something **attempt, effort** *Despite repeated attempts to contact the artist, he remained elusive.*
- use of something **application, exposure, use** *With repeated use, tolerance develops so that a person has to take more of the substance to achieve the desired effect.*
- something you do **act, action, attack, failure, movement, visit** *Regrettably, under the current Government it has all too often been a story of repeated failure.* • *Repeated visits to my doctor resulted in me being prescribed various types of antibiotics.*
- type of medical treatment **doses, injections, treatment** *There are still questions over the safety of giving patients repeated doses of cortisone.*

repercussions N

the bad effects that something has

- adj+N big and important **enormous, huge, huge,**

important, major, profound, serious, significant, wide *Industrial action will have major repercussions for the company.*
- ▶ especially bad **adverse, devastating, negative, severe** *The negative repercussions of alcohol abuse can affect the whole family.*
- ▶ possibly going to happen **possible, potential** *It's important to understand which risks you face and the potential repercussions for your business.*
- ▶ types of repercussions **economic, emotional, environmental, financial, legal, political, social** *France was badly affected by the economic repercussions of the Habsburg-Valois Wars.*
- v+N **cause, fear, have, suffer** *The incident could have major repercussions on Iraqi-Jordanian relations.*

repertoire N

the full range of things that a person can do or a performer can perform

- adj+N large **broad, extensive, huge, large, vast, wide, wide-ranging** *A singer in this type of band will need to have a wide repertoire.*
- ▶ small **limited, small** *We performed a small repertoire of unaccompanied songs.*
- ▶ of many different styles **diverse, rich, varied** *The band has a very diverse repertoire, ranging from the traditional to the modern.*
- ▶ involving different types of music **choral, classical, musical, operatic, orchestral, vocal** *In recent years she has extended her operatic repertoire into the area of popular musicals.*
- v+N have a repertoire **have** *The 6-piece band has a wide repertoire.*
- ▶ develop a repertoire **build, build up, create, develop** *Over the years, he has developed his repertoire of skills and tricks.*
- ▶ perform a repertoire **perform, play, sing** *We play a broad repertoire of classic jazz standards, blues and funky improvization.*
- ▶ make a repertoire bigger **add to, broaden, expand, extend, increase** *We were interested in expanding our dance repertoire and this competition gave us the perfect opportunity.*
- N+v **consist of sth, cover sth, encompass sth, extend from sth to sth, feature sth, include sth, range from sth to sth** *Her repertoire includes a variety of popular and lesser-known songs.*

repetitive ADJ

involving repeating the same action over long periods

- adv+ADJ very **highly, incredibly, overly, very** *It was very repetitive and got a little bit boring after a while.*
- ▶ rather **a little, quite, rather, somewhat** *You may find some of the questions a little repetitive.*
- and/or **boring, dull, long, monotonous, predictable, routine, simple, tedious** *I find their songs dull and repetitive.*

replacement N

someone or something that replaces another person or thing

- adj+N good or suitable **adequate, appropriate,**

good, ideal, perfect, suitable *If a suitable replacement is not available, we will provide a refund.*

▶ direct **direct** *Energy-saving light bulbs are available as direct replacements for incandescent ones.*

▶ permanent/temporary **long-term, permanent, temporary** *We appointed a temporary replacement, who has been excellent.*

▶ possible **possible, potential** *Mick McCarthy has been touted as a possible replacement.*

● v+N be a replacement **act as, be, be intended as, serve as** *This document will not act as a replacement for travel insurance .*

▶ look for a replacement **look for, search for, seek** *The band is now urgently seeking a replacement to take up the vacant slot.*

▶ find a replacement **find, get, obtain, purchase** *She left the company in June, and it has been very hard to find a replacement.* ● *If your card has been lost or stolen, you can get a replacement from the Student Services Information Desk.*

▶ provide a replacement **arrange, provide, supply** *If the item is faulty, call us and we will arrange a suitable replacement.*

▶ appoint a replacement for someone doing a job **appoint, nominate, recruit, select** *If a vacancy occurs, the Executive Committee must appoint a replacement as soon as possible.*

replica N
an accurate copy of something

● adj+N exact in every detail **accurate, authentic, detailed, exact, faithful, perfect** *The cenotaph was an exact replica of the one in France.*

▶ of the same size **full-scale, full-size, life-size** *There are also life-size replicas of various extinct species outside in the grounds.*

▶ smaller **miniature, scaled-down, small** *He built a miniature replica of the White House.*

● v+N **build, construct, create, make, produce** *This is an exciting project to build a replica of Captain Cook's famous ship.*

● N+n sports clothes **(football) kit, (football) shirt, strip** *He was dressed in a Chelsea replica football shirt.*

▶ weapons **firearm, gun, weapon** *A large percentage of gun crime is carried out by people using replica firearms.*

▶ vehicles **car, ship** *A replica ship was used in the filming of the movie.*

reply V
say or do something as an answer

● adv+V quickly **immediately, instantly, promptly, quickly** *Although some publishers reply quickly, others may take weeks, and some do not reply at all.*

▶ directly **directly** *We regret that we are unable to reply directly to individual queries.*

▶ personally **individually, personally** *If you provide an email address, we'll try to reply personally.*

▶ in a particular way **calmly, kindly, politely, quietly** *"At least I don't hide it from you," Tony replied calmly.*

reply N
something you say or write as answer

● adj+N happening quickly **early, immediate, instant, prompt, quick, rapid, speedy, swift** *We will ensure you receive a prompt reply.*

▶ happening after a long time **late** *Sorry for the late reply.*

▶ with a lot of details **detailed, full, substantive** *We aim to send a full reply to all complaints within 20 working days.*

▶ short **brief, curt, terse** *I can't do justice to the issues in a brief reply.*

▶ long **lengthy, long** *A week later, I received a rather lengthy reply to my letter of complaint.*

▶ positive **encouraging, favourable, positive** *I sent off ten letters asking for work and I've had two positive replies.*

▶ negative or unhelpful **inadequate, negative, unsatisfactory** *We emailed the company we bought it from, but got a very unsatisfactory reply.*

▶ formal or written **formal, written** *We hope that this formal reply will resolve the matter to your satisfaction.*

▶ personal **personal** *While he guarantees a personal reply, this might take a few days.*

● v+N give a reply **give, post, provide, publish, send, write** *You can't post a reply because you are not logged in.*

▶ get a reply **get, receive** *Half an hour later I got a reply to my email.*

▶ wait for a reply **await, expect, wait for** *Two weeks after our complaint, we are still awaiting a reply.*

● N+to to a letter, email etc **email, letter, message, post** *My colleague James Porter has written a reply to this letter.*

▶ to a question **enquiry, query, question, questionnaire** *The children were always so ready with replies to his questions.*

▶ to a request **request** *I have received no replies to my requests for information.*

▶ to a complaint or criticism **complaint, criticism, objection** *In some cases, you may still not be satisfied after receiving a reply to your complaint.*

▶ to a something that someone says or writes **article, comment, paper, point, report, review** *Another section, 'Forum', includes occasional short replies to articles appearing in recent issues.*

report N
1 a spoken or written description of an event or situation, especially in the news media

● adj+N written or spoken **oral, printed, verbal, written** *Any materials brought into the examination room will be confiscated, and a full written report will be made on the circumstances.*

▶ given while a situation or process is still continuing **early, initial, original** *Initial reports of high casualties turned out to be exaggerated.*

▶ giving different facts that do not agree with each other **conflicting, mixed** *We have heard conflicting reports concerning the company's performance and prospects.*

▶ likely to be true **accurate, credible, reliable** *There have been credible reports of human-rights abuses by US personnel.*

▶ not based on reliable evidence **anecdotal,**

unconfirmed *According to one unconfirmed report, three US soldiers have been killed by a roadside bomb.*

▸ given by someone who was present at an event **eyewitness, first-hand** *Thanks to an eyewitness report from the streets, we have strong evidence of police brutality.*

Usage *Report* is often plural in all of the *adj+N* combinations shown above.

● v+N give a report **carry, give, post, provide** *Today's Times carries an excellent report on the presidential debate.* ● *Each staff member gives a report on their current work at the monthly staff meeting.*

▸ hear or read a report **get, hear, read, receive, see** *We're getting reports of a serious train crash in Austria.* ● *You can read a full report on today's Olympic action on our website.*

▸ say that the facts in a report are untrue **deny, dismiss, reject** *Milan's coach denied reports that his star player was planning to leave.*

▸ say or show that the facts in a report are true **confirm, corroborate** *The other members of the crew confirmed Wilson's report.*

2 a document dealing with a particular subject, plan, event etc, especially in an official context

● adj+N complete and detailed **comprehensive, detailed, extensive, full, in-depth** *Accident investigators produced a detailed report, and recommended improved safety measures.*

▸ favourable **encouraging, excellent, favourable, glowing, good, positive** *The school has just received a glowing report from the inspectors.*

▸ full of criticism **adverse, bad, critical, damning, disturbing, negative** *There is a new and highly critical report on the administration's transport policy.*

▸ given regularly at particular times **annual, monthly, periodic, quarterly, weekly** *The final quarterly report for 2009 showed improvements in turnover and profits.*

▸ not available to the public **confidential, secret, unpublished** *A committee of ex-ministers has produced a confidential report on the terrorist threat.*

▸ recently published **new, recent** *A major new report from the National Center for Food and Agricultural Policy outlines the benefits of biotech crops.*

▸ important **authoritative, groundbreaking, influential, key, major** *Her influential report on drug abuse was published in 1996.*

▸ given when something is still in progress **initial, interim, preliminary** *An interim report will be published shortly, but we will have to wait until next year for the final version.*

▸ produced by someone who is not involved in a situation **independent** *An independent report published last week points to weaknesses in the administration's decision-making process.*

▸ on a particular subject **economic, environmental, financial, medical, psychiatric, scientific, statistical, technical** *The council's environmental report claims that the new road will reduce inner-city traffic.*

● v+N prepare a report **compile, draft, prepare, produce, write** *All buildings have been inspected by specialist surveyors, and a report is being compiled.*

▸ ask someone to write a report **commission, order** *Local healthcare providers commissioned an independent report into the care Stone had received.*

▸ make a report publicly available **circulate, issue, launch, publish, release** *The Trade and Industry Committee published its report on Employment Regulation.*

▸ give a report to the people who ordered it **deliver, present, submit** *The low-pay commission is due to deliver its report to Congress next month.*

● N+v a report says something **argue (for) sth, mention sth, note sth, point out sth, say sth, state sth, warn sth** *The report argues for all energy sectors to be back under one department.* ● *A report warns that the reputation of higher education is being put at risk by falling standards in literacy.*

▸ a report shows something **demonstrate sth, indicate sth, reveal sth, show sth** *Stern's report showed that a global temperature rise of 2 degrees was almost inevitable.*

▸ a report deals with something **address sth, consider sth, contain sth, cover sth, detail sth, discuss sth, examine sth, include sth, investigate sth, look at sth, outline sth** *The report covers a wide range of proposed reforms in higher education.*

▸ a report says something is true after considering facts **conclude sth, confirm sth, find sth** *The report found that the proportion of women in academic posts rose 9 percentage points to 36 per cent between 1995 and 2005.*

▸ a report uses information **draw on sth** *The report also draws on recent research to show the importance of pre-school education.*

▸ a report emphasizes something **emphasize sth, highlight sth** *The report highlights the importance of basic research.*

▸ a report suggests something **propose sth, recommend sth, suggest sth** *Last week a government report suggested that vehicle tax should be massively increased.*

report V

produce an official statement or document about something

● V+n **conclusion, figure, findings, outcome, progress, result** *The purpose of this paper is to document the study and to report the preliminary results.*

represent V

1 speak, act, or make decisions as a representative of someone

● adv+V well **adequately, effectively, fairly, properly, truly** *We need independent directors who can effectively represent the shareholders.*

▸ legally **legally** *It is not essential to be legally represented, but it may be in your best interest to consider this.*

2 be something

● V+n be a change **change, departure, development, shift, step, turning point** *Both products represented a big departure from their previous product line.* ● *This discovery represents a significant step forward for our research.*

▸ be an improvement **advance, improvement,**

progress *This paper represented a dramatic advance in our understanding of how the brain works.*
▶ be an important achievement **achievement, breakthrough, landmark, milestone, victory** *We believe these results represent an important milestone for the project.*
▶ be an opportunity **challenge, opportunity** *This new venture represented a fantastic opportunity for the business.*
▶ be a danger **danger, risk, threat** *He has not committed a serious offence and does not represent a threat to public safety.*

representative N
someone chosen to represent other people

● adj+N official **accredited, authorized, named, official** *Our authorized representative may enter any part of the hall at any time during the hire period.*
▶ chosen **appointed, designated, elected** *In theory, he is the elected representative and spokesman of the villagers.*
▶ important **chief, key, leading, senior** *The consultation was conducted with key representatives from the defence industry.*
▶ of a particular area **international, local, national, regional** *If you are in any doubt about this instruction, please contact your local representative.*
▶ only **only, sole** *With Davis injured, Majid is now the sole Canadian representative in the competition.*
▶ special **special** *The Duke of York is the special representative of UK Trade & Investment.*
▶ representing an important individual **personal** *We managed to get a meeting with the President's personal representative.*
▶ permanent **permanent** *The company has a permanent representative on the panel.*
▶ not linked to a particular organization **independent** *The group consists of a panel of independent representatives and a panel of industry practitioners.*
▶ types of representative **industrial, legal, parliamentary, political** *Many people are cynical about their political representatives.*

● v+N choose a representative **appoint, choose, elect, nominate, select** *Each network nominated a representative to be on WCEN Board of Directors.*
▶ talk to or meet a representative **consult, contact, meet** *Scottish Ministers may consult representatives of the profession before making their decision.*
▶ ask a representative to go somewhere for you **send** *It was proposed that we should send a representative to attend the International Congress of Librarians.*

representative ADJ
typical of people or things in group

● adv+ADJ very or truly **fully, genuinely, highly, properly, sufficiently, truly, very** *We must ensure that these groups are genuinely representative of ordinary working people.*
▶ rather **broadly, fairly, reasonably** *I think these opinions are broadly representative of the views of local residents.*
▶ not very **hardly, not entirely, not really** *The end result was a test of six or seven people – hardly representative of the target market.*

▶ in a way that is scientifically valid **demographically, geographically, statistically** *The interviewees are not statistically representative of these ethnic groups.*

● ADJ+n group **collection, cross-section, group, range, sample, section, selection** *A representative sample of 1,007 adults was interviewed.*
▶ study **study, survey** *In a representative study of the working population, it was shown that 26.5 per cent had suffered from a serious back problem.*
▶ impression **picture, view** *We do not claim that this is a comprehensive or representative picture of the problem.* ● *I am concerned that the commissioner will not receive a fair and representative view of the issues.*
▶ example **example** *Choose two authors, one from each period, and compare representative examples of their writing.*

● ADJ+of of a group **area, community, country, group, people, population, the public, range, sector, society** *We currently have 1,100 people on the panel, who are broadly representative of the population in the area in terms of age, gender and ethnicity.*
▶ of opinions **feelings, opinions, views** *The petition was still representative of local views.*

repress V
1 prevent yourself from showing a feeling

● V+n **anger, desire, emotion, feeling, memory, thought, urge** *He tried to repress his feelings of impatience.*

2 use force or violence to control people

● adv+V **brutally, ruthlessly, savagely, violently** *The police and army brutally repressed local people for over ten hours.*

● V+n repress opposition **dissent, opposition, rebellion, revolt** *At that time the President had banned and repressed all opposition to his regime.*
▶ repress people **people, population** *We campaign for changes in countries that torture and repress their people.*

repression N
the use of force to control people

● adj+N severe or violent **bloody, brutal, harsh, savage, severe, vicious, violent** *The brutal repression of whole ethnic groups will no longer be tolerated.*
▶ types of repression **military, political, religious** *Military repression was used against the peaceful demonstrators.*

● v+N suffer repression **face, meet with, suffer** *Its people suffered brutal repression.*
▶ use repression **mete out, unleash, use** *The regime is increasingly using repression to try and keep people quiet.*

● n+of+N **act, campaign, wave** *A new wave of repression against the students put an end to their revolt.*

● and/or **aggression, censorship, exploitation, fear, persecution, poverty, violence, war** *After 25 years* *of repression and persecution, the tiny country of East Timor was racked with poverty.*

reprieve N

a decision to stop or delay something bad

- adj+N **brief, eleventh-hour, last-minute, temporary** *The Education Secretary granted a last-minute reprieve, overturning the State Senate's decision.*
- v+N get a reprieve **earn, gain, get, have, win** *A school threatened with closure has won a reprieve after a judge gave local people permission to challenge the decision.*
- ► give someone or something a reprieve **give, grant** *Some lenders are granting a 30-day reprieve; some, six months.*

reprimand V

tell someone officially that they have done something wrong

- adv+V **formally, officially, publicly, severely** *He was severely reprimanded for disobeying an officer's orders.*

reprimand N

an official statement telling someone they have done something wrong

- adj+N **formal, official, public, severe** *I actually got an official reprimand at one point for being 'too nice' on the phone.*
- v+N get a reprimand **get, receive** *He had received a reprimand for a fight outside school.*
- ► give someone a reprimand **give, issue** *The police can give reprimands and warnings at the police station.*

reputable ADJ

generally considered to be honest and reliable

- ► ADJ+n business **agency, agent, brand, breeder, builder, business, company, dealer, firm, insurer, manufacturer, organization, retailer, shop, store, supplier** *Always buy a car from a reputable dealer.*
- ► person or thing giving information **journal, site, source** *Details of transactional security measures will be given on reputable sites.* • *The report came from a very reputable source.*

reputation N

people's opinion about how good someone or something is

- adj+N good **considerable, enviable, excellent, fearsome, fine, formidable, good, great, impressive, outstanding, positive, solid, strong, unrivalled, world-class** *The pub has an enviable reputation for good ale and excellent food.*
  bad **bad, dubious, poor, terrible, unenviable** *The software has a poor reputation and many people find it unstable.*
  that you deserve **well-deserved, well-earned** *The faculty has a well-earned reputation for research and enterprise.*
  that has existed for a long time **long-established, long-standing, well-established** *The Centre for Language and Communication Research has a well-*

established reputation in a number of teaching and research areas.

- ► becoming stronger **burgeoning, growing** *Throughout the 18th century, Bath's growing reputation as a health spa attracted both patients and doctors to the town.*
- ► national, international etc **global, international, local, national, wide, worldwide** *It is the region's best known cancer centre and has an international reputation for cancer treatment.*
- ► types of reputation **academic, corporate, professional** *Allegations of assault, even when unproved, can ruin a teacher's professional reputation.*
- v+N have a reputation **boast, enjoy, have, hold** *This family pub enjoys a reputation for good food and fine beer.*
- ► develop a reputation **build, carve, create, develop, establish, forge, make** *The company has built an enviable reputation based on service, quality and value for money.*
- ► get a reputation **achieve, acquire, earn, gain, get, win** *The college has gained a reputation for providing students with first class lectures.*
- ► make a reputation stronger **cement, confirm, consolidate, reinforce, secure, strengthen, uphold** *Tales of riots and imprisonment helped to cement their bad-boy reputation.*
- ► make a reputation better **boost, enhance, improve** *The car repair industry knows it must improve its reputation.*
- ► make a reputation worse **damage, destroy, harm, ruin, sully, tarnish** *His reputation was almost destroyed by lies.*
- ► do something that might make your reputation worse **compromise, risk, stake** *I am not prepared to risk my reputation by being associated with drugs.*

You can also use the phrase ***put your reputation on the line***: *She was willing to put her reputation on the line in order to get political progress.*

- ► keep the good reputation that you have **defend, maintain, preserve, protect, retain** *The Faculty of Engineering has maintained an excellent reputation over many years.*
- ► make a reputation better after it has been damaged **rebuild, re-establish, restore, salvage, save** *The company must be praying that its smart new product will restore its reputation.*
- ► lose the good reputation that you have **lose** *The party lost its reputation for economic competence.*
- N+as skilled or impressive person **artist, composer, employer, expert, leader, painter, performer, player, speaker, specialist, teacher, writer** *She has established her reputation as the best viola player of her generation.*
- ► place or organization **centre, destination, provider, resort, supplier, venue** *Throughout the 1990s, it built up its reputation as a centre for cancer research.*
- N+for a good quality **excellence, expertise, honesty, hospitality, innovation, integrity, performance, quality, reliability, service** *We pride ourselves on our reputation for quality, innovation and service.*
- ► the thing you do or make **cuisine, design, food, research, teaching, work** *The local café has a great*

reputation for vegetarian food. • *Birmingham University has an outstanding reputation for research and teaching.*

request N

an act of asking for something, especially by means of a formal or official process

- adj+N needing to be dealt with immediately **urgent** *With the new system, you can send in an urgent request for information about someone at 1 a.m., and get an answer.*
- ▶ reasonable **legitimate, reasonable, valid** *A valid request will be answered within 40 calendar days of being received.*
- ▶ not reasonable **unreasonable, vexatious** *I had to get very tough with this guy and say that his request was unreasonable.*
- ▶ formal **formal, official, written** *If you would like your credit refunded, please make a written request.*
- ▶ polite **polite** *The tenants received a polite request to stop causing excessive noise.*
- ▶ special **special** *When you book, if you have any special requests just let us know and we'll try to accommodate your wishes.*
- ▶ strange **odd, strange, unusual** *What is the strangest request you have ever received?*
- ▶ made for the first time **initial, original** *I received an email today (8 days after my original request) saying he would call me soon.*
- ▶ made several times **frequent, numerous, repeated** *I have still not received a refund, even after repeated requests.*
- ▶ made by one person **individual, personal** *The University cannot give preference to individual requests from students for specific dates for exams.*
- ▶ made by many people **common, frequent** *One of the most frequent requests we get to our site concerns programmes at Budapest's State Opera House.*
- ▶ easy to deal with **simple, straightforward** *A simple request to view the building was met with ready consent by the owner.*
- v+N make a request **file, issue, make, put in, send, submit, write** *You must make a formal request for a permit.*
- ▶ get a request **get, have, receive** *I receive many requests from visitors about good places to stay.*
- ▶ agree to do what someone has asked you to do **accommodate, comply with, fulfil, honour** *We will accommodate all requests where practicable and where it is not practicable will explain why.*
- ▶ give someone permission to do or have what they have asked for **accede to, accept, agree to, approve, grant** *After a stressful delay, her request for a work permit was eventually granted.*
- ▶ say 'no' to someone's request **decline, deny, refuse, reject** *She was dissatisfied with their explanation and asked for an independent review, but her request was refused.*
- ▶ deal with a request **answer, deal with, handle, process, reply to, respond to** *We will process your request within 24 hours and contact you should any additional information be required.*
- ▶ consider someone's request **assess, consider, discuss, review** *There is a duty on employers to consider requests for flexible working hours.*

request V

ask for something in a formal way

- adv+V in a polite way **kindly, politely, respectfully** *Hotel guests are respectfully requested to smoke outside only.*
- ▶ specifically **explicitly, expressly, particularly, specially, specifically** *Unless there have been extensive corrections you will not normally see revised pages unless you specifically request them.*
- ▶ many times **commonly, frequently, often, repeatedly** *Black is the most frequently requested colour.*
- ▶ formally **formally, officially** *Councillor Southby formally requested permission to set up a committee.*
- ▶ urgently **urgently** *Clarke claimed that he urgently requested a cabinet level meeting.*
- ▶ simply **merely, simply** *Over 50 per cent of calls were simply requesting information.*
- V+n documents **brochure, catalogue, copy, data, document, file, form, pack, report** *Click here to request a copy of the University prospectus.*
- ▶ information **data, details, evidence, information** *Using the Freedom of Information Act, we requested data on the number of people arrested for terrorist offences.*
- ▶ help or advice **advice, assistance, feedback, help, support** *The Coastguard requested assistance for a woman stuck in the mud near the Marina.*
- ▶ money **donation, funding, money, payment, refund** *Full payment is requested 8 weeks prior to the commencement of your vacation.*
- ▶ a meeting **appointment, call, interview, meeting, visit** *Several groups involved in the debate had requested meetings with officials.*
- ▶ permission to do something **access, permission** *You may request permission to use the images for other purposes by contacting the photographer.*

requirement N

something you must do, according to a law or rule [usually plural]

- adj+N according to a law, contract, or rule **contractual, legal, legislative, mandatory, regulatory, statutory** *They are responsible for ensuring that we meet the Housing Corporation's regulatory requirements.*
- ▶ strict **absolute, demanding, rigorous, strict, stringent** *The nuclear regulatory regime imposes stringent safety requirements on nuclear power stations.*
- ▶ basic **basic, critical, fundamental, key** *This is a fundamental requirement of the policy.*
- ▶ the least you can have or do **minimum** *The minimum requirement is a grade 1 in English and Maths.*
- ▶ official **formal, official** *While there are no formal entry requirements, candidates should be advised that this is a professional level qualification.*
- ▶ that you must do **compulsory, essential, necessary** *These courses are not a compulsory requirement, but they are recommended for all students.*
- ▶ types of requirement **academic, dietary, educational, environmental, financial, nutritional, technical** *We need a heating system that meets current and future environmental requirements.*
- v+N do what a requirement says you should

achieve, adhere to, comply with, conform to, fulfil, match, meet, satisfy *Failure to meet the requirements of this Act can result in prosecution.*

▸ say what the requirement is **define, determine, establish, lay down, outline, set out, specify, state** *Attendance requirements are determined by the relevant Head of Department.*

▸ introduce a requirement **implement, impose, introduce** *We will also implement the requirements of the proposed legislation on Freedom of Information.*

▸ get rid of a requirement **dispense with, relax, remove, waive** *Changes to safety legislation will remove the requirement for fire certificates for workplaces.*

▸ do more than a requirement says **exceed, go beyond** *It is our policy to create products which meet the latest European standards, and in most instances exceed the requirements.*

▸ make sure people do what a requirement says **enforce** *We have a duty to enforce the requirements of food hygiene legislation.*

rescue N

an act of saving someone from an unpleasant situation

▸ adj+N **daring, dramatic, heroic, successful** *Three police officers risked their lives in a dramatic rescue.*

▸ v+N carry out a rescue **carry out, come to sb's, effect, mount, perform** *A kayaker came to the rescue of a surfer, bringing him back to shore after seeing him in difficulty in Portland Harbour.* • *Davies jumped in, but was unable to effect the rescue and the man was drowned.*

try to rescue someone **attempt, go to sb's** *Three lifeboats went to the rescue, but the sea was so rough that only one reached the ship.*

wait for someone to rescue you **await** *He stayed on the boat, trying to attract attention, and awaiting rescue.*

N+n an attempt to perform a rescue **attempt, bid, effort, mission, operation** *A rescue operation was immediately organized, which took most of the day to recover the bodies.*

work done to perform a rescue **work** *Without their sterling rescue work, the South China Sea would have claimed many more lives that day.*

a group of people performing a rescue **crew, party, personnel, squad, team, unit, workers** *She was trapped for 15 minutes before being released by a rescue team.*

organization whose function it is to carry out rescues **organization, service** *We are working on a new TV drama based on the work of the mountain rescue service.*

equipment or vehicles used for performing a rescue **boat, craft, equipment, helicopter, ship, vehicle, vessel** *She was taken to hospital by RAF rescue helicopter.*

research N

detailed study that discovers new facts

adj+N done recently or being done now **current, the latest, new, ongoing, recent** *New research suggests that most trainee teachers feel confident that their training has prepared them well.*

▸ new and different **cutting-edge, groundbreaking, innovative, pioneering** *The pioneering research of Professor Donald and his team has given us a clearer picture of early pregnancy.*

▸ important **important, necessary, vital** *Money raised by the charity has funded some of the most important research into kidney conditions.*

▸ involving a lot of thorough and detailed work **detailed, extensive, in-depth, intensive, meticulous, painstaking, rigorous, thorough** *Many of the issues raised in the inquiry demand further detailed research.*

▸ done with someone else **collaborative, interdisciplinary, joint** *There is a strong tradition of collaborative research with colleagues in the Faculty of Medicine.*

▸ done on a particular subject **biological, biomedical, clinical, educational, environmental, genetic, historical, medical, scientific, social** *Recent scientific research has shown a link between poor oral health and conditions such as heart and lung disease.*

▸ using particular methods **academic, applied, comparative, empirical, qualitative, quantitative** *Much of the research is qualitative and based on both male and female samples.*

• v+N do research **carry out, conduct, do, perform, pursue, undertake** *She is continuing to do research into medieval European dress.*

▸ provide money for research **finance, fund, sponsor, support** *Every penny received goes directly to buy equipment or to fund research.*

▸ officially ask someone to do research **commission** *The government has commissioned further research to be carried out by The National Parenting and Families Institute.*

▸ tell people the results of research **deliver, present, publish, report** *Professor David Mellor is to present his research at a conference organised by Compassion in World Farming next month.*

▸ be in charge of a programme of research **co-ordinate, direct, lead, manage, supervise** *The research was led by Professor Dennis Parker.*

▸ look at other people's research **assess, evaluate, review** *This paper will review the research of the past decade and consider some of the gaps in our knowledge.*

▸ report or publish your research **disseminate, present, publicize, publish, report** *The monthly meeting provides a forum for team members to present their research.*

• N+v be about something **address sth, centre on sth, concentrate on sth, cover sth, examine sth, explore sth, focus on sth, include sth, investigate sth, involve sth, look at sth** *This research focuses on the experiences of people being discharged from psychiatric in-patient treatment.*

▸ show something **conclude sth, demonstrate sth, find sth, highlight sth, identify sth, indicate sth, report sth, reveal sth, show sth, suggest sth, uncover sth** *Recent research has found that regular physical activity can add two or more years to life expectancy.* • *As to how such challenges might be tackled, this research highlighted a number of areas in need of attention.*

▸ prove something **confirm sth, prove sth, support**

Recent research has confirmed that early diagnosis of hearing problems is very important.

▶ aim to do something **aim to do sth, seek to do sth** *My research aims to push the boundaries of both the above developments.*

● N+n someone doing research **assistant, group, scientist, staff, student, team** *We accept people as research students if there is clear evidence that they can work independently on a research question.*

▶ results of research **findings, results** *New research findings show that 47 per cent of us suffer from a headache at least once a month.*

▶ methods of research **methodology, methods, process, strategy** *You will be given a general introduction to research methods.*

▶ research work **activity, programme, project, study, work** *She is currently working on a research project looking at stresses in the lives of working parents.*

▶ organization or place doing research **centre, establishment, facility, institute, institution, laboratory, organization** *We are raising funds for a dedicated brain tumour research centre.*

▶ money for research **budget, funding, grant** *He holds a research grant to investigate attitudes to disability.*

▶ the subject you research **area, interest, topic** *My main research area is English phonetics and phonology, and the interface between the two.*

▶ a written plan of something you want to research **proposal** *Please make your research proposal as detailed and specific as you can.*

▶ something you use to help you do research **tool** *The book is an invaluable research tool.*

resemblance N
similarity between people or things

● adj+N great **close, distinct, great, marked, strong** *The software bore a strong resemblance to its predecessor.*

▶ great and surprising **remarkable, startling, striking, uncanny** *Lesley bears a striking resemblance to Catherine Zeta Jones.*

▶ slight **faint, passing, slight, superficial, vague** *Shinty has a passing resemblance to hockey though the rules are very different.*

▶ very little **little** *The article has been re-written so it bears little resemblance to the original.*

▶ physical **physical** *I was struck by the close physical resemblance between Billy and his brother.*

● v+N have a resemblance **bear, have, show** *Our lifestyle today has little resemblance to that of our ancestors.*

▶ notice a resemblance **note, notice, see, spot** *When I straighten my hair I can see the resemblance between us so much.*

resemble V
be similar to someone or something

● adv+V very much **closely, exactly, greatly, strongly** *He was named Peter after his grandfather, whom he strongly resembled.*

▶ rather **remotely, slightly, somewhat, vaguely** *The plant somewhat resembles Indian corn, or maize.*

▶ in physical appearance **physically, superficially** *Though it superficially resembles a wasp, a hover-fly is completely harmless.*

▶ increasingly **increasingly** *Crime and violence have increased, and the area increasingly resembles a war zone.*

resent V
experience angry unhappy feelings when treated unfairly

● adv+V bitterly, deeply, greatly, really, strongly** *I bitterly resented his criticisms.*

● V+n **attempt, criticism, fact, idea, implication, interference, intrusion, presence, sb's success, suggestion** *She resents the fact that she isn't able to work.*

resentful ADJ
angry because of being treated unfairly or without respect

● adv+ADJ **bitterly, deeply, increasingly** *Local people are deeply resentful of what they see as interference by central government.*

● v+ADJ **be, become, feel, seem** *Without the opportunity to learn and grow, children may become increasingly resentful.*

● and/or **angry, bitter, frustrated, jealous** *The Treaty of Versailles left the German people feeling bitter and resentful.*

resentment N
an angry unhappy feeling caused by unfair treatment

● adj+N great **bitter, considerable, deep, great, intense, much, strong** *There is deep resentment among many people in the local community about the ban.*

▶ becoming greater **growing, increasing** *It is clear that there is growing resentment among the people towards the occupation of their country.*

▶ felt, but not openly expressed **festering, latent, simmering, smouldering** *The tax rises led to simmering resentment among the lower-paid, who felt they were bearing most of the burden.*

▶ among many people **popular, widespread** *Widespread resentment of the system was seen as contributing to Ireland's social unrest.*

● v+N cause resentment **arouse, breed, cause, create, generate, lead to, provoke, stir** *When people were forced to take work home with them, it could sometimes cause resentment.*

▶ make resentment stronger **exacerbate, fuel, increase** *Giving greater power to traffic wardens could fuel resentment among drivers already angry about speed cameras.*

▶ feel resentment **feel, harbour** *He is envious of Donna's greater intellectual ability and feels some resentment towards her.*

▶ show resentment **express, show** *Members of the local population have at times expressed resentment over aid from donor agencies going only to the refugees.*

● n+of+N a feeling of resentment **feeling, sense** *If staff perceive that they are valued, then feelings of resentment can be minimised.*

▶ a cause of resentment **cause, source** *The abuses*

committed by many landlords was also a major cause of resentment.

● and/or **anger, bitterness, envy, fear, frustration, guilt, hatred, hostility, jealousy, suspicion** *Resentment and bitterness may breed new terrorists.*

reservation N

1 an arrangement to have or use something later

● n+N **accommodation, dinner, ferry, flight, hotel, restaurant, seat, table, ticket, travel** *The new cinema will also have a service desk to help patrons with calling a taxi or making a dinner reservation.*

● v+N make a reservation **make, place, secure** *We can handle your flight bookings and make reservations for hotels and restaurants.*

▶ cancel a reservation **cancel** *If you have to cancel your reservation more than 14 days before your visit, any deposit will be refunded.*

▶ say that a reservation is definite **confirm** *We will confirm your reservation by email as soon as we receive your deposit.*

■ N+n **agent, deposit, enquiry, fee, form, office, price, request, service, system, team** *We provide a high-quality travel reservation service.*

2 doubts about whether something is right [usually plural]

adj+N serious **deep, grave, major, serious, severe, strong** *Congress had expressed 'grave reservations' about the plans.*
minor **minor, slight** *Despite very slight reservations about the sound problems, I would have no hesitation in recommending this product.*

v+N tell people about your reservations **air, express, voice** *I took the liberty of voicing some personal reservations about the content or balance of the scientific programme.*
have reservations **harbour, have** *Given the enormity of these changes, it is unsurprising to learn that many people harbour some reservations about going ahead.*

If you want to say that you have no doubt that something is good, you can use the phrase **without reservation**: *The one poet whom I can recommend without reservation is T. S. Eliot.*

reserve N

supply of something that can be used when people need it [usually plural]

adj+N **enormous, finite, huge, substantial, untapped, vast** *The marshes happen to be on top of the some of the greatest untapped reserves of oil.*

n+N natural resources **coal, energy, fuel, gas, hydrocarbon, mineral, oil, ore, petroleum** *The main demand of the demonstrators is for the nationalisation of the country's gas reserves.*
financial resources **capital, cash, currency, dollar, euro, gold, sterling** *At that time, the US dollar accounted for over 70 per cent of global currency reserves.*

v+N use some of a reserve **dip into, draw on, exploit, tap into** *A strong and stable relationship will be able to draw on reserves of strength.*

▶ build up a reserve **accumulate, amass, build up, develop** *The enemy had amassed a great secret reserve of fighter aircraft.*

▶ have a reserve **have, hold, own** *There are queues at the gas stations – and this is in a country which holds the world's second largest oil reserves.*

▶ use all of a reserve **deplete, drain, exhaust** *By 1797 war with France had drained the gold reserves.*

▶ increase a reserve again after it has been used **replenish** *From mid-May to August, reserves of food are replenished.*

resign V

state formally that you are leaving a job permanently

● adv+V in a willing way **happily, voluntarily, willingly** *Employees who resign voluntarily in the first 6 months must repay any relocation fees.*

▶ suddenly **abruptly, forthwith, immediately, promptly, suddenly, unexpectedly** *When Bealle revealed this fact, Richards resigned forthwith.*

● V+as **captain, chair, chairman, director, editor, executive, head, leader, manager, minister, president, secretary, trustee** *Anyone wishing to apply for a remunerated position within a charity should immediately resign as a trustee.*

● V+from **board, cabinet, committee, council, government, job, office, party, position, post** *He resigned from the board when an agreement couldn't be reached.*

resignation N

1 the act of leaving a job permanently

● v+N tell your boss that you are leaving **hand in, offer, submit, tender** *However, he soon became disheartened with the Fund and tendered his resignation in 1886.*

▶ tell the public that you are leaving **announce** *Senator Jeffords of Vermont announced his resignation from the Republican Party to sit as an independent.*

▶ cause someone to leave **force, lead to, prompt, provoke, trigger** *The defeat had triggered the resignation of the party leader and precipitated a leadership contest.*

▶ say publicly that someone must resign **call for, demand** *There were articles in all the main newspapers calling for the resignation of the council leader.*

● N+n **letter, speech, statement** *Resignation letters should be addressed to the Human Resources department.*

2 the attitude of accepting something unpleasant

● adj+N **passive, quiet, weary** *She paused, and a look of quiet resignation crossed her features.*

● n+of+N **air, feeling, sense, sigh** *An air of resignation seemed to hang over the everyone in the office.*

● and/or **despair, patience, regret, sadness** *Scully doesn't answer, but the sadness and resignation on her face says it all.*

resilience N
the ability to become healthy, happy, or strong again, after illness, problems etc

- adj+N **emotional, mental, natural, physical** *The key to success lies in promoting better mental health through initiatives which improve emotional resilience.*

> People are often described as showing resilience *in the face of* something: *The report discusses other people's resilience in the face of difficulties.*

- v+N show resilience **demonstrate, display, prove, show** *During the war years the residents demonstrated their resilience in many ways.*
- ▶ make resilience stronger **build, develop, enhance, improve, increase, promote, strengthen** *We need to consider what promotes resilience in children, as well as how best to help them when things go wrong.*

resilient ADJ
quickly becoming healthy, happy, or strong again after illness, problems etc

- adv+ADJ **amazingly, extremely, highly, incredibly, remarkably, surprisingly, very** *Children can be amazingly resilient and positive.*

> People are often described as being resilient *in the face of* something: *Our government, our citizens and our way of life proved once again resilient in the face of evil.*

- v+ADJ **be, prove, remain** *Despite the financial crisis, the housing market remained remarkably resilient.*

resist V
1 stop yourself from doing or having something attractive

- adv+V **firmly, resolutely, steadfastly, stoutly** *Steadfastly resisting the sirens of Hollywood, Jarmusch has fashioned a series of stylish, worldly, and thoroughly hip movies.*
- V+n **allure, appeal, impulse, lure, pull, temptation, tendency, urge** *Will he be strong enough to resist the temptation to go back to a life of crime?*

2 oppose something or fight against something

- adv+V **actively, bravely, fiercely, resolutely, strenuously, strongly, stubbornly, vigorously** *The Finns resisted fiercely and fighting continued until March 1940.*
- V+n **aggression, arrest, attempt, eviction, imposition, invasion, occupation, onslaught, oppression, pressure** *She continually resisted our attempts to enlist her as a full-time member.*

resistance N
1 the ability not to be affected or weakened by something

- v+N make resistance weaker **decrease, lower, reduce, weaken** *A poor diet had weakened their resistance to illness.*
- ▶ make resistance stronger **build up, develop, enhance, improve, increase** *The substance is added*

in small quantities to a petroleum product to increase its oxidation resistance.

- ▶ provide resistance **confer, give, provide** *They are investigating a gene which appears to confer resistance to the HIV virus.*
- N+to disease **disease, infection, pathogen, virus** *Stress can lower the body's resistance to infection.*
- ▶ chemicals or chemical action **antibiotics, chemicals, corrosion, drug, herbicide, insecticide** *Bacteria can develop a resistance to chemicals and antibiotics.*

2 refusal to accept something new

- adj+N **fierce, stiff, stubborn, token** *Stiff resistance from the bosses threatens the implementation of these changes.*
- v+N **encounter, face, meet with** *The committee's recommendations had met with initial resistance in Cambridge.*

3 opposition to someone or something

- adj+N **armed, fierce, heroic, non-violent** *The Kosovar Albanians maintained an unbroken non-violent resistance despite mass arrests and torture.*
- v+N **break, crush, overcome, quell** *A successful attack broke the rebels' resistance.*
- N+v **collapse, crumble** *From 1812 onwards, Napoleon's resistance rapidly crumbled.*
- N+n **exercise, fighter, movement, training** *They join forces with a group of resistance fighters.*
- N+to **occupation, oppression, regime, tyranny** *The armed resistance to occupation has been growing by leaps and bounds.*

resistant ADJ
not harmed or affected by something

- adv+ADJ very **completely, extremely, highly, totally, very** *The disc is also highly resistant to dust, shock and scratches.*
- ▶ in a particular way **chemically, genetically, naturally** *The blocks can be made from chemically resistant plastic.*
- v+ADJ **appear, be, become, prove, remain, seem** *Some of the trees appear resistant to disease, and these grow normally.*
- N+to action or effect **abrasion, corrosion, degradation, drought, mildew, oxidation, pest, weathering** *Plaswood is resistant to weathering and ideal for marine furniture.*
- ▶ substance or drug **antibiotics, chemotherapy, disinfectant, herbicide, insecticide, penicillin** *Tubercle bacteria are more resistant to chemical disinfectants than other bacteria.*

resolution N
1 a formal proposal

- v+N make a resolution **propose, put forward, submit, table** *A resolution tabled by the European Union was backed by 54 members of the International Atomic Energy Agency.*
- ▶ accept a resolution **approve, endorse, enforce, pass, sign up to, vote for** *The United Reformed*

Church has passed a resolution to operate the Fairtrade scheme.

▸ discuss a resolution **consider, debate, negotiate** The European Parliament will debate an emergency resolution from the Fisheries Committee calling for more scientific evaluation.

▸ oppose a resolution **block, dispute, oppose, reject, veto** Russia has threatened to veto the resolution if it comes to a vote.

▸ take action on the basis of a resolution **adopt, implement** Bush claimed that Saddam had failed to implement several UN resolutions.

2 the solving of a problem or settling of an argument

▸ adj+N without violence or arguments **amicable, harmonious, non-violent, peaceful** South Korea believes that there are 'favourable grounds for a peaceful resolution' of the crisis.

▸ quick **speedy, swift** We hope that this offer of talks indicates that the employers share our desire for a swift resolution **to** the dispute.

▸ n+N **conflict, crisis, disagreement, dispute** Staff are trained in the basic tenets of good governance, and conflict resolution.

v+N **achieve, bring about, facilitate** How can I help facilitate a harmonious resolution for all concerned?

resolve V

solve a problem or disagreement

adv+V without violence or arguments **amicably, easily, fully, peacefully, satisfactorily, successfully** The majority of noise problems can be resolved amicably by talking to the person who is responsible.

quickly **immediately, promptly, quickly, speedily, swiftly** The whole affair – though speedily resolved – was bound up with the coming war with Germany.

V n disagreement or dispute **conflict, differences, disagreement, dispute** If the two sides cannot resolve their differences, it may be time to call in an adjudicator.

problem or bad situation **concern, crisis, impasse, issue, matter, problem, question, situation, tension** Kashmir holds the key to resolving the current security crisis in South Asia.

difficult question, where there seems to be no clear answer **ambiguity, contradiction, controversy, dilemma, inconsistency, paradox, uncertainty** They have to resolve the contradiction between their peaceful beliefs, and the actions of some of their followers.

resolve N

m determination to do something

v+N make someone's resolve stronger **fix, harden, reaffirm, reinforce, stiffen, strengthen** Each of the stories we heard from the refugees stiffened our resolve to create a safe future for them.

destroy someone's resolve **break, shake, undermine, weaken** Nothing seems to shake their resolve; problems are always seen as opportunities.

test someone's resolve **test** This challenge must have tested their resolve to the limit.

and/ or **commitment, courage, determination,**

spirit, strength They resisted the threats with great determination and resolve.

resort to PHR VB

do something extreme in order to solve a problem

● V+n dishonest or illegal **bribery, cheating, crime, subterfuge, trick, trickery** We discovered that some students had resorted to cheating in order to pass the test.

▸ method **expedient, means, measure, remedy, strategy, tactic** Refugees may resort to illegal means of escape.

▸ violence or threats **force, intimidation, terrorism, violence** These groups were not afraid to resort to intimidation or violence to achieve their aims.

resource N

something, such as money or materials, that you use to help you achieve something [usually plural]

● adj+N useful **excellent, invaluable, precious, useful, valuable** The database remains an invaluable resource for members without access to a major reference library.

▸ available only in small quantities **finite, limited, scarce** Refurbished historic buildings make an effective contribution to the sustainable use of finite resources.

▸ available in large or large enough quantities **abundant, adequate, extensive, rich, sufficient, vast** The area has fertile soil and rich mineral resources.

▸ types of resource **economic, educational, environmental, financial, genetic, human, legal, natural, technical** I would like to thank the previous sponsors of these series for providing much more than simply financial resources.

▸ relating to computers **digital, electronic, online, web-based** Look at the list of websites for more web-based resources on this area.

● v+N provide resources **allocate, commit, devote, distribute, divert, provide, target** Central government is failing to allocate adequate financial resources to the social care sector.

▸ use resources **access, deploy, exploit, use, utilise** All students are encouraged to utilise the centre's resources for study and research.

● N+n use **consumption, exploitation, usage, utilisation** This has brought about a reduction in resource consumption in traditional materials, but an attendant increase in the use of plastics.

▸ management **allocation, budgeting, management, mobilization, planning** The committee makes recommendations on long-term planning and resource allocation.

▸ place providing resources **base, centre** Lecturers of the courses you take may place materials for you in the resource centre.

▸ set of resources **file, library, pack** We produce a resource pack for 3 to 5 year olds and their parents.

Usage **Resource** is always singular in all of the **N+n** combinations shown above.

resourced ADJ

provided with money or materials to help you achieve things

- adv+ADJ well, or well enough **adequately, appropriately, fully, generously, properly, well** *We can deliver an appropriately resourced service with fully qualified personnel.*
▶ badly **inadequately, insufficiently, poorly** *Higher Education has been dogged by underfunding, with universities that are poorly resourced, and some on the brink of bankruptcy.*

respect N
the attitude of admiring something or considering it seriously

- adj+N much **deep, enormous, genuine, great, immense, profound, sincere, tremendous, utmost** *He always ensured that his musicians were treated with the utmost respect.*
▶ not much **grudging, little, scant** *The old building seems to have been regarded with scant respect.*

- v+N get or deserve people's respect **command, deserve, earn, gain, garner, inspire, regain, win** *He was a brilliant communicator who commanded immense respect.*
▶ show respect **demonstrate, have, show, treat with** *By using the language of ethnic communities in educational literature, authorities demonstrate their respect for these groups.*
▶ have the respect of other people **enjoy, receive, retain** *She enjoys enormous respect within the television industry.*
▶ lose respect **lose** *They blamed Gorbachev for destroying the Soviet Union, and rapidly lost respect for Yeltsin and his disastrous reforms.*
▶ cause people to lose respect **undermine** *The legislation is creating a rights culture that has undermined the respect for the law.*

- and/or **admiration, affection, appreciation, compassion, courtesy, dignity, fairness, friendship, love, tolerance, trust** *We affirm our desire to promote respect and tolerance for each other's beliefs, cultures and traditions.*

respect V
show that you understand the importance of something

- V+n **autonomy, belief, boundary, confidentiality, copyright, custom, difference, dignity, diversity, freedom, independence, individuality, integrity, obligation, opinion, privacy, right, sovereignty, tradition, wishes** *The company has respected the wishes of local people.*

respected ADJ
admired and approved of by people

- adv+ADJ well **deeply, enormously, fully, greatly, highly, hugely, immensely, much, well** *She is well known and greatly respected in the local community.*
▶ by many people **globally, internationally, nationally, universally, widely** *A group of internationally respected security experts has reviewed the system.*

respite N
a short rest from a difficult or unpleasant situation

- adj+N lasting a short time **brief, momentary,**

short, short-lived, temporary *His comrade's bravery had earned them a momentary respite.*
▶ enjoyable **much-needed, perfect, welcome** *The inn served great food and offered a welcome respite from the rain.*

- v+N give someone respite **afford, allow, bring, give, grant, offer, provide** *The building offered no respite from the bitter cold.*
▶ try to get respite **seek** *Seeking respite from her failing marriage, she embarked on a relationship with a neighbour.*
▶ get respite **enjoy, find, gain, obtain** *The house provided him with an environment in which he could find respite from the anxieties of war.*

respond V
react to something with a particular action

- adv+V in a positive or useful way **constructively, creatively, effectively, enthusiastically, favourably, flexibly, generously, magnificently, positively, sensitively, sympathetically, well** *Previous supporters are more likely to respond favourably to another approach.*
▶ in a suitable way **accordingly, appropriately** *We will continue to monitor the situation and respond accordingly.*
▶ quickly **immediately, instantly, promptly, quickly, rapidly, swiftly** *We will keep this guidance under review so we can respond swiftly to new issues as they arise.*
▶ in a negative way **angrily, negatively** *Friends of the Earth has responded angrily to today's decision to allow oil to be pumped between ships in the Firth of Forth.*

- V+to things that people say or ask for **appeal, call, challenge, complaint, concern, criticism, demand, enquiry, invitation, pressure, query, question, request** *The EU position on GMO labelling goes too far in responding to consumer concerns.*
▶ things that happen **crisis, disaster, emergency, incident, threat** *The Highways Agency has substantially strengthened its ability to detect and respond to incidents.*
▶ a new situation **change, opportunity** *The farming community has responded well to changes in people eating habits.*

response N
a reaction

- adj+N showing that you like something **encouraging, enthusiastic, favourable, positive** *This piece receives an enthusiastic response from th audience.*
▶ showing that you dislike something **negative** *These shows had a negative response from viewers*
▶ quick **fast, immediate, instant, prompt, quick, rapid, speedy, swift** *The University will facilitate swift responses to enquiries and applications.*
▶ given quickly without thinking properly **knee-jerk** *Some condemned this law as a knee-jerk respon to the events of September 11th.*

- v+N cause a response **bring, evoke, generate, induce, prompt, provoke, stimulate, trigger** *His comments prompted an angry response from environmentalists.*

- get a response **attract, elicit, get, receive** *An initial survey elicited an enthusiastic response from the members.*
- give a response **give, offer, submit** *The deadline for submitting your response is the end of next week.*

responsibility N
the state of being in charge or being to blame

- adj+N types of responsibility **administrative, individual, legal, managerial, ministerial, moral, parental, personal, social, statutory** *Owners have a statutory responsibility to ensure that these signs are maintained.*
- emphasizing who is really in charge **overall, prime, sole, ultimate** *The committee takes overall responsibility for finance and budgeting.*
- when responsibility belongs to a group rather than an individual **collective, corporate, joint** *The Cabinet takes collective responsibility for decisions like these.*
- v+N have or accept responsibility **accept, assume, bear, have, retain, share, shoulder, take, undertake** *Classroom assistants were shouldering much more responsibility than they should.*
- give responsibility to others **assign, charge sb with, delegate, devolve, hand over, pass, transfer** *The Convener had chosen to delegate these responsibilities to an assistant.*
- refuse to accept responsibility **abdicate, disclaim, shirk, shrink from** *He could not have been accused of shirking his responsibilities.*
- N+v **fall on, lie with, rest with** *A fundamental principle in maritime safety is that the ultimate responsibility rests with the shipowner.*

responsible ADJ
having a responsibility, and therefore able to be blamed if something goes wrong

- adv+ADJ emphasizing that only one person is in charge or to blame **directly, entirely, solely, ultimately** *The driver will be solely responsible for any damage or injury resulting from an accident.*
- when a group of people is responsible, rather than an individual **collectively, jointly** *The police and city council are jointly responsible for controlling crime and disorder in the area.*
- mainly **chiefly, largely, mainly, principally** *The postholder will be principally responsible for dealing directly with customers.*
- in a particular way **financially, legally, managerially, morally, professionally** *Landlords are legally responsible for maintaining gas appliances and must have regular safety inspections.*
- v+ADJ **consider sb/sth, deem sb/sth, find sb/sth, hold sb/sth, make sb/sth, regard sb/sth, think sb/sth** *Captains are deemed responsible for the actions of their teams.*

rest V
relax or sleep after a tiring activity

- v and/or **eat, enjoy, feed, recover, refresh, relax, sit, sleep, stop, unwind** *I play computer games as a way of resting and relaxing from a hard day's work.*

rest on PHR VB
depend on or be based on something

- adv+V **chiefly, entirely, largely, primarily, principally, solely, ultimately** *His place in physics rests chiefly on his researches in radiation.*
- V+n an assumption **assertion, assumption, presumption, presupposition** *But these hopes often rest on unrealistic assumptions.*
- a principle or belief **argument, belief, conviction, foundation, idea, premise, principle, proposition, tenet** *Our policy for sourcing goods rests on firm ethical principles.*
- a mistaken belief **misunderstanding** *Their position on the Middle East rests on a misunderstanding of recent history.*

restoration N
the process of bringing something back to its original condition

- adj+N done with care and respect **careful, meticulous, painstaking, sensitive, sympathetic, tasteful** *Now fitted with Pullman Seats throughout, the rest of the cinema is undergoing tasteful restoration.*
- complete and on a large scale **complete, extensive, major, thorough** *The castle has undergone extensive restoration in the last 15 years.*
- incomplete **cosmetic, partial** *In the short-term, the budget will only allow for cosmetic restoration – mainly a thorough clean of all the brickwork.*
- v+N experience restoration **undergo** *A number of landmark buildings are currently undergoing restoration.*
- do restoration **carry out, complete, perform, undertake** *The Heritage Trust also undertakes restoration of historic buildings.*
- need restoration **await, be in need of, need, require** *The college buildings were improved in 1980, but are now in need of further restoration.*

restore V
1 cause a particular situation or state to exist again

- V+n a positive feeling **confidence, dignity, faith, pride, sanity** *Will the tighter regulations help restore public confidence?*
- a positive situation **credibility, democracy, discipline, equilibrium, harmony, normality, peace, profitability, stability** *After the bombings, it was important to restore normality as soon as possible.*

2 return someone or something to a previous state

- V+to **beauty, elegance, fitness, glory, grandeur, health, splendour** *The town of Whitehaven is being restored to its Georgian splendour.*

> Usage ***Restore*** is often passive in these **V+to** combinations.

3 make something old and damaged look new again

- adv+V well **beautifully, carefully, completely, extensively, faithfully, fully, imaginatively, immaculately, lovingly, magnificently, meticulously, newly, painstakingly, sensitively, splendidly, superbly, sympathetically, tastefully, wonderfully** *The building has been thoroughly and sympathetically restored, maintaining its charm.*

▶ partly **cosmetically, partially, partly** *The nave clerestory and roof are of the 15th century but have been partly restored.*

Usage **Restore** is usually passive in all of these *adv+V* combinations.

restraint N
controls on people's behaviour or actions

● adj+N **budgetary, constitutional, dietary, fiscal, judicial, monetary, moral, regulatory** *Such budgetary restraints are common to all building projects.*

● v+N advise people to control their behaviour **advocate, recommend, urge** *He advocated restraint in eating, drinking and sexual behaviour.*

▶ control your own behaviour **apply, exercise, observe, practise, show** *The Presidency calls on all parties to exercise restraint and refrain from any action which would make the situation worse.*

▶ force people to control their behaviour **enforce, impose** *The Government will use these powers to enforce restraint.*

restrict V
keep something within strict limits

● adv+V unfairly **artificially, unduly, unfairly, unnecessarily, unreasonably** *Critics contend that current programmes unfairly restrict private landlords.*

▶ strictly **greatly, seriously, severely, tightly** *Severely restricting sports development and facilities will not improve the health of the nation.*

restriction N
a rule or action that limits something [usually plural]

● adj+N strict **severe, strict, stringent, tight, tough** *We would have to impose much tighter restrictions on motoring, but this is politically risky.*

▶ unfair **arbitrary, draconian, undue, unnecessary, unreasonable** *We urge members to resist arbitrary restrictions placed upon their activities.*

▶ imposed by a law or rule **contractual, legal, legislative, regulatory, statutory** *When employees are under 20, there are statutory restrictions on the number of hours they can work.*

▶ types of restriction **budgetary, commercial, dietary, environmental, financial, geographical, religious, technical** *Engines had to be modified to meet California's stringent environmental restrictions.*

● v+N make a restriction exist **apply, enforce, impose, introduce, place** *The nature of the building is such that we have to impose a few restrictions on visitors.*

▶ obey a restriction **comply with, meet, observe** *Some trucking companies had failed to comply with the restrictions on drivers' hours.*

▶ make a restriction stop existing **abolish, ease, lift, loosen, relax, remove, waive** *The major supermarkets wanted the Government to lift all restrictions on trading on a Sunday.*

▶ avoid or break a restriction **breach, bypass, circumvent, evade, ignore, overcome, override, violate** *Attempts to violate restrictions on producing electrical goods would no longer be tolerated.*

restrictive ADJ
strictly limiting or controlling someone or something

● adv+ADJ **excessively, extremely, highly, overly, too, unduly, unnecessarily, unreasonably, very** *Limiting the use of downloaded music to a single copy on a single PC seems unduly restrictive.*

● ADJ+n **law, legislation, measure, policy, practice, regime, regulation, rule** *This policy is more restrictive than the law requires.*

result N
1 something caused by something else

● adj+N good **excellent, good, positive, satisfactory** *Good results can be achieved through patience and regular daily treatments.*

If you want to emphasize that one thing happens because of another particular thing, you can use the phrase *as a direct result of*: *As a direct result of all the structural work undertaken leading up to the Expo, Lisbon now boasts an extended underground system.*

▶ bad **catastrophic, disappointing, disasterous, negative** *Poor yoga practices will likely produce disappointing results.*

▶ after considering everything **end, final, net, overall** *The net result of these changes is that postage costs will be cheaper.*

▶ clear and noticeable **concrete, real, tangible, visible** *The new policy has not yet produced concrete results.*

2 information obtained, for example from an experiment or piece of research [usually plural]

● adj+N good or useful **encouraging, impressive, outstanding, pleasing, promising** *The drug has been trialled on mice, and so far the results are impressive.*

▶ not yet final **first, initial, interim, preliminary** *In the next chapter, we discuss the preliminary results of our survey.*

▶ surprising **startling, surprising, unexpected** *When he did this, he got some interesting and unexpected results.*

▶ bad, or not good enough **disappointing, inconclusive, negative, poor, unsatisfactory** *Some of the statistical measures were abandoned because they produced unsatisfactory results.*

● v+N publish results **announce, disseminate, give, present, publish, release, report, show** *The paper presents the results of their research into carbon capture.*

▶ consider or analyze results **analyze, assess, collate, discuss, evaluate, interpret, review** *Predictably, the UK media has tried to find a way to interpret the result negatively.*

▶ produce results **generate, give, produce, return, yield** *Searching for titles with 'Zen' and 'Tao' in them will also yield good results.*

▶ obtain results **get, obtain, see** *We're seeing better results now that we've changed the formula we use for calculating scores.*

● N+v **confirm, demonstrate, highlight, imply, indicate, mean, prove, reflect, report, reveal, show, suggest** *The results clearly demonstrate a huge variation between species.*

resume v

start something again after stopping temporarily

- V+n discussion **conversation, deliberations, dialogue, negotiations, talks** *Union officials are to resume talks with bosses in an attempt to avert a strike on New Year's Eve.*
- fighting **attack, battle, fighting, hostilities, offensive, operations** *If the intense cold was not bad enough, they also had the threat of the Afghans resuming hostilities.*
- other activities **career, duties, journey, search, study, testing, work** *Borschette had a heart attack that night and never resumed his duties as a Commissioner.*

retain v

continue to have something

- V+n good qualities **atmosphere, character, charm, flexibility, identity, independence, integrity** *The village has retained its rural charm despite the onset of tourism.*
- right to do or have something **copyright, freedom, option, ownership, possession, right, status, title** *Under the contract, the artist retains ownership of his master tapes.*
- power or responsibility **control, power, responsibility** *The president retained control over defence policy.*

retaliation n

something unpleasant done to punish a bad action

- adj+N severe **devastating, harsh, massive, overwhelming, violent** *Nuclear states manage their relations by the threat of devastating retaliation.*
- types of retaliation **economic, military, nuclear** *This policy is intended to deter a major aggressor by threatening nuclear retaliation.*
- v+N cause retaliation **invite, prompt, provoke, trigger** *The attack undermines the progress we are making towards peace and is likely to provoke retaliation.*
- threaten retaliation **threaten** *Some officials in those countries have threatened retaliation against U.S. companies.*
- be afraid of retaliation **fear** *Residents had already fled their homes, fearing retaliation.*
- experience retaliation **face, suffer** *He warned Shia Muslims not to attack Sunnis, saying they could face retaliation.*
- N+for **attack, bombing, death, killing, murder** *Moscow decided not to use force in retaliation for the bombings.*

rethink n

act of considering something again in order to change it

- adj+N **complete, fundamental, major, radical, serious, thorough, urgent** *The housing crisis will only be solved by a radical rethink of current government policy.*
- v+N **cause, demand, force, prompt, require, urge** *These trends are forcing a rethink of the current business model.*

retirement n

the time when older people stop working

- adj+N before the planned or expected date **early, premature** *He is taking early retirement in order to concentrate his energies on teaching adults.*
- after a long period of hard work **well-deserved, well-earned** *She will be taking well-earned retirement from the company in August this year.*
- even if you do not want it **compulsory, forced, mandatory** *Their government was the first to abolish compulsory retirement at age 65.*
- about to happen **forthcoming, imminent, impending** *With Professor Welch's impending retirement, the department needs to find a new head.*

- v+N reach the age of retirement **reach** *When you reach retirement, you may want to move to a smaller home.*
- be about to reach retirement **approach, face, head towards, near** *If you are nearing retirement, these bonds could be a popular investment solution.*
- think about taking retirement **consider, contemplate, ponder, think about** *Officer Wilkins says he has pondered retirement, but will keep going as long as he has enthusiasm for the job.*
- take retirement **take** *Once you have taken retirement, there may be increased opportunity for visiting new countries and discovering new cultures.*
- decide to take retirement later than usual **defer, delay, postpone** *Members must not feel forced by pension scares to delay retirement indefinitely.*
- have enough money for your retirement **finance, fund, provide for, save for** *How much do you need to save in order to fund a comfortable retirement?*

retreat n

an act of leaving an unpleasant or dangerous place or situation

- adj+N done quickly, especially without planning **disorderly, hasty, headlong, hurried, quick, rapid** *The dog let out a yelp and beat a hasty retreat to his doghouse.*
- deliberate and well-planned **orderly, strategic, tactical** *To avoid losing the election, they made a tactical retreat on the issue of tax.*
- causing a loss of respect **humiliating** *The change of tactics forced his rivals into a humiliating retreat.*

- v+N **beat, be forced into, lead, make, sound** *This weakened and demoralized the Comintern and the leadership finally sounded the retreat.*
- N+from+n **politics, public life** *But Karadzic's public retreat from politics did not necessarily mean the end of his influence.*

retribution n

punishment that a bad person deserves

- adj+N quick **immediate, swift** *The chance for immediate retribution has been missed, so what can be done now?*
- violent **bloody, terrible, violent** *Seven killers each bring their own bloody retribution.*
- justified or from God **divine, just** *Vengeance is not our goal, nor do we seek merely a just retribution.*
- v+N seek retribution **seek, threaten** *He then threatened further retribution.*

▶ take retribution **bring, exact, inflict** *The victorious allies inflicted retribution on Germany.*

▶ deserve or suffer retribution **face, invite, suffer** *To take such a position in an election campaign would be to invite retribution from voters.*

▶ avoid retribution **avoid, escape** *Has he somehow faked his own death in order to avoid some terrible retribution?*

▶ fear retribution **fear** *They refused to give evidence because they feared retribution against them or their families.*

return N

1 when someone goes back to a place or situation

● adj+N welcome **happy, triumphant, welcome** *New World marked a welcome return to the studio for the Zombies after a twenty-year absence.*

▶ quick **prompt, quick, rapid, speedy, swift** *I wish to take this opportunity to wish the Liberal Democrat spokesman a speedy return to health.*

▶ soon/not soon **eventual, gradual, immediate, imminent, long-awaited** *We will intensify our search for Amber and we remain hopeful of her eventual safe return.*

▶ safe **safe** *Marianne went to church to light a candle to her favourite saint and pray for Yohan's safe return.*

● v+N want or expect a return **await, demand, expect** *The Law Lords have demanded a return to respect for human rights.*

▶ delay a return **delay** *We decided to delay our return, in the hope that the weather would improve.*

▶ indicate a return **announce, herald, signal** *Rumbles of thunder heralded our return.*

▶ welcome a return **celebrate, welcome** *The Thai community seemed largely to welcome the return of tourists.*

▶ see a return **see** *Attempts to clean up the river have seen the return of salmon and trout.*

● N+to a good state **fitness, normality, profitability** *Initially, Andrew seemed to make a rapid return to normality.*

▶ someone's home, origins or place **earth, homeland, mainland, roots, shore** *Would they one day return to their own homeland as prophesied in the Scriptures?*

2 a profit on money invested

● adj+N types of return **economic, equity, financial, investment, rental, stock** *I guess you have already started to experience lower rental returns.*

▶ amount of return **average, guaranteed, maximum, total, 2%, 3%, 5% etc** *The sector's average return was a shade less than 65% over the period.*

▶ good/bad **adequate, decent, fair, good, high, low, poor, reasonable** *His primary concern is to ensure an adequate return on his investment.*

▶ quick **immediate** *They look for long-term stability rather than immediate returns.*

● v+N give a return **achieve, deliver, earn, generate, guarantee, yield** *There was a sufficient quantity of good land to yield a good return in rent.*

▶ make a return bigger **increase, maximize, optimize** *Socially responsible funds try to maximize returns while staying within these self-imposed boundaries.*

reunion N

when people meet again after a long time

● n+N types of reunion **alumni, cast, class, college, family, school** *Join us at an alumni reunion and catch up with old friends and meet new ones.*

● adj+N happening at or after a particular time **annual, 20th, 30th, 50th etc, 25th anniversary, 40th anniversary, 50th anniversary etc, 25-year, 30-year etc** *The 40th reunion of the 1965 Dental Year was celebrated in Glasgow in October.*

▶ happy or emotional **emotional, happy, joyful, joyous, tearful** *Much to my surprise the show ended with their joyful reunion.*

▶ big **grand** *We are looking forward to a grand reunion*

● v+N plan a reunion **arrange, organize, plan, propose** *We will help arrange a great reunion here for you and all your extended family.*

▶ go to a reunion **attend, go to** *I attended the 50th anniversary reunion of the 509th Division in Utah.*

▶ hold a reunion **hold, host** *It is hoped that all departments will participate by hosting reunions for their alumni.*

reveal V

let something become known

● adv+V clearly **clearly, plainly, starkly** *The report revealed clearly that the Directive is failing to do it job of protecting animals.*

▶ publicly **openly, publicly** *To protect the witness, neither the place, the state, nor the sources will be publicly revealed.*

▶ slowly/quickly **gradually, methodically, progressively, slowly, suddenly** *The explanatory text is a fairly gentle guide that progressively revea what is going on.*

▶ accidentally **accidentally, inadvertently** *It appear the unsavory truth was accidentally revealed by a State Department employee.*

▶ in the end **eventually, finally, ultimately** *Twain's lively satire ultimately reveals just what it is that defines cultural identity.*

▶ exclusively **exclusively** *Research revealed exclusively to the Times shows that the union supports the Government's plans.*

● n+V survey **poll, survey** *Surveys revealed that gardeners were keen to encourage wildlife into thei gardens.*

▶ research **analysis, findings, report, research, results, study** *A study has revealed high levels of dissatisfaction among university staff.*

▶ investigation or examination **enquiry, examination, excavation, inspection, investigatio tests** *Excavations have revealed evidence of an earl cemetery.*

▶ medical examination **autopsy, post mortem, sca test, tests, x-ray** *The autopsy revealed that Kevin died from a heroin overdose.*

▶ figures **figures, statistics** *Job tenure statistics reve only a small decline in the length of time most peo spend in their jobs.*

revealing ADJ

providing new, surprising, or important information

● adv+ADJ very **especially, extremely, highly,**

particularly, **very** *One of these prose poems, 'The Visit', is particularly revealing.*

▸ rather **quite, rather** *The results have been rather revealing.*

● ADJ+n piece of work **autobiography, biography, interview, memoir, passage, portrait** *She also published a revealing autobiography, 'What's It All About?'*

▸ insight **glimpse, insight** *The letters offer revealing glimpses into Chekhov's preoccupations.*

▸ words **anecdote, remark** *There is a wonderfully revealing remark early on in the book.*

revelation N
surprising piece of information

adj+N surprising **startling, surprising** *Nick presents some startling revelations which will simply blow you away.*

very surprising **astonishing, astounding, earth-shattering, sensational, shattering** *She is confronted by a series of shattering revelations that threaten everything she believes in.*

shocking **embarrassing, shocking** *At age 32, he learned the shocking revelation that his sister was really his mother.*

revenge N
hurting or defeating someone who has hurt or defeated you

adj+N violent **bloody, brutal, cruel, murderous, terrible, violent** *As Titus plots his bloody revenge, he reflects that 'Rome is but a wilderness of tigers'.*

quick **immediate, swift** *In the meantime, the creditors' revenge was swift.*

enjoyable **sweet** *Revenge was sweet for the former champions.*

justified **just** *It is at this point that he articulates the notion of a just revenge.*

v+N plan revenge **plan, plot, threaten** *Jamie knows his guilty secret and is planning a terrible revenge.*

want revenge **seek, want** *Dawn felt angry towards Konzani and wanted revenge.*

promise revenge **swear, vow** *Fearing his son dead, Edward swears revenge on the French.*

take revenge **exact, gain, get, take, wreak** *Truro gained their revenge however, by beating Newquay to retain the Cup.*

N+for for a violent act **attack, death, killing, murder** *They reportedly took revenge for the killing of their relatives.*

for a defeat **defeat, loss** *Revenge for the nightmarish semi-final defeat in 1999 would be sweet.*

revenue N
income from business activities or taxes

adj+N net/gross **average, gross, net, taxation, total** *Net revenue in the first three months rose to £84m, an increase of 42 per cent.*

extra **additional, extra, increased, incremental** *It focuses business strategy on engaging staff with customers and thereby creating incremental revenues.*

lost **lost** *One clause allows companies to sue governments for lost revenue caused by strikes.*

▸ expected **anticipated, estimated, projected** *At a rate of £7 per day and 50 spaces available for stall owners, the anticipated revenue for this year is expected to reach £8,400.*

▸ in a particular period **annual, yearly** *Tourism is the world's largest industry, with an annual revenue of almost $500 billion.*

● n+N from business **advertising, export, oil, sale, sponsorship, subscription, tourism** *Advertising revenues are volatile, but overall continue to be around 1 per cent, up year-on-year.*

▸ from tax **custom, tax, toll** *He also increased tax revenues for infrastructure development.*

● v+N create revenue **create, generate, raise, yield** *The Library currently generates revenue in the order of £24 million annually.*

▸ get revenue **collect, derive, earn** *In the last two years, the company has been improving its performance and earning higher revenue.*

▸ increase revenue **boost, double, increase, maximize** *The investment was planned to bring cost savings and help to boost sales revenue.*

▸ expect revenue **anticipate, expect, project** *In the first year, net revenues were projected at £130m.*

▸ lose revenue **lose** *We are losing revenue as we cannot transport vehicles to Dunoon.*

● N+n creation or increase **funding, generation, growth, raising** *Revenue growth over the summer has continued the trend we saw at the beginning of the year.*

▸ something that earns revenue **earner, generator, raiser, stream** *Few archaeological publications are potential major revenue earners.*

▸ loss **leakage, shortfall** *Reducing revenue leakage and maximising profits is the aim of every operator in the market.*

▸ sharing **allocation, sharing** *At the moment remuneration is based on volume, but in the future it could move to revenue sharing.*

reverence N
a strong feeling of respect and admiration

● adj+N great **deep, great, profound** *Anna is enthusiastic about the process before them, having great reverence for her native African traditions.*

▸ proper **due, proper** *The party has renewed itself, but without proper reverence for its eternal principles.*

● v+N show reverence **pay, show** *He did not show reverence to anyone, not even to his parents.*

▸ cause reverence **command, inspire** *Despite his many achievements, he has never really inspired the same reverence as other innovators of his generation.*

● n+of+N **attitude, feeling, sense, spirit** *From her came the early and deep feelings of reverence that marked his life.*

● and/or love **affection, devotion, love** *Halley's writings show his reverence and affection for Newton to have been as keen and lively as ever.*

▸ fear or respect **awe, fear, humility, respect** *Traditional worship promotes awe and reverence, spirituality and thoughtfulness.*

▸ admiration **admiration, wonder** *My respect, my admiration, my reverence for you will be with me always.*

reversal N

a change that makes something into the opposite thing

- adj+N sudden **abrupt, dramatic, rapid, sharp, sudden** *There is no hint that Frank is unhappy with Martha, so why the sudden reversal?*
- ▶ surprising **astonishing, remarkable, unexpected** *How was such an astonishing reversal in constitutional practice justified?*
- ▶ complete/partial **complete, partial** *We need to have a complete reversal of the current situation.*
- v+N experience a reversal **experience, suffer, undergo** *The decline of goodwill was most precipitous in Mexico, where opinions underwent a complete reversal.*
- ▶ seek a reversal **demand, seek, suggest** *Climate change demands a reversal of our moral compass, for which we are plainly unprepared.*
- ▶ mark a reversal **mark, represent, see** *The decision in Scotland marks a reversal of previous Labour policy.*
- N+of of a tendency **decline, pattern, trend** *There must be a reversal of the trend of reduced levels of health service funding.*
- ▶ of a decision **decision, policy** *Customs and Excise are appealing to the High Court for reversal of the decision.*
- ▶ of roles **role** *Both commented that it was a very interesting and productive reversal of roles!*

  You can also talk about **role reversal**: *This was a total role reversal for both men.*

- ▶ of luck **fortunes** *There are two stories of dramatic reversals of fortune.*

reverse V

change a process or situation to the opposite process or situation

- adv+V suddenly **abruptly, dramatically, suddenly** *My opinions were soon to be dramatically reversed!*
- ▶ quickly/slowly **quickly, slowly** *The current trend in the opposite direction should at least be halted, if not slowly reversed.*
- ▶ completely/partly **completely, partially, partly** *Today that situation is completely reversed.*
- ▶ temporarily **temporarily** *The welfare state temporarily reversed this tendency by institutionalising the university as a public good.*
- ▶ in practice **effectively** *Having placed such individuals under suspicion, the burden of proof of guilt is effectively reversed.*
- ▶ simply **simply** *Many people think that an eating disorder can be reversed simply be eating normally again.*
- V+n a tendency **decline, situation, trend** *We shall be looking at various ways and means of reversing this trend.*
- ▶ a decision **decision, ruling** *In an 8–0 judgement, the court reversed the ruling of a Montreal school board, which banned Gurbaj Singh Multani from wearing his dagger, known as a kirpan.*
- ▶ someone's luck **fortunes** *He reversed the ailing fortunes of his previous school, and hopes to repeat his success.*
- ▶ damage **damage** *No amount of restoration can reverse damage on this scale.*

review N

1 the process of studying a situation or idea again

- adj+N full **complete, comprehensive, detailed, full, fundamental, in-depth, thorough** *It's now over 20 years since the last comprehensive review of housing.*
- ▶ after a particular period **annual, constant, monthly, periodic, quarterly, regular** *There is on annual review of this policy by the IT co-ordinator.*
- ▶ types of review **critical, ethical, expert, formal, independent, internal, judicial, strategic, systematic** *The extraction was done by a statistician experienced in systematic reviews.*
- n+N **governance, medication, pay, performance, rent, salary, spending** *These costs may well be considered as part of the spending review that will shortly be announced.*
- v+N ask or pay for a review **apply for, ask for, call for, commission, request, seek** *You have a right to request a review of this decision.*
- ▶ carry out a review **carry out, complete, conduct, undertake** *The Culture Committee is currently conducting a review of the impact of sport and the arts on regeneration.*
- ▶ announce or start a review **announce, initiate, institute, launch, order** *In Spring 2006 the University initiated a review of the Student Charter*
- ▶ have a review **be kept under, be subject to, be under, undergo** *It is advised that this situation be kept under constant review.*

2 an article giving someone's opinion of a book, film etc

- adj+N positive **excellent, favourable, glowing, good, positive, rave** INFORMAL *Elinor's books were read all over the world and she received glowing reviews.*
- ▶ negative or mixed **bad, critical, mixed** *It will be interesting to see what he will make of a film that has had mixed reviews so far.*
- ▶ short/long **brief, critical, detailed, in-depth, short** *In Musical Traditions they can find in-depth critical reviews of records and books by real experts*
- n+N types of review **album, book, CD, DVD, film, gig** *The journal also carries a bibliography of recent publications and book reviews.*
- ▶ by a person or in a place **consumer, customer, online, press, reader** *Check online reviews and user ratings.*

review V

study a situation, policy, or idea again

- adv+V at particular intervals or now **annually, currently, periodically, regularly** *Subscriptions to all journals will be reviewed annually.*
- ▶ all the time **constantly, continually, continuously** *The policy and procedures will be reviewed continuously and in line with the school's Action Plan.*
- ▶ carefully or thoroughly **carefully, comprehensively, systematically, thoroughly** *The system should be thoroughly reviewed and consideration given to providing a bi-lingual service.*
- ▶ in a particular way **critically, formally, independently** *This Code of Practice will be formally reviewed after a period of three years.*

revise v

change something such as a plan, law, or piece of writing

• adv+V up/down **downward, downwardly, downwards, upward, upwardly, upwards** *Forecasts for global oil demand have again been revised downwards.*
▸ a lot/a little **completely, comprehensively, extensively, fully, slightly, substantially, thoroughly** *This is a completely revised, updated and expanded edition of Training an Actor.*
▸ all the time **constantly, continually, continuously** *We are constantly revising and improving these resources following your feedback.*
▸ at particular intervals **annually, periodically** *We periodically revise the guidance notes and application forms to include changes and to improve clarity.*
▸ severely **drastically, radically** *To take full advantage of telecommuting, traditional organisational structures must be drastically revised.*
recently **newly** *The aim of this newly revised online database is to keep researchers informed of current research activities.*

V+n document **document, draft, edition, version** *This is a fully revised edition of the groundbreaking study on tourism.*
estimate **budget, estimate, figures, forecast, prediction** *It revised its estimate of the ship's cargo from 900 tons to 1,900 tons.*
plan or suggestion **plan, proposal, schedule, strategy, timetable** *Do we revise our plans to keep them relevant?*
rules **code, constitution, directive, legislation, regulations** *This is probably a good time to revise the constitution of the governing body in line with the new requirements.*
way of doing something **criteria, guidance, guidelines, procedure** *We know that companies will need to revise their procedures to take advantage of this change.*

and/or make better or more correct **amend, correct, edit, review, rewrite, update** *We continue to revise and update this site and to add new material.*
make bigger **enlarge, expand** *Now this indispensable reference volume has been enlarged and completely revised.*
publish or give again **reissue, relaunch, reprint, republish, resubmit** *The plan was revised and reissued at least four times.*

vision N

the process of changing a plan, law, or piece of writing

adj+N big/small **minor, substantial, thorough** *There was no really thorough revision of the text before the end of the sixteenth century.*
complete **drastic, radical, wholesale** *Singer concludes that morality requires a radical revision of our moral duties.*
all the time or not all the time **constant, continual, periodic** *As the game progresses, the player's estimate of her winning chances will undergo constant revision.*
upward or downward **downward, upward** *Building*

leases include a clause to enable upward revision of the rental charge to prevailing market conditions.

• v+N need or require revision **necessitate, need, require** *The authors have written an important book that will necessitate the revision of many traditional theories.*
▸ ask for revision **ask for, call for, request** *After discussion, members requested a further revision of the structure.*
▸ suggest revision **propose, recommend, suggest** *The report recommends revisions to the original plans.*
▸ have revision **undergo** *The law is currently undergoing revision to close a rather strange loophole.*
▸ carry out revision **complete, initiate, undertake** *Eliot undertook a thorough revision of his translation for the second edition.*

revival N

the process of becoming successful or popular again

• adj+N **brief, mini, modest, short-lived** *The World Cup coverage seems to be prompting a mini revival of the game at kids' level and above.*
• v+N cause a revival **inspire, kick-start, spark** *Harsh words at half time seemed to spark a mini revival and Leamington finally took the lead.*
▸ experience a revival **enjoy, experience, undergo, witness** *In recent years, the Cornish language has undergone a revival.*
▸ lead a revival **spearhead** *In the 1870s William Morris spearheaded a revival of block printing.*
▸ indicate a revival **herald, mark, signal** *The introduction of a National Short Story Prize marks a revival of interest in the UK.*
• N+of **interest, sb's fortunes, tradition** *There is currently an enormous revival of interest in herbal medicine.*

revive v

become or make something popular or successful again

• adv+V **briefly, miraculously, partially, single-handedly, successfully** *He retired to Thailand, where he almost single-handedly revived the Thai silk industry.*
• V+n a feeling **hope, interest, memory, sb's spirits** *A hearty breakfast of sausage rolls, orange juice and tea seem to revive the spirits.*
▸ the economy **economy** *Efforts have been made by international bodies to revive the economies of Africa.*
▸ aim or activity **ambitions, career, fortunes** *The local economy is putting its money into next year's Winter Olympics, which will, it hopes, revive its fortunes.*
▸ a tradition **custom, tradition** *The school has recently revived the tradition of academic scholarships.*

revolt N

an attempt to remove a government using force

• adj+N unsuccessful **abortive, attempted, unsuccessful** *The revolt was unsuccessful and their last attempt at regaining any control.*

▶ mass **mass, popular** *Presumably they would stage a mass revolt if there was any suggestion that major rigging of elections had taken place.*

▶ armed or bloody **armed, bloody** *By this time, the term 'revolution' had come to mean a bloody revolt.*

● v+N stop a revolt **crush, put down, quell, repress, suppress** *He commanded the French expedition that helped quell an anti-Bourbon revolt in Spain in 1823.*

▶ start a revolt **provoke, spark, trigger** *The Dissolution provoked an armed revolt which nearly cost Henry his throne.*

▶ organize or lead a revolt **foment, lead, organize, stage** *Traveling from church to church allowed Turner to gather the knowledge he needed to organize his revolt.*

revolution N

1 a situation in which people completely change their government

● adj+N political **bourgeois, communist, democratic, proletarian, socialist** *A socialist revolution cannot be carried through from above.*

▶ successful **glorious, permanent** *Their leaders know that there will be no glorious revolution.*

● v+N start a revolution **ignite, inaugurate, instigate, precipitate, spark** *In Belgium in 1830, an opera sparked a revolution.*

▶ have a revolution **accomplish, bring about, effect, foment** *The proletariat of a backward country was fated to accomplish the first socialist revolution.*

▶ lead a revolution **lead, spearhead** *They are the only class capable of leading a revolution.*

▶ defeat a revolution **defeat, overthrow** *They used every means they could to isolate and defeat the revolution.*

2 a sudden or major change in the way something is done

● adj+N **agrarian, biotech, biotechnology, broadband, communications, digital, genetics, industrial, media, scientific, technological, telecommunications** *There is currently a technological revolution taking place in higher education.*

● v+N start a revolution **herald, inaugurate, instigate, kick-start, precipitate, spark** *The knowledge of our genetic make-up will herald a revolution in new diagnostic tests.*

▶ bring about a revolution **accomplish, bring about, effect** *It has been claimed that T.S. Eliot effected a poetic revolution.*

▶ lead a revolution **lead, spearhead** *Monica spearheaded the aerobics revolution in this country.*

▶ experience a revolution **experience, undergo** *Language teaching has undergone a revolution during the past decade.*

● N+in in a subject or activity **agriculture, biology, communication, computing, healthcare, mathematics, medicine, physic, science, technology** *The first half of the nineteenth century saw a revolution in agriculture.*

▶ in thoughts or attitudes **attitude, taste, thinking, thought** *The 20th century has seen a revolution in our attitudes to mental problems.*

revulsion N

an extreme feeling of dislike

● adj+N felt by many people **popular, public, universal, widespread** *It coincides with growing and widespread revulsion for professional politicians.*

▶ strong **deep, utter** *Words cannot adequately express our utter revulsion and horror at this senseless act.*

● v+N cause revulsion **cause, provoke** *It was a case that would provoke revulsion in the mind of all decent people.*

▶ feel revulsion **feel, share** *Does he share my revulsion at yesterday's acts of violent thuggery?*

▶ express revulsion **express** *Words cannot express my revulsion at a law which would place anyone in that situation.*

● and/or **disgust, fear, horror, shock** *This vicious and cowardly crime has filled us all with horror and deepest revulsion.*

reward N

1 something good received for good behaviour

● adj+N large/small **ample, great, immense, rich, scant, substantial** *A one-goal lead at the break was scant reward for a dominant home display.*

▶ in heaven **eternal, heavenly** *Your eternal reward will directly reflect your suffering.*

▶ suitable **fair, fitting, just** *It was a fitting reward for many hours of hard work by our students.*

▶ now or later **immediate, instant, ultimate** *For many students, instant rewards for speaking English are much more motivating.*

▶ clear **obvious, tangible** *Many donors seek the tangible rewards and impact of giving locally.*

● v+N get a reward **enjoy, gain, get, obtain, reap, receive** *Meanwhile, a targeted approach to improving behaviour is already reaping rewards.*

▶ deserve a reward **deserve, earn, merit** *We both vowed that night that such tenacity and determination deserved its rewards.*

▶ offer or give a reward **bring, offer, promise, yield** *External motivation can be affected by offering appropriate rewards for success in language learning.*

▶ expect a reward **expect** *Albania certainly expects substantial rewards for having proven itself as a loyal and stable ally.*

● N+for for effort **effort, endeavour, labour** *Relegation to the Third Division was the only reward for their endeavours.*

▶ for success **achievement, excellence, success** *This is a reward for significant school achievements in the previous year.*

▶ for loyalty **loyalty** *The Order of the Garter is an honour presented by the British monarch as a reward for loyalty and for military merit.*

2 money you receive for working or giving information

● adj+N financial **financial, monetary, tangible** *Rice makes about two to three times what he made as a scientist, but the rewards aren't all monetary.*

▶ large **ample, great, handsome, immense, rich, substantial** *I am guessing the financial rewards are handsome.*

▶ fair **fair, just** *It is important that people receive a fair reward for their labours.*
▶ immediate **immediate, instant** *The first is the set up fee which is a one off payment and is an immediate reward for work done.*
● v+N get rewards **enjoy, gain, get, obtain, reap, receive** *They are concerned about developers gaining financial reward from those practices.*
▶ deserve reward **deserve, earn** *Teachers who consistently raise standards deserve fair reward.*
▶ offer or give a reward **bring, offer, promise, yield** *Information regarding the robbing of a house might yield a reward of 10 guineas.*
▶ expect or claim a reward **claim, expect** *Please contact us to claim your reward.*

rewarding ADJ
giving you satisfaction, pleasure, or profit
● adv+ADJ very **enormously, extremely, highly, hugely, immensely, incredibly, infinitely, particularly, richly, tremendously, very, wonderfully** *Research into Medieval English is complex but richly rewarding.*
▶ in a particular way **financially, intellectually, personally, professionally** *Being a roofer can be a financially rewarding profession.*
▶ ADJ+n career **career, employment, job, profession** *The job is rewarding and varied.*
▶ task **challenge, task** *Parenting today is a complex but rewarding challenge.*
▶ hobby **hobby, pastime, pursuit** *Candlemaking is an easy and rewarding hobby.*
▶ experience **experience** *This was to be a very intense but rewarding experience that I will never forget.*
▶ feature **aspect** *What is the most rewarding aspect of your job?*
▶ relationship **relationship** *Any dog owner should have a long and rewarding relationship with their dog.*
▷ v+ADJ **be, find, prove** *Strathclyde University has proved extremely rewarding and I am now enjoying my first job.*
▷ and/or enjoyable **enjoyable, exciting, pleasurable** *We are hopeful you will find your time as a volunteer with us enjoyable and rewarding..*
▷ interesting **fascinating, interesting, stimulating** *My history course is brilliant constantly challenging but also very interesting and rewarding.*
▷ challenging **challenging, demanding** *The role is both rewarding and challenging.*
▷ satisfying **satisfying, worthwhile** *Our graduates go on to secure rewarding and worthwhile careers.*

rhetoric N
style of speaking or writing that is intended to influence people
▷ adj+N exaggerated **exaggerated, high-flown, overblown** *I do not like this kind of overblown, exaggerated rhetoric.*
▷ empty **empty, hollow, mere** *You wrote with the same empty rhetoric as your other replies.*
▷ types of rhetoric **anti-imperialist, government, left-wing, nationalist, patriotic, populist, right-wing** *It is vital to avoid surrendering to populist rhetoric.*
▷ intended to stir emotion **alarmist, bellicose,**

emotive, inflammatory *Headlines scream out with emotive rhetoric, spreading fear within the community.*
● v+N use rhetoric **adopt, deploy, employ, spout** *You're repeating hearsay and spouting rhetoric with absolutely nothing to back it up.*
▷ challenge rhetoric **challenge, examine** *A Catholic apologist challenges the anti-Catholic rhetoric of some extreme fundamentalists.*
▷ avoid rhetoric **avoid** *We have successfully avoided flowery rhetoric.*
▷ believe rhetoric **believe** *You will not be surprised to hear that no one in the conference believed the rhetoric.*
▷ match rhetoric **match** *We must ensure that the reality is changed to match the rhetoric.*

rhythm N
1 a regular pattern in nature or in life
● adj+N regular/irregular **abnormal, irregular, steady** *My opinion is that his heart had a sudden abnormal rhythm.*
▷ types of rhythm **biological, cardiac, circadian, diurnal** *I suffer from insomnia, unless I am careful about my circadian rhythm.*
● v+N **disrupt, disturb, upset** *Damaged heart muscle can also upset the normal rhythm of the heart.*
2 a regular pattern of sounds in music
● adj+N repetitive **hypnotic, insistent, pulsing, repetitive** *The insistent rhythms of its music had drawn and were holding a large crowd.*
▷ not smooth **dotted, jerky, staccato, syncopated** *The irregular metre is interrupted by many pauses, creating a slow and rather jerky rhythm.*
▷ smooth or gentle **gentle, lilting, undulating** *As soon as the spoken part is over, the percussion starts beating out a gentle rhythm.*
▷ strong **drumming, funky, percussive, pounding, pulsating, throbbing** *There are now eight such groups across Europe playing the same funky rhythms.*
▷ appealing **catchy, infectious, upbeat** *These infectious rhythms are what make the band so popular among locals and visitors to the islands.*

rich ADJ
1 having a lot of money
● adv+ADJ very **enormously, exceedingly, extremely, fabulously, fantastically, immensely, incredibly** *They're not fabulously rich, or famous, or beautiful.*
▷ too **filthy, obscenely, stinking** *The Lydian King, Kroisos, was filthy rich, coining his own money at will.*
● and/or **beautiful, famous, powerful, privileged** *For the most part we didn't become rich and powerful through our own efforts.*
2 interesting, with many different qualities, experiences etc
● adv+ADJ very **amazingly, astonishingly, extraordinarily, fantastically, incredibly, infinitely, wonderfully** *Clara's songs, recently discovered, are wonderfully rich in their own right.*

▶ unusually **exceptionally, particularly, remarkably, unusually** *The valley has an unusually rich flora of over 600 species with many rarities.*

▶ in a particular way **biologically, botanically, culturally, ecologically, functionally, graphically, harmonically, visually** *Today this culturally rich area gives a wonderful view on its history.*

● ADJ+n history **heritage, history, legacy, tradition** *The cuisine reflects the region's rich heritage and tradition.*

▶ mixture **diversity, mix, tapestry, variety** *This is a rich tapestry of a book, researched with meticulous accuracy.*

▶ plants or animals **fauna, flora** *The Quantocks is noted for its rich flora and fauna set against stunning views across the Severn Estuary.*

● ADJ+in **biodiversity, birdlife, flora, fossils, wildflowers, wildlife** *The island is rich in wildlife.*

● and/or **colourful, diverse, fascinating, satisfying, stimulating, varied** *Oakley Court was built in 1859 and has a rich and colourful history.*

ridicule N
remarks that make someone or something seem silly

● v+N risk ridicule **face, invite, provoke, risk** *Of course, without a phone teenagers risk the ridicule of their peers.*

▶ use ridicule **heap on sth/sb** *The journalist joined the editor in the easy work of heaping ridicule **on** the whole thing.*

▶ avoid ridicule **avoid** *All the people involved had kept it quiet in order to avoid ridicule.*

▶ suffer ridicule **be the object of, be the subject of, endure, incur, suffer** *It treats the rich and powerful as objects of ridicule, rather than objects of reverence.*

▶ cause ridicule **attract** *Such policies have attracted widespread ridicule and non-compliance.*

● and/or **contempt, criticism, derision, hatred, hostility, insults, mockery, rejection, sarcasm, scorn** *All sympathy was immediately withdrawn and replaced by scorn and ridicule.*

ridiculous ADJ
silly or unreasonable

● adv+ADJ completely **absolutely, completely, downright, frankly, quite, simply, totally, utterly** *The church's minister said: 'I think this rule is utterly ridiculous.'*

▶ clearly **patently, plain** INFORMAL, **plainly** *The idea is patently ridiculous.*

▶ slightly **faintly, a little, slightly** *The nation at large may regard the British intellectual as slightly ridiculous.*

▶ rather **pretty** INFORMAL, **rather, somewhat** *The food was actually pretty good and the amounts somewhat ridiculous.*

● ADJ+n idea **idea, notion** *That would be a ridiculous notion.*

▶ statement **accusation, assertion, claim, excuse, lie, rumour** *U.S. officials have called the accusations ridiculous.*

▶ amount **amount** *People have been offering us ridiculous amounts of money for this.*

▶ situation **situation** *The whole situation is just ridiculous.*

rift N
a disagreement between two people or groups

● adj+N serious **big, deep, huge, serious** *There is a serious rift, though no reason is recorded.*

▶ getting worse **deepening, widening** *There appears to be a widening rift **between** the President and the Prime Minister.*

● v+N heal a rift **heal, mend, overcome, repair** *He worked hard behind the scenes to heal the rifts within the Party.*

▶ make a rift worse **deepen, widen** *The appointment of a woman Bishop has deepened rifts **within** the Anglican Communion.*

▶ cause a rift **cause** *Unfortunately, this caused rather a rift **with** his wife, Beryl.*

▶ reveal a rift **expose** *The crisis during March 1946 had already exposed a serious rift.*

right N
something that is allowed morally or legally

● adj+N legal **automatic, constitutional, contractual, legal, statutory** *This policy is in addition to your legal statutory rights.*

▶ basic **absolute, basic, fundamental, inalienable** *That statement proclaims that every child is unique and has a fundamental right to education.*

▶ types of rights **democratic, individual, moral, parental, public** *He had no moral right to be connected with business at all.*

● n+N rights to do or have something **abortion, borrowing, cancellation, pension, privacy, reproduction, resale, voting** *Although they have no voting rights if under 18, these members can include school students.*

▶ rights associated with something **citizenship, employment, maternity, patent, property, welfare** *New employment rights are now in force.*

▶ rights for different groups **animal, consumer, disability, gay, minority, women's** *None of the abou terms and conditions affects your statutory consume rights.*

● v+N have or claim a right **assert, claim, enforce, have** *You have a right to request a review within 28 days.*

> You can say that someone **reserves or retains the right to do something**: *We reserve the right to edit responses before publication.*

▶ get or keep a right **acquire, get, secure** *Time is running out for new residents to secure their right t vote.*

▶ give someone a right **confer, grant** *The charter conferred the right of a weekly market to be held or Wednesdays.*

▶ use/not use a right **exercise, waive** *You can waiv your moral rights via a release form.*

▶ defend a right **defend, guarantee, protect, uphol** *We will tell you what you can do to protect your rights to stay in your home.*

▶ attack or refuse a right **deny, infringe, violate** *The claimed it violated her right not to be denied education under the Convention.*

▶ affect a right **affect** *This return policy does not affect your statutory rights.*

▶ recognize a right **recognize, respect** *We respect your right to privacy.*

● N+to **abortion, compensation, confidentiality, education, a fair hearing, freedom, liberty, privacy, representation, self-defence, self-determination, trial** *Britain is a multi-faith society in which everyone has the right to religious freedom.*

rigid ADJ
difficult to change, or unwilling to change

● adv+ADJ too **excessively, overly, too** *European governments, especially, seem to have taken an overly rigid stand on the issue.*

▶ very **extremely, highly, very** *They have very rigid views about what helping strategies they are prepared to accept.*

▶ rather **fairly, quite, relatively, somewhat** *The system is relatively rigid in operation, with limited options for customisation.*

● completely **absolutely, completely, totally** *True, this was not an absolutely rigid society.*

● ADJ+n **adherence, categorisation, dogma, fixation, hierarchy, observance** *Rigid adherence by the parties to their past positions will simply continue the stalemate.*

● and/or **bureaucratic, dogmatic, hierarchical, inflexible** *His faults are a tendency to be rigid and inflexible, and too serious.*

rigorous ADJ
thorough or severe

● adv+ADJ in a particular way **academically, intellectually, mathematically, methodologically, scientifically, statistically** *In my opinion, the research presented is methodologically rigorous.*

▶ enough/not enough **insufficiently, sufficiently, suitably** *Assessment was not always sufficiently rigorous or accurate.*

▶ rather **fairly, quite** *In order for a qualification to have credibility, it helps if the test is fairly rigorous.*

▶ very **extremely, highly, very** *Due to extremely rigorous checking procedures, errors in the data are extremely rare.*

● ADJ+n testing **analysis, assessment, evaluation, examination, scrutiny, testing** *We went through a very rigorous testing and assessment process.*
method **approach, methodology, procedure, process** *The broad philosophy is to apply rigorous scientific methodologies to questions that are relevant to a wide range of human diseases.*
checks **checks, inspection, investigation, monitoring** *We enforce rigorous checks on the quality of our ingredients.*
proof **proof** *Mr Mitchell laid particular emphasis on the need for clear and rigorous proof.*
standards **criteria, standards** *The criteria are rigorous, and all criteria must be fulfilled to achieve the award.*

rigour N
the quality of being thorough and careful

● adj+N types of rigour **academic, analytical,**

conceptual, critical, intellectual, journalistic, mathematical, methodological, philosophical, scholarly, scientific, technical, theoretical *This course combines the intellectual rigour of a graduate programme with the delivery of a business school.*

▶ great **full, great, the utmost** *In the medical domain, everything is tested with the utmost rigour.*

● v+N bring rigour **apply, bring** *As far as possible, the research team apply academic rigour to their activity.*

▶ maintain rigour **ensure, maintain** *Are academic staff also involved to ensure that academic rigour is maintained?*

▶ lack rigour **lack** *Students found the peer assessment process lacked rigour due to peer pressure for 'good' grades.*

riot N
a violent protest by a crowd

● adj+N big **full-scale, widespread** *The night before, they had attended a full-scale riot in the area.*

▶ violent **bloody, violent** *These bloody riots lasted for several days and claimed the lives of many Welsh miners.*

▶ types of riot **communal, sectarian** *The same period saw the first outbreaks of sectarian riots, which have recurred regularly since.*

● n+N **prison, race, street** *There are genuine fears that prison riots could break out as a result of this policy.*

● v+N cause a riot **cause, incite, instigate, provoke, spark, trigger** *The riots were sparked by the G8 Leaders' Summit scheduled to start later in the week.*

▶ crush a riot **quell, suppress** *As an interim step, troops were sent in to quell riots.*

▶ start a riot **start** *Lenin had returned to Russia in April 1917 and he was blamed by the government for starting the riots.*

▶ stop a riot **prevent, stop** *Society is still incapable of preventing race riots in the streets of many countries.*

● N+v **break out, ensue, erupt, happen, occur** *His family moved to England shortly after the first riots erupted in 1969.*

ripple N

● v+N **cause, create, send, spread** *These announcements will cause ripples of displeasure across the public sector.*

● N+of of a sound **applause, laughter** *After a ripple of applause from the audience, Bob was able to continue with the show.*

▶ of an emotion **excitement, fear** *It will send unnecessary ripples of fear throughout one of the UK's most vulnerable communities.*

rise V
1 increase in size, amount, quality, or strength

● adv+V quickly or suddenly **dramatically, exponentially, fast, quickly, rapidly, sharply, steeply, suddenly** *Carbon emissions from aviation are rising sharply.*

▶ slowly or gradually **gradually, progressively, slowly, steadily** *Imports of Australian wine into Great Britain rose steadily.*

▶ a lot **considerably, markedly, significantly, strongly, substantially** *Trading profits in these businesses rose significantly in the first half of the year.*

▶ a little **marginally, slightly** *The annual amount given to charities rose slightly after 1998.*

▶ continually **consistently, constantly, continually, continuously, inexorably** *Our readership numbers seem to rise inexorably.*

2 achieve success, power, or higher status

● adv+V quickly **dramatically, fast, rapidly, swiftly** *Success followed, and he swiftly rose up the managerial ranks.*

▶ slowly **gradually, slowly, steadily** *She gradually rose to become a leading character in the series.*

● V+to **dominance, eminence, fame, greatness, heights, prominence, stardom** *The director of the Netherlands Architecture Institute explains how such a small nation rose to such prominence.*

rise N

1 an increase in size, amount, quality, or strength

● adj+N fast or sudden **abrupt, dramatic, exponential, fast, rapid, sharp, steep, sudden** *Customers are being urged to conserve water following a sharp rise in demand during the hot weather.*

▶ large or noticeable **big, huge, marked, massive, noticeable, significant, substantial** *Melting glaciers would lead to a massive rise in global sea levels.*

▶ slow **gradual, slow, steady** *There has been a steady rise in the number of voices supporting the 'open sourcing' of science.*

▶ small **modest, slight** *When the government announced a slight rise in social security payments, it provoked an outcry.*

▶ surprising or worrying **alarming, unprecedented, worrying** *The statistics show an unprecedented rise in arrests for cannabis possession.*

▶ expected **anticipated, expected, predicted, projected** *The new road will help to cope with a predicted rise in traffic volumes.*

▶ continuing **continued, inexorable, sustained** *The first six months of the year saw continued price rises.*

▶ as a result of something **consequent, corresponding, inevitable** *Expenditure on tobacco advertising increased, with a corresponding rise in consumption.*

● v+N cause a rise **accelerate, cause, fuel, trigger** *They fuel the rise in racism by attempting to blame immigrants for the government's shortcomings.*

▶ prevent or control a rise **combat, counter, curb, halt, offset, prevent, reverse, stem** *There is a growing recognition that medicine alone cannot halt the rise of mental illness.*

▶ expect a rise **anticipate, expect, forecast, predict** *The authority predicted a rise in the number of passengers using the airports over the next ten years.*

▶ see or experience a rise **experience, see, show, witness** *This is why we are witnessing the rise in terrorism around the world.*

▶ report a rise **announce, report** *The company reported a rise in profits.*

▶ explain a rise **attribute to sth, explain** *Scientists attributed the rise to an increase in solar activity.*

2 an increase in power or success

● adj+N fast or sudden **dramatic, exponential, meteoric, phenomenal, rapid, spectacular, sudden** *The Wars of Independence brought the meteoric rise of one of Scotland's most famous sons, William Wallace.*

▶ gradual **gradual, slow, steady** *The last ten years have seen a steady rise in the band's fortunes.*

▶ impossible to stop **inexorable, irresistible, relentless, unstoppable** *The inexorable rise of the car and the lorry produces huge problems.*

● v+N see a rise **see, witness** *This period also witnessed the rise of a new tradition of working-class autobiography.*

▶ describe or record someone's rise **chart, chronicle, document, record, trace** *The novel charts the rise to notoriety of the Ryans, a poor Irish family, who become one of the foremost crime families in London.*

● N+to **dominance, fame, greatness, power, prominence, stardom** *The exhibition will examine the whole of his life and work, from his beginnings through to his rise to fame.*

rising ADJ

becoming larger, greater in level, or more frequent

● ADV+n price **cost, price** *There are numerous steps you can take to combat rising petrol prices.*

▶ demand **demand, popularity** *We have benefited from the rising popularity of specialist wholefood stores.*

▶ frequency **incidence, level, prevalence, rate, trend** *There is a rising incidence of cervical cancer in young women.*

▶ problem **crime, inequality, inflation, tension, unemployment** *Consumers are putting off major purchases, partly because they are afraid of rising unemployment.*

▶ wealth **affluence, income, prosperity** *We want a fairer Britain, where everyone can share in rising prosperity.*

▶ expectation **expectation** *The pace of technological change brings ever rising expectations of what can be achieved.*

risk N

the possibility that something bad might happen

● adj+N great or high **big, considerable, great, high, significant, substantial** *Such trading would involve considerable risk to the charity's resources.*

▶ greater than usual **elevated, heightened, higher, increased** *Elevated levels of the protein have been associated with a higher risk of cardiovascular disease.*

▶ small or low **low, minimal, negligible, slight, smal** *People in professional jobs have lower risks of lifestyle-related diseases like heart disease.*

▶ serious **grave, serious** *There is a serious risk of injury to employees or members of the public.*

▶ real or immediate **immediate, imminent, real** *The is a real risk that an unusual tidal event could resu in floods.*

▶ possible **possible, potential, theoretical** *Individua workers must be aware of potential risks.*

▶ not necessary or acceptable **unacceptable, undu unnecessary** *A reckless minority of drivers continu to take unacceptable risks by drinking and driving*

▶ taken deliberately **calculated** *We need to encourage innovation and the taking of calculated risks in business.*

▶ associated with something **associated, attendant, inherent** *Trading over the Internet has certain inherent risks.*

▶ easy to predict **foreseeable, obvious** *The risks are obvious, and so are the solutions.*

▶ types of risk **credit, environmental, financial, health, occupational, operational, personal, political, security** *At great personal risk, John crawled under the debris and dragged him out.*

● n+N of a particular event **accident, avalanche, cancer, contamination, fire, flood, suicide** *Homes in areas of flood risk will be given improved flood protection.*

● v+N reduce the risk **address, control, cut, decrease, halve, lessen, limit, lower, manage, minimize, mitigate, reduce, spread** *In some cases, we can reduce the risk of getting the condition in the first place.*

▶ avoid or eliminate risk **avoid, eliminate, prevent, remove** *Whenever possible, avoid risks altogether by removing hazards.*

▶ increase the risk **double, increase** *If you smoke, you more than double your risk of having heart disease.*

▶ be or present a risk **carry, constitute, entail, involve, pose, present, represent** *The treatment carries the risk of side effects in the form of serious allergic reactions.* ● *It is absurd to say these people pose a terrorist risk.*

▶ take or accept a risk **accept, assume, bear, face, incur, run, take** *Its leaders now run the risk of bringing the country to the brink of economic collapse.* ● *Some people invest money in businesses and take risks.*

▶ understand or measure the risks **assess, calculate, consider, estimate, evaluate, identify, predict, quantify, understand** *A Code of Good Practice has been produced to help farmers identify the risks.* ● *They understand the health risks, but are unable to quit smoking without help.*

▶ report a risk **highlight** *The report highlights potential risks to children from toxic landfill sites.*

▶ be equal to or greater than a risk **balance, outweigh** *The benefit of the treatment may outweigh the risks at this stage of the disease.*

● N+v happen because of something **arise from, be associated with, be attached to, be involved in** *There are political risks attached to this course of action.*

▶ be equal to or greater than something **be balanced by, outweigh** *Transplantation is likely to be necessary in the future, but at present the risks outweigh the potential benefits.*

risky ADJ
involving the possibility of danger or failure

adv+ADJ very **extremely, highly, hugely, seriously, very** *This is an extremely risky strategy if you are unsure of how your colleagues will respond.* rather **fairly, a little, pretty** INFORMAL, **quite, rather, slightly, somewhat** *Home birth in the UK has been seen as an odd and slightly risky thing to do.* too **too, unacceptably** *To start their own business was considered too risky.*

▶ possibly **possibly, potentially** *A new way of diagnosing brain tumours without the need for potentially risky biopsies has been developed.*

▶ more than other things or than before **especially, increasingly, particularly** *Falls in blood pressure are particularly risky in the elderly.*

▶ in itself **inherently** *Combat is inherently risky, but the prudent leader takes measures to reduce the risk.*

▶ from a particular point of view **financially, physically, politically** *I prefer to work for myself, even though it is financially riskier.*

● ADJ+n **bet, business, enterprise, gamble, manoeuvre, move, proposition, strategy, tactic, undertaking, venture** *A business with a well-established management team is a less risky proposition to a purchaser.* ● *Waiting until you get to the interview to show them how good you are is a risky tactic.*

ritual N
something such as a formal ceremony that is always done in the same way

● adj+N religious or magic **magic, magical, occult, religious, sacred, satanic** *Perfumes have always been of great importance for religious rituals.*

▶ strange or complicated **arcane, bizarre, elaborate** *The Houses of Parliament seems to be full of bizarre rituals conducted in dated language.*

▶ ancient **ancient** *The influence of ancient ritual in shaping our landscape is well known.*

▶ regular **nightly** *Her children loved the nightly ritual of bedtime stories.*

▶ without meaning **meaningless** *He satirizes the meaningless social rituals of the upper middle class.*

▶ with a particular purpose **bathing, ceremonial, cleansing, funeral, funerary, healing, mating, purification, sacrificial, tribal** *The warriors would perform a cleansing ritual before going off to fight.*

● v+N perform a ritual **conduct, enact, observe, perform, practise** *People come together at Christmas and enact the family rituals of past years.*

▶ repeat a ritual **re-enact, repeat** *He pauses at each door and repeats the same ritual.*

rival N
a person, team, or business competing with another

● adj+N very great **big, bitter, deadly, fierce, hated, serious** *The two banks were in different political camps and for many years they were bitter rivals.*

▶ main **chief, closest, main, nearest** *They remain top of the league, with an eight-point lead over their closest rivals.*

▶ for a long time **longtime, long-time, perennial** *She has finally overtaken her long-time rival to become world number one.*

▶ difficult to beat **fancied, formidable, worthy** *The Earl of Leicester looked upon him as a formidable rival at court.*

▶ jealous **envious, jealous** *Protected by the emperors, he could work free from his jealous rivals.*

▶ possible **potential** *For her, everyone else was a potential rival.*

● v+N defeat a rival **beat, defeat, eliminate, overcome, trounce, vanquish** *We managed to beat our local rivals 3–2.*

▸ do better than a rival **leapfrog, outdo, outpace, outperform, outsell, outshine, outstrip, outwit, overtake, surpass** *The new model car has qualities that far outshine its traditional rivals.*

▸ be cheaper than a rival **undercut** *The tax loophole has enabled the company to undercut its rivals in the music, DVD and videogame markets.*

rivalry N
competition between people, businesses etc

● adj+N strong **bitter, fierce, intense** *The relationship between the firms is characterised by both cooperation and fierce rivalry.*

▸ friendly **friendly, good-natured** *This is part of the good-natured rivalry that exists between Australia and New Zealand.*

▸ over unimportant things **petty** *He describes the petty rivalries and bad reviews that marked his debut as an actor.*

▸ old **age-old, long-running, long-standing** *It was the age-old rivalry between the two ancient universities.*

▸ between groups **factional, inter-departmental, internecine, inter-professional, sectarian, tribal** *There were fears a referendum could inflame ethnic and sectarian rivalries.*

▸ and/or **competition, conflict, hatred, jealousy, tension** *There are rivalries and jealousies in every family.*

● v+N start or continue a rivalry **continue, encourage, ignite, intensify, renew, resume** *The match will renew an old sporting rivalry.*

▸ overcome rivalry **end, forget, overcome, settle, transcend** *His two daughters have to overcome their own rivalry to rescue their father.*

river N
an area of water flowing towards the sea

● adj+N flowing fast **fast-flowing, free-flowing, rushing** *Five fast-flowing rivers powered the city's water wheels.*

▸ large or deep **mighty, swollen** *They crossed the swollen river with the aid of a rope.*

▸ shallow **shallow** *He had to wade across a shallow river.*

▸ not straight **meandering, winding** *This is a landscape of rich pastures and meandering rivers.*

▸ clean/not clean **clean, muddy, polluted** *The Mersey was then one of the most polluted rivers in Europe.*

● N+v flow along a course **bend, flow, meander, run, rush, wind** *A long section of the river flows through privately-owned land.*

▸ flood **burst its banks, flood, overflow its banks** *Some of the garden had been washed away when the river flooded.*

▸ dry up **dry up** *Some of the rivers have dried up, as they are experiencing a long dry season.*

▸ move earth **deposit sth, erode sth** *The river has deposited over 2m of sand, gravel and alluvial silt.*

▸ start/finish somewhere **drain, rise** *The estuary has a lot of silt from the river draining into it.* ● *The river rises high in the Cairngorm mountains and reaches the sea at Aberdeen.*

▸ get wider/narrower **narrow, widen** *Where the river widens lies an island at its centre.*

road N
a way from one place to another

● adj+N important or busy **busy, main, major** *Note that this is a main road, often with heavy traffic.*

▸ not important or busy **minor, quiet, rural, unclassified, unmade** *The cottage is located in a quiet road in this charming village.*

▸ safe/not safe **dangerous, icy, narrow, safe, steep, wet** *You're on a narrow road with a sheer cliff on your side.*

▸ straight/not straight **straight, twisty, windy** *You will be travelling east on a very straight road.*

▸ with a bad surface **bumpy, dusty, rough** *This small seaside community lies about 10km west, along some fairly rough dirt roads.*

● N+v follow a course **go, head, lead, pass, run** *You eventually join a minor road leading back to the car park.*

▸ connect places **connect, link** *This was the main road linking London and Norwich.*

▸ bend **bend, curve, turn, wind** *Where the road bends sharply to the left, turn right into the gateway.*

▸ divide into two **fork, split** *Just before the railway, the road forks.*

▸ go higher/lower **climb, descend** *After this, the road climbs through tea and coffee plantations.*

▸ become wider/narrower **narrow, widen** *The road narrows and potholes increase, but our driver is patient.*

roar N
a loud sound made by a crowd or by something such as an engine or a storm

● adj+N very loud **almighty, deafening, ear-splitting, full-throated, loud, mighty, thundering, thunderous, tremendous, tumultuous** *The noise of the river is a thunderous roar and truly awe-inspiring.*

▸ not very loud **distant, dull, muffled, muted** *The dull roar of the traffic could be heard all day from the bridge.*

▸ deep **guttural, rumbling, throaty** *The guttural roar of the tractor shatters the peace of the countryside.*

▸ continuous **incessant** *They listen to loud music to drown out the incessant roar of the machines.*

▸ happy **rapturous, triumphant** *She stepped on stage and was greeted by a rapturous roar from the eager crowd.*

● N+of **applause, approval, defiance, delight, disapproval, laughter, rage** *A roar of laughter went up from the audience.*

robbery N
the crime of stealing money or property

● adj+N violent **armed, brutal, knifepoint, terrifying, violent** *This violent robbery was terrifying for customers and staff in the pub at the time.*

▸ failed or possible **alleged, attempted, botched, bungled** *Police are appealing for witnesses after an attempted robbery in the city.*

▸ daring **audacious, daring** *The gang planned a daring robbery of the prestigious train.*

● v+N commit or organize a robbery **commit,**

orchestrate, perpetrate, stage *He was only 17 when the robberies were committed.*
▶ see a robbery **witness** *Anyone who witnessed the robbery is asked to contact detectives.*
▶ stop a robbery **foil** *He became a local hero when he foiled a robbery at his diner.*
▶ investigate a robbery **investigate** *Police investigating a knife-point robbery have issued a picture of a man they are trying to trace.*

role N

1 someone's or something's purpose or job

● adj+N important **big, central, critical, crucial, decisive, dominant, enhanced, essential, fundamental, important, influential, key, lead, major, pivotal, prominent, significant, valuable, vital** *This new harbour played a key role in the supply and repair of military ships.*
▶ not important **diminished, limited, minor, small** *Many studies have shown that material goods play only a minor role in enhancing quality of life.*
▶ main **main, primary, principal** *Although resolving disputes is our primary role, ombudsmen have traditionally made a broader contribution.*
▶ active **active, positive, proactive** *Education can help people play an active role in their communities.*
▶ same/different **different, respective, similar** *We must ensure that individuals are competent to carry out their respective roles.*
▶ including different things **dual, varied, various** *Headteachers of small schools have a dual role, combining class teaching with management.*
▶ traditional **traditional** *He expected her to settle into the traditional role of wife and mother.*
▶ new or present **current, new** *My new role encompasses all management activities.*
▶ possible **future, potential** *These initiatives will help establish the future role of the pharmaceutical profession.*
▶ specific **clear, defined, distinct, specific, unique** *Sport had a specific role to play in this society.*
▶ difficult **challenging, demanding** *Her experience and local knowledge will be invaluable in this challenging role.*
▶ senior **senior** *Rich has taken up a new senior role as group MD.*
▶ types of role **administrative, advisory, caring, functional, managerial, professional, strategic, supervisory** *Ms Dale will stay with the School in a part-time advisory role.*

● n+N **admin, campaigning, coaching, consultancy, consulting, co-ordination, decision-making, enforcement, leadership, liaison, management, marketing, mentoring, monitoring, nursing, teaching, volunteer** *It will provide you with the skills and knowledge for business consultancy roles within IT.*

● v+N have a role **carry out, fill, fulfil, have, occupy, perform, play, take** *Both played key roles in the team's cup final victory.*
accept a role **accept, adopt, assume, move into, settle into, step into, take on, undertake** *The Church must learn to accept a less directly important role in everyday affairs.* ● *Geoff has taken on the role of caring for Jo.*
examine the role of someone or something **assess,**

consider, discuss, evaluate, examine, explore, identify, investigate *The author examines the role of ICT in the tourism industry.*
▶ define or explain the role of someone or something **clarify, define, describe, explain, outline** *The charter defined the roles and powers of the mayor and councillors.*
▶ understand the role of someone or something **acknowledge, recognize, understand** *Librarians must recognize their social role.*
▶ be given a role **be assigned, be given, be thrust into** *In most societies, men and women are assigned different roles.*
▶ emphasize the role of someone or something **emphasize, highlight, stress** *Today's report highlights the role of social inequality in increasing the risk of lung disease.*
▶ extend the role of someone or something **develop, enhance, expand, extend, increase, strengthen** *The regulations should strengthen the educational role of broadcasting.*
▶ exchange or combine roles **combine, reverse** *Tom combined the manager's role with being Secretary of the club.* ● *In this sculpture, the gender roles are reversed.*

2 the character someone plays in a film or show

● adj+N large or important **lead, leading, main, major, principal, starring** *He became well-known through his starring role in the TV series Lovejoy.*
▶ not large or important **minor, small** *The film features Sam Shepherd in a minor role.*
▶ difficult **challenging, demanding** *She has probably the most challenging role as Klara, a troubled intellectual.*

● v+N play a role **act in, have, perform, play, reprise, star in** *Actor Parry Shen plays the lead role of Ben in the film.* ● *She reprised her role as the overburdened mother in 'Cheaper By The Dozen 2'.*
▶ be given a role **be cast in, be given, get, land** *Following a string of commercials, she landed a role in the feature film Annie.*
▶ accept a role **accept, slip into, take, take on** *In accepting a role that was coveted by dozens of actresses, she felt considerable pressure to succeed.*

romance N

an exciting romantic relationship

● adj+N exciting **fairytale, heady, passionate, steamy, torrid** *This story of desperate love behind bars features intense drama and steamy romance.*
▶ sudden or short **brief, whirlwind** *They had a whirlwind romance, but the relationship broke down within a year.*
▶ sad or unsuccessful **bittersweet, doomed, failed, ill-fated, tragic** *It is the story of a doomed romance between a nobleman and a beautiful peasant girl.*
▶ new **budding, burgeoning** *The budding romance between the two teenagers blossomed.*
▶ involving young people **teen, teenage** *This spirited drama perfectly captures the excitement and passion of teen romance.*

romantic ADJ

connected to love and the excitement of love

● adv+ADJ very **beautifully, deeply, gloriously,**

highly, incredibly, irresistibly, terribly, truly, very, wildly, wonderfully Choosing to marry abroad can be wildly romantic, not to mention cheaper.
▸ excessively **hopelessly, impossibly, overly** You often have very naive, idealistic, or overly romantic attitudes towards people.
▸ rather **rather, somewhat** The house has a rather romantic history.
▸ in a mysterious or intense way **darkly, intensely** The songs have doomed, darkly romantic lyrics.
▸ without embarrassment **overtly, unashamedly** There's something to be said for a film that is so unashamedly romantic.

room N
the possibility for something to exist or happen

● N+for flexibility **flexibility, manoeuvre** Forcing doctors to tell the police would leave no room for manoeuvre.
▸ individual expression **creativity, experimentation, imagination, improvisation, individuality** Academic research must allow room for creativity and unexpected discovery.
▸ improvement **improvement** This was just a first attempt, so there's plenty of room for improvement.
▸ optimism **complacency, optimism** There is no room for complacency in a highly competitive market.
▸ misunderstanding **ambiguity, confusion, misinterpretation, misunderstanding** His address put across the message in a way that left no room for misunderstandings.
▸ discussion or compromise **compromise, debate, disagreement, negotiation** The political atmosphere is absolutely toxic, with very little room for compromise on either side.
▸ doubt **doubt** His remarks left little room for doubt about what he had decided.
▸ error **error** Everything happens live, which leaves little room for error.
▸ growth **expansion, growth** Adolescents must have room for emotional growth, yet know their parents are behind them.

root N
someone's or something's origins, background, or basic cause [usually plural]

● v+N find someone's or something's roots **discover, explore, rediscover, research, revisit, uncover** This is the story of the author's 25,000 mile journey to rediscover her roots in Ethiopia. ● The Family History Club is an informal gathering of those researching their family roots.
▸ have roots **have, trace** The Masons is a secretive society that traces its roots to medieval craft associations in Britain.
▸ forget your roots **betray, forget** What a shame he betrayed his musical roots in pursuit of money and fame.
▸ attack the roots **address, attack, strike at, tackle** A more holistic approach to tackling the roots of racism is needed.

● N+of **bitterness, conflict, crisis, evil, oppression, problem, racism, terrorism** We need to address the roots of the problem, not least by challenging economic inequalities.

rooted ADJ
based on or influenced by something

● adv+ADJ strongly **deep, deeply, firmly, profoundly, securely, solidly, soundly, strongly** His work is firmly rooted in the tradition of English landscape paintings.
▸ partly **partly** The legends surrounding Glastonbury's past are partly rooted in fact.
▸ basically **fundamentally, ultimately** His unionism is ultimately rooted in a wider tradition of conservative political philosophy.
▸ having a particular type of basis **biologically, culturally, historically, locally, socially** These studies suggest that severe obsessions and compulsions are biologically rooted.

rough ADJ
not complete or exact

● ADJ+n indication **guide, guideline, idea, indication** As a rough guide, we find that the cost of data handling is typically 10–15% of a total budget.
▸ estimate **calculation, estimate, estimation, guess** They will produce a rough estimate of what they think the work will cost.
▸ equivalent **approximation, equivalent, translation** A rough translation for the term is 'pawn shop'.
▸ drawing or writing **draft, outline, sketch** This documuent is a rough outline of some of the discussions we have had.

route N
1 a way that something or someone travels

● adj+N main **arterial, main, major** This used to be the main route from London to Nottinghamshire and Derbyshire.
▸ busy **busy, congested** Drivers using congested routes would pay the highest tolls.
▸ quick or easy **easy, fast, quick, short** The hovercraft service from Southsea is the quickest route to the Isle of Wight.
▸ direct **direct, through** The rail company had no direct through route from Birmingham to Bristol.
▸ not quick or direct **circuitous, long, roundabout, scenic, tortuous** This meant that mail had to go via Royston – a circuitous route. ● From here, you can take the scenic mountain route to Glenelg or you can continue along the A87.
▸ different **alternate, alternative, different** When walking with a dog, look for alternative routes around fields with animals.
▸ suggested or planned **intended, planned, proposed, suggested** The intelligent navigation system will guide you back on to the planned route.
▸ best or usual **obvious, popular, preferred, recommended, usual** Book early to ensure your preferred holiday route and starting point.
▸ marked or fixed **designated, marked, signposted, waymarked** Problems normally occur when helicopters stray from designated routes.
▸ circular **circular** Riders take a circular route which passes through many picturesque villages.
▸ possible **possible** It is important to have a map which covers all possible descent routes.
▸ new/old **ancient, existing, new, original** There's a new bit of dual carriageway, with the original route running to the east of this.

▶ strategic **strategic** *The M40 is a strategic route between London and Birmingham.*

● v+N take a route **climb, follow, rejoin, retrace, take, travel, use, walk** *The ride follows an easy route to a quaint country tearoom.* ● *Charity collectors walk the entire route collecting donations.*

▶ plan or choose a route **choose, plan, select** *You can find further information on planning your route using public transport online.*

▶ show or describe a route **describe, indicate, map out, mark, plot, show, trace** *Pupils are asked to plot their routes to school on a large map.*

▶ find a route **discover, establish, find, identify, navigate** *Most people, given a current map, can find a route that suits them.*

▶ explore a route **explore, survey** *This is ideal for mountaineers wanting to explore more adventurous routes of ascent.*

▶ be on someone's route **block, line, obstruct** *Thousands of people lined the route to the cemetery.*

▶ offer a route **operate, ply** *Highland Country Buses also operate many local routes.*

2 a way of doing something that produces a particular result

● adj+N quick or easy **direct, easy, fast, fast-track, principal, quick, short** *Penny has not had an easy route to the top.*

▶ usual **existing, main, normal, principal, traditional, usual** *The normal route is surgery.* ● *Running one's own business is a traditional route for migrant communities to better themselves.*

▶ good or best **favoured, obvious, preferred, recommended** *The government has made clear that it sees work, not benefits, as the preferred route out of poverty.*

▶ different **alternative, different, possible** *A number of possible design routes were examined.*

▶ types of route **educational, vocational** *There are a range of employment-based and educational routes into the teaching profession.*

● v+N take a route **choose, explore, follow, pursue, take** *You may also choose to pursue a clinical route by completing the Dispensing Opticians qualification.* ● *The musical follows the fortunes of Percival and Rooster, who are taking different routes through life.*

▶ offer a route **offer, provide** *The Rural Charter provides a route for companies to make a real contribution to rural life.*

▶ find a route **establish, find, identify** *Others found a route to the public sphere through voluntary work.*

▶ N+to success **prosperity, salvation, stardom, success, the top, victory** *For many young artists, this prize might be the route to stardom.*

▶ knowledge or power **empowerment, enlightenment, independence** *I believe the only real route to empowerment is enabling people to help themselves.*

▶ happiness **happiness** *Convention tells us the route to happiness is having children.*

▶ education or employment **accreditation, employment, qualification, self-employment** *Other changes include more use of modules and flexible routes to qualification.*

routine N
someone's usual way of doing things

● adj+N usual **familiar, normal, usual** *Respite services are provided to give carers a break from the usual routine.*

▶ boring **boring, dreary, dull, humdrum, monotonous, predictable, repetitive** *She wants to escape from the boring routine of work.*

▶ regular **day-to-day, everyday, regular, daily, weekly etc** *He has a nightly routine of checking locks and closing doors.*

▶ strict **rigid, strict** *By adhering to a strict routine, the risk of accidents is reduced.*

▶ busy **hectic** *She is settling into into the hectic routine of having a newborn baby.*

● n+N at a particular time of day **bedtime, night-time, morning, evening etc** *I was so determined to stop drinking I changed my whole weekend routine.*

▶ exercise **exercise, fitness, workout** *This should be part of a daily fitness routine.*

▶ cleaning **cleansing, disinfection, hygiene** *Use a face-mask occasionally alongside your normal cleansing routine.*

● v+N establish a routine **establish, get into, settle into** *Help your toddler learn to go to bed by establishing a bedtime routine.*

▶ disturb a routine **disrupt, disturb, interrupt, upset** *The building work will inevitably disrupt the normal routines of the office.*

● N+n task **chore, task** *He is able to live independently, completing many routine tasks without the help of a carer.*

▶ check **check, check-up, examination, inspection, monitoring, scan, screening, surveillance, testing** *I went for a routine check-up with my midwife and was told to go home and rest.*

▶ repair or care **cleaning, maintenance, repairs, servicing** *The rent normally includes the cost of routine repairs and maintenance.*

▶ visit **appointment, follow-up, patrol** *The clinician will then schedule routine follow-up appointments.*

▶ question **enquiry** *With fewer routine enquiries to handle, staff can now concentrate on more complex issues.*

▶ immunization **immunization, vaccination** *Pet insurance will generally not cover the cost of routine vaccinations.*

row N
an argument, or a serious disagreement

● adj+N angry **bitter, fierce, furious, heated, stand-up** *The two men had a furious row and never spoke to each other again.*

▶ very bad or serious **almighty, big, major, unholy, unseemly** *During an almighty row, the girl smacked her mother.*

▶ getting worse **escalating, growing** *The Union chief is at the centre of a growing row as firefighters get ready to strike.*

▶ continuing **endless, long-running, simmering** *There was no-one to back her up in the endless rows with her parents.*

▶ drunken **drunken** *Police tried to break up a drunken row between her and another woman.*

▶ types of row **diplomatic, political** *The extradition case erupted into a full-scale political row.*

- v+N start a row **ignite, provoke, reignite, spark, trigger** *The news sparked a national row and Government ministers promised to examine the case.*
- ▶ have a row **get into, have** *He got into a row with the landlady, and she threw him out.*
- ▶ make a row worse **escalate, fuel** *His comments will fuel the damaging row in Whitehall.*
- ▶ help stop a row **break up, defuse** *The Government is attempting to defuse the row over faith-based schools.*

- N+v start **blow up, break out, ensue, erupt** *A new row erupted last night over the lack of European Union aid for Scottish fisherman.*
- ▶ threaten to start **be brewing, be looming** *A major diplomatic row was brewing between India and America.*
- ▶ get worse **escalate, flare up** *The threat of this row escalating into an embarrassing incident has been averted.*
- ▶ continue **be raging, rumble on** *The road has been completed now, but the row still rumbles on.*

rub V
press and move your hands over a surface

- adv+V gently **gently, lightly, softly** *Gently rub your stomach as it can help relax the muscles.*
- ▶ firmly **briskly, firmly, hard, roughly, vigorously** *She vigorously rubbed her hands together muttering 'Brrrr, it's cold'.*
- ▶ all the time **constantly, continuously, repeatedly** *She developed a habit of constantly rubbing her face.*

rubbish N
1 things thrown away because they are no longer useful

- adj+N unwanted **unwanted** *The park had been used as a place to leave unwanted rubbish.*
- ▶ unpleasant **stinking, unsightly** *Beach rubbish is unsightly and can be dangerous to sea creatures.*
- ▶ not collected **uncollected** *Litter and uncollected rubbish create a perception that a street is uncared for.*
- ▶ possible/not possible to recycle etc **biodegradable, burnable, compostable, non-biodegradable, non-recyclable, recyclable** *You will be given two sacks: a black one for rubbish and a clear one for recyclable rubbish.*
- ▶ from a particular place **domestic, garden, household** *Fire extinguishers must not be disposed of with domestic rubbish.*

- v+N throw away **chuck** INFORMAL, **deposit, discard, dispose of, dump, throw away, tip** *But we are running out of space to dump our rubbish.*
- ▶ recycle **compost, recycle, reuse** *People in Wales are playing their part in recycling their rubbish.*
- ▶ burn **burn, incinerate** *It is permissible to burn garden rubbish.*
- ▶ bury **bury** *We are running out of space to bury our rubbish.*
- ▶ take away **clear, collect, remove** *Our task was to clear rubbish from the river.*

2 things that have no meaning or value

- adj+N complete **absolute, unadulterated, utter** *Some people say it's hard to mix with students on other courses, although I think this is utter rubbish!*

- stupid **inane, trite, vacuous** *Most older people think children's television today is inane rubbish.*
- ▶ trying to seem superior **patronizing, pretentious** *More cynical critics have suggested the film is nothing more than pretentious rubbish.*
- ▶ worthless **useless, worthless** *He just keeps churning out the same old worthless rubbish.*

- v+N **peddle, spout, talk** *Is he being deliberately dishonest or just talking rubbish?*

rude ADJ
not polite

- adv+ADJ very **abominably, downright, exceptionally, extremely, incredibly, plain, so, terribly, very** *Although appearing to behave as an impeccable hostess, she is actually abominably rude.* ● *Sending an unsolicited email to somebody calling them names is downright rude.*
- ▶ rather **a little, quite, rather, slightly, somewhat** *Blowing your nose in public is seen as rather rude in Japan.*

- v+ADJ **appear, be, be considered, seem, sound** *It is considered rude to cancel a meeting at the last minute.*

- and/or disrespectful **discourteous, dismissive, disrespectful, impolite, insolent** *Frankly, I found the staff insolent and rude.*
- ▶ unpleasant **abrupt, arrogant, impatient, obnoxious, sarcastic** *He was tired of solicitors being described as arrogant, rude, and patronizing.*
- ▶ insulting **abusive, insulting, offensive** *Letters that we consider to be rude and abusive will not receive a response.*
- ▶ thoughtless **ignorant, inconsiderate, thoughtless** *The police officer said that rude and thoughtless drivers were unfortunately part of the job.*
- ▶ unkind **hurtful, unfriendly, unhelpful, unkind** *There are people who use 'honesty' as a reason for simply being rude and hurtful.*
- ▶ crude **crude, lewd, uncouth, vulgar** *Account holders are asked to report any rude or lewd emails which get through the system.*

ruin V
destroy or severely damage something

- adv+V completely **completely, hopelessly, totally, utterly** *When there are floods, the rice crop is completely ruined.*
- ▶ permanently **forever, irreparably, irretrievably, permanently** *He felt that his life was ruined irretrievably.*
- ▶ partly **partially, partly** *They returned to find the city in chaos and their home partially ruined.*

Usage *Ruin* is usually passive in these combinations.

- ▶ almost **almost, nearly, practically** *I nearly ruined everyone's day by making a serious miscalculation.*
- ▶ eventually **effectively, eventually, potentially, ultimately** *Wells writes that technology will ultimately ruin human society.*
- ▶ unfortunately **sadly** *It was a pleasant spot, sadly ruined by rubbish which hadn't been picked up.*
- ▶ in a particular way **economically, financially** *Farmers are being ruined financially by falling livestock prices.*

- V+n chance **chance** *This ruined any chance I had of getting my work done on time.*
▶ life **life** *Terry goes into graphic detail about his addiction and how it almost ruined his life.*
▶ career **career, livelihood** *Companies should be held to account for decisions that ruin workers' livelihoods.*
▶ reputation **credibility, reputation** *He must be fully aware that serious allegations can ruin a person's professional reputation.*
▶ pleasure **appetite, enjoyment, surprise** *If I told you now, it would ruin the surprise.*
▶ everything **everything** *A tragic accident ruined everything she had worked for.*

ruin N

the remaining parts of a severely damaged building
[usually plural]

- adj+N old **ancient, prehistoric, venerable** *Remains of the ancient ruins can also be found underwater.*
▶ attractive **atmospheric, evocative, impressive, magnificent, majestic, picturesque, romantic** *The gardens were created around the romantic ruins of a medieval vicarage.*
▶ in bad condition **crumbling, mouldering, shattered** *Amid the shattered ruins were personal clothing and cooking utensils.*
▶ damaged by fire **blackened, burning, smoking, smouldering** *They were dismayed to see the village was now a collection of blackened ruins.*
▶ in good condition **well-preserved** *The Gedi National Park protects the well-preserved ruins of a Swahili city.*
▶ types of ruin **monastic, Roman, Mayan etc** *Islands with their monastic ruins are often still places of pilgrimage.* • *Crete boasts impressive Minoan ruins at Knossos and Phaestos.*

rule N

1 a statement explaining what someone can or cannot do

- adj+N strict **absolute, hard and fast, restrictive, rigid, strict, stringent, tough** *There are no hard and fast rules as to how risk assessments should be carried out.* • *In racing, there are strict rules about the length, width and weight of your boat.*
▶ basic or important **basic, cardinal, fundamental, ground** *Many consumers still don't follow basic hygiene rules.*

> You can also refer to a very important basic rule as *the golden rule*: *The golden rule is that you can make good soup only from good ingredients.*

▶ general **general** *Obviously, every situation is different, but there are some general rules to follow.*
▶ specific or detailed **detailed, specific** *These principles appeal to basic concepts rather than spelling out detailed rules.*
▶ complex **complex** *This is a simple guide to the complex new rules governing the licensing of bars and clubs.*
▶ clear or simple **clear, simple** *It is important to set clear ground rules at the start.*
▶ usual **normal, usual** *Each match was played according to normal indoor cricket rules.*
▶ relevant **applicable, relevant** *Each chapter presents the applicable grammar rule followed by examples.*
▶ existing **current, existing** *Under current rules they*

must wait six months before they are eligible for benefits.
▶ agreed **accepted, agreed, defined** *Their aim was to make sure countries abided by agreed rules.*
▶ new or different **different, new, special** *Click this link for a summary of the new pension rules.* • *In some cases special rules apply which mean that backpay can be claimed.*
▶ fair/not fair **arbitrary, fair, unfair** *Good manners, unlike the arbitrary rules of etiquette, do not change with the times.*
▶ not officially stated **unspoken, unwritten** *There is an unwritten wedding rule that no one should look more beautiful than the bride.*
▶ types of rule **disciplinary, fiscal, grammatical, legal, moral, procedural, statutory** *The vast majority of the grammatical rules used by Shakespeare still apply now.*

- v+N obey a rule **abide by, apply, follow, implement, obey, observe, play by, respect, satisfy, stick to, uphold** *You need to make sure that the children obey the school rules.*
▶ disobey a rule **breach, break, contravene, flout, ignore, infringe, violate** *Those who persist in breaking the club rules will be asked to leave.*
▶ make someone obey a rule **adopt, apply, enforce, implement, impose, uphold** *Schools must set and enforce clear rules on lateness, absence and bullying.*
▶ create or state a rule **define, establish, fix, formulate, introduce, lay down, lay out, set, set out, specify** *We are merely seeking justice within the rules laid down by the legal system.*
▶ change a rule **alter, amend, change, harmonize, modify, reform, revise, rewrite, simplify** *We propose to amend the rules for elections to the Assembly.*
▶ make a rule less strict **bend, relax, stretch** *She warned her not to bend the rules for her own benefit.*
▶ make a rule more strict **tighten** *Should trade rules be tightened to protect poorer countries?*
▶ explain a rule **clarify, explain, interpret** *The booklet clearly explains the rules of the game.*
▶ suggest a rule **propose** *We are proposing new rules on the disclosure of personal information.*

2 control of a place by a particular person, country or group

- adj+N by another country **colonial, British, Spanish etc** *They fought to free Mozambique from Portuguese colonial rule.* • *The island has been under French rule for 235 years.*
▶ by a particular regime **authoritarian, communist, military** *After half a century of authoritarian rule, we stand at the crossroad to democracy.*

rule V

1 officially control or govern a country or area

- adv+V well **justly, wisely** *He ruled wisely as King for many years.*
▶ not well **harshly, unjustly** *The Spanish viceroy fled to Panama, where he ruled harshly until his death in 1821.*
▶ with someone else **jointly** *Severus ruled jointly with his eldest son Caracalla.*
▶ in name/in reality **effectively, nominally** *The tsars effectively ruled over most of the territory belonging to what is now the Republic of Kazakhstan.* • *The*

Roman Empire was divided into provinces nominally ruled by the Senate.

2 make and announce a decision

- adv+V in a definite or permanent way **categorically, conclusively, definitively, explicitly, specifically** *The Court has already ruled definitively against the company on this issue.*
- ▸ rightly/wrongly **rightly, wrongly** *The government's actions were rightly ruled unconstitutional by the Supreme Court.*
- ▸ with everyone in agreement **unanimously** *Five Law Lords unanimously ruled that the case should be heard in the UK.*
- ▸ in a way that causes disagreement **controversially, harshly** *The pass was controversially ruled as offside.*

rule out PHR VB
stop considering something as a possibility

- adv+V in a clear or definite way **categorically, conclusively, definitely, definitively, explicitly, flatly, specifically** *The US has not categorically ruled out a nuclear attack.*
- ▸ completely **completely, entirely** *He completely rules out the notion that a woman could be the killer.*
- ▸ in practice **effectively** *This result effectively rules out a diagnosis of congestive heart failure.*
- ▸ almost **virtually** *He suffered an awful injury that virtually ruled him out for the rest of the season.*

- V+n **move, option, possibility** *The management have still not ruled out the possibility that he will sign a new contract.*

ruling N
a decision by a court or authority

- adj+N important because it changes things **ground-breaking, historic, landmark** *A landmark ruling has named a gay man as the sole heir to his late partner's estate.*
- ▸ definite and absolute **authoritative, binding, definitive** *The courts' rulings are binding.*
- ▸ agreed by all authorities **unanimous** *This unanimous ruling meant that the British government would have to redraft the law.*
- ▸ in someone's favour **favourable** *He obtained a favourable ruling from the Solicitor General.*
- ▸ that causes disagreement **absurd, controversial** *The Law Lords made a controversial ruling allowing the withdrawal of food and water from a patient.*
- ▸ temporary **interim, preliminary, provisional** *The case was referred to the European Court for a preliminary ruling.*
- ▸ legal **court, judicial, legal** *She fears that her claim is caught up in the confusion following the latest legal ruling.*

- v+N give a ruling **issue, make** *The court issued a historic ruling that schools must take steps to eliminate harassment on the grounds of sexuality.*
- ▸ disagree with and change a ruling **overturn, quash, reverse** *The justices voted by 8–1 to overturn a lower court ruling.*
- ▸ confirm a ruling **confirm, enforce, uphold** *The Court of Appeal has upheld a ruling against the Board.*
- ▸ consider changing a ruling **reconsider** *It was*

agreed that the Committee would reconsider this ruling.

- ▸ obey a ruling **accept, follow, obey** *The European Court can only work if member states agree to accept its rulings.*
- ▸ ask for a ruling to be changed **appeal, appeal against, challenge** *The government may appeal the ruling.*
- ▸ be glad about a ruling **hail, welcome** *She hailed the ruling as a victory for unmarried women.*
- ▸ be angry about a ruling **condemn** *Low pay campaigners have condemned the ruling.*
- ▸ ignore a ruling **disregard, ignore** *They deliberately ignored the ruling which the court made in August.*
- ▸ wait for a ruling **await** *Two requests are awaiting rulings by the Information Commissioner.*
- ▸ get a ruling in your favour **win** *The family won a ruling in the High Court to have the inquest verdict quashed.*

rumour N
unofficial information that may not be true

- adj+N false or untrue **baseless, false, groundless, unfounded, untrue** *Unfounded rumours of a financial link between his company and the campaign were circulated.*
- ▸ unpleasant or malicious **defamatory, malicious, nasty, scandalous, scurrilous, ugly, unkind, vicious, vile** *Malicious rumours from government sources have been spread by the mass media.*
- ▸ shocking **alarming, disturbing, scandalous** *He reported alarming rumours of a possible English attack on France.*
- ▸ not confirmed **unconfirmed, unsubstantiated** *There had been an unconfirmed rumour of him being seen alive in Scotland.*
- ▸ common or persistent **persistent, rife** *Rumours are rife that they are thinking of moving to LA.*
- ▸ exaggerated or silly **exaggerated, ridiculous, wild** *She was quick to dismiss these as ridiculous rumours.*
- ▸ vague **vague** *Report anything suspicious to the police, but only facts, not vague rumours.*
- ▸ in the press **press, tabloid** *Tabloid rumours that she was to rejoin the band proved baseless.*

- v+N stop a rumour **counter, dispel, quash, quell, scotch, squash** *The principal quashed rumours of racist activity at the college.*
- ▸ deny a rumour **contradict, counter, deny, discount, dismiss, refute, rubbish, slam** *I must counter these absurd rumours with the actual facts.* • *She has denied rumours that she will perform at the Commonwealth Games.*
- ▸ cause a rumour to start **fuel, prompt, spark** *She was photographed wearing an engagement ring, sparking rumours that she and Mr Doherty are engaged.*
- ▸ spread a rumour **circulate, propagate, spread** *She accused the other candidates of spreading scurrilous rumours to scupper her campaign.*
- ▸ hear a rumour **hear** *I heard rumours that someone was trying to get me disqualified.*
- ▸ confirm a rumour **confirm, substantiate** *He confirmed rumours that he will be making a sequel to the film.*
- ▸ be the subject of rumours **be dogged by** *The coupl*

have been dogged by rumours that their marriage is on the rocks.

● N+v be common **abound, circulate, float around, fly, go around, spread, sweep sth, swirl around** *Rumours abound that they had an affair during the shooting.* ● *There's a rumour going around that Kate has been working on a new album.*

▶ continue or return **persist, resurface** *But rumours persisted that he was somehow responsible for her disappearance.*

▶ begin **begin, start, surface** *As time passed, the questions and rumours began.*

▶ be about someone or something **surround** *Rumours were already surrounding the fate of the Princess.*

▶ say something **suggest** *But later rumours suggested he had been seen in France.*

▶ come from somewhere **emanate from** *The leaks and rumours emanating from Washington were not encouraging.*

● and/or things which may not be true **conjecture, gossip, half-truth, hearsay, innuendo, speculation, supposition, tittle-tattle, whisper** *Avoid accusations based on rumours or hearsay.*

▶ things which are not true **disinformation, lies, misinformation, myth, untruths** *Rumours and disinformation flourish during a conflict.*

run V
control and organize something such as a business, organization, or event

● adv+V well **efficiently, properly, smoothly, successfully, well** *Many thanks to all of the volunteers who helped make the competition run smoothly.*

▶ by a particular group **independently, privately, professionally** *Most day nurseries are privately-run.*

▶ by more than one person or group **jointly** *The course is run jointly by The University of Stirling and The University of Dundee.*

● V+n company or organization **business, clinic, club, company, school, shop** *Until recently, she ran her own travel agency business.*

▶ course or class **class, course, seminar, session, workshop** *We run workshops to help you improve your study skills.*

▶ event **competition, event** *Let us know if you want help with running an event in your area.*

▶ project or scheme **campaign, programme, project, scheme, service** *If your company runs this scheme, ask your human resources department for a form to fill in.*

run into PHR VB
start to have

▶ V+n problems **difficulty, glitch, obstacle, problems, snag, trouble** *However, the idea has already run into trouble with some councillors.*

▶ opposition **controversy, flak, opposition** *Even before the company announced the plans, it ran into controversy.*

run up PHR VB
get into a situation where you owe money

● V+n **bill, debt, losses, overdraft** *Ron proceeded to run up a huge phone bill which he never paid.*

rural ADJ
relating to or in the countryside

● adv+ADJ mostly **essentially, largely, mainly, mostly, overwhelmingly, predominantly** *Aylesbury Vale is a predominantly rural area.*

▶ very or completely **decidedly, deeply, entirely, exclusively, genuinely, purely, truly, wholly** *The holiday will appeal to those seeking a decidedly rural atmosphere.*

▶ in a pleasant way **delightfully** *This is a delightfully rural village, nestling amid lush green fields and wooded valleys.*

rush V
hurry to do something

● adv+V **blindly, eagerly, frantically, furiously, headlong, hurriedly, madly, suddenly, wildly** *She advised me not to rush headlong into anything.* ● *The team rushes hurriedly to prepare the rocket for launch.*

rush N
1 a sudden movement forward or a hurry to do something

● adj+N intense **desperate, frantic, frenzied, hectic, mad, unseemly** *We left in a frenzied rush because I set our alarm for 8 am instead of 6 am.*

▶ sudden **sudden** *Why this sudden rush to go there?*

▶ last-minute **last-minute, late** *Order early to avoid the last-minute rush.*

● v+N cause a rush **cause, precipitate, prompt, provoke, spark, trigger** *The heatwave has sparked a mad rush to buy barbecues and sun loungers.*

▶ avoid the rush **avoid, beat, escape** *Beat the Christmas rush – buy your calenders here!*

▶ stop the rush **halt, stem** *It may be too late to halt the rush towards climate catastrophe.*

▶ observe a rush **observe, witness** *This term, we have witnessed the great rush to find accommodation for next year.*

▶ expect a rush **expect** *The Inspector said they were expecting a large rush of traffic heading out of town.*

2 a sudden strong emotion

● adj+N emotional **breathless, euphoric, exhilarating, giddy, heady, impetuous** *I felt the heady rush of new love once again.*

▶ sudden **sudden** *She felt a sudden rush of hope when she heard his name.*

● v+N feel a rush **experience, feel, get** *I experienced a rush of anger which I found difficult to control.*

▶ cause a rush **cause, trigger** *Frustration produces anxiety, which triggers an adrenaline rush.*

● N+of particular emotion **energy, enthusiasm, excitement, happiness, love, relief, warmth** *I got a rush of excitement and a burst of energy and started walking much faster.*

▶ feelings **emotion, feelings** *Many children can be disturbed by this rush of feelings.*

▶ physical reaction **adrenalin, blood** *The rush of blood returning to the feet makes them feel warm to the touch.*

sacrifice V

give up something important or valuable

- adv+V **gladly, willingly** *He would have gladly sacrificed his life if he thought it would save Kathryn.*
- V+n personal asset **career, comfort, freedom, happiness, liberty, life** *He is the one who sacrifices his happiness to make sure I am happy.*
- ▶ good quality **accuracy, individuality, integrity, performance, quality** *All this is achieved without sacrificing the individuality of your company or its products.*

sacrifice N

the act of giving up something important or valuable

- adj+N big **big, considerable, enormous, great, huge, major, real** *History abounds with tales of men and women who made great sacrifices for love.*
- ▶ small **little, small** *There are small sacrifices that can be made to save money.*
- ▶ leading to death **final, supreme, ultimate** *These are the widows of soldiers who made the supreme sacrifice.*
- ▶ unselfish or good **courageous, heroic, noble, selfless** *Thanks to their courageous, selfless sacrifices, I was born and raised as a free, equal citizen.*
- ▶ personal **own, personal, self** *My act of self-sacrifice impresses my shipmates.*

saddened ADJ

sad

- adv+ADJ very **deeply, extremely, greatly, really INFORMAL, very** *The Prime Minister said he was deeply saddened by her death.*
- ▶ rather **quite, rather, somewhat** *We are somewhat saddened by this anti-French propaganda.*
- ADJ+by **death, loss, news, passing** *I have been deeply saddened by the loss of my friend.*
- ADJ+infinitive find out **hear, learn, read, see** *I was saddened to hear she had breast cancer.*
- ▶ report **announce, report** *We are saddened to announce that our club president has died.*
- and/or **angered, appalled, disappointed, shocked, surprised** *Police working on the investigation were shocked and saddened by the suffering this baby must have endured.*

sadness N

a feeling of being unhappy

- adj+N great **deep, extreme, great, immense, intense, much, overwhelming, profound, terrible** *Dona Rosita is a curious play in that it combines profound sadness with light comedy.*
- ▶ real **genuine, real** *The shock and the sadness is very real.*
- v+N express sadness **be tinged with, express, show** *His voice is tinged with sadness when he talks about his days as a hunter.* • *In her grief, Petra cannot find words to express her sadness.*
- ▶ feel sadness **ache with, be filled with, be overwhelmed with/by, experience, feel** *Under pale moonlight, filled with sadness, a tear rolls down her cheek.*
- ▶ cause sadness **bring, cause** *The war brought sadness and disruption to so many homes.*
- n+of+N **hint, note, tinge, touch** *I felt a tinge of sadness as we left Lisbon – I'd had a great time.*
- and/or bad feelings **anger, anguish, despair, frustration, gloom, grief, guilt, hopelessness, loneliness, longing, regret, sorrow, tear** *The closure of the factory has been greeted with a mixture of anger and sadness.*
- ▶ good feelings **happiness, joy** *We have journeyed together through times of joy and sadness.*

safe ADJ

protected from harm or not likely to cause harm

- adv+ADJ very or totally **absolutely, completely, entirely, extremely, perfectly, remarkably, totally, truly, very** *The Minister announced that GM food was perfectly safe.*
- ▶ fairly **comparatively, fairly, pretty INFORMAL, quite, reasonably, relatively** *Walking appears to be a relatively safe means of travel.*
- ▶ as part of its basic qualities **inherently, intrinsically** *These stores are provided with ventilation, artificial lighting and fire detection equipment that are intrinsically safe.*
- ▶ in a particular way **clinically, ecologically, electrically, environmentally** *The cleaning products we use are environmentally safe and biodegradable.*
- v+ADJ feel or seem safe **appear, feel, seem** *I went into a church where I felt safe.*
- ▶ be or become safe **be, become, get, prove** *As long as everyone is safe, I'm happy.* • *Nuclear waste is highly dangerous and can take tens of thousands of years to become safe.*
- ▶ stay safe **remain, stay** *We should teach our children how to stay safe on and near roads.*
- ▶ consider something safe **consider sth, deem sth** *The insulin was tested on animals and deemed safe.*
- ▶ say that something is safe **declare sth** *Forensic work cannot begin until the building has been made safe.*
- ▶ make something safe **make sth, render sth** *Several explosive devices were rendered safe by the mine disposal officers.*
- ▶ keep something safe **keep sth** *The Child Protection legislation is aimed at ensuring that children are kept safe.*
- ADJ+from **attack, crime, danger, harm, terrorism, threat** *It is a continuing struggle to keep our children safe from the dangers of drugs.*
- and/or of a person **happy, sound** *Nicolette arrived safe and sound, if slightly delayed.*
- ▶ of a method or product **affordable, cheap, clean, convenient, effective, efficient, hygienic, quick,**

reliable *Now, people have safe, clean water right in the heart of their village.*

▶ of a place or environment **accessible, caring, comfortable, friendly, secure, supportive, warm** *It is important to provide a safe and secure environment for the staff to park their vehicles.*

▶ of an activity **easy, enjoyable, healthy** *Walking to school is a safe and healthy option.*

safety N

the fact that something is safe

● adj+N of a group **child, community, consumer, passenger, pedestrian, public** *Does this man pose a threat to public safety?*

▶ of an individual **own, personal** *Never put your personal safety at risk.*

▶ better **better, enhanced** *For even better safety, consider using a wooden board as a base for each firework.*

▶ more **added, additional, extra, greater, more** *These devices are designed for greater patient safety.*

▶ complete **absolute, complete, maximum, perfect, total** *You can see whole families out on their bikes in complete safety.*

▶ relative **comparative, reasonable, relative** *Those who could left the city for the comparative safety of the countryside.*

▶ general **basic, general, overall** *The overall safety of the drug is still being tested.*

▶ future **future, long-term** *Our job is to develop a long-term safety strategy for the rail industry.*

▶ at work **occupational, workplace, work-related** *I deal with the occupational safety of personnel working offshore.*

▶ types of safety **clinical, drug, environmental, fire, food, nuclear, physical, road, structural** *There is no environmental safety information on 95 per cent of the chemicals on the market.*

● v+N ensure someone or something's safety **assure, ensure, guarantee, maintain, protect, safeguard, secure** *It is your responsibility to maintain and ensure the safety of all pipes and equipment.*

▶ risk someone or something's safety **affect, compromise, disregard, endanger, jeopardize, prejudice, risk, sacrifice, threaten, undermine** *Some people are willing to risk their own safety to help others.*

▶ improve safety **boost, enhance, improve, increase, maximize, promote** *Quite rightly, the rules are primarily to do with maximizing safety on the race.*

▶ assess something's safety **assess, check, evaluate, monitor, test** *The Fire Service carry out free home safety checks, where they assess fire safety in people's homes.*

▶ worry about someone's safety **be concerned about, fear for, worry about** *Residents are very concerned about the speed of traffic and rightly fear for the safety of pedestrians.*

▶ try to make something safe **address, consider, manage, tackle** *Hospital plans must address safety for staff, patients and visitors.*

N+n check **assessment, check, inspection** *Safety checks showed that lives are being put at risk by parents fitting child seats in the front of their vehicles.*

measure **feature, measure, precaution, procedure,**

system *We have installed carbon monoxide detectors as a safety precaution.*

▶ hazard **hazard, risk** *The small quantities of mica being handled shouldn't pose a safety hazard if handled carefully by adults.*

▶ rules or law **law, legislation, policy, regulation, requirement, rule** *Non-compliance with the safety regulations is a criminal offence.*

▶ information or advice **advice, guidelines, information, recommendation, tip** INFORMAL *People are being denied vital safety information.*

▶ course of action **campaign, initiative** *We feel it is important to organize road safety initiatives all year round.*

▶ issue **issue, matter** *It's not a safety issue, it's an image issue.*

▶ reasons or concerns **concerns, considerations, implications, reasons** *If, for safety reasons, you cannot have a pond, consider a bog garden.*

▶ level or standard **levels, limits, standards** *The nuclear regulatory regime imposes stringent safety requirements on the industry.*

saga N INFORMAL

a long series of events

● adj+N **continuing, long, long-running, ongoing, sorry, whole** *The long-running saga regarding the future of the old theatre has taken another turn.*

● N+v **begin, continue, drag on, end, rumble on, unfold** *Scientists around the world watched as a dramatic saga unfolded in the depths of space.*

salary N

a fixed amount of money earned by working

● adj+N high **big, excellent, exorbitant, fat, generous, good, high, inflated, six-figure, top** *The Council leaders rewarded themselves with inflated salaries and generous perks.*

▶ fairly high **attractive, competitive, decent** INFORMAL, **reasonable** *We offer competitive salaries and benefits.*

▶ low **low, meagre, minimum, modest, small** *They live on her meagre salary and some social security*

▶ before/after tax **gross, net** *You can borrow up to two thirds of your gross annual salary.*

▶ all **full** *When she was on maternity leave, she was paid her full salary.*

▶ before commission **basic** *You will benefit from a good basic salary plus commission.*

▶ paid every year, month etc **annual, monthly, weekly, yearly** *Monthly salaries at the company currently range from $130 to $280.*

▶ at the end/start of a career **final, starting** *MPs pensions will now be calculated on a 40th of their final salary.*

▶ now **current** *Please send your CV with details of your current salary to our Human Resources department.*

● v+N earn a salary **command, draw, earn, get, have, receive, take** *Due to their valuable skills, our graduates can command top salaries.*

▶ pay a salary **give sb, offer, pay, provide** *What salary is paid to the specialist carrying out the work?*

▶ increase a salary **augment, boost, double, increase, inflate, raise** *I was immediately offered a more responsible job, and my salary was doubled!*

▸ reduce a salary **cut, reduce, slash** *Some tutors are having their salaries reduced by 40 percent.*

▸ add to a salary **supplement** *He started writing fiction to supplement his newspaper salary.*

▸ fix a salary **determine, fix, negotiate** *As a partner in the business, she can negotiate her own salary.*

▸ review a salary **review** *We will review your salary on an annual basis.*

● N+v for saying how much a salary is **amount to sth, be sth, exceed sth, range from sth to sth, start at sth** *Typical salaries range from 8,000 – 12,000 pounds per annum.*

▸ increase **double, go up, increase, rise** *This year, his salary rose to $180,100.*

▸ decrease **drop, fall, go down** *You might find that your basic salary has gone down, but the total you are paid is still higher.*

▸ depend on something **be commensurate with sth, depend on sth, reflect sth** *Basic salary is commensurate with experience.*

sale N [usually plural]
the total sold within a period or the money earned

● adj+N high **good, high, huge, massive, record, strong** *Ticket sales have been much higher than expected.*

▸ low **disappointing, poor** *The company said it had disappointing sales in Europe.*

▸ total **overall, total** *In 2005, UKAI exported over 67 per cent of its total sales.*

▸ average **average** *The average sales for 1839 were 36,000 copies a week.*

▸ gross/net **gross, net** *The group has operations in 55 countries and net sales of 2.8 billion US dollars.*

▸ per year **annual, yearly** *Annual sales are up by 10 per cent.*

▸ per month **monthly, quarterly** *The company saw a 2.8 per cent rise in quarterly sales.*

▸ future **future, possible, potential** *If our customers are not happy, then we lose potential sales.*

▸ in shops **high street, over-the-counter, retail** *The company is restructuring its retail sales force.*

▸ not in shops **direct, online, private, telephone** *Is your goal to make direct sales via e-commerce on your website?*

▸ in the world **global, worldwide** *Total worldwide sales of her books are now at four million copies.*

▸ in other countries **export, foreign, international, overseas** *Overseas sales continued to be important.*

▸ in your own country **domestic, home, local** *The ban on advertising applies to export sales as well as to domestic sales.*

● v+N increase sales **boost, double, drive (up), expand, grow, improve, increase, maximise, push up** *The Louis Vuitton brand is helping to drive sales.*

▸ achieve sales **achieve, generate, get, notch up, secure** *The tour didn't seem to generate many sales for the band.*

▸ forecast or expect sales **anticipate, expect, forecast, predict, project** *The business has forecast sales of £100 million this year.*

▸ reduce sales **affect, hurt, impact on, reduce** *The 2p per litre price increase had not affected sales.*

▸ announce sales **announce, report** *Hyundai announced sales of 44,508 vehicles for the month, an all-time record.*

● N+v increase **go up, grow, increase, leap, rise, rocket, soar** *Sales are rising slowly as prices drop.*

▸ decrease **decline, decrease, dip, drop, fall, go down, plummet, slip, slow down, slump** *It is only when it becomes obvious that sales are declining that a firm might start to investigate the reasons why.*

▸ equal an amount **amount to sth, reach sth, total sth** *In the first six months of 2006, Ford's U.S. sales totalled 1.55 million.*

▸ be more than an amount **exceed sth, top sth** *Sales so far have exceeded initial forecasts.*

sample N
1 a small amount of a substance used for tests

● adj+N first **first, initial, original** *The orginal sample would be sent to another laboratory for analysis.*

▸ new **fresh, new** *She ran the tests again and sent fresh samples to three other labs.*

▸ of faeces **faecal, stool** *The most effective way of finding out whether it is food poisoning is for the ill person to provide a faecal sample for testing.*

● n+N from the body **blood, DNA, fluid, hair, tissue, urine** *200 patients had blood samples taken in their own homes.*

▸ from the earth **rock, soil, water** *Over 250 soil samples have been collected.*

▸ for comparison **control** *Control samples are taken from unaffected parts of the same field for comparison.*

● v+N collect a sample **collect, draw, extract, get, obtain, take** *How is the sample collected for testing?*

▸ test a sample **analyze, examine, peform sth on, process, test** *By testing blood samples, the laboratory can measure the hormones which control the ovaries.*

▸ provide a sample **give sb, provide, send in, submit** *Wildlife specialists submitted hair samples from captive lynx as evidence of their presence in Washington and Oregon forests.*

▸ damage a sample **contaminate** *If the sample is contaminated with blood we may be unable to provide a result.*

2 a group of people tested to find out about a larger group

● adj+N small **small, tiny** *Even with a small sample of six organisations visited, we observed significant differences in the way they were organised.*

▸ large **bulk, large** *We are confident that the methodology applied here is robust and 'portable' to larger samples of staff.*

▸ total **overall, total** *We asked our total sample to prioritise their interest in retailing across twelve product sectors.*

▸ first **first, original** *Just under half of the original sample were retained in the school system to the age of fourteen.*

▸ good **good, representative** *The aim is to select a representative sample of all posts within the University to act as benchmarks.*

▸ not specially chosen **random** *The study measured height in a random sample of 50 males and 50 females.*

▸ national **national** *In most examples, a national population sample does yield an approximately normal distribution.*

- v+N study a sample **examine, interview, study** *We interviewed samples of deaf people in five different regions.*
▶ choose a sample **choose, draw, select** *Dr Hill said the sample was randomly selected from hospital patients.*

sanction N [usually plural]
punishment of a country that has broken international law

- adj+N strict **comprehensive, crippling, draconian, harsh, severe, strict, stringent, tough** *The country was already in the midst of a humanitarian disaster caused by 12 years of crippling sanctions.*
▶ economic **economic, trade** *The League had imposed economic sanctions on Italy for the invasion of Abyssinia.*
▶ from one/more than one country **international, multilateral, unilateral** *Without international sanctions, they will be able to allocate greater financial and human resources to their nuclear program.*
▶ v+N impose sanctions **apply, implement, impose, introduce, slap** *United Nations trade sanctions were slapped on Baghdad after its 1990 invasion of Kuwait.*
▶ end sanctions **end, lift, suspend, waive** *The deals can not be implemented until sanctions are lifted.*
▶ make sanctions less strict **ease, loosen** *The President announced his decision to ease some sanctions against North Korea.*
▶ make sanctions more strict **strengthen, tighten** *When the West tightens sanctions against Iraq, the people suffer.*
▶ threaten sanctions **threaten** *The European Union threatened sanctions should they refuse to stop enriching uranium.*
▶ not obey sanctions **break, circumvent, evade, violate** *He refused to say whether Washington believed the visit had in fact violated the sanctions.*
▶ make sure someone obeys sanctions **enforce** *The ILO does not have the power to enforce sanctions to ensure that labour rights are recognised around the globe.*
▶ agree/disagree with sanctions **oppose, support** *I oppose the sanctions on humanitarian grounds.*

sanitation N
conditions and processes relating to people's health

- adj+N good **adequate, decent, effective, good, proper, safe** *Nearly half of the world's people lack access to adequate sanitation.*
- bad **bad, inadequate, non-existent, poor** *Conditions in barracks were very bad, with overcrowding, poor sanitation and little ventilation.*
- basic **basic** *A staggering 2.4 billion people don't even have basic sanitation.*

sanity N
the ability to think, speak and behave normally

- v+N lose your sanity **lose** *Grant is in danger of losing his sanity.*
- keep your sanity **keep, maintain, preserve, retain** *There's a way to get through this and maintain your sanity.*
- save someone's sanity **save** *She must have saved*

his sanity on many an occasion with her level-headed advice.
▶ get your sanity back **recover, regain, restore** *I eventually regained my sanity and that's when I realised the drugs had never been my primary addiction.*
▶ threaten someone's sanity **threaten** *Strange things start to happen that threaten her sanity.*
▶ doubt someone's sanity **doubt, question** *I began to doubt my own sanity.*

sap V
to make someone feel weak or unenthusiastic

- V+n **confidence, energy, enthusiasm, morale, strength, vitality, will** *Disruptive behaviour in the classroom has an adverse impact on all of the class and saps the morale of our teachers.*

sarcasm N
saying the opposite of what you mean

- adj+N **biting, bitter, heavy, withering** *Some people were offended by his biting sarcasm.*
- and/or **cynicism, humour, irony, mockery, ridicule, wit** *He was happy to employ ridicule and sarcasm in defence of free speech and reason.*

sarcastic ADJ
using sarcasm to upset someone

- ADJ+n comment **comment, put-down, remark, reply** *The judges are there to help, so will not be offering sarcastic put-downs to the contestants.*
▶ humour **humour, wit** *He uses his sarcastic wit to shield himself and his feelings.*
▶ tone **tone** *I don't like your sarcastic tone!*
- and/or **cynical, humorous, ironic, rude, witty** *He believes that everything I say is cynical, sarcastic and intended to hurt.*

satellite N
an object that travels around the Earth

- adj+N **artificial, astronomical, civilian, communications, meteorological, military, radar, reconnaissance, spy, weather** *Sputnik 1 was the first artificial satellite, launched by the Soviet Union in October 1957.*
- v+N launch a satellite **deploy, launch** *On board was the largest telecommunications satellite ever launched.*
▶ follow a satellite **follow, track** *The user's device must then track a satellite's movement across the sky.*
▶ find a satellite **find, locate** *Then move the dish to locate the required satellite.*
▶ operate a satellite **control, operate** *The satellites were operated from a remote ground station in Australia.*
- N+v go round something **circle sth, orbit sth** *These changes are now continually monitored by satellites orbiting the Earth.*
▶ broadcast something **broadcast sth, transmit sth** *These satellites transmit radio signals which the GPS receiver picks up.*
▶ notice or watch something **detect sth, monitor sth, observe sth** *Spy satellites then observed the vehicles turn around and return to the centre of the city.*

satire N

the use of humour to criticize someone, or something that uses this kind of humour

- adj+N strong or clever **biting, clever, savage, scathing, sharp** *'Popcorn' is a biting satire of America's litigation culture.*
- ▶ funny **comic, hilarious, witty** *I'm not expecting incisive social comment or witty satire.*
- ▶ types of satire **political, social** *Amidst the humour, there is some serious political satire.*
- and/or **comedy, farce, humour, irony, parody, ridicule, wit** *The film was a mix of comedy and satire, with elements of drama thrown in.*

satisfaction N

pleasure obtained from getting what you want

- adj+N great **considerable, deep, enormous, great, high, immense, much, real, tremendous, ultimate** *To my immense satisfaction, I landed beside a main road.*
- ▶ continuing for a long time **lasting** *Lasting satisfaction comes from helping others.*
- ▶ complete **complete, entire, full, total** *Our overall mission is complete customer satisfaction, whatever it takes.*
- ▶ little **little, low** *It was expected that restructuring would result in lower job satisfaction and greater job insecurity.*
- ▶ overall **general, overall** *The overall satisfaction of patients with most NHS services is high.*
- ▶ too happy **smug** *You could feel the smug satisfaction from all the men there.*
- ▶ of both people **mutual** *Safe and satisfactory anaesthesia can easily be obtained to the mutual satisfaction of the patient, surgeon and anaesthetist.*
- ▶ of yourself **own, personal, self** *When I have achieved a successful result for my client, that gives me great personal satisfaction.*
- ▶ of the public **public** *The survey shows high levels of public satisfaction with parks and open spaces across the country.*
- ▶ types of satisfaction **emotional, intellectual, marital, professional, sexual** *Couples who share household tasks find greater marital satisfaction.*
- n+N of a group of people **client, consumer, customer, employee, learner, patient, staff, student, tenant, user** *We aim to deliver customer satisfaction and the highest possible standards of service.*
- ▶ with something **career, job, life, service** *She would be able to have a direct impact on bringing about change, so job satisfaction would be high.*
- v+N feel satisfaction **achieve, experience, feel, find, have** *You'll have the satisfaction of doing something really worthwhile.*
- ▶ get satisfaction **derive, gain, get, take** *The cast probably derived more satisfaction out of the play than the audience.*
- ▶ express satisfaction **express, indicate, report, show** *He expressed satisfaction at the progres of the project.*
- ▶ give satisfaction **afford, bring, give, provide** *Every part of the book would afford satisfaction and information to the reader.*
- ▶ ensure someone's satisfaction **assure, ensure, guarantee** *We guarantee your complete satisfaction.*

- ▶ measure satisfaction **assess, gauge, measure, monitor** *The questionnaire is designed to measure the job satisfaction or dissatisfaction of teachers.*
- ▶ improve satisfaction **enhance, improve, increase** *The industry is working hard at improving customer satisfaction.*

satisfactory ADJ

good enough

- adv+ADJ completely **altogether, completely, entirely, equally, fully, perfectly, totally, wholly** *Neither of these solutions is entirely satisfactory, however.* • *A different approach might bring you equally satisfactory results.*
- ▶ very **highly, really** INFORMAL, **thoroughly, very** *The company concluded the financial year with highly satisfactory financial results.*
- ▶ mainly **broadly, generally** *In the sixth form, students' progress is broadly satisfactory.*
- ▶ fairly **fairly, quite, reasonably** *These methods are fairly satisfactory out of doors, but are unlikely to succeed in a cave.*
- ▶ almost not **barely, hardly, rarely** *The result was a barely satisfactory recording interrupted by family conversations.*
- ▶ for both people **mutually** *It is hoped that a mutually satisfactory approach will be found.*
- ADJ+n end or result **completion, conclusion, outcome, resolution, result, solution** *On satisfactory completion of this course, you will receive a diploma*
- ▶ answer **answer, explanation, reply, response** *There doesn't seem to be a satisfactory answer to this.* • *No satisfactory explanation was given for this delay*
- ▶ progress or performance **performance, progress** *The trainee must maintain satisfactory progress at all times.*
- ▶ arrangement **arrangement, compromise, settlement** *Both parties agreed to a satisfactory compromise.*
- ▶ alternative **alternative, substitute** *Semi-skimmed milk is a satisfactory alternative to full-fat milk.*
- ▶ standard or condition **condition, level, quality, standard** *All work must be undertaken to a satisfactory standard.*
- ▶ manner **manner** *We hope to be able to resolve the matter in a speedy and satisfactory manner.*
- v+ADJ consider something satisfactory **consider sth, deem sth, find sth, judge sth, rate sth** *Premises must not be opened to the public until the work is deemed satisfactory.*
- ▶ be or remain satisfactory **be, prove, remain** *Her condition seemed to remain satisfactory although she had some swelling in her legs.*
- ▶ seem satisfactory **appear, seem** *None of these explanations seems fully satisfactory.*

satisfied ADJ

pleased with what has happened

- adv+ADJ very or completely **completely, fully, perfectly, totally, very** *Please say if you are not perfectly satisfied with the service.*
- ▶ fairly **fairly, quite, reasonably** *We feel reasonably satisfied because the team finished, but it was a shame we didn't score any points.*

satisfy V

1 to provide something that someone wants

- adv+V completely **completely, entirely, perfectly, thoroughly, totally, wholly** *We strive to totally satisfy all our customers.*

- V+n wish or need **ambition, aspirations, demand, desire, expectation, need, request, urge, wish** *I was finally able to satisfy my ambition to travel around the world.*
- interest **curiosity** *To satisfy his own curiosity, Pemberton examines the family's history.*
- physical feeling **appetite, hunger, lust, thirst** *We don't only eat to satisfy hunger.*
- strong wish **craving, longing, yearning** *If you find you need to satisfy your cravings for big city shops and nightlife, London is close by.*

2 to have the qualities needed by a rule, condition etc

- adv+V more or less **generally, reasonably** *The report as a whole generally satisfies the requirements set out by the Council.*
- completely **completely, entirely, fully** *This practice fully satisfies the requirements of UK law.*

- V+n **condition, constraint, criterion, obligation, requirement, rule** *To study at the university, students must satisfy certain entry requirements.*

satisfying ADJ

making you feel pleased or happy

- adv+ADJ very **deeply, enormously, extremely, hugely, immensely, incredibly, intensely, really** INFORMAL, **richly, supremely, thoroughly, very, wholly** *After six years of anticipation, to hold a European trophy was immensely satisfying.*
- when something is surprising **strangely, surprisingly** *I found cleaning strangely satisfying!*
- in a particular way **aesthetically, emotionally, intellectually** *You learn to use other languages in an intellectually satisfying way.*

- and/or **challenging, enjoyable, entertaining, meaningful, productive, rewarding, stimulating, worthwhile** *Beethoven sonatas are among the most satisfying and rewarding to play.*

saunter V

walk in a slow and relaxed way

- adv+V **casually, gently, nonchalantly, slowly** *He casually sauntered down to the platform.*

savage ADJ

cruel or severe

- ADJ+n **ferocity, indictment, irony, onslaught, repression, reprisals** *The book is a fairly savage indictment of social workers.*

- and/or **barbaric, brutal, cruel, ignorant, primitive, wild** *The Greeks did not necessarily think that all foreigners were savage and ignorant.*

saving N [always plural]

money that you have saved or invested

- adj+N of a person **personal, private** *Through*

personal savings and a bank loan, she was able to purchase and install the required machines.

- that you have worked hard for **hard-earned** *It is quite outrageous that computer mistakes deprive pensioners of their hard-earned savings.*

- n+N **emergency, household, life, lifetime, retirement** *Don't put your entire life savings into an online account.*

- v+N build up savings **accumulate, build up, increase** *As you begin to accumulate savings, you can start to invest.*
- pay in savings **deposit, invest** *Encourage older children to deposit savings in a High Street savings account.*
- take out savings **take out, withdraw** *Click here for more information on how to withdraw your savings.*
- have savings **have** *Many households on lower incomes have no savings at all.*
- use savings **dip into, raid, use** *Britons have been dipping into savings to pay for luxury items such as gifts, holidays and shopping.*

say V

to express something using words

- adv+V aloud **aloud, out loud** *The irregular verbs can be said aloud in chorus whilst clapping.*
- clearly or carefully **clearly, loudly, plainly, precisely, slowly** *I said clearly that there would be no public statements made.*
- calmly/not calmly **calmly, casually, excitedly** *'My daughter has leukaemia', she said almost casually.*
- quickly **briefly, hastily, hurriedly, quickly** *'Yes,' Sam said hastily, before Kate or Gary could formulate their own questions.*
- quietly **gently, quietly, softly** *'I love you,' she said softly.*
- firmly or confidently **confidently, emphatically, firmly** *Firmly say the word 'no' when your dog jumps up at you.*
- definitely **categorically, certainly, definitely, definitively, genuinely, positively, safely, truly, unequivocally** *I could safely say that he was one of the best painters I had ever met.*
- specifically **explicitly, expressly, specifically** *I explicitly said that I would not attend any function at which he was even present.*
- angrily **angrily, shortly** *'Well,' he said shortly, 'people's private opinions can wait'.*
- happily **cheerfully, happily** *'Daisy, come and help me,' Margot said cheerfully.*
- seriously or sadly **gravely, grimly, ruefully, sadly, seriously, solemnly** *He stared at me hard, then he solemnly said, 'You shouldn't be out, you should be home in bed.'*
- directly or rudely **abruptly, bluntly, directly, flatly, pointedly, rudely** *'He's in his office,' said Mr Henchard bluntly.*
- proudly/not proudly **modestly, proudly** *Santa Cruz has become, they say proudly, the new Barcelona.*
- in a pleasant or useful way **helpfully, kindly, politely** *'Don't you hurry, sonny,' said the old lady kindly .*
- in a joking way **dryly, jokingly, sarcastically** *I said jokingly to the clerk 'I bet you hope that never happens'.*
- publicly/privately **openly, privately, publicly** *Many*

things which they say publicly show the extent of their ignorance.

▶ honestly **earnestly, frankly, honestly, truthfully** *I can honestly say that I have never been so nervous in my life.*

▶ basically **basically, effectively, essentially, really** *What I'm basically saying is that I disagree with you.*

▶ only **merely, simply** *I am simply saying that all the research that I have done has left me exasperated.*

▶ often **again and again, consistently, constantly, continually, frequently, often, repeatedly** *I have said repeatedly that I believe climate change is the major long-term threat facing our planet.*

▶ when someone is right **correctly, rightly** *As the Governor General rightly said, 'I knew too much'.*

▶ when people say someone said something **allegedly, apparently, reportedly** *He has reportedly said he will give away 95 per cent of the money.*

▶ when what someone says is well-known **famously** *Winston Churchill famously said of democracy: 'It is the worst form of government, except for all the others'.*

saying N

a well-known statement about what often happens

● adj+N clever or funny **wise, witty** *She paid little attention to his witty sayings and sparkling comments.*

▶ old or well-known **common, famous, old, popular, well-known** *'The price of liberty is eternal vigilance' is a well-known saying.*

▶ favourite **favourite** *'Neither a borrower nor a lender be' was my granny's favourite saying.*

▶ short and effective **pithy, proverbial** *Short pithy sayings become popular when they express something that the experience of life shows to be true.*

scale N

1 the size of something, especially when it is big

● adj+N large **big, broad, full, grand, great, large, sheer, wide** *We were indeed impressed by the grand scale of the building.*

▶ very large **colossal, enormous, huge, massive, unimaginable, unprecedented, vast** *Increasing population and consumption are altering the planet on an unprecedented scale.*

▶ small **modest, small** *Ben made the same mistake as Max but on a more modest scale.*

▶ world **global, international, worldwide** *Climatic chaos has reached a global scale.*

▶ country **national** *Crimestoppers has been in operation on a national scale since 1988.*

▶ region **local, regional** *A modern telecommunications system is essential for any business that seeks to operate on more than the local scale.*

▶ industry **commercial, industrial** *Criminals can now produce these fakes on an industrial scale.*

2 an ordered arrangement of people, figures, levels etc

● adj+N **fixed, incremental, sliding, standard** *The cost is on a sliding scale – 99 pence for the first four frames, then 50 pence for the rest, with a 10 pence charge to edit a frame.*

● n+N of people's pay **pay, salary, wage** *For the first*

time, one set of salary scales was introduced throughout all the railway companies.

▶ for measuring the level of something **intensity, length, temperature, time, wavelength** *Unless the council can come up with a definitive time scale for starting the work, the offer will be withdrawn.*

▶ with a specified number of levels **3-point, 5-point, 10-point etc** *Regular feedback on individual teaching sessions is provided by the students using a 5-point scale.*

scandal N

a situation in which important people behave badly

● adj+N big **big, huge, major, real** *An even bigger scandal, involving corrupt politicians and officials, is now gathering momentum.*

▶ small **minor** *He made many enemies and seemed to be dogged by minor scandals.*

▶ well-known **high-profile, national, notorious, public, tabloid** *When Stalin died in 1953 a notorious scandal erupted over Picasso's drawing of him.*

▶ alleged **alleged** *The Serious Fraud Office is investigating an alleged bribery scandal.*

▶ of a particular type **abuse, accounting, bribery, corporate, corruption, financial, match-fixing, mis-selling, political, sex, sexual, sleaze** *Sexual scandal in high places is no longer as shocking as it used to be.*

● v+N reveal a scandal **expose, reveal, uncover** *The scandal was uncovered by the Belgian newspaper De Morgen.*

▶ cause a scandal **bring, cause, create, lead to, provoke** *In 1918 Josiah Wedgwood caused a scandal by divorcing his wife of twenty-four years.*

▶ be involved in a scandal **be embroiled in, be implicated in, be involved in** *Edward was embroiled in a scandal which effectively ended his political career.*

● N+v happen **break, ensue, erupt, unfold** *The scandal broke at the end of December.*

▶ affect someone or something **dog sb/sth, engulf sb/sth, hit sb/sth, rock sb/sth, shake sb/sth** *His political career was dogged by scandal.*

● and/or **controversy, corruption, gossip, intrigue, scam, sleaze** *He was a somewhat flamboyant monarch and a faint whiff of scandal and intrigue was to accompany his reign.*

scapegoat N

someone who is wrongly blamed for something

● adj+N **convenient, easy, handy** *Jews were used as a convenient scapegoat, and were blamed for many of the country's problems.*

● v+N **become, find, make sb, need, seek** *He feels that he has been made a scapegoat.*

scarce ADJ

when there is not much of something

● adv+ADJ very **exceedingly, extremely, very** *Wartime pictures of the village are extremely scarce*

▶ rather **comparatively, fairly, pretty** INFORMAL, **quite, rather, relatively** *Carry a toilet roll with you on your travels, as they can be quite scarce in some countries*

▶ increasingly **increasingly** *Water is an increasingly scarce resource throughout the world.*

- v+ADJ **be, become, grow, remain** *Fresh water is now becoming scarce in many regions of the world.*

scarcity N
when there is not enough of something

- adj+N relative **comparative, relative** *The relative scarcity of land will continue to decline.*
- extreme **absolute, acute, extreme, severe** *Nationwide, there is a severe scarcity of allergy clinics.*
- economic **economic** *The dramatic increase in poverty across the globe is not caused by economic scarcity.*
- N+of **food, fuel, land, material, money, resources, water** *Wars and civil violence often arise from the scarcity of resources such as water and land.*

scare V
to make someone feel frightened or worried

- adv+V a lot **the (living) daylights out of** INFORMAL, **really** INFORMAL, **stiff** INFORMAL, **to death, witless** INFORMAL *You really scared me!* • *Many a brave person has been scared witless by attempting to ghost hunt here.*
- a little **a little, slightly** *I must admit he scares me a little.*

scare N
when people suddenly feel worried or frightened

- adj+N small **brief, minor, slight** *There was a slight scare at the end of the first lap as his wheel touched the trackside grass causing a serious wobble.*
- big **big, major, real** *She caused a major food scare by declaring that most eggs were contaminated with salmonella.*
- real/not real **false, genuine** *There were enough genuine scares to make me and the rest of the audience jump several times!*
- n+N **AIDS, bomb, cancer, food, health, injury, pregnancy, safety, security, terrorist** *Earlier in the year the online filing system was hit by a security scare.*
- v+N cause a scare **cause, create, generate, provoke, spark, trigger** *A suspicious package which sparked a bomb scare turned out to be a birthday present.*
- suffer a scare **suffer** *In January 1985, Margaret suffered a cancer scare and a section of lung was removed.*
- survive a scare **recover from, survive** *She's survived health scares, heartbreak and career lows but now she's back.*

scenario N
situation that could possibly happen

- adj+N possible **likely, plausible, possible, probable, realistic** *We have to tailor our advice to realistic scenarios in the everyday working environment.*
- bad **bad, pessimistic** *Even in our most pessimistic scenarios we couldn't imagine that human society would be so stupid.*
- good **best-case, ideal, optimistic, win-win** *The*

optimistic scenario of a quick victory over the IRA began to unravel rapidly.
- ▶ the worst possible **apocalyptic, doomsday, nightmare, worst-case** *The nightmare scenario for us is where the customer wants it all done by 2pm tomorrow afternoon.*
- ▶ different **alternative, different** *The user can also explore alternative scenarios.*
- ▶ imaginary **fictional, fictitious, hypothetical, imaginary, simulated** *Professionals were asked to state how they would react to a hypothetical scenario.*
- v+N imagine a scenario **consider, envisage, foresee, imagine, look at, think of, visualize** *It is possible to envisage other scenarios – say, one in which a Democratic administration becomes extremely unpopular.*
- ▶ describe a scenario **construct, depict, paint, present** *The press painted an apocalyptic scenario of disaffected working class voters switching to extremist parties.*
- ▶ cause a scenario **lead to, produce** *The terrorism laws could lead to a scenario in which the police are arresting innocent people.*
- N+v **arise, emerge, happen, occur, play out, unfold** *There is still time to stop this scheme before this disastrous scenario unfolds.*

scene N
1 a part of play, book, film etc

- adj+N **climactic, comic, dramatic, funny, hilarious, romantic, violent** *The play is interesting because of Miller's meaty dialogue and the repeated dramatic scenes.*
- n+N **battle, chase, fight, murder, rape, sex, street** *We were rehearsing a fight scene and my knee hit her nose accidentally.*
- v+N create a scene **act out, enact, film, improvise, rehearse, set, shoot** *They participate in drama games and improvise a key scene from the show.*
- ▶ get rid of a scene **cut, delete** *They decided to cut a scene in which Jack questions his government's policy.*
- N+v **depict sth, feature sth, include sth, involve sth** *What should I do if I wish to film scenes involving firearms?*

2 the place where something happens

- v+N leave a scene **depart from, escape from, flee, run from** *Jane flees the scene, but is soon caught and arrested.*
- ▶ go to or be at a scene **arrive at, attend, be at, be on, remain at, rush to, stay at, stop at** *Emergency services were on the scene within minutes.* • *A passing motorist stopped at the scene of the accident.*
- N+of **accident, battle, collision, crash, crime, disaster, fighting, incident, massacre, murder, riot, robbery, shooting, tragedy, violence** *The upper floor, scene of the murder and arson in 1893, is used as a store.*

3 an area of interest or activity, especially in the arts or politics

- adj+N in which interesting things happen **exciting, lively, vibrant** *The city still has a vibrant jazz scene.*

▶ active and successful **burgeoning, flourishing, thriving** *Scotland has a thriving art scene and Glasgow is a great platform for new artists.*

● n+N **art, dance, folk, hip-hop, indie, jazz, music, punk, rave** *Your main base is Cambridge. How big is the hip-hop scene there?*

● v+N become part of a scene, especially in a noticeable way **arrive on, burst onto, come onto, emerge onto** *We had an exclusive interview with a young rapper who had just burst onto the scene.*

▶ stop being involved in a scene **depart from, disappear from, fade from, retire from, vanish from, withdraw from** *For nearly a year he disappeared from the political scene.*

4 things that you see around you, especially when they involve death or suffering

● v+N **observe, survey, witness** *A falcon was sitting comfortably on its perch, surveying the scene.*

● N+of **bloodshed, carnage, chaos, desolation, devastation, horror, mayhem, suffering** *As the attacks came over with increasing intensity, our camp became a scene of chaos.*

scenery N
natural things that you see in a place

● adj+N very beautiful or impressive **amazing, beautiful, breathtaking, dramatic, fabulous, fantastic, glorious, gorgeous, lovely, magnificent, majestic, picturesque, spectacular, splendid, stunning, superb, unspoiled, wonderful** *With breathtaking scenery and long winding roads, Dorset is a paradise for bikes.*

▶ of a particular type **alpine, coastal, mountainous, rugged** *Hotel Les Chamois makes an ideal base from where to explore some dramatic alpine scenery.*

● n+N **desert, forest, highland, limestone, moorland, mountain, woodland** *Expeditions by sea kayak or on foot through spectacular highland scenery are also on offer.*

> If you want to talk about the scenery around a place, you can say that it is *set amid* or *set amidst* scenery of a particular type: *You could stay at the Grunenberg, a family hotel set amid beautiful Black Forest scenery.*

● v+N **admire, appreciate, discover, enjoy, experience, look at, savour, take in, view** *Once at the top, we took a little time to savour the stunning scenery.*

scent N
a particular smell

● adj+N strong **aromatic, heady, overpowering, pungent** *We sat there inhaling the heady scents of a hot African evening.*

▶ pleasant **alluring, delicious, heavenly, irresistible, refreshing** *By this time the fruits should be ready to release their heavenly scent.*

▶ types of scent **earthy, feminine, floral, fruity, masculine, musky, spicy, sweet** *Distilled from the fresh leaves, this oil has a sweet, floral, geranium-like scent.*

▶ slight **delicate, faint** *The faint scent attracts bees, which pollinate the flowers.*

● v+N smell a scent **enjoy, inhale, smell, sniff** *She draws a finger over the roll's shiny egg glaze, sniffing its warm yeasty scent.*

▶ produce a scent **emit, exude, give off, produce, release** *The leaves, when rubbed, exude a strong caraway scent and taste.*

sceptic N
someone who has doubts about things that other people accept

● adj+N **complete, extreme, hardened** *Only the most hardened sceptic could not find some sympathetic resonance within this book.*

● v+N persuade a sceptic to believe something **convert, convince, persuade, win over** *If they are to win over the sceptics, they need more evidence that these alternative medicines actually work.*

▶ prove that a sceptic is wrong **confound, prove sb wrong, silence** *The company's continued existence has proved many sceptics wrong.*

sceptical ADJ
having doubts about something that other people accept

● adv+ADJ which is easy to understand **justifiably, naturally, rightly, understandably** *People in the health profession are understandably sceptical about the benefits of drug therapy.*

▶ very **deeply, extremely, highly, very** *Many of us are deeply sceptical about the assurances that civilian casualties will be minimised.*

▶ slightly **a little, mildly, slightly, somewhat** *I hope the Secretary of State will forgive those of us who are mildly sceptical of the Government's performance.*

● ADJ+n **argument, attitude, stance, view, viewpoint** *The public was rejecting Bush's sceptical stance on climate change.*

● v+ADJ **appear, be, become, feel, grow, remain, seem** *Some politicians remain sceptical about climate science.*

scepticism N
doubts about things that other people accept

● adj+N great **considerable, deep, extreme, much, profound, strong, total** *Whether these victims will receive the justice they deserve is a matter for profound scepticism.*

▶ expressed by many people **general, public, universal, widespread** *Among the general public, there appears to be almost universal scepticism about the trial.*

● v+N express scepticism **demonstrate, express, greet sth with, regard sth with, reveal, share, treat sth with, view sth with, voice** *The plan was greeted with scepticism by the Disability Rights Commission* ● *A number of councillors have voiced scepticism about the move.*

▶ cause a reaction of scepticism **meet with, provoke** *Plans for a new 'state-of-the-art' market hall have met with scepticism from traders.*

● n+of+N amount of scepticism **deal, degree, dose, lot** *Her claims were treated with a considerable degree of scepticism.*

▶ feeling of scepticism **attitude, climate, mood, spirit**

In the current climate of scepticism, it is difficult to persuade people of the need to conserve energy.

schedule N
a plan of times for activities or events

● adj+N **busy, crowded, demanding, exhausting, gruelling, hectic, packed, punishing, relentless, rigorous, strict, tight** *Some presenters, feeling the strain of a hectic television schedule, might practise yoga.*

● v+N make a schedule **agree, plan, prepare, produce, set** *In an exchange of emails, we set a rough schedule for getting the work done.*

▸ make changes to a schedule **adjust, revise, update** *These IT projects have been poorly managed, with schedules that get revised on a regular basis.*

▸ follow a schedule **adhere to, conform to, keep to, stick to, work to** *Stick to the schedule and don't fall behind in your work!*

If you fail to follow a schedule, and things happen later than they should, you can say that *you are behind schedule* or *you have fallen behind schedule: After weeks of bad weather, the construction project is seriously behind schedule.*

cheme N
plan for achieving something

adj+N new and ambitious **ambitious, innovative, new, pioneering, radical** *Hundreds of young people have been helped to join the workforce thanks to this pioneering scheme.*

on a large scale **comprehensive, large, major** *The report gives details of major new road schemes which are being planned.*

effective **effective, successful** *The whole district has been transformed, following a successful regeneration scheme.*

n+N **award, bonus, housing, licensing, loyalty, quality-control, recycling, regeneration, stakeholder, training, transport** *In February 2005, the new kerbside recycling scheme was introduced.*

v+N begin to run a scheme **devise, establish, implement, introduce, launch, pilot, set up** *The school launched a new award scheme to get youngsters thinking up their own ideas.*

run or manage a scheme **administer, manage, operate, run** *Crime is lower here than in similar areas not operating this scheme.*

support a scheme **back, fund, support** *Other measures to be introduced to support the building schemes include action against anti-social behaviour.*

holarship N
ney that allows someone to study

v+N get a scholarship **gain, obtain, receive, secure, win** *She attended Brighton High School, where she won a scholarship to Newnham College, Cambridge.*

give someone a scholarship **award, grant, offer** *When I was 13, I was awarded a scholarship to Wakefield Art College.*

school N
a place where children are taught

● v+N begin to go to school **enter, start** *I passed the entrance examination and entered the school in 1931.*

▸ go to school **attend, be at, go to** *About 82 per cent of young entrants to undergraduate courses had attended such schools.*

▸ stop going to school **finish, leave** *After finishing secondary school, Eisenstein enrolled at an institute for civil engineering.*

▸ stop going to school before the usual age **drop out** *She got involved in drugs, and dropped out of high school before she graduated.*

▸ be forced to leave school because of bad behaviour **be booted out of** INFORMAL, **be expelled from, be kicked out of** INFORMAL *I was on the verge of being kicked out of school for missing classes.*

scope N
1 the things that an activity, organization, subject etc deals with

● v+N increase the scope of sth **broaden, enlarge, expand, extend, increase, widen** *Professor Sykes advised her to broaden the scope of her research.*

▸ decrease the scope of sth **curtail, delimit, limit, minimize, narrow, reduce, restrict** *These findings usefully restricted the scope of the investigation.*

▸ say exactly what the scope is **circumscribe, define, determine, explain** *We wanted to determine the scope of this problem.*

● N+of+n of a programme of work or study **analysis, investigation, programme, project, research, review, study, work** *The first task is to define the scope of your research.*

▸ of a written document **article, book, document, paper, report** *The costs of the proposals fall outside the scope of this paper.*

▸ of a law or rule **directive, law, legislation, regulations** *It is not clear whether live musical events fall within the scope of this legislation.*

2 the opportunity or freedom needed to do something

● adj+N great **ample, broad, considerable, endless, enormous, immense, tremendous, unlimited, wide** *Due to our unique patient population, there is ample scope for clinical research.*

▸ little **limited, little, narrow, restricted** *The limited scope for tax cuts meant that growth was much slower than in the 1990s.*

● v+N **afford, allow, give sb, offer, provide sb with** *Its aim is to allow maximum scope for you to innovate and develop unique solutions.*

score N
1 the number of points gained in a game or competition

● adj+N good **big, excellent, good, high, record, top** *They won by 12 goals to 2 – still a record score for this competition.*

▸ bad **bad, low, poor** *At this level, 36 is a pretty bad score.*

▸ average **aggregate, average, mean, median** *If each team has won an equal number of matches, the aggregate score of the two matches between the teams shall decide the issue.*

▶ total **combined, final, overall, total** *Robertson blocked a ten-yard shot to keep the final score 1–0 to Raith.*

● v+N make the score the same for each team or player **even, level, tie** *A superb goal from Charlie levelled the score at 1–1.*

▶ get a score **get, notch up, reach, record** *In an exciting game, they notched up their highest score of the season.*

● N+v **be, be at, reach, remain at, stand at** *At the moment, the score stands at 149 for the challenger against 126 for the incumbent.*

2 the number of points or marks gained in a test or examination

● adj+N good **excellent, good, high, maximum, top** *The school regularly produces some of the highest test scores in the country.*

▶ bad **bad, low, poor** *With scores as low as this, he is unlikely to gain a place at college.*

▶ average **average, mean** *The mean score for the class was 7.6, but the girls performed better than the boys.*

▶ total **aggregate, combined, final, overall, total** *A strong result in the final test gave him a combined score of 82 per cent.*

● v+N get a score **achieve, attain, gain, get, obtain, receive** *Candidates will need to achieve a score of 40 out of 75 in order to pass.*

▶ improve your score **boost, improve, increase** *A good oral test will boost your overall score significantly.*

scorn N

complete lack of respect for someone or something

● v+N **greet with, heap on, pour on, treat with** *He poured scorn on those who thought the general strike would be a peaceable economic weapon.*

● and/or **contempt, derision, ridicule** *The Kaiser now became an object of derision and scorn as the clouds of war gathered.*

scream N

a loud shout of pain, fear, or excitement

● adj+N **blood-curdling, high-pitched, loud, piercing, shrill, terrifying, wild** *A piercing scream rang out and the crowd suddenly parted.*

● v+N **emit, give, let out, utter** *Nelly uttered a wild scream, and rushed forward with outstretched arms.*

● N+v **cut through sth, pierce sth, ring out** *A high-pitched scream pierces the air.*

● N+of **agony, anguish, horror, pain, rage, terror** *Their screams of terror could be heard from outside the building.*

screen V

test someone to see if they have a particular illness

● adv+V **carefully, effectively, regularly, rigorously, systematically, thoroughly** *This way, the animals can be screened effectively for viruses.*

● V+for **cancer, condition, defect, diabetes, disease, disorder, infection, virus** *Since then, all blood donations have been screened for the virus.*

screening N

tests to check someone for disease

● adj+N done regularly **annual, regular, routine** *Routine screening for breast cancer has improved survival rates.*

▶ done very carefully **careful, rigorous, systematic** *Offenders can only be released after rigorous psychiatric screening.*

▶ when people must receive screeing **compulsory** *A controversial law introduced compulsory screeing for HIV for new employees.*

● v+N carry out screening **arrange, carry out, conduct, introduce, offer, organize, perform, undertake** *Some public and private institutions routinely perform screening for the virus.*

▶ receive screening **undergo** *Each donor undergoes rigorous screening for possible genetic and infectious risks.*

scrutinize V

examine something very carefully

● adv+V **carefully, closely, critically, rigorously, thoroughly** *Every fact he comes across is carefully scrutinized for accuracy.*

> Usage **Scrutinize** is usually passive in these combinations.

● V+n someone's work **performance, progress, work** *The body was set up to scrutinize the performance of family doctors.*

▶ a proposal or decision **decision, plan, policy, proposal** *The council leader says he will rigorously scrutinize all planning proposals.*

▶ financial details **accounts, budget, expenditure** *One of the tasks of the committee is scrutinizing star budgets.*

▶ a new law **bill, law, legislation** *Any proposed legislation will be carefully scrutinized by congressional committees.*

scrutiny N

careful examination of someone or something

● adj+N thorough **careful, close, constant, critical, detailed, in-depth, intense, proper, rigorous, strict, thorough, tough** *Jones came under intense scrutiny when he played against Australia this summer.*

▶ independent **democratic, external, independent** *This assessment is then subjected to external scrutiny by one of our neighbouring authorities.*

▶ carried out by politicians or lawyers **judicial, legislative, parliamentary, regulatory** *The Liberal Democrats made the case for parliamentary scrutiny of the commission's activities.*

● n+N **council, expert, government, peer, police, shareholder** *Without peer scrutiny, research data have very little scientific value.*

● v+N be examined carefully **be subjected to, come under, endure, face, undergo** *At the moment, the drug has not undergone any independent scrutiny.*

▶ still seem good after examination **bear, stand, withstand** *We need to make sure that our processes are sufficiently robust to withstand external scrutiny.*

▶ deserve to be examined **attract, deserve, merit, require, warrant** *The process nonetheless merits detailed scrutiny by this department.*

- avoid examination **avoid, bypass, escape, evade** *This was a cynical attempt to manipulate the procedures of the House to avoid proper scrutiny.*

sea N
he salt water that surrounds land

- adj+N with large waves **angry, choppy, foaming, heavy, raging, rough, stormy, treacherous, turbulent** *The rain and heavy seas made the work of the rescue crew very difficult.*
  with small waves or none **calm, glassy, smooth** *We had six days of unbroken bright sunshine, calm seas and exceptional visibility.*

> Usage **Sea** is often plural in all of these **adj+N** combinations.

  with light reflecting off it **glistening, glittering, shimmering, shining, sparkling** *He sat thoughtfully gazing out of the window across the glittering sea.*

- v+N **brave, cross, navigate, roam, sail, traverse** *And in the great ship they crossed the sea, and eventually came to Greenland.*

- N+v **batter, crash against, lap, pound, wash** *The sea was pounding the rocky coastline and there was a distinct chill in the air.*

seal V
ose a container or space tightly

- adv+V **completely, effectively, firmly, hermetically, permanently, properly, safely, securely, tightly** *The building is in effect hermetically sealed, with no opening windows.*

> Usage **Seal** is usually passive in all of these **adv+V** combinations.

search N
  attempt to find something or someone

- adj+N thorough **comprehensive, diligent, exhaustive, extensive, relentless, systematic, thorough** *The site was selected for development after an exhaustive search.*
  done by someone who is worried **desperate, frantic** *When Kyle discovers that her daughter is missing, she embarks on a frantic search for answers.*
  producing no useful result **fruitless, unsuccessful** *That night we had another fruitless search for a decent restaurant, so went back to the boat to eat.*

- v+N start a search **commence, initiate, launch** *After two drivers were reported missing, a sea and air search was initiated.*
  make a search **carry out, conduct, do, execute, perform, undertake** *The Police said they didn't have enough resources to undertake missing persons searches.*
  stop a search **abandon, call off** *This failure should not give us cause to abandon the search for clarity of thought.*

- N+v **elicit, find, result, return, reveal, uncover, yield** *An Internet search returned eight BBC articles on the murder.*

search V
look carefully in order to find something or someone

- adv+V thoroughly **actively, comprehensively, constantly, continually, diligently, efficiently, endlessly, exhaustively, systematically, thoroughly** *He would diligently search the noticeboard morning and evening for information.*
- with no useful result **fruitlessly, unsuccessfully, vainly** *While officials searched fruitlessly for the memory stick, the people whose data was compromised were not informed of the loss.*
- in a worried way **desperately, frantically** *She was frantically searching her pockets for the passport.*
- in many places **everywhere, far and wide, high and low** *The officers search everywhere for Anne, but in vain.*

season N
a particular period of the year when certain things happen

- adj+N busy **busy, high, peak** *During the peak season, the village can appear as busy as a railway station in the rush hour.*
- of particular weather **dry, rainy, wet** *The rainy season is from November to April.*
- n+N type of weather **hurricane, monsoon, typhoon** *The region is prone to serious flooding in the monsoon season of June to September.*
- animal activity **breeding, mating, migration, nesting** *The bird becomes very bold and confident during the breeding season.*
- farming activity **grazing, harvesting, planting** *The festival takes place at the end of the harvesting season.*
- hunting **fishing, hunting, salmon, shooting** *They want the hotel to be ready in time for the next shooting season.*
- tourist activity **holiday, tourist, vacation** *The road currently gets clogged with traffic during the tourist season.*
- sporting activity **baseball, basketball, cricket, football, hockey, racing, rugby, skiing, soccer** *There are 140 to 160 games in a typical baseball season.*
- illness **flu, hay-fever, pollen** *The health campaign will run over several weeks before the onset of the winter flu season.*

seasonal ADJ
in existence, or available, during a particular season

- ADJ+n changes or differences **adjustment, fluctuation, variability, variation** *There is a large seasonal fluctuation in mortality, with around 40,000 more deaths between December and March than in other periods.*
- food **fruit, ingredient, produce, refreshment, veg, vegetable** *This menu is updated each semester to reflect the seasonal produce available to our chefs.*
- illness **allergy, flu, rhinitis** *Most people tested for flu-like symptoms will be suffering from regular seasonal flu.*
- weather **conditions, flooding, rainfall, temperature** *The river was still wide and shallow, with*

marshland to the north where seasonal flooding occurred.

seat N
a position as member of an elected group such as a parliament or committee.

- adj+N easy to win or keep **safe, winnable** *The Liberal Democrats seized one of Labour's safest seats in a key north London by-election.*
- ▶ which any candidate might win **marginal** *The paper also reports from Cheadle constituency, the country's most marginal seat.*
- v+N win a seat **gain, pick up, take, win** *He won the seat at the 1906 General Election.*
- ▶ try to get or keep a seat **contest, defend, fight for** *Representatives had until Saturday to inform the party whether they intended to contest their seats.*
- ▶ keep a seat which you already have **hold, hold onto, keep, retain** *Despite a strong challenge, she held onto her seat with a small majority.*
- ▶ lose a seat **lose** *We lost many seats, but we won the election.*

secluded ADJ
private, peaceful, and not near other people

- adv+ADJ
- ADJ+n **corner, hideaway, location, retreat, setting, spot, surroundings** *You will have the chance to meet people and work in some beautiful, secluded spots.*
- and/or **peaceful, private, quiet, rural, sheltered, tranquil** *The park offers a number of tranquil and secluded spots for picnicking.*

second V
officially support a proposal in a meeting

- V+n **amendment, motion, nomination, proposal, resolution** *In seconding the proposal, Councillor McBride welcomed the provision of car parking spaces.*

secrecy N
a situation in which you keep something secret

- adj+N **absolute, complete, deep, extreme, great, perfect, strict, total, utmost** *This is a very confidential matter that requires the utmost secrecy.*
- v+N keep something secret **ensure, maintain, preserve, protect** *Maintaining the secrecy and mystery of the Order is one of the main strengths of the Freemasons.*

  If something is very secret, you can say that it is **shrouded in secrecy** or **cloaked in secrecy**: *The new inquiry has been shrouded in secrecy since it was quietly resumed last year.*

- ▶ require secrecy **demand, impose, require** *The administration imposed strict secrecy on the production process.*

  If you make someone promise to keep something secret, you **swear** them **to secrecy**: *The few people who knew of its existence were sworn to secrecy.*

- n+of+N **blanket, cloak, shroud, veil, wall** *Under a*

blanket of secrecy, almost a million soldiers were gathered for the attack.

secret N
a piece of information which must not become publicly known

- adj+N not told to anyone **closely-guarded, deep, hidden, well-guarded, well-kept** *All the liqueurs are made to our own recipes, which are closely-guarded family secrets.*
- ▶ concerning personal matters **innermost, intimate** *Our unconscious world has the power to reveal our innermost secrets.*
- ▶ concerning bad or illegal behaviour **dark, deadly, dirty, dreadful, guilty, shameful, shocking, sinister, sordid, terrible** *This has been the west's 'dirty little secret' ever since President Roosevelt's time.*
- v+N tell people a secret **betray, disclose, divulge, give away, leak, let slip, let sb in on, reveal, share** *Putin's government accused the former naval officer of divulging state secrets.*
- ▶ discover a secret **find out, learn, steal, uncover, unearth, unlock** *Retracing her path, he unearths a terrible secret about a woman he never truly knew.*
- ▶ not let others find out **bury, conceal, guard, harbour, hide, keep** *His eldest son harbours a guilt secret.*
- N+v come out, emerge, get out, leak out *Dark secrets emerge and hidden pasts are revealed.*

section N
a part of a book, document etc

- adj+N **central, concluding, first, following, introductory, last, main, next, preceding** *In the preceding section, several references were made to new drugs currently under development.*
- N+v **comprise, consist of, contain, cover, deal with, describe, detail, discuss, examine, explain, feature, focus on, highlight, include, list, outline, provide, refer to** *The next section outlines the main stages in the process.*

sector N
a part of a country's economic or business activity

- adj+N involving a particular type of business **agricultural, automotive, commercial, creative, cultural, financial, industrial, legal, medical, pharmaceutical, retail** *The industrial sector produc 0.5 million tonnes of plastic packaging waste per year.*
- ▶ running a business in a particular way **charitable, corporate, independent, non-profit, not-for-profit, private, public, regulated, voluntary** *Opinion on this is divided within the charitable sector.*
- n+N **banking, biotechnology, business, charity, construction, education, energy, engineering, finance, healthcare, hospitality, housing, leisure, manufacturing, property, telecommunications, tourism, transport** *The company's priority is to strengthen our position in the competitive leisure sector.*

secure V

get or achieve something

● adv+V **safely, successfully** *Thanks for all your help in successfully securing my personal loan.*

● V+n money **award, backing, finance, funding, funds, grant, investment, loan, mortgage, sponsorship** *The main task was securing the funding to deliver the project.*

▸ an agreement **agreement, contract, deal** *The union took national action over a year ago to secure a better pay deal.*

▸ a job **appointment, employment, job, placement, position, promotion, title** *She subsequently secured a position with the Darmstadt City Opera in Germany.*

▸ a victory **comfortably, victory, win** *Simon Downer secured the win by heading home Nick Crittenden's cross in the 52nd minute.*

secure ADJ

safe from attack, harm, or damage

● adv+ADJ very **absolutely, completely, extremely, fully, highly, perfectly, totally** *The system uses a simple yet highly secure web interface.*

● in a particular way **economically, emotionally, financially, physically, psychologically** *I am emotionally secure and have a loving relationship with my partner and family.*

● v+ADJ be secure **appear, be, become, feel, look, seem** *Here are some tips to ensure that your child's bike is secure against any attempt to steal it.*

● make something secure **keep, make** *This type of wireless network can be made almost as secure as a wired network.*

security N

safety from attack, harm, or damage

● adj+N strict **added, additional, enhanced, extra, heightened, maximum, strong, tight** *Prisons operate under incredibly tight security.*

● types of security **corporate, environmental, financial, internal, military, nuclear, personal, physical** *Individuals who make provision for their retirement are interested in financial security.*

● v+N make security certain **afford, assure, enforce, ensure, guarantee, maintain, protect, provide, safeguard** *We have frameworks in place to safeguard the security of the information we hold.*

● make security more certain **bolster, enhance, improve, increase, strengthen, tighten, upgrade** *Airports are employing facial recognition techniques to enhance security.*

● put security in doubt **breach, compromise, endanger, jeopardize, threaten, undermine** *The system offers fast Internet connectivity that doesn't compromise security.*

● N+n actions or systems to protect security **check, feature, issue, measure, mechanism, policy, procedure, solution, system** *You should change your password after you provide the information below, as a security measure.*

● something that threatens security **breach, concern, flaw, risk, threat** *If you have authorised someone else to trade on your account, this may constitute a security breach.*

2 a feeling of confidence and safety

● n+of+N **feeling, sense** *Ours is quite a small group, which possibly adds to the feeling of security when expressing some very personal thoughts.*

seed N

a part a plant produces that can grow into a new plant

● v+N plant seeds **plant, sow** *Most popular herbs can be raised from seed sown indoors during early spring.*

▸ spread seeds over an area **bear, disperse, scatter, shed, spread** *The sweet chestnut tree starts to bear its seeds when about 30 years old.* ● *The seeds are dispersed by the wind.*

▸ produce seeds **produce, set** *When plants are fertilized they produce seeds that can develop into new plants.*

▸ grow plants from seeds **grow sth from, raise sth from** *These trees were grown from seeds collected from a forest.*

● N+v grow **appear, develop, germinate, grow, sprout** *Water and then cover until the seeds have germinated.*

seek V

ask for or try to get something

● adv+V in an active way **actively, proactively** *Funding from commercial sources is also actively sought.*

▸ in a worried or urgent way **desperately, earnestly, urgently** *Police are urgently seeking information about the disappearance of two children.*

▸ in a keen or enthusiastic way **diligently, eagerly** *Tickets for the final are being eagerly sought.*

▸ always or regularly **always, constantly, continually** *We constantly seek to improve the quality of our teaching.*

▸ now **currently** *We are currently seeking applications for the position of Store Manager.*

▸ deliberately **deliberately** *Was she deliberately seeking to anger him?*

● V+n help or support **advice, assistance, clarification, guidance, help, reassurance, support** *You are strongly advised to seek professional legal advice.*

▸ protection **asylum, refuge** *Figures show a steep decline in the number of people seeking asylum.*

▸ permission or approval **access, approval, permission** *If you wish to use any part of this article for your coursework, you have to seek permission from the University.*

▸ opinion **opinion, views** *The report highlighted the positive contributions of our students when their views were sought.*

▸ answer or solution **answer, resolution, solution, way** *We are seeking answers to these questions.*

▸ information **information** *I am seeking information about my maternal grandfather.*

▸ work **employment, opportunity, work** *She spends a lot of time travelling overseas to seek business opportunities.*

▸ money or financial support **compensation, funding, funds, sponsorship** *We are actively seeking funding for a new research project.*

see off PHR VB

deal successfully with someone, especially by
defeating them

- V+n **challenge, competition, opposition, rivals,
  threat** *Alonso saw off a strong challenge from
  Raikkonen in yesterday's Canadian grand prix.*

seethe V

be extremely angry

- V+with **anger, discontent, frustration, hatred,
  indignation, rage, resentment** *I was seething with
  anger all the way home.*

see through PHR VB

not be tricked by something

- V+n **deception, disguise, illusion, lie, plan, ruse,
  scam, trick** *I could see through her lies straight
  away.*

segregation N

the policy of keeping different groups separate

- adj+N for particular reasons **ethnic, gender,
  occupational, racial, religious, residential, social**
  Apartheid was state-imposed racial segregation.
- ▶ strictly applied **complete, compulsory, rigid, strict**
  *Even during a period of rigid segregation, Robeson
  worked regularly with white musicians.*
- v+N deal with or oppose segregation **challenge,
  end, fight, reduce, resist, tackle** *One of our main
  tasks is to tackle gender segregation in the workplace.*
- ▶ cause segregation to exist or continue **contribute
  to, encourage, increase, lead to, promote, reinforce**
  *Segregation in housing leads to segregation in
  education.*
- ▶ make sure that segregation is obeyed **enforce,
  ensure, maintain** *Segregation was rigidly enforced in
  the city.*

seize V

gain control in a situation

- adv+V **eagerly, immediately, promptly, quickly** *A
  once-in-a-generation opportunity has presented itself:
  it must be seized immediately or lost.*
- V+n opportunity **advantage, chance, moment,
  opportunity, possession, power** *It was vital to seize
  this historic opportunity before it was lost.*
- ▶ control **control** *United began to seize control of the
  match.*
- ▶ opportunity to take action before others **initiative**
  *The Conservatives have seized the initiative on the
  key election issues of tax and immigration.*

select V

choose someone or something from a group

- adv+V with no particular pattern or method
  arbitrarily, at random, randomly *We surveyed twenty
  randomly selected websites.*
- ▶ carefully **carefully, meticulously** *In the second and
  third years students carry out project work with
  carefully selected clients.*
- ▶ for a particular purpose **exclusively, specially,
  specifically** *Accommodation is in a range of
  specially selected quality hotels.*

- ▶ automatically **automatically** *With Automatic
  Exposure, shutter speed and aperture are
  automatically selected.*
- ▶ by one person only **personally** *All plants are
  personally selected by Martin Gibbons to offer you
  consistent quality.*

Usage **Select** is often used in the passive in all of
the **adv+V** combinations shown above.

selection N

things to choose from, or things chosen

- adj+N large **broad, comprehensive, extensive,
  huge, large, vast, wide** *Our online delicatessen offers
  a wide selection of British gourmet food.*
- ▶ including very different things **diverse, varied,
  wide-ranging** *This guidebook includes a rich and
  varied selection of walks on the island.*
- ▶ good **excellent, fantastic, fine, good, great,
  interesting, rich, superb, wonderful** *In our
  restaurant you can enjoy great food, a stunning
  selection of wines and exceptional service.*
- ▶ small **limited, small** *This album is just a small
  selection of his vast output.*
- ▶ with no particular method or pattern **random** *A
  random selection of instruments was tested for
  accuracy by researchers.*
- ▶ representative **representative** *We asked a
  representative selection of drivers to tell us their
  opinions.*
- v+N have or provide a selection **carry, feature,
  have, offer, present, provide, serve, stock** *A market
  is held every Wednesday, offering a wide selection of
  goods and bargains.*
- ▶ include a selection **boast, contain, include** *The
  hotel's menu boasts a fantastic selection of seafood
  dishes. ● A museum within the building contains an
  interesting selection of historic banknotes and coins.*
- ▶ find a selection **find** *You'll find a selection of our
  current vacancies on this site.*
- ▶ choose from a selection **choose from** *Choose from
  a selection of ten hotels, three-star to five-star.*
- ▶ look at a selection **browse, view** *We spent the
  morning in the market, browsing the excellent
  selection of local products.*

self-confidence N

confidence in your own abilities

- adj+N great **enormous, great, supreme** *Miss
  Burgess exuded a supreme self-confidence.*
- ▶ low **low** *He seems to understand what it's like to be
  a teenager with low self-confidence and esteem.*
- v+N increase self-confidence **boost, build,
  develop, increase** *Students said that getting early
  feedback boosted their self-confidence.*
- ▶ have or get self-confidence **gain, have, rebuild,
  regain, restore** *You will gain more self-confidence
  as you deliver more speeches.*
- ▶ give someone self-confidence **give sb** *This is a
  fantastic project which has given self-confidence to
  many of our pupils.*
- ▶ not have self-confidence **lack, lose** *She admits that
  she lacks self-confidence in new situations.*

You can also talk about a person's *lack of self-confidence*: He suffered from a chronic lack of self-confidence.

▸ make someone's self-confidence weaker **destroy, undermine** She lost her temper all the time, and the constant rants started to undermine my self-confidence.

self-control N
the ability to control your behaviour

▸ v+N have or use self-control **exercise, have, possess, practise** The test is to see if you can exercise self-control under trying circumstances.
▸ not have self-control **lack, lose** For the first time I was really on the verge of losing my self-control.

You can also talk about a person's *lack of self-control*: Alcohol may lead to lack of self-control, unconsciousness, or even coma.

learn self-control **develop, learn** I've gained weight and need to learn more self-control.
need self-control **require, take** It took all my self-control to prevent me from breaking out into a cry of astonishment.

self-esteem N
the feeling that you have good qualities and deserve to be treated well

adj+N low **low, negative, poor** There is evidence to show that individuals with low self-esteem are more likely to be intolerant of others.
high **high, increased, positive** Such children generally have higher self-esteem than kids with absent or uninvolved fathers.
v+N increase self-esteem **bolster, boost, build, develop, enhance, foster, improve, increase, raise** These sessions help boost the children's self-esteem and confidence.
make self-esteem weaker **damage, erode, lower, undermine** Being out of work can lower your self-esteem and affect your confidence.
have self-esteem **have, suffer from** His wife suffered from low self-esteem and deep depression after the birth of her two sons.
not have self-esteem **lack, lose** The problem for many of these children is that they lack self-esteem.
make somone have self-esteem again **rebuild, restore** Our priority is to restore these addicts' self-esteem.
and/or **confidence, dignity, independence, motivation, self-confidence, self-worth** Youngsters on the course gain in confidence and self-esteem.

self-evident ADJ
obvious, and therefore not needing any explanation

adv+ADJ **almost, by no means, fairly** How the costs are calculated is by no means self-evident.
ADJ+n idea or statement **fact, principle, proposition, truth** It is a self-evident fact that what looks good on paper may not necessarily translate to the small screen.
answer or meaning **answer, meaning** The answer is not self-evident or simple.
v+ADJ **appear, be, seem** It might seem self-evident

that new technology will improve productivity, but this is not always the case.

selfish ADJ
thinking only about yourself

● adv+ADJ completely **completely, entirely, purely, totally, utterly** I was in favour of the ban for purely selfish reasons, because I don't smoke.
▸ very **extremely, incredibly, very** That's not only incredibly selfish, it's downright irresponsible.
● and/or **greedy, inconsiderate, irresponsible, lazy, rude, thoughtless** The emergency services complain that they get too many unecessary calls from thoughtless and selfish people.

semblance N
a situation in which a condition only exists to a small degree

● v+N keep a semblance **keep, maintain, preserve, retain** We must endeavour to maintain the semblance of unity.
▸ give a semblance **bring, give sth** His efforts to bring some semblance of order to his team never flagged.
▸ get a semblance again **regain, restore** Extra resources will be needed to restore some semblance of stability and equity.
▸ not have a semblance **lack, lose** We had lost all semblance of control.

● N+of **control, dignity, legitimacy, normality, order, sanity, unity** Eventually, the war came to an end and, again, a semblance of normality returned to the villages.

seminar N
a meeting where people discuss a subject

● adj+N at a regular time **annual, fortnightly, monthly, regular, weekly** The course is taught in ten weekly one-hour seminars in the first term.
▸ length of seminar **one-hour, two-day etc** Additionally, we run six one-day seminars each year at our Conference Centre.
▸ free **free** Businesses are being offered the chance to attend free training seminars on the Green Tourism Business Scheme.
▸ for people in part of a country or from several countries **international, regional** The study group organized ten international seminars, the proceedings of which have been published
▸ done online **interactive, online, virtual** Most students reported that they enjoyed the virtual seminars, and wanted more of them.
● n+N time of the day **afternoon, breakfast, evening, lunchtime, weekend** Regular evening and lunchtime seminars are held.
▸ for people doing an advanced degree **graduate, postgraduate** The Department also runs a series of staff and postgraduate seminars featuring regular presentations by scholars of international standing.
▸ subject of seminar **business, history, management, marketing, research, training** The Department holds a weekly research seminar for its staff and postgraduates.
● v+N be present at a seminar **attend, go to** As part of their formal training, all students at UCC attend seminars on project management.

▶ organize a seminar **convene, hold, host, organize, run, stage** *The first seminar was held at Keele in December 2005 and was attended by over 70 delegates.*

▶ give a seminar **conduct, deliver, give, present** *In March, Professor Philip Hanson gave a seminar on 'Economic Developments and Prospects in Russia'.*

▶ be in charge of a seminar **chair, facilitate, lead** *A senior member of staff chairs the seminar.*

● N+n set of seminars **programme, series** *An intercollegiate seminar programme is run by graduates in London.*

▶ what is said or written **discussion, paper, presentation, topic** *In June he presented a seminar paper on 'A Year of President Putin'.*

▶ room **facilities, room, space** *Sessions are generally held in the ground floor seminar room.*

▶ time seminar takes place **session** *The presentations should reflect the subject matter of the lectures and seminar sessions.*

▶ people **attendee, class, group, speaker, tutor** *Tuition takes place in seminar groups of up to 22 students.*

senior ADJ
with a high rank or position

● ADJ+n worker or workers **advisor, director, executive, judge, lecturer, manager, member of staff, officer, official, partner, professor, staff, vice-president** *These records should be regularly checked by a senior member of staff.*

▶ job **level, position, post, role** *Graduates from our courses occupy senior positions throughout the construction industry.*

sensation N
a physical feeling

● adj+N affecting your body **bodily, physical, tactile** *Standing in front of a band like that is a real physical sensation.*

▶ strange **odd, strange, weird** *I felt a strange sensation on top of my head.*

▶ unpleasant **painful, uncomfortable, unpleasant** *Giving an animal one mild electric shock to the paws causes a brief unpleasant sensation, but doesn't cause any lasting harm.*

▶ pleasant **pleasant, pleasurable** *Such drugs produce pleasurable sensations in those who use them.*

▶ stinging or burning **burning, prickling, stinging, tingling** *Some people may experience a tingling sensation in the fingers.*

▶ extreme **intense, overwhelming** *I returned to bed and after a few minutes became aware of an intense burning sensation.*

● v+N experience a sensation **experience, feel, have** *He felt a mild sensation, akin to an electric shock, down his side.*

▶ produce a sensation **cause, create, evoke, produce, trigger** *Too much adrenalin will have an effect on the brain and produce the sensation of tiredness.*

▶ enjoy a sensation **enjoy** *I enjoy the sensation of floating in water.*

sense N
a strong feeling or belief

● adj+N strong **deep, great, keen, overwhelming, powerful, profound, strong** *As he stood there looking out, he felt a deep sense of well-being.*

▶ real **genuine, palpable, proper, real, true** *They were proud of their work and had a real sense of achievement.*

▶ clear **clear** *Our UK staff work in a variety of locations, each with its own clear sense of purpose and identity.*

▶ growing **growing, heightened** *I watched them with a growing sense of unease.*

▶ shared **shared** *Co-operation between parents, staff and governors leads to a shared sense of purpose.*

● v+N give a sense **bring, convey, create, develop, encourage, engender, evoke, foster, generate, give sb, instill, produce** *A social centre helps to create a sense of community.*

▶ have or get a sense **experience, feel, gain, get, have** *Once he'd gone, I felt a profound sense of failure.*

▶ not have a sense **lack, lose** *Prison can make people feel hopeless, make them lose any sense of self-value.*

▶ keep a sense **keep, maintain, retain** *As a relatively small school, we strive to maintain a sense of community among students and staff.*

▶ share a sense **share** *I share your sense of disappointment with the film.*

● N+of belonging to a group **belonging, community, identity, involvement, solidarity** *For most of us, verbal language is central to our sense of identity.*

▶ good feeling **achievement, duty, excitement, pride, purpose, relief, responsibility, satisfaction, security, well-being, wonder** *I think everybody departed on Sunday evening with a great sense of achievement.*

▶ bad feeling **disappointment, failure, frustration, guilt, insecurity, isolation, loss** *He admitted that he felt an increasing sense of guilt.*

▶ being urgent **urgency** *There seemed to be little sense of urgency.*

▶ having a clear purpose **mission, purpose** *The aim of the talk was to give the group a clear sense of purpose.*

sense V
know about something through a natural ability or feeling

● V+n a feeling or mood **atmosphere, feeling, mood** *As we went into the stadium, we could sense the atmosphere of mounting excitement.*

▶ a negative feeling **anxiety, disappointment, discomfort, fear, frustration, hostility, tension, unease** *I sensed his unease as he struggled to justify his decision.*

▶ a positive feeling **excitement, relief** *At last they scored a goal, and you could sense the relief in the crowd.*

▶ possibility of danger **danger, threat, trouble** *Sensing the danger they were in, they started to run.*

senseless ADJ
happening or done for no purpose

● ADJ+n **act, death, destruction, killing, murder, slaughter, tragedy, violence, waste** *I shudder to think what this senseless act of aggression has done to the peace process.*

sensible ADJ
reasonable and practical

- adv+ADJ very **eminently, entirely, perfectly, quite, really, thoroughly, very** *The proposed approach seems eminently sensible.*
- in a particular way **commercially, economically, environmentally, politically** *For the company, it is no longer commercially sensible to work in this area.*
- ADJ+n action, method or plan **approach, arrangement, compromise, course of action, measure, policy, precaution, solution, step, strategy, way** *You should always take sensible precautions when downloading any information from the Internet.*
- choice or decision **choice, decision, option** *The employment market is difficult, so it may be a sensible option to take a Master's degree.*
- advice or suggestion **advice, proposal, suggestion** *A good financial adviser will give you sensible advice about saving.*
- v+ADJ **appear, be, look, seem, sound** *The plan is to run the factory on renewable energy, which sounds very sensible.*

sensitive ADJ
needing to be kept secret or dealt with carefully

- adv+ADJ very **exceptionally, extremely, highly, incredibly, particularly, very** *Clearly, factory closures were a highly sensitive issue with major political implications.*
- possibly, in the future **potentially** *The government eventually published the report, but only after removing potentially sensitive information.*
- from a particular point of view **commercially, culturally, ecologically, emotionally, environmentally, ethically, politically** *Correspondence may be edited if it contains material that it is confidential or commercially sensitive.*
- ADJ+n information **data, information, material** *Sensitive information such as credit card details and customer records are not held on our website.*
- subject or issue **case, issue, matter, subject, topic** *Most Internet users are worried about their online privacy, especially when it comes to the sensitive subject of their medical information.*
- nature **nature** *Public access to a conference on terrorism was barred due to the sensitive nature of the topic, the organizers said.*

sensitivities N
a tendency to have strong emotional reactions or be offended

- adj+N **cultural, local, political, religious** *As new massive re-construction of the area went ahead, it took little account of local sensitivities.*
- v+N show you understand someone's sensitivities **be aware of, respect, take account of** *When exhibiting your work you need to be aware of the sensitivities of others.*
- offend someone's sensitivities **offend** *Advertisers are warned to be careful about offending religious sensitivities, particularly when advertising in untargeted media.*

sentence N
a punishment given by a judge

- adj+N in prison/not in prison **custodial, non-custodial** *Both women are now serving custodial sentences.*
- most/least severe allowed **maximum, minimum** *Those found guilty of harassment now face a maximum five-year jail sentence.*
- long/short **brief, lengthy, long, short** *Anyone who breaches the injunction will face arrest and the possibility of a long prison sentence.*
- length of sentence **two-year, six-month etc** *Scott is nearing the end of a five-year prison sentence.*
- severe **harsh, heavy, tough** *If defendants feel that the sentence was too harsh, they can appeal against it in the Appeal Court.*
- not severe **lenient, light** *In my judgment, the sentence was unduly lenient.*
- ordered by law **mandatory** *The mandatory sentence for murder is life.*
- only if you commit another crime **conditional, suspended** *She received a two-year suspended sentence for bank fraud.*
- n+N **community, death, jail, life, prison** *He is serving a life sentence for murder.*
- v+N officially say what the sentence is **hand down, impose, pass, pronounce** *If the defendant is found guilty the judge may pass sentence immediately.*
- receive a sentence **be given, get, receive** *He was found guilty on two charges and received an 18-month sentence.*
- spend time in prison **complete, serve** *The vast majority of women in prison are serving sentences for non-violent offences.*
- when a sentence is likely **face** *If found guilty, she faces a prison sentence of 15–20 years.*
- reduce a sentence **commute, reduce** *His death sentence was commuted to life imprisonment.*
- lead to a particular sentence **attract, carry** *This offence carries a custodial sentence.*
- officially cancel a sentence **overturn, quash** *She initially got 8 years in jail, but the sentence was overturned in the Appeal Court.*

sentiment N [usually plural]
a belief or an attitude towards something

- adj+N positive **admirable, fine, generous, lofty, noble, positive** *What a pity such noble sentiments are married to such awful words and music.*
- negative **negative** *When children are constantly criticized, they begin to have negative sentiments about their own abilities.*
- felt by many people **common, general, popular, widespread** *During this period, there was widespread anti-American sentiment.*
- types of sentiment **anti-war, liberal, nationalist, patriotic, racist, religious** *Her policies appealed to the public's growing nationalist sentiment.*
- v+N express a sentiment **express, voice** *Other speakers expressed the same sentiments.*
- express or show the same sentiment **echo, reflect** *Many delegates echoed these sentiments.*
- agree with a sentiment **agree with, endorse, share, support** *We agree wholeheartedly with the sentiments in the article.*

If you are agreeing with someone, you can also say *my sentiments exactly*: 'If that's art, I give up.' 'My sentiments exactly!'

▶ understand a sentiment **appreciate, understand** *He said he appreciated the sentiments expressed by his colleague, but did not agree with them.*

sequence N
a set of related things in a particular order

● adj+N arranged by time, numbers, or the alphabet **alphabetical, chronological, numerical** *Can you place these events in a chronological sequence?*

▶ sensible and reasonable **logical** *The chapters follow a logical sequence.*

▶ with no particular pattern **random** *Create passwords that will be hard to guess – ideally a random sequence of letters and numbers.*

▶ with things following one after the other **linear** *Programs comprise a linear sequence of arguments and functions.*

▶ correct **correct, proper, right** *Pupils have to arrange the pictures in the correct sequence.*

▶ complete **complete, entire, whole** *I can't remember the whole sequence of events all these years later.*

▶ long/short **extended, lengthy, long, short** *They just avoided equalling the club record for the longest sequence of defeats.*

▶ complicated **complex, complicated** *The dance involves a complex sequence of movements.*

serious ADJ
bad or dangerous enough to cause problems, damage, or anxiety

● adv+ADJ very **exceptionally, extremely, incredibly, particularly, really, very** *The situation is now extremely serious.*

▶ rather **fairly, pretty** INFORMAL *He had a pretty serious crash yesterday and you never know how that affects someone.*

▶ possibly **potentially** *The drug can cause potentially serious side effects.*

▶ enough **enough, sufficiently** *Her injuries were considered sufficiently serious to require medical attention.*

● ADJ+n something causing physical harm **accident, condition, crash, disease, illness, incident, infection, injury** *Young drivers are most at risk of death and serious injury.*

▶ problem or mistake **difficulty, error, flaw, mistake, problem, weakness** *We all have a one-in-thirteen chance of developing a serious sight problem.*

▶ breaking a law or rule **breach, crime, offence, violation** *Throwing or letting off fireworks in a public place is a serious offence.*

▶ result or effect **consequences, effect, implication, side-effect** *Failure by employers and employees to complete the procedures will have serious consequences.*

▶ damage or risk **damage, danger, harm, risk, threat** *The city suffered serious damage.*

▶ situation **business, challenge, crisis, issue, situation** *The healthcare system is on the verge of a serious crisis.*

● v+ADJ be serious **appear, be, look, seem, sound**

He will have a scan to determine the full extent of the injury, but it is not looking too serious.

▶ become serious **become, get, grow** *The crisis became more serious by the day.*

▶ more and more **increasingly, more and more** *Drug taking among young teenagers was becoming an increasingly serious problem.*

seriousness N
the fact of being bad or dangerous enough to cause problems, damage, or anxiety

● adj+N potential **demonstrate, highlight, potential, show, underline** *Because of the potential seriousness of her injuries, she was airlifted to West Cumberland hospital.*

▶ great **deep, extreme, great, high, utmost** *There is no doubt this is a problem of great seriousness.*

● v+N realize or understand the seriousness of something **acknowledge, appreciate, realize, recognize, understand** *She did not seem to appreciate the seriousness of her condition.*

● show the seriousness of something **reflect** *The sentence must reflect the seriousness of the crime.*

● N+of illegal activity **crime, offence** *The restrictions on the liberty of the offender must be in line with the seriousness of the offence.*

▶ bad or dangerous situation **problem, risk, situation, threat** *John quickly realized the seriousness of the situation.*

▶ illness or injury **condition, disease, illness, injury symptoms** *It is too early to assess the seriousness of her injuries.*

serve V
be used for a particular purpose

● V+as way or showing or informing **indicator, lesson, reminder, warning** *This case should serve as a reminder that radiation protection should never be taken for granted.*

▶ way of doing or getting something **means, mechanism, resource, source** *Your driver's licence can serve as a means of identification.*

▶ way of explaining, or showing how something done **example, guide, introduction, model, reference** *This new publication serves as a complete guide to investment banking.*

● V+infinitive **demonstrate, emphasize, heighten, highlight, illustrate, indicate, reinforce, remind, strengthen, underline** *The above descriptions are brief, but they serve to illustrate what small amount of money can do when used imaginatively.*

service N
help given to or work done for someone

● adj+N very helpful **great, valuable** *The links on this website offer a valuable service for tourists in the British Isles.*

▶ of a high quality **efficient, excellent, good, professional, quality, reliable** *Many thanks for the fast and efficient service you provided.*

▶ of a low quality **atrocious, bad, poor** *The company is notorious for poor customer service.*

▶ friendly or personal **friendly, personal** *We aim to provide a friendly and personal service.*

- v+N provide a service **offer (sb), provide (sb with)** *She offered her services as his guide.*
- ▶ perform a service **be of, do sb, perform, render** *The authors have done the profession a great service by writing a textbook that makes these developments accessible to undergraduates.*
- ▶ need a service **need, require** *Any other faults really require the services of an engineer.*
- ▶ receive a service **receive** *I am usually quick to complain if I receive poor service, so I feel it only fair to compliment good service.*
- n+of+N **effectiveness, level, quality, standard** *The restaurant offers good standards of service and cuisine.*

session N
a period of time spent doing a particular activity, especially in a group

- adj+N regular **regular, weekly** *It was an idea which came to us during one of our regular brainstorming sessions.*
- ▶ length of session **two-hour, 30-minute etc** *The training will consist of three one-hour sessions.*
- ▶ long/short **long, short** *Meetings usually begin with a short business session, followed by a guest speaker.*
- ▶ taking part in a practical or active way **hands-on, interactive, practical** *Storyteller Bea Nicholson will be holding interactive storytelling sessions throughout the afternoon.*
- ▶ involving two people or a group **face-to-face, group, one-to-one** *Our poet-in-residence provides workshops and one-to-one sessions during the Summer Festival.*
- ▶ as an introduction **introductory, taster** *These introductory sessions are free to all library members.*
- n+N time of the day **afternoon, evening, morning** *The afternoon session commenced with Dr Keith Duff giving an informative talk on water and ecology.*
- ▶ training or teaching **coaching, feedback, practice, study, teaching, training, tutorial, workshop** *Each training session can be individually designed and tailored to meet the needs of every audience.*
- ▶ types of session **brainstorming, briefing, counselling, discussion, question-and-answer, recording, therapy** *The day was rounded off with a question-and-answer session.*
- v+N organize a session **conduct, hold, offer, organize, run** *We run training sessions for teachers as well as children.*
- ▶ take part in a session **attend, join, participate in, take part in** *Parents are welcome to attend these sessions.*
- ▶ miss a session **miss** *Adams has missed some training sessions this week.*
- ▶ arrange a time for a session **book, schedule** *No appointment is needed, and you can book further sessions if you need to.*
- ▶ be in charge of a session **chair, facilitate, lead, teach** *A question-and-answer session was chaired by Peter Hughes.*
- ▶ start a session **begin, introduce, open, start** *Suzanne opened the second session of the conference.*
- ▶ end a session **close, conclude, end, finish** *Once you have finished your session, please make sure you sign out again.*

set V
1 do something that influences something else

- V+n **mood, pattern, precedent, tone, trend** *This incident set the tone for the whole weekend.*

2 establish what must be done or followed

- V+n what must be achieved or done **challenge, goal, objective, priorities, target, task** *Accountability for health and safety performance should be strengthened by setting objectives and targets.*
- ▶ conditions or rules **agenda, conditions, criteria, guidelines, parameters, rules** *Final decisions taken at the summit will set the rules for international trade for years to come.*
- ▶ standard to be followed **benchmark, standard** *The successful candidate will lead by example and set high standards.*
- ▶ limit or amount **budget, ceiling, deadline, fee, level, limit, rate, threshold** *The President has set a ceiling of 4 per cent for pay increases in the public sector.*

set N
a group of things of the same type

- N+of **conditions, criteria, guidelines, instructions, parameters, principles, questions, recommendations, regulations, results, rules, standards, values** *Nearly every language has a complete set of rules for the writing down of its sounds.*

setback N
a problem that delays or stops progress

- adj+N big or serious **big, huge, major, serious, severe, significant** *United's promotion chances suffered a major setback at the weekend.*
- ▶ small **minor, slight** *This minor setback has only made him more determined.*
- ▶ for only a short time **temporary** *However, the Battle of Badon Hill was only a temporary setback for the Anglo-Saxon forces.*
- ▶ when a setback happens **early, latest, recent** *Despite this early setback, the flight test programme continued.*
- v+N experience a setback **encounter, experience, face, have, hit, receive, suffer** *The project has suffered several setbacks over the past year.*
- ▶ successfully deal with a setback **deal with, overcome, overcome** *As he had proved again and again, he had the emotional reserves needed to overcome any setback.*
- ▶ be a setback **be, constitute, represent** *There is no doubt that the election result represents a significant setback for the party.*

set out PHR VB
explain, describe, or arrange something clearly

- V+n plan or policy **framework, options, plan, policy, position, principles, proposal, strategy, vision** *The report sets out a framework for reforming the banking system.*
- ▶ aims **aims, objectives, priorities, targets** *Set out your objectives, matching them to the job description.*
- ▶ reasons **arguments, reasons** *We listened as she set out her reasons for refusing our application.*

settings N

1 a position that controls are at

● v+N change settings **adjust, alter, change, modify, tweak, update** *You will need to adjust your browser settings using these instructions.*

▶ arrange settings **configure, optimize, set, specify** *You can configure virtual memory settings manually.*

▶ make a computer keep its settings **save, store** *Your settings will be saved automatically.*

▶ check settings **check** *If you are using a firewall, check your settings.*

▶ choose settings **choose, select** *Most home cinema systems have a menu where you can choose various settings.*

2 the place, situation, or environment in which something happens

● adj+N beautiful or perfect **beautiful, ideal, idyllic, lovely, magnificent, perfect, picturesque, spectacular** *The setting is idyllic, with majestic views on all sides.*

▶ peaceful **peaceful, tranquil** *Enjoy a relaxing break in a tranquil setting.*

▶ in the country/city **rural, urban** *The academy is in a rural setting just outside the capital city of Abuja.*

▶ natural **natural** *The park is a great place to see outdoor sculpture in a natural setting.*

▶ informal/formal **formal, informal** *The Self-Directed Seminar provides students with the opportunity to present ideas and discuss their work with each other in a very informal setting.*

▶ social **social** *She is rarely comfortable in a social setting.*

▶ in a school or college **classroom, educational** *The conference is an opportunity to share information about the effective use of ICT in educational settings.*

● v+N **create, enjoy, provide** *The leafy grounds of Sudbury House Hotel provided an ideal setting for three performances of Shakespeare's Much Ado About Nothing.*

settle v

end an argument by making an agreement

● adv+V after a long time **eventually, finally, ultimately** *The case was eventually settled and the insurance company paid up.*

▶ in a friendly or peaceful way **amicably, peacefully** *If any dispute cannot be settled amicably through ordinary negotiations, the matter shall be referred to an arbitrator.*

▶ without going to a law court **out of court** *Libel cases will often be settled out of court in order to avoid the potentially huge legal costs.*

● V+n disagreement **argument, conflict, differences, dispute, lawsuit** *The University lecturers have finally settled their pay dispute.*

▶ something being discussed or dealt with **affair, case, issue, matter, question** *First of all, we need to settle the question of hours and pay.*

settle into PHR VB

become familiar with something new

● V+n way of doing things **groove, pattern, rhythm, role, routine** *I'm struggling to settle into a normal routine after studying day and night for a whole year.*

▶ new place or activity **community, home, job, life, school, surroundings** *The girls have settled into school and love being by the sea.*

settlement N

a formal agreement ending a disagreement

● adj+N friendly or peaceful **amicable, peaceful** *The two parties announced today that they have reached an amicable settlement.*

▶ lasting a long time **lasting, long-term, permanent** *She believes the peace process could bring a lasting settlement to the conflict.*

▶ final **final** *It took more than a decade to arrive at a final peace settlement.*

▶ made without asking a court to decide **mediated, out-of-court** *Parties should be encouraged to reach out-of-court settlements of their disputes.*

▶ after formal discussions **negotiated** *You will never get a peaceful situation there until you get a final negotiated settlement.*

▶ types of settlement **constitutional, financial, political** *We must re-double our efforts at finding a political settlement.*

▶ satisfactory **acceptable, satisfactory** *The chances of the two sides reaching an acceptable settlement now look remote.*

● n+N **dispute, divorce, marriage, pay, peace** *A typical divorce settlement takes more than a year to negotiate.*

● v+N reach a settlement **achieve, agree, broker, gain, reach, secure** *A mediator's role is to assist the parties in reaching a settlement.*

▶ have discussions to reach a settlement **negotiate** *The only way out of the never-ending violence is for both sides to negotiate a settlement.*

▶ accept a settlement **accept, approve** *There are rumours that he is willing to accept a peace settlement.*

▶ suggest a settlement **propose, suggest** *A divorce settlement was proposed with a one-off payment £45,000.*

▶ try to reach a settlement **seek, want** *Lawyers for both sides are seeking a settlement.*

▶ force someone to accept a settlement **impose** *Mediators are not authorized to impose a settlement on the parties.*

severe ADJ

a severe problem is very serious and worrying

● adv+ADJ rather **fairly, moderately, pretty INFORMAL, quite, rather** *The side effects can be quite severe.*

▶ very **exceptionally, extremely, particularly, unusually, very** *A score of 14 points out of a possible 24 was equivalent to extremely severe problems.*

● ADJ+n problem **damage, difficulty, disruption, distress, hardship, limitation, shortage** *Up to 8 million people face severe food shortages or starvation.*

▶ illness or injury **depression, disability, disease, illness, impairment, injury, pain, trauma** *He has nursed me through a severe illness, and is even now with me.*

severity N
the seriousness or strictness of something

- adj+N great or very great **exceptional, extreme, undue, unusual, the utmost** *After its eventual defeat, the Roman authorities treated the tribe with the utmost severity.*
- ▶ moderate or relative **moderate, relative** *In terms of relative severity, the vows may be divided into major and minor vows.*
- ▶ variable **variable, varying** *While it is known that the disease runs in families, severity is very variable.*
- v+N decrease severity **alleviate, decrease, lessen, mitigate, reduce** *The second option is to lessen the severity of the defect by gentle polishing.*
- ▶ increase severity **increase** *This cycle of bingeing and purging maintains and increases the severity of the condition.*
- ▶ assess severity **assess, evaluate, rate** *The ultrasound scan can help to assess the severity of disease.*

sewage N
waste substances removed by large underground pipes

- adj+N **crude, raw, treated, untreated** *Avoid swimming where water may be contaminated with untreated sewage.*
- v+N **discharge, dump, pump, treat** *The majority of boats do not discharge sewage into the water.*

sexuality N
sexual feelings, attitudes, and activities

- adj+N types of sexuality **adolescent, female, feminine, gay, human, infantile, male, teenage** *It was the worst caricature of Asian female sexuality I have ever seen.*
- ▶ open/not open **overt, repressed** *Though there is a touch of nudity, there is no overt sexuality shown.*
- v+N reveal or express one's sexuality **disclose, express, flaunt** *Alicia is a beautiful girl, but doesn't flaunt her sexuality.*
- ▶ hide one's sexuality **deny, hide** *He didn't hide his sexuality but it wasn't until the sexual freedom of the sixties that it became widely known.*
- ▶ discover one's sexuality **discover, explore** *Alma discovers her sexuality and Johnny grows up, but will they ever find happiness together?*
- ▶ accept one's sexuality **acknowledge, celebrate, come to terms with, embrace** *Many liberal Christians claim to find freedom and acceptance when they embrace their sexuality.*

shade N
a form of a colour

- adj+N pale **cool, light, muted, neutral, pale, pastel, soft** *The buildings are all painted in pastel shades, complementing the natural Mediterranean light.*
- dark **dark, deep, sombre** *The duller and darker shades of blue do not energise!*
- bright or intense **bright, rich, vibrant, vivid, warm** *The houses are clean and colourful, often painted in bright shades of blue and yellow.*
- delicate **delicate, soothing, subtle** *They had a delicate shade of pink at the base of each petal.*

- ▶ exact **exact** *I use a lot of colour, but colour has to be the exact right shade.*
- ▶ varied **various** *Various shades were achieved by mixing the pigments.*

2 [usually plural] a slightly different form or type of something

- N+of **belief, difference, meaning, opinion** *They represented every shade of opinion and belief.*

shadow N
a dark area created when something blocks light

- adj+N dark **dark, deep, dense, inky, murky** *Just then, the man emerged out of the dense shadows into the twilight.*
- ▶ frightening **eerie, ghostly, gloomy, ominous, sinister** *The shadows are quite eerie.*
- ▶ long **long** *The torch cast long shadows on the interior.*
- ▶ moving quickly **fleeting** *A fleeting shadow passed the chinks in the wall.*
- v+N **cast, fling, project, throw** *The autumn sun threw their shadows across the lawn beneath them.*
- N+v get bigger **lengthen, loom** *Returning down the lane, the shadows are lengthening over Wharfedale.*
- ▶ come or stay **fall, linger** *Just then, a huge shadow fell over the pair.*
- ▶ go **disappear, flee** *At the ping of the bell, the shadow disappeared.*
- ▶ move **creep, dance, flicker** *The shadows are already creeping in at 17.30 as autumn approaches.*
- ▶ get darker **darken, deepen** *The twilight was ebbing swiftly as shadows were darkening in the corners of my room.*

shake V
make lots of small, quick movements

- adv+V a lot **badly, severely, uncontrollably, violently, wildly** *I began to shake uncontrollably.*
- ▶ physically **literally, physically, visibly** *I was literally shaking all over, never in my life had I been this lucky!*
- V+with **anger, emotion, excitement, fear, fright, laughter, rage** *The picture showed a man literally shaking with fear.*

shaken ADJ
feeling nervous or frightened by something

- adv+V very **badly, deeply, profoundly, seriously, severely, terribly** *Badly shaken, they had made their way back to the hut.*
- ▶ obviously **clearly, visibly** *Every building around had lost its glass and people all around us were visibly shaken and upset.*
- ▶ rather **quite, rather, somewhat** *Stan looked somewhat shaken by the margin at the end of the game.*
- ▶ slightly **a little** *On that occasion, my helmet was slightly cracked, and I was a little shaken.*
- ▶ for a good reason **understandably** *When a member of staff was killed, the remaining people were understandably shaken.*

shake-up N

an important change in the way something is organized

- adj+N big **big, huge, major, massive** *Will this massive shake-up of support funding end up limiting services for the most vulnerable?*
- ▶ planned **planned, proposed** *Mr Bell welcomed the planned shake-up of secondary education proposed in the report.*
- ▶ making important changes **dramatic, fundamental, radical** *The report will lead to a radical shake-up of the way such cases are handled.*
- v+N need a shake-up **need** *To be blunt, the private sector also needs a shake-up.*
- ▶ suggest or plan a shake-up **call for, plan, propose, urge** *The Government is planning a major pension shake-up.*
- ▶ announce a shake-up **announce** *The Financial Services Authority today announced a radical shake-up of the way financial products are sold.*
- ▶ have a shake-up **face, undergo** *Britain's charity law is facing its biggest shake-up for 400 years.*

shape V

influence the way someone or something develops

- adv+V significantly **decisively, fundamentally, profoundly, significantly** *He clearly valued the biblical traditions and was profoundly shaped by them.*
- ▶ directly **actively, directly** *Political developments directly shaped military strategy.*
- ▶ increasingly **increasingly** *EU environmental policies are increasingly shaped by citizens.*
- ▶ in the end **ultimately** *His behavior will ultimately shape the marriage as well.*
- V+n attitudes and behaviour **attitude, behaviour, consciousness, identity, opinion, outlook, perception, thinking** *There has been a debate about how far language shapes our perceptions of the world.*

You can say that someone or something **plays** or **has a role** or **a part in shaping** something: *Tourism is beginning to play an increasing role in shaping the economic future of the area.*

- ▶ policy **agenda, debate, direction, policy** *The author's ideas have been influential in shaping public policy in the United States.*
- ▶ the future **destiny, future** *There are choices to be made in shaping our future and those choices are yours.*
- ▶ the world **culture, environment, landscape, society, world** *As well as shaping the landscape, landslides often cause large devastation.*

share N

1 a part of something that is divided up

- adj+N fair **equal, equitable, fair, proportionate, rightful** *Every person has the right to an equal share of Earth's limited ecological capacity.*
- ▶ unfair **disproportionate, unequal** *Microsoft has attracted a disproportionate share of US computer talent.*
- ▶ large **large, the lion's, sizeable, substantial** *Although Leeds Met had the lion's share of possession, John Moore's dogged defence held firm.*
- ▶ half or part **half, part** *I have a half share in a pony at my local riding school.*
- n+N audience, market, revenue **audience, market, revenue** *Low tar cigarettes began to take an increasing market share.*
- v+N get a share **capture, claim, gain, get, grab** INFORMAL, **receive, secure** *Education received increased attention and began to receive a larger share of the national budget.*
- ▶ increase a share **boost** INFORMAL, **increase** *Almost everywhere, we increased our share of the vote and we did this in spite of the media black-out.*
- ▶ keep a share **retain** *This has led to a price war with insurance companies battling to retain their share of the market.*
- ▶ lose a share **lose** *The reason for the concern lies in the fact that the UK is now losing market share in the global student market.*

2 one of the equal parts of a company that you can buy

- adj+N **deferred, equity, ordinary, outstanding, penny, preference, redeemable, voting** *Can I use spread bets to play penny shares?*
- v+N buy or sell shares **acquire, buy, purchase, sell, trade, transfer** *We sold our shares, which in a matter of a few weeks had lost us 13% of our investment.*
- ▶ issue or give shares **allocate, allot, issue** *Companies were formed by issuing shares.*
- ▶ have shares **hold, own** *Every member owns one share in RAMSAK Ltd.*
- ▶ say what the share price is **quote** *You can invest in stocks and shares quoted on the London Stock Exchange.*

share V

1 use or have something at the same time as someone else

- adv+V equally or fairly **equally, equitably, evenly, fairly, jointly** *It is expected that each member of a pair will co-operate with the other to ensure that the work is shared equitably.*
- ▶ kindly **generously, kindly** *I sat next to a nice man who kindly shared his sandwiches with me.*
- ▶ willingly **gladly, happily, voluntarily, willingly** *She has amassed a wealth of in-depth knowledge, which she will happily share with the learner.*
- ▶ without restrictions **easily, freely, globally, openly** *Documents may be freely shared between users from the same purchasing organisation.*
- ▶ illegally **illegally** *He stands accused of illegally sharing music online via P2P networks.*

2 have the same feeling or opinion as someone else

- adv+V **broadly, commonly, universally, widely** *That view was widely shared, so the draft rules were rejected and will be resubmitted at our next meeting later this month.*
- V+n opinions **concerns, views** *These concerns are shared by other regulators across Europe, and by the European Commission.*
- ▶ feelings **enthusiasm, interest, love, passion** *They all share our passion for trees and the UK's beautiful ancient woodland.*
- ▶ beliefs **belief, faith** *There was one close friend of mine who shared my belief and ideology.*

sharp ADJ
sudden and very big, strong, or severe

- ADJ+n rise **increase, rise** *The result was price increases and a sharp rise in unemployment.*
- ▶ fall **decline, downturn, drop, fall, slowdown** *After a sharp decline in numbers, the goldfinch is back.*
- ▶ angle **bend, corner, curve, turn** *On the way down, watch out for the sharp bends and narrow hump back bridge at the bottom!*
- ▶ pain **pain, shock** *I feel a sharp pain in the side of my arm.*

shatter V
destroy or seriously damage something

- adv+V suddenly **abruptly, rudely, suddenly, violently** *Whatever hopes he may have had in the direction of peace were soon rudely shattered by the Crimean war.*
- ▶ cruelly **brutally, cruelly** *Her return to Manchester cruelly shattered her dreams of a happy reunion.*
- ▶ completely **completely, totally** *My pre-conceived ideas of Greece were completely shattered.*
- ▶ for ever **irretrievably, irrevocably** *His scheme to gain mastery over the world has been irrevocably shattered.*

- V+n things that are not true or real **dream, illusion, myth, preconceptions, stereotype** *It's cruel to have illusions shattered like this.*
- ▶ peace **calm, peace, silence, tranquillity** *Minutes later, a massive car bomb shattered the afternoon calm.*
- ▶ feelings **complacency, hope, optimism** *Towards the end of the year, his optimism was rudely shattered by the first signs of his illness.*

sheer ADJ
used for emphasizing an amount or degree

- ADJ+n size **breadth, complexity, enormity, magnitude, quantity, scale, size, volume, weight** *One of our selling points is the sheer volume of readers we can offer advertisers.*
- good qualities **beauty, brilliance, determination, exuberance, genius, luck** *The organisation, hospitality and sheer brilliance of the event was simply superb.*
- pleasure **bliss, delight, enjoyment, exhilaration, joy, pleasure** *Her performance was sheer comic delight.*
- bad qualities **brutality, incompetence, madness, nonsense, stupidity** *He might have got away with it, apart from some sheer stupidity on his behalf.*
- bad feelings **boredom, desperation, exhaustion, terror** *Many men were suffering tremendously from diseases, hunger and sheer exhaustion.*

sheet N
a piece of something flat

- N+of wood **hardboard, plasterboard, plywood** *A sheet of plywood 70 x 150 x 1 cm is ideal.*
- metal **aluminium, foil, metal** *Line a roasting tin with a large, thick sheet of foil.*
- paper **cardboard, foolscap, notepaper, paper, parchment, A4, A5 etc** *No more than two illustrations may be placed on any one sheet of paper.*
- plastic **acetate, perspex, plastic, polythene** *The*

sound resembled two sharp flaps of a large sheet of polythene.
- ▶ glass **glass** *I use the straight cutter to cut down full sheets of glass.*
- ▶ food **filo, gelatine, pastry** *Arrange another three or four sheets of pastry on top, and brush with butter.*

2 a large area of something
- N+of **flame, ice, water** *Scotland was covered with large sheets of thick ice.*

shelter N
a place where people are protected

- adj+N temporary **makeshift, overnight, temporary** *Many survivors have set up makeshift shelters on top of the debris that used to be their homes.*
- ▶ very strong or safe **bomb-proof, deep, protective, underground, waterproof** *On the far side of the road by the factory there were deep shelters cut into the hillside.*
- ▶ rough **crude, rough** *Rough shelters were built for the herdsmen to stay with the animals.*
- ▶ heated **heated** *Many unstaffed stations have no heated shelter.*
- ▶ for many people **communal** *Communal shelters were built to house the residents from a block of tenement flats.*

shield V
protect someone from something unpleasant

- V+from physical things **glare, interference, light, radiation, ray, sight, sun, sunlight, wind** *The pond should be shielded from direct sunlight to minimise microbial growth.*
- ▶ non-physical things **criticism, harm, interference, intrusion, liability, reality, scrutiny** *Some government functions will be shielded from scrutiny.*

shift V
change an idea, attitude, or plan

- adv+V in big ways **decisively, dramatically, fundamentally, markedly, radically** *The balance of power has to shift decisively in favour of the patient.*
- ▶ In small ways **slightly, subtly** *Her understanding of the issue has subtly shifted with the passing of time.*
- ▶ quickly or suddenly **rapidly, suddenly** *They ask about the function of community in rapidly shifting geo-political contexts.*
- ▶ slowly **gradually** *Looking back I can see how my attention has gradually shifted.*
- ▶ all the time **all the time, constantly, continually, continuously** *The landscape of social care is constantly shifting.*
- ▶ without difficulty **effortlessly** *She found him an unprincipled politician, who shifted effortlessly from Liberal to Conservative.*

- V+n blame **blame, burden, responsibility** *This is not trying to shift the blame.*
- ▶ attention **attention, emphasis, focus** *The protestors have shifted the focus of their campaigns to schools.*
- ▶ loyalty **allegiance, loyalty** *That explains why these communities have been prepared to shift political allegiances.*
- ▶ position **position, stance** *These institutions have*

shifted their public stance in favour of poverty reduction.

▶ discussion **debate, discussion** *They are helping to shift the debate within Third World countries.*

▶ attitude **attitude, mindset, perception, perspective** *To take advantage of these opportunities, designers have to learn to shift their mindset.*

shine V
produce or reflect light

● adv+V brightly **brightly, brilliantly, gloriously, radiantly, resplendently** *The sun shone brilliantly and the Green was crowded with people.*

▶ dimly **dimly, faintly, softly, weakly** *It was raining heavily, and the light shone dimly through the streaked and dripping glass.*

shiver V
if you shiver, your body shakes

● adv+V a lot **uncontrollably, violently** *I am shivering uncontrollably and feel a little chilly.*

▶ a little **a little, slightly** *Thoughts of the past made me shiver a little, as they always did.*

● V+with **cold, fear, fright** *He was shivering with fright, and was in a very agitated state.*

shock N
surprise from something bad

● adj+N bad **nasty, severe, terrible, unpleasant** *Mrs Slocombe visits the farm to collect some eggs and gets a nasty shock.*

▶ big or very big **big, great, huge, major, massive, profound, real, tremendous, utter** *He was staring at the letter he had received with utter shock.*

▶ sudden **rude, sudden** *The doctors warn Alex that any sudden shock could be fatal to his mother's health.*

▶ initial **initial** *After the initial shock, I decided to find out exactly what our options were.*

● v+N give a shock **administer, cause, deliver, spring** INFORMAL *The format is the best of five games during the group stages, which could cause some shocks.*

▶ get a shock **experience, get, receive, suffer, sustain** *She has suffered a terrible shock.*

▶ recover from a shock **get over, overcome, recover from** *Gradually, we overcame the initial shock and just got on with things.*

▶ bear a shock **absorb, survive, withstand** *Although he has survived the shock, there is still a long way to go.*

▶ decrease a shock **cushion, lessen, soften** *Having found the truth, I must tell it, without any pretence of softening the shock.*

● N+n method **tactics, value** *Do they capture the reader's attention e.g. are shock tactics, puns or effective messages used?*

> The expression **shock horror** is used, often in a humorous way, to show that people think something is shocking: *Sometimes when I'm out exploring I will stop and buy a lemonade, shock horror!*

▶ news **announcement, news, revelation** *The stock market reacted swiftly to the shock announcements, which came late on Monday evening.*

▶ action **decision, departure, move, reaction, resignation** *The shock resignation of the Chief Executive was also a top story.*

▶ result **defeat, exit, result, victory, win** *Once the match had started, Derby removed all fears of a shock defeat.*

shocked ADJ
surprised and upset by an unexpected bad event

● adv+ADJ obviously **visibly** *Though visibly shocked and shaken, everyone was safe.*

▶ very **absolutely, completely, deeply, genuinely, greatly, profoundly, totally** *He seemed genuinely shocked that anyone would violate a position of trust in that way.*

▶ rather **quite, rather, somewhat** *Our supporters were left somewhat shocked at the final score.*

▶ slightly **a little, slightly** *Four days later, I'm still wandering around looking slightly shocked.*

● ADJ+n person **audience, everybody, everyone, onlookers, passers by** *Shocked onlookers rushed to help after the incident on Tuesday afternoon.*

▶ expression or reaction **disbelief, expression, face, reaction** *Matilda chuckled at her shocked expression.*

● v+ADJ **feel, look, seem** *They seemed really shocked by what I had to say.*

shore N
land on the edge of a lake, sea etc

● adj+N rocky, sandy etc **muddy, palm-fringed, pebbly, rocky, rugged, sandy, stony** *This is a coastline of high cliffs and rocky shores, rich in flowers and wildlife.*

▶ direction **east, eastern, north, northern, southern, west** *Aquarium of the Lakes is on the southern shore of Lake Windermere, near Newby Bridge.*

▶ near/far **far, lee, near, opposite** *In the afternoon, we went to a picnic area on the far shore of Clear Lake.*

▶ sunny or peaceful **sheltered, sunny, tranquil** *The more delicate red and green seaweeds will begin to decorate the pools on sheltered shores.*

● v+N be on or near the shore **border, fringe, hug, lap, line, litter, skirt** *The great glory of these islands is the incredible sea lapping their shores.*

▶ reach or nearly reach the shore **approach, near, reach, regain** *Upon reaching shore, he was evacuated by ambulance to the local hospital.*

shortage N
a lack of something you need or want

● adj+N serious **acute, crippling, critical, desperate, dire, drastic, extreme, grave, massive, serious, severe** *There are very few woods that will not find use if there is an acute shortage of timber.*

▶ in many places **national, nationwide, UK-wide, widespread, worldwide** *There is a nationwide shortage of doctors.*

▶ happening now or soon **current, impending, looming** *Towards the end of last year, we heard reports of an impending water shortage.*

▶ longlasting **chronic** *Chronic energy shortages pose the most significant challenge.*

● n+N of people **labour, manpower, nursing, staff,**

staffing, teacher, workforce *What are we going to do about our manpower shortage?*

▸ of goods **food, fuel, housing, petrol, water** *Food shortages were particularly grave in Somalia, eastern Kenya, and south eastern Ethiopia.*

▸ of skill **skills** *There is a national problem of skills shortages in the construction industry.*

● v+N relieve a shortage **alleviate, ease, overcome, redress, relieve, remedy, solve** *Helping healthcare assistants to gain higher qualifications could alleviate the serious shortage of nurses in Britain.*

▸ tackle a shortage **address, combat, counter, tackle** *We will tackle the shortage of staff through 7,500 more consultants and 20,000 extra nurses.*

▸ make a shortage worse **aggravate, exacerbate, worsen** *Refurbishment of the Library has exacerbated our shortage of shelf space.*

▸ experience a shortage **experience, face, suffer** *Up to 8 million people face severe food shortages or starvation.*

▸ point out a shortage **highlight, identify, report** *Our Local Housing Strategy has highlighted the shortage of affordable rented housing.*

▸ cause a shortage **cause** *There was a lot of panic buying when war started, which caused shortages.*

▸ prevent a shortage **avert, avoid** *The action is thought necessary to avert a crisis shortage of gas supplies this winter.*

shortcoming N [usually plural]
a fault or problem that reduces effectiveness

▸ adj+N serious **fundamental, major, serious, severe, significant** *This investigation has identified a series of serious shortcomings.*

▸ obvious **evident, obvious** *Taking the short-term view, obvious shortcomings have surfaced over the past week.*

▸ types of shortcoming **methodological, procedural** *Methodological shortcomings of some studies are discussed.*

▸ seeming **alleged, apparent, perceived** *The trustees became so concerned over alleged shortcomings that they shut the club down.*

v+N find shortcomings **expose, highlight, identify, reveal, uncover** *He then admitted that the inspection also highlighted some shortcomings.*

correct shortcomings **correct, overcome, rectify, remedy** *Attempts to rectify these shortcomings are currently taking place.*

admit shortcomings **acknowledge, admit, recognize** *We were impressed with the way in which he openly acknowledged his shortcomings.*

tackle shortcomings **address** *I believe that we must seriously address the manifest shortcomings in our procedures.*

shortlist N
list of suitable people or things

adj+N initial/final **final, initial, provisional** *The panel did confirm this week that it intended to reveal a provisional shortlist on Wednesday.*

with good people **impressive, strong** *The shortlist was so strong I didn't think I stood a chance.*

v+N make a shortlist **choose, compile, create, draw up, make, prepare, produce, select** *Decide*

where you want to live and make a shortlist of three or four possibilities.

▸ announce a shortlist **announce, reveal, unveil** *The shortlist was officially announced at a ceremony on Monday, January 19.*

▸ be on a shortlist **make, reach** *Two submissions from the BBC made the shortlist for this year's Innovative Application Award.* ● *We regret that we will be unable to contact those who do not reach the shortlist.*

● N+of of people **applicants, artists, candidates, finalists** *A shortlist of 3 finalists in each category has been drawn up.*

▸ of entries **entries, nominations** *The shortlist of nominations for awards is below.*

▸ of possibilities **options** *You may need to undertake research and talk to suppliers before producing a shortlist of options.*

▸ in business **bidders, developers, firms, suppliers** *A shortlist of three bidders for phase one will be announced in early July.*

shoulders N [always plural]
the part of the body between the neck and arms

● v+N move shoulders up **shrug** *They shrugged their shoulders and tried to think of a witty response.*

▸ move shoulders forward and down **droop, hunch, slump** *Posture is stooped: the head is bowed and the shoulders are drooped.*

▸ move shoulders back **roll, square** *He drew himself up sharply and squared his shoulders.*

● N+v move forwards and down **sag, slump** *His shoulders slumped, as if defeated.*

▸ move up and down **heave, shake, shrug** *Her round shoulders heaved, black mascara ran down her face.*

shout V
say something in a loud voice

● adv+V loudly **aloud, at the top of your lungs, at the top of your voice, loud** INFORMAL, **loudly** *It is often better just to shout loudly and run away.*

▸ with strong feelings **angrily, drunkenly, excitedly, furiously, gleefully, hysterically, incoherently, wildly** *He saw a lot of girls had formed a circle and were shouting excitedly.*

▸ many times **repeatedly** *I'll never forget hearing Sarah repeatedly shouting, 'It's Joe.'*

▸ suddenly **suddenly** *He suddenly shouted: 'There's only one body!'*

● V+n with anger **abuse, defiance, insults, obscenities, slogans** *They shook their fists, shouted obscenities, and threatened to kill her.*

▸ encouragement or praise **encouragement, praise** *People were shouting encouragement from windows of flats and offices.*

▸ telling someone something **a greeting, a warning** *You need to shout a warning if there is a hazard ahead such as a pot-hole.*

● and/or shout **bawl, groan, scream, shriek, yell** *If you are threatened, shout and scream or set off your personal attack alarm.*

▸ make gestures **gesticulate, gesture, wave** *I went to the lowest point of the headland, and gesticulated and shouted.*

▸ show pleasure or approval **chant, cheer, clap,**

laugh, sing, whistle *The Germans sang and shouted and cheered, and we sang and cheered.*
▶ show disapproval **boo, jeer** *Bristling with anger, they waved their arms, shouted and jeered at each other.*
▶ cry **cry, weep** *They were shouting and crying and many were covered in blood.*
▶ swear **curse, swear** *Buck was in a frightful state, cursing and shouting in his office.*

show V
1 prove something exists or is true

● adv+V clearly or definitely **certainly, clearly, conclusively, consistently, exactly** *National surveys have consistently shown that dental disease is strongly related to deprivation.*
▶ **previously, recently, repeatedly** *These methods have been previously shown to change clinical practice.*

2 let people know your feelings, opinions etc

● V+n interest or understanding **appreciation, interest, understanding** *He always showed a huge interest in music.*
▶ support **respect, solidarity, support** *The fans showed their support for the players and the things being done at the club.*
▶ enthusiasm **commitment, determination, enthusiasm, willingness** *He has shown great enthusiasm and awareness.*

shower N
a short period of rain or snow

● adj+N heavy/light **heavy, light, moderate, sharp, torrential** *Heavy showers were forecast, and duly appeared, complete with huge hailstones.*
▶ with wind, snow or thunder **blustery, squally, thundery, wintry** *Another fine day with wintry showers on the hills.*
▶ frequent/infrequent **frequent, occasional, scattered** *A few scattered light showers developing later in the evening.*
● n+N **hail, rain, sleet, snow, thunder** *Rain showers are brief, but thunderstorms can be violent.*

shred N
a very small amount of something

● N+of good quality **credibility, decency, dignity, legitimacy** *Only two of the cast emerge with any shred of dignity.*

> Usage **Shred** is almost always used in questions and broad negatives in this meaning: *Who here has a shred of decency?*

▶ evidence **evidence, proof** *The fact that there is not a shred of evidence to back the theory does not deter them.*

shrewd ADJ
able to judge people and situations well

● ADJ+n person **businessman, businesswoman, investor, judge, observer, operator, politician, tactician** *He was a brave guerilla soldier and a shrewd tactician.*
▶ act **decision, judgement, move, observation** *It is a shrewd move to begin offering tailored finance.*

> If you have a **shrewd suspicion** that something is true, you are fairly sure it is true but not completely sure: *I have a shrewd suspicion that the forthcoming government White Paper will give us much less protection than we need.*

shrink from PHR VB
be unwilling to do something difficult or unpleasant

● V+n **challenge, confrontation, duty, responsibility, task** *He was a rich man indulging private pleasures and shrinking from public responsibilities.*

shroud V [usually passive]
cover or hide something, so that it remains secret or unknown

● V+n+in+n **confusion, controversy, doubt, mystery, mystique, myth, obscurity, secrecy, uncertainty** *His early life is shrouded in mystery.*

shrug off PHR VB
deal with something easily because it does not worry or upset you

● V+n **challenge, complaint, criticism, injury, suggestion** *The bank shrugged off suggestions that the event was a gimmick to distract customers from slow service.*

shudder V
if you shudder, your body suddenly shakes, for example when you have an unpleasant thought

● V+at **memory, mention, prospect, recollection, sight, thought** *Even now, I shudder at the memory of what happened in that place.*

> If a thought gives you an unpleasant feeling, you can also say **I shudder to think**: *I shudder to think what would happen if I lost my job.*

shut ADJ
closed

● adv+ADJ **firmly, fully, properly, safely, securely** *Always make sure all the windows to the car are securely shut.*
● v+ADJ **bang, blow, click, slam** *We walked out and the door banged shut behind us.*

shy ADJ
nervous and embarrassed in other people's company

● adv+ADJ very **extremely, incredibly, painfully, terribly, very** *The presence of female company always makes him painfully shy and speechless.*
▶ rather **fairly, a little, quite, rather, somewhat** *She introduced her brother, an awkward and somewhat shy young man.*
● and/or **awkward, elusive, embarrassed, insecure, nervous, quiet, reserved, timid** *He had a shy, reserved nature.*

sick ADJ

1 suffering from an illness or medical condition

- adv+ADJ **acutely, chronically, desperately, mentally, pretty, terminally, very** *We often see people who are desperately sick **with** asthma or bronchitis.*
- ▶ v+ADJ **be, become, fall, get, grow, look** *If a worker fell sick, the problem could be quickly dealt with.*

2 vomiting or wanting to vomit

- adv+ADJ **horribly, physically, violently** *He regretted eating it immediately, for he was then violently sick.*

3 fed up with something that makes you angry or impatient

- adv+ADJ **absolutely, completely, heartily, thoroughly, utterly** *We are all heartily sick of her constant complaining.*

side N

an aspect of a situation or problem, or of someone's character or personality

- adj+N positive **bright, funny, humorous, plus, positive** *We apologized to the owner, and fortunately he was able to see the funny side of the incident.*
- ▶ negative **negative, sinister** *The film explores the sinister side of artificial intelligence.*
- ▶ other **flip, other** *The flip side of that is that white communities sometimes feel a black politician is only capable of dealing with black issues.*
- ▶ of someone's character **caring, creative, cynical, gentle, nasty, romantic, serious, spiritual, vulnerable** *He enjoys a laugh with his friends, but he has a more serious side too.*
- ▶ v+N **explore, reflect, reveal, see, show** *Fairy tales give children an opportunity to explore the darker side to human nature in a safe way.*

side effects N

the additional and unexpected effects of something, especially of a medical treatment

- adj+N unpleasant **adverse, damaging, dangerous, harmful, negative, serious, severe, undesirable, unpleasant, unwanted** *Biofuels have environmental benefits, but there are significant undesirable side-effects in terms of reduced food production.* ● *This is a widespread problem with oral antidiabetic drugs, due to its unpleasant side effects.*
- ➧ common **common** *The most common side effects are nausea and diarrhoea.*
- ➧ possible **possible, potential** *All medications have potential side effects.*
- ➧ positive **beneficial, positive** *One of the beneficial side-effects of the rise in online shopping is that road traffic has slightly reduced.*
- ➧ v+N **produce side effects cause, have, produce** *Many medications have side effects which cause the body to lose essential minerals.*
- ➧ experience side effects **develop, experience, suffer** *Significant numbers of patients suffered side effects from drug A.*

siege N

a situation in which a place is surrounded, so that the people inside cannot get out

- adj+N lasting a long time **lengthy, long, prolonged, protracted** *Eventually, after a lengthy siege, the city was defeated and its walls partially demolished.*
- ▶ violent **bitter, bloody, brutal, terrible** *After a bitter siege, John captured Rochester castle from the barons in December 1215.*
- ● v+N end a siege **abandon, break, end, lift, raise, relieve** *Dozens of people died when police stormed the building to end the siege.*
- ▶ survive a siege **resist, stand, survive, withstand** *The town resisted a siege of thirteen months.*

> If a place is experiencing a siege, you can say that it is **under siege**, or that someone is **laying siege** to it: *The ships had protected Gibraltar at a time when the island was under siege.* ● *She was virtually imprisoned in her hotel, as fans and reporters laid siege to the place.*

- N+v **begin, continue, end, last** *The siege had lasted nearly eight weeks.*

sift V

examine information, documents etc in order to find something

- adv+V **carefully, painstakingly, slowly** *Having carefully sifted all the available information, you must next discard anything you consider to be unreliable, irrelevant or trivial.*
- V+n **archives, documents, evidence, facts** *The role of journalism is to sift facts and give you a truthful and factual picture.*

> You can also **sift through** information, documents etc: *After sifting through the evidence, we conclude that British economic prospects are bright.*

sigh V

breathe out slowly making a long soft sound

- adv+V loudly **deeply, heavily** *Scully sighs heavily, and Mulder gently puts his hand to the side of her neck.*

> If someone sighs because they are pleased that something bad has not happened, you can say that they **sigh with relief** or **sigh in relief**: *He was glad to see them all safe and sighed with relief.*

- ▶ quietly **gently, quietly, slightly, softly** *Chris sighed softly, his eyes weighed down by sleep.*
- ▶ expressing annoyance, disappointment, or sadness **resignedly, sadly, wearily** *Sighing wearily, Barbara agreed to work over the weekend in order to complete the job.*

sigh N

a slow breath out that makes a long soft sound

- adj+N loud **audible, big, deep, great, heavy, huge, long, loud, profound** *It was with a heavy sigh that he slid the latch and opened the door.*
- ▶ expressing annoyance, disappointment or sadness **exasperated, sad, weary, wistful** *With a weary sigh, he begins to outline the latest problem.*

▶ quiet **gentle, little, silent, slight, small, soft**
*Elizabeth gave a gentle sigh and took up the
conversation.*

▶ when several people sigh at once **collective** *There
was a collective sigh of relief from the United fans
when the final whistle went.*

● v+N make a sigh **breathe, give, heave, let out,
utter** *'It was only a plastic glass,' said Mick, heaving
a huge sigh of relief.*

▶ stop yourself from making a sigh **hold back, stifle,
suppress** *He suppressed a sigh, as he did so often in
her company.*

● N+of **contentment, disappointment, pleasure,
regret, relief, resignation, satisfaction** *With a sigh
of contentment, Jane flopped into the armchair.*

sight N
a person or thing that you see

● adj+N beautiful or impressive **amazing,
awesome, breathtaking, impressive, incredible,
magnificent, spectacular, stunning, unforgettable,
wonderful** *There were hundreds of tents of all
colours and it was quite an impressive sight.*

▶ unusual **bizarre, curious, strange, unusual**
*Sometimes, there were bizarre sights, like a bed still
in position on an upper floor although the rest of the
house had been destroyed.*

● v+N **behold, be met with, be presented with,
enjoy, experience, savour, see, witness** *Suddenly,
he beheld a sight so alarming that he stood for a
moment motionless with surprise.*

● N+v **await sb, confront sb, greet sb, meet sb** *As
we emerged from the forest, an amazing sight greeted
us.*

▶ shocking or unpleasant **awful, horrible, pitiful,
shocking, terrible** *Police were met with the shocking
sight of two bodies covered in blood.*

▶ common **common, familiar** *In many parts of Spain,
wind turbines have become a familiar sight.*

● v+at+N **faint, gasp, laugh, marvel, shudder,
tremble** *The island is a prardise for nature lovers,
where you can marvel at the sight of dolphins and
seals in the bay.*

sighting N
an occasion when you see something, especially
something unusual

● adj+N which people claim to have seen **alleged,
recorded, reported, unconfirmed** *There were
several reported sightings of sharks near the beach.*

▶ of strange things **ghostly, paranormal, unexplained**
*That sighting was attributed to a balloon launch,
but other unexplained sightings followed the next
day.*

▶ uncommon or unusual **infrequent, occasional,
rare, strange, unusual** *Sightings of this species of
whale are now very rare.*

● v+N **describe, discuss, investigate, record, report**
*Most garden birdwatchers are also able to record
sightings of familiar mammals, butterflies, reptiles
and amphibians.*

sign N
a piece of evidence showing that something exists

● adj+N giving hope of success **encouraging,
hopeful, positive** *The latest unemployment figures
are the first positive sign that the economy is
improving.*

▶ obvious **clear, obvious, sure, visible** *There are
obvious signs that the style of newspapers is being
influenced by online journalism.*

▶ suggesting that bad things will happen **danger,
ominous, telltale, warning, worrying** *There were
ominous signs of strain and acrimony in US-North
Korea relations.* ● *Telltale signs of the illness include
becoming tired and frustrated.*

▶ understand what the evidence shows **interpret as,
read** *Troops could be seen on all the main roads,
which we interpreted as a sign that war was now
likely.*

● v+N show evidence **bear, display, exhibit, have,
show** *Once in office, the new president showed signs
of reneging on some of his pledges.*

▶ see evidence **detect, identify, notice, observe,
recognize, see, spot** *Some illnesses show no early
symptoms and simple checks at regular intervals can
sometimes detect any warning signs.*

▶ not see or pay attention to evidence **ignore, miss**
*If you start to get stressed or feverish, don't ignore
these warning signs.*

Usage **Sign** is usually plural in all of the **v+N**
combinations shown here.

● N+v **indicate, point to sth, show, suggest, warn**
All signs pointed to a classic case of envy.

signal N
an attitude, opinion, or intention that you
communicate

● adj+N with an obvious meaning **clear,
detectable, powerful, strong, unmistakable** *This
strong signal from the Government has helped to
focus minds on meeting the targets.*

▶ with a confusing meaning **conflicting, mixed,
wrong** *You might not know what the other person
is thinking. You may be giving out mixed signals.*

● v+N **give, send, send out** *We want to reduce
congestion and send out the right signals to car
owners.*

signatory N
a person or organization that signs an official
document

● N+to **agreement, charter, convention, letter,
petition, protocol, statement, treaty** *The United
States is a signatory to the treaty, which came into
force in June 2004.*

signature N
someone's name written by them formally

● v+N say officially that someone's signature is
really theirs **authenticate, authorize, certify,
verify, witness** *All applications should bear a
signature authenticated by a lawyer.*

▶ deceive people by writing someone else's
signature **fake, forge** *Doreen shows Helen how to*

forge her signature so she can take money out of her bank account.
▶ ask many people to sign a document, giving their support **collect, gather, obtain** *They are attempting to collect 1 million signatures in favour of a European citizenship of residence.*
▶ have someone's signature written on it **bear, carry** *Besides signing the Declaration of Independence, he was also influential in drawing up the Constitution, which bears his signature.*

significance N
the importance of something

● adj+N types of significance **archaeological, clinical, constitutional, cultural, ecological, historical, legal, mystical, political, religious, spiritual, statistical, strategic, symbolic** *Stirling was the lowest bridging point on the Forth, giving the town a great strategic significance.*
▶ great **considerable, crucial, enormous, great, immense, particular, profound, special** *These collections have immense significance for the history of medicine in the region.*

● v+N understand the significance of something **appreciate, grasp, perceive, realize, recognize, understand** *If you do not know that something is historically interesting, how can you appreciate its significance?*
▶ fail to understand the significance of something **miss, overlook** *It is easy to overlook the significance of these events.*
▶ show or emphasize the significance of something **emphasize, highlight, illustrate, stress, underline, underscore** *This chapter underlines the greater economic significance of tourism in rural areas of Scotland.*
▶ make something seem less important **diminish, downplay, underestimate** *The prime minister downplayed the significance of the report which inspectors are to deliver to the Security Council on Monday.*
▶ make something seem more significant **exaggerate, overestimate, overstate** *Have climate scientists exaggerated the significance of their findings?*
▶ consider something to be important **acknowledge, attach to, attribute to** *They made the mistake of attaching little significance to the company's falling UK market share.*
▶ become important **acquire, assume, attain, gain, take on** *In the last quarter of the 18th century, the area suddenly acquired great industrial significance.*

N+of information, or results of study **data, discovery, evidence, fact, findings, information, research, results** *In Chapter Four, we discuss the significance of our findings for future energy planning.*
event or change **change, decision, development, event** *The significance of this new development cannot be overstated.*
what someone says **observation, remark, speech, statement, words** *At the time, we didn't fully grasp the significance of this remark.*

significant ADJ
very important

● adv+ADJ very **deeply, especially, extremely, highly, hugely, increasingly, particularly, very** *The proposed introduction of the Code is hugely significant for the communications industry.*
▶ in a particular way **archaeologically, architecturally, biologically, clinically, commercially, culturally, economically, environmentally, historically, militarily, politically, socially, statistically, strategically** *Cave 6 is the most historically significant and artistically important of the 53 principal caves at Yungang.*

● ADJ+n event or change **action, change, decision, development, improvement, initiative, move, trend** *The most significant recent development has been the introduction of an integrated fares and ticketing structure.*
▶ increase **expansion, growth, increase, rise** *A notable success of the food management operations in India has been the significant expansion in rice production.*
▶ decrease **decline, decrease, drop, fall, reduction** *These measures have led to significant reductions in deaths and serious injuries on the roads.*
▶ achievement **achievement, boost, milestone, progress, stride, success** *A particularly significant milestone was the publication of his influential paper on genetics.*
▶ problem or challenge **challenge, concern, delay, difficulty, disadvantage, disruption, error, obstacle, problem, risk, threat** *The report concludes that aviation poses a significant threat to the world's climate.*
▶ amount or money **amount, extent, funding, gap, investment, loss, percentage, profit, proportion, resource, saving, sum** *In Australia, foreign students constitute a significant proportion of the higher education cohort.*
▶ someone's or something's part in something **contribution, contributor, involvement, part, player, role** *Cultural factors also play a significant role in the continued reliance of rural communities on traditional medicine.*
▶ difference **difference, discrepancy** *Even small inaccuracies in data collection may produce significant discrepancies in your figures.*
▶ effect or result **benefit, consequence, effect, impact, implications, influence** *As one of the largest employers in the city, we know that we can have a significant impact on the economy of the region.*

● v+ADJ be or become significant **appear, be, become, feel, prove, seem, sound** *There were so many questions that we wanted answering – and we didn't really know what data would prove significant.*
▶ consider something to be significant **consider sth to be, deem sth to be, regard sth as, think of sth as** *There was clearly blood on the shoes, but astonishingly this had not been regarded as significant.*
▶ rather **fairly, pretty INFORMAL, quite, rather** *These changes have brought fairly significant improvements in traffic flow.*

silence N
complete quiet

● adj+N complete **absolute, complete, profound, utter** *He was one of the few teachers who could command absolute silence with just a look.*

▶ causing or showing unpleasant or embarrassed feelings **awkward, brooding, deathly, eerie, embarrassed, ominous, resounding, shocked, stony, uncomfortable, uneasy** *We all listened in stony silence to what was a rather unusual song.*

▶ showing respect or polite behaviour by saying nothing **dignified, hushed, respectful, solemn** *He maintained what he hoped was a dignified silence.*

● v+N spoil silence by making noise **break, disturb, interrupt, pierce, shatter** *A piercing siren disturbs the silence of the village.*

▶ be quiet or say nothing **keep, maintain, observe, preserve** *The audience in the theatre maintained the respectful silence of a church congregation.*

▶ ask people to be quiet or say nothing **command, enforce, impose** *Robin applied his knuckles to the table to command silence.*

● N+v **descend, ensue, fall, follow, prevail, reign, surround sth** *This latter part of the journey had left them in dull spirits, and complete silence reigned in the car.*

silence v
stop people from speaking, or expressing their opinions or criticism

● V+n people who are criticizing or opposing you **critic, doubter, enemy, opponent, sceptic** *The policy was designed to silence former critics and unite people behind a shared belief.*

▶ people who are making a lot of noise **crowd** *Two goals after just six minutes soon silenced the home crowd.*

▶ people who have good things to say **voice** *It is important to ensure, in a People's Parliament, that no voices are silenced.*

▶ opposition or criticism **criticism, dissent, objections, opposition** *They will stop at nothing to silence dissent or criticism of their policies.*

silent ADJ
not talking, laughing, or making noise

● adv+ADJ completely **absolutely, completely, dead** INFORMAL**, totally, utterly** *The cave remains utterly silent, save for the quiet drip of water from somewhere nearby.*

▶ in a strange or frightening way **curiously, eerily, mysteriously, oddly, strangely** *The street itself is oddly silent for a summer night.*

● v+ADJ **be, become, fall, go, grow, keep, remain, seem, stay** *By sheer coincidence, as soon as the stadium falls silent, United begin to play better.*

similar ADJ
sharing some qualities but not exactly same

● adv+ADJ very **remarkably, strikingly, very** *Australia is strikingly similar in its road system to the UK.*

▶ rather **fairly, quite, rather, vaguely** *The three models all look fairly similar.*

▶ in a strange or surprising way **confusingly, curiously, eerily, surprisingly, uncannily** *Alfonso's reign ended in 1931 in an eerily similar manner to that of his grandmother, Isabella II.*

▶ in most important respects **basically, broadly, essentially, fundamentally, roughly, substantially** *The approach works in a broadly similar way to that of natural evolution.*

▶ in a particular way **conceptually, culturally, functionally, genetically, physically, structurally, visually** *In the tests, the patients were infected with a genetically similar strain of the virus.*

▶ apparently, but not really **externally, outwardly, seemingly, superficially** *Though they are outwardly similar, the two products differ significantly in the quality of their manufacture.*

● v+ADJ **appear, be, become, feel, look, prove, remain, seem, sound** *In life, his affairs were not uncomplicated, and in death they have proved somewhat similar.*

similarity N
qualities that make one thing similar to another

● adj+N when things are very similar **close, eerie, marked, obvious, remarkable, startling, striking, uncanny** *By comparing these two figures, a striking similarity becomes obvious.*

▶ in most important respects **basic, essential, fundamental** *There are certain fundamental similarities between the three artists' work.*

▶ apparent but not real **apparent, superficial** *Despite this superficial similarity, the two theories are essentially quite different.*

▶ in a particular way **conceptual, cultural, functional, stylistic** *The author notes some stylistic similarity between these sculptures and the ones in southern India.*

● v+N have similarities **bear, display, exhibit, reveal, share, show** *Not only do the faces bear remarkable similarities to each other, but they are basically identical.*

▶ see similarities **discern, note, notice, recognize, spot** *Take a look at a couple of these sites and note the similarities between their views of citizenship.*

▶ emphasize similarities **emphasize, highlight, stress, underline** *This section highlights similarities in how these different pollutants were thought to act.*

> Usage *Similarity* is often plural in all of the *v+N* combinations shown here.

simmering adjective
simmering feelings are very strong and likely to become stronger

● ADJ+n **anger, conflict, discontent, dispute, feud, resentment, row, tension, violence** *Simmering tensions between sections of the community had frequently boiled over.*

simple ADJ
easy to understand or do

● adv+ADJ very **brilliantly, elegantly, extremely, incredibly, perfectly, remarkably, so, very, wonderfully** *The software is powerful but incredibly simple to use.*

▶ in an impressive or pleasing way **beautifully, delightfully, elegantly, refreshingly, wonderfully** *She offers a wonderfully simple but seriously tasty recipe for this popular Indian dish.*

▶ less simple than it appears to be **apparently, seemingly** *This brief description hides the complexities of a seemingly simple operation.*

▸ rather **comparatively, fairly, pretty, quite, rather, reasonably, relatively** *The introduction of various, relatively simple measures would go some way to solving the problem.*

▸ in a surprising way **apparently, deceptively, seemingly, stunningly, surprisingly** *The game itself is deceptively simple.*

● v+ADJ **appear, be, become, look, prove, remain, seem, sound** *The solution proved deceptively simple.*

● and/or **convenient, easy, effective, efficient, fast, inexpensive, practical, quick, reliable, straightforward** *Steam inhalation is a simple and effective method of relieving cold symptoms.*

simplistic ADJ
treating something complicated as if it is simple

● adv+ADJ very **dangerously, extremely, highly, incredibly, overly** *They share an unrealistic and overly simplistic view of the way the world works.*

▸ rather **a little, pretty** INFORMAL, **quite, rather, relatively, somewhat** *Her analysis of the events leading up the the war is, if I may say so, somewhat simplistic.*

● ADJ+n **answer, approach, argument, assumption, conclusion, depiction, explanation, generalization, interpretation, notion, overview, stereotype, view** *The view that all financial advisors are bad is a stupidly simplistic generalization.*

sincere ADJ
showing that you really mean what you say

● adv+ADJ **clearly, completely, deeply, entirely, genuinely, obviously, perfectly, quite, really, thoroughly, totally, undoubtedly, utterly, very** *He is a genuinely sincere and generous human being.*

● v+ADJ **be, look, seem, sound** *His apology sounded sincere, but I'm not sure if I trust him.*

● and/or **earnest, frank, genuine, heartfelt, honest, truthful** *Be sincere and truthful in your search for peace.*

sincerity N
honesty in words or behaviour

● adj+N **complete** or genuine **absolute, complete, deep, evident, genuine, great, obvious, passionate, perfect, total, true, utmost, utter** *I was always struck by his absolute sincerity and commitment to his work.*

not genuine **fake, false, mock, seeming** *The British offer reeked of mock sincerity.*

● v+N doubt someone's sincerity **doubt, question, suspect** *We do not question the sincerity of our political opponents.*
show that you are sincere **demonstrate, prove** *Both these parties have to prove their sincerity and commitment to the partnership.*

sinister ADJ
threatening or suggesting something unpleasant

● adv+ADJ very **decidedly, deeply, extremely, increasingly, particularly, really, very** *Events take a decidedly sinister turn when a dead body crops up.*

▸ rather **faintly, a little, quite, rather, slightly, somewhat, vaguely** *The hidden viewing room feels faintly sinister.*

● ADJ+n atmosphere or impression **atmosphere, overtones, tone, undertones** *Sinister undertones resonate throughout the novel.*

▸ intentions or plans **agenda, attempt, conspiracy, intent, machinations, motive, plot, purpose, reason** *You have accused your partner of having sinister motives.*

▸ event or change **happenings, turn, twist** *After the killer is released from jail, events take a sinister turn.*

● v+ADJ **become, feel, seem, sound, turn** *What seems to be a routine job turns sinister when everyone connected to Johnny winds up dead.*

sister N
a daughter of your parents

● adj+N older than you **big, elder, eldest, older** *She was placed in the care of her Aunt Jessie, her father's elder sister.*

▸ younger than you **little, young** *I needed to stay strong for the sake of my little sister.*

sit V
rest your lower body on a seat or on the ground

● V+adv with your body in a particular position **back, cross-legged, straight, upright** *They are so sick that they can't sit upright.*

▸ without moving or speaking **immobile, motionless, quietly, silent, silently, still** *I neither spoke nor looked at anyone, but sat motionless.*

▸ in an uncomfortable position **awkwardly, uncomfortably** *The reason so many people have back pain is that they sit awkwardly, in bad chairs, slumped over their computers for hours on end.*

situated ADJ
in a particular place

● adv+ADJ in a place that is easy to get to **centrally, conveniently, ideally, perfectly, strategically** *The hotel is conveniently situated for short drives to the beaches at Fulrbourne and Barmouth.*

▸ in a beautiful place **beautifully, delightfully, idyllically, peacefully, pleasantly, superbly** *Duddon Hall is delightfully situated on the banks of the river.*

situation N
the conditions existing somewhere at a particular time

● adj+N difficult **awkward, complex, complicated, difficult, no-win, stressful, tricky** INFORMAL *This will help you approach difficult situations in a calmer and more confident fashion.*

You can refer to a situation in which everybody gains as a *win-win situation*: *It is in his interest to put both parties in a win-win situation when possible.*

▸ bad **bad, dangerous, desperate, dire** INFORMAL, **life-or-death, serious** *When a potentially dangerous situation comes up, I'll try to work it out.*

▸ getting worse **deteriorating, worsening** *The army is monitoring the deteriorating security situation in the area.*

▶ good **good, ideal** *In an ideal situation, this work would be done in the first year of the course.*

▶ affecting a particular person **individual, personal** *In the meeting, we will discuss your personal situation and how the changes will affect you.*

▶ present **current, present** *I believe the precautionary principle is the best approach to the current situation.*

▶ real/not real **hypothetical, real, real-life, real-world** *The package presents a variety of topics, which involve real-life situations.*

▶ of a particular type **economic, financial, humanitarian, political, social** *You will learn a great deal about your financial situation by taking this first step.*

● n+N involving an emergency **crisis, disaster, emergency, panic, rescue** *Remember that we are responding to a crisis situation.*

▶ in work or business **employment, merger, monopoly, redundancy, staffing** *A redundancy situation arises when an employer needs fewer people or closes altogether.*

▶ involving people **hostage, refugee** *The refugee situation continued to be highly problematic.*

▶ involving fighting or conflict **combat, conflict, security** *It is our role to intervene when conflict situations arise.*

● v+N cause a situation **bring about, create, lead to** *Low interest rates had created a situation where people were not afraid to get into debt.*

● consider a situation **analyse, assess, consider, monitor, review** *We shall assess the situation and take appropriate action.*

▶ deal with a situation **address, deal with, handle, manage, respond to** *Can you explain to me how you propose to handle the situation?*

▶ improve a situation **improve, rectify, remedy** *The council promised to do what it could to remedy the situation.*

▶ make a situation worse **exacerbate, worsen** *The war has exacerbated the already difficult situation in which the children are living.*

● N+v happen **arise, exist, occur** *I am glad that the past is behind us and I regret that such a situation ever arose.*

▶ continue **continue, persist, remain** *Changes will have to be made if this situation persists.*

▶ develop **change, evolve, unfold** *The situation changes year by year.*

▶ get better **improve, stabilize** *The situation had not improved by 1891, when a further problem arose.*

▶ get worse **deteriorate, escalate, worsen, become difficult, serious, problematic etc** *The situation had deteriorated to such an extent that it was difficult to reverse course.*

▶ require action **demand, necessitate, require, warrant** *They can act quickly when the situation demands it.*

size N

how large or small something is

● adj+N large/small **big, compact, great, large, small** *The hotel was far from full tonight, despite its relatively small size.*

You can also use the expression **in size**: *The farms were about 20 hectares in size.* ● *The flats in the block vary in size – some are very large, some quite small.*

▶ maximum/minimum **maximum, minimum** *Daytime conducted site tour and Museum Visit – maximum party size 25.*

▶ exact/not exact **actual, approximate, exact** *The actual size of the governing body depends on the size of the school.*

▶ correct/ not correct **correct, right, wrong** *Make sure your children's shoes are the right size.*

▶ best **optimum** *The optimum size for a group is about 10–12 students.*

▶ total **overall, total** *Although the total fleet size has remained the same, 9 per cent of all vehicles are now alternatively fuelled.*

▶ average or medium **average, mean, medium, normal, standard** *When I joined the theatre, our average cast size was three.* ● *The mean tumour size was 2.5 cm (range 1 to 5 cm)*

▶ full **full, life** *Dishwashers come in all shapes and sizes, you can get three main sizes which are full size, compact or slimline.*

▶ relative **relative** *Cartographers are referring to the relative size of the representative fraction.*

● v+N increase the size **double, enlarge, increase** *The aim is to double the size of the European operation without taking more space.*

▶ decrease the size **decrease, reduce, shrink** *A more radical option would be to reduce further the size of the current small windows.*

▶ choose or set the size **choose, determine, fix, select, set, specify** *You can also choose a preset size from the drop-down list.*

▶ estimate the size **calculate, estimate, measure** *There are very few techniques that are able to accurately measure the size of small particles.*

▶ limit the size **control, limit, restrict** *The parents have chosen to limit the size of their family.*

▶ change the size **adjust, alter, change, vary** *Remember that you can adjust the text size before printing if you wish.*

You can also say that you **cut something** to **size**: *The boards are then cut to size and nailed in place.*

sketch N

1 a drawing made quickly without many details

● adj+N not finished **rough, unfinished** *I attach a rough sketch of the layout of the place as I remember it.*

▶ quick **hasty, quick** *When I see a volcano I make a quick sketch and take notes.*

▶ done at the beginning **preliminary, preparatory** *This is pure watercolour painting: there was no preliminary pencil sketch.*

● n+N **chalk, charcoal, ink, pen-and-ink, pencil, watercolour** *Each project includes a detailed pencil sketch to introduce the flower.*

● v+N **do, draw, execute, make, paint** *Art historians believe that the sketch was painted between the 1820 and late 1830s.*

2 a short funny scene in a show

● adj+N **comic, funny, hilarious, humorous, satirical**

witty *The satirical sketches took place on a small stage on the ground floor of the club.*

- n+N **comedy, revue** *It combines songs, jokes, comedy sketches, and dance numbers.*
- v+N **film, perform, rehearse, write** *I always like to hang around and see them rehearsing the sketches I'm not in.*

3 a short description without many details

- adj+N types of sketch **autobiographical, biographic, biographical, historical** *The authors are asked to provide a short biographical sketch.*
- ► short **brief, rough, short, thumbnail** *I am including a brief thumbnail sketch of his life and would like permission to make reference to your work.*
- v+N **write** *Writing this sketch of my life has been a sobering educational experience.*

skill N
the ability to do something well; a particular ability that involves special training

- adj+N basic/advanced **advanced, basic, core, generic, specialist** *What core clinical skills can be learnt?*
- ► good **excellent, valuable** *Have you got excellent communication skills and a thirst to succeed?*
- ► necessary **essential, key, necessary, relevant, vital** *He also taught me key skills such as looking backwards for long periods while cycling.*
- ► new **new** *I enjoyed planning the trip and feel I have learnt new skills from the experience.*
- ► types of skill **analytical, clinical, cognitive, creative, interpersonal, managerial, mathematical, organizational, personal, practical, professional, social, technical, vocational** *Interpersonal skills should include the ability to communicate in non-technical terms.*
- ► that can be used in different situations **transferable** *We're looking for candidates who have transferable skills, such as the ability to work in a team.*
- ► n+N in a particular subject **keyboard, language, literacy, maths, numeracy, reading, writing** *These courses were aimed at adults who want to improve their literacy skills.*
- ► with computers **computer, computing, ICT, programming** *It is important that you develop programming skills through this module.*
- ► for teaching and studying **coaching, research, study, teaching, thinking** *Refresher courses are available for existing teachers to upgrade their teaching skills.*
- ► for dealing with people **communication, employability, leadership, management, negotiation, networking, presentation** *He has good negotiation skills and shows the ability to work with a range of peers.*
- ► physical **circus, motor, survival** *Elliot's fine motor skills improve all the time, but slowly.*

> Usage **Skill** is usually plural in all of the **adj+N** and **n+N** combinations above: *With this new scheme, we aim to improve the basic skills of over a million adults.* • *She recommended that I should attend a course on presentation skills.*

- v+N get or have a skill **acquire, gain, learn, master, possess** *E-learning is an effective and efficient method of acquiring a new skill.*
- ► develop a skill **develop, enhance, hone, improve, update** *I'll be back in September to hone the skills learnt in the course.*
- ► use or show a skill **apply, demonstrate, practise, use, utilize** *The school team will be practising their rugby skills with our coaches and players.*
- ► test a skill **assess, test** *We fully assess your skills and experience to ensure you get the assignment that suits you best.*
- ► need skill **need, require** *All this work requires great skill if you are going to get it right.*
- ► lack a skill **lack** *Fifty per cent of children start school lacking the vital skills that are needed to start learning.*

skilled ADJ
trained to do something well; needing someone who is trained

- adv+ADJ very **exceptionally, extremely, highly, incredibly, particularly** *This scheme is designed to allow exceptionally skilled individuals to stay in the UK.*
- ► enough **adequately, sufficiently** *He was a sufficiently skilled carpenter to construct a fine zither, which he also taught himself to play.*
- ► suitably **appropriately, suitably** *I believe the shortage of appropriately skilled graduates is serious.*
- ► in a particular area **professionally, technically** *Volunteers do not need to be technically skilled, but should be happy using computers.*
- ► and/ or **dedicated, experienced, knowledgeable, motivated, qualified, semi-skilled, trained, unskilled** *We offer skilled and experienced staff who are experts in their field.* • *He employed a small workforce of both skilled and unskilled labour.*
- ADJ+n worker **artisan, craftsman, operative, practitioner, professional, technician, tradesman, worker, workman** *He described how the old tradition of the skilled craftsman led to the first industrial revolution.*
- ► group of workers **labour, manpower, personnel, staff, workforce** *We're stressing the benefits of having a skilled workforce already available.*
- ► work **job, occupation, work** *The maintenance of this equipment is highly skilled work.*

skin N
the body's outer layer

- adj+N smooth or soft **silky, smooth, soft, supple** *The skin is once more supple, soft and silky.*
- ► with problems **dry, flaky, greasy, irritated, itchy, oily, scaly, sensitive, sore** *The protector is especially useful for people with sensitive skin.*
- ► light/dark **black, brown, dark, fair, light, olive, pale, tanned, white** *I have very pale skin, but the rest of my family is quite dark*
- ► healthy **glowing, healthy** *Tanned skin is a sign of sun-damaged skin, not healthy skin.*
- ► not covered **bare** *Avoid using powder blush on bare skin.*
- ► damaged **cracked, damaged, peeling, wrinkled** *It can improve the appearance of wrinkled skin over a period of time.*

▶ delicate/tough **delicate, leathery, thick, tough** *The body was protected by a leathery skin.*

● v+N damage the skin **burn, damage, dehydrate, dry, inflame, irritate** *Perfumed soaps, creams or deodorants may irritate the skin*

▶ care for the skin **cleanse, hydrate, moisturize, nourish, protect, soften, soothe** *Use plenty of moisturising cream to soothe and soften the skin.*

● N+n **allergy, condition, disease, disorder, infection, irritation, rash, reaction** *He had been cleaning out a barn and got a skin infection on his hands and arms.*

sky N
the space above the earth seen by looking upwards

● adj+N of a particular colour **azure, black, blue, crimson, grey, pale, red** *By 3pm, there were clear blue skies and a warm sun to dry the track.*

▶ cloudy or dull **clouded, cloudy, dark, dull, gloomy, hazy, heavy, leaden, overcast, stormy** *The sky was hazy and the sea as still as a millpond.*

▶ bright or without clouds **bright, clear, cloudless, empty** *The number of days per year with clear skies is 120–150.*

▶ with sun, moon or stars **moonlit, starlit, starry, sunny** *We eventually emerged to a starlit sky after about 15 hours underground.*

▶ northern, eastern etc **southern** *Just before midnight, the southern sky started to show the first signs of the impending storm.*

▶ when you can see a lot of sky **big, huge, vast, wide** *Now she has a small study, with a window that looks out on wide skies and fields.*

Usage **Sky** is often used in the plural, especially when talking about the weather: *The forecast for November 18th is showers but be prepared for stormy skies.*

● n+N at a particular time of day **afternoon, dawn, evening, midnight, morning, night, twilight** *Suddenly a rocket shrieks into the evening sky and explodes with a loud bang.*

▶ at a particular time of year **spring, summer etc** *The autumn sky, just above the horizon, had a scarlet glow.*

● N+v become darker **darken** *We had lunch while the sky darkened and then the heavens opened.*

▶ become lighter **brighten, clear, glow, lighten, light up** *The dark skies cleared and the sun came out to mark the event.*

▶ become cloudy **cloud over** *Looking up, I saw that the sky had clouded over.*

▶ change colour **glow red, pink etc, turn red, orange etc** *A mist hung over one mountain and the sky was turning pink.*

skyline N
the shapes of buildings or mountains against the sky

● adj+N exciting or beautiful **beautiful, breathtaking, dramatic, impressive, spectacular, stunning** *The rooms are south facing and reveal the city's dramatic skyline.*

▶ famous or special **distinctive, famous,**

recognizable, unique *Can anyone identify the location, with its distinctive skyline?*

▶ with mountains **jagged, mountainous** *Its mountainous skyline reminded him of the Scottish Highlands.*

▶ northern, eastern etc **southern** *A golden glow along the southern skyline throws the farm into silhouette.*

▶ of a city **city, downtown, high-rise, urban** *The tour offers many impressive views of the downtown skyline.*

● v+N break the skyline **break, interrupt, pierce, punctuate** *The skyline is punctuated by golden domes.*

▶ be the main feature of the skyline **dominate** *The most prominent landmark in the city, the Cathedral, dominates the skyline.*

▶ make the skyline beautiful **adorn, grace** *Architecturally unique in the whole of Mexico, the building graces the skyline of modern Pachuca.*

▶ fill the skyline **clutter, dot, litter** *Now skyscrapers and half-completed buildings litter the skyline.*

slam V
shut or hit something with great force

● adv+V **hard, quickly, suddenly, violently** *She left quickly, the large front doors slamming hard behind her.*

If you **slam** something **home**, you hit or push it forcefully to where you want it to go: *Up he stepped to slam home the goal.*

● V+n door etc **door, gate, lid, window** *She tried to slam the door, but he was too fast for her.*

If you **slam the brakes on**, you put your foot down hard on the brakes: *The child ran into the road and I slammed the brakes on just in time.*

▶ ball **ball, penalty, shot, volley** *He slammed the ball into the back of the net from 6 yards out.*

▶ hand etc **fist, hand** *She slammed her fist against the closed door.*

▶ phone **phone, receiver** *I said I refused to comment, and slammed the phone down.*

slant N
a particular way of showing or considering information

● adj+N new **contemporary, fresh, modern, new** *Do you want to find a fresh slant on a favourite destination?*

▶ positive/negative **negative, positive** *His agent tried to put a more positive slant on things.*

▶ types of slant **educational, feminist, humorous, political** *All of the games will have an educational slant.*

▶ personal **personal** *I tried to give a personal slant on things.*

▶ different or interesting **different, interesting, original, particular, unique, unusual** *Each film about the life of Christ puts a slightly different slant on his life and work.*

● v+N **add, bring, give, offer, put** *The electric violin certainly put a fresh slant on these songs in a very positive way.*

slash V

reduce something by a large amount

- adv+V **dramatically, drastically, in half** *In the next few years, interest rates were slashed dramatically.*

- V+n costs or charges **bills, charges, costs, fares, prices, tariffs, taxes, wages** *Unless public spending was slashed, taxes would have to rise.*

- spending **budget, expenditure, funding, spending** *Achieving a low tax economy isn't about slashing state spending.*

- rate **rate** *The bank has slashed the interst rate on personal loans.* ● *Hotels can often fill their empty beds by slashing the room rates.*

- jobs **jobs** *There are plans to slash 30,000 fishing jobs across the European Union.*

- in betting **the odds** *William Hill has slashed the odds for snow in Glasgow from 7–4 to 8–11.*

- crime **crime** *Mayor Giuliani slashed crime in New York, at one time the crime capital of the US.*

- substances that go into the air **emissions** *A further regulation on fuel efficiency could easily slash carbon emmisions from vehicles by as much as 30 per cent.*

slaughter N

the violent killing of many people

- adj+N unnecessary **needless, pointless, senseless, unnecessary, wanton** *In 1914, much of Europe was drawn into four years of senseless slaughter.*

- of people in large numbers **genocidal, indiscriminate, mass, wholesale** *Things go wrong, and it all ends in wholesale slaughter.*

- violent and cruel **barbaric, brutal, cold-blooded, cruel** *I can say nothing good about this brutal slaughter.*

- very bad **appalling, terrible** *The appalling slaughter in the area has led to calls for UN peacekeepers to be sent there.*

- v+N allow or justify slaughter **condone, justify, order, permit** *How could he permit this endless slaughter?*

- carry out slaughter **inflict** *Having inflicted enormous slaughter on the Danes, he almost put them to flight.*

- escape slaughter **escape** *Sir Humphrey escaped the slaughter of his clan.*

- see slaughter **witness** *These youngsters may have witnessed the terrifying slaughter of their mothers and families.*

- stop or criticize slaughter **condemn, end, halt, prevent, stop** *We want to stop the slaughter.*

- N+of **civilian, infant, innocent** *In fact, nothing could justify the slaughter of civilians, directly or indirectly.*

slaughter V

kill many people in a violent way

- adv+V cruelly **brutally, cruelly, mercilessly, ruthlessly** *They are ambushed by bandits who set about mercilessly slaughtering the group.*

- in an organized way **systematically** *In many of the camps, the inmates were systematically slaughtered.*

slavery N

the system of owning people as slaves

- v+N fight slavery **campaign against, combat, condemn, fight, fight against, oppose** *Her father, Lord Grey, opposed slavery.*

- end slavery **abolish, ban, end, outlaw, prohibit** *Slavery was abolished there in 1863.*

- escape slavery **escape, escape from** *Tulun converted to Islam in order to escape slavery.*

- support slavery **accept, defend, justify** *The Atlantic powers had to justify slavery and colonialism.*

- when someone is made a slave **force into, sell into** *They were transported and sold into slavery in the New World.*

- n+of+N **abolition, ending, prohibition** *The emancipation of women and the abolition of slavery are examples for how the attitudes of society have changed.*

sleep V

be in the natural state of unconsciousness when the body rests

- adv+V well **comfortably, like a baby, like a log INFORMAL, properly, soundly, well** *Thinking she was asleep, I fell asleep myself and slept soundly.*

- peacefully or safely **easy, peacefully, quietly, safely, sweetly** *You can sleep easy knowing that your conscience is clear.*

- badly **badly, fitfully** *I have never slept so badly.*

- not much or not at all **barely, hardly, not a wink INFORMAL** *I feel like I hardly slept again last night.*

- for longer than usual **late** *Jonathan enjoys travelling, meeting new people, playing and watching football, eating and sleeping late!*

- when someone sleeps outside because they have no home **rough** *An increasing number of young people are sleeping rough in London.*

sleep N

a natural unconscious state when the body rests

- adj+N difficult to wake from **deep, dreamless, sound** *The child lay quiet for a few moments, then fell into a deep sleep.*

- peaceful **good, peaceful, restful, sweet, undisturbed, uninterrupted** *Melatonin is a hormone which helps to aid restful sleep.*

> When you have slept well you can say you have had **a good night's sleep**: *I haven't had a good night's sleep for months.*

- not peaceful **broken, disrupted, disturbed, fitful, light, restless, troubled** *I finally gave up on my disturbed sleep and pulled the curtains open.*

- a lot/a little **extra, less, a little, little, not much** *They got little sleep in those first few weeks after the baby was born.* ● *She didn't get much sleep that night.*

> It is common to use the expression **...hours sleep** to say how long someone sleeps: *Eight hours sleep is considered the optimum to allow the body to operate well.* ● *After a couple of hours sleep, he got up and went to work.*

- enough **adequate, enough** *Are you getting enough sleep?*

- necessary **much-needed** *We settled into our tent, hoping to catch up on some much-needed sleep.*

• v+N get sleep **get, grab** INFORMAL, **snatch** INFORMAL *Let's go to our rooms now and get some sleep.*

▶ lose sleep **lose** *Woody was woken up and lost precious sleep.*

▶ go to sleep **drift into, drift off to, fall into, get to, go to, sink into, slip into** *I felt better and drifted into a restless sleep.* • *She didn't find it difficult to get to sleep, but she often woke early.*

▶ when something stops you sleeping, or sleeping well **disrupt, disturb, interrupt** *Tea or coffee, too close to bedtime, can disturb your sleep.*

▶ when something helps you sleep, or sleep well **aid** *The lavender aroma also aids restful sleep.*

• N+n problems **deficit, deprivation, disorder, disruption, disturbance, loss, problem** *Chronic sleep deprivation is a condition that affects most working adults.*

▶ pattern **cycle, habits, pattern, routine** *Appetite, sleep patterns and sexual interest may be disrupted and generally life becomes dull.*

slender ADJ
very small and only just enough

• ADJ+n advantage or difference **advantage, lead, majority, margin** *Peter's skills under pressure were tested as he maintained his slender lead.*

▶ resources **means, resources** *Much has been achieved on comparatively slender resources.*

▶ hope or chance **chance, hope** *There is a slender hope that the military operation may be brief.*

▶ evidence **evidence, foundation** *The evidence is too slender to sustain any very broad conclusions.*

slight ADJ
small in size, amount, or degree

• adv+ADJ rather **fairly, rather, somewhat** *Most of the modifications we will be making are fairly slight.*

▶ very **extremely, very** *Any difference is very slight.*

▶ comparatively **comparatively, relatively** *So far, the environmental and social impacts of tourism have been relatively slight.*

• ADJ+n change **adjustment, alteration, deviation, difference, improvement, modification, variation** *Often the effects are minor and can be overcome with a slight adjustment in dosage.*

▶ decrease **decline, decrease, dip** INFORMAL, **drop, fall, reduction** *There was a slight decrease in fuel efficiency during the early 1990s.*

▶ increase **increase, rise** *Please note, fees for future academic years may be subject to a slight annual increase.*

▶ amount or extent **amount, degree** *The value of the research was not affected in the slightest degree.*

▶ problem or mistake **difficulty, error, mistake, problem** *The first noticeable symptom is a slight difficulty in walking.*

▶ idea **idea** *I didn't have the slightest idea what they were talking about.*

> **Slight** is usually used in the <u>superlative</u> form in this combination.

▶ sign **hint, sign** *He learned to walk away if there was the slightest hint of trouble.*

> **slight** is usually used in the <u>superlative</u> form in these combinations.

▶ exaggeration **exaggeration** *That may be a slight exaggeration.*

slogan N
a short phrase that is easy to remember

• adj+N political **anti-government, anti-war, militant, nationalist, patriotic, revolutionary** *Some 100 anti-riot police formed a shield around the embassy as the protesters shouted anti-war slogans.*

▶ good **catchy, snappy** *The huge sums that political parties pay PR 'experts' to dream up catchy election slogans were revealed this week.*

▶ bad **meaningless, simplistic** *It declared itself the party of law and order and put forward meaningless slogans such as 'democratic modernisation'.*

▶ for a particular purpose **advertising, campaign, marketing** *She declined to reveal any advertising slogans she had written.*

• v+N say a slogan **chant, mouth, proclaim, repeat, shout** *Thousands of angry protesters burned flags and chanted slogans.*

▶ write a slogan **daub, paint** *Some protesters daubed slogans on the station with spray paint.*

▶ carry a slogan **bear, carry** *The protesters carried placards bearing the slogan 'No third runway'.*

▶ create a slogan **coin, come up with** *Some of the same feminists who coined this slogan have turned their backs on its intent.*

slope N
the side of a hill or mountain

• adj+N steep/not steep **gentle, gradual, precipitous, slight, steep** *The slope was very steep and we moved over gradually to some rocks.*

▶ high/low **high, higher, lower, upper** *A single pine clings to the upper slopes.*

▶ covered with something **forested, grassy, rocky, wooded** *There are wooded valleys, rocky slopes, cultivated terraces and impressive cliffs to explore.*

▶ in a particular direction or location **eastern, north, west-facing etc** *Four experimental sites were identified on the northern, western and southern slopes of Torr Fada.*

• v+N go up a slope **ascend, clamber up, climb, climb up, scramble up** *Bear right and climb the gentle slope until you come to a bench.*

▶ go round a slope **hug, skirt** *From here you skirt th⸌ northern slopes of the wild Cheviot Hills.*

▶ go down a slope **clamber down, descend, scramble⸌ down** *A few of the more agile clambered down the very steep slope to the bank of the Dowles Brook.*

• v+on+N **be built, be perched, be situated, lie, stand** *The UEA campus lies on the slopes of the beautiful Yare Valley.*

slow ADJ
not fast; taking a long time

• adv+ADJ too **disappointingly, excruciatingly, frustratingly, painfully, tediously, unacceptably** *This process has been painfully slow and time consuming.*

▶ very **extremely, incredibly, terribly, very**

Unfortunately, service was extremely slow and we were only checked on once during the meal.

▶ rather **fairly, noticeably, pretty** INFORMAL**, quite, rather, significantly, somewhat** *The problem with this software is that it is quite slow.* • *Drivers' reaction times were significantly slower when they were using a mobile phone.*

▶ a little **a little, slightly, a tad** INFORMAL *It used to be suggested that bilingual children were a little slower learning to speak than monolingual children.*

▶ relatively **comparatively, relatively** *A straightforward, but comparatively slow approach is the two-part correction described below.*

▶ ADJ+n speed **pace, rate, speed, tempo** *Away from the bustling crowds on the main beaches you can enjoy a slower pace.*

▶ progress **development, growth, progress, recovery** *The gender pay gap has narrowed, but progress is still painfully slow.*

▶ when something changes or gets worse **change, decline** *The onset of cataract is painless and is characterised by a slow decline in vision.*

▶ response **reaction, response** *There has been a high demand for the product but a slow response from suppliers.*

slump N

sudden fall; a period when an economy is unsuccessful

adj+N big **big, deep, dramatic, major** *There was a dramatic slump in Labour's share of the vote.*

bad **alarming, bad, disastrous, severe** *Japan is just beginning to recover from its worst slump since the 1930s.*

happening everywhere **global, worldwide** *The deal is in an attempt to cut costs and overcome the global slump in hi-tech industries.*

recent or current **current, recent** *United travel to London in the hope of ending their recent slump in form.*

types of slump **advertising, economic, housing, market, price, property, sales, trade** *Unless you are forced to, never sell during a property slump.*

v+N experience a slump **experience, face, hit** INFORMAL**, suffer** *While French remains the most popular language, it still suffered a slump of 19 per cent in four years.*

predict a slump **predict** *This time last year, experts predicted a slump in the housing market.*

cause a slump **cause, spark, trigger** *Downloading from the Internet has caused a slump in the sales of CDs*

avoid or end a slump **avoid, end, prevent** *It will require international co-operation both to curb inflation and to avoid a slump.*

slur N

remark that is intended to insult someone

adj+N types of slur **ethnic, personal, racial, racist** *There are strict laws against racial slurs.*

very bad **disgraceful, disgusting, outrageous, terrible** *That's an outrageous slur!*

v+N make a slur **cast, make** *The article has cast a slur on our organization.*

not accept a slur **refute, reject** *In her letter she*

*corrects the errors and refutes the slurs made **against** her.*

small ADJ

not large, important or difficult

• adv+ADJ too **ridiculously, too** *Use standardised fonts which are easy to read and are not too large or too small.*

▶ very **especially, extremely, incredibly, particularly, so, vanishingly, very** *The article examines the tax issues affecting a very small company.*

▶ surprisingly **surprisingly** *Although many of these coins were made, a surprisingly small number have survived.*

▶ rather **fairly, pretty** INFORMAL**, quite, rather** *Molines is a fairly small ski resort, with a total of 34 slopes distributed over 38kms.*

▶ comparatively **comparatively, relatively** *We are a relatively small and friendly group.*

▶ when something is a little or a lot smaller **considerably, far, a little, much, significantly, slightly** *Drill the hole slightly smaller than the bolt, and screw it in from the bottom.*

• v+ADJ **appear, be, become, feel, get, grow, keep sth, look, make sth, remain, seem, stay** *The cost per pupil rises as the school gets smaller.* • *The numbers in the groups will be kept small, so that people can get to know each other better.*

smile V

raise the corners of the mouth when you are happy, being friendly etc

• adv+V strongly or happily **brightly, broadly, happily, serenely, warmly** *In a very friendly manner he approached me, smiling broadly.*

▶ weakly or sadly **faintly, sadly, weakly** *She stood up before him, smiling faintly.*

▶ kindly **benignly, fondly, graciously, indulgently, kindly, pleasantly** *I found Renfield sitting placidly in his room with his hands folded, smiling benignly.*

▶ gently **gently, softly, sweetly** *I merely smiled sweetly and agreed.*

▶ shyly **shyly** *She giggled at my silly pose, wiping her eyes and smiling shyly.*

▶ politely **politely** *When questioned on the matter, she smiled politely and said she had no information.*

▶ showing some other emotion **encouragingly, grimly, knowingly, nervously, ruefully, smugly, wryly** *Most viewers will smile wryly at the film's conclusion.*

smile N

an expression that shows happiness, friendliness, or amusement

• adj+N big or happy **beaming, beatific, big, bright, cheerful, cheery, contented, dazzling, radiant** *A radiant smile broke through her clouded face.*

▶ small or weak **faint, slight, wan** *She looks calm and placid, a slight smile on her lips.*

▶ showing some other emotion **apologetic, mocking, rueful, satisfied, shy, sly, smug, wry** *The wry smile and glinting eyes hold the suggestion of mischief.*

▶ not real or sincere **bland, fake, grim** *He raised his eyebrows and gave me a grim smile.*

▶ cheeky **cheeky, mischievous** *It seems we just can't get enough of his cheeky smile.*

▶ attractive **sweet, winning** *The boy gave a winning smile.*

● v+N have or give a smile **break into, crack** INFORMAL, **flash** INFORMAL, **give, have, put on, wear** *The star flashed her famous smile and gave us some great poses.* ● *He sounded angry but he had a smile on his face.*

▶ cause a smile **provoke, raise** *These make perfect gifts, and are always guaranteed to raise a smile.*

▶ smile reluctantly **force, manage** *The accused barely turned their heads, though some managed wan smiles.*

> You can use the expression **with a smile** to say that someone is smiling when they do something: *'Yes of course!' she relplied with a smile.* ● *Make sure everyone leaves with a smile on their face.*

● N+v appear **appear, come over sth, cross sth, light up sth, play on sth, spread** *A faint smile crossed his face at the thought.* ● *Suddenly a smile lit up her face.*

▶ become wider **broaden, widen** *'Well, let's start then,' he said, his thin smile broadening into a big grin.*

▶ disappear **disappear, fade** *Her smile faded quickly when she realized who I was.*

● n+of+N **flicker, glimmer, hint, shadow** *'You'll see', she replied, with a hint of a smile playing on her lips.*

smoke N
a cloud produced by something that is burning

● adj+N with a strong smell **acrid, pungent** *The air was full of acrid smoke from the burning tyres.*

▶ thick **dense, thick** *Suddenly there was a terrific roar, followed by flames and dense smoke.*

▶ moving **billowing** *The ship was a mass of billowing smoke and flames.*

▶ poisonous or dangerous **choking, noxious, poisonous, suffocating, toxic** *Residents were urged to shut their windows and doors following fears of toxic smoke from the fire.*

▶ of a particular colour **black, dark, white etc** *Check the exhaust doesn't produce lots of blue smoke when you rev the engine.*

● n+N tobacco and similar substances **cannabis, cigar, cigarette, fag** INFORMAL, **marijuana, tobacco** *Tobacco smoke contains over 4000 different chemicals, many of which are poisons.*

▶ something else that is burning **barbecue, bonfire, chimney, coal, exhaust, incense, wood** *Barbecue smoke is a minor irritation when compared with bonfire smoke.*

● v+N **belch, belch forth, billow, blow, emit, puff** *The dockyard, with its chimneys belching forth smoke, was a hive of industry.*

● N+v come out in large amounts **belch, billow, pour** *The sky is noticeably darker because of the smoke still billowing from the volcano.*

▶ move gently **curl, drift, swirl, waft** *Dark smoke drifting from a chimney means the wood is not burning completely.*

▶ not move **hang** *Smoke hung over the village in the evening, sometimes mixing with fog.*

▶ rise **ascend, rise** *Five kilometres away, I could see smoke rising.*

● N+n containing or consisting of smoke **haze, particle, plume, trail** *There was a thick haze of smoke, but visibility was good.*

▶ breathing smoke **exposure, inhalation** *Both casualties were taken to hospital suffering from smoke inhalation.*

● n+of+N large amount **billow, cloud, column, haze, pall, plume, swirl, trail, wreath** *The fire and enormous plumes of smoke can be seen from the office.*

▶ small amount **puff, wisp** *Suddenly the Officer of the Watch thinks he sees a puff of smoke on the horizon.*

▶ smell **aroma, smell, whiff** *The gorgeous aroma of wood smoke on the air and the shorter days are signs of early winter.*

smoker N
someone who smokes cigarettes, pipe etc

● adj+N smoking a lot **chain, heavy, 20-a-day, 40-a-day etc** *I've been a heavy smoker for 40 years.*

▶ addicted **addicted, dependent** *The clinic tends to attract the more highly dependent smoker.*

▶ regular/occasional **habitual, occasional, regular** *Both regular and occasional smokers appear to hav underestimated how much they smoked.*

● and/or **ex-smoker, non-smoker** *Our aim is to improve the overall health of everyone – smokers and non-smokers alike.*

smoking N
the activity of breathing smoke from cigarettes et

● adj+N by particular groups of people **adolescent, maternal, parental, paternal, teenage, underage** *Another environmental influence strongly related to reduced birthweight is maternal smoking.*

▶ harmful or serious **addictive, harmful, heavy** *Thi survey shows just how wasteful and addictive smoking is.*

▶ when other people smoke **involuntary, passive** *Asthma in children will be aggravated by passive smoking.*

▶ when you smoke one cigarette immediately afte another **chain** *Chain smoking in front of daytime TV day after day is enough to make anyone depresse*

● v+N allow smoking **allow, permit** *The restaurant is a no smoking area (smoking is permitted in the special areas outside).*

▶ forbid smoking **ban** INFORMAL, **forbid, outlaw, prohibit** *Should smoking be banned completely in public places?*

▶ limit or discourage smoking **discourage, preven reduce, restrict, tackle** *Tackling smoking is centra to cutting deaths from cancer and heart disease.*

▶ start/stop smoking **give up, quit** INFORMAL, **refrair from, start, stop** *There will also be support for residents to help them quit smoking.* ● *Don't lose heart if you start smoking again.*

smug ADJ
too satisfied with your abilities or achievements

● adv+ADJ slightly **a little, slightly** *The tone is a little smug.*

▶ rather **pretty** INFORMAL, **quite, rather** *So I was feeli pretty smug, as you can imagine.*

▸ very or too **too, very** *We're very smug about the quality of our programmes.*

▸ in a way that annoys people **insufferably, unbearably** *You run the risk of appearing unbearably smug.*

● ADJ+n smile **grin, smile** *'I found it quite easy,' he said with a smug grin.*

● look **expression, look** *The smug look on his face disappeared as I accelerated away from him.*

▸ attitude **complacency, self-righteousness, self-satisfaction, superiority** *We looked down on them with an air of smug self-satisfaction.*

● v+ADJ **feel, look, sound** *I was feeling so very smug.*

● and/or **arrogant, complacent, pompous, self-righteous, self-satisfied, superior** *I found their attitude both smug and arrogant.*

snag N
a problem or disadvantage you did not expect

● adj+N small **minor, slight** *There's a slight snag: I can't get off work till about 6.*

▸ big **big, major** *We've only hit one major snag in the project so far.*

▸ possible **possible, potential** *It's better to be fully aware of any possible snags and problems before you take the decision.*

▸ v+N **encounter, hit, run into** *Here we hit a snag, as we found this footpath blocked and a notice saying 'closed for eight weeks'.*

snippet N
a small piece of something, for example information or news

▸ adj+N interesting **fascinating, interesting** that makes you want to hear more **tantalizing** *'You can't just give us that tantalizing snippet of information and then leave us hanging in the air!'*
small **brief, little, short, small, tiny** *The brief snippet of text mentions the city's ring of 'verdant hills'.*
types of snippet **audio, historical, interview, news, video, vocal** *There are video snippets of shows, presenters and adverts here going back to the fifites.*

▸ v+N **catch, hear, overhear** *I overheard a snippet of conversation as I walked past a neighbouring table.*

N+of piece of information **conversation, gossip, info INFORMAL, information, news** *I hear the odd snippet of news about you from your sister.*
piece of a larger thing **interview, song, text, tune** *You can download ringtones, which are snippets of your favourite tunes.*

snow N
pieces of ice that fall from the sky

▸ adj+N in large/small quantities **deep, heavy, light, thick** *Winters are cold, with heavy snows.*
recent **fresh, new** *The fresh snow increases the avalanche risk and makes the climb much more dangerous.*
soft or wet **melting, soft, wet** *They manhandled the sledges over ice hummocks and through soft snow.*
hard or dry **crisp, dry, frozen, hard, powdery** *Conditions were perfect, lovely powdery snow and clear blue skies.*

▸ being blown **drifting, driving, swirling** *Drifting snow caused the closure of many roads.*

▸ where no one has trodden **virgin** *I trudged on through the virgin snow, along the broad ridge to the summit.*

● N+v fall **blow, fall** *Several centimetres of snow had already fallen and it was coming down heavily*

▸ stay **lie** *There was snow lying on the ground all the way.*

▸ melt **disappear, melt, recede, retreat, thaw** *The forecast is good and the snow has melted.*

▸ pile up **drift, pile up** *The severe frost continued through until March, with snow drifting in the easterly wind.*

▸ cover or block things **blanket, block, cover** *Three or four inches of snow has blanketed the ground for over a week now.*

● N+n **flurry, shower, storm** *Heavy snow showers fell across Grampian and the Highlands throughout the day.*

● n+of+N **blanket, covering, fall, flurry, sprinkling** *There was just a sprinkling of snow in the valley, although higher up the ground was covered.*

snowfall N
the amount of snow that falls during a period

● adj+N big/small **considerable, heavy, light, significant** *Heavy snowfalls had made the roads impassable in places.*

▸ happening at night **overnight** *Heavy overnight snowfalls meant that skiing was not possible early in the day.*

▸ unusual or unexpected **infrequent, rare, uncommon, unexpected** *The whole class responded spontaneously to the unexpected snowfall.*

▸ average **average** *The average snowfall is around 5 inches.*

▸ annual **annual** *Annual snowfall at lower elevations is 160mm.*

▸ recent **fresh, recent** *Our departure on the trip was delayed for three days because of fresh snowfall.*

snub N
an action or remark that is intended to insult someone

● adj+N **calculated, deliberate, humiliating, massive** *The failure to proffer a hand to shake could be seen as a deliberate snub.*

● v+N give a snub **deliver** *On the Scottish King's arrival at Gloucester, William delivered a snub by refusing to receive him.*

▸ see something as a snub **perceive sth as, regard sth as, see sth as, take sth as** *If you don't see your name on the list please don't take this as a snub!*

soar V
to quickly increase to a high level

● n+V **costs, demand, inflation, popularity, prices, profits, sales, temperatures, unemployment** *Stores ran out of phones, as demand soared in the pre-Christmas period.* ● *The sun broke through and temperatures soared.*

sober ADJ

1 not drunk

- adv+ADJ completely **completely, entirely, perfectly, totally** *He seemed a bit excited but perfectly sober when I met him.*
- ▶ fairly **fairly, quite, reasonably, relatively** *Take a drink, by all means, but try to say relatively sober.*
- v+ADJ **keep sb, remain, stay** *If I stay sober, will I turn into a boring person?*

2 with a serious attitude

- ADJ+n **account, analysis, assessment, judgment, reflection, reminder, warning** *The report is a sober assessment of where we are and what we should do to meet our targets.*

social ADJ

1 relating to society and people's lives

- ADJ+n situation in which people are poor, alone, or treated unfairly **deprivation, disadvantage, exclusion, inequality, injustice, isolation** *Circles Network runs a number of projects that support children at risk of social exclusion.*
- ▶ situation in which people protest or break the law **breakdown, unrest, upheaval** *Unemployment and social unrest soon led to rioting on the streets.*
- ▶ good situation **cohesion, equality, inclusion, integration, justice, welfare, well-being** *As a rule, housing estates reveal a total lack of social cohesion.*
- ▶ negative feeling **disapproval, embarrassment, stigma** *AIDS still carries a social stigma in many places.*
- ▶ system or structure **hierarchy, network, order, stratification, structure, system** *A slowing down in social mobility is not just an issue for those at the bottom of the social order.*
- ▶ group you belong to **background, class, group, network** *Our school has students from many social backgrounds.* • *Life expectancy varies by social class.*
- ▶ ability to improve your social position **mobility, movement** *Education is the key to social mobility.*
- ▶ change **change, reform, revolution** *Social change is never easy.*
- ▶ usual behaviour **mores, norms** *Social norms dictate the extent to which women can speak out against corruption.*
- and/or **academic, cultural, ecological, economic, educational, emotional, environmental, moral, personal, physical, political, psychological, religious, spiritual** *The country was experiencing social and economic crisis.*

2 used about activities done with other people

- ADJ+n event **call, engagement, event, function, gathering, occasion** *We have several fundraising and social events taking place over the next few months.*
- ▶ interaction **contact, interaction** *From a stress management point of view, social contact is crucial.*
- ▶ skills **graces, skills** *This new approach seeks to improve students' social skills through shared discussion and collaborative activities.*
- ▶ activities **activities, life** *I have a great social life!*
- ▶ good or bad effects on society **benefits, consequences, costs, effects, impact** *Her book deals with the social costs of crime and unemployment.*

society N

people living together in organized communities

- adj+N modern or advanced **advanced, contemporary, industrial, modern, Western** *This is a novel approach to life in a Western society so fixated on personal achievement.*
- ▶ not modern **early, hunter-gatherer, peasant, post-modern, primitive, traditional** *Natural propensity to war is the motive force in primitive societies only.*
- ▶ diverse **diverse, multi-cultural, multi-faith, multi-racial** *Living in a multi-cultural society is an enriching experience.*
- ▶ not religious **secular** *To what degree is India a secular society?*
- ▶ civilized **civilized** *This is a level of poverty that is unacceptable in a civilised society.*
- ▶ rich **affluent, bourgeois, high** *He became a favourite of high society and used it to his advantage.*
- ▶ normal **mainstream** *Disabled young people have the right to be included in mainstream society.*
- ▶ where everyone is treated fairly or equally **classless, co-operative, egalitarian, fair, inclusive, just, tolerant** *To see a classless society in operation is unforgettable.*
- ▶ where people are free to live the way they want **free, open** *The idea is disgusting, and in a free society it is our right to say so.*
- ▶ wider **larger, wider** *We have been looking at the ideas that people hold about men's behaviour, both in families and in wider society.*
- ▶ with a particular political or economic system **capitalist, democratic, liberal, socialist** *For a few brief years, the working class set about creating a socialist society.*
- ▶ where there is an emphasis on shopping and buying things **consumer, consumerist** *We have become a consumer society.*
- ▶ with a particular kind of industry **agricultural, information, knowledge, scientific, technological** *We live in a rapidly changing information society.*
- ▶ where men have the power **male-dominated, patriarchal** *Women are always at the bottom of the pecking order in a patriarchal society.*
- v+N change a society **affect, change, reform, shape, transform** *The 19th century was dominated by the Industrial Revolution, and society was transformed by the economic changes which that revolution brought about.*
- ▶ create a society **build, create, establish, form, rebuild** *The Russian Revolution tried to build a society in which all productive work, and scientific knowledge would be entirely communal.*
- ▶ exist in a society **exist in, permeate, pervade** *The desire for luxury pervaded society from the courtier downwards.*
- ▶ have a bad effect on a society **destroy, divide, polarize, undermine** *Many societies are divided by conflict and violence.*
- ▶ have a good effect on a society **benefit, enrich, strengthen** *The voluntary sector enriches society and should be promoted and supported.*
- ▶ consisting of ordinary people, not politicians, the military etc **civic, civil** *We need a public debate on these issues which involves civil society as a whole.*

soft ADJ
1 not stiff, firm or rough

● adv+ADJ in a good way **beautifully, deliciously, luxuriously, wonderfully** *The current collection includes luxuriously soft baby wraps and blankets.*
▶ very **extremely, incredibly, really** INFORMAL**, so, very** *The leather is incredibly soft.*
▶ rather **fairly, pretty** INFORMAL**, quite, rather, relatively** *Lead, in particular, is a fairly soft metal.*
▶ slightly **a little, slightly** *Gently cook the leeks until lightly coloured and slightly soft.*
● and/or flexible **flexible, pliable, stretchy, supple** *The skin is once more supple, soft and silky.*
▶ pleasant to touch **cuddly, fluffy, silky, smooth, velvety** *A soft cuddly toy can be full of germs.*
▶ easy to press **spongy, springy, squishy** INFORMAL *Bone marrow is the soft, spongy tissue in the centre of the bones.*

2 not strict enough

v+ADJ be soft **be** *Some people thought the media was too soft on President Bush.*
become soft **become, get, go, grow, turn** *Labour was accused of going soft on criminals.*
appear soft **appear, look, sound** *Such is the mood that no one wants to risk looking soft on terrorism.*

N+on activities **crime, drugs, immigration, terrorism** *Governments regard it as electorally damaging to be seen as soft on drugs.*
people **criminals, terrorists** *Many people think the law is too soft on criminals.*

software N
programs used by computers

v+N install or download software **download, install, load** *After you order, we will send you instructions on how to download and install the software.*
design software **build, create, design, develop, make, produce, write** *Postcript is one of the most elegant and powerful pieces of software ever developed.*
use software **operate, run, use, utilize** *Will I need to buy and learn to use complicated software?*
upgrade software **update, upgrade** *How are you planning to upgrade the software?*
make software available **distribute, launch, release** *A Cambridge team is releasing free software designed for hand held computers too small to have keyboards.*
make software suitable for a particular user **configure, customize** *We will install and configure your flight simulation software to give you optimum performance.*

N+n product or system **application, program, solution, system, tool** *Apple supplies software tools which are useful for project management.*
set **bundle, package, product, suite** *My computer has the standard Microsoft office software suite.*
designer **designer, developer, engineer, maker** *Infomill was founded in 1996 by a team of software engineers, sales staff and managers.*
design **design, development, engineering** *Software development is fraught with problems.*
company **business, company, firm, house,**

manufacturer, provider, publisher, supplier, vendor *Check with your software provider for these updates regularly.*
▶ upgrade **update, upgrade** *The forums will be offline today for essential software upgrades.*
▶ permission to use legally **licence** *8 per cent of the department budget is spent on software licences.*

solace N
something that makes you feel better, especially in a time of sadness or disappointment

● v+N try to find solace **seek** *I often feel alienated and seek solace in music.*
▶ find solace **find, gain, take** *Victoria sank into deep depression after the death of her husband, before finding solace with John Brown.*
▶ bring solace **bring, offer** *His quiet unseen ministry amongst the sick, the elderly and the dying brought solace and hope to many.*

sole ADJ
existing as the only one of a particular type

● ADJ+n aim or reason **aim, basis, cause, intention, justification, objective, purpose, reason** *It wasn't the sole reason I moved here, but it helped.*
▶ responsibility **authority, charge, control, responsibility** *The project panel has the sole responsibility for assigning projects.*
▶ exception **exception** *With the sole exception of Diana, we all lived in London.*
▶ method **means** *CVs will not be accepted as a sole means of application.*

solemn ADJ
expressing serious intentions

● ADJ+n promise **commitment, oath, pledge, promise, undertaking, vow** *They all took a solemn oath to stand by each other.*
▶ responsibility **duty, obligation, responsibility** *Everyone has a solemn duty to assist in the search for a lasting peace.*
▶ statement **affirmation, appeal, declaration, expression, warning** *The declarations were solemn and heartfelt and moved me to tears every time.*

solicit V
to ask someone for money or support

● V+n information or opinions **comments, feedback, opinions, suggestions, views** *The History Department solicits feedback from students.*
▶ help **aid, assistance, help, support** *I was unable to do the work alone, so I solicited the help of two or three others.*
▶ money **contributions, donations, funds, money** *We do not solicit donations by telephone.*

solution N
a way to solve a problem

● adj+N good **effective, efficient, elegant, excellent, good** *If you are looking for flexible storage units, our products offer an excellent solution.*
▶ practical and likely to succeed **feasible, practical, pragmatic, viable, workable** *You need to get to the root of a problem quickly, and devise a workable solution for it.*

▶ not expensive **affordable, cost-effective, economical, inexpensive, low-cost** *We work with local businesses to provide affordable solutions to the environmental challenges they face.*

▶ satisfactory or suitable **acceptable, appropriate, right, satisfactory, suitable** *It could take months before a satisfactory solution is found.*

▶ best possible **ideal, optimal, perfect, ultimate** *For many, the ideal solution is to bring a carer into the person's own home.*

▶ easy **convenient, easy, simple** *The simplest solution is to use a plastic box!*

▶ new and imaginative **creative, imaginative, innovative, new, radical, unique** *The Tribunals have to come up with creative solutions to legal problems.*

▶ lasting for ever, or for a long time **lasting, long-term, permanent, sustainable** *There will be no long-term solution to these problems.*

▶ possible **possible, potential** *There are a couple of possible solutions to this issue.*

▶ total/partial **complete, comprehensive, partial, total** *Partial solutions to these dilemmas are suggested.*

▶ peaceful **peaceful** *He always sought a peaceful solution in conflict, only fighting after the enemy had refused all negotiation.*

▶ quick **immediate, quick** *She agreed that genetically-modified crops had great potential, but did not offer an immediate solution to world hunger.*

● v+N find a solution **achieve, arrive at, discover, find, hit upon, identify, obtain, reach, think of** *Consider all aspects of a situation, weighing up different options to arrive at the best solution.*

▶ provide a solution **deliver, generate, give, negotiate, produce, provide, supply** *If you find that off-the-peg garments do not fit you, we can almost always provide the solution.*

▶ suggest a solution **present, propose, recommend, suggest** *They can propose solutions and work with others to implement them.*

▶ be a solution **be, offer, represent** *If you do not have much space, a fold-up bed can offer the solution.*

▶ try to find a solution **look for, search for, seek, work on, work towards** *Both partners must be willing to work towards a solution to improve their marriage.*

▶ develop a solution **customize, design, develop, devise, tailor** *We help companies develop solutions that make a real difference to their business.*

▶ need or demand a solution **ask for, call for, demand, need** *I don't think that boys find it more difficult than girls to say what their problem is, they just tend to ask for a solution.*

▶ have a solution **have** *Some problems simply have no solution.*

● N+to general problem **challenge, crisis, difficulty, dilemma, issue, predicament, problem** *We can help you find a solution to your problems.*

▶ particular problem **climate-change, conflict, congestion, dispute, inequality, poverty, shortage, unemployment** *Education and training could be part of the solution to poverty in this community.*

solve V
to find the solution to something

● V+n problem **conflict, crisis, dilemma, dispute,** issue, problem, problem, shortage *We're also going to have to start thinking of other ways to solve the energy crisis.*

▶ game or calculation **clue, conundrum, equation, puzzle, riddle** *There are two relatively simple approaches to solve such equations.* ● *Ask the children to solve the riddle.*

▶ crime or mystery **case, crime, enigma, murder, mystery** *Being a police officer in Hertfordshire is not just about solving crime, it's also about being seen on the streets.*

sombre ADJ
serious, or sad

● ADJ+n **air, atmosphere, moment, mood, occasion, scene, tone** *The death of Queen Victoria cast a sombre mood over the nation.*

sophisticated ADJ
showing an impressive understanding of complicated issues

● adv+ADJ very **extremely, incredibly, remarkably, very** *Doctors have access to a remarkably sophisticated diagnostic program.*

▶ in a particular way **financially, intellectually, linguistically, mathematically, politically, technically, technologically, theoretically** *The have to deal with clients who are financially very sophisticated.* ● *The software offers a technically sophisticated solution.*

sorrow N
great sadness

● adj+N **bitter, deep, endless, great, inconsolable, overwhelming, profound, terrible, unspeakable, untold** *He tells of his inconsolable sorrow at the los of a friend who died.*

● v+N feel sorrow **bear, be filled with, carry, endure, experience, feel, suffer** *She has experience much sorrow in her life.*

▶ express sorrow **express** *I expressed my sorrow at Caroline's death and asked how things had been.*

▶ cause sorrow **bring, cause** *Success, however, brought sorrow to the Carter's personal lives.*

▶ ease sorrow **alleviate, assuage, ease, soothe** *At th sad time, may happy memories help ease our sorro*

● and/or bad feeling **anger, anguish, bitterness, grief, heartache, loneliness, misery, pain, regret, remorse, sadness, shame, suffering, tears** *A wave grief and sorrow swept across the country.*

▶ good feeling **happiness, joy** *They formed a relationship that would cause her great happiness and sorrow for the rest of her life.*

sorry ADJ
feeling sadness, disappointment, or regret

● adv+ADJ very **awfully, deeply, desperately, dreadfully, extremely, heartily, really** INFORMAL, s INFORMAL, **terribly, very** *I'm terribly sorry, but I've forgotten your name.*

▶ genuinely **genuinely, sincerely, truly** *I am genuine sorry if you found my remarks offensive.*

● v+ADJ **be, feel, look** *We are sorry if people are disappointed.*

- ADJ+infinitive find out about something **find, hear, learn, note, read, see**
▶ tell someone something **admit, announce, inform sb, report, say, tell sb** *We are sorry to announce that the 08.40 train service has been cancelled.*

sound N
something heard

- adj+N easy to hear **audible, clear** *With the new speakers, you get a much clearer sound.*
▶ difficult to hear **distant, faint, muffled, muted** *He moved as quickly as he dared, listening for the faintest sound.*
▶ easy to recognize **distinct, distinctive, familiar, unique, unmistakable** *His voice has that distinct English sound to it.*
▶ strange **eerie, haunting, strange, weird** *The church bell struck – it was an eerie, haunting sound.*
▶ pleasant **gentle, mellow, pure, rich, soft, soothing, warm** *A water feature can recreate the soothing sound of running water.*
▶ unpleasant **grating, harsh** *I found the amplified sound too harsh.*
▶ of a particular type **buzzing, clicking, drumming, hissing, humming, ringing, rumbling, screeching, whirring, whistling** *Tinnitus is a ringing or buzzing sound in the ears.*
▶ loud or very loud **deafening, loud, powerful** *I couldn't hear what she was saying over the deafening sound of the music.*

- v+N hear a sound **hear, listen to** *Now they could hear just the sound of someone rummaging through one of the nearby rooms.*
▶ make a sound **create, emit, make, produce** *Electronic devices can be bought which emit a sound that drives moles away.*
▶ make a sound louder **amplify** *He and his teachers use microphones to amplify sounds and he has his own sign interpreter.*

sound ADJ
involving the use of good judgment

- adv+ADJ basically **basically, essentially, fundamentally** *The report is fundamentally sound.*
▶ from a particular point of view **academically, ecologically, economically, educationally, environmentally, ergonomically, ethically, idealogically, mechanically, methodologically, nutritionally, pedagogically, scientifically, technically, theologically, theoretically** *They encourage the production of coffee using ecologically sound growing practices.*

- ADJ+n basis **base, basis, footing, foundation, grounding** *Thanks to her, family finances were placed on a sounder footing.*
▶ knowledge or understanding **grasp, knowledge, understanding** *The HR Assistant requires a sound knowledge of current recruitment issues.*
▶ thinking **analysis, assessment, judgment, reasoning** *Washington's business judgment was always sound.*
▶ reasons or ideas **argument, principles, reasons** *As for your ancestors, you have sound reasons for believing you had thousands of them.*
▶ advice **advice** *It's good to be able to see that clients have received sound advice.*

source N
1 a place or thing that provides something

- adj+N good **abundant, excellent, fruitful, good, invaluable, rich, useful, valuable** *Researchers in the US have found that baby teeth may be a rich source of stem cells.*
▶ important **important, key, major, vital** *Siberia has been a major source of diamonds for some time.*
▶ main or original **main, original, primary, prime, principal** *The principal source of internal noise in classrooms is the children!*
▶ possible **possible, potential** *Producers cannot ignore such a potential source of profit.*
▶ external **external, outside** *The City Council borrowed £5m from outside sources.*
▶ many **different, multiple, numerous, various** *There are multiple sources of error including illegible or incorrect prescriptions.*
▶ only **only, single, sole** *A tiny window would have been the only source of natural daylight.*
▶ constant **constant** *My colleagues are a constant source of pride to me.*
▶ of energy: environmentally friendly **alternative, clean, natural, renewable, sustainable** *The UK Government committed to meeting a target of 10 per cent of its electricity being generated from renewable sources by 2010.*

- n+N money **funding, income, revenue** *The rest of the money has been contributed by the other funding sources.*
▶ energy **carbon, energy, fuel, heat, light, oil, power** *Refrigerators should be sited in well ventilated areas away from heat sources.*
▶ food or water **food, water** *The scheme brings food supplies directly to villages and offers the people a vital food source.*
▶ something undesirable **emissions, noise, pollution, radiation** *These areas are far away from pollution sources such as cities and industries.*

- v+N be or provide a source of something **act as, be, become, constitute, offer, provide, remain, represent, serve as** *Trusts and Foundations are an important source of financial support.*
▶ find a source of something **access, discover, find, identify, locate, pinpoint, trace** *His particular passion is fixing problems, especially locating noise sources and working out ways of silencing them.*
▶ use a source **draw on/upon, tap into, use** *Her work draws upon many sources of inspiration.*
▶ show what the source of something is **indicate, reveal** *A brief message indicates the source of the error.*
▶ come from a source **arise from, come from, derive from, emanate from, originate from, spring from, stem from** *The West's energy imports come from many sources.*
▶ get something from a source **collect sth from, cull sth from, derive sth from, draw sth from, extract sth from, gather sth from, generate sth from, get sth from, obtain sth from, take sth from** *Pulp is often made from waste paper which is obtained from local sources.*

2 a person or publication that provides information

- adj+N reliable **authoritative, credible, independent, informed, reliable, reputable, trusted**

The most important and reliable source of information on the pupil's cultural background will be the parents.

▶ types of source **archival, documentary, electronic, official, online, printed, written** *Sometimes these printed sources are not entirely accurate.*

▶ directly from someone who is involved in something **first-hand, primary** *The book contains a useful collection of primary sources from 15th century England.*

▶ taking or mentioning information from primary sources **secondary** *The first chapter reviews secondary sources on the events leading up to the war.*

▶ secret or not named **anonymous, confidential, unnamed** *The information comes from unnamed sources in the Russian intelligence community.*

● n+N information **data, information, news, reference** *I found the number and range of news sources staggering.*

▶ type of source **business, government, industry, intelligence, Internet, radio** *A British intelligence source reported that the bombing had left the residents of a neighbouring town 'very frightened'.*

● v+N refer to a source **acknowledge, cite, credit, list, mention, publish, quote, reference, refer to** *How do you cite Internet sources?*

▶ say who a source is **disclose, document, identify, publish, reveal** *It wouldn't be fair to reveal my sources.*

▶ protect a source **protect** *It was important that we protected the sources of intelligence, the nature of intelligence and the pattern of intelligence that we had.*

▶ check or discuss a source **analyze, check, consult, examine, research, review** *Whenever I read a new report I check its sources.*

sovereignty N
the right to rule a country

● adj+N of a country **national** *The regime is obsessed with its national sovereignty, making it suspicious of foreign relations.*

▶ shared **joint, pooled, shared** *European construction in the post-war period was based on the idea of shared sovereignty.*

▶ complete **absolute, full** *The concept of absolute sovereignty within state borders has met increasing criticism.*

▶ of a particular type **economic, monetary, parliamentary, political, territorial** *At that time, Shanghai was a place where no territorial sovereignty reigned.*

● v+N have sovereignty **exercise, have** *Westminster exercises the sovereignty of England, Wales and Ulster.*

▶ maintain sovereignty **maintain, retain** *As president, I have the responsibility to maintain our national sovereignty.*

▶ lose sovereignty **cede, lose, relinquish, renounce, surrender** *Countries such as Czechoslovakia, Luxembourg, Denmark and Poland lost their national sovereignty under the Nazis.*

▶ regain sovereignty **regain, restore** *The majority of Iraqis viewed elections as means of restoring sovereignty.*

▶ publicly claim sovereignty **affirm, assert, claim, establish** *The new government asserted Parliamentary sovereignty over the colonies.* ● *Although the United Kingdom claims sovreignty over this region, there are overlapping claims by Argentina and Chile.*

▶ attack or weaken something's sovereignty **compromise, erode, undermine, usurp, violate** *Iraq blocked the inspections, saying they would violate its sovereignty.*

▶ defend something's sovereignty **defend, preserve, protect, safeguard** *The concept of a natural right to defend national sovereignty is born of weakness and insecurity.*

▶ respect something's sovereignty **acknowledge, recognize, respect** *We will make positive efforts to develop good relations with any country which respects our sovereignty.*

▶ transfer sovereignty **transfer** *Devolution is the transfer of substantial powers to regional bodies, but it does not transfer any sovereignty.*

space N
an empty or available area

● adj+N physical **physical** *Do libraries have physical spaces that could be used as meeting rooms for community groups?*

▶ not being used **available, empty, free, vacant** *Every available space was full of junk.*

▶ enough **adequate, ample, enough, sufficient** *The U-shaped main cabin has ample storage space.*

▶ not enough **insufficient, limited** *If there is insufficient space in any of the boxes please continue on a separate sheet.*

▶ small **confined, enclosed, little, small, tight** *You step through the doors into a vestibule, and beyond the inner doors is a small, square space.*

▶ large **enormous, huge, large, vast** *The sound echoe around the vast space.*

▶ outside **external, green, open, outdoor** *Only 9 per cent of the land is public green space, compared to 12 per cent for roads and parking.*

▶ inside **interior, internal, living** *3-D computer modelling is used to see the building and interior spaces during the design stages.*

▶ more **additional, extra, more** *Pearson is keen to claim the extra space for car parking.*

▶ provided for a specific person or use **designated** *Please smoke only in the designated areas.*

▶ shared with others **common, communal, shared** *The owners of the block are responsible for repairs in communal spaces.*

● v+N be in a space **be in, fill, occupy, take up, use** *The new library is being built in a space formerly occupied by administration buildings.*

▶ fit into a space **fit in, fit into, go in, go into** *Make sure the bed you choose will fit into the space you have.*

▶ put something into a space **cram sth into, pack s into, squeeze sth into** *Some 12,000 tombstones are located here, each crammed into a tiny space.*

▶ make a space **clear, create, leave, make** *Tie up th end with muslin or string, but leave enough space for the rice to at least double in volume.*

▶ save or provide a space for a specific person or use **allocate, allot, book, provide, reserve, save** *Ea user will be allocated storage space on the file serve* *hard disk.* • *The Market provides space for artists wishing to display and sell their work.*

▶ waste/not waste space **save, waste** *How can you have big icons and not waste screen space at the same time?*

span N
the amount of time something lasts

● v+N reduce the span of something **decrease, limit, reduce, shorten** *Reading blogs has shortened my attention span.*

▶ increase the span of something **extend, increase, lengthen, prolong** *The study builds on previous research that used antioxidants to lengthen the life span of nematode worms.*

▶ include a particular span **cover, encompass** *The illustrations cover the whole span of Tony's work, from childhood drawings to his later, well-produced water colours.*

spark V
o make something happen, especially violence, rouble or anger

▶ V+n anger or disagreement **anger, backlash, controversy, furore, fury, outcry, outrage, row, uproar** *His comments on race relations have frequently sparked outrage.*

worry or fear **concern, fear, frenzy, panic** *A powerful earthquake struck near the Indonesian island of Sumatra yesterday, sparking fears of another tsunami disaster.*

protests or public violence **protests, revolution, riot, unrest, uprising, violence** *In many cities over the past few decades, riots sparked by racial tensions have shattered community relations.*

rumours **rumours, speculation** *She has been wearing an engagement ring, sparking rumours that she is back with her former boyfriend.*

interest **curiosity, interest** *He's ultimately hoping to work with larger companies, but so far has been unable to spark their interest.*

discussion **debate, discussion** *Her remarks sparked a lively debate about how to tackle discrimination in bodies like the police.*

reaction **reaction, response** *The tackle sparked angry reactions from the Dutch players.*

series of events or actions **flurry, series, wave** *The story hit the headlines, sparking a wave of resignations from the government.*

ideas or imagination **idea, imagination** *The story is quite scary, but it might also spark young children's imaginations.*

spark N
short feeling or expression of something

N+of **brilliance, creativity, genius, inspiration, life, magic, originality, romance, talent** *What really harms this book is the lack of any spark of originality.*

speak V
talk to someone about something

adv+V quietly **quietly, softly** *Leaning toward him, I spoke softly and said, 'Peter – we need to talk about this'.*

▶ clearly or loudly **aloud, clearly, confidently, loudly, slowly** *When he spoke, he spoke loudly, his voice echoing like that of a minister.*

▶ openly or publicly **freely, openly, publicly** *Staff should encourage complainants to speak openly and freely about their concerns.*

▶ honestly **candidly, frankly, honestly, plainly** *Many people think that politicians don't speak plainly and tell the truth.*

▶ well or impressively **articulately, eloquently, fluently** *Dr Yusuf spoke very eloquently about the influence Lord Todd had on his career.*

▶ with enthusiasm or emotion **enthusiastically, passionately** *She is a slender, affable woman who speaks passionately and articulately about HIV/AIDS.*

▶ in a way that shows you know what you are talking about **authoritatively, knowledgeably** *I'm not familiar enough with the constitution to speak authoritatively on this one.*

▶ in a way that affects the emotions **movingly, powerfully** *The former prisoners spoke movingly about their years of incarceration.*

▶ in a way that shows you like someone **fondly, warmly** *The children speak very warmly of their new Scottish friends.*

▶ giving praise or compliments **favourably, glowingly, highly** *All the students we met spoke very highly of the school.*

speaker N
someone who gives speeches or lectures

● adj+N impressive **charismatic, confident, eloquent, excellent, fluent, inspirational, inspiring, outstanding** *Martin Luther King was one of the most inspirational speakers in the civil rights movement.*

▶ enjoyable to listen to **amusing, engaging, interesting, popular** *She's a very entertaining speaker, and kept everyone amused.*

▶ well-known **distinguished, eminent, high-profile, prominent, renowned, well-known** *The conference provides an opportunity to listen to a number of internationally renowned speakers.*

species N
plants or animals with the same features

● adj+N rare **elusive, exotic, rare, scarce, uncommon** *The area is home to a rare species of tree-frog.*

▶ in danger of no longer existing **endangered, protected, vulnerable** *Dormice are an endangered species.*

▶ no longer existing **extinct** *Jurassic Park was based on the idea that extinct species could be recreated.*

▶ common **abundant, common, widespread** *The yellow-legged gull is common species seen daily all along the coast.*

▶ belonging to an area **endemic, indigenous, native** *This species of dragonfly is native to the southeastern US.*

▶ from outside an area **alien, invasive, non-native** *Aren't wild horses a non-native species?*

▶ distinct **different, distinct, separate** *The classification of this new virus as a distinct species is justified.*

▶ main **dominant, main, predominant** *Humanity has become the dominant species on the planet.*

specific ADJ

relating to only one thing, or very exact

- adv+ADJ very **extremely, highly, really** INFORMAL, **very** *I am being very specific in what I say.*
- ▸ rather **fairly, quite, rather, reasonably, relatively** *Many students were fairly specific about the kind of job and organization they wanted, and were reluctant to apply for other posts.*
- ▸ too much **overly, too** *Avoid being overly specific when describing an audience's likely characteristics.*
- ▸ enough **enough, sufficiently** *Was the information sufficiently specific and detailed?*
- ▸ in location **geographically, regionally** *There are very few goods that can only be sourced from a few geographically-specific locations.*
- ▸ in a particular way **contextually, culturally, functionally, historically, politically** *We provide culturally specific information for those groups at increased risk of having diabetes.*
- ▸ actions designed to deal with something **initiatives, legislation, measures, proposals, strategy** *We are now developing specific measures to counter tax evasion.*
- ADJ+n needs **needs, requirements** *If you have specific requirements please call us.*
- ▸ subject or problem **area, difficulty, issue, problem, subject, theme, topic** *Each of the four public events will focus on a specific theme.*
- ▸ aim or reason **aim, focus, goal, objective, purpose, reason, target** *A best practice is simply a process that represents the most effective way of achieving a specific objective.*
- ▸ information or advice **advice, details, guidance, information, instructions, recommendations** *Please contact the college for specific advice on your particular situation.*
- ▸ question or comment **comment, enquiry, query, question, request** *First, look at the website, but if you have more specific questions you can email our helpline.*
- ▸ situation **case, circumstances, conditions, context, situation** *There is a lack of data on safety in these specific circumstances.*
- ▸ part or type of something **aspect, characteristic, component, element, feature, form, type** *The course then investigates specific aspects of culture from a maritime perspective.*
- ▸ example **example, instance** *Referees should be requested to include specific examples of the applicant's good practice.*
- ▸ time **date, period, term, time** *Term life insurance is only good for a specific period of time.*
- ▸ job **job, junction, responsibility, role, task** *I started out arguing that a phone only needed to perform a few very specific functions.*

specification N

a detailed plan for making or achieving something

- adj+N exact or detailed **comprehensive, correct, detailed, exact, precise** *A good designer will need detailed specifications before they can make anything.*
- ▸ asked for **recommended, required** *You will therefore need a computer of the recommended specification, together with Internet access.*
- ▸ complete **complete, full** *Please refer to the catalogue page for full specifications.*

- ▸ strict **exacting, rigorous, strict, stringent, tight** *The army had strict specifications regarding who could enlist and become soldiers.*
- ▸ minimum or standard **basic, minimum, standard** *You will require a computer that meets the minimum specification.*
- ▸ original/new **new, original** *The units will have to be returned to their original specification upon termination of the tenancy.*
- ▸ technical **functional, mechanical, technical** *Click here to check your technical specification or download the required software*
- v+N do what is necessary to fulfil a specification **adhere to, comply with, conform to, fulfil, match, meet, satisfy** *Because all of our products conform to European Community specifications, you can be assured of their quality.*
- ▸ be better than a specification **exceed** *Our new model exceeds the government's specifications for fuel efficiency.*
- ▸ change a specification **alter, amend, change, improve, refine, revise** *The tenders came in substantially over budget, so we revised the specification.*
- ▸ prepare or create a specification **develop, devise, draft, draw up, formulate, give, lay down, prepare, produce, set, write** *In 1979, the Army drafted specifications for a High Mobility Multipurpose Wheeled Vehicle.*
- ▸ state clearly what a specification is **define, describe, detail, establish** *The report defines the minimum specification for plasma used in television.*

spectacle N

an unusual, exciting, or impressive event or sight

- adj+N good and exciting **amazing, awe-inspiring, awesome, breathtaking, dazzling, glorious, great, magnificent, stunning, thrilling, unforgettable** *The 1950s Sports-Car Race is always a thrilling spectacle and this year was no exception.*
- ▸ bad **awful, ghastly, grim, gruesome, sad, sickening, sorry** *They rushed to the bottom of the hill, where a ghastly spectacle met their eyes.*
- ▸ strange **bizarre, strange** *I wandered over to be greeted by the bizarre spectacle of the Biggles Band*

spectacular ADJ

very impressive or attracting a lot of attention

- adv+ADJ very **absolutely, really** INFORMAL, **simply, truly, utterly, very** *The scenery was absolutely spectacular.*
- ▸ rather **fairly, pretty** INFORMAL, **quite, rather** *The marble columns supporting the domes are conspicuous and rather spectacular.*
- ▸ to look at **visually** *Spielberg's visually spectacular wartime epic is a testimony to the human will to survive.*
- ▸ ADJ+n scenery **backdrop, landscape, location, panorama, scenery, setting, sight, surroundings, view, vista** *There are several marked paths for hiking through spectacular scenery.*
- ▸ something you watch **display, peformance, production, show** *Several boats entered the illuminated parade on the Sunday night, making spectacular display.*
- ▸ accident **accident, crash, explosion** *The guns don*

get louder or explosions more spectacular than in this film.

▸ action in sport **goal, kick, shot, volley** *Parkhouse brought the ball down on his chest and fired a spectacular volley beyond Paul Murphy.*

▸ success/failure **achievement, collapse, failure, success, victory** *Our research innovations have achieved spectacular success.*

▸ way something happens or is done **fashion, manner, way** *The entertainment kicked off in spectacular fashion, with a wonderful display of fireworks.*

spectre N

he possibility that something unpleasant might happen

● adj+N **awful, grim, haunting, looming, terrifying** *Once again, the haunting spectre of mass unemployment threatened to destabilize the government.*

● N+of **death, famine, global warming, invasion, revolution, starvation, terrorism, unemployment, war** *The spectre of terrorism hangs over us all, as we are constantly reminded.*

spectrum N

whole range of possible ideas, qualities, or subjects

adj+N **large broad, diverse, huge, vast, wide** *The choir performs a broad spectrum of music.*
whole **complete, entire, full, whole** *This journal covers the entire spectrum of physiology, including human physiology.*
types of spectrum **cultural, economic, educational, emotional, musical, political, religious, social, theological** *Academics and politicians from across the political spectrum signed the statement of principles.*

v+N include a spectrum **comprise, cover, embrace, encompass, incorporate, range across, represent, span** *Her caseload covers the whole spectrum of family law.*
widen a spectrum **broaden, widen** *The loan will allow them to broaden the spectrum of products on offer to their existing and new clients.*

N+of **activities, disciplines, emotions, experiences, interests, issues, opinion, people, possibilities, topics** *You need the full spectrum of emotions to experience what it is to be human.*

speculate V

consider or discuss why something has happened what might happen

adv+V without any purpose or control **idly, wildly** *Newspapers were speculating wildly about who this mysterious woman was.*
only **merely, only** *As to why this is so, we can at present only speculate.*
by many people **widely** *It is widely speculated that a second pipeline will be built.*

V+about/on **cause, future, nature, origin, possibility, reason** *It is not our place to speculate on the causes of such a change.* ● *Almost exactly 500 years ago, Leonardo da Vinci speculated about the possibility of flying machines.*

speculation N

1 discussion about why something has happened or what might happen

● adj+N only or complete **mere, pure** *This is pure speculation, however.*

▸ great in amount or degree **considerable, constant, intense, much, widespread** *There was much speculation **over** the fate of the two men.*

▸ increasing **growing, increasing, mounting** *Flynn has admitted he is itching to get back into football **amid** mounting speculation that he is about to be unveiled as the new City manager.*

▸ seeming to have no end **endless** *There has been endless speculation **as to** her whereabouts.*

▸ recent **recent** *In response to recent speculation, I would like to make it clear that I am not resigning.*

▸ not accurate **wild** *His departure has led to wild speculation regarding the identity of his replacement.*

▸ without real purpose **idle** *I won't bore you with idle speculation.*

▸ that has a basis in fact **informed** *The job of the historian is to provide informed speculation **about** the past based on the available evidence.*

● n+N **media, press** *I am sure there will be a great deal of media speculation **about** what happens next.*

● v+N cause or increase speculation **encourage, fuel, give rise to, increase, invite, lead to, prompt, provoke, spark** *Todd was appointed as manager within days, fuelling speculation that a deal had already been done.*

▸ say that speculation is not true **deny, dismiss, quash** *He once again dismissed speculation **about** his leadership.*

▸ end speculation **end, put an end to** *Davies has ended all speculation surrounding his future by signing a new contract with the club.*

▸ take part in speculation **indulge in** *I would simply warn people against indulging in speculation.*

● N+v when there is a lot of speculation **abound, be rife** *Press speculation was rife that a compromise would be found.*

> You can use ***surrounding*** or ***regarding*** to say what speculation is about: *There was widespread speculation regarding the manager's future at the club.*

▸ increase **grow, mount** *Speculation is mounting that they are planning to get married.*

▸ be connected with something **surround** *Speculation still surrounds the player's future.*

▸ say that two things are related **link** *Burley has dismissed speculation linking him with the vacant Scotland manager's job.*

▸ suggest **suggest** *Recent press speculation has suggested that many local authorities are proposing cuts in their public library services.*

● n+of+N **flurry, frenzy, matter, subject** *This week has seen a flurry of speculation **as to** the future of the company.* ● *His personal history is still a matter of speculation.*

● and/or **conjecture, controversy, debate, gossip, rumour** *Monday's revelation brought to an end a whirlwind of rumour and speculation that had engulfed the club.*

2 buying and selling to make a large profit

- adj+N **financial** *Massive financial speculation on oil markets has added at least $15 a barrel to crude.*
- n+N **currency, land, market, property** *Steer clear of property speculation unless you know what you're doing.*

speech N
a formal occasion when someone speaks to an audience

- adj+N short **brief, short** *After the unveiling of the plaque and a short speech by HRH Princess Anne, afternoon tea was served.*
- ▶ long **long** *As promised, this is not going to be a long speech.*
- ▶ full of emotion **emotional, impassioned, passionate, powerful, rousing** *Janet gave an impassioned speech which might have swayed some of the committee members.*
- ▶ clear and effective **eloquent** *He delivered a very able and eloquent speech which was loudly cheered.*
- ▶ entertaining **entertaining** *She made an entertaining speech about Vikings.*
- ▶ done for the first time **inaugural, maiden** *Ten years ago this month, I made my maiden speech to the House of Commons.*
- ▶ at the beginning/end of something **closing, opening** *The ceremony will end with a closing speech and the playing of the national anthem.*
- n+N most important or main **keynote** *He was invited to give the keynote speech at America's biggest media conference.*
- ▶ on a particular occasion or for a particular purpose **acceptance, after-dinner, budget, conference, farewell, resignation, wedding** *Here is a full transcript of her Nobel Prize acceptance speech.*
- v+N make a speech **deliver, give, make** *He toured Britain, giving speeches on parliamentary reform.*
- ▶ end a speech **conclude, end, finish** *Before concluding my speech, I want to say a little about exam results.*
- ▶ write a speech **prepare, write** *Joe had been writing his speech on his place card through the meal.*
- ▶ read a speech **read** *To read the speech in full, click here.*
- ▶ when a speech contains something **punctuate with** *He punctuated his speech with references to his family.*

speed N
the rate at which someone or something moves, works, or happens

- adj+N fast **breakneck, fast, great, high, incredible, supersonic** INFORMAL, **tremendous** *Lava flows can move at very high speeds.*
- ▶ fastest possible **full, maximum, top** *The car has a top speed of 165mph.*
- ▶ faster than sound **supersonic** *At one time, supersonic speed seemed to be the future of air travel.*
- ▶ slow **low, slow** *Reduced road widths will encourage slower speeds through the junction.*
- ▶ average or normal **average, normal** *During a three-minute journey, 1.24km was covered at an average speed of 25km/h.*
- ▶ not changing **constant** *Using cruise control on highway trips can help you maintain a constant speed.*

- ▶ too fast **excessive** *A third of motorcycle deaths are caused by excessive speed.*
- ▶ at which something is done **cruising, operating, running, typing** *Overall, they were satisfied with the program's operating speed.*
- n+N **broadband, connection, download, traffic, wind** *Customers are invited to have their broadband speed upgraded.*
- v+N increase speed **gain, gather, increase, pick up** *The train began to pick up speed.*
- ▶ reduce speed **cut, reduce, slow** *Vehicle-activated signs appear to be very effective in reducing speeds.*
- ▶ reach a particular speed **achieve, attain, reach** *The cheetah can reach speeds of over 60 mph.*
- ▶ keep a particular speed **maintain** *It takes less energy to maintain your speed than it does to build it back after it is lost.*
- ▶ change, control, or measure speed **adjust, calculate, change, control, improve, measure, set, vary** *Sensors measure the speed of approaching vehicles.*
- v+at+N **drive, fly, move, run, travel, work** *These roads carry small amounts of motor traffic travelling at low speeds.*

speeding N
the offence of driving a vehicle faster than is allowed

- v+N **be booked for, be caught, be caught for, be done for** INFORMAL, **be fined for, be pulled over for, be stopped for** *Around 10 per cent of drivers caught speeding were prosecuted.* • *Have you been stopped for speeding in the last year?*
- N+n **conviction, fine, offence, ticket** *Drivers caught for minor speeding offences may be sent on a speed awareness course.*

speed limit N
the fastest speed allowed for vehicles in an area

- v+N go faster than the speed limit **break, exceed** *The Highways Agency says people breaking the speed limit represent the biggest danger.*
- ▶ obey the speed limit **keep to, keep within, observe, stick to** *Please observe the 5mph speed limit on all roads on the College site.*
- ▶ make sure the speed limit is obeyed **enforce** *Police have said they will rigorously enforce the speed limit.*
- ▶ reduce/increase the speed limit **lower, raise, reduce** *The Head has suggested lowering the speed limit outside the school.*

spell V
show something bad is going to happen

- V+n **danger, death, disaster, doom, end, misery, trouble** *The potential financial losses from accidents at work can spell disaster for many small firms.*

spell N
a period of time

- adj+N short **brief, short** *She dominated the match, apart from a brief spell at the start of the second set.*
- ▶ long **lengthy, long, prolonged** *We can expect a prolonged spell of wet weather across the county.*

▶ length of time **five-minute, three-month, two-year etc** *United bounced back with two goals in a ten-minute spell.*
▶ weather **cold, dry, hot, mild, sunny, warm, wet** *I hope the current cold spell doesn't go on too long.*
▶ with no success **barren, lean** *Every team goes through a lean spell during the season.*
● v+N **enjoy, go through, have, spend** *The area enjoyed a brief spell of prosperity during the 19th century.*
● N+as **chairman, coach, editor, manager** *He remained on the board, having a brief spell as chairman.*
● N+in **army, hospital, jail, prison, rehab** *I had a long spell in hospital with an eye problem.*
● N+of weather **rain, sunshine, weather** *We have taken advantage of a spell of good weather to get the roof repaired.*
▶ pressure **pressure** *There followed a spell of pressure from the home side.*

spelling N
the ability to spell, or how well someone spells

● adj+N **bad, poor** *Students will be penalized for poor spelling.*

> You can also say that someone is **good** or **bad at spelling**: *My brother is very good at spelling.*

● v+N **check, correct, improve** *Chloe has made a big effort to improve her spelling.*
● N+n mistake **error, mistake** *It is a well-written essay, apart from the odd spelling mistake.*
▶ test **test** *She always does well in spelling tests.*

spend V
use money to pay for things

▶ adv+V in a sensible way **wisely** *What money there is available needs to be spent wisely.*

> You can also talk about **money well spent**: *A good pair of walking boots are not cheap, but it is money well spent.*

· in large amounts **freely, heavily** *The company spends heavily on marketing and promotion.*

V+n **amount, fortune, a lot, money, sum** *It is up to you how you spend your money.*

spending N
money that is spent, especially by a government or large organization

adj+N by the government **public** *Taxes are essential for public spending.*
total **overall, total** *The table shows total spending on education.*
high/low **high, low** *Labour has pledged higher spending to extend out-of-hours schooling.*
extra **additional, extra, increased** *The additional health spending announced in the Budget gives a real opportunity to make successful changes.*
each year **annual** *Its marketing budget is four times greater than the UN's annual spending on combating child poverty.*
on particular activities **military, social** *This represents a massive increase in US military spending.*

● n+N by the government **government, state** *There is no simple relationship between Government spending and economic success.*
▶ on particular activities **aid, defence, education, health, social security, transport, welfare** *Overall, defence spending in the EU is still falling.*
▶ on equipment and buildings **capital** *The competition for public capital spending is fierce.*
● v+N increase spending **boost, increase, raise** *The government has chosen to boost spending on health and education.*
▶ reduce spending **cut, cut back on, reduce, slash** INFORMAL *Party leaders confirmed their plan to cut public spending by £80 billion to 35 per cent of GDP.*
▶ control spending **cap, control** *One of the Treasury's most important jobs is to control public spending.*
▶ provide money for spending **finance, fund** *The Government would have to finance any extra spending that would be required.*
● N+v increase **increase, rise** *Government spending has risen from 19 per cent to 31 per cent of GDP.*
▶ become less **fall** *Health spending has fallen over the last three years.*
● n+in+N **cut, growth, increase, reduction, rise, slowdown** *The government has announced a massive increase in spending on roads and motorways.*

sphere N
a particular area of interest, activity, or work; a particular part of society

● adj+N public/private **private, public** *All forms of violence, she says, whether perpetrated in the public or private sphere, are a violation of human rights.*
▶ particular area or activity **cultural, domestic, economic, international, political, social** *UNICEF places itself explicitly outside the political sphere.* ● *The book is about two girls from very different social spheres.*
● N+of **activity, competence, control, influence, interest, knowledge, life, responsibility, work** *She argued that the family should be outside the state's sphere of influence.* ● *In Ireland, the Church wielded tremendous influence in all spheres of life.*

spin N INFORMAL
a way of presenting information, especially to make something seem good or less bad

● adj+N positive/negative **negative, positive** *There is a way to put a positive spin on these figures.*
▶ new or different **different, fresh, new, sb's own, unique** *The only interesting remakes are those that put a new spin on a fairly pedestrian first-time effort.* ● *She has taken traditional stories, and put her own spin on them.*
▶ in politics **government, political** *Is there too much political spin?*
▶ modern **contemporary, modern** *Yet the story has been given a contemporary spin by the writers.*
● v+N **give (sth), put** *The company was eager to put its own spin on things.*

- and/or **hype, propaganda, rhetoric, substance** *The presentation was all spin and no substance.*

spirit N

1 your attitude to life or to other people, or the attitude of people in a group

- adj+N human **human** *This is a courageous tale of the strength of the human spirit and the power of love.*
- ▶ trying or doing new things **adventurous, creative, entrepreneurial, pioneering, restless** *The judges were looking for work that showed an adventurous spirit.*
- ▶ determined and difficult to defeat **competitive, fighting, indomitable** *The team is well known for its fighting spirit.*
- ▶ independent **independent** *She appreciated her cat's independent spirit.*
- ▶ strong **strong** *The village has a very strong community spirit.*
- ▶ good or right **excellent, generous, good, great, right** *The game was played in the right spirit, highly competitive and very entertaining.*
- n+N **community, team** *There is strong community spirit here and local people are justly proud of their local hospital.*
- v+N express the spirit of something **capture, convey, embody, epitomize, evoke** *In his novel, he captures the spirit of the period brilliantly.*
- ▶ create a particular spirit **bring, engender, foster** *The new development brought a spirit of pride to the community.*

> If you ***enter into the spirit*** of something, you take part in something with enthusiasm: *We all entered into the spirit of things and got dressed up in fancy dress.*

- N+of **adventure, cooperation, enquiry, enterprise, openness** *Progress is best achieved through working together in a spirit of cooperation.*

2 your mood or your attitude [always plural]

- adj+N **excellent, good, great, high** *I found the children in high spirits.*
- v+N improve someone's spirits **keep up, lift, raise, revive** *There is nothing like a bit of sun in the gloomy depths of winter to lift your spirits and cheer you up.*
- ▶ make someone's spirits worse **dampen** *Even a night in the rain hadn't dampened their spirits.*

spite N

a feeling of wanting to upset someone

- adj+N **pure, sheer** *Out of sheer spite, I almost stayed away.*
- and/or **anger, envy, hate, jealousy, malice** *The game was so full of spite and malice that it did no credit to either team.*

split N

a division of a large group into smaller groups because of a disagreement

- adj+N serious or large in degree **clear, deep,** **major, serious** *It is clear that there was a deep split between the two groups.*
- ▶ unpleasant **acrimonious, damaging** *The pair haven't spoken since their acrimonious split in 1994.*
- v+N cause a split **cause, create, lead to, provoke** *Peel's decision caused a split in the Conservative party.*
- ▶ avoid a split **avoid** *The party leaders fought to bring their members along with them and to avoid a split at all costs.*
- N+v **emerge, occur** *He judged that a damaging split had emerged between the President and his secretary of State.*

spoil V

make something worse, or less attractive

- adv+V completely or very much **completely, really** *The dreadful restaurant completely spoilt what should have been a fantastic evening.*
- ▶ rather **rather, slightly, somewhat** *It is a fine story, slightly spoiled by the ending.*
- V+n something enjoyable **enjoyment, fun, surprise** *I don't want to be more specific about the plot or it will spoil the surprise.*
- ▶ how something looks **appearance, look, view** *These masts are an eyesore and spoil the view.*
- ▶ group activity **game, party** *The wind was doing its best to spoil the game.*
- ▶ story **plot, story** *Please don't read on if this will spoil the story for you.*
- ▶ situation **everything, things** *The evening seemed to be going well, until Bob managed to spoil things.*

sponsor N

a business that supports an event or activity by giving money

- adj+N main **main, major, principal** *The brewery is our main sponsor.*
- ▶ official **official** *The promotion gave the misleading impression that the newspaper was an official sponsor of the competition.*
- ▶ generous **generous** *A big thank you again to our very generous sponsors.*
- ▶ possible **potential** *We have been in negotiations with a number of potential sponsors for next season.*
- ▶ involved in business **commercial, corporate, industrial, private** *These activities are supported by a wide range of commercial sponsors and funding agencies.* • *Should private sponsors be allowed to help fund state schools?*
- v+N get a sponsor **attract, find, get** *The event has attracted several sponsors.*
- ▶ try to get a sponsor **look for, need, seek** *The Club is seeking sponsors for its Charity Golf Day.*
- ▶ thank a sponsor **thank** *We would like to thank the many generous sponsors who have supported the team this year.*
- ▶ be a sponsor **act as, be, become** *Why not get a local business to act as sponsor?*

sponsorship N

money given to help pay for an event or activity; the fact of an organization giving money

- adj+N generous **generous** *The competition could*

not have taken place without the generous sponsorship of the following businesses and organizations.

▶ from businesses **commercial, corporate, private** *Her job is to raise funds from individual donations and corporate sponsorship.* ● *The museum had to raise private sponsorship in order to stage the exhibition.*

● n+N activity supported **arts, sports** *We are considering our involvement in sports sponsorship for 2011.*

▶ source of money **business, tobacco** *With the end of tobacco sponsorship looming, a new sponsor had to be found.*

● v+N get sponsorship **attract, gain, get, obtain, raise, receive, secure** *What is the best means of securing industrial sponsorship for an academic research programme?*

▶ try to get sponsorship **appeal for, apply for, ask for, look for, seek** *We are actively seeking sponsorship for next year's competition.*

▶ provide sponsorship **offer, provide** *The School is very grateful for the sponsorship provided by a number of public organizations and private individuals.*

● N+n arrangement **agreement, arrangement, deal, package, programme, scheme** *The team has just landed a three-year sponsorship deal worth a four-figure sum per year.*

▶ opportunities **opportunities** *Your company can benefit from a wide range of sponsorship opportunities at Southampton Football Club.*

▶ money **money** *I am a rugby fan and happy to put sponsorship money into the club.*

sport N
activity involving physical effort in which people compete against each other

▶ v+N **be involved in, compete in, do, participate in, play, pursue** *Almost a quarter of pupils are doing sport in local clubs.* ● *Playing sport can provide young people with a broad range of social skills.* ● *At the centre, you can pursue your favourite sports, on land or on the water.*

spot N
he particular place where someone or something s

adj+N very good or suitable **good, ideal, perfect, right, suitable** *The Abbey lies in a picturesque valley by a stream and is an ideal spot for a picnic on a sunny day.*

pleasant **beautiful, idyllic, lovely, nice, pleasant, sunny** *In the end, we found a lovely mooring spot and tied up for the night.*

sheltered from bad weather or hot sun **shady, sheltered** *The garden lies in a nice sheltered spot.*

peaceful **peaceful, quiet, secluded** *We parked the car in a secluded spot.*

favourite **favourite, popular** *This is one of France's most popular tourist spots.*

far away **remote** *In this remote spot there was no prospect of a speedy rescue.*

exact, or exactly the same **exact, particular, same, very** *Just ten minutes previously, she had been*

standing in the exact spot where the lightning struck.

● n+N **beauty, parking, picnic, tourist, trouble** *Dovedale is one of the most popular beauty spots in the UK.*

● v+N show the position of a spot **mark, point to** *He stuck a spade in the snow to mark the spot.*

▶ find a spot **find, pick** *We headed off to find a good spot to film from.*

▶ reach a spot **reach** *She reached a spot about twenty feet from the edge of the beach.*

▶ be in a particular spot **occupy** *The current church opened in 1969, although a Baptist church has occupied the same spot since 1671.*

▶ be unable to move from a spot **be rooted to** *I stood, rooted to the spot for a long time.*

spot V
notice someone or something

● V+n mistake **error, mistake, typo** *Please let us know if you spot a mistake in one of the listings.*

▶ opportunity **gap in the market, opportunity** *She's an excellent businesswoman, who can always spot a gap in the market.*

▶ what someone is capable of **potential, talent** *His artistic talent was spotted early on.*

▶ sign **pattern, sign, trend** *Her job involved spotting new fashion trends and writing about them for the magazine.*

▶ difference/similarity **difference, similarity** *Can you spot the difference between these two accounts?*

▶ space, or something missing **gap** *He spotted a gap in the defence and cruised through to score.*

spotlight N
the situation when someone or something gets a lot of public attention

● adj+N from a lot of people **international, national, public** *We try to protect the interests of people who are thrust into the public spotlight.*

▶ in politics **political** *These issues are very much under the political spotlight at the moment.*

▶ unpleasant **harsh** *The government's tax policies have recently come under a harsh spotlight.*

● n+N **media** *The couple are sick of living in the constant media spotlight.*

● v+N put the spotlight on someone **focus, put, shine, throw, turn** *Once again the spotlight has been thrown on the industry and its failings.*

▶ experience the spotlight **be put under, be thrust into, come under** *The party's spending plans have recently been put under the spotlight.*

▶ share the spotlight **share** *She was reluctant to let her co-stars share the spotlight with her.*

● N+v **fall on, shine on, turn to/on** *The media spotlight fell on so-called 'failing' schools again.*

spread V
affect a larger area or a larger number of people

● adv+V quickly **fast, quickly, rapidly, soon** *The campaign quickly spread to other European countries.*

You can also say that something **spreads like wildfire**: *Mass protests spread like wildfire across the country.*

▸ slowly **gradually, slowly** *The habit gradually spread to all sections of society.*

▸ over a large area **far, widely** *No one believes the infection will spread very far.*

You can also say that something **spreads far and wide**: *Her influence has spread far and wide.*

▸ easily **easily** *The virus can spread easily from one person to another.*

● V+n information **awareness, message, news, rumour, the word** *Somebody is spreading rumours about you.* ● *Posters helped spread the word about the campaign.*

▸ disease **disease, infection, virus** *The infection is spread by contaminated water.*

▸ a good way of doing things **good practice** *Our aim is to spread good practice across all our schools.*

● n+V disease **cancer, disease, epidemic, infection, virus** *It is not yet entirely clear how the disease is spreading.*

▸ information **news, rumour, the word** *The news spread quickly, and soon the concerts were sold out.*

▸ fire **fire, flames** *The quick thinking of the fire brigade prevented the fire spreading to adjoining buildings.*

▸ being famous **fame** *Her fame spread far and wide.*

spread N
when something grows and affects a larger area or a larger number of people

● adj+N fast **rapid** *The rapid spread of HIV/AIDS in the country is a growing problem for the government.*

▸ across the world **global, worldwide** *What factors have contributed to the worldwide spread of English over the past century?*

▸ not controlled **uncontrolled** *We are concerned about the uncontrolled spread of small arms and light weapons.*

● v+N stop the spread of something **halt, prevent, stop** *Handwashing is a vital part of routine practice on the ward to prevent the spread of infection.*

▸ reduce or control the spread of something **combat, control, curb, limit, reduce, slow** *Travel restrictions have been imposed to control the spread of the disease.*

▸ cause or help the spread of something **contribute to, encourage, facilitate, increase, lead to** *Straying livestock may have contributed to the spread of the disease.*

● N+of disease **disease, infection, virus** *All steps are being taken to minimize the spread of infection.*

▸ fire **fire** *It is important to keep fire doors closed to prevent the spread of fire.*

▸ weapons or technology **technology, weapons** *The treaty is designed to stop the spread of nuclear weapons.*

spree N
a short period spent doing something enjoyable

● n+N buying things **buying, shopping, spending** *After lunch, we went on a spending spree in the garden centre.*

▸ committing crime **crime, killing, murder** *She was arrested after a year-long killing spree that ended with seven men murdered.*

▸ drinking **drinking** *His response to the news was to go out on a drinking spree on his own.*

● v+N **go on** *They went on a shopping spree at the Frieze Art Fair.*

spring N
the season between winter and summer

● adj+N **early, last, late, next** *It was a great way to spend a bright afternoon in early spring.*

● N+n weather conditions **rain, sunshine, weather** *We sat outside to enjoy the spring sunshine.*

▸ time **break, day, equinox, morning, season, semester, term** *Those warm spring days still seem far away.* ● *The Society holds its AGM during the spring term of every academic year.*

squabble N
an argument about something that is not important

● adj+N not important **minor, petty** *This is a time for them to act together and forget their petty squabbles.*

▸ within a particular group or country **domestic, family, internal** *She has called on members of the parliamentary group to settle their internal squabbles.*

▸ in politics **political** *Political squabbles between the two factions have placed the entire framework of the plan in jeopardy.*

● v+N **resolve, settle** *It could be that there are old family squabbles that need to be resolved.*

squalor N
dirty and unpleasant conditions

● adj+N in towns etc **public, urban** *Cholera is a disease associated with urban squalor and extreme poverty.*

▸ very bad **appalling, indescribable, unimaginable** *They lived and worked in the slums, in conditions of appalling squalor.*

● and/or **depradation, deprivation, dirt, disease, filth, misery, poverty** *He seemed content to live in filth and squalor.*

squeeze V
1 press something firmly, especially with your hands

● adv+V gently **gently, lightly** *His finger gently squeezed the trigger.*

▸ tightly **hard, tightly** *She squeezed my hand so tight I yelled in pain.*

▸ recently **freshly** *I usually have a glass of freshly squeezed orange juice.*

Usage **Squeeze** is always <u>passive</u> in this combination.

2 when someone or something limits the supply money

● V+n money **budget, margins, profits, revenues** *Cheap imports have caused the prices of locally*

produced rice to plummet, squeezing the profits of
local producers.
▶ people **suppliers** *Major supermarkets squeeze
suppliers to maximize profits.*

squeeze N [always singular]
strict control over money or goods

● adj+N **financial** *The financial squeeze has hit staff
hard, with job cuts across the sector.*

● n+N **cash, credit, funding, profit, spending** *The
government's response was to tighten the credit
squeeze, which sent large parts of the economy into
full-blown recession.*

● v+N **face, feel** *Most big stores are feeling the squeeze
right now.*

stab V
kill or hurt someone using a sharp object

● adv+V **accidentally, brutally, fatally, repeatedly**
One of the men was fatally stabbed in neck.

● V+in **chest, neck, stomach** *The police officer was
stabbed in the chest and died soon afterwards.*

stability N
a situation with no unexpected or harmful changes

● adj+N financial **economic, financial, monetary,
price** *Wales has enjoyed a period of economic
stability not experienced for more than 30 years.*

▶ political or social **political, social** *In times of
political stability and strong economic growth, such
matters are easily forgotten.*

▶ affecting a region **global, regional** *Lack of water is
set to be the biggest threat to global stability in coming
decades.*

▶ more **greater, increased** *Here is an agreement which
can deliver industrial peace, fair wages, and greater
price stability.*

▶ compared to something else **relative** *There was a
widespread sense of crisis after the relative stability
of earlier decades.*

▶ as a whole **overall** *Ministers are committed to
maintaining overall economic stability.*

▶ over a long period **long-term** *What is required is a
fiscal framework that provides long-term stability.*

v+N bring stability **achieve, bring, create,
deliver, ensure, provide** *A core function of
government is to ensure economic stability.*
bring stability back **restore** *We've taken steps as a
government to restore stability to the economy.*
keep stability **maintain** *The country has a huge
interest in helping to maintain regional stability.*
increase stability **contribute to, enhance, improve,
increase, promote** *Reducing the violence and
enhancing political stability should be the first
priorities of the new government.*
harm stability **threaten, undermine** *There is
concern that the demonstrations could threaten
stability in this volatile region.*

n+of+N **degree, lack, measure, period** *The
elections brought a measure of stability to the area.*
● *What is needed now in education is a period of
stability, with no new initiatives to deal with.*

stable ADJ
not changing or becoming worse

● adv+ADJ unusually or surprisingly **amazingly,
exceptionally, extremely, incredibly, remarkably,
unusually** *Levels of customer satisfaction remain
remarkably stable from one area to another.*

▶ fairly **broadly, comparatively, fairly, pretty**
INFORMAL**, reasonably, relatively, sufficiently** *The
total number of Poles in the UK is now fairly stable.*

▶ in a particular way **clinically, economically,
emotionally, environmentally, financially,
medically, politically** *If you wish to fly in late
pregnancy, you must have a letter from your doctor
certifying you are medically stable.*

▶ apparently **apparently** *These were apparently stable
people with no history of violence.*

● ADJ+n rate or value **currency, funding, income,
inflation, population, price** *Inflation is falling and
the local currency becoming more stable.*

▶ condition **condition, state** *She is in a stable
condition but she remains in hospital.*

▶ economic situation **economy, growth, market**
*Business needs a strong, stable economy as the basis
for innovation and investment.*

▶ country or political situation **community, country,
democracy, government, regime, society** *In order
to join, they have had to demonstrate they are a
stable democracy.*

▶ situation **environment, situation** *They were
attempting to establish a stable political
environment in which democracy could flourish.*

▶ relationship **relationship** *The Government is
committed to supporting marriage and stable
relationships.*

● v+ADJ be or become stable **be, become, prove**
*There was less turnover of population, communities
were becoming more stable.*

▶ remain stable **be kept, remain, stay** *The price is
expected to stay stable for most of the coming weeks.*

▶ seem stable **appear, seem** *Things at the club seem
relatively stable at present.*

● and/or strong **durable, enduring, resilient, robust,
solid, strong, sturdy** *The new version of the software
is more robust and stable.*

▶ staying the same **steady, unchanging** *The world is
not and has never been a stable, unchanging place.*

▶ possible to predict **predictable, reliable** *To his
credit, he has delivered a stable, predictable
economy.*

▶ safe **safe, secure** *Children thrive in a stable, secure
and loving environment.*

▶ well organized **efficient, orderly** *Liberty and
enterprise can only flourish in stable, orderly and
strong communities.*

staff N
employees of a particular company or institution

● adj+N with a lot of skill or knowledge **aware,
competent, experienced, high-calibre,
knowledgeable, professional, qualified, skilled,
trained** *There may be opportunities for experienced
staff to work overseas.*

▶ hard-working **attentive, committed, dedicated,
enthusiastic, motivated, responsible** *Our team of
dedicated staff are experts in arranging the perfect
holiday for you.*

▶ pleasant **friendly, happy, helpful** *The staff were very friendly and cooperative.*

▶ important **key** *Offering flexible working can play a vital role in retaining key staff.*

▶ additional **additional, extra** *The NHS will not be able to take on as many additional staff as planned.*

▶ senior/junior **junior, senior** *Bids will be adjudicated by a panel of senior staff.*

▶ working full-time/part-time **full-time, part-time** *There was now a full-time staff of twenty auditors.*

▶ temporary/permanent **permanent, temporary** *The organization spends millions every year on temporary staff.*

▶ types of staff **academic, administrative, ancillary, clerical, clinical, departmental, editorial, secretarial, technical** *The theatre employs 60 backstage and administrative staff.*

● v+N employ staff **appoint, employ, hire, recruit, take on** *The agency employs around 20,000 staff at 80 locations.*

▶ train staff **train** *There have been difficulties in recruiting and training staff.*

▶ keep staff **attract, retain** *Firms have invested more in retaining their staff.*

▶ encourage staff **empower, enable, encourage, motivate, reward** *Motivate staff through involvement in the local community.*

▶ join a staff **join** *He left the Dover Express to join the editorial staff of the Deal Mercury.*

● N+n of or involving staff **absence, appointment, appraisal, development, expertise, induction, involvement, meeting, productivity, recruitment, retention, rota, shortage, supervision, survey, training, turnover, vacancy** *The complex is occasionally closed for staff training sessions.* ● *Retail has a bad reputation as a sector with poor career prospects and high staff turnover.*

▶ for the use or benefit of staff **canteen, discount, handbook, newsletter, pay, salary** *We offer facilities such as free parking and a staff canteen.*

▶ part of the staff **member, officer, representative** *Among those taking part in the course are senior staff members from engineering firms.*

▶ attitude **attitude, awareness, morale, motivation, satisfaction** *This has helped to keep absenteeism levels low and staff morale high.*

stage N
a particular point in a process or event

● adj+N early **beginning, developmental, early, initial, opening, preliminary, qualifying** *The training programme is still in the early stages.*

▶ very early or undeveloped **design, embryonic, experimental, formative, immature, larval, planning, preparatory, primitive, prototype** *A collaboration with the University of Sydney is currently at an embryonic stage.*

▶ late or advanced **advanced, closing, final, last, late, latter, mature, penultimate, terminal** *Clearly, their sole purpose in offering concessions at this late stage was to secure victory.*

▶ middle **halfway, interim, intermediate, middle, midway, transitional** *It is a halfway stage in the evolution of reptiles into birds.*

▶ important **critical, crucial, exciting, important, key, main, necessary, vital** *The basic framework of the lesson can be divided into three main stages.*

▶ serious **acute** *My illness was going through an acute stage at the time.*

▶ particular **certain, defined, distinct, particular** *There are three distinct stages to the job evaluation process.*

▶ in a particular place in the sequence **further, next, previous, subsequent, successive, first, second, third etc** *The next stage is to send us payment.* ● *In the fourth stage, your retina sends signals to your body asking for more oxygen.*

▶ current **current, present** *At the present stage of the project we have seen only a few employers.*

▶ various **different, various** *The documentary charts the evolution of the sport through its various stages of development.*

● v+N reach a stage **attain, enter, hit, reach** *Electric generators did not reach a stage when they could power indoor lighting until the late 1870s.*

▶ begin a stage **begin, initiate, undertake** *The company has been chosen to undertake the first stage of the refurbishment.*

▶ come near to reaching a stage **approach, near** *Repairs were approaching the midway stage.*

▶ finish a stage **complete, conclude, finish, pass** *Those who complete this stage are then offered a full membership.*

▶ experience stages **follow, go through, pass through, undergo** *Until last year, junior doctors underwent three stages of training.*

▶ represent a stage **characterise, constitute, form, mark, represent** *The land reclamation works form the first stage of the redevelopment scheme.* ● *Her appointment as High Commissioner marks an exciting new stage in her illustrious career.*

▶ include stages **comprise, involve** *The process comprises successive stages which allow for consultation and debate.*

▶ miss a stage **bypass, omit, skip** *They skipped the stage of learning to type, and began talking to their machines instead.*

▶ describe the stages of something **define, describe, document, explain, identify, outline** *This section outlines the main stages in extradition requests made to the UK.*

● N+of process **career, cycle, development, evolution, growth, life, lifecycle, procedure, proceedings, process** *It is a problem that can affect anyone, at any stage of their career.*

▶ undertaking **investigation, journey, negotiation, plan, planning, project** *Several new construction projects are in the final stages of negotiation.*

▶ medical condition **disease, illness, infection, labour, pregnancy** *The symptoms are associated with advanced stages of the disease.*

staggering ADJ
extremely surprising

● adv+ADJ **absolutely, frankly, quite, simply, truly** *They have won the series a frankly staggering twenty-two times.*

● ADJ+n achievement **achievement, feat** *Even people who could barely read and write seemed capable of staggering feats of memory.*

▶ amount or number **amount, array, proportion, statistic, sum, total, volume** *The cycling team added two more medals to an already staggering total.*

▸ quality **beauty, coincidence, complexity, disparity** *Tanzania is a land of staggering scenic beauty.*
▸ bad quality **hypocrisy, ignorance, incompetence** *Someone should be held to account for the staggering incompetence of the government.*

stagnation N
a situation in which there is no progress, development, or economic growth

● adj+N lasting for a long time **continued, prolonged** *There was a pattern of temporary surge followed by prolonged stagnation.*
▸ types of stagnation **cultural, economic, intellectual, political** *In the mid-1980s, Europe was gripped by economic stagnation.*

stain N
a mark left accidentally on clothes or surfaces

● adj+N ugly **dark, nasty, ugly, unsightly** *Avoid hair lotions coming into contact with the leather, as they can leave unsightly stains.*
▸ slight **faint** *The fine sea spray had left faint salt stains on his shoes.*
▸ greasy **greasy, oily** *Blu-tac can leave greasy stains on walls.*
▸ hard to remove **stubborn** *Stubborn stains can be removed using baking soda and vinegar.*

● v+N cause stains **cause, leave** *Stains caused by sticky tape are often impossible to remove.*
▸ remove stains **absorb, clean, loosen, remove, tackle, treat, wash, wipe** *Rub pieces of fresh lemon on your teeth to remove the stains.* ● *Good tip – wipe salt stains with diluted vinegar.*
▸ avoid stains **avoid, prevent, repel** *This product adds a protective layer that repels stains.*
▸ hide stains **hide** *She owns mostly dark clothes to hide stains.*

tairs N
set of steps between floors of a building

adj+N unsafe or difficult to climb **creaky, narrow, precipitous, rickety, slippery, steep, uneven, winding** *We were led up some rickety stairs to her studio.* ● *The stairs were steep and there was no elevator.*
made or decorated in a particular way **carpeted, concrete, painted, polished, uncarpeted, wooden** *They walked in and up the concrete stairs.*
inside/outside a building **external, internal, outside** *I saw the residents of the house leaving by the outside stairs.*
shared **communal** *He saw her bag at the bottom of their communal stairs.*

v+N go up stairs **ascend, climb, go up, mount, walk up** *By the time he was 74, it was getting difficult for him to climb stairs.*
go down stairs **come down, descend, go down, walk down** *As I descended the stairs of the hotel, a taxi drew up.*
use stairs **take, use** *Taking the stairs instead of the lift can make a positive difference.*
manage stairs **manage, negotiate** *Friends helped her to buy a specially-designed wheelchair which can negotiate stairs.*

stake N
part of a business that someone owns

● adj+N majority/minority **controlling, majority, minority** *Bates invested around £10 million, giving him a 50 per cent controlling stake.*
▸ large **significant, sizeable, substantial** *He has a sizeable financial stake in the biotechnology industry.*
▸ types of stake **financial, strategic** *If necessary the government will acquire a strategic stake in the company.*

● v+N own a stake **have, hold, own, retain** *BAA already owned a majority stake in Naples airport.*
▸ buy a stake **acquire, buy, gain, purchase, secure, take** *They were determined to prevent foreign buyers acquiring a controlling stake in the company.*
▸ sell your stake **offload, sell** *It has sold its 11.7 per cent stake in Australia's Seven Network for $87m.*
▸ increase your stake **increase** *Centrica made a further move to increase its stake in North Sea gas production.*
▸ reduce your stake **reduce** *Branson is planning to reduce his stake in the company through a public share offering.*

● N+in **bank, business, company, enterprise, firm, retailer, venture** *The fund also owns a substantial stake in fashion retailer French Connection.*

stalemate N
a situation in which progress or agreement is impossible

● adj+N hard to end **complete, continued, intractable, long-standing** *He was worried about the continued political stalemate in Northern Ireland.*
▸ uncomfortable **tense, uneasy** *There followed an uneasy stalemate in which the violence temporarily stopped.*
▸ current **current** *We will consider any measures to overcome the current stalemate.*
▸ of a particular type **military, nuclear, political** *The US was caught in a military stalemate in Iraq.*

● v+N reach stalemate **reach** *Casualties mounted on both sides as the situation reached stalemate.*
▸ end a stalemate **break, end, overcome, resolve** *One session of couples therapy can be enough to break the stalemate.*

stall V
stop making progress

● n+V **economy, investigation, negotiations, progress, recovery, reform, talks** *The latest information is that, for the time being, those negotiations have stalled.*

stamina N
the ability to work hard without getting tired

● adj+N great **amazing, considerable, extraordinary, immense, incredible, sheer, superior, tremendous** *His incredible stamina saw him through the 1500m and 5000m races.*
▸ enough **enough, sufficient** *He wondered if some of them had sufficient stamina to complete the journey.*
▸ types of stamina **emotional, mental, physical, vocal** *Physical stamina is a necessity because the hours are long and the pressure hard.*

- v+N have or show stamina **demonstrate, display, have, possess, regain, show** *He also showed great stamina to come third in the 3000m.*
- ▶ lack stamina **lack** *They often lack the stamina to deal with the mundane work.*
- ▶ increase stamina **boost, build, develop, enhance, improve, increase, restore** *Walking can improve stamina and increase energy levels.*
- ▶ decrease stamina **reduce, sap** *The sticky mud slowed the players down and sapped their stamina.*
- ▶ require stamina **demand, need, require, test** *It was a gruelling experience for the actors, requiring stamina and physical discipline.*
- ▶ admire someone's stamina **admire** *One has to admire the sheer stamina of the dancers.*

- and/or strength **courage, endurance, fitness, fortitude, resilience, strength, toughness, vitality** *This food will most certainly give you strength and stamina for shopping!*
- ▶ determination **determination, patience, perseverance, persistence, resolve, tenacity** *To become a surgeon, I think one needs stamina and tenacity.*
- ▶ other physical quality **agility, alertness, coordination, dexterity, flexibility, speed, suppleness** *Swimming is good all-round exercise, boosting strength, stamina and suppleness.*

stamp out PHR VB

end something bad by strong and determined action

- V+n **abuse, bullying, corruption, discrimination, fraud, poverty, prejudice, racism, terrorism, violence** *More measures are needed to stamp out election fraud.*

stance N

an attitude that you state clearly

- adj+N showing a determination to defend your view and never change it **adversarial, aggressive, confrontational, defensive, defiant, hardline, oppositional, rigid, uncompromising, unwavering** *We took a clear and uncompromising stance against collaboration with our persecutors.*
- ▶ strong or positive **firm, proactive, purposeful, strong, tough** *Companies are tempted to wait and see, when the market is calling for a more proactive stance.*
- ▶ neither positive nor negative **cautious, neutral** *The scientists of the day adopted a cautious stance.*
- ▶ based on moral principle **principled** *The outcome of his principled stance was imprisonment.*
- ▶ anti-war/pro-war **anti-war, hawkish, pro-war** *The government has reaffirmed its anti-war stance.*
- ▶ types of stance **ethical, fiscal, ideological, monetary, moral, philosophical, religious, theoretical** *Our ethical stance is very important to our customers.*

- v+N have a stance **adopt, assume, favor, maintain, take** *Our response to terrorism has largely been to assume a patriotic stance.* • *We are the only major Party that is prepared to take a firm stance on this issue.*
- ▶ change or review your stance **abandon, alter, change, modify, reassess, reconsider, rethink,**

reverse, shift *Experts are urging the Government to reconsider its stance on cannabis.*
- ▶ confirm your stance **affirm, clarify, reaffirm, reiterate, uphold** *The team reiterated their stance against drugs in football.*
- ▶ make your stance tougher **harden, tighten, toughen** *We believe that the local authority needs to toughen its stance and focus more on enforcement.*
- ▶ make your stance less tough **loosen, moderate, relax, soften** *The Premier has significantly softened his stance on climate change.*
- ▶ weaken someone's stance **compromise, contradict, undermine, weaken** *The US has often apparently compromised its stance on human rights.*
- ▶ show that someone's stance is right **justify, vindicate** *We believe this is excellent news that vindicates the stance we took.*
- ▶ support or praise someone's stance **admire, applaud, back, defend, endorse** *We applaud the brave stance of church leaders in calling for democracy in their country.*
- ▶ criticize someone's stance **criticize, deplore, oppose, question** *Customers have questioned the company's ethical stance.*

stand V

have your body upright supported by your feet

- V+adj straight **proud, straight, tall, upright** *The cells are not even tall enough to allow the prisoners to stand upright.*
- ▶ still **immobile, motionless** *Over to the left, a huge herd of elephants stood almost motionless.*
- ▶ silent **mute, silent, speechless** *The crowd stood silent, waiting for him to speak.*
- ▶ amazed or shocked **aghast, amazed, dumbfounded, helpless, open-mouthed** *The men stood aghast, looking at each other.* • *This is no consolation to those who stood helpless on their doorsteps as water streamed into their homes.*
- ▶ without help **unaided, unsupported** *Her legs had weakened to the point where she could no longer stand unaided.*

stand N

an attitude or opinion that you state publicly

- adj+N brave **brave, courageous, defiant, heroic, uncompromising, valiant** *He had taken a courageous stand on issues of national and international justice.*
- ▶ strong **firm, resolute** *It is time to take a firmer stand on racism towards Gypsies and Travellers.*
- ▶ based on moral principle **principled** *We took a principled stand against sending troops to Afghanistan.*

- v+N **adopt, make, mount, take** *Someone has to make a stand against those in power who are to blame.*

standard N [usually plural]

a level of quality or achievement

- adj+N good **excellent, exceptional, good, high** *Our reputation is your guarantee of the highest standards.*
- ▶ difficult to achieve **exacting, rigorous, robust, strict, stringent, tough** *We will work on your vehic until it meets our exacting standards.*

▶ not good **low, poor** *Internet-based review sites are generally of a very poor standard.*

▶ good enough **acceptable, adequate, decent, reasonable, satisfactory** *A teacher must ensure a reasonable standard of discipline.*

▶ required **mandatory, minimum, recommended, required** *Strict minimum standards for energy efficiency apply.*

▶ shared or agreed **accepted, agreed, appropriate, approved, common, harmonized, recognized, same** *The Consortium has agreed common standards of rented housing across its members.*

▶ usual **current, normal, usual** *I enjoyed the gig, but thought the sound wasn't up to the usual standard.*

▶ applying across a particular area **global, international, national** *National standards for food safety are being developed.*

▶ of a particular type **academic, educational, environmental, ethical, nutritional, occupational, professional, technical** *The role of the organization is to maintain professional standards.*

▶ improving **rising** *A big investment in education has led to rapidly rising standards in our schools.*

▶ getting worse **declining, falling** *With its corrupt government, weak economy, and declining standards of literacy, the country was in a mess.*

● v+N set or introduce a standard **adopt, define, develop, establish, introduce, lay down, promote, propose, set, specify** *Florence Nightingale was a nurse who set new standards for treatment and hygiene.*

▶ do what is necessary to achieve a standard **achieve, attain, comply with, conform to, match, meet, reach, satisfy** *Companies have been expelled from membership for failing to meet the standards required.*

▶ do better than a standard requires **exceed, surpass** *All our products far exceed the appropriate safety standards, giving you added peace of mind.*

▶ keep to a standard **keep to, maintain, uphold** *The company needs to maintain standards through a period of growth.*

▶ raise standards **improve, raise** *We work to raise standards in education and develop the skills of the nation.*

▶ lower standards **compromise, lower** *The nursing profession cannot afford to lower its standards.*

▶ impose a standard **apply, enforce, ensure, implement, impose, monitor** *The Environment Agency enforces water quality standards.*

▶ require a standard **demand, expect, require** *We expect the same academic standards of mature students and school leavers.*

standard ADJ
generally used or accepted as normal

ADJ+n method **formula, method, practice, procedure, protocol** *Brake tests will be carried out, a standard procedure in this sort of incident.*

amount or size **charge, fee, rate, size** *All calls are charged at standard rate.* • *The application must be accompanied with standard size original colour photographs.*

way of measuring or describing something **definition, notation, scale, specification, term, test** *This is a standard test for antibacterial activity.*

standing N
the status or reputation of someone or something

● adj+N good **excellent, good, high** *Pharmacists are warned not to sell products which may be detrimental to the good standing of the profession.*

▶ bad **low, poor** *Napoleon was at first very sensitive about his low social standing.*

▶ types of standing **academic, economic, legal, moral, political, professional, social** *Such activities could damage their own professional standing.*

▶ affect standing **affect** *Be careful not to get involved with people like this, as it could affect your standing in the business community.*

● v+N improve standing **bolster, boost, enhance, improve, strengthen** *This approach will enhance the standing of geography in the academic community.*

▶ damage standing **compromise, damage, diminish, erode, lower, undermine, weaken** *It exposes us as hypocrites and undermines our moral standing.*

standpoint N
a way of considering something

● adj+N not influenced by personal feelings **detached, independent, neutral, objective** *I can only say from an objective standpoint that I find her work lacks credibility.*

▶ influenced by personal feelings **personal, subjective** *People often retreat to the subjective standpoint of 'that's just your view'.*

▶ of a particular type **academic, aesthetic, cultural, environmental, ethical, feminist, historical, ideological, moral, pedagogical, philosophical, scientific, sociological, theological, theoretical** *A very different picture comes from exploring these issues from a specifically feminist standpoint.*

● v+N have a standpoint **adopt, analyze sth from, approach sth from, assume, represent, speak from, view sth from, write from** *This is an example of a judge adopting a political standpoint.*

▶ defend a standpoint **argue from, defend** *Students will have the opportunity to defend their own standpoint.*

staple ADJ
most basic and important

● ADJ+n food **diet, fare, fodder, food, foodstuff, ingredient** *Voles and small birds act as the staple diet for birds of prey such as hen harriers.*

▶ crop **cereal, crop, grain** *During the potato famine, millions died of starvation when their staple crop failed.*

▶ product **commodity, goods** *The price of staple goods in the country has soared in recent days.*

star N
a very famous, popular, or successful person or thing

● adj+N very famous **A-list, big, famous, international, major, massive, top** *Markova became the first British-born ballerina to become an international star.* • *I was shy being in the same room as all those massive stars!*

▶ genuine **real, true, undoubted** *The real stars of the*

day are the children themselves, many of whom create their own costumes.

▶ young **teenage, young** *A future young star, 14-year-old Laura Gemmell is the Number 1 seed in the Girls Under 15.*

▶ future **budding, future, rising, up-and-coming** *His show featured many up-and-coming stars of the time.*

▶ past **former** *Beckham is a former star of the legendary team Manchester United.*

● n+N **basketball, film, football, hip-hop, movie, pop, rap, rock, soap, soccer, tennis, TV** *He was a pop star in the early seventies, playing with the likes of David Bowie and Marc Bolan.*

● N+n **person chef, guest, name, performer, player, striker** *Yasu, their captain, was also their star striker.*

▶ attraction **attraction, turn** *One of the star attractions has always been the excellent refreshments on sale.*

▶ position **billing, role, status** *By 1938 he was getting star billing for his BBC broadcasts.* ● *She went from obscurity to movie star status.*

stare V
look directly at something for long time

● V+adj **aghast, open-mouthed, unblinking, wide-eyed** *The two of them stared open-mouthed at me as I sat down on the ground.*

● adv+V not understanding or thinking anything **blankly, glassily, helplessly, idly, stupidly, uncomprehendingly, vacantly** *We all scratch our heads and stare blankly at computer screens full of data.*

▶ without blinking or moving **fixedly, impassively, intently, unblinkingly** *No one talked or moved, they all just stood, staring intently at a closed door.*

▶ with surprise or interest **curiously, expectantly, incredulously** *The butler was staring incredulously at Des's ancient top hat.*

▶ in an angry or threatening way **coldly, hard, menacingly, moodily** *The large man stared menacingly into Martin's face.*

▶ sadly **forlornly, gloomily, longingly, mournfully** *The cows stare mournfully at us as we pass.*

▶ silently **silently** *Children gathered outside the shop, silently staring in.*

▶ in a particular direction **ahead, straight, upwards** *The boys just stared ahead at the whiteboard saying nothing.*

start V
begin

● adv+V again **afresh, again** *You can use that water and then fill it back up and start again.*

▶ quickly **immediately, instantly, promptly, quickly, soon** *The reader immediately starts to form a picture in the mind.*

▶ slowly or carefully **cautiously, gradually, slowly, sluggishly, tentatively** *If you decide to exercise after a period of relative inactivity, you should start very slowly.*

▶ well **brightly, hopefully, positively, promisingly, strongly, well** *The day started well, with a clear blue sky.*

▶ badly **badly, poorly** *In the Final, Italy started badly.*

▶ by itself **automatically** *If the player does not start automatically, double-click on the CD icon.*

start N
the way someone begins something

● adj+N good **auspicious, bright, brilliant, encouraging, excellent, explosive, fantastic, good, great, impressive, perfect, positive, promising, terrific** *Altogether, this was a promising start for the coming season.*

▶ fairly good **decent, modest, solid, steady** *David and Tom opened the innings and got us off to a steady start.*

▶ bad **bad, disappointing, disastrous, inauspicious, poor, terrible** *A bad start influences the audience, and is difficult to recover from.*

▶ uncertain **false, nervous, rocky, shaky** *After a rather shaky start, the side settled down to score some excellent goals.*

▶ difficult **tough** *He has had a tough start in life.*

▶ quick **immediate, prompt** *We will make an immediate start on that.*

▶ slow **slow, sluggish** *After a slow start, markets picked up significantly in May and June.*

▶ new **clean, fresh** *They asked me to stay, but I felt it was time for a fresh start.*

startled ADJ
suddenly frightened or surprised by something

● adv+ADJ rather **faintly, a little, mildly, quite, rather, slightly, somewhat** *He looked faintly startled to be addressed by a stranger on the bus.*

▶ for a moment **initially, momentarily** *She seemed momentarily startled, but then smiled happily.*

▶ easily **easily** *A baby is easily startled by loud or sudden noises.*

● ADJ+n **cry, exclamation, expression, look, reaction, response** *She gave a startled cry and dropped the tray she was carrying.*

starvation N
illness or death from lack of food

● adj+N among many people **mass, widespread** *This was a brutal process which caused mass starvation.*

▶ threatened **imminent, impending** *Millions of Afghans faced imminent starvation.*

● v+N prevent starvation **alleviate, avert, avoid, eliminate, prevent** *Too few planes could get throug. to avert starvation.*

▶ cause starvation **cause, lead to** *She said the U.N. sanctions are causing widespread starvation.*

▶ experience starvation **suffer** *Parisians suffered starvation, bombardments and disease.*

▶ risk starvation **be at risk of, be threatened with, face, risk** *12 million people are facing starvation in southern Africa.*

▶ escape from starvation **escape, flee** *Over 100,000 people are on the move, fleeing starvation over the harsh winter months.*

▶ die from starvation **die from, die of** *Soon, people began to die of starvation and disease.*

● n+of+N edge **brink, edge, verge** *There are million. of people in the world that are on the brink of starvation.*

▶ danger **danger, prospect, risk, spectre, threat** *The. found themselves alone in the world with the prospe. of starvation before them.*

▶ fear **fear, horror** *Why does half the world's population live with the ever-present fear of starvation?*

● and/or hunger **famine, hunger, malnutrition** *We want to end starvation and malnutrition, which affect billions of people.*

▶ thirst **dehydration, drought, thirst** *Without vitamins and water, tortoises die of starvation or dehydration.*

▶ poverty **deprivation, destitution, poverty, want** *The book tells a harsh tale of unemployment, poverty and starvation.*

▶ disease **disease, pestilence** *Those fortunate enough to escape still risked dying from starvation or disease.*

▶ tiredness **exhaustion, overwork** *Many more died in the camps, of overwork or starvation.*

▶ suffering **misery** *The people were suffering great misery and starvation following 6 years of war.*

▶ cold **cold, hypothermia** *Thousands of soldiers died of starvation and the cold.*

state N
the condition of something or someone

● adj+N present **actual, current, present** *Britain lifted itself from post-war austerity to its present state of relative affluence.*

▶ bad **fragile, parlous, poor, sad, sorry, terrible** *Something must be done about the poor state of the monument.*

> You can also say that someone or something is *in no fit state* or *not in a fit state*: *She had had too much to drink and was in no fit state to work.*

● all the time **constant, permanent** *These services are in a constant state of growth and change.*

● original **natural, normal, original** *The Castle in its original state covered a very large area.*

● different to normal **altered, heightened** *It is my belief that deep sleep is an altered state of consciousness.*

● types of state **emotional, financial, mental, physical, psychological** *They have been detained for almost three years without trial and we are deeply concerned about their health and mental state.*

● v+N create a state **bring about, cause, create, induce, produce, throw sb into** *These incidents induced a state of considerable anxiety.*

● reach a state **achieve, attain, be in, enter, experience, fall into, get into, reach** *Their case was unsatisfactory and should never have reached such a state.*

● keep or get back a state **maintain, restore** *How can it maintain its own state of equilibrium?*

● change a state **affect, change** *Colour can certainly affect your emotional state.*

● study or describe a state **assess, describe, determine, examine, review** *The purpose of this paper is to examine the current state of the evidence.*

● indicate a state **indicate, reflect** *These decisions reflect the state of the research at the time they were made.*

● N+of disorder or change **anarchy, chaos, crisis, disarray, flux, tension, turmoil** *The massive shake-up of the White House threw the administration into a state of disarray.*

● collapse **collapse, exhaustion** *She was found in a state of collapse and later died in hospital.*

▶ poor physical condition **decay, delapidation, dereliction, disrepair** *It was tragic that the mansion had fallen into such a state of disrepair.*

▶ being ready or aware **alert, awareness, preparedness, readiness** *A constant state of alert was to be maintained, because war could start at any moment.*

▶ shock or fear **agitation, anxiety, excitement, fear, panic, shock, terror** *Many homeowners are still in a state of shock at the scale of the damage caused by the floods.*

▶ happiness or calm **bliss, ecstasy, equilibrium, perfection, relaxation** *Hypnosis is a state of deep relaxation.*

▶ despair **depression, despair, distress** *He wandered the streets all night in a state of absolute despair.*

▶ uncertainty or lack of understanding **confusion, ignorance, limbo, uncertainty** *Students have been left in a state of confusion after receiving the letters.*

▶ affected by drink or drugs **inebriation, intoxication** *He came home in a state of intoxication.*

state V
express something in speech or writing

● adv+V clearly **baldly, bluntly, clearly, explicitly, expressly, flatly, plainly, specifically** *You should clearly state the complaint and the action you expect to put it right.*

▶ in a definite way **categorically, emphatically, firmly, unambiguously, unequivocably** *She stated categorically that that was not true.*

▶ in public **openly, overtly, publicly** *The Chairman of the Council has stated publicly that the shop is an asset to the town.*

▶ in a simple or brief way **briefly, simply, succinctly** *First, I will briefly state the nature of the question.*

▶ in a confident way **boldly, confidently, proudly** *The article boldly states that UK taxpayers are losing out.*

▶ in an official context **formally, officially** *In the document, they formally state their commitment to a democratic constitution.*

▶ many times **consistently, frequently, repeatedly** *The Bible repeatedly states that God is the creator of everything.*

▶ correctly **accurately, correctly, rightly** *He correctly stated that the blood must pass from the right ventricle to the left ventricle by way of the lungs.*

▶ incorrectly **erroneously, incorrectly, wrongly** *He was not the editor of the Economist in 1982, as this book wrongly states.*

● V+n fact **fact, truth** *I simply stated a fact.*

▶ intention **aim, commitment, intent, intention, objective, purpose, willingness** *She has stated her intention to step down next year.*

▶ opinion or belief **belief, conviction, hypothesis, opinion, position, theorem** *The author wishes to make it clear that the opinions stated in this article are entirely personal.*

▶ reason or argument **argument, case, criteria, grounds, principle, reason** *The Disciplinary Commission has not stated the reasons for its decision.*

▶ objection **objection, opposition** *Russia has already stated its objections to the proposal.*

▶ what you want **desire, preference, requirements,**

wish *Please state your preferences at time of ordering.*

stated ADJ
announced officially or in public

- ADJ+n intention **aim, ambition, commitment, goal, intent, intention, mission, objective, policy, purpose, strategy** *The Government's stated aim is to put consumers at the heart of policy making.*
- ▶ wish or preference **desire, preference, priority, willingness, wish** *There is a stated willingness to pay more for quality.*
- ▶ reason **criterion, justification, rationale** *What is the stated rationale behind the research?*
- ▶ limit **deadline, dose, timescale** *Applications must be received by the stated deadline: 1st of June 2011.*

statement N
a piece of writing or speech that makes a formal or public announcement

- adj+N official or public **formal, official, public** *An official statement from the board of directors is expected today.*
- ▶ clear or firm **categorical, clear, explicit, strongly-worded, unequivocal** *We need a clear statement of members' roles and responsibilities.*
- ▶ short **brief, concise, short, simple** *Mission statements are brief statements that summarise an organisation's key aims.*
- ▶ true or accurate **accurate, authoritative, correct, definitive, true** *Please treat the specification as a guide rather than a definitive statement. • Although this is a reasonable generalization, this statement is not true in all cases.*
- ▶ not true or accurate **ambiguous, contradictory, defamatory, false, incorrect, misleading, untrue** *In the face of contradictory statements **about** the safety of GM foods, the consumer must decide whom to believe. • She claimed that the memoranda contained defamatory statements **about** her mental health.*
- ▶ general **bold, general, sweeping, vague** *He made bold statements full of inaccuracies.*
- ▶ prepared in advance **carefully-worded, prepared, written** *The Chief Secretary read a prepared statement at a press conference.*
- ▶ legal **signed, statutory, sworn** *Affidavits are sworn statements made before the court.*
- ▶ shared **joint, shared** *The manufacturers issued a shared statement.*
- ▶ types of statement **environmental, financial, ministerial, personal, political** *The directors have a responsibility to deliver annual financial statements.*
- v+N make or publish a statement **issue, make, present, produce, publish, put out, release, send, submit** *The club had to issue a statement denying that the player was about to be sold.*
- ▶ write a statement **draft, formulate, prepare, write** *You should prepare a written statement including details of your business.*
- ▶ agree a statement **agree, approve, sign** *The parties agree a joint statement and present it to the Judge.*
- ▶ read a statement **read** *A White House spokesman read a statement from the President.*
- ▶ support or approve of a statement **accept, adopt, endorse, support, welcome** *The statement was welcomed by the Securities & Exchange Commission.*

- ▶ confirm a statement **confirm, verify** *I have been unable to verify his statement.*
- ▶ disagree with a statement **contradict** *The survey contradicts recent statements made by the Consumers' Union.*
- ▶ change a statement **amend, qualify, review, update** *In the light of Dr Hawkins' report, they might wish to amend their statement.*
- ▶ withdraw a statement **retract, withdraw** *There was a fall in the proportion of victims who retracted their statement.*
- ▶ understand a statement in a particular way **interpret, understand** *Felicity has no sense of irony and interprets the statement literally.*
- ▶ refer to a statement **quote, repeat** *Later, Defence Counsel quoted a statement made by the Judge.*
- ▶ receive a statement **obtain, receive** *Obtain an accurate statement from the supplier as to what it actually is.*
- ▶ contain a statement **contain, include** *The report may contain certain statements with which you disagree.*

- N+of intention, aim, or belief **aim, aspirations, belief, commitment, evidence, intent, intention, objective, position, principle, priorities, purpose** *The Corporate Policy contained a statement of intent on health and safety.*
- ▶ fact **fact, truth** *Science deals with statements of fact which can be proved or disproved.*
- ▶ reason **reason** *This was set down in their statement of the reasons for their decision.*
- ▶ objection or complaint **complaint, grievance, objection, opposition** *The first formal step is a written statement of your objection.*
- ▶ regret **regret** *Suppose his statements of regret and repentance are sincere?*

statistical ADJ
relating to statistics

- ADJ+n relating to the meaning of statistics **correlation, distribution, probability, significance** *The number of people in the study was too small to reach statistical significance.*
- ▶ analysing statistics **analysis, breakdown, evaluation** *We can provide training in statistical analysis and interpretation.*
- ▶ consisting of statistics **data, evidence** *Official statistical data shows that the return on the investment is approximately 18 per cent.*
- ▶ using statistics **algorithm, calculation, comparison, measure, method, methodology, model, procedure, sampling, technique** *He teaches statistical methods in epidemiology.*

statistics N
numbers that represent facts or a situation

- adj+N official **official** *A new study shows that the number of people who die suddenly could be much greater than is recorded in official statistics.*
- ▶ accurate or detailed **accurate, detailed, reliable** *There are no reliable statistics **on** the subject.*
- ▶ likely to make people believe something which is not true **misleading** *Although the figures sugge[st] that violent crime has fallen, the statistics can be misleading.*
- ▶ worrying or surprising **alarming, disturbing,**

frightening, grim, shocking, sobering, staggering, startling, worrying *These shocking accident statistics should serve as a wake-up call for the government.*

▶ comparing different things **comparative** *We produce comparative statistics to assist in performance management.*

▶ dealing with different topics **demographic, economic, environmental, financial, medical** *The course includes a lecture on the use of medical statistics.*

● v+N collect statistics **collate, collect, compile, gather, record** *Do schools compile statistics on this sort of thing?*

▶ analyse statistics **analyse, interpret** *I'll analyse these statistics and publish anything interesting.*

▶ calculate statistics **calculate, collate, compute** *If you want to know how statistics are calculated, please contact the R&D department.*

▶ publish statistics **issue, publish, release, report** *Statistics recently released show that the use of these services is on the increase.*

▶ produce statistics **generate, produce** *Statistics produced for the consortium show that prices have risen by 290 per cent.*

▶ quote statistics **cite, quote** *The magazine quoted annual statistics on aircraft production in the US.*

▶ make statistics inaccurate **manipulate, massage, skew** *The change in definition meant they were diagnosed earlier, and this skewed the statistics.*

● N+v show or prove something **confirm sth, demonstrate sth, highlight sth, illustrate sth, indicate sth, prove sth, reflect sth, reveal sth, show sth, tell sth** *Home Office statistics showed there were 2,000 fewer robberies in August.*

▶ suggest something **imply, point to sth, suggest sth** *The statistics point to a gradual slowdown in traffic speeds, but the effect is marginal.*

▶ concern something **concern sth, regard sth, relate to sth** *The website is a good source of facts and statistics relating to the USA.*

be inaccurate **mislead sb, underestimate sth** *Experts believe these statistics vastly underestimate the scale of the epidemic.*

status N
the legal, official or public position someone or something has

adj+N legal or official **legal, official, statutory** *If you have the legal status of an employee, you gain extra rights.*

high **high, top** *The Irish language commands high official status in the Irish Republic.*

low **inferior, low** *Women were more restricted and had an inferior legal status.*

with advantages or protection **favourable, preferential, preferred, privileged, protected, special** *The press have portrayed them as having a privileged status in society.*

considered very special by some **classic, cult, iconic, legendary** *After his death, numerous articles and books were written which expanded his legendary status.*

professional **professional, qualified** *The Summer Institute will start you on your way to gaining qualified status.*

equal **equal, same** *In 1910 women were permitted membership and equal status to men.*

▶ current **current** *We are writing to inform you about the current status of the merger discussions.*

▶ types of status **charitable, constitutional, ecological, employment, financial, marital, moral, nutritional, occupational, social, socioeconomic** *Smoking during pregnancy is associated with many factors, including age, social class, and marital status.*

● v+N have or achieve a status **achieve, acquire, attain, be accorded, be awarded, be granted, command, enjoy, gain, obtain, reach, secure** *The town was granted borough status in 1227. ● A majority of secondary schools now enjoy specialist status.*

▶ give status **confer on sb/sth** *Initiation is intended to confer the status of adulthood on the initiate.*

▶ keep or get back a status **maintain, preserve, regain, retain** *Moscow was not to regain its status as capital until 1918.*

▶ find out status **ascertain, assess, determine, evaluate** *What measures are used to determine the applicant's residency status?*

▶ improve status **elevate, enhance** *His intention was to elevate the international status of France.*

▶ check status **check, clarify, monitor, track** *Systems must be in place to check the registration status of nursing staff.*

▶ prove status **confirm, indicate, verify** *I need a letter to confirm my student status.*

▶ be appropriate for status **befit, reflect** *Both authors, as befits their status as key figures in the subject, write in a clear and accessible style.*

the status quo N
the present situation, or the way things usually are

● V+N keep the status quo **defend, keep, maintain, preserve, retain** *Had they wanted to maintain the status quo they would have voted no.*

▶ change the status quo **alter, change, disrupt, disturb, upset** *It's a conservative company, and employees who try to upset the status quo tend not to last.*

▶ accept the status quo **accept, conform to, support, uphold** *She is a woman who refuses to conform to the status quo.*

▶ not accept the status quo **challenge, question, threaten** *He challenged the status quo by initiating an investigation into the industry and seeking a means of bringing it under tighter control.*

statutory ADJ
controlled by a law or statute

● ADJ+n duty **duty, obligation, requirement, responsibility** *The Housing Act, 1977, gives local authorities a statutory duty to house the homeless.*

▶ right **entitlement, right** *These terms and conditions do not affect consumers' statutory rights.*

▶ power **control, power** *The Commission must have the statutory power to publish its advice to Ministers.*

▶ protection or recognition **protection, recognition** *It will call for legislation to confer equal rights and statutory protection against racial discrimination.*

▶ rule or set of rules **code, guidance, prohibition, provision, regulation, restriction, rule** *The statutory guidance on exclusion from schools has been revised to take into account recent changes in the law.*

▶ limit **limit, maximum, minimum** *If a notice period is not specified, the statutory minimum will apply.*

▶ organization or service **agency, authority, body, organization, service** *We work in partnership with other statutory agencies, including courts and local authorities.*

▶ document or statement **declaration, document, notice** *As with a civil wedding in a register office, you have a choice of which version of the statutory declaration you want to include.*

▶ name or definition **definition, designation** *There is no statutory definition of derelict land.*

▶ job or process **function, procedure, process** *Prior to 1 October 2004, there were no statutory procedures that had to be followed in relation to disciplinary action, dismissals or grievances.*

▶ system **framework, mechanism, system** *Community councils are voluntary bodies which exist within a statutory framework.*

▶ basis **basis, footing** *They needed to put the existing Code of Practice on a statutory footing.*

▶ payment or charge **charge, fee, funding, pay, payment, wage** *The new law will extend statutory maternity pay to cover the first year of a child's life.*

stay N
a period spent somewhere

● adj+N short **brief, minimum, overnight, short** *Thank you for your attention and understanding during my brief stay with you.*

▶ long **extended, lengthy, prolonged** *We found a nice campsite and settled down for a lengthy stay.*

▶ pleasant **comfortable, delightful, enjoyable, pleasant, pleasurable, relaxing** *There are a series of comfortable lodges where visitors can base themselves for a relaxing stay.*

▶ memorable **memorable, unforgettable** *As a family run hotel, we are dedicated to making your stay memorable for the right reasons.*

● v+N make a stay longer **extend, prolong** *He was trying to prolong his stay in Britain.*

▶ make a stay shorter **cut short, reduce, shorten** *The Rehabilitation Unit helps to shorten your stay in hospital.*

▶ arrange a stay **arrange, book, organize, plan** *We cater for vegetarians, but please remember to mention this when booking your stay with us.*

▶ enjoy a stay **enjoy** *We are sure that you will enjoy your stay here.*

> You can also use the pattern *make someone's stay* pleasant, comfortable etc: *We have a range of leisure facilities to make your stay even more enjoyable.*

steady ADJ
slow and gradual, or regular

● adv+ADJ rather **fairly, generally, pretty** INFORMAL, **quite, reasonably, relatively** *Graduates benefit from a reasonably steady pattern of earnings growth over their working lives.*

▶ very **remarkably, very** *Visitor numbers had remained remarkably steady throughout the year.*

● ADJ+n flow **drip, flow, influx, stream, supply, trickle** *Despite the wonderful new stadium, they've lost a steady trickle of players throughout the summer.*

▶ increase **climb, expansion, gain, growth, increase, rise** *The steady growth in traffic caused serious congestion at peak times.*

▶ decrease **decrease, drop, fall, reduction** *The data shows a steady reduction in road traffic deaths.*

▶ progress **advance, development, progress, progression** *He has made steady progress and his immune system is already better than it was.*

▶ when something gets better/worse **decline, deterioration, improvement** *This led to a steady decline of the empire after 1945.*

▶ speed or rate **beat, level, pace, rate, rhythm, speed** *Your heart beats with a slow but steady rhythm.*

● v+ADJ **hold, remain, stay** *The average number of trips per person has also held steady, at roughly 1000 per year.*

steep ADJ
1 rising quickly and difficult to climb

● adv+ADJ very **dangerously, extremely, impossibly, incredibly, really** INFORMAL, **very** *We saw spectacular glaciers and impossibly steep mountain peaks.*

▶ rather **fairly, moderately, pretty** INFORMAL, **quite, rather, relatively, slightly** *I can only recall a couple of fairly steep climbs, and these were very short.*

2 sudden and very big

● ADJ+n decrease **decline, dive, drop, drop-off, fall** *Figures show a steep decline in the number of people seeking asylum last year.*

▶ increase **hike** INFORMAL, **increase, rise** *Over the past ten years, we have seen a steep rise in the number of young people going into custody.*

stem V
stop something bad from spreading or increasing

● V+n flow **flood, flow, influx, tide** *Researchers are working to discover ways to stem the tide of deaths in hospitals as a result of medical errors.*

▶ increase **growth, proliferation, rise, spread** *Senegal and Uganda have shown the way to stemming the spread of HIV/AIDS.*

▶ decrease **decline, loss** *He has done incredible work in stemming the decline of church numbers.*

stench N
a very bad smell

● adj+N **acrid, awful, fetid, foul, horrible, nauseating, overpowering, putrid, rancid, terrible, unbearable, vile** *The whole area was engulfed in the putrid stench of decaying flesh.*

step N
one of a series of actions

● adj+N first/last **final, first, initial, preliminary** *Identifying the most important capabilities for your children is a first step to focusing on what we aim t improve.*

▶ next or more **another, further, next** *The next step is to work out how much you use your phone on average.*

▶ good **constructive, positive, progressive, sensible** *They have banned junk food in vending machines, so this is a positive step.*

▸ bad **dangerous, retrograde** *We believe that any policy to centralize children's care is a retrograde step.*

▸ big or important **big, critical, crucial, essential, giant, huge, important, key, major, necessary, significant, vital** *E-Passports are an important step forward in a larger effort to enhance security.*

▸ small **modest, small, tiny** *Thank you for all the people who help us take small steps to overcome our problems.*

▸ unusual **unprecedented, unusual** *Marie took the unusual step of employing only female nurses and doctors.*

▸ extreme **drastic, radical** *This would be a radical step to take.*

▸ brave **bold, decisive** *The album is a bold step forward musically and demonstrates how gifted this band is.*

▸ careful **faltering, tentative** *Now, for the first time, the two sides are finally taking tentative steps to reduce tension.*

● v+N take a step **take** *Take the first step towards fulfilling your career aspirations.*

▸ be a step **be, constitute, mark, represent** *This represents a major step forward.*

● N+towards making something happen **creation, establishment, implementation, realization** *The agreement represents a decisive step towards the realization of our dream of peace in the region.*

▸ an aim or solution **aim, goal, objective, solution** *Our technology centre opened last year, another step towards our objective of providing students with state-of-the-art facilities.*

step V
move or walk a short distance

● adv+V carefully **carefully, cautiously, gingerly, reluctantly, tentatively** *He stepped gingerly into the river and waded out to the centre.*

▸ confidently **boldly, bravely, calmly, confidently, coolly** *It was Mick who bravely stepped up to the door and rang the bell.*

▸ lightly or quietly **delicately, lightly, quietly, softly** *He stepped lightly and, to his amazement, directly in front of him sat the big bald bird on a high branch.*

step up PHR VB
increase something

▸ V+n **attack, campaign, efforts, fight, pace, pressure, production, search, security** *We need to step up our efforts to make road traffic greener and more efficient.*

stereotype N
fixed idea about a particular type of person or thing

● adj+N negative **crude, damaging, negative, unhelpful** *Their questions revealed confusion and negative stereotypes surrounding HIV and AIDS.*

offensive **ageist, offensive, racist, sexist** *Some TV programmes reinforce sexist stereotypes to children.*

common **common, familiar, popular, prevalent** *Professors are, according to the popular stereotype, absent-minded.*

▸ old-fashioned or traditional **conventional, old, outdated, outmoded, traditional** *But those involved in the sector say this is an outdated stereotype.*

▸ about a particular group of people **cultural, gender, national, racial, sexual, social** *It's not funny to use racial stereotypes in jokes.*

● v+N reinforce a stereotype **perpetuate, promote, reinforce** *Stereotypes are often perpetuated by the media.*

▸ show that a stereotype is not true **break, dispel, overcome, overturn, shatter, subvert**

▸ believe a stereotype **hold** *Stereotypes about ballet dancers are most strongly held by those who have never seen a ballet.*

▸ fit a stereotype **confirm, conform to, fall into, fit, fit into, match** *Only a minority of landlords fit this stereotype.*

▸ not fit a stereotype **defy, explode** *He is a Chinese student who has never ridden a bicycle before, defying all stereotypes.*

▸ refuse to accept a stereotype **challenge, combat, confront, counter, reject, tackle** *There is an opportunity for single parents to challenge negative stereotypes, and share their own positive experiences.*

● and/or **assumptions, caricature, cliches, generalizations, ignorance, misconceptions, myths, preconceptions, prejudice** *Discrimination is usually based on prejudice and stereotypes.*

stick to PHR VB
continue to do or use particular thing

● adv+V **closely, doggedly, faithfully, firmly, religiously, resolutely, rigidly, rigorously, slavishly, steadfastly, strictly, stubbornly** *People are changing careers several times in their working lifetime, instead of sticking rigidly to the same thing until they retire.*

● V+n beliefs **belief, idea, principle, view** *You have to admire her for sticking to her principles.*

▸ plan or decision **agreement, brief, budget, deadline, decision, plan, policy, schedule, strategy** *Despite provocation, the group stuck to its policy of non-violence.*

▸ rule or law **convention, guidelines, law, rule** *As long as you stick closely to the guidelines, you won't have any problems.*

stigma N
a feeling among people in general that something is wrong or embarrassing

● adj+N of a particular degree **considerable, huge, terrible, widespread** *There is still a huge stigma and misunderstanding about depression.*

▸ types of stigma **moral, religious, social** *There are two main areas of concern – the social stigma of having head lice, and worries over the effectiveness and safety of treatments.*

● v+N carry a stigma **bear, carry** *Mental health difficulties frequently carry a stigma.*

▸ fight against a stigma **challenge, combat, fight, fight against, tackle** *Help us to combat the stigma that surrounds HIV and AIDS.*

▸ remove or reduce a stigma **dispel, eliminate, end, eradicate, overcome, reduce, remove** *They aim to*

remove the stigma surrounding epilepsy by educating
other students about the illness.

▸ experience a stigma **bear, cope with, deal with,
experience, face, feel, suffer, suffer from** He wants
to remove the social stigmas faced by children with
mental health problems.

● N+v **affect sb/sth, be associated with sth, be
attached to sth, surround sth** Because of the stigma
associated with leprosy, it is estimated that many
cases go undetected.

still ADJ
not moving

● adv+ADJ **absolutely, completely, perfectly, quite,
stock** I stood there stock still, unable to move.

● v+ADJ **stay still be, hold, keep, sit, stand, stay**
Keep still and stop wriggling.

▸ make someone stay still **hold sb, keep sb** I couldn't
hold her still, she was struggling so much.

stimulate V
encourage something to happen, develop, or
improve

● V+n economic process **consumption, demand,
development, growth, investment, production**
Funds are needed to stimulate this growth, especially
in urban areas.

▸ new ideas **creativity, curiosity, imagination,
innovation** How do you stimulate creativity?

▸ new research or study **research, thinking, work**
The aim of the workshop is to stimulate fresh
thinking on this difficult topic.

▸ discussion **conversation, debate, dialogue,
discussion** The consultation paper may stimulate a
wider debate on landscape issues.

stimulus N
something that encourages something to happen,
develop etc

● adj+N important or large **great, important,
major, powerful, significant** The building of
railways was a major stimulus to the coal and iron
and steel industries.

▸ types of stimulus **economic, emotional,
environmental, fiscal, intellectual, social** Pre-
school education is of value in providing a child with
intellectual stimulus and social skills.

● v+N be a stimulus **act as, be, give sth, prove,
provide, represent, serve as** TV programmes can
sometimes provide a stimulus for group discussion.

▸ react to a stimulus **react to, respond to** We are all
different in our habits and in the way we react to
environmental stimuli.

● N+for discussion or research **debate, dialogue,
discussion, exploration, reflection** The lecture
series should act as a stimulus for further debate.

▸ development **development, growth, improvement,
innovation, regeneration** The new railway has the
potential to provide a stimulus for major
regeneration in the region.

stir V
1 move liquid or food around with a spoon

● adv+V thoroughly **thoroughly, well** The paint
must be stirred thoroughly before it is used.

▸ gently **carefully, gently, lightly** Add the cooked
carrots, potatoes and cauliflower and gently stir in.

▸ hard or fast **briskly, hard, vigorously** Drizzle in the
beaten egg, vigorously stirring the soup as you do
so.

▸ occasionally **occasionally, periodically** Cover and
cook for about 30 minutes on low heat, stirring
occasionally.

▸ continually or frequently **constantly, continually,
continuously, frequently, regularly** Now make the
roux sauce, firstly melting the margarine and then
mixing in the flour whilst stirring continuously.

2 make someone's feelings stronger

● V+n emotions or memories **emotions, feelings,
memories** The war stirred all kinds of emotions in
the young Neill.

▸ negative feelings **hatred, resentment** His
revolutionary impulse has stirred great resentment
abroad.

▸ excitement or interest **curiosity, excitement,
imagination, interest, passion** The event failed to
stir great excitement.

▸ disagreement or conflict **conflict, controversy,
disagreement, tension** He insisted that his article
was not intended to stir racial tension.

3 start to have a feeling, thought etc

● n+V **emotion, feeling, heart, memory, passion,
spirits** An unfamiliar feeling stirs within him; an
impulse other than his pure instinct for personal
survival.

stir N
a situation in which many people feel interested
or angry

● adj+N **big, considerable, great, real** They are
delighted with the campaign, which has created a
real stir in the media industry.

● v+N **cause, create** Her book should cause a stir
when it hits the shelves in June.

stock N
an available amount of something

● adj+N large **extensive, huge, large, vast** We hold
an extensive stock of organ music.

▸ small or getting smaller **declining, depleted,
dwindling, falling, limited** Order now – limited stock
available.

▸ enough **adequate, enough, sufficient** Does the
country have sufficient food stocks?

▸ total **entire, overall, total** These organizations have
a total stock of around 4,000 apartments and houses.

▸ new **fresh, new** Your order will be delivered as soon
as possible after fresh stocks arrive.

▸ old **existing, old** High house prices are putting
incredible strain on our existing stock of affordable
homes.

▸ unwanted **damaged, excess, redundant, unsold** The
company is extending its summer sale to clear excess
stock.

● v+N use up a stock **clear, decimate, diminish,
dispose of, exhaust, use up** Paper copies will be
amended when current stocks are exhausted.

▸ add to a stock **add to, replace, replenish** *Businesses need to increase production in order to replenish stocks to desired levels.*

▸ have a stock **have, hold, keep, maintain, retain** *The Glasgow Gallery holds a stock of over 1000 original paintings.*

▸ make sure you have enough stock **conserve, preserve** *In the current situation, everyone needs to use water wisely and help us conserve stocks.*

▸ get a stock **accumulate, acquire, purchase** *Over his lifetime, he has accumulated a stock of funny stories.*

stomach N
the organ in your body where food goes when you have eaten it

● adj+N empty/full **empty, full** *Some drugs should not be taken on an empty stomach.*

▸ sick **bad, dodgy** INFORMAL, **queasy, sore, upset** *But jet lag, holiday viruses and upset stomachs can take all the joy out of going abroad.*

▸ strong **(cast) iron, strong** *Next morning everyone was ill, except Jack whose cast iron stomach was unaffected.*

▸ weak **delicate, sensitive, weak** *Very acidic foods can upset sensitive stomachs, contributing to digestive problems such as heartburn.*

▸ sticking out **bloated, bulging, distended, enlarged, swollen** *The little boy's stomach was bloated, and his ribs were sticking out.*

● v+N cause pain in your stomach **irritate, turn** INFORMAL, **upset** *These tablets can irritate the stomach, and in some cases cause internal bleeding.*

▸ make your stomach feel less painful **calm, settle, soothe** *You can use ginger to soothe an upset stomach.*

N+v have a strong nervous feeling **churn, heave, lurch, tighten, turn over** *Does the thought of doing a parachute jump make your stomach churn?*

make a noise **growl, gurgle, rumble** *Her empty stomach rumbled one last time.*

N+n illness **bug, cancer, complaint, disorder, problem, trouble, ulcer, upset** *Unripe bananas can cause slight stomach upsets.*

pain **ache, cramps, discomfort, irritation, pain, spasm** *Chamomile tea is good for stomach ache.*

outer part **lining, wall** *Sometimes the ulcer can perforate the stomach, causing a hole in the stomach wall.*

top V
o longer do something or not continue

adv+V suddenly **abruptly, immediately, instantly, quickly, suddenly** *That was a big problem because the advertisers instantly stopped buying ads.*

finally **eventually, finally** *I finally stopped feeling sick some time on Friday morning.*

completely **altogether, completely, dead** *Of course the recovery programme does not stop dead in March 2011.*

early **early, prematurely** *Her trial had to be stopped prematurely.*

almost **almost, nearly, virtually** *Work on the house then virtually stopped for approximately 6 months.*

for some time, but not permanently **currently, momentarily, temporarily** *The work on the railway*

line has currently stopped, but should start up again in the spring.

stop N
a place where you stop on a journey or the period when you stop

● adj+N brief **brief, quick, short** *After a brief stop for lunch, we continued on our journey.*

▸ for one night **overnight** *It is possible to fly direct to and from the UK, but in many cases an overnight stop is needed.*

▸ planned/not planned **planned, scheduled, unplanned, unscheduled** *On any ride there are always unscheduled stops.*

▸ good or suitable **convenient, excellent, popular** *The hotel is about halfway between the two cities, so it makes a really convenient overnight stop.*

● n+N to eat or drink something **coffee, lunch, picnic, refreshment** *We had a lunch stop at an old Fifties-style diner.*

▸ to use the toilet **bathroom, comfort, toilet** *Our driver told us that because of our tight schedule there would be no comfort stop, but that basic toilet facilities would be made available on request.*

▸ to get fuel **fuel, refuelling** *He drove for 340 miles without a single fuel stop.*

● v+N **have, make, take** *It's about 4 hours from here by car, so it's a good place to make a stop.*

store V
to keep something in a particular place [usually passive]

● adv+V permanently **forever, indefinitely, permanently** *Balsamic vinegar can be stored indefinitely even when the bottle has been opened.*

▸ temporarily **temporarily** *They started moving the rail that had been temporarily stored by the side of the track.*

▸ safely or carefully **carefully, safely, securely** *Data should be stored securely with password protection.*

▸ well **conveniently, efficiently, neatly** *A waterproof zipped carrying bag keeps everything clean and neatly stored.*

▸ correctly **appropriately, correctly, properly** *All of the contents will keep, if stored correctly, for at least a year.*

▸ in electronic form **digitally, electronically** *Each order, receipt, invoice, fax, email, picture or presentation is stored electronically.*

▸ outside somewhere **elsewhere, externally, remotely** *Remote working can also help avoid problems of data loss or damage in the office by having data stored remotely.*

▸ inside somewhere **internally, locally** *a locally stored pdf file*

▸ together in one place **centrally** *The beauty of the system is that all data can be stored centrally, allowing easier maintenance.*

▸ not together **separately** *Some of the more valuable and fragile material is stored separately and can be requested from the Information Desk.*

store N
a large amount of something kept in your memory

● adj+N **big, enormous, large, phenomenal, rich,**

vast *Our staff have a vast store of knowledge in this type of work.*

- N+of **anecdotes, information, knowledge, memories, stories, wisdom** *Within all of us there is a phenomenal store of wisdom to be discovered.*

storm N

1 a period of much rain, strong winds etc

- adj+N severe **bad, devastating, ferocious, fierce, heavy, howling, huge, intense, mighty, severe, terrible, terrific, violent** *During a fierce thunder storm, a house at Pentlow was struck by lighting.*
- ▶ approaching **approaching, imminent, impending, impending, oncoming** *The island was in the direct path of an oncoming tropical storm.*
- ▶ types of storm **cyclonic, electrical, hail, lightning, magnetic, rain, snow, solar, thunder, tropical** *Last year, Rarotonga was hit by three separate tropical storms in two weeks.*
- ▶ unusual or unexpected **freak, unexpected** *Homeowners were clearing up the mess, after a freak storm caused local flooding.*
- N+v happen **blow, rage** *Storms raged in the Gulf of Biscay, and the English Channel was covered in ice.*
- ▶ get calmer **abate, ease, pass, subside** *Sailings didn't resume until Saturday afternoon when the storm had abated.*
- ▶ start to happen **break out, erupt** *As we settle down to sleep in our tent, a violent storm erupts outside.*
- ▶ be going to happen **approach, brew** *Perhaps a storm was brewing off shore.*
- ▶ affect a place **batter sth, hit sth, lash sth, sweep sth, wreck sth** *Bedfordshire was lashed by storms on Tuesday night.*

2 a situation in which many people are upset, angry, or excited

- v+N survive a storm **brave, ride, survive, weather, withstand** *By the early 1920s international capitalism had weathered the revolutionary storm that swept across Europe.*
- ▶ cause a storm **bring, cause, create, provoke, raise, spark, unleash, whip up** *The article sparked a predictable storm of protest.*
- ▶ calm a storm **calm, still** *How do you help to calm storms in the workplace?*
- ▶ experience a storm **encounter, endure, experience, face** *The Prime Minister is likely to encounter a storm of hostility.*
- N+of **complaints, controversy, criticism, indignation, outrage, protest, publicity** *They couldn't have known that the scheme would evoke a storm of protest amongst local people.*

story N

an account of real or imaginary events

- adj+N true **true** *Based on a true story, the movie is one of the best I have ever seen.*
- ▶ not true **apocryphal, fiction, fictional, imaginary** *This story was probably fictional, but there is no doubt that Walter had suffered during his service.*
- ▶ interesting **compelling, fascinating, gripping, interesting, intriguing** *Fukuzawa's autobiography is a fascinating story.*
- ▶ good **amazing, entertaining, exciting, good, great, incredible, powerful, remarkable, wonderful** *This is the remarkable story of a man who has become a legend in his own lifetime.*
- ▶ inspiring **heart-warming, inspirational, inspiring** *Read the inspiring story of how she became 5 stone lighter.*
- ▶ shocking or frightening **chilling, disturbing, harrowing, horrific, scary, shocking** *'Homeland' is the gripping and often chilling story of the interwoven lives of three characters.*
- ▶ strange **astonishing, bizarre, extraordinary, strange, unusual** *Someone at the magazine dreamed up a bizarre story involving David Beckham and Michael Jackson.*
- ▶ sad **poignant, sad, touching, tragic** *The touching story of one girl's migration from the Caribbean to England is explored in 'Weeding Cane'.*
- ▶ funny **amusing, comic, funny, hilarious, humorous** *Martin told an amusing story about camping in the New Forest.*
- ▶ complete **complete, entire, full, whole** *Only when we see the whole story of a person's life can we judge whether it went well.*
- ▶ well-known **familiar, famous, old, popular, well-known** *'Jungle Book, the Musical ' was adapted from Rudyard Kipling's famous story.*
- ▶ real **inside, real, untold** *Here's the inside story of what happened on 28/29 October.*
- ▶ traditional **classic, epic, fairy, traditional** *We take a fresh look at the traditional story of 'Red Riding Hood'.*
- ▶ about love **love, romantic** *Romeo and Juliet is one of the most famous love stories in the world.*
- ▶ in a newspaper **big, cover, front-page, lead, top** *While a front-page story on racism in the workplace may be more appealing to the paper's editorial team, it is soccer that sells newspapers.*
- n+N **adventure, bible, coming-of-age, detective, fantasy, ghost, gospel, horror, mystery, news, rags-to-riches, spy** *Becker stars in the rags-to-riches story of a young Latino player who journeys from the ghetto of East LA to the glamour of the English Premier league.*
- v+N tell a story **narrate, recount, share, tell** *Payday tells the story without leaving a thing out.*
- ▶ repeat a story **repeat, retell** *They believe every word even when she retells the story from someone else's viewpoint.*
- ▶ write or make up a story **concoct, dream up, fabricate, invent, make up, weave, write** *He concocted a story about seeing a UFO and its occupants to impress his 'superior,' a UFO enthusiast. • Johnson had children of his own and probably invented the story to make me feel better.*
- ▶ read or hear a story **hear, listen to, read** *This week I read the true story of an American called Gerald Barnes.*
- ▶ find out about a story **investigate, piece together, research, uncover, unravel** *Bit by bit, I pieced together the story.*
- ▶ of a newspaper: to include a story **cover, feature, get, print, publish, report, run** *The Evening News covered the story.*
- N+v progress **continue, evolve, progress, unfold** *As his story unfolds, we meet others in his world.*

► be about something or someone **be about sb/sth, centre on sb/sth, concern sb/sth, feature sb/sth, recount sth, revolve around sb/sth, tell of sb/sth** *The story revolves around Jack and Rebecca, two children who have been sent to stay with their unfriendly Aunt Caroline.*

straight ADJ
honest and true, with no attempt to hide anything

● adv+ADJ **absolutely, completely, dead, perfectly, pretty, quite, totally** *May I be quite straight with you?*

● ADJ+n **answer, talker, talking** *Can you give me a straight answer for once?*

straightforward ADJ
clear and honest or not complicated

● adv+ADJ fairly **comparatively, fairly, pretty INFORMAL, quite, rather, reasonably, relatively** *It is relatively straightforward to configure a PC as a dual-boot system.*

► very or completely **entirely, extremely, perfectly, very** *Getting the engine sorted out hasn't been entirely straightforward.*

► surprisingly **deceptively, remarkably, surprisingly** *This cotton sling is a deceptively straightforward and comfortable way of carrying your child.*

► apparently **apparently, seemingly** *These two seemingly straightforward tasks are getting ever more demanding and complex.*

► in a good way **refreshingly** *His approach is refreshingly straightforward.*

● ADJ+n something someone says or asks **account, answer, description, explanation, question, request, statement** *At the moment, I don't have any straightforward answers to these questions.*

► process or job **job, operation, procedure, process, task** *Graphic scales are simple to use and can make estimating distances a very straightforward task.*

► situation **affair, case, issue, matter** *It looked like a straightforward case of murder.*

► way of dealing with something **approach, fashion, method, route, solution, technique** *This approach is straightforward and logical.*

► information **advice, guide, information, instructions** *By following some straightforward advice, and working together, we can ensure that this type of crime keeps falling.*

● v+ADJ **appear, be, look, prove, seem, sound** *The planning process may sound straightforward, but it's actually rather complicated.*

● and/or **clear, concise, easy, factual, honest, logical, simple, transparent, unambiguous, uncomplicated** *Installation and maintenance are designed to be as simple and straightforward as possible.*

strain N
pressure caused by a difficult situation

● adj+N a lot **considerable, enormous, great, huge, immense, severe, tremendous, unbearable** *The number of strikers was approaching 30,000 and the nation's economy was under severe strain.*

► too much **excessive, undue, unnecessary** *A well-implemented system can deliver high productivity without putting undue strain on the workforce.*

► more **added, additional, extra, more** *A repeat of the heavy spring floods in recent years would put added strain on the insurance industry.*

► types of strain **economic, emotional, financial, psychological** *The emotional strain our family was under following my son's cancer diagnosis was immense.*

● v+N reduce strain **alleviate, ease, lessen, minimize, reduce, relieve** *Having plenty of visitors can ease the strain of being in hospital.*

► increase strain **add to, increase** *If you report the crime, a police investigation may add to the strain you are already feeling.*

► cause strain **cause, exert, impose, involve, lead to, place, put, result in, subject sth to** *Building an extension can put a severe strain on neighbour relations.*

► feel strain **come under, experience, feel, suffer** *When caring for a sick child, parents' relationships can come under intense strain.*

► successfully deal with strain **bear, cope with, deal with, stand, withstand** *I couldn't stand the strain of knowing he was in danger too.*

► be unable to deal with strain **break under, buckle under, collapse under, crack under, creak under, succumb to** *Ruth begins to buckle under the strain of her conflicting commitments.*

2 a type of disease, virus etc

● adj+N dangerous or spreading quickly **deadly, pandemic, virulent** *During 1918, there was a worldwide pandemic of a virulent strain of influenza.*

► not dangerous **mild** *The method involves infecting a plant with a mild strain of a virus to build its resistance to related, more harmful viruses.*

► unable to be treated by drugs **antibiotic-resistant, drug-resistant, resistant** *Treatment failed as a result of resistant strains of bacteria.*

► different from others of its type **mutant** *The project aims to produce mutant strains of yeast in which each of the 6000 genes is mutated.*

► types of strain **bacterial, pathogenic, recombinant, viral** *The H5N1 viral strain has been identified by global health authorities as being a potential cause of a pandemic.*

stranger N
someone who you do not know

● adj+N total **complete, perfect, total, utter** *Don't expect a long conversation with a total stranger at the bus stop or in the bus.*

► almost **comparative, relative, virtual** *This family's willingness to house a virtual stranger for two days is testament to the hospitality and friendliness of the Kiwis.*

strategic ADJ
carefully planned to achieve a particular aim

● ADJ+n action or decision **decision, initiative, manoeuvre, move, plan** *The committee will focus on strategic initiatives to reduce youth crime.*

► relationship **alliance, partnership** *It is believed that this strategic alliance will create a win-win situation for shareholders.*

► partner **ally, partner** *We are in a process of carefully selecting strategic partners that will allow us to provide an even better service.*

▶ aim **aim, direction, goal, objective, priority, target** *The strategy document sets out our strategic objectives for the future.*

▶ thinking **consideration, decision-making, planning, thinking, vision** *This book is the best compilation of strategic thinking regarding brand management.*

▶ examination of a problem or situation **analysis, assessment, overview, review** *The report provides a strategic assessment of our options for growing the business over the next five years.*

strategy N
a plan or method for achieving something

● adj+N overall or general **basic, general, overall, overarching** *Steroids are a useful treatment as part of an overall strategy to treat eczema.*

▶ for the future **five-year, forward, future, long-term** *The successful candidate will have an influential role in shaping the company's long-term strategy.*

▶ useful or sensible **cost-effective, practical, sensible, useful** *She offers practical strategies that can be used to escape negative thoughts.*

▶ effective or likely to be successful **effective, efficient, good, optimal, proven, robust, sound, successful, viable, winning** *The project is designed to help formulate an effective strategy for the promotion of internet connectivity in communities in southern Africa.*

▶ suitable **appropriate, correct, proper, right, suitable** *Academics need to recognise these learning types and develop appropriate strategies for dealing with them.*

▶ different **alternative, different** *Concern regarding the overuse of antibiotics has led to the need for alternative disease control strategies.*

▶ having different aspects **inclusive, integrated** *This is part of a well-planned, integrated transport strategy.*

▶ clear **clear, coherent, cohesive** *That is why we need a coherent national strategy to tackle the backlog of disrepair.*

▶ new **innovative, new, novel** *Brain experts have come up with a novel strategy for shedding excess flab.*

▶ detailed **comprehensive, detailed** *We need a comprehensive prevention strategy for breast cancer.*

▶ ambitious **ambitious, grand** *Did the US have a grand strategy?*

▶ complicated/simple **complex, simple, sophisticated** *The strategy was very complex and sophisticated.*

▶ dangerous **high-risk, risky** *Changing the appearance of a well-known range of products can be a risky strategy.*

▶ types of strategy **corporate, cultural, economic, educational, electoral, environmental, financial, industrial, institutional, instructional, military, organizational, political** *In 2000, he was named vice president of corporate strategy.*

▶ relating to a particular area **global, international, national, regional** *We need a global strategy for fighting terrorism.*

● n+N **business, communication, development, health, housing, investment, management, marketing, research, security, training, transport** *The new rail line forms part of an integrated transport strategy for the Olympic Games.*

● v+N develop a strategy **arrive at, come up with,**

deliver, design, determine, develop, devise, establish, formulate, identify, plan, prepare, produce, shape *Instead of exploiting the poor, we have developed strategies to address poverty.*

▶ define a strategy **define, outline, set out** *The Welfare Reform Green Paper outlined our strategy to enable people to overcome obstacles to work.*

▶ agree a strategy **agree, decide on, negotiate** *In January, the Programme Board agreed a new marketing strategy.*

▶ examine or consider a strategy **assess, consider, discuss, evaluate, examine, look at, monitor** *I needed to look at strategies to enable me to continue to live life to the full.*

▶ use a strategy **adopt, apply, embark on, employ, execute, follow, implement, launch, pursue, use** *The teacher employed positioning strategies to establish herself as the dominant voice in the classroom.*

▶ suggest a strategy **propose, recommend, suggest** *The President is responsible for diagnosing problems affecting the members and proposing strategies for dealing with these problems.*

▶ change a strategy **adapt, change, improve, rethink, review, revise** *We reviewed our research strategy in November 2005.*

▶ be the basis of a strategy **base, inform, underpin** *The strategy was underpinned by concrete objectives.*

streak N
part of someone's character that is different from the rest

● adj+N unpleasant or strict **authoritarian, jealous, mean, nasty, ruthless, sadistic, vicious, vindictive** *Moore was suave, cool, and witty, with a ruthless streak.*

▶ wanting to disobey rules or do exciting things **adventurous, mischievous, rebellious, stubborn** *My father's strictness brought out my rebellious streak.*

▶ competitive **competitive, entrepreneurial** *You need to be naturally confident, outgoing and have a competitive streak.*

stream N
a continuous flow of something

● adj+N **constant, continual, continuous, endless, relentless, steady, unbroken, unending** *We were kept busy explaining our work to the steady stream of visitors to the stand.*

● n+N **funding, income, profit, revenue** *There isn't a real revenue stream to attract mainstream reviews and media attention.*

streamline V
make business or process more modern or simple

● V+n **administration, bureaucracy, communication, decision-making, operations, paperwork, planning, procedure, process, processing, task, workflow** *We enable organisations to streamline workflow and therefore enhance productivity.*

● and/or **automate, enhance, improve, modernize, simplify, speed up, standardize** *The new service will streamline and modernise the process of recruitment*

street N

a road with buildings along it

- adj+N quiet/busy **busy, congested, crowded, deserted, quiet** *The hotel was located in a quiet street, not far from the city centre.*
- of a particular type, or with particular features **back, leafy, narrow, one-way, residential, suburban, tree-lined** *Take time to explore all the back streets of the city, away from the crowded centre.*
- most important **high, main** *You'll find the museum on the main street of the town.*
- N+n person **entertainer, performer, trader, vendor** *Liverpool City Council recently introduced a scheme to allow street entertainers to perform under licence in ten designated performance areas.*
- activity **theatre, trading** *People toured the city, stopping at various venues for talks and street theatre.*

strength N

the fact of somone or something being strong

- adj+N of the muscles **brute, muscular, physical** *These exercises will increase muscular strength and cardiovascular endurance.*
- great **considerable, great, superhuman, superior** *The outward appearance of the castle is still nearly entire, the great strength and solidity of its walls having resisted the ravages of time and man.*
- of the mind **inner, mental** *The task breaks some people, but I have an inner strength that allows me to continue.*

- v+N have strength **have, possess** *Yet these people possess the necessary mental strength to continue to practice.*
- get more strength **boost, gain in, gather, grow in, improve, increase, maximize** *The German economy is continuing to grow in strength.* • *Physical activity improves muscle strength and muscle mass.*
- take someone's strength away **exhaust, sap, use up** *This was back-breaking, disgusting work on your hands and knees that sapped your strength and destroyed your health.*
- get strength back **recover, regain, renew** *The animal regained the strength in both hind legs and had 5 more years of active life.*
- use strength **draw on, use** *She had enormous reserves of mental strength to draw on.*

- N+v **decline, decrease, ebb, fail, wane** *My strength was waning as I ran at a punishing pace.*

- N+of **argument, belief, character, conviction, feeling** *We didn't anticipate the strength of feeling that exists among workers on this issue.*

something that someone or something does very well

- adj+N important or main **great, key, main, major** *A key strength of the company is its ability to react quickly to changes in the market.* • *Make a list of your main strengths and weaknesses.*
- someone's or something's own **individual, own, particular** *We all have our own particular strengths.*

- v+N find out or show strengths **highlight, identify, recognize** *The questionnaire will help you identify your strengths and areas where you need more help.*

- make use of strengths **build on, capitalize on, draw on** *We need to build on these strengths and ensure that the university remains at the forefront of research in the field.*

strengthen V

make something stronger, more powerful, or more effective

- adv+V **considerably, dramatically, enormously, greatly, immeasurably, immensely, significantly, substantially** *The Highways Agency has substantially strengthened its ability to detect and respond to incidents.*

- V+n relationship **bond, cooperation, link, partnership, relationship, unity** *It involves consultation, cooperation and dialogue, strengthening bonds within the community.*
- political system or economy **democracy, economy, regime** *By respecting individual and minority rights, democracy is strengthened, not weakened as many people assume.*
- belief **belief, faith** *Illness can test, but also strengthen someone's faith.*
- ability **ability, capability, capacity** *The aim is to strengthen our ability to spot problems before they become critical.*
- power **control, power** *We shall vote to strengthen the power of the Mayor and the London Assembly.*
- confidence or determination **confidence, resolve** *The obvious injustice only strengthened their resolve to fight back.*
- argument or opinion **argument, view** *She used skilfully chosen quotations from the literature to strengthen her arguments.*

stress N

worried or nervous feelings that stop you relaxing

- adj+N in a particular situation **emotional, occupational, post-traumatic, psychological, workplace, work-related** *I was doing a highly specific yoga exercise to relieve work-related stress.*
- severe **acute, enormous, excessive, extreme, severe** *He was under enormous stress at work.* • *Lifestyle and excessive stress exaggerate these symptoms.*
- unnecessary **undue, unnecessary** *You must avoid all unnecessary stress and make sure you relax.*
- lasting for a long time **chronic, prolonged** *Prolonged stress can lead to depression.*

- v+N deal with or reduce stress **alleviate, avoid, combat, cope with, counteract, deal with, ease, eliminate, handle, lessen, manage, minimize, reduce, relieve, tackle, withstand** *The exercises can help to alleviate stress and mental ill-health.*
- cause stress **cause, create, induce, place on sb, put sb under** *It is important for non-smokers to understand the enormous stress that the new rules place on smokers.*
- feel stress **be under, experience, suffer from, undergo** *Managers experience stress not only from these activities, but also from the need to adhere to budgets and production schedules.*

- and/or **anxiety, burnout, depression, exhaustion, fatigue, frustration, hassle, insomnia, overwork, strain, tension, tiredness, trauma, worry** *The touring life has its stresses and strains, but it seems to suit Joss Stone.*

stress V

emphasize an idea, fact, detail etc

- adv+V **emphatically, heavily, repeatedly, rightly, strongly** *This point was heavily stressed in the article.*

> If you want to emphasize the importance of something, you can say that it **cannot be stressed enough**: *It cannot be stressed enough how important it is to watch what your young child eats.*

- V+n need or importance **benefit, centrality, desirability, importance, necessity, need, primacy, significance, urgency, value** *The advice stresses the need to review all relevant information about the medical history of the patient.*
- ▶ fact or point **fact, idea, point** *He stressed the fact that time was limited, as the deadline was only a few weeks away.*
- ▶ role **role** *This episode stresses the key role played by managers in helping to improve staff performance.*

stressful ADJ

involving or causing great pressure or worry

- adv+ADJ very **extremely, highly, incredibly, particularly, really, so, very** *A child might develop problems following an extremely stressful event.*
- ▶ rather **fairly, a little, pretty** INFORMAL, **quite, rather, slightly, somewhat** *We managed this task with ease, even if at times it proved somewhat stressful.*
- ▶ in a particular way **emotionally, personally** *People tend to seek comfort from chocolate under emotionally stressful conditions.*
- ADJ+n situation **circumstances, conditions, environment, situation** *Many animals react badly in new and stressful environments.* ● *We all face difficult and stressful situations throughout the course of our lives.*
- ▶ work **job, occupation** *Always remember that teaching can be a very stressful job.*
- ▶ time **day, moment, period, time, week** *Yoga has helped me deal with stressful times during my life.*
- ▶ experience or process **event, experience, process** *Moving home can be one of the most stressful experiences of your life.*
- ▶ life, or way of life **life, lifestyle** *These suggestions will help you to lead a healthier, less stressful life.*

stretch V

go beyond what can be expected

- V+n what people are willing to believe **credibility, credulity** *This story stretches credibility and is widely recognized as being mythical.*
- ▶ what people can imagine or achieve **boundaries, the bounds of sth, imagination, ingenuity** *We are aiming to expand our e-learning capacity and stretch the boundaries of education and learning.*

stretch N

an area of land or water

- adj+N of a particular size **endless, large, long, narrow, short, small, vast, wide, three-mile, half-mile etc** *This is one of the world's finest and longest stretches of sand.* ● *Vast stretches of forest have already been felled.* ● *The villa backs onto a two-mile stretch of sandy beach.*

- ▶ beautiful **beautiful, magnificent, picturesque, scenic, spectacular, unspoilt** *The Costa Smeralda is one of the most beautiful stretches of the Sardinian coastline.*
- ▶ with a particular feature **barren, coastal, gentle, navigable, open, sandy, straight, tidal, uphill** *The speed limit is too low on open stretches of road where there is good visibility.*
- N+of **beach, canal, coast, coastline, highway, moorland, motorway, river, road, sand, water, waterway** *Just outside Kuantan is Teluk Cempedak, a fabulous stretch of beach near the Karyaneka Handicraft Centre.*

strict ADJ

involving or demanding care in following rules

- adv+ADJ very or too **extremely, overly, so, too, very** *Overly strict enforcement of school rules can encourage truancy.*
- ▶ rather **fairly, a little, pretty** INFORMAL, **quite, rather, reasonably, relatively, somewhat** *The Inland Revenue rules are quite strict on this issue.*
- ADJ+n when people must follow rules strictly **adherence, compliance, enforcement, supervision** *We act in accordance with a code of practice which includes strict adherence to the rules about confidentiality.*
- ▶ rules **criteria, guidelines, regulations, rules** *There are strict rules that govern the import of meat.*
- ▶ limit **deadline, limit, time limit** *Strict limits are set on the levels of lead in drinking water.*
- ▶ control **control** *The report advocated maintaining strict controls on the use of biotechnology.*

stride V

walk with energy and confidence; make progress in a confident way

- adv+V **ahead, away, boldly, briskly, confidently, forth, forward, purposefully** *Our scientists were struggling to cope with poor facilities while our international competitors were striding ahead.* ● *Th band strode purposefully on stage.*

strife N

fighting or disagreement between people or group

- adj+N between groups **civil, factional, internal, internecine, sectarian** *The clan had played a prominent role in the warfare and internecine strif that wracked the border region.*
- ▶ types of strife **domestic, economic, ethnic, financial, industrial, marital, political, racial, religious, social** *She grew up in the 1970s, a decade torn by industrial strife and inflation.*
- v+N **cause, end, foment, provoke** *A responsible government must not allow anyone to succeed in fomenting strife and disorder.*

strike V

affect someone or something seriously and suddenly

- n+V general unpleasant event **calamity, disaste tragedy** *However, tragedy struck in 2007 when her husband died.*
- ▶ specific unpleasant event **earthquake, hurricane**

plague, tornado, tsunami *The hotel was under construction when the earthquake struck.*

strike N

1 when people refuse to work as a protest

- adj+N affecting many or all workers **all-out, general, mass, nationwide** *If the union held an all-out strike of depot workers, the company would be forced to shut down in days.*
- ▶ official/ not official **official, unofficial, wildcat** *By 1981, wildcat strikes were outlawed by the new Conservative government.*
- ▶ lasting a particular length of time **indefinite, two-hour, one-day etc** *The planned 48-hour strike is part of the ongoing dispute with the airline bosses.*

- v+N organize a strike **call, organize, stage** *The National Union of Teachers is staging a strike over pay on Tuesday and Wednesday of this week.*
- ▶ take part in a strike **be called out on, be involved in, be on, come out on, go on, take part in** *They went on strike against the proposed wage cuts.*

> You can also say that people **take strike action**: *We agreed to take strike action to defend our jobs.*

- ▶ be affected by a strike **be affected by, be disrupted by, be hit by** *The whole railway network will be hit by a strike next week.*
- ▶ avoid a strike **avert** *Talks are being held to try and avert a New Year's Eve strike by Tube station workers.*
- ▶ stop a strike **call off, end** *The strike was called off and the miners returned to work.*
- ▶ defeat a strike **break, crush, defeat, end** *Government troops were called out to crush strikes, at times firing on protesters.*
- ▶ threaten a strike **threaten** *At first, their leaders talked tough, for example threatening mass strikes.*

- N+n **action, ballot, pay, vote** *A site meeting has already called for a strike ballot in protest at company plans to cut wages.*

n+of+N **series, succession, wave** *A wave of strikes had brought down the government.*

a military attack

adj+N **air, long-range, massive, military, nuclear, pre-emptive, terrorist** *Modern warfare is dependent upon long-range strikes.*

v+N **launch, make, unleash** *We knew there would be far-reaching political and economic consequences if a strike was launched on the city.*

striking ADJ

very interesting or noticeable

adv+ADJ in a particular way **architecturally, visually** *The art deco buildings make Miami an architecturally striking place.*

very **especially, immediately, particularly, quite, really, so, truly, very** *What is immediately striking about the data in Figure 1 is the huge variation in reaction times.* • *The region offers splendid landscapes which are particularly striking.*

rather **rather, somewhat** *I noticed a rather striking absence of senior members at the meeting.*

ADJ+n similarity **likeness, parallel, resemblance,**

similarity *Lesley bears a striking resemblance to the actress Catherine Zeta Jones.*
- ▶ difference **contrast, difference** *While all of the economies in the region grew quickly during the period, there were some striking differences between them.*
- ▶ feature or example **example, feature, illustration** *The original building was a striking example of library architecture of the nineteen-thirties.* • *He offered a striking illustration of the point that I was making.*
- ▶ picture **illustration, image, picture, portrait** *His collection includes striking black-and-white images of the city in the snow.*
- ▶ result, or what someone has found out **finding, result** *One of the most striking findings was the way that excessive speed contributes to serious and fatal accidents.*

string N

a group or series of things

- N+of letters, numbers, words, or symbols **characters, digits, letters, numbers, symbols, words** *In the past, email addresses were anonymous strings of numbers or letters followed by the identifier of the ISP.*
- ▶ successes or performances **awards, hits, performances, successes, victories** *The team produced a string of fantastic performances to finish in the top four of the league.*
- ▶ results **results** *Some students have received strings of A* results for their exams.*
- ▶ failures **defeats** *He has sunk to number 10 in the world rankings after a string of defeats last year.*
- ▶ crimes **convictions, murders, offences** *There has been a string of high-profile child murders over the past few years.*
- ▶ geographical features **beaches, islands, villages** *The coast is very crowded but there is a string of unspoilt villages a few miles inland.*

strive V

make a great effort to achieve something

- adv+V all the time **always, consistently, constantly, continually, continuously** *We are continually striving towards improvement in our service.*
- ▶ with great effort **desperately, earnestly, hard, manfully, tirelessly, valiantly** *She strives tirelessly for excellence and her activities always lead to improvements in patient care.*
- ▶ with no useful result **in vain, vainly** *He strove vainly to have his enemies expelled from the party.*

stroke N

an unexpected but important event or action

- adj+N **bold, master** *His master stroke was to give his rival one of the top jobs, thereby silencing his opposition to the plan.*

- N+of bad luck, fate, fortune, good fortune, good luck, luck *By a stroke of luck, they happened to have a torch with them.*
- ▶ when someone has a good idea **brilliance, genius, inspiration** *It was a stroke of genius getting her to organize the meeting – she did an excellent job.*

stroll N
a slow walk for pleasure

- adj+N **easy, gentle, leisurely, pleasant, quiet, relaxing, short** *Whether you enjoy quiet strolls **through** idyllic countryside or all-night dance music extravaganzas, you could do a lot worse than visit the Balearic Islands.*
- v+N **enjoy, go for, take** *The rest of the group enjoyed a stroll **along** the canal.*

strong ADJ
1 firmly believed, or firmly based on facts

- ADJ+n feeling or opinion **commitment, convictions, desire, feeling, opinion, sense, view** *People admire your strong sense of responsibility, and know that you fulfill your commitments.*
- ▸ case or argument **argument, case, evidence** *There is a strong case for doing nothing in this situation.*

2 of a high degree or level

- ADJ+n **emphasis, focus, interest** *A strong emphasis on customer focus led to the huge success of telephone banking.*

3 unlikely to end or be defeated

- adv+ADJ **economically, financially, mentally, physically, spiritually, technically** *The club is financially strong and we want to keep our finances sound.*
- ADJ+n position **base, foundation, position, reputation, tradition** *Considerable on-going investment would be required to maintain the company's strong market position in the future.*
- ▸ relationship **connection, link, partnership, relationship** *There are strong connections with other departments working in the same area.*

structure N
the way something is organized or arranged

- adj+N connected with a particular area or feature **administrative, bureaucratic, corporate, democratic, economic, financial, institutional, legal, organizational, political, social** *The team found that there was a clear and effective organizational structure for risk management within the service.*
- ▸ complicated/not complicated **complex, complicated, simple** *In spoken English, the sentence structure is highly complex.*
- ▸ able/not able to be changed easily **flexible, rigid** *This more flexible structure will enable us to form partnerships with other organizations.*
- ▸ with different levels **hierarchical** *He argued that the 'top-down' hierarchical structure of the company was having a negative effect on staff morale.*
- n+N **career, class, family, management, pay, staffing** *When she left, it was an opportunity for the board to introduce a new management structure.*
- v+N create a structure **create, define, determine, develop, establish, form, implement, impose, reinforce** *These institutions are guaranteed the freedom to define their own internal structure.*
- ▸ change a structure **alter, change, review, revise, simplify** *The membership structure was revised to reflect the changes that took place in 1997.*

struggle V
try hard to deal with or obtain something

- adv+V with great effort **bravely, frantically, furiously, gamely, hard, heroically, manfully, mightily, valiantly** *For some time he struggled valiantly to find a new backer.*
- ▸ with little chance of success **desperately, unsuccessfully, vainly** *For the last decade we have been desperately struggling to overcome a crisis of identity and reputation.*
- V+against **adversity, capitalism, imperialism, injustice, the odds, oppression, poverty, racism** *It's a story of a working-class hero struggling against the odds to escape from the harsh reality of his surroundings.*
- V+for **democracy, freedom, independence, justice, liberation, recognition, survival** *The people are all struggling for survival and dignity.*
- V+with **addiction, alcoholism, conscience, debt, depression, emotion, fatigue, grief, guilt, injury, loneliness, temptation** *You struggle with your own conscience because people's lives are affected by your decision.*
- V+infinitive **cope, find, keep up, overcome, survive** *Many children are struggling to cope with the demands of the new curriculum.*

struggle N
1 an attempt involving a lot of effort [usually singular]

- adj+N **constant, continual, desperate, heroic, life-and-death, uphill** *We managed in the end, but it was an uphill struggle.*
- v+N **face, have** *They face the daily struggle of finding enough food to live on.*

2 a fight, war, or disagreement

- adj+N types of struggle **armed, factional, ideological, political, proletarian, revolutionary** *In 2000, the government passed a law giving all fighters who renounced the armed struggle complete amnesty. • The text reveals the ideological struggles within these early Christian communities.*
- ▸ serious or violent **bitter, desperate, fierce, life-and-death, titanic, violent** *After a violent struggle, he was shot in the head and fatally wounded.*
- ▸ when the people taking part are not equal **unequal** *He finally had to give up the unequal struggle and handed in his resignation.*
- v+N carry on a struggle **be embroiled in, be involved in, be locked in, conduct, fight, take part in, wage** *He joined forces with Mamontov, and for two years waged an armed struggle against the Soviet Government.*
- ▸ stop a struggle **abandon, renounce** *Many trade unions have abandoned the class struggle in favour of credit cards and private insurance.*
- N+v **begin, break out, commence, continue, ensue, erupt, intensify, rage** *A desperate struggle ensued, and the Congress was split in half.*
- N+against **apartheid, bourgeoisie, capitalism, colonialism, communism, dictatorship, domination, fascism, imperialism, injustice, militarism, oppression, racism, terrorism, tsarism,**

tyranny *There he became active in the struggle against apartheid and a close friend of Nelson Mandela.*

● N+for **autonomy, democracy, dominance, domination, emancipation, equality, freedom, independence, justice, liberation, liberty, peace, self-determination, suffrage, supremacy, survival** *We have to do this, otherwise the struggle for our independence will have been in vain.*

stubborn ADJ
not willing to change; difficult to defeat or persuade

● ADJ+n **conviction, defence, determination, insistence, opposition, persistence, pride, refusal, resistance, silence, will** *He was standing in the way of peace with his stubborn refusal to come to an agreement over land.*

If someone is stubborn, you can say that they have **a stubborn streak**: *We share the same values; pride, directness, generosity and, if I'm honest, a certain stubborn streak.*

● and/or **arrogant, determined, independent, obstinate, opinionated, persistent, proud, stupid** *He is a quiet, stubborn and determined man.*

student N
someone who goes to university, college, or school

● adj+N **good bright, brilliant, good, outstanding, promising, talented** *She received an award as the most promising student of the year.*

▶ average or not good **average, poor, weak** *Weaker students will find the course challenging.*

▶ types of student **doctoral, full-time, mature, part-time, PhD, postgraduate, research, undergraduate** *I am assisting a doctoral student in international management.*

▶ v+N attract or take students **admit, attract, recruit, welcome** *We welcome many overseas students to our programmes every year.*

▶ encourage students **encourage, engage, motivated, support** *Encouraging the student in this way is very good for their motivation.*

▶ teach or assess **assess, educate, mark, supervise, teach, train** *He currently supervises seven doctoral students.*

N+v **attend, be enrolled on, be registered on/ for, do, learn, study, take, work** *About 800 students are registered for our degrees each year.* ● *Students take a language option as an integral part of their programme.*

study N
research project

adj+N **academic, clinical, empirical, historical, in-depth, qualitative, scientific** *Scientific studies have enabled scholars to draw new conclusions on technology transfer.*

n+N **evaluation, feasibility, field, follow-up, laboratory, research** *The institute completed a detailed feasibility study on the development of a commercial mediation centre in Moscow.*

v+N carry out a study **carry out, conduct,**

perform, undertake *There is a need to undertake studies to assess, identify and quantify the possible impacts of climate change on tourism.*

▶ publish a study **present, publish** *In a study published in September, the department found a wide variation in prices charged by local authorities.*

▶ ask someone to carry out a study **commission** *The government has commissioned a study of budgeting models in schools.*

● N+v **conclude, confirm, demonstrate, evaluate, find, highlight, identify, illustrate, indicate, reveal, show, suggest** *Several studies suggest that these facilities can help reduce the incidence of fatal overdoses.*

● N+into **aspect, attitude, behaviour, cause, effect, effectiveness, feasibility, future, impact, nature, possibility, potential, use, viability** *They have recently commissioned a study into the feasibility of attracting artists and other creative businesses into Thurrock.*

study V
think or learn about something

● adv+V **carefully, closely, diligently, extensively, intensely, intensively, scientifically, systematically, thoroughly, widely** *A number of historians have intensively studied specific aspects of 'traditional' customs.*

stunned ADJ
very shocked, upset, or surprised

● adv+ADJ very or completely **absolutely, completely, totally, utterly** *I was totally stunned by the response to the appeal.*

▶ rather **a little, rather, somewhat** *I'm fine now, if a little stunned by what has happened.*

● ADJ+n **amazement, disbelief, reaction, silence** *My first reaction is stunned amazement.*

stunning ADJ
very impressive or beautiful

● adv+ADJ in a particular way **aesthetically, architecturally, aurally, graphically, scenically, technically, visually** *This debut film is visually stunning and emotionally powerful.*

▶ very **absolutely, just, particularly, quite, really, simply, totally, truly** *Their new album is just stunning.* ● *Acquiring footage in a high definition video format can result in the creation of some truly stunning imagery.*

▶ rather **pretty** INFORMAL, **rather** *The views from all directions are pretty stunning.*

● ADJ+n view or place **backdrop, beach, coastline, countryside, landscape, location, panorama, scenery, sunset, surroundings, view, vista** *The story is set against the stunning scenery of the South African bush.*

▶ piece of work **architecture, cinematography, costume, display, graphics, photograph, photography, visual** *The photography is absolutely stunning and there are some amazing close-ups.*

▶ what someone does **debut, performance, victory** *The singer is renowned for his stunning live performances.*

- v+ADJ **be, look, sound** *The bride will look stunning on the day, so it is important that the groom look his best.*

stunt N
something dangerous or unusual done to entertain or impress people

- adj+N **acrobatic, aerobatic, amazing, breathtaking, clever, crazy, dangerous, daredevil, daring, outrageous, silly, spectacular, stupid** *Branson is known as much for his daredevil stunts as for his business.*
- n+N **publicity** *Part of the campaign was a colourful publicity stunt outside Parliament, involving several well-known actors.*
- v+N **arrange, attempt, design, do, organize, perform, pull, stage, try** *He performed daredevil stunts, like hanging from power lines.* • *Don't try to pull a stunt like that again!*

stupid ADJ
not intelligent or sensible

- adv+ADJ very or completely **completely, downright, extraordinarily, incredibly, monumentally, plain, remarkably, ridiculously, terminally, unbelievably, utterly** *The government's view is completely misguided, naive or just plain stupid.*
- ► rather **pretty** INFORMAL, **rather** *You'd be pretty stupid not to agree with it.*
- v+ADJ **appear, be, feel, look, seem, sound** *I stood outside the door, feeling stupid.*

stupidity N
lack of intelligence or thought

- adj+N **blatant, blind, complete, crass, gross, plain, sheer, utter** *This performance thankfully refrains from the crass stupidity of his previous movie roles.*
- n+of+N **act, height, moment** *To give up now would be the height of stupidity.*
- and/ or **arrogance, greed, ignorance, incompetence** *There is a big difference between ignorance and stupidity – one is curable.*

style N
the individual way that something is done, played etc.

- adj+N typical **characteristic, distinctive, inimitable, personal, typical, unique** *Her distinctive style is immediately recognizable in her unusual use of colour.*
- ► traditional/ not traditional **classic, contemporary, modern, traditional** *The apartment is decorated in a contemporary style.*
- ► in a particular area **architectural, conversational, literary, musical, visual, vocal** *This album covers a wide range of musical styles and genres.*
- n+N **boardroom, dance, driving, jazz, leadership, learning, management, playing, prose, singing, teaching, writing** *The course enabled him to assess his leadership style.*
- v+N **adopt, choose, develop, emulate, establish,**

evolve, favour, have *The band has developed a style that is ideally suited to formal wedding receptions and hotel dinner dances.*

stylish ADJ
attractive and showing good taste

- adv+ADJ very **effortlessly, exceptionally, extremely, incredibly, seriously, supremely, truly, wonderfully** *This extremely stylish new residence was built in 2006.*
- ► in a particular way **visually** *But the film is so tightly edited and visually stylish that the events are always absorbing.*
- ► rather **pretty** INFORMAL, **quite, rather** *Although the coat looks pretty stylish, it's light and comfortable to wear.*
- and/ or **comfortable, compact, contemporary, elegant, modern, sleek, sophisticated** *This is arguably the most elegant and stylish hotel on the French Riviera.*

subject N
an idea, problem etc that people talk about or write about

- adj+N causing difficulties or strong feelings **complex, controversial, difficult, emotive, sensitive, serious, taboo** *This is one of the definitive texts on a very complex subject.*
- ► important **important, main** *The book contains two chapters on this important subject.*
- v+N start talking about a subject **approach, bring up, broach, get onto, touch on** *Somehow, we got onto the subject of education.*
- ► change/ not change a subject **change, stick to, wander off/ from** *They seemed annoyed, so Sophie discreetly changed the subject.*
- ► stop talking about a subject **drop** *I don't want to talk about it, so can we drop the subject?*
- ► talk or write about a subject **address, cover, deal with, debate, discuss, examine, explore, pursue, research, study, tackle, talk on/ about, treat, write on/ about** *The author tackles a particularly difficult subject here.*
- N+of **complaint, consultation, controversy, conversation, criticism, debate, discussion, dispute, inquiry, investigation, ridicule, scrutiny, speculation** *The exact relationship between the media and their audiences has been the subject of debate since the media were first seriously studied.*

subjective ADJ
based on your own feelings and ideas

- adv+ADJ very **extremely, highly, very** *We could argue forever, music is highly subjective.*
- ► rather **fairly, pretty** INFORMAL, **quite, rather, somewhat** *The nature of this type of research means that, to a point, data analysis is somewhat subjective.*
- ► mostly **essentially, largely** *In the past, therefore, evaluation of the quality of a translation has been largely subjective.*
- ► completely **entirely, purely, totally, wholly** *Our response to a great work of art is often spontaneous and purely subjective.*
- ADJ+n opinion or feeling **feeling, impression,**

opinion, response, view, viewpoint *These comments are purely my subjective opinion, not those of my employer.*

▸ judgement or analysis **assessment, evaluation, interpretation, judgement, perception** *Medical images are often complex, of poor visual quality and open to subjective interpretation.*

▸ quality **element, factor, nature** *The fact that quality of life is a purely subjective factor is given scant consideration.*

▸ experience **experience** *Fatigue is a subjective experience.*

subject to PHR VB
cause something or someone to be treated in a particular way

▸ V+n examination **criticism, scrutiny, testing** *This assessment is then subjected to external scrutiny by one of our neighbouring authorities.*

▸ something unpleasant **abuse, assault, beating, cross-examination, harassment, humiliation, indignity, interrogation, intimidation, ordeal, persecution, ridicule, stress, taunt, torture, violence** *Scores of journalists remain in prison, however, and many more continue to be subjected to intimidation and violence.*

submission N
document given to someone for their decision

adj+N formal or written **formal, written** *Some reports from Canada have been included in our written submission.*

spoken **oral** *Although he made no oral sumbissions, I am grateful for his assistance.*

by more than one person or a group **joint** *The Museum put forward a joint submission with several other historic societies.*

not asked for **unsolicited** *Never send unsolicited submissions, as these will probably never reach the right person.*

first and possibly changing later **draft, first, initial, original** *PDF is the preferred format, but other formats will be accepted for initial submissions.*

last **final** *Responses from the consultation will be considered and taken into account in our final submission to the Secretary of State.*

arriving late **late** *Late submissions will not be considered.*

done electronically **electronic, online** *Electronic submissions are preferred.*

involving a lot of details **detailed** *I would be very happy to make a more detailed submission on this issue.*

new **new** *Each new submission is compared with all the existing information.*

v+N prepare a submission **draft, prepare, produce, write** *The submission was written by their legal adviser.*

send a submission to someone **make, present, send, submit** *We request that submissions are sent to us as early as possible.*

receive a submission **receive** *Your tutor will grade each module within 24 hours of receiving your submission.*

want people to send a submission **encourage, invite, welcome** *We invite submissions for the Spring newsletter.*

▸ consider or discuss a submission **assess, consider, discuss, review** *Hundreds of submissions were carefully reviewed by the exhibition jurors.*

▸ accept/not accept a submission **accept, approve, reject** *A site administrator will review and approve the submission before publishing it on the website.*

submit V
formally give something to someone in authority

● V+n a request for something **application, bid, claim, form, order, request, tender** *You must read our Terms of Use Agreement before submitting your application.*

▸ information **data, details, evidence, information, material** *You will be asked to submit further written evidence to back up your claim.*

▸ a plan or idea **idea, plan, proposal** *Since submitting the original proposal, some modifications have been made.*

▸ written work you have done **abstract, article, assignment, copy, coursework, dissertation, document, entry, essay, manuscript, paper, report, review, thesis, work** *We have submitted a paper to the minister which draws upon evidence from the study.*

▸ question, answer, or opinion **comment, question, response, view** *You can also submit your own questions for use on the site.*

▸ more than one piece of work **portfolio** *You are required to submit a portfolio which demonstrates your academic knowledge.*

▸ by more than one person **petition** *They met the President and submitted a petition signed by over 8,000 pensioners.*

▸ for discussion in a meeting **motion** *If you would like to submit a motion that will be discussed and voted on, please submit it more than 48 hours before the meeting.*

● V+for **analysis, approval, assessment, consideration, discussion, examination, inclusion, publication, review, testing** *This article was submitted for publication earlier this year.*

subscribe to PHR VB
agree with an idea

● V+n **belief, doctrine, idea, notion, principle, theory, values, view** *I have long subscribed to the belief that we are all responsible for our own continuing good health.*

subscription N
an agreement to pay to receive something regularly

● adj+N continuing for a year, month etc **annual, full, monthly, one-year, quarterly, weekly, yearly** *The journal is issued quarterly at an annual subscription of £200.*

▸ continuing for your whole life **life, lifetime** *The life subscription traditionally payable on graduation has been suspended, so new graduates now automatically join.*

▸ who the subscription is for **corporate, individual, institutional, personal, single** *Each person nominated in a corporate subscription enjoys the same borrowing rights as an individual external member.*

▸ for a short period to see if you like it **trial** *All*

delegates will receive a 3 month trial subscription to the daily Energy Price Messenger report.

▸ free **free** *Take out a free subscription **to** SiteFinder for the latest news about education resources on the web.*

▸ for receiving something using the Internet **electronic, email, Internet, online** *The full text of each article is available through online subscription to the New York Review of Books.*

● n+N **journal, magazine, membership** *The membership subscription is £50 for a family for a year.*

● v+N give money for a subscription **activate, buy, have, pay, purchase, take out** *Islanders have to pay a yearly subscription for their ambulance service.*

▸ receive a subscription **get, receive** *All members receive a free subscription **to** the magazine 'School's Out'.*

▸ say that you no longer want a subscription **cancel, terminate** *Unless you cancel your subscription, payment will be taken from your account on an annual basis.*

▸ ask for a subscription to continue for longer **renew** *The summer issue of the magazine will be dispatched only to those members who have renewed their subscription by the end of May.*

● N+n cost or payment **charge, cost, fee, payment, price, rate** *Subscription charges are non-refundable.*

▸ service **package, scheme, service** *Both channels are available as part of Sky's subscription package.*

▸ list of people having a subscription **list** *To join our free subscription list, please send us your email address.*

subside V
become weaker, less violent, or less severe

● adv+V **eventually, gradually, quickly, slowly, somewhat** *The rain gradually subsided.*

● n+V feeling **anger, excitement, fear, pain, panic, symptoms** *Symptoms of a cold usually subside within 5–7 days.*

▸ bad weather **flood, rain, storm, wind** *By the time the wind subsided, over 40 ships were wrecked.*

subsidy N
an amount paid by government to reduce the cost of something

● adj+N large **generous, heavy, high, huge, large, massive, substantial** *The aviation industry gets huge public subsidies.*

▸ small **low, small** *A new report showed that relatively small subsidies would be needed to keep the Selby coalfields open.*

▸ paid for by ordinary people through taxes **public** *Huge public subsidies are routinely devoted towards the encouragement of rail use.*

▸ direct **direct** *There are no direct subsidies available for solar installations.*

▸ indirect **hidden, indirect** *Hidden subsidies to air transport in the form of tax exemptions on fuel and tickets cost the country an estimated $9.2 billion.*

▸ type of subsidy **agricultural, domestic** *We are committed to phasing out the agricultural subsidies that keep African goods out of our markets.*

● v+N get a subsidy **attract, get, receive** *All local authority funded public libraries are eligible to receive a subsidy on official publications.*

▸ give a subsidy **give, offer, pay, provide** *Large subsidies were given to EU farmers.*

▸ increase a subsidy **increase** *EU countries increased their subsidies to fishing fleets from $80 million to $580 million between 1983 and 1990.*

▸ reduce a subsidy **cut, reduce, scrap** *Norris also promises to increase bus fares by reducing subsidies*

▸ get rid of a subsidy **eliminate, end, remove, withdraw** *It is not politically feasible to remove subsidies to conventional energy sources overnight.*

● N+to **agriculture, employers, farmers, industry, producers** *The government stopped the subsidy to the mining industry.*

substance N
important ideas, or the basic meaning of something

● N+of **argument, book, case, complaint, concern, decision, discussion, evidence, matter, policy, report, work** *The substance of the complaints was wide-ranging, and related both to the care of residents and the state of the premises.*

substantial ADJ
large in amount or degree

● ADJ+n number or amount **amount, cost, discount, growth, increase, investment, loss, majority, minority, number, period, proportion, quantity, reduction, saving, sum** *He withdrew a substantial amount of cash.*

▸ improvement or advantage **benefit, boost, gain, growth, improvement, progress, reward, support** *Even a low-level activity, such as walking, can produce substantial health benefits.*

▸ problem **damage, disadvantage, loss, risk** *The accident caused substantial damage to the car.*

▸ change **alteration, change, difference** *We applied for planning permission to make substantial alterations to the building.*

▸ experience **experience** *He has had substantial experience of working with children.*

▸ effect **effect, impact** *Cuts in the funding of higher education will have a substantial impact on students.*

▸ evidence **evidence** *There is no really substantial evidence that many herbal remedies work.*

substitute N
something used instead of something else

● adj+N good or very good **effective, excellent, good, perfect** *Bert Tucker discovered that broomsticks are not a good substitute **for** ski stick*

▸ acceptable **acceptable, adequate, reasonable, satisfactory, suitable, useful** *If fresh peas are har to find, frozen peas make a reasonable substitute.*

▸ not good **imperfect, inadequate, poor** *Even a goo translation is a poor substitute **for** the original poe text.*

▸ cheap **cheap** *Black cardamom was originally use in India as a cheap substitute **for** green cardamor pods.*

▸ very similar to the thing replaced **close, direct** *the product you order is out of stock, we will offer you a close substitute.*

addgt;

v+N **be, become, provide, use** *A variety of substitutes can be used instead of milk products.*

subtle ADJ
not obvious

adv+ADJ very extremely, very *The book contains a very subtle blend of real life with a hint of magic.* **rather fairly, quite, rather, relatively** *His humour is usually quite subtle.*

ADJ+n change or difference change, difference, distinction, improvement, shift, variation *It's a subtle distinction, but it's a very important one.* **colour, flavour, light etc aroma, blend, colour, flavour, fragrance, lighting, shade, taste, tone** *Fennel seeds have a subtle, sweet anise-like flavour.* **something written or spoken argument, clue, detail, hint, humour, message, point, question, reference** *She spends the week dropping subtle hints, which I totally fail to notice.* **method or process approach, method, process, technique, way** *Other more sophisticated and subtle marketing techniques were employed successfully by the team.* **effect effect, influence** *Even subtle nutritional effects on the fetus may have longer term adverse effects on health.* **feature or quality aspect, feature, nuance, quality** *The film is full of subtle nuances.*

and/or clever, complex, delicate, effective, powerful, profound, sophisticated *The relationship between body and mind is subtle and complex.*

subtlety N
the quality of being complicated or difficult to notice

adj+N great, infinite *The English language is capable of great subtlety, and we have many and various way of expressing what we wish to say.*

v+N have subtlety have *She has such subtlety and style, she can switch to humour from high drama in a split second.* **understand subtlety appreciate, understand** *Adult filmgoers will appreciate the subtlety of the original film.* **not have subtlety lack** *They can lack subtlety in their presentation of both characters and plot.*

and/or complexity, delicacy, intricacy, nuance, sophistication *Open questions, where people respond in their own words, enable greater expression of subtlety and complexity of opinion.*

succeed V
achieve something planned or attempted

adv+V finally eventually, finally, ultimately *Morris swam out and eventually succeeded in saving him.* **in some way but not completely almost, largely, nearly, not entirely, partially** *They only partially succeeded.* **completely completely, fully** *For e-learning to succeed fully, we need people to be independent learners.* **in a way that people admire admirably, brilliantly, spectacularly, triumphantly, well** *The show succeeds admirably in being smart, funny and entertaining.*

▶ rarely **rarely** *People who try to lose weight by dieting alone rarely succeed.*
▶ definitely **certainly** *The exhibition has certainly succeeded, and has delighted buyers and press alike.*
● V+in **aim, endeavour, goal, mission, objective, quest** *We now know that the alchemists could never have suceeded in their endeavours to create gold.*

success N
1 achievement of something you planned to do

● adj+N great **amazing, considerable, extraordinary, great, huge, incredible, remarkable, significant** *I've been growing the plant with considerable success.*
▶ to some degree but not much **limited, little, mixed, modest, partial** *Researchers have attempted with limited success in the past to empirically measure outcomes of citizenship education.*
▶ continuing **continued, continuing** *Our continued success is a result of teamwork.*
▶ happening at the beginning/end **initial, ultimate** *After initial success, such screening programmes were subject to criticisms.*
▶ economic **economic** *The author believes that using language correctly is a key to economic success.*
● v+N have or achieve success **achieve, enjoy, experience, have, meet with** *I wanted to know if you had had any success dealing with the professionals.*

If something is the main factor in helping you have success, you can use the phrase *the key to success*: *Effort is the key to success.*

▶ make sure that you have success **assure, ensure, guarantee** *Even with more resources, success is not guaranteed.*
▶ judge whether someone or something has success **assess, determine, evaluate, gauge, measure, monitor** *The model allows us to assess the success of various reform proposals.*
▶ show that someone or something has had success **demonstrate, highlight, reflect, show** *Our growth record shows our success in meeting customer requirements.*
▶ say that you have had success **claim, report** *The Government has claimed success for its Street Crime initiative.*
▶ celebrate your success **celebrate** *Today is about celebrating the success of social enterprise and looking to the future.*
▶ result in success **lead to, result in** *The enhanced facilities in the Faculty of Science have already led to significant success in terms of attracting funding for projects.*
▶ repeat previous success **emulate, match, repeat, replicate** *How can the EU replicate this success in the wider region surrounding it?*
▶ use previous success to have more success **build on, capitalize on** *This event will build on the success of previous years.*
▶ guarantee success **guarantee** *It is hoped that they can guarantee the economic success of their business.*
● N+n **criteria, factors, indicator, rate** *Our personal injury solicitors have specialist experience and a 97 per cent success rate in holiday accident claims.*

2 a plan or attempt that achieves good results

- adj+N having extremely good results **big, enormous, fantastic, great, huge, major, massive, outstanding, overwhelming, phenomenal, real, resounding, roaring, spectacular, tremendous, unqualified** *The European Summit in Cardiff was a great success and established the city as a venue for major events.*
- ▶ good and surprising **amazing, extraordinary, incredible, remarkable, runaway, unprecedented** *The festival was, however, an amazing success.*
- ▶ having moderate results **modest, partial** *Initiatives to help poorer people into work have been a modest success.*
- ▶ having success very quickly **immediate, instant, overnight, runaway** *The campaign is a runaway success exceeding all expectations.*
- ▶ unusual or interesting enough to mention **notable** *Eurofoot has been a notable success, encouraging male and female football players to compete in European competitions.*
- ▶ complete **complete, total** *The operation has been a complete success and he doesn't need to have any follow-up treatment.*
- ▶ proved by facts **proven** *The project was piloted in 2002 and was a proven success.*
- v+N be a success **prove** *Students took part in a sailing trip and this proved a great success.*
- ▶ think or say that something is a success **consider sth, hail sth, judge sth** *A similar scheme was initially unpopular but was later hailed a success.*
- ▶ repeat a success **emulate, repeat, replicate** *We are hoping to repeat the successes of 2008.*

successful ADJ
achieving the result that you want

- adv+ADJ very **enormously, extremely, highly, hugely, immensely, incredibly, massively, outstandingly, phenomenally, really, remarkably, spectacularly, tremendously, truly, very, wildly** *The event was hugely successful and positively received by the industry.*
- ▶ rather **fairly, moderately, pretty** INFORMAL**, quite, reasonably, relatively** *We believe that the current system has been quite successful in achieving this aim.*
- ▶ completely **completely, totally, wholly** *The treatment was completely successful and he will not need an operation.*
- ▶ in most ways **broadly, generally, largely, mostly** *Mayor Bloomberg has been largely successful in winning the argument that passive smoking is dangerous for workers.*
- ▶ in some ways but not in others **not completely, not entirely, partially, partly** *Some of these strategies were not entirely successful.*
- ▶ in a particular way **academically, commercially, economically, financially** *All the shows were commercially successful.*
- ▶ at the end of something **eventually, ultimately** *Nuffield waged a robust and ultimately successful lobbying campaign.*
- v+ADJ be successful **prove** *Their campaign to bring Broadband to the village has proved successful.*
- ▶ to be judged as being successful **be considered, be deemed, be judged** *The experiment was deemed successful.*

- and/ or **ambitious, enjoyable, popular, profitable, respected, rewarding, unsuccessful** *I would like to thank Bob and his team for organizing a very successful and enjoyable show.* • *All candidates (whether successful or unsuccessful) receive helpful written comments.*

succession N
a series of things of the same type

- adj+N a lot, or for a long time **constant, continuous, endless, long, perpetual, unbroken, whole** *They quickly left the show, and were followed by a long succession of presenters.* • *From 1.30pm onwards there's a whole succession of shows.*
- ▶ happening quickly **rapid** *There was a rapid succession of songs.*
- ▶ confusing **bewildering** *The story unfurls through a bewildering succession of scenes.*

succumb V
lose your ability to fight against someone or something with the result that it controls you

- adv+V finally **eventually, finally, ultimately** *Sadly, the tree may be dead, having finally succumbed to years of assault.*
- ▶ quickly **easily, quickly, rapidly, soon** *Professor Longair exuded such infectious enthusiasm that we quickly succumbed to his charm.*
- ▶ slowly **gradually, slowly** *He gradually succumbed to the disease and died peacefully in his sleep.*
- V+to an attractive quality **charm, lure, temptation** *Sometimes a student succumbs to the temptation to cheat as the only means of catching up*
- ▶ an illness or injury **attack, cancer, disease, illness, infection, injury, wound** *Many men who survived the initial amputation succumbed later to bacterial infections.*
- ▶ an influence **effect, influence, power, pressure** *Three of them succumbed to the effects of the gas.*

sudden ADJ
happening very quickly and unexpectedly

- ADJ+n increase **growth, increase, influx, leap, rise, surge** *The data would indicate that genetics is unlikely to be the prime cause of this sudden increase in diabetes cases.*
- ▶ decrease or worsening **collapse, decline, deterioration, drop, fall, loss, reduction** *If there is a sudden pressure drop, the engine can stall.*
- ▶ change **change, reversal, shift, switch, transformation** *Be prepared for sudden changes in the weather.*
- ▶ appearance/disappearance **appearance, arrival, departure, disappearance, withdrawal** *Jack jumped, startled by Thor's sudden appearance.*
- ▶ movement **jerk, jump, movement** *Avoid sudden movements which can startle an animal.*
- ▶ stop **halt, stop** *Whenever he changed gear, the car would come to a sudden halt and we would all be thrown forwards.*
- ▶ strong amount of something **burst, explosion, flash, gust, outburst, rush, spurt** *She found a sudden burst of energy, and pulled herself out of the mud.*
- ▶ death or illness **attack, death, demise, illness** *Police are investigating the sudden death of a man.*

▶ thought or feeling **desire, fear, feeling, impulse, interest, pain, realisation, shock, thought, urge** *I had a sudden urge to see her, and tell her that I loved her.*

▶ noise **noise** *A sudden noise startled him.*

▶ silence **silence** *There was a sudden silence as he came into the room.*

▶ start/end **end, onset** *People who have a stroke experience a sudden onset of disability.*

▶ period of bad weather **downpour, shower, squall, storm** *Her sweatsuit was soaked by the sudden downpour that had caught her on her morning run.*

● and/or **dramatic, inexplicable, severe, sharp, unexpected, unexplained, violent** *Public liability insurance covers sudden and unexpected incidents that take place during the insured period.*

suffer V
feel pain in body or mind

▶ adv+V very much **badly, considerably, greatly, heavily, severely, terribly** *I suffered badly from allergies when I was younger.*

▶ in a way that is not necessary **needlessly, unnecessarily** *I feel that I was punished and made to suffer unnecessarily.*

experience something very unpleasant or painful

V+n damage or an injury **damage, hardship, harm, injury, loss** *The city suffered serious damage during the air-raids.*

a problem **blow, crisis, difficulties, problem, setback** *Phoebe's wedding plans suffered a setback when the reception venue went bankrupt.*

an attack or violence **abuse, attack, persecution, violence** *20 schools a week suffer an arson attack in the UK. • Thirty-one per cent of abused women suffered physical violence during pregnancy.*

a defeat or failure **defeat, failure** *Liverpool suffered a 4-2 defeat.*

unfair treatment **disadvantage, discrimination, harassment, indignity, injustice** *Many guide dog owners continue to suffer discrimination.*

bad effects or results **consequences, effects** *We offer support to families suffering the effects of separation and divorce.*

a decrease **decline, drop, fall** *The black rhino populations in Africa have suffered dramatic declines as a result of poaching to supply the illegal trade in rhino horn.*

adv+N too much **disproportionately, unbearably, unduly** *Research has shown that ethnic minorities suffer disproportionately from overcrowding and substandard housing.*

very much **badly, considerably, dreadfully, greatly, severely, terribly** *He suffered greatly from the loss of the coffee crop.*

suffering N
mental or physical pain or problems

adj+N great **appalling, enormous, extreme, great, immense, intense, massive, real, severe, terrible, tremendous, unbearable, unimaginable, untold** *There were harrowing tales both of unbearable suffering and remarkable survival.*

unnecessary **avoidable, needless, unnecessary** *Have children vaccinated to avoid unnecessary suffering.*

▶ physical, mental etc **emotional, mental, physical, psychological** *The report examines the human and emotional suffering caused by domestic violence.*

▶ human or animal **animal, human, personal** *The terrible human suffering continues to intensify in Darfur.*

▶ affecting many people **widespread** *Sanctions have caused widespread suffering.*

▶ long-lasting **prolonged** *I am comforted to know that he was spared prolonged suffering.*

● v+N cause suffering **cause, create, impose, inflict** *The war inflicted suffering on ordinary civilians.*

▶ make suffering less severe **alleviate, ameliorate, ease, lessen, mitigate, reduce, relieve** *Palliative care focuses on controlling pain and easing suffering.*

▶ reduce suffering to the lowest level **minimize** *Everything must be done to minimise the suffering of the Iraqi people.*

▶ end suffering **eliminate, end, stop** *The cat was put to sleep to end its suffering.*

▶ experience suffering **bear, endure, experience, face, undergo** *Her immense suffering was borne with incredible strength.*

▶ make suffering worse or last for longer **aggravate, increase, prolong** *What happens if saving a life means prolonging suffering in ways that do not seem to be in a child's best interests?*

▶ prevent suffering **avoid, prevent** *This kind of research could save lives and prevent unnecessary suffering.*

▶ see someone else's suffering **witness** *Over the years we have witnessed extreme suffering being imposed on sheep by the live export trade.*

● n+of+N amount **amount, degree, level, scale** *I have been appalled by the scale of the suffering.*

▶ cause **cause** *It is man's pride and greed and inhumanity that is the cause of the suffering.*

▶ the act of making suffering less severe **alleviation, relief** *The alleviation of suffering is a basic tenet of most people's morality.*

● and/or **death, distress, evil, hardship, loss, misery, pain, poverty, sorrow** *Oxfam works to overcome poverty and suffering throughout the world.*

sufficient ADJ
as much as is needed

● adv+ADJ usually **generally, normally, usually** *Good walking boots are usually sufficient, unless the weather has been excessively wet.*

▶ quite **quite** *The kitchen equipment provided is quite sufficient for basic self catering requirements.*

▶ almost **almost, nearly** *The royalties I received were almost sufficient to pay the solicitor.*

▶ only just **barely, hardly, scarcely** *The two lanterns were scarcely sufficient to light the way.*

▶ not usually **rarely** *A diagnosis of personality disorder is rarely sufficient to explain a serious offence.*

● ADJ+n information **data, detail, evidence, information, proof** *You will be prosecuted if there is sufficient evidence against you.*

▶ knowledge, understanding, skills **experience, knowledge, skill, training, understanding** *A legally*

sworn interpreter is required for the ceremony unless both parties have a sufficient understanding of German.
▶ strength, energy etc **energy, force, power, strength** *The country has sufficient military strength to defend itself.*
▶ reason **grounds, reason** *Adultery is considered to be sufficient grounds for divorce.*
▶ interest **attention, demand, interest, support** *If there is sufficient interest, we will run an extra course.*
▶ time **time** *You should allow sufficient time to get to the airport.*

● v+ADJ be sufficient **be, prove** *A thick envelope should prove sufficient.*
▶ be considered to be sufficient **be considered, be deemed, be regarded as, think** *Notification by telephone or electronic mail shall be deemed sufficient for these meetings.*

suggest V
1 offer someone an idea or plan to consider

● adv+V seriously/not seriously **jokingly, seriously** *She laughed, and jokingly suggested that I should make her grandfather happy.* ● *You're not seriously suggesting that I give up my job are you?*
▶ in a gentle way **gently, subtly, tentatively** *Andrea gently suggested I try turning around.*
▶ in a way that is helpful or kind **helpfully, kindly** *He has very kindly suggested putting our website address on the side of his car.*
▶ in a polite way **humbly, politely, respectfully** *May I respectfully suggest that the first thing you do is check your facts?*
▶ originally **initially, originally** *Harnad initially suggested an alternative approach.*
▶ strongly **strongly** *He strongly suggested that I ask for help.*
▶ correctly **rightly** *He rightly suggests that young people need to be treated with respect.*

2 say that something is likely to exist

● adv+V strongly **certainly, clearly, strongly** *Scientific research strongly suggests that the best way for athletes to increase fitness is to train a little faster than usual.*
▶ suggesting the opposite **otherwise** *Most people think this is true, but the evidence suggests otherwise.*

● n+V a study suggests something **analysis, paper, report, research, study, survey, work** *Research suggests it is excess consumption of fat rather than sugar that is linked to people putting on weight.*
▶ information or figures suggest something **data, estimate, evidence, figures, findings, results, statistics, theory** *Crimestoppers' own figures suggest that about 11 per cent of the calls result in actionable information.*
▶ a name suggests something **name, title** *The wines of Fleurie, as their name suggests, are fresh, fragrant and floral.*
▶ experience suggests something **experience** *Experience suggests that user error will be the cause of the problem.*

suggestion N
1 an idea you offer someone to consider

● adj+N good or helpful **constructive, excellent, good, great, helpful, interesting, positive, practical, sensible, useful, valuable** *The book offers practical suggestions for dealing with depression.*
▶ not good **absurd, bizarre, ludicrous, ridiculous** *Andreas laughed at such a ridiculous suggestion.*
▶ gentle **tentative** *These tentative suggestions are put forward to generate discussion.*
▶ with clear details **concrete, detailed, specific** *These detailed suggestions need to be studied very carefully.*
▶ likely to produce big changes **radical** *The most radical suggestion of all is the building of a new airport in the Warwickshire countryside.*

● v+N make a suggestion **give, make, offer, provide, put forward, submit** *They read each other work and made helpful suggestions.*
▶ have a suggestion **have** *If you would like to be involved or have any suggestions, please contact the director.*
▶ receive a suggestion **get, receive** *We are always pleased to receive any suggestions regarding the development of the school.*
▶ want suggestions from people **appreciate, invite, welcome** *We welcome suggestions from guests about how we can improve our service.*
▶ accept someone's suggestion **accept** *This suggestion was enthusiastically accepted.*
▶ say no to someone's suggestion **dismiss, reject** *The committee rejected a suggestion that money should spent to improve the clubhouse.*
▶ consider someone's suggestion **consider, discuss** *The School Council meets once a week to discuss suggestions and ideas for improving the school.*

2 a possibility that something is true

● v+N **deny, dismiss, refute, reject** *He dismissed suggestions of impropriety.*
● N+of **discrimination, impropriety, racism, violence** *There was no suggestion of deliberate racism.*

suicide N
the action of deliberately killing yourself

● adj+N involving a particular group of people **male, teenage, young, youth** *Papyrus is a voluntary organisation committed to the prevention of young suicide.*
▶ helped by another person **assisted, physician-assisted** *At present, euthanasia and assisted suicide are illegal under British law.*
▶ tried but not succeeded **attempted** *There have be several attempted suicides at the prison.*
▶ seeming to be a suicide **apparent** *His teenage daughter's been found dead in an apparent suicide*
▶ involving many people who all kill themselves **mass** *It was 1978 when the People's Temple cult committed mass suicide in the jungles of Guyana.*

● v+N commit suicide **commit** *Every 40 seconds, someone in the world commits suicide.*
▶ try to commit suicide **attempt** *Once a person ha attempted suicide, he or she is more at risk of tryi again.*
▶ think about committing suicide **consider, contemplate** *Her anxiety was very great, and the were times when she seriously contemplated suicide*

- say you will commit suicide **threaten** *He has threatened suicide on two occasions in the past.*
- reduce or prevent suicides **prevent, reduce** *If you can directly affect that pattern of thinking, then you have a better chance of preventing suicides in people in crisis.*
- **N+n** an attempt to commit suicide **attempt, bid** *He had rescued a man from a suicide bid in the River Seine.*
- the number of people who commit suicide **rate** *American whites have a suicide rate double that of blacks, and that has long puzzled sociologists.*
- someone who has committed suicide **victim** *Depression is present in the majority of suicide victims.*
- an agreement by two or more people to commit suicide **pact** *The couple had made a suicide pact and had both taken pills.*
- the risk of someone committing suicide **risk** *Alcohol abuse has long been associated with suicide risk.*
- a message left by someone who commits suicide **note** *The bullies were named in Marie's suicide note, which prompted an investigation.*
- attack **attack, bomb, bombing, terrorism** *At least 18 people were killed this morning in suicide attacks on Iraqi police stations.*

suit V
be convenient or suitable for someone

- **adv+V admirably, exactly, perfectly** *The holiday cottage is well equipped and would admirably suit those who wish to cook at home.*

> If you want to say that something suits you well, you can also use the phrase **suit sb down to the ground**: *This way of life suited me down to the ground.*

- **V+n** a need or purpose **needs, purpose, requirements** *I searched high and low for a camera that would suit my needs.*
- a situation or event **circumstances, condition, occasion, situation** *We have menus to suit every occasion.*
- the amount of money that someone has **budget, pocket** *The development will include houses and a range of apartments from loft style to studios to suit all pockets.*
- the things that someone likes **ability, interest, lifestyle, mood, preference, style, taste** *There are a choice of courses to suit all abilities.* • *There is a good selection of bars and restaurants available to suit all tastes.*
- a method **approach, method, way** *Customise how you view your inbox messages to suit your way of working.*

suit N
a claim or complaint made in court

- **v+N** start a suit **bring, file, initiate, institute, launch** *A lawyer for Gibson said the director was considering filing a civil suit in the matter.*
- win a suit **win** *Campbell's renown was further enhanced when he won a suit against the BBC.*
- decide not to continue with a suit **drop** *The team also dropped its defamation suit.*
- say officially that a suit cannot be continued

- **dismiss, reject** *The Taiwan High Court rejects the suit brought by Lien Chan and James Soong to nullify the election results.*
- reach an agreement about a suit **settle** *Eventually, the plagiarism suit was settled out of court.*
- lose a suit **lose** *They lost the suit and are now appealing.*

suitability N
how suitable someone or something is

- **v+N** examine and decide someone or something's suitability **ascertain, assess, check, consider, determine, discuss, establish, evaluate, gauge, investigate, judge, test** *We will assess the suitability of each candidate for this type of work.*
- make sure of someone or something's suitability **confirm, ensure** *People working with children must undergo police checks to ensure their suitability for working young people.*
- show someone or something's suitability **demonstrate, indicate** *Admission to all courses is open to any applicant who demonstrates suitability for it.*

suitable ADJ
right for a particular purpose, person, or situation

- **adv+ADJ** very **eminently, entirely, extremely, highly, ideally, perfectly, quite, very** *The Great Hall is eminently suitable for weddings, banquets and other celebrations.*
- especially **especially, particularly** *The story telling session is particularly suitable for ages 5 – 11.*
- not very **hardly, not really** *Her dainty shoes were hardly suitable for a boat trip.*
- possibly **potentially** *We will interview all potentially suitable candidates.*
- in most situations **generally, normally** *The route is generally suitable for all cyclists.*
- as suitable as another **equally** *These activities are designed for use in nursery schools but are equally suitable for use at home.*
- **v+ADJ** judge something to be suitable **be considered, be deemed, be judged, think** *The movie was deemed suitable for children.*
- be suitable **prove** *No existing system proved entirely suitable for our purposes.*
- seem suitable **appear, look, seem** *There are additional motels available if none of these appear suitable.*
- make something suitable **make sth suitable** *The hall has a sprung floor, making it suitable for recreational activities such as badminton.*
- and/ or **adequate, affordable, appropriate, convenient, sufficient, unsuitable** *It is important that the claim is handled by someone with appropriate and suitable experience.* • *The books given to charities are sorted and classified as either suitable or unsuitable for sale.*

suitcase N
a large container for carrying clothes when travelling

- **v+N** put clothes into a suitcase **fill, pack** *He packed his suitcase and left for Switzerland.*
- take clothes out of a suitcase **unpack** *When we got to the hotel, I unpacked our suitcases.*

▶ carry a suitcase **carry, drag, lug** INFORMAL, **wheel** *Dan left me to lug two heavy suitcases up to our room.*

suited ADJ
right for a particular purpose or situation

● adv+ADJ very **admirably, eminently, exactly, highly, ideally, perfectly, uniquely, well** *This process is also highly suited to mass production.*

▶ not very **ill, poorly** *They lived in a mountainous area, ill suited for agriculture.*

▶ especially **especially, particularly, peculiarly, specially** *Visa cards are especially suited to these kinds of transaction.*

▶ naturally **naturally** *The surrounding environment is naturally suited to outdoor activity.*

▶ suited to two different groups or situations **equally** *This hardwearing climbing boot is equally suited to novices or experts.*

▶ badly **ill, poorly** *The report showed that the trail was poorly suited to cycling and was dangerous.*

● ADJ+to needs **need, purpose, requirements** *We have an insurance package suited to your needs.*

▶ a job **job, role, task, work** *People who have worked in retail travel agencies are very suited to this role.*

▶ a situation **circumstances, conditions, environment, situation** *Crops and other plants can be bred to be particularly suited to their environments.*

▶ a use **application, use** *The chair is suited to regular office use.*

sum N
an amount of money

● adj+N large **considerable, enormous, fantastic, generous, handsome, hefty, huge, large, massive, not inconsiderable, significant, sizeable, staggering, substantial, tidy** INFORMAL, **vast** *Some items at auction fetch huge sums of money, far beyond their original purchase price.*

▶ small **insignificant, modest, nominal, small, trifling** *You may be able to get one for free, or for a small sum.*

▶ small and not enough **derisory, measly** INFORMAL, **paltry, princely** *For all that work, I received the princely sum of £10.*

▶ not known how much **undisclosed** *They have bought the company for an undisclosed sum.*

▶ total **total** *They requested a total sum of over $2,000,000.*

▶ spent or paid every year, month etc **annual, monthly, weekly, yearly** *Some providers charge a fixed monthly sum.*

▶ showing how many numbers make up the amount etc, **five-figure, six-figure** *Swansea paid a six-figure sum for the player.*

▶ not changing **fixed** *Statutory sick pay is a fixed sum covering absence for up to 28 weeks.*

● v+N get a sum **borrow, earn, get, receive** *Some doctors have borrowed large sums to train in the UK.*

▶ spend a sum **allocate, hand over, invest, pay, spend** *For many years schools have invested large sums in ICT suites.*

▶ cost a sum **cost** *The re-organisation of local government will cost substantial sums.*

▶ collect a sum for a particular purpose **collect,**

raise *They raised the magnificent sum of £10,000 for the Air Ambulance Trust.*

▶ give a sum **award, contribute, donate, give, grant, offer** *Smaller cash sums are awarded to runners-up.*

▶ get back a sum **recover** *There is no real prospect of the sum due being recovered.*

▶ ask someone to pay a sum **charge** *The fact that large sums are charged for these treatments he felt was exploitative.*

▶ pay back a sum **refund, repay** *This sum is later repaid with interest when the house is sold.*

▶ owe a sum **owe** *Overall, the average sum owed stood at $30,763.*

summarize V
provide a summary of something

● adv+V **accurately, briefly, neatly, succinctly** *The results are difficult to summarize neatly.*

● V+n information **content, data, information, points** *When summarizing the data, always include measures of variability and the number of students.*

▶ research and research results **conclusion, findings, research, results** *Here, I will briefly summarize the findings.*

▶ discussion **argument, discussion** *The report summarizes the discussions and conclusions of a workshop held in 2002.*

▶ evidence **evidence** *He summarized the evidence for and against the prisoner.*

summary N
a short account of something

● adj+N short **basic, brief, concise, quick, short, succinct** *This article provides a very brief summary of the changes in employment law.*

▶ good **clear, excellent, good, helpful, useful** *The chapter offers a useful summary of the available evidence.*

▶ having a lot of details **complete, comprehensive, detailed, full** *If a full transcript is unreasonable, a detailed summary would be a useful alternative.*

▶ general **general, overall** *'Greenside is a very good school' was the overall summary from the school inspectors.*

▶ correct or fair **accurate, fair** *The report is a fair summary of what was a very difficult process.*

▶ written **written** *A clear written summary of the results is given.*

▶ types of summary **biographical, descriptive, factual, statistical** *Your CV is a biographical summary of your life and is written to describe details of education and achievements in chronological order.*

● v+N write a summary **compile, draft, make, prepare, produce, publish, write** *Their task is to write a summary of the information they have gathered.*

▶ give someone a summary **give, offer, present, provide** *The booklet provides a basic summary of the regulations.*

▶ print a summary **print, publish** *We publish a summary every weekend of all events scheduled for the coming week.*

● N+v **contain sth, cover sth, describe sth, give sth**

highlight sth, include sth, outline sth, provide sth, show sth, state sth *The summary highlights the key findings of a survey into use of the scheme.*

● **N+of** a study or piece of work **presentation, project, research, study, work** *Download free reports and summaries of our research.*

▶ information **argument, content, data, evidence, information, news** *The following summary of the evidence is taken from the sheriff's report.*

▶ things people have said **comments, debate, discussion, meeting, points, response, views** *A summary of the meeting is now available to download.*

▶ results **conclusion, findings, results** *A summary of findings from the report is available here.*

▶ a document **article, document, paper, proceedings, report** *You can view summaries of this article.*

▶ a situation or problem **issue** *The Tax Faculty also published a summary of the key issues.*

▶ plans or suggestions **policy, proposal, recommendation** *A more detailed summary of proposals and papers is available on the website.*

▶ changes and development **changes, development, history, progress** *This is a concise summary of the history of jewellery.*

summer N
the warm season between spring and autumn

● adj+N last, next etc **last, next, previous** *We're going to Hawaii for our holidays next summer.*

▶ at the beginning/middle/end of summer **early, high, late** *Sometimes there are hurricanes in the late summer and early autumn.*

▶ describing the weather of summer **balmy, cool, dry, fine, glorious, hot, humid, sunny, warm, wet** *The tree is used to the hot Asian summers and cannot survive exposed cold areas.*

● v+N **spend** *They spent the summer at Padre Island.*

● N+v **approach, arrive, begin, come, end** *Summer has arrived!*

● N+n period **period, season, time** *Mare de Deu is a festival to officially mark the end of the island's summer season.*

- day, night etc **afternoon, day, evening, month, morning, night** *It was a fine summer afternoon.*

You can also say *a summer's day, a summer's evening* etc: *It was a glorious hot summer's afternoon.*

- holiday **break, holiday, hols** INFORMAL**, recess, vacation** *For some children returning to school after the summer break is a big dread.*

- weather **heat, sun, sunshine, temperatures, weather** *Here are some tips on how to enjoy the summer sun safely.*

- festival **festival, fete** *A yearly summer festival is held in the third week of June, in honour of Charles Dickens.*

summit N
series of meetings between countries' leaders

adj+N **global, international, major, world** *We began to develop our proposals for this White Paper with an international summit on smoking.* ● The

European Union is holding its major summit in Gothenburg, Sweden.

● v+N **have** a summit **hold, host** *The Minister hosted a summit at her Trafalgar Square offices to discuss the issues.*

▶ go to a summit **attend** *World leaders attended the summit.*

▶ organize a summit **convene, organize** *The two-day summit was organised by Mr Milburn before Iraq returned to the political agenda.*

summon V
1 officially order someone to come somewhere

● adv+V **duly, hastily, immediately, quickly** *He immediately summoned a servant to take the crystals to the awaiting jewellers.*

● V+infinitive **answer sb/sth, appear, assist (sb), attend (sth), help (sb), meet** *She was summoned to appear before the court.*

2 produce a quality or reaction needed for a situation

● V+n **courage, energy, enthusiasm, power, strength, will** *Some days I can barely summon the enthusiasm to get dressed.*

sun N
the star that provides light and warmth to the Earth

● adj+N bright or too bright **bright, glaring, glinting, glistening, glorious, golden, radiant** *The first week of September went by with a permanently radiant sun in the sky.*

▶ hot or warm **hot, intense, strong, warm** *Don't forget to use a sunscreen if the sun is intense.*

▶ too hot **baking hot, blazing, blistering, fierce, intense, pitiless, relentless, scorching, searing, sweltering** *Years of wind, rain, and relentless sun have shaped these dunes.*

▶ weak **hazy, watery, wintry** *It was bitterly cold out there, but a wintry sun was half smiling on us.*

▶ at a particular time of day **morning, afternoon etc** *They face east or west to avoid direct sunlight from the mid-day sun.*

▶ at a particular time of year **summer, winter etc** *The autumn sun threw their shadows across the lawn beneath them.*

▶ in a particular place **equatorial, tropical, Caribbean, Tuscan etc** *With the beach just 100 metres away and lots of African sun, it's a diver's dream!*

● N+v go down **dip somewhere, disappear, set, sink, sink somewhere, slip somewhere** *Many have live music entertainment, and provide the perfect setting for a cocktail as the sun slips down.*

You can say that *the sun dips, sinks* or *slips below the horizon*: *The sun sank beneath the horizon as we landed.*

▶ come up **appear, climb somewhere, come up, rise** *They woke up before the sun rose to go and queue up to vote.*

▶ shine **beam down, glint off sth, glint on sth, shine** *The sun is shining and I'm ready to make my way through this lovely city.*

▶ shine very strongly **beat down, blaze down, stream**

somewhere *In London the sun blazed down on us as the talks went on.*

▶ burn something **burn, scorch** *The sun scorched the desert sands, looking like a disk of fire which settled on people's heads.*

sunlight N

the light from the sun

● adj+N bright **blinding, bright, brilliant, dazzling, golden** *I climbed the hill and near the top entered dazzling sunlight.*

▶ strong **direct, full, harsh, intense, strong** *Try to stay out of strong sunlight.*

▶ weak **pale, weak** *Polished instruments gleam in the pale sunlight of the May Fair.*

▶ natural **natural** *In the sea, under natural sunlight, photosynthesis increases oxygen levels.*

▶ at a particular time of day **afternoon, midday etc** *The village, dappled in the early morning sunlight, was as pretty as a picture.*

▶ at a particular time of year **summer, autumn etc** *It sounds for all the world like icicles melting in the winter sunlight.*

● N+v shine **glint, shine** *I sat by the lake for a while delighting in the sunlight glinting off the water.*

▶ shine strongly **flood somewhere, pour somewhere, stream somewhere** *When he awoke, the sunlight was streaming in through the little windows of the cottage.*

▶ shine through something **filter through sth, penetrate sth, pierce sth** *The last thing he remembered was the first ray of sunlight piercing the sky.*

▶ make something visible **illuminate sth, light sth up** *The sky seemed to crack open and a stream of sunlight illuminated us.*

▶ reflect **reflect off sth** *She looked at the sunlight reflecting off the boats in the harbour.*

sunset N

when the sun goes down and night begins

● adj+N beautiful **beautiful, fabulous INFORMAL, fantastic INFORMAL, glorious, gorgeous INFORMAL, lovely, magnificent, nice, perfect, superb, wonderful** *Some say Santorini enjoys the most beautiful sunsets in the world.*

▶ dramatic **amazing, breathtaking, dramatic, spectacular, stunning** *Go there for beautiful beaches, great scenery, stunning sunsets and the wild surf.*

▶ of a particular colour **fiery, gold, pink etc** *From the edge of the road stretch flat fields towards the horizon, glowing with a red sunset.*

▶ in a particular place **tropical, African, Caribbean etc** *Yachting is not all about gin and tonics and tropical sunsets!*

● v+N see a sunset **admire, catch, enjoy, see, view, watch, witness** *Watch the sunset over Angkor Wat, a highlight of your journey.*

▶ miss a sunset **miss** *By the time I got back I'd almost missed the sunset.*

sunshine N

light from the sun

● adj+N pleasant **beautiful, glorious, gorgeous**

INFORMAL, **lovely, pleasant** *The rest of our time was spent climbing in glorious sunshine.*

▶ bright **blazing, bright, brilliant, dazzling, golden** *It was a lovely day, with brilliant sunshine and a blue sea.*

▶ warm or hot **baking, blistering, hot, scorching, tropical, warm** *After a Friday of blistering sunshine, Saturday dawned much cooler.* ● *We were blessed with warm sunshine and a slight breeze.*

▶ continuous/not continuous **constant, continuous, endless, intermittent, perpetual, unbroken, uninterrupted, wall-to-wall INFORMAL, year-round** *Many places in England and Wales will see unbroken sunshine.*

▶ at a particular time **morning, afternoon etc, spring, summer etc** *Short-lived high pressure on the 26th and 27th gave a couple of settled days with good autumnal sunshine by day, but some widespread ground frosts overnight.*

▶ weak **hazy, watery, weak** *24 June 2003 It was a warm day with hazy sunshine on Anglesey.*

▶ a lot **abundant, plentiful** *The islands enjoy plentiful sunshine with little airborne pollution.*

● v+N enjoy sunshine **bask in, catch, enjoy** *After basking in the sunshine on the summit, we headed for home.*

▶ have a lot of sunshine **be bathed in** *Entry into this haven of natural beauty bathed in year round sunshine comes at a price.*

● v+in+N enjoy sunshine **bask, laze, sit** *I had plenty of leisure to bask in the sunshine and sketch the scene.*

▶ sparkle in the sunshine **gleam, glint, glitter, sparkle** *Even in summer, skiers weave patterns on snowfields gleaming in the sunshine.*

superficial ADJ

affecting or involving only the surface or outside of something

● adv+ADJ rather **fairly, quite, rather, relatively, somewhat** *The whole process of learning and assessment becomes somewhat superficial.*

▶ very **extremely, very** *The book itself is extremely superficial, and has little to do with investing.*

▶ only or mainly **largely, merely, purely** *Water damage during the fire proved to be largely superficial.*

● ADJ+n similarity/difference **change, difference, resemblance, similarity** *These similarities are superficial.*

▶ knowledge **knowledge, understanding** *They give the impression of knowing something about the subject but their knowledge is very superficial.*

▶ examination **analysis, approach, examination, reading, view** *Present historians reject such a superficial view of the revolt.*

▶ appearance or manner **appearance, aspect, level, nature, way** *Reports also identified an interest in sociological themes, although at a fairly superficial level.*

superior ADJ

bigger, or better

● adv+ADJ very greatly **immeasurably, incomparably, infinitely, overwhelmingly, vastly**

All three had quickly surrendered to a vastly superior enemy.

▸ greatly **decidedly, far, greatly, markedly** *At the end of Warwick Street was a decidedly superior detached property known as Warwick House.*

▸ slightly **marginally** *This site proves that a very bad human translator is marginally superior to a very good computer one.*

▸ in a particular way **genetically, intellectually, militarily, morally, numerically, nutritionally, qualitatively, spiritually, technically, technologically** *If you need to feel intellectually superior, this is your book!*

▸ by nature **inherently, innately, intrinsically** *No race is inherently superior to any other.*

● v+ADJ be **be, prove, remain** *Can you recommend any make of wheel that has proved superior for touring?*

▸ seem **appear, seem** *These machines appear far superior to the remainder.*

▸ be thought **be considered, be regarded as** *In most of Europe, the grayling is considered far superior to the brown trout.*

▸ feel **feel, feel yourself** *They were despised, sneered at, and people felt superior to them.*

superiority N
when one thing is better than another

● adj+N great **absolute, marked, overwhelming** *A handful of British pilots fought off the overwhelming superiority of the German Air force.*

▸ natural **inherent, innate, intrinsic** *Their pride in their innate superiority justified the pursuing of such goals.*

▸ achieved without effort **effortless, smug** *This consciousness of effortless superiority on the part of Englishmen was intolerable.*

▸ types of superiority **intellectual, military, moral, numerical, political, racial, technological** *Consider the implications of our belief in the political and moral superiority of liberal democracy.*

● v+N claim superiority **assert, claim, proclaim** *Mill proclaims the superiority of Anglo-American civilisation.*

▸ show superiority **demonstrate, prove, show** *Precision-guided munitions demonstrated their superiority over conventional munitions on the battlefield.*

▸ stress superiority **emphasise, stress** *They stressed their superiority as the people who brought wealth, knowledge and civilisation to the region.*

▸ suggest superiority **assume, imply** *A position of leadership does not imply spiritual superiority.*

▸ get or keep superiority **achieve, establish, gain, maintain, retain** *We are champions of our products, consistently finding ways to achieve and maintain competitive superiority.*

● n+of+N **air, altitude, assumption, claim, feeling, position, sense** *It is easy to feel a sense of superiority over our ancestors and their societies and values.*

supervision N
the process of supervising someone or something

● adj+N intense or careful **careful, close, direct, intensive, strict** *Heads should look into facilitating*

closer supervision of new employees during probation.

▸ very little **minimal** *Candidates will also work well with minimal supervision and be highly motivated.*

▸ continual or regular **constant, continual, regular** *This product should not be used by minors without constant adult supervision.*

▸ adequate/inadequate **adequate, inadequate, proper** *Adequate supervision during swimming sessions is essential.*

▸ types of supervision **clinical, judicial, medical, parental, veterinary** *Any children on the track are there under parental supervision only.*

▸ of study **doctoral, fortnightly, joint, one-to-one, PhD, tutorial** *Students are offered up to six hours of one-to-one supervision.*

● v+N carry out supervision **conduct, ensure, exercise, offer, organize, provide** *I provide supervision for three hours at a voluntary project.*

▸ need supervision **need, require** *Alternative therapies are available but require specialist supervision.*

▸ include supervision **include** *The programme includes clinical supervision for six months.*

▸ in studies **arrange, conduct, provide, receive, undertake** *Personal supervision is arranged by the student's college and forms a feature of the course.*

● and/or in general **appraisal, guidance, inspection, management, mentoring, monitoring, regulation, support** *Monitoring and supervision of performance and training to develop a multi-skilled team will be vital.*

▸ in studies **instruction, teaching, training** *All teaching and supervision take place through the medium of English.*

supplement V
add something to make something better or bigger

● adv+V usefully **usefully** *In some circumstances, personal oxygen monitors may usefully supplement fixed ones.*

▸ sometimes **occasionally, often, sometimes** *It must be noted that money was often supplemented by wages in kind.*

▸ perhaps **perhaps, possibly** *He compiles a film from footage of a past event, perhaps supplemented by interviews and commentary about it.*

● V+n food **diet, nutrients, rations** *A Government campaign called Dig For Victory encouraged people to supplement their rations by growing their own vegetables.*

▸ income **earnings, grant, income, pension, salary, wages** *To supplement their income, the Hunters started a market stall.*

▸ supply **intake, supply** *The swimming baths were used to supplement the water supply in that area.*

supply N
an amount of something that is available to be used

● v+N obtain supply **obtain, procure, secure** *Many small or remote hospitals have difficulty obtaining a reliable oxygen supply.*

▸ increase supply **boost, increase, replenish, supplement** *The rain of the last few weeks should have done much to replenish supplies.*

▶ protect supply **assure, conserve, ensure, guarantee, maintain, safeguard** *We cannot guarantee immediate supply if demand is growing.*

▶ control supply **limit, reduce, regulate, restrict** *The aim must be to improve quality and achieve better value without further restricting supply.*

▶ interrupt supply **disrupt, interrupt** *The aim is to disrupt the supply of drugs into the city in the run-up to Christmas.*

▶ provide supply again **reconnect, restore** *The Ministry's first concern was to restore supplies of safe drinking water.*

▶ cut off supply **cut (off), withhold** *We don't realize how essential water is until our supply is cut off.*

▶ be greater than supply **exceed, outstrip** *Demand far outstrips supply for this product in Europe, Africa and Asia.*

▶ need supply **need** *People with liver damage need a regular supply of sugar.*

▶ finish supply **exhaust** *Their supplies were nearly exhausted when they reached their goal.*

● adj+N in large quantities **abundant, ample, endless, inexhaustible, limitless, plentiful, uninterrupted, unlimited** *There is a very plentiful supply of fish – the reservoir is stocked with trout.*

▶ adequate **adequate, sufficient** *Over 1 billion people lack access to an adequate supply of safe water.*

▶ available **constant, continuous, fresh, ready, regular, reliable** *Your body needs a constant supply of oxygen to function.*

▶ limited or inadequate **inadequate, insufficient, limited, scarce** *A key factor is the limited supply of accommodation.*

If there is not enough of something, you can say that it is **in short supply**: *Soldiers froze to death in their sleep, diesel froze in fuel tanks and food was in very short supply.*

support V

1 approve of and help someone or something

● adv+V strongly **actively, enthusiastically, fully, overwhelmingly, partially, partly, strongly, unanimously, vigorously, wholeheartedly, widely** *We strongly support this proposal.*

▶ broadly **broadly** *A climate of innovation and entrepreneurship should be broadly supported.*

▶ openly or directly **directly, officially, openly, publicly** *I told both Ron and Rhodri to their faces that I would publicly support neither of them.*

▶ properly **effectively, properly, well** *Parents cannot properly support the school if they don't know what the rules are.*

● V+n attempt or aim **aim, campaign, effort, idea, initiative, project, proposal** *A French-language newspaper was published to support the campaign.*

▶ people **children, family, learners, parents, pupils, staff, students, teachers** *The project supported children from age seven through to eleven years old.*

▶ activity **activity, development, growth, learning, work** *Purpose built laboratories and workshops ensure good facilities to support your learning.*

● and/or **assist, develop, encourage, help, promote, sustain** *The primary function of University is to support and encourage academic learning.*

2 prove an idea, statement etc is true or correct

● adv+V strongly **clearly, strongly** *The weight of evidence strongly supports evolution, and I think it would be misleading to suggest otherwise.*

▶ generally **broadly, generally** *The responses from the questionnaires broadly support the interview data.*

● V+n idea **hypothesis, idea, notion, theory, view** *A recent survey of employers in Wales supports this view.*

▶ statement **assertion, claim, statement** *Make sure you can support your statements with evidence.*

support N

help and approval that you give to someone

● adj+N types of support **administrative, emotional, financial, moral, mutual, pastoral, practical, public, secretarial, technical, tutorial** *We continue to rely on your financial support to keep going.*

▶ strong **active, enthusiastic, full, intensive, overwhelming, strong, widespread** *A poll seemed to show strong support of the use of animals in biomedical research.*

▶ continuing **continued, continuing, ongoing** *New developments can be fragile and need ongoing support if they are to be sustained.*

▶ suitable **appropriate, effective, necessary** *Before you begin your studies, ensure that adequate support is in place.*

▶ generous **generous** *The generous support available from this new scholarship scheme will help to achieve this end.*

▶ extra **additional, extra** *Bereavement is a normal life experience and not everyone needs additional support.*

● v+N give support **express, give, lend, offer, provide, show, voice** *A friend and neighbour, John, provides some support and care.*

▶ obtain support **access, attract, gain, get, obtain, secure, win** *It is a very balanced package which I hope will gain widespread support.*

▶ have support **command, enjoy, receive** *You will work as part of the project team whilst enjoying the support and training provided by an industry leader.*

▶ need support **deserve, need, require, seek** *Some groups also require additional support to overcome specific barriers to work.*

▶ stop support **withdraw** *The support was withdrawn gradually.*

▶ say thank you for support **acknowledge, appreciate** *Lastly, we wish to acknowledge the excellent support received from our colleagues in industry.*

▶ promise support **pledge, promise** *Other internationally renowned writers have pledged their support to the campaign.*

supporter N

someone who supports a particular idea, person or group

● adj+N loyal **faithful, loyal, stalwart, staunch, steadfast** *Freda was a staunch supporter of the Guild.*

▶ enthusiastic **active, ardent, avid, committed, enthusiastic, fanatical, fervent, keen, passionate, strong** *Lesley had been a keen participant in – and ardent supporter of – the sport for some years.*

▶ for a long time **lifelong, long-standing, long-**

suffering, long-time *Many of the club's long-time supporters have been left scratching their heads about what went wrong.*

▶ generous **generous** *Ron has been a most generous supporter for many years.*

▶ vocal **outspoken, vocal, vociferous** *Marcantonio was an outspoken supporter of African American Civil Rights.*

▶ in sport or politics **Arsenal, Liverpool etc, Conservative, Labour etc, rugby, football etc** *That message was designed to enthuse reluctant Lib Dem supporters to come out and vote.* ● *He is a keen football supporter of both Scotland and Dunfermline Athletic.*

supporting ADJ
helping to prove a theory or claim

● ADJ+n **arguments, documentation, documents, evidence** *The supporting documentation does not seem to have been checked adequately.*

suppose V
believe that something is probably true [usually passive]

● adv+V commonly **commonly, generally, popularly, traditionally** *These birds are popularly supposed to come forth only at night-time, but such is by no means the case.*

▶ wrongly **erroneously, mistakenly, wrongly** *Some authors have erroneously supposed that it was built out of the ruins of Old Penrith.*

suppress V
stop opposition or protest

▶ adv+V using violence **bloodily, brutally, forcibly, ruthlessly, violently** *Each rebellion was bloodily suppressed by the central authorities.*

▶ in an organized way **systematically** *Students organizing dissent are systematically and violently suppressed.*

completely **completely, entirely** *The King destroyed the Danish fortress at York in order to completely suppress any further Viking rebellions.*

V+n violence **insurrection, mutiny, rebellion, revolt, uprising** *Cromwell ruled as a dictator, suppressing uprisings in Wales, Scotland and Ireland with great military skill.*

disagreement **dissent, movement, opposition, protest** *We should not forget how the government used the courts to suppress dissent and protest.*

stop yourself feeling or showing an emotion

V+n an emotion **anger, excitement, rage** *It is no use suppressing our anger.*

an act **giggle, groan, laughter, sigh, yawn** *Marie suppressed a yawn.*

a feeling or desire **desire, emotion, feeling, urge** *He suppressed an urge to laugh hysterically.*

suppression N
the act of stopping opposition or protest

adj+N violent **bloody, brutal, forcible, forcible, ruthless, violent** *The Strike is the story of a strike by factory workers and its brutal suppression.*

organized **complete, deliberate, prolonged,**

systematic *Those means alone would not assure the complete suppression of all opponents and potential opponents of the regime.*

● N+of of revolt **mutiny, rebellion, resistance, revolt, uprising** *The suppression of the rebellion was completed on 29 April 1916.*

▶ of disagreement **debate, dissent, opposition, protest** *Pombal's whole program was executed by ruthless suppression of all opposition.*

▶ of rights **freedom, freedom of speech, free speech, rights** *Few media organisations like supporting the suppression of freedom of speech through the courts.*

sure ADJ
certain that something is real, true, or correct

● adv+ADJ completely or very **absolutely, completely, damn** INFORMAL, **damned** INFORMAL, **doubly, perfectly, quite, really, totally** *We will not go into battle until I am absolutely sure that the time is right.*

▶ rather **almost, fairly, pretty** INFORMAL, **reasonably** *I'm pretty sure the Furlings would oblige if we asked nicely.*

▶ not **never, not, not even, not exactly, not quite, not really, not terribly, not too, not very, not yet** *I was contemplating going over to Fiona's but wasn't too sure.*

▶ not completely **not altogether, not entirely** *Having not gone to university, I'm not entirely sure what a 2–1 really means.*

● v+ADJ be or become **be, become, feel** *If you are not sure about which method to use, ask your doctor.*

▶ seem **look, seem, sound** *'I think I did suffer depression,' she says slowly, not sounding too sure.*

surface N
the top layer or outside part of something

● adj+N rough/smooth **bumpy, flat, icy, rough, slippery, smooth, uneven** *There are no steps, but the ground surface is uneven.*

▶ hard/soft **hard, soft** *Run slower and on softer surface.*

▶ shiny **metallic, polished, reflective, shiny** *A frost smoke was rising from the polished steel surface of the loch.*

▶ wet/dry **dry, greasy, wet** *Their new tyres provide excellent performance on both wet and dry surfaces.*

surge N
a sudden increase in price, value, or interest

● adj+N sudden or unexpected **sudden, unexpected, unprecedented** *This recent period has seen an unprecedented surge of new ventures.*

▶ big **big, dramatic, great, huge, large, massive, strong, tremendous** *Gambling, and especially internet betting, is seeing a massive surge of interest at the moment.*

▶ upward **upward** *Motorhome sales have witnessed a great upward surge in recent years.*

▶ happening again **further, renewed** *A further rate hike would risk prompting a renewed surge in the value of the pound.*

▶ happening at a particular time **final, initial, late, recent** *The recent surge in internet enquiries is due to availability of on-line catalogues.*

- v+N cause a surge **bring, cause, create, produce, prompt, spark, trigger** *What created this surge of interest?*
▶ experience a surge **experience, see, witness** *The 18th century experienced a massive surge in the production and consumption of goods.*
▶ expect a surge **anticipate, expect** *We anticipate a surge in demand.*
▶ report a surge **report** *Several countries reported import surges in particular products, notably dairy products and meat.*

- N+in in the economy **demand, growth, imports, investment, prices, profits, sales, spending, supply** *Demand has been rising by more than five million tonnes per year, with the biggest surge in demand occurring in China.*
▶ good things **interest, popularity** *The brand has experienced a surge in popularity amongst consumers.*
▶ bad things **complaints, crime, violence** *What's to blame for the devastating surge in violence?*
▶ quantity **claim, number** *The surge in traveller numbers has been driven by the delays at UK airports.*

surge V
increase a lot very quickly

- n+V in the economy **demand, price, profits, sales, shares** *In the last five or six years, however, prices have surged.*
▶ population **population** *London's population surged during the 19th century.*

surgery N
medical operations

- adj+N major/minor **extensive, invasive, life-saving, major, minor, radical** *Surviving major surgery against all the odds, her recovery is a remarkable one.*
▶ on a part of the body **abdominal, cardiac, eye, facial, heart, oral, orthopaedic, spinal, vascular** *Achieving good results in cardiac surgery requires team work.*
▶ emergency/planned **day, elective, emergency, planned** *In emergency surgery almost all operations were performed by registrars.*
▶ types of surgery **corrective, keyhole, reconstructive** *I need a minor operation by keyhole surgery in October.*
▶ on children **paediatric** *Paediatric surgery involves working with children and their parents.*

- v+N need surgery **necessitate, need, require** *After consulting two specialists, it was decided the Hungarian player required extensive surgery.*
▶ have surgery **have, undergo** *Last year he underwent brain surgery to remove an aneurism.*
▶ do surgery **do, perform, practise, undertake** *Learn how surgery was performed without anaesthetic.*
▶ wait for surgery **await** *Patients awaiting surgery generally experience high levels of anxiety.*
▶ delay or cancel surgery **cancel, delay, postpone** *Elective surgery is postponed until the patient is ready.*
▶ refuse surgery **refuse** *The number of patients who refused surgery was lower than predicted.*

surpass V
be better or greater than something

- adv+V greatly **easily, far, greatly, truly** *We rely on the goodwill of the people of Chesterfield and this has far surpassed all expectations.*
▶ maybe/definitely **almost, certainly, perhaps, possibly, probably** *We use the word 'perfect' to describe anything which comes up to, or perhaps surpasses, our highest existing expectations.*
▶ with time expressions **already, finally, never, now, often, soon** *The first volume came out in 1848 and it soon surpassed all his other books in popularity.*
▶ even **actually, even** *Anxiety can surpass even smoking as a risk for certain heart problems.*

- V+n aim **figure, goal, mark, target** *I far surpassed my intended goals and more.*
▶ beauty **beauty, glory** *Sicily has many ancient ruins but none surpasses the glory that is Agrigento.*
▶ expectations **expectations, sb's wildest dreams** *Th flat surpassed my expectations.*
▶ achievement **achievement, performance, record, standard** *Both are hoping to surpass their past performance in their new roles.*
▶ limit **boundary, limit** *Sanchez is a musician that surpasses the boundaries of traditional sounds.*

surplus N
an amount that is left when someone has more than necessary

- adj+N large/small **big, healthy, huge, large, massive, significant, small, substantial, vast** *Villagers borrow rice, on the condition that they return a small surplus when times are good.*
▶ types of surplus **agricultural, budget, consumer, economic, financial, fiscal, trade** *Financial surpluses are reinvested into the business.*
▶ average or sufficient **average, modest, sufficient** *Nonetheless there was a modest surplus due to a decrease in expenses.*
▶ with time expressions **annual, current, future** *We expect the current surplus to be 1 billion pounds ne year.*
▶ total or net **net, overall, total** *Last year's overall deficit has been turned into a net surplus.*

- v+N create a surplus **accrue, accumulate, achieve, generate, yield** *Increasing social differentiation within the peasantry led some to accumulate a surplus.*
▶ invest a surplus **invest, plough back, reinvest** *A surplus is reinvested in next year's festival.*
▶ predict or report a surplus **declare, forecast, project, report** *Only one authority is projecting a surplus.*
▶ get rid of a surplus **dump, export** *These producer dump their surpluses overseas at less than the cost of production.*
▶ have or keep a surplus **have, retain, run** *They ca retain any surpluses they generate.*

surprise N
1 an unusual or unexpected event

- adj+N big **big, great, huge, major, real** *A big surprise was how much free info you can pick up.*
▶ pleasant **the best, delightful, lovely** INFORMAL, **nic** INFORMAL, **pleasant, welcome, wonderful** *It is alwc a pleasant surprise to see who turns up.*

▸ unpleasant **nasty** INFORMAL**, unpleasant, unwelcome**
▸ unexpected **complete, total, unexpected** *Looking through these log books often provides some unexpected surprises.*
▸ few/many **few, many** *Log in and expect to find a wealth of high quality academic resources with a few surprises along the way!*
▸ v+N be a surprise **be, bring, come as, contain, hold, offer, produce, provide** *As usual, this year's nominees offered a few surprises.*

> If something is not a surprise you can say that it *is no surprise*, *holds no surprises* or that it *comes as no surprise*: *The final verdict was no surprise to me.*

▸ give someone a surprise **give sb, spring** *Sometimes even descriptive poems work by springing surprises.*
▸ get a surprise **get, have, receive** *Did you have any surprises?*
▸ reveal or spoil a surprise **reveal, spoil** *I don't want to be more specific or it will spoil the surprise!*
▸ N+n event **appearance, attack, decision, move, party, visit** *Inspectors make surprise visits to the facilities each year.*
▸ result **defeat, result, success, victory** *It was a surprise victory for Kingston on Saturday night in a game that even they admitted they hadn't expected to win.*
▸ person **guest, visitor, winner** *We had a lovely lunch and our surprise guest was a great finale to the day.*
▸ statement **announcement** *Debbie makes a surprise announcement.*
▸ gift **gift** *We'll make the graduate feel extra special with a surprise gift!*

> You can refer to someone or something that is not expected as a *surprise package*: *Pang Weiguo also has three wins, as does surprise package Mohsen Abulaziz of Qatar.*

the feeling you have when something unexpected happens

v+N express surprise **express, show** *Dr Jones expressed some surprise at the low number of applications received.*
hide surprise **conceal, hide** *I concealed my surprise and sat down.*
pretend surprise **feign** *After shopping in the town I feigned surprise when we turned up outside the museum.*

ırprised ADJ
periencing a reaction to something unexpected :ppening

adv+**ADJ** rather **quite, rather, somewhat** *He was rather surprised and sad at the attitude of the people and the priests.*
very **extremely, greatly, very** *He looks very surprised when the management ask him to leave.*
slightly **a little, mildly, slightly** *Something I was a little surprised at is that all the cake shops in the town sell exactly the same things.*
n a pleasant way **agreeably, pleasantly** *In Britain one assumes things will go wrong, and is pleasantly surprised if they go right.*
really **genuinely, really** *They have no expectations, so whatever happens they are genuinely surprised and grateful.*

● v+**ADJ** appear, be, feel, look, seem, sound *Many people seem genuinely surprised that there is a difference between buying and selling.*
● and/or good feeling **amazed, delighted, entertained, impressed, pleased, thrilled** *Sara said: I'm both surprised and delighted to be named 'Young Woman Engineer of the Year'.*
▸ bad feeling **concerned, disappointed, dismayed, shocked, upset** *I am really surprised and disappointed by our principal's decision to censor us.*

surprising ADJ
unusual, or unexpected

● adv+**ADJ** not **hardly, not, scarcely** *If you think about it, this is hardly surprising.*
▸ not very **not altogether, not entirely, not particularly, not really, not terribly** *Their views were very interesting, but not altogether surprising.*
▸ slightly **a little, slightly** *What was a little surprising was the general support given to the European project.*
▸ rather **rather, somewhat** *It is somewhat surprising, then, that there aren't more books on the subject.*
▸ very **especially, genuinely, very** *The plot twists are genuinely surprising and, more importantly, consistent.*
▸ continually **constantly, continually** *The choreography is wonderfullly intricate, complex and continually surprising.*

● ADJ+n fact or conclusion **conclusion, discovery, fact, finding, outcome, result, revelation** *Geneticists have recently made a surprising discovery.*
▸ feature **aspect, feature** *Although much has been altered over the last 400 years, many fascinating and surprising features still remain.*
▸ similarity/difference **difference, similarity** *The similarities are possibly more surprising than the differences.*
▸ twist **twist** *The performance reveals surprising twists and turns along the paths that each character follows.*
▸ omission **omission** *There are several surprising omissions in most existing compilations.*
▸ v+**ADJ** appear, be, find, seem, sound *I've been studying Maths at university, something some people may find surprising.*
● and/ or **disappointing, interesting, shocking, unexpected, unpredictable, unusual** *The artist finds beauty in surprising and unusual places.*

surrender V
say you are defeated and stop fighting

● adv+V willingly **easily, meekly, peacefully, voluntarily, willingly** *More than a hundred Russians surrendered willingly.*
▸ completely **completely, totally, unconditionally** *On 7th May 1945, Grand Admiral Donitz surrendered unconditionally.*
▸ formally **formally** *Japanese forces in Singapore formally surrendered.*
▸ with time expressions **eventually, finally, immediately, quickly, soon** *In the summer of 1651 he resumed the siege of Limerick, which finally surrendered after another four months.*
▸ never **never** *Even though her struggle is hopeless, she will never surrender.*

surrender N

when you officially say you are defeated

- adj+N complete or partial **complete, full, partial, total, unconditional** *It becomes a fight to the finish with no alternative except unconditional surrender.*
- ▶ with time expressions **early, eventual, final, immediate** *On 3rd February the fleet appeared off the islands and demanded immediate surrender.*
- ▶ with nationality adjectives **British, Italian etc** *In 1801 he served in the 22nd Light Dragoons helping to force the French surrender of Egypt.*
- ▶ official **formal** *He accepted the formal surrender of the German military at Luneburg Heath on May 4th 1945.*
- ▶ cowardly **abject, craven** *The good news is there was no abject surrender this time, like last week against Australia when they lost 49–0.*
- ▶ peaceful **peaceful** *Local tribal leaders were attempting to negotiate a peaceful surrender.*
- ▶ voluntary **voluntary** *The Government of Columbia expected the voluntary surrender of more than 4,000 illegal armed militants.*

- v+N agree surrender **negotiate, sign** *He had little choice but to negotiate the surrender of the garrison.*
- ▶ get surrender **demand, force, secure** *In 389 B.C. the commander of Athens anchored off the coast of Aspendos in an effort to secure its surrender.*
- ▶ accept surrender **accept** *William accepted the surrender of the Anglo-Saxon nobles at Berkhamsted Castle, north-west of London.*

surround V

be closely connected with a situation or event

- n+V discussion **controversy, debate, discourse, furore, speculation** *Many of you will be aware of some of the controversy surrounding this company.*
- ▶ publicity **hype INFORMAL, publicity** *Perhaps Oxford University have learnt their lesson from the trial and the negative publicity surrounding it.*
- ▶ mystery **mystery, myth, secrecy** *The attempt to recreate Stonehenge may provide answers to some of the mysteries surrounding it.*
- ▶ confusion **confusion, misconception, uncertainty** *These terms are surrounded by confusion, self-deception and imagination.*
- ▶ reputation **stigma** *They would aim to remove the stigma surrounding epilepsy by educating other pupils about the illness.*
- ▶ rumour **rumour, scandal** *Christopher Marlowe's life was surrounded by rumour and mystery.*
- ▶ issues **issues** *The centre ran a programme of national seminars on the issues surrounding the development and use of information and communication technology.*

surrounding ADJ

near or all around a place

- ADJ+n area **area, counties, district, islands, neighbourhood, parishes, region** *Down the hill from Struthof lies prosperous Schirmeck and its surrounding district.*
- ▶ land **countryside, farmland, forests, hills, land, mountains, valleys, woodland** *The delicate drawing of the great cathedral indicated how it dominated the surrounding countryside.*
- ▶ places **houses, streets, towns, villages** *The school is also busy – taking in children from several surrounding villages.*
- ▶ scenery **landscape, scenery** *The village lies low, but the surrounding scenery is extremely beautiful.*

surroundings N

things in the place where you are

- adj+N beautiful **attractive, beautiful, delightful, lovely, picturesque, wonderful** *This year's conference will take place in the beautiful surroundings of Exeter University.*
- ▶ peaceful **idyllic, peaceful, quiet, serene, tranquil** *It was really great to get away from the hustle of London and relax in such peaceful surroundings.*
- ▶ dramatic **magnificent, spectacular, splendid, stunning** *After the service, the reception was in the spectacular surroundings of the banqueting hall of Cardiff Castle.*
- ▶ comfortable **comfortable, cosy, intimate, pleasant** *They spent a lot of time in relatively comfortable surroundings.*
- ▶ luxurious **elegant, luxurious, opulent, plush, stylish, sumptuous** *All rooms offer extreme comfort in elegant surroundings.*
- ▶ familiar/unfamiliar **familiar, new, unfamiliar** *He took to his new surroundings straight away and has become a regular little sun worshipper.*
- ▶ close **immediate, local** *If all you want is to relax in the immediate surroundings of the hotel, there's free admission to a local leisure centre.*

- v+N experience **absorb, appreciate, enjoy, experience, explore** *There is also a restaurant available so that visitors can relax and enjoy the surroundings.*
- ▶ match **be in harmony with, be in keeping with, blend into, blend in with, complement, fit into, match, suit** *The Grand Hotel offers genuine service to match its elegant surroundings.*
- ▶ dominate **dominate** *Photos can show the way a structure dominates its surroundings.*

surveillance N

the process of carefully watching for possible criminal activity

- adj+N hidden/open **covert, intrusive, overt, undercover** *One of the most fundamental themes of the TV series is that covert surveillance is wrong.*
- ▶ continuous or close **24-hour, close, constant, continuous, round-the-clock** *Where 24-hour surveillance is necessary, Closed Circuit Television (CCTV) may be appropriate.*
- ▶ types of surveillance **arial, CCTV, electronic, routine, satellite, video** *In video surveillance, we diagnose unusual or suspicious behaviour of people moving in an outdoor scene.*

- v+N carry out surveillance **conduct, keep under place under, undertake** *Their UK Headquarters at Basingstoke was placed under twenty-four hour surveillance.*
- ▶ allow surveillance **authorize, justify** *Police had authorised surveillance on the grounds that there was good reason to suppose Barnes was dealing in heroin.*
- ▶ avoid surveillance **evade** *It will become impossib to evade surveillance from satellites and sensors.*

▶ continue or increase surveillance **enhance, increase, maintain, strengthen** *As governments become less popular, they will be tempted to increase their surveillance to suppress the opposition.*
▶ carry out surveillance **carry out, conduct, perform** *Undercover police officers conduct covert surveillance of people protesting about the Iraq war.*

survey N
a study or examination of something

● adj+N detailed/not detailed **brief, comprehensive, detailed, extensive, systematic** *The initial survey identified a number of areas worthy of detailed survey.*
▶ involving many people **international, large, large-scale, major, national, nationwide** *The data in the figure is taken from a recent national survey of elderly people.*
▶ with time expressions **annual, new, previous, quarterly, recent, regular** *A recent survey has recorded over 116 species of plants.*
▶ types of survey **initial, online, postal, preliminary** *The BMA invited doctors to take part in an online survey to gather their views on retirement.*

● v+N carry out a survey **administer, carry out, conduct, undertake** *In January, the director conducted a survey to investigate how the programme was progressing.*
▶ produce a survey **compile, design** *The survey was designed and analysed using a system called Libra, which is widely used in university libraries.*
▶ publish a survey **launch, publish, release** *A recently published survey revealed what people across the UK really think about the homeless.*
▶ pay for a survey **commission, fund, sponsor** *English Heritage has taken a strong interest in coastal archaeology, funding several surveys.*
▶ do a survey **complete, fill in, participate in, take part in** *Students complete two university-sanctioned surveys at the end of the course.*

● N+v survey shows something **conclude, confirm, demonstrate, highlight, indicate, record, report, reveal, show** *A recent survey revealed that only 15 % of Labour Party members see themselves as working class.*
▶ survey suggests something **claim, suggest** *The quality of life really is as high as the surveys claim.*
▶ survey discovers something **discover, find, identify, uncover** *The survey found that two in five patients were unaware of the dangers of mixing natural and conventional remedies.*
▶ survey asks something **ask, examine** *The survey asked the drivers about their ways of avoiding police.*
▶ survey asks someone **ask, question** *The survey questioned people about their knowledge of art.*

survival N
the fact of continuing to live or exist

adj+N for a long/short time **indefinite, long-term, prolonged, short-term** *Against Breast Cancer is a charitable organisation that funds research work into long-term survival.*
future **continued, future** *As long as this demand continues, the future survival of this species remains under threat.*
types of survival **business, national, personal,** **physical, political** *What exactly do we mean when we talk about national survival?*

● v+N cause survival **assure, determine, ensure, guarantee, promote, secure** *Building in stone did not guarantee survival of the castle.*
▶ threaten or reduce survival **endanger, reduce, threaten** *Kangaroo killing now seriously threatens the long-term survival of the target species.*
▶ extend survival **enhance, extend, improve, increase, prolong** *Matluba's chances of survival were enhanced by what her midwives and obstetrician had learned only weeks before.*
▶ affect survival **affect, influence** *The type of surgery performed did not influence survival in this group of patients.*
▶ fight for survival **battle for, compete for, fight for, struggle for** *The people are all struggling for survival and dignity.*

> You can also talk about **a battle, a fight** or **a struggle for survival**: *The loss of one of his own men and most of his supplies turned a hazardous trek into a fight for survival.*

survive V
stay alive or continue to exist

● V+adj **intact, unchanged, unscathed** *This unique little church survived intact until 1757.*
● adv+V in a very lucky or unexpected way **miraculously** *The driver of the train miraculously survived the massive explosion.*
▶ in some way **somehow** *These scrubby tussocks of vegetation somehow survive in the desert dryness.*
▶ almost not **barely, just, only just** *Jones barely survived his sickly childhood.* ● *The firm was just surviving; in no way was it thriving.*
▶ not often **rarely** *Papyrus rarely survives the ravages of the centuries.*
▶ for a long time **long** *When the company was established, few would have predicted it would survive so long.*
▶ still **still** *The Association, originating as far back as 1807, still survives.*
▶ well **successfully, well** *Foxes who become used to humans do not survive well once released back in to the wild.*
▶ in a financial way **financially** *A significant minority of GPs' practices have been struggling to survive financially.*
● V+n **attack, attempt, battle, crash, fire, journey, onslaught, ordeal, scare, war, winter** *All the plants have survived the winter, and most are flourishing.*

susceptible ADJ
easily influenced or affected by something

● adv+ADJ **especially, extremely, highly, particularly, very** *Young chicks are particularly susceptible to extremes of temperature.*
● v+ADJ **be, become, prove, remain, seem** *Older trees become susceptible to disease and wind damage.*
● ADJ+to **attack, damage, disease, erosion, flooding, illness, infection, injury, interference, virus** *The map shows land areas susceptible to flooding.*

suspect V
believe that something is true

- adv+V strongly **strongly** *I strongly suspect you've heard all this before.*
- ▶ rather **rather** *Sometimes I rather suspect I'm just being humoured by those around me.*
- ▶ for a long time **always, long** *They had long suspected that they were distantly related.*
- ▶ never **never** *Her colleagues never suspected she was a spy.*
- ▶ by a lot of people **widely** *Smoking during pregnancy is widely suspected to increase the risk.*

Usage **Suspect** is always <u>passive</u> in this combination.

suspect N
someone who may have committed a crime

- adj+N main **chief, main, prime** *The prime suspect was never brought to court.*
- ▶ possible **likely, obvious, possible, potential** *The squad gathered evidence, interviewed potential suspects, and followed various leads.*
- ▶ types of suspect **criminal, terrorist** *Three men have been arrested as terrorist suspects.*
- n+N **murder, terror, terrorism** *Two murder suspects have been released due to lack of evidence.*
- v+N arrest a suspect **apprehend, arrest, detain, hold** *A young suspect has been detained for questioning.*
- ▶ give the name of a suspect **identify** *A number of suspects for the murder were identified.*
- ▶ ask a suspect questions **interrogate, interview, question** *Should police have extra powers to question suspects for longer?*
- ▶ accuse a suspect of a crime **charge** *In the end the police never charged any suspect with the murders.*
- ▶ let a suspect leave **release** *The suspect was released on police bail.*

suspect ADJ
that cannot be trusted or believed, or that may be dangerous or illegal

- adv+ADJ very **highly, very** *The figure of $600 million is highly suspect.*
- ▶ rather **a bit** INFORMAL, **rather, slightly, somewhat** *She spoke with a slightly suspect Spanish accent.*
- ▶ in a particular way **morally, politically** *The film is incredibly violent and morally suspect.*
- ADJ+n **device, package, vehicle** *If you identify a suspect package, do not touch it.*
- v+ADJ **be, become, consider sth, seem** *If one piece of information is found to be false, the rest of the data becomes suspect.* • *Any statment from his office is considered suspect until it is proved otherwise.*

suspense N
excitement or worry felt when waiting

- adj+N too extreme to deal with **agonizing, unbearable** *The story moves slowly, which makes the suspense almost unbearable.*
- ▶ connected with the mind **psychological** *Her new thriller is a gripping tale of psychological suspense.*
- v+N create or increase suspense **build, create,** **generate, heighten, maintain** *The music helps to build suspense.*
- N+v be difficult to deal with **be killing sb** *Tell me what happened, the suspense is killing me.*
- ▶ increase **build** *As the story progresses, the suspense builds gradually.*
- v+in+N **keep sb, leave sb** *Please do not keep me in suspense any longer.*
- and/ or **drama, excitement, horror, intrigue, mystery, tension** *This book has it all: suspense, mystery and love.*

suspicion N
a feeling that someone has done something wrong, or that you do not trust them; a feeling that something bad is likely to happen

- adj+N strong **deep, grave, great, strong** *Where there is an initial strong suspicion of fraud, the case is passed to the Fraud Investigation Service.*
- ▶ reasonable **reasonable** *The police should only be searching for drugs if they have reasonable suspicion.*

You can also talk about someone having **grounds for suspicion**: *The library staff may ask to inspect any bag where they have reasonable grounds for suspicion.*

- ▶ unpleasant and difficult to get rid of **dark, lingering, nagging, sneaking, sneaky, worst** *I can't seem to shake off this nagging suspicion that there's a selfish motive behind it all.*
- ▶ growing **growing** *There is growing suspicion that the government is about to pull the plug on this grant money.*
- ▶ very little **slightest** *I went home without the slightest suspicion that it was all a lie.*
- ▶ shared by two people or groups **mutual** *It will help to remove the culture of mutual suspicion that exists between landlords and students.*
- ▶ felt by many people **widespread** *There are widespread suspicions that profiteers are diverting some of the aid.*
- v+N cause suspicion **arouse, cast, create, fuel, give rise to, increase, lead to, raise** *We argued that his absence was only going to arouse suspicion.*
- ▶ have suspicions **harbour, have** *I didn't get close enough to smell alcohol on his breath, but I have my suspicions.*
- ▶ make suspicions stronger **confirm, reinforce** *I made a few inquiries, and they confirmed my worst suspicions.*
- ▶ get rid of suspicions **allay, dispel, remove** *One should declare any potential interest in advance to allay suspicion of bias.*
- ▶ avoid suspicion **avoid** *To avoid suspicion of plagiarism, you are advised to develop good study habits from the outset.*
- ▶ express suspicion **report, voice** *Before Riley could voice his suspicions, he was found strangled to death.*
- ▶ be the object of suspicion **be under, come under, fall under** *When a business tycoon is found murdered, his wife comes under suspicion.*
- N+v be aimed at someone **fall on sb** *Doreen finds all her money has been stolen, and Lizzie is upset when suspicion falls on her first.*

▶ exist **arise, grow, remain** *Gabriela's suspicions grew but she kept quiet.*

● v+with+N **regard sb, treat sb, view sb** *Candidates who are unable to come up with any weaknesses at all are often viewed with suspicion.*

● and/or **allegation, distrust, doubt, fear, hatred, hostility, mistrust** *A climate of fear and suspicion pervades many urban areas.*

suspicious ADJ

1 believing someone has probably done something wrong, or that they cannot be trusted

● adv+ADJ very **deeply, extremely, highly, very** *He became an egalitarian, deeply suspicious of unearned privilege.*

▶ rather **a bit INFORMAL, a little, rather, slightly** *I have always been a little suspicious of people who seem overly fond of their pets.*

▶ more and more **increasingly** *Police became increasingly suspicious of the woman's story and arrested her.*

● v+ADJ **become, feel, get, grow, make sb, remain, seem** *Staff became suspicious because he was wearing a doctor's coat.* ● *No one answered – and that made me a bit suspicious.*

● ADJ+of **intentions, motives** *We are suspicious of the motives behind these statements.*

2 making you believe something is wrong, dangerous, or illegal

● adv+ADJ very **extremely, highly, very** *The decision looked highly suspicious.*

▶ slightly **a bit INFORMAL, a little, rather, slightly** *Because of the circumstances, this death has to be regarded as slightly suspicious.*

● ADJ+n **activity, behaviour, circumstances, death, fire, incident, object, package** *Police have confirmed that there are no suspicious circumstances surrounding her death.*

● v+ADJ be suspicious **be, look, seem** *If anyone looks suspicious, make a note of their car registration number.*

▶ think something is suspicious **find sth, regard sth as, treat sth as** *The fire is not being treated as suspicious.*

sustain V

1 provide conditions for something to happen or exist

● adv+V with money **economically, financially** *The welfare benefits are proving increasingly difficult to sustain financially.*

▶ successfully or for a long time **indefinitely, on a long-term basis, successfully** *These policies could not be sustained idefinitely.* ● *Plants represent a*

lifeline that is essential for successfully sustaining life on Earth.

● V+n **community, economy, employment, growth, interest, life, population, relationship** *Australia's ability to sustain economic growth is likely to be compromised.*

2 experience loss, injury, damage etc

● V+n **casualties, damage, fracture, injury, loss, wound** *One man sustained severe head injuries in the car crash.*

sustainable ADJ

using methods that do not harm the environment

● adv+ADJ really or completely **fully, genuinely, truly** *The environmental campaign group highlighted the need for more investment in genuinely sustainable energy sources.*

▶ in a way that relates to the environment **ecologically, environmentally** *Cycling is an environmentally sustainable form of transport.*

● ADJ+n **agriculture, community, development, energy, farming, fishery, forestry, lifestyle, living, production, source, tourism, transport, use** *Her work centres on promoting biodiversity and sustainable agriculture.* ● *The concept of sustainable development has brought in its wake an increased awareness of energy, environmental and ecological issues.*

sway V

1 move gently from side to side

● adv+V gently **gently, slightly** *Tall trees were swaying gently in the breeze.*

▶ one way, then the other **back and forth, from side to side** *She began to sway from side to side in time with the music.*

▶ strongly **alarmingly, violently** *When the new bridge was first opened, it swayed alarmingly and had to be closed for several months.*

2 influence or change someone's opinion

● adv+V **easily** *He has a sense of fair play and justice, but he's not easily swayed by pleas for mercy.*

● V+n what someone decides or thinks **decision, opinion, vote** *Activists have been swaying public opinion through letter-writing campaigns and publicity stunts.*

▶ people **audience, crowd, voters** *The audience was swayed by the excellence of the sales pitch that the team made.*

swear V

use deliberately offensive words

● adv+V **loudly, profusely, softly, violently** *He has been known to swear profusely on live television.*

sweat V

produce liquid on the surface of your skin

● adv+V **copiously, heavily, a lot, profusely** *I was*

trying hard to keep up, sweating profusely and gulping litres of air.

You can also say informally that someone is **sweating buckets** or is **sweating like a pig**: *It gets so hot that you end up sweating buckets just from walking around.*

sweet ADJ
tasting like sugar, or smelling pleasant

- adv+ADJ very or too **overly, sickly, too, very** *Unlike many ginger wines, it is not too sickly sweet.*
- slightly **slightly** *I enjoyed the smooth, slightly sweet, tomato and garlic sauce.*
- pleasantly **deliciously, wonderfully** *It's wonderfully sweet but there's no added sugar!*
- v+ADJ **be, find sth, smell, taste** *Many people find these wines overly sweet.* • *The peas tasted really sweet.*

swift ADJ
happening quickly or immediately

- adv+ADJ **extremely, fairly, relatively, remarkably, very** *His recovery from the injury was remarkably swift.*
- ADJ+n **action, progress, recovery, reply, resolution, response, return** *Thank you for your swift response to my email enquiry.*
- and/or **decisive, effective, efficient** *Existing laws did not enable us to take swift and effective action to deal with the problem.*

swing V
change from one emotion, condition, or idea to another

- adv+V **dramatically, violently, wildly** *He began to swing violently between elation and despair.*
- n+V **balance, fortunes, game, match, momentum, mood, pendulum, (public) opinion** *The political mood is swinging firmly towards environmental protection.* • *The pendulum is swinging back in favour of home buyers again.*

swing N
a change from one emotion, idea, or condition to another

- adj+N large and easy to notice **big, dramatic, huge, large, massive, violent** *There have been some dramatic swings in the exchange rate.*
- small **small** *A small swing either way could determine a national trend.*
- sudden **sudden, wild** *As an actor Kinski was notorious for wild mood swings.*
- percentage **2 per cent, 10 per cent etc** *The seat was won with a massive 30 per cent swing to Labour.*
- involving the whole country **national** *A national swing of 8.5 per cent from Labour to the Liberal Democrats would result in a hung parliament.*
- n+N **mood** *Too many carbohydrates cause me to experience severe mood swings.*

switch V
change from one thing to another

- adv+V quickly or easily **easily, instantly, quickly,**

simply, suddenly *The patient may suddenly switch from an animated state to total immobility.*
- smoothly **effortlessly, seamlessly** *He can switch effortlessly between ballet, tap, jazz, and even gymnastics.*
- automatically **automatically** *The cameras switch automatically from colour, for daytime use, to ultra-sensitive black-and-white for night-time surveillance.*
- one way, then the other **back and forth** *The voiceover switches back and forth from Urdu to English.*
- V+n group you support **allegiance, sides** *Choosing the King initially, the Marquis of Argyll switched his allegiance to Cromwell.*
- attention **attention, focus** *She has difficulty in switching attention from one thing to another.*
- company supplying a service **provider, supplier** *You can switch your telephone supplier in a couple of days and you don't have to change your phone number.*

switch N
something that controls the electrical supply to equipment

- v+N **flick, flip, hit, operate, press, throw, turn off, turn on** *John crossed to the control console and flicked a switch.*

syllabus N
a list of the main subjects in an educational course

- n+N course **course** *A copy of the course syllabus is attached overleaf.*
- most important or basic **core** *You follow a core geology syllabus with specialized modules in the area of your choice.*
- for an examination **exam, examination** *Although students are required to refer to plays in detail, few exam syllabuses explicitly require extended direct quotation.*
- for a particular subject **Mathematics, Biology etc** *Teachers will be given the chance to hear about new research that can be tied to the A-level History syllabus.*
- v+N design or write a syllabus **design, develop, set, write** *The syllabus is designed to provide a wide understanding of all the major world religions.*
- include and deal with all of a syllabus **cover** *The mock tests are very useful as they cover the entire syllabus of each module.*
- teach or study a syllabus **follow, teach** *It is recommended that the syllabus be followed in the order given below.*
- N+v include **cover, include** *The syllabus covers all aspects of English for business purposes.*

symbol N
a picture, thing, or person that represents something

- adj+N powerful **potent, powerful** *The most powerful symbol of social exclusion is the sight of people sleeping rough on our streets.*
- used by everyone **standard, universal** *The dove is a universal symbol of peace and innocence.*
- that can be seen **graphic, visible, visual** *A logo is*

graphic symbol that visually communicates a company, product, or service.
- ▶ old or traditional **ancient, traditional** *The Mace is the traditional symbol of authority.*
- ▶ mark used in writing **chemical, mathematical, phonetic** *It is a computer algebra package for solving problems expressed in mathematical symbols and notation.*
- ▶ religious **religious** *The government there has banned the presence of religious symbols in public buildings.*
- ▶ of a country **national** *The red dragon is the national symbol of Wales.*

- ● N+v **denote, indicate, mean, represent** *A word is simply a symbol representing something in the real world.*

symbolic ADJ
representing something important
- ● adv+ADJ very **deeply, highly, very** *The colour red is highly symbolic in China.*
- ▶ only or completely **merely, purely** *The deployment of these troops was seen as merely symbolic.*
- ▶ mainly **largely** *Such a reform, then, would probably be largely symbolic.*
- ● ADJ+n something you do **act, gesture** *A Teaching Award is a symbolic gesture designed to celebrate and reward excellence in teaching.*
- ▶ importance or meaning **importance, meaning, significance, value** *This was a victory of considerable symbolic significance.*

sympathetic ADJ
kind to and sorry for someone with a problem; showing understanding
- ● adv+ADJ very **deeply, extremely, very** *My boss was very sympathetic and helpful.*
- ▶ in general **broadly, generally** *Most newspapers were generally sympathetic to the strikers.*
- ● ADJ+n **hearing, manner, portrayal, smile, tone** *They reported that they had received a sympathetic hearing from the minister.*
- ● v+ADJ **be, feel, find sb, remain, seem** *When they admitted experiencing difficulties it was not hard to feel sympathetic.* ◆ *She may find the public more sympathetic than she expects.*

sympathy N
a kind feeling towards someone experiencing something unpleasant
- adj+N great or sincere **considerable, deep, great, heartfelt, profound, sincere** *One can only feel heartfelt sympathy for residents affected by the flood waters.*
- not much **little** *If he's guilty, then we should have very little sympathy for him.*
- of the public **public** *There was little public sympathy for him in Spain.*
- human **human** *She is incapable of human sympathy.*

- v+N feel sympathy **feel, find, have** *However, we ought to have some sympathy for the director.*
- show sympathy **express, show (sb)** *She didn't show any sympathy for the victims of the bomb.*
- give or send sympathy **extend, offer (sb), send (sb)** *I wish to extend my deepest sympathies to the bereaved families.*

> Usage *Sympathy* is usually plural in these combinations.

- ▶ get sympathy **arouse, attract, elicit, evoke, gain, get, receive, win** *News of the tragedy spread at once all over the world and evoked sympathy everywhere.*
- ▶ deserve sympathy **deserve** *They should not have been put in that position and certainly deserved sympathy.*
- ▶ lose sympathy **lose** *She was so gratuitously aggressive that she lost the sympathy of the audience.*

2 agreement with or support of a group or idea
- ● N+with **aim, argument, cause, position, view** *I suspect many of us would have sympathy with these views.*

symptom N
a sign that someone has an illness
- ● adj+N severe **distressing, serious, severe, unpleasant** *The symptoms are generally more severe in males than females.*
- ▶ not severe **mild** *Some people also experience mild respiratory symptoms at the outset.*
- ▶ common or typical **classic, common, typical** *Headaches are a classic symptom of dehydration.*
- ▶ most important **main** *Stiff and painful joints are the main symptoms.*
- ▶ physical **physical** *Users do not suffer from physical withdrawal symptoms if they stop taking the drug.*

- ● v+N make symptoms less severe **alleviate, control, deal with, ease, improve, reduce, relieve, treat** *The drug is effective in relieving the symptoms of arthritis.*
- ▶ make symptoms more severe **aggravate, exacerbate, worsen** *Asthma symptoms can be aggravated by outdoor pollution.*
- ▶ have or show symptoms **display, exhibit, experience, have, show, suffer, suffer from** *Not everyone will experience these symptoms.*
- ▶ get symptoms **develop, get** *Help is offered to people when they first start to develop the symptoms of mental illness.*
- ▶ cause symptoms **cause, produce** *A dramatic increase in blood pressure occurs, causing symptoms such as severe headache and sweating.*
- ▶ notice or recognize symptoms **notice, recognize** *Only a quarter of the people who catch this virus will notice any symptoms at all.*
- ▶ describe symptoms **describe, report** *Survival rates would be even better if more women reported their symptoms to their doctor at an earlier stage.*
- ▶ deal successfully with your symptoms **manage** *Although there is currently no cure for this disease, there are ways to manage symptoms effectively.*

- ● N+v get more/less severe **improve, persist, subside, worsen** *If your symptoms persist, please contact your surgery.*
- ▶ appear/disappear **appear, develop, disappear, occur** *After several days, the symptoms disappeared.*
- ▶ when you say what different symptoms are **include sth, vary** *Symptoms include headaches, muscle and joint pain, and sleep disruption.*

system N

1 a method of organizing or doing things

- adj+N that works well **effective, efficient, good, proven, viable** *This is a proven system of storing data, which will serve you well.*
- ▶ usual or shared **common, standard** *It is helpful to use a standard system of reporting, so that results can be compared with each other.*
- ▶ complicated/ simple **complex, complicated, elaborate, simple** *Unfortunately the English spelling system is extremely complex, and caused learners a lot of problems.*
- v+N have a system **have** *The airline now has a new fares system.*
- ▶ use or run a system **maintain, run, use** *The election will be conducted through a postal ballot using the system of the single transferable vote.*
- ▶ invent or design a system **build, create, design, develop, devise, establish, set up** *We set about designing an alternative pension system for the UK.*
- ▶ start using a new system **adopt, implement, introduce** *A fairer charging system was introduced last October.*
- ▶ make a system better **improve, reform** *We have worked to improve our booking systems and offer even more quality to all our customers.*
- ▶ change a system **change, replace** *Since they changed the system there have been delays.*
- N+v exist or work **operate, work** *Find out how the voting system works and which MP is representing your local area.*

> You can also say that a system is **in operation**: *A booking system is in operation to use this facility.*

- ▶ not work **break down, fail** *On the first day chaos reigned and the system largely broke down.*

2 a set of things working together

- v+N put a system in **install** *We have installed a new central heating system.*
- ▶ design or put together a system **build, design, develop** *I helped to build a system to handle scanning and storing of engineering drawings.*
- ▶ use a system **use** *Using a secure log-on system, patients can view their medical records quickly and easily.*
- N+v work or operate **operate, run, work** *The city's transport system works extremely well.*
- ▶ not work **break down, fail, go down** *In the middle of all this, the school heating system failed.*

systematic ADJ

done thoroughly, according to a careful plan

- ADJ+n way of doing something **approach, attempt, manner, method, way** *Mathematics is helping me to develop a more logical and systematic approach to study.*
- ▶ studying or examining something **analysis, evaluation, examination, investigation, observation, review, search, study, survey** *Officials are to undertake a systematic review of the commission's recommendations.*
- and/ or **coherent, comprehensive, consistent, disciplined, methodical, rigorous, structured** *Unless the planning is carried out in a systematic and methodical way, it will be of limited benefit.*

Tt

table N
a set of information arranged in rows and lines

- adj+N **accompanying, comparative, statistical** *In the comparative tables you can find the cost of insurance cover from a range of insurers.*

- N+v **compare, give, illustrate, indicate, list, present, provide, show, summarize** *The following table indicates that smaller schools are experiencing the most serious financial problems.* • *The table below summarizes the most frequent responses given.*

taboo ADJ
not done or talked about because it is shocking

- adv+ADJ **absolutely, socially, strictly** *Mixed bathing was strictly taboo!*

- ADJ+n **subject, topic, word** *The series deals with the taboo subject of death and bereavement.*

- v+ADJ **be, be considered, remain** *Issues that were previously taboo are now the subject of open discussion.*

tackle V
make an organized attempt to deal with a problem

- adv+V successfully **effectively, successfully** *If bullying is to be effectively tackled, it first has to be known about.*

- directly **directly, head-on** *Waste management is a very serious issue for this council and one that we are committed to tackling head-on.*

- in a serious way **seriously, systematically** *They claim to be the only party committed to seriously tackling the environmental challenges the world faces.*

- V+n problem or subject **challenge, crisis, issue, problem, question, subject, task** *We are tackling the problem of overcrowding on our commuter trains.*

- particular issue **anti-social behaviour, climate change, crime, discrimination, inequality, poverty, social exclusion** *There is a new determination to tackle global poverty.*

tact N
are taken to avoid upsetting other people

- v+N need tact **need, require** *This situation requires tact.*

- have or use tact **employ, exercise, have, show, use** *She has shown great tact and patience.*

- not have tact **lack** *The remark lacks a little tact.*

- and/or **courtesy, diplomacy, discretion, patience, sensitivity** *We deal with each application with tact and sensitivity.*

tactic N
particular method or plan for achieving something [usually plural]

- adj+N using force or threats **aggressive, brutal, bully-boy INFORMAL, bullying, heavy-handed,** **intimidatory, strong-arm** *She complained that the union had been subjected to bullying tactics.*

- secret and dishonest **devious, underhand** *He had a reputation for underhand business tactics.*

- intended to frighten or shock **scare, shock, terror** *The Speed Awareness campaign does not employ shock tactics.*

- making a process slower **delaying, stalling** *The defence lawyers have run out of delaying tactics.*

- taking attention away **diversionary** *She has been a victim of quite deliberate diversionary tactics.*

- v+N use tactics **adopt, employ, resort to, try, use** *Schools have adopted several tactics to raise awareness of the issue.*

- change tactics **change** *As spammers change their tactics, so should industry.*

- discuss tactics **discuss** *Of course we will discuss tactics before the race.*

- N+v be unsuccessful **backfire, fail** *His campaign tactics of smearing the other candidate backfired when voters turned against him.*

- be successful **pay off, succeed, work** *The tactic worked well and they won the match easily.*

tailor V
make or change something especially for a particular person [usually passive]

- adv+V for a particular person or group **individually, personally, specially, specifically** *All tuition is one-to-one, and is personally tailored to the client's needs.*

- carefully or exactly **carefully, exactly, precisely** *The rehabilitation programme is carefully tailored to meet the needs of each patient.*

- V+n **activity, advice, approach, content, course, package, product, programme, service, session, solution, training, treatment** *There are opportunities for substituting other, relevant modules so that your course is tailored to you.*

- V+to what someone needs **circumstances, interests, needs, requirements** *Workshops are tailored to the needs of each group depending upon age range and previous musical experience.*

- person or people **audience, client, customer, individual, patient** *Your lecture must be tailored to your target audience.*

take on PHR VB
accept work or responsibility

- V+n **challenge, duty, job, responsibility, role, task, work** *They returned to their office feeling energized and ready to take on new challenges.*

take out PHR VB
get something officially

- V+n **cover, injunction, insurance, loan, mortgage, policy, subscription** *Every year we find that many of our students have not taken out any travel insurance and deeply regret it.*

take over PHR VB
begin doing something that someone else was doing

- V+n job or responsibility **duty, function, job, position, responsibility, role, task** *Mr Mason became Exams Officer, taking over the role from Mr Ewing.*
- ▶ being in charge of something **command, control, leadership, management, reins, running** *She took over the running of the school last year.*

takeover N
the act of taking control of another company

- adj+N opposed by the company **hostile** *The company could become the target of a hostile takeover.*
- ▶ planned or attempted **attempted, proposed** *The proposed takeover would reduce competition among supermarkets.*
- ▶ when a smaller company takes control of a larger one **reverse** *The acquisition of the business constitutes a reverse takeover.*
- ▶ involving large companies **company, corporate** *A corporate takeover squeezed out the old management.*
- v+N **agree, announce, complete, plan, prevent, stage** *The company may well try to stage a hostile takeover.*
- N+n relating to the takeover process **approach, attempt, battle, bid, deal, offer, talks** *He has tabled a £300m takeover bid for the entire car plant.*
- ▶ company you want to buy **target** *The company is also a likely takeover target.*
- ▶ talking about a possible takeover **rumours, speculation** *Her company is currently the subject of takeover speculation.*

tale N
a story about imaginary events or people

- adj+N sad **sad, sorry, tragic** *It is a tragic tale of love and grief.*
- ▶ strange or unusual **extraordinary, strange** *Strange tales are told about this awe-inspiring mountain.*
- ▶ upsetting or frightening **chilling, dark, harrowing** *This is a chilling tale of suspense and betrayal surrounding the gruesome murders at a school.*
- ▶ funny **amusing, comic, funny, hilarious, humorous** *It is a darkly humorous tale packed full of unexpected twists and turns.*
- ▶ exciting and interesting **fascinating, gripping** *'The Probability' is a gripping tale of chance, fate, and gambling.*
- ▶ making you feel happy or sympathetic **heart-warming, touching** *The film is a heart-warming tale of adventure and hope.*
- ▶ mysterious and attractive **enchanting, magical** *This magical tale of friendship, kindness, and generosity is told using story-telling, music, and puppetry.*
- ▶ having a moral **cautionary, moral, morality** *The last section includes several moral tales and fables.*
- ▶ old or traditional **ancient, classic, folk, traditional** *She begins by retelling a traditional Japanese folk tale.*
- v+N tell a tale **recount, relate, tell** *A story-teller will recount traditional Indian tales with elephant themes.*

- ▶ invent a tale **make up, spin, weave** *The author weaves a tale that is both engrossing and horrific.*
- ▶ read or write a tale **read, write** *Carroll wrote a modern fairy tale that follows the adventures of a little girl called Alice.*
- ▶ put a tale in a particular time or place **set** *Verne sets his tale in 1885.*

talent N
a natural ability in a particular activity

- adj+N great or unusual **amazing, considerable, exceptional, extraordinary, formidable, genuine, great, immense, incredible, obvious, outstanding, prodigious, rare, real, remarkable, undoubted, unique** *Chris has an undoubted talent for choreography.*
- ▶ basic and natural **natural, raw** *You find out about local classes where you can study acting and improve your natural talent.*
- ▶ not known about **hidden** *Whatever kind of writer you want to be, we'll help you to tap into your hidden talents.*
- ▶ of a particular type **acting, artistic, comic, creative, entrepreneurial, literary, musical, sporting, vocal, writing** *When he was a young man, his family and friends encouraged him to develop his artistic talents.*
- v+N encourage someone's talent **develop, encourage, foster, nurture** *Nurturing the talents of young people is his proudest achievement.*
- ▶ recognize someone's talent **discover, recognize, spot** *Her talent was soon spotted and she made her stage debut aged 10.*
- ▶ have or show talent **demonstrate, display, have, possess, reveal, show, showcase, use** *At our school he showed talent as an actor in the drama group.*
- ▶ waste talent **squander, waste** *The programme wasted the talent of its contributors.*
- ▶ use someone's talent **harness, utilize** *We need to harness the talent of every section of society.*

talented ADJ
very good at something

- adv+ADJ very **amazingly, exceptionally, extremely, highly, hugely, immensely, incredibly, outrageously, prodigiously, supremely, wonderfully** *Their star was Zico, an exceptionally talented player, and a great goal-scorer.*
- ▶ in a particular way **academically, artistically, musically** *Recognised immediately as artistically talented, Louis was awarded a scholarship in the following year.*
- ADJ+n in the arts **actor, artist, band, composer, dancer, designer, musician, painter, performer, photographer, poet, singer, songwriter, writer** *Johansson's performance shows why she is one of the most talented young actors working today.*
- ▶ in sport **athlete, footballer, player, rider, squad, team** *Wenger has built up one of the most talented squads in English football.*

talk N
1 discussions designed to help people reach an agreement [usually plural]

- adj+N **all-party, bilateral, high-level,**

international, multilateral, multi-party *There will undoubtedly be bilateral talks between the United States and Egypt and possibly also with other states in the region.*

- n+N **climate, crisis, disarmament, emergency, merger, pay, peace, takeover, trade** *Victims of violence are seeking representation in peace talks between the government and the rebels.*

- v+N have talks **conduct, have, hold** *The largest separatist group is at last holding peace talks with the Philippine government.*
- end talks because of disagreement **break off, pull out of, walk out of, withdraw from** *The union is threatening to pull out of talks if the package isn't substantially improved.*
- begin talks **begin, initiate, open, start** *The Council said Iraq would have to re-admit U.N. inspection teams before the chief inspector would open talks on what remains to be done.*

- N+v fail **break down, collapse, fail, falter, stall** *Despite the mediators' efforts, the talks failed, and the situation in eastern Congo remained unresolved.*
- begin **begin, commence, start** *Important peace talks were commencing in Northern Ireland.*

an informal lecture about something

- adj+N interesting **entertaining, fascinating, informative, inspirational, inspiring, interesting, lively** *We then enjoyed a very interesting talk on the history of the locality.*
- short **brief, short** *On arrival at the centre, your tour guide will first hold a brief talk with the group.*

- n+N **half-time, pep, pre-concert, pre-match, pre-performance** *He regularly gives pre-performance talks on operas from Handel to Stravinsky.*
- v+N give a talk **deliver, give, present** *The weavers give special talks about their work at scheduled times throughout the day.*
- attend a talk **attend, hear** *When I was 30 I heard a talk on the theory of reincarnation.*

alk through PHR VB

iscuss something in detail

- V+n feelings or problems **concerns, difficulty, feelings, issue, problem, worries** *The doctor will be available so that you can talk through any concerns about the operation.*
- plans or ideas **aspect, idea, option, proposal, requirement, situation** *You may wish to talk through your career options with our student advisors.*

all ADJ

aving greater height than average

- adv+ADJ **exceptionally, extremely, incredibly, particularly, unusually, very** *Long climbs and falls through mountains follow, with incredibly tall cactus plants to admire.*
- and/or **gaunt, lanky, lean, narrow, skinny, slender, slim, thin** *The tall lanky Crouch climbed magnificently to score against Trinidad.*

p V

uch someone or something gently

- adv+V gently **gently, lightly, quietly** *The mixture should drop off the spoon when you lightly tap the bowl.*
- quickly or repeatedly **furiously, impatiently, rapidly, repeatedly** *Guy fished out his mobile phone and tapped furiously on the keypad.*

target N

something that you try to achieve

- adj+N difficult to achieve **ambitious, challenging, stringent, tough, unrealistic** *Again this year we have set ourselves challenging targets to improve our performance in vital areas.*
- which it is possible to achieve **achievable, realistic** *These forecasts ensure that sales targets are realistic.*

- n+N relating to finance **budget, growth, inflation, poverty, profit, recruitment, revenue, sales** *Last year, both regions exceeded their sales targets.*
- relating to the environment **biodiversity, carbon, emissions reduction, landfill, leakage, recycling, renewables** *We have been calling for tougher CO2 emissions reduction targets and more investment in renewable energy.*
- relating to how well you work **efficiency, performance, quality** *The department says it has met its efficiency targets, and improved productivity by 15 per cent.*

- v+N achieve a target **achieve, attain, hit, meet, reach** *For individuals to meet their targets, they have to collaborate.*
- do better than a target **beat, exceed, surpass** *The final figures have yet to be completed, but it looks as though we have exceeded our targets.*
- decide on a target for yourself or someone else **agree, identify, impose, propose, set** *The Bill intends to set realistic targets for Local Authorities to increase home energy conservation.*
- change a target **increase, raise, reduce, review, revise** *We need to monitor progress and revise our sales targets if necessary.*

target V

try to persuade or influence a particular group

- adv+V mainly **mainly, primarily, principally** *Most legitimate music download sites have primarily targeted the youth and pop markets.*
- particularly **actively, aggressively, carefully, deliberately, directly, exclusively, explicitly, particularly, selectively, specifically** *These are sports programmes specifically targeting teenage girls.*

tariff N

a tax on some goods, especially when they are traded between countries

- n+N **customs, export, freight, import, trade** *When import tariffs on rice were eliminated, the market was flooded with cheap US rice.*
- v+N charge a tariff **apply, charge, impose, introduce, set** *The EU was to start to charge a tariff on Latin American fruits of 230 euros a tonne.*
- reduce a tariff **cut, lower, reduce, slash** *Developing countries will have to slash their tariffs by between 10 per cent and 40 per cent, leaving their farmers exposed to cheap, subsidised imports.*

▸ stop charging a tariff **abolish, eliminate, remove** *Sadly, removing tariffs without eliminating subsidy will continue to distort world prices.*

▸ change the level of a tariff **adjust, alter, review, revise** *There are no indications that the government is intending to adjust the tariff.*

tarnish V
make people's opinion of you worse

● adv+V **badly, heavily, seriously** *Ford's image was seriously tarnished in the US over the scandal involving Firestone tires.*

● V+n **brand, credibility, image, memory, name, reputation** *The risk of war between them has tarnished the international image of both countries.*

task N
something that you have to do

● adj+N difficult or unpleasant **arduous, challenging, complex, daunting, difficult, impossible, mammoth, onerous, thankless, tough, unenviable** *This may sound like a daunting task, especially if you haven't carried out this type of work before.*

▸ usual **daily, everyday, routine** *He required prompting and supervision even when performing routine tasks.*

▸ easy **easy, simple, straighforward, trivial** *At first, it looked like a straightforward task, but we soon ran into problems.*

▸ boring and requiring no skill **low-level, menial, mundane, repetitive, tedious** *They have used robots to automate most of the mundane tasks.*

● v+N do a task **approach, handle, perform, tackle, undertake** *The animals can be trained to perform simple tasks.*

▸ finish a task **accomplish, complete, execute, finish, fulfil** *Soldiers are trained to accomplish difficult tasks under dangerous circumstances.*

▸ give someone a task **allocate, assign, delegate, entrust, set** *He has proved to be a fine organiser and he successfully delegates tasks to others.*

taste N
the feeling of liking a particular type of thing

● v+N start to like something **acquire, cultivate, get** *Having acquired a taste for sushi in my home town, I wanted to try the real thing in Tokyo.*

▸ get something that you like **gratify, indulge, satisfy** *He finally had enough money to indulge his taste for expensive clothes.*

▸ have the same taste as someone else **share** *They soon realized that they shared similar tastes in classical music.*

tasty ADJ
tasty food or drink has a nice flavour

● adv+ADJ **amazingly, deliciously, extremely, incredibly, particularly, really, seriously, so** INFORMAL **truly, very, wonderfully** *Mild beers in good condition are deliciously tasty and come in a host of varieties.*

● and/ or **fresh, healthy, inexpensive, nutritious** *Soups like this are tasty, nutritious and easy to cook.*

tax N
money paid to the government

● adj+N considered to be unfair **regressive, unfair** *Petrol tax is a regressive tax.*

▸ considered to be fair **fair, progressive** *This would be a far more progressive tax than the existing flat-rate per household.*

▸ high/ low **high, low** *Their citizens pay some of the highest taxes in Europe.*

▸ with a single rate, rather than several rates **flat** *They replaced graduated income tax with a flat tax of 25 per cent.*

● n+N **business, capital gains, carbon, corporation, fuel, income, inheritance, land, property, road, tobacco** *The protests have led to increases in fuel tax being abandoned.*

● v+N charge a tax **apply, charge, impose, introduce, levy** *Honduras had joined other banana-exporting nations in an agreement to levy an export tax on that fruit.*

▸ pay a tax **pay** *It seems I didn't pay any tax on these bonuses.*

▸ take tax directly from someone's pay **deduct** *This rule applies to income tax deducted at source from gross income.*

▸ avoid paying tax **avoid, defer, evade** *This enables the seller of the property to evade tax, by artificially reducing the declared price of the property.*

▸ stop charging a tax **abolish, scrap** *We also propose to scrap council tax and replace it with a local income tax.*

taxable ADJ
on which tax must be paid

● ADJ+n **benefit, dividend, earnings, expense, income, pay, payment, profit, salary, turnover** *The total amount you pay into your pension cannot go over 15 per cent of your taxable pay.*

taxation N
the system that the government uses for collecting tax

● adj+N considered to be fair **fair, progressive, redistributive** *There were claims the party would restore the welfare state by introducing progressive taxation.*

▸ considered to be unfair **excessive, heavy, oppressive, penal, punitive, regressive, unfair, unjust** *Local taxation is too regressive and bears too heavily on those on low incomes.*

▸ charged directly on what you earn/indirectly on what you spend **direct, indirect** *Under this administration, direct taxation has been reduced, b[ut] taxes on goods have risen.*

● v+N change the taxation system **modernize, reform, simplify** *Their Election Manifesto promised both to reduce and reform taxation.*

▸ stop charging tax **abolish, eliminate** *While virtually eliminating taxation for millionaires, the Bush administration allowed the collapse of the social infrastructure.*

▸ increase the amount of tax charged **double, increase** *He supported green taxes only where they did not increase taxation overall.*

collect money from people in tax **collect, raise** *The Scottish Parliament does not raise its own taxation, but its legitimacy is not questioned.*

N+n agreement, law, legislation, measure, policy, regime, rule, system, treaty *The current taxation regime should continue to encourage enterprise and investment.*

axi N
car taking passengers who pay the driver

v+N take a taxi catch, get, grab INFORMAL**, jump in, take** *Get the train to Bourg St Maurice, then grab a taxi.*

book a taxi **arrange, book, order** *We can arrange a taxi to collect you from the airport.*

shout or wave to a taxi driver **flag down, hail** *Jane hails the first taxi that comes along.*

aching N
e job or work of a teacher

adj+N good effective, excellent, good, high-quality, outstanding, successful *The school provides high-quality teaching in music, art, and other creative subjects.*

using new methods **creative, innovative, modern** *Our university delivers innovative teaching and a student experience of the highest quality.*

types of teaching **face-to-face, one-to-one, research-led, text-based, web-based, whole-class** *All full-time staff are active in research and research-led teaching.*

n+N type of class, classroom, postgraduate, small-group, undergraduate, university *We use a Virtual Learning Environment to support classroom teaching.*

subjects **history, language, literacy, mathematics, music, numeracy, science** *For children from disadvantaged backgrounds, there is not enough access to music teaching.*

v+N improve the quality of teaching complement, enhance, enrich, improve, supplement *The use of ICT to enhance teaching and learning varies significantly from school to school.*

provide students with education **deliver, provide** *The mission statement of the University is to deliver teaching and research to world-class standards.*

d+n methods and materials aid, materials, method, methodology, practice, resources, strategy, style, tool *The teaching strategy we use is based firmly on interaction between the teacher and students.*

people **assistant, position, post, profession, staff** *He went into the teaching profession in 1947.*

am N
oup of people who work together

dj+N skilled crack INFORMAL**, experienced, expert, killed, talented** *A crack team of specially-trained explosives experts managed to prevent a potential disaster.*

ard-working **dedicated, enthusiastic, hard-working, professional** *We have a dedicated team of committed volunteers to help us.*

+N campaign, care, design, editorial, editorial,

inspection, management, marketing, nursing, production, project, rescue, research, sales, specialist *You will receive expert advice from a knowledgeable and experienced sales team.*

- **v+N become a member of a team join** *You will join a capable management team, and touch on all aspects of the business.*
- ▶ be the leader of a team **head, lead, manage, run** *The American businesswoman was a controversial choice to head the team when London initially decided to bid for the games.*
- ▶ develop a team **assemble, build, develop, establish, put together** *Our plan was to put together a team of top reporters, and start a news website.*

teamwork N
work done together with others

- adj+N involving people from different groups **collaborative, cross-professional, interdisciplinary, multidisciplinary** *Section 3 presents the factors which facilitate multidisciplinary teamwork.*
- ▶ good **close, effective, excellent, fantastic, good, great, outstanding, productive, real, strong, successful, superb** *The size and complexity of IT systems means that strong teamwork and carefully planned management are now essential.*
- v+N **build, develop, encourage, enhance, foster, improve, promote** *You'll enjoy a dynamic working environment that fosters teamwork.*
- and/or **camaraderie, collaboration, communication, co-operation, co-ordination** *The courses involve participants working on different skills, such as communication, teamwork and making decisions.*

tear N
a drop of liquid that comes from your eye when you cry [usually plural]

- v+N try not to cry or show that you are crying **blink back, choke back, control, fight back, hide, restrain, swallow** *I was blinking back tears as I lifted the phone.*
- ▶ cry **cry, shed, weep** *Many tears were shed as the old friends parted, in many cases never to see each other again.*
- N+v **drip, fall, flow, pour, roll, run, stream, trickle, well up** *I could feel tears welling up in my eyes.*
- N+of **agony, anger, anguish, compassion, despair, emotion, frustration, gratitude, grief, happiness, joy, laughter, mirth, pity, rage, regret, remorse, repentance, sadness, shame, sorrow, sympathy** *His whole body shook as tears of mirth poured down his cheeks.*

tearful ADJ
feeling, showing, or involving sadness

- ADJ+n involving people crying **departure, farewell, goodbye, moment, parting, reunion, scene, speech** *Tina says a tearful farewell to Darlene and Julie.*
- ▶ showing evidence of tears **eye, face** *With tearful eyes we watched them leave.*

tease v

have fun embarrassing or annoying someone

- adv+V in a cruel way **cruelly, mercilessly** *He can speak barely a word of English and is mercilessly teased by his fellow pupils.*
- ▶ in a friendly way **gently** *The other girls in the bridal shop gently tease her.*
- ▶ all the time **always, constantly, continually** *Her friends were constantly teasing her about her new boyfriend.*

technical ADJ

relating to, having, or involving special skill or knowledge

- adv+ADJ very **extremely, highly, really** INFORMAL, **very** *The successful candidate will enjoy the challenges of highly technical and advanced medical procedures.*
- ▶ only **essentially, merely, narrowly, purely, strictly** *Even when dealing with strictly technical areas, the text seems to have been lifted wholesale from marketing brochures.*
- ▶ rather **fairly, moderately, quite, rather, relatively, somewhat** *This is a moderately technical but well written book which analyses all sorts of practical and theoretical problems.*
- ADJ+n skill or knowledge **ability, capability, competence, excellence, experience, expertise, know-how, knowledge** *The software will be familiar to users of Microsoft Office applications and requires no technical expertise.*
- ▶ help or advice **advice, assistance, guidance, support** *We provide technical business guidance, with solutions that are cost-effective and tailored to your special needs.*
- ▶ problem or challenge **challenge, difficulty, hitch, issue, problem, question** *As a result of technical problems with our IT system, the whole project was delayed.*
- ▶ vocabulary **jargon, language, term** *The word 'nuisance' is used here in its technical, legal sense.*
- ▶ people **advisor, consultant, department, director, expert, manager, officer, specialist, staff, team** *Please contact our technical department if you have any problems installing the software.*
- v+ADJ **be, become, get, sound** *Give players clear advice – they don't need a coach getting too technical.*

technique N

a method of doing something using special skill

- adj+N good or effective **appropriate, effective, efficient, good, powerful, proven, sound** *To learn more about their customers, they use proven marketing techniques such as questionnaires and interviews.*
- ▶ modern or advanced **advanced, alternative, experimental, innovative, modern, new, novel, state-of-the-art** *It is an intensive course covering advanced navigation techniques.*
- ▶ traditional or usual **common, established, standard, traditional** *The hotel was built using traditional local techniques.*
- ▶ simple **basic, practical, simple** *Becoming a good cook means first mastering a few basic techniques.*
- ▶ types of technique **agricultural, analytical,** **computational, diagnostic, investigative, mathematical, photographic, scientific, statistical, surgical** *A variety of computational techniques are available for analysing electronic text.*
- v+N use a technique **apply, demonstrate, employ, exploit, practise, use, utilize** *The studio employed some brilliant marketing techniques prior to the movie's release.*
- ▶ develop a new technique **develop, devise, invent, pioneer** *They devised a new technique for predicting the eruptions of volcanoes.*
- ▶ learn a technique **acquire, adopt, learn** *Delegates at the seminar will acquire valuable techniques to improve their skill in motivating employees.*
- ▶ improve a technique **improve, master, perfect, refine** *If we can perfect this technique, it may eventually be possible to create artificial bone marrow.*

technological ADJ

relating to or involving technology

- ADJ+n progress **advance, advancement, breakthrough, change, development, improvement, innovation, leap, progress, revolution, transformation** *Recent technological advances in radiotherapy have improved survival rates for cancer patients.*
- ▶ knowledge or skill **capability, expertise, know-how, prowess, skill, sophistication, wizardry** *The auditorium seats about 2,700 people, and the revolving stages make this opera house a masterpiece of technological wizardry.*
- ▶ problem or challenge **barrier, challenge, constraints, limitations, problem** *The book provides an insight into warfare, and its technological advances and limitations in the 19th century.*
- ▶ method or solution **method, solution, tool** *They are seeking a technological solution to the problem capturing and storing carbon.*

technology N

advanced scientific knowledge used for practical purposes

- adj+N modern or advanced **advanced, current, innovative, latest, modern, new, revolutionary, sophisticated, state-of-the-art** *We have mixed the latest technology with body health knowledge to bring you our range of competitively priced equipment.*
- ▶ types of technology **agricultural, alternative, assistive, digital, educational, electronic, environmental, genetic, medical, military, mobile, nuclear, renewable, web-based** *It's a testament to how fast mobile technology is developing that manufacturers are now designing expansion cards for notebooks.*
- ▶ good or effective **effective, efficient, powerful, reliable, smart** *We are sceptical of their claims that the use of smart technology will minimize civilian casualties.*
- ▶ good for the environment **clean, green, low-carbon, renewable, solar, sustainable** *The project promotes the use of sustainable technologies in urban regeneration.*
- v+N use technology **adopt, apply, deploy, embrace, employ, exploit, harness, implement,**

use, utilize *Deploying this technology could have a larger impact on the business.*

▶ start to use technology **develop, introduce, pioneer** *The firm has continued to pioneer technology such as remote computing and the Internet.*

tedious ADJ
boring and continuing for too long

● adv+ADJ very **crushingly, exceedingly, excruciatingly, extremely, incredibly, seriously, unbearably, utterly, very** *The book is crushingly tedious and uninspiring nonsense.*

▶ rather **fairly, a little, pretty** INFORMAL, **quite, rather, slightly, somewhat, a tad** INFORMAL *I felt the second Lord of the Rings movie was a tad tedious.*

● ADJ+n **affair, chore, exercise, illness, job, journey, procedure, process, tale, task** *One of the most tedious tasks was stripping back the layers of brown paint from all the woodwork.*

● v+ADJ **be, become, get, prove, seem, sound** *The new job sounded exciting, but in the end proved just as tedious as the old one.*

telephone N
equipment for speaking to someone in a different place

● v+N make a telephone call **be on, call, dial, ring, use** *Hang on a minute – I'm on the telephone. ● Call 1471 to find out the last number to dial your telephone.*
answer a telephone call **answer, get** INFORMAL, **pick up** *After watching this movie I was frightened to answer my telephone for weeks.*

● N+v **go off, ring** *It was a bit embarrassing – my telephone went off in the middle of the interview.*

● N+n communication **call, conference, conversation, enquiry, interview, survey** *Following our telephone conversation yesterday, I write to confirm our agreement.*
service **advice line, answering, banking, booking, consultation, helpline, hotline** *A telephone hotline service will be set up to deal with enquiries.*

television N
electrical equipment for watching programmes

● adj+N **digital, free-to-air, high definition, interactive, satellite, terrestrial** *Each room has satellite television, hairdryer and free Wi-fi.*

● v+N watch programmes on television **be in front of, watch** *They spent most evenings slumped in front of the television. ● He would fall asleep watching television, and wake up in the middle of the night.*
switch on a television **put on, switch on, turn on** *He lay down on the sofa and switched the television on.*
switch off a television **put off, switch off, turn off** *Tell him I want the television turned off now.*

● N+n **adaptation, advert, broadcast, comedy, documentary, drama, interview, programme, report, serial, series, show** *It was the Princess's first television interview.*

temper N
tendency to get angry very quickly

● adj+N **bad, evil, explosive, ferocious, fierce, fiery, foul, nasty, quick, savage, uncontrollable, vicious, violent** *He becomes unpredictable and develops a violent temper.*

● v+N control your temper **calm, control, cool, curb, keep** *I reminded him that he should curb his temper and refrain from using strong language.*

▶ become angry **lose** *John lost his temper when he saw the damage.*

● N+v **boil, flare, fray, rise** *With tempers fraying towards the end of the game, there were bookings for several players.*

temperament N
a basic tendency to be happy, angry etc

● adj+N calm or happy **calm, docile, even, excellent, fantastic, gentle, lovely, loving, placid, sanguine, sweet** *The qualities you will need include an even temperament and a good sense of humour.*

▶ easily excited or made angry **excitable, fiery, lively** *A redhead with a fiery temperament, Marion knew her own mind.*

▶ changing quickly **mercurial, unpredictable, volatile** *He displayed a mercurial temperament which showed him to be irrational and vindictive.*

▶ tending to be sad or nervous **melancholic, nervous** *These dogs are bred simply to win shows, and this has given them a nervous temperament.*

● v+N **display, have, possess** *He possessed a temperament which sometimes made him seem much more mature than his years.*

temperature N
how hot or cold something is

● adj+N low **cold, cool, freezing, low, sub-zero** *The walls were covered with patches of snow, indicating relatively low temperatures.*

▶ hot or warm **high, hot, warm** *They had to work in extremely high temperatures for up to 14 hours a day.*

▶ neither too hot nor too cold **comfortable, mild, moderate, pleasant** *Mrs Henry had thrown open the shutters and even the window, for the temperature was mild.*

▶ average or usual **average, normal** *The city has a comfortable climate, with normal daytime temperatures of about 25 degrees in Summer.*

● N+v become higher **climb, creep up, go up, increase, rise, soar** *It was a hot summer's evening in London and the temperature soared.*

▶ reach a particular level **hover around sth, nudge sth, peak at sth, reach sth, top sth** *In the Basra region of south-east Iraq, temperatures nudged 50 degrees.*

▶ become lower **decrease, dip, drop, fall, go down, plummet, plunge** *An Arctic cold front has seen temperatures plummet to minus 30 Celsius this month.*

● N+n **difference, fluctuation, variation** *The garage will provide protection against the temperature fluctuations throughout winter.*

temporary ADJ
existing, done, or used for a limited period

- adv+ADJ **just, merely, only, purely** *The entire policy was intended to be purely temporary – a transitional arrangement.*
- ADJ+n job **appointment, employment, job, position, post, vacancy, work** *It was only a temporary post to cover her maternity leave, but we got over a hundred applicants.*
- ▶ worker **employee, replacement, staff, worker** *We usually recruit temporary staff to cover our peak period in the Summer.*
- ▶ building or place to stay or work in **accommodation, building, classroom, housing, shelter, structure** *Their main task was to find temporary accommodation for the earthquake victims.*
- ▶ arrangement or decision **absence, arrangement, ban, closure, contract, restriction, solution** *My office is in the basement, but this is just a temporary arrangement while the building is being renovated.*

temptation N
a strong feeling of wanting to have or do something

- adj+N difficult to control **great, irresistible, powerful, seductive, strong, tremendous** *For the inexperienced runner, there is a strong temptation to set off at a hard pace.*
- ▶ always present **constant, continual, perennial** *The attempt to control history has been a perennial political temptation.*
- v+N try to stop feeling temptation **avoid, combat, escape, fight, guard against, ignore, resist, struggle with, wrestle with** *We are taught to stand clear of and to resist temptation.*
- ▶ succeed in resisting temptation **conquer, overcome, withstand** *I managed to overcome the temptation to accept a cigarette from her.*
- ▶ feel temptation **experience, feel** *You may experience temptation to a degree that others do not feel.*
- ▶ be unable to control temptation **fall into, give in to, succumb to, yield to** *We must not yield to the temptation to opt for a quick solution to this complex problem.*

tenancy N
the right to use a rented building or land

- adj+N secure or legal **assured, contractual, protected, regulated, secure** *He lived in a modest cottage, subject to a secure tenancy.*
- ▶ alone/with others **joint, sole** *Some contracts are joint tenancies, which all housemates sign together, and some are individual.*
- ▶ for a particular length of time **lifetime, shorthold, short-term, weekly, yearly** *She has a short-term tenancy on a flat.* • *The Association hires the Hall on a yearly tenancy.*
- v+N give someone a tenancy **grant (sb)** *All the terms on which the tenancy was granted were in writing.*
- ▶ have a tenancy **have, hold** *The 'new tenant survey' is sent to all residents after they have held a tenancy for three months.*
- ▶ end a tenancy **end, relinquish, surrender** *This page contains items on tenants' rights, including ending your tenancy.*
- ▶ continue a tenancy **maintain, renew** *His landlord was threatening not to renew his tenancy.*

tendency N
the fact that something is likely to happen or someone is likely to do something in a particular way

- adj+N strong **clear, marked, pronounced, strong** *He shows a marked tendency to give up when things go wrong.*
- ▶ not strong **slight** *In most people there is a slight tendency to gain weight with age.*
- ▶ bad or worrying **alarming, unfortunate, worrying** *There is an unfortunate tendency to treat myth as history.*
- ▶ aggressive or harmful **aggressive, authoritarian, destructive, psychopathic, self-destructive, suicidal, violent** *She works with people who suffer from depression or have suicidal tendencies.*
- ▶ natural **inherent, inherited, innate, instinctive, natural** *The book reflects his belief in the inherent tendency of capitalism to raise living standards.*
- ▶ different or mixed **contradictory** *Her view of history aims to show the contradictory tendencies at work.*
- v+N have a tendency **demonstrate, display, exhibit, have, manifest, show** *He begins having terrible nightmares and exhibiting violent tendencies.*
- ▶ try to prevent a tendency **avoid, combat, counter, counteract** *Our concern is to counter the tendency to drop out of school at 16 or 17.*
- ▶ overcome a tendency **curb, overcome, resist, suppress** *Nathan suppressed his more aggressive tendencies.*
- ▶ make a tendency stronger **aggravate, encourage, reinforce** *This reinforces a tendency we all have to look at the world in a blinkered way.*
- ▶ notice a tendency **notice** *She also noticed a tendency to shut himself in and refuse to communicate.*
- ▶ show that someone or something may have a tendency **indicate, reflect, reveal, suggests** *The language he used suggested a tendency towards authoritarianism.*

tense ADJ
making you feel nervous and not relaxed

- adv+ADJ very **extremely, genuinely, incredibly, particularly, really, unbearably, unbelievably, very** *The way these scenes are filmed makes them unbearably tense.*
- ▶ rather **a bit INFORMAL, fairly, a little, pretty INFORMAL, quite, rather, slightly, somewhat** *When you're stuck in traffic and feeling a little tense, music can be very soothing.*
- ADJ+n ending **climax, ending, finale, finish** *They narrowly defeated their rivals in a tense finale.*
- ▶ period of time **moment, wait** *During the incredibly tense moments that followed, I read a mixture of emotions in his eyes.*
- ▶ situation in which there is angry disappointment **encounter, showdown, standoff** *The crowding led to a tense standoff between UN officials and local police.*
- ▶ atmosphere **atmosphere, mood** *The atmosphere is tense with the impending elections.*
- ▶ silence **silence** *The curtain closed behind them, leaving a tense silence.*
- ▶ game, film etc **affair, competition, drama, game, scene, thriller** *In the tense thriller 'Inside Man', a*

bank robbery leads to a number of people being taken hostage.

◆ v+ADJ be or become tense **become, feel, get, grow** *Try not to become tense, as your baby will sense this.*

▸ seem tense **look, seem** *She seems very tense, even nervous.*

▸ remain tense **remain** *The situation in the country remains extremely tense.*

⁀ension N
nervous or worried feeling, or a feeling that people do not trust each other

▸ adj+N getting stronger **escalating, growing, heightened, increased, mounting** *At this time of heightened tension in the world, we need to do all we can to show the power of nonviolence.*

▸ obvious **clear, palpable** *The runners waited, the tension palpable.*

unbearable **unbearable** *In the closing minutes of the game the tension was almost unbearable.*

all the time **constant, ongoing** *While the common people were Protestant, their leaders were Catholic and there was constant religious tension.*

not yet expressed **inner, pent-up, simmering, smouldering, underlying, unresolved** *Many unresolved tensions found expression on the football field.*

impossible to avoid **inevitable, inherent, irresolvable** *There is an inherent tension between his utopian socialist politics and his work creating luxury goods for the upper middle classes.*

unnecessary **undue, unnecessary** *Rewarding individuals at the expense of the team can only create unnecessary tensions.*

between particular groups **communal, ethnic, racial, sectarian** *In 1979 Thatcher had just been elected and there was a lot of racial tension around.*

types of tension **creative, dramatic, emotional, political, psychological, religious, sexual** *New parents are affected by lack of sleep and emotional tensions.*

▾ v+N reduce tension **alleviate, defuse, ease, lessen, reconcile, reduce, relax, release, relieve, resolve** *He spoke of the need to reconcile the tension between the goals of seeking peace and seeking justice.* • *There are a range of treatments designed to relieve tension.*

increase tension **aggravate, exacerbate, fuel, heighten, increase, inflame, ratchet up** *The move will heighten tension between Moscow and Washington, who both have interests in the region's oilfields.*

create tension **cause, create, give rise to, result in** *All of this creates further tension in a fragile political situation.*

feel tension **feel, sense** *I sensed a tension in the room.*

N+v increase **build, escalate, grow, increase, mount, rise** *Tensions were escalating in the Middle East over the weekend.*

decrease **ease, subside** *Fortunately there were signs that tension was easing.*

be violently expressed **erupt, explode, flare** *All the pent-up tensions finally erupt into bloody slaughter.*

exist **arise, emerge, exist, simmer** *In recent years a*

tension has arisen between science and society. • *In many societies tensions simmer below the surface.*

● n+of+N cause **cause, source** *They believe that water is likely to become a growing source of tension between nations.*

▸ feeling or state **atmosphere, feeling, period, sense, state** *Threats of closure have created an atmosphere of unbearable tension among the workforce.*

▸ increase **build-up, escalation** *One of the best things about the film is the build-up of tension.*

▸ decrease **easing, reduction, relaxation, resolution** *Both sides in the conflict welcomed the easing of tensions in the border regions.*

terminate V
end something

● adv+V suddenly or quickly **abruptly, speedily, suddenly** *A stroke abruptly terminated his political career.*

▸ sooner than expected **early, prematurely, unexpectedly** *The study was terminated prematurely, before all subjects had reached the intended three years follow up.*

▸ immediately **automatically, forthwith, immediately** *Your membership will be terminated automatically if you stop the payments.* • *This exploitation of impoverished peoples must be terminated forthwith.*

▸ officially **formally, lawfully, officially** *The current bus service will be formally terminated on the 1st January 2012.*

▸ in a friendly way **amicably** *The best way forward for all the parties involved is to amicably terminate the contract.*

▸ by one side only **unilaterally** *He alleged that any treaty ratified by the Senate could not be terminated unilaterally by the President.*

● V+n legal agreement **agreement, arrangement, contract, lease, licence, membership, tenancy, treaty** *Either party may terminate the contract by giving the other party 28 days notice in writing.*

▸ employment **appointment, employment** *Employers sometimes offer an employee a compromise agreement when terminating their employment.*

▸ event or process **operation, proceedings, process, study** *Eventually heavy rain terminated the proceedings.*

termination N
the end of an agreement, job, or situation

● adj+N allowed/not allowed by law **lawful, wrongful** *Anyone subjected to wrongful termination of employment has the right to claim compensation.*

▸ sudden **abrupt, immediate, speedy, sudden** *This led to the abrupt termination of his career as finance minister.*

▸ earlier than expected **early, premature, unexpected** *There was an unexpected termination of the network connection.*

● N+of legal agreement **agreement, contract, lease, licence, membership, tenancy** *The apartment must be returned to its original condition upon termination of the tenancy.*

▸ employment **appointment, employment** *Payment will be made only for work done up to the time of the termination of the appointment.*

▶ relationship **engagement, marriage, relationship** *Their children may suffer financial hardship following the termination of their relationship.*

▶ war **hostilities, war** *With the termination of hostilities, our society can look to the future.*

▶ court case **proceedings, trial** *It is in the interests of justice that there is a speedy termination of proceedings.*

terms N

the conditions of an agreement

● v+N agree terms **accept, agree, negotiate** *A spokesman for the broadcaster said it had agreed terms for the matches to be shown.*

▶ change terms **amend, change, modify, vary** *We reserve the right to amend the terms of this competition at any time without prior notice.*

▶ check terms **check, read, review** *Every part-timer should check their contract and review their terms and conditions.*

▶ say what the terms are **define, dictate, impose, set, specify, state** *The UN security council passed a resolution dictating the terms of the ceasefire.*

▶ make someone obey terms **apply, enforce** *If the parties cannot agree, the Patent Office can enforce the terms of the licence.*

▶ explain terms **clarify, explain** *The Chairman explained the terms on which the Council were willing to let them use the hall.*

▶ obey terms **abide by, follow, keep to, stick to** INFORMAL *It is your responsibility to abide by the terms of the licence.*

▶ not obey terms **breach, violate** *Breaching the terms of the licence is a criminal offence.*

● N+of legal agreement **agreement, contract, engagement, lease, licence, settlement, tenancy, treaty** *Under the terms of the agreement, Care UK will provide three doctors and seven nurses.*

▶ business arrangement **trade, use** *Fair trade looks to provide improved terms of trade for producers.*

▶ employment **appointment, employment** *Make sure you are clear about the terms of employment before you accept the job.*

▶ relationship **relationship** *Partners have a wide discretion to decide for themselves the terms of their relationship .*

▶ debate **debate** *Opponents of the plan have successfully set the terms of the debate.*

terrain N

an area of land with particular physical features

● adj+N with mountains **hilly, mountainous, steep, upland** *The city was hidden from the world for centuries by the mountainous terrain around it. ● They were built in exposed positions on very steep terrain.*

▶ with gentle slopes **rolling, sloping, undulating** *The golf course is set in perfect rolling terrain.*

▶ flat **flat** *Barcelona benefits from an exceptional situation on the flat terrain between the sea and the mountains.*

▶ not smooth **bumpy, rocky, rough, rugged, uneven, varied** *The terrain is rough and unsuitable for wheelchairs. ● We went for a 12 mile run over varied terrain.*

▶ soft and wet **boggy, marshy, muddy** *The animals happily graze on flat and often boggy terrain.*

▶ dangerous or difficult **arduous, challenging, dangerous, difficult, harsh, hostile, inhospitable, tough, treacherous, tricky, unforgiving** *They live in arguably the world's harshest and most inhospitable terrain.*

▶ unknown **unfamiliar** *Darkness was beginning to fall, and he was lost in unfamiliar terrain.*

▶ without features **barren, featureless** *They flew for hours over featureless terrain.*

● v+N **cross, explore, navigate, negotiate, tackle, traverse** *The low gears allow the vehicle to negotiate very rough terrain.*

terrified ADJ

extremely frightened

● adv+ADJ completely **absolutely, completely, utterly** *My dog is absolutely terrified of fireworks.*

▶ truly **genuinely, truly** *Many are genuinely terrified about the future.*

▶ rather **pretty** INFORMAL, **somewhat** *I feel somewhat terrified at the prospect of doing it again.*

▶ obviously **clearly, obviously** *The fox, obviously terrified, sought refuge down a rabbit hole.*

▶ secretly **secretly** *They must have been secretly terrified of being rejected.*

▶ in a way that is easy to understand **naturally, understandably** *She is understandably terrified by the incident and is upgrading the security at her home.*

● v+ADJ **be, feel, look, seem, sound** *'I have to speak to you right now', she said, sounding genuinely terrified.*

territory N

an area of land controlled by a particular group or country

● adj+N controlled by the enemy **enemy, hostile** *The area where the helicopter crashed is regarded as hostile territory.*

▶ ruled by a group somewhere else **colonial, occupied, overseas** *They continue to subjugate the population of these occupied territories in defiance of the United Nations.*

▶ whose ownership is not clear **border, disputed, frontier** *The company had begun to extend its rail lines into disputed territory along the Guatemalan border.*

▶ not controlled by any of the groups in a disagreement **neutral** *The two sides will meet on neutral territory, usually in central London.*

▶ with the right to rule itself **sovereign** *The bombings of the embassies were seen as direct assaults on U.S. sovereign territory.*

▶ controlled by a particular group **tribal** *The hill forts were built around 400 BC to defend tribal territories.*

● v+N take or control territory **acquire, annex, colonise, conquer, invade, occupy, rule, seize** *They were Polish territories annexed in the German invasion. ● The British Empire was not the first instance of English sovereigns ruling overseas territories.*

▶ protect territory **defend, guard, patrol, protect** *Popular movements are growing up in the region defend territory, cultural identity and natural resources.*

▶ mark territory **demarcate, mark** *The city had 14 boundary stones that demarcated its territory.*

▶ get territory back **recapture, reclaim, regain** *The territory was regained by the English crown under Edward I.*

▶ live in territory **inhabit** *There were approximately 20 million Indians inhabiting this territory before the Conquest.*

▶ give up territory **cede to sb, give up, surrender** *In 1947, the Finns agreed to cede territory to the then USSR.*

▶ say that you own territory **claim** *With both states claiming the disputed border territory, war was inevitable.*

▶ gain more territory **expand, extend** *Over the next ten years Genghis Khan expanded his territory to the west and north.*

terror N
◀ a strong feeling of fear

● adj+N very great **abject, absolute, downright, mortal, outright, sheer, stark, unimaginable, unspeakable, utter** *The Vikings' merciless raids struck abject terror into Saxon hearts.* • *They watched in sheer terror as the train came towards them.*

▶ not based on sensible reasons **nameless, primal, superstitious, unreasoning, visceral** *Epileptic fits have often evoked superstitious terror rather than sympathy.*

● v+N create terror **cause, create, evoke, excite, induce, inspire, instil in sb, sow, strike into sb** *She instils terror in all those who work for her.*

▶ experience terror **endure, experience, feel** *We endured the terror of being trapped with no escape.*

▶ overcome terror **overcome** *Some have to overcome terror at the idea of speaking in public.*

◀ violence used to frighten people for political aims

● adj+N against all people **indiscriminate, mass, random** *His aim was to rule the country without relying upon indiscriminate terror.*

▶ by a particular group **state, Stalinist, Nazi, fascist etc** *The dictator is the symbol of state terror and aggression.*

● v+N use terror **inflict on sb, perpetrate, spread, unleash, wage on sb** *The violence and terror they unleashed shocked the international commmunity.*

▶ fight against terror **combat, confront, defeat, fight, oppose, tackle** *We have to stand together in our efforts to combat terror.*

▶ condemn terror **condemn, renounce** *The country had to show that it was doing everything possible to renounce terror.*

▶ support terror **sponsor** *States that sponsor terror must be warned against it.*

▶ escape terror **flee** *We stand up for those fleeing terror and persecution.*

terrorism N
◀ the use of violence to achieve political aims

● adj+N between different countries **cross-border, global, international, transnational** *The threat posed by the former Soviet Union has been replaced by ethnic conflict and global terrorism.*

▶ within a country **domestic, home-grown** *The war abroad fuelled home-grown terrorism in Britain.*

▶ against all and any people **indiscriminate, mass** *The atrocities of indiscriminate terrorism must not be tolerated.*

● v+N fight against terrorism **combat, confront, counter, curb, deter, fight, oppose, prevent, tackle** *We do not believe this war is the most effective means of combating international terrorism.*

▶ stop terrorism **defeat, eliminate, eradicate** *Eradicating terrorism is a much more daunting task than most people realize.*

▶ speak publicly against terrorism **abhor, condemn, denounce, renounce** *The Panamanian government repeatedly condemned terrorism.*

▶ support or encourage terrorism **abet, condone, finance, foment, glorify, incite, promote, sponsor** *Freedom of speech never should be an excuse for inciting terrorism and fostering hatred.*

▶ commit acts of terrorism **perpetrate** *We are not in any way associated with the evil people who perpetrate terrorism.*

● n+against+N **battle, campaign, fight, stand, struggle, war** *It is not quite clear how ID cards will help in the fight against terrorism.*

● n+of+N **evil, menace, scourge, spectre, threat** *We must be consistent and tackle the scourge of terrorism wherever it is present.*

terrorist N
someone using violence to achieve political aims

● adj+N possible **alleged, suspected, wanted, would-be** *Thanks to the hard work of intelligence services, we have seen arrests of suspected terrorists around the world.*

▶ dangerous or crazy **armed, cowardly, fanatical, fundamentalist, notorious, suicidal** *Cowardly terrorists killed 182 innocent civilians.* • *This is a time when fanatical terrorists are plotting mass murder.*

▶ from within a country **homegrown** *The film examines homegrown terrorists like the Weathermen, who grew out of Chicago university activist groups.*

● N+n **act, attack, murder, plot, strike, threat** *Participants paid tribute to the victims of the terrorist acts.*

test N
1 a set of questions or tasks to check someone's knowledge or ability

● adj+N difficult **demanding, difficult, rigorous, tough** *If she passes the rigorous tests then she will go on to the next interview stage.*

▶ simple **simple** *All students are given a simple numeric and literacy test.*

▶ fair **fair, objective, reliable, standardized** *Objective tests of reading ability can be an important aid for measuring literacy.*

▶ using a particular format **computer-based, multiple-choice, online, oral, paper-based, practical, written** *Although most of the assessments are practical, there are some written tests.*

▶ testing a particular thing **aptitude, intelligence, listening, personality, proficiency, psychological,** psychometric, spelling, writing *We offer advice on using psychometric tests in recruitment.*

- v+N do a test **complete, do, retake, sit, take, undergo** *Candidates for sports scholarships will be expected to undergo a practical test of their abilities.*
- ▶ give someone a test **administer, set** *The materials include a teacher's manual about how to administer the test.*
- ▶ pass a test **pass** *Taxi drivers are required to pass a topographical test.*
- ▶ fail a test **fail** *If you fail the test we will usually consider further training to correct the faults identified by the examiner.*
- ▶ prepare for a test **cram for, prepare for, revise for, study for** *This is a useful vocabulary book when studying for a test.*

2 an examination of something to find out what it is or whether it works

- adj+N giving a particular result **abnormal, negative, positive** *After many months, the much awaited positive pregnancy test arrived.*
- ▶ strict **rigorous, stringent, thorough** *In order that we earn the Quality Mark, our document has to pass their stringent tests.*
- ▶ fair or reliable **fair, reliable, sensitive** *A reliable blood test for the diagnosis of subclinical BSE would have been extremely valuable.*
- ▶ simple or standard **common, routine, simple, standard** *Some routine blood tests were undertaken and it was discovered that she has an underactive thyroid gland.*
- ▶ random **random** *Norwegian police can carry out random roadside breath tests for alcohol.*
- ▶ done at first **first, initial, preliminary** *Initial tests are based on the child's ability to hear sounds made by the assessor.*
- ▶ types of test **biochemical, diagnostic, forensic, genetic, medical, nuclear, predictive, screening, statistical** *A person may be faced with important ethical factors to consider when they are offered a genetic test.*
- ● v+N carry out a test **administer, apply, carry out, complete, conduct, do, perform, repeat, run, undertake, use** *If we want to store samples, or do any other tests on them, we will have to get permission.* ● *The specialist will perform tests to determine whether surgery could help.*
- ▶ be given a test **have, undergo** *Medicines which are found to cause unacceptable side effects will not undergo further tests.*
- ▶ pass a test **meet, pass, satisfy** *The employer must satsify a test of fairness in dismissing an employee.*
- ▶ fail a test **fail** *He was the first athlete to fail a drug test at the Olympics.*
- ▶ devise a test **design, develop, devise** *The Professor has devised a test which gives a score for risk.*
- ▶ ask for a test **arrange, book, order, request** *You can book an eye test online.*

3 a difficult situation

- ● adj+N **gruelling, real, stern, stiff, tough** *This weekend the team face another stern test when they play Arsenal.*
- ● v+N cope with a test **meet, stand, survive, withstand** *Will the agreement stand the test of recent events?*

- ▶ face a test **face** *He faces a test of his maturity and character.*
- ● N+of+N **character, commitment, endurance, loyalty, nerve, patience, resolve, stamina, strength, will** *The expedition was a gruelling test of strength for the new recruits.*

test V
examine something to see what it is or whether it works

- ● adv+V thoroughly **adequately, exhaustively, extensively, fully, properly, rigorously, stringently, systematically, thoroughly** *The system has been rigorously tested to ensure security.*
- ▶ scientifically **clinically, empirically, experimentally, scientifically** *Using new DNA techniques, these speculations can be tested experimentally.*
- ▶ objectively **independently, objectively** *It has been independently tested and proven to work.*
- ▶ regularly **annually, periodically, regularly, routinely** *The only way to tell whether the ammonia levels are acceptable is to regularly test the water.*

> **Usage** *Test* is usually passive in all of the *adv+V* combinations shown above: *Our designs have been extensively tested by outdoor experts.* ● *The efficacy of disinfectants is routinely tested in laboratories.*

- ● V+n theory **assumption, hypothesis, prediction, theory** *Linguists can test their own hypotheses against information in the database.*
- ▶ how effective or good something is **accuracy, effectiveness, efficacy, feasibility, performance, robustness, validity, viability** *The overall aim was to test the effectiveness of conference participation in changing behaviour.*
- ▶ someone's knowledge or skill **ability, knowledge, skill, understanding** *The Quiz section gives you the chance to test your knowledge.*
- ▶ product **formula, model, product, prototype, vaccine** *Are any of your products tested on animals*
- ▶ sample **sample** *In seed samples tested in 2008–09, 12 per cent were found to contain contaminants.*
- ▶ study the results of a test **analyse, evaluate, interpret** *The workshop is for anyone who wants to learn more about evaluating diagnostic tests.*

testament N
evidence that something exists or is true

- ● adj+N true or appropriate **eloquent, fitting, powerful, real, true** *The exhibition is a fitting testament to the students' hard work.*
- ▶ lasting **enduring, lasting** *The record remains a lasting testament to his unique guitar style.*
- ▶ wonderful or impressive **fantastic, fine, glowing, great, impressive, magnificent, remarkable, wonderful** *The Museum is a magnificent testament to the Victorian neo-Gothic movement.*
- ▶ sad **sad** *There were very few present at the funeral, a sad testament to his inability to let people get close to him.*
- ● N+to hard work or determination **commitment, dedication, determination, devotion, efforts, professionalism, reliability, teamwork, tenacity** *Our recent good report was a testament to the dedication of the whole school.*

▶ strength or courage **bravery, courage, durability, endurance, resilience, strength** *The book is a haunting testament to the resilience of the human spirit.*

▶ generosity **generosity** *The success of the Visitor Centre is testament to the generosity of the public.*

▶ popularity **popularity** *The fact that we now have over 80,000 members is testament to the popularity of eating out in the North.*

▶ talent or skill **ability, genius, ingenuity, talent, versatility** *The album is a testament to their extreme versatility and talent.*

▶ high quality **greatness, quality, success** *That it should still be read by so many people forty years after its publication is a testament to its greatness.*

▶ fact **fact** *Today the pier is testament to the fact that pleasure piers can still be operated successfully.*

testimony N

1 a formal statement about something you saw or know

▶ adj+N from personal experience **expert, first-hand, personal** *A doctor giving expert medical testimony said it was impossible for her to have shot herself.* • *Many of those people contributed first-hand testimony of what happened in the camps.*

▶ sworn in court to be true **sworn** *There is sworn testimony from many sources that the leadership knew about this.*

▶ seeming to be true **convincing, credible** *Calling him a murderer simply made Kumar's testimony more credible.*

▶ false **false** *Any person giving a false testimony is subject to punishment by law.*

▶ making you upset or angry **damning, harrowing, poignant** *The inquiry heard harrowing testimony from victims.*

▶ v+N give testimony **give, submit** *Several sources gave testimony in which they said explosions went off in the building.*

▶ listen to testimony **hear** *They claim the court refused to hear their testimony.*

▶ believe someone's testimony **accept, believe** *We are inclined to believe the testimony of eyewitnesses.*

▶ reject someone's testimony **discredit, reject** *Historians have discredited this testimony.*

▶ support testimony **confirm, corroborate** *Mr Crab corroborated the testimony given by Mr Crocker.*

▶ contradict testimony **contradict, retract** *This statement contradicts your testimony that you telephoned after 11pm.* • *There are only two trial witnesses who have not retracted their testimony.*

▶ collect testimony **collect, gather** *He said he had gathered testimony about all kinds of racism going on inside football.*

2 evidence that something exists or is true

▶ adj+N true or great **ample, fitting, glowing** *They are a glowing testimony to the spirit of resilience in the face of terrorism.*

▶ strong **eloquent, emphatic, powerful, vivid** *Many letters bear eloquent testimony to the joy this music brings.*

▶ silent **mute, silent** *The stones stand in mute testimony to the monument's essential mystery.*

▶ sad **poignant** *The film is a lasting and at times poignant testimony to these musicians and their achievements.*

▶ agreed by all **unanimous** *The unanimous testimony of ancient records describes the destruction of the library.*

● v+N **bear, furnish, offer, provide, stand as** *It is 5000 years old and bears testimony to the great understanding our ancestors had of the stars.*

● N+to fact **fact, truth** *These findings bear testimony to the truth of Darwin's theories.*

▶ strong personal quality **character, commitment, courage, determination, faith, resilience** *This award is a powerful testimony to the commitment of everyone in the school.*

▶ skill or ability **ability, professionalism, skill, talent** *All our offices remained open during the crisis, a testimony to the professionalism of our staff.*

text N

a written document or book, or the written part of something

● adj+N complete or original **actual, authentic, complete, complete, entire, full, original** *The full text of her presentation can be downloaded here.* • *There is evidence that someone has tampered with the original text.*

▶ main/not main **accompanying, main** *The footnotes are quite long, so there are probably about as many words in the footnotes as in the main text.*

▶ in a particular format **electronic, printed, written** *There are many ways to make electronic text easier to read.*

▶ recommended or required for study **canonical, core, introductory, key, prescribed, recommended, set** *This book should be a core text on any nursing degree program.* • *Students will find it useful to look at introductory texts such as Economics of the Public Sector.*

▶ one of the most important or well-known **authoritative, canonical, classic, definitive, key, seminal, standard** *She co-authored the seminal text on eating disorders in young women.*

▶ old **ancient, classical, early, medieval** *This is a digital library that provides a wide range of ancient texts with translations, images and a very useful links section.*

▶ types of text **biblical, descriptive, explanatory, historical, literary, philosophical, religious, sacred** *There may be a paragraph of descriptive text associated with an item of news.* • *We explore the study of literary texts in the classroom.*

● v+N produce or show text **display, print, produce, publish, reproduce, type** *It would be great to see the text displayed in a slightly larger font to make it easier to read.* • *She has generously given her permission to reproduce this text.*

▶ read or study text **analyse, read, study** *Blind children read braille at about a third of the pace that sighted children read printed text.*

▶ interpret text **interpret, translate** *Readers use implicit grammatical knowledge as they interpret a text.*

▶ edit text **edit, revise** *There is no indication as to who edited this text.*

▶ cut, paste or move text **add, copy, cut, delete, enter, format, import, insert, paste** *If emailing, cut and paste the text into the body of the email.*

▶ select or highlight text **highlight, select, underline** *Click the button to underline the selected text.*

texture N
the way something feels when you touch or eat it

● adj+N smooth **creamy, silky, smooth, soft, velvety** *Creme fraiche has a smooth thick texture, similar to cream cheese.*

▶ rough **coarse, crumbly, crunchy, grainy, rough** *Rub the fat into the flour until a crumbly texture is achieved.*

▶ that you have to chew **chewy, meaty, rubbery** *For a chewy, meaty texture, tofu can be frozen, then thawed.*

▶ firm **dense, firm** *Rye produces breads with a dense texture.*

▶ rich **rich** *The Cabernet Sauvignon is a blend of rich textures and subtle flavours.*

▶ typical and easy to recognize **characteristic, distinctive, unique** *The structure of muscle is made up of segments of short fibres, and this is what gives fish its characteristic texture.*

● v+N create a texture **achieve, add, create, give, produce, provide** *A sea grass mat can add texture to a room.*

▶ have a texture **have** *When the stone is first quarried, it has a very rough texture.*

● n+of+N **combination, mixture, range, variety** *Serve with rice and tortilla chips to create a superb combination of textures and flavours.*

● and/or **colour, flavour, taste** *Washing mushrooms damages their texture and flavour.*

thank V
tell someone you are grateful for something

● adv+V in a sincere or enthusiastic way **heartily, profusely, sincerely, warmly, wholeheartedly** *At the last meeting, Mr Shortland was warmly thanked for his work as Secretary.*

▶ publicly **formally, publicly** *I would also like to thank publicly those who worked so hard on the project.*

▶ in a direct way; yourself **personally** *We would like to take this opportunity to personally thank you for all your help and support.*

● V+for **assistance, contribution, effort, generosity, help, support, work** *Both Clive and Colin were thanked for their efforts over the years.*

● v+V **want, would like** *We would like to thank you for your assistance.*

thanks N
words or actions to show you are grateful

● adj+N sincere or strongly felt **big** INFORMAL, **grateful, heartfelt, hearty, huge** INFORMAL, **many, sincere, warm** *My sincere thanks go out to all those people who sent in articles.*

▶ particular **especial, particular** *We owe especial thanks to the office staff for all their help.*

▶ deserved **due** *Many thanks are due to all our members for their kindness and generosity.*

● v+N express thanks **convey, express, extend, give, offer** *I would like to express my thanks to all those who have hosted events.*

▶ send a message of thanks **pass on, send** *Could you please pass our thanks on to all the staff who helped us achieve our goal.*

theft N
the crime of stealing

● adj+N minor **minor, petty** *Petty theft should be the main focus of crime prevention.*

▶ common or involving large amounts **common, large-scale, massive, rife, wholesale** *Mobile phone theft is particularly rife amongst students.*

▶ committed by someone taking an opportunity **opportunistic, walk-in** *Laptops are easy to steal, and they are open to opportunistic theft.*

▶ attempted **attempted** *He appeared in court in Peterborough, and admitted attempted theft.*

▶ claimed to be true **alleged** *The five men face charges of alleged theft.*

▶ relating to a particular area **corporate, intellectual, retail, vehicle-related** *Ten per cent of vehicle owners had experienced at least one vehicle-related theft.*

● n+N **bicycle, bike, car, computer, credit card, cycle, handbag, ID, identity, motorcycle, phone, phone, vehicle** *Clearly, identity theft is a major concern for consumers.*

● v+N prevent theft **combat, curb, deter, discourage, prevent, reduce, tackle** *The company uses CCTV to deter theft.*

▶ report a theft **report** *If your licence plate is stolen, it is essential that you report the theft to the police.*

▶ protect yourself against theft **guard (sb/sth) against, insure (sb/sth) against, protect (sb/sth) against, safeguard against** *The documents are fully insured against theft and fire.*

● n+of+N **rash, series, spate, string** *There has been a recent spate of computer thefts from schools.*

theme N
the main subject of a book, speech, exhibition etc

● adj+N main **central, core, dominant, key, main, major, overall, overarching, principal** *The key theme of the report was the success of the pharmaceutical industry.*

▶ shared **broad, common, underlying, unifying, universal** *Although the book uses Christian terminology, it deals with universal spiritual theme*

▶ appearing several times **constant, continuing, persistant, recurrent, recurring** *Age discrimination is a recurrent theme in studies of social care.*

● v+N study a theme **address, cover, deal with, discuss, examine, explore, focus on, investigate, pursue, reflect on, tackle, touch on** *His paintings tackle the themes of war and conflict.*

▶ draw attention to a theme **highlight, identify, illustrate, outline** *Rousseau highlights an importa theme: the notion of self-improvement.*

▶ arrange something into themes **arrange sth into, categorize sth into, divide sth into, group sth into, organize sth into, split sth into** *The photo gallery grouped into four main themes.*

● N+v be in many parts of something **dominate**

sth, **permeate sth, pervade sth, run through sth** *All good stories have a strong theme running through them.*

▶ include **encompass sth, include** *The project theme encompassed most of the students' study areas.*

▶ slowly appear **emerge** *The main theme emerging from the study relates to social responsibility in the workplace.*

● N+of occasion where people formally discuss a subject **conference, congress, lecture, sermon, symposium, workshop** *The theme of the conference was 'The future is networked'.*

● piece of study or literature **article, chapter, novel, paper, play, report, research** *The theme of the play is revealed through the characters and their interaction.*

▶ particular subject **alienation, friendship, identity, innocence, loneliness, love** *How does Steinbeck present the theme of loneliness in his novel 'Of Mice and Men'?*

theoretical ADJ

based on theories or ideas

● adv+ADJ mainly **essentially, largely, mainly, mostly, primarily** *Many courses at university level are essentially theoretical in nature.*

● completely **entirely, just, only, purely, strictly** *The course is project-oriented: it calls for design proposals rather than purely theoretical work.*

● very **highly, very** *Philosophy is often focused on highly theoretical discussions.*

● ADJ+n ideas or facts from which theory develops **assumption, background, basis, foundation, grounding, underpinnings** *Einstein's most famous equation, $E = mc2$, is the theoretical basis for nuclear fission.*

way of thinking about something **approach, concept, construct, framework, model, perspective** *We propose a theoretical framework for action research.*

knowledge **knowledge, understanding** *I learnt to apply the theoretical knowledge to real-life practice.*

idea **concept, construct, idea, notion, question** *Scientists had to develop new theoretical constructs to account for the effects of dark matter.*

study **analysis, investigation, research, study, work** *This group carries out experimental and theoretical research in artificial intelligence.*

discussion **argument, debate, discourse, discussion** *Her paper makes a significant contribution to the theoretical debate around the origins of language.*

and/or **abstract, applied, empirical, experimental, practical** *Courses at the Academy include practical and theoretical training.*

theory N

an idea or principle that explains something

adj+N relating to particular subjects or ideas **cultural, economic, ethical, evolutionary, linguistic, literary, mathematical, moral, political, scientific, social, sociological** *Next, I shall outline some developments in recent social theory.*

disagreeing with one another **competing, conflicting** *The report covers the various competing theories in a fair and balanced way.*

▶ sensible and likely to be useful **coherent, consistent, logical, plausible, sound** *The Administration's policies no longer conformed to any coherent theory of socio-economic development.*

▶ well-established **accepted, classical, conventional, established, mainstream, standard, traditional** *According to accepted scientific theory, the core of a planet as small as Mercury should have cooled down by now.*

▶ important or major **dominant, key, major** *A belief in unrestrained free markets was the dominant economic theory for almost 30 years.*

▶ different from what is generally accepted **alternative, new, novel, revolutionary** *The position is unsatisfactory, but so far no alternative theory has emerged to explain this phenomenon.*

● v+N develop a theory **construct, develop, formulate** *The aim of the research is to develop a theory that can account for all situations.*

▶ offer a theory for people to consider **advance, expound, outline, propose, propound, put forward** *This theory was first put forward in a paper at a conference.*

▶ show or suggest that a theory is wrong **contradict, disprove, refute** *When a theory is refuted by scientists, the community tries to find another, better theory.*

▶ apply a theory **apply, test** *Assignments are designed to help you to apply theory to practice.*

▶ combine theory with practice **combine, integrate** *On the Nursing degree, you will learn to integrate theory and practice.*

● N+v suggest that something is true **assume, imply, posit, postulate, predict, suggest** *Narrative theory suggests that our 'selves' are products of the stories we tell about ourselves.*

▶ state that something is true **argue, assert, claim, state** *This theory claims that living beings have evolved by means of a struggle for life.*

▶ develop from particular ideas or facts **arise from sth, be based on sth, build on sth** *Our theory is based on sound thinking and practice.*

therapy N

a form of treatment for an illness or emotional problem

● adj+N using methods not used by most doctors **alternative, complementary, holistic** *If conventional medicine is unsuccessful, it may be worth trying an alternative therapy.*

▶ using established methods **conventional, standard, traditional** *The trials compared the effects of homeopathic remedies with conventional drug therapies.*

▶ relating to a person's mind or behaviour **behavioural, cognitive, hormonal, nutritional, occupational, psychological** *Cognitive therapy is widely used in the treatment of anxiety and depression.*

● n+N relating to medical treatments **drug, gene, hormone replacement, laser, radiation** *Radiation therapy can often cause a permanently dry mouth.*

▶ relating to human behaviour **art, behaviour, language, music, speech** *Matthew attends speech therapy sessions on Friday mornings.*

▶ group/individual **family, group, individual** *Each*

patient attends a group therapy session once a week.

- v+N need therapy **need, require, seek** *Many of these children require therapy in later life.*
- ▶ receive therapy **be given, get, receive, try, undergo** *All candidates must undergo personal therapy.*
- ▶ provide therapy **administer, offer, provide** *Your family doctor can recommend a clinic offering appropriate therapies.*

thesis N

1 a long piece of writing done for an advanced degree

- adj+N type of thesis **doctoral, master's, postgraduate, research-based, undergraduate** *His doctoral thesis was a detailed study of the music of the French composer Henri Dutilleux.*
- ▶ published/not published **published, unpublished** *Even a quote from another author's unpublished thesis without full acknowledgement can constitute plagiarism.*
- v+N write a thesis **do, prepare, produce, write, write up** *The candidate must produce a written thesis of between 4,000 and 5,000 words.*
- ▶ formally give a thesis to someone who will make a decision about it **present, submit** *By the time students submit their thesis, they will be an expert in their chosen area of study.*
- ▶ formally support ideas presented in a thesis **defend** *She has completed a Master's degree, but she has not yet defended her thesis.*
- ▶ finish a thesis **complete, finish** *I'm hoping to complete my doctoral thesis by July next year.*
- ▶ publish a thesis **publish** *He graduated in 1865, and in the same year published his thesis.*

2 an idea or opinion used to explain something

- adj+N **basic, central, fundamental, main, principal** *Chapter 2 presents the book's central thesis – the anomalous origins of Homo sapiens.*
- v+N suggest an idea for people to consider **advance, expound, offer, present, propose** *Isaiah Berlin advanced the thesis that intellectuals and artists tend to be of two types: hedgehogs and foxes.*
- ▶ say or prove that a thesis is wrong **contradict, disprove, refute, reject, undermine** *An experimental project may prove, or disprove the original thesis.*

thief N

someone who steals something

- adj+N frequently stealing things **determined, habitual, notorious, persistent, professional, prolific** *Persistent thieves will spend time looking for things to steal.*
- ▶ hoping or trying to be **potential, would-be** *Police are urging people in the village to lock their doors and deter would-be thieves.*
- ▶ minor **petty** *For many years the building was used as a prison for petty thieves and criminals.*
- ▶ not planning to steal, but taking the opportunity to steal something **casual, opportunistic** *Most burglaries are carried out by opportunistic thieves.*
- ▶ showing no sympathy **callous, heartless, ruthless, unrepentant** *These heartless thieves are even returning to people they have already robbed before.*

- v+N catch a thief **apprehend, arrest, catch, stop** *They informed us that they had apprehended the thieves and located the vehicle.*
- ▶ make a thief decide not to steal **beat, deter, discourage, put off, thwart** *Well lit areas deter car thieves.*
- n+of+N **band, bunch, gang** *One night in January, a gang of thieves broke into the church and stole the statues.*

thin ADJ

with little fat on your body

- adv+ADJ **dangerously, extremely, incredibly, painfully, really, very** *She was painfully thin, with a pale complexion.*
- v+ADJ be, or look **be, look, seem** *He looked thinner than when I had last seen him, and very worried.*
- ▶ become **become, get, grow** *I got so thin that I had to leave my job, and I was in bed for quite a long time time.*

think V

consider facts carefully

- adv+V with your full attention **carefully, deeply, hard, long and hard, seriously** *Frederick leant back in his chair and thought hard for a moment.*
- ▶ in an intelligent or original way **creatively, laterally, outside the box, strategically** *The pupils had to think creatively and work as a team.* • *Employees are encouraged to think outside the box and find creative solutions.*
- ▶ clearly, critically, logically, rationally *I could think clearly, I could stay focused, I had more energy*
- ▶ quickly **fast, on your feet** *The car was rolling backwards; I had to think fast.*

> If you **think twice** about something, you carefully consider whether what you are planning to do is a good idea: *You should think twice before you hop on a plane.*

thinker N

someone thinking and developing ideas about important subjects

- adj+N important or influential **eminent, foremost, great, influential, leading, prominent, seminal** *Time magazine named her one of the most influential thinkers of our time.*
- ▶ believing in the need for social change **feminist, liberal, progressive, radical, socialist, utopian** *He was a progressive thinker, with sympathy for the anti-slavery campaign.*
- ▶ with imagination and new ideas **creative, innovative, lateral, original, strategic** *Each team needs a keen leader and at least one creative thinker.*
- ▶ modern **contemporary, modern** *Jean Baudrillard is one of the world's most celebrated contemporary thinkers.*

thinking N

an opinion or set of ideas

- adj+N modern **contemporary, current, latest, modern, new, recent** *New thinking on transport must form part of our plan for the future of Britain's cities.*

▶ original and creative **creative, fresh, imaginative, innovative, lateral, leading-edge, original, radical** *Over the years, they have built up a reputation for innovative thinking in the field of urban transport.*

▶ relating to developments in the future **blue-sky, long-term, strategic** *The policy unit's job is to do blue-sky thinking on the country's future energy needs.*

▶ in which different parts of a system are considered together **joined-up** *The problem with the government's environmental policies is the lack of joined-up thinking.*

▶ about a particular subject **economic, educational, mathematical, philosophical, political, scientific, theological** *His job is to bring the journal in line with current political thinking.*

● v+N influence someone's thinking **develop, guide, influence, inform, shape** *We researched the processes involved, and used this knowledge to inform our thinking.*

▶ make thinking clear **articulate, clarify, explain, outline** *The article outlines the latest scientific thinking about where all the water on Earth came from.*

▶ be the most important influence on thinking **dominate** *Three broad areas will dominate Christian thinking in the immediate future.*

● N+behind **decision, initiative, proposal** *What is the thinking behind these decisions?*

think through PHR VB

consider the facts about something in an organized way

▶ V+n problem **issue, problem, question** *This unit attempts to help children to think through difficult questions about equality.*

▶ what might happen as a result **consequences, implications** *Regrettably, nobody thought through the implications of this decision.*

▶ possible actions or ways of dealing with something **alternatives, options, possibilities, response** *Our careers service will help you to think through your options and make the right decision.*

thirst N [always singular]

a strong feeling of wanting something

adj+N strong **great, incredible, powerful** *As a child, I had a great thirst for books and learning.*

that cannot be satisfied **insatiable, unquenchable** *Young children have an insatiable thirst for knowledge.*

becoming stronger **growing** *Is the world's growing thirst for energy sustainable?*

v+N satisfy thirst **satisfy** *This book will satisfy the reader's thirst for more knowledge in the field.*

experience thirst **develop, experience, have, suffer from** *Milan and its shoppers have a thirst for designer labels.*

N+for knowledge **knowledge, learning, truth** *The curriculum aims to develop intellectual curiosity and a thirst for learning in children.*

hurting or punishing someone because they have hurt you **justice, revenge, vengeance** *A thirst for revenge also played its part in the attacks.*

▶ power **power** *A thirst for power caused a small group to break away and form their own people.*

▶ exciting experiences **adventure** *No sailing experience is necessary – all you need is a thirst for adventure and a willingness to learn new skills.*

2 the feeling that you want or need to drink something

● adj+N **excessive, extreme, great, intense, raging, severe** *Symptoms include excessive thirst, tiredness, and weight loss.*

● v+N satisfy thirst **quench, satisfy, slake** *Having bought a bottle of lemonade to quench our thirst, we continued on our way.*

▶ die because of thirst **die of** *She was dying of thirst and prayed for water.*

▶ do physical activity that causes thirst **develop, work up** *Two-and-a-half miles was just about right to work up a thirst.*

thirsty ADJ

feeling you want to drink something

● adv+ADJ **desperately, extremely, really, so** INFORMAL, **very** *After two hours of climbing, we were desperately thirsty.*

● v+ADJ **be, feel, get** *It was a hot long day, and I got really thirsty.*

● and/or **hot, hungry, tired, weary** *By lunchtime we were very tired, hot and thirsty.*

thorough ADJ

including everything that is possible or necessary

● adv+ADJ very **exceptionally, extremely, incredibly, particularly, really, remarkably, very** *This is an extremely thorough and well-balanced book on software construction.*

▶ fairly **fairly, pretty** INFORMAL, **quite, reasonably** *Using these techniques, you can do a pretty thorough search in about fifteen minutes.*

● ADJ+n knowledge **grasp, grounding, knowledge, understanding** *This course aims to give students a thorough understanding of the principles of criminal law.*

▶ check **assessment, check, check-up, evaluation, examination, inspection, testing** *The safety of your bike is your responsibility, and thorough checks are essential.*

▶ research or analysis **analysis, appraisal, exploration, investigation, research, review, study** *We carry out a thorough investigation before offering any property to our clients.*

▶ description of the main features of something **description, overview, survey** *The programme is designed to provide a thorough overview of the topic.*

▶ change **overhaul, reform, revision** *The report recommends a thorough overhaul of the current system.*

▶ preparation **preparation, warm-up** *All classes begin with a thorough warm-up for the entire body.*

● and/ or **careful, comprehensive, detailed, full, professional, rigorous, systematic** *The department has completed a thorough and systematic review of its recruitment practices.*

thought N

1 an idea, opinion, word or image that you have in your mind

- adj+N unexpected or for no reason **random, sudden** *A random thought passed through my head.*
- ▶ bad **anxious, evil, frightening, horrible, negative, scary, suicidal** *It was a scary thought, but I took a deep breath and did it anyway.*
- ▶ changing the way you feel **comforting, sobering** *Now there's a comforting thought.*
- ▶ private **inner, innermost** *Their body language can reveal their inner thoughts.*
- ▶ first/not first **final, first, initial, original, second** *As soon as I got here, my first thought was how big my new school was.* ● *The paper sets out some initial thoughts for consideration.*
- v+N have thoughts about something **echo, entertain, harbour, have, think** *There will many who will echo those thoughts.* ● *I always harboured thoughts of being a writer.*
- ▶ stop having thoughts about something **banish, dismiss** *I banished thoughts of football from my mind.* ● *He dismissed the thought with a gesture of the hand.*

> When someone starts thinking about something new, they **turn their thoughts to** the new thing: *I can now turn my thoughts to training for the next big challenge.*

- ▶ organize your thoughts **clarify, collect, gather** *He paused to gather his thoughts.*
- ▶ express your thoughts **articulate, communicate, convey, express, give, let sb know/have, share, tell sb, voice** *He often struggled to articulate his thoughts.* ● *I was asked to give my thoughts on this subject on a web forum.*
- ▶ record your thoughts **put down on paper/in writing, record** *If she finds it hard to talk, encourage her to put her thoughts and feelings down on paper.*
- ▶ like/not like a particular thought **cannot bear, like, relish** *I didn't relish the thought of getting soaked for no reason.*
- ▶ welcome someone else's thoughts **appreciate, welcome** *We would appreciate your thoughts on the new design.*

> Usage **Thought** is usually plural in all of the v+N combinations shown above.

- N+v arrive **arise, come to sb, cross sb's mind, flash through sb's mind, hit sb, occur to sb, pass through sb's mind, strike sb** *A sudden thought struck her.*
- ▶ have an effect on someone **haunt sb, inspire sb, trouble sb** *He was haunted by the thought that justice would not be done.*
- ▶ start to be about something else **drift, race, stray, turn to sth, wander** *Her thoughts had wandered far from the subject.*

2 the action or effort of thinking, or the ability to think

- adj+N serious **careful, considerable, serious** *Throughout the writing, give careful thought to the structure of the chapters.* ● *It is a matter that requires considerable thought.*

> You can also say that someone gives something *a lot of*, *a great deal of*, or *much thought*.

- ▶ types of thought **abstract, conscious, critical, logical, rational** *Our capacity for rational thought has placed human life at the top of nature's hierarchy.*
- v+N when someone thinks about doing something **give to sth, put into sth** *The programme continued without any thought being given to wider issues.*
- ▶ when someone thinks with sympathy about someone else **spare for sb** *Spare a thought for those without clean water.*
- ▶ make someone think about something **prompt, provoke, require** *Concerns over fossil fuels and landfill space have prompted much thought on new ways of treating waste.*
- ▶ be grateful that someone thinks about something **appreciate** *We all really appreciated the thought, especially as you are so busy.*

thoughtful ADJ

1 showing that you consider what people want or need

- ADJ+n thing given or done **extras, gesture, gift, present, touch** *Facilities include tea- and coffee-making facilities, and lots of other thoughtful extras*
- ▶ behaviour **manner** *Children are encouraged to work and play in a thoughtful manner with those about them.*
- and/or **caring, considerate, generous, kind** *She is kind, thoughtful and considerate.*

2 showing careful thought

- ADJ+n behaviour or activity **approach, consideration, mood, reflection** *This decision is the result of much thoughtful consideration.*
- ▶ things written or said **analysis, comment, contribution, discussion, essay, insight, lyrics, piece** *Thank you for your thoughtful comments.*
- and/or **informed, insightful, measured, perceptive, provocative, reflective, thought-provoking, well-informed** *I would like to thank her for writing such a measured and thoughtful review*

thread N

an idea connecting all the different parts of something

- adj+N **common, disparate, multiple, narrative, unbroken, unifying** *Will he be able to bring all the disparate threads of the mystery together?*
- N+v **connect sth, emerge, link sth, run through sth, weave through sth** *This theme was a constant thread running through our stay.*

threat N

1 a situation or activity that could cause harm

- adj+N serious **big INFORMAL, constant, global, grave, great, heightened, major, real, serious, severe, significant** *No major threats to the species are currently known.* ● *Their future is under sever threat.*
- ▶ likely to cause harm soon, or in the future

credible, immediate, imminent, potential *Firearms were allowed if there was an imminent threat of death or serious injury.* • *This poses a potential threat.*

▶ types of threat **economic, environmental, legal, military, nuclear, strategic** *There is no military threat from this region.*

● n+N **bomb, cyber, missile, security, terror, terrorist** *Recently we have seen a wide range of cyber threats.*

● v+N fight a threat **address, avert, combat, counter, eliminate, reduce, tackle** *We hope to reduce the threat of accidental poisoning.*

▶ be a threat **constitute, pose** *These problems are very serious and pose a real threat to the future of the Library.*

▶ be affected by a threat **face** *The country faces the threat of race riots.*

● N+v **come from sth, emerge, face sb, hang over sb** *Lately, a more sinister threat has emerged.*

2 a statement that you will cause someone harm

▶ v+N **face, receive** *Staff received threats, and at times violence broke out.*

threaten V
1 tell someone you might cause them harm

▶ V+n **action, invasion, strike, violence** *The company threatened court action if she did not pay.*

> **Usage** You can also **threaten** someone **with** something, or t**hreaten to** do something: *The family is being threatened **with** deportation.* • *The boss threatened **to** sack him.*

and/or **abuse, assault, bully, harass, humiliate, insult, intimidate** *He accused us of bullying and threatening him.*

2 be likely to harm or destroy something

V+n **situation, system, or process existence, future, integrity, livelihood, peace, security, stability, supply, survival, viability** *The new requirements could threaten the viability of the service.*

living things **existence, habitat, species** *We will work to save threatened species.*

threatening ADJ
likely to harm you

ADJ+n **attitude, behaviour, gesture, language, letter, message, phone call** *We will not accept rude and threatening behaviour.*

and/or violent **abusive, aggressive, confrontational, violent** *The courts will act to stop violent and threatening behaviour.*

insulting **abusive, defamatory, insulting, libellous, obscene, offensive, rude** *Threatening, insulting or abusive language must not be used.*

threshold N
limit at which arrangements or rules change

adj+N high/low **high, low, lower, maximum, minimum, upper** *Do you have a high pain threshold?*

significant **certain, critical, indicative** *When the level*

of hormone is above a critical threshold, special treatment is used to reduce it.

▶ established by law **legal, statutory** *Where the combination of crops exceeds the statutory threshold, farmers are automatically compensated.*

● n+N needed in order to do something **age, audit, eligibility, income, tax** *There should be an additional income threshold for top earners.*

▶ feelings **boredom, pain, stress** *There is considerable variation in individual pain threshold.*

● v+N set or change the threshold **establish, fix, increase, lower, propose, raise, set, specify** *The government promised to raise the tax threshold.*

▶ pass the threshold **breach, cross, exceed, pass, reach** *Some large-scale projects which exceed the agreed thresholds may not be significant.*

thrill N
a sudden feeling of being very excited and pleased

● adj+N big **big, great, huge, real, tremendous, ultimate** *Winning the award was a great thrill.*

▶ real **sheer, visceral** *The sheer thrill of speed is what I love.*

● v+N have a thrill **experience, feel, get, share** *I get a huge thrill from discovering new things.*

▶ give someone a thrill **deliver, send** *Her voice sent a thrill through me.*

▶ enjoy a thrill **enjoy, love** *They love the thrill of the races.*

▶ think about a thrill **imagine, remember, not forget** *Imagine the the thrill as your hot air balloon takes off.*

thriller N
a book, play, or film telling an exciting story

● adj+N exciting or frightening **action-packed, chilling, edgy, fast-paced, gripping, gritty, stylish, suspenseful, taut, tense** *She was the heroine in a number of tense thrillers.*

▶ types of thriller **comic, erotic, futuristic, psychological, supernatural** *This is a classic supernatural thriller where no-one is sure what is real and what is illusion.*

thrive V
become very successful, happy, or healthy

● n+V business **business, company, economy, enterprise, industry, tourism** *Tourism is thriving here.*

▶ living things **creature, plant, species, tree, wildlife** *Very few plants thrive in very wet or very dry soil.*

▶ places and people **church, city, community, population, region** *Recent history shows how remote communities can thrive, culturally and economically, when they are given the power to make their own decisions.*

throne N
the position of being king or queen

● v+N take the throne **accede to, ascend (to), assume, come to, inherit, occupy, regain, succeed (to)** *As tradition requires, the monarch accedes to the throne instantly.* • *He ascended the throne of Spain in 1700.*

▶ take the throne from someone **claim, reclaim, seize, usurp** *He seized the throne from Richard II.*
▶ give up the throne **abdicate, renounce** *She was forced to abdicate her throne in favour of her son, James.*
● n+to+N person who will take the throne **claimant, heir, pretender, successor** *There was no clear successor to the Scottish throne.*

> Usage Someone who is *in line to the throne* may become king or queen in the future: *Princes William and Harry are second and third in line to the throne*.

▶ claiming or taking the throne **accession, ascension, claim, right, succession** *He was ready to give up his right to the throne.*

thrust N
the main idea or intention of a document, speech etc

● adj+N **basic, broad, central, general, main, major, overall, whole** *We agree with the general thrust of the report.*
● N+of document **article, book, chapter, document, paper, report** *The thrust of the article remains unchanged.*
▶ set of ideas **argument, debate, policy, proposal, recommendation, strategy** *The basic thrust of his argument is that stress causes people to under-perform.*

thud N
a low sound made by a heavy object hitting something

● adj+N loud **almighty, loud, mighty, resounding, terrific** *I fell with a mighty thud.*
▶ not loud **dull, heavy, muffled, soft** *They heard a heavy thud, as though something had struck the ship.*
▶ frightening **ominous, sickening** *All we heard was an ominous thud.*

thug N
a man who is violent, especially a criminal

● adj+N violent **armed, brutal, murderous, sadistic, vicious, violent** *Armed thugs attacked his family.*
▶ without feelings or morals **callous, drunken, hardened, lawless, mindless** *The mindless thugs who caused this damage must be punished.*
▶ with extreme beliefs **fascist, racist** *He was attacked by racist thugs.*
● n+of+N **band, bunch, gang** *We will not be intimidated by a bunch of thugs.*

thunder N
a loud noise heard in the sky during a storm

● adj+N **booming, distant, heavy, loud** *In the afternoon the sky grew overcast, and distant thunder could be heard during the evening.*
● N+v **boom, crash, roar, roll, rumble** *Thunder crashed overhead.*
● n+of+N **clap, crack, crash, peal, roll, rumble, sound** *There was a massive clap of thunder.*

● and/or **lightning, rain** *Last night we had torrential rain, and thunder and lightning.*

thunderstorm N
a heavy storm with thunder

● adj+N **heavy, massive, severe, spectacular, violent** *Heavy thunderstorms brought torrential rain to the area.*

thwart V
prevent someone from doing what they want

● adv+V **continually, cruelly, repeatedly, successfully** *Activists successfully thwarted ministers' plans.*
● V+n **ambition, aspirations, attack, attempt, effort, plan, plot** *Further attempts to mount attacks were thwarted by the Security Service.*

tide N
1 the regular rise and fall of the level of the sea

● adj+N strong and possibly dangerous **extreme, powerful, strong, treacherous** *This area is known for its treacherous tides.*
▶ higher/lower **high, incoming, low, outgoing, rising** *Be aware of tide times, and avoid being trapped by an incoming tide.* ● *At low tide you can walk along the bay.*
● N+v become higher **come in, rise** *The tide was coming in very quickly.*
▶ become lower **ebb, go out, recede** *The tide goes out furthest when there is a full moon or a new moon.*
▶ change direction **turn** *The tide had turned.*
▶ flow **flood, flow, sweep, wash** *The tide sweeps into the estuary.*

2 the way events or opinions are developing

● v+N **halt, reverse, stem, turn, unleash** *The government was failing to halt the tide of university closures.*
● N+of events **crime, democracy, fiction, globalization, history, struggle, violence, war** *In the current tide of globalization, no country can develop and prosper in isolation.*
▶ opinions **anger, emotion, feeling, opinion, sentiment** *The anti-terror law was rushed through Congress on a tide of anger after the bombings.*

tidy ADJ
with everything in the correct place

● ADJ+n place **bedroom, desk, garden, house, kitchen, kitchen, office, yard** *The rest of the house is perfectly tidy.*
▶ condition **appearance, condition, look** *You must leave your property in a clean and tidy condition.*
● v+ADJ **keep sth, leave sth, look** *Work areas must be kept tidy.* ● *We cleaned and painted the kitchen, and it looks a lot tidier now.*

tight ADJ
controlled very carefully, so as to allow no freedom or extra time or money

● adv+ADJ very **extremely, impossibly, incredibly,**

really INFORMAL, **ridiculously, so** INFORMAL, **too, very** *The time constraints are extremely tight.*

▸ **rather fairly, pretty** INFORMAL *Security was fairly tight.*

● ADJ+n controls **constraint, control, regulations, restrictions, security** *This could lead to tighter controls on industrial waste.*

▸ time **deadline, schedule, timescale, timetable** *The ability to cope with tight deadlines is essential.*

▸ money **budget, margin** *Small businesses, whose margins are much tighter, face greater problems.*

Usage If *time* or *money is tight*, there is not enough, or only just enough.

time N

the quantity that is measured in hours, days, years etc

● v+N use time **pass, spend, use, waste** *I have spent a lot of time in his company.*

▸ use less time **reduce, save** *We can show you how to save time and money.*

▸ have enough time to do something **find, get, have, leave** *Will you be able to find time to have a coffee with us?* ● *I didn't have time to talk to him.*

▸ need time **need, require** *This will require time and energy.*

▸ make time available for a purpose **allocate, allow, devote, divide, give, invest, set aside** *The deadline allows time for a full consultation.* ● *She divides her time between teaching and research.*

timetable N

a plan of the times at which something will happen

▸ adj+N fixed or clear **detailed, rigid, strict, structured, tight** *You will follow a structured study timetable for each module.*

▸ not yet fixed **provisional** *The provisional timetable for the application and assessment process is as follows.*

needing a lot of effort **ambitious, demanding** *We have an ambitious timetable and a frightening volume of work.*

v+N set a timetable **co-ordinate, devise, finalize, fix, impose, set** *We have devised a timetable for the switchover, to be phased in on a region-to-region basis.* ● *As soon as they have been finalized, the examination timetables appear on the website.*

propose or agree a timetable **agree, outline, propose** *This will allow the Agency to meet with those involved and to agree a timetable of support.*

change a timetable **adjust, alter, amend, disrupt, juggle, personalise, revise, suspend** *The normal timetable is suspended for two days each year, as students take part in a range of charitable activities.*

follow a timetable **follow, operate to, run to** *It was a great success, not least because it ran to a strict timetable.*

N+n information **enquiry, information** *For bus timetable enquiries, visit our website.*

the way a timetable is organized **change, clash, constraint, slot** *They may not be able to take the course because of timetable clashes.*

timing N

1 the date or time when something happens

● v+N affect the timing **affect, constrain, determine, dictate, influence** *The individual analyst determines the timing and content of the research.*

▸ change the timing **alter, change** *The feasibility of changing the timing and duration of the event should be investigated.*

● adj+n good **opportune, optimal, optimum, perfect** *The timing was perfect.*

▸ lucky **fortuitous, opportune, uncanny** *He was helped by fortuitous timing.*

▸ bad **bad, inconvenient, poor, unfortunate** *The proximity of the broadcast to Christmas was bad timing.*

▸ not yet final or exact **approximate, provisional** *Provisional timings are as follows.*

2 the skill of doing something at the best moment

● adj+N very good **deft, exquisite, razor-sharp, split-second, superb** *Her poems, with their exquisite timing and wonderful stories, are captivating.*

▸ perfect **faultless, immaculate, impeccable, perfect, spot-on** *With impeccable timing, we arrived back just in time to hear the result.* ● *His timing is spot-on.*

tinge N

a small amount of a colour, feeling, or quality

● adj+N colour **greenish, bluish etc, purple, rosy etc** *Some of the white flowers have a pinkish tinge.* ● *This beautiful fish has a golden tinge to its body.*

▸ pale **faint, pale, slight** *I could see a faint tinge of colour in her cheeks.*

● N+of **bitterness, disappointment, jealousy, regret, sadness** *It is with a tinge of regret that I have asked the board to accept my resignation.*

Usage You can also say that *there is a tinge of* something: *There was a tinge of sadness in his voice.*

tip N

a useful suggestion

● adj+N useful **handy** INFORMAL, **helpful, practical, useful, valuable** *Here are some helpful tips on spotting the signs and how to deal with them.* ● *The guidelines contain some practical tips to help with weight loss.*

▸ most useful **hot** INFORMAL, **invaluable, top** INFORMAL *Here are ten top tips for buyers.*

▸ simple **quick, simple** *By following a few simple tips, you will be able to dramatically reduce the energy you use.*

● v+N give tips **contain, give, offer** *The coaches offered tips on technique.*

▸ get tips **get** *You can get fundraising tips from us.*

▸ follow tips **follow** *Follow our simple safety tips.*

▸ share tips **exchange, share, swap** *You can swap tips and share problems.*

● and/or **advice, cheats** INFORMAL, **hints, how-tos** INFORMAL, **ideas, shortcuts, suggestions, tricks** *For tips and hints, click here.*

tired ADJ
needing to rest or sleep

- adv+ADJ very **dead, extremely, really** INFORMAL, **so** INFORMAL, **very** *The sun was hot again and we were very tired.*
- ▶ rather **fairly, pretty** INFORMAL, **quite, rather** *She was looking quite tired.*
- ADJ+n **bones, brain, eyes, feet, legs, limbs, muscles** *They couldn't wait to bathe their tired feet in the river.*
- v+ADJ **become, feel, get, grow, look, seem, sound** *When I got home I felt tired and had a headache.*
- and/or without energy **lethargic, listless, sleepy, weary** *During your treatment you may start to feel tired and listless.*
- ▶ unhappy **bored, depressed, irritable, jaded** *He was tired and irritable after a tough day at work.*

title N
the position of a winner in competition

- v+N win **claim, clinch, come away/ walk away/ leave with, earn, scoop, secure, win** *He went on to win the title in 2007.*
- ▶ try to win **battle for, compete for, defend** *They will battle for one of the European Tour's most prestigious titles.*
- ▶ win again **regain, retain, successfully defend** *Can he maintain his form to regain the title?*

token ADJ
done in order to pretend that you are dealing with something, or that you take something seriously

- ADJ+n action **attempt, force, gesture, pretence, protest, resistance** *The public consultation was a token gesture – the decision had already been made.*
- ▶ money paid or received **amount, economy, fine, gift, payment, sum** *The richer nations promised billions of dollars in aid, but have so far only paid token amounts.*

tolerance N
the ability to accept someone else's beliefs, way of life, or mistakes

- adj+N **cultural, political, racial, religious** *As a nation, we pride ourselves on our racial tolerance and cultural awareness.*
- v+N **advocate, encourage, foster, preach, promote, show, teach** *We want to teach people tolerance and respect for the rights of others.*
- and/or **diversity, fairness, kindness, openness, patience, respect, understanding** *Many thanks to my wife for all her patience and tolerance.*

tolerant ADJ
willing to accept someone else's beliefs, way of life, or mistakes

- adv+ADJ **extremely, incredibly, remarkably, very** *Most people are extremely tolerant of other people's religious beliefs.*
- ADJ+of mistakes **faults, mistakes, shortcomings** *They are not very tolerant of shortcomings.*

- ▶ differences **differences, diversity, minorities** *They were tolerant of religious differences.*
- ▶ opinions **beliefs, faith, opinions, views** *We should all be more tolerant of others' beliefs.*
- and/or used about a person **compassionate, easy-going, forgiving, humane, liberal, moderate, open-minded, patient, peace-loving, respectful** *Be respectful and tolerant of everyone you meet, even if you disagree with their opinions.*
- ▶ used about an organization or community **cosmopolitan, inclusive, multi-cultural, multi-ethnic, peaceful, pluralist, pluralistic** *This is an important part of developing a tolerant multi-cultural society.*

tolerate V
allow someone to do something you dislike

- V+n unfair treatment **discrimination, harassment, homophobia, injustice, racism** *The Association will not tolerate harassment in any form.*
- ▶ bad behaviour **behaviour, blasphemy, corruption, dissent, rudeness** *Residents will not tolerate this behaviour.*

> Usage ***Tolerate*** is often used with a negative in all of these combinations.

toll N
the total number of people killed or hurt

- adj+N **appalling, devastating, dreadful, enormous, grim, heavy, high, horrific, huge, terrible** *In an effort to reduce the devastating toll of heart disease, new guidelines have been released for doctors treating people at risk.*
- n+N **accident, casualty, death, injury** *The US death toll rose to 24 after two marines were killed by a home-made bomb.*
- v+N result in a toll **exact, inflict, result in** *Deaths from occupational causes inflict a greater toll on men than on women.*
- ▶ reduce the toll **lower, reduce** *The way to reduce thi toll is to change attitudes before an accident occurs.*
- ▶ increase the toll **add to, increase** *Months of fighting between rival rebel factions has added to the toll of the dead and displaced.*

tone N
the general character of a place, event, or a piece of writing or film

- adj+N general **general, overall, whole** *The audience praised the humour of the speakers, the interesting nature of the subjects tackled, and the overall tone of the event.*
- ▶ moral **moral** *The moral tone of the New Testament is so high that it could not possibly be fiction.*
- ▶ suggesting something bad **dark, harsh, menacing** *The ending also creates the dark tone the new series has, making the programme more serious.*
- ▶ sad or serious **serious, solemn, sombre** *The movement of the water and the haze which filters through the harbour, all contribute to the sombre tone of the sequence.*
- ▶ not serious **light** *There are a number of moments where real life horror impinges on the otherwise light tone of the novel.*

▶ showing strong opinions **strident** *What strikes one about these texts is the somewhat strident disciplinarian tone of much of them.*

▶ positive **hopeful, optimistic, positive, upbeat** *The book takes a very upbeat tone about your potential for success.*

● v+N create a tone **create, give sth, set, strike** *Your choice of appliances will set the tone of your kitchen and highlight the style you have chosen.*

▶ have a tone **have** *The story has a tone that varies between playful wit and pathos which excites sympathy in the reader for Mrs Henley.*

▶ change the tone **alter, change** *That would certainly alter the tone of many of these debates.*

▶ make the tone worse/better **lower, raise** *Is it really necessary to lower the tone of an otherwise excellent magazine with a double page spread of a character throwing up on the cover?*

▶ make the tone less serious or angry **lighten, soften** *People of faith can make a valuable contribution by softening the tone of often strident secular debate.*

tool N

something used to do or achieve something

● adj+N good **effective, efficient, excellent, great, innovative, powerful, practical, sophisticated** *When it works, such personalisation is a powerful and sophisticated tool.*

▶ useful **handy, helpful, useful, valuable** *The integrity test is a useful tool for monitoring purposes.*

▶ important or essential **essential, ideal, important, indispensable, invaluable, key, necessary, perfect, vital** *He acknowledged that the internet was an important tool to disseminate information.*

▶ for many situations **flexible, versatile** *This complex system thus creates an extremely versatile assessment tool with a wide range of test possibilities.*

▶ basic **basic, standard** *E-mail, electronic data transfer, and websites are all accepted as being standard business tools.*

▶ on a computer **automated, computational, digital, electronic, ICT, interactive, online, software, technological, web-based** *There are many electronic tools for translators.*

▶ for finding information **investigative, reference, research** *A comprehensive glossary provides an invaluable reference tool.*

▶ for teaching **educational, teaching** *Such a board would be a useful teaching tool.*

▶ for testing or checking something **analysis, analytical, assessment, diagnostic, evaluation, measurement, monitoring, screening, testing** *This technique is not purely a research technique, but is also a valuable diagnostic tool.*

▶ mathematical or scientific **mathematical, scientific, statistical** *The mere fact that cosmology makes use of scientific and mathematical tools does not make it a science.*

for selling something or doing business **business, marketing, promotional** *We were asked to produce a website that would act as a promotional tool for the show.*

for creating an idea **conceptual, creative, visualization** *Alexander's patterns are conceptual tools for helping people design buildings which might themselves have that quality.*

n+N for planning or designing something

design, development, planning *Designed to be a planning tool, this publication consists of a series of maps showing the various routes to the Mediterranean through the French canals and rivers.*

▶ for managing people **management** *Users can create their own reports quickly and easily, making it the ideal management tool.*

tooth N

a hard white object inside your mouth [usually plural]

● adj+N in good condition **clean, healthy, perfect, strong** *I noticed he had perfect straight teeth.*

▶ in bad condition **bad, rotten** *The tooth was so rotten, it broke.*

▶ white **pearly, white** *Smiling a broad smile of pearly teeth, she waved him forward.*

▶ straight/not straight **crooked, straight** *When she smiles, her teeth are endearingly crooked.*

▶ sticking out **buck, prominent, protruding** *He had huge buck teeth that looked like they belonged on Goofy.*

▶ sensitive **sensitive** *There are special toothpastes for sensitive teeth.*

▶ sharp **jagged, pointed, razor sharp, sabre, sharp** *Chimps are extremely strong and have sharp teeth.*

● v+N keep your teeth tightly together **clench, grit** *I gritted my teeth and tried to enjoy all the attention I was getting.*

▶ move your top teeth on top of your bottom teeth **gnash, grind** *She did not realize she had been grinding her teeth in the night when she was asleep.*

▶ clean your teeth **brush, clean** *The worst thing you can do is to brush your teeth with an abrasive toothpaste after eating or drinking acidic foods.*

▶ make your teeth whiter **bleach, whiten** *There are several toothpastes on the market which claim to whiten teeth.*

▶ stain your teeth **discolour, stain, yellow** *Teeth are easily stained, especially by tobacco, certain foods and beverages.*

▶ damage your teeth **break, chip, crack, damage, knock out** *Apparently, Viduka chipped a tooth in last night's game.*

▶ decay your teeth **decay, rot** *Do not give them carbonated water as this has carbolic acid which rots teeth.*

▶ show your teeth **bare, flash, show** *'ARRR, ARRR, ARRR,' it snarled as it flashed its huge teeth.*

▶ remove someone's tooth **extract, pull, remove, take out** *An instant solution is to extract the tooth, thereby removing the infection, but leaving you with a gap.*

▶ repair or clean someone's teeth **drill, fill, polish, straighten** *Can my crooked or twisted teeth be straightened?*

▶ when a new tooth comes up through your gum **cut, get** *Most babies will let you know they're cutting new teeth loud and clear.*

▶ when a tooth falls out **lose** *When Jessica loses her first tooth, Granny tells her to watch out for the tooth fairy.*

topic N

a subject that you write or speak about

● adj+N that people have strong feelings about **emotive, sensitive** *The issue of asylum seekers remains one of the most emotive topics facing Britons today.*

▸ that people disagree about **contentious, controversial, thorny** *No essays about such a controversial topic can be truly without bias.*

▸ that people do not talk about **off-limits, taboo** *Sex is still seen as a taboo topic, but we showed that it is not something to be embarrassed about.*

▸ that many people want to talk about **hot** *Seeing as my boy is such a hot topic, here are some more pictures of him.*

▸ interesting **fascinating, interesting** *A number of interesting topics were discussed.*

▸ important **central, important, key, main, major, priority** *There is no doubt that globalisation is an important topic.*

▸ difficult **challenging, complex, complicated, difficult, tricky** INFORMAL *This is a fun way to learn about a complex topic.*

▸ specialized **specialist, specialized** *In the final year, you will do a piece of professional research in a specialist topic.*

▸ with many parts **broad, diverse, substantive, weighty, wide-ranging** *Work life balance is a broad topic.*

▸ relevant **pertinent, relevant** *The introduction will help you identify which topics are pertinent to your situation.*

▸ types of topic **environmental, health, historical, history, legal, mathematical, philosophical, science, scientific** *Each child will cover six historical topics in the year.*

● v+N deal with a topic **address, cover, deal with, tackle** *This book covers many topics, so you may find it useful.*

▸ study a topic **examine, explore, investigate, look at, pursue, research, study** *Candidates will study one topic in-depth.*

▸ talk about a topic **debate, discuss, speak on, talk about** *Jobs and careers were the main topic discussed.*

▸ talk about something for the first time **bring up, broach, raise** *I had not broached this topic with my young child yet.*

▸ mention a topic **mention, touch on** *She briefly touches on other topics that affect the lives of disabled people.*

▸ choose a topic **choose, decide on, identify, pick, select** *Students pick a research topic in Semester 1.*

▸ suggest a topic **propose, suggest** *Among the suggested topics for research is examining the needs of people who face multiple barriers in accessing information and services.*

● N+of **conversation, debate, discussion, research** *Food quickly became the main topic of conversation.*

torment N
severe physical or mental pain

● adj+N lasting forever **constant, endless, eternal, everlasting, unending** *Hell is a place of unending torment.*

▸ bad **dreadful, terrible, unspeakable** *How many more animals have to suffer unspeakable torment before those in power are made to be accountable for this cruelty?*

▸ affecting someone's mind **emotional, inner, mental, psychological** *His highly emotional music mirrors his inner torment.*

▸ v+N suffer torment **endure, suffer** *People continue to suffer mental torment and the misery and pain of physical illness.*

▸ end someone's torment **end, free sb from** *How long will it be until I am freed from this torment?*

torrent N
a large amount of something

● N+of **abuse, criticism, emotions, invective, words** *Four men in a car pulled up beside her and hurled a torrent of racial abuse.*

torture N
extreme physical pain caused to someone

● adj+N bad **brutal, cruel, horrible, severe, terrible, unspeakable** *Some prisoners suffered severe torture and were denied any legal counsel.*

▸ affecting someone's mind **emotional, mental, psychological** *He was kidnapped, battered, drugged and then subjected to extraordinary psychological torture for over 11 years.*

● v+N suffer torture **endure, face, suffer** *He was a prisoner of war, suffering torture and interrogation at the hands of his captors.*

▸ torture someone **engage in, inflict, subject sb to** *He experienced the keenest delight in inflicting torture upon defenceless animals.*

▸ get something using torture **extract sth under, obtain sth by, obtain sth under** *Her confession was obtained under torture.*

torture V
hurt a person or animal deliberately and cruelly

● adv+V badly **brutally, cruelly, horribly, mercilessly, savagely, severely, terribly** *Jesus knows that in the next 24 hours he will be brutally tortured and executed.*

▸ regularly or thoroughly **repeatedly, routinely, systematically** *Prisoners are routinely tortured, sometimes by immersion into boiling water.*

▸ in a way that affects someone's mind **emotionally, mentally, psychologically** *The 28 men were abducted from their homes then beaten and psychologically tortured.*

total N
an amount obtained by adding things together

● adj+N when other totals are added together **combined, cumulative, final, grand, overall** *We raised a grand total of £700.*

▸ large **amazing, formidable, good, high, impressive, large, magnificent, respectable, staggering** *The sailors added two more medals to an already staggering total.*

▸ small **low, meagre, modest** *In most regions where groundwater levels are least healthy, rainfall totals were especially meagre.*

● v+N be a total **bring, equal, make, reach, take** *The service added 206,000 subscribers, bringing its total to 35.3m.* ● *In addition, 34 non military staff such a servants etc. lived there, thus making a grand total of 204 people.*

▸ be more than a total **exceed** *Andrew hopes to rais more than 30,000 pounds for our Hospice Challenge.*

but he's hoping more people will join him on the walk so he can exceed even that total.

▸ bring together a total **accumulate, amass** *The European Champion will be the person who accumulates the highest total of points from all 5 competitions.*

▸ increase a total **boost, increase, raise, swell** *In the run up to Christmas, our fundraising committee is holding a Grand Draw to boost the appeal total further.*

▸ have a total **boast, have** *The La Quinta Golf Club boasts a total of 27 holes.*

▸ calculate or guess a total **calculate, estimate** *Please use the following form to calculate your order total.*

● N+v be an amount **amount to sth, be sth, reach sth, stand at sth** *By 2003, the global unemployment total had reached 180 million.*

▸ be more than sth **exceed sth** *Our total had now exceeded 300.*

▸ rise **go up, rise** *Within the first month, 80 new members had joined, and in the past year the total has risen to 250.*

▸ fall **decline, fall, go down** *We were astounded to find out that our photocopying total went down from an average of 167 sheets per day to 135.*

touch N

a small feature or quality

● adj+N final **final, finishing** *Her guitar and piano work was excellent, giving the perfect finishing touches to her exquisite poetry.*

▸ small **delicate, little, subtle** *Masses of wild roses add their delicate touch to the beauty of the overhanging trees.*

▸ pleasant **delightful, homely, lovely, nice, thoughtful** *The accounts of why it was a good thing were a nice touch .*

▸ funny or clever **clever, comic, humorous** *The man has a nice comic touch, but an hour after watching the film I can't bring to mind any of them.*

▸ special **magic, personal, special** *We are small enough to add that personal touch to your enquiries.*

▸ for decorating something **decorative** *The well equipped kitchen combines up to date appliances with pretty decorative touches.*

▸ typical of women **feminine** *There's a cute, sweetheart shaped neckline for an extra feminine touch.*

touching ADJ

making you feel emotional or sympathetic

▸ adv+ADJ very **deeply, really, very** *The attitude of the women was deeply touching.*

▸ rather **quite, rather** *This last episode is in fact quite touching.*

▸ truly **genuinely, truly** *She manages to bring out her characters' vulnerabilities in some genuinely touching scenes.*

● ADJ+n **gesture, moment, scene, story, tale, tribute** *On his web site, Mac pays touching tribute to Kim: 'She is my shining light and always will be'.*

touch on PHR VB

mention something when talking or writing

● V+on **aspect, issue, matter, point, question,** **subject, theme, topic** *This was the first time that Isaac had expressed a desire to touch on religious subjects.*

tough ADJ

1 difficult

● ADJ+n game or race **battle, challenge, draw, encounter, fight, fixture, game, match, race** *Completing the course was one of the toughest psychological challenges I've taken.*

▸ decision **choice, decision** *She always chickened out of tough decisions.*

▸ job **assignment, job, task** *I personally think this is a tough task.*

▸ exercise **climb, workout** *The view from the top of the hill is certainly worth the somewhat tough climb.*

▸ talks or question **negotiations, question** *You should therefore be prepared for some tough negotiations to get what you may feel is a fair deal.*

2 very strict or severe

● v+ADJ become tough **become, get** *The police are getting tough on illegal traders.*

▸ be tough **be, remain** *The Prime Minister says he will be tough on crime.*

▸ behave in a tough way **talk** *At first, their leaders talked tough, for example threatening mass strikes and disobedience.*

▸ seem tough **appear, seem** *The Church's rule of celibacy for priests might seem tough, but in previous times it was not seen to be such a difficult option.*

● ADJ+on behaviour **crime, drugs, immigration, terror, terrorism** *From here on, the two main political parties were to compete as to which would be toughest on immigration.*

▸ people **criminals, offenders** *The Government should be tougher on criminals imposing tougher sentences.*

3 strong, confident and determined

● adv+ADJ rather **fairly, pretty INFORMAL, quite, rather** *He had been in the business twenty years, and thought he was pretty tough.*

▸ very **exceptionally, extremely, incredibly, really INFORMAL, remarkably, very** *Few women have this combination of characteristics – being both immensely beautiful and incredibly tough.*

▸ mentally **emotionally, mentally** *Some athletes are mentally tough enough not to need additional support in this area.*

● and/or **determined, gritty, resilient, resourceful, rough, streetwise, tenacious, tough, uncompromising** *We know how tough and resilient the Russian people are and always have been.*

tour N

a journey to several different places

● adj+N around a country **national, nationwide** *The stars will now embark on a nationwide tour of schools to spread the message to youngsters across the country.*

▸ around the world **world, worldwide** *The singer is planning a worldwide tour for next year.*

▸ abroad **overseas** *They will be making their first overseas tour with the senior squad.*

▸ quick **quick, whirlwind** *They're just back from a whirlwind tour of America's top northeast colleges.*

▶ short **brief, mini, short** *Then they were taken on a short tour around Westminster.*

▶ slow **leisurely** *Our leisurely tour gives you time to enjoy all 3 resorts to the full.*

▶ long **extended, extensive, full, grand, long** *We offer short or extended tours throughout the UK and Europe.*

▶ to see beautiful places **panoramic, scenic** *After the excitement of Race Day, what better than a scenic tour of Donegal?*

▶ to see things you do not usually see **behind-the-scenes** *Behind-the-scenes tours of the Olympic Park are available.*

▶ interesting **fascinating, informative** *This is a relaxing and highly informative tour, offering a welcome escape from the hustle and bustle of the city.*

▶ organized **guided, organized, package** *The first time I read this book, I was on an organized bus tour in Europe.*

▶ starting and finishing in the same place **circular** *This circular tour of the city wall starts in Castle Street.*

▶ on computer **interactive, virtual** *Explore colliery buildings and go on a virtual tour of a modern mine.*

tourism N
the business of providing holiday services for people

● adj+N by a lot of people **mass** *The island of Kythira, only 12 miles off the southern tip of the Peloponnese but somehow unaffected by mass tourism, is a wonderfully restful place.*

▶ for a particular purpose **business, cultural, leisure, sex** *Leisure and business tourism are vital to the economy of the region.*

▶ to a particular place **rural, space** *I attended a meeting to promote rural tourism.*

▶ abroad/in your own country **domestic, international** *Both domestic and international tourism are responsible for beachfront urbanization in the Dominican Republic.*

▶ not harming a place **ethical, responsible** *Ethical tourism worldwide is, of course, not something that can just happen overnight.*

▶ not harming the environment **eco, green** *We look forward to your visit to this 'little golden part of Devon' where green tourism is encouraged.*

● v+N increase tourism **boost, enhance, improve, increase** *The Olympic games will create jobs and boost tourism.*

▶ encourage tourism **attract, bring, develop, encourage, promote, revive, stimulate, support** *The railway also brought the first mass tourism to the Yorkshire Dales in the 19th century.*

▶ affect tourism **affect** *High travel costs are also affecting tourism.*

● N+n business **business, industry, sector** *Some 10 % of all new jobs created are in the tourism industry.*

▶ place **attraction, destination** *He will work with the Australian Tourist Commission to promote Australia as a tourism destination to the Japanese market.*

▶ development **development, marketing, promotion** *Recent tourism marketing campaigns have been a huge success.*

▶ plan **initiative, strategy** *A new tourism initiative for*

the North Highlands of Scotland was launched on 1 August.

▶ increase **boom** *Prague was enjoying a tourism boom.*

tourist N
someone visiting place on holiday

● v+N attract tourists **attract, bring in, draw in, encourage, entice, lure, pull in, welcome** *With its lush, beautiful scenery and tropical climate, Jamaica has long been luring tourists from all over the world.*

▶ discourage tourists **discourage** *Beggars may even discourage foreign tourists from visiting London, he moans.*

▶ be full of tourists **be crowded with, be overrun with, be swarming with, be thronged with** *Miraculously, this place doesn't seem to be overrun with tourists.*

● N+n place **attraction, centre, destination, haven, hotspot, magnet, resort, sight, spot, trap** *Without doubt, the Grand Palace is the best of Bangkok's many tourist attractions.*

▶ route **route, trail** *Cat Island is off the normal tourist trail of the Bahamas, one of the outer islands.*

▶ organization or information office **board, bureau, information, office** *Ask at tourist information offices for detailed programmes.*

▶ information book **brochure, guide, leaflet** *It features on all the island tourist brochures.*

tournament N
a series of games producing one final winner

● v+N win a tournament **win** *They then became the first team to win the tournament twice.*

▶ hold or organize a tournament **hold, host, organize, stage** *The tournament was first staged in 1877.*

▶ enter or play in a tournament **compete in, enter, participate in, play in** *I was told that they were paying to enter a poker tournament in which they would then play for their own money.*

▶ leave a tournament **be disqualified from, exit, leave, withdraw from** *He should have been disqualified from the tournament.*

trace V
discover or desribe something from the past

● V+n people who used to be in your family **ancestors, ancestry, descendants, descent, genealogy, lineage, pedigree** *Those of us who spend a lot of time tracing our pedigree take for granted that the records we find are true.*

▶ beginnings **emergence, genesis, origins, roots** *The club can actually trace its origins back to 1903.*

▶ history or development **development, evolution, history, progress** *This exhibition traces the history of the fast-fading tradition of Punjabi wrestling.*

trace N
1 a small sign that someone has been present or that something has happened

● v+N remove or hide traces of something **destroy, eliminate, eradicate, erase, hide, obliterate, remove** *The system has a stealth mode that eliminates all traces of itself on any machine it's plugged into.*

▶ leave or keep traces of something **leave, preserve** *These nomadic peoples left traces of their cultural activity on rocks, paths and hills.*

▶ find traces of something **detect, discover, find** *Amongst the modern buildings you will still find traces of the pre-war city.*

▶ look for traces of something **look for, search for** *Tegan peered closely at the face in the poor light, searching for some trace of her inner disquiet.*

▶ show traces of something **bear, reveal** *The linoleum-covered floor bore abundant traces of a busy morning.*

● N+v disappear **disappear, vanish** *Of Thunderley church, all traces disappeared many years ago.*

▶ remain **exist, linger, remain, survive** *No trace survives of settlements, but there are a number of Bronze Age burial cairns.*

● v+without+N **be lost, disappear, sink, vanish** *We shall be selling all the remaining club equipment, all proceeds to vanish without a trace.*

2 a slight sign of an emotion

● N+of **bitterness, irony, self-pity, sentimentality** *There is not a single trace of irony in the rest of this sentence.*

tract N
a large area of land

● adj+N **extensive, great, huge, large, vast** *Canada has vast tracts of stunning, unspoilt scenery.*

● N+of land **country, ground, land, landscape, territory** *Vineyards were no longer confined to a few places, but extended over large tracts of country.*

▶ woods or forest **forest, rainforest, woodland** *It is an ancient tract of woodland running along a deep rocky cleft.*

▶ fields and countryside **countryside, farmland, meadow** *There are extensive and productive tracts of meadow in the parish.*

▶ exposed land **grassland, heathland, moor, moorland, wilderness** *Its vast tracts of wilderness and miles of spectacular coastline mean that it is a magnet for those who enjoy the big outdoors.*

trade N
the activities of buying and selling goods

▶ adj+N fair **ethical, fair** *He heard a first-hand account of how fair trade is helping to lift whole communities out of poverty.*

▶ unfair **unfair** *For every dollar the West gives in aid to developing countries, it takes two back through unfair trade.*

▶ illegal **illegal, illicit** *Many small carnivores in Vietnam are threatened due to illegal trade.*

▶ without restrictions **free** *The message was that the advantage of joining the EEC was to become a member of a common market in which free trade was encouraged between the countries.*

▶ between countries **cross-border, foreign, global, international, overseas** *He devoted himself to the internal security of his land and promoted domestic and foreign trade.*

▶ in your own country **domestic** *The riverfront became increasingly important as overseas and domestic trade expanded.*

▶ between two groups or countries **bilateral, two-way** *In terms of economy and trade, Taiwan's bilateral trade with Japan in 2004 totaled US$56.83 billion.*

● v+N control trade **control, govern, regulate** *The government must continue activities to regulate cross-border trade.*

▶ increase trade **boost, expand, increase** *The historic bridge is set to reopen to traffic in a few weeks, which should further boost trade.*

▶ make trade easier **facilitate, liberalize** *It is not intended to facilitate online trade.*

▶ encourage trade **encourage, promote, stimulate** *In January 1699, towns were allowed to elect their own officials, collect revenue and stimulate trade.*

▶ make trade harder **affect, disrupt, hinder, impede, restrict, suppress** *The new barriers hinder trade and investment.* ● *It emerged that rules that have existed in Britain for many years were on shaky ground under EU law because they may restrict free trade between member states.*

tradition N
a very old custom, belief, or story

● adj+N old **age-old, ancient, long, long-standing, old, time-honoured** *The true charm of the country runs beyond the wonder of ancient traditions.*

▶ good **fine, proud, rich, strong** *Bournemouth has a proud tradition of horticultural excellence.*

▶ types of tradition **classical, cultural, family, folk, literary, musical, religious, spiritual** *As C. S. Lewis has observed: once you have rejected a part of a religious tradition, you have rejected the entire tradition.*

● v+N follow a tradition **continue in, follow, keep with, uphold** *The 7th Earl, following family tradition, lives in Kenya.*

▶ continue a tradition **carry on, continue, maintain, perpetuate, preserve** *They in turn will continue the tradition with their own children and remember those special times.*

▶ honour a tradition **celebrate, honour, respect** *We want to show the older generation that we honour their traditions and value their memories and wisdom.*

▶ start following a tradition again **re-establish, revive** *The school has recently revived the tradition of academic scholarships.*

▶ receive a tradition from someone **inherit** *Inheriting the Greek traditions and knowledge, the ancient Romans also valued Ginger for its 'culinary and medicinal uses.'*

▶ establish a tradition **establish, invent** *ATTIK has established a tradition of working with students throughout their studies to globally showcase the opportunities there are in Yorkshire.*

▶ stop following a tradition **abandon, break, reject** *Left to our own devices, we readily abandon our traditions.*

▶ not follow tradition **break with, depart from** *She broke with family tradition by marrying and staying married to the same person for 34 years!*

▶ have a lot of tradition **be steeped in** *The village of Visa is located in Mezoseg, Transylvania, and is steeped in tradition.*

▶ come from tradition **be based on, be built on,**

belong to, be rooted in, come from, derive from, stem from *'Halloween' on the last night of October is thought to have derived from an ancient Celtic tradition.*

traditional ADJ
relating to or based on old things

- adv+ADJ very **deeply, highly, really** INFORMAL, **strictly, truly, very** *This is a very traditional and beautiful Savoyard restaurant.*
- ▶ rather **fairly, pretty** INFORMAL, **quite, rather, relatively, somewhat** *Kershaw's painting style is relatively traditional.*
- ▶ in a pleasant way **charmingly, delightfully, wonderfully** *For many people, holiday cottages in Spain conjure up images of charmingly traditional buildings nestling in the wild and unspoilt countryside of Andalucia.*

- ADJ+n **form, method, model, practice, style, system, technique, view, way** *Rooms are simply furnished in traditional style.*

traffic N
vehicles travelling in an area at a particular time

- adj+N coming towards you **oncoming** *I feel like a rabbit caught in the headlights of oncoming traffic.*
- ▶ when there is a lot of traffic **busy, dense, heavy, horrendous** *The traffic was horrendous.*
- ▶ when there is not much traffic **light** *Local diversions, suitable for light traffic, will also be set up.*
- ▶ at the busiest time of the day **peak, rush-hour** *Rush-hour traffic might flow better if traffic lights were set at random.*
- ▶ slow **slow, slow-moving** *The majority of these accidents occur when motorbikes collide with stationary or slow-moving traffic.*
- ▶ fast **fast-moving, speeding** *People are fed up with speeding traffic on their roads.*
- ▶ not moving **congested, gridlocked, stationary** *I was faced with around 2 miles of almost stationary traffic!*
- ▶ passing through a place **through** *All through traffic would be directed onto a network of arterial roads.*

- v+N direct traffic somewhere **direct, rout** *At present, traffic was directed away from, and not through, the village.*
- ▶ send traffic in a different direction **divert, redirect, reroute** *For three hours there was chaos, with traffic diverted.*
- ▶ slow or control traffic **calm, control, regulate, slow (down)** *Can anything be done to slow the traffic in this area of the town?*
- ▶ block or stop traffic **block, disrupt, halt, obstruct, stop** *Traffic was severely disrupted throughout the area as lakes formed across main roads.*
- ▶ increase traffic **attract, generate, increase, induce** *All the evidence shows that building more roads generates more traffic.*
- ▶ reduce traffic **curb, cut, discourage, reduce, restrict** *They need a relief road to reduce traffic through the narrow country roads.*
- ▶ be in traffic **be in, be stuck in** *No one enjoys being stuck in traffic.*
- ▶ drive through traffic **dodge, drive through, weave**

through *Cyclists dash through intersections, dodging traffic.*

- N+v move in a direction **head for, travel** *Priority is given to traffic travelling from the south.*
- ▶ move continuously **flow, keep moving** *Police have to try and keep traffic flowing at road traffic accidents.*
- ▶ slow down or stop **slow (down), stop** *Traffic slowed down considerably whilst drivers gawped at this unusual sight.*
- ▶ not move **queue** *Buses were delayed by traffic queuing at the traffic lights.*
- ▶ move quickly or noisily **roar, rumble, speed, thunder, whiz** *The traffic thunders down the Cold Ash Hill and can barely stop at the roundabout.*
- ▶ move slowly **crawl** *The snow fell during the day, while traffic was crawling along the roads.*
- ▶ obstruct a place **choke sth, clog sth** *Transport 2000 believes congestion charging offers a new way forward for cities choked by traffic.*

- N+n when there is too much traffic **congestion, jam, queue** *Do expect traffic jams during rush hour.*
- ▶ control **control, management, monitoring, reduction, regulation** *We need new approaches to transportation, traffic management and parking.*
- ▶ movement **flow, movement** *Despite schemes to improve traffic flows, motorists are still spending a lot of time in traffic jams.*
- ▶ pollution **fumes, pollution** *Traffic fumes are a major cause of breathing problems.*
- ▶ delays **delays, disruption** *There are special delivery 'windows' to minimise traffic disruption and nuisance.*
- ▶ amount **density, volume** *Lower traffic volumes could potentially result in fewer casualties.*

tragedy N
a very sad event causing people to suffer

- adj+N very bad **appalling, awful, horrific, terrible, unspeakable** *Our thoughts and prayers are with those affected by this week's terrible tragedies.*
- ▶ affecting people's lives **human, humanitarian** *War will cause a humanitarian tragedy and a political crisis.*
- ▶ affecting a particular person **personal** *He experienced a personal tragedy when his son Hamnet died in 1596.*
- ▶ going to happen soon **impending** *A mood of impending tragedy hangs over their lives.*

- v+N avoid or prevent a tragedy **avert, avoid, prevent** *What actions might have averted the tragedies that rate among the worst in human history?*
- ▶ experience a tragedy **be affected by, be blighted by, be devastated by, be hit by, be touched by, experience, suffer** *In 1881, he suffered a tragedy when his brother Dante died suddenly.*
- ▶ end in tragedy **end in, lead to, result in, turn into** *The gang corners Jim and challenges him to take part in a car race which ends in tragedy.*
- ▶ deal with tragedy **cope with, deal with, react to, respond to** *We humans use different ways to cope with a tragedy.*

- N+v **happen, occur, strike, unfold** *We should be using the world-wide coalition to address the humanitarian tragedy unfolding before us.*

tragic ADJ
causing or involving great sadness

● adv+ADJ very or particularly **absolutely, deeply, particularly, really** INFORMAL, **so** INFORMAL, **truly, utterly, very** *It was particularly tragic that such an accident occurred following what was a happy family occasion.* ● *The death of this beautiful young woman is truly tragic.*

▶ rather **quite, rather, somewhat** *It's rather tragic that the band were at their very best just as the lead singer was mentally disintegrating.*

▶ possibly **potentially** *When automatic gates to these lakes open, a potentially tragic situation could arise.*

● ADJ+n event **accident, death, event, incident, loss, murder** *At first, they thought he died in a tragic accident.*

▶ situation **circumstances** *Michael died under tragic circumstances in a hotel room in Sydney.*

▶ ending or result **consequences, ending, fate** *The play tells the story of a young arsonist and the tragic consequences of his crimes.*

▶ mistake **miscalculation, mistake, misunderstanding** *The police said that Mr de Menezes' death was a tragic mistake that will not be repeated.*

trained ADJ
with all the necessary skills and qualifications

● adv+ADJ well **highly, well** *The review found that staff are well trained and have a high level of awareness of the needs of patients.*

▶ in the right way **adequately, appropriately, properly, suitably** *Make sure that your operator is properly trained and confident in the application of eartags.*

▶ badly **inadequately, poorly** *Poorly trained or unscrupulous firms often won out at the expense of quality and the consumer.*

▶ completely **fully** *Every windscreen is replaced by fully trained fitters.*

▶ specially **specially** *This service is staffed by specially trained volunteers.*

having proper qualifications **professionally** *Our professionally trained advisers can also assist with dispute resolution on equality and diversity issues.*

of actors or musicians, traditionally **classically** *Michael is a classically trained actor.*

in medicine **medically** *Whilst not medically trained, Alex has combat medical experience from Iraq and West Africa.*

training N
the process of training people for a job or activity

adj+N thorough **comprehensive, extensive, full, in-depth, intensive, rigorous, thorough** *Previous experience is not essential as full training will be given relevant to the role.*

good **effective, excellent** *The effective use of any information system requires effective training.*

suitable or enough **adequate, appropriate, proper, relevant, sufficient, suitable** *The need to offer appropriate training to staff cannot be understated.*

not suitable or enough **inadequate, minimal** *Insufficient employer support and inadequate training are the most common complaints.*

basic **basic, essential, necessary** *They need to invest much more heavily in basic training in IT for all the staff.*

▶ more or continuing **additional, continuous, extra, further, more, ongoing** *If the institution would like ongoing training, it can be arranged.*

▶ formal **formal, professional** *NYDC is a company for young dancers that have not yet gone through professional training.*

▶ special **special, specialist, specialized, specific** *Certain dangerous machines require special training and may not be used by persons under 18 years of age.*

▶ in your company **in-house, in-service, on-site** *When a non-officer is due for promotion, he or she has to undergo in-service training for two months and pass an exam in order to be promoted to the level of officer.*

▶ involving actual work **hands-on, on-the-job, work-based** *There is no substitute for hands-on training.*

▶ for a job **vocational** *The course is of benefit both to those coming fresh from undergraduate degrees or vocational training.*

● v+N do training **attend, do, engage in, go through, participate in, pursue, undergo, undertake** *Managers are currently undergoing training on work-life balance.*

▶ receive training **get, receive** *Here he received training for the priesthood.*

▶ give training **conduct, deliver, give, offer, provide** *The Masters in Financial Economics (MFE) is a full-time nine-month programme that will provide outstanding training in the tools of financial economics.*

▶ organize training **arrange, organize** *Staff can come in and work on their own or we can arrange group training to suit.*

▶ start training **begin, commence, embark on, start** *She would like to embark on further training.*

▶ complete training **complete, finish** *Those who successfully complete their training may be suitable for employment in many areas of the sport, leisure or recreation industry.*

▶ not have enough training **lack, need** *Many teachers lack training to properly teach sports to disabled pupils.*

● N+n course **course, initiative, module, package, plan, programme, scheme** *We have run training courses in many hospitals.*

▶ meeting or event **day, event, seminar, session, workshop** *This was a really inspiring and well thought out training session.*

▶ place **centre, establishment** *The building was previously a training centre to teach women how to bricklay.*

▶ organization **organization, provider** *You can gain useful knowledge through talking to the training providers.*

▶ books, videos etc **aid, manual, materials, pack, resources, video** *The training materials can be used again and again, providing a cost-effective way for staff to gain new skills.*

▶ activity **activity, exercise** *Below is a planning worksheet taken from a recent training exercise.*

trait N
a particular quality in someone's character

● adj+N good **admirable, desirable, endearing,**

good *You seem to be a bit apologetic for being judgemental, and that is, in general an admirable trait.*

▶ bad **annoying, bad, undesirable** *He was displaying all the annoying traits that his father displayed during their marriage.*

▶ characteristic **characteristic, distinctive, distinguishing** *His most distinctive trait was a deep, incredibly gravelly voice.*

▶ in someone's behaviour or thinking **behavioural, character, personality, psychological** *Individuals may show obsessive behavioural traits.*

▶ typical of a type of person **autistic, masculine, psychopathic** *Eight years later, Luke has severe learning disabilities, chronic epilepsy and autistic traits.*

● v+N have a trait **display, exhibit, have, possess, show** *Pilots tend to possess such traits as leadership, dominance, alertness, achievement, and consistency of behaviour.*

▶ when a trait is passed on from someone **acquire, inherit** *Of course she inherits other traits from me – her cooking, her humour, her allergy to housework!*

tranquil ADJ
calm, still, and quiet

● adv+ADJ very **so** INFORMAL, **truly, very** *Surrounded by wonderful countryside with a huge variety of wildlife on site, it is truly tranquil.*

▶ in a good way **beautifully, delightfully, wonderfully** *The hotel occupies a wonderfully tranquil spot amongst the olive and pine trees.*

▶ rather **fairly, relatively** *The eastern coast contrasts with the western and southern coasts as it is fairly tranquil.*

● ADJ+n place **countryside, haven, oasis, retreat, setting, spot, surroundings** *It is a small farm, set in the beautiful and tranquil surroundings of the Blackmore Vale.*

▶ atmosphere **ambience, atmosphere** *Take a moment to sit down and enjoy the tranquil atmosphere.*

● and/or quiet or calm **calm, peaceful, quiet, relaxing, secluded, serene** *The manicured garden offers a tranquil and peaceful setting.*

▶ beautiful **beautiful, idyllic, picturesque, scenic, unspoilt** *Whilst the setting is tranquil and picturesque, access to major road, rail and airport links are close by.*

transaction N
an action of buying or selling something

● adj+N dishonest **fraudulent, suspicious** *It's easier for a human to spot fraudulent transactions than a machine.*

▶ honest **legitimate** *I confirm that the transaction is legitimate.*

▶ involving money **cash, currency, finance, financial, monetary** *Banks use encryption methods all around the world to process financial transactions.*

▶ between businesses **commercial, corporate** *She specialises in commercial property transactions.*

▶ using the Internet **electronic, online** *Encryption is at the heart of secure electronic transactions.*

● v+N make a transaction **carry out, conduct, do,**

enter into, execute, make, perform, undertake *Many people are still wary about using the Internet when making financial transactions.*

▶ complete a transaction **complete, conclude, finalise, settle** *Press F5 to complete the transaction.*

▶ deal with a transaction **deal with, handle, manage, process** *The Service handles financial transactions totalling around 0.5 billion pounds annually.*

▶ cancel a transaction **cancel, clear, void, withdraw from** *I'm trying to take steps to cancel the transaction.*

▶ allow a transaction **allow, authenticate, authorise** *The use of signatures to authorise credit card transactions was phased out.*

▶ record a transaction **log, record** *Record all transactions as you spend so that there are no surprises when your bank statement arrives.*

transcript N
a written copy of the exact words someone said

● adj+N complete/not complete **complete, full, partial, uncorrected, unedited, verbatim** *You can read a full transcript of her interview here.*

▶ not published or official **unofficial, unpublished** *The Society's unpublished transcripts can be consulted in the Archives section.*

▶ official **certified, official** *You will need to bring with you an official transcript from the overseas institution showing your results.*

● N+of **conference, conversation, debate, interview, lecture, presentation, proceedings, session, speech, tape** *Some scenes present authentic dialogue from transcripts of conversations.*

transfer N
the process of moving to a different job in the same organization

● adj+N easy **easy, seamless, smooth, successful** *There has been a smooth transfer of staff into PASA.*

▶ permanent **permanent** *He joined Chesterfield originally on loan, but with a view to a permanent transfer.*

▶ inside a company **internal** *Where possible, the company will provide opportunities for internal transfer.*

● v+N make a transfer **make** *His transfer was made at the request of Dr. Richard Kracowski.*

▶ ask for a transfer **request** *Mark requested a transfer in February 2002.*

▶ get a transfer **get** *In 2005, he got his next transfer when he was made checker in the same department.*

▶ offer or give someone a transfer **give sb, offer sb** *She was offered a transfer to another department.*

▶ give permission for someone's transfer **approve, authorize** *If the transfer is approved, it is the supervisor's responsibility to ensure that the necessary paperwork is done.*

transform V
make something completely different and much better [usually passive]

● adv+V completely **completely, dramatically, fundamentally, radically, totally, utterly** *The company has radically transformed its employment practices over the last 3 years.*

▸ quickly **immediately, instantly, quickly, rapidly, suddenly** *Perceptions of the region are being rapidly transformed as a result.*

▸ slowly **gradually, slowly** *People saw the empty butcher's shop being slowly transformed.*

▸ with successful results **successfully** *Sue and Mike have successfully transformed an old barn into a delightful family home.*

▸ in a way that seems impossible **magically, miraculously** *Your document will be magically transformed into a beautiful and legible HTML document.*

transformation N

a change into someone or something completely different

● adj+N big **complete, dramatic, fundamental, great, major, massive, profound, radical, real, significant, total** *The main shopping area has undergone a major transformation.*

▸ surprising **amazing, magical, miraculous, remarkable** *I first visited the reserve when it still looked like a construction site, since then I have visited twice a year and the transformation is remarkable.*

▸ quick **rapid, sudden** *Visitors can witness first-hand the rapid transformation of a country that has only recently crept from under the doormat of history.*

▸ slow **gradual** *I believe we will see a gradual transformation in cares services with further investment.*

▸ types of transformation **cultural, economic, organizational, personal, physical, political, social, spiritual** *He was a key figure in Poland's post-communist political transformation.*

● v+N make or achieve a transformation **achieve, effect, make, perform** *A two-pronged strategy will be necessary to achieve this transformation.*

▸ experience a transformation **experience, undergo** *As you can see, the website has undergone a transformation.*

▸ notice a transformation **see, witness** *It's amazing to see the transformation in people who come to the workshop in despair and without hope.*

▸ complete a transformation **complete** *There was a rush to finish before the end of the day, but the transformation was completed and it looks amazing.*

▸ make a transformation easier **facilitate** *Road freight has facilitated the transformation of business activity through the reduction in business costs.*

transition N

the process of changing to a new situation

● adj+N successful **easy, effective, seamless, smooth, successful** *The location of the new nursery has been carefully chosen to present a seamless transition between the private nursery care and that provided by the school.*

▸ difficult **difficult, painful** *She's made the difficult transition from comedy actress to being taken seriously.*

▸ quick **abrupt, quick, rapid, sudden** *After approximately 20 minutes of slow wave sleep there is a quick transition back to stage 2 sleep.*

▸ slow **gradual, slow** *I would have preferred a more gradual transition.*

▸ involving big changes **important, major** *Adolescence is a major life transition.*

▸ without any trouble or violence **orderly, painless, peaceful** *The country was lauded for its peaceful transition to democracy.*

▸ types of transition **cultural, democratic, demographic, economic, historical, political, social** *Comparatively, within Europe, the demographic transition in Finland took place relatively recently.*

● v+N make a transition **achieve, complete, effect, make** *He is an actor who has successfully made the transition from television to the stage.*

▸ make a transition easier **aid, ease, enable, facilitate, help, smooth** *This information can help ease the transition from school to university.*

▸ be in charge of a transition **manage, oversee** *She will oversee the transition from the old to the new system.*

▸ experience a transition **experience, undergo** *The field of Radiation Oncology has undergone a radical transition in the last decade.*

▸ show that a transition is happening **mark** *Two pictures in the exhibition mark the transition from Munnings' youthful watercolours to the more mature oils.*

● N+n **period, phase, process, stage** *The new measures aim to provide people with additional financial support during the transition period.*

translate V

change words into another language

● adv+V in a way that gives the general meaning **freely, loosely, roughly** *The motto 'Vocati Veniemus' may be freely translated as 'when summoned we shall be there'.*

▸ in a way that gives the exact meaning of each word **literally** *The title of Proust's masterpiece, if translated literally into English, is not 'The Remembrance of Things Past', but 'The Search for Past Time'.*

▸ correctly **accurately, correctly** *Getting your business cards accurately translated and properly typeset is absolutely essential.*

▸ usually **usually** *'Carpe Diem' is usually translated from the Latin as 'seize the day'.*

translation N

words changed into different language

● adj+N exact **direct, exact, faithful, literal** *Its literal translation from its original Latin is 'to make into a thing'.*

▸ not exact **free, rough** *In a rough translation, 'grk' means brave, generous and foolish, all at the same time.*

▸ good **accurate, correct, good** *Even a good translation is a poor substitute for the original poetic text.*

▸ bad **bad, poor** *The explanations of symbols are in German, with a poor English translation.*

▸ types of translation **automatic, computer-assisted, machine, simultaneous, technical** *Although there remain many outstanding problems, some degree of automatic translation is now a daily reality.*

● v+N **do, find, make, produce, provide** *Some difficult terms may require lengthy research in order to find a suitable translation.* ● *Translations are* made *into* Russian, Egyptian Arabic, Spanish and Portuguese.

transmit V
spread something from one person to another

- adv+V easily **easily, readily** *The disease is easily transmitted by skin contact, so keep affected areas covered.*
- ▶ in a physical way **genetically, orally, sexually** *Cystic fibrosis is genetically transmitted.* • *His work was transmitted orally for over 200 years.*
- ▶ in an electronic way **electronically** *They issued a weekly bulletin which was transmitted electronically to library staff across the country.*
- V+n disease **disease, infection, virus** *The disease is transmitted from one dog to another by contact with infected faeces.*
- ▶ information or ideas **data, idea, information, knowledge, message, values** *How are we to transmit religious values to the next generation?*

transparent ADJ
not hiding information

- adv+ADJ **completely, entirely, fully, highly, sufficiently, totally** *We found that the committee's policies and procedures were not sufficiently transparent.*
- ADJ+N system or method **approach, manner, mechanism, procedure, process, system, way** *A fair and transparent system of paying employees reduces the risks of being taken to a costly tribunal.*
- ▶ information **criterion, decision, information, policy** *It's important that such decisions are transparent and can be justified publicly.*
- ▶ management or government **government, management** *At a public level, the G8 demand transparent government and an end to corruption.*
- and/or **accountable, clear, consistent, democratic, effective, efficient, equitable, fair, honest, inclusive, open, simple** *More serious complaints will be managed by us in an open and transparent way.*

transplant N
an operation to put a new organ into the body

- v+N have a transplant **get, have, receive, undergo** *I had a kidney transplant in 1996.*
- ▶ do a transplant **carry out, do, perform** *The hospital performs several transplants every month and donors are drawn from a national list.*
- ▶ need a transplant **await, need, require** *He is awaiting a liver transplant.*
- ▶ react badly to a transplant **reject** *Drugs are used to prevent your immune system from rejecting the transplant.*
- N+n person who has a transplant **patient, recipient** *Transplant patients are typically referred to the transplant unit at Aberdeen Royal Infirmary.*
- ▶ operation **operation, surgery** *Pat's transplant operation was carried out at the Royal Liverpool Hospital.*
- ▶ person or people who do the transplant **surgeon, team** *A specialist transplant surgeon will look at all your test results and decide whether you are likely to make a good recovery from the surgery.*

- ▶ person who gives the organ **donor** *Time was running out for Steve, as the search for a transplant donor failed.*
- ▶ rejection **rejection** *Our goal is to identify the factors underlying organ transplant rejection.*

transport N
the business of moving people using vehicles

- adj+N for anyone to use **public** *We hope that providing accurate information will encourage more people to use public transport.*
- ▶ good **accessible, affordable, efficient, excellent, good, reliable** *Efficient, fast, reliable transport is vital to our future prosperity.*
- ▶ bad **inadequate, poor** *City centre shops suffer if transport is poor.*
- ▶ in a particular area **local, rural, urban** *Improved funding of rural transport is required to address the social exclusion of people living in rural areas.*
- ▶ free or cheap **cheap, free** *Offering cheap transport is one way of encouarging people to use buses and trains.*
- ▶ that can continue without harming the environment **sustainable** *Leeds has campaigned within Europe for the need to develop sustainable transport.*
- ▶ local **local** *The area is well served by local public transport.*
- v+N **arrange, improve, offer, organize, provide, use** *The government has promised to improve transport in our cities.* • *A trolley bus service offers transport around the main tourist areas.*
- N+n system **facilities, infrastructure, network, provision, service, system** *The county has a reliable public transport network.*
- ▶ connection **connection, link** *The town has excellent public transport links.*
- ▶ company that provides transport **company, operator, provider** *Arriva is a successful public transport operator in many European countries.*
- ▶ businesses that provide transport **industry, sector** *The research investigates the effects of privatising the transport industry.*
- ▶ plans **plan, planning, policy, scheme, strategy** *Transport policy is now high up on the political agenda.*
- ▶ person using transport **user** *The study aims to seek the views of transport users.*
- ▶ a place where you can get transport to many places **hub** *Santiago-Benitez International Airport is the main transport hub for Chile.*

transportation N
the activity or system of moving people or things

- adj+N **easy, efficient, safe** *Many options exist for the storage and safe transportation of rifles and handguns.*
- v+N **arrange, provide** *All items are sold as seen and the buyer will be required to arrange transportation.*
- N+n **infrastructure, link, network, service, system** *The reality is that today's transportation infrastructure can no longer cope with the demands we are placing on it.*

trap N
a trick

- v+N set a trap **lay, set, spring** *So, the police set a trap to catch their murderer.*
- ▶ be deceived by a trap **be lured into, walk into** *They walked into a trap they should have seen.*
- ▶ avoid **avoid, escape, evade** *He won through, avoiding the trap set for him.*

trappings N
possessions showing someone is rich or powerful

- adj+N **traditional, usual** *Despite international success, she had none of the usual trappings of fame.*
- v+N have trappings **acquire, enjoy, have** *He has the trappings of a multimillionaire – 5 luxury homes, a Ferrari, a Rolls-Royce, a private jet and a yacht in the south of France.*
- ▶ not have trappings **avoid, eschew, shun** *He had a BMW but otherwise shunned the trappings of capitalism.*
- N+of **fame, life, power, success, wealth** *Cruise is a rich man who enjoys all the trappings of wealth.*

trauma N
a bad experience that upsets someone

- adj+N types of trauma **emotional, mental, personal, psychological** *Anyone being routinely abused is likely to experience emotional trauma that can cause depression.*
- severe **acute, deep, major, serious, severe, significant, terrible** *The victims have suffered a significant trauma as a result of the attack.*
- happening recently/in the past **past, recent** *Counselling can help you to resolve any past traumas that have contributed to your current thinking.*
- v+N suffer a trauma **experience, face, suffer, undergo** *Many victims of child abuse have to face the trauma of describing personal details of their abuse in front of strangers.*
- cause a trauma for someone **inflict** *Divorce can inflict trauma on children.*
- successfully deal with a trauma **heal, overcome, survive** *Happily, our small household has survived the traumas of an international move, and we are settling into our new lifestyle.*
- avoid a trauma **avoid, prevent** *To avoid the trauma of appearing in court, the victim was allowed to give evidence by a remote link.*
- make a trauma less bad **lessen, minimize, reduce** *We offer counselling to soldiers to reduce the trauma and long term effects of being in a war zone.*

traumatic ADJ
making you feel very upset or shocked

- adv+ADJ very **deeply, extremely, particularly, very** *The death of a child is extremely traumatic for parents.*
- rather **fairly, pretty** INFORMAL, **quite** *Searching for a lost pet can be quite traumatic.*
- in a particular way **emotionally, psychologically** *Domestic abuse is a psychologically traumatic experience.*
- ADJ+n situation or experience **change,**

circumstances, episode, event, experience, incident, situation *Memories of the traumatic event may surface in the form of flashbacks.*
- ▶ time **childhood, period, time, week, year** *James had many insecurities, probably derived from his traumatic childhood.* • *This was a traumatic time, from which we shall never totally recover.*
- ▶ effect **effect, impact** *Never underestimate the traumatic effects of a major crisis on people's lives.*
- ▶ memory **memory** *It is a strange thing that you can suppress a traumatic memory for decades and then it comes back in the form of nightmares.*
- and/or **difficult, painful, stressful** *The breakdown of any marriage is bound to be a painful and traumatic time.*

travel V
go to different places

- adv+V to many places **extensively, far and wide, widely** *Jamie travels extensively to support youth projects in Europe and Lebanon.*
- ▶ to foreign countries **abroad, internationally, overseas, worldwide** *They are based in Lancashire, U.K., but are prepared to travel worldwide for gigs.*
- ▶ without any legal limits **freely** *We Americans cherish our ability to travel freely.*
- ▶ without someone else's help **alone, independently** *Many people prefer to travel independently rather than take package holidays.*
- ▶ often **frequently, often, regularly** *If you travel frequently, for business or for pleasure, these new language courses might be of interest to you.*

traveller N
someone who is travelling

- adj+N having travelled often **experienced, frequent, regular, seasoned** *Like many seasoned travellers, Buerk has learned to cope with jet-lag.*
- ▶ who enjoys travelling **avid, great, keen** *Spottiswoode was always a keen traveller and he visited several countries.*
- ▶ having good judgement **discerning** *Summerwood is a luxury hotel offering stylish accommodation for the discerning traveller.*
- ▶ going to places that not many people go to **adventurous, intrepid** *For many years, Cambodia was off limits to all but the most intrepid travellers.*
- ▶ travelling without other people **lone, single, solo** *We have as many single travellers as we do couples, so don't feel worried about booking on your own.*
- ▶ travelling to foreign countries **foreign, international, overseas** *For international travellers, Birmingham is served by two airports: Birmingham International and East Midlands.*
- ▶ travelling to the same place as you **fellow** *You can use the website to check hotel and resort reviews posted by fellow travellers.*
- ▶ tired **weary** *The hotel offers a high standard of comfort for the weary traveller.*
- ▶ making your own arrangements and not using a travel company **independent** *The 'Peru Traveller Guide' is an excellent source of information for the independent traveller to Peru.*
- ▶ similar to you **like-minded** *Volunteer holidays are a great way to meet other like-minded travellers.*
- n+N a traveller for work/pleasure **business,**

holiday, leisure *The New Yorker, with its excellent location, represents excellent value for money for both the business and leisure traveller.*
▸ a traveller using a particular method of transport **air, bus, coach, rail, train** *Bad weather brought delays and cancellations for rail travellers.*
▸ a traveller who wants to travel cheaply **budget** *For budget travellers, cheap accommodation is widely available throughout Malaysia.*

treason N
the crime of helping your country's enemies

- v+N **commit** *Any baron who disobeyed this royal command would be committing treason, which carried the death penalty.*
- n+of+N **accusation, act, charge, offence** *He was put on trial on charges of treason.*

treat V
1 deal with someone or something in a particular way

- adv+V in a good or fair way **appropriately, correctly, equally, equitably, fairly, humanely, properly, sensitively** *The FSA has a general duty to ensure consumers are treated fairly.*
▸ in a bad or unfair way **badly, harshly, inadequately, poorly, unfairly, unjustly** *If you think you have been treated unfairly, you're entitled to make a complaint.*
▸ in a different or separate way **differently, individually, separately** *Why is death caused by driving treated differently from death caused in any other circumstance?*
▸ in a secret way **confidentially** *All information will be treated confidentially.*
▸ in a special or better way **favourably, specially** *Employers must ensure that male employees are not treated less favourably than female employees, and vice versa.* • *They should stop expecting to be treated specially.*
▸ in a serious way **seriously** *Dreams are treated seriously in many cultures and are often assumed to be messages from the spirit world.*
- V+with kindness, politeness, or fairness **care, compassion, consideration, courtesy, dignity, fairness, kindness, respect, reverence, sensitivity** *Refugees and asylum seekers must be treated with dignity and human respect.*
▸ doubt and suspicion **caution, scepticism, suspicion** *Any offer that does not give you a chance to think about it should be treated with suspicion.*
▸ a lack of respect **contempt, derision, disdain, disrespect, scorn** *He treats his parents with complete contempt.*
▸ an assurance that something will be kept secret **confidence, confidentiality** *All enquiries are treated with the strictest confidence.*

2 cure a patient or illness using medical methods

- adv+V successfully **adequately, effectively, successfully** *Many types of cancer can be successfully treated if caught early enough.*
▸ quickly **promptly, quickly** *These diseases can be fatal if not recognized and treated quickly.*
▸ by an operation or drugs **medically, surgically** *All microadenomas should be treated surgically.*

- V+n an illness or injury **addiction, condition, disease, disorder, illness, infection, injury, pain, problem, symptom** *Some optometrists may also recommend and prescribe drops to treat eye conditions.*
▸ a particular illness **cancer, depression, arthritis** etc *Zispin belongs to the group of medicines called antidepressants that are used to treat depression.*
▸ a person **casualty, patient** *A doctor has no authority to treat the patient unless consent is given.*

treat N
something special that you do or buy

- adj+N tasting nice **delicious, indulgent, sweet, tasty** *There's ice cream and food galore, with tasty treats to tempt all the family.*
▸ real **absolute, big, great, real, special, wonderful** *Our biggest treat as kids was to enjoy a pork pie with baked beans for our lunch.*
▸ because it is a particular time of year **festive, seasonal** *Festive treats will be available in the form of mulled wine and mince pies.*
▸ done or happening only rarely **occasional, rare** *We didn't have much money, so going to the theatre was a rare treat.*
▸ small **little, small** *I bought my daughter a little treat because she'd been so brave.*
▸ that you were not expecting **unexpected** *The opportunity to visit Tokyo was an unexpected treat.*

treatment N
1 the process of providing medical care

- adj+N done immediately **emergency, immediate, prompt, urgent** *These are signs of severe liver damage and require urgent medical treatment.*
▸ involving drugs or operations **conventional, traditional** *Conventional treatment is usually by anti inflammatory drugs.*
▸ involving methods not used by most doctors **complementary, holistic** *The idea behind complementary treatment is that the body is capable of healing itself naturally.*
▸ involving many different things to achieve success **aggressive, intensive** *Aggressive treatment of sudden and severe pain may reduce the odds of developing chronic pain.*
▸ continuing for a long time **long-term** *Long-term treatment with beta-blockers may reduce the risks of further bleeding.*
▸ successful **effective** *Without long term research we are never going to find a cure or effective treatments*
▸ types of treatment **clinical, dental, medical, psychiatric, psychological, specialist, surgical, therapeutic** *In most cases, surgical treatment permanently corrects the disease.*
- n+N **hospital, in-patient, outpatient** *Radiotherapy can be given as inpatient or outpatient treatment.*
- v+N get treatment **get, have, obtain, receive, undergo** *Before you receive any treatment, the doctor will explain to you what he or she intends do.*
▸ give someone treatment **administer, carry out, give, offer, provide** *No treatment is carried out without your consent.*
▸ ask for treatment **seek** *An infected abscess won't go away on its own, you really need to seek medical treatment.*

▶ start/stop treatment **begin, discontinue, initiate, start, stop, withdraw** *When treatment was stopped, the hair loss recurred.*

▶ need treatment **need, require** *She received cuts to her right leg requiring hospital treatment.*

▶ say you do not want treatment **refuse** *His parents refused treatment on religious grounds.*

▶ say someone should have a particular treatment **prescribe** *One of the treatments now prescribed for CFS is graded exercise therapy.*

▶ have a good result from treatment **respond to** *Some cancers respond to treatment such as chemotherapy and others do not.*

● N+n plan **package, plan, programme, regime, regimen, schedule, strategy** *Your age will be taken into account when deciding on the best treatment plan.*

▶ method **method, technique** *The centre helps heroin addicts who are not responding to conventional treatment methods.*

▶ place where treatment is done **centre, room** *There are twelve massage rooms and two treatment rooms.*

▶ choice **option** *The doctor will discuss treatment options with you.*

▶ time when treatment is given **session** *A normal treatment session costs £35.*

▶ prevent somone getting treatment **deny, withhold** *Older patients should not be denied treatment because of their age.*

2 the general way in which people are dealt with

● adj+N **degrading, fair, favourable, humane, inhuman, special, unfair, unfavourable** *There can be no circumstances in which torture or degrading treatment can be excused or justified.*

● v+N **deserve, mete out, receive** *A major form of discrimination is the unequal treatment meted out to agency staff, compared with those on fixed-term contracts.*

treaty N

an official written agreement between countries

● adj+N international **global, international** *There are international treaties concerning good stewardship of the Earth's resources.*

▶ involving two/several countries **bilateral, multilateral** *There have been calls for a multilateral treaty on nuclear disarmament.*

▶ that a country must legally obey **binding** *48 countries have now ratified the first legally binding treaty on biodiversity for food and agriculture.*

▶ formal and official **formal** *Under a formal peace treaty signed in 1947, the Finns agreed to cede territory to the then USSR.*

▶ types of treaty **arms, climate, constitutional, environmental, extradition, human rights, nuclear non-proliferation, peace** *Several of those countries do not have extradition treaties with the United States.*

▶ v+N sign a treaty **conclude, enter into, join, make, sign** *In 1783, the Americans and the British signed a peace treaty in Paris, France.*

▶ accept a treaty **accept, agree, approve, ratify** *Denmark had to be granted opt-outs from these provisions before the treaty was approved in 1993.*

▶ not agree a treaty **oppose, reject, withdraw from** *The treaty was opposed by the Christian majority.*

▶ start to use a treaty **adopt, implement** *Failure to implement the treaty would result in the United Kingdom being in breach of its international obligations.*

▶ not obey a treaty **breach, break, violate** *Severe penalties will be imposed on anybody involved in activities that violate the treaty.*

▶ change the details of a treaty **alter, amend, renegotiate** *The Commission should ask the member-states to amend the treaties.*

▶ discuss things before making a treaty **negotiate** *He later became Earl of Strafford and negotiated the treaty of Utrecht in 1713.*

▶ get rid of a treaty **abrogate** *Britain agreed to abrogate a treaty which stated that the US and Britain would share control of the canal*

▶ start to write the details of a treaty which may be changed **draft** *These problems could hardly have been imagined when the original UN drug control treaties were drafted.*

● N+v **allow sth, ban sth, establish sth, give sth, govern sth, prohibit, provide, require sth** *In December 1988, an international treaty banning the dumping of plastics from ships went into effect.*

tremble V

shake, for example because of fear

● adv+V a lot **uncontrollably, violently, visibly** *I thought he had been taken ill, his face was a shade of grey and he shook visibly.*

If someone is trembling a lot, you can also use the phrase ***tremble like a leaf***: *When I got out of the glider I was trembling like a leaf.*

▶ a little **slightly, somewhat** *Davis, his hand shaking somewhat, had begun to pour drinks.*

● V+with **anger, emotion, excitement, fear, fright, laughter, rage** *He was shaking with fright.*

tremendous ADJ

extremely great, important, or strong

● adv+ADJ **absolutely, really, truly** *The response of the audience was really tremendous.*

● ADJ+n amount **amount, number, range, value, variety** *It has taken a tremendous amount of hard work to get me to this stage.*

▶ success or achievement **achievement, success, victory** *Dalglish enjoyed tremendous success as both a player and a manager.*

▶ strength or speed, or effort **effort, energy, force, pace, power, pressure, speed, strength** *The car hit the tree with tremendous force.*

▶ feeling or quality **enthusiasm, fun, importance, interest, respect, spirit** *I also retain a tremendous sense of achievement from the whole thing.*

▶ advantage **advantage, benefit, privilege** *The English language offers the UK a tremendous advantage for the development of content provision over the Internet.*

▶ help and support **contribution, help, support** *I want to thank everyone in the community for the tremendous support I've had.*

▸ result or effect **effect, impact, influence, result** *Our buying habits have a tremendous impact on the environment.*

▸ change, especially to something bigger or better **advance, boost, change, difference, growth, improvement, increase, progress** *Healthcare has undergone tremendous changes during the last decade.*

trend N

a gradual change or development producing a particular result

● adj+N becoming bigger or better **accelerating, growing, increasing, positive, rising, upward** *There is a growing trend towards online shopping.*

▸ becoming less or worse **declining, downward, negative** *This marked the beginning of a downward trend in property prices.*

▸ happening now or recently **contemporary, current, the latest, modern, new, present, prevailing, recent** *On current trends, we are confident of another year of progress.*

▸ happening in the future **future** *This research seeks to identify future crime trends.*

▸ happening over a long period of time **longer-term, long-term** *Figures reveal a long-term trend towards greater inclusion of disabled students in mainstream schools.*

▸ happening in a particular place **global, international, local, national** *Crime detection rates have bucked national trends.*

▸ clear **clear, definite, dominant, strong** *There was a strong trend for a large section of the male population to remain unpartnered.*

▸ making you feel worried **disturbing, worrying** *The rise in votes for fascist parties was a worrying trend.*

▸ important **important, key, main, major, significant** *The most significant trend is the growth in the sale of organic foods.*

▸ general **broad, general, overall, underlying** *The population has fluctuated, but the underlying trend is not easy to discern.*

▸ more general **wider** *The figures do not necessarily reflect wider trends in the industry.*

▸ starting to exist **emerging** *Chapter 10 looks at emerging trends in social behaviour.*

▸ types of trend **cultural, demographic, economic, historical, political, social** *Business surveys provided factual information on economic trends.*

● n+N business **business, consumer, employment, growth, industry, market, price, sales, technology** *Last year, Skoda sold almost 38,000 new cars in the UK, a record for the company and bucking market trends.*

▸ weather and climate **climate, temperature** *The study could shed new light on present climate trends.*

▸ people and society **crime, design, fashion, health, lifestyle, population, shopping** *On the whole, health trends are improving.*

● v+N find or notice a trend **detect, establish, find, identify, notice, observe, see, spot** *All this information is reviewed to identify trends and, where appropriate, early action is taken on specific problems.*

▸ show a trend **highlight, illustrate, indicate, reflect, represent, reveal, show** *The latest figures show a downward trend.*

▸ study a trend **analyse, assess, examine, explore, monitor, review, study, track** *The study examined trends in employment.*

▸ try to guess what a trend will be **anticipate, determine, forecast, predict** *Dynamical seasonal forecast models are used to predict major climate trends up to four months ahead.*

▸ do something that is different from the trend **buck, counter** *Most towns suffered a downturn in shopping over Christmas, but shops in Bedford bucked the national trend.*

▸ to stop a trend and make it change **halt, reverse** *More people are abandoning city centres in favour of out-of-town shopping malls, and we want to reverse this trend.*

▸ be the same as a trend **continue, follow, mirror** *The city has followed the national trend of the decline in the mining and manufacturing sectors.*

▸ make a trend seem stronger **confirm, reinforce, support** *International mergers have reinforced this trend.*

▸ make a trend happen more quickly **accelerate**

● N+v a trend shows something **indicate sth, show sth, suggest sth** *Demographic trends show that British people are living longer and having fewer children.*

▸ a trend increases **grow, increase** *There are more elderly people in the country than ever before, and the trend is increasing.*

▸ a trend stops and becomes the opposite **reverse** *Since 1999, however, this trend has reversed.*

▸ a trend starts **begin, develop, emerge, start** *Over the last few years, a rather disturbing trend has emerged.*

▸ a trend continues **continue, persist** *These trends have continued and, in some cases, have accelerated over the past year.*

▸ a trend changes **change** *Shopping trends have changed.*

trial N

1 the process of examining a court case

● adj+N fair/unfair **fair, unfair** *In the absence of a fair trial, these men should be released.*

▸ types of trial **civil, criminal, full, public** *She has experience of handling long serious criminal trials in the Crown Court.*

● v+N appear in court for a trial **be on, go on, stand** *He is due to stand trial for murder later this month.*

▸ be going to appear in court for a trial in the future **await, face** *She's facing trial on a charge of assault*

▸ go to a trial **attend** *Parents of the murdered girl attended the trial.*

▸ hold a trial **hold** *The trial was held at Newcastle Crown Court.*

▸ make someone have a trial **commit sb for, put sb on** *He was put on trial for rape.*

▸ stop a trial and arrange for it to happen at a later time **adjourn** *The trial was adjourned until Monday*

● N+v **collapse** *The trial collapsed when the prosecution refused to produce witnesses in court.*

● N+n **court, judge, lawyer** *Whether this action was legal is a matter for the trial judge after hearing all the evidence.*

2 the process of testing a product or plan

- adj+N involving a lot of people or products **extensive, large, large-scale, major** *Extensive trials conducted by our research centre complement work from our manufacturer partners.*
- ▶ involving only a few people or products **small, small-scale** *One small trial looked at magnetic treatment plus heat and exercise, and reported no benefit compared with heat and exercise alone.*
- ▶ involving people rather than animals **human** *They were about to start human trials of a cancer vaccine.*
- ▶ done before other larger trials **initial, preliminary** *Preliminary trials have suggested that 50 to 200 mg per day of the vitamin improved symptoms.*
- ▶ types of trial **clinical, commercial, controlled, double-blind, medical, randomized, scientific, therapeutic** *Clinical trials are a scientific way to assess the safety and effectiveness of new drugs.*
- v+N do a trial **carry out, conduct, do, perform, run, undertake** *Several trials were conducted to investigate vitamin therapies.*
- ▶ have a trial done **undergo** *The device is undergoing trials and could cost as little as £300 if mass-produced.*
- ▶ organize a trial **organize, plan, set up** *The researchers are now planning a small human trial to test the effects of the vaccine.*
- ▶ provide money for a trial **fund** *Most clinical trials are funded by pharmaceutical companies who are testing new products.*
- N+v a trial shows something **confirm sth, demonstrate sth, find sth, indicate sth, prove sth, provide sth, report sth, reveal sth, show sth, suggest sth, support sth** *Many trials suggest a benefit of low doses of aspirin in reducing risk from a second stroke.*
- ▶ a trial examines something **assess, compare sth, evaluate, examine, investigate, test** *There is a new clinical trial investigating aspects of the treatment of venous leg ulcers.*

N+n **basis, copy, design, period, programme, project, result, scheme, service, session, version** *The council is running a two-year trial battery collection scheme for households.*

ribute N
omething showing you respect and admire
omeone

adj+N good or suitable **beautiful, fantastic, fine, fitting, glowing, good, great, real, special, ultimate, unique, wonderful, worthy** *The creation of this garden in remembrance of Jill is a fitting tribute to her life.* • *The Beatles Story is the ultimate tribute to the City's most famous sons – John, Paul, George and Ringo.*
sincere **heartfelt, sincere** *The family has paid a heartfelt tribute to the son they lost in a tragic road crash last week.*
making you feel emotional **moving, touching** *The poem is a moving tribute to a dead comrade.*
showing you like someone **affectionate, loving, warm** *After his death, affectionate tributes poured in from around the world.*
lasting for a very long time **lasting** *As a lasting tribute, the Young Player of the Year award will be renamed in Daphne's memory.*

- ▶ sent to a funeral **floral, funeral** *Thank you for all the floral tributes received on the death of a much-loved husband.*
- v+N give a tribute **add, give, offer, pay, provide, send, write** *Hundreds of well-wishers paid tribute to Fred's career in education.*
- ▶ receive a tribute **receive** *She received many tributes for her work.*
- ▶ be the first to give a tribute **lead** *Leading the tributes was the Washington Post, which described the film as 'one of the most winning movie creations in years'.*

trickle N
a small amount of liquid flowing slowly

- adj+N small **gentle, little, mere, slow, small, thin, tiny** *A small trickle of blood dribbled from his nose.*
- ▶ happening in a steady way **constant, steady** *The well had a constant trickle of water which fell in a pool.*

trigger V
make something happen

- V+n an illness **asthma, attack, condition, disease, migraine, seizure, symptom** *Excess alcohol can trigger a seizure, even in people without epilepsy.*
- ▶ an event or situation **action, attack, change, collapse, crisis, crisis, event, explosion, investigation, problem, war** *A small spark could trigger another war.*
- ▶ a feeling, thought, or memory **feeling, idea, interest, memory, need, thought** *This book will trigger children's interest in where they come from.*
- ▶ a discussion **debate, discussion, review** *His comments have triggered a debate about constitutional issues.*
- ▶ a process **development, process, production, release** *This reactive state then triggers a process known as oxidation.*
- ▶ a reaction **effect, reaction, response** *Running, playing, screaming kids can trigger an instinctive predator-prey reaction in some dogs.*

trip N
an occasion when you go somewhere and return

- adj+N good, interesting, or enjoyable **enjoyable, excellent, exciting, fantastic, good, great, interesting, memorable, pleasant, special, successful, wonderful, worthwhile** *It was a great trip during which we caught plenty of fish.* • *Overall, it was a very enjoyable and memorable trip.*
- ▶ long/short **brief, extended, long, quick, short** *We took a short boat trip along the river.*
- ▶ how often you make the trip **annual, daily, frequent, occasional, regular, weekly** *We organize regular trips for our international students to local places of interest.*
- ▶ to a foreign country **foreign, overseas** *Britons are forecast to take 101 million foreign trips by 2020.*
- ▶ in which nothing unusual happens **uneventful** *The trip down was comparatively uneventful.*
- n+N the activity you do or the place you visit **business, camping, caving, dive, fishing, hunting, sailing, shopping, sightseeing, ski, skiing, study, theatre, walking** *The children went on camping trips in the mountains.*

▶ the time that the trip lasts for **afternoon, day, evening, morning, night, overnight, weekend, two-hour/three-hour, etc, two-week/three-week, etc** *One of the highlights of the holiday was a day trip to the town of Takarazuka.*

▶ the method of transport or the type of travel **boat, bus, car, coach, ferry, river, road, sea, train** *In the afternoon, there was a coach trip to Highcliffe Castle and Christchurch Priory.* ● *They went on a road trip around eastern Europe.*

▶ the people who are going on the trip **family, school, tourist** *A family trip to South Africa means an amazing adventure for Mandy and James.*

▶ the trip there and back **return, round, round-the-world** *The airline will offer twice daily return trips between London and Prague.*

● v+N go on a trip **do, go on, have, make, take, undertake** *Many fans made the trip to Donington to see the band play.* ● *You can take a boat trip along the river.*

▶ arrange a trip **arrange, organize, plan** *We organize regular trips to the coast for our students.*

▶ offer a trip **offer, operate, provide, run** *In addition, we are also running trips to Paris and New York.*

▶ buy tickets for a trip **book** *John has booked another trip out to Almeria.*

▶ not go on a trip that you have tickets for **cancel, postpone** *Take out insurance in case you need to cancel your trip due to illness.*

▶ be in charge of a trip **lead** *I have been leading trips in Orkney since 1975.*

▶ make a trip longer than planned **extend** *We were having such a good time that we decided to extend our trip.*

triumph N

a great victory or success

● adj+N great **big, complete, glorious, great, major, real** *This is not his first major triumph of the year.*

▶ types of triumph **artistic, electoral, military, Olympic, personal, political** *The President was asked what he considered to be his greatest political triumph.*

▶ small **minor, small** *Individual victories, small triumphs, can still be achieved even in the context of defeat.*

▶ coming at the end of something **eventual, final, ultimate** *I was pleased with my eventual triumph against every difficulty.*

▶ better than others **biggest, greatest, supreme** *Rodney regarded this battle as his greatest triumph.*

● v+N have a triumph **achieve, have, score, secure** *In 1948, he scored his greatest triumph with the show 'Kiss Me, Kate'.*

▶ celebrate a triumph **celebrate, mark** *Harold celebrated his triumph at York.*

▶ be a triumph **represent** *This represents a triumph for the food industry in its long battle with perishability.*

● N+of **capitalism, democracy, design, engineering, evil, hope, love, revolution, spirit, style, technology, will** *'Alive' is a film about the triumph of the human spirit in the face of overwhelming odds.*

● n+of+N **feeling, look, moment, sense** *He had a look of triumph as he walked away with his stack of passports.* ● *My moment of triumph came later.*

triumphant ADJ

very pleased or excited about a success

● ADJ+n **conclusion, debut, march, moment, performance, return, success, team, tour, victory** *The player made a triumphant return to the game with a performance that helped his team win 26–10.*

● v+ADJ **emerge, feel, return** *Pete vanished into the office, and ten minutes later emerged triumphant.*

trivial ADJ

not very important, serious, or valuable

● adv+ADJ rather **fairly, pretty INFORMAL, quite, rather, somewhat** *If you are depressed, you may cry for reasons that seem quite trivial to other people.*

▶ very **utterly, very** *It seemed to her a very trivial offence.*

▶ when compared to other things **comparatively, relatively** *Most injuries were relatively trivial, involving nothing more than cuts and bruises.*

▶ appearing to be trivial **apparently, seemingly** *He was too anxious about seemingly trivial details.*

● ADJ+n subject or situation **issue, matter, nature, problem, question, reason, thing** *He is indecisive even in trivial matters.*

▶ fact or detail **detail, example, fact, point** *I didn't want to know all the trivial details.*

▶ mistake **error, mistake** *It was only a trivial mistake*

▶ injury **injury** *The injuries were trivial and no hospital treatment was required.*

▶ amount **amount, sum** *The amounts were trivial.*

▶ event **event, incident, offence** *Trivial offences don't generally lead to a prison sentence.*

▶ change or difference **change, difference** *There have been a few trivial changes to the document.*

▶ thing you have to do **exercise, task** *Fortunately, it is a relatively trivial task to modify the software.*

● v+ADJ **appear, be, become, seem, sound** *A broken wrist or sprained ankle may seem trivial until you try to fasten a button or climb the stairs.*

troops N

soldiers, especially in large numbers [always plural]

● n+N **coalition, combat, enemy, front-line, government, ground, occupation, shock** *The government has ruled out sending combat troops.*

● v+N use or send troops **deploy, dispatch, send, send in** *Although there was a 78-day air war, ground troops were not deployed.*

▶ promise to send troops **commit** *No decision to commit British troops has been taken.*

▶ move troops into a place **land, march in(to), transport** *Soviet troops marched into Prague in 196*

▶ troops go into a place **advance, arrive, enter, invade, land, liberate, march, occupy** *The village was occupied by British troops in March 1917.*

▶ troops leave a place **flee, retreat, surrender, withdraw** *As British troops withdrew from Tiberia the Jews took their place.*

▶ make troops leave a place **evacuate, pull out, retreat, withdraw** *Protesters are demanding the government pull its troops out of the region.*

▶ be in charge of troops **command, order** *Troops were ordered to disperse the crowd*

● N+v troops use force **attack, battle, fight, fire,**

kill, massacre, raid, seize, shoot, storm *It's now over 60 years since troops stormed ashore on the beaches of Normandy.*

trophy N
a large silver cup or similar object given as a prize

- adj+N **coveted, magnificent, major, prestigious** *Celtic became the first British club to win Europe's most coveted trophy.*
- v+N win a trophy **claim, clinch, lift, receive, scoop, take, win** *Brazil are favourites to lift the trophy.*
- ▶ give someone a trophy **award, present** *The overall competition winner will be awarded a trophy.*
- ▶ be the last winner of a trophy **hold** *England currently holds the trophy.*
- ▶ keep a trophy **defend, retain** *This is the first ever Irish team to retain the trophy.*

tropical ADJ
in or from the hottest parts of the world

- ▶ ADJ+n region or place **beach, forest, island, jungle, paradise, rainforest, region, sea** *These bats come from the tropical forests of central and south America.*
- ▶ plants or trees **flower, foliage, fruit, garden, greenery, hardwood, plant, tree, vegetation** *There are also greenhouses full of tropical plants.*
- ▶ animals **fish, species** *She keeps tropical fish.*
- ▶ weather **climate, clime, cyclone, depression, monsoon, rainstorm, storm, sun** *Tobago enjoys a tropical climate.*
- diseases **disease, medicine** *Our research laboratories are dedicated to the study of tropical medicine.*

trouble N
problems or difficulties

- adj+N serious **big, considerable, deep, desperate, dire, real, serious, terrible** *I could tell from his face that we were in serious trouble.*
- little **less, little** *You can put a website together with little trouble.*

> If you say that **nothing is too much trouble** for someone, you mean that they will do it however difficult or however many problems there are: *We offer a family service where nothing is too much trouble.*

- types of trouble **financial, mechanical, political** *Her father had run into financial trouble.*
- n+N **car, engine, family, money, heart/back/knee etc** *His plane was turned back owing to engine trouble.*
- v+N experience trouble **experience, have** *I was having trouble sleeping.*
- cause trouble **bring (sb), cause (sb), foment, give (sb), incite, lead to, make, provoke** *The virus can cause trouble by consuming your computer's storage space and memory.* ● *Her eyes were giving her trouble that summer.*
- mean trouble **mean, spell** *If these trends continue, it will spell trouble for property markets.*
- be in trouble **be in, get in, get into, run into** *Small*

businesses can get into trouble because they have to pay VAT before their customers have paid them.
- ▶ be likely to cause trouble **be asking for** *If you borrow more than you can afford to pay back, you are asking for trouble.*
- ▶ avoid trouble **avoid** *Recruiting the right person first time will avoid trouble later.*
- n+of+N **cause, source** *A computer virus seems to have been the cause of the trouble.*

troubled ADJ
worried about or affected by problems

- adv+ADJ very **deeply, particularly, very** *This is the story of a young, deeply troubled man.*
- ▶ about money **financially** *Investors bought the financially troubled company in 1937.*
- ADJ+n person **genius, soul** *Matt is a troubled soul.*
- ▶ young person **teen, teenager, youngster, youth** *She became an angry, troubled teenager.*
- ▶ life or events **childhood, history, life, marriage, past, relationship, time, world** *Due to its troubled past, the country has unique challenges to its development.*
- ▶ mind **conscience, mind** *From his writings you can see he had a very troubled mind.*
- v+ADJ seem to be troubled **look, seem** *All morning, Alan seemed quite troubled.*
- ▶ feel troubled **become, feel** *I wonder if I am alone in feeling deeply troubled by this news.*

truancy N
the act of staying away from school

- adj+N **persistent** *There are stong links between persistent truancy and a child's life chances.*
- v+N do something about truancy **combat, tackle** *The Government has recently announced measures to tackle truancy.*
- ▶ reduce truancy **curb, cut, reduce** *The Government's target is to reduce school truancies by 10% from 2002 levels.*
- ▶ allow truancy **condone** *It is not for us to condone truancy and absences from school.*

truce N
a temporary agreement to stop arguing or fighting

- adj+N **fragile, temporary, uneasy** *Union leaders informally agreed upon an uneasy truce with the government.*
- v+N agree to have a truce **agree, agree to, arrange, call, conclude, declare, negotiate, reach** *Let's just call a truce for now and talk when you get back.*
- ▶ sign a document agreeing a truce **sign** *Eventually, a truce was signed between the two countries.*
- ▶ break a truce **break, violate** *By that time, a wave of strikes had broken the truce with the management.*

trudge V
walk somewhere with slow heavy steps

- adv+V slowly **slowly, wearily** *He left his office and wearily trudged home through the rain.*

▶ back **back, home** *With the rain pouring down, the players trudged reluctantly back on to the pitch.*

true ADJ

1 based on fact

● adv+ADJ very **especially, particularly, very** *This is particularly true for girls.*

▶ without a doubt **certainly, obviously, undoubtedly** *It is certainly true that there are striking similarities between the two passages.*

▶ completely **absolutely, all, completely, entirely, literally, perfectly, quite** *What you say is perfectly true.*

▶ not completely **not actually, not completely, not entirely, not necessarily, not really, not strictly, partly** *That is not strictly true.*

▶ really **actually, indeed, really** *In one sense, this is indeed true.*

> You can also say that something is **in fact true**: *There is evidence to suggest that this may in fact be true.*

▶ mostly or probably **generally, probably** *It is probably true to say that he is nearing the end of his playing career.*

▶ equally **equally** *While mistakes have been made, this was equally true of the old system.*

● v+ADJ be or sound true **be, hold, remain, ring, seem** *Her explanation doesn't quite ring true.*

▶ be true in the future **become, come, prove** *The first of his wishes looks as though it may come true.*

2 always loyal

● v+ADJ **be, keep, remain, stay** *Firstly, stay true to yourself.*

● N+to **principles, roots, spirit, word** *Despite everything he has achieved, he remains true to his roots.*

3 real, or actual

● ADJ+n cost or value **cost, value** *The true value of what was lost is difficult to estimate.*

▶ meaning or nature **meaning, nature, sense** *Human beings are prone to lose sight of their true nature.*

▶ who someone really is or what they feel **feelings, identity, self** *She reveals her true feelings in her diary.*

▶ love or happiness **happiness, love** *He feels that this is his only chance of true happiness.*

▶ friend **friend** *Thank you for being a true friend.*

▶ potential **potential** *In the game against Germany, Ireland showed their true potential with a superb display.*

▶ amount **extent, value, worth** *These figures do not reflect the true extent of homelessness in England.*

trust N

a belief that someone is honest and reliable

● adj+N **absolute, complete, mutual, public** *She had complete trust in him to always act in her best interests.*

● v+N show you have trust in someone **place, put** *It's not easy to put our trust in someone we don't understand.*

▶ develop or create trust **build, build up, create, develop, engender, establish** *Businesses need to*

build public trust by showing their concern for local communities.

▶ get someone's trust **earn, gain, inspire, win** *Local newspapers have earned the trust of their communities through decades of service to readers.*

▶ make trust exist again **rebuild, re-establish, restore** *The industry must rebuild trust.*

▶ treat someone badly who has trust in you **abuse, betray** *He trusted her implicitly and she never betrayed that trust.*

▶ damage trust **breach, destroy, erode, undermine** *This could undermine the trust between doctor and patient.*

▶ lose trust **lose** *When the trust and support of senior players is lost, the authority of a captain goes.*

● n+of+N when trust is broken or does not exist **betrayal, breach, breakdown, lack** *Quite frankly, there was a lack of trust on both sides.*

▶ when there is trust **bond, position, relationship** *Little by little, a bond of trust developed between them.*

▶ atmosphere **atmosphere, climate** *It takes time to build a climate of trust and acceptance.*

trust V

be confident that someone is honest and reliable

● adv+V really **absolutely, completely, fully, implicitly, really, totally, truly** *How many people in your life do you trust implicitly?*

▶ not really **never, not enough, not entirely, not really** *The parties are reluctant to talk because they don't entirely trust one another.*

trusted ADJ

that you can trust

● ADJ+n information **information, source** *Our database is continually updated from trusted sources.*

▶ person **adviser, friend, partner** *You may have a trusted friend you can confide in.*

▶ product **brand** *If you stick with well-known and trusted brands, you'll be safe.*

truth N

the actual facts about something, or the quality of being true

● adj+N complete **absolute, real, whole** *Jennifer wa. not telling the whole truth.*

▶ clear, perhaps unpleasant **naked, plain, simple** *T! plain truth is that a motorbike is not as safe as a car.*

▶ not pleasant **awful, brutal, sad, shocking, terrible uncomfortable, unpalatable** *The sad truth is that the exact number of victims will never be known.*

▶ based on facts **literal, objective** *She does not thin. that science is getting nearer to an objective truth.*

▶ believed by everyone, or for all time **eternal, fundamental, profound, self-evident, ultimate, universal** *Fairy tales deal with universal truths, which fascinate us all, whatever our age.*

● v+N tell the truth **admit, confess, proclaim, reveal, speak, tell** *If the witnesses really are tellin. the truth, then he must be guilty.*

▶ discover or know the truth **discover, expose, fin. get at, get to, know, learn, realize, uncover** *She* *cannot risk her husband discovering the truth about her past life.*

▶ try to discover the truth **search for, seek** *He never stopped searching for truth.*

▶ accept the truth **accept, face** *The majority of the party cannot face the truth.*

▶ hide the truth **conceal, hide, suppress** *She decided that she could hide the truth no longer, and told David everything.*

▶ change the truth **distort** *The company have distorted the truth in their public statements about the success of the research.*

▶ not admit the truth **deny, doubt** *It's no good denying the truth.*

▶ n+of+N small amount of truth **element, germ, grain, kernel, shred** *It's a romantic story but there may be a grain of truth in it.*

▶ trying to find the truth **pursuit** *Our common puropse is the search for peace and the pursuit of truth and wisdom.*

▶ changing the truth, or denying it **denial, distortion, perversion, travesty** *Any distortion of the truth will be picked up at an interview.*

ruthful ADJ
. truthful person says what is true

adv+ADJ **absolutely, completely, not entirely, totally, very** *Please be completely truthful when you fill in the application form.*

ADJ+n **account, answer communication, statement** *The truthful answer to this question is – we don't know.*

and/or **accurate, honest, sincere** *Employers are realizing that a CV isn't always necessarily truthful or accurate.*

y V
tempt to do something

adv+V with a lot of effort **desperately, frantically, hard** *He was desperately trying to keep himself hidden.*

without being successful **unsuccessfully, vainly** *United spent the second half unsuccessfully trying to break down the Milan defence.*

You can also say that someone tries *in vain*: *I tried in vain to persuade her to come.*

always, or again and again **always, constantly, continually, repeatedly** *Scientists are constantly trying to find new ways to protect people from this disease.*

deliberately **actively, deliberately** *She found out that her business partner was deliberately trying to defraud her.*

only **merely, simply** *I could see that Virginia was merely trying to preserve an aura of hospitality.*

y N
attempt to do something

adj+N good **good, nice** *That's a nice try, but it's not the right answer.*

first, second etc **first, second etc** *Marion was successful in picking out the right card, first try, 11 times.*

▶ unsuccessful **unsuccessful** *Mandy made a number of unsuccessful tries to climb the tree.*

● v+N have a try **give sth, have** *Shall I give it a try?* ● *Here, let me have a try.*

▶ be worth a try **be worth** *This isn't easy, but it is worth a try.*

tuition N
the work of teaching, especially to one person or a small group

● adj+N to one person **face-to-face, individual, one-on-one, one-to-one, personal** *You will receive one-to-one tuition via email.*

▶ given to one person for payment **private** *More and more parents are paying for additional private tuition for their children.*

▶ expert **expert** *We offer expert tuition in all aspects of computing.*

▶ extra **extra** *Throughout your training, the Technical Director will monitor your progress and will arrange extra tuition if it is required.*

▶ free **free** *Free English language tuition is offered throughout the year.*

● v+N receive tuition **get, receive, undergo** *The course offers the opportunity to receive professional tuition from experienced writers.*

▶ give tuition **deliver, give (sb), offer (sb), provide (sb with), undertake** *Tuition is provided by qualified ski school instructors.*

● N+n **fee** *You will need to complete a form to apply for a student loan and help with your tuition fees.*

tumour N
a mass of cells growing not in normal way

● adj+N that can cause death **cancerous, inoperable, malignant** *Cancer is the name given to a malignant tumour.*

▶ harmless **benign** *These tumours are almost always benign.*

▶ in the first/second stage of development **primary, secondary** *He suspects that there is something wrong with his liver, possibly a secondary tumour there.*

▶ types of tumour **ovarian, pituitary, testicular, pancreatic etc** *Any patient with a suspected testicular tumour is seen urgently.*

● n+N **bladder, bone, brain, breast, liver, lung, prostate, skin** *In March, she went into hospital for a third brain tumour operation.*

● v+N treat or remove a tumour **cure, erradicate, excise, remove, shrink, treat** *She had a tumour successfully removed from her leg.*

▶ have a tumour **be diagnosed with, develop, have** *He was diagnosed with a brain tumour.* ● *She had developed malignant ovarian tumours.*

▶ cause a tumour **cause, induce** *What causes brain tumours?*

tune N INFORMAL
a song or piece of music

● adj+N easy to remember **catchy, memorable** *The show is full of catchy tunes.*

▶ well-known or popular **classic, familiar, favourite, old, popular, traditional, well-known** *Our steel*

band will be bringing a Caribbean flavour to some
popular tunes.
▶ making you feel happy **bouncy, infectious, jaunty,
jolly, lively, merry, rousing** *'Don't Listen to the
Radio' is a happy, bouncy tune with some rock
moments.*
● n+N type of music **dance, folk, hymn, pop, rock,
show** *It is an adaptation of a traditional Irish folk
tune.*
▶ played at the beginning of a programme or film
signature, theme *This CD is full of your favourite
Wild West theme tunes.*
● v+N make a tune with your voice **hum, sing,
whistle** *She was humming a tune under her breath.*
▶ play a tune **play** *Every Friday night, street musicians
play the latest tunes.*
▶ write a tune **compose, write** *He writes some pretty
good tunes.*
▶ know a tune **know, learn** *I'm afraid I don't know
the tune.*
▶ hear a tune **hear** *Every time I hear that tune, I think
of summer holidays.*

turmoil N
a state of excitement or uncontrolled activity

● adj+N mental **emotional, inner, mental** *He
suffered emotional turmoil, not knowing what was
happening to his family.*
▶ type of turmoil **economic, financial, political,
religious, social** *They will recover after a period, but
only after considerable political and economic
turmoil.*
▶ great **great, much** *She managed to secure the town's
future prosperity at a time of great turmoil.*
● v+N **cause, create, throw sb/sth into** *The country
is only just recovering from the turmoil caused by the
civil war.* ● *Nina's feelings are thrown into turmoil
when she realizes that she is falling in love.*

turn V
change and do or become something else

● V+adj unpleasant **bad, nasty, sour, ugly, violent**
Then the atmosphere in the bar turned nasty.
▶ colours **pink, yellow, blue etc** *His face started to
turn pale.*
▶ professional **professional** *Since turning professional
in 1990, Rick has had a career in most areas of the
music business.*
▶ weather **chilly, cloudy, cold, showery, wintry** *The
afternoon turned cloudy, with the temperature
falling to 8 degrees.*

turn N
a change in a situation

● adj+N unexpected **strange, surprising,
unexpected** *Life took an unexpected turn for Rick
when he met Jess.*
▶ sudden **dramatic, sudden** *We were so upset at the
sudden turn of events.*
▶ harmful or unpleasant **sinister, unfortunate** *Events
took a decidedly sinister turn when a dead body was
found in the garden.*
▶ when a situation gets worse/better **downward,
upward** *From that moment on, things took a
downward turn.*

You can also say that things **take a turn for the
worse/better**: *Fortunately his life then took a turn for
the better.*

turn down PHR VB
not accept an offer or request

● V+n request for something **appeal, application,
claim, request** *It can be difficult to find out exactly
why a particular application has been turned down.*
▶ offer or invitation **invitation, offer** *She has turned
down all invitations to be interviewed.*
▶ work **job, work** *I'm not in a financial position to
turn down jobs.*

turning point N
a time of important change in a situation

● adj+N **big, crucial, decisive, historic, important,
key, major, real, significant** *Winning the 2005
championship was a major turning point in his
career.*
● v+N be or represent a turning point **be, become,
mark, prove, represent** *The events of that day marked
a turning point in South Africa's political history.*
▶ believe that something is a turning point **see sth
as** *The decision may come to be seen as a turning
point by historians.*
▶ reach a turning point **reach** *I believe we have
reached a turning point in our campaign.*

turnout N
the number of people coming to an event or voting
in an election

● adj+N few people **disappointing, low, poor** *Two of
the shows had a very poor turnout.*
▶ many people **big, excellent, fantastic, good, great,
high, huge, impressive, large, massive** *We are
expecting a massive turnout, so book your tickets
now.*
▶ in an election **electoral** *Steps need to be taken to
encourage greater electoral turnout.*
● n+N **election, voter** *Voter turnout at local elections
appears to be declining.*
● v+N get a particular turnout **get, have** *The class
reunion sounded as if it would have a good turnout.*
▶ expect a particular turnout **expect** *We expect a
good turnout over the New Year period.*
▶ increase the turnout **boost, increase** *The
government has looked at ways of boosting voter
turnout.*

turnover N
the value of a company's sales in a particular
period

● adj+N in a year **annual** *The company has an
annual turnover of about £10 million.*
▶ high/low **high, low, rapid** *We are a small enterprise
with a low turnover.* ● *It is a clean, well-organized
shop with a rapid turnover and helpful staff.*
▶ total **combined, total** *Total turnover increased by
2.8 per cent.*
● v+N have a particular turnover **achieve,
generate, have** *The Group achieved a half-year
turnover of $600 million.*

▶ increase turnover **boost, double, increase** *The company has ambitious plans to double its turnover over the next four years.*

▶ predict turnover **anticipate, estimate, expect, forecast** *The company expects turnover and profit to increase even further this year.*

● N+v increase **grow, increase, rise** *Our overall business turnover rose by over 10 per cent to about £160k.*

▶ fall **fall** *Over the past three years, turnover has fallen from £15m to £10m.*

▶ be a particular amount **approach sth, exceed sth, reach sth** *Turnover exceeded £500m, with profits in excess of £20m.*

twilight N

he evening time when the sky begins to get dark

▶ adj+N **deepening, gathering** *We climbed to the top of the hill in the gathering twilight.*

▶ N+v **deepen, fall** *It was ten o' clock and the twilight was deepening into night.*

winge N

sudden short feeling of an unpleasant emotion

adj+N slight **little, slight** *I must admit to a slight twinge of disappointment.*
not frequent **occasional, odd** *She did experience the occasional twinge of regret.*

N+of **conscience, guilt, jealousy, sympathy** *As I walked away, I felt another twinge of guilt.*

wist N

sudden unexpected change in a situation

adj+N unexpected or unusual **bizarre, dramatic, ironic, strange, surprising, unexpected** *The story then takes an unexpected twist.*
that seems unfair **cruel** *It was a cruel twist of fate that his wife died a year later.*
clever or interesting **clever, interesting, intriguing, neat, nice** *The end of the play has very neat twist.*
slight **little, slight** *There is a slight twist at the end of the film.*
recent **latest, new** *The prime minister had to answer questions about the latest twist in the scandal.*
final **final** *This is an interesting film right up to the final twist.*
modern **contemporary, modern** *His designs draw their inspiration from the 1960's but he gives them a contemporary twist.*
strange and sometimes frightening **macabre, sinister, strange, unusual** *The CD consists of four children's fairy tales, each with an unusual twist at the end.*

coon N

ich and powerful business person

n+N **business, media, newspaper, oil, property** *She is the daughter of the billionaire media tycoon, Rupert Murdoch.*

pical ADJ

e most similar people or things

dv+ADJ rather **fairly, pretty** INFORMAL, **quite,**

rather, somewhat *Our house was fairly typical of those in the street.*

▶ very **absolutely, so, very** *This was very typical of Jim's attitude to his work.*

● ADJ+n example or case **case, example** *The painting we illustrate here is a typical example of his later work.*

▶ feature **characteristic, feature** *Spam messages contain typical features which can be calculated and detected.*

▶ comment or reaction **comment, question, reaction, response** *These views are represented by the following typical comments.*

tyranny N

a government that controls people by force and cruel treatment

● adj+N **brutal, cruel, political, religious** *This was one of the cruellest tyrannies the world has ever known.*

● v+N escape from tyranny **be freed from, escape, escape from** *These people have fled to our shores to escape tyranny and poverty.*

▶ fight tyranny **end, fight, oppose, overthrow, resist** *If we seek to end tyranny on a global level, we have to show that peaceful alternatives exist at a local level.*

▶ impose tyranny **impose** *He constantly fought the regime that was trying to impose an intolerant tyranny.*

● and/or **cruelty, injustice, oppression, persecution, terror, war** *They are fleeing from tyranny and persecution.*

tyrant N

a person ruling a country in a cruel and unfair way

● adj+N cruel **bloodthirsty, bloody, brutal, cruel, evil, murderous, vicious** *The country is ruled by an evil tyrant.*

▶ minor **petty** *He is a petty tyrant whose misdeeds reflect on the government which supports him.*

● v+N **depose, overthrow, remove, topple** *They led a successful coup to overthrow the tyrant.*

tyre N

a thick rubber cover fitting around a wheel

● v+N fit or replace a tyre **change, fit, fit sth with, replace** *How many of you struggle to change your tyres?* ● *The vehicle has been fitted with extra wide tyres.*

▶ put air into a tyre **inflate, pump (up)** *You need to pump your tyres up.*

▶ let air come out of a tyre **deflate, let down** *Someone has let her tyres down as a joke.*

▶ damage a tyre **puncture, slash** *Youths were laying broken glass bottles in the road to try to puncture car tyres.*

▶ check a tyre **check** *Check the tyres for wear, damage, and tread depth.*

U u

ugly ADJ
1 unpleasant to look at

- adv+ADJ very **downright** INFORMAL, **extremely, hideously, incredibly, plain** INFORMAL, **really, so** INFORMAL, **very** *She was reputed to be hideously ugly, with a long hooked nose.*
- ▸ rather **quite, rather** *In spite of its rather ugly appearance, it's a wonderful library.*

2 very unpleasant or threatening

- adv+ADJ **a little, pretty, quite, rather, really, very** *Things soon got quite ugly, with a fair bit of shouting.*
- v+ADJ **get, look, turn** *The demonstration could turn ugly at any moment.*

ultimate ADJ
happening at the end of a long process

- ADJ+n aim **aim, ambition, goal, objective, purpose** *The ultimate aim of this research remains a cure.*
- ▸ responsibility for something **decision, responsibility** *Chief executives bear the ultimate responsibility for the actions of their staff.*
- ▸ where someone or something is going **destination** *The ultimate destination of the drugs was Spain.*
- ▸ what happens **destiny, fate, outcome** *The mystery of Sonia's ultimate fate is never settled explicitly.*
- ▸ success **success, victory, winner** *We needed four more points for ultimate victory.*

ultimatum N
a threat to punish someone if something is not done

- v+N issue an ultimatum **deliver, issue, present, send** *On 26 April, the Action Council delivered an ultimatum to Roy Mason.*
- ▸ accept/reject an ultimatum **accept, comply with, ignore, reject** *His ultimatum was ignored.*
- ▸ get an ultimatum **be given, get, receive** *After this time, he was given an ultimatum to either get a job, or leave!*

unacceptable ADJ
wrong or harmful

- adv+ADJ completely **absolutely, completely, entirely, totally, utterly, wholly** *Her public criticism of an elected representative is totally unacceptable.*
- ▸ clearly **clearly, frankly, quite, simply** *It is simply unacceptable for the situation to stay as it is.*
- ▸ in a particular context **culturally, environmentally, ethically, morally, politically, socially** *It remained socially unacceptable for women to smoke until the Suffragette movement in the 1920s.*
- v+ADJ be considered unacceptable **be considered, be deemed, be regarded as** *The public health risks are considered unacceptable.*
- ▸ be or become unacceptable **be, become, prove, remain, seem** *This document proved unacceptable*

to the King because it went too far, by giving too much power to Parliament.
- ▸ think something is unacceptable **find sth** *These migrants come to the UK to work, to do the jobs we won't, for wages we find unacceptable.*

unaffected ADJ
not changed or influenced by something

- adv+ADJ mainly **essentially, largely, relatively, virtually** *Even if one of the generating stations fails, the system copes and is virtually unaffected.*
- ▸ completely **completely, entirely, totally** *Few of us nowadays can remain totally unaffected by change.*
- ▸ apparently **apparently, seemingly** *Studies have shown that apparently unaffected twins may go on to develop the disease later.*
- v+ADJ remain unaffected **continue, remain** *All other passengers travelling to and from Gatwick will remain unaffected.*
- ▸ be or seem unaffected **appear, be, be left, seem** *The test scores were unaffected.*

unanimous ADJ
agreed with and supported by everybody

- adv+ADJ almost **almost, near, nearly, practically, virtually** *There was near unanimous agreement with the general approach adopted in the document.*
- ▸ completely **absolutely, completely, quite** *They are completely unanimous both as to diagnosis and prognosis.*
- ADJ+n decision **adoption, conclusion, decision, opinion, resolution, ruling, verdict, vote** *The inquest jury recorded a unanimous verdict of unlawful killing.*
- ▸ agreement **agreement, consensus, consent, endorsement** *Lack of unanimous agreement occurred in 24 cases (62 per cent).*
- ▸ approval **acceptance, acclaim, approval, praise** *His recent solo recording of Handel's Organ concertos has received unanimous critical acclaim.*
- ADJ+in approval/disapproval **condemnation, disapproval, opposition, praise** *Members are unanimous in their praise for this confidential service.*
- ▸ opinion **belief, opinion, view** *We are unanimous in our views.*

unavoidable ADJ
impossible to stop from happening

- adv+ADJ almost **almost, virtually** *We recognise that alterations are virtually unavoidable.*
- ▸ completely **absolutely, completely** *Please do not put your bin out any earlier than the morning of collection unless absolutely unavoidable.*
- ADJ+n problem **absence, cancellation, damage, delay, disruption, emissions, problem, risk** *I apologise for this unavoidable delay.*
- ▸ result **conclusion, consequence** *Such disasters were an unavoidable consequence of scientific progress.*

▶ situation **circumstances, necessity** *I confirm that I am unable to attend the appeal due to unavoidable circumstances.*

▶ cost **cost, expense, increase** *The war lead to disruptions in the supply of gas, making price increases unavoidable.*

● v+ADJ **appear, be, become, prove, seem** *Crowded lectures and shared flats are unavoidable for most students.*

unaware ADJ
not realizing that something is happening

● adv+ADJ completely or mainly **completely, entirely, genuinely, largely, quite, totally, wholly** *I drove off to town, wholly unaware that I had been observed by anyone.*

▶ apparently **apparently, seemingly** *Her parents are seemingly unaware of her hobby.*

▶ happily **blissfully, blithely** *One department was blithely unaware that the laptops were not PCs.*

● v+ADJ **appear, be, remain, seem** *They seem blissfully unaware of the impending oil crisis.*

unbearable ADJ
so extreme that you cannot deal with it

● adv+ADJ almost **almost, nearly** *The temperature in the room was stifling, the conditions nearly unbearable.*

▶ completely **completely, quite, truly, utterly** *As the evening closed in, her impatience was quite unbearable.*

ADJ+n pain or difficulty **burden, pain, strain, stress, suffering** *The physical and mental pain is unbearable.*

something that affects your senses **heat, noise, smell, stench** *The stench was unbearable.*

tension **pressure, suspense, tension** *The suspense is nearly unbearable.*

unbeatable ADJ
impossible to defeat in a competition

adv+ADJ almost **almost, nearly, virtually** *Radcliffe and Taylor were virtually unbeatable in mountain marathons.*

completely **absolutely, simply, truly** *It is only a matter of time before the machines become absolutely unbeatable.*

apparently **seemingly** *With one match remaining, they look certain to eclipse the seemingly unbeatable total set last year.*

better than anything else of the same type

adv+ADJ almost **almost, nearly** *We think you'll agree this offer is almost unbeatable and too tempting to miss.*

completely **absolutely, simply, truly** *It's a superb product at an absolutely unbeatable price!* ● *Our prices are simply unbeatable.*

ADJ+n price **deal, discount, offer, price, value** *We supply a wide range of quality wiring accessories, indoor and outdoor lighting at unbeatable prices!*

combination **combination, package** *We offer an unbeatable package with superior performance and support.*

▶ place **atmosphere, location, scenery** *Situated in the town of Masnou, the Port Masnou marina is in an unbeatable location.*

unbelievable ADJ INFORMAL
used for emphasizing how good, bad etc something is

● adv+ADJ completely **absolutely, completely, just, quite, simply, totally, truly** *The hype and buzz around this product is absolutely unbelievable.*

▶ rather **pretty** *The last two gigs we've played have been pretty unbelievable.*

uncertain ADJ
1 not clearly known or understood

● adv+ADJ very **decidedly, extremely, highly, substantially, very** *The scale of these effects, and their general direction, is highly uncertain.*

▶ rather **rather, slightly, somewhat** *The long-term funding of the services remained somewhat uncertain.*

▶ basically **inherently** *The future is, of course, inherently uncertain.*

▶ increasingly **increasingly** *It was increasingly uncertain where government and the law resided.*

● ADJ+n origin **derivation, origin, provenance** *Many of the documents are of uncertain provenance.*

▶ future **fate, future, outcome, outlook, prognosis, prospects** *He argues that the Party faces an uncertain future.*

▶ situation **circumstances, climate, conditions, environment, situation** *The uncertain political situation meant that no students were admitted.*

● v+ADJ be or become **be, become, remain** *According to some analysts, the outcome remains uncertain.*

▶ seem **appear, look, seem** *The date of these relics seems quite uncertain.*

2 not sure about something

● adv+ADJ very **extremely, very** *He left Beryl feeling extremely uncertain about whether she would ever see him again.*

▶ rather or slightly **a little, quite, rather, somewhat** *I was at times a little uncertain about the target audience for this book.*

● v+ADJ be or become **be, be left, feel** *Archaeologists are uncertain as to when the first stone tools came in to being.*

▶ seem **appear, look, seem** *Many seem uncertain just what they mean by federation.*

uncertainty N
when people are not sure about something

● adj+N great **considerable, deep, great, major, much, real, significant** *There should be no approvals for new power stations of this type, as long as there is significant uncertainty about their environmental impact.*

▶ types of uncertainty **environmental, financial, legal, political, scientific, statistical** *The current budget proposals will increase costs for industry, and add to the mood of financial uncertainty.*

● v+N cause uncertainty **cause, create, generate,**

introduce, mean, result in *All this introduces major uncertainties, particularly at the regional level.*
▶ increase uncertainty **add to, compound, prolong** *Events in the Middle East have led to a rise in oil prices, compounding uncertainty about the strength of global demand.*
▶ reduce or remove uncertainty **eliminate, minimize, reduce, remove, resolve** *Resolving this uncertainty could take several years.*
▶ measure uncertainty **calculate, estimate, model, quantify** *Our aim is to quantify uncertainty in flow performance prediction due to uncertainty in a reservoir description.*
▶ face uncertainty **face** *Your concerns are understandable as we face uncertainty and challenge.*

● N+v exist **arise, characterize sth, exist, hang over sth, prevail, surround sth** *A mood of complete uncertainty prevails among the workers.*
▶ continue **continue, persist, remain** *This matter has never been tested, leaving a void in which uncertainty persists.*

● n+of+N amount **degree, element, measure** *The problem is interesting because of the large degree of uncertainty about what might happen.*
▶ feeling or state **climate, feeling, mood, sense, state** *Users acknowledged feelings of uncertainty and ignorance.*
▶ time **period, time** *Advertisers faced a long period of uncertainty, as revenues from TV and newspapers continued to fall.*

● and/or not being sure **ambiguity, confusion, instability, risk, unpredictability, vagueness, variability, volatility** *Psychiatrists must be able to tolerate ambiguity and uncertainty.*
▶ fear or worry **anxiety, doubt, fear, insecurity, unease, worry** *All changes bring uncertainty and anxiety, and the management of this change must be sensitive.*

unchanged ADJ
remaining the same

● adv+ADJ mainly **basically, broadly, essentially, fundamentally, largely, mostly, practically, relatively, remarkably, substantially** *A year after that, the situation was essentially unchanged.*
▶ completely **completely, entirely** *The interest rate has remained completely unchanged at 6 per cent.*
▶ almost **almost, virtually** *The Treasurer reported that finances were virtually unchanged from his last statement.*

● v+ADJ **be left, continue, remain, stay, survive** *The reduction for students, the unemployed and old age pensioners stays unchanged at 50 per cent.*

unclear ADJ
not obvious, definite, or easy to understand

● adv+ADJ with time expressions **currently, extremely, frequently, often, presently, sometimes, still** *It is often unclear who should be responsible for conducting the debriefing.*
▶ slightly **a little, slightly** *The structure of the book is a little unclear.*
▶ rather **largely, quite, rather, somewhat** *The position on chapters in edited volumes is rather unclear.*

▶ very **particularly, very** *In the current system, the role of the independent regulator is very unclear.*
▶ completely **completely, entirely, totally** *It is entirely unclear what the scope of these freedoms will be in practice.*

● ADJ+n language **details, diagnosis or information, evidence, meaning, wording** *The wording is unclear and the notion of 'Hypothesis' is not clearly developed.*
▶ cause **cause, motive, origins, reason** *Their cultural origins are unclear.*
▶ situation **position, situation, status** *60 per cent or more of books have unclear copyright status.*
▶ result **future, outcome, result** *The longer-term results are still unclear.*
▶ purpose **function, purpose, role** *A number of stone-built tanks were also found, although their function is unclear.*

> Usage ***Unclear*** usually comes after the noun in all of the ADJ+n combinations shown above.

● v+ADJ be or become **be, become, be left, remain** *At present, the results of this change in approach remain unclear.*
▶ seem **appear, seem** *This point still appears unclear*

uncomfortable ADJ
1 with an unpleasant or slightly painful feeling

● adv+ADJ very **acutely, exceedingly, extremely, incredibly, profoundly, terribly, very** *These foods are highly acidic and may make the eater profoundly uncomfortable.*
▶ rather **decidedly, distinctly, rather, somewhat** *For someone of his height, the seating is somewhat uncomfortable.*
▶ slightly **a little, mildly, slightly, vaguely** *The process is only mildly uncomfortable, and only takes a minute or so.*

● ADJ+n **feeling, sensation** *I felt the uncomfortable sensation of sweat trickling down my back where I pressed against the seat.*

● v+ADJ be **be, feel, prove** *Unfortunately, the boots proved too uncomfortable for some of us.*
▶ seem **appear, look, seem** *I pass many hot people, looking uncomfortable in their sticky seats.*
▶ become **become, get, grow** *Her knees stiffen up in the evenings, and get uncomfortable after walking for too long.*

2 feeling embarrassed or nervous

● adv+ADJ very **acutely, deeply, exceedingly, extremely, incredibly, profoundly, terribly, very** *There's stuff in here which I find acutely uncomfortable.*
▶ rather **decidedly, distinctly, rather, somewhat** *'Come on, Jack,' Daniel urged, beginning to look distinctly uncomfortable.*
▶ slightly **faintly, a little, slightly, vaguely** *Naomi is the first one to admit that she found doing the scene a little uncomfortable.*

● ADJ+n truth **fact, reality, truth** *She gradually unravels her own difficult story, and her own uncomfortable truth.*

If something you watch, listen to or read makes you feel uncomfortable, you can say that *it makes **uncomfortable reading, viewing** or **listening***: *The programme demonstrated how this was done and it made very uncomfortable viewing.*

▶ silence **pause, silence** *There was a moment or two of uncomfortable silence.*
▶ understanding **realization, reminder** *If we force ourselves to step back and take a look at the supporting data, we are faced with two uncomfortable realizations.*
▶ situation **experience, position, situation** *Dining solo does not have to be an uncomfortable experience.*
▶ subject **issue, subject** *The book raises uncomfortable issues about immigration and religious extremism, and deals with them very honestly.*

● v+ADJ be **be, feel, prove, remain** *Many men and women remain deeply uncomfortable **with** the notion of feminism.*
▶ seem **appear, look, seem** *Participants knew they were being video-taped but did not appear uncomfortable.*
▶ become **become, get, grow** *Harry grew increasingly uncomfortable at the press conference.*
▶ find something **find sth** *Euphemisms are coined to avoid talking directly about things we find uncomfortable.*

unconcerned ADJ
not worried about a situation or event

● adv+ADJ completely **completely, entirely, quite, totally, utterly, wholly** *Most of them don't see God as a part of their existence and are totally unconcerned **about** the afterlife.*
▶ apparently **apparently, seemingly** *A group of horses remained near the center of the pasture, seemingly unconcerned **by** the approach of night.*
▶ strangely **curiously, strangely, surprisingly** *His boss seems strangely unconcerned.*
▶ mainly or partly **generally, largely, relatively** *The British public seem to be relatively unconcerned **about** the circulation of their personal information.*

● v+ADJ **appear, remain, seem** *The prison service appear unconcerned **at** the continual loss of able and experienced staff.*

unconscious ADJ
not conscious, and therefore unable to think, feel, or see anything

● adv+ADJ completely **completely, totally**
almost **almost, not quite** *He was rushed to the local hospital, where he was almost unconscious on arrival.*
apparently **apparently, seemingly** *He saw Symonds lying apparently unconscious next to him.*

● v+ADJ be or remain unconscious **be found, be left, be slumped, lie, remain** *Amy was left lying unconscious in the road after the accident.*
be made unconscious **be beaten, be knocked, be rendered** *Andrew was thrown back across the compartment and knocked unconscious instantly.*
become unconscious **become, collapse, fall** *Clive fell unconscious onto Des's front lawn.*

when you do not realize something

● adv+ADJ completely or very **completely, deeply, quite, totally, wholly** *By this time, it was clear to me that Eric was quite unconscious of my presence.*
▶ almost or partly **almost, largely, partly** *They relate to the viewer in a spiritual, almost unconscious way.*
▶ apparently **apparently, seemingly** *He continued to talk, apparently unconscious of her return.*

● ADJ+n wish **desire, impulse, motivation, motive, urge, wish** *He argued that unconscious motivation is by far the most determinate part of our minds.*
▶ mind or feeling **fear, feeling, memory, mind, psyche** *This language of the unconscious mind is characterized by its use of metaphors.*
▶ idea or belief **assumption, belief, bias, idea, racism** *The student sought judicial review, alleging unconscious bias on the part of the decision-making body.*
▶ action **action, behaviour, habit, imitation, reaction** *He took his left hand out of his pocket and scratched his eyebrow, in completely unconscious imitation of his father.*

● v+ADJ **appear, be, seem** *The husband seems unconscious of his wife's emotional needs.*

uncontrollable ADJ
impossible to control or stop

● adv+ADJ almost **almost, virtually** *He decided that his anger was making his life almost uncontrollable.*
▶ completely **completely, totally** *I feel very sorry for you, you have a child who is totally uncontrollable.*
▶ apparently **apparently, seemingly** *You are worried about expensive, seemingly uncontrollable litigation costs.*

● ADJ+n laughter **giggles, laughter, mirth** *We all burst into uncontrollable giggles, and it is a wonder I didn't get a detention on the spot.*
▶ anger **anger, emotion, fury, passion, rage, temper, violence** *I half expected him to fly into an uncontrollable rage over a slip of the tongue.*
▶ desire **desire, urge** *Users have an uncontrollable desire to feel the high that is brought on by the drug.*

uncover V
find out about something hidden or secret

● V+n information **details, evidence, evidence, facts, identity, information, story, truth** *Recent evidence uncovered in the library of Rouen Cathedral sheds new light on these matters.* ● *It was an idle internet search that uncovered the truth.*
▶ secret **mystery, secret** *How do you think I've not had my secret uncovered before now?*
▶ crime or bad act **conspiracy, fraud, plot, racket, scam, scandal** *They were accused of treason whenever a national conspiracy was uncovered.*
▶ fault or difference **discrepancies, flaws, inconsistencies, irregularities, shortcomings** *Police were called into council offices after mystery accounting discrepancies were uncovered.* ● *Our investigation uncovered serious flaws in the asylum system.*

underestimate V
think that something is smaller or less important than it really is

● adv+V very much **drastically, greatly, grossly,**

hugely, massively, seriously, severely, totally, vastly, wildly *Official statistics grossly underestimate the work-related contribution to deaths and illness in the UK.*

▶ considerably **considerably, significantly, substantially** *She significantly underestimated her ability to control others.*

▶ all the time **consistently, systematically** *The world has consistently underestimated the threat of terrorist attacks.*

▶ completely **completely, totally** *I completely underestimated how much work would be involved!*

▶ with time expressions **frequently, never, not ever, often, sometimes, usually** *Never underestimate the power of being bored!*

● V+n importance **impact, importance, power, seriousness, significance** *We should not underestimate the significance of this agreement.*

▶ size **extent, incidence, level, magnitude, prevalence, scale, strength** *Their only failure was to underestimate the magnitude of the disaster.*

▶ problem **challenge, complexity, danger, difficulty, risk, severity** *We should not underestimate the difficulty of organising such a project.*

▶ ability **ability, intelligence** *Did I underestimate your abilities?*

underestimate N
the belief that something is less than it really is

● adj+N big **considerable, gross, massive, serious, significant, substantial** *We believe that figure to be a gross underestimate.*

▶ small **slight** *The mean retirement age is currently 61, although it may be a slight underestimate.*

undergo V
experience something

● V+n change **alteration, change, metamorphosis, modification, overhaul, restructuring, revision, transformation** *The area will undergo a transformation through the sustainable regeneration housing initiative.*

▶ improvement or repair **makeover, redesign, redevelopment, refit, refurbishment, renaissance, renovation, repair, restoration** *Their shop has recently undergone a refurbishment and has doubled in size.*

▶ medical treatment **chemotherapy, operation, procedure, radiotherapy, resection, surgery, treatment** *The staff on this ward are specialists in caring for patients who have undergone transplant surgery.*

▶ testing **assessment, check, examination, inspection, review, screening, testing** *Candidates undergo formal psychometric testing using accredited systems.*

▶ training **training** *Our solicitors undergo annual training and assessment to ensure that our customers are getting the very best service possible.*

▶ bad experience **crisis, hardship, pain, persecution, stress, suffering, trauma** *All of the soldiers had undergone great hardship during this campaign.*

undergrowth N
small thick bushes covering the ground

● adj+N **deep, dense, heavy, impenetrable, lush,**

tangled, thick *Trees fall, rot and re-grow amidst a dense tangled undergrowth rich in wild flora.*

● v+N **clear, cut, remove** *Boaters have cleared the undergrowth between the towpath and the fence.*

underline V
show clearly that something is important

● adv+V **just, merely, only, simply** *The ambiguity of the ending merely underlines the closeness between the two men.*

▶ problem or danger **concern, danger, difficulty, problem, risk, threat** *The report once again underlines the treat posed by the uncontrolled rise in carbon emissions.*

● V+n importance **importance, seriousness, significance, value** *The latest pictures on international television screens underline the seriousness of the situation.*

▶ need **necessity, need, urgency, usefulness** *She underlined the need for patience and the investment of time.*

▶ fact **fact, truth** *Professor Bain had underlined the fact that this package was self-financing.*

▶ belief or commitment **belief, commitment, position** *The two sides underlined their commitment to the protection and promotion of human rights.*

▶ superiority **superiority** *The Knights underlined their superiority with two tries from Chris Langley in the last five minutes.*

▶ determination **determination** *Operation Justice has underlined our determination to make Staffordshire as unwelcoming as possible to the criminal.*

underlying ADJ
real or basic, but not obvious

● ADJ+n idea **assumption, concept, logic, philosophy, principle, theme** *Key concepts and their underlying assumptions are rigorously analysed.*

▶ reason **cause, motive, rationale, reason** *The underlying causes of anti-social behaviour should be addressed.*

▶ change **change, trend** *The population has fluctuated but the underlying trend is not easy to discern.*

undermine V
make someone or something gradually less confident or successful

● V+n trust or credibility **accountability, credibility, dignity, integrity, legitimacy, trust, validity** *Turnouts this low could undermine the legitimacy of the result and the Parliament itself.*

▶ confidence **confidence, morale, self-confidence** *Critics say the revelations undermine confidence in the criminal justice system.*

▶ freedom or power **autonomy, democracy, independence, liberty, power, sovereignty** *A number of MPs have expressed fears that a total ban on smoking would undermine civil liberties.*

▶ effectiveness **competitiveness, effectiveness, viability, vitality** *Attempting change without an understanding of the cultural dynamics will undermine its effectiveness.*

▶ stability **cohesion, stability** *By undermining social cohesion, inequality provides a breeding ground for crime and disorder.*

▶ idea or belief **belief, concept, idea, principle, values** *The secret trials undermine the fundamental principles of an independent judiciary.*

underscore V
emphasize something or show it is important

● adv+V brilliantly **brilliantly, dramatically, emphatically, neatly, repeatedly** *The opening line neatly underscored the entire episode and set the tone for the next 30 minutes.*

● V+n importance **importance, relevance, seriousness, significance** *Nozick (1981) underscores the significance of this decision*
▶ need **necessity, need, urgency** *The work of Chatzi et al underscores the need to reevaluate these presumptions.*
▶ commitment **commitment** *This acquisition underscores our commitment to excellence.*
▶ fact **fact, point** *Recent efforts in Europe on cybercrime underscore this point.*

understand V
know what someone or something means

● adv+V completely **completely, fully, perfectly, precisely, properly, really, thoroughly, totally, truly** *It is important to fully understand what is going on.*
▶ easily **clearly, easily** *The lectures are given by researchers eminent in their field, but in a manner that is easily understood by all.*
▶ correctly **correctly, rightly** *These, if understood rightly, are certainly worthwhile questions.*
▶ not much or not at all **imperfectly, little, not, not even, not quite, poorly** *This groundbreaking book addresses a widespread but poorly understood problem.*
▶ by most or all people **commonly, generally, universally** *Brainwashing, as it is commonly understood, does not really exist.*

● V+n importance **importance, relevance, significance, value** *As an organisation, we understand the importance of joined up thinking.*
meaning **issues, meaning, nature** *Potential exporters need to understand the nature of the country to succeed.*
reason or cause **cause, rationale, reason** *I apologise about this in advance and I hope you understand my reasons.*
need **needs, requirements** *The hardest challenge was understanding dealers' requirements.*
idea or concept **concept, idea, notion, principle, reasoning, view** *Students will be expected to show that they are capable of understanding complex philosophical ideas.*
effects **consequences, effects, impact, implications** *It is clear that he doesn't really understand the full consequences of his policies.*
problem or difficulty **challenge, complexity, danger, difficulty, problem, risk, threat** *The public needs to understand the threat that these terrorists pose.*
someone's feelings **anger, fear, feelings, frustration, reluctance** *The programme is designed to help children understand their own feelings.*

understandable ADJ
normal and reasonable in a particular situation

● adv+ADJ completely **completely, entirely, perfectly, quite, totally, wholly** *It is completely understandable that people should feel nervous and frightened for their futures.*
▶ rather **perhaps, somewhat** *The defensive stance taken by many in the music industry towards the loss of revenue is somewhat understandable.*

● ADJ+n worry **anxiety, caution, concern, confusion, reluctance** *Such anxieties are perfectly understandable under the circumstances.*

> If you understand why someone does something, you can say that they do it *for understandable reasons*: *The newspapers wanted to protect the anonymity of their sources for understandable reasons, so we could not force them to reveal any details.*

▶ anger **anger, frustration, outrage** *Ian's efforts were appreciated and his frustration understandable.*
▶ reaction **reaction, response** *Fear was an understandable reaction.*
▶ wish **desire** *There is an understandable desire to put off the day of reckoning.*

understanding N
knowledge about a subject, process, or situation

● adj+N good **clear, complete, full, good, great, proper, real, solid, sound, thorough** *The Education Authority had a clear understanding of their operational policies.*
▶ basic **basic, fundamental, limited** *This unit aims to give the student a basic understanding of the rules and principles of international law.*
▶ deep **deep, detailed, in-depth, profound, sophisticated** *They can only be talking about a superficial familiarity, not a deep understanding.*
▶ broad **broad, comprehensive** *The volume guides readers towards a broad understanding of the history of the Classical period.*
▶ shared **common, mutual, shared** *It was about ensuring a common understanding of guidelines.*
▶ types of understanding **conceptual, critical, cultural, mathematical, scientific, technical, theoretical** *I guess my theoretical understanding was quite a bit of help.*

● v+N get understanding **achieve, acquire, form, gain, obtain** *Graduates acquire a sound understanding of the fundamentals of IT.*
▶ increase or improve understanding **broaden, build, deepen, develop, enhance, enrich, extend, improve, increase, reinforce** *It deepened my understanding in every way.*
▶ encourage understanding **advance, aid, foster, further, promote** *The main objective of the event is to promote a better understanding of science.*
▶ show understanding **communicate, demonstrate, reflect, reveal, show** *Does the literature review demonstrate understanding?*
▶ need understanding **call for, need, require** *The degree programme requires an understanding of basic statistical techniques.*
▶ test someone's understanding **assess, check, monitor, test** *There is a comprehension test which assesses students' understanding of the reading passage.*

understatement N
a statement that does not express how large, serious etc something really is

- adj+N big **big, dramatic, gross, huge, massive** *To say that I was surprised would be a gross understatement.*

  You can refer to a very big understatement as **the understatement of the century, the year, or the decade**: *Hidden away near the end was a single, cautious sentence which scientists regard as the understatement of the century.*

- ▶ small **slight** *To say that I am a bit anxious about this birth is a slight understatement!*

  You can describe what someone says as **something of an understatement** or **a bit of an understatement** to indicate that you actually think it is quite a big understatement: *To say her life had been colourful would be something of an understatement.*

- ▶ typical **characteristic, classical, typical** *'That wasn't a great idea' is a characteristic understatement from a student friend.*
- ▶ striking **masterly** *'It was an interesting race for me this afternoon,' said Alonso, **with** masterly understatement.*

  You can also refer to someone as **a master of understatement**, or to something they say as **a masterpiece of understatement**: *When he hasn't been silent, he's been a master of understatement.*

undertake V
agree to do something

- V+n study **project, research, review, study** *You choose your area of investigation and undertake your own research under the supervision of a member of staff.*
- ▶ survey **audit, consultation, enquiry, exercise, inspection, investigation, monitoring, survey** *We undertook a survey of voluntary action in two rural areas.*
- ▶ work or activity **activity, assignment, commission, fieldwork, placement, task, training, work** *Students also have opportunities to undertake short placements in organisations that hold particular interest for them.*
- ▶ analysis **analysis, assessment, evaluation** *It is part of their function to undertake risk/benefit analysis of research proposals.*

undertaking N
something difficult or complicated that you do

- adj+N very big **enormous, great, huge, immense, major, mammoth, massive** *In terms of pavement area alone, this project is a mammoth undertaking.*
- ▶ difficult **ambitious, arduous, complex, difficult, formidable** *Outlining the history of sculpture from pre-history to the present day in sixty pages is an ambitious undertaking.*
- ▶ dangerous **hazardous, risky** *In these conditions, even crossing the bridges can be a risky undertaking.*

undertone N
something suggesting an idea or feeling indirectly
[usually plural]

- adj+N unpleasant **dark, disturbing, sinister, unpleasant** *Sinister undertones resonate throughout the novel.*
- ▶ strong **deep, heavy, serious, strong** *This is a superbly crafted film, with powerful images and a strong sexual undertone.*
- ▶ weak **subtle** *Subtle undertones and delicate suggestions mean nothing to them.*
- ▶ types of undertone **homoerotic, melancholy, political, racial, racist, religious, sexual** *The history of the topic will be discussed, including its political undertones.*

underworld N
criminals in a community, considered as a group

- adj+N unpleasant **dangerous, seedy, sinister, sordid, violent** *Drug Wars is an addictive game of buying and selling in a seedy underworld.*
- ▶ dark **dark, murky, shadowy, shady** *In this riveting thriller, Dublin's shady underworld is brought to life in all its raw and chilling detail.*
- ▶ criminal **criminal** *Donna finds herself drawn further into a dark, menacing criminal underworld.*

undesirable ADJ
bad or harmful

- adv+ADJ very **extremely, highly, particularly, very, wholly** *Prison makes many criminals worse in one sense and is highly undesirable.*
- ▶ clearly **clearly, inherently, obviously** *This kind of attack is obviously undesirable.*
- ▶ possibly **possibly, potentially, probably** *Measuring individual performance is very difficult, and possibly undesirable, in a hospital environment.*
- ▶ in a particular way **environmentally, politically, socially** *Does he agree that this would be politically undesirable?*
- v+ADJ **be considered, be deemed, be regarded as, be seen as, seem** *The Parish Council believes that further building in any of the villages is considered undesirable.*

undue ADJ
not necessary, reasonable, or suitable

- ADJ+n difficulty **burden, disruption, disturbance, hardship, inconvenience** *Our consultants can help to ensure that your problems are resolved without undue disruption to your business.*
- ▶ stress **distress, pressure, strain, stress, wear, wear and tear** *If you are subjected to prolonged or undue stress, your body will be affected in some way.*
- ▶ influence **bias, influence, interference** *Any undue interference would be in breach of Article 10 of the European Convention on Human Rights.*
- ▶ emphasis **attention, emphasis, prominence, weight** *All movements are accomplished in an easy and playful way, without effort or undue emphasis.*
- ▶ speed/slowness **delay, haste** *Are the government acting with undue haste?*

unease N
a nervous, uncomfortable, or unhappy feeling about a situation

- adj+N great **considerable, deep, much, profound** *We should not underestimate the feeling of deep unease which this development causes.*

▶ among many people **general, public, widespread** *Numerous surveys worldwide report growing public unease **about** GM foods.*

▶ slight **a certain, slight, vague** *There was a slight unease between soloist and accompaniments, but a good performance nevertheless.*

▶ increasing **growing, increasing** *The move reflects growing unease **about** the impact of turbines on sensitive sites.*

● v+N cause unease **cause, create, generate, provoke** *I write this hoping not to cause any more unease.*

● feel or express unease **express, feel, sense** *On the country's programme of privatization, the report expresses some unease.*

uneasy ADJ

1 feeling slightly nervous, worried, or upset

● adv+ADJ very **deeply, distinctly, extremely, profoundly, very** *Alice began to feel very uneasy.*

▶ rather **quite, rather, somewhat** *I'm rather uneasy that 93 per cent of people are more right-wing than I am.*

▶ slightly **a bit** INFORMAL**, a little, slightly, vaguely** *I felt slightly uneasy as it was the first time I'd spoken to them.*

▶ more and more **increasingly** *On the way to the summit, I became increasingly uneasy **about** the guy.*

● ADJ+n **feeling, sensation, sense** *They had had an uneasy feeling throughout the day that they were being watched.*

● v+ADJ feel or seem uneasy **feel, look, seem** *Many airlines felt distinctly uneasy **about** the whole project.*

▶ be or become uneasy **become, grow, remain** *Animals can become uneasy **about** sounds they've never heard before.*

2 not settled or calm

● ADJ+n relationship **alliance, co-existence, friendship, partnership, relationship** *There is always an uneasy relationship between art and commerce.*

▶ agreement **coalition, compromise, truce** *After much diplomatic coming and going, a rather uneasy compromise was reached.*

▶ mixture **mix, mixture** *Today Ponders End is an uneasy mixture of old and new.*

▶ balance **balance, equilibrium** *It is true that we are striking an uneasy balance.*

▶ quiet or peace **peace, silence** *Mrs. Johnson was the first to break the uneasy silence.*

unemployment N

situation where people have no work or income

adj+N high/low **high, low, mass, massive, widespread** *He was brought up in a community in which there was mass unemployment.*

lasting for a long time **chronic, long-term, persistent** *We need new ways of tackling the old problems of persistent unemployment, family breakdown, and low expectations.*

getting higher/lower **falling, growing, increasing, rising, soaring** *Consumers are putting off major purchases, partly because they are afraid of rising unemployment.*

types of unemployment **graduate, hidden, involuntary, male, seasonal, structural, youth** *Keynes had great difficulty persuading the economics profession that there could be structural unemployment.*

● v+N reduce unemployment **alleviate, combat, cut, halve, lower, reduce, relieve, tackle** *New Deal was launched in order to tackle long-term unemployment.*

▶ end unemployment **abolish, eliminate** *This economic growth will create new jobs and eliminate unemployment.*

▶ experience unemployment **experience, face, suffer** *Young people are more likely to experience unemployment than older age groups.*

▶ increase unemployment **increase** *This will make the country less competitive and may increase unemployment.*

● cause unemployment **cause, create, lead to** *Factories closed, causing widespread unemployment.*

● N+v rise **double, increase, rise, soar** *Unemployment rose unexpectedly in the three months to August, according to official figures.*

> You can say that unemployment *hits* or *reaches* a certain figure: *We see miserable workers leaving a factory and the caption 'Unemployment hits 3 million'.*

▶ fall **decline, decrease, drop, fall, halve** *As a result, youth unemployment has fallen dramatically, down 90 per cent since 1997.*

● N+n **figures, levels, rates, statistics** *The published unemployment figures only tell part of the story.*

● n+in+N increase **increase, rise** *The result was price increases and a sharp rise in unemployment.*

▶ reduction **drop, fall, reduction** *We have seen a massive drop in unemployment.*

unexpected ADJ

surprising, because you did not expect it

● adv+ADJ completely **completely, entirely, quite, totally, wholly** *These incidents usually appear out of the blue, i.e. are totally unexpected.*

> If something is not completely unexpected, you can say that it is *not entirely unexpected* or *not altogether unexpected*: *We were questioned for a very long time, which was not altogether unexpected.*

▶ very **very** *There was one very unexpected request.*

▶ rather or slightly **rather, slightly, somewhat** *Then, something rather unexpected happened.*

● ADJ+n surprise **surprise, twist** *It is a darkly humorous tale packed full of unexpected twists and turns.*

> You can say that events *take an unexpected turn* or go *in an unexpected direction*, or that something *comes from an unexpected quarter*: *His marriage is in a crisis and he seeks help from an unexpected quarter.*

▶ result or discovery **consequence, discovery, ending, finding, outcome, result, side-effect** *An unexpected finding was that the mouse and rat were resistant.*

▶ event **arrival, death, event** *His unexpected death has shocked the German rowing world.*

▶ person **ally, caller, guest, visitor** *This folding bed is great for when you have an unexpected guest.*
▶ benefit **benefit, bonus, treat, windfall** *We also have access to a smaller conference hall for exhibitor presentations, which is an unexpected bonus.*
▶ meeting **encounter, visit** *Each new and unexpected encounter can evoke new ways of thinking and acting.*

unfair ADJ
not fair or reasonable

● adv+ADJ very **deeply, grossly, terribly, very** *The guys spent a year doing it and I get all the credit, it's grossly unfair.*
▶ slightly or rather **a bit INFORMAL, a little, rather, slightly** *This criticism is a little unfair.*
▶ clearly **blatantly, manifestly, obviously, patently** *Her primary submission is that the procedure adopted at the trial was manifestly unfair.*
▶ by its nature **fundamentally, inherently, intrinsically** *The application of a uniform tariff is inherently unfair in that it favours those who consume most.*
▶ completely **completely, totally, wholly** *To equate this great religion with backwardness and reaction is totally unfair.*

● v+ADJ consider something unfair **consider sth as, perceive sth as, regarded sth as** *Parents may be less willing to engage in a process that they perceive as unfair.*
▶ seem unfair **appear, be deemed, be felt to be, feel, seem** *A few complained that the distribution of classroom assistants among schools appeared unfair.*
▶ be unfair **be** *A City victory would have been perhaps unfair, but it almost came.*

unfit ADJ
below the accepted quality or standard

● adv+ADJ in a particular way **medically, mentally, permanently, physically** *Jimmy was found to be medically unfit for the Armed Services during the Second World War.*
▶ completely **quite, totally, utterly, wholly** *This junction is utterly unfit for the hundreds of thousands of vehicles that pass through it each day.*
▶ clearly **clearly** *By early 1997, this architecture was clearly unfit for our expansion plans.*

● v+ADJ be or become unfit **be, become, be found, be rendered** *The old-style notes are then withdrawn from circulation as they became unfit to be re-issued.*
▶ be considered unfit **be considered, be declared, be deemed, be judged** *Grants may be available if your home is deemed unfit to live in.*
▶ make sth unfit **make sth** *Years of neglect had made the buildings unfit for human habitation.*

unforgettable ADJ
remembered for a very long time afterwards

● adv+ADJ completely **absolutely, completely, quite, totally, utterly** *The thrill of hand-feeding these beautiful creatures is utterly unforgettable.*
▶ really **simply, truly** *Suitable for any regular hillwalker, this is a simply unforgettable alpine holiday.*

● ADJ+n experience **experience, holiday, journey, moment, sight** *The gourmet cuisine is an unforgettable experience.*

unfortunate ADJ
unlucky or that you wish had not happened

● adv+ADJ very **doubly, especially, extremely, particularly, very** *I have been extremely unfortunate in having three operations within the space of a year.*
▶ rather **rather, somewhat** *Note the rather unfortunate printing error on the top line.*
▶ slightly **a little, slightly** *The timing of the marriage was a little unfortunate.*

● ADJ+n event **accident, event, experience, incident** *The details that led up to this unfortunate incident are available from the Dundee Courier.*
▶ situation **circumstances, situation** *It was just a set of unfortunate circumstances which I think could have been dealt with a little better.*
▶ result **consequence, effect, result, side-effect** *The unfortunate consequence of an ageing population is that many more people will suffer from dementia.*

unfounded ADJ
not supported with facts or evidence

● adv+ADJ completely **completely, entirely, quite, totally, wholly** *After contacting the farmer, we found that the rumour was entirely unfounded.*
▶ mainly **largely** *The criticism of the music is largely unfounded.*
▶ clearly **clearly, manifestly** *The majority of claims were clearly unfounded.*

● ADJ+n accusing someone **accusation, allegation, charge, criticism, suspicion** *Tell them that their client's allegations are completely unfounded.*
▶ statement **assertion, claim** *It is hard to know how any honest man can present such a mishmash of unfounded assertion as evidence.*
▶ belief **assumption, belief** *The argument rests on an unfounded assumption.*
▶ talking about someone or something **rumour, speculation** *I think that this is simply an unfounded rumour!*
▶ worry **concern, fear, worry** *In the event, my fears were largely unfounded.*

● v+ADJ be unfounded **be, prove** *Sadly, their hopes had proved unfounded.*
▶ seem unfounded **appear, seem** *Fears of increased cannabis usage would thus appear unfounded.*

unhappy ADJ
feeling sad or upset

● adv+ADJ very **deeply, desperately, distinctly, extremely, profoundly, terribly, very** *It is made quite clear to us that she is deeply unhappy.*
▶ clearly **clearly, obviously** *She is obviously unhappy about her marriage.*

● v+ADJ be or become unhappy **be, become, feel** *I felt extremely unhappy, anxious, and lonely.*
▶ seem unhappy **look, seem** *The poor girl looks so unhappy.*
▶ make someone unhappy **make sb unhappy** *The only thing that makes me unhappy is the idea of returning there.*

uniform ADJ
the same everywhere

- adv+ADJ very **extremely, remarkably, very**
*Although there is a wide variation in height over
this area, the general pattern of the sections is very
uniform.*
▸ rather **fairly, quite, reasonably, relatively** *Coffee
beans are of fairly uniform size and proportion.*
▸ completely **completely, perfectly** *In many cases, an
atomic nucleus is shaped like a perfectly uniform
sphere.*
▸ almost **almost, nearly** *Jupiter has a single ring that
is almost uniform in its structure.*
- ADJ+n size or level **density, rate, size, standard,
temperature, thickness** *Slices are assumed to have
uniform thickness of arbitrary dimension.*
▸ way something is spread **distribution** *Underfloor
heating is one of the most effective methods of
obtaining uniform heat distribution.*
▸ movement **flow, motion, velocity** *In Section 2 we
apply Newton's second law to uniform circular
motion.*
▸ appearance **appearance, colour** *This type of picture
format is best suited for images containing blocks of
uniform colour.*

uniformity N
the state of being the same as others

- adj+N dull **bland, drab, dull** *The problem is the
supermarkets like bland uniformity.*
- great **great, remarkable** *There is a remarkable
uniformity in the customs of this night all through
the British Isles.*
- complete **absolute, complete, perfect, rigid, strict**
*He would say that the enemy of opportunity was
rigid uniformity.*
- types of uniformity **cultural, genetic, religious** *Only
in Europe was there a consistent policy of enforcing
religious uniformity.*
- v+N achieve uniformity **achieve, bring, create,
ensure, establish, introduce** *The first step must be
to create a uniformity of judging.*
- make sure uniformity happens **encourage,
enforce, impose, promote** *Guidelines on diagnosing
are issued to doctors to try to promote uniformity in
the diagnoses.*
- keep or increase uniformity **improve, increase,
maintain** *More recently the history of the landscape
is one of gradually increased uniformity.*

unimportant ADJ
not important or relevant

adv+ADJ completely **completely, totally** *I talk to
you about totally unimportant things that have
happened.*
rather **fairly, quite** *Even things that seem quite
unimportant might be significant to someone.*
when compared to other things **comparatively,
relatively** *For long-range search radars, this 'blind'
area is relatively unimportant.*
when something seems to be unimportant
apparently, seemingly *It's the seemingly
unimportant people who determine the course of
history.*

v+ADJ be or seem unimportant **appear, become,**

seem *Information that initially appears
unimportant may become valuable when used with
other information.*
▸ think something is unimportant **consider sth,
deem sth** *One matter that this paper considers
unimportant is the manner of collecting samples for
DNA testing.*
▸ feel unimportant **feel** *Consequently, we will avoid
circumstances that make us feel unimportant.*

unintelligible ADJ
impossible to understand

- adv+ADJ almost **almost, largely, virtually** *I have
to say here that the writing style was virtually
unintelligible.*
▸ completely **completely, quite, totally** *Sanskrit itself
uses a non-Roman script that is totally unintelligible
without some serious study.*
▸ between each other **mutually** *China is home to eight
mutually unintelligible spoken Chinese dialects.*

uninterested ADJ
not interested

- adv+ADJ completely **completely, entirely,
singularly, totally, utterly** *I was and still am totally
uninterested in competitive sport.*
▸ rather **largely, quite** *Current energy suppliers are
largely uninterested in small-scale energy generation.*
- v+ADJ **appear, seem** *The company seemed
uninterested in rectifying their mistake.*

unique ADJ
very unusual, or not like anything else

- adv+ADJ completely **absolutely, completely,
entirely, genuinely, quite, totally, truly, utterly,
wholly** *We are happy to provide a service which is
totally unique to you.*
▸ almost **almost, virtually** *Skara Brae, by the shore of
the Bay of Skaill, is virtually unique.*
▸ possibly **perhaps, possibly, probably** *The manner
of his progress to the final heat was remarkable,
possibly unique.*
▸ not at all **hardly** *She lived to 90 – unusual, but
hardly unique.*

> You can also say that something is **by no means
> unique** or **far from unique**: *Sadly, Roz's story is far
> from unique.*

united ADJ
if people are united, they all have the same aims
or beliefs

- adv+ADJ completely **completely, fully, really**
*Senior Tories are completely united on the issue of
ID cards.*
▸ strongly **closely, firmly** *Our countries have never
been so closely united.*
▸ in politics **politically** *Real black freedom will only
come when the region is politically united.*
- ADJ+in opposition **condemnation, opposition** *We
are united in opposition to further violence and
military retaliation.*
▸ support **praise, solidarity, support** *The angling
community is united in its support for these changes
to the law.*

▶ wish or intention **aim, commitment, desire, determination, resolve** *We are united in our resolve to confront and defeat this terrorism.*

▶ belief or opinion **belief, view** *Above all, they are united in their belief in the project and each other.*

unity N
a situation where people join together or agree

● v+N create unity **achieve, attain, bring, build, create, forge, restore** *Let us look for ways to forge stronger unity in the future.*

▶ keep or increase unity **foster, maintain, preserve, promote, strengthen** *To preserve national unity, he agreed to relinquish the presidency.*

▶ damage or destroy unity **destroy, disrupt, shatter, threaten, undermine** *The rift now threatens to undermine the unity of NATO itself.*

▶ try to create unity **call for, seek** *At his inauguration the governor called for political unity.*

universal ADJ
involving or affecting everyone

● adv+ADJ almost **almost, fairly, near, nearly, practically, pretty** INFORMAL, **pretty much** INFORMAL, **virtually** *There was almost universal agreement for these principles.*

> If something is not universal at all, you can say that it is *far from universal* or *by no means universal*: *Unfortunately, this flexibility is far from universal.*

▶ in a real way **genuinely, truly** *This site can be read in practically all languages, making it a truly universal site.*

▶ seeming to be **apparently** *Our ability to use language to communicate and think develops in stages that are apparently universal.*

▶ possibly **potentially, supposedly** *It is a move from targeted to potentially universal surveillance.*

● ADJ+n agreement or approval **acceptance, acclaim, agreement, appeal, approval** *There is still no universal agreement on the classification of the marsupials.*

▶ idea or value **principle, theme, truth, value** *Rules need to be rigorous and based on agreed universal principles.*

university N
an institution where people study for degrees and do research

● adj+N quality **elite, good, leading, prestigious, top** INFORMAL, **world-class** *Cambridge is a world-class university.*

▶ age **modern, new, old, redbrick, traditional** *Founded in 1881, the University of Liverpool is the original redbrick university.*

● v+N study at university **attend, enter, go to, study at** *At the age of 20, she attended university.*

▶ leave university **finish, graduate from, leave** *I don't know what he did after leaving university.*

▶ apply to university **apply to** *I didn't have any idea about how to prepare for applying to university.*

● N+n places **campus, department, faculty, library** *The School of Electronics and Computer Science is the largest and most successful university department of its kind in the UK.*

▶ teacher **academic, lecturer, professor, researcher, staff, teacher, tutor** *Two university academics have recently published books in their fields of expertise.*

▶ student **graduate, student, undergraduate** *Do I have to be a university graduate?*

▶ education **course, degree, education, teaching, tuition** *Include any advanced university degrees on your business card.*

▶ joining a university **admission, entrance** *We help students decide on the right subjects for university entrance.*

unknown ADJ
which people do not know about

● adv+ADJ completely **completely, entirely, quite, totally, utterly, wholly** *Most of the names were completely unknown to me.*

▶ mainly **largely, mostly** *The longer-term risks of the drug are still largely unknown.*

▶ compared to others **comparatively, relatively** *Eric Bana, best known as The Hulk, leads the relatively unknown cast.*

▶ almost **almost, practically, virtually** *As the twentieth century began, Antarctica had been barely visited and was virtually unknown.*

▶ with time expressions **as yet, currently, hitherto, presently, previously, still** *This enabled cotton output to be increased to levels as yet unknown.*

▶ except for one fact **otherwise** *An unusual edition of Euclid was published in 1847 in England, edited by an otherwise unknown mathematician named Oliver Byrne.*

● v+ADJ **be, remain** *Other possible causes of the disease remain unknown.*

unlikely ADJ
not likely to happen

● adv+ADJ very **exceedingly, extremely, highly, incredibly, very** *The extent of these similarities make a mere coincidence highly unlikely.*

▶ rather **fairly, pretty** INFORMAL, **quite, rather, relatively, somewhat** *It is quite unlikely that they will manage to fill all the spaces in that time.*

▶ by its nature **inherently** *It was inherently unlikely that the document could have been written without the involvement of lawyers.*

▶ more and more **increasingly** *With all the key players pursuing their own successful careers, a major reunion is increasingly unlikely.*

● v+ADJ seem unlikely **appear, look, seem, sound** *It seemed very unlikely that Jack's body would ever be recovered.*

▶ be considered unlikely **be considered, be deemed, be thought** *The city was not provided with anti-aircraft defences because an attack was considered unlikely.*

▶ be unlikely **be, remain** *Without new evidence, it remains unlikely that Strauss's suggestion can be validated.*

> If you think something is unlikely to happen, you can use the expression *in the unlikely event*: *In the unlikely event that an order is not received, please contact us as soon as possible so that we can arrange another delivery.*

unlimited ADJ
not stopped or made less by anything

● adv+ADJ almost **almost, nearly, potentially, practically, virtually** *Modern information technology allows us practically unlimited access to each other's languages.*
▶ in effect **effectively, essentially** *Electricity backup capabilities at our data center are essentially unlimited.*
▶ seeming to be **apparently, seemingly** *Each entry is extensively cross-referenced, giving the reader seemingly unlimited avenues to explore.*

unlucky ADJ
if you are unlucky, something bad happens to you

● adv+ADJ very **desperately** INFORMAL, **extremely, particularly, really, so, very** *Unless you are really unlucky, rain should not stop play.*
▶ slightly **a bit** INFORMAL, **a little** *We felt a little unlucky to be losing at half time.*
▶ rather **pretty** INFORMAL, **rather, somewhat** *I think he was pretty unlucky never to get a contract in Australia.*
● v+ADJ **be, feel, prove** *I always feel so depressed because I feel so unlucky.*

unmoved ADJ
feeling no sympathy or sadness

● adv+ADJ **completely, quite, totally, utterly** *What will move one of us to tears will leave the other totally unmoved.*
● v+ADJ be unmoved **be, remain** *Despite passionate lobbying and entreaties, the BBC remained unmoved.*
▶ seem unmoved **appear, seem** *So far, the council appears unmoved.*
▶ make someone feel unmoved **leave sb** *The devastation and escalating death toll in the region can leave no one unmoved.*

unnecessary ADJ
possible to avoid

● adv+ADJ completely **completely, entirely, quite, totally, wholly** *Spraying the plant with chemical sprays is wholly unnecessary because it is so disease-resistant.*
▶ mainly **generally, largely** *This conclusion was eventually reached, but only after a tiresome and largely unnecessary discussion.*
▶ perhaps **perhaps, probably** *She realized that the test was probably unnecessary.*

● ADJ+n difficulties or problems **barriers, burden, bureaucracy, complications, delay, duplication, paperwork, regulation, restrictions, risk** *The staff is kept small to avoid unnecessary bureaucracy.*
suffering **distress, pain, pressure, stress, suffering** *How can this unnecessary suffering be stopped?*
costs **cost, expense, waste** *We have streamlined the whole process to eliminate any unnecessary costs.*

v+ADJ be or become unnecessary **be, become, prove** *The IMF demanded cuts in public expenditure that proved unnecessary.*
be considered unnecessary **be considered, be deemed, be thought** *It was thought unnecessary to go into great depth.*
▶ seem unnecessary **appear, seem** *The idea of a consumer boycott seems unnecessary.*
▶ make something unnecessary **make sth, render sth** *Pensions should be raised high enough to make it unnecessary for people to ask for extra help.*

unnoticed ADJ
not seen or noticed by anyone

● adv+ADJ completely **completely, entirely, quite, totally** *Eating disorders can, in the early stages, go completely unnoticed.*
▶ mainly **largely, mostly** *These conditions can lead to major visual impairment, mostly unnoticed by parents and teachers.*
▶ almost **almost, practically, virtually** *The quaint town remains, virtually unnoticed, in the shadow of its urban neighbour.*
▶ until now **hitherto, previously** *Previously unnoticed, the leaves are beginning to turn yellow.*
● v+ADJ be unnoticed **go, lie, pass, remain** *Sadly this important anniversary appeared to pass unnoticed.*
▶ go somewhere unnoticed **escape, slip, slip away** *While the hostages are rounded up, McClane slips away unnoticed.*

unorthodox ADJ
not following the usual rules or beliefs

● adv+ADJ very **highly** *The central hypothesis, and the various interpretations that follow from it, are highly unorthodox.*
▶ rather **rather, somewhat** *He was a most capable, if somewhat unorthodox, architect.*
▶ slightly **slightly** *When I graduated, I chose a slightly unorthodox career path.*

● ADJ+n method **approach, method, style, tactics** *He resigned from the school in 1991, following allegations about his unorthodox teaching methods.*
▶ beliefs or ideas **beliefs, ideas, views** *Her unorthodox views created much controversy.*

unpleasant ADJ
not liked or enjoyed

● adv+ADJ very **decidedly, deeply, distinctly, downright, extremely, particularly, thoroughly, very** *Your demeanour is arrogant, impatient, and downright unpleasant.*
▶ rather or slightly **fairly, pretty** INFORMAL, **quite, rather, slightly, somewhat** *The weather stayed fairly unpleasant, so we were grateful to be in sheltered waters.*

● ADJ+n situation **conditions, situation** *Conditions were very unpleasant during this campaign.*
▶ experience **experience, incident, memory** *I do often get recognized but so far I've never had an unpleasant experience.*
▶ surprise **shock, surprise** *It is important to fix the price at the beginning in order to avoid unpleasant surprises.*
▶ feeling **feeling, sensation, side-effect, symptom** *Diarrhoea is an unpleasant symptom and can be very debilitating.*
▶ smell or taste **odour, smell, taste** *The slime which*

covers the skin has a strong but not unpleasant smell.

unpopular ADJ
disliked by many people

- adv+ADJ **very deeply, extremely, highly, hugely, massively, very** *A six-month pay freeze was not only hugely unpopular but failed to do the trick.*
- with many people **universally** *His wife, Ingrid, was a disagreeable and universally unpopular woman.*
- possibly **potentially** *Regulating the movement of people is highly political and potentially unpopular.*
- more and more **increasingly** *The war grew increasingly unpopular in the US, and troops began to withdraw in 1970.*
- relating to politics **politically** *This solution is likely to prove politically unpopular in the UK.*

- ADJ+n decision **choice, decision** *Pensions are another area where any Government is likely to face tough and unpopular decisions.*
- action **measure, move, policy, proposal, scheme** *The first Budget of a new parliamentary term is often an occasion to announce unpopular measures.*
- opinion **cause, opinion, view** *Rainsborough's radical views were unpopular in the Navy.*

- v+ADJ **be, become, prove, remain** *Though necessary, the measure is likely to prove unpopular with the electorate.*

unprecedented ADJ
never having happened or existed before

- adv+ADJ almost **almost, virtually** *This season will see a level of competition almost unprecedented in recent years.*
- completely **absolutely, completely, quite, totally, truly** *The next century was to see changes whose scale and pace was to be quite unprecedented.*
- in history **historically** *In absolute terms, armies reached historically unprecedented sizes in the twentieth century.*
- until now **hitherto, previously** *Businesses now cooperate with each other in a way that was previously unprecedented.*
- not **hardly** *While this is an unusual example, such a collapse of law-and-order is hardly unprecedented.*
- perhaps **perhaps, probably** *The appeal judges described the challenge to the Act as 'unusual, and in modern times probably unprecedented'.*

- ADJ+n level or amount **amount, degree, demand, level, number, rate, scale, speed** *We are currently experiencing unprecedented levels of business.*
- increase **growth, increase, rise** *Recent years have seen an unprecedented increase in the numbers of undergraduate medical students in the UK.*
- action **action, move, step** *In an unprecedented move, the force decided to issue the images of 31 protesters they wanted to interview.*
- opportunity **opportunity** *For schools, this is an unprecedented opportunity to consider their future.*

unpredictable ADJ
involving changes you cannot prepare for

- adv+ADJ very **extremely, highly, very** *We operate in a highly unpredictable and quickly changing business environment.*

- completely **completely, entirely, quite, totally, utterly, wholly** *Depression is totally unpredictable and irrational.*
- rather **largely, rather, sometimes, somewhat** *Training in Africa is always somewhat unpredictable.*
- by nature **essentially, inherently** *Auctions are inherently unpredictable.*
- more and more **increasingly** *His behaviour became increasingly unpredictable and violent, resulting in divorce from his first wife.*

- ADJ+n result **change, consequences, effect, outcome, result** *The outcome is unpredictable at best.*
- way **manner, way** *It can be difficult for customers to budget when their income fluctuates in such an unpredictable manner.*
- behaviour **behaviour, nature, pattern** *The boy's unpredictable behaviour has put him and others in danger.*
- situation **conditions, situation** *Tomorrow's race is going to be exciting, especially as the unpredictable weather conditions are set to continue.*

unprovoked ADJ
an unprovoked attack is made for no reason

- adv+ADJ completely **completely, entirely, totally** *The massacre was entirely unprovoked.*
- apparently **apparently, seemingly** *This was a violent and apparently unprovoked attack and we need to find those responsible.*

- ADJ+n attack **act of aggression, aggression, assault, attack, violence, war** *While revenge and unprovoked aggression are condemned, self defence is justified.*
- killing **killing, murder** *It is for the prosecution to prove that the killing was unprovoked.*
- and/or violent **brutal, vicious, violent** *This appears to have been an unprovoked and vicious attack on vulnerable members of the community.*
- illegal or without reason **illegal, unjustified** *The assault was totally unprovoked and unjustified and it was racially motivated.*
- because of someone's race **racist** *Satpal suffered an unprovoked racist attack.*

unqualified ADJ
complete and total, without any doubts

- ADJ+n success **success** *The Bulletin was instituted as an experiment and has become an unqualified success.*
- approval **approval, praise** *Her work is cited in a footnote with unqualified approval.*
- agreement or support **acceptance, support** *I am giving this project my unqualified support and commitment.*
- apology **apology** *Unless you publish an immediate unqualified apology, I shall never buy another copy.*

unreasonable ADJ
not fair

- adv+ADJ very **completely, entirely, quite, totally, very, wholly** *The regulations are being applied in a totally unreasonable way.*
- clearly and without any doubt **clearly, manifestly**

obviously *An appeal will only be appropriate where the judge's ruling is manifestly unreasonable.*

● v+ADJ **appear, be, consider sth, seem** *It seems unreasonable to some of Brazil's landless that approximately 217.5 million acres are given to about 250,000 individuals.*

unreliable ADJ
impossible to trust completely

● adv+ADJ **very extremely, highly, increasingly, totally, very, wholly** *Reliable empirical data is extremely limited, and casual anecdotal evidence highly unreliable.*
▶ rather **rather, somewhat** *The figures are rather unreliable before that time.*
▶ possibly **potentially** *Maps are potentially unreliable.*
▶ in a way that most people know **notoriously** *Such information is notoriously unreliable.*
▶ in a way that cannot be avoided **inherently** *Any information obtained by means of torture is inherently unreliable.*

● ADJ+n information **data, evidence, figures, guide, information, results, statistics** *The Tribunal concluded that her evidence was unreliable and inconsistent.*
▶ method, system etc **indicator, method, service, supply, system, test** *Take some candles with you, as the electricity supply is unreliable.*
▶ person providing information **narrator, source, witness** *Arouca claimed that Kumar is an unreliable witness who has lied to the court.*

● v+ADJ **be, consider sth, prove, seem** *Data are presented in tables and graphs throughout this report, except in cases where it is considered unreliable.*

unrest N
angry or violent protests

● adj+N involving many people **considerable, great, massive, serious, widespread** *In many parts of the country, there was widespread unrest as rival armies fought for supremacy.*
▶ becoming more serious **growing, increasing** *Despite growing unrest, the presidential elections were relatively peaceful and fair.*
▶ violent **violent** *Violent unrest necessitated the evacuation of embasssy employees.*
▶ types of unrest **civil, general, industrial, internal, political, popular, public, racial, religious, social, urban** *Social unrest brought chaos to the country.*
▶ v+N cause unrest **cause, create, foment, fuel, lead to, provoke, spark** *The news of Eluay's death sparked unrest in his home town.*
▶ stop unrest **deal with, quell** *The government agreed to provide 700–800 soldiers to quell the unrest.*

n+of+N **cause, outbreak, period, state, wave** *The rail industry is already suffering the worst wave of industrial unrest since the 1980s.*

and/or **conflict, instability, riot, tension, violence, war** *By 1995, it was estimated that 1,500 people had been killed in the violence and unrest.*

unscathed ADJ
not harmed or damaged by a dangerous event

● adv+ADJ **largely, relatively, totally, virtually** *Coulthard emerged virtually unscathed from a plane crash in France.*
● v+ADJ **come through, emerge, escape, leave, remain, survive, walk away** *The one time capital of Japan emerged largely unscathed from the Pacific War.*

unstable ADJ
changing often and having problems

● adv+ADJ **very extremely, highly, very** *A new and very unstable situation has opened up in Gaza and the West Bank.*
▶ rather **quite, rather, relatively, somewhat** *The situation in Taiwan was rather unstable at the time.*
▶ possibly **potentially** *The report suggests that current productivity is very dependent upon a few successful individuals, and is potentially unstable.*
▶ becoming more unstable **increasingly** *The Roman Republic became increasingly unstable.*
▶ in a way that is dangerous **dangerously** *The position in this country remains dangerously unstable.*
▶ in a way that is well known **notoriously** *It is hard to attract investment because the region is notoriously unstable.*
▶ in a basic way **fundamentally, inherently, intrinsically, structurally** *Some economists believe that price-fixing cartels are inherently unstable.*
▶ in a particular way **economically, emotionally, financially, politically** *We want to reduce dependence on energy imports from politically unstable countries.*

● v+ADJ **appear, be, become, prove, remain** *Financial markets will become more unstable as international economic co-operation breaks down further.*
● and/or **dangerous, difficult, uncertain, unpredictable, unreliable, weak** *Economic growth is too weak and unstable to revive the labour market.*

unsuccessful ADJ
not achieving what you want

● adv+ADJ **very singularly, spectacularly, totally, very** *If the intention of these churchmen is to encourage better community relations, then they are being singularly unsuccessful.*
▶ rather **largely, rather, relatively** *This effort was largely unsuccessful.*
▶ at the end **ultimately** *The argument is ingenious, but ultimately unsuccessful.*

● v+ADJ **be, prove, remain** *Attempts to find an operator for the mine have proved unsuccessful.*
● ADJ+in **application, attempt, bid** *If you are unsuccessful in your application, you will be notified.*

unsuitable ADJ
not suitable for situation or purpose

● adv+ADJ **very completely, entirely, highly, quite, totally, very, wholly** *We need to resolve the problem* *of these juggernauts using narrow and highly unsuitable country lanes.*

▶ in most situations **generally, often** *Ports and harbours which had been built in a pre-railway age were often unsuitable for rail access.*

▶ clearly **clearly, obviously** *Such an open channel is obviously unsuitable for secure business communications.*

● v+ADJ be or seem unsuitable **be, prove, seem** *As motorised transport developed, the town's narrow streets proved unsuitable for trucks and buses to negotiate.*

▶ consider something unsuitable **consider, deem, judge** *Some images in this section may be deemed unsuitable for viewing by young children.*

unsure ADJ
not certain about something

● adv+ADJ rather **a bit, a little, quite, rather, slightly** *There was a silence and I was a little unsure what to say.*

▶ very **completely, very** *Many people are still very unsure of their rights.*

▶ at first **initially** *Because of my relatively low grades, I was initially unsure about my ability to study for a physics degree.*

● v+ADJ **appear, be, feel, remain, seem** *Mothers may also feel unsure about how long they should breastfeed.*

untouched ADJ
not harmed or spoiled

● adv+ADJ **almost, completely, largely, relatively, virtually** *Antarctica is one of the few areas of the world that has been left relatively untouched.*

● ADJ+n **area, beach, beauty, forest, landscape, rainforest, wilderness** *The hotel rooms have views over the garden, to the untouched beauty of the Lakeland hills.* ● *Alberta still has huge expanses of untouched wilderness and open plains.*

● v+ADJ **be left, lie, remain, seem, survive** *The tiny narrow Moorish back streets have remained untouched by modern tourism.* ● *Stonehenge and its landscape survived relatively untouched for thousands of years.*

unusual ADJ
not normal, common, or ordinary

● adv+ADJ very **extremely, highly, really, truly, very** *The college is also highly unusual in having a fully equipped purpose-built theatre.*

▶ rather **fairly, a little, pretty** INFORMAL, **quite, rather, relatively, slightly, somewhat** *If you visit this city from the 5th to the 16th July, you will be in for a rather unusual treat.*

▶ very and more than others **especially, particularly** *The sword dated back to the Napoleonic era and was particularly unusual because of its size.*

▶ certainly/possibly **certainly, perhaps** *The rules are not complex, but the concepts are certainly unusual.*

● v+ADJ seem unusual **appear, look, seem, strike sb as** *The conversation might have seemed unusual to an outsider.*

▶ think that something is unusual **consider sth,**

find sth *We were quite quiet on the journey, which I found unusual.*

● and/or **attractive, beautiful, complex, different, exciting, exotic, innovative, interesting, new, rare, special, strange, unexpected, unique** *If you have an interesting or unusual hobby, let us know.*

● V+infinitive **come across, encounter, find, have, hear, see** *It is unusual to find such a regular landscape so close to the coast.*

unveil V
announce something that was previously secret

● adv+V officially **formally, officially** *The Lancashire Carers Charter was officially unveiled this week.*

▶ recently **just, recently, today** *The firm has just unveiled its new management structure.*

▶ after a long time **finally** *The Department of Health finally unveiled its plans for dealing with smoking in public places.*

● V+n a plan **campaign, initiative, package, plan, policy, programme, project, proposal, scheme, strategy, system, vision** *The company has unveiled an ambitious expansion plan.*

▶ information **detail, mystery, result, secret** *BT has unveiled details of a new product that could revolutionize broadband.*

unwarranted ADJ
not fair or necessary

● ADJ+n **assumption, attack, criticism, damage, disclosure, infringement, interference, intrusion, restriction** *Tenants must be free from unwarranted intrusion by anyone, including the landlord.*

unwell ADJ
ill

● adv+ADJ very **acutely, extremely, seriously, very** *I woke up feeling very unwell.*

▶ rather **a little, quite, slightly** *Children are often sick and can feel quite unwell.*

▶ in your mind/body **mentally, physically** *Older people may feel depressed because they are isolated, on a low income or physically unwell.*

▶ in all parts of your body **generally** *The infection may make you feel generally unwell and give you a fever.*

● v+ADJ **become, feel, look** *He became unwell with diarrhoea and vomiting.*

unwilling ADJ
not wanting to do something

● adv+ADJ **clearly, generally, increasingly, simply, understandably, very** *People are simply unwilling to accept orders from above.*

● v+ADJ **appear, be, become, prove, remain, seem** *The government appears unwilling to accept that the problem is as least partly of their own making.*

● and/or **incapable, unable** *He seemed unable or unwilling to make a real commitment to any relationship.*

upbringing N

the way parents look after and teach children

- adj+N good **good, proper, stable** *Love, affection and a good stable upbringing are seen as the most important factors in raising children.*
- ▶ difficult, or without much money **difficult, humble, poor, tough** *We had a very difficult upbringing, and my brother suffered the most.*
- ▶ easy, or with plenty of money **comfortable, privileged** *He was born into an aristocratic family and had a highly privileged upbringing.*
- ▶ not unusual in any way **conventional, normal, traditional** *She had a conventional middle-class upbringing.*
- ▶ protected from unpleasant events and experiences **sheltered** *Having had a sheltered upbringing, I saw little of the effects of gambling in my early years.*
- ▶ having strict rules of behaviour **strict** *Our upbringing was very strict indeed, and often I rebelled against this.*
- ▶ involving religion **religious** *Some people become atheists in reaction to a strict religious upbringing.*

upgrade N

equipment or software making a computer more powerful

- adj+N **automatic, easy, free, minor, simple** *Please download the free upgrade by clicking on the link below.* • *It is only a minor upgrade, the system should be back up in a few hours.* • *A simple upgrade to your line is required.*
- v+N get an upgrade **do, download, get, install, perform** *By installing the latest OS upgrades, the speed and stability of your system can be significantly improved.*
- need an upgrade **need, require** *New technical opportunities and platforms will require upgrades to existing systems.*

upheaval N

a sudden or violent change affecting people's lives

- adj+N big or violent **big, considerable, enormous, great, huge, major, massive, tremendous, violent** *This was a time of great upheaval.*
- types of upheaval **domestic, economic, emotional, political, religious, revolutionary, social** *Since the start of the project, Fiji has experienced serious political and social upheaval.*
- v+N cause upheaval **cause, create, lead to, mean** *The entry of Chandni into the lives of Rishi and Mohan causes a huge upheaval in their relationship.*
- experience or deal with upheaval **cope with, experience, face, go through, survive, undergo** *The country has experienced very few political upheavals since the end of World War II, creating a stable environment for business and investment.*
- n+of+N **period, time** *The companies have both been undergoing periods of major upheaval.*
- and/or **change, disruption, turmoil, uncertainty, war** *The industry must prepare itself for a period of upheaval and change.*

uphold V

support an idea, decision etc

- V+n a decision, especially a legal one **appeal, authority, ban, conviction, decision, finding, order, policy, ruling** *This Committee upheld the decision of the LSC.*
- ▶ a right **freedom, interest, right** *Laws have been revised to uphold press freedom.*
- ▶ a complaint **complaint, objection** *The Federal Radio Commission (FRC) upheld the objection.*
- ▶ a belief **belief, claim, ideal, position, principle, values, view** *They promoted themselves as a party upholding Christian values.*
- ▶ a standard **dignity, integrity, justice, reputation, standard, truth** *It upholds standards and maintains our commitment to the very best of public service broadcasting.*
- ▶ a rule or law **law, rule** *The University is committed to upholding the law relating to racial equality.*
- ▶ a tradition **tradition** *He admired artists who upheld the classical traditions of painting.*

uplifting ADJ

making you feel happier or more hopeful

- adv+V very **really, truly, very** *The survivors' stories are very uplifting and helped me a great deal.*
- ▶ in a particular way **morally, spiritually** *This series of pictures depicts the artist's internal journey, the culmination of which is a beautiful, spiritually uplifting painting entitled 'Back Home'*
- V+n music **chorus, melody, music, piece, song, sound, track, tune** *Filled with the energy of joy, these uplifting songs are accompanied by African harps and drums.*
- ▶ story **message, story, tale** *Here, she tells her heartbreaking, but ultimately uplifting, story.*
- ▶ experience **experience** *It is always a pleasing and uplifting experience to see students perform well.*
- ▶ feeling or effect **effect, feeling** *Neroli oil is believed to have a soothing, peaceful and uplifting effect.*

uprising N

an attempt by a group to defeat a government or ruler

- adj+N involving many people **general, major, mass, national, popular** *There are fears that there will be a mass uprising if the election is rigged.* • *He moved to Jakarta after the popular uprising that overthrew President Suharto.*
- ▶ involving violence or weapons **armed, bloody, violent** *The perceived lack of action on the part of the government led to a series of armed uprisings.*
- ▶ starting suddenly, without being planned **spontaneous** *We have witnessed a spontaneous uprising of disaffected youth.*
- ▶ unsuccessful **abortive, failed, unsuccessful** *In July 1917, after an abortive uprising in Petrograd, Lenin was forced to flee to Finland.*
- ▶ types of uprising **military, nationalist, political, revolutionary** *Seven years later, there was a nationalist uprising, the Orabi Rebellion of September 1881, with the slogan of 'Egypt for the Egyptians'.*
- v+N lead an uprising **lead, organize** *Thomas Wyatt led an uprising **against** Queen Mary.*

▶ cause an uprising **cause, lead to, provoke, spark, trigger** *Insensitive treatment of Tibet's ancient culture provoked a further uprising in 1959.*
▶ start an uprising **launch, stage, start** *They staged many uprisings and so managed to draw Rome's attention to this city.*
▶ stop an uprising **crush, defeat, quell, suppress** *Despite the enormous heroism of the workers, the uprising was crushed.*

uproar N
angry public criticism of something

● adj+N **great, huge, public** *When Hicks announced that the campaign was due to close, there was a huge uproar.* ● *If the airlines tried to do something similar with air crew, there would be public uproar.*
● v+N **cause, create, end in, provoke, spark** *This ruling has created uproar.*

upset ADJ
very sad, worried, or angry about something

● adv+ADJ very **deeply, extremely, incredibly, really, terribly, very** *She was really offended and very upset.*
▶ rather **pretty INFORMAL, quite, rather** *I could see that he was rather upset at having his supposed expertise called into doubt.*
▶ in a way that is easy to see **clearly, obviously, visibly** *He was obviously upset, but that's no excuse for petulantly walking off stage.*
▶ in a way that is easy to understand. **understandably** *The woman was understandably upset at this very hurtful comment.*
▶ often **easily** *I get upset very easily.*

● v+ADJ become upset **become, get** *There's no point in getting upset about things you cannot change.*
▶ feel upset **feel** *Anybody who has reported a person missing will be feeling upset, anxious and worried about that person's welfare.*
▶ seem upset **look, seem, sound** 'No, no, no,' she claimed, looking quite upset at my reaction.*

● and/or **angry, annoyed, confused, hurt, shocked, worried** *If you are worried or upset about something, you can ask to speak to your head of department.*
● V+infinitive **find, hear, learn, see** *I was upset to see how rundown in appearance the whole area had become.*

upset N
a defeat of an opponent considered to be better

● adj+N **big, major, notable** *They had the best team, and anything other than a win would have been a major upset.*
● v+N **cause, create, produce** *Chuah, the fifth seed, produced the upset of the day as she defeated the third seed, Hansen.*

upsurge N
a sudden increase in something

● adj+N big or sudden **big, dramatic, great, huge, major, massive, sudden, tremendous** *There has been a huge upsurge in street crime.* ● *Parliament was concerned about the sudden upsurge in demands for reform.*

▶ happening now or recently **current, new, recent** *The current upsurge in strikes has exposed the weaknesses of some of the current trade union leaders.*
● v+N **experience, see, witness** *The 1830s saw a tremendous upsurge in interest in the occult.*
● N+in interest or popularity **activity, demand, interest, popularity** *There has been an upsurge in interest in a more intensive study of the Baha'i Faith.*
▶ violence or crime **attacks, crime, violence** *A dramatic upsurge in violence in the country prompted fears of a return to full-scale civil war.*

up-to-date ADJ
including the most recent news and information

● adv+ADJ completely **bang INFORMAL, completely, fully, right, very** *While there is a huge database of survey details, it is not fully up-to-date.*
▶ in most ways **reasonably** *Most people need to review their will at least every five years, to check that it is still reasonably up-to-date.*
● v+ADJ stay up-to-date **remain, stay** *We can work with you to ensure that your website remains up-to-date.*
▶ make something up-to-date **bring sth, keep sth** *This latest edition of the book has been brought right up-to-date to reflect the changing face of business.*

upturn N
an increase in business or economic activity

● adj+N big **dramatic, major, marked, sharp, significant** *The market has shown a significant upturn this year, with a steady increase in prices over that period.*
▶ small **modest, slight** *In the US, there are some early signs of a modest upturn in levels of corporate finance activity.*
▶ recent **recent** *Property sellers are coming to the market – perhaps encouraged by the recent upturn in prices.*
▶ economic **economic** *Russia enjoyed an economic upturn last year.*
● v+N **experience, result in, see, show, take** *The run-up to the Christmas period saw an upturn in consumer spending.* ● *The company's fortunes were about to take an upturn.*
● N+in **business, demand, economy, fortunes, market, number, sales** *Abraham's appointment as manager resulted in an upturn in the club's fortunes.*

urban ADJ
relating to towns and cities

● adv+ADJ **largely, mainly, mostly, particularly, predominantly, very** *In industrialized countries, like the UK, the population is largely urban.*
● ADJ+n area **area, environment, landscape, setting, space, sprawl** *The Adelphi, which was demolished in the 1930s, was a highly symbolic site in London's urban landscape.*
▶ people **community, dweller, population** *This is an urban community with limited opportunity to access green space.* ● *I was an urban dweller, a resident of London, who knew nothing about farming.*

▸ improvement **development, redevelopment, regeneration, renaissance, renewal** *The Government considers that the urban renaissance will benefit everyone, making towns and cities vibrant and successful.*

▸ design or planning **design, planning** *Lack of urban planning allows unsafe development on floodplains, unstable slopes or ravines.*

urge N
a strong feeling of wanting to do something

● adj+N strong or sudden **deep, desperate, great, irresistible, overwhelming, powerful, strong, sudden, uncontrollable** *He had a strong urge to travel.* ● *I had a sudden urge to see her, and tell her that I did love her, really.*

▸ natural **natural** *Children have a natural urge to explore and learn about the environment.*

▸ types of urge **competitive, creative, sexual** *I have a real creative urge to do something, and to create my own greeting cards is one of the ideas I've had.*

● v+N have an urge **experience, feel, get, have** *Our store is online 24 hours a day, for whenever you feel the urge to shop.*

▸ try to stop an urge **control, fight, overcome, resist, stifle, suppress** *I'm not a smoker myself, but my husband is currently fighting the urge to light up again.*

▸ satisfy an urge **satisfy** *If you do crave chocolate, satisfy the urge with a little dark, bitter chocolate.*

urgency N
the need to deal with something quickly

● adj+N great **extreme, great, particular, real, utmost** *This is a matter of the utmost urgency.*

▸ extra **added, increased, new, special** *It is a real and growing problem, and has given new urgency to the debate about national missile defenses.*

▸ v+N emphasize urgency **emphasize, highlight, stress, underline** *He stressed the urgency of revising the legislation, since elections for provincial assemblies are due next year.*

▸ understand urgency **recognize, see, understand** *The British government has recognized the urgency of the HIV/AIDS epidemic and has already increased overseas aid.*

▸ have or make something have urgency **give sth, have, inject, lend, take on** *Understanding the climate system is a major research challenge given urgency by global warming.* ● *Other repairs may have some urgency, such as a broken water pipes.*

N+of **case, issue, matter, need, problem, situation, task, threat** *She became concerned that the man did not understand the urgency of the situation.*

n+of+N **degree, matter, sense** *That is the task that the government needs to return to with a degree of urgency.* ● *They told her that they were dealing with her case as a matter of urgency.*

urgent ADJ
which needs to be dealt with immediately

adv+ADJ **desperately, extremely, increasingly, particularly, really, very** *It is increasingly urgent that food and other emergency supplies reach people in need in remote areas, as winter sets in.*

● v+ADJ **be, become, consider sth, remain, seem, sound** *With each passing hour, the need becomes more urgent.*

useless ADJ
not effective in any way

● adv+ADJ completely **absolutely, completely, entirely, quite, really, seemingly, totally, utterly** *These theories were absolutely useless when it came to explaining why.*

▸ almost **almost, effectively, essentially, largely, mostly, nearly, practically, virtually** *The cheap and once very effective anti-malarial drug chloroquine is now almost useless in large parts of the world due to the development of resistance.* ● *So here we have a well publicized list of companies running what is now effectively useless security software.*

▸ rather **fairly, pretty INFORMAL, rather** *A program may be magnificent in all ways, but if it doesn't help the user learn what they need to know, it is rather useless.*

● v+ADJ be or become useless **be, become, prove** *The access software soon becomes useless if the latest applications are not included.*

▸ seem useless **seem** *Everything he had learnt before seemed useless when faced with such real life issues.*

▸ make something useless **render sth** *In some cities, cycle lanes have been rendered completely useless by parked cars.*

utilize V
use something

● adv+V **effectively, efficiently, fully, properly, successfully** *Teachers must be able to efficiently utilize school resources relative to the needs of students with disabilities.*

● V+n information, knowledge, or skills **data, experience, expertise, information, knowledge, material, resource, service, skill, technology** *We must be smart and create new opportunities to utilize this knowledge.*

▸ a method **approach, method, methodology, process, strategy, system, technique, tool** *They utilized new methods of campaigning.*

▸ energy **energy, power** *Photovoltaics modules utilize solar power to generate useable amounts of electricity.*

▸ space or place **area, building, land, site, space** *They want to utilize the space by creating an oasis and a refuge from the daily stresses of life.*

U-turn N
a sudden and complete change of policy

● adj+N complete or big **complete, dramatic, major** *The scheme looks set to go ahead after a dramatic U-turn by the government.*

▸ embarrassing **embarrassing, humiliating** *The humiliating U-turn follows yesterday's legal challenge by Friends of the Earth.*

● v+N do a U-turn **do, make, perform** *A determined campaign by locals forced the council to do a U-turn on the pool's closure.*

▸ make someone do a U-turn **force sb into** *The government may be forced into an embarrassing U-turn following a barrage of criticism.*

Vv

vacancy N
a job available for someone to do

- adj+N available now **available, current, immediate, the latest, new** *For more of our current vacancies, please go to the vacancies page.*
- ▸ suitable **appropriate, suitable** *Once you've registered, you'll be able search for suitable vacancies.*
- ▸ permanent/temporary **casual, permanent, temporary** *During your training, you will be in a position to apply for suitable permanent vacancies within the council.* • *Our client has a 3-month temporary vacancy for an experienced Quality Engineer to work in the Portsmouth area.*
- ▸ part-time/full-time **full-time, part-time** *The college currently has a part-time vacancy for an experienced Early Years lecturer.*
- ▸ that nobody is doing **unfilled** *One in five vacancies is unfilled because of skill shortages.*
- ▸ in the company that you are working for **internal** *Internal vacancies are advertised on our intranet.*

- n+N **graduate, job, management, staff** *The competition for graduate vacancies is likely to be tough, so you'll need to stand out from the crowd.* • *Get details of job vacancies by email or text.*
- v+N have a vacancy **have** *We currently have a vacancy for a Customer Service Officer.*
- ▸ create a vacancy **create, leave** *His transfer to another office has created a vacancy within the department.*
- ▸ advertise a vacancy **advertise, list, post, publicize** *We advertise most vacancies externally, mainly using newspapers and professional magazines.*
- ▸ find a vacancy **find** *Recruitment agencies can save you valuable time in finding a suitable vacancy.*
- ▸ fill a vacancy **fill** *Research indicates that the average cost of filling a vacancy is £4,800.*

- N+v **arise, come up, exist, occur** *A vacancy has arisen for a Clerical Assistant within our Clerical Services Department.*

vacuum N
a feeling or the fact that something is missing

- adj+N **moral, political, spiritual** *He does not think that scientific enquiry should take place in a moral vacuum.*
- n+N **policy, power, security** *The withdrawal of troops could create a security vacuum.*
- v+N create a vacuum **create, leave** *Her departure left a power vacuum at the campaign's headquarters.*
- ▸ fill a vacuum **fill** *There is an urgent need to fill the political vacuum which is fast developing.*
- ▸ be in a vacuum **exist in, operate in** *The writer does not exist in a vacuum.*

vague ADJ
not clear or fully formed

- adv+ADJ rather **fairly, pretty** INFORMAL, **quite,**

rather, somewhat *My memories of 30 years ago are rather vague.*
- ▸ slightly **a bit** INFORMAL, **a little** *Some of these descriptions are a little vague.*
- ▸ very **extremely, very** *My own recollections are extremely vague.*
- ▸ deliberately **deliberately** *This review is deliberately vague because I don't want to give anything away.*

- ADJ+n idea or thought **concept, idea, impression, notion** *I have only a vague idea of what I want to do when I leave university.*
- ▸ feeling **feeling, sense, suspicion** *She had the vague feeling that something was wrong.*
- ▸ memory **memory, recollection** *I have a vague memory of the restaurant.*
- ▸ something said or written **answer, description, hint, promise, reference, statement, term, wording** *The government has given a rather vague promise that it will aim to increase funding per pupil.*

- v+ADJ **be, leave sth, remain, seem** *Details were left vague, including how people might be compensated.* • *Estimates of the cost remain vague.*

vain ADJ
unsuccessful or useless

- ADJ+n attempt **attempt, effort, endeavour** *A vain attempt was made to attract the attention of the train driver.*
- ▸ hope **hope** *I stayed until the end, in the vain hope that things would improve.*
- ▸ feelings of sadness **regrets** *We do not want to waste these precious moments with vain regrets or bitterness.*

valid ADJ
reasonable and generally accepted

- adv+ADJ **equally, perfectly, scientifically, statistically, still, universally, very** *This is a perfectly valid point of view.*
- ADJ+n reason **excuse, reason** *You must have a valid reason for not attending.*
- ▸ idea or opinion **argument, comment, opinion, point** *It is a valid point to raise.*
- ▸ statement that something is wrong **complaint, criticism, objection** *There were some valid criticisms of the website, which we'll take on board.*
- ▸ something you decide is true **assumption, conclusion, inference, interpretation** *If it ever was a valid assumption, which I doubt, it is certainly out of date.*
- ▸ comparison **comparison** *We do not believe that this comparison is valid.*

- v+ADJ be valid **be, remain, seem** *These criticisms remain valid.*
- ▸ think something is valid **accept sth as, consider sth, deem sth, regard sth as** *The appeal may be rejected if these reasons are not considered valid.*

validity N
the state of being reasonable and generally accepted

- adj+N using science or numbers **scientific, statistical** *It must be stressed that these figures have little statistical validity.*
- ▶ possibly not existing **questionable** *The presumption that a country is safe is of questionable validity.*
- ▶ in all cases **universal** *It is difficult to formulate simple principles of human behaviour that have a universal validity.*
- ▶ equal **equal** *These statements are not all of equal validity.*

- v+N question the validity of something **challenge, deny, doubt, question** *Many researchers now question the validity of these findings.*
- ▶ check or consider the validity of something **assess, check, examine, investigate, test, verify** *We will need to assess your complaint to check its validity.*
- ▶ prove or show the validity of something **confirm, demonstrate, determine, establish, prove** *There remains no medical test to clearly demonstrate the validity of the diagnosis.*
- ▶ accept the validity of something **accept, recognize** *She finally accepted the validity of his argument.*
- ▶ have validity **have** *These measures had no scientific validity.*
- ▶ give something validity **give sth** *Should we give all these points of view equal validity?*

- n+about+N **concerns, doubts, questions** *However, doubts about the validity of such tests remain.*
- N+of results or information **data, findings, results** *We are in no position to determine the validity of the findings.*
- statement or argument **argument, assumption, claim, statement** *I'm not sure of the validity of that argument.*
- theory or method **approach, method, model, theory** *The validity of this approach was tested using data from three previously published studies.*

valley N
a low area of land between mountains or hills

- adj+N with trees and plants growing **fertile, forested, green, lush, wooded** *You now follow a path through a wooded valley.*
- ▶ deep or wide **broad, deep, wide** *Massive glaciers carve their way through deep valleys.*
- ▶ steep **steep, steep-sided** *The route crossed a series of high moors and steep valleys.*
- ▶ not deep or wide **narrow, shallow, small** *The town nestles in a narrow dry valley.*
- ▶ peaceful or far from other places **peaceful, quiet, remote, secluded, sheltered, tranquil** *The hotel is situated in a secluded valley with mountains to the rear.*
- ▶ beautiful **beautiful, picturesque, scenic** *The Abbey lies in a picturesque valley by a stream.*

- n+N **mountain, river** *Perched on a small hill, the church has pleasant views over the river valley.*

valuable ADJ
very useful and important

- adv+ADJ very **especially, extremely, highly, immensely, particularly, very** *This is an extremely valuable blog for anyone interested in journalism.*
- ▶ more and more **increasingly** *The committee is an increasingly valuable source of information to universities.*
- ▶ equally **equally** *Fathers may have a different, but equally valuable, view to offer.*
- ▶ possibly in the future **potentially** *Some potentially valuable contributions may be lost.*

- ADJ+n something you learn **information, insight, lesson** *There are valuable lessons to be learned from this case.*
- ▶ something done or used **addition, asset, contribution, resource, service, source, tool, work** *I found it a very valuable resource, with some useful hints and tips.*
- ▶ help or support **advice, assistance, help, support** *Many people provided very valuable assistance during the planning stage.*
- ▶ skill or experience **experience, skill** *This allows students to gain valuable experience in a relevant sector of the computing industry.*
- ▶ opportunity **opportunity** *The tournament will provide a valuable opportunity for the team to compete against the top European nations.*
- ▶ being involved in something **part, role** *By raising much-needed funds, you can play a valuable part in the continuing care of our residents.*

- v+ADJ **be, become, consider sth, find sth, prove** *It was an illuminating experience which we all found valuable.* • *Video footage has proven highly valuable when such cases come to court.*

value N
1 the amount that something is worth

- adj+N high/low **high, low** *We recommend you obtain proof of posting, particularly for high-value items.*
- ▶ total **full, total** *Two stolen cars with a total value of £100,000 were recovered by police.*
- ▶ real **real, true** *Before that question can be answered, the true value of these goods must be established.*
- ▶ in money **monetary** *Gardening books are becoming more and more collectable – but more for the interest of the topic than for the monetary value of the books.*

- n+N when sold at a particular time **market** *The player's market value must be at least £30 million.*
- ▶ property or land **land, property** *Lenders will often only lend to 75 or 80 per cent of the property value.*

- v+N have a value **have** *The goods have a total value of around £32,500.*
- ▶ put a value on something **place, put, set** *It is impossible to put a monetary value on our greatest asset, the team spirit.*
- ▶ add value to something **add** *Here are some tips on adding value to your property.*
- ▶ increase value **enhance, increase, maximize** *We would increase the value of the basic state pension in line with earnings.*
- ▶ reduce value **reduce** *This may cause the wood to be discoloured and reduce its value.*

▶ when the value increases **increase in, rise in** *These shares have risen greatly in value.*
▶ when the value decreases **fall in, lose** *Your car is losing value every day.*
▶ when the value stays the same **hold** *Luxury cars are likely to hold their value.*

● N+v increase **go up, increase, rise** *The value of the company's shares has risen by 12 per cent in the last quarter.*
▶ decrease **decrease, fall, go down** *Property values have gone down recently.*

● n+in+N **change, decline, decrease, fall, increase, reduction, rise** *There was a decline in the value of the rouble, which had a marked effect on trade.*

2 how important or useful someone or something is

● adj+N great value **considerable, great, high, immense** *I am sure this publication will be of immense value to military historians and researchers.*
▶ additional value **added** *There is added value in coming together to learn alongside and from each other.*
▶ in itself **intrinsic** *Biodiversity is of intrinsic value as well as contributing to education, quality of life, and the local economy.*
▶ real **main, real, true** *Be persistent – anything of real value takes time.*
▶ not much **limited, low** *Although each piece of evidence on its own was of very limited value, together they built into a very powerful case.*
▶ types of value **educational, entertainment, nutritional** *We need to be sure that a school trip has a clear educational value.*

● v+N have a value **have** *Alcohol has no nutritional value.*
▶ put a value on something **place, put** *Although Hilda never married she placed great value on family life.*
▶ realize the value of something **appreciate, know, realize, recognize, see, understand** *Most early childhood professionals recognize the value of books to young children.*
▶ when somebody thinks something may not be valuable **question** *Head teachers question the value of these exams as qualifications.*
▶ show the value of something **demonstrate, prove, show** *This shows the value of forward planning and organization.*

● N+v **be, lie (in)** *The book's value lies in its comprehensive coverage of these two important topics.*

3 principles or beliefs [always plural]

● adj+N most important or basic **core, fundamental** *The European Union is built on a set of fundamental values.*
▶ shared **common, shared, universal** *We operate as eight distinct organizations governed by shared values.*
▶ types of value **aesthetic, cultural, ethical, moral, social** *It is important that the moral and ethical values which inform our work are promoted.*
▶ traditional **traditional** *There is a tension between traditional values and a modern society.*

● n+N **family** *The party claims to support family values.*

● v+N have values **have, hold** *She holds essentially liberal values.*
▶ have the same values **share** *Our employees share the same basic values.*
▶ show what values someone or something has **reflect** *All the merchandising is designed to reflect the values of the brand.*
▶ encourage others to have values **promote** *The values promoted in schools depend to a large extent on the social structures within which we all operate.*

value v
consider someone or something to be important

● adv+V very much **greatly, highly, particularly, really** *Your feedback is greatly valued.*
▶ equally **equally** *All students at the school are equally valued.*

● V+n someone's help or opinion **contribution, feedback, input, opinion, support** *We value your opinion and suggestions to help us improve.*
▶ skill or experience **experience, skill** *Within a global economy, employers increasingly value overseas experience.*
▶ opportunity **opportunity** *They valued the opportunity to spend time in discussion with other international students.*

vandalism N
deliberate damage or destruction to property

● adj+N done for no reason or without thinking **mindless, wanton** *Acts of mindless vandalism are common occurrences in all the major cities of the world.*
▶ not serious **minor, petty** *The only crime in recent years has been minor vandalism and burglary.*

● v+N reduce or try to prevent vandalism **combat, deter, prevent, reduce, tackle** *CCTV cameras have been installed to combat vandalism.*
▶ commit vandalism **cause, commit** *Two youths were charged with committing vandalism.*

● n+of+N **act, incident, level, problem, spate** *The head teacher is very concerned about the level of vandalism at the school. ● A spate of vandalism has been causing problems at local stations.*

● and/or **anti-social behaviour, crime, damage, graffiti, litter, theft** *Vandalism and graffiti continue to be a major problem.*

vanish v
disappear or stop existing

● adv+V suddenly or quickly **quickly, suddenly** *My guide suddenly vanished, and left me alone in the darkness.*
▶ completely or for all time **altogether, completely, forever** *This once familiar term has now vanished altogether.*

> You can also say that a person or thing *vanishes into thin air, vanishes without a trace*, or *vanishes from sight*: *Kate appears to have vanished into thin air.* ● *Her husband had vanished without a trace.* ● *The aircraft suddenly exploded in a shower of blue and green sparks, and then vanished from sight.*

▶ just **just, simply** *The man seems to have simply vanished off the face of the Earth.*

▶ in a mysterious way **mysteriously** *The baffling sickness vanished as mysteriously as it appeared.*
▶ almost **all but, almost** *The iron industry too has all but vanished.*

variation N
the existence of differences in amount etc

● adj+N much **considerable, great, huge, large, marked, significant, substantial, wide** *The great rivers of the Amazon Basin show considerable variation in their rates of flow.*
▶ slight **minor, slight, subtle** *Note that these are general instructions – there will be slight variations among different manufacturers.*
▶ from place to place **geographical, local, regional** *There is a full analysis of the results below, including regional variations.*
▶ according to the season **seasonal** *There was significant seasonal variation in weekly death rates.*
▶ relating to a particular subject or area **climatic, cultural, genetic** *The distribution of species may change in response to climatic variation.*
▶ having no limit **endless** *Scotland's great hillwalking strength lies in the endless variation in landscape, light, and weather.*
▶ without any pattern **random** *What is the impact of random variation on these results?*
▶ natural **natural** *This timber grows with a natural variation in grain and texture.*
▶ individual **individual** *While there was a general pattern of development, there was wide individual variation.*

● v+N show variation **exhibit, reflect, reveal, show** *Local trends show considerable variation from year to year.*
▶ explain variation **account for, explain** *This may help explain variations in operating costs.*
▶ find or notice variation **detect, find, identify, observe** *The study found a wide variation in prices charged.*
▶ study variation **investigate, study** *Pupils can study the variations in brightness of these objects as they 'tumble' through space.*
▶ cause variation **cause, create, introduce, lead to, produce** *Physical and physiological differences between the sexes may cause a variation in toxic response.*

● N+in **colour, level, pattern, performance, price, quality, rate, response, size, standard, temperature** *There is too much variation in the quality of the training.*

varied ADJ
including a wide range of things or people

adv+ADJ **extremely, highly, infinitely, richly, very, widely, wonderfully** *The region has an extremely varied landscape.*

and/or **diverse, extensive, many, rich, wide** *The article reflects the many and varied business opportunities available in this field. ● Each year we offer a rich and varied programme of musical events.*

variety N
collection of different things, or the fact that there are different things

● adj+N great **amazing, bewildering, broad, endless, enormous, good, great, huge, infinite, large, rich, vast, wide, wonderful** *University students come from a wide variety of backgrounds.*
▶ emphasizing the degree of variety **sheer, whole** *The food is famous for the sheer variety of spices, vegetables, and fruit.*

● v+N provide variety **offer, provide** *The resort offers a wide variety of hotels, restaurants, bars, shops, and boutiques.*
▶ add variety **add** *Use these methods to add variety to your workouts.*
▶ include a variety of things **contain, cover, include** *Our short courses cover a variety of IT skills.*

vary V
be different in different situations

● adv+V very much **considerably, dramatically, enormously, greatly, hugely, markedly, significantly, substantially, tremendously, widely, wildly** *Women go into business for all sorts of reasons, and the goals for their business can vary enormously.*
▶ slightly **a little, slightly, somewhat** *Dyes vary slightly from batch to batch.*
▶ in a suitable way **accordingly** *Students learn in a variety of ways and teaching methods must vary accordingly.*
▶ in the opposite way **inversely** *Dolphin presence throughout the day varied inversely with boat traffic.*

● V+in **colour, degree, intensity, length, price, quality, shape, size, style** *Golf courses vary in size.*

vast ADJ
extremely large

● ADJ+n amount **amount, collection, number, quantity** *People can use their mobile phones to access the vast amount of information on the Internet.*
▶ range of things **array, range** *Ginger is used in a vast array of sweet and savoury dishes around the world.*
▶ amount of money **resources, sum** *Vast sums of public money are being wasted on this scheme.*
▶ area or distance **area, distance, expanse, space** *To the north is only the vast expanse of the sea.*
▶ most of something **bulk, majority** *The vast majority of victims of climate change are in developing countries.*
▶ experience or knowledge **experience, knowledge** *He has vast experience across many business sectors.*
▶ change or difference **difference, improvement** *This was a vast improvement on their last performance.*

veer V
suddenly move in a different direction

● adv+V by a large amount or in an uncontrolled way **sharply, wildly** *Suddenly, the car veered sharply to the left-hand side of the road.*
▶ away **away, off** *After a few hundred yards, the path veers away from the road.*
▶ right/left **left, right** *If you veer too far right, you encounter a stream.*

vegetation N
plants and trees

- adj+N growing close together in large amounts **dense, lush, thick** *The land in the east was very fertile, with lush vegetation.*
- ▶ green **green** *The island has a warm tropical climate with a rich landscape covered in lush green vegetation.*
- ▶ natural **natural, semi-natural** *Great care has been taken to preserve the natural vegetation in the area.*
- ▶ growing in a particular type of place **aquatic, tropical** *Tropical vegetation covers the rugged landforms.*
- ▶ growing in small amounts **sparse** *It is a desert region with sparse vegetation.*
- ▶ decaying **decaying, rotting** *The larvae feed largely on decaying vegetation.*

veil N
a situation in which there is a lack of knowledge or information [usually singular]

- v+N when someone discovers or reveals the truth **lift, pierce, remove** *I feel it's important to remove the veil of ignorance and fear that still surrounds this illness.*
- ▶ when someone avoids talking about something **draw, throw** *I think maybe we had better draw a veil over that.*
- N+of **ignorance, mystery, secrecy** *The new system has been developed **under** a veil of secrecy.*

veiled ADJ
a veiled threat, or attack etc which is not direct but is understood

- adv+**ADJ** **thinly** *The play is a thinly veiled attack on the Prime Minister.*
- ADJ+n **attack, attempt, criticism, reference, threat** *Many people protested on the streets, despite veiled threats of repercussions.*

vendetta N
a situation in which someone keeps trying to harm someone else

- adj+N **personal** *This is beginning to feel like a personal vendetta.*
- v+N **conduct, have, pursue, wage** *She believes the paper has been pursuing a vendetta **against** her.*

veneer N
a pleasant or acceptable appearance, or polite way of behaving that is not sincere [always singular]

- adj+N **superficial, thin** *They had concealed some of the facts, and this managed to give their actions a thin veneer of legality.*
- N+of **civilization, democracy, legality, legitimacy, normality, respectability** *They sought to legitimize their wealth with the veneer of respectability.*

vengeance N
harming or killing someone who harmed you

- v+N take vengeance on someone **exact, take, wreak** *She escapes and wreaks terrible vengeance **on** the perpetrators of this crime.*
- ▶ promise or want to take vengeance **seek, swear, vow, want** *He seeks vengeance **against** the family who killed his father.*

vent V
express your feelings of anger very strongly

- V+n **anger, emotions, feelings, frustration, fury, rage, spleen, wrath** *This is an online forum where people can go to get support and vent their anger.*

ventilation N
the movement of fresh air around a building

- adj+N good enough **adequate, good, proper, sufficient** *Make sure the bathroom has adequate ventilation.*
- ▶ not good enough **inadequate, poor** *Breathing these fumes in can be harmful, especially in small confined spaces with poor ventilation.*
- ▶ using fresh air **natural** *Each building will use natural ventilation on the upper floors.*
- v+N provide or allow ventilation **allow, ensure, give, provide** *These relatively cheap structures allow good ventilation whilst offering protection against wet weather.*
- ▶ improve ventilation **improve, increase** *Some of these damp problems can be solved by improving the ventilation of your property.*

venture N
a new business or activity

- adj+N involving people or groups working together **collaborative, cooperative, joint** *This new engine was the first result of Volvo's joint venture with Renault and Peugeot for the development of car engines.*
- ▶ in business **business, commercial, entrepreneurial, money-making** *Most banks will lend money for a business venture if they believe it will be profitable.*
- ▶ exciting **exciting** *As part of the team, you will be involved in this exciting new venture from the outset.*
- ▶ successful/unsuccessful **failed, profitable, successful, unsuccessful** *The venture was highly successful, but had its critics.*
- ▶ worth doing **worthwhile** *I hope you will support this very worthwhile venture.*
- ▶ new **latest, new** *We are delighted to be able to support this latest venture.*
- ▶ involving new ideas **innovative** *This is a very exciting and innovative venture that will bring together staff with shared interests in both universities.*
- ▶ not using public money **private** *The railway line has been reopened as a private venture.*
- v+N start a venture **embark on, establish, launch, start, undertake** *We want to give people the skills and confidence to consider starting their own venture*
- ▶ give money to a venture **finance, fund, invest in, support** *At some time in the future, we will obviously require money, but at present I am funding this venture myself.*
- ▶ join in a venture with someone else **enter into, form** *Toshiba and Schneider Electric are forming a joint venture that they say will make them global leaders in this market.*

venue N
the place where an activity or event happens

- adj+N suitable **excellent, great, ideal, perfect, suitable** *The inn is an ideal venue for private parties.*
- ▶ important or respected **major, premier, prestigious, top** *Our dancers have performed at prestigious venues across the UK.*
- ▶ popular **favourite, popular** *The Octagon Theatre is a popular live entertainment venue.*
- ▶ large **big, large** *Those who need a bigger venue can use the lecture hall, which seats 174 people.*
- ▶ small **intimate, small** *Personally, I prefer music in smaller, more intimate venues.*
- ▶ used instead **alternative** *If the Council building is not open when an organization wishes to hold a meeting, the library is suggested as an alternative venue.*
- ▶ very unusual **unique** *The old court room is a unique venue for book fairs, parties, wedding receptions, and meetings.*
- ▶ local **local** *We have performed at various local venues.*
- n+N **arts, concert, conference, entertainment, music, sporting, wedding** *The city also features an international sporting venue, the Millennium Stadium.*
- v+N provide or be a venue **offer, provide** *The hall also provides a venue for many corporate conferences, dinners, and weddings.*
- ▶ find or choose a venue **choose, find** *A brand new website has been launched to help event organisers find the perfect venue.*
- ▶ arrange to use a venue **arrange, book, hire** *You should start thinking about booking a venue for the Christmas party.*
- ▶ change a venue **change** *The organizers changed the venue to avoid traffic problems.*
- ▶ fill a venue with people **fill, pack** *There was sufficient interest to fill the conference venue to capacity.*
- ▶ play music at a venue **play** *The band has been playing venues all over the country.*

verbal ADJ
using words, or relating to words; using speech rather than writing

- ADJ+n skill or ability **ability, dexterity, fluency, skill** *You will need to have excellent writing and verbal skills.*
- criticizing or being offensive to someone **abuse, attack** *The survey showed that 16 per cent of respondents had experienced verbal abuse on public transport.*
- telling something to someone else **agreement, communication, description, explanation, feedback, instruction, presentation, warning** *Verbal feedback from his students confirms that they find the recordings useful.*

verdict N
an official judgment made in a court of law, or by a person in authority

- adj+N guilty/not guilty **guilty, not guilty** *She directed the jury to return a not guilty verdict.*

- ▶ with everyone/most people agreeing **majority, unanimous** *The jury took just three hours to return a unanimous verdict.*
- ▶ saying that the cause of a death is unknown **open** *The inquest returned an open verdict.*
- n+N **court, inquest, jury** *He was convicted of possession of drugs on a majority jury verdict.*
- v+N give a verdict **bring in, deliver, give, pass, pronounce, record, return** *The jury returned a verdict of not guilty.*
- ▶ agree or decide what the verdict is **reach** *The jury has now been discharged after failing to reach a verdict.*
- ▶ accept a verdict **accept** *His family and friends found it hard to accept a verdict of suicide.*
- ▶ think about a verdict **consider** *The jury then retired to consider its verdict.*
- ▶ say that a verdict is wrong and change it **overturn** *This verdict was later overturned on appeal.*

2 an opinion that you have, or a decision that you take

- adj+N saying something is good/not good **damning, favourable** *The commission has now published its damning verdict on the state of education for the disabled.*
- ▶ passed by everybody **unanimous** *There is a unanimous verdict on the high quality of music in London.*
- ▶ considering everything **overall** *Our overall verdict on the restaurant: it's worth a visit.*
- ▶ final **final** *It's too early for a final verdict on his acting ability.*
- v+N **give, pass** *History will pass its verdict as to whether the theory is correct or not.*

verge N
you are on the verge of something when you are about to do or experience it

- N+of **bankruptcy, breakdown, breakthrough, collapse, death, extinction, starvation, tears, war** *By September, the world economy was, it was said, on the verge of collapse.*
- v+on+N **be, seem, stand, teeter** *At that time, the shipbuilding industry seemed on the verge of collapse.* ● *He was teetering on the verge of a nervous breakdown.*

verification N
checking or proving that something is true or correct

- adj+N from other people, not directly involved **external, independent, third-party** *There is no independent verification of these findings.*
- ▶ using scientific methods **empirical, experimental, scientific** *It is important for medical data to go through the process of scientific verification.*
- v+N need verification **need, require** *The Governors may require verification of applicants' residential addresses.*
- ▶ when information needs verification before it is accepted **be subject to** *The details in the application are subject to verification.*
- ▶ try to get verification **seek** *We are in the process of*

seeking verification from the seller that the details of this property are correct.

▶ get verification **obtain** *It was not until Friday that we were able to obtain verification.*

▶ give verification **provide** *You should provide verification of all the qualifications you hold.*

versatile ADJ
able to be used in many ways; having a range of different skills

● adv+ADJ **extremely, highly, incredibly, truly, very** *Climbers are incredibly versatile plants.*

● ADJ+n device or system **device, instrument, product, system, tool** *This versatile tool can be used in many ways to create stunningly different painting effects.*

▶ way of doing something **approach, option, solution** *This technology provides a versatile solution to your data storage needs.*

▶ person **actor, artist, musician, performer, player** *This talented and versatile performer is one of the few British actresses to develop a large fan base in both the UK and the US.*

version N
a form of something that is different from others or the original

● adj+N new **current, latest, modern, new, recent** *You should download the latest version of the software.*

▶ early or original **draft, early, old, original, previous** *As a part of the consultative process, the draft version of the document has been made available for comment.*

▶ later **later** *According to a later version of the story, this was the moment when they fell in love.*

▶ final **final** *The final version of the report will be sent to the committee in May.*

▶ complete **complete, full** *Click here to download the full version of the article.*

▶ large/small **large, small** *Please click on an image for a larger version.*

▶ changed or improved **edited, improved, modifed, revised, simplified, updated** *We are about to produce an updated version of the guide.*

▶ made shorter **abridged, shortened** *This is an abridged version of a much longer review.*

▶ printed **print, printed, published** *If you require a printed version, please contact me.*

▶ available through a computer **electronic, online** *An online version of the form is not yet available.*

● v+N make a version available **create, develop, launch, produce, release** *Most of the large journal publishers, particularly in the science and business area, already produce electronic versions.*

▶ put a version on a computer **download, install** *To install the latest version of software, see the download site here.*

▶ use a version on a computer **run** *PCs must run the latest version of the appropriate virus protection software.*

vestige N
a very small sign of something that existed previously

● adj+N **last, remaining** *The committee has lost any last vestiges of credibility as an independent body.*

● v+N destroy or remove vestige of something **destroy, remove** *The rebellion has destroyed the last vestiges of his diminished authority.*

▶ keep vestige of something **retain** *We have been attempting to retain some vestige of normality.*

▶ lose vestige of something **lose** *It has lost every vestige of having ever been a prison.*

veteran N
someone with a lot of experience doing something

● adj+N **experienced, grizzled, hardened, seasoned, 10-year, 20-year etc** *By that time, he was already a seasoned veteran, having played competitively since the age of eight.* ● *He was a 30-year veteran of the teaching profession.*

veto N
an official refusal to approve or allow something; the right to refuse to approve or allow something

● v+N use a veto **exercise, use, wield** *Both parties can exercise a single veto to obtain an alternative mediator.*

▶ have or keep a veto **have, keep, retain** *They were determined to retain the veto on taxation matters.*

▶ give up a veto **surrender** *The governement refused to surrender its veto on border control issues.*

● n+of+N **power, right** *As a full member-state, it has the right of veto over any agreement.*

viable ADJ
able to be done, or worth doing

● adv+ADJ completely **perfectly** *Both software and hardware solutions are perfectly viable options.*

▶ really **really, truly** *Neither of these explanations seems to be truly viable.*

▶ possibly **potentially** *From a number of potentially viable ideas put forward, eighteen have been selected.*

▶ in a particular way **commercially, economically, environmentally, financially, politically, technically** *These online services are starting to become commercially viable.*

● ADJ+n method or plan **means, method, option, plan, proposition, solution, strategy** *The cart survived as a viable means of transport until well into the twentieth century.*

▶ different choice **alternative, substitute** *In most circles, online learning is hailed as a viable alternative to traditional classroom settings.*

▶ project or business **business, enterprise, project** *It was obvious that the project was not viable.*

● v+ADJ be or become viable **be, become, prove, remain** *How can the industry remain viable in such a climate?*

▶ seem viable **appear, seem** *The County Council considered that the project did not appear financially viable.*

▶ consider something viable **consider sth, deem sth** *Option three is not considered viable as a method of limiting biodegradable waste.*

vicious ADJ
extremely violent or unkind

- adv+ADJ extremely **downright, extremely, particularly, really** INFORMAL *The tribunal described the treatment she had received as 'inhumane' and 'downright vicious'.*
▶ rather **pretty** INFORMAL**, quite, rather** *From what I was told, I was quite vicious to the nurses because I thought I was being tortured.*
▶ more and more **increasingly** *Her notes are getting increasingly vicious.*

- ADJ+n physical attack or crime **assault, attack, beating, crime, fighting, murder** *He and seven colleagues were subjected to three days of vicious beatings.*
▶ things people say **attack, campaign, rumours** *These vicious rumours have no truth in them at all.*
▶ person **dictator, killer, tyrant** *Hollywood has shown them as vicious killers, ready to attack humans at the slightest provocation.*
▶ political system **dictatorship, regime** *Its people have been fighting a revolutionary war for the past forty years against a vicious, imperialistic regime.*

victim N
someone who has been harmed by a crime or badly affected by an accident or illness

- adj+N innocent or unlucky **hapless, helpless, innocent, passive, poor, tragic, unfortunate, unsuspecting, unwitting, vulnerable** *A wreath was laid in memory of the innocent victims of terrorism.*
▶ intended **intended, potential** *Bogus doorstep callers are very accomplished in selecting potential victims.*

- n+N of a crime **abuse, bomb, burglary, crime, homicide, murder, rape** *The murder victim was a student at Queen's University in Belfast.*
▶ of an accident **accident, burns, crash** *Firefighters demonstrated how a road crash victim is safely removed from the wreckage of their car.*
▶ of a natural disaster **disaster, earthquake, famine, flood, hurricane, tsunami** *A young man was so moved by the plight of tsunami victims that he spent six months as volunteer in Sri Lanka.*
▶ of an illness **cancer, stroke** *His mouth is slightly slanted, like that of a stroke victim.*

- N+of crime **abuse, burglary, crime, fraud, murder, offence, rape, terrorism, theft** *Almost 25 per cent of independent retailers or their staff have been victims of violent crime at work.*
violence **assault, attack, conflict, violence, war** *We provide support for victims of domestic violence.*
terrible situation **disaster, tragedy** *People across the world have been pulling together to try and help the victims of the disaster.*
accident **accident, crash** *We specialize in acting for victims of accidents and medical negligence.*

victory N
the fact of winning a competition or battle

adj+N definite or complete **comfortable, comprehensive, convincing, crushing, decisive, emphatic, landslide, outright, overwhelming, resounding, runaway, sweeping** *The outcome so far has been a stand-off rather than a decisive victory for either side.*
almost not won **hard-fought, last-gasp** INFORMAL**, narrow** *Robins clinched a narrow victory by 101 points to 90.*

▶ impressive or exciting **dramatic, great, impressive, remarkable, sensational, stunning, thrilling, tremendous, well-deserved** *In hockey, the Women's 1st team recorded another impressive victory away at Durham.*
▶ famous or that will be remembered **epic, famous, historic, landmark, memorable, notable** *The Romans built triumphal arches as reminders of famous victories.*
▶ not seeming like a victory **hollow, Pyrrhic** *The company's prime objective will be to find an acceptable solution rather than to score a victory (which, in financial terms, may be a Pyrrhic victory) in the employment tribunal.*
▶ very surprising **shock, surprise** *Mrs Gandhi led the Congress party to a shock victory in the world's largest democracy.*
▶ types of victory **election, electoral, military, moral, naval** *She was the only one who could lead the party to electoral victory.*

- v+N win a victory **achieve, complete, gain, record, score, seal, secure, win** *The final whistle blew and we had secured a fine victory.*
▶ only just win a victory **clinch, grab, snatch** *With only eight days to go, the polls suggested that the Tories might snatch a sensational victory.*
▶ win a victory easily **coast to, cruise to, romp to, storm to, sweep to** *They romped to a 5–2 victory.*
▶ announce a victory **claim, declare, hail sth as, proclaim** *The Conservative candidate declared victory on Monday after Sunday's hotly contested election.*
▶ deserve a victory **deserve, earn** *City were always better than Watford and thoroughly deserved their victory.*
▶ celebrate or enjoy a victory **celebrate, commemorate, enjoy** *I do hope as many as possible of the supporters will stay to celebrate our victory.*
▶ know that victory is close **scent, taste** *Safely over the first seven fences, the huge crowd started to scent victory.*
▶ make someone win a victory **assure, ensure, give sb, guarantee (sb), hand sb** *If you can break the opponent's spirit so that they lose their will to fight, you are guaranteed victory.* • *Two fine goals handed them victory.*
▶ stop someone winning a victory **deny sb, rob sb of** *Brand was denied the victory that many had assumed would be his.*
▶ try to win a victory **chase, fight for, hope for, strive for** *Keep striving for victory!*

view N
a personal opinion, belief, or attitude

- adj+N personal **individual, own, personal, private** *The governing body and headteacher will have their own views about punishment for unacceptable behaviour.*
▶ considering all aspects of a situation **broad** *We need to take a broad view and look at the things that make people take part in physical exercise.*
▶ not considering all aspects of a situation **narrow, simplistic** *This seems to be a very narrow view of what science should be doing.*
▶ traditional **accepted, classical, conservative, conventional, historical, orthodox, traditional** *All*

the mothers in the study had strong, traditional views **about** what being a 'good mother' was about.
▶ different **alternative, contrary, different, opposing, opposite** I want to present an alternative view.
▶ positive **favourable, optimistic, positive** As an employer, L&C takes a positive view of gap-year graduates.
▶ negative **cynical, negative, pessimistic, sceptical** Another respondent echoed this pessimistic view of government's willingness to introduce legislation likely to prove unpopular.
▶ influenced/not influenced by personal feelings **objective, subjective** Therapists use their expertise to develop an objective view of the problem.
▶ reasonable **balanced, common sense, informed, objective, pragmatic, realistic, reasonable, rounded, unbiased** It is important that a balanced view is taken in assessing individual proposals.
▶ strong **clear, strong** Some employers expressed strong views **about** the government's failure to understand small business.
▶ extreme **extreme, extremist, outspoken, racist, radical** The expression of extreme views would alienate people.
▶ accepting of different opinions **liberal** His views were less liberal than Hunt's.
▶ that most people have **common, consensus, dominant, general, majority, popular, public, unanimous, widespread** I think the general view is that this isn't the radical change that we thought it was going to be.
▶ that not many people have **minority** However, this was a minority view.
▶ wrong **distorted, mistaken, wrong** This argument fails because it relies on a mistaken view of what the standards of mathematics require.
▶ current **current, modern, prevailing** The prevailing view is that such droughts are brought about and ended by random fluctuations.
▶ on a particular subject **political, religious, scientific** Public housing was largely responsible for forming my political views.

• v+N tell people your view **air, articulate, express, give, offer, present, put forward, state, submit, tell sb, voice** She appears in public only to express her passionate views **on** the subject of animal rights.
▶ when people tell each other their views **exchange, share** You can exchange views with others at any time by popping over to the discussion forum.
▶ ask for or want to know someone's view **ask for, gather, invite, seek, welcome** We would welcome your views **on** any of these issues.
▶ be someone's view **be, reflect, represent** All material published on these pages represents the personal views of the individual columnists.
▶ have a particular view **adhere to, be inclined to, cling to, form, have, hold, subscribe to, take** So it seems that I am not the only one to hold these views.
▶ have the same view **share** Do you share the same view, Miss Hunter?
▶ agree with someone's view **accept, agree with, coincide with, concur with, confirm, echo, endorse, reinforce, support** I support the view put forward by Tim Kirkhope MEP.
▶ disagree with someone's view **argue against, challenge, disagree with, oppose, reject** We disagree with the view that choice is good in itself.

▶ get someone's view **get, hear, listen to, obtain** It is important that we hear your views to keep this process moving forward.
▶ change your view **change** They changed their views **about** the Bible.

view V
think about a subject in a particular way

• V+with worry or fear **alarm, caution, concern, horror, scepticism, suspicion, trepidation** This claim by the government has to be viewed with some scepticism.
▶ negative feeling **contempt, disdain, disfavour, dismay** The move will be viewed with dismay by anti-arms campaigners.
▶ positive feeling **favour, respect** The two major political parties are viewed with less respect by the public than at any time in this century.

viewpoint N
a way of considering something

• adj+N different **alternative, conflicting, different, differing, opposing** In the evening there was no conflicting viewpoint put across.
▶ types of viewpoint **own, particular, personal** They made it clear they were expressing a personal viewpoint.
▶ that most/few people have **majority, minority** I would take issue with your contention that we represent only a minority viewpoint.
▶ influenced/not influenced by personal feelings **objective, subjective** Although not impossible, this is a very subjective viewpoint.
▶ expressing doubt or not accepting change **conservative, sceptical** They were, rightly, approaching the situation **from** a sceptical viewpoint.
▶ on a particular subject **philosophical, political, religious, scientific, theological, theoretical** From a theological viewpoint, it makes little sense to look at the existence of God merely as a matter of opinion

• v+N express a viewpoint **express, offer, present, put** Many interesting and varied viewpoints were expressed during the discussion.
▶ have a viewpoint **have, hold** Those who hold minority viewpoints must be given their due respect.
▶ start to have a viewpoint **adopt, formulate** It usually best not to adopt an extreme viewpoint – a balanced answer is best.
▶ look at something from a viewpoint **tell sth from, view sth from, write sth from** The story is written from the viewpoint of a child.
▶ respect or agree with someone's viewpoint **respect, support, understand** Personal expression of views is encouraged and all viewpoints are respected.
▶ be or show someone's viewpoint **reflect, represent** Mr Paisley represents the viewpoint of an increasing number of police officers.
▶ have the same viewpoint as someone **share** Do you share the viewpoint that children should not be allowed to play computer games?

vigil N
a time when you wait in a place, often to give support to someone or make a protest

- adj+N all night **all-night, overnight** *They had elected to maintain an all-night vigil rather than sleep.*
▶ all day and all night **24-hour, constant, round-the-clock** *Workers maintained a round-the-clock vigil in front of the factory for 10 weeks.*
▶ quiet or peaceful **peaceful, silent** *All are welcome to join a silent vigil for peace and justice and in memory of all the victims of violence.*
▶ lit by candles **candlelit** *They followed up their campaign with a candlelit vigil.*
▶ for a particular reason **anti-war, peace, prayer, protest, solidarity** *Anti-war vigils were happening around Britain.*
- v+N hold a vigil **hold, keep, maintain, mount, stage, stand** *Eleanor kept a vigil by his bedside as the doctors tried to save him.*
▶ organize a vigil **organize, plan** *The Green Party organized a candlelit vigil in protest against the war.*
▶ be present at a vigil **attend, join** *We are asking everyone who can to join the vigil outside the Town Hall.*

vigilance N
the state of watching a person or situation very carefully

- adj+N continuous **constant, continued, continuing, continuous, eternal** *The price of e-mail is constant vigilance.*
▶ more than usual **extra, greater, heightened, increased** *Customers will notice a heightened vigilance for baggage left unattended in the airport.*
▶ v+N show vigilance **exercise** *All police officers will exercise vigilance during this time, to try to reduce the grief caused by drink-driving.*
▶ encourage vigilance **call for, urge** *He also called for continued vigilance against ongoing terrorism.*
▶ increase/decrease vigilance **increase, relax** *As soon as his mother relaxed her vigilance for a moment, he vanished.*
▶ continue vigilance **maintain** *It is always necessary to maintain the utmost vigilance in regard to administrative expenses.*
▶ need vigilance **need, require** *Fraud threats are constantly changing and require constant vigilance.*

vigilant ADJ
watching something carefully to check for danger

- adv+ADJ always **always, constantly, ever** *We must remain ever vigilant against attempts to undermine our traditions.*
▶ more than usual **especially, particularly** *Be especially vigilant with any horse that has a history of colic.*
▶ very **extremely, very** *Dog owners should be extremely vigilant and wary of anyone showing an unusual interest in their pet.*
- v+ADJ **be, remain, stay** *To help us tackle fraud, always be aware of the risks and remain vigilant.*

vigorous ADJ
full of energy, enthusiasm, or determination

- ADJ+n activity or effort **action, activity, effort, exercise, exertion, pursuit** *Since the war, vigorous efforts have been made to rebuild the collection.* • *As little as 30 minutes vigorous exercise once a week will significantly reduce the risk of heart attack.*
▶ protest **opposition, protest** *I did not expect the extremely vigorous opposition to which I was subjected.*
▶ discussion or argument **debate, defence, discussion** *There was vigorous debate on the question of whether the party should participate in elections.*
▶ course of action **campaign, programme** *A vigorous campaign to save the School of Architecture attracted overwhelming support.*

vigour N
mental energy, enthusiasm, and determination

- adj+N new or more **fresh, increased, increasing, more, new, renewed** *Rosie had to take a break from work, but she has come back with renewed vigour and enthusiasm.*
▶ large amount **great, much, utmost** *She fought the election with great vigour.*

> You can also say that someone is **full of vigour**: *We were all in our early twenties, full of youth and vigour.*

▶ equal **equal, same** *Both views seem to be held with equal vigour, by academics and practitioners alike.*
▶ typical of an intelligent person **intellectual** *His intellectual vigour makes him a bracing writer.*
▶ typical of a young person **youthful** *Despite his youthful vigour, Martin was born almost 75 years ago.*
- v+N give someone vigour **bring, restore** *For all the claims of anti-ageing creams and therapies, nothing has so far restored the vigour of youth.*
▶ keep vigour **maintain, retain** *He retained his vigour to extreme old age.*
▶ try to achieve something with vigour **pursue sth with** *The report was the start of a campaign we are pursuing with vigour.*
▶ lose vigour **lose** *Self-doubt starts to eat him up, and he loses his vigour and business instincts.*
▶ not have vigour **lack** *The Socialist Party won the election but their leader lacked the vigour to introduce the necessary reforms.*

village N
a very small town in the countryside

- adj+N attractive **attractive, beautiful, charming, delightful, idyllic, lovely, picturesque, pleasant, pretty, quaint, unspoilt** *Visit the picturesque village of Perithia and enjoy the wonderful scenery of the Ropa Valley.*
▶ small **little, small, tiny** *This tiny village nestles in the heart of the hills.*
▶ quiet **peaceful, quiet, sleepy, tranquil** *North of the Algarve, you will find sleepy white-washed villages and the Monchique mountains.*
▶ old **ancient, historic, medieval, old** *Walton-Le-Dale is an ancient village situated in close proximity to the Rivers Ribble and Darwen.*
▶ traditional **native, traditional** *Holidays in Larnaca are not complete without a trip to one of the more traditional Cypriot villages.*
▶ in the countryside **country, rural** *This five-bedroomed home is set in a sought-after rural village.*

▶ close to a place **adjacent, local, nearby, neighbouring, surrounding** *Messengers were used to deliver post to nearby villages.*

▶ far from other places **isolated, outlying, remote** *We are helping to build a new classroom in a remote village in Thailand.*

▶ near the sea **coastal, seaside** *The Old Byre sits in the delightful coastal village of Morston.*

● n+N with a particular kind of industry **farming, fishing, mining** *The black-and-white films tell the story of a young lad growing up in a tough mining village.*

▶ in a particular location **highland, hill, hillside, hilltop, lakeside, mountain, riverside** *Holiday rentals in Mallorca can be easily found situated near to sleepy, hilltop villages.*

violate V
do something that breaks a law or principle

● adv+V in an obvious way **blatantly, clearly, flagrantly** *The ban has been flagrantly violated.*

▶ in a serious way **grossly, seriously** *Their human rights in general have been grossly violated.*

▶ deliberately **deliberately, knowingly** *He didn't knowingly violate the terms of his parole.*

▶ many times **consistently, frequently, persistently, repeatedly, routinely, systematically** *International arms embargoes are systematically violated with impunity.*

● V+n law or agreement **agreement, constitution, copyright, law, principle, rule, terms, treaty** *Drivers frequently violate traffic laws.*

▶ rights **privacy, rights, sovereignty** *Human rights are being violated, day in, day out, in countries around the world.*

▶ usual behaviour **convention, norm** *Eighty five companies in total were charged with violating international norms by such trading.*

violation N
an action that breaks a law, agreement, principle etc

● adj+N obvious **blatant, clear, direct, flagrant, obvious** *It is obvious that a flagrant violation of International Law occurred.*

▶ serious **grave, gross, massive, serious** *This is a shameful attempt to silence him and a gross violation of his human rights.*

▶ not serious **minor** *What may seem a minor traffic violation to the driver is perceived as aggressive or inconsiderate by others.*

▶ possible **alleged, apparent, possible, potential, suspected** *Alleged violations of the ceasefire shall be reported to international observers.*

▶ happening often **continued, persistent, repeated, systematic, widespread** *Systematic violations of human rights, wherever they may take place, should not be allowed to stand.*

● v+N commit a violation **commit, perpetrate** *The player was found to have committed two separate anti-doping regulation violations.*

▶ be a violation **amount to, be, constitute** *This clearly constitutes a violation of the country's sovereignty.*

▶ prevent a violation **prevent, stop** *The new Copyright Act aims to prevent copyright violation in the digital age.*

▶ find or examine a violation **detect, find, investigate, report** *The Ombudsman is charged with the task of investigating alleged violations of human rights.*

● N+of law or principle **copyright, law, obligation, principle, regulation, rule** *Any attack or threat of attack against peaceful nuclear facilities constitutes a grave violation of international law.*

▶ agreement **agreement, ceasefire, convention, terms, treaty** *Refusal to withdraw the troops would be a clear violation of the treaty.*

▶ rights **freedom, human rights, liberty, privacy, rights, sovereignty** *Are the new anti-terror measures a violation of civil liberties?*

violence N
violent behaviour

● adj+N serious **bloody, brutal, excessive, extreme, graphic, horrific, serious, terrible** *Some people have criticized the film for its extreme violence.*

▶ with no reason **gratuitous, indiscriminate, mindless, random, senseless, wanton** *There is far too much mindless violence on TV.*

▶ getting worse **escalating, increasing** *There is deep unease about escalating violence in the region.*

▶ using weapons **armed, gun** *One person dies from armed violence every minute.*

▶ in many places **widespread** *There have been reports of widespread violence, vote-rigging, and electoral malpractice.*

▶ by a particular group **gang, paramilitary, terrorist** *They want lasting peace in a just society in which paramilitary violence plays no part.*

▶ types of violence **alcohol-related, domestic, ethnic, homophobic, physical, political, racial, racist, sectarian, sexual, street, work-related** *Anyone can experience domestic violence – it can happen in all kinds of relationships.*

● v+N commit violence **commit, inflict, perpetrate, resort to, turn to, unleash, use** *Last year, we strengthened the law against those who perpetrate domestic violence.*

▶ say that you will commit violence **threaten** *Using or threatening violence to get what you want is not acceptable.*

▶ cause or result in violence **end in, fuel, incite, instigate, lead to, provoke, result in, spark** *He denies that his lyrics incite violence against the gay community.*

▶ experience or see violence **be exposed to, experience, suffer, witness** *The results show that witnessing violence in the real world is strongly correlated with aggressive behaviour.*

▶ escape violence **escape, flee** *Refugees were fleeing the violence in Darfur.*

▶ stop or reduce violence **combat, curb, deal with, end, prevent, quell, stop, tackle** *Police fired tear gas at the rampaging crowds to quell the violence.*

▶ say that violence is acceptable **advocate, condone, justify** *But the ASA disagreed, ruling that the poster condoned violence and was irresponsible.*

▶ say that violence is not acceptable **condemn, denounce, oppose, reject, renounce** *The whole international community must condemn this violence.*

▶ make violence seem attractive **glamorize, glorify** *Hollywood blockbusters glorify violence.*

- N+v start to happen **break out, erupt, flare (up)** *This is a time when there is unprecedented violence erupting in the area.*

You can talk about an **act of violence**. An occasion when a number of people behave violently is an **outbreak of violence**: *The region has seen outbreaks of violence in recent days and weeks.*

- happen **continue, occur, rage, take place** *The worst violence occurred in Montepuez.*
- happen after something **ensue** *More resentment followed, regrettable violence ensued, and the dispute still continues.*
- get worse **escalate, increase, intensify** *As violence has escalated, a number of bomb attacks have also occurred.*
- affect someone or something **affect sb/sth, mar sth, plague sb/sth** *Those islands were as plagued by violence as much as war-torn Europe was.*

violent ADJ

using or containing physical force

- adv+ADJ very **brutally, dangerously, extremely, incredibly, really** INFORMAL **shockingly, very** *Romans did sometimes put Christians to death in shockingly violent ways.*
- rather **pretty** INFORMAL **quite, rather** *It was a rather violent attack.*
- particularly **especially, particularly** *This was a particularly violent episode in English history.*
  more and more **increasingly** *She became increasingly violent and unstable.*
  too much **excessively, too** *The only criticism that can be levelled at this movie is that it is sometimes excessively violent.*
  in a way that is unnecessary **gratuitously** *The film was banal and gratuitously violent.*
  possibly **potentially** *A police officer should attempt to defuse any potentially violent situation.*
  as part of something's nature **inherently** *Conflict is not inherently violent.*

  ADJ+n fight or argument **clash, conflict, confrontation, disorder, riot, struggle** *People cleared the streets and a lot of violent confrontation was avoided.*
  attack **act, action, assault, attack, incident** *He was the victim of a violent assault.*
  crime **crime, offence, robbery** *Many of these prisoners are in jail for violent offences.*
  protest **demonstration, protest** *Other students were shouting, arguing that the protest was not violent.*
  reaction **outburst, reaction** *She has violent outbursts, is unsettled during the night, and is very clingy.*
  behaviour **behaviour, conduct, temper** *He was sent off later in the match for violent conduct.*
  means of control **repression, suppression** *Indeed, the violent repression of the Albanian population of Kosova escalated.*
  person **criminal, extremist, offender, thug** *We do not want personal contact information getting into the hands of violent criminals.*

virtual ADJ

almost the same as the thing mentioned

  ADJ+n person **dictator, prisoner, recluse,**

stranger, unknown *He has been living the life of a virtual recluse since the death of his wife.*
- situation **collapse, monopoly, silence, slavery, standstill** *The event was a huge success, bringing the shopping centre to a virtual standstill.*
- when something is not present **absence, disappearance, elimination, extinction** *The virtual absence of medical supplies meant doctors had to resort to unconventional methods of treatment.*
- when talking about possibility **certainty, impossibility** *It is a virtual certainty that war will be fought in space one day.*

2 created by computers, or appearing on computers

- ADJ+n reality **reality** *Over the last ten years, the use of virtual reality systems has become widespread.*
- places **classroom, environment, gallery, laboratory, library, office, space, university, world** *Players get to create fantasy characters and explore a virtual 3D environment in order to build up a story.*
- events **exhibition, seminar, tour** *Explore colliery buildings and go on a virtual tour of a modern mine.*
- people or companies **community, enterprise, marketplace, network** *I have been in close contact with several of the members of the virtual community since then.*

virtue N

a good quality in someone or something

- v+N talk about the virtues of something **espouse, expound, extol, praise, preach, proclaim, trumpet** *Lunch meetings are a highly productive way to extol the virtues of online marketing to advertisers.*
- have or develop virtues **cultivate, embody, have, possess, practise** *Different cultures embody different virtues.*

virus N

1 a simple living thing that makes you ill

- v+N spread a virus **circulate, pass on, spread, transmit** *We could be passing on the virus to other people.*
- catch a virus **be exposed to, catch, contract, get** *No one knows how the viruses are contracted.*
- get rid of a virus **destroy, eliminate, eradicate, kill** *A programme of vaccination was started with the aim of completely eradicating the smallpox virus.*
- have a virus **be affected by, be infected by, be infected with, have, live with, suffer from** *Nursing people infected with the HIV virus can be a challenging and rewarding job.*
- carry a virus **carry, harbour** *Which animals typically harbour the rabies virus?*
- get better after a virus **recover from** *Sarah is still recovering from a throat virus.*
- fight a virus **combat, fight** *Each species uses its immune system to combat different viruses in different ways.*
- prevent a virus **prevent, protect against** *Vaccine programs can prevent viruses before they start.*
- N+v affect someone or something **affect sb/sth, attack sb/sth, infect sb, invade sth** *Do bird flu viruses infect humans?*
- spread **circulate, spread** *Chickenpox can be caught by the virus spreading in the air.*
- change **evolve, mutate** *The HIV virus mutates at a*

rapid rate and there are numerous strains found in different areas of the world.

▶ increase **multiply, replicate, reproduce** *Viruses typically replicate for a long period of time before they activate, allowing plenty of time to spread.*

▶ kill sb **kill sb, wipe out sth** *In the film, a deadly virus has wiped out almost all of humanity.*

2 a program that can damage your computer

● v+N spread a virus **introduce, spread, transmit** *Studies have shown that 98 per cent of viruses are transmitted through e-mails.*

▶ find a virus **detect, discover, identify, spot** *Make sure that you update your antivirus software regularly so that it can detect even the newest viruses.*

▶ contain a virus **be infected with, carry, contain** *Special software blocks incoming messages that may contain viruses.*

▶ get rid of a virus **destroy, disinfect, remove** *It is very important that this virus is removed from any computers.*

▶ stop a virus **block, prevent, protect against, stop** *Take steps to prevent viruses, even if you do not visit unknown or untrusted websites.*

▶ look for a virus **check for, scan for** *Files with the suffix .rtf may not be scanned for viruses.*

● N+v affect or damage something **affect sth, attack sth, damage sth, hit sth, infect sth** *Computer viruses are a constant threat and lead to a lot of wasted time if a virus infects a PC.*

▶ spread or go round **circulate, go round, spread** *A particularly nasty email virus is circulating which will delete all your files.*

● N+n software **checker, scanner, software** *Run a virus scanner to see if your PC is infected.*

▶ finding or protecting against viruses **checking, detection, protection, scanning** *No virus checking can be 100 per cent effective.*

▶ when a virus enters or might enter your computer **attack, infection, threat, warning** *Virus infections are spread by sloppy computing practice.*

visa N
an official document allowing you to enter a country

● adj+N that can be used **appropriate, correct, necessary, valid** *U.S. citizens require a valid visa for travel to Brazil and Paraguay.*

If a visa is no longer valid, you say that it has **expired**: *You cannot remain in the UK once your student visa has expired.*

▶ temporary **short-term, temporary** *There are still large numbers of students or other people on temporary visas.*

▶ permanent **long-term, permanent** *To apply for a permanent visa, you have to be under 45 years old.*

▶ used now **current** *My current visa expires in July 2012.*

● n+N for entering or passing through a country **entry, exit, transit** *Transit visas are valid for up to three days.*

▶ purpose **student, tourist, work** *British passport holders require a tourist visa for entry into Turkey.*

● v+N need a visa **need, require** *Please note that*

nationals of some countries require visas in order to visit Turkey.

▶ get a visa **get, obtain, receive, secure** *Before you set off, get a visa from the Chinese Embassy in London.*

▶ have a visa **have, hold** *He was deported from Chicago even though he held a valid visa.*

▶ arrange a visa **apply for, arrange** *Make sure you apply for a visa that covers the whole period of your stay in Britain.*

▶ give a visa **give (sb), grant (sb), issue (sb)** *About one and a half million visas were issued in 2004.*

▶ not give a visa **deny sb, refuse (sb)** *It was just possible that my visa was refused for military reasons.*

▶ take back a visa **revoke** *The U.S. Department of Homeland Security has revoked her visa.*

▶ stay longer than a visa allows **overstay** *She was arrested for overstaying her visa.*

▶ make your visa last longer **extend, renew** *I visited Singapore every few months to renew my visa when I lived in Malaysia.*

● N+n form **application, form** *A visa form will not be issued without this documentation.*

▶ rules or arrangements **arrangements, policy, procedures, regulations, requirements, restrictions, rules** *It is not normally possible for full-time students to change to part-time status because of visa requirements.*

▶ problem **problem, violation** *He was detained for a minor visa violation.*

▶ when a visa lasts for longer **extension, renewal** *Can I request a visa extension in case I decide to continue my internship?*

▶ when someone does not need a visa **waiver** *Currently, British travellers can visit the US for up to three months without a visa under the visa waiver scheme.*

visibility N
the distance that you can see or a situation in which something can be seen

● adj+N good **clear, excellent, good, high, superb** *The large wraparound rear windscreen provides excellent visibility.*

▶ bad **limited, low, poor, reduced, restricted, zero** *Keep together in conditions of poor visibility.*

▶ medium **moderate** *Cloud was low and visibility on moderate.*

● v+N reduce visibility **impair, limit, obscure, obstruct, reduce, restrict** *The silty sea bed can quickly reduce visibility to a few metres.*

▶ increase visibility **aid, enhance, improve, increase, maximize** *Luminous accessories such as armbands or buttons increased visibility even more.*

▶ provide visibility **ensure, give, provide** *The screen provide the best brightness and viewing angle, ensuring clear visibility even in direct sunlight.*

visible ADJ
able to be seen

● adv+ADJ clearly **clearly, distinctly, easily, highly, plainly, readily** *The joy and skill of all the pupils clearly visible.*

▶ faintly **dimly, faintly** *A mountain is faintly visible in the far background.*

▶ almost not **barely, hardly, just, scarcely** *The hills*

on either side of the road were barely visible because of a dust storm.
▶ completely **fully, quite** *Costs are high and the benefits are not fully visible.*
▶ partly **partially, partly** *An inscription in the top stone is still partly visible.*
▶ still/no longer **no longer, still** *The remains of some of the fortifications are still visible.*
● v+ADJ be or become visible **be, become** *The darkness lifts and the boat crew becomes visible.*
▶ stay visible **remain, stay** *Very little of the ancient stonework remains visible.*
▶ make something visible **leave sth, make sth, render sth** *The walnut-wood rafters are left visible, and the intervening spaces filled with a kind of white plaster.*

vision N
the ability to plan for the future, or someone's idea or hope of what something will be like in the future

● adj+N clear **clear, coherent, strategic** *We've a clear vision of where we want to be.*
▶ good or positive **compelling, extraordinary, good, great, inspiring, optimistic, positive, strong, utopian** *In conclusion, let me offer a more positive vision of the purpose of educational research.*
▶ ambitious **ambitious, bold, grand** *He had a grand vision, but he knew he needed to give himself a kick-start to turn this into reality.*
▶ different, special, or new **alternative, different, new, original, radical, unique** *Instead, I shall try to present an alternative vision of computers in education.*
▶ broad **broad, overall, wide** *There is no overall vision for land use in the area, no grand plan to improve the environment.*
▶ of one person **own, personal** *Librarians have to develop their own entrepreneurial vision so that they take the lead in these initiatives.*
▶ of two or more people **collective, common, shared** *A single shared vision in a divided society is unattainable.*
▶ for the future **future, long-term** *We need policies and programmes with long-term vision.*
▶ types of vision **artistic, creative, political** *They gleefully blend and blur musical genres in pursuit of their artistic vision.*
▶ v+N tell people about a vision **articulate, communicate, describe, express, give, offer, outline, present, provide, set out, share** *They must communicate that vision to their colleagues in their parent organizations.*
▶ achieve a vision **achieve, deliver, fulfil, implement, realize** *Achieving this vision will require radical, innovative thinking.*

> You can also say that someone *turns a vision into (a) reality*: *Over the next five years we intend to turn this vision into reality.*

▶ try to achieve a vision **embrace, pursue, work towards** *He saluted their courage and faith in pursuing a vision that has now become a reality.*
▶ develop a vision **create, develop, shape** *We help customers shape their vision into a feasible and successful Internet strategy.*

▶ have vision **be blessed with, have** *He is a true pioneer, blessed with a far-seeing vision.*
▶ not have vision **lack** *Critics say that the protesters lack vision.*

visit N
an occasion when you visit a person or place

● adj+N regular **frequent, regular** *Regular visits to your dentist will help to prevent gum disease.*
▶ not regular **occasional, periodic** *She enjoys keeping fit by cycling and occasional visits to the gym.*
▶ special/not special **routine, special** *The tumour was discovered during a routine visit to the doctor.*
▶ recent **recent** *At a recent visit to a hotel in Nottingham, we were looked after extremely well.*
▶ happening soon **forthcoming** *We are all excited about our forthcoming visit to Torbay.*
▶ next **next, subsequent** *She is already planning her next visit to Asia.*
▶ previous **last, previous** *We had had good weather on previous visits.*
▶ first **first, initial, preliminary** *After an initial visit, we concluded that the Baltic States were an ideal place to do business.*
▶ not planned or expected **unannounced, unexpected** *On occasions, the Inspectorate may decide that it is necessary to make unannounced visits.*
▶ planned **planned** *Frequent planned visits were made to the patient's home.*
▶ short **brief, fleeting, flying, quick, short** *Except for a brief visit to England, he never travelled extensively outside of continental Europe.*
▶ long **extended, long** *I have recently returned from a long visit to Jamaica.*
▶ official **formal, official** *She is on a private business trip to make money, and not an official visit.*
▶ not official **informal, personal, social** *To arrange an informal visit, call the senior engineer.*
▶ useful or enjoyable **enjoyable, memorable, worthwhile** *I would like to express our thanks to all concerned for making our visit so enjoyable.*
▶ for a particular purpose **educational, fact-finding** *This will be a fact-finding visit.*
▶ to a foreign country **foreign, overseas** *The capital accounts for five per cent of all overseas visits to the UK.*
● v+N arrange a visit **arrange, organize, plan, schedule** *We are pleased to arrange visits at home if you cannot come to the office.*
▶ go on a visit **come for, conduct, do, go for, go on, make, pay (sb)** *Between 1885 and 1893 he paid several visits to Egypt.*
▶ receive a visit **get, have, receive** *From time to time, we received visits from people who knew our father.*
▶ cancel or delay a visit **cancel, postpone** *Unfortunately, she had to cancel this visit at the last moment.*
▶ be worth a visit **be worth** *Ludlow Castle is certainly worth a visit.*

vital ADJ
very important or necessary

● adv+ADJ completely or very **absolutely, really** INFORMAL, **so** INFORMAL, **truly, very** *It's absolutely vital that our teams have a passionate belief in the importance of their work.*

▶ particularly **especially, particularly** *Correct spelling of individual and company names is particularly vital!*

▶ more and more **increasingly** *IT employees constitute an increasingly vital component of the labour force.*

▶ in a particular way **economically, strategically** *Colombia is very close to the strategically vital Panama Canal.*

● v+ADJ be, become, or stay vital **be, become, prove, remain** *Your letters to politicians and the press remain vital!*

▶ seem vital **seem** *The things that seem so vital when we are young are completely missing from our lives in middle age.*

▶ consider something to be vital **consider sth (as), deem sth (as), recognize sth as, regard sth as, see sth as** *Good training is considered absolutely vital.*

● N+to **development, growth, health, prosperity, security, success, survival, understanding, well-being** *Your participation is vital to the success of the project.*

vitality N
energy or enthusiasm

● adj+N great **extraordinary, great, sheer, tremendous** *This unique collection provides an insight into the sheer vitality and depth of Classical Arabic literature.*

▶ more **added, continued, new, renewed** *The most common sensations after hypnosis are feelings of renewed vitality and a greater sense of well-being.*

▶ types of vitality **cultural, economic, intellectual, physical, religious, rhythmic, spiritual** *We will continue to encourage the economic vitality of town centres.*

● v+N increase vitality **improve, increase, promote, strengthen** *Such major investment will further increase the vitality of the city.*

▶ give vitality **add, bring, contribute to, inject, restore** *Our new policies for competition will inject fresh vitality into British industry.*

▶ get back vitality **regain** *Her passion lies in helping people regain their vitality.*

▶ keep vitality **maintain, retain, sustain** *We need to sustain the economic vitality of the City Centre as a commercial, shopping, and tourist centre.*

▶ reduce vitality **harm, sap, threaten, undermine** *We have a system of regulation that is in grave danger of sapping the natural vitality and energy of entrepreneurs in this country.*

▶ lose vitality **lose** *The General Assembly had lost its vitality and often failed to focus effectively on the most compelling issues of the day.*

▶ have vitality **be brimming with, be bursting with, be full of, demonstrate, have** *His style of playing is exciting and full of vitality.*

▶ not have vitality **lack** *Almost all of the early 21st-century developments for apartment buildings lack the vitality of earlier designs.*

● and/or **attractiveness, dynamism, energy, freshness, originality, richness, vibrancy, vigour** *The whole show has a freshness and vitality that reminds you of the long-gone days when musicals were fun.*

vivid ADJ
very clear and detailed

● adv+ADJ very **exceptionally, extraordinarily, extremely, incredibly, really INFORMAL, remarkably, so INFORMAL, very, wonderfully** *She is renowned for her extraordinarily vivid recreations of historical events.*

▶ rather **pretty INFORMAL, quite** *Memories of my childhood are quite vivid.*

▶ particularly **especially, particularly** *It was a particularly vivid dream.*

▶ still **still** *Her memories of that time are still vivid.*

● ADJ+n memory, recollection, reminder **memory, recollection, reminder** *Eileen has vivid memories of her father's shop.*

▶ image in your mind **dream, image, picture, scene** *I still have a very vivid image of his tearful face.*

▶ description or acting **account, depiction, description, imagery, portrait, portrayal** *This is a vivid account of a young teacher coming to terms with the horrors of life in an inner-city school.*

▶ ability to imagine **imagination, insight** *Children have vivid imaginations.*

▶ example **example, illustration** *This is a vivid example of just how important it is to get architecture right.*

▶ experience or feeling **experience, impression, sense** *He describes his vivid experience of visiting Chernobyl in 1996.*

▶ detail **detail** *Every nuance and subtlety is described in vivid detail.*

vocabulary N
all the words that a person knows or words used in a particular language or subject

● adj+N small **limited, small** *This activity was designed to include all members of the class, including four with an extremely limited vocabulary.*

▶ large **extensive, good, large, rich, varied, wide** *This method enables learners to develop a wide vocabulary in the target language.*

▶ only including certain words **controlled, core, restricted** *They propose a core vocabulary, organized in areas of meaning which are of interest to young learners.*

▶ easy **basic, simple** *The children enjoy learning basic French vocabulary.*

▶ important or useful **essential, important, key, useful** *Teachers will be able to highlight key vocabulary in English.*

▶ difficult **complex, difficult** *Tell the students to focus on noting down simple words, not any complex technical vocabulary the speaker uses.*

▶ not known **new, unfamiliar** *Don't use unfamiliar vocabulary in your questions.*

▶ suitable **appropriate, relevant** *Pupils learn how to comment on works of art, using appropriate vocabulary.*

▶ that you understand **passive, receptive** *Rises in receptive vocabulary resulted from reading performance, rather than the other way round.*

▶ that you can use **active, expressive** *The successful student will possess a minimum active vocabulary of about 1,000 Russian words.*

▶ special **domain-specific, special, specialist, specialized, subject-specific, technical** *Education, like all professions, has a specialized vocabulary.*

▶ used by most people **common, everyday, general, standard** *The words 'guilt' and 'conscience' are common words in everyday vocabulary.*
▶ of a subject area **geographical, mathematical, musical, political, scientific, theatrical** *Opportunities are also provided for children to develop mathematical vocabulary.*
● v+N have a vocabulary **have** *You really don't have a very varied vocabulary, do you?*
▶ improve your vocabulary **broaden, build, develop, enlarge, enrich, expand, extend, improve, increase, widen** *A dictionary of synonyms and antonyms will allow you to write more effectively and enrich your vocabulary.*
▶ learn or practise vocabulary **acquire, learn, practise** *You will acquire appropriate vocabulary for shopping in supermarkets, clothes shops, and the pharmacy.*
▶ teach vocabulary **introduce, teach** *Cooking instructions can be used at a very simple level to teach vocabulary.*
▶ not have a large vocabulary **lack** *Young children lack the vocabulary to express their fears, memories, or distress.*
▶ use vocabulary **employ, use** *Rachel writes in an appropriately impersonal style, using varied vocabulary.*
▶ become part of a vocabulary **enter** *Recently, she has found lots of new words entering her vocabulary.*
● N+n word **item, term, word** *The list of vocabulary items put together was selected so as to reflect the needs and interests of the prospective learners.*
▶ learning **acquisition, building, development, extension, learning, recognition** *The course includes classes on academic writing, grammar, and vocabulary development.*
▶ knowledge or skills **knowledge, skills** *This game helps kids to develop spelling and vocabulary skills.*
▶ list **list** *Lesson 1 begins with a vocabulary list covering Basic Expressions.*
▶ activity **exercise, test** *We had to have a vocabulary test.*

vocal ADJ
expressing opinions frequently and strongly

▶ adv+ADJ very **extremely, highly, particularly, very** *We are extremely vocal in warning music fans not to buy tickets from unofficial outlets.*
▶ rather **quite, rather** *Government has been egged on by the media and by some rather vocal members of Parliament.*
▶ more and more **increasingly** *Non-smokers were becoming increasingly vocal in their demands for the right to work in a smoke-free environment.*
▶ ADJ+n person or group **advocate, critic, minority, opponent, proponent, supporter** *She has been a persistent and vocal critic of the scheme.*
▶ behaviour **encouragement, opposition, support** *There has been vocal opposition to the plan.*

vocation N
job that is your purpose in life

▶ adj+N true **real, true** *There are undoubtedly people working within the nursing profession who see it as a true vocation.*

▶ chosen **chosen** *We need to be continually monitoring how good we are at our chosen vocation.*
● v+N fulfil your vocation **follow, fulfil, pursue** *Warwick left college at the age of 21 to pursue his vocation full-time as a painter.*
▶ not fulfil your vocation **miss** *The man has missed his vocation – he should be on the stage.*
▶ find your vocation **discover, find** *After a brief nursing career, she found her true vocation as a musician.*

vocational ADJ
teaching the skills necessary for a particular job

● ADJ+n course or qualification **course, curriculum, degree, programme, qualification, scheme** *Vocational qualifications should be valued in their own right.*
▶ part of a course or qualification **element, option** *All its courses have a strong vocational element.*
▶ teaching or learning **education, learning, training** *The college gives young people vocational training in things like computing and mechanics.*
▶ subject **specialism, subject** *Our students study a wide range of both academic and vocational subjects.*
▶ skills **experience, skills** *The purpose of the course is to teach occupational skills (life skills) or vocational skills (work-related skills).*
▶ emphasis **emphasis, focus** *We pride ourselves on the vocational focus of our courses.*

voice N
the sound made when someone speaks or sings

● adj+N loud **big, booming, clear, loud, strident** *I could hear Brian's booming voice drawing ever closer.*
▶ quiet **calm, gentle, quiet, small, soft** *Speak in a very soft gentle voice.*
▶ low or harsh **deep, gravelly, gruff, harsh, hoarse, husky, low, rasping** *'I've got something for you,' he said in his low husky voice.*
▶ high **high, high-pitched, shrill, squeaky** *She put on a squeaky voice and did an impression of Michael Jackson.*
▶ pleasant **beautiful, fine, rich, soulful, sweet, velvet** *'I'll look after you', she said in a sweet voice.*
▶ of a singer: good **amazing, good, great, incredible, powerful, strong** *The lead singer has a great voice.*
▶ different to others **distinctive** *Apollo possesses a distinctive rasping voice.*
▶ going up and down in pitch **sing-song** *In a sing-song voice, the flight attendant runs throught he safety procedures.*
▶ staying the same in pitch **flat, monotone** *She delivered her dialogue in a monotone voice.*
● N+v gradually stop **drift off, trail off** *His voice trails off quickly as the procession approaches.*
▶ when a voice is loud **boom (out), echo, ring out** *When he spoke, he spoke loudly, his voice echoing like that of a minister.*
▶ shake **crack, falter, shake, tremble** *The old man's eyes filled and his voice trembled.*
▶ change **break, change** *When boys' voices break, they become deeper in tone.*

▶ get higher **rise** *Her voice rose to a squeak as she went on.*

▶ get lower **drop** *Her voice dropped to a conspiratorial whisper.*

voice V
express your opinions or feelings about something

● adv+V clearly **clearly, loudly, strongly** *The crowd began loudly voicing its displeasure at some of the referee's calls.*

▶ in public **openly, publicly** *After the war, Oppenheimer openly voiced his opposition to the development of the more powerful hydrogen bomb.*

▶ often **frequently, often, regularly, repeatedly** *The Union has repeatedly voiced its concerns over the decline in the services and facilities available to rural communities.*

● V+n feeling or opinion **feelings, idea, opinion, sentiments, thoughts, view** *This will be an opportunity for all participants to voice their opinions on the possible regeneration.*

▶ worry or fear **anxieties, concern, disquiet, fears, worries** *Significant people from within the UN system have regularly voiced their concerns.*

▶ disagreement or disapproval **complaint, criticism, disapproval, discontent, disgust, displeasure, dissent, objection, opposition, protest** *Members of the public have voiced their disapproval through the local press.*

▶ disappointment **disappointment, dismay, dissatisfaction** *Davies was quick to voice his disappointment with the referee.*

▶ anger **anger, frustration, outrage** *He insisted the visiting supporters had every right to voice their anger at the way his team are playing.*

▶ doubt **doubts, misgivings, reservations, scepticism, suspicion** *Motoring organizations voiced doubts about the scheme.*

▶ support **approval, support** *The public voiced universal approval.*

▶ hope or wish **desire, hope** *The forum is an opportunity for people to voice their hopes and concerns.*

volunteer N
someone who does useful work but is not paid for it

● v+N need, want, or get volunteers **ask for, attract, enlist, invite, need, recruit, seek, train, welcome** *We may also need volunteers to staff each polling station.* ● *We are currently recruiting up to 100 volunteers to become Community Health Outreach workers.*

▶ thank volunteers **reimburse, reward, thank** *The programme is designed to reward volunteers for their good work and practices.*

● N+n **counsellor, crew, driver, firefighter, fundraiser, helper, mentor, tutor** *We have between 15 and 20 permanent staff and a number of volunteer helpers.*

vote V
formally express your opinion by officially choosing

● adv+V clearly, by most or all people **decisively,** **massively, overwhelmingly, resoundingly, solidly, unanimously** *The union voted overwhelmingly to ditch its no-strike policy.*

▶ by only a few people **narrowly** *The Turkish parliament narrowly voted against this proposal.*

● V+on a proposal **amendment, bill, constitution, legislation, motion, proposal, resolution** *We need to vote on the motion as it stands.*

▶ an issue **issue, matter, question, topic** *Finally, the audience was invited to vote on the question of whether there should be a referendum.*

vote N
the formal expression of a choice by voting

● adj+N in a particular contest **democratic, electoral, parliamentary, presidential** *Winning the parliamentary vote on Friday 10 March will be crucial, but not easy.*

▶ made in a particular way **electronic, postal, proxy** *People must request a postal vote far enough in advance of the ballot.*

▶ showing strong support for an opinion or proposal **affirmative, decisive, overwhelming, resounding, unanimous** *We will be working together to secure an affirmative vote.*

▶ made in order to influence the result of an election, not to show support for someone **tactical** *The Liberal Democrats fought a good campaign, and clearly grabbed a large number of tactical votes.*

● v+N make your choice by voting **cast, exercise, register** *At the last general election, only 46.5% of eligible voters cast their vote.*

▶ gain votes **attract, gain, garner, get, poll, receive, secure, win** *Helen Cumming stood for the Socialist Party and polled 647 votes.*

▶ count votes **count, record** *The inVote interactive voting system instantly records the votes as they come in.*

voter N
someone who votes in an election

● adj+N not sure who to vote for **floating, swing, undecided** *It seems that this message had at least swayed some of the floating voters.*

▶ not enthusiastic about voting **disaffected, disenchanted, disillusioned** *The overwhelming majority of disaffected voters live in urban areas.*

● v+N persuade or attract voters **attract, convince, persuade, sway, tempt, win, woo** *The leadership adopted a more left-wing image in order to win back their core voters.* ● *He was appointed by Hague to woo new voters.*

▶ make voters choose other people or things **alienate, scare off** *The Democrats were unwilling to use her in too prominent a role for fear of alienating non-white voters.*

▶ treat voters in an unfair way **deceive, disenfranchise, fool, intimidate, mislead** *Many thousands of voters would be effectively disenfranchised by paramilitary intimidation.*

● N+n negative feelings **apathy, confusion, cynicism, dissatisfaction, fatigue** *Voter apathy has also increased due to a perceived lack of conviction amongst politicians.*

▶ being involved in voting **engagement,**

participation, registration, turnout *The Electoral Commission produced a report entitled 'Voter engagement and young people'.*

vow N
a serious, official, or religious promise

- adj+N **binding, formal, holy, irrevocable, religious, sacred, solemn, strict, unbreakable** *I made a solemn vow that I would read every submission from beginning to end.*
- v+N make a vow **make, swear, take** *They took a solemn vow to perform the obligations of the office they now held.*
- ▶ keep a vow **fulfil, keep, observe, remember** *I promised to go, and I'm determined to keep my vow.*
- ▶ break a vow **break, forget** *When he got well, he did not forget his earlier vow.*
- N+of **abstinence, celibacy, chastity, obedience, poverty, secrecy, silence, virginity** *He started to live the life of an ascetic, taking a vow of celibacy and living a life of great hardship.*

voyage N
a long journey

- adj+N dangerous or disastrous **arduous, dangerous, fateful, ill-fated, perilous** *'Titanic' is the fictional tale of a rich girl and poor boy who meet on the ill-fated voyage of the famous ship.*
- ▶ exciting **eventful, exciting, extraordinary, fantastic** *He produced a remarkable series of paintings inspired by his fantastic voyage and spectacular surroundings.*
- v+N **commence, complete, make, undertake**

According to old Irish tales, St Brendan made a voyage to the Faroe Islands, Iceland, Greenland and North America sometime in the 6th century.

vulnerable ADJ
1 easy to harm physically or mentally

- adv+ADJ very **especially, exceptionally, extremely, highly, increasingly, particularly** *The report presents new findings on why children run away, and makes recommendations for helping this highly vulnerable group of young people.*
- ▶ in emotions **emotionally, mentally, psychologically** *Many religious cults deliberately target people who are emotionally vulnerable.*
- ▶ in particular ways **economically, financially, nutritionally, socially** *Even before the disaster, the island community included thousands of economically vulnerable households.*
- v+ADJ **appear, be, become, feel, leave sb, look, remain, seem** *Stick with groups of friends if you feel vulnerable.* ● *Our charity supports and children who have been left vulnerable by the HIV/AIDS epidemic in South Africa.*

2 easily damaged by negative influences or events

- ADJ+to other people's actions **accusation, attack, exploitation, takeover, theft, vandalism** *Which retailers are vulnerable to takeover and who are the likely investors?*
- ▶ events that cannot be controlled **downturn, drought, erosion, flooding, fluctuations, infection, vagaries, whim** *Such farmers are very vulnerable to the vagaries of an economic system beyond their control.*

Ww

wage N
an amount of money earned for working

- adj+N fair or reasonable **average, decent, fair, just, living** *We want these women to be able to work for a decent wage without being exploited.*
- ► low **low, meagre, modest** *Out of his meagre wages, very little was left with which to buy food.*
- ► set by law **minimum** *They are calling for an immediate rise in the minimum wage for 16–18 year-olds.*
- ► too low to live on **poverty, starvation** *This obsession with low prices has led to poverty wages and ever-worsening working conditions.*

- v+N get a wage **command, demand, earn, receive** *Knowing a foreign language means you can earn better wages and have the possibility of international travel.*
- ► increase wages **increase, raise** *The labour shortages following the Black Death forced employers to raise workers' wages.*
- ► reduce wages **cut, deduct, depress, dock, freeze, lower, slash, undercut** *Luckily, they were not docked any wages for being late.*
- ► earn extra money **supplement** *He supplemented his wages by selling details of the company's secret 'recipe'.*

> Usage **Wage** is usually plural in all of the **v+N** combinations shown above.

- N+n reduction **cut, freeze, restraint** *Of course, that will mean wage restraint for the lower grades in the civil service.*
- ► increase **increase, inflation, rise** *This means that the economy can sustain a lower rate of unemployment without triggering off a renewed burst of wage inflation.*
- ► differences between people's wages **differential, inequality** *Economists claim that globalisation did not cause the rise in wage inequality.*

waist N
the middle part of the human body

- adj+N **narrow, slender, slim, small, thin, tiny** *He came up beside her and placed an arm about her slim waist.*

wait V
expect or hope that something will happen

- adv+V with particular feelings **anxiously, eagerly, expectantly, impatiently, nervously, passively, patiently, quietly** *Everyone is nervously waiting to hear what plans the Glazer family has for the club.*
- ► for a long time **awhile, forever, long** *They were willing to work hard and wait long.*

wait N
a period when you expect or hope that something will happen

- adj+N long **extended, interminable, lengthy, long,** longish, prolonged, protracted *After an interminable wait, instructions were given to board the train.*
- ► short **brief, short** *After a brief wait in an outer office, I was called in for the interview.*
- ► making you feel anxious or irritated **agonizing, anxious, frustrating, tense** *Laura needed a liver transplant as a toddler, and her family faced an agonizing wait while a donor was found.*

walk N
a journey on foot

- adj+N short/long **brief, long, short** *My cousin arrived in the afternoon, and we went for a brief walk around the neighbourhood and did a bit of window shopping.*
- ► enjoyable **beautiful, delightful, enjoyable, lovely, nice, pleasant** *We reached the little fishing town after a delightful walk along a coastal path.*
- ► involving a lot of effort **arduous, brisk, challenging, hard, strenuous, uphill** *Revitalise yourself by going for a brisk walk at any time of the day.*
- ► not involving much effort **easy, leisurely** *If you like, you can take a leisurely walk through the hotel's stunning gardens, enjoy a dip in the pool, or relax with a good book in the library.*

wander V
1 travel without purpose

- adv+V **aimlessly, casually, happily, idly, lazily, leisurely, randomly** *He wandered aimlessly about the streets, feeling depressed.*

2 stop concentrating or focussing on something

- n+V attention wanders **attention, imagination, mind, thoughts** *If your attention wanders, gently bring it back to the task.*
- ► eyes wander **eyes, gaze** *For a moment, he allowed his gaze to wander over the sea of faces surrounding him on all sides.*

wane V
become weaker or less important

- adv+V a lot **considerably, somewhat** *Now that he is no longer a part of the show, his interest in it was waned considerably.*
- ► quickly **fast, quickly, rapidly** *Support and enthusiasm for the campaign was rapidly waning.*
- ► finally **eventually, finally** *As with many teen bands, their popularity eventually waned.*

- n+V power or influence **dominance, influence, power, strength** *By about the year 1700, Dutch sea power and influence was waning, as Britain's power rose.*
- ► positive feelings **confidence, enthusiasm, hope, interest, optimism** *After several hours of hard work, our initial enthusiasm for the job was beginning to wane.*
- ► luck or popularity **fortunes, popularity, star** *With a career spanning some 30 years, Paul's popularity has never waned.*

want V
feel that you would like something

- adv+V **definitely, desperately, genuinely, obviously, particularly, really** *Mourinho only had respect for European winners, and he desperately wanted to win with Chelsea.*

war N
1 serious fighting between countries

- v+N fight a war **fight, prosecute, wage** *This was a highly effective method of waging war in Afghanistan.*
- ▶ start a war **declare, launch, start, unleash** *We need to ask whether it was actually the Prime Minister who declared war on Iraq.*
- ▶ end a war **end, stop** *Wellington defeated Napoleon at Waterloo (1815), thus ending the Napoleonic Wars.*
- ▶ avoid a war **avert, avoid, prevent** *The two states narrowly averted a full-scale war in Kashmir in 1999.*
- ▶ cause a war **cause, lead to, provoke, spark, trigger** *The terrorists are determined to stoke sectarian tension and are attempting to spark a civil war.*

2 an organized effort to control or stop something

- N+on **crime, drugs, graffiti, hunger, obesity, poverty, terror, terrorism** *Political reforms will count for just as much as agricultural innovation in the war on hunger.*

warm ADJ
fairly hot in a comfortable, pleasant way

- adv+**ADJ** to a pleasant degree **comfortably, delightfully, gloriously, pleasantly, wonderfully** *It was a delightfully warm evening on the longest night of the year.*
- ▶ to a surprising degree **amazingly, exceptionally, surprisingly, unseasonably, unusually** *The year started cold before becoming unseasonably warm and dry.*
- ▶ fairly **moderately, quite, reasonably, relatively** *The Alps region has harsh winters and moderately warm summers with abundant rainfall.*
- v+**ADJ** be, become, or remain warm **be, become, get, grow, remain, stay, turn** *After a long winter, the weather was at last turning warmer.*
- ▶ keep yourself warm **keep, stay, wrap up** *In the winter the office is very cold, so you'll want to wrap up warm.*

warmth N
a kind and friendly quality

- adj+N **genuine, great, personal, real** *The strong tradition of desert hospitality lives on in the genuine warmth and friendliness that welcomes any visitor.*
- v+N **bring, convey, exude, radiate, spread** *He exuded warmth and kindness; it was impossible not to be charmed by him.*
- N+of **affection, applause, feeling, friendship, hospitality, personality, reception, smile, welcome** *The warmth of the applause was indicative of the respect and popularity that this master deserves.*
- and/or **affection, friendliness, generosity, hospitality, humanity, humour** *A big man with a big personality, who exudes warmth and good humour, Dara is a delight to be entertained by.*

warn V
make someone conscious of a possible problem or danger

- adv+V seriously **earnestly, ominously, solemnly, sternly** *Party members were solemnly warned not to indulge in internal arguments.*
- ▶ urgently or with emphasis **emphatically, urgently** *Answering the phone, he heard his wife's voice urgently warning him to stay away from the city centre.*
- ▶ very clearly **clearly, explicitly, expressly, specifically** *A terrorist gang has explicitly warned that it will target tourists during this year's summer season.*
- ▶ more than once **consistently, constantly, regularly, repeatedly** *He had been repeatedly warned by his doctor of the damage his lifestyle was causing.*
- V+of **consequences, crisis, dangers, hazards, perils, pitfalls, risk, threat** *While the demand for tobacco grew, some physicians began to warn of the potential dangers.*

warning N
a statement that warns of possible problems or danger

- adj+N serious **chilling, dire, grim, solemn, stark, stern** *His stark warnings about the consequences of ignoring climate change are spot on.*
- ▶ enough **adequate, ample, fair, sufficient** *The local population was given ample warning of the impending attack and people were sufficiently familiar with the procedure for evacuating the area.*
- ▶ helpful, because given when it is needed **salutary, timely** *The oil crises of the 1970s had been a salutary warning to Americans accustomed to cheap gasoline and gas-guzzling cars.*
- ▶ clear or urgent **explicit, urgent** *Earlier in the year, the world's leading climate scientists issued the most urgent warning yet about the need to reduce carbon emissions.*
- n+N **air-raid, bomb, cyclone, flood, gale, hurricane, storm, tornado, typhoon, virus** *For the latest information on flood warnings, contact the Environment Agency.*
- v+N give a warning **carry, echo, give, issue, reiterate, renew, sound, utter** *Our leaders have issued stark warnings about the dangers of terrorism.*
- ▶ take particular action because of a warning **heed** *Like so many fools before me, I failed to heed the warnings about the dangers of prolonged exposure to the sun.*
- ▶ ignore a warning **disregard, ignore** *Government ministers are accused of ignoring warnings of electoral fraud.*
- N+n **bell, flag, light, notice, sign, signal, siren** *In children, these warning signs mean you should get medical advice immediately.*

warrant N
a judge's document allowing the police to do something

- n+N **arrest, death, detention, extradition, search, seizure** *Even with a search warrant, the police still cannot forcibly enter your house.*
- v+N **grant, issue, serve** *When he failed to appear in court on the appointed day, a warrant wss issued for his arrest.*

wary ADJ
careful or nervous about someone or something

- adv+ADJ very **extremely, increasingly, particularly, very** *Be very wary of a club where staff or volunteers behave in those ways.*
- ▶ slightly **a little, pretty** INFORMAL**, quite, rather, slightly, somewhat** *I was somewhat wary of what I was letting myself in for.*
- ▶ in a way that seems normal and sensible **naturally, rightly, understandably** *Some staff are naturally wary **about** their ability to support a pupil with a medical condition.*
- v+ADJ **be, become, feel, grow, remain, seem** *Aid organisations and the US military remain wary of working together on relief operations for Iraq.*

waste N
1 failure to make effective use of something valuable

- adj+N complete **appalling, colossal, complete, total, utter** *Overall, this has been a colossal waste of everybody's time.*
- ▶ sad **terrible, tragic** *Young people are far more likely to be killed on the road than older people, meaning road deaths are often a tragic waste of young lives.*
- ▶ unnecessary **needless, pointless, unnecessary** *Protesters criticized the new runway as a needless waste of public money.*
- N+of **effort, energy, funds, life, money, potential, resources, talent, time** *The movie is an awful waste of Meryl Streep's talent.*

2 useless materials or parts left after using something

- adj+N dangerous **contaminated, hazardous, high-level, nuclear, radioactive, toxic** *The rules relate to the disposal of hazardous waste in landfill sites.*
- ▶ not dangerous **biodegradable, inert, low-level, non-hazardous, organic** *These are the targets for reducing the amount of biodegradable waste transported to landfill sites.*
- ▶ types of waste **agricultural, chemical, clinical, domestic, industrial, municipal** *The local authority provides a collection of commercial clinical waste on request.*
- n+N from a particular place **farm, garden, hospital, household, kitchen, slaughterhouse** *A total of 20.6 per cent of household waste was recycled in 1999/2000 in Orkney.*
- ▶ types of waste **asbestos, food, mineral, packaging, plastic, sewage, vegetable** *Use these baskets for collecting vegetable waste for composting.*
- ▶ from a particular activity **catering, construction, demolition, mining** *The new scheme turns catering waste into top quality organic fertiliser.*
- v+N process waste **bury, compost, incinerate, manage, recycle, reprocess, reuse** *Just over 25% of this waste is currently being recycled.*

- ▶ reduce or get rid of waste **eliminate, minimize, reduce** *By initiating a recycling programme, your canteen can drastically reduce waste with minimal effort.*
- ▶ spoil a place by leaving waste there **dump, tip** *The company was continuing to tip clay waste on the moors.*
- ▶ collect waste and take it away **collect, dispose of, remove, transport** *We will collect almost any commercial waste.*

watch V
look at someone or something for some time

- adv+V with a lot of attention **attentively, avidly, carefully, closely, eagerly, intently, keenly** *Journalists and press officers alike are avidly watching the post-match analysis.*
- ▶ in a worried way **anxiously, nervously** *All the speculation about where rates are going has left many homeowners nervously watching house prices.*
- ▶ without reacting **idly, impassively, passively, quietly, silently** *A police officer was still silently watching our movements from the doorway.*
- V+in **amazement, awe, disbelief, fascination, horror, silence, wonder** *My brother watched in disbelief as government troops completely destroyed a house belonging to someone he knew.*

watch N
an act of carefully looking at or checking something

- adj+N **24-hour, careful, close, constant, round-the-clock, vigilant** *We have to keep a constant watch **on** the temperatures of the engines.*
- v+N **keep, maintain** *Analysts will be keeping a close watch **on** what happens.*

watchdog N
an organization whose purpose is to make sure that organizations act lawfully

- adj+N having particular status **independent, international, local, national, official, public, statutory** *The Financial Services Authority is the independent watchdog that regulates the finance industry.*
- ▶ in a particular industry **civil, corporate, environmental, financial, medical, nuclear, postal** *The construction industry is under pressure from environmental watchdogs to improve its environmental performance.*
- n+N **advertising, broadcasting, consumer, electricity, exams, media, passenger, press, prison, telecoms** *The exams watchdog, the Qualifications and Curriculum Authority, wants a ban on pupils taking coursework home to stamp out cheating.*

watershed N
an event that causes an important change

- adj+N **critical, crucial, historical, major** *These workshops will be an informal opportunity to discuss these matters at a critical watershed **in** European history and governance.*
- v+N be a watershed **be, mark, prove, represent** *The TV series represents a fascinating watershed in the history of mass communication.*

▶ reach a watershed **approach, reach** *Like many scientists, she felt the planet was approaching a watershed when it would be too late to reverse this devastation.*

wave N

1 a raised line of moving water

● N+v **batter sth, break, buffet sth, crash, engulf sth, hit sth, lap sth, lash sth, pound sth, roll, wash (sth)** *Huge waves were crashing over the top of the pier.* ● *Massive waves pounded the coast of Florida today as Hurricane Wilma swept across the state.*

2 a large number of things that happen or people that go somewhere

● v+N **generate, herald, provoke, spark, trigger, unleash** *The talks have triggered a wave of speculation about a possible merger.*

way N

a method or manner of doing something

● adj+N effective **effective, efficient, excellent, good, practical** *She came up with an excellent way of presenting the course material.*

▶ easy **convenient, easy, simple, straightforward** *Interested in finding a cheap and easy way to work and travel abroad next summer?*

▶ different **alternative, different, other, possible** *A major concern is finding alternative ways of using the premises to provide income.*

▶ new or original **creative, innovative, new, novel, original** *They came up with some novel ways of raising money for charity.*

● v+N find or try to find a way **come up with, discover, find, identify, investigate, look for, seek** *Employers and employees have to find ways to bring a level of personal control back into the workplace.*

▶ change a way **change, improve, revolutionize, transform** *The technology is going to change the way we teach.* ● *Over the past few years, email and smartphones have revolutionized the way we live and work.*

▶ develop a way **create, develop, devise, establish** *One of our goals will be to devise cleaner ways of making chemicals, replacing the conventional oil-based solvents used in chemical reactions.*

▶ consider a way **consider, discuss, examine, explore, review** *The case study will focus on schools with broadband connections, and will explore the ways in which connectivity is being used in teaching and learning.*

weak ADJ

not strong enough to succeed or be effective

▶ adv+ADJ in a particular way **academically, economically, financially, militarily, morally, politically, structurally** *These students are academically weak.*

▶ rather **fairly, pretty** INFORMAL**, rather** *The analysis is pretty weak.*

▶ very **extremely, inherently, too, very** *This argument is inherently weak.*

▶ compared to others **comparatively, considerably, much, relatively** *The party has a considerably weaker position in England.* ● *The law in this respect is much weaker than in the UK.*

● ADJ+n part or aspect **area, aspect, point, spot** *This is the weak spot in his book.*

▶ idea or explanation **argument, excuse, explanation, idea, policy** *This, of course, is a relatively weak argument.*

▶ understanding **grasp, knowledge, understanding** *The author clearly has a weak grasp of historical matters.*

▶ evidence **analysis, evidence** *The evidence in support of this idea seems very weak.*

▶ government or leadership **administration, authority, government, leadership, regime** *In the late 8th Century, Northumbria was plagued by weak leadership and collapsed into a state of anarchy.*

▶ economic system or performance **currency, demand, economy, growth, market** *The advertising market remains very weak, for the third year running.*

● v+ADJ **appear, be, become, grow, remain, seem** *The role of the voluntary sector remains comparatively weak.*

● and/or **ineffective, ineffectual, unstable, vacillating, vulnerable** *Their policies were weak and ineffective.*

weaken V

make something weaker

● adv+V **considerably, drastically, fatally, gravely, greatly, seriously, severely, significantly** *The economy has been gravely weakened by the civil war.*

> Usage ***Weaken*** is usually <u>passive</u> in all these ***adv+V*** combinations.

● V+n someone's ability to do something **ability, capacity, credibility, effectiveness, position** *The President's position was severely weakened.*

▶ power or control **authority, grip, hold, influence, power** *The new technologies are gradually weakening the hold of the traditional television channels.*

▶ belief or determination **confidence, morale, resolve, will** *A salary cut would weaken staff morale.*

▶ connections **bonds, solidarity, ties, union** *Anything that weakens those bonds of trust weakens us as a fighting force.*

▶ an argument **argument** *Unsubstantiated claims such as these weaken an argument that is compelling enough based on the facts.*

weakness N

a problem or fault that makes something weak

● adj+N basic **fundamental, inherent, intrinsic, methodological, structural, systemic, underlying** *The recent banking crisis has highlighted some inherent structural weaknesses in the financial system.*

▶ major or serious **fatal, key, serious, significant** *This was the most significant weakness in the design of the experiment.*

▶ lasting a long time **long-standing** *The Government must address long-standing weaknesses.*

▶ obvious to others **apparent, evident, glaring, perceived** *The film has many glaring weaknesses.*

▶ possible **potential** *Senior managers are good at identifying potential weaknesses.*

● v+N find a weakness **detect, find, identify,**

pinpoint, see, spot *Auditors can spot weaknesses and advise your company on improvements.*

▶ show a weakness **demonstrate, expose, highlight, reflect, reveal** *It exposed fundamental weaknesses in the European economy.*

▶ deal with a weakness **acknowledge, address, correct, eliminate, overcome, rectify, remedy, tackle** *Subsequent reforms sought to address weaknesses in education.*

▶ use a weakness for your own advantage **exploit** *Enemies will exploit these weaknesses.*

● N+in **approach, argument, leadership, management, process, system** *Some of the weaknesses in his argument come from over-generalizing from particular cases.*

● n+of+N **area, sign, source** *Asking for help is so often viewed as a sign of weakness.*

wealth N

1 a large amount of money

● adj+N very great **abundant, considerable, enormous, fabulous, great, immense, obscene, tremendous, untold, vast** *He amassed considerable wealth.*

▶ hard to imagine **incredible, unimaginable** *You see incredible wealth and significant poverty.*

▶ obvious **conspicuous, obvious, ostentatious** *There was a lot of ostentatious wealth.*

▶ gained in a particular way **ill-gotten, new-found** *How do they intend to use their new-found wealth?*

▶ so much that it is regarded as wrong **obscene** *A small minority at the top enjoy obscene wealth while a massive majority exists in abject poverty and misery.*

● v+N get or have wealth **accumulate, acquire, amass, enjoy, inherit, possess** *During the nineteenth century, the family acquired great wealth.*

▶ create wealth **create, generate, increase** *Well-managed investments can be a good way of increasing your wealth.*

▶ share wealth **distribute, redistribute, share** *He believed that the rich should distribute their wealth for the benefit of society.*

▶ use wealth **flaunt, squander, use** *He was rich and had no qualms about flaunting his wealth in public.* ● *We should use our wealth to help others.*

● N+n **creation, distribution, management, redistribution, tax** *In the next Parliament, we shall introduce an annual wealth tax.*

● n+of+N sharing **distribution, redistribution** *This has prevented any effective redistribution of wealth and income.*

▶ getting wealth **accumulation, creation, pursuit** *There was a rapid accumulation of wealth.*

● and/or **fame, influence, power, prestige, privilege, status** *He relied on his family's wealth and influence to get everything he got in life.*

2 a large supply of something

● v+N **amass, boast, bring, contain, gain, have, increase, possess** *She has amassed a wealth of experience and her views are widely respected.* ● *The region boasts a wealth of attractions.*

● N+of information **data, details, evidence,**

information, material *There is a wealth of anecdotal evidence.*

▶ skills **experience, expertise, knowledge, talent** *She has gained a wealth of experience from working on these projects.*

▶ things you can do, use, or see **attractions, features, opportunities, possibilities, resources, treasures** *Broadband opens up a wealth of creative opportunities.* ● *You'll encounter a wealth of historic treasures.*

wealthy ADJ

with a large amount of money, land etc

● adv+ADJ **fabulously, immensely, independently, obscenely, very** *He is independently wealthy and does not need the cash.*

● v+ADJ **be, become, grow** *As societies grow wealthy, differences in well-being are less frequently due to income, and more frequently due to factors such as social relationships and enjoyment at work.*

● and/or **aristocratic, influential, powerful, privileged, well-connected** *She was born into a wealthy and influential Anglo-Irish family.*

weather N

conditions in the atmosphere relating to temperature, rain etc

● adj+N with sun, rain etc **cloudy, frosty, icy, rainy, snowy, stormy, sunny, windy** *The weather was sunny and warm.*

▶ hot or warm **boiling (hot), hot, scorching, warm** *The weather ranged from boiling to freezing.*

▶ cold **chilly, cold, cool, freezing (cold), frosty, wintry** *Wintry weather causes problems on the roads.*

▶ wet or dull **cloudy, damp, dismal, dull, humid, overcast, rainy, wet** *Be prepared for some hot and very humid weather.* ● *The weather was overcast but warm.*

▶ good **beautiful, favourable, fine, glorious, good, lovely, nice, perfect** *It was perfect weather for a picnic.*

▶ bad **adverse, atrocious, awful, bad, foul, inclement, miserable** *The weather was awful.*

▶ extreme **extreme, freak, rough, severe, stormy, wild** *We have all experienced freak weather over the last few years.*

▶ not staying the same **changeable, unpredictable, unsettled** *The weather was very changeable, one day beautiful and sunny, the next cold, wet and windy.*

● v+N talk about expected weather **check, expect, forecast, predict** *Climate models can successfully forecast the weather.*

▶ have good/bad weather **enjoy, have** *The March event usually enjoys better weather than the autumn one.*

▶ do something despite the weather **brave, withstand** *A few people had chosen to brave the weather and were looking around outside.*

● N+v change **change, turn colder, warmer etc** *The weather then turned cooler, with nasty showers.*

▶ get better **brighten (up), clear (up), improve, warm up** *After a gloomy start, the weather gradually improved.*

▶ get worse **close in, deteriorate, set in, turn, worse**

The weather closed in on us again. • *By this time, the weather was deteriorating rapidly.*

weather V
manage a difficult experience without being seriously harmed

- V+n **challenge, crisis, downturn, recession, storm** *The economy has weathered the storm relatively well.*

web N
1 a complicated set of related things

- adj+N **complex, complicated, intricate, tangled** *He becomes trapped in a tangled web of deceit.*
- v+N **create, spin, untangle, weave** *Others are better qualified to untangle this complex web.*
- N+of lies **conspiracy, corruption, deceit, deception, intrigue, lies** *Every day, he becomes more entangled in the web of deceit that he and his supporters have spun.*
- ▶ connections **connections, interconnections, relations, relationships** *Understanding this complex web of relationships is crucial.*

2 the Internet

- v+N use the web **access, use** *Not everyone can access the web.*
- ▶ search the web **browse, scour, search, surf, trawl** *I've trawled the web, but have not found the answer.*
- N+n space **address, log, page, site, space** *There is free web space and online customer support.*
- ▶ information available **content, directory, resources, version** *Click here to download a web version.*
- ▶ use **access, accessibility, traffic, use** *Check your mail from anywhere that you have web access.*
- ▶ activities **browsing, conferencing, design, development, hosting, publishing, search, streaming** *The programs cover tasks such as word processing, e-mail and web browsing.*
- ▶ tool or service **browser, cam, host, server, service, tool** *Your web browser must be able to accept cookies for you to log-in.*

website N
a space on the Internet providing information about a particular thing

- v+N start or develop a website **build, create, design, develop, launch, update** *We ensure that your website is built with accessibility in mind.*
- ▶ run a website **host, maintain, manage, own, run** *They will charge you a monthly fee to host your website.*
- ▶ look at a website **access, browse, check, find, navigate, search, see, view, visit** *Check this website for details.*

wedding N
ceremony in which two people get married

- adj+N types of wedding **civil, religious, traditional, white** *We can host both civil and religious weddings.* • *She likes the idea of a traditional white wedding.*
- large **grand, large, lavish** *She wanted a lavish wedding.*
- ▶ small **intimate, simple, small** *It's the perfect setting for small, intimate weddings.*
- ▶ very nice **dream, fairytale, lovely, perfect, romantic** *We can make your dream wedding into a reality.* • *It was the most romantic wedding I've ever been to.*
- v+N arrange a wedding **announce, arrange, book, organize, plan** *We can arrange weddings in a number of different destinations.*
- ▶ perform or have a ceremony for a wedding **celebrate, conduct, hold, host, officiate at** *Some ministers will not conduct a church wedding if one partner is divorced.*
- ▶ go to a wedding **attend, be invited to, go to** *He did not attend her wedding.*
- ▶ stop or delay a wedding **cancel, postpone** *We have had to postpone the wedding.*
- N+n date **anniversary, day** *They've just celebrated their 20th wedding anniversary.*
- ▶ event **breakfast, ceremony, reception** *It is a beautiful setting for wedding receptions.*
- ▶ gifts **gift, present** *He gave us a lovely wedding present.*
- ▶ clothes **attire, dress, gown, outfit** *Most men hire their wedding attire.*

weep V
cry because of sadness or strong emotion

- adv+V a lot **bitterly, copiously, hysterically, inconsolably, uncontrollably** *Tears rolled down his face and he wept uncontrollably.*
- ▶ letting people see **openly, unashamedly** *When I was told the news, I wept unashamedly.*
- ▶ quietly **quietly, silently, softly** *Weeping softly, she leant against my shoulder.*

weight N
1 a measurement of how heavy someone is

- v+N lose weight and become less heavy **lose, reduce, shed** *The aim of the procedure is not to reduce weight but to improve your figure.* • *Patients with arthritis should shed any excess weight.*
- ▶ gain weight **gain, put on, regain** *Diets are soon discarded, and often the lost weight is regained.*
- ▶ keep your weight the same **control, keep off, maintain** *This will help you keep the weight off permanently.*

2 importance or influence

- adj+N **considerable, equal, great, sufficient, (too) much, undue** *The reporter had not given sufficient weight to the positive aspects of the scheme.*
- v+N have weight **carry, have, hold** *The information comes from a variety of sources, some of which carry more weight in our analysis.*
- ▶ give weight to something **add, assign, attach, give, lend** *We attach great weight to this argument.* • *He goes on to explain the concept of the balance of nature, and how this lends weight to the Gaia theory of the Earth as an organism.*
- N+of **argument, evidence, history, opinion, tradition** *Despite the weight of scientific evidence, not enough has been done.*

weigh up PHR VB

consider good and bad aspects before reaching a decision

- V+n information **arguments, evidence, information** *You will be weighing up all the arguments and solving problems as they crop up.*
- ▶ choices **choices, considerations, options** *I have to weigh up my options.*
- ▶ advantages/disadvantages **advantages, benefits, costs, disadvantages, good and bad points, merits, pros and cons, risks** *He must have weighed up the risks.*
- ▶ effects **consequences, effects** *Weigh up the consequences of leaving your friends and family.*
- ▶ situation **factors, issues, situation** *Only you can weigh up all the emotional and social factors involved.*

weird ADJ INFORMAL

strange and unusual

- adv+**ADJ downright, kinda, kind of, a little, plain, pretty, really** *I was staying at this really weird old hotel where the hallways made no sense and I kept getting lost trying to find my room.*
- v+**ADJ act, be, feel, get, look, seem, sound** *He has been acting pretty weird lately.* • *Things just get plain weird from here onwards.*

welcome V

1 greet someone arriving, in a polite friendly way

- adv+**V** with enthusiasm **enthusiastically, heartily, warmly** *We were then all warmly welcomed by the Mayor.*
- ▶ formally **formally, officially** *After registration, we were formally welcomed by the General Secretary.*

2 react to something in a positive way

- adv+**V** with enthusiasm **genuinely, greatly, positively, warmly, wholeheartedly** *We genuinely welcome all your comments – positive or negative.* • *I wholeheartedly welcome this initiative.*
- ▶ generally **broadly, generally, universally, widely** *Their views have not been universally welcomed.*
- ▶ not strongly **cautiously** *Members cautiously welcomed the initiative.*
- V+n new development **appointment, arrival, decision, initiative, introduction, launch, move, publication** *We welcome the launch of the campaign.*
- ▶ proposal **application, proposal, recommendation, submission, suggestion** *Everyone on the committee welcomes this proposal from our friends in the U.S.*
- ▶ opportunity **chance, opportunity** *We welcome the opportunity to work with you on this important project.*
- ▶ information **announcement, fact, findings, information, news** *The announcement was welcomed by environmentalists.*
- ▶ comments or questions **comments, enquiries, feedback, input, queries, questions, views** *We would welcome your feedback.* • *We welcome your input and, and there is a feedback page where you can contact us.*

welcome ADJ

received in a positive way

- ▶ ADJ+n comments **comments, contributions, enquiries, feedback, suggestions** *Your comments are always welcome.*
- ▶ something that makes you feel better **boost, break, development, distraction, news, relief, respite** *It was a welcome break for all of us.* • *This was very welcome news.*

welcome N

a greeting or reaction

- adj+**N** friendly **cordial, friendly, good, gracious, hospitable** *We received a very cordial welcome from the landlord.*
- ▶ enthusiastic or positive **enthusiastic, genuine, rapturous, tremendous, warm** *In June 1461, Edward entered London, where he was given a rapturous welcome and hailed as King.*
- ▶ not strong **cautious, guarded, lukewarm, qualified** *There has been a qualified welcome for the recent White Paper.*
- v+**N** offer a welcome **accord, extend, give, offer** *The new novel has been accorded a warm welcome.*
- ▶ receive a welcome **enjoy, find, get, have, receive** *At the hotel, we enjoyed a very cordial welcome.* • *Her proposal got a rather lukewarm welcome from the press.*
- ▶ make sure someone receives a good welcome **assure, ensure, guarantee, promise** *Please come and join us – a warm welcome is ensured.*

welfare N

people's health and happiness

- adj+**N** relating to an individual **emotional, general, mental, personal, physical, psychological** *Our main concern is her physical and emotional welfare.* • *We will closely monitor your academic progress and general welfare.*
- ▶ relating to society **human, public, social** *Projects in the fields of education, health and social welfare will also be considered.*
- ▶ financial **economic** *This is important for the economic welfare of many households.*
- ▶ future **future, long-term** *They leave with our best wishes for their future welfare.*
- v+**N** improve someone's welfare **advance, enhance, further, improve, promote** *The unit was set up to promote the welfare of the most vulnerable children in our local community.*
- ▶ protect someone's welfare **ensure, guarantee, protect, safeguard, secure** *My role is concerned primarily with ensuring the welfare of postgraduate students.*
- ▶ threaten someone's welfare **compromise, endanger, jeopardize, neglect, sacrifice, threaten, undermine** *They claimed their mother had neglected their welfare by putting her career first.*
- ▶ affect someone's welfare **affect** *There are several factors which may affect the welfare of residents.*
- ▶ be responsible for someone's welfare **assess, be responsible for, monitor, oversee** *Your tutor will visit you and monitor your welfare during your year in industry.*

well-being N

the satisfactory state of being happy, healthy etc

- adj+**N** mental **emotional, mental, psychological,**

spiritual *The aim is to develop emotional well-being in school.*

▶ physical **nutritional, physical** *You will soon notice changes in your physical wellbeing.*

▶ general **general, overall, personal, social** *The book explains how yoga can contribute to general well-being.* ● *Personal well-being also includes mental health.*

▶ financial **economic, financial** *The Directorate has a shared responsibility for the financial well-being of the University.*

▶ future **future, long-term** *This is an important issue for the future wellbeing of our children.*

● v+N improve someone's well-being **advance, enhance, improve, promote** *Exercise can help lift your mood and enhance wellbeing.*

▶ protect someone's well-being **ensure, guarantee, maintain, safeguard** *The panel works exceptionally well to ensure the wellbeing of children.*

▶ threaten someone's well-being **endanger, jeopardize, threaten** *Anyone who jeopardises the well-being of others is bad news.*

▶ affect someone's well-being **affect, influence** *Getting a good night's sleep influences our psychological well-being.*

▶ check someone's well-being **assess, measure, monitor** *To measure the well-being of a region, quality-of-life and economic indicators are required.*

● and/or **contentment, happiness, health, independence, safety, self-esteem, vitality** *The Centre's focus is the safety and well-being of vulnerable groups within society.* ● *You should also experience feelings of vitality and well-being after treatment.*

well-known ADJ
known by many people

● adv+ADJ rather **fairly, quite, reasonably, relatively** *I am fairly well-known as a critic of his newspaper.*

▶ in a particular area **internationally, locally** *She is an internationally well-known and respected children's author.*

● and/or admired **popular, reputable, respected, well-loved** *He was a well-known and respected musician.*

▶ successful **eminent, influential, prominent, well-established** *She has become a well-known and influential food writer.*

wet ADJ
1 covered with or full of liquid

● adv+ADJ very **dripping, extremely, soaking, sopping, thoroughly, very** *The cave can become extremely wet in bad weather.* ● *The children came back soaking wet.*

▶ rather **rather, slightly** *It can be rather wet underfoot.*

● v+ADJ **be, become, get** *You should wear old trainers and socks that you do not mind getting wet.*

● and/or people **bedraggled, cold, miserable, tired** *We finished the walk very wet and bedraggled.*

▶ surfaces **muddy, slimy, slippery, soggy** *It is unusually wet and muddy along the path.*

2 with a lot of rain

● adv+ADJ **exceptionally, rather, unseasonably, unusually, very** *The weather was still unseasonably wet and cool.*

● and/or dull **cloudy, dreary, dull, grey, miserable, misty, rainy** *It was a wet, miserable afternoon in late November.*

▶ cold/not cold **cold, cool, mild, warm** *The forecast is wetter and milder at the weekend.*

▶ with wind **blustery, stormy, windy** *The weather was wet and windy.*

whereabouts N
the place where someone or something is

● adj+N exact **exact, precise** *He did not know his exact whereabouts.*

▶ now **current, present** *Their current whereabouts is unknown.*

▶ known/not known **last known, unknown** *His last known whereabouts was in the Chicago area.*

● v+N find someone's whereabouts **ascertain, discover, find, identify, locate, trace, track** *Police are trying to locate the whereabouts of her husband, who has been missing for three days.*

▶ become certain of someone's whereabouts **ascertain, confirm, determine, establish, know** *Nobody has been able to confirm his whereabouts.*

▶ show someone's whereabouts **disclose, reveal** *For security reasons, I am unable to reveal my exact whereabouts.*

whiff N
a slight amount or sign of something

● adj+N slight **faint, mere, slight** *Though nothing has been proved, a faint whiff of scandal is in the air, with all kinds of questionable land deals and allocations of contracts.*

▶ definite **definite, distinct, strong, unmistakable** *His conversation was always suffused with a strong whiff of irony.*

● v+N **catch, detect, get, smell** *Do I detect a whiff of hypocrisy here?*

whim N
a sudden feeling that you must have something or do something

● adj+N not lasting **fickle, passing, sudden** *He left his job on a sudden whim.*

▶ not based on good reasons **arbitrary, capricious, strange** *Nature should not be subject to our arbitrary whim.*

▶ not important **idle, mere, slightest** *It was no idle whim which took him there.* ● *The hotel staff will satisfy your slightest whim.*

● v+N **cater to, indulge, pander to, satisfy** *It is the most perfect place, where your every whim is indulged.* ● *Politicians are too ready to pander to the whims of any minority that shouts the loudest.*

whisper V
speak very quietly so others cannot hear

● adv+V **conspiratorially, gently, hoarsely, quietly, softly** *He bent his head, and she whispered very softly into his ear.*

whisper N
a very quiet way of speaking

● adj+N **conspiratorial, faint, gentle, hoarse, low, quiet, soft** *Across the stillness came a soft whisper.*

white ADJ
1 of the same colour as milk

● adj+ADJ pure **plain, pure** *There are miles of pure white beaches here.*

▶ bright **blinding, bright, brilliant, dazzling, gleaming, sparkling** *I saw a flash of brilliant white light.*

2 pale because ill or upset

● v+ADJ **be, go, grow, look, turn** *He suddenly went as white as a sheet and had to sit down* ● *She turned white with fear.*

wide ADJ
1 involving many different things or people

● adv+ADJ in a way that is noticeable **exceptionally, extraordinarily, impressively, remarkably, surprisingly, unusually** *Students choose from an exceptionally wide range of modules.*

▶ very **enormously, extremely, very** *There is an extremely wide diversity of views on this issue.*

▶ rather **fairly, quite a** *Your work shows quite a wide range of techniques.*

● ADJ+n range **array, choice, cross-section, diversity, network, range, scope, selection, spectrum, variety** *The book gives a good idea of the wide scope of philosophical thought in Islam.* ● *Students will study a wide variety of applied problems.*

▶ responsibility **remit, responsibility** *The group has a wide remit, with members taking an interest in all policy issues.*

▶ support **backing, support** *The recommendations have won wide support across the sector.*

2 general rather than specific

● ADJ+n issue or situation **agenda, context, implications, issue, question** *We wanted to challenge managers to think about the wider agenda within the healthcare system.* ● *The Bill should be seen not in isolation, but in its wider context.*

▶ opinion **perspective, view** *They could be relied upon to take a wider view of things.*

▶ discussion **debate, discussion** *There should be a much wider debate on this issue.*

▶ people **audience, community, public, society** *The indicators will also be of interest to a wider audience.* ● *The college plays a pivotal role in supporting the needs of the wider community.*

> Usage **Wide** is usually used in the comparative form in all these **ADJ+n** combinations.

widen V
increase

● adv+V a lot **alarmingly, considerably, dramatically, greatly, rapidly, significantly** *The gap between rich and poor widened dramatically.*

▶ gradually **gradually, progressively, steadily** *The aim is to gradually widen the appeal of our game.*

▶ V+n difference **disparity, divide, division, gap, gulf, inequality, rift** *This further widens the gap between those on average income and those in poverty.*

▶ group of people **base, circle, net, pool** *Opening up to additional markets has widened their customer base.*

▶ possibilities **access, appeal, choice, horizons, participation, scope** *Less advantaged households have been targeted in an effort to widen the scope of the scheme.*

▶ discussion or description **debate, definition** *It is important that the energy debate is widened.*

▶ area of work or responsibility **agenda, focus, remit** *The committee has now widened its focus from monitoring costs of public services to improving performance.*

● n+V **divide, gap, gulf, inequality** *The bottom two-fifths of humanity share less than 4% of the world's wealth, while the top one-fifth share about 85%. This gulf has actually widened in the last ten years.*

wide-ranging ADJ
dealing with a large variety of subjects

● V+n discussion or study **analysis, consultation, debate, discussion, report, research, review, study, survey** *There will be wide-ranging consultation with the community.*

▶ set of subjects or issues **agenda, curriculum, issues, programme, subjects, topics** *He writes on wide-ranging topics, from the Spanish Civil War to English cooking.*

▶ experience or knowledge **experience, expertise, interests, knowledge** *Having access to lecturers with wide-ranging expertise and experience has been a great bonus.*

▶ effects **consequences, effects, impact, implications** *This will have wide-ranging implications for the curriculum.*

▶ changes **changes, reform** *The administration has embarked on a programme of wide-ranging reform.*

▶ powers **policy, powers, remit, responsibilities** *He had wide-ranging powers bestowed on him by the emperor.*

widespread ADJ
happening or existing in many places

● adv+ADJ more **ever more, increasingly, more, more and more** *The use of calculators in examinations is becoming an increasingly widespread practice.*

▶ now **already, now, still** *There is still widespread famine, poverty, disease and suffering.*

● ADJ+n belief **assumption, belief, consensus, feeling, perception, speculation** *Our research indicates that this perception is widespread.*

▶ worry **concern, confusion, fear, panic, unease** *There is widespread unease about this proposal.*

▶ anger or criticism **anger, condemnation, criticism, discontent, dissatisfaction, opposition, protest, resentment, unrest** *The research programme found evidence of widespread dissatisfaction.*

▶ lack of trust **cynicism, disillusionment, scepticism, suspicion** *This has produced widespread disillusionment among workers.*

▶ lack of knowledge **ignorance, misconception,**

misunderstanding *There is a widespread misconception that genetics is a difficult subject.*

▶ support **acceptance, acclaim, popularity, praise, recognition, support** *Several films were produced, to widespread critical acclaim.* • *There is widespread recognition of the need for accountability.*

▶ use **abuse, adoption, deployment, practice, uptake, usage, use** *The widespread use of pesticides upsets the natural balance.*

▶ publicity **consultation, coverage, dissemination, distribution, publicity** *There has been widespread coverage in many national newspapers.*

▶ damage **contamination, damage, destruction, devastation** *The widespread destruction of woodland has made life harder for many animals.*

▶ social problems **corruption, deprivation, disease, famine, illiteracy, malnutrition, poverty, suffering, unemployment** *Widespread corruption was brought to light.*

wildlife N
animals, birds, and plants in natural conditions

● adj+N a lot of **abundant, prolific** *Costa Rica boasts forests, rivers, mountains, volcanoes, and prolific wildlife.*

▶ various forms of **diverse, rich, varied** *Watch out for the varied wildlife, including deer and herons.*

▶ local **indigenous, local, native** *Our native wildlife is at risk.*

▶ rare **endangered, exotic, rare, unique** *The Amazon is home to lush vegetation and exotic wildlife.*

● v+N protect wildlife **conserve, preserve, protect, safeguard** *Raising awareness of biodiversity is necessary to conserve wildlife.*

▶ harm wildlife **disturb, endanger, harm, threaten** *Please respect the peace and quiet and do not disturb the wildlife.*

▶ watch wildlife **observe, see, spot, view, watch** *The park has many seats where visitors can rest and observe the wildlife.*

▶ be full of wildlife **be home to, be teeming with, support** *The island is teeming with wildlife.*

● N+v **abound, flourish, thrive** *A wide variety of wildlife now flourishes in what was once almost a desert.*

● N in **habitat, haven, park, refuge, reserve, sanctuary** *Call a wildlife sanctuary for advice.*

will N
determination to do what you want

● adj+N strong **indomitable, iron, strong** *There has been strong political will to involve Barcelona in a series of EU Research projects.*

▶ shared by many people **collective, general, popular** *The collective will of the people can change things despite the odds stacked against.*

▶ types of will **democratic, political** *To continue the process of ratification of the Constitution is in direct defiance of the democratic will of the people.*

● v+N act according to your will **assert, enforce, exercise, exert, impose** *They are providing revolutionary leadership to the working class, not imposing the will of a small elite on the majority.*

If two people are both strongly determined to do what they want, you can say that there is **a battle** (or **clash**) **of wills**.

▶ express your will **express** *Did the result of the election truly express the will of the people?*

▶ obey someone's will **obey, submit to** *It is always a man's duty to obey the will of God.*

▶ weaken someone's will **break, sap, weaken** *They trap the unsuspecting victim by sapping their will to resist.*

▶ not have or lose the will to do something **lack, lose** *Drug problems are most serious in communities where people lack the will or resources to manage their addiction.*

▶ not obey someone's will **defy, thwart** *They were accused of defying the will of the international community.*

willing ADJ
agreeing to do what someone asks you

● adv+ADJ **always, increasingly, only too, perfectly, quite, very** *Outside school, some of the pupils were often perfectly willing to speak to me.*

● v+ADJ **appear, be, become, prove, remain, seem, show yourself** *More and more schools are becoming willing to involve local parents in education and prevention activities.* • *Consumers have shown themselves willing to spend more than ever before on communications hardware.*

If you **show willing**, your behaviour proves to other people that you are enthusiastic or willing to help: *For example, they will often be at work on a Saturday in an attempt to show willing in a new job.*

● and/or **able, capable, competent, eager, enthusiastic, friendly, helpful, keen, knowledgeable, motivated, ready, supportive** *This post would best suit someone who is willing and eager to learn new skills.* • *She enjoys working with enthusiastic and willing children.*

willingness N
the fact that a person agrees to do what someone asks

● adj+N real **genuine, real** *The key is genuine willingness to learn more about other people's lives.*

▶ increasing **greater, growing, increasing** *Landlords are showing an increasing willingness to make lease terms more flexible.*

▶ seeming to exist **apparent** *Davis has shown no apparent willingness to fight the decision.*

▶ among people in general **general** *There is a general willingness among staff to support each other.*

● v+N show a willingness **demonstrate, indicate, show, signal** *Both sides have indicated a willingness to participate in this process.*

▶ express a willingness **confirm, declare, express, state** *The union has expressed a willingness to negotiate.*

● and/or **ability, capacity, desire, enthusiasm, openness** *The key to the success of this project is your openness and willingness to share information with us.*

win V

1 defeat others by being best or finishing first

- adv+V clearly or easily **comfortably, convincingly, decisively, easily, outright** *Sam collected a gold medal for the 4x2 Lap Relay, which the team won convincingly.*

> You can also say that a person or thing wins ***hands down***: *If I had to choose one place I would like to live, Verona wins hands down.*

- ▶ by only a small amount **just, narrowly** *He had a much closer semi-final, narrowly winning 15–12.*
- ▶ finally **at last, eventually, finally, ultimately** *After four decades in films, he finally won an Oscar for best supporting actor in The Untouchables.*
- ▶ almost **almost, nearly** *I almost won a medal, coming in 4th.*
- ▶ when it is right that someone wins **deservedly** *Wills deservedly won the race.*

2 succeed in getting something by work or ability

- V+n praise or approval **acclaim, accolade, approval, honour, plaudits, praise, recognition** *Peter Sellers went on to win world-wide acclaim with a succession of famous movie roles.*
- ▶ support **backing, support** *She won massive public support for her case.*

win N

an instance of winning, especially in sports

- adj+N easy or clear **big, comfortable, convincing, decisive, easy, emphatic, impressive, outright, resounding** *The year started for the first team with a convincing win over rivals St. Anne's.*
- ▶ almost not won **hard-fought, narrow** *Spurs held on for a narrow win.*
- ▶ one after the other **back-to-back, consecutive, straight, successive** *The Berlin side's rough start to the season looks to be over, following three straight wins in the UEFA Cup.*
- v+N achieve a win **claim, earn, gain, grab, notch up, record, register, score, seal, secure** *And it was a relief for the home side when Beevers sealed the win with the goal of the game.*
- ▶ only just achieve a win **clinch, scrape, snatch, sneak** *Cardiff came from a goal behind to snatch a 3–2 win over Rhyl.*
- ▶ deserve a win **deserve** *Bristol can argue they did just enough to deserve the win.*
- ▶ celebrate a win **celebrate** *How did you celebrate your first win?*

wind N

the natural movement of air

- adj+N blowing hard **blustery, brisk, fierce, gusty, high, howling, strong, swirling** *Sunday brought gusty winds, which caused one or two problems for some of the flyers.*
- ▶ cold **biting, bitter, chilly, cold, icy** *Biting winds blew through her long, dark brown hair.*
- ▶ not blowing hard **light** *Light winds are coming from the east.*
- ▶ direction **easterly, northerly, southerly, westerly** *It was the worst possible start to the day, with very strong northerly winds.*
- ▶ that blows most frequently **prevailing** *If you cycle*

the traditional route of east to west, then you will be cycling against the prevailing wind.

- N+v make a noise **howl, moan, roar, sigh, whistle** *A bitter wind whistled through the bare branches of the trees in the park.*
- ▶ blow or blow hard **blow, pick up, rage, rush, sweep** *Outside, a bitingly cold wind was blowing.*
- ▶ keep hitting something **batter sth, buffet sth, rattle sth, whip sth** *The wind buffeted the car mercilessly as we drove round to the north shore of the Firth.*
- ▶ become less strong **die down, drop, ease** *However, by five o'clock the wind was easing and we set off.*

windy ADJ

with a lot of wind

- adv+ADJ very **extremely, increasingly, particularly, really** INFORMAL, **so, very** *It was extremely windy in the square.*
- ▶ rather or slightly **a bit** INFORMAL, **fairly, a little, pretty** INFORMAL, **quite, rather, slightly** *The afternoon was fairly windy and cool.*
- and/or with rain **damp, rainy, showery, wet** *An angry sky threatens to make the experience a wet and windy one.*
- ▶ with clouds **cloudy, dull, miserable, overcast** *It remained heavily overcast and very windy.*
- ▶ cold **chilly, cool** *The weather is windy and cool and she pulls her small wool coat more tightly around her.*

wing N

the part of a bird, insect etc that makes it fly

- v+N move wings up and down **beat, flap, flutter** *The little bird gave a startled squawk and flapped its wings at him.*
- ▶ spread wings out **open, spread, stretch, unfurl** *The crane momentarily unfurled its wings.*
- ▶ no longer spread wings out **fold** *Gannets plummet out of the sky, folding their wings just before their beaks break the surface of the sea.*

winner N

someone who wins a race, competition, or prize

- adj+N winning easily **clear, comfortable, convincing, outright, runaway** *The legendary Ethiopian was the runaway winner in 28 mins and 12 seconds.*
- ▶ winning finally **eventual, ultimate** *She was beaten by the eventual winner of the gold medal.*
- ▶ deserving to win **deserving, worthy** *We have been impressed by the high quality of the entries and congratulate the worthy winners.*
- ▶ likely to win **likely, potential** *United began to look the more likely winners.*
- ▶ with someone else **joint** *He was a joint winner of the 1996 Nobel prize for Chemistry.*
- ▶ considered as a whole **overall** *Choosing the overall winner was a difficult task for the judging panel.*

win over PHR VB

persuade someone to agree or be friendly

- V+n **audience, critics, crowd, fans, majority, public, voters** *His barnstorming campaign performances have won over new voters.*

winter N
the cold season after autumn and before spring

- adj+N cold and unpleasant **bad, bitter, bleak, chilly, cold, cool, dark, hard, harsh, severe** *It was a most severe winter in England that year.*
- ▶ less cold than people expect **mild, warm** *This semi-evergreen plant will come through a mild winter without too much trouble.*
- ▶ with/without a lot of rain **dry, wet** *It was one of the wettest winters on record.*
- ▶ long **long** *After a long, cold winter, we can start looking forward to some warmer weather at last.*
- ▶ time **early, last, late, next** *They flower in late winter to early spring.*
- N+n weather conditions **rainfall, snow, storm, sun, sunshine, weather** *The plants looked tattered after winter storms.*
- ▶ time **months, period, season** *Low light levels can be a hazard during the winter months.*

wipe out PHR VB
destroy sth or kill sb

- V+adv completely **completely, totally** *The indigenous population was completely wiped out by the rapid spread of new diseases.*
- ▶ almost **all but, almost, nearly, virtually** *The population of the village was all but wiped out by plague in 1645.*

> Usage **Wipe out** is usually passive in these combinations.

wisdom N
knowledge and good judgment

- adj+N traditional **ancient, folk, timeless, traditional** *This is timeless wisdom, and will hold up long after the trendy methodologies have gone out of fashion.*
- ▶ generally accepted **accepted, conventional, perceived, prevailing, received** *His views on public space have now become part of accepted wisdom.*
- ▶ collected over time or from many people **accumulated, collective** *This book is a compendium of accumulated wisdom.*
- ▶ types of wisdom **practical, spiritual, worldly** *The book examines Ninja spiritual wisdom.*
- v+N say or write wise things **dispense, impart, share** *The roving rock pundit has been dispensing wisdom to world potentates for years.*

> People often use the word **wisdom** to suggest that someone's words or actions are not sensible at all: *Hordes of moaning maniacs were keen to impart their wisdom on how the Net should be run.*

- ▶ doubt the wisdom of something **challenge, doubt, question** *Local people doubted the wisdom of having a weapons museum in a church.*
- ▶ have or get wisdom **acquire, gain, have, possess** *Stories are an excellent way of helping children acquire wisdom.*
- n+of+N wise words **gem, nugget, pearl, piece, words** *Mr Brownlow has a pearl of wisdom which he brings out at critical moments.*
- ▶ person, book etc **font, fount, fountain, repository, source** *They need to shed the old image of the teacher being the fount of wisdom and replace it with the teacher as facilitator.*

wise ADJ
sensible in the current situation

- ADJ+n advice **advice, counsel, words** *His long experience and knowledge have been particularly helpful, and we thank him for giving us the benefit of his wise counsel.*
- ▶ action or decision **choice, decision, move, precaution** *As any financial advisor will tell you, investing in a fast depreciating asset is not a wise move.*
- v+ADJ be or seem wise **be, look, prove, seem, sound** *If you're not sure, it seems wisest not to eat it.*
- ▶ think something is wise **consider sth, think sth** *It might be considered wiser to stick to a smaller project.*

wish V
want something to happen

- adv+V very much **desperately, earnestly, fervently, genuinely, heartily, really** INFORMAL, **sincerely** *I wished fervently that he might not discover my hiding-place.*
- ▶ only **just, merely, only, simply** *I only wish I had attended this course sooner.*

wish N
the feeling of wanting to do or have something

- adj+N which someone feels strongly **ardent, cherished, dear, earnest, fervent, genuine, heartfelt, sincere, strong** *It is my sincere wish that as many members as possible take part in the discussion.*
- ▶ which someone states clearly **express, expressed, stated** *It was at the express wish of Mr. Kirby that the band did not play at the funeral.*
- ▶ before someone dies **dying, final, last** *His dying wish was to be taken to his native land to be buried.*
- v+N do or give what someone wants **accommodate, carry out, fulfil, grant, gratify, honour, meet, obey, respect, satisfy** *Thank you for being so flexible in accommodating our wishes.*
- ▶ tell people what you want **confirm, declare, express, indicate, make known, state** *Several major companies have expressed their wish to participate in the programme.* • *It is also a good idea to make your wishes known to relatives or friends.*
- ▶ ignore someone's wishes **disregard, frustrate, go against, ignore, override** *Should the law disregard people's wishes about how they want to die?*

> Usage **Wish** is often plural in these combinations: *By having such inadequate regulation, the government is ignoring the wishes of the public.*

- ▶ be or show someone's wish **reflect, represent** *It is important to update your will every few years so that it still reflects your wishes.*

wit N
1 the use of words in a clever, funny way

- adj+N slightly unkind **acerbic, barbed, biting, caustic, ironic, mordant, sarcastic, sardonic,** satirical *Wilder's caustic wit was famous, but he wasn't above bullying.*

▶ showing a quick mind **incisive, quick, razor-sharp, ready, sharp, sparkling** *John Fortune's razor-sharp wit will expertly draw out the absurdity of what was a terribly serious situation.*

▶ funny but without smiles or laughter **deadpan, dry, laconic, sly, wry** *When he takes to the microphone, he entertains the audience with his dry wit.*

● and/or **charm, humour, intelligence, wisdom** *She was known for her intelligence and wit.*

2 the ability to think quickly and make sensible decisions [always plural]

● v+N **collect, gather, recover, use** *I was shocked, but before I could gather my wits he had fled the house.*

To **keep** (or **have**) **your wits about you** is to be ready to think and act quickly: *Fishing from a boat is not as hard as it seems, as long as you keep your wits about you.* You can also use **wits** in expressions about being frightened: *This movie will scare the wits out of you.* If you are competing against someone, you can say that you **pit your wits against** them: *The game that lets you pit your wits against football lovers from all around the world.*

withdraw V
stop providing or offering something

● adv+V completely **altogether, completely** *The danger was that the unions could withdraw their support altogether.*

▶ immediately **abruptly, hastily, immediately, instantly, promptly, quickly, suddenly, swiftly** *This was the last straw for the commissioner, who immediately withdrew funding.*

● V+n permission **approval, consent, permission** *Patients have the right to withdraw consent for use of their images at any time.*

▶ help or money **funding, subsidy, support** *They became unconvinced that the venture would work and withdrew their support.*

▶ offer or invitation **invitation, offer** *We will withdraw the offer of a place if we find that you have given fraudulent or misleading information.*

withdrawal N
the decision to stop providing or offering something

● adj+N quick **abrupt, immediate, rapid, sudden** *Training has continued despite a sudden withdrawal of funding.*

▶ complete **complete, total** *The statement was tantamount to a complete withdrawal of backing, financial and moral.*

● N+of **approval, consent, funding, service, subsidy, support, treatment** *You are, of course, aware that the withdrawal of your support would have a serious effect on the club?*

withhold V
deliberately not give something to someone

● adv+V unfairly **unreasonably, wrongly** *We agree that the consent will not be withheld unreasonably.*

▶ deliberately **deliberately, knowingly** *When people knowingly withhold this information, they are being cruel.*

● V+n permission or approval **approval, blessing, consent, permission** *The National Committee reserves the right to withhold approval of events.*

▶ money or support **aid, deposit, money, payment, rent, support** *Larger companies may withhold payment for many months.*

▶ information **address, information, name** *You are able to withhold all personal information that is not required to complete your order transaction.*

▶ medical treatment **treatment** *Decisions to withdraw or withhold treatment should not be taken with the sole intention of causing death.*

withstand V
be strong enough not to be harmed or damaged

● V+n an attack, or something that seems like an attack **assault, attack, barrage, blow, onslaught, shock, siege** *Harlech Castle withstood a Welsh attack at the very end of the 13th century.*

▶ a physical force **blast, cold, drought, earthquake, extremes, forces, frost, heat, pressure, storm, stress, temperature, wear, wind** *The plant thrives in sun or partial shade and withstands frost and wind damage.*

witness N
someone who sees a crime or other event, or tells a court about it

● adj+N who can be trusted **credible, independent, reliable, truthful** *He was a straightforward, consistent and reliable witness.*

▶ who cannot be trusted **unreliable** *The evidence was shaky, the witnesses unreliable, and both men had strong alibis.*

▶ important **chief, key, principal, star, vital** *The investigation was hampered because a key witness had gone missing.*

▶ with expert knowledge **expert** *An expert witness might be brought in by the defence.*

● n+N **defence, prosecution** *She was called as a prosecution witness.*

● N+n **account, evidence, statement, testimony** *The case relied entirely on witness testimony.*

witness V
see a crime or other event happen

● adv+V **actually, firsthand, personally** *Several of the firefighters witnessed firsthand the carnage of this brutal attack.*

witty ADJ
clever and funny

● adv+ADJ in a way that people admire **brilliantly, deliciously, delightfully, sharply, wonderfully** *Wilde's deliciously witty satire lays bare the moral contradictions of Victorian society.*

▶ very **extremely, incredibly, very** *This is a light read but highly entertaining and extremely witty.*

● ADJ+n comment **aside, comment, observation,**

one-liner, quip, remark, retort, saying *Tony prefers to take a back seat, interjecting witty one-liners now and again just to prove he's still listening.*

▶ conversation **banter, dialogue, repartee** *The movie sparkles with witty banter and delightful comedic situations.*

▶ piece of writing **lyrics, script** *The characters were well thought out and the script is witty and sharp.*

● and/or **charming, clever, entertaining, funny, intelligent, sharp, wise** *It is a song with witty and clever lyrics and, once it arrives, a great chorus.*

wonder N
surprise, admiration, or pleasure

● v+in+N **be lost, gasp, gaze, stand, stare, watch** *Go whale watching and gaze in wonder at these fabulously impressive creatures.*

word N
a remark

● N+of **advice, caution, comfort, congratulations, consolation, encouragement, explanation, praise, thanks, warning, welcome, wisdom** *He is always ready with a word of advice and some emotional support.*

> Usage **Word** is often plural in these combinations: *There were no words of comfort I could offer her.*

word V
use words to express something in particular way [usually passive]

● adv+V in a way that is not clear **ambiguously, badly, poorly, vaguely** *Vaguely worded questions encourage vaguely worded answers.*

▶ in a clear or skilful way **carefully, clearly, cleverly, well** *These documents have been carefully worded to ensure that they comply with current legislation.*

▶ in a suitable way **appropriately, properly, suitably** *If questions aren't worded properly, the debate will lack validity.*

▶ showing strong feelings **strongly** *I have written them a rather strongly worded letter demanding an explanation.*

wording N
the words used in a particular piece of writing

● adj+N exact **actual, exact, precise, specific** *The publishers had to agree the precise wording for the questionnaires.*

▶ original **original** *The original wording has been simplified in places.*

▶ not clear **ambiguous, imprecise, loose, unclear, vague** *Some companies are exploiting loose wording in the agreements.*

▶ clear or careful **careful, clear** *Careful wording of terms and conditions is essential.*

● v+N change wording **alter, amend, change, revise** *The publishers also reserve the right to amend the wording of an advertisement when considered necessary.*

▶ write or suggest wording **draft, finalize, propose, suggest** *The following wording is suggested for Reg. 16 (3).*

▶ give permission for wording **agree, approve** *The*

USA had refused to agree the wording in the preparatory meetings.*

▶ use wording **use** *Is that wording used anywhere in other legislation?*

work V
1 use effort to achieve something

● adv+V with a lot of effort **hard, tirelessly** *She worked tirelessly in charity and social work.*

▶ effectively **effectively, well** *During this period, he worked effectively* **with** *other churches.*

▶ with other people **closely, collaboratively, together** *Senior managers work closely* **with** *members of the Cabinet.*

2 operate well

● adv+V **correctly, effectively, efficiently, normally, perfectly, properly, smoothly, well** *The house is warm now that the radiator thermostats are working properly.*

work N
activity that involves physical or mental effort

● adj+N involving a lot of effort **extensive, hard** *All that hard work was worth it.*

▶ done at the beginning **initial, preliminary, preparatory** *The next stage in the preparatory work involved searching for primary sources on the Internet.*

▶ more **additional, extra, further** *We have no objection to such a plan, but we feel it needs further work.*

▶ good **excellent, good, great, nice INFORMAL** *Richard Brown has done some excellent work with the website.*

worker N
someone who has a job

● adj+N doing practical work **blue-collar, manual, unskilled** *The scheme is designed for unskilled and other manual workers.*

▶ having a particular working arrangement **casual, full-time, part-time, temporary** *The company has agreed limits on the use of agency and casual workers.*

▶ having skills or experience **experienced, professional, qualified, skilled, trained, white-collar** *The machine needed a skilled worker to operate it.*

workforce N
the people who work somewhere

● adj+N with good skills and qualifications **competent, educated, highly-skilled, multi-skilled, qualified, skilled, trained, well-educated, well-trained, world-class** *Running a boatyard that takes on a wide range of work requires a skilled workforce.*

▶ willing to work hard **committed, dedicated, loyal, motivated, productive, well-motivated** *A well-trained and motivated local workforce is crucial.*

▶ able to change jobs easily **flexible, mobile** *Our economic future depends on a highly skilled and flexible workforce.*

▶ all the workforce **entire, total, whole** *Our only stipulation is that it really must be shares for all, offered across the company's entire workforce.*

- v+N employ a workforce **employ** *There is a clear business case for recruiters employing a more diverse workforce in terms of age.*
- ▶ enter/leave the workforce **enter, leave** *This is a time of year when many young people are entering the workforce.*
- ▶ increase/reduce a workforce **cut, expand, increase, reduce** *This section outlines the strategies the NHS is using to expand its workforce.*

workload N
the amount of work to be done

- adj+N large amount **busy, challenging, demanding, enormous, excessive, heavy, huge, increasing** *Nurses have to fight for their wages and always face heavy workloads.*
- ▶ extra **additional, extra, increased** *Some 7,000 staff from other parts of the Department have been drafted in to cope with the extra workloads.*
- v+N deal with the workload **balance, cope with, deal with, handle, juggle, manage, tackle** *How will I be able to cope with the workload?*
- ▶ reduce the workload **ease, lessen, lighten, minimize, reduce** *A number of sub-committees help to lighten the workload for the board.*
- ▶ increase the workload **increase** *The implementation of compulsory cost-benefit analyses of experiments would increase the workload of many researchers.*
- ▶ share the workload among people **share, spread** *A larger team helps to spread the workload and new faces will help to develop fresh ideas.*

workout N
an occasion when you do physical exercise

- adj+N requiring a lot of effort **athletic, energetic, good, gruelling, hard, intense, strenuous, thorough, tough, vigorous** *If you would prefer to have a more intense workout, why not have a go in the fitness suite?*
- ▶ affecting a particular part of your body **abdominal, aerobic, cardiovascular, full-body, upper-body** *If you often find yourself breathless, a cardiovascular workout would be beneficial to your heart and lungs.*
- v+N **complete, do, get, have, perform** *The dog can really get a workout in a relatively small space.*

workshop N
a meeting where people learn about a particular subject

- adj+N involving practical experience **hands-on, interactive, practical** *Guest educators teach modules which include theory work and hands-on workshops.*
- ▶ involving a lot of work **intensive** *The festival programme was made up of two days of intensive workshops, followed by three days of public performances.*
- ▶ how long it lasts **two-day, half-day, weekend etc** *The one-day workshop will enable participants to meet colleagues and provide an opportunity for professional development.*
- v+N organize a workshop **arrange, hold, host, organize, run** *He is an international best-selling author who hosts writing workshops in his New York loft.*

- ▶ teach a workshop **conduct, deliver, do, lead, present, teach** *The project directors will lead workshops based on themes arising from their projects.*
- ▶ design a workshop **design, plan, tailor** *She tailors inclusive dance workshops for groups of children and adults.*
- ▶ go to a workshop **attend, go to, participate in, take part in** *More than 60 participants from EU countries attended this workshop.*
- N+n what is done during a workshop **discussion, presentation, session** *These notes are based on a workshop session on budgeting and project management.*
- ▶ person **attendee, delegate, facilitator, leader, participant, presenter** *A proposal to initiate the formation of a national research institute received strong support from the workshop participants.*

worried ADJ
anxious about bad things that could happen

- adv+ADJ very **deeply, extremely, increasingly, particularly, really, seriously, very** *Her teachers became extremely worried about her.*
- ▶ slightly **a bit, a little, slightly** *I was a little worried about it being sent in the mail, but it was fine.*
- ▶ rather **quite, rather** *I was quite worried about getting everything right.*
- ▶ clearly **clearly** *By Sunday evening, he was clearly worried.*
- ADJ+n **expression, glance, look, tone** *She had a worried look on her face.*
- v+ADJ be worried **be, feel, look, seem** *I'm not asking for money, don't look so worried.*
- ▶ become worried **become, get** *I began to get very worried.*

worry V
feel anxious about something, or make someone feel anxious

- adv+V very much **particularly, really** *What really worries people is violent crime.*
- ▶ slightly **a little, slightly** *I had no new ideas, which slightly worried me.*
- ▶ more than is necessary **excessively, needlessly, too much, unduly, unnecessarily** *Assume you will accumulate some debt over your period of study, but don't worry unduly about it.*
- ▶ all the time **always, constantly, continually** *She worries constantly about her health.*

worry N
a problem or possibility that makes you worried

- adj+N serious **big, great, main, major, real, serious** *Credit card security is a major worry for Internet shoppers.*
- ▶ continuous **constant** *They live with the constant worry that comes from having a sick child.*
- ▶ unpleasant and difficult to get rid of **nagging, niggling** *This gave him confidence about his speed, but a nagging worry remained over his stamina.*
- ▶ not necessary **needless, unfounded, unnecessary** *Telling them would only cause unnecessary worry.*
- ▶ financial **financial, money** *She found a job, and some of the financial worries were lifted.*

- v+N have a worry **have** *I'm a bit too old to have any worries **about** what people think of me.*
▶ express or talk about a worry **discuss, express, share, talk about** *Industry professionals have also expressed their worries.* ● *Women are more likely to share their worries with someone else than men.*
▶ cause a worry **cause, lead to** *It would only cause unnecessary worry.*
▶ remove a worry or make it less serious **alleviate, ease, relieve, remove, take away** *You have eased my worries slightly.*
▶ forget a worry **forget** *This is a chance to relax, unwind, and forget your worries for a while.*

Usage *Worry* is often plural in all of the *v+N* combinations shown above.

worrying ADJ
making you feel worried

- adv+ADJ very **deeply, extremely, particularly, very** *It is a deeply worrying situation.*
▶ rather **quite, rather** *In 2005, she faced a rather worrying time when her son Thomas became ill.*
▶ slightly **a bit, a little, slightly** *It was getting a little worrying.*

- ADJ+n change or development **decline, development, increase, rise, tendency, trend** *The latest figures show a worrying rise in reported cases of the life-threatening MRSA bug.* ● *The number of deaths of motorcyclists in our region has increased for the last three years, a worrying trend.*
▶ sign of something **sign, symptom** *Children involved in domestic accidents or who show worrying symptoms of illness are very often taken by parents to their local hospital.*
▶ fact **aspect, fact, figures, findings, statistic** *The survey revealed the worrying statistic that 47 per cent of respondents had made no provision at all for their retirement.*

worse ADJ
more unpleasant or bad than something else or than before

- adv+ADJ even **even, still** *There is a danger that the planned job cuts will make the situation even worse.*
▶ much **considerably, far, a lot, much, significantly** *It became apparent that the situation is far worse than we realized.*
▶ slightly or rather **a bit, a little, rather, slightly** *Their finances are in a rather worse state this year.*
▶ steadily **progressively, steadily** *The weather looked as though it would get steadily worse.*

- v+ADJ be worse **be, feel, look** *If you start to feel worse, call the doctor.*
▶ become worse **become, get, grow** *The problem appears to be getting worse.*
▶ make something worse **make sth** *Matters had been made worse by the poor weather.*

worsen V
become worse

- adv+V a lot **considerably, dramatically, markedly, significantly** *The problem of homelessness has worsened considerably.*

▶ steadily **gradually, progressively, steadily** *The unemployment figures have worsened steadily since the party came to power.*
▶ quickly **rapidly** *Weather conditions rapidly worsened.*

- n+V **conditions, crisis, position, problem, situation, symptoms, weather** *If the situation worsens, the matter will be considered further.*

worst N
something or someone worse than all others

- v+N expect or fear the worst **assume, expect, fear** *When we found her gone, we did a frantic search, fearing the worst.*
▶ think the worst **believe, think** *I always imagine that people think the worst of me.*
▶ be prepared for the worst **be prepared for, prepare for** *When he turned to me to tell me the result, I was prepared for the worst.*
▶ avoid the worst **avoid, escape** *We managed to avoid the worst of the weather.*

worth N
how good, useful, or important someone or something is

- adj+N in itself **inherent, intrinsic** *She has a belief in the intrinsic worth of education.*
▶ real **real, true** *We never had a chance to show our true worth.*
▶ relating to a person's qualities **human, own, personal, self** *A job title and salary are not the sole measure of human worth.*
▶ equal **equal** *All the children are of equal worth and ought to be treated as such.*
▶ of a particular type **artistic, commercial, cultural, historical, intellectual, moral, social** *How can we assess the moral worth of a course of action?* ● *Bankers were criticized for making vast amounts of money from transactions which were of little social worth.*

- v+N show worth **demonstrate, prove, show** *He lacks experience but he has to be given his chance to prove his worth.*
▶ have worth **have** *Most of us are brought up to believe that all human beings have equal worth.*
▶ realize or know worth **appreciate, know, realize, recognize** *He is a man who knows his true worth.*
▶ make a judgement about worth **assess, evaluate, measure** *Students are invited to assess the worth of their own work according to specified criteria.*

worthless ADJ
not having any value, or not useful

- adv+ADJ completely **absolutely, completely, totally, utterly** *Some sections of this book are quite interesting while others are utterly worthless.*
▶ almost **almost, effectively, practically, virtually** *In court he sounded convincing, but his evidence was virtually worthless.*

- v+ADJ be worthless **be, become, feel, prove** *His promises proved worthless.*
▶ make something worthless **make sth, render sth** *Just because it is a very right-wing book doesn't make it worthless.*

worthwhile ADJ

worth spending time, money, or effort on

- adv+ADJ very **extremely, really, truly, very, well** *It was a long journey but it was well worthwhile.*
- ▶ definitely **certainly, definitely** *The wait was definitely worthwhile, though.*
- ADJ+n **activity, addition, cause, charity, contribution, effort, event, exercise, experience, investment, job, project, trip, visit** *The concert will raise money for some very worthwhile causes.*
- v+ADJ be worthwhile **be, prove, seem** *A few minutes spent on the website could prove worthwhile.*
- ▶ think something is worthwhile **consider sth, find sth, think sth** *Students, parents, and teachers all found the session worthwhile.*
- ▶ make something worthwhile **make sth** *The benefits for both employers and staff make the effort worthwhile.*

worthy ADJ

1 deserving something

- v+ADJ think that something is worthy **consider sth, deem sth, think sth** *These popular customs were so commonplace that they were rarely considered worthy of mention.*
- ▶ be worthy **be, prove, seem** *These results proved worthy of further investigation.*
- ADJ+of being mentioned or discussed **attention, discussion, mention, note, notice, remark** *Two minor incidents in 2007 are the only other safety problems worthy of mention.*
- ▶ being considered or examined **consideration, examination, exploration, inclusion, investigation, research** *There are also practical issues here which are worthy of consideration.*
- ▶ being admired **admiration, praise, respect** *The whole production is worthy of the highest praise.*
- ▶ being protected **conservation, preservation, protection** *Only documents which are judged to be of historical value and worthy of preservation will be retained.*

2 with qualities that make people respect them

- adv+ADJ very **certainly, particularly, truly, very, well** *She is a truly worthy champion.*
- ▶ equally **equally** *The reader will almost certainly think of others – equally worthy – that I have not had the space to mention.*
- ADJ+n someone who wins or takes part in a competition **adversary, candidate, champion, opponent, recipient, winner** *We congratulate the worthy winners.*
- ▶ attempt to do or achieve something **attempt, effort, initiative, project** *The building has its share of flaws but, but it is a very worthy effort and the good points far outweigh the bad.*
- ▶ aim **aim, goal** *We need to ensure that the worthy aims of the bill are achieved.*
- ▶ charity **cause, charity** *This annual event helps support many local worthy causes.*
- ▶ addition **addition** *This is still a very worthy addition to your DVD collection.*

wound N

1 an injury when your skin or flesh is damaged

- adj+N very bad **deep, serious, severe** *The victim sustained serious head wounds.*
- ▶ resulting in death **fatal, mortal** *He continued to fire at the retreating enemy until he received a fatal wound in the head.*
- ▶ not serious **minor, superficial** *We were taught how to treat minor wounds such as burns and cuts.*
- ▶ open **gaping, open** *Blood was pouring out of a gaping wound.*
- ▶ infected **infected** *Infected wounds had caused many deaths in previous wars.*
- n+N cause of a wound **bite, bullet, gunshot, shrapnel, stab** *He was found dead from gunshot wounds at his home.*
- ▶ part of the body **chest, head, leg, neck, stomach** *One diver required five stitches to a head wound.*
- ▶ received in a war **war** *He died of war wounds in October 1918.*
- v+N cause a wound **cause, inflict** *Police do not know who inflicted the fatal wound.*
- ▶ treat or cover a wound **bandage, clean, cleanse, cover, dress, treat** *I was seen relatively quickly and the wound was dressed.*
- ▶ receive a wound **receive, suffer, sustain** *She had suffered multiple stab wounds.*
- ▶ die from a wound **die from, die of** *He died of wounds received in battle.*

2 emotional damage caused by something bad

- adj+N **deep, emotional, festering, old, open, self-inflicted** *For many people, those events of ten years ago are still an open wound.*
- v+N when people feel happier **heal** *Time heals all wounds.*
- ▶ cause a wound **cause, inflict** *The break-up of a home always inflicts a lasting wound on the personalities of all involved in it.*
- ▶ when people are made to think again about a bad experience **open, reopen** *It's been very distressing to open these wounds, even though it's been two years since it happened.*

wound V

injure someone, damaging their skin or flesh
[usually passive]

- adv+V so badly that someone dies **fatally, mortally** *Nelson was fatally wounded during the battle.*
- ▶ badly **badly, critically, seriously, severely** *Eight were killed and 13 were badly wounded.*
- ▶ slightly **lightly, slightly** *He was slightly wounded in the leg by a splinter.*

wrath N

very great anger

- v+N cause wrath **arouse, bring, incur, kindle, provoke** *Last-minute requests to meet imminent deadlines risk incurring my wrath.*
- ▶ experience wrath **endure, experience, face, feel, suffer** *At the next home game, the manager faced the wrath of the supporters.*
- ▶ not experience wrath **avoid, escape** *Somehow, the movie escaped the wrath of the censors.*

▸ when someone might experience wrath **fear, risk** *They feared the wrath of their gods.*

wreck V
severely damage or destroy a vehicle or building

● adv+V completely **completely, totally** *Vandals had totally wrecked the interior of the building.*
▸ almost **almost, nearly** *People started fighting and almost wrecked the place.*

wreckage N
parts remaining after something has been damaged

● adj+N twisted **mangled, twisted** *Firefighters cut free people trapped in the mangled wreckage of their cars.*
▸ on fire **burning** *At least 10 bodies lay strewn around the burning wreckage.*
▸ spread over a large area **scattered** *Divers have found the scattered wreckage of an aircraft that went missing in the Indian Ocean.*
● v+N **be trapped in, clear, cling to, cut sb from, pull sb from** *One of the passengers had to be cut from the wreckage.*
● N+v **be scattered, be spread, be strewn** *Wreckage was strewn over a wide area.*

write V
create a story, letter, article etc

● adv+V very well **beautifully, brilliantly, elegantly, eloquently, superbly, well** *The play is witty, well-constructed, and elegantly written.* ● *She writes well, but somehow her characters don't seem very sympathetic.*
▸ not well **badly, poorly** *Badly written letters could be costing firms millions in lost customers.*
▸ in a clear way **clearly, lucidly, simply** *There are many clearly written books dealing with this subject.*
▸ a lot **extensively, prolifically** *She has written extensively on China and its global relationships.*
▸ replying to someone **back** *Please write back to me when you can.*

writer N
someone who writes books, stories, or articles

adj+N good **accomplished, brilliant, fine, gifted, good, talented** *Joolz is a very talented writer and performer.*
famous or admired **acclaimed, award-winning, distinguished, famous, great, leading, respected, well-known** *Conrad has been called one of the greatest writers of the English novel.*
popular or successful **bestselling, favourite, popular, successful** *Nigella Lawson is one of the UK's most popular food writers.*
modern **contemporary, modern** *This course looks at the work of three major contemporary writers.*
writing many books **prolific** *He was a prolific writer on military affairs.*
wanting to be a writer **aspiring, budding, would-be** *What advice would you give to aspiring writers?*

writing N
books, poems, newspaper articles etc

● adj+N involving imagination **creative, descriptive, experimental, imaginative, original** *We offer workshops on storytelling and creative writing.*
▸ of the present time **contemporary, current, modern** *The feelings of the characters are portrayed with an intelligence and sensitivity that is rarely seen in contemporary writing.*
▸ relating to education or study **academic, critical, historical, scientific, technical** *There are a number of referencing systems used in academic writing.*
▸ long **extended** *Students were asked to do a piece of extended writing, such as writing a letter home or a diary entry.*

wrong ADJ
incorrect, unacceptable, or causing problems

● adv+ADJ completely **absolutely, all, completely, entirely, fundamentally, plain, quite, totally, utterly** *I believe that analysis is completely wrong.*
▸ extremely **badly, disastrously, horribly, seriously, spectacularly, terribly** *This is where things started to go horribly wrong.*
▸ when it is obvious **clearly, obviously, plainly** *The overturned decision was clearly wrong in the light of the evidence available at the time it was made.*
▸ when there is no doubt **just, simply** *But this contention is simply wrong.*
● v+ADJ be or seem wrong **be, feel, look, seem, sound** *That seems wrong to me.*
▸ go wrong **go** *We cannot afford for anything to go wrong.*
▸ be wrong about something **get sth, guess** *Make a note of the answers that you got wrong.*
▸ show that someone is wrong **prove sb** *I hope I'm proved wrong, but I don't think I will be.*
▸ think something is wrong **consider sth, find sth, think sth** *This a kind of behaviour which many Christians would consider wrong.*
● V+infinitive **argue, assume, claim, conclude, say, suggest, think** *It would be wrong to assume, however, that this hostility was shared by everyone.*

wrong N
immoral behaviour

● adj+N serious **great, grievous, serious, terrible** *A great wrong has been done here.*
▸ in the past **ancient, historic, past** *We demand that past wrongs are put right.*
● v+N correct a wrong **address, put right, redress, right** *We all want to see justice done and wrongs righted.*
▸ commit a wrong **commit, do (sb), inflict, perpetrate** *They sought vengeance for wrongs done to them years ago.*
▸ punish someone for a wrong **avenge** *She was determined to avenge wrongs inflicted on her family.*

Yy

yawning ADJ
very wide

- ADJ+n **chasm, gap, gulf** *There is a yawning gap between what the Government says in public and its actions.*

yearn V
want something a lot

- adv+V **always, deeply, desperately, secretly, still** *She had always yearned to live in Australia.*
- V+for **freedom, justice, love, peace, return** *It is clear that the overwhelming majority of the population yearns for peace.*

yearning N
a feeling of wanting something very much

- adj+N **strong deep, intense** *There is a deep yearning in the region for change.*
- ▶ types of yearning **nostalgic, romantic, spiritual** *Her dancing captured the romantic yearning of the music.*
- v+N **express, feel, have, satisfy** *These Gothic-style castle ruins seem to satisfy a nostalgic yearning for the romance and chivalry of the past.*

yellow ADJ
the colour of the middle of an egg

- adj+ADJ bright **bright, brilliant, flourescent, vibrant, vivid** *The mustard is produced from seed grown in brilliant yellow fields surrounding the region's capital.*
- ▶ light **light, pale** *The walls are pale yellow.*
- ▶ dark **dark, deep, dull, rich** *When you enter the secure area of the site, the background of the address bar will turn dark yellow.*
- ▶ types of yellow **creamy, golden, lemon, mustard, straw** *The leaves become golden yellow in the fall.*
- v+ADJ **become, flash, glow, go, turn** *As evening fell, small fishing boats chugged softly into the harbour, their cabin windows glowing yellow in the fragile light.*

yield V
1 produce something useful

- V+n result or benefit **benefit, conclusion, dividends, improvement, insight, result, rewards** *This research is already yielding good results.*
- ▶ profit or money **gain, income, profit, return, revenue, saving** *Investment is concentrated in those areas which will yield a quick profit.*
- ▶ useful information **answer, clue, data, evidence, information** *Since then, excavations of the site have yielded important new evidence of human occupation.*

2 finally do what someone wants or what you were trying not to do

- adv+V **easily, eventually, finally, readily** *Reg finally yielded to their demands.*
- V+to **demand, impulse, pressure, request,**

temptation, wish *Try not to yield to the temptation to skip parts of this long book.*

yield N
an amount of something that is produced

- adj+N high **excellent, good, high, large** *The breeding programme is designed to produce dairy cows with high milk yields.*
- ▶ low **low, poor** *Poor yields from harvests have led to widespread food shortages in these areas.*
- ▶ particular amount **average, gross, maximum, net, total** *The average yield was 470 kilos of cotton per hectare.*
- n+N in farming **cereal, crop, grain, maize, milk, rice, wheat** *Changes in agricultural practices were introduced to increase crop yields.*
- ▶ in business **bond, dividend, income, investment** *Does a high dividend yield indicate a strong company?*
- v+N produce a yield **achieve, deliver, generate, give, produce** *Organic food is more expensive because it produces smaller yields and is more labour intensive.*
- ▶ increase a yield **boost, improve, increase, maximize** *New irrigation projects are set to boost yields.*
- ▶ reduce a yield **compromise, depress, reduce** *A drought a year earlier had reduced Europe's potato yields significantly.*

young ADJ
having lived for only a short time

- v+ADJ be or look young **be, feel, look, seem, sound** *Her gravelly voice is a surprising sound for one who looks so young.* • *She sounded very young on the phone, but she turned out to be about 45.*
- ▶ seem to remain young **keep (sb), remain, stay** *My grandchildren keep me young.*
- ▶ seem to become younger **get** *Our students seem to be getting younger every year.*
- ▶ die at a young age **die** *Three of her children died young.*

youth N
the time when someone is young

- adj+N no longer existing **lost** *As he turns 40, he laments his lost youth and searches for meaning in his life.*
- ▶ in which time and opportunites were wasted **misspent** *In my misspent youth, I went to greyhound tracks.*
- v+N spend your youth **spend** *He spent his youth working on a farm.*
- ▶ feel you are in your youth again **recapture, reliv** *The 1970s disco night was a chance for some to reliv their youth.*
- ▶ not make good use of your youth **waste** *They sa he was wasting his youth playing computer games.*

Zz

zeal N
great energy, effort, and enthusiasm

- adj+N great or too much **excessive, fanatical, great, tremendous** *He embarked upon this project with great zeal.*
- ▶ types of zeal, especially for changing things **crusading, evangelical, evangelistic, missionary, reforming, religious, revolutionary** *She had a crusading zeal.*